Cost Accounting
A Managerial Emphasis

Fifteenth Edition

Charles T. Horngren
Stanford University

Srikant M. Datar
Harvard University

Madhav V. Rajan
Stanford University

 Pearson

Authorized adaptation from the United States edition, entitled *Cost Accounting: A Managerial Emphasis, 15th Edition,* ISBN 9780133428704 by Horngren, Charles T., Datar, Srikant M., Rajan, Madhav V., published by Pearson Education, Inc., Copyright © 2015.

Indian Subcontinent Adaptation

ISBN 978-93-325-4221-1

First Impression

This edition is manufactured in India and is authorized for sale only in India, Bangladesh, Bhutan, Pakistan, Nepal, Sri Lanka and the Maldives. Circulation of this edition outside of these territories is UNAUTHORIZED.

Published by Pearson India Education Services Pvt. Ltd, CIN: U72200TN2005PTC057128, formerly known as TutorVista Global Pvt. Ltd, licensee of Pearson Education in South Asia.

Head Office: A-8 (A), 7th Floor, Knowledge Boulevard, Sector 62, Noida 201 309, Uttar Pradesh, India.
Registered Office: 4th Floor, Software Block, Elnet Software City, TS-140, Block 2 & 9, Rajiv Gandhi Salai, Taramani, Chennai 600 113, Tamil Nadu, India.
Fax: 080-30461003, Phone: 080-30461060
www.pearson.co.in, Email: companysecretary.india@pearson.com

Printed in India by Thomson Press India Ltd.

Brief Contents

Contents

About the Authors

Charles T. Horngren was the Edmund W. Littlefield Professor of Accounting, Emeritus, at Stanford University. A Graduate of Marquette University, he received his MBA from Harvard University and his PhD from the University of Chicago. He was also the recipient of honorary doctorates from Marquette University and DePaul University.

A certified public accountant, Horngren served on the Accounting Principles Board for six years, the Financial Accounting Standards Board Advisory Council for five years, and the Council of the American Institute of Certified Public Accountants for three years. For six years, he served as a trustee of the Financial Accounting Foundation, which oversees the Financial Accounting Standards Board and the Government Accounting Standards Board. Horngren was a member of the Accounting Hall of Fame.

A member of the American Accounting Association, Horngren had been its president and its director of research. He received its first Outstanding Accounting Educator Award. The California Certified Public Accountants Foundation gave Horngren its Faculty Excellence Award and its Distinguished Professor Award. He was the first person to have received both awards.

The American Institute of Certified Public Accountants presented its first Outstanding Educator Award to Horngren. Horngren was named Accountant of the Year, Education, by the national professional accounting fraternity, Beta Alpha Psi. Professor Horngren was also a member of the Institute of Management Accountants, from whom he received its Distinguished Service Award. He was also a member of the Institutes' Board of Regents, which administers the Certified Management Accountant examinations.

Horngren is the author of other accounting books published by Pearson Education: *Introduction to Management Accounting,* 15th ed. (2011, with Sundem, and Stratton); *Introduction to Financial Accounting,* 10th ed. (2011, with Sundem and Elliott); *Accounting,* 8th ed. (2010, with Harrison and Bamber); and *Financial Accounting,* 8th ed. (2010, with Harrison).

Horngren was the Consulting Editor for the Charles T. Horngren Series in Accounting.

Srikant M. Datar is the Arthur Lowes Dickinson Professor at the Harvard Business School. He served as Senior Associate Dean from 2000 to 2010. A graduate with distinction from the University of Bombay, he received gold medals upon graduation from the Indian Institute of Management, Ahmedabad, and the Institute of Cost and Works Accountants of India. A chartered accountant, he holds two master's degrees and a PhD from Stanford University.

Datar has published his research in leading accounting, marketing, and operations management journals, including *The Accounting Review, Contemporary Accounting Research, Journal of Accounting, Auditing and Finance, Journal of Accounting and Economics, Journal of Accounting Research,* and *Management Science.* He has served as an associate editor and on the editorial board of several journals and has presented his research to corporate executives and academic audiences in North America, South America, Asia, Africa, Australia, and Europe. He is a coauthor of three other books: *Managerial Accounting: Making Decisions and Motivating Performance, Rethinking the MBA: Business Education at a Crossroads*, and *Rethinking Graduate Management Education in Latin America*.

Cited by his students as a dedicated and innovative teacher, Datar received the George Leland Bach Award for Excellence in the Classroom at Carnegie Mellon University and the Distinguished Teaching Award at Stanford University.

Datar is a member of the board of directors of Novartis A.G., ICF International, T-Mobile US, and Stryker Corporation and has worked with many organizations, including Apple Computer, Boeing, DuPont, Ford, General Motors, Morgan Stanley, PepsiCo, Visa, and the World Bank. He is a member of the American Accounting Association and the Institute of Management Accountants.

Madhav V. Rajan is the Robert K. Jaedicke Professor of Accounting and Senior Associate Dean for Academic Affairs at Stanford University's Graduate School of Business. He is also Professor of Law (by courtesy) at Stanford Law School. Rajan oversees the MBA and MSx programs as well as the Marketing and Organizational Behavior faculty areas at the GSB.

Rajan received his undergraduate degree in commerce from the University of Madras, India, and his MS in accounting, MBA, and PhD degrees from Carnegie Mellon University. In 1990, his dissertation won the Alexander Henderson Award for Excellence in Economic Theory.

Rajan's primary area of research interest is the economics-based analysis of management accounting issues, especially as they relate to internal control, capital budgeting, quality management, supply chain and performance systems in firms. He has published his research in a variety of leading journals, including *The Accounting Review, Journal of Accounting Research, Management Science*, and *Review of Financial Studies*. In 2004, he received the Notable Contribution to Management Accounting Literature award. He is a coauthor of *Managerial Accounting: Making Decisions and Motivating Performance*.

Rajan has served as the Departmental Editor for Accounting at *Management Science* as well as associate editor for both the accounting and operations areas. From 2002 to 2008, Rajan served as an editor of *The Accounting Review*. Rajan has twice been a plenary speaker at the AAA Management Accounting Conference.

Rajan has received several teaching honors at Wharton and Stanford, including the David W. Hauck Award, the highest undergraduate teaching award at Wharton. He has taught in a variety of executive education programs, including the Stanford Executive Program and the National Football League Program for Managers, as well as custom programs for firms, including Genentech, Hewlett-Packard, and nVidia.

Rajan is a director of Cavium, Inc., and iShares, Inc., and a trustee of the iShares Trust.

Preface

Studying Cost Accounting is one of the best business investments a student can make. Why? Because success in any organization—from the smallest corner store to the largest multinational corporation—requires the use of cost accounting concepts and practices. Cost accounting provides key data to managers for planning and controlling, as well as costing products, services, even customers. This book focuses on how cost accounting helps managers make better decisions, as cost accountants are increasingly becoming integral members of their company's decision-making teams. In order to emphasize this prominence in decision making, we use the "different costs for different purposes" theme throughout this book. By focusing on basic concepts, analyses, uses, and procedures instead of procedures alone, we recognize cost accounting as a managerial tool for business strategy and implementation.

We also prepare students for the rewards and challenges they face in the professional cost accounting world of today and tomorrow. For example, we emphasize both the development of analytical skills such as Excel to leverage available information technology and the values and behaviors that make cost accountants effective in the workplace.

New to This Edition

Deeper Consideration of Global Issues

Businesses today have no choice but to integrate into an increasingly global ecosystem. Virtually all aspects, including supply chains, product markets, and the market for managerial talent, have become more international in their outlook. To illustrate this, we incorporate global considerations into many of the chapters. For example, Chapter 6 talks about the special challenges of budgeting in multinational companies while Chapter 23 discusses the challenges of evaluating the performance of divisions located in different countries. The opener for Chapter 17 highlights the differences in the way process flows are accounted for under U.S. and international accounting rules and the impact of these differences on companies' margins and after-tax income. Chapter 22 examines the importance of transfer pricing in minimizing the tax burden faced by multinational companies. Several new examples of management accounting applications in companies are drawn from international settings.

Increased Focus on Merchandising and Service Sectors

In keeping with the shifts in the U.S. and world economy, this edition makes greater use of merchandising and service sector examples, with corresponding de-emphasis of traditional manufacturing settings. For example, Chapter 10 illustrates linear cost functions in the context of payments for cloud computing services. Chapter 20 highlights inventory management in retail organizations and has a revised example based on a seller of sunglasses. Chapter 21 now incorporates a new running example that looks at capital budgeting in the context of a transportation company.

Greater Emphasis on Sustainability

This edition places significant emphasis on sustainability as one of the critical managerial challenges of the coming decades. Many managers are promoting the development and implementation of strategies to achieve long-term financial, social, and environmental performance as key imperatives. We highlight this in Chapter 1 and return to the theme in several subsequent chapters. Chapter 12 discusses the benefits to companies from measuring social and environmental performance and how such measures can be incorporated in a balanced scorecard. Chapter 23 provides several examples of companies that mandate disclosures and evaluate managers on environmental and social metrics. A variety of chapters, including Chapters 4, 10, and 15, contain vignettes that stress themes of energy independence, using cost analysis to reduce environmental footprints, and constructing "green" homes in a cost-effective manner.

New Cutting-Edge Topics

The pace of change in organizations continues to be rapid. The fifteenth edition of *Cost Accounting* reflects changes occurring in the role of cost accounting in organizations.

- We have introduced sustainability strategies and the methods companies use to implement sustainability with business goals.
- We have added ideas based on academic research regarding the weights to be placed on performance measures in a balanced scorecard.
- We have provided details on the transfer pricing strategies used by multinational technology firms such as Apple and Google to minimize income taxes.
- We discuss current trends in the regulation of executive compensation.
- We describe the evolution of enterprise resource planning systems and newer simplified costing systems that practice lean accounting.
- We discuss the role of accounting concepts and systems in fostering and supporting innovation and entrepreneurial activities in firms.

Streamlined Presentation

We continue to try to simplify and streamline our presentation of various topics to make it as easy as possible for students to learn the concepts, tools, and frameworks introduced in different chapters. A major change in this edition is the reorganization of Chapters 12 and 13. Chapter 13 in the fourteenth edition, "Strategy, Balanced Scorecard, and Strategic Profitability Analysis," has been moved to Chapter 12, and Chapter 12 in the fourteenth edition, "Pricing Decisions and Cost Management," has been moved to Chapter 13. As a result of the switch, Chapter 13 is the first of four chapters on cost allocation. We introduce the purposes of cost allocation in Chapter 13 and discuss cost allocation for long-run product costing and pricing. Continuing the same example, Chapter 14 discusses cost allocation for customer costing. Chapter 15 builds on the Chapter 4 example to discuss cost-allocation for support departments. Chapter 16 discusses joint cost allocation. As a result of the reorganization, we have also made major revisions in the structure and writing of each of these chapters as we discuss in detail in the next section.

Other examples of more streamlined presentations can be found in:

- Chapter 2 on the discussion of fundamental cost concepts and the managerial framework for decision making.
- Chapter 8, which has a comprehensive chart that lays out all of the variances described in Chapters 7 and 8.
- Chapter 9, which uses a single two-period example to illustrate the impact of various inventory costing methods and denominator level choices.

Selected Chapter-by-Chapter Content Changes

Thank you for your continued support of Cost Accounting. *In every new edition, we strive to update this text thoroughly. To ease your transition from the fourteenth edition, here are selected highlights of chapter changes for the fifteenth edition.*

Chapter 1 has been rewritten to include greater discussion of sustainability and why this issue has become increasingly critical for managers. It also includes more material on the importance of ethics, values, and behaviors as well as the role of the Sarbanes–Oxley act in improving the quality of financial reporting.

Chapter 2 has been updated and revised to make it easier for students to understand core cost concepts and to provide a framework for how cost accounting and cost management help managers make decisions.

Chapter 3 now includes greater managerial content, using examples from real companies to illustrate the value of cost–volume–profit analysis in managerial decision making.

Chapter 4 has been revised with the addition of substantial new material to the section discussing end-of-period adjustments for the difference between Manufacturing Overhead Control and Manufacturing Overhead Allocated. The chapter also now discusses criteria for allocating costs and relates them to real examples to highlight why managers need allocated cost information to make decisions.

Chapter 5 has been reorganized with a new section on first-stage allocation to help students understand how costs from the standard accounting classifications (salaries, depreciation, rent, and so on) are allocated to activity-cost pools. The discussion of behavioral considerations in implementing activity-based costing has been moved to a new section and integrated with other material in the chapter. There is also new material on the tradeoffs related to allocating facility-sustaining costs to products or not allocating them at all because these costs do not have good cost drivers.

Chapter 6 has been significantly rewritten with the addition of more managerial content.

Chapter 7 and 8 now provides a revised comprehensive summary of the variances in both the chapters.

Chapter 9 has been simplified substantially by a change in the integrated example from three to two periods. This retains the pedagogical value of the example while making it much easier for students to read and understand. Exhibit 9-4 and the material around it have been simplified further, and the self-study problem has also been revised.

Chapter 10 provides a practical guide to the use of various cost estimation techniques with many illustrative examples. The opening vignette has been revised, and we include a new discussion of the difference between correlation and causation, as well as a more streamlined description of inference and hypothesis testing when using regression analysis.

Chapter 11 has been revised substantially; the material on "Theory of Constraints and Throughput Contribution Margin" from Chapter 19 has now been incorporated into a new section in this chapter. The text and numbers have been rewritten to link with the Power Recreation problem already in Chapter 11. The chapter has been made easier for students to follow by replacing paragraphs with tables. Throughout, there is greater emphasis on understanding why relevant costs and revenues are important when making decisions.

The new Chapter 12 (on the balanced scorecard) has been rewritten with a completely new section on using the balanced scorecard to achieve environmental and social goals. This section describes the motivations for companies to focus on sustainability goals (such as the concept of shared value), sustainability strategies, and the methods companies use to implement sustainability with business goals. There is also a new exhibit extending the Chipset balanced scorecard to include environmental and social objectives and measures.

The new Chapter 13 focuses on cost allocation for long-run pricing decisions. The material on short-run costing and pricing (from Chapter 12 in the fourteenth edition) has been moved to Chapter 11.

Chapter 14 has been completely rewritten. It continues the same example of Astel Computers from Chapter 13 but switches the context from cost allocation for pricing to cost allocation for customer profitability. The order of presentation, the content, the examples, and the exhibits are all new. The chapter now starts with customer profitability based on customer-level costs and discusses the hierarchical operating income statement. It then motivates why corporate, division, and distribution channel costs need to be allocated and the criteria that can be used to allocate them. The chapter closes with sales variances and market-share and market-size variances (moved here from Chapter 7). The example is new and builds on the Astel Computers example that is used throughout Chapters 13 and 14.

Chapter 15 is also heavily revised, with new content, examples, and exhibits. It continues the example of Robinson Company from Chapter 4 but adds more issues around cost allocation—single rate, dual rate, and support-department cost allocations using direct, step-down, and reciprocal methods. Using the same example helps link and integrate normal costing and support department cost allocation.

Chapter 16 now provides an in-depth discussion of the rationale for joint-cost allocation and the merits and demerits of various joint-cost allocation methods. It also uses real-world examples to highlight the preferred method of joint-cost allocation in various settings.

Chapters 17 and 18 present actual costing with the material on standard costing. We have added a discussion of managerial issues when estimating equivalent units and choosing between the FIFO and weighted-average costing methods. Chapter 18 emphasizes the importance of reducing spoilage and scrap and more generally the theme of striving for a sustainable production and service environment.

As a result of moving material on the theory of constraints to Chapter 11, Chapter 19 now focuses on quality and time. We use the same Photon example throughout the chapter to discuss both quality and time-based competition. This helps to integrate and streamline the chapter.

Chapter 20 contains revised content and presentation comparing traditional and just-in-time purchasing (and a changed Exhibit 20-5). The sections on supplier evaluation, relevant costs of quality, and timely deliveries have also been rewritten, as well as the material on enterprise resource planning systems and lean accounting.

Chapter 21 has been completely redone with an entirely new example and a set of revised (and clearer) exhibits. The focus has shifted from a manufacturing setting to a transportation firm evaluating the purchase of a new hybrid-engine bus.

Chapter 22 has been significantly revised to reflect the latest developments in the controversial use of transfer prices for tax minimization by multinational corporations, with several real-world examples. The revision also highlights the costs and benefits of decentralization and the tradeoffs involved in setting a transfer pricing policy.

Chapter 23 includes a description of the use of environmental, social, and ethical objectives by companies as part of top management's pay structures. It discusses the new SEC regulations on disclosure of executive compensation and the Dodd-Frank "say on pay" rules. The chapter also incorporates research findings on the relative weight to be placed on different measures of the balanced scorecard.

Hallmark Features of Cost Accounting

- Exceptionally strong emphasis on managerial uses of cost information
- Clarity and understandability of the text
- Excellent balance in integrating modern topics with traditional coverage
- Emphasis on human behavior aspects
- Extensive use of real-world examples
- Ability to teach chapters in different sequences
- Excellent quantity, quality, and range of assignment material

The first thirteen chapters provide the essence of a one-term (quarter or semester) course. There is ample text and assignment material in the book's twenty-three chapters for a two-term course. This book can be used immediately after the student has had an introductory course in financial accounting. Alternatively, this book can build on an introductory course in managerial accounting.

Deciding on the sequence of chapters in a textbook is a challenge. Because every instructor has a unique way of organizing his or her course, we utilize a modular, flexible organization that permits a course to be custom tailored. *This organization facilitates diverse approaches to teaching and learning.*

As an example of the book's flexibility, consider our treatment of process costing. Process costing is described in Chapters 17 and 18. Instructors interested in filling out a student's perspective of costing systems can move directly from job-order costing described in Chapter 4 to Chapter 17 without interruption in the flow of material. Other instructors may want their students to delve into activity-based costing and budgeting and more decision-oriented topics early in the course. These instructors may prefer to postpone discussion of process costing.

Resources

In addition to this textbook and MyAccountingLab, a companion website is available for students at www.pearsoned.co.in/charlesthorngren.

The following resources are available for instructors in MyAccountingLab and on the Instructors Rescource Center at www.pearsoned.co.in/charlesthorngren.

- Solutions Manual
- Test Bank in word and TestGen, including algorithmic questions
- Instructors Manual
- PowerPoint Presentations
- Image Library

Acknowledgments

We are indebted to many people for their ideas and assistance. Our primary thanks go to the many academics and practitioners who have advanced our knowledge of cost accounting. The package of teaching materials we present is the work of skillful and valued team members developing some excellent end-of-chapter assignment material. Tommy Goodwin and Tola Lawal provided outstanding research assistance on technical issues and current developments. We would also like to thank the dedicated and hard-working supplement author team and Integra. The book is much better because of the efforts of these colleagues.

In shaping this edition, we would like to thank a group of colleagues who worked closely with us and the editorial team. This group provided detailed feedback and participated in focus groups that guided the direction of this edition:

Wagdy Abdallah
Seton Hall University

David Alldredge
Salt Lake Community College

Felicia Baldwin
Richard J. Daley College

Molly Brown
James Madison University

Shannon Charles
Brigham Young University

David Franz
San Francisco State University

Anna Jensen
Indiana University

Donna McGovern
Custom Business Results, Inc.

Cindy Nye
Bellevue University

Glenn Pate
Florida Atlantic University

Kelly Pope
DePaul University

Jenice Prather-Kinsey
University of Missouri

Melvin Roush
Pittsburgh State University

Karen Shastri
Pittsburgh University

Frank Stangota
Rutgers University

Patrick Stegman
College of Lake County

We would also like to extend our thanks to those

professors who provided detailed written reviews or comments on drafts. These professors include the following:

Robyn Alcock
Central Queensland University

Robert Alford
DePaul University

T. S. Amer
Northern Arizona University

David S. Baglia
Grove City College

Charles Bailey
University of Central Florida

Robert Bauman
Allan Hancock Joint Community College

David Bilker
University of Maryland, University College

Marvin Bouillon
Iowa State University

Laurie Burney
Mississippi State University

Dennis Caplan
Columbia University

A. J. Cataldo II
West Chester University

Karl E. Dahlberg
Rutgers University

Kenneth Danko
San Francisco State University

Kreag Danvers
Clarion University of Pennsylvania

Jennifer Dosch
Metro State University

Joe Dowd
Eastern Washington University

Michael Eames
Santa Clara University

Thomas D. Fields
Washington University in St. Louis

Patrick J. Fiorelli
Columbus State Community College

Michael Flores
Wichita University

Ralph Greenberg
Temple University

Donald W. Gribbin
Southern Illinois University

Ronald N. Guymon
Georgia State University

Rosalie Hallbauer
Florida International University

Robert Hartman
University of Iowa

John Haverty
St. Joseph's University

Jean Hawkins
William Jewell College

Rodger Holland
Francis Marion University

Jiunn C. Huang
San Francisco State University

Constance Hylton
George Mason University

Zafar U. Khan
Eastern Michigan University

Larry N. Killough
Virginia Polytechnic Institute & State University

Keith Kramer
Southern Oregon University

Leslie Kren
University of Wisconsin–Madison

Benjamin Lansford
Penn State University

Jay Law
Central Washington University

Sandra Lazzarini
University of Queensland

Gary J. Mann
University of Texas at El Paso

Ronald Marshall
Michigan State University

Maureen Mascha
Marquette University

Michele Matherly
Xavier University

Pam Meyer
University of Louisiana at Lafayette

Mike Morris
Notre Dame University

Cinthia Nye
Bellevue University

Marjorie Platt
Northeastern University

Roy W. Regel
University of Montana

Diane Satin
California State University East Bay

Karen Schoenebeck
Southwestern College

Pradyot K. Sen
University of Cincinnati

Gim S. Seow
University of Connecticut

Margaret Shackell-Dowel
Notre Dame University

Rebekah A. Sheely
Northeastern University

Robert J. Shepherd
University of California, Santa Cruz

Kenneth Sinclair
Lehigh University

John Stancil
Florida Southern College

Vic Stanton
California State University, Hayward

Carolyn Streuly
Marquette University

Diane L. Tanner
University of North Florida

Gerald Thalmann
North Central College

Paul Warrick
Westwood College

James Williamson
San Diego State University

Peter D. Woodlock
Youngstown State University

Sung-Soo Yoon
UCLA at Los Angeles

We also would like to thank our colleagues who helped us greatly by accuracy checking the text and supplements, including Molly Brown, Barbara Durham, Anna Jensen, and Sandra Cereola.

We thank the people at Pearson for their hard work and dedication, including Donna Battista, Ellen Geary, Nicole Sam, Roberta Sherman, Christine Donovan, and Martha LaChance. We extend special thanks to Lena Buonanno and Amy Ray, the development editors on this edition, who took charge of this project and directed it across the finish line. This book would not have been possible without their dedication and skill. Amanda Zagnoli at Integra expertly managed the production aspects of the manuscript's preparation with superb skill and tremendous dedication. We are deeply appreciative of their good spirits, loyalty, and ability to stay calm in the most hectic of times.

Appreciation also goes to the American Institute of Certified Public Accountants, the Institute of Management Accountants, the Society of Management Accountants of Canada, the Certified General Accountants Association of Canada, the Financial Executive Institute of America, and many other publishers and companies for their generous permission to quote from their publications. Problems from the Uniform CPA examinations are designated (CPA); problems from the Certified Management Accountant examination are designated (CMA); problems from the Canadian examinations administered by the Society of Management Accountants are designated (SMA); and problems from the Certified General Accountants Association are designated (CGA). Many of these problems are adapted to highlight particular points. We are grateful to the professors who contributed assignment material for this edition. Their names are indicated in parentheses at the start of their specific problems. Comments from users are welcome.

Srikant M. Datar
Madhav V. Rajan

In memory of Charles T. Horngren 1926–2011

Chuck Horngren revolutionized cost and management accounting. He loved new ideas and introduced many new concepts. He had the unique gift of explaining these concepts in simple and creative ways. He epitomized excellence and never tired of details, whether it was finding exactly the right word or working and reworking assignment materials. He combined his great intellect with genuine humility and warmth and a human touch that inspired others to do their best. He taught us many lessons about life through his amazing discipline, his ability to make everyone feel welcome, and his love of family. It was a great privilege, pleasure, and honor to have known Chuck Horngren. Few individuals will have the enormous influence that Chuck had on the accounting profession. Fewer still will be able to do it with the class and style that was his hallmark. He was unique, special, and amazing in many, many ways and, at once, a role model, teacher, mentor, and friend. He will be deeply missed.

SRIKANT M. DATAR
Harvard University

MADHAV V. RAJAN
Stanford University

To Our Families
Swati, Radhika, Gayatri, Sidharth (SD)
Gayathri, Sanjana, Anupama (MVR)

Cost Accounting
A Managerial Emphasis

The Manager and Management Accounting

1

Learning Objectives ▼

1. Distinguish financial accounting from management accounting

2. Understand how management accountants affect strategic decisions

3. Describe the set of business functions in the value chain and identify the dimensions of performance that customers are expecting of companies

4. Explain the five-step decision-making process and its role in management accounting

5. Describe three guidelines management accountants follow in supporting managers

6. Understand how management accounting fits into an organization's structure

7. Understand what professional ethics mean to management accountants

Learning Objective 1

Distinguish financial accounting

. . . . reporting on past performance to external users

from management accounting

. . . helping managers make decisions

All businesses are concerned about revenues and costs.

Managers at companies small and large must understand how revenues and costs behave or risk losing control of the performance of their firms. Managers use cost accounting information to make decisions about research and development, budgeting, production planning, pricing, and the products or services to offer customers. Sometimes these decisions involve tradeoffs.

Financial Accounting, Management Accounting, and Cost Accounting

As many of you have already learned in your financial accounting class, accounting systems are used to record economic events and transactions, such as sales and materials purchases, and process the data into information helpful to managers, sales representatives, production supervisors, and others. Processing any economic transaction means collecting, categorizing, summarizing, and analyzing. For example, costs are collected by category, such as materials, labor, and shipping. These costs are then summarized to determine a firm's total costs by month, quarter, or year. Accountants analyze the results and together with managers evaluate, say, how costs have changed relative to revenues from one period to the next. Accounting systems also provide the information found in a firm's income statement, balance sheet, statement of cash flow, and performance reports, such as the cost of serving customers or running an advertising campaign. Managers use this information to make decisions about the activities, businesses, or functional areas they oversee. For example, a report that shows an increase in sales of laptops and iPads at an Apple store may prompt Apple to hire more salespeople at that location. Understanding accounting information is essential for managers to do their jobs.

Individual managers often require the information in an accounting system to be presented or reported differently. Consider, for example, sales order information. A sales manager at Porsche may be interested in the total dollar amount of sales to determine the commissions paid to salespeople. A distribution manager at Porsche may be interested in the sales order quantities by geographic region and by customer-requested delivery dates to ensure vehicles get delivered to customers on time. A manufacturing manager at Porsche may be interested in the quantities of various products and their desired delivery dates so that he or she can develop an effective production schedule.

To simultaneously serve the needs of all three managers, Porsche creates a database, sometimes called a data warehouse or infobarn, consisting of small, detailed bits of information that can be used for multiple purposes. For instance, the sales order database will contain detailed information about a product, its selling price, quantity ordered, and delivery details (place and date) for each sales order. The database stores information in a way that allows different managers to access the information they need. Many companies are building their own enterprise resource planning (ERP) systems. An ERP system is a single database that collects data and feeds them into applications that support a company's business activities, such as purchasing, production, distribution, and sales.

Financial accounting and management accounting have different goals. As you know, **financial accounting** focuses on reporting financial information to external parties such as investors, government agencies, banks, and suppliers based on Generally Accepted Accounting Principles (GAAP). The most important way financial accounting information affects managers' decisions and actions is through compensation, which is often, in part, based on numbers in financial statements.

Management accounting is the process of measuring, analyzing, and reporting financial and nonfinancial information that helps managers make decisions to fulfill the goals of an organization. Managers use management accounting information to:

1. Develop, communicate, and implement strategies
2. Coordinate product design, production, and marketing decisions and evaluate a company's performance

Management accounting information and reports do not have to follow set principles or rules. The key questions are always (1) how will this information help managers do their jobs better, and (2) do the benefits of producing this information exceed the costs?

	Management Accounting	Financial Accounting
Purpose of information	Help managers make decisions to fulfill an organization's goals	Communicate an organization's financial position to investors, banks, regulators, and other outside parties
Primary users	Managers of the organization	External users such as investors, banks, regulators, and suppliers
Focus and emphasis	Future-oriented (budget for 2014 prepared in 2013)	Past-oriented (reports on 2013 performance prepared in 2014)
Rules of measurement and reporting	Internal measures and reports do not have to follow GAAP but are based on cost-benefit analysis	Financial statements must be prepared in accordance with GAAP and be certified by external, independent auditors
Time span and type of reports	Varies from hourly information to 15 to 20 years, with financial and nonfinancial reports on products, departments, territories, and strategies	Annual and quarterly financial reports, primarily on the company as a whole
Behavioral implications	Designed to influence the behavior of managers and other employees	Primarily reports economic events but also influences behavior because manager's compensation is often based on reported financial results

Exhibit 1-1

Major Differences Between Management Accounting and Financial Accounting

3

Exhibit 1-1 summarizes the major differences between management accounting and financial accounting. Note, however, that reports such as balance sheets, income statements, and statements of cash flows are common to both management accounting and financial accounting.

Cost accounting provides information for both management accounting and financial accounting professionals. **Cost accounting** is the process of measuring, analyzing, and reporting financial and nonfinancial information related to the costs of acquiring or using resources in an organization. For example, calculating the cost of a product is a cost accounting function that meets both the financial accountant's inventory-valuation needs and the management accountant's decision-making needs (such as deciding how to price products and choosing which products to promote). However, today most accounting professionals take the perspective that cost information is part of the management accounting information collected to make management decisions. Thus, the distinction between management accounting and cost accounting is not so clear-cut, and we often use these terms interchangeably in the book.

Businesspeople frequently use the term *cost management*. Unfortunately, the term does not have an exact definition. In this book we use **cost management** to describe the activities managers undertake to use resources in a way that increases a product's value to customers and achieves an organization's goals. In other words, cost management is not only about reducing costs. Cost management also includes making decisions to incur additional costs—for example, to improve customer satisfaction and quality and to develop new products—with the goal of enhancing revenues and profits. Whether or not to enter new markets, implement new organizational processes, and change product designs are also cost management decisions. Information from accounting systems helps managers to manage costs, but the information and the accounting systems themselves are not cost management.

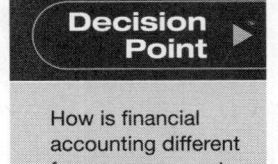

Decision Point ▶

How is financial accounting different from management accounting?

Strategic Decisions and the Management Accountant

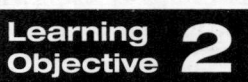

Learning Objective 2

Understand how management accountants help firms make strategic decisions

. . . they provide information about the sources of competitive advantages

A company's **strategy** specifies how the organization matches its own capabilities with the opportunities in the marketplace. In other words, strategy describes how an organization will compete and the opportunities its managers should seek and pursue. Businesses follow one of two broad strategies. Some companies, such as Southwest Airlines and Vanguard (the mutual fund company), follow a cost leadership strategy. They have been profitable and have grown over the years by providing quality products or services at low prices and by judiciously managing their costs. Other companies such as Apple and the pharmaceutical giant Johnson & Johnson follow a product differentiation strategy. They generate their profits and growth because they offer differentiated or unique products or services that appeal to their customers and are often priced higher than the less-popular products or services of their competitors.

Deciding between these strategies is a critical part of what managers do. Management accountants work closely with managers in various departments to formulate strategies by providing information about the sources of competitive advantage, such as (1) the company's cost, productivity, or efficiency advantage relative to competitors or (2) the premium prices a company can charge relative to the costs of adding features that make its products or services distinctive. **Strategic cost management** describes cost management that specifically focuses on strategic issues.

Management accounting information helps managers formulate strategy by answering questions such as the following:

- *Who are our most important customers, and how can we be competitive and deliver value to them?* After Amazon.com's success selling books online, management accountants at Barnes & Noble outlined the costs and benefits of several alternative approaches for enhancing the company's information technology infrastructure and developing the capability to sell books online. A similar cost–benefit analysis led Toyota to build flexible computer-integrated manufacturing plants that enable it to use the same equipment efficiently to produce a variety of cars in response to changing customer tastes.

- *What substitute products exist in the marketplace, and how do they differ from our product in terms of features, price, cost, and quality?* Hewlett-Packard, for example, designs, costs, and prices new printers after comparing the functionality and quality of its printers to other printers available in the marketplace.

- *What is our most critical capability? Is it technology, production, or marketing? How can we leverage it for new strategic initiatives?* Kellogg Company, for example, uses the reputation of its brand to introduce new types of cereals with high profit margins.

- *Will adequate cash be available to fund the strategy, or will additional funds need to be raised?* Procter & Gamble, for example, issued new debt and equity to fund its strategic acquisition of Gillette, a maker of shaving products.

The best-designed strategies and the best-developed capabilities are useless unless they are effectively executed. In the next section, we describe how management accountants help managers take actions that create value for their customers.

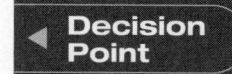

◀ Decision Point

How do management accountants support strategic decisions?

Value-Chain and Supply-Chain Analysis and Key Success Factors

Customers demand much more than just a fair price; they expect quality products (goods or services) delivered in a timely way. The entire customer experience determines the value a customer derives from a product. In this section, we explore how a company goes about creating this value.

Learning Objective 3

Describe the set of business functions in the value chain and identify the dimensions of performance that customers are expecting of companies

. . . R&D, design, production, marketing, distribution, and customer service supported by administration to achieve cost and efficiency, quality, time, and innovation

Value-Chain Analysis

The **value chain** is the sequence of business functions by which a product is made progressively more useful to customers. Exhibit 1-2 shows six primary business functions: research and development (R&D), design of products and processes, production, marketing, distribution, and customer service. We illustrate these business functions with Sony Corporation's television division.

1. **Research and development (R&D)**—generating and experimenting with ideas related to new products, services, or processes. At Sony, this function includes research on alternative television signal transmission and on the picture quality of different shapes and thicknesses of television screens.

2. **Design of products and processes**—detailed planning, engineering, and testing of products and processes. Design at Sony includes deciding on the number of component parts in a television set and determining the effect alternative product designs will have on the set's quality and manufacturing costs. Some representations of the value chain collectively refer to the first two steps as technology development.[1]

---

[1]M. Porter, Competitive Advantage (New York: Free Press, 1998).

3. **Production**—procuring, transporting, and storing ("inbound logistics") and coordinating and assembling ("operations") resources to produce a product or deliver a service. The production of a Sony television set includes the procurement and assembly of the electronic parts, the cabinet, and the packaging used for shipping.

4. **Marketing (including sales)**—promoting and selling products or services to customers or prospective customers. Sony markets its televisions at tradeshows, via advertisements in newspapers and magazines, on the Internet, and through its sales force.

5. **Distribution**—processing orders and shipping products or services to customers ("outbound logistics"). Distribution for Sony includes shipping to retail outlets, catalog vendors, direct sales via the Internet, and other channels through which customers purchase new televisions.

6. **Customer service**—providing after-sales service to customers. Sony provides customer service on its televisions in the form of customer-help telephone lines, support on the Internet, and warranty repair work.

In addition to the six primary business functions, Exhibit 1-2 shows an administration function, which includes accounting and finance, human resource management, and information technology and supports the six primary business functions. When discussing the value chain in subsequent chapters of the book, we include the administration function within the primary functions. For example, included in the marketing function is the function of analyzing, reporting, and accounting for resources spent in different marketing channels, whereas the production function includes the human resource management function of training frontline workers. Each of these business functions is essential to companies satisfying their customers and keeping them satisfied (and loyal) over time.

To implement their corporate strategies, companies such as Sony and Procter & Gamble use **customer relationship management (CRM),** a strategy that integrates people and technology in all business functions to deepen relationships with customers, partners, and distributors. CRM initiatives use technology to coordinate all customer-facing activities (such as marketing, sales calls, distribution, and after-sales support) and the design and production activities necessary to get products to customers.

Different companies create value in different ways. Lowe's (the home-improvement retailer) does so by focusing on cost and efficiency. Toyota Motor Company does so by focusing on quality. Fast response times at eBay create quality for the online auction giant's customers, whereas innovation is primarily what creates value for the customers of the biotech company Roche-Genentech. The Italian apparel company Gucci creates value for its customers by building a prestigious brand. As a result, at different times and in different industries, one or more of these functions is more critical than others. For example, a company such as Roche-Genentech will emphasize R&D and the design of products and processes. In contrast, a company such as Gucci will focus on marketing, distribution, and customer service to build its brand.

| **Exhibit 1-2** | Different Parts of the Value Chain |

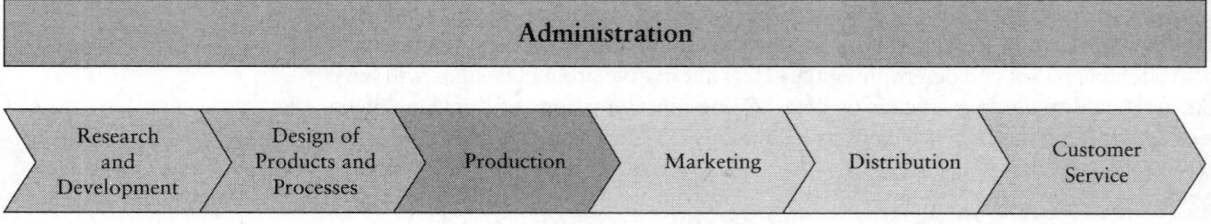

Exhibit 1-2 depicts the usual order in which different business-function activities physically occur. Do not, however, interpret Exhibit 1-2 to mean that managers should proceed sequentially through the value chain when planning and managing their activities. Companies gain (in terms of cost, quality, and the speed with which new products are developed) if two or more of the individual business functions of the value chain work concurrently as a team. For example, a company's production, marketing, distribution, and customer service personnel can often reduce a company's total costs by providing input for design decisions.

Managers track the costs incurred in each value-chain category. Their goal is to reduce costs and to improve efficiency. Management accounting information helps managers make cost–benefit tradeoffs. For example, is it cheaper to buy products from a vendor or produce them in-house? How does investing resources in design and manufacturing reduce costs of marketing and customer service?

Supply-Chain Analysis

The parts of the value chain associated with producing and delivering a product or service—production and distribution—are referred to as the *supply chain*. The **supply chain** describes the flow of goods, services, and information from the initial sources of materials and services to the delivery of products to consumers, regardless of whether those activities occur in one organization or in multiple organizations. Consider Coke and Pepsi: Many companies play a role in bringing these products to consumers as the supply chain in Exhibit 1-3 shows. Part of cost management emphasizes integrating and coordinating activities across all companies in the supply chain to improve their performance and reduce costs. For example, to reduce materials-handling costs, both the Coca-Cola Company and Pepsi Bottling Group require their suppliers (such as plastic and aluminum companies and sugar refiners) to frequently deliver small quantities of materials directly to their production floors. Similarly, to reduce inventory levels in the supply chain, Walmart requires its suppliers, such as Coca-Cola, to directly manage its inventory of products to ensure the right amount of them are in its stores at all times.

Key Success Factors

Customers want companies to use the value chain and supply chain to deliver ever-improving levels of performance when it comes to several (or even all) of the following:

- **Cost and efficiency**—Companies face continuous pressure to reduce the cost of the products they sell. To calculate and manage the cost of products, managers must first understand the activities (such as setting up machines or distributing products) that cause costs to arise as well as monitor the marketplace to determine the prices customers

---

Exhibit 1-3   Supply Chain for a Cola Bottling Company

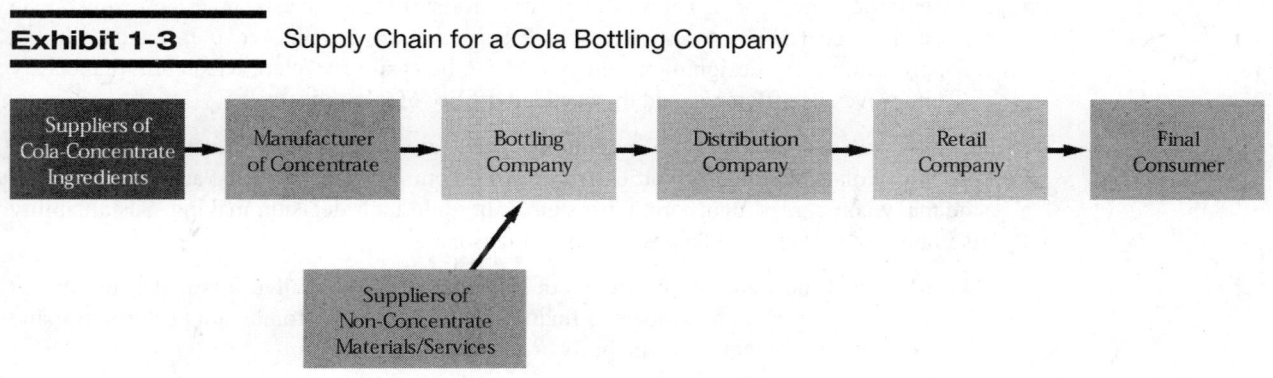

are willing to pay for products or services. Management accounting information helps managers calculate a target cost for a product by subtracting from the "target price" the operating income per unit of product that the company wants to earn. To achieve the target cost, managers eliminate some activities (such as rework) and reduce the costs of performing activities in all value-chain functions—from initial R&D to customer service. Many U.S. companies have cut costs by outsourcing some of their business functions. Nike, for example, has moved its manufacturing operations to China and Mexico, and Microsoft and IBM are increasingly doing their software development in Spain, Eastern Europe, and India.

- **Quality**—Customers expect high levels of quality. **Total quality management (TQM)** is an integrative philosophy of management for continuously improving the quality of products and processes. Managers who implement TQM believe that each and every person in the value chain is responsible for delivering products and services that exceed customers' expectations. Using TQM, companies design products or services to meet customer needs and wants, to make these products with zero (or very few) defects and waste, and to minimize inventories. Managers use management accounting information to evaluate the costs and revenue benefits of TQM initiatives.

- **Time**—Time has many dimensions. Two of the most important dimensions are new-product development time and customer-response time. New-product development time is the time it takes for companies to create new products and bring them to market. The increasing pace of technological innovation has led to shorter product life cycles and more rapid introduction of new products. To make new-product development decisions, managers need to understand the costs and benefits of a product over its life cycle.

  Customer-response time describes the speed at which an organization responds to customer requests. To increase the satisfaction of their customers, organizations need to meet their promised delivery dates as well as reduce their delivery times. Bottlenecks are the primary cause of delays. For example, a bottleneck can occur when the work to be performed on a machine exceeds its available capacity. To deliver the product on time, managers need to increase the capacity of the machine to produce more output. Management accounting information can help managers quantify the costs and benefits of doing so.

- **Innovation**—A constant flow of innovative products or services is the basis for the ongoing success of a company. Managers rely on management accounting information to evaluate alternative investment and R&D decisions.

- **Sustainability**—Companies are increasingly applying the key success factors of cost and efficiency, quality, time, and innovation to promote **sustainability**—the development and implementation of strategies to achieve long-term financial, social, and environmental goals. The sustainability efforts of the Japanese copier company Ricoh include energy conservation, resource conservation, product recycling, and pollution prevention. By designing products that can be easily recycled, Ricoh simultaneously improves its efficiency and the cost and quality of its products.

The interest in sustainability appears to be intensifying among companies. General Electric, Poland Springs (a bottled-water manufacturer), and Hewlett-Packard are among the many companies incorporating sustainability into their decision making. Sustainability is important to these companies for several reasons:

- More and more investors care about sustainability. These investors make investment decisions based on a company's financial, social, and environmental performance and raise questions about sustainability at shareholder meetings.

- Companies that emphasize sustainability find that sustainability goals attract and inspire employees.

- Customers prefer the products of companies with good sustainability records and boycott companies with poor sustainability records.

- Society and activist nongovernmental organizations, in particular, monitor the sustainability performance of firms and take legal action against those that violate environmental laws. Countries with fast-growing economies, such as China and India, are now either requiring or encouraging companies to develop and report on their sustainability initiatives.

Management accountants help managers track the key success factors of their firms as well as those of their competitors. Competitive information such as this serves as a *benchmark* managers use to continuously improve their operations. Examples of continuous improvement include Southwest Airlines' efforts to increase the number of its flights that arrive on time, eBay's efforts to improve the access its customers have to online auctions, and Lowe's efforts to continuously reduce the cost of its home-improvement products. Sometimes, more fundamental changes in operations, such as redesigning a manufacturing process to reduce costs, may be necessary. To successfully implement their strategies, firms have to do more than analyze their value chains and supply chains and execute key success factors. They also have to have good decision-making processes.

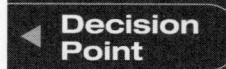

Decision Point

How do companies add value, and what are the dimensions of performance that customers are expecting of companies?

Decision Making, Planning, and Control: The Five-Step Decision-Making Process

We illustrate a five-step decision-making process using the example of the *Daily News,* a newspaper in Mumbai. Subsequent chapters of the book describe how managers use this five-step decision-making process to make many different types of decisions.

The *Daily News* differentiates itself from its competitors by using (1) highly respected journalists who write well-researched news articles, (2) color to enhance attractiveness to readers and advertisers, and (3) a Web site that delivers up-to-the-minute news, interviews, and analyses. The newspaper has the following resources to deliver on this strategy: an automated, computer-integrated, state-of-the-art printing facility; a Web-based information technology infrastructure; and a distribution network that is one of the best in the newspaper industry.

To keep up with steadily increasing production costs, Anita Guha, manager of the *Daily News,* needs to increase the company's revenues. To decide what she should do, Anita works through the five-step decision-making process.

1. **Identify the problem and uncertainties.** Anita has two main choices:
   a. increase the selling price of the newspaper or
   b. increase the rate per page charged to advertisers.
   The key uncertainty is the effect any increase in prices or rates will have on demand. A decrease in demand could offset the price or rate increases and lead to lower rather than higher revenues.

2. **Obtain information.** Gathering information before making a decision helps managers gain a better understanding of uncertainties. Anita asks her marketing manager to talk to some representative readers to gauge their reaction to an increase in the newspaper's selling price. She asks her advertising sales manager to talk to current and potential advertisers to assess demand for advertising. She also reviews the effect that past price

Learning Objective 4

Explain the five-step decision-making process

. . . identify the problem and uncertainties; obtain information; make predictions about the future; make decisions by choosing among alternatives; implement the decision, evaluate performance, and learn

and its role in management accounting

. . . planning and control of operations and activities

increases had on readership. Amit Choksi, management accountant at the *Daily News,* presents information about the effect of past increases or decreases in advertising rates on advertising revenues. He also collects and analyzes information on advertising rates competing newspapers and other media outlets charge.

3. **Make predictions about the future.** Based on this information, Anita makes predictions about the future. She concludes that increasing prices would upset readers and decrease readership. She has a different view about advertising rates. She expects a marketwide increase in advertising rates and believes that increasing rates will have little effect on the number of advertising pages sold.

   Anita recognizes that making predictions requires judgment. She looks for biases in her thinking. Has she correctly judged reader sentiment or is the negative publicity of a price increase overly influencing her decision making? How sure is she that competitors will increase their advertising rates? Is her thinking in this respect biased by how competitors have responded in the past? Have circumstances changed? How confident is she that her sales representatives can convince advertisers to pay higher rates? After retesting her assumptions and reviewing her thinking, Anita feels comfortable with her predictions and judgments.

4. **Make decisions by choosing among alternatives.** When making decisions, a company's strategy serves as a vital guidepost for the many individuals in different parts of the organization making decisions at different times. Consistent strategies provide a common purpose for these disparate decisions. Only if these decisions can be aligned with its strategy will an organization achieve its goals. Without this alignment, the company's decisions will be uncoordinated, pull the organization in different directions, and produce inconsistent results.

   Consistent with a product differentiation strategy, Anita decides to increase advertising rates by 4% to ₹52,000 per page in March 2014, but not increase the selling price of the newspaper. She is confident that the *Daily News*'s distinctive style and Web presence will increase readership, creating value for advertisers. She communicates the new advertising rate schedule to the sales department. Amit estimates advertising revenues of ₹4,16,00,000 (₹52,000 per page × 800 pages predicted to be sold in March 2014).

Steps 1 through 4 are collectively referred to as *planning.* **Planning** consists of selecting an organization's goals and strategies, predicting results under various alternative ways of achieving those goals, deciding how to attain the desired goals, and communicating the goals and how to achieve them to the entire organization. Management accountants serve as business partners in these planning activities because they understand the key success factors and what creates value.

The most important planning tool when implementing strategy is a *budget.* A **budget** is the quantitative expression of a proposed plan of action by management and is an aid to coordinating what needs to be done to execute that plan. For March 2014, the budgeted advertising revenue of the *Daily News* equals ₹4,16,00,000. The full budget for March 2014 includes budgeted circulation revenue and the production, distribution, and customer-service costs to achieve the company's sales goals; the anticipated cash flows; and the potential financing needs. Because multiple departments help prepare the budget, personnel throughout the organization have to coordinate and communicate with one another as well as with the company's suppliers and customers.

5. **Implement the decision, evaluate performance, and learn.** Managers at the *Daily News* take action to implement the March 2014 budget. The firm's management accountants then collect information on how the company's actual performance compares to planned or budgeted performance (also referred to as scorekeeping). The information on the actual results is different from the *predecision* planning information

Anita collected in Step 2, which enabled her to better understand uncertainties, to make predictions, and to make a decision. Allowing managers to compare actual performance to budgeted performance is the *control* or *postdecision* role of information. **Control** comprises taking actions that implement the planning decisions, evaluating past performance, and providing feedback and learning to help future decision making.

Measuring actual performance informs managers how well they and their subunits are doing. Linking rewards to performance helps motivate managers. These rewards are both intrinsic (recognition for a job well done) and extrinsic (salary, bonuses, and promotions linked to performance). We discuss this in more detail in a later chapter (Chapter 23). A budget serves as much as a control tool as a planning tool. Why? Because a budget is a benchmark against which actual performance can be compared.

Consider performance evaluation at the *Daily News*. During March 2014, the newspaper sold advertising, issued invoices, and received payments. The accounting system recorded these invoices and receipts. Exhibit 1-4 shows the *Daily News*'s advertising revenues for March 2014. This performance report indicates that 760 pages of advertising (40 pages fewer than the budgeted 800 pages) were sold. The average rate per page was ₹50,800, compared with the budgeted ₹52,000 rate, yielding actual advertising revenues of ₹3,86,08,000. The actual advertising revenues were ₹29,92,000 less than the budgeted ₹4,16,00,000. Observe how managers use both financial and nonfinancial information, such as pages of advertising, to evaluate performance.

The performance report in Exhibit 1-4 spurs investigation and **learning,** which involves examining past performance (the control function) and systematically exploring alternative ways to make better-informed decisions and plans in the future. Learning can lead to changes in goals, strategies, the ways decision alternatives are identified, and the range of information collected when making predictions and sometimes can lead to changes in managers.

The performance report in Exhibit 1-4 would prompt the management accountant to raise several questions directing the attention of managers to problems and opportunities. Is the strategy of differentiating the *Daily News* from other newspapers attracting more readers? Did the marketing and sales department make sufficient efforts to convince advertisers that, even at the higher rate of ₹52,000 per page, advertising in the *Daily News* was a good buy? Why was the actual average rate per page (₹50,800) less than the budgeted rate (₹52,000)? Did some sales representatives offer discounted rates? Did economic conditions cause the decline in advertising revenues? Are revenues falling because editorial and production standards have declined? Are more readers getting their news online?

Answers to these questions could prompt the newspaper's publisher to take subsequent actions, including, for example, adding more sales personnel, making changes in editorial policy, or putting more resources into expanding its presence online and on mobile devices. Good implementation requires the marketing, editorial, and production departments to work together and coordinate their actions.

	Actual Result (1)	Budgeted Amount (2)	Difference: (Actual Result – Budgeted Amount) (3) = (1) – (2)	Differences Percentage of Budgeted Amount (3) = (1) ÷ (2)
Advertising pages sold	760 pages	800 pages	40 pages unfavorable	5.0% Unfavorable
Average rate per page	₹50,800	₹52,000	₹1,200 unfavorable	2.3% Unfavorable
Advertising revenues	₹3,86,08,000	₹4,16,00,000	₹29,92,000 unfavorable	7.2% Unfavorable

Exhibit 1-4

Performance Report of Advertising Revenues at the *Daily News* for March 2014

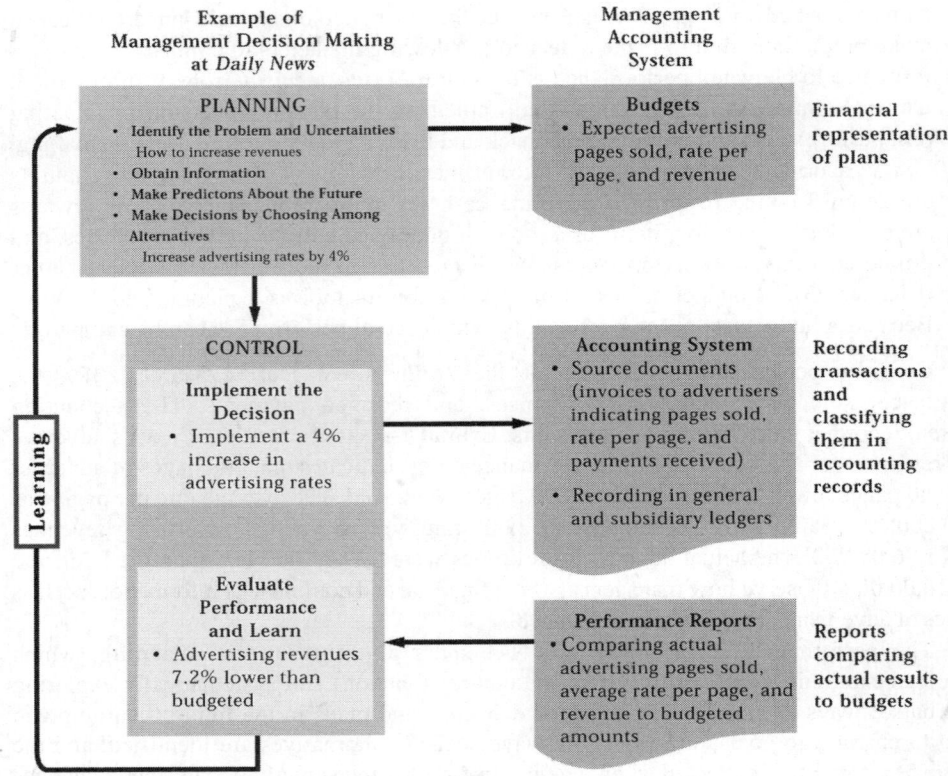

The management accountant could go further by identifying the specific advertisers that cut back or stopped advertising after the rate increase went into effect. Managers could then decide when and how sales representatives should follow up with these advertisers.

Planning and control activities must be flexible enough so that managers can seize opportunities unforeseen at the time the plan was formulated. In no case should control mean that managers cling to a plan when unfolding events (such as a sensational news story) indicate that actions not encompassed by that plan (such as spending more money to cover the story) would offer better results for the company (from higher newspaper sales).

The left side of Exhibit 1-5 provides an overview of the decision-making processes at the *Daily News*. The right side of the exhibit highlights how the management accounting system aids in decision making.

**Decision
Point** ▶

How do managers
make decisions to
implement strategy?

**Learning
Objective 5**

Describe three guide-
lines management
accountants follow in
supporting managers

. . . employing a
cost-benefit approach,
recognizing behavioral
as well as technical
considerations, and
calculating different
costs for different
purposes

Key Management Accounting Guidelines

Three guidelines help management accountants provide the most value to the strategic and operational decision making of their companies: (1) employ a cost–benefit approach, (2) give full recognition to behavioral and technical considerations, and (3) use different costs for different purposes.

Cost–Benefit Approach

Managers continually face resource-allocation decisions, such as whether to purchase a new software package or hire a new employee. They use a **cost–benefit approach** when making these decisions. Managers should spend resources if the expected benefits to the company exceed the expected costs. Managers rely on management accounting information to quantify expected benefits and expected costs (although all benefits and costs are not easy to quantify).

Consider the installation of a consulting company's first budgeting system. Previously, the company used historical recordkeeping and little formal planning. A major benefit of installing a budgeting system is that it compels managers to plan ahead, compare actual to budgeted information, learn, and take corrective action. Although the system leads to better decisions and consequently better company performance, the exact benefits are not easy to measure. On the cost side, some costs, such as investments in software and training, are easier to quantify. Others, such as the time spent by managers on the budgeting process, are more difficult to quantify. Regardless, senior managers compare expected benefits and expected costs, exercise judgment, and reach a decision, in this case to install the budgeting system.

Behavioral and Technical Considerations

When utilizing the cost–benefit approach, managers need to keep in mind a number of technical and behavioral considerations. The technical considerations help managers make wise economic decisions by providing them with the desired information (for example, costs in various value-chain categories) in an appropriate format (for example, actual results versus budgeted amounts) and at the preferred frequency (for example, weekly or quarterly). However, management is not confined to technical matters. Management is primarily a human activity that should focus on encouraging individuals to do their jobs better. Budgets have a behavioral effect by motivating and rewarding employees for achieving an organization's goals. So, when workers underperform, for example, behavioral considerations suggest that managers need to discuss ways to improve their performance with them rather than just sending them a report highlighting their underperformance.

Different Costs for Different Purposes

This book emphasizes that managers use alternative ways to compute costs in different decision-making situations because there are different costs for different purposes. A cost concept used for the purposes of external reporting may not be appropriate for internal, routine reporting.

Consider the advertising costs associated with Microsoft Corporation's launch of a product with a useful life of several years. For external reporting to shareholders, Generally Accepted Accounting Principles (GAAP) require television advertising costs for this product to be fully expensed in the income statement in the year they are incurred. However, the television advertising costs could be capitalized and then amortized or written off as expenses over several years if Microsoft's management team believed that doing so would more accurately and fairly measure the performance of the managers that launched the new product.

We now discuss the relationships and reporting responsibilities among managers and management accountants within a company's organization structure.

> **◀ Decision Point**
>
> What guidelines do management accountants use?

Organization Structure and the Management Accountant

We focus first on broad management functions and then look at how the management accounting and finance functions support managers.

Line and Staff Relationships

Organizations distinguish between line management and staff management. **Line management**, such as production, marketing, and distribution management, is directly responsible for achieving the goals of the organization. For example, managers of manufacturing divisions are responsible for meeting particular levels of budgeted operating income, product quality and safety, and compliance with environmental laws. Similarly, the pediatrics department in a hospital is responsible for quality of service, costs, and patient billings. **Staff management**, such as management accountants and information technology and human-resources management, provides advice, support, and assistance to line management. A plant manager (a line function) may be responsible for investing in new equipment. A management accountant (a staff function) works as a business partner of the plant manager by preparing detailed operating-cost comparisons of alternative pieces of equipment.

Increasingly, organizations such as Honda and Dell are using teams to achieve their objectives. These teams include both line and staff management so that all inputs into a decision are available simultaneously.

The Chief Financial Officer and the Controller

The **chief financial officer (CFO)**—also called the **finance director** in many countries—is the executive responsible for overseeing the financial operations of an organization. The responsibilities of the CFO vary among organizations, but they usually include the following areas:

- **Controllership**—provides financial information for reports to managers and shareholders and oversees the overall operations of the accounting system.
- **Treasury**—oversees banking and short- and long-term financing, investments, and cash management.
- **Risk management**—manages the financial risk of interest-rate and exchange-rate changes and derivatives management.
- **Taxation**—plans income taxes, sales taxes, and international taxes.
- **Investor relations**—communicates with, responds to, and interacts with shareholders.
- **Strategic planning**—defining strategy and allocating resources to implement strategy.

An independent internal audit function reviews and analyzes financial and other records to attest to the integrity of the organization's financial reports and to adherence to its policies and procedures.

The **controller** (also called the *chief accounting officer*) is the financial executive primarily responsible for management accounting and financial accounting. This book focuses on the controller as the chief management accounting executive. Modern controllers have no line authority except over their own departments. Yet the controller exercises control over the entire organization in a special way. By reporting and interpreting relevant data, the controller influences the behavior of all employees and helps line managers make better decisions.

Exhibit 1-6 shows an organization chart of the CFO and the corporate controller at Nike, the leading footwear and sports apparel company. The CFO is a staff manager who reports to and supports the chief executive officer (CEO). As in most organizations, the corporate controller at Nike reports to the CFO. Nike also has regional controllers who support regional managers in the major geographic regions in which the company operates, such as the United States, Asia Pacific, Latin America, and Europe. Because they support the activities of the regional manager, for example, by managing budgets and analyzing costs, regional

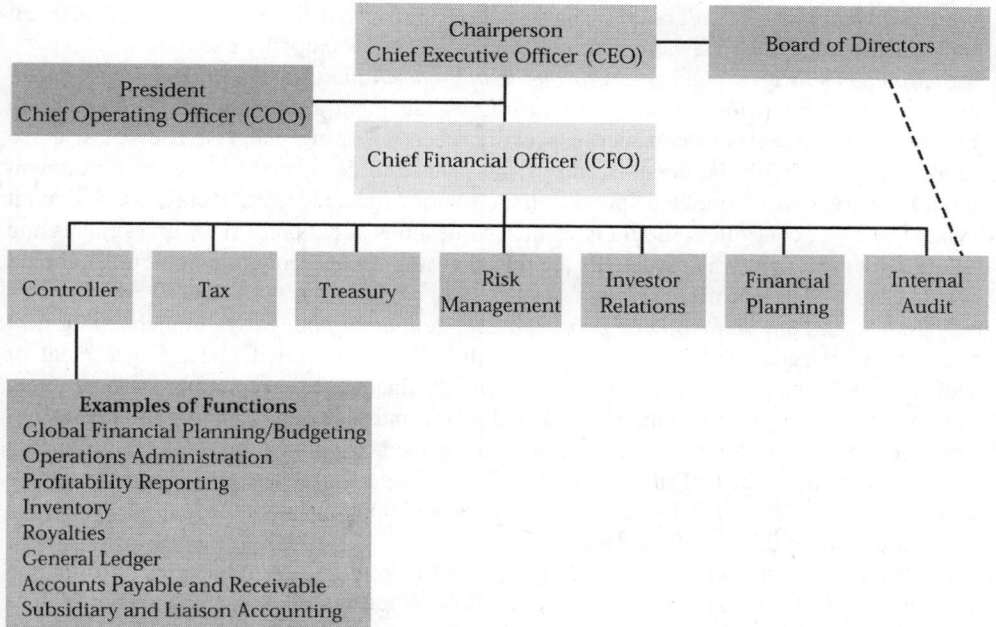

controllers report to the regional manager rather than the corporate controller. At the same time, to align accounting policies and practices for the whole organization, regional controllers have a functional (often called a dotted-line) responsibility to the corporate controller. Individual countries sometimes have a country controller.

Organization charts such as the one in Exhibit 1-6 show formal reporting relationships. In most organizations, there also are informal relationships that must be understood when managers attempt to implement their decisions. Examples of informal relationships are friendships among managers (friendships of a professional or personal kind) and the personal preferences of top management about the managers they rely on when making decisions.

Think about what managers do to design and implement strategies and the organization structures within which they operate. Then think about the management accountants' and controllers' roles. It should be clear that the successful management accountant must have technical and analytical competence *as well as* behavioral and interpersonal skills.

Management Accounting Beyond the Numbers[2]

To people outside the profession, it may seem like accountants are just "numbers people." It is true that most accountants are adept financial managers, yet their skills do not stop there. The successful management accountant possesses several skills and characteristics that reach well beyond basic analytical abilities.

Management accountants must work well in cross-functional teams and as a business partner. In addition to being technically competent, the best management accountants

---

[2] United States Senate Permanent Subcommittee on Investigations. *JPMorgan Chase Whale Trades: A Case History of Derivatives Risks and Abuses.* Washington, DC: Government Printing Office, March 15, 2013; Wendy Garling, "Winning the Transformation Battle at the Defense Finance and Accounting Service," Balanced Scorecard Report, May–June 2007; Nixon, Bill, Burns, John, and Mostafa Jazayeri. The role of management accounting in new product design and development decisions. Volume 9, Issue 1. London: Chartered Institute of Management Accountants, November 2011; and Ben Worthen, "H-P Says It Was Duped, Takes $8.8 Billion Charge," The Wall Street Journal (November 12, 2012).

work well in teams, learn about business issues, understand the motivations of different individuals, respect the views of their colleagues, and show empathy and trust.

Management accountants must promote fact-based analysis and make tough-minded, critical judgments without being adversarial. Management accountants must raise tough questions for managers to consider, especially when preparing budgets. They must do so thoughtfully and with the intent of improving plans and decisions. Before the investment bank JP Morgan lost more than ₹60 billion on "exotic" financial investments (credit-default swaps) in 2012, controllers should have raised questions about these risky investments and the fact that the firm was essentially betting that improving economic conditions abroad would earn it a large profit.

They must lead and motivate people to change and be innovative. Implementing new ideas, however good they may be, is difficult. When the United States Department of Defense (DoD) began consolidating more than 320 finance and accounting systems into a common platform, the accounting services director and his team of management accountants held meetings to make sure everyone in the agency understood the goal for such a change. Ultimately, the DoD aligned each individual's performance with the transformative change and introduced incentive pay to encourage personnel to adopt the platform and drive innovation within this new framework.

They must communicate clearly, openly, and candidly. Communicating information is a large part of a management accountant's job. When premium car companies such as Rolls Royce and Porsche design new models, management accountants work closely with engineers to ensure that each new car supports a carefully defined balance of commercial, engineering, and financial criteria. These efforts are successful because management accountants clearly communicate the information that multi-disciplinary teams need to deliver new innovations profitably.

They must have a strong sense of integrity. Management accountants must never succumb to pressure from managers to manipulate financial information. They must always remember that their primary commitment is to the organization and its shareholders.

Decision Point ▶

Where does the management accounting function fit into an organization's structure?

Professional Ethics

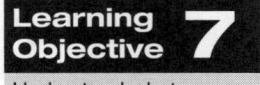

Learning Objective 7

Understand what professional ethics mean to management accountants

. . . for example, management accountants must maintain integrity and credibility in every aspect of their job

At no time has the focus on ethical conduct been sharper than it is today. Corporate scandals at Arthur Andersen, a public accounting firm; Countrywide Financial, a home mortgage company; Enron, an oil and gas company; Lehman Brothers, an investment bank; Olympus, a Japanese optical equipment company; Satyam Computers in India; and Bernie Madoff Investment Securities have seriously eroded the public's confidence in corporations. All employees in a company must comply with the organization's—and more broadly, society's—expectations of ethical standards.

Ethics are the foundation of a well-functioning economy. When ethics are weak, suppliers bribe executives to win supply contracts rather than invest in improving quality or lowering costs. Because customers have very little confidence in the quality of products produced, they can become reluctant to buy them, causing markets to fail. Costs are higher because of higher prices paid to suppliers and fewer products being produced and sold. Investors are unsure about the integrity of financial reports, affecting their ability to make investment decisions, resulting in a reluctance to invest and a misallocation of resources. The scandals at Ahold, an international supermarket operator, and Tyco International, a diversified global manufacturing company, and others make clear that value is quickly destroyed by unethical behavior.

Institutional Support

Accountants have special ethical obligations, given that they are responsible for the integrity of the financial information provided to internal and external parties. The Sarbanes–Oxley legislation in the United States was passed in 2002 in response to a series of corporate scandals. The act focused on improving internal control, corporate governance, monitoring of managers, and disclosure practices of public corporations. These regulations impose tough ethical standards and criminal penalties on managers and accountants who don't meet the standards. The regulations also delineate a process for employees to report violations of illegal and unethical acts (these employees are called whistleblowers).

As part of the Sarbanes–Oxley Act, CEOs and CFOs must certify that the financial statements of their firms fairly represent the results of their operations. In order to increase the independence of auditors, the act empowers the audit committee of a company's board of directors (which is composed exclusively of independent directors) to hire, compensate, and terminate the public accounting firm to audit a company. To reduce their financial dependency on their individual clients and increase their independence, the act limits auditing firms from providing consulting, tax, and other advisory services to the companies they are auditing. The act also authorizes the Public Company Accounting Oversight Board to oversee, review, and investigate the work of the auditors.

Professional accounting organizations, which represent management accountants in many countries, offer certification programs indicating that those who have completed them have management accounting and financial management technical knowledge and expertise. These organizations also advocate high ethical standards. In the United States, the Institute of Management Accountants (IMA) has also issued ethical guidelines. Exhibit 1-7 presents the IMA's guidance on issues relating to competence, confidentiality, integrity, and credibility. To provide support to its members to act ethically at all times, the IMA runs an ethics hotline service. Members can call professional counselors at the IMA's

---

Exhibit 1-7

Ethical Behavior for Practitioners of Management Accounting and Financial Management

Practitioners of management accounting and financial management have an obligation to the public, their profession, the organizations they serve, and themselves to maintain the highest standards of ethical conduct. In recognition of this obligation, the Institute of Management Accountants has promulgated the following standards of ethical professional practice. Adherence to these standards, both domestically and internationally, is integral to achieving the Objectives of Management Accounting. Practitioners of management accounting and financial management shall not commit acts contrary to these standards nor shall they condone the commission of such acts by others within their organizations.

IMA STATEMENT OF ETHICAL PROFESSIONAL PRACTICE

Practitioners of management accounting and financial management shall behave ethically. A commitment to ethical professional practice includes overarching principles that express our values and standards that guide our conduct.

PRINCIPLES

IMA's overarching ethical principles include: Honesty, Fairness, Objectivity, and Responsibility. Practitioners shall act in accordance with these principles and shall encourage others within their organizations to adhere to them.

STANDARDS

A practitioner's failure to comply with the following standards may result in disciplinary action.

COMPETENCE

Each practitioner has a responsibility to:

1. Maintain an appropriate level of professional expertise by continually developing knowledge and skills.

2. Perform professional duties in accordance with relevant laws, regulations, and technical standards.

3. Provide decision support information and recommendations that are accurate, clear, concise, and timely.

4. Recognize and communicate professional limitations or other constraints that would preclude responsible judgment or successful performance of an activity.

CONFIDENTIALITY

Each practitioner has a responsibility to:

1. Keep information confidential except when disclosure is authorized or legally required.

2. Inform all relevant parties regarding appropriate use of confidential information. Monitor subordinates' activities to ensure compliance.

3. Refrain from using confidential information for unethical or illegal advantage.

INTEGRITY

Each practitioner has a responsibility to:

1. Mitigate actual conflicts of interest. Regularly communicate with business associates to avoid apparent conflicts of interest. Advise all parties of any potential conflicts.

2. Refrain from engaging in any conduct that would prejudice carrying out duties ethically.

3. Abstain from engaging in or supporting any activity that might discredit the profession.

CREDIBILITY

Each practitioner has a responsibility to:

1. Communicate information fairly and objectively.

2. Disclose all relevant information that could reasonably be expected to influence an intended user's understanding of the reports, analyses, or recommendations.

3. Disclose delays or deficiencies in information, timeliness, processing, or internal controls in conformance with organization policy and/or applicable law.

Source: *IMA Statement of Ethical Professional Practice*, 2005. Montvale, NJ: Institute of Management Accountants. Reprinted with permission from the Institute of Management Accountants, Montvale, NJ, www.imanet.org.

Ethics Counseling Service to discuss their ethical dilemmas. The counselors help identify the key ethical issues and possible alternative ways of resolving them, and confidentiality is guaranteed. The IMA is just one of many institutions that help navigate management accountants through what could be turbulent ethical waters.

Typical Ethical Challenges

Ethical issues can confront management accountants in many ways. Here are two examples:

■ **Case A:** A management accountant is concerned about the commercial potential of a software product for which development costs are currently being capitalized as an asset rather than being shown as an expense for internal reporting purposes. The firm's division manager, whose bonus is based, in part, on the division's profits, argues that showing development costs as an asset is justified because the new product will generate profits. However, he presents little evidence to support his argument. The last two products from the division have been unsuccessful. The management accountant wants to make the right decision while avoiding a difficult personal confrontation with his boss, the division manager.

■ **Case B:** A packaging supplier, bidding for a new contract, offers a management accountant of the purchasing company an all-expenses-paid weekend to the Super Bowl. The supplier does not mention the new contract when extending the invitation. The management accountant is not a personal friend of the supplier. He knows cost issues are critical when it comes to approving the new contract and is concerned that the supplier will ask for details about the bids placed by competing packaging companies.

In each case, the management accountant is faced with an ethical dilemma. Ethical issues are not always clear-cut. Case A involves competence, credibility, and integrity. The management accountant should request that the division manager provide credible evidence that the new product is commercially viable. If the manager does not provide such evidence, expensing development costs in the current period is appropriate.

Case B involves confidentiality and integrity. The supplier in Case B may have no intention of asking questions about competitors' bids. However, the appearance of a conflict of interest in Case B is sufficient for many companies to prohibit employees from accepting Case B involves confidentiality and integrity. The supplier in Case B may have no intention of asking questions about competitors' bids. However, the appearance of a conflict of interest in Case B is sufficient for many companies to prohibit employees from accepting "favors" from suppliers. Exhibit 1-8 presents the IMA's guidance on "Resolution of Ethical Conflict." The accountant in Case B should discuss the invitation with his or her immediate supervisor. If the visit is approved, the accountant should inform the supplier that the invitation has been officially approved subject to following corporate policy (which includes not disclosing confidential company information).

Most professional accounting organizations around the globe issue statements about professional ethics. These statements include many of the same issues discussed by the IMA in Exhibits 1-7 and 1-8. For example, the Chartered Institute of Management Accountants (CIMA) in the United Kingdom advocates the same four ethical principles shown in Exhibit 1-7: competency, confidentiality, integrity, and credibility.

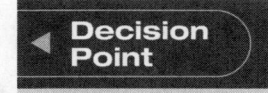

◄ Decision Point

What are the ethical responsibilities of management accountants?

In applying the Standards of Ethical Professional Practice, you may encounter problems identifying unethical behavior or resolving an ethical conflict. When faced with ethical issues, you should follow your organization's established policies on the resolution of such conflict. If these policies do not resolve the ethical conflict, you should consider the following courses of action:

1. Discuss the issue with your immediate supervisor except when it appears that the supervisor is involved. In that case, present the issue to the next level. If you cannot achieve a satisfactory resolution, submit the issue to the next management level. If your immediate superior is the chief executive officer or equivalent, the acceptable reviewing authority may be a group such as the audit committee, executive committee, board of directors, board of trustees, or owners. Contact with levels above the immediate superior should be initiated only with your superior's knowledge, assuming he or she is not involved. Communication of such problems to authorities or individuals not employed or engaged by the organization is not considered appropriate, unless you believe there is a clear violation of the law.

2. Clarify relevant ethical issues by initiating a confidential discussion with an IMA Ethics Counselor or other impartial advisor to obtain a better understanding of possible courses of action.

3. Consult your own attorney as to legal obligations and rights concerning the ethical conflict.

Source: IMA Statement of Ethical Professional Practice, 2005. Montvale, NJ: Institute of Management Accountants. Reprinted with permission from the Institute of Management Accountants, Montvale, NJ, www.imanet.org.

Exhibit 1-8

Resolution of Ethical Conflict

Problem for Self-Study

Campbell Soup Company incurs the following costs:

a. Purchase of tomatoes by a canning plant for Campbell's tomato soup products
b. Materials purchased for redesigning Pepperidge Farm biscuit containers to make biscuits stay fresh longer
c. Payment to Backer, Spielvogel, Bates, the advertising agency, for advertising work on Healthy Request line of soup products
d. Salaries of food technologists researching feasibility of a Prego pizza sauce that has minimal calories
e. Payment to Safeway for redeeming coupons on Campbell's food products
f. Cost of a toll-free telephone line used for customer inquiries about using Campbell's soup products
g. Cost of gloves used by line operators on the Swanson Fiesta breakfast-food production line
h. Cost of handheld computers used by Pepperidge Farm delivery staff serving major supermarket accounts

Required

Classify each cost item (a–h) as one of the business functions in the value chain in Exhibit 1-2.

Solution

a. · Production
b. Design of products, services, or processes
c. Marketing
d. Research and development
e. Marketing
f. Customer service
g. Production
h. Distribution

Decision Points

The following question-and-answer format summarizes the chapter's learning objectives. Each decision presents a key question related to a learning objective. The guidelines are the answer to that question.

Decision	Guidelines
1. How is management accounting different from financial accounting?	Financial accounting reports to external users on past financial performance using GAAP. Management accounting provides future-oriented information to help managers (internal users) make decisions and achieve organizational goals.
2. How do management accountants support strategic decisions?	Management accountants contribute to strategic decisions by providing information about the sources of competitive advantage.

3. How do companies add value, and what are the dimensions of performance that customers are expecting of companies?

Companies add value through R&D; design of products, services, or processes; production; marketing; distribution; and customer service. Customers want companies to deliver performance through cost and efficiency, quality, timeliness, and innovation.

4. How do managers make decisions to implement strategy?

Managers use a five-step decision-making process to implement strategy: (1) identify the problem and uncertainties; (2) obtain information; (3) make predictions about the future; (4) make decisions by choosing among alternatives; and (5) implement the decision, evaluate performance, and learn. The first four steps are the planning decisions, which include deciding on organization goals, predicting results under various alternative ways of achieving those goals, and deciding how to attain the desired goals. Step 5 is the control decision, which includes taking actions to implement the planning decisions and deciding on performance evaluation and feedback that will help future decision making.

5. What guidelines do management accountants use?

Three guidelines that help management accountants increase their value to managers are (a) employ a cost-benefit approach, (b) recognize behavioral as well as technical considerations, and (c) identify different costs for different purposes.

6. Where does the management accounting function fit into an organization's structure?

Management accounting is an integral part of the controller's function in an organization. In most organizations, the controller reports to the chief financial officer, who is a key member of the top management team.

7. What are the ethical responsibilities of management accountants?

Management accountants have ethical responsibilities that are related to competence, confidentiality, integrity, and credibility.

TERMS TO LEARN

Each chapter will include this section. Like all technical terms, accounting terms have precise meanings. Learn the definitions of new terms when you initially encounter them. The meaning of each of the following terms is given in this chapter and in the Glossary at the end of this book.

budget (p. 10)

chief financial officer (CFO)
 (p. 14)

control (p. 11)

controller (p. 14)

cost accounting (p. 4)

cost–benefit approach (p. 12)

cost management (p. 4)

customer relationship management (CRM) (p. 6)

customer service (p. 6)

design of products and processes
 (p. 5)

distribution (p. 6)

finance director (p. 14)

financial accounting
 (p. 3)

learning (p. 11)

line management (p. 14)

management accounting (p. 3)

marketing (p. 6)

planning **(p. 10)**

production **(p. 6)**

research and
  development (R&D)
  (p. 5)

staff management **(p. 14)**

strategic cost management **(p. 4)**

strategy **(p. 4)**

supply chain **(p. 7)**

sustainability **(p. 8)**

total quality management (TQM)
  (p. 8)

value chain **(p. 5)**

ASSIGNMENT MATERIAL

Questions

1-1 How does management accounting differ from financial accounting?

1-2 "Management accounting should not fit the straitjacket of financial accounting." Explain and give an example.

1-3 How can a management accountant help formulate a strategy?

1-4 Describe the business functions in the value chain.

1-5 Explain the term "supply chain" and its importance to cost management.

1-6 "Management accounting deals only with costs." Do you agree? Explain.

1-7 How can management accountants help improve quality and achieve timely product deliveries?

1-8 Describe the five-step decision-making process.

1-9 Distinguish planning decisions from control decisions.

1-10 What three guidelines help management accountants provide the most value to managers?

1-11 "Knowledge of technical issues such as computer technology is a necessary but not sufficient condition to becoming a successful management accountant." Do you agree? Why?

1-12 As a new controller, reply to this comment by a plant manager: "As I see it, our accountants may be needed to keep records for shareholders and Uncle Sam, but I don't want them sticking their noses in my day-to-day operations. I do the best I know how. No bean counter knows enough about my responsibilities to be of any use to me."

1-13 As used in accounting, what do IMA and CMA stand for?

1-14 Name the four areas in which standards of ethical conduct exist for management accountants in the United States. What organization sets forth these standards?

1-15 What steps should a management accountant take if established written policies provide insufficient guidance on how to handle an ethical conflict?

Solved Examples

1-16 Planning and control decisions. Rupa is a book retailing company. Most of its sales are made at its own stores, located in shopping malls or in central business districts. A small but increasing percentage of sales is made via BarnesandNoble.com, in which its major competitor is Amazon.com.

The following five reports were recently prepared by the management accounting group at Rupa:

1. Annual financial statements.
2. Weekly report to Vice President of operations for each Rupa store – includes revenues, gross margin, and operating costs.

3. Study for Vice President of new business development of the expected revenues and costs of BarnesandNoble.com, selling music products (CDs, cassettes, etc.) as well as books.

4. Weekly report to book publishers and trade magazines on the sales of the top 10 selling fiction and non-fiction books at both its own stores and BarnesandNoble.com.

5. Report to insurance company on losses Rupa suffered at its three Gujarat stores due to an earthquake.

For each report, identify both a planning-decision and a control-decision used by a Rupa manager.

Required

Solution

Planning and control decisions

1. (a) Planning—decision by Rupa about cash needs for the future.
   (b) Control—performance evaluation of Rupa for the year.
2. (a) Planning—decision to increase or decrease local marketing support.
   (b) Control—decision on whether recent sales promotion led to an increase in revenues.
3. (a) Planning—decision about whether or not to expand Rupa's internet lines of business.
   (b) Control—evaluation by Vice President of New Business Development of the performance of managers of individual lines of business.
4. (a) Planning—decision on which books to advertise more or which books to include in a special chat-room site.
   (b) Control—decision by publisher to pay additional bonuses to authors due to their book being on a bestseller list.
5. (a) Planning—decision by Rupa on the amount and type of insurance to purchase next year.
   (b) Control—follow up by Rupa with the insurance company regarding cash payment to Rupa.

1-17 Problem solving, scorekeeping, and attention direction. For each of the following activities, identify the main role the accountant is performing—problem solving, scorekeeping, or attention directing.

Required

1. Preparing a monthly statement of Indian sales for the IBM marketing Vice President.
2. Interpreting differences between actual results and budgeted amounts on a performance report for the Customer Warranty Department of General Electric.
3. Analyzing, for a Mitsubishi international-manufacturing manager, the desirability of having some auto parts made in India.
4. Interpreting why a New Delhi distribution center exceeded its delivery-costs budget.
5. Explaining a Xerox Corporation Shipping Department's performance report.
6. Preparing for the manager of production control of an Indian steel plant, a cost comparison of two computerized-manufacturing control systems.
7. Preparing a scrap report for the Finishing Department of a Toyota parts plant.
8. Preparing the budget for the Maintenance Department of Appolo Hospital.
9. Analyzing for a General Motors product designer the impact on product costs of a new headlight.

Solution

Problem solving, scorekeeping, and sttention directing.

1. Scorekeeping
2. Attention directing

3. Problem solving
4. Attention directing
5. Attention directing
6. Problem solving
7. Scorekeeping (depending on the extent of the report) or attention directing.
8. This question is intentionally vague. The give-and-take of the budgetary process usually encompasses all three functions, but it emphasizes scorekeeping the least. The main function is attention directing, but problem solving is also involved.
9. Problem solving

Note: Because the accountant's duties are often not sharply defined, some of these answers might be challenged.

1-18 Value chain and classification of costs, fast-food restaurant. Mc Donald, a burger fast food restaurant, incurs the following costs:

a. Cost of oil for the deep fryer.
b. Wages of the counter help who give customers the food they order.
c. Cost of the costume for the Mc Donald on the television commercials.
d. Cost of children's toys given away free with kids' meals.
e. Cost of the posters indicating the special "two cheeseburgers for ₹250".
f. Costs of frozen onion rings and French fries.
g. Salaries of the food specialists who create new sandwiches for the restaurant chain.
h. Cost of "to-go" bags requested by customers who could not finish their meals in the restaurant.

Required Classify each of the cost items (a–h) as one of the business functions of the value chain shown in Exhibit 1-2 (in text).

Solution

Cost Item	Value Chain Business Function
a.	Production
b.	Distribution
c.	Marketing
d.	Marketing
e.	Marketing
f.	Production
g.	Design of products and processes (or research and development)
h.	Customer service

1-19 Key success factors. Deloitte Consulting has issued a report recommending changes for its newest manufacturing client, Kirloskar Engines. Kirloskar Engines currently manufactures a single product, which is sold and distributed nationally. The report contains the following suggestions for enhancing business performance:

a. Develop a hybrid engine to stay ahead of competitors.
b. Increase training hours of assembly-line personnel to decrease the currently high volumes of scrap and waste.
c. Reduce lead times (time from customer order of product to customer receipt of product) by 20% in order to increase customer retention.
d. Negotiate faster response times with direct material suppliers to allow for lower material inventory levels.
e. Benchmark the company's gross margin percentages against its major competitors.

Required Link each of these changes to the key success factors that are important to managers.

Solution

Change in Operations/Management Accounting	Key Success Factor
a.	Innovation
b.	Cost and efficiency and quality
c.	Time
d.	Time and cost and efficiency
e.	Cost and efficiency

1-20 Key success factors. Ansal Construction Company provides construction services for major projects. Managers at the company believe that construction is a people-management business, and they list the following as factors critical to their success:

a. Provide tools to simplify and complete construction sooner.
b. Foster cooperative relationships with suppliers that allow for more frequent deliveries as and when products are needed.
c. Integrate tools and techniques that reduce errors in construction projects.
d. Provide continuous training for employees on new tools and equipment.
e. Benchmark the company's gross margin percentages against its major competitors.

Required

Match each of the above factors to the key success factors that are important to managers.

Solution

Change in Operations/Management Accounting	Key Success Factor
a.	Time and cost and efficiency
b.	Time and cost and efficiency
c.	Quality and cost and efficiency
d.	Innovation and quality
e.	Cost and efficiency

1-21 Five-step decision-making process, manufacturing. KFC Foods makes frozen dinners that it sells through grocery stores. Typical products include turkey, pot roast, fried chicken, and meatloaf. The managers at KFC have recently proposed a line of frozen chicken pies. They take the following actions to help decide whether to launch the line.

a. KFC's test kitchen prepares a number of possible recipes for a consumer focus group.
b. Sales managers estimate they will sell more chicken pies in their northern sales territory than in their southern sales territory.
c. Managers discuss the possibility of introducing a new chicken pie.
d. Managers compare actual costs of making chicken pies with their budgeted costs.
e. Costs for making chicken pies are budgeted.
f. The company decides to introduce a new chicken pie.
g. To help decide whether to introduce a new chicken pie, the company researches the costs of potential ingredients.

Required

Classify each of the actions (a–g) as a step in the five-step decision-making process (identify the problem and uncertainties; obtain information; make predictions about the future; make decisions by choosing among alternatives; implement the decision, evaluate performance, and learn). The actions are not listed in the order they are performed.

Solution

Action	Step in Decision-Making Process
a.	Obtain information
b.	Make predictions about the future
c.	Identify the problem and uncertainties
d.	Implement the decision, evaluate performance, and learn
e.	Make predictions about the future
f.	Make decisions by choosing among alternatives
g.	Obtain information

1-22 Five-step decision-making process, service firm. Birla Exteriors is a firm that provides house-painting services. Aditya Birla, the owner, is trying to find new ways to increase revenues. Mr Birla performs the following actions, not in the order listed.

a. Mr Birla decides to buy the paint sprayers rather than hire additional painters.
b. Mr Birla discusses with his employees the possibility of using paint sprayers instead of hand painting to increase productivity and thus profits.
c. Mr Birla learns of a large potential job that is about to go out for bids.
d. Mr Birla compares the expected cost of buying sprayers to the expected cost of hiring more workers who paint by hand and estimates profits from both alternatives.
e. Mr Birla estimates that using sprayers will reduce painting time by 20%.
f. Mr Birla researches the price of paint sprayers online.

Required
Classify each of the actions (a–f) according to its step in the five-step decision-making process (identify the problem and uncertainties; obtain information; make predictions about the future; make decisions by choosing among alternatives; implement the decision, evaluate performance, and learn).

Solution

Action	Step in Decision-Making Process
a.	Make decisions by choosing among alternatives
b.	Identify the problem and uncertainties
c.	Obtain information and/or make predictions about the future
d.	Obtain information and/or make predictions about the future
e.	Make predictions about the future
f.	Obtain information

1-23 Professional ethics and reporting division performance. Rahul Gupta is division controller and Ravi Gupta is division manager of the Punjab Shoe Company. Rahul has line responsibility to Ravi, but he also has staff responsibility to the company controller.

Ravi is under severe pressure to achieve the budgeted division income for the year. He has asked Rahul to book ₹2,00,000 of revenues on December 31. The customers' orders are firm, but the shoes are still in the production process. They will be dispatched on or around January 4. Ravi says to Rahul, "The key event is getting the sales order, not dispatching the shoes. You should support me, not obstruct my reaching division goals."

Required
1. Describe Rahul's ethical responsibilities.
2. What should Rahul do if Ravi gives him a direct order to book the sales?

Solution

1. Rahul's ethical responsibilities are well summarized in the IMA's "Standards of Ethical Conduct for Management Accountants" (Exhibit 1-7 of text). Areas of ethical responsibility include the following:
   - Competence
   - Confidentiality
   - Integrity
   - Credibility

The ethical standards related to Rahul's current dilemma are integrity, competence, and credibility. Using the integrity standard, Rahul should carry out duties ethically and communicate unfavorable as well as favorable information and professional judgments or opinions. Competence demands that Rahul perform his professional duties in accordance with relevant laws, regulations, and technical standards and provide decision support information that is accurate. Credibility requires that Rahul report information fairly and objectively and disclose deficiencies in internal controls in conformance with organizational policy and/or applicable law. Rahul should refuse to book the ₹2,00,000 of sales until the goods are dispatched. Both financial accounting and management accounting principles maintain that sales are not complete until the title is transferred to the buyer.

2. Rahul should refuse to follow Ravi's orders. If Ravi persists, the incident should be reported to the corporate controller. Support for line management should be wholehearte, but it should not require unethical conduct.

1-24 Strategic decisions and management accounting. Consider the following series of independent situations in which a firm is about to make a strategic decision.

Decisions

a. Micromax Phones is about to decide whether to launch production and sale of a cell phone with standard features.

b. Acer Computers is trying to decide whether to produce and sell a new home computer software package that includes the ability to interface with a sewing machine and a vacuum cleaner. There is no such soft- ware currently on the market.

c. L'oreal Cosmetics has been asked to provide a "store brand" lip gloss that will be sold at discount retail stores.

d. Kasim Meats is considering developing a special line of gourmet bologna made with sun-dried tomatoes, pine nuts, and artichoke hearts.

Required

1. For each decision, state whether the company is following a cost leadership or a product differentiation strategy.

2. For each decision, discuss what information the management accountant can provide about the source of competitive advantage for these firms.

Solution

1. The strategies the companies are following in each case are:
   a. Cost leadership or low price strategy.
   b. Product differentiation strategy.
   c. Cost leadership or low price strategy.
   d. Product differentiation strategy.

2. Examples of information the management accountant can provide for each strategic decision follow:
   a. Cost to manufacture and sell the cell phone.
      Productivity, efficiency, and cost advantages relative to competition.

Prices of competitive cell phones.

Sensitivity of target customers to price and quality.

The production capacity of Micromax Phones and its competitors.

How the market for cell phones with standard features is growing.

b. Cost to develop, produce, and sell new software.

Premium price that customers would be willing to pay due to product uniqueness.

Price of basic software.

Price of closest competitive software.

Cash needed to develop, produce, and sell new software.

c. Cost of producing the "store-brand" lip gloss.

Productivity, efficiency, and cost advantages relative to competition.

Prices of competitive products.

Sensitivity of target customers to price and quality.

The production capacity of L'oreal Cosmetics and its competitors.

How the market for lip gloss is growing.

d. Cost to produce and sell new line of gourmet bologna.

Premium price that customers would be willing to pay due to product uniqueness.

Price of basic meat product.

Price of closest competitive product.

Cash available to develop, produce, and sell special line of gourmet bologna.

1-25 Pharmaceutical company, budgeting, ethics. Nitin Jain was recently promoted to Controller of Research and Development (R&D) for Abott, a *Fortune* 500 pharmaceutical company that manufactures prescription drugs and nutritional supplements. The company's total R&D cost for 2015 was expected (budgeted) to be ₹500 crore. During the company's midyear budget review, Nitin realized that current R&D expenditures were already at ₹350 crore, nearly 40% above the midyear target. At this current rate of expenditure, the R&D division was on track to exceed its total year-end budget by ₹200 crore!

In a meeting with CFO later that day, Nitin delivered the bad news. CFO was both shocked and outraged that the R&D spending had gotten out of control. CFO wasn't any more understanding when Nitin revealed that the excess cost was entirely related to research and development of a new drug, Vyacon, which was expected to go to market next year. The new drug would result in large profits for Abott, if the product could be approved by year-end.

The CFO had already announced his expectations of third-quarter earnings to the press. If the R&D expenditures weren't reduced by the end of the third quarter, CFO was certain that the targets he had announced publicly would be missed and the company's stock price would tumble. CFO instructed Nitin to make up the budget shortfall by the end of the third quarter using "whatever means necessary."

Nitin was new to the controller's position and wanted to make sure that CFO's orders were followed. Nitin came up with the following ideas for making the third-quarter budgeted targets:

a. Stop all research and development efforts on the drug Vyacon until after year-end. This change would delay the drug going to market by at least 6 months. It is possible that in the meantime a Abott competitor could make it to market with a similar drug.

b. Sell off rights to the drug Martek. The company had not planned on doing this because, under current market conditions, it would get less than fair value. It would, however, result in a one-time gain that could offset the budget shortfall. Of course, all future profits from Martek would be lost.

c. Capitalize some of the company's R&D expenditures, reducing R&D expense on the income statement. This transaction would not be in accordance with GAAP, but Nitin thought it was justifiable because the Vyacon drug was going to market early next year.

Nitin would argue that capitalizing R&D costs this year and expensing them next year would better match revenues and expenses.

Required

1. Referring to the "Standards of Ethical Behavior for Practitioners of Management Accounting and Financial Management," Exhibit 1-7 (in text), which of the preceding items (a–c) are acceptable to use? Which are unacceptable?

2. What would you recommend Nitin do?

Solution

1. The overarching principles of the IMA Statement of Ethical Professional Practice are Honesty, Fairness, Objectivity and Responsibility. The statement's corresponding "Standards for Ethical Conduct…" require management accountants to:

   - Perform professional duties in accordance with relevant laws, regulations, and technical standards.
   - Refrain from engaging in any conduct that would prejudice carrying out duties ethically.
   - Communicate information fairly and objectively.
   - Disclose all relevant information that could reasonably be expected to influence an intended user's understanding of the reports, analyses, or recommendations.

The idea of capitalizing some of the company's R&D expenditures is a direct violation of the IMA's ethical standards above. This transaction would not be "in accordance with relevant laws, regulations, and technical standards." GAAP requires research and development costs to be expensed as incurred. Even if Nitin believes his transaction is justifiable, it violates the profession's technical standards and would be unethical.

The other "year-end" actions occur in many organizations and fall into the "gray" to "acceptable" area. Much depends on the circumstances surrounding each one, however, such as the following:

   a. *Stop all research and development efforts on the drug Vyacon until after year-end. This change would delay the drug going to market by at least six months. It is also possible that in the meantime a Abott competitor could make it to market with a similar drug.* While this solution may solve the budget shortfall in this year, it could result in a significant loss of future profits for Abott in the long run, especially if a competitor is able to obtain a patent on a similar drug before Abott.

   b. *Sell off rights to the drug, Martek. The company had not planned on doing this because, under current market conditions, it would get less than fair value. It would, however, result in a onetime gain that could offset the budget shortfall. Of course, all future profits from Martek would be lost.* Again, this solution may solve the company's short-term budget crisis, but could result in the loss of future profits for Abott in the long run.

2. While it is not uncommon for companies to sacrifice long-term profits for short-term gains, it may not be in the best interest of the company's shareholders. In the case of Abott, the CFO is primarily concerned with "maximizing shareholder wealth" in the immediate future (third quarter only) but not in the long term. Because this executive's incentive pay and even employment may be based on his ability to meet short-term targets, he may not be acting in the best interest of the shareholders in the long run.

Nitin definitely faces an ethical dilemma. It is not unethical on Nitin's part to want to please his new boss, nor is it unethical that Nitin wants to make a good impression on his first days at his new job; however, Nitin must still act within the ethical standards required by his profession. Taking illegal or unethical action by capitalizing R&D to satisfy the demands of his new supervisor, is unacceptable. Although not strictly unethical, I would recommend that Nitin not agree to slow down the R&D efforts on Vyacon or sell off the rights to Martek. Each of these appears to sacrifice the overall economic interests of Abott for short-run gain. Nitin should argue against doing this but not resign if CFO insists that these actions be taken. If, however, CFO asks Nitin to capitalize R&D, he should raise this issue with the chair of the audit committee after informing CFO that he is doing so. If the CFO still insists on Nitin capitalizing R&D, he should resign rather than engage in unethical behavior.

1-26 Professional ethics and end-of-year actions. Pearson Publishing House produces consumer magazines. The house and home division, which sells home-improvement and home-decorating magazines, has seen a 20% reduction in operating income over the past 9 months, primarily due to an economic recession and a depressed consumer housing market. The division's controller, Raza, has felt pressure from the CFO to improve his division's operating results by the end of the year. Raza is considering the following options for improving the division's performance by year-end:

a. Cancelling two of the division's least profitable magazines, resulting in the layoff of 25 employees.

b. Selling the new printing equipment that was purchased in January and replacing it with discarded equipment from one of the company's other divisions. The previously discarded equipment no longer meets current safety standards.

c. Recognizing unearned subscription revenue (cash received in advance for magazines that will be delivered in the future) as revenue when cash is received in the current month (just before fiscal year-end) instead of showing it as a liability.

d. Reducing the division's Allowance for Bad Debt Expense. This transaction alone would increase operating income by 5%.

e. Recognizing advertising revenues that relate to January in December.

f. Switching from declining balance to straight-line depreciation to reduce depreciation expense in the current year.

Required

1. What are the motivations for Raza to improve the division's year-end operating earnings?

2. From the point of view of the "Standards of Ethical Behavior for Practitioners of Management Accounting and Financial Management," Exhibit 1-7, which of the preceding items (a–f) are acceptable? Which are unacceptable?

3. What should Raza do about the pressure to improve performance?

Solution

1. The possible motivations for Controller Raza to modify the division's year-end earnings are:

   (i) Job security and promotion. The company's CFO will likely reward him for meeting the company's performance expectations. Alternately, the Raza may be penalized, perhaps even by losing his job if the performance expectations are not met.

   (ii) Management incentives. Raza's bonus may be based on the division's ability to meet certain profit targets. If the House and Home division has already met its profit target for the year, the Controller may personally benefit if new printing equipment is sold off and replaced with the discarded equipment that no longer meets current safety standards, or if operating income is manipulated by questionable revenue and/or expense recognition.

2. The overarching principles of the IMA Statement of Ethical Professional Practice are Honesty, Fairness, Objectivity and Responsibility. The statement's corresponding "Standards for Ethical Conduct…" require management accountants to:

   • Perform professional duties in accordance with relevant laws, regulations, and technical standards.

   • Refrain from engaging in any conduct that would prejudice carrying out duties ethically.

   • Communicate information fairly and objectively.

   • Disclose all relevant information that could reasonably be expected to influence an intended user's understanding of the reports, analyses, or recommendations.

Several of the "year-end" actions are clearly are in conflict with the statement's principles and required standards and should be viewed as unacceptable.

(c) Subscription revenue received in December in advance for magazines that will be sent out in January is a liability. Showing it as revenue falsely reports next year's revenue as this year's revenue.

(d) Reversing the division's Allowance for Bad Debt Expense would violate Generally Accepted Accounting Principles unless the bad debt allowance is currently overstated. Recording this transaction would result in an overstatement of income and could potentially mislead investors.

(e) Booking advertising revenues that relate to January in December falsely reports next year's revenue as this year's revenue.

The other "year-end" actions occur in many organizations and fall into the "gray" to "acceptable" area. Much depends on the circumstances surrounding each one, however, such as the following:

(a) *Cancelling two of the division's least profitable magazines, resulting in the layoff of twenty-five employees.* While employee layoffs may be necessary for the business to survive, the layoff decision could result in economic hardship for those employees who lose their jobs, as well as result in employee morale problems for the rest of the division. Most companies would prefer to avoid causing hardship for their existing employees due to layoffs unless absolutely necessary for the survival of the business as a whole.

(b) *Selling the new printing equipment that was purchased in January and replacing it with discarded equipment from one of the company's other divisions.* The previously discarded equipment no longer meets current safety standards. Again, while this method may result in a short-term solution for the Controller and the Production Manager personally, this decision may actually harm the corporation financially as a whole, not to mention the potential resulting injuries to production workers from hazardous equipment. This method would be also be ethically questionable and would likely violate the IMA's ethical standards of integrity and credibility.

(f) *Switching from declining balance to straight line depreciation to reduce depreciation expense in the current year.* Many companies switch their depreciation policy from one method to another. Macon Publishing could argue that straight-line depreciation better represents the decrease in the economic value of the asset compared to the declining balance method. Straight-line depreciation may also be more in line with what its competitors do. If, however, the company changes to straight-line depreciation with the sole purpose of reducing expenses to meet its profit goals, such behavior would be unacceptable. The Standards of Ethical Behavior require management accountants to communicate information fairly and objectively and to carry out duties ethically.

3. Raza should directly raise his concerns first with the CFO, especially if the pressure from the CFO is so great that the only course of action on the part of the controller is to otherwise behave unethically. If the CFO refuses to change his direction, then the controller should raise these issues with the CEO, and next to the Audit Committee and the Board of Directors, after informing the CFO that he is doing so. The Controller could also initiate a confidential discussion with an IMA Ethics Counselor, other impartial adviser, or his/her own attorney. In the extreme, the Controller may want to resign if the corporate culture of Vikas Publishing is to reward executives who take year-end actions that the Controller views as unethical and possibly illegal. It was precisely actions along the lines of (c), (d) and (e) that caused, an accountant at WorldCom, to be indicted for falsifying WorldCom's books and misleading investors.

1-27 Ethical challenges, global company. Great Eastern Logistics, an Indian shipping company, has just begun distributing goods across the Atlantic to Norway. The company began operations in 2015, transporting goods to South America. The company's earnings are currently trailing behind its competitors and Great Eastern's investors are becoming anxious. Some of the company's largest investors are even talking of selling their interest in the shipping newcomer. Great Eastern's CEO, Rohan, calls an emergency meeting with his executive team. Rohan needs a plan before his upcoming conference call with uneasy investors. Great Eastern's executive staff make the following suggestions for salvaging the company's short-term operating results:

a. Stop all transatlantic shipping efforts. The startup costs for the new operations are hurting current profit margins.

b. Make deep cuts in pricing through the end of the year to generate additional revenue.

c. Pressure current customers to take early delivery of goods before the end of the year so that more revenue can be reported in this year's financial statements.

d. Sell off distribution equipment prior to year-end. The sale would result in one-time gains that could offset the company's lagging profits. The owned equipment could be replaced with leased equipment at a lower cost in the current year.

e. Record executive year-end bonus compensation for the current year in the next year when it is paid after the December fiscal year-end.

f. Recognize sales revenues on orders received but not shipped as of the end of the year.

g. Establish corporate headquarters in Ireland before the end of the year, lowering the company's corporate tax rate from 28% to 12.5%.

Required

1. As the management accountant for Great Eastern, evaluate each of the preceding items (a–g) in the context of the "Standards of Ethical Behavior for Practitioners of Management Accounting and Financial Management," Exhibit 1-7 (in text). Which of the items are in violation of these ethics standards and which are acceptable?

2. What should the management accountant do with regard to those items that are in violation of the ethical standards for management accountants?

Solution

1. The overarching principles of the IMA Statement of Ethical Professional Practice are Honesty, Fairness, Objectivity, and Responsibility. The statement's corresponding "Standards for Ethical Conduct…" require management accountants to:

- Perform professional duties in accordance with relevant laws, regulations, and technical standards.
- Refrain from engaging in any conduct that would prejudice carrying out duties ethically.
- Communicate information fairly and objectively.
- Disclose all relevant information that could reasonably be expected to influence an intended user's understanding of the reports, analyses, or recommendations.

Several of the suggestions made by Rohan's staff are clearly in conflict with the statement's principles and required standards and should be viewed as unacceptable.

c. *Pressure current customers to take early delivery of goods before the end of the year so that more revenue can be reported on this year's financial statements.* This tactic, commonly known as channel stuffing, merely results in shifting future period revenues into the current period. The overstatement of revenue in the current period may mislead investor's to believe that the company's financial well-being is better than the actual results achieved. This practice would violate the IMA's standards of credibility and integrity. Channel stuffing is frequently considered a fraudulent practice.

e. *Record the executive year-end bonus compensation for the current year in the next year when it is paid until after the December fiscal year-end.* GAAP requires expenses to be recorded (accrued) when incurred, not when paid (cash basis accounting). Therefore, failure to record the executives' year-end bonus would violate the IMA's standards of credibility and integrity.

f. *Recognize sales revenues on orders received but not shipped as of the end of the year.* GAAP requires income to be recorded (accrued) when the four criteria of revenue recognition have been met:

1. The company has completed a significant portion of the production and sales effort.

2. The amount of revenue can by objectively measured.

3. The major portion of the costs has been incurred, and the remaining costs can be reasonably estimated.

4. The eventual collection of the cash is reasonably assured.

Because criteria 1 and 3 have not been met at the time the order is placed, the revenue should not be recognized until after year-end. Therefore, recording next year's revenue in the current year would be a violation of GAAP and would be falsifying revenue. This would be a violation of the IMA's standards of credibility and integrity and may be considered fraudulent.

The other "year-end" actions occur in many organizations and fall into the "gray" to "acceptable" area. Much depends on the circumstances surrounding each one, however, such as the following:

a. *Stop all transatlantic shipping efforts. The start-up costs for the new operations are hurting current profit margins.* While this method may result in better short-term financial results for Great Eastern, it may do harm to the long-term financial condition of the corporation as a whole.

b. *Make deep cuts in pricing through the end of the year to generate additional revenue.* Again, this is only a short-term tactic to improve this year's financial results. Investors may be content in the short run, but in the long run, the new shipping company will see reduced margins from these actions.

d. *Sell-off distribution equipment prior to year-end. The sale would result in one-time gains that could offset the company's lagging profits. The owned equipment could be replaced with leased equipment at a lower cost in the current year.* While this course of action does not necessarily violate the IMA's code of ethical standards, it may be only a short-term tactic to improve this year's financial results. Chang will need to weigh his options long term to make the most cost effective decision for his company.

g. *Establish corporate headquarters in Ireland before the end of the year, lowering the company's corporate tax rate from 28 percent to 12.5 percent.* Rohan may have other legitimate reasons for relocating his company abroad, but doing so only to reduce his tax liability would likely be considered an evasion of taxes in the company's home country. Rohan should seek the advice of skilled consultants in the area of international tax before making any such move. The company could face large fines and even criminal charges for evading corporate income taxes of the home country.

2. It is possible that any of the "year-end" actions that fall into the "gray" area may be good for investors, depending on the credible evidence that supports the management decision. For example, replacing owned equipment with leased equipment may result in both short-term gains for the company and long-term cost reduction. If so, this decision would be in the best interest of the investors. If the decision only results in short-term gains, but higher costs in the long-run, then the decision may not be in the best long-term interest of the company's investors and should not be implemented solely to prop up short-term earnings.

Those decisions that clearly violate the IMA code of ethical standards (c, e, and f) would never be in the best interest of the investor. These options would result in misleading financial statements and could result in the demise of the company or even in criminal charges, as was the case with companies such as Enron and WorldCom. If Rohan asks the management accountant to take any of the actions that are clearly unethical, he should raise this issue with the chair of the Audit Committee after informing Rohan that he is doing so. If Rohan still insists on the management accountant taking these actions, he should resign rather than engage in unethical behavior.

Exercises

[Comprehensive solutions to all exercises are available on the companion website www.pearsoned.co.in/charlesthorngren]

1-28 Problem solving, scorekeeping, and attention directing. For each of the following activities, identify the main role the accountant is performing—problem solving, scorekeeping, or attention directing.

1. Interpreting differences between actual results and budgeted amounts on a shipping manager's performance report at a Maruti distribution center.
2. Preparing a report showing the benefits from leasing motor vehicles rather than owning them.
3. Preparing journal entries for depreciation on the personnel manager's office equipment at Citibank.
4. Preparing a customer's monthly statement for a Ranbaxy store.
5. Processing the weekly payroll for the Bombay University Maintenance Department.
6. Analyzing the costs of different ways to blend materials in the foundry of a TISCO plant.
7. Tallying sales, by branches, for the Vice President of Hindustan Levers, sales.
8. Analyzing, for the President of Microsoft, the impact of a contemplated new product on the net income.
9. Interpreting why an IBM sales district did not meet its sales quota.

1-29 Value chain and classification of costs, pharmaceutical company. Indian Drugs and Pharmaceutical Corp., a pharmaceutical company, incurs the following costs:

1. Cost of redesigning blister packs to make drug containers more tamper-proof.
2. Cost of videos sent to doctors to promote sales of a new drug.
3. Cost of a toll-free telephone line used for customer inquiries about usage, side effects of drugs, and so on.
4. Equipment purchased to conduct experiments on drugs yet to be approved by the government.
5. Payment to actors on an infomercial to be shown on television promoting a new hair-growing product for balding men.
6. Labor costs of workers in the packaging area of a production facility.
7. Bonus paid to a salesperson for exceeding monthly sales quota.
8. Cost of Desk to Desk Courier service to deliver drugs to hospitals.

Required Classify each of the cost items (1-8) as one of the business functions of the value chain shown in Exhibit 1-4.

1-30 Management themes and changes in management accounting. A survey on ways organizations are changing their management accounting systems reported the following:

1. Company A now prepares a value-chain income statement for each brand it sells.
2. Company B now presents in a single report all costs related to achieving high quality levels of its products.
3. Company C now presents in its performance report estimates of the manufacturing costs of its two most important competitors, in addition to its own manufacturing costs.
4. Company D reduces by 1 percent each month the budgeted labor-assembly cost of a product while evaluating the performance of a plant manager.
5. Company E now reports profitability and satisfaction measure (as assessed by a third party) on a customer-by-customer basis.

Required Link each of these changes to one of the key themes that are important to managers attaining success (see Exhibit 1-3).

2 An Introduction to Cost Terms and Purposes

Learning Objectives

1. Define and illustrate a cost object
2. Distinguish between direct costs and indirect costs
3. Explain variable costs and fixed costs
4. Interpret unit costs cautiously
5. Distinguish inventoriable costs from period costs
6. Illustrate the flow of inventoriable and period costs
7. Explain why product costs are computed in different ways for different purposes
8. Describe a framework for cost accounting and cost management

What does the word cost mean to you?

Is it the price you pay for something of value, like a cell phone? A cash outflow, like monthly rent? Something that affects profitability, like salaries? Organizations, like individuals, deal with different types of costs. At different times organizations put more or less emphasis on these costs. When times are good, companies often focus on selling as much as they can, with costs taking a backseat. But when times get tough, companies shift their emphasis from selling to cutting costs. Unfortunately, when times are really bad, companies may find that they are unable to cut costs fast enough, leading to bankruptcy,.

Costs and Cost Terminology

Learning Objective 1

Define and illustrate a cost object

. . . examples of cost objects are products, services, activities, processes, and customers

A **cost** is a resource sacrificed or forgone to achieve a specific objective. A cost (such as the cost of labor or advertising) is usually measured as the monetary amount that must be paid to acquire goods or services. An **actual cost** is the cost incurred (a historical or past cost), as distinguished from a **budgeted cost,** which is a predicted, or forecasted, cost (a future cost).

When you think of cost, you invariably think of it in the context of finding the cost of a particular thing. We call this thing a **cost object**, which is anything for which a measurement of costs is desired. Suppose that you were a manager at BMW's Chennai plant. BMW makes several different types of cars and sport activity vehicles (SAVs) at this plant. What cost objects can you think of? Now look at Exhibit 2-1.

You will see that BMW managers want to know the cost of various products, such as the BMW X5, but that they also want to know the costs of things such as projects, services, and departments. Managers use their knowledge of these costs to guide decisions, for example, about product innovation, quality, and customer service.

Now think about whether a manager at BMW might want to know the *budgeted* cost of a cost object, or the *actual cost*. Managers almost always need to know both types of costs when making decisions. Comparing budgeted costs to

Exhibit 2-1

Examples of Cost Objects at BMW

Cost Object	Illustration
Product	A BMW X5 sports activity vehicle
Service	Telephone hotline providing information and assistance to BMW dealers
Project	R&D project providing information and assistance to BMW dealers
Customer	Herb Chambers Motors, the BMW dealer that purchases a broad range of BMW vehicles
Activity	Settting up machines for production or maintaining production equipment
Department	Environmental, Health, and Safety Department

actual costs helps managers evaluate how well they did and learn about how they can do better in the future.

How does a cost system determine the costs of various cost objects? Typically in two basic stages: accumulation, followed by assignment. *Cost accumulation* is the collection of cost data in some organized way by means of an accounting system. For example, at its Chennai plant, BMW collects (accumulates) costs in various categories such as different types of materials, different classifications of labor, and costs incurred for supervision. Managers and management accountants then *assign* these accumulated costs to designated cost objects, such as the different models of cars that BMW manufactures at that plant. BMW managers use this cost information in two main ways:

1. when *making* decisions, for instance, on how to price different models of cars or how much to invest in R&D and marketing and

2. for *implementing* decisions, by influencing and motivating employees to act and learn, for example, by rewarding employees for reducing costs.

Now that we know why it is useful to assign costs, we turn our attention to some concepts that will help us do it. Again, think of the different types of costs that we just discussed—materials, labor, and supervision. You are probably thinking that some costs, such as costs of materials, are easier to assign to a cost object than others, such as costs of supervision. As you will see, this is indeed the case.

◄ **Decision Point**

What is the cost object?

Direct Costs and Indirect Costs

We now describe how costs are classified as direct and indirect costs and the methods used to assign these costs to cost objects.

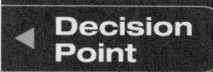

Learning Objective 2

Distinguish between direct costs

. . . costs that are traced directly to the cost object and indirect costs

. . . costs that are allocated to the cost object

- **Direct costs of a cost object** are related to the particular cost object and can be traced to it in an economically feasible (cost-effective) way. For example, the cost of steel or tires is a direct cost of BMW X6s. The cost of the steel or tires can be easily traced to or identified with the BMW X6. The workers on the BMW X6 line request materials from the warehouse and the material requisition document identifies the cost of the materials supplied to the X6. In a similar vein, individual workers record the time spent working on the X6 on time sheets. The cost of this labor can easily be traced to the X6 and is another example of a direct cost. The term **cost tracing** is used to describe the assignment of direct costs to a particular cost object.

- **Indirect costs of a cost object** are related to the particular cost object but cannot be traced to it in an economically feasible (cost-effective) way. For example, the salaries of plant administrators (including the plant manager) who oversee production of the many different types of cars produced at the Chennai plant are an indirect cost of the X6s. Plant administration costs are related to the cost object (X6s) because plant administration is necessary for managing the production of X6s. Plant administration costs are indirect costs because plant administrators also oversee the production of other products, such as the Z4 Roadster. Unlike the cost of steel or tires, there is no requisition of plant

Exhibit 2-2

Cost Assignment to a
Cost Object

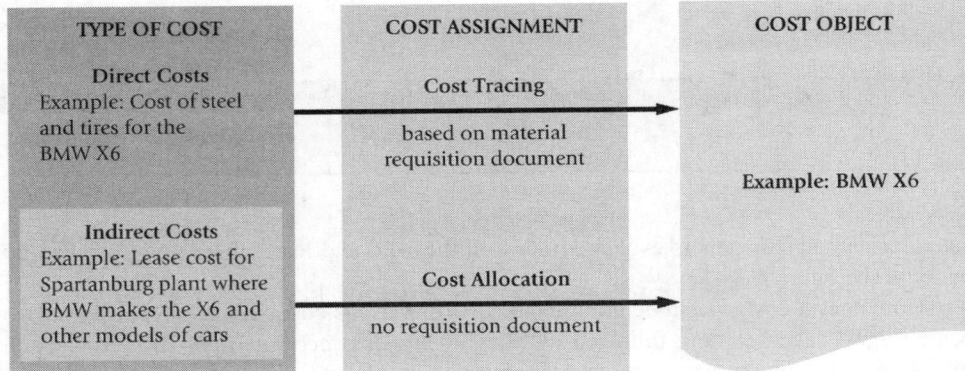

administration services and it is virtually impossible to trace plant administration costs to the X6 line. The term **cost allocation** is used to describe the assignment of indirect costs to a particular cost object. **Cost assignment** is a general term that encompasses both (1) tracing direct costs to a cost object and (2) allocating indirect costs to a cost object. Exhibit 2-2 depicts direct costs and indirect costs and both forms of cost assignment—cost tracing and cost allocation—using the example of the BMW X6.

Cost Allocation Challenges

Managers want to assign costs accurately to cost objects because inaccurate product costs will mislead managers about the profitability of different products. This, for example, could result in the managers unknowingly working harder to promote less-profitable products instead of more-profitable products. Generally, managers are more confident about the accuracy of the direct costs of cost objects, such as the cost of steel and tires of the X6.

Consider the cost to lease the Chennai plant. This cost is an indirect cost of the X6—there is no separate lease agreement for the area of the plant where the X6 is made. Nonetheless, BMW *allocates* to the X6 a part of the lease cost of the building—for example, on the basis of an estimate of the percentage of the building's floor space occupied for the production of the X6 relative to the total floor space used to produce all models of cars. This approach measures the building resources used by each car model reasonably and accurately. The more floor space a car model occupies, the greater the lease costs assigned to it. Accurately allocating other indirect costs, such as plant administration, to the X6, however, is more difficult. For example, should these costs be allocated on the basis of the number of employees working on each car model or the number of cars produced of each model? Measuring the share of plant administration used by each car model is not clear-cut.

Factors Affecting Direct/Indirect Cost Classifications

Several factors affect the classification of a cost as direct or indirect:

- **The materiality of the cost in question**. The smaller the amount of a cost—that is, the more immaterial the cost is—the less likely that it is economically feasible to trace that cost to a particular cost object. Consider a mail-order catalog company. It would be economically feasible to trace the courier charge for delivering a package to an individual customer as a direct cost. In contrast, the cost of the invoice paper included in the package would be classified as an indirect cost. Why? Because although the cost of the paper can be traced to each customer, it is not cost-effective to do so. The benefits of knowing that, say, exactly ₹0.50 worth of paper is included in each package do not exceed the data processing and administrative costs of tracing the cost to each package. The time of the sales administrator, who earns a salary of ₹4,50,000 a year, is better spent organizing customer information to help with a company's marketing efforts than tracking the cost of paper.

- **Available information-gathering technology.** Improvements in information-gathering technology make it possible to consider more and more costs as direct costs. Bar codes, for example, allow manufacturing plants to treat certain low-cost materials such as clips and screws, which were previously classified as indirect costs, as direct costs of products. At Dell, component parts such as the computer chip and the CD-ROM drive display a bar code that can be scanned at every point in the production process. Bar codes can be read into a manufacturing cost file by waving a "wand" in the same quick and efficient way supermarket checkout clerks enter the cost of each item purchased by a customer.

- **Design of operations.** Classifying a cost as direct is easier if a company's facility (or some part of it) is used exclusively for a specific cost object, such as a specific product or a particular customer. For example, the cost of the General Chemicals facility that is dedicated to manufacturing soda ash is a direct cost of soda ash.

Be aware that a specific cost may be both a direct cost of one cost object and an indirect cost of another cost object. *That is, the direct/indirect classification depends on the choice of the cost object.* For example, the salary of an Assembly Department supervisor at BMW is a direct cost if the cost object is the Assembly Department, However, because the assembly department assembles many different models, the supervisor's salary is an indirect cost if the cost object is a product such as the BMW X6 sports activity vehicle. A useful rule to remember is that the broader the cost object definition is—the assembly department rather than the X6—the higher the proportion direct costs are of total costs and the more confident a manager will be about the accuracy of the resulting cost amounts.

> ◀ **Decision Point**
>
> How do managers decide whether a cost is a direct or an indirect cost?

Cost-Behavior Patterns: Variable Costs and Fixed Costs

Costing systems record the cost of resources acquired, such as materials, labor, and equipment, and track how those resources are used to produce and sell products or services. Recording the costs of resources acquired and used allows managers to see how costs behave. Consider two basic types of cost-behavior patterns found in many accounting systems. A **variable cost** changes *in total* in proportion to changes in the related level of total activity or volume. A **fixed cost** remains unchanged *in total* for a given time period, despite wide changes in the related level of total activity or volume. Costs are defined as *variable or fixed with respect to a specific activity* and for *a given time period*. Identifying a cost as variable or fixed provides valuable information for making many management decisions and is an important input when evaluating performance. To illustrate these two basic types of costs, again consider costs at the Chennai plant of BMW.

> **Learning Objective 3**
>
> Explain variable costs and fixed costs
>
> . . . the two basic ways in which costs behave

Number of X6s Produced (1)	Variable Cost per Steering Wheel (2)	Total Variable Cost of Steering Wheels (3) = (1) × (2)
1	₹600	₹600
1,000	600	6,00,000
3,000	600	18,00,000

Exhibit 2-3

Graphs of Variable and
Fixed Costs

**PANEL A: Variable Cost of Steering Wheels
at ₹600 per BMW X6 Assembled**

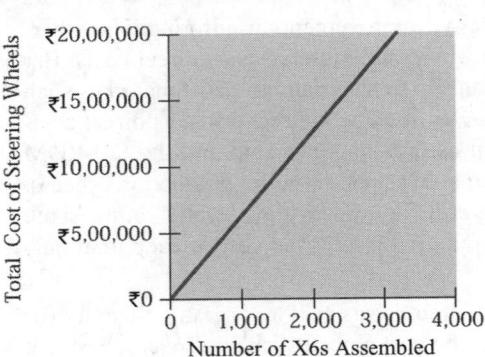

**PANEL B: Supervision Costs for the BMW X6
assembly line (in millions)**

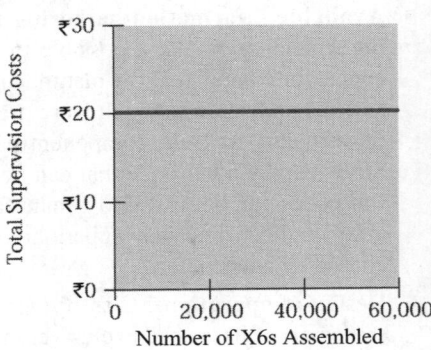

1. **Variable costs:** If BMW buys a steering wheel at ₹600 for each of its BMW X6 vehicles, then the total cost of steering wheels should be ₹600 times the number of vehicles produced, as the following table illustrates.

The steering wheel cost is an example of a variable cost because *total cost* changes in proportion to changes in the number of vehicles produced. However, the cost per unit of a variable cost is constant. For example, the variable cost per steering wheel in column 2 is the same regardless of whether 1,000 or 3,000 X6s are produced. As a result, the total variable cost of steering wheels in column 3 changes proportionately with the number of X5s produced in column 1. When considering how variable costs behave, always focus on total costs.

Panel A in Exhibit 2-3 shows a graph of the total variable cost of steering wheels. The cost is represented by a straight line that climbs from left to right. The phrases "strictly variable" and "proportionately variable" are sometimes used to describe the variable cost in this Panel.

Now, consider an example of a variable cost with respect to a different activity—the ₹200 hourly wage paid to each worker to set up machines at the Chennai plant. Setup labor cost is a variable cost with respect to setup hours because setup cost changes in total in proportion to the number of setup hours used.

2. **Fixed costs:** Suppose BMW incurs a total cost of ₹2,00,00,000 per year for supervisors who work exclusively on the X6 line. These costs are unchanged in total over a designated range of the number of vehicles produced during a given time span (see Exhibit 2-3, Panel B). Fixed costs become smaller and smaller on a per unit basis as the number of vehicles assembled increases, as the following table shows.

Annual Total Fixed Supervision Costs for BMW X6 Assembly Line (1)	Number of X6s Produced (2)	Fixed Supervision Cost per X6 (3) = (1) ÷ (2)
₹2,00,00,000	10,000	₹2,000
₹2,00,00,000	25,000	800
₹2,00,00,000	50,000	400

It is precisely because *total* line supervision costs are fixed at ₹2,00,00,000 that fixed supervision cost per X6 decreases as the number of X6s produced increases; the same fixed cost is spread over a larger number of X6s. Do not be misled by the change in fixed cost per unit. Just as in the case of variable costs, when considering fixed costs, always focus on total costs. Costs are fixed when total costs remain unchanged despite significant changes in the level of total activity or volume.

Why are some costs variable and other costs fixed? Recall that a cost is usually measured as the amount of money that must be paid to acquire goods and services. The total cost of steering wheels is a variable cost because BMW buys the steering wheels only when they are needed. As more X6s are produced, proportionately more steering wheels are acquired and proportionately more costs are incurred.

Contrast the description of variable costs with the ₹2,00,00,000 of fixed costs per year incurred by BMW for supervision of the X6 assembly line. This level of supervision is acquired and put in place well before BMW uses it to produce X6s and before BMW even knows how many X6s it will produce. Suppose that BMW puts in place supervisors capable of supervising the production of 60,000 X6s each year. If the demand is for only 55,000 X6s, there will be idle capacity. Supervisors on the X6 line could have supervised the production of 60,000 X6s but will supervise only 55,000 X6s because of the lower demand. However, BMW must pay for the unused line supervision capacity because the cost of supervision cannot be reduced in the short run. If demand is even lower—say only 50,000 X6s—line supervision costs will continue to be ₹2,00,00,000, and idle capacity will increase.

Unlike variable costs, fixed costs of resources (such as for line supervision) cannot be quickly and easily changed to match the resources needed or used. Over time, however, managers can take actions to reduce fixed costs. For example, if the X6 line needs to be run for fewer hours because of low demand for X6s, BMW may lay off supervisors or move them to another production line. Unlike variable costs that go away automatically if the resources are not used, reducing fixed costs requires active intervention on the part of managers.

Do not assume that individual cost items are inherently variable or fixed. Consider labor costs. Labor costs can be purely variable for units produced when workers are paid on a piece-unit basis (for each unit they make). For example, some companies pay garment workers on a per-shirt-sewed basis, so the firms' labor costs are variable. That is, the costs depend on how many shirts each worker makes. In contrast, other companies negotiate labor union agreements with set annual salaries that contain no-layoff clauses for workers. At a company such as this, the salaries would appropriately be classified as fixed. For decades, Japanese companies provided their workers a lifetime guarantee of employment. Although such a guarantee entails higher fixed labor costs, a firm can benefit from it because workers are more loyal and dedicated, which can improve productivity. However, during an economic downturn, the company risks losing money if its revenues decrease while its fixed costs remain unchanged. The recent global economic crisis has made companies very reluctant to lock in fixed costs.

A particular cost item could be variable with respect to one level of activity and fixed with respect to another. Consider annual registration and license costs for a fleet of planes owned by an airline company. Registration and license costs would be a variable cost with respect to the number of planes owned. But registration and license costs for a particular plane are fixed with respect to the miles flown by that plane during a year.

Some costs have both fixed and variable elements and are called *mixed* or *semivariable* costs. For example, a company's telephone costs may have a fixed monthly payment and a charge per phone-minute used. We discuss mixed costs and techniques to separate out their fixed and variable components in Chapter 10.

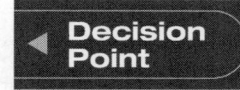

Decision Point

How do managers decide whether a cost is a variable or a fixed cost?

Cost Drivers

A cost driver is a variable, such as the level of activity or volume, that causally affects costs over a given time span. An *activity* is an event, task, or unit of work with a specified purpose—for example, designing products, setting up machines, or testing products.

The level of activity or volume is a cost driver if there is a cause-and-effect relationship between a change in the level of activity or volume and a change in the level of total costs. For example, if product-design costs change with the number of parts in a product, the number of parts is a cost driver of product-design costs. Similarly, miles driven is often a cost driver of distribution costs.

The cost driver of a variable cost is the level of activity or volume whose change causes proportionate changes in the variable cost. For example, the number of vehicles assembled is the cost driver of the total cost of steering wheels. If setup workers are paid an hourly wage, the number of setup hours is the cost driver of total (variable) setup costs.

Costs that are fixed in the short run have no cost driver in the short run but may have a cost driver in the long run. Consider the costs of testing, say, 0.1% of the color printers at Hewlett-Packard. These costs consist equipment and staff costs of Testing Department that are difficult to change Consequently, they are fixed in the short run with respect to changes in the volume of production. In this case, volume of production is not a cost driver of testing costs in the short run. In the long run, however, Hewlett-Packard will increase or decrease the Testing Department's equipment and staff to the levels needed to support future production volumes. In the long run, volume of production is a cost driver of testing costs. Costing systems that identify the cost of each activity such as testing, design, or set up are called *activity-based costing systems*.

Relevant Range

Relevant range is the band or range of normal activity level or volume in which there is a specific relationship between the level of activity or volume and the cost in question. For example, a fixed cost is fixed only in relation to a given wide range of total activity or volume (at which the company is expected to operate) and only for a given time span (usually a particular budget period). Suppose that BMW contracts with Jaipur Golden Transport Company (JGTC) to transport X6s to BMW dealerships. Jaipur Golden Transport Company (JGTC), rents two trucks, and each truck has annual fixed rental costs of ₹4,00,000. The maximum annual usage of each truck is 1,20,000 kms. In the current year (2014), the predicted combined total hauling of the two trucks is 1,70,000 kms.

Exhibit 2-4 shows how annual fixed costs behave at different levels of miles of hauling. Up to 1,20,000 kms, JGTC can operate with one truck; from 1,20,001 to 2,40,000 kms, it operates with two trucks; from 2,40,001 to 3,60,000 kms, it operates with three trucks. This pattern will continue as JGTC adds trucks to its fleet to provide more miles of hauling. Given the predicted 1,70,000-km usage for 2014, the range from 1,20,001 to 2,40,000 kms hauled is the range in which JGTC expects to operate, resulting in fixed rental costs

Exhibit 2-4

Fixed-Cost Behavior at Thomas Transport Company

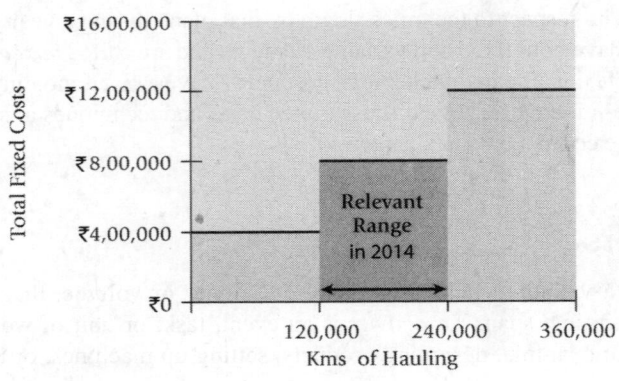

CHAPTER 2   AN INTRODUCTION TO COST TERMS AND PURPOSES ■ 43

of ₹8,00,000. Within this relevant range, changes in miles hauled will not affect the annual fixed costs.

Fixed costs may change from one year to the next. For example, if the total rental fee of the two trucks is increased by ₹20,000 for 2015, the total level of fixed costs will increase to ₹8,20,000 (all else remaining the same). If that increase occurs, total rental costs will be fixed at this new level of ₹8,20,000 for 2015 for kms hauled in the 1,20,001 to 2,40,000 range.

The relevant range also applies to variable costs. Outside the relevant range, variable costs, such as direct materials, may not change proportionately with changes in production volume. For example, above a certain volume, direct material costs may increase at a lower rate because a firm may be able to negotiate price discounts for purchasing greater amounts of materials from its suppliers.

Relationships of Types of Costs

We have introduced two major classifications of costs: direct/indirect and variable/fixed. Costs may simultaneously be:

- Direct and variable
- Direct and fixed
- Indirect and variable
- Indirect and fixed

Exhibit 2-5 shows examples of costs in each of these four cost classifications for the BMW X6.

Total Costs and Unit Costs

The preceding section concentrated on the behavior patterns of total costs in relation to activity or volume levels. We now consider unit costs.

		Assignment of Costs to Cost Object	
		Direct Costs	**Indirect Costs**
Cost-Behavior Pattern	**Variable Costs**	• Cost object: BMW X6s produced Example: Tires used in assembly of automobile	• Cost object: BMW X6s produced Example: Power costs at Chennai plant. Power usage is metered only to the plant, where multiple products are assembled.
	Fixed Costs	• Cost object: BMW X6s produced Example: Salary of supervisor on BMW X6 assembly line	• Cost object: BMW X6s produced Example: Annual lease costs at Chennai plant. Lease is for whole plant, where multiple products are produced.

Exhibit 2-5

Examples of Costs in Combinations of the Direct/Indirect and Variable/Fixed Cost Classifications for a Car Manufacturer

Unit Costs

A **unit cost**, also called an **average cost**, is calculated by dividing the total cost by the related number of units produced. In many decision contexts, calculating a unit cost is essential. Consider the booking agent who has to make the decision to book Paul McCartney to play at Shea Stadium. She estimates the cost of the event to be ₹4,00,00,000. This knowledge is helpful for the decision, but it is not enough.

Before reaching a decision, the booking agent also must predict the number of people who will attend. Without knowing the number of attendees, she cannot make an informed decision about the admission price she needs to charge to recover the cost of the event or even on whether to have the event at all. So he computes the unit cost of hiring the musical group by dividing the total cost (₹4,00,00,000) by the expected number of people who will attend. If 50,000 people attend, the unit cost is ₹800 (₹4,00,00,000 ÷ 50,000) per person; if 20,000 attend, the unit cost increases to ₹2,000 (₹4,00,00,000 ÷ 20,000).

Unless the total cost is "unitized" (that is, averaged with respect to the level of activity or volume), the ₹4,00,00,000 cost is difficult to interpret. The unit cost combines the total cost and the number of people in a simple and understandable way.

Accounting systems typically report both total-cost amounts and average-cost-per-unit amounts. . The units might be expressed in various ways. Examples are automobiles assembled, packages delivered, or hours worked. Consider LG Products, a manufacturer of speaker systems with a plant in Pune. Suppose that, in 2014, its first year of operations, the company incurs ₹40,00,00,000 of manufacturing costs are incurred to produce 5,00,000 speaker systems. Then the unit cost is ₹800:

$$\frac{\text{Total manufacturing costs}}{\text{Number of units manufactured}} = \frac{₹40,00,00,000}{5,00,000\ \text{units}} = ₹800\ \text{per unit}$$

If 4,80,000 units are sold and 20,000 units remain in ending inventory, the unit-cost concept helps in the determination of total costs in the income statement and balance sheet and, hence, the financial results reported by LG Products to shareholders, banks, and the government.

Cost of goods sold in the income statement, 4,80,000 units × ₹800 per unit	₹38,40,00,000
Ending inventory in the balance sheet, 20,000 units × ₹800 per unit	1,60,00,000
Total manufacturing costs of 5,00,000 units	₹40,00,00,000

Unit costs are found in all areas of the value chain—for example, unit cost of product design, of sales visits, and of customer-service calls. By summing unit costs throughout the value chain, managers calculate the unit cost of the different products or services they deliver and determine the profitability of each product or service. Managers use this information, for example, to decide the products in which they should invest more resources, such as R&D and marketing, and the prices they should charge.

Use Unit Costs Cautiously

Although unit costs are regularly used in financial reports and for making product mix and pricing decisions, *managers should think in terms of total costs rather than unit costs for many decisions*. Consider the manager of the Pune plant of LG Products. Assume the ₹40,00,00,000 in costs in 2014 consist of ₹10,00,00,000 of fixed costs and ₹30,00,00,000 of variable costs (at ₹600 variable cost per speaker system produced). Suppose the total fixed cost and the variable cost per speaker system in 2015 are expected to be unchanged from 2014. The budgeted costs for 2015 at different production levels, calculated on the basis of total variable costs, total fixed costs, and total costs, are:

Units Produced (1)	Variable Cost per Unit (₹) (2)	Total Variable Costs (₹) (3) = (1) × (2)	Total Fixed Costs (₹) (4)	Total Costs (₹) (5) = (3) + (4)	Unit Cost (₹) (6) = (5) ÷ (1)
1,00,000	600	6,00,00,000	10,00,00,000	16,00,00,000	1,600.00
2,00,000	600	12,00,00,000	10,00,00,000	22,00,00,000	1,100.00
5,00,000	600	30,00,00,000	10,00,00,000	40,00,00,000	800.00
8,00,000	600	48,00,00,000	10,00,00,000	58,00,00,000	725.00
10,00,000	600	60,00,00,000	10,00,00,000	70,00,00,000	700.00

A plant manager who uses the 2014 unit cost of ₹800 per unit will underestimate actual total costs if 2015 output is below the 2014 level of 5,00,000 units. If actual volume is 2,00,000 units due to, say, the presence of a new competitor, actual costs would be ₹22,00,00,000. The unit cost of ₹800 times 2,00,000 units equals ₹16,00,00,000, which underestimates the actual total costs by ₹6,00,00,000 (₹22,00,00,000 – ₹16,00,00,000). *In other words, The unit cost of ₹800 applies only when 5,00,000 units are produced.*

An overreliance on unit cost in this situation could lead to insufficient cash being available to pay costs if volume declines to 2,00,000 units. As the table indicates, for making this decision, managers should think in terms of total variable costs, total fixed costs, and total costs rather than unit cost. As a general rule, first calculate total costs, then compute a unit cost, if it is needed for a particular decision.

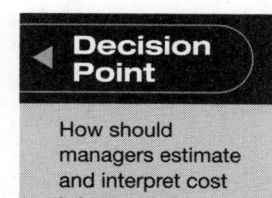

◀ Decision Point

How should managers estimate and interpret cost information?

Business Sectors, Types of Inventory, Inventoriable Costs, and Period Costs

In this section, we describe the different sectors of the economy, the different types of inventory that companies hold, and some commonly used classifications of manufacturing costs.

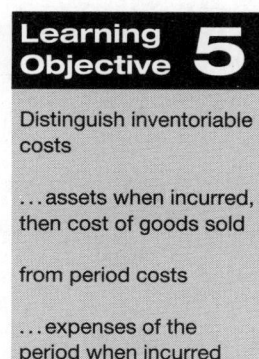

Learning Objective 5

Distinguish inventoriable costs

...assets when incurred, then cost of goods sold from period costs

...expenses of the period when incurred

Manufacturing-, Merchandising-, and Service-Sector Companies

We define three sectors of the economy and provide examples of companies in each sector.

1. **Manufacturing-sector companies** purchase materials and components and convert them into various finished goods. Examples are automotive companies such as Jaguar, cellular phone producers such as Nokia, food-processing companies such as Heinz, and computer companies such as Toshiba.

2. **Merchandising-sector companies** purchase and then sell tangible products without changing their basic form. This sector includes companies engaged in retailing (for example, bookstores such as Barnes and Noble or department stores such as Target), distribution (for example, a supplier of hospital products, such as Owens and Minor), or wholesaling (for example, a supplier of electronic components, such as Arrow Electronics).

3. **Service-sector companies** provide services (intangible products)—for example, legal advice or audits—to their customers. Examples are law firms, such as Wachtell, Lipton, Rosen & Katz, accounting firms such as Ernst and Young, banks such as Barclays, mutual fund companies such as Fidelity, insurance companies such as Aetna, transportation companies such as Singapore Airlines, advertising agencies such as Saatchi & Saatchi, television stations such as Turner Broadcasting, Internet service providers such as Comcast, travel agencies such as American Express, and brokerage firms such as Merrill Lynch.

Types of Inventory

Manufacturing-sector companies purchase materials and components and convert them into various finished goods. These companies typically have one or more of the following three types of inventory:

1. **Direct materials inventory.** Direct materials in stock and awaiting use in the manufacturing process (for example, computer chips and components needed to manufacture cellular phones).

2. **Work-in-process inventory.** Goods partially worked on but not yet completed (for example, cellular phones at various stages of completion in the manufacturing process). Also called **work in progress**.

3. **Finished goods inventory.** Goods (for example, cellular phones) completed but not yet sold.

Merchandising-sector companies purchase tangible products and then sell them without changing their basic form. They hold only one type of inventory, which is products in their original purchased form, called *merchandise inventory*. Service-sector companies provide only services or intangible products and so do not hold inventories of tangible products.

Commonly Used Classifications of Manufacturing Costs

Three terms commonly used when describing manufacturing costs are direct material costs, direct manufacturing labor costs, and indirect manufacturing costs. These terms build on the direct versus indirect cost distinction we described earlier in the context of manufacturing costs.

1. **Direct material costs** are the acquisition costs of all materials that eventually become part of the cost object (work in process and then finished goods) and can be traced to the cost object in an economically feasible way. The steel and tires used to make the BMW X6 and the computer chips used to make cellular phones are examples of direct material costs. Note that the costs of direct materials include not only the cost of the materials themselves but the freight-in (inward delivery) charges, sales taxes, and customs duties that must be paid to acquire them.

2. **Direct manufacturing labor costs** include the compensation of all manufacturing labor that can be traced to the cost object (work in process and then finished goods) in an economically feasible way. Examples include wages and fringe benefits paid to machine operators and assembly-line workers who convert direct materials purchased to finished goods.

3. **Indirect manufacturing costs** are all manufacturing costs that are related to the cost object (work in process and then finished goods) but cannot be traced to that cost object in an economically feasible way. Examples include supplies, indirect materials such as lubricants, indirect manufacturing labor such as plant maintenance and cleaning labor, plant rent, plant insurance, property taxes on the plant, plant depreciation, and the compensation of plant managers. This cost category is also referred to as **manufacturing overhead costs** or **factory overhead costs**. We use *indirect manufacturing costs* and *manufacturing overhead costs* interchangeably in this book.

We now describe the distinction between inventoriable costs and period costs.

Inventoriable Costs

Inventoriable costs are all costs of a product that are considered as assets in the balance sheet when they are incurred and that become cost of goods sold only when the product is sold. For manufacturing-sector companies, all manufacturing costs are inventoriable costs. The costs first accumulate as work-in-process inventory assets (in other words, they are "inventoried") and then as finished goods inventory assets. Consider Cellular Products, a manufacturer of cellular phones. The cost of the company's direct materials, such as computer chips, direct manufacturing labor costs, and manufacturing overhead costs create new assets. They start out as work in process inventory and become finished goods inventory (the cellular phones). When the cellular phones are sold, the costs move from being assets to cost of goods sold expense. This cost is matched against **revenues**, which are inflows of assets (usually cash or accounts receivable) received for products or services customers purchase.

Note that the cost of goods sold includes all manufacturing costs (direct materials, direct manufacturing labor, and manufacturing overhead costs) incurred to produce them. The cellular phones may be sold during a different accounting period than the period in which they were manufactured. Thus, inventorying manufacturing costs in the balance sheet during the accounting period when the phones are manufactured and expensing the manufacturing costs in a later income statement when the phones are sold matches revenues and expenses.

For merchandising-sector companies such as Bharti Wal-Mart, inventoriable costs are the costs of purchasing the goods that are resold in their same form. These costs comprise the costs of the goods themselves plus any incoming freight, insurance, and handling costs for those goods. Service-sector companies provide only services or intangible products. The absence of inventories of tangible products for sale means there are no inventoriable costs.

Period Costs

Period costs are all costs in the income statement other than cost of goods sold. Period costs, such as marketing, distribution, and customer service costs, are treated as expenses of the accounting period in which they are incurred because managers expect these costs to increase revenues in only that period and not in future periods. Some costs such as R&D costs are treated as period costs because, although these costs may increase revenues in a future period if the R&D efforts are successful, it is highly uncertain if and when these increased revenues will occur. Expensing period costs as they are incurred best matches expenses to revenues.

For manufacturing-sector companies, period costs in the income statement are all non-manufacturing costs (for example, design costs and distribution costs). For merchandising-sector companies, period costs in the income statement are all costs not related to the cost of goods purchased for resale. Examples of these period costs are labor costs of sales floor personnel and advertising costs. Because there are no inventoriable costs for service-sector companies, all costs in the income statement are period costs.

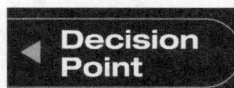

◄ **Decision Point**

What are the differences in the accounting for inventoriable versus period costs?

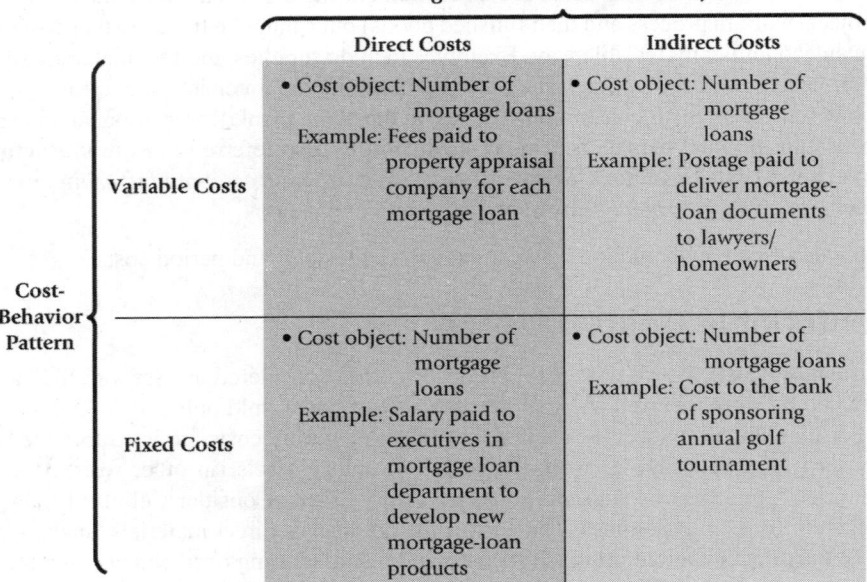

Exhibit 2-5 showed examples of inventoriable costs in direct/indirect and variable/fixed cost classifications for a car manufacturer. Exhibit 2-6 shows examples of period costs in direct/indirect and variable/fixed cost classifications at a bank.

Illustrating the Flow of Inventoriable Costs and Period Costs

Learning Objective 6

Illustrate the flow of inventoriable and period costs

...in manufacturing settings, inventoriable costs flow through work-in-process and finished goods accounts and are expensed when goods are sold; period costs are always expensed as incurred

We illustrate the flow of inventoriable costs and period costs through the income statement of a manufacturing company, for which the distinction between inventoriable costs and period costs is most detailed.

Manufacturing-Sector Example

Follow the flow of costs for Cellular Products in Exhibit 2-7 and Exhibit 2-8. Exhibit 2-7 visually highlights the differences in the flow of inventoriable and period costs for a manufacturing-sector company. Note how, as described in the previous section, inventoriable costs go through the balance sheet accounts of work-in-process inventory and finished goods inventory before entering cost of goods sold in the income statement. Period costs are expensed directly in the income statement. Exhibit 2-8 takes the visual presentation in Exhibit 2-7 and shows how inventoriable costs and period expenses would appear in the income statement and schedule of cost of goods manufactured of a manufacturing company.

We start by tracking the flow of direct materials shown on the left of Exhibit 2-7 and in Panel B of Exhibit 2-8. To keep things simple, all numbers are expressed in thousands, except for the per unit amounts.

Step 1: Cost of direct materials used in 2014. Note how the arrows in Exhibit 2-7 for beginning inventory, ₹1,10,000, and direct material purchases, ₹7,30,000, "fill up" the direct material inventory box and how direct material used, ₹7,60,000 "empties out" direct material inventory leaving an ending inventory of direct materials of ₹80,000 that becomes the beginning inventory for the next year.

The cost of direct materials used is calculated in Exhibit 2-8, Panel B (light blue shaded area) as

Beginning inventory of direct materials, January 1, 2014	₹1,10,000
+ Purchases of direct materials in 2014	7,30,000
− Ending inventory of direct materials, December 31, 2014	80,000
= Direct materials used in 2014	₹7,60,000

Step 2: Total manufacturing costs incurred in 2014. Total manufacturing costs refers to all direct manufacturing costs and manufacturing overhead costs incurred during 2014 for all goods worked on during the year. Cellular Products classifies its manufacturing costs into the three categories described earlier.

(i) Direct materials used in 2014 (shaded light blue in Exhibit 2-8, Panel B)	₹7,60,000
(ii) Direct manufacturing labor in 2014 (shaded blue in Exhibit 2-8, Panel B)	90,000
(iii) Manufacturing overhead costs (shaded dark blue in Exhibit 2-8, Panel B)	2,00,000
Total manufacturing costs incurred in 2014	₹10,50,000

Note how in Exhibit 2-7, these costs increase work-in-process inventory.

Step 3: Cost of goods manufactured in 2014. Cost of goods manufactured refers to the cost of goods brought to completion, whether they were started before or during the current accounting period.

Exhibit 2-7   Flow of Revenue and Costs for a Manufacturing-Sector Company, Cellular Products (in thousands)

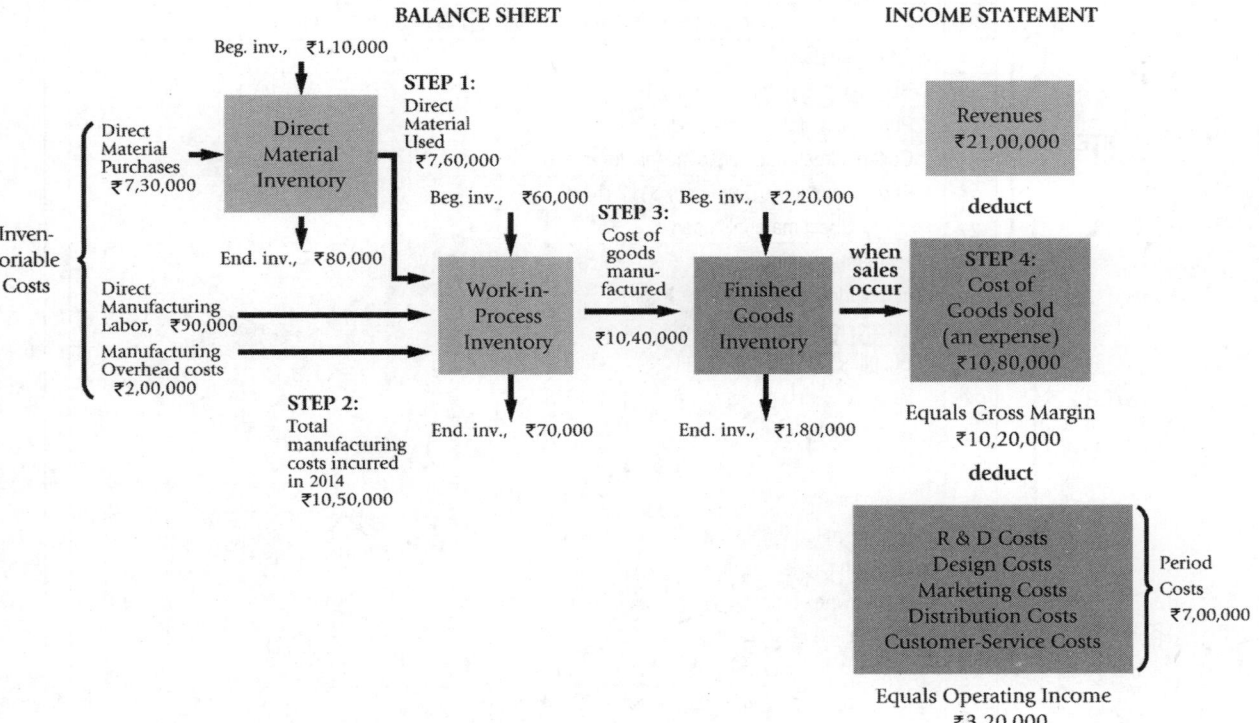

Exhibit 2-8 Income Statement and Schedule of Cost of Goods Manufactured of a Manufacturing-Sector Company, Cellular Products

	A	B	C	D
	File Edit View Insert Format Tools Data Window Help			
1	**PANEL A: INCOME STATEMENT**			
2	**Cellular Products**			
3	**Income Statement**			
4	**For the Year Ended December 31, 2014 (in thousands)**			
5	Revenues		₹21,00,000	
6	Cost of goods sold:			
7	Beginning finished goods inventory, January 1, 2014	₹2,20,000		
8	Cost of goods manufactured (see Panel B)	₹10,40,000	◄	
9	Cost of goods available for sale	₹12,60,000		
10	Ending finished goods inventory, December 31, 2014	₹1,80,000		
11	Cost of goods sold		₹10,80,000	
12	Gross margin (or gross profit)		₹10,20,000	
13	Operating costs:			
14	R&D, design, mktg., dist., & cust.-service cost	₹7,00,000		
15	Total operating costs		₹7,00,000	
16	Operating income		₹3,20,000	
17				
18	**PANEL B: COST OF GOODS MANUFACTURED**			
19	**Cellular Products**			
20	**Schedule of Cost of Goods Manufactured**[a]			
21	**For the Year Ended December 31, 2014 (in thousands)**			
22	Direct materials:			
23	Beginning inventory, January 1, 2014	₹1,10,000		
24	Purchases of direct materials	7,30,000		
25	Cost of direct materials available for use	8,40,000		
26	Ending inventory, December 31, 2014	80,000		
27	Direct materials used		₹7,60,000	
28	Direct manufacturing labor		90,000	
29	Manufacturing overhead costs:			
30	Indirect manufacturing labor	₹70,000		
31	Supplies	20,000		
32	Heat, light, and power	50,000		
33	Depreciation--plant building	20,000		
34	Depreciation--plant equipment	30,000		
35	Miscellaneous	10,000		
36	Total manufacturing overhead costs		2,00,000	
37	Manufacturing costs incurred during 2014		10,50,000	
38	Beginning work-in-process inventory, January 1, 2014		60,000	
39	Total manufacturing costs to account for		11,10,000	
40	Ending work-in-process inventory, December 31, 2014		70,000	
41	Cost of goods manufactured (to Income Statement)		₹10,40,000	
42	[a]Note that this schedule can become a Schedule of Cost of Goods Manufactured and Sold simply by including the beginning and ending finished goods inventory figures in the supporting schedule rather than in the body of the income statement.			

STEP 4 (rows 6–11)

STEP 1 (rows 22–26)

STEP 2 (rows 27–36)

STEP 3 (rows 37–41)

Note how the work-in-process inventory box in Exhibit 2-7 has a very similar structure to the direct material inventory box described in Step 1. Beginning work-in-process inventory of ₹60,000 and total manufacturing costs incurred in 2014 of ₹10,50,000 "fill-up" the work-in-process inventory box. Some of the manufacturing costs incurred during 2014 are held back as the cost of the ending work-in-process inventory. The ending work-in-process inventory of ₹70,000 becomes the beginning inventory for the next year, and the cost of goods manufactured during 2014 of ₹10,40,000 "empties out" the work-in-process inventory while "filling up" the finished goods inventory box.

The cost of goods manufactured in 2014 (shaded teal) is calculated in Exhibit 2-8, Panel B as:

Beginning work-in-process inventory, January 1, 2014	₹60,000
1 Total manufacturing costs incurred in 2014	10,50,000
5 Total manufacturing costs to account for	11,10,000
2 Ending work-in-process inventory, December 31, 2014	70,000
5 Cost of goods manufactured in 2014	₹10,40,000

Step 4: Cost of goods sold in 2014. The cost of goods sold is the cost of finished goods inventory sold to customers during the current accounting period. Looking at the finished goods inventory box in Exhibit 2-7, we see that the beginning inventory of finished goods of ₹2,20,000 and cost of goods manufactured in 2014 of ₹10,40,000 "fill up" the finished goods inventory box. The ending inventory of finished goods of ₹1,80,000 becomes the beginning inventory for the next year, and the cost of goods sold during 2014 of ₹10,80,000 "empties out" the finished goods inventory.

This cost of goods sold is an expense that is matched against revenues. The cost of goods sold for Cellular Products (shaded brown) is computed in Exhibit 2-8, Panel A, as:

Beginning inventory of finished goods, January 1, 2014	₹2,20,000
+ Cost of goods manufactured in 2014	10,40,000
− Ending inventory of finished goods, December 31, 2014	1,80,000
= Cost of goods sold in 2014	₹10,80,000

Exhibit 2-9 shows related general-ledger T-accounts for Cellular Products' manufacturing cost flow. Note how the cost of goods manufactured (₹10,40,000) is the cost of all goods completed during the accounting period. These costs are all inventoriable costs. Goods completed during the period are transferred to finished goods inventory. These costs become cost of goods sold in the accounting period when the goods are sold. Also note that the direct materials, direct manufacturing labor, and manufacturing overhead costs of the units in work-in-process inventory (₹70,000) and finished goods inventory (₹1,80,000) as of December 31, 2014, will appear as an asset in the balance sheet. These costs will become expenses next year, when these units are sold.

We can now prepare Cellular Products' income statement for 2014. The income statement of Cellular Products is shown on the right-hand side of Exhibit 2-7 and in Exhibit 2-8, Panel A. Revenues of Cellular Products are (in thousands) ₹21,00,000.

Exhibit 2-9   General-Ledger T-Accounts for Cellular Products' Manufacturing Cost Flow

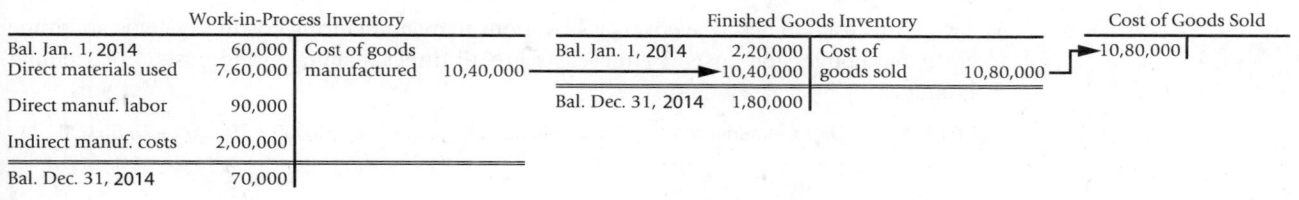

Inventoriable costs expensed during 2014 equal cost of goods sold of ₹10,80,000. Gross margin = Revenues − Cost of goods sold = ₹21,00,000 − ₹10,80,000 = ₹10,20,000.

The ₹7,00,000 comprising R&D, design, marketing, distribution, and customer-service costs are period costs of Cellular Products. These period costs include, for example, salaries of salespersons, depreciation on computers and other equipment used in marketing, and the cost of leasing warehouse space for distribution. Period costs help to calculate **operating income**, which is total revenues from operations minus cost of goods sold and operating costs (excluding interest expense and income taxes). The operating income of Cellular Products is ₹3,20,000 (gross margin, ₹10,20,000 − period costs, ₹7,00,000). If you are familiar with financial accounting, recall that period costs are typically called selling, general, and administrative expenses in the income statement.

Newcomers to cost accounting frequently assume that indirect costs such as rent, telephone, and depreciation are always costs of the period in which they are incurred and are not associated with inventories. When these costs are incurred in marketing or in corporate headquarters, they are period costs. However, when these costs are incurred in manufacturing, they are manufacturing overhead costs and are inventoriable.

Because costs that are inventoried are not expensed until the units associated with them are sold, a manager can produce more units than are expected to be sold in a period without reducing a firm's net income. In fact, building up inventory in this way defers the expensing of the current period's fixed manufacturing costs as manufacturing costs are inventoried and not expensed until the units are sold in a subsequent period. This in turn actually *increases* the firm's gross margin and operating income even though there is no increase in sales, causing outsiders to believe that the company is more profitable than it actually is. We will discuss this risky accounting practice in greater detail in Chapter 9.

Recap of Inventoriable Costs and Period Costs

Exhibit 2-7 highlights the differences between inventoriable costs and period costs for a manufacturing company. The manufacturing costs of finished goods include direct materials, other direct manufacturing costs such as direct manufacturing labor, and manufacturing overhead costs such as supervision, production control, and machine maintenance. All these costs are inventoriable: They are assigned to work-in-process inventory until the goods are completed and then to finished goods inventory until the goods are sold. All non-manufacturing costs, such as R&D, design, and distribution costs, are period costs.

Inventoriable costs and period costs flow through the income statement at a merchandising company similar to the way costs flow at a manufacturing company. At a merchandising company, however, the flow of costs is much simpler to understand and track. Exhibit 2-10 shows the distribution between inventoriable costs and period costs for a retailer or wholesaler who buys goods for resale. The only inventoriable cost is the cost of merchandise. (This corresponds to the cost of finished goods manufactured for a manufacturing company.) Purchased goods are held as merchandise inventory, the cost of which is shown as an asset in the balance sheet. As the goods are sold, their costs are shown in the income statement as cost of goods sold. A retailer or wholesaler also has a variety of marketing, distribution, and customer-service costs, which are period costs. In the income statement, period costs are deducted from revenues without ever having been included as part of inventory.

Prime Costs and Conversion Costs

Two terms used to describe cost classifications in manufacturing costing systems are prime costs and conversion costs. **Prime costs** are all direct manufacturing costs. For Cellular Products,

Prime costs = Direct material costs + Direct manufacturing labor = ₹7,60,000 + ₹90,000 = ₹8,50,000

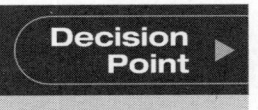

Decision Point ▶

What is the flow of inventoriable and period costs in manufacturing and merchandising settings?

Exhibit 2-10   Merchandising Company (Retailer or Wholesaler)

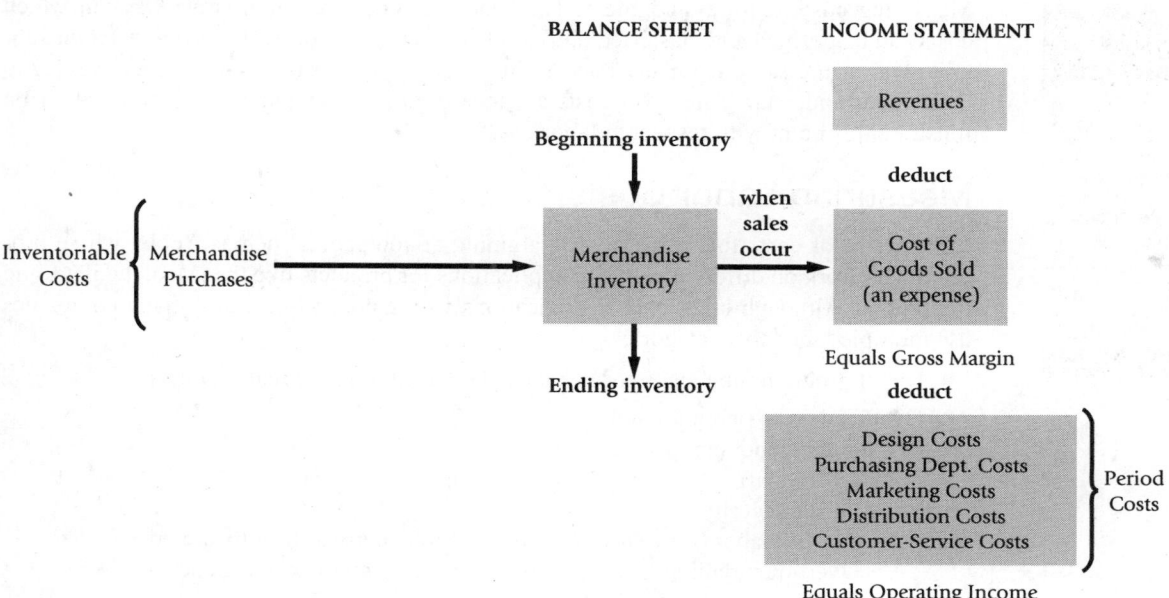

As we have already discussed, the greater the proportion of prime costs in a company's cost structure, the more confident managers can be about the accuracy of the costs of products. As information-gathering technology improves, companies can add more and more direct-cost categories. For example, power costs might be metered in specific areas of a plant and identified with specific products. In this case, prime costs would include direct materials, direct manufacturing labor, and direct metered power. Furthermore, if a production line were dedicated to the manufacture of a specific product, the depreciation on the production equipment would be a direct manufacturing cost and would be included in prime costs. Computer software companies often have a "purchased technology" direct manufacturing cost item. This item, which represents payments to suppliers who develop software algorithms for a product, is also included in prime costs. **Conversion costs** are all manufacturing costs other than direct material costs. Conversion costs represent all manufacturing costs incurred to convert direct materials into finished goods. For Cellular Products,

$$\text{Conversion costs} \frac{\text{Direct manufacturing}}{\text{labor costs}} + \frac{\text{manufacturing}}{\text{overhead costs}} = ₹90,000 + ₹2,00,000 = ₹2,90,000$$

Note that direct manufacturing labor costs are a part of both prime costs and conversion costs.

Some manufacturing operations, such as computer-integrated manufacturing (CIM) plants, have very few workers. The workers' roles are to monitor the manufacturing process and to maintain the equipment that produces multiple products. Costing systems in CIM plants do not have a direct manufacturing labor cost category because direct manufacturing labor cost is relatively small and because it is difficult to trace this cost to products. In CIM plants, the only prime cost is direct material costs, and conversion costs consist only of manufacturing overhead costs.

Measuring Costs Requires Judgment

Measuring costs requires judgment. That's because there are alternative ways in which costs can be defined and classified. Different companies or sometimes even different subunits within the same company may define and classify costs differently. Be careful to define and understand the ways costs are measured in a company or situation. We first illustrate this point with respect to labor cost.

Measuring Labor Costs

Consider labor costs for software programming at companies such as Apple, where programmers work on different software applications for products like the iMac, the iPad, and the iPhone. Although labor cost classifications vary among companies, many companies use multiple labor cost categories:

- Direct programming labor costs that can be traced to individual products
- Overhead costs (labor related)
  - Indirect labor compensation for
    Office staff
    Office security
    Rework labor (time spent by direct laborers correcting software errors)
    Overtime premium paid to software programmers (explained next)
    Idle time (explained next)
  - Salaries for managers, department heads, and supervisors
  - Payroll fringe costs, for example, health care premiums and pension costs (explained later)

To retain information on different categories, *indirect labor costs* are commonly divided into many subclassifications, for example, office staff and idle time costs. Note that managers' salaries usually are not classified as indirect labor costs. Instead, the compensation of supervisors, department heads, and all others who are regarded as management is placed in a separate classification of labor-related overhead.

Overtime Premium and Idle Time

Managers need to pay special attention to two classes of indirect labor—overtime premium and idle time. **Overtime premium** is the wage rate paid to workers (for both direct labor and indirect labor) in *excess* of their straight-time wage rates. Overtime premium is usually considered to be a part of indirect costs or overhead. Consider the example of Govind Chopra, a junior software programmer who writes software for multiple products. He is paid ₹400 per hour for straight-time and ₹600 per hour (time and a half) for overtime. His overtime premium is ₹200 per overtime hour. If he works 44 hours, including 4 overtime hours, in one week, his gross compensation would be classified as follows:

Direct programming labor: 44 hours × ₹400 per hour	₹17,600
Overtime premium: 4 hours × ₹200 per hour	800
Total compensation for 44 hours	₹18,400

In this example, why is the overtime premium of direct programming labor usually considered an overhead cost rather than a direct cost? After all, the premium can be traced to specific products that Govind worked on while working overtime. Overtime premium is generally not considered a direct cost because the particular job that Govind worked on during the overtime hours is a matter of chance. For example, assume that Govind worked on two products for 5 hours each on a specific workday that lasted 10 hours, including 2 overtime hours. Should the product Govind worked on during hours 9 and 10 be assigned the overtime premium? Or should the premium be prorated over both products? Prorating the overtime premium does not "penalize"—add to the cost of—a particular product solely because it happened to be worked on during the overtime hours. *Instead, the overtime premium is considered to be attributable to the heavy overall volume of work. Its cost is regarded as part of overhead, which is borne by both products.*

Sometimes, though, overtime can definitely be attributed to a single product. For example, the overtime needed to meet the launch deadline for a new product may clearly be the sole source of overtime. In such instances, the overtime premium is regarded as a direct cost of that product.

Another subclassification of indirect labor is the idle time of both direct and indirect labor. **Idle time** refers to the wages paid for unproductive time caused by lack of orders, machine or computer breakdowns, work delays, poor scheduling, and the like. For example, if Govind had no work for 3 hours during that week while waiting to receive code from another colleague, Govind's earnings would be classified as follows:

Direct programming labor: 41 hours × ₹400/hour	₹16,400
Idle time (overhead): 3 hours × ₹400/hour	1,200
Overtime premium (service overhead): 4 hours × ₹200/hour	800
Total earnings for 44 hours	₹18,400

Clearly, in this case, the idle time is not related to a particular product, nor, as we have already discussed, is the overtime premium. Both the overtime premium and the costs of idle time are considered overhead costs.

Benefits of Defining Accounting Terms

Managers, accountants, suppliers, and others will avoid many problems if they thoroughly understand and agree on the classifications and meanings of the cost terms introduced in this chapter and later in this book. Consider the classification of programming labor *payroll fringe costs,* which include employer payments for employee benefits such as Social Security, life insurance, health insurance, and pensions. Consider, for example, a software programmer who is paid a wage of ₹400 an hour with fringe benefits totaling, say, ₹100 per hour. Some companies classify the ₹400 as a direct programming labor cost of the product for which the software is being written and the ₹100 as overhead cost. Other companies classify the entire ₹500 as direct programming labor cost. The latter approach is preferable because the stated wage and the fringe benefit costs together are a fundamental part of acquiring direct software programming labor services.

Caution: In every situation, it is important for managers and management accountants to pinpoint clearly what direct labor includes and what direct labor excludes. This clarity will help prevent disputes regarding cost-reimbursement contracts, income tax payments, and labor union matters, which often can take a substantial amount of time for managers to resolve. Consider that some countries, such as Costa Rica and Mauritius, offer substantial income tax savings to foreign companies that generate employment within their borders. In some cases, to qualify for the tax benefits, the direct labor costs must at least equal a specified percentage of a company's total costs.

When managers do not precisely define direct labor costs, disputes can arise about whether payroll fringe costs should be included as part of direct labor costs when calculating the direct labor percentage for qualifying for such tax benefits. Companies have sought to classify payroll fringe costs as part of direct labor costs to make direct labor costs a higher percentage of total costs. Tax authorities have argued that payroll fringe costs are part of overhead. In addition to payroll fringe costs, other debated items are compensation for training time, idle time, vacations, sick leave, and overtime premium. To prevent disputes, contracts and laws should be as specific as possible about accounting definitions and measurements.

Different Meanings of Product Costs

Many cost terms found in practice have ambiguous meanings. Consider the term *product cost*. A **product cost** is the sum of the costs assigned to a product for a specific purpose. Different purposes can result in different measures of product cost, as the brackets on the value chain in Exhibit 2-11 illustrate:

- **Pricing and product-mix decisions.** For the purposes of making decisions about pricing and which products provide the most profits, the manager is interested in the overall (total) profitability of different products and, consequently, assigns costs incurred in all business functions of the value chain to the different products.

- **Reimbursement under government contracts.** Government contracts often reimburse contractors on the basis of the "cost of a product" plus a prespecified margin of profit. A contract such as this is referred to as a "cost-plus" agreement. Cost-plus agreements are typically used for services and development contracts when it is not easy to predict the amount of money required to design, fabricate, and test items. Because these contracts transfer the risk of cost overruns to the government, agencies such as the Department of Defense and the Department of Energy provide detailed guidelines on the cost items they will allow (and disallow) when calculating the cost of a product. For example, many government agencies explicitly exclude marketing, distribution, and customer-service costs from product costs that qualify for reimbursement, and they may only partially reimburse R&D costs. These agencies want to reimburse contractors for only those costs most closely related to delivering products under the contract. The second bracket in Exhibit 2-11 shows how the product-cost calculations for a specific contract may allow for all design and production costs but only part of R&D costs.

- **Preparing financial statements for external reporting under GAAP.** Under GAAP, only manufacturing costs can be assigned to inventories in the financial statements. For purposes of calculating inventory costs, product costs include only inventoriable (manufacturing) costs.

As Exhibit 2-11 illustrates, product-cost measures range from a narrow set of costs for financial statements—a set that includes only inventoriable costs—to a broader set of costs for reimbursement under a government contract to a still broader set of costs for pricing and product-mix decisions.

Exhibit 2-11

Different Product Costs for Different Purposes

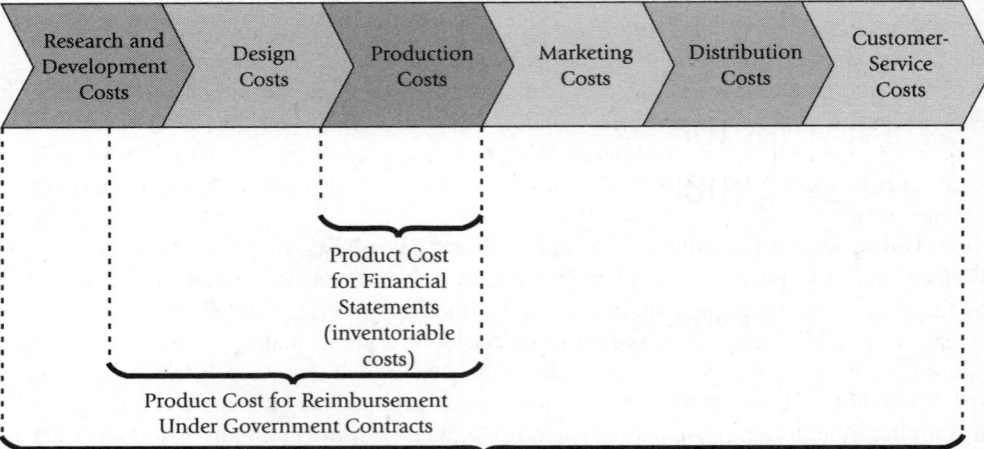

1. Business function
   a. Research and development
   b. Design of products, services, or processes
   c. Production
   d. Marketing
   e. Distribution
   f. Customer service
2. Assignment to a cost object
   a. Direct cost
   b. Indirect cost

3. Behavior pattern in relation to the level of activity or volume
   a. Variable cost
   b. Fixed cost
4. Aggregate or average
   a. Total cost
   b. Unit cost
5. Assets or expenses
   a. Inventoriable cost
   b. Period cost

Exhibit 2-12

Alternative Classifications of Costs

This section focused on how different purposes result in the inclusion of different cost items of the value chain of business functions when product costs are calculated. The same caution about the need to be clear and precise about cost concepts and their measurement applies to each cost classification introduced in this chapter. Exhibit 2-12 summarizes the key cost classifications.

Using the five-step process described in Chapter 1, think about how these different classifications of costs are helpful to managers when making decisions and evaluating performance.

1. **Identify the problem and uncertainties.** Consider a decision about how much to price a product. This decision often depends on how much it costs to make the product.

2. **Obtain information.** Managers identify direct and indirect costs of a product in each business function. Managers also gather other information about customers, competitors, and prices of substitute products.

3. **Make predictions about the future.** Managers estimate what it will cost to make the product in the future. This requires predictions about the quantity of product that managers expect to sell and an understanding of fixed and variable costs.

4. **Make decisions by choosing among alternatives.** Managers choose a price to charge based on a thorough understanding of costs and other information.

5. **Implement the decision, evaluate performance, and learn.** Managers control costs and learn by comparing actual total and unit costs against predicted amounts.

The next section describes how the basic concepts introduced in this chapter lead to a framework for understanding cost accounting and cost management that can then be applied to the study of many topics, such as strategy evaluation, quality, and investment decisions.

A Framework for Cost Accounting and Cost Management

Three features of cost accounting and cost management across a wide range of applications are:

1. Calculating the cost of products, services, and other cost objects
2. Obtaining information for planning and control and performance evaluation
3. Analyzing the relevant information for making decisions

We develop these ideas in Chapters 3 through 12. The ideas also form the foundation for the study of various topics later in the book.

Learning Objective 9

Describe a framework for cost accounting and cost management

. . . three features that help managers make decisions

Calculating the Cost of Products, Services, and Other Cost Objects

We have already seen the different purposes and measures of product costs. Whatever the purpose, the costing system traces direct costs and allocates indirect costs to products. Chapters 4 and 5 describe systems, such as activity-based costing systems, used to calculate total costs and unit costs of products and services. The chapters also discuss how managers use this information to formulate strategy and make pricing, product-mix, and cost-management decisions.

Obtaining Information for Planning and Control and Performance Evaluation

Budgeting is the most commonly used tool for planning and control. A budget forces managers to look ahead, to translate strategy into plans, to coordinate and communicate within the organization, and to provide a benchmark for evaluating performance. Budgeting often plays a major role in affecting behavior and decisions because managers strive to meet budget targets. Chapter 6 describes budgeting systems.

At the end of a reporting period, managers compare actual results to planned performance. The manager's tasks are to understand why differences (called variances) between actual and planned performances arise and to use the information provided by these variances as feedback to promote learning and future improvement. Managers also use variances as well as nonfinancial measures, such as defect rates and customer satisfaction ratings, to control and evaluate the performance of various departments, divisions, and managers. Chapters 7 and 8 discuss variance analysis. Chapter 9 describes planning, control, and inventory-costing issues relating to capacity. Chapters 6, 7, 8, and 9 focus on the management accountant's role in implementing strategy.

Analyzing the Relevant Information for Making Decisions

When making decisions about strategy design and strategy implementation, managers must understand which revenues and costs to consider and which ones to ignore. Management accountants help managers identify what information is relevant and what information is irrelevant. Consider a decision about whether to buy a product from an outside vendor or to make it in-house. The costing system indicates that it costs ₹250 per unit to make the product in-house. A vendor offers the product for ₹220 per unit. At first glance, it seems it will cost less for the company to buy the product rather than make it. Suppose, however, that of the ₹250 to make the product in-house, ₹50 consists of plant lease costs that the company will have to pay whether the product is made or bought. That is, if the product is bought, the plant will remain idle and the ₹50 in lease costs will still be incurred. Under this condition, it will cost less to make the product than to buy it. That's because making the product costs only an *additional* ₹200 per unit (₹250 − ₹50), compared with an *additional* ₹220 per unit if it is bought. The ₹50 per unit of lease cost is irrelevant to the decision because it will be incurred whether the product is made or bought. Analyzing relevant information is a key aspect of making decisions.

When making strategic decisions about which products to produce, managers must know how revenues and costs vary with changes in output levels. For this purpose, managers need to distinguish fixed costs from variable costs. Chapter 3 analyzes how operating income changes with changes in units sold and how managers use this information to make decisions such as how much to spend on advertising. Chapter 10 describes methods to estimate the fixed and variable components of costs. Chapter 11 applies the concept of relevance to decision making in many different situations and describes methods managers use to maximize income given the resource constraints that they face.

Later chapters in the book discuss topics such as strategy evaluation, customer profitability, quality, just-in-time systems, investment decisions, transfer pricing, and performance evaluation. Each of these topics invariably has product costing, planning and control, and decision-making perspectives. A command of the first 12 chapters will help you master these topics. For example, Chapter 13 on strategy describes the balanced score-card, a set of financial and nonfinancial measures used to implement strategy that builds on the planning and control functions. The section on strategic analysis of operating income builds on ideas of product costing and variance analysis. The section on downsizing and managing capacity builds on ideas of relevant revenues and relevant costs.

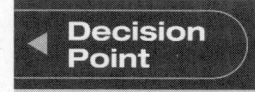

◄ **Decision Point**

What are the three key features of cost accounting and cost management?

Problem for Self-Study

Campbell Company is a metal- and woodcutting manufacturer, selling products to the home construction market. Consider the following data for 2014:

Sandpaper	₹20,000
Materials-handling costs	7,00,000
Lubricants and coolants	50,000
Miscellaneous indirect manufacturing labor	4,00,000
Direct manufacturing labor	30,00,000
Direct materials inventory Jan. 1, 2014	4,00,000
Direct materials inventory Dec. 31, 2014	50,00,000
Finished goods inventory Jan. 1, 2014	10,00,000
Finished goods inventory Dec. 31, 2014	15,00,000
Work in process inventory Jan. 1, 2014	1,00,000
Work in process inventory Dec. 31, 2014	1,40,000
Plant-leasing costs	5,40,000
Depreciation—plant equipment	3,60,000
Property taxes on plant equipment	40,000
Fire insurance on plant equipment	₹30,000
Direct materials purchased	46,00,000
Revenues	1,36,00,000
Marketing promotions	6,00,000
Marketing salaries	10,00,000
Distribution costs	7,00,000
Customer-service costs	10,00,000

Required

1. Prepare an income statement with a separate supporting schedule of cost of goods manufactured. For all manufacturing items, classify costs as direct costs or indirect costs and indicate by V or F whether each is basically a variable cost or a fixed cost (when the cost object is a product unit). If in doubt, decide on the basis of whether the total cost will change substantially over a wide range of units produced.

2. Suppose that both the direct material costs and the plant-leasing costs are for the production of 9,00,000 units. What is the direct material cost of each unit produced? What is the plant-leasing cost per unit? Assume that the plant-leasing cost is a fixed cost.

3. Suppose Campbell Company manufactures 10,00,000 units next year. Repeat the computation in requirement 2 for direct materials and plant-leasing costs. Assume the implied cost-behavior patterns persist.

4. As a management consultant, explain concisely to the company president why the unit cost for direct materials did not change in requirements 2 and 3 but the unit cost for plant-leasing costs did change.

Solution

1.

Campbell Company
Income Statement

For the Year Ended December 31, 2014

Revenues		₹1,36,00,000
Cost of goods sold		
Beginning finished goods inventory January 1, 2014	₹10,00,000	
Cost of goods manufactured (see schedule below)	96,00,000	
Cost of goods available for sale	1,06,00,000	
Deduct ending finished goods inventory		
December 31, 2014	15,00,000	91,00,000
Gross margin (or gross profit)		45,00,000
Operating costs		
Marketing promotions	6,00,000	
Marketing salaries	10,00,000	
Distribution costs	7,00,000	
Customer-service costs	10,00,000	33,00,000
Operating income		₹12,00,000

Campbell Company
Schedule of Cost of Goods Manufactured
For the Year Ended December 31, 2014

Direct materials		
Beginning inventory, January 1, 2014		₹4,00,000
Purchases of direct materials		46,00,000
Cost of direct materials available for use		50,00,000
Ending inventory, December 31, 2014		5,00,000
Direct materials used		45,00,000 (V)
Direct manufacturing labor		30,00,000 (V)
Indirect manufacturing costs		
Sandpaper	₹20,000 (V)	
Materials-handling costs	7,00,000 (V)	
Lubricants and coolants	50,000 (V)	
Miscellaneous indirect manufacturing labor	4,00,000 (V)	
Plant-leasing costs	5,40,000 (F)	
Depreciation—plant equipment	3,60,000 (F)	
Property taxes on plant equipment	40,000 (F)	
Fire insurance on plant equipment	30,000 (F)	21,40,000
Manufacturing costs incurred during 2014		96,40,000
Beginning work in process inventory, January 1, 2014		1,00,000
Total manufacturing costs to account for		97,40,000
Ending work in process inventory, December 31, 2014		1,40,000
Cost of goods manufactured (to Income Statement)		₹96,00,000

2. Direct material unit cost = Direct materials used ÷ Units produced

$$= 45,00,000 \div 9,00,000 \text{ units} = ₹5 \text{ per unit}$$

Plant-leasing unit cost = Plant-leasing costs ÷ Units produced

$$= 5,40,000 \div 9,00,000 \text{ units} = ₹6 \text{ per unit}$$

3. The direct material costs are variable, so they would increase in total from ₹45,00,000 to ₹50,00,000 (10,00,000 units × ₹5 per unit). However, their unit cost would be unaffected: ₹50,00,000 ÷ 10,00,000 units = ₹5 per unit.

In contrast, the plant-leasing costs of ₹5,40,000 are fixed, so they would not increase in total. However, the plant-leasing cost per unit would decline from ₹6 to ₹5.40: ₹5,40,000 ÷ 10,00,000 units = ₹5.4 per unit.

4. The explanation would begin with the answer to requirement 3. As a consultant, you should stress that the unitizing (averaging) of costs that have different behavior patterns can be misleading. A common error is to assume that a total unit cost, which is often a sum of variable unit cost and fixed unit cost, is an indicator that total costs change in proportion to changes in production levels. The next chapter demonstrates the necessity for distinguishing between cost-behavior patterns. You must be wary, especially about average fixed cost per unit. Too often, unit fixed cost is erroneously regarded as being indistinguishable from unit variable cost.

Decision Points

The following question-and-answer format summarizes the chapter's learning objectives. Each decision presents a key question related to a learning objective. The guidelines are the answer to that question.

Decision	Guidelines
1. What is a cost object?	A cost object is anything for which a separate measurement of cost is needed. Examples include a product, a service, a project, a customer, a brand category, an activity, and a department.
2. How do managers decide whether a cost is a direct or an indirect cost?	A direct cost is any cost that is related to a particular cost object and can be traced to that cost object in an economically feasible way. Indirect costs are related to the particular cost object but cannot be traced in an economically feasible way. The same cost can be direct for one cost object and indirect for other cost objects. This book uses *cost tracing* to describe the assignment of direct costs to a cost object and cost *allocation* to describe the assignment of indirect costs to a cost object.
3. How do managers decide whether a cost is a variable or a fixed cost?	A variable cost changes *in total* in proportion to changes in the related level of total activity or volume. A fixed cost remains unchanged *in total* for a given time period despite wide changes in the related level of total activity or volume.
4. How should managers estimate and interpret cost information?	In general, focus on total costs, not unit costs. When making total cost estimates, think of variable costs as an amount per unit and fixed costs as a total amount. The unit cost of a cost object should be interpreted cautiously when it includes a fixed-cost component.
5. What are the differences in the accounting for inventoriable versus period costs?	Inventoriable costs are all costs of a product that a company regards as an asset in the accounting period in which they are incurred and which become cost of goods sold in the accounting period in which the product is sold. Period costs are expensed in the accounting period in which they are incurred and are all of the costs in an income statement other than cost of goods sold.

6. What is the flow of inventoriable and period costs in manufacturing and merchandising settings?

In manufacturing settings, inventoriable costs flow through work-in-process and finished goods accounts, and are expensed as cost of goods sold. Period costs are expensed as they are incurred. In merchandising settings, only the cost of merchandise is treated as inventoriable.

7. Why do managers assign different costs to the same cost objects?

Managers can assign different costs to the same cost object depending on the purpose. For example, for the external reporting purpose in a manufacturing company, the inventoriable cost of a product includes only manufacturing costs. In contrast, costs from all business functions of the value chain often are assigned to a product for pricing and product-mix decisions.

8. What are the three key features of cost accounting and cost management?

Three features of cost accounting and cost management are (1) calculating the cost of products, services, and other cost objects; (2) obtaining information for planning and control and performance evaluation; and (3) analyzing relevant information for making decisions.

TERMS TO LEARN

This chapter contains more basic terms than any other in this book. Do not proceed before you check your understanding of the following terms. Both the chapter and the Glossary at the end of the book contain definitions.

actual cost **(p. 36)**
average cost **(p. 44)**
budgeted cost **(p. 36)**
conversion
  costs **(p. 53)**
cost allocation **(p. 38)**
cost assignment **(p. 38)**
cost object **(p. 36)**
cost tracing **(p. 37)**
direct costs of a cost
  object**(p. 37)**
direct manufacturing labor
  costs **(p. 46)**
direct material
  costs **(p. 46)**
direct materials
  inventory **(p. 46)**

factory overhead
  costs **(p. 46)**
finished goods
  inventory **(p. 46)**
fixed cost **(p. 39)**
idle time **(p. 55)**
indirect costs of a cost
  object **(p. 37)**
indirect manufacturing
  costs **(p. 46)**
inventoriable costs **(p. 46)**
manufacturing overhead
  costs **(p. 46)**
manufacturing-sector
  companies **(p. 45)**
merchandising-sector
  companies **(p. 45)**

operating
  income **(p. 52)**
overtime
  premium **(p. 54)**
period costs **(p. 46)**
product cost **(p. 56)**
relevant
  range **(p. 42)**
revenues **(p. 46)**
service-sector
  companies **(p. 46)**
unit cost **(p. 44)**
variable cost **(p. 39)**
work-in-process
  inventory **(p. 46)**
work in
  progress **(p. 46)**

ASSIGNMENT MATERIAL

Questions

2-1 Define cost object and give three examples.

2-2 Define direct costs and indirect costs.

2-3 Why do managers consider direct costs to be more accurate than indirect costs?

2-4 Name three factors that will affect the classification of a cost as direct or indirect.

2-5 Define variable cost and fixed cost. Give an example of each.

2-6 What is a cost driver? Give one example.

2-7 What is the relevant range? What role does the relevant-range concept play in explaining how costs behave?

2-8 Explain why unit costs must often be interpreted with caution.

2-9 Describe how manufacturing-, merchandising-, and service-sector companies differ from each other.

2-10 What are three different types of inventory that manufacturing companies hold?

2-11 Distinguish between inventoriable costs and period costs.

2-12 Do service-sector companies have inventoriable costs? Explain.

2-13 Define the following: direct material costs, direct manufacturing-labor costs, manufacturing overhead costs, prime costs, and conversion costs.

2-14 Describe the overtime-premium and idle-time categories of indirect labor.

2-15 Define product cost. Describe three different purposes for computing product costs.

Solved Examples

2-16 Computing and interpreting manufacturing unit costs. J.K. Paper Products (JKPP) produces three different paper products - Supreme, Deluxe, and Regular. Each product has its own dedicated production line at the plant. It currently uses the following three-part classification for its manufacturing costs: direct materials, direct manufacturing labor, and indirect manufacturing costs. Total indirect manufacturing costs of the plant for July, current year are ₹150 million (₹20 million of which is fixed). This total amount is allocated to each product line on the basis of direct manufacturing labor costs of each line. Summary data (in millions) for July are as follows:

Particulars	Supreme	Deluxe	Regular
Direct material costs	₹84.00	₹54.00	₹62.00
Direct manufacturing labor costs	14.00	28.00	8.00
Manufacturing overhead costs	42.00	84.00	24.00
Units produced	80.00	120.00	100.00

Required

1. Compute the manufacturing cost per unit for each product produced in July.

2. Suppose that in August production was 120 million units of Supreme, 160 million units of Deluxe, and 180 million units of Regular. Why might the July manufacturing unit cost information be misleading when predicting total manufacturing costs in August?

Solution

1. Computation of manufacturing cost per unit (in millions)

Particulars	Supreme	Deluxe	Regular
Direct materials costs	₹84.00	₹54.00	₹62.00
Direct manufacturing labor costs	14.00	28.00	8.00
Indirect manufacturing costs	42.00	84.00	24.00
Total manufacturing costs	140.00	166.00	94.00
Units produced (millions)	80	120	100
Cost per unit (Total manufacturing costs ÷ Units produced)	₹1.7500	₹1.3833	₹0.9400

2. The unit costs in requirement 1 includes ₹20 million of indirect manufacturing costs that are fixed irrespective of changes in the volume of output per month, while the remaining variable indirect manufacturing costs change with the production volume. Given the unit volume changes for August, the use of unit costs from the past month at a different unit volume level (both in aggregate and at the individual product level) will yield incorrect estimates of total costs in August.

2-17 Direct, indirect, fixed, and variable costs. Everbake Bakery manufactures two types of bread, which it sells as wholesale products to various specialty retail bakeries. Each loaf of bread requires a three-step process. The first step is mixing. The mixing department combines all of the necessary ingredients to create the dough and processes it through high-speed mixers. The dough is then left to rise before baking. The second step is baking, which is an entirely automated process. The baking department molds the dough into its final shape and bakes each loaf of bread in a high-temperature oven. The final step is finishing, which is an entirely manual process. The finishing department coats each loaf of bread with a special glaze, allows the bread to cool, and then carefully packages each loaf in a specialty carton for sale in retail bakeries.

Required

1. Costs involved in the process are listed next. For each cost, indicate whether it is a direct variable, direct fixed, indirect variable, or indirect fixed cost, assuming "units of production of each kind of bread" is the cost object.

Costs:
Yeast	Mixing department manager
Flour	Materials handlers in each department
Packaging materials	Custodian in factory
Depreciation on ovens	Night guard in factory
Depreciation on mixing machines	Machinist (running the mixing machine)
Rent on factory building	Machine maintenance personnel in each department
Fire insurance on factory building	Maintenance supplies for factory
Factory utilities	Cleaning supplies for factory
Finishing department hourly laborers	

2. If the cost object were the "mixing department" rather than units of production of each kind of bread, which preceding costs would now be direct instead of indirect costs?

Solution

1. Yeast—direct, variable
   Flour—direct, variable
   Packaging materials—direct (or could be indirect if small and not traced to each unit), variable
   Depreciation on ovens—indirect, fixed (unless "units of output" depreciation, which then would be variable)

Depreciation on mixing machines—indirect, fixed (unless "units of output" depreciation, which then would be variable)

Rent on factory building—indirect, fixed

Fire Insurance on factory building—indirect, fixed

Factory utilities—indirect, probably some variable and some fixed (e.g., electricity may be variable but heating costs may be fixed)

Finishing department hourly laborers—direct, variable (or fixed if the laborers are under a union contract)

Mixing department manager—indirect, fixed

Materials handlers—depends on how they are paid. If paid hourly and not under union contract, then indirect, variable. If salaried or under union contract, then indirect, fixed

Custodian in factory—indirect, fixed

Night guard in factory—indirect, fixed

Machinist (running the mixing machine)—depends on how they are paid. If paid hourly and not under union contract, then indirect, variable. If salaried or under union contract, then indirect, fixed

Machine maintenance personnel—indirect, probably fixed, if salaried, but may be variable if paid only for time worked and maintenance increases with increased production

Maintenance supplies—indirect, variable

Cleaning supplies—indirect, most likely fixed because the custodians probably do the same amount of cleaning every night

2. If the cost object is Mixing Department, then anything directly associated with the Mixing Department will be a direct cost. This will include:
   • Depreciation on mixing machines
   • Mixing Department manager
   • Materials handlers (of the Mixing Department)
   • Machinist (running the mixing machines)
   • Machine Maintenance personnel (of the Mixing Department)
   • Maintenance supplies (if separately identified for the Mixing Department)

Of course the yeast and flour will also be a direct cost of the Mixing Department, but it is already a direct cost of each kind of bread produced.

2-18 Classification of costs, service sector. Consumer Focus is a marketing research firm that organizes focus groups for consumer-product companies. Each focus group has eight individuals who are paid ₹1,000 per session to provide comments on new products. These focus groups meet in hotels and are led by a trained, independent, marketing specialist hired by Consumer Focus. Each specialist is paid a fixed retainer to conduct a minimum number of sessions and per session fee of ₹5,000. A Consumer Focus staff member attends each session to ensure that all the logistical aspects run smoothly.

Classify each of the following cost items as:

Required

   a. Direct or indirect (D or I) costs with respect to each individual focus group.
   b. Variable or fixed (V or F) costs with respect to how the total costs of Consumer Focus change as the number of focus groups conducted changes. (If in doubt, select on the basis of whether the total costs will change substantially if there is a large change in the number of groups conducted.)

You will have two answers (D or I; V or F) for each of the following items:

Cost Item

   A. Payment to individuals in each focus group to provide comments on new products.
   B. Annual subscription of Consumer Focus to Consumer Reports magazine.

C. Phone calls made by Consumer Focus staff member to confirm individuals will attend a focus group session (records of individual calls are not kept).

D. Retainer paid to focus group leader to conduct 20 focus groups per year on new medical products.

E. Meals provided to participants in each focus group.

F. Lease payment by Consumer Focus for corporate office.

G. Cost of tapes used to record comments made by individuals in a focus group session. (These tapes are sent to the company whose products are being tested.)

H. Petrol/diesel costs of Consumer Focus staff for company-owned vehicles (staff members submit monthly bills with no mileage breakdowns).

Solution

Cost object: Each individual focus group.

Cost variability: With respect to changes in the number of focus groups.

There may be some debate over classifications of individual items. Debate is more likely as regards to cost variability.

Cost Item	D or I	V or F
A	D	V
B	I	F
C	I	V[a]
D	I	F
E	D	V
F	I	F
G	D	V
H	I	V[b]

[a]Some students will note that phone call costs are variable when each call has a separate charge. It may be a fixed cost if Consumer Focus has a flat monthly charge for a line, irrespective of the amount of usage.

[b]Petrol/diesel costs are likely to vary with the number of focus groups. However, vehicles are likely to serve multiple purposes, and detailed records may be required to examine how costs vary with changes in one of the many purposes served.

2-19 Classification of costs, manufacturing sector. Skoda Octavia, plant of New United Motor Manufacturing, Ltd. (NUMML), a joint venture of General Motors and Toyota, assembles two types of cars (Corollas and Geo Prisms). Separate assembly lines are used for each type of car.

a. Direct or indirect (D or I) costs with respect to the type of car assembled (Corolla or Geo Prism).

b. Variable or fixed (V or F) costs with respect to how the total costs of the plant change as the number of cars assembled changes. (If in doubt, select on the basis of whether the total costs will change substantially if there is a large change in the number of cars assembled.)

You will have two answers (D or I; V or F) for each of the following items:

Cost Item	D or I	V or F
A. Cost of tires used on Geo Prisms		
B. Salary of public relations manager for NUMML plant		

C. Annual awards dinner for Corolla suppliers

D. Salary of engineer who monitors design changes on Geo Prism

E. Freight costs of Corolla engines shipped from Toyota City, Japan, to Fremont, California

F. Electricity costs for NUMML plant (single bill covers entire plant)

G. Wages paid to temporary assembly-line workers hired in periods of high production (paid on hourly basis)

H. Annual fire-insurance policy cost for NUMML plant

Solution

Cost object: Type of car assembled (Corolla or Geo Prism)

Cost variability: With respect to changes in the number of cars assembled

There may be some debate over classifications of individual items. Debate is more likely as regards cost variability.

Cost Item	D or I	V or F
A	D	V
B	I	F
C	D	F
D	D	F
E	D	V
F	I	V
G	D	V
H	I	F

2-20 Variable costs, fixed costs, total costs. Akshita Jain is getting ready to open a small restaurant. She is on a tight budget and must choose between the following long-distance phone plans:

Plan A: Pay ₹1 per minute of long-distance calling.

Plan B: Pay a fixed monthly fee of ₹150 for up to 240 long-distance minutes and ₹0.8 per minute thereafter (if she uses fewer than 240 minutes in any month, she still pays ₹150 for the month).

Plan C: Pay a fixed monthly fee of ₹220 for up to 510 long-distance minutes and ₹0.5 per minute there- after (if she uses fewer than 510 minutes, she still pays ₹220 for the month).

Required

1. Draw a graph of the total monthly costs of the three plans for different levels of monthly long-distance calling.

2. Which plan should Akshita choose if she expects to make 100 minutes of long-distance calls? 240 minutes? 540 minutes?

Solution

1.

Minutes/month	0	50	100	150	200	240	300	327.5	350	400	450	510	540	600	650
Plan A (₹/month)	0	50	100	150	200	240	300	327.5	350	400	450	510	540	600	650
Plan B (₹/month)	150	150	150	150	150	150	198	220	238	278	318	366	390	438	478
Plan C (₹/month)	220	220	220	220	220	220	220	220	220	220	220	220	235	265	290

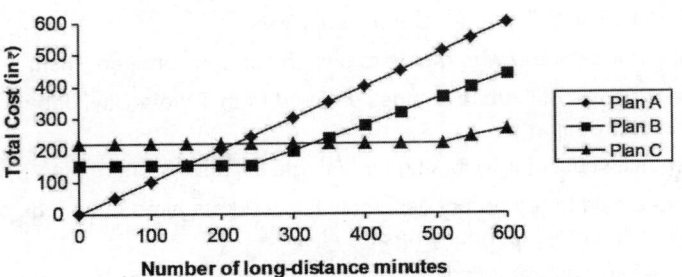

2. In each region, Askhita chooses the plan that has the lowest cost. From the graph (or from calculations)*, we can see that if Askhita expects to use 0–150 minutes of long-distance each month, she should buy Plan A; for 150–327.5 minutes, Plan B; and for more than 327.5 minutes, Plan C. If Askhita plans to make 100 minutes of long-distance calls each month, she should choose Plan A; for 240 minutes, choose Plan B; for 540 minutes, choose Plan C.

*Let x be the number of minutes when Plan A and Plan B have equal cost

$$₹1x = ₹150$$

$$x = ₹150 ÷ ₹1 \text{ per minute} = 150 \text{ minutes.}$$

Let y be the number of minutes when Plan B and Plan C have equal cost

$$₹150 + ₹0.8 (y − 240) = ₹220$$

$$₹0.8 (y − 240) = ₹220 − ₹150 = ₹70$$

$$y − 240 = \frac{₹70}{₹0.8} = 87.5$$

$$y = 87.5 + 240 = 327.5 \text{ minutes}$$

2-21 Variable costs and fixed costs. Mahindra & Mahindra Ltd specializes in producing one specialty vehicle. It is called Surfer and is styled to easily fit multiple surfboards in its back area and top-mounted storage racks. Mahindra & Mahindra Ltd has the following manufacturing costs:

Plant management costs, ₹1,200 lakh per year

Cost of leasing equipment, ₹1,800 lakh per year

Workers' wages, ₹70,000 per Surfer vehicle produced

Direct materials costs: Steel, ₹1,50,000 per Surfer; Tires, ₹12,500 per tire, each Surfer takes 5 tires (one spare).

City license, which is charged monthly based on the number of tires used in production:

0–500 tires	₹50 lakh
501–1,000 tires	₹74.5 lakh
more than 1,000 tires	₹200 lakh

Mahindra & Mahindra Ltd currently produces 110 vehicles per month.

Required

1. What is the variable manufacturing cost per vehicle? What is the fixed manufacturing cost per month?

2. Plot a graph for the variable manufacturing costs and a second for the fixed manufacturing costs per month. How does the concept of relevant range relate to your graphs? Explain.

3. What is the total manufacturing cost of each vehicle if 100 vehicles are produced each month? 225 vehicles? How do you explain the difference in the manufacturing cost per unit?

Solution

1. Variable manufacturing cost per vehicle

Steel	₹1,50,000 per Surfer
Tires	62,500 per Surfer
Direct manufacturing labor	70,000 per Surfer
Total	₹2,82,500 per Surfer

Fixed manufacturing costs per month

Plant management costs (₹1,200 lakh ÷ 12)	₹100 lakh
Cost of leasing equipment (₹1,800 lakh ÷ 12)	150 lakh
City license (for 110 surfers or 550 tires)	74.5 lakh
Total fixed manufacturing costs	₹324.5 lakh

Fixed costs per month (1 surfer takes 5 tires)

0 to 100 surfers per month = ₹100 lakh + ₹150 lakh + ₹50 lakh
= ₹300 lakh

101 to 200 surfers per month = ₹100 lakh + ₹150 lakh + ₹74 lakh
= ₹324.5 lakh

More than 200 surfers per month = ₹100 lakh + ₹150 lakh + ₹200 lakh
= ₹450 lakh

2.

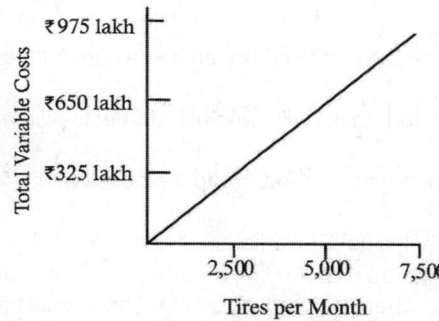
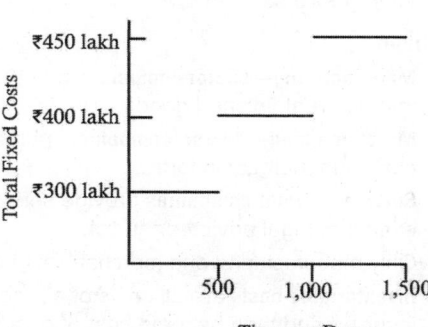

The concept of relevant range is potentially relevant for both graphs. However, the question does not place restrictions on the unit variable costs. The relevant range for the total fixed costs is from 0 to 100 surfers; 101 to 200 surfers; more than 200 surfers. Within these ranges, the total fixed costs do not change in total.

3.

Vehicles Produced per Month	Tires Produced per Month (₹)	Fixed Cost per Month (₹)	Unit Fixed Cost per Vehicle (₹)	Unit Variable Cost per Vehicle (₹)	Unit Total Cost per Vehicle (₹)
(1)	(2) = (1) × 5	(3)	(4) = FC ÷ (1)	(5)	(6) = (4) + (5)
(a) 100	500	300 lakh	300 lakh ÷ 100 = 3 lakh	2,82,500	5,82,500
(b) 225	1,125	450 lakh	450 lakh ÷ 225 = 2 lakh	2,82,500	4,82,500

The unit cost for 100 vehicles produced per month is ₹5,82,500, while for 225 vehicles it is only ₹4,82,500. This difference is caused by the fixed cost increment of ₹150 lakh (an increase of 50%, ₹150 lakh ÷ ₹300 lakh = 50%) being spread over an increment of 125 (225 – 100) vehicles (an increase of 125%, 125 ÷ 100). The fixed cost per unit is therefore lower.

2-22 Inventoriable costs versus period costs. Each of the following cost items pertains to one of these companies. General Electric (a manufacturing-sector company), Tata Industries (a merchandising-sector company), and Infosys (a service-sector company):

- **a.** Perrier mineral water purchased by Tata Industries for sale to its customers.
- **b.** Electricity used to provide lighting for assembly-line workers at a General Electric refrigerator-assembly plant.
- **c.** Depreciation on Infosys computer equipment used to update directories of Web sites.
- **d.** Electricity used to provide lighting for Tata Industries store aisles.
- **e.** Depreciation on General Electric's computer equipment used for quality testing of refrigerator components during the assembly process.
- **f.** Salaries of Tata Industries marketing personnel planning local-newspaper advertising campaigns.
- **g.** Perrier mineral water purchased by Infosys for consumption by its software engineers.
- **h.** Salaries of Infosys marketing personnel selling banner advertising.

Required

1. Distinguish between manufacturing-sector, merchandising-sector, and service-sector companies.
2. Distinguish between inventoriable costs and period costs.
3. Classify each of the cost items (a-h) as an inventoriable cost or a period cost. Explain your answers.

Solution

1. **Manufacturing—sector companies** purchase materials and components and convert them into different finished goods.

   Merchandising—sector companies purchase and then sell tangible products without changing their basic form.

   Service—sector companies provide services or intangible products to their customers–for example, legal advice or audits.

   Only manufacturing and merchandising companies have inventories of goods for sale.

2. **Inventoriable costs** are all costs of a product that are regarded as an asset when they are incurred and then become cost of goods sold when the product is sold. These costs for a manufacturing company are included in work-in-process and finished goods inventory (they are "inventoried") to build up the costs of creating these assets.

   Period costs are all costs in the income statement other than cost of goods sold. These costs are treated as expenses of the period in which they are incurred because they are presumed not to benefit future periods (or because there is not sufficient evidence to conclude that such benefit exists). Expensing these costs immediately best matches expenses to revenues.

3. **(a)** Mineral water purchased for resale by Tata Industries–inventoriable cost of a merchandising company. It becomes part of cost of goods sold when the mineral water is sold.

   (b) Electricity used at GE assembly plant–inventoriable cost of a manufacturing company. It is part of the manufacturing overhead that is included in the manufacturing cost of a refrigerator finished good.

   (c) Depreciation on Infosys computer equipment–period cost of a service company. Infosys has no inventory of goods for sale and, hence, no inventoriable cost.

   (d) Electricity for Tata Industries store aisles–period cost of a merchandising company. It is a cost that benefits the current period and is not traceable to goods purchased for resale.

   (e) Depreciation on GE's assembly testing equipment–inventoriable cost of a manufacturing company. It is part of the manufacturing overhead that is included in the manufacturing cost of a refrigerator finished good.

(f) Salaries of Tata Industries marketing personnel–period cost of a merchandising company. It is a cost that is not traceable to goods purchased for resale. It is presumed not to benefit future periods (or at least not to have sufficiently reliable evidence to estimate such future benefits).

(g) Water consumed by Infosys engineers–period cost of a service company. Infosys has no inventory of goods for sale and, hence, no inventoriable cost.

(h) Salaries of Infosys marketing personnel–period cost of a service company. Infosys has no inventory of goods for sale and, hence, no inventoriable cost.

2-23 Variable costs, fixed costs, relevant range. Everbake manufactures jaw-breaker candies in a fully automated process. The machine that produces candies was purchased recently and can make 4,400 per month. The machine costs ₹95,000 and is depreciated using straight-line depreciation over 10 years assuming zero residual value. Rent for the factory space and warehouse and other fixed manufacturing overhead costs total ₹13,000 per month.

Everbake currently makes and sells 3,100 jaw-breakers per month. Everbake buys just enough materials each month to make the jaw-breakers it needs to sell. Materials cost ₹1 per jawbreaker.

Next year Everbake expects demand to increase by 100%. At this volume of materials purchased, it will get a 10% discount on price. Rent and other fixed manufacturing overhead costs will remain the same.

1. What is Everbake's current annual relevant range of output? **Required**

2. What is Everbake's current annual fixed manufacturing cost within the relevant range? What is the annual variable manufacturing cost?

3. What will Everbake's relevant range of output be next year? How, if at all, will total annual fixed and variable manufacturing costs change next year? Assume that if it needs to Everbake could buy an identical machine at the same cost as the one it already has.

Solution

1. The production capacity is 4,400 jaw breakers per month. Therefore, the current annual relevant range of output is 0 to 4,400 jaw breakers × 12 months = 0 to 52,800 jaw breakers.

2. Current annual fixed manufacturing costs within the relevant range are ₹13,000 × 12 = ₹1,56,000 for rent and other overhead costs, plus ₹95,000 ÷ 10 = ₹9,500 for depreciation, totaling ₹1,65,500.

The variable costs, the materials, are ₹1 per jaw breaker, or ₹37,200 (₹1 per jaw breaker × 3,100 jaw breakers per month × 12 months) for the year.

3. If demand changes from 3,100 to 6,200 jaw breakers per month, or from 3,100 × 12 = 37,200 to 6,200 × 12 = 74,400 jaw breakers per year, Everbake will need a second machine. Assuming Everbake buys a second machine identical to the first machine, it will increase capacity from 4,400 jaw breakers per month to 8,800. The annual relevant range will be between 4,400 × 12 = 52,800 and 8,800 × 12 = 1,05,600 jaw breakers.

Assume the second machine costs ₹95,000 and is depreciated using straight-line depreciation over 10 years and zero residual value, just like the first machine. This will add ₹9,500 of depreciation per year.

Fixed costs for next year will increase to ₹1,75,000 from ₹1,65,500 for the current year + ₹9,500 (because rent and other fixed overhead costs will remain the same at ₹1,56,000). That is, total fixed costs for next year equal ₹9,500 (depreciation on first machine) + ₹9,500 (depreciation on second machine) + ₹1,56,000 (rent and other fixed overhead costs).

The variable cost per jaw breaker next year will be 90% × ₹1.0 = ₹0.9. Total variable costs equal ₹0.9 per jaw breaker × 74,400 jaw breakers = ₹66,960.

If Everbake decides not to increase capacity and meet only that amount of demand for which it has available capacity (4,400 jaw breakers per month or 4,400 × 12 = 52,800 jaw breakers per year), the variable cost per unit will be the same at ₹1 per jaw breaker. Annual total variable manufacturing costs will increase to ₹1 × 4,400 jaw breakers per month × 12 months = ₹52,800. Annual total fixed manufacturing costs will remain the same, ₹1,65,500.

2-24 Cost drivers and value chain. Nokia is developing a new touch-screen smartphone to compete in the cellular phone industry. The company will sell the phones at wholesale prices to cell phone companies, which will in turn sell them in retail stores to the final customer. Nokia has undertaken the following activities in its value chain to bring its product to market:

Identify customer needs (What do smartphone users want?)
Perform market research on competing brands
Design a prototype of the Nokia smartphone
Market the new design to cell phone companies
Manufacture the Nokia smartphone
Process orders from cell phone companies
Package the Nokia smartphones
Deliver the Nokia smartphones to the cell phone companies
Provide online assistance to cell phone users for use of the Nokia smartphone
Make design changes to the smartphone based on customer feedback

During the process of product development, production, marketing, distribution, and customer service, Nokia has kept track of the following cost drivers:
Number of smartphones transported by Nokia
Number of design changes
Number of deliveries made to cell phone companies
Engineering hours spent on initial product design
Hours spent researching competing market brands
Customer-service hours
Number of smartphone orders processed
Number of cell phone companies purchasing the Nokia smartphone
Machine hours required to run the production equipment
Number of surveys returned and processed from competing smartphone users

Required

1. Identify each value chain activity listed at the beginning of the exercise with one of the following value-chain categories:
   a. Design of products and processes
   b. Production
   c. Marketing
   d. Distribution
   e. Customer service

2. Use the list of preceding cost drivers to find one or more reasonable cost drivers for each of the activities in Nokia's value chain.

Solution

1. Identify customer needs (what do smartphone users want?)—Design of products and processes
   Perform market research on competing brands—Design of products and processes
   Design a prototype of the Nokia smartphone—Design of products and processes
   Market the new design to cell phone companies—Marketing
   Manufacture the Nokia smartphone—Production
   Process orders from cell phone companies—Distribution

Package the Nokia smartphones—Production

Deliver the Nokia smartphones to the cell phone companies—Distribution

Provide online assistance to cell phone users for use of the Nokia smartphone—Customer Service

Make design changes to the Nokia smartphone based on customer feedback—Design of products and processes

2.

Value Chain Category	Activity	Cost Driver
Design of products and processes	Identify customer needs	Number of surveys returned and processed from competing smart-phone users
	Perform market research on competing brands	Hours spent researching competing market brands
		Number of surveys returned and processed from competing smart-phone users
	Design a prototype of the Nokia smartphone	Engineering hours spent on initial product design
	Make design changes to the smartphone based on cus-tomer feedback	Number of design changes
Production	Manufacture the Nokia smart-phones	Machine hours required to run the production equipment
	Package the Nokia smart-phones	Number of smartphones transported by Nokia
Marketing	Market the new design to cell phone companies	Number of cell phone companies purchasing the Nokia smartphone
Distribution	Process orders from cell phone companies	Number of smartphone orders pro-cessed
		Number of deliveries made to cell phone companies
	Deliver the Nokia smart-phones to cell phone compa-nies	Number of deliveries made to cell phone companies
Customer service	Provide on-line assistance to cell phone users for use of the Nokia smartphone	Number of smartphones transported by Nokia
		Customer service hours

2-25 Total costs and unit costs The Big Event (TBE) recently started a business organiz-ing food and music at weddings and other large events in a small city. In order to better understand the profitability of the business, the owner has asked you for an analysis of costs—what costs are fixed, what costs are variable, and so on, for each event. You have the following cost information:

Music costs: ₹10,000 per event

Catering costs:

    Food: ₹65 per guest

    Setup/cleanup: ₹15 per guest

    Fixed fee: ₹4,000 per event

The Big Event has allowed the caterer, who is also new in business, to place business cards on each table as a form of advertising. This has proved quite effective, and the caterer gives TBE a discount of ₹5 per guest in exchange for allowing the caterer to advertise.

Required

1. Draw a graph depicting fixed costs, variable costs, and total costs for each event versus the number of guests.
2. Suppose 150 persons attend the next event. What is TBE's total net cost and the cost per attendee?
3. Suppose instead that 200 persons attend. What is TBE's total net cost and the cost per attendee.
4. How should TBE charge customers for its services? Explain briefly.

Solution

1.

Number of guests	0	50	100	150	200	250	300
Variable cost per guest (₹80 caterer charge – ₹5 discount for advertising)	₹75	₹75	₹75	₹75	₹75	₹75	₹75
Fixed Costs	₹14,000	₹14,000	₹14,000	₹14,000	₹14,000	₹14,000	₹14,000
Variable costs (number of guests × variable cost per guest)	0	3,750	7,500	11,250	15,000	18,750	22,500
Total costs (fixed + variable)	₹14,000	₹17,750	₹21,500	₹25,250	₹29,000	₹32,750	₹36,500

2.

Number of guests	0 (₹)	50 (₹)	100 (₹)	150 (₹)	200 (₹)	250 (₹)	300 (₹)
Total costs (fixed + variable)	14,000	17,750	21,500	25,250	29,000	32,750	36,500
Costs per guest (total costs ÷ number of guests)		355	215	168.33	145	131	121.67

As shown in the table above, for 150 attendees the total cost will be ₹25,250, and the cost per attendee will be ₹168.33.

2. As shown in the table in requirement 2, for 200 attendees, the total cost will be ₹29,000, and the cost per attendee will be ₹145.

3. TBE should charge customers based on the number of guests. As the number of guests increase, TBE could offer price discounts because its fixed costs would be spread over a larger number of guests.

Alternatively, TBE could charge a flat fee of ₹10,000 plus a margin for the music. The catering costs would then vary less with the number of guests because only ₹4,000 of fixed costs would be spread over the number of guests. For 100 guests, the fixed catering cost per guest would be ₹40 (₹4,000 ÷ 100 guests); for 200 guests, it would be ₹20 (₹4,000 ÷ 200 guests). TBE's total cost would be ₹115 (variable cost per guest of ₹75 + fixed catering cost per guest of ₹40) for 100 guests and ₹95 (variable cost per guest of ₹75 + fixed catering cost per guest of ₹20) for 200 guests.

2-26 Cost of goods purchased, cost of goods sold, and income statement. The following data are for Montgomery Retail Outlet Stores. The account balances (in thousands) are for 2015.

Marketing and advertising costs	₹48,000
Merchandise inventory, January 1, 2015	90,000
Shipping of merchandise to customers	4,000
Building depreciation	8,400
Purchases	5,20,000
General and administrative costs	64,000
Merchandise inventory, December 31, 2015	1,04,000
Merchandise freight-in	20,000
Purchase returns and allowances	22,000
Purchase discounts	18,000
Revenues	6,40,000

Required

1. Compute (a) the cost of goods purchased and (b) the cost of goods sold.
2. Prepare the income statement for 2015.

Solution

1a.

Reliable Retail Outlet Stores Schedule of Cost of Goods Purchased For the Year Ended December 31, 2015 (in thousands)

Purchases		₹5,20,000
Add freight—in		20,000
		5,40,000
Deduct:		
Purchase returns and allowances	₹22,000	
Purchase discounts	18,000	40,000
Cost of goods purchased		₹5,00,000

1b.

Reliable Retail Outlet Stores Schedule of Cost of Goods Sold For the Year Ended December 31, 2015 (in thousands)

Beginning merchandise inventory, January 1, 2015	₹90,000
Cost of goods purchased (see above)	5,00,000
Cost of goods available for sale	5,90,000
Ending merchandise inventory, December 31, 2015	1,04,000
Cost of goods sold	₹4,86,000

2.

Reliable Retail Outlet Stores IncomeStatement Year Ended December 31, 2015 (in thousands)

Revenues		₹6,40,000
Cost of goods sold (see 1b)		4,86,000
Gross margin		1,54,000
Operating costs		
Marketing and advertising costs	₹48,000	
Building depreciation	8,400	

Shipping of merchandise to customers	4,000
General and administrative costs	64,000
Total operating costs	1,24,400
Operating income	₹29,600

2-27 Flow of Inventoriable Costs. Electric Heaters selected data for March, 2015 are presented here (in lakh):

Direct materials inventory March 1, 2015	₹105
Direct materials purchased	365
Direct materials used	385
Total manufacturing overhead costs	450
Variable manufacturing overhead costs	265
Total manufacturing costs incurred during March 2015	1,610
Work-in-process inventory March 1, 2015	230
Cost of goods manufactured	1,660
Finished goods inventory March 1, 2015	130
Cost of goods sold	1,770

Required Calculate the following costs:

1. Direct materials inventory March 31, 2015
2. Fixed manufacturing overhead costs for March, 2015
3. Direct manufacturing labor costs for March, 2015
4. Work-in-process inventory March 31, 2015
5. Cost of finished goods available for sale in March, 2015
6. Finished goods inventory March 31, 2015

Solution

(All numbers below are in lakh of rupees).

1.

Direct materials inventory March 1, 2015	₹105
Direct materials purchased	365
Direct materials available for production	470
Direct materials used	(385)
Direct materials inventory March 31, 2015	₹85

2.

Total manufacturing overhead costs	₹450
Subtract: Variable manufacturing overhead costs	(265)
Fixed manufacturing overhead costs for March, 2015	₹185

3.

Total manufacturing costs	₹1,610
Subtract: Direct materials used (from requirement 1)	(385)
Total manufacturing overhead costs	(450)
Direct manufacturing labor costs for March, 2015	₹775

4.

Work-in-process inventory March 1, 2015	₹230

Total manufacturing costs	1,610
Work-in-process available for production	1,840
Subtract: Cost of goods manufactured (moved into FG)	(1,660)
Work-in-process inventory March 31, 2015	₹180

5.

Finished goods inventory March 1, 2015	₹130
Cost of goods manufactured (moved from WIP)	1,660
Cost of finished goods available for sale in March, 2015	₹1,790

6.

Finished goods available for sale in March, 2015 (from requirement 5)	₹1,790
Subtract: Cost of goods sold	(1,770)
Finished goods inventory March 31, 2015	₹20

2-28 Cost of goods manufactured, income statement, manufacturing company. Consider the following account balances (in thousands) for the Bajaj Corporation:

Bajaj Corporation	Beginning of 2014	End of 2014
Direct materials inventory	₹1,30,000	₹68,000
Work-in-process inventory	1,66,000	1,44,000
Finished goods inventory	2,46,000	2,04,000
Purchases of direct materials		2,56,000
Direct manufacturing labor		2,12,000
Indirect manufacturing labor		96,000
Indirect materials		28,000
Plant insurance		4,000
Depreciation—plant, building, and equipment		42,000
Plant utilities		24,000
Repairs and maintenance—plant		16,000
Equipment leasing costs		64,000
Marketing, distribution, and customer-service costs		1,24,000
General and administrative costs		68,000

Required

1. Prepare a schedule for the cost of goods manufactured for 2014.
2. Revenues (in thousands) for 2014 were ₹12,00,000. Prepare the income statement for 2014.

Solution

Bajaj CorporationSchedule of Cost of Goods ManufacturedYear Ended December 31, 2015 (in thousands)

Direct materials costs		
Beginning inventory, January 1, 2015	₹1,30,000	
Purchases of direct materials	2,56,000	
Cost of direct materials available for use	3,86,000	
Ending inventory, December 31, 2015	68,000	
Direct materials used		₹3,18,000

Direct manufacturing labor costs		2,12,000
Indirect manufacturing costs		
Indirect manufacturing labor	96,000	
Indirect materials	28,000	
Plant insurance	4,000	
Depreciation—plant building & equipment	42,000	
Plant utilities	24,000	
Repairs and maintenance—plant	16,000	
Equipment lease costs	64,000	
Total indirect manufacturing costs		2,74,000
Manufacturing costs incurred during 2015		8,04,000
Add beginning work-in-process inventory, January 1, 2015		1,66,000
Total manufacturing costs to account for		9,70,000
Deduct ending work-in-process inventory, December 31, 2015		1,44,000
Cost of goods manufactured (to Income Statement)		₹8,26,000

Bajaj Corporation Income Statement
Year Ended December 31, 2015
(in thousands)

Revenues		₹12,00,000
Cost of goods sold:		
Beginning finished goods, January 1, 2015	₹2,46,000	
Cost of goods manufactured	8,26,000	
Cost of goods available for sale	10,72,000	
Ending finished goods, December 31, 2015	2,04,000	
Cost of goods sold		8,68,000
Gross margin		3,32,000
Operating costs:		
Marketing, distribution, and customer-service costs	1,24,000	
General and administrative costs	68,000	
Total operating costs		1,92,000
Operating income		₹1,40,000

2-29 Labor cost, overtime and idle time. Ajay works in the production department of Supreme Plasticworks as a machine operator. Ajay, a long-time employee of Supreme, is paid on an hourly basis at a rate of ₹40 per hour. Ajay works five 8-hour shifts per week Monday–Friday (40 hours). Any time Ajay works over and above these 40 hours is considered overtime for which he is paid at a rate of time and a half (₹60 per hour). If the overtime falls on weekends, Ajay is paid at a rate of double time (₹80 per hour). Ajay is also paid an additional ₹40 per hour for any holidays worked, even if it is part of his regular 40 hours. Ajay is paid his regular wages even if the machines are down (not operating) due to regular machine maintenance, slow order periods, or unexpected mechanical problems. These hours are considered "idle time." During October Ajay worked the following hours:

	Hours worked including machine downtime	Machine downtime
Week 1	48	6.4
Week 2	44	2.0
Week 3	43	5.8
Week 4	46	3.5

Included in the total hours worked are two company holidays (Deepawali peroid) during Week 4. All overtime worked by Ajay was Monday–Friday, except for the hours worked in Week 3; all of the Week 3 overtime hours were worked on a Saturday.

1. Calculate (a) direct manufacturing labor, (b) idle time, (c) overtime and holiday premium, and (d) total earnings for Ajay in October.   **Required**
2. Is idle time and overtime premium a direct or indirect cost of the products that Ajay worked on in October? Explain.

Solution

1.(a) Total cost of hours worked at regular rates

48 hours × ₹40 per hour	₹1,920
44 hours × ₹40 per hour	1,760
43 hours × ₹40 per hour	1,720
46 hours × ₹40 per hour	1,840
	7,240
Minus idle time	
(6.4 hours × ₹40 per hour)	256
(2.0 hours × ₹40 per hour)	80
(5.8 hours × ₹40 per hour)	232
(3.5 hours × ₹40 per hour)	140
Total idle time	708
Direct manufacturing labor costs	₹6,532

(b) Idle time = 17.7 hours × ₹40 per hour =   ₹708

(c) Overtime and holiday premium.

Week 1: Overtime (48 – 40) hours × Premium, ₹20 per hour	₹160
Week 2: Overtime (44 – 40) hours × Premium, ₹20 per hour	80
Week 3: Overtime (43 – 40) hours × Premium, ₹40 per hour	120
Week 4: Overtime (46 – 40) hours × Premium, ₹20 per hour	120
Week 4: Holiday 8 hours × 2 days × Premium, ₹40 per hour	640
Total overtime and holiday premium	₹1,120

(d) Total earnings in October

Direct manufacturing labor costs	₹6,532
Idle time	708
Overtime and holiday premium	1,120
Total earnings	₹8,360

2. Idle time caused by regular machine maintenance, slow order periods, or unexpected mechanical problems is an indirect cost of the product because it is not related to a specific product.

Overtime premium caused by the heavy overall volume of work is also an indirect cost because it is not related to a particular job that happened to be worked on during the overtime hours. If, however, the overtime is the result of a demanding "rush job," the overtime premium is a direct cost of that job.

2-30 Cost analysis, litigation risk, ethics. Singhania is the manager of new product development of Lakme Lever (LL). Singhania is currently considering E nhance, which would be (LL's) next major product. All LL's current products are cosmetics applied to the skin by the consumer. In contrast, Enhance is inserted via a needle into the skin by a doctor. Each treatment is planned to cost patients ₹3,000 and will last three months. Enhance fills out the skin so that fewer wrinkles are observable.

LL plans to sell Enhance to doctors for ₹1,200 per treatment, providing the doctor with a large incentive to promote the product. However, Singhania questions the economics of this product. At present all the costs recognized, including manufacturing by a third party, are ₹1,000 per treatment. Singhania's main concern is that the current costing proposal excludes potential litigation costs in defending lawsuits related to Enhance. Kareena the CEO of the company, totally disagrees with Singhania. She maintains she has total confidence in her medical research team and directs Singhania not to include any amount from his potential litigation cost of ₹1,100 per treatment in his upcoming presentation to the board of directors on the economics and pricing of the Enhance product. Singhania was previously controller of LL.

Required

1. What reasons might Kareena have for not wanting Singhania to include potential litigation costs on the product in a presentation on Enhance's economics and pricing?

2. LL sets prices by adding 20 percent to total costs. What would be the selling price per unit if Singhania's proposal for including potential litigation costs are also included? How might this price affect promotion of Enhance?

3. Kareena directs Singhania to drop any further discussion of the litigation issue. Singhania is to focus on making Enhance the blockbuster product that field research has suggested it will be. Singhania is uneasy with this directive. He tells Kareena "it is an ostrich approach" (head-in-the-sand) to a real problem that could potentially bankrupt the company. Kareena tells Singhania to go and think about her directive. What should Singhania do next?

Solution

1. Reasons for Kareena not wanting Singhania to include the potential litigation costs include:

   (a) Genuine belief that the product has no risk of future litigation. Note that she asserts "she has total confidence in her medical research team".

   (b) Concern that the uncertainties about litigation are sufficiently high to make any numerical estimate "meaningless".

   (c) Concern that inclusion of future litigation costs would cause the board of directors to vote against the project. Kareena may be "overly committed" to the project and wants to avoid showing information that prompts questions she prefers not to be raised.

   (d) Kareena may believe that if subsequent litigation occurs, the plaintiffs will "inappropriately" use a litigation cost line item as "proof" (LL) "knew the product had health problems" that were known to management at the outset.

2.

Unit costs excluding litigation costs	₹1,000
Add unit litigation costs	1,100
Total unit costs	2,100
Add 20% markup	420
Selling price per unit	2,520

Since each treatment is planned to cost patients ₹3,000, the new selling price of ₹2,520 will drop the doctors' margin to only ₹480 from the planned margin of ₹1,800 based on the planned selling price of ₹1,200. This would probably result in the doctors not having much incentive to promote the product. In fact, it may be quite possible that the doctors may not attempt to prescribe the treatment at such a low margin because of their own exposure to liability.

3. Singhania has already registered his concern to Kareena. The difficulty is that Kareena asked Singhania not to include the possible litigation in his presentation. If there is no record of this presentation, then Singhania may have several concerns.

(a) He may be accused at a later stage of not anticipating the costs of litigation. If litigation does occur, some people will try to distance themselves from the problems. It may be to Singhania's advantage to have a record of his early concerns. (Although plaintiffs may make Singhania's life very difficult if they get access to Singhania's files.) Singhania may want to keep some record of his presentation to Kareena.

(b) He may be portrayed as not being a "team player" if he continues his objections. Kareena may have to silence his concerns if he decides to stay at LL.

(c) He may have difficult ethical objections with Kareena's behavior. If he thinks she is acting unethically, his main options are to speak to her first (at least one time), speak to her supervisor (probably chairman of the company), or, as a final resort, resign.

Exercises

[Comprehensive solutions to all exercises are available on the companion website www.pearsoned.co.in/charlesthorngren]

2-31 Classification of costs, merchandising sector. Home Entertainment Centre (HEC) operates a large store in Mumbai. The store has both a video section and a musical (compact disks, and tapes) section. HEC reports revenues for the video section separately from the musical section.

Classify each of tn he following cost items as:

Required

    a. Direct or indirect (D or I) costs with respect to the video section.

    b. Variable or fixed (V or F) costs with respect to how the total costs of the video section change as the number of videos sold changes. (If in doubt, select on the basis of whether the total costs will change substantially if there is a large change in the number of videos sold.)

You will have two answers (D or I; V or F) for each of the following items:

Cost Item	D or I	V or F
A. Annual retainer paid to a video distributor		
B. Electricity costs of HEC store (single bill covers entire store)		
C. Costs of videos purchased for sale to customers		
D. Subscription to video trends magazine		
E. Leasing of computer software used for financial budgeting at HEC		
F. Cost of popcorn provided free to all customers of HEC		
G. Earthquake insurance policy for HEC store		
H. Freight-in costs of videos purchased by HEC		

2-32 Cost drivers and functions. The list of representative cost drivers in the right column below are randomized with respect to the list of functions in the left column. That is, they do not match.

Function	Representative Cost Driver
1. Accounting	**A.** Number of invoices sent
2. Personnel	**B.** Number of purchase orders
3. Data Processing	**C.** Number of research scientists
4. Research and Development	**D.** Hours of computer processing unit (CPU)
5. Purchasing	**E.** Number of new hires
6. Billing	**F.** Number of transactions processed

1. Match each function with its representative cost driver.
2. Give a second example of a cost driver for each function.

2-33 Total cost and unit costs. A student association has hired a musical group for a graduation party. The cost will be a fixed amount of ₹4,000.

1. Suppose 500 people attend the party. What will be the total cost of the musical group? The unit cost per person?
2. Suppose 2,000 people attend. What will be the total cost of the musical group? The unit cost per person?
3. For prediction of total costs, should the manager of the party use the unit cost in requirement 1? The unit cost in requirement 2? What is the major lesson of this exercise?

2-34 Total costs and unit costs. Ms Thomas is a well-known software engineer. Her specialty is writing software code used in maintaining the security of credit-card information. Thomas is approached by the Electronic Commerce Group (ECG). It offers to pay her ₹1,00,000 for the right to use her code under license in their e.procurement software package. Thomas rejects this offer because it provides her with no upside if the e.procurement package is a runaway success. Both parties eventually agree to a contract in which ECG pays Thomas a flat fee of ₹1,00,000 for the right to use her code in up to 10,000 packages. If e.procurement sells more than 10,000 packages, Thomas receives an additional ₹8 for each package sold beyond the 10,000 level.

1. What is the unit cost to ECG of Thomas software code included in its e.procurement package if it sells (a) 2,000 packages, (b) 6,000 packages, (c) 10,000 packages, and (d) 20,000 packages? Comment on the results.
2. To predict ECG's total cost of using Thomas software code in e.procurement, which unit cost (if any) of (a) to (d) in requirement 1 would you recommend ECG use? Explain.

2-35 Computing cost of goods purchased and cost of goods sold. The data below are for Big Bazaar Department Store. The account balances (in thousands) are for current year.

Marketing, distribution, and customer service costs	₹3,70,000
Merchandise inventory, January 1, current year	2,70,000
Utilities	1,70,000
General and administrative costs	4,30,000
Merchandise inventory, December 31, current year	3,40,000
Purchases	15,50,000
Miscellaneous expenses	40,000
Freight on purchases	70,000
Purchase returns and allowances	40,000
Purchase discounts	60,000

Compute (a) cost of goods purchased and (b) cost of goods sold.

2-36 Income statement and schedule of cost of goods manufactured. The following items (in millions) pertain to NTPC Ltd.

For Specific Date		For Current Year	
Work in process, Jan. 1. current year	₹1,000	Plant utilities	₹500
Direct materials, Dec. 31, current year	500	Indirect manufacturing labor	2,000
Finished goods, Dec. 31, current year	1,200	Depreciation-pant, building, and equipment	900
Accounts payable, Dec. 31, current year	2,000	Revenues	35,000
Accounts receivable, Jan. 1. current year	5,000	Miscellaneous manufacturing overhead	1,000
Work in process, Dec. 31, current year	200	Marketing, distribution, and customer-service costs	9,000
Finished goods, Jan. 1. current year	4,000	Direct materials purchased	8,000
Accounts receivable, Dec. 31, current year	3,000	Direct manufacturing labor	4,000
Accounts payable, Jan. 1. current year	4,000	Plant supplies used	600
Direct materials, Jan. 1. current year	3,000	Property taxes on plant	100

NTPC's manufacturing costing system uses a three-part classification of direct materials, direct manufacturing labor, and indirect manufacturing costs.

Prepare an income statement and a supporting schedule of cost of goods manufactured.   **Required**
(For additional questions regarding these facts, see the next problem).

2-37 Terminology, interpretation of statements (continuation of the previous question).

1. Calculate total prime costs and total conversion costs.
2. Compute total inventoriable costs and period costs.
3. Design costs and R&D costs are not considered product costs for financial reporting purposes. When might some of these costs be regarded as product costs? Give an example.
4. Suppose that both the direct materials used and the plant depreciation are related to the manufacture of 1 million units of product. Determine the unit cost for the direct materials assigned to those units and the unit cost for plant, building, and equipment depreciation. Assume that yearly depreciation is computed on a straight-line basis.
5. Assume that the implied cost-behavior patterns in requirement 4 persist. That is, direct materials costs behave as a variable cost and plant depreciation behaves as a fixed cost. Repeat the computations in requirement 4, assuming that the costs are being predicted for the manufacturing of 1.5 million units of product. Determine the effect on total cost.
6. Assume depreciation on the equipment (but not the plant and building) is computed based on number of units produced because the equipment deteriorates with units produced. The depreciation rate is ₹4 per unit. Calculate the equipment depreciation assuming (a) 1 million units of product are produced and (b) 1.5 million units of product are produced.

2-38 Finding unknown amounts. An author for the Internal Revenue Service is trying to reconstruct some partially destroyed records of two taxpayers. For each of the cases in the accompanying list, find the unknowns designated by the letters A through D.

	Case 1	Case 2 (in thousands)
Accounts receivable, 12/31	₹6,000	₹2,100
Cost of goods sold	A	20,000
Accounts payable, 1/1	3,000	1,700
Accounts payable, 12/31	1,800	1,500
Finished goods inventory, 12/31	B	5,300
Gross margin	11,300	C
Work in process, 1/1	0	800
Work in process, 12/31	0	3,000
Finished goods inventory, 1/1	4,000	4,000
Direct material used	8,000	12,000
Direct manufacturing labor	3,000	5,000
Indirect manufacturing costs	7,000	D
Purchases of direct material	9,000	7,000
Revenues	32,000	31,800
Accounts receivable, 1/1	2,000	1,400

2-39 Fire loss, computing inventory costs. A distraught employee, Mr Unsatisfied, put a torch to a manufacturing plant on a blustery February 26. The resulting blaze destroyed the plant and its contents. Fortunately, certain accounting records were kept in another building. They reveal the following for the period from January 1 to February 28, current year.

Direct materials purchased	₹1,60,000
Work in process, 1st January	3,40,000

Direct materials, 1st January	1,60,000
Finished goods, 1st January	3,00,000
Indirect manufacturing costs	40% of conversion costs
Revenues	50,00,000
Direct manufacturing labor	18,00,000
Prime costs	29,40,000
Gross margin percentage based on revenues	20%
Cost of goods available for sale	45,00,000

The loss is fully covered by insurance. The insurance company wants to know the historical cost of the inventories as a basis for negotiating a settlement, although the settlement is actually to be based on replacement cost, not historical cost.

Calculate the cost of

Required

1. Finished goods inventory, 28th February.
2. Work-in-process inventory, 28th February.
3. Direct materials inventory, 28th February.

2-40 Comprehensive problem on unit costs, product costs. Godrej office equipment manufactures and sells metal shelving. It began operations on January 1. Costs incurred for the current year are as follows(V stands for variable; F stands for fixed):

Direct material costs	₹1,40,000 V
Direct manufacturing-labor costs	30,000 V
Plant energy costs	5,000 V
Indirect manufacturing-labor costs	10,000 V
Indirect manufacturing-labor costs	16,000 F
Other indirect manufacturing costs	8,000 V
Other indirect manufacturing costs	24,000 F
Marketing, distribution, and customer-service costs	1,22,850 V
Marketing, distribution, and customer-service costs	40,000 F
Administrative costs	50,000 F

Variable manufacturing costs are variable with respect to units produced. Variable marketing, distribution, and customer-service costs are variable with respect to units sold.

Inventory data are	Beginning, January 1	Ending, December 31
Direct materials	0 kg	2,000 kg
Work in process	0 units	0 units
Finished goods	0 units	? units

Production in the current year was 1,00,000 units. Two kgs of direct materials are used to make one unit of finished product.

Revenues in the current year were ₹4,36,800. The selling price per unit and the purchase price per kg of direct materials were stable throughout the year. The company's ending inventory of finished goods is carried at the average unit manufacturing costs for the current year. Finished-goods inventory at December 31, current year was ₹20,970.

Required

1. Calculate direct materials inventory, total cost, as on December 31.
2. Calculate finished-goods inventory, total units, as on December 31.
3. Calculate selling price per unit.
4. Calculate operating income.

2-41 Product costs, effect of changing the cost classification (continuation of previous problem).
Assume the same facts as in the previous problem, except that fixed indirect manufacturing costs are not considered inventoriable costs. There are 9,000 units of finished goods inventory on December 31.

Required

1. Calculate finished goods inventory, total costs, December 31.
2. Calculate operating income of the year.

2-42 Missing data. Shaheen Plastics, Ltd's selected data for the month of August related to current year are presented below (in millions):

Beginning work-in-process inventory	₹2,000
Beginning direct materials inventory	900
Direct materials purchased	3,600
Direct materials used	3,750
Variable manufacturing overhead	2,500
Total manufacturing overhead	4,800
Total manufacturing costs	16,000
Cost of goods manufactured	16,500
Cost of goods sold	17,000
Ending finished goods inventory	1,250

Calculate the following costs:

Required

1. Direct materials inventory as on 31st August.
2. Fixed manufacturing overhead costs for August.
3. Direct manufacturing labor costs for August.
4. Work-in-process inventory as on 31st August.
5. Goods available for sale in August.
6. Finished-goods inventory as on 31st August.

③ Cost-Volume-Profit Analysis

Learning Objective 1

Explain the features of cost–volume–profit (CVP) analysis

. . .how operating income changes with changes in output level, selling prices, variable costs, or fixed costs

All managers want to know how profits will change as the units sold of a product or service change.

Home Depot managers, for example, might wonder how many units of a new power drill must be sold to break even or make a certain amount of profit. Procter & Gamble managers might ask themselves how expanding their business in Nigeria would affect costs, revenues, and profits. These questions have a common "what-if" theme: What if we sold more power drills? What if we started selling in Nigeria? Examining the results of these what-if possibilities and alternatives helps managers make better decisions.

Managers must also decide how to price their products and understand the effect of their pricing decisions on revenues and profits.

Essentials of CVP Analysis

In Chapter 2, we discussed total revenues, total costs, and income. Managers use **cost–volume–profit (CVP) analysis** to study the behavior of and relationship among these elements as changes occur in the number of units sold, the selling price, the variable cost per unit, or the fixed costs of a product. Consider this example:

Example: Neeta Ambani is a young entrepreneur who recently used *GMAT Success*, a test-prep book and software package for the business school admission test. Neeta loved the book and program so much that after graduating she signed a contract with *GMAT Success*'s publisher to sell the learning materials. She recently sold them at a college fair in New Delhi and is now thinking of selling them at a college fair in Mumbai. Neeta knows she can purchase each package (book and software) from the publisher for ₹1,200 per package, with the privilege of returning all unsold packages and receiving a full ₹1,200 refund per package. She also knows that she must pay ₹20,000 to rent a booth at the fair. She will incur no other costs. Should she rent the booth or not?

Neeta, like most managers who face such a situation, will need to work through the series of steps introduced in Chapter 1 to make the most profitable decisions.

1. **Identify the problem and uncertainties.** Every managerial decision involves selecting a course of action. The decision to rent the booth hinges on how Neeta resolves two important uncertainties: the price she can charge and the number of packages she can sell at that price. Neeta must decide knowing that the outcome of the action she chooses is uncertain. The more confident she is about selling a large number of packages at a high price, the more willing she will be to rent the booth.

2. **Obtain information.** When faced with uncertainty, managers obtain information that might help them understand the uncertainties more clearly. For example, Neeta gathers information about the type of individuals likely to attend the

fair and other test-prep packages that might be sold at the fair. She also gathers data from her experience selling the packages at the New Delhi fair.

3. **Make predictions about the future.** Managers make predictions using all the information available to them. Neeta predicts she can charge ₹2,000 for the *GMAT Success* package. At that price, she is reasonably confident that she will be able to sell at least 30 packages and possibly as many as 60. Neeta must be realistic and exercise judgment when making these predictions. If they are too optimistic, she will rent the booth when she should not. If they are too pessimistic, she will not rent the booth when she should.

    Neeta's predictions rest on the belief that her experience at the Mumbai fair will be similar to her experience at the New Delhi fair 4 months earlier. Yet Neeta is uncertain about several aspects of her prediction. Are the fairs truly comparable? For example, will attendance at the two fairs be the same? Have market conditions changed over the past 4 months? Are there any biases creeping into her thinking? She is keen on selling at the Mumbai fair because sales in the last couple of months have been lower than expected. Is this experience making her predictions overly optimistic? Has she ignored some of the competitive risks? Will the other test-prep vendors at the fair reduce their prices? If they do, should she? How many packages can she expect to sell if she does?

    Neeta rethinks her plan and retests her assumptions. She obtains data about student attendance and total sales in past years from the organizers of the fair. In the end, she feels quite confident that her predictions are reasonable, accurate, and carefully thought through.

4. **Make decisions by choosing among alternatives.** Neeta uses the CVP analysis that follows and decides to rent the booth at the Chicago fair.

5. **Implement the decision, evaluate performance, and learn.** Thoughtful managers never stop learning. They compare their actual performance to predicted performance to understand why things worked out the way they did and what they might learn. At the end of the Mumbai fair, for example, Neeta would want to evaluate whether her predictions about price and the number of packages she could sell were correct. This will help her make better decisions about renting booths at future fairs.

How does Neeta use CVP analysis in Step 4 to make her decision? She begins by identifying which costs are fixed and which costs are variable and then calculates *contribution margin*.

Contribution Margins

The booth-rental cost of ₹20,000 is a fixed cost because it will not change no matter how many packages Neeta sells. The total cost of the package is a variable cost because it increases in proportion to the number of packages sold and she can return whatever she doesn't sell for a full refund. To understand how operating income will change by selling different quantities of packages, Neeta calculates operating income if sales are 5 packages and if sales are 40 packages.

	5 packages sold	40 packages sold
Revenues	₹10,000 (₹2,000 per package × 5 packages)	₹80,000 (₹2,000 per package × 40 packages)
Variable purchase costs	6,000 (₹1,200 per package × 5 packages)	48,000 (₹1,200 per package × 40 packages)
Fixed costs	20,000	20,000
Operating income	₹(16,000)	₹12,000

The only numbers that change from selling different quantities of packages are *total revenues* and *total variable costs*. The difference between total revenues and total variable costs is called **contribution margin**. That is,

Contribution margin = Total revenues − Total variable costs

Contribution margin indicates why operating income changes as the number of units sold changes. The contribution margin when Neeta sells 5 packages is ₹4,000 (₹10,000 in total revenues minus ₹6,000 in total variable costs); the contribution margin when Neeta sells 40 packages is ₹32,000 (₹80,000 in total revenues minus ₹48,000 in total variable costs). When calculating the contribution margin, be sure to subtract all variable costs. For example, if Neeta had variable selling costs because she paid a commission to salespeople for each package they sold at the convention, variable costs would include the cost of each package plus the sales commission paid on it.

Contribution margin per unit is a useful tool for calculating contribution margin and operating income. It is defined as,

Contribution margin per unit = Selling price − Variable cost per unit

In the *GMAT Success* example, contribution margin per package, or per unit, is ₹2,000 − ₹1,200 = ₹800. Contribution margin per unit recognizes the tight coupling of selling price and variable cost per unit. Unlike fixed costs, Neeta will only incur the variable cost per unit of ₹1,200 when she sells a unit of GMAT success. Contribution per unit provides a second way to calculate contribution margin:

Contribution margin = Contribution margin per unit × Number of units sold

For example, when 40 packages are sold, contribution margin = ₹800 per unit 3 40 units = ₹32,000.

Even before she gets to the fair, Neeta incurs ₹20,000 in fixed costs. Because the contribution margin per unit is ₹800 for each package she sells at the fair, Neeta will recover ₹800 for each package that she sells at the fair. Neeta hopes to sell enough packages to fully recover the ₹20,000 she spent for renting the booth and to then make a profit.

Exhibit 3-1 presents contribution margins for different quantities of packages sold. The income statement in Exhibit 3-1 is called a **contribution income statement** because it groups costs into variable costs and fixed costs to highlight contribution margin.

Operating income = Contribution margin − Fixed costs

Each additional package sold from 0 to 1 to 5 increases contribution margin by ₹800 per package, and helps Neeta recover more and more of her fixed cost and reduce her operating loss. If Neeta sells 25 packages, contribution margin equals ₹20,000 (₹800 per packag × 25 packages). This quantity exactly recovers her fixed costs and results in ₹0 operating income. If Neeta sells 40 packages, contribution margin increases by another ₹12,000 (₹32,000 − ₹20,000), all of which becomes operating income. As you look across Exhibit 3-1 from left to right, you see that the increase in contribution margin exactly equals the increase in operating income (or the decrease in operating loss).

When companies, such as Samsung and Prada, sell multiple products, calculating contribution margin per unit is cumbersome. Instead of expressing contribution margin in dollars per unit, these companies express it as a percentage called **contribution margin percentage** (or **contribution margin ratio**):

$$\text{Contribution margin percentage (or contribution margin ratio)} = \frac{\text{Contribution margin}}{\text{Revenues}}$$

Consider a sales level such as 40 units sold in Exhibit 3-1:

$$\text{Contribution margin percentage} = \frac{₹800}{₹2,000} = 0.40, \text{ or } 40\%$$

Contribution margin percentage is the contribution margin per rupee of revenue. Neeta earns 40% of each rupee of revenue (equal to 40 paise) she takes in.

Contribution margin percentage is a handy way to calculate contribution margin for different dollar amounts of revenue. Rearranging terms in the equation defining contribution margin percentage, we get:

Contribution margin = Contribution margin percentage × Revenues (in rupees)

To derive the relationship between operating income and contribution margin percentage, recall that:

$$\text{Operating income} = \text{Contribution margin} - \text{Fixed costs}$$

Substituting for contribution margin in the above equation:

$$\text{Operating income} = \text{Contribution margin percentage} \times \text{Revenues} - \text{Fixed costs}$$

For example, in Exhibit 3-1, if Neeta sells 40 packages:

Revenues	₹80,000
Contribution margin percentage	40%
Contribution margin, 40% × ₹80,000	₹32,000
Fixed costs	20,000
Operating income	₹12,000

When there is only one product, as in our example, we can divide both the numerator and denominator of the contribution margin percentage equation by the quantity of units sold and calculate contribution margin percentage as follows:

$$\text{Contribution margin percentage} = \frac{\text{Contribution margin/Quantity of units sold}}{\text{Revenues/Quantity of units sold}}$$

$$= \frac{\text{Contribution margin per unit}}{\text{Selling price}}$$

In our example,

$$\text{Contribution margin percentage} = \frac{₹800}{₹2,000} = 0.40, \text{ or } 40\%$$

Contribution margin percentage is a useful tool for calculating how a change in revenues changes contribution margin. As Neeta's revenues increase by ₹30,000 from ₹50,000 to ₹80,000, her contribution margin increases from ₹20,000 to ₹32,000 (by ₹12,000):

Contribution margin at revenue of ₹80,000, 0.40 × ₹80,000	₹32,000
Contribution margin at revenue of ₹50,000, 0.40 × ₹50,000	₹20,000
Change in contribution margin when revenue increases by ₹30,000, 0.40 × ₹30,000	₹12,000

Change in Contribution margin = Contribution margin percentage × Change in Revenues

Contribution margin analysis is a widely used technique. For example, managers at Home Depot use contribution margin analysis to evaluate how sales fluctuations during a recession will affect the company's profitability.

Expressing CVP Relationships

How was the Excel spreadsheet in Exhibit 3-1 constructed? Underlying the Exhibit are some equations that express the CVP relationships. To make good decisions using CVP analysis, we must understand these relationships and the structure of the contribution income statement in Exhibit 3-1. There are three related ways (we will call them methods) to think more deeply about and model CVP relationships:

1. The equation method
2. The contribution margin method
3. The graph method

As we shall see later in the chapter, different methods are useful for different decisions. The equation method and the contribution margin method are most useful when managers want to determine operating income at few specific levels of sales (for example $-5, 15, 25$, and 40 units sold). The graph method helps managers visualize the relationship between units sold and operating income over a wide range of quantities.

Equation Method

Each column in Exhibit 3-1 is expressed as an equation.

Revenues = Variable costs − Fixed costs = Operating income

How are revenues in each column calculated?

Revenues = Selling price (SP) × Quantity of units sold (Q)

How are variable costs in each column calculated?

Variable costs = Variable cost per unit (VCU) × Quantity of units sold (Q)

So,

$$\left[\left(\begin{array}{c}\text{Selling}\\ \text{price}\end{array} \times \begin{array}{c}\text{Quantity of}\\ \text{units sold}\end{array}\right) - \left(\begin{array}{c}\text{Variable cost}\\ \text{per unit}\end{array} \times \begin{array}{c}\text{Quantity of}\\ \text{units sold}\end{array}\right)\right] - \begin{array}{c}\text{Fixed}\\ \text{costs}\end{array} = \begin{array}{c}\text{Operating}\\ \text{income}\end{array} \quad \textbf{(Equation 1)}$$

Equation 1 becomes the basis for calculating operating income for different quantities of units sold. For example, if you go to cell F7 in Exhibit 3-1, the calculation of operating income when Neeta sells 5 packages is

(₹2,000 × 5) − (₹1,200 × 5) − (₹20,000 = ₹10,000 − ₹6,000 − ₹20,000 = − ₹16,000

Exhibit 3-1

Contribution Income Statement for Different Quantities of Do-All Software Packages Sold

	A	B	C	D	E	F	G	H
	File Edit View Insert Format Tools Data Window Help							
1				Number of Packages Sold				
2				0	1	5	25	40
3	Revenues	₹2,000	per package	₹0	₹ 2,000	₹10,000	₹50,000	₹80,000
4	Variable costs	₹1,200	per package	0	1,200	6,000	30,000	48,000
5	Contribution margin	₹800	per package	0	800	4,000	20,000	32,000
6	Fixed costs	₹20,000		20,000	20,000	20,000	20,000	20,000
7	Operating income			₹(20,000)	₹(19,200)	₹(16,000)	₹0	₹2,000

Contribution Margin Method

Rearranging equation 1,

$$\left[\left(\begin{array}{c}\text{Selling}\\\text{price}\end{array}-\begin{array}{c}\text{Variable cost}\\\text{per unit}\end{array}\right)\times\left(\begin{array}{c}\text{Quantity of}\\\text{units sold}\end{array}\right)\right]-\begin{array}{c}\text{Fixed}\\\text{costs}\end{array}=\begin{array}{c}\text{Operating}\\\text{income}\end{array}$$

$$\left(\begin{array}{c}\text{Contribution margin}\\\text{per unit}\end{array}\times\begin{array}{c}\text{Quantity of}\\\text{units sold}\end{array}\right)-\begin{array}{c}\text{Fixed}\\\text{costs}\end{array}=\begin{array}{c}\text{Operating}\\\text{income}\end{array}\quad(\text{ Equation 2})$$

In our Do-All Software example, contribution margin per unit is ₹800 (₹2,000 − ₹1,200), so when Neeta sells 5 packages,

Operating income = (₹800 × 5) − ₹20,000 = −₹16,000

Equation 2 expresses the basic idea we described earlier—each unit sold helps Neeta recover ₹800 (in contribution margin) of the ₹20,000 in fixed costs.

Graph Method

The graph method helps managers visualize the relationships between total revenues and total costs. The graph shows each relationship as a line. Exhibit 3-2 illustrates the graph method for selling *GMAT Success*. Because we have assumed that total costs and total revenues behave in a linear fashion, we need only two points to plot the line representing each of them.

1. **Total costs line.** The total costs line is the sum of fixed costs and variable costs. Fixed costs are ₹20,000 at all quantities of units sold within the relevant range. To plot the total costs line, use as one point the ₹20,000 fixed costs at zero units sold (point A), because variable costs are ₹0 when no units are sold. Select a second point

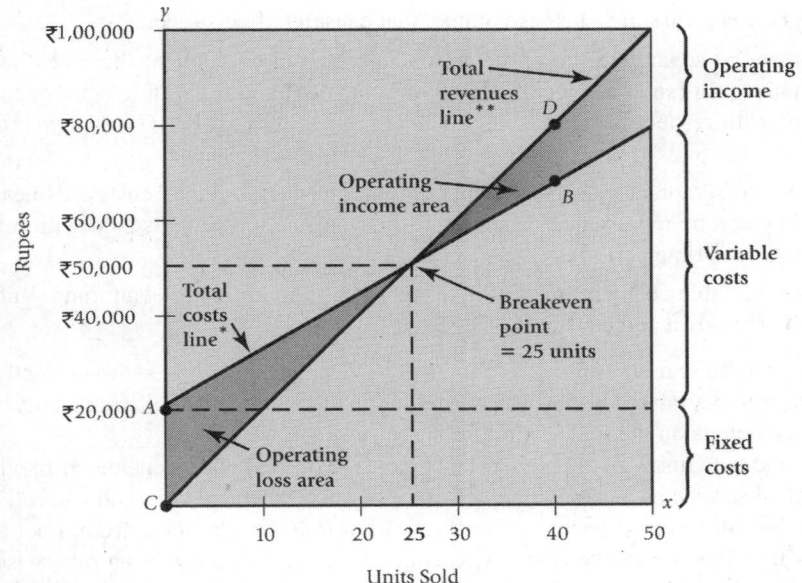

Exhibit 3-2

Cost-Volume Graph for Do-All Software

*Slope of the total costs line is the variable cost per unit =   ₹1,200
**Slope of the total revenues line is the selling price =   ₹2,000

by choosing any other convenient output level (say, 40 units sold) and determine the corresponding total costs. Total variable costs at this output level are ₹48,000 (40 units × ₹1,200 per unit). Remember, fixed costs are ₹20,000 at all quantities of units sold within the relevant range, so total costs at 40 units sold equal ₹68,000 (₹20,000 + ₹48,000), which is point B in Exhibit 3-2. The total costs line is the straight line from point A through point B.

2. **Total revenues line.** One convenient starting point is ₹0 revenues at 0 units sold, which is point C in Exhibit 3-2. Select a second point by choosing any other convenient output level and determining the corresponding total revenues. At 40 units sold, total revenues are ₹80,000 (₹2,000 per unit × 40 units), which is point D in Exhibit 3-2. The total revenues line is the straight line from point C through point D.

The profit or loss at any sales level can be determined by the vertical distance between the two lines at that level in Exhibit 3-2. For quantities fewer than 25 units sold, total costs exceed total revenues, and the purple area indicates operating losses. For quantities greater than 25 units sold, total revenues exceed total costs, and the blue-green area indicates operating incomes. At 25 units sold, total revenues equal total costs. Neeta will break even by selling 25 packages.

Decision Point ▶

How can CVP analysis help managers?

Like Neeta, many companies, particularly small- and medium-sized companies, use the graph method to see how their revenues and costs will change as the quantity of units sold changes. The graph helps them understand their regions of profitability and unprofitability.

Cost-Volume-Profit Assumptions

Now that you have seen how CVP analysis works, think about the following assumptions we made during the analysis:

1. Changes in the levels of revenues and costs arise only because of changes in the number of product (or service) units sold. The number of units sold is the only revenue driver and the only cost driver. Just as a cost driver is any factor that affects costs, a **revenue driver** is a variable, such as volume, that causally affects revenues.

2. Total costs can be separated into two components: a fixed component that does not vary with units sold (such as Neeta's ₹20,000 booth fee) and a variable component that changes with respect to units sold. (such as the ₹1,200 cost per *GMAT Success* package).

3. When represented graphically, the behaviors of total revenues and total costs are linear (meaning they can be represented as a straight line) in relation to units sold within a relevant range (and time period).

4. Selling price, variable cost per unit, and total fixed costs (within a relevant range and time period) are known and constant.

As you can tell from these assumptions, to conduct a CVP analysis, you need to correctly distinguish fixed from variable costs. Always keep in mind, however, that whether a cost is variable or fixed depends on the time period for a decision.

The shorter the time horizon, the higher the percentage of total costs considered fixed. Suppose a Kingfisher Airlines plane will depart from its gate in the next hour and currently has 20 seats unsold. A potential passenger arrives with a transferable ticket from a competing airline. Kingfisher's variable costs of placing one more passenger in an otherwise empty seat (such as the cost of providing the passenger with a free beverage) is negligible.

With only an hour to go before the flight departs, virtually all costs (such as crew costs and baggage-handling costs) are fixed.

Alternatively suppose Kingfisher must decide whether to continue to offer this particular flight next year. If Kingfisher Airlines decides to cancel this flight because very few passengers during the last year have taken it, many more of its costs, including crew costs, baggage-handling costs, and airport fees for the flight, would be considered variable: Over this longer 1-year time period, Kingfisher Airlines would not have to incur these costs if the flight were no longer operating. Always consider the relevant range, the length of the time horizon, and the specific decision situation when classifying costs as variable or fixed.

Breakeven Point and Target Operating Income

Managers and entrepreneurs like Neeta always want to know how much they must sell to earn a given amount of income. Equally important, they want to know how much they must sell to avoid a loss.

Breakeven Point

The **breakeven point (BEP)** is that quantity of output sold at which total revenues equal total costs—that is, the quantity of output sold that results in ₹0 of operating income. You have already learned how to use the graph method to calculate the breakeven point. Recall from Exhibit 3-1 that operating income was ₹0 when Neeta sold 25 units, this is the breakeven point. But by understanding the equations underlying the calculations in Exhibit 3-1, we can calculate the breakeven point directly for selling *GMAT Success* rather than trying out different quantities and checking when operating income equals ₹0.

Recall the equation method (equation 1):

$$\left(\begin{array}{c}\text{Selling} \\ \text{price}\end{array} \times \begin{array}{c}\text{Quantity of} \\ \text{units sold}\end{array}\right) - \left(\begin{array}{c}\text{Variable costs} \\ \text{per unit}\end{array} \times \begin{array}{c}\text{Quantity of} \\ \text{units sold}\end{array}\right) - \begin{array}{c}\text{Fixed} \\ \text{costs}\end{array} = \begin{array}{c}\text{Operating} \\ \text{income}\end{array}$$

Setting operating income equal to ₹0 and denoting quantity of output units that must be sold by Q,

$$(₹2,000 \times Q) - (₹1,200 \times Q) - ₹20,000 = ₹0$$

$$₹800 \times Q = ₹20,000$$

$$Q = ₹20,000 \div ₹800 \text{ per unit} = 25 \text{ units}$$

Recall the contribution margin method (equation 2):

$$\left(\begin{array}{c}\text{Contribution} \\ \text{margin per unit}\end{array} \times \begin{array}{c}\text{Quantity of} \\ \text{units sold}\end{array}\right) - \text{Fixed costs} = \text{Operating income}$$

At the breakeven point, operating income is by definition ₹0 and so:

Contribution margin per unit × Breakeven number of units = Fixed cost   **(Equation 3)**

Rearranging equation 3 and entering the data,

$$\frac{\text{Breakeven}}{\text{number of units}} = \frac{\text{Fixed costs}}{\text{Contribution margin per unit}} = \frac{₹20,000}{₹800 \text{ per unit}} = 25 \text{ units}$$

$$\frac{\text{Breakeven}}{\text{revenues}} = \frac{\text{Fixed costs}}{\text{Contribution margin}\%} = \frac{₹20,000}{0.40} = ₹50,000$$

In practice (because companies have multiple products), management accountants usually calculate the breakeven point directly in terms of revenues using contribution margin percentages. Recall that in the *GMAT Success* example, at revenues of ₹80,000, contribution margin is ₹32,000:

$$\frac{\text{Contribution margin}}{\text{Percentage}} = \frac{\text{Contribution margin}}{\text{Revenues}} = \frac{₹32,000}{₹80,000} = 0.40, \text{ or } 40\%$$

That is, 40% of each dollar of revenue, or 40 cents, is the contribution margin. To break even, contribution margin must equal Neeta's fixed costs, which are ₹20,000. To earn ₹20,000 of contribution margin, when ₹1 of revenue results in a ₹0.40 contribution margin, revenues must equal ₹20,000 ÷ 0.40 = ₹50,000.

$$\frac{\text{Breakeven}}{\text{revenues}} = \frac{\text{Fixed costs}}{\text{Contribution margin}\%} = \frac{₹20,000}{0.40} = ₹50,000$$

While the breakeven point tells managers how much they must sell to avoid a loss, managers are equally interested in how they will achieve the operating income targets underlying their strategies and plans. In our example, selling 25 units at a price of ₹2,000 (equal to revenue of ₹50,000) assures Neeta that she will not lose money if she rents the booth. While this news is comforting, how does Neeta determine how much she needs to sell to achieve a targeted amount of operating income?

Target Operating Income

Suppose Neeta wants to earn an operating income of ₹12,000? How many units must she sell? One approach is to keep plugging in different quantities into Exhibit 3-1 and check when operating income equals ₹12,000. Exhibit 3-1 shows that operating income is ₹12,000 when 40 packages are sold. A more convenient approach is to use equation 1.

$$\left[\left(\begin{array}{c}\text{Selling} \\ \text{price}\end{array} \times \begin{array}{c}\text{Quantity of} \\ \text{units sold}\end{array}\right) - \left(\begin{array}{c}\text{Variable costs} \\ \text{per unit}\end{array} \times \begin{array}{c}\text{Quantity of} \\ \text{units sold}\end{array}\right)\right] - \begin{array}{c}\text{Fixed} \\ \text{costs}\end{array} = \begin{array}{c}\text{Operating} \\ \text{income}\end{array} \quad \text{(Equation 1)}$$

We denote by Q the unknown quantity of units Neeta must sell to earn an operating income of ₹12,000. Selling price is ₹2,000, variable cost per package is ₹1,200, fixed costs are ₹20,000, and target operating income is ₹12,000. Substituting these values into equation 1, we have

$$(₹2,000 \times Q) - (₹1,200 \times Q) - ₹20,000 = ₹12,000$$
$$₹800 \times Q = ₹20,000 + ₹12,000 = ₹32,000$$
$$Q = ₹32,000 \div ₹800 \text{ per unit} = 40 \text{ units}$$

Alternatively, we could use equation 2,

$$\left(\begin{array}{c}\text{Contribution margin} \\ \text{per unit}\end{array} \times \begin{array}{c}\text{Quantity of} \\ \text{units sold}\end{array}\right) - \begin{array}{c}\text{Fixed} \\ \text{costs}\end{array} = \begin{array}{c}\text{Operating} \\ \text{income}\end{array} \quad \textbf{(Equation 2)}$$

Given a target operating income (₹12,000 in this case), we can rearrange terms to get equation 4.

$$\text{Quantity of units required to be sold} = \frac{\text{Fixed costs} + \text{Target operating income}}{\text{Contribution margin per unit}}$$

$$\text{Quantity of units required to be sold} = \frac{₹20,000 + ₹12,000}{₹800 \text{ per unit}} = 40 \text{ units} \qquad \textbf{(Equation 4)}$$

Proof:

Revenues, ₹2,000 per unit × 40 units	₹80,000
Variable costs, ₹1,200 per unit × 40 units	48,000
Contribution margin, ₹800 per unit × 40 units	32,000
Fixed costs	20,000
Operating income	₹12,000

The revenues needed to earn an operating income of ₹12,000 can also be calculated directly by recognizing (1) that ₹32,000 of contribution margin must be earned (fixed costs of ₹20,000 plus operating income of ₹12,000) and (2) that each rupee of revenue earns 40 paise of contribution margin. To earn ₹32,000 of contribution margin, revenues must equal ₹32,000 ÷ 0.40 = ₹80,000. That is,

$$\text{Revenues needed to earn target operating income} = \frac{\text{Fixed costs} + \text{Target operating income}}{\text{Contribution margin percentage}}$$

$$\text{Revenues needed to earn ₹12,000} = \frac{₹20,000 + ₹12,000}{0.40} = \frac{₹32,000}{0.40} = ₹80,000$$

Could we use the graph method and the graph in Exhibit 3-2 to figure out how many units Neeta must sell to earn an operating income of ₹12,000? Yes, but it is not easy to determine from the graph the precise point at which the difference between the total revenues line and the total costs line equals ₹12,000. Recasting Exhibit 3-2 in the form of a profit-volume (PV) graph makes it easier to answer this question.

A **PV graph** shows how changes in the quantity of units sold affect operating income. Exhibit 3-3 is the PV graph for Do-All Software (fixed costs, ₹20,000; selling price, ₹2,000; and variable cost per unit, ₹1,200). The PV line can be drawn using two points. One convenient point (M) is the operating loss at 0 units sold, which is equal to the fixed costs of ₹20,000, shown at −₹20,000 on the vertical axis. A second convenient point (N) is the breakeven point, which is 25 units in our example. The PV line is the straight line from point M through point N. To find the number of units Neeta must sell to earn an operating income of ₹12,000, draw a horizontal line parallel to the x-axis corresponding to ₹12,000 on the vertical axis (that's the y-axis). At the point where this line intersects the PV line, draw a vertical line down to the horizontal axis (that's the x-axis). The vertical line intersects the x-axis at 40 units, indicating that by selling 40 units Neeta will earn an operating income of ₹12,000.

Just like Neeta, managers at larger companies such as Pizza Kitchen use profit−volume analyses to understand how profits change with sales volumes. They use this understanding to target the sales levels they need to achieve to meet their profit plans.

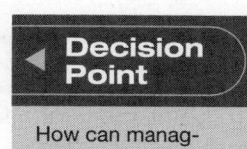

Decision Point

How can managers determine the breakeven point or the output needed to achieve a target operating income?

Target Net Income and Income Taxes

Net income is operating income plus nonoperating revenues (such as interest revenue) minus nonoperating costs (such as interest cost) minus income taxes. For simplicity,

Learning Objective 3

Understand how income taxes affect CVP analysis

. . . focus on net income

throughout this chapter we assume nonoperating revenues and nonoperating costs are zero. So, our net income equation will simply be:

$$\text{Net income} = \text{Operating income} - \text{Income taxes}$$

Until now, we have ignored the effect of income taxes in our CVP analysis. In many companies, the income targets for managers in their strategic plans are expressed in terms of net income because the company's top executives want them to consider the effect their decisions have on the firm's operating income *after* income taxes. Some decisions might not result in a large operating income, but their tax consequences make them attractive because they have a positive effect on net income—the measure that drives shareholders' dividends and returns.

To make net income evaluations, CVP calculations for target income must be stated in terms of target net income instead of target operating income. For example, Neeta may be interested in knowing the quantity of units of *GMAT Success* she must sell to earn a net income of ₹9,600, assuming an income tax rate of 40%.

$$\text{Target net income} = \left(\begin{array}{c}\text{Target}\\\text{operating income}\end{array}\right) - \left(\begin{array}{c}\text{Target}\\\text{operating income}\end{array} \times \text{Tax rate}\right)$$

$$\text{Target net income} = (\text{Target operating income}) \times (1 - \text{Tax rate})$$

$$\text{Target operating income} = \frac{\text{Target net income}}{1 - \text{Tax rate}} = \frac{₹9,600}{1 - 0.40} = ₹16,000$$

In other words, to earn a target net income of ₹9,600, Neeta's target operating income is ₹16,000.

Proof:

Target operating income	₹16,000
Tax at 40% (0.40 × ₹16,000)	6,400
Target net income	₹9,600

The key step is to take the target net income number and convert it into the corresponding target operating income number. We can then use equation 1 for target operating income and substitute numbers from our of *GMAT Success* example.

Exhibit 3-3

Profit-Volume Graph for Do-All Software

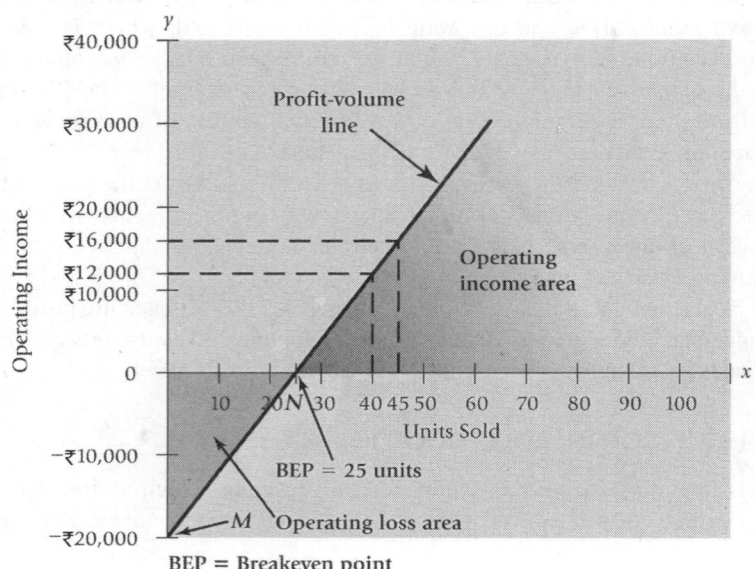

Exhibit 3-3: Profit-Volume Graph for Do-All Software

BEP = Breakeven point

$$\left[\left(\begin{matrix}\text{Selling}\\\text{price}\end{matrix}\times\begin{matrix}\text{Quantity of}\\\text{units sold}\end{matrix}\right)-\left(\begin{matrix}\text{Variable cost}\\\text{per unit}\end{matrix}\times\begin{matrix}\text{Quantity of}\\\text{units sold}\end{matrix}\right)\right]-\begin{matrix}\text{Fixed}\\\text{costs}\end{matrix}=\begin{matrix}\text{Operating}\\\text{income}\end{matrix}\quad\textbf{(Equation)}$$

$$(₹2,000\times Q)-(₹1,200\times Q)-₹20,000=\frac{₹9,600}{1-0.40}$$
$$(₹2,000\times Q)-(₹1,200\times Q)-₹20,000=₹16,000$$
$$₹800\times Q=₹36,000$$
$$Q=₹36,000\div₹800\text{ per unit}=45\text{ units}$$

Alternatively we can calculate the number of units Neeta must sell by using the contribution margin method and equation 4:

$$\begin{matrix}\text{Quantity of units}\\\text{required to be sold}\end{matrix}=\frac{\text{Fixed costs}+\text{Target operating income}}{\text{Contribution margin per unit}}\qquad\textbf{(Equation 4)}$$

$$=\frac{₹20,000+₹16,000}{₹800\text{ per unit}}=45\text{ units}$$

Proof:

Revenues, ₹2,000 per unit × 45 units	₹90,000
Variable costs, ₹1,200 per unit × 45 units	54,000
Contribution margin	36,000
Fixed costs	20,000
Operating income	16,000
Income taxes, ₹16,000 × 0.40	6,400
Net income	₹9,600

Neeta can also use the PV graph in Exhibit 3-3. To earn target operating income of ₹16,000, Neeta needs to sell 45 units.

Focusing the analysis on target net income instead of target operating income will not change the breakeven point. That's because, by definition, operating income at the breakeven point is ₹0, and no income taxes are paid when there is no operating income.

◄ **Decision Point**

How can managers incorporate income taxes into CVP analysis?

Using CVP Analysis for Decision Making

You have learned how CVP analysis is useful for calculating the units that need to be sold to break even or to achieve a target operating income or target net income. A manager can also use CVP analysis to make other strategic decisions. Consider a decision about choosing the features for a product, such as the engine size, transmission system, or steering system for a new car model. Different choices will affect the vehicle's selling price, variable cost per unit, fixed costs, units sold, and operating income. CVP analysis helps managers make product decisions by estimating the expected profitability of these choices. We return to our *GMAT Success* example to show how Neeta can use a CVP analysis to make decisions about advertising and selling price.

Learning Objective 4

Explain how managers use CVP analysis in decision making

. . . choose the alternative that maximizes operating income

Decision to Advertise

Suppose Neeta anticipates selling 40 units of the *GMAT Success* package at the fair. Exhibit 3-3 indicates that Neeta's operating income will be ₹12,000. Neeta is considering advertising the product and its features in the fair brochure. The advertisement will be a fixed cost of ₹5,000. Neeta thinks that advertising will increase sales by 10% to 44 packages. Should Neeta advertise? The following table presents the CVP analysis.

	40 Packages Sold with No Advertising (1)	44 Packages Sold with Advertising (2)	Difference (3) = (2) − (1)
Revenues (₹2,000 × 40; ₹2,000 × 44)	₹80,000	₹88,000	₹8,000
Variable costs (₹1,200 × 40; ₹1,200 × 44)	48,000	52,800	4,800
Contribution margin (₹800 × 40; ₹800 × 44)	32,000	35,200	3,200
Fixed costs	−20,000	−25,000	5,000
Operating income	₹12,000	₹10,200	₹(1,800)

Operating income decreases from ₹12,000 to ₹10,200, so Neeta should not advertise. Note that Neeta could focus only on the difference column and come to the same conclusion: If Neeta advertises, contribution margin will increase by ₹3,200 (revenues, ₹8,000-variable costs, ₹4,800), and fixed costs will increase by ₹5,000, resulting in a ₹1,800 decrease in operating income.

When using CVP analysis, try evaluating decisions based on differences rather than mechanically working through the contribution income statement. What if advertising costs were ₹4000 or ₹6000 instead of ₹5000? Analyzing differences gets to the heart of CVP analysis and sharpens intuition by focusing only on the revenues and costs that will change by implementing new decisions.

Decision to Reduce Selling Price

Having decided not to advertise, Neeta is contemplating whether to reduce the selling price to ₹1,750. At this price, she thinks she will sell 50 units. At this quantity, the test-prep package that supplies *GMAT Success* will sell the packages to Neeta for ₹1,150 per unit instead of ₹1,200. Should Neeta reduce the selling price?

Contribution margin from lowering price to ₹1,750:
(₹1,750 − ₹1,150) per unit × 50 units   ₹30,000
Contribution margin from maintaining price at ₹2,000:
(₹2,000 − ₹1,200) per unit × 40 units   32,000
Change in contribution margin from lowering price   ₹(2,000)

Decreasing the price will reduce contribution margin by ₹2,000 and, because the fixed costs of ₹20,000 will not change, it will also reduce operating income by ₹2,000. Neeta should not reduce the selling price.

Determining Target Prices

Neeta could also ask "At what price can I sell 50 units (purchased at ₹1,150 per unit) and continue to earn an operating income of ₹12,000?" The answer is ₹1,790, as the following calculations show.

Target operating income	₹12,000
Add fixed costs	20,000
Target contribution margin	₹32,000
Divided by number of units sold	÷ 50 units
Target contribution margin per unit	₹640
Add variable cost per unit	1,150
Target selling price	₹1,790

Proof:		
	Revenues, ₹1,790 per unit × 50 units	₹89,500
	Variable costs, ₹1,150 per unit × 50 units	57,500
	Contribution margin	32,000
	Fixed costs	20,000
	Operating income	₹12,000

Neeta should also examine the effects of other decisions, such as simultaneously increasing advertising costs and lowering prices of *GMAT Success* packages. In each case, Neeta will estimate the effects these actions are likely to have on the demand for *GMAT Success*. She will then compare the changes in contribution margin (through the effects on selling prices, variable costs, and quantities of units sold) to the changes in fixed costs, and she will choose the alternative that provides the highest operating income.

Strategic decisions invariably entail risk. Managers can use CVP analysis to evaluate how the operating income of their companies will be affected if the outcomes they predict are not achieved—say, if sales are 10% lower than they estimated. Evaluating this risk affects other strategic decisions a manager might make. For example, if the probability of a decline in sales seems high, a manager may take actions to change the cost structure to have more variable costs and fewer fixed costs.

Decision Point

How do managers use CVP analysis to make decisions?

Sensitivity Analysis and Margin of Safety

Sensitivity analysis is a "what-if" technique managers use to examine how an outcome will change if the original predicted data are not achieved or if an underlying assumption changes. The analysis answers questions such as "What will operating income be if the quantity of units sold decreases by 5% from the original prediction?" and "What will operating income be if variable cost per unit increases by 10%?" This helps visualize the possible outcomes that might occur *before* the company commits to funding a project. For example, companies such as Boeing and Airbus use CVP analysis to evaluate how many airplanes they need to sell in order to recover the multibillion-dollar costs of designing and developing new ones. The managers then do a sensitivity analysis to test how sensitive their conclusions are to different assumptions, such as the size of the market for the airplane, its selling price, and the market share they think it can capture.

Using the spreadsheet, Neeta can immediately see how many units she needs to sell to achieve particular operating-income levels, given alternative levels of fixed costs and variable cost per unit that she may face. For example, she must sell 32 units to earn an operating income of ₹12,000 if fixed costs are ₹20,000 and variable cost per unit is ₹1,000. Neeta can also use Exhibit 3-4 to determine that she needs to sell 56 units to break even (earn operating income of ₹0) if the booth rental at the New Delhi fair is raised to ₹28,000 and if the variable cost per unit charged by the test-prep package supplier increases to ₹1500, Neeta can use information about costs and sensitivity analysis, together with realistic predictions about how much she can sell to decide if she should rent a booth.

Another aspect of sensitivity analysis is **margin of safety**:

Learning Objective **5**

Explain how sensitivity analysis helps managers cope with uncertainty

. . . determine the effect on operating income of different assumptions

Margin of safety = Budgeted (or actual) revenues − Breakeven revenues

Margin of safety (in units) = Budgeted (or actual) sales quantity − Breakeven quantity

Exhibit 3-4

Spreadsheet Analysis of CVP Relationships for Do-All Software

	File	Edit	View	Insert	Format	Tools	Data	Window	Help
	D5	▼			fx	= (₹ A5+D₹3)/(₹ F₹1-₹B5)			

	A	B	C	D	E	F
1			Number of units required to be sold at ₹ 200			
2			Selling Price to Earn Target Operating Income of			
3		**Variable Costs**	₹0	₹12,000	₹16,000	₹20,000
4	**Fixed Costs (₹)**	**per Unit (₹)**	(Breakeven point)			
5	20,000	1,000	20	32[a]	36	40
6	20,000	1,200	25	40	45	50
7	20,000	1,500	40	64	72	80
8	24,000	1,000	24	36	40	44
9	24,000	1,200	30	45	50	55
10	24,000	1,500	48	72	80	88
11	28,000	1,000	28	40	44	48
12	28,000	1,200	35	50	55	60
13	28,000	1,500	56	80	88	96
14						
15	[a]Number of units	=	$\dfrac{\text{Fixed costs} + \text{Target operating income}}{\text{Contribution margin per unit}}$	=	$\dfrac{₹20,000 + ₹12,000}{₹2,000 - ₹1,000}$	=32
16	required to be sold					

The margin of safety answers the "what-if" question: If budgeted revenues are above breakeven and drop, how far can they fall below budget before the breakeven point is reached? Sales might decrease as a result of factors such as a poorly executed marketing program or a competitor introducing a better product. Assume that Neeta has fixed costs of ₹20,000, a selling price of ₹2,000, and variable cost per unit of ₹1,200. From Exhibit 3-1, if Neeta sells 40 units, the budgeted revenues are ₹80,000 and the budgeted operating income is ₹12,000. The breakeven point is 25 units or ₹50,000 in total revenues.

$$\text{Margin of safety} = \frac{\text{Budgeted}}{\text{revenues}} - \frac{\text{Breakeven}}{\text{revenues}} = ₹80,000 - ₹50,000 = ₹30,000$$

$$\frac{\text{Margin of}}{\text{safety (in units)}} = \frac{\text{Budgeted}}{\text{sales (units)}} - \frac{\text{Breakeven}}{\text{sales (units)}} = 40 - 25 = 15 \text{ units}$$

Sometimes margin of safety is expressed as a percentage:

$$\text{Margin of safety percentage} = \frac{\text{Margin of safety in rupees}}{\text{Budgted (or actual) revenues}}$$

In our example, margin of safety percentage $= \dfrac{₹30,000}{₹80,000} = 37.5\%$

This result means that revenues would have to decrease substantially, by 37.5%, to reach breakeven revenues. The high margin of safety gives Neeta confidence that she is unlikely to suffer a loss.

If, however, Neeta expected to sell only 30 units, budgeted revenues would be ₹60,000 (₹2,000 per unit × 30 units) and the margin of safety would equal:

Budgeted revenues − Breakeven revenues = ₹60,000 − ₹50,000 = ₹10,000

$$\frac{\text{Margin of}}{\text{safety percentage}} = \frac{\text{Margin of safety in rupees}}{\text{Budgeted (or actual) revenues}} = \frac{₹10,000}{₹60,000} = 16.67\%$$

The analysis implies that if revenues fall by more than 16.67%, Neeta would suffer a loss. A low margin of safety increases the risk of a loss, which means Neeta would need to look for ways to lower the breakeven point by reducing fixed costs or increasing contribution margin. For example, she would need to evaluate if her product is attractive enough to customers to allow her to charge a higher price without reducing the demand for it or if she could purchase the software at a lower cost. If Neeta can neither reduce her fixed costs nor increase contribution margin and if she does not have the tolerance for this level of risk, she will prefer not to rent a booth at the fair.

   Sensitivity analysis gives managers a good feel for a decision's risks. It is a simple approach to recognizing **uncertainty**, which is the possibility that an actual amount will deviate from an expected amount. A more comprehensive approach to recognizing uncertainty is to compute expected values using probability distributions.

Decision Point

What can managers do to cope with uncertainty or changes in underlying assumptions?

Cost Planning and CVP

Managers have the ability to choose the levels of fixed and variable costs in their cost structures. This is a strategic decision. In this section, we describe various factors that managers and management accountants consider as they make this decision.

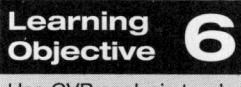

Learning Objective 6

Use CVP analysis to plan variable and fixed costs

. . . compare risk of losses versus higher returns

Alternative Fixed-Cost/Variable-Cost Structures

CVP-based sensitivity analysis highlights the risks and returns as fixed costs are substituted for variable costs in a company's cost structure. In Exhibit 3-4, compare line 6 and line 11.

	Fixed Cost ₹0 (Breakeven point)	Variable Cost ₹20,000	Number of units required to be sold at ₹2,000 selling price to earn target operating income	
Line 6	₹20,000	₹1,200	25	50
Line 11	₹28,000	₹1,000	28	48

Line 11, which has higher fixed costs, and lower variable costs than line 6, has a higher breakeven point but requires fewer units to be sold (48 versus 50) to earn operating income of ₹20,000. CVP analysis can help managers evaluate various fixed-cost/variable-cost structures. We next consider the effects of these choices in more detail. Suppose the Mumbai fair organizers offers Neeta three rental alternatives:

- Option 1: ₹20,000 fixed fee
- Option 2: ₹8,000 fixed fee plus 15% of *GMAT Success* revenues
- Option 3: 25% of *GMAT Success* revenues with no fixed fee

Neeta is interested in how her choice of a rental agreement will affect the income she earns and the risks she faces. Exhibit 3-5 graphically depicts the profit-volume relationship for each option.

- The line representing the relationship between units sold and operating income for Option 1 is the same as the line in the PV graph shown in Exhibit 3-3 (fixed costs of ₹20,000 and contribution margin per unit of ₹800).

- The line representing Option 2 shows fixed costs of ₹8,000 and a contribution margin per unit of ₹500 [selling price, ₹2,000, minus variable cost per unit, ₹1,200, minus variable rental fees per unit, ₹300, (0.15 × ₹2,000)].
- The line representing Option 3 has fixed costs of ₹0 and a contribution margin per unit of ₹300 [₹2,000 − ₹1,200 − ₹500 (0.25 × ₹2,000)].

Option 3 has the lowest breakeven point (0 units), and Option 1 has the highest breakeven point (25 units). Option 1 has the highest risk of loss if sales are low, but it also has the highest contribution margin per unit (₹800) and hence the highest operating income when sales are high (greater than 40 units).

The choice among Options 1, 2, and 3 is a strategic decision that Neeta faces. As in most strategic decisions, what Neeta decides now will significantly affect her operating income (or loss), depending on the demand for the product. Faced with this uncertainty, Neeta's choice will be influenced by her confidence in the level of demand for the *GMAT Success* packages and her willingness to risk losses if demand is low. For example, if Neeta's tolerance for risk is high, she will choose Option 1 with its high potential rewards. If, however, Neeta is averse to taking risk, she will prefer Option 3, where the rewards are smaller if sales are high but where she never suffers a loss if sales are low.

Operating Leverage

The risk-return trade-off across alternative cost structures can be measured as operating leverage. **Operating leverage** describes the effects that fixed costs have on changes in operating income as changes occur in units sold and contribution margin. Organizations with a high proportion of fixed costs in their cost structures, as is the case under Option 1, have high operating leverage. The line representing Option 1 in Exhibit 3-5 is the steepest of the three lines. Small increases in sales lead to large increases in operating income. Small decreases in sales result in relatively large decreases in operating income, leading to a greater risk of operating losses. *At any given level of sales,*

$$\frac{\text{Degree of}}{\text{operating leverage}} = \frac{\text{Contribution margin}}{\text{Operating income}}$$

The following table shows the **degree of operating leverage** at sales of 40 units for the three rental options.

	Option 1	Option 2	Option 3
1. Contribution margin per unit	₹800	₹500	₹300
2. Contribution margin (Row 1 × 40 units)	₹32,000	₹20,000	₹12,000
3. Operating income (from Exhibit 3–5)	₹12,000	₹12,000	₹12,000
4. Degree of operating leverage (Row 2 ÷ Row 3)	$\frac{₹32,000}{₹12,000} = 2.67$	$\frac{₹20,000}{₹12,000} = 1.67$	$\frac{₹12,000}{₹12,000} = 1.00$

These results indicate that, when sales are 40 units, a 1% change in sales and contribution margin will result in 2.67% times that 1% change in operating income for Option 1. For Option 3, a 1% change in sales and contribution margin will result in only a 1% change in operating income. Consider, for example, a sales increase of 50% from 40 to 60 units. Contribution margin will increase by 50% under each option. Operating income,

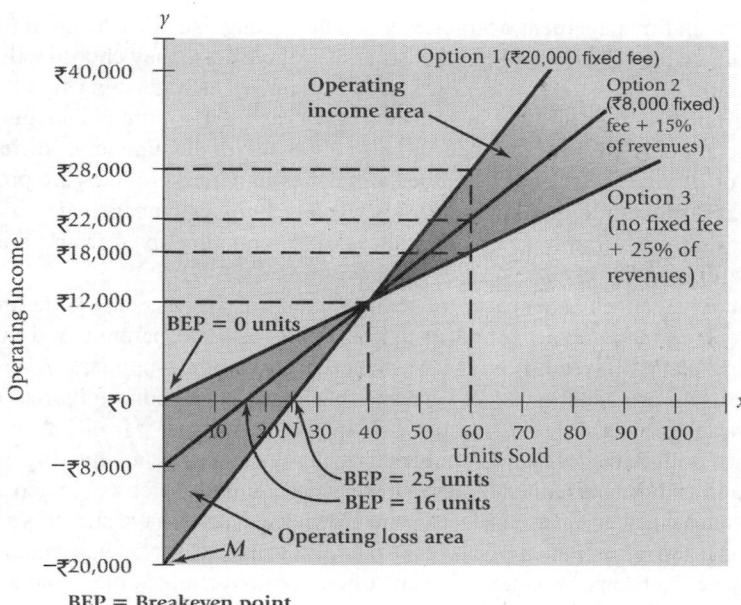

Exhibit 3-5

Profit-Volume Graph for
Alternative Rental Options
for Do-All Software

however, will increase by $2.67 \times 50\% = 133\%$ from ₹12,000 to ₹28,000 in Option 1, but it will increase by only $1.00 \times 50\% = 50\%$ from ₹12,000 to ₹18,000 in Option 3 (see Exhibit 3-5). The degree of operating leverage at a given level of sales helps managers calculate the effect of fluctuations in sales on operating income.

Keep in mind that, in the presence of fixed costs, the degree of operating leverage is different at different levels of sales. For example, at sales of 60 units, the degree of operating leverage under each of the three options is as follows:

	Option 1	Option 2	Option 3
1. Contribution margin per unit	₹800	₹500	₹300
2. Contribution margin (Row 1 × 60 units)	₹48,000	₹30,000	₹18,000
3. Operating income (from Exhibit 3 − 5)	₹28,000	₹22,000	₹18,000
4. Degree of operating leverage (Row 2 ÷ Row 3)	$\dfrac{₹48,000}{₹28,000}=1.71$	$\dfrac{₹30,000}{₹22,000}=1.36$	$\dfrac{₹18,000}{₹18,000}=1.00$

The degree of operating leverage decreases from 2.67 (at sales of 40 units) to 1.71 (at sales of 60 units) under Option 1 and from 1.67 to 1.36 under Option 2. In general, whenever there are fixed costs, the degree of operating leverage decreases as the level of sales increases beyond the breakeven point. If fixed costs are ₹0 as in Option 3, contribution margin equals operating income, and the degree of operating leverage equals 1.00 at all sales levels.

It is important for managers to monitor operating leverage carefully. Consider companies such as General Motors and Kingfisher Airlines. Their high operating leverage was a major reason for their financial problems. Anticipating high demand for their services, these companies borrowed money to acquire assets, resulting in high fixed costs. As their sales declined, these companies suffered losses and could not generate enough cash to service their interest and debt, causing them to seek bankruptcy protection.

Managers and management accountants should distinguish fixed from variable costs and then evaluate how the level of fixed costs and variable costs they choose will affect the risk-return tradeoffs of their firms. As we have explained, distinguishing fixed from variable costs is fairly straightforward in some cases. In others it's more challenging because costs do not vary only with the number of units sold but with the number of different types of products or services offered, the number of batches in which products are produced, or the complexity of operations. Chapter 10 describes techniques managers can use to separate fixed costs from variable costs. Regardless, differentiating fixed from variable costs requires careful judgment.

What actions can managers take to reduce fixed costs? Nike, the shoe and apparel company, does no manufacturing and incurs no fixed costs of operating and maintaining manufacturing plants. Instead, it buys its products from various suppliers. As a result, all of Nike's costs of producing products are variable costs. Nike reduces its risk of loss by increasing variable costs and reducing fixed costs.

To reduce both fixed costs and variable costs, many companies are moving their manufacturing facilities from the United States to lower-cost countries, such as Mexico and China. Other companies, such as General Electric and Hewlett-Packard, have shifted service functions, such as after-sales customer service, to their customer call centers in countries such as India. These decisions by companies are often controversial. Some economists argue that outsourcing helps keep costs, and therefore prices, low and enables U.S. companies to remain globally competitive. Others argue that outsourcing reduces job opportunities in the United States and hurts working-class families.

Decision Point

How should managers choose among different variable-cost/ fixed-cost structures?

Learning Objective 7

Apply CVP analysis to a company producing multiple products

. . . assume sales mix of products remains constant as total units sold changes

Effects of Sales Mix on Income

Sales mix is the quantities (or proportion) of various products (or services) that constitute total unit sales of a company. Suppose Neeta is now budgeting for a subsequent college fair in Chennai. She plans to sell two different test-prep packages—*GMAT Success and GRE Guarantee*—and budgets the following:

	GMAT Success	GRE Guarantee	Total
Expected sales	60	40	100
Revenues, ₹2,000 and ₹1,000 per unit	₹1,20,000	₹40,000	₹1,60,000
Variable costs, ₹1,200 and ₹700 per unit	72,000	28,000	1,00,000
Contribution margin, ₹800 and ₹300 per unit	₹48,000	₹12,000	60,000
Fixed costs			45,000
Operating income			₹15,000

What is the breakeven point for Neeta's business now? The total number of units that must be sold to break even in a multiproduct company depends on the sales mix. For Neeta, this is the combination of the number of units of *GMAT Success* sold and the number of units of *GRE Guarantee* sold. We assume that the budgeted sales mix (60 units of *GMAT Success* sold for every 40 units of *GRE Guarantee* sold, that is, a ratio of 3:2) will not change at different levels of total unit sales. That is, we think of Neeta selling a bundle of 3 units of *GMAT Success* and 2 units of *GRE Guarantee*. (Note that this does not mean that Neeta physically bundles the two products together into one big package.)

Each bundle yields a contribution margin of ₹3,000 calculated as follows:

	Number of Units of GMAT Success and GRE Guarantee Bundle	Contribution Margin per GMAT Success and GRE Guarantee	Contribution Margin of the Bundle
GMAT Success	3	₹800	₹2,400
GRE Guarantee	2	300	600
Total			₹3,000

To compute the breakeven point, we calculate the number of bundles Neeta needs to sell.

$$\text{Breakeven point in bundles} = \frac{\text{Fixed costs}}{\text{Contribution margin per bundle}} = \frac{₹45,000}{₹3,000 \text{ per bundle}} = 15 \text{ bundles}$$

Breakeven point in units of *GMAT Success* and *GRE Guarantee* is:

GMAT Success : 15 bundles × 3 units of GMAT Success per bundle 5		45 units
GRE Guarantee : 15 bundles × 2 units of GRE Guarantee per bundle 5		30 units
Total number of units to breakeven		75 units

Breakeven point in rupees for *GMAT Success* and *GRE Guarantee* is:

GMAT Success : 45 units × ₹2,000 per unit		₹90,000
GRE Guarantee : 30 units × ₹1,000 per unit		30,000
Breakeven revenues		₹1,20,000

When there are multiple products, it is often convenient to use the contribution margin percentage. Under this approach, Neeta also calculates the revenues from selling a bundle of 3 units of *GMAT Success* and 2 units of *GRE Guarantee*:

	Number of Units of GMAT Success and GRE Guarantee in Each Bundle Bundle	Selling Price for GMAT Success and GRE Guarantee	Revenue of the Bundle
GMAT Success	3	₹2,000	₹6,000
GRE Guarantee	2	1,000	2,000
Total			₹8,000

$$\text{Contribution margin percentage for the bundle} = \frac{\text{Contribution margin of the bundle}}{\text{Revenue of the bundle}} = \frac{₹3,000}{₹8,000} = 0.375 \text{ or } 37.5\%$$

$$\text{Breakeven revenues} = \frac{\text{Fixed costs}}{\text{Contribution margin \% for the bundle}} = \frac{₹45,000}{0.375} = ₹1,20,000$$

$$\text{Number of bundles required to be sold to break even} = \frac{\text{Breakeven revenues}}{\text{Revenue per bundle}} = \frac{₹1,20,000}{₹8,000 \text{ per bundle}} = 15 \text{ bundles}$$

The breakeven point in units and rupees for *GMAT Success* and *GRE Guarantee* are:

GMAT Success: 15 bundles × 3 units of GMAT Success per bundle =
                               45 units × ₹2,000 per unit = ₹90,000

GRE Guarantee: 15 bundles × 2 units of GRE Guarantee per bundle =
                                30 units × ₹1,000 per unit = ₹30,000

Recall that in all our calculations, we have assumed that the budgeted sales mix (3 units of *GMAT Success* for every 2 units of GRE Guarantee) will not change at different levels of total unit sales.

Of course, there are many different sales mixes (in units) that result in a contribution margin of ₹45,000 and cause Neeta to break even, as the following table shows:

Sales Mix (Units)		Contribution Margin from		Total Contribution Margin
GMAT Success (1)	GRE Guarantee (2)	GMAT Success (3) = ₹800 × (1)	GRE Guarantee (4) = ₹300 × (2)	(5) = (3) + (4)
48	22	₹38,400	₹6,600	₹45,000
36	54	28,800	16,200	45,000
30	70	24,000	21,000	45,000

If for example, the sales mix changes to 3 units of GMAT Success for every 7 units of GRE Guarantee, you can see in the preceding table that the breakeven point increases from 75 units to 100 units, comprising 30 units of GMAT Success and 70 units of GRE Guarantee. The breakeven quantity increases because the sales mix has shifted toward the lower-contribution-margin product, GRE Guarantee (₹300 per unit compared to GMAT Success's ₹800 per unit). In general, for any given total quantity of units sold, as the sales mix shifts toward units with lower contribution margins (more units of Superword compared to GMAT Success), operating income will be lower.

How do companies choose their sales mix? They adjust their mix to respond to demand changes. For example, as gasoline prices increase and customers want smaller cars, auto companies, such as Ford, Volkswagen, and Toyota, shift their production mix to produce smaller cars. This shift to smaller cars might result in an increase in the breakeven point because the sales mix has shifted toward lower-contribution-margin products. Despite this increase in the breakeven point, shifting the sales mix to smaller cars is the correct decision because the demand for larger cars has fallen. At no point should a manager focus on changing the sales mix to lower the breakeven point without taking into account customer preferences and demand. Of course, the shift in sales mix to smaller cars prompts managers at Ford, Volkswagen, and Toyota to take other actions such as reducing fixed costs and increasing contribution margins on smaller cars by charging higher prices for features that customers are willing to pay for or lowering variable costs.

The multi-product case has two cost drivers, GMAT Success and GRE Guarantee. It shows how CVP and breakeven analysis can be adapted to the case of multiple cost drivers. The key point is that many different combinations of cost drivers can result in a given contribution margin.

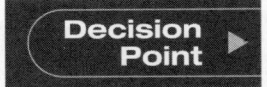

Decision Point ▶

How can managers apply CVP analysis to a company producing multiple products?

Learning Objective 8

Apply CVP analysis in service and not-for-profit organizations

. . . define appropriate output measures

CVP Analysis in Service and Not-for-Profit Organizations

So far, our CVP analysis has focused on Neeta's merchandising company. Of course, managers at manufacturing companies such as BMW, service companies such as Bank of America, and not-for-profit organizations such as the United Way also use CVP analysis to make decisions. To apply CVP analysis in service and nonprofit organizations, we need to focus on measuring their output, which is different from the tangible units sold by manufacturing and merchandising companies. Examples of output measures in various service industries (for example, airlines, hotels/motels, and hospitals) and nonprofit organizations (for example, Universities) are as follows:

Industry	Measure of Output
Airlines	Passenger miles
Hotels/motels	Room-nights occupied
Hospitals	Patient days
Universities	Student credit-hours

Consider an agency of the Delhi Muncipal Corporation's Social Welfare Department that helps disabled people seeking employment with a ₹90,00,000 budget appropriation (its revenues) for 2014. This nonprofit agency's purpose is to assist handicapped people seeking employment. On average, the agency supplements each person's income by ₹50,000 annually. The agency's only other costs are fixed costs of rent and administrative salaries equal to ₹27,00,000. The agency manager wants to know how many people could be assisted in 2014. We can use CVP analysis here by setting operating income to ₹0. Let Q be the number of handicapped people to be assisted:

$$\text{Revenues} - \text{Variable costs} - \text{Fixed costs} = 0$$
$$₹90,00,000 - ₹50,000\, Q - ₹27,00,000 = 0$$
$$₹50,000\, Q = ₹90,00,000 - ₹27,00,000 = ₹63,00,000$$
$$Q = ₹63,00,000 \div ₹50,000 \text{ per person} = 126 \text{ people}$$

Suppose total budget appropriation for 2015 will be reduced by 15% to ₹90,00,000 × (1 − 0.15) = ₹76,50,000. The manager wants to know how many handicapped people could be assisted with this reduced budget. Assume the same amount of monetary assistance per person and no change in fixed cost:

$$₹76,50,000 - ₹50,000\, Q - ₹27,00,000 = 0$$
$$₹50,000\, Q = ₹76,50,000 - ₹27,00,000 = ₹49,50,000$$
$$Q = ₹49,50,000 \div ₹50,000 \text{ per person} = 99 \text{ people}$$

So, in 2015, instead of assisting 126 people, the agency can assist only 99. Note the following two characteristics of the CVP relationships in this nonprofit situation:

1. The percentage drop in the number of people assisted, (126 − 99) ÷ 126, or 21.4%, is greater than the 15% reduction in the budget appropriation. It is greater because the ₹27,00,000 in fixed costs still must be paid, leaving a proportionately lower budget to assist people. In other words, the percentage drop in service exceeds the percentage drop in budget appropriation.

2. Given the reduced budget appropriation (revenues) of ₹76,50,000, in 2015 the manager can adjust operations to stay within this appropriation in one or more of three ways: (a) by reducing the number of people assisted from the current 126, (b) by reducing the variable cost (the extent of assistance per person) from the current ₹50,000 per person, or (c) by reducing the total fixed costs from the current ₹27,00,000.

Decision Point

How do managers apply CVP analysis in service and not-for-profit organizations?

Contribution Margin Versus Gross Margin

So far, we have developed two important concepts relating to profit margin—contribution margin, which was introduced in this chapter, and gross margin, which was discussed in Chapter 2. Is there a relationship between these two concepts? In the following equations, we clearly distinguish contribution margin, which provides information for CVP analysis, from gross margin, a measure of competitiveness, described in Chapter 2.

$$\text{Gross margin} = \text{Revenues} - \text{Cost of goods sold}$$
$$\text{Contribution margin} = \text{Revenues} - \text{All variable costs}$$

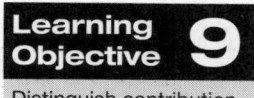

Learning Objective 9

Distinguish contribution margin

...revenues minus all variable costs

from gross margin

...revenues minus cost of goods sold

The gross margin measures how much a company can charge for its products over and above the cost of acquiring or producing them. Companies, such as brand-name pharmaceuticals producers, have high gross margins because their products are often patented and provide unique and distinctive benefits to consumers. In contrast, manufacturers of generic medicines and basic chemicals have low gross margins because the market for these products is highly competitive. Contribution margin indicates how much of a company's revenues are available to cover fixed costs. It helps in assessing the risk of losses. For example, the risk of loss is low if the contribution margin exceeds a company's fixed costs even when sales are low. Gross margin and contribution margin are related but give different insights. For example, a company operating in a competitive market with a low gross margin will have a low risk of loss if its fixed costs are small.

Contribution Income Statement Emphasizing Contribution Margin (in 000s)			Financial Accounting Income Statement Emphasizing Gross Margin (in 000s)	
Revenues		₹10,000	Revenues	₹10,000
Variable manufacturing costs	₹2,500		Cost of goods sold (₹2,500 + ₹1,600)	4,100
Variable nonmanufacturing costs	2,700	5,200		
Contribution margin		4,800	Gross margin	5,900
Fixed manufacturing costs	1,600		Nonmanufacturing costs	
Fixed nonmanufacturing costs	1,380	2,980	(₹2,700 + ₹1,380)	4,080
Operating income		₹1,820	Operating income	₹1,820

Consider the distinction between gross margin and contribution margin in the manufacturing sector. The concepts differ in two ways: fixed manufacturing costs and variable nonmanufacturing costs. The following example (figures assumed) illustrates this difference: Fixed manufacturing costs of ₹16,00,000 are not deducted from revenues when computing contribution margin but are deducted when computing gross margin. The cost of goods sold in a manufacturing company includes all variable manufacturing costs and all fixed manufacturing costs (₹25,00,000 + ₹16,00,000). The company's variable nonmanufacturing costs (such as commissions paid to salespersons) of ₹27,00,000 are deducted from revenues when computing contribution margin but are not deducted when computing gross margin.

Like contribution margin, gross margin can be expressed as a total, as an amount per unit, or as a percentage. For example, the **gross margin percentage** is the gross margin divided by revenues—59% (₹5,900 ÷ ₹10,000) in our manufacturing-sector example.

One reason why gross margin and contribution margin are confused with each other is that the two are identical in the case of merchandising companies. That's because cost of goods sold equals the variable cost of goods purchased (and subsequently sold).

Decision Point ▶

What is the difference between contribution margin and gross margin?

Problem for Self-Study

National Travel Agency specializes in flights between New Delhi and Dubai. It books passengers on Indian Airlines at ₹9,000 per round-trip ticket. Until last month, Indian Airlines paid National a commission of 10% of the ticket price paid by each passenger. This commission was National's only source of revenues. National's fixed costs are ₹1,40,000 per month (for salaries, rent, and so on), and its variable costs are ₹200 per ticket purchased for a passenger. This ₹200 includes a ₹150 per ticket delivery fee paid to Desk-to-Desk Couriers. (To keep the analysis simple, we assume each round-trip ticket purchased is delivered in a separate package. Thus, the ₹150 delivery fee applies to each ticket.)

Indian Airlines has just announced a revised payment schedule for all travel agents. It will now pay travel agents a 10% commission per ticket up to a maximum of ₹500. Any ticket costing more than ₹5,000 generates only a ₹500 commission, regardless of the ticket price.

Required

1. Under the old 10% commission structure, how many round-trip tickets must National sell each month (a) to break even and (b) to earn an operating income of ₹70,000?
2. How does Indian's revised payment schedule affect your answers to (a) and (b) in requirement 1?

Solution

1. National receives a 10% commission on each ticket: 10% × ₹9,000 = ₹900. Thus,

$$
\begin{aligned}
\text{Selling price} &= ₹900 \text{ per ticket} \\
\text{Variable cost per unit} &= ₹200 \text{ per ticket} \\
\text{Contribution margin per unit} &= ₹900 - ₹200 = ₹700 \text{ per ticket} \\
\text{Fixed costs} &= ₹1,40,000 \text{ per month}
\end{aligned}
$$

a. $$\dfrac{\text{Breakeven number}}{\text{of tickets}} = \dfrac{\text{Fixed costs}}{\text{Contribution margin per unit}} = \dfrac{₹1,40,000}{₹700 \text{ per ticket}} = 200 \text{ tickets}$$

b. When target operating income = ₹70,000 per month:

$$\dfrac{\text{Quantity of tickets}}{\text{required to be sold}} = \dfrac{\text{Fixed costs} + \text{Target operating income}}{\text{Contribution margin per unit}}$$

$$= \dfrac{₹1,40,000 + ₹70,000}{₹700 \text{ per ticket}} = \dfrac{₹2,10,000}{₹700 \text{ per ticket}} = 300 \text{ tickets}$$

2. Under the new system, National would receive only ₹500 on the ₹9,000 ticket. Thus,

$$
\begin{aligned}
\text{Selling price} &= ₹500 \text{ per ticket} \\
\text{Variable cost per unit} &= ₹200 \text{ per ticket} \\
\text{Contribution margin per unit} &= ₹500 - ₹200 = ₹300 \text{ per ticket} \\
\text{Fixed costs} &= ₹1,40,000 \text{ per month}
\end{aligned}
$$

a. $$\dfrac{\text{Breakeven number}}{\text{of tickets}} = \dfrac{₹1,40,000}{₹300 \text{ per ticket}} = 467 \text{ tickets (rounded up)}$$

b. $$\dfrac{\text{Quantity of tickets}}{\text{required to be sold}} = \dfrac{₹2,10,000}{₹300 \text{ per ticket}} = 700 \text{ tickets}$$

The ₹500 cap on the commission paid per ticket causes the breakeven point to more than double (from 200 to 467 tickets) and the tickets required to be sold to earn ₹70,000 per month to also more than double (from 300 to 700 tickets). As would be expected, travel agents reacted very negatively to the Indian Airlines announcement to change commission payments. Unfortunately for travel agents, other airlines also changed their commission structure in similar ways.

Decision Points

The following question-and-answer format summarizes the chapter's learning objectives. Each decision presents a key question related to a learning objective. The guidelines are the answer to that question.

Decision	Guidelines
1. How can CVP analysis help managers?	CVP analysis assists managers in understanding the behavior of a product's or service's total costs, total revenues, and operating income as changes occur in the output level, selling price, variable costs, or fixed costs.
2. How can managers determine the breakeven point or the output needed to achieve a target operating income?	The breakeven point is the quantity of output at which total revenues equal total costs. The three methods for computing the breakeven point and the quantity of output to achieve target operating income are the equation method, the contribution margin method, and the graph method. Each method is merely a restatement of the others. Managers often select the method they find easiest to use in a specific decision situation.
3. How can managers incorporate income taxes into CVP analysis?	Income taxes can be incorporated into CVP analysis by using the target net income to calculate the target operating income. The breakeven point is unaffected by income taxes because no income taxes are paid when operating income equals zero.
4. How do managers use CVP analysis to make decisions?	Managers compare how revenues, costs, and contribution margins change across various alternatives. They then choose the alternative that maximizes operating income.
5. What can managers do to cope with uncertainty or changes in underlying assumptions?	Sensitivity analysis is a "what-if" technique that examines how an outcome will change if the original predicted data are not achieved or if an underlying assumption changes. When making decisions, managers use CVP analysis to compare contribution margins and fixed costs under different assumptions. Managers also calculate the margin of safety equal to budgeted revenues minus breakeven revenues.
6. How should manaers choose among different variable-cost/fixed-cost structures?	Choosing the variable-cost/fixed-cost structure is a strategic decision for companies. CVP analysis helps managers compare the risk of losses when revenues are low and the upside profits when revenues are high for different proportions of variable and fixed costs in a company's cost structure.
7. How can managers apply CVP analysis to a company producing multiple products?	Managers apply CVP analysis in a company producing multiple products by assuming the sales mix of products sold remains constant as the total quantity of units sold changes.
8. How do managers apply CVP analysis in service and not-for-profit organizations?	Managers define output measures such as passenger-miles in the case of airlines or patient-days in the context of hospitals and identify costs that are fixed and those that vary with these measures of output.
9. What is the difference between contribution margin and gross margin?	Contribution margin is revenues minus all variable costs whereas gross margin is revenues minus cost of goods sold. Contribution margin measures the risk of a loss, whereas gross margin measures the competitiveness of a product.

TERMS TO LEARN

This chapter and the Glossary at the end of the book contain definitions of the following important terms:

breakeven point (BEP) **(p. 93)**
contribution income
  statement **(p. 88)**
contribution margin **(p. 88)**
contribution margin
  percentage **(p. 89)**

contribution margin
  ratio **(p. 89)**
gross margin
  percentage **(p. 108)**
margin of safety **(p. 99)**
operating leverage **(p. 102)**

PV graph **(p. 95)**
revenue driver **(p. 92)**
sales mix **(p. 104)**
sensitivity analysis **(p. 99)**
uncertainty **(p. 101)**

ASSIGNMENT MATERIAL

Note: To underscore the basic CVP relationships, the assignment material ignores income taxes unless stated otherwise.

Questions

3-1 Define cost-volume-profit analysis.

3-2 Describe the assumptions underlying CVP analysis.

3-3 Distinguish between operating income and net income.

3-4 Define contribution margin, contribution margin per unit, and contribution margin percentage.

3-5 Describe three methods that can be used to express CVP relationships.

3-6 Why is it more accurate to describe the subject matter of this chapter as CVP analysis rather than as breakeven analysis?

3-7 "CVP analysis is both simple and simplistic. If you want realistic analysis to underpin your decisions, look beyond CVP analysis." Do you agree? Explain.

3-8 How does an increase in the income tax rate affect the breakeven point?

3-9 Describe sensitivity analysis. How has the advent of the electronic spreadsheet affected the use of sensitivity analysis?

3-10 Give an example of how a manager can decrease variable costs while increasing fixed costs.

3-11 Give an example of how a manager can increase variable costs while decreasing fixed costs.

3-12 What is operating leverage? How is knowing the degree of operating leverage helpful to managers?

3-13 "There is no such thing as a fixed cost. All costs can be 'unfixed' given sufficient time." Do you agree? What is the implication of your answer for CVP analysis?

3-14 How can a company with multiple products compute its breakeven point?

3-15 "In CVP analysis, gross margin is a less-useful concept than contribution margin." Do you agree? Explain briefly.

Solved Examples

3-16 CVP computations. Jain Manufacturing sold 20,000 units of its product for ₹100 per unit in the current year. Variable cost per unit is ₹60 and total fixed costs are ₹2,00,000.

Required

1. Calculate (a) contribution margin (b) operating income.

2. Jain's current manufacturing process is labour intensive. Rahul, Jain's production manager, has proposed investing in state-of-the-art manufacturing equipment, which will increase the annual fixed costs to ₹7,00,000. The variable costs are expected to decrease to ₹30 per unit. Jain expects to maintain the same sales volume and selling price next year. How would acceptance of Rahul's proposal affect your answers to (a) and (b) in requirement (1)?

3. Should Jain accept Rahul's proposal? Explain.

Solution

1. **a.** Calculation of Contribution MarginSales − Variable costs = Contribution margin(20,000 × ₹100 − (₹60 × 20,000) = Contribution margin (₹20,00,000 − ₹12,00,000) = Contribution margin ₹8,00,000 = Contribution margin

2. **b.** Calculation of Operating IncomeContribution margin − Fixed costs = Operating income ₹8,00,000 − ₹2,00,000 = ₹6,00,000 = Operating income

1. **a.** Impact of Acceptance of Proposal on Contribution MarginFixed costs = ₹7,00,000 Variable cost per unit = ₹30 per unitSales Variable costs = Contribution margin(20,000 × ₹100) − (₹30 × 20,000) ₹20,00,000 − ₹6,00,000 = ₹14,00,000

2. **b.** Impact of Acceptance of Proposal on Operating IncomeFixed costs = ₹7,00,000 Contribution margin × Fixed costs = Operating income = ₹14,00,000 − ₹7,00,000 = ₹7,00,000 = Operating income

3. Rahul's proposal should be accepted as it is expected to increase operating income by ₹1,00,000.

3-17 CVP exercises. The Bata owns and operates an outlet in Gurgaon City. You are given the following corporate budget data for next year:

Revenues	₹1,04,00,000
Fixed costs	₹21,00,000
Variable costs	₹79,00,000

Variable costs change based on the number of shoes sold.

Compute the budgeted operating income for each of the following deviations from the original budget data. (Consider each case independently.)

Required

1. An 11% increase in contribution margin, holding revenues constant
2. An 11% decrease in contribution margin, holding revenues constant
3. A 4% increase in fixed costs
4. A 4% decrease in fixed costs
5. A 7% increase in units sold
6. A 7% decrease in units sold
7. An 11% increase in fixed costs and a 11% increase in units sold
8. A 4% increase in fixed costs and a 4% decrease in variable costs
9. Which of these alternatives yields the highest budgeted operating income? Explain why this is the case.

Solution

	Revenues	Variable Costs	Contribution Margin	Fixed Costs	Budgeted Operating Income
Orig.	₹1,04,00,000[G]	₹79,00,000[G]	₹25,00,000	₹21,00,000[G]	₹4,00,000
1.	1,04,00,000	76,25,000	27,75,000[a]	21,00,000	6,75,000
2.	1,04,00,000	81,75,000	22,25,000[b]	21,00,000	1,25,000
3.	1,04,00,000	79,00,000	25,00,000	21,84,000[c]	3,16,000
4.	1,04,00,000	79,00,000	25,00,000	20,16,000[d]	4,84,000
5.	1,11,28,000[e]	84,53,000[f]	26,75,000	21,00,000	5,75,000
6.	96,72,000[g]	73,47,000[h]	23,25,000	21,00,000	2,25,000
7.	1,15,44,000[i]	87,69,000[j]	27,75,000	23,31,000[k]	4,44,000
8.	1,04,00,000	75,84,000[l]	28,16,000	21,84,000[m]	6,32,000

[G]stands for given.

[a]₹25,00,000 × 1.11; [b]₹25,00,000 × 0.89; [c]₹21,00,000 × 1.04; [d]₹21,00,000 × 0.96; [e]₹1,04,00,000 × 1.07; [f]₹79,00,000 × 1.07; [g]₹1,04,00,000 × 0.93; [h]₹79,00,000 × 0.93; [i]₹1,04,00,000 × 1.11; [j]₹79,00,000 × 1.11; [k]₹21,00,000 × 1.11; [l]₹79,00,000 × 0.96; [m]₹21,00,000 × 1.04

9. Alternative 1, a 11% increase in contribution margin holding revenues constant, yields the highest budgeted operating income because it has the highest increase in contribution margin without increasing fixed costs.

3-18 CVP analysis, income taxes. Reliable Motors is a small car dealership. On average, it sells a car for ₹2,70,000, which it purchases from the manufacturer for ₹2,30,000. Each month, Reliable Motors pays ₹4,82,000 in rent and utilities and ₹6,80,000 for salespeople's salaries. In addition to their salaries, salespeople are paid a commission of ₹6,000 for each car they sell. Reliable Motors also spends ₹1,30,000 each month for local advertisements. Its tax rate is 40%

1. How many cars must Reliable Motors sell each month to break even?
2. Reliable Motors has a target monthly net income of ₹5,10,000. What is its target monthly operating income? How many cars must be sold each month to reach the target monthly net income of ₹5,10,000?

Solution

1. Monthly fixed costs = ₹4,82,000 + ₹6,80,000 + ₹1,30,000 = ₹12,92,000

Contribution margin per unit = ₹2,70,000 − ₹2,30,000 − ₹6,000 = ₹34,000

$$\text{Breakeven units per month} = \frac{\text{Monthly fixed costs}}{\text{Contribution margin per unit}} = \frac{₹12,92,000}{₹34,000 \text{ per car}} = 38 \text{ cars}$$

2. Tax rate   40%
   Target net income   ₹5,10,000

$$\text{Target operating income} = \frac{\text{Target net income}}{1 - \text{tax rate}} = \frac{₹5,10,000}{(1 - 0.40)} = \frac{₹5,10,000}{0.60} = ₹8,50,000$$

$$\text{Quantity of output units required to be sold} =$$

$$\frac{\text{Fixed costs} + \text{Target operating income}}{\text{Contribution margin per unit}} = \frac{₹12,92,000 + ₹8,50,000}{₹34,000} = 63 \text{ cars}$$

3-19 CVP analysis, sensitivity analysis. Levis Jeans Co. sells blue jeans wholesale to major retailers across the country. Each pair of jeans has a selling price of ₹3,000 with ₹2,100 in variable costs of goods sold. The company has fixed manufacturing costs of ₹120 lakh and fixed marketing costs of ₹30 lakh. Sales commissions are paid to the wholesale sales reps at 5% of revenues. The company has an effective income tax rate of 25%

Required

1. How many jeans must company sell in order to break even?
2. How many jeans must the company sell in order to reach:
   a. a target operating income of ₹45 lakh?
   b. a net income of ₹45 lakh?
3. How many jeans would company have to sell to earn the net income in part 2b if (consider each requirement independently).
   a. The contribution margin per unit increases by 10%
   b. The selling price is increased to ₹3,250
   c. The company outsources manufacturing to an overseas company increasing variable costs per unit by 200 and saving 60% of fixed manufacturing costs.

Solution

1. CMU = ₹3,000 − ₹2,100 − (0.05 × ₹3,000) = ₹750

$$Q = \frac{FC}{CMU} = \frac{₹1,50,00,000}{₹750 \text{ per pair}}$$

$$= 20,000 \text{ pairs}$$

Note: No income taxes are paid at the breakeven point because operating income is zero.

2a.

$$Q = \frac{FC + TOI}{CMU} = \frac{₹150 \text{ lakh} + ₹45 \text{ lakh}}{₹750 \text{ per pair}}$$

$$= \frac{₹195 \text{ lakh}}{₹750 \text{ per pair}} = 26,000 \text{ pairs}$$

2b. Target operating income $= \frac{\text{Target net income}}{1 - \text{tax rate}} = \frac{₹45 \text{ lakh}}{(1 - 0.25) = 0.75} = ₹60 \text{ lakh}$

$$\frac{\text{Quantity of output units}}{\text{required to be sold}} = \frac{\text{Fixed costs} + \text{Target operating income}}{\text{Contribution margin per unit}} = \frac{₹150 \text{ lakh} + ₹60 \text{ lakh}}{₹750}$$

$$= 28,000 \text{ pairs}$$

3a. Contribution margin per unit increases by 10%

Contribution margin per unit = ₹750 × 1.10 = ₹825

$$\frac{\text{Quantity of output units}}{\text{required to be sold}} = \frac{\text{Fixed costs} + \text{Target operating income}}{\text{Contribution margin per unit}} = \frac{₹150 \text{ lakh} + ₹60 \text{ lakh}}{₹825}$$

$$= 25,455 \text{ pairs (rounded)}$$

The net income target in units decreases from 28,000 pairs in requirement 2b to 25,455 pairs.

3b. Increasing the selling price to ₹3,250

Contribution margin per unit = ₹3,250 − ₹2,100 − (0.05 × ₹3,250) = ₹987.50

$$\frac{\text{Quantity of output units}}{\text{required to be sold}} = \frac{\text{Fixed costs} + \text{Target operating income}}{\text{Contribution margin per unit}} = \frac{₹150 \text{ lakh} + ₹60 \text{ lakh}}{₹987.50}$$

$$= 21,266 \text{ pairs (rounded)}$$

The net income target in units decreases from 28,000 pairs in requirement 2b to 21,266 pairs.

3c. Increase variable costs by ₹200 per unit and decrease fixed manufacturing costs by 60%.

Contribution margin per unit = ₹3,000 − ₹2,300 (₹2,100 + ₹200) − (0.05 × ₹3,000) = ₹550

Fixed manufacturing costs = (1 − 0.6) × ₹120 lakh = ₹48 lakh

Fixed marketing costs = ₹30 lakh

Total fixed costs = ₹48 lakh + ₹30 lakh = ₹78 lakh

$$\frac{\text{Quantity of output units}}{\text{required to be sold}} = \frac{\text{Fixed costs} + \text{Target operating income}}{\text{Contribution margin per unit}} = \frac{₹78\ \text{lakh} + ₹60\ \text{lakh}}{₹550}$$

= 25,091 pairs (rounded)

The net income target in units decreases from 28,000 pairs in requirement 2b to 25,091 pairs.

3-20 CVP analysis, margin of safety. Suppose Aggarwal Brothers breakeven point is revenues of ₹15,00,000. Fixed costs are ₹7,20,000.

1. Compute the contribution margin percentage.
2. Compute the selling price if variable costs are ₹13 per unit.
3. Suppose 90,000 units are sold. Compute the margin of safety in units and dollars.
4. What does this tell you about the risk of firm making a loss? What are the most likely reasons for this risk to increase?

Required

Solution

1. Breakeven point revenues = $\dfrac{\text{Fixed costs}}{\text{Contribution margin percentage}}$

Contribution margin percentage = $\dfrac{₹7,20,000}{₹15,00,000}$ = 0.48 or 48%

2. Contribution margin percentage = $\dfrac{\text{Selling} - \text{Variable cost per unit}}{\text{Selling price}}$

$$0.48 = \frac{\text{SP} - ₹13}{\text{SP}}$$

0.48 SP = SP − ₹13

0.52 SP = ₹13

SP = ₹25

3. Breakeven sales in units = Revenues ÷ Selling price = ₹15,00,000 ÷ ₹25 = 60,000 units

Margin of safety in units = Sales in units − Breakeven sales in units

= 90,000 − 60,000 = 30,000 units

Revenues, 90,000 units × ₹25	₹22,50,000
Breakeven revenues	15,00,000
Margin of safety	₹7,50,000

4. The risk of making a loss is low. Sales would need to decrease by 30,000 units ÷ 90,000 units = 33.33% before Aggarwal Brothers. will make a loss. The most likely reasons for this risk to increase competition, weakness in the economy, or bad management.

3-21 CVP, Not for profit Sound Well Music Society is a not-for-profit organization that brings guest artists to the community's greater metropolitan area. The music society just bought a small concert hall in the center of town to house its performances. The lease payments on the concert hall are expected to be ₹40,000 per month. The organization pays its guest performers ₹18,000 per concert and anticipates corresponding ticket sales to be ₹45,000 per concert. The music society also incurs costs of approximately ₹10,000 per concert for marketing and advertising. The organization pays its part-time artistic director ₹3,30,000 per year and expects to receive ₹3,00,000 in donations in addition to its ticket sales.

Required

1. If the Sound Well Music Society just breaks even, how many concerts does it hold?
2. In addition to the organization's part-time artistic director, the music society would like to hire a part-time marketing director for ₹2,55,000 per year. What is the breakeven point? The music society anticipates that the addition of a marketing director would allow the organization to increase the number of concerts to 41 per year. What is the music society's operating income/(loss) if it hires the new marketing director?
3. The music society expects to receive a grant that would provide the organization with an additional ₹1,70,000 toward the payment of the marketing director's salary. What is the breakeven point if the music society hires the marketing director and receives the grant?

Solution

1. Ticket sales per concert   ₹45,000
   Variable costs per concert:
      Guest performers   ₹18,000
      Marketing and advertising   10,000
        Total variable costs per concert   28,000
   Contribution margin per concert   ₹17,000

   Fixed costs
      Salaries   ₹3,30,000
      Lease payments (₹40,000 × 12)   4,80,000
        Total fixed costs   ₹8,10,000
   Less donations   3,00,000
   Net fixed costs   ₹5,10,000

$$\text{Breakeven point in units} = \frac{\text{Net fixed costs}}{\text{Contribution margin per concert}} = \frac{₹5,10,000}{₹17,000} = 30 \text{ concerts}$$

Check

Donations   ₹3,00,000
Revenue (₹45,000 × 30)   13,50,000
Total revenue   16,50,000

Less variable costs
   Guest performers (₹18,000 × 30)   ₹5,40,000
   Marketing and advertising (₹10,000 × 30)   3,00,000
     Total variable costs   8,40,000

Less fixed costs
   Salaries   ₹3,30,000
   Mortgage payments   4,80,000
     Total fixed costs   8,10,000
Operating income   ₹0

2. Ticket sales per concert   ₹45,000
   Variable costs per concert:
   Guest performers   ₹18,000
      Marketing and advertising   10,000
      Total variable costs per concert   28,000

Contribution margin per concert		₹17,000
Fixed costs		
Salaries (₹3,30,000 + ₹2,55,000)	₹5,85,000	
Lease payments (₹40,000 × 12)	4,80,000	
Total fixed costs		₹10,65,000
Less donations		3,00,000
Net fixed costs		₹7,65,000

$$\text{Breakeven point in units} = \frac{\text{Net fixed costs}}{\text{Contribution margin per concert}} = \frac{₹7,65,000}{₹17,000} = 45 \text{ concerts}$$

Check

Donations		₹3,00,000
Revenue (₹45,000 × 45)		20,25,000
Total revenue		23,25,000
Less variable costs		
Guest performers (₹18,000 × 45)	₹8,10,000	
Marketing and advertising (₹10,000 × 45)	4,50,000	
Total variable costs		12,60,000
Less fixed costs		
Salaries	₹5,85,000	
Lease payments	4,80,000	
Total fixed costs		10,65,000
Operating income		₹0

Operating Income if 41 concerts are held

Donations		₹3,00,000
Revenue (₹45,000 × 41)		18,45,000
Total revenue		21,45,000
Less variable costs		
Guest performers (₹18,000 × 41)	₹7,38,000	
Marketing and advertising (₹10,000 × 41)	4,10,000	
Total variable costs		11,48,000
Less fixed costs		
Salaries	₹5,85,000	
Lease payments	4,80,000	
Total fixed costs		10,65,000
Operating income (loss)		₹(68,000)

The Music Society would not be able to afford the new marketing director if the number of concerts were to increase to only 41 events. The addition of the new marketing director would require the Music Society to hold at least 45 concerts in order to breakeven. If only 41 concerts were held, the organization would lose ₹68,000 annually. The Music Society could look for other contributions to support the new marketing director's salary or perhaps increase the number of attendees per concert if the number of concerts could not be increased beyond 41.

3. Ticket sales per concert ₹45,000

Variable costs per concert:

Guest performers	₹18,000	
Marketing and advertising	10,000	
Total variable costs per concert		28,000
Contribution margin per concert		₹17,000

Fixed costs

Salaries (₹3,30,000 + ₹2,55,000)	₹5,85,000	
Lease payments (₹40,000 × 12)	4,80,000	
Total fixed costs		₹10,65,000
Deduct donations		4,70,00
Net fixed costs		₹5,95,000

$$\text{Breakeven point in units} = \frac{\text{Net fixed costs}}{\text{Contribution margin per concert}} = \frac{₹5,95,000}{₹17,000} = 35 \text{ concerts}$$

Check

Donations		₹4,70,000
Revenue (₹45,000 × 35)		15,75,000
Total revenue		20,45,000

Less variable costs

Guest performers (₹18,000 × 35)	₹6,30,000	
Marketing and advertising (₹10,000 × 35)	3,50,000	
Total variable costs		9,80,000

Less fixed costs

Salaries	₹5,85,000	
Mortgage payments	4,80,000	
Total fixed costs		10,65,000
Operating income		₹0

3-22 Sales mix, three products. The Lee Company has three product lines of belts: X, Y and Z with contribution margins of ₹15, ₹10 and ₹5 = respectively. The president foresees sales of 1,00,000 units in the coming period, consisting of 10,000 units of X, 50,000 units of Y and 40,000 units of Z. The company's fixed costs for the period are ₹5,10,000.

Required

1. What is the company's breakeven point in units, assuming that the given sales mix is maintained?

2. If the sales mix is maintained, what is the total contribution when 1,00,000 units are sold? What is the operating income?

3. What would operating income be if 10,000 units of X, 40,000 units of Y and 50,000 units of Z were sold? What is the new breakeven point in units if these relationships persist in the next period?

Solution

1. Sales of X, Y and Z are in the ratio 10,000:50,000:40,000. So for every 1 unit of X, = units of Y are sold, and 4 units of Z are sold.

   Let Q = Number of units of X to breakeven

   5Q = Number of units of Y to breakeven

4Q = Number of units of Z to breakeven

Total Contribution Fixed costs = Zero operating income

₹15 × Q + ₹10 (5Q) + ₹5 (4Q) − ₹5,10,000 = 0

85Q − ₹5,10,000 = 0

Q = 5,10,000/85 = 6,000 units

Q = 6,000 units of X

5Q = 30,000 units of Y

4Q = 24,000 units of Z

Total 60,000 units

2. **Total Contribution and Operating Income**

X: 10,000 × ₹15	₹1,50,000
Y: 50,000 × ₹10	5,00,000
Z: 40,000 × ₹5	2,00,000
Total contribution	8,50,000
Fixed costs	5,10,000
Operating income	3,40,000

3. **Operating Income**

X: 10,000 × 15	₹1,50,000	
Y: 40,000 × 10	4,00,000	
Z: 50,000 × 5	2,50,000	
Total contribution		₹8,00,000
Fixed costs		5,10,000
Operating income		2,90,000

Let   Q = Number of units of X to breakeven

4Q = Number of units of Y to breakeven

5Q = Number of units of Z to breakeven

Contribution margin − Fixed costs = Breakeven point

₹15 (Q) + ₹10 (4Q) + ₹= (5Q) − ₹5,10,000 = 0

80 Q = ₹5,10,000

Q = 6,375 units of X

4Q = 25,500 units of Y

5Q = 31,875 units of Z

Total = 63,750 units

Breakeven point increases because the new mix contains less of the higher contribution margin per unit, product Y, and more of the lower contribution margin per unit, product Z.

3-23 **CVP analysis, multiple cost drivers.** Ritu is a distributor of brass picture frames. For current year, she plans to purchase frames for ₹60 each and sell them for ₹90 each. Ritu's fixed costs for current year are expected to be ₹4,80,000. Ritu's only other costs will be variable costs of ₹120 per shipment for preparing the invoice and delivery documents, organizing the delivery, and following up for collection accounts receivable. The ₹120 cost will be incurred each time Ritu ships an order of picture frames, regardless of the number of frames in the order.

Required

1. **a.** Suppose Ritu sells 40,000 picture frames in 1,000 shipments in current year. Calculate Ritu's current year operating income.

   b. Suppose Ritu sells 40,000 picture frames in 800 shipments in current year. Calculate Ritu's current year operating income.

2. Suppose Ritu anticipates making 500 shipments in current year. How many picture frames must Ritu sell to breakeven in current year?

3. Calculate another breakeven point for current year different from the one described in requirement 2. Explain briefly why Ritu has multiple break even points.

Solution

1. **a.** Operating income = Revenues − (Cost of picture frames × Quantity of picture frames) − (Cost of shipment × Number of shipments) − Fixed costs
   = (₹90 × 40,000) − (₹60 × 40,000) − (₹120 × 1,000) − ₹4,80,000
   = ₹36,00,000 − 24,00,000 − 1,20,000 − 4,80,000 = ₹6,00,000
   b. Operating income = (₹90 × 40,000) − (₹60 × 40,000) − (₹120 × 800) − ₹4,80,000
   = ₹36,00,000 − 24,00,000 − 96,000 − ₹4,80,000 = ₹6,24,000

2. Denote the number of picture frames sold by Q, then ₹90Q ₹60Q 500 × ₹120 ₹4,80,000 = 0
   ₹30Q − ₹60,000 − ₹4,80,000 = 0
   ₹30Q = ₹5,40,000
   Q = 5,40,000/30 = 18,000 picture frames

3. Suppose Ritu had 1,000 shipments
   ₹90Q − ₹60Q − (1,000 × ₹120) − ₹4,80,000 = 0
   30Q = 1,20,000 = 4,80,000
   Q = 6,00,000/30 = 20,000 picture frames.

There are multiple BEP, as there are two cost drivers quantity of picture frames and number of shipments. Various combinations of the two cost drivers can yield zero operating income.

3-24 Sales mix, new and upgrade customers. Far Point Spread is a top-selling electronic spreadsheet product. Far Point Technologies India is about to release version 5.0. It divides its customer into two groups: new customers and upgrade customers (those who previously purchased Far Point Spread 4.0 or earlier versions) Although the same physical product is provided to each customer group, sizable differences exist in selling prices and variable marketing costs:

Particulars	New Customers		Upgrade Customers	
Selling price		₹10,500		₹6,000
Variable costs				
Manufacturing	₹1,250		₹1,250	
Marketing	3,250	4,500	750	2,000
Contribution margin		₹6,000		₹4,000

The fixed costs of Far Point Spread 5.0 are ₹1,40,00,000. The planned sales mix in units is 60 percent new customers and 40 percent upgrade customers.

Required

1. What is the Far Point Spread 5.0 breakeven point in units, assuming that the planned 60 percent/40 percent sales mix is attained?
2. If the sales mix is attained, what is the operating income when 2,00,000 units are sold?
3. Show how the breakeven point in units changes with the following customer mixes:
   a. New 50 percent/Upgrade 50 percent
   b. New 90 percent/Upgrade 10 percent
   c. Comment on the results

Solution

1.

	New Customers	Upgrade Customers
Selling Price	₹10,500	₹6,000
Variable Cost per unit	4,500	2,000
Contribution Margin per unit	6,000	4,000

Let S = Number of units sold to upgrade customers
1.5S = Number of units sold to new customers

Operating Income = Revenues Variable Costs Fixed Costs
Operating Income = [₹10,500 (1.5S) + 6,000S] − [₹4,500 (1.5S) + 2000S] − 1,40,00,000
Operating Income = ₹21,750S − 8,750S − ₹1,40,00,000
Operating Income = ₹13,000S -- ₹1,40,00,000
S = ₹1,40,00,000/13,000 = ₹1,077 units (rounded up)
S = 1,077 units sold to upgrade customers
1.5S = 1,615 units sold to new customers
Breakeven point is 2,692 units when operating income = 0
We can check the value:

Check

Revenues (₹10,500 × 1,615; ₹6,000 × 1,077)	₹2,34,19,500
Variable costs (₹4,500 × 1,615; ₹2,000 × 1,077)	94,21,500
Contribution margin	1,39,98,000
Fixed costs	1,40,00,000
Operating income (subject to rounding)	0

2. When 2,00,000 units are sold, mix is:

Units sold to new customers (60% × 2,00,000)	1,20,000
Units sold to upgrade customers (40% × 2,00,000	80,000
Revenues (₹10,500 × 1,20,000; ₹6,000 × 80,000)	₹1,74,00,00,000
Variable costs (₹4,500 × 1,20,000; ₹2,000 × 80,000)	70,00,00,000
Contribution margin	1,04,00,00,000
Fixed cost	1,40,00,000
Operating income	1,02,60,00,000

3. a. Let S = Number of units sold to upgrade customers
then S = Number of units sold to new customers
(₹10,500S + 6,000S) − (₹4,500S + 2,000S) − ₹1,40,00,000 = Operating Income
16,500S − 6,500S − ₹1,40,00,000 = Operating Income
10,000S = ₹1,40,00,000
    S = 1,40,00,000/10,000 = 1,400 units
    S = 1,400 units sold to upgrade customers
    S = 1,400 units sold to new customers
    Total unit = 2800 unit

Check

Revenues (₹10,500 × 1,400; ₹6,000 × 1,400)	₹2,31,00,000
Variable costs (₹4,500 × 1,400; ₹2,000 × 1,400)	91,00,000
Contribution margin	1,40,00,000
Fixed costs	1,40,00,000
Operating income	0

3. b. Let S = Number of units sold to upgrade customers
then 9S = Number of units sold to new customers
(₹10,500 (9S) + 6,000 S) − (₹4,500 × (9S) + 2,000 × S) − ₹1,40,00,000 × Operating income
1,00,500 S − 42,500 S − ₹1,40,00,000 = Operating income
58,000 S = ₹1,40,00,000
    S = 241 units
    S = 241 units sold to upgrade customers

$$9S = \frac{2169}{2410} \quad \text{units sold to new customer}$$

Total units

Check:

Revenues (₹10,500 × 2,169; ₹6,000 × 241)	₹2,42,20,500
Variable costs (₹4,500 × 2,169; ₹2,000 × 241)	1,02,42,500
Contribution margin	1,39,78,000
Fixed costs	1,40,00,000
Operating income (subject to rounding)	0

3. **c.** As Far Point Technologies India increases its percentage of new customers, which have a higher contribution margin per unit than upgrade customers, the number of units required to breakeven decreases.

	New Customers	Upgrade Customers	Breakeven Point
Requirement 3 (a)	50%	50%	2,800 units
Requirement 1	60	40	2,692 units
Requirement 3 (b)	90	10	2,410 units

3-25 Contribution margin, decision making. Well Knit Men's Clothing's revenues and cost data for 2015 are as follows:

Revenues		₹50,00,000
Cost of goods sold		25,00,000
Gross margin		25,00,000
Operating costs:		
Salaries fixed	₹16,00,000	
Sales commissions (11% of sales)	5,50,000	
Depreciation of equipment and fixtures	1,50,000	
Store rent (₹40,000 per month)	4,80,000	
Other operating costs	4,00,000	31,80,000
Operating income (loss)		₹(6,80,000)

Mr Raman, the owner of the store, is unhappy with the operating results. An analysis of other operating costs reveals that it includes ₹3,50,000 variable costs, which vary with sales volume, and ₹50,000 (fixed) costs.

Required

1. Compute the contribution margin of Well Knit Men's Clothing.
2. Compute the contribution margin percentage.
3. Mr Raman estimates that he can increase units sold, and hence revenues by 20% by incurring additional advertising costs of ₹1,20,000. Calculate the impact of the additional advertising costs on operating income.
4. What other actions can Mr Raman take to improve operating income?

Solution

1.
Revenues		₹50,00,000
Deduct variable costs:		
Cost of goods sold	₹25,00,000	
Sales commissions	5,50,000	
Other operating costs	3,50,000	34,00,000
Contribution margin		₹16,00,000

$$\text{Contribution margin percentage} = \frac{₹16,00,000}{₹50,00,000} = 32\%$$

Incremental revenue (20% × ₹50,00,000) = ₹10,00,000

Incremental contribution margin

(32% × ₹10,00,000)	₹3,20,000
Incremental fixed costs (advertising)	1,20,000
Incremental operating income	₹2,00,000

If Mr Raman spends ₹1,20,000 more on advertising, the operating income will increase by ₹2,00,000, decreasing the operating loss from ₹6,80,000 to an operating loss of ₹4,80,000.

Proof (Optional):

Revenues (120% × ₹50,00,000)	₹60,00,000
Cost of goods sold (50% of sales)	30,00,000
Gross margin	30,00,000

Operating costs:

Salaries and wages	₹16,00,000	
Sales commissions (11% of sales)	6,60,000	
Depreciation of equipment and fixtures	1,50,000	
Advertising	1,20,000	
Other operating costs:		
Variable $\left(\dfrac{₹3,50,000}{₹50,00,000} \times ₹60,00,000 \right)$	4,20,000	
Fixed	50,000	34,80,000
Operating income		₹(4,80,000)

4. To improve operating income, Mr Raman must find ways to decrease variable costs, decrease fixed costs, or increase selling prices.

3-26 Contribution margin, gross margin and margin of safety. Lakme manufactures and sells a face cream to small ethnic stores in Northern India. It presents the monthly operating income statement shown here to Amit, a potential investor in the business. Help Amit understand Lakme's cost structure.

	A	B	C	D
1		Lakme Cosmetics		
2		Operating Income Statement, June 2015		
3	Units sold			10,000
4	Revenues			₹10,00,000
5	Cost of goods sold			
6	Variable manufacturing costs		₹5,50,000	
7	Fixed manufacturing costs		2,00,000	
8	Total			7,50,000
9	Gross margin			2,50,000
10	Operating costs			
11	Variable marketing costs		₹50,000	
12	Fixed marketing & administration costs		1,00,000	
13	Total operating costs			1,50,000
14	Operating income			₹1,00,000

Required

1. Recast the income statement to emphasize contribution margin.
2. Calculate the contribution margin percentage and breakeven point in units and revenues for June 2015.
3. What is the margin of safety (in units) for June 2015?
4. If sales in June were only 8,000 units and Lakme's tax rate is 30%, calculate its net income.

Solution

1.

Lakme Cosmetics

Operating Income Statement, June 2015

Units sold		1,00,000
Revenues		₹10,00,000
Variable costs		
Variable manufacturing costs	₹5,50,000	
Variable marketing costs	50,000	
Total variable costs		6,00,000
Contribution margin		4,00,000
Fixed costs		
Fixed manufacturing costs	₹2,00,000	
Fixed marketing & administration costs	1,00,000	
Total fixed costs		3,00,000
Operating income		₹1,00,000

2. Contribution margin per unit = $\dfrac{₹4,00,000}{10,000 \text{ units}}$ = ₹40 per unit

Breakeven quantity = $\dfrac{\text{Fixed costs}}{\text{Contribution margin per unit}} = \dfrac{₹3,00,000}{₹40 \text{ per unit}}$ = 7,500 units

Selling price = $\dfrac{\text{Revenues}}{\text{Units sold}} = \dfrac{₹10,00,000}{10,000 \text{ units}}$ = ₹100 per unit

Breakeven revenues = 7,500 units × ₹100 per unit = ₹7,50,000

Alternatively,

Contribution margin percentage = $\dfrac{\text{Contribution margin}}{\text{Revenues}} = \dfrac{₹4,00,000}{₹10,00,000}$ = 40%

Breakeven revenues = $\dfrac{\text{Fixed costs}}{\text{Contribution margin percentage}} = \dfrac{₹3,00,000}{0.40}$ = ₹7,50,000

3. Margin of safety (in units) = Units sold − Breakeven quantity
                               = 10,000 units − 7,500 units = 2,500 units

4.		
Units sold		8,000
Revenues (Units sold × Selling price = 8,000 × ₹100)		₹8,00,000
Contribution margin (Revenues × CM percentage = ₹8,00,000 × 40%)		₹3,20,000
Fixed costs		3,00,000
Operating income		20,000
Taxes (30% × ₹20,000)		6,000
Net income		₹14,000

3.27 CVP, target operating income, service firm. KinderKids provides daycare for children Mondays through Fridays. Its monthly variable costs per child are as follows:

Lunch and snacks	₹1,000
Educational supplies	300
Other supplies (paper products, toiletries, etc.)	200
Total	₹1,500

Monthly fixed costs consist of the following:

Rent	₹15,000
Utilities	1,500
Insurance	2,000
Salaries	17,000
Miscellaneous	4,500
Total	₹40,000

KinderKids charges each parent ₹4,000 per child per month.

Required

1. Calculate the breakeven point.
2. KinderKids' target operating income is ₹50,000 per month. Compute the number of children who must be enrolled to achieve the target operating income.
3. KinderKids lost its lease and had to move to another building. Monthly rent for the new building is ₹22,000. At the suggestion of parents, KinderKids plans to take children on field trips. Monthly costs of the field trips are ₹11,000. By how much should KinderKids increase fees per child to meet the target operating income of ₹50,000 per month, assuming the same number of children as in requirement 2?

Solution

1.

Revenue per child	₹4,000
Variable costs per child	1,500
Contribution margin per child	₹2,500

$$\text{Breakeven quantity} = \frac{\text{Fixed costs}}{\text{Contribution margin per child}}$$

$$= \frac{₹40,000}{₹2,500} = 16 \text{ children}$$

2. $$\text{Target quantity} = \frac{\text{Fixed costs} + \text{Target operating income}}{\text{Contribution margin per child}}$$

$$= \frac{₹40,000 + ₹50,000}{₹2,500} = 36 \text{ children}$$

3.

Increase in rent (₹22,000 − ₹15,000)	₹7,000
Field trips	11,000
Total increase in fixed costs	₹18,000
Divide by the number of children enrolled	÷ 36
Increase in fee per child	₹500

Therefore, the fee per child will increase from ₹4,000 to ₹4,500.

Alternatively,

$$\text{New contribution margin per child} = \frac{₹40,000 + ₹18,000 + ₹50,000}{36} = ₹3,000$$

New fee per child = Variable costs per child + New contribution margin per child
$$= ₹1,500 + ₹3,000 = ₹4,500$$

3-28 CVP analysis, margin of safety. (CMA, adapted) Singhania Tax Preparation Services has total budgeted revenues for 2015 of ₹61,80,000, based on an average price of ₹20,600 per tax return prepared. The company would like to achieve a margin of safety percentage of at least 45%. The company's current fixed costs are ₹32,76,000, and variable costs average ₹2,400 per customer. (Consider each of the following separately).

Required

1. Calculate Singhania's breakeven point and margin of safety in units.
2. Which of the following changes would help Singhania achieve its desired margin of safety?
   a. Average revenue per customer increases to ₹22,400.
   b. Planned number of tax returns prepared increases by 15%
   c. Singhania purchases new tax software that results in a 5% increase to fixed costs but e-files all tax returns, which reduces mailing costs an average ₹200 per customer.

Solution

1.
Selling price	₹20,600
Variable costs per unit:	2,400
Contribution margin per unit (CMU)	₹18,200

$$\text{Breakeven point in units} = \frac{\text{Fixed costs}}{\text{Contribution margin per unit}}$$

$$\text{Breakeven point in units} = \frac{₹32,76,000}{₹18,200} = 180 \text{ returns (units)}$$

Margin of safety (units) = 300* − 180 = 120 units

*₹61,80,000 budgeted revenue ÷ ₹20,600 = 300 units
Breakeven revenues = ₹20,600 × 180 = ₹37,08,000
Margin of safety percentage = (₹61,80,000 − ₹37,08,000) ÷ ₹61,80,000 = 40%

2a. Increase selling price to ₹22,400

Selling price	₹22,400
Variable costs per unit:	2,400
Contribution margin per unit (CMU)	₹20,000

$$\text{Breakeven point in units} = \frac{\text{Fixed costs}}{\text{Contribution margin per unit}}$$

$$\text{Breakeven point in units} = \frac{₹32,76,000}{₹20,000} = 163.8(164) \text{ returns (units)}$$

Breakeven revenues = ₹22,400 × 164 units = ₹36,73,600
Margin of safety percentage = (₹61,80,000 − ₹36,73,600) ÷ ₹61,80,000 = 40.56%
This change will not help Singhania achieve its desired margin of safety of 45%.

2b.
Selling price	₹20,600
Variable costs per unit:	2,400
Contribution margin per unit (CMU)	₹18,200

$$\text{Breakeven point in units} = \frac{\text{Fixed costs}}{\text{Contribution margin per unit}}$$

$$\text{Breakeven point in units} = \frac{₹32,76,000}{₹18,200} = 180 \text{ returns (units)}$$

Breakeven revenues = ₹20,600 × 180 = ₹37,08,000

Budgeted revenues = ₹61,80,000 × 1.15 = ₹71,07,000
Margin of safety percentage = (₹71,07,000 − ₹37,08,000) ÷ ₹71,07,000 = 47.8%
This change will help Singhania achieve its desired margin of safety of 45%.

2c.

Selling price	₹20,600
Variable costs per unit ₹2,400 − ₹200):	2,200
Contribution margin per unit (CMU)	₹18,400

Fixed costs = ₹32,76,000 × 1.05 = ₹34,39,800

$$\text{Breakeven point in units} = \frac{\text{Fixed costs}}{\text{Contribution margin per unit}}$$

$$\text{Breakeven point in units} = \frac{₹34,39,800}{₹18,400} = 187 \text{ returns/units (rounded up)}$$

Breakeven revenues = ₹20,600 × 187 units = ₹38,52,200
Margin of safety percentage = (₹61,80,000 − ₹38,52,200) ÷ ₹61,80,000 = 37.7%
This change will not help Singhania achieve its desired margin of safety of 45%.

Options 2a and 2b improve the margin of safety, but only option 2b exceeds the company's desired margin of safety. Option 2c actually lowers the company's margin of safety.

3-29 CVP, sensitivity analysis. Kid Shoe Company produces its famous shoe, the Divine Loafer that sells for ₹700 per pair. Operating income for 2015 is as follows:

Sales revenue (₹700 per pair)	₹35,00,000
Variable cost (₹300 per pair)	15,00,000
Contribution margin	20,00,000
Fixed cost	10,00,000
Operating income	₹10,00,000

Kid Shoe Company would like to increase its profitability over the next year by at least 25%. To do so, the company is considering the following options:

Required

1. Replace a portion of its variable labor with an automated machining process. This would result in a 20% decrease in variable cost per unit but a 15% increase in fixed costs. Sales would remain the same.
2. Spend ₹2,50,000 on a new advertising campaign, which would increase sales by 10%.
3. Increase both selling price by ₹100 per unit and variable costs by ₹80 per unit by using a higher-quality leather material in the production of its shoes. The higher-priced shoe would cause demand to drop by approximately 20%.
4. Add a second manufacturing facility that would double Company's fixed costs but would increase sales by 60%.

Evaluate each of the alternatives considered by Company Shoes. Do any of the options meet or exceed Company's targeted increase in income of 25%? What should Company do?

Solution
Contribution margin per pair of shoes = ₹700 − ₹300 = ₹400
Fixed costs = ₹10,00,000
Units sold = Total sales ÷ Selling price = ₹35,00,000 ÷ ₹700 per pair = 5,000 pairs of shoes

1. Variable costs decrease by 20%; Fixed costs increase by 15%
   Sales revenues 5,000 × ₹700   ₹35,00,000

Variable costs 5,000 × ₹300 × (1 − 0.20)	12,00,000
Contribution margin	23,00,000
Fixed costs ₹10,00,000 × 1.15	11,50,000
Operating income	₹11,50,000

2. Increase advertising (fixed costs) by ₹2,50,000; Increase sales 20%

Sales revenues 5,000 × 1.10 × ₹700	₹38,50,000
Variable costs 5,000 × 1.10 × ₹300	16,50,000
Contribution margin	22,00,000
Fixed costs (₹10,00,000 + ₹2,50,000)	12,50,000
Operating income	₹9,50,000

3. Increase selling price by ₹100; Sales decrease 20%; Variable costs increase by ₹80

Sales revenues 5,000 × 0.80 × (₹700 + ₹100)	₹32,00,000
Variable costs 5,000 × 0.80 × (₹300 + ₹80)	15,20,000
Contribution margin	16,80,000
Fixed costs	10,00,000
Operating income	₹6,80,000

4. Double fixed costs; Increase sales by 60%

Sales revenues 5,000 × 1.60 × ₹700	₹56,00,000
Variable costs 5,000 × 1.60 × ₹300	24,00,000
Contribution margin	32,00,000
Fixed costs ₹10,00,000 × 2	20,00,000
Operating income	₹12,00,000

Alternative 4 yields the highest operating income. Choosing alternative 4 will give Company a 20% increase in operating income [(₹12,00,000 − ₹10,00,000)/ ₹10,00,000 = 20%], which is less than the company's 25% targeted increase. Alternative 1also generates more operating income for Company, but it too does not meet Company's target of 25% increase in operating income. Alternatives 2 and 3 actually result in lower operating income than under Company's current cost structure. There is no reason, however, for Company to think of these alternatives as being mutually exclusive. For example, Company can combine actions 1 and 4, automate the machining process and decrease variable costs by 20% while increasing fixed costs by 15%. This will result in a 38% increase in operating income as follows:

Sales revenue 5,000 × 1.60 × ₹700	₹56,00,000
Variable costs 5,000 × 1.60 × ₹300 × (1 − 0.20)	19,20,000
Contribution margin	36,80,000
Fixed costs ₹2,00,000 × 1.15	23,00,000
Operating income	₹13,80,000

The point of this problem is that managers always need to consider broader rather than narrower alternatives to meet ambitious or stretch goals.

3-30 Alternative cost structures, uncertainty, and sensitivity analysis. Fine Printing Company currently leases its only copy machine for ₹12,000 a month. The company is considering replacing this leasing agreement with a new contract that is entirely commission based. Under the new agreement, Fine would pay a commission for its printing at a rate of ₹200 for every 500 pages printed. The company currently charges ₹1.5 per page to its customers. The paper used in printing costs the company ₹0.4 per page and other variable costs, including hourly labor amounting to ₹0.5 per page.

1. What is the company's breakeven point under the current leasing agreement? What is it under the new commission-based agreement?

2. For what range of sales levels will Fine prefer (a) the fixed lease agreement (b) the commission agreement?

Solution

1. Contribution margin per page assuming current fixed leasing agreement $= ₹1.5 - ₹0.4 - ₹0.5 = ₹0.6$ per page

Fixed costs = ₹12,000

$$\text{Breakeven point} = \frac{\text{Fixed costs}}{\text{Contribution margin per page}} = \frac{₹12,000}{₹0.6 \text{ per page}} = 20,000 \text{ pages}$$

Contribution margin per page assuming ₹200 per 500 page commission agreement $= ₹1.5 - ₹0.4a - ₹0.4 - ₹0.5 = ₹0.2$ per page

Fixed costs = ₹0

$$\text{Breakeven point} = \frac{\text{Fixed costs}}{\text{Contribution margin per page}} = \frac{₹0}{₹0.2 \text{ per page}} = 0 \text{ pages}$$

(i.e., Company makes a profit no matter how few pages it sells)

[a]₹200 ÷ 500 pages = ₹0.4 per page

2. Let x denote the number of pages Company must sell for it to be indifferent between the fixed leasing agreement and commission based agreement.

To calculate x we solve the following equation.

$₹1.5x - ₹0.4x - ₹0.5x - ₹12,000 = ₹1.5x - ₹0.4x - ₹0.4x - ₹0.5x$

$₹0.6x - ₹12,000 = ₹0.2x$

$₹0.4x = ₹12,000$

$x = ₹12,000 ÷ ₹0.4 = 30,000$

For sales between 0 to 30,000 pages, Company prefers the commission-based agreement because in this range, $₹0.2x > ₹0.6x - ₹12,000$. For sales greater than 30,000 pages, Company prefers the fixed leasing agreement because in this range, $₹0.6x - ₹12,000 > ₹0.2x$.

3-31 Multi-product CVP and decision making. Crystal Clear Products produces two types of water filters. One attaches to the faucet and cleans all water that passes through the faucet. The other is a pitcher-cum-filter that only purifies water meant for drinking.

The unit that attaches to the faucet is sold for ₹1,000 and has variable costs of ₹350.

The pitcher-cum-filter sells for ₹1,200 and has variable costs of ₹300.

Crystal Clear sells two faucet models for every three pitchers sold. Fixed costs equal ₹120 lakh.

1. What is the breakeven point in unit sales and rupees for each type of filter at the current sales mix?

2. Crystal Clear is considering buying new production equipment. The new equipment will increase fixed cost by ₹20.8 lakh per year and will decrease the variable cost of the faucet and the pitcher units by ₹50 and ₹100, respectively. Assuming the same sales mix, how many of each type of filter does Crystal Clear need to sell to break even?

3. Assuming the same sales mix, at what total sales level would Crystal Clear be indifferent between using the old equipment and buying the new production equipment? If total sales are expected to be 24,000 units, should Crystal Clear buy the new production equipment?

Solution

1. Faucet filter:

Selling price	₹1,000
Variable cost per unit	350
Contribution margin per unit	₹650

Pitcher-cum-filter:

Selling price	₹1,200
Variable cost per unit	300
Contribution margin per unit	₹900

Each bundle contains two faucet models and three pitcher models.

So contribution margin of a bundle = 2 × ₹650 + 3 × ₹900 = ₹4,000

$$\text{Breakeven point in bundles} = \frac{\text{Fixed costs}}{\text{Contribution margin per bundle}} = \frac{₹1,20,00,000}{₹4,000} = 3,000 \text{ bundles}$$

Breakeven point in units of faucet models and pitcher models is:
Faucet models: 3,000 bundles × 2 units per bundle = 6,000 units
Pitcher models: 3,000 bundles × 3 units per bundle = 9,000 units
Total number of units to breakeven   5,000 units

Breakeven point in rupees for faucet models and pitcher models is:
Faucet models: 6,000 units × ₹1,000 per unit = ₹60,00,000
Pitcher models: 9,000 units × ₹1,200 per unit = 1,08,00,000
Breakeven revenues   ₹1,68,00,000

Alternatively, weighted average contribution margin per unit = $\dfrac{(2 \times ₹650) + (3 \times ₹900)}{5} = ₹800$

$$\text{Breakeven point} = \frac{₹1,20,00,000}{`800} = 15,000 \text{ units}$$

Faucet filter : $\dfrac{2}{5} \times 15,000 \text{ units} = 6,000 \text{ units}$

Pitcher – cum – filter : $\dfrac{3}{5} \times 15,000 \text{ units} = 9,000 \text{ units}$

Breakeven point in rupees
Faucet filter: 6,000 units × ₹1,000 per unit = ₹60,00,000
Pitcher-cum-filter: 9,000 units × ₹1,200 per unit = ₹1,08,00,000

2. Faucet filter:

Selling price	₹1,000
Variable cost per unit	300
Contribution margin per unit	₹700

Pitcher-cum-filter:

Selling price	₹1,200
Variable cost per unit	200
Contribution margin per unit	₹100

Each bundle contains two faucet models and three pitcher models.
So contribution margin of a bundle = 2 × ₹700 + 3 × ₹1,000 = ₹4,400

$$\text{Breakeven point in bundles} = \frac{\text{Fixed costs}}{\text{Contribution margin per bundle}} = \frac{₹1,20,00,000 + ₹20,80,000}{₹4,400} = 3,200 \text{ bundles}$$

Breakeven point in units of faucet models and pitcher models is:

Faucet models: 3,200 bundles × 2 units per bundle = 6,400 units

Pitcher models: 3,200 bundles × 3 units per bundle = 9,600 units

Total number of units to breakeven   16,000 units

Breakeven point in dollars for faucet models and pitcher models is:

Faucet models: 6,400 bundles × ₹1,000 per unit = ₹64,00,000

Pitcher models: 9,600 bundles × ₹1,200 per unit = 1,15,20,000

Breakeven revenues   ₹1,79,20,000

Alternatively, weighted average contribution margin per unit $= \dfrac{(2 \times ₹700) + (3 \times ₹1,000)}{5} = ₹880$

$$\text{Breakeven point} = \frac{₹1,20,00,000 + ₹20,80,000}{₹880} = 16,000 \text{ units}$$

Faucet filter : $\dfrac{2}{5} \times 16,000$ units $= 6,400$ units

Pitcher $-$ cum $-$ filter : $\dfrac{3}{5} \times 16,000$ units $= 9,600$ units

Breakeven point in rupees:

Faucet filter: 6,400 units × ₹1,000 per unit = ₹64,00,000

Pitcher-cum-filter: 9,600 units × ₹1,200 per unit = ₹1,15,20,000

3. Let *x* be the number of bundles for Crystal Clear Products to be indifferent between the old and new production equipment.

Operating income using old equipment = ₹4,000*x* − ₹1,20,00,000

Operating income using new equipment = ₹4,400*x* − ₹1,20,00,000 − ₹20,80,000

At point of indifference:

₹4,000*x* − ₹1,20,00,000 = ₹4,400*x* − ₹1,40,80,000

₹4,400*x* − ₹4,000*x* = ₹1,40,80,000 − ₹1,20,00,000

₹400*x* = ₹20,80,000

x = ₹20,80,000 ÷ ₹400 = 5,200 bundles

Faucet models = 5,200 bundles × 2 units per bundle = 10,400 units

Pitcher models = 5,200 bundles × 3 units per bundle = 15,600 units

Total number of units   26,000 units

Let x be the number of bundles,

When total sales are less than 26,000 units (5,200 bundles), ₹4000*x* − ₹1,20,00,000>

₹4,400*x* − ₹1,40,80,000, so Crystal Clear Products is better off with the old equipment.

When total sales are greater than 26,000 units (5,200 bundles), ₹4000*x* − ₹1,40,80,000>

₹4,400*x* − ₹1,20,00,000, so Crystal Clear Products is better off buying the new equipment.

At total sales of 24,000 units (4,800 bundles), Crystal Clear Products should keep the old production equipment.

Check

₹4,000 × 4,800 − ₹1,20,00,000 = ₹72,00,000 is greater than ₹4,400 × 4,800 − ₹1,40,80,000 = ₹70,40,000.

3-32 Ethics, CVP analysis. Milton Ltd. produces a molded plastic casing, LX 201, for desktop computer. Summary data from its current year income statement are as follows:

Revenues	₹50,00,000
Variable costs	30,00,000
Fixed costs	21,60,000
Operating income	₹(1,60,000)

Kamna, Milton's president, is very concerned about Milton's poor profitability. She asks Amit, production manager, and Sudhir, controller, to see if there are ways to reduce costs.

After two weeks Amit returns with a proposal to reduce variable costs to 52 percent of revenues by reducing the costs Milton currently incurs for safe disposal of wasted plastic. Sudhir is concerned that this would expose the company to potential environmental liabilities. He tells Amit, We would need to estimate some of these potential environmental costs and include them in our analysis. You can't do that," Amit replies. "We are not violating any laws. There is some possibility that we may have to incur environmental costs in the future, but if we ring it up now, this proposal will not go through because our senior management always assumes these costs to be larger than they turn out to be. The market is very tough, and we are in danger of shutting down the company. We don't want all our colleagues to lose their jobs. The only reason our competitors are making money is because they are doing exactly what I am proposing".

Required

1. Calculate Milton's break even revenues for the current year.
2. Calculate Milton's break even revenues if variable costs are 52 percent of revenues.
3. Calculate Milton's operating income in current year if variable costs had been 52 percent of revenues.
4. Given Amit's comments, what should Sudhir do?

Solution

1. Contribution margin percentage = (Revenues − Variable costs)/Revenues
   = (₹50,00,000 − ₹30,00,000)/₹50,00,000
   = ₹20,00,000/₹50,00,000 = 40 percent
   Breakeven revenues = Fixed costs/Contribution margin percentage
   = ₹21,60,000/0.40 = ₹54,00,000
2. If variable costs are 52 percent of revenues, contribution margin percentage equals 48 percent (100% − 52%)
   Break even revenues = Fixed costs/Contribution margin percentage
   = ₹21,60,000/0.48 = ₹45,00,000
3.

Revenues	₹50,00,000
Variable costs (0.52 × ₹50,00,000)	26,00,000
Fixed costs	21,60,000
Operating income	₹2,40,000

4. Incorrect reporting of environmental costs with the goal of continuing operations is unethical.

Sudhir should indicate to Kamna that estimates of environmental costs and liabilities should be included in the analysis. If Kamna still insists on modifying the numbers and reporting lower environmental costs, Sudhir should raise the matter with one of Kamna's superiors. If after taking all these steps, there is continued pressure to understate environmental costs, Sudhir should consider resigning from the company and not engage in unethical behavior.

Exercises

[*Comprehensive solutions to all exercises are available on the companion website www. pearsoned.co.in/charlesthorngren*]

3-33 The Digital Company has fixed costs of ₹3,00,000 and a variable cost percentage of 75 percent. The company earns net income after taxes of ₹80,000 in current year. The income tax rate is 40 percent.

Compute (1) Operating income (2) Contribution margin (3) Total revenues (4) Breakeven revenues.

3-34 CVP exercises. The Reynolds Company manufactures and sells pens. Currently 6,00,000 units are sold per year at ₹10 per unit. Fixed costs are ₹15,00,000 per year. Variable costs are ₹6 per unit.

Consider each case separately:

1. (a) What is the present operating income for a year? **Required**
   (b) What is the present breakeven point in revenues?
   Compute the new operating income for each of the following changes.
2. A ₹0.50 per unit increase in variable costs.
3. A 10 percent increase in fixed costs and a 10 percent increase in units sold.
4. A 20 percent decrease in fixed costs, a 20 percent decrease in selling price, a 10 percent decrease in variable cost per unit and a 40 percent increase in units sold.
   Compute the new breakeven point in units for each of the following changes:
5. A 15 percent increase in fixed costs.
6. A 10 percent increase in selling price and a ₹1,00,000 increase in fixed costs.

3-35 Gross margin and contribution margin, making decision. Big Jos clothing's revenues and cost data for 2015 appear below:

Revenues	₹10,00,000
Cost of goods sold (40 percent of sales)	4,00,000
Gross margin	6,00,000

Operating costs

Salaries	₹3,00,000	
Sales commissions (10 percent of sales)	1,00,000	
Depreciation of equipment and fixtures	24,000	
Store rent (₹8,000 per month)	96,000	
Other operating costs	1,00,000	6,20,000
Operating income (loss)		₹(20,000)

Mr Nitin, the owner of the store is unhappy with the operating results. An analysis of other operating costs reveals that it includes ₹80,000 variable costs, which vary with sales volume, and ₹20,000 fixed costs.

1. Compute the contribution margin of Big Jos Clothing.
2. Compute the contribution margin percentage.
3. Mr Nitin estimates he can increase revenues by 20 percent by incurring additional advertising costs of ₹20,000. Calculate the impact on operating income.

3-36 CVP analysis, service firm. Thomas Cook India generates average revenue of ₹20,000 per person on its five-day package tours to Goa. The variable costs per person are as follows:

Airfare	₹5,000
Hotel accommodation	2,000
Meals	3,000
Ground transportation	3,000
Park tickets and other costs	1,000
Total	₹14,000

Annual fixed costs total ₹18,00,000

1. Calculate the number of package tours that must be sold to breakeven.
2. Calculate the revenue needed to earn a target operating income of ₹6,00,000
3. If fixed costs increase by ₹3,00,000 what decrease in variable costs must be achieved to maintain the breakeven point calculated in requirement 1?

3-37 CVP analysis, income taxes. The Grand Plaza has two restaurants that are open 24 hours a day. Fixed costs for the two restaurants together total ₹10,00,000 per year. Service varies from a cup of tea to full meals. The average sales revenue per customer is ₹20. The average cost of food and other variable costs for each customer is ₹8. The income tax rate is 30 percent. Target net income is ₹3,50,000.

Required

1. Compute the revenues needed to obtain the target net income.
2. How many customers are needed to breakeven? To earn net income of ₹3,50,000?
3. Compute net income if the number of customer is 2,00,000.

3-38 CVP analysis, international cost structure differences. Vardhman Spinning is considering three countries for the sole manufacturing site of its new sweater: Singapore, Thailand and the Unites States. All sweaters are to be sold to retail outlets in the United States at ₹32 per unit. These retail outlets add their own markup when selling to final customers. The three countries differ in their fixed cost and their variable cost per sweater.

Country	Annual Fixed Costs	Variable Manufacturing Cost per Sweater	Variable Marketing and Distribution Cost per Sweater
Singapore	₹6.5 million	₹8.00	₹11.00
Thailand	4.5 million	5.50	11.50
United States	12.0 million	13.00	9.00

Required

1. Compute the breakeven point of Vardhman Spinning in (a) units sold for each country and (b) revenues for each country.
2. If Vardhman Spinning sells 8,00,000 sweaters in current year, what is the budgeted operating income for each country? Comment on the result.

3-39 Gross margin and contribution margin. Ramesh Fork Pvt. Ltd's. income statement for current year at the level of production and sales of 2,00,000 units is as follows:

Revenues	₹26,00,000
Cost of goods sold	16,00,000
Gross margin	10,00,000
Marketing and distribution costs	11,50,000
Operating income (loss)	₹(1,50,000)

Ramesh's fixed manufacturing costs are ₹5,00,000 and variable marketing and distribution costs are ₹4 per unit.

Required

1. a. Calculate Ramesh's variable manufacturing cost per unit in current year.
   b. Calculate Ramesh's fixed marketing and distribution costs in current year.
2. Ramesh's gross margin per unit is ₹ = (₹10,00,000/2,00,000 units). Sudhir, Ramesh's president, believes that if production and sales had been 2,30,000 units, it would have also recovered ₹1,50,000 of marketing and distribution costs (₹11,50,000/5 = 2,30,000) and enabled Ramesh's to breakeven for the year. Calculate Ramesh's operating income if production and sales equal 2,30,000 units, Explain briefly why Sudhir is wrong.
3. Calculate the breakeven point for current year in units and in revenues.

3-40 Athletic scholarships, CVP analysis. Delhi University has an annual budget of ₹1,00,00,000 for athletic scholarships. Each athletic scholarship is for ₹40,000 per year. Fixed operating costs of the athletic scholarship program are ₹12,00,000 and variable operating costs are ₹4,000 per scholarship offered.

1. Determine the number of athletic scholarships Delhi University can offer each year.

2. Suppose the total budget for next year is reduced by 22 percent. Fixed costs are to remain the same. Calculate the number of athletic scholarships that Delhi University can offer next year.

3. As in requirement 2, assume a budget reduction of 22 percent and the same fixed costs. If Delhi University wanted to offer the same number of athletic scholarships as it did in requirement 1, calculate the amount that will be paid to each student who receives a scholarship.

3-41 CVP analysis, income taxes, sensitivity. (CMA, adapted) Birla Company manufactures and sells adjustable canopies that attach to motor homes and trailers. For its current year budget, Birla estimated the following:

Selling price	₹20,000
Variable cost per canopy	10,000
Annual fixed costs	50,00,000
Net income	1,20,00,000
Income tax rate	40%

The May financial statements reported that sales were not meeting expectations. For the first five months of the year, only 350 units had been sold at the established price, with variable costs as planned, and it was clear that the net income projection for current year would not be reached unless some actions were taken. A management committee presented the following mutually exclusive alternatives to the president.

Reduce the selling price by ₹2,000. The sales organization forecasts that at this significantly reduced price, 2,700 units can be sold during the remainder of the year. Total fixed costs and variable cost per unit will stay as budgeted.

Lower variable cost per unit by ₹500 through the use of less expensive direct materials and slightly modified manufacturing techniques. The selling price will also be reduced by ₹1,500 and sales of 2,200 units are expected for the remainder of the year.

Reduce fixed costs by ₹5,00,000 and lower the selling price by = percent. Variable cost per unit will be unchanged. Sales of 2,000 units are expected for the remainder of the year.

1. If no changes are made to the selling price or cost structure, determine the number of units that Birla Company must sell (a) to break even and (b) to achieve its net income objective.

2. Determine which alternative Birla should select to achieve its net income objective. Show your calculations.

3-42 Sales mix, two products. The VIP company retails two products, a standard and a deluxe version of a luggage carrier. The budgeted income statement for next period is as follows:

Particulars	Standard Carrier	Deluxe Carrier	Total
Units sold	1,50,000	5,00,000	2,00,000
Revenues at ₹1,000 and ₹1;500 per unit	₹15,00,00,000	₹7,50,00,000	₹22,50,00,000
Variable costs at ₹700 and ₹900 per unit	10,50,00,000	4,50,00,000	15,00,00,000
Contribution margins at ₹300 and ₹600 per unit	4,50,00,000	30,00,000	7,50,00,000
Fixed costs			6,00,00,000
Operating income			1,50,00,000

1. Compute the breakeven point, in units, assuming that the planned sales mix is attained.
2. Compute the breakeven point in units (a) if only standard carriers are sold and (b) if only deluxe carriers are sold.
3. Suppose 2,00,000 units are sold, but only 20,000 of them are deluxe. Compute the operating income. Compute the breakeven point in units. Compare your answer with the answer to requirement 1. What is the major lesson of this problem?

3-43 CVP analysis under uncertainty. The Jindal Company is considering two new colors for their umbrella products: emerald green and shocking pink. Either can be produced using present facilities. Each product requires an increase in annual fixed costs of ₹40,00,000. The products have the same ₹100 selling price and the same ₹80 variable cost per unit.

Management, after studying past experience with similar products, has prepared the following probability distribution:

| | Probability for | |
Even (Units Demanded)	Emerald Green Umbrella	Shocking Pink Umbrella
50,000	0.0	0.1
1,00,000	0.1	0.1
2,00,000	0.2	0.1
3,00,000	0.4	0.2
4,00,000	0.2	0.4
5,00,000	0.1	0.1
	1.0	1.0

1. What is the breakeven point units for each product?
2. Which product should be chosen, assuming the objective is to maximize expected operating income? Why? Show your computations.
3. Suppose management is absolutely certain that 3,00,000 units of shocking pink will be sold, but it still faces the same uncertainty about the demand for emerald green as outlined in the problem. Which product should be chosen? Why? What benefits are available to management from having the complete probability distribution instead of just an expected value?

3-44 CVP analysis, shoe stores. The Liberty Shoe Company operates a chain of shoe stores. The stores sell 10 different styles of inexpensive men's shoes with identical unit costs and selling prices. A unit is defined as a pair of shoes. Each store has a store manager who is paid a fixed salary. Individual salespeople receive a fixed salary and a sales commission. Liberty is trying to determine whether to open another store, which is expected to have the following revenue and cost relationships:

Unit variable data (per pair of shoe)

Selling price	₹300
Cost of shoes	195
Sales commissions	15
Variable costs per unit	210

Annual fixed costs

Rent	1,20,000
Salaries	4,00,000
Advertising	1,60,000
Other fixed costs	40,000
Total fixed costs	7,20,000

Consider each question independently.

1. What is the annual breakeven point in (a) units sold and (b) revenues?
2. If 35,000 units are sold, what will be the store's operating income (loss)?

3. If sales commissions were discontinued for individual salespeople in favor of ₹1,62,000 increase in fixed salaries, what would be the annual breakeven point in (a) units sold and (b) revenues?

4. Refer to the original data. If the store manager were paid ₹0.3 per unit sold in addition to his current fixed salary, what would be the annual breakeven point in (a) units sold and (b) revenues?

5. Refer to the original data. If the store manager were paid ₹0.3 per unit commission on each unit sold in excess of the breakeven point, what would be store's operating income if 50,000 units were sold? (This ₹0.3 is in addition to both the commission paid to the sales staff and the store manager's fixed salary.)

3-45 CVP analysis, shoe stores (continuation of 3-44). Refer to requirement 3 of 3-44.

1. Calculate the number of units sold at which the operating income under the fixed-salary plan and the lower fixed-salary-and-commission plan (for sales people only) would be equal. Above that number of units sold, one plan would be more profitable than the other; below that number of units sold, the reverse would occur.   **Required**

2. Compute the operating income or loss under each plan in requirement 1 at sales levels of (a) 50,000 units and (b) 60,000 units.

3. Suppose the target operating income is ₹16,80,000. How many units must be sold to reach the target under (a) the fixed-salary plan and (b) the lower fixed-salary-and-commission plan?

3-46 Sensitivity and inflation (continuation of previous question). As president of Liberty shoe Co., you are concerned that inflation may squeeze your profitability. Specifically, you feel committed to the ₹300 selling price and fear that decreasing the quality of the shoes in the face of rising costs would be an unwise move. You expect the cost of shoes to rise by 10 percent during the coming year. You are tempted to avoid the cost increase by placing a non-cancelable order with a large supplier that would provide 50,000 units of the specified quality for each store at ₹195 per units. (to simplify this analysis, assume that all stores will face identical demands.) These shoes could be acquired and paid for as delivered throughout the year. However, all shoes must be delivered to the stores by the end of the year.

As a shrewd merchandiser, you foresee some risks. If sales were less than 50,000 units, you feel that markdowns of the unsold merchandise would be necessary to sell the goods. You predict that the average selling price of the leftover units would be ₹180. The regular commission of = percent of revenues would be paid to salespeople.

1. Suppose that actual sales for the year are 48,000 units at ₹300 per unit and that you contracted for 50,000 units, what is the operating income for the Liberty Shoe Company?   **Required**

2. If you had perfect forecasting ability, you would have contracted for 48,000 units rather than 50,000 units. What would the operating income have been if you had ordered 48,000 units.

3. Given actual sales of 48,000 units, by how much would the average cost per unit have had to rise before the Shoe Company would have been indifferent to having the contract for 50,000 units or not having the contract?

4 Job Costing

Learning Objective 1

Describe the building-block concepts of costing systems

. . . the building blocks are cost object, direct costs, indirect costs, cost pools, and cost-allocation bases

No one likes to lose money.

Whether a company is a new startup venture providing marketing consulting services or an established manufacturer of custom-built motorcycles, knowing how to job cost—that is, knowing how much it costs to produce an individual product—is critical if a company is to generate a profit.

Building-Block Concepts of Costing Systems

Before we begin our discussion of costing systems, let's review the cost-related terms from Chapter 2 and introduce the new terms we will need to discuss the topics in this chapter.

1. A *cost object* is anything for which a measurement of costs is desired—for example, a product, such as an iMac computer, or a service, such as the cost of repairing an iMac computer.

2. The *direct costs of a cost object* are costs related to a particular cost object that can be traced to that cost object in an economically feasible (cost-effective) way—for example the cost of purchasing the main computer board or the cost of parts used to make an iMac computer.

3. The *Indirect costs of a cost object* are costs related to a particular cost object that cannot be traced to that cost object in an economically feasible (cost-effective) way—for example, the costs of supervisors who oversee multiple products, one of which is the iMac, or the rent paid for the repair facility that repairs many different Apple computer products besides the iMac. Indirect costs are allocated to the cost object using a cost-allocation method.

Recall that *cost assignment* is a general term for assigning costs, whether direct or indirect, to a cost object. *Cost tracing* is the process for assigning direct costs. *Cost allocation* is the process of assigning indirect costs. The relationship among these three concepts can be graphically represented as

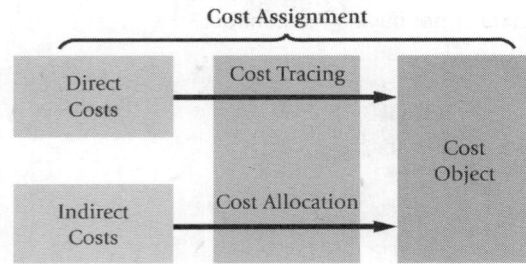

Throughout this chapter, the costs assigned to a cost object such as a BMW Mini Cooper car, or a service, such as an audit of the MTV network, include

138

both variable and fixed costs that are fixed in the short run. Managers use costs of products and services to guide long-run strategic decisions (for example, what mix of products and services to produce and sell and what prices to charge for them). In the long run, managers want revenues to exceed total (variable plus fixed) costs.

We need to introduce and explain two more terms to discuss costing systems:

4. **Cost pool.** A **cost pool** is a grouping of individual indirect cost items. Cost pools can range from broad, such as all manufacturing-plant costs, to narrow, such as the costs of operating metal-cutting machines. Cost pools are often organized in conjunction with cost-allocation bases.

5. **Cost-allocation base.** How should a company allocate costs to operate metal-cutting machines among different products? One way would be to allocate the costs based on the number of machine-hours used to produce the different products. The **cost-allocation base** (in our example, the number of machine-hours) is a systematic way to link an indirect cost or group of indirect costs (in our example, operating costs of all metal-cutting machines) to a cost object (in our example, different products). For example, if overhead costs of operating metal-cutting machines is ₹50,00,000 based on running these machines for 10,000 hours, the cost allocation rate is ₹50,00,000 ÷ 10,000 hours = ₹500 per machine-hour, where machine-hours is the cost allocation base. If a product uses 800 machine-hours, it will be allocated ₹4,00,000, ₹500 per machine-hour × 800 machine hours. The ideal cost-allocation base is the cost driver of the indirect costs because there is a cause-and-effect relationship between the cost-allocation base and the indirect costs. A cost-allocation base can be either financial (such as direct labor costs) or nonfinancial (such as the number of machine-hours). When the cost object is a job, product, or customer, the cost-allocation base is also called a **cost-application base**. For example, when the cost object is a department or another cost pool, the cost-allocation base is not called a cost-application base.

Sometimes a cost may need to be allocated when the cause-and-effect relationship is not clear-cut. Consider a corporatewide advertising program that promotes the general image of a company and its various divisions, rather than the image of an individual product. Many companies, such as PepsiCo, allocate costs like these to their individual divisions on the basis of revenues: The higher a division's revenue, the higher the business's allocated cost of the advertising program. Allocating costs this way is based on the criterion of *benefits received* rather than cause-and-effect. Divisions with higher revenues benefit from the advertising more than divisions with lower revenues and therefore ought to be allocated more of the advertising costs.

Another criterion for allocating some costs is the cost object's *ability to bear* the costs allocated to it. The city government of Houston, Texas, for example, distributes the costs of the city manager's office to other city departments—including the police department, fire department, library system, and others—based on the size of their budgets. The city's rationale is that larger departments should absorb a larger share of the costs. Organizations generally use the cause-and-effect criterion to allocate costs, followed by benefits received, and finally, and more rarely, by ability to bear.

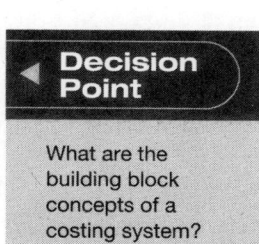

Decision Point

What are the building block concepts of a costing system?

The concepts represented by these five terms constitute the building blocks we will use to design the costing systems described in this chapter.

Job-Costing and Process-Costing Systems

Management accountants use two basic types of costing systems to assign costs to products or services:

1. **Job-costing system.** In a job costing system, the cost object is a unit or multiple units of a distinct product or service called a **job**. Each job generally uses different amounts of resources. The product or service is often a single unit, such as a specialized machine made at Hitachi, a construction project managed by Larsen and Toubro, a repair job done at an Honda Service Center, or an advertising campaign produced by Saatchi & Saatchi. Each special machine made by Hitachi is unique and distinct from the other machines made at the plant. An advertising campaign for one client at Saatchi and Saatchi is unique and distinct from advertising campaigns for other clients. Job costing is also used to cost multiple identical units of a distinct product, such as the costs incurred by Hindustan Aeronautics Ltd. to manufacture multiple units of the Agni missile for the ministry of Defense. Because the products and services are distinct, job-costing systems accumulate costs separately for each product or service.

2. **Process-costing system.** In a process costing system, the cost object is masses of identical or similar units of a product or service. For example, Citibank provides the same service to all its customers when processing customer deposits. Intel provides the same product (say, a Pentium 4 chip) to each of its customers. All Reliance Fresh customers receive the same frozen orange juice product. In each period, process-costing systems divide the total costs of producing an identical or similar product or service by the total number of units produced to obtain a per-unit cost. This per-unit cost is the average unit cost that applies to each of the identical or similar units produced in that period.

Exhibit 4-1

Examples of Job Costing and Process Costing in the Service, Merchandising, and Manufacturing Sectors

	Service Sector	Merchandising Sector	Manufacturing Sector
Job Costing Used	• Audit engagements done by Price Waterhouse Coopers • Consulting engagements done by McKinsey & Co. • Advertising-agency campaigns run by Ogilvy and Mather • Individual legal cases argued by Hale & Dorr • Computer-repair jobs done by Intel India • Movies produced by RK Studios	• Sending individual items by mail order • Special promotion of new products by Shoppers' shop	Assembly of individual aircrafts at Boeing • Construction of ships at Mazgaon Dock
Process Costing Used	• Bank-check clearing at Bank of America • Postal delivery (standard items) by Indian Postal Service	• Grain dealing • Lumber dealing	• Oil refining by Indian Oil • Beverage production by PepsiCo

Exhibit 4-1 presents examples of job costing and process costing in the service, merchandising, and manufacturing sectors. These two types of costing systems are best considered as opposite ends of a continuum; in between, one type of system can blur into the other to some degree.

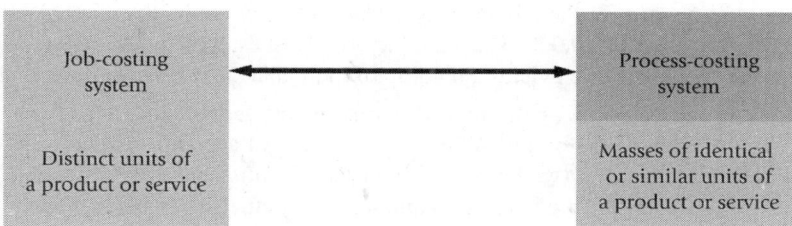

Many companies have costing systems that are neither pure job costing nor pure process costing but have elements of both tailored to the underlying operations. For example, Kellogg Corporation uses job costing to calculate the total cost to manufacture each of its different and distinct types of products— such as Corn Flakes, Crispix, and Froot Loops— and process costing to calculate the per-unit cost of producing each identical box of Corn Flakes. In this chapter, we focus on job-costing systems. **Chapters 17 and 18** discuss process-costing systems.

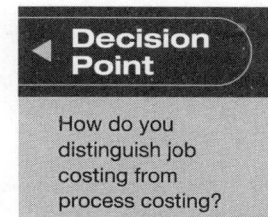

How do you distinguish job costing from process costing?

Job Costing: Evaluation and Implementation

We illustrate job costing using the example of Heavy Engineering Corporation (HEC), a company that manufactures and installs specialized machinery for the paper-making industry at its Ranchi plant. In early 2013, HEC receives a request to bid for the manufacturing and installation of a new paper-making machine for the Western Pulp and Paper Company (WPP). HEC has never made a machine quite like this one, and its managers wonder what to bid for the job. In order to make decisions about the job, HEC's management works through the five-step decision-making process.

Describe the approaches to evaluating and implementing job-costing systems

. . . to determine costs of jobs in a timely manner

1. **Identify the problems and uncertainties.** The decision of whether and how much to bid for the WPP job depends on how management resolves two critical uncertainties: (1) what it will cost to complete the job; and (2) the prices that HEC's competitors are likely to bid.

2. **Obtain information.** HEC's managers first evaluate whether doing the WPP job is consistent with the company's strategy. Do they want to do more of these kinds of jobs? Is this an attractive segment of the market? Will Robinson be able to develop a competitive advantage over its competitors and satisfy customers such as WPP? After completing their research, Robinson's managers conclude that the WPP job fits well with the company's strategy.

   HEC's managers study the drawings and engineering specifications provided by WPP and decide on technical details of the machine. They compare the specifications of this machine to similar machines they have made in the past, identify competitors who might bid on the job and speculate on what these bids might be.

3. **Make predictions about the future.** HEC's managers estimate the cost of direct materials, direct manufacturing labor, and overhead for the WPP job. They also consider qualitative factors and risk factors and think through any biases they might have. For

example, do engineers and employees working on the WPP job have the necessary skills and technical competence? How accurate are the cost estimates, and what is the likelihood of cost overruns? What biases do HEC's managers have to be careful about?

4. **Make decisions by choosing among alternatives.** HEC's managers consider several alternative bids based on what they believe competing firms will bid, the technical expertise needed for the job, business risks, and other qualitative factors. Ultimately HEC decides to bid ₹1,50,000. The manufacturing cost estimate is ₹97,050 (as described later in the chapter), which yields a markup of more than 50% on manufacturing cost.

5. **Implement the decision, evaluate performance, and learn.** HEC wins the bid for the WPP job. As Hec works on the WPP job, management accountants carefully track all the costs it has incurred (which are detailed later in this chapter). Ultimately, HEC's managers compare the predicted amounts against actual costs to evaluate how well they did on the WPP job.

In its job-costing system, HEC accumulates costs incurred on a job in different parts of the value chain, such as manufacturing, marketing, and customer service. We focus here on HEC's manufacturing function (which also includes product installation). To make a machine, HEC purchases some components from outside suppliers and makes others itself. Each of HEC's jobs also has a service element: installing a machine at a customer's site, integrating it with the customer's other machines and processes, and ensuring the machine meets customer expectations.

One form of a job-costing system that HEC can use is *actual costing*, which is a costing system that traces direct costs to a cost object based on the actual direct-cost rates times the actual quantities of the direct-cost inputs used. It allocates indirect costs based on the actual indirect-cost rates times the actual quantities of the cost-allocation bases. The *actual indirect-cost rate* is calculated by dividing actual total indirect costs by the actual total quantity of the cost-allocation base.

$$\frac{\text{Actual indirect}}{\text{cost rate}} = \frac{\text{Actual annual indirect costs}}{\text{Actual annual quantity of the cost-allocation base}}$$

As its name suggests, actual costing systems calculate the actual costs of jobs. Yet, actual costing systems are not commonly found in practice because actual costs cannot be computed in a *timely* manner[1]. The problem is not with computing direct-cost rates for direct materials and direct manufacturing labor. For example, HEC records the actual prices paid for materials. As it uses these materials, the prices paid serve as actual direct-cost rates for charging material costs to jobs. As we discuss next, calculating actual indirect-cost rates on a timely basis each week or each month is, however, a problem. HEC can only calculate actual indirect-cost rates at the end of the fiscal year. However, the firm's managers are unwilling to wait that long to learn the costs of various jobs because they need cost information to monitor and manage the cost of jobs while they are in progress. Ongoing cost information about jobs also helps managers bid on new jobs while old jobs are in progress.

Time Period Used to Compute Indirect-Cost Rates

There are two reasons for using longer periods, such as a year, to calculate indirect-cost rates.

1. **The numerator reason (indirect-cost pool).** The shorter the period, the greater is the influence of seasonal patterns on the amount of costs. For example, if indirect-cost rates were calculated each month, costs of heating (included in the numerator) would

---

[1] Actual costing is presented in more detail on pages (pages 149–151).

be charged to production only during the winter months. An annual period incorporates the effects of all four seasons into a single, annual indirect-cost rate.

Levels of total indirect costs are also affected by nonseasonal erratic costs. Nonseasonal erratic costs are the costs incurred in a particular month that benefit operations during future months, such as equipment-repair costs and the costs of vacation and holiday pay for employees. If monthly indirect-cost rates were calculated, the jobs done in a month in which there were high, nonseasonal erratic costs would be charged with these higher costs. Pooling all indirect costs together over the course of a full year and calculating a single annual indirect-cost rate helps smooth some of the erratic bumps in costs associated with shorter periods.

2. **The denominator reason (quantity of the cost-allocation base).** Another reason for longer periods is to avoid spreading monthly fixed indirect costs over fluctuating levels of monthly output and fluctuating quantities of the cost-allocation base. Consider the following example.

Choksi & Choksi is a firm of tax accountants whose work follows a highly seasonal pattern. Tax season (January–April) is very busy. Other times of the year are less busy. The firm has both variable indirect costs and fixed indirect costs. Variable indirect costs (such as supplies, power, and indirect support labor) vary with the quantity of the cost-allocation base (direct professional labor-hours). Fixed indirect costs (depreciation and general administrative support) do not vary with short-run fluctuations in the quantity of the cost-allocation base:

| | Indirect Costs | | | Direct Professional Labor-Hours (4) | Variable Indirect Cost Rate per Direct Professional Labor-Hour (5) = (1) ÷ (4) | Fixed Indirect Cost Rate per Direct Professional Labor-Hour (6) = (2) ÷ (4) | Total Allocation Rate per Direct Professional Labor-Hour (7) = (3) ÷ (4) |
	Variable (1)	Fixed (2)	Total (3)				
High-output month	₹4,00,000	₹6,00,000	₹10,00,000	3,200	₹125.0	₹187.5	₹312.6
Low-output month	1,00,000	6,00,000	7,00,000	800	₹125.0	₹750	875.0

Variable indirect costs change in proportion to changes in direct professional labor-hours. Therefore, the variable indirect-cost rate is the same in both the high-output months and the low-output months (₹125 in both as the table shows). Sometimes overtime payments can cause the variable indirect-cost rate to be higher in high-output months. In such cases, variable indirect costs will be allocated at a higher rate to production in high-output months relative to production in low-output months.

Now consider the fixed costs of ₹6,00,000. The fixed costs cause monthly total indirect-cost rates to vary considerably—from ₹312.5 per hour to ₹875.0 per hour. Few managers believe that identical jobs done in different months should be allocated such significantly different indirect-cost charges per hour (₹875.0 ÷ ₹312.5 = 2.80, or 280%) because of fixed costs. Furthermore, if fees for preparing tax returns are based on costs, fees would be high in low-output months leading to lost business, when in fact management wants to accept more bids to utilize idle capacity during these months (for more details, see Chapter 9).

Choksi & Choksi chose a specific level of capacity based on a time horizon far beyond a mere month. An average, annualized rate based on the relationship of total annual indirect costs to the total annual level of output smoothes the effect of monthly variations in output levels. This rate is more representative of the total costs and total output that management

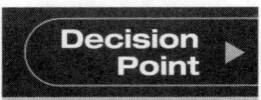

Decision Point ▶

What is the main challenge in implementing job-costing systems?

considered when choosing the level of capacity and, hence, fixed costs. Another denominator reason for using annual overhead rates is that the calculation of monthly indirect-cost rates is affected by the number of Monday-to-Friday workdays in a month. The number of workdays per month varies from 20 to 23 during a year. Because February has the fewest workdays (and consequently labor-hours), if separate rates are computed each month, jobs done in February would bear a greater share of the firm's indirect costs (such as depreciation and property taxes) than identical jobs in other months. An annual period reduces the effect that the number of working days per month has on unit costs.

Normal Costing

Learning Objective 4

Outline the seven-step approach to job costing

. . . the seven-step approach is used to compute direct and indirect costs of a job

As we indicated, because it's hard to calculate actual indirect-cost rates on a weekly or monthly basis, managers cannot calculate the actual costs of jobs as they are completed. Nonetheless, managers want a close approximation of the costs of various jobs regularly during the year, not just at the end of the fiscal year. They want to know manufacturing costs (and other costs, such as marketing costs) to price jobs, monitor and manage costs, evaluate the success of jobs, learn about what did and did not work, bid on new jobs, and prepare interim financial statements. Because companies need immediate access to job costs, few wait to allocate overhead costs until the end of the accounting year. Instead, a *predetermined* or *budgeted* indirect-cost rate is calculated for each cost pool at the beginning of a fiscal year, and overhead costs are allocated to jobs as work progresses. For the numerator and denominator reasons already described, the **budgeted indirect-cost rate** for each cost pool is computed as follows:

$$\frac{\text{Budgeted indirect}}{\text{cost rate}} = \frac{\text{Budgeted annual indirect costs}}{\text{Budgeted annual quantity of the cost-allocation base}}$$

Using budgeted indirect-cost rates gives rise to normal costing.

Normal costing is a costing system that (1) traces direct costs to a cost object by using the actual direct-cost rates times the actual quantities of the direct-cost inputs and (2) allocates indirect costs based on the *budgeted* indirect-cost rates times the actual quantities of the cost-allocation bases.

General Approach to Job Costing Using Normal Costing

We illustrate normal costing for the HEC example using the following seven steps to assign costs to an individual job. This approach is commonly used by companies in the manufacturing, merchandising, and service sectors.

Step 1: Identify the Job That Is the Chosen Cost Object. The cost object in the Hec example is Job WPP 298, manufacturing a paper-making machine for the Western Pulp and Paper Company in 2013. HEC's managers and management accountants gather information to cost jobs through source documents. A **source document** is an original record (such as a labor time card on which an employee's work hours are recorded) that supports journal entries in an accounting system. The main source document for Job WPP 298 is a job-cost record. A **job-cost record**, also called a **job-cost sheet,** records and accumulates all the costs assigned to a specific job, starting when work begins. Exhibit 4-2 shows the job-cost record for the paper-making machine ordered by Western Pulp and Paper Company. Follow the various steps in costing Job WPP 298 on the job-cost record in Exhibit 4-2.

Exhibit 4-2   Source Documents at Hec Company: Job-Cost Record

	File Edit View Insert Format Tools Data Window Help					
	A	B	C	D	E	
1			JOB-COST RECORD			
2	JOB NO:	WPP 298		CUSTOMER:	Western Pulp and Paper	
3	Date Started:	Feb. 4, 2013		Date Completed	Feb. 28, 2013	
4						
5						
6	DIRECT MATERIALS					
7	Date	Materials		Quantity	Unit	Total
8	Received	Requisition No.	Part No.	Used	Cost	Costs
9	Feb. 4, 2013	2013: 198	MB 468-A	8	Rs 140	₹1,120
10	Feb. 4, 2013	2013: 199	TB 267-F	12	630	7,560
11						•
12						•
13	Total					₹46,060
14						
15	DIRECT MANUFACTURING LABOR					
16	Period	Labor Time	Employee	Hours	Hourly	Total
17	Covered	Record No.	No.	Used	Rate	Costs
18	Feb. 4-10, 2013	LT 232	551-87-3076	25	₹180	₹4,500
19	Feb. 4-10, 2013	LT 247	287-31-4671	5	190	950
20						•
21						•
22	Total					₹15,790
23						
24	MANUFACTURING OVERHEAD*					
25		Cost Pool		Allocation-Base	Allocation-	Total
26	Date	Category	Allocation-Base	Quantity Used	Base Rate	Costs
27	Dec. 31, 2013	Manufacturing	Direct Manufacturing	88 hours	₹400	₹35,200
28			Labor-Hours			
29						
30	Total					35,200
31	TOTAL MANUFACTURING COST OF JOB					₹97,050
32						
33						
34	*The HEC uses a single manufacturing-overhead cost pool. The use of multiple overhead cost pools					
35	would mean multiple entries in the "Manufacturing Overhead" section of the job-cost record.					
36						

Step 2:   Identify the Direct Costs of the Job. Hec identifies two direct-manufacturing cost categories: direct materials and direct manufacturing labor.

■ **Direct materials:** On the basis of the engineering specifications and drawings provided by WPP, a manufacturing engineer orders materials from the storeroom using a basic source document called a **materials-requisition record,** which contains information about the cost of direct materials used on a specific job and in a specific department. Exhibit 4-3, Panel A, shows a materials-requisition record for the Hec. See how the record specifies the job for which the material is requested (WPP 298), the description of the material (Part Number MB 468-A, metal brackets), the actual quantity (8), the actual unit cost (₹140), and the actual total cost (₹1,120). The ₹1,120 actual total cost also appears on the job-cost record in Exhibit 4-2. If we add the cost of all material requisitions, the total actual direct material cost is ₹46,060, which is shown in the Direct Materials panel of the job-cost record in Exhibit 4-2.

■ **Direct manufacturing labor:** Accounting for direct manufacturing labor is similar to the accounting described for direct materials. The source document for direct manufacturing labor is a **labor-time record**, which contains information about the amount of labor time used for a specific job in a specific department. Exhibit 4-3, Panel B, shows a typical weekly labor-time record for a particular employee (Ram Prasad). Each day Prasad records the time spent on individual jobs (in this case WPP 298 and JL 256), as well as the time spent on other tasks, such as maintenance of machines or cleaning, that are not related to a specific job.

The 25 hours that Prasad spent on Job WPP 298 appears on the job-cost record in Exhibit 4-2 at a cost of ₹4,500 (25 hours × ₹180 per hour). Similarly, the job-cost record for Job JL 256 will carry a cost of ₹2,160 (12 hours × ₹180 per hour). The three hours of time spent on maintenance and cleaning at ₹180 per hour equals ₹540. This cost is part of indirect manufacturing costs because it is not traceable to any particular job. This indirect cost is included as part of the manufacturing-overhead cost pool allocated to jobs. The total direct manufacturing labor costs of ₹15,790 for the papermaking machine that appears in the Direct Manufacturing Labor panel of the job-cost record in Exhibit 4-2 is the sum of all the direct manufacturing labor costs charged to this job by different employees.

All costs other than direct materials and direct manufacturing labor are classified as indirect costs.

Step 3: Select the Cost-Allocation Bases to Use for Allocating Indirect Costs to the Job. Recall that indirect manufacturing costs are costs that are necessary to do a job but that cannot be traced to a specific job. It would be impossible to complete a job without incurring indirect costs such as supervision, manufacturing engineering, utilities, and repairs. Moreover, different jobs require different quantities of indirect resources. The objective is to allocate the costs of indirect resources in a systematic way to their related jobs. Because

| **Exhibit 4-3** | Source Documents at HEC: Materials Requisition Record and Labor-Time Record. |

PANEL A:

MATERIALS-REQUISITION RECORD				
Materials-Requisition Record No.			2008: 198	
Job No. WPP 298		Date:	FEB. 4, 2008	
Part No.	Part Description	Quantity	Unit Cost	Total Cost
MB 468-A	Metal Brackets	8	₹140	₹1,120
Issued By: B. Clyde		Date:	Feb. 7, 2011	
Received By: L. Daley		Date:	Feb. 7, 2011	

PANEL B:

LABOR-TIME RECORD								
Labor-Time Record No:		LT 232						
Employee Name: Ram Prasad			Employee No: 551-87-3076					
Employee Classification Code:			Grade 3 Machinist					
Hourly Rate: ₹180								
Week Start: Feb. 4, 2011			Week End: Feb. 13, 2011					
Job. No.	M	T	W	Th	F	S	Su	Total
WPP 298	4	8	3	6	4	0	0	25
JL 256	3	0	4	2	3	0	0	12
Maintenance	1	0	1	0	1	0	0	3
Total	8	8	8	8	8	0	0	40
Supervisor: R. Stuart			Date: Feb. 7, 2011					

these costs cannot be traced to a specific job, they must be allocated to all jobs in a systematic way.

Companies often use multiple cost-allocation bases to allocate indirect costs because different indirect costs have different cost drivers. For example, some indirect costs such as depreciation and repairs of machines are more closely related to machine-hours. Other indirect costs such as supervision and production support are more closely related to direct manufacturing labor-hours. HEC, however, chooses direct manufacturing labor-hours as the sole allocation base for linking all indirect manufacturing costs to jobs. The managers do so because, in HEC's labor-intensive environment, they believe the number of direct manufacturing labor-hours drives the manufacturing overhead resources required by individual jobs. (We will see in Chapter 5 that managers in many manufacturing environments often need to broaden the set of cost drivers.) In 2013, HEC budgets 28,000 direct manufacturing labor-hours.

Step 4:   Identify the Indirect Costs Associated with Each Cost-Allocation Base. Because Hec believes that a single cost-allocation base—direct manufacturing labor-hours—can be used to allocate indirect manufacturing costs to jobs, Hec creates a single cost pool called manufacturing overhead costs. This pool represents all indirect costs of the Manufacturing Department that are difficult to trace directly to individual jobs. In 2013, actual manufacturing overhead costs total ₹1,12,00,000.

As we saw in Steps 3 and 4, managers first identify cost-allocation bases and then identify the costs related to each cost-allocation base, not the other way around. They choose this order because managers must first understand the cost driver, (the reasons why costs are being incurred) before they can determine the costs associated with each cost driver. Otherwise, there is nothing to guide the creation of the cost pools. Of course, Steps 3 and 4 can be done almost simultaneously.

Step 5:   Compute the Rate per Unit of Each Cost-Allocation Base Used to Allocate Indirect Costs to the Job. For each cost pool, the **budgeted indirect-cost rate** is calculated by dividing budgeted total indirect costs in the pool (determined in Step 4) by the budgeted total quantity of the cost-allocation base (determined in Step 3). HEC calculates the allocation rate for its single manufacturing overhead cost pool as follows:

$$\frac{\text{Actual manufacturing}}{\text{overhead rate}} = \frac{\text{Actual annual manufacturing overhead costs}}{\text{Actual annual quantity of the cost-allocation base}}$$

$$= \frac{₹1,21,50,000}{2,70,000 \text{ direct manufacturing labor-hours}}$$

$$= ₹450 \text{ per direct manufacturing labor-hour}$$

Step 6:   Compute the Indirect Costs Allocated to the Job. The indirect costs of a job are computed by multiplying the actual quantity of each different allocation base (one allocation base for each cost pool) associated with the job by the budgeted indirect cost rate of each allocation base (computed in Step 5). Recall that HEC's managers selected direct manufacturing labor-hours as the only cost-allocation base. HEC uses 88 direct manufacturing labor-hours on the WPP 298 job. Consequently, the manufacturing overhead costs allocated to WPP 298 equal ₹35,200 (₹400 per direct manufacturing labor-hour × 88 hours) and appear in the Manufacturing Overhead panel of the WPP 298 job-cost record in Exhibit 4-2.

Step 7:   Compute the Total Cost of the Job by Adding All Direct and Indirect Costs Assigned to the Job. Exhibit 4-2 shows that the total manufacturing costs of the WPP job are ₹97,050

Direct manufacturing costs		
Direct materials	₹46,060	
Direct manufacturing labor	15,790	₹61,850
Manufacturing overhead costs		
(₹400 per direct manuf. labor-hour × 88 hours)		35,200
Total manufacturing costs of job WPP 298		₹97,050

Recall that Hec bid a price of ₹1,50,000 for the job. At that revenue, the actual-costing system shows a gross margin of ₹52,950 (₹1,50,000 – ₹97,050) and a gross-margin percentage of 35.3% (₹52,950 ÷ ₹1,50,000 = 0.35).

HEC's manufacturing managers and sales managers can use the gross-margin and gross-margin percentage calculations to compare the different jobs to try to understand why some jobs aren't as profitable as others. Were direct materials wasted? Was the direct manufacturing labor cost of the jobs too high? Were the jobs simply underpriced? A job-cost analysis provides the information managers needed to gauge the manufacturing and sales performance of their firms.

Exhibit 4-4 is an overview of HEC's job-costing system. This exhibit represents the concepts comprising the five building blocks of job-costing systems introduced at the beginning of this chapter: (1) cost objects, (2) the direct costs of a cost object, (3) the indirect (overhead) costs of a cost object, (4) the indirect-cost pool, and (5) the cost-allocation base. (The symbols in the exhibit are used consistently in the costing-system overviews

Exhibit 4-4

Job-Costing Overview
for Determining
Manufacturing Costs of
Jobs at Hec Company

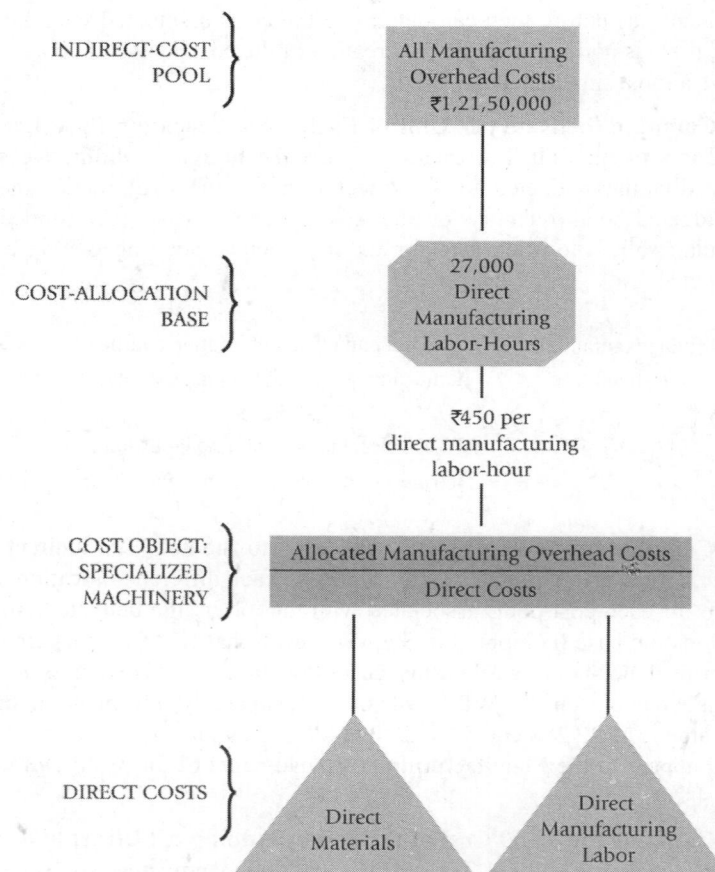

presented in this book. A triangle always identifies a direct cost, a rectangle represents the indirect-cost pool, and an octagon describes the cost-allocation base.) Costing-system overviews such as Exhibit 4-4 are important learning tools. We urge you to sketch one when you need to understand a costing system.

Note the similarities between Exhibit 4-4 and the cost of the WPP 298 job described in Step 7. Exhibit 4-4 shows two direct-cost categories (direct materials and direct manufacturing labor) and one indirect-cost category (manufacturing overhead) used to allocate indirect costs. The costs in Step 7 also have three dollar amounts, each corresponding respectively to the two direct-cost and one indirect-cost categories.

The Role of Technology

Information technology gives managers quick and accurate job-costing information, making it easier for them to manage and control jobs. Consider, for example, the direct materials charged to jobs. Managers control these costs as materials are purchased and used. Using Electronic Data Interchange (EDI) technology, companies like Robinson order materials from their suppliers by clicking a few keys on a computer keyboard. EDI, an electronic computer link between a company and its suppliers, ensures that the order is transmitted quickly and accurately with minimal paperwork and costs. A bar code scanner records the receipt of incoming materials, and a computer matches the receipt with the order, prints out a check to the supplier, and records the materials received. When an operator on the production floor transmits a request for materials via a computer terminal, the computer prepares a materials-requisition record, instantly recording the issue of materials in the materials and job-cost records. Each day, the computer sums the materials-requisition records charged to a particular job or manufacturing department. A performance report is then prepared monitoring the actual costs of direct materials. The use of direct materials can be reported hourly if managers believe the benefits exceed the cost of such frequent reporting.

Similarly, information about direct manufacturing labor is obtained as employees log into computer terminals and key in the job numbers, their employee numbers, and start and end times of their work on different jobs. The computer automatically prints the labor time record and, using hourly rates stored for each employee, calculates the direct manufacturing labor costs of individual jobs. Information technology also provides managers with instantaneous feedback to help control manufacturing overhead costs, jobs in process, jobs completed, and jobs shipped and installed at customer sites.

Actual Costing

How would the cost of Job WPP 298 change if HEC had used actual costing rather than normal costing? Both actual costing and normal costing trace direct costs to jobs in the same way because source documents identify the actual quantities and actual rates of direct materials and direct manufacturing labor for a job as the work is being done. The only difference between costing a job with normal costing and actual costing is that normal costing uses *budgeted* indirect-cost rates, whereas actual costing uses *actual* indirect-cost rates calculated annually at the end of the year. Exhibit 4-5 distinguishes actual costing from normal costing.

	Actual Costing	Normal Costing
Direct Costs	*Actual direct-cost rates ×* actual quantities of direct-cost inputs	*Actual direct-cost rates ×* actual quantities of direct-cost inputs
Indirect Costs	*Actual indirect-cost rates ×* actual quantities of cost-allocation bases	*Budgeted indirect-cost rates ×* actual quantities of cost-allocation bases

Learning Objective 5

Distinguish actual costing

. . . actual costing uses actual indirect-cost rates

from normal costing

. . . normal costing uses budgeted indirectcost rates

Exhibit 4-5

Actual Costing and Normal Costing Methods

The following actual data for 2013 are for HEC's manufacturing operations:

	Actual
Total manufacturing overhead costs	₹1,21,50,000
Total direct manufacturing labor-hours	2,70,000

Steps 1 and 2 are exactly as before: Step 1 identifies WPP 298 as the cost object; Step 2 calculates actual direct material costs of ₹46,060, and actual direct manufacturing labor costs of ₹15,790. Recall from Step 3 that HEC uses a single cost-allocation base, direct manufacturing labor-hours, to allocate all manufacturing overhead costs to jobs. The actual quantity of direct manufacturing labor-hours for 2013 is 27,000 hours. In Step 4, HEC groups all actual indirect manufacturing costs of ₹1,21,50,000 into a single manufacturing overhead cost pool. In Step 5, the **actual indirect-cost rate** is calculated by dividing actual total indirect costs in the pool (determined in Step 4) by the actual total quantity of the cost-allocation base (determined in Step 3). HEC calculates the actual manufacturing overhead rate in 2013 for its single manufacturing overhead cost pool as follows:

$$\text{Actual manufacturing overhead rate} = \frac{\text{Actual annual manufacturing overhead costs}}{\text{Actual annual quantity of the cost-allocation base}}$$

$$= \frac{₹1,21,50,000}{2,70,000 \text{ direct manufacturing labor-hours}}$$

$$= ₹450 \text{ per direct manufacturing labor-hour}$$

In Step 6, under an actual-costing system,

$$\text{Manufacturing overhead costs allocated to WPP 298} = \text{Actual manufacturing overhead rate} \times \text{Actual quantity of direct manufacturing labor-hours}$$

$$= ₹450 \text{ per direct manuf. labor-hour} \times 88 \text{ direct manufacturing labor-hours}$$

$$= ₹39,600$$

In Step 7, the cost of the job under actual costing is ₹1,01,450, calculated as follows:

Direct manufacturing costs		
Direct materials	₹46,060	
Direct manufacturing labor	15,790	₹61,850
Manufacturing overhead costs		
(₹450 per direct manufacturing labor-hour × 88 actual direct manufacturing labor-hours)		39,600
Total manufacturing costs of job		₹1,01,450

The manufacturing cost of the WPP 298 job is higher by ₹4,400 under actual costing (₹1,01,450) than it is under normal costing (₹97,050) because the actual indirect-cost rate is ₹450 per hour, whereas the budgeted indirect-cost rate is ₹400 per hour. That is, (₹450 – ₹400) × 88 actual direct manufacturing labor-hours = ₹4,400.

As we discussed previously, manufacturing costs of a job are available much earlier under a normal-costing system. Consequently, HEC's manufacturing and sales managers can evaluate the profitability of different jobs, the efficiency with which the jobs are done, and the pricing of different jobs as soon as the jobs are completed, while the experience is still fresh in everyone's mind. Another advantage of normal costing is that it provides managers with information earlier—while there is still time to take corrective actions, such as improving the company's labor efficiency or reducing the company's overhead costs. At the end of the year, though, costs allocated using normal costing will not, in general, equal actual costs incurred. If material, adjustments will need to be made so that the cost of jobs and the costs in various inventory accounts are based on actual rather that normal costing. We describe these adjustments later in the chapter.

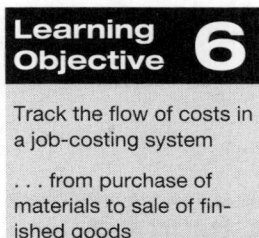

A Normal Job-Costing System in Manufacturing

The following example looks at events that occurred at HEC in February 2013. Before getting into details, study Exhibit 4-6, which provides a broad framework for understanding the flow of costs in job costing.

The upper part of Exhibit 4-6 shows the flow of inventoriable costs from the purchase of materials and other manufacturing inputs, to their conversion into work-in-process and finished goods, to the sale of finished goods.

Direct materials used and direct manufacturing labor can be easily traced to jobs. They become part of work-in-process inventory on the balance sheet because direct manufacturing labor transforms direct materials into another asset, work-in-process inventory. HEC also incurs manufacturing overhead costs (including indirect materials and indirect manufacturing labor) to convert direct materials into work-in-process inventory. These overhead (indirect) costs, however, cannot be easily traced to individual jobs. Manufacturing overhead costs, therefore, are first accumulated in a manufacturing overhead account and then allocated to individual jobs. As manufacturing overhead costs are allocated, they become part of work-in-process inventory.

As individual jobs are completed, work-in-process inventory becomes another balance sheet asset, finished goods inventory. Only when finished goods are sold is an expense, cost of goods sold, recognized in the income statement and matched against revenues earned.

The lower part of Exhibit 4-6 shows the period costs—marketing and customer-service costs. These costs do not create any assets on the balance sheet because they are not incurred

Learning Objective 6

Track the flow of costs in a job-costing system

. . . from purchase of materials to sale of finished goods

Exhibit 4-6   Flow of Costs in Job Costing

◄——————————————— BALANCE SHEET ———————————————►   INCOME STATEMENT
Revenues

| Inventoriable Costs: | Purchases of Direct Materials Direct Manufacturing Labor | Traced to → | Conversion into Work-in-Process Inventory | → | Conversion into Finished Goods Inventory | When sales occur → | Cost of Goods Sold |
| | Manufacturing Overhead including Indirect Materials and Indirect Manufacturing Labor | Allocated to → | | | | | |

Period Costs: Marketing Expense
Customer-service Expense

to transform materials into a finished product. Instead, they are expensed in the income statement as they are incurred to best match revenues.

We next describe the entries made in the general ledger.

General Ledger

You know by this point that a job-costing system has a separate job-cost record for each job. A summary of the job-cost record is typically found in a subsidiary ledger. The general ledger account Work-in-Process Control presents the total of these separate job-cost records pertaining to all unfinished jobs. The job-cost records and Work-in-Process Control account track job costs from when jobs start until they are complete. When jobs are completed or sold, they are recorded in the finished goods inventory records of jobs in the subsidiary ledger. The general ledger account Finished Goods Control records the total of these separate job-cost records for all jobs completed and subsequently for all jobs sold.

Exhibit 4-7 shows T-account relationships for HEC's general ledger. The general ledger gives a "bird's-eye view" of the costing system. The amounts shown in Exhibit 4-7 are

---

Exhibit 4-7　　Manufacturing Job-Costing System Using Normal Costing: Diagram of General Ledger Relationships for February 2013.

GENERAL LEDGER

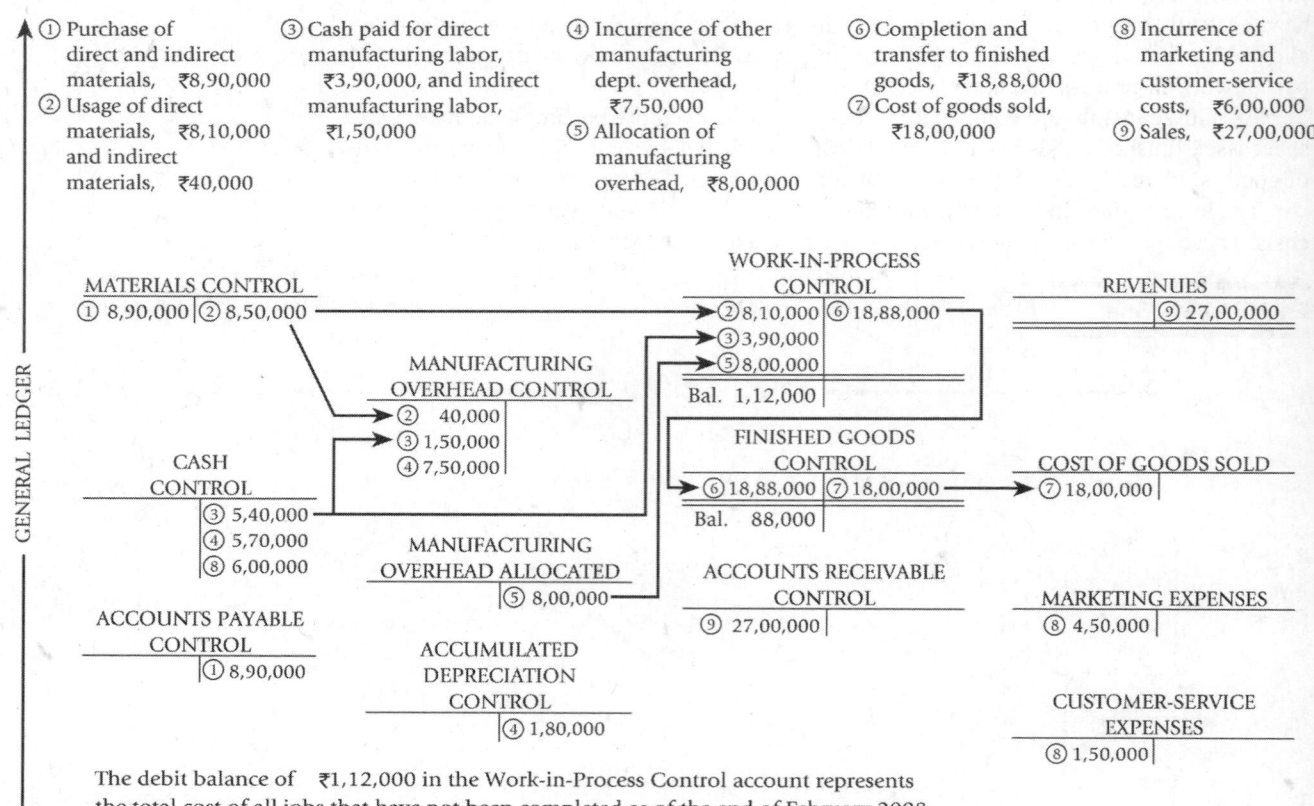

① Purchase of direct and indirect materials, ₹8,90,000
② Usage of direct materials, ₹8,10,000 and indirect materials, ₹40,000
③ Cash paid for direct manufacturing labor, ₹3,90,000, and indirect manufacturing labor, ₹1,50,000
④ Incurrence of other manufacturing dept. overhead, ₹7,50,000
⑤ Allocation of manufacturing overhead, ₹8,00,000
⑥ Completion and transfer to finished goods, ₹18,88,000
⑦ Cost of goods sold, ₹18,00,000
⑧ Incurrence of marketing and customer-service costs, ₹6,00,000
⑨ Sales, ₹27,00,000

The debit balance of ₹1,12,000 in the Work-in-Process Control account represents the total cost of all jobs that have not been completed as of the end of February 2008.

The debit balance of ₹88,000 in the Finished Goods Control account represents the cost of all jobs that have been completed but not sold as of the end of February 2013.

based on the monthly transactions and journal entries that follow. As you go through each journal entry, use Exhibit 4-7 to see how the various entries being made come together. General ledger accounts with "Control" in the titles (for example, Materials Control and Accounts Payable Control) have underlying subsidiary ledgers that contain additional details, such as each type of material in inventory and individual suppliers that HEC must pay.

Some companies simultaneously make entries in the general ledger and subsidiary ledger accounts. Others, such as HEC, make entries in the subsidiary ledger when transactions occur and entries in the general ledger less frequently, often on a monthly basis.

A general ledger should be viewed as only one of many tools that assist management in planning and control. To control operations, managers rely on not only the source documents used to record amounts in the subsidiary ledgers, but also nonfinancial information such as the percentage of jobs requiring rework.

Explanations of Transactions

We next look at a summary of Hec's transactions for February 2013 and the corresponding journal entries for those transactions.

1. Purchases of materials (direct and indirect) on credit, ₹8,90,000

Materials Control	8,90,000	
Accounts Payable Control		8,90,000

2. Usage of direct materials, ₹8,10,000 and indirect materials, ₹40,000

Work-in-Process Control	8,10,000	
Manufacturing Overhead Control	40,000	
Materials Control		8,50,000

3. Manufacturing payroll for February: direct labor, ₹3,90,000 and indirect labor, ₹1,50,000 paid in cash

Work-in- Process Control	3,90,000	
Manufacturing Overhead Control	1,50,000	
Cash Control		5,40,000

4. Other manufacturing overhead costs incurred during February, ₹7,50,000, consisting of supervision and engineering salaries, ₹4,40,000 (paid in cash); plant utilities, repairs, and insurance, ₹1,30,000 (paid in cash); and plant depreciation, ₹1,80,000

Manufacturing Overhead Control	7,50,000	
Cash Control		5,70,000
Accumulated Depreciation Control		1,80,000

5. Allocation of manufacturing overhead to jobs, ₹8,00,000

Work-in-Process Control	8,00,000	
Manufacturing Overhead Allocated		8,00,000

Under normal costing, **manufacturing overhead allocated**—also called **manufacturing overhead applied**—is the amount of manufacturing overhead costs allocated to individual jobs based on the budgeted rate multiplied by actual quantity used of the allocation base. Manufacturing overhead allocated contains all manufacturing overhead costs. They are assigned to jobs using a cost-allocation base because these costs cannot be traced specifically to jobs in an economically feasible way.

Keep in mind the distinct difference between transactions 4 and 5. In transaction 4, actual overhead costs incurred throughout the month are added (debited) to the Manufacturing Overhead Control account. These costs are not debited to

Work-in-Process Control. Manufacturing overhead costs are added (debited) to Work-in-Process Control *only when* manufacturing overhead costs are allocated in transaction 5. At the time these costs are allocated, Manufacturing Overhead Control is, *in effect,* decreased (credited) via its contra account, Manufacturing Overhead Allocated. Overhead Control account. Having Manufacturing Overhead Allocated as a contra account allows the job-costing system to separately retain information about the manufacturing overhead costs the company has *incurred* (in the Manufacturing Overhead Control account) as well as the amount of manufacturing overhead costs it has *allocated* (in the Manufacturing Overhead Allocated account). If the allocated manufacturing overhead had been credited to manufacturing overhead control, the company would lose information about the actual manufacturing overhead costs it is incurring.

Under the normal costing system described in our illustration, the budgeted manufacturing overhead rate of ₹400 per direct manufacturing labor-hour is calculated at the beginning of the year on the basis of predictions of annual manufacturing overhead costs and the annual quantity of the cost-allocation base. Almost certainly, the actual amounts allocated will differ from the predictions. In a later section, we discuss what to do with this difference.

6. Completion and transfer of individual jobs to finished goods in February 2013 is, ₹18,88,000

Finished Goods Control	18,88,000	
Work-in- Process Control		18,88,000

7. Cost of goods sold, ₹18,00,000

Cost of Goods Sold	18,00,000	
Finished Goods Control		18,00,000

8. Marketing costs for February 2013, ₹4,50,000 and customer service costs for February 2013, ₹1,50,000, paid in cash

Marketing Expenses	4,50,000	
Customer Service Expenses	1,50,000	
Cash Control		6,00,000

9. Sales revenues, from all jobs and delivered in February 2013, all on credit, ₹27,00,000

Accounts Receivable Control	27,00,000	
Revenues		27,00,000

Subsidiary Ledgers

Exhibits 4-8 and 4-9 present subsidiary ledgers that contain the underlying details—the "worm's-eye view"—that help HEC's managers keep track of the WPP 298 job, as opposed to the "bird's-eye view" of the general ledger. The sum of all entries in underlying subsidiary ledgers equals the total amount in the corresponding general ledger control accounts.

Material Records by Type of Materials   The subsidiary ledger for materials at HEC— called *Materials Records*—is used to continuously record the quantity of materials received, issued to jobs, and inventory balances for each type of material. Panel A of Exhibit 4-8 shows the Materials Record for Metal Brackets (Part No. MB 468-A). In many companies, the source documents supporting the receipt and issue of materials are scanned into a computer. Software programs then automatically update the Materials Records and make all the necessary accounting entries in the subsidiary and general ledgers. The cost of materials received across all types of direct and indirect material records for February 2013 is

Exhibit 4-8   Subsidiary Ledger for Materials, Labor, and Manufacturing Department Overhead[1]

PANEL A: Materials Records by Type of Materials	PANEL B: Labor Records by Employee	PANEL C: Manufacturing Department Overhead Records by Month
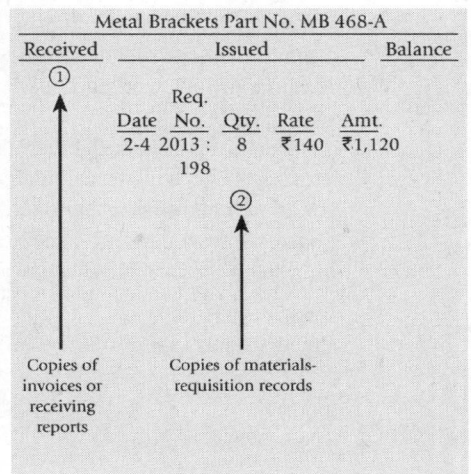	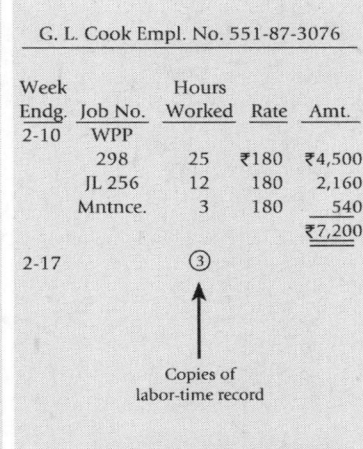	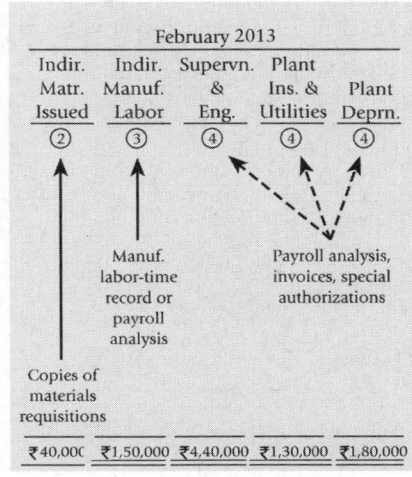
Total cost of all types of materials received in February, ₹8,90,000 Total cost of all types of materials issued in February, ₹8,50,000	Total cost of all direct and indirect manufacturing labor incurred in February, ₹5,40,000 (₹3,90,000 + ₹1,50,000)	Other manufacturing overhead costs incurred in February, ₹7,50,000

[1]The arrows show how the supporting documentation (for example, copies of materials requisition records) results in the journal entry number shown in circles (for example, journal entry number 2) that corresponds to the entries in Exhibit 4-7.

₹8,90,000 (Exhibit 4-8, Panel A). The cost of materials issued across all types of direct and indirect material records for February 2013 is ₹8,50,000 (Exhibit 4-8, Panel A)

As direct materials are used, they are recorded as issued in the Materials Records (see Exhibit 4-8, Panel A, for a record of the Metal Brackets issued for the Western Pulp and Paper [WPP] machine job). Direct materials are also charged to Work-in-Process inventory records for Jobs, which are the subsidiary ledger accounts for the Work-in-Process Control account in the general ledger. For example, the metal brackets used in the WPP machine job appear as direct material costs of ₹1,120 in the subsidiary ledger under the work-in-process inventory record for WPP 298 [Exhibit 4-9, Panel A, which is based on the job-cost record source document in Exhibit 4-2, (page 145)]. The cost of direct materials used across all job-cost records for February 2013 is ₹8,10,000 (Exhibit 4-9, Panel A).

As indirect materials (for example, lubricants) are used, they are charged to the Manufacturing Department overhead records (Exhibit 4-8, Panel C), which comprise the subsidiary ledger for Manufacturing Overhead Control account. The Manufacturing Department overhead records are used to accumulate actual costs in individual overhead categories by each indirect-cost-pool account in the general ledger. Recall that HEC has only one indirect-cost pool: Manufacturing Overhead. The cost of indirect materials used is not added directly to individual job records. Instead, the cost of these indirect materials is allocated to individual job records as a part of manufacturing overhead.

Exhibit 4-9   Subsidiary Ledger for Individual Jobs[1]

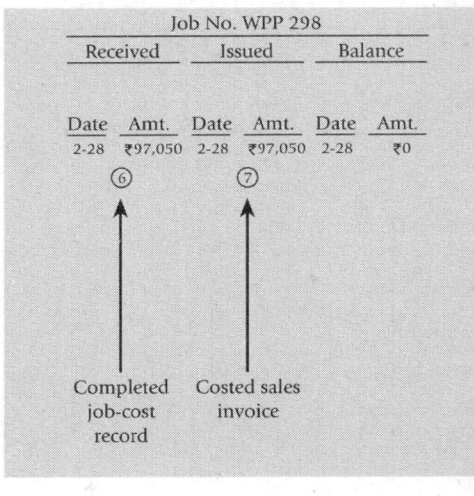

PANEL A: Work-in-Process Inventory Records by Jobs

Job No. WPP 298

		In-Process			Completed		Balance	
Date	Direct Materials	Direct Manuf. Labor	Allocated Manuf. Overhead	Total Cost	Date	Total Cost	Date	Total Cost
2-4	₹1,120			₹1,120				
2-10		₹4,500		₹4,500				
	•	•						
2-28	₹46,060	₹15,790	₹35,200	₹97,050	2-28	₹97,050	2-28	₹0
	②	③	⑤			⑥		

Copies of materials-requisition records ↑②

Copies of labor-time records ↑③

Budgeted rate × actual direct manuf. labor-hours ↑⑤

Completed job-cost record ↑⑥

Total cost of direct materials issued to all jobs in Feb., ₹8,10,000

Total cost of direct manuf. labor used on all jobs in Feb., ₹3,90,000

Total manuf. overhead allocated to all jobs in Feb., ₹8,00,000

Total cost of all jobs completed and transferred to finished goods in Feb., ₹18,88,000

PANEL B: Finished Goods Inventory Records by Job

Job No. WPP 298

Received		Issued		Balance	
Date	Amt.	Date	Amt.	Date	Amt.
2-28	₹97,050	2-28	₹97,050	2-28	₹0
	⑥		⑦		

Completed job-cost record ↑⑥

Costed sales invoice ↑⑦

Total cost of all jobs transferred to finished goods in Feb., ₹18,88,000

Total cost of all jobs sold and invoiced in Feb., ₹18,00,000

[1]The arrows show how the supporting documentation (for example, copies of materials requisition records) results in the journal entry number shown in circles (for example, journal entry number 2) that corresponds to the entries in Exhibit 4-7.

Labor Records by Employee Labor-time records (see Exhibit 4-8, Panel B for Ram Prasad are used to trace direct manufacturing labor to individual jobs and to accumulate the indirect manufacturing labor in Manufacturing Department overhead records (Exhibit 4-8, Panel C). The labor records are based on the labor-time sheet source documents (see Exhibit 4-3, Panel B, (page 146)). The subsidiary ledger for employee labor records (Exhibit 4-8, Panel B) shows the different jobs that Ram Prasad, Employee No. 551-87-3076 worked on and the ₹7,200 of wages owed to Prasad, for the week ending February 10. The sum of total wages owed to all employees for February 2013 is ₹40,000. The job-cost record for WPP 298 shows direct manufacturing labor costs of ₹4,500 for the time Prasad spent on the WPP machine job during that week (Exhibit 4-9, Panel A). Total direct manufacturing labor costs recorded in all job-cost records (the subsidiary ledger for Work-in-Process Control) for February 2013 is ₹3,90,000.

Ram Prasad's employee record shows ₹540 for maintenance, which is an indirect manufacturing labor cost. The total indirect manufacturing labor costs of ₹1,50,000 for February 2013 appear in the Manufacturing Department overhead records in the subsidiary ledger (Exhibit 4-8, Panel C). These costs, by definition, are not traced to an individual job. Instead, they are allocated to individual jobs as a part of manufacturing overhead.

Manufacturing Department Overhead Records by Month The Manufacturing Department overhead records (see Exhibit 4-8, Panel C) that make up the subsidiary ledger for Manufacturing Overhead Control show details of different categories of overhead costs such as indirect materials, indirect manufacturing labor, supervision and engineering, plant insurance and utilities, and plant depreciation. The source documents for these entries include invoices (for example, a utility bill) and special schedules (for example, a depreciation schedule) from the responsible accounting officer. Manufacturing department overhead for February 2013 is indirect materials, ₹40,000; indirect manufacturing labor, ₹1,50,000; and other manufacturing overhead, ₹7,50,000 (Exhibit 4-8, Panel C).

Work-in-Process Inventory Records by Jobs As we have already discussed, the job-cost record for each individual job in the subsidiary ledger is debited by the cost of direct materials and direct manufacturing labor used by individual jobs. In HEC's normal-costing system, the job-cost record for each individual job in the subsidiary ledger is also debited for manufacturing overhead allocated based on the budgeted manufacturing overhead rate times the actual direct manufacturing labor-hours used in that job. For example, the job-cost record for Job WPP 298 (Exhibit 4-9, Panel A) shows Manufacturing Overhead Allocated of ₹35,200 (budgeted rate of ₹400 per labor-hour × 88 actual direct manufacturing labor-hours used). For the 2,000 actual direct manufacturing labor-hours used for all jobs in February 2013, the total manufacturing overhead allocated equals ₹400 per labor-hour × 2,000 direct manufacturing labor-hours = ₹8,00,000.

Finished Goods Inventory Records by Jobs Exhibit 4-9, Panel A, shows that Job WPP 298 was completed at a cost of ₹97,050 Job WPP 298 also simultaneously appears in the finished goods records of the subsidiary ledger. The total cost of all jobs completed and transferred to finished goods in February 2013 is ₹18,88,000 (Exhibit 4-9, Panels A and B). Exhibit 4-9, Panel B, indicates that Job WPP 298 was sold and delivered to the customer on February 28, 2013, at which time ₹97,050 was transferred from finished goods to cost of goods sold. The total cost of all jobs sold and invoiced in February 2013 is ₹18,00,000 (Exhibit 4-9, Panel B).

Other Subsidiary Records Just as it does for manufacturing payroll, Hec maintains employee labor records in subsidiary ledgers for marketing and customer service payroll as well as records for different types of advertising costs (print, television, and radio). An accounts receivable subsidiary ledger is also used to record the February 2013 amounts due from each customer, including the ₹1,50,000 due from the sale of Job WPP 298.

Revenues		₹27,00,000
Cost of goods sold (₹18,00,000 + ₹1,40,000)		19,40,000
Gross margin		7,60,000
Operating costs		
Marketing costs	₹4,50,000	
Customer-service costs	1,50,000	
Total operating costs		6,00,000
Operating income		₹1,60,000

[1]Cost of goods sold has been increased by ₹1,40,000 the difference between the Manufacturing overhead control account (₹9,40,000) and the Manufacturing overhead allocated (₹8,00,000). In a later section of this chapter, we discuss this adjustment, which represents the amount by which actual manufacturing overhead cost exceeds the manufacturing overhead allocated to jobs during February 2013.

Exhibit 4-10

HEC Income Statement for the Month Ending February 2013

At this point, pause and review the nine entries in this example. Exhibit 4-7 is a handy summary of all nine general-ledger entries presented in T-account form. Be sure to trace each journal entry, step-by-step, to T-accounts in the general ledger presented in Exhibit 4-7.

HEC's managers will use this information to evaluate how HEC has performed on the WPP job.

Exhibit 4-10 provides HEC's income statement for February 2013 using information from entries 7, 8, and 9. Managers could further subdivide the cost of goods sold calculations and present them in the format of Exhibit 2-8 [(page 50)]. The benefit of using the subdivided format is that it allows managers to discern detailed performance trends that can help them improve the efficiency on future jobs.

Nonmanufacturing Costs and Job Costing

In Chapter 2 (pages 56–57), you learned that companies use product costs for different purposes. The product costs reported as inventoriable costs to shareholders may differ from the product costs reported to managers to guide their pricing and product-mix decisions. Managers must keep in mind that even though marketing and customer-service costs are expensed when incurred for financial accounting purposes, companies often trace or allocate these costs to individual jobs for pricing, product-mix, and cost-management decisions.

HEC can trace direct marketing costs and customer-service costs to jobs the same way in which it traces direct manufacturing costs to jobs. Assume these costs have the same cost-allocation base, revenues, and are included in a single cost pool. HEC can then calculate a budgeted indirect-cost rate by dividing budgeted indirect marketing costs plus budgeted indirect customer-service costs by budgeted revenues. HEC can use this rate to allocate these indirect costs to jobs. For example, if this rate were 15% of revenues, HEC would allocate ₹22,500 to Job WPP 298 (0.15 × ₹1,50,000, the revenue from the job). By assigning both manufacturing costs and nonmanufacturing costs to jobs, Hec can compare all costs against the revenues that different jobs generate.

Budgeted Indirect Costs and End-of-Accounting-Year Adjustments

Managers try to closely approximate actual manufacturing overhead costs and actual direct manufacturing labor-hours when calculating the budgeted indirect cost rate. However, for the numerator and denominator reasons explained earlier in the chapter, under normal costing, a company's actual overhead costs incurred each month are not likely to equal its overhead costs allocated each month. Even at the end of the year, allocated costs are unlikely to equal actual costs because they are based on estimates made up to 12 months before actual costs are incurred. We now describe adjustments that management accountants need to make when, at the end of the fiscal year, indirect costs allocated differ from actual indirect costs incurred. These adjustments affect the reported income numbers used to evaluate managerial performance.

Underallocated and Overallocated Indirect Costs

Underallocated indirect costs occur when the allocated amount of indirect costs in an accounting period is less than the actual (incurred) amount. **Overallocated indirect costs** occur when the allocated amount of indirect costs in an accounting period is greater than the actual (incurred) amount.

Underallocated (overallocated) indirect costs = Actual indirect costs incurred - Indirect costs allocated

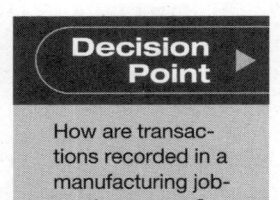

Decision Point

How are transactions recorded in a manufacturing job-costing system?

Learning Objective 7

Dispose of under- or overallocated manufacturing overhead costs at the end of the fiscal year using alternative methods

. . . for example, writing off this amount to the Cost of Goods Sold account

Underallocated (overallocated) indirect costs are also called **underapplied (overapplied) indirect costs** and **underabsorbed (overabsorbed) indirect costs**.

Consider the manufacturing overhead indirect-cost pool at Hec. There are two indirect-cost accounts in the general ledger that have to do with manufacturing overhead:

1. Manufacturing Overhead Control, the record of the actual costs in all the individual overhead categories (such as indirect materials, indirect manufacturing labor, supervision, engineering, utilities, and plant depreciation)

2. Manufacturing Overhead Allocated, the record of the manufacturing overhead allocated to individual jobs on the basis of the budgeted rate multiplied by actual direct manufacturing labor-hours

At the end of the year, the overhead accounts show the following amounts.

Manufacturing Overhead Control		Manufacturing Overhead Allocated	
Bal. Dec 31, 2011	1,21,50,000	Bal. Dec 31, 2011	1,08,00,000

The ₹1,08,00,000 credit balance in Manufacturing Overhead Allocated results from multiplying the 27,000 actual direct manufacturing labor-hours worked on all jobs in 2008 by the budgeted rate of ₹400 per direct manufacturing labor-hour.

The ₹13,50,000 difference (a net debit) is an underallocated amount because actual manufacturing overhead costs are greater than the allocated amount. This difference arises from two reasons related to the computation of the ₹400 budgeted hourly rate:

1. **Numerator reason (indirect-cost pool).** Actual manufacturing overhead costs of ₹1,21,50,000 are greater than the budgeted amount of ₹1,12,00,000.

2. **Denominator reason (quantity of allocation base).** Actual direct manufacturing labor-hours of 27,000 are fewer than the budgeted 28,000 hours.

There are three main approaches to accounting for the ₹13,50,000 underallocated manufacturing overhead caused by HEC underestimating manufacturing overhead costs and overestimating the quantity of the cost-allocation base: (1) adjusted allocation-rate approach, (2) proration approach, and (3) write-off to cost of goods sold approach.

Adjusted Allocation-Rate Approach

The **adjusted allocation-rate approach** restates all overhead entries in the general ledger and subsidiary ledgers using actual cost rates rather than budgeted cost rates. First, the actual manufacturing overhead rate is computed at the end of the fiscal year. Then, the manufacturing overhead costs allocated to every job during the year are recomputed using the actual manufacturing overhead rate (rather than the budgeted manufacturing overhead rate). Finally, end-of-year closing entries are made. The result is that at year-end, every job-cost record and finished goods record—as well as the ending Work-in-Process Control, Finished Goods Control, and Cost of Goods Sold accounts—represent actual manufacturing overhead costs incurred.

The widespread adoption of computerized accounting systems has greatly reduced the cost of using the adjusted allocation-rate approach. In our HEC example, the actual manufacturing overhead (₹1,21,50,000) exceeds the manufacturing overhead allocated (₹1,08,00,000) by 12.5% [(₹1,21,50,000 − ₹1,08,00,000) ÷ ₹1,08,00,000]. At year-end,

HEC could increase the manufacturing overhead allocated to each job in 2013 by 12.5% using a single software command. The command would adjust both the subsidiary ledgers and the general ledger.

Consider the Western Pulp and Paper machine job, WPP 298. Under normal costing, the manufacturing overhead allocated to the job is ₹35,200 (the budgeted rate of ₹400 per direct manufacturing labor-hour × 88 hours). Increasing the manufacturing overhead allocated by 12.5%, or ₹4,400 (₹35,200 × 0.125), means the adjusted amount of manufacturing overhead allocated to Job WPP 298 equals ₹39,600 (₹35,200 + ₹4,400). Note from page 149 that using actual costing, manufacturing overhead allocated to this job is also ₹39,600 (the actual rate of ₹450 per direct manufacturing labor-hour × 88 hours). Making this adjustment under normal costing for each job in the subsidiary ledgers ensures that all ₹1,21,50,000 of manufacturing overhead is allocated to jobs.

The adjusted allocation-rate approach yields the benefits of both the *timeliness and convenience of normal costing during the year and the allocation of actual manufacturing overhead costs at year-end.* Each individual job-cost record and the end-of-year account balances for inventories and cost of goods sold are adjusted to actual costs. These adjustments, in turn, will affect the income HEC reports. Knowing the actual profitability of individual jobs after they are completed provides managers with accurate and useful insights for future decisions about which jobs to undertake, how to price them, and how to manage their costs.

Proration Approach

The proration approach spreads underallocated overhead or overallocated overhead among ending work in process inventory, finished goods inventory, and cost of goods sold. Materials inventory is not included in this proration because no manufacturing overhead costs have been allocated to it. We illustrate end-of-year proration in the HEC Company example. Assume the following actual results for HEC Company in 2013:

	A	B	C
			Allocated Manufacturing Overhead Included in Each
1	Account	Account Balance (Before Proration)	Account Balance (Before Proration)
2	Work in process control	₹5,00,000	₹1,62,000
3	Finished goods control	7,50,000	3,13,200
4	Cost of goods sold	2,37,50,000	1,03,24,800
5		₹2,50,00,000	₹1,08,00,000

How should Hec prorate the underallocated ₹13,50,000 of manufacturing overhead at the end of 2013?

Hec prorates underallocated or overallocated amounts on the basis of the total amount of manufacturing overhead allocated in 2013 (before proration) in the ending balances of

	File	Edit	View	Insert	Format	Tools	Data	Window	Help			

	A	B	C	D	E	F	G
10		Account Balance (Before Proration)	Allocated Manufacturing Overhead Included in Each Account Balance (Before Proration)	Allocated Manufacturing Overhead Included in Each Account Balance as a Percent of Total	Proration of ₹13,50,000 of Underallocated Manufacturing Overhead		Account Balance (After Proration)
11	Account	(1)	(2)	(3) = (2) / ₹1,08,00,000	(4) = (3) x ₹13,50,000		(5) = (1) + (4)
12	Work in process control	₹5,00,000	₹1,62,000	1.5%	0.015 x ₹13,50,000 =	₹20,250	₹5,20,250
13	Finished goods control	7,50,000	3,13,200	2.9%	0.029 x 13,50,000 =	39,150	7,89,150
14	Cost of goods sold	2,37,50,000	1,03,24,800	95.6%	0.956 x 13,50,000 =	12,90,600	2,50,40,600
15	Total	₹2,50,00,000	₹1,08,00,000	100.0%		₹13,50,000	₹2,63,50,000

Work-in-Process Control, Finished Goods Control, and Cost of Goods Sold accounts. The ₹13,50,000 underallocated overhead is prorated over the three affected accounts in proportion to their total amount of manufacturing overhead allocated (before proration) in column 2 of the following table, resulting in the ending balances (after proration) in column 5 at actual costs.

Prorating on the basis of the manufacturing overhead allocated (before proration) results in allocating manufacturing overhead based on actual manufacturing overhead costs. Recall that HEC's actual manufacturing overhead (₹1,21,50,000) exceeds the manufacturing overhead allocated (₹1,08,00,000) in 2013 by 12.5%. The proration amounts in column 4 can also be derived by multiplying the balances in column 2 by 0.125. For example, the ₹39,150 proration to Finished Goods is 0.125 × ₹3,13,200. Adding these amounts effectively means allocating manufacturing overhead at 112.5% of what had been allocated before. The journal entry to record this proration is:

Work-in-Process Control	20,250	
Finished Goods Control	39,150	
Cost of Goods Sold	12,90,600	
Manufacturing Overhead Allocated	1,08,00,000	
Manufacturing Overhead Control		1,21,50,000

If manufacturing overhead had been overallocated, the Work-in-Process Control, Finished Goods Control, and Cost of Goods Sold accounts would be decreased (credited) instead of increased (debited).

This journal entry closes (brings to zero) the manufacturing overhead-related accounts and restates the 2013 ending balances for Work-in-Process Control, Finished Goods Control, and Cost of Goods Sold to what they would have been if actual manufacturing overhead rates had been used rather than budgeted manufacturing overhead rates. This method reports the same 2013 ending balances in the general ledger as the adjusted allocation-rate approach does. However, unlike the adjusted allocation-rate approach, the sum of the amounts shown in the subsidiary ledgers will not match the amounts shown in the general ledger after proration because no adjustments from budgeted to actual manufacturing overhead rates are made in the individual job-cost records. The objective of the proration approach is to only adjust the general ledger to actual manufacturing overhead rates for purposes of financial reporting. The increase in cost of goods sold expense by ₹12,90,600

	File Edit View Insert Format Tools Data Window Help					
	A	B	C	D	E	F
1		**Account Balance (Before Proration)**	**Account Balance as a Percent of Total**	**Proration of ₹13,50,000 of Underallocated Manufacturing Overhead**		**Account Balance (After Proration)**
2	**Account**	**(1)**	**(2) = (1) / ₹2,50,00,000**	**(3) = (2) x ₹13,50,000**		**(4) = (1) + (3)**
3	Work in process control	₹5,00,000	2.0%	0.02 x ₹13,50,000 =	₹27,000	₹5,27,000
4	Finished goods control	7,50,000	3.0%	0.03 x 13,50,000 =	40,500	7,90,500
5	Cost of goods sold	2,37,50,000	95.0%	0.95 x 13,50,000 =	12,82,500	2,50,32,500
6	Total	₹2,50,00,000	100.0%		₹13,50,000	₹2,63,50,000

as a result of the proration causes HEC's reported operating income to decrease by the same amount.

Some companies use the proration approach but base it on the ending balances of Work-in-Process Control, Finished Goods Control, and Cost of Goods Sold prior to proration (see column 1 of the preceding table). The following table shows that prorations based on ending account balances are not the same as the more-accurate prorations calculated earlier based on the amount of manufacturing overhead allocated to the accounts because the proportions of manufacturing overhead costs to total costs in these accounts are not the same.

However, proration based on ending balances is frequently justified as being an expedient way of approximating the more-accurate results from using indirect costs allocated.

Write-off to Cost of Goods Sold Approach

Under the write-off approach, the total under- or overallocated manufacturing overhead is included in this year's Cost of Goods Sold. For Hec, the journal entry would be:

Cost of Goods Sold	13,50,000	
Manufacturing Overhead Allocated	1,08,00,000	
Manufacturing Overhead Control		1,21,50,000

HEC's two Manufacturing Overhead accounts —Manufacturing Overhead Control and Manufacturing Overhead Allocated—are closed with the difference between them included in cost of goods sold. The Cost of Goods Sold account after the write-off equals ₹2,51,00,000, the balance before the write-off of ₹2,37,50,000 *plus the underallocated* manufacturing overhead amount of ₹13,50,000. This results in operating income decreasing by ₹1,35,000.

Choice Among Approaches

Which of the three approaches of dealing with underallocated overhead and overallocated overhead is the best one to use? When making this decision, managers should consider the amount of underallocated or overallocated overhead and the purpose of the adjustment, as the following table indicates.

If the purpose of the adjustment is to . . .	and the total amount of underallocation or overallocation is . . .	then managers prefer to use the . . .
state the balance sheet and income statements based on actual rather than budgeted manufacturing overhead rates	big, relative to total operating income, and inventory levels are high	proration method because it is the most accurate method of allocating actual manufacturing overhead costs to the general ledger accounts.
state the balance sheet and income statements based on actual rather than budgeted manufacturing overhead rates	small, relative to total operating income, or inventory levels are low	writeoff to cost of goods sold approach because it is a good approximation of the more accurate proration method.
provide an accurate record of actual individual job costs in order to conduct a profitability analysis, learn how to better manage the costs of jobs, and bid on future jobs	big, relative to total operating income,	adjusted-allocation rate method because it makes adjustments in individual job records in addition to the general ledger accounts.

Many management accountants and managers argue that to the extent that the underallocated overhead cost measures inefficiency during the period, it should be written off to the Cost of Goods Sold account instead of being prorated to the Work-in-Process or Finished Goods inventory accounts. This line of reasoning favors applying a combination of the writeoff and proration methods. For example, the portion of the underallocated overhead cost that is due to inefficiency (say, because of excessive spending or idle capacity) and that could have been avoided should be written off to the Cost of Goods Sold account, whereas the portion that is unavoidable should be prorated. Unlike full proration, this approach avoids making the costs of inefficiency part of inventory assets.

As our discussion suggests, choosing which method to use and determining the amount to be written off is often a matter of judgment. The method managers choose affects the operating income a company reports. In the case of underallocated overhead, the method of writing it off to cost of goods sold results in lower operating income compared to proration. In the case of overallocated overhead, proration results in lower operating income compared to writing the overhead off to cost of goods sold. Reporting lower operating income lowers the company's taxes, saving the company cash and increasing the company's value. Reporting higher operating income, however, can increase the compensation managers earn even though it results in higher taxes for the company. Top managers design compensation plans to encourage managers to take actions that increase a company's value. For example, the compensation plan might reward the managers for after-tax cash flow metrics, in addition to achieving various levels of operating income, to align decision making and performance evaluation. Occasionally, if a company is experiencing financial difficulty, its managers may prefer to report higher operating income to avoid showing losses that could affect the firm's credit rating and result in its loans being called. In general, however, managers should choose the method that increases the company's value and best represents its performance, while consistently applying the same method year after year. At no time should managers make choices that are illegal or unethical. We discuss these issues in more detail in another chapter (Chapter 23).

HEC's managers believed that a single manufacturing overhead cost pool with direct manufacturing labor-hours as the cost-allocation base was appropriate for allocating all

Decision Point

How should managers dispose of under- or overallocated manufacturing overhead costs at the end of the accounting year?

manufacturing overhead costs to jobs. Had Robinson's managers felt that different manufacturing departments (for example, machining and assembly) used overhead resources differently, they would have assigned overhead costs to each department and calculated a separate overhead allocation rate for each department based on the cost driver of the overhead costs in each department. The general ledger would contain Manufacturing Overhead Control and Manufacturing Overhead Allocated accounts for each department, resulting in end-of-year adjustments for underallocated or overallocated overhead costs for each department.

Instructors and students interested in exploring these more detailed allocations can go to Chapter 15, where we continue the HEC example.

Variations from Normal Costing: A Service-Sector Example

Job costing is also very useful in service organizations such as accounting and consulting firms, advertising agencies, auto repair shops, and hospitals. In an accounting firm, each audit is a job. The costs of each audit are accumulated in a job-cost record, much like the document used by Hec, based on the seven-step approach described earlier. On the basis of labor-time sheets, direct labor costs of the professional staff—audit partners, audit managers, and audit staff—are traced to individual jobs. Other direct costs such as travel, out-of-town meals and lodging, phone, fax, and copying are also traced to jobs. The costs of secretarial support, office staff, rent, and depreciation of furniture and equipment are indirect costs because these costs cannot be traced to jobs in an economically feasible way. Indirect costs are allocated to jobs, for example, using a cost-allocation base such as number of professional labor-hours.

In some service organizations, a variation from normal costing is helpful because actual direct-labor costs—the largest component of total costs—can be difficult to trace to jobs as they are completed. For example, in our audit illustration, the actual direct-labor costs may include bonuses that become known only at the end of the year (a numerator reason). Also, the hours worked each period might vary significantly depending on the number of working days each month and the demand for services (a denominator reason) while the direct-labor costs remain largely fixed. It would be inappropriate to charge a job with higher actual direct labor costs simply because a month had fewer working days or demand for services was low in that month. Using budgeted rates gives a better picture of the direct labor cost per hour that the company had planned when it hired the workers. In situations like these, a company needing timely information during the progress of an audit (and not wanting to wait until the end of the fiscal year) will use budgeted rates for some direct costs and budgeted rates for indirect costs. All budgeted rates are calculated at the start of the fiscal year. In contrast, normal costing uses actual cost rates for all direct costs and budgeted cost rates only for indirect costs.

The mechanics of using budgeted rates for direct costs are similar to the methods employed when using budgeted rates for indirect costs in normal costing. We illustrate this for Batliboi & Co, a public accounting firm. For 2013, Batliboi budgets total direct-labor costs of ₹14,40,00,000, total indirect costs of ₹12,96,00,000, and total direct (professional) labor-hours of 288,000. In this case,

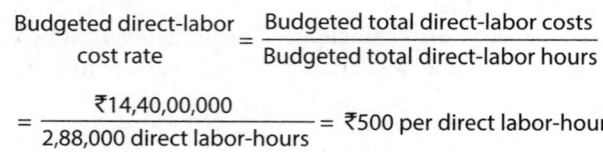

$$\frac{\text{Budgeted direct-labor}}{\text{cost rate}} = \frac{\text{Budgeted total direct-labor costs}}{\text{Budgeted total direct-labor hours}}$$

$$= \frac{₹14,40,00,000}{2,88,000 \text{ direct labor-hours}} = ₹500 \text{ per direct labor-hour}$$

Assuming only one indirect-cost pool and total direct-labor costs as the cost-allocation base,

$$\frac{\text{Budgeted indirect}}{\text{cost rate}} = \frac{\text{Budgeted total costs in indirect cost pool}}{\text{Budgeted total quantity of cost-allocation base (direct-labor costs)}}$$

$$= \frac{₹12,96,00,000}{₹14,40,00,000} = 0.90, \text{ or } 90\% \text{ of direct-labor costs}$$

Suppose that in March 2013, an audit of Tracy Transport, a client of Batliboi, uses 800 direct labor-hours. Batliboi calculates the direct-labor costs of the Jaipur Golden Transport audit by multiplying the budgeted direct-labor cost rate, ₹500 per direct labor-hour, by 800, the actual quantity of direct labor-hours. The indirect costs allocated to the Jaipur Golden Transport audit are determined by multiplying the budgeted indirect-cost rate (90%) by the direct-labor costs assigned to the job (₹4,00,000). Assuming no other direct costs for travel and the like, the cost of the Jaipur Golden Transport audit is:

Direct-labor costs, ₹500 × 800	₹4,00,000
Indirect costs allocated, 90% × ₹4,00,000	3,60,000
Total	₹7,60,000

At the end of the fiscal year, the direct costs traced to jobs using budgeted rates will generally not equal actual direct costs because the actual rate and the budgeted rate are developed at different times using different information. End-of-year adjustments for under- or overallocated direct costs would need to be made in the same way that adjustments are made for under- or overallocated indirect costs.

The Batliboi & Co example illustrates that all costing systems do not exactly match either the actual-costing system or the normal-costing system described earlier in the chapter. As another example, engineering consulting firms such as Tata Consulting services (TCS) often use budgeted rates to allocate indirect costs (such as engineering and office-support costs) as well as some direct costs (such as professional labor-hours) and trace some actual direct costs (such as the cost of making blueprints and fees paid to outside experts). Users of costing systems should be aware of the different systems that they may encounter.

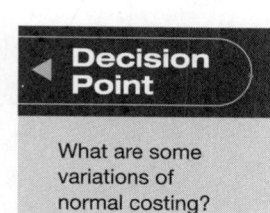

Decision Point

What are some variations of normal costing?

Problem for Self-Study

Your manager asks you bring the following incomplete accounts of Thomson Press Ltd., up-to-date through January 31, 2014. Consider the data that appear in the T-accounts as well as the following information in items (a) through (j).

Thomson's normal-costing system has two direct-cost categories (direct material costs and direct manufacturing labor costs) and one indirect-cost pool (manufacturing overhead costs, which are allocated using direct manufacturing labor costs).

Materials Control

12-31-2013 Bal.	1,50,000

Work-in-Process Control

Finished Goods Control

12-31-2013 Bal.	2,00,000

Wages Payable Control

1-31-2014 Bal.	30,000

Manufacturing Overhead Control

1-31-2014 Bal.	5,70,000

Costs of Goods Sold

Additional Information:

a. Manufacturing overhead is allocated using a budgeted rate that is set every December. Management forecasts next year's manufacturing overhead costs and next year's direct manufacturing labor costs. The budget for 2014 is ₹60,00,000 for manufacturing overhead costs and ₹40,00,000 for direct manufacturing labor costs.

b. The only job unfinished on January 31, 2014, is No. 419, on which direct manufacturing labor costs are ₹20,000 (125 direct manufacturing labor-hours) and direct material costs are ₹80,000.

c. Total direct materials issued to production during January 2014 are ₹9,00,000.

d. Cost of goods completed during January is ₹18,00,000.

e. Materials inventory as of January 31, 2014, is ₹2,00,000.

f. Finished goods inventory as of January 31, 2014, is ₹1,50,000.

g. All plant workers earn the same wage rate. Direct manufacturing labor-hours used for January total 2,500 hours. Other labor costs total ₹1,00,000.

h. The gross plant payroll paid in January equals ₹5,20,000. Ignore withholdings.

i. All "actual" manufacturing overhead incurred during January has already been posted.

j. All materials are direct materials.

Required   **Calculate:**

1. Materials purchased during January
2. Cost of Goods Sold during January
3. Direct manufacturing labor costs incurred during January
4. Manufacturing Overhead Allocated during January
5. Balance, Wages Payable Control, December 31, 2013
6. Balance, Work-in-Process Control, January 31, 2014
7. Balance, Work-in-Process Control, December 31, 2013
8. Manufacturing Overhead Underallocated or Overallocated for January 2014

Solution

Amounts from the T-accounts are labeled "(T)"

1. From Materials Control T-account, Materials purchased: ₹9,00,000 (c) + ₹2,00,000 (e) − ₹1,50,000 (T) = ₹9,50,000

2. From Finished Goods Control T-account, Cost of Goods Sold: ₹2,00,000 (T) + ₹18,00,000 (d) − ₹1,50,000 (f) = ₹18,50,000

3. Direct manufacturing wage rate: ₹20,000 (b) ÷ 125 direct manufacturing labor-hours (b) = ₹160 per direct manufacturing labor-hour
   Direct manufacturing labor costs: 2,500 direct manufacturing labor-hours (g) × ₹160 per hour = ₹4,00,000

4. Manufacturing overhead rate: ₹60,00,000 (a) × ₹40,00,000 (a) = 150%
   Manufacturing Overhead Allocated: 150% of ₹4,00,000 = 1.50 × ₹4,00,000 (see 3) × ₹6,00,000

5. From Wages Payable Control T-account, Wages Payable Control, December 31, 2011: ₹5,20,000 (h) + ₹30,000 (T) − ₹4,00,000 (see 3) − ₹1,00,000 (g) = ₹50,000

6. Work-in-Process Control, January 31, 2012: ₹80,000 (b) + ₹20,000 (b) + 150% of ₹20,000 (b) = ₹1,30,000 (This answer is used in item 7.)

7. From Work-in-Process Control T-account, Work-in-Process Control, December 31, 2011: ₹18,00,000 (d) + ₹1,30,000 (see 6) − ₹9,00,000 (c) − ₹4,00,000 (see 3) − ₹6,00,000 (see 4) = ₹30,000

8. Manufacturing overhead overallocated: ₹6,00,000 (see 4) + ₹5,70,000 (T) = ₹30,000.

Letters alongside entries in T-accounts correspond to letters in the preceding additional information. Numbers alongside entries in T-accounts correspond to numbers in the requirements above.

Materials Control

December 31,2013 Bal.	(given)	1,50,000			
	(1)	9,50,000[1]	(c)	9,00,000
January 31, 2014 Bal.	(e)	2,00,000			

[1] Can be computed only after all other postings in the account have been found.

Work-in-Process Control

December 31, 2013 Bal.	(7)	30,000	(d) 18,00,000	
Direct materials	(c)	9,00,000		
Direct manufacturing labor(b) (g)	(3)	4,00,000		
Manufacturing overhead allocated	(3) (a) (4)	6,00,000		
January 31, 2014 Bal.	(b) (6)	1,30,000		

Finished Goods Control

December 31, 2013 Bal.	(given)	2,00,000	(2) 18,50,000	
	(d)	18,00,000		
January 31, 2014 Bal.	(f)	1,50,000		

Wages Payable Control

	(h)	5,20,000	December 31,2013 Bal.	(5)	50,000
			(g) (3)	4,00,000
			(g)	1,00,000
			January 31, 2014	(given)	30,000

Manufacturing Overhead Control

Total January charges	(given)	5,70,000	

Manufacturing Overhead Allocated

		(3) (a) (4)	6,00,000

Cost of Goods Sold

(d) (f) (2)	18,50,000	

Decision Points

The following question-and-answer format summarizes the chapter's learning objectives. Each decision presents a key question related to a learning objective. The guidelines are the answer to that question.

Decision	Guidelines
1. What are the building-block concepts of a costing system?	The building-block concepts of a costing system are cost object, direct costs of a cost object, indirect costs of a cost object, cost pool, and cost-allocation base. Costing-system overview diagrams represent these concepts in a systematic way. Costing systems aim to report cost numbers that reflect the way chosen cost objects (such as products or services) use the resources of an organization.
2. How do you distinguish job costing from process costing?	Job-costing systems assign costs to distinct units of a product or service. Process-costing systems assign costs to masses of identical or similar units and compute unit costs on an average basis. These two costing systems represent opposite ends of a continuum. The costing systems of many companies combine some elements of both job costing and process costing.
3. What is the main challenge of implementing job-costing systems?	The main challenge of implementing job-costing systems is estimating actual costs of jobs in a timely manner.
4. How do you implement a job-costing system?	A general seven-step approach to job costing requires identifying (1) the job, (2) the direct-cost categories, (3) the cost-allocation bases, (4) the indirect-cost categories, (5) the cost-allocation rates, (6) the allocated indirect costs of a job, and (7) the total direct and indirect costs of a job.
5. How do you distinguish actual costing from normal costing?	Actual costing and normal costing differ in the type of indirect-cost rates used:

	Actual Costing	**Normal Costing**
Direct-cost rates	Actual rates	Actual rates
Indirect-cost rates	Actual rates	Budgeted rates

Both systems use actual quantities of inputs for tracing direct costs and actual quantities of the allocation bases for allocating indirect costs.

Decision	Guidelines
6. How are transactions recorded in a manufacturing job-costing system?	A job-costing system in manufacturing records the flow of inventoriable costs: (a) acquisition of materials and other manufacturing inputs; (b) their conversion into work in process; (c) their conversion into finished goods; and (d) the sale of finished goods. The job costing system also expenses period costs such as marketing costs as these costs are incurred.

7. How should you dispose of under- or overallocated manufacturing overhead costs at the end of the fiscal year?

The two theoretically correct approaches to disposing of under- or overallocated manufacturing overhead costs at the end of the fiscal year are (1) to adjust the allocation rate and (2) to prorate on the basis of the total amount of the allocated manufacturing overhead cost in the ending balances of Work-in-Process Control, Finished Goods Control, and Cost of Goods Sold. Many companies, however, simply write off amounts of under- or overallocated manufacturing overhead to Cost of Goods Sold when amounts are immaterial.

8. What are some variations of normal costing?

In some variations from normal costing, organizations use budgeted rates to assign direct costs, as well as indirect costs, to jobs.

TERMS TO LEARN

This chapter and the Glossary at the end of the book contain definitions of the following important terms:

actual costing **(p. 149)**
actual indirect-cost
  rate **(p. 150)**
adjusted allocation-rate
  approach **(p. 159)**
budgeted indirect-cost
  rate **(p. 144, 147)**
cost-allocation
  base **(p. 139)**
cost-application
  base **(p. 139)**
cost pool **(p. 139)**
job **(p. 140)**
job-cost record **(p. 144)**

job-cost sheet **(p. 144)**
job-costing
  |system **(p. 140)**
labor-time
  record **(p. 146)**
manufacturing overhead
  applied **(p. 153)**
materials-requisition
  record **(p. 145)**
normal costing **(p. 144)**
overabsorbed indirect
  costs **(p. 159)**
overallocated indirect
  costs **(p. 158)**

overapplied indirect
  costs **(p. 159)**
process-costing
  system **(p. 140)**
proration **(p. 160)**
source
  document **(p. 144)**
underabsorbed indirect
  costs **(p. 159)**
underallocated indirect
  costs **(p. 158)**
underapplied indirect
  costs **(p. 159)**

ASSIGNMENT MATERIAL

Questions

4-1 Define cost pool, cost tracing, cost allocation, and cost-allocation base.

4-2 How does a job-costing system differ from a process-costing system?

4-3 Why might an advertising agency use job costing for an advertising campaign by Pepsi, whereas a bank might use process costing to determine the cost of checking account deposits?

4-4 Describe the seven steps in job costing.

4-5 What are the two major cost objects that managers focus on in companies using job costing?

4-6 Describe three major source documents used in job-costing systems.

4-7 What is the main concern about source documents used to prepare job-cost records?

4-8 Give two reasons why most organizations use an annual period rather than a weekly or monthly period to compute budgeted indirect-cost rates.

4-9 Distinguish between actual costing and normal costing.

4-10 Describe two ways in which a house construction company may use job-cost information.

4-11 Comment on the following statement: "In a normal-costing system, the amounts in the Manufacturing Overhead Control account will always equal the amounts in the Manufacturing Overhead Allocated account."

4-12 Describe three different debit entries to the Work-in-Process Control T-account under normal costing.

4-13 Describe three alternative ways to dispose of under- or overallocated overhead costs.

4-14 When might a company use budgeted costs rather than actual costs to compute direct-labor rates?

4-15 Describe briefly why modern technology such as Electronic Data Interchange (EDI) is helpful to managers.

Solved Examples

4-16 **Job order costing, process costing**. In each of the following situations, determine whether job-costing or process costing would be more appropriate.

a. ACA firm	**l.** A software company
b. An oil refinery	**m.** A cola-drink-concentrate producer
c. A custom furniture manufacturer	**n.** A movie studio
d. A tyre manufacturer	**o.** A law firm
e. A textbook publisher	**p.** A commercial aircraft manufacturer
f. A pharmaceutical company	**q.** A management consulting firm
g. An advertising agency	**r.** A biscuit manufacturing
h. An apparel manufacturing plant	**s.** A catering service
i. A flour mill	**t.** A paper mill
j. A paint manufacturer	**u.** An auto repair garage
k. A hospital	

Solution

a.	Job Costing	**l.**	Job Costing
b.	Process Costing	**m.**	Process Costing
c.	Job Costing	**n.**	Job Costing
d.	Process Costing	**o.**	Job Costing
e.	Job Costing	**p.**	Job Costing
f.	Process Costing	**q.**	Job Costing
g.	Job Costing	**r.**	Process Costing
h.	Job Costing (but some process costing)	**s.**	Job Costing
i.	Process Costing	**t.**	Process Costing
j.	Process Costing	**u.**	Job Costing
k.	Job Costing		

4-17 Time period used to compute indirect cost rates. Plunge Manufacturing produces outdoor wading and slide pools. The company uses a normal-costing system and allocates manufacturing overhead on the basis of direct manufacturing labor-hours. Most of the company's production and sales occur in the first and second quarters of the year. The company is in danger of losing one of its larger customers, Royal Industries, due to large fluctuations in price. The owner of Plunge has requested an analysis of the manufacturing cost per unit in the second and third quarters. You have been provided the following budgeted information for the coming year:

	Quarter			
	1	2	3	4
Pools manufactured and sold	565	490	245	100

It takes 1 direct manufacturing labor-hour to make each pool. The actual direct material cost is ₹140 per pool. The actual direct manufacturing labor rate is ₹200 per hour. The budgeted variable manufacturing overhead rate is ₹150 per direct manufacturing labor-hour. Budgeted fixed manufacturing overhead costs are ₹1,22,500 each quarter.

Required

1. Calculate the total manufacturing cost per unit for the second and third quarters assuming the company allocates manufacturing overhead costs based on the budgeted manufacturing overhead rate determined for each quarter.

2. Calculate the total manufacturing cost per unit for the second and third quarters assuming the company allocates manufacturing overhead costs based on an annual budgeted manufacturing overhead rate.

3. Plunge Manufacturing prices its pools at manufacturing cost plus 30%. Why might Royal Industries be seeing large fluctuations in the prices of pools? Which of the methods described in requirements 1 and 2 would you recommend Plunge use? Explain.

Solution

1.

	Quarter				
	1	2	3	4	Annual
(1) Pools sold	565	490	245	100	1,400
(2) Direct manufacturing labor hours (1 × Row 1)	565	490	245	100	1,400
(3) Fixed manufacturing overhead costs	₹1,22,500	₹1,22,500	₹1,22,500	₹1,22,500	₹4,90,000
(4) Budgeted fixed manufacturing overhead rate per direct manufacturing labor hour (₹1,22,500 ÷ Row 2)	₹216.80	₹250	₹500	₹1,225	₹350

	Budgeted Costs Based on Quarterly Manufacturing Overhead Rate	
	2nd Quarter	3rd Quarter
Direct material costs (₹140 × 490 pools; 245 pools)	₹68,600	₹34,300
Direct manufacturing labor costs (₹200 × 490 hours; 245 hours)	98,000	49,000
Variable manufacturing overhead costs (₹150 × 490 hours; 245 hours)	73,500	36,750
Fixed manufacturing overhead costs (₹250 × 490 hours; ₹500 × 245 hours)	1,22,500	1,22,500

Total manufacturing costs	₹3,62,600	₹2,42,550
Divided by pools manufactured each quarter	÷ 490	÷ 245
Manufacturing cost per pool	₹740	₹990

2.

	Budgeted Costs Based on Annual Manufacturing Overhead Rate	
	2nd Quarter	**3rd Quarter**
Direct material costs (₹140×490 pools; 245 pools)	₹68,600	₹34,300
Direct manufacturing labor costs (₹200×490 hours; 245 hours)	98,000	49,000
Variable manufacturing overhead costs (₹150 × 490 hours; 245 hours)	73,500	36,750
Fixed manufacturing overhead costs (₹350×490 hours; 75 hours)	1,71,500	85,750
Total manufacturing costs	₹4,11,600	₹2,05,800
Divided by pools manufactured each quarter	÷ 490	÷ 245
Manufacturing cost per pool	₹840	₹840

3.

	2nd Quarter	3rd Quarter
Prices based on quarterly budgeted manufacturing overhead rates calculated in requirement 1 (₹740×130%; ₹990×130%)	₹962	₹1,287
Price based on annual budgeted manufacturing overhead rates calculated in requirement 2 (₹840×130%; ₹840×130%)	₹1,092	₹1,092

Royal might be seeing large fluctuations in the prices of its pools because Plunge is determining budgeted manufacturing overhead rates on a quarterly rather than an annual basis. Plunge should use the budgeted annual manufacturing overhead rate because capacity decisions are based on longer annual periods rather than quarterly periods. Prices should not vary based on quarterly fluctuations in production. Plunge could vary prices based on market conditions and demand for its pools. In this case, Plunge would charge higher prices in quarter 2 when demand for its pools is high. Pricing based on quarterly budgets would cause Plunge to do the opposite—to decrease rather than increase prices!

4-18 Accounting for manufacturing overhead. Ratan Woodworking uses normal costing and allocates manufacturing overhead to jobs based on a budgeted labor-hour rate and actual direct labor-hours. Under- or overallocated overhead, if immaterial, is written off to Cost of Goods Sold. During 2015, Ratan recorded the following:

Budgeted manufacturing overhead costs	₹44,00,000
Budgeted direct labor-hours	20,000
Actual manufacturing overhead costs	₹46,50,000
Actual direct labor-hours	21,200

Required

1. Compute the budgeted manufacturing overhead rate.
2. Prepare the summary journal entry to record the allocation of manufacturing overhead.
3. Compute the amount of under- or overallocated manufacturing overhead. Is the amount significant enough to warrant proration of overhead costs, or would it be permissible to write it off to cost of goods sold? Prepare the journal entry to dispose of the under- or overallocated overhead.

Solution

1. Budgeted manufacturing overhead rate = $\dfrac{₹44,00,000}{20,000 \text{ labor} - \text{hours}}$

= ₹220 per direct labor-hour

2. Work-in-Process Control   46,64,000

     Manufacturing Overhead Allocated   46,64,000

  (21,200 direct labor-hours × ₹220 per direct labor-hour = ₹46,64,000)

3. ₹46,50,000 – ₹46,64,000 = ₹14,000 overallocated, an insignificant amount of difference compared to manufacturing overhead costs allocated ₹14,000 ÷ ₹46,64,000 = 0.3%. If the quantities of work-in-process and finished goods inventories are small, the difference between proration and write off to Cost of Goods Sold account would be very small compared to net income.

  Manufacturing Overhead Allocated   ₹46,64,000

     Manufacturing Department Overhead Control   ₹46,50,000

     Cost of Goods Sold   ₹14,000

4-19 Journal entries, T-accounts, and source documents. Bajaj produces gadgets for the coveted small appliance market. The following data reflect activity for the year 2016:

Costs incurred:

Purchases of direct materials (net) on credit	₹122,000
Purchases of direct materials (net) on credit	₹1,22,000
Direct manufacturing labor cost	83,000
Indirect labor	54,000
Depreciation, factory equipment	32,000
Depreciation, office equipment	7,900
Maintenance, factory equipment	29,000
Miscellaneous factory overhead	9,900
Rent, factory building	78,000
Advertising expense	94,000
Sales commissions	33,000

Inventories:

	January 1, 2016	December 31, 2016
Direct materials	₹9,800	₹13,000
Work in process	6,300	23,000
Finished goods	68,000	27,000

The Company uses a normal-costing system and allocates overhead to work in process at a rate of 2.6 times direct manufacturing labor cost. Indirect materials are insignificant so there is no inventory account for indirect materials.

Required

1. Prepare journal entries to record the transactions for 2016 including an entry to close out over- or underallocated overhead to cost of goods sold. For each journal entry indicate the source document that would be used to authorize each entry. Also note which subsidiary ledger, if any, should be referenced as backup for the entry.

2. Post the journal entries to T-accounts for all of the inventories, Cost of Goods Sold, the Manufacturing Overhead Control Account, and the Manufacturing Overhead Allocated Account.

Solution

1.

i. Direct Materials Control   ₹1,22,000
    Accounts Payable Control   ₹1,22,000
Source Document: Purchase Invoice, Receiving Report
Subsidiary Ledger: Direct Materials Record, Accounts Payable

ii. Work in Process Controla   ₹1,18,800
    Direct Materials Control   ₹1,18,800
Source Document: Material Requisition Records, Job Cost Record
Subsidiary Ledger: Direct Materials Record, Work-in-Process Inventory Records by Jobs

iii. Work in Process Control   ₹83,000
Manufacturing Overhead Control   ₹54,000
    Wages Payable Control   ₹1,37,000
Source Document: Labor Time Sheets, Job Cost Records
Subsidiary Ledger: Manufacturing Overhead Records, Employee Labor Records, Work-in-Process Inventory Records by Jobs

iv. Manufacturing Overhead Control   ₹1,48,900
    Salaries Payable Control   ₹29,000
    Accounts Payable Control   9,900
    Accumulated Depreciation Control   32,000
    Rent Payable Control   78,000
Source Document: Depreciation Schedule, Rent Schedule, Maintenance wages due, Invoices for miscellaneous factory overhead items
Subsidiary Ledger: Manufacturing Overhead Records

v. Work in Process Control   ₹2,15,800
    Manufacturing Overhead Allocated   ₹2,15,800
    (₹83,000 × 2.60)
Source Document: Labor Time Sheets, Job Cost Record
Subsidiary Ledger: Work-in-Process Inventory Records by Jobs

vi. Finished Goods Controlb   ₹4,00,900
    Work in Process Control   ₹4,00,900
Source Document: Job Cost Record, Completed Job Cost Record
Subsidiary Ledger: Work-in-Process Inventory Records by Jobs, Finished Goods Inventory Records by Jobs

vii. Cost of Goods Soldc   ₹4,41,900
    Finished Goods Control   ₹4,41,900

Source Document: Sales Invoice, Completed Job Cost Record
Subsidiary Ledger: Finished Goods Inventory Records by Jobs

viii. Manufacturing Overhead Allocated	₹2,15,800	
Manufacturing Overhead Control (₹54,000 + ₹148,900)		₹2,02,900
Cost of Goods Sold		12,900

Source Document: Prior Journal Entries

ix. Administrative Expenses	₹7,900	
Marketing Expenses	1,27,000	
Salaries Payable Control		₹33,000
Accounts Payable Control		94,000
Accumulated Depreciation, Office Equipment		7,900

Source Document: Depreciation Schedule, Marketing Payroll Request, Invoice for Advertising, Sales Commission Schedule.

Subsidiary Ledger: Employee Salary Records, Administration Cost Records, Marketing Cost Records.

[a] $\text{Materials used} = \text{Beginning direct materials inventory} + \text{Purchases} - \text{Ending direct materials inventory}$

$$= ₹9,800 + ₹1,22,000 - ₹13,000 = ₹1,18,800$$

[b] $\text{Cost of goods manufactured} = \text{Beginning WIP inventory} + \text{Manufacturing cost} - \text{Ending WIP inventory}$

$$= ₹6,300 + (₹1,18,800 + ₹83,000 + ₹2,15,800) - ₹23,000 = ₹4,00,900$$

[c] $\text{Cost of goods sold} = \text{Beginning finished goods inventory} + \text{Cost of goods manufactured} - \text{Ending finished goods inventory}$

$$= ₹68,000 + ₹4,00,900 - ₹27,000 = ₹4,41,900$$

1. T-accounts

Direct Materials Control

Bal. 1/1/2014	₹9,800	(2) Work-in-Process Control (Materials used)	₹1,18,800
(1) Accounts Payable Control (Purchases)	1,22,000		
Bal. 12/31/2014	13,000		

Work-in-Process Control

Bal. 1/1/2014	₹6,300	(6) Finished Goods Control (Cost of goods manufactured)	₹4,00,900
(2) Materials Control (Direct materials used)	1,18,800		
(3) Wages Payable Control (Direct manuf. labor)	83,000		
(5) Manuf. Overhead Allocated	2,15,800		
Bal. 12/31/2014	23,000		

Finished Goods Control

Bal. 1/1/2014	₹68,000	(7) Cost of Goods Sold	₹4,41,900
(6) WIP Control(Cost of goods manuf.)	4,00,900		
Bal. 12/31/2014	₹27,000		

Cost of Goods Sold

(7) Finished Goods Control (Goods sold)	₹4,41,900	(8) Manufacturing Overhead Allocated (Adjust for over-allocation)	₹12,900

Manufacturing Overhead Control

(3) Wages Payable Control (Indirect manuf. labor)	₹54,000	(8) To close	₹2,02,900
(4) Salaries Payable Control (Maintenance)	29,000		
(4) Accounts Payable Control (Miscellaneous)	9,900		
(4) Accum. Deprn. Control (Depreciation)	32,000		
(4) Rent Payable Control (Rent)			
	78,000		
Bal.	0		

Manufacturing Overhead Allocated

(8) To close	₹2,15,800	(5) Work-in-Process Control (Manuf. overhead allocated)	₹2,15,800
		Bal.	0

4-20 Job costing, journal entries. Container Transport assembles prestige manufactured homes. Its job-costing system has two direct-cost categories (direct materials and direct manufacturing labor) and one indirect-cost pool (manufacturing overhead allocated at a budgeted ₹310 per machine-hour in 2016). The following data (in lakh of rupees) show operation costs for 2016:

Materials Control, beginning balance, January 1, 2016	₹180
Work-in-Process Control, beginning balance, January 1, 2016	90
Finished Goods Control, beginning balance, January 1, 2016	100
Materials and supplies purchased on credit	1,540
Direct materials used	1,520
Indirect materials (supplies) issued to various production departments	190
Direct manufacturing labor	960
Indirect manufacturing labor incurred by various production departments	340
Depreciation on plant and manufacturing equipment	280
Miscellaneous manufacturing overhead incurred (ordinarily would be detailed as repairs, utilities, etc., with a corresponding credit to various liability accounts)	130
Manufacturing overhead allocated, 3,00,000 actual machine-hours	?
Cost of goods manufactured	2,980
Revenues	4,100
Cost of goods sold	2,940

1. Prepare an overview diagram of Container Transport's job-costing system.
2. Prepare journal entries. Number your entries. Explanations for each entry may be omitted. Post to T-accounts. What is the ending balance of Work-in-Process Control?
3. Show the journal entry for disposing of under- or overallocated manufacturing overhead directly as a year-end writeoff to Cost of Goods Sold. Post the entry to T-accounts.
4. How did Container Transport perform in 2016?

Solution

Some instructors may wish to assign Problem 4-25. It demonstrates the relationships of journal entries, general ledger, subsidiary ledgers, and source documents.

1. An overview of the product-costing system is

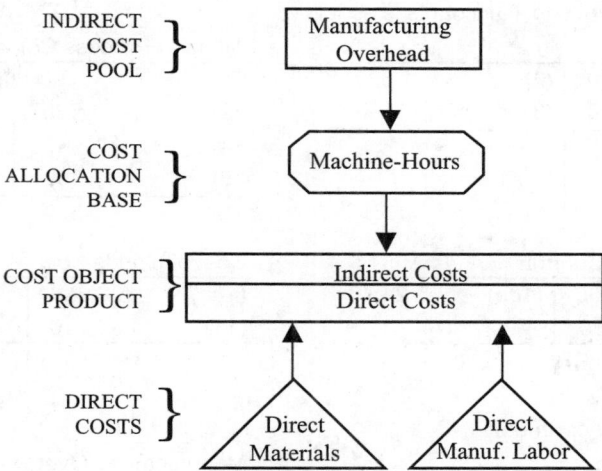

2. Amounts in lakh of rupees.

(1) Materials Control	1,540	
Accounts Payable Control		1,540
(2) Work-in-Process Control	1,520	
Materials Control		1,520
(3) Manufacturing Department Overhead Control	190	
Materials Control		190
(4) Work-in-Process Control	960	
Wages Payable Control		960
(5) Manufacturing Department Overhead Control	340	
Wages Payable Control		340
(6) Manufacturing Department Overhead Control	280	
Accumulated Depreciation		280
(7) Manufacturing Department Overhead Control	130	
Various liabilities		130

(8) Work-in-Process Control	930
Manufacturing Overhead Allocated	930
(9) Finished Goods Control	2,980
Work-in-Process Control	2,980
(10a) Cost of Goods Sold	2,940
Finished Goods Control	2,940
(10b) Accounts Receivable Control (or Cash)	4,100
Revenues	4,100

The posting of entries to T-accounts is as follows:

Materials Control

Bal	180	(2)	1,520
(1)	1,540	(3)	190
Bal.	1		

Work-in-Process Control

Bal.	90	(9)	2,980
(2)	1,520		
(4)	960		
(8)	930		
Bal.	520		

Finished Goods Control

Bal.	100	(10a)	2,940
(9)	2,980		
Bal.140			

Cost of Goods Sold

(10a)	2,940		
(11)	10		

Manufacturing Department Overhead Control

(3)	190	(11)	940
(5)	340		
(6)	280		
(7)	130		

Manufacturing Overhead Allocated

(11)	930	(8)	930

Accounts Payable Control

		(1)	1,540

Wages Payable Control

		(4)	960
		(5)	340

Accumulated Depreciation

		(6)	280

Various Liabilities

		(7)	130

Accounts Receivable Control

(10b)	4,100		

Revenues

		(10b)	4,100

The ending balance of Work-in-Process Control is ₹520 lakhs.

3. (11) Manufacturing Overhead Allocated   930

        Cost of Goods Sold   10

              Manufacturing Department Overhead Control   940

    Entry posted to T-accounts in Requirement 2.

4. Gross margin = Revenues − Cost of goods sold = ₹4,100 lakhs − ₹2,950 lakhs = ₹1,150 lakhs.

Container Transport's gross margin of 28% (₹1,150 ÷ ₹4,100) is relatively small, indicating Container Transport did fine but not particularly well in 2016. (Gross margins below 30% are generally considered small.) A company manufacturing prestige manufactured homes should have higher gross margins.

4-21 Job costing; actual, normal, and variation from normal costing. Creative Solutions designs Web pages for clients in the education sector. The company's job-costing system has a single direct cost category (Web-designing labor) and a single indirect cost pool composed of all overhead costs. Overhead costs are allocated to individual jobs based on direct labor-hours. The company employs six Web designers. Budgeted and actual information regarding Creative Solutions follows:

Budget for 2016:

Direct labor costs	₹27,30,000
Direct labor-hours	10,500
Overhead costs	₹15,75,000

Actual results for 2016:

Direct labor costs	₹28,50,000
Direct labor-hours	11,400
Overhead costs	₹15,96,000

Required

1. Compute the direct cost rate and the indirect cost rate per Web-designing labor-hour for 2016 under (a) actual costing, (b) normal costing, and (c) the variation from normal costing that uses budgeted rates for direct costs.
2. Which method would you suggest Creative Solutions use? Explain.
3. Creative Solutions' Web design for Greenville Day School was budgeted to take 86 direct labor-hours. The actual time spent on the project was 79 hours. Compute the cost of the Greenville Day School job using (a) actual costing, (b) normal costing, and (c) the variation from normal costing that uses budgeted rates for direct cost.

Solution

1. Actual direct-labor hour rate = $\dfrac{₹28,50,000}{11,400}$ = ₹250 per direct labor-hour

   Actual indirect cost rate = $\dfrac{₹15,96,000}{11,400}$ = ₹140 per direct labor-hour

   = $\dfrac{₹27,30,000}{10,500}$ = ₹260 per direct labor-hour

   Budgeted indirect cost rate = $\dfrac{₹15,75,000}{10,500}$ = ₹150 per direct labor-hour

	(a) Actual Costing	(b) Normal Costing	(c) Variation of Normal Costing
Direct-Cost Rate	₹250 (Actual rate)	₹250 (Actual rate)	₹260 (Budgeted rate)
Indirect-Cost Rate	₹140 (Actual rate)	₹150 (Budgeted rate)	₹150 (Budgeted rate)

2. Creative Solutions should choose a job-costing system based on the direct cost information available to them. If Creative Solutions knows direct costs as the jobs are being done,

I would recommend Creative Solutions use normal costing over actual costing by calculating a budgeted indirect cost rate to cost jobs. Normal costing enables Creative Solutions to use the budgeted indirect cost rate calculated at the beginning of the year to estimate the cost of a job as soon as the job is completed. Creative Solutions can use knowledge of job costs for ongoing uses, including pricing jobs, monitoring and managing costs, evaluating the success of the job, learning about what did and did not work, bidding on new jobs, and preparing interim financial statements. Under actual costing, Creative Solutions would only determine the cost of a job at the end of the year when actual indirect costs are known. To be useful, of course, the budgeted indirect cost rate and the allocated costs need to reasonably approximate the actual indirect cost rate and the actual costs.

If Creative Solutions does not know direct costs as the jobs are being completed, I would recommend that Creative Solutions use the variation of normal costing that calculates a budgeted direct cost rate. This would allow Creative Solutions to estimate costs on a more-timely basis and gain all the benefits discussed earlier in the context of indirect costs. However, if Creative Solutions does use the variation of normal costing, it needs to continue to do a good job of estimating the budgeted direct cost rate. Currently, the budgeted direct cost rate (₹260) is very close to the actual rate of ₹250 per direct labor-hour.

3.

	(a) Actual Costing	(b) Normal Costing	(c) Variation of Normal Costing
Direct Costs	₹250×79 = ₹19,750	₹250×79 = ₹19,750	₹260×79 = ₹20,540
Indirect Costs	₹140×79 = 11,060	₹150×79 = 11,850	₹150×79 = 11,850
Total Job Costs	₹30,810	₹31,600	₹32,390

All three costing systems use the actual direct labor-hours of 79 hours. The budgeted 86 hours for the Greenville Day School job is not used in job costing. However, Creative Solutions may have used the budgeted number of hours in bidding for the job.

4-22 Job costing, unit cost, ending work in process. Raymond Ltd. worked on only two jobs during May. Information on the jobs is given below:

Particulars	Job M1	Job M2
Direct materials	₹75,000	₹50,000
Direct manufacturing labor	2,70,000	2,10,000
Direct manufacturing labor-hours	6,000	5,000

Manufacturing overhead costs are allocated at the budgeted rate of ₹30 per direct manufacturing labor-hour. Job M1 was completed in May.

Required

1. Compute the total cost of Job M1.
2. Calculate per unit cost for Job M1 assuming it has 15,000 units.
3. Prepare the journal entry transferring Job M1 to Finished goods.
4. Determine the ending balance in the Work-in-process account

Solution

1. **Cost of Job M1:**

Direct materials	₹75,000
Direct manufacturing labor	2,70,000
Manufacturing overhead allocated	1,80,000
Total cost	₹5,25,000

Budgeted rate ₹30 × 6,000 direct manufacturing labor-hours = ₹1,80,000

2. Per unit cost = Total cost of the job/Number of units in the job
   = ₹5,25,000/15,000 units = ₹35 per unit

3. Finished goods control   ₹5,25,000

   Work-in-process control   ₹5,25,000

4. **The work-in-process consists of Job M2 only:**

Direct materials	₹50,000
Direct manufacturing labor	2,10,000
Manufacturing overhead allocated	1,50,000
Work-in-process May 31	₹4,10,000

   Budgeted rate of ₹30 × 5,000 direct manufacturing labor-hours.

4-23 Job costing, accounting for manufacturing overhead, budgeted rates. The Hero Honda Motors uses a job-costing system at its Gurgaon plant. The plant has a Machining Department and a Finishing Department. Hero Honda uses normal-costing with two direct-cost categories (direct materials and direct machine-hours as the allocation base, and the Finishing Department, with direct manufacturing labor costs as the allocation base). The current year budget for the plant is as follows:

Particulars	Machining Department	Assembly Department
Manufacturing overhead	₹1,00,00,000	₹80,00,000
Direct manufacturing labor cost	₹9,00,000	₹10,00,000
Direct manufacturing labor-hours	30,000	1,60,000
Machine-hours	2,00,000	33,000

Required

1. Present an overview diagram of Hero Honda Motor's job-costing system.
2. What is the budgeted overhead rate that should be used in the Machining Department? In the Finishing Department?
3. During the month of January, the job-cost record for Job 431 shows the follows:

Particulars	Machining Department	Assembly Department
Direct materials used	₹14,000	₹3,000
Direct manufacturing labor costs	₹600	₹1,250
Direct manufacturing labor-hours	30	50
Machine-hours	130	10

Compute the total manufacturing overhead allocated to Job 431.

4. Assuming that Job 431 consisted of 200 units of product, what is the unit product cost of Job 431?
5. Amounts at the end of current year are as follows:

Particulars	Machining Department	Finishing Department
Manufacturing overhead incurred	₹1,12,00,000	₹79,00,000
Direct manufacturing labor costs	₹9,50,000	₹41,00,000
Machine-hours	2,20,000	32,000

Compute the under or allocated manufacturing overhead for each department and for the Gurgaon plant as a whole.

6. Why might Hero Honda use two different manufacturing overhead cost pools in its job-costing system?

Solution

1. An overview of the job-costing system is:

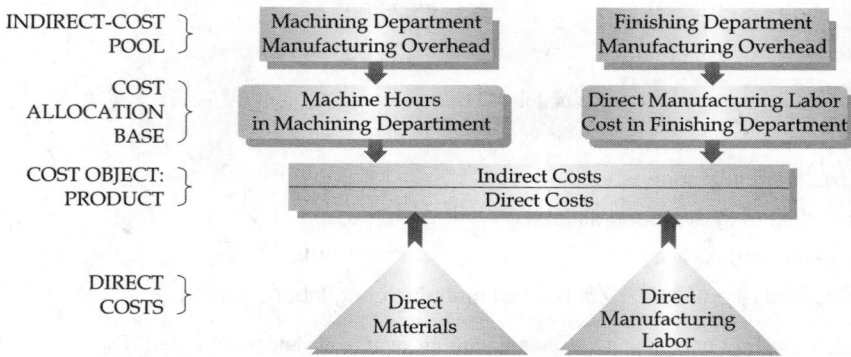

2. Budgeted manufacturing overhead divided by allocation base:

   a. Machining Department:

   ₹1,00,00,000/2,00,000 = ₹50 per machine hour

   b. Finishing Department:

   ₹80,00,000/40,00,000 = 200% of direct manufacturing labor costs

3.
Machining Department overhead, ₹50 × 130 hours	= ₹6,500
Finishing Department overhead, 200 percent of ₹1,250	= 2,500
Total manufacturing overhead allocated	9,000

4. **Total costs of Job 431:**

   Direct costs

Direct materials - Machining department	₹14,000
- Finishing department	3,000
Direct manufacturing labor - Machining department	600
- Finishing department	1,250
	18,850

   Indirect costs

Machining department overhead, ₹50 × 130	6,500
Finishing department overhead, 200% of ₹1,250	2,500
	9,000
Total costs	₹27,850

   The per unit product cost of job 431 is ₹27,850/200 units = ₹139.25 per unit

   The point of this part is (a) to get the definitions straight multiplying the actual amount of the allocation base by the budgeted rate.

5.
Particulars	Machining	Finishing
Manufacturing overhead incurred (actual)	₹1,12,00,000	₹79,00,000
Manufacturing overhead allocated		
2,20,000 hours × ₹50	1,10,00,000	
200% of ₹41,00,000		82,00,000
Underallocated manufacturing overhead	2,00,000	
Overallocated manufacturing overhead		3,00,000
Total overallocated overhead = (₹3,00,000 – ₹2,00,000)		1,00,000

6. A homogeneous cost pool is one where all costs have the same or a similar cause-and-effect or benefits-received relationship with the cost-allocation base. Hero Honda Motors likely assumes that all its manufacturing overhead cost items are not homogeneous. Specifically, those in the Machining Department have a cause-and-effect relationship with machine-hours, while those in the Finishing Department have a cause-and-effect relationship with direct manufacturing labor costs. Hero Honda Motors believes that the benefits of using two cost pools (more accurate product costs and better ability to manage costs) exceeds the costs of implementing a more complex system.

4-24 Proration of overhead. The Ride-On-Wave Company (ROW) produces a line of non-motorized boats. ROW uses a normal-costing system and allocates manufacturing overhead using direct manufacturing labor cost. The following data are for 2016:

Budgeted manufacturing overhead cost	₹1,25,000
Budgeted direct manufacturing labor cost	₹2,50,000
Actual manufacturing overhead cost	₹1,17,000
Actual direct manufacturing labor cost	₹2,28,000

Inventory balances on December 31, 2016, were as follows:

Account	Ending balance	2016 direct manufacturing labor cost in ending balance
Work in process	₹50,700	₹20,520
Finished goods	2,45,050	59,280
Cost of goods sold	5,49,250	1,48,200

Required

1. Calculate the manufacturing overhead allocation rate.
2. Compute the amount of under- or overallocated manufacturing overhead.
3. Calculate the ending balances in work in process, finished goods, and cost of goods sold if under- or overallocated manufacturing overhead is as follows:
   a. Written off to cost of goods sold
   b. Prorated based on ending balances (before proration) in each of the three accounts
   c. Prorated based on the overhead allocated in 2016 in the ending balances (before proration) in each of the three accounts
4. Which method would you choose? Justify your answer.

Solution

1. $\dfrac{\text{Budgeted manufacturing}}{\text{overhead rate}} = \dfrac{\text{Budgeted manufacturing overhead cost}}{\text{Budgeted direct manufacturing labor cost}}$

$$= \frac{₹1,25,000}{₹2,50,000} = 50\% \text{ of direct manufacturing labor cost}$$

2. Overhead allocated = 50% × Actual direct manufacturing labor cost
   = 50% × ₹2,28,000 = ₹1,14,000

$\dfrac{\text{Underallocated}}{\text{manufacturing}}_{\text{overhead}} = \dfrac{\text{Actual}}{\text{manufacturing}}_{\text{overhead costs}} - \dfrac{\text{Allocated plant}}{\text{overhead costs}}$

= ₹1,17,000 − ₹1,14,000 = ₹3,000
Underallocated manufacturing overhead = ₹3,000

3a. All underallocated manufacturing overhead is written off to cost of goods sold. Both work-in-process (WIP) and finished goods inventory remain unchanged.

Account	Dec. 31, 2016 Balance (Before Proration) (1)	Proration of ₹3,000 Underallocated Manuf. Overhead (2)	Dec. 31, 2016 Balance (After Proration) (3) = (1) + (2)
WIP	₹50,700	₹0	₹50,700
Finished Goods	2,45,050	0	2,45,050
Cost of Goods Sold	5,49,250	3,000	5,52,250
Total	₹8,45,000	₹3,000	₹,8,48,000

3b. Underallocated manufacturing overhead prorated based on ending balances:

Account	Dec. 31, 2016 Account Balance (Before Proration) (1)	Account Balance as a Percent of Total (2) = (1) ÷ ₹8,45,000	Proration of ₹3,000 Underallocated Manuf. Overhead (3) = (2) × ₹3,000	Dec. 31, 2016 Account Balance (After Proration) (4) = (1) + (3)
WIP	₹50,700	0.06	0.06 × ₹3,000 = ₹180	₹50,880
Finished Goods	2,45,050	0.29	0.29 × ₹3,000 = 870	2,45,920
Cost of Goods Sold	5,49,250	0.65	0.65 × ₹3,000 = 1,950	5,51,200
Total	₹8,45,000	1.00	₹3,000	₹8,48,000

3c. Underallocated manufacturing overhead prorated based on 2016 overhead in ending balances:

Account	Dec. 31, 2016 Account Balance (Before Proration) (1)	Allocated Manuf. Overhead in Dec. 31, 2016 Balance (Before Proration) (2)	Allocated Manuf. Overhead in Dec. 31, 2016 Balance as a Percent of Total (3) = (2) ÷ ₹114,000	Proration of ₹3,000 Underallocated Manuf. Overhead (4) = (3) × ₹3,000	Dec. 31, 2016 Account Balance (After Proration) (5) = (1) + (4)
WIP	₹50,700	₹10,260[a]	0.09	0.09 × ₹3,000 = ₹270	₹50,970
Finished Goods	2,45,050	29,640[b]	0.26	0.26 × ₹3,000 = 780	2,45,830
Cost of Goods Sold	5,49,250	74,100[c]	0.65	0.65 × ₹3,000 = 1,950	5,51,200
Total	₹8,45,000	₹1,14,000	1.00	₹3,000	₹8,48,000

[a,b,c] Overhead allocated = Direct manuf. labor cost × 50% = ₹20,520; ₹59,280; ₹1,48,200 × 50%

4. Writing off all of the underallocate6d manufacturing overhead to Cost of Goods Sold (CGS) is usually warranted when CGS is large relative to Work-in-Process and Finished Goods Inventory and the underallocated manufacturing overhead is immaterial. Both these conditions apply in this case. ROW should write off the ₹3,000 underallocated manufacturing overhead to Cost of Goods Sold Account.

4-25 Proration of overhead with two indirect cost pools. Premier Golf Carts makes custom golf carts that it sells to dealers across the Southeast. The carts are produced in two departments, fabrication (a mostly automated department) and custom finishing (a mostly manual department). The company uses a normal-costing system in which overhead in the fabrication department is allocated to jobs on the basis of machine-hours and overhead in the finishing department is allocated to jobs based on direct labor-hours. During May, Premier Golf Carts reported actual overhead of ₹4,95,000 in the fabrication department and ₹2,22,000 in the finishing department. Additional information follows:

Manufacturing overhead rate (fabrication department)	₹200 per machine-hour
Manufacturing overhead rate (finishing department)	₹160 per direct labor-hour
Machine-hours (fabrication department) for May	2,000 machine-hours
Direct labor-hours (finishing department) for May	1,200 labor-hours
Work in process inventory, May 31	₹5,00,000
Finished goods inventory, May 31	₹15,00,000
Cost of goods sold, May	₹30,00,000

Premier Golf Carts prorates under- and overallocated overhead monthly to work in process, finished goods, and cost of goods sold based on the ending balance in each account.

Required

1. Calculate the amount of overhead allocated in the fabrication department and the finishing department in May.
2. Calculate the amount of under-or overallocated overhead in each department and in total.
3. How much of the under-or overallocated overhead will be prorated to (a) work in process inventory, (b) finished goods inventory, and (c) cost of goods sold based on the ending balance (before proration) in each of the three accounts? What will be the balance in work in process, finished goods, and cost of goods sold after proration?
4. What would be the effect of writing off under- and overallocated overhead to cost of goods sold? Would it be reasonable for Premier Golf Carts to change to this simpler method?

Solution

1. Fabrication department:
   Overhead allocated = ₹200 per machine-hour × 2,000 machine-hours = ₹4,00,000
   Finishing department:
   Overhead allocated = ₹160 per direct labor-hour × 1,200 direct labor-hours = ₹1,92,000

2. Under- or overallocated overhead in each department and in total follows:
   Fabrication department:
   ₹4,95,000 actual overhead – ₹4,00,000 allocated = ₹95,000 underallocated
   Finishing department:
   ₹2,22,000 actual overhead – ₹1,92,000 allocated = ₹30,000 underallocated
   Total underallocated overhead = ₹95,000 + ₹30,000 = ₹1,25,000

3. Underallocated overhead prorated based on ending balances:

Account	Account Balance (Before Proration) (1)	Account Balance as a Percent of Total (2) = (1) ÷ ₹50,00,000	Proration of ₹1,25,000 Underallocated Overhead (3) = (2) × ₹1,25,000	Account Balance (After Proration) (4) = (1) + (3)
Work in Process	₹5,00,000	0.10	0.10 × ₹1,25,000 = ₹12,500	₹5,12,500
Finished Goods	15,00,000	0.30	0.30 × ₹1,25,000 = 37,500	15,37,500
Cost of Goods Sold	30,00,000	0.60	0.60 × ₹1,25,000 = 75,000	30,75,000
Total	₹50,00,000	1.00	₹1,25,000	₹51,25,000

Because Premier Golf Carts is disposing of underallocated costs based on the ending balance in Work in Process, Finished Goods, and Cost of Goods Sold accounts, it does not have to allocate the underallocated overhead from each department separately. Had Premier Golf Carts disposed of the underallocated overhead based on the overhead allocated in the ending balances in each of the three accounts, it would have to dispose of the underallocated overhead in the Fabrication Department and the underallocated overhead in the Finishing Department separately.

4. The ending balance in Cost of Goods Sold would be ₹31,25,000 instead of ₹30,75,000 if the entire ₹1,25,000 amount of underallocated overhead was written off to Cost of Goods Sold account. Cost of Goods Sold would increase by 1.6% (₹31,25,000 − ₹30,75,000) ÷ ₹30,75,000. Because this is an insignificant amount, it would be reasonable to use the simpler method of charging off to Cost of Goods Sold.

4-26 Allocation and proration of overhead. Zee Company prints custom training material for corporations. The business was started January 1, 2016. The company uses a normal-costing system. It has two direct cost pools, materials and labor, and one indirect cost pool, overhead. Overhead is charged to printing jobs on the basis of direct labor cost. The following information is available for 2016.

Budgeted direct labor costs	₹2,25,000
Budgeted overhead costs	₹3,15,000
Costs of actual material used	₹1,48,500
Actual direct labor costs	₹2,13,500
Actual overhead costs	₹3,02,100

There were two jobs in process on December 31, 2016: Job 11 and Job 12. Costs added to each job as of December 31 are as follows:

	Direct materials	Direct labor
Job 11	₹4,870	₹5,100
Job 12	₹5,910	₹6,800

Zee Company has no finished goods inventories because all printing jobs are transferred to cost of goods sold when completed.

Required

1. Compute the overhead allocation rate.
2. Calculate the balance in ending work in process and cost of goods sold before any adjustments for under-or overallocated overhead.
3. Calculate under-or overallocated overhead.

4. Calculate the ending balances in work in process and cost of goods sold if the under-or overallocated overhead amount is as follows:

   a. Written off to cost of goods sold

   b. Prorated using the overhead allocated in 2016 (before proration) in the ending balances of cost of goods sold and work-in-process control accounts

5. Which of the methods in requirement 4 would you choose? Explain.

Solution

Budgeted overhead rate = Budgeted overhead costs ÷ Budgeted labor costs

= ₹3,15,000 ÷ ₹2,25,000 = 140% of labor cost

2. Ending work in process

	Job 11	Job 12	Total
Direct material costs	₹4,870	₹5,910	₹10,780
Direct labor costs	5,100	6,800	11,900
Overhead			
(1.40 × Direct labor costs)	7,140	9,520	16,660
Total costs	₹17,110	₹22,230	₹39,340

Cost of goods sold = Beginning WIP + Manufacturing costs − Ending WIP

= ₹0 + ₹1,48,500 + ₹2,13,500 + (₹2,13,500 × 1.40) − ₹39,340 = ₹6,21,560

3. Overhead allocated   = 1.40 × ₹2,13,500 = ₹2,98,900

Underallocated overhead = Actual overhead − Allocated overhead

= ₹3,02,100 − ₹2,98,900 = ₹3,200 underallocated

4a. All underallocated overhead is written off to cost of goods sold.

WIP inventory remains unchanged.

Account (1)	Dec. 31, 2016 Account Balance (Before Proration) (2)	Write-off of ₹3,200 Underallocated overhead (3)	Dec. 31, 2016 Account Balance (After Proration) (4) = (2) + (3)
Work in Process	₹39,340	₹0	₹39,340
Cost of goods sold	6,21,560	3,200	6,24,760
	₹6,60,900	₹3,200	₹6,64,100

4b. Underallocated overhead prorated based on overhead allocated before proration.

Account (1)	Dec. 31, 2016 Account Balance (Before Proration) (2)	Allocated Overhead Included in Dec. 31, 2016 Account Balance (Before Proration) (3) (4)		Proration of ₹32,000 Underallocated Manufacturing Overhead (5)	Dec. 31, 2016 Account Balance (After Proration) (6) = (2) + (5)
Work in Process	₹39,340	₹16,660[a]	(5.57%)	0.0557 × ₹3,200 = ₹178	₹39,518
Cost of Goods Sold	6,21,560	2,82,240[b]	(94.43%)	0.9443 × ₹3,200 = 3,022	6,24,582
Total	₹6,60,900	₹2,98,900	100%	₹3,200	₹6,64,100

[a]₹11,900 × 1.40; [b](₹2,13,500 − ₹11,900) × 1.40

5. Writing off all of the underallocated overhead to Cost of Goods Sold (CGS) is warranted when CGS is large relative to Work-in-Process Inventory and Finished Goods Inventory and the underallocated overhead is immaterial. Both these conditions apply in this case. Zee Company should write off the ₹3,200 underallocated overhead to Cost of Goods Sold account.

4-27 General ledger relationships, under and overallocation. (S.Sridhar, adapted) Neelam Company uses normal costing in its job-costing system. Partially completed T-accounts and additional information for Neelam for current year are as follows:

Materials Control			Work-in-process Control		
Beginning	₹30,000	₹3,80,000	Beginning		₹20,000
	4,00,000		Direct manufacturing labor	3,60,000	

Finished Goods Control			Manufacturing Overhead Control		
Beginning	₹10,000	₹9,00,000		₹5,40,000	
	9,40,000				

Additional information

a. Direct manufacturing labor wage rate was ₹30 per hour.

b. Manufacturing overhead was allocated at ₹40 per direct manufacturing-labor hour.

c. During the year, sales revenues were ₹10,90,000, and marketing and distribution costs were ₹1,40,000.

Required

1. What was the amount of direct materials issued to production during current year?

2. What was the amount of manufacturing overhead allocated to jobs during current year?

3. What was the cost of jobs completed during current year?

4. What was the balance of ending work-in-process inventory on December 31, current year?

5. What was the cost of goods sold before proration of under-or overallocated overhead?

6. What was the under-allocated or overallocated manufacturing overhead in current year?

7. Dispose of the under-allocated or overallocated manufacturing overhead using

   a. Write-off to cost of goods sold.

   b. Proration based on ending balances (before proration) in work-in-process, finished goods, and cost of goods sold.

8. Using each of the approaches in requirement 7, calculate Neelam's operating income for the current year.

9. Which approach in requirement 7 do you recommend Neelam use? Explain your answer briefly.

Solution

The solution assumes all materials used are direct material. A summary of the T-accounts for Neelam Company before adjusting for under- or overallocation of overhead follows:

Direct Materials Control

Beginning	₹30,000	Materials used for manufacturing	₹3,80,000
Purchases	4,00,000		
Ending	50,000		

Work-in-process Control

Beginning	₹20,000	Transferred to finished goods	₹9,40,000
Direct materials	3,80,000		
Direct manufacturing labor	3,60,000		
Manufacturing overhead allocated	4,80,000		
Ending	3,00,000		

Finished Goods Control

Beginning	₹10,000	Cost of goods sold	₹9,00,000
Transferred from work-in-process	9,40,000		
Ending	50,000		

Cost of Goods Sold

Finished goods sold	₹9,00,000

Manufacturing Overhead Control

Manufacturing overhead costs	₹5,40,000

Manufacturing Overhead Allocated

Manufacturing overhead allocated to work-in-process	₹4,80,000

1. From Direct Material Control T-account
   Direct material issued to production = ₹3,80,000 that appears as a credit.

2. Direct manufacturing labor-hours = Direct manufacturing labor costs/Direct manufacturing wage rate per hour
   = ₹3,60,000/₹30 per hour = 12,000 hours

3. From the debit entry to Finished Goods T-account
   Cost of jobs completed and transferred from Work-in-Process = ₹9,40,000

4. From Work-in-Process T-account, Work-in-Process inventory
   On 31st December = ₹20,000 + ₹3,80,000 + 3,60,000 + 4,80,000 —
   ₹9,40,000 = ₹3,00,000

5. From the credit entry to Finished Goods Control T-account, Cost of goods sold (before proration) = ₹9,00,000

6. Manufacturing overhead underallocated = Debit to Manufacturing Overhead Control — Credit to Manufacturing Overhead Allocated = ₹5,40,000-₹4,80,000 = ₹60,000 underallocated.

7. a. Write-off to Cost of Goods Sold will increase (debit) Cost of Goods Sold by ₹60,000. Hence, Cost of Goods Sold = ₹9,00,000 + 60,000 = ₹9,60,000

   b. Proratioin based on ending balances (before proration) in Work-in-Process, Finished Goods and Cost of Goods Sold.

Account balances in each account after proration follows:

Account	Account Balance (before proration)	Proration of ₹60,000 Underallocated Manufacturing Overhead	Account Balance (after proration)
(1)	(2)	(3)	(4) = (2) + (3)
Work in process	₹3,00,000 (24%)	0.24 × ₹60,000 = ₹14,400	₹3,14,400
Finished goods	50,000 (4%)	0.04 × 60,000 = 2,400	52,400
Cost of goods sold	9,00,000 (72%)	0.72 × 60,000 = 43,200	9,43,200
	₹12,50,000 (100%)	60,000	13,10,000

8. Neelam's Operating Income under the write off to Cost of Goods Sold and Proration based on ending balances (before proration) follows

Particulars	Write off to Cost of Goods Sold	Proration Based on Ending Balances
Revenues	₹10,90,000	₹10,90,000
Cost of goods sold	9,60,000	9,43,200
Gross margin	1,30,000	1,46,800
Marketing and distribution costs	1,40,000	1,40,000
Operating income/floss)	₹(10,000)	₹6,800

9. If the purpose is to report the most accurate inventory and cost of goods sold figures, the preferred method is to prorate based on the manufacturing overhead allocated component in the inventory and cost of goods sold accounts. Proration based on the balances in work in process, finished goods, and cost of goods sold will equal the proration based on the manufacturing overhead allocated component if the proportions of direct costs to manufacturing overhead costs are constant in the work in process, finished goods and cost of goods sold accounts. Even if this is not the case, the prorations based on work in process, finished goods, and cost of goods sold will better approximate the results if actual cost rates had been used rather than the write-off to cost of goods sold method.

Another consideration in Neelam's decision about how to dispose of underallocated manufacturing overhead is the effects on operating income. The write-off to cost of goods sold will lead to an operating loss, proration based on the balances in work in process, finished goods, and cost of goods sold will help Neelam avoid the loss and show an operating income.

The main merit of the write-off to cost of goods sold method is its simplicity. However, accuracy and the effect on operating income favor the preferred and recommended proration approach.

4-28 Job costing, contracting, ethics. Ansal manufactures modular homes. The company has two main products that it sells commercially: a 1,000-square-foot, one-bedroom model and a 1,500-square-foot, two-bedroom model. The company recently began providing emergency housing (huts) to the State Emergency Management Agency (SEMA). The emergency housing is similar to the 1,000-square-foot model.

SEMA has requested Ansal to create a bid for 150 emergency huts to be sent for J&K victims in the North. Your manager has asked that you prepare this bid. In preparing the bid, you find a recent invoice to SEMA for 200 huts provided. You also have a standard cost sheet for the 1,000-square-foot model sold commercially. Both are provided as follows:

Standard cost sheet: 1,000-sq.-ft., one-bedroom model

Direct materials		₹95,000
Direct manufacturing labor	32 hour	7,040

Manufacturing labor*	₹3.5 per rupee of direct labor cost	24,640
Total cost		₹1,26,680
Retail markup on total cost		25%
Retail price		₹1,58,350

INVOICE

DATE: September 15, 2016
BILL TO: SEMA
FOR: 200 Emergency Hunts

Direct materials	₹2,09,00,000
Direct manufacturing labor**	16,44,000
Manufacturing overhead	57,54,000
Total cost	2,82,98,000
Government contract markup on total cost	20%
Total	₹3,39,57,600

Required

1. Calculate the total bid if you base your calculations on the standard cost sheet assuming a cost plus 20% government contract.
2. Calculate the total bid if you base your calculations on the September 15, 2016, invoice assuming a cost plus 20% government contract.
3. What are the main discrepancies between the bids you calculated in requirements 1 and 2?

*Overhead cost pool includes inspection labor (₹150 per hour), setup labor (₹120 per hour), and other indirect costs associated with production.

**Direct manufacturing labor includes 30 production hours per unit, 4 inspection hours per unit, and 6 setup hours per unit.

Solution

1. Direct manufacturing costs:

Direct materials (₹95,000 × 150 huts)	₹1,42,50,000	
Direct manufacturing labor (₹7,040 × 150 huts)	10,56,000	
Manufacturing overhead (3.50 × ₹10,56,000)	36,96,000	
Total costs		₹1,90,02,000
Markup (20% × ₹1,90,02,000)		38,00,400
Total bid price		₹2,28,02,400

2. Direct manufacturing costs:

Direct materials	₹1,56,75,000	
Direct manufacturing labor	12,33,000	
Manufacturing overhead	43,15,500	
Total costs		₹2,12,23,500
Markup (20% of ₹2,12,23,500)		42,44,700
Total bid price		₹2,54,68,200

Direct materials = (₹2,09,00,000/200) × 150 = ₹1,56,75,000

$$\text{Direct manufacturing labor} = \frac{₹16,44,000}{200 \text{ huts}} \times 150 \text{ huts} = ₹12,33,000$$

Manufacturing overhead = (3.50 × ₹12,33,000) = ₹43,15,500

3. The main discrepancies in costs (before the mark up) in requirements 1 and 2 are as follows:
   a. Materials are marked up by 10% in the Sept. 15, 2016, invoice. (₹1,56,75,000 − ₹1,42,50,000)/₹1,42,50,000 = 10%.
   b. Costs are double-counted based on the Sept. 15, 2016, invoice (inspection and setup costs are included as both a direct cost as part of direct manufacturing labor and in manufacturing overhead allocated at 3.5 times direct manufacturing labor cost).
   c. The standard cost sheet includes 32 direct manufacturing labor hours, while the Sept. 15, 2016, invoice includes 30 hours of production labor.

Exercises

[*Comprehensive solutions to all exercises are available on the companion website www. pearsoned.co.in/charlesthorngren*]

4-29 Job-costing, normal and actual costing. Ansal Construction assembles residential houses. It uses a job-costing system with two direct-cost categories (direct materials and direct labor) and one indirect-cost pool (assembly support). Direct labor-hours is the allocation base for assembly support costs. In December Year 1, Ansal budgets Year 2 assembly-support costs to be ₹40,00,000 and Year 2 direct labor-hours to be ₹80,000.

At the end of Year 2, Ansal is comparing the costs of several jobs that were started and completed in Year 2.

Particulars	Gurgaon Model	Noida Model
Construction period	Feb-June 2004	May-Oct. 2004
Direct materials	₹2,12,900	₹2,55,208
Direct labor	₹72,552	₹82,820
Direct labor-hours	1,800	2,020

Direct materials and direct labor are paid for on a contract basis. The costs of each are known when direct materials are used or direct labor-hours are worked. The Year 2 actual assembly-support costs were ₹1,37,76,000, and the actual direct labor-hours were 3,28,000.

Required
1. Compute the (a) budgeted and (b) actual indirect-cost rates. Why do they differ?
2. What is the job cost of the Gurgaon Model and the Noida Model using (a) normal costing and (b) actual costing?
3. Why might Ansal construction prefer normal costing over actual costing?

4-30 Job-costing, consulting firm. Vaish and Associates, a consulting firm, has the following condensed budget for Year 1.

Revenues		₹4,00,00,000
Total costs		
Direct costs		
Professional labor	₹1,00,00,000	
Indirect costs		
Consulting support	2,60,00,000	3,60,00,000
Operating income		40,00,000

Vaish has a single direct-cost category (professional labor) and a single indirect-cost pool (client support). Indirect costs are allocated to jobs on the basis of professional labor costs.

Required
1. Present an overview diagram of the job-costing system. Compute the Year 1 budgeted indirect-cost rate of Vaish and Associates.
2. The markup rate for pricing jobs is intended to produce operating income equal to 10 percent of revenues. Compute the markup rate as a percentage of professional labor costs.

3. Vaish is bidding on a consulting job for Karim's, a fast-food chain. The budgeted breakdown of professional labor on the job is as follows:

Professional labor category	Budgeted Rate per hour	Budgeted Hours
Director	₹2,000	3
Partner	1,000	16
Associate	500	40
Assistant	300	160

Compute the budgeted cost of the Karim's job. How much will Vaish bid for the job if it is to earn its target operating income of 10 percent of revenues?

4-31 Job costing, journal entries. The University of Delhi Press is wholly owned by the university. It performs the bulk of its work for other university departments, which pay as though the press were an outside business enterprise. The press also publishes and maintains a stock of books for general sale. Ajob-costing system is used to cost each job. There are two direct-cost categories (direct materials and direct manufacturing labor) and one indirect-cost pool (manufacturing overhead, allocated on the basis of direct manufacturing labor costs).

The following data (in thousands) pertain to current year

Direct materials and supplies purchased on account	₹8,000
Direct materials used	7,100
Indirect materials issued to various production departments	1,000
Direct manufacturing labor	13,000
Indirect manufacturing labor incurred by various departments	9,000
Depreciation on building and manufacturing equipment	4,000
Miscellaneous manufacturing overhead* incurred by various	5,500

departments (ordinarily would be detailed as repairs, photocopying, utilities, etc.) Manufacturing overhead allocated at 160 percent of direct manufacturing labor costs

Cost of goods manufactured	41,200
Revenues	80,000
Cost of goods sold	40,200
Beginning inventories	
Materials control	10,000
Work-in-process control	600
Finished goods control	5,000

*The term manufacturing overhead is not used uniformly. Other terms that are often encountered in printing companies include job overhead and shop overhead.

Required

1. Present an overview diagram of the job-costing system at the University of Delhi Press.

2. Prepare journal entries to summarize current year transactions. As your final entry, dispose of the year-end under or overallocated manufacturing overhead as a write-off to Cost of goods sold. Number your entries. Explanations for each entry may be omitted.

3. Show posted T-accounts for all inventories, Cost of goods sold, Manufacturing overhead control, and Manufacturing overhead allocated.

4-32 Job costing; actual, normal, and variation from normal costing. S R Batliboi and Co. is a Delhi-based public accounting partnership specializing in audit services. Its job-costing system has a single direct-cost category (professional labor) and a single indirect-cost pool (audit support, which contains all the costs in the Audit Support Department). Audit support costs are allocated to individual jobs using actual professional labor-hours. S R Batliboi and Co. employs ten professionals who are involved in their auditing services.

Budgeted and actual amounts for current year are as follows:

Budget for current year

Professional labor compensation	₹9,60,000
Audit Support Department costs	7,20,000
Professional labor-hours billed to clients	6,000 hours

Actual Results for current year

Audit Support Department costs	₹7,44,000
Professional labor-hours billed to clients	5,500 hours
Actual professional labor cost rate	58 per hour

Required

1. Compute the direct-cost rate per professional labor-hour and the indirect-cost rate per professional labor-hour for current year under (a) actual costing, (b) normal costing, and (c) the variation of normal costing that uses budgeted rates for direct costs.

2. The audit of the Gupta Entreprises, done in current year, was budgeted to take 110 hours of professional labor time. The actual professional labor time on the audit was 120 hours. Compute the current year job cost using (a) actual costing, (b) normal costing, and (c) the variation of normal costing that uses budgeted rates for direct costs. Explain any differences in the job cost.

4-33 Service industry, job costing, law firm. Viash & Associates is a law firm specializing in labor relations and employee-related work. It employs 50 professionals (10 partners and 40 associates) who work directly with its clients. The average budgeted total compensation per professional for current year is ₹2,08,000. Each professional is budgeted to have 3,200 billable hours to clients in current year. Viash & Associates is a highly respected firm; all professional work for clients to their maximum 3,200 billable hours available. All professional labor costs are included in a single direct-cost category and are traced to jobs on a per-hour basis.

All costs of Viash & Associates other than professional labor costs are included in a single indirect-cost pool (legal support) and are allocated to jobs using professional labor-hours as the allocation base. The budgeted level of indirect costs in current year is ₹44,00,000.

Required

1. Present an overview diagram of Vaish's job-costing system.

2. Compute the current year budgeted direct-cost rate per hour of professional labor.

3. Compute the current year budgeted indirect-cost rate per hour of professional labor.

4. Viash & Associates is considering bidding on two jobs:

a. Litigation work for Saw Pipes Ltd. which requires 100 budgeted hours of professional labor.

b. Labor contract work for J K Paper Ltd. which requires 150 budgeted hours of professional labor. Prepare a cost estimate for each job.

4-34 Service industry, job costing two direct and two indirect-cost categories, law firm (continuation of 4-33) Vaish has just completed a review of its job-costing system. This review included a detailed analysis of how past jobs used the firm's resources and interviews with personnel about what factors drive the level of indirect costs. Management concluded that a system with two direct-cost categories (professional partner labor and professional associate labor) and two indirect-cost categories (general support and secretarial support) would yield more accurate job costs. Budgeted information for current year related to the two direct-cost categories is as follows:

Particulars	Professional Partner Labor	Professional Associate Labor
Number of professionals	10	40
Hours of billable time per professional	3,200 per year	3,200 per year
Total compensation (average per professional)	₹4,00,000	₹1,60,000

Budgeted information for current year relating to the two indirect-cost categories is

Particulars	General Support	Secretarial Support
Total costs	₹36,00,000	₹8,00,000
Cost-allocation base	Professional labor-hours	Partner labor-hours

Required

1. Compute the current year budgeted direct-cost rates for (a) professional partners and (b) professional associates.
2. Compute the current year budgeted indirect-cost rates for (a) general support and (b) secretarial support.
3. Compute the budgeted costs for the Saw Pipes and J K Paper jobs, given the following information:

	Saw Pipes	J.K. Paper
Professional partners	120 hours	60 hours
Professional associates	80 hours	240 hours

4. Comment on the results in requirement 3. Why are the job costs different from those computed in Problem 4-31?

4-35 Normal costing, overhead allocation, working backwards. (M. Rajan, adapted) Tata Company uses normal costing. Its job-costing system has two direct-cost categories (direct materials and direct manufacturing labor) and one indirect-cost category (manufacturing overhead). The following information is obtained from the company's records for current year:

- Total manufacturing costs ₹1,60,00,000.
- Cost of finished goods manufactured ₹1,58,40,000.
- Manufacturing overhead allocated ₹72,00,000.
- Manufacturing overhead was allocated to production at a rate of 200 percent of direct manufacturing labor costs.
- The rupee amount of work-in-process inventory on January 1, current year was ₹6,40,000.

Required

1. Compute the total direct manufacturing labor costs in current year.
2. Calculate the total cost of direct materials used in current year.
3. Determine work-in-process inventory on December 31, current year.

4-36 General ledger relationships, under and overallocation, service industry. ICT International Enginneering consulting firm, uses a variation from normal costing in its job-costing system. It charges jobs for fees paid to outside experts at actual costs, professional direct-labor costs at a budgeted direct-labor rate, and engineering support overhead costs at a budgeted indirect-cost rate.

ICT maintains a "Jobs-in-Process Control" account in its general ledger that accumulates all costs of jobs. As a job is completed, ICT immediately bills the client and transfers the cost of the completed job to a "Cost of Jobs Billed" account.

The following data pertain to current year:

1. Direct costs of fees (all cash)	₹3,00,000
2. Actual direct professional labor costs (all cash)	30,00,000
3. Direct professional labor allocated at ₹100 per actual	29,00,000
4. Actual engineering support overhead costs (all cash)	23,60,000
5. Engineering support overhead allocated at 80% of actual direct professional labor costs	24,00,000
6. Cost of jobs billed	50,00,000

Required

1. Prepare summary journal entries for the above transactions using these accounts: Jobs-in-Process control, Cost of jobs billed, Direct professional labor control, Direct professional labor allocated, Engineering support overhead control, Engineering support overhead allocated, and Cash control.

2. As your final entry, dispose of the year-end under or overallocated account balances as direct writeoffs to cost of jobs billed.

4-37. Amitabh Company is a small machine shop that uses normal costing in its job-costing system. The total debits and credits in certain accounts one day before current year-end are as follows:

	December 30	
Particulars	**Total Debits**	**Total Credits**
Materials control	₹1,00,000	₹70,000
Work-in-process control	3,20,000	3,05,000
Manufacturing department overhead control	85,000	3,00,000
Finished goods control	3,25,000	–
Cost of goods sold	3,00,000	–
Manufacturing overhead allocated	–	90,000

All materials purchased are direct material. Note that "total debits" in the inventory accounts would include beginning inventory balances, if any.
The total debits and total credits above do not include the following:

a. The manufacturing labor costs for the December 31 working day: direct manufacturing labor, ₹5,000 and indirect manufacturing labor, ₹1,000

b. Miscellaneous manufacturing overhead incurred on December 31, ₹1,000.

Additional information

a. Manufacturing overhead has been allocated as a percentage of direct manufacturing labor costs through December 30.

b. Direct materials purchased during the current year were ₹85,000.

c. No direct materials were returned to suppliers.

d. Direct manufacturing labor costs during the current year totaled ₹1,50,000, not including the December 31 working day described previously.

Required

1. Compute the inventories (December 31, previous year) of Materials control, Work-in-process control, and Finished goods control. Show T-accounts.

2. Prepare all adjusting and closing journal entries for the preceding accounts. Assume that all under- or overallocated manufacturing overhead is closed directly to cost of goods sold.

3. Compute the ending inventories (December 31), after adjustments and closing of materials control, Work-in-process control, and Finished goods control.

4-38 Service industry, job costing, accounting for overhead costs, budgeted rates. Sinhgama's Company, a painting contractor, uses normal costing to cost each job. Sinhgama's job costing system has two direct-cost categories (direct materials and direct labor) and one indirect-cost pool called overhead costs. Sinhgama's budgeted overhead rate for allocating overhead costs to jobs is 80 percent of direct labor costs. Sinhgama's provides the following additional information:

1. As of January 31, current year, Job A21 was the only job in process, with direct materials costs of ₹30,000 and direct labor costs of ₹50,000.
2. Jobs A22, A23, and A24 were started during February.
3. Direct materials used during February were ₹50,000.
4. Direct-labor costs for February were ₹20,000.
5. Actual overhead costs for February were ₹1,02,000.
6. The only job still in process as of February 29, current year, was job A24, with direct materials costs of ₹20,000 and direct labor costs of ₹40,000.

Sinhgama maintains a "Jobs-in-process control" account in its general ledger. When a job is completed, Sinhgama transfers the cost of the completed job to "Cost of jobs billed" account. Each month, Sinhgama closes any underallocated or overallocated overhead to "Cost of jobs billed".

Required

1. Calculate the overhead allocated to Job A21 as of January 31, current year and the overhead allocated to job A24 as of February 29, current year.
2. Calculate the underallocated or overallocated overhead for February current year.
3. Calculate the cost of jobs billed for February current year.

4-39 Allocation and proration of manufacturing overhead. (SMA, heavily adapted) Usha Limited is a company that produces machinery to customer order. Its job-costing system (using normal costing) has two direct-cost categories (direct materials and direct manufacturing labor) and one indirect-cost pool (manufacturing overhead, allocated using a budgeted rate based on direct manufacturing labor costs). The budget for the current year was

Direct manufacturing labor	₹8,40,000
Manufacturing overhead	5,04,000

At the end of current year, two jobs were incomplete: No. 1768B (total direct manufacturing labor costs were ₹22,000) and No. 1819C (total direct manufacturing labor costs were ₹78,000). Machine time totaled 287 hours for No 1768B and 647 hours for No. 1819C. Direct materials issued to No. 1768B amounted to ₹44,000. Direct materials for No. 1819C were ₹84,000.

Total charges to the Manufacturing overhead control account for the year were ₹3,73,680. Direct manufacturing labor costs of all jobs were ₹8,00,000, representing 20,000 direct manufacturing labor-hours.

There were no beginning inventories. In addition to the ending work in process, the ending finished goods showed a balance of ₹3,12,000 (including direct manufacturing labor costs of ₹80,000). Revenues for current year totaled ₹54,01,360, cost of goods sold was ₹32,00,000 and marketing costs were ₹17,15,740. Usha prices on a cost-plus basis. It currently uses a guideline of cost plus 40 percent of cost.

Required

1. Prepare a detailed schedule showing the ending balances in the inventories and Cost of Goods Sold (before considering any under- or overallocated manufacturing overhead). Show also the manufacturing overhead allocated in these ending balances.
2. Compute the under- or overallocated manufacturing overhead for current year.

3. Prorate the amount computed in requirement 2 on the basis of:
   a. The ending balances (before proration) of Work-in-Process Control, Finished Goods Control, and Cost of Goods Sold.
   b. The allocated overhead amount (before proration) in the ending balances of Work-in-Process Control, Finished Goods Control, and Cost of Goods Sold.

4. Assume Usha decides to write off to Cost of Goods Sold any under- or overallocated manufacturing overhead. Will operating income be higher or lower than the operating income that would have resulted from the proration in requirements 3a and 3b?

5. Calculate the cost of job No. 1819C if Usha Limited had used the adjusted allocation-rate approach to dispose of under- or overallocated manufacturing overhead in current year.

5 Activity-Based Costing and Activity-Based Management

Learning Objectives ▼

1. Explain how broad averaging undercosts and overcosts products or services

2. Present three guidelines for refining a costing system

3. Distinguish between simple and activity-based costing systems

4. Describe a four-part cost hierarchy

5. Cost products or services using activity-based costing

6. Evaluate the costs and benefits of implementing activity-based costing systems

7. Explain how managers use activity-based costing in activity-based management

8. Compare activity-based costing systems and department costing systems

Learning Objectives 1

Explain how broad averaging undercosts and overcosts products or services

. . . this problem arises when reported costs of products do not equal their actual costs

A good mystery never fails to capture the imagination.

Money is stolen or lost, property disappears, or someone meets with foul play. On the surface, many people may view these cases as typical. Someone with a trained eye, however, may uncover hidden facts, details, and patterns. Getting to the bottom of the case, understanding what happened and why, and taking action can make the difference between a solved case and an unsolved one. Business and organizations face similar cases. Their costing systems are often mysteries with unresolved questions: Why are we bleeding red ink? Are we pricing our products accurately? Activity-based costing can help unravel the mystery and result in improved operations.

Broad Averaging and Its Consequences

Historically, companies (such as television and automobile manufacturers) produced a limited variety of products. These companies used few overhead resources to support these simple operations, so indirect (or overhead) costs were a relatively small percentage of total costs. Managers used simple costing systems to allocate overhead costs broadly in an easy, inexpensive, and reasonably accurate way. But as product diversity and indirect costs increased, broad averaging led to inaccurate product costs. That's because simple *peanut-butter costing* (yes, that's what it's called) broadly averages or spreads the cost of resources uniformly to cost objects (such as products or services) when, in fact, the individual products or services use those resources in nonuniform ways.

Undercosting and Overcosting

The following example illustrates how averaging can provide inaccurate and misleading cost data. Consider the cost of a restaurant bill for four colleagues who meet monthly to discuss business developments. Each diner orders separate entrees, desserts, and drinks. The restaurant bill for the most recent meeting is as follows:

	Anita	Anurag	Ajit	Anshul	Total	Average
Entree	₹110	₹200	₹150	₹140	₹600	₹150
Dessert	0	80	40	40	160	40
Drinks	40	140	80	60	320	80
Total	₹150	₹420	₹270	₹240	₹1,080	₹270

If the ₹1,080 total restaurant bill is divided evenly, ₹270 is the average cost per diner. This cost-averaging approach treats each diner the same. When costs are averaged across all four diners, both Anita and Anshul are overcosted, Anurag is undercosted, and Ajit is (by coincidence) accurately costed. Anita, especially, may object to paying the average bill of ₹270 because her individual bill is only ₹150.

Broad averaging can lead to undercosting or overcosting of products or services:

- **Product undercosting**—a product consumes a high level of resources but is reported to have a low cost per unit (Anurag's dinner).

- **Product overcosting**—a product consumes a low level of resources but is reported to have a high cost per unit (Anita's dinner).

What are the strategic consequences of product undercosting and overcosting? Suppose a manager uses cost information about products to guide pricing decisions. Undercosted products will be underpriced and may even lead to sales that actually result in losses because the sales may bring in less revenue than the cost of resources they use. Overcosted products will lead to overpricing, causing those products to lose market share to competitors producing similar products. But what if prices are determined by the market based on consumer demand and competition among companies? In this case, product undercosting and overcosting cause managers to focus on the wrong products. Managers give greater attention to overcosted products that show low profits when in fact costs and profits from these products are perfectly reasonable. They give less attention to undercosted products thinking they are highly profitable, when in fact these products consume large amounts of resources and are far less profitable than they appear.

Product-Cost Cross-Subsidization

Product-cost cross-subsidization means that if a company undercosts one of its products, it will overcost at least one of its other products. Similarly, if a company overcosts one of its products, it will undercost at least one of its other products. Product-cost cross-subsidization is very common in situations in which a cost is uniformly spread—meaning it is broadly averaged—across multiple products without recognizing the amount of resources consumed by each product.

In the restaurant-bill example, the amount of cost cross-subsidization of each diner can be readily computed *because all cost items can be traced as direct costs to each diner*. If all diners pay ₹270, Anita is paying ₹120 more than her actual cost of ₹150. She is cross-subsidizing Anurag who is paying ₹150 less than his actual cost of ₹420. Calculating the amount of cost cross-subsidization takes more work when there are indirect costs to be considered. Why? Because when two or more diners use the resources represented by indirect costs, we need to find a way to allocate costs to each diner. Consider, for example, a ₹400 bottle of wine whose cost is shared equally. Each diner would pay ₹100 (₹400 ÷ 4). Suppose Anshul drinks 2 glasses of wine while Anita, Anurag and Ajit drink one glass each for a total of 5 glasses. Allocating the cost of the bottle of wine on the basis of the glasses of wine that each diner drinks would result in Anshul paying ₹160 (₹400) and each of the others paying ₹80 (₹400 1/5). In this case, sharing the cost equally, Anita, Anurag and Ajit are each paying ₹20 (₹100 – ₹80) more and are cross-subsidizing Anshul who is paying ₹60 (₹160 – ₹100) less for the wine he consumes.

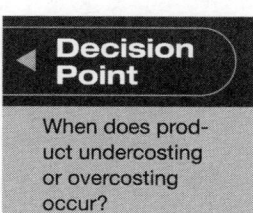

Decision Point

When does product undercosting or overcosting occur?

To see the effects of broad averaging on direct and indirect costs, we consider Plastim Corporation's costing system.

Simple Costing System at Plastim Corporation

Plastim Corporation manufactures lenses for the rear taillights of automobiles. A lens, made from black, red, orange, or white plastic, is the part of the lamp visible on the automobile's exterior. Lenses are made by injecting molten plastic into a mold to give the lamp its desired shape. The mold is cooled to allow the molten plastic to solidify, and the lens is removed.

Plastim has a contract with Tata Motors, a major automobile manufacturer, to make two types of lenses: a complex lens, C5, and a simple lens, S3. The complex lens is a large lens with special features, such as multicolor molding (when more than one color is injected into the mold) and a complex shape that wraps around the corner of the car. Manufacturing C5 lenses is more complex because various parts in the mold must align and fit precisely. The S3 lens is simpler to make because it has a single color and few special features.

Design, Manufacturing, and Distribution Processes

Whether lenses are simple or complex, Plastim follows this sequence of steps to design, produce, and distribute them:

- **Design products and processes.** Each year Tata Motors specifies details of the simple and complex lenses it needs for its new models of cars. Plastim's Design Department designs the molds from which the lenses will be made and specifies the manufacturing process to make the lenses.
- **Manufacture lenses.** The lenses are molded, finished, cleaned, and inspected.
- **Distribute lenses.** Finished lenses are packed and sent to Tata Motors.

Plastim is operating at capacity and incurs very low marketing costs. Because of its high-quality products, Plastim has minimal customer-service costs. Plastim competes with several other companies who also manufacture simple lenses. At a recent meeting, Tata's purchasing manager informed Plastim's sales manager that Jain Motors, which makes only simple lenses, is offering to supply the S3 lens to Tata at a price of ₹530, well below Plastim's ₹630 price. Unless Plastim can lower its selling price, it will lose the Tata business for the simple lens for the upcoming model year. Fortunately, the same competitive pressures do not exist for the complex lens, which Plastim currently sells to Tata at ₹1,370 per lens.

Plastim's managers have two primary options:

- Give up the Tata business in simple lenses if it is unprofitable. Jain Motors makes only simple lenses and perhaps, therefore, uses simpler technology and processes than Plastim. The simpler operations may give Jain Motors a cost advantage that Plastim cannot match. If so, it is better for Plastim to not supply the S3 lens to Tata.
- Reduce the price of the simple lens and either accept a lower margin or aggressively seek to reduce costs.

To make these long-run strategic decisions, management needs to first understand the costs to design, make, and distribute the S3 and C5 lenses.

Jain Motors makes only simple lenses and can fairly accurately calculate the cost of a lens by dividing total costs by the number of simple lenses produced. Plastim's costing environment is more challenging because the manufacturing overhead costs support the production of both simple and complex lenses. Plastims' managers and management accounts need to find a way to allocate overhead costs to each type of lense.

In computing costs, Plastim assigns both variable costs and costs that are fixed in the short run to the S3 and C5 lenses. Managers cost products and services to guide long-run strategic decisions, such as what mix of products and services to produce and sell and what prices to charge for them. In the long run, managers have the ability to influence all costs. The firm will only survive in the long run if revenues exceed total costs, regardless of whether these costs are variable or fixed in the short run.

To guide pricing and cost-management decisions, Plastim's managers assign both manufacturing and nonmanufacturing costs to the S3 and C5 lenses. If managers had wanted to calculate the cost of inventory, Plastim's management accountants would have assigned only manufacturing costs to the lenses, as required by Generally Accepted Accounting Principles. Surveys of company practice across the globe indicate that the vast majority of companies use costing systems not just for inventory costing but also for strategic purposes, such as pricing and product-mix decisions and decisions about cost reduction, process improvement, design, and planning and budgeting. Managers of these companies assign all costs to products and services. Even merchandising-sector companies (for whom inventory costing is straightforward) and service-sector companies (who have no inventory) expend considerable resources in designing and operating their costing systems to allocate costs for strategic purposes.

Simple Costing System Using a Single Indirect-Cost Pool

Plastim currently has a simple costing system that allocates indirect costs using a single indirect-cost rate, the type of system described in Chapter 4. The only difference between these two chapters is that Chapter 4 focuses on jobs while here the cost objects are products. Exhibit 5-1 shows an overview of Plastim's simple costing system. Use this exhibit as a guide as you study the following steps, each of which is marked in Exhibit 5-1.

Step 1: Identify the Products That Are the Chosen Cost Objects. The cost objects are the 60,000 simple S3 lenses and the 15,000 complex C5 lenses that Plastim will produce in 2014. Plastim's management accountants first calculate the total costs and then the unit cost of designing, manufacturing, and distributing these lenses.

Step 2: Identify the Direct Costs of the Products. The direct costs are direct materials and direct manufacturing labor. Exhibit 5-2 shows the direct and indirect costs for the S3 and the C5 lenses using the simple costing system. The direct cost calculations appear on lines 5, 6, and 7 in Exhibit 5-2. Plastim's simple costing system classifies all costs other than direct materials and direct manufacturing labor as indirect costs.

Step 3: Select the Cost-Allocation Bases to Use for Allocating Indirect (or Overhead) Costs to the Products. A majority of the indirect costs consist of salaries paid to supervisors, engineers, manufacturing support, and maintenance staff, all supporting direct manufacturing labor. Plastim's managers use direct manufacturing labor-hours as the only allocation base to allocate all manufacturing and nonmanufacturing indirect costs to S3 and C5. In 2014, Plastim's managers budget 39,750 direct manufacturing labor-hours.

Step 4: Identify the Indirect Costs Associated with Each Cost-Allocation Base. Because Plastim uses only a single cost-allocation base, Plastim's management accountants group all budgeted indirect costs of ₹2,38,50,000 for 2014 into a single overhead cost pool.

Step 5:   Compute the Rate per Unit of Each Cost-Allocation Base.

$$\text{Budgeted indirect-cost rate} = \frac{\text{Budgeted total costs in indirect-cost pool}}{\text{Budgeted total quantity of cost-allocation base}}$$

$$= \frac{₹2,38,50,000}{39,750 \text{ direct manufacturing labour-hours}}$$

$$= ₹600 \text{ per direct manufacturing labor-hour}$$

Step 6:   Compute the Indirect Costs Allocated to the Products. Plastim's managers budget 30,000 total direct manufacturing labor-hours to make the 60,000 S3 lenses and 9,750 total direct manufacturing labor-hours to make the 15,000 C5 lenses. Exhibit 5-2 shows indirect costs of ₹1,80,00,000 (₹600 per direct manufacturing labor-hour × 30,000 direct manufacturing labor-hours) allocated to the simple lens and ₹58,50,000 (₹600 per direct manufacturing labor-hour × 9,750 direct manufacturing labor-hours) allocated to the complex lens.

Step 7:   Compute the Total Cost of the Products by Adding All Direct and Indirect Costs Assigned to the Products. Exhibit 5-2 presents the product costs for the simple and complex lenses. The direct costs are calculated in step 2 and the indirect costs in step 6. Be sure you see the parallel between the simple costing system overview diagram (Exhibit 5-1) and the costs calculated in step 7. Exhibit 5-1 shows two direct-cost categories

Exhibit 5-1

Overview of Plastim's
Simple Costing System

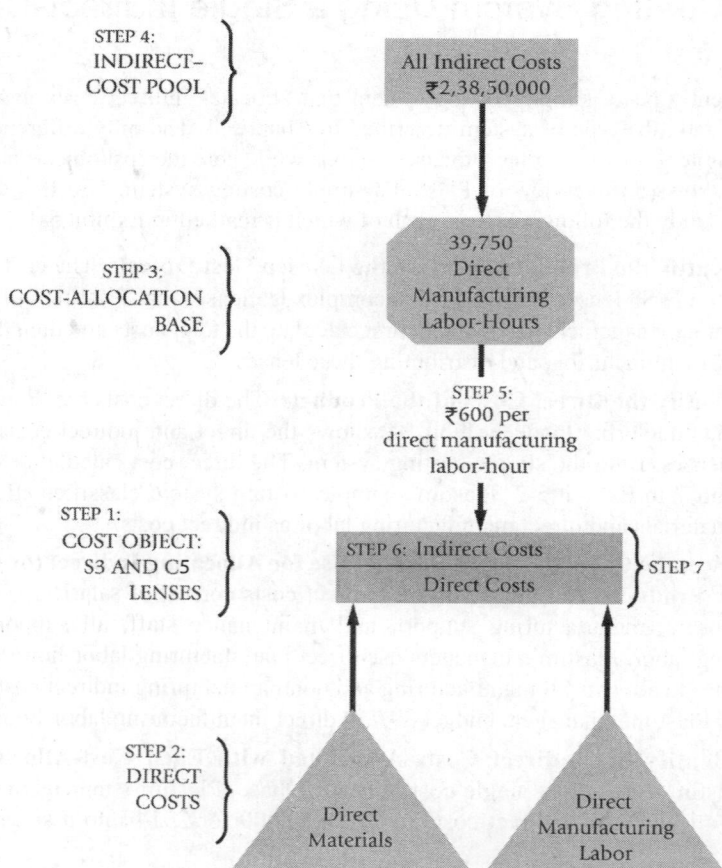

Exhibit 5-2   Plastim's Product Costs Using the Simple Costing System

	A	B	C	D	E	F	G
		File Edit View Insert Format Tools Data Window Help					
1		60,000			15,000		
2		Simple Lenses (S3)			Complex Lenses (CL5)		
3		Total	per Unit		Total	per Unit	Total
4		(1)	(2) = (1) ÷ 60,000		(3)	(4) = (3) ÷ 15,000	(5) = (1) + (3)
5	Direct materials	₹1,12,50,000	₹187.50		₹67,50,000	₹450.00	₹1,80,00,000
6	Direct manufacturing labor	60,00,000	100.00		19,50,000	130.00	79,50,000
7	Total direct costs (Step 2)	1,72,50,000	287.50		87,00,000	580.00	₹2,59,50,000
8	Indirect costs allocated (Step 6)	1,80,00,000	300.00		58,50,000	390.00	2,38,50,000
9	Total costs (Step 7)	₹3,52,50,000	₹587.50		₹1,45,50,000	₹970.00	₹4,98,00,000
10							

and one indirect-cost category. Therefore, the budgeted cost of each type of lens in step 7 (Exhibit 5-2) has three line items: two for direct costs and one for allocated indirect costs. It is very helpful to draw overview diagrams to see the big picture of costing systems before getting into the detailed costing of products and services. The budgeted cost per S3 lens is ₹587.5, well above the ₹530 selling price quoted by Jain Motors. The budgeted cost per C5 lens is ₹970.

Applying the Five-Step Decision-Making Process at Plastim

To decide how it should respond to the threat that Jain Motors poses to its S3 lens business, Plastim's managers works through the five-step decision-making process introduced in Chapter 1.

Step 1:   Identify the problem and uncertainties. The problem is clear—if Plastim wants to retain the Tata business for S3 lenses and make a profit, it must find a way to reduce the price and costs of the S3 lens. The two major uncertainties Plastim faces are (1) whether it's technology and processes for the S3 lens are competitive with Jain's and (2) whether Plastim's S3 lens is overcosted by the simple costing system.

Step 2:   Obtain information. Management asks a team of its design and process engineers to analyze and evaluate the design, manufacturing, and distribution operations for the S3 lens. The team is very confident that the technology and processes for the S3 lens are not inferior to those of Jain and other competitors because Plastim has many years of experience in manufacturing and distributing simple lenses like the S3 with a history and culture of continuous process improvements. The team is less certain about Plastim's capabilities in manufacturing and distributing complex lenses because it only recently started making this type of lens. Given these doubts, senior management is happy that Tata Motors considers the price of the CL5 lens to be competitive. Plastim's managers are puzzled, though, by how, at the currently budgeted prices, Plastim is expected to earn a very large profit margin percentage (operating income ÷ revenues) on the C5 lenses and a small profit margin on the S3 lenses:

	60,000 Simple Lenses (S3)		15,000 Complex Lenses (CL5)		
	Total (1)	per Unit (2) = (1) ÷ 60,000	Total (3)	per Unit (4) = (3) ÷ 5,000	Total (5) = (1) + (3)
Revenues	₹3,78,00,000	₹630.00	₹2,05,50,000	₹1370.00	₹5,83,50,000
Total costs	3,52,50,000	587.50	1,45,50,000	970.00	4,98,00,000
Operating income	₹25,50,000	42.50	₹60,00,000	₹400	₹85,50,000
Profit margin percentage		6.75%		29.20%	

As it continues to gather information, Plastim's management begins to ponder why the profit margin percentage is low for the S3 lens, where the company has strong capabilities, but high on the newer, less-established C5 lens. Plastim is not deliberately charging a low price for S3, so managers begin to evaluate the costing system. Plastim's simple costing system may be overcosting the simple S3 lens (assigning too much cost to it) and undercosting the complex C5 lens (assigning too little cost to it).

Step 3: Make predictions about the future. Plastim's key challenge is to get a better estimate of what it will cost to design, make, and distribute the S3 and C5 lenses. Managers are fairly confident about the direct material and direct manufacturing labor costs of each lens because these costs are easily traced to the lenses. But managers are quite concerned about how accurately the simple costing system measures the indirect resources used by each type of lens. They believe the costing system can be substantially improved.

Even as they come to this conclusion, managers want to avoid biased thinking. In particular, they want to be careful that the desire to be competitive on the S3 lens does not lead to assumptions that bias them in favor of lowering costs of the S3 lens.

Step 4: Make decisions by choosing among alternatives. On the basis of predicted costs, and taking into account how Jain Motors might respond, Plastim's managers must decide whether to bid for the Tata Motors' S3 lens business and if it does bid, what price it should offer.

Step 5: Implement the decision, evaluate performance, and learn. If Plastim wins Tata's S3 lens business, it must compare actual costs, as it makes and ships S3 lenses, to predicted costs and learn why actual costs deviate from predicted costs. Such evaluation and learning form the basis for future improvements.

The next few sections focus on Steps 3, 4 and 5 (3): how Plastim improves the allocation of indirect costs to the S3 and C5 lenses, (4) how it uses these predictions to bid for the S3 lens business, and (5) how it evaluates performance, makes product design and process improvements and learns using the new system.

Learning Objective 2

Present three guidelines for refining a costing system

. . . classify more costs as direct costs, expand the number of indirect-cost pools, and identify cost drivers

Refining a Costing System

A **refined costing system** reduces the use of broad averages for assigning the cost of resources to cost objects (such as jobs, products, and services) and provides better measurement of the costs of indirect resources used by different cost objects—no matter how differently various cost objects use indirect resources. Refining a costing system helps managers make better decisions about how to allocate resources and which products to produce.

Reasons for Refining a Costing System

Three principal reasons have accelerated the demand for refinements to the costing system.

1. **Increase in product diversity.** The growing demand for customized products has led managers to increase the variety of products and services companies offer. Banks, offer many different types of accounts and services: special passbook accounts, ATMs, credit cards, and electronic banking products. Producing these products places different demands on resources because of differences in volume, process, technology, and complexity. For example, the computer and network resources needed to support electronic banking products are much greater than the computer and network resources needed to support a passbook savings account. The use of broad averages fails to capture these differences in demand and leads to distorted and inaccurate cost information.

2. **Increase in indirect costs.** The use of product and process technology such as computer-integrated manufacturing (CIM) and flexible manufacturing systems (FMS), has led to an increase in indirect costs and a decrease in direct costs, particularly direct manufacturing labor costs. In CIM and FMS, computers on the manufacturing floor give instructions to set up and run equipment quickly and automatically. The computers accurately measure hundreds of production parameters and directly control the manufacturing processes to achieve high-quality output. Managing more complex technology and producing very diverse products also requires committing an increasing amount of resources for various support functions, such as production scheduling and product and process design and engineering. Because direct manufacturing labor is not a cost driver of these costs, allocating indirect costs on the basis of direct manufacturing labor (which was the common practice) often does not accurately measure how resources are being used by different products.

3. **Competition in product markets.** As markets have become more competitive, managers have felt the need to obtain more accurate cost information to help them make important strategic decisions, such as how to price products and which products to sell. Making correct pricing and product mix decisions is critical in competitive markets because competitors quickly capitalize on a manager's mistakes. For example, if Plastim overcosts the S3 lens and charges a higher price, a competitor aware of the true costs of making the lens could charge a lower price and gain the S3 business.

    The preceding factors explain why managers want to refine cost systems. Refining costing systems requires gathering, validating, analyzing, and storing vast quantities of data. Advances in information technology have drastically reduced the costs of performing these activities.

Guidelines for Refining a Costing System

There are three main guidelines for refining a costing system.

1. **Direct-cost tracing.** Identify as many direct costs as is economically feasible. This guideline aims to reduce the amount of costs classified as indirect, thereby minimizing the extent to which costs have to be allocated, rather than traced.

2. **Indirect-cost pools.** Expand the number of indirect-cost pools until each of these pools is more homogeneous. All costs a *homogeneous cost pool,* have the same or a similar cause-and-effect (or benefits-received) relationship with a single cost driver that is used as the cost-allocation base. Consider, for example, a single indirect-cost pool containing both indirect machining costs and indirect distribution costs that are allocated to products using machine-hours. This pool is not homogeneous because machine-hours

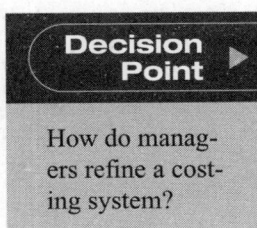

Decision Point ▶

How do managers refine a costing system?

are a cost driver of machining costs but not of distribution costs, which has a different cost driver, number of shipments. If, instead, machining costs and distribution costs are separated into two indirect-cost pools, with machine-hours as the cost-allocation base for the machining cost pool and number of shipments as the cost-allocation base for the distribution cost pool, each indirect-cost pool would become homogeneous.

3. **Cost-allocation bases.** As we describe later in the chapter, whenever possible, managers should use the cost driver (the cause of indirect costs) as the cost-allocation base for each homogenous indirect-cost pool (the effect).

Activity-Based Costing Systems

Learning Objective 3

Distinguish between simple and activity-based costing systems

. . . unlike simple systems, ABC systems calculate costs of individual activities to cost products

One of the best tools for refining a costing system is activity-based costing. **Activity-based costing (ABC)** refines a costing system by identifying individual activities as the fundamental cost objects. An **activity** is an event, task, or unit of work with a specified purpose—for example, designing products, setting up machines, operating machines, and distributing products. More informally, activities are verbs; they are things that a firm does. To help make strategic decisions, ABC systems identify activities in all functions of the value chain, calculate costs of individual activities and assign costs to cost objects such as products and services on the basis of the mix of activities needed to produce each product or service:[1]

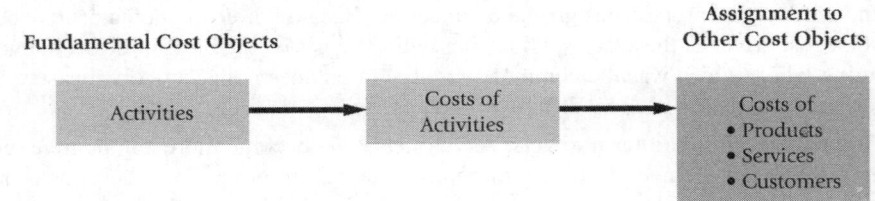

Plastim's ABC System

After reviewing its simple costing system and the potential miscosting of product costs Plastim decides to implement an ABC system. Direct costs can be traced to products easily, so the ABC system focuses on refining the assignment of indirect costs to departments processes, products, or other cost objects. To identify activities, Plastim organizes a team of managers from design, manufacturing, distribution, accounting, and administration Plastim's ABC system then uses these activities to break down its current single indirect cost pool into finer pools of costs related to the various activities.

Defining activities is difficult. The team evaluates hundreds of tasks performed at Plastim. It must decide which tasks should be classified as separate activities and which should be combined. For example, should maintenance of molding machines, operations of molding machines, and process control be regarded as separate activities or combined into a single activity? An activity-based costing system with many activities becomes overly detailed and unwieldy to operate. An activity-based costing system with too few activities may not be refined enough to measure cause-and-effect relationships between cost

---

[1] For more details on ABC systems, see R. Cooper and R. S. Kaplan, The Design of Cost Management Systems (Upper Saddle River, NJ: Prentice Hall, 1999); G. Cokins, *Activity-Based Cost Management: An Executive's Guide* (Hoboken, NJ: John Wiley & Sons, 2001); and R. S. Kaplan and S. Anderson, *Time-Driven Activity-Based Costing: A Simpler and More Powerful Path to Higher Profits* (Boston: Harvard Business School Press, 2007).

drivers and various indirect costs. To achieve an effective balance, Plastim's team focuses on activities that account for a sizable fraction of indirect costs and combines activities that have the same cost driver into a single activity. For example, the team decides to combine maintenance of molding machines, operations of molding machines, and process control into a single activity—molding machine operations—because all these activities have the same cost driver: molding machine-hours.

The team identifies the following seven activities by developing a flowchart of all the steps and processes needed to design, manufacture, and distribute S3 and C5 lenses.

a. Design products and processes

b. Set up molding machines to ensure that the molds are properly held in place and parts are properly aligned before manufacturing starts

c. Operate molding machines to manufacture lenses

d. Clean and maintain the molds after lenses are manufactured

e. Prepare batches of finished lenses for shipment

f. Distribute lenses to customers

g. Administer and manage all processes at Plastim

These activity descriptions (or *activity list* or *activity dictionary*) form the basis of the activity-based costing system. Compiling the list of tasks, however, is only the first step in implementing activity-based costing systems. Plastim must also identify the cost of each activity and the related cost driver by using the three guidelines for refining a costing system described on pages 206–208.

1. **Direct-cost tracing.** Plastim's ABC system subdivides the single indirect cost pool into seven smaller cost pools related to the different activities. The costs in the cleaning and maintenance activity cost pool (item d) consist of salaries and wages paid to workers who clean the mold. These costs are direct costs because they can be economically traced to a specific mold and lens.

2. **Indirect-cost pools.** The remaining six activity cost pools are indirect cost pools. Unlike the single indirect cost pool of Plastim's simple costing system, each of the activity-related cost pools is homogeneous. That is, each activity cost pool includes only those narrow and focused set of costs that have the same cost driver. For example, the distribution cost pool includes only those costs (such as wages of truck drivers) that, over time, increase as the cost driver of distribution costs, cubic feet of packages delivered, increases. In the simple costing system, Plastim lumped all indirect costs together and the cost-allocation base, direct manufacturing labor-hours, was not a cost driver of the indirect costs. Managers were therefore unable to measure how different cost objects used resources.

   To determine the costs of activity pools, managers assign costs accumulated in various account classifications (such as salaries, wages, maintenance, and electricity) to each of the activity cost pools. This process is commonly called *first-stage allocation*. For example, as we will see later in the chapter, of the ₹2,38,50,000 in the total indirect-cost pool, Plastim identifies setup costs of ₹30,00,000. Setup costs include depreciation and maintenance costs of setup equipment, wages of setup workers, and allocated salaries of design engineers, process engineers, and supervisors. We discuss *first-stage allocation* in more detail in Chapters 14 and 15. We focus here on the *second-stage allocation*, the allocation of costs of activity cost pools to products.

3. **Cost-allocation bases.** For each activity cost pool, Plastim uses the cost driver (whenever possible) as the cost-allocation base. To identify cost drivers, Plastim's managers consider various alternatives and use their knowledge of operations to choose among

them. For example, Plastim's managers choose setup-hours rather than the number of setups as the cost driver of setup costs, because Plastim's managers believe that more complex setups take more time and are more costly. Over time, Plastim's managers can use data to test their beliefs. (Chapter 10 discusses several methods to estimate the relationship between a cost driver and costs.)

The logic of ABC systems is twofold. First, when managers structure activity cost pools more finely with cost drivers for each activity cost pool as the cost-allocation base, it leads to more accurate costing of activities. Second, allocating these costs to products by measuring the cost-allocation bases of different activities used by different products leads to more accurate product costs. We illustrate this logic by focusing on the setup activity at Plastim.

Setting up molding machines frequently entails trial runs, fine-tuning, and adjustments. Improper setups cause quality problems such as scratches on the surface of the lens. The resources needed for each setup depend on the complexity of the manufacturing operation. Complex lenses require more setup resources (set-up hours) per setup than simple lenses. Furthermore, complex lenses can be produced only in small batches because the molds for complex lenses need to be cleaned more often than molds for simple lenses. Relative to simple lenses, complex lenses, therefore, not only use more set-up hours per setup, but they also require more frequent setups.

Setup data for the simple S3 lens and the complex C5 lens are:

		Simple S3 Lens	Complex C5 Lens	Total
1	Quantity of lenses produced	60,000	15,000	
2	Number of lenses produced per batch	240	50	
3 = (1) ÷ (2)	Number of batches	250	300	
4	Setup time per batch	2 hours	5 hours	
5 = (3) × (4)	Total setup-hours	500 hours	1,500 hours	2,000 hours

Recall that in its simple costing system, Plastim uses direct manufacturing labor-hours to allocate all ₹2,38,50,000 of indirect costs (which includes ₹30,00,000 of indirect setup costs) to products. The following table compares how setup costs allocated to simple and complex lenses will be different if Plastim allocates setup costs to lenses based on setup-hours rather than direct manufacturing labor-hours. Of the ₹600 total rate per direct manufacturing labor-hour, the setup cost per direct manufacturing labor-hour amounts to ₹75.4717 (₹30,00,000 ÷ 39,750 total direct manufacturing labor-hours). The setup cost per setup-hour equals ₹1,500 (₹30,00,000 ÷ 2,000 total setup-hours).

	Simple S3 Lens	Complex C5 Lens	Total
Setup cost allocated using direct manufacturing labor-hours: ₹75.4717 × 30,000; ₹75.4717 × 9,750	₹22,64,150	₹7,35,850	₹30,00,000
Setup cost allocated using setup-hours: ₹1,500 × 500; ₹1,500 × 1,500	₹7,50,000	₹22,50,000	₹30,00,000

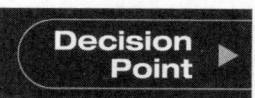

Decision Point

What is the difference between the design of a simple costing system and an activity-based costing (ABC) system?

ABC systems that use available time (setup-hours in our example) to calculate the cost of a resource and to allocate costs to cost objects are sometimes called *time-driven activity-based costing (TDABC) systems*. As we have already discussed when presenting guidelines 2 and 3, setup-hours, not direct manufacturing labor-hours, are the cost driver of setup costs. The C5 lens uses substantially more setup-hours than the S3 lens (1,500 hours ÷ 2,000 hours = 75% of the total setup-hours) because the C5 requires a greater number of setups (batches) and each setup is more challenging and requires more setup-hours.

The ABC system therefore allocates significantly more setup costs to C5 than to S3. When direct manufacturing labor-hours rather than setup-hours are used to allocate setup costs in the simple costing system, the S3 lens is allocated a very large share of the setup costs because the S3 lens uses a larger proportion of direct manufacturing labor-hours ($30,000 \div 39,750 = 75.47\%$). As a result, the simple costing system overcosts the S3 lens with regard to setup costs.

As we will see later in the chapter, ABC systems provide valuable information to managers beyond more accurate product costs. For example, identifying setup-hours as the cost driver correctly orients managers' cost reduction efforts on reducing setup-hours and cost per setup-hour. Note that setup-hours are related to batches (or groups) of lenses made, not the number of individual lenses. Activity-based costing attempts to identify the most relevant cause-and-effect relationship for each activity pool without restricting the cost driver to only units of output or variables related to units of output (such as direct manufacturing labor-hours). As our discussion of setups illustrates, limiting cost-allocation bases to only units of output weakens the cause-and-effect relationship between the cost-allocation base and the costs in a cost pool.

Cost Hierarchies

A **cost hierarchy** categorizes various activity cost pools on the basis of the different types of cost drivers, or cost-allocation bases, or different degrees of difficulty in determining cause-and-effect (or benefits-received) relationships. ABC systems commonly use a cost hierarchy having four levels—(1) output unit–level costs, (2) batch-level costs, (3) product-sustaining costs, and (4) facility-sustaining costs—to identify cost-allocation bases that are, whenever possible, drivers of costs in activity cost pools.

Output unit-level costs are the costs of activities performed on each individual unit of a product or service. Machine operations costs (such as the cost of energy, machine depreciation, and repair) related to the activity of running the automated molding machines are output unit-level costs because, over time, the cost of this activity increases with additional units of output produced (or machine-hours used). Plastim's ABC system uses molding machine-hours, an output-unit level cost-allocation base, to allocate machine operations costs to products.

Batch-level costs are the costs of activities related to a group of units of products or services rather than to each individual unit of product or service. In the Plastim example, setup costs are batch-level costs because, over time, the cost of this setup activity increases with setup-hours needed to produce batches of lenses. As described in the table on page 210, the S3 lens requires 500 setup-hours (2 setup-hours per batch × 250 batches). The C5 lens requires 1,500 setup-hours (5 setup-hours per batch × 300 batches). The total setup costs allocated to S3 and C5 depend on the total setup-hours required by each type of lens, not on the number of units of S3 and C5 produced. (Setup costs being a batch-level cost cannot be avoided by producing one less unit of S3 or C5.) Plastim's ABC system uses setup-hours, a batch-level cost-allocation base, to allocate setup costs to products.

Other examples of batch-level costs are material-handling and quality-inspection costs associated with batches (not the quantities) of products produced, and costs of placing purchase orders, receiving materials, and paying invoices related to the number of purchase orders placed rather than the quantity or value of materials purchased.

Product-sustaining costs (service-sustaining costs) are the costs of activities undertaken to support individual products or services regardless of the number of units or batches in which the units are produced. In the Plastim example, design costs are product-sustaining costs. Over time, design costs depend largely on the time designers spend on designing and modifying the product, the mold, and the process. These design costs are a function of the complexity of the mold, measured by the number of parts in the mold multiplied by the area (in square feet) over which the molten plastic must flow (12 parts × 2.5 square feet, or 30 parts-square feet for the S3 lens, and 14 parts × 5 square feet, or 70 parts-square feet for the C5 lens). As a result, the total design costs allocated to S3 and C5 depend on the complexity of the mold, regardless of the number of units or batches of production. Plastim can't avoid design costs by producing fewer units or running fewer batches. Plastim's ABC system uses parts-square feet—a product-sustaining cost-allocation base—to allocate design costs to products. Other examples of product-sustaining costs are product research and development costs, costs of making engineering changes, and marketing costs to launch new products.

Facility-sustaining costs are the costs of activities that cannot be traced to individual products or services but that support the organization as a whole. In the Plastim example, and at companies such as Samsung, and General Electric, the general administration costs (including top management compensation, rent, and building security) are facility-sustaining costs. It is usually difficult to find a good cause-and-effect relationship between these costs and the cost-allocation base, so some companies deduct facility-sustaining costs as a separate lump-sum amount from operating income rather than allocate them to products. Managers who follow this approach need to keep in mind that when making decisions based on costs (such as pricing), some lump-sum costs have not been allocated. They must set prices that are much greater than the allocated costs to recover some of the unallocated facility-sustaining costs. Other companies, such as Plastim, allocate facility-sustaining costs to products on some basis—for example, direct manufacturing labor-hours—because management believes all costs should be allocated to products even if it's done in a somewhat arbitrary way. Allocating all costs to products or services ensures that managers have taken into account all costs when making decisions based on costs (such as pricing). So long as managers are aware of the nature of facility-sustaining costs and the pros and cons of allocating them, which method a manager chooses is a matter of personal preference.

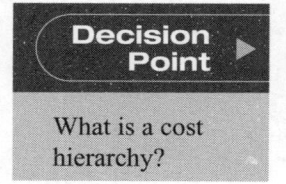

Decision Point

What is a cost hierarchy?

Implementing Activity-Based Costing at Plastim

Now that you understand the basic concepts of ABC, let's see how Plastim's managers refine the simple costing system, evaluate the two systems, and identify the factors to consider when deciding whether to develop the ABC system.

Learning Objective 5

Cost products or services using activity-based costing

. . . use cost rates for different activities to compute indirect costs of a product

Implementing ABC at Plastim

To implement ABC, Plastim's managers follow the seven-step approach to costing and the three guidelines for refining costing systems (increasing direct-cost tracing, creating homogeneous indirect-cost pools, and identifying cost-allocation bases that have cause-and-effect relationships with costs in the cost pool). Exhibit 5-3 shows an overview of Plastim's ABC system. Use this exhibit as a guide as you study the following steps, each of which is marked in Exhibit 5-3.

Step 1: Identify the Products That Are the Chosen Cost Objects. The cost objects are the 60,000 S3 and the 15,000 C5 lenses that Plastim will produce in 2014. Plastim's managers want to determine the total costs and then the per-unit cost of designing, manufacturing, and distributing these lenses.

Step 2: Identify the Direct Costs of the Products. The managers identify the following direct costs of the lenses because these costs can be economically traced to a specific mold and lens: direct material costs, direct manufacturing labor costs, and mold cleaning and maintenance costs.

Exhibit 5-3   Overview of Plastim's Activity-Based Costing System

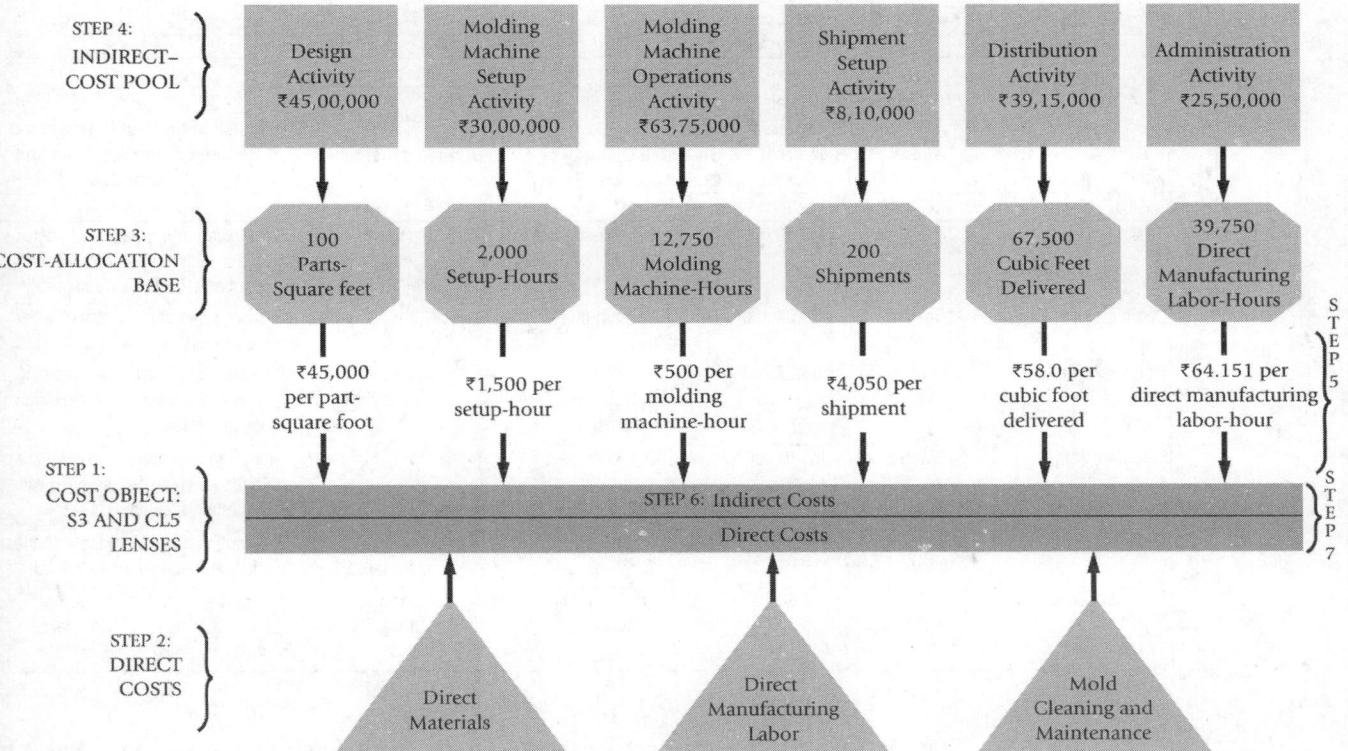

Exhibit 5-5 shows the direct and indirect costs for the S3 and C5 lenses using the ABC system. The direct costs calculations appear on lines 6, 7, 8 and 9 of Exhibit 5-5. Plastim's managers classify all other costs as indirect costs, as we will see in Exhibit 5-4.

Step 3: Select the Activities and Cost-Allocation Bases to Use for Allocating Indirect Costs to the Products. Following guidelines 2 and 3 for refining a costing system, Plastim identifies six activities for allocating indirect costs to products. (a) design, (b) molding machine setups, (c) machine operations, (d) shipment setup, (e) distribution, and (f) administration. Exhibit 5-4, column 2, shows the cost hierarchy category, and column 4 shows the cost-allocation base and the budgeted quantity of the cost-allocation base for each activity described in column 1.

Identifying the cost-allocation bases defines the number of activity pools into which costs must be grouped in an ABC system. For example, rather than define the design activities of product design, process design, and prototyping as separate activities, Plastim defines these three activities together as a combined "design" activity and forms a homogeneous design cost pool. Why? Because the same cost driver— the complexity of the mold— drives the costs of each design activity. A second consideration for choosing a cost-allocation base is the availability of reliable data and measures. For example, in its ABC system, Plastim's managers measure mold complexity in terms of the number of parts in the mold and the surface area of the mold (parts-square feet). If these data are difficult to obtain or measure, Plastim's managers may be forced to use some other measure of complexity, such as the amount of material flowing through the mold that may only be weakly related to the cost of the design activity.

Exhibit 5-4   Activity-Cost Rates for Indirect-Cost Pools

	File Edit View Insert Format Tools Data Window Help						
	A	B	C	D	E	F G	H
1			**(Step 4)**	**(Step 3)**		**(Step 5)**	
2	**Activity**	**Cost Hierarchy Category**	**Total Budgeted Indirect Costs**	**Budgeted Quantity of Cost-Allocation Base**		**Budgeted Indirect Cost Rate**	**Cause-and-Effect Relationship Between Allocation Base and Activity Cost**
3	**(1)**	**(2)**	**(3)**	**(4)**		**(5) = (3) ÷ (4)**	**(6)**
4	Design	Product-sustaining	₹45,00,000	100	parts-square feet	₹45,000 per part-square foot	Design Department indirect costs increase with more complex molds (more parts, larger surface area).
5	Setup molding machines	Batch-level	₹30,00,000	2,000	setup-hour	₹1,500 per setup-hour	Indirect setup costs increase with setup-hours.
6	Machine operations	Output unit-level	₹63,75,000	12,750	molding machine-hours	₹500 per molding machine-hour	Indirect costs of operating molding machines increases with molding machine-hours.
7	Shipment setup	Batch-level	₹8,10,000	200	shipments	₹4,050 per shipment	Shipping costs incurred to prepare batches for shipment increase with the number of shipments.
8	Distribution	Output-unit-level	₹39,15,000	67,500	cubic feet delivered	₹58.0 per cubic foot delivered	Distribution costs increase with the cubic feet of packages delivered.
9	Administration	Facility sustaining	₹25,50,000	39,750	direct manuf. labor-hours	₹64.151 per direct manuf. labor-hour	The demand for Administrative resources increases with direct manufacturing labor-hours.

Step 4: Identify the Indirect Costs Associated with Each Cost-Allocation Base. In this step, Plastim's managers try to assign budgeted indirect costs for 2014 to activities (see Exhibit 5-4, column 3), on the basis of a cause-and-effect relationship between the cost-allocation base for an activity and the costs. For example, all costs that have a cause-and-effect relationship to cubic feet of packages moved are assigned to the distribution cost pool. Of course, the strength of the cause-and-effect relationship between the cost-allocation base and the respective cost of the activity varies across cost pools. For example, the cause-and-effect relationship between direct manufacturing labor-hours and administration activity costs is not as strong as the relationship between setup-hours and setup activity costs.

Some costs can be directly identified with a particular activity. For example, salaries paid to design engineers, and depreciation of equipment used in the design department are directly identified with the design activity. Other costs need to be allocated across activities. For example, on the basis of interviews or time records, manufacturing engineers and supervisors estimate the time they will spend on design, molding machine setup, and machine operations. If a manufacturing engineer spends 15% of her time on design, 45% of her time managing molding machine setups, and 40% of her time on molding operations, the company will allocate the manufacturing engineer's salary to each of these activities in proportion to the time spent. Still other costs are allocated to activity-cost pools using allocation bases that measure how these costs support different activities. For example, rent costs are allocated to activity cost pools on the basis of square-feet area used by different activities.

As you can see, all costs do not fit neatly into activity categories. Often, costs may first need to be allocated to activities (Stage 1 of the two-stage cost-allocation model) before the costs of the activities can be allocated to products (Stage 2).

The following table shows the assignment of costs to the seven activities identified earlier. Recall that Plastim's management accountants reclassify mold cleaning costs as a direct cost because these costs can be easily traced to a specific mold and lens.

	Design	Molding Machine Setups	Molding Operations	Mold Cleaning	Shipment Setup	Distribution	Administration	Total
Salaries (supervisors, design engineers, process engineers)	₹32,00,000	₹10,50,000	₹13,75,000	₹0	₹2,10,000	₹6,15,000	₹16,50,000	₹81,00,000
Wages of support staff	6,50,000	11,50,000	7,00,000	23,40,000	3,40,000	12,50,000	4,00,000	68,30,000
Depreciation	2,40,000	3,00,000	29,00,000	1,80,000	1,10,000	14,00,000	1,50,000	52,80,000
Maintenance	1,30,000	1,60,000	4,50,000	1,20,000	60,000	2,50,000	50,000	12,20,000
Power and fuel	1,80,000	2,00,000	3,50,000	60,000	50,000	3,00,000	1,00,000	12,40,000
Rent	1,00,000	1,40,000	6,00,000	0	40,000	1,00,000	2,00,000	11,80,000
Total	₹45,00,000	₹30,00,000	₹63,75,000	₹27,00,000	₹8,10,000	₹39,15,000	₹25,50,000	₹2,38,50,000

Step 5: Compute the Rate per Unit of Each Cost-Allocation Base. Exhibit 5-4, column 5, summarizes the calculation of the budgeted indirect cost rates using the budgeted quantity of the cost-allocation base from step 3 and the total budgeted indirect costs of each activity from step 4.

Step 6: Compute the Indirect Costs Allocated to the Products. Exhibit 5-5 shows total budgeted indirect costs of ₹1,15,39,530 allocated to the simple lens and ₹96,10,470 allocated to the complex lens. Follow the budgeted indirect cost calculations for each lens in Exhibit 5-5. For each activity, Plastim's operations personnel indicate the total quantity of the cost-allocation base that will be used for each lens (recall that Plastim operates at capacity). For example, lines 15 and 16 of Exhibit 5-5 show that of the 2,000 total setups hours, the S3 lens is budgeted to use 500 hours and the C5 lens 1,500 hours. The budgeted indirect cost rate is ₹1,500 per setup hour (Exhibit 5-4, column 5, line 5). Therefore, total budgeted cost of setup activity allocated to the S3 lens is ₹7,50,000 (500 setup-hours × ₹1,500 per setup-hour) and to the C5 lens is ₹22,50,000 (1,500 setup-hours × ₹1,500 per setup-hour). Budgeted setup cost per unit equals ₹12.50 (₹7,50,000 ÷ 60,000 units) for the S3 lens and ₹150 (₹22,50,000 ÷ 15,000 units) for the C5 lens.

Step 7: Compute the Total Cost of the Products by Adding All Direct and Indirect Costs Assigned to the Products. Exhibit 5-5 presents the product costs for the simple and complex lenses. The direct costs are calculated in step 2, and the indirect costs are calculated in step 6. The ABC system overview in Exhibit 5-3 shows three direct-cost categories and six indirect-cost categories. The budgeted cost of each lens type in Exhibit 5-5 has nine line items, three for direct costs and six for indirect costs. The differences between the ABC product costs of S3 and C5 calculated in Exhibit 5-5 highlight how each of these products uses different amounts of direct and indirect costs in each activity area.

We emphasize two features of ABC systems. First, these systems identify all costs used by products, whether the costs are variable or fixed in the short run. When making long-run strategic decisions using ABC information, managers want revenues to exceed total costs.

Exhibit 5-5　　Plastim's Product Costs Using Activity-Based Costing System

File	Edit	View	Insert	Format	Tools	Data	Window	Help

	A	B	C	D	E	F	G	H	I	J	K	L	M	N
1			Manufacturing cost information							Manufacturing cost information				
2			for 200,000 units of Provalue II for 2010							for 200,000 units of Provalue III for 2010				
3	Cost Category	Cost Driver	Details of Budgeted Cost Driver Quantities				Budgeted Total Quantity of Cost Driver	Budgeted Cost per Unit of Cost Driver	Details of Budgeted Cost Driver Quantities				Budgeted Total Quantity of Cost Driver	Budgeted Cost per Unit of Cost Driver
4	(1)	(2)	(3)		(4)		(5)=(3)x(4)	(6)	(7)		(8)		(9)=(7)x(8)	(10)
5	Direct materials	No. of kits	1	kit per unit	2,00,000	units	2,00,000	₹3,850	1	kit per unit	2,00,000	units	2,00,000	₹3,750
6	Direct manuf. labor (DML)	DML hours	2.65	DML hours per unit	2,00,000	units	5,30,000	₹200	2.65	DML hours per unit	2,00,000	units	5,30,000	₹200
7	Direct machining (fixed)	Machine-hours					3,00,000	₹380					3,00,000	₹380
8	Ordering and receiving	No. of orders	50	orders per component	425	components	21,250	₹800	50	orders per component	400	components	20,000	₹600
9	Test and inspection	Testing-hours	15	testing-hours per unit	2,00,000	units	30,00,000	₹20	14	testing-hours per unit	2,00,000	units	28,00,000	₹17
10	Rework				6.5%	defect rate						6.5%	defect rate	
11		Rework-hours	2.5	rework-hours per defective unit	13,000[a]	defective units	32,500	₹400	2.5	rework-hours per defective unit	13,000[a]	defective units	32,500	₹320
12														
13	[a]6.5% defect rate x 200,000 units = 13,000 defective units													

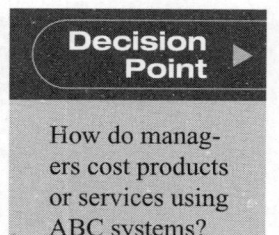

Decision Point ▶

How do managers cost products or services using ABC systems?

Otherwise, a company will make losses and will be unable to continue in business. Second, recognizing the hierarchy of costs is critical when allocating costs to products. Management accountants use the cost hierarchy to first calculate the total costs of each product. They then derive per-unit costs by dividing total costs by the number of units produced.

Comparing Alternative Costing Systems

Exhibit 5-6 compares the simple costing system using a single indirect-cost pool (Exhibit 5-1 and Exhibit 5-2) that Plastim had been using and the ABC system (Exhibit 5-3 and Exhibit 5-5). Note three points in Exhibit 5-6, consistent with the guidelines for refining a costing system: (1) ABC systems trace more costs as direct costs; (2) ABC systems create homogeneous cost pools linked to different activities; and (3) for each activity-cost pool,

ABC systems seek a cost-allocation base that has a cause-and-effect relationship with costs in the cost pool.

The homogeneous cost pools and the choice of cost-allocation bases, tied to the cost hierarchy, give Plastim's managers greater confidence in the activity and product cost numbers from the ABC system. The bottom part of Exhibit 5-6 shows that allocating costs to lenses using only an output unit-level allocation base—direct manufacturing labor-hours, as in the single indirect-cost pool system used prior to ABC—overcosts the simple S3 lens by ₹87.70 per unit and undercosts the complex C5 lens by ₹350.7 per unit. The C5 lens uses a disproportionately larger amount of output unit-level, batch-level, and product-sustaining costs than is represented by the direct manufacturing labor-hour cost-allocation base. The S3 lens uses a disproportionately smaller amount of these costs.

The benefit of an ABC system is that it provides information to make better decisions. But this benefit must be weighed against the measurement and implementation costs of an ABC system.

Considerations in Implementing Activity-Based-Costing Systems

Managers choose the level of detail to use in a costing system by evaluating the expected costs of the system against the expected benefits that result from better decisions.

Benefits and Costs of Activity-Based Costing Systems

Here are some of the telltale signs of when an ABC system is likely to provide the most benefits:

- Significant amounts of indirect costs are allocated using only one or two cost pools.
- All or most indirect costs are identified as output unit-level costs (few indirect costs are described as batch-level costs, product-sustaining costs, or facility-sustaining costs).
- Products make diverse demands on resources because of differences in volume, process steps, batch size, or complexity.
- Products that a company is well-suited to make and sell show small profits; whereas products that a company is less suited to produce and sell show large profits.
- Operations staff has substantial disagreement with the reported costs of manufacturing and marketing products and services.

When managers decide to implement ABC, they must make important choices about the level of detail to use. Should managers choose many finely specified activities, cost drivers, and cost pools, or would a few suffice? For example, Plastim's managers could identify a different molding machine-hour rate for each different type of molding machine. In making such choices, managers weigh the benefits against the costs and limitations of implementing a more detailed costing system.

The main costs and limitations of an ABC system are the measurements necessary to implement it. ABC systems require managers to estimate costs of activity pools and to identify and measure cost drivers for these pools to serve as cost-allocation bases. Even basic ABC systems require many calculations to determine costs of products and services. These measurements are costly. Activity cost rates also need to be updated regularly.

As ABC systems get very detailed and more cost pools are created, more allocations are necessary to calculate activity costs for each cost pool which increases the chances of misidentifying the costs of different activity cost pools. For example, supervisors are more

Exhibit 5-6		Simple Costing System Using a Single Indirect-Cost Pool (1)	ABC System (2)	Difference (3) = (2) − (1)
Comparing Alternative Costing Systems	Direct-cost categories	2	3	1
		Direct materials	Direct materials	
		Direct manufacturing labor	Direct manufacturing labor	
			Direct mold cleaning and maintenance labor	
	Total direct costs	₹2,59,50,000	₹2,86,50,000	₹27,00,000
	Indirect-cost pools	1	6	5
		Single indirect-cost pool allocated using direct manufacturing labor-hours	Design (parts-square feet)[1]	
			Molding machine setup (setup-hours)	
			Machine operations (molding machine-hours)	
			Shipment setup (number of shipments)	
			Distribution (cubic feet delivered)	
			Administration (direct manufacturing labor-hours)	
	Total indirect costs	₹2,38,50,000	₹2,11,50,000	(₹27,00,000)
	Total costs assigned to simple (S3) lens	₹3,52,50,000	₹2,99,89,530	(₹52,60,470)
	Cost per unit of simple (S3) lens	₹587.5	₹499.80	(₹87.70)
	Total costs assigned to complex (CL5) lens	₹1,45,50,000	₹1,98,10,470	₹52,60,470
	Cost per unit of complex (CL5) lens	₹970.0	₹1,320.7	₹350.7

[1]Cost drivers for the various indirect-cost pools are shown in parentheses.

prone to incorrectly identify the time they spent on different activities if they have to allocate their time over five activities rather than only two activities.

Occasionally, managers are also forced to use allocation bases for which data are readily available rather than allocation bases they would have liked to use. For example, a manager might be forced to use the number of loads moved, instead of the degree of difficulty and distance of different loads moved, as the allocation base for material-handling costs, because data on degree of difficulty and distance of moves are difficult to obtain. When incorrect cost-allocation bases are used, activity-cost information can be misleading. For example, if the cost per load moved decreases, a company may conclude that it has become more efficient in its materials-handling operations. In fact, the lower cost per load move may have resulted solely from moving many lighter loads over shorter distances.

Many companies, such as Kanthal, the Swedish manufacturer of heating elements, have found the strategic and operational benefits of a less-detailed ABC system to be good enough to not warrant incurring the costs and challenges of operating a more-detailed system. Other organizations, such as Hewlett-Packard, have implemented ABC in certain divisions or functions. As improvements in information technology and accompanying declines in measurement costs continue, more-detailed ABC systems have become a practical alternative in many companies. As these advancements become more widespread, more detailed ABC systems will be better able to pass the cost–benefit test.

Global surveys of company practice suggest that ABC implementation varies among companies. Nevertheless, its framework and ideas provide a standard for judging whether any simple costing system is good enough for a particular management's purposes. ABC thinking can help managers improve any simple costing system.

Behavioral Issues in Implementing Activity-Based Costing Systems

Successfully implementing ABC systems requires more than an understanding of the technical details. ABC implementation often represents a significant change in the costing system and, as the chapter indicates, requires a manager to choose how to define activities and the level of detail. What then are some of the behavioral issues that managers and management accountants must be sensitive to?

1. **Gaining support of top management and creating a sense of urgency for the ABC effort.** This requires managers and management accountants to clearly communicate the strategic benefits of ABC, such as improvements in product and process design. For example, at USAA Federal Savings Bank, managers calculated the cost of individual activities such as opening and closing accounts and demonstrated how the information gained from ABC provided insights into the efficiency of bank operations, which were previously unavailable.

2. **Creating a guiding coalition of managers throughout the value chain for the ABC effort.** ABC systems measure how the resources of an organization are used. Managers responsible for these resources have the best knowledge about activities and cost drivers. Getting managers to cooperate and take the initiative for implementing ABC is essential for gaining the required expertise, the proper credibility, greater commitment, valuable coordination, and the necessary leadership.

3. **Educating and training employees in ABC as a basis for employee empowerment.** Management accountants must disseminate information about ABC throughout the organization to enable employees in all areas of a business to use their knowledge of ABC to make improvements. For example, WS Industries, an Indian manufacturer of insulators, not only shared ABC information with its workers but also established an incentive plan that gave them a percentage of the cost savings. The results were dramatic because employees were empowered and motivated to implement numerous cost-saving projects.

4. **Seeking small short-run successes as proof that the ABC implementation is yielding results.** Too often, managers and management accountants seek big results and major changes far too quickly. In many situations, achieving a significant change overnight is difficult. However, showing how ABC information has helped improve a process and save costs, even if only in small ways, motivates the team to stay on course and build momentum. The credibility gained from small victories leads to additional and bigger improvements involving larger numbers of people and different parts of the organization. Eventually ABC becomes rooted in the culture of the organization. Sharing short-term successes also helps motivate employees to be innovative. At USAA Federal Savings Bank, managers created a "process improvement" mailbox in Microsoft Outlook to facilitate the sharing of process improvement ideas.

5. **Recognizing that ABC information is not perfect because it balances the need for better information against the costs of creating a complex system that few managers and employees can understand.** The management accountant must help managers recognize both the value and the limitations of ABC and not oversell it. Open and honest communication about ABC ensures that managers use ABC thoughtfully to make

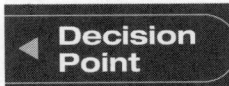

◄ **Decision Point**

What should managers consider when deciding to implement ABC systems?

good decisions. Managers can then make critical judgments without being adversarial and can ask tough questions to help drive better decisions about the system.

Activity-Based Management

Learning Objective 7

Explain how managers use activity-based costing systems in activity-based management

. . . such as pricing decisions, product-mix decisions, and cost reduction

The emphasis of this chapter so far has been on the role of ABC systems in obtaining better product costs. However, Plastim's managers must now use this information to make decisions (step 4 of the 5-step decision process) and to implement the decision, evaluate performance, and learn (step 5). **Activity-based management (ABM)** is a method of management decision-making that uses activity-based costing information to improve customer satisfaction and profitability. We define ABM broadly to include decisions about pricing and product mix, cost reduction, process improvement, and product and process design.

Pricing and Product-Mix Decisions

An ABC system gives managers information about the costs of making and selling diverse products. With this information, managers can make pricing and product-mix decisions. For example, the ABC system indicates that Plastim can match its competitor's price of ₹530 for the S3 lens and still make a profit because the ABC cost of S3 is ₹499.8 (see Exhibit 5-5).

Plastim's managers offer Tata Motors a price of ₹520 for the S3 lens. Plastim's managers are confident that they can use the deeper understanding of costs that the ABC system provides to improve efficiency and further reduce the cost of the S3 lens. Without information from the ABC system, Plastim managers might have erroneously concluded that they would incur an operating loss on the S3 lens at a price of ₹530. This incorrect conclusion would have probably caused Plastim to reduce its business in simple lenses and focus instead on complex lenses, where its single indirect-cost-pool system indicated it is very profitable.

Focusing on complex lenses would have been a mistake. The ABC system indicates that the cost of making the complex lens is much higher—₹1,320.7 versus ₹970 under the direct manufacturing labor-hour-based costing system Plastim had been using. As Plastim's operations staff had thought all along, Plastim has no competitive advantage in making C5 lenses. At a price of ₹1,370 per lens for C5, the profit margin is very small (₹1,370 − ₹1,320.7 = ₹49.3). As Plastim reduces its prices on simple lenses, it would need to negotiate a higher price for complex lenses with Tata Motors.

Cost Reduction and Process Improvement Decisions

Managers use ABC systems to focus on how and where to reduce costs. They set cost reduction targets for the cost per unit of the cost-allocation base in different activity areas. For example, the supervisor of the distribution activity area at Plastim could have a performance target of decreasing distribution cost per cubic foot of products delivered from ₹58.0 to ₹54.0 by reducing distribution labor and warehouse rental costs. The goal is to reduce these costs by improving the way the work is done without compromising customer service or the actual or perceived value (usefulness) customers obtain from the product or service. That is, the supervisor will attempt to take out only those costs that are *nonvalue added*.

Controlling physical cost drivers, such as setup-hours or cubic feet delivered is another fundamental way that operating personnel manage costs. For example, Plastim can decrease distribution costs by packing the lenses in a way that reduces the bulkiness of the packages delivered.

The following table shows the reduction in distribution costs of the S3 and C5 lenses as a result of actions that lower cost per cubic foot delivered (from ₹58.0 to ₹54.0) and total cubic feet of deliveries (from 45,000 to 40,000 for S3 and 22,500 to 20,000 for C5).

	60,000 (S3) Lenses		15,000 (C5) Lenses	
	Total	per Unit	Total	per Unit
	(1)	(2) = (1) ÷ 60,000	(3)	(4) = (3) ÷ 15,000
Distribution costs (from Exhibit 5-5)				
S3, 45,000 cubic feet × ₹58.0/cubic foot	₹26,10,000	₹43.5		
C5, 22,500 cubic feet × ₹58.0/cubic foot			₹13,05,000	₹87.0
Distribution costs as a result of process improvements				
S3, 40,000 cubic feet × ₹58.0/cubic foot	₹26,10,000	36.0	10,80,000	72.0
C5, 20,000 cubic feet × ₹58.0/cubic foot				
Savings in distribution costs from process improvements	₹4,50,000	₹7.50	₹22,50,000	₹15.0

In the long-run, total distribution costs will decrease from ₹39,15,000 (₹26,10,000 + ₹13,05,000) to ₹32,40,000 (₹21,60,000 + ₹10,80,000). In the short run, however, distribution costs may be fixed and may not decrease. Suppose all ₹39,15,000 of distribution costs are fixed costs in the short run. The efficiency improvements (using less distribution labor and space) mean that the same ₹39,15,000 of distribution costs can now be used to distribute 72,500 $\left(\dfrac{₹39,15,000}{₹54.0 \text{ per cubic feet}} \right)$ cubic feet of lenses. In this case, how should costs be allocated to the S3 and C5 lenses?

ABC systems distinguish *costs incurred* from *resources used* to design, manufacture, and deliver products and services. For the distribution activity, after process improvements,

Costs incurred = ₹39,15,000

Resources used = ₹21,60,000 (for S3 lens) + ₹10,80,000 (for C5 lens) = ₹32,40,000

On the basis of the resources used by each product, Plastim's ABC system allocates ₹21,60,000 to S3 and ₹10,80,000 to C5 for a total of ₹32,40,000. The difference of ₹6,75,000 (₹39,15,000 − ₹32,40,000) is shown as costs of unused but available distribution capacity. Plastim's ABC system does not allocate the costs of unused capacity to products so as not to burden the product costs of S3 and C5 with the cost of resources not used by these products. Instead, the system highlights the amount of unused capacity as a separate line item to signal to managers the need to reduce these costs, such as by redeploying labor to other uses or laying off workers. Chapter 9 discusses issues related to unused capacity in more detail.

Design Decisions

ABC systems help managers to evaluate the effect of current product and process designs on activities and costs and to identify new designs to reduce costs. For example, design decisions that decrease the complexity of the mold reduce costs of design, but also materials, labor, machine setups, machine operations, and mold cleaning and maintenance because a less-complex design reduces scrap and the time for setups and operations of the molding machine. Plastim's customers may be willing to give up some features of the lens in exchange for a lower price.

Note that Plastim's previous costing system, which used direct manufacturing labor-hours as the cost-allocation base for all indirect costs, would have mistakenly signaled that Plastim choose those designs that most reduce direct manufacturing labor-hours when, in fact, there is a weak cause-and-effect relationship between direct manufacturing labor-hours and indirect costs.

Planning and Managing Activities

Most managers implementing ABC systems for the first time start by analyzing actual costs to identify activity-cost pools and activity-cost rates. Managers then calculate a budgeted rate (as in the Plastim example) that they use for planning, making decisions, and managing activities. At year-end, managers compare budgeted costs and actual costs to evaluate how well activities were managed. Management accountants make adjustments for underallocated or overallocated indirect costs for each activity using methods described in Chapter 4. As activities and processes change, managers calculate new activity-cost rates.

We will return to activity-based management in later chapters. Management decisions that use activity-based costing information are described in Chapter 6, where we discuss activity-based budgeting; Chapter 11, where we discuss outsourcing and adding or dropping business segments; in Chapter 12, where we evaluate alternative design choices to improve efficiency and reduce nonvalue-added costs; in Chapter 13, where we cover reengineering and downsizing; in Chapter 14, where we explore managing customer profitability; in Chapter 19, where we explain quality improvements; and in Chapter 20, where we describe how to evaluate suppliers.

Decision Point ▶

How can ABC systems be used to manage better?

Activity-Based Costing and Department Costing Systems

Learning Objective 8

Compare activity-based costing systems and department costing systems

. . . activity-based costing systems are a refinement of department costing systems into more-focused and homogenous cost pools

Companies often use costing systems that have features of ABC systems—such as multiple cost pools and multiple cost-allocation bases—but that do not emphasize individual activities. Many companies have evolved their costing systems from using a single indirect cost rate system to using separate indirect cost rates for each department (such as design, manufacturing, distribution,) or each subdepartment (such as machining and assembly departments within manufacturing) that can represent broad tasks. ABC systems, with its focus on specific activities, are a further refinement of department costing systems. In this section, we compare ABC systems and department costing systems.

Plastim uses the Design Department indirect cost rate to cost its design activity. Plastim calculates the design activity rate by dividing total Design Department costs by total parts-square feet, a measure of the complexity of the mold and the driver of Design Department costs. Plastim does not find it worthwhile to calculate separate activity rates within the Design Department for the different design activities, such as designing products, making temporary molds, and designing processes. The complexity of a mold is an appropriate cost-allocation base for costs incurred in each design activity because Design Department costs are homogeneous with respect to this cost-allocation base.

In contrast, the Manufacturing Department identifies two activity cost pools—a setup cost pool and a machine operations cost pool—instead of using a single Manufacturing Department overhead cost pool. It identifies these activity cost pools for two reasons. First, each of these activities within manufacturing incurs significant costs and has a different cost driver setup-hours for the setup cost pool and machine-hours for the machine operations cost pool. Second, the S3 and C5 lenses do not use resources from these two activity areas in the same proportion. For example, C5 uses 75% (1,500 ÷ 2,000) of the setup-hours but only 29.4% (3,750 ÷ 12,750) of the machine-hours. Using only machine-hours, say, to allocate all Manufacturing Department costs at Plastim would result in C5 being undercosted because it would not be charged for the significant amounts of setup resources it actually uses.

For the reasons we just explained, using department indirect cost rates to allocate costs to products results in similar information as activity cost rates if: (1) a single activity accounts for a sizable proportion of the department's costs; or (2) significant costs are incurred on different activities within a department but each activity has the same cost driver and hence cost-allocation base (as was the case in Plastim's Design Department). From a purely product costing standpoint, department and activity indirect cost rates will also result the same product costs if (1) significant costs are incurred for different activities with different cost-allocation bases within a department but (2) different products use resources from the different activity areas in the same proportions (for example, if C5 had used 65%, say, of the setup-hours and 65% of the machine-hours). In this case, though, not identifying activities and cost drivers within departments conceals activity cost information that would help managers manage costs and improve design and processes.

We close this section with a note of caution. Do not assume that because department costing systems require the creation of multiple indirect cost pools that they properly recognize the drivers of costs within departments as well as how resources are used by products. As we have indicated, in many situations, department costing systems can be refined using ABC. Emphasizing activities leads to more-focused and homogeneous cost pools, aids in identifying cost-allocation bases for activities that have a better cause-and-effect relationship with the costs in activity cost pools, and leads to better design and process decisions. But the benefits of an ABC system must be balanced against its costs and limitations.

◀ **Decision Point**

When can department costing systems be used instead of ABC systems?

ABC in Service and Merchandising Companies

Although many of the early examples of ABC originated in manufacturing, ABC has many applications in service and merchandising companies. For instance, the Plastim example includes the application of ABC to a service activity—design—and to a merchandising activity—distribution. Some banks, hospitals, telecom companies and wholesale/retail companies have used ABC System. As we describe in Chapter 14, a large number of financial services companies (as well as other companies) employ variations of ABC systems to analyze and improve the profitability of their customer interactions.

The widespread use of ABC systems in service and merchandising companies reinforces the idea that ABC systems are used by managers for strategic decisions rather than for inventory valuation. (Inventory valuation is fairly straightforward in merchandising companies and not needed in service companies.) Service companies, in particular, find great value from ABC because a vast majority of their cost structure comprises indirect costs. After all, there are few direct costs when a bank makes a loan, or when a representative answers a phone call at a call center. As we have seen, a major benefit of ABC is its ability to assign indirect costs to cost objects by identifying activities and cost drivers. As a result, ABC systems provide greater insight than traditional systems into the management of these indirect costs. The general approach to ABC in service and merchandising companies is similar to the ABC approach in manufacturing.

The Cooperative Bank followed the approach described in this chapter when it implemented ABC in its retail baking operations. Managers calculated the costs of various activities, such as performing ATM transactions, opening and closing accounts, administering mortgages, and processing Visa transactions by dividing the cost of these activities by the time available to do them. Managers used these time-based rates to cost individual products, such as checking accounts, mortgages, and Visa cards, and to calculate the costs of supporting different types of customers. Information from this time-driven activity-based costing system helped the USAA Cooperative Bank to improve its processes and to identify profitable products and customer segments.

Activity-based costing raises some interesting issues when it is applied to a public service institution such as the Postal Service. The costs of delivering mail to remote locations are far greater than the costs of delivering mail within urban areas. Howerver, for fairness and community-building reasons, the Postal Service cannot charge customers in remote areas higer prices. In this case, activity-based coosting is valuable for understanding, managing, and reducing costs but not for pricing decisions.

Problem for Self-Study

Family Supermarkets (FS) has decided to increase the size of its NOIDA store. It wants information about the profitability of individual product lines: soft drinks, fresh produce, and packaged food. FS provides the following data for 2014 for each product line:

	Soft Drinks	Fresh Produce	Packaged Food
Revenues	₹31,74,000	₹84,02,400	₹48,39,600
Cost of goods sold	₹24,00,000	₹60,00,000	36,00,000
Cost of bottles returned	₹4,800	₹0	₹0
Number of purchase orders placed	144	336	144
Number of deliveries received	120	876	264
Hours of shelf-stocking time	216	2,160	1,080
Items sold	50,400	441,600	122,400

FS also provides the following information for 2010:

Activity (1)	Description of Activity (2)	Total Support Costs (3)	Cost-Allocation Base (4)
1. Bottle returns	Returning of empty bottles to store	₹48,000	Direct tracing to soft-drink line
2. Ordering	Placing of orders for purchases	₹6,24,000	624 purchase orders
3. Delivery	Physical delivery and receipt of merchandise	₹10,08,000	1,260 deliveries
4. Shelf-stocking	Stocking of merchandise on store shelves and ongoing restocking	₹6,91,200	3,456 hours of shelf-stocking time
5. Customer support	Assistance provided to customers, including checkout and bagging	₹12,28,800	614,400 items sold
Total		₹36,00,000	

Required

1. Family Supermarkets currently allocates store support costs (all costs other than cost of goods sold) to product lines on the basis of cost of goods sold of each product line. Calculate the operating income and operating income as a percentage of revenues for each product line.
2. If Family Supermarkets allocates store support costs (all costs other than cost of goods sold) to product lines using an ABC system, calculate the operating income and operating income as a percentage of revenues for each product line.
3. Comment on your answers in requirements 1 and 2.

Solution

1. The following table shows the operating income and operating income as a percentage of revenues for each product line. All store support costs (all costs other than cost of goods sold) are allocated to product lines using cost of goods sold of each product line as the cost-allocation base. Total store support costs equal ₹36,00,000 (cost of bottles returned, ₹48,000 + cost of purchase orders, ₹6,24,000 + cost of deliveries, ₹10,08,000 + cost of shelf-stocking, ₹6,91,200 + cost of customer support, ₹12,28,200). The allocation rate for store support costs = ₹36,00,000 ÷ ₹1,20,00,000 (soft drinks ₹24,00,000 + fresh produce ₹60,00,000 + packaged food, ₹36,00,000)

= 30% of cost of goods sold. To allocate support costs to each product line, FS multiplies the cost of goods sold of each product line by 0.30.

	Soft Drinks	Fresh Produce	Packaged Food	Total
Revenues	₹31,74,000	₹84,02,400	₹48,39,600	₹1,64,16,000
Cost of goods sold	24,00,000	60,00,000	36,00,000	1,20,00,000
Store support cost (₹24,00,000; ₹60,00,000; ₹36,00,000) × 0.30	7,20,000	18,00,000	10,80,000	36,00,000
Total costs	31,20,000	78,00,000	46,80,000	1,56,00,000
Operating income	₹ 54,000	₹6,02,400	₹1,59,600	₹8,16,000
Operating income ÷ Revenues	1.70%	7.17%	3.30%	4.97%

2. Under an ABC system, FS identifies bottle-return costs as a direct cost because these costs can be traced to the soft drink product line. FS then calculates cost-allocation rates for each activity area (as in step 5 of the seven-step costing system, described in the chapter). The activity rates are as follows:

Activity (1)	Cost Hierarchy (2)	Total Costs (3)	Quantity of Cost-Allocation Base (4)	Overhead Allocation Rate (5) = (3) ÷ (4)
Ordering	Batch-level	₹6,24,000	624 purchase orders	₹1,000 per purchase order
Delivery	Batch-level	₹10,08,000	1,260 deliveries	₹800 per delivery
Shelf-stocking	Output unit-level	₹6,91,200	3,456 shelf-stocking-hours	₹200 per stocking-hour
Customer support	Output unit-level	₹12,28,800	614,400 items sold	₹2.0 per item sold

Store support costs for each product line by activity are obtained by multiplying the total quantity of the cost-allocation base for each product line by the activity cost rate. Operating income and operating income as a percentage of revenues for each product line are as follows:

	Soft Drinks	Fresh Produce	Packaged Food	Total
Revenues	₹31,74,000	₹84,02,400	₹48,39,600	₹1,6416,000
Cost of goods sold	24,00,000	60,00,000	36,00,000	1,20,00,000
Bottle-return costs	48,000	0	0	4,800
Ordering costs (144; 336; 144) purchase orders × ₹1,000	1,44,000	3,36,000	1,44,000	6,24,000
Delivery costs (120; 876; 264) deliveries × ₹800	96,000	7,00,800	2,11,200	10,08,000
Shelf-stocking costs (216; 2,160; 1,080) stocking-hours × ₹200	43,200	4,32,000	2,16,000	6,91,200
Customer-support costs (50,400; 441,600; 122,400) items sold × ₹2.0	10,08,000	8,83,200	2,44,800	12,28,800
Total costs	28,32,000	83,52,000	44,16,000	1,56,00,000
Operating income	₹3,42,000	₹50,400	₹4,23,600	₹8,16,000
Operating income ÷ Revenues	10.78%	0.60%	8.75%	4.97%

3. Managers believe the ABC system is more credible than the simple costing system. The ABC system distinguishes the different types of activities at FS more precisely. It also tracks more accurately how individual product lines use resources. Rankings of relative profitability—operating income as a percentage of revenues—of the three product lines under the simple costing system and under the ABC system are:

Simple Costing System		ABC System	
1. Fresh produce	7.17%	1. Soft drinks	10.78%
2. Packaged food	3.30%	2. Packaged food	8.75%
3. Soft drinks	1.70%	3. Fresh produce	0.60%

The percentage of revenues, cost of goods sold, and activity costs for each product line are as follows:

	Soft Drinks	Fresh Produce	Packaged Food
Revenues	19.34%	51.18%	29.48%
Cost of goods sold	20.00	50.00	30.00
Bottle returns	100.00	0	0
Activity areas:			
Ordering	23.08	53.84	23.08
Delivery	9.53	69.52	20.95
Shelf-stocking	6.25	62.50	31.25
Customer-support	8.20	71.88	19.92

Soft drinks consume fewer resources than either fresh produce or packaged food. Soft drinks have fewer deliveries and require less shelf-stocking time than required for either fresh produce or packaged food. Most major soft-drink suppliers deliver merchandise to the store shelves and stock the shelves themselves. In contrast, the fresh produce area has the most deliveries and consumes a large percentage of shelf-stocking time. It also has the highest number of individual sales items. The simple costing system assumed that each product line used the resources in each activity area in the same ratio as their respective individual cost of goods sold to total cost of goods sold. Clearly, this assumption is incorrect. The simple costing system is an example of averaging that is too broad.

FS managers can use the ABC information to guide decisions such as how to allocate a planned increase in floor space. An increase in the percentage of space allocated to soft drinks is warranted. Note, however, that ABC information should be but one input into decisions about shelf-space allocation. FS may have minimum limits on the shelf space allocated to fresh produce because of shoppers' expectations that supermarkets will carry products from this product line. In many situations, companies cannot make product decisions in isolation but must consider the effect that dropping a product might have on customer demand for other products.

Pricing decisions can also be made in a more informed way with ABC information. For example, suppose a competitor announces a 5% reduction in soft-drink prices. Given the 10.77% margin FS currently earns on its soft-drink product line, it has flexibility to reduce prices and still make a profit on this product line. In contrast, the simple costing system erroneously implied that soft drinks only had a 1.70% margin, leaving little room to counter a competitor's pricing initiatives.

Decision Points

The following question-and-answer format summarizes the chapter's learning objectives. Each decision presents a key question related to a learning objective. The guidelines are the answer to that question.

Decision	Guidelines
1. When does product undercosting or overcosting occur?	Product undercosting (overcosting) occurs when a product or service consumes a high (low) level of resources but is reported to have a low (high) cost. Broad averaging, or peanut-butter costing, a common cause of undercosting or overcosting, is the result of using broad averages that uniformly assign, or spread, the cost of resources to products when the individual products use those resources in a nonuniform way. Product-cost cross-subsidization exists when one undercosted (overcosted) product results in at least one other product being overcosted (undercosted).
2. How do managers refine a costing system?	Refining a costing system means making changes that result in cost numbers that better measure the way different cost objects, such as products, use different amounts of resources of the company. These changes can require additional direct-cost tracing, the choice of more-homogeneous indirect cost pools, or the use of different cost-allocation bases.
3. What is the difference between the design of a simple costing system and an activity-based costing (ABC) system?	The ABC system differs from the simple system by its fundamental focus on activities. The ABC system typically has more-homogeneous indirect-cost pools than the simple system, and more cost drivers are used as cost-allocation bases.
4. What is a cost hierarchy?	A cost hierarchy categorizes costs into different cost pools on the basis of the different types of cost-allocation bases or different degrees of difficulty in determining cause-and-effect (or benefits-received) relationships. A four-part cost hierarchy consists of output unit-level costs, batch-level costs, product-sustaining or service-sustaining costs, and facility-sustaining costs.
5. How do managers cost products or services using ABC systems?	In ABC, costs of activities are used to assign costs to other cost objects such as products or services based on the activities the products or services consume.
6. What should managers consider when deciding to implement ABC systems?	ABC systems are likely to yield the most decision-making benefits when indirect costs are a high percentage of total costs or when products and services make diverse demands on indirect resources. The main costs of ABC systems are the difficulties of the measurements necessary to implement and update the systems.
7. How can ABC systems be used to manage better?	Activity-based management (ABM) is a management method of decision making that uses ABC information to satisfy customers and improve profits. ABC systems are used for such management decisions as pricing, product-mix, cost reduction, process improvement, product and process redesign, and planning and managing activities.
8. When can department costing systems be used instead of ABC systems?	Activity-based costing systems are a refinement of department costing systems into more-focused and homogeneous cost pools. Cost information in department costing systems approximates cost information in ABC systems only when each department has a single activity (or a single activity accounts for a significant proportion of department costs) or a single cost driver for different activities or when different products use the different activities of the department in the same proportions.

TERMS TO LEARN

This chapter and the Glossary at the end of the book contain definitions of the following important terms:

activity **(p. 8)**
activity-based costing
  (ABC) **(p. 208)**
activity-based management
  (ABM) **(p. 220)**
batch-level
  costs **(p. 211)**
cost hierarchy **(p. 211)**

facility-sustaining
  costs **(p. 212)**
output unit–level
  costs **(p. 211)**
product-cost cross-
  subsidization **(p. 201)**
product overcosting
  (p. 201)

product-sustaining
  costs **(p. 211)**
product undercosting
  (p. 201)
refined costing
  system **(p. 206)**
service-sustaining
  costs **(p. 211)**

ASSIGNMENT MATERIAL

Questions

5-1 What is broad averaging and what consequences can it have on costs?

5-2 Why should managers worry about product overcosting or undercosting?

5-3 What is costing system refinement? Describe three guidelines for refinement.

5-4 What is an activity-based approach to designing a costing system?

5-5 Describe four levels of a cost hierarchy.

5-6 Why is it important to classify costs into a cost hierarchy?

5-7 What are the key reasons for product cost differences between simple costing systems and ABC systems?

5-8 Describe four decisions for which ABC information is useful.

5-9 "Department indirect-cost rates are never activity-cost rates." Do you agree? Explain.

5-10 Describe four signs that help indicate when ABC systems are likely to provide the most benefits.

5-11 What are the main costs and limitations of implementing ABC systems?

5-12 "ABC systems only apply to manufacturing companies." Do you agree? Explain.

5-13 "Activity-based costing is the wave of the present and the future. All companies should adopt it." Do you agree? Explain.

5-14 "Increasing the number of indirect-cost pools is guaranteed to sizably increase the accuracy of product or service costs." Do you agree? Why?

5-15 The controller of a retail company has just had a ₹5,00,000 request to implement an ABC system quickly turned down. A senior vice president, in rejecting the request, noted, "Given a choice, I will always prefer a ₹5,00,000 investment in improving things a customer sees or experiences, such as our shelves or our store layout. How does a customer benefit by our spending ₹5,00,000 on a supposedly better accounting system?" How should the controller respond?

Solved Examples

5-16 ABC, distribution. (W. Bruns, adapted) Shaw Wallace makes two wines: a regular wine and a premium wine. Shaw Wallace distributes the regular wine and the premium wine through different distribution channels. It distributes 2,40,000 cases of regular wine through

10 general distributors and 1,60,000 cases of the premium wine through 30 specialty distributors. Shaw Wallace incurs ₹42,60,000 in distribution costs. Under its existing costing system, Shaw Wallace allocates distribution costs to products on the basis of cases shipped.

To understand better the demands on its resources in the distribution area, Shaw Wallace identifies three activities and related activity costs.

a. Promotional costs–Shaw Wallace estimates it incurs ₹16,000 per distributor.

b. Order handling costs–Shaw Wallace estimates costs of ₹600 pertaining to each order. Shaw Wallace records show that distributors of regular wine place an average of 10 orders per year, whereas distributors of premium wine place an average of 20 orders per year.

c. Delivery costs–₹8 per case.

Required

1. Using Shaw Wallace existing costing system, calculate the total distribution costs and distribution cost per case for the regular wine and the premium wine.
2. Using Shaw Wallace activity-based costing system, calculate the total distribution costs and distribution cost per case for the regular wine and the premium wine.
3. Explain the cost differences and the accuracy of the product costs calculated using the existing costing system and the ABC system. How might Shaw Wallace management use the information from the ABC system to manage its business better?

Solution

1. Total distribution costs (given), ₹42,60,000

$$\text{Distribution cost per case under existing system} = \frac{\text{Total distribution cost}}{\text{Total cases of premium and regular wine shipped}}$$

$$= ₹42,60,000/4,00,000 = ₹10.65 \text{ per case}$$

	Regular Per Case		Premium Per Case	
	Total (1)	(2) (1) ÷ 2,40,000	Total (3)	(4) 3 ÷ 1,60,000
Distribution costs				
₹10.65 × 2,40,000 and	₹25,56,000	₹10.65	₹17,04,000	₹10.65
₹10.65 × 1,60,000				

2.

Particulars	Regular Per Case		Premium Per Case	
	Total (1)	(2) 1 ÷ 2,40,000	Total (3)	(4) 3 ÷ 1,60,000
Delivery costs				
₹8 × 2,40,000 cases	₹19,20,000	₹8.00	₹12,80,000	₹8.00
₹8 × 1,60,000 cases				
Ordering costs				
₹600 × 10 orders/year ×				
10 distributors	60,000	0.25	3,60,000	2.25
₹600 × 20 orders/year ×				
30 distributors				
Promotion costs				
₹16,000 × 10 distributors	1,60,000	0.67	4,80,000	3.00
₹16,000 × 30 distributors			—	
Total costs	21,40,000	8.92	21,20,000	13.25

3. The existing costing system uses cases shipped as the only cost allocation base for distribution costs. As a result, the distribution cost per case is the same for premium and regular wines (₹10.65). In fact, premium wine uses distribution resources more intensively than regular wine: (a) Shaw Wallace spends ₹16,000 on promotional costs at each distributor independent of cases sold. Premium wine distributors sell fewer cases a year than regular wine distributors. As a result the promotional cost per case of wine sold is higher for premium wine than for regular wine. (b) Shaw Wallace's cost per order

is ₹600 regardless of the number of cases sold in each order. Because premium wine distributors order fewer cases per order, the ordering costs per case are higher for premium wines than for regular wines.

The existing costing system undercosts distribution costs per case for premium wine and overcosts distribution costs per case for regular wine.

Shaw Wallace's management can use the information from the ABC system to make better pricing and product mix decisions, to reduce costs by eliminating processes and activities that do not add value, to reduce the costs of doing various activities, and to plan and manage activities.

5-17 Plant-wide, department, and ABC indirect cost rates. Automotive Products (AP) designs and produces automotive parts. In 2015, actual variable manufacturing overhead is ₹30,86,000. AP's simple costing system allocates variable manufacturing overhead to its three customers based on machine-hours and prices its contracts based on full costs. One of its customers has regularly complained of being charged noncompetitive prices, so AP's controller Ajay Jain realizes that it is time to examine the consumption of overhead resources more closely. He knows that there are three main departments that consume overhead resources: design, production, and engineering. Interviews with the department personnel and examination of time records yield the following detailed information.

Home	Insert	Page Layout	Formulas	Data	Review	View	

	A	B	C	D	E	F
1				Usage of Cost Drivers by Customer Contract		
2	Department	Cost Driver	Manufacturing Overhead in 2015	United Motors	Holden Motors	Leland Auto
3	Design	CAD-design-hours	₹3,90,000	110	200	80
4	Production	Engineering-hours	2,96,000	70	60	240
5	Engineering	Machine-hours	24,00,000	120	2,800	1,080
6	Total		₹30,86,000			

Required

1. Compute the manufacturing overhead allocated to each customer in 2015 using the simple costing system that uses machine-hours as the allocation base.

2. Compute the manufacturing overhead allocated to each customer in 2015 using department-based manufacturing overhead rates.

3. Comment on your answers in requirements 1 and 2. Which customer do you think was complaining about being overcharged in the simple system? If the new department-based rates are used to price contracts, which customer(s) will be unhappy? How would you respond to these concerns?

4. How else might AP use the information available from its department-by-department analysis of manufacturing overhead costs?

5. AP's managers are wondering if they should further refine the department-by-department costing system into an ABC system by identifying different activities within each department. Under what conditions would it not be worthwhile to further refine the department costing system into an ABC system?

Solution

1.

Actual plantwide variable MOH rate
based on machine hours,
₹30,86,000 ÷ 4,000   ₹771.50 per machine hour

	United Motors	Holden Motors	Leland Auto	Total
Variable manufacturing overhead, allocated based on machine hours (₹771.50 × 120; ₹771.50 × 2,800; ₹771.50 × 1,080)	₹92,580	₹21,60,200	₹8,33,220	₹30,86,000

2.

Department	MOH in 2015	Total Driver Units	Rate	
Design	₹3,90,000	390	₹1,000	per CAD-design hour
Production	2,96,000	370	₹800	per engineering hour
Engineering	24,00,000	4,000	₹600	per machine hour

	United Motors	Holden Motors	Leland Auto	Total
Design-related overhead, allocated on CAD-design hours (110 × ₹1,000; 200 × ₹1,000; 80 × ₹1,000)	₹1,10,000	₹2,00,000	₹80,000	₹3,90,000
Production-related overhead, allocated on engineering hours (70 × ₹800; 60 × ₹800; 240 × ₹800)	56,000	48,000	1,92,000	2,96,000
Engineering-related overhead, allocated on machine hours (120 × ₹600; 2,800 × ₹600; 1,080 × ₹600)	72,000	16,80,000	6,48,000	24,00,000
Total	₹2,38,000	₹19,28,000	₹9,20,000	₹30,86,000

3.

	United Motors	Holden Motors	Leland Auto
a. Department rates (Requirement 2)	₹2,38,000	₹19,28,000	₹9,20,000
	₹92,580	₹21,60,200	₹8,33,220
b. Plantwide rate (Requirement 1)			
Ratio of (a) ÷ (b)	2.57	0.89	1.10

The manufacturing overhead allocated to United Motors increases by 157% under the department rates, the overhead allocated to Holden decreases by about 11%, and the overhead allocated to Leland increases by about 10%.

The three contracts differ sizably in the way they use the resources of the three departments.

The percentage of total driver units in each department used by the companies is:

Department	Cost Driver	United Motors	Holden Motors	Leland Auto
Design	CAD-design hours	28%	51%	21%
Engineering	Engineering hours	19	16	65
Production	Machine hours	3	70	27

The United Motors contract uses only 3% of total machines hours in 2015, yet uses 28% of CAD design-hours and 19% of engineering hours. The result is that the plantwide rate, based on machine hours, will greatly underestimate the cost of resources used on the United Motors contract. This explains the 157% increase in indirect costs assigned to the United Motors contract when department rates are used. The Leland Auto contract also uses far fewer machine-hours than engineering-hours and is also undercosted.

In contrast, the Holden Motors contract uses less of design (51%) and engineering (16%) than of machine-hours (70%). Hence, the use of department rates will report lower indirect costs for Holden Motors than does a plantwide rate.

Holden Motors was probably complaining under the use of the simple system because its contract was being overcosted relative to its consumption of MOH resources. United and Leland, on the other hand, were having their contracts undercosted and underpriced by the simple system. Assuming that AP is an efficient and competitive supplier, if the new department-based rates are used to price contracts, United and Leland will be unhappy. AP should explain to United and Leland how the calculation was done, and point out United's high use of design and engineering resources and Leland's high use of engineering resources relative to production machine hours. Discuss ways of reducing the consumption of those resources, if possible, and show willingness to partner with them to do so. If the price rise is going to be steep, perhaps offer to phase in the new prices.

4. Other than for pricing, AP can also use the information from the department-based system to examine and streamline its own operations so that there is maximum value-added from all indirect resources. It might set targets over time to reduce both the consumption of each indirect resource and the unit costs of the resources. The department-based system gives AP more opportunities for targeted cost management.

5. It would not be worthwhile to further refine the cost system into an ABC system if (1) a single activity accounts for a sizable proportion of the department's costs or (2) significant costs are incurred on different activities within a department, but each activity has the same cost driver or (3) there wasn't much variation among contracts in the consumption of activities within a department. If, for example, most activities within the design department were, in fact, driven by CAD-design hours, then the more refined system would be more costly and no more accurate than the department-based cost system. Even if there was sufficient variation, considering the relative sizes of the three department cost pools, it may only be cost-effective to further analyze the engineering cost pool, which consumes 78% (₹24,00,000 ÷ ₹30,86,000) of the manufacturing overhead.

5-18 Plant-wide, department, and activity-cost rates. Triumph Trophies makes trophies and plaques and operates at capacity. Triumph does large custom orders, such as the participant trophies for the Mohan Began League. The controller has asked you to compare plant-wide, department, and activity- based cost allocation.

Triumph Trophies Budgeted Information for the Year Ended March 31, 2015

Forming Department	Trophies	Plaques	Total
Direct materials	₹26,000	₹22,500	₹48,500
Direct manufacturing labor	31,200	18,000	49,200
Overhead costs			
Set up			24,000
Supervision			20,772

Assembly Department	Trophies	Plaques	Total
Direct materials	₹5,200	₹18,750	₹23,950
Direct manufacturing labor	15,600	21,000	36,600
Overhead costs			
Setup			46,000
Supervision			21,920

Other information follows:

Setup costs in each department vary with the number of batches processed in each department. The budgeted number of batches for each product line in each department is as follows:

	Trophies	Plaques
Forming department	40	116
Assembly department	43	103

Supervision costs in each department vary with direct manufacturing labor costs in each department.

Required

1. Calculate the budgeted cost of trophies and plaques based on a single plant-wide overhead rate, if total overhead is allocated based on total direct costs.
2. Calculate the budgeted cost of trophies and plaques based on departmental overhead rates, where forming department overhead costs are allocated based on direct manufacturing labor costs of the forming department and assembly department overhead costs are allocated based on total direct costs of the assembly department.
3. Calculate the budgeted cost of trophies and plaques if Triumph allocates overhead costs in each department using activity-based costing.
4. Explain how the disaggregation of information could improve or reduce decision quality.

Solution

1.

	Trophies	Plaques	Total
Direct materials			
Forming	₹26,000	₹22,500	
Assembly	5,200	18,750	
Total	31,200	41,250	
Direct manufacturing labor			
Forming	31,200	18,000	
Assembly	15,600	21,000	
Total	46,800	39,000	
Total direct costs	₹78,000	₹80,250	₹158,250

$$\text{Budgeted overhead rate} = \frac{(₹24,000 + ₹20,772 + ₹46,000 + ₹21,920)}{₹1,58,250} = \frac{₹1,12,692}{₹1,58,250}$$

$$= \frac{₹0.712114}{\text{per rupee of direct cost}}$$

	Trophies	Plaques	Total
Direct materials	₹31,200	₹41,250	₹72,450
Direct labor	46,800	39,000	85,800
Total direct cost	78,000	80,250	1,58,250
Allocated overhead*	55,544	57,148	1,12,692
Total costs	₹1,33,544	₹1,37,398	₹2,70,942

*Allocated overhead = Total direct cost × Budgeted overhead rate (0.712114).

2. $\text{Budgeted overhead rate Forming Dept.} = \dfrac{\text{Budgeted Forming Department overhead costs}}{\text{Budgeted Forming Department direct manufacturing labor costs}}$

$$= \frac{₹24,000 + ₹20,772}{₹31,200 + ₹18,000}$$

$$= \frac{₹44,772}{₹49,200} = ₹0.91 \text{ per Forming Department direct manuf.-labor cost}$$

Budgeted overhead rate Assembly Dept. $= \dfrac{\text{Budgeted Assembly Department overhead costs}}{\text{Budgeted Assembly Department direct costs}}$

$$= \frac{₹46,000 + ₹21,920}{(₹5,200 + ₹18,750 + ₹15,600 + ₹21,000)}$$

$$= \frac{₹67,920}{₹60,550} = 1.121718 \text{ times Assembly Department direct cost}$$

	Trophies	Plaques	Total
Direct materials	₹31,200	₹41,250	₹72,450
Direct labor	46,800	39,000	85,800
Total direct cost	78,000	80,250	1,58,250
Allocated overhead			
Forming Dept.[a]	28,392	16,380	44,772
Assembly Dept.[b]	23,332	44,588	67,920
Total costs	₹1,29,724	₹1,41,218	₹2,70,942

	Trophies	Plaques	Total
[a]Forming Dept.			
Direct manufacturing labor costs	₹31,200	₹18,000	₹49,200
Allocated overhead			
(0.91 × ₹31,200; ₹18,000)	₹28,392	₹16,380	₹44,772
[b]Assembly Dept.			
Total direct costs			
(₹5,200 + ₹15,600; ₹18,750 + ₹21,000)	₹20,800	₹39,750	₹60,550
Allocated overhead			
(1.121718 × ₹20,800; ₹39,750)	₹11,666	₹22,294	₹33,960

3.

Forming Department

Budgeted setup rate $= \dfrac{₹24,000}{156 \text{ batches}} = ₹1,53.84615 \text{ per batch}$

Budgeted supervision rate $= \dfrac{₹20,772}{₹49,200} = ₹0.422195 \text{ per direct-labor cost}$

Assembly Department

Budgeted set up rate $= \dfrac{₹46,000}{146 \text{ batches}} = ₹315.06849 \text{ per batch}$

Budgeted supervision rate $= \dfrac{₹21,920}{₹36,600} = ₹0.598907 \text{ per direct manuf.-labor cost}$

	Trophies	Plaques	Total
Direct material costs	₹31,200	₹41,250	₹72,450
Direct labor costs	46,800	39,000	85,800
Total direct costs	78,000	80,250	1,58,250

Forming Dept. overhead
Set up

₹153.84615 × 40; 116		6,154	17,846	24,000

Supervision

0.422195 × ₹31,200; ₹18,000		13,172	7,600	20,772

Assembly Department overhead
Set up

₹315.06849 × 43; 103		13,548	32,452	46,000

Supervision

0.598907 × ₹15,600; ₹21,000		9,343	12,577	21,920

Total costs		₹1,20,217	₹1,50,725	₹2,70,942

4. As Triumph uses more refined cost pools, the costs of trophies decreases, and costs of plaques increases. This is because plaques use a higher proportion of cost drivers (batches of set ups and direct manufacturing labor costs) than trophies, whereas the direct costs (the allocation base used in the simple costing system) are slightly smaller for plaques compared to trophies. This results in plaques being undercosted and trophies overcosted in the simple costing system.

Department costing systems increase the costs of plaques relative to trophies because the forming department costs are allocated based on direct manufacturing labor costs in the forming department and plaques use more direct manufacturing labor in this department compared to trophies.

Disaggregated information can improve decisions by allowing managers to see the details that help them understand how different aspects of cost influence total cost per unit. Managers can also understand the drivers of different cost categories and use this information for pricing and product-mix decisions, cost reduction and process-improvement decisions, design decisions, and to plan and manage activities. However, too much detail can overload managers who don't understand the data or what it means. Also, managers looking at per-unit data may be misled when considering costs that aren't unit-level costs.

5-19 Department costing, service company. S.S.Kothari is an architectural firm that designs and builds buildings. It prices each job on a cost plus 20% basis. Overhead costs in 2015 are ₹40,11,780. S.S.Kothari's simple costing system allocates overhead costs to its jobs based on number of jobs. There were three jobs in 2015. One customer, Bharti, has complained that the cost of its building in Gurgaon was not competitive. As a result, the controller has initiated a detailed review of the overhead allocation to determine if overhead costs are charged to jobs in proportion to consumption of overhead resources by jobs. She gathers the following information.

			Quantity of cost Drivers Used by Each Project		
Department	**Cost Driver**	**Overhead Cost in 2015**	**Bharti**	**Vinod**	**Arham**
Design	Design department hours	₹15,00,000	1,000	5,000	4,000
Engineering	Number of engineers	₹5,00,030	2,000	2,000	2,200
Construction	Labor-hours	₹20,11,750	20,800	21,500	19,600
		₹40,11,780			

Required

1. Compute the overhead allocated to each project in 2015 using the simple costing system.
2. Compute the overhead allocated to each project in 2015 using department overhead cost rates.

3. Do you think Bharti had a valid reason for dissatisfaction with the cost? How does the allocation based on department rates change costs for each project?

4. What value, if any, would S.S.Kothari get by allocating costs of each department based on the activities done in that department?

Solution

Note: The cost driver for engineering is number of engineering-hours, not number of engineers. This change does not, however, affect the solution itself.

1. Using the simple costing system, total overhead costs are equally allocated to projects. There were 3 projects in 2015, so the overhead cost per project is

$$\frac{\text{Overhead cost}}{\text{per project in } 2015} = \frac{₹40,11,780}{3} = ₹13,37,260 \text{ per project}$$

2. Rates per unit cost driver.

Activity	Cost Driver	Rate
Design	Design department hours	₹15,00,000 ÷ (1,000 + 5,000 + 4,000)
		= ₹150 per design-hour
Engineering	Engineering dept. hours	₹5,00,030 ÷ (2,000 + 2,000 + 2,200)
		= ₹80.65 per engineering-hour
Construction	Labor-hours	₹20,11,750 ÷ (20,800 + 21,500 + 19,600)
		= ₹32.50 per labor-hour

Overhead cost allocated to each project using department overhead cost rates:

	Bharti	Vinod	Arham
Design: ₹150 × 1,000; 5,000; 4,000	₹1,50,000	₹7,50,000	₹6,00,000
Engineering: ₹80.65 × 2,000; 2,000; 2,200	1,61,300	1,61,300	1,77,430
Construction: ₹32.50 × 20,800; 21,500; 19,600	6,76,000	6,98,750	6,37,000
Total overhead costs	₹9,87,300	₹16,10,050	₹14,14,430

3.

	Bharti	Vinod	Arham
a. Department rates			
(Requirement 2)	₹9,87,300	₹16,10,050	₹14,14,430
b. Plantwide rate			
(Requirement 1)	₹13,37,260	₹13,37,260	₹13,37,260
Ratio of (a) ÷ (b)	0.74	1.20	1.06

The overhead allocated to Bharti decreases by 26% under the department rates, the overhead allocated to Vinod increases by about 20%, and the overhead allocated to Arham increases by about 6%.

The three projects differ sizably in the way they use the resources of the three departments. The percentage of total driver units in each department used by the companies is:

Department	Cost Driver	Bharti	Vinod	Arham
Design	Design-hours	10%	50%	40%
Engineering	Engineering-hours	32	32	36
Construction	Labor-hours	33	35	32

The Bharti project uses only 10% of design-hours in 2015 and uses 32% of engineering-hours and 33% of construction hours. The result is that the overhead rate, based on allocating costs equally to all projects (33%), will greatly overestimate the cost of resources used on the Bharti project, which uses very few design-hours. This explains the 26% decrease in indirect costs assigned to the Bharti project when department rates are used.

In contrast, the Vinod and Arham projects use more of design (50% and 40%, respectively). Hence, the use of department rates will report higher indirect costs for Vinod and Arham than does a single overhead rate.

Bharti was probably complaining about the costs resulting from using the simple system because its project was being overcosted relative to its consumption of overhead resources. Vinod and Arham, on the other hand, were having their projects undercosted and underpriced by the simple system. If the new department-based rates are used to price projects, Vinod and Arham will be unhappy. S.S.Kothari should explain to Vinod and Arham how the calculations were done and point out their high use of design resources. S.S.Kothari should discuss ways of reducing the consumption of design resources, if possible, and show willingness to partner with them to do so. S.S.Kothari could even offer to phase in the new prices.

4. It would not be worthwhile to further refine the cost system into an ABC system if (1) a single activity accounts for a sizable proportion of the department's costs or (2) significant costs are incurred on different activities within a department, but each activity has the same cost driver or (3) there wasn't much variation among contracts in the consumption of activities within a department. If, for example, most activities within the design department were, in fact, driven by design-hours, then the more refined system would be more costly and no more accurate than the department-based cost system.

5-20 Activity-based costing, service company. Metro Corporation owns a small printing press that prints leaflets, brochures, and advertising materials. Metro classifies its various printing jobs as standard jobs or special jobs. Metro's simple job-costing system has two direct-cost categories (direct materials and direct labor) and a single indirect-cost pool. Metro operates at capacity and allocates all indirect costs using printing machine-hours as the allocation base.

Metro is concerned about the accuracy of the costs assigned to standard and special jobs and therefore is planning to implement an activity-based costing system. Metro's ABC system would have the same direct-cost categories as its simple costing system. However, instead of a single indirect-cost pool there would now be six categories for assigning indirect costs: design, purchasing, setup, printing machine operations, marketing, and administration. To see how activity-based costing would affect the costs of standard and special jobs, Metro collects the following information for the fiscal year 2016 that just ended.

	A	B	C	D	E F G H
1		Standard Job	Special Job	Total	Cause-and-Effect Relationship Between Allocation Base and Activity Cost
2	Number of printing jobs	400	200		
3	Price per job	₹6,000	₹7,500		
4	Cost of supplies per job	₹1,000	₹1,250		
5	Direct labor costs per job	₹900	1,000		
6	Printing machine-hours per job	10	10		
7	Cost of printing machine operations			₹7,50,000	Indirect costs of operating printing machines
8					increase with printing machine-hours
9	Setup-hours per job	4	7		
10	Setup costs			₹4,50,000	Indirect setup costs increase with setup-hours
11	Total number of purchase orders	400	500		
12	Purchase order costs			₹1,80,000	Indirect purchase order costs increase with
13					number of purchase orders
14	Design costs	₹40,000	₹1,60,000	2,00,000	Design costs are allocated to standard and special
15					jobs based on a special study of the design department
16	Marketing costs as a percentage of revenues	5%	5%	1,95,000	
17	Administration costs			₹2,40,000	Demand for administrative resources increases with direct labor costs

<u>**Required**</u>

1. Calculate the cost of a standard job and a special job under the simple costing system.
2. Calculate the cost of a standard job and a special job under the activity-based costing system.
3. Compare the costs of a standard job and a special job in requirements 1 and 2. Why do the simple and activity-based costing systems differ in the cost of a standard job and a special job?
4. How might Metro use the new cost information from its activity-based costing system to better manage its business?

Solution

1. Total indirect costs = ₹7,50,000 + ₹4,50,000 + ₹1,80,000 + ₹2,00,000 + ₹1,95,000 + ₹2,40,000

	= ₹20,15,000
Total machine-hours	= (400 × 10) + (200 × 10) = 6,000
Indirect cost rate per machine-hour	= ₹20,15,000 ÷ 6,000
	= ₹335.83 per machine-hour

Simple Costing System	Standard Job	Special Job
Cost of supplies per job	₹1,000	₹1,250
Direct labor cost per job	900	1,000
Indirect cost allocated to each job		
(10 machine hours × ₹335.83 per machine hour)	3,358.30	3,358.30
Total costs	₹5,258.30	₹5,608.30

2. Activity-based costing system

		Quantity of Cost Driver Consumed during 2015 (see column (1))			
Activity (1)	Cost Driver (2)	Standard Job (3)	Special Job (4)	Total Cost of Activity (given) (5)	Allocation Rate (6) = (5) ÷ ((3) + (4)), or given
Machine operations (400 jobs × 10 mach. hrs. per job; 200 jobs × 10 mach. hrs. per job)	machine hours	4,000	2,000	₹7,50,000 ₹125	per machine hour
Setups (4 × 400; 7 × 200)	setup hours	1,600	1,400	₹4,50,000 ₹150	per setup hour
Purchase orders (given)	no. of purchase orders	400	500	₹1,80,000 ₹200	per purchase order
Design				₹2,00,000	
Marketing	Percentage of revenue			₹1,95,000 ₹0.5	per rupee of sales
Administration (₹900 × 400; ₹1,000 × 200)	dir. labor costs	₹3,60,000	₹2,00,000	₹2,40,000 ₹4.2857	per rupee of direct manuf. labor cost

	Total Costs	
	Standard Job	Special Job
Cost of supplies (₹1,000 × 400; ₹1,250 × 200)	₹4,00,000	₹2,50,000
Direct labor costs (₹900 × 400; ₹1,000 × 200)	3,60,000	2,00,000
Indirect costs allocated:		
Machine operations (₹125 per mach. hr. × 4,000; 2,000)	5,00,000	2,50,000
Setups (₹150 per setup hr. × 1,600; 1,400)	2,40,000	2,10,000
Purchase orders (₹200 per order × 400; 500)	80,000	1,00,000

Design	40,000	1,60,000
Marketing (0.5 × ₹6,000 × 400; 0.5 × ₹7,500 × 200)	1,20,000	75,000
Administration (4.2857 × ₹3,60,000; ₹2,00,000)	1,54,290	85,710
Total costs	₹18,94,290	₹13,30,710
Cost of each job (₹18,94,290 ÷ 400; ₹13,30,710 ÷ 200)	₹4,735.70	₹6,653.60

3.

Cost per job	Standard Job	Special Job
Simple Costing System	₹5,258.30	₹5,608.30
Activity-based Costing System	₹4,735.70	₹6,653.60
Difference (Simple – ABC)	₹522.60	₹(1,045.30)

Relative to the ABC system, the simple costing system overcosts standard jobs and under-costs special jobs. Both types of jobs need 10 machine hours per job, so in the simple system, they are each allocated ₹3,358.30 in indirect costs. But, the ABC study reveals that each standard job consumes less of the indirect resources such as setups, purchase orders, and design costs than a special job, and this is reflected in the lower indirect costs allocated to the standard jobs and higher indirect costs allocated to special jobs in the ABC system.

4. Metro can use the information revealed by the ABC system to change its pricing based on the ABC costs. Under the simple system, Metro was making a gross margin of 12% on each standard job ([₹6,000 – ₹5,258.30] ÷ ₹6,000) and 25% on each special job ([₹7,500 – ₹5608.30] ÷ ₹7,500). But, the ABC system reveals that it is actually making a gross margin of 21% ([₹6,000 – ₹4,735.70] ÷ ₹6,000) on each standard job and about 11% ([₹7,500 – ₹6,653.60] ÷ ₹7,500) on each special job. Depending on the market competitiveness, Metro may either want to reprice the different types of jobs, or it may choose to market standard jobs more aggressively than before.

Metro can also use the ABC information to improve its own operations. It could examine each of the indirect cost categories and analyze whether it would be possible to deliver the same level of service, but consume fewer indirect resources, or find a way to reduce the per-unit-cost-driver cost of some of those indirect resources.

5-21 Activity-based costing, manufacturing. Fancy Doors, Inc., produces two types of doors, interior and exterior. The company's simple costing system has two direct cost categories (materials and labor) and one indirect cost pool. The simple costing system allocates indirect costs on the basis of machine-hours. Recently, the owners of Fancy Doors have been concerned about a decline in the market share for their interior doors, usually their biggest seller. Information related to Fancy Doors production for the most recent year follows:

	Interior	Exterior
Units sold	3,200	1,800
Selling price	₹2,500	₹4,000
Direct material cost per unit	₹600	₹900
Direct manufacturing labor cost per hour	₹320	₹320
Direct manufacturing labor-hours per hour	1.50	2.25
Production runs	40	85
Material moves	72	168
Machine setups	45	155
Machine-hours	5,500	4,500
Number of inspection	250	150

The owners have heard of other companies in the industry that are now using an activity-based costing system and are curious how an ABC system would affect their product costing decisions. After analyzing the indirect cost pool for Fancy Doors, the owners identify six activities as generating indirect costs: production scheduling, material handling, machine setup, assembly, inspection, and marketing. Fancy Doors collected the following data related to the indirect cost activities:

Activity	Activity Cost	Activity Cost Driver
Production scheduling	₹19,00,000	Production runs
Material handling	₹9,00,000	Material moves
Machine setup	₹5,00,000	Machine setups
Assembly	₹12,00,000	Machine-hours
Inspection	₹1,60,000	Number of inspections

Marketing costs were determined to be 3% of the sales revenue for each type of door.

Required

1. Calculate the cost of an interior door and an exterior door under the existing simple costing system.
2. Calculate the cost of an interior door and an exterior door under an activity-based costing system.
3. Compare the costs of the doors in requirements 1 and 2. Why do the simple and activity-based costing systems differ in the cost of an interior and exterior door?
4. How might Fancy Door, Inc., use the new cost information from its activity-based costing system to address the declining market share for interior doors?

Solution

1. Simple costing system:

$$\text{Total indirect costs} = ₹19,00,000 + ₹9,00,000 + ₹5,00,000 + ₹12,00,000 + ₹1,60,000 +$$
$$3\%[(₹2,500 \times 3,200) + (₹4,000 \times 1,800)]$$
$$= ₹51,16,000$$

$$\text{Total machine-hours} = 5,500 + 4,500 = 10,000$$

$$\text{Indirect cost rate per machine-hour} = ₹51,16,000 \div 10,000$$
$$= ₹511.60 \text{ per machine-hour}$$

Simple Costing System	Interior	Exterior
Direct materials[a]	₹19,20,000	₹16,20,000
Direct manufacturing labor[b]	15,36,000	12,96,000
Indirect cost allocated to each job		
(₹511.60 × 5,500; 4,500 machine hours)	28,13,800	23,02,200
Total costs	₹62,69,800	₹52,18,200
Total cost per unit		
(₹62,69,800 ÷ 3,200; ₹52,18,200 ÷ 1,800)	₹1,959.30	₹2,899

[a] ₹600 × 3,200 units; ₹900 × 1,800 units
[b] ₹320 × 1.5 × 3,200 units; ₹320 × 2.25 × 1,800 units

2. Activity-based costing system

Activity	Total Cost of Activity	Cost Driver	Cost Driver Quantity	Allocation Rate	
(1)	(2)	(3)	(4)	(5) = (2) ÷ (4)	
Product scheduling	₹19,00,000	production runs	125[c]	₹15,200	per production run
Material handling	₹9,00,000	material moves	240[d]	₹3,750	per material move
Machine setup	₹5,00,000	machine setups	200[e]	₹2,500	per setup
Assembly	₹12,00,000	machine hours	10,000	₹120	per machine hour
Inspection	₹1,60,000	inspections	400[f]	₹400	per inspection
Marketing		Percentage of revenues		₹0.03	per rupee of sales

[c] 40 + 85 = 125; [d] 72 + 168 = 240; [e] 45 + 155 = 200; [f] 250 + 150 = 400

ABC System	Interior	Exterior
Direct materials	₹19,20,000	₹16,20,000
Direct manufacturing labor	15,36,000	12,96,000
Indirect costs allocated:		
Product scheduling (₹15,200 per run × 40; 85)	6,08,000	12,92,000
Material handling (₹3,750 per move × 72; 168)	2,70,000	6,30,000
Machine setup (₹2,500 per setup × 45; 155)	1,12,500	3,87,500
Assembly (₹120 per MH × 5,500; 4,500)	6,60,000	5,40,000
Inspection (₹400 per inspection × 250; 150)	1,00,000	60,000
Marketing (0.03 × ₹2,500 × 3,200; 0.03 × ₹4,000 × 1,800)	2,40,000	2,16,000
Total costs	₹54,46,500	₹60,41,500
Total cost per unit		
₹54,46,500 ÷ 3,200 units; ₹60,41,500 ÷ 1,800 units)	₹1,702	₹3,356.4

3.

Cost per unit	Interior	Exterior
Simple Costing System	₹1,959.30	₹2,899
Activity-based Costing System	₹1,702.00	₹3,356.40
Difference (Simple − ABC)	₹257.30	₹(457.40)

Relative to the ABC system, the simple costing system overcosts interior doors and under-costs exterior doors. Interior doors require 1.72 machine-hours per unit while exterior doors require 2.5 machine-hours per unit. In the simple-costing system, overhead costs are allocated to the interior and exterior doors on the basis of the machine-hours used by each type of door. The ABC study reveals that the ratio of the cost of production runs, material moves, and setups for each exterior door versus each interior door is even higher than the ratio of 2.5 to 1.72 machine-hours for each exterior relative to each interior door. This higher ratio results in higher indirect costs allocated to exterior doors relative to interior doors in the ABC system.

4. Fancy Doors, Inc. can use the information revealed by the ABC system to change its pricing based on the ABC costs. Under the simple system, Fancy Doors was making an operating margin of 21.6% on each interior door ([₹2,500 − ₹1,959.30] ÷ ₹2,500) and 27.5% on each exterior door ([₹4,000 − ₹2,899] ÷ ₹4,000). But, the ABC system reveals that it is actually making an operating margin of about 32% ([₹2,500 − ₹1,702] ÷ ₹2,500) on each interior door and about 16% ([₹4,000 − ₹3,356.40] ÷ ₹4,000) on each exterior door. Fancy Doors, Inc., should consider decreasing the price of its interior doors to be more competitive. Fancy Doors should also consider increasing the price of its exterior doors, depending on the competition it faces in this market.

Fancy Doors can also use the ABC information to improve its own operations. It could examine each of the indirect cost categories and analyze whether it would be possible to deliver the same level of service, but consume fewer indirect resources, or find a way to reduce the per-unit-cost-driver cost of some of those indirect resources. Making these operational improvements can help Fancy Doors to reduce costs, become more competitive, and reduce prices to gain further market share while increasing its profits.

5-22 ABC, process costing. Citizen Company produces mathematical and financial calculators. Data related to the two products is presented below.

	Mathematical	Financial
Annual production in units	50,000	1,00,000
Direct materials costs	₹1,50,000	₹3,00,000
Direct manufacturing labor costs	₹50,000	₹1,00,000
Direct manufacturing labor-hours	2,500	5,000

Machine-hours	25,000	50,000
Number of production runs	50	50
Inspection hours	1,000	500

Both products pass through Department 1 and Department 2. The departments' combined manufacturing overhead costs are

	Total
	Total
Machining costs	₹3,75,000
Setup costs	1,20,000
Inspection costs	1,05,000

Required

1. Compute the manufacturing overhead cost per unit for each product.
2. Compute the manufacturing cost per unit for each product.

Solution

Rates per unit cost driver.

Activity	Cost Driver	Rate
Machining	Machine-hours	₹3,75,000 ÷ (25,000 + 50,000) = ₹5 per machine-hour
Set up	Production runs	₹1,20,000 ÷ (50 + 50) = ₹1,200 per production run
Inspection	Inspection-hours	₹1,05,000 ÷ (1,000 + 500) = ₹70 per inspection-hour

Overhead cost per unit:

Particulars	Mathematical	Financial
Machining: ₹5 × 25,000; 50,000 × ₹5 ₹2,50,000	₹1,25,000	₹1,25,000
Set up: ₹1,200 × 50; ₹1,200 × 50	60,000	60,000
Inspection: ₹70 × 1,000; ₹70 × 500	70,000	35,000
Total manufacturing overhead costs	2,55,000	3,45,000
Divide by number of units	÷ 50,000	÷ 1,00,000
Manufacturing overhead cost per unit	₹5.10	₹3.45

Particulars	Mathematical	Financial
Manufacturing cost per unit		
Direct materials ₹1,50,000 ÷ 50,000	₹3	
₹3,00,000 ÷ 1,00,000		₹3
Direct manufacturing labor ₹50,000 ÷ 50,000	1	
₹100,000 ÷ 100,000		1
Manufacturing overhead (from Requirement 1)	5.10	3.45
Manufacturing cost per unit	9.10	7.45

5-23 ABC, activity area cost-driver rates, product cross-subsidization. Indian Potatoes (IP) operates at capacity and processes potatoes into potato cuts at its highly automated Punjab plant. It sells potatoes to the retail consumer market and to the institutional market, which includes hospitals, cafeterias, and university dormitories.

IP's simple costing system, which does not distinguish between potato cuts processed for retail and institutional markets, has a single direct-cost category (direct materials; that is, raw potatoes) and a single indirect-cost pool (production support). Support costs, which include packaging materials, are allocated on the basis of Kilograms (kgs) of potato cuts processed. The company uses 18,00,000 Kgs of raw potatoes to process 16,00,000 Kgs of potato cuts. At the end of 2015, IP unsuccessfully bid for a large institutional contract. Its bid was reported to be 30% above the winning bid. This feedback came as a shock because IP included only a minimum profit margin on its bid, and the Punjab plant was acknowledged as the most efficient in the industry.

As a result of its review process of the lost contract bid, IP decided to explore ways to refine its costing system. The company determined that 90% of the direct materials (raw potatoes) related to the retail market and 10% to the institutional market. In addition, the company identified that packaging materials could be directly traced to individual jobs (₹19,00,000 for retail and ₹90,000 for institutional). Also, the company used ABC to identify three main activity areas that generated support costs: cleaning, cutting, and packaging.

- **Cleaning Activity Area**—The cost-allocation base is Kgs of raw potatoes cleaned.
- **Cutting Activity Area**—The production line produces (a) 150 Kgs of retail potato cuts per cutting-hour and (b) 200 Kgs of institutional potato cuts per cutting-hour. The cost-allocation base is cutting-hours on the production line.
- **Packaging Activity Area**—The packaging line packages (a) 25 Kgs of retail potato cuts per pack- aging-hour and (b) 80 Kgs of institutional potato cuts per packaging-hour. The cost-allocation base is packaging-hours on the production line.

The following table summarizes the actual costs for 2015 before and after the preceding cost analysis.

	Before the Cost Analysis	After the Cost Analysis Production Support	Retail	Institutional	Total
Direct materials used	₹23,10,000		₹20,79,000	₹2,31,000	₹23,10,000
Potatoes			19,00,000	90,000	19,90,000
Packaging					
Production support	1,68,90,000				
Cleaning		₹27,00,000			27,00,000
Cutting		62,40,000			62,40,000
Packaging		59,60,000			59,60,000
Total	₹1,92,00,000	₹1,49,00,000	₹39,79,000	₹3,21,000	₹1,92,00,000

Required

1. Using the simple costing system, what is the cost per Kg of potato cuts produced by IP?
2. Calculate the cost rate per unit of the cost driver in the (a) cleaning, (b) cutting, and (c) packaging activity areas.
3. Suppose IP uses information from its activity cost rates to calculate costs incurred on retail potato cuts and institutional potato cuts. Using the ABC system, what is the cost per Kg of (a) retail potato cuts and (b) institutional potato cuts?
4. Comment on the cost differences between the two costing systems in requirements 1 and 3. How might IP use the information in requirement 3 to make better decisions?

Solution

1. Direct costs

Direct materials	₹23,10,000
Indirect costs	
Product support	1,68,90,000
Total costs	₹1,92,00,000

$$\text{Cost per kilogram of potato cuts} = \frac{₹1,92,00,000}{16,00,000} = ₹12$$

2.

Cost Pool	Costs in Pool	Number of Driver Units	Costs per Driver Unit
Cleaning	₹27,00,000	18,00,000 raw kilograms	₹1.50
Cutting	₹62,40,000	10,400 hours*	₹600.00
Packaging	₹59,60,000	59,600 hours**	₹100.00

*((16,00,000 × 90%) ÷ 150) + ((16,00,000 × 10%) ÷ 200) = 9,600 + 800 = 10,400 hours

**(14,40,000 ÷ 25) + (1,60,000 ÷ 80) = 57,600 + 2,000 = 59,600 hours

3.

	Retail Potato Cuts		Institutional Potato Cuts	
Direct costs				
Direct materials	₹20,79,000		₹2,31,000	
Packaging	19,00,000	₹39,79,000	90,000	₹3,21,000
Indirect costs				
Cleaning				
₹1.5 × 90% × 18,00,000	24,30,000			
₹1.5 × 10% × 18,00,000			2,70,000	
Cutting				
₹600 × 9,600 hours	57,60,000			
₹600 × 800 hours			4,80,000	
Packaging				
₹100 × 57,600; ₹100 × 2,000	57,60,000	1,39,50,000	2,00,000	9,50,000
Total costs	₹1,79,29,000		₹12,71,000	
Kilograms produced	14,40,000		1,60,000	
Costs per kg	₹12.45		₹7.94	

Note: The total costs of ₹1,92,00,000 (₹1,79,29,000 + ₹12,71,000) are the same as those in Requirement 1.

4. There is much evidence of product-cost cross-subsidization.

Cost per Kg	Retail	Institutional
Simple costing system	₹12	₹12
ABC system	₹12.45	₹7.94

Assuming the ABC numbers are more accurate, potato cuts sold to the retail market are undercosted, while potato cuts sold to the institutional market are overcosted.

The simple costing system assumes each product uses all the activity areas in a homogeneous way. This is not the case. Institutional sales use sizably less resources in the cutting area and the packaging area. The percentages of total costs for each cost category are as follows:

	Retail	Institutional	Total
Direct costs			
Direct materials	90.0%	10.0%	100.0%
Packaging	95.5	4.5	100.0
Indirect costs			
Cleaning	90.0	10.0	100.0
Cutting	92.3	7.7	100.0
Packaging	96.6	3.4	100.0
Units produced	90.0%	10.0%	100.0%

IP can use the revised cost information for a variety of purposes:

a. *Pricing/product emphasis decisions.* The sizable drop in the reported cost of potatoes sold in the institutional market makes it possible that IP was overpricing potato products in this market. It lost the bid for a large institutional contract with a bid 30% above the winning bid. With its revised product cost dropping from ₹12.0 to ₹7.94, IP could have bid much lower and still made a profit. An increased emphasis on the institutional market appears warranted.

b. *Product design decisions.* ABC provides a road map as to how to reduce the costs of individual products. The relative components of costs are:

	Retail	Institutional
Direct costs		
Direct materials	11.6%	18.2%
Packaging	10.6	7.1
Indirect costs		
Cleaning	13.6	21.2
Cutting	32.1	37.8
Packaging	32.1	15.7
Total costs	100.0%	100.0%

Packaging-related costs constitute 42.7% (10.6% + 32.1%) of total costs of the retail product line. Design efforts that reduce packaging costs can have a big impact on reducing total unit costs for retail.

c. *Process improvements.* Each activity area is now highlighted as a separate cost. The three indirect cost areas comprise over 70% of total costs for each product, indicating the upside from improvements in the efficiency of processes in these activity areas.

5-24 Activity-based costing, job-costing system. The job costing system at Nancy's Custom Framing has five indirect cost pools (purchasing, material handling, machine maintenance, product inspection, and packaging). The company is in the process of bidding on two jobs: Job 215, an order of 15 intricate personalized frames, and Job 325, an order of 6 standard personalized frames. The controller wants you to compare overhead allocated under the current simple job-costing system and a newly designed activity-based job-costing system. Total budgeted costs in each indirect cost pool and the budgeted quantity of activity driver are as follows.

	Budgeted Overhead	Activity Driver	Budgeted Quantity of Activity Driver
Purchasing	₹3,50,000	Purchase orders processed	2,000
Material handling	4,37,500	Material moves	5,000
Machine maintenance	11,86,500	Machine-hours	10,500
Product inspection	94,500	Inspections	1,200
Packaging	1,99,500	Units produced	3,800
	₹22,68,000		

Information related to Job 215 and Job 325 follows. Job 215 incurs more batch-level costs because it uses more types of materials that need to be purchased, moved, and inspected relative to Job 325.

	Job 215	Job 325
Number of purchase orders	25	8
Number of material moves	10	4
Machine-hours	40	60
Number of inspections	9	3
Units produced	15	6

Required

1. Compute the total overhead allocated to each job under a simple costing system, where overhead is allocated based on machine-hours.
2. Compute the total overhead allocated to each job under an activity-based costing system using the appropriate activity drivers.
3. Explain why Nancy's Custom Framing might favor the ABC job-costing system over the simple job-costing system, especially in its bidding process.

Solution

1. Overhead allocation using a simple job-costing system, where overhead is allocated based on machine hours:

Overhead allocation rate = ₹22,68,000 ÷ 10,500 machine-hours = ₹216 per machine-hour

	Job 215	Job 325
Overhead allocated[a]	₹8,640	₹12,960

[a] ₹216 per machine-hour × 40 hours; 60 hours

2. Overhead allocation using an activity-based job-costing system:

	Budgeted Overhead (1)	Activity Driver (2)	Budgeted Activity Driver (3)	Activity Rate (4) = (1) ÷ (3)
Purchasing	₹3,50,000	Purchase orders pro-cessed	2,000	₹175.00
Material handling	₹4,37,500	Material moves	5,000	₹87.50
Machine maintenance	₹11,86,500	Machine hours	10,500	₹113.00
Product inspection	₹94,500	Inspections	1,200	₹78.75
Packaging	₹1,99,500	Units produced	3,800	₹52.50
	₹22,68,000			

	Job 215	Job 325
Overhead allocated		
Purchasing (₹175 × 25; 8 orders)	₹4,375	₹1,400
Material handling (₹87.5 × 10; 4 moves)	875	350
Machine maintenance (₹113.0 × 40; 60 hours)	4,520	6,780
Product inspection (₹78.75 × 9; 3 inspections)	708.80	236.30
Packaging (₹52.50 × 15; 6 units)	787.50	315.00
Total	₹11,266.30	₹9,081.30

3. The manufacturing manager likely would find the ABC job-costing system more useful in cost management. Unlike direct manufacturing labor costs, the five indirect cost pools are systematically linked to the activity areas at the plant. The result is more accurate product costing. The manufacturing manager can seek to reduce both the level of activity (fewer purchase orders, less material handling) and the cost of each activity (such as the cost per inspection).

Marketing managers can use ABC information to bid for jobs more competitively because ABC provides managers with a more accurate reflection of the resources used for and the costs of each job.

5-25 First stage allocation, activity-based costing, manufacturing sector. Precision Devices uses activity-based costing to allocate overhead costs to customer orders for pricing purposes. Many customer orders are won through competitive bidding. Direct material and direct manufacturing labor costs are traced directly to each order. Precision's direct manufacturing labor rate is ₹200 per hour. The company reports the following yearly overhead costs:

Wages and salaries	₹48,00,000
Depreciation	6,00,000
Rent	12,00,000
Other overhead	24,00,000
Total overhead costs	₹90,00,000

Precision has established four activity cost pools:

Activity Cost Pool	Activity Measure	Total Activity for the Year
Direct manufacturing labor support	Number of direct manufacturing labor-hours	30,000 direct manufacturing labor-hours
Order processing	Number of customer orders	500 orders
Design support	Number of custom designs	100 custom designs
Other	Facility-sustaining costs allocated to orders based on direct manufacturing labor-hours	30,000 direct manufacturing labor-hours

Only about 20% of Precision's yearly orders require custom designs.

Mr Paul, Precision's controller, has prepared the following estimates for distribution of the over- head costs across the four activity cost pools:

	Direct Manufacturing Labor Support	Order Processing	Design Support	Other	Total
Wages and salaries	40%	25%	30%	5%	100%
Depreciation	25%	10%	15%	50%	100%
Rent	30%	25%	10%	35%	100%
Other overhead	20%	30%	35%	15%	100%

Order 4,48,200 required ₹45,500 of direct materials, 80 direct manufacturing labor-hours, and one custom design.

Required

1. Allocate the overhead costs to each activity cost pool. Calculate the activity rate for each pool.
2. Determine the cost of Order 4,48,200.
3. How does activity-based costing enhance Precision's ability to price its orders? Suppose Precision used a traditional costing system to allocate all overhead costs to orders on the basis of direct manufacturing labor-hours. How might this have affected Precision's pricing decisions?

Solution

1.

	Direct Manuf. Labor Support	Order Processing	Design Support	Other	Total
Wages and salaries	₹19,20,000	₹12,00,000	₹14,40,000	₹2,40,000	₹48,00,000
Depreciation	1,50,000	60,000	90,000	3,00,000	6,00,000
Rent	3,60,000	3,00,000	1,20,000	4,20,000	12,00,000
Other overhead	4,80,000	7,20,000	8,40,000	3,60,000	24,00,000
Total	₹29,10,000	₹22,80,000	₹24,90,000	₹13,20,000	₹90,00,000

	Cost	Allocation Base	Allocation Rate
Direct Manuf. Labor Support	₹29,10,000	30,000 DMLHs	₹97/DMLH
Order Processing	₹22,80,000	500 orders	₹4,560/order
Design Support	₹24,90,000	100 custom designs	₹24,900/custom design
Other	₹13,20,000	30,000 DMLHs	₹44/DMLH

2.

Direct materials	₹45,500
Direct manuf. labor (80 hrs. × ₹200/hr.)	16,000

Direct manuf. labor support (80 dir. manuf. lbr-hrs. × ₹97/hr.)	7,760
Order processing (1 order × ₹4,560/order)	4,560
Design support (1 custom design × ₹24,900/custom design)	24,900 3,520
Other overhead (80 dir. manuf. lbr-hrs. × ₹44/hr.)	
Total overhead costs	₹1,02,240

3. Because only about 20% of the orders that Precision receives require custom designs, it is important that the costs generated by custom designs are not allocated to non-custom orders. Activity-based costing allows Precision to only assign resources used by orders to the orders. Similarly, order processing costs of ₹4,560/order are assigned to each order, regardless of the size of the order. Activity-based costing leads to more accurate costing of orders. This, in turn, leads to more competitive pricing. If Precision allocated all overhead costs to orders on the basis of direct manufacturing labor hours, they would tend to over-price larger, non-custom orders and underprice smaller, custom orders. They would likely lose bids on the overpriced orders and win the underpriced orders, but then lose money on the bids they won because the actual costs would be much greater than the estimated costs. The underpriced bids have small direct manufacturing labor hours relative to the resources needed to support custom designs and order processing costs for small orders.

5-26 First stage allocation, activity-based costing, service sector. LawnCare India provides lawn care and landscaping services to commercial clients. LawnCare uses activity-based costing to bid on jobs and to evaluate their profitability. LawnCare reports the following annual costs:

Wages and Salaries	₹36,00,000
Depreciation	7,20,000
Supplies	12,00,000
Other overhead	28,80,000
Total overhead costs	₹84,00,000

John controller of LawnCare, has established four activity cost pools:

Activity Cost Pool	Activity Measure	Total Activity for the Year
Estimating jobs	Number of job estimates	250 estimates
Lawn care	Number of direct labor-hours	10,000 direct labor-hours
Landscape design	Number of design hours	500 design hours
Other	Facility-sustaining costs that are not allocated to jobs	Not applicable

John Estimates that LawnCare's costs are distributed to the activity-cost pools as follows:

	Estimating Jobs	Lawn Care	Landscape Design	Other	Total
Wages and salaries	5%	70%	15%	10%	100%
Depreciation	10%	65%	10%	15%	100%
Supplies	0%	100%	0%	0%	100%
Other overhead	15%	50%	20%	15%	100%

Sunset Office Park, a new development in a nearby community, has contacted LawnCare to provide an estimate on landscape design and annual lawn maintenance. The job is esti-mated to require a single landscape design requiring 40 design hours in total and 250 direct labor-hours annually. LawnCare has a policy of pricing estimates at 150% of cost.

Required

1. Allocate LawnCare's costs to the activity-cost pools and determine the activity rate for each pool.
2. Estimate total cost for the Sunset Office Park job.
3. How much should LawnCare bid to perform the job?
4. Sunset Office Park asks LawnCare to give an estimate for providing its services for a 2-year period. What are the advantages and disadvantages for LawnCare to provide a 2-year estimate?

Solution

1.

	Estimating Jobs	Lawn Care	Landscape Design	Other	Total
Wages and salaries	₹1,80,000	₹25,20,000	₹5,40,000	₹3,60,000	₹36,00,000
Depreciation	72,000	4,68,000	72,000	1,08,000	7,20,000
Supplies	0	12,00,000	0	0	12,00,000
Other overhead	4,32,000	14,40,000	5,76,000	4,32,000	28,80,000
Total	₹6,84,000	₹56,28,000	₹11,88,000	₹9,00,000	₹84,00,000

2 and 3.

	Cost	Allocation Base	Allocation Rate
Estimating Jobs	₹6,84,000	250 estimates	₹2,736/estimate
Lawn Care	₹56,28,000	10,000 DMLHs	₹562.80/DMLH
Landscape Design	₹11,88,000	500 design hours	₹2,376/design hour

Estimating jobs (1 estimate × ₹2,736/estimate.)	₹2,736
Lawn care (250 DLHs × ₹562.80/DLH)	1,40,700
Landscape design (40 design hours × ₹2,376/design hour)	95,040
Total costs	₹2,38,476
Markup	× 150%
Bid price	₹3,57,714

4. Because the landscape design and estimating costs are only incurred once for the entire job, bidding on 2 years of service may allow LawnCare to be more competitive on a yearly basis. However, submitting an estimate for 2 years would lock LawnCare into the same price for both years, regardless of possible increases in their costs.

5-27 Department and activity-cost rates service sector. Must & More Radiology Center (MRC) performs X-rays, ultrasounds, computer tomography (CT) scans, and magnetic resonance imaging (MRI). MRC has developed a reputation as a top radiology center in the state. MRC has achieved this status because it constantly reexamines its processes and procedures. MRC has been using a single, facility-wide overhead allocation rate. The vice president of finance believes that MRC can make better process improvements if it uses more disaggregated cost information. She says, "We have state-of-the-art medical imaging technology. Can't we have state-of-the-art accounting technology?"

Must and More Radiology Center Budgeted Information for the Year March 31, 2015

	X-rays	Ultrasound	CT Scan	MRI	Total
Technician labor	₹6,20,000	₹10,10,000	₹15,50,000	₹10,30,000	₹42,10,000
Depreciation	4,22,400	25,60,000	42,49,600	87,68,000	1,60,00,000
Materials	2,26,000	1,64,000	2,36,000	3,15,000	9,41,000
Administration					2,00,000
Maintenance					25,00,000
Sanitation					25,25,000
Utilities					15,11,000
	₹12,68,400	₹37,34,000	₹60,35,600	₹1,01,13,000	₹2,78,87,000
Number of Procedures	3,842	4,352	2,924	2,482	
Minutes to clean after each procedure	5	5	15	35	
Minutes of each procedure	5	15	25	40	

MRC operates at capacity. The proposed allocation bases for overhead are:

Administration	Number of procedures
Maintenance (including parts)	Capital cost of the equipment (use Depreciation)
Sanitation	Total cleaning minutes
Utilities	Total procedure minutes

Required

1. Calculate the budgeted cost per service for X-rays, ultrasounds, CT scans, and MRI using direct technician labor costs as the allocation basis.
2. Calculate the budgeted cost per service of X-rays, ultrasounds, CT scans, and MRI if MRC allocated overhead costs using activity-based costing.
3. Explain how the disaggregation of information could be helpful to MRC's intention to continuously improve its services.

SOLUTION

1. Overhead costs = ₹2,00,000 + ₹25,00,000 + ₹25,25,000 + ₹15,11,000 = ₹67,36,000

$$\text{Budgeted overhead rate} = \frac{₹67,36,000}{₹42,10,000} = ₹1.6 \text{ per rupee of direct labor cost}$$

	X-rays	Ultrasound	CT scan	MRI	Total
Technician labor	₹6,20,000	₹10,10,000	₹15,50,000	₹10,30,000	₹42,10,000
Depreciation	4,22,400	25,60,000	42,49,600	87,68,000	1,60,00,000
Materials	2,26,000	1,64,000	2,36,000	3,15,000	9,41,000
Allocated overhead*	9,92,000	16,16,000	24,80,000	16,48,000	67,36,000
Total budgeted costs	₹22,60,400	₹53,50,000	₹85,15,600	₹1,17,61,000	₹2,78,87,000
Budgeted number of procedures	÷ 3,842	÷ 4,352	÷ 2,924	÷ 2,482	
Budgeted cost per service	₹588.3	₹1,229.3	₹2,912.3	₹4,738.5	

*Allocated overhead = Budgeted overhead rate × Technician labor costs = ₹1.60 × Technician labor costs

2. Budgeted Information

	X-rays	Ultrasound	CT scan	MRI	Total
Number of procedures	3,842	4,352	2,924	2,482	13,600
Cleaning minutes per procedure	× 5	× 5	× 15	× 35	
Total cleaning minutes	19,210	21,760	43,860	86,870	171,700
Number of procedures	3,842	4,352	2,924	2,482	13,600
Minutes for each procedure	× 5	× 15	× 25	× 40	
Total procedure minutes	19,210	65,280	73,100	99,280	256,870

Activity	Budgeted Cost (1)	Cost Driver (2)	Units of Cost Driver (3)	Activity Rate (4) = (1) ÷ (3)
Administration	₹2,00,000	Total number of procedures	13,600	₹14.7059 per procedure
Maintenance	₹25,00,000	Total depreciation	₹1,60,00,000	₹1.5625 per rupee of depreciation
Sanitation	₹25,25,000	Total cleaning minutes	1,71,700	₹14.7059 per cleaning minute
Utilities	₹15,11,000	Total procedure minutes	2,56,870	₹5.88235 per procedure minute

	X-rays	Ultrasound	CT Scan	MRI	Total
Technician labor	₹6,20,000	₹10,10,000	₹15,50,000	₹10,30,000	₹42,10,000
Depreciation	4,22,400	25,60,000	42,49,600	87,68,000	1,60,00,000
Materials	2,26,000	1,64,000	2,36,000	3,15,000	9,41,000
Allocated activity costs:					
Administration					
($14.7059 × 3,842; 4,352; 2,924; 2,482)	56,500	64,000	43,000	36,500	2,00,000
Maintenance					
₹1.5625 × ₹4,22,400;					
₹25,60,000; 42,49,600; 87,68,000)	66,000	4,00,000	6,64,000	13,70,000	25,00,000
Sanitation					
(₹14.7059 × 19,210; 21,760; 43,860; 86,870)	2,82,500	3,20,000	6,45,000	12,77,500	25,20,000
Utilities					
(₹5.88235 × 19,210; 65,280; 73,100; 99,280)	1,13,000	3,84,000	4,30,000	5,84,000	15,11,000
Total budgeted cost	₹17,86,400	₹49,02,000	₹78,17,600	₹1,33,81,000	₹2,78,87,000
Budgeted number of procedures	÷ 3,842	÷ 4,352	÷ 2,924	÷ 2,482	
Budgeted cost per service	₹465	₹1,126.4	₹2,673.6	₹5,391.20	

3. Using the disaggregated activity-based costing data, managers can see that the MRI actually costs substantially more and x-rays, ultrasounds, and CT scans substantially less than the traditional system indicated. In particular, the MRI activity generates a lot of maintenance activity and sanitation activity. Managers should examine the use of these two activities to search for ways to reduce the activity consumption and ultimately its cost.

5-28 Choosing cost drivers, activity-based costing, activity-based management. Samsonite Bags (SB) is a designer of high-quality backpacks and purses. Each design is made in small batches. Each spring, Samsonite comes out with new designs for the backpack and for the purse. The company uses these designs for a year and then moves on to the next trend. The bags are all made on the same fabrication equipment that is expected to operate at capacity. The equipment must be switched over to a new design and set up to prepare for the production of each new batch of products. When completed, each batch of products is immediately transported to a wholesaler. Transportation costs vary with the number of consignments. Budgeted information for the year is as follows:

Samsonite Bags
Budget for Costs and Activities
For the Year Ended March 31, 2015

Direct materials—purses	₹3,19,155
Direct materials—backpacks	4,54,995
Direct manufacturing labor—purses	99,000
Direct manufacturing labor—backpacks	1,13,000
Setup	64,000
Shipping	73,000
Design	1,69,000
Plant utilities and administration	2,21,000
Total	₹15,13,150

Other budget information follows:

	Backpacks	Purses	Total
Number of bags	6,175	3,075	9,250
Hours of production	1,665	2,585	4,250
Number of batches	120	80	200
Number of designs	2	2	4

1. Identify the cost hierarchy level for each cost category.
2. Identify the most appropriate cost driver for each cost category. Explain briefly your choice of cost driver.
3. Calculate the budgeted cost per unit of cost driver for each cost category.
4. Calculate the budgeted total costs and cost per unit for each product line.
5. Explain how you could use the information in requirement 4 to reduce costs.

Solution

1.

Direct materials—purses	Output unit-level costs
Direct materials—backpacks	Output unit-level costs
Direct manufacturing labor—purses	Output unit-level costs
Direct manufacturing labor—backpacks	Output unit-level costs
Setup	Batch-level costs
Transportation	Batch-level costs
Design	Product-sustaining costs
Plant utilities and administration	Facility-sustaining costs

2.

Direct materials—purses	Number of purses
Direct materials—backpacks	Number of backpacks
Direct manufacturing labor—purses	Number of purses
Direct manufacturing labor—backpacks	Number of backpacks
Setup	Number of batches
Transportation	Number of batches
Design	Number of designs
Plant utilities and administration	Hours of production

Direct material and direct manufacturing labor are costs that can be easily traced to output, which in this case is the number of purses or backpacks produced.

Setup and Transportation costs are both a function of the number of batches produced.

Design is related to the number of designs created for each product.

Plant utilities and administration result from general activity level in the plant. Thus, hours of production seems to be an appropriate cost driver.

3.

Direct materials—purses	₹3,19,155 ÷ 3,075 purses = ₹103.79 per purse
Direct materials—backpacks	₹4,54,995 ÷ 6,175 backpacks = ₹73.68 per backpack
Direct manufacturing labor—purses	₹99,000 ÷ 3,075 purses = ₹32.20 per purse
Direct manufacturing labor—backpacks	₹1,13,000 ÷ 6,175 backpacks = ₹18.30 per backpack
Setup	₹64,000 ÷ 200 batches = ₹320 per batch
Transportation	₹73,000 ÷ 200 batches = ₹365 per batch
Design	₹1,69,000 ÷ 4 designs = ₹42,250 per design
Plant utilities and administration	₹2,21,000 ÷ 4,250 hours = ₹52 per hour

4.

	Backpacks	Purses	Total
Direct materials	₹4,54,995	₹3,19,155	₹7,74,150
Direct manufacturing labor	1,13,000	99,000	2,12,000
Setup			
(₹320 × 120; 80 batches)	38,400	25,600	64,000

Transportation			
(₹365 × 120; 80 batches)	43,800	29,200	73,000
Design			
(₹42,250 × 2; 2 designs)	84,500	84,500	1,69,000
Plant utilities and administration			
(₹52 × 1,665; 2,585 hours)	86,580	1,34,420	2,21,000
Budgeted total costs	₹8,21,275	₹6,91,875	₹15,13,150
Divided by number of backpacks/purses	÷ 6,175	÷ 3,075	
Budgeted cost per backpack/purse	₹133.00	₹225.00	

5. Based on this analysis, more than 50% of product cost relates to direct material. Managers should determine whether the material costs can be reduced. Producing in small lots increases the setup and Transportation costs. While both are relatively small components of product cost, management may want to evaluate ways to reduce the number of setups and the cost per setup. Of the indirect costs, the product- and facility-sustaining costs are the highest. Management should review the design process for cost savings and examine why it takes so long to produce purses relative to backpacks.

5-29 Unused capacity, activity-based costing, activity-based management. Cosco is a manufacturer of high-quality basketballs and volleyballs. Setup costs are driven by the number of batches. Equipment and maintenance costs increase with the number of machine-hours, and lease rent is paid per square foot. Capacity of the facility is 14,000 square feet, and Cosco is using only 80% of this capacity. Cosco records the cost of unused capacity as a separate line item and not as a product cost. The following is the budgeted information for Cosco:

Cosco
Budgeted Costs and Activities
For the Year Ended March 31, 2015

Direct materials—basketballs	₹16,81,000
Direct materials—volleyballs	30,32,800
Direct manufacturing labor—basketballs	11,18,000
Direct manufacturing labor—volleyballs	10,08,200
Setup	15,75,000
Equipment and maintenance costs	11,52,000
Lease rent	21,00,000
Total	₹1,16,67,000

Other budget information follows:

	Basketballs	Volleyballs
Number of balls	58,000	85,000
Machine-hours	13,500	10,500
Number of batches	450	300
Square footage of production space used	3,200	8,000

Required

1. Calculate the budgeted cost per unit of cost driver for each indirect cost pool.
2. What is the budgeted cost of unused capacity?
3. What is the budgeted total cost and the cost per unit of resources used to produce (a) basketballs and (b) volleyballs?
4. Why might excess capacity be beneficial for Cosco? What are some of the issues Cosco should consider before increasing production to use the space?

Solution

1.

	Basketballs	Volleyballs	Total
Number of batches	450	300	750
Machine-hours	13,500	10,500	24,000

Setup cost per batch = ₹15,75,000 ÷ 750 batches = ₹2,100 per batch.

Equipment and maintenance = ₹1,15,200 ÷ 24,000 machine-hours + ₹4.80 per machine-hour.

Lease rent, insurance, utilities = ₹21,00,000 ÷ 14,000 sq. ft. of capacity = ₹150 per sq. ft.

2.

$$\text{Unused capacity} = \text{Total capacity} - \frac{\text{Capacity used for}}{\text{basketball production}} - \frac{\text{Capacity used for}}{\text{volleyball production}}$$

$$= 14,000 - 3,200 - 8,000 = 2,800 \text{ sq. ft.}$$

Cost of unused capacity = ₹150 per sq. ft × 2,800 sq. ft. = ₹4,20,000

3.

	Basketballs	Volleyballs	Total
Direct materials	₹16,81,000	₹30,32,800	₹47,13,800
Direct manufacturing labor	11,18,000	10,08,200	21,26,200
Setup			
(₹2,100 × 450; 300)	9,45,000	6,30,000	15,75,000
Equipment and maintenance			
(₹48 × 13,500; 10,500)	6,48,000	5,04,000	11,52,000
Lease rent, etc.			
(₹150 × 3,200; 8,000)	4,80,000	12,00,000	16,80,000
Budgeted total costs	₹48,72,000	₹63,75,000	₹1,12,47,000
Divided by number of units	÷ 58,000	÷ 85,000	
Budgeted cost per unit	₹84	₹75	

4. Currently, Cosco only utilizes 80% of its available capacity. Managers should consider whether the excess capacity is sufficient to produce footballs. Other issues to consider include demand for the proposed product, the competition, capital investment needed to start and support this product line, and the availability of skilled and unskilled labor needed to manufacture footballs.

5-30 Unused capacity, activity-based costing, activity-based management. Whitewater Adventures manufactures two models of kayaks, Basic and Deluxe, using a combination of machining and hand finishing. Machine setup costs are driven by the number of setups. Indirect manufacturing labor costs increase with direct manufacturing labor costs. Equipment and maintenance costs increase with the number of machine-hours, and facility rent is paid per square foot. Capacity of the facility is 6,250 square feet, and Whitewater is using only 80% of this capacity. Whitewater records the cost of unused capacity as a separate line item and not as a product cost. For the current year, Whitewater has budgeted the following:

Whitewater Adventures
Budgeted Costs and Activities
For the Year Ended March 31, 2015

Direct materials—Basic Kayaks	₹32,50,000
Direct materials—Deluxe Kayaks	24,00,000
Direct manufacturing labor—Basic Kayaks	11,00,000

Direct manufacturing labor—Deluxe Kayaks	13,00,000
Indirect manufacturing labor costs	7,20,000
Machine setup costs	4,05,000
Equipment and maintenance costs	23,50,000
Facility rent	20,00,000
Total	₹1,35,25,000

Other budget information follows:

	Basic	Deluxe
Number of kayaks	5,000	3,000
Machine-hours	11,000	12,500
Number of setups	300	200
Square footage of production space used	2,860	2,140

Required

1. Calculate the cost per unit of each cost-allocation base.
2. What is the budgeted cost of unused capacity?
3. Calculate the budgeted total cost and the cost per unit for each model.
4. Why might excess capacity be beneficial for Whitewater? What are some of the issues Whitewater should consider before increasing production to use the space?

Solution

1.

	Cost	Allocation Base	Allocation Rate
Indirect manufacturing labor costs	₹7,20,000	₹24,00,000 direct labor cost	30% of direct labor cost
Machine setup costs	₹4,05,000	500 batches	₹810/batch
Equipment and maintenance costs	₹23,50,000	23,500 MH	₹100/MH
Facility rent costs	₹20,00,000	6,250 sq. ft.	₹320/sq. ft.

2. Budgeted cost of unused capacity = ₹320 per sq. ft. (6,250 − 2,860 − 2,140) sq. ft.

= ₹320 × 1,250 sq. ft. = ₹4,00,000

3.

	Basic	Deluxe
Direct materials	₹32,50,000	₹24,00,000
Direct manufacturing labor	11,00,000	13,00,000
Indirect manuf. labor (₹11,00,000 and ₹13,00,000 × 30%)	3,30,000	3,90,000
Machine setup (300 and 200 batches × ₹810/batch)	2,43,000	1,62,000
Equipment and maintenance costs (11,000 and 12,500 MH × ₹100/MH)	11,00,000	12,50,000
Facility rent (2,860 and 2,140 sq. ft. × ₹320/sq. ft.)	9,15,200	6,84,800
Total cost	₹69,38,200	₹61,86,800
Divided by number of units	÷ 5,000	÷ 3,000
Cost per unit	₹1,387.60	₹2,062.30

4. Although the excess capacity is currently costing Whitewater ₹4,00,000 annually, having excess capacity allows for the company to accept special orders if they are received, expand production of either of the existing models, or add a new product line in the future. Whitewater should consider if there is available labor and machine hours before increasing production to use the space, as well as demand for the product. Whitewater may also consider renting out the available space to a compatible outside user, with the option to take the space back if needed.

5-31 Activity-based costing, cost hierarchy. Om Books and Café (OBC) is a large city bookstore that sells books and music CDs and has a café. OBC operates at capacity and allocates selling, general, and administration (S, G & A) costs to each product line using the cost of merchandise of each product line. OBC wants to optimize the pricing and cost management of each product line. OBC is wondering if its accounting system is providing it with the best information for making such decisions.

Om Books and Café
Product Line Information
For the Year Ended March 31,2015

	Books	CDs	Café
Revenuses	₹3,72,04,800	₹2,31,53,600	₹73,62,160
Cost of Merchandise	2,65,67,270	1,72,23,110	55,66,850
Cost of Café Cleaning	—	—	₹1,82,500
Number of purchase orders placed	2,800	2,500	2,000
Number of deliveries received	1,400	1,700	1,600
Hours of shelf stocking time	15,000	14,000	10,000
Items sold	1,24,016	1,15,768	3,68,108

Om Books and Café incurs the following selling, general, and administration costs:

Om Books and Café
Selling, General, and Administration (S, G & A) Costs
For the Year Ended March 31, 2015

Purchasing department expense	₹47,45,000
Receiving department expense	43,24,000
Shelf stocking labor expense	48,75,000
Customer support expense (cashiers and floor employees)	9,11,840
	₹1,48,55,840

Required

1. Suppose OBC uses cost of merchandise to allocate all S, G & A costs. Prepare product line and total company income statements.

2. Identify an improved method for allocating costs to the three product lines. Explain. Use the method for allocating S, G & A costs that you propose to prepare new product line and total company income statements. Compare your results to the results in requirement 1.

3. Write a memo to OBC management describing how the improved system might be useful for managing the store.

Solution

1.

Om Books and Café
Income Statement
For the Year Ended March 31, 2015

	Books	CDs	Café	Total
Revenues	₹3,72,04,800	₹2,31,53,600	₹73,62,160	₹6,77,20,560
Cost of Merchandise	2,65,67,270	1,72,23,110	55,66,850	4,93,57,230
Cost of Café Cleaning			1,82,500	1,82,500

Allocated Selling, General and Administration Costs (0.300986 × ₹2,65,67,270; ₹1,72,23,110; ₹55,66,850)	79,96,380	51,83,920	16,75,540	1,48,55,840
Operating income		₹26,41,150	₹7,46,570	₹(62,730)	₹33,24,990

Overhead rate = ₹1,48,55,840 ÷ ₹4,93,57,230 = 0.300986 per rupee cost of merchandise

2. Selling, general, and administration (S, G, & A) is comprised of a variety of costs that are unlikely to be consumed uniformly across product lines based on the cost of merchandise. Om Books and Café should consider an activity-based costing system to clarify how each product line uses these S, G, & A resources.

	Books	CDs	Café	Total
Number of purchase orders	2,800	2,500	2,000	7,300
Number of deliveries received	1,400	1,700	1,600	4,700
Hours of shelf-stocking time	15,000	14,000	10,000	39,000
Items sold	1,24,016	1,15,768	3,68,108	6,07,892

Purchasing	₹47,45,000 ÷ 7,300 orders placed = ₹650 per purchase order
Receiving	₹43,24,000 ÷ 4,700 deliveries = ₹920 per delivery
Stocking	₹48,75,000 ÷ 39,000 hours = ₹125 per stocking hour
Customer support	₹9,11,840 ÷ 6,07,892 items sold = ₹1.50 per item sold

	Books	CDs	Café	Total
Revenues	₹3,72,04,800	₹2,31,53,600	₹73,62,160	₹6,77,20,560
Cost of Merchandise	2,65,67,270	1,72,23,110	55,66,850	4,93,57,230
Gross margin	1,06,37,530	59,30,490	17,95,310	1,83,63,330
Cost of Café Cleaning			1,82,500	1,82,500
Purchasing (₹650 × 2,800; 2,500; 2,000)	18,20,000	16,25,000	13,00,000	47,45,000
Receiving (₹920 × 1,400; 1,700; 1,600)	12,88,000	15,64,000	14,72,000	43,24,000
Shelf-stocking (₹125 × 15,000; 14,000; 10,000)	18,75,000	17,50,000	12,50,000	48,75,000
Customer support (₹1.5 × 124,016; 115,768; 368,108	1,86,030	1,73,650	5,52,160	9,11,840
Total S, G, & A costs	51,69,030	51,12,650	47,56,660	1,50,38,340
Operating income	₹54,68,500	₹8,17,840	₹(29,61,350)	₹33,24,990

Comparing product line income statements in requirements 1 and 2, it appears that books are much more profitable and café loses a lot more money under the ABC system compared to the simple system. The reason is that books use far fewer S,G, & A resources relative to its merchandise costs, and café uses far greater S, G, & A resources relative to its merchandise costs.

3. **To: Om Books and Café Management Team**
   From: Cost Analyst
   Re: Costing System

The current accounting system allocates indirect costs (S,G, & A) to product lines based on the Cost of Merchandise sold. Using this method, the S, G, & A costs are assigned 54%, 35%, 11%, to the Books, CDs, and Café product lines, respectively.

I recommend that the organization switch to an activity-based costing (ABC) method. With ABC, the product lines are assigned indirect costs based on their consumption of the activities that give rise to the costs. An ABC analysis reveals that the Café consumes considerably more than 11% of indirect costs. Instead, the café generally requires 25–35% of the purchasing, receiving, and stocking activity and 60% of the customer support.

The current accounting technique masks the losses being produced by the café because it assumes all indirect costs are driven by the rupee amount of merchandise sold. By adopting ABC, management can evaluate the costs of operating the three product lines and make more informed pricing and product mix decisions. For example, management may want to consider increasing prices of the food and drinks served in the café. Before deciding whether to increase prices or to close the café, management must consider the beneficial effect that having a cafe has on the other product lines.

An ABC analysis can also help Om Books and Café manage its costs by reducing the number of activities that each product line demands and by reducing the cost of each activity. These actions will improve the profitability of each product line. ABC analysis can also be used to plan and manage the various activities.

5-32 ABC, implementation, ethics. (CMA, adapted) Sony Electronics, a division of Sony Corporation, manufactures two large-screen television models the Flatron, which has been produced since 2005 and sells for ₹45,000 and the Wega, a newer model introduced in early 2008 that sells for ₹57,000. Based on the following income statement for the current year ended March 31, senior management at Sony have decided to concentrate Sony's marketing resources on the Wega and to phase out the Flatron model.

Sony Electronics

Income Statement

For the Current Fiscal Year Ended March 31

Particulars	Flatron	Wega	Total
Revenues	₹1,98,00,000	₹45,60,000	₹2,43,60,000
Cost of goods sold	1,25,40,000	31,92,000	1,57,32,000
Gross margin	72,60,000	13,68,000	86,28,000
Selling and administrative expenses	58,30,000	9,78,000	68,08,000
Operating income	14,30,000	3,90,000	18,20,000
Units produced and sold	440	80	
Net income per unit sold	₹3,250	₹4,875	

Unit Cost for Flatron and Wega are as follows:

Particulars	Flatron	Wega
Direct materials	₹10,400	₹29,200
Direct manufacturing labor		
Flatron (1.5 hours × ₹600)		900
Wega (3.5 hours × ₹600)		2,100
Machine costs[a]		
Flatron (8 hours × ₹900)		7,200
Wega (4 hours × ₹900)		3,600
Manufacturing overhead other than machine costs[b]	10,000	5,000
Total cost	28,500	39,900

[a]Machine costs include lease costs of the machine, repairs, and maintenance.
[b]Manufacturing overhead was allocated to products based on machine-hours at the rate of ₹1,250 per hour.

Sony's controller, Susan Thomas, is advocating the use of activity-based costing and activity-based management and has gathered the following information about the company's manufacturing overhead costs for the current year ended March 31.

Activity Center (Cost-allocation Base)	Total Activity Costs	Units of the Cost-allocation Base		
		Flatron	Wega	Total
Soldering (number of solder points)	₹9,42,000	11,85,000	3,85,000	15,70,000
Shipments (number of shipments)	8,60,000	16,200	3,800	20,000
Quality control (number of inspection)	12,40,000	56,200	21,300	77,500
Purchase orders (number of orders)	9,50,400	80,100	1,09,980	1,90,080
Machine power (machine-hours)	57,600	1,76,000	16,000	1,92,000
Machine setups (number of setups)	7,50,000	16,000	14,000	30,000
Total manufacturing overhead	48,00,000			

After completing her analysis Thomas shows the result to Fred Duval, the Sony division president. Duval does not like what he sees. "If you show headquarters this analysis, they are going to ask us to phase out the Wega line which we have just introduced. This whole costing stuff has been a major problem for us. First Flatron was not profitable and now Wega."

"Looking at the ABC analysis, I see two problems. First, we do many more activities than the ones you have listed. If you had included all activities, maybe your conclusions would be different. Second, you used number of setups and number of inspections as allocation bases. The numbers would be different had you used setup-hours and inspection-hours instead. I know that measurement problems precluded you from using these other cost-allocation bases, but I believe you ought to make some adjustments to our current numbers to compensate for these issues. I know you can do better. We can't afford to phase out either product."

Thomas knows her numbers are fairly accurate. On a limited sample, she calculated the profitability of Wega and Flatron using more and different allocation bases. The set of activities and activity rates she had used resulted in numbers that closely approximate those based on more detailed analyses. She is confident that headquarters, knowing that Wega was introduced only recently, will not ask Sony to phase it out. She is also aware that a sizable portion of Duval's bonus is based on division revenues. Phasing out either product would adversely affect his bonus. Still, she feels some pressure from Duval to do something.

Required

1. Using activity-based costing, calculate the profitability of the Wega and Flatron models.
2. Explain briefly why these numbers differ from the profitability of the Wega and Flatron models calculated using Sony's existing costing system.
3. Comment on Duval's concerns about the accuracy and limitations of ABC.

Solution

1. Sony Electronics should not emphasize the Wega model and phase out the Flatron model. Under activity-based costing, the Wega model has an operating income percentage of less than 3%, while the Flatron model has an operating income percentage of nearly 43%.

Cost driver rates for the various activities identified in the activity-based costing (ABC) system are as follows:

Soldering	₹9,42,000	÷	15,70,000	= ₹0.60 per solder point
Shipments	8,60,000	÷	20,000	= 43.00 per shipment
Quality control	12,40,000	÷	77,500	= 16.00 per inspection
Purchase orders	9,50,400	÷	1,90,080	= 5.00 per order
Machine power	57,600	÷	1,92,000	= 0.30 per machine-hour
Machine setups	7,50,000	÷	30,000	= 25.00 per setup

Sony Electronics

Calculation of costs of each model under activity-based costing

Particulars	Flatron	Wega
Direct costs		
Direct materials (₹10,400 × 440; 80 × ₹29,200)	₹45,76,000	₹23,36,000
Direct manufacturing labor (₹900 × 440; ₹2,100 × 80)	3,96,000	1,68,000
Machine costs ₹7,200 × 440; ₹3,600 × 80)	31,68,000	2,88,000
Total direct costs	81,40,000	27,92,000
Indirect costs		
Soldering (₹0.60 × 11,85,000; 0.60 × 3,85,000)	7,11,000	2,31,000
Shipments (₹43 × 16,200; 43 × 3,800)	6,96,600	1,63,400
Quality control (16 × 56,200; ₹(6 × 21,300)	8,99,200	3,40,800
Purchase orders (₹5 × 80,100; 5 × 1,09,980)	4,00,500	5,49,900
Machine power (₹0.30 × 1,76,000; 0.30 × 16,000)	52,800	4,800
Machine setups (25 × 16,000; 25 × 14,000)	4,00,000	3,50,000
Total indirect costs	31,60,100	16,39,900
Total costs	1,13,00,100	44,31,900

Profitability analysis

Particulars	Flatron	Wega	Total
Revenues	₹1,98,00,000	₹45,60,000	₹2,43,60,000
Cost of goods sold	1,13,00,100	44,31,900	1,57,32,000
Gross margin	84,99,900	1,28,100	86,28,000
Per-unit calculations:			
Units sold	440	80	
Selling price (₹1,98,00,000/440; ₹45,60,000/80)	45,000	57,000	
Cost of goods sold			
(₹1,13,00,100/440; ₹44,31,900/80)	25,682	55,399	
Gross margin	19,318	1,601	
Gross margin percentage	42.9%	2.8%	

2. Sony's existing costing system allocates all manufacturing overhead other than machine costs on the basis of machine-hours, an output unit-level cost driver. Consequently, the more machine-hours per unit that a product needs, the greater the manufacturing overhead allocated to it. Because Flatron uses twice the number of machine-hours per unit compared to Wega, a large amount of manufacturing overhead is allocated to Flatron.

   The ABC analysis recognizes several batch-level cost drivers such as purchase orders, shipments, and setups. Wega uses these resources much more intensively than Flatron. The ABC system recognizes Wega's use of these overhead resources. Consider, for example, purchase order costs. The existing system allocates these costs on the basis of machine-hours. As a result, each unit of Flatron is allocated twice the purchase order costs of each unit of Wega. The ABC system allocates ₹4,00,500 of purchase order costs to Flatron (equal to ₹910.22 (₹4,00,500 ÷ 440) per unit) and ₹5,49,900 of purchase order costs to Wega (equal to ₹6,873.75 (₹5,49,900 ÷ 80) per unit). Each unit of Wega uses ₹7.55 (₹6,873.75 ÷ 910.22) times the purchases order costs of each unit of Flatron.

   Recognizing Wega's more intensive use of manufacturing overhead results in Regal showing a much lower profitability under the ABC system. By the same token, the ABC analysis shows that Flatron is quite profitable. The existing costing system overcosted Flatron, and so made it appear less profitable.

3. Duval's comments about ABC implementation are valid. When designing and implementing ABC systems, managers and management accountants need to trade off

the costs of the system against its benefits. Adding more activities makes the system harder to understand and more costly to implement but would probably improve the accuracy of cost information, which, in turn, would help Sony make better decisions.

4. Incorrect reporting of ABC costs with goal of retaining both the Flatron and Wega Product lines is unethical.

Thomas should indicate to Duval that the product cost calculations are, indeed, appropriate. If Duval still insists on modifying the product cost numbers, Thomas should raise the matter with one of Duval's superiors. If, after taking all these steps, there is continued pressure to modify product cost numbers, Thomas should consider resigning from the company, rather than engage in unethical behavior.

Exercises

[Comprehensive solutions to all exercises are available on the companion website www. pearsoned.co.in/charlesthorngren]

5-33 Cost smoothing or peanut-butter costing, cross-subsidization. For many years five former classmates – Aashish, Amit, Nitin, Ankur and Aakash – have had a reunion dinner at the annual meeting of the College Alumni Association. The details of the bill for the most recent dinner at the Parikrama Restaurant break down as follows:

Diner	Entree	Dessert	Drinks	Total
Aashish	₹270	₹80	₹240	₹590
Amit	240	30	0	270
Nitin	210	60	130	400
Ankur	310	60	120	490
Aakash	150	40	60	250

For at least the last 10 dinners, Nitin has put the total restaurant bill on his ICICI Bank card. He then mails the other four bills for the average cost. Nitin continued this practice for the Parikrama dinner. However, just before he sent the bill to the other diners, Aakash phoned him to complain. He was livid at Ankur for ordering the steak and lobster entrée ("he always does that") and at Aashish for having three glasses of imported champagne ("What's wrong with domestic beer?").

Required

1. Why is the average-cost approach in the context of the reunion dinner an example of cost smoothing or peanut-butter costing?

2. Compute the average cost to each of the five diners. Who is undercharged and who is overcharged under the average-cost approach? Is Aakash's complaint justified?

3. Give an example of a dining situation in which Nitin would find it more difficult to compute the amount of under or overcosting. How might the behavior of the diners be affected if each person paid his or her own bill instead of continuing with the average cost approach?

5-34 Cost hierarchy. Telecom Ltd. manufactures boom boxes (music systems with radio, cassette, and compact disc players) for several well-known companies. The boom boxes differ significantly in their complexity and their manufacturing batch sizes. The following costs were incurred in current year.

a. Designing processes, drawing process charts, making engineering process changes for products, ₹8,00,000.

b. Procurement costs of placing purchase orders, receiving materials, and paying suppliers related to the number of purchase orders placed, ₹5,00,000.

c. Direct materials costs, ₹60,00,000.

d. Costs incurred to set up machines each time a different product needs to be manufactured, ₹6,00,000.

e. Direct manufacturing labor costs, ₹10,00,000.

f. Machine-related overhead costs such as depreciation, maintenance, production engineering, ₹11,00,000. (These resources relate to the activity of running the machines.)

g. Plant management, plant rent, and plant insurance, ₹9,00,000.

Required

1. Classify each of the preceding costs as output unit-level, batch-level, product-sustaining, or facility sustaining. Explain each answer.
2. Consider two types of boom boxes made by Telecom. Ltd. One boom box is complex to make and is produced in many batches. The other boom box is simple to make and is produced in few batches. Suppose that Telecom needs the same number of machine-hours to make each type of boom box and that Telecom allocates all overhead costs using machine-hours as the only allocation base. How, if at all, would the boom boxes be miscosted? Briefly explain why.
3. How is the cost hierarchy helpful to Telecom in managing its business?

5-35 Plant wide indirect-cost rates. Delphi Automotive Systems Ltd. (DASL) designs, manufactures, and sells automotive parts. It has three main operating departments: design, engineering, and production.

- Design-the design of parts, using state of the art, computer aided design (CAD) equipments.
- Engineering- the prototyping of parts and testing of their specifications.
- Production-the manufacture of parts.

For many years, (DASL) had long-term contracts with major automobile assembly companies. These contracts had large production runs DASL's costing system allocates variable manufacturing overhead on the basis of machine-hours. Actual variable manufacturing overhead costs for current year were ₹6,17,200. DASL had three contracts in current year, and its machine-hours used in current year were assigned as follows:

Tata Motors	240
Maruti Udyog	5,600
Hyundai Motors	2,160
	8,000

Required

1. Compute the plantwide variable manufacturing overhead rate for current year.
2. Compute the variable manufacturing overhead allocated to each contract in current year.
3. What conditions must hold for machine-hours to provide an accurate estimate of the variable manufacturing overhead incurred on each individual contract at DASL in current year?

5-36 Department indirect-cost rates as activity rates (continuation of 5-35). The controller of Delphi Automotive Systems Ltd decides to interview key managers of the Design, Engineering, and Production departments. Each manager is to indicate the consensus choice among department personnel of the cost driver of variable manufacturing overhead costs for his or her department. Summary data are

Department	Variable Manufacturing Overhead	Cost Driver
Design	₹78,000	CAD design-hours
Engineering	59,200	Engineering-hours
Production	4,80,000	Machine-hours
	6,17,200	

Details pertaining to usage of these cost drivers for each of the three contracts are:

Department	Cost Driver	Tata Motors	Maruti Udyog	Hyundai Motors
Design	CAD design-hours	220	400	160
Engineering	Engineering-hours	140	120	480
Production	Machine-hours	240	5,600	2,160

1. What is the variable manufacturing overhead rate for each department in current year?
2. What is the variable manufacturing overhead allocated to each contract in current year using department variable manufacturing overhead rates?
3. Compare your answer in requirement 2 to that in requirement 2 of Exercise 5-31. Comment on the results.

5-37 ABC, activity area cost-driver rates, product cross-subsidization. Lays Potatoes (LP) processes potatoes into potato cuts at its highly automated Noida Plant. It sells potatoes to the retail consumer market and to the institutional market, which includes hospitals, cafeterias, and university dormitories.

LP's existing costing system has a single direct-cost category (direct materials, which are the raw potatoes) and a single indirect-cost pool (production support). Support costs are allocated on the basis of kgs of potato cuts processed. Support costs include packaging materials. The current year total actual costs for producing 10,00,000 kgs of potato cuts (9,00,000 for the retail market and 1,00,000 for the institutional market) are

Direct materials used	₹1,50,000
Production support	9,83,000

The existing costing system does not distinguish between potato cuts produced for the retail and the institutional markets.

At the end of current year, LP unsuccessfully bid for a large institutional contract. Its bid was reported to be 30 percent above the winning bid. This feedback came as a shock because LP included only a minimum profit margin on its bid. Moreover, the Noida plant was acknowledged as the most efficient in the industry.

As a result of its review process of the lost contract bid, LP decided to explore ways to refine its costing system. First, it identified that ₹88,000 of the ₹9,83,000 pertaining to packaging materials could be traced to individual jobs ₹1,80,000 for retail and ₹8,000 for institutional). These costs will now be classified as direct material. The ₹1,50,000 of direct materials used were classified as ₹1,35,000 for retail and ₹15,000 for institutional. Second, it used ABC to examine how the two products (retail potato cuts and institutional potato cuts) used indirect support resources. The finding was that three activity areas could be distinguished.

- Cleaning Activity Area – LP uses 12,00,000 kgs of raw potatoes to yield 10,00,000 kgs of potato cuts. The cost-allocation base is kgs of raw potatoes cleaned. Costs in the cleaning activity area are ₹1,20,000.
- Cutting Activity Area – Lp processes raw potatoes for the retail market independently of those processed for the institutional market. The production line produces (a) 250 kgs of retail potato cuts per cutting-hour and (b) 400 kgs of institutional potato cuts per cutting-hour. The cost-allocation base is cutting-hours on the production line. Costs in cutting activity area are ₹2,31,000.
- Packaging Activity Area – LP packages potato cuts for the retail market independently of those packaged for the institutional market. The packaging line packages (a) 25 kgs of retail potato cuts per packaging-hour and (b) 100 kgs of institutional potato cuts per packaging-hour. The cost-allocation based is packaging-hours on the production line. Costs in the packaging activity area are ₹4,44,000.

1. Using the existing costing system, what is the cost per kg of potato cuts produced by LP.
2. Calculate the cost rate per unit of the cost driver in the (a) cleaning, (b) cutting, and (c) packaging activity areas.
3. Suppose LP uses information from its activity-cost rates to calculate costs incurred on retail potato cuts and institutional potato cuts. Using the ABC system, what is the cost per kg of (a) retail potato cuts and (b) institutional potato cuts?
4. Comment on the cost differences between the two costing system in 1 and 3. How might LP use the information in 3 to make better decisions?

5-38 **Job costing with single direct-cost category, single indirect-cost pool, law firm.** Ramesh Associates is a recently formed law partnership. Ramesh, the managing partner of Ramesh Associates, has just finished a tense phone call with Harish, president of Coal India Ltd. Harish strongly complained about the price Ramesh charged for some legal work done for Coal India.

Ramesh also received a phone call from its only other client (Asahi Glass), which was very pleased with both the quality of the work and the price charged on its most recent job.

Ramesh Associates uses a cost-based approach to pricing (billing) each job. Currently it uses a single direct-cost category (professional labor-hours) and a single indirect-cost pool (general support). Indirect costs are allocated to cases on the basis of professional labor-hours per case. The job files show the following:

	Coal India	Asahi Glass
Professional labor	104 hours	96 hours

Professional labor costs at Ramesh Associates are ₹700 an hour. Indirect costs are allocated to cases at ₹1,050 an hour. Total indirect costs in the most recent period were ₹2,10,000.

Required

1. Why is it important for Ramesh Associates to understand the costs associated with individual jobs?
2. Compute the costs of the Coal India and Asahi Glass jobs using Ramesh's existing job-costing system.

5-39 **Job costing with multiple direct-cost categories, single indirect-cost pool, law firm (continuation of 5-38).** Ramesh asks his assistant, Ratan to collect details on those costs included in the ₹10,000 indirect-cost pool that can be traced to each individual job. After analysis, Ratan is able to reclassify ₹1,40,000 of the ₹10,000 as direct costs:

Other direct costs	Coal India	Asahi Glass
Research support labor	₹16,000	₹34,000
Computer time	5,000	13,000
Travel and allowances	6,000	44,000
Telephones/faxes	2,000	10,000
Photocopying	2,500	7,500
Total	31,500	1,08,500

Ramesh decides to calculate the costs of each job. Ratan used six direct-cost pools and a single indirect-cost pool. The single indirect-cost pool would have ₹70,000 of costs and would be allocated to each case using the professional labor-hours base.

Required

1. What is the revised indirect-cost allocation rate per professional labor-hour for Ramesh Associates when total indirect costs are ₹70,000?
2. Compute the costs of the Coal India and Asahi Glass jobs if the firm in question had used its refined costing system with multiple direct-cost categories and one indirect-cost pool.
3. Compare the costs of Coal India and Asahi Glass jobs in 2 above with those in requirement 2 of Problem 5-34. Comment on the results.

5-40 **Job costing with multiple direct-cost categories, multiple indirect-cost pools, law firm (continuation of 5-37 and 5-38).** Ramesh has two classifications of professional staff: partners and associates. Ramesh asks his assistant to examine the relative use of partners and associates on the recent Coal India and Asahi Glass jobs. The Coal India job used 24 partner-hours and 80 associate-hours. The Asahi glass job used 56 partner-hours and 40 associates-hours. Therefore, totals of the two jobs together were 80 partner-hours and 120 associate-hours. Ramesh decides to examine how using separate direct-cost rates for partners and associates and using separate indirect-cost pools for partners and associates would have affected the costs of the Coal India and Asahi Glass jobs. Indirect costs in each indirect-cost pool would be allocated on the basis of total hours of that category of professional labor. From the total indirect-cost pool would be allocated on the basis of total hours of that category of professional labor. From the total indirect-cost pool of ₹70,000, ₹46,000 is attributable to the activities of partners, and ₹24,000 is attributable to the activities of associates.

The rates per category of professional labor are as follows:

Category of Professional Labor	Direct Cost Per Hour	Indirect Cost Per Hour
Partner	₹1,000	₹46,000/80 hours = ₹575
Associate	500	₹24,000/120 hours = ₹200

Required

1. Compute the costs of the Coal India and Asahi Glass cases using Ramesh's further refined system, with multiple direct-cost categories and multiple indirect-cost pools.
2. For what decisions might Ramesh Associates find it more useful to use this job-costing approach rather than the approaches in problems 5-33 or 5-34?

5-41 Plantwide versus department overhead cost rates. (CMA, adapted) The Samsonite Ltd. manufactures a complete line of fiberglass suitcases. Samsonite has three manufacturing departments (molding, component, and assembly) and two support departments (maintenance and power).

The sides of the cases are manufactured in the Molding Department. The frames, hinges, locks, and so forth are manufactured in the Component Department. The cases are completed in the Assembly Department. Varying amounts of materials, time, and effort are required for each of the various cases. The maintenance Department and Power Department provide services to the three manufacturing departments.Samsonite has always used a plantwide manufacturing overhead rate. Direct manufacturing labor-hours are used to allocate the overhead to each product. The budgeted rate is calculated dividing the company's total budgeted manufacturing overhead cost by the total budgeted direct manufacturing labor-hours to be worked in the three manufacturing departments.

Aditya, manager of Cost Accounting, has recommended that Samsonite use department overhead rates. Aditya has projected operating costs and production levels for the coming year. They are presented (in thousands) by department in the following table:

Particulars	Manufacturing Department		
	Molding	Component	Assembly
Department operating data			
Direct manufacturing labor-hours	500	2,000	1,500
Machine-hours	875	125	–
Department costs			
Direct manufacturing materials	₹24,800	60,000	₹2,500
Direct manufacturing labor	7,000	40,000	24,000
Manufacturing overhead	42,000	32,400	45,200
Total department costs	73,800	1,32,400	71,700
Uses of support departments			
Estimated usage of maintenance resources in labor-hours for coming year	90	25	10
Estimated usage of power (in kilowatt-hours) for coming year	360	320	120

Estimated costs are ₹8,000 for the Maintenance Department and ₹36,800 for the Power Department.

Required

1. Calculate the plantwide overhead rate for Samsonite Ltd. for the coming year using the same method as used in the past.
2. Aditya has been asked to develop department overhead rates for comparison with the plantwide rate. Follow these steps in developing the department rates:

a. Allocate the Maintenance Department and Power Department costs to the three manufacturing departments.

b. Calculate department overhead rates for the three manufacturing departments using a machine-hour allocation based for the Molding Department and a direct manufacturing labor-hour allocation base for the Component Department and Assembly Department.

3. Should the Samsonite Ltd. use a plantwide rate or department rates to allocate overhead cost to its products? Explain your answer.

4. Under what conditions should Samsonite Ltd. further subdivide the department cost pools into activity-cost pools?

5-42 Activity-based costing, product-cost cross-subsidization. Ever Bake (EB) has been in the food processing business for three years. For its first two years (year 1 and year 2), its sole product was raisin cake. All cakes were manufactured and packaged in one-kg units. EB used a normal costing system. The two direct-cost categories were direct materials and direct manufacturing labor. The sole indirect manufacturing cost category-manufacturing overhead-was allocated to products using units of production as the allocation base.

In its year 3, EB added a second product-layered carrot cake-which was packaged in one-kg units. This product-differs from raisin cake in several ways:

- More expensive ingredients are used.
- More direct manufacturing labor time is required.
- More-complex manufacturing processing is required.

In year 3, EB continued to use its existing costing system, in which it allocated manufacturing overhead using total units produced of raisin and layered carrot cakes.

Direct materials, costs in year 3 were ₹120 per kg of raisin cake and ₹180 per kg of layered carrot cake. Direct manufacturing labor cost in year 3 was ₹28 per kg of raisin cake and ₹40 per kg layered carrot cake.

During year 3, EB sales staff reported greater-than-expected sales of layered carrot cake and less-than-expected sales of raisin cake. The budgeted and actual sales volume for year 3 is as follows:

	Budgeted	Actual
Raisin cake	1,60,000 kgs	1,20,000 kgs
Layered carrot cake	40,000 kgs	80,000 kgs

The budgeted manufacturing overhead for year 3 is ₹42,16,000.

At the end of year 3, Manish, the controller of EB, decided to investigate how an activity-based costing system would affect the product-cost numbers. After consultation with operating personnel the single manufacturing overhead cost pool was subdivided into five activity areas. These activity areas, the cost-allocation base, the budgeted year 3 cost-allocation rate, and the quantity of the cost-allocation base used by the raisin and layered carrot cakes are as follows:

Activity	Cost-allocation Base	Budgeted Year 3 Cost per Unit of Cost-allocation Base	Quantity of Cost-Allocation Base Raising Cake	Layered Carrot Cake
Mixing	Labor-hours	₹0.80	6,00,000	6,40,000
Cooking	Over-hours	2.80	2,40,000	2,40,000
Cooling	Cool room-hours	0.40	3,60,000	4,00,000
Creaming/Icing	Machine-hours	5.00	0	2,40,000
Packaging	Machine-hours	1.60	3,60,000	5,60,000

Required

1. Compute the year 3 unit-product cost of raisin cake and layered carrot cake using the existing costing system used in the year 3 to year 3 period.

2. Compute the year 3 unit-product cost of raisin cake and layered carrot cake using the activity-based costing system.

3. Explain the differences in unit-product costs computed in requirements 1 and 2.

4.   Describe three uses Ever Bake might make of the activity-based cost numbers.

5-43 ABC, health care. Max Health Center runs three programs: (1) alcoholic rehabilitation, (2) drug addict rehabilitation, and (3) after care (counseling and support of patients after release from a mental hospital).

The center's budget for current year follows:

Professional salaries		
4 physicians ? ₹6,00,000	₹24,00,000	
18 psychologists ? ₹3,00,000	54,00,000	
20 nurses ? ₹1,20,000	24,00,000	₹1,02,00,000
Medical supplies		6,00,000
General overhead (administrative salaries, rent, utilities, etc.)		17,60,000
		1,25,60,000

Amitabh, the director of the Center, is keen on determining the cost of each program. Amitabh compiled the following data describing employee allocations to individual programs:

	Alcohol	Drug	Aftercare	Total Employees
Physicians		4		4
Psychologists	6	4	8	18
Nurses	4	6	10	20

Eighty patients are in residence in the alcohol program, each staying about six months. Thus, the clinic provides 40 patient-years of service in the alcohol program. Similarly, 100 patients are involved in the drug program for about six months each. Thus, the clinic provides 50 patient-years of service in the drug program.

Amitabh has recently become aware of activity-based costing as a method to refine costing systems. He asks his accountant, Suresh, how he should apply this new technique. Suresh obtains the following information:

1.   Consumption of medical supplies depends on the number of patient-years.

2.   General overhead costs consists of

Rent and clinic maintenance	₹3,60,000
Administrative costs to manage patient charts, food, laundry	12,00,000
Laboratory services	2,00,000
Total	17,60,000

3.   Other information about individual departments:

	Alcohol	Drug	Aftercare	Total Employees
Square feet of space occupied by each program	9,000	9,000	12,000	30,000
Patient-years of service	40	50	60	150
Number of laboratory tests	400	1,400	70	2,500

Required

1. **a.** Select cost-allocation bases that you believe are the most appropriate for allocating indirect costs to programs, calculate the indirect-cost rates for medical supplies, rent, and clinic maintenance; administrative costs for patient charts, food, and laundry; and laboratory services.

   b. Using an activity-based costing approach to cost analysis, calculate the cost of each program and the cost per patient-year of the alcohol and drug programs.

   c. What benefits can Max Health Center obtain by implementing the ABC system?

2. What factors, other than cost, do you think Max Health Center should consider in allocating resources to its programs?

5-44 Activity-based costing, cost hierarchy. (CMA, adapted) Basista Coffee Ltd. (BCL) buys coffee beans from around the world and roasts, blends, and packages them for resale. The major cost is direct materials; however, there is substantial manufacturing overhead in the predominantly automated roasting and packing process. The company uses relatively little direct labor.

Some of the coffees are very popular and sell in large volumes, whereas a few of the newer blends sell in very low volumes. BCL prices its coffee at budgeted cost, including allocated overhead, plus a markup on cost of 30 percent.

Data for the current year budget include manufacturing overhead of ₹30,00,000, which has been allocated on the basis of each product's budgeted direct-labor cost. The budget direct-labor cost for current year totals ₹6,00,000. Purchases and use of materials (mostly coffee beans) are budgeted to total ₹60,00,000.

The budgeted direct costs for one-kg bags of two of the company's products are

	Indian	Malaysian
Direct materials	₹42	₹32
Direct labor	3	3

BCL's controller believes the existing costing system may be providing misleading cost information. She has developed an activity-based analysis of current year budgeted manufacturing overhead costs shown in the following table.

Activity	Cost Driver	Cost Driver Rate
Purchasing	Purchase orders	₹5,000
Materials handling	Setups	4,000
Quality control	Batches	2,400
Roasting	Roasting-hours	100
Blending	Blending-hours	100
Packaging	Packaging-hours	100

Data regarding the current year production of the Indian and Malaysian coffee follow. There will be no beginning or ending materials inventory for either of these coffees.

Particulars	Indian	Malaysian
Expected sales	1,00,000 kg	2,000 kg
Purchase orders	4	4
Batches	10	4
Setups	30	12
Roasting-hours	1,000	20
Blending-hours	500	10
Packaging-hours	100	2

Required

1. Using BCL's existing costing system:
   a. Determine the company's current year budgeted manufacturing overhead rate using direct-labor cost as the single allocation base.
   b. Determine the current year budgeted costs and selling prices of 1 kg of Indian coffee and 1 kg of Malaysian coffee.
2. Use the controller's activity-based approach to estimate the current year budgeted cost for 1 kg of:
   a. Indian coffee
   b. Malaysian coffee
   Allocate all costs to the 1,00,000 kg of Indian and the 2,000 kg of Malaysian coffee. Compare the results with those in requirement 1.
3. Examine the implications of your answers to requirement 2 for BCL's pricing and product-mix strategy.

6 Master Budget and Responsibility Accounting

No one likes to run out of cash.

During the global recession of 2007–2009, both households and businesses faced economic hardships. Among the hottest innovations to emerge during the recession were Web sites that enabled users to get a snapshot of their financial data, including checking accounts, investment statements, and loans, and to create budgets to manage their spending and saving. Mint.com was one of these Web sites. In 2009, Intuit, the developer of the Quicken and TurboTax products, recognized the growing popularity of these financial Web sites and acquired Mint.com for $170 million.

Businesses, like individuals, need budgets. Without budgets, it's difficult for managers and their employees to know whether they're on target for their growth and spending goals. Adhering to budgets is important for all types of companies: large financial institutions, large retailers, profitable computer companies, and luxury hotels.

Budgets and the Budgeting Cycle

A *budget* is (a) the quantitative expression of a proposed plan of action by management for a specified period and (b) an aid to coordinate what needs to be done to implement that plan. The budget generally includes both financial and non-financial aspects of the plan, and it serves as a blueprint for the company to follow in an upcoming period. A financial budget quantifies management's expectations regarding income, cash flows, and financial position. Just as financial statements are prepared for past periods, financial statements can be prepared for future periods—for example, a budgeted income statement, a budgeted statement of cash flows, and a budgeted balance sheet. Managers develop financial budgets using supporting information from nonfinancial budgets for, say, units manufactured or sold, number of employees, and number of new products being introduced to the marketplace.

Strategic Plans and Operating Plans

Budgeting is most useful when it is integrated with a company's strategy. *Strategy* specifies how an organization matches its own capabilities with the opportunities in the marketplace to accomplish its objectives. To develop successful strategies, managers must consider questions such as the following:

- What are our objectives?
- How do we create value for our customers while distinguishing ourselves from our competitors?
- Are the markets for our products local, regional, national, or global? What trends affect our markets? How do the economy, our industry, and our competitors affect us?

- What organizational and financial structures serve us best?
- What are the risks and opportunities of alternative strategies, and what are our contingency plans if our preferred plan fails?

A company, such as Reliance Retail, can have a strategy of providing quality products or services at a low price. Another company, such as Pfizer or Porsche, can have a strategy of providing a unique product or service that is priced higher than the products or services of competitors. Exhibit 6-1 shows that strategic plans are expressed through long-run budgets and operating plans are expressed via short-run budgets. But there is more to the story! The exhibit shows arrows pointing backward as well as forward. The backward arrows are a way of graphically indicating that budgets can lead to changes in plans and strategies. Budgets help managers assess strategic risks and opportunities by providing them with feedback about the likely effects of their strategies and plans. Sometimes the feedback prompts managers to revise their plans and possibly their strategies.

Boeing's experience with the 747-8 program illustrates how budgets can help managers rework their operating plans. Boeing believed that utilizing some of the design concepts it was implementing in its 787 Dreamliner program would be a relatively inexpensive way to reconfigure its 747-8 jet. However, continued cost overruns and delays undermined that strategy: In early 2012, the 747-8 program was already ₹2,000 crore over budget and a year behind schedule. As a result, the company expected to earn no profit on any of the more than 100 orders for 747-8 planes it had on its books. And with the budget revealing higher-than-expected costs in design, rework, and production, Boeing postponed production plans for the 747-8 program.

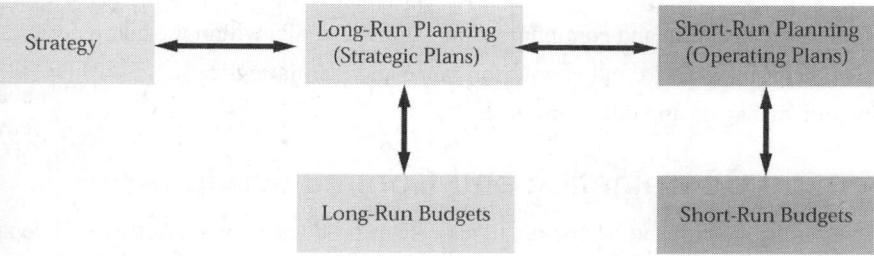

Exhibit 6-1

Strategy, Planning, and Budgets

Budgeting Cycle and Master Budget

Well-managed companies usually cycle through the following budgeting steps during the course of the fiscal year:

1. Before the start of the fiscal year, managers at all levels take into account the company's past performance, market feedback, and anticipated future changes to initiate plans for the next period. For example, an anticipated economic recovery from a recession may cause managers to plan for sales increases, higher production, and greater promotion expenses. Managers and management accountants work together to develop plans for the company as a whole and the performance of its subunits, such as departments or divisions.

**Learning
Objective** **1**

Describe the master
budget

. . . The master budget
is the initial budget prepared before the start of
a period

and explain its benefits

. . . benefits include
planning, coordination,
and control

2. At the beginning of the fiscal year, senior managers give subordinate managers a frame of reference, a set of specific financial or nonfinancial expectations against which they will compare actual results.

3. During the course of the year, management accountants help managers investigate any deviations from the plans, such as an unexpected decline in sales. If necessary, corrective action follows, such as changes in a product's features, a reduction in prices to boost sales, or cutting of costs to maintain profitability.

The preceding three steps describe the ongoing budget-related process. The working document at the core of this process is called the master budget. The **master budget** expresses management's operating and financial plans for a specified period (usually a fiscal year), and it includes a set of budgeted financial statements. The master budget is the initial plan of what the company intends to accomplish in the budget period and evolves from both operating and financing decisions managers make along the way.

- Operating decisions deal with how to best use the limited resources of an organization.
- Financing decisions deal with how to obtain the funds to acquire those resources.

The terminology used to describe budgets varies among companies. For example, budgeted financial statements are sometimes called **pro forma statements**. Some companies such as Hewlett-Packard, refer to budgeting as *targeting*. And many companies refer to the budget as a *profit plan*. Microsoft refers to goals as *commitments* and distributes firm level goals across the company, connecting them to organizational, team, and ultimately individual commitments.

This book focuses on how management accounting helps managers make operating decisions, which is why operating budgets are emphasized here. Managers spend a significant part of their time preparing and analyzing budgets because budgeting yields many advantages.

**Decision
Point** ▶

What is the master
budget and why is
it useful?

Advantages and Challenges of Implementing Budgets

Budgets are an integral part of management control systems. As we have discussed at the start of this chapter, when administered thoughtfully by managers, budgets do the following:

- Promote coordination and communication among subunits within the company
- Provide a framework for judging performance and facilitating learning
- Motivate managers and other employees

**Learning
Objective** **2**

Describe the advantages
of budgets

. . . advantages
include coordination,
communication, perfor-
mance evaluation, and
managerial motivation

Promoting Coordination and Communication

Coordination is meshing and balancing all aspects of production or service and all departments in a company in the best way for the company to meet its goals. *Communication* is making sure all employees understand those goals. Coordination forces executives to think about the relationships among individual departments within the company, as well as between the company and its supply chain partners.

Consider budgeting at Samsung, a South Korea–based manufacturer of electronic products. A key product is Samsung's digital set-top box for decoding satellite broadcasts. The production manager can achieve more timely production by coordinating and communicating with the company's marketing team to understand when set-top boxes need to be shipped to customers. In turn, the marketing team can make better predictions of future demand for set-top boxes by coordinating and communicating with Samsung's customers.

Suppose BSkyB, one of Samsung's largest customers, is planning to launch a new high definition personal video recorder service. If Samsung's marketing group is able to obtain information about the launch date for the service, it can share this information with Samsung's manufacturing group. The manufacturing group must then coordinate and communicate with Samsung's materials-procurement group, and so on. The point to understand is that Samsung is more likely to have personal video recorders in the quantities customers demand if Samsung coordinates and communicates both within its business functions and with its customers and suppliers during the budgeting process as well as during the production process.

Providing Framework for Judging Performance and Facilitating Learning

Budgets enable a company's managers to measure actual performance against predicted performance. Budgets can overcome two limitations of using past performance as a basis for judging actual results. One limitation is that past results often incorporate past miscues and substandard performance. Suppose the cellular telephone company Airtel Communications is examining the current-year (2014) performance of its sales force. The sales force's 2013 performance incorporated the efforts of an unusually high number of salespeople who have since left the company because they did not have a good understanding of the marketplace. The president of Airtel said of those salespeople, "They could not sell ice cream in a heat wave." Using the sales record of those departed employees would set the performance bar for 2014 much too low.

The other limitation of using past performance is that future conditions can be expected to differ from the past. Consider again Airtel Communications. Suppose, in 2014, Airtel had a 20% revenue increase, compared with a 10% revenue increase in 2013. Does this increase indicate outstanding sales performance? Not if the forecasted and actual 2014 industry growth rate was 40%. In this case, Airtel's 20% actual revenue gain in 2014 doesn't look so good, even though it exceeded the 2013 actual growth rate of 10%. Using the 40% budgeted growth rate for the industry provides Airtel Communications with a better benchmark against which to evaluate its 2014 sales performance than using the 2013 actual growth rate of 10%. This is why many companies also evaluate their performance relative to their peers. Using only the budget to evaluate performance creates an incentive for subordinates to set targets that are relatively easy to achieve.[1] Of course, managers at all levels recognize this incentive and therefore work to make the budget more challenging to achieve for the individuals who report to them. Still, the budget is the end product of negotiations among senior and subordinate managers. At the end of the year, senior managers gain information about the performance of competitors and external market conditions. This is valuable information senior managers can use to judge the performance of subordinate managers.

One of the most valuable benefits of budgeting is that it helps managers learn. When actual performance falls short of budgeted or planned performance, it prompts thoughtful senior managers to ask questions about what happened and why, and how performance can be improved in the future. This probing and learning is one of the most important reasons why budgeting helps improve performance.

Motivating Managers and Other Employees

Research shows that the performance of employees improves when they receive a challenging budget. Why? Because they view not meeting it as a failure. Most employees are motivated to work more intensely to avoid failure than to achieve success. As employees get closer to a goal, they work harder to achieve it. Creating a little anxiety improves performance. However, overly ambitious and unachievable budgets can actually de-motivate employees

---

[1] For several examples, see Jeremy Hope and Robin Fraser, *Beyond Budgeting* (Boston: Harvard Business School Press, 2003). The authors also criticize the tendency for managers to administer budgets rigidly even when changing market conditions have rendered the budgets obsolete.

because they see little chance of avoiding failure. As a result, many executives like to set demanding but achievable goals for their subordinate managers and employees.[2] General Electric's former CEO Jack Welch describes challenging yet achievable budgets as energizing, motivating, and satisfying for managers and other employees and capable of unleashing out-of-the-box and creative thinking. We will return to the topic of setting difficult-to-achieve targets and how it affects employees later in the chapter.

Challenges in Administering Budgets

The budgeting process involves all levels of management. Top managers want lower-level managers to participate in the budgeting process because lower-level managers have more specialized knowledge and first-hand experience with day-to-day aspects of running the business. Participation creates greater commitment and accountability toward the budget among lower-level managers. This is the bottom-up aspect of the budgeting process.

The budgeting process, however, is time-consuming. Estimates suggest that senior managers spend about 10% to 20% of their time on budgeting, and finance planning departments spend as much as 50% of their time on it.[3] For most organizations, the annual budget process is a months-long exercise that consumes a tremendous amount of resources.

The widespread use of budgets in companies ranging from major multinational corporations to small local businesses indicates that the advantages of budgeting systems outweigh the costs. To gain the benefits of budgeting, management at all levels of a company should understand and support the budget and all aspects of the management control system. This is critical for obtaining lower-level management's participation in the formulation of budgets and for successful administration of budgets. Lower-level managers who feel that top management does not "believe" in a budget are unlikely to be active participants in a budget process.

Budgets should not be administered rigidly. Attaining the budget is not an end in itself, especially when conditions change dramatically. A manager may commit to a budget, but if a situation arises in which some unplanned repairs or an unplanned advertising program would serve the long-run interests of the company, the manager should undertake the additional spending. On the flip side, the dramatic decline in consumer demand during the 2007–2009 recession led designers such as Gucci to slash their ad budgets and put on hold planned new boutiques. Macy's and other retailers, stuck with shelves of merchandise ordered before the financial crisis, had no recourse but to slash prices and cut their workforce. JCPenney eventually missed its sales projections for 2009 by ₹2,000 crores. However, its aggressive actions during the year enabled it to survive the recession. Unfortunately, in 2012, J. C. Penney suffered steep declines in sales as a result of changing its strategy away from offering discounts and deals to everyday low pricing.

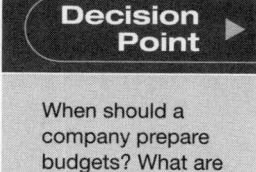

Decision Point ▶

When should a company prepare budgets? What are the advantages of preparing budgets?

Developing an Operating Budget

Budgets are typically developed for a set period, such as a month, quarter, year, and so on. The set period can itself be broken into subperiods. For example, a 12-month cash budget may be broken into 12 monthly periods so that cash inflows and outflows can be better coordinated.

---

[2] For a detailed discussion and several examples of the merits of setting specific hard goals, see Gary P. Latham, "The Motivational Benefits of Goal-Setting," *Academy of Management Executive* 18, no. 4 (2004).

[3] See P. Horvath and R. Sauter, "Why Budgeting Fails: One Management System is Not Enough," *Balanced Scorecard* Report, (September 2004).

Time Coverage of Budgets

The motive for creating a budget should guide a manager in choosing the period for the budget. For example, consider budgeting for a new Bajaj 500-cc motorcycle. If the purpose is to budget for the total profitability of this new model, a five-year period (or more) may be suitable and long enough to cover the product from design through to manufacture, sales, and after-sales support. In contrast, consider budgeting for a seasonal theater production, which is expected to run for a few months. If the purpose is to estimate all cash outlays, a six-month period from the planning stage to the final performance may suffice.

The most frequently used budget period is one year, which is often subdivided into months and quarters. The budgeted data for a year are frequently revised as the year goes on. At the end of the second quarter, management may change the budget for the next two quarters in light of new information obtained during the first six months. For example, Amerigroup, a health insurance firm, had to make substantial revisions to its third-quarter and annual cost projections for 2009 because of higher-than-expected costs related to the H1N1 virus.

Businesses are increasingly using rolling budgets. A **rolling budget,** also called a **continuous budget** or rolling forecast, is a budget that is always available for a specified future period. It is created by continually adding a month, quarter, or year to the period that just ended. Consider Electrolux, the global appliance company, which has a three- to five-year strategic plan and a four-quarter rolling budget. A four-quarter rolling budget for the April 2013 to March 2014 period is superseded in the next quarter—that is in June 2013—by a four-quarter rolling budget for July 2013 to June 2014, and so on. There is always a 12-month budget (for the next year) in place. Rolling budgets constantly force Electrolux's management to think about the forthcoming 12 months, regardless of the quarter at hand.

Learning Objective 3

Prepare the operating budget

. . . the budgeted income statement

and its supporting schedules

. . . such as cost of goods sold and non-manufacturing costs

Steps in Preparing an Operating Budget

The best way to explain how to prepare an operating budget is by walking through the steps a company would take to do this. Consider Stylistic Furniture, a company that makes two types of granite-top coffee tables—Casual and Deluxe. It is late 2013 and Stylistic's CEO, Usha Thorat, is very concerned about how he is going to respond to the Board of Directors' mandate to increase profits by 10% in the coming year. Usha goes through the five-step decision-making process introduced in Chapter 1.

1. **Identify the problem and uncertainties.** The problem is to identify a strategy and to build a budget to achieve a 10% profit growth. There are several uncertainties. Can Stylistic dramatically increase sales of its more profitable Deluxe tables? What price pressures is Stylistic likely to face? Will the cost of materials increase? Can Stylistic reduce costs through efficiency improvements?

2. **Obtain information.** Stylistic's managers gather information about sales of Deluxe tables in the current year. They are delighted to learn that sales of Deluxe have been stronger than expected. Moreover, one of Stylistic's key competitors in its line of Casual tables has had quality problems that are unlikely to be resolved until early 2014. Unfortunately, Stylistic's managers also discover that the prices of direct materials have increased slightly during 2013.

3. **Make predictions about the future.** Stylistic's managers feel confident that with a little more marketing, they will be able to grow the Deluxe tables business and even increase prices slightly relative to 2013. They also do not expect significant price pressures on Casual tables in the early part of the year because of the quality problems faced by a key competitor.

The purchasing manager anticipates that prices of materials will be about the same as in 2013. The manufacturing manager believes that efficiency improvements would allow costs of manufacturing tables to be maintained at 2013 costs despite an increase in prices of other inputs. Achieving these efficiency improvements is important if Stylistic is to maintain its 12% operating margin (that is, operating income ÷ sales = 12%) and to grow sales and operating income.

4. **Make decisions by choosing among alternatives.** Usha and her managers feel confident in their strategy to increase the sales of Deluxe tables. This decision has some risks but is easily the best option available for Stylistic to increase profits by 10%.

5. **Implement the decision, evaluate performance, and learn.** As we will discuss in Chapters 7 and 8, managers compare a company's actual performance to its predicted performance to learn why things turned out the way they did and how to do things better. Stylistic's managers would want to know whether their predictions about prices of Casual and Deluxe tables were correct. Did the prices of direct materials increase more or less than anticipated? Did efficiency improvements occur? Such learning would be very helpful as Stylistic plans its budgets in subsequent years.

Stylistic's managers begin their work toward the 2014 budget. Exhibit 6-2 shows the various parts of the *master budget,* which is composed of the financial projections for Stylistic's operating and financial budgets for 2014. The light, medium and dark purple boxes in Exhibit 6-2 represent the budgeted income statement and its supporting budget schedules—together called the **operating budget**.

We show the revenues budget box in a light gray to indicate that it is often the starting point of the operating budget. The supporting schedules—shown in medium green—quantify the budgets for various business functions of the value chain, from research and development to distribution costs. These schedules build up to the budgeted income statement—the key summary statement in the operating budget—shown in dark green.

The orange and purple boxes in the exhibit are the **financial budget**, which is that part of the master budget made up of the capital expenditures budget, the cash budget, the budgeted balance sheet, and the budgeted statement of cash flows. A financial budget focuses on how operations and planned capital outlays affect cash—shown in orange.

Management accountants use the cash budget and the budgeted income statement to prepare two other summary financial statements—the budgeted balance sheet and the budgeted statement of cash flows, which are shown in purple.

Top managers and line managers responsible for various business functions in the value chain finalize the master budget after several rounds of discussions among them. We next present the steps in preparing an operating budget for Stylistic Furniture for 2014. Use Exhibit 6-2 as a guide for the steps that follow. The following details are needed to prepare the budget:

- Stylistic sells two models of granite-top coffee tables—Casual and Deluxe. Revenue unrelated to sales, such as interest income, is zero.
- Work-in-process inventory is negligible and is ignored.
- Direct materials inventory and finished goods inventory are costed using the first-in, first-out (FIFO) method. The unit costs of direct materials purchased and unit costs of finished goods sold remain unchanged throughout each budget year but can change from year to year.
- There are two types of direct materials: red oak (RO) and granite slabs (GS). Direct material costs are variable with respect to units of output—coffee tables.
- Direct manufacturing labor workers are hired on an hourly basis; no overtime is worked.

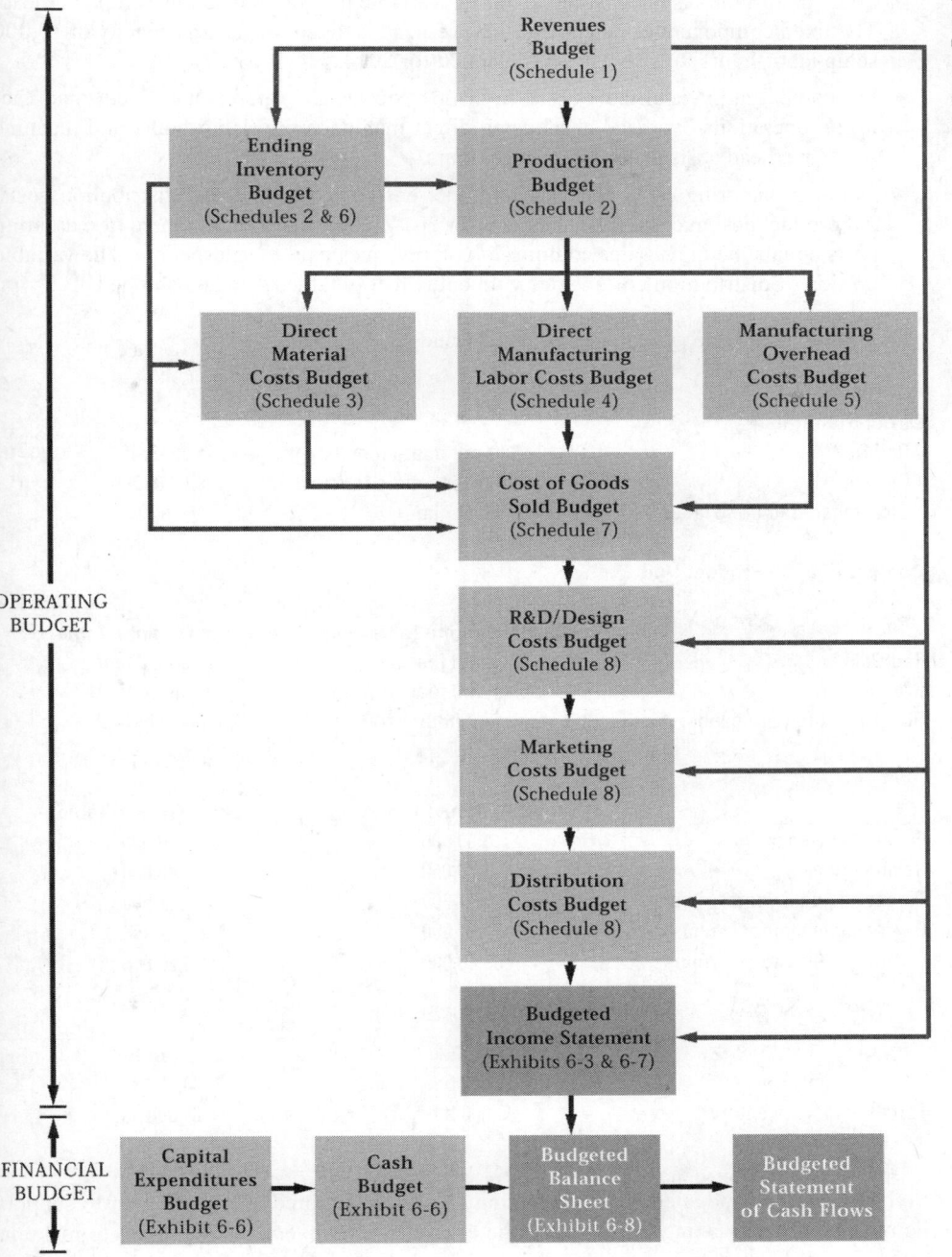

Exhibit 6-2

Overview of the Master
Budget for Stylistic
Furniture

- There are two cost drivers for manufacturing overhead costs—direct manufacturing labor-hours and setup labor-hours, and two manufacturing overhead cost pools—manufacturing operations overhead and machine setup overhead.

- Direct manufacturing labor-hours is the cost driver for the variable portion of manufacturing operations overhead. The fixed component of manufacturing operations overhead is tied to the manufacturing capacity of 3,00,000 direct manufacturing labor-hours Stylistic has planned for 2014.

- Setup labor-hours is the cost driver for the variable portion of machine setup overhead. The fixed component of machine setup overhead is tied to the setup capacity of 15,000 setup labor-hours that Stylistic has planned for 2014.

- For computing inventoriable costs, Stylistic allocates all (variable and fixed) manufacturing operations overhead costs using direct manufacturing labor-hours and machine setup overhead costs using setup labor-hours.

- Nonmanufacturing costs consist of product design, marketing and distribution costs. All product design costs are fixed costs for 2014. The variable component of marketing costs equals the 6.5% sales commission on revenues paid to salespeople. The variable portion of distribution costs varies with cubic feet of tables sold and shipped.

The following data are available for the 2014 budget:

Direct materials

Red Oak	₹70 per board foot (b.f.) (same as in 2013)
Granite	₹100 per square foot (s.f.) (same as in 2013)
Direct manufacturing labor	₹200 per hour

Content of Each Product Unit

	Product	
	Casual Granite Table	**Deluxe Granite Table**
Red Oak	12 board feet	12 board feet
Granite	6 square feet	8 square feet
Direct manufacturing labor	4 hours	6 hours

	Product	
	Casual Granite Table	**Deluxe Granite Table**
Expected sales in units	50,000	10,000
Selling price	₹6,000	₹8,000
Target ending inventory in units	11,000	500
Beginning inventory in units	1,000	500
Beginning inventory in rupees	₹38,40,000	₹26,20,000

	Direct Materials	
	Red Oak	**Granite**
Beginning inventory	70,000 b.f.	60,000 s.f.
Target ending inventory	80,000 b.f.	20,000 s.f.

Stylistic bases its budgeted cost information on the costs it predicts it will incur to support its revenue budget, taking into account the efficiency improvements it expects to make in 2014. Recall from step 3 in the decision-making process that efficiency improvements are critical to offset anticipated increases in direct materials prices and to maintain Stylistic's 12% operating margin. Some companies rely heavily on past results when developing budgeted amounts; others rely on detailed engineering studies. Companies differ in how they compute their budgeted amounts.

Most companies have a budget manual that contains a company's particular instructions and relevant information for preparing its budgets. Although the details differ among companies, the following basic steps are common for developing the operating budget for a manufacturing company. Beginning with the revenues budget, each of the other budgets follows step-by-step in logical fashion. As you go through the details for preparing a budget, think about two things: (1) the information needed to prepare each budget and (2) the actions managers can plan to take to improve the company's performance.

Step 1:   Prepare the Revenues Budget. Stylistic currently sells two models of granite-top coffee tables: Casual and Deluxe. During 2013, Stylistic's managers had considered introducing a third coffee-table model but decided against it. They must now budget for the quantities and prices of Casual and Deluxe tables in 2014.

A revenues budget is the usual starting point for the operating budget. Why? Because the forecasted level of unit sales or revenues has a major impact on the production capacity and the inventory levels planned for 2014—and therefore manufacturing and nonmanufacturing costs. Many factors affect the sales forecast, including the sales volume in recent periods, general economic and industry conditions, market research studies, pricing policies, advertising and sales promotions, competition, and regulatory policies. The key to Stylistic achieving its goal of growing its profits by 10% is to grow its sales of Deluxe tables from 8,000 tables in 2013 to 10,000 tables in 2014.

Sales managers and sales representatives build the revenues budget by gathering detailed information about customer needs, market potential, and competitors' products. They debate how best to position, price, and promote Casual and Deluxe tables relative to competitors' products. Together with top management, they consider various actions, such as adding product features, digital advertising, and changing sales incentives, to increase revenues. The cost of these actions are included in the various cost budgets.

Managers often gather information through a customer response management (CRM) or sales management system. Statistical approaches such as regression and trend analysis also help with sales forecasting. These techniques use indicators of economic activity and past sales data to forecast future sales. Managers use statistical analysis only as one input to forecast sales. In the final analysis, the sales forecast represents the collective experience and judgment of managers.

After much discussion, top managers decide on the budgeted sales quantities and prices shown in the revenues budget in Schedule 1. These are difficult targets designed to motivate the organization to achieve higher levels of performance.

Schedule 1: Revenues Budget
For the Year Ending December 31, 2014

	Units	Selling Price	Total Revenues
Casual	50,000	₹6,000	₹30,00,00,000
Deluxe	10,000	8,000	8,00,00,000
Total			₹38,00,00,000

The ₹38,00,00,000 is the amount of revenues in the budgeted income statement. Revenues budgets are usually based on expected demand because demand for a company's products is invariably the limiting factor for achieving profit goals. Occasionally, other factors, such as available production capacity (being less than demand) or a manufacturing input in short supply, limit budgeted revenues. In these cases, managers base the revenues budget on the maximum units that can be produced because sales will be limited by that amount.

Step 2:   Prepare the Production Budget (in Units). After budgeting revenues, the logical next step is to plan the production of Casual and Deluxe tables so that the product is available when customers need it. The only new information managers need to prepare the production budget is the level of finished goods inventory Stylistic wants to maintain. High inventory levels increase the cost of carrying inventory, the costs of quality, and shrinkage costs. On the flip side, keeping inventory levels too low increases setup costs and results in lost sales from holding inadequate inventory. Over the course of the year, Stylistic's management decides to increase the inventory of Casual tables to avoid some of the supply shortages the company had encountered in the current year but to maintain the inventory level of Deluxe tables.

The manufacturing manager then prepares the production budget, shown in Schedule 2. The total finished goods units to be produced depend on budgeted unit sales (calculated in Step 1), the target ending finished goods inventory, and the beginning finished goods inventory:

$$\begin{array}{l} \text{Budget} \\ \text{production} \\ \text{(units)} \end{array} = \begin{array}{l} \text{Budget} \\ \text{sales} \\ \text{(units)} \end{array} + \begin{array}{l} \text{Target ending} \\ \text{finished goods} \\ \text{inventory} \\ \text{(units)} \end{array} - \begin{array}{l} \text{Beginning} \\ \text{finished goods} \\ \text{inventory} \\ \text{(units)} \end{array}$$

Schedule 2: Production Budget (in Units)
For the Year Ending December 31, 2014

	Product	
	Casual	Deluxe
Budgeted unit sales (Schedule 1)	50,000	10,000
Add target ending finished goods inventory	11,000	500
Total required units	61,000	10,500
Deduct beginning finished goods inventory	1,000	500
Units of finished goods to be produced	60,000	10,000

The production budget drives the various budgeted costs (for example, direct materials, direct manufacturing labor, and manufacturing overhead) Stylistic plans to incur in 2014 to support its revenues budget, taking into account the efficiency improvements it plans to make.

Managers are always looking for opportunities to reduce costs, for example, by redesigning products, improving processes, streamlining manufacturing, and reducing the time it takes to complete various activities such as setting up machines or transporting materials. Making these changes improves a company's competitiveness, but it also requires investment. The budgeting exercise is an ideal time for managers to evaluate their plans and request any financial resources that they might need. We start with the budget for direct materials.

Step 3: Prepare the Direct Material Usage Budget and Direct Material Purchases Budget. The number of units to be produced, calculated in Schedule 2, is the key to computing the usage of direct materials in quantities and in rupees. The direct material quantities used depend on the efficiency with which materials are consumed to produce a table. In determining budgets, managers are constantly anticipating ways to make process improvements that increase quality and reduce waste, thereby reducing direct material usage and costs. Senior managers set budgets that motivate production managers to reduce direct material costs and keep negligible work-in-process inventory. We ignore work-in-process inventory when preparing Stylistic's budgets for 2014.

Like many companies, Stylistic has a *bill of materials,* stored and updated in its computer systems that it constantly updates for efficiency improvements. This document identifies how each product is manufactured, specifying all materials (and components), the sequence in which the materials are used, the quantity of materials in each finished unit, and the work centers where the operations are performed. For example, the bill of materials would indicate that 12 board feet of red oak and 6 square feet of granite are needed to produce each Casual coffee table, and 12 board feet of red oak and 8 square feet of granite to produce each Deluxe coffee table. This information is then used to calculate the amounts in Schedule 3A.

Schedule 3A: Direct Material Usage Budget in Quantity and Rupees
For the Year Ending December 31, 2014

| | Material | | |
	Red Oak	Granite	Total
Physical Units Budget			
Direct materials required for			
Casual tables (60,000 units × 12 b.f. and 6 s.f.)	7,20,000 b.f.	3,60,000 s.f.	
Direct materials required for			
Deluxe tables (10,000 units × 12 b.f. and 8 s.f.)	1,20,000 b.f.	80,000 s.f.	
Total quantity of direct materials to be used	8,40,000 b.f.	4,40,000 s.f.	
Cost Budget			
Available from beginning direct materials inventory			
(under a FIFO cost-flow assumption)			
Red Oak: 70,000 b.f. × ₹70 per b.f.	₹49,00,000		
Granite: 60,000 s.f. × ₹100 per s.f.		₹60,00,000	
To be purchased this period			
Red Oak: (8,40,000 – 70,000) b.f. × ₹70 per b.f.	5,39,00,000		
Granite: (4,40,000 – 60,000) s.f. × ₹100 per s.f.		3,80,00,000	
Direct materials to be used this period	₹5,88,00,000	₹4,40,00,000	₹10,28,00,000

The only new information needed to prepare the direct materials purchases budget is the level of direct materials inventory Stylistic wants to maintain. Over the course of the year, Stylistic's managers decide to increase the inventory of red oak but reduce the inventory of granite to the planned levels of ending inventory. The purchasing manager then prepares the budget for direct material purchases, shown in Schedule 3B:

Schedule 3B: Direct Material Purchases Budget
For the Year Ending December 31, 2014

| | Material | | |
	Red Oak	Granite	Total
Physical Units Budget			
To be used in production (from Schedule 3A)	8,40,000 b.f.	4,40,000 s.f.	
Add target ending inventory	80,000 b.f.	20,000 s.f.	
Total requirements	9,20,000 b.f.	4,60,000 s.f.	
Deduct beginning inventory	70,000 b.f.	60,000 s.f.	
Purchases to be made	8,50,000 b.f.	4,00,000 s.f.	
Cost Budget			
Red Oak: 8,50,000 b.f. × ₹70 per b.f.	₹5,95,00,000		
Granite: 4,00,000 s.f × ₹100 per s.f.		₹4,00,00,000	
Purchases	₹5,95,00,000	₹4,00,00,000	₹9,95,00,000

Step 4:   Prepare the Direct Manufacturing Labor Costs Budget. To create the budget for direct manufacturing labor costs, Stylistic's managers estimate wage rates, production methods, process and efficiency improvements, and hiring plans. The company hires direct manufacturing labor workers on an hourly basis. These workers do not work overtime. Manufacturing managers use *labor standards,* the time allowed per unit of output, to calculate the direct manufacturing labor costs budget in Schedule 4 based on the information.

Schedule 4: Direct Manufacturing Labor Costs Budget
For the Year Ending December 31, 2014

	Output Units Produced (Schedule 2)	Direct Manufacturing Labor-Hours per Unit	Total Hours	Hourly WageRate	Total
Casual	60,000	4	2,40,000	₹200	₹4,80,00,000
Deluxe	10,000	6	60,000	200	1,20,00,000
Total			3,00,000		₹6,00,00,000

Step 5: Prepare the Manufacturing Overhead Costs Budget. Stylistic's managers next budget for manufacturing overhead costs such as supervision, depreciation, maintenance, supplies, and power. Managing overhead costs is important but also challenging because it requires managers to understand the various activities needed to manufacture products and the cost drivers of those activities. As we described earlier (page 276), Stylistic's managers identify two activities for manufacturing overhead costs in its activity-based costing system: manufacturing operations and machine setups. The following table presents the activities and their cost drivers.

Manufacturing Overhead Costs	Cost Driver of Variable Component of Overhead Costs	Cost Driver of Fixed Component of Overhead Costs	Manufacturing and Setup Capacity in 2014
Manufacturing Operations Overhead Costs	Direct manufacturing labor-hours	Manufacturing capacity	3,00,000 direct manufacturing labor-hours
Machine Setup Overhead Costs	Setup labor-hours	Setup capacity	15,000 setup labor-hours

The use of activity-based cost drivers gives rise to **activity-based budgeting (ABB),** a budgeting method that focuses on the budgeted cost of the activities necessary to produce and sell products and services.

In its activity-based costing system, Stylistic's manufacturing managers estimate various line items of overhead costs that comprise manufacturing operations overhead (that is, all costs for which direct manufacturing labor-hours is the cost driver). Managers identify opportunities for process and efficiency improvements, such as reducing defect rates and the time to manufacture a table, and then calculate budgeted manufacturing operations overhead costs in the operating department. They also determine the resources that they will need from the two support departments—kilowatt-hours of energy from the power department and hours of maintenance service from the maintenance department. The support department managers, in turn, plan the costs of personnel and supplies that they will need in order to provide the operating department with the support services it requires. The costs of the support departments are then allocated (first-stage cost allocation) as part of manufacturing operations overhead. Chapter 15 describes the allocation of support department costs to operating departments when support departments provide services to each other and to operating departments. The first half of Schedule 5 shows the various line items of costs that constitute manufacturing operations overhead costs—that is, all variable and fixed overhead costs (in the operating and support departments) that are caused by the 3,00,000 direct manufacturing labor-hours (the cost driver).

Stylistic budgets costs differently for variable and fixed overhead costs. Consider variable overhead costs of supplies: Stylistic's managers use past historical data and their knowledge of operations to estimate the cost of supplies per direct manufacturing labor-hour, which is ₹50. The total budgeted cost of supplies for 2014 is therefore ₹50 multiplied by the 3,00,000 budgeted direct manufacturing labor-hours, for a total of

₹1,50,00,000. The total variable manufacturing operations overhead cost equals ₹216.0 per direct manufacturing labor-hour multiplied by the 3,00,000 budgeted direct manufacturing labor-hours, for a total of ₹6,48,00,000.

For fixed overhead costs, Stylistic's managers start the budgeting process by determining the total fixed manufacturing operations overhead costs of ₹2,52,00,000 needed to support the 3,00,000 direct manufacturing labor-hours of capacity Stylistic's managers have planned. (Stylistic may not operate at full capacity each year, but its fixed manufacturing operations costs will still be ₹2,52,00,000.) Its fixed manufacturing overhead cost is ₹2,52,00,000 ÷ 3,00,000 = ₹84 per direct manufacturing labor-hour (regardless of the budgeted direct manufacturing labor-hours, which may be less than 3,00,000 in a particular year). That is, each direct manufacturing labor-hour will absorb ₹216 of variable manufacturing operations overhead plus ₹84 of fixed manufacturing operations overhead for a total of ₹300 of manufacturing operations overhead cost per direct manufacturing labor-hour.

Next, Stylistic's managers determine how setups should be done for the Casual and Deluxe line of tables, taking into account past experiences and potential improvements in setup efficiency.

For example, managers consider:

- Increasing the number of tables produced per batch so that fewer batches (and therefore fewer setups) are needed for the budgeted production of tables.
- Decreasing the setup time per batch.
- Reducing the supervisory time needed, for instance by increasing the skill base of workers.

Stylistic's managers forecast the following setup information for the Casual and Deluxe tables:

	Casual Tables	Deluxe Tables	Total
1. Quantity of tables to be produced	60,000 tables	10,000 tables	
2. Number of tables to be produced per batch	50 tables/batch	40 tables/batch	
3. Number of batches (1) ÷ (2)	1,200 batches	250 batches	
4. Setup time per batch	10 hours/batch	12 hours/batch	
5. Total setup-hours (3) ÷ (4)	12,000 hours	3,000 hours	15,000 hours
6. Setup-hour per table (5) × (1)	0.2 hour	0.3 hour	

Using an approach similar to the one described for manufacturing operations overhead costs, Stylistic's managers estimate various line items of costs that comprise machine setup overhead costs (supplies, indirect manufacturing labor, power, depreciation, and supervision)—that is, all costs that are caused by the 15,000 setup labor-hours (the cost driver). The second half of Schedule 5 summarizes (1) total variable machine setup overhead costs per setup labor-hour = ₹880 (₹260 + ₹560 + ₹60) × the budgeted 15,000 setup labor-hours = ₹1,32,00,000 and (2) fixed machine setup overhead costs of ₹1,68,00,000 needed to support the 15,000 setup labor-hours of capacity that Stylistic's managers have planned. (Again, Stylistic may not operate at full capacity each year. However, the fixed machine setup costs will still be ₹1,68,00,000.) The fixed machine setup cost is ₹1,68,00,000 ÷ 15,000 = ₹1,120 per setup labor-hour (regardless of the budgeted setup labor-hours, which may be less than 15,000 in a particular year). That is, each setup labor-hour will absorb ₹880 of variable machine setup overhead cost plus ₹1,120 of fixed machine setup overhead cost for a total of ₹2,000 of machine setup overhead cost per setup labor-hour. Note how using activity-based cost drivers provides more-detailed information that improves decision making compared with budgeting based solely on output-based cost drivers. Of course, managers must always evaluate whether

Schedule 5: Manufacturing Overhead Costs Budget
For the Year Ending December 31, 2014
Manufacturing Operations Overhead Costs

Variable costs (for 3,00,000 direct manufacturing labor-hours)		
Supplies (₹50 per direct manufacturing labor-hour)	₹1,50,00,000	
Indirect manufacturing labor (₹56 per direct manufacturing labor-hour)	1,68,00,000	
Power (support department costs) (₹70 per direct manufacturing labor-hour)	2,10,00,000	
Maintenance (support department costs) (₹40 per direct manufacturing labor-hour)	1,20,00,000	₹6,48,00,000
Fixed costs (to support capacity of 3,00,000 direct manufacturing labor-hours)		
Depreciation	1,02,00,000	
Supervision	39,00,000	
Power (support department costs)	63,00,000	
Maintenance (support department costs)	48,00,000	2,52,00,000
Total manufacturing operations overhead costs		₹9,00,00,000

Machine Setup Overhead Costs

Variable costs (for 15,000 setup labor-hours)		
Supplies (₹260 per setup labor-hour)	₹39,00,000	
Indirect manufacturing labor (₹560 per setup labor-hour)	84,00,000	
Power (support department costs) (₹60 per setup labor-hour)	9,00,000	₹1,32,00,000
Fixed costs (to support capacity of 15,000 setup labor-hours)		
Depreciation	60,30,000	
Supervision	1,05,00,000	
Power (support department costs)	2,70,000	1,68,00,000
Total machine setup overhead costs		₹3,00,00,000
Total manufacturing operations overhead costs		₹12,00,00,000

the expected benefit of adding more cost drivers exceeds the expected cost.[4] The bottom half of Schedule 5 summarizes these costs.

Note that Stylistic is scheduled to operate at capacity. Therefore, the budgeted quantity of the cost allocation base/cost driver is the same for variable overhead costs and fixed overhead costs—3,00,000 direct manufacturing labor-hours for manufacturing operations overhead costs and 15,000 setup labor-hours for machine setup overhead costs. In this case, the budgeted rate for the manufacturing operations overhead cost does not have to be calculated separately for variable costs and for fixed costs. It can be calculated directly by estimating total budgeted manufacturing operations overhead: ₹9,00,00,000 ÷ 3,00,000 direct manufacturing labor-hours = ₹300 per direct manufacturing labor-hour. Similarly, the budgeted rate for machine setup overhead cost can be calculated as total budgeted machine setup overhead: ₹3,00,00,000 ÷ 15,000 budgeted setup hours = ₹2,000 per setup-hour.

Step 6: Prepare the Ending Inventories Budget. Schedule 6A shows the computation of the unit cost of coffee tables started and completed in 2014. These calculations are needed to calculate the ending inventories budget and the budgeted cost of goods sold. In accordance with Generally Accepted Accounting Principles, Stylistic treats both variable and fixed manufacturing overhead as inventoriable (product) costs. Manufacturing operations overhead costs are allocated to finished goods inventory at the budgeted rate of ₹300

---

[4] The Stylistic example illustrates ABB using setup costs included in Stylistic's manufacturing overhead costs budget. ABB implementations in practice include costs in many parts of the value chain. For an example, see S. Borjesson, "A Case Study on Activity-Based Budgeting," *Journal of Cost Management*, Vol. 10, No. 4, pp. 7–18.

per direct manufacturing labor-hour. Machine setup overhead costs are allocated to finished goods inventory at the budgeted rate of ₹2,000 per setup-hour.

Schedule 6A: Unit Costs of Ending Finished Goods Inventory December 31, 2014

		Product			
		Casual Tables		Deluxe Tables	
	Cost per Unit of Input	Input per Unit of Output	Total	Input per Unit of Output	Total
Red Oak	₹70	12 b.f.	₹840	12 b.f.	₹840
Granite	100	6 s.f.	600	8 s.f.	800
Direct manufacturing labor	200	4 hrs.	800	6 hrs.	1,200
Manufacturing overhead	300	4 hrs.	1,200	6 hrs.	1,800
Machine setup overhead	2,000	0.2 hrs.	400	0.3 hrs	600
Total			₹3,840		₹5,240

Schedule 6B: Ending Inventories Budget
December 31, 2014

	Quantity	Cost per Unit	Total	
Direct Materials				
Red Oak	80,000*	₹70	₹56,00,000	
Granite	20,000*	100	20,00,000	₹76,00,000
Finished Goods				
Casual	11,000**	₹3,840***	₹4,22,40,000	
Deluxe	500**	5,240***	26,20,000	4,48,60,000
Total ending inventory				₹5,24,60,000

*Data are from page 284. **Data are from page 284. ***From Schedule 6A, this is based on 2014 costs of manufacturing finished goods because under the FIFO costing method, the units in finished goods ending inventory consists of units that are produced during 2014.

Under the FIFO method, managers use this unit cost is used to calculate the cost of target ending inventories of finished goods in Schedule 6B.

Step 7: Prepare the Cost of Goods Sold Budget. The manufacturing and purchase managers, together with the management accountant, use information from Schedules 3 through 6 to prepare Schedule 7—the cost of goods sold expense that will he matched against revenues to calculate stylistic's budgeted gross margin for 2014.

Schedule 7: Cost of Goods Sold Budget
For the Year Ending December 31, 2014

	From Schedule		Total
Beginning finished goods inventory, January 1, 2012	Given*		₹64,60,000
Direct materials used	3A	₹10,28,00,000	
Direct manufacturing labor	4	6,00,00,000	
Manufacturing overhead	5	12,00,00,000	
Cost of goods manufactured			28,28,00,000
Cost of goods available for sale			28,92,60,000
Deduct ending finished goods inventory, December 31, 2012	6B		4,48,60,000
Cost of Goods Sold			₹24,44,00,000

*Based on beginning inventory values in 2014 for Casual tables, ₹38,40,000, and Deluxe tables, ₹26,20,000 (page 205).

Step 8:   Prepare the Nonmanufacturing Costs Budget. Schedules 2–7 represent budgets for Stylistic's manufacturing costs. Stylistic also incurs nonmanufacturing costs in other parts of the value chain—product design, marketing, and distribution. Just as in the case of manufacturing costs, the key to managing nonmanufacturing overhead costs is to understand the various activities that will be needed to support the design, marketing, and distribution of Deluxe and Casual tables in 2014 and the cost drivers of those activities. Managers in these functions of the value chain build in process and efficiency improvements and prepare nonmanufacturing cost budgets on the basis of the quantities of cost drivers planned for 2014.

The number of design changes is the cost driver for product design costs. Product design costs of ₹1,02,40,000 are fixed costs for 2014 and adjusted at the start of the year based on the number of design changes planned for 2014.

Total revenue is the cost driver for the variable portion of marketing (and sales) costs. The commission paid to salespeople equals 6.5 cents per dollar (or 6.5%) of revenues. Managers budget the fixed component of marketing costs, ₹1,33,00,000, at the start of the year based on budgeted revenues for 2014.

Cubic feet of tables sold and shipped (Casual: 18 cubic feet × 50,000 tables + Deluxe: 24 cubic feet × 10,000 tables = 11,40,000 cubic feet) is the cost driver of the variable component of budgeted distribution costs. Variable distribution costs equal ₹20 per cubic foot. The fixed component of budgeted distribution costs equal to ₹1,59,60,000 varies with the company's distribution capacity, which in 2014 is 1,140,000 cubic feet (to support the distribution of 50,000 Casual tables and 10,000 Deluxe tables). For brevity, Schedule 8 shows the product design, marketing, and distribution costs budget for 2014 in a single schedule.

Schedule 8: Nonmanufacturing Costs Budget
For the Year Ending December 31, 2014

Business Function	Variable Costs	Fixed Costs	Total Costs
Product Design	—	₹1,02,40,000	₹1,02,40,000
Marketing			
(Variable cost: ₹38,00,00,000 × 0.065)	₹2,47,00,000	1,33,00,000	3,80,00,000
Distribution			
(Variable cost: ₹20 × 1,140,000 cu. ft.)	2,28,00,000	1,59,60,000	3,87,60,000
	₹4,75,00,000	₹3,95,00,000	₹8,70,00,000

Step 9:   Prepare the Budgeted Income Statement. The CEO and managers of various business functions, with help from the management accountant, use information in Schedules 1, 7, and 8 to finalize the budgeted income statement, shown in Exhibit 6-3. The style used in Exhibit 6-3 is typical, but managers and accountants could include more details in the income statement. As more details are put in the income statement, fewer supporting schedules are needed.

Budgeting is a cross-functional activity. The strategies developed by top managers for achieving a company's revenue and operating income goals affect the costs planned for the different business functions of the value chain. For example, the budgeted increase in sales at Stylistic based on spending more for marketing must be matched with higher production costs to ensure there is an adequate supply of tables and with higher distribution costs to ensure the timely delivery of tables to customers. Pramod Thorat, the CEO of Stylistic Furniture, is very pleased with the 2014 budget. It calls for a 10% increase in operating income compared with 2013. The keys to achieving a higher operating income are a significant increase in sales of Deluxe tables and process improvements and efficiency gains throughout the value chain. As Pramod studies the budget more carefully, however, he is

	File Edit View Insert Format Tools Data Window Help		
	A	B	C	D
1	**Budgeted Income Statement for Stylistic Furniture**			
2	**For the Year Ending December 31, 2012**			
3	Revenues	Schedule 1		₹38,00,00,000
4	Cost of goods sold	Schedule 7		24,44,00,000
5	Gross margin			13,56,00,000
6	Operating costs			
7	Product design costs	Schedule 8	₹1,02,40,000	
8	Marketing costs	Schedule 8	3,80,00,000	
9	Distribution costs	Schedule 8	3,87,60,000	8,70,00,000
10	Operating income			₹4,86,00,000

Exhibit 6-3

Budgeted Income Statement for Stylistic Furniture

struck by two comments appended to the budget: First, to achieve the budgeted number of tables sold, Stylistic may need to reduce its selling prices by 3% to ₹5,820 for Casual tables and to ₹7,760 for Deluxe tables. Second, a supply shortage in direct materials may result in a 5% increase in the prices of direct materials (red oak and granite) above the material prices anticipated in the 2014 budget. Even if direct materials prices increase, selling prices are anticipated to remain the same. He asks Tina Muneem, a management accountant, to use Stylistic's financial planning model to evaluate how these outcomes will affect budgeted operating income.

◀ **Decision Point**

What is the operating budget and what are its components?

Financial Planning Models and Sensitivity Analysis

Financial planning models are mathematical representations of the relationships among operating activities, financing activities, and other factors that affect the master budget. Managers can use computer-based systems, such as enterprise resource planning (ERP) systems, to perform calculations for these planning models. Managers use budgeting tools within ERP systems to simplify budgeting, reduce the need to re-input data, and reduce the time required to prepare budgets. ERP systems store vast quantities of information about the materials, machines and equipment, labor, power, maintenance, and setups needed to manufacture different products. Once managers identify sales quantities for different products, the software can quickly compute the budgeted costs for manufacturing these products. ERP systems also help managers budget for nonmanufacturing costs.

As they prepare operating budgets, managers do not focus only on what they can achieve. They also identify the risks they face such as a potential decline in demand for the company's products, the entry of a new competitor, or an increase in the prices of different inputs. Sensitivity analysis is a useful tool that helps managers evaluate these risks. *Sensitivity analysis* is a "what-if" technique that examines how a result will change if the original predicted data are not achieved or if an underlying assumption changes. Software packages typically have a sensitivity analysis module managers can use in their planning and budgeting activities.

To see how sensitivity analysis works, we consider two scenarios identified as possibly affecting Stylistic Furniture's budget model for 2012.

Scenario 1: A 3% decrease in the selling price of the Casual table and a 3% decrease in the selling price of the Deluxe table.

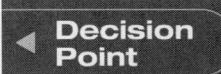

Learning Objective 4

Use computer-based financial planning models in sensitivity analysis

. . . for example, understand the effects of changes in selling prices and direct material prices on budgeted income

Exhibit 6-4	Effect of Changes in Budget Assumptions on Budgeted Operating Income for Stylistic Furniture

	A	B	C	D	E	F	G	H	I
1	Key Assumptions								
2		Units Sold		Selling Price		Direct Material Cost		Budgeted Operating Income	
3	What-If Scenario	Casual	Deluxe	Casual	Deluxe	Red Oak (₹)	Granite (₹)	Amount	Change from Master Budget
4	Master budget	50,000	10,000	₹6,000	₹8,000	70.0	100	₹4,86,00,000	
5	Scenario 1	50,000	10,000	5,820	7,760	70.0	100	3,79,41,000	22% decrease
6	Scenario 2	50,000	10,000	6,000	8,000	73.5	105	4,48,38,000	9% decrease

Scenario 2: A 5% increase in the price per board foot of red oak and a 5% increase in the price per square foot of granite.

Exhibit 6-4 presents the budgeted operating income for the two scenarios.

Note that under Scenario 1, a change in selling prices per table affects revenues (Schedule 1) as well as variable marketing costs (sales commissions, Schedule 8). The Problem for Self-Study at the end of the chapter shows the revised schedules for Scenario 1. Similarly, a change in the price of direct materials affects the direct material usage budget (Schedule 3A), the unit cost of ending finished goods inventory (Schedule 6A), the ending finished goods inventories budget (in Schedule 6B) and the cost of goods sold budget (Schedule 7). Sensitivity analysis is especially useful in incorporating such interrelationships into budgeting decisions by managers.

Exhibit 6-4 shows that operating income decreases substantially if selling prices decrease but declines much less if direct materials prices increase by 5%. The sensitivity analysis prompts Stylistic's managers to put in place contingency plans. For example, should selling prices decline in 2014, Stylistic may choose to postpone some product development programs that it had included in its 2014 budget but that could be deferred to a later year. More generally, when the success or viability of a venture is highly dependent on attaining one or more targets, managers should frequently update their budgets as uncertainty is resolved. These updated budgets can help managers to adjust expenditure levels as circumstances change.

Earlier in this chapter we described a rolling budget as a budget that is always available for a specified future period. Rolling budgets are constantly updated to reflect the latest cost and revenue information and make managers responsive to changing conditions and market needs.

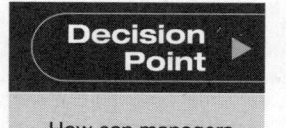

Decision Point ▶

How can managers plan for changes in the assumptions underlying the budget and manage risk?

Budgeting and Responsibility Accounting

To attain the goals described in the master budget, top managers must coordinate the efforts of all of the firm's employees—from senior executives through middle levels of management to every supervised worker. To coordinate the company's efforts, top managers assign a certain amount of responsibility to lower-level managers and then hold them accountable for how they perform. Consequently, how each company structures its organization significantly shapes how it coordinates its actions.

Organization Structure and Responsibility

Organization structure is an arrangement of lines of responsibility within the organization. A company such as Bharat Petroleum is organized primarily by business function—exploration, refining, and marketing—with the president of each business function having decision-making authority over his or her function. Another company, such as Procter & Gamble, the household-products giant, is organized by product line or brand. The managers of the individual divisions (toothpaste, soap, and so on) would each have decision-making authority concerning all the business functions (manufacturing, marketing, and so on) within that division.

Each manager, regardless of level, is in charge of a responsibility center. A **responsibility center** is a part, segment, or subunit of an organization whose manager is accountable for a specified set of activities. Higher-level managers supervise centers with broader responsibility and larger numbers of subordinates. **Responsibility accounting** is a system that measures the plans, budgets, actions, and actual results of each responsibility center. There are four types of responsibility centers:

1. **Cost center**—the manager is accountable for costs only.
2. **Revenue center**—the manager is accountable for revenues only.
3. **Profit center**—the manager is accountable for revenues and costs.
4. **Investment center**—the manager is accountable for investments, revenues, and costs.

The Maintenance Department of a Oberoi hotel is a cost center because the maintenance manager is responsible only for costs, and the budget is based on costs. The Sales Department is a revenue center because the sales manager is responsible primarily for revenues, and the department's budget is primarily based on revenues. The hotel manager is in charge of a profit center because the manager is accountable for both revenues and costs, and the hotel's budget is based on revenues and costs. The regional manager responsible for determining the amount to be invested in new hotel projects and for revenues and costs generated from these investments is in charge of an investment center. So this center's budget is based on revenues, costs, and the investment base.

A responsibility center can be structured to promote better alignment of individual and company goals. For example, until recently, Godrej, an office products distributor, operated its Sales Department as a revenue center. Each salesperson received a commission of 3% of the revenues per order, regardless of its size, the cost of processing it, or the cost of delivering the office products. Upon analyzing customer profitability, Godrej found that many customers were unprofitable. The main reason was the high ordering and delivery costs of small orders. Godrej's managers decided to make the Sales Department a profit center, accountable for revenues and costs, and to change the incentive system for salespeople to 15% of the monthly profits per customer. The costs for each customer included the ordering and delivery costs. The effect of this change was immediate. The Sales Department began charging customers for ordering and delivery, and salespeople at Godrej actively encouraged customers to consolidate their purchases into fewer orders. As a result, each order began producing larger revenues. Customer profitability increased because of a 40% reduction in ordering and delivery costs in one year.

Learning Objective 5

Describe responsibility centers

. . . a part of an organization that a manager is accountable for

and responsibility accounting

. . . measurement of plans and actual results that a manager is accountable for

Feedback

Budgets coupled with responsibility accounting provide feedback to top management about the performance relative to the budget of different responsibility center managers.

Differences between actual results and budgeted amounts—called *variances* can help managers implement and evaluate strategies in three ways:

1. ***Early warning.*** Variances alert managers early to events not easily nor immediately evident. Managers can then take corrective actions or exploit the available opportunities. For example, after observing a small decline in sales during a period, managers may want to investigate if this is an indication of an even steeper decline to follow later in the year.

2. ***Performance evaluation.*** Variances prompt managers to probe how well the company has performed in implementing its strategies. Were materials and labor used efficiently? Was R&D spending increased as planned? Did product warranty costs decrease as planned?

3. ***Evaluating strategy.*** Variances sometimes signal to managers that their strategies are ineffective. For example, a company seeking to compete by reducing costs and improving quality may find that it is achieving these goals but that it is having little effect on sales and profits. Top management may then want to re-evaluate the strategy.

Responsibility and Controllability

Controllability is the degree of influence that a specific manager has over costs, revenues, or related items for which he or she is responsible. A **controllable cost** is any cost that is primarily subject to the influence of a given *responsibility center manager* for a given *period*. A responsibility accounting system could either exclude all uncontrollable costs from a manager's performance report or segregate such costs from the controllable costs. For example, a machining supervisor's performance report might be confined to direct materials, direct manufacturing labor, power, and machine maintenance costs and might exclude costs such as rent and taxes paid on the plant.

In practice, controllability is difficult to pinpoint for at least two reasons:

1. Few costs are clearly under the sole influence of one manager. For example, prices of direct materials may be influenced by a purchasing manager, but these prices also depend on market conditions beyond the manager's control. Similarly, the decisions production managers make can affect the quantities of direct materials used but also depend on the quality of materials purchased. Moreover, managers often work in teams. Think about how difficult it is to evaluate individual responsibility in a team situation.

2. With a long enough time span, all costs will come under somebody's control. However, most performance reports focus on periods of a year or less. A current manager may benefit from a predecessor's accomplishments or may inherit a predecessor's problems and inefficiencies. For example, present managers may have to work under undesirable contracts with suppliers or labor unions that were negotiated by their predecessors. How can we separate what the current manager actually controls from the results of decisions made by others? Exactly what is the current manager accountable for? The answers may not be clear-cut.

Executives differ in how they embrace the controllability notion when evaluating people reporting to them. Some CEOs regard the budget as a firm commitment subordinates must meet and that "numbers always tell the story." Failing to meet the budget is viewed unfavorably. An executive once noted, "You can miss your plan once, but you wouldn't want to miss it twice." Such an approach forces managers to learn to perform under adverse circumstances and to deliver consistent results year after year. It removes the need to discuss which costs are controllable and which are noncontrollable because it does not matter whether the performance was due to controllable or uncontrollable factors. The disadvantage of this approach is that it subjects a manager's compensation to greater risk. It also de-motivates managers when uncontrollable factors adversely affect their performance evaluations even though they have performed well in terms of factors they can control.

Other CEOs believe that focusing on making the numbers in a budget puts excessive pressure on managers. These CEOs adjust for noncontrollable factors and evaluate managers only on what they can control, such as their performance relative to competitors. Using relative performance measures takes out the effects of favorable or unfavorable business conditions that are outside the manager's control and affect all competing managers in the same way. The challenge is in finding the correct benchmarks. Relative performance measures, however, reduce the pressure on managers to perform when circumstances are difficult.

Managers should avoid thinking about controllability only in the context of performance evaluation. Responsibility accounting is more far-reaching. It focuses on gaining *information and knowledge,* not only on control. *Responsibility accounting helps managers to first focus on whom they should ask to obtain information and not on whom they should blame.* Comparing the shortfall of actual revenues to budgeted revenues is certainly relevant when evaluating the performance of the sales managers of Oberoi hotels. But the more fundamental purpose of responsibility accounting is to gather information from the sales managers to enable future improvement. Holding them accountable for sales motivates them to learn about market conditions and dynamics outside of their personal control but relevant when deciding the actions the hotels might take to increase their future sales. Similarly, purchasing managers may be held accountable for total purchase costs, not because of their ability to control market prices, but because of their ability to predict and respond to uncontrollable prices and understand their causes.

Performance reports for responsibility centers are sometimes designed to change managers' behavior in the direction top managers desire even if the reports decrease controllability. Consider a manufacturing department. If the department is designated as a cost center, the manufacturing manager may emphasize efficiency and deemphasize the pleas of sales personnel for faster service and rush orders that reduce efficiency and increase costs. Evaluating the department as a profit center decreases the manufacturing manager's controllability (because the manufacturing manager has limited influence on sales) but it motivates the manager to look more favorably at rush orders that benefit sales. She will weigh the impact of decisions on costs and revenues rather than on costs alone.

Call centers provide another example. If designated as a cost center, the call-center manager will focus on controlling operating costs, for example, by decreasing the time customer representatives spend on each call. If designed as a profit center, the call-center manager will encourage customer-service representatives to balance efficiency with better customer service and efforts to upsell and cross-sell other products. Hewlett-Packard, Microsoft, Oracle, and others offer software platforms designed to prompt and help call center personnel turn their cost centers into profit centers. The new adage is, "Every service call is a sales call."

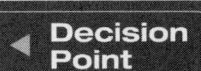

Decision Point

How do companies use responsibility centers? Should performance reports of responsibility center managers include only costs the manager can control?

Human Aspects of Budgeting

Why did we discuss the two major topics, the master budget and responsibility accounting, in the same chapter? Primarily to emphasize that human factors are crucial in budgeting. Too

Learning Objective 6

Recognize the human aspects of budgeting

. . . to engage subordinate managers in the budgeting process

often, budgeting is thought of as a mechanical tool. The budgeting techniques themselves are free of emotion. However, the administration of budgeting requires education, persuasion, and intelligent interpretation.

Budgetary Slack

As we discussed earlier in this chapter, budgeting is most effective when lower-level managers actively participate and meaningfully engage in the budgeting process. Participation adds credibility to the budgeting process and makes employees more committed and accountable for meeting the budget. But participation requires "honest" communication about the business from subordinates and lower-level managers to their bosses.

At times, subordinates may try to "play games" and build in *budgetary slack*. **Budgetary slack** is the practice of underestimating budgeted revenues, or overestimating budgeted costs, to make budgeted targets more easily achievable. This practice frequently occurs when budget variances (the differences between actual results and budgeted amounts) are used to evaluate the performance of line managers and their subordinates. Line managers are also unlikely to be fully honest in their budget communications if top management mechanically institutes across-the-board cost reductions (say, a 10% reduction in all areas) in the face of projected revenue reductions.

Budgetary slack provides managers with a hedge against unexpected adverse circumstances. But budgetary slack also misleads top management about the true profit potential of the company, which leads to inefficient resource planning and allocation and poor coordination of activities across different parts of the company.

To avoid problems of budgetary slack, some companies use budgets primarily for planning and to a lesser extent for performance evaluation. They evaluate the performance of managers using multiple indicators that take into account various factors that become known during the course of the year, such as the prevailing business environment and performance of their industry or their competitors. Evaluating performance in this way takes time and requires careful exercise of judgment.

One approach to dealing with budgetary slack is to obtain good benchmark data when setting the budget. Consider the plant manager of a beverage bottler. Suppose top managers could purchase a consulting firm's study of productivity levels—such as the number of bottles filled per hour—at a number of comparable plants owned by other bottling companies. The managers could then share this independent information with the plant manager and use it to set the operations budget. Using external benchmark performance measures reduces a manager's ability to set budget levels that are easy to achieve.

Rolling budgets are another approach to reducing budgetary slack. As we discussed earlier in the chapter, companies that use rolling budgets always have a budget for a defined period, say 12 months, by adding, at the end of each quarter, a budget for one more quarter to replace the quarter just ended. The continuous updating of budget information and the richer information it provides reduce the opportunity to create budgetary slack relative to when budgeting is done only annually.

Some companies, such as IBM, have designed innovative performance evaluation measures that reward managers based on the subsequent accuracy of the forecasts used in preparing budgets. For example, the *higher and more accurate* the budgeted profit forecasts of division managers, the higher their incentive bonuses.[5] Another approach to

---

[5] For an excellant discussion of these issuesm, see Chapter 14 (" Formal Models in Budgeting and Incentive Contracts") of R. S. Kaplan and A. A. Atkinson, *Advanced Management Accounting*, 3rd ed. (Upper Saddle River, NJ: Prentice Hall, 1998).

reducing budgetary slack is for managers to involve themselves regularly in understanding what their subordinates are doing. Such involvement should not result in managers dictating the decisions and actions of subordinates. Rather, a manager's involvement should take the form of providing support, challenging in a motivational way the assumptions subordinates make, and enhancing mutual learning about the operations. Regular interaction with their subordinates allows managers to become knowledgeable about the operations and diminishes the ability of subordinates to create slack in their budgets. Instead, the subordinates and their superiors have in-depth dialogues about the budgets and performance goals. Managers then evaluate the performance of subordinates using both subjective (and objective) measures. Of course, using subjective measures requires subordinates to trust their managers to evaluate them fairly.

In addition to developing their organization's strategies, top managers are responsible for defining a company's core values and norms and building employee commitment toward adhering to them. These values and norms describe what constitutes acceptable and unacceptable behavior. For example, Johnson & Johnson (J & J) has a credo that describes its responsibilities to doctors, patients, employees, communities, and shareholders. Employees are trained in the credo to help them understand the behavior that is expected of them. J & J managers are often promoted from within and are therefore very familiar with the work of the employees reporting to them. J & J also has a strong culture of mentoring subordinates. J & J's values and employee practices create an environment where managers know their subordinates well, which helps to reduce budgetary slack.

Stretch Targets

Many of the best performing companies, such as General Electric, Microsoft, and Novartis, set "stretch" targets. Stretch targets are challenging but achievable levels of expected performance, intended to create a little discomfort. Creating some performance anxiety motivates employees to exert extra effort and attain better performance, but setting targets that are very difficult or impossible to achieve hurts performance because employees give up on trying to achieve them. Organizations such as Goldman Sachs also use "horizontal" stretch goal initiatives. The aim is to enhance professional development of employees by asking them to take on significantly different responsibilities or roles outside their comfort zone.

A major rationale for stretch targets is their psychological motivation. Consider the following two compensation arrangements offered to a salesperson:

- In the first arrangement, the salesperson is paid ₹8,00,000 for achieving a sales target of ₹1,00,00,000 and 8 paise for every dollar of sales above ₹1,00,00,000 up to ₹1,10,00,000.
- In the second arrangement, the salesperson is paid ₹8,80,000 for achieving a sales target of ₹1,10,00,000 (a stretch target) with a reduction in compensation of 8 paise for every dollar of sales less than ₹1,10,00,000 up to ₹1,00,00,000.

For simplicity we assume that sales will be between ₹1,00,00,000 and ₹1,10,00,000.

The salesperson receives the same level of compensation under the two arrangements for all levels of sales between ₹1,00,00,000 and ₹1,10,00,000. The question is whether the psychological motivation is the same in the two compensation arrangements. Many executives who favor stretch targets point to the asymmetric way in which salespeople psychologically perceive the two compensation arrangements. In the first arrangement, achieving the sales target of ₹1,00,00,000 is seen as good, and everything above it as a bonus. In the second arrangement, not reaching the stretch sales target of ₹1,10,00,000 is seen as a failure. If salespeople are loss averse, that is, they feel the pain of loss more than the joy of success, they will work harder under the second arrangement to achieve sales of ₹1,10,00,000 and not fail.

Ethics

At no point should the pressure for performance embedded in stretch targets push employees to engage in illegal or unethical practices. The more a company tries to push performance, the greater the emphasis it must place on training employees to follow its code of conduct to prohibit behavior that is out of bounds (for example, no bribery, side payments, or dishonest dealings) and its norms and values (for example, putting customers first and not compromising on quality).

Ethical questions are sometimes subtle and not clear-cut. Consider, for example, a division manager, faced with the choice of doing maintenance on a machine at the end of 2013 or early in 2014. It is preferable to do the maintenance in 2013 because delaying maintenance increases the probability of the machine breaking down. But doing so would mean that the manager will not reach his 2013 stretch target for operating income and lose some of his bonus. If the risks of a breakdown and loss are substantial, many observers would view delaying maintenance as unethical. If the risk is minimal, there may be more debate as to whether delaying maintenance is unethical.

Many managers regard budgets negatively. To them, the word *budget* is about as popular as, say, *downsizing, layoff,* or *strike.* Top managers must convince their subordinates that the budget is a tool designed to help them set and reach goals. As with all tools of management, it has its benefits and challenges. Budgets must be used thoughtfully and wisely, but whatever the manager's perspective on budgets—pro or con—they are not remedies for weak management talent, faulty organization, or a poor accounting system.

Kaizen Budgeting

Chapter 1 noted the importance of continuous improvement, or *kaizen* in Japanese. **Kaizen budgeting** explicitly incorporates continuous improvement anticipated during the budget period into the budget numbers. Many companies that have cost reduction as a strategic focus, including General Electric in the United States and Toyota in Japan, use kaizen budgeting to continuously reduce costs. Much of the cost reduction associated with kaizen budgeting arises from many small improvements rather than "quantum leaps."

The improvements tend to come from employee suggestions as a result of managers creating a culture that values, recognizes, and rewards these suggestions. Employees who actually do the job, whether in manufacturing, sales, or distribution, have the best information and knowledge of how the job can be done better.

As an example, throughout our nine budgeting steps for Stylistic Furniture, we assumed four hours of direct labor time to manufacture each Casual coffee table. A Kaizen budgeting approach would incorporate continuous improvement by prescribing 4.00 direct manufacturing labor-hours per table for the first quarter of 2014, 3.95 hours for the second quarter, 3.90 hours for the third quarter, and so on. The implications of these reductions would be lower direct manufacturing labor costs, as well as lower variable manufacturing overhead costs, because direct manufacturing labor is the driver of these costs. If Stylistic Furniture doesn't meet continuous improvement goals, its managers will explore the reasons behind the failure to meet the goals and either adjust the targets or seek input from employees to implement process improvements. Of course, top managers should encourage managers and employees at all levels to try to find a way to achieve bigger (if periodic) cost reductions as well by changing operating processes and supply-chain relationships.

Managers can also apply Kaizen budgeting to activities such as setups with the goal of reducing setup time and setup costs or distribution with the goal of reducing the cost per cubic foot of shipping tables. Kaizen budgeting for specific activities is a key building block of the master budget for companies that use the Kaizen approach.

A growing number of cash-strapped states and agencies in the United States are using Kaizen techniques to bring together government workers, regulators, and end users of government processes to identify ways to reduce inefficiencies and eliminate bureaucratic procedures. Several state environmental agencies, for example, have conducted a Kaizen session or are planning one.[6] The U.S. Postal Service has identified many different programs to reduce its costs. The success of these efforts will depend heavily on human factors such as the commitment and engagement of managers and other employees to make these changes.

> **◄ Decision Point**
>
> Why are human factors crucial in budgeting?

Budgeting in Multinational Companies

Multinational companies, such as Federal Express, Kraft, and Pfizer, have operations in many countries. An international presence has benefits—access to new markets and resources—and drawbacks—operating in less-familiar business environments and exposure to currency fluctuations. Multinational companies earn revenues and incur expenses in many different currencies, and they must translate their operating performance into a single currency (say, U.S. dollars) for reporting results to their shareholders each quarter. This translation is based on the average exchange rates that prevail during the quarter. As a result, managers of multinational companies budget in different currencies and also budget for foreign exchange rates. This requires managers and management accountants to anticipate potential changes in exchange rates that might occur during the year. To reduce the possible negative impact a company could experience as a result of unfavorable exchange rate movements, finance managers frequently use sophisticated techniques such as forward, future, and option contracts to minimize exposure to foreign currency fluctuations (see Chapter 11). Besides currency issues, managers at multinational companies need to understand the political, legal, and, in particular, economic environments of the different countries in which they operate when preparing budgets. For example, in countries such as Turkey, Zimbabwe, and Guinea, annual inflation rates are very high, resulting in sharp declines in the value of the local currency. Managers also need to consider differences in tax regimes, especially when the company transfers goods or services across the many countries in which it operates (see Chapter 22).

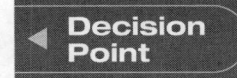

> **Learning Objective 7**
>
> Appreciate the special challenges of budgeting in multinational companies
>
> . . . exposure to currency fluctuations and to different legal, political, and economic environments

When there is considerable business and exchange rate uncertainty related to global operations, a natural question to ask is: "Do the managers of multinational companies find budgeting to be a helpful tool?" The answer is yes. However, in these circumstances the budgeting is not done so much to evaluate the firm's performance relative to its budgets—which can be meaningless when conditions are so volatile—as it is to help managers adapt their plans and coordinate the actions a company needs to take. Senior managers evaluate performance more subjectively, based on how well subordinate managers have managed in these constantly changing and volatile environments.

> **◄ Decision Point**
>
> What are the special challenges involved in budgeting at multinational companies?

---

[6] For details, see "state governments, including Ohio's, embrace Kaizen to seek efficiency via Japanese methods," www.cleveland.com (December 12, 2008).

Problem for Self-Study

Consider the Stylistic Furniture example described earlier. Suppose that to maintain its sales quantities, Stylistic needs to decrease selling prices to ₹5,820 per Casual table and ₹7,760 per Deluxe table, a 3% decrease in the selling prices used in the chapter illustration. All other data are unchanged.

Prepare a budgeted income statement, including all necessary detailed supporting budget schedules that are different from the schedules presented in the chapter. Indicate those schedules that will remain unchanged.

Solution

Schedules 1 and 8 will change. Schedule 1 changes because a change in selling price affects revenues. Schedule 8 changes because revenues are a cost driver of marketing costs (sales commissions). The remaining schedules will not change because a change in selling price has no effect on manufacturing costs. The revised schedules and the new budgeted income statement follow.

Schedule 1: Revenue Budget
For the Year Ending December 31, 2014

	Selling Price	Units	Total Revenues
Casual tables	₹5,820	50,000	₹29,10,00,000
Deluxe tables	7,760	10,000	7,76,00,000
Total			₹36,86,00,000

Schedule 8: Nonmanufacturing Costs Budget
For the Year Ending December 31, 2014

Business Function	Variable Costs	Fixed Costs (as in Schedule 8)	Total Costs
Product Design		₹1,02,40,000	₹1,02,40,000
Marketing			
(Variable cost: ₹36,86,00,000 × 0.065)	₹2,39,59,000	1,33,00,000	3,72,59,000
Distribution			
(Variable cost: ₹20 × 11,40,000 cu. ft.)	2,28,00,000	1,59,60,000	3,87,60,000
	₹4,67,59,000	₹3,95,00,000	₹8,62,59,000

Stylistic Furniture
Budgeted Income Statement
For the Year Ending December 31, 2014

Revenues	Schedule 1		₹36,86,00,000
Cost of goods sold	Schedule 7		24,44,00,000
Gross margin			12,42,00,000
Operating costs			
Product design	Schedule 8	₹1,02,40,000	
Marketing costs	Schedule 8	3,72,59,000	
Distribution costs	Schedule 8	3,87,60,000	8,62,59,000
Operating income			₹3,79,41,000

Decision Points

The following question-and-answer format summarizes the chapter's learning objectives. Each decision presents a key question related to a learning objective. The guidelines are the answer to that question.

Decision	Guidelines
1. What is the master budget, and why is it useful?	The master budget summarizes the financial projections of all the company's budgets. It expresses management's operating and financing plans—the formalized outline of the company's financial objectives and how they will be attained. Budgets are tools that, by themselves, are neither good nor bad. Budgets are useful when administered skillfully.
2. When should a company prepare budgets? What are the advantages of preparing budgets?	Budgets should be prepared when their expected benefits exceed their expected costs. There are four key advantages of budgets: (a) they compel strategic analysis and planning, (b) they promote coordination and communication among subunits of the company, (c) they provide a framework for judging performance and facilitating learning, and (d) they motivate managers and other employees.
3. What is the operating budget and what are its components?	The operating budget is the budgeted income statement and its supporting budget schedules. The starting point for the operating budget is generally the revenues budget. The following supporting schedules are derived from the revenues budget and the activities needed to support the revenues budget: production budget, direct material usage budget, direct material purchases budget, direct manufacturing labor cost budget, manufacturing overhead costs budget, ending inventories budget, cost of goods sold budget, R&D/product design cost budget, marketing cost budget, distribution cost budget, and customer-service cost budget.
4. How can managers plan for changes in the assumptions underlying the budget and manage risk?	Managers can use financial planning models—mathematical statements of the relationships among operating activities, financing activities, and other factors that affect the budget. These models make it possible for managers to conduct a what-if (sensitivity) analysis of the risks that changes in the original predicted data or changes in underlying assumptions would have on the master budget and to develop plans to respond to changed conditions.
5. How do companies use responsibility centers? Should performance reports of responsibility center managers include only costs the manager can control?	A responsibility center is a part, segment, or subunit of an organization whose manager is accountable for a specified set of activities. Four types of responsibility centers are cost centers, revenue centers, profit centers, and investment centers. Responsibility accounting systems are useful because they measure the plans, budgets, actions, and actual results of each responsibility center. Controllable costs are costs primarily subject to the influence of a given responsibility center manager for a given time period. Performance reports of responsibility center managers often include costs, revenues, and investments that the managers cannot control. Responsibility accounting associates financial items with managers on the basis of which manager has the most knowledge and information about the specific items, regardless of the manager's ability to exercise full control.
6. Why are human factors crucial in budgeting?	The administration of budgets requires education, participation, persuasion, and intelligent interpretation. When wisely administered, budgets create commitment, accountability, and honest communication among employees and can be used as the basis for continuous improvement efforts. When badly managed, budgeting can lead to game-playing and budgetary slack—the practice of making budget targets more easily achievable.
7. What are the special challenges involved in budgeting at multinational companies?	Budgeting is a valuable tool for multinational companies but is challenging because of the uncertainties posed by operating in multiple countries. In addition to budgeting in different currencies, managers in multinational companies also need to budget for foreign exchange rates and consider the political, legal, and economic environments of the different countries in which they operate. In times of high uncertainty, managers use budgets more to help the organization learn and adapt to its circumstances than to evaluate performance.

TERMS TO LEARN

This chapter and the Glossary at the end of the book contain definitions of the following important terms:

activity-based budgeting
  (ABB) **(p. 276)**
budgetary slack **(p. 292)**
cash budget **(p. 276)**
continuous
  budget **(p. 275)**
controllability **(p. 290)**
controllable cost **(p. 290)**
cost center **(p. 289)**
financial budget **(p. 276)**

financial planning
  models **(p. 287)**
investment
  center **(p. 289)**
Kaizen
  budgeting **(p. 294)**
master budget **(p. 272)**
operating budget **(p. 276)**
organization
  structure **(p. 289)**

pro forma
  statements **(p. 272)**
profit center **(p. 289)**
responsibility
  accounting **(p. 289)**
responsibility
  center **(p. 289)**
revenue center **(p. 289)**
rolling budget **(p. 275)**
rolling forecast **(p. 275)**

ASSIGNMENT MATERIAL

Questions

6-1 What are the four elements of the budgeting cycle?

6-2 Define master budget.

6-3 "Strategy, plans, and budgets are unrelated to one another." Do you agree? Explain.

6-4 "Budgeted performance is a better criterion than past performance for judging managers." Do you agree? Explain.

6-5 "Production managers and marketing managers are like oil and water. They just don't mix." How can a budget assist in reducing battles between these two areas?

6-6 "Budgets meet the cost-benefit test. They force managers to act differently." Do you agree? Explain.

6-7 Define rolling budget. Give an example.

6-8 Outline the steps in preparing an operating budget.

6-9 "The sales forecast is the cornerstone for budgeting." Why?

6-10 How can sensitivity analysis be used to increase the benefits of budgeting?

6-11 Define kaizen budgeting.

6-12 Describe how nonoutput-based cost drivers can be incorporated into budgeting.

6-13 Explain how the choice of the type of responsibility center (cost, revenue, profit, or investment) affects behavior.

6-14 What are some additional considerations that arise when budgeting in multinational companies?

6-15 "Cash budgets must be prepared before the operating income budget." Do you agree? Explain.

Solved Examples

6-16 Sales and production budget. The Royal Industries expects sales in current year of 1,00,000 units of serving trays. Royal's beginning inventory for current year is 7,000 trays, target ending inventory, 11,000 trays. Compute the number of trays budgeted for production in current year.

Solution

Production Budget

Budgeted sales in units	1,00,000
Add target ending finished goods inventory	11,000
Total requirements	1,11,000
Deduct beginning finished goods inventory	7,000
Units to be produced	1,04,000

6-17 Sales budget, service setting. In 2014, Gupta & Sons, a small environmental-testing firm, performed 12,200 radon tests for ₹290 each and 16,400 lead tests for ₹240 each. Because newer homes are being built with lead-free pipes, lead-testing volume is expected to decrease by 10% next year. However, awareness of radon-related health hazards is expected to result in a 6% increase in radon-test volume each year in the near future. Ajit Gupta feels that if he lowers his price for lead testing to ₹230 per test, he will have to face only a 7% decline in lead-test sales in 2015.

1. Prepare a 2015 sales budget for Gupta & Sons assuming that Gupta holds prices at 2014 levels.   **Required**

2. Prepare a 2015 sales budget for Gupta & Sons assuming that Gupta lowers the price of a lead test to ₹230. Should Gupta lower the price of a lead test in 2015 if the company's goal is to maximize sales revenue?

Solution

1.

Gupta & Sons	2014 Volume	At 2014 Selling Prices (₹)	Expected 2015 Change in Volume	Expected 2015 Volume
Radon Tests	12,200	290	+6%	12,932
Lead Tests	16,400	240	−10%	14,760

Gupta & Sons Sales Budget
For the Year Ended December 31, 2015

	Selling Price (₹)	Units Sold	Total Revenues
Radon Tests	290	12,932	₹37,50,280
Lead Tests	240	14,760	35,42,400
			₹72,92,680

2.

Gupta & Sons	2014 Volume	Planned 2015 Selling Prices (₹)	Expected 2015 Change in Volume	Expected 2015 Volume
Radon Tests	12,200	290	+6%	12,932
Lead Tests	16,400	230	−7%	15,252

Gupta & Sons Sales Budget
For the Year Ended December 31, 2015

	Selling Price (₹)	Units Sold	Total Revenues
Radon Tests	290	12,932	₹37,50,280
Lead Tests	230	15,252	35,07,960
			₹72,58,240

Expected revenues at the new 2015 prices are ₹72,58,240, which is lower than the expected 2015 revenues of ₹72,92,680 if the prices are unchanged. So, if the goal is to maximize sales revenue and if Jim Gupta's forecasts are reliable, the company should not lower its price for a lead test in 2015.

6-18 Budgeting: direct material usage, manufacturing cost, and gross margin. Woolworth Manufacturing Company manufactures blue rugs, using wool and dye as direct materials. One rug is budgeted to use 36 skeins of wool at a cost of ₹20 per skein and 0.8 gallons of dye at a cost of ₹60 per gallon. All other materials are indirect. At the beginning of the year Woolworth has an inventory of 4,58,000 skeins of wool at a cost of ₹96,18,000 and 4,000 gallons of dye at a cost of ₹2,36,800. Target ending inventory of wool and dye is zero. Woolworth uses the FIFO inventory cost flow method.

Woolworth blue rugs are very popular and demand is high, but because of capacity constraints the firm will produce only 2,00,000 blue rugs per year. The budgeted selling price is ₹20,000 each. There are no rugs in beginning inventory. Target ending inventory of rugs is also zero.

Woolworth makes rugs by hand, but uses a machine to dye the wool. Thus, overhead costs are accumulated in two cost pools—one for weaving and the other for dyeing. Weaving overhead is allocated to products based on direct manufacturing labor-hours (DMLH). Dyeing overhead is allocated to products based on machine-hours (MH).

There is no direct manufacturing labor cost for dyeing. Woolworth budgets 62 direct manufacturing labor-hours to weave a rug at a budgeted rate of ₹130 per hour. It budgets 0.2 machine-hours to dye each skein in the dyeing process.

The following table presents the budgeted overhead costs for the dyeing and weaving cost pools:

	Dyeing (based on 14,40,000 MH)	Weaving (based on 1,24,00,000 DMLH)
Variable costs		
Indirect materials	₹0	₹15,40,00,000
Maintenance	6,56,00,000	5,54,00,000
Utilities	7,55,00,000	2,89,00,000
Fixed costs		
Indirect labor	34,70,000	1,70,00,000
Depreciation	2,10,00,000	27,40,000
other	72,30,000	5,81,60,000
Total budgeted	₹17,28,00,000	₹31,62,00,000

Required

1. Prepare a direct material usage budget in both units and dollars.
2. Calculate the budgeted overhead allocation rates for weaving and dyeing.
3. Calculate the budgeted unit cost of a blue rug for the year.
4. Prepare a revenues budget for blue rugs for the year, assuming Woolworth sells (a) 2,00,000 or (b) 1,85,000 blue rugs (that is, at two different sales levels).
5. Calculate the budgeted cost of goods sold for blue rugs under each sales assumption.
6. Find the budgeted gross margin for blue rugs under each sales assumption.
7. What actions might you take as a manager to improve profitability if sales drop to 1,85,000 blue rugs?
8. How might top management at Woolworth use the budget developed in requirements 1–6 to better manage the company?

Solution

1.

Direct Material Usage Budget in Quantity and Rupees

	Material		
	Wool	Dye	Total
Physical Units Budget			
Direct materials required for			

Blue Rugs (2,00,000 rugs × 36 skeins and 0.8 gal.)   72,00,000 skeins   1,60,000 gal.

Cost Budget
Available from beginning direct materials inventory:
(a)

Wool: 4,58,000 skeins	₹96,18,000		
Dye: 4,000 gallons		₹2,36,800	
To be purchased this period: (b)			
Wool: (72,00,000 – 4,58,000) skeins × ₹20 per skein	13,48,40,000		
Dye: (1,60,000 – 4,000) gal. × ₹60 per gal.		93,60,000	
Direct materials to be used this period: (a) + (b)	₹14,44,58,000	₹95,96,800	₹15,40,54,800

2.

$$\text{Weaving budgeted overhead rate} = \frac{₹31,62,00,000}{1,24,00,000\ \text{DMLH}} = ₹25.50\ \text{per DMLH}$$

$$\text{Dyeing budgeted overhead rate} = \frac{₹17,28,00,000}{14,40,000\ \text{MH}} = ₹120\ \text{per MH}$$

3.

Budgeted Unit Cost of Blue Rug

	Cost per Unit of Input	Input per Unit of Output	Total
Wool	₹20	36 skeins	₹720
Dye	60	0.8 gal.	48
Direct manufacturing labor	130	62 hrs.	8,060
Dyeing overhead	120	7.2¹ mach-hrs.	864
Weaving overhead	25.50	62 DMLH	1,581
Total			₹11,273

¹0.2 machine hour per skein × 36 skeins per rug = 7.2 machine-hrs. per rug.

4.

Revenue Budget

	Units	Selling Price (₹)	Total Revenues (₹)
Blue Rugs	2,00,000	20,000	4,00,00,00,000
Blue Rugs	1,85,000	20,000	3,70,00,00,000

5a.

Sales = 2,00,000 rugs
Cost of Goods Sold Budget

	From Schedule	Total
Beginning finished goods inventory		₹0
Direct materials used	₹15,40,54,800	
Direct manufacturing labor (₹8,060 × 2,00,000)	1,61,20,00,000	
Dyeing overhead (₹864 × 2,00,000)	17,28,00,000	
Weaving overhead (₹1,581 × 2,00,000)	31,62,00,000	2,25,50,54,800
Cost of goods available for sale		2,25,50,54,800
Deduct ending finished goods inventory		0
Cost of goods sold		₹2,25,50,54,800

5b.

Sales = 1,85,000 rugs
Cost of Goods Sold Budget

	From Schedule	Total
Beginning finished goods inventory		₹0
Direct materials used	₹15,40,54,800	
Direct manufacturing labor (₹8,060 × 2,00,000)	1,61,20,00,000	
Dyeing overhead (₹864 × 2,00,000)	17,28,00,000	
Weaving overhead (₹1,581 × 2,00,000)	31,62,00,000	2,25,50,54,800
Cost of goods available for sale		2,25,50,54,800
Deduct ending finished goods inventory		
(₹11,273 × 15,000)		16,90,95,000
Cost of goods sold		₹2,08,59,59,800

6.

	2,00,000 rugs sold	1,85,000 rugs sold
Revenue	₹4,00,00,00,000	₹3,70,00,00,000
Less: Cost of goods sold	2,25,50,54,800	2,08,59,59,800
Gross margin	₹1,74,49,45,200	₹1,61,40,40,200

7. If sales drop to 1,85,000 blue rugs, Woolworth should look to reduce fixed costs and produce less to reduce variable costs and inventory costs.

8. Top management can look for ways to increase (stretch) sales and improve quality, efficiency, and input prices to reduce costs in each cost category such as direct materials, direct manufacturing labor, and overhead costs. Top management can also use the budget to coordinate and communicate across different parts of the organization, create a framework for judging performance and facilitating learning, and motivate managers and employees to achieve "stretch" targets of higher revenues and lower costs.

6-19 Revenue and production budgets. (CPA, adapted) The Lakshmi Corporation manufactures and sells two products, Royal Bucket and Royal Drum. In July 2015, Lakshmi's Budget Department gathered the following data to prepare budgets for 2016:

2016-17 Projected Sales

Product	Units	Price
Royal Bucket	60,000	₹165
Royal Drum	40,000	₹250

2016-17 Inventories (in Units)

Product	Expected April 1, 2016	Target March 31, 2017
Royal Bucket	20,000	25,000
Royal Drum	8,000	9,000

The following direct materials are used in the two products:

Amount Used per Unit

Direct Materials	Unit	Royal Bucket	Royal Drum
A	kg	4	5
B	kg	2	3
C	kg	0	1

Projected data for 2016-17 with respect to direct materials are as follows:

Direct Materials	Anticipated Purchase Price	Expected Inventories April 1, 2016	Target Inventories March 31, 2017
A	₹12	32,000 kg	36,000 kg
B	5	29,000 kg	32,000 kg
C	3	6,000 units	7,000 units

Projected direct manufacturing labor requirements and rates for 2016-17 are as follows:

Product	Hours per Unit	Rate per Hour
Royal Bucket	2	₹12
Royal Drum	3	₹16

Manufacturing overhead is allocated at the rate of ₹20 per direct manufacturing labor hour. Based on the preceding projections and budget requirements for Royal Bucket and Royal Drum, prepare the following budgets for 2016-17:

Required

1. Revenues budget (in rupees)
2. Production budget (in units)
3. Direct materials purchases budget (in quantities)
4. Direct materials purchases budget (in rupees)
5. Direct manufacturing labor budget (in rupees)
6. Budgeted finished goods inventory at March 31, 2016-17 (in rupees)

Solution

The key to its solution is to compute the correct *quantities* of finished goods and direct materials. Use the following general formula:

$$\begin{pmatrix} \text{Budgeted} \\ \text{production} \\ \text{or pruchases} \end{pmatrix} = \begin{pmatrix} \text{Target} \\ \text{ending} \\ \text{inventory} \end{pmatrix} + \begin{pmatrix} \text{Budgeted} \\ \text{sales or} \\ \text{materials used} \end{pmatrix} - \begin{pmatrix} \text{Beginning} \\ \text{inventory} \end{pmatrix}$$

1.

Lakshmi Corporation
Revenue Budget for 2016-17

	Units	Price	Total
Royal bucket	60,000	₹165	₹99,00,000
Royal drum	40,000	250	1,00,00,000
Budgeted revenues			₹1,99,00,000

2. Production Budget (in units) for 2016-17

	Royal Bucket	Royal Drum
Budgeted sales in units	60,000	40,000
Add target finished goods inventories, March 31, 2017	25,000	9,000
Total requirements	85,000	49,000
Deduct finished goods inventories, April 1, 2016	20,000	8,000
Units to be produced	65,000	41,000

3. Direct Materials Purchases Budget (in quantities) for 2016-17

	Direct Materials		
	A	B	C
Direct materials to be used in production			
• Royal Bucket (budgeted production of 65,000 units times 4 kg of A, 2 kg of B)	2,60,000	1,30,000	—
• Royal Drum (budgeted production of 41,000 units times 5 kg of A, 3 kg of B, 1 kg of C)	2,05,000	1,23,000	41,000
Total	4,65,000	2,53,000	41,000
Add target ending inventories, March 31, 2017	36,000	32,000	7,000
Total requirements in units	5,01,000	2,85,000	48,000
Deduct beginning inventories, April 1, 2016	32,000	29,000	6,000
Direct materials to be purchased (units)	4,69,000	2,56,000	42,000

4. Direct Materials Purchases Budget (in rupees) for 2016-17

	Budgeted Purchases (kgs)	Expected Purchases Price per kg	Total
Direct material A	4,69,000	₹12	₹56,28,000
Direct material B	2,56,000	5	12,80,000
Direct material C	42,000	3	1,26,000
Budgeted purchases			₹70,34,000

5. Direct Manufacturing Labor Budget (in rupees) for 2016-17

	Budgeted Production (Units)	Direct Manu-facturing Labor-Hours per Unit	Total Hours	Rate per Hour	Total
Royal Bucket	65,000	2	1,30,000	₹12	₹15,60,000
Royal Drum	41,000	3	1,23,000	16	19,68,000
Total					₹35,28,000

6. Budgeted Finished Goods Inventory At March 31, 2017

Royal Bucket:

Direct materials costs:

A, 4 kg × ₹12	₹48	₹58
	10	₹58
Direct manufacturing labor costs, 2 hours × ₹12		24
Manufacturing overhead costs at ₹20 per direct manufacturing labor-hour (2 hours × ₹20)		40
Budgeted manufacturing costs per unit		₹122
Finished goods inventory (₹122 × 25,000 units)		
		₹30,50,000

Royal Drum:

Direct materials costs:

A, 5 kg × ₹12	₹60	
B, 3 kg × ₹5	15	
C, 1 kg × ₹3	3	₹78
Direct manufacturing labor costs 3 hours ? ₹16		48
Manufacturing overhead costs at ₹20 per direct manufacturing labor-hour (3 hours × ₹20)		60
Budgeted manufacturing costs per unit		₹186
Finished goods inventory of (₹186 × 9,000 units)		
		16,74,000
Budgeted finished goods inventory, March 31, 2017		₹47,24,000

6-20 Budgeted income statement. (CMA, adapted) Polycom Company is a manufacturer of video-conferencing products. Regular units are manufactured to meet marketing projections, and specialized units are made after an order is received. Maintaining the video-conferencing equipment is an important area of customer satisfaction. With the recent downturn in the computer industry, the video-conferencing equipment segment has suffered, leading to a decline in Polycom's financial performance. The following income statement shows results for 2015.

Polycom Company
Income Statement
For the Year Ended December 31, 2015 (in thousands)

Revenues		
Equipment	₹6,00,000	
Maintenance contracts	1,80,000	
Total revenues		₹7,80,000
Cost of goods sold		4,60,000
Gross margin		3,20,000
Operating costs		
Marketing	60,000	
Distribution	15,000	
Customer maintenance	1,00,000	
Administration	90,000	
Total operating costs		2,65,000
Operating income		55,000

Polycom's management team is in the process of preparing the 2016 budget and is studying the following information:

1. Selling prices of equipment are expected to increase by 10% as the economic recovery begins. The selling price of each maintenance contract is unchanged from 2015.
2. Equipment sales in unit are expected to increase by 6%, with a corresponding 6% growth in units of maintenance contracts.
3. Cost of each units sold is expected to increase by 3% to pay for the necessary technology and quality improvements.
4. Marketing costs are expected to increase by ₹2,50,00,000, but administration costs are expected to remain at 2015 levels.
5. Distribution costs vary in proportion to the number of units of equipment sold.
6. Two maintenance technicians are to be added at a total cost of ₹1,30,00,000, which covers wages and related travel costs. The objective is to improve customer service and shorten response time.
7. There is no beginning or ending inventory of equipment.
   Prepare a budgeted income statement for 2016.

Solution

Polycom Company
Budgeted Income Statement for 2016
(in thousands)

Revenues		
Equipment (₹6,00,000 × 1.06 × 1.10)	₹6,99,600	
Maintenance contracts (₹1,80,000 × 1.06)	1,90,800	
Total revenues		₹8,90,400
Cost of goods sold (₹4,60,000 × 1.03 × 1.06)		5,02,228
Gross margin		3,88,172
Operating costs:		
Marketing costs (₹60,000 + ₹25,000)	85,000	
Distribution costs (₹15,000 × 1.06)	15,900	
Customer maintenance costs (₹1,00,000 + ₹13,000)	1,13,000	
Administrative costs	90,000	
Total operating costs		3,03,900
Operating income		₹84,272

6-21 Budgeting: service company. Sunshine Window Washers (SWW) provides window-washing services to commercial clients. The company has enjoyed considerable growth in recent years due to a successful marketing campaign and favorable reviews on service-rating Web sites. Sunshine owner Shyam makes sales calls himself and quotes on jobs based on square footage of window surface. Sunshine hires college students to drive the company vans to jobs and wash the windows. A part-time bookkeeper takes care of billing customers and other office tasks. Overhead is accumulated in two cost pools, one for travel to jobs, allocated based on miles driven, and one for window washing, allocated based on direct labor-hours (DLH).

Shyam estimates that his window washers will work a total of 2,000 jobs during the year Each job averages 2,000 square feet of window surface and requires 5 direct labor-hours and 12.5 miles of travel. Shyam pays his window washers ₹120 per hour. Taxes and benefits equal 20% of wages. Wages, taxes, and benefits are considered direct labor costs. The following table presents the budgeted overhead costs for the Travel and Window Washing cost pools:

	Travel (based on 25,000 miles driven)	Window Washing (based on 10,000 DLH)
Variable costs		
Supplies (₹44 per DLH)	₹0	₹4,40,000
Fuel (₹6 per mile)	1,50,000	0

Fixed costs (to support capacity of 30,000 miles driven and 12,000 direct labor-hours)		
Indirect labor	0	2,00,000
Depreciation	4,00,000	3,50,000
other	50,000	2,30,000
Total budgeted costs	₹6,00,000	₹12,20,000

Required

1. Prepare a direct labor budget in both hours and rupees. Calculate the direct labor rate.
2. Calculate the budgeted overhead allocation rates for travel and window washing based on the budgeted quantity of the cost drivers.
3. Calculate the budgeted total cost of all jobs for the year and the budgeted cost of an average 2,000-square-foot window-washing job.
4. Prepare a revenues budget for the year, assuming that Sunshine charges customers ₹1 per square foot.
5. Calculate the budgeted operating income.
6. Shyam believes that spending ₹1,50,000 in additional advertising will lead to a 20% increase in the number of jobs. Recalculate the budgeted revenue and operating income assuming this change is made. Calculate expenses by multiplying the existing budgeted cost per job calculated in requirement 3 by the number of jobs and adding the ₹1,50,000 advertising cost. Based on the change in budgeted operating income, would you recommend the investment?
7. Do you see any flaw in this analysis? How could the analysis be improved? Should SWW spend ₹1,50,000 in additional advertising?
8. What is SWW's profitability if sales should decline to 1,800 jobs annually? What actions can Shyam take to improve profitability?

Solution

1.

Direct Labor Budget in Hours and Rupees		**Total**
Hours Budget		
Direct labor hours required		
(2,000 jobs × 5 hours per job)		10,000 hours
Cost Budget		
Wages (10,000 hours × ₹120/hr.)	₹12,00,000	
Taxes and benefits (10,000 hours × ₹120/hr. × 20%)	2,40,000	
		₹14,40,000
Cost per direct-labor hour (₹14,40,000/10,000 DLH)		₹144/DLH

2.

$$\text{Travel budgeted overhead rate} = \frac{₹6,00,000}{25,000 \text{ miles}} = ₹24 \text{ per mile}$$

$$\text{Window washing budgeted overhead rate} = \frac{₹12,20,000}{10,000 \text{ DLH}} = ₹122 \text{ per DLH}$$

3.

Budgeted Cost of Average 2,000 Square-Foot Window Washing Job	
Direct labor	₹14,40,000
Travel ove rhead	6,00,000
Window washing overhead	12,20,000
Total Cost per Job	₹32,60,000
Total Cost of 2,000 jobs	₹32,60,000

Budgeted cost of average 2,000 square foot window washing job = ₹32,60,000 ÷ 2,000 = ₹1,630 per job.

4.

	Revenue Budget		
Square Feet		**Price per Square Foot**	**Total Revenues**
2,000 jobs × 2,000 sq. ft./job = 40,00,000 sq. ft.		₹1	₹40,00,000

5.

	2,000 jobs
Revenue	40,00,000
Expenses	32,60,000
Operating Income	7,40,000

6.

	Revenue Budget		
Square Feet		**Price per Square Foot**	**Total Revenues**
2,400 jobs × 2,000 sq. ft./job = 48,00,000 sq. ft.		₹1	₹48,00,000

	2,400 jobs
Revenue	48,00,000
Expenses (₹1,630 × 2,400 jobs) + ₹1,50,000	40,62,000
Operating Income	₹7,38,000

Decrease in net operating income: ₹7,40,000 – ₹7,38,000 = ₹2,000. According to this analysis, the increase in revenue would not warrant the ₹1,50,000 of additional advertising cost. Therefore, the investment should not be made.

7. Using the budgeted cost per job of ₹1,630 ignores the fact that ₹12,30,000 of the company's overhead costs are fixed. Because those costs will not increase with an increase in activity from 2,000 to 2,400 jobs, the fixed costs should not be considered in the analysis, and Sunshine's management should examine only incremental costs versus incremental revenues.

Revenues		₹48,00,000
Wages (₹144 × 12,000)	₹17,28,000	
Supplies (₹44 × 12,000)	5,28,000	
Fuel (₹6 × 30,000)	1,80,000	
Fixed travel costs	4,50,000	
Fixed window washing costs	7,80,000	
Advertising costs	1,50,000	38,16,000
Operating income		₹9,84,000

Sunshine's operating income increases by ₹2,44,000 (₹9,84,000 – ₹7,40,000) as a result of advertising, and so Sunshine should incur the ₹1,50,000 in additional advertising costs.

8. The following table shows Sunshine's profitability if sales decline to 1,800 jobs.

Revenue (1,800 jobs × 2,000 sq. ft. × ₹1/sq. ft.		₹36,00,000
Wages (₹144 × 9,000)	₹12,96,000	
Supplies (₹44 × 9,000)	3,96,000	
Fuel (₹6 × 22,500)	1,35,000	

Fixed travel costs	4,50,000	
Fixed window washing costs	7,80,000	30,57,000
		₹5,43,000

If revenue should fall to 1,800 jobs, Sunshine's management should examine the company's fixed overhead costs to determine if any cuts are possible. Variable product costs will naturally decline with a decline in jobs, but fixed costs will not decline without management taking action. While depreciation cost is not likely something that management can reduce, the "other" fixed overhead costs are significant and should be examined.

6-22 Cash flow analysis, sensitivity analysis. Game Depot is a retail store selling video games. Sales are uniform for most of the year but pick up in June and December both because new releases come out and because consumers purchase games in anticipation of summer or winter holidays. Game Depot also sells and repairs game systems. The forecast of sales and service revenue for the March–June 2015 is as follows:

Sales and Service Revenues Budget March – June 2015

Month	Expected Sales Revenue	Expected Services Revenue	Total Revenue
March	₹90,000	₹15,000	₹1,05,000
April	1,10,000	20,000	1,30,000
May	1,24,000	28,000	1,52,000
June	1,94,000	52,000	2,46,000

Almost all the service revenue is paid for by bank credit card, so Game Depot budgets this as 100% bank card revenue. The bank cards charge an average fee of 3% of the total. Half of the sales revenue is also paid for by bank credit card, for which the fee is also 3% on average. About 10% of the sales are paid in cash, and the rest (the remaining 40%) are carried on a store account. Although the store tries to give store credit only to the best customers, it still averages about 2% for uncollectible accounts; 90% of store accounts are paid in the month following the purchase, and 8% are paid 2 months after purchase.

Required

1. Calculate the cash that Game Depot expects to collect in May and in June 2015. Show calculations for each month.

2. Game Depot has budgeted expenditures for May of ₹87,000 for the purchase of games and game systems, ₹28,000 for rent and utilities and other costs, and ₹20,000 in wages for the two part-time employees.

   a. Given your answer to requirement 1, will Game Depot be able to cover its payments for May?

   b. The projections for May are a budget. Assume (independently for each situation) that May revenues might also be 5% less and 10% less and that costs might be 8% higher. Under each of those three scenarios, show the total net cash for May and the amount Game Depot would have to borrow if cash receipts are less than cash payments. Assume the beginning cash balance for May is ₹2,000.

3. Why do Game Depot's managers prepare a cash budget in addition to the revenue, expenses, and operating income budget? Has preparing the cash budget been helpful? Explain briefly.

4. Suppose the costs for May are as described in requirement 2, but the expected cash receipts for May are ₹1,24,000 and beginning cash balance is ₹2,000. Game Depot has the opportunity to purchase the games and game systems on account in May, but the supplier offers the company credit terms of 2/10 net 30, which means if Game Depot pays within 10 days (in May) it will get a 2% discount on the price of the merchandise. Game Depot can borrow money at a rate of 24%. Should Game Depot take the purchase discount?

Solution

1. The cash that Game Depot can expect to collect during May and June is calculated below.

Cash collected in	May	June
From service revenue		
May (₹28,000 × 0.97)	₹27,160	
June (₹52,000 × 0.97)		₹50,440
From sales revenue		
Cash sales		
From credit card sales		
May (0.5 × ₹1,24,000 × 0.97)	60,140	
June (0.5 × ₹1,94,000 × 0.97)		94,090
From cash sales		
May (0.1 × ₹1,24,000)	12,400	
June (0.1 × ₹1,94,000)		19,400
Credit sale collections		
From March (0.4 × ₹90,000 × 0.08)	2,880	
From April (0.4 × ₹1,10,000 × 0.9)	39,600	
(0.4 × ₹1,10,000 × 0.08)		3,520
From May (0.4 × ₹1,24,000 × 0.9)		44,640
Total collections	₹1,42,180	₹2,12,090

2. (a) Budgeted expenditures for May are as follows.

	Costs
Inventory purchases	₹87,000
Rent, utilities, etc.	28,000
Wages	20,000
Total	₹1,35,000

Yes, Game Depot will be able to cover its May costs because receipts are ₹1,42,180 and expenditures are only ₹1,35,000.

(b)

	Original numbers	May Revenues decrease 10%	May Revenues decrease 5%	May Costs increase 8%
Beginning cash	₹2,000.00	₹2,000.00	₹2,000.00	₹2,000.00
Collections	1,42,180.00	1,32,210.00[a]	1,37,195[b]	1,42,180.00[c]
Cash Costs	1,35,000.00	1,35,000.00	1,35,000.00	1,45,800.00
Total	₹9,180.00	₹(790)	₹4,195	₹(1,620)

[a]From requirement 1, this is 0.90 × (₹27,160 + ₹60,140 + ₹12,400) + ₹2,880 + ₹39,600
= ₹1,32,210

[b]From requirement 1, this is 0.95 × (₹27,160 + ₹60,140 + ₹12,400) + ₹2,880 + ₹39,600
= ₹1,37,195

[c]₹1,35,000 × 1.08 = ₹1,45,800.

3. Game Depot's managers prepare a cash budget in addition to the operating income budget to plan cash flows to ensure that the company has adequate cash to pay vendors, meet payroll, and pay operating expenses as these payments come due. Game Depot could be very profitable on an accrual accounting basis, but the pattern of cash receipts from revenues might be delayed and result in insufficient cash being available to make scheduled payments for its expenses. Game Depot's managers may then need to initiate a plan to borrow money to finance any shortfall. Building a profitable operating plan does not guarantee that adequate cash will be available, so Game Depot's managers need to prepare a cash budget in addition to an operating income budget.

4. The cost of inventory purchases without the discount is ₹87,000, which Game Depot would not have to pay until June if it buys the inventory on account in May. However, if it takes the discount and pays in May, the cost will be ₹87,000 × (100% − 2%) = ₹85,260. This means it will save ₹1,740.

This makes total expenditures for May

	Costs
Inventory purchases	₹85,260.00
Rent, utilities, etc.	28,000.00
Wages	20,000.00
Total	₹1,33,260.00

Game Depot's total cash available is ₹2,000 (cash balance) + ₹1,24,000 (cash receipts), so it will have to borrow ₹7,260 (₹1,33,260 − ₹1,26,000) at a rate of 24 percent (or 2 percent per month.) Based on the information from #1, it will be able to pay this back in June (assuming cash expenditures do not increase dramatically), so it will incur interest costs of ₹7,260 × 0.02 = ₹145.20. Because it will cost them less than ₹150 to save ₹1,740, it makes sense to go ahead and take the short-term loan to pay the account payable early.

Some students might interpret the question to mean that the cost of inventory purchases after taking the 2 percent discount in May is ₹87,000. Under this interpretation, the cost of the inventory is ₹87,000 ÷ 0.98 = ₹88,780. If Game Depot takes the discount and pays in May, it will save ₹88,780 − ₹87,000 = ₹1,780

Total expenditures in May:

Inventory purchases	₹87,000
Rent, utilities, etc.	28,000
Wages	20,000
Total	₹1,35,000

Total cash available is ₹2,000 + ₹1,24,000 = ₹1,26,000, so Game Depot will borrow ₹9,000 (₹1,35,000 − ₹1,26,000) at a rate of 24 percent (or 2 percent per month). The company can repay in June, so interest cost = ₹9,000 × 0.02 = ₹180. It will cost ₹180 to save ₹1,780, so Game Depot should take the short-term loan to pay the accounts payable early.

6-23 Budgeted costs, Kaizen improvements. Trendy T-Shirt Factory manufactures plain white and solid- colored T-shirts. Inputs include the following:

	Price	Quantity	Cost per unit of output
Fabric	₹70 per meter	1 meter per unit	₹70 per unit
Labor	₹140 per DMLH	0.25 DMLH per unit	₹35 per unit

Additionally, the colored T-shirts require 3 packets (of 30 grams each) of dye per shirt at a cost of ₹4 per packet. The shirts sell for ₹140 each for white and ₹180 each for colors. The company expects to sell 12,000 white T-shirts and 60,000 colored T-shirts uniformly over the year.

Trendy has the opportunity to switch from using the dye it currently uses to using an environmentally friendly dye that costs ₹12.5 per packet (of 30 grams). The company would still need 3 packets of dye per shirt. Trendy is reluctant to change because of the increase in costs (and decrease in profit), but the Environmental Protection Agency has threatened to fine the company ₹12,00,000 if it continues to use the harmful but less expensive dye.

Required

1. Given the preceding information, would Trendy be better off financially by switching to the environmentally friendly dye? (Assume all other costs would remain the same.)
2. Assume Trendy chooses to be environmentally responsible regardless of cost, and it switches to the new dye. The production manager suggests trying Kaizen costing. If Trendy can reduce fabric and labor costs each by 1% per month, how close will it be at the end of 12 months to the profit it would have earned before switching to the more expensive dye? (Round to the nearest rupees for calculating cost reductions.)

3. Refer to requirement 2. How could the reduction in material and labor costs be accomplished? Are there any problems with this plan?

Solution

1.

Increase in Costs for the Year
Assume Trendy uses New Dye

Units to dye	60,000
Cost differential (₹12.50 – ₹4.0) per packet (of 30 grams) × 3 packets	× ₹25.50
Increase in costs	₹15,30,000

Because the fine is only ₹12,00,000, Trendy would be financially better off by not switching.

2. If Trendy switches to the new dye, costs will increase by ₹15,30,000.If Trendy implements Kaizen costing, costs will be reduced as follows:

Original monthly costs

Input	Unit cost	Number of units	Total cost	Annual cost
Fabric	₹70	6,000*	₹4,20,000	₹50,40,000
Labor	₹35	6,000*	2,10,000	25,20,000
Total			₹6,30,000	₹75,60,000

* (12,000 + 60,000)/12 months = 6,000 units

Monthly decrease in costs

Fabric		Labor cost		
Month 1	₹4,20,000	Month 1	₹2,10,000	
Month 2	4,15,800	Month 2	2,07,900	
Month 3	4,11,640	Month 3	2,05,820	
Month 4	4,07,530	Month 4	2,03,760	
Month 5	4,03,450	Month 5	2,01,730	
Month 6	3,99,420	Month 6	1,99,710	
Month 7	3,95,420	Month 7	1,97,710	
Month 8	3,91,470	Month 8	1,95,730	
Month 9	3,87,550	Month 9	1,93,780	
Month 10	3,83,680	Month 10	1,91,840	
Month 11	3,79,840	Month 11	1,89,920	
Month 12	3,76,040	Month 12	1,88,020	
	₹47,71,840		₹23,85,920	₹71,57,760

TOTAL

Difference between costs with and without Kaizen improvements

(₹75,60,000 – ₹71,57,760)   ₹4,02,240

This means costs increase a net amount of ₹15,30,000 – ₹4,02,240 = ₹11,27,760

3. Reduction in materials can be accomplished by reducing waste and scrap. Reduction in direct labor can be accomplished by improving the efficiency of operations and decreasing down time.

Employees who make and dye the T-shirts may have suggestions for ways to do their jobs more efficiently. For instance, employees may recommend process changes that reduce idle time, setup time, and scrap. To motivate workers to improve efficiency, many companies have set up programs that share productivity gains with the workers. Trendy must be careful that productivity improvements and cost reductions do not in any way compromise product quality.

6-24 Responsibility of purchasing agent. Pranay Kumar owns a restaurant franchise that is part of a chain of "southern homestyle" restaurants. One of the chain's popular breakfast items is biscuits and gravy. Central Warehouse makes and freezes the biscuit dough, which it then sells to the franchise stores where it is thawed and baked in the individual stores by the cook. Each franchise also has a purchasing agent who orders the biscuits (and other items) based on expected demand. In March 2015, one of the freezers in Central Warehouse breaks down and biscuit production is reduced by 25% for 3 days. During those 3 days, Pranay's franchise runs out of biscuits but demand does not slow down. Pranay's franchise cook, Baker, sends one of the kitchen helpers to the local grocery store to buy refrigerated ready-to-bake biscuits. Although the customers are kept happy, the refrigerated biscuits cost Pranay's franchise three times the cost of the Central Warehouse frozen biscuits, and the franchise loses money on this item for those 3 days. Pranay is angry with the purchasing agent for not ordering enough biscuits to avoid running out of stock and with Baker for spending too much money on the replacement biscuits.

Required

Who is responsible for the cost of the biscuits? At what level is the cost controllable? Do you agree that Pranay should be angry with the purchasing agent? With Baker ? Why or why not?

Solution

The cost of the biscuits is usually the responsibility of the purchasing agent, and usually controllable by the Central Warehouse. However, in this scenario, Baker the cook has taken the responsibility for the cost of the replacement biscuits from the purchasing agent by making a purchasing decision. Because Pranay holds the purchasing agent responsible for biscuit costs, and presuming that Baker knew this, Baker should have discussed his decision with the purchasing agent before sending the kitchen helper to the store.

Pranay should not be angry because his employees acted to satisfy the customers on a short-term emergency basis. Presuming the Central Warehouse does not consistently have problems with their freezer, there is no way the purchasing agent could foresee the biscuit shortage and plan accordingly. Also, the problem only lasted three days, which, in the course of the year (or even the month) will not seriously harm the profits of a restaurant that sells a variety of foods. However, had they run out of biscuits for three days, this could have long-term implications for customer satisfaction and customer loyalty, and in the long run could harm profits as customers find other restaurants at which to eat breakfast.

6-25 Comprehensive problem with ABC costing Animal Gear Company makes two pet carriers, the Cat-allac and the Dog-eriffic. They are both made of plastic with metal doors, but the Cat-allac is smaller. Information for the two products for the month of April is given in the following tables:

Input prices
Direct materials

Plastic	₹50 per kg
Metal	₹40 per kg
Direct manufacturing labor	₹100 per direct manufacturing labor-hour

Input Quantities per Unit of Output

	Cat - allac	Dog – eriffic
Direct materials		
Plastics	4 kg	6 kg
Metals	0.5 kg	1 kg
Direct manufacturing labor – hours	3 hours	5 hours
Machine – hours (MH)	11 MH	19 MH

Inventory information, Direct Materials

	Plastic	Metals
Beginning inventory	290 kg	70 kg
Target ending inventory	410 kg	65 kg
Cost of beginning inventory	₹11,020	₹2,170

Animal Gear accounts for direct materials using a FIFO cost flow assumption.

Sales and Inventory Information, Finished Goods

	Cat – allac	Dog – eriffic
Expected sales in units	530	225
Selling price	₹2,050	₹3,100
Target ending inventory in units	300	100
Beginning inventory in units	100	250
Beginning inventory in rupees	₹10,000	₹46,500

Animal Gear uses a FIFO cost flow assumption for finished goods inventory.

Animal Gear uses an activity-based costing system and classifies overhead into three activity pools: Setup, Processing, and Inspection. Activity rates for these activities are ₹1,050 per setup-hour, ₹100 per machine-hour, and ₹150 per inspection-hour, respectively. Other information follows:

Cost-Driver Information

	Cat-allac	Dog-eriffic
Number of units per batch	25	9
Setup time per batch	1.50 hours	1.75 hours
Inspection time per batch	0.5 hour	0.7 hour

Nonmanufacturing fixed costs for March equal ₹3,20,000, half of which are salaries. Salaries are expected to increase 5% in April. The only variable nonmanufacturing cost is sales commission, equal to 1% of sales revenue.

Prepare the following for April:

Required

1. Revenues budget
2. Production budget in units
3. Direct material usage budget and direct material purchases budget
4. Direct manufacturing labor cost budget
5. Manufacturing overhead cost budgets for each of the three activities
6. Budgeted unit cost of ending finished goods inventory and ending inventories budget
7. Cost of goods sold budget
8. Nonmanufacturing costs budget
9. Budgeted income statement (ignore income taxes)
10. How does preparing the budget help Animal Gear's management team better manage the company?

Solution

1.

Revenue Budget
For the Month of April

	Units	Selling Price	Total Revenues
Cat-allac	530	₹2,050	₹10,86,500
Dog-eriffic	225	3,100	6,97,500
Total			₹17,84,000

2.

Production Budget
For the Month of April

	Product	
	Cat-allac	Dog-eriffic
Budgeted unit sales	530	225
Add target ending finished goods inventory	30	10
Total required units	560	235
Deduct beginning finished goods inventory	10	25
Units of finished goods to be produced	550	210

3.

Direct Material Usage Budget in Quantity and Rupees
For the Month of April

	Material		
	Plastic	Metal	Total
Physical Units Budget			
Direct materials required for			
Cat-allac (550 units × 4 kgs. and 0.5 kg.)	2,200 kgs.	275 kgs.	
Dog-eriffic (210 units × 6 kgs. and 1 kg.)	1,260 kgs.	210 kgs.	
Total quantity of direct material to be used	3,460 kgs.	485 kgs.	
Cost Budget			
Available from beginning direct materials inventory (under a FIFO cost-flow assumption)			
Plastic: 290 kg. × ₹38 per kg.	₹11,020		
Metal: 70 kgs. × ₹31 per kg.		₹2,170	
To be purchased this period			
Plastic: (3,460 – 290) kgs. × ₹50 per kg.	1,58,500		
Metal: (485 – 70) kgs. × ₹40 per kg.		16,600	
Direct materials to be used this period	₹1,69,520	₹18,770	₹1,88,290

Direct Material Purchases Budget
For the Month of April

	Material		
	Plastic	Metal	Total
Physical Units Budget			
To be used in production (requirement 3)	3,460 kgs.	485 kgs.	
Add target ending inventory	410 kgs.	65 kgs.	
Total requirements	3,870 kgs.	550 kgs.	
Deduct beginning inventory	290 kgs.	70 kgs.	
Purchases to be made	3,580 kgs.	480 kgs.	
Cost Budget			
Plastic: 3,580 kgs. × ₹50	₹1,79,000		
Metal: 480 kgs. × ₹40		₹19,200	
Purchases	₹1,79,000	₹19,200	₹1,98,200

4.

Direct Manufacturing Labor Costs Budget
For the Month of April

	Output Units Produced (requirement 2)	DMLH per Unit	Total Hours	Hourly Wage Rate	Total
Cat-allac	550	3	1,650	₹100	₹1,65,000
Dog-eriffic	210	5	1,050	100	1,05,000
Total					₹2,70,000

5. Machine Setup Overhead

	Cat-allac	Dog-eriffic	Total
Units to be produced	550	210	
Units per batch	÷25	÷9	
Number of batches (rounded up)	22	24	
Setup time per batch	×1.50 hrs.	×1.75 hrs.	
Total setup time	33 hrs.	42 hrs.	75 hrs.

Budgeted machine setup costs = ₹1,050 per setup hour × 75 hours
$$= ₹78,750$$

Processing Overhead

Budgeted machine-hours (MH) = (11 MH per unit × 550 units) + (19 MH per unit × 210 units)
$$= 6,050 \text{ MH} + 3,990 \text{ MH} = 10,040 \text{ MH}$$
Budgeted processing costs = ₹100 per MH × 10,040 MH
$$= ₹10,04,000$$

Inspection Overhead

Budgeted inspection-hours = (0.5 × 22 batches) + (0.7 × 24 batches)
$$= 11 + 16.8 = 27.8 \text{ inspection hrs.}$$
Budgeted inspection costs = ₹150 per inspection hr. × 27.8 inspection hours
$$= ₹4,170$$

Manufacturing Overhead Budget
For the Month of April

Machine setup costs	₹78,750
Processing costs	10,04,000
Inspection costs	4,170
Total costs	₹10,86,920

6.

Unit Costs of Ending Finished Goods Inventory
April 30

		Product			
		Cat-allac		Dog-eriffic	
	Cost per Unit of Input	Input per Unit of Output	Total	Input per Unit of Output	Total
Plastic	₹50	4 kgs	₹200	6 kgs	₹300
Metal	40	0.5 kgs	20	1 kg.	40

Direct manufacturing labor	100	3 hrs.	300	5 hrs.	500
Machine setup	1,050	0.06 hr[1]	63	0.2 hr[1]	210
Processing	100	11 MH	1,100	19 MH	1,900
Inspection	150	0.02 hr[2]	3	0.08 hr[2]	12
Total			₹1,686		₹2,962

[1] 33 setup-hours ÷ 550 units = 0.06 hours per unit; 42 setup-hours ÷ 210 units = 0.2 hours per unit

[2] 11 inspection hours ÷ 550 units = 0.02 hours per unit; 16.8 inspection hours ÷ 210 units = 0.08 hours per unit

Ending Inventories Budget
April 30

	Quantity	Cost per unit	Total	
Direct Materials				
Plastic	410	₹50	₹20,500	
Metals	65	40	2,600	₹23,100
Finished goods				
Cat-allac	30	₹1,686	₹50,580	
Dog-eriffic	10	2,962	29,620	80,200
Total ending inventory				₹1,03,300

7.

Cost of Goods Sold Budget
For the Month of April

Beginning finished goods inventory, April, 1 (₹10,000 + ₹46,500)		₹56,500
Direct materials used (requirement 3)	₹1,88,290	
Direct manufacturing labor (requirement 4)	2,70,000	
Manufacturing overhead (requirement 5)	10,86,920	
Cost of goods manufactured		15,45,210
Cost of goods available for sale		16,01,710
Deduct: Ending finished goods inventory, April 30 (requirement 6)		80,200
Cost of goods sold		₹15,21,510

8.

Nonmanufacturing Costs Budget
For the Month of April

Salaries (₹3,20,000 ÷ 2 × 1.05)	₹1,68,000
Other fixed costs (₹3,20,000 ÷ 2)	1,60,000
Sales commissions (₹17,84,000 × 1%)	17,840
Total nonmanufacturing costs	₹3,45,840

9.

Budgeted Income Statement
For the Month of April

Revenues	₹17,84,000
Cost of goods sold	15,21,510

Gross margin	2,62,490
Operating (nonmanufacturing) costs	3,45,840
Operating income	₹(83,350)

10. Preparing a budget helps Animal Gear manage costs based on revenues and production needs, look for opportunities to increase efficiencies, reduce costs, particularly in areas where costs are high, coordinate and communicate across different parts of the organization, create a framework for judging performance and facilitating learning, and motivate management and employees to achieve "stretch" targets of higher revenues and lower costs.

6-26 Cash budget (Continuation of 6-25) Refer to the information in Problem 6-25. Assume the following: Animal Gear (AG) does not make any sales on credit. AG sells only to the public and accepts cash and credit cards; 90% of its sales are to customers using credit cards, for which AG gets the cash right away, less a 2% transaction fee.

Purchases of materials are on account. AG pays for half the purchases in the period of the purchase and the other half in the following period. At the end of March, AG owes suppliers ₹80,000.

AG plans to replace a machine in April at a net cash cost of ₹1,30,000.

Labor, other manufacturing costs, and nonmanufacturing costs are paid in cash in the month incurred except of course depreciation, which is not a cash flow. Depreciation is ₹2,50,000 of the manufacturing cost and ₹1,00,000 of the nonmanufacturing cost for April.

AG currently has a ₹20,000 loan at an annual interest rate of 24%. The interest is paid at the end of each month. If AG has more than ₹1,00,000 cash at the end of April it will pay back the loan. AG owes ₹50,000 in income taxes that need to be remitted in April. AG has cash of ₹59,000 on hand at the end of March.

Required

1. Prepare a cash budget for April for Animal Gear.
2. Why do Animal Gear's managers prepare a cash budget in addition to the revenue, expenses, and operating income budget?

Solution

Cash Budget
April 30

Cash balance, April 1	₹59,000
Add receipts	
Cash sales (₹17,84,000 × 10%)	1,78,400
Credit card sales (₹17,84,000 × 90% × 98%)	15,73,490
Total cash available for needs (x)	₹18,10,890
Deduct cash disbursements	
Direct materials (₹80,000 + ₹1,98,200 × 50%)	₹1,79,100
Direct manufacturing labor	2,70,000
Manufacturing overhead (₹10,86,920 – ₹2,50,000 depreciation)	8,36,920
Nonmanufacturing salaries	1,68,000
Sales commissions	17,840
Other nonmanufacturing fixed costs (₹1,60,000 – ₹1,00,000 depreciation)	60,000
Machinery purchase	1,30,000
Income taxes	50,000
Total disbursements (y)	₹17,11,860
Financing	
Repayment of loan	₹20,000
Interest at 24% (₹20,000 × 24% × $\frac{1}{12}$)	400

Total effects of financing (z)	₹20,400
Ending cash balance, April 30 (x) — (y) — (z)	₹78,630

Note: The solution assumes that the loan is repaid. Some students may point out that the cash balance at the end of April is anticipated to be slightly less than ₹1,00,000 [₹99,030 (₹18,10,890 – ₹17,11,860)], and so Animal Gear would not repay the loan. Under this assumption, the ₹20,000 repayment would not be shown.

2. Animal Gear's managers prepare a cash budget in addition to the operating income budget to plan cash flows to ensure that the company has adequate cash to pay vendors, meet payroll, and pay operating expenses as these payments come due. Animal Gear could be very profitable on an accrual accounting basis, but the pattern of cash receipts from revenues might be delayed and result in insufficient cash being available to make scheduled payments for its expenses. Animal Gear's managers may then need to initiate a plan to borrow money to finance any shortfall. Building a profitable operating plan does not guarantee that adequate cash will be available, so Animal Gear's managers need to prepare a cash budget in addition to an operating income budget.

6-27 Budgeting and ethics. Jaypee Company manufactures a variety of products in a variety of departments and evaluates departments and departmental managers by comparing actual cost and output relative to the budget. Departmental managers help create the budgets and usually provide information about input quantities for materials, labor, and overhead costs.

Kamal is the manager of the department that produces product Z. Kamal has estimated these inputs for product Z:

Input	Budget Quantity per Unit of Output
Direct materials	8 kgs
Direct manufacturing labor	30 minutes
Machine time	24 minutes

The department produces about 100 units of product Z each day. Kamal's department always gets excellent evaluations, sometimes exceeding budgeted production quantities. For each 100 units of product Z produced, the company uses, on average, about 48 hours of direct manufacturing labor (eight people working 6 hours each), 790 kgs of material, and 39.5 machine-hours.

Top management of Jaypee Company has decided to implement budget standards that will challenge the workers in each department, and it has asked Kamal to design more challenging input standards for product Z. Kamal provides top management with the following input quantities:

Input	Budget Quantity per Unit of Output
Direct materials	7.9 kgs
Direct manufacturing labor	29 minutes
Machine time	23.6 minutes

Discuss the following:

1. Are these budget standards challenging for the department that produces product Z?
2. Why do you suppose Kamal picked these particular standards?
3. What steps can Jaypee Company's top management take to make sure Kamal's standards really meet the goals of the firm?

Solution

1 The standards proposed by Kamal are not challenging. In fact, he set the target at the level his department currently achieves.

Direct materials: 7.9 kgs × 100 units = 790 kgs.

Direct manufacturing labor: 29 min.×100 units = 2,900 min ÷ 60 = 48.33 hrs.

Machine time: 23.6 min × 100 units = 2,360 min. ÷ 60 = 39.33 hrs. approx

2. Kamal probably chose these standards so that his department would be able to make the goal and receive any resulting reward. With a little effort, his department can likely beat these goals.

3. Top management should point out that the targets set by Kamal are targets that the department already achieves. Top management is seeking targets that are slightly difficult to achieve, a stretch target that would challenge workers.

As discussed in the chapter, benchmarking might also be used to highlight the easy targets set by Kamal and to determine more challenging targets. Perhaps, the organization has multiple plant locations that could be used as comparisons. Alternatively, management could use industry averages. Also, management should work with Kamal to better understand his department and encourage him to set more realistic targets. Finally, the reward structure should be designed to encourage increasing productivity, not beating the budget. Management could also set continuous improvement standards.

6-28 Comprehensive budgeting problem; activity-based costing, operating and financial budgets.
Ritu makes a very popular undyed cloth sandal in one style, but in Regular and Deluxe. The Regular sandals have cloth soles and the Deluxe sandals have cloth-covered wooden soles. Ritu is preparing its budget for June 2016 and has estimated sales based on past experience.

Other information for the month of June follows:

Input prices
Direct materials
Plastic	₹52.50 per meter
Metal	₹75 per board foot (b.f.)
Direct manufacturing labor	₹150 per direct manufacturing labor hour

Input Quantities per Unit of Output (per pair of sandals)

	Regular	Deluxe
Direct materials		
Cloth	1.3 meters	1.5 meters
Wood	0	2 b.f.
Direct manufacturing labor – hours(DMLH)	5 hours	7 hours
Setup – hours per batch	2 hours	3 hours

Inventory information, Direct Materials

	Cloth	Wood
Beginning inventory	610 meters	800 b.f.
Target ending inventory	386 meters	295 b.f.
Cost of beginning inventory	₹32,190	₹60,600

Ritu accounts for direct materials using a FIFO cost flow assumption.

Sales and Inventory Information, Finished Goods

	Regular	Deluxe
Expected sales in units	2,000	3,000
Selling price	₹1,200	₹1,950
Target ending inventory in units	4,000	6,000
Beginning inventory in units	2,500	6,500
Beginning inventory in rupees	₹2,32,500	₹9,26,250

Ritu uses a FIFO cost flow assumption for finished goods inventory.

All the sandals are made in batches of 50 pairs of sandals. Ritu incurs manufacturing overhead costs, marketing and general administration, and transportation costs. Besides materials and labor, manufacturing costs include setup, processing, and inspection costs. Ritu transports 40 pairs of sandals per consignment. Ritu uses activity-based costing and has classified all overhead costs for the month of June as shown in the following chart:

Cost type	Denominator Activity	Rate
Manufacturing		
Setup	Setup – hours	₹180 per setup – hour
Processing	Direct manufacturing labor – hours	₹18 per DMLH
Inspection	Number of pairs of sandals	₹13.50
Nonmanufacturing		
Marketing and general administration	Sales revenue	8%
Shipping	Number of consignment	₹150 per consignment

Required

1. Prepare each of the following for June:
   a. Revenues budget
   b. Production budget in units
   c. Direct material usage budget and direct material purchases budget in both units and rupees; round to rupees
   d. Direct manufacturing labor cost budget
   e. Manufacturing overhead cost budgets for setup, processing, and inspection activities
   f. Budgeted unit cost of ending finished goods inventory and ending inventories budget
   g. Cost of goods sold budget
   h. Marketing and general administration and shipping costs budget
2. Ritu 's balance sheet for May 31 follows.

Ritu Balance Sheet as of May 31

Assets		
Cash		₹94,350
Accounts receivable	₹32,40,000	
Less: Allowance for bad debts	1,62,000	30,78,000
Inventories		
Direct materials		92,790
Finished goods		11,58,750
Fixed assets	₹87,00,000	
Less: Accumulated depreciation	13,63,350	73,36,650
Total assets		₹1,17,60,540
Liabilities and equity		
Accounts payable		₹1,56,000
Taxes payable		1,08,000
Interest payable		7,500
Long – term debt		15,00,000
Common stock		30,00,000
Retained earnings		69,89,040
Total liabilities and equity		₹1,17,60,540

Use the balance sheet and the following information to prepare a cash budget for Ritu for June. Round to rupees.

- All sales are on account; 60% are collected in the month of the sale, 38% are collected the following month, and 2% are never collected and written off as bad debts.
- All purchases of materials are on account. Ritu pays for 80% of purchases in the month of purchase and 20% in the following month.
- All other costs are paid in the month incurred, including the declaration and payment of a ₹1,50,000 cash dividend in June.
- Ritu is making monthly interest payments of 0.5% (6% per year) on a ₹15,00,000 long-term loan.
- Ritu plans to pay the ₹1,08,000 of taxes owed as of May 31 in the month of June. Income tax expense for June is zero.
- 30% of processing, setup, and inspection costs and 10% of marketing and general administration and shipping costs are depreciation.

3. Prepare a budgeted income statement for June and a budgeted balance sheet for Ritu as of June 30, 2016.

Solution

1a.

Revenues Budget
For the Month of June, 2016

	Units	Selling Price	Total Revenues
Regular	2,000	₹1,200	₹24,00,000
Deluxe	3,000	1,950	58,50,000
Total			₹82,50,000

b.

Production Budget
For the Month of June, 2016

	Product	
	Regular	Deluxe
Budgeted unit sales	2,000	3,000
Add: target ending finished goods inventory	400	600
Total required units	2,400	3,600
Deduct: beginning finished goods inventory	250	650
Units of finished goods to be produced	2,150	2,950

c.

Direct Material Usage Budget in Quantity and Rupees
For the Month of June, 2016

	Material		
	Cloth	Wood	Total
Physical Units Budget			
Direct materials required for			
Regular (2,150 units × 1.3 meter.; 0 b.f.)	2,795 meters.	0 b.f.	
Deluxe (2,950 units × 1.5 meter.; 2 b.f.)	4,425 meters.	5,900 b.f.	
Total quantity of direct materials to be used	7,220 meters.	5,900 b.f.	
Cost Budget			
Available from beginning direct materials inventory			
(under a FIFO cost-flow assumption)	₹32,190	₹60,600	

To be purchased this period

Cloth: (7,220 meters − 610 meters) × ₹52.50 per meter.	3,47,030	
Wood: (5,900 − 800) × ₹75 per b. f.		3,82,500
Direct materials to be used this period	₹3,79,220	₹4,43,100	₹8,22,320

Direct Materials Purchases Budget
For the Month of June, 2016

	Material		
	Cloth	Wood	Total
Physical Units Budget			
To be used in production	7,220 meters.	5,900 ft	
Add: Target ending direct material inventory	386 meters.	295 ft	
Total requirements	7,606 meters.	6,195 ft	
Deduct: beginning direct material inventory	610 meters.	800 ft	
Purchases to be made	6,996 meters.	5,395 ft	
Cost Budget			
Cloth: (6,996 meters. × ₹52.50 per meter.)	₹3,67,290		
Wood: (5,395 ft × ₹75 per b.f.)		₹4,04,630	
Total	₹3,67,290	₹4,04,630	₹7,71,920

d.

Direct Manufacturing Labor Costs Budget
For the Month of June, 2016

	Output Units Produced	Direct Manufacturing Labor-Hours per Unit	Total Hours	Hourly Wage Rate	Total
Regular	2,150	5	10,750	₹150	₹16,12,500
Deluxe	2,950	7	20,650	150	30,97,500
Total			31,400		₹47,10,000

e.

Manufacturing Overhead Costs Budget
For the Month of June 2016

	Total
Machine setup	
(Regular 43 batches[1] × 2 hrs./batch + Deluxe 59 batches[2] × 3 hrs./batch) × ₹180/hour	₹47,340
Processing (31,400 DMLH × ₹18)	5,65,200
Inspection (5,100 pairs × ₹13.50 per pair)	68,850
Total	₹6,81,390

[1]Regular: 2,150 pairs ÷ 50 pairs per batch = 43; [2]Deluxe: 2,950 pairs ÷ 50 pairs per batch = 59

f.

Unit Costs of Ending Finished Goods Inventory
For the Month of June, 2016

		Regular		Deluxe	
	Cost per Unit of Input	Input per Unit of Output	Total	Input per Unit of Output	Total
Cloth	₹52.5	1.3 meter	₹68.30	1.5 meter	₹78.8
Wood	75.0	0 b.f.	0.00	2 b.f.	150.0

Direct manufacturing					
labor	150.0	5 hr	750.00	7 hrs.	1,050.0
Machine setup	180.0	0.04 hr[1]	7.20	0.06 hr[1]	10.8
Processing	18.0	5 hrs	90.00	7 hrs	126.0
Inspection	13.50	1 pair	13.50	1 pair	13.5
Total			₹929.00		₹1,429.1

[1] 2 hours per setup ÷ 50 pairs per batch = 0.04 hr. per unit;
3 hours per setup ÷ 50 pairs per batch = 0.06 hr. per unit.

Ending Inventories Budget
June, 2016

	Quantity	Cost per unit		Total
Direct Materials				
Cloth	386 meters	₹52.50	₹20,265	
Wood	295 b.f.	₹75	22,125	₹42,390
Finished goods				
Regular	400	₹929	₹3,71,600	
Deluxe	600	1,429.10	8,57,460	12,29,060
Total ending inventory				₹12,71,450

g.

Cost of Goods Sold Budget
For the Month of June, 2016

Beginning finished goods inventory, June 1 (₹2,32,500 + ₹9,26,250)		₹11,58,750
Direct materials used (requirement c)	₹8,22,320	
Direct manufacturing labor (requirement d)	47,10,000	
Manufacturing overhead (requirement e)	6,81,390	
Cost of goods manufactured		62,13,710
Cost of goods available for sale		73,72,460
Deduct ending finished goods inventory, June 30 (requirement f)		12,29,060
Cost of goods sold		₹61,43,400

h.

Nonmanufacturing Costs Budget
For the Month of June, 2016

	Total
Marketing and general administration	
8% × ₹82,50,000	₹6,60,000
Shipping	
(5,000 pairs ÷ 40 pairs per consignment) × ₹150	18,750
Total	₹6,78,750

2.

Cash Budget
June 30, 2016

Cash balance, June 1 (from Balance Sheet)	₹94,350
Add receipts	
Collections from May accounts receivable	30,78,000

Collections from June accounts receivable (₹82,50,000 × 60%)	49,50,000
Total collection from customers	80,28,000
Total cash available for needs (x)	₹81,22,350
Deduct cash disbursements	
Direct material purchases in May	₹1,56,000
Direct material purchases in June (₹7,71,920 × 80%)	6,17,540
Direct manufacturing labor	47,10,000
Manufacturing overhead (₹6,81,390 × 70% because 30% is depreciation)	4,76,970
Nonmanufacturing costs (₹6,78,750 × 90% because 10% is depreciation)	6,10,880
Taxes	1,08,000
Dividends	1,50,000
Total disbursements (y)	₹68,29,390
Financing	
Interest at 6% (₹15,00,000 × 6% × 1 ÷ 12) (z)	₹7,500
Ending cash balance, June 30 (x) – (y) – (z)	₹12,85,460

3.

Budgeted Income Statement
For the Month of June, 2016

Revenues	₹82,50,000	
Bad debt expense (₹82,50,000 × 2%)	1,65,000	
Net revenues		₹80,85,000
Cost of goods sold		61,43,400
Gross margin		19,41,600
Operating (nonmanufacturing) costs	₹6,78,750	
Interest expense (for June)	7,500	6,86,250
Net income		₹12,55,350

Budgeted Balance Sheet
June 30, 2016
Assets

Cash		₹12,85,460
Accounts receivable (₹82,50,000 × 40%)	₹33,00,000	
Less: allowance for doubtful accounts	1,65,000	31,35,000
Inventories		
Direct materials	₹42,390	
Finished goods	12,29,060	12,71,450
Fixed assets	₹87,00,000	
Less: accumulated depreciation (₹13,63,350 + ₹6,81,390 × 30% + ₹6,78,750 × 10%))	16,35,640	70,64,360
Total assets		₹1,27,56,270

Liabilities and Equity

Accounts payable (₹7,71,920 × 20%)	₹1,54,380
Interest payable	7,500
Long-term debt	15,00,000
Common stock	30,00,000
Retained earnings (₹69,89,040 + ₹12,55,350 − ₹1,50,000)	80,94,390
Total liabilities and equity	₹1,27,56,270

Exercises

[Comprehensive solutions to all exercises are available on the companion website www.pearsoned.co.in/charlesthorngren]

6-29 Direct materials budget. Shaw Walace Company produces liquor. The company expects to produce 15,00,000 two-liter bottles of Royal Challenge in 2015. Shaw Walace purchases empty glass bottles from an outside vendor. Its target ending inventory of such bottles is 50,000; its beginning inventory is 20,000. For simplicity, ignore breakage. Compute the number of bottles to be purchased in 2015.

6-30 Budgeting material purchases. The Sunrise Company has prepared a sales budget of 4,20,000 finished units for a three-month period. The company has an inventory of 2,20,000 units of finished goods on hand at December 31 and has a target finished goods inventory of 2,40,000 units at the end of the succeeding quarter.

It takes 3 gallons of direct materials to make one unit of finished product. The company has an inventory of 9,00,000 gallons of direct materials at December 31 and has a target ending inventory of 11,00,000 gallons at the end of the succeeding quarter. How many gallons of direct materials should be purchased during the three months ending March 31?

6-31 Revenue, production, and purchases budgets. The Honda Co. in India has a division that manufactures two-wheel motorcycles. Its budgeted sales for Model G in 2013 are 80,00,000 units. Honda's target ending inventory is 10,00,000 units, and its beginning inventory is 12,00,000 units. The company's budgeted selling price to its distributors and dealers is ₹40,000 per motorcycle.

Honda buys all its wheels from an outside supplier. No defective wheels are accepted. Honda's needs for extra wheels for replacement parts are ordered by a separate division of the company. The company's target ending inventory is 3,00,000 wheels, and its beginning inventory is 2,00,000 wheels. The budgeted purchase price is ₹1,600 per wheel.

Required

1. Compute the budgeted revenues in rupees.
2. Compute the number of motorcycles to be produced.
3. Compute the budgeted purchases of wheels in units and in rupees.

6-32 Budgets for production and direct manufacturing labor. (CMA, adapted) Archies Company makes and sells artistic frames for pictures of weddings, graduations, and other special events. Rahul, the controller, is responsible for preparing Archies master budget and has accumulated the following information for 2016.

Particulars	January	February	March	April	May
Estimated sales in units	1,00,000	1,20,000	80,000	90,000	90,000
Selling price	₹540	₹515	₹515	₹515	₹515
Direct manufacturing labor-hours per unit	2	2	1.5	1.5	1.5
Wage per direct manufacturing labor-hour	₹10	₹10	₹10	₹11	₹11

Besides wages, direct manufacturing labor-related costs include pension contributions of ₹0.50 per hour, worker's compensation insurance of ₹0.15 per hour, employee medical insurance of ₹0.40 per hour, and social security taxes. Assume that as of January 1, 2016, the social security tax rates are 7.5% for employers and 7.5% for employees. The cost of employee benefits paid by Archies on its employees is treated as a direct manufacturing labor cost.

Archies has a labor contract that calls for a wage increase to ₹11 per hour on April 1, 2016. New labor-saving machinery has been installed and will be fully operational by March 1, 2016. Archies expects to have 1,60,000 frames on hand at December 31, 2015, and it has a policy of carrying an end-of-month inventory of 100% of the following month's sales plus 50% of the second following month's sales.

Prepare a production budget and a direct manufacturing labor budget for Archies Company by month and for the first quarter of 2016. Both budgets may be combined in one schedule. The direct manufacturing labor budget should include labor-hours and show the details for each labor cost category.

6-33 Budget schedules for a manufacturer. Delite Furniture is an elite desk manufacturer. It makes two products:
- Executive desks – 3 × 5 oak desks
- Chairman desks – 6 × 4 red oak desks

The budgeted direct-cost inputs for each product in 2016 are

	Executive Line	Chairman Line
Oak top	16 square feet	0
Red oak top	0	25 square feet
Oak legs	4	0
Red oak legs	0	4
Direct manufacturing labor	3 hours	5 hours

Unit data pertaining to the direct materials for March 2016 are

Actual-beginning Direct Materials Inventory (3/1/2016)

	Executive Line	Chairman Line
Oak top (square feet)	320	0
Red oak top (square feet)	0	150
Oak legs	100	0
Red oak legs	0	40

Target Ending Direct Materials Inventory (3/31/2016)

	Executive Line	Chairman Line
Oak top (square feet)	192	0
Red oak top (square feet)	0	200
Oak legs	80	0
Red oak legs	0	44

Unit cost data for direct-cost inputs pertaining to February 2016 and March 2016 are

	February (actual)	March V2P (budgeted)
Oak top (per square feet)	₹18	₹20
Red oak top (per square feet)	23	25
Oak legs (per leg)	11	12
Red oak legs (per leg)	17	18
Manufacturing labor cost per hour	30	30

Manufacturing overhead (both variable and fixed) is allocated to each desk on the basis of budgeted direct manufacturing labor-hours per desk. The budgeted variable manufacturing overhead rate for March 2016 is ₹35 per direct manufacturing labor-hour. The budgeted fixed manufacturing overhead for March 2016 is ₹42,500. Both variable and fixed manufacturing overhead cost are allocated to each unit of finished goods.

Data relating to finished goods inventory for March 2016 are

	Executive Line	Chairman Line
Beginning inventory in units	20	5
Beginning inventory in rupees (cost)	₹10,480	₹4,850
Target ending inventory in units	30	15

Budgeted sales for March 2016 are 740 units of the executive line and 390 units of the chairman line. The budgeted selling prices per unit in March 2016 are ₹1,020 for the executive line desk and ₹1,600 for the chairman line desk. Assume the following in your answer:

- Work-in-process inventories are negligible and ignored.
- Direct materials inventory and finished goods inventory are costed using the first-in-first-out (FIFO) method.
- Unit costs of direct materials purchased and finished goods are constant in March 2016.

1. Prepare the following budgets for March 2016:

    Required

    a. Revenues budget
    b. Production budget in units
    c. Direct materials usage budget and direct materials purchases budget
    d. Direct manufacturing labor budget
    e. Manufacturing overhead budget
    f. Ending inventory budget
    g. Cost of goods sold budget

2. Suppose Delite Furniture decides to incorporate continuous improvement into its budgeting process. Describe two areas where Delite could incorporate continuous improvement into the budget schedules in requirement 1.

6-34 Responsibility of purchasing agent. (Adapted from a description by R. Villers) Aashish Jain is the purchasing agent for the Birla Manufacturing Company, Sanjay Gupta is head of the Production Planning and Control Department. Every six months, Sanjay gives Aashish a general purchasing program. Aashish gets specifications from the Engineering Department. He then selects suppliers and negotiates prices. When he took this job, Aashish was informed very clearly that he bore responsibility for meeting the general purchasing program once he accepted it from Sanjay.

During week 24, Aashish is advised that Part No. 1234 – a critical part – Would be needed for assembly on Tuesday morning of week 32. He found that the regular supplier could not deliver. He called everywhere and finally found a supplier in Bombay who accepted the commitment.

He followed up by e-mail. Yes, the supplier assured him the part would be ready. The matter was so important that on Thursday of week 31, Aashish checked by phone. Yes, the shipment had left in time. Aashish was reassured and did not check further. But on Tuesday of week 32, the part had not arrived. Inquiry revealed that the shipment had been misdirected by the railroad and was still in Bombay.

What department should bear the costs of time lost in the plant due to the delayed shipment? Why? As purchasing agent, do you think it fair that such costs be charged to your department?

Required

6-35 Activity-based budgeting. Anderson Manufacturing, Inc, uses activity-based costing and activity-based budgeting. Budgetary information for selected activities for 2016 is provided below.

Activity	Cost Driver	Items Cost Pool (fixed cost + cost per unit of cost driver)
Machining	Machine hours	Indirect materials ₹0 + ₹10 per hour Indirect labor ₹20,000 + ₹15 per hour Utilities ₹0 + ₹5 per hour
Setups and quality assurance	Production runs	Indirect materials ₹0 + ₹1,000 per run Indirect labor ₹0 + ₹1,200 per run Inspection ₹80,000 + ₹2,000 per run
Procurement	Purchase orders	Indirect materials ₹0 + ₹4 per order Indirect labor ₹45,000 + ₹0 per order
Design Material handling	Design hours	Engineering ₹75,000 + ₹50 per hour

	Square feet of materials handled	Indirect materials ₹0 + ₹2 per square feet
		Indirect labor ₹30,000 + ₹0 per square feet

Additional budget for 2016

Activity	Cost Driver Budgeted Volume
a. Machining	10,000 machine hours
b. Setups and quality assurance	40 production runs
c. Procurement	15,000 purchase orders
d. Design	100 engineering hours
e. Material handling	1,00,000 square feet

Calculate the budgeted amount for each activity in 2016

6-36 Comprehensive operating budget, budgeted balance sheet. J. K. Wood Company is promoted by an entrepreneur. It manufactures and sells snowboards. In the summer of 2011 its accountant gathered the following data to prepare budgets for 2016:
Materials and labor requirements

Direct materials

Wood	5 board feet per snowboard
Fiberglass	6 yards per snowboard
Direct manufacturing labor	5 hours per snowboard

J.K.'s CEO expects to sell 1,000 snowboards during 2016 at an estimated retail price of ₹1,000 per board. Further, he expects 2016 beginning inventory of 100 boards and would like to end 2016 with 200 snowboards in stock.
Direct materials inventories

	Beginning Inventory 1/1/2016	Ending Inventory 12/31/2016
Wood	2,000	1,500
Fiberglass	1,000	2,000

Variable manufacturing overhead is allocated at the rate of ₹14 per direct manufacturing labor-hour. There are also ₹1,32,000 in fixed manufacturing overhead costs budgeted for 2016. J. K. combines both variable and fixed manufacturing overhead into a single rate based on direct manufacturing labor-hours. Variable marketing costs are allocated at the rate of ₹2,500 per sales visit. The marketing plan calls for 30 sales visits during 2016. Finally, there are ₹60,000 in fixed nonmanufacturing costs budgeted for 2016.

Other data includes:

	2015 Unit Price	2012 Unit Price
Wood	₹56 per b.f.	60 per b.f.
Fiberglass	9.60 per yard	10 per yard
Direct manufacturing labor	24.00 per hour	25.00 per hour

The inventoriable unit cost for ending finished goods inventory on December 31, 2015, is ₹647.60. Assume J. K. uses a FIFO inventory method for both direct materials and finished goods. Ignore work in process in your calculations.

Required

1. Prepare the 2016 revenues budget (in Rupees).
2. Prepare the 2016 production budget (in units).
3. Prepare the direct materials usage and purchases budgets.
4. Prepare a direct manufacturing labor budget.
5. Prepare a manufacturing overhead budget.
6. What is the budgeted manufacturing overhead rate?
7. What is the budgeted manufacturing overhead cost per output unit?
8. Calculate the cost of a snowboard manufactured in 2016.
9. Prepare an ending inventory budget for both direct materials and finished goods.

10. Prepare a cost of goods sold budget.
11. Prepare the budgeted income statement for J. K. for 2016.

6-37 Comprehensive budget; fill in schedules. The following information is for Retail Stationery Store:

1. **Balance sheet information as of December 31, 2014**

Current assets	
Cash	₹12,000
Accounts receivable	10,000
Inventory	63,600
Equipment – net	1,00,000
Liabilities as of December 31, 2014	None

2. **Recent and anticipated sales:**

December	₹40,000
January	48,000
February	60,000
March	80,000
April	36,000

3. Credit sales: Sales are 75% cash and 25% on credit. Assume that credit accounts are all collected within 30 days from sale. The accounts receivable on December 31 are the result of the credit sales for December (25% of ₹40,000).
4. Gross margin averages 30% of revenues. Store treats cash discounts on purchases in the income statement as "other income."
5. Operating costs: Salaries and wages average 15% of monthly revenues; rent, 5%; other operating costs, excluding depreciation, 4%. Assume that these costs are disbursed each month. Depreciation is ₹1,000 per month.
6. Purchases: Store keeps a minimum inventory of ₹30,000. The policy is to purchase each month additional inventory in the amount necessary to provide for the following month's sales. Terms on purchases are 2/10, net/30. (payments on purchases are to be made in 30 days; a 2% discount is available if the payment is made within 10 days after purchase.) Assume that payments are made in the month of purchase and that all discounts are taken.
7. Light fixtures: in January, ₹600 is spent for light fixtures, and in February, ₹400 is to be expended for this purpose. These amounts are to be capitalized.

Assume that a minimum cash balance of ₹8,000 must be maintained. Assume also that all borrowing is effective at the beginning of the month and all repayments are made at the end of the month of repayment. Loans are repaid when sufficient cash is available. Interest is paid only at the time of repaying principal. The interest rate is 18% per year. The owner of store does not want to borrow any more cash than is necessary and wants to repay as soon as cash is available.

On the basis of the preceding facts

Required

1. Complete Schedule A.

Schedule A: Budgeted Monthly Cash Receipts

Item	December	January	February	March
Total sales	₹40,000	₹48,000	₹60,000	₹80,000
Credit sales (25%)	10,000	12,000		
Cash sales (75%)	_____	_____	_____	_____
Receipts:	_____	_____	_____	_____
Cash sales		₹36,000		
Collections on accounts receivable		10,000		
Total		46,000		

2. Complete Schedule B. Note that purchases are 70% of next month's sales.

   Schedule B: Budgeted Monthly Cash Disbursements for Purchases

Item	January	February	March	4th Quarter
Purchases	₹42,000			
Deduct 2% cash discount	840			
Disbursements	₹41,160			

3. Complete Schedule C.

   Schedule C: Budgeted Monthly Cash Disbursements for Operating Costs

Item	January	February	March	4th Quarter
Salaries and wages	₹7,200			
Rent	2,400			
Other cash operating costs	1,920			
Total	11,520			

4. Complete Schedule D.

   Schedule D: Budgeted Total Monthly Cash Disbursements

Item	January	February	March	4th Quarter
Purchases	₹41,160			
Cash operating costs	11,520			
Light fixtures	600			
Total	₹53,280			

5. Complete Schedule E.

   Schedule E: Budgeted Cash Receipts and Disbursements

Item	January	February	March	4th Quarter
Receipts	₹46,000			
Disbursements	53,280			
Net cash increase				
Net cash decrease	₹7,280			

6. Complete Schedule F (assume that borrowings must be made in multiples of ₹1,000).

   Schedule F: Financing Required

Item	January	February	March	4th Quarter
Beginning cash balance	₹12,000			
Net cash increase				
Net cash decrease	7,280			
Cash position before borrowing (a)	4,720			
Minimum cash balance required	8,000			
Excess (Deficiency)	(3,280)			
Borrowing required (b)	4,000			
Interest payments (c)				
Borrowing repaid (d)				
Ending cash balance	8,720			

7. What do you think is the most logical type of loan needed by Retail Stationery Store?

8. Prepare a budgeted income statement for the fourth quarter and a budgeted balance sheet as of March, 2015. Ignore income taxes.

9. Some simplifications have been included in this problem. What complicating factors might arise in a typical business situation?

7 Flexible Budgets, Direct-Cost Variances, and Management Control

Every organization, regardless of its profitability or growth, has to step back and take a hard look at its spending decisions.

And when customers are affected by a recession, the need for managers to use budgeting and variance analysis tools for cost control becomes especially critical. By studying variances, managers can focus on where specific performances have fallen short and use the information they learn to make corrective adjustments and achieve significant savings for their companies. The drive to achieve cost reductions might seem at odds with the growing push for organizations to pursue environmentally sound business practices. To the contrary, managers looking to be more efficient with their plants and operations have found that cornerstones of the sustainability movement, such as reducing waste and power usage, offer fresh ways to help them manage risk and control costs.

Static Budgets and Variances

A **variance** is the difference between actual results and expected performance. The expected performance is also called budgeted performance, which is a point of reference for making comparisons.

The Use of Variances

Variances bring together the planning and control functions of management and facilitate management by exception. **Management by exception** is a practice whereby managers focus more closely on areas that are not operating as expected and less closely on areas that are. Consider the scrap and rework costs at a NOIDA appliances plant. If the plant's actual costs are much higher than originally budgeted, the variances will prompt managers to find out why and correct the problem so future operations result in less scrap and rework. Sometimes a large positive variance may occur, such as a significant decrease in the manufacturing costs of a product. Managers will try to understand the reasons for the decrease (better operator training or changes in manufacturing methods, for example) so these practices can be continued and implemented by other divisions within the organization.

Variances are also used for evaluating performance and to motivate managers. Production-line managers at NOIDA may have quarterly efficiency incentives linked to achieving a budgeted amount of operating costs.

Sometimes variances suggest that the company should consider a change in strategy. For example, large negative variances caused by excessive defect rates for a new product may suggest a flawed product design. Managers may then want to investigate the product design and potentially change the mix of products being offered. Variances also help managers make more informed predictions about the future and thereby improve the quality of the five-step decision-making process.

The benefits of variance analysis are not restricted to companies. In today's difficult economic environment, public officials have realized that the ability to make timely tactical changes based on variance information can result in their having to make fewer draconian adjustments later. For example, the city of Scottsdale, Arizona, monitors its tax and fee performance against expenditures monthly. Why? One of the city's goals is to keep its water usage rates stable. By monitoring the extent to which the city's water revenues are matching its current expenses, Scottsdale can avoid sudden spikes in the rate it charges residents for water as well as finance water-related infrastructure projects.[1]

How important of a decision-making tool is variance analysis? Very. A recent survey by the United Kingdom's Chartered Institute of Management Accountants found that it was easily the most popular costing tool used by organizations of all sizes.

Static Budgets and Static-Budget Variances

We will take a closer look at variances by examining one company's accounting system. As you study the exhibits in this chapter, note that "level" followed by a number denotes the amount of detail shown by a variance analysis. Level 1 reports the least detail, level 2 offers more information, and so on.

Consider Color Plus Company, a firm that manufactures and sells jackets. The jackets require tailoring and many hand operations. Color Plus sells exclusively to distributors, who in turn sell to independent clothing stores and retail chains. For simplicity, we assume the following: (1) Color Plus's only costs are in the manufacturing function; Color Plus incurs no costs in other value-chain functions, such as marketing and distribution; (2) All units manufactured in April 2014 are sold in April 2014; (3) There is no direct materials inventory at either the beginning or the end of the period. No work-in-process or finished goods inventories exist at either the beginning or the end of the period. Color Plus has three variable-cost categories. The budgeted variable cost per jacket for each category is:

Cost Category	Variable Cost per Jacket
Direct material costs	₹600
Direct manufacturing labor costs	160
Variable manufacturing overhead costs	120
Total variable costs	₹880

The number of units manufactured is the cost driver for direct materials, direct manufacturing labor, and variable manufacturing overhead. The relevant range for the cost driver is from 0 to 12,000 jackets. Budgeted and actual data for April 2014 follow:

Budgeted fixed costs for production between 0 and 12,000 jackets	₹27,60,000
Budgeted selling price	₹1,200 per jacket
Budgeted production and sales	12,000 jackets
Actual production and sales	10,000 jackets

---

[1] For an excellent discussion and other related examples from governmental settings, see Kavanagh S., and C. Swanson. 2009. Tactical financial management: Cash flow and budgetary variance analysis. *Government Finance Review*, October 1.

The **static budget**, or master budget, is based on the level of output planned at the start of the budget period. The master budget is called a static budget because the budget for the period is developed around a single (static) planned output level. Exhibit 7-1, column 3, presents the static budget for Color Plus Company for April 2014 that was prepared at the end of 2013. For each line item in the income statement, Exhibit 7-1, column 1, displays data for the actual April results. For example, actual revenues are ₹1,25,00,000, and the actual selling price is ₹1,25,00,000 ÷ 10,000 jackets = ₹1,250 per jacket—compared with the budgeted selling price of ₹1,200 per jacket. Similarly, actual direct material costs are ₹62,16,000, and the direct material cost per jacket is ₹621.6 ÷ 10,000 = ₹621.6 per jacket—compared with the budgeted direct material cost per jacket of ₹600. We describe potential reasons and explanations for these differences as we discuss different variances throughout the chapter.

The **static-budget variance** (see Exhibit 7-1, column 2) is the difference between the actual result and the corresponding budgeted amount in the static budget.

A **favorable variance**—denoted F in this book—has the effect, when considered in isolation, of increasing operating income relative to the budgeted amount. For revenue items, F means actual revenues exceed budgeted revenues. For cost items, F means actual costs are less than budgeted costs. An unfavorable variance—denoted U in this book—has the effect, when viewed in isolation, of decreasing operating income relative to the budgeted amount. Unfavorable variances are also called adverse variances in some countries.

The unfavorable static-budget variance for operating income of ₹9,31,000 in Exhibit 7-1 is calculated by subtracting static-budget operating income of ₹10,80,000 from actual operating income of ₹1,49,000:

$$\text{Static-budget variance for operating income} = \text{Actual result} - \text{Static-budget amount}$$

$$= ₹1,49,000 - ₹10,80,000$$
$$= ₹9,31,000 \text{ U.}$$

Exhibit 7-1

Static-Budget-Based Variance Analysis for Color Plus Company for April 2014[a]

Level 1 Analysis

	Actual Results (1)	Static-Budget Variances (2) = (1) − (3)	Static Budget (3)
Units sold	10,000	2,000 U	12,000
Revenues	₹1,25,00,000	₹19,00,000 U	₹1,44,00,000
Variable costs			
Direct materials	62,16,000	9,84,000 F	72,00,000
Direct manufacturing labor	19,80,000	60,000 U	19,20,000
Variable manufacturing overhead	13,05,000	1,35,000 F	14,40,000
Total variable costs	95,01,000	10,59,000 F	1,05,60,000
Contribution margin	29,99,000	8,41,000 U	38,40,000
Fixed costs	28,50,000	90,000 U	27,60,000
Operating income	₹1,49,000	₹9,31,000 U	₹10,80,000

₹9,31,000 U

Static-budget variance

[a]F = favorable effect on operating income; U = unfavorable effect on operating income.

The analysis in Exhibit 7-1 provides managers with additional information on the static-budget variance for operating income of ₹9,31,000 U. The more detailed breakdown indicates how the line items that comprise operating income—revenues, individual variable costs, and fixed costs—add up to the static-budget variance of ₹9,31,000.

Recall that Color Plus produced and sold only 10,000 jackets, although managers anticipated an output of 12,000 jackets in the static budget. *Managers want to know how much of the static-budget variance is because of inaccurate forecasting of output units sold and how much is due to Color Plus's performance in manufacturing and selling 10,000 jackets.* Managers, therefore, create a flexible budget, which enables a more in-depth understanding of deviations from the static budget.

Decision Point

What are static budgets and static-budget variances?

Flexible Budgets

A **flexible budget** calculates budgeted revenues and budgeted costs based on the *actual output in the budget period*. The flexible budget is prepared at the end of the period (April 2014 for Color Plus), after the managers know the actual output of 10,000 jackets. The flexible budget is the *hypothetical* budget that Color Plus would have prepared at the start of the budget period if it had correctly forecast the actual output of 10,000 jackets. In other words, the flexible budget is not the plan Color Plus initially had in mind for April 2014 (remember Color Plus planned for an output of 12,000 jackets). Rather, it is the budget Color Plus *would have* put together for April if it knew in advance that the output for the month would be 10,000 jackets. In preparing the flexible budget note that:

Learning Objective 2

Examine the concept of a flexible budget

. . . the budget that is adjusted (flexed) to recognize the actual output level

and learn how to develop it

. . . proportionately increase variable costs; keep fixed costs the same

- The budgeted selling price is the same ₹1,200 per jacket used in preparing the static budget.
- The budgeted variable costs are the same ₹880 per jacket used in the static budget.
- The budgeted fixed costs are the same static-budget amount of ₹27,60,000. Why? Because the 10,000 jackets produced falls within the relevant range of 0 to 12,000 jackets. Therefore, Color Plus would have budgeted the same amount of fixed costs, ₹27,60,000, whether it anticipated making 10,000 or 12,000 jackets.

The *only* difference between the static budget and the flexible budget is that the static budget is prepared for the planned output of 12,000 jackets, whereas the flexible budget is based on the actual output of 10,000 jackets. In other words, the static budget is being "flexed," or adjusted, from 12,000 jackets to 10,000 jackets.[2] The flexible budget for 10,000 jackets assumes that all costs are either completely variable or completely fixed with respect to the number of jackets produced.

Color Plus develops its flexible budget in three steps.

Step 1:   Identify the Actual Quantity of Output. In April 2014, Color Plus produced and sold 10,000 jackets.

Step 2:   Calculate the Flexible Budget for Revenues Based on Budgeted Selling Price and Actual Quantity of Output.

$$\text{Flexible-budget variable} = ₹1{,}200 \text{ per jacket} \times 10{,}000 \text{ jackets}$$
$$= ₹1{,}20{,}00{,}000$$

Step 3:   Calculate the Flexible Budget for Costs Based on Budgeted Variable Cost per Output Unit, Actual Quantity of Output, and Budgeted Fixed Costs.

---

[2] Suppose Color Plus, when preparing its next year's budget at the end of 2013, had perfectly anticipated that its output in April 2014 would equal 10,000 jackets. Then, the flexible budget for April 2014 would be identical to the static budget.

Flexible-budget variable costs	
Direct materials, ₹600 per jacket × 10,000 jackets	₹60,00,000
Direct manufacturing labor, ₹160 per jacket × 10,000 jackets	16,00,000
Variable manufacturing overhead, ₹120 per jacket × 10,000 jackets	12,00,000
Total flexible-budget variable costs	88,00,000
Flexible-budget fixed costs	27,60,000
Flexible-budget total costs	₹1,15,60,000

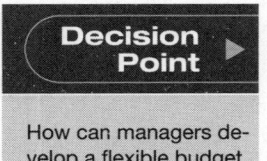

Decision Point ▶

How can managers develop a flexible budget and why is it useful to do so?

These three steps enable Color Plus to prepare a flexible budget, as shown in Exhibit 7-2, column 3. The flexible budget allows for a more detailed analysis of the ₹9,31,000 unfavorable static-budget variance for operating income.

Flexible-Budget Variances and Sales-Volume Variances

Exhibit 7-2 shows the flexible-budget-based variance analysis for Color Plus, which subdivides the ₹9,31,000 unfavorable static-budget variance for operating income into two parts: a flexible-budget variance of ₹2,91,000 U and a sales-volume variance of ₹6,40,000 U. The **sales-volume variance** is the difference between a flexible-budget amount and the corresponding static-budget amount. The **flexible-budget variance** is the difference between an actual result and the corresponding flexible-budget amount.

Exhibit 7-2   Level 2 Flexible-Budget-Based Variance Analysis for Color Plus Company for April 2014[a]

Level 2 Analysis

	Actual Results (1)	Flexible-Budget Variances (2) = (1) − (3)	Flexible Budget (3)	Sales-Volume Variances (4) = (3) − (5)	Static Budget (5)
Units sold	10,000	0	10,000	2,000 U	12,000
Revenues	₹1,25,00,000	₹5,00,000 F	₹1,20,00,000	₹24,00,000 U	₹1,44,00,000
Variable costs					
Direct materials	62,16,000	2,16,000 U	60,00,000	12,00,000 F	72,00,000
Direct manufacturing labor	19,80,000	3,80,000 U	16,00,000	3,20,000 F	19,20,000
Variable manufacturing overhead	13,05,000	1,05,000 U	12,00,000	2,40,000 F	14,40,000
Total variable costs	95,01,000	7,01,000 U	88,00,000	17,60,000 F	1,05,60,000
Contribution margin	29,99,000	2,01,000 U	32,00,000	6,40,000 U	38,40,000
Fixed manufacturing costs	28,50,000	90,000 U	27,60,000	0	27,60,000
Operating income	₹1,49,000	₹2,91,000 U	₹4,40,000	₹6,40,000 U	₹10,80,000

Level 2   ₹2,91,000 U   ₹6,40,000 U

Flexible-budget variance   Sales-volume variance

Level 1   ₹9,31,000 U

Static-budget variance

[a]F = favorable effect on operating income; U = unfavorable effect on operating income.

Sales-Volume Variances

Keep in mind that the flexible-budget amounts in column 3 of Exhibit 7-2 and the static-budget amounts in column 5 are both computed using budgeted selling prices, budgeted variable cost per jacket, and budgeted fixed costs. The difference between the static-budget and the flexible-budget amounts is called the sales-volume variance because it arises *solely* from the difference between the 10,000 actual quantity (or volume) of jackets sold and the 12,000 quantity of jackets expected to be sold in the static budget.

Learning Objective 3

Calculate flexible-budget variances

. . . each flexible-budget variance is the difference between an actual result and a flexible-budget amount

and sales-volume variances

. . . each sales-volume variance is the difference between a flexible-budget amount and a static-budget amount

$$\begin{aligned} \text{Sales-budget variance for operating income} &= \text{Flexible-budget amount} - \text{Static-budget amount} \\ &= ₹4,40,000 - ₹10,80,000 \\ &= ₹6,40,000 \text{ U} \end{aligned}$$

The sales-volume variance in operating income for Color Plus measures the change in budgeted contribution margin because Color Plus sold only 10,000 jackets rather than the budgeted 12,000.

$$\begin{aligned} \text{Sales-volume variance for operating income} &= \left(\begin{array}{c} \text{Budgeted contribution} \\ \text{margin per unit} \end{array} \right) \times \left(\begin{array}{c} \text{Actual units} \\ \text{sold} \end{array} - \begin{array}{c} \text{Static-budget} \\ \text{units sold} \end{array} \right) \\ &= \left(\begin{array}{c} \text{Budgeted selling} \\ \text{price} \end{array} - \begin{array}{c} \text{Budgeted variable} \\ \text{cost per unit} \end{array} \right) \times \left(\begin{array}{c} \text{Actual units} \\ \text{sold} \end{array} - \begin{array}{c} \text{Static-budget} \\ \text{units sold} \end{array} \right) \\ &= (₹1,200 \text{ per jacket} - ₹880 \text{ per jacket}) \times (10,000 \text{ jackets} - 12,000 \text{ jackets}) \\ &= ₹320 \text{ per jacket} \times (2,000 \text{ jackets}) \\ &= ₹6,40,000 \text{ U} \end{aligned}$$

Exhibit 7-2, column 4, shows the components of this overall variance by identifying the sales-volume variance for each of the line items in the income statement. The unfavorable sales-volume variance in operating income could be because of one or more of the following reasons:

1. Failure of Color Plus's managers to execute the sales plans.
2. Weaker than anticipated overall demand for jackets.
3. Competitors taking away market share from Color Plus.
4. Unexpected changes in customer tastes and preferences away from Color Plus's designs.
5. Quality problems leading to customer dissatisfaction with Color Plus's jackets.

How Color Plus responds to the unfavorable sales-volume variance will be influenced by what management believes to be the cause of the variance. For example, if Color Plus's managers believe the unfavorable sales-volume variance was caused by market-related reasons (reasons 1, 2, 3, or 4), the sales manager would be in the best position to explain what happened and to suggest corrective actions, such as sales promotions, that may be needed. If, however, managers believe the unfavorable sales-volume variance was caused by quality problems (reason 5), the production manager would be in the best position to analyze the causes and to suggest strategies for improvement, such as changes in the manufacturing process or investments in new machines.

The static-budget variances compared actual revenues and costs for 10,000 jackets against budgeted revenues and costs for 12,000 jackets. A portion of this difference, the sales-volume variance, reflects the effects of selling fewer units or inaccurate forecasting of sales. By removing this component from the static-budget variance, managers can compare their firm's revenues earned and costs incurred for April 2014 against the flexible budget—the revenues and costs Color Plus would have budgeted for the 10,000 jackets actually produced and sold. *Flexible-budget variances are a better measure of operating performance than static-budget variances because they compare actual revenues to budgeted revenues and actual costs to budgeted costs for the same 10,000 jackets of output.*

Flexible-Budget Variances

The first three columns of Exhibit 7-2 compare Color Plus's actual results with flexible-budget amounts. The flexible-budget variances for each line item in the income statement are shown in column 2:

$$\text{Flexible-budget variance} = \text{Actual result} - \text{Flexible-budget amount}$$

The operating income line in Exhibit 7-2 shows the flexible-budget variance is ₹2,91,000 U (₹1,49,000 – ₹4,40,000). The ₹2,91,000 U arises because actual selling price, actual variable cost per unit, and actual fixed costs differ from their budgeted amounts. The actual results and budgeted amounts for the selling price and variable cost per unit are as follows:

	Actual Result	**Budgeted Amount**
Selling price	₹1,250 (₹1,25,00,000 ÷ 10,000 jackets)	₹1,200 (₹1,20,00,000 ÷ 10,000 jackets)
Variable cost per jacket	₹950.1 (₹95,01,000 ÷ 10,000 jackets)	₹880 (₹88,00,000 ÷ 10,000 jackets)

The flexible-budget variance for revenues is called the **selling-price variance** because it arises solely from the difference between the actual selling price and the budgeted selling[3/4] price:

$$\text{Selling-price variance} = \left(\begin{array}{c} \text{Actual} \\ \text{selling price} \end{array} - \begin{array}{c} \text{Budgeted} \\ \text{selling price} \end{array} \right) \times \begin{array}{c} \text{Actual} \\ \text{units sold} \end{array}$$

$$= (₹1,250 \text{ per jacket} - ₹1,250 \text{ per jacket}) \times 10,000 \text{ jackets}$$

$$= ₹5,00,000$$

Color Plus has a favorable selling-price variance because the ₹1,250 actual selling price exceeds the ₹1,200 budgeted amount, which increases operating income. Marketing managers are generally in the best position to understand and explain the reason for this selling price difference. For example, was the difference due to better quality? Or was it due to an overall increase in market prices? Color's managers concluded it was due to a general increase in prices.

The flexible-budget variance for total variable costs is unfavorable (₹7,01,000 U) for the actual output of 10,000 jackets. It's unfavorable because of one or both of the following:

■ Color Plus used greater quantities of inputs (such as direct manufacturing labor-hours) compared to the budgeted quantities of inputs.

■ Color Plus incurred higher prices per unit for the inputs (such as the wage rate per direct manufacturing labor-hour) compared to the budgeted prices per unit of the inputs.

Higher input quantities and/or higher input prices relative to the budgeted amounts could be the result of Color Plus's deciding to produce a better product than what was planned or the result of inefficiencies in Color Plus's manufacturing and purchasing, or both. *You should always think of variance analysis as providing suggestions for further investigation rather than as establishing conclusive evidence of good or bad performance.*

The actual fixed costs of ₹28,50,000 are ₹90,000 more than the budgeted amount of ₹27,60,000. This unfavorable flexible-budget variance reflects unexpected increases in the cost of fixed indirect resources, such as factory rent or supervisory salaries.

In the rest of this chapter, we will focus on variable direct-cost input variances. Chapter 8 emphasizes indirect (overhead) cost variances.

Decision Point ◀

What are static budgets and static-budget variances?

Standard Costs for Variance Analysis

To gain further insight, almost all companies subdivide the flexible-budget variance for direct-cost inputs into two more-detailed variances:

1. A price variance that reflects the difference between an actual input price and a budgeted input price
2. An efficiency variance that reflects the difference between an actual input quantity and a budgeted input quantity

We will call these level 3 variances. Managers generally have more control over efficiency variances than price variances because the quantity of inputs used is primarily affected by factors inside the company (such as the efficiency with which operations are performed), whereas changes in the price of materials or in wage rates may be largely dictated by market forces outside the company.

Obtaining Budgeted Input Prices and Budgeted Input Quantities

To calculate price and efficiency variances, Color Plus needs to obtain budgeted input prices and budgeted input quantities. Color's three main sources for this information are: (1) past data, (2) data from similar companies, and (3) standards. Each source has its advantages and disadvantages.

Learning Objective 4

Explain why standard costs are often used in variance analysis

. . . standard costs exclude past inefficiencies and take into account expected future changes

1. **Actual input data from past periods.** Most companies have past data on actual input prices and actual input quantities. These historical data could be analyzed for trends or patterns using some of the techniques we will discuss in another chapter (Chapter 10) to obtain estimates of budgeted prices and quantities.

   Advantages: Past data represent quantities and prices that are real rather than hypothetical, so they can be very useful benchmarks for measuring improvements in performance. Moreover, past data are typically easy to collect at a low cost.

   Disadvantages: A firm's inefficiencies, such as the wastage of direct materials, are incorporated in past data. Consequently, the data do not represent the performance the firm could have ideally attained, only the performance it achieved in the past. Past data also do not incorporate any changes expected for the budget period, such as improvements resulting from new investments in technology.

2. **Data from other companies that have similar processes.** Another source of information is data from peer companies or companies that have similar processes, which can serve as a benchmark. For example, Fortis Healthcare System benchmarks its labor performance data against those of similar top-ranked hospitals.

Advantages: Data from other companies can provide a firm useful information about how it's performing relative to its competitors.

Disadvantages: Input-price and input-quantity data from other companies are often not available or may not be comparable to a particular company's situation. Consider Indian Apparel, which makes more than 1 million articles of clothing a week. At its sole factory, in NOIDA, workers receive hourly wages, piece rates, and medical benefits well in excess of those paid by its competitors, virtually all of whom are offshore and have significantly lower production costs. (We will discuss benchmarking in more detail later in the chapter.)

3. **Standards developed by the firm itself.** A **standard** is a carefully determined price, cost, or quantity that is used as a benchmark for judging performance. Standards are usually expressed on a per-unit basis. Consider how Color Plus determines its direct manufacturing labor standards. Color Plus conducts engineering studies to obtain a detailed breakdown of the steps required to make a jacket. Each step is assigned a standard time based on work performed by a *skilled* worker using equipment operating in an *efficient* manner. Similarly, Color Plus determines the standard quantity of square yards of cloth based on what is required by a skilled operator to make a jacket.

Advantages: Standard times (1) aim to exclude past inefficiencies and (2) take into account changes expected to occur in the budget period. An example of the latter would be a decision by Color Plus's managers to lease new, faster, and more accurate sewing machines. Color Plus would incorporate the resulting higher level of efficiency into the new standards it sets.

Disdvantages: Because they are not based on realized benchmarks, the standards might not be achievable, and workers could get discouraged trying to meet them.

The term "standard" refers to many different things.

■ A standard input is a carefully determined quantity of input—such as square yards of cloth or direct manufacturing labor-hours—required for one unit of output, such as a jacket.

■ A standard price is a carefully determined price that a company expects to pay for a unit of input. In the Color Plus example, the standard wage rate that Color Plus expects to pay its operators is an example of a standard price of a direct manufacturing labor-hour.

■ A standard cost is a carefully determined cost of a unit of output—for example, the standard direct manufacturing labor cost of a jacket at Color Plus.

$$\text{Standard cost per output unit for} \atop \text{each variable direct-cost input} = {\text{Standard input allowed} \atop \text{for one output unit}} \times {\text{Standard price} \atop \text{per input unit}}$$

Standard direct material cost per jacket: 2 square yards of cloth input allowed per output unit (jacket) manufactured, at ₹300 standard price per square yard

Standard direct material cost per jacket = 2 Square yards × ₹300 per square yard = ₹600

Standard direct manufacturing labor cost per jacket: 0.8 manufacturing labor-hour of input allowed per output unit manufactured, at ₹200 standard price per hour

Standard direct manufacturing labor cost per jacket = 0.8 labor-hours × ₹160 per labor-hour = ₹160

How are the words "budget" and "standard" related? Budget is the broader term. To clarify, budgeted input prices, input quantities, and costs need *not* be based on standards. However, when standards are used to obtain budgeted input quantities and prices, the terms "standard" and "budget" are used interchangeably. The standard cost of each input required for one unit of output is determined by the standard quantity of each input required for one unit of output and the standard price per input unit. Notice how the standard-cost computations shown previously for direct materials and direct manufacturing labor equal the budgeted direct material cost per jacket of ₹600 and the budgeted direct manufacturing labor cost of ₹160 referred to earlier.

In its standard costing system, Color Plus uses standards that are attainable by operating efficiently but that allow for normal disruptions. A normal disruption could include, for example, a short delay in the receipt of materials needed to produce the jackets or a production delay because a piece of equipment needed a minor repair. An alternative is to set more-challenging standards that are more difficult to attain. As we discussed in Chapter 6, setting challenging standards can increase the motivation of employees and a firm's performance. However, as we have indicated, if workers believe the standards are unachievable, they can become frustrated and the firm's performance could suffer.

Decision Point

What is a standard cost and what are its purposes?

Price Variances and Efficiency Variances for Direct-Cost Inputs

Consider Color's two direct-cost categories. The actual cost for each of these categories for the 10,000 jackets manufactured and sold in April 2014 is:

Learning Objective 5

Compute price variances

. . . each price variance is the difference between an actual input price and a budgeted input price

and efficiency variances

. . . each efficiency variance is the difference between an actual input quantity and a budgeted input quantity for actual output

for direct-cost categories

Direct materials purchased and used[3]

1.	Square yards of cloth input purchased and used	22,200
2.	Actual price incurred per square yard	₹280
3.	Direct material costs (22,200 × ₹280) [shown in Exhibit 7-2, column 1]	₹62,16,000

Direct manufacturing labor

1.	Direct manufacturing labor-hours	9,000
2.	Actual price incurred per direct manufacturing labor-hour	₹220
3.	Direct manufacturing labor costs (9,000 × ₹220) [shown in Exhibit 7-2, column 1]	₹19,80,000

Let's use the Color Plus data to illustrate the price variance and the efficiency variance for direct-cost inputs.

A price variance is the difference between actual price and budgeted price multiplied by actual input quantity, such as direct materials purchased. A price variance is sometimes called a rate variance, especially when referring to a price variance for direct manufacturing labor. An efficiency variance is the difference between actual input quantity used—such as square yards of cloth and budgeted input quantity allowed for actual output, multiplied by budgeted price. An efficiency variance is sometimes called a usage variance. Let's explore price and efficiency variances in greater detail so we can see how managers use them.

Price Variances

The formula for computing the price variance is:

$$\text{Price variance} = \left(\begin{array}{c} \text{Actual price} \\ \text{of input} \end{array} - \begin{array}{c} \text{Budgeted price} \\ \text{of input} \end{array} \right) \times \begin{array}{c} \text{Actual quanity} \\ \text{of input} \end{array}$$

[3] The Problem for Self-Study later in this chapter relaxes the assumption that the quantity of direct materials used equals the quantity of direct materials purchased.

Price variances for Color Plus's two direct-cost categories are:

Direct-Cost Category	$\left(\begin{array}{cc}\text{Actual price} & \text{Budgeted price}\\ \text{of input} & \text{of input}\end{array}\right)$	×	Actual quantity of input	=	Price Variance
Direct materials	(₹280 per sq. yard – ₹300 per sq. yard)	×	22,200 square yards	=	₹4,44,000 F
Direct manufac- turing labor	(₹220 per hour – ₹200 per hour)	×	9,000 hours	=	₹1,80,000 U

The direct materials price variance is favorable because actual price of cloth is less than budgeted price, resulting in an increase in operating income. The direct manufacturing labor price variance is unfavorable because actual wage rate paid to labor is more than the budgeted rate, resulting in a decrease in operating income.

Managers should always consider a broad range of possible causes for a price variance. For example, Color Plus's favorable direct materials price variance could be due to one or more of the following:

- Color's purchasing manager negotiated the direct materials prices more skillfully than was planned for in the budget.
- The purchasing manager changed to a lower-price supplier.
- The purchasing manager ordered larger quantities than the quantities budgeted, thereby obtaining quantity discounts.
- Direct material prices decreased unexpectedly because of an oversupply of materials in the industry.
- The budgeted purchase prices of direct materials were set too high without careful analysis of market conditions.
- The purchasing manager received favorable prices because he was willing to accept unfavorable terms on factors other than prices (such as lower-quality material).

How Color Plus's managers respond to the direct materials price variance depends on what they believe caused it. For example, if they believe the purchasing manager received quantity discounts by ordering a larger amount of materials than budgeted, Color Plus could investigate whether the larger quantities resulted in higher storage costs for the firm. If the increase in storage and inventory holding costs exceeds the quantity discounts, purchasing in larger quantities is not beneficial. Some companies have reduced their materials storage areas to prevent their purchasing managers from ordering in larger quantities.

Efficiency Variance

For any actual level of output, the efficiency variance is the difference between actual quantity of input used and the budgeted quantity of input allowed to produce actual output, multiplied by budgeted price:

$$\text{Efficiency Variance} = \left(\begin{array}{cc}\text{Actual} & \text{Budgeted quantity}\\ \text{quantity of} - \text{of unput allowed}\\ \text{input used} & \text{for actual output}\end{array}\right) \times \begin{array}{c}\text{Budgeted price}\\ \text{of input}\end{array}$$

The idea here is that, given a certain output level, a company is inefficient if it uses a larger quantity of input than the budgeted. Conversely, the company is efficient if it uses a smaller quantity of inputs than was budgeted for that output level.

The efficiency variances for each of Color's direct-cost categories are:

Direct-Cost Category	Actual quantity of input used	−	Budgeted quantity of input allowed for actual output	×	Budgeted price of input	=	Efficiency Variance
Direct materials	[22,200 sq. yds. − (10,000 units × 2 sq. yds./unit)]				× ₹300 per sq. yard		
	= (22,200 sq. yds − 20,000 sq. yds.)				× ₹300 per sq. yard	=	₹6,60,000 U
Direct manufacturing	[9,000 hours − (10,000 units × 0.8 hour/unit)]				× ₹200 per hour		
labor	= (9,000 hours − 8,000 hours) × ₹200 per hour				× ₹200 per hour	=	2,00,000 U

The two manufacturing efficiency variances—direct materials efficiency variance and direct manufacturing labor efficiency variance—are each unfavorable, why? Because given the firm's actual output, more of these inputs were used than were budgeted for. This lowered Color Plus's operating income.

As with price variances, there is a broad range of possible causes for these efficiency variances. For example, Color Plus's unfavorable efficiency variance for direct manufacturing labor could be because of one or more of the following:

- Color Plus's workers took longer to make each jacket because they worked more slowly or made poor-quality jackets that required reworking

- Color's personnel manager hired underskilled workers.

- Color's production scheduler inefficiently scheduled work, resulting in more manufacturing labor time than budgeted being used per jacket.

- Color's maintenance department did not properly maintain machines, resulting in more manufacturing labor time than budgeted being used per jacket.

- Color Plus's budgeted time standards were too tight because the skill levels of employees and the environment in which they operated weren't accurately evaluated.

Suppose Color's managers determine that the unfavorable variance is due to poor machine maintenance. Color could then establish a team consisting of plant engineers and machine operators to develop a maintenance schedule to reduce future breakdowns and prevent adverse effects on labor time and product quality[4].

Exhibit 7-3 provides an alternative way to calculate price and efficiency variances. It shows how the price variance and the efficiency variance subdivide the flexible-budget variance. Consider direct materials. The direct materials flexible-budget variance of ₹2,16,000 U is the difference between actual costs incurred (actual input quantity × actual price) of ₹62,16,000 shown in column 1 and the flexible budget (budgeted input quantity allowed for actual output × budgeted price) of ₹60,00,000 shown in column 3. Column 2 (actual input quantity × budgeted price) is inserted between column 1 and column 3. The difference between columns 1 and 2 is the price variance of ₹4,44,000 F. This price variance occurs because the same actual input quantity (22,200 sq. yds.) is multiplied by *actual price* (₹280) in column 1 and *budgeted price* (₹300) in column 2. The difference between columns 2 and 3 is the efficiency variance of ₹6,60,000 U because the same budgeted price (₹300) is multiplied by *actual input quantity* (22,200 sq. yds) in column 2 and *budgeted*

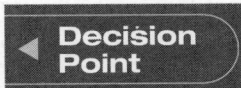

Decision Point

Why should a company calculate price and efficiency variances?

---

[4] When there are multiple inputs, such as different types of materials, that can be substituted for one another, the efficiency variance can be further decomposed into mix and yield variances.

input quantity allowed for actual output (20,000 sq. yds.) in column 3. The sum of the direct materials price variance, ₹4,44,000 F, and the direct materials efficiency variance, ₹6,60,000 U, equals the direct materials flexible budget variance, ₹2,16,000 U.

Exhibit 7-4 provides a summary of the different variances. Note how the variances at each higher level provide disaggregated and more detailed information for evaluating performance.

We now present Color Plus's journal entries under its standard costing system.

Journal Entries Using Standard Costs

Chapter 4 illustrated journal entries when normal costing is used. We will now illustrate journal entries for Color's Company using standard costs. Our focus is on direct materials and direct manufacturing labor. All the numbers included in the following journal entries are found in Exhibit 7-3.

Note: In each of the following entries, unfavorable variances are always debits (they decrease operating income), and favorable variances are always credits (they increase operating income).

JOURNAL ENTRY 1A

Isolate the direct materials price variance at the time the materials were purchased. This is done by increasing (debiting) Direct Materials Control account by the standard prices. This is the earliest time possible to isolate this variance.

Exhibit 7-3	Columnar Presentation of Variance Analysis: Direct Costs for Color Plus Company for April 2014[a]

Level 3 Analysis

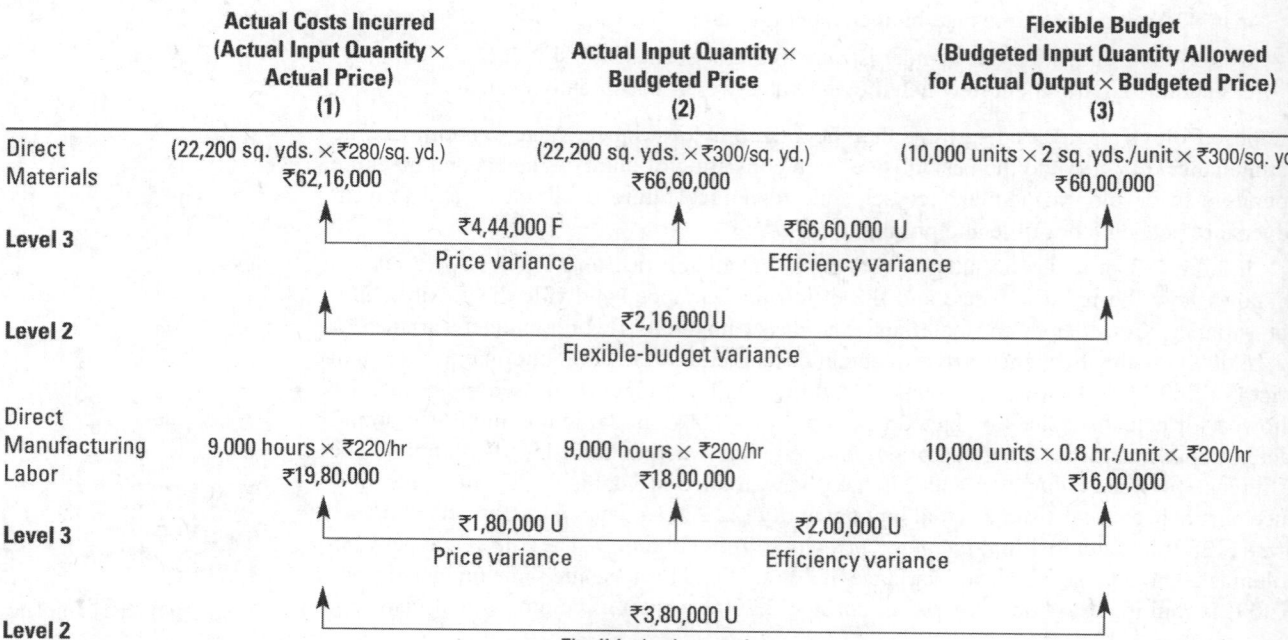

	Actual Costs Incurred (Actual Input Quantity × Actual Price) (1)	Actual Input Quantity × Budgeted Price (2)	Flexible Budget (Budgeted Input Quantity Allowed for Actual Output × Budgeted Price) (3)
Direct Materials	(22,200 sq. yds. × ₹280/sq. yd.) ₹62,16,000	(22,200 sq. yds. × ₹300/sq. yd.) ₹66,60,000	(10,000 units × 2 sq. yds./unit × ₹300/sq. yd.) ₹60,00,000
Level 3		₹4,44,000 F Price variance	₹66,60,000 U Efficiency variance
Level 2		₹2,16,000 U Flexible-budget variance	
Direct Manufacturing Labor	9,000 hours × ₹220/hr ₹19,80,000	9,000 hours × ₹200/hr ₹18,00,000	10,000 units × 0.8 hr./unit × ₹200/hr ₹16,00,000
Level 3		₹1,80,000 U Price variance	₹2,00,000 U Efficiency variance
Level 2		₹3,80,000 U Flexible-budget variance	

[a]F = favorable effect on operating income; U = unfavorable effect on operating income.

Exhibit 7-4 Summary of Levels 1, 2, and 3 Variance Analysis

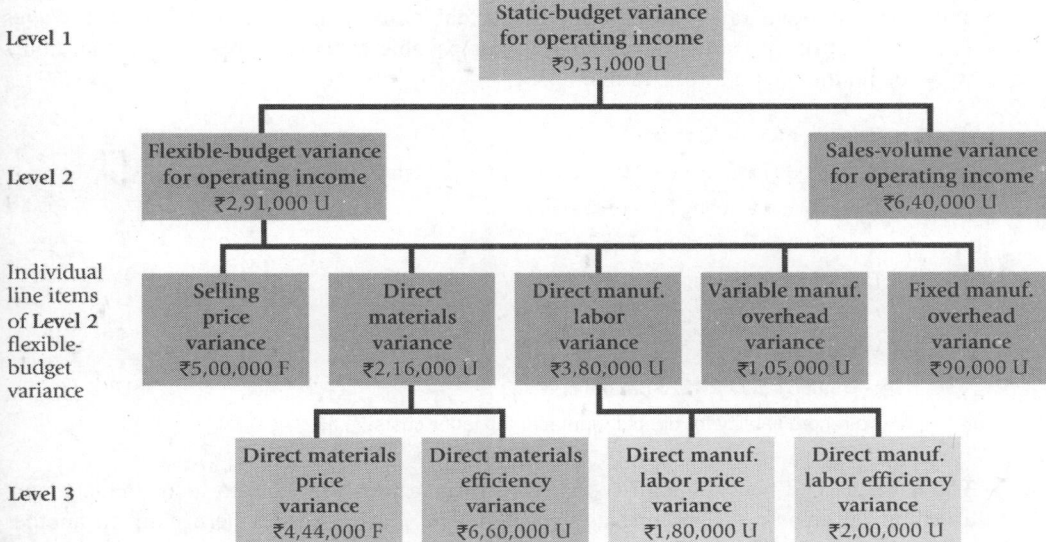

1a. Direct Materials Control

(22,200 square yards × ₹300 per square yard)	66,60,000	
Direct Materials Price Variance		
(22,200 square yards × ₹20 per square yard)		4,44,000
Accounts Payable Control		
(22,200 square yards × ₹280 per square yard)		62,16,000
To record direct materials purchased.		

JOURNAL ENTRY 1B

Isolate the direct materials efficiency variance at the time the direct materials are used by increasing (debiting) Work-in-Process Control account. Use the standard quantities allowed for actual output units manufactured times standard purchase prices.

1b. Work-in-Process Control

(10,000 jackets × 2 yards per jacket × ₹300 per square yard)	60,00,000	
Direct Materials Efficiency Variance		
(2,200 square yards × ₹300 per square yard)	6,60,000	
Direct Materials Control		
(22,200 square yards × ₹300 per square yard)		66,60,000
To record direct materials used.		

JOURNAL ENTRY 2

Isolate the direct manufacturing labor price variance and efficiency variance at the time this labor is used by increasing (debiting) Work-in-Process Control by the standard hours and standard wage rates allowed for the actual units manufactured. Note that Wages Payable Control measures the actual amounts payable to workers based on actual hours worked and their actual wage rates.

2.	Work-in-Process Control		
	(10,000 jackets × 0.80 hour per jacket × ₹200 per hour)	16,00,000	
	Direct Manufacturing Labor Price Variance		
	(9,000 hours × ₹20 per hour)	1,80,000	
	Direct Manufacturing Labor Efficiency Variance		
	(1,000 hours × ₹200 per hour)	2,00,000	
	Wages Payable Control		
	(9,000 hours × ₹220 per hour)		19,80,000
	To record liability for direct manufacturing labor costs.		

You have learned how standard costing and variance analysis help to focus management attention on areas not operating as expected. The journal entries here point to another advantage of standard costing systems—standard costs simplify product costing. As each unit is manufactured, costs are assigned to it using the standard cost of direct materials, the standard cost of direct manufacturing labor and, as you will see in Chapter 8, standard manufacturing overhead cost.

From the perspective of control, all variances should be isolated at the earliest possible time. For example, by isolating the direct materials price variance at the time materials are purchased, managers can take, corrective actions—such as trying to obtain cost reductions from the current supplier or obtaining price quotes from other potential suppliers—immediately when a large unfavorable variance is first known rather than waiting until after the materials are used in production.

If the variance accounts are immaterial in amount at the end of the fiscal year, they are written off to the cost of goods sold. For simplicity, we assume that the balances in the different direct cost variance accounts as of April 2014 are also the balances at the end of 2014 and therefore immaterial in total. Color Plus would record the following journal entry to write off the direct cost variance accounts to Cost of Goods Sold.

Cost of Goods Sold	5,96,000	
Direct Materials Price Variance	4,44,000	
Direct Materials Efficiency Variance		6,60,000
Direct Manufacturing Labor Price Variance		1,80,000
Direct Manufacturing Labor Efficiency Variance		2,00,000

Alternatively, assuming Color Plus has inventories at the end of the fiscal year, and the variances are material in their amounts, the variance accounts will be prorated between cost of goods sold and various inventory accounts using the methods described in Chapter 4. For example, Direct Materials Price Variance will be prorated among Materials Control, Work-in-Process Control, Finished Goods Control and Cost of Goods Sold on the basis of the standard costs of direct materials in each account's ending balance. Direct Materials Efficiency Variance is prorated among Work-in-Process Control, Finished Goods Control and Cost of Goods Sold on the basis of the direct material costs in each account's ending balance (after proration of the direct materials price variance).

As discussed in Chapter 4, many accountants, industrial engineers, and managers argue that to the extent variances measure inefficiency during the year, they should be written off against income for that period instead of being prorated among inventories and the cost of goods sold. These people believe it's better to apply a combination of the write-off and proration methods for each individual variance. That way, unlike full proration, the firm doesn't end up carrying the costs of inefficiency as part of its inventoriable costs. Consider the efficiency variance: The portion of the variance due to avoidable inefficiencies should be written off to cost of goods sold. In contrast, the portion that is unavoidable should be prorated. Likewise, if a portion of the direct materials price variance is unavoidable because it is entirely caused by general market conditions, it too should be prorated.

Implementing Standard Costing

Standard costing provides valuable information for the management and control of materials, labor, and other activities related to production.

Standard Costing and Information Technology

Both large and small firms are increasingly using computerized standard costing systems. Companies such as Sandoz (the manufacturer of generic pharmaceuticals) store standard prices and standard quantities in their computer systems. A bar code scanner records the receipt of materials, immediately costing each material using its stored standard price. The receipt of materials is then matched with the firm's purchase order and recorded in accounts payable and the direct materials price variance is isolated.

The direct materials efficiency variance is calculated as output is completed by comparing the standard quantity of direct materials that should have been used with the computerized request for direct materials submitted by an operator on the production floor. Labor variances are calculated as employees log into production-floor terminals and punch in their employee numbers, start and end times, and the quantity of product they helped produce. Managers use this instantaneous feedback from variances to immediately detect and correct any cost-related problem.

Wide Applicability of Standard Costing

Manufacturing firms as well as firms in the service sector find standard costing to be a useful tool. Companies implementing total quality management programs use standard costing to control materials costs. Service-sector companies such as McDonald's are labor intensive and use standard costs to control labor costs. Companies that have implemented computer-integrated manufacturing (CIM), such as Toyota, use flexible budgeting and standard costing to manage activities such as materials handling and setups. The growing use of Enterprise Resource Planning (ERP) systems, as described in Chapter 6, has made it easy for firms to keep track of the standard, average, and actual costs of items in inventory and to make real-time assessments of variances. Managers use variance information to identify areas of the firm's manufacturing or purchasing process that most need attention.

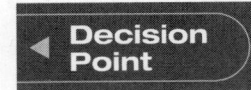

Decision Point

Why should a company calculate price and efficiency variances?

Management's Use of Variances

Managers and management accountants use variances to evaluate performance after decisions are implemented, to trigger organization learning, and to make continuous improvements. Variances serve as an early warning system to alert managers to existing problems

or to prospective opportunities. When done well, variance analysis enables managers to evaluate the effectiveness of the actions and performance of personnel in the current period, as well as to fine-tune strategies for achieving improved performance in the future.

Multiple Causes of Variances

To interpret variances correctly and make appropriate decisions based on them, managers need to recognize that variances can have multiple causes. Managers must not interpret variances in isolation of each other. The causes of variances in one part of the value chain can be the result of decisions made in another part of the value chain. Consider an unfavorable direct materials efficiency variance on Color's production line. Possible operational causes of this variance across the value chain of the company are:

1. Poor design of products or processes
2. Poor work on the production line because of underskilled workers or faulty machines
3. Inappropriate assignment of labor or machines to specific jobs
4. Congestion due to scheduling a large number of rush orders placed by Color's sales representatives
5. Color's cloth suppliers not manufacturing materials of uniformly high quality

Item 5 offers an even broader reason for the cause of the unfavorable direct materials efficiency variance by considering inefficiencies in the supply chain of companies—in this case, by the cloth suppliers for Color's jackets. Whenever possible, managers must attempt to understand the root causes of the variances.

When to Investigate Variances

Because a standard is not a single measure but rather a range of possible acceptable input quantities, costs, output quantities, or prices, managers should expect small variances to arise. A variance within an acceptable range is considered to be an "in control occurrence" and calls for no investigation or action by managers. So when would managers need to investigate variances?

Frequently, managers investigate variances based on subjective judgments or rules of thumb. For critical items, such as product defects, even a small variance may prompt investigations. For other items, such as direct material costs, labor costs, and repair costs, companies generally have rules such as "investigate all variances exceeding ₹50,000 or 25% of budgeted cost, whichever is lower." The idea is that a 4% variance in direct material costs of ₹1,00,00,000—a ₹4,00,000 variance—deserves more attention than a 20% variance in repair costs of ₹1,00,000—a ₹20,000 variance. In other words, variance analysis is subject to the same cost-benefit test as all other phases of a management control system.

Using Variances for Performance Measurement

Managers often use variance analysis when evaluating the performance of their subordinates. Two attributes of performance are commonly evaluated:

1. Effectiveness: the degree to which a predetermined objective or target is met—such as the sales, market share, and customer satisfaction, ratings of Nokia's new line of cell phones.
2. Efficiency: the relative amount of inputs used to achieve a given output level. For example, the smaller the quantity of Arabica beans used to make a given number of VIA packets or the greater the number of VIA packets made from a given quantity of beans, the greater the efficiency.

As we discussed earlier, it is important to understand the causes of a variance before using it for performance evaluation. Suppose a purchasing manager for Starbucks has just negotiated a deal that results in a favorable price variance for direct materials. The deal could have achieved a favorable variance for any or all of the following reasons:

1. The purchasing manager bargained effectively with suppliers.

2. The purchasing manager secured a discount for buying in bulk with fewer purchase orders. (However, buying larger quantities than necessary for the short run resulted in excessive inventory.)

3. The purchasing manager accepted a bid from the lowest-priced supplier without fully checking the supplier's quality-monitoring procedures.

If the purchasing manager's performance is evaluated solely on price variances, then the evaluation will be positive. Reason 1 would support this conclusion: The purchasing manager bargained effectively. Reasons 2 and 3, buying in bulk or buying without checking the supplier's quality-monitoring procedures, will lead to short-run gains. But should these lead to a positive evaluation for the purchasing manager? Not necessarily. These short-run gains could be offset by higher inventory storage costs or higher inspection costs and defect rates. Starbucks may ultimately lose more money because of reasons 2 and 3 than it gains from the favorable price variance.

Bottom line: Managers should not automatically interpret a favorable variance as "good news" or assume it means their subordinates performed well.

Firms benefit from variance analysis because it highlights individual aspects of performance. However, if any single performance measure (for example, achieving a certain labor efficiency variance or a certain consumer rating) is overemphasized, managers will tend to make decisions that will cause the particular performance measure to look good. These actions may conflict with the company's overall goals, inhibiting the goals from being achieved. This faulty perspective on performance usually arises when top management designs a performance evaluation and reward system that does not emphasize total company objectives.

Organization Learning

The goal of variance analysis is for managers to understand why variances arise, to learn, and to improve future performance. For instance, to reduce the unfavorable direct materials efficiency variance, Color's managers may attempt to improve the design of its jackets, the commitment of workers to do the job right the first time, and the quality of materials. Sometimes an unfavorable direct materials efficiency variance may signal a need to change product strategy, perhaps because the product cannot be made at a low enough cost. Variance analysis should not be used to "play the blame game" (find some one to blame for every unfavorable variance). but to help managers learn about what happened and how to perform better in the future.

Companies need to strike a delicate balance between using variances to evaluate the performance of managers and employees and improve learning within the organization. If the performance evaluation aspect is overemphasized, managers will focus on setting and meeting targets that are easy to attain rather than targets that are challenging, require creativity and resourcefulness, and result in continuous improvement. For example, Color Plus's manufacturing manager will prefer an easy standard that allows workers ample time to manufacture a jacket. But that will provide the manufacturing department little incentive to improve processes and identify methods to reduce production times and costs. Alternatively, the manufacturing manager might urge workers to produce jackets within the time allowed, even if this leads to poorer quality jackets being produced, which would later hurt revenues. If variance analysis is seen as a way to promote learning within the organization, negative effects such as these can be minimized.

˙Continuous Improvement

Managers can also use variance analysis to create a virtuous cycle of continuous improvement. How? By repeatedly identifying the causes of variances, taking corrective actions, and evaluating the results. Improvement opportunities are often easier to identify when the company first produces a product. Once managers identify easy improvements, much more ingenuity may be required to identify successive ones. Some companies use kaizen budgeting (Chapter 6) to specifically target reductions in budgeted costs over successive periods. The advantage of kaizen budgeting is that it makes continuous improvement goals explicit.

Financial and Nonfinancial Performance Measures

Almost all companies use a combination of financial and nonfinancial performance measures for planning and control rather than relying exclusively on either type of measure. To control a production process, supervisors cannot wait for an accounting report with variances reported in rupees. Instead, timely nonfinancial performance measures are frequently used for control purposes. For example, Nissan and many other manufacturers display real-time defect rates and production levels on large LED screens throughout their plants for workers and managers to see.

In Color's cutting room, cloth is laid out and cut into pieces, which are then matched and assembled. Managers exercise control in the cutting room by observing workers and by focusing on *nonfinancial measures*, such as number of square yards of cloth used to produce 1,000 jackets or percentage of jackets started and completed without requiring any rework. Color Plus production workers find these nonfinancial measures easy to understand. Color Plus managers also use *financial measures* to evaluate the overall cost efficiency with which operations are being run and to help guide decisions about, say, changing the mix of inputs used in manufacturing jackets. Financial measures are often critical in a company because they indicate the economic impact of diverse physical activities. This knowledge allows managers to make trade-offs such as increasing the costs of one physical activity (say, cutting) to reduce the costs of another physical measure (say, defects).

Decision Point

How do managers use variances?

Benchmarking and Variance Analysis

Color Plus Company based its budgeted amounts on analysis of its own operations. We now turn to the situation in which companies develop standards based on an analysis of operations at other companies. **Benchmarking** is the continuous process of comparing the levels of performance in producing products and services and executing activities against the best levels of performance in competing companies or in companies having similar processes. When benchmarks are used as standards, managers and management accountants know that the company will be competitive in the marketplace if it can meet or beat those standards.

Companies develop benchmarks and calculate variances on items that are the most important to their businesses. A common unit of measurement used to compare the efficiency of airlines is cost per available seat mile. Available seat mile (ASM) is a measure of airline size and equals the total seats in a plane multiplied by the distance the plane traveled. Consider the cost per available seat mile for United. Assume United uses data from each of six competing U.S. airlines in its benchmark cost comparisons. Summary data are in Exhibit 7-5. The benchmark companies are in alphabetical order in column A. Also

Learning Objective 7

Describe benchmarking and explain its role in cost management

. . . benchmarking compares actual performance against the best levels of performance

Exhibit 7-5   Available Seat Mile (ASM) Benchmark Comparison of United Airlines with Six Other Airlines

	A	B	C	D	E	F	G
1		Operating Cost (Cents per ASM)	Operating Revenue (Cents per ASM)	Operating Income (Cents per ASM)	Fuel Cost (Cents per ASM)	Labor Cost (Cents per ASM)	Total ASMs (Millions)
2							
3	Airline	(1)	(2)	(3) = (2) – (1)	(4)	(5)	(6)
4							
5	United Airlines	14.19	13.10	- 1.09	4.90	4.24	2,16,299
6	Airlines used as benchmarks:						
7	Alaska Airlines	11.90	13.09	1.19	4.10	3.53	28,185
8	American Airlines	14.26	13.47	-0.79	4.90	4.28	1,52,627
9	Delta Airlines	13.80	14.48	0.68	5.00	3.86	2,00,880
10	JetBlue Airways	11.42	11.96	0.54	4.40	2.76	40,095
11	Southwest Airlines	12.83	13.29	0.46	4.60	3.90	1,28,272
12	U.S. Airways	13.25	13.49	0.24	4.60	3.54	74,204
13	Average of airlines						
14	used as benchmarks	12.91	13.30	0.39	4.60	3.65	1,04,044
15							
16	Source: 2012 data from the MIT Global Airline Industry Program						

reported in Exhibit 7-5 are operating cost per ASM, operating revenue per ASM, operating income per ASM, fuel cost per ASM, labor cost per ASM, and total available seat miles for each airline. The slow recovery of the travel industry from the recession induced by the financial crisis is evident in the fact that only five of the seven airlines have positive levels of operating income.

How well did United manage its costs? The answer depends on which specific benchmark is being used for comparison. United's actual operating cost of 14.19 cents per ASM is above the average operating cost of 12.91 cents per ASM of the six other airlines. Moreover, United's operating cost per ASM is 24.2% higher than JetBlue Airways, the lowest-cost competitor at 11.42 cents per ASM [(14.19 – 11.42) ÷ 11.42 = 0.242]. So why is United's operating cost per ASM so high? Columns E and F suggest that both fuel cost and labor cost are possible reasons. These benchmarking data alert management at United that it needs to become more efficient in its use of both material and labor inputs to become more cost competitive.

It can be difficult for firms to find appropriate benchmarks such as those in Exhibit 7-5. Many companies purchase benchmark data from consulting firms. Another problem is ensuring the benchmark numbers are comparable. In other words, there needs to be an "apples to apples" comparison. Differences can exist across companies in their strategies, inventory costing methods, depreciation methods, and so on. For example, JetBlue serves fewer cities and flies mostly long-haul routes compared with United, which serves almost all major U.S. cities and several international cities and flies both long-haul and short-haul routes. Southwest Airlines differs from United because it specializes in short-haul direct flights and offers fewer services on board its planes. Because United's strategy is different from the strategies of JetBlue and Southwest, one might expect its cost per ASM to be different, too. United's strategy is more comparable to the strategies of American, Delta, and U.S. Airways. Note that its costs per ASM are relatively more competitive with these airlines. But United competes head to head with JetBlue and Southwest in several cities and markets, so it still needs to benchmark against these carriers as well.

United's management accountants can use benchmarking data to address several questions. How do factors such as plane size and type or the duration of flights affect the cost per ASM? Do airlines differ in their fixed cost/variable cost structures? To what extent can United's performance be improved by rerouting flights, using different types of aircraft on different routes, or changing the frequency or timing of specific flights? What explains revenue differences per ASM across airlines? Is it differences in the service quality passengers perceive or differences in an airline's competitive power at specific airports? Management accountants are more valuable to managers when they use benchmarking data to provide insight into *why* costs or revenues differ across companies or within plants of the same company, as distinguished from simply reporting the magnitude of the differences.

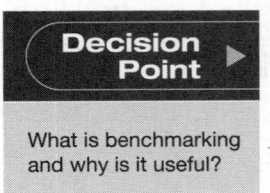

Decision Point ▶

What is benchmarking and why is it useful?

Problem for Self-Study

Somani Pilkingston Company manufactures ceramic vases. It uses its standard costing system when developing its flexible-budget amounts. In April 2014, 2,000 finished units were produced. The following information relates to its two direct manufacturing cost categories: direct materials and direct manufacturing labor.

Direct materials used were 4,400 kilograms (kg). The standard direct materials input allowed for one output unit is 2 kilograms at ₹150 per kilogram. Somani purchased 5,000¾ kilograms of materials at ₹165.0 per kilogram, a total of ₹8,25,000. (This Problem for Self-Study illustrates how to calculate direct materials variances when the quantity of materials *purchased* in a period differs from the quantity of materials *used* in that period.)

Actual direct manufacturing labor-hours were 3,250, at a total cost of ₹6,63,000. Standard manufacturing labor time allowed is 1.5 hours per output unit, and the standard direct manufacturing labor cost is ₹200 per hour.

Required

1. Calculate the direct materials price variance and efficiency variance, and the direct manufacturing labor price variance and efficiency variance. Base the direct materials price variance on a flexible budget for actual quantity purchased, but base the direct materials efficiency variance on a flexible budget for actual quantity used.

2. Prepare journal entries for a standard costing system that isolates variances at the earliest possible time.

Solution

1. Exhibit 7-6 shows how the columnar presentation of variances introduced in Exhibit 7-3 can be adjusted for the difference in timing between purchase and use of materials. Note, in particular, the two sets of computations in column 2 for direct materials—the ₹7,50,000 for direct materials purchased and the ₹6,60,000 for direct materials used. The direct materials price variance is calculated on purchases so that managers responsible for the purchase can immediately identify and isolate reasons for the variance and initiate any desired corrective action. The efficiency variance is the responsibility of the production manager, so this variance is identified only at the time materials are used.

2.
Materials Control (5,000 kg × ₹150 per kg)	7,50,000
Direct Materials Price Variance (5,000 kg × ₹15 per kg)	75,000

Accounts Payable Control (5,000 kg × ₹165 per kg)	
Work in Process Control (2,000 units × 2 kg per uni × ₹150 per kg)	6,00,000
Direct Materials Efficiency Variance (400 kg × ₹150 per kg)	60,000
Materials Control (4,400 kg × ₹150 per kg)	
Work in Process Control (2,000 units × 1.5 hours per unit × ₹200 per hour)	6,00,000
Direct Manufacturing Labor Price Variance (3,250 hours × ₹4 per hour)	13,000
Direct Manufacturing Labor Efficiency Variance (250 hours × ₹200 per hour)	50,000
Wages Payable Control (3,250 hours × ₹204 per hour)	

Note: All the variances are debits because they are unfavorable and thereforeduce operating income.

Exhibit 7-6   Columnar Presentation of Variance Analysis for Somani Pilkingston Company: Direct Materials and Direct Manufacturing Labor for April 2014[a]

Level 3 Analysis

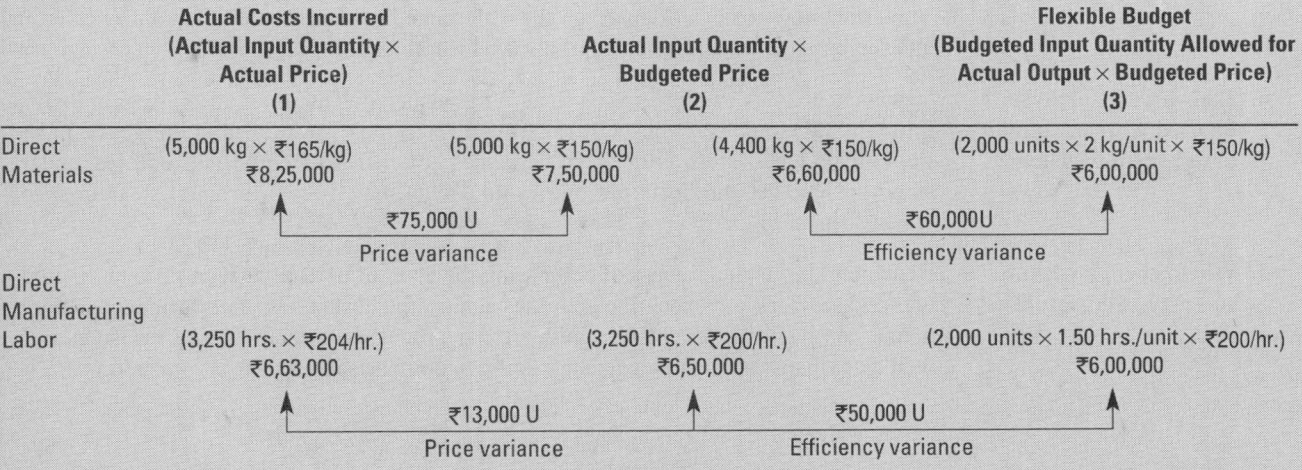

	Actual Costs Incurred (Actual Input Quantity × Actual Price) (1)	Actual Input Quantity × Budgeted Price (2)	Flexible Budget (Budgeted Input Quantity Allowed for Actual Output × Budgeted Price) (3)
Direct Materials	(5,000 kg × ₹165/kg) ₹8,25,000 (5,000 kg × ₹150/kg) ₹7,50,000	(4,400 kg × ₹150/kg) ₹6,60,000	(2,000 units × 2 kg/unit × ₹150/kg) ₹6,00,000
	₹75,000 U — Price variance	₹60,000U — Efficiency variance	
Direct Manufacturing Labor	(3,250 hrs. × ₹204/hr.) ₹6,63,000	(3,250 hrs. × ₹200/hr.) ₹6,50,000	(2,000 units × 1.50 hrs./unit × ₹200/hr.) ₹6,00,000
	₹13,000 U — Price variance	₹50,000 U — Efficiency variance	

[a]F = favorable effect on operating income; U = unfavorable effect on operating income.

Decision Points

The following question-and-answer format summarizes the chapter's learning objectives. Each decision presents a key question related to a learning objective. The guidelines are the answer to that question.

Decision

1. What are static budgets and static-budget variances?

Guidelines

A static budget is based on the level of output planned at the start of the budget period. The static-budget variance is the difference between the actual result and the corresponding budgeted amount in the static budget.

2. How can managers develop a flexible budget, and why is it useful to do so?

A flexible budget is adjusted (flexed) to recognize the actual output level of the budget period. Managers use a three-step procedure to develop a flexible budget. When all costs are either variable or fixed with respect to output, these three steps require only information about the budgeted selling price, budgeted variable cost per output unit, budgeted fixed costs, and actual quantity of output units. Flexible budgets help managers gain more insight into the causes of variances than is available from static budgets.

3. How are flexible-budget and sales-volume variances calculated?

The static-budget variance can be subdivided into a flexible-budget variance (the difference between the actual result and the corresponding flexible-budget amount) and a sales-volume variance (the difference between the flexible-budget amount and the corresponding static-budget amount).

4. What is a standard cost and what are its purposes?

A standard cost is a carefully determined cost used as a benchmark for judging performance. The purposes of a standard cost are to exclude past inefficiencies and to take into account changes expected to occur in the budget period.

5. Why should a company calculate price and efficiency variables?

The computation of price and efficiency variances helps managers gain insight into two different—but not independent—aspects of performance. The price variance focuses on the difference between the actual input price and the budgeted input price. The efficiency variance focuses on the difference between the actual quantity of input and the budgeted quantity of input allowed for actual output.

6. Can variance analysis be used with an activity-based costing system?

Variance analysis can be applied to activity costs (such as setup costs) to gain insight into why actual activity costs differ from activity costs in the static budget or in the flexible budget. Interpreting cost variances for different activities requires understanding whether the costs are output unit-level, batch-level, product-sustaining, or facility-sustaining costs.

7. What is benchmarking and why is it useful?

Benchmarking is the process of comparing the level of performance in producing products and services and executing activities against the best levels of performance in competing companies or companies with similar processes. Benchmarking measures how well a company and its managers are doing in comparison to other organizations.

TERMS TO LEARN

This chapter and the Glossary at the end of the book contain definitions of:

ASSIGNMENT MATERIAL

Questions

7-1 What is the relationship between management by exception and variance analysis?

7-2 What are two possible sources of information a company might use to compute the budgeted amount in variance analysis?

7-3 Distinguish between a favorable variance and an unfavorable variance.

7-4 What is the key difference between a static budget and a flexible budget?

7-5 Why might managers find a flexible-budget analysis more informative than a static-budget analysis?

7-6 Describe the steps in developing a flexible budget.

7-7 List four reasons for using standard costs.

7-8 How might a manager gain insight into the causes of a flexible-budget variance for direct materials?

7-9 List three causes of a favorable direct materials price variance.

7-10 Describe three reasons for an unfavorable direct manufacturing labor efficiency variance.

7-11 How does variance analysis help in continuous improvement?

7-12 Why might an analyst examining variances in the production area look beyond that business function for explanations of those variances?

7-13 Comment on the following statement made by a plant manager: "Meetings with my plant accountant are frustrating. All he wants to do is pin the blame on someone for the many variances he reports."

7-14 How can variances be used to analyze costs in individual activity areas?

7-15 "Benchmarking against other companies enables a company to identify the lowest-cost producer. This amount should become the performance measure for next year." Do you agree?

Solved Examples

7-16 Flexible budget. Bridgestone Limited manufactures tires. For August 2016, it budgeted to manufacture and sell 3,000 tires at a variable cost of ₹740 per tire and total fixed costs for ₹5,40,000. The budgeted selling price was ₹1,100 per tire. Actual results in August 2016 were 2,800 tires manufactured and sold at a selling price of ₹1,120 per tire. The actual total variable costs were ₹22,96,000, and the actual total fixed costs were ₹5,00,000.

Required

1. Prepare a performance report that uses a flexible budget and a static budget.
2. Comment on the results in requirement 1.

Solution

2. The total static-budget variance in operating income is ₹2,00,000 U. There is both an unfavorable total flexible-budget variance (₹1,28,000) and an unfavorable sales-volume variance (₹72,000).

The unfavorable sales-volume variance arises solely because actual units manufactured and sold were 200 less than the budgeted 3,000 units. The unfavorable flexible-budget variance of ₹1,28,000 in operating income is due primarily to the v80 increase in unit variable costs. This increase in unit variable costs is only partially offset by the ₹20 increase in unit selling price and ₹40,000 decrease in fixed costs.

1. Flexible budget.

	Actual Results (1)	Flexible-Budget Variances (2) = (1) — (3)	Flexible Budget (3)	Sales-Volume Variances (4) = (3) — (5)	Static Budget (5)
Units sold	2,800[G]	0	2,800	200 U	3,000[G]
Revenues	₹31,36,000[a]	₹56,000 F	₹30,80,000[b]	₹2,20,000 U	₹33,00,000[c]
Variable costs	22,96,000[d]	2,24,000 U	20,72,000[e]	1,48,000 F	22,20,000[f]
Contribution margin	8,40,000	1,68,000 U	10,08,000	72,000 U	10,80,000
Fixed costs	5,00,000[G]	40,000 F	5,40,000[G]	0	5,40,000[G]
Operating income	₹3,40,000	₹1,28,000 U	₹4,68,000	₹72,000 U	₹5,40,000

₹1,28,000 U   ₹72,000 U

Total flexible-   Total sales-
budget variance   volume variance

₹20,0000 U
Total static-budget variance

[a]₹1,120 × 2,800 = ₹31,36,000
[b]₹1,100 × 2,800 = ₹30,80,000
[c]₹1,100 × 3,000 = ₹33,00,000
[d]Given. Unit variable cost = ₹22,96,000 ÷ 2,800 = ₹820 per tire
[e]₹740 × 2,800 = ₹20,72,000
[f]₹740 × 3,000 = ₹22,20,000
[G]Given

7-17 Flexible budget, working backward. Eicher Motors produces engine parts for car manufacturers. A new accountant intern at Eicher has accidentally deleted the calculations on the company's variance analysis calculations for the year ended December 31, 2015. The following table is what remains of the data.

	Home	Insert	Page Layout	Formulas	Data	Review	View

	A	B	C	D	E	F
1	Performance Report, Year Ended December 31, 2015					
2						
3		Actual Results	Flexible-Budget Variances	Flexible Budget	Sales-Volume Variances	Static Budget
4	Units sold	1,30,000				1,20,000
5	Revenues (sales)	₹7,15,000				₹4,20,000
6	Variable costs	5,15,000				2,40,000
7	Contribution margin	2,00,000				1,80,000
8	Fixed costs	1,40,000				1,20,000
9	Operating income	₹ 60,000				₹60,000

Required

1. Calculate all the required variances. (If your work is accurate, you will find that the total static-budget variance is ₹0.)

2. What are the actual and budgeted selling prices? What are the actual and budgeted variable costs per unit?

3 Review the variances you have calculated and discuss possible causes and potential problems. What is the important lesson learned here?

Solution

1. Variance Analysis for Eicher Motors for the year ended December 31, 2015

	Actual Results (1)	Flexible-Budget Variances (2) = (1) – (3)	Flexible Budget (3)	Sales-Volume Variances (4) = (3) – (5)	Static Budget (5)
Units sold	1,30,000	0	1,30,000	10,000 F	1,20,000
Revenues	₹7,15,000	₹2,60,000 F	₹4,55,000[a]	₹35,000 F	₹4,20,000
Variable costs	5,15,000	2,55,000 U	2,60,000[b]	20,000 U	2,40,000
Contribution margin	2,00,000	5,000 F	1,95,000	15,000 F	1,80,000
Fixed costs	1,40,000	20,000 U	1,20,000	0	1,20,000
Operating income	₹60,000	₹15,000 U	₹75,000	₹15,000 F	₹60,000

₹15,000 U

Total flexible-budget variance

₹15,000 F

Total sales volume variance

₹0

Total static-budget variance

[a] 1,30,000 × ₹3.50 = ₹4,55,000; ₹4,20,000 ÷ 1,20,000 = ₹3.50

[b] 1,30,000 × ₹2.00 = ₹2,60,000; ₹2,40,000 ÷ 1,20,000 = ₹2.00

2. Actual selling price: ₹7,15,000 ÷ 1,30,000 = ₹5.50
   Budgeted selling price: 4,20,000 ÷ 1,20,000 = ₹3.50
   Actual variable cost per unit: 5,15,000 ÷ 1,30,000 = ₹3.96
   Budgeted variable cost per unit: 2,40,000 ÷ 1,20,000 = ₹2.00

3. A zero total static-budget variance may be due to offsetting total flexible-budget and total sales-volume variances. In this case, these two variances exactly offset each other:

   Total flexible-budget variance   ₹15,000 Unfavorable
   Total sales-volume variance   ₹15,000 Favorable

A closer look at the variance components reveals some major deviations from plan. Actual variable costs increased from ₹2.00 to ₹3.96, causing an unfavorable flexible-budget variable cost variance of ₹2,55,000. Such an increase could be a result of, for example, a jump in direct material prices. Eicher was able to pass most of the increase in costs onto their customers—actual selling price increased by 57% [(₹5.50 – ₹3.50) ÷ ₹3.50], bringing about an offsetting favorable flexible-budget revenue variance in the amount of ₹2,60,000. An increase in the actual number of units sold also contributed to more favorable results. The company should examine why the units sold increased despite an increase in direct material prices. For example, Eicher's customers may have stocked up, anticipating future increases in direct material prices. Alternatively, Eicher's selling price increases may have been lower than competitors' price increases. Understanding the reasons why actual results differ from budgeted amounts can help Eicher better manage its costs and pricing decisions in the future. The important lesson learned here is that a superficial examination of summary level data (Levels 0 and 1) may be insufficient. It is imperative to scrutinize data at a more detailed level (Level 2). Had Eicher not been able to pass costs on to customers, losses would have been considerable.

7-18 Flexible budget and sales volume variances, market-share and market-size variances. Marico Ltd., produces the basic fillings used in many popular frozen desserts and treats— vanilla and chocolate ice creams, puddings, meringues, and fudge. Marico uses standard costing and carries over no inventory from one month to the next. The ice-cream product group's results for June 2016 were as follows:

	A	B	C
1	**Performance Report, June 2016**		
2		**Actual Results**	**Static Budget**
3	Units (Kgs)	33,500	33,500
4	Revenues	₹20,12,500	₹19,76,500
5	Variable manufacturing costs	11,37,500	10,38,500
6	Contribution margin	₹8,75,000	₹9,38,000

(Excel ribbon tabs: Home, Insert, Page Layout, Formulas, Data)

Shyam, the business manager for ice-cream products, is pleased that more kgs of ice cream were sold than budgeted and that revenues were up. Unfortunately, variable manufacturing costs went up, too. The bottom line is that contribution margin declined by ₹63,000, which is less than 3% of the budgeted revenues of ₹19,76,500. Overall, Shyam feels that the business is running fine.

Required

1. Calculate the static-budget variance in units, revenues, variable manufacturing costs, and contribution margin. What percentage is each static-budget variance relative to its static-budget amount?

2. Break down each static-budget variance into a flexible-budget variance and a sales-volume variance.

3. Calculate the selling-price variance.

4. Assume the role of management accountant at Marico. How would you present the results to Shyam? Should he be more concerned? If so, why?

Solution

1. and 2.

Performance Report for Marico Ltd., June 2016

	Actual (1)	Flexible Budget Variances (2) = (1) − (3)	Flexible Budget (3)	Sales Volume Variances (4) = (3) − (5)	Static Budget (5)	Static Budget Variance (6) = (1) − (5)	Static Budget Variance as % of Static Budget (7) = (6) ÷ (5)
Units (Kgs)	35,000	−	33,500	1,500 F	33,500	1,500 F	4.48%
Revenues	₹20,12,500	₹52,500 U	₹20,65,000[a]	₹88,500 F	₹19,76,500	₹36,000 F	1.82%
Variable mfg. costs	11,37,500	52,500 U	10,85,000[b]	46,500 U	10,38,500	99,000 U	9.53%
Contribution margin	₹8,75,000	₹1,05,000 U	₹9,80,000	₹42,000 F	₹9,38,000	₹63,000 U	6.72%

₹1,05,000 U — Flexible-budget variance ↑

₹42,000 F — Sales-volume variance ↑

₹63,000 U — Static-budget variance

[a] Budgeted selling price = ₹19,76,500 ÷ 33,500 Kgs = ₹59 per Kg.
Flexible-budget revenues = ₹59 per Kg. × 35,000 Kgs. = ₹20,65,000

[b] Budgeted variable mfg. cost per unit = ₹10,38,500 ÷ 33,500 Kgs. = ₹31
Flexible-budget variable mfg. costs = ₹31 per Kg. × 35,000 Kgs. = ₹10,85,000

3. The selling price variance, caused solely by the difference in actual and budgeted selling price, is the flexible-budget variance in revenues = ₹52,500 U.

4. The flexible-budget variances show that for the actual sales volume of 35,000 Kgs selling prices were lower and costs per Kg were higher. The favorable sales volume variance in revenues (because more Kgs of ice cream were sold than budgeted) helped offset the unfavorable variable cost variance and shored up the results in June 2016. Shyam should be more concerned because the static-budget variance in contribution margin of ₹63,000 U is actually made up of a favorable sales-volume variance in contribution margin of ₹42,000, an unfavorable selling-price variance of ₹52,500 and an unfavorable variable manufacturing costs variance of ₹52,500. Shyam should analyze why each of these variances occurred and the relationships among them. Could the efficiency of variable manufacturing costs be improved? The sales volume appears to have increased due to the lower average selling price per Kilogram.

7-19 Price and efficiency variances. Bikaner Foods makes milk cake. For January it budgeted to purchase and use 15,000 kg of milk at ₹17.80 a kg. Actual purchase and usage for January was 16,000 kg at ₹16.40 a kg. It budgets for 3,750 kg milk cake. Actual output was 3,800 kg milk cake. Ignore, other ingredients inputs used to make milk-cake.

Required

1. Compute the 1 flexible-budged variance and (2) price and efficiency variances.
2. Comment on the results in requirements 1 and 2.

Solution

Price and efficiency variances.

1. The key information items are:

	Actual	Budgeted
Output units (scones)	3,800	3,750
Input units (kg of pumpkin)	16,000	15,000
Cost per input unit	₹16.40	₹17.80

Bikaner budgets to obtain one-four kg of milk-cake from each kg of milk used.

2. The favorable flexible-budget variance of ₹8,160 has two offsetting components:
   (a) favorable price variance of ₹22,400—reflects the ₹16.40 actual purchase cost being lower than the ₹17.80 budgeted purchase cost per kg.
   (b) unfavorable efficiency variance of ₹14,240—reflects the actual materials yield of 0.2375 per kg of milk (3,800 ÷ 16,000 = 0.2375) being less than the budgeted yield of 0.25 (3,750 ÷ 15,000 = 0.25). (The company used more milk to make the milk-cake than was budgeted.)

One explanation may be that Bikaner Foods purchased lower quality milk at a lower cost per kg.

7-20 Price and efficiency variances. Idea is a cellular phone service reseller. Idea contracts with major cellular operators for airtime in bulk and then resells service to retail customers. Idea budgeted to sell, 78,00,000 minutes in the month ended March 31, 2016. Actual minutes sold totaled only 75,00,000. Due to fluctuations in hourly usage, Idea "overbuys" airtime from cellular operators. Idea plans to buy 10% more airtime than it plans to sell. For example, Idea's budgets called for the purchase of 85,80,000 minutes, based on the plan to sell 78,00,000 minutes. In what follows, think of purchased airtime as direct materials.

Idea budgets purchased airtime to cost 45 paise per minute. Actual purchased airtime in 2016 averaged 50 paise per minute. Idea incurs direct labor costs due to the employment of technicians. One hour of technical support is required for every 5,000 minutes of airtime sold. In practice, only 1,600 hours of technical support were used. Technical support was planned at ₹600 per hour. Actual technical support costs averaged ₹620 per hour.

Required

1. Calculate the flexible-budget variance for direct materials and direct labor costs. (Use 82,50,000 (75,00,000 × 1.10) minutes in the flexible budget).
2. Calculate the price and efficiency variances for direct materials and labor costs.

Solution

Flexible budget variance.

1.

	Actual Results (1)	Flexible-Budget Variances (2) = (1) – (3)	Flexible-Budget (3)
Direct materials	₹42,90,000	₹5,77,500 U	₹37,12,500[a]
Direct labor	9,92,000	92,000 U	9,00,000[c]

Actual Results

Direct materials: 85,80,000[b] minutes × ₹0.50 per minute = ₹42,90,000
Direct labor: 1,600 hours × ₹620 per hour = ₹9,92,000

[a]75,00,000 minutes sold × 110% purchase × ₹0.45 = ₹37,12,500
[b]78,00,000 minutes × 110% purchase = 85,80,000
[c]75,00,000 minutes sold × 5,000 minutes per hour = 1,500 hours × ₹600 = ₹9,00,000

Idea commits to purchase 110% of the budgeted amount of time. Due to the forward commitment of time purchase, the actual time purchased will be the same as the budgeted amount of time to be purchased.

7-21 Direct materials and direct manufacturing labor variances. Raymond, designs and manufactures T-shirts. It sells its T-shirts to brand-name clothes retailers in lots of one dozen. Raymond's May 2014 static budget and actual results for direct inputs are as follows:

Static Budget	
Number of T-shirt lots (1 lot = 1 dozen)	400

Per Lot of T-shirts:	
Direct materials	14 meters at ₹17 per meter = ₹238
Direct manufacturing labor	1.6 hours at ₹81 per hour = ₹129.6

Actual Results	
Number of T-shirt lots sold	450

Total direct Inputs	
Direct materials	6,840 meters at ₹19.50 per meter = ₹1,33,380
Direct manufacturing labor	675 hours at ₹82 per hour = ₹55,350

Raymond has a policy of analyzing all input variances when they add up to more than 10% of the total cost of materials and labor in the flexible budget, and this is true in May 2014. The production manager discusses the sources of the variances: "A new type of material was purchased in May. This led to faster cutting and sewing, but the workers used more material than usual as they learned to work with it. For now, the standards are fine."

Required

1. Calculate the direct materials and direct manufacturing labor price and efficiency variances in May 2014. What is the total flexible-budget variance for both inputs (direct

materials and direct manufacturing labor) combined? What percentage is this variance of the total cost of direct materials and direct manufacturing labor in the flexible budget?

2. Azra, the CEO, is concerned about the input variances. But she likes the quality and feel of the new material and agrees to use it for one more year. In May 2015, Raymond again produces 450 lots of T-shirts. Relative to May 2014, 2% less direct material is used, direct material price is down 5%, and 2% less direct manufacturing labor is used. Labor price has remained the same as in May 2014. Calculate the direct materials and direct manufacturing labor price and efficiency variances in May 2015. What is the total flexible-budget variance for both inputs (direct materials and direct manufacturing labor) combined? What percentage is this variance of the total cost of direct materials and direct manufacturing labor in the flexible budget?

3. Comment on the May 2015 results. Would you continue the "experiment" of using the new material?

Solution

1.

May 2014	Actual Results (1)	Price Variance (2) = (1) – (3)		Actual Quantity × Budgeted Price (3)	Efficiency Variance (4) = (3) – (5)		Flexible Budget (5)
Units	450						450
Direct materials	₹1,33,380.00	₹17,100	U	₹1,16,280[a]	₹9,180	U	₹1,07,100.00[b]
Direct labor	₹55,350.00	₹675	U	₹54,675[c]	₹3,645	F	₹58,320.00[d]
Total price variance		₹17,775	U				
Total efficiency variance					₹5,535	U	

[a] 6,840 meters × ₹17 per meter = ₹1,16,280

[b] 450 lots × 14 meters per lot × ₹17 per meter = ₹1,07,100

[c] 675 hours × ₹81 per hour = ₹54,675

[d] 450 lots × 1.6 hours per lot × ₹81 per hour = ₹58,320

Total flexible-budget variance for both inputs = ₹17,775 U + ₹5,535 U = ₹23,310U

Total flexible-budget cost of direct materials and direct labor = ₹1,07,100 + ₹58,320 = ₹1,65,420

Total flexible-budget variance as % of total flexible-budget costs = ₹23,310 ÷ ₹1,65,420 = 14.09%

2.

May 2015	Actual Results (1)	Price Variance (2) = (1) – (3)		Actual Quantity × Budgeted Price (3)	Efficiency Variance (4) = (3) – (5)		Flexible Budget (5)
Units	450						450
Direct materials	₹1,24,009.2[a]	₹10,054.80	U	₹1,13,954.40[b]	₹6,854.40	U	₹1,07,100[c]
Direct manuf. labor	₹54,243[d]	₹661.50	U	₹53,581.50[e]	₹4,738.50	F	₹58,320[c]
Total price variance		₹10,716.30	U				
Total efficiency variance					₹2,115.9	U	

[a] Actual dir. mat. cost, May 2015 = Actual dir. mat. cost, May 2014 × 0.98 × 0.95 = ₹1,33,380 × 0.98 × 0.95 = ₹1,24,009.2

Alternatively, actual dir. mat. cost, May 2015

= (Actual dir. mat. quantity used in May 2014 × 0.98) × (Actual dir. mat. price in May 2014 × 0.95)

= (6,840 meters × 0.98) × (₹19.5/meter × 0.95)

= 6,703.20 × ₹18.52 = ₹1,24,009.2

[b] (6,840 meters × 0.98) × ₹17 per meter = ₹1,13,954.4

[c] Unchanged from 2014.

[d] Actual dir. labor cost, May 2015 = Actual dir. manuf. cost May 2014 × 0.98 = ₹55,350 × 0.98 = ₹54,243

Alternatively, actual dir. labor cost, May 2015

= (Actual dir. manuf. labor quantity used in May 2014 × 0.98) × Actual dir. labor price in 2014

= (675 hours × 0.98) × ₹82 per hour

= 661.50 hours × ₹82 per hour = ₹54,243

[e] (675 hours × 0.98) × ₹81 per hour = ₹53,581.50

Total flexible-budget variance for both inputs = 10,716.30U + 2,115.9U = 12,832.2 U

Total flexible-budget cost of direct materials and direct labor = 1,07,100 + 58,320 = 1,65,420

Total flexible-budget variance as % of total flexible-budget costs = 12,832.20 ÷ 1,65,420 = 7.76%

3. Efficiencies have improved in the direction indicated by the production manager—but, it is unclear whether they are a trend or a one-time occurrence. Also, overall, variances are still 7.8 percent of flexible input budget. Company should continue to use the new material, especially in light of its superior quality and feel, but it may want to keep the following points in mind:

- The new material costs substantially more than the old (19.5 in 2014 and 18.52 in 2015 versus 17 per meter). Its price is unlikely to come down even more within the coming year. Standard material price should be reexamined and possibly changed.

- Azra should continue to work to reduce direct materials and direct manufacturing labor content. The reductions from May 2014 to May 2015 are a good development and should be encouraged.

7-22 Price and efficiency variances, benchmarking. Supreme Industries. produces molded plastic garden pots and other plastic containers. In June 2014, Supreme produces 1,000 lots (each lot is 12 dozen pots) of its most popular line of pots, the 14-inch "Grecian urns," at each of its two plants, which are located in Mumbai and Baroda. The production manager, Ritu, asks her assistant, Neha, to find out the precise per-unit budgeted variable costs at the two plants and the variable costs of a competitor, Royal Art, who offers similar-quality pots at cheaper prices. Neha pulls together the following information for each lot:

Per lot	Mumbai Plant	Baroda Plant	Royal Art
Direct materials	13.50 kgs @ ₹92 per kg	14.00 kgs @ ₹90 per kg	13.00 kgs @ ₹88 per kg
Direct labor	3 hrs.@ ₹101.5 per hr.	2.7 hrs @102 per hr.	2.5 hrs @ 100 per hr
Variable overhead	₹120 per lot	₹110 per lot	₹110 per lot

Required

1. What is the budgeted variable cost per lot at the Mumbai Plant, the Baroda Plant, and at Royal Art?

2. Using the Royal Art data as the standard, calculate the direct materials and direct labor price and efficiency variances for the Mumbai and Baroda plants.

3. What advantage does supreme get by using Royal Art's benchmark data as standards in calculating its variances? Identify two issues that Ritu should keep in mind in using the Royal Art data as the standards.

Solution

1.

Mumbai Plant

	Prices and quantities					Cost per lot
Direct materials	13.50	kgs	@	₹92	per kg	₹1,242
Direct labor	3	hrs	@	₹101.50	per hr	304.50
Variable overhead						120.00
Budgeted variable cost						₹1,666.50

Baroda Plant

	Prices and quantities					Cost per lot
Direct materials	14.00	kgs	@	₹90	per kg	₹1,260
Direct labor	2.7	hrs	@	₹102	per hr	275.40
Variable overhead						110.00
Budgeted variable cost						₹1,645.40

Royal Art

	Prices and quantities					Cost per lot
Direct materials	13.00	kgs	@	₹88	per kg	₹1,144
Direct labor	2.5	hrs	@	₹100	per hr	250
Variable overhead						110
Budgeted variable cost						₹1,504

2.   Mumbai Plant

	Actual Results (1)	Price Variance (2) = (1) – (3)		Actual Quantity × Budgeted Price (3)	Efficiency Variance (4) = (3) – (5)		Flexible Budget (5)
Lots	1,000						1,000
Direct materials	₹12,42,000	₹54,000	U	₹11,88,000[b]	₹44,000	U	₹11,44,000
Direct labor	₹3,04,500	₹4,500	U	₹3,00,000[c]	₹50,000	U	₹2,50,000

[a]Using Royal Art's prices and quantities as the standard:

Direct materials: (13 kgs./lot × 1,000 lots) × ₹88/kg. = ₹11,44,000

(2.5 hrs./lot × 1,000 lots) × ₹100.00/hr. = ₹2,50,000

[b](13.50 kgs./lot × 1,000 lots) × ₹88 per kg. = ₹11,88,000

[c](3 hours/lot × 1,000 lots) × ₹100/hr. = ₹3,00,000

Baroda Plant

	Actual Results (1)	Price Variance (2) = (1) – (3)		Actual Quantity × Budgeted Price (3)	Efficiency Variance (4) = (3) – (5)		Flexible Budget (5)
Lots	1,000						1,000
Direct materials	₹12,60,000	₹28,000	U	₹12,32,000[b]	₹88,000	U	₹11,44,000
Direct labor	₹2,75,400	₹5,400	U	₹2,70,000[c]	₹20,000	U	₹2,50,000

[a]Using Royal Art's prices and quantities as the standard:

Direct materials: (13 kg./lot ×1,000 lots) × ₹88/kg. = ₹11,44,000

(2.5 hrs./lot ×1,000 lots) × ₹100/kg. = ₹2,50,000

[b](14 kgs./lot × 1,000 lots) × ₹88 per kg. = ₹12,32,000

[c](2.7 hours/lot × 1,000 lots) × ₹100/hr. = ₹2,70,000

3. Using an objective, external benchmark, like that of a competitor, will preempt the possibility of any one plant feeling that the other is being favored. That this competitor, Royal Art, is successful will also put positive pressure on the two plants to improve (note that all variances are unfavorable). Issues that Supreme industries should keep in mind include the following:

- Ensure that Royal Art is indeed the best and most relevant standard (for example, is there another competitor in the marketplace which should be considered?).
- Ensure that the data is reliable.
- Ensure that Royal Art is similar enough to use as a standard (if Royal Art has a different business model, for example, it may be following a strategy of lowering costs that the company may not want to emulate because the company is trying to differentiate its products).

7-23 Activity-based costing, flexible-budget variances for finance function activities. John is the chief financial officer of Flowers.com, an Internet company that enables customers to order deliveries of flowers by accessing its Web site. John is concerned with the efficiency and effectiveness of the finance function. He collects the following information for three finance activities in 2015.

Activity	Activity Level	Cost Driver	Rate per unit of Cost Driver	
			Static Budget	Actual
Receivables	Output unit	Remittances	₹6.39	₹7.5
Payables	Batch	Invoices	29.00	28.0
Travel expenses	Batch	Travel claims	76.00	74.0

The output measure is the number of deliveries, which is the same as the number of remittances. The following is additional information.

	Static-Budget Amounts	Actual Amounts
Number of deliveries	10,00,000	9,48,000
Batch size in terms of deliveries:		
Payables	5	4.468
Travel expenses	500	501.587

Required

1. Calculate the flexible-budget variance for each activity in 2015.
2. Calculate the price and efficiency variances for each activity in 2015.

Solution

Activity-based costing, flexible-budget variances for finance function activities.

1. Receivables

   Receivables is an output unit level activity. Its flexible-budget variance can be calculated as follows:

$$\text{Flexible - budget variance} = \text{Actual costs} - \text{Flexible - budget costs}$$

$$= (₹7.5 \times 9,48,000) - (₹6.39 \times 9,48,000)$$

$$= ₹71,10,000 - ₹60,57,720$$

$$= ₹10,52,280 \text{ U}$$

Payables

Payables is a batch level activity.

	Static-Budget Amounts	Actual Amounts
a. Number of deliveries	10,00,000	9,48,000
b. Batch size (units per batch)	5	4.468
c. Number of batches (a ÷ b)	2,00,000	2,12,175
d. Cost per batch	₹29	₹28
e. Total payables activity cost (c × d)	₹58,00,000	₹59,40,900

Step 1: The number of batches in which payables should have been processed = 9,48,000 actual units · 5 budgeted units per batch = 1,89,600 batches

Step 2: The flexible-budget amount for payables

= 1,89,600 batches × ₹29 budgeted cost per batch = ₹54,98,400

The flexible-budget variance can be computed as follows:

$$\text{Flexible-budget variance} = \text{Actual costs} - \text{Flexible-budget costs}$$
$$= (2,12,175 \times ₹28) - (1,89,600 \times ₹29)$$
$$= ₹59,40,900 - ₹54,98,400 = ₹4,42,500 \text{ U}$$

Travel expenses

Travel expenses is a batch level activity.

	Static-Budget Amounts	Actual Amounts
a. Number of deliveries	10,00,000	9,48,000
b. Batch size (units per batch)	500	501.587
c. Number of batches (a ÷ b)	2,000	1,890
d. Cost per batch	₹76	₹74
e. Total travel expenses activity cost (c × d)	₹1,52,000	₹1,39,860

Step 1: The number of batches in which the travel expense should have been processed 5 9,48,000 actual units ÷ 500 budgeted units per batch = 1,896 batches

Step 2: The flexible-budget amount for travel expenses

= 1,896 batches × ₹76 budgeted cost per batch = ₹1,44,096

The flexible budget variance can be calculated as follows:

$$\text{Flexible budget variance} = \text{Actual costs} - \text{Flexible-budget costs}$$
$$= (1,890 \times ₹74) - (1,896 \times ₹76)$$
$$= ₹1,39,860 - ₹1,44,096 = ₹4,236 \text{ F}$$

$$\text{Price variance} = \left[\begin{array}{c} \text{Actual price} \\ \text{of input} \end{array} - \begin{array}{c} \text{Budgeted price} \\ \text{of input} \end{array} \right] \times \begin{array}{c} \text{Actual quantity} \\ \text{of input} \end{array}$$

$$\text{Efficiency variance} = \left[\begin{array}{c} \text{Actual quantity} \\ \text{of input used} \end{array} - \begin{array}{c} \text{Budgeted quantity of} \\ \text{input allowed for} \\ \text{actual output} \end{array} \right] \times \begin{array}{c} \text{Budgeted price} \\ \text{of input} \end{array}$$

2. The flexible budget variances can be subdivided into price and efficiency variances.

Receivables

Price Variance   = (₹7.50 − ₹6.39) × 9,48,000 = ₹10,52,280 U

Efficiency variance = (9,48,000 − 9,48,000) × ₹6.39 = Zero

Payables

Price variance = (₹28 − ₹29) × 2,12,175 = ₹2,12,175 F

Efficiency variance = (2,12,175 − 1,89,600) × ₹29 = ₹6,54,675 U

Travel expenses

Price variance = (₹74 − ₹76) × 1,890 = ₹3,780 F

Efficiency variance = (1,890 − 1,896) × ₹76 = ₹456 F

7-24 Finance function activities, benchmarking (continuation of 7-23) John, CFO of Flowers. com, engages the BCG Group, a consulting firm specializing in benchmarking. He asks BCG to provide benchmark data of the finance function at "world-class" retail companies (both traditional retail and Internet-based retail). BCG's cost benchmarks for Flowers.com's three finance activities are

Finance Activity	"World-Class" Cost Performance
Payables	₹7.1 per invoice
Receivables	₹1.0 per remittance
Travel expenses	₹15.80 per travel claim

Required

1. What new insight might arise with the BCG benchmark data using the amounts in Solved Example 7-22?

2. Assume you are in charge of travel-claim processing. What concerns might you have with John using the BCG benchmark of ₹15.80 per travel claim as the key to evaluate your performance next period?

Solution

Finance function fctivities, benchmarking.

1. The key new insight is how Flowers.com compares with "world-class" organizations. At face value, there is much room for improvement. The per unit cost differences are dramatic:

	Flowers.com		
	Budgeted	Actual	"World-Class" Cost Performance
Receivables	₹6.39	₹7.50	₹1.0 per remittance
Payables	₹29.00	₹28.0	₹7.1 per invoice
Travel	₹76.00	₹74.0	₹15.8 per travel claim

2. For any meaningful comparison, the figures being compared must be compara- ble. John should first determine whether there is an "apples to apples" compari- son with these figures. Are costs of the finance department activities measured the same across Flowers.com and the company with "world-class" cost performance? Suppose Flowers.com allocates other costs into the finance area (such as the President's salary), while the ₹15.80 per travel claim figure is for finance department costs only.

John should consider whether the benchmark company also obtains information on why the large cost differences occur. For example, is it because the "world-class" performer is using new technologies in the finance area? If this is the case, then is John willing to invest in new technologies in the same way that "world-class" finance function organizations do? If not, then the ₹15.80 benchmark could be unattainable, no matter how hard and smart the travel claim processing group performs.

In addition, John should consider whether the benchmark company provides a valid comparison point. The benchmark company is a world-class retail company that has tra- ditional retail and Internet-based retail functions. Flowers.com is an Internet company. Costs and activities of Internet companies are going to differ from those of traditional retailers.

7-25 Variance analysis, nonmanufacturing setting. Mr Amar has run In-A-Flash Car Detailing for the past 10 years. His static budget and actual results for June 2016 are provided next. Amar has one employee who has been with him for all 10 years that he has been in business. In addition, at any given time he also employs two other less experienced workers. It usually takes each employee 2 hours to detail a vehicle, regardless of his or her experience. Amar pays his experienced employee ₹300 per vehicle and the other two employees ₹150 per vehicle. There were no wage increases in June.

In A Flash car Detailing
Actual and Budgeted Income Statements
For the Month Ended June 30,2016

	Budget	Actual
Cars detailed	280	320
Revenue	₹5,32,000	₹7,20,000
Variable costs		
Costs of supplies	12,600	13,600
Labor	67,200	84,000
Total variable costs	79,800	97,600
Contribution margin	4,52,200	6,22,400
Fixed costs	98,000	98,000
Operating income	₹3,54,200	₹5,24,400

Required

1, How many cars, on average, did Amar budget for each employee? How many cars did each employee actually detail?

2 Prepare a flexible budget for June 2016.

3 Compute the sales price variance and the labor efficiency variance for each labor type.

4 What information, in addition to that provided in the income statements, would you want Amar to gather, if you wanted to improve operational efficiency?

Solution

1. This is a problem of two equations and two unknowns. The two equations relate to the number of cars detailed and the labor costs (the wages paid to the employees).

    X = number of cars detailed by the experienced employee
    Y = number of cars detailed by the less experienced employees (combined)

    Budget: $X + Y$ = 280   Actual: $X + Y$ = 320
    ₹300X + ₹150Y = ₹67,200   ₹300X + ₹150Y = ₹84,000

    Substitution: Substitution:
    300X + 150(280 – X) = 67,200   300X + 150(320 – X) = 84,000
    150X = 25,200   150X = 36,000
    X= 168 cars   X = 240 cars
    Y = 112 cars   Y = 80 cars

Budget: The experienced employee is budgeted to detail 168 cars (and earn ₹50,400), and the less experienced employees are budgeted to detail 56 cars each and earn ₹8,400 apiece.

Actual: The experienced employee details 240 cars (and grosses ₹72,000 for the month), and the other two wash 40 each and gross ₹6,000 apiece.

2.

	Actual Results (1)	Flexible-Budget Variances (2) = (1) – (3)	Flexible Budget (3)	Sales - Volume Variance (4) = (3) – (5)	Static Budget (5)
Units sold	320		320		280
Revenues	₹7,20,000	₹1,12,000 F	₹6,08,000[a]	₹76,000 F	₹5,32,000
Variable costs					
Supplies	13,600	800 F	14,400[b]	1,800 U	12,600
Labor – Experienced	72,000	14,400 U	57,600[c]	7,200 U	50,400
Labor – Less experienced	12,000	7,200 F	19,200d	2,400 U	16,800
Total variable costs	97,600	6,400 U	91,200	11,400 U	79,800
Contribution Margin	6,22,400	1,05,600 F	5,16,800	64,600 F	4,52,200
Fixed costs	98,000	0	98,000	0	98,000
Operating income	₹5,24,400	₹1,05,600 F	₹4,18,800	₹64,600 F	₹3,52,400

[a] 320 × (₹5,32,000/280)
[b] 320 × (₹12,600/280)
[c] 320 × (₹50,400/280)
[d] 320 × (₹16,800/280)

3. Actual sales price = ₹7,20,000 ÷ 320 = ₹2,250
Sales Price Variance
= (Actual sales price – Budgeted sales price) × Actual number of cars detailed:
= (₹2,250 – ₹1,900) × 320
= ₹1,12,000 Favorable

Labor efficiency for experienced worker:
Standard cars expected to be completed by experienced worker based on actual number of cars detailed = (168 ÷ 280) × 320 = 192 cars
Labor efficiency variance = Budgeted wage rate per car × (Actual cars detailed – budgeted cars detailed)
= ₹300 × (240 – 192)
= ₹14,400 Unfavorable

Labor efficiency for less-experienced workers:
Standard cars expected to be completed by less-experienced workers based on actual number of cars detailed = (112 ÷ 280) × 320 = 128 cars
Labor efficiency variance = Budgeted wage rate per car × (Actual cars detailed – budgeted cars detailed)
= ₹150 × (80 – 128)
= ₹7,200 Favorable

4. In addition to understanding the variances computed above, Amar should attempt to keep track of the number of cars worked on by each employee, as well as the number of hours actually spent on each car. In addition, Amar should look at the prices charged for detailing, in relation to the hours spent on each job. It should also be considered whether the experienced worker should be asked to take less time per car, given his prior years at work and the fact that he is paid twice the wage rate of the less-experienced employees.

7-26 Material cost variances, use of variances for performance evaluation. Mr Hansraj is the owner of Best Bikes, a company that produces high-quality cross-country bicycles. Best Bikes participates in a supply chain that consists of suppliers, manufacturers, distributors, and elite bicycle shops. For several years Best Bikes has purchased titanium from suppliers in the supply chain. Best Bikes uses titanium for the bicycle frames because it is stronger and lighter than other metals and therefore increases the quality of the bicycle. Earlier this year, Best Bikes hired Vivek, a recent graduate from IIM, as purchasing manager. Vivek believed that he could reduce costs if he purchased titanium from an online marketplace at a lower price.

Best Bikes established the following standards based upon the company's experience with previous suppliers. The standards are as follows:

Cost of titanium	₹360 per kg
Titanium used per bicycle	4 kgs

Actual results for the first month using the online supplier of titanium are as follows:

Bicycles produced	400
Titanium produced	2,600 kgs for ₹8,84,000
Titanium used in production	2,350 kgs

Required

1. Compute the direct materials price and efficiency variances.
2. What factors can explain the variances identified in requirement 1? Could any other variances be affected?
3. Was switching suppliers a good idea for Best Bikes? Explain why or why not.
4. Should Vivek's performance evaluation be based solely on price variances? Should the production manager's evaluation be based solely on efficiency variances? Why is it important for Hansraj to understand the causes of a variance before she evaluates performance?
5. Other than performance evaluation, what reasons are there for calculating variances?
6. What future problems could result from Best Bikes' decision to buy a lower quality of titanium from the online marketplace?

Solution

1. Materials Variances

	Actual Costs Incurred (Actual Input Qty. × Actual Price)	Actual Input Qty. × Budgeted Price		Flexible Budget (Budgeted Input Qty. Allowed for Actual Output × Budgeted Price)
		Purchases	Usage	
Direct	(2,600 kgs × ₹340a)	(2,600 kgs × ₹360)	(2,350×₹360)	(400 × 4 × ₹360)
Materials	₹8,84,000			(1,600 × ₹360)
		₹9,36,000	₹8,46,000	₹5,76,000
	↑___₹52,000 F___↑		↑___₹2,70,000 U___↑	
	Price variance		Efficiency variance	

a ₹8,84,000 ÷2,600 = ₹340

2. The favorable price variance is due to the ₹20 difference (₹360 – ₹340) between the standard price based on the previous suppliers and the actual price paid through the

online marketplace. The unfavorable efficiency variance could be due to several factors including inexperienced workers and machine malfunctions. But the likely cause here is that the lower-priced titanium was lower quality or less refined, which led to more waste. The labor efficiency variance could be affected if the lower quality titanium caused the workers to use more time.

3. Switching suppliers was not a good idea. The ₹52,000 savings in the cost of titanium was outweighed by the ₹2,70,000 extra material usage. In addition, the ₹2,70,000 U efficiency variance does not recognize the total impact of the lower quality titanium because, of the 2,600 kgs pounds purchased, only 2,350 kgs pounds were used. If the quantity of materials used in production is relatively the same, Best Bikes could expect the remaining 250 kgs to produce approximately 40 more units. At standard, 40 more units should take 40 × 4 = 160 kgs. There could be an additional unfavorable efficiency variance of

$$
\begin{array}{ccc}
(250 \times ₹360) & & (40 \times 4 \times ₹360) \\
₹90,000 & & ₹57,600 \\
& \uparrow \quad ₹32,400\ \text{U} \quad \uparrow &
\end{array}
$$

4. The purchasing manager's performance evaluation should not be based solely on the price variance. The short-run reduction in purchase costs was more than offset by higher usage rates. His evaluation should be based on the total costs of the company as a whole. In addition, the production manager's performance evaluation should not be based solely on the efficiency variances. In this case, the production manager was not responsible for the purchase of the lower-quality titanium, which led to the unfavorable efficiency scores. In general, it is important for Hansraj to understand that not all favorable material price variances are "good news" because of the negative effects that can arise in the production process from the purchase of inferior inputs. They can lead to unfavorable efficiency variances for both materials and labor. Hansraj should also understand that efficiency variances may arise for many different reasons and he needs to know these reasons before evaluating performance.

5. Variances should be used to help Best Bikes understand what led to the current set of financial results, as well as how to perform better in the future. They are a way to facilitate the continuous improvement efforts of the company. Rather than focusing solely on the price of titanium, Hansraj can balance price and quality in future purchase decisions.

6. Future problems can arise in the supply chain. Vivek may need to go back to the previous suppliers. But Best Bikes' relationship with them may have been damaged, and they may now be selling all their available titanium to other manufacturers. Lower quality bicycles could also affect Best Bikes' reputation with the distributors, the bike shops, and customers, leading to higher warranty claims and customer dissatisfaction, and decreased sales in the future.

7-27 Direct materials efficiency, mix, and yield variances. Nature's Best Nuts produces specialty nut products for the gourmet and natural foods market. Its most popular product is Zesty Zingers, a mixture of roasted nuts that are seasoned with a secret spice mixture and sold in half litre tins. The direct materials used in Zesty Zingers are almonds, cashews, pistachios, and seasoning. For each batch of 100 tins, the budgeted quantities and budgeted prices of direct materials are as follows:

	Quantity for One Batch	Price of Input
Almonds	180 cups	₹10 per cup
Cashews	300 cups	₹20 per cup
Pistachios	90 cups	₹30 per cup
Seasoning	30 cups	₹60 per cup

Changing the standard mix of direct material quantities slightly does not significantly affect the overall end product, particularly for the nuts. In addition, not all nuts added to production end up in the finished product, as some are rejected during inspection.

In the current period, Nature's Best made 2,500 tins of Zesty Zingers in 25 batches with the following actual quantity, cost, and mix of inputs:

	Actual Quality	Actual Cost	Actual Mix
Almonds	5,280 cups	₹52,800	33%
Cashews	7,520 cups	1,50,400	47%
Pistachios	2,720 cups	81,600	17%
Seasoning	480 cups	28,800	3%
Total actual	16,000 cups	₹3,13,600	100%

Required

1. What is the budgeted cost of direct materials for the 2,500 tins?
2. Calculate the total direct materials efficiency variance.
3. Why is the total direct materials price variance zero?
4. Calculate the total direct materials mix and yield variances. What are these variances telling you about the 2,500 tins produced this period? Are the variances large enough to investigate?

Solution

1.

Almonds (₹10 × 180 cups)		₹1,800
Cashews (₹20 × 300 cups)		6,000
Pistachios (₹30 × 90 cups)		2,700
Seasoning (₹60 × 30 cups)		1,800
Budgeted cost per batch		₹12,300
Number of batches		× 25
Budgeted Cost		₹3,07,500

2. Solution Exhibit A presents the total price variance (₹0), the total efficiency variance (₹6,100 U), and the total flexible-budget variance (₹6,100 U).

Total direct materials efficiency variance can also be computed as:

$$\text{Direct materials efficiency variance for each input} = \left(\begin{array}{c} \text{Actual quantity} \\ \text{of input} \end{array} - \begin{array}{c} \text{Budgeted quantity} \\ \text{of input allowed} \\ \text{for actual output} \end{array} \right) \times \begin{array}{c} \text{Budgeted price} \\ \text{of input} \end{array}$$

Almonds	=	(5,280 − 4,500) × ₹10 =	₹7,800 U
Cashews	=	(7,520 − 7,500) × ₹20 =	400 U
Pistachios	=	(2,720 − 2,250) × ₹30 =	14,100 U
Seasoning	=	(480 − 750) × ₹60 =	6,200 F
Total direct materials efficiency variance			₹6,100 U

Solution Exhibit A

Columnar Presentation of Direct Materials Price and Efficiency Variances for Nature's Best Company.

	Actual Costs Incurred (Actual Input Quantity × Actual Price) (1)		Actual Input Quantity × Budgeted Price (2)		Flexible Budget (Budgeted Input Quantity Allowed for Actual Output × Budgeted Price) (3)	
Almonds	5,280 × ₹10 =	₹52,800	5,280 × ₹10 =	₹52,800	4,500 × ₹10 =	₹45,000
Cashews	7,520 × ₹20 =	1,50,400	7,520 × ₹20 =	1,50,400	7,500 × ₹20 =	1,50,000
Pistachios	2,720 × ₹30 =	81,600	2,720 × ₹30 =	8,16,000	2,250 × ₹30 =	67,500
Seasoning	480 × ₹60 =	28,800	480 × ₹60 =	28,800	750 × ₹60 =	45,000
		₹3,13,600		₹3,13,600		₹3,07,500

↑_____₹0_____↑_____₹6,100 U_____↑

Total price variance   Total efficiency variance

↑_____₹6,100 U_____↑

Total flexible-budget variance

F = favorable effect on operating income; U = unfavorable effect on operating income

3. The total direct materials price variance equals zero because, for all four inputs, actual price per cup equals the budgeted price per cup.

4. Solution Exhibit B presents the total direct materials yield and mix variances.

   The total direct materials yield variance can also be computed as the sum of the direct materials yield variances for each input:

$$\begin{pmatrix} \text{Direct materials} \\ \text{yield variance} \\ \text{for each input} \end{pmatrix} = \begin{pmatrix} \text{Actual total quantity} \\ \text{of all direct materials} - \text{of all direct materials inputs} \\ \text{inputs used} \end{pmatrix} \times \begin{pmatrix} \text{Budgeted total quantity} \\ \text{allowed for actual output} \end{pmatrix} \times \begin{pmatrix} \text{Budgeted direct} \\ \text{materials input mix} \\ \text{percentage} \end{pmatrix} \times \begin{pmatrix} \text{Budgeted price} \\ \text{of direct} \\ \text{materials inputs} \end{pmatrix}$$

Almonds	= (16,000 − 15,000) × 0.30a × ₹10 = 1,000 × 0.30 × ₹10 =	₹3,000 U
Cashews	= (16,000 − 15,000) × 0.50b × ₹20 = 1,000 × 0.50 × ₹20 =	10,000 U
Pistachios	= (16,000 − 15,000) × 0.15c × ₹30 = 1,000 × 0.15 × ₹30 =	4,500 U
Seasoning	= (16,000 − 15,000) × 0.05d × ₹60 = 1,000 × 0.05 × ₹60 =	3,000 U
Total direct materials yield variance		₹20,500 U

[a] 180 ÷ 600; [b] 300 ÷ 600; [c] 90 ÷ 600; [d] 30 ÷ 600

The total direct materials mix variance can also be computed as the sum of the direct materials mix variances for each input:

$$\begin{pmatrix} \text{Direct materials} \\ \text{mix variance} \\ \text{for each input} \end{pmatrix} = \begin{pmatrix} \text{Actual direct} \\ \text{materials input mix} - \text{materials input mix} \\ \text{percentage} \end{pmatrix} \times \begin{pmatrix} \text{Budgeted direct} \\ \text{percentage} \end{pmatrix} \times \begin{pmatrix} \text{Actually total} \\ \text{quantity of all direct} \\ \text{materials inputs used} \end{pmatrix} \times \begin{pmatrix} \text{Budgeted price} \\ \text{of direct} \\ \text{materials inputs} \end{pmatrix}$$

Almonds	= (0.33 − 0.30) × 16,000 × ₹10 = 0.03 × 16,000 × ₹10 =	₹4,800 U
Cashews	= (0.47 − 0.50) × 16,000 × ₹20 = −0.03 × 16,000 × ₹20 =	9,600 F
Pistachios	= (0.17 − 0.15) × 16,000 × ₹30 = 0.02 × 16,000 × ₹30 =	9,600 U
Seasoning	= (0.03 − 0.05) × 16,000 × ₹60 = −0.02 × 16,000 × ₹60 =	19,200 F
Total direct materials mix variance		₹14,400 F

Solution Exhibit B

Columnar Presentation of Direct Materials Yield and Mix Variances for Nature's Best Company.

	Actual Total Quantity of All Inputs Used × Actual Input Mix × Budgeted Price (1)	Actual Total Quantity of All Inputs Used × Budgeted Input Mix × Budgeted Price (2)	Flexible Budget: Budgeted Total Quantity of All Inputs Allowed for Actual Output × Budgeted Input Mix × Budgeted Price (3)
Almonds	16,000 × 0.33 × ₹10 ≈ ₹52,800	16,000 × 0.30 × ₹10 = ₹48,000	15,000 × 0.30 × ₹10 = ₹45,000
Cashews	16,000 × 0.47 × ₹20 = 1,50,400	16,000 × 0.50 × ₹20 = 1,60,000	15,000 × 0.50 × ₹20 = 1,50,000
Pistachios	16,000 × 0.17 × ₹30 = 81,600	16,000 × 0.15 × ₹30 = 72,000	15,000 × 0.15 × ₹30 = 67,500
Seasoning	16,000 × 0.03 × ₹60 = 28,800	16,000 × 0.05 × ₹60 = 48,000	15,000 × 0.05 × ₹60 = 45,000
	₹3,13,600	₹3,28,000	₹3,07,500

↑————————————— ₹14,400 F —————————————↑————————————— ₹20,500 U —————————————↑

Total mix variance   Total yield variance

↑————————————————————————— ₹6,100 U —————————————————————————↑

Total efficiency variance

F = favorable effect on operating income; U = unfavorable effect on operating income.

The direct materials mix variance of ₹14,400 F indicates that the actual product mix uses relatively more of less-expensive ingredients than planned. In this case, the actual mix contains slightly more almonds and pistachios while using fewer cashews and substantially less seasoning.

The direct materials yield variance of ₹20,500 U occurs because the amount of total inputs needed (16,000 cups) exceeded the budgeted amount (15,000 cups) expected to produce 2,500 tins.

The direct materials yield variance is significant enough to be investigated. The mix variance may be within expectations but should be monitored since it is favorable largely due to the use of less seasoning, which is considered an important element of the product's appeal to customers.

7-28 Use of materials and manufacturing labor variances for benchmarking. You are a new junior accountant at In Focus Corporation, maker of lenses for eyeglasses. Your company sells generic-quality lenses for a moderate price. Your boss, the controller, has given you the latest month's report for the lens trade association. This report includes information related to operations for your firm and three of your competitors within the trade association. The report also includes information related to the industry benchmark for each line item in the report. You do not know which firm is which, except that you know you are Firm A.

		Unit Variable Costs Member Firms For the Month Ended September 30, 2015					
	Firm A	Firm B	Firm C	Firm D	Industry	Benchmark	
Materials input	2.15	2.00	2.20	2.60	2.15	Oz. of glass	
Materials price	₹50	₹52.5	₹51	₹45	₹51	Per oz.	
Labor hours used	0.75	1.00	0.65	0.70	0.70	hours	
Wage rate	₹145	₹140	₹142.5	₹152.5	₹125	Per DLH	
Variable overhead rate	₹92.5	₹140	₹77.5	₹117.5	₹122.50	Per DLH	

1. Calculate the total variable cost per unit for each firm in the trade association. Computer the percent of total for the material, labor, and variable overhead components.

2. Using the trade association's industry benchmark, calculate direct materials and direct manufacturing labor price and efficiency variances for the four firms. Calculate the percent over standard for each firm and each variance.

3. Write a brief memo to your boss outlining the advantages and disadvantages of belonging to this trade association for benchmarking purposes. Include a few ideas to improve productivity that you want your boss to take to the department heads' meeting.

Solution

1. Unit variable cost (rupees) and component percentages for each firm:

	Firm A		Firm B		Firm C		Firm D	
DM	₹107.5	37.6%	₹105	27.3%	₹112.20	44.0%	₹117.0	38.2%
DL	108.8	38.1%	140	36.3%	92.6	36.3%	106.8	34.9%
VOH	69.4	24.3%	140	36.4%	50.4	19.7%	82.3	26.9%
Total	₹285.7	100.0%	₹385	100.0%	₹255.20	100.0%	₹306.10	100.0%

2. Variances and percentage over/under standard for each firm relative to the Industry Benchmark:

	Firm A		Firm B		Firm C		Firm D	
	Variance	% over standard	Variance	% over standard	Variance	% over standard	Variance	% over standard
DM Price Variance	₹2.2 F	−1.96%	₹3 U	2.94%	—	—	₹15.6 F	−11.76%
DM Efficiency Variance	—	—	₹7.7 F	−6.98%	₹2.6 U	2.33%	₹23.0 U	20.93%
DL Price Variance	₹15 U	16.00%	₹15 U	12.00%	₹11.4 U	14.00%	₹19.3 U	22.00%
DL Efficiency Variance	₹6.3 U	7.14%	₹37.5 U	42.86%	₹6.3 F	−7.14%	—	—

We illustrate these calculations for Firm A.

The DM Price Variance is computed as:

(Firm A Price − Benchmark Price) × Firm A Usage
= (₹50 − ₹51) × 2.15 oz.
= ₹2.2 F

The DM Efficiency Variance is computed as follows:

(Firm A Usage − Benchmark Usage) × Benchmark Price
= (2.15 oz. − 2.15 oz.) × ₹51
= ₹0

The DL Price Variance is computed as:

(Firm A Rate − Benchmark Rate) × Firm A Hours
= (₹145 − ₹125) × 0.75
= ₹15 u

The DL Efficiency Variance is computed as follows:

$$\text{(Firm A Usage} - \text{Benchmark Usage)} \times \text{Benchmark Rate}$$

= (0.75 hrs. − 0.70 hrs.) × ₹125

= ₹6.3 U

The % over standard is the percentage difference in prices relative to the Industry Benchmark. Again using the DM Price Variance calculation for Firm A, the % over standard is given by:

$$\text{(Firm A Price} - \text{Benchmark Price)/Benchmark Price}$$

= (₹50 − ₹51)/₹51

= 1.96% under standard.

3.

To: Controller

From: Junior Accountant

Re: Benchmarking & productivity improvements

Date: October 15, 2015

Benchmarking advantages

- We can see how productive we are relative to our competition and the industry benchmark.

- We can see the specific areas in which there may be opportunities for us to reduce costs.

Benchmarking disadvantages

- Some of our competitors are targeting the market for high-end and custom-made lenses. I'm not sure that looking at their costs helps with understanding ours better.

- We may focus too much on cost differentials and not enough on differentiating ourselves, maintaining our competitive advantages, and growing our margins.

Areas to discuss

- We may want to find out whether we can get the same lower price for glass as Firm D.

- We may want to re-evaluate the training our employees receive given our level of unfavorable labor efficiency variance compared to the benchmark.

- Can we use Firm B's materials efficiency and Firm C's variable overhead consumption levels as our standards for the coming year?

- It is unclear why the trade association is still using ₹125 for the labor rate benchmark. Given the difficulty of hiring qualified workers, real wage rates are now substantially higher. We pay our workers ₹20 more per hour, and at least one of our competitors pays even higher wages than we do! Firm B does pay ₹5 less than we do per hour and that may be worth looking into.

7-29 Direct labor variances: price, efficiency, mix and yield. Mr Faraz employs two workers in his guitar-making business. The first worker, Amar, has been making guitars for 20 years and is paid ₹150 per hour. The second worker, Rahman, is less experienced and is paid ₹100 per hour. One guitar requires, on average, 10 hours of labor. The budgeted direct labor quantities and prices for one guitar are as follows:

	Quality	**Price per Hour of Labor**	**Cost for One Guitar**
Amar	6 hours	150 per hour	₹900
Rahman	4 hours	100 per hour	400

That is, each guitar is budgeted to require 10 hours of direct labor, composed of 60% of Amar's labor and 40% of Rahman's, although sometimes Rahman works more hours on a particular guitar and Amar less, or vice versa, with no obvious change in the quality or function of the guitar.

During the month of August, Faraz manufactures 25 guitars. Actual direct labor costs are as follows:

Amar (145 hours)	₹21,750
Rahman (108 hours)	10,800
Total actual direct labor cost	₹32,550

Required

1. What is the budgeted cost of direct labor for 25 guitars?
2. Calculate the total direct labor price and efficiency variances.
3. For the 25 guitars, what is the total actual amount of direct labor used? What is the actual direct labor input mix percentage? What is the budgeted amount of Amar's and Rahman's labor that should have been used for the 25 guitars?
3. Calculate the total direct labor mix and yield variances. How do these numbers relate to the total direct labor efficiency variance? What do these variances tell you?

Solution

1.

Amar (₹150 × 6 hrs.)	₹900
Rahman (₹100 × 4 hrs.)	400
Cost per guitar	₹1,300
Number of guitars	×25 units
Total budgeted cost	₹32,500

2. Solution Exhibit A presents the total price variance (₹0), the total efficiency variance (₹50 U), and the total flexible-budget variance (₹50 U).

Total direct labor price variance can also be computed as:

$$\begin{array}{c} \text{Direct labor} \\ \text{price variance} \\ \text{for each input} \end{array} = \left(\begin{array}{c} \text{Actual price} \\ \text{of input} \end{array} - \begin{array}{c} \text{Budgeted price} \\ \text{of input} \end{array} \right) \times \begin{array}{c} \text{Actual quantity of} \\ \text{input} \end{array}$$

Amar	= (₹150 − ₹150) × 145 =	₹0
Rahman	= (₹100 − ₹100) × 108 =	0
Total direct labor price variance		₹0

Total direct labor efficiency variance can also be computed as:

$$\begin{array}{c} \text{Direct labor} \\ \text{efficiency} \\ \text{variance for} \\ \text{each input} \end{array} = \left(\begin{array}{c} \text{Actual quantity} \\ \text{of input} \end{array} - \begin{array}{c} \text{Budgeted quantity of input} \\ \text{allowed for actual output} \end{array} \right) \times \begin{array}{c} \text{Budgeted price} \\ \text{of input} \end{array}$$

Amar	= (145 − 150) × ₹150 =	₹750 F
Rahman	= (108 − 100) × ₹100 =	800 U
Total direct labor efficiency variance		₹50 U

Solution Exhibit A

Columnar Presentation of Direct Labor Price and Efficiency Variances for Faraz Guitars

	Actual Costs Incurred (Actual Input Quantity × Actual Price) (1)		Actual Input Quantity × Budgeted Price (2)		Flexible Budget (Budgeted Input Quantity Allowed for Actual Output × Budgeted Price) (3)	
Amar	145 × ₹150 = ₹21,750		145 × ₹150 = ₹21,750		150 × ₹150 = ₹22,500	
Rahman	108 × ₹100 = 10,800		108 × ₹100 = 10,800		100 × ₹100 = 10,000	
	₹32,550		₹32,550		₹32,500	

$$\underbrace{\hspace{4cm}}_{\text{₹0}}$$
Total price variance

$$\underbrace{\hspace{4cm}}_{\text{₹50 U}}$$
Total efficiency variance

$$\underbrace{\hspace{8cm}}_{\text{₹50 U}}$$
Total flexible-budget variance

F = favorable effect on operating income; U = unfavorable effect on operating income

3.

	Actual Quantity of Input	Actual Mix	Budgeted Quantity of Input for Actual Output		Budgeted Mix
Amar	145 hours	57.3%	6 hours × 25 units =	150 hours	60%
Rahman	108 hours	42.7%	4 hours × 25 units =	100 hours	40%
Total	253 hours	100.0%		250 hours	100%

4. Solution Exhibit B presents the total direct labor yield and mix variances for Faraz Guitars.

The total direct labor yield variance can also be computed as the sum of the direct labor yield variances for each input:

$$\text{Direct labor yield variance for each input} = \left(\begin{array}{c}\text{Actual total quantity} \\ \text{of all direct labor} \\ \text{inputs used}\end{array} - \begin{array}{c}\text{Budgeted total quantity} \\ \text{of all direct labor inputs} \\ \text{allowed for actual output}\end{array}\right) \times \begin{array}{c}\text{Budgeted direct} \\ \text{labor input mix} \\ \text{percentage}\end{array} \times \begin{array}{c}\text{Budgeted price} \\ \text{of direct labor} \\ \text{inputs}\end{array}$$

Amar   = (253 – 250) × 0.60 × ₹150 = 3 × 0.60 × ₹150 = ₹270 U
Rahman = (253 – 250) × 0.40 × ₹100 = 3 × 0.40 × ₹100 =   120 U
Total direct labor yield variance   ₹390 U

The total direct labor mix variance can also be computed as the sum of the direct labor mix variances for each input:

$$\text{Direct labor mix variance for each input} = \left(\begin{array}{c}\text{Actual direct} \\ \text{labor input mix} \\ \text{percentage}\end{array} - \begin{array}{c}\text{Budgeted direct} \\ \text{labor input mix} \\ \text{percentage}\end{array}\right) \times \begin{array}{c}\text{Actual total quantity} \\ \text{of all direct labor} \\ \text{inputs used}\end{array} \times \begin{array}{c}\text{Budgeted price of} \\ \text{direct labor inputs}\end{array}$$

Amar   = (0.573 – 0.60) × 253 × ₹150 = 0.027 × 253 × ₹150 = ₹1,025 F
Rahman = (0.427 – 0.40) × 253 × ₹100 = – 0.027 × 253 × ₹100 =   685 U
Total direct labor mix variance   ₹340 F

The sum of the direct labor mix variance and the direct labor yield variance equals the direct labor efficiency variance. The favorable mix variance arises from using more of the cheaper labor (and less of the costlier labor) than the budgeted mix. The yield variance indicates that the guitars required more total inputs (253 hours) than expected (250 hours) for the production of 25 guitars. Both variances are relatively small and probably within tolerable limits. It is likely that Rahman, who is less experienced, worked more slowly than Amar, which caused the unfavorable yield variance. Faraz should be careful that using more of the cheaper labor does not reduce the quality of the guitar or how customers perceive it.

Solution Exhibit B

Columnar Presentation of Direct Labor Yield and Mix Variances for Faraz Guitars

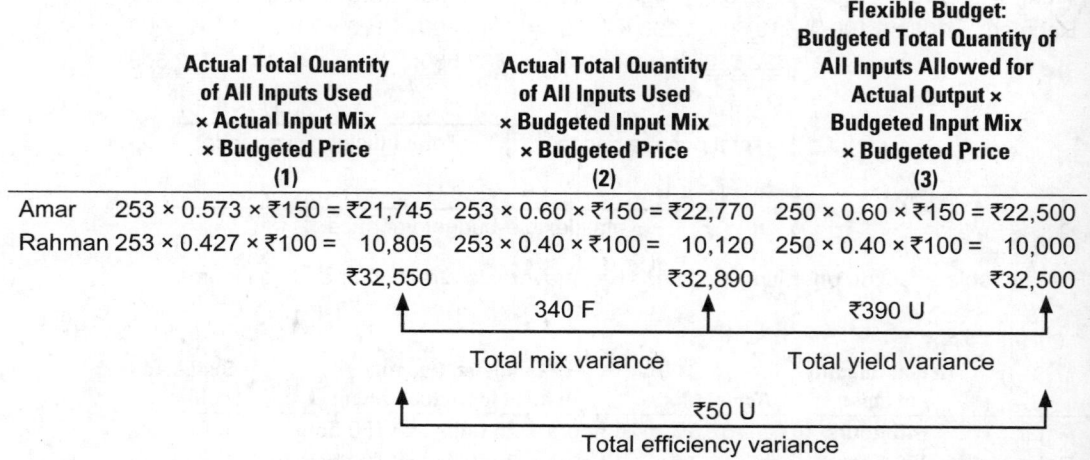

	Actual Total Quantity of All Inputs Used × Actual Input Mix × Budgeted Price (1)	Actual Total Quantity of All Inputs Used × Budgeted Input Mix × Budgeted Price (2)	Flexible Budget: Budgeted Total Quantity of All Inputs Allowed for Actual Output × Budgeted Input Mix × Budgeted Price (3)
Amar	253 × 0.573 × ₹150 = ₹21,745	253 × 0.60 × ₹150 = ₹22,770	250 × 0.60 × ₹150 = ₹22,500
Rahman	253 × 0.427 × ₹100 = 10,805	253 × 0.40 × ₹100 = 10,120	250 × 0.40 × ₹100 = 10,000
	₹32,550	₹32,890	₹32,500

340 F   ₹390 U

Total mix variance   Total yield variance

₹50 U

Total efficiency variance

F = favorable effect on operating income; U = unfavorable effect on operating income.

7-30 Comprehensive variance analysis review. Royal Industries manufactures diskettes. The CFO has provided you with the following budgeted standards for the month of February 2016:

Average selling price per diskette	₹40.00
Total direct material cost per diskette	₹8.50
Direct manufacturing labor	
Direct manufacturing labor cost per hour	₹150.00
Average labor productivity rate (diskettes per hour)	300
Direct marketing cost per unit	₹3.00
Fixed overhead	₹90,00,000

Sales of 15,00,000 units are budgeted for February. Actual February results are as follows:
- Units sales totaled 80% of plan.
- Actual average selling price declined to ₹37.
- Productivity dropped to 250 diskettes per hour.
- Actual direct manufacturing labor cost is ₹150 per hour.
- Actual total direct material cost per unit dropped to ₹8.0.
- Actual direct marketing costs were ₹3 per unit.
- Fixed costs were ₹3,00,000 below plan.

Required

Calculate the following
1. Static-budget and actual operating income
2. Total static-budget variance
3. Flexible-budget operating income
4. Total flexible-budget variance
5. Total sales-volume variance

6. Total static-budget variance
7. Price and efficiency variances for direct manufacturing labor
8. Flexible-budget variance for direct manufacturing labor.

Solution

Comprehensive variance analysis review.

1. **Actual Results**

Units sold (80 percent × 15,00,000)	12,00,000
Selling price per unit	₹37
Revenues (12,00,000 × ₹3.70)	₹4,44,00,000
Direct materials purchased and used:	
Direct materials per unit	₹8
Total direct materials cost (12,00,000 × ₹8)	₹96,00,000
Direct manufacturing labor:	
Actual manufacturing rate per hour	₹15
Labor productivity per hour in units	250
Manufacturing labor-hours of input (12,00,000 ÷ 250)	4,800
Total direct manufacturing labor costs (4,800 × ₹150)	₹7,20,000
Direct marketing costs:	
Direct marketing cost per unit	₹3
Total direct marketing costs (12,00,000 × ₹3)	₹36,00,000
Fixed costs (₹90,00,000 – ₹3,00,000)	₹87,00,000

Static Budgeted Amounts

Units sold	15,00,000
Selling price per unit	₹40
Revenues (15,00,000 × ₹40)	₹6,00,00,000
Direct materials purchased and used:	
Direct materials per unit	₹8.5
Total direct materials costs (15,00,000 × ₹8.5)	₹1,27,50,000
Direct manufacturing labor:	
Direct manufacturing rate per hour	₹150
Labor productivity per hour in units	300
Manufacturing labor-hours of input (15,00,000 × 300)	5,000
Total direct manufacturing labor cost (5,000 × ₹150)	₹7,50,000
Direct marketing costs:	
Direct marketing cost per unit	₹3
Total direct marketing cost (15,00,000 × ₹3)	₹45,00,000
Fixed costs	₹90,00,000

	Actual Results	Static-Budgeted Amounts
Revenues		
Variable costs	₹4 ,44,00,000	₹6,00,00,000
Direct materials	96,00,000	1,27,50,000
Direct manufacturing labor	7,20,000	7,50,000
Direct marketing costs	36,00,000	45,00,000
Total variable costs	1,39,20,000	1,80,00,000
Contribution margin	3,04,80,000	4,20,00,000
Fixed costs	87,00,000	90,00,000
Operating income	₹2,17,80,000	₹3,30,00,000

2. Actual operating income   ₹2,17,80,000

    Static-budget operating income   3,30,00,000

    Total static-budget variance   ₹1,12,20,000 U

7-31 Comprehensive variance analysis. (CMA) Meghraj Cookies bakes cookies for retail stores. The Company's best-selling cookie is Chocolate Nut Supreme, which is marketed as a gourmet cookie and regularly sells for ₹80 per kg. The standard cost per kg of Chocolate Nut Supreme, based on Meghraj's normal monthly production of 4,00,000 kg, follows:

Cost Item	Quantity	Standard Unit Costs	Total Standard Cost
Direct materials			
Cookie mix	10 oz.	₹0.2/oz.	₹2.0
Milk chocolate	5 oz.	1.5/oz.	7.5
Almonds	1 oz.	5.0/oz.	5.0
			14.5
Direct manufacturing labora			
Mixing	1 min.	144/hr.	2.4
Baking	2 min.	180/hr.	6.0
			8.4
Variable			
Overheadb	3 min.	324/hr.	16.2
Total standard cost per kg			₹39.1

aDirect manufacturing labor rates include employee benefits.

bAllocated on the basis of direct labor-hours.

Meghraj's management accountant, Zaheer, prepares monthly budget reports based on these standard costs. Presented below is April-June report.

Performance Report, April-June 2016

	Actual	Budget	Variance
Units (in kg)	4,50,000	4,00,000	50,000 F
Revenues	₹3,55,50,000	₹3,20,00,000	₹35,50,000 F
Direct materials	86,50,000	58,00,000	28,50,000 U
Direct manufacturing labor	34,80,000	33,60,000	1,20,000 U

Abbas, president of the company, is disappointed with the results. Despite a sizable increase in the number of cookies sold, the product's expected contribution to the overall profitability of the company decreased. Abbas has asked Zaheer to identify the reasons why the contribution margin decreased. Zaheer has gathered the following information to help in his analysis of the decrease.

Usage Report, April–June 2016

Cost Item	Quantity	Actual Cost
Direct materials:		
Cookie mix	46,50,000 ounces	₹9,30,000
Milk chocolate	26,60,000 ounces	53,20,000
Almonds	4,80,000 ounces	24,00,000
Direct manufacturing labor		
Mixing	4,50,000 minutes	10,80,000
Baking	8,00,000 minutes	24,00,000

Required   Compute and comment on the following variances:

    1. Selling-price variance.

    2. Direct material price variance.

3. Direct material efficiency variance.
4. Direct manufacturing labor efficiency variance

Solution

Comprehensive variance analysis.

1. Computing unit selling prices and unit costs of inputs:

Actual selling price　　 = ₹3,55,50,000 ÷ 4,50,000 = ₹79

Budgeting selling price = ₹3,20,00,000 ÷ 4,00,000 = ₹80

$$\text{Selling - price variance} = \left(\begin{array}{c} \text{Actual} \\ \text{selling price} \end{array} - \begin{array}{c} \text{Budgeted} \\ \text{selling price} \end{array} \right) \times \begin{array}{c} \text{Actual} \\ \text{units sold} \end{array}$$

= (₹79/unit − ₹80/unit)　 × 4,50,000 units

= ₹4,50,000 U

2., 3., and 4.

The actual and budgeted unit costs are:

	Actual	Budgeted
Direct materials		
Cookie mix	₹0.20 (₹9,30,000 ÷ 46,50,000)	₹0.20
Milk chocolate	2.0 (₹53,20,000 ÷ 26,60,000)	1.50
Almonds	5.0 (₹24,00,000 ÷ 4,80,000)	5.00
Direct manufacturing labor		
Mixing	144 (₹10,80,000 ÷ 4,50,000 × 60)	144.00
Baking	180 (₹24,00,000 ÷ 8,00,000 × 60)	180.00

The actual output achieved is 4,50,000 kg of chocolate Nut Supreme.

The direct cost price and efficiency variances are:

	Actual Costs Incurred (Actual Input Qty. × Actual Price)	Price Variance	Actual Input Qty. × Budgeted Price	Efficiency Variance	Flexible Budget (Budgeted Input Qty. Allowed for Actual Output × Budgeted Price)
Direct materials	(1)	(2) = (1) − (3)	(3)	(4) = (3) − (5)	(5)
Cookie mix	₹9,30,000	₹0	₹9,30,000[a]	₹30,000 U	₹9,00,000[f]
Milk chocolate	53,20,000	13,30,000 U	39,90,000[b]	6,15,000 U	33,75,000[g]
Almonds	24,00,000	0	24,00,000[c]	1,50,000 U	22,50,000[h]
	₹86,50,000	₹13,30,000 U	₹73,20,000	₹7,95,000 U	₹65,25,000
Direct manufacturing labor costs					
Mixing	₹10,80,000	₹0	₹10,80,000[d]	₹0	₹10,80,000[i]
Baking	24,00,000	0	24,00,000[e]	3,00,000 F	27,00,000[j]
	₹34,80,000	₹0	₹34,80,000	₹3,00,000 F	₹37,80,000

[a]₹0.20 × 46,50,000　　 = ₹9,30,000

[b]₹1.50 × 26,60,000　　 = ₹39,90,000

[c]₹5.0 × 4,80,000　　　 = ₹24,00,000

[d]₹144 × (4,50,000 ÷ 60)　 = ₹10,80,000

[e]₹180 × (8,00,000 ÷ 60)　 = ₹24,00,000

[f]₹0.20 × 10 × 4,50,000　 = ₹9,00,000

[g]₹1.50 × 5 × 4,50,000　　 = ₹33,75,000

[h]₹5.0 × 1 × 4,50,000　　 = ₹22,50,000

[i]₹144 × (4,50,000 ÷ 60)　 = ₹10,80,000

[j]₹180 × (4,50,000 ÷ 30)　 = ₹27,00,000

Comments on the variances include:

- **Selling price variance.** This may arise from a proactive decision to reduce price to expand market share or from a reaction to a price reduction by a competitor.
- **Material price variance.** The ₹0.50 increase in the price per ounce of milk chocolate could arise from uncontrollable market factors or from poor contract negotiations.
- **Material efficiency variance.** For all three material inputs, usage is greater than budgeted. Possible reasons include lower quality inputs, use of lower quality workers, and the mixing and baking equipment not being maintained in a fully operational mode.
- **Labor efficiency variance.** The favorable efficiency variance for baking could be due to workers eliminating nonvalue-added steps in production.

7-32 Procurement costs, variance analysis, ethics. Vijay is the manager of the athletic shoe division of Action Shoes. Action Shoes is a company that has just purchased Relaxo, a leading shoe company. Relaxo has long-term production contracts with suppliers in two States, Uttar Pradesh and Bihar. Vijay receives a request from Anil, president of Action Shoes. Vijay and his controller, Mohan, are to make a presentation to the next Board of Directors meeting on the cost competitiveness of the Relaxo. This report should include budgeted and actual procurement costs for 2015 at its Uttar Pradesh and Bihar supply sources.

Mohan decides to visit the two supply operations. The budgeted average procurement cost for 2015 was ₹120 per pair of shoes. This cost includes payments to the shoe manufacturer and all other payments to conduct business in each state. Mohan reports the following to Vijay:

- **Uttar Pradesh.** Total 2015 procurement costs for 2,50,000 pairs of shoes were ₹3,32,50,000. Payment to the shoe manufacturer was ₹2,65,00,000. Very few receipts existed for the remaining ₹67,50,000. Kickback payments are viewed as common in Uttar Pradesh.
- **Bihar.** Total 2015 procurement costs for 9,00,000 pairs of shoes were ₹10,48,50,000. Payment to the shoe manufacturer was ₹8,64,00,000. Receipts existed for ₹70,50,000 of the other costs, but Mohan said he is skeptical of their validity. Kickback payments are a "way of business" at Bihar.

At both Uttar Pradesh and Bihar plants, Mohan was disturbed by the employment of young children (many of them younger than 15 years). He was told that all major shoe-producing companies had similar low-cost employment practices in both states.

Vijay is uncomfortable about the upcoming presentation to the board. He was a leading advocate of the acquisition. A recent business magazine reported that Relaxo acquisition would make Action Shoes the global low-cost producer in its market lines. The stock price of Action Shoes jumped 21% the day Relaxo acquisition was announced. Mohan likewise is widely identified as a proponent of the acquisition. He is seen as a "rising star" due for a promotion to a division manager in the near future.

Required

1. What summary procurement cost variances could be reported to the Board of Directors of Action Shoes?
2. What ethical issues do (a) Vijay and (b) Mohan face when preparing and making a report to the Board of Directors?
3. How should Mohan address the issues you identify in requirement 2?

Solution

Procurement costs, variance analysis, ethics.

1. Purchase price variances can be computed for each country.

$$\text{Purchase price variance} = \left[\begin{array}{c}\text{Actual price} \\ \text{of input}\end{array} - \begin{array}{c}\text{Budgeted price} \\ \text{of input}\end{array}\right] \times \begin{array}{c}\text{Actual quantity} \\ \text{of input}\end{array}$$

Uttar Pradesh

$$= (₹133^a – ₹120) \times 2,50,000 = ₹32,50,000 \text{ U}$$

^{a}₹3,32,50,000 ÷ 250,000 × ₹133

On a per-unit basis, there is a ₹106 payment to the shoe manufacturer and a ₹27 payment for "other costs."

Bihar

$$= (₹116.5^a – ₹120) \times 9,00,000 = ₹31,50,000 \text{ F}$$

^{a}₹10,48,50,000 ÷ 9,00,000 = ₹116.50

On a per-unit basis, there is a ₹96 payment to the shoe manufacturer and a ₹20.5 payment for "other costs."

Vijay and Mohan face many ethical issues:

(a) Reliability of cost information to be presented to the board of directors. There are minimal or questionable receipts for ₹67,50,000 in Uttar Pradesh and ₹1,84,50,000 in Bihar.

(b) Potential existence of kickback payments in both Uttar Pradesh and Bihar.

(c) Employment of young children (many of them under 15 years).

Should Vijay and Mohan be forthright and present all their concerns on (a), (b), and (c)?

Both Vijay and Mohan face the dilemma that any discussion of (a), (b), or (c) will raise questions about their own behavior at the time the acquisitions were made. Board members may ask "When did they first know about (a), (b), and (c)?," and "Why did they not undertake examination of these issues at the time they supported the acquisitions?"

3. Mohan has very high standards of ethical conduct to meet. He should not make presentations to the Board based on information he has strong doubts about. If he decides to make the presentation, all his concerns and caveats should be presented.

He should require detailed documentation for all payments. No future payments should be made without adequate documentation. Investigation of kickback allegations should be made, however difficult that may be. Mohan should be able to make a good-faith effort to ensure kickback payments are not an ongoing practice in Uttar Pradesh or Bihar.

Exercises

[*Comprehensive solutions to all exercises are available on the companion website www. pearsoned.co.in/charlesthorngren*]

7-33 Flexible budget. Haldiram Company sells sweets. Its budgeted operating income for the year ended December 31, 2014, was ₹31,50,000. As a result of continued explosive growth in its sales, actual operating income totaled ₹65,56,000.

Required

1. Calculate the total static-budget variances.
2. Flexible-budget operating income was ₹69,30,000. Calculate the total flexible-budget and total sales-volume variances.
3. Comment on the total flexible-budget variance in light of the explosive growth in its sales.

7-34 Materials and manufacturing labor variances. Consider the following data collected (for March) for Alps Industries Limited.

Particulars	Direct Materials	Direct Manufacturing Labor
Cost incurred: actual inputs × actual prices	₹2,00,000	₹90,000
Actual inputs × standard prices	2,14,000	86,000
Standard inputs allowed for actual outputs × standard prices	2,25,000	80,000

Required

Compute the price, efficiency, and flexible-budget variances for direct materials and direct manufacturing labor.

7-35 Flexible budgets, variance analysis. You have been hired as a consultant by Sandeep, the president of a small manufacturing company that makes automobile parts. Sandeep is an excellent engineer, but he has been frustrated by working with inadequate cost data.

You helped install flexible budgeting and standard costs. Sandeep has asked you to consider the following May data and recommend how variances might be computed and presented in performance reports:

Static budget in output units	20,000
Actual output units produced and sold	23,000
Budgeted selling price per output unit	₹40
Budgeted variable costs per output unit	₹25
Budgeted total fixed costs per month	₹2,00,000
Actual revenue	₹8,74,000
Actual variable costs	₹6,30,000
Favorable variance in fixed costs	₹5,000

Sandeep was disappointed. Although output units sold exceeded expectations, operating income did not. Assume that there was no beginning or ending inventory.

Required

1. You decide to present Sandeep with alternative ways to analyze variances so that he can decide what level of detail he prefers. The reporting system can then be designed accordingly. Prepare an analysis similar to Levels 0, 1, and 2 in Exhibit 7-1 and Exhibit 7-2.

2. What are some likely causes for the variances you report in requirement 1?

7-36 Flexible-budget preparation and analysis. Bank Printers Limited, produces luxury checkbooks with three checks and stubs per page. Each checkbook is designed for an individual customer and is ordered through the customer's bank.

The company's operating budget for September included these data:

Number of checkbooks	15,000
Selling price per book	₹20
Variable cost per book	₹8
Fixed costs for the month	₹1,45,000

The actual results for September were:

Number of checkbooks produced and sold	12,000
Average selling price per book	₹21
Variable cost per book	₹7
Fixed costs for the month	₹1,50,000

The executive Vice-president of the company observed that the operating income for September was much less than anticipated, despite a higher-than-budgeted selling price and a lower-than-budgeted variable cost per unit. You have been asked to provide explanations for the disappointing September results.

Bank Printer Limited develops its flexible budget on the basis of budgeted per-output-unit revenue and per-output-unit variable costs without detailed analysis of budgeted inputs.

1. Prepare a Level 1 analysis of the September performance.
2. Prepare a Level 2 analysis of the September performance.
3. Why might Bank Printer find the Level 2 analysis more informative than the Level 1 analysis? Explain your answer.

7-37 Materials and manufacturing labor variances, standard costs. Consider the following selected data regarding the manufacture of a line of upholstered chairs:

	Standards per Chair
Direct materials	2 square yards of input at ₹100 per square yard
Direct manufacturing labor	0.5 hour of input at 40 per hour

The following data were compiled regarding actual performance:

Actual output units (chairs) produced, 20,000; square yards of input purchased and used, 37,000; price per square yard, ₹102; direct manufacturing labor costs, ₹3,52,800; actual hours of input 9,000; labor price per hour, ₹39.20.

Required

Show computations of price and efficiency variances for direct materials and direct manufacturing labor. Give a plausible explanation of why the variances occurred.

7-38 Flexible budget. (Refer to Exercise 7-35) Suppose the static budget was for 24,000 units of output. The general manager is thrilled about the following report:

	Actual Results	Static Budget	Variance
Direct materials	₹37,74,000	₹48,00,000	₹10,26,000 F
Direct manufacturing labor	₹3,52,800	₹4,80,000	₹1,27,200 F

Required

Is the manager's glee warranted? Prepare a report that provides a more detailed explanation of why the static budget was not achieved. Actual output was 20,000 units.

7-39 Flexible budget, direct materials and direct manufacturing labor variances. TNT manufactures bust statues of famous historical figures. All statues are the same size. Each unit requires the same amount of resources. The following information is from the static budget for 2015:

Expected production and sales	5,000 units
Direct materials	50,000 kgs
Direct manufacturing labor	20,000 hours
Total fixed costs	₹10,00,000

Standard quantities, standard prices, and standard unit costs follow for direct materials and direct manufacturing labor.

	Standard Quantity	Standard Price	Standard Unit Cost
Direct material	10 kgs	₹100 per kg	₹1,000
Direct manufacturing labor	4 hours	₹40 per hour	₹160

During 2014, actual number of units produced and sold was 6,000. Actual cost of direct materials used was ₹59,40,000, based on 54,000 kgs purchased at ₹110 per kg. Direct manufacturing labor-hours actually used were 25,000, at the rate of ₹38 per hour. This resulted in actual direct manufacturing labor cost of ₹9,50,000. Actual fixed costs were ₹10,05,000. There were no beginning or ending inventories.

Required

1. Calculate sales-volume variance and flexible-budget variance.
2. Compute price and efficiency variances for direct materials and direct manufacturing labor.

7-40 Level 2 variance analysis, solve for unknowns. Home Sports manufactures and distributes baseball caps to ballparks and other sports venues. Home's plan for 2016 forecast sales of 6,00,000 caps. However, only 5,00,000 caps were sold. Based on the following data, calculate the missing numbers and complete the analysis.

Required

1. Calculate the budgeted and actual selling prices.
2. Assuming that the driver for variable costs is units sold, what are the budgeted and actual variable costs per unit?
3. Calculate the flexible-budget operating income.
4. Calculate the total flexible-budget variance.
5. Calculate the total sales-volume variance.
6. Calculate the total static-budget variance.

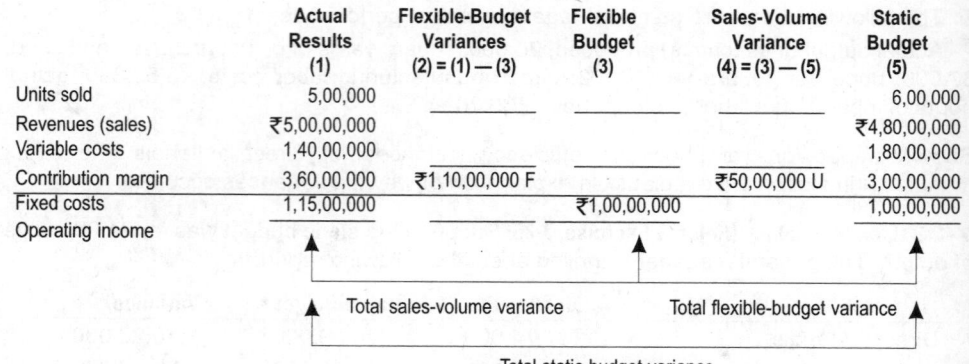

	Actual Results (1)	Flexible-Budget Variances (2) = (1) — (3)	Flexible Budget (3)	Sales-Volume Variance (4) = (3) — (5)	Static Budget (5)
Units sold	5,00,000				6,00,000
Revenues (sales)	₹5,00,00,000				₹4,80,00,000
Variable costs	1,40,00,000				1,80,00,000
Contribution margin	3,60,00,000	₹1,10,00,000 F		₹50,00,000 U	3,00,00,000
Fixed costs	1,15,00,000		₹1,00,00,000		1,00,00,000
Operating income					

Total sales-volume variance   Total flexible-budget variance

Total static-budget variance

7-41 Direct labor and direct materials variances, missing data (CMA, heavily adapted). Amit Surfboards manufactures fiberglass surfboards. The standard cost of direct materials and direct manufacturing labor is ₹500 per board. This includes 20 kg of direct materials, at the budgeted price of ₹10 per kg, and five hours of direct manufacturing labor, at the budgeted rate of ₹60 per hour. Following are the data for the month of July:

Units completed	6,000 units
Direct material purchases	1,50,000 kgs
Cost of direct material purchases	₹14,62,500
Actual direct manufacturing labor-hours	32,000 hours
Actual direct-labor cost	₹18,40,000
Direct materials efficiency variance	₹62,500 U

There were no beginning inventories.

Required

1. Compute direct manufacturing labor variances for July.
2. Compute the actual kg of direct materials used in production in July.
3. Calculate the actual price per kg of direct materials purchased.
4. Calculate direct materials price variance.

7-42 Direct materials and manufacturing labor variances, solving unknowns. (CPA, adapted) On May 1, 2015, First Call Company began the manufacture of a new product. The company installed a standard-costing system to account for manufacturing costs. The standard costs per unit is:

Direct materials (3 kg. at ₹5 per kg.)	₹15.00
Direct manufacturing labor (1/2 hour at ₹20 per hour)	10.00
Manufacturing overhead (75 percent of direct manufacturing labor costs)	7.50
	₹32.50

The following data were obtained from the records for the month of May:

Particulars	Debit	Credit
Revenues		₹1,25,000
Accounts payable control (for May's purchases of direct materials)		68,250
Direct materials price variance	₹3,250	
Direct materials efficiency variance	2,500	
Direct manufacturing labor price variance	1,900	
Direct manufacturing labor efficiency variance		2,000

Actual production in May was 4,000 units and actual sales in May were 2,500 units.

The amount shown earlier for direct materials price variance applies to materials purchased during May. There was no beginning inventory of materials on May 1, 2015.

Compute each of the following items for First Call for the month of May. Show your computations.   **Required**

1. Standard direct manufacturing labor-hours allowed for actual output produced.
2. Actual direct manufacturing labor-hours worked.
3. Actual direct manufacturing labor wage rate.
4. Standard quantity of direct materials allowed (in kg).
5. Actual quantity of direct materials used (in kg).
6. Actual quantity of direct materials purchased (in kg).
7. Actual direct materials price per kg.

7-43 Flexible budgeting, activity-based costing, variance analysis. Toymaster Limited produces a toy car, TGC, in batches. After each batch of TGC is run, the molds are cleaned. The labor costs of cleaning the molds can be traced to TGC because TGC can only be produced for a specific mold. The following information pertains to June 2015:

Particulars	Static-Budget Amounts	Actual Amounts
Units of TGC produced and sold	30,000	22,500
Batch size (units per batch)	250	225
Cleaning labor-hours per batch	3	3.5
Cleaning labor cost per hour	₹140	₹125

1. Calculate the flexible-budget variance for total cleaning labor costs in June 2015.   **Required**
2. Calculate the price and efficiency variances for total cleaning labor costs in June 2015. Comment on the results.

8 Flexible Budgets, Overhead Cost Variances, and Management Control

Learning Objectives ▼

1. Explain the similarities and differences in planning variable overhead costs and fixed overhead costs

2. Develop budgeted variable overhead cost rates and budgeted fixed overhead cost rates

3. Compute the variable overhead flexible-budget variance, the variable overhead efficiency variance, and the variable overhead spending variance

4. Compute the fixed overhead flexible-budget variance, the fixed overhead spending variance, and the fixed overhead production-volume variance

5. Show how the 4-variance analysis approach reconciles the actual overhead incurred with the overhead amounts allocated during the period

6. Explain the relationship between the sales-volume variance and the production-volume variance

7. Calculate variances in activity-based costing

8. Examine the use of overhead variances in nonmanufacturing settings

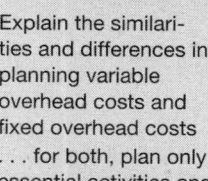

Learning Objective 1

Explain the similarities and differences in planning variable overhead costs and fixed overhead costs
. . . for both, plan only essential activities and be efficient; fixed overhead costs are usually determined well before the budget period begins

What do this week's weather forecast and an organization's performance have in common?

Much of the time, reality doesn't match what people expect. Rain that results in a little league game being canceled may suddenly give way to sunshine. Business owners expecting to "whistle their way to the bank" may change their tune after tallying their monthly bills and discovering that skyrocketing operational costs have significantly reduced their profits. Differences, or variances, are all around us.

Analyzing variances is a valuable activity for firms because the process highlights the areas where performance most lags expectations. By using this information to make corrective adjustments, companies can achieve significant savings. Furthermore, the process of setting up standards requires firms to have a thorough understanding of their fixed and variable overhead costs, which brings its own benefits.

Planning of Variable and Fixed Overhead Costs

We'll use the Color Plus Company example again to illustrate the planning and control of variable and fixed overhead costs. Recall that Color Plus manufactures jackets that are sold to distributors, who in turn sell to independent clothing stores and retail chains. Because we assume Color Plus's only costs are *manufacturing* costs, for simplicity we use the term overhead costs instead of manufacturing overhead costs. Color's variable overhead costs include energy, machine maintenance, engineering support, and indirect materials. Color's fixed overhead costs include plant leasing costs, depreciation on plant equipment, and the salaries of the plant managers.

Planning Variable Overhead Costs

To effectively plan variable overhead costs for a product or service, managers must focus on the activities that create a superior product or service for their customers and eliminate activities that do not add value. For example, customers expect Color Plus's jackets to last. So managers at Color Plus consider sewing to be an essential activity. Therefore, maintenance activities for sewing machines which are included in Color's variable overhead costs are also essential activities for which management must plan. Such maintenance should be done in a cost-effective way such as by scheduling periodic equipment maintenance rather than waiting for sewing machines to break down. For many companies today, it is critical to plan for ways to become more efficient in the use of energy, a rapidly growing component of variable overhead costs. Color Plus installs smart meters in order to monitor energy use in real time and steer production operations away from peak consumption periods.

Planning Fixed Overhead Costs

Planning fixed overhead costs is similar to planning variable overhead costs—undertake only essential activities and then plan to be efficient in that undertaking. But there is an additional strategic issue when it comes to planning fixed overhead costs: choosing the appropriate level of capacity or investment that will benefit the company in the long run. Consider Color's leasing of sewing machines, each of which has a fixed cost per year. Leasing too many machines will result in overcapacity and unnecessary fixed leasing costs. Leasing too few machines will result in an inability to meet demand, lost sales of jackets, and unhappy customers. Consider AT&T, which did not initially foresee the iPhone's appeal or the proliferation of "apps" and consequently did not upgrade its network sufficiently to handle the resulting data traffic. AT&T subsequently had to impose limits on how customers could use the iPhone (such as by curtailing tethering and the streaming of Webcasts). This explains why following the iPhone's release, at one point AT&T had the lowest customer satisfaction ratings among all major carriers.

The planning of fixed overhead costs differs from the planning of variable overhead costs in another regard as well: timing. At the start of a budget period, management will have made most of the decisions determining the level of fixed overhead costs to be incurred. But it's the day-to-day, ongoing operating decisions that mainly determine the level of variable overhead costs incurred in that period. For example, the variable overhead costs of hospitals, which include the costs of disposable supplies, doses of medication, suture packets, and medical waste disposal, are a function of the number and nature of procedures carried out, as well as the practice patterns of the physicians. However, most of the costs of providing hospital service are fixed overhead costs—those related to buildings, equipment, and salaried labor. These costs are unrelated to a hospital's volume of activity.[1]

◀ **Decision Point**

How do managers plan variable overhead costs and fixed overhead costs?

Standard Costing at Color Plus Company

Webb uses standard costing. Chapter 7 explained how the standards for Color's direct manufacturing costs were developed. This chapter explains how the standards for Color's manufacturing overhead costs are developed. **Standard costing** is a costing system that (1) traces direct costs to output produced by multiplying the standard prices or rates by the standard quantities of inputs allowed for actual outputs produced and (2) allocates overhead costs on the basis of the standard overhead-cost rates times the standard quantities of the allocation bases allowed for the actual outputs produced.

The standard cost of Color's jackets can be computed at the start of the budget period. This feature of standard costing simplifies record keeping because no record is needed of the actual overhead costs or of the actual quantities of the cost-allocation bases used for making the jackets. What managers do need are the standard overhead cost rates for Color's variable and fixed overhead. Management accountants calculate these cost rates based on the planned amounts of variable and fixed overhead and the standard quantities of the allo-

Learning Objective 2

Develop budgeted variable overhead cost rates

. . . budgeted variable costs divided by quantity of cost-allocation base

and budgeted fixed overhead cost rates

. . . budgeted fixed costs divided by quantity of cost-allocation base

---

[1] Free-standing surgery centers have thrived because they have lower fixed overhead costs compared to traditional hospitals. For an enlightening summary of costing issues in health care, see A. Macario. 2010. "What does one minute of operating room time cost?" Journal of Clinical Anesthesia, June.

cation bases. We describe these computations next. Note that once standards have been set, the costs of using standard costing are low relative to the costs of using actual costing or normal costing.

Developing Budgeted Variable Overhead Rates

Budgeted variable overhead cost-allocation rates can be developed in four steps. Throughout the chapter, we use the broader term "budgeted rate" rather than "standard rate" to be consistent with the term used in describing normal costing in earlier chapters. When standard costing, is used, the budgeted rates are standard rates.

Step 1: Choose the Period to Be Used for the Budget. Color Plus uses a 12-month budget period. Chapter 4 (page 144) provided two reasons for using annual overhead rates rather than, say, monthly rates. The first relates to the numerator, such as reducing the influence of seasonality on the firm's cost structure. The second relates to the denominator, such as reducing the effect of varying output and number of days in a month. In addition, setting overhead rates once a year rather than 12 times a year saves managers time.

Step 2: Select the Cost-Allocation Bases to Use in Allocating Variable Overhead Costs to Output Produced. Color's operating managers select machine-hours as the cost-allocation base because they believe that machine-hours is the only cost driver of variable overhead. Based on an engineering study, Color Plus estimates it will take 0.40 of a machine-hour per actual output unit. For its budgeted output of 1,44,000 jackets in 2014, Color Plus budgets 57,600 (0.40 × 1,44,000) machine-hours.

Step 3: Identify the Variable Overhead Costs Associated with Each Cost-Allocation Base. Color Plus groups all of its variable overhead costs, including costs of energy, machine maintenance, engineering support, indirect materials, and indirect manufacturing labor in a single cost pool. Color's total budgeted variable overhead costs for 2014 are ₹1,72,80,000.

Step 4: Compute the Rate per Unit of Each Cost-Allocation Base Used to Allocate Variable Overhead Costs to Output Produced. Dividing the amount in step 3 (₹1,72,80,000) by the amount in step 2 (57,600 machine-hours), Color Plus estimates a rate of ₹300 per standard machine-hour for allocating its variable overhead costs.

When standard costing is used, the variable overhead rate per unit of the cost-allocation base (₹300 per machine-hour for Color Plus) is generally expressed as a standard rate per output unit. Color Plus calculates the budgeted variable overhead cost rate per output unit as follows:

$$
\begin{aligned}
\text{Budgeted variable overhead cost} &= \text{Budgeted input allowed} \times \text{Budgeted variable overhead cost} \\
\text{rate per output unit} & \text{per output unit} \quad\quad \text{rate per input unit} \\
&= \text{0.40 hour per jacket} \times \text{₹300 per hour} \\
&= \text{₹120 per jacket}
\end{aligned}
$$

The ₹120 per jacket is the budgeted variable overhead cost rate in Color's static budget for 2014 as well as in the monthly performance reports the firm prepares during 2014.

The ₹120 per jacket represents the amount by which managers expect Color's variable overhead costs change when the amount of output changes. As the number of jackets manufactured increases, the variable overhead costs allocated to output (for the inventory costing) increase at the rate of ₹120 per jacket. The ₹120 per jacket represents the firm's total variable overhead costs, per unit of output, including energy, repairs, indirect labor, and so on. Managers help control variable overhead costs by budgeting each of these line items and then investigating possible causes for any significant variances.

Developing Budgeted Fixed Overhead Rates

Fixed overhead costs are, by definition, a lump sum of costs that remains unchanged in total for a given period, despite wide changes in the level of total activity or output. Fixed costs are included in flexible budgets, but they remain the same total amount within the relevant range of activity regardless of the output level chosen to "flex" the variable costs and revenues. Recall from Exhibit 7-2 and the steps in developing a flexible budget, that Color's monthly fixed overhead costs of ₹27,60,000 are the same in the static budget as they are in the flexible budget. Do not assume, however, that these costs can never be changed. Managers can reduce them by selling equipment or by laying off employees, for example. But the costs are fixed in the sense that, unlike variable costs such as direct material costs, fixed costs do not automatically increase or decrease with the level of activity within the relevant range.

The process of developing the budgeted fixed overhead rate is the same as that detailed earlier for calculating the budgeted variable overhead rate. The steps are as follows:

Step 1:   Choose the Period to Use for the Budget. As with variable overhead costs, the budget period for fixed overhead costs is typically 12 months to help smooth out seasonal effects.

Step 2:   Select the Cost-Allocation Bases to Use in Allocating Fixed Overhead Costs to Output Produced. Color Plus uses machine-hours as the only cost-allocation base for fixed overhead costs. Why? Because Color Plus's managers believe that, in the long run, fixed overhead costs will increase or decrease to the levels needed to support the amount of machine-hours. Therefore, in the long run, the amount of machine-hours used is the only cost driver of fixed overhead costs. The number of machine-hours is the denominator in the budgeted fixed overhead rate computation and is called the **denominator level**. For simplicity, we assume Color Plus expects to operate at capacity in fiscal year 2014 with a budgeted usage of 57,600 machine-hours for a budgeted output of 1,44,000 jackets.[2]

Step 3:   Identify the Fixed Overhead Costs Associated with Each Cost-Allocation Base. Because Color Plus identifies only a single cost-allocation base—machine-hours—to allocate fixed overhead costs, it groups all such costs into a single cost pool. Costs in this pool include depreciation on plant and equipment, plant and equipment leasing costs, and the plant manager's salary. Color Plus's fixed overhead budget for 2014 is ₹3,31,20,000.

Step 4:   Compute the Rate per Unit of Each Cost-Allocation Base Used to Allocate Fixed Overhead Costs to Output Produced. By dividing the ₹3,31,20,000 from Step 3 by the 57,600 machine-hours from Step 2, Color Plus estimates a fixed overhead cost rate of ₹575.0 per machine-hour:

$$\frac{\text{Budgeted fixed overhead cost per unit of cost-allocation base}} = \frac{\text{Budgeted total costs in fixed overhead cost pool}}{\text{Budgeted total quantity of cost-allocation base}} = \frac{₹3,31,20,000}{57,600} = ₹575.0 \text{ per machine-hour}$$

Under standard costing, the ₹575.0 fixed overhead cost per machine-hour is usually expressed as a standard cost per output unit. Recall that Color Plus's engineering study estimates that it will take 0.40 machine-hour per output unit. Color Plus can now calculate the budgeted fixed overhead cost per output unit as follows:

---

[2] Because Color Plus plans its capacity over multiple periods, anticipated demand in 2011 could be such that budgeted output for 2014 is less than capacity. Companies very in the denominator levels they choose; some may choose budgeted output and other may choose capacity. In either case, the basic approach and analysis presented in this chapter is unchanged. Chapter 9 discusses in more detail implication of choosing a denominator level.

$$\begin{array}{ccc}
\text{Budgeted fixed} & \text{Budgeted quantity of} & \text{Budgeted fixed} \\
\text{overhead cost per} = & \text{cost-allocation} & \times & \text{overhead cost} \\
\text{output unit} & \text{base allowed per} & \text{per unit of} \\
 & \text{output unit} & \text{cost-allocation base}
\end{array}$$

$$= \text{0.40 of a machine-hour per jacket} \times ₹575.0 \text{ per machine-hour}$$

$$= ₹230.0 \text{ per jacket}$$

When preparing monthly budgets for 2014, Color Plus divides the ₹3,31,20,000 annual total fixed costs into 12 equal monthly amounts of ₹27,60,000.

Variable Overhead Cost Variances

We now illustrate how the budgeted variable overhead rate is used in computing Color's variable overhead cost variances. The following data are for April 2014, when Color Plus produced and sold 10,000 jackets:

	Actual Result	Flexible-Budget Amount
1. Output units (jackets)	10,000	10,000
2. Machine-hours per output unit	0.45	0.40
3. Machine-hours (1 × 2)	4,500	4,000
4. Variable overhead costs	₹13,05,000	₹12,00,000
5. Variable overhead costs per machine-hour (4 ÷ 3)	₹90	₹300
6. Variable overhead costs per output unit (4 ÷ 1)	₹130.5	₹120

As we saw in Chapter 7, the flexible budget enables Color Plus to highlight the differences between actual costs and actual quantities versus budgeted costs and budgeted quantities for the actual output level of 10,000 jackets.

Flexible-Budget Analysis

The **variable overhead flexible-budget variance** measures the difference between actual variable overhead costs incurred and flexible-budget variable overhead amounts.

$$\begin{array}{ccc}
\text{Variable overhead} & \text{Actual costs} & \text{Flexible-budget} \\
\text{flexible-budget variance} = & \text{incurred} & - & \text{amount}
\end{array}$$

$$= ₹13,05,000 - ₹12,00,000$$

$$= ₹1,05,000 \text{ U}$$

This ₹1,05,000 unfavorable flexible-budget variance means Color's actual variable overhead exceeded the flexible-budget amount by ₹1,05,000 for the 10,000 jackets actually produced and sold. Color's managers would want to know why. Did Color Plus use more machine-hours than planned to produce the 10,000 jackets? If so, was it because workers were less skilled than expected in using machines? Or did Color Plus spend more on variable overhead costs, such as maintenance?

Just as we illustrated in Chapter 7 with the flexible-budget variance for direct-cost items, Color's managers can get further insight into the reason for the ₹1,05,000 unfavorable variance by subdividing it into the efficiency variance and spending variance.

Variable Overhead Efficiency Variance

The **variable overhead efficiency variance** is the difference between actual quantity of the cost-allocation base used and budgeted quantity of the cost-allocation base that should have been used to produce actual output, multiplied by budgeted variable overhead cost per unit of the cost-allocation base.

$$\begin{matrix} \text{Variable} \\ \text{overhead} \\ \text{efficiency} \\ \text{variance} \end{matrix} = \left(\begin{matrix} \text{Actual quantity of} \\ \text{variable overhead} \\ \text{cost-allocation base} \\ \text{used for actual} \\ \text{output} \end{matrix} - \begin{matrix} \text{Budgeted quantity of} \\ \text{variable overhead} \\ \text{cost-allocation base} \\ \text{allowed for} \\ \text{actual output} \end{matrix} \right) \times \begin{matrix} \text{Budgeted variable} \\ \text{overhead cost per unit} \\ \text{of cost-allocation base} \end{matrix}$$

= (4,500 hours – 0.40 hr/unit × 10,000 units) × ₹300 per hour

= (4,500 hours – 4,000 hours) × ₹300 per hour

= 1,50,000 U

Columns 2 and 3 of Exhibit 8-1 depict the variable overhead efficiency variance. Note the variance arises solely because of the difference between actual quantity (4,500 hours) and budgeted quantity (4,000 hours) of the cost-allocation base. The variable overhead efficiency variance is computed the same way as the efficiency variance for direct-cost items (Chapter 7). However, the interpretation of the variance is somewhat different. Efficiency variances for direct-cost items are based on differences between actual inputs used and budgeted inputs allowed for actual output produced. a forensic laboratory (the kind popularized by television shows such as *CSI* and *Dexter*) would calculate a direct labor efficiency variance based on whether the lab used more or fewer hours than the standard hours allowed for the actual number of DNA tests. In contrast, the efficiency variance for variable overhead cost is based on the efficiency with which the cost-allocation base is used. Color's unfavorable variable overhead efficiency variance of ₹1,50,000 means that the actual machine-hours (the cost-allocation base) of 4,500 hours turned out to be higher than the budgeted machine-hours of 4,000 hours allowed to manufacture 10,000 jackets

---

Exhibit 8-1 Columnar Presentation of Variable Overhead Variance Analysis: Color Plus Company for April 2014[a]

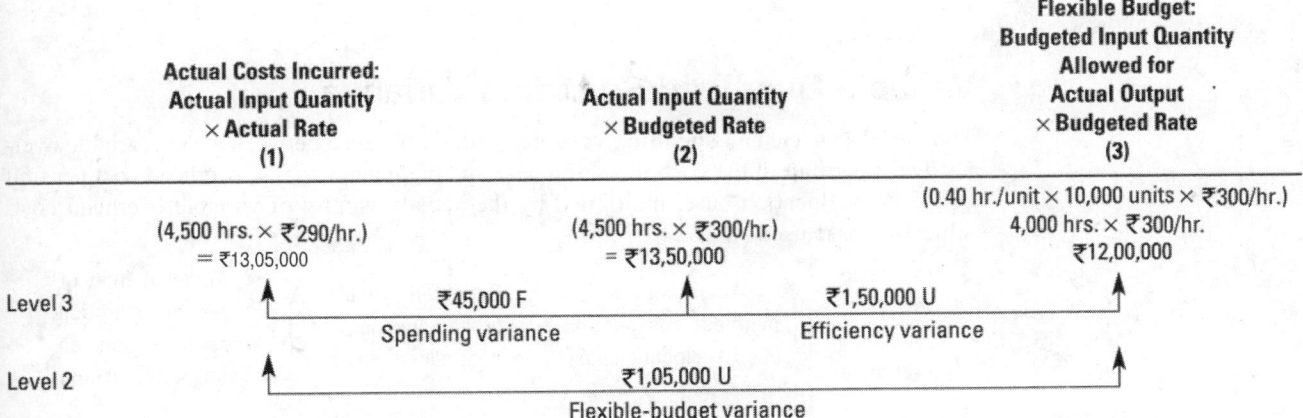

	Actual Costs Incurred: Actual Input Quantity × Actual Rate (1)		Actual Input Quantity × Budgeted Rate (2)		Flexible Budget: Budgeted Input Quantity Allowed for Actual Output × Budgeted Rate (3)
					(0.40 hr./unit × 10,000 units × ₹300/hr.)
	(4,500 hrs. × ₹290/hr.)		(4,500 hrs. × ₹300/hr.)		4,000 hrs. × ₹300/hr.
	= ₹13,05,000		= ₹13,50,000		₹12,00,000
Level 3		₹45,000 F		₹1,50,000 U	
		Spending variance		Efficiency variance	
Level 2			₹1,05,000 U		
			Flexible-budget variance		

---

[a]F = favorable effect on operating income; U = unfavorable effect on operating income.

Possible Causes for Exceeding Budget	Potential Management Responses
1. Workers were less skilled than expected in using machines.	1. Encourage the human resources department to implement better employee-hiring practices and training procedures.
2. Production scheduler inefficiently scheduled jobs, resulting in more machine-hours used than budgeted.	2. Improve plant operations by installing production scheduling software.
3. Machines were not maintained in good operating condition.	3. Ensure preventive maintenance is done on all machines.
4. Color's sales staff promised a distributor a rush delivery, which resulted in more machine-hours used than budgeted.	4. Coordinate production schedules with sales staff and distributors and share information with them.
5. Budgeted machine time standards were set too tight.	5. Commit more resources to develop appropriate standards.

and this, to the extent machine-hours are a cost driver for variable overhead, pushed up the potential spending on variable overhead.

The following table shows possible causes for Color's actual machine-hours exceeding budgeted machine-hours and Color's potential responses to each of these causes.

Note how, depending on the cause(s) of the variance, corrective actions may need to be taken not just in manufacturing but also in other business functions of the value chain, such as sales and distribution.

Color's managers discovered that one reason for the unfavorable variance was that workers were underskilled. As a result, Color is improving its hiring and training practices. Insufficient maintenance performed in the 2 months prior to April 2014 was another reason. A former plant manager had delayed the maintenance in an attempt to meet Color's monthly cost targets. As we discussed in Chapter 6, managers should not focus on meeting short-run cost targets if they are likely to result in harmful long-run consequences. For example, if Color's employees were to hurt themselves while operating poorly maintained machinery, the consequences would not only be harmful, they could be deadly. Color is now strengthening its internal maintenance procedures so that failure to do monthly maintenance as needed will raise a "red flag" that must be immediately explained to management. Color is also taking a hard look at its evaluation practices to determine if they inadvertently pressure managers to fixate on short-term targets to the long-run detriment of the firm.

Variable Overhead Spending Variance

The **variable overhead spending variance** is the difference between actual variable overhead cost per unit of the cost-allocation base and budgeted variable overhead cost per unit of the cost-allocation base, multiplied by the actual quantity of variable overhead cost-allocation base used.

$$\begin{pmatrix} \text{Variable} \\ \text{overhead} \\ \text{spending} \\ \text{variance} \end{pmatrix} = \begin{pmatrix} \text{Actual variable} \\ \text{overhead cost per unit} \\ \text{of cost-allocation base} \end{pmatrix} - \begin{pmatrix} \text{Budgeted variable} \\ \text{overhead cost per unit} \\ \text{of cost-allocation base} \end{pmatrix} \times \begin{pmatrix} \text{Actual quantity of} \\ \text{variable overhead} \\ \text{cost-allocation base} \\ \text{used for actual output} \end{pmatrix}$$

$= ₹(290 \text{ per machine-hour} - ₹300 \text{ per machine-hour}) \times 4{,}500 \text{ machine-hour}$

$= (- ₹10 \text{ per machine-hour}) \times 4{,}500 \text{ machine-hour}$

$= ₹45{,}000 \text{ F}$

Color Plus operated in April 2014 with a lower-than-budgeted variable overhead cost per machine-hour, so there is a favorable variable overhead spending variance. Columns 1 and 2 in Exhibit 8-1 depict this variance.

To understand why the favorable variable overhead spending variance occurred, Color's managers need to recognize why *actual* variable overhead cost per unit of the cost-allocation base (₹290 per machine-hour) is *lower* than *budgeted* variable overhead cost per unit of the cost-allocation base (₹300 per machine-hour).

Overall, Color Plus used 4,500 machine-hours, which is 12.5% greater than the flexible-budget amount of 4,000 machine hours. However, actual variable overhead costs of ₹13,05,000 are only 8.75% greater than the flexible-budget amount of ₹12,00,000. Thus, relative to the flexible budget, the percentage increase in actual variable overhead costs is less than the percentage increase in machine-hours. Consequently, the actual variable overhead cost per machine-hour is lower than the budgeted amount, resulting in a favorable variable overhead spending variance.

Recall that variable overhead costs include costs of energy, machine maintenance, indirect materials, and indirect labor. Two possible reasons why the percentage increase in actual variable overhead costs is less than the percentage increase in machine-hours are as follows:

1. The actual prices of individual inputs included in variable overhead costs, such as the price of energy, indirect materials, or indirect labor, are lower than budgeted prices of these inputs. For example, the actual price of electricity may only be ₹0.90 per kilowatt-hour, compared with a price of ₹1.0 per kilowatt-hour in the flexible budget.

2. Relative to the flexible budget, the percentage increase in the actual use of individual items in the variable overhead-cost pool is less than the percentage increase in machine-hours. Compared with the flexible-budget amount of 30,000 kilowatt-hours, suppose the actual energy use was 32,400 kilowatt-hours, or 8% higher. The fact that this is a smaller percentage increase than the 12.5% increase in machine-hours (4,500 actual machine-hours versus a flexible budget of 4,000 machine-hours) will lead to a favorable variable overhead spending variance, which can be partially or completely traced to the efficient use of energy and other variable overhead items.

As part of the last stage of the five-step decision-making process, Color's managers will need to examine the signals provided by the variable overhead variances to *evaluate the firm's performance and learn*. By understanding the reasons for these variances, Color Plus can take appropriate actions and make more precise predictions in order to achieve improved results in future periods.

For example, Color's managers must examine why actual prices of variable overhead cost items are different from budgeted prices. The differences could be the result of skillful negotiation on the part of the purchasing manager, oversupply in the market, or lower quality of inputs such as indirect materials. Color's response depends on what is believed to be the cause of the variance. If the concerns are about quality, for instance, Color Plus may want to put in place new quality management systems.

Similarly, Color's managers should understand the possible causes for the efficiency with which variable overhead resources are used. These causes include skill levels of workers, maintenance of machines and the efficiency of the manufacturing process. Color's managers discovered that Color Plus used fewer supervision resources per machine hour because of manufacturing process improvements. As a result, they began organizing cross-functional teams to see if more process improvements could be achieved.

We emphasize that a favorable variable overhead spending variance is not always desirable. For example, the variable overhead spending variance would be favorable if Color's managers purchased lower-priced, poor-quality indirect materials, hired less-talented supervisors, or performed less machine maintenance. These decisions, however, are likely to hurt product quality and harm the long-run prospects of the business.

To clarify the concepts of variable overhead efficiency variance and variable overhead spending variance, consider the following example. Suppose that (a) energy is the only item of variable overhead cost and machine-hours is the cost-allocation base, (b) actual machine-hours used equals the number of machine-hours under the flexible budget, and (c) actual price of energy equals budgeted price. From (a) and (b), it follows that there is no efficiency variance—the company has been efficient with respect to the number of machine-hours (the cost-allocation base) used to produce the actual output. However, and despite (c), there could still be a spending variance. Why? Because even though the company used the correct number of machine-hours, the energy consumed *per machine-hour* could be higher than budgeted (for example, because the machines have not been maintained correctly). The cost of this higher energy usage would be reflected in an unfavorable spending variance.

Journal Entries for Variable Overhead Costs and Variances

We now prepare journal entries for Variable Overhead Control account and the contra account Variable Overhead Allocated.

Entries for variable overhead for April 2014 (data from Exhibit 8-1) are:

1.	Variable Overhead Control	13,05,000	
	Accounts Payable and various other accounts	13,05,000	
	To record actual variable overhead costs incurred.		
2.	Work-in-Process Control	12,00,000	
	Variable Overhead Allocated		12,00,000
	To record variable overhead cost allocated		
	(0.40 machine-hour/unit × 10,000 units ×		
	₹300/machine-hour). (The costs accumulated in		
	Work-in-Process Control are transferred to Finished		
	Goods Control when production is completed and to		
	Cost of Goods Sold when the products are sold.)		
3.	Variable Overhead Allocated	12,00,000	
	Variable Overhead Efficiency Variance	15,000	
	Variable Overhead Control		13,05,000
	Variable Overhead Spending Variance		45,000
	To record variances for the accounting period.		

These variances are the underallocated or overallocated variable overhead costs. At the end of the fiscal year, the variance accounts are written off to cost of goods sold if immaterial in amount. If the variances are material in amount, they are prorated among Work-in-Process Control, Finished Goods Control, and Cost of Goods Sold on the basis of the variable overhead allocated to these accounts, as described in Chapter 4. As we discussed in Chapter 7, only unavoidable costs are prorated. Any part of the variances attributable to avoidable inefficiency are written off in the period. Assume that the balances in the variable overhead variance accounts as of April 2014 are also the balances at the end of the 2014 fiscal year and are immaterial in amount. The following journal entry records the write-off of the variance accounts to cost of goods sold.

Cost of Goods Sold	1,05,000	
Variable Overhead Spending Variance	45,000	
Variable Overhead Efficiency Variance		1,50,000

Next we demonstrate how to calculate fixed overhead cost variances.

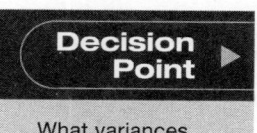

Decision Point ▶

What variances can be calculated for variable overhead costs?

Fixed Overhead Cost Variances

The flexible-budget amount for a fixed-cost item is also the amount included in the static budget prepared at the start of the period. No adjustment is required for differences between actual output and budgeted output for fixed costs because fixed costs are unaffected by changes in the output level within the relevant range. At the start of 2014, Color Plus budgeted its fixed overhead costs to be ₹27,60,000 per month. The actual amount for April 2014 turned out to be ₹28,50,000. The **fixed overhead flexible-budget variance** is the difference between actual fixed overhead costs and fixed costs in the flexible budget:

$$\text{Fixed overhead flexible-budget variance} = \text{Actual costs incurred} - \text{Flexible-budget amount}$$

$$= ₹28,50,000 - ₹27,60,000$$

$$= ₹90,000 \text{ U}$$

The variance is unfavorable because ₹28,50,000 actual fixed overhead costs exceed the ₹27,60,000 budgeted for April 2014, which decreases that month's operating income by ₹90,000.

The variable overhead flexible-budget variance described earlier in this chapter was subdivided into a spending variance and an efficiency variance. There is not an efficiency variance for fixed overhead costs. That's because a given lump sum of fixed overhead costs will be unaffected by how efficiently machine-hours are used to produce output in a given budget period. As we will see later on, this does not mean that a company cannot be efficient or inefficient in its use of fixed-overhead-cost resources. As Exhibit 8-2 shows, because there is no efficiency variance, the **fixed overhead spending variance** is the same amount as the fixed overhead flexible-budget variance:

$$\text{Fixed overhead spending variance} = \text{Actual costs incurred} - \text{Flexible-budget amount}$$

$$= ₹28,50,000 - ₹27,60,000$$

$$= ₹90,000 \text{ U}$$

Exhibit 8-2

Columnar Presentation of Fixed Overhead Variance Analysis: Color Plus Company for April 2014[a]

Actual Costs Incurred (1)	Flexible Budget: Same Budgeted Lump Sum (as in Static Budget) Regardless of Output Level (2)	Allocated: Budgeted Input Quantity Allowed for Actual Output × Budgeted Rate (3)
		(0.40 hr./unit × 10,000 units × ₹575.0/hr.)
		(4,000 hrs. × ₹575.0/hr.)
₹28,50,000	₹27,60,000	₹23,00,000

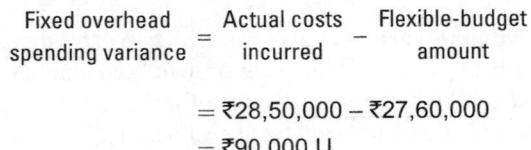

Level 3   ↑——— 90,000 U ———↑   ↑——— ₹4,60,000 U ———↑
              Spending variance   Production-volume variance

Level 2   ↑——————— ₹90,000 U ———————↑
                 Flexible-budget variance

[a]F = favorable effect on operating income; U = unfavorable effect on operating income.

Reasons for the unfavorable spending variance could be higher plant-leasing costs, higher depreciation on plant and equipment, or higher administrative costs such as a higher-than-budgeted salary paid to the plant manager. Color Plus investigated this variance and found that there was a ₹90,000 per month unexpected increase in its equipment-leasing costs. However, managers concluded that the new lease rates were competitive with lease rates available elsewhere. If this were not the case, Color Plus would look to lease equipment from other suppliers.

Production-Volume Variance

The **production-volume variance** arises only for fixed costs. It is the difference between the budgeted fixed overhead and the fixed overhead allocated on the basis of actual output produced. Recall that at the start of the year, Webb calculated a budgeted fixed overhead rate of ₹575.0 per machine-hour based on monthly budgeted fixed overhead costs of ₹27,60,000. Under standard costing, Color's fixed overhead costs are allocated to the actual output produced during each period at the rate of ₹575.0 per standard machine-hour, which is equivalent to a rate of ₹230 per jacket (0.40 machine-hour per jacket × ₹575.0 per machine-hour). If Color Plus produces 1,000 jackets, ₹2,30,000 (₹230 per jacket × 1,000 jackets) out of April's budgeted fixed overhead costs of ₹27,60,000 will be allocated to the jackets. If Color Plus produces 10,000 jackets, ₹23,00,000 (₹230 per jacket × 10,000 jackets) will be allocated. Only if Color Plus produces 12,000 jackets (that is, operates at capacity), will all ₹27,60,000 (₹230 per jacket × 12,000 jackets) of the budgeted fixed overhead cost be allocated to the jacket output. The key point here is that even though Color Plus budgets fixed overhead costs to be ₹27,60,000 it does not necessarily allocate all these costs to output. The reason is that Color Plus budgets ₹27,60,000 of fixed costs to support its planned production of 12,000 jackets. If Color Plus produces fewer than 12,000 jackets, it only allocates the budgeted cost of capacity actually needed and used to produce the jackets.

The **production-volume variance, also** referred **to as the denominator-level variance**, is the difference between budgeted and allocated fixed amount overheads. Note that the allocated overhead can be expressed in terms of allocation-base units (machine-hours for Color Plus) or in terms of the budgeted fixed cost per unit:

$$\begin{array}{rcl} \text{Production} & = & \text{Budgeted} \\ \text{volume variance} & & \text{fixed overhead} \end{array} - \begin{array}{l} \text{Fixed overhead allocated} \\ \text{for actual output units produced} \end{array}$$

= ₹27,60,000 – (0.40 hour per jacket × ₹575.0 per hour × 10,000 jackets)
= ₹27,60,000 – ₹230 per jacket × 10,000 jackets)
= ₹27,60,000 – ₹23,00,000
= ₹4,60,000 U

As shown in Exhibit 8-2, the budgeted fixed overhead (₹27,60,000) will be the lump sum shown in the static budget and also in any flexible budget within the relevant range. Fixed overhead allocated (₹23,00,000) is the amount of fixed overhead costs allocated; it is calculated by multiplying the number of output units produced during the budget period (10,000 units) by the budgeted cost per output unit (₹230). The ₹4,60,000 U production-volume variance can also be thought of as ₹230 per jacket × 2,000 jackets that were *not* produced. We will explore possible causes for the unfavorable production-volume variance and its management implications in the following section.

Exhibit 8-3 shows Color's production-volume variance. For planning and control purposes, Color's fixed (manufacturing) overhead costs do not change in the 0 to 12,000 unit relevant range. Contrast this behavior of fixed costs with how these costs are depicted for the inventory costing purpose in Exhibit 8-3. Under generally accepted accounting principles, fixed (manufacturing) overhead costs are allocated as an inventoriable cost to the output units produced. Every output unit that Color Plus manufactures will increase the fixed overhead allocated to products by ₹230. That is, for purposes of allocating fixed overhead costs to jackets, these costs are viewed as if they had a variable-cost behavior pattern. As the graph in Exhibit 8-3 shows, the difference between the fixed overhead costs budgeted of ₹27,60,000 and the ₹23,00,000 of costs allocated is the ₹4,60,000 unfavorable production-volume variance.

Managers should always be careful to distinguish the true behavior of fixed costs from the manner in which fixed costs are assigned to products. In particular, although fixed costs are unitized and allocated for inventory costing purposes, managers should be wary of using the same unitized fixed overhead costs for planning and control purposes. When forecasting fixed costs, managers should concentrate on total lump-sum costs instead of unitized costs. Similarly, when managers are looking to assign costs for control purposes or identify the best way to use capacity resources fixed in the short run, we will see in Chapter 9 and Chapter 11 that the use of unitized fixed costs often leads to incorrect decisions.

Interpreting the Production-Volume Variance

Lump-sum fixed costs represent costs of acquiring capacity. These costs do not decrease automatically if the capacity needed turn out to be less than the capacity acquired. Sometimes costs are fixed for a specific time period for contractual reasons such as an annual lease contract for a plant. At other times, costs are fixed because capacity has to be acquired or disposed of in fixed increments, or lumps. For example, suppose that acquiring a sewing machine gives Color Plus the ability to produce 1,000 jackets. If it is not possible to buy or lease a fraction of a machine, Color Plus can add capacity only in increments of 1,000 jackets. That is, Color Plus may choose capacity levels of 10,000, 11,000, or 12,000 jackets, but nothing in between.

Color's management would want to analyze the ₹4,60,000 unfavorable production-volume variance. Why did this overcapacity occur? Why were 10,000 jackets produced instead

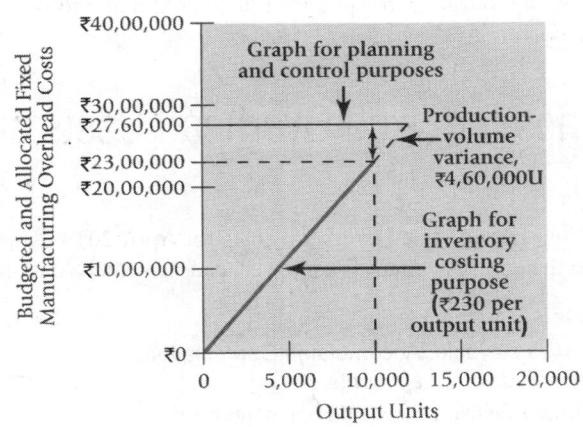

Exhibit 8-3

Behavior of Fixed Manufacturing Overhead Costs: Budgeted for Planning and Control Purposes and Allocated for Inventory Costing Purposes for Color Plus Company for April 2014

of 12,000? Is demand weak? Should Color Plus reevaluate its product and marketing strategies? Is there a quality problem? Or did Color Plus make a strategic mistake by acquiring too much capacity? The causes of the ₹4,60,000 unfavorable production-volume variance will determine the actions Color's managers take in response to the variance.

In contrast, a favorable production-volume variance indicates an overallocation of fixed overhead costs. That is, the overhead costs allocated to the actual output produced exceed the budgeted fixed overhead costs of ₹27,60,000. The favorable production-volume variance comprises the fixed costs recorded in excess of ₹27,60,000.

Be careful when drawing conclusions about a company's capacity planning whether the production-volume variance is either favorable or unfavorable. To correctly interpret Color Plus's ₹4,60,000 unfavorable production-volume variance, its managers should consider why it sold only 10,000 jackets in April. Suppose a new competitor gained market share by pricing its jackets lower than Color's. To sell the budgeted 12,000 jackets, Color Plus might have had to reduce its own selling price on all 12,000 jackets. Suppose it decided that selling 10,000 jackets at a higher price yielded higher operating income than selling 12,000 jackets at a lower price. The production-volume variance does not take into account such information. That's why Color Plus should not interpret the ₹4,60,000 U amount as the total economic cost of selling 2,000 jackets fewer than the 12,000 jackets budgeted. If, however, Color's managers anticipate they will not need capacity beyond 10,000 jackets, they may reduce the excess capacity, say, by canceling the lease on some of the machines.

Companies plan their plant capacity strategically on the basis of market information about how much capacity will be needed over some future time horizon. For 2014, Color's budgeted quantity of output is equal to the maximum capacity of the plant for that budget period. Actual demand (and quantity produced) turned out to be below the budgeted quantity of output, so Color Plus reports an unfavorable production-volume variance for April 2014. However, it would be incorrect to conclude that Color's management made a poor planning decision regarding plant capacity. The demand for Color's jackets might be highly uncertain. Given this uncertainty and the cost of not having sufficient capacity to meet sudden demand surges (including lost contribution margins and reduced follow-on business), Color's management may have made a wise capacity choice for 2014.

So what should Color Plus's managers ultimately do about the unfavorable variance in April? Should they try to reduce capacity, increase sales, or do nothing? Based on their analysis of the situation, Color's managers decided to reduce some capacity but continued to maintain some excess capacity to accommodate unexpected surges in demand. Chapter 9 and Chapter 13 examine these issues in more detail.

Next we describe the journal entries Color Plus would make to record fixed overhead costs using standard costing.

Journal Entries for Fixed Overhead Costs and Variances

We illustrate journal entries for fixed overhead costs for April 2014 using Fixed Overhead Control account and the contra account Fixed Overhead Allocated (data from Exhibit 8-2).

1.	Fixed Overhead Control	28,50,000
	Salaries Payable, Accumulated Depreciation,	
	and various other accounts	28,50,000
	To record actual fixed overhead costs incurred.	

2. Work-in-Process Control   23,00,000
        Fixed Overhead Allocated   23,00,000
    To record fixed overhead costs allocated,
        (0.40 machine-hour/unit × 10,000 units × ₹575.0/machine-hour).
        (The costs accumulated in Work-in-Process Control are transferred
        to Finished Goods Control when production is completed and to
        Cost of Goods Sold when the products are sold.)

3. Fixed Overhead Allocated   23,00,000
    Fixed Overhead Spending Variance   90,000
    Fixed Overhead Production-Volume Variance   4,60,000
        Fixed Overhead Control   28,50,000
    To record variances for the accounting period.

Overall, ₹28,50,000 of fixed overhead costs were incurred during April, but only ₹23,00,000 were allocated to jackets. The difference of ₹5,50,000 is precisely the underallocated fixed overhead costs that we introduced when studying normal costing in Chapter 4. The third entry illustrates how the fixed overhead spending variance of ₹90,000 and the fixed overhead production-volume variance of ₹4,60,000 together record this amount in a standard costing system.

At the end of the fiscal year, the fixed overhead spending variance is written off to cost of goods sold if it is immaterial in amount, or prorated among Work-in-Process Control, Finished Goods Control and Cost of Goods Sold on the basis of the fixed overhead allocated to these accounts as described in Chapter 4. Some companies combine the write-off and proration methods—that is, they write off the portion of the variance that is due to inefficiency and could have been avoided and prorate the portion of the variance that is unavoidable. Assume that the balance in the Fixed Overhead Spending Variance account as of April 2014 is also the balance at the end of 2014 and is immaterial in amount. The following journal entry records the write-off to Cost of Goods Sold.

    Cost of Goods Sold   90,000
        Fixed Overhead Spending Variance   90,000

We now consider the production-volume variance. Assume that the balance in Fixed Overhead Production-Volume Variance as of April 2014 is also the balance at the end of 2014. Also assume that some of the jackets manufactured during 2014 are in work-in-process and finished goods inventory at the end of the year. Many management accountants make a strong argument for writing off to Cost of Goods Sold and not prorating an unfavorable production-volume variance. Proponents of this argument contend that the unfavorable production-volume variance of ₹4,60,000 measures the cost of resources expended for 2,000 jackets that were not produced (₹230 per jacket × 2,000 jackets = ₹4,60,000). Prorating these costs would inappropriately allocate fixed overhead costs incurred for the 2,000 jackets that were not produced to the jackets that were produced. The jackets produced already bear their representative share of fixed overhead costs of ₹230 per jacket. Therefore, this argument favors charging the unfavorable production-volume variance against the year's revenues so that fixed costs of unused capacity are not carried in work-in-process inventory and finished goods inventory.

There is, however, an alternative view. This view regards the denominator level chosen as a "soft" rather than a "hard" measure of the fixed resources required and needed to produce each jacket. Suppose that either because of the design of the jacket or the functioning of the machines, it took more machine-hours than previously thought to manufacture each jacket. Consequently, Color Plus could make only 10,000 jackets rather than the planned 12,000 in April. In this case, the ₹27,60,000 of budgeted fixed overhead costs support the production of the 10,000 jackets manufactured. Under this reasoning, prorating the fixed overhead production-volume variance would appropriately spread fixed overhead costs among Work-in-Process Control, Finished Goods Control, and Cost of Goods Sold.

What about a favorable production-volume variance? Suppose Color Plus manufactured 13,800 jackets in April 2014.

$$\text{Production-volume variance} = \begin{array}{c}\text{Budgeted}\\\text{fixed}\\\text{overhead}\end{array} - \begin{array}{c}\text{Fixed overhead allocated using}\\\text{budgeted cost per output unit overhead}\\\text{allowed for actual output produced}\end{array}$$

$$= ₹27,60,000 - (₹230 \text{ per jacket} \times 13,800 \text{ jackets})$$

$$= ₹27,60,000 - ₹31,74,000 = ₹4,14,000 \text{ F}$$

Because actual production exceeded the planned capacity level, clearly the fixed overhead costs of ₹27,60,000 supported the production of all 13,800 jackets and should therefore be allocated to them. Prorating the favorable production-volume variance achieves this outcome and reduces the amounts in Work-in-Process Control, Finished Goods Control, and Cost of Goods Sold. Proration is also the more conservative approach in the sense that it results in a lower operating income than if the entire favorable production-volume variance were credited to Cost of Goods Sold.

Another point relevant to this discussion is that if variances are always written off to cost of goods sold, a company could set its standards to either increase (for financial reporting purposes) or decrease (for tax purposes) operating income. In other words, always writing off variances invites gaming behavior. For example, Color Plus could generate a favorable production-volume variance by setting the denominator level used to allocate fixed overhead costs low and thereby increase operating income. Or the firm could do just the opposite if it wanted to decrease its operating income to lower its taxes. The proration method has the effect of approximating the allocation of fixed costs based on actual costs and actual output so it is not susceptible to this type of manipulation.

There is no clear-cut or preferred approach for closing out the production-volume variance. The appropriate accounting procedure is a matter of judgment and depends on the circumstances of each case. Variations of the proration method may be desirable. For example, a company may choose to write off a portion of the production-volume variance and prorate the rest. The goal is to write off that part of the production-volume variance that represents the cost of capacity not used to support the production of output during the period. The rest of the production-volume variance is prorated to Work-in-Process Control, Finished Goods Control, and Cost of Goods Sold.

If Color Plus were to write off the production-volume variance to cost of goods sold, it would make the following journal entry.

Cost of Goods Sold	4,60,000	
Fixed Overhead Production-Volume Variance		4,60,000

Integrated Analysis of Overhead Cost Variances

As our discussion indicates, the variance calculations for variable overhead and fixed overhead differ.

- Variable overhead has no production-volume variance.
- Fixed overhead has no efficiency variance.

Decision Point ▶

What variances can be calculated for fixed overhead costs?

Learning Objective 5

Show how the 4-variance analysis approach reconciles the actual overhead incurred with the overhead amounts allocated during the period

. . . the 4-variance analysis approach identifies spending and efficiency variances for variable overhead costs and spending and production-volume variances for fixed overhead costs

Exhibit 8-4 presents an integrated summary of the variable overhead variances and the fixed overhead variances computed using standard costs for April 2014. Panel A shows the variances for variable overhead, while Panel B contains the fixed overhead variances. As you study Exhibit 8-4, note how the columns in Panels A and B are aligned to measure the different variances. In both Panels A and B,

Exhibit 8-4	Columnar Presentation of Integrated Variance Analysis: Color Plus Company for April 2011[a]

PANEL A: Variable (Manufacturing) Overhead

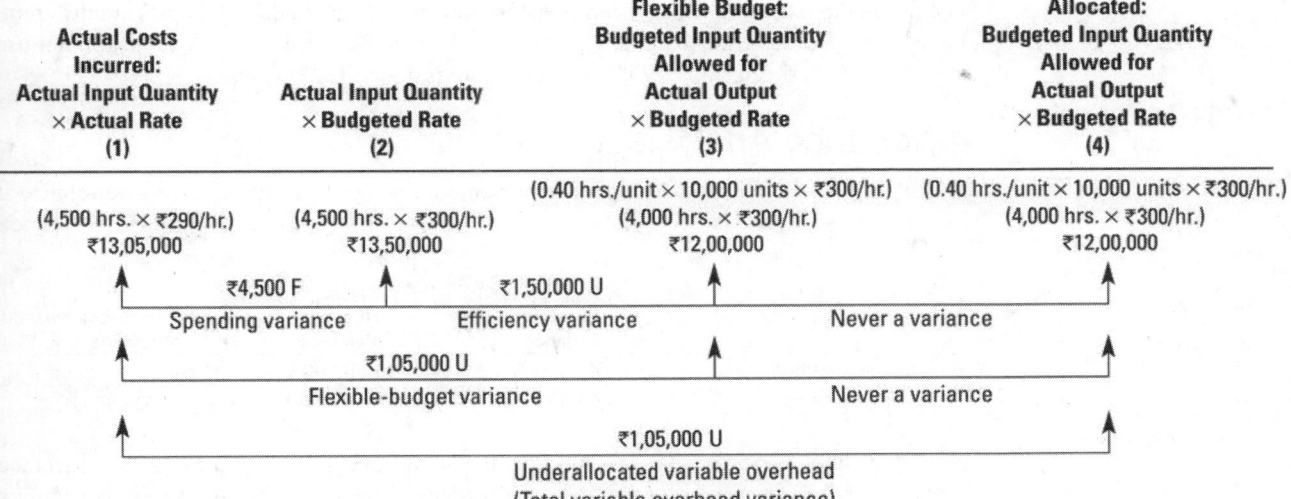

PANEL B: Fixed (Manufacturing) Overhead

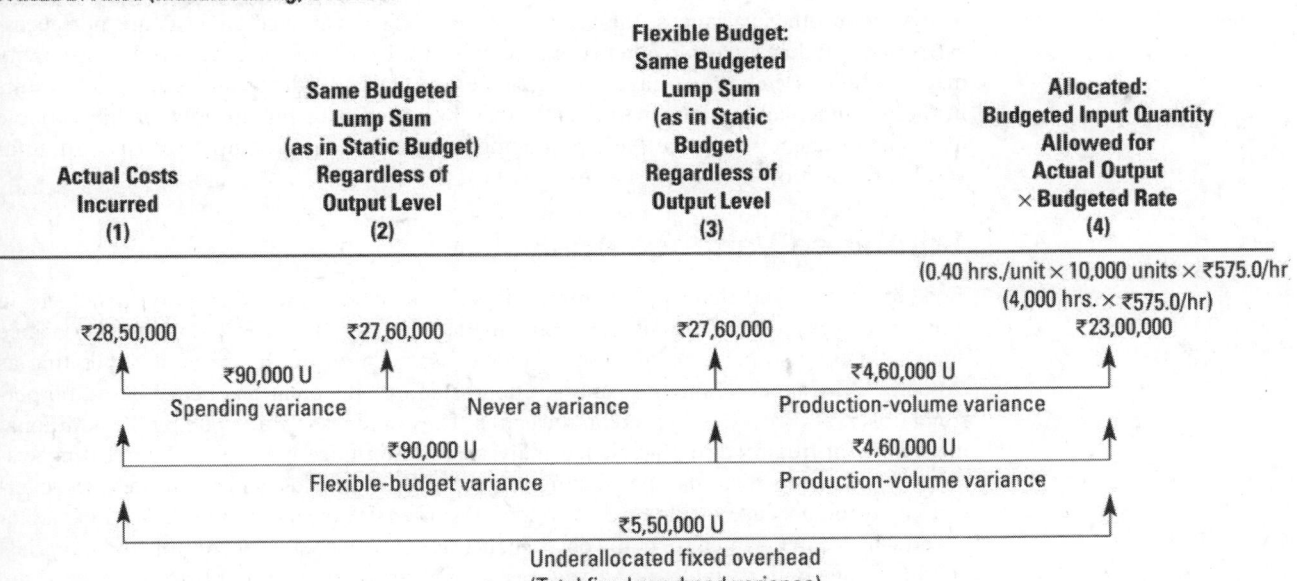

[a]F = favorable effect on operating income; U = unfavorable effect on operating income.

- the difference between columns 1 and 2 measures the spending variance.
- the difference between columns 2 and 3 measures the efficiency variance (if applicable).
- the difference between columns 3 and 4 measures the production-volume variance (if applicable).

Panel A contains an efficiency variance; Panel B has no efficiency variance for fixed overhead. As discussed earlier, a lump-sum amount of fixed costs will be unaffected by the degree of operating efficiency in a given budget period.

Panel A does not have a production-volume variance because the amount of variable overhead allocated is always the same as the flexible-budget amount. Variable costs never have any unused capacity. When production and sales decline from 12,000 jackets to 10,000 jackets, budgeted variable overhead costs proportionately decline. Fixed costs are different. Panel B has a production-volume variance (see Exhibit 8-3) because Color Plus did not use some of the overhead capacity it had acquired to produce 12,000 jackets.

4-Variance Analysis

When all of the overhead variances are presented together as in Exhibit 8-4, we refer to it as a 4-variance analysis:

	Spending Variance	**Efficiency Variance**	**Production-Volume Variance**
Variable overhead	₹45,000 F	₹1,50,000 U	Never a variance
Fixed overhead	₹90,000 U	Never a variance	₹4,60,000 U

4-Variance Analysis

Note that the 4-variance analysis provides the same level of information as the variance analysis carried out earlier for variable overhead and fixed overhead separately (in Exhibits 8-1 and 8-2, respectively), but it does so in a unified presentation that also indicates those variances that are never present.

As with other variances, the variances in Color's 4-variance analysis are not necessarily independent of each other. For example, Color Plus may purchase lower-quality machine fluids (leading to a favorable variable overhead spending variance), which results in the machines taking longer to operate than budgeted (causing an unfavorable variable overhead efficiency variance), and producing less than budgeted output (causing an unfavorable production-volume variance).

Combined Variance Analysis

To keep track of all that is happening within their areas of responsibility, managers in large, complex businesses, such as General Electric and Disney, use detailed 4-variance analysis. Doing so helps them identify and focus attention on the areas not operating as expected. Managers of small businesses understand their operations better based on personal observations and nonfinancial measures. They find less value in doing the additional measurements required for 4-variance analyses. For example, to simplify their costing systems, small companies may not distinguish variable overhead incurred from fixed overhead incurred because making this distinction is often not clear-cut. As we saw in Chapter 2 and will see in Chapter 10, many costs such as supervision, quality control, and materials handling have both variable- and fixed-cost components that may not be easy to separate.

Managers may therefore use a less detailed analysis that combines the variable overhead and fixed overhead into a single total overhead cost.

When a single total overhead cost category is used, it can still be analyzed in depth. The variances are now the sums of the variable overhead and fixed overhead variances for that level, as computed in Exhibit 8-4. The combined variance analysis looks as follows:

Combined 3-Variance Analysis

	Spending Variance	Efficiency Variance	Production-Volume Variance
Total overhead	₹45,000 U	₹1,50,000 U	₹4,60,000 U

The accounting for 3-variance analysis is simpler than for 4-variance analysis, but some information is lost because the variable and fixed overhead spending variances are combined into a single total overhead spending variance.

Finally, the overall **total-overhead variance** is given by the sum of the preceding variances. In the Color Plus example, this equals ₹6,55,000 U. Note that this amount, which aggregates the flexible-budget and production-volume variances, equals the total amount of underallocated (or underapplied) overhead costs. (Recall our discussion of underallocated overhead costs in normal costing from Chapter 4.) Using figures from Exhibit 8-4, the ₹6,55,000 U total-overhead variance is the difference between (a) the total actual overhead incurred (₹13,05,000 + ₹28,50,000 = ₹41,55,000) and (b) the overhead allocated (₹12,00,000 + ₹23,00,000 = ₹35,00,000) to the actual output produced. If the total-overhead variance were favorable, it would have corresponded instead to the amount of overapplied overhead costs.

> **◄ Decision Point**
>
> What is the most detailed way for a company to reconcile actual overhead incurred with the amount allocated during a period?

Production-Volume Variance and Sales-Volume Variance

As we complete our study of variance analysis for Color Plus Company, it is helpful to step back to see the "big picture" and to link the accounting and performance evaluation functions of standard costing. Exhibit 7-1, page 334, first identified a static-budget variance of ₹9,31,000 U as the difference between the static budget operating income of ₹10,80,000 and the actual operating income of ₹1,49,000. Exhibit 7-2 then subdivided the static-budget variance of ₹9,31,000 U into a flexible-budget variance of ₹2,91,000 U and a sales-volume variance of ₹6,40,000 U. In both Chapter 7 and this chapter, we presented more detailed variances that subdivided, whenever possible, individual flexible-budget variances for selling price, direct materials, direct manufacturing labor and variable overhead. For the fixed overhead, we noted that the flexible-budget variance is the same as the spending variance. Where does the production-volume variance belong then? As you shall see, the production-volume variance is a component of the sales-volume variance.

Under our assumption of actual production and sales of 10,000 jackets, Color's costing system debits to Work-in-Process Control the standard costs of the 10,000 jackets produced. These amounts are then transferred to Finished Goods account and finally to Cost of Goods Sold account:

> **Learning Objective 6**
>
> Explain the relationship between the sales-volume variance and the production-volume variance
>
> . . . the production-volume and operating-income volume variances together comprise the sales-volume variance

Direct materials (Chapter 7, Entry 1b)
   (₹600 per jacket × 10,000 jackets)   ₹60,00,000
Direct manufacturing labor (Chapter 7, Entry 2)

(₹160 per jacket × 10,000 jackets)	16,00,000
Variable overhead (Chapter 8, Entry 2)	
(₹120 per jacket × 10,000 jackets)	12,00,000
Fixed overhead (Chapter 8, Entry 2)	
(₹230 per jacket × 10,000 jackets)	23,00,000
Cost of goods sold at standard cost	
(₹1,110 per jacket × 10,000 jackets)	₹1,11,00,000

Color's costing system also records the revenues from the 10,000 jackets sold at the budgeted selling price of ₹1,200 per jacket. The net effect of these entries on Color's budgeted operating income is as follows:

Revenues at budgeted selling price	
(₹1,200 per jacket × 10,000 jackets)	₹1,20,00,000
Cost of goods sold at standard cost	
(₹1,110 per jacket × 10,000 jackets)	1,11,00,000
Operating income based on budgeted profit per jacket	
(₹90 per jacket × 10,000 jackets)	₹9,00,000

A crucial point to keep in mind is that under standard costing, fixed overhead costs are treated as if they are a variable cost. That is, in determining the budgeted operating income of ₹9,00,000 only ₹23,00,000 (₹230 per jacket × 10,000 jackets) of fixed overhead is considered, whereas the budgeted fixed overhead costs are ₹27,60,000. Color's accountants then record the ₹4,60,000 unfavorable production-volume variance (the difference between budgeted fixed overhead costs, ₹27,60,000, and allocated fixed overhead costs, ₹23,00,000, Entry 2), as well as the various flexible-budget variances (including the fixed overhead spending variance) that total ₹2,91,000 unfavorable (see Exhibit 7-2). This results in actual operating income of ₹1,49,000 as follows:

Operating income based on budgeted profit per jacket	
(₹90 per jacket × 10,000 jackets)	₹9,00,000
Unfavorable production-volume variance	(4,60,000)
Flexible-budget operating income (Exhibit 7-2)	4,40,000
Unfavorable flexible-budget variance for operating income (Exhibit 7-2)	(2,91,000)
Actual operating income (Exhibit 7-2)	₹1,49,000

In contrast, the static-budget operating income of ₹10,80,000 is not entered in Color's costing system because standard costing records budgeted revenues, standard costs, and variances only for the 10,000 jackets actually produced and sold, not for the 12,000 jackets that were *planned* to be produced and sold. As a result, the sales-volume variance of ₹6,40,000 U, which is the difference between static-budget operating income, ₹10,80,000, and flexible-budget operating income, ₹4,40,000 (Exhibit 7-2), is never actually recorded under standard costing. Nevertheless, the sales-volume variance is useful because it helps managers understand the lost contribution margin from selling 2,000 fewer jackets (the sales-volume variance assumes fixed costs remain at the budgeted level of ₹27,60,000).

The sales-volume variance has two components. They are as follows:

1. A difference between the static-budget operating income of ₹10,80,000 for 12,000 jackets and budgeted operating income of ₹9,00,000 for 10,000 jackets. This is the **operating-income volume variance** of ₹1,80,000 U (₹10,80,000 − ₹9,00,000), and reflects the fact that Color Plus produced and sold 2,000 fewer units than budgeted.

2. A difference between the budgeted operating income of ₹9,00,000 and the flexible budget operating income of ₹4,40,000 (Exhibit 7-2) for the 10,000 actual units. This difference arises because Color Plus's costing system treats fixed costs as if they behave in a variable manner and so assumes fixed costs equal the allocated amount of ₹23,00,000, rather than the budgeted fixed costs of ₹27,60,000. Of course, the difference between the allocated and budgeted fixed costs is precisely the production-volume variance of ₹4,60,000 U.

In summary, we have the following:

	Operating-income volume variance	₹1,80,000 U
(+)	Production-volume variance	4,60,000 U
	Equals Sales-volume variance	₹6,40,000 U

We can now provide a summary (see Exhibit 8-5) that formally disaggregates the static-budget variance of ₹9,31,000 U into its components. Note how the comprehensive chart incorporates all of the variances you have studied in Chapters 7 and 8.

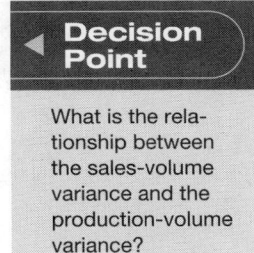

Decision Point

What is the relationship between the sales-volume variance and the production-volume variance?

Exhibit 8-5   Summary of Levels 1, 2, and 3 Variance Analysis: Webb Company for April 2014

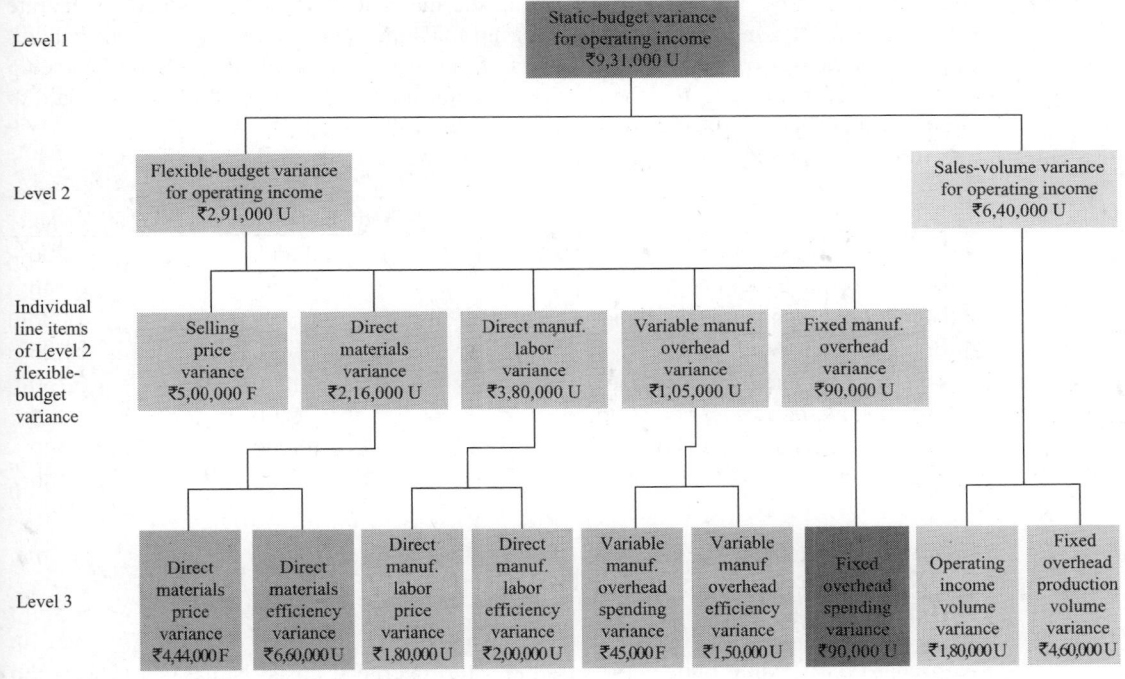

We next describe the use of variance analysis in activity-based costing systems.

Variance Analysis and Activity-Based Costing

Activity-based costing (ABC) systems focus on individual activities as the fundamental cost objects. ABC systems classify the costs of various activities into a cost hierarchy—

output unit-level costs, batch-level costs, product-sustaining costs, and facility-sustaining costs. In this section, we show how a company that has an ABC system and batch-level costs can benefit from variance analysis. Batch-level costs are the costs of activities related to a group of units of products or services rather than to each individual unit of product or service. We illustrate variance analysis for variable batch-level direct costs and fixed batch-level setup overhead costs.[3]

Consider Nanak Brass Works, which manufactures many different types of faucets and brass fittings. Because of the wide range of products it produces, Nanak uses an activity-based costing system. In contrast, Color Plus uses a simple costing system because it makes only one type of jacket. One of Nanak's products is Elegance, a decorative brass faucet for home spas. Nanak produces Elegance in batches.

For each product Nanak makes, it uses dedicated materials-handling labor to bring materials to the production floor, transport work in process from one work center to the next, and take the finished goods to the shipping area. Therefore, materials-handling labor costs for Elegance are direct costs of Elegance. Because the materials for a batch are moved together, materials-handling labor costs vary with number of batches rather than with number of units in a batch. Materials-handling labor costs are variable direct batch-level costs.

To manufacture a batch of Elegance, Nanak must set up the machines and molds. Employees must be highly skilled to set up the machines and molds. Hence, a separate setup department is responsible for setting up machines and molds for different batches of products. Setup costs are overhead costs of products. For simplicity, assume that setup costs are fixed with respect to the number of setup-hours. They consist of salaries paid to engineers and supervisors and costs of leasing setup equipment.

Information regarding Elegance for 2012 follows:

	Static-Budget Amount	Actual Amount
1. Units of Elegance produced and sold	1,80,000	1,51,200
2. Batch size (units per batch)	150	140
3. Number of batches (Line 1 ÷ Line 2)	1,200	1,080
4. Setup-hours per batch	6	6.25
5. Total setup-hours (Line 3 × Line 4)	7,200	6,750
6. Variable overhead cost per setup-hour	₹200	₹210
7. Variable setup overhead costs (Line 5 × Line 6)	₹14,40,000	₹14,17,500
8. Total fixed setup overhead costs	₹21,60,000	₹22,00,000

Flexible Budget and Variance Analysis for Direct Labor Costs

To prepare the flexible budget for variable setup overhead costs, Nanak starts with the actual units of output produced, 1,51,200 units, and proceeds using the following steps..

Step 1: Using Budgeted Batch Size, Calculate the Number of Batches that Should Have Been Used to Produce Actual Output. At the budgeted batch size of 150 units per batch, Nanak should have produced 1,51,200 units of output in 1,008 batches (1,51,200 units ÷ 150 units per batch).

Step 2: Using Budgeted Materials-Handling Labor-Hours per Batch, Calculate the Number of Materials-Handling Labor-Hours that Should Have Been Used. At the budgeted

---

[3] The techniques we demonstrate can be applied to analyze variable batch-level overhead costs as well.

quantity of 5 hours per batch, 1,008 batches should have required 5,040 materials-handling labor-hours (1,008 batches × 5 hours per batch).

Step 3: Using Budgeted Cost per Materials-Handling Labor-Hour, Calculate the Flexible-Budget Amount for Materials-Handling Labor-Hours. The flexible-budget amount is 5,040 materials-handling labor-hours × ₹140 budgeted cost per materials-handling labor-hour = ₹7,05,600.

Note how the flexible-budget calculations for materials-handling labor costs focus on batch-level quantities (materials-handling labor-hours per batch rather than per unit). The flexible-budget quantity computations focus at the appropriate level of the cost hierarchy. For example, because materials handling is a batch-level cost, the flexible-budget quantity calculations are made at the batch level—the quantity of materials-handling labor-hours that Nanak should have used based on the number of batches it should have used to produce the actual quantity of 151,200 units. If a cost had been a product-sustaining cost—such as product design cost—the flexible-budget quantity computations would focus at the product-sustaining level, for example, by evaluating the actual complexity of product design relative to the budget.

The flexible-budget variance for materials-handling labor costs can now be calculated as follows:

$$\text{Flexible-budget variance} = \text{Actual costs} - \text{Flexible-budget costs}$$

$$= (5{,}670 \text{ hours} \times ₹145.0 \text{ per hour}) - (5{,}040 \text{ hours} \times ₹140 \text{ per hour})$$

$$= ₹8{,}22{,}150 - ₹7{,}05{,}600$$

$$= ₹1{,}16{,}550 \text{ U}$$

The unfavorable variance indicates that materials-handling labor costs were ₹1,16,550 higher than the flexible-budget target. We can get some insight into the possible reasons for this unfavorable outcome by examining the price and efficiency components of the flexible-budget variance. Exhibit 8-6 presents the variances in columnar form.

$$\text{Price variance} = \left(\begin{array}{c} \text{Actual price} - \text{Budgeted price} \\ \text{of input} \quad\quad \text{of input} \end{array} \right) \times \begin{array}{c} \text{Actual quantity} \\ \text{of input} \end{array}$$

$$= (₹145.0 \text{ per hour} - ₹140 \text{ per hour}) \times 5{,}670 \text{ hours}$$

$$= ₹5.0 \text{ per hour} \times 5{,}670 \text{ hours}$$

$$= ₹28{,}350 \text{ U}$$

Actual Costs Incurred: Actual Input Quantity × Actual Rate (1)	Actual Input Quantity × Budgeted Rate (2)	Flexible Budget: Budgeted Input Quantity Allowed for Actual Output × Budgeted Rate (3)
(5,670 hours × ₹145.0 per hour) ₹8,22,150	(5,670 hours × ₹140 per hour) ₹7,93,800	(5,040 hours × ₹140 per hour) ₹7,05,600

Level 3 ↑————— ₹28,350 U —————↑————— ₹88,200 U —————↑
         Price variance   Efficiency variance

Level 2 ↑——————————————— ₹1,16,550 U ———————————————↑
                        Flexible-budget variance

Exhibit 8-6

Columnar Presentation of Variance Analysis for Direct Materials-Handling Labor Costs: Nanak Brass Works for 2014[a]

[a]F = favorable effect on operating income; U = unfavorable effect on operating income.

The unfavorable price variance for materials-handling labor indicates that the ₹145.0 actual cost per materials-handling labor-hour exceeds the ₹140.0 budgeted cost per materials-handling labor-hour. This variance could be the result of Nanak's human resources manager negotiating wage rates less skillfully or of wage rates increasing unexpectedly due to scarcity of labor.

$$\text{Efficiency variance} = \left(\begin{array}{c} \text{Actual} \\ \text{quantity of} \\ \text{input used} \end{array} - \begin{array}{c} \text{Budgeted quantity} \\ \text{of input allowed} \\ \text{for actual output} \end{array} \right) \times \begin{array}{c} \text{Budgeted price} \\ \text{of input} \end{array}$$

$$= (5{,}670 \text{ hours} - 5{,}040 \text{ hours}) \times ₹140 \text{ per hour}$$

$$= 630 \text{ hours} \times ₹140 \text{ per hour}$$

$$= ₹88{,}200 \text{ U}$$

The unfavorable efficiency variance indicates that the 5,670 actual materials-handling labor-hours exceeded the 5,040 budgeted materials-handling labor-hours for actual output. Possible reasons for the unfavorable efficiency variance are as follows:

- Smaller actual batch sizes of 140 units, instead of the budgeted batch sizes of 150 units, resulting in Nanak producing the 1,51,200 units in 1,080 batches instead of 1,008 (1,51,200 ÷ 150) batches
- The actual materials-handling labor-hours per batch of 5.25 hours were higher than the budgeted materials-handling labor-hours per batch (5 hours)

Reasons for smaller-than-budgeted batch sizes could include quality problems when batch sizes exceed 140 faucets and high costs of carrying inventory.

Possible reasons for larger actual materials-handling labor-hours per batch are as follows:

- Inefficient layout of the Elegance production line
- Materials-handling labor having to wait at work centers before picking up or delivering materials
- Unmotivated, inexperienced, and underskilled employees
- Very tight standards for materials-handling time

Identifying the reasons for the efficiency variance helps Nanak's managers develop a plan for improving materials-handling labor efficiency and to take corrective action that will be incorporated into future budgets.

We now consider fixed setup overhead costs.

Flexible Budget and Variance Analysis for Fixed Setup Overhead Costs

Exhibit 8-7 presents the variances for fixed setup overhead costs in columnar form.

Nanak's fixed setup overhead flexible-budget variance is calculated as follows:

$$\begin{array}{c} \text{Fixed-setup} \\ \text{overhead} \\ \text{flexible-budget} \\ \text{variance} \end{array} = \begin{array}{c} \text{Actual costs} \\ \text{incurred} \end{array} - \begin{array}{c} \text{Flexible-budget} \\ \text{costs} \end{array}$$

$$= ₹22{,}00{,}000 - ₹21{,}60{,}000$$

$$= ₹40{,}000 \text{ U}$$

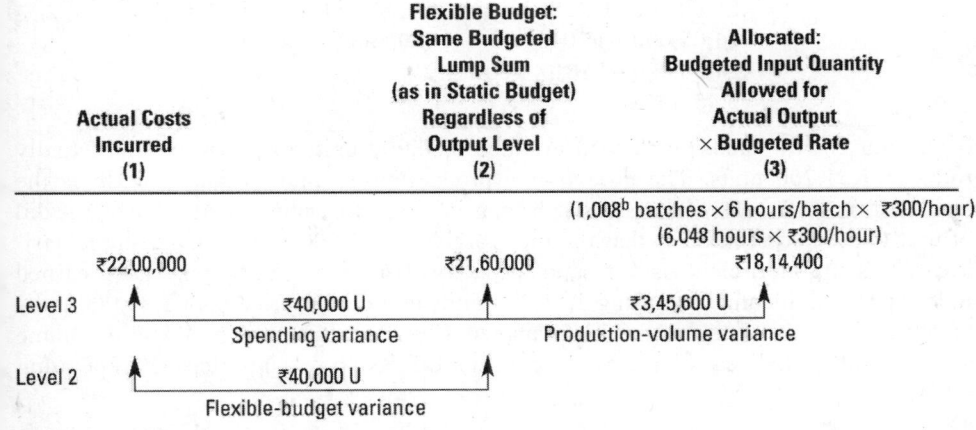

Exhibit 8-7

Columnar Presentation of Fixed Setup Overhead Variance Analysis: Nanak Brass Works for 2014[a]

[a]F = favorable effect on operating income; U = unfavorable effect on operating income.

[b]1,008 batches = 151,200 units ÷ 150 units per batch.

Note that the flexible-budget amount for fixed setup overhead costs equals the static-budget amount of ₹21,60,000. That's because there is no "flexing" of fixed costs. Moreover, because fixed overhead costs have no efficiency variance, the fixed setup overhead spending variance is the same as the fixed overhead flexible-budget variance. The spending variance could be unfavorable because of higher leasing costs of new setup equipment or higher salaries paid to engineers and supervisors. Nanak may have incurred these costs to alleviate some of the difficulties it was having in setting up machines.

To calculate the production-volume variance, Nanak first computes the budgeted cost-allocation rate for fixed setup overhead costs using the same four-step approach described under 'Developing Budgeted Variable Overhead cost Rates' earlier in this chapter.

Step 1: Choose the Period to Use for the Budget. Nanak uses a period of 12 months (the year 2014).

Step 2: Select the Cost-Allocation Base to Use in Allocating Fixed Overhead Costs to Output Produced. Nanak uses budgeted setup-hours as the cost-allocation base for fixed setup overhead costs. Budgeted setup-hours in the static budget for 2014 are 7,200 hours.

Step 3: Identify the Fixed Overhead Costs Associated with the Cost-Allocation Base. Nanak's fixed setup overhead cost budget for 2014 is ₹21,60,000.

Step 4: Compute the Rate per Unit of the Cost-Allocation Base Used to Allocate Fixed Overhead Costs to Output Produced. Dividing the ₹21,60,000 from step 3 by the 7,200 setup-hours from step 2, Nanak estimates a fixed setup overhead cost rate of ₹300 per setup-hour:

$$\frac{\text{Budgeted fixed setup overhead cost per unit of cost-allocation base}}{} = \frac{\text{Budgeted total costs in fixed overhead cost pool}}{\text{Budgeted total quantity of cost-allocation base}} = \frac{₹21,60,000}{7,200 \text{ setup costs}}$$

$$= ₹300 \text{ per setup-hour}$$

$$\frac{\text{Production-volume variance for fixed setup overhead costs}}{} = \frac{\text{Budgeted fixed setup overhead costs}}{} - \frac{\text{Fixed setup overhead allocated using budgeted input allowed for actual output units produced}}{}$$

$$= ₹21,60,000 - (1,008 \text{ batches} \times 6 \text{ hours/batch} \times ₹300 \text{ hour}$$
$$= ₹21,60,000 - (6,048 \text{ hours} \times ₹300/\text{hour}$$
$$= ₹21,60,000 - ₹18,14,400$$
$$= ₹3,45,600 \text{ U}$$

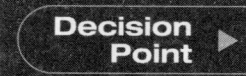

Decision Point ▶

How can variance analysis be used in an activity-based costing system?

During 2014, Nanak planned to produce 1,80,000 units of Elegance but actually produced 1,51,200 units. The unfavorable production-volume variance measures the amount of extra fixed setup costs that Nanak incurred for setup capacity it had it did not use. One interpretation is that the unfavorable ₹3,45,600 production-volume variance represents inefficient use of setup capacity. However, Nanak may have earned higher operating income by selling 1,51,200 units at a higher price than 1,80,000 units at a lower price. As a result, Nanak's managers should interpret the production-volume variance cautiously because it does not consider effects on selling prices and operating income.

Overhead Variances in Nonmanufacturing Settings

Learning Objective 8

Examine the use of overhead variances in nonmanufacturing settings

. . . analyze nonmanufacturing variable overhead costs for decision making and cost management; fixed overhead variances are especially important in service settings

Our Color Plus Company example examines variable and fixed manufacturing overhead costs. Managers can also use variance analysis to examine the overhead costs of the nonmanufacturing areas of the company and to make decisions about (1) pricing, (2) managing costs, and (3) the mix of products to make. For example, when product distribution costs are high, as they are in the automobile, consumer durables, cement, and steel industries, standard costing can provide managers with reliable and timely information on variable distribution overhead spending variances and efficiency variances.

What about service-sector companies such as airlines, hospitals, hotels, and railroads? How can they benefit from variance analyses? The output measures these companies commonly use are passenger-miles flown, patient days provided, room-days occupied, and ton-miles of freight hauled, respectively. Few costs can be traced to these outputs in a cost-effective way. Most of these costs are fixed overhead costs, such as the costs of equipment, buildings, and staff. Using capacity effectively is the key to profitability, and fixed overhead variances can help managers in this task. Retail businesses, such as Kmart, also have high capacity-related fixed costs (lease and occupancy costs).

Consider the following data United Airlines for selected years from the past decade. Available seat miles (ASMs) are the actual seats in an airplane multiplied by the distance traveled.

Year	Total ASMs (Millions) (1)	Operating Revenue per ASM (2) (₹)	Operating Cost per ASM (3) (₹)	Operating Income per ASM (4) = (2) − (3) (₹)
2000	1,75,493	10.2	10.0	0.2
2003	1,36,566	8.6	9.8	−1.2
2006	1,43,085	10.6	10.8	−0.2
2008	1,35,859	11.9	13.6	−1.4
2011	1,18,973	13.1	13.5	−0.4

When air travel declined after terrorists hijacked a number of commercial jets on September 11, 2001, United's revenues fell. However most of the company's fixed costs—for its airport facilities, equipment, personnel, and so on—did not. United had a large unfavorable production-volume variance because its capacity was underutilized. As column 1 of the table indicates, United responded by reducing its capacity substantially over the next few years. Available seat miles (ASMs) declined from 1,75,493 million in 2000 to 1,36,566 million in 2003. Yet United was unable to fill even the planes it had retained, so its revenue per ASM declined (column 2) and its cost per ASM stayed roughly the same (column 3). United filed for Chapter 11 bankruptcy in December 2002 and began seeking government guarantees to obtain the loans it needed. Subsequently, strong demand for airline travel, as well as productivity improvements resulting from the more efficient use of resources and networks, led to increased traffic and higher average ticket prices. By maintaining a disciplined approach to capacity and tight control over growth, United saw over a 20% increase in its revenue per ASM between 2003 and 2006. The improvement in performance allowed United to come out of bankruptcy on February 1, 2006. In the past few years, however, the global recession and soaring jet fuel prices have had a significant negative impact on United's performance, as reflected in the continued negative operating incomes and the further decline in capacity. In May 2010, a merger agreement was reached between United and Continental Airlines, and Continental was dissolved in 2012.

Financial and Nonfinancial Performance Measures

The overhead variances discussed in this chapter are examples of financial performance measures. As the preceding examples illustrate, nonfinancial measures such as those related to capacity utilization and physical measures of input usage also provide useful information. The nonfinancial measures that managers of Color Plus would likely find helpful in planning and controlling its overhead costs include the following:

1. Quantity of actual indirect materials used per machine-hour, relative to quantity of budgeted indirect materials used per machine-hour

2. Actual energy used per machine-hour, relative to budgeted energy used per machine-hour

3. Actual machine-hours per jacket, relative to budgeted machine-hours per jacket

These performance measures, like the financial variances discussed in this chapter and Chapter 7, alert managers' attention to problems and probably would be reported daily or hourly on the production floor. The overhead variances we discussed in this chapter capture the financial effects of items such as the three factors listed, which in many cases first appear as nonfinancial performance measures. An especially interesting example along these lines comes from Japan: Some Japanese companies have begun reining in their CO_2 emissions in part by doing a budgeted-to-actual variance analysis of the emissions. The goal is to make employees aware of the emissions and reduce them in advance of greenhouse-gas reduction plans being drawn up by the Japanese government.

Finally, both financial and nonfinancial performance measures are used to evaluate the performance of managers. Exclusive reliance on either is always too simplistic because each gives a different perspective on performance. Nonfinancial measures (such as those described previously) provide feedback on individual aspects of a manager's performance, whereas financial measures evaluate the overall effect of and the tradeoffs among different nonfinancial performance measures. We provide further discussion of these issues in Chapters 13, 19, and 23.

Decision Point

How are overhead variances useful in nonmanufacturing settings?

Problem for Self-Study

Nina Ganotra is the newly appointed president of Laser Products. She is examining the May 2014 results for the Aerospace Products Division. This division manufactures wing parts for satellites. Nina's current concern is with manufacturing overhead costs at the Aerospace Products Division. Both variable and fixed overhead costs are allocated to the wing parts on the basis of laser-cutting-hours. The following budget information is available:

Budgeted variable overhead rate	₹2,000 per hour
Budgeted fixed overhead rate	₹2,400 per hour
Budgeted laser-cutting time per wing part	1.5 hours
Budgeted production and sales for May 2009	5,000 wing parts
Budgeted fixed overhead costs for May 2009	₹1,80,00,000

Actual results for May 2014 are:

Wing parts produced and sold	4,800 units
Laser-cutting-hours used	8,400 hours
Variable overhead costs	₹1,47,84,000
Fixed overhead costs	₹1,83,22,000

Required
1. Compute the spending variance and the efficiency variance for variable overhead.
2. Compute the spending variance and the production-volume variance for fixed overhead.
3. Give two explanations for each of the variances calculated in requirements 1 and 2.

Solution

1. and 2. See Exhibit 8-8.
3. a. Variable overhead spending variance, ₹20,16,000 F. One possible reason for this variance is that the actual prices of individual items included in variable overhead (such as cutting fluids) are lower than budgeted prices. A second possible reason is that the percentage increase in the actual quantity usage of individual items in the variable overhead cost pool is less than the percentage increase in laser-cutting-hours compared to the flexible budget.
   b. Variable overhead efficiency variance, ₹24,00,000 U. One possible reason for this variance is inadequate maintenance of laser machines, causing them to take more laser-cutting time per wing part. A second possible reason is use of undermotivated, inexperienced, or underskilled workers with the laser-cutting machines, resulting in more laser-cutting time per wing part.
   c. Fixed overhead spending variance, ₹3,22,000 U. One possible reason for this variance is that the actual prices of individual items in the fixed-cost pool unexpectedly increased from the prices budgeted (such as an unexpected increase in machine leasing costs). A second possible reason is that the Aerospace Products Division had to lease more machines or hire more supervisors than had been budgeted.
   d. Production-volume variance, ₹7,20,000 U. Actual production of wing parts is 4,800 units, compared with 5,000 units budgeted. One possible reason for this variance is demand factors, such as a decline in an aerospace program that led to

a decline in demand for aircraft parts. A second possible reason is supply factors, such as a production stoppage due to labor problems or machine breakdowns.

Exhibit 8-8   Columnar Presentation of Integrated Variance Analysis: Laser Products for May 2014a

PANEL A: Variable (Manufacturing) Overhead

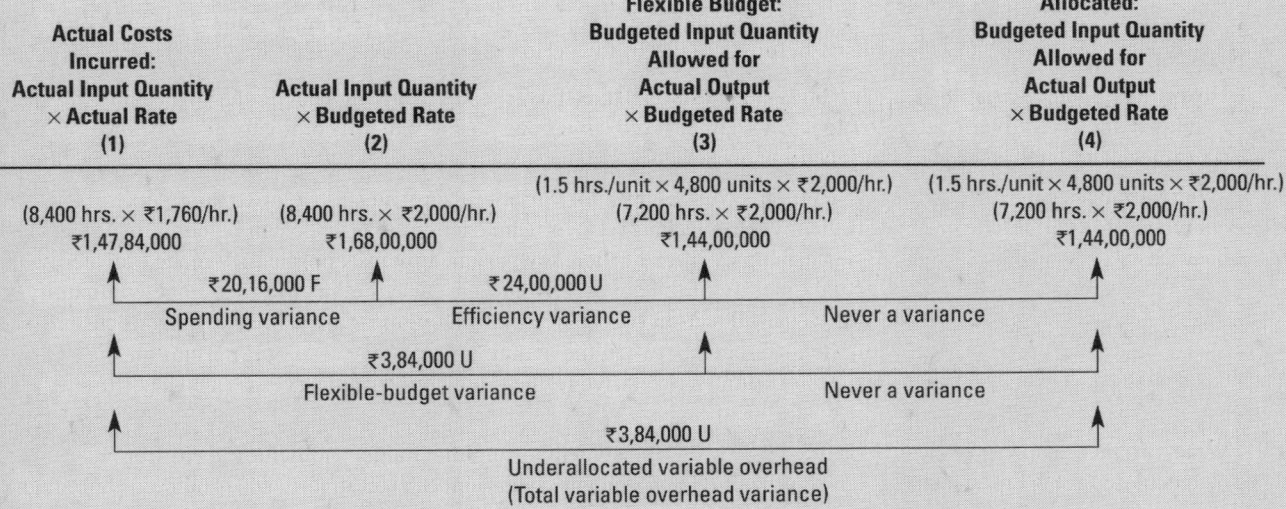

Actual Costs Incurred: Actual Input Quantity × Actual Rate (1)	Actual Input Quantity × Budgeted Rate (2)	Flexible Budget: Budgeted Input Quantity Allowed for Actual Output × Budgeted Rate (3)	Allocated: Budgeted Input Quantity Allowed for Actual Output × Budgeted Rate (4)
		(1.5 hrs./unit × 4,800 units × ₹2,000/hr.)	(1.5 hrs./unit × 4,800 units × ₹2,000/hr.)
(8,400 hrs. × ₹1,760/hr.)	(8,400 hrs. × ₹2,000/hr.)	(7,200 hrs. × ₹2,000/hr.)	(7,200 hrs. × ₹2,000/hr.)
₹1,47,84,000	₹1,68,00,000	₹1,44,00,000	₹1,44,00,000

₹20,16,000 F ← Spending variance | ₹24,00,000 U ← Efficiency variance | Never a variance

₹3,84,000 U ← Flexible-budget variance | Never a variance

₹3,84,000 U ← Underallocated variable overhead (Total variable overhead variance)

PANEL B: Fixed (Manufacturing) Overhead

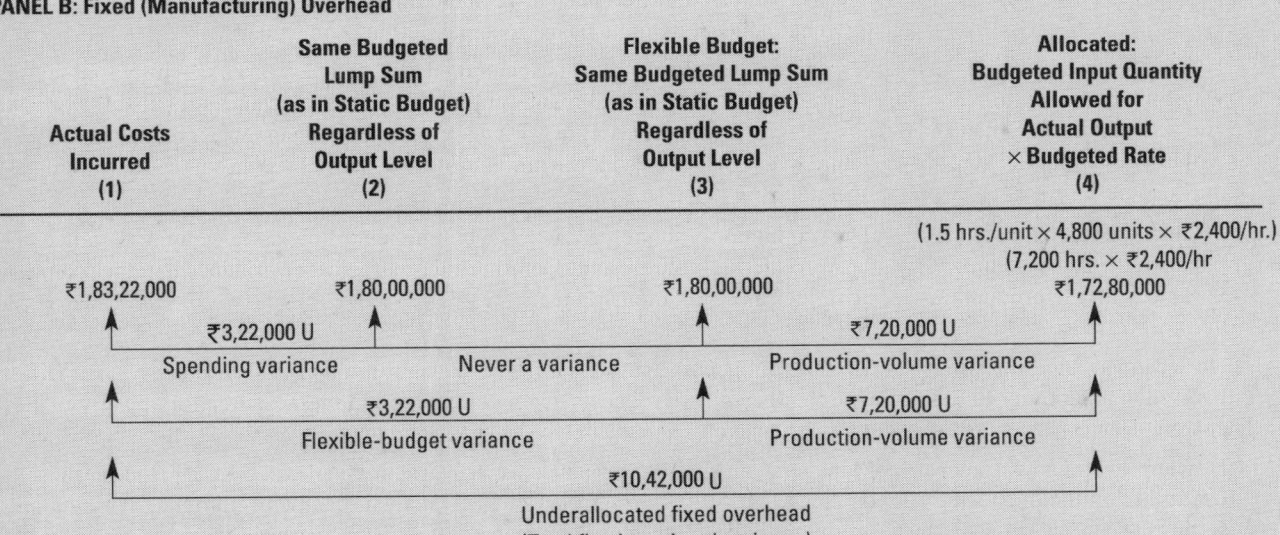

Actual Costs Incurred (1)	Same Budgeted Lump Sum (as in Static Budget) Regardless of Output Level (2)	Flexible Budget: Same Budgeted Lump Sum (as in Static Budget) Regardless of Output Level (3)	Allocated: Budgeted Input Quantity Allowed for Actual Output × Budgeted Rate (4)
			(1.5 hrs./unit × 4,800 units × ₹2,400/hr.)
			(7,200 hrs. × ₹2,400/hr
₹1,83,22,000	₹1,80,00,000	₹1,80,00,000	₹1,72,80,000

₹3,22,000 U ← Spending variance | Never a variance | ₹7,20,000 U ← Production-volume variance

₹3,22,000 U ← Flexible-budget variance | ₹7,20,000 U ← Production-volume variance

₹10,42,000 U ← Underallocated fixed overhead (Total fixed overhead variance)

---

aF = favorable effect on operating income; U = unfavorable effect on operating income.

Source: Republished with permission of Strategic Finance by Paul Sherman. Copyright 2003 by Institute of Management Accountants. Permission conveyed through Copyright Clearance Center, Inc

Decision Points

The following question-and-answer format summarizes the chapter's learning objectives. Each decision presents a key question related to a learning objective. The guidelines are the answer to that question.

Decision	Guidelines
1. How do managers plan variable overhead costs and fixed overhead costs?	Planning of both variable and fixed overhead costs involves undertaking only activities that add value and then being efficient in that undertaking. The key difference is that for variable-cost planning, ongoing decisions during the budget period play a much larger role; for fixed-cost planning, most key decisions are made before the start of the period.
2. How are budgeted variable overhead and fixed overhead cost rates calculated?	The budgeted variable (fixed) overhead cost rate is calculated by dividing the budgeted variable (fixed) overhead costs by the denominator level of the cost-allocation base.
3. What variances can be calculated for variable overhead costs?	When the flexible budget for variable overhead is developed, an overhead efficiency variance and an overhead spending variance can be computed. The variable overhead efficiency variance focuses on the difference between the actual quantity of the cost-allocation base used relative to the budgeted quantity of the cost-allocation base. The variable overhead spending variance focuses on the difference between the actual variable overhead cost per unit of the cost-allocation base relative to the budgeted variable overhead cost per unit of the cost-allocation base.
4. What variances can be calculated for fixed overhead costs?	For fixed overhead, the static and flexible budgets coincide. The difference between the budgeted and actual amount of fixed overhead is the flexible-budget variance, also referred to as the spending variance. The production-volume variance measures the difference between the budgeted fixed overhead and the fixed overhead allocated on the basis of actual output produced.
5. What is the most detailed way for a company to reconcile actual overhead incurred with the amount allocated during a period?	A 4-variance analysis presents spending and efficiency variances for variable overhead costs and spending and production-volume variances for fixed overhead costs. By analyzing these four variances together, managers can reconcile the actual overhead costs with the amount of overhead allocated to the output produced during a period.
6. What is the relationship between the sales-volume variance and the production-volume variance?	The production-volume variance is a component of the sales-volume variance. The production-volume and operating-income volume variances together comprise the sales-volume variance.
7. How can variance analysis be used in an activity-based costing system?	Flexible budgets in ABC systems give insight into why actual activity costs differ from budgeted activity costs. Using output and input measures for an activity, a comprehensive variance analysis can be conducted.
8. How are overhead variances useful in nonmanufacturing settings?	Managers can analyze variances for all variable overhead costs, including those outside the manufacturing function. The analysis can be used to make pricing and product mix decisions and to manage costs. Fixed overhead variances are especially important in service settings, where using capacity effectively is the key to profitability. In all cases, the information provided by variances can be supplemented by the use of suitable nonfinancial metrics.

TERMS TO LEARN

The chapter and the Glossary at the end of the book contain definitions of the following important terms:

denominator level **(p. 391)**
denominator-level variance **(p. 398)**
fixed overhead flexible-budget
  variance **(p. 397)**
fixed overhead spending
  variance **(p. 397)**

operating-income volume variance
  (p. 406)
production-volume variance
  (p. 398)
standard costing **(p. 389)**
total-overhead variance **(p. 405)**

variable overhead efficiency
  variance **(p. 393)**
variable overhead flexible-budget
  variance **(p. 392)**
variable overhead spending
  variance **(p. 394)**

ASSIGNMENT MATERIAL

Questions

8-1 How do managers plan for variable overhead costs?

8-2 How does the planning of fixed overhead costs differ from the planning of variable overhead costs?

8-3 How does standard costing differ from actual costing?

8-4 What are the steps in developing a budgeted variable overhead cost-allocation rate?

8-5 What are the factors that affect the spending variance for variable manufacturing overhead?

8-6 Assume variable manufacturing overhead is allocated using machine-hours. Give three possible reasons for a favorable variable overhead efficiency variance.

8-7 Describe the difference between a direct materials efficiency variance and a variable manufacturing overhead efficiency variance.

8-8 What are the steps in developing a budgeted fixed overhead rate?

8-9 Why is the flexible-budget variance the same amount as the spending variance for fixed manufacturing overhead?

8-10 Explain how the analysis of fixed manufacturing overhead costs differs for (a) planning and control on the one hand and (b) inventory costing for financial reporting on the other hand.

8-11 Provide one caveat that will affect whether a production-volume variance is a good measure of the economic cost of unused capacity.

8-12 "The production-volume variance should always be written off to Cost of Goods Sold." Do you agree? Explain.

8-13 What are the variances in a 4-variance analysis?

8-14 "Overhead variances should be viewed as interdependent rather than independent." Give an example.

8-15 Describe how flexible-budget variance analysis can be used in the control of costs of activity areas.

Solved Examples

8-16 Fixed manufacturing overhead variance analysis. The Harvest Gold Bread Company bakes baguettes for distribution to upscale grocery stores. The company has two direct-cost categories, direct materials and direct manufacturing labor. Fixed manufacturing overhead is allocated to products on the basis of standard direct manufacturing labor-hours. Following is some pertinent budgeted data for the Harvest Gold Bread Company:

| Direct manufacturing labor use | 0.02 hours per baguette |
| Variable manufacturing overhead | ₹40 per direct labor-hour |

The Harvest Gold Bread Company recorded the following additional data for the current year ended December 31:

Planned (budgeted) output	32,00,000 baguettes
Actual production	28,00,000
Direct manufacturing labor	50,400 hours
Actual variable manufacturing overhead	₹27,20,000

Required

1. Prepare a variance analysis of fixed manufacturing overhead cost. Use Exhibit 8-3 as a guide.
2. Is fixed overhead underallocated or overallocated? By what amount?
3. Comment on your results. Discuss the variances and explain what may be driving them.

Solution

Fixed manufacturing overhead variance analysis.

1. Budgeted standard direct manufacturing labor used = 0.02 hours per baguette
   Budgeted output = 32,00,000 baguettes
   Budgeted standard direct manufacturing labor-hours: = 32,00,000 × 0.02 = 64,000 hours
   Budgeted fixed manufacturing overhead costs: = 64,000 × ₹40 per hour = ₹25,60,000
   Actual output   = 28,00,000 baguettes
   Allocated fixed manufacturing overhead
           = 28,00,000 × 0.02 × ₹40 = ₹22,40,000
2. The fixed manufacturing overhead is underallocated by ₹4,80,000.
3. The production-volume variance captures the difference between the budgeted 32,00,0000 baguettes and the actual 28,00,000 baguettes. The spending variance of ₹1,60,000 unfavorable means that the actual aggregate of fixed costs (₹27,20,000)

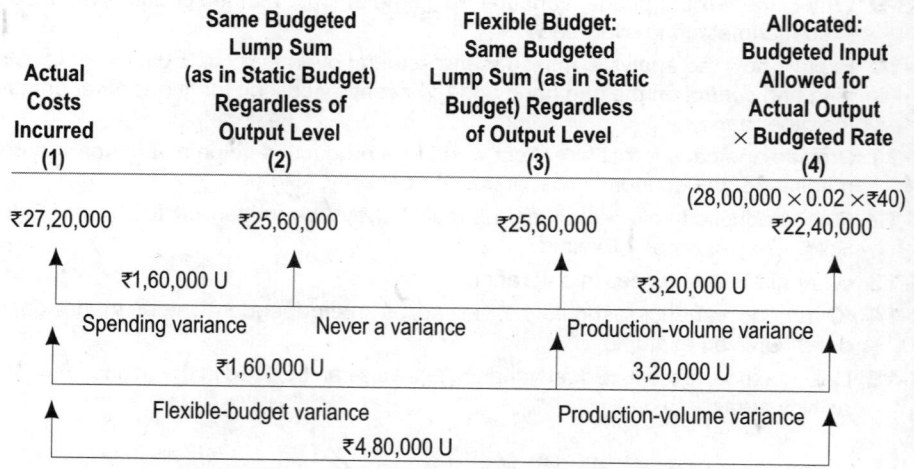

exceeds the budget amount (₹25,60,000). For example, monthly leasing rates for baguette-making machines may have increased above those in the budget for current year.

8-17 Manufacturing overhead, variance analysis. The Bajaj Electricals is a manufacturer of centrifuges. Fixed and variable manufacturing overheads are allocated to each centrifuge using budgeted assembly-hours. Budgeted assembly time is 2 hours per unit. The following table shows the budgeted amounts and actual results related to overhead for June 2016.

	Home	Insert	Page Layout	Formulas	Data	Review	View	
	A	B	C	D	E		F	G
							Actual	Static
1			Bajaj Electricals (June 2016)				Results	Budget
2	Number of centrifuges assembled and sold						225	110
3	Hours of assembly time						360	
4	Variable manufacturing overhead cost per hour of assembly time							₹320
5	Variable manufacturing overhead costs						₹1,19,330	
6	Fixed manufacturing overhead costs						₹1,21,800	₹1,07,800

Required

1. Prepare an analysis of all variable manufacturing overhead and fixed manufacturing overhead variances using the columnar approach in Exhibit 8-4 (in text).
2. Prepare journal entries for Bajaj's June 2016 variable and fixed manufacturing overhead costs and variances; write off these variances to cost of goods sold for the quarter ending June 30, 2016.
3. How does the planning and control of variable manufacturing overhead costs differ from the planning and control of fixed manufacturing overhead costs?

Solution

1. The summary information is:

The Bajaj Electricals (June 2016)	Actual	Flexible Budget	Static Budget
Outputs units (number of assembled units)	225	225	110
Hours of assembly time	360	450	220[a]
Assembly hours per unit	1.60[b]	2.00	2.00
Variable mfg. overhead cost per hour of assembly time	₹331.50[d]	₹320	₹320
Variable mfg. overhead costs	₹1,19,330	₹1,44,000[e]	₹70,400[f]
Fixed mfg. overhead costs	₹1,21,800	₹1,07,800	₹1,07,800
Fixed mfg. overhead costs per hour of assembly time	₹338.30[g]		₹490[h]

[a] 110 units × 2 assembly hours per unit = 220 hours
[b] 360 hours ÷ 225 units = 1.60 assembly hours per unit
[c] 225 units × 2 assembly hours per unit = 450 hours
[d] ₹1,19,330 × 360 assembly hours = ₹331.50 per assembly hour
[e] 450 assembly hours × ₹320 per assembly hour = ₹1,44,000
[f] 220 assembly hours × ₹320 per assembly hour = ₹70,400
[g] ₹1,21,800 ÷ 360 assembly hours = ₹338.30 per assembly hour
[h] ₹1,07,800 ÷ 220 assembly hours = ₹490 per assembly hour

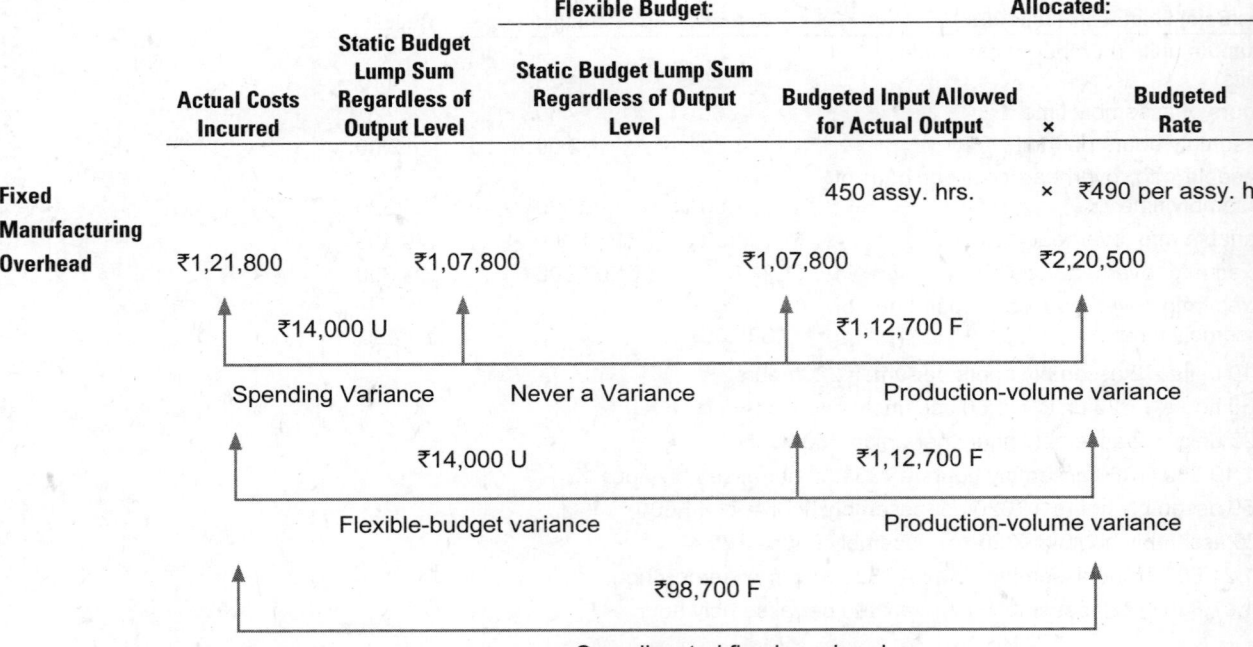

	Actual Costs Incurred	Actual Input Qty. × Budgeted Rate	**Flexible Budget:** Budgeted Input Qty. Allowed for Actual Output	×	Budgeted Rate	**Allocated:** Budgeted Input Qty. Allowed for Actual Output	×	Budgeted
		360 assy. hrs. × ₹320 per assy. hr.	450 assy. hrs.	×	₹320 per assy. hr.	450 assy. hrs.	×	₹320 per assy. hr.
Variable Manufacturing Overhead	₹1,19,330	₹1,15,200			₹1,44,000	₹1,44,000		

₹4,130 U   ₹28,800 F

Spending variance   Efficiency variance   Never a variance

₹24,670 F

Flexible-budget variance   Never a variance

₹24,670 F

Overallocated variable overhead

	Actual Costs Incurred	Static Budget Lump Sum Regardless of Output Level	**Flexible Budget:** Static Budget Lump Sum Regardless of Output Level	Budgeted Input Allowed for Actual Output	×	**Allocated:** Budgeted Rate
				450 assy. hrs.	×	₹490 per assy. hr.
Fixed Manufacturing Overhead	₹1,21,800	₹1,07,800	₹1,07,800			₹2,20,500

₹14,000 U   ₹1,12,700 F

Spending Variance   Never a Variance   Production-volume variance

₹14,000 U   ₹1,12,700 F

Flexible-budget variance   Production-volume variance

₹98,700 F

Overallocated fixed overhead

The summary analysis is:

	Spending Variance	Efficiency Variance	Production-Volume Variance
Variable Manufacturing Overhead	₹4,130 U	₹28,800 F	Never a variance
Fixed Manufacturing Overhead	₹14,000 U	Never a variance	₹1,12,700 F

2. Variable Manufacturing Costs and Variances

a. Variable Manufacturing Overhead Control   ₹1,19,330
    Accounts Payable Control and various other accounts   ₹1,19,330
  To record actual variable manufacturing overhead costs incurred.

b. Work-in-Process Control   1,44,000
    Variable Manufacturing Overhead Allocated   1,44,000
  To record variable manufacturing overhead allocated.

c. Variable Manufacturing Overhead Allocated   1,44,000
  Variable Manufacturing Overhead Spending Variance   4,130
    Variable Manufacturing Overhead Control   1,19,330
    Variable Manufacturing Overhead Efficiency Variance   28,800
  To isolate variances for the accounting period.

d. Variable Manufacturing Overhead Efficiency Variance   28,800
    Variable Manufacturing Overhead Spending Variance   4,130
    Cost of Goods Sold   24,670
To write off variable manufacturing overhead variances to cost of goods sold.

Fixed Manufacturing Costs and Variances

a. Fixed Manufacturing Overhead Control   ₹ 1,21,800
    Salaries Payable, Acc. Depreciation, various other accounts   ₹1,21,800
  To record actual fixed manufacturing overhead costs incurred.

b. Work-in-Process Control   2,20,500
    Fixed Manufacturing Overhead Allocated   2,20,500
  To record fixed manufacturing overhead allocated.

c. Fixed Manufacturing Overhead Allocated   2,20,500
  Fixed Manufacturing Overhead Spending Variance   14,000

    Fixed Manufacturing Overhead Production-Volume Variance   1,12,700
    Fixed Manufacturing Overhead Control   1,21,800
  To isolate variances for the accounting period.

d. Fixed Manufacturing Overhead Production-Volume Variance   1,12,700
    Fixed Manufacturing Overhead Spending Variance   14,000
    Cost of Goods Sold   98,700
To write off fixed manufacturing overhead variances to cost of goods sold.

3. Planning and control of variable manufacturing overhead costs have both a long-run and a short-run focus. It involves Principles planning to undertake only value-added overhead activities (a long-run view) and then managing the cost drivers of those activities in the most efficient way (a short-run view). Planning and control of fixed manufacturing overhead costs at Principles have primarily a long-run focus. It involves undertaking only value-added fixed-overhead activities for a budgeted level of output. Principles make most of the key decisions that determine the level of fixed-overhead costs at the start of the accounting period.

8-18 Overhead variances, service sector. Easy Meals Now (EMN) operates a meal home-delivery service. It has agreements with 20 restaurants to pick up and deliver meals to customers who phone or fax orders to EMN. EMN allocates variable and fixed overhead costs on the basis of delivery time. EMN's owner, Raghav obtains the following information for May 2016 overhead costs:

	Home	Insert	Page Layout	Formulas	Data	Review
	A				B	C
1	**Easy Meals Now (May 2016)**				**Actual Results**	**Static Budget**
2	Output units (number of deliveries)				8,600	12,000
3	Hours per delivery					0.70
4	Hours of delivery time				5,660	
5	Variable overhead cost per hour of delivery time					₹17.5
6	Variable overhead costs				₹1,13,200	
7	Fixed overhead costs				₹3,96,000	₹3,36,000

Required

1. Compute spending and efficiency variances for EMN's variable overhead in May 2016.
2. Compute the spending variance and production-volume variance for EMN's fixed overhead in May 2016.
3. Comment on EMN's overhead variances and suggest how Raghav might manage EMN's variable overhead differently from its fixed overhead costs.

Solution

1.

Easy Meals Now (May 2016)	Actual Results	Flexible Budget	Static Budget
Output units (number of deliveries)	8,600	8,600	12,000
Hours per delivery	0.66[a]	0.70	0.70
Hours of delivery time	5,660	6,020[b]	8,400[c]
Variable overhead costs per delivery hour	₹20[d]	₹17.50	₹17.50
Variable overhead (VOH) costs	₹1,13,200	₹1,05,350[e]	₹1,47,000[f]
Fixed overhead costs	₹3,96,000	₹3,36,000	₹3,36,000
Fixed overhead cost per hour			₹46.70[g]

[a] 5,660 hours ÷ 8,600 deliveries = 0.66 hours per delivery
[b] hrs. per delivery × actual number of deliveries = 0.70 × 8,600 = 6,020 hours
[c] hrs. per delivery × expected number of deliveries = 0.70 × 12,000 = 8,400 hours
[d] ₹1,13,200 VOH costs ÷ 5,660 delivery hours = ₹20 per delivery hour
[e] 8,600 deliveries × 0.70 hours per delivery × ₹17.50 VOH cost per delivery hour = ₹1,47,000

[f] 12,000 deliveries × 0.70 hours per delivery × ₹17.50 VOH cost per delivery hour = ₹1,47,000
[f] Static budget delivery hours = 12,000 units × 0.70 hours/unit = 8,400 hours;
[g] Fixed overhead rate = Fixed overhead costs ÷ Static budget delivery hours = ₹3,36,000 ÷ 8,400 hours = ₹40 per hour

VARIABLE OVERHEAD

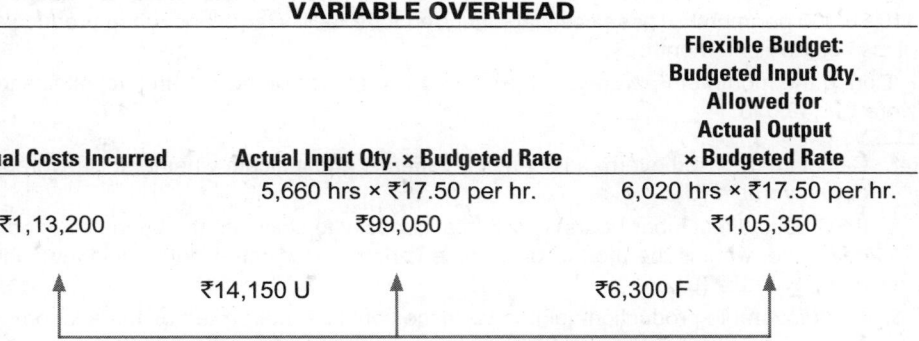

Actual Costs Incurred	Actual Input Qty. × Budgeted Rate	Flexible Budget: Budgeted Input Qty. Allowed for Actual Output × Budgeted Rate
	5,660 hrs × ₹17.50 per hr.	6,020 hrs × ₹17.50 per hr.
₹1,13,200	₹99,050	₹1,05,350
	₹14,150 U	₹6,300 F
	Spending variance	Efficiency variance

2.

FIXED OVERHEAD

Actual Costs Incurred	Flexible Budget: Same Budgeted Lump Sum (as in Static Budget) Regardless of Output Level	Allocated: Budgeted Input Qty. Allowed for Actual Output × Budgeted Rate
		6,020 hrs. × ₹40/hr.
₹3,96,000	₹3,36,000	₹2,40,800
	₹60,000 U	₹95,200 U
	Spending variance	Production-volume variance

3. The spending variances for variable and fixed overhead are both unfavorable. This means that EMN had increases over budget in either or both the cost of individual items (such as telephone calls and gasoline) in the overhead cost pools, or the usage of these individual items per unit of the allocation base (delivery time). The favorable efficiency variance for variable overhead costs results from more efficient use of the cost allocation base—each delivery takes 0.66 hours versus a budgeted 0.70 hours.

EMN can best manage its fixed overhead costs by long-term planning of capacity rather than day-to-day decisions. This involves planning to undertake only value-added fixed-overhead activities and then determining the appropriate level for those activities. Most fixed overhead costs are committed well before they are incurred. In contrast, for variable overhead, a mix of long-run planning and daily monitoring of the use of individual items is required to manage costs efficiently. EMN should plan to undertake only value-added variable-overhead activities (a long-run focus) and then manage the cost drivers of those activities in the most efficient way (a short-run focus).

There is no production-volume variance for variable overhead costs. The unfavorable production-volume variance for fixed overhead costs arises because EMN has unused fixed overhead resources that it may seek to reduce in the long run.

8-19 Production-volume variance analysis and sales volume variance. PC Jeweller Ltd, makes jewelry in the shape of geometric patterns. Each piece is handmade and takes an average of 1.5 hours to produce because of the intricate design and scrollwork. PC uses direct labor-hours to allocate the overhead cost to production. Fixed overhead costs, including rent, depreciation, supervisory salaries, and other production expenses, are budgeted at ₹10,80,000 per month. These costs are incurred for a facility large enough to produce 1,200 pieces of jewelry a month.

During the month of February, PC produced 720 pieces of jewelry and actual fixed costs were ₹11,40,000.

Required

1. Calculate the fixed overhead spending variance and indicate whether it is favorable (F) or unfavorable (U).

2. If PC uses direct labor-hours available at capacity to calculate the budgeted fixed overhead rate, what is the production-volume variance? Indicate whether it is favorable (F) or unfavorable (U).

3. An unfavorable production-volume variance could be interpreted as the economic cost of unused capacity. Why would PC be willing to incur this cost?

4. PC's budgeted variable cost per unit is ₹2,500, and it expects to sell its jewelry for ₹5,500 apiece. Compute the sales-volume variance and reconcile it with the production-volume variance calculated in requirement 2. What does each concept measure?

Solution

1. and 2.   Fixed Overhead Variance Analysis for PC Jewellers for February

Actual Fixed Overhead	Static Budget Fixed Overhead	Standard Hours × Budgeted Rate
		(720 × 1.5 × ₹600*)
₹11,40,000	₹10,80,000	₹6,48,000
⬆	⬆	⬆
₹ 60,000 U	₹ 4,32,000 U	
Spending variance	Production-volume variance	

* fixed overhead rate = (budgeted fixed overhead)/(budgeted DL hours at capacity)

               = ₹10,80,000/(1,200 × 1.5 hours)

               = ₹10,80,000/1,800 hours

               = ₹ 600/hour

3. An unfavorable production-volume variance measures the cost of unused capacity. Production at capacity would result in a production-volume variance of zero because the fixed overhead rate is based on expected hours at capacity production. However, the existence of an unfavorable volume variance does not necessarily imply that management is doing a poor job or incurring unnecessary costs. Two reasons can be identified.

a. For most products, demand varies from month to month while commitment to the factors that determine capacity, e.g., size of the workshop or supervisory staff, tends to remain relatively constant. If PC wants to meet demand in high demand months, it will have excess capacity in low demand months. In addition, forecasts of future demand contain uncertainty due to unknown future factors. Having some excess capacity would allow PC to produce enough to cover peak demand as well as slack to deal with unexpected demand surges in non-peak months.

b. Basic economics provides a demand curve that shows a tradeoff between price charged and quantity demanded. Potentially, PC could have a lower net revenue if they produce at capacity and sell at a lower price than if they sell at a higher price at some level below capacity.

In addition, the unfavorable production-volume variance may not represent a feasible cost savings associated with lower capacity. Even if PC could shift to lower fixed costs by lowering capacity, the fixed cost may behave as a step function. If so, fixed costs would decrease in fixed amounts associated with a range of production capacity, not a specific production volume. The production-volume variance would only accurately identify potential cost savings if the fixed cost function is continuous, not discrete.

4. The static-budget operating income for February is:

Revenues ₹5,500 × 1,200	₹66,00,000
Variable costs ₹2,500 × 1,200	30,00,000
Fixed overhead costs	10,80,000
Static-budget operating income	₹25,20,000

The flexible-budget operating income for February is:

Revenues ₹5,500 × 720	₹39,60,000
Variable costs ₹2,500 × 720	18,00,000
Fixed overhead costs	10,80,000
Flexible-budget operating income	₹10,80,000

The sales-volume variance represents the difference between the static-budget operating income and the flexible-budget operating income:

Static-budget operating income	₹25,20,000
Flexible-budget operating income	10,80,000
Sales-volume variance	₹14,40,000 U

Equivalently, the sales-volume variance captures the fact that when PC sells 720 units instead of the budgeted 1,200, only the revenue and the variable costs are affected. Fixed costs remain unchanged. Therefore, the shortfall in profit is equal to the budgeted contribution margin per unit times the shortfall in output relative to budget.

$$\text{Sales-volume variance} = \left[\begin{array}{c} \text{Budgeted selling price} \end{array} - \begin{array}{c} \text{Budgeted variable cost per unit} \end{array} \right] \times \begin{array}{c} \text{Difference in quantity of units sold relative to the static budget} \end{array}$$

$$=(₹5,500 - ₹2,500) \times 480 = ₹3,000 \times 480 = ₹14,40,000 \text{ U}$$

In contrast, we computed in requirement 2 that the production-volume variance was ₹4,32,000 U. This captures only the portion of the budgeted fixed overhead expected to be unabsorbed because of the 480-unit shortfall. To compare it to the sales-volume variance, consider the following:

Budgeted selling price		₹5,500
Budgeted variable cost per unit	₹2,500	
Budgeted fixed cost per unit (₹10,80,000 ÷ 1,200)	900	
Budgeted cost per unit		3,400
Budgeted profit per unit		₹2,100
Operating income based on budgeted profit per unit		
₹2,100 per unit × 720 units		₹15,12,000

The ₹4,32,000 U production-volume variance explains the difference between operating income based on the budgeted profit per unit and the flexible-budget operating income:

Operating income based on budgeted profit per unit	₹15,12,000
Production-volume variance	− 4,32,000 U
Flexible-budget operating income	₹10,80,000

Because the sales-volume variance represents the difference between the static- and flexible-budget operating incomes, the difference between the sales-volume and production-volume variances, which is referred to as the operating-income volume variance, is:

Operating-income volume variance

= Sales-volume variance − Production-volume variance

= Static-budget operating income − Operating income based on budgeted profit per unit

= ₹25,20,000 U − ₹15,12,000 U = ₹10,08,000 U.

The operating-income volume variance explains the difference between the static-budget operating income and the budgeted operating income for the units actually sold. The static-budget operating income is ₹25,20,000 and the budgeted operating income for 720 units would have been ₹15,12,000 (₹2,100 operating income per unit × 720 units). The difference, ₹10,08,000 U, is the operating-income volume variance, i.e., the 480 unit drop in actual volume relative to budgeted volume would have caused an expected drop of ₹10,08,000 in operating income, at the budgeted operating income of ₹2,100 per unit. The operating-income volume variance assumes that ₹4,32,000 in fixed cost (₹900 per unit × 480 units) would be saved if production and sales volumes decreased by 480 units.

8-20 **Straightforward 4-variance overhead analysis.** The Omax Auto Company uses a standard-costing system in its manufacturing plant for auto parts. Its standard cost of an auto part, based on a denominator level of 4,000 output units per year, included 6 machine-hours of variable manufacturing overhead at ₹80 per hour and 6 machine-hours of fixed manufacturing overhead at ₹150 per hour. Actual output produced was 4,400 units. Variable manufacturing overhead incurred was ₹24,50,000. Fixed manufacturing overhead incurred was ₹37,30,000. Actual machine-hours were 28,400.

Required

1. Prepare an analysis of all variable manufacturing overhead variances, using the 4-variance analysis in Exhibit 8-3.
2. Prepare journal entries using the 4-variance analysis.
3. Describe how individual variable manufacturing overhead items are controlled from day to day. Also, describe how individual fixed manufacturing overhead items are controlled.

Solution

Straightforward 4-variance overhead analysis.

1. The budget for fixed manufacturing overhead is 4,000 × 6 × ₹150 = ₹36,00,000.

An overview of the 4-variance analysis is:

4-Variance Analysis	Spending Variance	Efficiency Variance	Production-Volume
Variable manufacturing overhead	₹1,78,000 U	₹1,60,000 U	Never a Variance
Fixed manufacturing overhead	₹1,30,000 U	Never a Variance	₹3,60,000 F

Solution Exhibit 8-20 has details of these variances.
A detailed comparison of actual and flexible budgeted amounts is:

	Actual	Flexible Budget
Output units (auto parts)	4,400	4,400
Allocation base (machine-hours)	28,400	26,400[a]
Allocation base per output unit	6.45[b]	6.00
Variable MOH	₹24,50,000	₹21,12,000[c]
Variable MOH per hour	₹86.30[d]	₹80
Fixed MOH	₹37,30,000	₹36,00,000[e]
Fixed MOH per hour	₹131.30[f]	—

⁴4,400 units × 6.00 machine-hours/unit = 26,400 machine-hours
²28,400 ÷ 4,400 = 6.45 machine-hours per unit
⁻4,400 units × 6.00 machine-hours per unit × ₹80 per machine-hour = ₹21,12,000
⁴₹24,50,000 ÷ 28,400 = ₹86.30
⁴4,000 units × 6.00 machine-hours per unit × ₹150 per machine-hour = ₹36,00,000
₹37,30,000 ÷ 28,400 = ₹131.30

2.

Variable Manufacturing Overhead Control	₹24,50,000	
Accounts payable control and other accounts		₹24,50,000
Work-in-process control	21,12,000	
Variable manufacturing overhead allocated		21,12,000
Variable manufacturing overhead allocated	21,12,000	
Variable manufacturing Overhead spending variance	1,78,000	
Variable manufacturing overhead efficiency variance	1,60,000	
Variable manufacturing overhead control		24,50,000
Fixed manufacturing overhead control	37,30,000	
Wages payable control, accumulated depreciation control, etc.		37,30,000
Work-in-process control	39,60,000	
Fixed manufacturing overhead allocated		39,60,000
Fixed manufacturing overhead allocated	39,60,000	
Fixed manufacturing overhead spending variance	1,30,000	
Fixed manufacturing overhead production-volume variance		3,60,000
Fixed manufacturing overhead control		37,30,000

3. The control of variable manufacturing overhead requires the identification of the cost drivers for such items as energy, supplies, and repairs. Control often entails monitoring nonfinancial measures that affect each cost item, one by one. Examples are kilowatt used, quantities of lubricants used, and repair parts and hour used. The most convincing way to discover why overhead performance did not agree with a budget is to investigate possible causes, line item by line item.

Individual fixed manufacturing overhead items are not usually affected very much by day-to-day control. Instead, they are controlled periodically through planning decisions and budgeting procedures that may sometimes have horizons covering six months or a year (for example, management salaries) and sometimes covering many years (for example, long-term leases and depreciation on plant and equipment).

Solution Exhibit 8-20

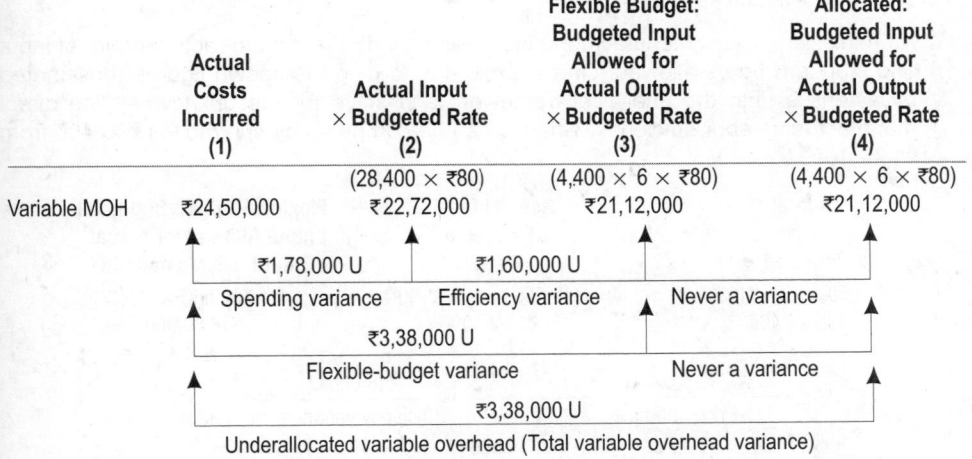

	Actual Costs Incurred (1)	Actual Input × Budgeted Rate (2)	Flexible Budget: Budgeted Input Allowed for Actual Output × Budgeted Rate (3)	Allocated: Budgeted Input Allowed for Actual Output × Budgeted Rate (4)
		(28,400 × ₹80)	(4,400 × 6 × ₹80)	(4,400 × 6 × ₹80)
Variable MOH	₹24,50,000	₹22,72,000	₹21,12,000	₹21,12,000

₹1,78,000 U   ₹1,60,000 U

Spending variance   Efficiency variance   Never a variance

₹3,38,000 U

Flexible-budget variance   Never a variance

₹3,38,000 U

Underallocated variable overhead (Total variable overhead variance)

	Actual Costs Incurred (1)	Same Budgeted Lump Sum (as in Static Budget) Regardless of Output Level (2)	Flexible Budget: Same Budgeted Lump Sum (as in Static Budget) Regardless of Output Level (3)	Allocated: Budgeted Input Allowed for Actual Output × Budgeted Rate (4)
Fixed MOH	₹37,30,000	(4,000 × 6 × ₹150) ₹36,00,000	(4,000 × 6 × ₹150) ₹36,00,000	(4,400 × 6 × ₹150) ₹39,60,000

₹1,30,000 U
Spending variance   Never a variance   Production-volume variance   ₹3,60,000 F

₹1,30,000 U   ₹3,60,000 F
Flexible-budget variance   Production-volume variance

₹2,30,000 F
Overallocated fixed overhead (Total fixed overhead variance)

8-21 Total overhead, 3-variance analysis. Delhi Cantt Air Force Base has an extensive repair facility for jet engines. It developed standard costing and flexible budgets to account for this activity. Budgeted variable overhead at a level of 8,000 standard monthly direct labor-hours was ₹6,40,000; budgeted total overhead at 10,000 standard direct labor-hours was ₹19,76,000. The standard cost allocated to repair output included a total overhead rate of 120 percent of standard direct labor costs. Total overhead incurred for October was ₹24,90,000. Direct labor costs incurred were ₹20,24,400. The direct labor price variance was ₹96,400 unfavorable. The direct labor flexible-budget variance was ₹1,44,400 unfavorable. The standard labor price was ₹160 per hour. The production-volume variance was ₹1,40,000 favorable.

Required

1. Compute the direct labor efficiency variance and the spending, efficiency, and production-volume variances for overhead. Also, compute the denominator level.
2. Describe how individual variable manufacturing overhead items are controlled from day to day. Also, describe how individual fixed manufacturing overhead items are controlled.

Solution

Total overhead, 3-variance analysis.

1. An analysis of direct manufacturing labor will provide the data for actual hours of input and standard hours allowed. One approach is to plug the known figures (designated by asterisks) into the analytical framework and solve for the unknowns. The direct manufacturing labor efficiency variance can be computed by subtracting ₹96,400 from ₹1,44,400.

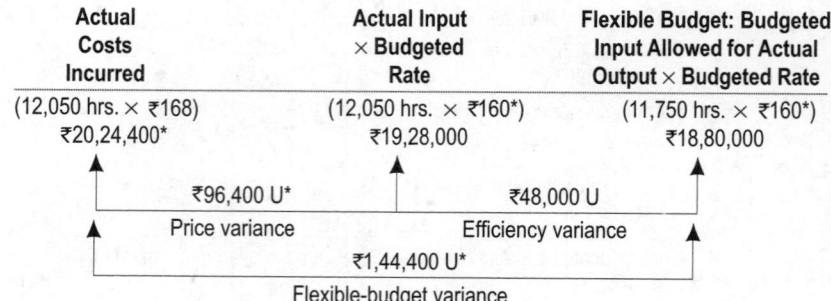

Actual Costs Incurred	Actual Input × Budgeted Rate	Flexible Budget: Budgeted Input Allowed for Actual Output × Budgeted Rate
(12,050 hrs. × ₹168) ₹20,24,400*	(12,050 hrs. × ₹160*) ₹19,28,000	(11,750 hrs. × ₹160*) ₹18,80,000

₹96,400 U*   ₹48,000 U
Price variance   Efficiency variance

₹1,44,400 U*
Flexible-budget variance

The complete picture is:

*Given

Direct Labor calculations

Actual input × Budgeted rate = Actual costs – Price variance
$$= ₹20,24,400 – ₹96,400 = ₹19,28,000$$

Actual input
$$= ₹19,28,000 ÷ \text{Budgeted rate} = ₹19,28,000 ÷ ₹160 = 12,050 \text{ hours}$$

Budgeted input × Budgeted rate = ₹19,28,000 – Efficiency variance
$$= ₹19,28,000 – ₹48,000 = ₹18,80,000$$

Budgeted input
$$= ₹18,80,000 ÷ \text{Budgeted rate} = ₹18,80,000 ÷ 160 = 11,750 \text{ hours}$$

Repair Overhead

Variable overhead rate
$$= ₹6,40,000* ÷ 8,000* \text{ hrs.} = ₹80 \text{ per standard labor-hour}$$

Budgeted fixed overhead costs = ₹19,76,000* – 10,000*(₹80) = ₹11,76,000

If total overhead is allocated at 120% of direct labor-cost, the single overhead rate must be 120% of ₹160, or ₹192 per hour. Therefore, the fixed overhead component of the rate must be ₹192 – ₹80, or ₹112 per direct labor-hour.

Let D = denominator level in input units

$$\text{Budgeted fixedoverhead rateper input unit} = \frac{\text{Budgeted fixed oerhead costs}}{\text{Denominator level in input units}}$$

$$₹112 = ₹11,76,000/D$$
$$D = 10,500 \text{ direct labor-hours}$$

A summary 3-variance analysis for October follows:

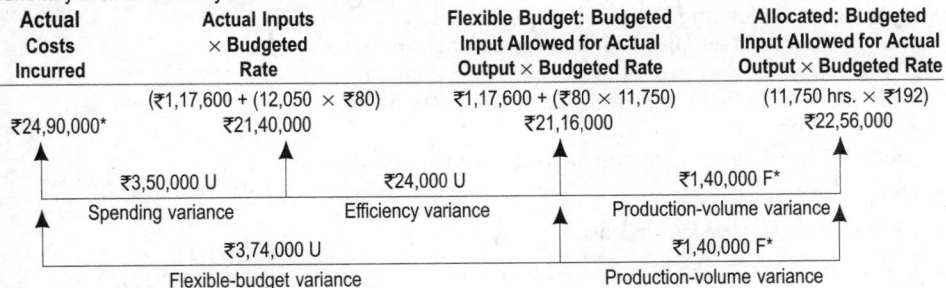

Actual Costs Incurred	Actual Inputs × Budgeted Rate	Flexible Budget: Budgeted Input Allowed for Actual Output × Budgeted Rate	Allocated: Budgeted Input Allowed for Actual Output × Budgeted Rate
	(₹1,17,600 + (12,050 × ₹80)	₹1,17,600 + (₹80 × 11,750)	(11,750 hrs. × ₹192)
₹24,90,000*	₹21,40,000	₹21,16,000	₹22,56,000

₹3,50,000 U — Spending variance

₹24,000 U — Efficiency variance

₹1,40,000 F* — Production-volume variance

₹3,74,000 U — Flexible-budget variance

₹1,40,000 F* — Production-volume variance

A summary 3-variance analysis for October follows:

*Known figure

An overview of the 3-variance analysis using the block format in the text is:

3-Variance Analysis	Spending Variance	Efficiency Variance	Production-Volume Variance
Total Overhead	₹3,50,000 U	₹24,000 U	₹1,40,000 F

2. The control of variable manufacturing overhead requires the identification of the cost drivers for such items as energy, supplies, equipment, and maintenance. Control often entails monitoring nonfinancial measures that affect each cost item, one by one. Examples are kilowatt used, quantities of lubricants used, and equipment parts and hours used. The most convincing way to discover why overhead performance did not agree with a budget is to investigate possible causes, line item by line item.

Individual fixed manufacturing overhead items are not usually affected very much by day-to-day control. Instead, they are controlled periodically through planning decisions and budgeting that may sometimes have horizons covering six months or a year (for example, management salaries) and sometimes covering many years (for example, long-term leases and depreciation on plant and equipment).

8-22 Flexible budgets, 4-variance analysis. (CMA, adapted) Essel Products use a standard-costing system. It allocates manufacturing overhead (both variable and fixed) to products on the basis of standard direct manufacturing labor-hours (DLH). Essel develops its manufacturing overhead rate from the current annual budget. The manufacturing overhead budget for 2015 is based on budgeted output of 7,20,000 units, requiring 36,00,000 DLH. The company is able to schedule production uniformly throughout the year.

A total of 66,000 output units requiring 3,15,000 DLH was produced during May 2015. Manufacturing overhead (MOH) costs incurred for May amounted to ₹37,50,000. The actual costs, compared with the annual budget and 1/12 of the annual budget are as follows:

Annual Manufacturing Overhead Budget 2015:

	Total Amount	Per Output Unit	Per DLH Input Unit	Monthly MOH Budget May 2012	Actual MOH Costs for May 2012
Variable MOH					
Indirect manufacturing labor	₹90,00,000	₹12.5	₹2.5	₹7,50,000	₹7,50,000
Supplies	1,22,40,000	17.0	3.4	10,20,000	11,10,000
Fixed MOH					
Supervision	64,80,000	9.0	1.8	5,40,000	5,10,000
Utilities	54,00,000	7.5	1.5	4,50,000	5,40,000
Depreciation	1,00,80,000	14.0	2.8	8,40,000	8,40,000
Total	4,32,00,000	60.0	12	36,00,000	37,50,000

Required

Calculate the following amounts for Essel Products for May 2015:

1. Total manufacturing overhead costs allocated.
2. variable manufacturing overhead spending variance.
3. Fixed manufacturing overhead spending variance.
4. variable manufacturing overhead efficiency variance.
5. Production-volume variance.

Be sure to identify each variance as favorable (F) or unfavorable (U).

Solution

Flexible budgets, 4-variance analysis.

1. Budgeted hours allowed per unit of output = $\dfrac{\text{Budgeted DLH}}{\text{Budgeted actual output}}$

= 36,00,000/7,20,000 = 5 hours per unit

Budgeted DLH allowed for May output = 66,000 units × 5 hrs./unit = 3,30,000 hrs.

Allocated total MOH = 3,30,000 × Total MOH rate per hour

= 3,30,000 × ₹12 = ₹39,60,000

2,3, 4, 5. See Solution Exhibit 8-26

Variable overhead rate per DLH = ₹2.5 + ₹3.4 = ₹5.9

Fixed overhead rate per DLH = ₹1.8 + ₹1.5 + ₹2.8 = ₹6.1

Fixed overhead budget for May = (₹64,80,000 + ₹54,00,000 + ₹1,00,80,000) ÷ 12

= ₹2,19,60,000 ÷ 12 = ₹18,30,000

Using the format of Exhibit 8-3 for variable overhead and then fixed overhead:

Actual variable overhead: ₹7,50,000 + ₹11,10,000 = ₹18,60,000

Actual fixed overhead: ₹5,10,000 + ₹5,40,000 + ₹8,40,000 = ₹18,90,000

An overview of the 4-variance analysis using the block format of the text is:

4-Variance Analysis	Spending Variance	Efficiency Variance	Production-Volume Variance
Variable manufacturing overhead	₹1,500 U	₹88,500 F	Never a variance
Fixed manufacturing overhead	₹60,000 U	Never a variance	₹1,83,000 F

Solution Exhibit 8-26

Variable Manufacturing Overhead

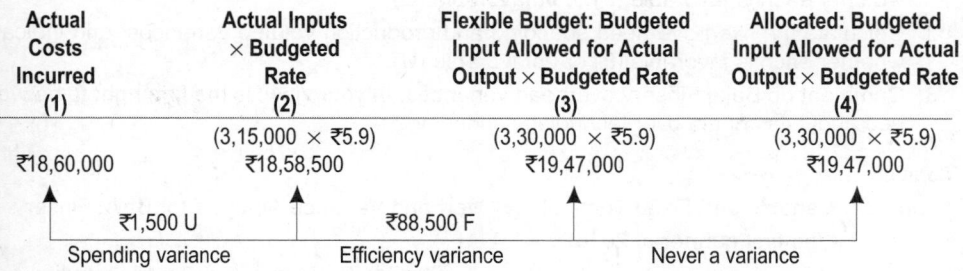

Actual Costs Incurred (1)	Actual Inputs × Budgeted Rate (2)	Flexible Budget: Budgeted Input Allowed for Actual Output × Budgeted Rate (3)	Allocated: Budgeted Input Allowed for Actual Output × Budgeted Rate (4)
	(3,15,000 × ₹5.9)	(3,30,000 × ₹5.9)	(3,30,000 × ₹5.9)
₹18,60,000	₹18,58,500	₹19,47,000	₹19,47,000

₹1,500 U ← Spending variance

₹88,500 F ← Efficiency variance

Never a variance

Fixed Manufacturing Overhead

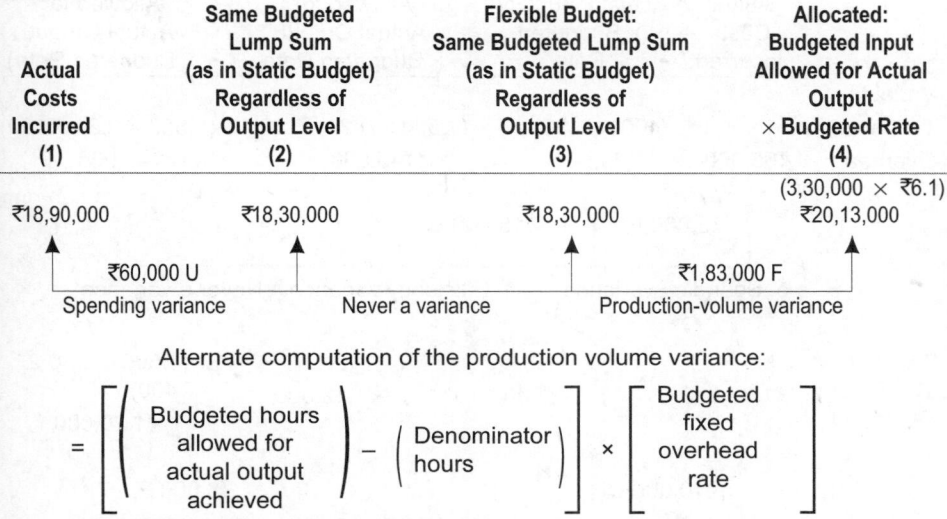

Actual Costs Incurred (1)	Same Budgeted Lump Sum (as in Static Budget) Regardless of Output Level (2)	Flexible Budget: Same Budgeted Lump Sum (as in Static Budget) Regardless of Output Level (3)	Allocated: Budgeted Input Allowed for Actual Output × Budgeted Rate (4)
			(3,30,000 × ₹6.1)
₹18,90,000	₹18,30,000	₹18,30,000	₹20,13,000

₹60,000 U ← Spending variance

Never a variance

₹1,83,000 F ← Production-volume variance

Alternate computation of the production volume variance:

$$= \left[\left(\begin{array}{c} \text{Budgeted hours} \\ \text{allowed for} \\ \text{actual output} \\ \text{achieved} \end{array} \right) - \left(\begin{array}{c} \text{Denominator} \\ \text{hours} \end{array} \right) \right] \times \left[\begin{array}{c} \text{Budgeted} \\ \text{fixed} \\ \text{overhead} \\ \text{rate} \end{array} \right]$$

= [(3,30,000) − (36,00,000/12) × ₹6.10

= [(3,30,000 − 3,00,000) × ₹6.10 = ₹1,83,000 F

8-23 Overhead variances, service setting. Bajaj Finserv provides a diverse array of back office services to its clients in the financial services industry, ranging from record keeping and compliance to order processing and trade settlement. Bajaj has grown increasingly reliant on technology to acquire, retain, and serve its clients. Worried that its spending on information technology is getting out of control, Bajaj has recently embraced variance analysis as a tool for cost management.

After some study, Bajaj determines that its variable and fixed technology overhead costs are both driven by the processing time involved in meeting client requests. This is typically measured in CPU units of usage of a high-performance computing cluster. Bajaj's primary measure of output is the number of client interactions its partners have in a given period. The following information pertains to the first quarter of 2016:

Budgeted Output Units	1,400 client interaction
Budgeted Fixed Technology Overhead	₹1,12,000
Budgeted Variable Technology Overhead	₹150 per CPU Unit
Budgeted CPU Units	0.2 units per client interaction
Fixed Technology Overhead incurred	₹1,22,000
CPU Units Based	400
Variable Technology Overhead incurred	₹55,000
Actual Output Units	1,500 client interaction

Required

1. Calculate the variable overhead spending and efficiency variances, and indica
   whether each is favorable (F) or unfavorable (U).
2. Calculate the fixed overhead spending and production volume variances, and indica
   whether each is favorable (F) or unfavorable (U).
3. Comment on Bajaj Finserv overhead variances. In your view, is the firm right to be wo
   ried about its control over technology spending?

Solution

1. and 2.   Variable and Fixed Technology Overhead Variance Analysis for Bajaj Finserv
   for the first quarter of 2016

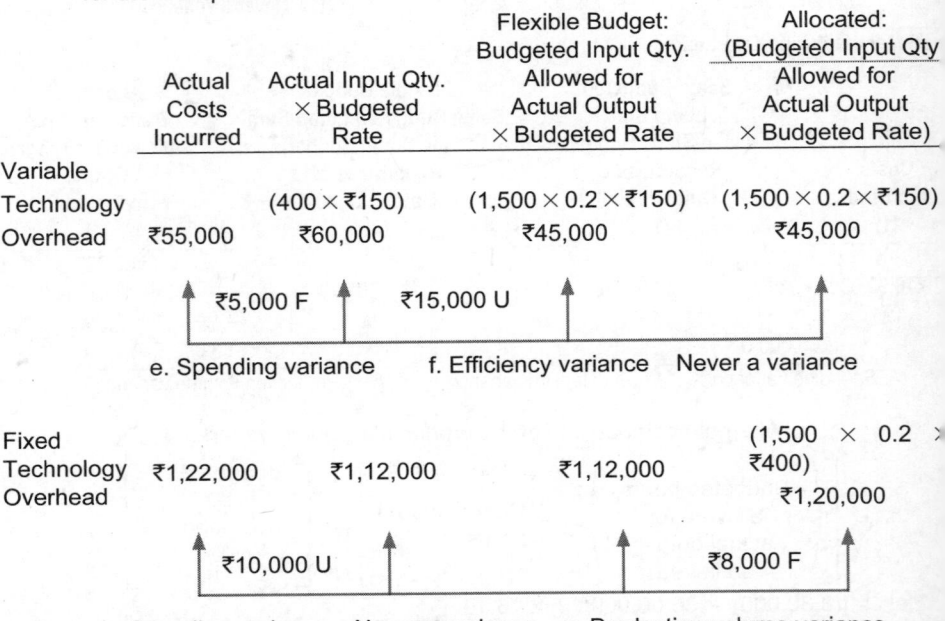

3. Bajaj has done a reasonable job overall of managing its technology overhead costs.
   has an unfavorable variable overhead efficiency variance because it used too many CF
   units of processing time relative to the number of client interactions it had. This is not a
   issue if the goal was to meet the high-performance computing needs of clients and result
   in higher levels of client satisfaction or revenues. For the 4,000 CPU units used, Bajaj spe
   ₹137.50 per unit relative to the budgeted ₹150, so the price/spending variance on variab
   technology overhead was favorable.

   From the standpoint of capacity utilization, the company was successful at managing th
   fixed technology overhead resources. They handled 1,500 client interactions, compared
   an expected output of 1,400. It would be useful to know what the firm views as the maximu
   attainable level of capacity given its current spending on technology. This is particularly s
   nificant because Bajaj spent an additional ₹10,000 more than the expected expenditure
   fixed resources for the period. The firm should attempt to identify the causes of this negati
   spending variance and assess whether this higher spending level is likely to persist in futu
   years.

8-24 Identifying favorable and unfavorable variances. Apollo Tyres Ltd, manufactures tires f
large auto companies. It uses standard costing and allocates variable and fixed manufacturing overhead based on machine-hours. For each independent scenario given, indicate
whether each of the manufacturing variances will be favorable or unfavorable or, in case
insufficient information, indicate "CBD" (cannot be determined).

Scenario	Variable Overhead Spending Variance	Variable Overhead Efficiency Variance	Fixed Overhead Spending Variance	Fixed Overhead Production-Volume Variance
Production output is 6% less than budgeted, and actual fixed manufacturing overhead costs are 5% more than budgeted				
Production output is 13% less than budgeted; actual machine-hours are 7% more than budgeted				
Production output is 10% more than budgeted				
Actual machine-hours are 20% less than flexible-budget machine-hours				
Relative to the flexible budget, actual machine-hours are 15% less, and actual variable manufacturing overhead costs are 20% greater				

Solution

Scenario	VOH Spending Variance	VOH Efficiency Variance	FOH Spending Variance	FOH Production-Volume Variance
Production output is 6% less than budgeted, and actual fixed manufacturing overhead costs are 5% more than budgeted.	Cannot be determined; no information on actual versus budgeted VOH rates.	Cannot be determined; no information on actual versus flexible-budget machine-hours.	Unfavorable:;actual fixed costs are more than budgeted fixed costs.	Unfavorable; output is less than budgeted causing FOH costs to be underallocated.
Production output is 13% less than budgeted; actual machine-hours are 7% more than budgeted.	Cannot be determined; no information on actual versus budgeted VOH rates.	Unfavorable; actual machine-hours more than flexible-budget machine-hours.	Cannot be determined; no information on actual versus budgeted FOH costs.	Unfavorable; output is less than budgeted causing FOH costs to be underallocated.
Production output is 10% more than budgeted.	Cannot be determined; no information on actual versus budgeted VOH rates.	Cannot be determined; no information on actual machine-hours versus flexible-budget machine-hours.	Cannot be determined; no information on actual versus budgeted FOH costs.	Favorable; output more than budgeted will cause FOH costs to be overallocated.

Actual machine-hours are 20% less than flexible-budget machine-hours.	Cannot be determined; no information on actual versus budgeted VOH rates.	Favorable; less machine-hours used relative to flexible budget.	Cannot be determined; no information on actual versus budgeted FOH costs.	Cannot be determined; no information on flexible-budget machine-hours relative to static-budget machine-hours.
Relative to the flexible budget, actual machine-hours are 15% less, and actual variable manufacturing overhead costs are 20% greater.	Unfavorable; actual VOH rate greater than budgeted VOH rate.	Favorable; actual machine-hours less than flexible-budget machine-hours.	Cannot be determined; no information on actual versus budgeted FOH costs.	Cannot be determined; no information on actual output relative to budgeted output.

8-25 Overhead variance, missing information. Consider the following two situations—cases A and B—independently. Data refer to operations for March, 2016. For each situation, assume standard costing. Also assume the use of a flexible budget for control of variable and fixed manufacturing overhead based machine-hours.

		Cases	
		A	B
(1)	Fixed manufacturing overhead incurred	₹84,920	₹23,180
(2)	Variable manufacturing overhead incurred	₹1,20,400	—
(3)	Denominator level in machine-hours	—	1,000
(4)	Standard machine-hours allowed for actual output achieved	6,200	—
(5)	Fixed manufacturing overhead (per standard machine-hour)	—	—
Flexible-Budget Data:			
(6)	Variable manufacturing overhead (per standard machine-hour)	—	₹42.00
(7)	Budgeted fixed manufacturing overhead	₹88,200	₹20,000
(8)	Budgeted variable manufacturing overhead[a]	—	—
(9)	Total budgeted manufacturing overhead[a]	—	—
Additional Data:			
(10)	Standard variable manufacturing overhead allocated	₹1,24,000	—
(11)	Standard fixed manufacturing overhead allocated	₹86,800	—
(12)	Production-volume variance	—	₹4,000 F
(13)	Variable manufacturing overhead spending variance	₹5,000 F	₹2,282 F
(14)	Variable manufacturing overhead efficiency variance	—	₹2,478 F
(15)	Fixed manufacturing overhead spending variance	—	—
(16)	Actual machine-hours used	—	—

[a]For standard machine-hours allowed for actual output produced.

Required

Fill in the blanks under each case. [Hint: Prepare a worksheet similar to that in Exhibit 8-4 (In Text). Fill in the knowns and then solve for the unknowns.]

Solution

Known figures denoted by an *

Case A:

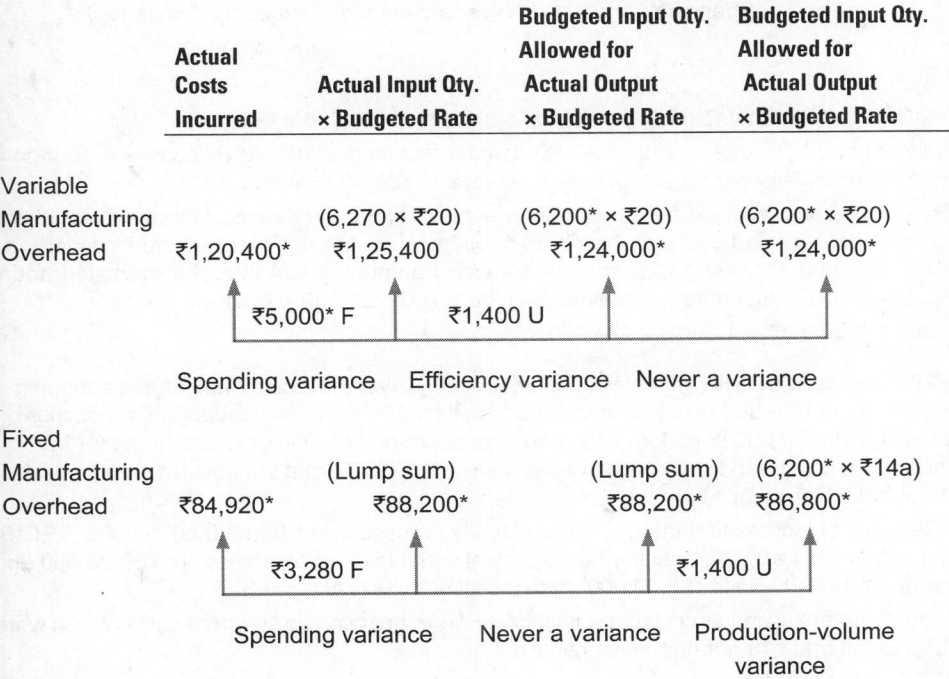

Total budgeted manufacturing overhead = ₹1,24,000 + ₹88,200 = ₹2,12,200

Case B:

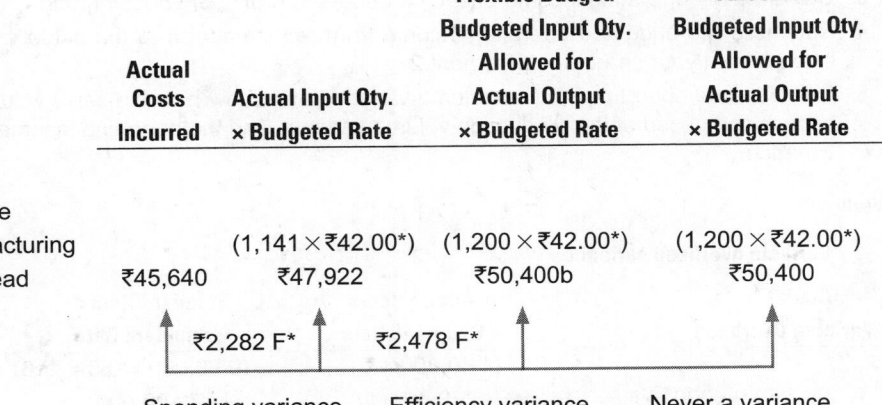

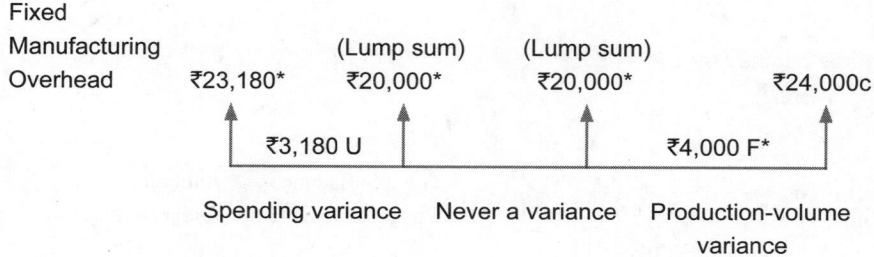

Spending variance   Never a variance   Production-volume variance

Total budgeted manufacturing overhead = ₹50,400 + ₹20,000 = ₹70,400

[a]Budgeted FMOH rate = Standard fixed manufacturing overhead allocated ÷ Standard machine-hours allowed for actual output achieved =₹86,800 ÷ 6,200 = ₹14.

[b] Budgeted hours allowed for actual output achieved must be derived from the output level variance before this figure can be derived, or because the fixed manufacturing overhead rate is ₹20,000 ÷ 1,000 = ₹20 and the allocated amount is ₹24,000, the budgeted hours allowed for the actual output achieved must be 1,200 (₹24,000 ÷ ₹20).

[c]1,200 × (₹20,000* ÷ 1,000*) = ₹24,000.

8-26 Overhead variances and sales volume variance Royal Plastics manufactures shopping bags made of recycled plastic that it plans to sell for ₹50 each. Royal budgets production and sales of 8,00,000 bags for 2016, with a standard of 4,00,000 machine-hours for the whole year. Budgeted fixed overhead costs are ₹50,00,000, and variable overhead cost is ₹16 per machine-hour.

Because of increased demand, Royal actually produced and sold 9,00,000 bags in 2016, using a total of 4,40,000 machine-hours. Actual variable overhead costs are ₹69,96,000 and actual fixed overhead is ₹50,19,000. Actual selling price is ₹60 per bag.

Direct materials and direct labor actual costs were the same as standard costs, which were ₹12 per unit and ₹18 per unit, respectively.

Required

1. Calculate the variable overhead and fixed overhead variances (spending, efficiency, spending, and volume).

2. Create a chart like that in Exhibit 7-2 showing Flexible Budget Variances and Sales Volume Variances for revenues, costs, contribution margin, and operating income.

3. Calculate the operating income based on budgeted profit per shopping bag.

4. Reconcile the budgeted operating income from requirement 3 to the actual operating income from your chart in requirement 2.

5. Calculate the operating income volume variance and show how the sales volume variance is composed of the production volume variance and the operating income volume variance.

Solution

1 Variable overhead variances

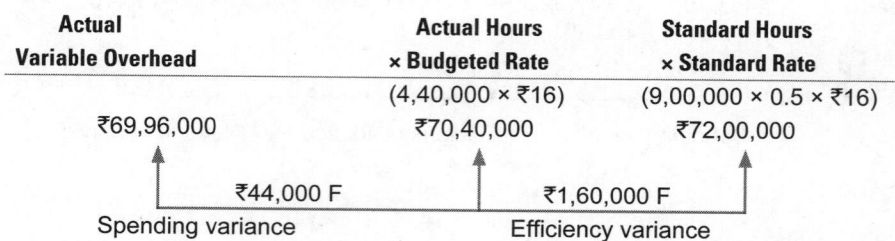

Actual Variable Overhead	Actual Hours × Budgeted Rate	Standard Hours × Standard Rate
	(4,40,000 × ₹16)	(9,00,000 × 0.5 × ₹16)
₹69,96,000	₹70,40,000	₹72,00,000

₹44,000 F   ₹1,60,000 F

Spending variance   Efficiency variance

Fixed overhead variances

Actual Fixed Overhead	Static Budget Fixed Overhead	Standard Hours × Budgeted Rate
		(9,00,000 × 0.5 × ₹12.50*)
₹50,19,000	₹50,00,000	₹56,25,000

₹19,000 U — Spending variance

₹6,25,000 F — Production-volume variance

*FOH rate is ₹50,00,000 / 40,00,000 std hours = ₹12.50 per hour

2.

	Actual Results (1)	Flexible-Budget Variances (2) = (1) – (3)	Flexible Budget (3)	Sales-Volume Variances (4) = (3) – (5)	Static Budget (5)
Units sold	9,00,000		9,00,000		8,00,000
Unit price	₹60		₹50		₹50
Revenues	₹5,40,00,000	₹90,00,000 F	₹4,50,00,000	₹50,00,000 F	₹4,00,00,000
Variable costs					
Direct materials	1,08,00,000	0	1,08,00,000	12,00,000 U	96,00,000
Direct labor	1,62,00,000	0	1,62,00,000	18,00,000 U	1,44,00,000
Variable overhead	69,96,000	2,04,000 F	72,00,000	8,00,000 U	64,00,000
Total variable costs	3,39,96,000	2,04,000 F	3,42,00,000	38,00,000 U	3,04,00,000
Contribution margin	2,00,04,000	92,04,000 F	1,08,00,000	12,00,000 F	96,00,000
Fixed manufacturing costs	50,19,000	19,000 U	50,00,000	0	50,00,000
Operating income	₹1,49,85,000	₹91,85,000 F	₹58,00,000	₹12,00,000 F	₹46,00,000

3 Budgeted cost per shopping bag:

Direct materials per bag (given)	₹12
Direct labor per bag (given)	18
Variable overhead (₹16 per hour × 0.5 MH)	8.0
Fixed overhead (₹12.5 per hour × 0.5 MH)	6.25
Total	₹44.25

Budgeted sales revenue, 9,00,000 actual units sold	
9,00,000 × ₹50	₹4,50,00,000
Budgeted Cost of Goods sold	
9,00,000 × ₹44.25	3,98,25,000
Budgeted operating income	₹51,75,000

4. Budgeted operating income (from #3)	₹51,75,000
Add: favorable volume variance (from #1)	5,87,500
Flexible budget operating income	₹58,00,000

Add: Favorable flexible budget variance	91,85,000
Actual operating income	₹1,49,85,000

5. Operating income volume variance:

Budgeted operating income for actual output − static budget operating income
= ₹51,75,000 − ₹46,00,000 = ₹5,75,000 F

Sales volume variance = ₹11,62,500 F

= production volume variance + operating income volume variance
= ₹5,87,500 + ₹5,75,000 = ₹11,62,500 F

Solution Exhibit 8-26
Variable Manufacturing Overhead

8-27 Activity-based costing, batch-level variance analysis Pearson Publishing Company specializes in printing specialty textbooks for a small but profitable college market. Due to the high setup costs for each batch printed, Pearson holds the book requests until demand for a book is approximately 520. At that point Pearson will schedule the setup and production of the book. For rush orders, Pearson will produce smaller batches for an additional charge of ₹9,870 per setup.

Budgeted and actual costs for the printing process for 2015 were as follows:

	Static-Budget Amounts	Actual Results
Number of books produced	1,97,600	2,25,680
Average number of books per setup	520	496
Hours to set up printers	7 hours	7.5 hours
Direct variable cost per setup-hour	₹1,300	₹700
Total fixed setup overhead costs	₹5,32,000	₹6,80,000

Required

1. What is the static budget number of setups for 2015?
2. What is the flexible budget number of setups for 2015?
3. What is the actual number of setups in 2015?
4. Assuming fixed setup overhead costs are allocated using setup-hours, what is the predetermined fixed setup overhead allocation rate?
5. Does Pearson's charge of ₹9,870 cover the budgeted direct variable cost of an order? The budgeted total cost?
6. For direct variable setup costs, compute the price and efficiency variances.
7. For fixed setup overhead costs, compute the spending and the production-volume variances.
8. What qualitative factors should Pearson consider before accepting or rejecting a special order?

Solution

Static budget number of setups = Budgeted books produced/ Budgeted books per setup
= 1,97,600 ÷ 520 = 380 setups

Flexible budget number of setups = Actual books produced / Budgeted books per setup
= 2,25,680 ÷ 520 = 434 setups

Actual number of setups = Actual books produced / Actual books per setup
= 2,25,680/496 = 455 setups

Static budget number of hours = Static budget # of setups × Budgeted hours per setup
= 380 × 7 = 2,660 hours

Fixed overhead rate = Static budget fixed overhead / Static budget number of hours

= ₹5,32,000/2,660 = ₹200 per hour

Budgeted direct variable cost of a setup

= Budgeted variable cost per setup-hour × Budgeted number of setup-hours

= ₹1,300 × 7 = ₹9,100.

Budgeted total cost of a setup

= Budgeted direct variable cost + Fixed overhead rate × Budgeted number of setup – hours

= ₹9,100 + ₹200 × 7 = ₹10,500.

So, the charge of ₹9,870 covers the budgeted incremental (i.e., variable) cost of a setup but not the budgeted full cost.

6. Direct Variable Variance Analysis for Pearson Publishing Company for 2015

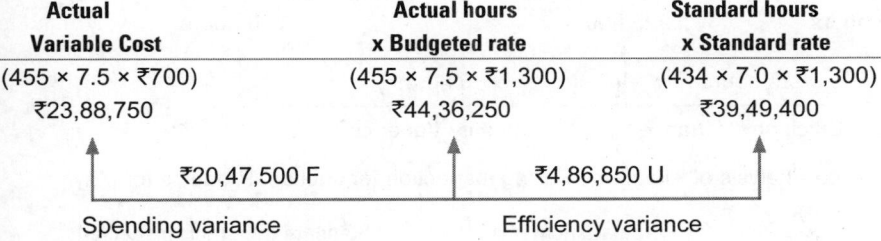

Actual Variable Cost	Actual hours x Budgeted rate	Standard hours x Standard rate
(455 × 7.5 × ₹700)	(455 × 7.5 × ₹1,300)	(434 × 7.0 × ₹1,300)
₹23,88,750	₹44,36,250	₹39,49,400

₹20,47,500 F   ₹4,86,850 U

Spending variance   Efficiency variance

7. Fixed Setup Overhead Variance Analysis for Pearson Publishing Company for 2015

Actual Fixed Overhead	Static Budget Fixed Overhead	Standard hours × Budgeted Rate
		(434 × 7.0 × ₹200)
₹6,80,000	₹5,32,000	₹6,07,600

₹1,48,000 U   ₹75,600 F

Spending variance   Production-volume variance

8. Rejecting an order may have implications for future orders (i.e., professors would be reluctant to order books from this publisher again). Pearson should consider factors such as prior history with the customer and potential future sales.

If a book is relatively new, Pearson might consider running a full batch and holding the extra books in case of a second special order or just hold the extra books until next semester.

If the special order comes at heavy volume times, Pearson should look at the opportunity cost of filling it, i.e., accepting the order may interfere with or delay the printing of other books.

8-28 Non-financial variances. Jubilant Products produces high-quality dog food distributed only through veterinary offices. To ensure that the food is of the highest quality and has taste appeal, Jubilant has a rigorous inspection process. For quality control purposes, Jubilant has a standard based on the Kilograms of food inspected per hour and the number of Kilograms that pass or fail the inspection.

Jubilant expects that for every 13,000 Kilograms of food produced, 1,300 Kilograms of food will be inspected. Inspection of 1,300 Kilograms of dog food should take 1 hour. Jubilant also expects that 5% of the food inspected will fail the inspection. During the month of May, Jubilant produced 29,90,000 Kilograms of food and inspected 2,92,500 Kilograms of food in 200 hours. Of the 2,92,500 Kilograms of food inspected, 15,625 Kilograms of food failed to pass the inspection.

Required

1. Compute two variances that help determine whether the time spent on inspections was more or less than expected. (Follow a format similar to the one used for the variable overhead spending and efficiency variances, but without prices.)

2. Compute two variances that can be used to evaluate the percentage of the food that fails the inspection.

Solution

1. Variance Analysis of Inspection Hours for Jubilant Products for May

Actual Hours For Inspections	Actual Kilograms Inspected/Budgeted Kilograms per hour	Standard Kilograms Inspected for Actual Output /Budgeted Kilograms per hour
	2,92,500 kgs/1,300 kgs/hr	(29,90,000 × 0.1) kgs/(1,300 kgs/hr)
200 hours	225 hours	230 hours

25 hours F   5 hours F

Efficiency Variance   Quantity Variance

2. Variance Analysis of Kilograms Failing Inspection for Jubilant Products for May

Actual Kilograms Failing Inspections	Actual Kilograms Inspected × Budgeted Inspection Failure Rate	Standard Kilograms Inspected for Actual Output × Budgeted Inspection Failure Rate
	(2,92,500 kgs × 0.05)	(29,90,000 × 0.1 × 0.05)
15,625 kgs	14,625 kgs	14,950 kgs

1,000 kgs U   325 kgs F

Quality Variance   Quantity Variance

8-29 Overhead variances, service sector. Infosys Ltd, is a cloud service provider that offers computing resources to handle enterprise-wide applications. For March 2015, Infosys estimates that it will provide 18,000 RAM hours of services to clients. The budgeted variable overhead rate is ₹60 per RAM hour.

At the end of March, there is a ₹5,000 favorable spending variance for variable overhead and a ₹15,750 unfavorable spending variance for fixed overhead. For the services actually provided during the month, 14,850 RAM hours are budgeted and 15,000 RAM hours are actually used. Total actual overhead costs are ₹11,98,750.

Required

1. Compute efficiency and flexible-budget variances for Infosys's variable overhead in March 2015. Will variable overhead be over- or underallocated? By how much?

2. Compute production-volume and flexible-budget variances for Infosys's fixed overhead in March 2015. Will fixed overhead be over- or underallocated? By how much?

Solution

1. In the columnar presentation of variable overhead variance analysis, all numbers shown in bold are calculated from the given information, in the order (a)–(e).

VARIABLE MANUFACTURING OVERHEAD

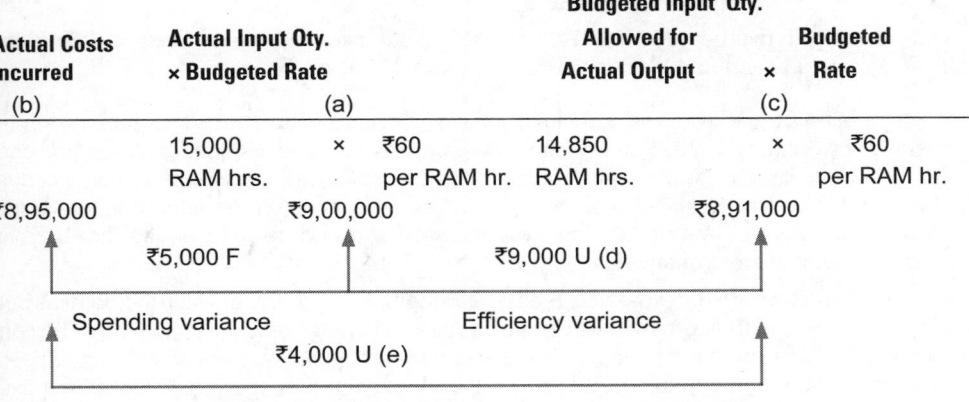

Actual Costs Incurred (b)	Actual Input Qty. × Budgeted Rate (a)	Flexible Budget: Budgeted Input Qty. Allowed for Actual Output ×	Budgeted Rate (c)
	15,000 RAM hrs. × ₹60 per RAM hr.	14,850 RAM hrs. ×	₹60 per RAM hr.
₹8,95,000	₹9,00,000		₹8,91,000

₹5,000 F .... ₹9,000 U (d)

Spending variance .... Efficiency variance

₹4,000 U (e)

Flexible-budget variance

a. 15,000 RAM hours × ₹60 per RAM hour = ₹9,00,000
b. Actual VMOH = ₹9,00,000 – ₹5,000F (VOH spending variance) = ₹8,95,000
c. 14,850 RAM hours × ₹60 per RAM hour = ₹8,91,000
d. VOH efficiency variance = ₹9,00,000 – ₹8,91,000 = ₹9,000 U
e. VOH flexible budget variance = ₹9,000U – ₹5,000F = ₹4,000 U

Allocated variable overhead will be the same as the flexible budget variable overhead of ₹8,91,000. The actual variable overhead cost is ₹8,95,000. Therefore, variable overhead is underallocated by ₹4,000.

2. In the columnar presentation of fixed overhead variance analysis, all numbers shown in bold are calculated from the given information, in the order (a)–(e).

FIXED MANUFACTURING OVERHEAD

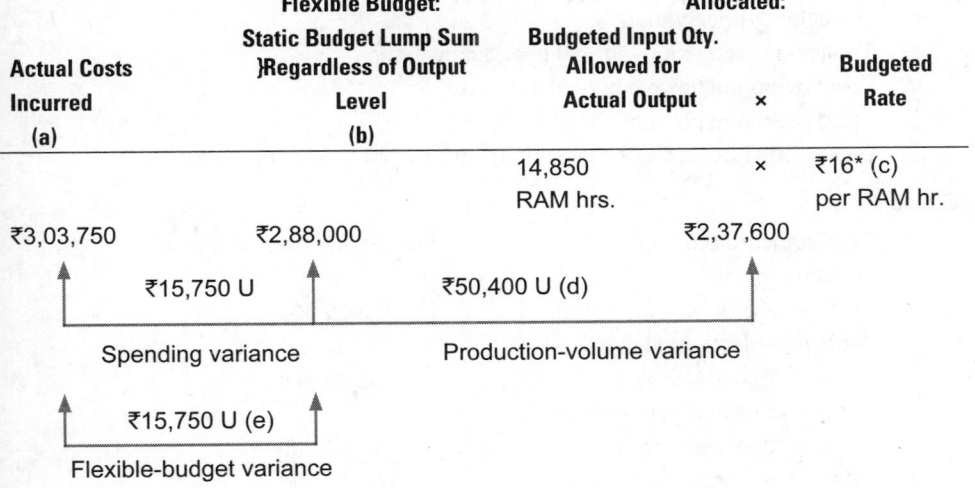

Actual Costs Incurred (a)	Flexible Budget: Static Budget Lump Sum)Regardless of Output Level (b)	Allocated: Budgeted Input Qty. Allowed for Actual Output ×	Budgeted Rate
		14,850 RAM hrs. ×	₹16* (c) per RAM hr.
₹3,03,750	₹2,88,000		₹2,37,600

₹15,750 U .... ₹50,400 U (d)

Spending variance .... Production-volume variance

₹15,750 U (e)

Flexible-budget variance

a. Actual FOH costs = ₹11,98,750 total overhead costs – ₹8,95,000 VOH costs = ₹3,03,750
b. Static budget FOH lump sum = ₹3,03,750 – ₹15,750 spending variance = ₹2,88,000
c. *FOH allocation rate = ₹2,88,000 FOH static-budget lump sum ÷ 18,000 static-budget RAM-hours

= ₹16 per RAM hour

d. Allocated FOH = 14,850 RAM hours × ₹16 per RAM hour = ₹2,37,600

e. PVV = ₹2,88,000 – ₹2,37,600 = ₹50,400 U

f. FOH flexible budget variance = FOH spending variance = ₹15,750 U

Allocated fixed overhead is ₹2,37,600. The actual fixed overhead cost is ₹3,03,750. Therefore, fixed overhead is underallocated by ₹66,150.

8-30 Direct-cost and overhead variances, income statement. The Kordell Company started business on January 1, 2015, in Raleigh. The company adopted a standard absorption costing system for its one product—a football for use in collegiate intramural sports. Because of the extensive handcrafting needed to do quality assurance on the final product, Kordell chose direct labor as the application base for overhead and decided to use the proration method to account for variances at year-end.

Kordell expected to make and sell 80,000 footballs the first year; each football was budgeted to use one half kilogram of leather and require 15 minutes of direct labor work. The company expected to pay ₹20 for each kg of leather and compensate workers at an hourly wage of ₹160. Kordell has no variable overhead costs, but expected to spend ₹20,00,000 on fixed manufacturing overhead in 2015.

In 2015, Kordell actually made 1,00,000 footballs and sold 80,000 of them for a total revenue of ₹1 lakh.

The expenses incurred were as follows:

Fixed manufacturing costs	₹30,00,000
Leather costs (55,000 kgs bought and used)	₹12,10,000
Direct labor costs(30,000 hours)	₹46,50,000

Required

1. Compute the following variances for 2015, and indicate whether each is favorable (F) or unfavorable (U):
   a. Direct materials efficiency variance
   b. Direct materials price variance
   c. Direct labor efficiency variance
   d. Direct labor price variance
   e. Total manufacturing overhead spending variance
   f. Fixed overhead flexible budget variance
   g. Fixed overhead production-volume variance
2. Compute Kordell Company's gross margin for its first year of operation.

Solution

Total standard production costs are based on 80,000 units of output.

Direct materials,	
80,000 × ½ kg. × ₹20	₹ 8,00,000
Direct manufacturing labor	
80,000 × 0.25 hrs. × ₹160	32,00,000
Fixed manufacturing overhead	
Lump-sum	20,00,000
Total	₹60,00,000

Standard cost per unit = ₹60,00,000/80,000 = ₹75 per unit

Fixed manufacturing overhead rate =

=₹20,00,000/(80,000 × 0.25 hrs.)

= ₹20,00,000/ 20,000 hours

=₹100 per labor hour

1. Solution Exhibit 8-30 presents a columnar presentation of the variances. Based on the exhibit, the variances are as follows:

a. Direct materials efficiency variance = ₹1,00,000 U

b. Direct materials price variance = ₹1,10,000 U

c. Direct labor efficiency variance = ₹8,00,000 U

d. Direct labor price variance = ₹1,50,000 F

e. Total manufacturing overhead spending variance = ₹10,00,000 U

f. Fixed overhead flexible budget variance = Spending variance = ₹10,00,000 U

g. Fixed overhead production-volume variance = ₹5,00,000 F

Note that the total variances for the period equal:

₹1,00,000 U + ₹1,10,000 U + ₹8,00,000 U + ₹1,50,000 F + ₹10,00,000 U + ₹5,00,000 F = ₹13,60,000 U.

This represents the cumulative amount by which costs were under applied during the year.

Solution Exhibit 8-30

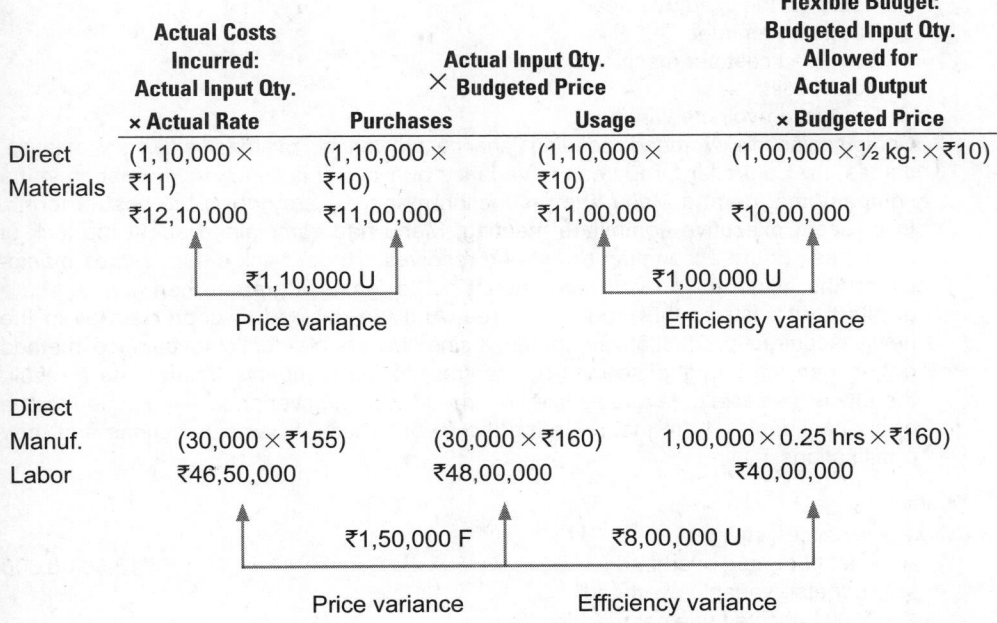

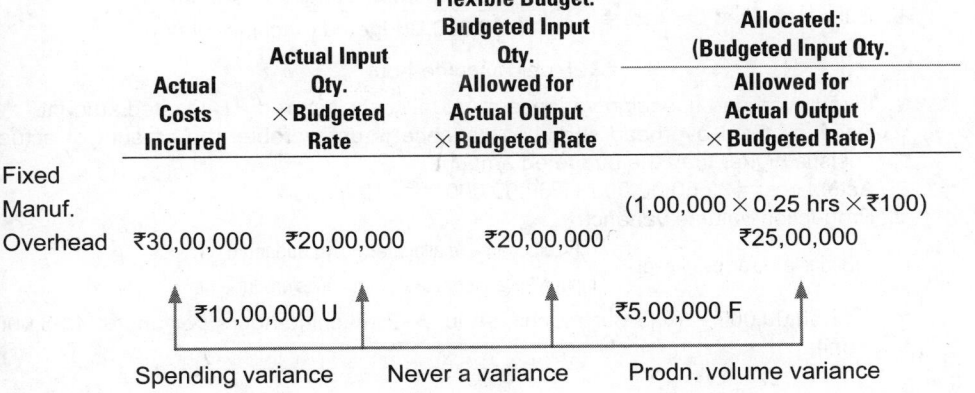

2. Sales Revenue = 80,000 units sold × ₹125   = ₹1,00,00,000

Cost of Goods sold: At standard: 80,000 × ₹75   = ₹ 60,00,000

(+) Prorated share of underapplied cost: ₹13,60,000 × (80,000/1,00,000)   = ₹ 10,88,000

Total   ₹ 70,88,000

Gross Margin = ₹1,00,00,000 – ₹70,88,000

= ₹29,12,000

8-31 Overhead variances, ethics. New India Company uses a standard-costing system. The company prepared its static budget for 2015 at 1,000,000 machine-hours for the year. Total budgeted overhead cost is ₹12,50,00,000. The variable overhead rate is ₹100 per machine-hour (₹200 per unit). Actual results for 2015 are as follows:

Machine-hours	9,60,000 hours
Output	4,98,000 hours
Variable overhead	₹10,08,00,000
Fixed overhead spending variance	₹60,00,000 U

Required

1. Compute for the fixed overhead
   a. Budgeted amount
   b. Budgeted cost per machine-hour
   c. Actual cost
   d. Production-volume variance
2. Compute variable overhead spending variance and variable overhead efficiency variance.
3. James, the controller, prepares the variance analysis. It is common knowledge in the company that he and Manu, the production manager, are not on the best of terms. In a recent executive committee meeting, Manu had complained about the lack of usefulness of the accounting reports he receives. To get back at him James manipulated the actual fixed overhead amount by assigning a greater-than-normal share of allocated costs to the production area. And, he decided to depreciate all of the newly acquired production equipment using the double-declining balance method rather than the straight-line method, contrary to the company practice. As a result, there was a sizable unfavorable fixed overhead spending variance. He boasted to one of his confidants, "I am just returning the favor." Discuss James's actions and their ramifications.

Solution

Overhead variances, ethics.

1. a. Total budgeted overhead   ₹12,50,00,000

Budgeted variable overhead
(₹100 budgeted rate per machine-hour ×
10,00,000 budgeted machine-hours)   10,00,00,000

Budgeted fixed overhead   ₹2,50,00,000

   b. Budgeted fixed OH rate = $\dfrac{\text{₹2,50,00,000 Budgeted amount}}{\text{10,00,000 Budgeted machine – hours}}$

= ₹25 per machine-hour

   c. Fixed overhead spending variance = Actual costs incurred – Budgeted amount. Because fixed overhead spending variance is unfavorable, the amount of actual costs is higher than the budgeted amount.
   Actual cost = ₹2,50,00,000 + ₹60,00,000 = ₹3,10,00,000

   d. Production-volume variance

= [Budgeted fixed overhead] – $\left[\begin{array}{l}\text{Fixed overhead allocated using budgeted}\\\text{input allowed for actual output units produced}\end{array}\right]$

= ₹2,50,00,000 – (₹25 per machine-hour × 2 machine-hours per unit* × 4,98,000 units)

= ₹2,50,00,000 − ₹2,49,00,000

= ₹1,00,000 U

*Budgeted variable overhead per unit = ₹200

Budgeted variable overhead rate = ₹100 per machine-hour

Therefore, budgeted machine hours allowed per unit = $\dfrac{₹200}{₹100}$

$$= 2 \text{ machine-hours}$$

2. Variable overhead spending variance:

$$\begin{bmatrix} \text{Actual variable} \\ \text{overhead cost} \\ \text{per unit of cost} \\ \text{actual output} \end{bmatrix} - \begin{bmatrix} \text{Budgeted variable} \\ \text{overhead cost} \\ \text{cost-allocation base} \\ \text{actual output} \end{bmatrix} \times \begin{bmatrix} \text{Actual quantity} \\ \text{of variable overhead} \\ \text{cost-allocation base} \\ \text{used for actual output} \end{bmatrix}$$

$$= \left(\frac{₹10,08,00,000 \text{ Budgeted amount}}{9,60,000 \text{ actual machine-hours}} - ₹100 \text{ per machine-hour} \right) \times 9,60,000 \text{ machine-hours}$$

$$= (₹105 - ₹100) \times 9,60,000 = ₹48,00,000 \text{ U}$$

Variable overhead efficiency variance:

$$\begin{bmatrix} \text{Actual units of} \\ \text{variable overhead} \\ \text{cost-allocation} \\ \text{base used for} \\ \text{actual output} \end{bmatrix} - \begin{bmatrix} \text{Budgeted units of} \\ \text{variable overhead} \\ \text{cost-allocation base} \\ \text{allowed for} \\ \text{actual output} \end{bmatrix} \times \begin{bmatrix} \text{Budgeted} \\ \text{variable} \\ \text{overhead} \\ \text{rate} \end{bmatrix}$$

$$= (9,60,000 - (2 \times 4,98,000)) \times ₹100$$

$$= (9,60,000 - 9,96,000) \times 100 = ₹36,00,000 \text{ F}$$

3. By manipulating, James has created a sizable unfavorable fixed overhead spending variance or, at least, has increased its magnitude. James's action is clearly unethical. Variances draw attention to the areas which need management attention. If the top management relies on James, due to his expertise, to interpret and explain the reasons for the unfavorable variance, it is likely that his report will be biased and misleading to the top management. The top management may erroneously conclude that Manu is not able to manage his fixed overhead costs effectively. Another probable adverse outcome of James's actions will be that Manu will have even less confidence in the usefulness of accounting reports. This, of course, defeats the purpose of preparing the reports. In summary, James's unethical actions will waste top management's time and may lead to wrong decisions.

Exercises

[*Comprehensive solutions to all exercises are available on the companion website www.pearsoned.co.in/charlesthorngren*]

8-32 Variable manufacturing overhead variance analysis. The Harvest Gold Bread Company bakes baguettes for distribution to upscale grocery stores. The company has two direct-cost categories, direct materials and direct manufacturing labor. Variable manufacturing overhead is allocated to products on the basis of standard direct manufacturing labor-hours. Following is some pertinent data for the Harvest Gold:

Direct manufacturing labor use	0.02 hour per baguette
Variable manufacturing overhead	₹100 per direct manufacturing labor-hour

The Harvest Gold Company recorded the following additional data for the current year ended December 31:

Planned (budgeted) output	32,00,000 baguettes

Actual production	28,00,000
Direct manufacturing labor	50,400 hours
Actual variable manufacturing overhead	₹68,04,000

Required

1. What is the denominator used for allocating variable manufacturing overhead? (That is, for how many direct manufacturing labor-hour is Harvest Gold Bread budgeting?).
2. Prepare a variance analysis of variable manufacturing overhead. Use Exhibit 8-3 for reference.
3. Discuss the variances you have calculated and give possible explanations for them.

8-33 4-variance analysis, fill in the blanks. Use the following manufacturing overhead data to fill in the
following blanks:

	Variable	Fixed
Actual costs incurred	₹1,19,000	₹60,000
Costs allocated to products	90,000	45,000
Flexible budget: Budgeted input allowed for actual output produced x Budgeted rate	90,000	50,000
Actual input x Budgeted rate	1,00,000	50,000

Use F for favorable and U for unfavorable:

	Variable	Fixed
	(₹)	(₹)
1. Spending variance		
2. Efficiency variance		
3. Production-volume variance		
4. Flexible-budget variance		
5. Underallocated (overallocated) manufacturing overhead		

8-34 Straightforward coverage of manufacturing overhead, standard-costing system. The Indian division of a Canadian telecommunications company uses a standard-costing system for its machine-paced production of telephone equipment. Data regarding production during June are as follows:

Variable manufacturing overhead costs incurred	₹15,51,000
Variable manufacturing overhead cost rate	₹120 per standard machine-hour
Fixed manufacturing overhead costs incurred	₹40,10,000
Fixed manufacturing overhead budgeted	₹39,00,000
Denominator level in machine-hours	13,000
Standard machine-hour allowed per unit of output	0.30
Units of output	41,000
Actual machine-hours used	13,300
Ending work-in-process inventory	0

Required

1. Prepare an analysis of all manufacturing overhead variances. Use the 4-variance analysis framework illustrated in Exhibit 8-3.
2. Prepare journal entries for manufacturing overhead.
3. Describe how individual variable manufacturing overhead items are controlled from day to day. Also, describe how individual fixed manufacturing overhead items are controlled.

8-35 Overhead variances, missing information. Aasbi Printing prepared its budget at 10,000 machine hours. Aasbi reported a ₹7,500 unfavorable spending variance for fixed overhead and a ₹2,500 unfavorable spending variance for variable overhead. The budgeted variable overhead rate is ₹50 per machine hour. The input allowed for actual output was 9,900 machine hours. Actual machine hours were 9,800, and actual total overhead costs were ₹8,00,000.

1. Compute variable overhead efficiency variance, flexible-budget variance, and the amount underallocated or overallocated.
2. Calculate fixed overhead production-volume variance, flexible-budget variance, and the amount underallocated or overallocated.

8-36 Flexible-budget variances. The Times of India budgets to produce 3,00,000 copies of its monthly magazine (the output unit) for August. It is budgeted to have 50 print pages per magazine. Actual production was 3,20,000 copies, with 17,280,000 print pages run. Each magazine had only 50 print pages, but quality problems with paper led to many pages being unusable.

Variable costs are direct materials, direct labor, and variable indirect costs. Variable and fixed indirect costs are allocated to each copy on the basis of good print pages. The driver for all variable costs is the number of print pages.
Data pertaining to August are:

	Budgeted	Actual
Direct materials	₹5,40,000	₹6,73,920
Direct labor	1,35,000	1,50,336
Variable indirect	1,80,000	1,91,808
Fixed indirect	2,70,000	2,91,000

The actual direct labor rate was ₹87 per hour. Actual and budgeted pages produced per direct labor-hour were 10,000 print pages. Data pertaining to revenues for Times of India in August are

	Budgeted	Actual
Circulation revenue	₹4,20,000	₹4,62,000
Advertising revenue	10,80,000	11,83,800

The Magazine sells for ₹1.50 per copy. Copies produced but not sold have no value. Advertising revenues covers receipts from all advertising sources.

1. Prepare a comprehensive set of flexible-budget variances for the two direct-cost items (using Exhibit 7-3) and the two indirect-cost items (using Exhibit 8-3) for The Times of India.
2. Comment on the results in requirement 1.

8-37 Variance analysis, graphs. Hindalco Industries budgets and allocates overhead costs using machine-hours. Hindalco's budget for 2016 was 10,000 machine-hours. Following is additional information relating to overhead for 2016:

Budgeted fixed overhead	₹60,00,000
Actual fixed overhead	59,00,000
Budgeted variable overhead	1,00,00,000
Actual variable overhead	1,10,00,000
Budgeted machine-hours allowed for actual output	9,800
Actual machine-hours used	9,500

1. Compute the variable overhead spending variance and efficiency variance.
2. Compute the fixed overhead spending variance and production-volume variance.
3. Draw graphs similar to those in Exhibit 8-4.

8-38 4-variance analysis, find the unknowns. Consider each of the following situations—cases A, B, and C – independently. Data refers to operations for April. For each situations, assume a standard-costing system. Also assume the use of a flexible budget for control of variable and fixed manufacturing overhead based on machine-hours.

	Cases		
	A	B	C
1. Fixed manufacturing overhead incurred	₹1,06,000	—	₹1,20,000
2. Variable manufacturing overhead incurred	₹70,000	—	—
3. Denominator level in machine-hours	500	—	1,100
4. Standard machine-hours allowed for actual output achieved	—	650	—
Flexible-budget data:			
5. Fixed manufacturing overhead	—	—	—
6. Variable manufacturing overhead (per standard machine-hour)	—	₹85	₹50
7. Budgeted fixed manufacturing overhead	₹1,00,000	—	₹1,10,000
8. Budgeted variable manufacturing overhead[a]			
9. Total budgeted manufacturing overhead[a]	—	₹1,25,250	—
Additional data:			
10. Standard variable manufacturing overhead allocated	₹75,000	—	—
11. Standard Fixed manufacturing overhead allocated	₹1,00,000		
12. Production-volume variance	₹5,000 U	₹5,000 U	
13. Variable manufacturing overhead spending variance	₹9,500 F	0	₹3,500 U
14. Variable manufacturing overhead efficiency variance	0	₹1,000 U	
15. Fixed manufacturing overhead spending variance	₹3,000		
16. Actual machine-hours used			

[a]For standard machine-hours allowed for actual output produced.

Required

Fill in the blanks under each case. (Hint: Prepare a worksheet similar to that in Exhibit 8-3. Fill in the knowns and then solve for the unknowns.)

8-39 Overhead analysis. Hyundai Motors uses standard costing. The following information is for 2015:

Static-budget machine-hours	33,000
Fixed overhead budget costs	₹49,50,000
Fixed overhead actual costs	₹45,00,000
Variable overhead actual costs	₹96,00,000
Variable overhead rate per machine-hour	₹300
Actual machine-hours used	30,000
Budgeted machine-hours allowed for actual output	35,000

Required

1. Calculate variable overhead spending variance and efficiency variance.
2. Compute fixed overhead spending variance and production-volume variance.

8-40 Activity-based costing, variance analysis. Precision Surgical Instruments, Ltd. makes a special line of forceps, SFA, in batches. Precision randomly selects forceps from each SFA batch for quality-testing purposes. Quality testing costs consist of some variable and some fixed costs in relation to the quality-testing hours. The following information is for 2015:

	Static-Budget Amounts	Actual Amounts
Units of SFA produced and sold	21,000	22,000
Batch size (number of units per batch)	500	550

Testing-hours per batch	5.5	5.4
Variable overhead cost per testing-hour	₹400	₹420
Total fixed testing overhead costs	₹2,88,750	₹2,72,160

Required

1. For variable testing overhead costs, compute the efficiency and spending variances. Comment on the results.
2. For fixed testing overhead costs, compute the spending and the production-volume variances. Comment on the results.

8-41 Comprehensive review, working backward from given variances. Maruti company uses a flexible budget and standard costs to aid planning and control of its machining manufacturing operations. Its normal-costing system for manufacturing has two direct-cost categories (direct materials and direct manufacturing labor-both variable) and two indirect-cost categories (variable manufacturing overhead and fixed manufacturing overhead, both allocated using direct manufacturing labor-hours).

At the 40,000 budgeted direct manufacturing labor-hour level for August, budgeted direct manufacturing labor is ₹40,00,000, budgeted variable manufacturing overhead is ₹24,00,000, and budgeted fixed manufacturing overhead is ₹32,00,000.
The following actual results for August are:

Direct materials price variance (based on purchases)	₹8,80,000 F
Direct materials efficiency variance	3,45,000 U
Direct manufacturing labor costs incurred	26,13,750
Variable manufacturing overhead flexible-budget variance	51,750 U
Variable manufacturing overhead efficiency variance	90,000 U
Fixed manufacturing overhead incurred	29,87,300
Fixed manufacturing overhead spending variance	2,12,700 F

The standard cost per kg of direct materials is ₹57.5. The standard allowance is three kg of direct materials for each unit of product. During August 30,000 units of product were produced. There was no beginning inventory of direct materials. There was no beginning or ending work in process. In August, the direct materials price variance was ₹5.5 per kg.

In July, labor unrest caused a major slowdown in the pace of production, resulting in an unfavorable direct manufacturing labor efficiency variance of ₹2,25,000. There was no direct manufacturing labor price variance. Labor unrest persisted into August. Some workers quit. Their replacements had to be hired at higher rates, which had to be extended to all workers. The actual average wage rate in August exceeded the standard average wage rate by ₹2.50 per hour.

1. Compute the following for August
   a. Total kg of direct materials purchased
   b. Total number of kg of excess direct materials used
   c. Variable manufacturing overhead spending variance
   d. Total number of actual direct manufacturing labor-hours used
   e. Total number of standard direct manufacturing labor-hours allowed for the units produced
   f. Production-volume variance
2. Describe how Maruti's control of variable manufacturing overhead items differs from its control of fixed manufacturing overhead items.

8-42 Review 3-variance analysis. (CPA, adapted) The Ajanta Manufacturing Company's job-costing system has two direct-cost categories: direct materials and direct manufacturing labor. Manufacturing overhead (both variable and fixed) is allocated to products on the basis of standard direct manufacturing labor-hours (DLH). At the beginning of 2015, Ajanta adopted the following standards for its manufacturing costs:

	Input	Cost per Output Unit
Direct materials	3 kgs. At ₹5 per kg	₹15.00
Direct manufacturing labor	5 hrs. at ₹15 per hr	75.00
Manufacturing overhead:		
Variable	₹6 per DLH	30.00
Fixed	₹8 per DLH	40.00
Standard manufacturing cost per output unit		₹160.00

The denominator level for total manufacturing overhead per month in 2013 is 40,000 direct manufacturing labor-hours. Ajanta's flexible budget for January 2014 was based on this denominator level. The records for January indicated the following:

Direct materials purchased	25,000	kgs. At ₹5.20 per kg
Direct materials used	23,100	kgs.
Direct manufacturing labor	40,100	hrs. at ₹14.60 per hr
Total actual manufacturing overhead		
(variable and fixed)	₹6,00,000	
Actual production	7,800	output units

Required

1. Prepare a schedule of total standard manufacturing costs for the 7,800 output units in January 2015.
2. For the month of January 2015, compute the following variances, indicating whether each is favorable (F) or unfavorable (U):
   a. Direct materials price variance, based on purchases
   b. Direct materials efficiency variance
   c. Direct manufacturing labor price variance
   d. Direct manufacturing labor efficiency variance
   e. Total manufacturing overhead spending variance
   f. Variable manufacturing overhead efficiency variance
   g. Production-volume variance

9 Inventory Costing and Capacity Analysis

Learning Objectives ▼

1. Identify what distinguishes variable costing from absorption costing

2. Compute income under absorption costing and variable costing, and explain the difference in income

3. Understand how absorption costing can provide undesirable incentives for managers to build up inventory

4. Differentiate throughput costing from variable costing and absorption costing

5. Describe the various capacity concepts that can be used in absorption costing

6. Examine the key factors in choosing a capacity level to compute the budgeted fixed manufacturing cost rate

7. Understand other issues that play an important role in capacity planning and control

Few numbers capture the attention of managers and shareholders more than operating profits.

In industries that require significant upfront investments in capacity, two key decisions have a substantial impact on corporate profits: (1) How much money a firm spends on fixed investments and (2) the extent to which the firm eventually utilizes capacity to meet customer demand. Unfortunately, the compensation and reward systems of a firm, as well as the choice of inventory-costing methods, may induce managers to make decisions that benefit short-term earnings at the expense of a firm's long-term health. It may take a substantial external shock, like a sharp economic slowdown, to motivate managers to make the right capacity and inventory choices.

Variable and Absorption Costing

The two most common methods of costing inventories in manufacturing companies are *variable costing* and *absorption costing*. We describe each in this section and then discuss them in detail, using a hypothetical telescope-manufacturing company as an example.

Variable Costing

Variable costing is a method of inventory costing in which all variable manufacturing costs (direct and indirect) are included as inventoriable costs. All fixed manufacturing costs are excluded from inventoriable costs and are instead treated as costs of the period in which they are incurred. Note that *variable costing* is imprecise term to describe this inventory-costing method, because only variable manufacturing costs are inventoried; variable nonmanufacturing costs are still treated as period costs and are expensed. Another common term used to describe this method is **direct costing**. This term is also a misnomer because variable costing considers variable manufacturing overhead (an indirect cost) as inventoriable, while excluding direct marketing costs, for example.

Absorption Costing

Absorption costing is a method of inventory costing in which all variable manufacturing costs and all fixed manufacturing costs are included as inventoriable costs. That is, inventory "absorbs" all manufacturing costs. The job costing system you studied in Chapter 4 is an example of absorption costing.

Under both variable costing and absorption costing, all variable manufacturing costs are inventoriable costs and all nonmanufacturing costs in the value chain (such as research and development and marketing), whether variable or fixed, are period costs and are recorded as expenses when incurred.

Learning Objective 1

Identify what distinguishes variable costing

. . . fixed manufacturing costs excluded from inventoriable costs

from absorption costing

. . . fixed manufacturing costs included in inventoriable costs

Comparing Variable and Absorption Costing

The easiest way to understand the difference between variable costing and absorption costing is with an example. In this chapter, we will study Stassen Company, an optical consumer-products manufacturer. We focus in particular on its product line of high-end telescopes for aspiring astronomers.

Stassen uses standard costing:

- Direct costs are traced to products using standard prices and standard inputs allowed for actual outputs produced.

- Indirect (overhead) manufacturing costs are allocated using standard indirect rates times standard inputs allowed for actual outputs produced.

Stassen's management wants to prepare an income statement for 2014 (the fiscal year just ended) to evaluate the performance of the telescope product line. The operating information for the year is as follows:

	File Edit View Insert Format Tools Data Window Help	
	A	B
1		**Units**
2	Beginning Inventory	0
3	Production	8,000
4	Sales	6,000
5	Ending Inventory	2,000

Actual price and cost data for 2014 are:

	File Edit View Insert Format Tools Data Window Help	
	A	B
10	Selling price	₹10,000
11	Variable manufacturing cost per unit	
12	Direct material cost per unit	₹1,100
13	Direct manufacturing labor cost per unit	400
14	Manufacturing overhead cost per unit	500
15	Total variable manufacturing cost per unit	₹2,000
16	Variable marketing cost per unit sold	₹1,850
17	Fixed manufacturing costs (all indirect)	₹1,08,00,000
18	Fixed marketing costs (all indirect)	₹1,38,00,000

For simplicity and to focus on the main ideas, we assume the following about Stassen:

- Stassen incurs manufacturing and marketing costs only. The cost driver for all variable manufacturing costs is units produced; the cost driver for variable marketing costs is units sold. There are no batch-level costs and no product-sustaining costs.
- There are no price variances, efficiency variances, or spending variances. Therefore, the budgeted (standard) price and cost data for 2014 are the same as the actual price and cost data.
- Work-in-process inventory is zero.
- Stassen budgeted production of 8,000 units for 2014. This was used to calculate the budgeted fixed manufacturing cost per unit of ₹1,350 (₹1,08,00,000/8,000 units).[1]
- Stassen budgeted sales of 6,000 units for 2014, which is the same as the actual sales for 2014.
- The actual production for 2014 is 8,000 units. As a result, there is no production-volume variance for manufacturing costs in 2014. A later examples, based on data for 2015 does include production-volume variances. However, even in that case, the income statements contain no variances other than the production-volume variance.
- Variances are written off to cost of goods sold in the period (year) in which they occur.

Based on the preceding information, Stassen's inventoriable costs per unit produced in 2014 under the two inventory costing methods are as follows:

	Variable Costing		Absorption Costing	
Variable manufacturing cost per unit produced:				
Direct materials	₹1,100		₹1,100	
Direct manufacturing labor	400		400	
Manufacturing overhead	500	₹2,000	500	₹2,000
Fixed manufacturing cost per unit produced		—		₹1,350
Total inventoriable cost per unit produced		₹2,000		₹3,350

Decision Point ▶

How does variable costing differ from absorption costing?

To summarize, the main difference between variable costing and absorption costing is the accounting for fixed manufacturing costs:

- Under variable costing, fixed manufacturing costs are not inventoried; they are treated as an expense of the period.
- Under absorption costing, fixed manufacturing costs are inventoriable costs. In our example, the standard fixed manufacturing cost is ₹1350 per unit (₹1,08,00,000 ÷ 8,000 units) produced.

Variable vs. Absorption Costing: Operating Income and Income Statements

When comparing variable and absorption costing, we must also take into account whether we are looking at short-or long-term numbers. How does the data for a one-year period differ from that of a two-year period under variable and absorption costing?

---

[1] Throughout this section, we use budgeted output as the basis for calculating the fixed manufacturing cost per unit for ease of exposition. In the latter half of this chapter, we consider the relative merits of alternative denominator-level choices for calculating this unit cost

Comparing Income Statements for One Year

What will Stassen's operating income be if it uses variable costing or absorption costing? The differences between these methods are apparent in Exhibit 9-1. Panel A shows the variable costing income statement and Panel B the absorption-costing income statement for Stassen's telescope product line for 2014. The variable-costing income statement uses the contribution-margin format (introduced in Chapter 3). The absorption-costing income statement uses the gross-margin format (introduced in Chapter 2). Why these different formats? The distinction between variable costs and fixed costs is central to variable costing, and it is highlighted by the contribution-margin format. Similarly, the distinction between manufacturing and nonmanufacturing costs is central to absorption costing, and it is highlighted by the gross-margin format.

Absorption-costing income statements do not need to differentiate between variable and fixed costs. However, we will make this distinction between variable and fixed costs in the Stassen example to show how individual line items are classified differently under variable costing and absorption costing. In Exhibit 9-1, Panel B, note that inventoriable cost is ₹3,350 per unit under absorption costing: allocated fixed manufacturing costs of ₹1,350 per unit plus variable manufacturing costs of ₹2,000 per unit.

Notice how the fixed manufacturing costs of ₹1,08,00,000 are accounted for under variable costing and absorption costing in Exhibit 9-1. The income statement under variable costing deducts the ₹1,08,00,000 lump sum as an expense for 2014. In contrast, under absorption costing the ₹1,08,00,000 (₹1,350 per unit × 8,000 units) is initially treated as an inventoriable cost in 2014. Of this, ₹81,00,000 (₹1,350 per unit × 6,000 units sold) subsequently becomes a part of cost of goods sold in 2014, and ₹27,00,000 (₹ 1,350 per unit × 2,000 units) remains an asset—part of ending finished goods inventory on December 31, 2014.

Operating income is ₹27,00,000 higher under absorption costing compared with variable costing, because only ₹81,00,000 of fixed manufacturing costs are expensed under absorption costing, whereas all ₹1,08,00,000 of fixed manufacturing costs are expensed

Learning Objective 2

Compute income under absorption costing

. . . using the gross-margin format

and variable costing,

. . . using the contribution-margin format

and explain the difference in income

. . . affected by the unit level of production and sales under absorption costing, but only the unit level of sales under variable costing

Exhibit 9-1 Comparison of Variable Costing and Absorption Costing for Stassen Company: Telescope Product-Line Income Statements for 2014

	A	B	C	D	E	F	G
1	**Panel A: VARIABLE COSTING**				**Panel B: ABSORPTION COSTING**		
2	Revenues: ₹10,000 × 6,000 units		₹6,00,00,000		Revenues: ₹10,000 × 6,000 units		₹6,00,00,000
3	Variable cost of goods sold:				Cost of goods sold:		
4	Beginning inventory	₹0			Beginning inventory	₹0	
5	Variable manufacturing costs: ₹2,000 × 8,000 units	1,60,00,000			Variable manufacturing costs: ₹2,000 × 8,000 units	1,60,00,000	
6					Allocated fixed manufacturing costs: ₹1,350 × 8,000 units	1,08,00,000	
7	Cost of goods available for sale	1,60,00,000			Cost of goods available for sale	2,68,00,000	
8	Deduct ending inventory: ₹2,000 × 2,000 units	(4,00,000)			Deduct ending inventory: ₹3,350 × 2,000 units	(67,00,000)	
9	Variable cost of goods sold		1,20,00,000		Cost of goods sold		2,01,00,000
10	Variable marketing costs: ₹1,850 × 6,000 units sold		1,11,00,000				
11	Contribution margin		3,69,00,000		Gross Margin		3,99,00,000
12	Fixed manufacturing costs		1,08,00,000		Variable marketing costs: ₹1,850 × 6,000 units sold		1,11,00,000
13	Fixed marketing cost		1,38,00,000		Fixed marketing costs		13,80,00,000
14	Operating income		₹1,23,00,000		Operating Income		₹1,50,00,000
15							
16	Manufacturing costs expensed in Panel A:		₹1,20,00,000		Manufacturing costs expensed in Panel B:		
17	Variable cost of goods sold		1,08,00,000				
18	Fixed manufacturing costs						
19	Total		₹2,28,00,000		Cost of goods sold		₹2,01,00,000

under variable costing. Note that the variable manufacturing cost of ₹2,000 per unit is accounted for the same way in both income statements in Exhibit 9-1.

These points can be summarized as follows:

	Variable Costing	Absorption Costing
Variable manufacturing costs: ₹2,000 per telescope produced	Inventoriable	Inventoriable
Fixed manufacturing costs: ₹1,08,00,000 per year	Deducted as an expense of the period	Inventoriable at ₹1,350 per telescope produced using budgeted denominator level of 8,000 units produced per year (₹1,080,00,00 ÷ 8,000 units ÷ ₹1,350 per unit)

The basis of the difference between variable costing and absorption costing is how fixed manufacturing costs are accounted for. If inventory levels change, operating income will differ between the two methods because of the difference in accounting for fixed manufacturing costs. To see this difference, let's compare telescope sales of 6,000, 7,000, and 8,000 units by Stassen in 2014, when 8,000 units were produced. Of the ₹1,08,00,000 total fixed manufacturing costs, the amount expensed in the 2014 income statement under each of these scenarios would be:

File	Edit	View	Insert	Format	Tools	Data	Window	Help

	A	B	C	D	E	G	H
1			Variable Costing			Absorption Costing	
2						Fixed Manufacturing Costs	
3	**Units**	**Ending**	**Fixed Manufacturing Costs**			**Included in Inventory (₹)**	**Amount Expensed (₹)**
4	**Sold**	**Inventory**	Included in Inventory (₹)	Amount Expensed (₹)		= ₹1,350 × Ending Inv.	≠ ₹1,350 × Units Sold
5	6,000	2,000	0	1,08,00,000		27,00,000	81,00,000
6	7,000	1,000	0	1,08,00,000		13,50,000	94,50,000
7	8,000	0	0	1,08,00,000		0	1,08,00,000

In the last scenario, where 8,000 units are produced and sold, both variable and absorption costing report the same net income because inventory levels are unchanged.

Comparing Income Statements for Multiple Years

To get a more-comprehensive view of the effects of variable costing and absorption costing, Stassen's management accountants prepare income statements for two years of operations, starting with 2014.

The data are given in units in the following table.

Home	Insert	Page Layout	Formulas

	E	F	G
1		**2014**	**2015**
2	Budgeted production	8,000	8,000
3	Beginning inventory	0	2,000
4	Actual production	8,000	5,000
5	Sales	6,000	6,500
6	Ending inventory	2,000	500

All other 2014 data given earlier for Stassen also apply for 2015.

In 2015, Stassen has a production-volume variance because actual telescope production differs from the budgeted level of production of 8,000 units per year used to calculate the budgeted fixed manufacturing cost per unit. The actual quantity sold for 2015 is 6,500 units, which is the same as the sales quantity budgeted for that year.

Exhibit 9-2 presents the income statement under variable costing in Panel A and the income statement under absorption costing in Panel B for 2014 and 2015. As you study Exhibit 9-2, note that the 2014 columns in both Panels A and B show the same figures

---

Exhibit 9-2　Comparison of Variable Costing and Absorption Costing for Stassen Company: Telescope Product-Line Income Statements for 2012, 2013, and 2014

	Home　Insert　Page Layout　Formulas　Data　Review　View				
	A	B	C	D	E
1	Panel A: VARIABLE COSTING				
2			2014		2015
3	Revenues: ₹1,000 × 6,000; 6,500 units		₹60,00,000		₹65,00,000
4	Variable cost of goods sold:				
5	Beginning inventory: ₹200 × 0; 2,000 units	₹0		₹4,00,000	
6	Variable manufacturing costs: ₹200 × 8,000; 5,000 units	16,00,000		10,00,000	
7	Cost of goods available for sale	16,00,000		14,00,000	
8	Deduct ending inventory: ₹200 × 2,000; 500 units	(4,00,000)		(1,00,000)	
9	Variable cost of goods sold		12,00,000		13,00,000
10	Variable marketing costs: ₹185 × 6,000; 6,500 units		11,10,000		12,02,500
11	Contribution margin		36,90,000		39,97,500
12	Fixed manufacturing cost		10,80,000		10,80,000
13	Fixed marketing costs		13,80,000		13,80,000
14	Operating income		₹12,30,000		₹15,37,500
15					
16	Panel B: ABSORPTION COSTING				
17			2014		2015
18	Revenues: ₹1,000 × 6,000; 6,500 units		₹60,00,000		₹6,500,000
19	Cost of goods sold:				
20	Beginning inventory: ₹335 × 0; 2,000 units	0		6,70,000	
21	Variable manufacturing costs: ₹200 × 8,000; 5,000 units	16,00,000		10,00,000	
22	Allocated fixed manufacturing costs: ₹135 × 8,000; 5,000 units	10,80,000		6,75,000	
23	Cost of goods available for sale	26,80,000		23,45,000	
24	Deduct ending inventory: ₹335 × 2,000; 500 units	(6,70,000)		(1,67,500)	
25	Adjustment for production-volume variance[a]	₹0		₹4,05,000	U
26	Cost of goods sold		20,10,000		25,82,500
27	Gross Margin		39,90,000		39,17,500
28	Variable marketing costs: ₹185 × 6,000; 6,500 units		11,10,000		12,02,500
29	Fixed marketing costs		13,80,000		13,80,000
30	Operating Income		₹15,00,000		₹13,35,000
31					
32	[a]Production-volume variance = Budgeted fixed manufacturing costs – Fixed manufacturing overhead allocated using budgeted cost per output unit allowed for actual output produced (Panel B, line 22)				
33	2014: ₹10,80,000 – (₹135 × 8,000) = ₹10,80,000 – ₹10,80,000 = ₹0				
34	2015:₹10,80,000 – (₹135 × 5,000) = ₹10,80,000 – ₹6,75,000 =₹4,05,000 U				
35					
36	Production-volume variance can also be calculated as follows:				
37	Fixed manufacturing cost per unit × (Denominator level – Actual output units produced)				
38	2014: ₹135 × (8,000 – 8,000) units = ₹135 × 0 = ₹0				
39	2015: ₹135 × (8,000 – 5,000) units = ₹135 × 3,000 = ₹4,05,000 U				

as Exhibit 9-1. The 2015 columns is similar to 2014 *except for the production-volume variance line item under absorption costing in Panel B*. Keep in mind the following points about absorption costing as you study Panel B of Exhibit 9-2:

1. The ₹1,350 fixed manufacturing cost rate is based on the budgeted denominator capacity level of 8,000 units in 2014, and 2015 (₹1,08,00,000 ÷ 8,000 units ₹1,350 per unit). Whenever production (that's the quantity produced, not the quantity sold) deviates from the denominator level, there will be a production-volume variance. The amount of Stassen's production-volume variance is determined by multiplying ₹1,350 per unit by the difference between the actual level of production and the denominator level.

   Recall how standard costing works under absorption costing. Each time a unit is manufactured, ₹1,350 of fixed manufacturing costs is included in the cost of goods manufactured and available for sale. In 2015, when 5,000 units are manufactured, ₹67,50,000 (₹1,350 per unit × 5,000 units) of fixed manufacturing costs is included in the cost of goods available for sale (see Exhibit 9-2, Panel B, line 22). Total fixed manufacturing costs for 2015 are ₹1,08,00,000. The production-volume variance of ₹40,50,000 U equals the difference between ₹1,08,00,000 and ₹67,50,000. In Panel B, note how, for each year, the fixed manufacturing costs included in the cost of goods available for sale plus the production-volume variance always equals ₹1,08,00,000.

2. As a result of the production-volume variance, note that the absorption costing income is lower in 2015 than in 2014 even though Stassen sold 500 more units. We explore the impact of production levels on income under absorption costing in greater detail later in this chapter.

3. The production-volume variance, which relates only to fixed manufacturing overhead, exists under absorption costing but not under variable costing. Under variable costing, fixed manufacturing costs of ₹1,08,00,000 are always treated as an expense of the period, regardless of the level of production (and sales).

Here's a summary (using information from Exhibit 9-2) of the operating-income differences for Stassen Company during the 2014 and 2015:

	2014	2015
1. Absorption-costing operating income	₹1,50,00,000	₹1,33,50,000
2. Variable-costing operating income	1,23,00,000	1,53,75,000
3. Difference: (1) – (2)	27,00,000	(20,25,000)

The sizeable differences in the preceding table illustrate why managers whose performance is measured by reported income are concerned about the choice between variable costing and absorption costing.

Why do variable costing and absorption costing usually report different operating income numbers? In general, if inventory increases during an accounting period, less operating income will be reported under variable costing than absorption costing. Conversely, if inventory decreases, more operating income will be reported under variable costing than absorption costing. The difference in reported operating income is due solely to (a) moving fixed manufacturing costs into inventories as inventories increase and (b) moving fixed manufacturing costs out of inventories as inventories decrease under absorption costing.

The difference between operating income under absorption costing and variable costing can be computed by formula 1, which focuses on fixed manufacturing costs in beginning inventory and ending inventory:

Fixed manufacturing costs in ending inventory are deferred to a future period under absorption costing. For example, ₹27,00,000 of fixed manufacturing overhead is deferred to 2015 at December 31, 2014. Under variable costing, all ₹1,08,00,000 of fixed manufacturing costs are treated as an expense of 2014.

File   Edit   View   Insert   Format   Tools   Data   Window   Help

	A	B	C	D	E	F	G	H
1	Formula 1							
2						Fixed manufacturing		Fixed manufacturing
3		Absorption-costing	-	Variable-costing	=	costs in ending inventory	-	costs in beginning inventory
4		operating income		operation income		under absorption costing		under absorption costing
5	2009	₹1,50,00,000	-	₹1,23,00,000	=	(₹1,350 × 2,000 units)	-	(₹1,350 × 0 units)
6				₹27,00,000	=	₹27,00,000		
7								
8	2010	₹1,33,50,000	-	₹1,53,75,000	=	(₹1,350 × 500 units)	-	(₹1,350 × 2,000 units)
9				₹20,25,000	=	₹20,25,000)		
10								
11	2011	₹2,49,00,000	-	₹2,15,25,000	=	(₹1,350 × 3,000 units)	-	(₹1,350 × 500 units)
12				₹33,75,000	=	₹33,75,000		

Recall that,

$$\text{Beginning inventory} + \text{Cost of goods manufactured} = \text{Cost of goods sold} + \text{Ending Inventory}$$

Therefore, instead of focusing on fixed manufacturing costs in ending and beginning inventory (as in formula 1), we could alternatively focus on fixed manufacturing costs in units produced and units sold. This later approach (see formula 2) highlights how fixed manufacturing costs move between units produced and units sold during the fiscal year.

File   Edit   View   Insert   Format   Tools   Data   Window   Help

	A	B	C	D	E	F	G	H
16	Formula 2							
17						Fixed manufacturing costs		Fixed manufacturing costs
18		Absorption-costing	-	Variable-costing	=	inventoried in units produced	-	in cost of goods sold
19		operating income (₹)		operation income (₹)		under absorption costing (₹)		under absorption costing (₹)
20		1,50,00,000	-	1,23,00,000	=	(1,350 × 8,000 units)	-	(1,350 × 6,000 units)
21				27,00,000	=	27,00,000		
22								
23		1,33,50,000	-	1,53,75,000	=	(1,350 × 5,000 units)	-	(1,350 × 6,500 units)
24				(20,25000)	=	(20,25000)		
25								
26		2,49,00,000	-	2,15,25,000	=	(1,350 × 10,000 units)	-	(1,350 × 7,500 units)
27				33,75,000	=	33,75,000		

Managers face increasing pressure to reduce inventory levels. Some companies are achieving steep reductions in inventory levels using policies such as just-in-time production—a production system under which products are manufactured only when needed. Formula 1 illustrates that, as Stassen reduces its inventory levels, operating income differences between absorption costing and variable costing become immaterial. Consider, for example, the formula for 2014. If instead of 2,000 units in ending inventory, Stassen had only 2 units in ending inventory, the difference between absorption-costing operating income and variable-costing operating income would drop from ₹27,00,000 to ₹2,700.

Variable Costing and the Effect of Sales and Production on Operating Income

Given a constant contribution margin per unit and constant fixed costs, the period-to-period change in operating income under variable costing is *driven solely by changes in the quantity of units actually sold*. Consider the variable-costing operating income of Stassen in 2015 versus 2014. Recall the following:

$$\text{Contribution margin per unit} = \text{Selling price} - \text{Variable manufacturing cost per unit} - \text{Variable marketing cost per unit}$$

$$= ₹10,000 \text{ per unit} - ₹2,000 \text{ per unit} - ₹1,850 \text{ per unit}$$
$$= ₹6,150 \text{ per unit}$$

$$\text{Change in variable-costing operating income} = \text{Contribution margin per unit} \times \text{Change in quantity of units sold}$$

2015 vs. 2014: ₹1,53,75,000 − ₹1,23,00,000 = ₹6,150 per unit × (6,500 units − 6,000 units)
₹30,75,000 = ₹30,75,000

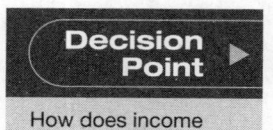

Decision Point ▶

How does income differ under variable and absorption costing?

Under variable costing, Stassen managers cannot increase operating income by "producing for inventory." Why not? Because, as you can see from the preceding computations, when using variable costing, only the quantity of units sold drives operating income. We'll explain later in this chapter that absorption costing enables managers to increase operating income by increasing the unit level of sales, as well as by producing more units. Before you proceed to the next section, make sure that you examine Exhibit 9-3 for a detailed comparison of the differences between variable costing and absorption costing.

Exhibit 9-3   Comparative Income Effects of Variable Costing and Absorption Costing

Question	Variable Costing	Absorption Costing	Comment
Are fixed manufacturing costs inventoried?	No	Yes	Basic theoretical question of when these costs should be expensed
Is there a production-volume variance?	No	Yes	Choice of denominator level affects measurement of operating income under absorption costing only
Are classifications between variable and fixed costs routinely made?	Yes	Infrequently	Absorption costing can be easily modified to obtain subclassifications for variable and fixed costs, if desired (for example, see Exhibit 9-1, Panel B)
How do changes in unit inventory levels affect operating income?[a]			Differences are attributable to the timing of when fixed manufacturing costs are expensed
Production = sales	Equal	Equal	
Production > sales	Lower[b]	Higher[c]	
Production < sales	Higher	Lower	
What are the effects on cost-volume-profit relationship (for a given level of fixed costs and a given contribution margin per unit)?	Driven by unit level of sales	Driven by (a) unit level of sales, (b) unit level of production, and (c) chosen denominator level	Management control benefit: Effects of changes in production level on operating income are easier to understand under variable costing

[a]Assuming that all manufacturing variances are written off as period costs, that no change occurs in work-in-process inventory, and no change occurs in the budgeted fixed manufacturing cost rate between accounting periods.

[b]That is, lower operating income than under absorption costing.

[c]That is, higher operating income than under variable costing.

Absorption Costing and Performance Measurement

Absorption costing is the required inventory method for external financial reporting in most countries (we provide potential reasons for this rule later in the chapter). Many companies use absorption costing for internal accounting as well because:

- It is cost-effective and less confusing for managers to use one common method of inventory costing for both external and internal reporting and performance evaluation.
- It can help prevent managers from taking actions that make their performance measure look good but that hurt the income they report to shareholders.
- It measures the cost of all manufacturing resources, whether variable or fixed, necessary to produce inventory. Many companies use inventory costing information for long-run decisions, such as pricing and choosing a product mix. For these long-run decisions, inventory costs should include both variable *and* fixed costs.

An important attribute of absorption costing is that it enables a manager to increase margins and operating income by producing more ending inventory. Producing for inventory is justified when a firm's managers anticipate rapid growth in demand and want to produce and store additional units to deal with possible production shortages in the next year. For example, with the recent improvement in the national economy, manufacturers of energy-efficient doors and windows are stepping up production in order to take advantage of an anticipated rebound in the housing market. But, under absorption costing, Stassen's managers may be tempted to produce inventory even when they *do not* anticipate customer demand to grow. The reason is that this production leads to higher operating income, which can benefit managers in two ways: directly, because higher incomes typically result in a higher bonus for the manager, and indirectly, because greater income levels have a positive effect on stock price, which increases managers' stock-based compensation. But higher income results in the company paying higher taxes. Shareholders and supporters of good corporate governance would also argue that it is unethical for managers to take actions that are intended solely to increase their compensation rather than to improve the company. Producing for inventory is a risky strategy, especially in industries with volatile demand or high risk of product obsolescence because of the pace at which innovation is occuring. For example, the new BlackBerry Z10 smartphone has seen declining sell-through rates and higher levels of inventory and is being sold at deeply discounted prices.

To reduce the undesirable incentives to build up inventories that absorption costing can create, a number of companies use variable costing for internal reporting. Variable costing focuses attention on distinguishing variable manufacturing costs from fixed manufacturing costs. This distinction is important for short-run decision making (as in cost-volume-profit analysis in Chapter 3 and in planning and control in Chapters 6, 7, and 8).

Companies that use both methods for internal reporting—variable costing for short-run decisions and performance evaluation and absorption costing for long-run decisions—benefit from the different advantages of both. Surveys have shown that while most organizations employ absorption costing systems, more than 75% indicate the use of variable costing information as either the most important or second most important measure for decision-making purposes.

In the next section, we explore in more detail the challenges that arise from absorption costing.

Undesirable Buildup of Inventories

If a manager's bonus is based on reported absorption-costing operating income, that manager may be motivated to build up an undesirable level of inventories. Assume that

Learning Objective 3

Understand how absorption costing can provide undesirable incentives for managers to build up inventory

. . . producing more units for inventory absorbs fixed manufacturing costs and increases operating income

Stassen's managers have such a bonus plan. Exhibit 9-4 shows how Stassen's absorption-costing operating income for 2015 changes as the production level changes. This exhibit assumes that the production-volume variance is written off to cost of goods sold at the end of each year. Beginning inventory of 2,000 units and sales of 6,500 units for 2015are unchanged from the case shown in Exhibit 9-2. *As you review Exhibit 9-4, keep in mind that the computations are basically the same as those in Exhibit 9-2.*

Exhibit 9-4 shows that production of 4,500 units meets the 2015 sales budget of 6,500 units (2,000 units from beginning inventory + 4,500 units produced). Operating income at this production level is ₹1,26,75,000. By producing more than 4,500 units, commonly referred to as *producing for inventory*, Stassen increases absorption-costing operating income. Each additional unit in 2015 ending inventory will increase operating income by ₹1,350. For example, if 9,000 units are produced (column H in Exhibit 9-4), ending inventory will be 4,500 units and operating income increases to ₹1,87,50,000. This amount is ₹60,75,000 more than he operating income with zero ending inventory (₹1,87,50,000 − ₹1,26,75,000, or 4,500 units × ₹1,350 per unit 5 ₹60,75,000). By producing 4,500 units for inventory, the company using absorption costing, includes ₹60,75,000 of fixed manufacturing costs in finished goods inventory, so those costs are not expensed in 2015.

The scenarios outlined in Exhibit 9-4 raise three other important points. First, column D is the base-case setting and just restates the 2015 absorption costing results from Panel B of Exhibit 9-2. Second, column F highlights that when inventory levels are unchanged, that is, production equals sales, the absorption costing income equals the income under variable costing (see Panel A of Exhibit 9-2 for comparison). Third, the example in Exhibit 9-4 focuses on one year, 2015. A Stassen manager who built up an inventory of 4,500 telescopes at the end of 2015 would have to further increase ending inventories in 2016 to increase that

Exhibit 9-4	Effect on Absorption-Costing Operating Income of Different Production Levels for Stassen Company: Telescope Product-Line Income Statement for 2015 at Sales of 6,500 Units

	A	B	C	D	E	F	G	H	I
1	**Unit Data**								
2	Beginning inventory	2,000		2,000		2,000		2,000	
3	Production	4,500		5,000		6,500		9,000	
4	Goods available for sale	6,500		7,000		8,500		11,000	
5	Sales	6,500		6,500		6,500		6,500	
6	Ending inventory	0		500		2,000		4,500	
7									
8	**Income Statement**								
9	Revenues	₹65,00,000		₹65,00,000		₹65,00,000		₹65,00,000	
10	Cost of goods sold:								
11	Beginning inventory: ₹335 × 2,000	6,70,000		6,70,000		6,70,000		6,70,000	
12	Variable manufacturing costs: ₹200 × production	9,00,000		10,00,000		13,00,000		18,00,000	
13	Allocated fixed manufacturing costs: ₹135 × production	6,07,500		6,75,000		8,77,500		12,15,000	
14	Cost of goods available for sale	21,77,500		23,45,000		28,47,500		36,85,000	
15	Deduct ending inventory: ₹335 × ending inventory	0		(1,67,500)		(6,70,000)		(15,07,500)	
16	Adjustment for production-volume variance[a]	4,72,500	U	4,05,000	U	2,02,500	U	(1,35,000)	F
17	Cost of goods sold	26,50,000		25,82,500		23,80,000		20,42,500	
18	Gross Margin	38,50,000		39,17,500		41,20,000		44,57,500	
19	Marketing costs: ₹13,80,000 + (₹185 per unit × 6,500 units sold)	25,82,500		25,82,500		25,82,500		25,82,500	
20	Operating Income	₹12,67,500		₹13,35,000		₹15,37,500		₹18,75,000	
21									
22	[a]Production-volume variance = Budgeted fixed manufacturing costs − Allocated fixed manufacturing costs (Income Statement, line 13)								
23	At production of 4,500 units: ₹10,80,000 − ₹6,07,500 = ₹4,72,500 U								
24	At production of 5,000 units: ₹10,80,000 − ₹6,75,000 = ₹4,05,000 U								
25	At production of 6,500 units: ₹10,80,000 − ₹8,77,500 = ₹2,02,500 U								
26	At production of 9,000 units: ₹10,80,000 − ₹12,15,000 = (₹1,35,000) F								

year's operating income by producing for inventory. There are limits to how much inventory levels can be increased over time because of physical constraints on storage space and management controls. Such limits reduce the likelihood of incurring some of absorption costing's undesirable effects. Nevertheless, managers do have the ability and incentive to move costs in and out of inventory in order to manage operating income under absorption costing.

Top management can implement checks and balances that limit managers from producing for inventory under absorption costing. However, the practice cannot be completely prevented. There are many subtle ways a manager can produce for inventory that may not be easy to detect. For example, consider the following scenarios:

- A plant manager may switch to manufacturing products that absorb the highest amount of fixed manufacturing costs, regardless of the customer demand for these products (called "cherry picking" the production line). Production of items that absorb the least or lower fixed manufacturing costs may be delayed, resulting in failure to meet promised customer delivery dates (which, over time, can result in unhappy customers).

- A plant manager may accept a particular order to increase production, even though another plant in the same company is better suited to handle that order.

- To increase production, a manager may defer maintenance beyond the current period. Although operating income in this period may increase as a result, future operating income could decrease by a larger amount if repair costs increase and equipment becomes less efficient.

Proposals for Revising Performance Evaluation

Top management, with help from the controller and management accountants, can take several steps to reduce the undesirable effects of absorption costing.

- Focus on careful budgeting and inventory planning to reduce management's freedom to build up excess inventory. For example, the budgeted monthly balance sheets have estimates of the rupee amount of inventories. If actual inventories exceed these rupee amounts, top management can investigate the inventory buildups.

- Incorporate a carrying charge for inventory in the internal accounting system. For example, the company could assess an inventory carrying charge of 1% per month on the investment tied up in inventory and for spoilage and obsolescence when it evaluates a manager's performance. An increasing number of companies are beginning to adopt this inventory carrying charge.

- Change the period used to evaluate performance. Critics of absorption costing give examples in which managers take actions that maximize quarterly or annual income at the potential expense of long-run income. When their performance is evaluated over a three- to five-year period, managers will be less tempted to produce for inventory.

- Include nonfinancial as well as financial variables in the measures used to evaluate performance. Examples of nonfinancial measures that can be used to monitor the performance of Stassen's managers in 2014 are:

$$(a) \quad \frac{\text{Ending inventory in units in 2014}}{\text{Beginning inventory in units in 2014}} = \frac{3,000}{500} = 6$$

$$(b) \quad \frac{\text{Units produced in 2014}}{\text{Units sold in 2014}} = \frac{10,000}{7,500} = 1.33$$

Top management would want to see production equal to sales and relatively stable levels of inventory. Companies that manufacture or sell several products could report these two measures for each of the products they manufacture and sell.

Decision Point

Why might managers build up finished goods inventory if they use absorption costing?

Besides the formal performance measurement systems, companies develop codes of conduct to discourage behavior that benefits managers but not the company and build values and cultures that focus on behaving ethically. We discuss these topics in Chapter 23.

Comparing Inventory Costing Methods

Before we begin our discussion of capacity, we will look at *throughput costing*, a variation of variable costing, and compare the various costing methods.

Throughput Costing

Some managers believe that even variable costing promotes an excessive amount of costs being inventoried. They argue that only direct materials, such as the lenses, casing, scope, and mount in the case of Stassen's telescopes, are "truly variable" in output. Throughput costing, which also is called **super-variable costing,** such as lense casing, scope and mount in the case of Stassen's Telescope is an extreme form of variable costing, is a method of inventory costing in which only direct material costs are included as inventoriable costs. All other costs are costs of the period in which they are incurred. In particular, variable direct manufacturing labor costs and variable manufacturing overhead costs are regarded as period costs and are deducted as expenses of the period.

Exhibit 9-5 is the throughput-costing income statement for Stassen Company for 2014 and 2015. *Throughput margin* equals revenues minus all direct material cost of the goods sold. Compare the operating income amounts reported in Exhibit 9-5 with those for absorption costing and variable costing:

Exhibit 9-5

Throughput Costing for Stassen Company: Telescope Product-Line Income Statements for 2014 and 2015

	A	B	C
1		**2014**	**2015**
2	Revenues: ₹1,000 × 6,000; 6,500 units	₹6,000,000	₹65,00,000
3	Direct material cost of goods sold		
4	Beginning inventory: ₹110× 0 ; 2,000 units	0	2,20,000
5	Direct materials:₹110 × 8,000; 5,000 units	8,80,000	5,50,000
6	Cost of goods available for sale	8,80,000	7,70,000
7	Deduct ending inventory:₹110 × 2,000; 500 units	(2,20,000)	(55,000)
8	Direct material cost of goods sold	6,60,000	7,15,000
9	Throughput margin[a]	53,40,000	57,85,000
10	Manufacturing costs (other than direct materials)[b]	18,00,000	15,30,000
11	Marketing costs[c]	24,90,000	25,82,500
12	Operating income	₹10,50,000	₹16,72,500
13			
14	[a]Throughput margin equals revenues minus all direct material cost of goods sold		
15	[b]Fixed manuf. costs + [(variable manuf. labor cost per unit + variable manuf. overhead cost per unit) × units produced];		
16	[c]Fixed marketing costs + (variable marketing cost per unit × units sold);		
17	₹1,380,000 + (₹185 × 6,000; 6,500 units)		

	2014	2015
Absorption-costing operating income	₹1,50,00,000	₹1,33,50,000
Variable-costing operating income	₹1,23,00,000	₹1,53,75,000
Throughput-costing operating income	₹1,05,00,000	₹1,67,25,000

Only the ₹1,100 direct material cost per unit is inventoriable under throughput costing, compared with ₹3,350 per unit for absorption costing and ₹2,000 per unit for variable costing. When the production quantity exceeds sales as in 2014, throughput costing results in the largest amount of expenses in the current period's income statement. Advocates of throughput costing say it provides managers less incentive to produce for inventory than either variable costing or, especially, absorption costing. Throughput costing is a more recent phenomenon in comparison with variable costing and absorption costing and has avid supporters, but so far it has not been widely adopted.[2]

A Comparison of Alternative Inventory-Costing Methods

Variable costing and absorption costing may be combined with actual, normal, or standard costing. Exhibit 9-6 compares product costing under six alternative inventory-costing systems. Variable costing has been controversial among accountants because of how it affects *external reporting*, not because of disagreement about the need to delineate between variable and fixed costs for internal planning and control, Accountants who favor variable costing

Exhibit 9-6	Comparison of Alternative Inventory-Costing Systems

		Actual Costing	**Normal Costing**	**Standard Costing**
Variable Costing	**Variable Direct Manufacturing Cost**	Actual prices × Actual quantity of inputs used	Actual prices × Actual quantity of inputs used	Standard prices × Standard quantity of inputs allowed for actual output achieved
	Variable Manufacturing Overhead Costs	Actual variable overhead rates × Actual quantity of cost-allocation bases used	Budgeted variable overhead rates × Actual quantity of cost-allocation bases used	Standard variable overhead rates × Standard quantity of cost-allocation bases allowed for actual output achieved
	Fixed Direct Manufacturing Costs	Actual prices × Actual quantity of inputs used	Actual prices × Actual quantity of inputs used	Standard prices × Standard quantity of inputs allowed for actual output achieved
	Fixed Manufacturing Overhead Costs	Actual fixed overhead rates × Actual quantity of cost-allocation bases used	Budgeted fixed overhead rates × Actual quantity of cost-allocation bases used	Standard fixed overhead rates × Standard quantity of cost-allocation bases allowed for actual output achieved

(Absorption Costing brackets the entire set; Variable Costing brackets the Variable Direct Manufacturing Cost and Variable Manufacturing Overhead Costs rows.)

---

[2] See E. Goldratt, *The Theory of Constraints* (New York: North River Press, 1990); E. Noreen, D. Smith, and J. Mackey, *The Theory of Constraints and Its Implications for Management Accounting* (New York: North River Press, 1995).

for external reporting maintain that the fixed portion of manufacturing costs is more closely related to the capacity to produce than to the actual production of specific units. Fixed costs should therefore be expensed, not inventoried.

Accountants who support absorption costing for *external reporting* maintain that inventories should carry a fixed-manufacturing-cost component because both variable manufacturing costs and fixed manufacturing costs are necessary to produce goods. Therefore, both types of costs should be inventoried in order to match all manufacturing costs to revenues, regardless of their different behavior patterns. For external reporting to shareholders, companies around the globe tend to follow the generally accepted accounting principle that all manufacturing costs are inventoriable. This also eases the burden on firms and auditors to attempt to disentangle fixed and variable costs of production, a distinction that is not always clear-cut in practice.

Similarly, for tax reporting in the United States, direct production costs, as well as fixed and variable indirect production costs, managers must take taken into account in the computation of inventoriable costs in accordance with the "full absorption" method of inventory costing. Indirect production costs include items such as rent, utilities, maintenance, repair expenses, indirect materials, and indirect labor. For other indirect cost categories (including depreciation, insurance, taxes, officers' salaries, factory administrative expenses, and strike-related costs), the portion of the cost that is "incident to and necessary for production or manufacturing operations or processes" is inventoriable for tax purposes if (and only if) it is treated as inventoriable for the purposes of financial reporting. Accordingly, managers must often allocate costs between those portions related to manufacturing activities and those not related to manufacturing.[3]

DENOMINATOR-LEVEL CAPACITY CONCEPTS AND FIXED-COST CAPACITY ANALYSIS

We have seen that the difference between variable and absorption costing methods arises solely from the treatment of fixed manufacturing costs. Spending on fixed manufacturing costs enables firms to obtain the scale or capacity needed to satisfy the expected demand from customers. Determining the "right" amount of spending, or the appropriate level of capacity is one of the most strategic and most difficult decisions managers face. Having too much capacity to produce relative to that needed to meet market demand means incurring some costs of unused capacity. Having too little capacity to produce means that demand from some customers may be unfilled. These customers may go to other sources of supply and never return. Both managers and accountants must understand these issues that arise with capacity costs.

We start this section by analysing a key question in absorption costing: Given a firm's level of spending on fixed manufacturing costs, what capacity level should managers and accounts use to compute the fixed manufacturing cost per unit produced? We then study the broader question of how a firm should decide on its level of capacity investment.

Absorption Costing and Alternative Denominator-Level Capacity Concepts

Earlier chapters, especially Chapters 4, 5, and 8, have highlighted how normal costing and standard costing report costs in an ongoing timely manner throughout a fiscal year. The choice of the capacity level used to allocate budgeted fixed manufacturing costs to prod-

---

[3] Details regarding tax rules can be found in Section 1.471-11 of the U.S. Internal Revenue Code: Inventories of Manufacturers (see http://ecfr.gpoaccess.gov). Recall from Chapter 2 that costs not related to production, such as marketing, distribution, or research expenses, are treated as period expenses for financial reporting. Under U.S. tax rules, a firm can still consider these costs as inventoriable for tax purposes provided that it does so consistently.

ucts can greatly affect the operating income reported under normal costing or standard costing and the product-cost information available to managers.

Consider the Stassen Company example again. Recall that the annual fixed manufacturing costs of the production facility are ₹1,08,00,000. Stassen currently uses absorption costing with standard costs for external reporting purposes, and it calculates its budgeted fixed manufacturing rate on a per unit basis. We will now examine four different capacity levels used as the denominator to compute the budgeted fixed manufacturing cost rate:theoretical capacity, practical capacity, normal capacity utilization, and master-budget capacity utilization.

Theoretical Capacity and Practical Capacity

In business and accounting, *capacity* ordinarily means a "constraint," an "upper limit." **Theoretical capacity** is the level of capacity based on producing at full efficiency all the time. Stassen can produce 25 units per shift when the production lines are operating at maximum speed. If we assume 360 days per year, the theoretical annual capacity for two shifts per day is:

$$\text{25 units per shift} \times \text{2 shifts per day} \times \text{360 days} = \text{18,000 units}$$

Theoretical capacity is theoretical in the sense that it does not allow for any slowdowns due to plant maintenance, shutdown periods, or interruptions because of downtime on the assembly lines. Theoretical capacity levels are unattainable in the real world but they represent the real goal of capacity utilization a company can aspire to.

Practical capacity is the level of capacity that reduces theoretical capacity by considering unavoidable operating interruptions, such as scheduled maintenance time, shutdowns for holidays. Assume that practical capacity is the practical production rate of 20 units per shift (as opposed to 25 units per shift under theoretical capacity) for two shifts per day for 300 days a year (as distinguished from 360 days a year under theoretical capacity). The practical annual capacity is:

$$\text{25 units per shift} \times \text{2 shifts per day} \times \text{300 days} = \text{12,000 units}$$

Engineering and human resource factors are both important when estimating theoretical or practical capacity. Engineers at the Stassen facility can provide input on the technical capabilities of machines for cutting and polishing lenses. Human resources can evaluate employeesafety factors, such as increased injury risk when the line operates at faster speeds.

Normal Capacity Utilization and Master-Budget Capacity Utilization

Both theoretical capacity and practical capacity measure capacity levels in terms of what a plant can *supply*—available capacity. In contrast, normal capacity utilization and master-budget capacity utilization measure capacity levels in terms of *demand* for the output of the plant, that is, the amount of available capacity the plant expects to use based on the demand for its products. In many cases, budgeted demand is well below production capacity available.

Normal capacity utilization is the level of capacity utilization that satisfies average customer demand over a period (say, two to three years) that includes seasonal, cyclical, and trend factors. **Master-budget capacity utilization** is the level of capacity utilization that managers expect for the current budget period, which is typically one year. These two capacity-utilization levels can differ quite significantly in industries that face cyclical demand patterns. For example:

- The automobile industry may have a period of high demand due to low interest rates or a period of low demand due to a recession.

- The semiconductor industry may have a period of high demand if companies update employee computers or a period of low demand if companies downsize.

Consider Stassen's master budget for 2014, based on production of 8,000 telescopes per year. Despite using this master-budget capacity-utilization level of 8,000 telescopes for 2014, top management believes that over the next three years the normal (average) annual production level will be 10,000 telescopes. It view 20142's budgeted production level of 8,000 telescopes to be "abnormally" low because a major competitor has been sharply reducing its selling price and spending a lot of money on advertising. Stassen expects that the competitor's lower price and advertising blitz will not be a long-run phenomenon and that, by 2015 and beyond, Stassen's production and sales will be higher.

Effect on Budgeted Fixed Manufacturing Cost Rate

We now illustrate how each of these four denominator levels affects the budgeted fixed manufacturing cost rate. Stassen has budgeted (standard) fixed manufacturing overhead costs of ₹1,08,00,000 for 2014. This lump-sum is incurred to provide the capacity to produce telescopes. The amount includes, among other costs, leasing costs for the facility and the compensation of the facility managers. The budgeted fixed manufacturing cost rates for 2014 for each of the four capacity-level concepts are as follows:

	A	B	C	D
	Denominator-Level Capacity Concept (1)	**Budgeted Fixed Manufacturing Costs per Year (₹)** (2)	**Budget Capacity Level (in units)** (3)	**Budgeted Fixed Manufacturing Cost per Unit (₹)** (4) = (2) / (3)
5	Theoretical capacity	1,08,00,000	18,000	600
6	Practical capacity	1,08,00,000	12,000	900
7	Normal capacity utilization	1,08,00,000	10,000	1,080
8	Master-budget capacity utilization	1,08,00,000	8,000	1,350

The significant difference in cost rates (from ₹600 to ₹1,350) arises because of large differences in budgeted capacity levels under the different capacity concepts.

Budgeted (standard) variable manufacturing cost is ₹2,000 per unit. The total budgeted (standard) manufacturing cost per unit for alternative capacity-level concepts is as follows:

	A	B	C	D
	Denominator-Level Capacity Concept (1)	**Budgeted Variable Manufacturing Cost per unit (₹)** (2)	**Budgeted Fixed Manufacturing Cost per unit (₹)** (3)	**Budgeted Total Manufacturing Cost per unit (₹)** (4) = (2) + (3)
5	Theoretical capacity	2,000	600	2,600
6	Practical capacity	2,000	900	2,900
7	Normal capacity utilization	2,000	1,080	3,080
8	Master-budget capacity utilization	2,000	1,350	3,350

Decision Point ▶

What are the various capacity levels a company can use to compute the budgeted fixed manufacturing cost rate?

Because different denominator-level capacity concepts yield different budgeted fixed manufacturing costs per unit, Stassen must decide which capacity level to use. Stassen is not required to use the same capacity-level concept, say, for management planning and control, external reporting to shareholders, and income tax purposes.

Choosing a Capacity Level

As we just saw, at the start of each fiscal year, managers determine different denominator levels for the different capacity concepts and calculate different budgeted fixed manufacturing costs per unit. We now discuss different denominator-level choices for different purposes, including (a) product costing and capacity management, (b) pricing, (c) performance evaluation, (d) external reporting, and (e) tax requirements.

Product Costing and Capacity Management

Data from normal costing or standard costing are often used in pricing or product-mix decisions. As the Stassen example illustrates, use of theoretical capacity results in an unrealistically small fixed manufacturing cost per unit because it is based on an idealistic and unattainable level of capacity. Theoretical capacity is rarely used to calculate budgeted fixed manufacturing cost per unit because it departs significantly from the real capacity available to a company.

Many companies favor practical capacity as the denominator to calculate budgeted fixed manufacturing cost per unit. Practical capacity in the Stassen example represents the maximum number of units (12,000) that Stassen can reasonably expect to produce per year for the ₹1,08,00,000 it will spend annually on capacity. If Stassen had consistently planned to produce fewer units, say 6,000 telescopes each year, it would have built a smaller plant and incurred lower costs.

Stassen budgets ₹900 in fixed manufacturing cost per unit based on the ₹1,08,00,000 it costs to acquire the capacity to produce 12,000 units. This level of plant capacity is an important strategic decision that managers make well before Stassen uses the capacity and even before Stassen knows how much of the capacity it will actually use. That is, budgeted fixed manufacturing cost of ₹900 per unit measures the *cost per unit of supplying the capacity*.

Demand for Stassen's telescopes in 2014 is expected to be 8,000 units, which is 4,000 units lower than the practical capacity of 12,000 units. However, it costs Stassen ₹1,08,00,000 per year to acquire the capacity to make 12,000 units, so the cost of *supplying* the capacity needed to make 12,000 units is still ₹900 per unit. The capacity and its cost are fixed *in the short run*; unlike variable costs, the capacity supplied does not automatically reduce to match the capacity needed in 2014. As a result, not all of the capacity supplied at ₹900 per unit will be needed or used in 2014. Using practical capacity as the denominator level, managers can subdivide the cost of resources supplied into used and unused components. At the supply cost of ₹900 per unit, the manufacturing resources that Stassen will use equal ₹72,00,000 (₹900 per unit × 8,000 units). Manufacturing resources that Stassen will not use are ₹36,00,000 [₹900 per unit × (12,000 − 8,000) units].

Using practical capacity as the denominator level sets the cost of capacity at the cost of supplying the capacity, regardless of the demand for the capacity. Highlighting the cost of capacity acquired but not used directs managers' attention toward managing unused capacity, perhaps by designing new products to fill unused capacity, by leasing unused capacity to others, or by eliminating unused capacity. In contrast, using either of the capacity levels based on the demand for Stassen's telescopes—master-budget capacity utilization or normal capacity utilization—hides the amount of unused capacity. If Stassen had used master-budget capacity utilization as the capacity level, it would have calculated budgeted fixed manufacturing cost per unit as ₹1,350 (₹1,08,00,000 ÷ 8,000 units). This calculation does not use data about practical capacity, so it does not separately identify the cost of unused capacity. Note, however, that the cost of ₹1,350 per unit includes a charge for unused capacity: it is composed of the ₹900 fixed manufacturing resource that would be used to produce each unit at practical capacity plus the cost of unused capacity allocated to each unit, ₹450 per unit (₹36,00,000 ÷ 8,000 units).

Learning Objective 6

Examine the key factors in choosing a capacity level to compute the budgeted fixed manufacturing cost rate

. . . managers must consider the effect a capacity level has on product costing, capacity management, pricing decisions, and financial statements

From the perspective of long-run product costing, which cost of capacity should Stassen use for pricing purposes or for benchmarking its product cost structure against competitors: ₹900 per unit based on practical capacity or ₹1,350 per unit based on master-budget capacity utilization? Probably the ₹900 per unit based on practical capacity. Why? Because ₹900 per unit represents the budgeted cost per unit of only the capacity used to produce the product, and it explicitly excludes the cost of any unused capacity. Stassen's customers will be willing to pay a price that covers the cost of the capacity actually used but will not want to pay for unused capacity that provides no other benefits to them. Customers expect Stassen to manage its unused capacity or to bear the cost of unused capacity, not pass it along to them. Moreover, if Stassen's competitors manage unused capacity more effectively, the cost of capacity in the competitors' cost structures (which guides competitors' pricing decisions) is likely to approach ₹900. In the next section we show how the use of normal capacity utilization or master-budget capacity utilization can result in setting selling prices that are not competitive.

Pricing Decisions and the Downward Demand Spiral

The **downward demand spiral** for a company is the continuing reduction in the demand for its products that occurs when competitor prices are not met; as demand drops further, higher and higher unit costs result in greater reluctance to meet competitors' prices.

The easiest way to understand the downward demand spiral is with an example. Assume Stassen uses master-budget capacity utilization of 8,000 units for product costing in 2014. The resulting manufacturing cost is ₹3,350 per unit (₹2,000 variable manufacturing cost per unit 1 + ₹1,350 fixed manufacturing cost per unit). Assume that in December 2013, a competitor offers to supply a major customer of Stassen (a customer who was expected to purchase 2,000 units in 2014) telescopes at ₹3,000 per unit. The Stassen manager, doesn't want to show a loss on the account and wants to recoup all costs in the long run, so the manager declines to match the competitor's price. The account is lost. The loss means budgeted fixed manufacturing costs of ₹1,08,00,000 will be spread over the remaining master-budget volume of 6,000 units at a rate of ₹1,800 per unit (₹1,08,00,000 ÷ 6,000 units).

Suppose yet another Stassen customer who also accounts for 2,000 units of budgeted volume receives a bid from a competitor at a price of ₹3,500 per unit. The Stassen manager compares this bid with his revised unit cost of ₹3,800 (₹2,000 + ₹1,800), declines to match the competition, and the account is lost. Planned output would shrink further to 4,000 units. Budgeted fixed manufacturing cost per unit for the remaining 4,000 telescopes would now be ₹2,700 (₹1,08,00,000 ÷ 4,000 units). The following table shows the effect of spreading fixed manufacturing costs over a shrinking amount of master-budget capacity utilization:

	File Edit View Insert Format Tools Data Window Help		
	A	B	C	D
1	Master-Budget		Budgeted Fixed	
2	Capacity Utilization	Budgeted Variable	Manufacturing	Budgeted Total
3	Denominator Level	Manufacturing Cost	Cost per Unit (₹)	Manufacturing
4	(Units)	per Unit (₹)	[₹1,08,00,000 ÷ (1)]	Cost per Unit (₹)
5	(1)	(2)	(3)	(4) = (2) + (3)
6	8,000	2,000	1,350	3,350
7	6,000	2,000	1,800	3,800
8	4,000	2,000	2,700	4,700
9	3,000	2,000	3,600	5,600

Practical capacity, by contrast, is a stable measure. The use of practical capacity as the denominator to calculate budgeted fixed manufacturing cost per unit avoids the recalculation of unit costs when expected demand levels change because the fixed cost rate is calculated based on *capacity available* rather than *capacity used to meet demand*. Managers who use reported unit costs in a mechanical way to set prices are less likely to promote a downward demand spiral when they use practical capacity than when they use normal capacity utilization or master-budget capacity utilization.

Using practical capacity as the denominator level also gives the manager a more accurate idea of the resources needed and used to produce a unit by excluding the cost of unused capacity. As discussed earlier, the cost of manufacturing resources supplied to produce a telescope is ₹2,900 (₹2,000 variable manufacturing cost per unit plus ₹900 fixed manufacturing cost per unit). This cost is lower than the prices offered by Stassen's competitors and would have correctly led the manager to match the prices and retain the accounts (assuming for purposes of this discussion that Stassen has no other costs). If, however, the prices offered by competitors were lower than ₹2,900 per unit, the Stassen manager would not recover the cost of resources used to supply telescopes. This would signal to the manager that Stassen was noncompetitive even if it had no unused capacity. The only way then for Stassen to be profitable and retain customers in the long run would be to reduce its manufacturing cost per unit.[4]

Performance Evaluation

Consider how the choice among normal capacity utilization, master-budget capacity utilization, and practical capacity affects how a company evaluates its marketing manager. Normal capacity utilization is often used as a basis for long-run plans. Normal capacity utilization depends on the time span selected and the forecasts made for each year. *However, normal capacity utilization is an average that provides no meaningful feedback to the marketing manager for a particular year.* Using normal capacity utilization as a reference for judging current performance of a marketing manager is an example of misusing a long-run measure for a short-run purpose. The company should use master-budget capacity utilization, rather than normal capacity utilization or practical capacity, to evaluate a marketing manager's performance in the current year because the master budget is the principal short-run planning and control tool. Managers feel more obligated to reach the levels specified in the master budget, which should have been carefully set in relation to the maximum opportunities for sales in the current year.

When large differences exist between practical capacity and master-budget capacity utilization, several companies (such as Texas Instruments, Polysar, and Sandoz) classify the difference as *planned unused capacity*. One reason for this approach is performance evaluation. Consider our Stassen telescope example. The managers in charge of capacity planning usually do not make pricing decisions. Top management decided to build a production facility with 12,000 units of practical capacity, focusing on demand over the next five years. But Stassen's marketing managers, who are mid-level managers, make the pricing decisions. These marketing managers believe they should be held accountable only for the manufacturing overhead costs related to their potential customer base in 2014. The master-budget capacity utilization suggests a customer base in 2014 of 8,000 units (2/3 of the 12,000 practical capacity). Using responsibility accounting principles (see Chapter 6), only 2/3 of the budgeted total fixed manufacturing costs (₹1,08,00,000 × 2/3 = ₹72,00,000) would be attributed to the fixed capacity costs of meeting 2014 demand. The

---

[4] The downward demand spiral is currently at work in the traditional landline phone industry. As more telephone customers shift services to wireless or Internet-based options, Verizon and AT&T, the two largest telephone service providers in the United States, are reducing their focus on providing copper-wire telephone service to homes and business. As AT&T told the U.S. Federal Communications Commission, "The business model for legacy phone services is in a death spiral."

remaining 1/3 of the numerator (₹1,08,00,000 × 1/3 = ₹36,00,000) would be separately shown as the capacity cost of meeting increases in long-run demand expected to occur beyond 2014.[5]

External Reporting

The magnitude of the favorable/unfavorable production-volume variance under absorption costing is affected by the choice of the denominator level used to calculate the budgeted fixed manufacturing cost per unit. Assume the following actual operating information for Stassen in 2014:

	A	B	C
1	Beginning inventory	0	
2	Production	8,000	units
3	Sales	6,000	units
4	Ending inventory	2,000	units
5	Selling price	₹10,000	per unit
6	Variable manufacturing cost	₹2,000	per unit
7	Fixed manufacturing costs	₹1,08,00,000	
8	Variable marketing cost	₹1,850	per unit sold
9	Fixed marketing costs	₹1,38,00,000	

Note that this is the same data used to calculate the income under variable and absorption costing for Stassen in Exhibit 9-1. As before, we assume that there are no price, spending, or efficiency variances in manufacturing costs.

Recall from Chapter 8 the equation used to calculate the production-volume variance:

$$\begin{matrix} \text{Production-volume} \\ \text{variance} \end{matrix} = \left(\begin{matrix} \text{Budgeted} \\ \text{fixed} \\ \text{manufacturing} \\ \text{overhead} \end{matrix} \right) - \left(\begin{matrix} \text{Fixed manufacturing overhead allocated using} \\ \text{budgeted cost per output unit} \\ \text{allowed for acutal output produced} \end{matrix} \right)$$

The four different capacity-level concepts result in four different budgeted fixed manufacturing overhead cost rates per unit. The different rates will result in different amounts of fixed manufacturing overhead costs allocated to the 8,000 units actually produced and different amounts of production-volume variance. Using the budgeted fixed manufacturing costs of ₹1,08,00,000 (equal to actual fixed manufacturing costs) and the rates calculated earlier for different denominator levels, the production-volume variance computations are as follows:

Production-volume variance (theoretical capacity) = ₹1,08,00,000 − (8,000 unitd × ₹600 per unit)
= ₹1,08,00,000 − 48,00,000
= 60,00,000 U

Production-volume variance (practical capacity) = ₹1,08,00,000 − (8,000 unitd × ₹900 per unit)
= ₹1,08,00,000 − 72,00,000
= 36,00,000 U

---

[5] For further discussion, see T. Klammer, *Capacity Measurement and Improvement* (Chicago: Irwin, 1996). This research was facilitated by CAM-I, an organization promoting innovative cost management practices. CAM-I's research on capacity costs explores ways in which companies can identify types of capacity costs that can be reduced (or eliminated) without affecting the required output to meet customer demand. An example is improving processes to successfully eliminate the costs of capacity held in anticipation of handling difficulties due to imperfect coordination with suppliers and customers.

Production-volume variance (normal capacity) utilization	= ₹1,08,00,000 − (8,000 unitd × ₹1,080 per unit) = ₹1,08,00,000 − 86,40,000 = 21,60,000 U
Production-volume variance (master-budget) capacity utilization)	= ₹1,08,00,000 − (8,000 unitd × ₹1,350 per unit) = ₹1,08,00,000 − 1,08,00,000 = ₹0

How Stassen disposes of its production-volume variance at the end of the fiscal year will determine the effect this variance has on the company's operating income. We now discuss the three alternative approaches Stassen can use to dispose of the production-volume variance. These approaches were first discussed in Chapter 4.

1. **Adjusted allocation-rate approach.** This approach restates all amounts in the general and subsidiary ledgers by using actual rather than budgeted cost rates. Given that actual fixed manufacturing costs are ₹1,08,00,000 and actual production is 8,000 units, the recalculated fixed manufacturing cost is ₹1,350 per unit (₹1,08,00,000 ÷ 8,000 actual units). Under the adjusted allocation-rate approach, the choice of the capacity level used to calculate the budgeted fixed manufacturing cost per unit has no effect on year-end financial statements. In effect, actual costing is adopted at the end of the fiscal year.

2. **Proration approach.** The underallocated or overallocated overhead is spread among ending balances in Work-in-Process Control, Finished Goods Control, and Cost of Goods Sold. The proration restates the ending balances in these accounts to what they would have been if actual cost rates had been used rather than budgeted cost rates. The proration approach also results in the choice of the capacity level used to calculate the budgeted fixed manufacturing cost per unit having no effect on year-end financial statements.

3. **Write-off variances to cost of goods sold approach.** Exhibit 9-7 shows how use of this approach affects Stassen's operating income for 2014. Recall that the ending inventory on December 31, 2014, is 2,000 units. Using master-budget capacity utilization as the denominator level results in assigning the highest amount of fixed manufacturing cost per unit to the 2,000 units in ending inventory (see the line item "deduct ending inventory" in Exhibit 9-7). Accordingly, operating income is highest using master-budget capacity utilization. The differences in operating income for the four denominator-level concepts in Exhibit 9-7 are due to different amounts of fixed manufacturing overhead being inventoried at the end of 2014:

Fixed Manufacturing Overhead		
in Dec. 31, 2014 Inventory		
Theoretical capacity	2,000 units × ₹600 per unit	= ₹12,00,000
Practical capacity	2,000 units × ₹900 per unit	= ₹18,00,000
Normal capacity utilization	2,000 units × ₹1,080 per unit	= ₹21,60,000
Master-budget capacity utilization	2,000 units × ₹1,350 per unit	= ₹27,00,000

In Exhibit 9-7, for example, the ₹5,40,000 difference (₹1,50,00,000 − ₹1,44,60,000) in operating income between master-budget capacity utilization and normal capacity utilization is due to the difference in fixed manufacturing overhead inventoried (₹27,00,000 − ₹21,60,000).

To summarize, the common factor behind the increasing operating-income numbers in Exhibit 9-4 and Exhibit 9-7 is the increasing amount of fixed manufacturing costs incurred that is included in ending inventory. The amount of fixed manufacturing costs inventoried depends on two factors: the number of units in ending inventory and the rate at which fixed manufacturing costs are allocated to each unit. Exhibit 9-4 shows the effect on operating income of increasing the number of units in ending inventory (by increasing production).

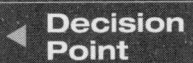

◀ **Decision Point**

What are the major factors managers consider in choosing the capacity level to compute the budgeted fixed manufacturing cost rate?

Exhibit 9-7 shows the effect on operating income of increasing the fixed manufacturing cost allocated per unit (by decreasing the denominator level used to calculate the rate).

Chapter 8 discusses the various issues managers and management accountants must consider when deciding whether to prorate the production-volume variance among inventories and cost of goods sold or to simply write off the variance to cost of goods sold. The objective is to write off the portion of the production-volume variance that represents the cost of capacity not used to support the production of output during the period. Determining this amount is almost always a matter of judgment.

Planning and Control of Capacity Costs

In addition to the issues previously discussed, managers must take a variety of other factors into account when planning capacity levels and in deciding how best to control and assign capacity costs. These other factors include the level of uncertainty about both the expected costs and the expected demand for the installed capacity; the presence of capacity-related issues in nonmanufacturing settings; and the potential use of activity-based costing techniques in allocating capacity costs.

Exhibit 9-7 Income-Statement Effects of Using Alternative Capacity-Level Concepts: Stassen Company for 2014

		Theoretical Capacity		Practical Capacity		Normal Capacity Utilization		Master-Budget Capacity Utilization	
2	Denominator level in cases	18,000		12,000		10,000		8,000	
3	Revenues[a]	₹6,00,00,000		₹6,00,00,000		₹6,00,00,000		₹6,00,00,000	
4	Cost of goods sold								
5	Beginning inventory	₹0		₹0		₹0		₹0	
6	Variable manufacturing costs[b]	₹1,60,00,000		₹1,60,00,000		₹1,60,00,000		₹1,60,00,000	
7	Fixed manufacturing costs[c]	₹48,00,000		₹72,00,000		₹86,40,000		₹1,08,00,000	
8	Cost of goods available for sale	₹2,08,00,000		₹2,32,00,000		₹2,46,40,000		₹2,68,00,000	
9	Deduct ending inventory[d]	(₹52,00,000)		(₹58,00,000)		(₹61,60,000)		(₹67,00,000)	
10	Cost of goods sold (at standard cost)	₹1,56,00,000		₹1,74,00,000		₹1,84,80,000		₹2,01,00,000	
11	Adjustment for production-volume variance	₹60,00,000	U	₹36,00,000	U	₹21,60,000	U	0	
12	Cost of goods sold	₹2,16,00,000		₹2,10,00,000		₹2,06,40,000		₹2,01,00,000	
13	Gross margin	₹3,84,00,000		₹3,90,00,000		₹3,93,60,000		₹3,99,00,000	
14	Marketing costs[e]	₹2,49,00,000		₹2,49,00,000		₹2,49,00,000		₹2,49,00,000	
15	Operating income	₹1,35,00,000		₹1,41,00,000		₹1,44,60,000		₹1,50,00,000	

17 [a]₹10,000 x 6,000 units = ₹6,00,00,000   [d]Ending inventory costs:

18 [b]₹2,000 x 8,000 units = ₹1,60,00,000   (₹2,000+ ₹600) x 2,000 units = ₹52,00,000

19 [c]Fixed manufacturing overhead costs: (₹2,000+ ₹900) x 2,000 units = ₹58,00,000

20 ₹600 x 8,000 units = ₹48,00,000   (₹2,000+ ₹1,080) x 2,000 units = ₹61,60,000

21 ₹900 x 8,000 units = ₹72,00,000   (₹2,000+ ₹1,350) x 2,000 units = ₹67,00,000

22 ₹1,080 x 8,000 units = ₹86,40,000   [e]Marketing costs:

23 ₹1,350 x 8,000 units = ₹1,08,00,000   ₹1,38,00,000+ ₹1,850 x 6,000 units = ₹24,90,000

Difficulties in Forecasting Chosen Denominator-Level Concept

Practical capacity measures the available supply of capacity. Managers can usually use engineering studies and human-resource considerations (such as worker safety) to obtain a reliable estimate of this denominator level for the budget period. It is more difficult to obtain reliable estimates of demand-side denominator-level concepts, especially longer-term normal capacity utilization figures. For example, many U.S. steel companies in the 1980s believed they were in the downturn of a demand cycle that would have an upturn within two or three years. After all, steel had been a cyclical business in which upturns followed downturns, making the notion of normal capacity utilization appear reasonable. Unfortunately, the steel cycle in the 1980s did not turn up resulting in some companies and numerous plants closing. The recent global economic slowdown demonstrated the extent to which demand projections could be inaccurate. Consider that in 2006, the forecast for the Indian automotive market was that annual demand for cars and passenger vehicles would hit 1.92 million in the year 2009–2010. In early 2009, the forecast for the same period was revised downward to 1.37 million vehicles. Even ignoring the vagaries of economic cycles, another problem is that marketing managers of firms are often prone to overestimate their ability to regain lost sales and market share. Their estimate of "normal" demand for their product may consequently reflect an overly optimistic outlook. Master-budget capacity utilization focuses only on the expected demand for the next year. Therefore, master-budget capacity utilization can be more reliably estimated than normal capacity utilization. However, it is still just a forecast, and the true demand realization can be either higher or lower than this estimate.

It is important to understand that costing systems, such as normal costing or standard costing, do not recognize uncertainty the way managers recognize it. A single amount, rather than a range of possible amounts, is used as the denominator level when calculating the budgeted fixed manufacturing cost per unit in absorption costing. Consider Stassen's facility, which has an estimated practical capacity of 12,000 units. The estimated master-budget capacity utilization for 2014 is 8,000 units. However, there is still substantial doubt about the actual number of units Stassen will have to manufacture in 2014 and in future years. Managers recognize uncertainty in their capacity-planning decisions. Stassen built its current plant with a 12,000 unit practical capacity in part to provide the capability to meet possible demand surges. Even if such surges do not occur in a given period, do not conclude that capacity unused in a given period is wasted resources. The gains from meeting sudden demand surges may well require having unused capacity in some periods.

Difficulties in Forecasting Fixed Manufacturing Costs

The fixed manufacturing cost rate is based on a numerator (budgeted fixed manufacturing costs) and a denominator (some measure of capacity or capacity utilization). Our discussion so far has emphasized issues concerning the choice of the denominator. Challenging issues also arise in measuring the numerator. For example, deregulation of the U.S. electric utility industry has resulted in many electric utilities becoming unprofitable. This situation has led to write-downs in the values of the utilities' plants and equipment. The write-downs reduce the numerator because there is less depreciation expense included in the calculation of fixed capacity cost per kilowatt-hour of electricity produced. The difficulty that managers face in this situation is that the amount of write-downs is not clear-cut but, rather, a matter of judgment. In several industries, the increased emphasis on sustainability and attention to the environment has led to unexpected increases in the fixed costs of operations. On the other hand, infrastructure costs for information technology have continued to plummet and have moved from fixed to variable costs in many cases because of the capabilities offered by providers such as Amazon Web Services.

Nonmanufacturing Costs

Capacity costs also arise in nonmanufacturing parts of the value chain. Stassen may acquire a fleet of vehicles capable of distributing the practical capacity of its production facility. When actual production is below practical capacity, there will be unused-capacity cost issues with the distribution function, as well as with the manufacturing function.

As you saw in Chapter 8, capacity cost issues are prominent in many service-sector companies, such as airlines, hospitals, and railroads—even though these companies carry no inventory and so have no inventory costing problems. For example, in calculating the fixed overhead cost per patient-day in its obstetrics and gynecology department, a hospital must decide which denominator level to use: practical capacity, normal capacity utilization, or master-budget capacity utilization. The hospital's decision may have implications for capacity management, as well as pricing and performance evaluation.

Activity-Based Costing

To maintain simplicity, the Stassen example in this chapter assumed that all costs were either variable or fixed. In particular, there were no batch-level costs and no product-sustaining costs. It is easy to see that the distinction between variable and absorption costing carries over directly into activity-based costing systems, with batch-level costs acting as variable costs and product-sustaining ones as fixed costs, as a function of the number of units produced.

In order to focus on the choice of denominator to calculate the budgeted fixed manufacturing cost rate, our Stassen example assumed that all fixed manufacturing costs had a single cost driver: telescope units produced. As you saw in Chapter 5, activity-based costing systems have multiple overhead cost pools at the output-unit, batch, product-sustaining, and facility-sustaining levels—each with its own cost driver. In calculating activity cost rates (for fixed costs of setups and material handling, say), management must choose a capacity level for the quantity of the cost driver (setup-hours or loads moved). Should management use practical capacity, normal capacity utilization, or master-budget capacity utilization? For all the reasons described in this chapter (such as pricing and capacity management), most proponents of activity-based costing argue that managers should use practical capacity as the denominator level to calculate activity cost rates.

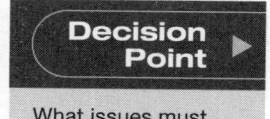

Decision Point ▶

What issues must managers take into account when planning capacity levels and for assigning capacity costs?

Problem for Self-Study

Assume Stassen Company on January 1, 2014, decides to contract with another company to preassemble a large percentage of the components of its telescopes. The revised manufacturing cost structure during the 2014–2015 period is as follows:

Variable manufacturing cost per unit produced	
Direct materials	₹2,500
Direct manufacturing labor	200
Manufacturing overhead	50
Total variable manufacturing cost per unit produced	₹2,750
Fixed manufacturing costs	₹48,00,000

Under the revised cost structure, a larger percentage of Stassen's manufacturing costs are variable with respect to units produced. The denominator level of production used to calculate budgeted fixed manufacturing cost per unit in 2014 and 2015 is 8,000 units. Assume no other change from the data underlying Exhibits 9-1 and 9-2. Summary information pertaining to absorption-costing operating income and variable-costing operating income with this revised cost structure is as follows:

	2014	2015
Absorption-costing operating income	₹1,50,00,000	₹1,56,00,000
Variable-costing operating income	1,38,00,000	1,65,00,000
Difference	₹12,00,000	₹(9,00,000)

1. Compute the budgeted fixed manufacturing cost per unit in 2014 and 2015.
2. Explain the difference between absorption-costing operating income and variable-costing operating income in 2014 and 2015, focusing on fixed manufacturing costs in beginning and ending inventory.
3. Why are these differences smaller than the differences in Exhibit 9-2?
4. Assume the same preceding information, except that for 2014, the master-budget capacity utilization is 10,000 units instead of 8,000. How would Stassen's absorption-costing income for 2014 differ from the ₹1,50,00,000 shown previously? Show your computations.

Solution

1. $$\text{Budgeted fixed manufacturing cost per unit} = \frac{\text{Budgeted fixed manufacturing costs}}{\text{Budgeted production units}}$$

$$= \frac{₹48,00,000}{8,000 \text{ units}}$$

$$= ₹600 \text{ per unit}$$

2. $$\begin{array}{c}\text{Absorption-costing} \\ \text{operating} \\ \text{income}\end{array} - \begin{array}{c}\text{Variable-costing} \\ \text{operating} \\ \text{income}\end{array} = \begin{array}{c}\text{Fixed manufacturing} \\ \text{costs in ending inventory} \\ \text{under absorption costing}\end{array} - \begin{array}{c}\text{Fixed manufacturing costs} \\ \text{in beginning inventory under} \\ \text{absorption costing}\end{array}$$

2014: ₹1,50,00,000 − ₹1,38,00,000 = (₹60 per unit × 20,000 units) − (₹6,000 per unit × 0 units)

₹12,00,000 = ₹12,00,000

2015: ₹1,56,00,000 − ₹1,65,00,000 = (₹600 per unit × 500 units) − (₹600 per unit × 2,000 units)

− ₹9,00,000 = − ₹9,00,000

3. Subcontracting a large part of manufacturing has greatly reduced the magnitude of fixed manufacturing costs. This reduction, in turn, means differences between absorption costing and variable costing are much smaller than in Exhibit 9-2.
4. Given the higher master-budget capacity utilization level of 10,000 units, the budgeted fixed manufacturing cost rate for 2014 is now as follows:

$$\frac{₹48,00,000}{10,000 \text{ units}} = ₹480 \text{ per unit}$$

The manufacturing cost per unit is ₹3,230 (₹2,750 + ₹480). So, the production-volume variance for 2014 is

(10,000 units − 8,000 units) × ₹480 per unit = ₹9,60,000 U

The absorption-costing income statement for 2014 is as follows:

Revenues: ₹10,000 per unit × 6,000 units	₹6,00,00,000
Cost of goods sold:	
Beginning inventory	0
Variable manufacturing costs: ₹2,750 per unit × 8,000 units	2,20,00,000
Fixed manufacturing costs: ₹480 per unit × 8,000 units	38,40,000
Cost of goods available for sale	2,58,40,000
Deduct ending inventory: ₹3,230 per unit × 2,000 units	(64,60,000)
Cost of goods sold (at standard costs)	1,93,80,000
Adjustment for production-volume variance	9,60,000 U
Cost of goods sold	20,34,000
Gross margin	2,03,40,000
Marketing costs: ₹1,38,00,000 fixed + (₹1,850 per unit × 6,000 units sold)	2,49,00,000
Operating income	₹1,47,60,000

The higher denominator level used to calculate the budgeted fixed manufacturing cost per unit means that fewer fixed manufacturing costs are inventoried (₹480 per unit × 2,000 units = ₹9,60,000) than when the master-budget capacity utilization was 8,000 units (₹600 per unit × 2,000 units = ₹12,00,000). This difference of ₹2,40,000 (₹12,00,000 – ₹9,60,000) results in operating income being lower by ₹2,40,000 relative to the prior calculated income level of ₹1,50,00,000.

Decision Points

The following question-and-answer format summarizes the chapter's learning objectives. Each decision presents a key question related to a learning objective. The guidelines are the answer to that question.

Decision	Guidelines
1. How does variable costing differ from absorption costing?	Variable costing and absorption costing differ in only one respect: how to account for fixed manufacturing costs. Under variable costing, fixed manufacturing costs are excluded from inventoriable costs and are a cost of the period in which they are incurred. Under absorption costing, fixed manufacturing costs are inventoriable and become a part of cost of goods sold in the period when sales occur.
2. How does income differ under variable and absorption costing?	The variable-costing income statement is based on the contribution-margin format. Under it, operating income is driven by the unit level of sales. Under absorption costing, the income statement follows the gross-margin format. Operating income is driven by the unit level of production, the unit level of sales, and the denominator level used for assigning fixed costs.
3. Why might managers build up finished goods inventory if they use absorption costing?	When absorption costing is used, managers can increase current operating income by producing more units for inventory. Producing for inventory absorbs more fixed manufacturing costs into inventory and reduces costs expensed in the period. Critics of absorption costing label this manipulation of income as the major negative consequence of treating fixed manufacturing costs as inventoriable costs.

4. How does throughput costing differ from variable costing and absorption costing?

Throughput costing treats all costs except direct materials as costs of the period in which they are incurred. Throughput costing results in a lower amount of manufacturing costs being inventoried than either variable or absorption costing.

5. What are the various capacity levels a company can use to compute the budgeted fixed manufacturing cost rate?

Capacity levels can be measured in terms of capacity supplied—theoretical capacity or practical capacity. Capacity can also be measured in terms of output demanded—normal capacity utilization or master-budget capacity utilization.

6. What are the major factors managers consider in choosing the capacity level to compute the budgeted fixed manufacturing cost rate?

The major factors managers consider in choosing the capacity level to compute the budgeted fixed manufacturing cost rate are (a) effect on product costing and capacity management, (b) effect on pricing decisions, (c) effect on performance evaluation, (d) effect on financial statements, (e) regulatory requirements.

7. What issues must managers take into account when planning capacity levels and for assigning capacity costs?

Critical factors when planning capacity levels and for assigning capacity costs include the uncertainty about the expected spending on capacity costs and the demand for the installed capacity; the role of capacity-related issues in nonmanufacturing areas; and the possible use of activity-based costing techniques in allocating capacity costs.

TERMS TO LEARN

This chapter and the Glossary at the end of the book contain definitions of the following important terms:

absorption costing **(p. 452)**

direct costing **(p. 452)**

downward demand spiral **(p. 470)**

master-budget capacity
   utilization **(p. 467)**

normal capacity
   utilization **(p. 467)**

practical capacity **(p. 467)**

super-variable
   costing **(p. 464)**

theoretical capacity **(p. 467)**

throughput
   costing **(p. 464)**

variable costing **(p. 452)**

ASSIGNMENT MATERIAL

Questions

9-1 Differences in operating income between variable costing and absorption costing are due solely to accounting for fixed costs. Do you agree? Explain.

9-2 Why is the term *direct costing* a misnomer?

9-3 Do companies in either the service sector or the merchandising sector make choices about absorption costing versus variable costing?

9-4 Explain the main conceptual issue under variable costing and absorption costing regarding the timing for the release of fixed manufacturing overhead as expense.

9-5 "Companies that make no variable-cost/fixed-cost distinctions must use absorption costing, and those that do make variable-cost/fixed-cost distinctions must use variable costing." Do you agree? Explain.

9-6 The main trouble with variable costing is that it ignores the increasing importance of fixed costs in manufacturing companies. Do you agree? Why?

9-7 Give an example of how, under absorption costing, operating income could fall even though the unit sales level rises.

9-8 What are the factors that affect the breakeven point under (a) variable costing and (b) absorption costing?

9-9 Critics of absorption costing have increasingly emphasized its potential for leading to undesirable incentives for managers. Give an example.

9-10 What are two ways of reducing the negative aspects associated with using absorption costing to evaluate the performance of a plant manager?

9-11 What denominator-level capacity concepts emphasize the output a plant can supply? What denominator-level capacity concepts emphasize the output customers demand for products produced by a plant?

9-12 Describe the downward demand spiral and its implications for pricing decisions.

9-13 Will the financial statements of a company always differ when different choices at the start of the accounting period are made regarding the denominator-level capacity concept?

9-14 What is the IRS's requirement for tax reporting regarding the choice of a denominator-level capacity concept?

9-15 "The difference between practical capacity and master-budget capacity utilization is the best measure of management's ability to balance the costs of having too much capacity and having too little capacity." Do you agree? Explain.

Solved Examples

9-16 Variable and absorption costing, explaining operating income differences. Saya Motors assembles and sells motor vehicles. Data relating to April and May of current year are:

	April	May
Unit data		
Beginning inventory	0	150
Production	500	400
Sales	350	520
Variable costs		
Manufacturing cost per unit produced	₹1,00,000	1,00,000
Operating cost per unit sold	30,000	30,000
Fixed costs		
Manufacturing costs	₹2,00,00,000	₹2,00,00,000
Operating costs	60,00,000	60,00,000

The selling price per motor vehicle (excluding government taxes) is ₹2,40,000.

Required

1. Present income statements for Saya Motors in April and May under (a) variable costing and (b) absorption costing.

2. Prepare a numerical reconciliation and explanation of the difference between operating income for each month under absorption costing and variable costing.

Solution

Variable and absorption costing, explaining operating income differences.

1. Key inputs for income statement computations are:

	April	May
Beginning inventory	0	150
Production	500	400
Goods available for sale	500	550
Units sold	350	520
Ending inventory	150	30

The fixed cost per unit and total manufacturing costs per unit under absorption costing are:

		April	May
(a)	Fixed manufacturing costs	₹2,00,00,000	₹2,00,00,000
(b)	Units produced	500	400
(c) = (a) ÷ (b)	Fixed manufacturing costs per unit	₹40,000	₹50,000
(d)	Variable manufacturing costs per unit	₹1,00,000	₹1,00,000
(e) = (c) + (d)	Total manufacturing costs per unit	₹1,40,000	₹1,50,000

(a) Variable costing

	April		May	
Revenues^a	₹8,40,00,000	₹12,48,00,000		
Variable costs:				
Beginning inventory	₹0		₹1,50,00,000	
Variable manufacturing costs^b	5,00,00,000		4,00,00,000	
Cost of goods available for sale	5,00,00,000		5,50,00,000	
Deduct ending inventory^c	1,50,00,000		30,00,000	
Variable cost of goods sold	3,50,00,000		5,20,00,000	
Variable operating costs^d	1,05,00,000		1,56,00,000	
Total variable costs		4,55,00,000	6,76,00,000	
Contribution margin		3,85,00,000	5,72,00,000	
Fixed costs				
Fixed manufacturing costs	2,00,00,000		2,00,00,000	
Fixed operating costs	60,00,000		60,00,000	
Total fixed costs		2,60,00,000		2,60,00,000
Operating income		₹1,25,00,000		₹3,12,00,000

^{a}₹2,40,000 × 350; ₹2,40,000 × 520 ^{c}₹1,00,000 × 150; ₹1,00,000 × 30
^{b}₹1,00,000 × 500; ₹1,00,000 × 400 ^{d}₹30,000 × 350; ₹30,000 × 520

(b) Absorption costing

	April		May	
Revenues^a		₹8,40,00,000		₹12,48,00,000
Cost of goods sold				
Beginning inventory	₹0		₹2,10,00,000	
Variable manufacturing costs^b	5,00,00,000		4,00,00,000	
Fixed manufacturing costs^c	2,00,00,000		2,00,00,000	
Cost of goods available for sale	7,00,00,000		8,10,00,000	
Deduct ending inventory^d	2,10,00,000		45,00,000	
Cost of goods sold		4,90,00,000		7,65,00,000
Gross margin		3,50,00,000		4,83,00,000
Operating costs				
Variable operating costs^e	1,05,00,000		1,56,00,000	
Fixed operating costs	60,00,000		60,00,000	
Total operating costs		1,65,00,000		2,16,00,000
Operating income		₹1,85,00,000		₹2,67,00,000

^{a}₹2,40,000 × 350; ₹2,40,000 × 520 ^{d}(₹1,40,000 × 150; ₹1,50,000 × 30)
^{b}₹1,00,000 × 500; ₹1,00,000 × 400 ^{e}(₹30,000 × 350; ₹30,000 × 520)
^{c}(₹40,000 × 500); (₹50,000 × 400)

$$\textbf{2.} \begin{pmatrix} \text{Absorption - costing} \\ \text{operating income} \end{pmatrix} - \begin{pmatrix} \text{Variable - costing} \\ \text{operating income} \end{pmatrix} = \begin{pmatrix} \text{Fixed manufacturing} \\ \text{costs in} \\ \text{ending inventory} \end{pmatrix} - \begin{pmatrix} \text{Fixed manufacturing} \\ \text{costs in} \\ \text{beginning inventory} \end{pmatrix}$$

April:

$$₹1,85,00,000 - ₹1,25,00,000 \quad = \quad (₹40,000 \times 150) - (₹0)$$
$$₹60,00,000 \quad = \quad ₹60,00,000$$

May:

$$₹2,67,00,000 - ₹3,12,00,000 \quad = \quad (₹50,000 \times 30) - (₹40,000 \times 150)$$
$$- ₹45,00,000 \quad = \quad ₹15,00,000 - ₹60,00,000$$
$$- ₹45,00,000 \quad = \quad - ₹45,00,000$$

The difference between absorption and variable costing is due solely to moving fixed manufacturing costs into inventories as inventories increase (as in April) and out of inventories as they decrease (as in May).

9-17 Throughput costing (continuation of 9-16). The variable manufacturing costs per unit of Saya Motors are

	April	May
Direct materials	₹67,000	₹67,000
Direct manufacturing labor	15,000	15,000
Manufacturing overhead	18,000	18,000

Required

1. Present income statements for Saya Motors in April and May under throughput costing.
2. Contrast the results in requirement 1 with those in requirement 1 of 9-16.
3. Give one motivation for Saya Motors to adopt throughput costing.

Solution

Throughput costing (continuation of 9-16).

1.	**April**		**May**
Revenues[a]	₹8,40,00,000		₹12,48,00,000
Direct material cost of goods sold			
Beginning inventory			
Direct materials in goods manufactured[b]	₹0	₹1,00,50,000	
	3,35,00,000	2,68,00,000	
Cost of goods available for sale	3,35,00,000	3,68,50,000	
Deduct ending inventory[c]	1,00,50,000	20,10,000	
Total direct material cost of goods sold	2,34,50,000		3,48,40,000
Throughput contribution	6,05,50,000		8,99,60,000
Other costs			
Manufacturing costs	3,65,00,000[d]	3,32,00,000[e]	
Other operating costs	1,65,00,000[f]	2,16,00,000[g]	
Total other costs	5,30,00,000		5,48,00,000
Operating income	₹75,50,000		₹3,51,60,000

[a]₹2,40,000 × 350; ₹2,40,000 × 520
[b]₹67,000 × 500; ₹67,000 × 400
[c]₹67,000 × 150; ₹67,000 × 30
[d](₹33,000 × 500) + ₹2,00,00,000

[e](₹33,000 × 400) + ₹2,00,00,000
[f](₹30,000 × 350) + ₹60,00,000
[g](₹30,000 × 520) + ₹60,00,000

2. Operating income under:

	April	May
Absorption costing	₹1,85,00,000	₹2,67,00,000
Variable costing	1,25,00,000	3,12,00,000
Throughput costing	75,50,000	3,51,60,000

In April, throughput costing has the lowest operating income, whereas in May throughput costing has the highest operating income. Throughput costing puts greater emphasis on sales as the source of operating income than does either absorption or variable costing.

9-18 Variable versus absorption costing. The Timex Company manufactures trendy, high-quality moderately priced watches. As Timex's senior financial analyst, you are asked to recommend a method of inventory costing. The CFO will use your recommendation to construct Timex's current year income statement. The following data are for the current year ended December 31:

Beginning inventory, January 1	85,000 units
Ending inventory, December 31	34,500 units
Current year sales	3,45,400 units
Selling price (to distributor)	₹200 per unit
Variable manufacturing cost per unit, including direct materials	₹51 per unit
Variable operating cost per unit sold	₹11 per unit
Fixed manufacturing overhead	₹1,44,00,000
Denominator-level machine-hours	6,000
Standard production rate	50 units per machine-hour
Fixed operating costs	₹1,08,00,000

Assume standard costs per unit are the same for units in beginning inventory and units produced during the year. Also, assume no price, spending, or efficiency variances.

Required

1. Prepare income statements under variable and absorption costing for the current year ended December 31.
2. What is Timex's operating income under each costing method (in percentage terms)?
3. Explain the difference in operating income between the two methods.
4. Which costing method would you recommend to the CFO? Why ?

Solution
Variable vs absorption costing.

　1.

Income Statement for Timex Company, Variable Costing
For the Current Year Ended December 31

Revenues: ₹220 × 3,45,400		₹7,59,88,000
Variable costs		
Beginning inventory: ₹51 × 85,000	₹43,35,000	
Variable manufacturing costs: ₹51 × 2,94,900	1,50,39,900	
Cost of goods available for sale	1,93,74,900	
Deduct ending inventory: ₹51 × 34,500	17,59,500	
Variable cost of goods sold	1,76,15,400	

Variable operating costs: ₹11 × 3,45,400	37,99,400	
Total variable costs (at standard costs)	2,14,14,800	
Adjustment for variances	0	
Total variable costs		2,14,14,800
Contribution margin		5,45,73,200
Fixed costs		
Fixed manufacturing overhead costs	1,44,00,000	
Fixed operating costs	1,08,00,000	
Adjustment for fixed cost variances	0	
Total fixed costs		2,52,00,000
Operating income		2,93,73,200

Absorption Costing Data

Fixed manufacturing overhead allocation rate =

Fixed manufacturing overhead/Denominator level machine-hours = ₹1,44,00,000/6,000

= ₹2,400 per machine-hour

Fixed manufacturing overhead allocation rate per unit =

Fixed manufacturing overhead allocation rate/standard production rate = ₹2,400/50

= ₹48 per unit

Income Statement for Timex Company, Absorption Costing

For the Year Ended December 31

Revenues: ₹220 × 3,45,400		₹7,59,88,000
Cost of goods sold		
Beginning inventory: (₹51 + ₹48) × 85,000	₹84,15,000	
Variable manufacturing costs: ₹51 × 2,94,900	1,50,39,900	
Fixed manufacturing costs: ₹48 × 2,94,900	1,41,55,200	
Cost of goods available for sale	₹3,76,10,100	
Deduct ending inventory: (₹51 + ₹48) × 34,500	(34,15,500)	
Adjust for manufacturing variances (₹48 × 5,100)[a]	2,44,800	
Cost of goods sold		3,44,39,400
Gross margin		4,15,48,600
Operating costs		
Variable operating costs: ₹110 × 345,400	₹37,99,400	
Fixed operating costs	1,08,00,000	
Adjust for operating cost variances	0	
Total operating costs		1,45,99,400
Operating income		₹2,69,49,200

[a]Production volume variance

= [(6,000 hours × 50) – 2,94,900) × ₹48

= (3,00,000 – 2,94,900) × ₹48

= ₹2,44,800

2. Timex's pre-tax profit margins Under variable costing:

Revenues	₹7,59,88,000
Operating income	2,93,73,200
Pre-tax profit margin	38.7%
Under absorption costing:	
Revenues	₹7,59,88,000
Operating income	2,69,49,200
Pre-tax profit margin	35.5%

3. Operating income using variable costing is about 9% higher than operating income calculated using absorption costing.

Variable costing operating income − Absorption costing operating income
$$= ₹2,93,73,200 - ₹2,69,49,200 = ₹24,24,000$$

Fixed manufacturing costs in beginning inventory under absorption costing − Fixed manufacturing costs in ending inventory under absorption costing
$$= (₹48 \times 85,000) - (₹48 \times 34,500) = ₹24,24,000$$

4. The factors the CFO should consider include:
   a. Effect on managerial behavior, and
   b. Effect on external users of financial statements.

   Absorption costing has many critics. However, the dysfunctional aspects associated with absorption costing can be reduced by:
   - Careful budgeting and inventory planning,
   - Adding a capital charge to reduce the incentives to build up inventory, and
   - Monitoring nonfinancial performance measures.

9-19 Absorption versus variable costing. Bajaj Electricals manufacturers a professional-grade vacuum cleaner and began operations in 2015. For 2015, Bajaj budgeted to produce and sell 20,000 units. The company had no price, spending, or efficiency variances and writes off production-volume variance to cost of goods sold. Actual data for 2015 are given as follows:

	A	B
	Home Insert Page Layout Formulas Data	
1	Units produced	18,000
2	Units sold	17,500
3	Selling price	₹4,500
4	Variable costs:	
5	Manufacturing cost per unit produced	
6	Direct materials	₹ 300
7	Direct manufacturing labor	250
8	Manufacturing overhead	600
9	Marketing cost per unit sold	450
10	Fixed costs:	
11	Manufacturing costs	₹1,20,00,000
12	Administrative costs	96,54,500
13	Marketing	1,36,64,000

Required

1. Prepare a 2015 income statement for Bajaj Electricals using variable costing.
2. Prepare a 2015 income statement for Bajaj Electricals using absorption costing.

3. Explain the differences in operating incomes obtained in requirements 1 and 2.
4. Company's management is considering implementing a bonus for the supervisors based on gross margin under absorption costing. What incentives will this bonus plan create for the supervisors? What modifications could Company management make to improve such a plan? Explain briefly.

Solution

1. The variable manufacturing cost per unit is ₹300 + ₹250 + ₹600 = ₹1,150.

2015 Variable-Costing Based Income Statement

Revenues (17,500 × ₹4,500 per unit)		₹7,87,50,000
Variable costs		
Beginning inventory	₹0	
Variable manufacturing costs (18,000 units × ₹1,150 per unit)	2,07,00,000	
Cost of goods available for sale	2,07,00,000	
Deduct: Ending inventory (500 units × ₹1,150 per unit)	(5,75,000)	
Variable cost of goods sold	2,01,25,000	
Variable marketing costs (17,500 units × ₹450 per unit)	78,75,000	
Total variable costs		2,80,00,000
Contribution margin		5,07,55,000
Fixed costs		
Fixed manufacturing costs	1,20,00,000	
Fixed administrative costs	96,54,500	
Fixed marketing	1,36,64,000	
Total fixed costs		3,53,18,500
Operating income		₹1,54,31,500

2. Fixed manufacturing overhead rate = ₹1,20,00,000 / 20,000 units = ₹600 per unit

2015 Absorption-Costing Based Income Statement

Revenues (17,500 units × ₹4,500 per unit)		₹7,87,55,000
Cost of goods sold		
Beginning inventory	₹0	
Variable manufacturing costs (18,000 units × ₹1,150 per unit)	2,07,00,000	
Allocated fixed manufacturing costs (18,000 units × ₹600 per unit)	1,08,00,000	
Cost of goods available for sale	3,15,00,000	
Deduct ending inventory [500 units × (₹1,150 + ₹600) per unit]	(8,75,000)	
Add unfavorable production volume variance	12,00,000[a] U	
Cost of goods sold		3,18,25,000
Gross margin		4,69,25,000
Operating costs		

Variable marketing costs (17,500 units × ₹450 per unit)	78,75,000
Fixed administrative costs	96,54,500
Fixed marketing	1,36,64,000
Total operating costs	3,11,93,500
Operating income	₹1,57,31,500

[a] PVV = ₹1,20,00,000 budgeted fixed mfg. costs – ₹1,08,00,000 allocated fixed mfg. costs = ₹12,00,000 U

3. 2015 operating income under absorption costing is greater than the operating income under variable costing because in 2015 inventory increased by 500 units. As a result, under absorption costing, a portion of the fixed overhead remained in the ending inventory and led to a lower cost of goods sold (relative to variable costing). As shown below, the difference in the two operating incomes is exactly the same as the difference in the fixed manufacturing costs included in ending versus beginning inventory (under absorption costing).

Operating income under absorption costing	₹1,57,31,500
Operating income under variable costing	1,54,31,500
Difference in operating income under absorption versus variable costing	₹3,00,000
Under absorption costing:	
Fixed mfg. costs in ending inventory (500 units × ₹600 per unit)	₹3,00,000
Fixed mfg. costs in beginning inventory (0 units × ₹600 per unit)	0
Change in fixed mfg. costs between ending and beginning inventory	₹3,00,000

4. Relative to the alternative of using contribution margin (from variable costing), the absorption-costing based gross margin has some pros and cons as a performance measure for Bajaj's supervisors. It takes into account both variable costs and fixed costs—costs that the supervisors should be able to control in the long run—and therefore is a more complete measure than contribution margin, which ignores fixed costs (and may cause the supervisors to pay less attention to fixed costs). The downside of using absorption-costing-based gross margin is the supervisor's temptation to use inventory levels to control the gross margin—in particular, to shore up a sagging gross margin by building up inventories. This can be offset by specifying, or limiting, the inventory build-up that can occur, charging the supervisor a carrying cost for holding inventory, and using nonfinancial performance measures such as the ratio of ending to beginning inventory.

9-20 Variable and absorption costing, sales, and operating-income changes. Smart Safety, a three- year-old company, has been producing and selling a single type of bicycle helmet. Smart Safety uses standard costing. After reviewing the income statements for the first three years, Mr Prateek, president of Smart Safety, commented, "I was told by our accountants—and in fact, I have memorized—that our breakeven volume is 52,000 units. I was happy that we reached that sales goal in each of our first two years. But here's the strange thing: In our first year, we sold 52,000 units and indeed we broke even. Then in our second year we sold the same volume and had a positive operating income. I didn't complain, of course. . . but here's the bad part. In our third year, we *sold 20% more* helmets, but our *operating income fell by more than 80%* relative to the second year! We didn't change our selling price or cost structure over the past three years and have no price, efficiency, or spending variances. . . so what's going on?!"

	A	B	C	D
		Home Insert Page Layout Formulas Data Review View		
	A	B	C	D
1	**Absorption Costing**			
2		**2013**	**2014**	**2015**
3	Sales (units)	52,000	52,000	62,400
4	Revenues	₹2,23,60,000	₹2,23,60,000	₹2,68,32,000
5	Cost of goods sold			
6	Beginning inventory	0	0	40,56,000
7	Production	2,02,80,000	2,43,36,000	2,02,80,000
8	Available for sale	2,02,80,000	2,43,36,000	2,43,36,000
9	Deduct ending inventory	0	(40,56,000)	0
10	Adjustment for production-volume variance	0	(26,06,000)	0
11	Cost of goods sold	2,02,80,000	1,76,80,000	2,43,36,000
12	Gross margin	20,80,000	46,86,000	24,96,000
13	Selling and administrative expenses (all fixed)	2080,000	20,80,000	20,80,000
14	Operating income	₹ 0	₹ 26,00,000	₹ 4,16,000
15				
16	Beginning inventory	0	0	10,400
17	Production (units)	52,000	62,400	52,000
18	Sales (units)	52,000	52,000	62,400
19	Ending inventory	0	10,400	0
20	Variable manufacturing cost per unit	₹140	₹140	₹ 140
21	Fixed manufacturing overhead costs	₹1,30,00,000	₹1,30,00,000	₹1,30,00,000
22	Fixed manuf. costs allocated per unit produced	₹ 250	₹250	₹250

Required

1. What denominator level is Smart Safety using to allocate fixed manufacturing costs to the bicycle helmets? How is Smart Safety disposing of any favorable or unfavorable production-volume variance at the end of the year? Explain your answer briefly.

2. How did Smart Safety's accountants arrive at the breakeven volume of 52,000 units?

3. Prepare a variable costing-based income statement for each year. Explain the variation in variable costing operating income for each year based on contribution margin per unit and sales volume.

4. Reconcile the operating incomes under variable costing and absorption costing for each year, and use this information to explain to the president the positive operating income in 2014 and the drop in operating income in 2015.

Solution

1. Smart Safety's annual fixed manufacturing costs are ₹1,30,00,000. It allocates ₹250 of fixed manufacturing costs to each unit produced. Therefore, it must be using ₹1,30,00,000 ÷ ₹250 = 52,000 units (annually) as the denominator level to allocate fixed manufacturing costs to the units produced.

We can see from Smart Safety's income statements that it disposes of any production volume variance against cost of goods sold. In 2014, 62,400 units were produced instead of the budgeted 52,000 units. This resulted in a favorable production volume variance of ₹26,00,000 F [(62,400 − 52,000) units × ₹250 per unit], which, when written off against cost of goods sold, increased gross margin by that amount.

2. The breakeven calculation, same for each year, is shown below:

Calculation of breakeven volume	2013	2014	2015
Selling price (₹2,23,60,000 ÷ 52,000; ₹2,23,60,000 ÷ 59,000; ₹2,68,30,000 ÷ 62,400)	₹430	₹430	₹430
Variable cost per unit (all manufacturing)	140	140	140
Contribution margin per unit	₹290	₹290	₹290
Total fixed costs (fixed mfg. costs + fixed selling & admin. costs)	₹1,50,80,000	₹1,50,80,000	₹1,50,80,000
Breakeven quantity = Total fixed costs ÷ contribution margin per unit	52,000	52,000	52,000

3.

Variable Costing

	2013	2014	2015
Sales (units)	52,000	52,000	62,400
Revenues	₹2,23,60,000	₹2,23,60,000	₹2,68,30,000
Variable cost of goods sold			
Beginning inventory ₹140 × 0; 0; 10,400	0	0	14,56,000
Variable manuf. costs ₹140 × 52,000; 62,400; 52,000	72,80,000	87,36,000	72,80,000
Deduct ending inventory ₹140 × 0; 10,400; 0	0	(14,56,000)	0
Variable cost of goods sold	72,80,000	72,80,000	87,36,000
Contribution margin	₹1,50,80,000	₹1,50,80,000	₹1,80,96,000
Fixed manufacturing costs	₹1,30,00,000	₹1,30,00,000	₹1,30,00,000
Fixed selling and administrative expenses	20,80,000	20,80,000	20,80,000
Operating income	₹0	₹0	₹30,16,000

Explaining variable costing operating income			
Contribution margin (₹260 contribution margin per unit × sales units)	₹1,50,80,000	₹1,50,80,000	₹1,80,96,000
Total fixed costs	1,50,80,000	1,50,80,000	1,50,80,000
Operating income	₹0	₹0	₹30,16,000

4.

Reconciliation of absorption/variable costing operating incomes	2013	2014	2015
(1) Absorption costing operating income	₹0	₹26,00,000	₹4,16,000
(2) Variable costing operating income	0	0	30,16,000

(3) Difference in operating incomes = (1) – (2)	₹0	₹26,00,000	₹(26,00,000)
(4) Fixed mfg. costs in ending inventory under absorption costing (ending inventory in units × ₹250 per unit)	₹0	₹26,00,000	₹0
(5) Fixed mfg. costs in beginning inventory under absorption costing (beginning inventory in units × ₹250 per unit)	0	0	26,00,000
(6) Difference = (4) – (5)	₹0	₹26,00,000	₹(26,00,000)

In the table above, row (3) shows the difference between the operating income under absorption costing and the operating income under variable costing, for each of the three years. In 2013, the difference is ₹0; in 2014, absorption costing income is greater by ₹26,00,000; and in 2015, it is less by ₹26,00,000. Row (6) above shows the difference between the fixed costs in ending inventory and the fixed costs in beginning inventory under absorption costing; this figure is ₹0 in 2013, ₹26,00,000 in 2014, and – ₹26,00,000 in 2015. Row (3) and row (6) explain and reconcile the operating income differences between absorption costing and variable costing.

The President is surprised at the non-zero, positive net income (reported under absorption costing) in 2014, when sales were at the 'breakeven volume' of 52,000; further, he is concerned about the drop in operating income in 2015, when, in fact, sales increased to 62,400 units. In 2014, starting with zero inventories, 62,400 units were produced and 52,000 were sold, i.e., at the end of the year, 10,400 units remained in inventory. These 10,400 units had each absorbed ₹250 of fixed costs (total of ₹26,00,000), which would remain as assets on Smart Safety's balance sheet until they were sold. Cost of goods sold, representing only the costs of the 52,000 units sold in 2014, was accordingly reduced by ₹26,00,000, the production volume variance, resulting in a positive operating income even though sales were at breakeven levels. The following year, in 2015, production was 52,000 units, sales were 62,400 units, i.e., all of the fixed costs that were included in 2014 ending inventory flowed through COGS in 2015. Contribution margin in 2015 was ₹1,80,96,000 (62,400 units × ₹290), but in absorption costing, COGS also contains the allocated fixed manufacturing costs of the units sold, which were ₹1,56,00,000 (62,400 units × ₹250), resulting in an operating income of ₹4,16,000 = ₹1,80,96,000 – ₹1,56,00,000 – ₹20,80,000 (fixed sales and admin.) Hence the drop in operating income under absorption costing, even though sales were greater than the computed breakeven volume: inventory levels decreased sufficiently in 2015 to cause 2015's operating income to be lower than 2014 operating income.

Note that beginning and ending with zero inventories during the 2013–2015 period, under both costing methods, Smart Safety's total operating income was ₹30,16,000.

9-21 Capacity management, denominator-level capacity concepts. Match each of the following numbered descriptions with one or more of the denominator-level capacity concepts by putting the appropriate letter(s) by each item:

a. Theoretical capacity

b. Practical capacity

c. Normal capacity utilization

d. Master-budget capacity utilization

1. Measures the denominator level in terms of what a plant can supply

2. Is based on producing at full efficiency all the time

3. Represents the expected level of capacity utilization for the next budget period

4. Measures the denominator level in terms of demand for the output of the plant

5. Takes into account seasonal, cyclical, and trend factors

6. Should be used for performance evaluation in the current year

7. Represents an ideal benchmark

8. Highlights the cost of capacity acquired but not used
9. Should be used for long-term pricing purposes
10. Hides the cost of capacity acquired but not used
11. If used as the denominator-level concept, would avoid the restatement of unit costs when expected demand levels change

Solution

1. a, b
2. a
3. d
4. c, d
5. c
6. d
7. a
8. b (or a)
9. b
10. c, d
11. a, b

9-22 Effects of differing production levels on absorption costing income: Metrics to minimize inventory buildups. Pearson Press produces textbooks for college courses. The company recently hired a new editor, Neeraj, to handle production and sales of books for an introduction to accounting course. Neeraj's compensation depends on the gross margin associated with sales of this book. Neeraj needs to decide how many copies of the book to produce. The following information is available for the fall semester 2014:

Estimated sales	26,000	books
Beginning inventory	0	
Average selling price	₹810	per books
Variable production costs	₹450	per books
Fixed production costs	₹41,60,000	per semester

The fixed cost allocation rate is based on expected sales and is therefore equal to ₹41,60,000/26,000 books = ₹160 per book

Neeraj has decided to produce either 26,000, 32,500, or 33,800 books.

Required

1. Calculate expected gross margin if Neeraj produces 26,000, 32,500, or 33,800 books. (Make sure you include the production-volume variance as part of cost of goods sold.)
2. Calculate ending inventory in units and in rupees for each production level.
3. Managers who are paid a bonus that is a function of gross margin may be inspired to produce a product in excess of demand to maximize their own bonus. The chapter suggested metrics to discourage managers from producing products in excess of demand. Do you think the following metrics will accomplish this objective? Show your work.

   a. Incorporate a charge of 5% of the cost of the ending inventory as an expense for evaluating the manager.
   b. Include nonfinancial measures when evaluating management and rewarding performance.

Solution

1.

	26,000 Books	32,500 Books	33,800 Books
Revenues	₹2,10,60,000	₹2,10,60,000	₹2,10,60,000
Cost of goods sold	1,58,60,000[a]	1,58,60,000	1,58,60,000

Production-volume variance	0[b]	(10,40,000)[c]	(12,48,000)[d]
Net cost of goods sold	1,58,60,000	1,48,20,000	1,46,12,000
Gross Margin	₹52,00,000	₹62,40,000	₹64,48,000

[a] Cost per unit = (₹450 + ₹41,60,000/26,000 books sold) = ₹610 per book
   CGS = ₹610 ₹26,000 = ₹1,58,60,000

[b] volume variance = Budgeted fixed cost − fixed overhead rate × production
   ₹41,60,000 − (₹160 × 26,000 books) = ₹0

[c] volume variance = Budgeted fixed cost − fixed overhead rate × production
   ₹41,60,000 − (₹160 × 32,500 books) = − ₹10,40,000

[d] volume variance = Budgeted fixed cost − fixed overhead rate × production
   ₹41,60,000 − (₹160 × 33,800 books) = − ₹12,48,000

2.

	26,000 Books	32,500 Books	33,800 Books
Beginning inventory	0	0	0
+ Production	26,000 books	32,500 books	33,800 books
	26,000	32,500	33,800
− Books sold	26,000	26,000	26,000
Ending inventory	0 books	6,500 books	7,800 books
×Cost per book	×₹610	×₹610	×₹610
Cost of Ending Inventory	₹0	₹39,65,000	₹47,58,000

3a.

	26,000 Books	32,500 Books	33,800 Books
Gross margin	₹52,00,000	₹62,40,000	₹64,48,000
Less 10% × Ending inventory	0	(1,98,250)	(2,37,900)
Adjusted gross margin	₹52,00,000	₹60,41,750	₹62,10,100

While adjusting for ending inventory does to some degree mitigate the increase in inventory associated with excess production, it may be difficult to mechanically compensate for all of the increased income. In addition, it does nothing to hold the manager responsible for the poor decisions from the organization's standpoint.

3b.

	26,000 Books	32,500 Books	33,800 Books
1) Inventory change: End inventory − begin inventory	0		7,800 books
2) Excess production (%) Production ÷ sales	26,000 ÷ 26,000	32,500 ÷ 26,000	33,800 ÷ 26,000
	1.0	1.25	1.3

- A ratio of ending inventory to beginning inventory, as suggested in the book, is not possible because beginning inventory was zero, so we substituted change in inventory level.

For these nonfinancial measures to be useful they must be incorporated into the reward function of the manager.

9-23 Alternative denominator-level capacity concepts, effect on operating income. Castle Lager has just purchased the New Brewery. The brewery is two years old and uses absorption costing. It will "sell" its product to Castle Lager at ₹470 per barrel. Shaw, Castle Lager's controller, obtains the following information about New Brewery's capacity and budgeted fixed manufacturing costs for 2015:

	Home	Insert	Page Layout	Formulas	Data	Review	View	
	A		B		C	D	E	
1			**Budgeted Fixed**		**Days of**	**Hours of**		
2	**Denominator-Level**		**Manufacturing**		**Production**	**Production**	**Barrels**	
3	**Capacity Concept**		**Overhead per Period**		**per Period**	**per Day**	**per Hour**	
4	Theoretical capacity		₹ 27,90,00,000		358	22	545	
5	Practical capacity		₹ 27,90,00,000		348	20	510	
6	Normal capacity utilization		₹ 27,90,00,000		348	20	410	
7	Master-budget capacity for each half year							
8	(a) January–June 2015		₹ 13,95,00,000		174	20	315	
9	(b) July–December 2015		₹ 13,95,00,000		174	20	505	

Required

1. Compute the budgeted fixed manufacturing overhead rate per barrel for each of the denominator-level capacity concepts. Explain why they are different.

2. In 2015, the New Brewery reported these production results:

	Home	Insert	Page Layout	Formulas	Data	
	A			B		
12	Beginning inventory in barrels, 1-1-2015			0		
13	Production in barrels			26,70,000		
14	Ending inventory in barrels, 12-31-2015			2,10,000		
15	Actual variable manufacturing costs			₹ 80,63,40,000		
16	Actual fixed manufacturing overhead costs			₹ 26,70,00,000		

There are no variable cost variances. Fixed manufacturing overhead cost variances are written off to cost of goods sold in the period in which they occur. Compute the Jacksonville Brewery's operating income when the denominator-level capacity is (a) theoretical capacity, (b) practical capacity, and (c) normal capacity utilization.

Solution

1.

Denominator-Level Capacity Concept	Budgeted Fixed Manuf. Overhead per Period (1)	Days of Production per Period (2)	Hours of Production per Day (3)	Barrels per Hour (4)	Budgeted Denominator Level (Barrels) (5) = (2) × (3) × (4)	Manufacturing Overhead Rate per Barrel (6) = (1) ÷ (5)
Theoretical capacity	₹27,90,00,000	358	22	545	42,92,420	₹65
Practical capacity	27,90,00,000	348	20	510	35,49,600	78.60
Normal capacity utilization	27,90,00,000	348	20	410	28,53,600	97.80
Master-budget utilization						
(a) January–June 2015	13,95,00,000	174	20	315	10,96,200	127.30
(b) July–December 2015	13,95,00,000	174	20	505	17,57,400	79.40

The differences arise for several reasons:

a. The theoretical and practical capacity concepts emphasize supply factors and are consequently higher, while normal capacity utilization and master-budget utilization emphasize demand factors.

b. The two separate six-month rates for the master-budget utilization concept differ because of seasonal differences in budgeted production.

2. Using column (6) from above,

Per Barrel

Denominator-Level Capacity Concept	Budgeted Fixed Mfg. Overhead Rate per Barrel	Budgeted Variable Mfg. Cost Rate	Budgeted Total Mfg Cost Rate	Fixed Mfg. Overhead Costs Allocated	Fixed Mfg. Overhead Variance
	(6)	(7)	(8) = (6) + (7)	(9) = 26,70,000 × (6)	(10) = ₹26,70,00,000 – (9)
Theoretical capacity	₹65	₹302[a]	₹367	₹17,35,50,000	₹9,34,50,000
Practical capacity	78.60	302	380.6	20,98,62,000	5,71, 38,000 U
Normal capacity utilization	97.80	302	399.8	26,11,26,000	58,74,000 U

[a] ₹80,63,40,000 ÷ 26,70,000 barrels

Absorption-Costing Income Statement

	Theoretical Capacity	Practical Capacity	Normal Capacity Utilization
Revenues (24,60,000 bbls. × ₹470 per bbl.)	₹1,15,62,00,000	₹1,15,62,00,000	₹1,15,62,00,000
Cost of goods sold			
Beginning inventory	0	0	0
Variable mfg. costs	80,63,40,000	80,63,40,000	80,63,40,000
Fixed mfg. overhead costs allocated (26,70,000 units × ₹65; ₹78.6; ₹97.8 per unit)	17,35,50,000	20,98,62,000	26,11,26,000
Cost of goods available for sale	97,98,90,000	1,01,62,02,000	1,06,74,66,000
Deduct ending inventory (2,10,000 units × ₹367; ₹380.6; ₹399.8 per unit)	(7,70,70,000)	(7,99,26,000)	(8,39,58,000)
Adjustment for variances (add: all unfavorable)	9,34,50,000 U	5,71,38,000 U	58,74,000 U
Cost of goods sold	99,62,70,000	99,34,14,000	98,93,82,000
Gross margin	15,99,30,000	16,27,86,000	16,68,18,000
Other costs	0	0	0
Operating income	₹15,99,30,000	₹16,27,86,000	₹16,68,18,000

9-24 Denominator-level choices, changes in inventory levels, effect on operating income. Arhant Corporation is a manufacturer of computer accessories. It uses absorption costing based on standard costs and reports the following data for 2015:

	A	B	C
	Home Insert Page Layout Formulas Data Review		
1	Theoretical capacity	2,75,000	unit
2	Practical capacity	2,65,000	unit
3	Normal capacity utilization	2,33,200	unit
4	Selling price	₹390	Per unit
5	Beginning inventory	35,000	unit
6	Production	2,35,000	unit
7	Sales volume	2,50,000	unit
8	Variable budgeted manufacturing cost	₹80	Per unit
9	Total budgeted fixed manufacturing costs	₹2,91,50,000	
10	Total budgeted operating (nonmanuf.) costs (all fixed)	₹20,00,000	

There are no price, spending, or efficiency variances. Actual operating costs equal budgeted operating costs. The production-volume variance is written off to cost of goods sold. For each choice of denominator level, the budgeted production cost per unit is also the cost per unit of beginning inventory.

Required

1. What is the production-volume variance in 2015 when the denominator level is (a) theoretical capacity, (b) practical capacity, and (c) normal capacity utilization?
2. Prepare absorption costing–based income statements for Arhant Corporation using theoretical capacity, practical capacity, and normal capacity utilization as the denominator levels.
3. Why is the operating income under normal capacity utilization lower than the other two scenarios?
4. Reconcile the difference in operating income based on theoretical capacity and practical capacity with the difference in fixed manufacturing overhead included in inventory.

Solution

1.

	Theoretical Capacity	Practical Capacity	Normal Capacity Utilization
Denominator level in units	2,75,000	2,65,000	2,33,200
Budgeted fixed manuf. costs	₹2,91,50,000	₹2,91,50,000	₹2,91,50,000
Budgeted fixed manuf. cost allocated per unit	₹106	₹110	₹125
Production in units	2,35,000	2,35,000	2,35,000
Allocated fixed manuf. costs (production in units × budgeted fixed manuf. cost allocated per unit)	₹2,49,10,000	₹2,58,50,000	₹2,93,75,000
Production volume variance (budgeted fixed manuf. costs – allocated fixed manuf. costs)[a]	₹42,40,000 U	₹33,00,000 U	₹2,25,000 F

[a]PVV is unfavorable if budgeted fixed manuf. costs are greater than allocated fixed costs

2.

	Theoretical Capacity	Practical Capacity	Normal Capacity Utilization
Units produced	2,35,000	2,35,000	2,35,000
Budgeted fixed mfg. cost allocated per unit	₹106	₹110	₹125
Budgeted var. mfg. cost per unit	₹50	₹50	₹50
Budgeted cost per unit of inventory or production	₹156	₹165	₹175
Absorption-Costing Based Income Statements			
Revenues (₹390 selling price per unit × units sold)	₹9,75,00,000	₹9,75,00,000	₹9,75,00,000
Cost of goods sold			
Beginning inventory (35,000 units × budgeted cost per unit of inventory)	65,10,000	66,50,000	71,75,000
Variable manufacturing costs (2,35,000 units × ₹80 per unit)	1,88,00,000	1,88,00,000	1,88,00,000
Allocated fixed manufacturing overhead (2,35,000 units × budgeted fixed mfg. cost allocated per unit)	2,49,10,000	2,58,50,000	2,93,70,000
Cost of goods available for sale	5,02,20,000	5,13,00,000	5,53,50,000
Deduct ending inventory (20,000[b] units × budgeted cost per unit of inventory)	(37,20,000)	(38,00,000)	(41,00,000)
Adjustment for production-volume variance	42,40,000	33,00,000	(2,25,000)
Total cost of goods sold	5,07,40,000	5,08,00,000	5,10,25,000
Gross margin	4,67,60,000	4,67,00,000	4,64,75,000
Operating costs	20,00,000	20,00,000	20,00,000
Operating income	₹4,47,60,000	₹4,47,00,000	₹4,44,75,000

[b]Ending inventory = Beginning inventory + production – sales = 35,000 + 2,35,000 – 2,50,000
= 20,000 units
20,000 × ₹186; 20,000 × ₹190; 20,000 × ₹205

3. Arhant's 2015 beginning inventory was 35,000 units; its ending inventory was 20,000 units. So, during 2015, there was a drop of 15,000 units in inventory levels (matching the 15,000 more units sold than produced). The smaller the denominator level, the larger is the budgeted fixed cost allocated to each unit of production, and when those units are sold (all the current production is sold, and then some), the larger is the cost of each unit sold, and the smaller is the operating income. Normal capacity utilization is the smallest capacity of the three; hence, in this year, when production was less than sales, the absorption-costing based operating income is the smallest when normal capacity utilization is used as the denominator level.

4.

Reconciliation

Theoretical Capacity Operating Income— Practical Capacity Operating Income	₹60,000
Decrease in inventory level during 2015	15,000
Fixed mfg cost allocated per unit under practical capacity—fixed mfg. cost allocated per unit under theoretical capacity (₹110 – ₹106)	₹4
Additional allocated fixed cost included in COGS under practical capacity = 15,000 units × ₹4 per unit =	₹60,000

More fixed manufacturing costs are included in inventory under practical capacity, so when inventory level decreases (as it did in 2015), more fixed manufacturing costs are included in COGS under practical capacity than under theoretical capacity, resulting in a lower operating income.

9-25 ABC and capacity usage. The controller of Dabur Ltd. has collected the following data for two activities. Harris calculates activity cost rates based on cost driver capacity.

Activity	Cost Driver	Capacity	Cost
Power	Kilowatt hours	50,000 kilowatt hours	₹20,00,000
Quality inspection	Number of inspections	10,000 inspections	30,00,000

The company makes two products: Hajmola and Ambla oil. For the year just ended, the following consumption of cost drivers was reported:

Product	Kilowatt hour	Quality Inspections
Hajmola	10,000	5,000
Amla oil	35,000	4,000

Required

1. Compute the costs allocated to each product from each activity.
2. Calculate the cost of unused capacity for each activity.

Solution

ABC and capacity usage.

1. Activity   Rate per Unit of Cost Driver

Power   ₹20,00,000 activity costs 4 50,000 kilowatt hours = ₹40 per kilowatt hour

Quality inspection   ₹30,00,000 activity costs 4 10,000 inspections = ₹300 per inspection

Cost allocation:
Power

Hajmola (10,000 kilowatt hours × ₹40)	₹4,00,000
Amla oil (35,000 kilowatt hours × ₹40)	14,00,000
Total power costs allocation	₹18,00,000

Quality inspection

Hajmola (5,000 inspections × ₹300)		₹15,00,000
Amla oil (4,000 inspections × ₹300)		12,00,000
Total quality inspection costs allocation		₹27,00,000

2. Cost of unused capacity:

Power (₹20,00,000 – ₹18,00,000)		₹2,00,000
Quality inspection (₹30,00,000 – ₹27,00,000)		3,00,000
Total cost of unused capacity		₹5,00,000

9-26 Variable and absorption costing and breakeven points Whistler, Ltd., manufactures a specialized snowboard made for the advanced snowboarder. Whistler began 2014 with an inventory of 240 snowboards. During the year, it produced 900 boards and sold 995 for ₹7,500 each. Fixed production costs were ₹28,00,000, and variable production costs were ₹3,250 per unit. Fixed advertising, marketing, and other general and administrative expenses were ₹11,20,000, and variable transportation costs were ₹150 per board. Assume that the cost of each unit in beginning inventory is equal to 2014 inventory cost.

1. Prepare an income statement assuming Whistler uses variable costing.   **Required**
2. Prepare an income statement assuming Whistler uses absorption costing. Whistler uses a denominator level of 1,000 units. Production-volume variances are written off to cost of goods sold.
3. Compute the breakeven point in units sold assuming Whistler uses the following:
   a. Variable costing   **b.** Absorption costing (Production = 900 boards)
4. Provide proof of your preceding breakeven calculations.
5. Assume that ₹2,00,000 of fixed administrative costs were reclassified as fixed production costs. Would this reclassification affect breakeven point using variable costing? What if absorption costing were used? Explain.
6. The company that supplies Whistler with its specialized impact-resistant material has announced a price increase of ₹300 for each board. What effect would this have on the breakeven points previously calculated?

Solution

1.

2014 Variable-Costing Based Operating Income Statement

Revenues (995 boards × ₹7,500 per board)		₹74,62,500
Variable costs		
Beginning inventory (240 boards × ₹3,250 per board)	₹7,80,000	
Variable manufacturing costs (900 boards × ₹3,250 per board)	29,25,000	
Cost of goods available for sale	37,05,000	
Deduct: Ending inventory (145 boards × ₹3,250 per board)	(4,71,250)	
Variable cost of goods sold	32,33,750	
Variable transportation costs (995 boards × ₹150 per board)	1,49,250	
Total variable costs		33,83,000
Contribution margin		40,79,500
Fixed costs		
Fixed manufacturing costs	28,00,000	
Fixed selling and administrative	11,20,000	
Total fixed costs		39,20,000
Operating income		₹1,59,500

2.

2014 Absorption-Costing Based Operating Income Statement

Revenues (995 boards × ₹7,500 per board)		₹74,62,500
Cost of goods sold		
Beginning inventory (240 boards × ₹6,050[a] per board)	₹14,52,000	
Variable manufacturing costs (900 boards × ₹3,250 per board)	29,25,000	
Allocated fixed manufacturing costs (900 boards × ₹2,800 per board)	25,20,000	
Cost of goods available for sale	68,97,000	
Deduct ending inventory (145 boards × ₹6,050 per board)	(8,77,250)	
Cost of goods sold at standard cost	60,19,750	
Production-volume variance [₹2,800 × (1,000 – 900)]	2,80,000 U	62,99,750
Gross margin		1,62,750
Operating costs		
Variable transportation costs (995 boards × ₹150 per board)	1,49,250	
Fixed selling and administrative	11,20,000	
Total operating costs		12,69,250
Operating income		₹(1,06,500)

[a]Fixed manufacturing cost per unit   = Fixed manufacturing cost/denominator level of production

$$= ₹28,00,000/1,000 \text{ snowboards}$$

$$= ₹2,800 \text{ per snowboard}$$

₹2,800 fixed manufacturing cost + ₹3,250 variable manufacturing cost = ₹6,050 per board

3. Breakeven point in units:

a. Variable Costing:

$$Q = \frac{\text{Total Fixed Costs} + \text{Target Operating Income}}{\text{Contribution Margin Per Unit}}$$

$$Q = \frac{₹39,20,000}{₹4,100}$$

$$Q = \frac{₹39,20,000}{₹4,100}$$

Q = 956 snowboards

b. Absorption costing:

Fixed manufacturing cost rate = ₹28,00,000 ÷ 1,000 = ₹2,800 per snowboard

$$Q = \frac{\begin{array}{c}\text{Total} \\ \text{fixed} \\ \text{costs}\end{array} + \begin{array}{c}\text{Target} \\ \text{operating} \\ \text{income}\end{array} + \left[\begin{array}{c}\text{Fixed} \\ \text{manufacturing} \\ \text{cost rate}\end{array} \times \left(\begin{array}{c}\text{Breakeven} \\ \text{sales} \\ \text{in units}\end{array} - \begin{array}{c}\text{Units} \\ \text{produced}\end{array} \right) \right]}{\text{Contribution margin per unit}}$$

$$Q = \frac{(₹28,00,000 + ₹11,20,000) + ₹0 + [₹2,800(Q-900)]}{₹4,100}$$

₹4,100Q = ₹39,20,000 + ₹2,800Q – ₹25,20,000

₹4,100Q = ₹2,800Q = ₹39,20,000 – ₹25,20,000

₹1,300Q = ₹1,40,00,000

Q = 1,077 snowboards

4. Proof of breakeven point:

a. Variable Costing:

Revenues, ₹7,500 × 956 units	₹71,70,000
Variable costs, ₹3,400 × 956	32,50,400
Contribution margin, ₹4,100 × 956	39,20,000
Fixed costs	39,19,600
Operating income	₹400*

b. Absorption costing:

Revenues, ₹7,500 × 1,077 units		₹80,77,500
Cost of goods sold:		
Cost of goods @ standard cost, ₹6,050 × 1,077 units	65,15,850	
Production-volume variance, ₹2,800 × (1,000 – 900)	2,80,000 U	67,95,850
Gross margin		12,81,650
Variable transportation costs, ₹150 × 1,077 units	1,61,550	
Fixed selling and administrative costs	11,20,000	12,81,550
Operating income		₹100*

*This is not zero due to rounding to 956 and 1,077 whole units sold.

5. If ₹2,00,000 of fixed administrative costs were reclassified as production costs, there would be no change in breakeven sales using variable costing. This is because all fixed costs, regardless of whether they are for production or administrative activities, are treated the same way in a variable costing system. However, this is not true for absorption costing. The change in classification would impact the fixed manufacturing overhead rate that is applied to units of production. If sales and production are unequal, the additional fixed overhead would either increase or decrease breakeven sales.

6. The additional ₹300 per unit variable production cost will cause unit contribution margin to decrease from ₹4,100 to ₹3,800. This decrease will cause the breakeven point to increase.

In the case of variable costing:

$Q = ₹39,20,000 ÷ ₹3,800$

$Q = 1,032$ units (rounded)

In the case of absorption costing:

$₹3,800Q = ₹39,20,000 + ₹2,800Q – ₹25,20,000$

$₹3,800Q – ₹2,800Q = ₹39,20,000 – ₹25,20,000$

$₹1,000Q = ₹14,00,000$

$Q = 1,400$ units

9-27 Downward demand spiral. Godrej Company is about to enter the highly competitive personal electronics market with a new optical reader. In anticipation of future growth, the company has leased a large manufacturing facility and has purchased several expensive pieces of equipment. In 2014, the company's first year, Godrej budgets for production and sales of 24,000 units, compared with its practical capacity of 48,000. The company's cost data are as follows:

	A	B
1	Variable manufacturing costs per unit:	
2	Direct materials	₹200
3	Direct manufacturing labor	350
4	Manufacturing overhead	90
5	Fixed manufacturing overhead	₹57,60,000

1. Assume that Godrej uses absorption costing and uses budgeted units produced as the denominator for calculating its fixed manufacturing overhead rate. Selling price is set at 130% of manufacturing cost. Compute Godrej's selling price.

2. Godrej enters the market with the selling price computed previously. However, despite growth in the overall market, sales are not as robust as the company had expected, and a competitor has priced its product ₹160 lower than Godrej's. The company's president, insists that the competitor must be pricing its product at a loss and that the competitor will be unable to sustain that. In response, Godrej makes no price adjustments but budgets production and sales for 2015 at 18,000 units. Variable and fixed costs are not expected to change. Compute Godrej's new selling price. Comment on how Godrej's choice of budgeted production affected its selling price and competitive position.

3. Recompute the selling price using practical capacity as the denominator level of activity. How would this choice have affected Godrej's position in the marketplace? Generally, how would this choice affect the production-volume variance?

Solution

1. Fixed manufacturing overhead rate = ₹57,60,000/24,000 units = ₹240 per unit

Manufacturing cost per unit:

₹200 direct materials + ₹350 direct mfg. labor + ₹90 var. mfg. OH + ₹240 fixed mfg. OH = ₹880

Selling price: ₹880 × 130% = ₹1,144

2. Fixed manufacturing overhead rate = ₹57,60,000/18,000 units = ₹320 per unit

Manufacturing cost per unit:

₹200 direct materials + ₹350 direct mfg. labor + ₹90 var. mfg. OH + ₹320 fixed mfg. OH = ₹960

Selling price: ₹960 × 130% = ₹1,248

By using budgeted units produced, and not practical capacity, as the denominator level, Godrej is burdening its products with the cost of unused capacity. Apparently, the competitor has not done this, and because of its higher selling price, Godrej's sales decline. Consequently, 2015 budgeted quantities are even lower, which increases the unit cost and selling price. This phenomenon is known as the downward demand spiral, and it causes Godrej to continually inflate its selling price, which in turn leads to progressively lower sales.

3. Fixed manufacturing overhead rate = ₹57,60,000/48,000 units = ₹120 per unit

Manufacturing cost per unit:

₹200 direct materials + ₹350 direct mfg. labor + ₹90 var. mfg. OH + ₹120 fixed mfg. OH = ₹760

Selling price: ₹760 × 130% = ₹988

If Godrej had used practical capacity as its denominator level of activity, its initial selling price of ₹986 would have been virtually in line with the ₹984 selling price of Godrej's competitor, and it would likely have resulted in higher sales. Using practical capacity will result in a higher unfavorable production-volume variance, which will most likely be written off to cost of goods sold and reduce operating income. However, as sales and production increase in future years and the company "grows into" its capacity, the amount of unused capacity will be lower, resulting in future cost savings.

9-28 Absorption costing and production volume variance—alternative capacity bases. Planet Light First (PLF), a producer of energy-efficient light bulbs, expects that demand will increase markedly in coming years. Due to the high fixed costs involved in the business, PLF has decided to evaluate its financial performance using absorption costing income. The production-volume variance is written off to cost of goods sold. The variable cost of production is ₹24 per bulb. Fixed manufacturing costs are ₹1,17,00,000 per year. Variable and fixed selling and administrative expenses are ₹2 per bulb sold and ₹22,00,000, respectively. Because its light bulbs are currently popular with environmentally conscious customers, PLF can sell the bulbs for ₹98 each.

PLF is deciding among various concepts of capacity for calculating the cost of each unit produced. Its choices are as follows:

Theoretical capacity	9,00,000 bulbs
Practical capacity	5,20,000 bulbs
Normal capacity	2,60,000 bulbs(average expected output for the next three years)
Master budget capacity	2,25,000 bulbs expected production this year

Required

1. Calculate the inventoriable cost per unit using each level of capacity to compute fixed manufacturing cost per unit.
2. Suppose PLF actually produces 3,00,000 bulbs. Calculate the production-volume variance using each level of capacity to compute the fixed manufacturing overhead allocation rate.
3. Assume PLF has no beginning inventory. If this year's actual sales are 2,25,000 bulbs, calculate operating income for PLF using each type of capacity to compute fixed manufacturing cost per unit.

Solution

1. Inventoriable cost per unit = Variable production cost + Fixed manufacturing overhead/ Capacity

Capacity Type	Capacity Level	Fixed Mfg. Overhead	Fixed Mfg. Overhead Rate	Variable Production Cost	Inventoriable Cost Per Unit
Theoretical	9,00,000	₹1,17,00,000	₹13	₹24	₹37
Practical	5,20,000	₹1,17,00,000	₹22.5	₹24	₹46.5
Normal	2,60,000	₹1,17,00,000	₹45.0	₹24	₹69.0
Master Budget	2,25,000	₹1,17,00,000	₹52.0	₹24	₹76.0

2. PLF's actual production level is 3,00,000 bulbs. We can compute the production-volume variance as:

Production Volume Variance = Budgeted Fixed Mfg. Overhead
− (Fixed Mfg. Overhead Rate × Actual Production Level)

Capacity Type	Capacity Level	Fixed Mfg. Overhead	Fixed Mfg. Overhead Rate	Fixed Mfg. Overhead Rate × Actual Production	Production Volume Variance
Theoretical	9,00,000	₹1,17,00,000	₹13.0	₹39,00,000	₹78,00,000 U
Practical	5,20,000	₹1,17,00,000	₹22.5	₹67,50,000	₹49,50,000 U
Normal	2,60,000	₹1,17,00,000	₹45.0	₹1,35,00,000	₹18,00,000 F
Master Budget	2,25,000	₹1,17,00,000	₹52	₹1,56,00,000	₹39,00,000 F

3. Operating Income for PLF given production of 3,00,000 bulbs and sales of 2,25,000 bulbs @ ₹98 apiece:

	Theoretical	Practical	Normal	Master Budget
Revenue [a]	₹2,20,50,000	₹2,20,50,000	₹2,20,50,000	₹2,20,50,000
Less: Cost of goods sold [b]	83,25,000	1,04,62,500	1,55,25,000	1,71,00,000

Production-volume variance	78,00,000 U	49,50,000 U	(18,00,000) F	(39,00,000) F
Gross margin	59,25,000	66,37,500	83,25,000	88,50,000
Variable selling [c]	4,50,000	4,50,000	4,50,000	4,50,000
Fixed selling	22,00,000	22,00,000	22,00,000	22,00,000
Operating income	₹32,75,000	₹39,87,500	₹56,75,000	₹62,00,000

[a]2,25,000 × ₹98

[b]2,25,000 × ₹37, × ₹46.5, × ₹69.0, × ₹76.0

[c]2,25,000 × ₹2

9-29 Operating income effects of denominator-level choice and disposal of production-volume variance (continuation of 9-28).

Required

1. If PLF sells all 3,00,000 bulbs produced, what would be the effect on operating income of using each type of capacity as a basis for calculating manufacturing cost per unit?

2. Compare the results of operating income at different capacity levels when 2,25,000 bulbs are sold and when 3,00,000 bulbs are sold. What conclusion can you draw from the comparison?

Solution

1. Because no beginning inventories exist, if PLF sells all 3,00,000 bulbs manufactured, its operating income will be the same under all four capacity options. Calculations are provided below:

	Theoretical	Practical	Normal	Master Budget
Revenue [a]	₹2,94,00,000	₹2,94,00,000	₹2,94,00,000	₹2,94,00,000
Less: Cost of goods sold [b]	1,11,00,000	1,39,50,000	2,07,00,000	2,28,00,000
Less: Production volume variance	78,00,000 U	49,50,000 U	(18,00,000) F	(39,00,000) F
Gross margin	1,05,00,000	1,05,00,000	1,05,00,000	1,05,00,000
Variable selling [c]	6,00,000	6,00,000	6,00,000	6,00,000
Fixed selling	22,00,000	22,00,000	22,00,000	22,00,000
Operating income	₹77,00,000	₹77,00,000	₹77,00,000	₹77,00,000

[a]3,00,000 × ₹98

[b]3,00,000 × ₹37, × ₹46.5, × ₹69.0, × ₹76.0

[c]3,00,000 × ₹2

2. If the manager of PLF produces and sells 3,00,000 bulbs, then all capacity levels will result in the same operating income of ₹77,00,000 (see requirement 1 above). If the manager of PLF is able to sell only 2,25,000 of the bulbs produced and if the production-volume variance is closed to cost of goods sold, then the operating income is given as in requirement 3 of 9-36. Both sets of numbers are reproduced below.

	Theoretical	Practical	Normal	Master Budget
Income with sales of 3,00,000 bulbs	₹77,00,000	₹77,00,000	₹77,00,000	₹77,00,000
Income with sales of 2,25,000 bulbs	32,75,000	39,87,500	56,75,000	62,00,000
Decrease in income when there is over-production	₹44,25,000	₹37,12,500	₹20,25,000	₹15,00,000

Comparing these results, it is clear that for a given level of overproduction relative to sales, the manager's performance will appear better if he/she uses as the denominator a level that is lower. In this example, setting the denominator to equal the master budget (the lowest of the four capacity levels here), minimizes the loss to the manager from being unable to sell the entire production quantity of 3,00,000 bulbs.

9-30 Variable and absorption costing, actual costing. The Dabur Company started business on January 1, 2014. Dabur manufactures a specialty honey beer, which it sells directly to state-owned distributors in Northern India. Honey beer is produced and sold in six-packs, and in 2014, Dabur produced more six-packs than it was able to sell. In addition to variable and fixed manufacturing overhead, Dabur incurred direct materials costs of ₹88,00,000, direct manufacturing labor costs of ₹40,00,000, and fixed marketing and administrative costs of ₹29,50,000. For the year, Dabur sold a total of 1,80,000 six-packs for a sales revenue of ₹2,25,00,000.

Dabur's CFO is convinced that the firm should use an actual costing system but is debating whether to follow variable or absorption costing. The controller notes that Dabur's operating income for the year would be ₹43,80,000 under variable costing and ₹46,10,000 under absorption costing. Moreover, the ending finished goods inventory would be valued at ₹71.50 under variable costing and ₹83 under absorption costing.

Dabur incurs no variable nonmanufacturing expenses.

Required

1. What is Dabur's total contribution margin for 2014?
2. Dabur incurs fixed manufacturing costs in addition to its fixed marketing and administrative costs. How much did Dabur incur in fixed manufacturing costs in 2014?
3. How many six-packs did Dabur produce in 2014?
4. How much in variable manufacturing overhead did Dabur incur in 2014?
5. For 2014, how much in total manufacturing overhead is expensed under variable costing, either through Cost of Goods Sold or as a period expense?

Solution

1. Because no beginning inventories exist, the cost of the ending inventory must be the same as the cost of goods sold for the period. So, the unit cost of goods sold under variable costing is ₹71.50.

Variable cost of goods sold	= Units sold × Unit variable cost of goods sold
	= 1,80,000 × ₹71.50
	= ₹1,28,70,000
Variable nonmanufacturing expenses	= ₹0
Sales Revenues	= ₹2,25,00,000
Contribution Margin	= ₹2,25,00,000 (–) ₹1,28,70,000 (–) ₹0
	= ₹96,30,000

2. The profit under variable costing is given as ₹43,80,000. We just calculated the contribution margin of Dabur as ₹96,30,000. The difference, ₹52,50,000 (₹96,30,000 − ₹43,80,000) must represent the total fixed costs incurred by Dabur in 2014.

Fixed marketing and administrative costs are given as ₹29,50,000. The remainder, ₹23,00,000 (₹52,50,000 − ₹29,50,000) is therefore the fixed manufacturing costs for 2014.

3. The unit cost of ending inventory, as well as the unit cost of goods produced and sold, is ₹71.50 under variable costing and ₹83 under absorption costing. The difference, ₹11.50 (₹83 − ₹71.50) is the unit fixed manufacturing cost of goods produced during the period.

In requirement 2, we calculated that the total fixed manufacturing costs are ₹23,00,000. So, Units produced = Total manufacturing costs/Unit fixed manufacturing cost of production

= ₹23,00,000/₹11.50

= 2,00,000 six-packs.

4. In 2014, Dabur incurred a total of 2,00,000 × ₹71.50 = ₹1,43,00,000 in variable manufacturing costs. This includes ₹88,00,000 in direct materials costs (given), ₹40,00,000 in
direct manufacturing labor costs (given), and the rest in variable manufacturing overhead.
So, variable manufacturing overhead = ₹1,43,00,000 (–) ₹88,00,000 (–) ₹40,00,000
= ₹15,00,000.

5. Under variable costing, the proportion of variable manufacturing overhead corresponding to the units sold, relative to units produced, is expensed as variable cost of goods
sold. This equals:

₹15,00,000 × (1,80,000 units produced)/(2,00,000 units sold) = ₹13,50,000.

Moreover, the entire amount of fixed manufacturing overhead, totaling ₹23,00,000, is
expensed.

So, total manufacturing overhead expensed = ₹13,50,000 (+) ₹23,00,000 = ₹36,50,000.

9-31 Costing methods and variances, comprehensive. Kapil, the controller of Asian Paint Supply
Company, has been exploring a variety of internal accounting systems. Kapil hopes to get
the input of Asian's board of directors in choosing one. To prepare for his presentation to the
board, Kapil applies four different cost accounting methods to the firm's operating data for
2015. The four methods are actual absorption costing, normal absorption costing, standard
absorption costing, and standard variable costing.

With the help of a junior accountant, Kapil prepares the following alternative income
statements:

	A	B	C	D
Sales Revenue	₹9,00,000	₹9,00,000	₹9,00,000	₹9,00,000
Cost of Goods Sold	₹3,75,000	₹2,50,000	₹4,20,000	₹3,95,000
(+) Variances:				
Direct Materials	15,000	15,000	—	—
Direct Labor	5,000	5,000	—	—
Manufacturing Overhead	25,000	—	—	25,000
(+) Other Costs (All Fixed)	3,50,000	4,75,000	3,50,000	3.50,000
Total Costs	₹7,70,000	₹7,45,000	₹7,70,000	₹7,70,000
Net Income	₹1,30,000	₹1,55,000	₹1,30,000	₹1,30,000

Where applicable, Kapil allocates both fixed and variable manufacturing overhead using
direct labor hours as the driver. Company carries no work-in-process inventory. Standard
costs have been stable over time, and Kapil writes off all variances to cost of goods sold. For
2015, there was no flexible budget variance for fixed overhead. In addition, the direct labor
variance represents a price variance.

Required

1. Match each method below with the appropriate income statement (A, B, C, or D):

   Actual Abosorption costing   _____
   Normal Abosorption costing   _____
   Standard Abosorption costing _____
   Standard Variable costing   _____

2. During 2015, how did Company's level of finished goods inventory change? In other
words, is it possible to know whether Company's finished goods inventory increased,
decreased, or stayed constant during the year?

3. From the four income statements, can you determine how the actual volume of production during the year compared to the denominator (expected) volume level?

4. Did Asian Paints have a favorable or unfavorable variable overhead spending variance
during 2015?

Solution

1. Actual Absorption costing   C

   Normal Absorption costing   D

   Standard Absorption costing   A

   Standard Variable costing   B

   Statement C, with no variances, is clearly actual costing. Statement D, which contains variances for overhead but not for direct materials and direct labor, must be normal costing. Finally, A has a higher figure for Cost of Goods Sold and so must represent standard absorption costing (where fixed manufacturing overhead is also treated as a product cost), while B is standard variable costing.

2. The net income under standard variable costing (B; ₹1,55,000) exceeds that under standard absorption costing (A; ₹1,30,000). Because there are no work-in-process inventories, this reflects a higher level of fixed overhead expensed from opening inventory under absorption costing than the amount trapped in ending inventory. With stable standard costs, this implies that the level of finished goods inventory has decreased in 2015.

3. From statement B, the aggregate variance for variable overhead is zero. So, the ₹25,000 variance for total overhead in A must all be for fixed overhead. We are told that there is no flexible budget variance for fixed overhead. The ₹25,000 variance in statement A (standard absorption costing) must therefore be the production volume variance. As it is added to cost of goods sold, the variance is unfavorable. This implies that fixed manufacturing overhead costs were underapplied, or that fewer units were produced than the denominator (expected) level.

4. The aggregate variable overhead variance of zero is the sum of the spending and efficiency variances. Note that variable overhead is applied using direct labor hours as the driver. We are told that there is no direct labor efficiency variance (because the direct labor variance is a price variance), which implies that the variable overhead efficiency variance is also zero. Therefore, the variable overhead spending variance must also be zero, i.e., it is neither favorable nor unfavorable.

Exercises

[*Comprehensive solutions to all exercises are available on the companion website www. pearsoned.co.in/charlesthorngren*]

9-32 Variable and absorption costing, explaining operating income differences. Sony Corporation manufactures and sells 50-inch television sets. Data relating to January, February, and March are:

	January	February	March
Unit data			
Beginning inventory	0	300	300
Production	1,000	800	1,250
Sales	700	800	1,500
Variable costs			
Manufacturing cost per unit produced	₹9,000	₹9,000	₹9,000
Operating cost per unit sold	6,000	6,000	6,000
Fixed costs			
Manufacturing costs	₹40,00,000	₹40,00,000	₹40,00,000
Operating costs	14,00,000	14,00,000	14,00,000

The selling price per unit is ₹25,000.

Required

1. Present income statements Sony in January, February, and March under (a) variable costing and (b) absorption costing.
2. Explain differences between (a) and (b) for January, February, and March.

9-33 Throughput costing (continuation of 9-32). The variable manufacturing costs per unit of Sony Corporation are:

	January	February	March
Direct materials	₹5,000	₹5,000	₹5,000
Direct manufacturing labor	1,000	1,000	1,000
Manufacturing overhead	3,000	3,000	3,000
	9,000	9,000	9,000

Required

1. Present income statements for Sony in January, February, and March under throughput costing.
2. Contrast the results in requirement 1 with those in requirement 1 of 9-29.
3. Give one motivation for Sony to adopt throughput costing.

9-34 Absorption and variable costing. (CMA) Ashoka Ltd. planned and actually manufactured 2,00,000 units of its single product in 2015, its first year of operation. Variable manufacturing cost was ₹20 per unit produced. Variable operating cost was ₹10 per unit sold. Planned and actual fixed manufacturing costs were ₹6,00,000. Planned and actual fixed operating costs totaled ₹4,00,000 in 2015. Ashoka sold 1,20,000 units of product in 2015 at ₹40 per unit.

Required

1. Ashoka's 2015 operating income using absorption costing is (a) ₹4,40,000, (b) ₹2,00,000, (c) ₹6,00,000, (d) ₹8,40,000, (e) none of these.
2. Ashoka's 2015 operating income using variable costing is (a) ₹8,00,000, (b) ₹4,40,000, (c) ₹2,00,000, (d) ₹6,00,000, (e) none of these.

9-35 Comparison of actual-costing methods. The Razor India sells its razors at ₹30 per unit. The company uses a first-in, first-out actual-costing system. A new fixed manufacturing overhead rate is computed each year dividing the actual fixed manufacturing overhead cost by the actual production units. The following simplified data are related to its first two years of operation:

	2014	2015
Sales	1,000 units	1,200 units
Production	1,400 units	1,000 units
Costs:		
Variable manufacturing	₹7,000	₹5,000
Fixed manufacturing	7,000	7,000
Variable operating	10,000	12,000
Fixed operating	4,000	4,000

Required

1. Prepare income statements based on variable costing for each of the two years.
2. Prepare income statements based on absorption costing for each of the two years.
3. Prepare a numerical reconciliation and explanation of the difference between operating income for each year under absorption-costing and variable costing.
4. Critics have claimed that a widely used accounting system has led to undesirable buildups of inventory levels. (a) Is variable costing or absorption costing more likely to lead to such buildups? Why? (b) What can be done to counteract undesirable inventory buildups?

9-36 ABC and capacity usage. Engineering Company has identified the following activities and cost drivers for its manufacturing overhead. The company calculates activity cost rates based on cost driver capacity.

Machine setup	₹50,00,000	5,000 setup-hours
Material handling	20,00,000	1,00,000 kg of material

The Company makes only two products:.A and B. During 2015, A required 3,000 machine setup-hours and handling of 40,000 kgs of materials. B production required 1,500 setup-hours and handling of 50,000 kg of materials.

Required

1. Calculate the costs allocated to each product from each activity.
2. Compute the cost of unused capacity for each activity.

9-37 Cost behavior, activity-based costing, capacity usage. John & Charles Company employs five individuals for its bill processing activity. Each of the employees is paid fixed annual salary of ₹3,00,000. The budgeted annual activity output of bill processing is 6,000 bills per employee. All other costs in the bill processing activity are variable and are budgeted at ₹2,25,000 for the year. During the year, 26,000 bills were actually processed. There are no price, efficiency, or spending variances for variable costs and there is no spending variance for fixed costs.

Required

1. Calculate the budgeted fixed rate, budgeted variable rate, and the budgeted total rate for bill processing activity.
2. Compute the total capacity available in bill processing activity in units.
3. Compute the unused capacity in bill processing activity in units.
4. For (a) fixed costs and (b) variable costs, calculate the cost of bill processing activity supplied, the cost of capacity used for the bill processing activity, and the cost of unused capacity, if any, for the bill processing activity. Are there any differences between fixed costs and variable costs with respect to unused capacity. Explain.

9-38 Variable costing versus absorption costing. The Neelkamal Plastics Company uses an absorption-costing system based on standard costs. Total variable manufacturing cost, including direct material cost, is ₹30 per unit; the standard production rate is 10 units per machine-hour. Total budgeted and actual fixed manufacturing overhead costs are ₹42,00,000. Fixed manufacturing overhead is allocated at ₹70 per machine-hour (₹42,00,000 ÷ 60,000 machine-hours of denominator level). Selling price is ₹50 per unit. Variable operating cost, which is driven by units sold, is ₹10 per unit. Fixed operating costs are ₹12,00,000. Beginning inventory in 2014 is 30,000 units; ending inventory is 40,000 units. Sales in 2015 are 5,40,000 units. The same standard unit costs persisted throughout 2014 and 2015. For simplicity, assume that there are no price, spending, or efficiency variances.

Required

1. Prepare an income statement for 2015 assuming that all underallocated or overallocated overhead is written off at year-end as an adjustment to Cost of Goods Sold.
2. The President has heard about variable costing. He asks you to recast the 2015 statement as it would appear under variable costing.
3. Explain the difference in operating income as calculated in requirements (1) and (2).
4. Critics have claimed that a widely used accounting system has led to undesirable buildups of inventory levels. (a) Is variable costing or absorption costing more likely to lead to such buildups? Why? (b) What can be done to counteract undesirable inventory buildups?

9-39 Breakeven under absorption costing. Refer to Solved Example 9-38.

Required

1. Compute the breakeven point (in units) under variable costing.
2. Compute the breakeven point (in units) under absorption costing.
3. Suppose that production is exactly equal to the denominator level, but no units are sold. Fixed manufacturing costs are unaffected. Assume, however, that all operating costs are avoided. Compute operating income under (a) variable costing and (b) absorption costing. Explain the difference between your answers.

9-40 The All-Fixed Company. (R. Marple, adapted) It is the end of 2015. The All-Fixed Company began operations in January 2014. The company is so named because it has no variable costs. All its costs are fixed; they do not vary with output.

The All-Fixed Company is located on the bank of a river and has its own hydroelectric plant to supply power, light, and heat. The company manufactures a synthetic fertilizer from air and river water and sells its product at a price that is not expected to change. It has a small staff of employees all hired on a fixed annual salary. The output of the plant can be increased or decreased by adjusting a few dials on a control panel.

The following data are for the operations of the All-Fixed Company:

	2014	2015[a]
Sales	10,000 tons	10,000 tons
Production	20,000 tons	–
Selling price	₹300 per ton	₹300 per ton
Costs (all fixed):		
Manufacturing	₹28,00,000	₹28,00,000
Operating	₹4,00,000	₹4,00,000

[a]Management adopted the policy, effective January 1, 2015, of producing only as much product as needed to fill sales orders. During 2015, sales were the same as for 2015 and were filled entirely from inventory at the start of 2015.

1. Prepare income statements with one column for 2014, one column for 2015, and one column for the two years together, using (a) variable costing and (b) absorption costing.
2. What is the breakeven point under (a) variable costing and (b) absorption costing?
3. What inventory costs would be carried on the balance sheet on December 31, 2014 and 2015, under each method?
4. Assume that the performance of the top manager of the company is evaluated and rewarded largely on the basis of reported operating income. Which costing method would the manager prefer? Why?

9-41 Alternative denominator-level concepts. Lucky Ali recently purchased a brewing plant from a bankrupt company. The brewery is in Warangal, Andhar Pradesh. It was constructed only two years ago. The plant has budgeted fixed manufacturing overhead of ₹4,200 lakh (₹350 lakh each month) in 2015. Amitabh, the controller of the brewery, must decide on the denominator-level concept to use in its absorption costing system for 2015. The options available to him are

a. Theoretical capacity for 2015: 600 barrels an hour for 24 hours per day × 365 days = 5,256,000 barrels
b. Practical capacity for 2015: 500 barrels an hour for 20 hours per day × 350 days = 3,500,000 barrels
c. Normal capacity utilization for 2015: 400 barrels an hour for 20 hours per day × 350 days = 2,800,000 barrels
d. Master-budget capacity utilization for 2015 (separate rates computed for each half-year)
   • January-June 2015 budget: 320 barrels an hour for 20 hours a day × 175 days = 1,120,000 barrels
   • July- December 2015 budget: 480 barrels an hour for 20 hours a day × 175 days = 1,680,000 barrels

Variable standard manufacturing costs per barrel are ₹450 (variable direct materials, ₹320; variable manufacturing labor, ₹60; and variable manufacturing overhead, ₹70). The Warangal brewery "sells" its output to the sales division of Lucky Ali at a budgeted price of ₹680 per barrel.

1. Compute the budgeted fixed manufacturing overhead rate using each of the four denominator-level concepts for (a) beer produced in March 2015 and (b) beer produced in September 2015. Explain why any differences arise.
2. Explain why the theoretical capacity and practical capacity concepts are different.
3. Which denominator-level concept would the plant manager of the Warangal brewery prefer when senior management of Lucky Ali is judging plant manager performance during 2015? Explain.

9-42 Operating income effects of alternative denominator-level concepts (continuation of Problem 9-41). In 2015, the Warangal brewery of Lucky Ali showed these results:

Beginning inventory, January 1, 2015	0 barrels
Production	26,00,000 barrels
Ending inventory, December 31, 2015	2,00,000 barrels

The Warangal brewery had actual costs of:

Variable manufacturing costs	₹1,20,38,00,000
Fixed manufacturing overhead costs	40,63,20,000

The sales division of Lucky Ali purchased 24,00,000 barrels in 2015 at the ₹680 per barrel rate. All manufacturing variances are written off to cost of goods sold in the period in which they are incurred.

1. Compute the operating income of the Warangal brewery using the denominator-level concepts of (a) theoretical capacity, (b) practical capacity, and (c) normal capacity utilization. Explain any differences among (a), (b), and (c).
2. What denominator-level concept would Lucky Ali prefer for income tax reporting, assuming he has the choice? Explain.

9-43 Downward demand spiral. Moser beer Company manufactures 1 terabyte optical mini-disk systems. The current year's monthly production and sales are budgeted at 10,000 units. Moser beer's variable manufacturing cost per unit is ₹2,000, and its monthly fixed manufacturing overhead costs total ₹1,00,00,000. Moser beer sets the selling price of its product by adding a 100% markup to the full product cost per unit. The full product cost per unit includes variable manufacturing cost per unit plus the fixed manufacturing overhead cost per unit based on fully allocating total fixed manufacturing overhead costs to the units produced.

1. Compute Moser beer's Company's budgeted selling price.
2. Due to intense competition, Moser beer had to revise its budgeted monthly production and sales downward to 8,000 units. Compute Moser beer Company's revised budgeted selling price.
3. Comment on your results in (1) and (2) above.

9-44 Denominator level, production-volume variance. Mirc Electronics Ltd. acquired plant assets based on forecasts of long-range demand for its products. Its budgeted manufacturing overhead costs for 2016 are ₹10,50,00,000. For each of the four alternative denominator-level capacities, Mirc's capacity is:

Denominator-Level Capacity	Denominator-Level (in machine-hours)
Theoretical capacity	21,00,000
Practical capacity	15,00,000
Normal capacity utilization	13,12,500
Master-budget capacity utilization	10,00,000

1. Calculate budgeted fixed manufacturing overhead rate per machine-hour for each denominator-level capacity.
2. For 2016 actual output, 11,00,000 budgeted machine-hours were allowed. Compute production-volume variance under each of the denominator-level capacity assumptions.

10 Determining How Costs Behave

Learning Objective 1

Describe linear cost functions

. . . graph of cost function is a straight line

and three common ways in which they behave

. . . variable, fixed, and mixed

What is the value of looking at the past?

Perhaps it is to recall fond memories of family and friends or help you understand historical events. Maybe recalling the past helps you better understand and predict the future. An organization looks at the past to analyze its performance and make the best decisions for improving its future performance. This activity requires managers to gather information about costs and how they behave so that managers can predict what they will be "down the road." Understanding how costs behave is a valuable technical skill, and the knowledge gained in this process can motivate an organization to reorganize its operations in innovative ways and tackle important challenges. Managers look to management accountants to help them identify cost drivers, estimate cost relationships, and determine the fixed and variable components of costs. To be effective, management accountants must have a clear understanding of the business's strategy in order to identify new opportunities to reduce costs and increase profitability.

Basic Assumptions and Examples of Cost Functions

Managers are able to understand cost behavior through cost functions , which are the basic building blocks for estimating costs. A **cost function** is a mathematical description of how a cost changes with changes in the level of an activity relating to that cost. Cost functions can be plotted on a graph by measuring the level of an activity, such as number of batches produced or number of machine-hours used, on the horizontal axis (called the x-axis). The amount of total costs corresponding to—or, preferably, dependent on—the levels of that activity are measured on the vertical axis (called the y-axis).

Basic Assumptions

Managers often estimate cost functions based on two assumptions:

1. Variations in the level of a single activity (the cost driver) explain the variations in the related total costs.

2. Cost behavior is approximated by a linear cost function within the relevant range. Recall from Chapter 2 that a relevant range is the range of the activity in which there is a relationship between total cost and the level of activity. For a **linear cost function,** total cost versus the level of a single activity related to that cost is a straight line within the relevant range.

We use these two assumptions throughout most, but not all, of this chapter. Not all cost functions are linear and can be explained by a single activity. Later sections will discuss cost functions that do not rely on these assumptions.

Linear Cost Functions

To understand three basic types of linear cost functions and to see the role of cost functions in business decisions, consider the negotiations between StoreBox, a technology startup, and Forest Web Services (FWS) for enterprise-class cloud computing services.

- **Alternative 1:** ₹5 per CPU hour used. Total cost to StoreBox changes in proportion to the number of CPU hours used. The number of CPU hours used is the only factor whose change causes a change in total cost.

   Panel A in Exhibit 10-1 presents this *variable cost* for StoreBox. Under alternative 1, there is no fixed cost for cloud services. We write the cost function in Panel A of Exhibit 10-1 as

$$Y = ₹5\ X$$

   where X measures the number of CPU hours used (on the x-axis) and y measures the total cost of the CPU hours used (on the y-axis), calculated using the cost function. Panel A illustrates the ₹5 **slope coefficient**, the amount by which total cost changes when a one-unit change occurs in the level of activity (one hour of CPU usage in the StoreBox example). *Throughout the chapter, uppercase letters, such as X, refer to the actual observations, and lowercase letters, such as y, represent estimates or calculations made using a cost function.*

- **Alternative 2:** The total cost will be fixed at ₹10,000 per month, regardless of the number of CPU hours used. (We use the same activity measure, number of CPU hours used, to compare cost-behavior patterns under the three alternatives.)

   Panel B in Exhibit 10-1 shows the fixed cost alternative for StoreBox. We write the cost function in Panel B as

$$Y = ₹10,000$$

Exhibit 10-1　　　Examples of Linear Cost Functions

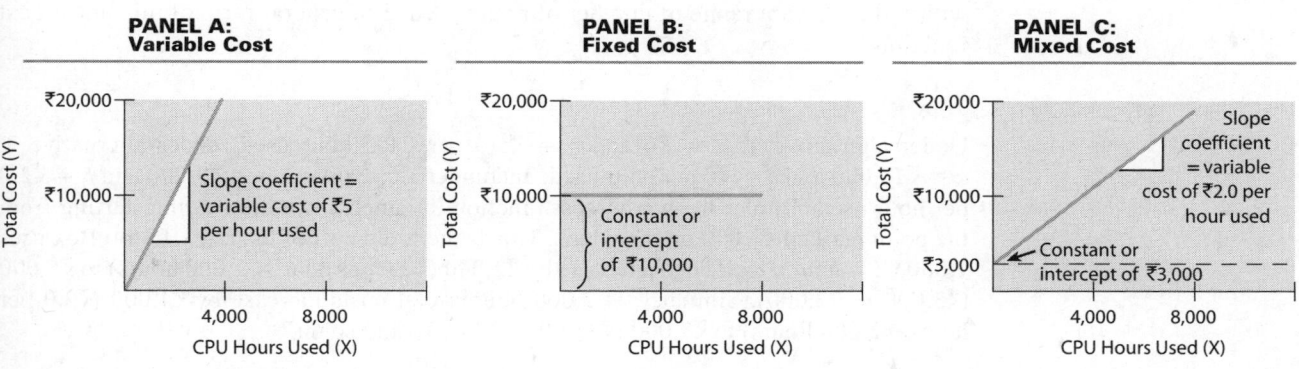

| PANEL A: Variable Cost | PANEL B: Fixed Cost | PANEL C: Mixed Cost |

The fixed cost of ₹10,000 is called a **constant**; it is the component of the total cost that does not vary with changes in the level of the activity. The constant accounts for all the cost because there is no variable cost. Graphically, the slope coefficient of this cost function is zero; this cost function intersects the *y*-axis at a constant value. Therefore, the *constant* is also called the **intercept**.

■ **Alternative 3:** ₹3,000 per month plus ₹2 per CPU hour used. This is an example of a mixed cost. A **mixed cost**—also called a **semivariable cost**—is a cost that has both fixed and variable elements.

Panel C in Exhibit 10-1 shows the mixed cost alternative for StoreBox. We write the cost function in Panel C of Exhibit 10-1 as

$$Y = ₹3,000 + ₹2.0X$$

Unlike the graphs for alternatives 1 and 2, Panel C has both a constant, or intercept, value of ₹3,000 and a slope coefficient of ₹2.0. In the case of a mixed cost, the total cost in the relevant range increases as the number of CPU hours used increases. Note that the total cost does not vary strictly in proportion to the number of CPU hours used within the relevant range. For example, when 4,000 hours are used, the total cost equals ₹11,000 [₹3,000 + (₹2.0 per hour × 4,000 hours)], but when 8,000 hours are used, the total cost equals ₹19,000 [₹3,000 + (₹2.0 per hour × 8,000 hours)]. Although the usage in terms of hours has doubled, the total cost has increased by only about 73% [(₹19,000 − ₹11,000) ÷ ₹11,000].

StoreBox's managers must understand the cost-behavior patterns in the three alternatives to choose the best deal with FWS. Suppose StoreBox expects to use at least 4,000 hours of CPU time each month. Its cost for 4,000 hours under the three alternatives would be as follows:

■ **Alternative 1:** ₹20,000 (₹5.0 per hour × 4,000 hours)]
■ **Alternative 2:** ₹10,000
■ **Alternative 3:** ₹11,000 [₹3,000 + (₹2.0 per hour × 4,000 hours)]

Alternative 2 is the least costly. Moreover, if StoreBox were to use more than 4,000 hours, as is likely to be the case, alternatives 1 and 3 would be even more costly. StoreBox's managers, therefore, should choose alternative 2.

Note that the graphs in Exhibit 10-1 are linear. That is, they appear as straight lines. We simply need to know the constant, or intercept, amount (commonly designated *a*) and the slope coefficient (commonly designated *b*). For any linear cost function based on a single activity (recall our two assumptions discussed at the start of this section), knowing *a* and *b* is sufficient to describe and graphically plot all the values within the relevant range of number of hours used. The general form of this linear cost function is

$$y = a + bX$$

Under alternative 1, a = ₹0 and b = ₹5.0 per CPU hour used; under alternative 2, a = ₹10,000 and b = ₹0 per hour used; and under alternative 3, a = ₹3,000 and b = ₹2.0 per hour used. To plot the mixed-cost function in Panel C, we draw a line starting from the point marked ₹3,000 on the *y*-axis. This is the fixed part of the rate. If StoreBox uses 1,000 CPU hours, total costs increase by ₹2,000 (₹2.0 per hour × 1,000 hours) to ₹5,000 (₹3,000 + ₹2,000). Similarly, at 2,000 hours, total costs increase by ₹4,000 (₹2.0 per hour × 2,000 hours) to ₹7,000 (₹3,000 + ₹4,000), and so on.

Review of Cost Classification

Before we discuss issues related to the estimation of cost functions, we briefly review the three criteria laid out in Chapter 2 for classifying a cost into its variable and fixed components.

Choice of Cost Object   A particular cost item could be variable with respect to one cost object and fixed with respect to another cost object. Consider Super Shuttle, an airport transportation company. If the fleet of vans it owns is the cost object, then the annual van registration and license costs would be variable costs with respect to the number of vans owned. But if a particular van is the cost object, then the registration and license costs for that van are fixed costs with respect to the miles driven during a year.

Time Horizon   Whether a cost is variable or fixed with respect to a particular activity depends on the time horizon being considered in the decision situation. The longer the time horizon, all other things being equal, the more likely that the cost will be variable. For example, inspection costs at Boeing Company are typically fixed in the short run with respect to inspection-hours used because inspectors earn a fixed salary in a given year regardless of the number of inspection-hours of work done. But, in the long run, Boeing's total inspection costs will vary with the inspection-hours required: More inspectors will be hired if more inspection-hours are needed, and some inspectors will be reassigned to other tasks or laid off if fewer inspection-hours are needed.

Relevant Range   Managers should never forget that variable and fixed cost-behavior patterns are valid for linear cost functions only within the given relevant range. Outside the relevant range, variable and fixed cost-behavior patterns change, causing costs to become nonlinear (nonlinear means the plot of the relationship on a graph is not a straight line). For example, Exhibit 10-2 plots the relationship (over several years) between total direct manufacturing labor costs and the number of snowboards produced each year by Ski Authority. In this case, the nonlinearities outside the relevant range occur because of labor and other inefficiencies (first because workers are learning to produce snowboards and later because capacity limits are being stretched). Knowing the relevant range is essential to properly classify costs.

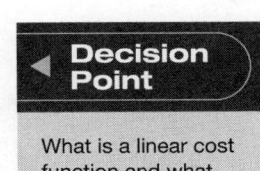

Decision Point

What is a linear cost function and what types of cost behavior can it represent?

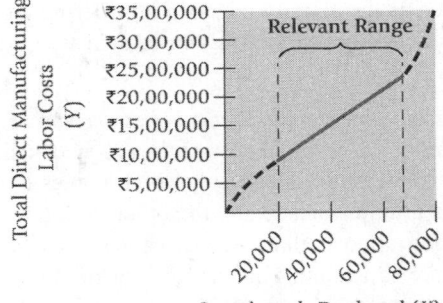

Snowboards Produced (X)

Exhibit 10-2

Linearity Within Relevant Range for Ski Authority, is. Ltd

Identifying Cost Drivers

In the StoreBox/FWS example, we discussed variable-, fixed-, and mixed-cost functions using information about *future* cost structures StoreBox was considering. Often, however, cost functions are estimated from *past* cost data. Managers use **cost estimation** to measure a relationship based on data from past costs and the related level of an activity. Managers are interested in estimating past cost functions primarily because they can help them make more accurate **cost predictions**, or forecasts, of future costs. For example, to choose the design features for its new TV models, Sony's managers use past cost functions to evaluate the costs of alternative designs and combine this information with insights about what customers are willing to pay. Similarly, marketing managers at Volkswagen use cost estimation to understand what causes their customer-service costs to change from year to year (for example, the number of new car models introduced or the total number of cars sold) and the fixed and variable components of these costs. Better cost predictions help Volkswagen's managers make more informed planning and control decisions, such as preparing next year's customer-service budget. But better management decisions, cost predictions, and estimation of cost functions can be achieved only if managers correctly identify the factors that affect costs.

The Cause-and-Effect Criterion

The most important issue in estimating a cost function is determining whether a cause-and-effect relationship exists between the level of an activity and the costs related to it. Without a cause-and-effect relationship, managers will be less confident about their ability to estimate or predict costs. Recall from Chapter 2 that when a cause-and-effect relationship exists between a change in the level of an activity and a change in the level of total costs, we refer to the activity measure as a *cost driver*. We use the terms *level of activity* and *level of cost driver* interchangeably when estimating cost functions. Understanding the drivers of costs is crucially important for managing costs. The cause-and-effect relationship might arise as a result of the following:

- **A physical relationship between the level of activity and the costs.** Direct materials costs and production are an example. Producing more snowboards requires more plastic, which results in higher total direct materials costs.

- **A contractual arrangement.** Consider the contract between StoreBox and FWS. The contract specifies the number of CPU hours used as the level of activity that affects the cloud services costs. Consequently, there is a direct cause and effect between the two.

- **Knowledge of operations.** An example of knowledge of operations is when the number of parts is used as the activity measure of ordering costs. A Lenovo computer with many parts will incur higher ordering costs than will a newer model that has fewer parts.

Managers must be careful not to interpret a high correlation, or connection, between two variables to mean that either variable causes the other. Consider the total direct materials costs and labor costs for Winston Furniture, which makes two types of (otherwise identical) tables, one with a granite surface and the other with a wooden surface. Granite tables have higher direct material costs than wooden tables because granite is a more expensive input. However, granite is available in precut blocks, so the granite tables require less direct manufacturing labor costs than the wooden tables. Winston currently sells 10,000 granite tables and 30,000 wooden ones.

If Winston sells 20% more of each type of table, then the total direct materials costs and total direct manufacturing labor costs for each type will increase by 20%. The two cost categories are highly correlated in this case. However, it is important to note that neither causes the other, so using one cost to predict the other is problematic.

To see why, suppose Winston sells 20% more tables (or a total of 48,000 again), but now 4,000 of them are granite tables and 44,000 are wooden tables. The direct manufacturing labor costs are higher for wooden tables compared with granite ones, so Winston's total direct manufacturing labor costs will increase by more than 20%. In contrast, because granite is so much more expensive than wood, Winston's total direct materials costs will actually decrease. Consequently, using Winston's total direct manufacturing labor costs to predict its total direct materials costs would be a mistake. Other factors, such as the number of each type of table produced, would have more accurately predicted the changes in the company's total direct materials costs.

Only a cause-and-effect relationship—not merely correlation—establishes an economically plausible relationship between the level of an activity and its costs. Economic plausibility is critical because it gives analysts and managers confidence that the estimated relationship will appear again and again in other sets of data. Identifying cost drivers also gives managers insights into ways to reduce costs and the confidence that reducing the quantity of the cost drivers will lead to a decrease in costs.

Cost Drivers and the Decision-Making Process

To correctly identify cost drivers in order to make decisions, managers should always use a long time horizon. Why? Because costs may be fixed in the short run (during which time they have no cost driver), but they are usually variable and have a cost driver in the long run. Focusing on the short run may inadvertently cause a manager to believe that a cost has no cost driver.

Consider Elegant Rugs, which uses state-of-the-art automated weaving machines to produce carpets for homes and offices. Management has altered manufacturing processes and wants to introduce new styles of carpets. Elegant Rugs' managers follow the five-step decision-making process outlined in Chapter 1 to evaluate how these changes have affected costs and what styles of carpets they should introduce.

Step 1: Identify the problem and its uncertainties. The manufacturing process was changed to reduce Elegant Rugs' indirect manufacturing labor costs. Now managers want to know whether the firm's supervision, maintenance, and quality control costs did, in fact, decrease. One option is to simply compare the firm's indirect manufacturing labor costs before and after the process change. The problem with this approach, however, is that the volume of activity and the style of carpets produced before and after the process change are very different, so the costs need to be compared after taking into account these changes.

Elegant Rugs' managers are fairly confident about the direct materials and direct manufacturing labor costs of the new styles of carpets. They are less certain about the impact that the choice of different styles would have on indirect manufacturing costs.

Step 2: Obtain information. Managers gather information about potential cost drivers—such as machine-hours or direct manufacturing labor-hours—that cause indirect manufacturing labor costs to be incurred. They also begin to consider different techniques (discussed in the next section) for estimating the magnitude of the effect a cost driver has on the firm's indirect manufacturing labor costs. Their goal is to identify the best possible single cost driver.

Step 3: Make predictions about the future. Managers use past data to estimate the relationship between the cost drivers and costs and use this relationship to predict future costs.

Decision Point ▶

What is the most important issue in estimating a cost function?

Step 4: Make decisions by choosing among alternatives. As we will describe later, the managers chose machine-hours as the cost driver. Using a regression analysis, they estimated the indirect manufacturing labor costs per machine-hour of alternative styles of carpets and chose to produce the most profitable styles.

Step 5: Implement the decision, evaluate performance, and learn. A year later the managers evaluated the results of their decision. Comparing predicted to actual costs helped them determine how accurate the estimates were, set targets for continuous improvement, and seek ways to improve Elegant Rugs' efficiency and effectiveness.

Cost Estimation Methods

Learning Objective 3

Understand various methods of cost estimation

. . . for example, the regression analysis method determines the line that best fits past data

Four methods of cost estimation are (1) the industrial engineering method, (2) the conference method, (3) the account analysis method, and (4) the quantitative analysis method (which takes different forms). These methods differ with respect to how expensive they are to implement, the assumptions they make, and the information they provide about the accuracy of the estimated cost function. The methods are not mutually exclusive, and many organizations use a combination of these methods.

Industrial Engineering Method

Description of method

The **industrial engineering method**, also called the **work-measurement method**, estimates cost functions by analyzing the relationship between inputs and outputs in physical terms. Elegant Rugs uses inputs of cotton, wool, dyes, direct manufacturing labor, machine time, and power. Production output is square yards of carpet. Time-and-motion studies analyze the time required to perform the various operations to produce the carpet. For example, a time-and-motion study may conclude that to produce 10 square yards of carpet requires one hour of direct manufacturing labor. Standards and budgets transform these physical input measures into costs. The result is an estimated cost function relating direct manufacturing labor costs to the cost driver, square yards of carpet produced.

Advantages and challenges

The industrial engineering method is a very thorough and detailed way to estimate a cost function when there is a physical relationship between inputs and outputs. Although it can be time-consuming, some government contracts mandate its use. Many organizations, such as Bose and Nokia, use it to estimate direct manufacturing costs but find it too costly or impractical for analyzing their entire cost structure. For example, physical relationships between inputs and outputs are difficult to specify for some items, such as indirect manufacturing costs, R&D costs and advertising costs.

Conference Method

Description of method

The **conference method** estimates cost functions on the basis of analysis and opinions about costs and their drivers gathered from various departments of a company (purchasing, process engineering, manufacturing, employee relations, and so on). Some banks, for example, develops cost functions for its retail banking products (checking accounts, VISA cards, mortgages), based on the consensus of estimates from personnel of the particular departments. Relying on the collective judgment of experts is the most popular strategy for estimating the cost of software development projects. Elegant Rugs gathers opinions from supervisors and production engineers about how indirect manufacturing labor costs vary with machine-hours and direct manufacturing labor-hours.

Advantages and challenges

The conference method encourages interdepartmental cooperation. The pooling of expert knowledge from different business functions of the value chain gives the conference method credibility. Because the conference method does not require detailed analysis of data, cost functions and cost estimates can be developed quickly. However, because opinions are being used, the accuracy of the cost estimates depends largely on the care and skill of the people providing the inputs.

Account Analysis Method

Description of method

The **account analysis method** estimates cost functions by classifying various cost accounts as variable, fixed, or mixed with respect to the identified level of activity. Typically, managers use qualitative rather than quantitative analysis when making these cost-classification decisions.

Consider indirect manufacturing labor costs for a small production area (or cell) at Elegant Rugs. These include the wages paid for supervision, maintenance, quality control, and setups. During the most recent 12-week period, Elegant Rugs ran the machines in the cell for a total of 862 hours and incurred total indirect manufacturing labor costs of ₹1,25,010. Using qualitative analysis, the manager and the cost analyst determine that over this 12-week period indirect manufacturing labor costs are mixed costs with only one cost driver—machine hours. As machine-hours vary, one component of the cost (such as supervision cost) is fixed, whereas another component (such as maintenance cost) is variable. The manager and management accountant want to estimate a linear cost function for the cell's indirect manufacturing labor costs using the number of machine-hours as the cost driver. To do so, they must distinguish between the variable and fixed cost components. Using their experience and judgment they separate total indirect manufacturing labor costs (₹1,25,010) into costs that are fixed (₹21,570, based on 950 hours of machine capacity for the cell over a 12-week period) and costs that are variable (₹1,03,440) with respect to the number of machine-hours used. Variable cost per machine-hour is ₹1,03,440 ÷ 862 machine-hours = ₹120 per machine-hour. Therefore, the linear cost equation, $y = a + bX$, is:

Indirect manufacturing labor cost = ₹21,570 + (₹120 per machine-hour × Number of machine-hours)

Elegant Rugs' managers can use the cost function to estimate the indirect manufacturing labor costs of using, say, 950 machine-hours to produce carpet in the next 12-week period. The estimated costs equal ₹21,570 + (950 machine-hours × ₹120 per machine-hour) = ₹1,35,570. The indirect manufacturing labor cost per machine-hour decreases to ₹1,35,570 ÷ 950 machine-hours = ₹142.7 per machine-hour, as fixed costs of ₹21,570 are spread over a greater number of machine-hours.

Advantages and challenges

The account analysis approach is widely used because it is reasonably accurate, cost-effective, and easy to use. To obtain reliable estimates of the fixed and variable components of cost, organizations must take care to ensure that individuals thoroughly knowledgeable about the operations make the cost-classification decisions. Supplementing the account analysis method with the conference method improves credibility. The accuracy of the account analysis method depends on the accuracy of the qualitative judgments that managers and management accountants make about which costs are fixed and which are variable.

Quantitative Analysis Method

Description of method

What are the different methods that can be used to estimate a cost function?

Quantitative analysis uses a formal mathematical method to fit cost functions to past data observations. Excel is a useful tool for performing quantitative analysis. Columns B and C of Exhibit 10-3 show the breakdown of Elegant Rugs's total machine-hours (862) and total indirect manufacturing labor costs (₹1,25,010) into weekly data for the most recent 12-week period. Note that the data are paired: for each week there is data for the number of machine-hours and corresponding indirect manufacturing labor costs. For example, week 12 shows 48 machine-hours and indirect manufacturing labor costs of ₹9,630. The next section uses the data in Exhibit 10-3 to illustrate how to estimate a cost function using quantitative analysis. We examine two techniques: the relatively simple high-low method as well as the more common quantitative tool used to examine and understand data, regression analysis.

Exhibit 10-3

Weekly Indirect Manufacturing Labor Costs and Machine-Hours for Elegant Rugs

	A	B	C
		Cost Driver:	Indirect Manufacturing
1	Week	Machine-Hours	Labor Costs
2		(X)	₹(Y)
3	1	68	₹11,900
4	2	88	12,110
5	3	62	10,040
6	4	72	9,170
7	5	60	7,700
8	6	96	14,560
9	7	78	11,800
10	8	46	7,100
11	9	82	13,160
12	10	94	10,320
13	11	68	7,520
14	12	48	9,630
15	Total	862	₹1,25,010
16			

Advantages and challenges

Quantitative analysis is the most rigorous approach to estimate costs. Computer programs have made performing quantitative analysis and, in particular, regression analysis much easier. However, regression analysis requires more detailed information about costs, cost drivers, and cost functions and is therefore more time consuming to implement.

Estimating a Cost Function Using Quantitative Analysis

There are six steps in estimating a cost function using a quantitative analysis of a past data. We illustrate the steps as follows using the Elegant Rugs example.

Step 1:   Choose the dependent variable. Which **dependent variable** (the cost to be predicted and managed) managers choose will depend on the cost function being estimated. In the Elegant Rugs example, the dependent variable is indirect manufacturing labor costs.

Step 2:   Identify the independent variable, or cost driver. The **independent variable** (level of activity or cost driver) is the factor used to predict the dependent variable (costs). When the cost is an indirect cost, as with Elegant Rugs, the independent variable is also called a cost-allocation base. Although these terms are sometimes used interchangeably, we use the term *cost driver* to describe the independent variable. Frequently, the management accountant, working with the management team, will cycle through the six steps several times, trying alternative economically plausible cost drivers to identify a cost driver that best fits the data.

Recall that cost driver should be measurable and have an economically plausible relationship with the dependent variable and be measurable. Economic plausibility means that the relationship (describing how changes in the cost driver lead to changes in the costs being considered) is based on a physical relationship, a contract, or knowledge of operations and makes economic sense to the operating manager and the management accountant. As we learned in Chapter 5, all the individual items of costs included in the dependent variable should have the same cost driver, that is, the cost pool should be homogenous. When all items of costs in the dependent variable do not have the same cost driver, the cost analyst should investigate the possibility of creating homogenous cost pools and estimating more than one cost function, one for each cost item/cost driver pair.

As an example, consider several types of fringe benefits paid to employees and the cost drivers of the benefits:

Fringe Benefit	Cost Driver
Health benefits	Number of employees
Cafeteria meals	Number of employees
Pension benefits	Salaries of employees
Life insurance	Salaries of employees

The costs of health benefits and cafeteria meals can be combined into one homogenous cost pool because they have the same cost driver—the number of employees. Pension benefits and life insurance costs have a different cost driver—the salaries of employees—and, therefore, should not be combined with health benefits and cafeteria meals. Instead, pension benefits and life insurance costs should be combined into a separate homogenous cost pool. The cost pool comprising pension benefits and life insurance costs can be estimated using salaries of employees receiving these benefits as the cost driver.

Step 3:   Collect data on the dependent variable and the cost driver. This is usually the most difficult step in cost analysis. Management accountants obtain data from company documents, from interviews with managers, and through special studies. These data may be time-series data or cross-sectional data.

Time-series data pertain to the same entity (such as on organization or plant or activity,) over successive past periods. Weekly observations of indirect manufacturing labor costs and number of machine-hours of Elegant Rugs are examples of time-series data. The ideal time-series database would contain numerous observations for a company whose operations have not been affected by economic or technological change. A stable economy

Learning Objective 4

Outline six steps in estimating a cost function using quantitative analysis

. . . the end result (step 6) is to evaluate the cost driver of the estimated cost function

and technology ensure that data collected during the estimation period represent the same underlying relationship between the cost driver and the dependent variable. Moreover, the periods used to measure the dependent variable and the cost driver should be consistent throughout the observations.

Cross-sectional data pertain to different entities during the same period. For example, studies of loans processed and the related personnel costs at 50 individual, yet similar branches of a bank during March 2014 would produce cross-sectional data for that month. The cross-sectional data should be drawn from entities that, within each entity, have a similar relationship between the cost driver and costs. Later in this chapter, we describe the problems that arise in data collection.

Step 4: Plot the data. The general relationship between the cost driver and costs can be readily seen in a plot of the data once it's graphed. The plot provides insight into the relevant range of the cost function and reveals whether the relationship between the driver and costs is approximately linear. Moreover, the plot highlights extreme observations (observations outside the general pattern) that analysts should check. Was there an error in recording the data or an unusual event, such as a work stoppage, that makes these observations unrepresentative of the normal relationship between the cost driver and the costs?

Exhibit 10-4 is a plot of the weekly data from columns B and C of the Excel spreadsheet in Exhibit 10-3. This graph provides strong visual evidence of a positive linear relationship between Elegant Rugs' number of machine-hours and indirect manufacturing labor costs (when machine-hours go up, so do indirect manufacturing labor costs). There do not appear to be any extreme observations in Exhibit 10-4. The relevant range is from 46 to 96 machine-hours per week (weeks 8 and 6, respectively).

Step 5: Estimate the cost function. The two most common forms of quantitative analysis managers and accountants use to estimate a cost function are the high-low method and regression analysis. Even though computer programs such as Excel make regression analysis much easier, we will describe the high-low method to provide some basic intuition for the idea of drawing a line to "fit" a number of data points. We present these methods after Step 6.

Step 6: Evaluate the cost driver of the estimated cost function. In this step, we describe the criteria for evaluating the cost driver of the estimated cost function. But to do so you first need to understand both the high-low method and regression analysis. Identifying cost drivers is a critical aspect of managing costs and improving profitability and therefore a vital component in a manager's toolkit.

Exhibit 10-4

Plot of Weekly Indirect Manufacturing Labor Costs and Machine-Hours for Elegant Rugs

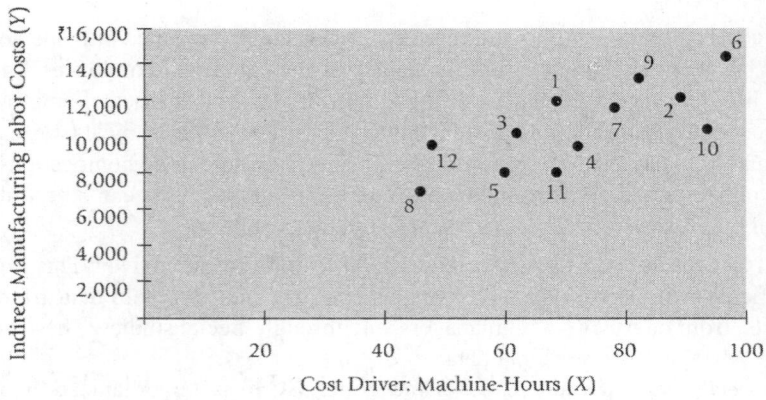

High-Low Method

The simplest form of quantitative analysis to "fit" a line to data points is the **high-low method**. It uses only the highest and lowest observed values of the cost driver within the relevant range and their respective costs to estimate the slope coefficient and the constant of the cost function. It provides a quick first look at the relationship between a cost driver and costs. We illustrate the high-low method using data from Exhibit 10-3.

	Cost Driver: Machine-Hours (X)	Indirect Manufacturing Labor Costs (Y)
Highest observation of cost driver (week 6)	96	₹14,560
Lowest observation of cost driver (week 8)	46	7,100
Difference	50	₹7,460

The slope coefficient, b, is calculated as:

$$\text{Slope coefficient} = \frac{\text{Difference between costs associated with highest and lowest observations of the cost driver}}{\text{Difference between highest and lowest observations of the cost driver}}$$

$$= ₹7,460 \div 50 \text{ machine-hours} = ₹149.2 \text{ per machine-hour}$$

To compute the constant, we can use either the highest or the lowest observation of the cost driver. Both calculations yield the same answer because the solution technique solves two linear equations with two unknowns, the slope coefficient and the constant. Because

$$Y = a + bX$$
$$a = y - bX$$

At the highest observation of the cost driver, the constant, a, is calculated as:

$$\text{Constant} = ₹14,560 - ₹149.2 \text{ per machine-hours} \times 96 \text{ machine-hours} = ₹236.8$$

And at the lowest observation of the cost driver, a is:

$$\text{Constant} = ₹7,100 - ₹149.2 \text{ per machine-hours} \times 46 \text{ machine-hours} = ₹236.8$$

Thus, the high-low estimate of the cost function is:

$$a = y + bX$$
$$Y = ₹236.8 + (₹149.2 \text{ per machine-hours} \times \text{Number of machine-hours})$$

The black line in Exhibit 10-5 shows the estimated cost function using the high-low method (based on the data in Exhibit 10-3). The estimated cost function is a straight line joining the observations with the highest and lowest values of the cost driver (number of machine-hours). Note how this simple high-low line falls "in-between" the data points with three observations on the line, four above it and five below it. The intercept ($a = ₹236.8$), the point where the dashed extension of the maroon line meets the y-axis, is the constant component of the equation that provides the best linear approximation of how a cost behaves *within the relevant range* of 46 to 96 machine-hours. Managers should *not* intercept as an estimate of the fixed costs if no machines were run. The reason is that running no machines and shutting down the plant—that is, using zero machine-hours—is *outside the relevant range*.

Suppose Elegant Rugs' indirect manufacturing labor costs in week 6 were ₹12,800, instead of ₹14,560, and that 96 machine-hours were used. In this case, the highest observation of the cost driver (96 machine-hours in week 6) will not coincide with the newer highest observation of the costs (₹13,160 in week 9). How would this change affect our high-low calculation? Given that the cause-and-effect relationship runs *from* the cost driver *to* the costs in a cost function, we choose the highest and lowest observations of the cost driver (the factor that causes the costs to change). The high-low method would still estimate the new cost function using data from weeks 6 (high) and 8 (low).

The high-low method is simple to compute and easy to understand. It gives the managers of Elegant Rugs quick initial insight into how the cost driver—the number

Exhibit 10-5

High-Low Method
for Weekly Indirect
Manufacturing Labor
Costs and Machine-
Hours for Elegant Rugs

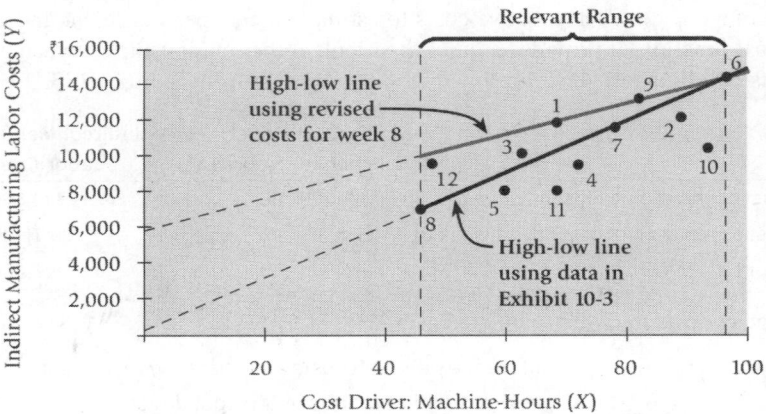

of machine-hours—affects the firm's indirect manufacturing labor costs. However, i
is dangerous for managers to rely on only two observations to estimate a cost function. Suppose that because a labor contract guarantees certain minimum payments in
week 8, indirect manufacturing labor costs in week 8 were ₹10,000, instead of ₹7,100
when only 46 machine-hours were used. The green line in Exhibit 10-5 shows the cos
function that would be estimated by the high-low method using this revised cost. Other
than the two points used to draw the line, all other data lie on or below the line! In this
case, choosing the highest and lowest observations for machine-hours would result in
an estimated cost function that poorly describes the underlying linear cost relationship
between number of machine-hours and indirect manufacturing labor costs. In such a
situation, managers can modify the high-low method so that the two observations chosen to estimate the cost function are a *representative high* and a *representative low*. By
making this adjustment, managers can avoid having extreme observations, which arise
from abnormal events, influence the estimate of the cost function. The modification
allows managers to estimate a cost function that is representative of the relationship
between the cost driver and costs and, therefore, is more useful for making decisions
(such as pricing and performance evaluation). Next we describe the regression analysis
method. Rather than just high and low values, it uses all available data to estimate the
cost function.

Regression Analysis Method

Regression analysis is a statistical method that measures the average amount of change in
the dependent variable associated with a unit change in one or more independent variables
The method is widely used because it helps managers "get behind the numbers" so they
understand why costs behave the way they do and what managers can do to influence them
For example, at Analog Devices, a maker of digital and analog integrated circuits, managers
use regression analysis to evaluate how and why defect rates and product quality change
over time. Managers who understand these relationships gain greater insight into their businesses, make more judicious decisions, and manage more effectively.

Simple regression analysis estimates the relationship between the dependent variable
and *one* independent variable. In the Elegant Rugs example, the dependent variable is total
indirect manufacturing labor costs; the single independent variable, or cost driver, is the
number of machine-hours. **Multiple regression** analysis estimates the relationship between
the dependent variable and *two or more* independent variables. Multiple regression analysis
for Elegant Rugs might use as the independent variables the number of machine-hours and
number of batches.

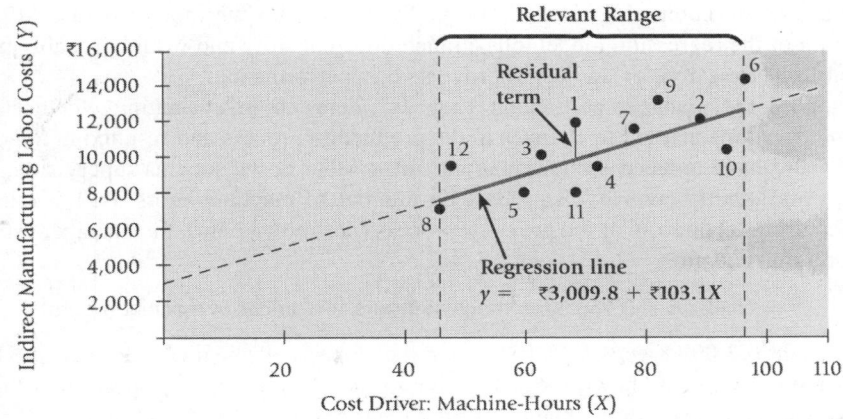

Exhibit 10-6

Regression Model
for Weekly Indirect
Manufacturing Labor
Costs and Machine-
Hours for Elegant Rugs

In later sections, we will explain how to use Excel to do regression analysis. Here we will discuss how managers interpret and use the output from programs such as Excel to make critical strategic decisions. Exhibit 10-6 shows the line developed using regression analysis that best fits the data in columns B and C of Exhibit 10-3. Excel estimates the cost function to be

$$Y = ₹3,009.8 + ₹103.1X$$

The regression line in Exhibit 10-6 is derived using the least-squares technique. The least-squares technique determines the regression line by minimizing the sum of the squared vertical differences from the data points (the various points in the graph) to the regression line. The vertical difference, called **residual term**, measures the distance between actual cost and estimated cost for each observation of the cost driver. Exhibit 10-6 shows the residual term for the week 1 data. The line from the observation to the regression line is drawn perpendicular to the horizontal axis, or *x*-axis. The smaller the residual terms, the better the fit between actual cost observations and estimated costs. *Goodness of fit* indicates the strength of the relationship between the cost driver and costs. The regression line in Exhibit 10-6 rises from left to right. The positive slope of this line and small residual terms indicate that, on average, indirect manufacturing labor costs increase as the number of machine-hours increases. The vertical dashed lines in Exhibit 10-6 indicate the relevant range, the range within which the cost function applies.

The estimate of the slope coefficient, *b*, indicates that indirect manufacturing labor costs vary at the average amount of ₹103.1 for every machine-hour used within the relevant range. Managers can use the regression equation when budgeting for future indirect manufacturing labor costs. For instance, if 90 machine-hours are budgeted for the upcoming week, the predicted indirect manufacturing labor costs would be

$$Y = ₹3,009.8 + (₹103.1 \text{ per machine-hours} \times \text{Number of machine-hours}) = ₹12,288.8$$

As we have already mentioned, the regression method is more accurate than the high-low method because the regression equation estimates costs using information from all observations, whereas the high-low equation uses information from only two observations. The inaccuracies of the high-low method can mislead managers. Consider the high-low method equation in the preceding section, $y = ₹236.8 + ₹149.2$ per machine-hour × Number of machine-hours. For 90 machine-hours, the predicted weekly cost based on the high-low method equation is ₹236.8 + (₹149.2 per machine-hour × 90 machine-hours) = ₹13,664.8. Suppose that for 7 weeks over the next 12-week period, Elegant Rugs runs its machines for 90 hours each week. Assume the average indirect manufacturing labor costs for those 7 weeks are ₹13,000. Based on the high-low method prediction of ₹13,664.8, Elegant Rugs would conclude it has performed well because actual costs are less than predicted costs. But comparing the ₹13,000 performance with the more-accurate ₹12,288.8 prediction of the regression model tells a much different story and would probably prompt Elegant Rugs to search for ways to improve its cost performance.

Suppose the manager at Elegant Rugs is interested in evaluating whether recent strategic decisions that led to changes in the production process and resulted in the data in Exhibit 10-3 have reduced indirect manufacturing labor costs, such as supervision, maintenance, and quality control. Using data on number of machine-hours used and indirect manufacturing labor costs of the previous process (not shown here), the manager estimates the regression equation,

$$Y = ₹5,452.6 + (₹158.6 \text{ per machine-hours} \times \text{Number of machine-hours})$$

The constant (₹3,009.8 versus ₹5,452.6) and the slope coefficient (₹103.1 versus ₹158.6) are both smaller for the new process relative to the old process. It appears that the new process has decreased indirect manufacturing labor costs.

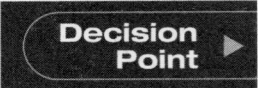

Decision Point ▶

What are the steps to estimate a cost function using quantitative analysis?

Learning Objective 5

Describe three criteria used to evaluate and choose cost drivers

. . . economically plausible relationships, goodness of fit, and significant effect of the cost driver on costs

Evaluating and Choosing Cost Drivers

How does a company determine the best cost driver when estimating a cost function? In many cases, managers must understand both operations and cost accounting. To see why understanding operations is needed, consider the costs to maintain and repair metal-cutting machines at Helix Company Ltd., a manufacturer of treadmills. Helix schedules repairs and maintenance at a time when production is at a low level to avoid having to take machines out of service when they are needed most. An analysis of the monthly data will then show high repair costs in months of low production and low repair costs in months of high production. Someone unfamiliar with operations might conclude that there is an inverse relationship between production and repair costs. The engineering link between units produced and repair costs, however, is usually clear-cut. Over time, there is a cause-and-effect relationship: the higher the level of production, the higher the repair costs. To estimate the relationship correctly, operating managers and analysts will recognize that repair costs will tend to lag behind periods of high production, and hence, they will use production of prior periods as the cost driver.

In other cases, choosing a cost driver is more subtle and difficult. Consider again indirect manufacturing labor costs at Elegant Rugs. Although both the number of machine-hours and the number of direct manufacturing labor-hours are plausible cost drivers of indirect manufacturing labor costs, managers are not sure which is the better cost driver. Exhibit 10-7 presents weekly data (in Excel) on indirect manufacturing labor costs and number of machine-hours for the most recent 12-week period from Exhibit 10-3, together with data on the number of direct manufacturing labor-hours for the same period.

What guidance do the different cost-estimation methods provide for choosing among cost drivers? The industrial engineering method relies on analyzing physical relationships between cost drivers and costs, relationships that are difficult to specify in this case. The conference method and the account analysis method use subjective assessments to choose a cost driver and to estimate the fixed and variable components of the cost function. In these cases, managers must rely on their best judgment. Managers cannot use these methods to test and try alternative cost drivers. The major advantages of quantitative methods are that they are objective—a given data set and estimation method result in a unique estimated cost function—and managers can use them to evaluate different cost drivers. We use the regression analysis approach to illustrate how to evaluate different cost drivers.

First, the cost analyst at Elegant Rugs enters data in columns C and D of Exhibit 10-7 in Excel and estimates the following regression equation of indirect manufacturing labor

	File Edit View Insert Format Tools Data Window Help			
	A	B	C	D
1	Week	Original Cost Driver: Machine-Hours	Alternate Cost Driver: Direct Manufacturing Labor-Hours (X)	Indirect Manufacturing Labor Costs (Y)
2	1	68	30	₹11,900
3	2	88	35	12,110
4	3	62	36	10,040
5	4	72	20	9,170
6	5	60	47	7,700
7	6	96	45	14,560
8	7	78	44	11,800
9	8	46	38	7,100
10	9	82	70	13,160
11	10	94	30	10,320
12	11	68	29	7,520
13	12	48	38	9,630
14	Total	862	462	₹1,25,010
15				

Exhibit 10-7

Weekly Indirect Manufacturing Labor Costs, Machine-Hours, and Direct Manufacturing Labor-Hours for Elegant Rugs

costs based on number of direct manufacturing labor-hours:

$$Y = ₹7,446.7 + ₹77.2X$$

Exhibit 10-8 shows the plot of the data points for number of direct manufacturing labor-hours and indirect manufacturing labor costs, and the regression line that best fits the data. Recall that Exhibit 10-6 shows the corresponding graph when number of machine-hours is the cost driver. To decide which of the two cost drivers Elegant Rugs should choose, the analyst compares the machine-hour regression equation and the direct manufacturing labor-hour regression equation. There are three criteria used to make this evaluation.

1. **Economic plausibility.** Both cost drivers are economically plausible. However, in the state-of-the-art, highly automated production environment at Elegant Rugs, managers

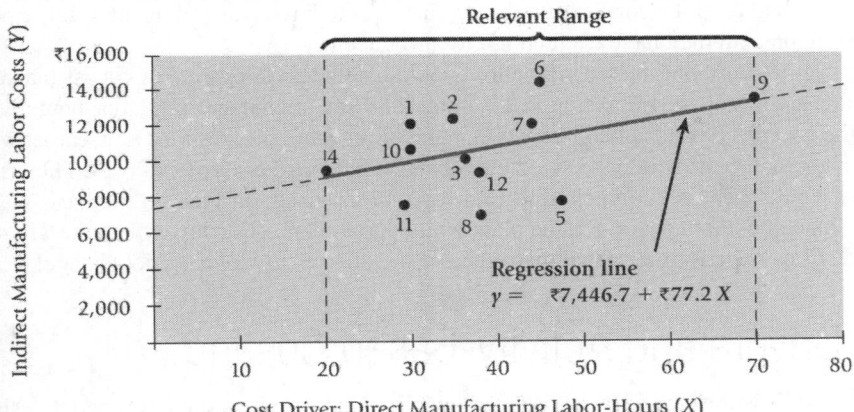

Exhibit 10-8

Regression Model for Weekly Indirect Manufacturing Labor Costs and Direct Manufacturing Labor-Hours for Elegant Rugs

familiar with the operations believe that costs such as machine maintenance are likely to be more closely related to number of machine-hours used than to number of direct manufacturing labor-hours used.

2. **Goodness of fit.** Compare Exhibits 10-6 and 10-8. The vertical differences between actual costs and predicted costs are much smaller for the machine-hours regression than for the direct manufacturing labor-hours regression. The number of machine-hours used, therefore, has a stronger relationship—or goodness of fit—with indirect manufacturing labor costs.

3. **Significance of independent variable.** Again compare Exhibits 10-6 and 10-8 (both of which have been drawn to roughly the same scale). The machine-hours regression line has a steep slope relative to the slope of the direct manufacturing labor-hours regression line. *For the same (or more) scatter of observations about the line (goodness of fit)*, a flat, or slightly sloped regression line indicates a weak relationship between the cost driver and costs. In our example, changes in direct manufacturing labor-hours appear to have a small influence or effect on indirect manufacturing labor costs.

Based on this evaluation, managers at Elegant Rugs select number of machine-hours as the cost driver and use the cost function $y = ₹3,009.8 + (₹10.31$ per machine-hour $\times$ Number of machine-hours) to predict future indirect manufacturing labor costs.

Why is choosing the correct cost driver to estimate indirect manufacturing labor costs important? Because identifying the wrong drivers or misestimating cost functions can lead management to incorrect (and costly) decisions along a variety of dimensions. Consider the following strategic decision that management at Elegant Rugs must make. The company is thinking of introducing a new style of carpet that, from a manufacturing standpoint, is similar to the carpets it has manufactured in the past. The company expects to sell 650 square yards of this carpet each week. Managers estimates 72 machine-hours and 21 direct manufacturing labor-hours are be required per week to produce this amount of output. Using the machine-hour regression equation, Elegant Rugs would predict indirect manufacturing labor costs of $y = ₹3,009.8 + (₹103.1$ per machine-hour $\times$ 72 machine-hours$) = ₹10,433.0$. If the company used direct manufacturing labor-hours as the cost driver, it would incorrectly predict costs of $₹7,446.7 + (₹77.2$ per labor-hour $\times$ 21 labor-hours$) = ₹9,067.9$. If Elegant Rugs chose similarly incorrect cost drivers for other indirect costs as well and systematically underestimated costs, it would conclude that the costs of manufacturing the new style of carpet would be low and basically fixed (fixed because the regression line is nearly flat). But the actual costs driven by number of machine-hours used and other correct cost drivers would be higher. By failing to identify the proper cost drivers, managers would be misled into believing the new style of carpet would be more profitable than it actually is. If the managers had used the correct cost driver, they would have realized the new carpet was not as profitable and may have decided not to introduce it.

Incorrectly estimating the cost function would also affect Elegant Rugs' cost management and cost control activities. Suppose number of direct manufacturing labor-hours were used as the cost driver, and actual indirect manufacturing labor costs for the new carpet were ₹9,700. The actual costs would then be higher than the predicted costs of ₹9,067.9. The firm's managers would then feel compelled to find ways to cut costs. In fact, on the basis of the preferred machine-hour cost driver, the plant would have actual costs lower than the ₹10,433 predicted costs—a performance that management should seek to replicate, not change!

Cost Drivers and Activity-Based Costing

Activity-based costing (ABC) systems focus on individual activities such as product design, machine setup, materials handling, distribution, and customer service as the fundamental cost objects. To implement ABC systems, managers must identify a cost driver for each activity. Consider, for example, a manager at Westronics, a manufacturer of electronic products. Using methods described in this chapter, the manager must decide whether the number of loads moved or the weight of loads moved is the cost driver of materials-handling costs.

To choose the cost driver, the manager collects data on materials-handling costs and the quantities of the two competing cost drivers over a reasonably long period. Why a long period? Because in the short run, materials-handling costs may be fixed and, therefore, will not vary with changes in the level of the cost driver. In the long run, however, there is a clear cause-and-effect relationship between materials-handling costs and the cost driver. Suppose number of loads moved is the cost driver of materials-handling costs. Increases in the number of loads moved will require more materials-handling labor and equipment; decreases in the number of loads moved will result in equipment being sold and labor being reassigned to other tasks.

ABC systems have a great number and variety of cost drivers and cost pools. That means ABC systems require many cost relationships to be estimated. When estimating the cost function for each cost pool, the manager must pay careful attention to the cost hierarchy. For example, if a cost is a batch-level cost such as setup cost, the manager must only consider batch-level cost drivers like number of setup-hours. In some cases, the costs in a cost pool may have more than one cost driver from different levels of the cost hierarchy. The cost drivers for Elegant Rugs' indirect manufacturing labor costs could be machine-hours and the number of production batches of carpet manufactured. Furthermore, it may be difficult to subdivide the indirect manufacturing labor costs into two cost pools and to measure the costs associated with each cost driver. In these cases, companies use multiple regression to estimate costs based on more than one independent variable.

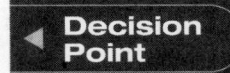

Decision Point

How should a company evaluate and choose cost drivers?

Nonlinear Cost Functions

As we explained, cost functions are not always linear. A **nonlinear cost function** is a cost function for which the graph of total costs (based on the level of a single activity) is not a straight line within the relevant range. To see what a nonlinear cost function looks like, return to Exhibit 10-2. The relevant range is currently set at 20,000 to 65,000 snowboards. But if we extend the relevant range to cover the region from 0 to 80,000 snowboards produced, it is evident that the cost function over this expanded range is graphically represented by a line that is not straight.

Consider another example. Economies of scale in advertising may enable an advertising agency to produce double the number of advertisements for less than double the costs. Even direct material costs are not always linear. As shown in Exhibit 10-9, Panel A, total direct material costs rise as the units of direct materials purchased increase. But, because of quantity discounts, these costs rise more slowly (as indicated by the slope coefficient) as the units of direct materials purchased increase. This cost function has $b = ₹250$ per unit for 1 to 1,000 units purchased, $b = ₹150$ per unit for 1,001 to 2,000 units purchased, and $b = ₹100$ per unit for 2,001 to 3,000 units purchased. The direct material cost per unit falls at each price. The cost function is nonlinear over the relevant range from 1 to 3,000 units. the direct materials cost per unit falls with each price cut Over a more narrow relevant range (for example, from 1 to 1,000 units), the cost function is linear.

Step cost functions are also nonlinear cost functions. A **step cost function** is a cost function in which the cost remains the same over various ranges of the level of activity, but the cost increases by discrete amounts—that is, increases in steps—as the level of activity increases from one range to the next. Panel B in Exhibit 10-9 shows a *step variable-cost function*, a step cost function in which cost remains the same over *narrow* ranges of the

Learning Objective 6

Explain nonlinear cost functions

. . . graph of cost function is not a straight line, for example, because of quantity discounts or costs changing in steps

in particular those arising from learning curve effects

. . . either cumulative average-time learning, where cumulative average time per unit declines by a constant percentage, as units produced double

. . . or incremental unit-time learning, in which incremental time to produce last unit declines by constant percentage, as units produced double

Exhibit 10-9   Examples of Nonlinear Cost Functions

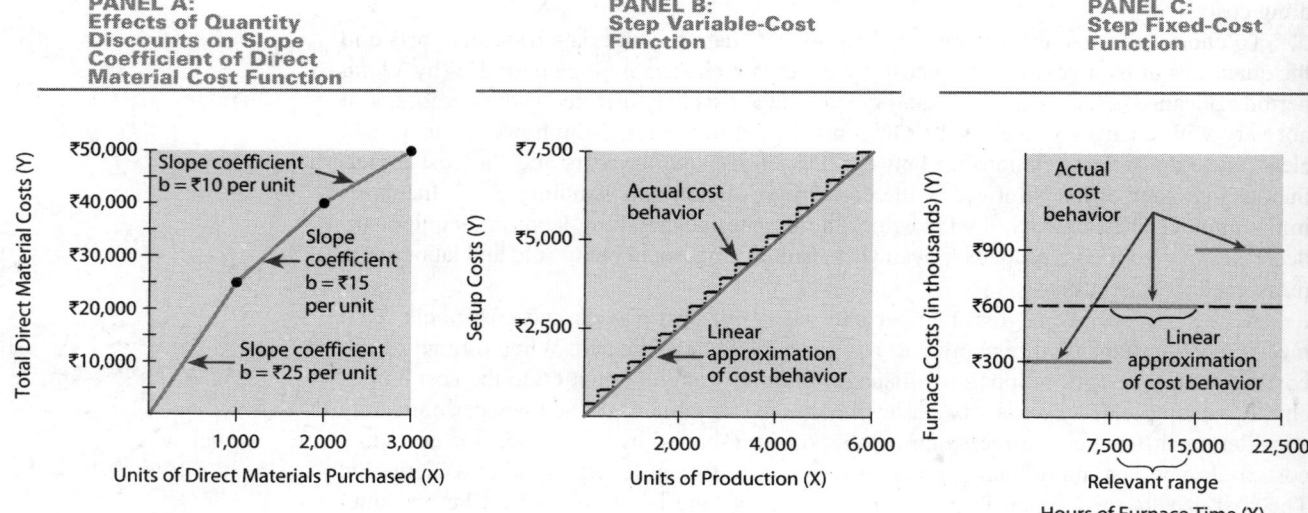

PANEL A:
Effects of Quantity Discounts on Slope Coefficient of Direct Material Cost Function

PANEL B:
Step Variable-Cost Function

PANEL C:
Step Fixed-Cost Function

level of activity in each relevant range. Panel B presents the relationship between units of production and setup costs. The pattern is a step cost function because, as we described in Chapter 5 on activity-based costing, setup costs are related to each production batch started. If the relevant range is considered to be from 0 to 6,000 production units, the cost function is nonlinear. However, as shown by the gray line in Panel B, managers often approximate step variable costs with a continuously-variable cost function. This type of step cost pattern also occurs when production inputs such as materials-handling labor, supervision, and process engineering labor are acquired in discrete quantities but used in fractional quantities.

Panel C in Exhibit 10-9 shows a *step fixed-cost function* for Crofton Steel, a company that operates large heat-treatment furnaces to harden steel parts. Looking at Panel C and Panel B, you can see that the main difference between a step variable-cost function and a step fixed-cost function is that the cost in a step fixed-cost function remains the same over *wide* ranges of the activity in each relevant range. The ranges indicate the number of furnaces being used (each furnace costs ₹30,00,000). The cost increases from one range to the next higher range when another furnace is used. The relevant range of 7,500 to 15,000 hours of furnace time indicates that the company expects to operate with two furnaces at a cost of ₹60,00,000. Managers considers the cost of operating furnaces as a fixed cost within this relevant range of operation. However, if the relevant range is considered to be from 0 to 22,500 hours, the cost function is nonlinear: The graph in Panel C is not a single straight line; it is three broken lines.

Learning Curves

Nonlinear cost functions also result from learning curves. A **learning curve** is a function that measures how labor-hours per unit decline as units of production increase because workers are learning and becoming better at their jobs. Managers use learning curves to predict how labor-hours, or labor costs, will increase as more units are produced.

The aircraft-assembly industry first documented the effect that learning has on efficiency. In general, as workers become more familiar with their tasks, their efficiency improves. Managers learn how to improve the scheduling of work shifts and how to operate the plant better. As a result, unit costs decrease as productivity increases, and the unit-cost function behaves nonlinearly. These nonlinearities must be considered when estimating and predicting unit costs.

The term *experience curve* describes a broader application of the learning curve—one that extends to other business functions in the value chain, such as marketing, distribution, and customer service. An **experience curve** measures the decline in cost per unit in various business functions as the amount of these activities increases. For companies such as Dell Computer, Wal-Mart, and McDonald's, learning curves and experience curves are key elements of their profit-maximization strategies. These companies use learning curves and experience curves to reduce costs and increase customer satisfaction, market share, and profitability.

We now describe two learning-curve models: the cumulative average-time learning model and the incremental unit-time learning model.

Cumulative Average-Time Learning Model

In the **cumulative average-time learning model**, cumulative average time per unit declines by a constant percentage each time the cumulative quantity of units produced doubles. Consider Rayburn Company, a radar systems manufacturer. Rayburn has an 80% learning curve. This means that when Rayburn doubles the quantity of units produced is doubled from X to $2X$, the cumulative average time *per unit* for $2X$ units is 80% of cumulative average time *per unit* the X units. In other words, the average time per unit has dropped by 20% (100% − 80%). Exhibit 10-10 shows (in Excel) the calculations for the cumulative average-time learning model for Rayburn Company. Note that as the number of units produced doubles from 1 to 2 in column A, the cumulative average time per unit declines from 100 hours to 80% of 100 hours (0.80 × 100 hours = 80 hours) in column B. As the number of units doubles from 2 to 4, the cumulative average time per unit declines to 80% of 80 hours = 64 hours, and so on. To obtain the cumulative total time in column D, multiply cumulative average time per unit by the cumulative number of units produced. For example, to produce 4 cumulative units would require 256 labor-hours (4 units × 64 cumulative average labor-hours per unit).

Incremental Unit-Time Learning Model

In the **incremental unit-time learning model**, incremental time needed to produce the last unit declines by a constant percentage each time the cumulative quantity of units produced doubles. Again, consider Rayburn Company and an 80% learning curve. With this model, the 80% means that when the quantity of units produced is doubled from X to $2X$, the time needed to produce the unit corresponding to $2X$ is 80% of the time needed to produce the Xth unit. Exhibit 10-11 shows the Excel calculations for the incremental unit-time learning model for Rayburn Company based on an 80% learning curve. Note how when units produced double from 2 to 4 in column A, the time to produce unit 4 (the last unit when 4 units are produced) is 64 hours in column B, which is 80% of the 80 hours needed to produce unit 2 (the last unit when 2 units are produced). We obtain the cumulative total time in column D by summing individual unit times in column B. For example, to produce 4 cumulative units would require 314.21 labor-hours (100.00 + 80.00 + 70.21 + 64.00).

Exhibit 10-10   Cumulative Average-Time Learning Model for Rayburn Company

	File Edit View Insert Format Tools Data Window Help

	A	B	C	D	E	F	G	H	I
1	Cumulative Average-Time Learning Model for Rayburn Company								
2									
3		80% Learning Curve							
4									
5	Cumulative	Cumulative		Cumulative	Individual Unit				
6	Number	Average Time		Total Time:	Time for X th				
7	of Units (X)	per Unit (y)*: Labor Hours		Labor-Hours	Unit: Labor Hours				
8									
9				D = Col A x Col B					
10									
11	1	100.00		100.00	100.00				
12	2	80.00	=(100x0.8)	160.00	60.00				
13	3	70.21		210.63	50.63				
14	4	64.00	=(80x0.8)	256.00	45.37				
15	5	59.56		297.82	41.82				
16	6	56.17		337.01	39.19				
17	7	53.45		374.14	37.13				
18	8	51.20	=(64x0.8)	409.60	35.46				
19	9	49.29		443.65	34.05				
20	10	47.65		476.51	32.86				
21	11	46.21		508.32	31.81				
22	12	44.93		539.22	30.89				
23	13	43.79		569.29	30.07				
24	14	42.76		598.63	29.34				
25	15	41.82		627.30	28.67				
26	16	40.96	=(51.2x0.8)	655.36	28.06				
27									

E13 = D13 - D12
= 210.63 - 160.00

*The mathematical relationship underlying the cumulative average-time learning model is:

$$y = aX^b$$

where y = Cumulative average time (labor-hours) per unit
X = Cumulative number of units produced
a = Time (labor-hours) required to produce the first unit
b = Factor used to calculate cumulative average time to produce units

The value of b is calculated as

$$\frac{\ln (\text{learning-curve \% in decimal form})}{\ln 2}$$

For an 80% learning curve, b = ln 0.8/ln 2 = -0.2231/0.6931 = -0.3219
when X = 3, a = 100, b = -0.3219,

$$y = 100 \times 3^{-0.3219} = 70.21 \text{ labor hours}$$

Numbers in table may not be exact because of rounding.

Exhibit 10-12 shows the cumulative average-time learning model (using data from Exhibit 10-10) and the incremental unit-time learning model (using data from Exhibit 10-11). Panel A illustrates the cumulative average time per unit as a function of cumulative units produced for each model (column A in Exhibit 10-10 or 10-11). The curve for the cumulative average-time learning model is plotted using the data from Exhibit 10-10, column B, whereas the curve for the incremental unit-time learning model is plotted using the data from Exhibit 10-11, column E. Panel B graphically illustrates the cumulative total labor-hours again as a function of cumulative units produced for each model. The curve for the cumulative average-time learning model is plotted using the data from Exhibit 10-10, column D, while that for the incremental unit-time learning model is plotted using the data from Exhibit 10-11, column D.

Assuming the learning rate is the same for both models, the cumulative average-time learning model represents a faster pace of learning. This is evidenced by the fact that in Exhibit 10-12, Panel B, the cumulative total labor-hours graph for the 80% incremental unit-time learning model lies above the graph for the 80% cumulative average-time learning model. If we compare the results in Exhibit 10-10 (column D) with the results in Exhibit 10-11 (column D), to produce 4 cumulative units, the 80% incremental unit-time learning model predicts 314.21 labor-hours whereas the 80% cumulative average-time learning

Exhibit 10-11   Incremental Unit-Time Learning Model for Rayburn Company

	A	B	C	D	E	F	G	H	I
1	Incremental Unit-Time Learning Model for Rayburn Company								
2									
3		80% Learning Curve							
4									
5	Cumulative	Individual Unit Time		Cumulative	Cumulative				
6	Number	for Xth Unit (y)*:		Total Time:	Average Time				
7	of Units (X)	Labor Hours		Labor-Hours	per Unit:				
8					Labor-Hours				
9									
10					E = Col D ÷ Col A				
11									
12	1	100.00		100.00	100.00		D14 = D13 + B14		
13	2	80.00	=(100x0.8)	180.00	90.00		= 180.00 + 70.21		
14	3	70.21		250.21	83.40				
15	4	64.00	=(80x0.8)	314.21	78.55				
16	5	59.56		373.77	74.75				
17	6	56.17		429.94	71.66				
18	7	53.45		483.39	69.06				
19	8	51.20	=(64x0.8)	534.59	66.82				
20	9	49.29		583.89	64.88				
21	10	47.65		631.54	63.15				
22	11	46.21		677.75	61.61				
23	12	44.93		722.68	60.22				
24	13	43.79		766.47	58.96				
25	14	42.76		809.23	57.80				
26	15	41.82		851.05	56.74				
27	16	40.96	=(51.2x0.8)	892.01	55.75				
28									

*The mathematical relationship underlying the incremental unit-time learning model is:

$$y = aX^b$$

where y = Time (labor-hours) taken to produce the last single unit
X = Cumulative number of units produced
a = Time (labor-hours) required to produce the first unit
b = Factor used to calculate incremental unit time to produce units
$$= \frac{\text{ln (learning-curve \% in decimal form)}}{\text{ln2}}$$

For an 80% learning curve, $b = \ln 0.8 \div \ln 2 = -0.2231 \div 0.6931 = -0.3219$
Where $X = 3$, $a = 100$, $b = -0.3219$,
$$y = 100 \times 3^{-0.3219} = 70.21 \text{ labor hours}$$
The cumulative total time when $X = 3$ is 100+80+70.21=250.21 labor-hours.
Numbers in the table may not be exact because of rounding.

Exhibit 10-12   Plots for Cumulative Average-Time Learning Model and Incremental Unit-Time Learning Model for Rayburn Company

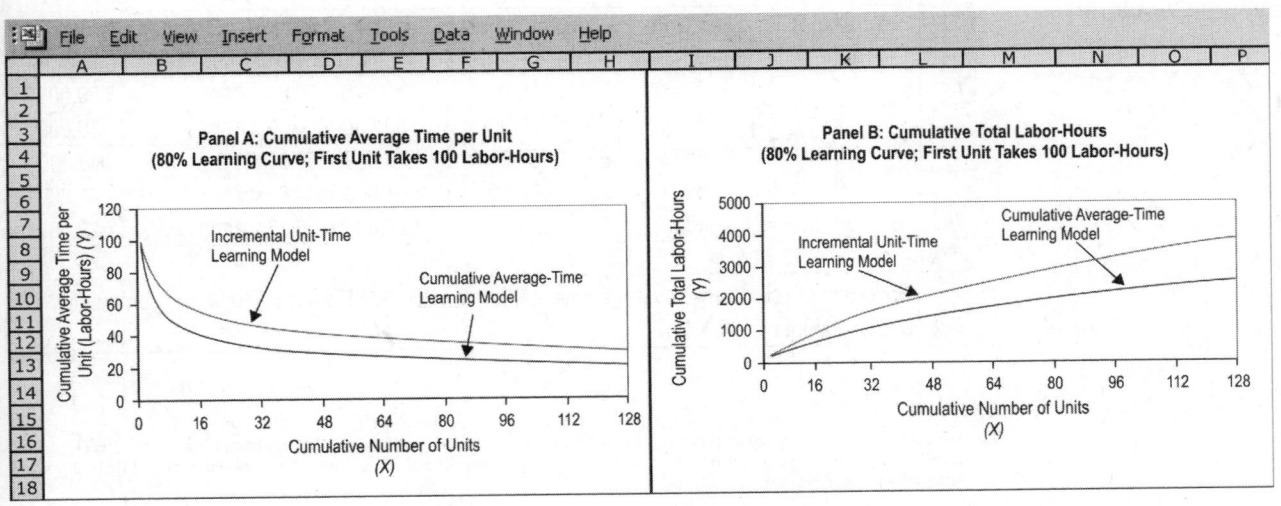

model predicts 256.0 labor-hour. That's because under the cumulative average-time learning model *average labor-hours needed to produce all 4 units* is 64 hours; the labor-hour amount needed to produce unit 4 is much less than 64 hours—it is 45.37 hours (see Exhibit 10-10). Under the incremental unit-time learning model, the labor-hour amount needed to produce unit 4 is 64 hours, and the labor-hours needed to produce the first 3 units are more than 64 hours, so average time needed to produce all 4 units is more than 64 hours.

How do managers choose which model and what percent learning curve to use? They do so on a case-by-case basis. For example, if the behavior of manufacturing labor-hour usage as production levels increase follows a pattern like the one predicted by the 80% learning curve cumulative average-time learning model, then the 80% learning curve cumulative average-time learning model should be used. Engineers, plant managers, and workers are good sources of information on the amount and type of learning actually occurring as production increases. Plotting this information and estimating the model that best fits the data is helpful in selecting the appropriate model.[1]

Incorporating Learning-Curve Effects into Prices and Standards

How do companies use learning curves? Consider the data in Exhibit 10-10 for the cumulative average-time learning model at Rayburn Company. Suppose the variable costs subject to learning effects are direct manufacturing labor, at ₹200 per hour, and related overhead, at ₹300 per direct manufacturing labor-hour. Managers should predict the costs shown in Exhibit 10-13.

These data show that the effects of the learning curve could have a major influence on the decisions Rayburn's managers make. For example, the managers might price the firm's radar systems extremely low to generate high demand. As production of the system increases to meet this growing demand, the cost per unit drops and Rayburn "rides the product down the learning curve" as it gains market share. Although it may have earned

Exhibit 10-13

Predicting Costs Using Learning Curves at Rayburn Company

	File Edit View Insert Format Tools Data Window Help					
	A	B	C	D	E	F
1		Cumulative				
2	Cumulative	Average Time	Cumulative	Cumulative Costs		Additions to
3	Number of	per Unit:	Total Time:	at ₹500 per		Cumulative
4	Units	Labor-Hours[a]	Labor-Hours[a]	Labor-Hour		Costs
5	1	100.00	100.00	₹50,000	(100.00 x ₹500	₹50,000
6	2	80.00	160.00	80,000	(160.00 x ₹500	30,000
7	4	64.00	256.00	1,28,000	(256.00 x ₹500	48,000
8	8	51.20	409.60	2,04,800	(409.60 x ₹500	76,800
9	16	40.96	655.36	3,27,680	(655.36 x ₹500	1,22,880
10						
11	[a]Based on the cumulative average-time learning model. See Exhibit 10-10 for the computations					
12	of these amounts.					

---

[1] For details, see C. Bailey, 2000 "Learning Curve Estimation of Production Costs and Labor-Hours Using a Free Excel Add-In," *Management Accounting Quarterly*, Summer: 25–31. Free software for estimating learning curves is available at Dr Bailey's Web site (www.profbailey.com).

little operating income on its first unit sold—it may actually have lost money on that unit—Rayburn earns more operating income per unit as output increases.

Alternatively, subject to legal and other considerations, Rayburn's managers might set a low price on just the final 8 units. After all, the total labor and related overhead costs per unit for these units are predicted to be only ₹1,22,880 (₹3,27,680 − ₹2,04,800). On these final 8 units, the ₹15,360 cost per unit (₹1,22,880 ÷ 8 units) is much lower than the ₹50,000 cost per unit of the first unit produced. Employees are expected to learn on the job, and their performance is evaluated accordingly.

Many companies, such as Pizza Hut and Home Depot, incorporate learning-curve effects when evaluating performance levels. The Nissan Motor Company sets assembly-labor efficiency standards for new models of cars after taking into account the learning that will occur as more units are produced. Employees are expected to learn on the job and their performance is evaluated accordingly.

The learning-curve models examined in Exhibits 10-10 to 10-13 assume that learning is driven by a single variable (production output). Other models of learning have been developed (by companies such as Hewlett-Packard) that focus on how quality—rather than manufacturing labor-hours—will change over time, regardless of whether more units are produced. Studies indicate that factors other than production output, such as job rotation and organizing workers into teams, contribute to learning that improves quality.

◄ **Decision Point**

What is a nonlinear cost function and in what ways do learning curves give rise to nonlinearities?

Data Collection and Adjustment Issues

Learning Objective 7

Be aware of data problems encountered in estimating cost functions

. . . for example, unreliable data and poor recordkeeping, extreme observations, treating fixed costs as if they are variable, and a changing relationship between a cost driver and cost

The ideal database for estimating cost functions quantitatively has two characteristics:

1. **The database should contain numerous reliably measured observations of the cost driver (the independent variable) and the related costs (the dependent variable).** Errors in measuring the costs and the cost driver are serious. They result in inaccurate estimates of the effect of the cost driver on costs.

2. **The database should consider many values spanning a wide range for the cost driver.** Using only a few values of the cost driver that are grouped closely considers too small a segment of the relevant range and reduces the accuracy of the estimates obtained.

Unfortunately, management accountants typically do not have the advantage of working with a database having both characteristics. This section outlines some frequently encountered data problems and steps the cost you can take to overcome these problems. Managers should ask about these problems and assess how they have been resolved before they rely on cost estimates generated from the data.

- The time period for measuring the dependent variable does not properly match the period for measuring the cost driver. This problem often arises when a company does not keep accounting records on the accrual basis. Consider a cost function for a transportation company with engine-lubricant costs as the dependent variable and number of truck-hours as the cost driver. Assume that the lubricant is purchased sporadically and stored for later use. Records maintained on the basis of lubricants purchased will indicate small lubricant costs in many months and large lubricant costs in other months. These records present an obviously inaccurate picture of what is actually taking place. The analyst should use accrual accounting to measure the cost of lubricants consumed to better match costs with the truck-hours cost driver in this example.

- Fixed costs are allocated as if they are variable. For example, costs such as depreciation, insurance, or rent may be allocated to products to calculate cost per unit of output.

The danger for managers is to regard these costs as variable rather than as fixed. The costs appear to be variable but that is related to the allocation methods used, not the actual behavior of the costs. To avoid this problem, the analyst should distinguish carefully fixed costs from variable costs and not treat allocated fixed cost per unit as a variable cost.

■ Data are either not available for all observations or are not uniformly reliable. Missing cost observations often arise because they haven't been recorded or haven't been classified correctly. For example, a firm's marketing costs may be understated because costs of sales visits to customers may be incorrectly recorded as customer-service costs. Recording data manually rather than electronically tends to result in a higher percentage of missing observations and erroneously entered observations. Errors also arise when data on cost drivers originate outside the internal accounting system. For example, the Accounting Department may obtain data on testing-hours for medical instruments from the company's Manufacturing Department and data on number of items shipped to customers from the Distribution Department. One or both of these departments might not keep accurate records. To minimize these problems, the cost analyst should design data collection reports that regularly and routinely obtain the required data and should follow up immediately whenever data are missing.

■ Extreme values of observations occur. These values arise from (a) errors in recording costs (for example, a misplaced decimal point), (b) nonrepresentative periods (for example, from a period in which a major machine breakdown occurred or from a period in which a delay in delivery of materials from an international supplier curtailed production), or (c) observations outside the relevant range. Analysts should adjust or eliminate unusual observations before estimating a cost relationship.

■ There is no homogeneous relationship between the cost driver and the individual cost items in the dependent variable-cost pool. A homogeneous relationship exists when each activity whose costs are included in the dependent variable has the same cost driver. In this case, a single cost function can be estimated. As discussed in step 2 for estimating a cost function using quantitative analysis when the cost driver for each activity is different, separate cost functions, (each with its own cost driver) should be estimated for each activity. Alternatively, as discussed, the analyst should estimate the cost function with more than one independent variable using multiple regression.

■ The relationship between the cost driver and the cost is not stationary. This occurs when the underlying process that generated the observations has not remained stable over time. For example, the relationship between number of machine-hours and manufacturing overhead costs is unlikely to be stationary when the data cover a period in which new technology was introduced. One way to see if the relationship is stationary is to split the sample into two parts and estimate separate cost relationships—one for the period before the technology was introduced and one for the period after the technology was introduced. Then, if the estimated coefficients for the two periods are similar, the analyst can pool the data to estimate a single cost relationship. When feasible, pooling data provides a larger data set for the estimation, which increases confidence in the cost predictions being made.

■ Inflation has affected costs, the cost driver, or both. For example, inflation may cause costs to change even when there is no change in the level of the cost driver. To study the underlying cause-and-effect relationship between the level of the cost driver and costs, the analyst should remove purely inflationary price effects from the data by dividing each cost by the price index on the date the cost was incurred.

In many cases, a cost analyst must expend considerable effort to reduce the effect of these problems before estimating a cost function on the basis of past data. Before making any decisions, a manager should carefully review any data that seem suspect and work closely with the company's analysts and accountants to obtain and process the correct and relevant information.

Decision Point ▶

What are the common data problems a company must watch for when estimating costs?

Problem for Self-Study

The Helicopter Division of GLD, Ltd. is examining helicopter assembly costs at its Indiana plant. It has received an initial order for eight of its new land-surveying helicopters. GLD can adopt one of two methods of assembling the helicopters:

	A	B	C	D	E
		Labor-Intensive Assembly Method		**Machine-Intensive Assembly Method**	
1					
2	Direct material cost per helicopter	₹40,000		₹36,000	
3	Direct-assembly labor time for first helicopter	2,000	labor-hours	800	labor-hours
4	Learning curve for assembly labor time per helicopter	85%	cumulative average time*	₹90%	incremental unit time**
5	Direct-assembly labor cost	₹30	per hour	₹30	per hour
6	Equipment-related indirect manufacturing cost	₹12	per direct-assembly labor-hour	45	per direct-assembly labor-hour
7	Material-handling-related indirect manufacturing cost	50%	of direct material cost	50%	of direct material cost
8					
9					
10	*Using the formula (page 529), for an 85% learning curve, $b = \dfrac{\ln 0.85}{\ln 2} = \dfrac{-0.162519}{0.693147} = -0.234465$				
11					
12					
13					
14					
15	**Using the formula (page 529), for a 90% learning curve, $b = \dfrac{\ln 0.90}{\ln 2} = \dfrac{-0.105361}{0.693147} = -0.152004$				
16					
17					

Required

1. How many direct-assembly labor-hours are required to assemble the first eight helicopters under (a) the labor-intensive method and (b) the machine-intensive method?
2. What is the total cost of assembling the first eight helicopters under (a) the labor-intensive method and (b) the machine-intensive method?

Solution

1. a. The following calculations show the labor-intensive assembly method based on an 85% cumulative average-time learning model (using Excel):

	G	H	I	J	K
1	Cumulative	Cumulative		Cumulative	Individual
2	Number	Average Time		Total Time:	time for
3	of Units	per Unit (y):		Labor-Hours	Xth unit:
4		Labor Hours			Labor-Hours
5				Col J = Col G x Col H	
6	1	2,000		2,000	2,000
7	2	1,700	(2,000 x 0.85)	3,400	1,400
8	3	1,546		4,637	1,237
9	4	1,445	(1,700 x 0.85)	5,780	1,143
10	5	1,371		6,857	1,077
11	6	1,314		7,884	1,027
12	7	1,267		8,871	987
13	8	1,228.25	(1,445 x 0.85)	9,826	955
14					

Cumulative average-time per unit for the Xth unit in column H is calculated as $y = aX^b$; see Exhibit 10-10. For example, when $X = 3$, $y = 2,000 \times 3^{-0.234465} = 1,546$ labor-hours.

b. The following calculations show the machine-intensive assembly method based on a 90% incremental unit-time learning model:

	G	H	I	J	K
	File Edit View Insert Format Tools Data Window Help				
1	Cumulative	Individual		Cumulative	Cumulative
2	Number	Unit Time		Total Time:	Average Time
3	of Units	for Xth Unit (y):		Labor-Hours	Per Unit:
4		Labor Hours			Labor-Hours
5					Col K = Col J ÷ Col G
6	1	800		800	800
7	2	720	(800 x 0.9)	1,520	760
8	3	677		2,197	732
9	4	648	(720 x 0.9)	2,845	711
10	5	626		3,471	694
11	6	609		4,081	680
12	7	595		4,676	668
13	8	583	(648 x 0.9)	5,258	657

Individual unit time for the Xth unit in column H is calculated as $y = aX^b$; see Exhibit 10-11. For example, when $X = 3$, $y = 800 \times 3^{-0.152004} = 677$ labor-hours.

2. Total costs of assembling the first eight helicopters are:

	O	P	Q
	File Edit View Insert Format Tools Data Window Help		
1		Labor-Intensive	Machine-Intensive
2		Assembly Method	Assembly Method
3		(using data from part 1a) (₹)	(using data from part 1b)
4	Direct materials:		
5	8 helicopters x ₹4,00,000; ₹3,60,00 per helicopte	32,00,000	₹28,80,000
6	Direct-assembly labor:		
7	9,826 hrs.; 5,258 hrs. x ₹300/hr.	29,47,800	15,77,400
8	Indirect manufacturing costs		
9	Equipment related		
10	9,826 hrs. x ₹120/hr.; 5,258 hrs. × ₹450/hr.	11,79,120	23,66,100
11	Materials-handling related		
12	0.50 x ₹32,00,000; ₹28,80,000	16,00,000	14,40,000
13	Total assembly costs	89,26,920	₹82,63,500

The machine-intensive method's assembly costs are ₹6,63,420 lower than the labor-intensive method (₹89,26,920 − ₹82,63,500).

Decision Points

The following question-and-answer format summarizes the chapter's learning objectives. Each decision presents a key question related to a learning objective. The guidelines are the answer to that question.

Decision	Guidelines
1. What is a linear cost function, and what types of cost behavior can it represent?	A linear cost function is a cost function in which, within the relevant range, the graph of total costs based on the level of a single activity is a straight line. Linear cost functions can be described by a constant, a, which represents the estimate of the total cost component that, within the relevant range, does not vary with changes in the level of the activity; and a slope coefficient, b, which represents the estimate of the amount by which total costs change for each unit change in the level of the activity within the relevant range. Three types of linear cost functions are variable, fixed, and mixed (or semivariable).
2. What is the most important issue in estimating a cost function?	The most important issue in estimating a cost function is determining whether a cause-and-effect relationship exists between the level of an activity and the costs related to it. Only a cause-and-effect relationship—not merely correlation—establishes an economically plausible relationship between the level of an activity and its costs.
3. What are the different methods that can be used to estimate a cost function?	Four methods for estimating cost functions are the industrial engineering method, the conference method, the account analysis method, and the quantitative analysis method (which includes the high-low method and the regression analysis method). If possible, the cost analyst should use more than one method. Each method is a check on the others.
4. What are the steps to estimate a cost function using quantitative analysis?	Six steps need to be taken to estimate a cost function using quantitative analysis: (a) Choose the dependent variable; (b) identify the cost driver; (c) collect data on the dependent variable and the cost driver; (d) plot the data; (e) estimate the cost function; and (f) evaluate the cost driver of the estimated cost function. In most situations, working closely with operations managers, the cost analyst will cycle through these steps several times before identifying an acceptable cost function.
5. How should a company evaluate and choose cost drivers?	Three criteria for evaluating and choosing cost drivers are (a) economic plausibility, (b) goodness of fit, and (c) the significance of the independent variable.
6. What is a nonlinear cost function, and in what ways do learning curves give rise to nonlinear costs?	A nonlinear cost function is one in which the graph of total costs based on the level of a single activity is not a straight line within the relevant range. Nonlinear costs can arise because of quantity discounts, step cost functions, and learning-curve effects. Due to learning curves, labor-hours per unit decline as units of production increase. With the cumulative average-time learning model, the cumulative average-time per unit declines by a constant percentage each time the cumulative quantity of units produced doubles. With the incremental unit-time learning model, the time needed to produce the last unit declines by a constant percentage each time the cumulative quantity of units produced doubles.
7. What are the common data problems a company must watch for when estimating costs?	The most difficult task in cost estimation is collecting high-quality, reliably measured data on the costs and the cost driver. Common problems include missing data, extreme values of observations, changes in technology, and distortions resulting from inflation.

TERMS TO LEARN

This chapter and the Glossary at the end of this book contain definitions of the following important terms:

account analysis
  method **(p. 517)**
conference method **(p. 516)**
constant **(p. 512)**
cost estimation **(p. 514)**
cost function **(p. 510)**
cost predictions **(p. 514)**
cumulative average-time
  learning model **(p. 529)**
dependent variable **(p. 519)**
experience curve **(p. 529)**
high-low method **(p. 520)**

incremental unit-time
  learning model **(p. 529)**
independent variable **(p. 519)**
industrial engineering
  method **(p. 516)**
intercept **(p. 512)**
learning curve **(p. 529)**
linear cost function **(p. 510)**
mixed cost **(p. 512)**
multiple regression **(p. 522)**
nonlinear cost
  function **(p. 527)**

regression analysis **(p. 522)**
residual term **(p. 523)**
semivariable
  cost **(p. 512)**
simple regression **(p. 522)**
slope coefficient **(p. 511)**
step cost
  function **(p. 527)**
time horizon **(p. 513)**
work-measurement
  method **(p. 516)**

ASSIGNMENT MATERIAL

Questions

10-1 What two assumptions are frequently made when estimating a cost function?

10-2 Describe three alternative linear cost functions.

10-3 What is the difference between a linear and a nonlinear cost function? Give an example of each type of cost function.

10-4 "High correlation between two variables means that one is the cause and the other is the effect." Do you agree? Explain.

10-5 Name four approaches to estimating a cost function.

10-6 Describe the conference method for estimating a cost function. What are two advantages of this method?

10-7 Describe the account analysis method for estimating a cost function.

10-8 List the six steps in estimating a cost function on the basis of an analysis of a past cost relationship. Which step is typically the most difficult for the cost analyst?

10-9 When using the high-low method, should you base the high and low observations on the dependent variable or on the cost driver?

10-10 Describe three criteria for evaluating cost functions and choosing cost drivers.

10-11 Define learning curve. Outline two models that can be used when incorporating learning into the estimation of cost functions.

10-12 Discuss four frequently encountered problems when collecting cost data on variables included in a cost function.

10-13 What are the four key assumptions examined in specification analysis in the case of simple regression?

10-14 "All the independent variables in a cost function estimated with regression analysis are cost drivers." Do you agree? Explain.

10-15 "Multicollinearity exists when the dependent variable and the independent variable are highly correlated." Do you agree? Explain.

Solved Examples

10-16 Estimating a cost function. The CFO of the Colgate Co. wants you to estimate a cost function from the following two observations in a general ledger account called maintenance:

Month	Machine-Hours	Maintenance Costs Incurred
January	4,000	₹3,00,000
February	7,000	3,90,000

Required

1. Estimate the cost function for maintenance.
2. Can the constant in the cost function be used as an estimate of fixed maintenance cost per month? Explain.

Solution
Estimating a cost function.

1. Slope coefficient $=\dfrac{\text{Difference in costs}}{\text{Difference in machine-hours}}$

   (₹3,90,000 − ₹3,00,000)/(7,000 − 4,000)

₹90,000/3,000	=	₹30 per machine-hour
Constant	=	Total cost − (Slope coefficient × Quantity of cost driver)
	=	₹3,90,000 − (₹30 × 7,000) = ₹1,80,000
	=	₹3,00,000 − (₹30 × 4,000) = ₹1,80,000

The cost function based on the two observations is

   Maintenance costs   =   ₹1,80,000 + (₹30 × Machine-hours)

2. The cost function in requirement 1 is an estimate of how costs behave within the relevant range, not at cost levels outside the relevant range. If there are no months with zero machine-hours represented in the maintenance account, data in that account cannot be used to estimate the fixed costs at the zero machine-hours level. Rather, the constant component of the cost function provides the best available starting point for a straight line that approximates how a cost behaves within the relevant range.

10-17 Identifying variable, fixed, and mixed-cost functions. The Avis Ltd. operates car rental agencies at more than 20 airports. Customers can choose from one of three contracts for car rentals of one day or less:

Required

1. Contract 1: ₹600 for the day
2. Contract 2: ₹300 for the day plus ₹6 per mile traveled
3. Contract 3: ₹10 per mile traveled

1. Express each contract as a linear cost function of the form $y = a + bX$.
2. Identify each contract as a variable, fixed, or mixed-cost function.

Solution
Identifying variable, fixed, and mixed-cost functions.

1. Contract 1: $y = ₹600$
   Contract 2: $y = ₹300 + ₹6X$
   Contract 3: $y = ₹10X$
   where X is the number of miles traveled in the day.

2.

Contract	Cost Function
1	Fixed
2	Mixed
3	Variable

10-18 Matching graphs with descriptions of cost and revenue behavior. (D. Green. Adapted) Given below are a number of graphs.

If the horizontal axis represents the units produced over the year and the vertical axis represents total cost or revenue, indicate by number which graph best fits the situation or item described. Some graphs may be used more than once; some may not apply to any of the situations.

(a) Direct materials costs

(b) Supervisors' salaries for one shift and two shifts

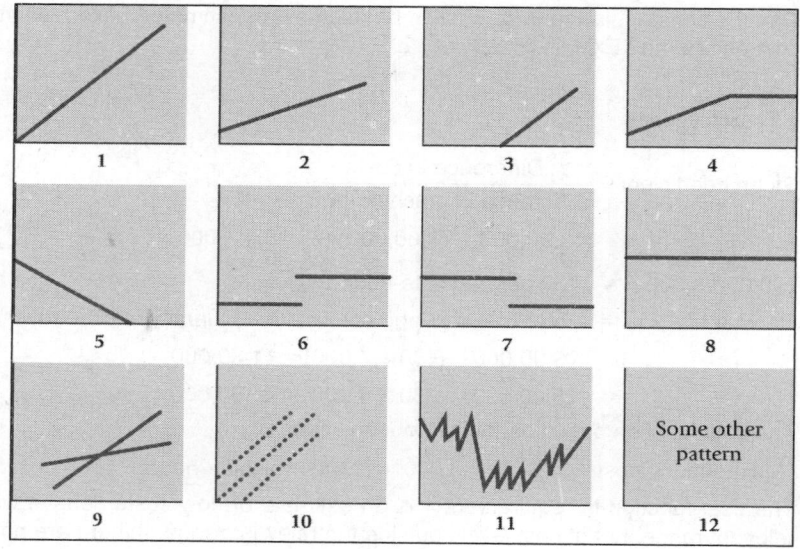

(c) A cost-volume-profit graph

(d) Mixed costs-for example, car rental fixed charge plus variable rate for miles driven

(e) Depreciation of plant, computed on a straight-line basis

(f) Data supporting the use of a variable-cost rate, such as manufacturing labor cost of ₹14 per unit produced

(g) Incentive bonus plan that pays manages ₹1 for every unit produced above some level of production

(h) Interest expense on ₹20 lakh borrowed at a fixed rate of interest

Solution

Matching graphs with descriptions of cost and revenue behavior.

    a. (1)

    b. (6)   A step-cost function.

    c. (9)

    d. (2)

    e. (8)

    f. (10)   It is data plotted on a scatter diagram showing a linear variable cost function with constant variance of residuals. The constant variance of residuals implies that there is a uniform dispersion of the data points about the regression line.

    g. (3)

    h. (8)

10-19 Account analysis method. Supreme Industries, a manufacturer of plastic products, reports the following manufacturing costs and account analysis classification for the current year ended December 31, 2015:

Account	Classification	Amount
Direct materials	All variable	₹30,00,000
Direct manufacturing labor	All variable	22,50,000
Power	All variable	3,75,000
Supervision labor	20% variable	5,62,500
Materials-handling labor	50% variable	6,00,000
Maintenance labor	40% variable	7,50,000
Depreciation	0% variable	9,50,000
Rent, property taxes, and administration	0% variable	10,00,000

Supreme Industries produced 75,000 units of product in 2015. Supreme's management is estimating costs for 2016 on the basis of 2015 numbers. The following additional information is available for 2016.

a. Direct materials prices in 2016 are expected to increase by 5% compared with 2015.

b. Under the terms of the labor contract, direct manufacturing labor wage rates are expected to increase by 10% in 2016 compared with 2015.

c. Power rates and wage rates for supervision, materials handling, and maintenance are not expected to change from 2015 to 2016.

d. Depreciation costs are expected to increase by 5% and rent, property taxes, and administration costs are expected to increase by 7%.

e. Supreme Industries expects to manufacture and sell 80,000 units in 2016.

Required

1. Prepare a schedule of variable, fixed, and total manufacturing costs for each account category in 2016. Estimate total manufacturing costs for 2016.

2. Calculate Supreme's total manufacturing cost per unit in 2015, and estimate total manufacturing cost per unit in 2016.

3. How can you obtain better estimates of fixed and variable costs? Why would these better estimates be useful to Supreme Industries?

Solution

Account analysis method.

1. Manufacturing cost classification for 2015

Account	Total Costs (1)	Percentage of Total Costs That Is Variable (2)	Variable Costs (3) = (1) × (2)	Fixed Costs (4) = (1) − (3)	Unit Variable Costs (5) = (3) ÷ 75,000
Direct materials	₹30,00,000	100%	₹30,00,000	₹0	₹40.0
Direct manufacturing labor	22,50,000	100	22,50,000	0	30.0
Power	3,75,000	100	3,75,000	0	5.0
Supervision labor	5,62,500	20	1,12,500	4,50,000	1.5
Materials-handling labor	6,00,000	50	3,00,000	3,00,000	4.0
Maintenance labor	7,50,000	40	30,00,000	4,50,000	4.0
Depreciation	9,50,000	0	0	9,50,000	0
Rent, property taxes, and administration	10,00,000	0	0	10,00,000	0
Total	₹94,87,500		₹63,37,500	₹31,50,000	₹84.5

Total manufacturing cost for 2015 = ₹94,87,500

Variable costs in 2016

Account	Unit Variable Cost for 2015 (6)	Percentage Increase (7)	Increase in Variable Costs per Unit (8) = (6) × (7)	Unit Variable Cost for 2016 (9) = (6) + (8)	Total Variable Costs for 2016 (10) = (9) × 80,000
Direct materials	₹40.0	5%	₹2.0	₹42.0	₹33,60,000
Direct manufacturing labor	30.0	10	3.0	33.0	26,40,000
Power	5.0	0	0	5.0	4,00,000
Supervision labor	1.5	0	0	1.5	1,20,000
Materials-handling labor	4.0	0	0	4.0	3,20,000
Maintenance labor	4.0	0	0	4.00	32,00,000
Depreciation	0	0	0	0	0
Rent, property taxes, administration	0	0	0	0	0
Total	₹84.5		₹5.0	₹89.5	₹71,60,000

Fixed and total costs in 2016

Account	Fixed Costs for 2015 (11)	Percentage Increase (12)	Rupee Increase in Fixed Costs (13) = (11) × (12)	Fixed Costs for 2016 (14) = (11) + (13)	Variable Costs for 2016 (15)	Total Costs (16) = (14) + (15)
Direct materials	₹0	0%	₹0	₹0	₹33,60,000	₹33,60,000
Direct manufacturing labor	0	0	0	0	26,40,000	26,40,000
Power	0	0	0	0	4,00,000	4,00,000
Supervision labor	4,50,000	0	0	4,50,000	1,20,000	5,70,000
Materials-handling labor	3,00,000	0	0	3,00,000	3,20,000	6,20,000
Maintenance labor	4,50,000	0	0	4,50,000	3,20,000	7,70,000
Depreciation	9,50,000	5	47,500	9,97,500	0	9,97,500
Rent, property taxes, administration	10,00,000	7	70,000	10,70,000	0	10,70,000
Total	31,50,000		1,17,500	32,67,500	71,60,000	1,04,27,500

Total manufacturing costs for 2016 = ₹1,04,27,500

2. Total cost per unit, 2015 = $\dfrac{₹94,87,500}{75,000}$ = ₹126.5

Total cost per unit, 2016 = $\dfrac{₹1,04,27,500}{80,000}$ = ₹130.3

3. Cost classification into variable and fixed costs is based on qualitative, rather than quantitative, analysis. How good the classifications are depends on the knowledge of individual managers who classify the costs. Supreme Industries may want to undertake quantitative analysis of costs, using regression analysis on time-series or cross-sectional data to better estimate the fixed and variable components of costs. Better knowledge of fixed and variable costs will help Supreme Industries to better price its products, know when he is getting a positive contribution margin, and to better manage costs.

10-20 High-low, regression Sohan is the new manager of the materials storeroom for Crompton Greaves Ltd. Sohan has been asked to estimate future monthly purchase costs for small part #696, used in two of Crompton's products. Sohan has purchase cost and quantity data for the past 9 months as follows:

Month	Cost of Purchase	Quantity Purchased
January	₹12,468	2,700 parts
February	12,660	2,820
March	17,280	4,068
April	15,816	3,744
May	13,164	2,988
June	13,896	3,216
July	15,228	3,636
August	10,272	2,316
September	14,940	3,552

Estimated monthly purchases for this part based on expected demand of the two products for the rest of the year are as follows:

Month	Purchase Quantity Expected
October	3,360 parts
November	3,720
December	3,000

Required

1. The computer in Sohan's office is down, and Sohan has been asked to immediately provide an equation to estimate the future purchase cost for part #696. Sohan grabs a calculator and uses the high- low method to estimate a cost equation. What equation does he get?

2. Using the equation from requirement 1, calculate the future expected purchase costs for each of the last 3 months of the year.

3. After a few hours Sohan's computer is fixed. Sohan uses the first 9 months of data and regression analysis to estimate the relationship between the quantity purchased and purchase costs of part #696. The regression line Sohan obtains is as follows:

$$Y = ₹2,135.5 + 3.67X$$

Evaluate the regression line using the criteria of economic plausibility, goodness of fit, and significance of the independent variable. Compare the regression equation to the equation based on the high-low method. Which is a better fit? Why?

4. Use the regression results to calculate the expected purchase costs for October, November, and December. Compare the expected purchase costs to the expected purchase costs calculated using the high-low method in requirement 2. Comment on your results.

Solution

1. Sohan will pick the highest point of activity, 4,068 parts (March) at ₹17,280 of cost, and the lowest point of activity, 2,316 parts (August) at ₹10,272.

	Cost driver: Quantity Purchased	Cost
Highest observation of cost driver	4,068	₹17,280
Lowest observation of cost driver	2,316	10,272
Difference	1,752	₹7,008

Purchase costs = $a + b \times$ Quantity purchased

Slope Coefficient = ₹7,008/1,752 = ₹4 per part

Constant (a) = ₹17,280 − (₹4 × 4,068) = ₹1,008

The equation Sohan gets is:

Purchase costs = ₹1,008 + (₹4 × Quantity purchased)

2. Using the equation above, the expected purchase costs for each month will be:

Month	Purchase Quantity Expected	Formula	Expected cost
October	3,360 parts	y = ₹1,008 + (₹4 × 3,360)	₹14,448
November	3,720	y = ₹1,008 + (₹4 × 3,720)	15,888
December	3,000	y = ₹1,008 + (₹4 × 3,000)	13,008

3. Economic Plausibility: Clearly, the cost of purchasing a part is associated with the quantity purchased.

Goodness of Fit: As seen in Solution Exhibit 10-27, the regression line fits the data well. The vertical distance between the regression line and observations is small. An r-squared value of greater than 0.98 indicates that more than 98 percent of the change in cost can be explained by the change in quantity.

Significance of the Independent Variable: The relatively steep slope of the regression line suggests that the quantity purchased is correlated with purchasing cost for part #696.

Solution Exhibit 10-27

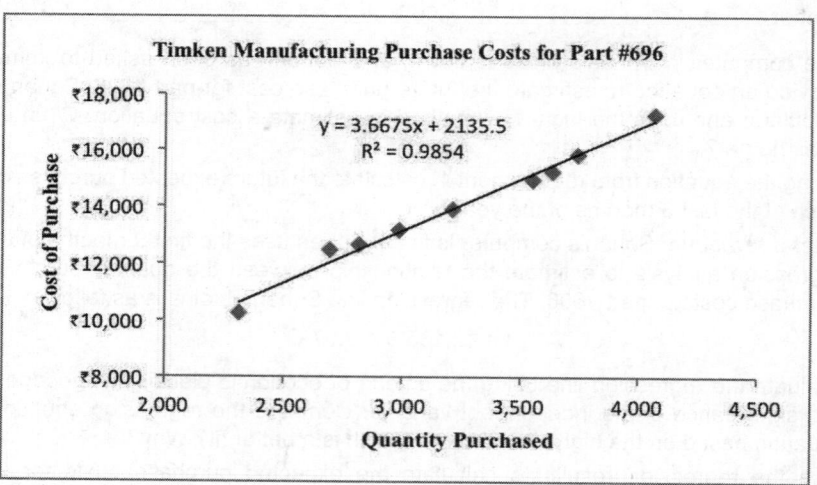

According to the regression, Sohan's original estimate of fixed cost is too low given all the data points. The original slope is too steep but only by 33 paise. So, the variable rate is lower, but the fixed cost is higher for the regression line than for the high-low cost equation.

The regression is the more accurate estimate because it uses all available data (all nine data points), while the high-low method only relies on two data points and may therefore miss some important information contained in the other data.

4. Using the regression equation, the purchase costs for each month will be:

Month	Purchase Quantity Expected	Formula	Expected cost
October	3,360 parts	y = ₹2,135.50 + (₹3.67 × 3,360)	₹14,466.70
November	3,720	y = ₹2,135.50 + (₹3.67 × 3,720)	15,787.90
December	3,000	y = ₹2,135.50 + (₹3.67 × 3,000)	13,145.50

Although the two equations are different in both fixed element and variable rate, within the relevant range they give similar expected costs. This implies that the high and low points of the data are a reasonable representation of the total set of points within the relevant range.

10-21 Regression, activity-based costing, choosing cost drivers. Parker Manufacturing has been using activity-based costing to determine the cost of product X-678. One of the activities, "Inspection," occurs just before the product is finished. The company inspects every 10th unit and has been using "number of units inspected" as the cost driver for inspection costs. A significant component of inspection costs is the cost of the test kit used in each inspection.

Sharon, the line manager, is wondering if inspection labor-hours might be a better cost driver for inspection costs. Sharon gathers information for weekly inspection costs, units inspected, and inspection labor-hours as follows:

Week	Units Inspected	Inspection Labor-Hours	Inspection Costs
1	1,800	210	₹3,600
2	800	90	1,700
3	2,100	250	4,400
4	2,800	260	5,700
5	2,500	230	5,200
6	1,100	110	2,300
7	1,300	130	2,800

Sharon runs regressions on each of the possible cost drivers and estimates these cost functions:

Inspection Costs = ₹98.79 + (₹2.02 × Number of units inspected

Inspection Costs = ₹3.89 + (₹20.02 × Inspection labor-hours)

Required

1. Explain why number of units inspected and inspection labor-hours are plausible cost drivers of inspection costs.
2. Plot the data and regression line for units inspected and inspection costs. Plot the data and regression line for inspection labor-hours and inspection costs. Which cost driver of inspection costs would you choose? Explain.
3. Sharon expects inspectors to work 160 hours next period and to inspect 1,500 units. Using the cost driver you chose in requirement 2, what amount of inspection costs should Sharon budget? Explain any implications of Sharon choosing the cost driver you did not choose in requirement 2 to budget inspection costs.

Solution

1. Both number of units inspected and inspection labor-hours are plausible cost drivers for inspection costs. The number of units inspected is likely related to test-kit usage, which is a significant component of inspection costs. Inspection labor-hours are a plausible cost driver if labor hours vary per unit inspected because costs would be a function of how much time the inspectors spend on each unit. This is particularly true if the inspectors are paid a wage, and if they use electric or electronic machinery to test the units of product (cost of operating equipment increases with time spent).

2. Solution Exhibit 10-21A presents (a) the plots and regression line for number of units inspected versus inspection costs and (b) the plots and regression line for inspection labor-hours and inspection costs.

Solution Exhibit 10-21A

Plot and Regression Line for Units Inspected versus Inspection Costs for Parker Manufacturing

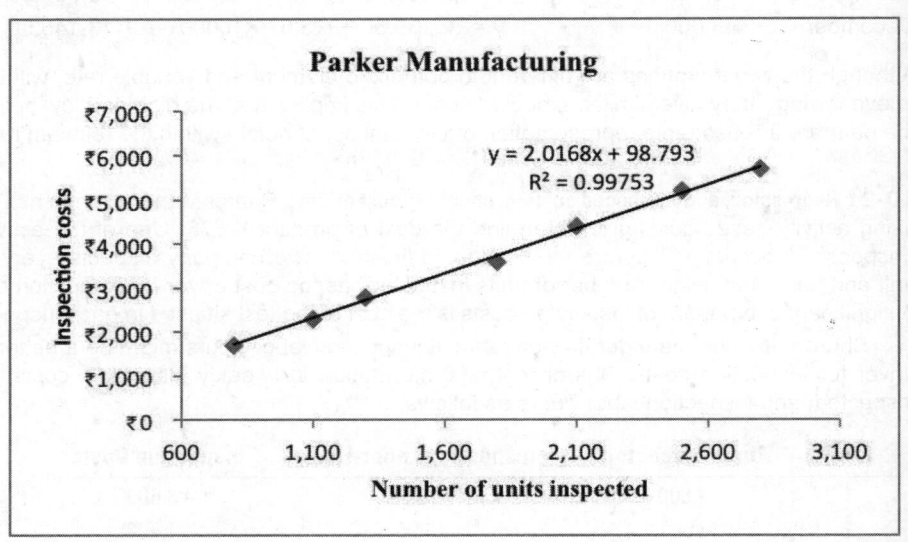

Solution Exhibit 10-21B

Plot and Regression Line for Inspection Labor-Hours and Inspection Costs for Parker Manufacturing

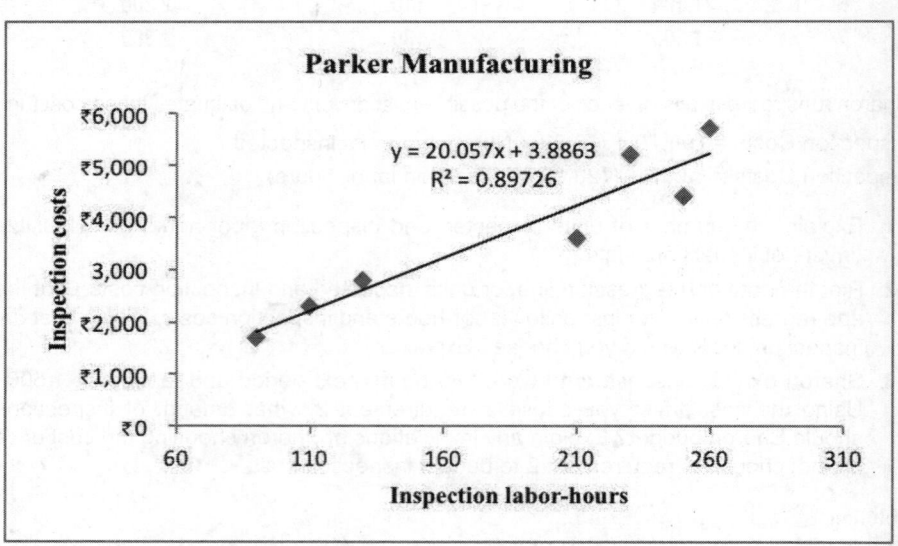

Goodness of fit. As you can see from the two graphs, the regression line based on number of units inspected better fits the data (has smaller vertical distances from the points to the line) than the regression line based on inspection labor-hours. The activity of inspection appears to be more closely linearly related to the number of units inspected than inspection labor-hours. Hence number of units inspected is a better cost driver. This is probably because the number of units inspected is closely related to test-kit usage, which is a significant component of inspection costs.

Significance of independent variable. It is hard to visually compare the slopes because the graphs are not the same size, but both graphs have steep positive slopes indicating a strong relationship between number of units inspected and inspection costs, and inspection labor-hours and inspection costs. Indeed, if labor-hours per inspection do not vary much, number of units inspected and inspection labor-hours will be closely related. Overall, it is the significant cost of test-kits that is driven by the number of units inspected (not the inspection labor-hours spent on inspection) that makes units inspected the preferred cost driver.

3. At 160 inspection labor hours and 1,500 units inspected:

Inspection costs using units inspected = ₹98.79 + (₹2.02 × 1,500) = ₹3,128.79

Inspection costs using inspection labor-hours = ₹3.89 + (₹20.06 × 160) = ₹3,213.49

If Sharon uses inspection-labor-hours she will estimate inspection costs to be ₹3,213.49, ₹84.70 (₹3,213.49 — ₹3,128.79) higher than if she had used number of units inspected. If actual costs equaled, say, ₹3,160, Sharon would conclude that Parker has performed efficiently in its inspection activity because actual inspection costs would be lower than budgeted amounts. In fact, based on the more accurate cost function, actual costs of ₹3,160 exceeded the budgeted amount of ₹3,128.79. Sharon should find ways to improve inspection efficiency rather than mistakenly conclude that the inspection activity has been performing well.

10-22 Cost-volume-profit and regression analysis. Hero Cycles manufactures a children's bicycle, Model C18. Hero Cycles currently manufactures the bicycle frame. During 2015, Hero Cycles made 30,000 frames at a total cost of ₹90,00,000. Rehman Ltd. has offered to supply as many frames as Hero Cycle wants at a cost of ₹285 per frame. Hero Cycles anticipates needing 36,000 frames each year for the next few years.

Required

1. (a) What is the average cost of manufacturing a bicycle frame in 2015? How does it compare to Rehman's offer. (b) Can Hero Cycles use the answer in requirement (a) to determine the cost of manufacturing 36,000 bicycle/frames? Explain.
2. Hero Cycles cost analyst uses annual data from past years to estimate the following regression equation with total manufacturing costs of the bicycle frame as the dependent variable and bicycle frames produced as the independent variable

$$y = ₹43,20,000 + ₹150X$$

During the years used to estimate the regression equation, the production of bicycle frames had varied from 28,000 to 36,000. Using this equation, estimate how much it would cost Hero Cycles to manufacture 36,000 bicycle frames. How much more or less costly is it to manufacture the frames rather than to acquire them from Rehman. (3) What other information would you need in order to be confident that the equation in requirement 2 accurately predicts the cost of manufacturing bicycle frames?

Solution

Cost-volume-profit and regression analysis.

1a. Average cost of manufacturing = $\dfrac{\text{Total manufacturing costs}}{\text{Number of bicycle frames}}$

$$= \frac{₹90,00,000}{30,000} = ₹300 \text{ per frame}$$

This cost is greater than the ₹285 per frame that Rehman has quoted.

1b. Hero Cycles cannot take the average manufacturing cost in 2015 of ₹300 per frame and multiply it by 36,000 bicycle frames to determine the total cost of manufacturing 36,000 bicycle frames. The reason is that some of the ₹90,00,000 (or equivalently the ₹300 cost per frame) are fixed costs and some are variable costs. Without distinguishing fixed from variable costs, Hero Cycles cannot determine the cost of manufacturing 36,000 frames. For example, if all costs are fixed, the manufacturing costs of 36,000 frames will continue to be ₹90,00,000. If, however, all costs are variable, the cost of manufacturing 36,000 frames would be ₹300 × 36,000 = ₹1,08,00,000. If some costs are fixed and some are variable, the cost of manufacturing 36,000 frames will be somewhere between ₹90,00,000 and ₹1,08,00,000.

Some students could argue that another reason for not being able to determine the cost of manufacturing 36,000 bicycle frames is that not all costs are output unit-level costs. If some costs are, for example, batch-level costs, more information would be needed on the number of batches in which the 36,000 bicycle frames would be produced, in order to determine the cost of manufacturing 36,000 bicycle frames.

2. Expected cost to make 36,000 bicycle frames = ₹43,20,000 + ₹150 × 36,000

$$= ₹43,20,000 + ₹54,00,000 = ₹97,20,000$$

Purchasing bicycle frames from Ryan will cost ₹285 × 36,000 = ₹1,02,60,000. Hence it will cost Hero Cycles ₹1,02,60,000 − ₹97,20,000 = ₹5,40,000 more to purchase the frames from Hero Cycles rather than manufacture them in-house.

3. Hero Cycles would need to consider several factors before being confident that the equation in requirement 2 accurately predicts the cost of manufacturing bicycle frames.

a. Is the relationship between total manufacturing costs and quantity of bicycle frames economically plausible? For example, is the quantity of bicycles made the only cost driver or are there other cost-drivers (for example batch-level costs of setups, production-orders or material handling) that affect manufacturing costs?

b. How good is the goodness of fit? That is, how well does the estimated line fit the data?

c. Is the relationship between the number of bicycle frames produced and total manufacturing costs linear?

d. Does the slope of the regression line indicate that a strong relationship exists between manufacturing costs and the number of bicycle frames produced?

e. Are there any data problems such as, for example, errors in measuring costs, trends in prices of materials, labor or overheads that might affect variable or fixed costs over time, extreme values of observations, or a nonstationary relationship over time between total manufacturing costs and the quantity of bicycles produced?

f. How is inflation expected to affect costs?

g. Will Rehman supply high-quality bicycle frames on time?

10-23 Regression analysis, service company. (CMA, adapted) Paul owns a catering company that prepares banquets and parties. For a standard cocktail party the cost on a per-person basis is:

Food and beverages	₹150
Labor (0.5 hour × ₹100 per hour)	50
Overhead (0.5 hour × ₹140 per hour)	70
Total cost per person	₹270

Paul is quite certain about his estimates of the food, beverages, and labor costs but is not as, comfortable with the overhead estimate. The overhead estimate was based on the actual data for the past 12 months presented below. These data indicate that overhead costs vary with the direct labor-hours used. The ₹140 estimate was determined dividing total overhead costs for the 12 months by total labor-hours.

Month	Labor-Hours	Overhead Costs
January	2,500	₹5,50,000
February	2,700	5,90,000
March	3,000	6,00,000
April	4,200	6,40,000
May	7,500	7,70,000

June	5,500	7,10,000
July	6,500	7,40,000
August	4,500	6,70,000
September	7,000	7,50,000
October	4,500	6,80,000
November	3,100	6,20,000
December	6,500	7,30,000
Total	57,500	₹80,50,000

Paul has recently become aware of regression analysis. He estimated the following regression equation with overhead costs as the dependent variable and labor-hours as the independent variable.

$$y = ₹4,82,710 + ₹39.40X$$

Required

1. Plot the relationship between overhead costs and labor-hours. Draw the regression line and evaluate it using the criteria of economic plausibility, goodness of fit, and slope of the regression line.
2. Using data from the regression analysis, what is the variable cost per person for a cocktail party?
3. Paul has been asked to prepare a bid for a 200-person cocktail party to be given next month. Determine the minimum bid price that Paul would be willing to submit to recoup variable costs.

Solution

Regression analysis, service company.

1. Solution Exhibit 10-23 plots the relationship between labor-hours and overhead costs and shows the regression line.

   $y = ₹4,82,710 + ₹39.40X$

   Economic plausibility. Labor-hours appears to be an economically plausible driver of overhead costs for a catering company. Overhead costs such as scheduling, hiring and training of workers, and managing the workforce are largely incurred to support labor.

   Goodness of fit. The vertical differences between actual and predicted costs are extremely small, indicating a very good fit. The good fit indicates a strong relationship between the labor-hour cost driver and overhead costs.

   Slope of regression line. The regression line has a reasonably steep slope from left to right. Given the small scatter of the observations around the line, the positive slope indicates that, on average, overhead costs increases as labor-hours increase.

2. The regression analysis indicates that, within the relevant range of 2,500 to 7,500 labor-hours, the variable cost per person for a cocktail party equals:

Food and beverages	₹150.0
Labor (0.5 hr × ₹100 per hour)	50.0
Variable overhead (0.5 hr × ₹39.40 per labor-hour)	19.7
Total variable cost per person	₹219.7

3. To earn a positive contribution margin, the minimum bid for a 200-person cocktail party would be any amount greater than ₹43,940. This amount is calculated multiplying the variable cost per person of ₹219.70 by the 200 people. At a price above the variable costs of ₹43,940, Paul will be earning a contribution margin towards coverage of his fixed costs.

Of course, Paul will consider other factors in developing his bid including (a) an analysis of the competition—vigorous competition will limit Paul's ability to obtain a higher price (b) a determination of whether or not his bid will set a precedent for lower prices—overall, the prices Paul charges should generate enough contribution to cover fixed costs and earn a reasonable profit, and (c) a judgment of how representative past historical data (used in the regression analysis) is about future costs.

Solution Exhibit 10-23

Regression Line of Labor-Hours on Overhead Costs for Paul's Catering Company

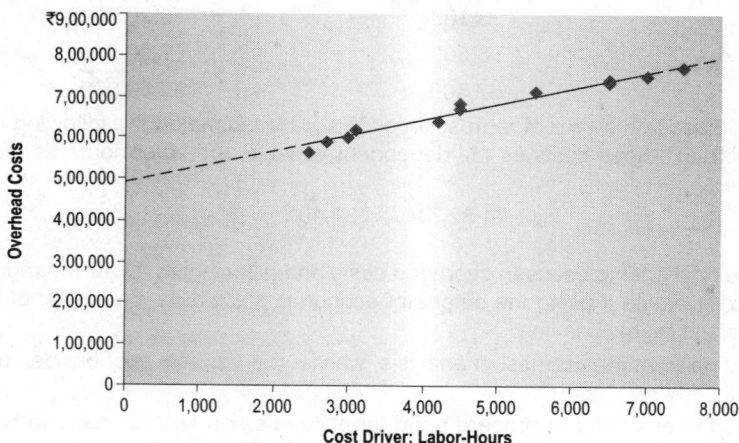

10-24 Cost estimation. Nokia Electronics started production on a sophisticated new smartphone running the Android operating system in January 2016. Given the razor-thin margins in the consumer electronics industry, Nokia's success depends heavily on being able to produce the phone as economically as possible.

At the end of the first year of production, Nokia's controller, Alok, gathered data on its monthly levels of output, as well as monthly consumption of direct labor-hours (DLH). Alok views labor-hours as the key driver of Nokia's direct and overhead costs. The information collected by Alok is provided below:

	Home	Insert	Page Layout	Formulas
	A	B	C	
1	**Month**	**Output (Units)**	**Direct Labor-Hours**	
2	January	684	1,400	
3	February	492	820	
4	March	660	875	
5	April	504	670	
6	May	612	760	
7	June	636	765	
8	July	648	735	
9	August	600	660	
10	September	648	695	
11	October	696	710	
12	November	672	690	
13	December	675	700	

1. Alok is keen to examine the relationship between direct labor consumption and output levels. He decides to estimate this relationship using a simple linear regression based on the monthly data. Verify that the following is the result obtained by Alok:

Regression 1: Direct labor-hours $= a + (b \times$ Output units)

Variable	Coefficient	Standard Error	t-Value
Constant	345.24	589.07	0.59
Independent variable: Output units	0.71	0.93	0.76

$r^2 = 0.054$; Durbin-Watson statistic $= 0.50$

2. Plot the data and regression line for the above estimation. Evaluate the regression using the criteria of economic plausibility, goodness of fit, and slope of the regression line.
3. Alok estimates that Nokia has a variable cost of ₹17.50 per direct labor-hour. He expects that Nokia will produce 650 units in the next month, January 2015. What should he budget as the expected variable cost? How confident is he of her estimate?

Solution

1. Here is the summary output for the monthly regression of Direct Labor Hours on Output Units for Nokia Electronics:

SUMMARY OUTPUT

Regression Statistics	
Multiple R	0.2333602
R Square	0.054457
Adjusted R Square	–0.0400973
Standard Error	206.18345
Observations	12

ANOVA

	df	SS	MS	F	Significance F
Regression	1	24,483.86	24,483.86	0.575933	0.465422344
Residual	10	4,25,116.1	42,511.61		
Total	11	4,49,600			

	Coefficients	Standard Error	t Stat	P-value	Lower 95%	Upper 95%
Intercept	345.24	589.07	0.59	0.57	–967.29	1,657.77
X Variable 1	0.71	0.93	0.76	0.47	–1.37	2.79

2. The plot and regression line for monthly direct labor hours on monthly output for Nokia Electronics are given below:

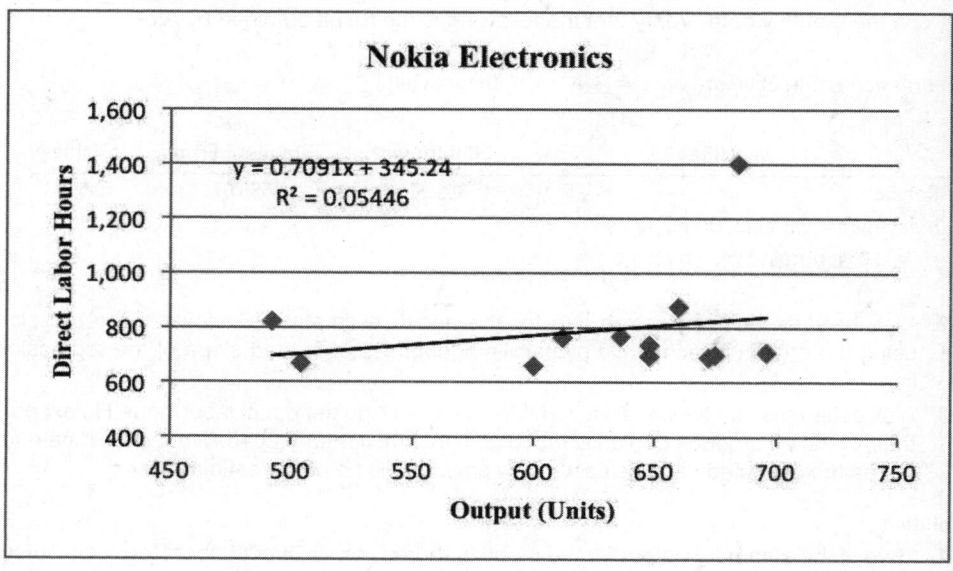

Economic plausibility

A positive relationship between direct labor hours and monthly output is economically plausible because increased levels of production should lead to the consumption of greater amounts of direct labor.

Goodness of fit $r^2 = 5.45\%$, Adjusted $r^2 = -4\%$

Standard error of regression = 206.18

Terrible fit; in fact, there is no evidence of a linear relationship between the dependent and independent variables. At least one data point represents a significant outlier.

Significance of independent variables

The t-value of 0.76 for output units is not significant at the 0.05 level.

3. Given Alok's expectation that Nokia will produce 650 units in January 2016, his best estimate given the linear regression above is that Nokia will use:

$$345.24 + (0.71 \times 650 \text{ units}) = 806.74 \text{ direct labor hours.}$$

At an estimated variable cost of ₹17.50 per direct labor-hour, this implies that Alok should budget

$$806.74 \times ₹17.50 = ₹14,118$$

for direct labor costs for January 2016.

Note that 650 units is in the range of output values that were used to find the regression equation and therefore falls in the range of predictability for this model. However, there is substantial uncertainty around the cost estimate of ₹14,118. In particular, this predicted value relies on the regression point estimate of 0.71 for the marginal impact of output on labor hours. But, the 95 percent confidence interval for the slope of the regression ranges all the way from −1.37 to 2.79, and the predicted cost would vary accordingly. One cannot reject the null hypothesis that output levels have no impact on labor consumption, leaving the budgeted cost estimate a highly speculative one!

10-25 Cost estimation, learning curves (continuation of 10-24). Alok is concerned that he still does not understand the relationship between output and labor consumption. He consults with Amar, the head of engineering, and shares the results of his regression estimation. He indicates that the production of new smartphone models exhibits significant learning effects—as Nokia gains experience with production, it can produce additional units using less time. He suggests that it is more appropriate to specify the following relationship:

$$y = ax^b$$

where x is cumulative production in units, y is the cumulative average direct labor-hours per unit (i.e., cumulative DLH divided by cumulative production), and a and b are parameters of the learning effect.

To estimate this, Alok and Amar use the original data to calculate the cumulative output and cumulative average labor-hours per unit for each month. They then take natural logarithms of these variables in order to be able to estimate a regression equation. Here is the transformed data:

	A	B	C	D	E	F
		Insert	Page Layout	Formulas	Data	Review
21	Month	Cumulative Output (x)	Cumulative DLH	Cumulative Avg DLH (y)	LN (y)	LN (x)
22	January	684	1,400	2.047	0.716	6.528
23	February	1,176	2,220	1.888	0.635	7.070
24	March	1,836	3,095	1.686	0.522	7.515
25	April	2,340	3,765	1.609	0.476	7.758
26	May	2,952	4,525	1.533	0.427	7.990
27	June	3,588	5,290	1.474	0.388	8.185
28	July	4,236	6,025	1.422	0.352	8.351
29	August	4,836	6,685	1.382	0.324	8.484
30	September	5,484	7,380	1.346	0.297	8.610
31	October	6,180	8,090	1.309	0.269	8.729
32	November	6,852	8,780	1.281	0.248	8.832
33	December	7,527	9,480	1.259	0.231	8.926

Required

1. Estimate the relationship between the cumulative average direct labor-hours per unit and cumulative output (both in logarithms). Verify that the following is the result obtained by Alok and Amar:

Regression 1: Ln (Cumulative avg DLH per unit) $= a + [b \times$ Ln(Cumulative Output)]

Variable	Coefficient	Standard Error	t-Value
Constant	2.087	0.024	85.44
Independent variable: Ln (Cum Output)	−0.208	0.003	−69.046

$r^2 = 0.054$; Durbin-Watson statistic $= 2.66$

2. Plot the data and regression line for the above estimation. Evaluate the regression using the criteria of economic plausibility, goodness of fit, and slope of the regression line.

3. Verify that the estimated slope coefficient corresponds to an 86.6% cumulative average-time learning curve.

4. Based on this new estimation, how will Alok revise his budget for Nokia's variable cost for the expected output of 650 units in January 2016? How confident is he of this new cost estimate?

Solution

1. Here is the summary output for the monthly regression of the natural log of Cumulative Average Direct Labor-Hours per Unit on the natural logarithm of Cumulative Output:

SUMMARY OUTPUT

Regression Statistics	
Multiple R	0.9989528
R Square	0.9979068
Adjusted R Square	0.9976975
Standard Error	0.0074326
Observations	12

ANOVA

	df	SS	MS	F	Significance F
Regression	1	0.263368	0.263368	4,767.34	9.89803E-15
Residual	10	0.000552	5.52E-05		
Total	11	0.26392			

	Coefficients	Standard Error	t Stat	P-value	Lower 95%	Upper 95%
Intercept	2.09	0.02	85.44	0.00	2.03	2.14
X Variable 1	−0.21	0.00	−69.05	0.00	−0.21	−0.20

2. The plot of the data and the regression line estimated above are provided next.

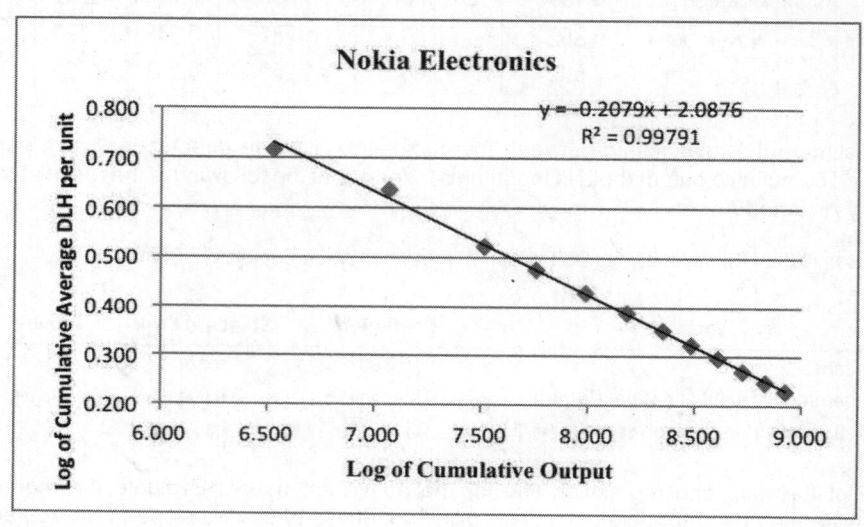

Nokia Electronics

$y = -0.2079x + 2.0876$
$R^2 = 0.99791$

Economic plausibility	A negative relationship between cumulative average direct-labor hours per unit and cumulative output (in natural logarithms) is economically plausible and reflects the presence of learning effects. Specifically, as the firm gains experience from production, it becomes more efficient and is able to use fewer direct labor hours to make each unit of product.
Goodness of fit	r^2 = 99.8%, Adjusted r^2 = 99.8% Standard error of regression = 0.007 Unparalleled goodness of fit. Virtually perfect linear fit in logarithms.
Significance of independent variables	The t-value of –69.05 for the logarithm of cumulative output is significant at all conventional levels. The t-value for the intercept (85.44) is highly significant as well.

3. The original learning curve specification, $y = ax^b$ is mathematically identical to the following log-linear specification:

$$Ln\ y = Ln\ a + b \times Ln\ x$$

The regression equation we have estimated,

$$Ln\ (Cumulative\ avg\ DLH\ per\ unit) = a + (b \times Ln\ (Cumulative\ Output))$$

is precisely the above specification, and in particular, the slope coefficient directly yields the "b" from the learning curve equation. We know, therefore, that for Nokia electronics, $b =$ –0.208. As explained in Exhibit 10-10, this value is related to the learning curve percentage as follows:

$$b = Ln\ (learning\text{-}curve\ \%\ in\ decimal\ form)/Ln\ 2,\ or$$

$$-0.208 = Ln\ (learning\text{-}curve\ \%\ in\ decimal\ form)/0.693,\ or$$

$$Ln(learning\text{-}curve\ \%\ in\ decimal\ form) = -0.208 \times 0.693 = -0.144.$$

As the exponent of –0.144 is 0.8659, this implies that Nokia is experiencing an 86.6 percent cumulative average-time learning curve.

4. With an additional 650 units in January 2016, Nokia's cumulative output will go from 7,527 at the end of December 2014 to 8,177 (7,527 + 650). As Ln (8,177) = 9.0091, the cumulative average direct-labor hours in logarithmic terms are given by:

$$2.0876 - 0.2079 \times 9.0091 = 0.2146.$$

The cumulative direct-labor hours per unit therefore equals Exp (0.2146) = 1.2394. This implies a total direct labor hours of 1.2394 × 8,177 = 10,134 by the end of January. As Nokia has used a total of 9,480 direct labor hours at the end of December 2015, the incremental hours needed in January therefore are 654 (10,134 – 9,480). At ₹17.50 per labor hour, this suggests that Alok should budget

$$654 \times ₹17.50 = ₹11,445$$

for direct labor costs for January 2016.

Although 9.0091 is outside the range of cumulative output values (measured in logarithms) used to find the regression equation, unless there has been a structural break in the experience curve Nokia is facing, it is highly likely that its January costs will be in the neighborhood of ₹11,445. The reason is that the estimated regression line is close to perfect and has a standard error close to zero. There is virtually no uncertainty around the coefficient estimates. The slope coefficient, for example, has a point estimate of – 0.2079, and a narrow 95 percent confidence interval between – 0.2146 and – 0.2012. Using either of those estimates would make barely any difference to the predicted cost for the month of January 2016.

10-26 Purchasing Department cost drivers, activity-based costing, simple regression analysis. Designer Wear operates a chain of 10 retail department stores. Each department store makes its own purchasing decisions. Amit, assistant to the president of Designer Wear, is interested in better understanding the drivers of purchasing department costs. For many years, Designer Wear has allocated purchasing department costs to products on the basis of the rupee value of merchandise purchased. A ₹100 item is allocated 10 times as many overhead costs associated with the purchasing department as a ₹10 item.

Amit recently attended a seminar titled "Cost Drivers in the Retail Industry." In a presentation at the seminar, Design Fabrics, a leading competitor that has implemented activity-based costing, reported number of purchase orders and number of suppliers to be the two most important cost drivers of purchasing department costs. The rupee value of merchandise purchased in each purchase order was not found to be a significant cost driver. Amit interviewed several members of the purchasing department at the Designer Wear store Mumbai. They believed that Design Fabrics' conclusions also applied to their purchasing department.

Amit collects the following data for the most recent year for Designer Wear's 10 retail department stores:

	Home	Insert	Page Layout	Formulas	Data	Review	View	
	A		B	C	D	E		
1	Department Store		Purchasing Department Costs (PDC)	Rupee Value of Merchandise Purchased (MPRs)	Number of Purchase Orders (No. of POs)	Number of Suppliers (No. of Ss)		
2	Delhi		₹15,25,000	₹6,83,25,000	4,350	130		
3	Chennai		11,20,000	3,34,50,000	2,555	225		
4	Kanpur		5,35,000	12,11,00,000	1,438	12		
5	Mumbai		20,42,000	11,95,50,000	5,940	193		
6	Kolkutta		10,50,000	3,35,20,000	2,795	20		
7	Banglore		5,22,000	2,98,47,000	1,315	39		
8	Lucknow		15,33,000	10,28,86,000	7,592	112		
9	Hyderabad		17,48,000	3,86,65,000	3,610	124		
10	Patna		16,18,000	13,93,15,000	1,710	215		
11	Jaipur		12,51,000	13,09,40,000	4,725	208		

Amit decides to use simple regression analysis to examine whether one or more of three variables (the last three columns in the table) are cost drivers of purchasing department costs. Summary results for these regressions are as follows:

Regression 1: PDC $= a + (b \times$ MPRs$)$

Variable	Coefficient	Standard Error	t-Value
Constant	₹10,40,594	₹3,44,830	3.02
Independent variable 1: MPRs)	₹0.0031	0.0037	0.83

$r^2 = 0.08$; Durbin-Watson statistic $= 2.42$

Regression 2: PDC $= a (b \times$ No. of POs$)$

Variable	Coefficient	Standard Error	t-Value
Constant	₹7,31,687	₹2,67,395	2.74
Independent variable 1: No. of POs	₹156.18	₹65.19	2.40

$r^2 = 0.42$; Durbin-Watson statistic $= 1.99$

Regression 3: PDC $= a + (b \times$ No. of Ss$)$

Variable	Coefficient	Standard Error	t-Value
Constant	₹8,02,629	₹2,48,566	3.23
Independent variable 1: No. of Ss	3,848	1,660	2.32

$r^2 = 0.40$; Durbin-Watson statistic $= 2.00$

1. Compare and evaluate the three simple regression models estimated by Amit. Graph each one. Also, use the format employed in Exhibit 10-18 to evaluate the information.
2. Do the regression results support the Design Fabrics' presentation about the purchasing department's cost drivers? Which of these cost drivers would you recommend in designing an ABC system?
3. How might Amit gain additional evidence on drivers of purchasing department costs at each of Designer Wear's stores?

Solution

The problem reports the exact t-values from the computer runs of the data. Because the coefficients and standard errors given in the problem are rounded to three decimal places, dividing the coefficient by the standard error may yield slightly different *t*-values.

1. Plots of the data used in Regressions 1 to 3 are in Solution Exhibit 10-26A. See Solution Exhibit 10-26B for a comparison of the three regression models.
2. Both Regressions 2 and 3 are well-specified regression models. The slope coefficients on their respective independent variables are significantly different from zero. These results support the Couture Fabrics' presentation in which the number of purchase orders and the number of suppliers were reported to be drivers of purchasing department costs.

In designing an activity-based cost system, Designer Wear should use number of purchase orders and number of suppliers as cost drivers of purchasing department costs. As the chapter describes, Designer Wear can either (a) estimate a multiple regression equation for purchasing department costs with number of purchase orders and number of suppliers as cost drivers, or (b) divide purchasing department costs into two separate cost pools, one for costs related to purchase orders and another for costs related to suppliers, and estimate a separate relationship for each cost pool.

3. Guidelines presented in the chapter could be used to gain additional evidence on cost drivers of purchasing department costs.

    1. Use physical relationships or engineering relationships to establish cause-and-effect links. Amit could observe the purchasing department operations to gain insight into how costs are driven.
    2. Use knowledge of operations. Amit could interview operating personnel in the purchasing department to obtain their insight on cost drivers.

Solution Exhibit 10-26A

Regression Lines of Various Cost Drivers for Purchasing Dept. Costs for Designer Wear

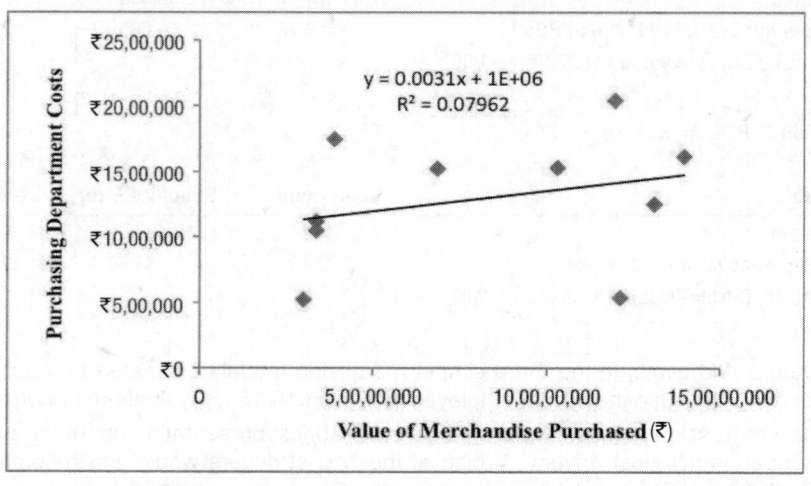

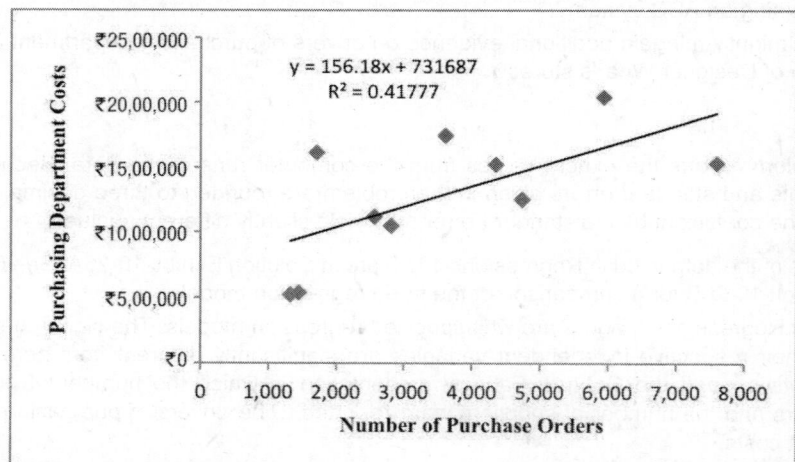

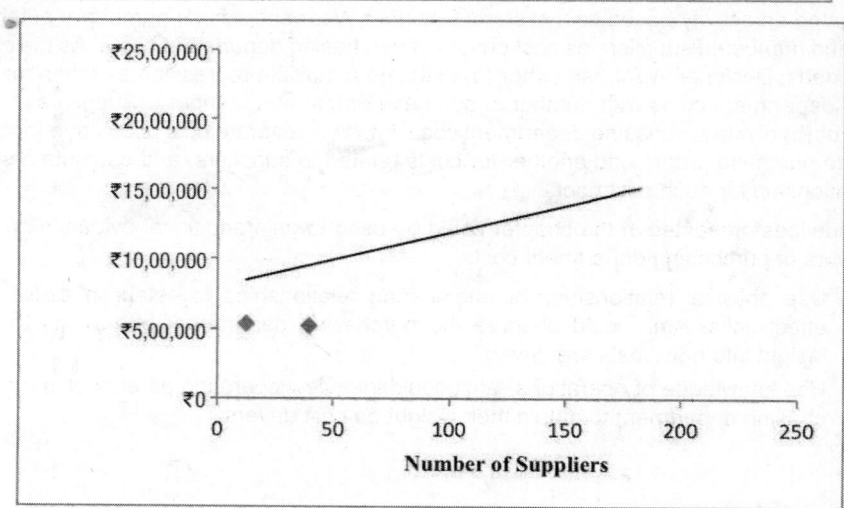

Solution Exhibit 10-26B

Comparison of Alternative Cost Functions for Purchasing Department
Costs Estimated with Simple Regression for Designer Wear

Criterion	Regression 1 PDC = a + (b × MPRs)	Regression 2 PDC = a + (b × # of POs)	Regression 3 PDC = a + (b × # of Ss)
1. Economic plausibility	Result presented at seminar by Design Fabrics found little support for MPRs as a driver. Purchasing personnel at the Mumbai store believe MPRs is not a significant cost driver.	Economically plausible. The higher the number of purchase orders, the more tasks undertaken.	Economically plausible. Increasing the number of suppliers increases the costs of certifying vendors and managing the Designer Wear-supplier relationship.
2. Goodness of fit	$r^2 = 0.08$. Poor goodness of fit.	$r^2 = 0.42$. Reasonable goodness of fit.	$r^2 = 0.40$. Reasonable goodness of fit.
3. Significance of independent variables	t-value on MPRs of 0.83 is insignificant.	t-value on # of POs of 2.40 is significant.	t-value on # of Ss of 2.32 is significant.
4. Specification analysis			
A. Linearity within the relevant range	Appears questionable but no strong evidence against linearity.	Appears reasonable.	Appears reasonable.
B. Constant variance of residuals	Appears questionable, but no strong evidence against constant variance.	Appears reasonable.	Appears reasonable.
C. Independence of residuals	Durbin-Watson Statistic = 2.42. Assumption of independence is not rejected.	Durbin-Watson Statistic = 1.99. Assumption of independence is not rejected.	Durbin-Watson Statistic = 2.00. Assumption of independence is not rejected.
D. Normality of residuals	Database too small to make reliable inferences.	Database too small to make reliable inferences.	Database too small to make reliable inferences.

10-27 Purchasing Department cost drivers, multiple regression analysis (continuation of 10-26).
Amit decides that the simple regression analysis used in Problem 10-26 could be extended to a multiple regression analysis. He finds the following results for two multiple regression analyses:

Regression 4: PDC $= a + (b_1 \times$ No. of POs$) + (b_2 \times$ No. of Ss$)$

Variable	Coefficient	Standard Error	t-Value
Constant	₹4,81,186	₹2,59,020	1.86
Independent variable 1: No. of POs	₹121.37	₹58.04	2.09
Independent variable 2: No. of Ss	₹2,941	₹1,458	2.02

$r^2 = 0.63$; Durbin-Watson statistic $= 1.91$

Regression 5: PDC $= a + (b_1 \times$ No. of POs$) + (b_2 \times$ No. of Ss$) + (b_3 \times$ MPRs$)$

Variable	Coefficient	Standard Error	t-Value
Constant	₹4,96,544	₹3,11,137	1.60
Independent variable 1: No. of POs	₹122.73	₹63.79	1.92
Independent variable 2: No. of Ss	₹2,996	₹1,646	1.82
Independent variable 3: MPRs	−0.00002	−0.0030	−0.11

$r^2 = 0.63$; Durbin-Watson statistic $= 1.92$

The coefficients of correlation between combinations of pairs of the variables are as follows:

	PDC	MPRs	No. of POs
MPRs	0.28		
No. of POs	0.65	0.27	
No. of Ss	0.63	0.35	0.30

Required

1. Evaluate regression 4 using the criteria of economic plausibility, goodness of fit, significance of independent variables, and specification analysis. Compare regression 4 with regressions 2 and 3 in Problem 10-26. Which one of these models would you recommend that Amit use? Why?

2. Compare regression 5 with regression 4. Which one of these models would you recommend that Amit use? Why?

3. Amit estimates the following data for the Delhi store for next year: rupee value of merchandise purchased, ₹7,70,00,000; number of purchase orders, 4,200; number of suppliers, 120. How much should Amit budget for purchasing department costs for the Delhi store for next year?

4. What difficulties do not arise in simple regression analysis that may arise in multiple regression analysis? Is there evidence of such difficulties in either of the multiple regressions presented in this problem? Explain.

5. Give two examples of decisions in which the regression results reported here (and in Problem 10-26) could be informative.

Solution

The problem reports the exact t-values from the computer runs of the data. Because the coefficients and standard errors given in the problem are rounded to three decimal places, dividing the coefficient by the standard error may yield slightly different t-values.

1. Regression 4 is a well-specified regression model:

Economic plausibility: Both independent variables are plausible and are supported by the findings of the Design Fabrics study.

Goodness of fit: The r^2 of 0.63 indicates an excellent goodness of fit.

Significance of independent variables: The *t*-value on # of POs is 2.09 while the *t*-value on # of Ss is 2.02. These *t*-values are either significant or border on significance.

Specification analysis: Results are available to examine the independence of residuals assumption. The Durbin-Watson statistic of 1.91 indicates that the assumption of independence is not rejected.

Regression 4 is consistent with the findings in Problem 10-26 that both the number of purchase orders and the number of suppliers are drivers of purchasing department costs. Regressions 2, 3, and 4 all satisfy the four criteria outlined in the text. Regression 4 has the best goodness of fit (0.63 for Regression 4 compared to 0.42 and 0.40 for Regressions 2 and 3, respectively). Most importantly, it is economically plausible that both the number of purchase orders and the number of suppliers drive purchasing department costs. We would recommend that Amit use Regression 4 over Regressions 2 and 3.

2. Regression 5 adds an additional independent variable (MPRs) to the two independent variables in Regression 4. This additional variable (MPRs) has a *t*-value of −0.11, implying its slope coefficient is insignificantly different from zero. The r^2 in Regression 5 (0.63) is the same as that in Regression 4 (0.63), implying the addition of this third independent variable adds close to zero explanatory power. In summary, Regression 5 adds very little to Regression 4. We would recommend that Amit use Regression 4 over Regression 5.

3. Budgeted purchasing department costs for the Delhi store next year are

$$₹4,81,186 + (₹121.37 \times 4,200) + (₹2,941 \times 120) = ₹13,43,860$$

4. Multicollinearity is a frequently encountered problem in cost accounting; it does not arise in simple regression because there is only one independent variable in a simple regression. One consequence of multicollinearity is an increase in the standard errors of the coefficients of the individual variables. This frequently shows up in reduced *t*-values for the independent variables in the multiple regression relative to their *t*-values in the simple regression:

Variables	*t*-value in Multiple Regression	*t*-value from Simple Regressions in Problem 10-42
Regression 4:		
# of POs	2.09	2.40
# of Ss	2.02	2.32
Regression 5:		
# of POs	1.92	2.40
# of Ss	1.82	2.32
MPRs	-0.11	0.83

The decline in the *t*-values in the multiple regressions is consistent with some (but not very high) collinearity among the independent variables. Pairwise correlations between the independent variables are:

	Correlation
# of POs and # of Ss	0.30
# of POs and MPRs	0.27
# of Ss and MPRs	0.28

There is no evidence of difficulties due to multicollinearity in Regressions 4 and 5.

5. Decisions in which the regression results in Problems 10-26 and 10-27 could be useful are as follows:

Cost management decisions: Designer Wear could restructure relationships with the suppliers so that fewer separate purchase orders are made. Alternatively, it may aggressively reduce the number of existing suppliers.

Purchasing policy decisions: Designer Wear could set up an internal charge system for individual retail departments within each store. Separate charges to each department could be made for each purchase order and each new supplier added to the existing ones. These internal charges would signal to each department ways in which their own decisions affect the total costs of Designer Wear.

Accounting system design decisions: Designer Wear may want to discontinue allocating purchasing department costs on the basis of the rupee value of merchandise purchased. Allocation bases better capturing cause-and-effect relations at Designer Wear are the number of purchase orders and the number of suppliers.

10-28 **Learning curve, incremental unit-time learning model.** Assume the same information for Global Defense as in Exercise 10-23, except that Global Defense uses a 90% incremental unit-time learning model as a basis for predicting direct manufacturing labor-hours. (A 90% learning curve means $b = -0.1520$)

1. Calculate the total variable costs of producing 2, 3, and 4 units.
2. If you having solved Exercise 10-23, compare your cost predictions in the two exercises for 2 and 4 units. Why are the predictions different?

Solution

Learning curve, incremental unit-time learning model.

1. The direct manufacturing labor-hours (DMLH) required to produce the first 2, 3, and 4 units, given the assumption of an incremental unit-time learning curve of 90%, is as follows:

Cumulative Number of Units (1)	Individual Unit Time for Xth Unit (2)	Cumulative Total Time (3)
1	3,000	3,000
2	2,700 (3,000 × 0.90)	5,700
3	2,539	8,239
4	2,430 (2,700 × 0.90)	10,669

Values in column 2 are calculated using the formula $y = aX^b$

where a = 3,000, X = 2, 3, or 4, and $b = -0.1520$, which gives

when X = 2, $y = 3,000 \times 2 - 0.1520 = 2,700$

when X = 3, $y = 3,000 \times 3 - 0.1520 = 2,539$

when X = 4, $y = 3,000 \times 4 - 0.1520 = 2,430$

	Variable Costs of Producing		
	2 Units	4 Units	8 Units
Direct materials ₹8,00,000 × 2; 3; 4	₹16,00,000	₹24,00,000	₹32,00,000
Direct manufacturing labor ₹250 × 5,700; 8,239; 10,669	14,25,000	20,59,750	26,67,250
Variable manufacturing overhead ₹150 × 5,700; 8,239;10669	8,55,000	12,35,850	16,00,350
Total variable costs	₹38,80,000	₹56,95,600	₹74,67,600

2.

	Variable Costs of Producing	
	2 Units	4 Units
Incremental unit-time learning model (from requirement 1)	₹38,80,000	₹74,67,600
Cumulative average-time learning model (from Exercise 10-23)	37,60,000	70,88,000
Difference	1,20,000	₹3,79,600

Total variable costs for manufacturing 2 and 4 units are lower under the cumulative average-time learning curve relative to the incremental unit-time learning curve. Direct manufacturing labor-hours required to make additional units decline more slowly in the incremental unit-time learning curve relative to the cumulative average-time learning curve when the same 90% factor is used for both curves. The reason is that, in the incremental unit-time learning curve, as the number of units double, only the last unit produced has a cost of 90% of the initial cost. In the cumulative average-time learning model, doubling the number of units causes the average cost of all the additional units produced (not just the last unit) to be 90% of the initial cost.

10-29 Time lag consideration in interpreting regression results. Lily Put Company manufactures apparel for young adults. It has four peak-load periods, one each for manufacturing the clothing suitable for spring, summer, fall, and winter. Each of these periods lasts for two months. In off-peak period, Lily Put schedules equipment maintenance and runs advertising campaigns to introduce new lines of clothing.

Lily Put wanted to study the cost-behavior pattern of its equipment maintenance costs and the relationship between its sales and advertising costs. Using monthly data and linear regression analysis, the following results were obtained:

Maintenance costs = ₹3,80,000 − (₹12 per Machine-hour × Number of Machine - hours)

Sales revenue = ₹2,50,000 − (2.10 × Advertising costs)

Required

Interpret the regression results.

Solution

Time lag consideration in interpreting regression results. The relationship between machine-hours and maintenance costs is negative because Lily Put Company schedules maintenance during slow production periods. There is a time lag between heavy machine usage during peak production months, and maintenance in later months when the production volume is low. To correctly understand the relationship between machine-hours and maintenance costs, Lily Put should estimate the regression equation of maintenance costs on lagged machine-hours (that is, machine-hours in prior months).

The explanation for the relationship between sales revenue and advertising costs is that the result of advertising is often not instantaneous. Generally advertising generates increased sales revenue in subsequent month(s), so Lily Put should estimate the relationship between advertising costs in a particular period and sales in future periods. Another explanation is that Lily Put increases its advertising costs during periods of declining sales in an attempt to increase sales volume of the clothing lines that will soon be out of season. For example, Lily Put may increase its advertising on winter clothing during late winter before the customers start purchasing spring clothes.

Exercises

[Comprehensive solutions to all exercises are available on the companion website www. pearsoned.co.in/charlesthorngren]

10-30 Various cost-behavior patterns. (CPA, adapted) Select the graph that matches the numbered manufacturing cost data. Indicate by letter which graph best fits the situation or item described.

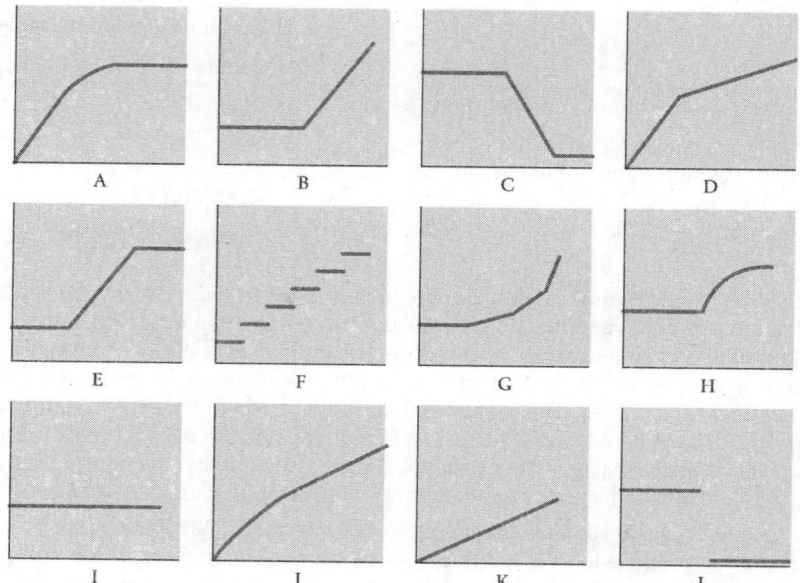

The vertical axes of the graphs represent total cost, and the horizontal axes represent units produced during a calendar year. In each case, the zero point of rupees and production is at the intersection of the two axes. The graphs may be used more than once.

a. Annual depreciation of equipment, where the amount of depreciation charged is computed by the machine-hours method.

b. Electricity bill – a flat fixed charge, plus a variable cost after a certain number of kilowatt-hours are used, in which the quantity of kilowatt-hours used varies proportionately with quantity of units produced.

c. City water bill, which is computed as follows:

First 1,00,000 gallons or less	₹10,000 flat fee
Next 10,000 gallons	₹3 per gallon used
Next 10,000 gallons	₹6 per gallon used
Next 10,000 gallons and so on	₹9 per gallon used and so on

The gallons of water used vary proportionately with the quantity of production output.

d. Cost of direct materials, where direct material cost per unit produced decreases with each kg of material used (for example, if 1 kg is used, the cost is ₹10; if 2 kg are used, the cost is ₹19.98; if 3 kg are used, the cost is ₹29.94), with a minimum cost per unit of ₹9.20.

e. Annual depreciation of equipment, where the amount is computed by the straight-line method. When the depreciation schedule was prepared, it was anticipated that the obsolescence factor would be greater than the wear-and-tear factor.

f. Rent on a manufacturing plant donated by the city, where the agreement calls for a fixed-fee payment unless 200,000 labor-hours are worked, in which case no rent is paid.

g. Salaries of repair personnel, where one person is needed for every 1,000 machine-hours or less (that is, 0-1,000 hours requires one person, 1,001-2,000 hours requires two people, and so on).

h. Cost of direct materials used (assume no quantity discounts).

i. Rent on a manufacturing plant donated by the county, where the agreement calls for rent of ₹10,00,000 to be reduced by ₹10 for each direct manufacturing labor-hour worked in excess of 20,00,000 hours, but a minimum rental fee of ₹2,00,000 must be paid.

10-31 Account analysis method. Johnson operates a car wash. Incoming cars are put on an automatic conveyor belt. Cars are washed as the conveyor belt carries the car from the start station to the finish station. After the car moves off the conveyor belt, the car is dried manually. Workers then clean and vacuum the inside of the car. Johnson serviced 80,000 cars in 2015. Johnson reports the following costs for 2015:

Account Description	Costs
Car wash labor	₹24,00,000
Soap, cloth, and supplies	3,20,000
Water	2,80,000
Electric power to move conveyor belt	7,20,000
Depreciation	6,40,000
Salaries	4,60,000

Required

1. Classify each account as variable or fixed with respect to the number of cars washed. Explain.
2. Johnson expects to wash 90,000 cars in 2016. Use the cost classification You developed in requirement 1 to estimate Johnson's total costs in 2016. Depreciation is computed on a straight-line basis.

10-32 Linear cost approximation. Rajeev Menon, managing director of the Ernst & Young Consulting is examining how overhead costs behave with changes in monthly professional labor-hours billed to clients. Assume the following historical data:

Total Overhead Costs	Professional Labor-Hours Billed to Clients
₹34,00,000	3,000
40,00,000	4,000
43,50,000	5,000
47,70,000	6,000
52,90,000	7,000
58,70,000	8,000

Required

1. Compute the linear cost function, relating total overhead cost to professional labor-hours, using the representative observations of 4,000 and 7,000 hours. Plot the linear cost function. Does the constant component of the cost function represent the fixed overhead costs of the Ernst & Young Consulting? Why?
2. What would be the predicted total overhead costs for (a) 5,000 hours and (b) 8,000 hours using the cost function estimated in requirement 1? Plot the predicted costs and actual costs for 5,000 and 8,000 hours.
3. Rajeev had a chance to accept a special job that would have boosted professional labor-hours from 4,000 to 5,000 hours. Suppose Rajeev guided by the linear cost function, rejected this job because it would have brought a total increase in contribution margin of ₹3,80,000, before deducting the predicted increase in total overhead cost, ₹4,30,000. What is the total contribution margin actually forgone?

10-33 Regression analysis, activity-based costing, choosing cost drivers. Akshita collects the following data to identify cost drivers of distribution costs at Container Corporation. Distribution costs includes the costs of organizing shipments and moving packaged units. Akshita thinks that because the product is heavy, the number of units moved will affect distribution costs significantly, but she is uncertain.

Month	Distribution Costs	Number of Packaged Units Moved	Number of Shipments Made
January	₹2,80,000	51,000	200
February	2,00,000	43,000	210
March	1,70,000	28,000	185
April	3,20,000	67,000	315
May	4,00,000	73,000	335
June	2,40,000	54,000	225
July	2,20,000	37,000	190
August	3,50,000	72.000	390
September	4,20,000	71,000	280
October	2,30,000	56,000	360
November	3,30,000	52,000	380
December	2,20,000	45,000	270
Total	₹33,80,000	6,49,000	3,340

Required

Akshita estimates the following regression equations:

$y = ₹13,490 + (₹4.96 × \text{Number of packaged units moved})$

$y = ₹1,04,170 + (₹637.7 × \text{Number of shipments made})$

1. Plot the monthly data and the regression lines for each of the following cost functions:

   a. Distribution costs = $a + (b × \text{Number of packaged units moved})$
   b. Distribution costs = $a + (b × \text{Number of shipments made})$

   Which cost driver for distribution costs would you choose? Explain briefly.

2. Akshita anticipates moving 40,000 units in 220 shipments next month. Using the preferable cost function, what amount of distribution costs should Akshita budget?

10-34 High-low method. Faraz, financial analyst at J B Chemicals (JVC) is examining the behavior of quarterly maintenance costs for budgeting purposes. Faraz collects the following data on machine-hours worked and maintenance costs for the past 12 quarters:

Quarter	Machine-Hours	Maintenance Costs
1	90,000	₹18,50,000
2	1,10,000	22,00,000
3	1,00,000	20,00,000
4	1,20,000	24,00,000
5	85,000	17,00,000
6	1,05,000	21,50,000
7	95,000	19,50,000
8	1,15,000	23,50,000
9	95,000	19,00,000
10	1,15,000	22,50,000
11	1,05,000	18,00,000
12	1,25,000	25,00,000

Required

1. Estimate the cost function for the quarterly data using the high-low method.
2. Plot and comment on the estimated cost function.

3. Faraz anticipates that JVC will operate machines for 90,000 hours in quarter 13. Calculate the predicted maintenance costs in quarter 13 using the cost function estimated in requirement 1.

10-35 High-low method; regression analysis. (CIMA, adapted) Ruha the financial manager at the Casa restaurant, is checking if there is any relationship between newspaper advertising and sales revenue at the restaurant. She obtains the following monthly data for the past 10 months.

Month	Revenues	Advertising Costs
March	₹5,00,000	₹20,000
April	7,00,000	30,000
May	5,50,000	15,000
June	6,50,000	35,000
July	5,50,000	10,000
August	6,50,000	20,000
September	4,50,000	15,000
October	8,00,000	40,000
November	5,50,000	25,000
December	6,00,000	25,000

They estimate the following regression equation:
Monthly revenues = ₹3,95,020 + (8.723 × Advertising costs)

Required

1. Plot the relationship between advertising costs and revenues.
2. Draw the regression line and evaluate it using the criteria of economic plausibility, goodness of fit, and slope of the regression line.
3. Use the high-low method to compute the cost function, relating advertising costs and revenues.
4. Using (a) the regression equation and (b) the high-low equation, what is the increase in revenues for each ₹1,000 spent on advertising within the relevant range? Which method should Ruha use to predict the effect of advertising costs on revenues? Explain briefly.

10-36 Cost estimation, cumulative average-time learning curve. The Bharat Company, which is under contract to the Indian Navy, assembles troop deployment boats. As part of its research program, it completes the assembly of the first of a new model (PT109) of deployment boats. The Navy is impressed with the PT109. It requests that Bharat submit a proposal on the cost of producing another seven PT109s.

Bharat reports the following cost information for the first PT109 assembled by Bharat:

Direct materials	₹3,00,000
Direct manufacturing labor (10,000 labor-hours × ₹90)	9,00,000
Tooling cost[a]	1,50,000
Variable manufacturing overhead[b]	6,00,000
Other manufacturing overhead[c]	2,25,000
	₹21,75,000

[a]Tooling can be reused at no extra cost, because all of its cost has been assigned to the first deployment boat.

[b]Variable manufacturing overhead is proportional to direct manufacturing labor-hours; a rate of ₹60 per hour is used for purposes of bidding on contracts.

cOther manufacturing overhead is allocated at a flat rate of 25% of direct manufacturing labor costs for purposes of bidding on contracts.

Bharat uses an 85% cumulative average-time learning model as a basis for forecasting direct manufacturing labor-hours on its assembling operations. (An 85% learning curve means $b = -0.2345$)

Required

1. Calculate predicted total costs of producing seven PT109s for the Navy. (Bharat will keep the first deployment boat assembled, costed at ₹21,75,000, as a demonstration model for potential customers)

2. What is the rupee amount of difference between (a) the predicted total costs for producing the seven PT109s in requirement 1, and (b) the predicted total costs for producing the seven PT109s assuming that there is no learning curve for direct manufacturing labor? That is, for (b) assume a linear function for units produced and direct manufacturing labor-hours.

Decision Making and Relevant Information

Learning Objectives ▼

1. Use the five-step decision-making process to make decisions

2. Distinguish relevant from irrelevant information in decision situations

3. Explain the concept of opportunity cost and why managers should consider it when making insourcing-versus-outsourcing decisions

4. Know how to choose which products to produce when there are capacity constraints

5. Explain how to manage bottlenecks

6. Discuss the factors managers must consider when adding or dropping customers or business units

7. Explain why book value of equipment is irrelevant for managers making equipment-replacement decisions

8. Explain how conflicts can arise between the decision model a manager uses and the performance-evaluation model top management uses to evaluate managers

How many decisions have you made today?

Maybe you made a big decision today, such as accepting a job offer. Or maybe your decision was as simple as making plans for the weekend or choosing a restaurant for dinner. Regardless of whether decisions are significant or routine, most people follow a simple, logical process when making them. This process involves gathering information, making predictions, making a choice, acting on the choice, and evaluating results. The process also includes evaluating the costs and benefits of each choice. For decisions that involve costs, some costs are irrelevant. For example, once you purchase a coffee maker, its cost is irrelevant when calculating how much money you save each time you brew coffee at home versus buy it at Starbucks. You incurred the cost of the coffee maker in the past, and you can't recoup that cost. This chapter will explain which costs and benefits are relevant and which are not—and how you should think of them when choosing among alternatives.

Information and the Decision Process

Managers usually follow a *decision model* for choosing among different courses of action. A **decision model** is a formal method of making a choice that often involves both quantitative and qualitative analyses. Management accountants analyze and present relevant data to guide managers' decisions.

Consider a strategic decision facing managers at Precision Sporting Goods, a manufacturer of golf clubs: Should the company reorganize its manufacturing operations to reduce manufacturing labor costs? Precision Sporting Goods has only two alternatives: do not reorganize or reorganize.

Reorganization will eliminate all manual handling of materials. Current manufacturing labor consists of 20 workers: 15 workers operate machines and 5 workers handle materials. The 5 materials-handling workers have been hired on contracts that permit layoffs without additional payments. Each worker works 2,000 hours annually. Reorganization is predicted to cost ₹9,00,000 each year (mostly for new equipment leases). The reorganization will not affect the production output of 25,000 units, the selling price of ₹2,500, the direct material cost per unit of ₹500, manufacturing overhead of ₹75,00,000, or marketing costs of ₹2,00,00,000.

Managers use the five-step decision-making process presented in Exhibit 11-1 and first introduced in Chapter 1 to make this decision. Study the sequence of the steps in this exhibit and note how Step 5 evaluates performance to provide feedback about actions taken in the previous steps. This feedback might affect future predictions, the prediction methods used, the way choices are made, or the implementation of the decision.

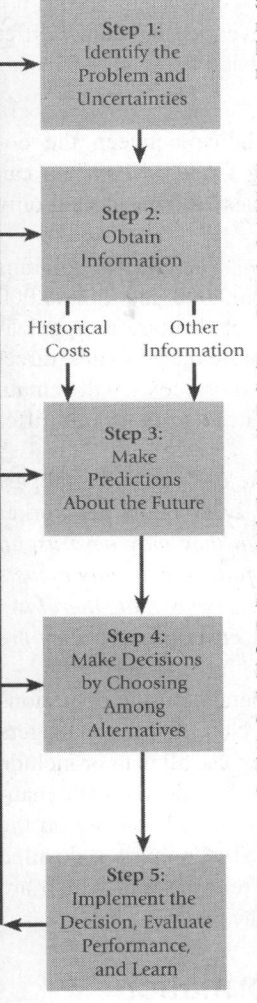

Step 1:
Identify the
Problem and
Uncertainties

Should Precision Sporting Goods reorganize its
manufacturing operations to reduce manufacturing
labor costs? An important uncertainty is how the
reorganization will affect employee morale.

Step 2:
Obtain
Information

Historical hourly wage rates are ₹140 per hour. However, a
recently negotiated increase in employee benefits of ₹20 per
hour will increase wages to ₹160 per hour. The reorganization
of manufacturing operations is expected to reduce the number
of workers from 20 to 15 by eliminating all 5 workers who
handle materials. The reorganization is likely to have negative
effects on employee morale.

Historical   Other
Costs   Information

Step 3:
Make
Predictions
About the Future

Managers use information from step 2 together with an
assessment of probability as a basis for predicting future
manufacturing labor costs. Under the existing do-not-
reorganize alternative, costs are predicted to be ₹64,00,000
(20 workers × 2,000 hours per worker per year × ₹160 per
hour), and under the reorganize alternative, costs are predicted
to be ₹48,00,000 (15 workers × 2,000 hours per worker per
year × ₹160 per hour). Recall, the reorganization is predicted
to cost ₹9,00,000 per year.

Step 4:
Make Decisions
by Choosing
Among
Alternatives

Managers compare the predicted benefits calculated in step 3
(₹64,00,000 − ₹48,00,000 = ₹16,00,000—that is, savings from
eliminating materials-handling labor costs, 5 workers × 2,000
hours per worker per year × ₹160 per hour = ₹16,00,000) against
the cost of the reorganization (9,00,000) along with other
considerations (such as likely negative effects on employee
morale). Management chooses the reorganize alternative
because the financial benefits are significant and the effects on
employee morale are expected to be temporary and relatively small.

Step 5:
Implement the
Decision, Evaluate
Performance,
and Learn

Evaluating performance after the decision is implemented
provides critical feedback for managers, and the five-step
sequence is then repeated in whole or in part. Managers
learn from actual results that the new manufacturing labor
costs are ₹54,00,000, rather than the predicted ₹48,00,000,
because of lower-than-expected manufacturing labor
productivity. This (now) historical information can
help managers make better subsequent predictions that
allow for more learning time. Alternatively, managers may
improve implementation via employee training and better
supervision.

**Learning
Objective** **1**

Use the five-step deci-
sion-making process to
make decisions

. . . the five steps are
identify the problem and
uncertainties, obtain
information, make pre-
dictions about the future,
make decisions by
choosing among alterna-
tives, and implement
the decision, evaluate
performance, and learn

◄ **Decision
Point**

What is the five-step
process that manag-
ers can use to make
decisions?

The Concept of Relevance

Much of this chapter focuses on Step 4 in Exhibit 11-1 and on the concepts of relevant
costs and relevant revenues when choosing among alternatives.

**Learning
Objective 2**

Distinguish relevant from
irrelevant information in
decision situations

. . . only costs and rev-
enues that are expected
to occur in the future
and differ among alter-
native courses of action
are relevant

Relevant Costs and Relevant Revenues

Relevant costs are *expected future costs* and **relevant revenues** are *expected future revenues* that differ among the alternative courses of action being considered. Costs and revenues that are *not relevant* are said to be *irrelevant*. It is important to recognize that relevant costs and relevant revenues *must*:

- **Occur in the future**—every decision deals with a managers selecting a course of action based on its expected future results.

- **Differ among the alternative courses of action**—costs and revenues that do not differ will not matter and, therefore, will have no bearing on the decision being made.

The question is always, "What difference will an action make?"

Exhibit 11-2 presents the financial data underlying the choice between the do-not-reorganize and reorganize alternatives for Precision Sporting Goods. Managers can analyze the data in two ways: by considering "all costs and revenues" or considering only "relevant costs and revenues."

The first two columns describe the first way and present *all data*. The last two columns describe the second way and present *only relevant costs*: the ₹64,00,000 and ₹48,00,000 expected future manufacturing labor costs and the ₹9,00,000 expected future reorganization costs that differ between the two alternatives. Managers can ignore the revenues, direct materials, manufacturing overhead, and marketing items because these costs will remain the same whether or not Precision Sporting Goods reorganizes. These costs do not differ between the alternatives and, therefore, are irrelevant.

Notice that the past (historical) manufacturing hourly wage rate of ₹140 and total past (historical) manufacturing labor costs of ₹56,00,000 (20 workers × 2,000 hours per worker per year × ₹140 per hour) do not appear in Exhibit 11-2. *Although they may be a useful basis for making informed predictions of the expected future manufacturing labor costs of ₹64,00,000 and ₹48,00,000, historical costs themselves are past costs that, therefore, are irrelevant to decision making.* Past costs are also called **sunk costs** because they are unavoidable and cannot be changed no matter what action is taken.

The analysis in Exhibit 11-2 indicates that reorganizing the manufacturing operations will increase predicted operating income by ₹7,00,000 each year. Note that the managers at Precision Sporting Goods reach the same conclusion whether they use all data or include only relevant data in the analysis. By confining the analysis to only the relevant data, managers can clear away the clutter of potentially confusing irrelevant data. Focusing on the relevant data is especially helpful when all the information needed to prepare a detailed income statement is unavailable. Understanding which costs are relevant and which are irrelevant helps the decision maker concentrate on obtaining only the pertinent data.

Qualitative and Quantitative Relevant Information

Managers divide the outcomes of decisions into two broad categories: *quantitative* and *qualitative*. **Quantitative factors** are outcomes that are measured in numerical terms. Some quantitative factors are financial; they can be expressed in monetary terms. Examples include the cost of direct materials, direct manufacturing labor, and marketing. Other quantitative factors are nonfinancial; they can be measured numerically, but they are not expressed in monetary terms. Examples include reduction in new product-development time for a manufacturing company such as Microsoft and the percentage of on-time flight arrivals for an airline company such as Jet line. *Qualitative factors* are outcomes that are difficult to measure accurately in numerical terms. Employee morale is an example.

Relevant-cost analysis generally emphasizes quantitative factors that can be expressed in financial terms. *Although qualitative factors and quantitative nonfinancial factors are*

Exhibit 11-2

Determining Relevant Revenues and Relevant Costs for Precision Sporting Goods

| | All Revenues and Costs | | Relevant Revenues and Costs | |
	Alternative 1: Do Not Reorganize (₹)	Alternative 2: Reorganize (₹)	Alternative 1: Do Not Reorganize (₹)	Alternative 2: Reorganize (₹)
Revenues[a]	6,25,00,000	6,25,00,000	—	—
Costs:				
Direct materials[b]	1,25,00,000	1,25,00,000	—	—
Manufacturing labor	64,00,000[c]	48,00,000[d]	64,00,000[c]	48,00,000[d]
Manufacturing overhead	75,00,000	75,00,000	—	—
Marketing	2,00,00,000	2,00,00,000	—	—
Reorganization costs	—	9,00,000	—	9,00,000
Total costs	4,64,00,000	4,57,00,000	64,00,000	57,00,000
Operating income	1,61,00,000	1,68,00,000	(64,00,000)	(57,00,000)
	⎵ ₹7,00,000 Difference		⎵ ₹7,00,000 Difference	

[a]25,000 units × ₹2,500 per unit = ₹6,25,00,000   [c]20 workers × 2,000 hours per worker × ₹160 per hour = ₹64,00,000
[b]25,000 units × ₹500 per unit = ₹1,25,00,000   [d]15 workers × 2,000 hours per worker × ₹160 per hour = ₹48,00,000

difficult to measure in financial terms, they are important for managers to consider. In the Precision Sporting Goods example, managers carefully considered the negative effect on employee morale of laying off materials-handling workers, a qualitative factor, before choosing the reorganize alternative. It is often challenging for managers to compare and trade off nonfinancial and financial considerations.

Exhibit 11-3 summarizes the key features of relevant information. The concept of relevance applies to all decision situations. We present some of these decision situations in this chapter. Later chapters describe other decision situations that require managers to apply the relevance concept, such as joint costs (Chapter 16); quality and timeliness (Chapter 19); inventory management and supplier evaluation (Chapter 20); capital investment (Chapter 21); and transfer pricing (Chapter 22). We start our discussion on relevance by considering managerial decisions that affect output levels, such as whether to introduce a new product or to try to sell more units of an existing product.

One-Time-Only Special Orders

One type of decision that affects output levels is accepting or rejecting special orders when there is idle production capacity and the special orders have no long-run implications. We use the term **one-time-only special order** to describe these conditions.

Example 1: Surf Gear manufactures quality beach towels at its highly automated Mumbai plant. The plant has a production capacity of 48,000 towels each month. Current monthly production is 30,000 towels. Retail department stores account for all existing sales. Exhibit 11-4 shows the expected results for the coming month (August). (These amounts are predictions based on past costs.) We assume all costs can be classified as either fixed or variable with respect to a single cost driver (units of output).

Azelia is a luxury hotel chain that purchases towels from Mugar Corporation. The workers at Mugar are on strike, so Azelia must find a new supplier. In August, Azelia contacts Surf Gear and offers to buy 5,000 towels from them at ₹110 per towel. Based on the following facts, should Surf Gear's managers accept Azelia's offer?

Exhibit 11-3

Key Features of
Relevant Information

- Past (historical) costs may be helpful as a basis for making *predictions*. However, past costs themselves are always irrelevant when making *decisions*.
- Different alternatives can be compared by examining differences in expected total future revenues and expected total future costs.
- Not all expected future revenues and expected future costs are relevant. Expected future revenues and expected future costs that do not differ among alternatives are irrelevant and, hence, can be eliminated from the analysis. The key question is always, What difference will an action make?
- Appropriate weight must be given to qualitative factors and quantitative nonfinancial factors.

The management accountant gathers the following additional information.

- No subsequent sales to Azelia are anticipated.
- Fixed manufacturing costs are based on the 45,000-towel production capacity. That is, fixed manufacturing costs relate to the production capacity available and not the actual capacity used. If Surf Gear accepts the special order, it will use existing idle capacity to produce the 5,000 towels and fixed manufacturing costs will not change.
- No marketing costs will be necessary for the 5,000-unit one-time-only special order.
- Accepting this special order is not expected to affect the selling price or the quantity of towels sold to regular customers.

The management accountant prepares the data shown in Exhibit 11-4 on an absorption-costing basis (both variable and fixed manufacturing costs are included in inventoriable costs and cost of goods sold). In this exhibit, the manufacturing cost of ₹120 per unit and the marketing cost of ₹70 per unit include both variable and fixed costs. The sum of all costs (variable and fixed) in a particular business function of the value chain, such as manufacturing costs or marketing costs, are called business function costs. Full costs of the product, in this case ₹190 per unit, are the sum of all variable and fixed costs in all business functions of the value chain (R&D, design, production, marketing, distribution, and customer service). For Surf Gear,

Exhibit 11-4

Budgeted Income
Statement for August,
Absorption-Costing
Format for Surf Gear[a]

	A	B	C	D
		Total	**Per Unit**	
1				
2	Units sold	30,000		
3				
4	Revenues	₹60,00,000	₹200.0	
5	Cost of goods sold (manufacturing costs)			
6	Variable manufacturing costs	22,50,000	75.0[b]	
7	Fixed manufacturing costs	13,50,000	45.0[c]	
8	Total cost of goods sold	36,00,000	120.0	
9	Marketing costs			
10	Variable marketing costs	15,00,000	50.0	
11	Fixed marketing costs	6,00,000	20.0	
12	Total marketing costs	21,00,000	70.0	
13	Full costs of the product	57,00,000	190.0	
14	Operating income	₹3,00,000	₹10.0	
15				
16	[a]Surf Gear incurs no R&D, product-design, distribution or customer-service costs			
17	[b]Variable manufacturing	Direct material	Direct manufacturing	Variable manufacturing
18	cost per unit =	cost per unit +	labor cost per unit +	overhead cost per unit
19	= ₹60.0 + ₹5.0 + ₹10.0 = ₹75.0			
20	[c]Fixed manufacturing	Fixed direct manufacturing	Fixed manufacturing	
21	cost per unit =	labor cost per unit +	overhead cost per unit	
22	= ₹15.0 + ₹30.0 = ₹45.0			

Exhibit 11-5

One-Time-Only Special-Order Decision for Surf Gear: Comparative Contribution Income Statements

		A	B	C	D	E	F	G	H
					Without the Special Order		With the Special Order		Difference: Relevant Amounts
1									
2					30,000		35,000		for the
3					Units to be Sold		Units to be Sold		5,000
4			Per Unit (₹)		Total		Total		Units Special Order
5			(1)		(2) = (1) x 30,000		(3)		(4) = (3) − (2)
6	Revenues		200.0		₹60,00,000		₹65,50,000		₹5,50,000[a]
7	Variable costs:								
8	Manufacturing		75.0		22,50,000		26,25,000		3,75,000[b]
9	Marketing		50.0		15,00,000		15,00,000		0[c]
10	Total variable costs		125.0		37,50,000		41,25,000		3,75,000
11	Contribution margin		75.0		22,50,000		24,25,000		1,75,000
12	Fixed costs:								
13	Manufacturing		45.0		13,50,000		13,50,000		0[d]
14	Marketing		20.0		6,00,000		6,00,000		0[d]
15	Total fixed costs		65.0		19,50,000		19,50,000		0
16	Operating income		10.0		₹3,00,000		₹4,75,000		₹1,75,000
17									
18	[a]5,000 units x ₹110 per unit = ₹5,50,000.								
19	[b]5,000 units x ₹75 per unit = ₹3,75,000.								
20	[c]No variable marketing costs would be incurred for the 5,000-unit one-time-only special order.								
21	[d]Fixed manufacturing costs and fixed marketing costs would be unaffected by the special order.								

full costs of the product consist of costs in manufacturing and marketing because these are the only business functions. Because no marketing costs are necessary for the special order, the manager of Surf Gear will focus only on manufacturing costs. Based on the manufacturing cost per unit of ₹120, which is greater than the ₹110-per-unit price offered by the hotel chain, the manager might decide to reject the offer.

In Exhibit 11-5 the management accountant separates manufacturing and marketing costs into their variable- and fixed-cost components and presents data in the format of a contribution income statement. The relevant revenues and costs are the expected future revenues and costs that differ as a result of accepting the special offer: revenues of ₹5,50,000 (₹110 per unit × 5,000 units) and variable manufacturing costs of ₹3,75,000 (₹75.0 per unit × 5,000 units). The fixed manufacturing costs and all marketing costs (*including variable marketing costs*) are irrelevant in this case because these costs will not change in total whether the special order is accepted or rejected. Surf Gear would gain an additional ₹1,75,000 (relevant revenues, ₹5,50,000—relevant costs, ₹3,75,000) in operating income by accepting the special order. In this example, by comparing total amounts for 30,000 units versus 35,000 units or focusing only on the relevant amounts in the difference column in Exhibit 11-5, the manager avoids a misleading implication to: reject the special order because the ₹110-per-unit selling price is lower than the manufacturing cost per unit of ₹120 (Exhibit 11-4), which includes both variable and fixed manufacturing costs.

The assumption of no long-run or strategic implications is crucial to a manager's analysis of the one-time-only special-order decision. Suppose the manager concludes that the retail department stores (Surf Gear's regular customers) will demand a lower price if Surf

Gear sells towels at ₹110 apiece to Azelia. In this case, revenues from regular customers will be relevant. Why? Because the future revenues from regular customers will differ depending on whether Surf Gear accepts the special order. The Surf Gear manager would need to modify the relevant-revenue and relevant-cost analysis of the Azelia order to consider both the short-run benefits from accepting the order and the long-run consequences on profitability if Surf Gear lowered prices to all regular customers.

Potential Problems in Relevant-Cost Analysis

Managers should avoid two potential problems in relevant-cost analysis. First, they must watch for incorrect general assumptions, such as all variable costs are relevant and all fixed costs are irrelevant. In the Surf Gear example, the variable marketing cost of ₹50 per unit is irrelevant because Surf Gear will incur no extra marketing costs by accepting the special order. But fixed manufacturing costs could be relevant. The extra production of 5,000 towels per month from 30,000 towels to 35,000 towels does not affect fixed manufacturing costs because we assumed that the existing level of fixed manufacturing cost can support any level of production in the relevant range from 30,000 to 45,000 towels per month. In some cases, however, producing the extra 5,000 towels might increase fixed manufacturing costs. (and also increase variable manufacturing cost per unit). Suppose Surf Gear would need to run three shifts of 15,000 towels per shift to achieve full capacity of 45,000 towels per month. Increasing the monthly production from 30,000 to 45,000 would require a partial third shift because two shifts (or overtime payments) could produce only 32,000 towels. The partial shift would increase fixed manufacturing costs, thereby making these additional fixed manufacturing costs relevant for this decision.

Second, unit-cost data can potentially mislead decision makers in two ways:

1. **When irrelevant costs are included.** Consider the ₹45 of fixed manufacturing cost per unit (direct manufacturing labor, ₹15 per unit, plus manufacturing overhead, ₹30 per unit) included in the ₹120-per-unit manufacturing cost in the one-time-only special-order decision (see Exhibits 11-4 and 11-5). This ₹45-per-unit cost is irrelevant, because this cost will not change if the one-time-only special order is accepted, and so managers should not consider it.

2. **When the same unit costs are used at different output levels.** Generally, managers use total costs rather than unit costs because total costs are easier to work with and reduce the chance for erroneous conclusions. Then, if desired, the total costs can be unitized. In the Surf Gear example, total fixed manufacturing costs remain at ₹13,50,000 even if the company accepts the special order and produces 35,000 towels. Including the fixed manufacturing cost per unit of ₹45 as a cost of the special order would lead to the erroneous conclusion that total fixed manufacturing costs would increase to ₹15,75,000 (₹45 per towel × 35,000 towels).

The best way for managers to avoid these two potential problems is to keep focusing on (1) total fixed costs (rather than unit fixed cost) and (2) the relevance concept. Managers should always require all items included in an analysis to be expected total future revenues and expected total future costs that differ among the alternatives.

Short-Run Pricing Decisions

In the one-time-only special-order decision in the previous section, Surf Gear's managers had to decide whether to accept or reject Azelia's offer to supply towels at ₹110 each. Sometimes managers must decide how much to bid on a one-time-only special order. This

Decision Point

When is a revenue or cost item relevant for a particular decision and what potential problems should be avoided in relevant cost analysis?

is an example of a short-run pricing decision—decisions that have a time horizon of only a few months.

Consider a short-run pricing decision facing managers at Surf Gear. Cranston Corporation has asked Surf Gear to bid on supplying 5,000 towels in September after Surf Gear has fulfilled its obligation to Azelia in August. Cranston is unlikely to place any future orders with Surf Gear. Cranston will sell Surf Gear's towels under its own brand name in regions and markets where Surf Gear does not sell its towels. Whether Surf Gear accepts or rejects this order will not affect Surf Gear's revenues—neither the units sold nor the selling price—from existing sales channels.

Relevant Costs for Short-Run Pricing Decisions

As before, Surf Gear's managers estimate how much it will cost to supply the 5,000 towels. There are no incremental marketing costs, so the relevant costs are the variable manufacturing costs of ₹75 calculated in the previous section. As before, the extra production of 5,000 towels in September from 30,000 to 35,000 towels does not affect fixed manufacturing costs because the relevant range is from 30,000 to 45,000 towels per month. Any selling price above ₹75 will improve Surf Gear's profitability in the short run. What price should Surf Gear's managers bid for the order of 5,000 towels?

Strategic and Other Factors in Short-Run Pricing

Based on market intelligence, Surf Gear's managers believe that competing bids will be between ₹100 and ₹110 per towel, so they decide to bid ₹100 per towel. If Surf Gear wins this bid, operating income will increase by ₹1,25,000 (relevant revenues, ₹100 × 5,000 = ₹5,00,000 − relevant costs, ₹75 × 5,000 = ₹3,75,000). In light of the extra capacity and strong competition, management's strategy is to bid as high above ₹75 as possible while remaining lower than competitors' bids. Note how Surf Gear chooses the price after looking at the problem through the eyes of its competitors, not based on just its own costs.

What if Surf Gear was the only supplier and Cranston could undercut Surf Gear's selling price in Surf Gear's current markets? The relevant cost of the bidding decision would then include the contribution margin lost on sales to existing customers. What if there were many parties eager to bid and win the Cranston contract? In this case, the contribution margin lost on sales to Surf Gear's existing customers would be irrelevant to the decision because Cranston would undercut the existing business regardless of whether Surf Gear wins the contract.

In contrast to the Surf Gear case, in some short-run situations, a company may experience strong demand for its products or have limited capacity. In these circumstances, managers will strategically increase prices in the short run to as much as the market will bear. We observe high short-run prices in the case of new products or new models of older products, such as microprocessors, computer chips, cellular telephones, and software.

Insourcing-versus-Outsourcing and Make-versus-Buy Decisions

We now apply the concept of relevance to another strategic decision: whether a company should make a component part or buy it from a supplier. We again assume idle capacity.

Outsourcing and Idle Facilities

Outsourcing is purchasing goods and services from outside vendors rather than **insourcing**, producing the same goods or providing the same services within the organization. For example, Kodak prefers to manufacture its own film (insourcing), but has IBM do its data processing (outsourcing). Honda relies on outside vendors to supply some component parts (outsourcing) but chooses to manufacture other parts internally (insourcing).

Decisions about whether a producer of goods or services will insource or outsource are called **make-or-buy decisions**. Surveys of companies indicate that managers consider quality, dependability of suppliers, and costs as the most important factors in the make-or-buy decision. Sometimes, however, qualitative factors dominate management's make-or-buy decision. For example, Dell Computer buys the Pentium chip for personal computers from Intel because Dell does not have the know-how and technology to make the chip itself. In contrast, to maintain the secrecy of its formula, Coca-Cola does not outsource the manufacture of its concentrate.

Example 2: The Soho Company manufactures a two-in-one video system consisting of a DVD player and a digital media receiver (that downloads movies and video from internet sites such as NetFlix). Columns 1 and 2 of the following table show the expected total and per-unit costs for manufacturing the DVD-player. Soho plans to manufacture the 2,50,000 units in 2,000 batches of 125 units each. Variable batch-level costs of ₹6,250 per batch vary with the number of batches, not the total number of units produced.

Broadfield, Inc., a manufacturer of DVD players, offers to sell Soho 2,50,000 DVD players next year for ₹640 per unit on Soho's preferred delivery schedule. Assume that financial factors will be the basis of this make-or-buy decision. Should Soho make or buy the DVD player?

Columns 1 and 2 of the preceding table indicate the expected total costs and expected cost per unit of producing 2,50,000 DVD players next year. The expected manufacturing cost per unit for next year is ₹720. At first glance, it appears that the company should buy DVD players because the expected ₹720-per-unit cost of making the DVD player is more than the ₹640 per unit to buy it. But a make-or-buy decision is rarely obvious. To make a decision, managers needs to answer the question, "What is the difference in relevant costs between the alternatives?"

For the moment, suppose (1) the capacity now used to make the DVD players will become idle next year if the DVD players are purchased; (2) the ₹3,00,00,000 of fixed manufacturing overhead will continue to be incurred next year regardless of the decision made; and the ₹75,00,000 in fixed salaries to support materials handling and setup will not be incurred if the manufacture of DVD players is completely shut down.

Exhibit 11-6 presents the relevant-cost computations which show that Soho will save ₹1,00,00,000 by making DVD players rather than buying them from Broadfield. Based on this analysis, Soho's managers decide to make the DVD players.

Note how the key concepts of relevance presented in Exhibit 11-3 apply here:

- Exhibit 11-6 compares differences in expected total future revenues and expected total future costs. Past costs are always irrelevant when making decisions.
- Exhibit 11-6 shows ₹2,00,00,000 of future materials-handling and setup costs under the make alternative but not under the buy alternative. Why? Because buying

Relevant Items	Total Relevant Costs		Relevant Cost Per Unit	
	Make	**Buy**	**Make**	**Buy**
Outside purchase of parts (₹640 × 250,000 units)		₹16,00,00,000		₹640
Direct materials	₹9,00,00,000		₹360	
Direct manufacturing labor	2,50,00,000		100	
Variable manufacturing overhead	1,50,00,000		60	
Mixed (variable and fixed) materials-handling and setup overhead	2,00,00,000		80	
Total relevant costs[a]	₹15,00,00,000	₹16,00,00,000	₹580	₹640
Difference in favor of making DVD players	₹1,00,00,000		₹40	

Exhibit 11-6

Relevant (Incremental) Items for Make-or-Buy Decision for DVD Players at Soho Company

[a]The ₹3,00,00,000 of plant-lease, plant-insurance, and plant-administration costs could be included under both alternatives. Conceptually, they do not belong in a listing of relevant costs because these costs are irrelevant to the decision. Practically, some managers may want to include them in order to list all costs that will be incurred under each alternative.

- DVD players and not manufacturing them will save ₹2,00,00,000 in future variable costs per batch and avoidable fixed costs. The ₹2,00,00,000 represents future costs that differ between the alternatives and so is relevant to the make-or-buy decision.

- Exhibit 11-6 excludes the ₹3,00,00,000 of plant-lease, insurance, and administration costs under both alternatives. Why? Because these future costs will not differ between the alternatives, so they are irrelevant.

A common term in decision making is *incremental* cost. An **incremental cost** is the additional total cost incurred for an activity. In Exhibit 11-6, the incremental cost of making DVD players is the additional total cost of ₹15,00,00,000 that Soho will incur if it decides to make DVD players. The ₹3,00,00,000 of fixed manufacturing overhead is not an incremental cost because Soho will incur these costs whether or not it makes DVD players. Similarly, the incremental cost of buying DVD players from Broadfield is the additional total cost of ₹16,00,00,000 that Soho will incur if it decides to buy DVD players. A **differential cost** is the difference in total (relevant) cost between two alternatives. In Exhibit 11-6, the differential cost between the make-DVD-players and buy-DVD-players alternatives is ₹1,00,00,000 (₹16,00,00,000 − ₹15,00,00,000). Note that *incremental* cost and *differential* cost are sometimes used interchangeably in practice. When faced with these terms, always be sure to clarify what they mean.

We define *incremental revenue* and *differential revenue* similarly to incremental cost and differential cost. **Incremental revenue** is the additional total revenue from an activity. **Differential revenue** is the difference in total revenue between two alternatives.

Strategic and Qualitative Factors

Strategic and qualitative factors affect outsourcing decisions. For example, Soho may prefer to manufacture CD players in-house to retain control over the design, quality, reliability, and delivery schedules. Conversely, despite the cost advantages documented in Exhibit 11-6, Soho may prefer to outsource, become a leaner organization, and focus on areas of its core competencies, the manufacture and sale of video systems. For example, advertising companies, such as J. Walter Thompson, only focus on the creative and planning aspects of advertising (their core competencies), and they outsource production activities, such as film, photographs, and illustrations.

Outsourcing is risky. As a company's dependence on its suppliers increases, suppliers could increase prices and let quality and delivery performance slip. To minimize these risks, companies generally enter into long-run contracts specifying costs, quality, and delivery schedules with their suppliers. Wise managers build close partnerships or alliances with a few key suppliers. For example, Toyota sends its own engineers to improve processes of suppliers. Suppliers of companies such as Ford, Hyundai, Panasonic, and Sony have researched and developed innovative products, met demands for increased quantities, maintained quality and on-time delivery, and lowered costs—actions that the companies themselves would not have had the competencies to achieve.

Outsourcing decisions invariably have a long-run horizon in which the financial costs and benefits of outsourcing become more uncertain. Almost always, strategic and qualitative factors such as those described here become important determinants of the outsourcing decision. Weighing all these factors requires the exercise of considerable management judgment and care.

International Outsourcing

What additional factors would Soho have to consider if the supplier of DVD players was based in India? One important factor would be exchange-rate risk. Suppose the Indian supplier offers to sell Soho 2,50,000 DVD players for ₹19,20,00,000. Should Soho make or buy? The answer depends on the exchange rate that Soho's managers expects next year. If they forecasts an exchange rate of ₹48 per $, Soho's expected purchase cost equals ₹16,00,00,000 (₹19,20,00,000/₹48 per $) greater than the ₹15,00,00,000 relevant costs for making the DVD players. If, however, Soho's managers anticipate an exchange rate of ₹54 per $, Soho's expected purchase cost equals ₹15,00,00,000 (₹19,20,00,000/₹54 per $), which is less than the ₹1,42,22,222 relevant costs for making the DVD players, so Soho's managers would prefer to buy rather than make the DVD players.

Soho's managers have yet another option. Soho could enter into a forward contract to purchase ₹19,20,00,000. A forward contract allows Soho to contract today to purchase rupees next year at a predetermined, fixed cost, thereby protecting itself against exchange rate risk. If Soho's managers choose decides to go this route, they would make (buy) DVD players if the cost of the contract is greater (less) than ₹1,50,00,000.

International outsourcing requires managers to evaluate manufacturing and transportation costs, exchange-rate risks, and the other strategic and qualitative factors discussed earlier such as quality, reliability, and efficiency of the supply chain.

The Total Alternatives Approach

In the simple make-or-buy decision in Exhibit 11-6, we assumed that the capacity currently used to make DVD players will remain idle if Soho purchases the parts from Broadfield. Often, however, the released capacity can be used for other, more-profitable purposes. In the case, Soho's managers must choose whether to make or buy. based on how best to use available production capacity.

Example 3: If Soho decides to buy DVD players for its video systems from Broadfield, then Soho's best use of the capacity that becomes available is to produce 1,00,000 Digitecks, a portable, stand-alone DVD player. From a manufacturing standpoint, Digitecks are similar DVD players made from the video system. With help from operating managers, Soho's management accountant, estimates the following future revenues and costs if Soho decides to manufacture and sell Digitecks:

Incremental future revenues		₹8,00,00,000
Incremental future costs		
Direct materials	₹3,40,00,000	
Direct manufacturing labor	1,00,00,000	
Variable overhead (such as power, utilities)	60,00,000	
Materials-handling and setup overheads	50,00,000	
Total incremental future costs		5,50,00,000
Incremental future operating income		₹2,50,00,000

Because of capacity constraints, Soho can make either DVD players for its video system unit or Digitecks, but not both. Which of the two alternatives should Soho's managers choose: (1) Make video system DVD players and do not make Digitecks (2) Buy video system DVD players and make Digitecks:

(1) Make video system DVD player and do not make Digiteks or

(2) Buy video system DVD and make Digiteks

Exhibit 11-7, Panel A, summarizes the "total-alternatives" approach—the future costs and revenues for *all* alternatives. Soho's managers will choose Alternative 2, buying video-system DVD players and use the available capacity to make and sell Digitecks. The future incremental costs of buying video-system DVD players from an outside supplier (₹16,00,00,000) exceed the future incremental costs of making video-system DVD players in-house (₹15,00,00,000). But Soho can use the capacity freed up by buying video-system DVD players to gain ₹2,50,00,000 in operating income (incremental future revenues of ₹8,00,00,000 minus total incremental future costs of ₹5,50,00,000) by making and selling Digitecks. The *net relevant* costs of buying video-system DVD players and making and selling Digitecks are ₹16,00,00,000 − ₹2,50,00,000 = ₹13,50,00,000.

The Opportunity-Cost Approach

Deciding to use a resource in a particular way causes a manager to forgo the opportunity to use the resource in any other ways. This lost opportunity is a cost that the manager must consider when making a decision. **Opportunity cost** is the contribution to operating income that is forgone by not using a limited resource in its next-best alternative use. For example, the (relevant) cost of going to school for a BS in accounting degree is not only the cost of tuition, books, lodging, and food, but also the income sacrificed (opportunity cost) by not working. Presumably, however, the estimated future benefits of obtaining a BS in accounting degree (such as, higher-paying career) will exceed these out-of-pocket and opportunity costs.

Exhibit 11-7, Panel B, displays the opportunity-cost approach for analyzing the alternatives Soho faces. *Note that the alternatives are defined differently under the two approaches:*

In the total alternatives approach:	In the opportunity cost approach:
1. Make video-system DVD players and do not make Digitek	1. Make video-system DVD players
2. Buy video-system DVD players and make Digitek	2. Buy video-system DVD players

The opportunity cost approach does not reference Digitecks. Under the opportunity-cost approach, the cost of each alternative includes (1) the incremental costs and (2) the opportunity cost, the profit forgone from not making Digitecks. This opportunity cost arises because Digitek is excluded from formal consideration in the alternatives.

Exhibit 11-7

Total-Alternatives
Approach and
Opportunity-Cost
Approach to
Make-or-Buy Decisions
for Soho Company

Relevant Items	Alternatives for Soho	
	1. Make Video-System DVD Players and Do Not Make Digitecks	2. Buy Video-System DVD Players and Make Digitecks
PANEL A Total-Alternatives Approach to Make-or-Buy Decisions		
Total incremental future costs of making/buying video-system DVD players (from Exhibit 11-6)	₹1,50,00,000	₹1,60,00,000
Deduct excess of future revenues over future costs from Digitek	0	(25,00,000)
Total relevant costs under total-alternatives approach	₹1,50,00,000	₹1,35,00,000
	1. Make Video-System DVD Players	**2. Buy Video-System DVD Players**
PANEL B Opportunity-Cost Approach to Make-or-Buy Decisions		
Total incremental future costs of making/buying video-system DVD players (from Exhibit 11-6)	₹1,50,00,000	₹1,60,00,000
Opportunity cost: Profit contribution forgone because capacity will not be used to make Digitek, the next-best alternative	25,00,000	0
Total relevant costs under opportunity-cost approach	₹1,75,00,000	₹1,60,00,000

Note that the differences in costs across the columns in Panels A and B are the same: The cost of alternative 2 is ₹15,00,000 less than the cost of alternative 1.

Consider alternative 1, making video-system DVD players. What are all the costs of making video-system DVD players? Certainly Soho will incur ₹15,00,00,000 of incremental costs to make video-system DVD players, but is this the entire cost? No, because by deciding to use limited manufacturing resources to make video-system DVD players, Soho will give up the opportunity to earn ₹2,50,00,000 by not using these resources to make Digitecks. Therefore, the relevant costs of making video-system DVD players are the incremental costs of ₹15,00,00,000 plus the opportunity cost of ₹2,50,00,000.

Next consider alternative 2, buy video-system DVD players. The incremental cost of buying video-system DVD players is ₹16,00,00,000. The opportunity cost is zero. Why? Because by choosing this alternative, Soho will not forgo the profit it can earn from making and selling Digitecks.

Panel B leads managers to the same conclusion as Panel A: buying video-system DVD players and making Digitecks is the preferred alternative.

Panels A and B of Exhibit 11-7 describe two consistent approaches to decision making with capacity constraints. The total-alternatives approach in Panel A includes all future incremental costs and revenues. For example, under alternative 2, the additional future operating income from *using capacity to make and sell Digitecks* (₹2,50,00,000) is subtracted from the future incremental cost of buying stereo DVD (₹16,00,00,000). The opportunity-cost analysis in Panel B takes the opposite approach. It focuses on stereo DVD players. *Whenever capacity is not going to be used to make and sell Digitecks*, the future forgone operating income is added as an opportunity cost of making or buying stereo DVD players, as in alternative 1. (Note that when Digitecks are made, as in alternative 2, there is no "opportunity cost of not making Digitecks.") Therefore, whereas Panel A *subtracts* ₹2,50,00,000 under alternative 2, Panel B *adds* ₹2,50,00,000 under alternative 1. *Panel B highlights the idea that when capacity is constrained, the relevant revenues and costs of any alternative equal (1) the incremental future revenues and costs plus (2) the opportunity cost*. However, when managers are considering more than two alternatives simultaneously, it is generally easier to use the total-alternatives approach.

Opportunity costs are not incorporated into formal financial accounting records. Why? Because historical record keeping is limited to transactions involving alternatives that managers *actually selected*, rather than alternatives that they rejected. Rejected alternatives do not produce transactions and are not recorded. If Soho makes stereo DVD players, it will not make Digitecks, and it will not record any accounting entries for Digitecks. Yet the opportunity cost of making stereo DVD players, which equals the operating income that Soho forgoes by not making Digitecks, is a crucial input into the make-or-buy decision. Consider again Exhibit 11-7, Panel B. On the basis of only the incremental costs systematically recorded in the accounting system, it is less costly for Soho to make rather than buy video system DVD players. Recognizing the opportunity cost of ₹2,50,00,000 leads to the different conclusion: buying video system DVD players is preferable.

Suppose Soho has sufficient capacity to make Digitecks even if it makes video system DVD players. In this case, the opportunity cost of making video system DVD players is ₹0 because Soho does not give up the ₹2,50,00,000 operating income from making Digitecks even if it chooses to make video system DVD players. The relevant costs are ₹15,00,00,000 (incremental costs of ₹15,00,00,000 plus opportunity cost of ₹0). Under these conditions, Soho's managers would prefer to make video system DVD players, rather than buy them, and also make Digitecks.

Besides quantitative considerations, managers also consider strategic and qualitative factors in make-or-buy decisions. In deciding to buy video-system DVD players from an outside supplier, Soho's managers consider factors such as the supplier's reputation for quality and timely delivery. They also consider the strategic consequences of selling Digitecks. For example, will selling Digitecks take Soho's focus away from its video-system business?

Carrying Costs of Inventory

To see another example of an opportunity cost, consider the following data for Soho's DVD player purchasing decision:

Annual estimated video-system DVD player requirements for next year	2,50,000 units
Cost per unit when each purchase is equal to 2,500 units	₹640
Cost per unit when each purchase is equal to or greater than 30,000 units (₹640 − 0.5% discount)	₹636.8
Cost of a purchase order	₹1,500

Soho's managers are evaluating the following alternatives:

A. Make 100 purchases (twice a week) of 2,500 units each during next year

B. Make 8 purchases (twice a quarter) of 31,250 units during the year

Average investment in inventory:	
A. (2,500 units × ₹640 per unit) ÷ 2[a]	₹8,00,000
B. (31,250 units × ₹636.8 per unit) ÷ 2[a]	₹99,50,000
Annual rate of return if cash is invested elsewhere (for example, bonds or stocks) at the same level of risk as investment in inventory	12%

[a] The example assumes that video-system-DVD-player purchases will be used uniformly throughout the year. The average investment in inventory during the year is the cost of the inventory when a purchase is received plus the cost of inventory just before the next purchase is delivered (in our example, zero) divided by 2.

Soho will pay cash for the video-system DVD players it buys. Which purchasing alternative is more economical for Soho?

The management accountant presents the following analysis to the company's managers using the total alternatives approach, recognizing that Soho has, on average, ₹99,50,000 of cash available to invest. If Soho invests only ₹8,00,000 in inventory as in alternative A, it will have ₹91,50,000 (₹99,50,000 − ₹8,00,000) of cash available to invest elsewhere, which at a 12% rate of return will yield a total return of ₹10,98,000. This income is subtracted from the ordering and purchasing costs incurred under alternative A. If Soho invests all ₹99,50,000 in inventory as in alternative B, it will have ₹0 (₹99,50,000 − ₹99,50,000) available to invest elsewhere and will earn no return on the cash.

	Alternative A: Make 100 Purchases of 2,500 Units Each During the Year and Invest Any Excess Cash (1)	Alternative B: Make 8 Purchases of 31,250 Units Each During the Year and Invest Any Excess Cash (2)	Difference (3) = (1) − (2)
Annual purchase-order costs (100 purch. orders × ₹1,500/purch. order; 8 purch. orders × ₹1,500/purch. order)	₹1,50,000	₹12,000	₹1,38,000
Annual purchase costs (2,50,000 units × ₹640/unit; 2,50,000 units × ₹636.8/unit)	16,00,00,000	15,92,00,000	8,00,000
Deduct annual rate of return earned by investing cash not tied up in inventory elsewhere at the same level of risk [0.12 × (₹99,50,000 − ₹8,00,000); 0.12 × (₹99,50,000 − ₹99,50,000)]	(10,98,000)	0	(10,98,000)
Relevant costs	₹1,59,05,200	₹1,59,21,200	₹(1,60,000)

Consistent with the trends toward holding smaller inventories, it is more economical for Soho's managers to purchase smaller quantities of 2,500 units 100 times a year than to purchase 31,250 units 8 times a year by ₹6,00,00.

The following table presents the management accountant's analysis of the two alternatives using the opportunity cost approach. Each alternative is defined only in terms of the two purchasing choices with no explicit reference to investing the excess cash.

	Alternative A: Make 100 Purchases of 2,500 Units Each During the Year (1)	Alternative B: Make 8 Purchases of 31,250 Units Each During the Year (2)	Difference (3) = (1) − (2)
Annual purchase-order costs (100 purch. orders × ₹1,500/purch. order; 8 purch. orders × ₹1,500/purch. order)	₹1,50,000	₹12,000	₹1,38,000

	Alternative A: Make 100 Purchases of 2,500 Units Each During the Year (1)	Alternative B: Make 8 Purchases of 31,250 Units Each During the Year (2)	Difference (3) = (1) – (2)
Annual purchase costs (2,50,000 units × ₹640/unit; 2,50,000 units × ₹636.8/unit)	16,00,00,000	15,92,00,000	8,00,000
Opportunity cost: Annual rate of return that could be earned if investment in inventory were invested elsewhere at the same level of risk (0.12 × ₹8,00,000; 0.12 × ₹99,50,000)	96,000	11,94,000	(10,98,000)
Relevant costs	₹16,02,46,000	₹16,04,06,000	₹(1,60,000)

Recall that under the opportunity-cost approach, the relevant cost of any alternative is (1) the incremental cost of the alternative plus (2) the opportunity cost of the profit forgone from choosing that alternative. The opportunity cost of holding inventory is the income forgone by tying up money in inventory and not investing it elsewhere. The opportunity cost would not be recorded in the accounting system because, once the money is invested in inventory, there is no money available to invest elsewhere and so no return related to this investment to record. On the basis of the costs recorded in the accounting system (purchase-order costs and purchase costs), Soho's managers would erroneously conclude that making eight purchases of 31,250 units each is the less costly alternative. Column 3, however, indicates that, as in the total-alternatives approach, purchasing smaller quantities of 2,500 units 100 times a year is more economical than purchasing 31,250 units eight times during the year by ₹1,60,000. Why? Because the lower opportunity cost of holding smaller inventory exceeds the higher purchase and ordering costs. If the opportunity cost of money tied up in inventory were greater than 12% per year, or if other incremental benefits of holding lower inventory were considered, such as lower insurance, materials-handling, storage, obsolescence, and breakage cost, making 100 purchases would be even more economical.

Decision Point

What is an opportunity cost and why should managers consider it when making insourcing-versus-outsourcing decisions?

Product-Mix Decisions with Capacity Constraints

We now examine how the concept of relevance applies to **product-mix decisions**, the decisions managers make about which products to sell and in what quantities. These decisions usually have only a short-run focus because they typically arise in the context of capacity constraints that can be relaxed in the long run. For example, BMW, the German car manufacturer, continually adapts the mix of its different models of cars (for example, 325i, 525i, and 740i) to fluctuations in selling prices and demand.

To determine product mix, managers maximizes operating income, subject to constraints such as capacity and demand. Throughout this section, we assume that as short-run changes in product mix occur, the only costs that change are costs that are variable with the number of units produced (and sold). Under this assumption, the analysis of individual product contribution margins provides insight into the product mix that maximizes operating income.

Learning Objective 4

Know how to choose which products to produce when there are capacity constraints

. . . select the product with the highest contribution margin per unit of the limiting resource

Example 4: Power Recreation assembles two engines, a snowmobile engine and a boat engine. The following table shows the selling prices, costs, and contribution margins of these two engines:

	Snowmobile Engine	Boat Engine
Selling price	₹8,000	₹10,000
Variable cost per unit	5,600	6,250
Contribution margin per unit	₹2,400	₹3,750
Contribution margin percentage (₹2,400 ÷ ₹8,000; ₹3,750 ÷ ₹10,000)	30%	37.5%

Only 600 machine-hours are available daily for assembling engines. Additional capacity cannot be obtained in the short run. Power Recreation can sell as many engines as it produces. The constraining resource, then, is machine-hours. It takes two machine-hours to produce one snowmobile engine and five machine-hours to produce one boat engine. What product mix should Power Recreation's managers choose to maximize its operating income?

In terms of contribution margin per unit and contribution margin percentage, the data in Example 4 shows that boat engines are more profitable than snowmobile engines. The product that Power Recreation should produce and sell, however, is not necessarily the product with the higher individual contribution margin per unit or contribution margin percentage. As the following table shows, managers should choose the product with *the highest contribution margin per unit of the constraining resource (factor)*. That's the resource that restricts or limits the production or sale of products.

	Snowmobile Engine	Boat Engine
Contribution margin per unit	₹2,400	₹3,750
Machine-hours required to produce one unit	2 machine-hours	5 machine-hours
Contribution margin per machine-hour ₹2,400 per unit ÷ 2 machine-hours/unit ₹3,750 per unit ÷ 5 machine-hours/unit	₹1,200/machine-hour	₹750/machine-hour
Total contribution margin for 600 machine-hours ₹1,200/machine-hour × 600 machine-hours ₹750/machine-hour × 600 machine-hours	₹7,20,000	₹4,50,000

The number of machine-hours is the constraining resource in this example, and snowmobile engines earn more contribution margin per machine-hour (₹1,200/machine-hour) compared with boat engines (₹750/machine-hour). Therefore, choosing to produce and sell snowmobile engines maximizes *total* contribution margin (₹7,20,000 vs. ₹4,50,000 from producing and selling boat engines) and operating income. Other constraints in manufacturing settings can be the availability of direct materials, components, or skilled labor, as well as financial and sales factors. In a retail department store, the constraining resource may be linear feet of display space. Regardless of the specific constraining resource, managers should always focus on maximizing *total* contribution margin by choosing products that give the highest contribution margin per unit of the constraining resource.

In many cases, a manufacturer or retailer has the challenge of trying to maximize total operating income for a variety of products, each with more than one constraining resource. Some constraints may require a manufacturer or retailer to stock minimum quantities of products even if these products are not very profitable. For example, supermarkets must stock less-profitable products such as paper towels and toilet paper because customers will be willing to shop at a supermarket only if it carries a wide range of products. To determine the most profitable production schedule and the most profitable product mix, the manufacturer or retailer needs to determine the maximum total contribution margin in the face of many constraints. Optimization techniques, such as linear programming, help solve these more-complex problems.

Finally, there is the question of managing the bottleneck constraint to increase output and, therefore, contribution margin. Can the available machine-hours for assembling engines be increased beyond 600, for example, by reducing idle time? Can the time needed to assemble each snowmobile engine (two machine-hours) or each boat engine (five machine-hours) be reduced, for example, by reducing setup time and processing time of assembly? Can some of the assembly operations be outsourced to allow more engines to be built?

In the following section, we examine how managers can deal with the bottleneck constraint to increase output and, therefore, the contribution margin when some operations are bottlenecks and others are not.

> ◄ **Decision Point**
>
> When resources are constrained, how should managers choose which of multiple products to produce and sell?

Bottlenecks, Theory of Constraints, and Throughput-Margin Analysis

Suppose Power Recreation's snowmobile engine must go through a forging operation before it goes to the assembly operation. The company has 1,200 hours of daily forging capacity dedicated to the manufacture of snowmobile engines. The company takes 3 hours to forge each snowmobile engine, so Power Recreation can forge 400 snowmobile engines per day (1,200 hours ÷ 3 hours per snowmobile engine). Recall that it can assemble only 300 snowmobile engines per day (600 machine-hours ÷ 2 machine-hours per snowmobile engine). The production of snowmobile engines is constrained by the assembly operation, not the forging operation.

The **theory of constraints (TOC)** describes methods to maximize operating income when faced with some bottleneck and some nonbottleneck operations.[1] The TOC defines these three measures:

1. **Throughput margin** equals revenues minus the direct material costs of the goods sold.

2. *Investments* equal the sum of (a) material costs in direct materials, work-in-process, and finished goods inventories; (b) R&D costs; and (c) capital costs of equipment and buildings.

3. *Operating costs* equal all costs of operations (other than direct materials) incurred to earn throughput margin. Operating costs include costs such as salaries and wages, rent, utilities, and depreciation.

> **Learning Objective 5**
>
> Explain how to manage bottlenecks
>
> …keep bottlenecks busy and increase their efficiency and capacity by increasing throughput (contribution) margin

The objective of the TOC is to increase throughput margin while decreasing investments and operating costs. *The TOC considers a short-run time horizon of a few months and assumes operating costs are fixed and direct material costs are the only variable costs. In a situation where some of the operating costs are also variable in the short run, throughput margin is replaced by contribution margin.* In the Power Recreation example, each snowmobile engine sells for ₹8,000. We assume that the variable costs of ₹600 consist only

---

[1] See Eliyahu M. Goldratt and Jeff Cox, *The Goal* (New York: North River Press, 1986); Eliyahu M. Goldratt, *The Theory of Constraints* (New York: North River Press, 1990); Eric W. Noreen, Debra A. Smith, and James T. Mackey, *The Theory of Constraints and Its Implications for Management Accounting* (New York: North River Press, 1995); and Mark J. Woeppel, *Manufacturers' Guide to Implementing the Theory of Constraints* (Boca Raton, FL: Lewis Publishing, 2000).

of direct material costs (incurred in the forging department), so throughput margin equals contribution margin. For ease of exposition and consistency with the previous section, we use the term *contribution margin* instead of *throughput margin* throughout this section.

TOC focuses on managing bottleneck operations, as explained in the following steps:

Step 1: Recognize that the bottleneck operation determines the contribution margin of the entire system. In the Power Recreation example, output in the assembly operation determines the output of snowmobile engines.

Step 2: Identify the bottleneck operation by identifying operations with large quantities of inventory waiting to be worked on. As snowmobile engines are produced at the forging operation, inventories will build up at the assembly operation because daily assembly capacity of 300 snowmobile engines is less than the daily forging capacity of 400 snowmobile engines.

Step 3: Keep the bottleneck operation busy and subordinate all nonbottleneck operations to the bottleneck operation. That is, the needs of the bottleneck operation determine the production schedule of the nonbottleneck operations. To maximize operating income, the manager must maximize contribution margin of the constrained or bottleneck resource. The bottleneck assembly operation must always be kept running; the workers should not be waiting to assemble engines. To achieve this objective, Power Recreation's managers maintain a small buffer inventory of snowmobile engines that have gone through the forging operation and are waiting to be assembled. The bottleneck assembly operation sets the pace for the nonbottleneck forging operations. Operating managers maximize contribution margin by ensuring the assembly operation is operating at capacity by developing a detailed production schedule at the forging operation to ensure that the assembly operation is not waiting for work. At the same time, forging more snowmobile engines that cannot be assembled does not increase output or contribution margin; it only creates excess inventory of unassembled snowmobile engines.

Step 4: Take actions to increase the efficiency and capacity of the bottleneck operation as long as the incremental contribution margin exceeds the incremental costs of increasing efficiency and capacity.

We illustrate Step 4 using data from the forging and assembly operations of Power Recreation.

	Forging	Assembly
Capacity per day	400 units	300 units
Daily production and sales	300 units	300 units
Other fixed operating costs per day (excluding direct materials)	₹2,40,000	₹1,80,000
Other fixed operating costs per unit produced (₹2,40,000 ÷ 300 units; ₹1,80,000 ÷ 300 units)	₹800 per unit	₹600 per unit

Power Recreation's output is constrained by the capacity of 300 units in the assembly operation. What can Power Recreation's managers do to relieve the bottleneck constraint of the assembly operation?

Desirable actions include the following:

1. **Eliminate idle time at the bottleneck operation (time when the assembly machine is neither being set up to assemble nor actually assembling snowmobile engines).** Power Recreation's manager is evaluating permanently positioning two workers at the assembly operation to unload snowmobile engines as soon as they are assembled and to set up the machine to begin assembling the next batch of snowmobile engines. This action will cost ₹3,200 per day and bottleneck output will increase by 3 snowmobile engines per day. Should Power Recreation's managers incur the additional costs? Yes,

because Power Recreation's contribution margin will increase by ₹7,200 per day (₹2,400 per snowmobile engine × 3 snowmobile engines), which is greater than the incremental cost of ₹3,200 per day. All other costs are irrelevant.

2. **Shift products that do not have to be made on the bottleneck machine to nonbottleneck machines or to outside processing facilities.** Suppose Spartan Corporation, an outside contractor, offers to assemble 5 snowmobile engines each day at ₹750 per snowmobile engine from engines that have gone through the forging operation at Power Recreation. Spartan's quoted price is greater than Power Recreation's own operating costs in the assembly department of ₹600 per snowmobile engine. Should Power Recreation's managers accept the offer? Yes, because assembly is the bottleneck operation. Getting Spartan to assemble additional snowmobile engines will increase contribution margin by ₹12,000 per day (₹2,400 per snowmobile engine × 5 snowmobile engines), while the relevant cost of increasing capacity will be ₹3,750 per day (₹750 per snowmobile engine × 5 snowmobile engines). The fact that Power Recreation's unit cost is less than Spartan's quoted price is irrelevant.

   Suppose Gemini Industries, another outside contractor, offers to do the forging operation for 8 snowmobile engines per day for ₹650 per snowmobile engine from direct materials supplied by Power Recreation. Gemini's price is lower than Power Recreation's operating cost of ₹800 per snowmobile engine in the forging depart ment. Should Power Recreation's managers accept Gemini's offer? No, because other operating costs are fixed costs. Power Recreation will not save any costs by subcon tracting the forging operations. Instead, its costs will increase by ₹5,200 per day (₹650 per snowmobile engine × 8 snowmobile engines) with no increase in contribution margin, which is constrained by assembly capacity.

3. **Reduce setup time and processing time at bottleneck operations (for example, by simplifying the design or reducing the number of parts in the product).** Suppose Power Recreation can assemble 10 more snowmobile engines each day at a cost of ₹10,000 per day by reducing setup time at the assembly operation. Should Power Recreation's managers incur this cost? Yes, because the contribution margin will increase by ₹24,000 per day (₹2,400 per snowmobile engine × 10 snowmobile engines), which is greater than the incremental costs of ₹10,000 per day. Will Power Recreation's managers find it worthwhile to incur costs to reduce machining time at the nonbottleneck forging opera tion? No. Other operating costs will increase, while the contribution margin will remain unchanged because bottleneck capacity of the assembly operation will not increase.

4. **Improve the quality of parts or products manufactured at the bottleneck operation.** Poor quality is more costly at a bottleneck operation than at a nonbottleneck operation. The cost of poor quality at a nonbottleneck operation is the cost of materials wasted. If Power Recreation produces 5 defective snowmobile engines at the forging operation, the cost of poor quality is ₹28,000 (direct material cost per snowmobile engine, ₹5,600 × 5 snowmobile engines). No contribution margin is forgone because forging has unused capacity. Despite the defective production, forging can produce and trans fer 300 good-quality snowmobile engines to the assembly operation. At a bottleneck operation, the cost of poor quality is the cost of materials wasted *plus* the opportunity cost of lost contribution margin. Bottleneck capacity not wasted in producing defective snowmobile engines could be used to generate additional contribution margin. If Power Recreation produces 5 defective units at the assembly operation, the cost of poor qual ity is the lost revenue of ₹40,000 (₹8,000 per snowmobile engine × 5 snowmobile engines) or, alternatively stated, direct material costs of ₹28,000 (direct material cost per snowmobile engine, ₹5,600 × 5 snowmobile engines) plus the forgone contribu tion margin of ₹12,000 (₹2,400 per snowmobile engine × 5 snowmobile engines).

The high cost of poor quality at the bottleneck operation means that bottleneck time should not be wasted processing units that are defective. That is, engines should be inspected before the bottleneck operation to ensure that only good-quality parts are processed at the bottleneck operation. Furthermore, quality-improvement programs should place special emphasis on minimizing defects at bottleneck machines.

If successful, the actions in Step 4 will increase the capacity of the assembly operation until it eventually exceeds the capacity of the forging operation. The bottleneck will then shift to the forging operation. Power Recreation would then focus continuous-improvement actions on increasing forging operation efficiency and capacity. For example, the contract with Gemini Industries to forge 8 snowmobile engines per day at ₹650 per snowmobile engine from direct material supplied by Power Recreation will become attractive because the contribution margin will increase by ₹19,200 per day (₹2,400 per snowmobile engine × 8 snowmobile engines), which is greater than the incremental costs of ₹5,200 (₹650 per snowmobile engine × 8 snowmobile engines).

The theory of constraints emphasizes management of bottleneck operations as the key to improving performance of production operations as a whole. It focuses on short-run maximization of contribution margin. Because TOC regards operating costs as difficult to change in the short run, it does not identify individual activities and drivers of costs. Therefore, TOC is less useful for the long-run management of costs. In contrast, activity-based costing (ABC) systems take a long-run perspective and focus on improving processes by eliminating non-value-added activities and reducing the costs of performing value-added activities. ABC systems are therefore more useful than TOC for long-run pricing, cost control, and capacity management. The short-run TOC emphasis on maximizing contribution margin by managing bottlenecks complements the long-run strategic-cost-management focus of ABC.[2]

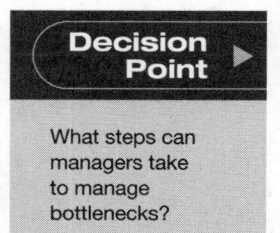

Decision Point ▶

What steps can managers take to manage bottlenecks?

Customer Profitability and Relevant Costs

Learning Objective 6

Discuss factors managers must consider when adding or dropping customers or segments

. . . managers should focus on how total costs differ among alternatives and ignore allocated overhead costs

We have seen how managers make choices about which products and how much of each product to produce, In addition, managers must often make decisions about adding or dropping a product line or a business segment. Similarly, if the cost object is a customer, companies must make decisions about adding or dropping customers (analogous to a product line) or a branch office (analogous to a business segment). We illustrate relevant-revenue and relevant-cost analysis for these kinds of decisions using customers rather than products as the cost object.

Example 5: Allied West, the West zone sales office of Allied Furniture, a wholesaler of specialized furniture, supplies furniture to three local retailers: Vijay, Amit, and Ankush. Exhibit 11-8 presents expected revenues and costs of Allied West by customer for the upcoming year using its activity-based costing system. Allied West's management accountant assigns costs to customers based on the activities needed to support each customer. Information on Allied West's costs for different activities at various levels of the cost hierarchy are:

---

[2] For an excellent evaluation of TOC, operations management, cost accounting, and the relationship between TOC and activity-based costing, see Anthony Atkinson, *Cost Accounting, the Theory of Constraints, and Costing* (Issue Paper, CMA Canada, December 2000).

| | Customer | | | |
	Vijay	Amit	Ankush	Total
Revenues	₹50,00,000	₹30,00,000	₹40,00,000	₹1,20,00,000
Cost of goods sold	37,00,000	22,00,000	33,00,000	92,00,000
Furniture-handling labor	4,10,000	1,80,000	3,30,000	9,20,000
Furniture-handling equipment cost written off as depreciation	1,20,000	40,000	90,000	2,50,000
Rent	1,40,000	80,000	1,40,000	3,60,000
Marketing support	1,10,000	90,000	1,00,000	3,00,000
Sales-order and delivery processing	1,30,000	70,000	1,20,000	3,20,000
General administration	2,00,000	1,20,000	1,60,000	4,80,000
Allocated corporate-office costs	1,00,000	60,000	80,000	2,40,000
Total costs	49,10,000	28,40,000	43,20,000	1,20,70,000
Operating income	₹90,000	₹1,60,000	₹(3,20,000)	₹(70,000)

Exhibit 11-8

Customer Profitability Analysis for Allied West

- Furniture-handling labor costs vary with the number of units of furniture shipped to customers.
- Allied West reserves different areas of the warehouse to stock furniture for different customers. For simplicity, assume that furniture-handling equipment in an area and depreciation costs on the equipment that Allied West has already acquired are identified with individual customers (customer-level costs). Any unused equipment remains idle. The equipment has a one-year useful life and zero disposal value.
- Allied West allocates rent to each customer on the basis of the amount of warehouse space reserved for that customer.
- Marketing costs vary with the number of sales visits made to customers.
- Sales-order costs are batch-level costs that vary with the number of sales orders received from customers. Delivery-processing costs are batch-level costs that vary with the number of shipments made.
- Allied West allocates fixed general-administration costs (facility-level costs) to customers on the basis of customer revenues.
- Allied Furniture allocates its fixed corporate-office costs to sales offices on the basis of the square feet area of each sales office. Allied West then allocates these costs to customers on the basis of customer revenues.

In the following sections, we consider several decisions that Allied West's managers face: Should Allied West drop the Ankush account? Should it add a fourth customer, Anurag? Should Allied Furniture close down Allied West? Should it open another sales office, Allied South zone, whose revenues and costs are identical to those of Allied West?

Relevant-Revenue and Relevant-Cost Analysis of Dropping a Customer

Exhibit 11-8 indicates a loss of ₹3,20,000 on the Ankush account. Allied West's manag ers believe the reason for the loss is that Ankush places low-margin orders with Allied, and has relatively high sales-order, delivery-processing, furniture-handling, and market- ing costs. Allied West's managers is considering several possible actions for the Ankush

Exhibit 11-9

Relevant-Revenue and
Relevant-Cost Analysis
for Dropping the Ankush
Account and Adding the
Anurag
Account

	(Loss in Revenues) and Savings in Costs from Dropping Ankush Account (1)	Incremental Revenues and (Incremental Costs) from Adding Anurag Account (2)
Revenues	₹(40,00,000)	₹40,00,000
Cost of goods sold	33,00,000	(33,00,000)
Furniture-handling labor	3,30,000	(3,30,000)
Furniture-handling equipment cost written off as depreciation	0	(90,000)
Rent	0	0
Marketing support	1,00,000	(1,00,000)
Sales-order and delivery processing	1,20,000	(1,20,000)
General administration	0	0
Corporate-office costs	0	0
Total costs	38,50,000	(39,40,000)
Effect on operating income (loss)	₹(1,50,000)	₹60,000

account: reducing the costs of supporting Ankush by becoming more efficient, cutting back on some of the services it offers Ankush, asking Ankush to place larger, less frequent orders, charging Ankush higher prices, or dropping the Ankush account. The following analysis focuses on the operating-income effect of dropping the Ankush account.

Allied West's managers first identify the relevant revenues and relevant costs. Dropping the Ankush account will:

- Save cost of goods sold, furniture-handling labor, marketing support, sales-order, and delivery-processing costs incurred on the account.

- Leave idle the warehouse space and furniture-handling equipment currently used to supply products to Ankush.

- Not effect fixed rent costs, general-administration costs or corporate-office costs.

Exhibit 11-9, column 1, presents the relevant-revenue and relevant-cost analysis using data from the Ankush column in Exhibit 11-8. The ₹38,50,000 cost savings from drop ping the Ankush account will not be enough to offset the ₹40,00,000 loss in revenues. Because Allied West's operating income will be ₹1,50,000 lower if it drops the Ankush account, Allied West's managers decide to keep the Ankush account. They will, of course, continue to find ways to become more efficient, change Ankush's ordering patterns, or charge higher prices.

Depreciation on equipment that Allied West has already acquired is a past cost and therefore irrelevant. Rent, general-administration, and corporate-office costs are future costs that will not change if Allied West drops the Ankush account and are also irrelevant.

Overhead costs allocated to the sales office and individual customers are always irrelevant. The only question is, will expected total corporate office costs decrease as a result of dropping the Ankush account? In our example, they will not, so these costs are irrelevant. *If expected total corporate-office costs* were to decrease by dropping the Ankush account, those savings would be relevant even if *the amount allocated to Ankush did not change.*

Note that there is no opportunity cost of using warehouse space and equipment for Ankush because there is no alternative use for them. That is, the space and equipment will remain idle if managers drop the Ankush account. But suppose Allied West could lease the available extra space and equipment to Sanchez Corporation for ₹2,00,000 per year. Then ₹2,00,000 would be Allied West's opportunity cost of continuing to use the warehouse to service Ankush. Allied West would gain ₹50,000 by dropping the Ankush account (₹2,00,000 from lease revenue minus lost operating income of ₹1,50,000). Under the total alternatives approach, the revenue loss from dropping the Ankush account would be ₹38,00,000 (₹40,00,000 − 2,00,000) versus the savings in costs of ₹38,50,000 (Exhibit 11-9, column 1). Before reaching a decision, Allied West's managers must examine whether Ankush can be made more profitable so that supplying products to Ankush earns more than the ₹2,00,000 from leasing to Sanchez. The managers must also consider strategic factors such as the effect of dropping the Ankush account on Allied West's reputation for developing stable, long-run business relationships with its customers.

Relevant-Revenue and Relevant-Cost Analysis of Adding a Customer

Suppose that Allied West's managers are evaluating the profitability of adding another customer, Anurag, to its existing customer base of Vijay, Amit, and Ankush. There is no other alternative use of the Allied West facility. Anurag has a customer profile much like Ankush's. Suppose Allied West's managers predict revenues and costs of doing business with Anurag to be the same as the revenues and costs described under the Ankush column in Exhibit 11-8. In particular, Allied West would have to acquire furniture-handling equipment for the Anurag account costing ₹90,000, with a one-year useful life and zero disposal value. If Anurag is added as a customer, warehouse rent costs (₹3,60,000), general-administration costs (₹4,80,000), and *actual total* corporate-office costs will not change. Should Allied West's managers add Anurag as a customer?

Exhibit 11-9, column 2, shows relevant revenues exceed relevant costs by ₹60,000. The opportunity cost of adding Anurag is ₹0 because there is no alternative use of the Allied West facility. On the basis of this analysis, Allied West's managers would recommend adding Anurag as a customer. Rent, general-administration, and corporate-office costs are irrelevant because these costs will not change if Anurag is added as a customer. However, the cost of new equipment to support the Anurag order (written off as depreciation of ₹90,000 in Exhibit 11-9, column 2) is relevant. That's because this cost can be avoided if Allied West decides not to add Anurag as a customer. Note the critical distinction here: *Depreciation cost is irrelevant in deciding whether to drop Ankush as a customer because depreciation on equipment that has already been purchased is a past cost, but the cost of purchasing new equipment in the future that will then be written off as depreciation is relevant in deciding whether to add Anurag as a customer.*

Relevant-Revenue and Relevant-Cost Analysis of Closing or Adding Branch Offices or Business Divisions

Companies periodically confront decisions about closing or adding branch offices or business divisions. For example, given Allied West's expected loss of ₹70,000 (see Exhibit 11-8),should Allied Furniture's managers close Allied West for the year? Closing Allied West will save all costs currently incurred at Allied West. Recall that there is no disposal value for the equipment that Allied West has already acquired. Closing Allied West will have no effect on total corporate-office costs and there is no alternative use for the Allied West spaces.

Exhibit 11-10, column 1, presents the relevant-revenue and relevant-cost analysis using data from the Total column in Exhibit 11-8. The revenue losses of ₹1,20,00,000 will exceed the cost savings of ₹1,15,80,000, leading to a decrease in operating income of ₹4,20,000. Allied West should not be closed. The key reasons are that closing Allied West will not save depreciation cost or actual total corporate-office costs. Depreciation

Exhibit 11-10

Relevant-Revenue and Relevant-Cost Analysis for Closing Allied West and Opening Allied South

	(Loss in Revenues) and Savings in Costs from Closing Allied West (1)	Incremental Revenues and (Incremental Costs) from Opening Allied South (2)
Revenues	₹(1,20,00,000)	₹1,20,00,000
Cost of goods sold	92,00,000	(92,00,000)
Furniture-handling labor	9,20,000	(9,20,000)
Furniture-handling equipment cost written off as depreciation	0	(2,50,000)
Rent	3,60,000	(3,60,000)
Marketing support	3,00,000	(3,00,000)
Sales-order and delivery processing	3,20,000	(3,20,000)
General administration	4,80,000	(4,80,000)
Corporate-office costs	0	0
Total costs	1,15,80,000	(1,18,30,000)
Effect on operating income (loss)	₹(4,20,000)	₹1,70,000

Decision Point ▶

In deciding to add or drop customers or to add or discontinue branch offices or segments, what should managers focus on and how should they take into account allocated overhead costs?

cost is past or sunk because it represents the cost of equipment that Allied West has already purchased. Corporate-office costs allocated to various sales offices will change *but the total amount of these costs will not decline.* The ₹2,40,000 no longer allocated to Allied West will be allocated to other sales offices. Therefore, the ₹2,40,000 of allocated corporate-office costs should not be included as expected cost savings from closing Allied West.

Finally suppose Allied Furniture has the opportunity to open another sales office, Allied South, whose revenues and costs would be identical to Allied West's costs, including a cost of ₹2,50,000 to acquire furniture-handling equipment with a one-year useful life and zero disposal value. Opening this office will have no effect on total corporate-office costs. Should Allied Furniture open Allied South? Exhibit 11-10, column 2, indicates that it should do so because opening Allied South will increase operating income by ₹1,70,000. As before, the cost of new equipment to be purchased in the future (and written off as depreciation) is relevant and *allocated* corporate-office costs are irrelevant because total corporate-office costs will not change if Allied South is opened.

Irrelevance of Past Costs and Equipment-Replacement Decisions

Learning Objective 7

Explain why book value of equipment is irrelevant in equipment-replacement decisions

. . . it is a past cost

At several points in this chapter, we reasoned that past (historical or sunk) costs are irrelevant to decision making. That's because a decision cannot change something that has already happened. We now apply this concept to decisions about replacing equipment. We stress the idea that **book value**—original cost minus accumulated depreciation—of existing equipment is a past cost that is irrelevant.

Example 6: Toledo Company is considering replacing a metal-cutting machine with a newer model. The new machine is more efficient than the old machine, but it has a shorter life. Revenues from aircraft parts (₹1,10,00,000 million per year) will be unaffected by the replacement decision. Here are the data the management accountant prepares for the existing (old) machine and the replacement (new) machine:

	Two Years Together			
	Keep (1)	Replace (2)	Difference (3) = (1) – (2)	
Revenues	2,20,00,000	₹2,20,00,000	—	
Operating costs				
Cash operating costs				
(₹80,00,000/yr. × 2 years;				
(₹46,00,000/yr. × 2 years)	1,60,00,000	92,00,000	₹68,00,000	
Book value of old machine				
Periodic write-off as depreciation or	40,00,000	—	—	
Lump-sum write-off	—	40,00,000[a]		
Current disposal value of old machine	—	(4,00,000)[a]	4,00,000	
New machine cost, written off periodically				
as depreciation	—	60,00,000	(60,00,000)	
Total operating costs	2,00,00,000	1,88,00,000	12,00,000	
Operating income	₹20,00,000	₹32,00,000	₹(12,00,000)	

Exhibit 11-11

Operating Income Comparison: Replacement of Machine, Relevant and Irrelevant Items for Toledo Company

[a] In a formal income statement, these two items would be combined as "loss on disposal of machine" of ₹36,00,000.

	Old Machine	New Machine
Original cost	₹1,00,00,000	₹60,00,000
Useful life	5 years	2 years
Current age	3 years	0 years
Remaining useful life	2 years	2 years
Accumulated depreciation	₹60,00,000	Not acquired yet
Book value	₹40,00,000	Not acquired yet
Current disposal value (in cash)	₹4,00,000	Not acquired yet
Terminal disposal value (in cash 2 years from now)	₹0	₹0
Annual operating costs (maintenance, energy, repairs, coolants, and so on)	₹80,00,000	₹46,00,000

Toledo Corporation uses straight-line depreciation. To focus on relevance, we ignore the time value of money and income taxes.[3] Should Toledo replace its old machine?

Exhibit 11-11 presents a cost comparison of the two machines. Consider why each of the four items in Toledo's equipment-replacement decision are relevant or irrelevant:

1. **Book value of old machine, ₹40,00,000.** Irrelevant, because it is a past or sunk cost. All past costs are "down the drain." Nothing can change what has already been spent or what has already happened.

2. **Current disposal value of old machine, ₹4,00,000.** Relevant, because it is an expected future benefit that will only occur if the machine is replaced.

3. **Loss on disposal, ₹36,00,000.** This is the difference between amounts in items 1 and 2. This amount is a meaningless combination blurring the distinction between the irrelevant book value and the relevant disposal value. Managers should consider each value separately, as was done in items 1 and 2.

4. **Cost of new machine, ₹60,00,000.** Relevant, because it is an expected future cost that will only occur if the machine is purchased.

Exhibit 11-11 should clarify these four assertions. Column 3 in Exhibit 11-11 shows that the book value of the old machine does not differ between the alternatives and could be ignored

---

[3] See Chapter 21 for a discussion of time-value-of-money and income-tax considerations in capital investment decisions.

Exhibit 11-12

Cost Comparison:
Replacement of
Machine, Relevant
Items Only, for Toledo
Company

| | Two Years Together | | |
	Keep (1)	Replace (2)	Difference (3) = (1) – (2)
Cash operating costs	₹1,60,00,000	₹92,00,000	₹68,00,000
Current disposal value of old machine	—	(4,00,000)	4,00,000
New machine, written off periodically as depreciation	—	60,00,000	(60,00,000)
Total relevant costs	₹1,60,00,000	₹1,48,00,000	₹12,00,000

for decision-making purposes. No matter what the timing of the write-off—whether a lump-sum charge in the current year or depreciation charges over the next two years—the total amount is still ₹40,00,000 because it is a past (historical) cost. In contrast, the ₹60,00,000 cost of the new machine and the current disposal value of ₹4,00,000 for the old machine are relevant because they would not arise if Toledo's managers decided not to replace the machine. Considering the cost of replacing the machine and savings in cash operating costs, Toledo's managers should replace the machine because the operating income from replacing it is ₹12,00,000 higher for the 2 years together.

Exhibit 11-12 concentrates only on relevant items and leads to the same answer—replacing the machine leads to lower costs and higher operating income of ₹12,00,000—even though book value is omitted from the calculations. The only relevant items are the cash operating costs, the disposal value of the old machine, and the cost of the new machine, which is represented as depreciation in Exhibit 11-12.

Decision Point ▶

Is book value of existing equipment relevant in equipment replacement decisions?

Decisions and Performance Evaluation

Learning Objective 8

Explain how conflicts can arise between the decision model used by a manager and the performance-evaluation model used to evaluate the manager

. . . tell managers to take a multiple-year view in decision making but judge their performance only on the basis of the current year's operating income

Consider our equipment-replacement example in light of the five-step sequence in Exhibit 11-1.

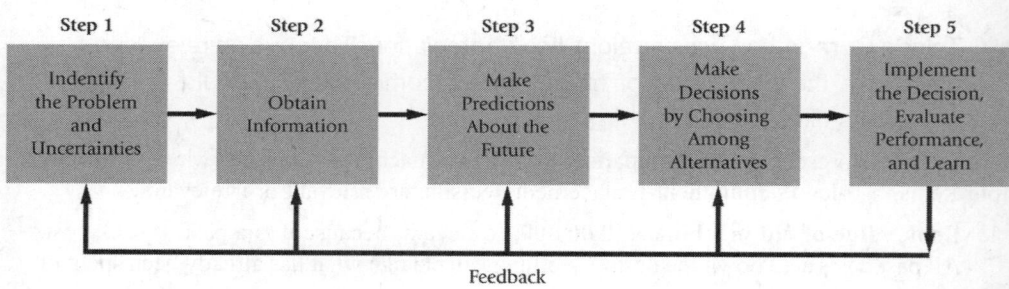

The decision model analysis (step 4), which is presented in Exhibits 11-11 and 11-12, dictates replacing the machine rather than keeping it. In the real world, however, would the manager replace? An important factor in replacement decisions is the manager's perception of whether the decision model is consistent with how the company will judge his or her performance after the decision is implemented (the performance-evaluation model in step 5).

From the perspective of their own careers, it is no surprise that managers tend to favor the alternative that makes their performance look better. In our examples throughout this chapter, the decision model and the performance-evaluation model were consistent. If, however, the performance-evaluation model conflicts with the decision model, the performance-evaluation model often prevails in influencing managers' decisions. The following table compares Toledo's accrual accounting income for the first year and the second year when the manager decides to keep the machine versus when the manager decides to replace the machine.

	Accrual Accounting First-Year Results		Accrual Accounting Second-Year Results	
	Keep	Replace	Keep	Replace
Revenues	₹1,10,00,000	₹1,10,00,000	₹1,10,00,000	₹1,10,00,000
Operating costs				
Cash-operating costs	₹80,00,000	46,00,000	80,00,000	46,00,000
Depreciation	20,00,000	30,00,000	20,00,000	30,00,000
Loss on disposal	—	36,00,000	—	—
Total operating costs	1,00,00,000	1,12,00,000	1,00,00,000	76,00,000
Operating income (loss)	₹10,00,000	₹(2,00,000)	₹10,00,000	₹34,00,000

Total accrual accounting income for the 2 years together is ₹12,00,000 higher if the machine is replaced, as in Exhibit 11-11. But if the promotion or bonus of the manager at Toledo hinges on his or her first year's operating income performance under accrual accounting, the manager would be very tempted to keep the old machine. Why? Because the accrual accounting model for measuring performance will show a first-year operating income of ₹10,00,000 if the old machine is kept versus an operating loss of ₹2,00,000 if the machine is replaced. Even though top management's goals encompass the 2-year period (consistent with the decision model), the manager will focus on first-year results if top management evaluates his or her performance on the basis of short-run measures such as the first-year's operating income.

Managers frequently find it difficult to resolve the conflict between the decision model and the performance-evaluation model. In theory, resolving the difficulty seems obvious: Managers should design models that are consistent. Consider our replacement example. Year-by-year effects on operating income of replacement can be budgeted for the 2-year planning horizon. The manager then would be evaluated on the expectation that the first year would be poor and the next year would be much better. Doing this for every decision, however, makes the performance-evaluation model very cumbersome. As a result of these practical difficulties, accounting systems rarely track each decision separately. Performance evaluation focuses on responsibility centers for a specific period, not on projects or individual items of equipment over their useful lives. Thus, the effects of many different decisions are combined in a single performance report and evaluation measure, say operating income. Lower-level managers make decisions to maximize operating income, and top management—through the reporting system—is rarely aware of particular desirable alternatives that lower-level managers did *not* choose because of conflicts between the decision and performance-evaluation models.

Consider another conflict between the decision model and the performance-evaluation model. Suppose a manager buys a particular machine only to discover shortly afterward that he or she could have purchased a better machine instead. The decision model may suggest replacing the machine that was just bought with the better machine, but will the manager do so? Probably not. Why? Because replacing the machine so soon after its purchase will reflect badly on the manager's capabilities and performance. If the manager's bosses have no knowledge of the better machine, the manager may prefer to keep the recently purchased machine rather than alert them to the better machine.

Many managers consider it unethical to take actions that make their own performance look good when these actions are not in the best interests of the firm. Critics believe that it was precisely these kinds of behaviors that contributed to the recent global financial crisis. To discourage such behaviors, managers develop codes of conduct, emphasize values, and build cultures that focus on doing the right things.

Chapter 23 discusses performance-evaluation models, ethics, and ways to reduce conflict between the decision model and the performance-evaluation model in more detail.

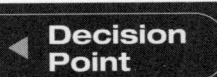

Decision Point

How can conflicts arise between the decision model used by a manager and the performance-evaluation model used to evaluate that manager?

Problem for Self-Study

Praveen Singh is manager of the engineering development division of Goldcoast Products. Praveen has just received a proposal signed by all 15 of his engineers to replace the workstations with networked personal computers (networked PCs). Praveen is not enthusiastic about the proposal.

Data on workstations and networked PCs are:

	Workstations	Networked PCs
Original cost	₹30,00,000	₹13,50,000
Useful life	5 years	3 years
Current age	2 years	0 years
Remaining useful life	3 years	3 years
Accumulated depreciation	₹12,00,000	Not acquired yet
Current book value	₹18,00,000	Not acquired yet
Current disposal value (in cash)	₹9,50,000	Not acquired yet
Terminal disposal value (in cash 3 years from now)	₹0	₹0
Annual computer-related cash operating costs	₹4,00,000	₹1,00,000
Annual revenues	₹1,00,00,000	₹1,00,00,000
Annual noncomputer-related operating costs	₹88,00,000	₹88,00,000

Praveen's annual bonus includes a component based on division operating income. He has a promotion possibility next year that would make him a group vice president of Goldcoast Products.

Required

1. Compare the costs of workstations and networked PCs. Consider the cumulative results for the three years together, ignoring the time value of money and income taxes.
2. Why might Praveen be reluctant to purchase the networked PCs?

Solution

1. The following table considers all cost items when comparing future costs of workstations and networked PCs:

	Three Years Together		
All Items	**Workstations** **(1)**	**Networked PCs** **(2)**	**Difference** **(3) = (1) − (2)**
Revenues	₹3,00,00,000	₹3,00,00,000	—
Operating costs			
Noncomputer-related operating costs	2,64,00,000	2,64,00,000	—
Computer-related cash operating costs	12,00,000	3,00,000	₹9,00,000
Workstations' book value			
Periodic write-off as depreciation or	18,00,000	—	—
Lump-sum write-off	—	18,00,000	
Current disposal value of workstations	—	(9,50,000)	9,50,000
Networked PCs, written off periodically as depreciation	—	13,50,000	(13,50,000)
Total operating costs	2,94,00,000	2,89,00,000	5,00,000
Operating income	₹6,00,000	₹11,00,000	₹(5,00,000)

Alternatively, the analysis could focus on only those items in the preceding table that differ between the alternatives.

Relevant Items	Three Years Together		
	Workstations	Networked PCs	Difference
Computer-related cash operating costs	₹12,00,000	₹3,00,000	₹9,00,000
Current disposal value of workstations	—	(9,50,000)	9,50,000
Networked PCs, written off periodically as depreciation	—	13,50,000	(13,50,000)
Total relevant costs	₹12,00,000	₹7,00,000	₹5,00,000

The analysis suggests that it is cost-effective to replace the workstations with the networked PCs.

2. The accrual-accounting operating incomes *for the first year* under the keep-workstations versus the buy-networked-PCs alternatives are:

	Keep Workstations	Buy Networked PCs
Revenues	₹1,00,00,000	₹1,00,00,000
Operating costs		
Noncomputer-related operating costs	₹88,00,000	₹88,00,000
Computer-related cash operating costs	4,00,000	1,00,000
Depreciation	6,00,000	4,50,000
Loss on disposal of workstations	—	8,50,000a
Total operating costs	98,00,000	1,02,00,000
Operating income (loss)	₹2,00,000	₹(2,00,000)

a ₹8,50,000 = Book value of workstations, ₹18,00,000 − Current disposal value, ₹9,50,000.

Praveen would be less happy with the expected operating loss of ₹2,00,000 if the networked PCs are purchased than he would be with the expected operating income of ₹2,00,000 if the workstations are kept. Buying the networked PCs would eliminate the component of his bonus based on operating income. He might also perceive the ₹2,00,000 operating loss as reducing his chances of being promoted to a group vice president.

Decision Points

The following question-and-answer format summarizes the chapter's learning objectives. Each decision presents a key question related to a learning objective. The guidelines are the answer to that question.

Decision	Guidelines
1. What is the five-step process that managers can use to make decisions?	The five-step decision-making process is (a) identify the problem and uncertainties, (b) obtain information, (c) make predictions about the future, (d) make decisions by choosing among alternatives, and (e) implement the decision, evaluate performance, and learn.
2. When is a revenue or cost item relevant for a particular decision, and what potential problems should managers avoid in relevant-cost analysis?	To be relevant for a particular decision, a revenue or cost item must meet two criteria: (a) It must be an expected future revenue or expected future cost and (b) it must differ among alternative courses of action. Relevant revenue and relevant cost analysis only consider quantitative outcomes that can be expressed in financial terms. Quantitative outcomes are outcomes that can be measured in numerical terms. The outcomes of alternative actions can also have nonfinancial quantitative and qualitative effects. Qualitative factors, such as employee morale, are difficult to measure accurately in numerical terms. But managers must consider both qualitative factors and nonfinancial quantitative factors when making decisions.
	Two potential problems to avoid in relevant-cost analysis are (a) making incorrect general assumptions—such as all variable costs are relevant and all fixed costs are irrelevant—and (b) losing sight of total fixed costs and focusing instead on unit fixed costs.
3. What is an opportunity cost, and why should managers consider it when making insourcing-versus-outsourcing decisions?	Opportunity cost is the contribution to income that is forgone by not using a limited resource in its next-best alternative use. Opportunity cost is included in decision making because the relevant cost of any decision is (a) the incremental cost of the decision plus (b) the opportunity cost of the profit forgone from making that decision. When capacity is constrained, managers must consider the opportunity cost of using the capacity when deciding whether to produce the product in-house versus outsourcing it.
4. When a resource is constrained, how should managers choose which of multiple products to produce and sell?	When a resource is constrained, managers should select the product that yields the highest contribution margin per unit of the constraining or limiting resource (factor). In this way, total contribution margin will be maximized.
5. What steps can managers take to manage bottlenecks?	Managers can take four steps to manage bottlenecks: (a) recognize that the bottleneck operation determines throughput (contribution) margin, (b) identify the bottleneck, (c) keep the bottleneck busy and subordinate all nonbottleneck operations to the bottleneck operation, and (d) increase bottleneck efficiency and capacity.
6. In deciding to add or drop customers or to add or discontinue branch offices or business divisions, what should managers focus on and how should they take into account allocated overhead costs?	When making decisions about adding or dropping customers or adding or discontinuing branch offices and business divisions, managers should focus on only those costs that will change and any opportunity costs. Managers should ignore allocated overhead costs.
7. Is book value of existing equipment relevant in equipment-replacement decisions?	Book value of existing equipment is a past (historical or sunk) cost and, therefore, is irrelevant in equipment-replacement decisions.
8. How can conflicts arise between the decision model a manager uses and the performance-evaluation model top management uses to evaluate that manager?	Top management faces a persistent challenge: making sure that the performance-evaluation model of lower-level managers is consistent with the decision model. A common inconsistency is to tell these managers to take a multiple-year view in their decision making but then to judge their performance only on the basis of the current year's operating income.

TERMS TO LEARN

This chapter and the Glossary at the end of the book contain definitions of the following important terms:

book value **(p. 594)**
business function costs **(p. 574)**
constraint **(p. 587)**
decision model **(p. 570)**
differential cost **(p. 579)**
differential revenue **(p. 579)**
full costs of the product **(p. 574)**
incremental cost **(p. 579)**

incremental revenue **(p. 579)**
insourcing **(p. 578)**
make-or-buy decisions **(p. 578)**
one-time-only special order **(p.573)**
opportunity cost **(p. 581)**
outsourcing **(p. 578)**
product-mix decisions **(p. 585)**
qualitative factors **(p. 572)**

quantitative factors **(p. 572)**
relevant costs **(p. 572)**
relevant
 revenues **(p. 572)**
sunk costs **(p. 572)**
theory of constraints
 (TOC) **(p. 587)**
throughput margin **(p. 587)**

ASSIGNMENT MATERIAL

Questions

11-1 Outline the five-step sequence in a decision process.

11-2 Define relevant costs. Why are historical costs irrelevant?

11-3 "All future costs are relevant." Do you agree? Why?

11-4 Distinguish between quantitative and qualitative factors in decision making.

11-5 Describe two potential problems that should be avoided in relevant-cost analysis.

11-6 "Variable costs are always relevant, and fixed costs are always irrelevant." Do you agree? Why?

11-7 "A component part should be purchased whenever the purchase price is less than its total manufacturing cost per unit." Do you agree? Why?

11-8 Define opportunity cost.

11-9 "Managers should always buy inventory in quantities that result in the lowest purchase cost per unit." Do you agree? Why?

11-10 "Management should always maximize sales of the product with the highest contribution margin per unit." Do you agree? Why?

11-11 "A branch office or business segment that shows negative operating income should be shut down." Do you agree? Explain briefly.

11-12 "Cost written off as depreciation on equipment already purchased is always irrelevant." Do you agree? Why?

11-13 "Managers will always choose the alternative that maximizes operating income or minimizes costs in the decision model." Do you agree? Why?

11-14 Describe the three steps in solving a linear programming problem.

11-15 How might the optimal solution of a linear programming problem be determined?

Solved Examples

11-16 Relevant and irrelevant costs. Answer the following questions.

1. HCL Computers makes 5,200 units of a circuit board, CB76, at a cost of ₹5,600 each. Variable cost per unit is ₹3,800 and fixed cost per unit is ₹1,800. New Electronics offers to supply 5,200 units of CB76 for ₹5,200. If HCL buys from New Electronics it will be able to save ₹200 per unit in fixed costs but continue to incur the remaining ₹1,600 per unit. Should HCL accept New Electronics's offer? Explain.

2. LN Manufacturing is deciding whether to keep or replace an old machine. It obtains the following information:

	Old Machine	New Machine
Original cost	₹10,70,000	₹9,00,000
Useful life	10 years	3 years
Current age	7 years	0 years
Remaining useful life	3 years	3 years
Accumulated depreciation	₹7,49,000	Not acquired yet
Book value	₹3,21,000	Not acquired yet
Current disposal value(in cash)	₹2,20,000	Not acquired yet
Terminal disposal value(3 years from now)	₹0	₹0
Annual cash operating costs	₹17,50,000	₹15,50,000

LN Manufacturing uses straight-line depreciation. Ignore the time value of money and income taxes. Should LN Manufacturing replace the old machine? Explain.

Solution

1.

	Make	Buy
Relevant costs		
Variable costs	₹3,800	
Avoidable fixed costs	200	
Purchase price		₹5,200
Unit relevant cost	₹4,000	₹5,200

HCL Computers should reject New Electronics offer. The ₹1,600 of fixed costs is irrelevant because it will be incurred regardless of this decision. When comparing relevant costs between the choices, New Electronics's offer price is higher than the cost to continue to produce.

2.

	Keep	Replace	Difference
Cash operating costs (3 years)	₹52,50,000	₹46,50,000	₹6,00,000
Current disposal value of old machine		(₹2,20,000)	₹2,20,000
Cost of new machine		₹9,00,000	₹(9,00,000)
Total relevant costs	₹52,50,000	₹53,30,000	₹(80,000)

LN Manufacturing should keep the old machine. The cost savings are less than the cost to purchase the new machine.

11-17 Special order, activity-based costing. (CMA, adapted) The Tanisque Company manufactures medals for winners of athletic events and other contests. Its manufacturing plant has the capacity to produce 10,000 medals each month. Current production and sales are 7,500 medals per month. The company normally charges ₹150 per medal. Cost information for the current activity level is as follows:

Variable costs that vary with number of units produced

Direct materials	₹2,62,500
Direct manufacturing labor	3,00,000
Variable costs (for setup materials handling quality control and so on)	
that vary with number of batches 150 batches x ₹500 per batch	75,000
Fixed manufacturing costs	2,75,000
Fixed marketing costs	1,75,000
Total costs	10,87,500

Tanisque has just received a special one-time-only order for 2,500 medals at ₹100 per medal. Accepting the special order would not affect the company's regular business.

Tanisque makes medals for its existing customers in batch sizes of 50 medals (150 batches × 50 medals per batch = 7,500 medals). The special order requires Tanisque to make medals in 25 batches of 100 each.

Required

1. Should Tanisque accept this special order? Show your calculations.
2. Suppose plant capacity were only 9,000 medals instead of 10,000 medals each month. The special order must either be taken in full or rejected completely. Should Tanisque accept the special order? Show your calculations.
3. As in requirement (1), assume that monthly capacity is 10,000 medals. Tanisque is concerned that if it accepts the special order, its existing customers will immediately demand a price discount of ₹10 in the month in which the special order is being filled. They would argue that Tanisque's capacity costs are now being spread over more units and that existing customers should get the benefit of these lower costs should Tanisque accept the special order under these conditions? Show your calculations.

Solution

Special order, activity-based costing (CMA, adapted).

1. Tanisque's operating income under the alternatives of accepting/rejecting the special order are:

	Without One-Time Only Special Order 7,500 Units	With One-Time Only Special Order 10,000 Units	Difference 2,500 Units
Revenues	₹11,25,000	₹13,75,000	₹2,50,000
Variable costs:			
Direct materials	2,62,500	35,00,00[1]	87,500
Direct manufacturing labor	3,00,000	40,00,00[2]	1,00,000
Batch manufacturing costs	75,000	8,75,00[3]	12,500
Fixed costs:			
Fixed manufacturing costs	2,75,000	2,75,000	—
Fixed marketing costs	1,75,000	1,75,000	—
Total costs	10,87,500	12,87,500	2,00,000
Operating income	₹37,500	₹87,500	₹50,000

$$[1]\frac{₹2,62,500}{7,500} \times 10,000 \quad [2]\frac{₹3,00,000}{7,500} \times 10,000 \quad [3]₹75,000 + (25 \times ₹500)$$

Alternatively, we can calculate the incremental revenue and the incremental costs of the additional 2,500 units as follows:

Incremental revenue ₹100 × 2,500	₹2,50,000
Incremental direct manufacturing costs (₹2,62,500/7,500) × 2,500	87,500
Incremental direct manufacturing costs (₹3,00,000/7,500) × 2,500	1,00,000
Incremental batch manufacturing costs ₹500 × 25	12,500
Total incremental costs	2,00,000
Total incremental operating income from accepting the special order	₹50,000

Tanisque should accept the one-time-only special order if it has no long-term implications because accepting the order increases Tanisque's operating income by ₹50,000. If, however, accepting the special order would cause the regular customers to be dissatis fied or to demand lower prices, then Tanisque will have to trade off the ₹50,000 gain from accepting the special order against the operating income it might lose from regular customers.

2. Tanisque has a capacity of 9,000 medals. Therefore, if it accepts the special one-time order of 2,500 medals, it can sell only 6,500 medals instead of the 7,500 medals that it currently sells to existing customers. That is, by accepting the special order, Tanisque must forgo sales of 1,000 medals to its regular customers. Alternatively, Tanisque can reject the special order and continue to sell 7,500 medals to its regular customers. Tanisque's operating income from selling 6,500 medals to regular customers and 2,500 medals under one-time special order follows:

Revenues (6,500 × ₹150) + (2,500 × ₹100)	₹12,25,000
Direct materials (6,500 × ₹35[1]) + (2,500 × ₹35[1])	3,15,000

Direct manufacturing labor $(6{,}500 \times ₹40^2) + (2{,}500 \times ₹40^2)$	3,60,000
Batch manufacturing costs $(130^3 \times ₹500) + (25 \times ₹500)$	77,500
Fixed manufacturing costs	2,75,000
Fixed marketing costs	1,75,000
Total costs	12,02,500
Operating income	₹22,500

$$^1₹35 = \frac{₹2{,}62{,}500}{7{,}500} \qquad ^2₹40 = \frac{₹3{,}00{,}000}{7{,}500}$$

[3]Tanisque makes regular medals in batch sizes of 50. To produce 6,500 medals requires 130 (6,500 ÷ 50) batches.

Accepting the special order will result in a decrease in operating income of ₹15,000 (₹37,500 – ₹22,500). The special order should, therefore, be rejected.

A more direct approach would be to focus on the incremental effects—the benefits of accepting the special order of 2,500 units versus the costs of selling 1,000 fewer units to regular customers. Increase in operating income from the 2,500-unit special order equals ₹50,000 (requirement 1). The loss in operating income from selling 1,000 fewer units to regular customers equals:

Lost revenue ₹150 × 1,000	₹(1,50,000)
Savings in direct materials costs ₹35 × 1,000	35,000
Savings in direct manufacturing labor costs ₹40 × 1,000	40,000
Savings in batch manufacturing costs ₹500 × 20	10,000
Operating income lost	₹(65,000)

Accepting the special order will result in a decrease in operating income of ₹15,000 (₹50,000 – ₹65,000). The special order should, therefore, be rejected.

3. Tanisque should not accept the special order.

Increase in operating income by selling 2,500 units under the special order (requirement 1)	₹50,000
Operating income lost from existing customers (₹10 × 7,500)	(75,000)
Net effect on operating income of accepting special order	₹(25,000)

The special order should, therefore, be rejected.

11-18 Make versus buy, activity-based costing. The Bharti Televentures manufactures cellular modems. It manufactures its own cellular modem circuit boards (CMCB), an important part of the cellular modem. It reports the following cost information about the costs of making CMCBs in 2015 and the expected costs in 2016:

	Current Costs in 2015	Expected Costs in 2016
Variable manufacturing costs		
Direct material cost per CMCB	₹1,800	₹1,700
Direct manufacturing labor cost per CMCB	500	450
Variable manufacturing cost per batch for setups, material handling, and quality control	16,000	15,000
Fixed manufacturing cost		
Fixed manufacturing overhead costs that can be avoided if CMCBs are not made	32,00,000	32,00,000
Fixed manufacturing overhead costs of plant depreciation, insurance, and administration that cannot be avoided even if CMCBs are not made	80,00,000	80,00,000

Bharti manufactured 8,000 CMCBs in 2015 in 40 batches of 200 each. In 2016, Bharti anticipates a requirement of 10,000 CMCBs. The CMCBs would be needed in 80 batches of 125 each.

The Reliance Infocom has approached Bharti about supplying CMCBs to Bharti in 2016 at ₹3,000 per CMCB on whatever delivery schedule Bharti wants.

Required

1. Calculate the total expected manufacturing cost per unit of making CMCBs in 2016.

2. Suppose the capacity currently used to make CMCBs will become idle if Bharti purchases CMCBs from Reliance. On the basis of financial considerations alone, should Bharti make CMCBs or buy them from Reliance? Show your calculations.

3. Now suppose that if Bharti purchases CMCBs from Reliance, its best alternative use of the capacity currently used for CMCBs is to make and sell special circuit boards (CB3s) to the Airtel Corporation.

Bharti estimates the following incremental revenues and costs from CB3s:

Total expected incremental future revenues	₹2,00,00,000
Total expected incremental future costs	₹2,15,00,000

On the basis of financial considerations alone, should Bharti make CMCBs or buy them from Reliance? Show your calculations.

Solution

Make versus buy, activity-based costing.

1. The expected manufacturing cost per unit of CMCBs in 2016 is as follows:

	Total Manufacturing Costs of CMCB (1)	Manufacturing Cost per Unit (2) = (1) ÷ 10,000
Direct materials ₹1,700 × 10,000	₹1,70,00,000	₹1,700
Direct manufacturing labor ₹450 × 10,000	45,00,000	450
Variable batch manufacturing costs ₹15,000 × 80	12,00,000	120
Fixed manufacturing costs		
Avoidable fixed manufacturing costs	32,00,000	320
Unavoidable fixed manufacturing costs	80,00,000	800
Total manufacturing costs	₹3,39,00,000	₹3,390

2. The following table identifies the incremental costs in 2016 if Bharti (a) made CMCBs and (b) purchased CMCBs from Reliance.

	Total Incremental Costs		Per-Unit Incremental Costs	
Incremental Items	Make	Buy	Make	Buy
Cost of purchasing CMCBs from Reliance		₹3,00,00,000		₹3,000
Direct materials	₹1,70,00,000		₹1,700	
Direct manufacturing labor	45,00,000		450	
Variable batch manufacturing costs	12,00,000		120	
Avoidable fixed manufacturing costs	32,00,000		320	
Total incremental costs	₹2,59,00,000	₹3,00,00,000	₹2,590	₹3,000
Difference in favor of making	↑ ₹41,00,000 ↑		↑ ₹410 ↑	

Note that the opportunity cost of using capacity to make CMCBs is zero since Bharti would keep this capacity idle if it purchases CMCBs from Reliance.

Bharti should continue to manufacture the CMCBs internally since the incremental costs to manufacture are ₹2,590 per unit compared to the ₹3,000 per unit that Reliance has quoted. Note that the unavoidable fixed manufacturing costs of ₹80,00,000 (₹800 per unit) will continue to be incurred whether Bharti makes or buys CMCBs. These are not incremental costs under either the make or the buy alternative and are, hence, irrelevant.

3. Bharti should continue to make CMCBs. The simplest way to analyze this problem is to recognize that Bharti would prefer to keep any excess capacity idle rather than use it to make CB3s. Why? Because expected incremental future revenues from CB3s, ₹2,00,00,000 are less than expected incremental future costs, ₹2,15,00,000. If Bharti keeps its capacity idle, we know from requirement 2 that it should make CMCBs rather than buy them.

An important point to note is that, because Bharti forgoes no contribution by not being able to make and sell CB3s, the opportunity cost of using its facilities to make CMCBs is zero. It is, therefore, not forgoing any profits by using the capacity to manufacture CMCBs. If it does not manufacture CMCBs, rather than lose money on CB3s, Bharti will keep capacity idle.

A longer and more detailed approach is to use the total alternatives or opportunity cost analyses shown in Exhibit 11-7 of the chapter.

Relevant Items	Make CMCBs and Do Not Make CB3s	Buy CMCBs and Do Not Make CB3s	Buy CMCBs and Make CB3s
		Choices for Bharti	
Total-alternatives approach to make-or-buy decisions			
Total incremental costs of making/buying CMCBs (from requirement 2)	₹2,59,00,000	₹3,00,00,000	₹3,00,00,000
Excess of future costs over future revenues from CB3s	0	0	15,00,000
Total relevant costs	₹2,59,00,000	₹3,00,00,000	₹3,15,00,000
Bharti will minimize manufacturing costs by making CMCBs.			
Opportunity-cost approach to make-or-buy decisions			
Total incremental costs of making/buying CMCBs (from requirement 2)	₹2,59,00,000	₹3,00,00,000	₹3,00,00,000
Opportunity cost: profit contribution forgone because capacity will not be used to make CB3s	0*	0*	0
Total relevant costs	2,59,00,000	3,00,00,000	3,00,00,000

*Opportunity cost is 0 because Bharti does not give up anything by not making CB3s. Bharti is best off leaving the capacity idle (rather than manufacturing and selling CB3s).

11-19 Selection of most profitable product. Children Toy Company produces two models of toy Car, Deluxe and Super. Pertinent data are as follows:

	Deluxe	Per Unit Super
Selling price	₹100.00	₹70.00
Costs		
Direct material	28.00	13.00
Direct manufacturing labor	15.00	25.00
Variable manufacturing overhead*	25.00	12.50
Fixed manufacturing overhead*	10.00	5.00
Marketing (all variable)	14.00	10.00
Total cost	92.00	65.50
Operating income	8.00	4.50

* Allocated on the basis of machine-hours.

The car craze is such that enough of either Deluxe or Super can be sold to keep the plant operating at full capacity. Both products are processed through the same production departments.

Required Which products should be produced? Briefly explain your answer.

Solution

Selection of most profitable product.

Only Super model should be produced. The key to this problem is the relationship of manufacturing overhead to each product. Note that it takes twice as long to produce Deluxe; machine-hours for Deluxe model are twice that for Super model. Management should choose the product mix that maximizes operating income for a given production capacity (the scarce resource in this situation). In this case, Super model will yield a ₹9.50 contribution to fixed costs per machine hour, and Deluxe model will yield ₹9.00:

	Deluxe	Super
Selling price	₹100.00	₹70.00
Variable costs per unit	82.00	60.50
Contribution margin per unit	₹18.00	₹9.50
Relative use of machine-hours per unit of product	÷ 2	÷ 1
Contribution margin per machine hour	₹9.00	₹9.50

11-20 Which base to close, relevant-cost analysis, opportunity costs. The Indian Defense Department has the difficult decision of deciding which military bases to shut down. Military and political factors obviously matter, but cost savings are also an important factor. Consider two naval bases one located on the West Coast and the other on South Coast. The Navy has decided that it needs only one of those two bases permanently, so one must be shut down. The decision regarding which base to shut down will be made on cost considerations alone. The following information is available:

a. The West Coast base was built at a cost of ₹100 crore. The operating costs of the base are ₹400 crore per year. The base is built on land owned by the Navy, so the Navy pays nothing for the use of the property. If the base is closed, the land will be sold to developers for ₹500 crore.

b. The South Coast base was built at a cost of ₹150 crore on land leased by the Navy from private citizens. The Navy can choose to lease the land permanently for a lease payment of ₹3 crore per year. If it decides to keep the South Coast base open, the Navy plans to invest ₹60 crore in a fixed income note, which at 5% interest will earn the ₹3 crore the government needs for the lease payments. The land and buildings will immediately revert back to the owner if the base is closed. The operating costs of the base, excluding lease payments, are ₹300 crore per year.

c. If the West Coast base is shut down, the Navy will have to transfer some personnel to the South Coast facility. As a result, the yearly operating costs at South Coast will increase by ₹100 crore per year. If the South Coast facility is closed down, no extra costs will be incurred to operate the West Coast facility.

Required

The Defense Department argues that it is cheaper to shut down the South Coast base for two reasons:

1. It would save ₹100 crore per year in additional costs required to operate the South Coast base, and

2. it would save the lease payment of ₹3 crore per year. (Recall that he West Coast base requires no cash payments for use of the land because the land is owned by the Navy). Do you agree with the Defense Department's arguments and conclusions? In your answer, identify and explain all costs that you consider relevant and all costs that you consider irrelevant for the base-closing decision.

Solution

Which base to close, relevant-cost analysis, opportunity costs.

The future outlay operating costs will be ₹400 crore regardless of which base is closed, given the additional ₹100 crore in costs at South Coast if West Coast is closed. Further, one of the bases will permanently remain open while the other will be shut down. The only relevant revenue and cost comparisons are:

a. ₹500 crore from sale of the West Coast base. Note that the historical cost of building the West Coast base (₹100 crore) is irrelevant. Note, also, that future increases in the value of the land at the West Coast base is also irrelevant. One of the bases must be kept open, so if it is decided to keep the West Coast base open, the Defense Department will not be able to sell this land at a future date.

b. ₹60 crore in savings in fixed income note if the South Coast base is closed. Again, the historical cost of building the South Coast base (₹150 crore) is irrelevant.

The relevant costs and benefits analysis favors closing the West Coast base despite the objections raised by the Defense Department. The net benefit equals ₹440 (₹500 – ₹60) crore.

11-21 Theory of constraints, throughput contribution, relevant costs. The Pierce Corporation manufactures filing cabinets in two operations: machining and finishing. It provides the following information:

	Machining	Finishing
Annual capacity	1,10,000 units	90,000 units
Annual production	90,000 units	90,000 units
Fixed operating costs(excluding direct materials)	₹5,40,00,000	₹2,70,00,000

Fixed operating costs per unit produced ₹600 per unit ₹300 per unit
(₹5,40,00,000 ÷ 90,000; ₹2,70,00,000 ÷ 90,000)

Each cabinet sells for ₹7,000 and has direct material costs of ₹3,000 incurred at the start of the machining operation. Pierce has no other variable costs. Pierce can sell whatever output it produces. The following requirements refer only to the preceding data. There is no connection between the requirements.

Required

1. Pierce is considering using some modern jigs and tools in the finishing operation that would increase annual finishing output by 1,150 units. The annual cost of these jigs and tools is ₹35,00,000. Should Pierce acquire these tools? Show your calculations.

2. The production manager of the Machining Department has submitted a proposal to do faster setups that would increase the annual capacity of the Machining Department by 9,000 units and would cost ₹4,00,000 per year. Should Pierce implement the change? Show your calculations.

3. An outside contractor offers to do the finishing operation for 9,500 units at ₹900 per unit, triple the ₹300 per unit that it costs Pierce to do the finishing in-house. Should Pierce accept the subcontractor's offer? Show your calculations.

4. The Reliable company offers to machine 5,000 units at ₹300 per unit, half the ₹600 per unit that it costs Pierce to do the machining in-house. Should Pierce accept Reliable's offer? Show your calculations.

5. Pierce produces 1,700 defective units at the machining operation. What is the cost to Pierce of the defective items produced? Explain your answer briefly.

6. Pierce produces 1,700 defective units at the finishing operation. What is the cost to Pierce of the defective items produced? Explain your answer briefly.

Solution

1. Finishing is a bottleneck operation. Therefore, producing 1,150 more units will generate additional contribution (throughput) margin and operating income.

Increase in contribution (throughput) margin (₹7,000 – ₹3,000) × 1,150	₹46,00,000
Incremental costs of the jigs and tools	35,00,000
Increase in operating income investing in jigs and tools	₹11,00,000

Pierce should invest in the modern jigs and tools because the benefit of higher contribution (throughput) margin of ₹46,00,000 exceeds the cost of ₹35,00,000.

2. The Machining Department has excess capacity and is not a bottleneck operation. Increasing its capacity further will not increase contribution (throughput) margin. There is, therefore, no benefit from spending ₹4,00,000 to increase the Machining Department's capacity by 9,000 units. Pierce should not implement the change to do setups faster.

3. Finishing is a bottleneck operation. Therefore, getting an outside contractor to produce 9,500 units will increase contribution (throughput) margin.

Increase in contribution (throughput) margin ₹7,000 – ₹3,000) × 9,500	₹3,80,00,000
Incremental contracting costs ₹900 × 9,500	85,50,000
Increase in operating income by contracting 9,500 units of finishing	₹2,94,50,000

Pierce should contract with an outside contractor to do 9,500 units of finishing at ₹900 per unit because the benefit of higher throughput margin of ₹3,80,00,000 exceeds the cost of ₹85,50,000. The fact that the cost of ₹900 per unit is three times Pierce's finishing cost of ₹300 per unit is irrelevant.

4. Operating costs in the Machining Department of ₹5,40,00,000, or ₹600 per unit, are fixed costs. Pierce will not save any of these costs by subcontracting machining of 5,000 units to Reliable Corporation. Total costs will be greater by ₹15,00,000 (₹300 per unit × 5,000 units) under the subcontracting alternative. Machining more filing cabinets will not increase contribution (throughput) margin, which is constrained by the finishing capacity. Pierce should not accept Reliable's offer. The fact that Reliable's costs of machining per unit are half of what it costs Pierce in-house is irrelevant.

5. The cost of 1,700 defective units in the Machining Operation is ₹3,000 per unit × 1,700 units = ₹51,00,000. Because the Machining Operation has a capacity of 1,10,000 units, it can still produce and transfer 90,000 good units to the Finishing Operation. There is, therefore, no opportunity cost of producing defective units in the Machining Operation.

6. The cost of 1,700 defective units in the Finishing Operation is:

Cost of direct materials used in the defective units ₹3,000 per unit × 1,700 units ₹51,00,000

Opportunity cost, lost contribution (throughput) margin ₹4,000 per unit × 1,700 units 68,00,000

Total cost of defective unit in the Finishing Operation   ₹1,19,00,000

Alternatively, the cost of 1,700 defective units in the Finishing Operation equals the revenues lost by selling 1,700 fewer units = ₹7,000 per unit × 1,700 units = ₹1,19,00,000. The cost of the defective unit at a bottleneck operation is much higher than at a non-bottleneck operation because of the opportunity cost of lost contribution margin at the bottleneck operation.

11-22 Short-run pricing, capacity constraints. Mother Dairy, maker of specialty cheeses, produces a soft cheese from the milk of cows raised on a special corn-based diet. One kilogram of soft cheese, which has a contribution margin of ₹80, requires 4 liters of milk. A well-known gourmet restaurant has asked Mother Dairy to produce 2,000 kilograms of a hard cheese from the same milk of cows. Knowing that the dairy has sufficient unused capacity, CFO of Mother Dairy calculates the costs of making one kilogram of the desired hard cheese:

Milk (10 liters × ₹30 per liter)	₹300
Variable direct manufacturing labor	80
Variable manufacturing overhead	40
Fixed manufacturing cost allocated	100
Total manufacturing cost	₹520

Required

1. Suppose Mother Dairy can acquire all the milk that it needs. What is the minimum price per kilogram the company should charge for the hard cheese?
2. Now suppose that the milk is in short supply. Every kilogram of hard cheese Mother Dairy produces will reduce the quantity of soft cheese that it can make and sell. What is the minimum price per kilogram the company should charge to produce the hard cheese?

Solution

1. Per kilogram of hard cheese:

Milk (10 liters × ₹30 per liter)	₹300
Direct manufacturing labor	80
Variable manufacturing overhead	40
Fixed manufacturing cost allocated	100
Total manufacturing cost	₹520

If Mother Dairy can get all the cow milk it needs and has sufficient production capacity, then the minimum price per kilo it should charge for the hard cheese is the variable cost per kilo = ₹300 + ₹80 + ₹40 = ₹420 per kilo.

2. If milk is in short supply, then each kilo of hard cheese displaces 2.5 kilos of soft cheese (10 liters of milk per kilo of hard cheese versus 4 liters of milk per kilo of soft cheese). Then, for the hard cheese, the minimum price Mother Dairy should charge is the variable cost per kilo of hard cheese plus the contribution margin from 2.5 kilos of soft cheese, or,

$$₹420 + (2.5 × ₹80 \text{ per kilo}) = ₹620 \text{ per kilo}$$

That is, if milk is in short supply, Mother Dairy should not agree to produce any hard cheese unless the buyer is willing to pay at least ₹620 per kilo.

11-23 Opportunity costs and relevant costs Ratan operates Exclusive Deluxe taxis, a fleet of 10 Deluxe taxis used for weddings, proms, and business events in NCR region. Ratan charges customers a flat fee of ₹2,500 per car taken on contract plus an hourly fee of ₹40. His income statement for May follows:

Revenue(200 contracts × ₹2,500 + (1,250 hours × ₹40)	₹5,50,000
Operating expenses:	
Driver wages and benefits (₹60 per hour × 1,250 hours)	75,000
Depreciation on Deluxe Taxis	19,000
Fuel costs (₹180 per hour × 1,250 hours)	2,25,000
Maintenance	18,400
Liability and casualty insurance	2,500
Advertising	10,500
Administrative expenses	24,200
Total expenses	3,74,600
Operating income	₹1,75,400

All expenses are fixed, with the exception of driver wages and benefits and fuel costs, which are both variable per hour. During May, Ratan's Deluxe taxis were fully booked. In June, Ratan expects that Deluxe taxis will be operating near capacity. At this stage, Ratan has been asked to bid for new offer requiring the service of five Deluxe taxis for four hours each. The customer will only hire Deluxe taxis if they take the entire job. Ratan checks his schedule and finds that he only has three Deluxe taxis available that day.

Required

1. If Ratan accepts the contract, he would either have to (a) cancel two prom contracts each for 1 car for 6 hours or (b) cancel one business event for three cars contracted for two hours each. What are the relevant opportunity costs of accepting the New contract in each case? Which contract should he cancel?

2. Ratan would like to win the bid on the New job because of the potential for lucrative future business. Assume that Ratan cancels the contract in part 1 with the lowest opportunity cost, and assume that the three currently available cars would go unrented if the company does not win the bid. What is the lowest amount he should bid on the New job?

3. Another Deluxe taxis company has offered to rent Deluxe taxis two additional cars for ₹3,000 each per day. Ratan would still need to pay for fuel and driver wages on these cars for the New job. Should Ratan rent the two cars to avoid canceling either of the other two contracts?

Solution

1. If Ratan cancels the two prom contracts, the opportunity cost of accepting the New job would be ₹2,600, as follows:

Lost revenue (2 × ₹2,500) + (12 hrs. × ₹40)	₹5,480
Less variable costs	
Driver wages and benefits (₹60 × 12 hrs.)	720
Fuel costs (₹180 × 12 hrs.)	2,160
Opportunity cost	₹2,600

If Ratan cancels the business event contract, the opportunity cost would be ₹6,300, as follows:

Lost revenue (3 × ₹2,500) + (6 hrs. × ₹40)	₹7,740
Less variable costs	
Driver wages and benefits (₹60 × 6 hrs.)	360
Fuel costs (₹180 × 6 hrs.)	1,080
Opportunity cost	₹6,300

Ratan should cancel the prom contracts because the opportunity cost would be lower by ₹3,700 (₹6,300 − ₹2,600).

2. If Ratan cancels the two prom contracts, opportunity cost equals ₹2,600. In addition, variable costs of the 20-hour New job would be (20 hrs. × ₹60) + (20 hrs. × ₹180) = ₹4,800. Therefore, the minimum amount Ratan would bid is ₹7,400 (₹2,600 + 4,800).

3. No, it would not be in Ratan's interest to lease the additional cars for a total of ₹6,000.

11-24 Product mix, constrained resource. Small Manufacturing Company produces three products: A110, B382, and C657. All three products use the same direct material. Unit data for the three products are:

	Product		
	A110	**B382**	**C657**
Selling price	₹1,680	₹1,120	₹1,400
Variable costs			
Direct materials	480	300	180
Labor and other costs	560	540	800
Quantity of material per unit	8 kgs	5 kgs	3 kgs

The demand for the products far exceeds the direct materials available to produce the products. Material costs ₹60 per kg, and a maximum of 5,000 kgs is available each month. Company must produce a minimum of 200 units of each product.

Required

1. How many units of product A110, B382, and C657 should company produce?
2. What is the maximum amount company would be willing to pay for another 1,200 kgs of material?

Solution

1.

	A110	**B382**	**C657**
Selling price	₹1,680	₹1,120	₹1,400
Variable costs:			
Direct materials (DM)	480	300	180
Labor and other costs	560	540	800
Total variable costs	1,040	840	980
Contribution margin	₹640	₹280	₹420
kgs of DM per unit	÷ 8 kgs.	÷ 5 kgs.	÷ 3 kgs.
Contribution margin per kg.	₹80 per kg.	₹56 per kg.	₹140 per kg.

First, satisfy minimum requirements.

	A110	**B382**	**C657**	**Total**
Minimum units	200	200	200	
Times kgs per unit	×8 kgs. per unit	×5 kgs. per unit	×3 kgs. per unit	
kgs needed to produce minimum units	1,600 kgs.	1,000 kgs.	600 kgs.	3,200 kgs.

The remaining 1,800 kgs (5,000 − 3,200) should be devoted to C657 because it has the highest contribution margin per kg of direct material. Because each unit of C657 requires 3 kgs of material, the remaining 1,800 kgs can be used to produce another 600 units of C657. The following combination yields the highest contribution margin given the 5,000 kgs constraint on availability of material.

A110: 200 units
B382: 200 units
C657: 800 units (200 minimum + 600 extra)

2. The demand for Company's products exceeds the materials available. Assuming that fixed costs are covered by the original product mix, Company would be willing to pay up to an additional ₹140 per kg (the contribution margin per kg of C657) for another 1,200 kgs of material. That is, Company would be willing to pay ₹60 + ₹140 = ₹200 per kg of material that will be used to produce C657. If sufficient demand does not exist for 400 units (1,200 kgs ÷ 3 kgs per unit) of C657, then the maximum price company would be willing to pay is an additional ₹80 per kg (the contribution margin per kg of A110) for the kgs of company that will be used to produce A110. In this case company would be willing to pay ₹60 + ₹80 = ₹140 kg. If all the 1,200 kgs of Company are not used to satisfy the demand for C657 and A110, then the maximum price it would be willing to pay is an additional ₹56 per kg (the contribution margin per kg of B382) for the kgs of material that will be used to produce B382. Company would be willing to pay ₹56 + ₹60 = ₹116 per kg of material.

[1]An alternative calculation focuses on column 3 for C657 of the table in requirement 1.

Selling price	₹1,400
Variable labor and other costs (excluding direct materials)	800
Contribution margin	₹600
Divided by kgs of direct material per unit	÷3 kgs.
Direct material cost per kg that company can pay without contribution margin becoming negative	₹200

11-25 Product mix, relevant costs. (N. Melumad, adapted) Reliable Precision Tools makes cutting tools for metalworking operations. It makes two types of tools: A6, a regular cutting tool, and EX4, a high-precision cutting tool. A6 is manufactured on a regular machine, but EX4 must be manufactured on both the regular machine and a high-precision machine. The following information is available:

	A6	EX4
Selling price	₹200	₹300
Variable manufacturing cost per unit	₹120	₹200
Variable marketing cost per unit	₹30	₹70
Budgeted total fixed overhead costs	₹7,00,000	₹11,00,000
Hours required to produce one unit on the regular machine	1.0	0.5

Additional information includes the following:

a. Company faces a capacity constraint on the regular machine of 50,000 hours per year.
b. The capacity of the high-precision machine is not a constraint.
c. Of the ₹11,00,000 budgeted fixed overhead costs of EX4, ₹6,00,000 are lease payments for the high-precision machine. This cost is charged entirely to EX4 because Reliable uses the machine exclusively to produce EX4. The company can cancel the lease agreement for the high-precision machine at any time without penalties.
All other overhead costs are fixed and cannot be changed.

Required

1. What product mix—that is, how many units of A6 and EX4—will maximize company's operating income? Show your calculations.
2. Suppose company can increase the annual capacity of its regular machines by 15,000 machine-hours at a cost of ₹3,00,000. Should company increase the capacity of the regular machines by 15,000 machine-hours? By how much will company's operating income increase or decrease? Show your calculations.
3. Suppose that the capacity of the regular machines has been increased to 65,000 hours. Company has been approached to supply 20,000 units of another cutting tool, V2, for ₹240 per unit. Company must either accept the order for all 20,000 units or reject it totally. V2 is exactly like A6 except that its variable manufacturing cost is ₹140 per unit.

(It takes 1 hour to produce one unit of V2 on the regular machine, and variable marketing cost equals ₹30 per unit) What product mix should company choose to maximize operating income? Show your calculations.

Solution

1.

	A6	EX4
Selling price	₹200	₹300
Variable manufacturing cost per unit	120	200
Variable marketing cost per unit	30	70
Total variable costs per unit	150	270
Contribution margin per unit	₹50	₹30
Contribution margin per hour of the constrained resource	$\frac{₹50}{1}$ = ₹50	$\frac{₹30}{0.5}$ = ₹60
Total contribution margin from selling only A6 or only EX4		
A6: ₹50 × 50,000; EX4: ₹60 × 50,000	₹25,00,000	₹30,00,000
Less Lease costs of high-precision machine to produce and sell EX4	0	6,00,000
Net relevant benefit	₹25,00,000	₹24,00,000

Even though EX4 has the higher contribution margin per unit of the constrained resource, the fact that company must incur additional costs of ₹6,00,000 to achieve this higher contribution margin means that company is better off using its entire 50,000-hour capacity on the regular machine to produce and sell 50,000 units (50,000 hours × 1 hour per unit) of A6. The additional contribution from selling EX4 rather than A6 is ₹5,00,000 (₹30,00,000 – ₹25,00,000), which is not enough to cover the additional costs of leasing the high-precision machine. Note that, because all other overhead costs are fixed and cannot be changed, they are irrelevant for the decision. Company produces 50,000 units of A6, which increases operating income by ₹25,00,000.

2. If capacity of the regular machines is increased by 15,000 machine-hours to 65,000 machine-hours (50,000 originally + 15,000 new), the net relevant benefit from producing A6 and EX4 is as follows:

	A6	EX4
Total contribution margin from selling only A6 or only EX4		
A6: ₹50 × 65,000; EX4: ₹60 × 65,000	₹32,50,000	₹39,00,000
Less Lease costs of high-precision machine that would be incurred if EX4 is produced and sold	—	6,00,000
Less Cost of increasing capacity by 15,000 hours on regular machine	3,00,000	3,00,000
Net relevant benefit	₹29,50,000	₹30,00,000

Adding 15,000 machine-hours of capacity for regular machines and using all the capacity to produce EX4 increases operating income by ₹30,00,000.

Investing in the additional capacity increases Company's operating income by ₹5,00,000 (₹30,00,000 calculated in requirement 2 minus ₹25,00,000 calculated in requirement 1), so Company should add 15,000 hours to the regular machine. With the extra capacity available to it, Company should use its entire capacity to produce EX4. Using all 65,000 hours of capacity to produce EX4 rather than to produce A6 generates additional contribution margin of ₹6,50,000 (₹39,00,000 – ₹32,50,000), which is more than the additional cost of ₹6,00,000 to lease the high-precision machine. Company should therefore produce and sell 1,30,000 units of EX4 (65,000 hours × 0.5 hours per unit of EX4) and zero units of A6.

3.

	A6	EX4	V2
Selling price	₹200	₹300	₹240
Variable manufacturing costs per unit	120	200	140
Variable marketing costs per unit	30	70	30
Total variable costs per unit	150	270	170
Contribution margin per unit	₹50	₹30	₹70

Contribution margin per unit of the constrained resource $\dfrac{₹50}{1} = ₹50; \dfrac{₹30}{0.5} = ₹60; \dfrac{₹70}{1} = ₹70$

The first step is to compare the operating profits that Company could earn if it accepted the new offer for 20,000 units with the operating profits Company is currently earning. V2 has the highest contribution margin per hour on the regular machine and requires no additional investment such as leasing a high-precision machine. To produce the 20,000 units of V2 requested by new order, Company would require 20,000 hours on the regular machine resulting in contribution margin of ₹70 × 20,000 = ₹14,00,000.

Company now has 45,000 hours available on the regular machine to produce A6 or EX4.

	A6	EX4
Total contribution margin from selling only		
A6 or only EX4		
A6: ₹50 × 45,000; EX4: ₹60 × 45,000	₹22,50,000	₹27,00,000
Less Lease costs of high-precision machine		
to produce and sell EX4	–	6,00,000
Net relevant benefit	₹22,50,000	₹21,00,000

Company should use all the 45,000 hours of available capacity to produce 45,000 units of A6. Thus, the product mix that maximizes operating income is 20,000 units of V2, 45,000 units of A6, and zero units of EX4. This optimal mix results in a contribution margin of ₹36,50,000 (₹14,00,000 from V2 and ₹22,50,000 from A6). Relative to requirement 2, operating income increases by ₹6,50,000 (₹36,50,000 minus ₹30,00,000 calculated in requirement 2). Hence, Company should accept the new business and supply 20,000 units of V2.

11-26 Product mix, relevant costs. Hindustan Machine Tools (HMT) makes cutting tools for metalworking operations. It makes two types of tools: R3, a regular cutting tool, and HP6, a high-precision cutting tool. R3 is manufactured on a regular machine, but HP6 must be manufactured on both the regular machine and a high-precision machine. The following information is available:

	R3	HP6
Selling price	₹1,000	₹1,500
Variable manufacturing cost per unit	600	1,000
Variable marketing cost per unit	150	350
Budgeted total fixed overhead costs	35,00,000	55,00,000
Hours required to produce 1 unit on the regular machine	1.0	0.5

Additional information includes:
a. HMT faces a capacity constraint on the regular machine of 50,000 hours per year.
b. The capacity of the high-precision machine is not a constraint
c. Of the ₹55,00,000 budgeted fixed overhead costs of HP6, ₹30,00,000 are lease payments for the high-precision machine. This cost is charged entirely to HP6 because HMT uses the machine exclusively to produce HP6. The lease agreement for the high-precision machine can be canceled at any time with out penalties.
d. All other overhead costs are fixed and cannot be changed.

Required
1. What product mix-that is, how many units of R3 and HP6-will maximize HMT's operating income?

2. Suppose HMT can increase the annual capacity of regular machines by 15,000 machine-hours at a cost of ₹15,00,000. Should HMT increase the capacity of regular machines by 15,000 machine hours? By how much will HMT's operating income increase? Show your calculations.

3. Suppose that the capacity of the regular machines has been increased to 65,000 hours. HMT has been approached by Titan to supply 20,000 units of another cutting tool, S3, for ₹1,200 per unit. HMT must either accept the order for all 20,000 units or reject it totally. S3 is exactly like R3 except that its variable manufacturing costs are ₹700 per unit (It takes one hour to produce one unit of S3 on the regular machine, and variable marketing costs equal ₹150 per unit) What product mix should HMT choose to maximize operating income? Show your calculations.

Solution
Product mix, relevant costs

1.

	R3	HP6
Selling price	₹1,000	₹1,500
Variable manufacturing cost per unit	600	1,000
Variable marketing cost per unit	150	350
Total variable costs per unit	750	1,350
Contribution margin per unit	₹250	₹150

Contribution margin per hour of the constrained resource (the regular machine)

$$\frac{₹250}{1} = ₹250 \qquad \frac{₹15}{1} = ₹300$$

	R3	HP6
Total contribution margin from selling only R3 or only HP6		
R3: ₹250 × 50,000; HP6: ₹300 × 50,000	₹1,25,00,000	₹1,50,00,000
Less Lease costs of high-precision machine to produce and sell HP6	–	30,00,000
Net relevant benefit	₹1,25,00,000	₹1,20,00,000

Even though HP6 has the higher contribution margin per unit of the constrained resource, the fact that HMT must incur additional costs of ₹30,00,000 to achieve this higher contribution margin means that HMT is better off using its entire 50,000-hour capacity on the regular machine to produce and sell 50,000 units (50,000 hours ÷ 1 hour per unit) of R3. The additional contribution from selling HP6 rather than R3 is ₹25,00,000 (₹1,50,00,000 − ₹1,25,00,000), which is not enough to cover the additional costs of leasing the high-precision machine. Note that, because all other overhead costs are fixed and cannot be changed, they are irrelevant for the decision.

2. If capacity of the regular machines is increased by 15,000 machine-hours to 65,000 machine-hours (50,000 originally + 15,000 new), the net relevant benefit from producing R3 and HP6 is as follows:

	R3	HP6
Total contribution margin from selling only R3 or only HP6		
R3: ₹250 × 65,000; HP6: ₹300 × 65,000	₹1,62,50,000	₹1,95,00,000
Less Lease costs of high-precision machine that would be incurred if HP6 is produced and sold	–	30,00,000
Less Cost of increasing capacity by 15,000 hours on regular machine	15,00,000	15,00,000
Net relevant benefit	₹1,47,50,000	₹1,50,00,000

Investing in the additional capacity increases HMT's operating income by ₹25,00,000 (₹1,50,00,000 calculated in requirement 2 minus ₹1,25,00,000 calculated in requirement 1), so HMT should add 15,000 hours to the regular machine. With the extra capacity available to it, HMT should use its entire capacity to produce HP6. Using all 65,000 hours of capacity to produce HP6 rather than to produce R3 generates additional contribution margin of ₹32,50,000 (₹1,95,00,000 − ₹1,62,50,000) which is more than the additional cost of ₹30,00,000 to lease the high-precision machine. HMT should therefore produce and sell 1,30,000 units of HP6 (65,000 hours ÷ 0.5 hours per unit of HP6) and zero units of R3.

3.

	R3	HP	S3
Selling price	₹1,000	₹1,500	₹1,200
Variable manufacturing costs per unit	600	1,000	700
Variable marketing costs per unit	150	350	150
Total variable costs per unit	750	1,350	850
Contribution margin per unit	₹250	₹150	₹350

Contribution margin per hour of the constrained resource (the regular machine)

$$\frac{₹250}{1} = ₹250 \quad \frac{₹15}{0.5} = ₹300 \quad \frac{₹350}{1} = ₹350$$

The first step is to compare the operating profits that HMT could earn if it accepted the Titan Corporation offer for 20,000 units with the operating profits HMT is currently earning. S3 has the highest contribution margin per hour on the regular machine and requires no additional investment such as leasing a high-precision machine. To produce the 20,000 units of S3 requested by Titan Corporation, HMT would require 20,000 hours on the regular machine resulting in contribution margin of ₹350 × 20,000 = ₹70,00,000. HMT now has 45,000 hours available on the regular machine to produce R3 or HP6.

	R3	HP6
Total contribution margin from only selling		
R3 or only HP6		
R3: ₹250 × 45,000; HP6: ₹300 × 45,000	₹1,12,50,000	₹1,35,00,000
Less Lease costs of high-precision machine to produce and sell HP 6	–	30,00,000
Net relevant benefit	₹1,12,50,000	₹1,05,00,000

HMT should use all the 45,000 hours of available capacity to produce 45,000 units of R3. Thus, the product mix that maximizes operating income is 20,000 units of S3, 45,000 units of R3, and zero units of HP6. This optimal mix results in a contribution margin of ₹1,82,50,000 (₹70,00,000 from S3 and ₹1,12,50,000 from R3). Relative to requirement 2, operating income increases by ₹32,50,000 (₹1,82,50,000 minus ₹1,50,00,000 calculated in requirement 2). Hence, HMT should accept the Titan business and supply 20,000 units of S3.

11-27 Discontinuing a product line, selling more units. The Northern Division of Steel Craft and Furnishings makes and sells tables and beds. The following estimated revenue and cost information from the division's activity-based costing system is available for 2016.

	4,000 Tables	5,000 Beds	Total
Revenues (₹1,250 × 4,000; ₹2,000 × 5,000)	₹50,00,000	₹1,00,00,000	₹1,50,00,000
Variable direct materials and direct manufacturing labor costs (₹750 × 4,000; ₹1,050 × 5,000)	30,00,000	52,50,000	82,50,000
Depreciation on equipment used exclusively by each product line	4,20,000	5,80,000	10,00,000
Marketing and distribution costs ₹4,00,000 (fixed) + ₹7,500 per consignment × 40 consignments ₹6,00,000 (fixed) + ₹7,500 per consignment × 100 consignments	7,00,000	13,50,000	20,50,000
Fixed general administration costs of the division allocated to product lines on the basis of revenues	11,00,000	22,00,000	33,00,000
Allocated corporate-office costs allocated to product lines on the basis of revenues	5,00,000	10,00,000	15,00,000
Total costs	57,20,000	1,03,80,000	1,61,00,000
Operating income (loss)	₹(7,20,000)	₹(3,80,000)	₹(11,00,000)

Additional information includes:

a. On January I, 2016, the equipment has a book value of ₹10,00,000 and zero disposal value. Any equipment not used will remain idle.

b. Fixed marketing and distribution costs of a product line can be avoided if the line is discontinued.

c. Fixed general administration costs of the division and corporate-office costs will not change if sales of individual product lines are increased or decreased or if product lines are added or dropped.

Required

1. On the basis of financial considerations alone, should the Northern Division discontinue the tables product line, assuming the released facilities remain idle? Show your calculations.

2. What would be the effect on Northern Division's operating income if it were to sell 4,000 more tables? Assume that to do so the division would have to acquire additional equipment costing ₹4,20,000 with a one-year useful life and zero terminal disposal value. Assume further that the fixed marketing and distribution costs would not change but that the number of consignments would double. Show your calculations.

Solution

Discontinuing a product line, selling more units.

1. The incremental revenue losses and incremental savings in cost by discontinuing the Tables product line follows:

	Difference: Incremental(Loss in Revenues) and Savings in Costs from Dropping Tables Line
Revenues	₹(50,00,000)
Direct materials and direct manufacturing labor	30,00,000
Depreciation on equipment	0
Marketing and distribution	7,00,000
General administration	0
Corporate office costs	0
Total costs	37,00,000
Operating income (loss)	₹(13,00,000)

Dropping the Tables product line results in revenue losses of ₹50,00,000 and cost savings of ₹37,00,000. Hence, Steel Craft's and Furnishing's operating income will be ₹13,00,000 higher if it does not drop the Tables line.

Note that, by dropping the Tables product line, Steel Craft and Furnishings will save none of the depreciation on equipment, general administration costs, and corporate office costs, but it will save variable manufacturing costs and all marketing and distribution costs on the Tables product line.

2. Steel Craft's will generate incremental operating income of ₹12,80,000 from selling 4,000 additional tables and, hence, should try to increase table sales. The calculations follow:

Incremental Revenues (Costs) and Operating Income	
Revenues	₹50,00,000
Direct materials and direct manufacturing labor	(30,00,000)
Cost of equipment written off as depreciation	(4,20,000)*
Marketing and distribution costs	(3,00,000)†
General administration costs	0**
Corporate office costs	0**
Operating income	₹12,80,000

*Note that the additional costs of equipment are relevant future costs for the "selling more tables decision" because they represent incremental future costs that differ between the alternatives of selling and not selling additional tables.

†Current marketing and distribution costs which varies with number of consignments = ₹7,00,000 – ₹4,00,000 = ₹3,00,000. As the sales of tables double, the number of consignments will double, resulting in incremental marketing and distribution costs of (2 × ₹3,00,000) – ₹3,00,000 = ₹3,00,000.

**General administration and corporate office costs will be unaffected if Steel Craft and Furnishings decides to sell more tables. Hence, these costs are irrelevant for the decision.

11-28 Discontinuing or adding division (continuation of 11-27). Refer to the information presented in Solved Example 11-27.

Required

1. Given the Northern Division's expected operating loss of ₹11,00,000, should Steel Craft and Furnishings shut it down? Assume that shutting down the Northern Division will have no effect on corporate-office costs but will lead to savings of all general administration costs of the division. Show your calculations.

2. Suppose the manager at corporate headquarters responsible for making the decision of whether to shut down the Northern Division will be evaluated in 2016 on the Northern Division's operating income after allocating' corporate-office costs. Will the manager prefer to shut down the division? Show your calculations. Is the decision model consistent with the performance evaluation model? Explain.

3. Suppose Steel Craft has the opportunity to open another division, the Southern Division, whose revenues and costs are expected to be identical to the Northern Division's revenues and costs (including a cost of ₹10,00,000 to acquire equipment with a one-year useful life and zero terminal disposal value). Opening the new division will have no effect on corporate office costs. Should Steel Craft open the Southern Division? Show your calculations.

Solution

Discontinuing or adding another division (continuation of 11-27).

1. Solution Exhibit 11-28, Column 1, presents the relevant loss of revenues and the relevant savings in costs from closing the Northern Division. As the calculations show, Steel Craft's operating income would decrease by ₹14,00,000 if it shuts down the Northern Division (loss in revenues of ₹1,50,00,000 versus savings in costs of ₹1,36,00,000).

   Steel Craft will save variable manufacturing costs, marketing and distribution costs, and division general administration costs by closing the Northern Division but equipment related depreciation and corporate office allocations are irrelevant to the decision. Equipment related costs are irrelevant because they are past costs (and the equipment has zero disposal price). Corporate office costs are irrelevant because Steel Craft will not save any actual corporate office costs by closing the Northern Division. The corporate office costs that used to be allocated to the Northern Division will be allocated to other divisions.

2. The manager at corporate headquarters responsible for making the decision is evaluated on Northern Division's operating income after allocating corporate office costs. The manager will evaluate the options as follows: If the manager does not close the Northern Division in 2015, the division is expected to show an operating loss of ₹11,00,000 after allocating all corporate office costs. If the manager closes the Northern Division, the division would show an operating loss of ₹10,00,000 from the write off of equipment. It would show no revenues and, hence, would not attract any corporate office costs. It would also not incur any manufacturing, marketing and distribution, and general administration costs.

   From the viewpoint of maximizing the operating income against which the manager is evaluated, the manager would prefer to shut down Northern Division (and show an operating loss of ₹10,00,000 instead of an operating loss of ₹11,00,000 by operating it). In fact, the manager might argue that even the ₹10,00,000 operating loss is more a consequence of accounting write offs rather than a "real" operating loss.

   Recall from requirement 1 that the decision model favored keeping the Northern Division open. The performance evaluation model of the manager making the decision suggests that the Northern Division be closed. Hence, the performance evaluation model is inconsistent with the decision model.

3. Solution Exhibit 11-28, Column 2, presents the relevant revenues and relevant costs of opening the Southern Division (a division whose revenues and costs are expected to be identical to the revenues and costs of the Northern Division). Steel Craft should open the

Southern Division because it would increase operating income by ₹4,00,000 (increase in relevant revenues of ₹1,50,00,000 and increase in relevant costs of ₹1,46,00,000). The relevant costs include direct materials, direct manufacturing labor, marketing and distribution, equipment, and division general administration costs but not corporate office costs. Note, in particular, that the cost of equipment written off as depreciation is relevant because it is an expected future cost that Steel Craft will incur only if it opens the Southern Division. Corporate office costs are irrelevant because actual corporate office costs will not change if Steel opens the Southern Division. The current corporate staff will be able to oversee the Southern Division's operations. Steel Craft will allocate some corporate office costs to the Southern Division but this allocation represents corporate office costs that are already currently being allocated to some other division. Because actual total corporate office costs do not change, they are irrelevant to the division.

Solution Exhibit 11-28

Relevant-Revenue and Relevant-Cost Analysis for Closing Northern Division and Opening Southern Division

	(Loss in Revenues) and Savings in Costs from Closing Northern Division (1)	Incremental Revenues and (Incremental Costs) from Opening Southern Division (2)
Revenues	₹(1,50,00,000)	₹1,50,00,000
Variable direct materials and direct manufacturing labor costs	82,50,000	(82,50,000)
Equipment cost written off as depreciation	0	(10,00,000)
Marketing and distribution costs	20,50,000	(20,50,000)
Division general administration costs	33,00,000	(33,00,000)
Corporate office costs	0	0
Total costs	1,36,00,000	(1,46,00,000)
Effect on operating income (loss)	₹(14,00,000)	₹4,00,000

11-29 Theory of constraints, throughput contribution, relevant costs. Bajaj Electricals manufactures electronic testing equipment. Bajaj also installs the equipment at customers' sites and ensures that it functions smoothly. Additional information on the manufacturing and installation departments is as follows (capacities are expressed in terms of the number of units of electronic testing equipment):

	Equipment Manufactured	Equipment Installed
Annual capacity	310 units per year	275 units per year
Equipment manufactured and installed	275 units per year	275 units per year

Bajaj manufactures only 275 units per year because the installation department has only enough capacity to install 275 units. The equipment sells for ₹4,50,000 per unit (installed) and has direct material costs of ₹2,00,000. All costs other than direct material costs are fixed. The following requirements refer only to the preceding data. There is no connection between the requirements.

1. Bajaj's engineers have found a way to reduce equipment manufacturing time. The new method would cost an additional ₹500 per unit and would allow Bajaj to manufacture 20 additional units a year. Should Bajaj implement the new method? Show your calculations.

2. Bajaj's designers have proposed a change in direct materials that would increase direct material costs by ₹20,000 per unit. This change would enable Bajaj to install 310 units of equipment each year. If Bajaj makes the change, it will implement the new design on all equipment sold. Should Bajaj use the new design? Show your calculations.

3. A new installation technique has been developed that will enable Bajaj's engineers to install 7 additional units of equipment a year. The new method will increase installation

costs by ₹5,50,000 each year. Should Bajaj implement the new technique? Show your calculations.

4. Bajaj is considering how to motivate workers to improve their productivity (output per hour). One proposal is to evaluate and compensate workers in the manufacturing and installation departments on the basis of their productivities. Do you think the new proposal is a good idea? Explain briefly.

Solution

1. It will cost Bajaj ₹500 per unit to reduce manufacturing time. But manufacturing is not a bottleneck operation; installation is. Therefore, manufacturing more equipment will not increase sales and throughput margin. Bajaj should not implement the new manufacturing method.

2. Increase in throughput margin, ₹2,50,000 × 35 units,   ₹87,50,000
Additional relevant costs of new direct materials, ₹20,000 × 310 units,   62,00,000
Increase/(Decrease) in operating income   ₹25,50,000
Alternatively, compare throughput margin under each alternative.
With the modification, throughput margin is ₹2,30,000 × 310   ₹7,13,00,000
Current throughput margin is ₹2,50,000 × 275   6,87,50,000
Increase/(Decrease) in operating income   ₹25,50,000

The throughput margin resulting from the proposed change in direct materials is greater than the current throughput margin. Therefore, Bajaj should implement the new design.

3. Increase in throughput margin, ₹2,50,000 × 7 units   ₹17,50,000
Increase in relevant costs   5,50,000
Increase in operating income   ₹12,00,000

The additional throughput margin exceeds incremental costs by ₹12,00,000, so Bajaj should implement the new installation technique.

4. Motivating installation workers to increase productivity is worthwhile because installation is a bottleneck operation, and any increase in productivity at the bottleneck will increase throughput margin. On the other hand, motivating workers in the manufacturing department to increase productivity is not worthwhile. Manufacturing is not a bottleneck operation, so any increase in output will result only in extra inventory of equipment. Bajaj should encourage manufacturing to produce only as much equipment as the installation department needs, not to produce as much as it can. Under these circumstances, it would not be a good idea to evaluate and compensate manufacturing workers on the basis of their productivity.

11-30 Closing down divisions. Vivek Industries has four operating divisions. The budgeted revenues and expenses for each division for 2016 follows:

	Division			
	A	**B**	**C**	**D**
Sales	₹5,04,000	₹9,48,000	₹9,60,000	₹12,40,000
Cost of goods sold	4,40,000	9,30,000	7,65,000	9,25,000
Selling, general, and administrative expenses	96,000	2,02,500	1,44,000	2,10,000
Operating income/loss	₹(32,000)	₹(1,84,500)	₹51,000	₹1,05,000

Further analysis of costs reveals the following percentages of variable costs in each division:

Cost of goods sold	90%	80%	90%	85%
Selling, general, and administrative expenses	50%	50%	60%	60%

Closing down any division would result in savings of 40% of the fixed costs of that division.

Top management is very concerned about the unprofitable divisions (A and B) and is considering closing them for the year.

Required

1. Calculate the increase or decrease in operating income if Vivek closes division A.
2. Calculate the increase or decrease in operating income if Vivek closes division B.
3. What other factors should the top management of Vivek consider before making a decision?

Solution

1. and 2.

	Division A	Division B
Sales	₹5,04,000	₹9,48,000
Variable costs of goods sold		
(₹4,40,000 × 0.90; ₹9,30,000 × 0.80)	3,96,000	7,44,000
Variable S,G & A		
(₹96,000 × 0.50; ₹2,02,500 × 0.50)	48,000	1,01,250
Total variable costs	4,44,000	8,45,250
Contribution margin	₹60,000	₹1,02,750

	Division A	Division B
Fixed costs of goods sold		
(₹4,40,000 × 0.10; ₹9,30,000 × 0.20)	₹44,000	₹1,86,000
Fixed S,G & A		
(₹96,000 × 0.50; ₹2,02,500 × 0.50)	48,000	1,01,250
Total fixed costs	₹92,000	₹2,87,250
Fixed costs savings if shutdown		
(₹92,000 × 0.40; ₹2,87,250 × 0.40)	₹36,800	₹1,14,900

Division A's contribution margin of ₹60,000 more than covers its avoidable fixed costs of ₹36,800. The difference of ₹23,200 helps cover the company's unavoidable fixed costs. Because ₹36,800 of Division A's fixed costs are avoidable, the remaining ₹55,200 is unavoidable and will be incurred regardless of whether Division A continues to operate. Division A's ₹32,000 loss is the rest of the unavoidable fixed costs (₹55,200 –₹23,200). If Division A is closed, the remaining divisions will need to generate sufficient profits to cover the entire ₹55,200 unavoidable fixed cost. Consequently, Division A should not be closed because it helps defray ₹23,200 of this cost.

Division B earns a positive contribution margin of ₹1,02,750. Division B also generates ₹1,14,900 of avoidable fixed costs. Based strictly on financial considerations, Division B should be closed because the company will save ₹12,150 (₹1,14,900 – ₹1,02,750). Division B is currently incurring ₹1,14,900 in fixed costs that it could have avoided while earning only ₹1,02,750 in contribution margin.

An alternative set of calculations is as follows:

	Division A	Division B
Total variable costs	₹4,44,000	₹8,45,250
Avoidable fixed costs if shutdown	36,800	1,14,900
Total cost savings if shutdown	4,80,800	9,60,150
Loss of revenues if shutdown	(5,04,000)	(9,48,000)
Cost savings minus loss of revenues	₹(23,200)	₹12,150

Division A should not be shut down because loss of revenues if Division A is shut down exceeds cost savings by ₹23,200. Division B should be shut down because cost savings from shutting down Division B exceeds loss of revenues by ₹12,150.

3. Before deciding to close Division B, management should consider the role that the Division's product line plays relative to other product lines. For instance, if the product manufactured by Division B attracts customers to the company, then dropping Division B may have a detrimental effect on the revenues of the remaining divisions. Management may also want to consider the impact on the morale of the remaining employees if Division B is closed. Talented employees may become fearful of losing their jobs and seek employment elsewhere.

11-31 Make versus buy, ethics. (CMA, adapted) Harish Aggarwal, a management accountant with the Maruti Udyog, is evaluating whether a component MTR.2000 should continue to manufactured by Maruti or purchased from Outside Vendor Company. Outside Vendor has submitted a bid to manufacture and supply the 32,000 units of MTR.2000 that Maruti Udyog will need for 2016 at a selling price of ₹173.

Harish has gathered the following information regarding Maruti's costs to manufacture 30,000 units of MTR-2000 in 2015:

Direct materials	₹19,50,000
Direct manufacturing labor	12,00,000
Plant space rental	8,40,000
Equipment leasing	3,60,000
Other manufacturing overhead	22,50,000
Total manufacturing costs	66,00,000

Harish has also collected the following information related to manufacturing MTR 2000:

- Prices of direct materials used in the production of MTR.2000 are expected to increase by 8% in 2016.
- Maruti Udyog's direct manufacturing labor contract calls for a 5% increase in 2016.
- Maruti Udyog can withdraw from the plant space rental agreement without any penalty. Maruti Udyog will have no need for this space if MTR.2000 is not manufactured.
- The equipment lease can be terminated by paying ₹60,000.
- 40% of the other manufacturing overhead is considered variable. Variable overhead changes proportionately with the number of units produced. The fixed component of other manufacturing overhead costs is expected to remain the same whether or not MTR.2000 is manufactured.

Pradeep, plant manager at Maruti Udyog, indicates to Harish that the current performance of the plant can be significantly improved and that the cost increases he is assuming are unlikely to occur. Hence, the analysis should be done assuming costs will be considerably below current levels, Harish knows that Pradeep is concerned about outsourcing MTR.2000 because it will mean that some of his close friends will be laid off.

Harish believes that it is unlikely that the plant will achieve the lower costs as Pradeep describes. He is very confident about the accuracy of the information he has collected, but he is also unhappy about laying off employees.

Required

1. On the basis of the financial information Harish has obtained, should Maruti Udyog make MTR.2000 or buy it in 2016? Show your calculations.
2. What other factors should Maruti Udyog consider before making a decision?
3. What should Harish do in response to Pradeep's comments?

Solution

Make versus buy, ethics (CMA, adapted).

1. An analysis of relevant costs that shows whether Maruti Udyog should make MTR.2000 or purchase it from Outside Vendor Company for 2016 follows:

	Total Costs for 32,000 Units
Cost to purchase MTR.2000 from Outside Vendor	
Bid price from Outside Vendor, ₹173 × 32,000	₹55,36,000

Equipment lease penalty	60,000
Total incremental cost to purchase	55,96,000
Cost for Maruti Udyog to make MTR.2,000 in 2016	
Direct materials (₹19,50,000 × 1.08) × 32,000/32,000	22,46,400
Direct manufacturing labor (₹12,00,000 × 1.05) × 32,000/32,000	13,44,000
Factory space rental	8,40,000
Equipment leasing costs	3,60,000
Variable manufacturing overhead (₹22,50,000 × 40%) × $\dfrac{32,000}{30,000}$	9,60,000
Fixed manufacturing overhead (not relevant)	–
Total incremental cost to make MTR.2000	57,50,400
Savings if purchased from Outside Vendor	₹1,54,400

2. Based solely on the financial results, the 32,000 units of MTR.2000 for 2016 should be purchased from Outside Vendor. The total cost from Outside Vendor would be ₹55,96,000, or ₹1,54,400 less than if the units were made by Maruti.

At least three other factors that Maruti Udyog should consider before agreeing to purchase MTR.2000 from Outside Vendor Company include the following:

- The quality of the Outside Vendor component should be equal to, or better than, the quality of the internally made component. Otherwise, the quality of the final product might be compromised and Maruti Udyog's reputation affected.
- Outside Vendor's reliability as an on-time supplier is important, since late deliveries could hamper Maruti Udyog's production schedule and delivery dates for the final product.
- Layoffs may result if the component is outsourced to Outside Vendor. This could impact Maruti Udyog's other employees and cause labor problems or affect the company's position in the community. In addition, there may be termination costs, which have not been factored into the analysis.

Exercises

[Comprehensive solutions to all exercises are available on the companion website www. pearsoned.co.in/charlesthorngren]

11-32 Multiple choice. (CPA) Choose the best answer.

1. The Bata Company manufactures slippers and sells them at ₹100 a pair. Variable manufacturing cost is ₹45 a pair, and allocated fixed manufacturing cost is ₹15 a pair. It has enough idle capacity available to accept a one-time-only special order of 20,000 pairs of slippers at ₹60 a pair. Bata will not incur any marketing costs as a result of the special order. What would the effect on operating income be if the special order could be accepted without affecting normal sales? (a) ₹0, (b) ₹3,00,000 increase, (c) ₹9,00,000 increase, or (d) ₹12,00,000 increase.

2. The Sona Steering manufactures Part No. 498 for use in its production line. The manufacturing cost per unit for 20,000 units of Part No. 498 is as follows:

Direct material	₹6
Direct manufacturing labor	30
Variable manufacturing overhead	12
Fixed manufacturing overhead allocated	16
Total manufacturing cost per unit	64

The Sundaram Fastners Company has offered to sell 20,000 units of Part No. 498 to Sona Steering for ₹60 per unit. Sona Steering will make the decision to buy the part from Sundaram Fastners if there is an overall savings of at least ₹25,000 for Sona Steering. If Sona Steering accepts Sundaram Fastners's offer, ₹9 per unit of the fixed overhead allocated would be eliminated. Furthermore, Sona Steering has determined that the released facilities could be used to save relevant costs in the manufacture of Part No. 575. For Sona

Steering to achieve an overall savings of ₹25,000, the amount of relevant costs that would have to be saved by using the released facilities in the manufacture of Part No. 575 would be (a) ₹80,000 (b) ₹85,000 (c) ₹1,25,000 or (d) ₹1,40,000.

11-33 Inventory decision, opportunity costs. Maharaja, a manufacturer of lawn mowers predicts that 2,40,000 spark plugs will have to be purchased next year. Maharaja estimate that 20,000 spark plugs will be required each month. A supplier quotes a price of ₹80 per spark plug. The supplier also offers a special discount option: If all 2,40,000 spark plugs are purchased at the start of the year, a discount of 5% off the ₹80 price will be given. Maharaja can invest its cash at 8% per year. It costs Maharaja ₹2,000 to place each purchase order.

Required

1. What is the opportunity cost of interest forgone from purchasing all 2,40,000 units at the start of the year instead of in 12 monthly purchases of 20,000 units per order?
2. Would this opportunity cost ordinarily be recorded in the accounting system? Why?
3. Should Maharaja purchase 2,40,000 units at the start of the year or 20,000 units each month? Show your calculations.

11-34 Relevant costs, contribution margin, product emphasis. The Rainbows is a take-out food store, at a popular beach resort. Sudhir, owner of the Rainbows, is deciding how much refrigerator space to devote to four different drinks. Pertinent data on these four drinks are as follows:

	Cola	Lemonade	Punch	Natural Orange Juice
Selling price per case	₹180	₹192	₹264	₹384
Variable cost per case	135	152	201	302
Cases sold per foot of shelf space per day	25	24	4	5

Sudhir has a maximum front shelf-space of 12 feet to devote to the four drinks. He wants a minimum of 1 foot and a maximum of 6 feet of front shelf-space for each drink.

Required

1. Compute the contribution margin per case of each type of drink?
2. A co-worker of Sudhir's recommends that he maximize the shelf space devoted to those drinks with the highest contribution margin per case. Evaluate this recommendation.
3. What shelf-space allocation for the four drinks would you recommend for the Rainbows Show your calculations.

11-35 Choosing customers. Sharma Printers operates a printing press with a monthly capacity of 2,000 machine-hours. Sharma has two main customers, Hyundai and Maruti Data on each customer for January follows:

	Hyundai	Maruti	Total
Revenues	₹12,00,000	₹8,00,000	₹20,00,000
Variable costs	4,20,000	4,80,000	9,00,000
Contribution margin	7,80,000	3,20,000	11,00,000
Fixed costs (allocated)	6,00,000	4,00,000	10,00,000
Operating income	₹1,80,000	₹(80,000)	₹1,00,000
Machine-hours required	1,500 hours	500 hours	2,000 hours

Maruti indicates that it wants Sharma to do an additional ₹8,00,000 worth of printing jobs during February. These jobs are identical to the existing business Sharma did for Maruti in January in terms of variable costs and machine-hours required. Sharma anticipates that the business from Hyundai in February would be the same as that in January. Sharma can choose to accept as much of the Hyundai and Maruti business for February as its capacity allows Assume that total machine-hours and fixed costs for February will be the same as in January.

Required

What action should Sharma take to maximize its operating income? Show your calculations

11-36 Equipment upgrade versus replacement (A. Spero, adapted) The Steel Authority of India (SAIL) makes steel table lamps. It is considering either upgrading its existing production line or replacing it The production equipment was purchased two years ago for

₹60,00,000. It has an expected useful life of five years, a terminal disposal value of ₹0, and is depreciated on a straight-line basis at the rate of ₹12,00,000 per year. The equipment has a current book value of ₹36,00,000 and a current disposal value of ₹9,00,000. The following table presents expected costs under the upgrade and replace alternatives:

	Upgrade	Replace
Expected one-time-only equipment costs	₹30,00,000	₹75,00,000
Variable manufacturing cost per lamp	₹120	₹90
Expected production and sales of lamps per year	60,000 units	60,000 units
Selling price of lamps	₹250	₹250

The expected useful life after the machine is upgraded or replaced is three years, and the expected terminal disposal value is ₹0. If the machine is upgraded, the ₹30,00,000 would be added to the current book value of ₹36,00,000 and depreciated on a straight-line basis. The new equipment, if purchased, will also be depreciated on a straight-line basis.
For simplicity, ignore income taxes and the time value of money.

Required

1. Should SAIL upgrade its production line or replace it? Show your calculations.
2. Now suppose the capital expenditure needed to replace the production line is not known. All other data are as given previously. What is the maximum price that SAIL would be willing to pay for the new line to prefer replacing the existing line to upgrading it?
3. Consider again the basic information given in this exercise. Suppose Rohan, the manager of the SAIL, is evaluated on operating income. The coming year's operating income is crucial to Rohan's bonus. What alternative would Rohan choose? Explain.

11-37 Opportunity costs. (H. Schaefer) The Bajaj is working at full production capacity producing 10,000 units of a unique product, Rosebo. Manufacturing cost per unit for Rosebo is as follows:

Direct material	₹20
Direct manufacturing labor	30
Manufacturing overhead	50
Total manufacturing cost	100

Manufacturing overhead cost per unit is based on variable cost per unit of ₹20 and fixed costs of ₹3,00,000 (at full capacity of 10,000 units). Marketing cost, all variable, is ₹40 per unit, and the selling price is ₹200.

A customer, the Royal Company, has asked Bajaj to produce 2,000 units of Orangebo, a modification of Rosebo. Orangebo would require the same manufacturing processes as Rosebo. Royal has offered to pay Bajaj ₹150 for a unit of Orangebo and half the marketing cost per unit.

Required

1. What is the opportunity Cost to Bajaj of producing the 2,000 units of Orangebo? (Assume that no overtime is worked.)
2. The Reliable Corporation has offered to produce 2,000 units of Roseba for Bajaj so that Bajaj may accept the Royal offer. That is, if Bajaj accepts the Reliable offer, Bajaj would manufacture 8,000 units of Rosebo and 2,000 units of Orangebo and purchase 2,000 units of Rosebo from Reliable. Reliable would charge Bajaj ₹140 per unit to manufacture Rosebo. On the basis of financial considerations alone, should Bajaj accept the Reliable offer? Show your calculations.
3. Suppose Bajaj had been working at less than full capacity, producing 8,000 units of Rosebo at the time the Royal offer was made. Calculate the minimum price Bajaj should accept far Orangebo under these conditions. (Ignore the previous ₹150 selling price.)

11-38 Make or buy, unknown level of volume. (A. Atkinson) Hindustan Motors manufactures small engines. The engines are sold to manufacturers who install them in such products as lawn mowers. The company currently manufactures all the parts used in these engines but is considering a proposal from an external supplier who wishes to supply the starter assemblies used in these engines.

The starter assemblies are currently manufactured in Division 3 of Hindustan Motors. The costs relating to the starter assemblies for the past 12 months were as follows:

Direct materials	₹20,00,000
Direct manufacturing labor	15,00,000
Manufacturing overhead	40,00,000
Total	75,00,000

Over the past year, Division 3 manufactured 1,50,000 starter assemblies. The average cost for each starter assembly is ₹50 (₹75,00,000 ÷ 1,50,000).

Further analysis of manufacturing overhead revealed the following information. Of the total manufacturing overhead, only 25% is considered variable. Of the fixed portion, ₹15,00,000 is an allocation of general overhead that would remain unchanged for the company as a whole if production of the starter assemblies is discontinued. A further ₹10,00,000 of the fixed overhead is avoidable if production of the starter assemblies is discontinued. The balance of the current fixed overhead, ₹5,00,000, is the division manager's salary. If production of the starter assemblies is discontinued, the manager of Division 3 will be transferred to Division 2 at the same salary. This move will allow the company to save the ₹4,00,000 salary that would otherwise be paid to attract an outsider to this position.

Required

1. Bharat Electronics, a reliable supplier, has offered to supply starter assembly units at ₹40 per unit. Since this price is less than the current average cost of ₹50 per unit, the vice-president of manufacturing is eager to accept this offer. On the basis of financial considerations alone, should the outside offer be accepted? Show your calculations. (Hint: Production output in the coming year may be different from production output in the last year.)

2. How, if at all, would your response to requirement 1 change if the company could use the vacated plant space for storage and, in so doing, avoid ₹5,00,000 of outside storage charges currently incurred? Why is this information relevant or irrelevant?

11-39 Make versus buy, activity-based costing, opportunity costs. (N. Melumad and S. Reichelstein, adapted) The Atlas Company produces bicycles. This year's expected production is 10,000 units. Currently, Atlas makes the chains for its bicycles. Atlas's management accountant reports the following costs for making the 10,000 bicycle chains:

	Cost per Unit	Costs for 10,000 Units
Direct materials	₹40	₹4,00,000
Direct manufacturing labor	20	2,00,000
Variable manufacturing overhead (power and utilities)	15	1,50,000
Inspection setup materials handling'		20,000
Machine rent		30,000
Allocated fixed costs of plant administration taxes and insurance	3,00,000	
Total costs		11,00,000

Atlas has received an offer from an outside vendor to supply any number of chains. Atlas requires ₹82 per chain. The following additional information is available:

a. Inspection, setup, and materials handling costs vary with the number of batches in which the chains, are produced. Atlas produces chains in batch sizes of 1,000 units. Atlas estimates that it will produce the 10,000 units in 10 batches.

b. Atlas rents the machine used to make the chains. If Atlas buys all of its chains from the outside vendor, it does not need to pay rent on this machine.

Required

1. Assume that if Atlas purchases the chains from the outside supplier, the facility where the chains are currently made will remain idle. On the basis of financial considerations alone, should Atlas accept the outside supplier's offer at the anticipated production (and sales) volume of 10,000 units? Show your calculations.

2. For this question, assume that if the chains are purchased outside, the facilities where the chains are currently made will be used to upgrade the bicycles by adding mud flaps and reflectors. As a consequence, the selling price of bicycles will be raised by ₹200. The variable cost per unit of the upgrade would be ₹180, and additional tooling costs of ₹1,60,000 would be incurred. On the basis of financial considerations alone, should Atlas make or buy the chains, assuming that 10,000 units are produced (and sold)? Show your calculations.

3. The sales manager at Atlas is concerned that the estimate of 10,000 units may be high and believes that only 6,200 units will be sold. Production will be cut back, freeing up work space. This space can be used to add the mud flaps and reflectors whether Atlas goes outside for the chains or makes them in-house. At this lower output, Atlas will produce the chains in eight batches of 775 units each. On the basis of financial considerations alone, should Atlas purchase the chains from the outside vendor? Show your calculations.

11-40 Multiple choice, comprehensive problem on relevant costs. The following are the Parkar Company's unit cost of manufacturing and marketing a high-style pen at an output level of 20,000 units per month:

Manufacturing cost	
Direct material	₹10
Direct manufacturing labor	12
Variable manufacturing indirect cost	8
Fixed manufacturing indirect cost	5
Marketing cost	
Variable	15
Fixed	9

The following situations refer only to the preceding data; there is no connection between the situations. Unless stated otherwise, assume a regular selling price of ₹60 per unit. Choose the best answer to each question. Show your calculations.

Required

1. In an inventory of 10,000 units of the high-style pen presented in the balance sheet, the appropriate unit cost to use is (a) ₹30, (b) ₹35, (c) ₹50, (d) ₹22, or (e) ₹59.

2. The pen is usually produced and sold at the rate of 2,40,000 units per year (an average of 20,000 per month). The selling price is ₹60 per unit, which yields total annual revenues of ₹1,44,00,000. Total costs are ₹1,41,60,000, and operating income is ₹2,40,000, or ₹1 per unit. Market research estimates that unit sales could be increased by 10% if prices were cut to ₹58. Assuming the implied cost-behavior patterns continue, this action, if taken, would

   a. Decrease operating income by ₹72,000.

   b. Decrease operating income by ₹2 per unit (₹4,80,000) but increase operating income by 10% of revenues (₹14,40,000), for a net increase of ₹9,60,000.

   c. Decrease fixed cost per unit by 10%, or ₹1.4, per unit, and thus decrease operating income by ₹0.6 (₹2.0 − ₹1.4) per unit.

   d. Increase unit sales to 2,64,000 units, which at the ₹58 price would give total revenues of ₹1,53,12,000 and lead to costs of ₹59 per unit for 2,64,000 units, which would equal ₹1,55,76,000, and result in an operating loss of ₹2,64,000.

   e. None of these.

3. A contract with the government for 5,000 units of the pens calls for the reimbursement of all manufacturing costs plus a fixed fee of ₹10,000. No variable marketing costs are incurred on the government contract. You are asked to compare the following two alternatives:

Sales Each Month to	Alternative A	Alternative B
Regular customers	15,000 units	15,000 units
Government	0 units	5,000 units

Operating income under alternative B is greater than that under alternative A by (a) ₹10,000, (b) ₹25,000, (c) ₹35,000, (d) ₹3,000, or (e) none of these.

4. Assume the same data with respect to the government contract as in requirement 3 except that the two alternatives to be compared are

Sales Each Month to	Alternative A	Alternative B
Regular customers	20,000 units	15,000 units
Government	0 units	5,000 units

Operating income under alternative B relative to that under alternative A is (a) ₹40,000 less, (b) ₹30,000 greater, (c) ₹65,000 less, (d) ₹5,000 greater, or (e) none of these.

5. The company wants to enter a foreign market in which price competition is keen. The company seeks a one-time-only special order for 10,000 units on a minimum-unit-price basis. It expects that shipping costs for this order will amount to only ₹7.5 per unit, but the fixed costs of obtaining the contract will be ₹40,000. The company incurs no variable marketing costs other than shipping costs. Domestic business will be unaffected. The selling to break-even is (a) ₹35, (b) ₹41.5, (c) ₹42.5, (d) ₹30 or (e) ₹50.

6. The company has an inventory of 1,000 units of pens that must be sold immediately at reduced prices. Otherwise, the inventory will be worthless. The unit cost that is relevant for establishing the minimum selling price is (a) ₹45, (b) ₹40, (c) ₹30, (d) ₹59, or (e) ₹15.

7. A proposal is received from an outside supplier who will make and transport these high-style pens directly to the Parkar Company's customers as sales orders are forwarded from Parkar's sales staff. Parkar's fixed marketing costs will be unaffected, but its variable marketing costs will be slashed by 20%. Parkar's plant will be idle, but its fixed manufacturing overhead will continue at 50% of present levels. How much per unit would the company be able to pay the supplier without decreasing operating income? (a) ₹47.5, (b) ₹39.5, (c) ₹29.5, (d) ₹53.5, or (e) none of these.

11-41 Make or buy (continuation of 11-40). Assume that, as in requirement 7 of Exercise 11-40, a proposal is received from an outside supplier who will make and transport high-style pens directly to the Parkar Company's customers as sales orders are forwarded from Parkar's sales staff. If the supplier's offer is accepted, the present plant facilities will be used to make a new pen whose unit costs will be

Variable manufacturing cost	₹50
Fixed manufacturing cost	10
Variable marketing cost	20
Fixed marketing cost	5

Total fixed manufacturing overhead will be unchanged from the original level given at the beginning of Problem 11-39. Fixed marketing costs for the new pens are over and above the fixed marketing costs incurred for marketing the high-style pens at the beginning of Problem 11-39. The new pen will sell for ₹90. The minimum desired operating income on the two pens taken together is ₹5,00,000 per year.

What is the maximum purchase cost per unit that the Parkar Company would be willing to pay for subcontracting the production of the high-style pens?

11-42 Optimal product mix. (CMA, adapted) Royal Sport's Plastics Department is currently manufacturing 5,000 pairs of skates annually, making full use of its machine capacity. The selling price and total cost per unit associated with Royal Sport's skates are

Selling price per pair of skates		₹980
Cost per pair of skates		
Direct material,	₹200	
Variable machine operating cost (₹160 per machine-hour)	240	
Manufacturing overhead cost	180	
Marketing and administrative cost	210	830
Operating income per pair of skates		150

Royal Sport believes it could sell 8,000 pairs of skates annually if it had sufficient manufacturing capacity. Outside vendor has offered to provide up to 6,000 pairs of skates per year at a price of ₹750 per pair delivered at Royal place.

Krishna, Royal Sport product manager, has suggested that the company can make better use of its Plastics Department by manufacturing snowboard bindings. Krishna believes that Royal Sport could expect to sell up to 12,000 snowboard bindings annually. Krishna's estimate of the selling price and total cost per unit to manufacture 12,000 snowboard bindings are:

Selling price per snowboard binding		₹600
Cost per snowboard binding		
Direct material	₹200	
Variable machine operating cost (₹160 per machine-hour)	80	
Manufacturing overhead cost	60	
Marketing and administrative cost	100	440
Operating income per snowboard binding		160

Other information pertinent to Royal Sport's operations includes the following:

- In the Plastics Department, Royal Sport uses machine-hours as the allocation base for manufacturing overhead costs. The fixed manufacturing overhead component of these costs for the current year is the ₹3,00,000 of fixed plantwide manufacturing overhead that has been allocated to the Plastics Department. These costs will not be affected by the product-mix decision.

- Variable marketing and administrative cost per unit for the various products are as follows:

Manufactured in-line skates	₹90
Purchased in-line skates	40
Manufactured snowboard bindings	80

Required

Fixed marketing and administrative costs of ₹6,00,000 are not affected by the product-mix decision.

Calculate the quantity of each product that Royal Sport should manufacture and/or purchase to maximize operating income. Show your calculations.

12 Strategy, Balanced Scorecard, and Strategic Profitability Analysis

Learning Objectives ▼

1. Recognize which of two generic strategies a company is using

2. Understand what comprises reengineering

3. Understand the four perspectives of the balanced scorecard

4. Analyze changes in operating income to evaluate strategy

5. Identify unused capacity and how to manage it

Learning Objective 1

Recognize which of two generic strategies a company is using

. . . product differentiation or cost leadership

Olive Garden wants to know

So do Barnes and Noble, PepsiCo, and L.L. Bean. Even your local car dealer and transit authority are curious. They all want to know if they are meeting their goals. Many companies have successfully used the balanced scorecard approach to measure their progress. Volkswagen do Brasil is one of them.

What Is Strategy?

Strategy specifies how an organization matches its own capabilities with the opportunities in the marketplace to accomplish its objectives. In other words, strategy describes how an organization can create value for its customers while differentiating itself from its competitors. For example, Wal-Mart, the retail giant, creates value for its customers by locating stores in suburban and rural areas, and by offering low prices, a wide range of product categories, and few choices within each product category. Consistent with its strategy, Wal-Mart has developed the capability to keep costs down by aggressively negotiating low prices with its suppliers in exchange for high volumes and by maintaining a no-frills, cost-conscious environment with minimum sales staff.

In formulating its strategy, an organization must first thoroughly understand its industry. Industry analysis focuses on five forces: (1) competitors, (2) potential entrants into the market, (3) equivalent products, (4) bargaining power of customers, and (5) bargaining power of input suppliers.[1] The collective effect of these forces shapes an organization's profit potential. In general, profit potential decreases with greater competition, stronger potential entrants, products that are similar, and more-demanding customers and suppliers. Below we illustrate these five forces for Chipset, Inc., maker of linear integrated circuit devices (LICDs) used in modems and communication networks. Chipset produces a single specialized product, CX1. This standard, high-performance microchip can be used in multiple applications. Chipset designed CX1 with extensive input from its customers base.

1. **Competitors.** The CX1 model faces severe competition with respect to price, timely delivery, and quality. Companies in the industry have high fixed costs, and persistent pressures to reduce selling prices and utilize capacity fully. Price reductions spur growth because it makes LICDs a cost-effective option in new applications such as digital subscriber lines (DSLs).

2. **Potential entrants into the market.** The small profit margins and high capital costs discourage new entrants. Moreover, incumbent companies such as Chipset are further down the learning curve with respect to lowering costs and building close relationships with customers and suppliers.

---

[1] M. Porter, *Competitive Strategy* (New York: Free Press, 1980); M. Porter, *Competitive Advantage* (New York: Free Press, 1985); and M. Porter, "What Is Strategy?" Harvard Business Review (November–December 1996): 61–78.

3. **Equivalent products.** Chipset tailors CX1 to customer needs and lowers prices by continuously improving CX1's design and processes to reduce production costs. This reduces the risk of equivalent products or new technologies replacing CX1.

4. **Bargaining power of customers.** Customers, such as EarthLink and Verizon, negotiate aggressively with Chipset and its competitors to keep prices down because they buy large quantities of product.

5. **Bargaining power of input suppliers.** To produce CX1, Chipset requires high-quality materials (such as silicon wafers, pins for connectivity, and plastic or ceramic packaging) and skilled engineers, technicians, and manufacturing labor. The skill-sets suppliers and employees bring gives them bargaining power to demand higher prices and wages.

In summary, strong competition and the bargaining powers of customers and suppliers put significant pressure on Chipset's selling prices. To respond to these challenges, Chipset must choose one of two basic strategies: *differentiating its product* or *achieving cost leadership.*

Product differentiation is an organization's ability to offer products or services perceived by its customers to be superior and unique relative to the products or services of its competitors. Apple has successfully differentiated its products in the electronics industry, as have Johnson & Johnson in the pharmaceutical industry and Coca-Cola in the soft drink industry. These companies have achieved differentiation through innovative product R&D, careful development and promotion of their brands, and the rapid push of products to market. Managers use differentiation to increase brand loyalty and charge higher prices.

Cost leadership is an organization's ability to achieve lower costs relative to competitors through productivity and efficiency improvements, elimination of waste, and tight cost control. Cost leaders in their respective industries include Wal-Mart (consumer retailing), Home Depot and Lowe's (building products), Texas Instruments (consumer electronics), and Emerson Electric (electric motors). These companies all provide products and services that are similar to—not differentiated from—those of their competitors, but they are provided at a lower cost to the customer. Lower selling prices, rather than unique products or services, provide a competitive advantage for these cost leaders.

To evaluate the success of its strategy, a company must trace the sources of its profitability to product differentiation or cost leadership. For example, an analysis of Porsche's profitability shows that the increase in its profitability is due to successful implementation of its product-differentiation strategy. Product differentiation enabled Porsche to increase its profit margins and grow sales. Changes in Home Depot's profitability are due to successful implementation of its cost-leadership strategy through productivity and quality improvements.

What strategy should Chipset follow? In order to make this decision, Chipset develops the customer preference map shown in Exhibit 12-1. The *y*-axis describes various attributes of the product desired by customers. The *x*-axis describes how well Chipset and Visilog, a competitor of Chipset that follows a product-differentiation strategy, do along the various attributes desired by customers from 1 (poor) to 5 (very good). The

Exhibit 12-1

Customer Preference
Map for LICDs

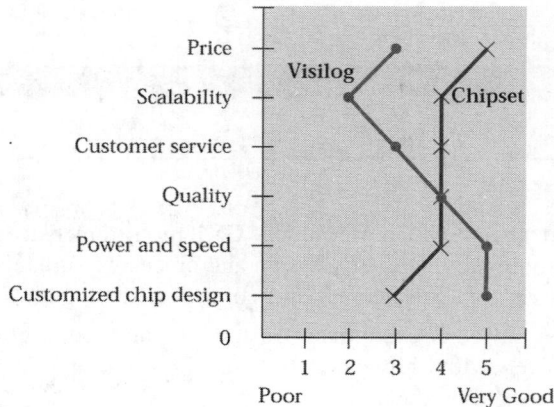

map highlights the trade-offs in any strategy. It shows the advantages CX1 enjoys in terms of price, scalability,[2] and customer service. Visilog's chips are, however, faster and more powerful and are customized for various applications such as different types of modems and communication networks.

CX1 is somewhat differentiated from competing products. Differentiating CX1 further would be costly, but Chipset may be able to charge a higher price. Conversely, reducing the cost of manufacturing CX1 would allow the Chipset to lower price, spur growth, and increase market share. The scalability of CX1 makes it an effective solution for meeting varying customer needs. Also, consistent with its strategy, Chipset has, over the years, recruited an engineering staff that is more skilled at making product and process improvements than at creatively designing new products and technologies. The market benefit from lowering prices by improving manufacturing efficiency through process improvements leads Chipset to choose a cost-leadership strategy.

To achieve its cost-leadership strategy, Chipset must improve its own internal capabilities. It must enhance quality and reengineer processes to downsize and eliminate excess capacity. At the same time, Chipset's management team does not want to make cuts in personnel that would hurt company morale and hinder future growth. We explore these in the next section.

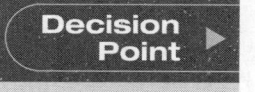

Decision Point ▶

What are two generic strategies a company can use?

Learning Objective 2

Understand what comprises reengineering

. . . redesigning business processes to improve performance by reducing cost and improving quality

Building Internal Capabilities: Quality Improvement and Reengineering at Chipset

To improve product quality—that is, to reduce defect rates and improve manufacturing yields—Chipset must maintain process parameters within tight ranges based on real-time data about manufacturing-process parameters, such as temperature and pressure. Chipset must also train its workers in quality-management techniques to identify the root causes of defects to take actions to improve quality.

The second component of Chipset's strategy is to reengineer its order-delivery process. Some of Chipset's customers have complained about the lengthening time span between ordering products and receiving them. **Reengineering** is the fundamental rethinking and

---

[2] The ability to achieve different performance levels by altering the number of CX1 units in a product.

redesign of business processes to achieve improvements in critical measures of performance, such as cost, quality, service, speed, and customer satisfaction.[3] To illustrate reengineering, consider the order-delivery system at Chipset in 2012. When Chipset received an order from a customer, a copy was sent to manufacturing, where a production scheduler began planning the manufacturing of the ordered products. Frequently, a considerable amount of time elapsed before equipment became available for production to begin. After manufacturing was complete, CX1 chips moved to the Shipping Department, which matched the quantities of CX1 to be shipped against customer orders. Often, completed CX1 chips stayed in inventory until a truck became available for shipment. If the quantity to be shipped was less than the number of chips the customer requested, the shipping department made a special shipment of the balance of the chips. Shipping documents moved to the Billing Department for issuing invoices. Special staff in the Accounting Department followed up with customers for payments.

The many transfers of CX1 chips and information across departments (sales, manufacturing, shipping, billing, and accounting) to satisfy a customer's order created delays. Moreover, no single individual was responsible for fulfilling each customer order. To respond to these challenges, Chipset formed a cross-functional team in late 2012 and implemented a reengineered order-delivery process in 2013.

Under the new system, each customer has a customer-relationship manager who negotiates long-term contracts with customers specifying quantities and prices. The customer-relationship manager works closely with the customer and with manufacturing to specify delivery schedules for CX1 one month in advance of shipment and sends the schedule of customer orders and delivery dates electronically to manufacturing. Completed chips are shipped directly from the manufacturing plant to customer. Each shipment automatically triggers an electronic invoice and customers electronically transfer funds to Chipset's bank.

Companies, such as AT&T, PepsiCo, and Siemens, have benefited significantly by reengineering their processes across design, production, and marketing (just as in the Chipset example). Reengineering has only limited benefits when reengineering efforts focus on only a single activity such as shipping or invoicing rather than the entire order-delivery process. To be successful, reengineering efforts must focus on changing roles and responsibilities, eliminating unnecessary activities and tasks, using information technology, and developing employee skills.

Take another look at Exhibit 12-1 and note the interrelatedness and consistency in Chipset's strategy. To help meet customer preferences for price, quality, and customer service, Chipset decides on a cost-leadership strategy. And to achieve cost leadership, Chipset builds internal capabilities by reengineering its processes. Chipset's next challenge is to effectively implement its strategy.

> ◀ **Decision Point**
>
> What is reengineering?

Strategy Implementation and the Balanced Scorecard

Many organizations, such as BP, and Dow Chemical, have introduced a *balanced scorecard* approach to manage the implementation of their strategies.

---

[3] See M. Hammer and J. Champy, *Reengineering the Corporation: A Manifesto for Business Revolution* (New York: Harper, 1993); E. Ruhli, C. Treichler, and S. Schmidt, "From Business Reengineering to Management Reengineering—A European Study," *Management International Review* (1995): 361–371; and K. Sandberg, "Reengineering Tries a Comeback—This Time for Growth, Not Just for Cost Savings," *Harvard Management Update* (November 2001).

**Learning
Objective 3**

Understand the four
perspectives of the bal-
anced scorecard

. . . financial, customer,
internal business pro-
cess, learning and
growth

The Balanced Scorecard

The **balanced scorecard** translates an organization's mission and strategy into a set of performance measures that provides the framework for implementing its strategy.[4] Not only
does the balanced scorecard focus on achieving financial objectives, it also highlights the
nonfinancial objectives that an organization must achieve to meet and sustain its financial
objectives. The scorecard measures an organization's performance from four perspectives:

1. **Financial**: the profits and value created for shareholders
2. **Customer**: the success of the company in its target market
3. **Internal business processes**: the internal operations that create value for customers
4. **Learning and growth**: the people and system capabilities that support operations

The measures that a company uses to track performance depend on its strategy. This set
of measures is called a "balanced scorecard" because it balances the use of financial and
nonfinancial performance measures to evaluate short-run and long-run performance in a
single report. The balanced scorecard reduces managers' emphasis on short-run financial
performance, such as quarterly earnings, because the key strategic nonfinancial and operational indicators, such as product quality and customer satisfaction, measure changes that a
company is making for the long run. The financial benefits of these long-run changes may
not appear immediately in short-run earnings; however, strong improvement in nonfinancial
measures usually indicates the creation of future economic value. For example, an increase
in customer satisfaction, as measured by customer surveys and repeat purchases, signals a
strong likelihood of higher sales and income in the future. By balancing the mix of financial and nonfinancial measures, the balanced scorecard broadens management's attention to
short-run *and* long-run performance. In many for-profit companies, the primary goal of the
balanced scorecard is to sustain long-term financial performance. Nonfinancial measures simply serve as leading indicators for the hard-to-measure long-run financial performance. Other
companies explicitly set long-term financial, social, and environmental goals. As we discuss
in a later section, these companies use the balanced scorecard to implement multiple goals.

Strategy Maps and the Balanced Scorecard

In this section, we use the Chipset example to develop strategy maps and the four perspectives of the balanced scorecard. The objectives and measures Chipset's managers choose
for each perspective relates to the action plans for furthering Chipset's cost leadership
strategy: *improving quality* and *reengineering processes*.

Strategy Maps

A useful first step in designing a balanced scorecard is a *strategy map*. A **strategy map** is a
diagram that describes how an organization creates value by connecting strategic objectives
in explicit cause-and-effect relationships with each other in the financial, customer, internal
business process, and learning and growth perspectives. Exhibit 12-2 presents Chipset's

---

[4] See R. S. Kaplan and D. P. Norton, *The Balanced Scorecard* (Boston: Harvard Business School Press, 1996); R. S. Kaplan and
D. P. Norton, *The Strategy-Focused Organization: How Balanced Scorecard Companies Thrive in the New Business Environment*
(Boston: Harvard Business School Press, 2001); R. S. Kaplan and D. P. Norton, *Strategy Maps: Converting Intangible Assets
into Tangible Outcomes* (Boston: Harvard Business School Press, 2004); R. S. Kaplan and D. P. Norton, *Alignment: Using the
Balanced Scorecard to Create Corporate Synergies* (Boston: Harvard Business School Press, 2006).

For simplicity, this chapter, and much of the literature, emphasizes long-run financial objectives as the primary goal of for-
profit companies. For-profit companies interested in long-run financial, environmental, and social objectives adapt the balanced
scorecard to implement all three objectives, as we discuss in a later section.

strategy map. Follow the arrows to see how a strategic objective affects other strategic objectives. For example, empowering the workforce helps align employee and organization goals and improves processes which, improves manufacturing quality and productivity, reduce customer delivery time, meet specified delivery dates, and improve post-sales service, all of which increase customer satisfaction. Improving manufacturing quality and productivity grows operating income directly and also increases customer satisfaction that, in turn, increases market share, operating income, and shareholder value.

To compete successfully, Chipset invests in its employees, implements new technology and process controls, improves quality, and reengineers processes. The strategy map helps Chipset evaluate whether these activities are generating financial returns.

Chipset could include many other cause-and-effect relationships in the strategy map in Exhibit 12-2. But, Chipset, like other companies implementing the balanced scorecard, focuses on only those relationships that it believes to be the most significant so that the scorecard does not become unwieldy and difficult to understand.

Exhibit 12-2   Strategy Map for Chipset, Inc., for 2013

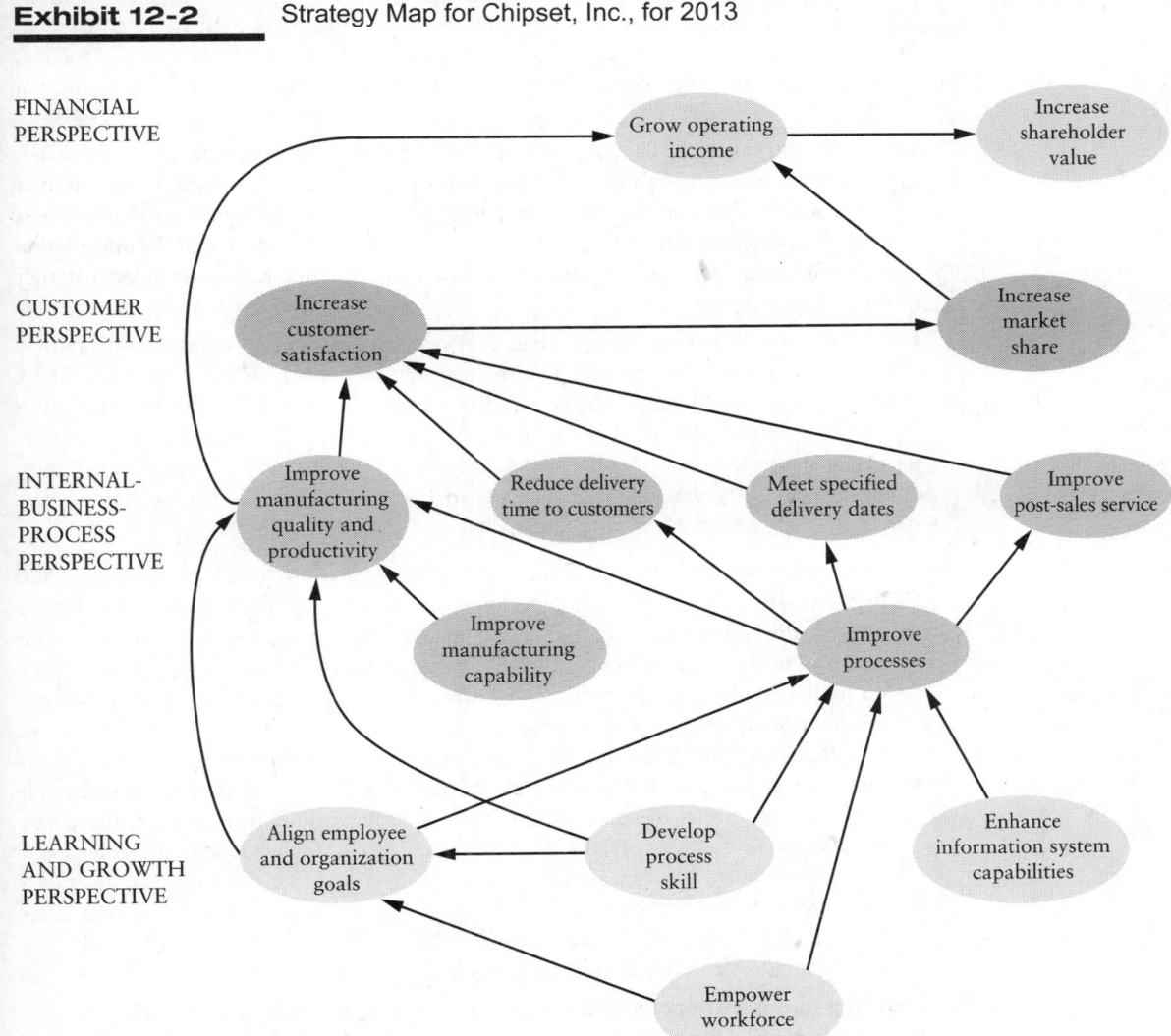

Chipset uses the strategy map from Exhibit 12-2 to build the balanced scorecard presented in Exhibit 12-3. The scorecard highlights the four perspectives of performance: financial, customer, internal business process, and learning and growth. The first column presents the strategic objectives from the strategy map in Exhibit 12-2. At the beginning of 2013, the company's managers specify the strategic objectives, measures, initiatives (the actions necessary to achieve the objectives), and target performance (the first four columns of Exhibit 12-3).

Chipset wants to use the balanced scorecard targets to drive the organization to higher levels of performance. Managers therefore set targets at a level of performance that is achievable, yet distinctly better than competitors. Chipset's managers complete the fifth column, reporting actual performance at the end of 2013. This column compares Chipset's performance relative to target.

Four Perspectives of the Balanced Scorecard

We next describe the perspectives in general terms and illustrate each perspective using the measures chosen by Chipset in the context of its strategy.

1. **Financial perspective.** This perspective evaluates the profitability of the strategy and the creation of shareholder value. Because Chipset's key strategic initiatives are cost reduction relative to competitors' costs and sales growth, the financial perspective focuses on how much operating income results from reducing costs and selling more units of CX1.

2. **Customer perspective.** This perspective identifies targeted customer and market segments and measures the company's success in these segments. To monitor its customer objectives, Chipset's managers use (a) market research such as surveys and interviews to determine market share in the communication-networks segment, and (b) information about the number of new customers, and customer-satisfaction ratings from its customer management systems.

3. **Internal-business-process perspective.** This perspective focuses on internal operations that create value for customers that, in turn, help achieve financial performance. Managers at Chipset determine internal-business-process improvement targets after benchmarking against its main competitors. Benchmarking involves getting information about competitors from published financial statements, prevailing prices, customers, suppliers, former employees, industry experts, and financial analysts. The internal-business-process perspective comprises three subprocesses:

   - **Innovation process:** Creating products, services, and processes that will meet the needs of customers. This is a very important process for companies that follow a product-differentiation strategy and must constantly design and develop innovative new products to remain competitive in the marketplace. Chipset's innovation focuses on improving its manufacturing capability and process controls to lower costs and improve quality. Chipset measures innovation by the number of improvements in manufacturing processes and percentage of processes with advanced controls.
   - **Operations process:** Producing and delivering existing products and services that will meet the needs of customers. Chipset's strategic initiatives are (a) improving manufacturing quality, (b) reducing delivery time to customers, and (c) meeting specified delivery dates so it measures yield, order-delivery time, and on-time deliveries.
   - **Postsales-service process:** Providing service and support to the customer after the sale of a product or service. Chipset monitors how quickly and accurately it is responding to customer-service requests.

4. **Learning-and-growth perspective.** This perspective identifies the capabilities necessary for organization to learn, improve and grow. These capabilities help achieve superior

| **Exhibit 12-3** | The Balanced Scorecard for Chipset, Inc., for 2013 |

Strategic Objectives	Measures	Initiatives	Target Performance	Actual Performance
Financial Perspective				
Grow operating income	Operating income from productivity gain	Manage costs and unused capacity	₹1,85,00,000	₹1,91,25,000
	Operating income from growth	Build strong customer relationships	₹2,50,00,000	₹2,82,00,000
Increase shareholder value	Revenue growth		9%	10%[a]
Customer Perspective				
Increase market share	Market share in communication-networks segment	Identify future needs of customers	6%	7%
Increase customer satisfaction	Number of new customers	Identify new target-customer segments	1	1[b]
	Customer-satisfaction ratings	Increase customer focus of sales organization	90% of customers give top two ratings	87% of customers give top two ratings
Internal-Business-Process Perspective				
Improve postsales service	Service response time	Improve customer-service process	Within 4 hours	Within 3 hours
Improve manufacturing quality and productivity	Yield	Identify root causes of problems and improve quality	78%	79.3%
Reduce delivery time to customers	Order-delivery time	Reengineer order-delivery process	30 days	30 days
Meet specified delivery dates	On-time delivery	Reengineer order-delivery process	92%	90%
Improve processes	Number of major improvements in manufacturing and business processes	Organize teams from manufacturing and sales to modify processes	5	5
Improve manufacturing capability	Percentage of processes with advanced controls	Organize R&D/manufacturing teams to implement advanced controls	75%	75%
Learning-and-Growth Perspective				
Align employee and organization goals	Employee-satisfaction ratings	Employee participation and suggestions program to build teamwork	80% of employees give top two ratings	88% of employees give top two ratings
Empower workforce	Percentage of line workers empowered to manage processes	Have supervisors act as coaches rather than decision makers	85%	90%
Develop process skill	Percentage of employees trained in process and quality management	Employee training programs	90%	92%
Enhance information-system capabilities	Percentage of manufacturing processes with real-time feedback	Improve online and offline data gathering	80%	80%

[a](Revenues in 2013 + Revenues in 2012) ÷ Revenues in 2012 = (₹25,30,00,000 + ₹23,00,00,000) ÷ ₹23,00,00,000 = 10%.

[b]Number of customers increased from seven to eight in 2013.

internal processes that in turn create value for customers and shareholders. Chipset's learning and growth perspective emphasizes three capabilities:

- information-system capabilities, measured by the percentage of manufacturing processes with real-time feedback;
- employee capabilities, measured by the percentage of employees trained in process and quality management; and
- motivation, measured by employee satisfaction and the percentage of manufacturing and sales employees (line employees) empowered to manage processes.

The arrows in Exhibit 12-3 indicate the *broad* cause-and-effect linkages: how gains in the learning-and-growth perspective lead to improvements in internal business processes, which lead to higher customer satisfaction and market share, and finally lead to superior financial performance. Note how the scorecard describes elements of Chipset's strategy implementation. Worker training and empowerment improve employee satisfaction and lead to manufacturing and business-process improvements that improve quality and reduce delivery time, which, in turn, results in increased customer satisfaction and higher market share. Exhibit 12-3 indicates that Chipset's actions have been successful from a financial perspective. Chipset has earned significant operating income from its cost leadership strategy, and that strategy has also led to growth.

To sustain long-run financial performance, a company must strengthen all links across its different balanced scorecard perspectives. For example, Indigo Airlines' high employee satisfaction levels and low employee turnover (learning-and-growth perspective) lead to greater efficiency and customer-friendly service (internal-business-process perspective) that enhances customer satisfaction (customer perspective) and boosts profits and return on investment (financial perspective).

A major benefit of the balanced scorecard is that it promotes causal thinking as described in the previous paragraph—where improvement in one activity causes an improvement in another. Think of the balanced scorecard as a *linked scorecard* or a *causal scorecard*. Managers must search for empirical evidence (rather than rely on faith alone) to test the validity and strength of the various connections. A causal scorecard enables a company to focus on the key drivers that steer the implementation of the strategy. Without convincing links, the scorecard loses much of its value.

Implementing a Balanced Scorecard

To successfully implement a balanced scorecard, subordinate managers and executives require commitment and leadership from top management. At Chipset, the vice president of strategic planning headed the team building the balanced scorecard. The team conducted interviews with senior managers, asked executives about customers, competitors, and technological developments, and sought proposals for balanced scorecard objectives across the four perspectives. The team then met to discuss the responses and to build a prioritized list of objectives.

In a meeting with all senior managers, the team sought to achieve consensus on the scorecard objectives. The vice president of strategic management than divided senior management into four groups, with each group responsible for one of the perspectives. In addition, each group broadened the base of inputs by including representatives from the next-lower levels of management and key functional managers. The groups identified measures for each objective and the sources of information for each measure. The groups then met to finalize scorecard objectives, measures, targets, and the initiatives to achieve the targets. Management accountants played an important role in the design and implementation of the balanced scorecard, particularly in determining measures to represent the realities of the business. This required management accountants to understand the economic environment of the industry, Chipset's customers and competitors, and internal business issues such as human resources, operations, and distribution.

Managers made sure that employees understood the scorecard and the scorecard process. The final balanced scorecard was communicated to all employees. Sharing the scorecard allowed engineers and operating personnel, for example, to understand the reasons for customer satisfaction and dissatisfaction and to make suggestions for improving internal processes directly aimed at satisfying customers and implementing Chipset's strategy. Too often, scorecards are seen by only a select group of managers. By limiting the scorecard's exposure, an organization loses the opportunity for widespread organization engagement and alignment. Companies likes Citibank share their scorecards widely across their departments and divisions.

Chipset also encourages each department to develop its own scorecard that ties into Chipset's main scorecard described in Exhibit 12-3. For example, the quality control department's scorecard has measures that its department managers use to improve quality—number of quality circles, statistical process control charts, Pareto diagrams, and root-cause analyses (see Chapter 19 for more deatils). Department scorecards help align actions that each department needs to perform to implement Chipset's strategy.

Companies frequently use balanced scorecards to evaluate and reward managerial performance and to thereby influence a managerial behavior. Using the balanced scorecard for performance evaluation widens the performance management lens and motivates managers to give greater attention to nonfinancial drivers of performance. Surveys indicate, however, that companies continue to assign more weight to the financial perspective (55%) than to the other perspectives—customer (19%), internal business process (12%), and learning and growth (14%). Companies cite several reasons for this—difficulty evaluating the relative importance of different measures, challenges in measuring and quantifying qualitative, nonfinancial data, and problems in compensating managers despite poor financial performance (see Chapter 23 for a more detailed discussion of performance evaluation). More and more companies in the manufacturing, merchandising, and service sectors are giving greater weight to nonfinancial measures when promoting employees because they believe that nonfinancial measures—such as customer satisfaction, process improvements, and employee motivation—better assess a manager's potential to succeed at senior levels of management. As this trend continues, operating managers will put more weight on nonfinancial factors when making decisions even though these factors carry smaller weights when determining their annual compensation. For the balanced scorecard to be effective, managers must view it as fairly assessing and rewarding all important aspects of a manager's performance and promotion prospects.

Different Strategies Lead to Different Scorecards

Recall that while Chipset follows a cost-leadership strategy, its competitor Visilog, follows a product-differentiation strategy by designing custom chips for modems and communication networks. Visilog designs its balanced scorecard to fit its strategy. For example, in the financial perspective, Visilog evaluates how much of its operating income comes from charging premium prices for its products. In the customer perspective, Visilog measures the percentage of its revenues from new products and new customers. In the internal-business-process perspective, Visilog measures the number of new products introduced and new product development time. In the learning-and-growth perspective, Visilog measures the development of advanced manufacturing capabilities to produce custom chips. Visilog also uses some of the measures described in Chipset's balanced scorecard in Exhibit 12-3. For example, revenue growth, customer satisfaction ratings, order-delivery time, on-time

Exhibit 12-4 Frequently Cited Balanced Scorecard Measures	***Financial Perspective*** *Income measures:* Operating income, gross margin percentage *Revenue and cost measures:* Revenue growth, revenues from new products, cost reductions in key ar *Income and investment measures:* Economic value added (EVA)[a] Return on investment ***Customer Perspective*** Market share, customer satisfaction, customer-retention percentage, time taken to fulfill customers' requests, number of customer complaints ***Internal-Business-Process Perspective*** *Innovation Process:* Operating capabilities, number of new products or services, new-product development times, and number of new patents *Operations Process:* Yield, defect rates, time taken to deliver product to customers, percentage of on- deliveries, average time taken to respond to orders, setup time, manufacturing downtime *Postsales Service Process:* Time taken to replace or repair defective products, hours of customer trai for using the product ***Learning-and-Growth Perspective*** *Employee measures:* Employee education and skill levels, employee-satisfaction ratings, employee turnover rates, percentage of employee suggestions implemented, percentage of compensation base individual and team incentives *Technology measures:* Information system availability, percentage of processes with advanced contr

[a] This measure is described in Chapter 23.

delivery, percentage of frontline workers empowered to manage processes, and employee-satisfaction ratings are also important measures under the product-differentiation strategy. The goal is to align the balanced scorecard with company strategy.[5] Exhibit 12-4 presents some common measures found on company scorecards in the service, retail, and manufacturing sectors.

Environmental and Social Performance and the Balanced Scorecard

Companies are increasingly recognizing that they must continually earn the right to operate in the communities and countries in which they do business. Failure to perform adequately on environmental and social processes puts at risk a company's ability to deliver future value to shareholders. Citizens and governments are becoming much more active in pushing companies to live up to and to report on what they see as their environmental and social obligations.

As we discussed in Chapter 1, many managers are promoting sustainability—the development and implementation of strategies to achieve:

- Long-term financial performance
- Social performance, such as minimizing employee injuries, improving product safety, and eliminating corruption
- Environmental performance, such as reducing greenhouse gas emissions and non-recycled waste

There are a wide variety of opinions on this issue. Some believe that managers should only focus on long-run financial performance and not be distracted by pursuing social and environmental goals beyond the minimum levels required by law. Others believe that

---

[5] For simplicity, we have presented the balanced scorecard in the context of companies that have followed either a cost-leadership or a product-differentiation strategy. Of course, a company may have some products for which cost leadership is critical and other products for which product differentiation is important. The company will then develop separate scorecards to implement the different product strategies. In still other contexts, product differentiation may be of primary importance, but some cost leadership must also be achieved. The balanced scorecard measures would then be linked in a cause-and-effect way to this strategy.

managers must act to attain environmental and social objectives beyond what is legally required, while achieving good financial performance—often called the *triple bottom line*—as part of a company's social responsibility. Still others believe that there is no conflict between achieving social and environmental goals and long-run financial performance.

Many managers recognize that good environmental and social performance helps to attract and inspire outstanding employees, improves employee safety and health, increases productivity, and lowers operating costs. Environmental and social performance also enhances a company's reputation with socially conscious customers and investors and boosts its image with governments and citizens, all contributing to long-run financial performance. Experienced financial analysts are publishing favorable reports about companies with strong environmental and social performance because of their greater transparency and engagement with multiple stakeholders. A distinguishing organizational characteristic of companies that emphasize environmental and social performance is their long-term orientation. Some recent research suggests that taking the long-term view and engaging with multiple stakeholders results in superior financial performance. Companies, such as Natura, China Light & Power, and Dow Chemical, that focus on the triple bottom line of financial, environmental, and social performance benefit from innovating in technologies, processes, products, and business models to reduce the trade-offs between financial and sustainability goals. These companies also build transformational and transitional leadership and change capabilities needed to implement the strategies to achieve the triple bottom line.

Managers interested in measuring environmental and social performance are incorporating these factors into their balanced scorecards to set priorities for initiatives, guide decisions and actions, and fuel discussions around strategies and business models to improve performance. Suppose Chipset decides to emphasize environmental and social goals in its balanced scorecard. What measures might it add to the balanced scorecard presented in Exhibit 12-3? Chipset, like all companies that emphasize environmental and social goals, integrates its sustainability goals and measures presented in Exhibit 12-5 with the business goals and measures presented in Exhibit 12-3 into a single scorecard. Chipset gains the following benefits from measuring environmental and social performance.

1. **Creating shared value.** A major benefit of measuring environmental and social performance is the opportunity it provides to create shared value[6]—recognizing that the competitiveness of Chipset and its social activities are mutually dependent. In this view, achieving environmental and social objectives is seen as providing strategic advantage to the business. For example, reducing greenhouse gas emissions motivates Chipset to redesign its product and processes to reduce energy consumption. Measuring non-recycled hazardous and nonhazardous waste prompts Chipset to work with its suppliers to redesign and reduce packaging and toxic substances in its materials and components. Measuring worker-related injuries and illnesses motivates Chipset to redesign processes to lessen the number of such incidents. In each of these initiatives, Chipset achieves environmental and social goals as well as gains competitive advantage by pushing itself to innovate and building a social and environmental value proposition into its business strategy.

2. **Identifying cause-and-effect relationships to evaluate benefits.** Together with developing the kinds of skills in processes and information systems described in Exhibit 12-3, Chipset's top management creates a culture that encourages hiring employees from a wide variety of backgrounds, particularly women and minorities. This furthers

[6] Porter, M., and M. Kramer. 2011. Creating shared value: Redefining capitalism and the role of the corporation in society. *Harvard Business Review*, January/February, Volume 89, Issue 1/2, pp. 62–77.

Exhibit 12-5	Environmental and Social Balanced Scorecard Measures for Chipset, Inc., for 2013

Strategic Objectives	Measures	Initiatives	Target Performance	Actual Performance
Financial Perspective				
Reduce waste	Cost savings from reducing energy use and waste	Quality improvement programs	₹40,00,000	₹41,50,000
Reduce cost of time lost from work injuries and illness	Cost savings from fewer work injuries and illness	Train workers in safety methods and hygiene	₹5,00,000	₹5,50,000
Customer Perspective				
Enhance reputation for sustainability with customers	Percentage of customers giving top two ratings for environmental and social performance	Communicate environmental and social goals and performance	90%	92%
Internal-Business-Process Perspective				
Reduce greenhouse gas emissions	Greenhouse gas emissions per million dollars of sales	Increase energy efficiency and reduce carbon footprint by planting trees	27 grams/₹10 million of sales	25.6 grams/₹10 million of sales
Reduce operational waste not recycled	Hazardous and non-hazardous waste not recycled per million dollars of sales	Increase recycling programs and redesign products	130 grams/₹10 million of sales	126 grams/₹10 million of sales
Reduce work-related injuries and illnesses	Days of lost time per worker per year due to injury or illness	Redesign processes to improve worker safety and hygiene	0.20 days per worker per year	0.18 days per worker per year
Learning-and-Growth Perspective				
Inspiring employees through environmental and social goals	Percentage of employees giving top two ratings for environmental and social performance	Training employees about environmental and social benefits	87%	90%
Diversity of employees	Percentage of women and minorities in managerial positions	Develop human resource practices to support mentoring and coaching for women and minorities	40%	42%

the company's social goals but also gives it access to top talent from a broad cross-section of society. The company trains and mentors employees to create shared value. This training improves internal business processes to decrease greenhouse gases, hazardous and nonhazardous waste, and work-related injuries. These actions, in turn, improve customer measures such as Chipset's reputation for sustainability with customers and customer satisfaction. The financial benefits are the cost savings from shared value such as lower energy consumption and waste. If Chipset can measure growth in revenue or operating income from customers attracted to Chipset's environmental and social actions with reasonable accuracy, the company might add that measure in its financial perspective. The scorecard shows that Chipset has achieved all its environmental and social goals, indicating that its environmental and social actions are translating into financial gains. These results would encourage Chipset to continue its environmental and social efforts.

3. **Reducing risks.** A final benefit of measuring environmental and social performance is to help manage downside risk by acting as a good corporate citizen. This involves being responsive to different stakeholders and reducing any adverse environmental or social effects of business activities. For example, reducing greenhouse gases might ward off fines or more stringent carbon emission caps from the U.S. environmental protection agency. Increase in greenhouse gases or waste might result in fines and lawsuits and lead to negative media attention and stakeholder activism that damages a company's reputation.

Companies use a variety of measures for environmental and social performance in addition to the ones described in the Chipset example:

1. **Financial perspective.** Cost of preventing and remediating environmental damage (training, cleanup, legal costs, and costs of consumer boycotts); cost of recycled materials to total cost of materials

2. **Customer perspective.** Brand image (percentage of survey respondents who rate the company high on trust)

3. **Internal-business perspective.** Energy consumption (joules per ₹10,000 of sales), water use (millions of cubic meters); waste water discharge (thousands of cubic meters); individual quantities of different greenhouse gases, for example, carbon dioxide, nitrous oxide, sulphur dioxide (grams per ₹10 million in sales); number of environmental incidents (such as unexpected discharge of air, water, or solid waste); codes of conduct violations (percentage of total employees); contributions to community-based nonprofit organizations; number of joint ventures and partnerships between the company and community organizations

4. **Learning-and-growth perspective.** Implementation of ISO 14000 environmental management standards (subjective score); employees trained and certified in codes of conduct (percentage of total employees); employees trained in United Nations global compact, for example, human rights, fair wage, no child labor, corruption and bribery prevention (percentage of total employees)

Features of a Good Balanced Scorecard

A well-designed balanced scorecard has several features:

1. It tells the story of a company's strategy, articulating a sequence of cause-and-effect relationships—the links among the various perspectives that align implementation of the strategy. In for-profit companies, each measure in the scorecard is part of a cause-and-effect chain leading to financial outcomes. Not-for-profit organizations such as World Bank design the cause-and-effect chain to achieve their strategic service objectives—for example, reducing the number of people in poverty, or raising high school graduation rates.

2. The balanced scorecard helps to communicate the strategy to all members of the organization by translating the strategy into a coherent and linked set of understandable

and measurable operational targets. Guided by the scorecard, managers and employees take actions and make decisions to achieve the company's strategy. Companies that have distinct strategic business units (SBUs)—such as consumer products and pharmaceuticals at Johnson & Johnson—develop their balanced scorecards at the SBU level. Each SBU has its own unique strategy and implementation goals, so building separate scorecards allows managers of each SBU to choose measures that help implement its distinctive strategy.

3. In for-profit companies, the balanced scorecard must motivate managers to take actions that eventually result in improvements in financial performance. Managers sometimes tend to focus too much on quality, and customer satisfaction as ends in themselves. For example, Xerox discovered that higher customer satisfaction, through service guarantees, did not increase customer loyalty and financial returns because customers also wanted product innovations, such as high-speed color printing, that met their needs. Some companies use statistical methods, such as regression analysis, to test the anticipated cause-and-effect relationships among various nonfinancial measures and financial measures. The data for this analysis can come from either time series data (collected over time) or cross-sectional data (collected, for example, across multiple stores of a retail chain). In the Chipset example, improvements in nonfinancial factors have, in fact, already led to improvements in financial factors.

4. The balanced scorecard limits the number of measures, identifying only the most critical ones. Chipset's scorecard, for example, has 16 measures, between 3 and 6 measures for each perspective. Limiting the number of measures focuses managers' attention on those that most affect strategy implementation. Using too many measures makes it difficult for managers to process relevant information.

5. The balanced scorecard highlights less-than-optimal trade-offs that managers may make when they fail to consider operational and financial measures together. For example, a company with a strategy of innovation and product differentiation spends a lot of money on R&D. That company could achieve superior short-run financial performance by reducing spending on R&D. A good balanced scorecard would signal that the short-run financial performance might have been achieved by taking actions that hurt future financial performance because a leading indicator of that performance, R&D spending and R&D output, has declined.

Pitfalls in Implementing a Balanced Scorecard

Pitfalls to avoid in implementing a balanced scorecard include the following:

1. Managers should not assume the cause-and-effect linkages are precise. These linkages are merely hypotheses. Over time, a company must gather evidence of the strength and timing of the linkages among the nonfinancial and financial measures. With experience, organizations should alter their scorecards to include those nonfinancial objectives and measures that are the best leading indicators (the causes) of financial performance (a lagging indicator or effect). Understanding that the scorecard evolves over time helps managers to avoid unproductively spending time and money trying to design the "perfect" scorecard at the outset. Moreover, as the business environment and strategy change over time, the measures in the scorecard will also need to change. For example, when Sandoz, a manufacturer of generic pharmaceutical chemicals, shifted its strategy to produce biologic medicines that required significant investment in new technologies and patient trials, its balanced scorecard also changed from only emphasizing productivity and cost efficiency to also measuring innovation.

2. Managers should not seek improvements across all of the measures all of the time. For example, strive for quality and on-time performance but not beyond a point at which further improvement in these objectives is so costly that it is inconsistent with long-run profit maximization. Cost-benefit considerations should always be a central element when designing a balanced scorecard.

3. Managers should not use only objective measures in the balanced scorecard. Chipset's balanced scorecard includes both objective measures (such as operating income from cost leadership, market share, and manufacturing yield) and subjective measures (such as customer- and employee-satisfaction ratings). When using subjective measures, however, managers must be careful that the benefits of this potentially rich information are not lost by using measures that are inaccurate or that can be easily manipulated.

4. Despite challenges of measurement, top management should not ignore nonfinancial measures when evaluating managers and other employees. Managers tend to focus on the measures used to reward their performance. Excluding nonfinancial measures (such as customer satisfaction or product quality) when evaluating performance will reduce the significance and importance that managers give to nonfinancial measures.

> **◀ Decision Point**
>
> How can an organization translate its strategy into a set of performance measures?

Evaluating the Success of Strategy and Implementation

To evaluate how successful Chipset's strategy and its implementation have been, its management compares the target- and actual-performance columns in the balanced scorecard (Exhibit 12-3). Chipset met most targets set on the basis of competitor benchmarks in 2013 itself because, improvements in Chipset's learning and growth perspective quickly ripple through to the financial perspective. While Chipset will continue to seek improvements to achieve the targets it did not achieve, managers were satisfied that the strategic initiatives that Chipset identified and measured for learning and growth resulted in improvements in internal business processes, customer measures, and financial performance.

How would Chipset know if it had problems in strategy implementation? If it did not meet its targets on the two perspectives that are more internally focused: learning and growth and internal business processes.

What if Chipset performed well on learning and growth and internal business processes, but customer measures and financial performance in this year and the next still did not improve? Chipset's managers would then conclude that Chipset did a good job of implementation as the various internal nonfinancial measures it targeted improved, but that its strategy was faulty (there was no effect on customers or on long-run financial performance and value creation). In this case, management failed to identify the correct causal links and it did a good job implementing the wrong strategy. Management would then reevaluate the strategy and the factors that drive it.

Strategic Analysis of Operating Income

As we have discussed, Chipset performed well on its various nonfinancial measures, and operating income over this year and the next also increased. Chipset's managers might be tempted to declare the cost-leadership strategy a success, but, in fact, they cannot conclude with any confidence that Chipset successfully formulated and implemented its intended strategy. Operating income could have increased simply because prices of inputs decreased

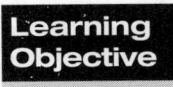

Learning Objective 4

Analyze changes in operating income to evaluate strategy

...growth, price recovery, and productivity

or the entire market expanded. Alternatively, a company that has chosen a cost-leadership strategy, like Chipset, may find that its operating-income increase actually resulted from some degree of product differentiation. *To evaluate the success of a strategy, managers and management accountants need to link strategy to the sources of operating-income increases.* These are the kinds of details that top management and boards of directors routinely discuss in their meetings when evaluating performance. Managers who have mastered the strategic analysis of operating income changes gain an understanding of the levers of strategy and strategy implementation that help them deliver sustained operating performance.

For Chipset managers to conclude that they were successful in implementing their strategy, they must demonstrate that improvements in the company's financial performance and operating income over time resulted from achieving targeted cost savings and growth in market share. Fortunately, the top two rows of Chipset's balanced scorecard in Exhibit 12-3 show that operating-income gains from productivity (₹1,91,25,000) and growth (₹2,82,00,000) exceeded targets. (The next section of this chapter describes how these numbers were calculated.) Because its strategy has been successful, Chipset's management can be more confident that the gains will be sustained in subsequent years.

Chipset's management accountants subdivide changes in operating income into components that can be identified with product differentiation, cost leadership, and growth. Managers look to growth because successful product differentiation or cost leadership generally increases market share and helps a company to grow. Subdividing the change in operating income to evaluate the success of a strategy is conceptually similar to the variance analysis discussed in Chapters 7 and 8. One difference, however, is that management accountants compare actual operating performance over *two different periods,* not actual to budgeted numbers in the *same time period* as in variance analysis.[7] A second difference is that the analysis in this section breaks down changes in operating income rather than focusing on differences in individual categories of costs (direct materials, direct manufacturing labor, and overheads) as we did in Chapters 7 and 8.

We next explain how the change in operating income from one period to *any* future period can be subdivided into product differentiation, cost leadership, and growth components.[8] We illustrate the analysis using data from 2012 and 2013 because Chipset implemented key elements of its strategy in late 2012 and early 2013 and expects the financial consequences of these strategies to occur in 2013. Suppose the financial consequences of these strategies had been expected to affect operating income in only 2014. Then we could just as easily have compared 2012 to 2014. If necessary, we could also have compared 2012 to 2013 and 2014 taken together.

Chipset's data for 2012 and 2013 follow:

		2012	2013
1.	Units of CX1 produced and sold	10,00,000	11,50,000
2.	Selling price	₹270	₹250
3.	Direct materials (square centimeters of silicon wafers)	30,00,000	29,00,000
4.	Direct material cost per square centimeter	₹14	₹15
5.	Manufacturing processing capacity (in square centimeters of silicon wafer)	37,50,000	35,00,000
6.	Conversion costs (all manufacturing costs other than direct material costs)	₹16,05,00,000	₹15,22,50,000
7.	Conversion cost per unit of capacity (Row 6 ÷ Row 5)	₹42.8	₹3.5

---

[7] Other examples of focusing on actual performance over two periods rather than comparisons of actuals with budgets can be found in J. Hope and R. Fraser, *Beyond Budgeting* (Boston, MA: Harvard Business School Press, 2003).

[8] For other details, see R. Banker, S. Datar, and R. Kaplan, "Productivity Measurement and Management Accounting," *Journal of Accounting, Auditing and Finance* (1989): 528–554; and A. Hayzen and J. Reeve, "Examining the Relationships in Productivity Accounting," *Management Accounting Quarterly* (2000): 32–39.

Chipset provides the following additional information.

1. Conversion costs for each year depend on production capacity defined in terms of the quantity of square centimeters of silicon wafers that can be processed. These costs do not vary with the actual quantity of silicon wafers processed.

2. Chipset incurs no R&D costs. Its marketing, sales, and customer-service costs are small relative to the other costs. Chipset has 8 customers, each purchasing roughly the same quantities of CX1. Because of the highly technical nature of the product, Chipset uses a cross-functional team for its marketing, sales, and customer-service activities. This cross-functional approach ensures that, although marketing, sales, and customer-service costs are small, the entire Chipset organization, including manufacturing engineers, remains focused on increasing customer satisfaction and market share. (The Problem for Self-Study at the end of this chapter describes a situation in which marketing, sales, and customer-service costs are significant.)

3. Chipset's asset structure is very similar in 2012 and 2013.

4. Operating income for each year is as follows:

	2012	2013
Revenues		
(₹230 per unit × 10,00,000 units; ₹220 per unit × 11,50,000 units) Costs	₹23,00,00,000	₹25,30,00,000
Direct material costs		
(₹14/sq. cm. × 30,00,000 sq. cm.; ₹15/sq. cm. × 29,00,000 sq. cm.) Conversion costs	4,20,00,000	4,35,00,000
(₹42.8/sq. cm. × 37,50,000 sq. cm.; ₹43.5/sq. cm. × 35,00,000 sq. cm.)	16,05,00,000	15,22,50,000
R&D costs (₹10,00,000 × 40 employees; ₹10,00,000 × 39 employees)	4,00,00,000	3,90,00,000
Total costs	20,25,00,000	19,57,50,000
Operating income	₹2,75,00,000	₹5,72,50,000
Change in operating income	₹2,97,50,000 F	

The goal of Chipset's managers is to evaluate how much of the ₹2,97,50,000 increase in operating income was caused by the successful implementation of the company's cost-leadership strategy. To do this, management accountants analyze three main factors: (1) growth, (2) price recovery, and (3) productivity.

The **growth component** measures the change in operating income attributable solely to the change in the quantity of output sold between 2012 and 2013. The **price-recovery component** measures the change in operating income attributable solely to changes in Chipset's prices of inputs and outputs between 2012 and 2013. The **price-recovery component** measures change in output price compared with changes in input prices. A company that has successfully pursued a strategy of product differentiation will be able to increase its output price faster than the increase in its input prices, boosting profit margins and operating income: The company will show a large positive price-recovery component.

The **productivity component** measures the change in costs attributable to a change in the quantity of inputs used in 2013 relative to the quantity of inputs that would have been used in 2012 to produce the 2013 output. The productivity component measures the amount by which operating income increases by using inputs efficiently to lower costs. A company that has successfully pursued a strategy of cost leadership will be able to produce a given quantity of output with a lower cost of inputs and will show a large positive productivity component. Given Chipset's strategy of cost leadership, managers expect the increase in operating income to be attributable to the productivity and growth components, not to price recovery. We now examine these three components in detail.

Growth Component of Change in Operating Income

The growth component of the change in operating income measures the increase in revenues minus the increase in costs from selling more units of CX1 in 2013 (11,50,000 units) than in 2012 (10,00,000 units), *assuming nothing else has changed.*

Revenue effect of growth

$$\text{Revenue effect of growth} = \left(\begin{array}{c}\text{Actual units of}\\\text{output sold}\\\text{in 2013}\end{array} - \begin{array}{c}\text{Actual units of}\\\text{output sold}\\\text{in 2012}\end{array}\right) \times \begin{array}{c}\text{Selling}\\\text{price}\\\text{in 2010}\end{array}$$

$$= (11,50,000 \text{ units} - 10,00,000 \text{ units}) \times ₹230 \text{ per unit}$$

$$= ₹34,50,000 \text{ F}$$

This growth component is favorable (F) because the increase in output sold in 2013 increases operating income. Components that decrease operating income are unfavorable (U).

Note that Chipset uses the 2012 price of CX1 here and focuses only on the increase in units sold between 2012 and 2013, because the objective of the revenue effect of the growth component measures how much revenues would have changed in 2012 if Chipset had sold 11,50,000 units instead of 10,00,000 units.

Cost effect of growth

The cost effect of growth measures how much costs would have changed in 2012 if Chipset had produced 11,50,000 units of CX1 instead of 10,00,000 units. To measure the cost effect of growth, Chipset's managers distinguish variable costs such as direct material costs from fixed costs such as conversion costs and R&D costs because as units produced (and sold) increase, variable costs increase proportionately but fixed costs, generally, do not change.

$$\text{Cost effect of growth for variable costs} = \left(\begin{array}{c}\text{Units of input}\\\text{required to}\\\text{produce 2013}\\\text{output in 2012}\end{array} - \begin{array}{c}\text{Actual units of}\\\text{input used}\\\text{to produce}\\\text{2012 output}\end{array}\right) \times \begin{array}{c}\text{Input}\\\text{price}\\\text{in 2012}\end{array}$$

$$\text{Cost effect of growth for direct materials} = \left(30,00,000 \text{ sq. cm.} \times \frac{11,50,000 \text{ units}}{10,00,000 \text{ units}} - 30,00,000 \text{ sq. cm. }\right) \times ₹14 \text{ per sq.cm.}$$

$$= (34,50,000 \text{ sq. cm.} - 30,00,000 \text{ sq.cm.}) \times ₹14 \text{ per sq.cm.} = ₹63,00,000 \text{ U}$$

The units of input required to produce 2013 output in 2012 can also be calculated as follows:

$$\text{Units of input per unit of output in 2012} = \frac{30,00,000 \text{ sq. cm.}}{10,00,000 \text{ units}} = 3 \text{ sq. cm/unit}$$

Units of input required to produce 2013 output of 11,50,000 units in 2012 = 3 sq. cm. per unit × 11,50,000 units = 34,50,000 sq. cm.

$$\begin{pmatrix} \text{Cost effect of} \\ \text{growth for} \\ \text{fixed costs} \end{pmatrix} = \begin{pmatrix} \text{Actual units of capacity in} \\ \text{2010 because adequate capacity} \\ \text{exists to produce 2013 output in 2012} \end{pmatrix} - \begin{pmatrix} \text{Actual units} \\ \text{of capacity} \\ \text{in 2012} \end{pmatrix} \times \begin{pmatrix} \text{Price per} \\ \text{unit of} \\ \text{capacity} \\ \text{in 2012} \end{pmatrix}$$

$$\begin{array}{l} \text{Cost effect of} \\ \text{growth for} \\ \text{conversion costs} \end{array} = (37{,}50{,}000 \text{ sq. cm.} - 37{,}50{,}000 \text{ sq. cm.}) \times ₹42.8 \text{ per sq. cm.} = ₹0$$

Conversion costs are fixed costs at a given level of capacity. Chipset has manufacturing capacity to process 37,50,000 square centimeters of silicon wafers in 2012 at a cost of ₹16,05,00,000, or ₹42.8 per square centimeter. To produce 11,50,000 units of output in 2012, Chipset would have needed to process 34,50,000 square centimeters of direct materials. which is less than the available capacity of 37,50,000 sq. cm. Throughout this chapter, we assume adequate capacity exists in the current year (2012) to produce next year's (2013) output. Under this assumption, the cost effect of growth for capacity-related fixed costs is, by definition, ₹0. Had 2012 capacity been inadequate to produce 2013 output in 2012, we would need to calculate the additional capacity required to produce 2013 output in 2012. These calculations are beyond the scope of the book.

In summary, the net increase in operating income attributable to growth equals:

Revenue effect of growth		₹3,45,00,000 F
Cost effect of growth		
Direct material costs	₹63,00,000 U	
Conversion costs	0	
R&D costs	0	63,00,000 U
Change in operating income due to growth		₹2,82,00,000 F

Price-Recovery Component of Change in Operating Income

Assuming that the 2012 relationship between inputs and outputs continued in 2013, the price-recovery component of the change in operating income measures solely the effect of price changes on revenues and costs to produce and sell the 11,50,000 units of CX1 in 2013.

Revenue effect of price recovery

$$\begin{array}{l} \text{Revenue effect of} \\ \text{price recovery} \end{array} = \begin{pmatrix} \text{Selling price} \\ \text{in 2013} \end{pmatrix} - \begin{array}{l} \text{Selling price} \\ \text{in 2012} \end{array} \times \begin{array}{l} \text{Actual units} \\ \text{of output} \\ \text{sold in 2013} \end{array}$$

$$= (₹220 \text{ per unit} - ₹230 \text{ per unit}) \times 11{,}50{,}000 \text{ units}$$

$$= ₹1{,}15{,}00{,}000 \text{ U}$$

Note that the calculation focuses on revenue changes caused by changes in the selling price of CX1 between 2012 (₹230) and 2013 (₹220).

Cost effect of price recovery

Chipset's management accountants calculate the cost effects of price recovery separately for variable costs and for fixed costs, just as they did when calculating the cost effect of growth.

$$\begin{matrix} \text{Cost effect of} \\ \text{price recovery for} \\ \text{variable costs} \end{matrix} = \left(\begin{matrix} \text{Input price} \\ \text{in 2013} \end{matrix} - \begin{matrix} \text{Input price} \\ \text{in 2012} \end{matrix} \right) \times \begin{matrix} \text{Units of input} \\ \text{required to} \\ \text{produce 2013} \\ \text{output in 2012} \end{matrix}$$

$$\begin{matrix} \text{Cost effect of} \\ \text{price recovery for} \\ \text{direct materials} \end{matrix} = (₹15 \text{ per sq.cm.} - ₹14 \text{ per sq.cm.}) \times 34,50,000 \text{ sq.} = ₹34,50,000 \text{ U}$$

Recall that the direct materials of 34,50,000 square centimeters required to produce 2011 output in 2010 had already been calculated when computing the cost effect of growth.

$$\begin{matrix} \text{Cost effect of} \\ \text{price recovery for} \\ \text{fixed costs} \end{matrix} = \left(\begin{matrix} \text{Price per} \\ \text{unit of} \\ \text{capacity} \\ \text{in 2013} \end{matrix} - \begin{matrix} \text{Price per} \\ \text{unit of} \\ \text{capacity} \\ \text{in 2012} \end{matrix} \right) \times \begin{matrix} \text{Actual units of capacity in} \\ \text{2012, if adequate} \\ \text{to produce} \\ \text{2013 output in 2012} \end{matrix}$$

Cost effects of price recovery for fixed costs are:

Conversion costs: (₹43.5 per sq. cm. − ₹42.8 per sq. cm.) × 37,50,000 sq. cm. = ₹26,25,000 U

Recall that the detailed analyses of capacities were presented on the previous page when computing the cost effect of growth.

In summary, the net decrease in operating income attributable to price recovery equals:

Revenue effect of price recovery		₹1,15,00,000 U
Cost effect of price recovery		
Direct material costs	₹34,50,000 U	
Conversion costs	26,25,000 U	
R&D costs	0	60,75,000 U
Change in operating income due to price recovery		₹1,75,75,000 U

The price-recovery analysis indicates that, even as the prices of its inputs increased, the selling prices of CX1 decreased and Chipset could not pass on input-price increases to its customers.

Productivity Component of Change in Operating Income

The productivity component of the change in operating income uses 2013 input prices to measure how costs have decreased as a result of using fewer inputs, a better mix of inputs, and/or less capacity to produce 2013 output, compared with the inputs and capacity that would have been used in 2012.

The productivity-component calculations use 2013 prices and output. That's because the productivity component isolates the change in costs between 2012 and 2013 caused solely by the change in the quantities, mix, and/or capacities of inputs.[9]

---

[9] Note that the productivity-component calculation uses actual 2013 input prices, whereas its counterpart, the efficiency variance in Chapters 7 and 8, uses budgeted prices. (In effect, the budgeted prices correspond to 2012 prices). Year 2013 prices are used in the productivity calculation because Chipset wants its managers to choose input quantities to minimize costs in 2013 based on currently prevailing prices. If 2012 prices had been used in the productivity calculation, managers would choose input quantities based on irrelevant input prices that prevailed a year ago! Why does using budgeted prices in Chapters 7 and 8 not pose a similar problem? Because, unlike 2012 prices that describe what happened a year ago, budgeted prices represent prices that are expected to prevail in the current period. Moreover, budgeted prices can be changed, if necessary, to bring them in line with actual current-period prices.

$$\text{Cost effect of productivity for variable costs} = \left(\begin{array}{cc} \text{Actual units of} & \text{Units of input} \\ \text{input used} & \text{required to} \\ \text{to produce} & - \text{produce 2013} \\ \text{2013 output} & \text{output in 2012} \end{array} \right) \times \begin{array}{c} \text{Input} \\ \text{price} \\ \text{in 2013} \end{array}$$

Using the 2013 data and the calculation of units of input required to produce 2013 output in 2012 when discussing the cost effects of growth,

$$\text{Cost effect of productivity for direct materials} = (29,00,000 \text{ sq. cm.} - 34,50,000 \text{ sq. cm.}) \times ₹15 \text{ per sq. cm}$$

$$= 5,50,000 \text{ sq. cm.} \times ₹15 \text{ per sq. cm.} = ₹82,50,000 \text{ F}$$

Chipset's quality and yield improvements reduced the quantity of direct materials needed to produce output in 2013 relative to 2012.

$$\text{Cost effect of productivity for fixed costs} = \left(\begin{array}{cc} \text{Actual units of} & \text{Actual units of capacity in} \\ \text{capacity} & 2012, \text{ if adequate} \\ \text{in 2013} & - \text{ to produce} \\ & 2013 \text{ output in 2012} \end{array} \right) \times \begin{array}{c} \text{Price per} \\ \text{unit of} \\ \text{capacity} \\ \text{in 2013} \end{array}$$

To calculate the cost effect of productivity for fixed costs, we use the 2013 data, and the analyses of capacity required to produce 2013 output in 2012 when discussing the cost effect of growth,

Cost effects of productivity for fixed costs are

Conversion costs: $(35,00,000 \text{ sq. cm.} - 37,50,000 \text{ sq. cm.} \times ₹43.5 \text{ per sq. cm.} = ₹1,08,75,000 \text{ F}$

Chipset's managers decreased manufacturing capacity in 2013 to 35,00,000 square centimeters by selling off old equipment and reducing the work force using a combination of retirements and layoffs.

In summary, the net increase in operating income attributable to productivity equals

Cost effect of productivity	
Direct material costs	₹82,50,000 F
Conversion costs	1,08,75,000 F
Change in operating income due to productivity	1,91,25,000 F

The productivity component indicates that Chipset was able to increase operating income by improving quality and productivity and eliminating capacity, to reduce costs. Note that the productivity component focuses exclusively on costs, so there is no revenue effect for this component.

Exhibit 12-6 summarizes the growth, price-recovery, and productivity components of the changes in operating income. Generally, companies that have been successful at cost leadership will show favorable productivity and growth components. Companies that have successfully differentiated their products will show favorable price-recovery and growth components. In Chipset's case, consistent with its strategy and its implementation, productivity contributed ₹1,91,25,000 to the increase in operating income, and growth contributed ₹2,82,00,000. Price-recovery decreased operating income by ₹1,75,75,000 because, even as input prices increased, the selling price of CX1 decreased. Had Chipset been able to differentiate its product and charge a higher price, the price-recovery effects might have been less unfavorable or perhaps even favorable. As a result, Chipset's managers plan to evaluate some modest changes in product features that might help differentiate CX1 somewhat from competing products.

Exhibit 12-6   Strategic Analysis of Profitability

	Income Statement Amounts in 2012 (1)	Revenue and Cost Effects of Growth Component in 2013 (2)	Revenue and Cost Effects of Price-Recovery Component in 2013 (3)	Cost Effect of Productivity Component in 2013 (4)	Income Statement Amounts in 2013 (5) = (1) + (2) + (3) + (4)
Revenues	₹23,00,00,000	₹3,45,00,000 F	₹1,15,00,000 U	—	₹25,30,00,000
Costs	20,25,00,000	63,00,000 U	60,75,000 U	₹1,91,25,000 F	19,57,50,000
Operating income	₹2,75,00,000	₹2,82,00,000 F	₹1,75,75,000 U	₹1,91,25,000 F	₹5,72,50,000
			₹2,97,50,000 F		

Change in operating income

Further Analysis of Growth, Price-Recovery, and Productivity Components

As in all variance and profit analysis, Chipset's managers want to more closely analyze the change in operating income. For example, Chipset's growth might have been helped, by an increase in industry market size. Therefore, at least part of the increase in operating income may be attributable to favorable economic conditions in the industry rather than to any successful implementation of strategy. Some of the growth might relate to the management decision to decrease selling price, made possible by the productivity gains. In this case, the increase in operating income from cost leadership must include operating income from productivity-related growth in market share in addition to the productivity gain.

We illustrate these ideas, using the Chipset example and the following additional information. *Instructors who do not wish to cover these detailed calculations can go to the next section on "Applying the Five-Step Decision-Making Framework to Strategy" without any loss of continuity.*

- The market growth rate in the industry is 8% in 2013. Of the 1,50,000 (11,50,000 − 10,00,000) units of increased sales of CX1 between 2012 and 2013, 8,00,000 (0.10 × 8,00,000) units are due to an increase in industry market size (which Chipset should have benefited from regardless of its productivity gains), and the remaining 70,000 units are due to an increase in market share.

- During 2013, Chipset could have maintained the price of CX1 at the 2012 price of ₹230 per unit. But management decided to take advantage of the productivity gains to reduce the price of CX1 by ₹10 to grow market share leading to the 70,000-unit increase in sales.

The effect of the industry-market-size factor on operating income (rather than any specific strategic actions) is:

Change in operating income due to growth in industry market size

$$\frac{₹2,82,00,000 \text{ (Exibit 12-5, column 2)} \times 80,000 \text{ units}}{1,50,000 \text{ units}} = ₹1,50,40,000 \text{ F}$$

Lacking a differentiated product, Chipset could have maintained the price of CX1 at ₹230 per unit even while the prices of its inputs increased.

The effect of product differentiation on operating income is:

Change in prices of inputs (cost effect of price recovery)	60,75,000 U
Change in operating income due to product differentiation	₹60,75,000 U

To exercise cost and price leadership, Chipset made the strategic decision to cut the price of CX1 by ₹10. This decision resulted in an increase in market share and 70,000 units of additional sales.

The effect of cost leadership on operating income is:

Productivity component	₹1,91,25,000 F
Effect of strategic decision to reduce price	
(₹10/unit × 11,50,000 units)	11,50,000 U
Growth in market share due to productivity improvement	
and strategic decision to reduce prices	
₹2,82,00,000 (Exibit 12-5, column 2) × $\frac{70,000 \text{ units}}{1,50,000 \text{ units}}$	1,31,60,000 F
Change in operating income due to cost leadership	₹2,07,85,000

A summary of the change in operating income between 2012 and 2013 follows.

Change due to industry market size	₹1,50,40,000 F
Change due to product differentiation	60,75,000 U
Change due to cost leadership	2,07,85,000 F
Change in operating income	₹2,97,50,000 F

Consistent with its cost-leadership strategy, the productivity gains of ₹1,91,25,000 in 2013 were a big part of the increase in operating income from 2012 to 2013. Chipset took advantage of these productivity gains to decrease price by ₹10 per unit at a cost of ₹1,15,00,000 to gain ₹1,31,60,000 in operating income by selling 70,000 additional units. The Problem for Self-Study later in this chapter describes the analysis of the growth, price-recovery, and productivity components for a company following a product-differentiation strategy.

Under different assumptions about the change in selling price, the analysis will attribute different amounts to the different strategies.

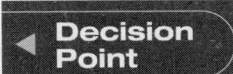

Decision Point

How can a company analyze changes in operating income to evaluate the success of its strategy?

Applying the Five-Step Decision-Making Framework to Strategy

We next briefly describe how the five-step decision-making framework, introduced in Chapter 1, is also useful in making decisions about strategy.

1. *Identify the problem and uncertainties.* Chipset's strategy choice depends on resolving two uncertainties: (1) whether Chipset can add value to its customers that its competitors cannot copy, and (2) whether Chipset can develop the necessary internal capabilities to add this value.

2. *Obtain information.* Chipset's managers develop customer preference maps to identify various product attributes customers want and the competitive advantage or disadvantage it has on each attribute relative to competitors. The managers also gather data on Chipset's internal capabilities. How good is Chipset in designing and developing innovative new products? How good are its process and marketing capabilities?

3. *Make predictions about the future.* Chipset's managers conclude that they will not be able to develop innovative new products in a cost-effective way. They believe that Chipset's strength lies in improving quality, reengineering processes, reducing costs, and delivering products faster to customers.

4. *Make decisions by choosing among alternatives.* Chipset's management decide to follow a cost-leadership rather than a product-differentiation strategy. They decide to introduce a balanced scorecard to align and measure Chipset's quality improvement and process reengineering efforts.

5. *Implement the decision, evaluate performance, and learn.* On its balanced scorecard, Chipset's managers compare actual and targeted performance and evaluate possible cause-and-effect relationships. They learn, for example, that increasing the percentage of processes with advanced controls improves yield. As a result, just as they had anticipated, productivity and growth initiatives result in increases in operating income in 2013. The one change Chipset's managers plan for 2014 is to make modest changes in product features that might help differentiate CX1 somewhat from competing products. In this way, feedback and learning help in the development of future strategies and implementation plans.

Downsizing and the Management of Capacity

Learning Objective 5

Identify unused capacity

. . . capacity available minus capacity used for engineered costs but difficult to determine for discretionary costs

and how to manage it

. . . downsize to reduce capacity

As we saw in our earlier discussion of the productivity component, fixed costs are tied to capacity. Unlike variable costs, fixed costs do not change automatically with changes in activity level (for example, fixed conversion costs do not change with changes in the quantity of silicon wafers started into production). How then can managers reduce capacity-based fixed costs? By measuring and managing **Unused capacity** which is the amount of productive capacity available over and above the productive capacity employed to meet consumer demand in the current period. To understand unused capacity, it is necessary to distinguish *engineered costs* from *discretionary costs*.

Engineered and Discretionary Costs

Engineered costs result from a cause-and-effect relationship between the cost driver—output—and the (direct or indirect) resources used to produce that output. Engineered costs have a detailed, physically observable, and repetitive relationship with output. In the Chipset example, direct material costs are *direct engineered costs*. Conversion costs are an example of *indirect engineered costs*. Consider 2013. The output of 11,50,000 units of CX1 and the efficiency with which inputs are converted into outputs result in 29,00,000 square centimeters of silicon wafers being started into production. Manufacturing-conversion-cost resources used equal ₹12,61,50,000 (₹43.5 per sq. cm. × 29,00,000 sq. cm.), but actual conversion costs (₹15,22,50,000) are higher because Chipset has manufacturing capacity to process 35,00,000 square centimeters of silicon wafer (₹43.5 per sq. cm. × 35,00,000 sq. cm. = 15,22,50,000). Although these costs are fixed in the short run, over the long run there is a cause-and-effect relationship between output and manufacturing capacity required (and conversion costs needed). In the long run, Chipset will try to match its capacity to its needs.

In general, cost leadership requires managers to pay special attention to engineered costs and capacity. Companies such as Jet Airlines have struggled to achieve profitability because of the difficulties they have had in managing capacity-related engineered costs. Jet's cost structure varies with the number of flights on its schedule. For a given number of flights, most of Jet's costs such as the cost of airplane leases, fuel, and wages are fixed. Jet must anticipate future revenues and decide on a level of capacity and the related costs. If revenues fall short, it is difficult for Jet Airlines to reduce its costs quickly.

Discretionary costs have two important features: (1) They arise from periodic (usually annual) decisions regarding the maximum amount to be incurred; and (2) they have no measurable cause-and-effect relationship between output and resources used. Examples of discretionary costs include advertising, executive training, R&D, and corporate-staff department costs such as legal, human resources, and public relations. Unlike engineered costs, the relationship between discretionary costs and output is weak and unclear because the relationship is nonroutine. A noteworthy aspect of discretionary costs is that managers are seldom confident that the "correct" amounts are being spent. The founder of Lever Brothers, an international consumer-products company, once noted, "Half the money I spend on advertising is wasted; the trouble is, I don't know which half!"[10].

Identifying Unused Capacity for Engineered and Discretionary Overhead Costs

Identifying unused capacity is very different for engineered costs compared to discretionary costs. Consider engineered conversion costs.

At the start of 2013, Chipset had capacity to process 37,50,000 square centimeters of silicon wafers. Quality and productivity improvements made during 2013 enabled Chipset to produce 11,50,000 units of CX1 by processing 29,00,000 square centimeters of silicon wafers. Unused manufacturing capacity as 8,50,000 (37,50,000 − 29,00,000) square centimeters of silicon-wafer processing capacity at the beginning of 2013. At the 2013 conversion cost of ₹43.5 per square centimeter,

$$\begin{array}{c}\text{Cost of}\\\text{unused capacity}\end{array} = \begin{array}{c}\text{Cost of capacity}\\\text{at the beginning}\\\text{of the year}\end{array} - \begin{array}{c}\text{Manufacturing resources}\\\text{used during the year}\end{array}$$

$$= (37,50,000 \text{ sq. cm.} \times ₹43.5 \text{ per sq. cm.}) - (29,00,000 \text{ sq. cm.} \times ₹43.5 \text{ per sq. cm.})$$

$$= ₹16,31,25,000 - ₹12,61,50,000 = ₹3,69,75,000$$

The absence of a cause-and-effect relationship makes identifying unused capacity for discretionary costs difficult. For example, management cannot determine the R&D resources used for the actual output produced to compare to R&D capacity. And without a measure of capacity used, it is not possible to compute unused capacity.

Managing Unused Capacity

What actions can Chipset management take when it identifies unused capacity? In general, it has two alternatives: eliminate the unused capacity, or grow output to utilize the unused capacity.

---

[10] Managers also describe some costs as infrastructure costs—costs that arise from having property, plant, and equipment and a functioning organization. Examples are depreciation, long-run lease rental, and the acquisition of long-run technical capabilities. These costs are generally fixed costs because a company purchases property, plant, and equipment before using them. Infrastructure costs can be engineered or discretionary. For instance, manufacturing-overhead cost incurred at Chipset to acquire manufacturing capacity is an infrastructure cost that is an example of an engineered cost. In the long run, there is a cause-and-effect relationship between output and manufacturing-overhead costs needed to produce that output. R&D cost incurred to acquire technical capability is an infrastructure cost that is an example of a discretionary cost. There is no measurable cause-and-effect relationship between output and R&D cost incurred.

In recent years, many companies have *downsized* in an attempt to eliminate their unused capacity. **Downsizing** (also called **rightsizing**) is an integrated approach of configuring processes, products, and people to match costs to the activities that need to be performed to operate effectively and efficiently in the present and future. Companies such as Ford Motors and IBM, have downsized to focus on their core businesses and have instituted organization changes to increase efficiency, reduce costs, and improve quality. However, downsizing often means eliminating jobs, which can adversely affect employee morale and the culture of a company.

Consider Chipset's alternatives dealing with unused manufacturing capacity. Because it needed to process 29,00,000 square centimeters of silicon wafers in 2013, the company could have reduced capacity to 30,00,000 square centimeters (Chipset can add or reduce manufacturing capacity in increments of 2,50,000 sq. cm.), resulting in cost savings of ₹3,26,25,000 [(37,50,000 sq. cm. – 30,00,000 sq. cm.) × ₹43.5 per sq. cm.]. Chipset's strategy, however, is not just to reduce costs but also to grow its business. So early in 2013, Chipset reduces its manufacturing capacity by only 2,50,000 square centimeters—from 37,50,000 square centimeters to 35,00,000 square centimeters—saving ₹1,08,75,000 (₹43.5 per sq. cm. × 2,50,000 sq. cm.). It retainssome extra capacity for future growth. By avoiding greater reductions in capac ity, it also maintains the morale of its skilled and capable workforce. The success of this Identifying unused capacity for discretionary costs such as R&D costs, is difficult, so downsizing or otherwise, managing this unused capacity is also difficult. Management must exercise considerable judgment in deciding the level of R&D costs that would generate the needed product and process improvements. Unlike engineered costs, there is no clear-cut way to know whether management is spending too much (or too little) on R&D.

Problem for Self-Study

Following a strategy of product differentiation, Westwood Company makes a high-end kitchen range hood, KE8. Westwood's data for 2012 and 2013 follow:

	2012	2013
1. Units of KE8 produced and sold	40,000	42,000
2. Selling price	₹1,000	₹1,100
3. Direct materials (square feet)	1,20,000	1,23,000
4. Direct material cost per square foot	₹100	₹110
5. Manufacturing capacity for KE8	50,000 units	50,000 units
6. Conversion costs	₹1,00,00,000	₹1,10,00,000
7. Conversion cost per unit of capacity (Row 6 ÷ Row 5)	₹200	₹220
8. Selling and customer-service capacity	30 customers	29 customers
9. Selling and customer-service costs	₹72,00,000	₹72,50,000
10. Cost per customer of selling and customer-service capacity (Row 9 ÷ Row 8)	₹2,40,000	₹2,50,000

Westwood produced no defective units and reduced direct material usage per unit of KE8 in 2013. Conversion costs in each year are tied to manufacturing capacity. Selling and customer service costs are related to the number of customers that the selling and service functions are designed to support. Westwood has 23 customers (wholesalers) in 2012 and 25 customers in 2013.

Required

1. Describe briefly the elements you would include in Westwood's balanced scorecard.
2. Calculate the growth, price-recovery, and productivity components that explain the change in operating income from 2012 to 2013.
3. Suppose during 2013, the market size for high-end kitchen range hoods grew 3% in terms of number of units and all increases in market share (that is, increases in the number of units sold greater than 3%) are due to Westwood's product-differentiation strategy. Calculate how much of the change in operating income from 2012 to 2013 is due to the industry-market-size factor, cost leadership, and product differentiation.
4. How successful has Westwood been in implementing its strategy? Explain.

Solution

1. The balanced scorecard should describe Westwood's product-differentiation strategy. Elements that should be included in its balanced scorecard are:

   - **Financial perspective** Increase in operating income from higher margins on KE8 and from growth
   - **Customer perspective** Market share in the high-end market and customer satisfaction
   - **Internal business process perspective** Manufacturing quality, order-delivery time, on-time delivery, new product features added, development time for new products, and improvements in manufacturing processes
   - **Learning-and-growth perspective** Percentage of employees trained in process and quality management and employee satisfaction ratings

2. Operating income for each year is:

	2012	2013
Revenues		
(₹1,000 per unit × 40,000 units; ₹1,100 per unit × 42,000 units)	₹4,00,00,000	₹4,62,00,000
Costs		
Direct material costs		
(₹100 per sq. ft. × 1,20,000 sq. ft.; ₹110 per sq. ft. × 1,23,000 sq. ft.)	1,20,00,000	1,35,30,000
Conversion costs		
(₹200 per unit × 50,000 units; ₹220 per unit × 50,000 units)	1,00,00,000	1,10,00,000
Selling and customer-service cost		
(₹2,40,000 per customer × 30 customers; ₹2,50,000 per customer × 29 customers)	72,00,000	72,50,000
Total costs	2,92,00,000	3,17,80,000
Operating income	₹1,08,00,000	₹1,44,20,000
Change in operating income	₹36,20,000 F	

Growth Component of Operating Income Change

$$\text{Revenue effect of growth} = \left(\begin{array}{c} \text{Actual units of} \\ \text{output sold} \\ \text{in 2013} \end{array} - \begin{array}{c} \text{Actual units of} \\ \text{output sold} \\ \text{in 2012} \end{array} \right) \times \begin{array}{c} \text{Selling} \\ \text{price} \\ \text{in 2012} \end{array}$$

= (42,000 units – 40,000 units) × ₹1,000 per unit = ₹20,00,000 F

$$\begin{pmatrix} \text{Cost effect} \\ \text{of growth for} \\ \text{variable costs} \end{pmatrix} = \begin{pmatrix} \text{Units of input} \\ \text{required to produce} \\ \text{2013 output in 2012} \end{pmatrix} - \begin{pmatrix} \text{Actual units of input} \\ \text{used to produce} \\ \text{2012 output} \end{pmatrix} \times \begin{pmatrix} \text{Input} \\ \text{price} \\ \text{in 2012} \end{pmatrix}$$

$$\begin{pmatrix} \text{Cost effect} \\ \text{of growth for} \\ \text{direct materials} \end{pmatrix} = \frac{(1,20,000 \text{sq. ft} \times 42,000 \text{ units} - 1,20,000 \text{sq. ft.}) ₹100 \text{per sq.ft}}{40,000 \text{ units}}$$

$$= (1,26,000 \text{sq. ft} - 1,20,000 \text{sq. ft.}) \times ₹100 \text{per sq.ft} = ₹6,00,000 \text{ U}$$

$$\begin{pmatrix} \text{Cost effect} \\ \text{of growth for} \\ \text{fixed costs} \end{pmatrix} = \begin{pmatrix} \text{Actual units of capacity in} \\ \text{2012, because adequate capacity} \\ \text{exists to produce 2013 output in 2012} \end{pmatrix} - \begin{pmatrix} \text{Actual units of capacity in} \\ \text{2012} \end{pmatrix} \times \begin{pmatrix} \text{Price per} \\ \text{unit of} \\ \text{capacity} \\ \text{in 2012} \end{pmatrix}$$

Cost effects of growth for fixed costs are:

Conversion costs: $(50,000 \text{ units} - 50,000 \text{ units}) \times ₹200 \text{ per unit} = ₹0$

Selling and customer-service costs: $(30 \text{ costomers} - 30 \text{ customers}) \times ₹2,40,000 \text{ per customer} = ₹0$

In summary, the net increase in operating income attributable to growth equals:

Revenue effect of growth		₹20,00,000 F
Cost effect of growth		
Direct material costs	₹6,00,000 U	
Conversion costs	0	
Selling and customer-service costs	0	6,00,000 U
Change in operating income due to growth		₹14,00,000 F

Price-Recovery Component of Operating-Income Change

$$\begin{pmatrix} \text{Revenue effect of} \\ \text{price recovery} \end{pmatrix} = \begin{pmatrix} \text{Selling price} \\ \text{in 2013} \end{pmatrix} - \begin{pmatrix} \text{Selling price} \\ \text{in 2012} \end{pmatrix} \times \begin{pmatrix} \text{Actual units} \\ \text{of output} \\ \text{sold in 2013} \end{pmatrix}$$

$$= (₹1,110 \text{ per unit} - ₹1,000 \text{ per unit}) \times 42,000 \text{ units} = ₹42,00,000 \text{ F}$$

$$\begin{pmatrix} \text{Cost effect of} \\ \text{price recovery} \\ \text{for variable costs} \end{pmatrix} = \begin{pmatrix} \text{Input} \\ \text{price} \\ \text{in 2013} \end{pmatrix} - \begin{pmatrix} \text{Input} \\ \text{price} \\ \text{in 2012} \end{pmatrix} \times \begin{pmatrix} \text{Units of input} \\ \text{required to produce} \\ \text{2013 outputs in 2012} \end{pmatrix}$$

Direct material costs: $(₹110 \text{ per sq. ft.} - ₹100 \text{ per sq. ft.}) \times 1,26,000 \text{ sq. ft.} = ₹12,60,000 \text{ U}$

$$\begin{pmatrix} \text{Cost effect of} \\ \text{price recovery} \\ \text{for fixed costs} \end{pmatrix} = \begin{pmatrix} \text{Price per} \\ \text{unit of} \\ \text{capacity} \\ \text{in 2013} \end{pmatrix} - \begin{pmatrix} \text{Price per} \\ \text{unit of} \\ \text{capacity} \\ \text{in 2012} \end{pmatrix} \times \begin{pmatrix} \text{Actual units of capacity in} \\ \text{2012 because asequate capacity} \\ \text{exists to produce 2013 output in 2012} \end{pmatrix}$$

Cost effects of price recovery for fixed costs are:

Conversion cots: $(₹220 \text{ per unit} - ₹200 \text{ per unit}) \times 50,000 \text{ units} = ₹10,00,000 \text{ U}$

Selling and cust. – service costs: $(₹2,50,000 \text{ per cust} - ₹2,40,000 \text{ per cust.}) \times 30 \text{ customers} \times ₹3,00,000 \text{ U}$

In summary, the net increase in operating income attributable to price recovery equals:

Revenue effect of price recovery		₹42,00,000 F
Cost effect of price recovery		
Direct material costs	₹12,60,000 U	
Conversion costs	10,00,000 U	
Selling and customer-service costs	3,00,000 U	25,60,000 U
Change in operating income due to price recovery		₹16,40,000 F

Productivity Component of Operating-Income Change

$$\begin{pmatrix} \text{Cost effect of} \\ \text{productivity for} \\ \text{variable costs} \end{pmatrix} = \begin{pmatrix} \text{Actual units of} \\ \text{input used to produce} \\ \text{2013 output} \end{pmatrix} - \begin{pmatrix} \text{Units of input} \\ \text{required to produce} \\ \text{2013 output in 2012} \end{pmatrix} \times \begin{pmatrix} \text{Input} \\ \text{price in} \\ \text{2013} \end{pmatrix}$$

$$\begin{array}{l} \text{Cost effect of} \\ \text{productiity for} \\ \text{direct materials} \end{array} = (1{,}23{,}000 \text{ sq. ft.} - 1{,}26{,}000 \text{ sq. ft.}) \times ₹110 \text{ per sq. ft.} = ₹3{,}30{,}000F$$

$$\begin{pmatrix} \text{Cost effect of} \\ \text{productivity for} \\ \text{fixed costs} \end{pmatrix} = \begin{pmatrix} \text{Actual units} \\ \text{of capacity} \\ \text{in 2013} \end{pmatrix} - \begin{pmatrix} \text{Actual Units of capacity in} \\ \text{2008, because asequate} \\ \text{capacity exists to produce} \\ \text{2013 output in 2012} \end{pmatrix} \times \begin{pmatrix} \text{price per} \\ \text{unit of} \\ \text{capacity} \\ \text{in 2013} \end{pmatrix}$$

Cost effects of productivity for fixed costs are:

Conversion cots: (50,000 unit − 50,000 unit) × ₹220 per unit = ₹0

Selling and customer − service costs: (29 customers − 30 customers) × ₹2,50,000/customer = ₹2,50,000 F

In summary, the net increase in operating income attributable to productivity equals:

Cost effect of productivity:	
Direct material costs	₹3,30,000 F
Conversion costs	0
Selling and customer-service costs	2,50,000 F
Change in operating income due to productivity	₹5,80,000 F

A summary of the change in operating income between 2012 and 2013 follows:

	Income Statement Amounts in 2012 (1)	Revenue and Cost Effects of Growth Component in 2013 (2)	Revenue and Cost Effects of Price-Recovery Component in 2013 (3)	Cost Effect of Productivity Component in 2013 (4)	Income Statement Amounts in 2013 (5) = (1) + (2) + (3) + (4)
Revenue	₹4,00,00,000	₹20,00,000 F	₹42,00,000 F	—	₹4,62,00,000
Costs	2,92,00,000	6,00,000 U	25,60,000 U	₹5,80,000 F	3,17,80,000
Operating income	₹1,08,00,000	₹14,00,000 F	₹16,40,000 F	₹5,80,000 F	₹1,44,20,000
			36,20,000 F		
		Change in operating income			

3. *Effect of the industry-market-size factor on operating income* Of the increase in sales from 40,000 to 42,000 units, 3%, or 1,200 units (0.03 × 40,000), is due to growth in market size, and 800 units (2,000 – 1,200) are due to an increase in market share. The change in Westwood's operating income from the industry-market-size factor rather than specific strategic actions is:

$$₹14,00,000 \text{ (column 2 of precedig table)} \times \frac{1,200 \text{ units}}{2,000 \text{ units}} \qquad ₹8,40,000 \text{ F}$$

Effect of product differentiation on operating income

Increase in the selling price of KE8 (revenue effect of the price-recovery component)	₹42,00,000 F
Increase in prices of inputs (cost effect of the price-recovery component)	25,60,000 U
Growth in market share due to product differentiation	5,60,000 F
$₹14,00,000 \text{ (column 2 of precedig table)} \times \dfrac{800, \text{units}}{2,000 \text{ units}}$	
Change in operating income due to product differentiation	₹22,00,000 F

Effect of cost leadership on operating income

Productivity component	₹5,80,000 F

A summary of the net increase in operating income from 2012 to 2013 follows:

Change due to the indust ry-market-size factor	₹8,40,000 F
Change due to product differentiation	22,00,000 F
Change due to cost leadership	5,80,000 F
Change in operating income	₹36,20,000 F

4. The analysis of operating income indicates that a significant amount of the increase in operating income resulted from Westwood's successful implementation of its product-differentiation strategy (operating income attributable to product differentiation, ₹22,00,000 F). The company was able to continue to charge a premium price for KE8 while increasing market share. Westwood was also able to earn additional operat ing income through productivity improvement (operating income attributable to cost leadership, ₹5,80,000 F).

Decision Points

The following question-and-answer format summarizes the chapter's learning objectives. Each decision presents a key question related to a learning objective. The guidelines are the answer to that question.

Decision	Guidelines
1. What are two generic strategies a company can use?	Two generic strategies are product differentiation and cost leadership. Product differentiation is offering products and services that customers perceive as superior and unique. Cost leadership is achieving low costs relative to competitors. A company chooses its strategy based on an understanding of customer preferences and its own internal capabilities, while differentiating itself from its competitors.

2. What is reengineering?

Reengineering is the rethinking of business processes, such as the order-delivery process, to improve critical performance measures such as cost, quality, and customer satisfaction.

3. How can an organization translate its strategy into a set of performance measures?

An organization can develop a balanced scorecard that provides the framework for a strategic measurement and management system. The balanced scorecard measures performance from four perspectives: (1) financial, (2) customer, (3) internal business processes, and (4) learning and growth. To build their balanced scorecards, organizations often create strategy maps to represent the cause-and-effect relationships across various strategic objectives.

4. How can a company analyze changes in operating income to evaluate the success of its strategy?

To evaluate the success of its strategy, a company can subdivide the change in operating income into growth, price-recovery, and productivity components. The growth component measures the change in revenues and costs from selling more or less units, assuming nothing else has changed. The price-recovery component measures changes in revenues and costs solely as a result of changes in the prices of outputs and inputs. The productivity component measures the decrease in costs from using fewer inputs, using a better mix of inputs, and reducing capacity. If a company is successful in implementing its strategy, changes in components of operating income align closely with strategy.

5. How can a company identify and manage unused capacity?

A company must first distinguish engineered costs from discretionary costs. Engineered costs result from a cause-and-effect relationship between output and the resources needed to produce that output. Discretionary costs arise from periodic (usually annual) management decisions regarding the amount of cost to be incurred. Discretionary costs are not tied to a cause-and-effect relationship between inputs and outputs. Identifying unused capacity is easier for engineered costs and more difficult for discretionary costs. Downsizing is an approach to managing unused capacity that matches costs to the activities that need to be performed to operate effectively.

TERMS TO LEARN

This chapter and the Glossary at the end of the book contain definitions of the following important terms:

balanced scorecard **(p. 634)**
cost leadership **(p. 631)**
discretionary costs **(p. 655)**
downsizing **(p. 656)**
engineered costs **(p. 654)**

growth component **(p. 647)**
price-recovery
   component **(p. 647)**
product differentiation **(p. 631)**
productivity component **(p. 647)**

reengineering **(p. 632)**
rightsizing **(p. 656)**
strategy map **(p. 634)**
unused capacity **(p. 654)**

ASSIGNMENT MATERIAL

Questions

12-1 Define strategy.
12-2 Describe the five key forces to consider when analyzing an industry.
12-3 Describe two generic strategies.

12-4 What is a customer preference map and why is it useful?

12-5 What is reengineering?

12-6 What are four key perspectives in the balanced scorecard?

12-7 What is a strategy map?

12-8 Describe three features of a good balanced scorecard.

12-9 What are three important pitfalls to avoid when implementing a balanced score-card?

12-10 Describe three key components in doing a strategic analysis of operating income.

12-11 Why might an analyst incorporate the industry-market-size factor and the interre-lationships among the growth, price-recovery, and productivity components into a strategic analysis of operating income?

12-12 How does an engineered cost differ from a discretionary cost?

12-13 What is downsizing?

12-14 What is a partial-productivity measure?

12-15 "We are already measuring total factor productivity. Measuring partial productivities would be of no value." Do you agree? Comment briefly.

Solved Examples

12-16 Strategy, balanced scorecard, merchandizing operation. Octave buys T-shirts in bulk, applies its own trendsetting silk-screen designs, and then sells the T-shirts to a number of retailers. Octave wants to be known for its trendsetting designs, and it wants every teenager to be seen in a distinctive Octave T-shirt. Octave presents the following data for its first two years of operations, 2014 and 2015.

A		B	C
		2014	**2015**
1	Number of T-shirts purchased	2,00,000	2,50,000
2	Number of T-shirts discarded	2,000	3,300
3	Number of T-shirts sold	1,98,000	2,46,700
4	Average selling price	₹250	₹260
5	Average cost per T-shirt	₹100	₹85
6	Administrative capacity (number of customers)	4,000	3,750
7	Administrative cost	₹1,20,00,000	₹1,16,25,000
8	Administrative cost per customer	₹3,000	₹3,100
9	Design staff	5	5
10	Total design costs	₹25,00,000	₹27,50,000
11	Design cost per employee	₹5,00,000	₹5,50,000

Administrative costs depend on the number of customers that Octave has created as capac-ity to support, not on the actual number of customers served. Octave had 3,600 customers in 2014 and 3,500 customers in 2015. At the start of each year, the management uses its discretion to determine the number of employees on the design staff for the year. The design staff and its costs have no direct relationship with the number of T-shirts purchased and sold, or the number of customers to whom T-shirts are sold.

Required

1. Is Octave's strategy one of product differentiation or cost leadership? Explain briefly.

2. Describe briefly the key elements Octave should include in its balanced scorecard and the reasons it should do so.

Solution

Strategy, balanced scorecard, merchandizing operation.

1. Octave follows a product differentiation strategy. Octave's designs are "trendsetting" and its T-shirts are distinctive, and it aims to make its T-shirts a "must have" for each and every teenager. These are all clear signs of a product differentiation strategy, and, to succeed, Octave must continue to innovate and be able to charge a premium price for its product.

2. Possible key elements of Octave's balance scorecard, given its product differentiation strategy are:

Financial Perspective

(1) Increase in operating income from charging higher margins and (2) price premium earned on products.

These measures will indicate whether Octave has been able to charge premium prices and achieve operating-income increases through product differentiation.

Customer Perspective

(1) Market share in distinctive, name-brand T-shirts, (2) customer satisfaction, (3) new customers, (4) number of mentions of Octave's T-shirts in the leading fashion magazines.

Octave's strategy should result in improvements in these customer measures that help evaluate whether Octave's product differentiation strategy is succeeding with its customers. These measures are, in turn, leading indicators of superior financial performance.

Internal-Business-Process Perspective

(1) Quality of silk-screening (number of colors, use of glitter, durability of the design),

(2) frequency of new designs, and (3) time between concept and delivery of design.

Improvements in these measures are expected to result in more distinctive and trendsetting designs delivered to its customers and in turn, superior financial performance.

Learning-and-Growth Perspective

(1) Ability to attract and retain talented designers (2) improvements in silk-screening processes, (3) continuous education and skill levels of marketing and sales staff, and (4) employee satisfaction.

Improvements in these measures are expected to improve Octave's capabilities to produce distinctive designs that have a cause-and-effect relationship with improvements in internal business processes, which in turn lead to customer satisfaction and financial performance.

12-17 **Strategic analysis of operating income (continuation of 12-16). Refer to Exercise 12-16.**
If you want to use Excel to solve this exercise, go to the Excel Lab at www.prenhall.com/horngren/cost13e and download the template for Exercise 12-16.

Required

1. Calculate Octave's operating income in both 2014 and 2015.
2. Calculate the growth, price-recovery, and productivity components that explain the change in operating income from 2014 to 2015.
3. Comment on your answers in requirement 2. What do each of these components indicate?

Solution

Strategic analysis of operating income (continuation of 12-16).

1. **Operating–Income Statement**

	2014	2015
Revenues (₹250 × 1,98,000; ₹260 × 2,46,700)	₹4,95,00,000	₹6,41,42,000
Costs		

T-shirts purchased (₹100 × 2,00,000; ₹85 × 2,50,000)	2,00,00,000	2,12,50,000
Administrative costs	1,20,00,000	1,16,25,000
Design costs	25,00,000	27,50,000
Total costs	3,45,00,000	3,56,25,000
Operating income	₹1,50,00,000	₹2,85,17,000
Change in operating income	₹1,35,17,000 F	

2. The Growth Component

$$\text{Revenue effect of growth} = \left(\begin{array}{c} \text{Actual units of} \\ \text{output sold in 2015} \end{array} - \begin{array}{c} \text{Actual units of} \\ \text{output sold in 2014} \end{array} \right) \times \begin{array}{c} \text{Selling price} \\ \text{in 2014} \end{array}$$

$$= (20,46,700 - 1,98,000) \times ₹250 = ₹1,21,75,000F$$

$$\text{Cost effect of growth for variable costs} = \left(\begin{array}{c} \text{Units of input} \\ \text{required to produc} \\ \text{2015 output in 2014} \end{array} - \begin{array}{c} \text{Actual units of} \\ \text{input used to produce} \\ \text{2014 output} \end{array} \right) \times \begin{array}{c} \text{Input price} \\ \text{in 2014} \end{array}$$

$$\text{Cost effect of growth for fixed costs} = \left(\begin{array}{c} \text{Actual units of capacity in 2014} \\ \text{if adequate to produce 2015} \\ \text{output in 2014 OR} \\ \text{In 2014 capacity inadequate to} \\ \text{produce 2015 output in 2014, units} \\ \text{of capacity required to} \\ \text{produce 2015 output in 2014} \end{array} - \begin{array}{c} \text{Actual units of} \\ \text{capacity in} \\ 2014 \end{array} \right) \times \begin{array}{c} \text{Price per} \\ \text{unit of} \\ \text{capacity in} \\ 2014 \end{array}$$

Direct materials (purchased T-shirts) costs that would be required in 2015 to sell 2,46,700 T-shirts instead of the 1,98,000 sold in 2014, assuming the 2014 input–output relationship continued into 2015, would equal 2,49,192

purchased T-shirts ($\frac{2,46,700}{1,98,000} \times 2,00,000$).

Administrative costs will not change as adequate capacity exists in 2014 to support year 2015 output and customers. Design capacity is discretionary and adequate to support output in year 2015.

The cost effects of growth component are

Direct materials costs	(2,49,192 – 2,00,000)	×	₹100	=	₹49,19,200 U
Administrative costs	(4,000 – 4,000)	×	₹3,000	=	0
Design costs	(5 – 5)	×	₹5,00,000	=	0
Cost effect of growth					₹49,19,200 U

In summary, the net increase in operating income as a result of the growth component equals:

Revenue effect of growth	₹1,21,75,000 F
Cost effect of growth	49,19,200 U
Change in operating income due to growth	₹72,55,800 F

The Price-Recovery Component

$$\text{Revenue effect of price-recovery} = \left(\text{Selling price in 2015} - \text{Selling price in 2014} \right) \times \text{Actual units of output sold in 2015}$$

$$= (₹260 - ₹250) \times 2,46,700 = ₹24,67,000 \text{ F}$$

$$\text{Cost effect of price-recovery for variable costs} = \left(\text{Input price in 2015} - \text{Input price in 2014} \right) \times \text{Units of input required to produce 2015 output in 2014}$$

$$\text{Cost effect of price-recovery for fixed costs} = \left(\begin{array}{c} \text{Price per unit} \\ \text{of capacity} \\ \text{in 2015} \end{array} - \begin{array}{c} \text{Price per unit} \\ \text{of capacity} \\ \text{in 2014} \end{array} \right) \times \begin{array}{c} \text{Actual Units of capacity in} \\ \text{2014, if adequate} \\ \text{to produce 2015 output in 2014} \\ \text{OR} \\ \text{If 2014 capacity inadeqaute} \\ \text{to produce 2015} \\ \text{output in 2014, then units} \\ \text{of capacity required to} \\ \text{produce 2015 outpuit in 2014} \end{array}$$

Direct materials costs	(₹85 – ₹100) ×	2,49,192 =	₹37,37,880 F
Administrative costs	(₹3,100 – ₹3,000) ×	4,000 =	4,00,000 U
Design costs	(₹5,50,000 – ₹5,00,000) ×	5 =	2,50,000 U
Total cost effect of price-recovery component			₹30,87,880 F

In summary, the net increase in operating income as a result of the price-recovery component equals:

Revenue effect of price-recovery	₹24,67,000 F
Cost effect of price-recovery	30,87,880 F
Change in operating income due to price-recovery	₹55,54,880 F

The Productivity Component

$$\text{Cost effect of productivity for variable costs} = \left(\begin{array}{c} \text{Actual units of input} \\ \text{used produce 2015} \\ \text{output} \end{array} - \begin{array}{c} \text{Units in input} \\ \text{required to produce} \\ \text{2015 output in 2014} \end{array} \right) \times \begin{array}{c} \text{Input price in} \\ \text{2015} \end{array}$$

$$\text{Cost effect of productivity for fixed costs} = \left(\begin{array}{c} \text{Actual units} \\ \text{of capacity} \\ \text{in 2015} \end{array} - \begin{array}{c} \text{Actual units of capacity in} \\ \text{2014, if adequate to} \\ \text{produce 2015 output} \\ \text{in 2014} \\ \text{OR} \\ \text{If 2014 capacity inadequate} \\ \text{to produce 2015} \\ \text{output in 2014, than units} \\ \text{of capacity required to} \\ \text{produce 2015 output in 2014} \end{array} \right) \times \begin{array}{c} \text{price per} \\ \text{unit of} \\ \text{capacity} \\ \text{in 2015} \end{array}$$

The productivity component of cost changes are

Direct materials costs	$(2,50,000 - 2,49,192)$	×	₹85	=	₹68,680 U
Administrative costs	$(4,000 - 3,750)$	×	₹3,100	=	7,75,000 F
Design costs	$(5 - 5)$	×	₹5,50,000	=	0
Change in operating income due to productivity					₹7,06,320 F

The change in operating income between 2014 and 2015 can be analyzed as follows:

	Income Statement Amounts in 2014 (1)	Revenue-and-Cost Effects of Growth in 2015 (2)	Revenue-and-Cost Effects of Price-Recovery in 2015 (3)	Cost Effect of Productivity in 2015 (4)	Income Statement Amounts in 2015 (5) = (1) + (2) + (3) + (4)
Revenues	₹4,95,00,000	₹1,21,75,000 F	₹24,67,000 F	–	₹6,41,42,000
Costs	3,45,00,000	49,19,200 U	30,87,880 F	₹7,06,320 F	3,56,25,000
Operating income	₹1,50,00,000	₹72,55,800 F	₹55,54,880 F	₹7,06,320 F	₹2,85,17,000

₹1,35,17,000 F

Change in operating income

3. The analysis of operating income indicates that growth, price-recovery, and productivity, all resulted in favorable changes in operating income in 2015. Further, a significant amount of the increase in operating income resulted from Octave's product differentiation strategy. The company was able to continue to charge a premium price while growing sales. It was also able to earn an additional operating income by improving its productivity.

12-18 Analysis of growth, price-recovery, and productivity components (continuation of 12-17).
Refer to Exercise 12-17. Suppose that the market for silk-screened T-shirts grew by 10% during 2015. All other increases in Octave's sales were the result of its own strategic actions.
If you want to use Excel to solve this exercise, go to the Excel Lab at **www.prenhall.com/ horngren/cost13e** and download the template for Exercise 12-16.

Required   Calculate the change in operating income from 2014 to 2015, due to growth in market size, cost leadership, and product differentiation. How successful has Octave been in implementing its strategy? Explain.

Solution

Analysis of growth, price-recovery, and productivity components (continuation of 12-17).
Effect of the industry-market-size factor on operating income
Of the 48,700-unit (2,46,700 – 1,98,000) increase in sales between 2014 and 2015, 19,800 (10% × 1,98,000) units are due to the growth in market size, and 28,900 units are due to an increase in market share.
The change in Octave's operating income from the industry-market-size factor rather than from specific strategic actions is:

₹72,55,800 (the growth component in Exercise 12-17) × $\dfrac{19,800}{48,700}$ ₹29,50,000 F

Effect of product differentiation on operating income
The change in operating income due to:

Increase in the selling price (revenue effect of price-recovery)	₹24,67,000 F
Increase in price of inputs (cost effect of price-recovery)	30,87,880 F
Growth in market share due to product differentiation	
₹72,55,800 (the growth component in Exercise 12-17) × $\dfrac{28,900}{48,700}$	43,05,800 F
Change in operating income due to product differentiation	₹98,60,680 F

Effect of cost leadership on operating income

The change in operating income from cost leadership is:

Productivity component	₹7,06,320 F

The change in operating income between 2014 and 2015 can be summarized as follows:

Change due to industry-market size	₹29,50,000 F
Change due to product differentiation	98,60,680 F
Change due to cost leadership	7,06,320 F
Change in operating income	₹1,35,17,000 F

Octave has been very successful in implementing its product differentiation strategy. Nearly 73% (₹98,60,680 ÷ ₹1,35,17,000) of the increase in operating income during 2015 was due to product differentiation, that is, the distinctiveness of its T-shirts. It was able to raise prices of its products despite a decline in the cost of the T-shirts purchased. Octave's operating-income increase in 2015 was also helped by a growth in the overall market and a small productivity improvement, which it did not pass on to its customers in the form of lower prices.

12-19 Identifying and managing unused capacity (continuation of 12-16). Refer to Exercise 12-16.

1. Calculate the amount and cost of (a) unused administrative capacity and (b) unused design capacity at the beginning of 2015, based on the information for 2015. If you are unable to calculate the amount and cost of a particular unused capacity, then indicate why not.   **Required**

2. Suppose Octave can only add or reduce administrative capacity in increments of 200 customers. What is the maximum amount of costs that Octave can save in 2015 by down-sizing administrative capacity?

3. What factors, other than cost, should Octave consider before it downsizes the administrative capacity?

Solution

Identifying and managing unused capacity (continuation of 12-16).

1. The amount and cost of unused capacity at the beginning of year 2015 based on year 2015 production follows:

	Amount of Unused Capacity	Cost of Unused Capacity
Administrative, 4,000 − 3,500; (4,000 − 3,500) × ₹3,100 Design	500	₹15,50,000
	Discretionary cost, so cannot determine unused capacity*	Discretionary cost so cannot be calculated*

*The absence of a cause-and-effect relationship makes identifying the unused capacity for discretionary costs difficult. Management cannot determine the design resources used for the actual output produced against which to compare design capacity.

2. Octave can at most reduce the administrative capacity by another 200 customers (3,750 − 200 = 3,550 × 3,500 = actual customers; but 3,750 − 400 = 3,350 × 3,500 = actual customers). Octave will save another 200 × ₹3,100 = ₹6,20,000. This is the maximum amount of costs Octave can save in 2015.

3. Before Octave downsizes the administrative capacity, it should consider whether sales increases in future would lead to a greater demand for and utilization of capacity as new customers are drawn to Octave's distinctive products—at that point, customer service may be the key to new customer retention and further growth. Also, the market feedback often provided by customer service staff is probably a key to Octave's cutting-edge fashion strategy; some of this may be lost if the adminis-

trative capacity is cut back. Additionally, significant reductions in capacity usually mean laying off people which can hurt employee morale.

12-20 Balanced scorecard and strategy. Sony Company manufactures a DVD player. The company sells the player to discount stores throughout the country. This player is significantly less expensive than similar products sold by Sony's competitors, but the Sony offers just DVD playback, compared with DVD and Blu-ray playback offered by competitor LG. Furthermore, the Sony has experienced production problems that have resulted in significant rework costs. LG's model has an excellent reputation for quality.

Required

1. Draw a simple customer preference map for Sony and LG using the attributes of price, quality, and playback features. Use the format of Exhibit 12-1.
2. Is Sony's current strategy that of product differentiation or cost leadership?
3. Sony would like to improve quality and decrease costs by improving processes and training workers to reduce rework. Sony's managers believe the increased quality will increase sales. Draw a strategy map as in Exhibit 12-2 describing the cause-and-effect relationships among the strategic objectives you would expect to see in Sony's balanced scorecard.
4. For each strategic objective, suggest a measure you would recommend in Sony's balanced scorecard.

Solution

1. Solution Exhibit 12-20A shows the customer preference map for DVD players for Sony Company and LG Manufacturing on price, playback features, and quality.

Solution Exhibit 12-20A

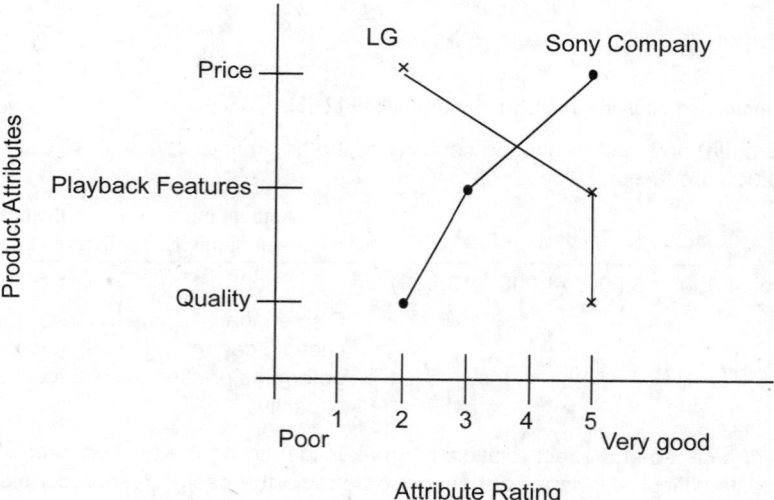

Customer Preference Map for DVD Players

2. Sony currently follows a cost leadership strategy, which is reflected in its lower price compared to LG. The DVD player is similar to products offered by competitors.

3. Solution Exhibit 12-20B presents Sony's strategy map explaining cause-and-effect relation-ships in its balanced scorecard.

Solution Exhibit 12-20B

Strategy Map for Sony Company

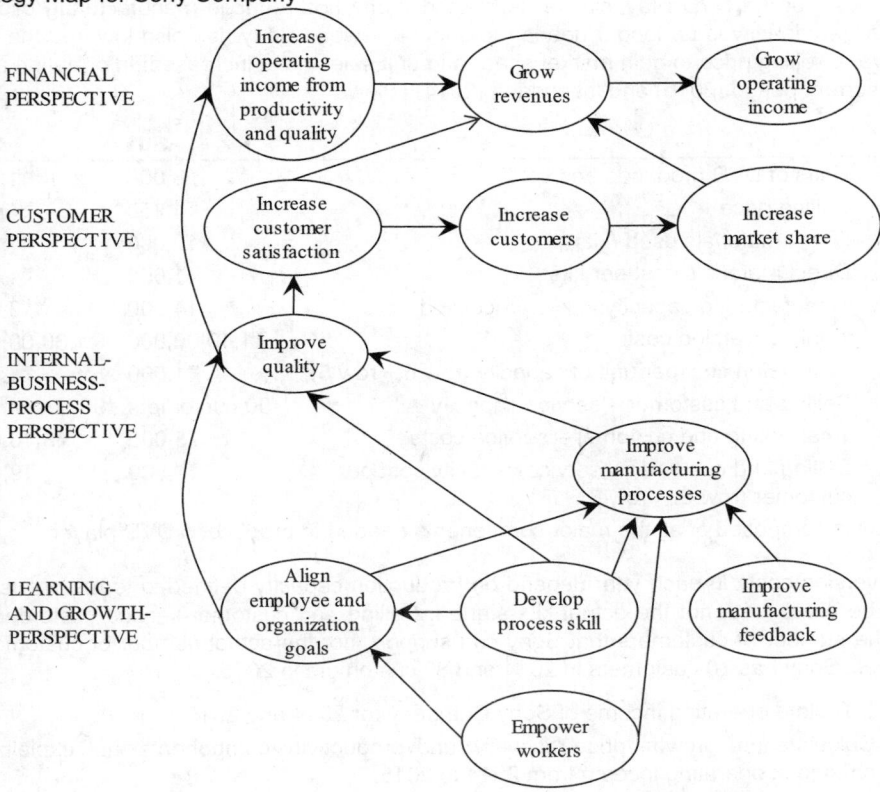

In the learning and growth perspective, Sony measures the percentage of employees trained in quality management and the percentage of manufacturing processes with real-time feedback. These objectives improve manufacturing processes and quality in the internal-business process perspective. Improvements in these measures increase customer satisfaction and market shares, which in turn increase revenues and operating income. To see if the increases in operating income are coming from productivity improvements, Sony measures the changes in operating income specifically attributable to productivity and quality improvements.

4. To achieve its goals, Sony could include the following measures under each perspective of the balanced scorecard related to its strategy map:

Financial Perspective	Operating income from productivity and quality improvement
	Operating income from growth
	Revenue growth
Customer Perspective	Market share
	Number of additional customers
	Customer-satisfaction ratings
Internal-Business-Process Perspective	Percentage of defective products sold
	Number of major improvements in manufacturing process
Learning-and-Growth Perspective	Employee-satisfaction ratings
	Percentage of employees trained in quality management
	Percentage of line workers empowered to manage processes
	Percentage of manufacturing processes with real-time feedback

12-21 Strategic analysis of operating income (continuation of 12-20). Refer to Problem 12-20. As a result of the actions taken, quality has significantly improved in 2015 while rework and unit costs of the DVD Player have decreased. Sony has reduced manufacturing capacity because capacity is no longer needed to support rework. Sony has also lowered the DVD Player's selling price to gain market share and unit sales have increased. Information about the current period (2015) and last period (2014) follows.

		2014	2015
1.	Units of DVD produced and sold	8,000	11,000
2.	Selling price	₹4,750	₹4,000
3.	Direct materials used (kits*)	10,000	11,000
4.	Direct materials cost per kits*	₹1,600	₹1,600
5.	Manufacturing capacity in kits processed	14,000	13,000
6.	Total conversion costs	₹1,40,00,000	₹1,30,00,000
7.	conversion cost per unit of capacity (row 6 ÷ row 5)	₹1,000	₹1,000
8.	Selling and customer – service capacity	90 customers	90 customers
9.	Total selling and customer – service costs	₹6,75,000	₹8,10,000
10.	Selling and customer – service capacity cost per customer (row 6 ÷ row 8)	₹7,500	₹9,000

*A kit is composed of all the major components needed to produce a DVD player

Conversion costs in each year depend on production capacity defined in terms of kits that can be processed, not the actual kits started. Selling and customer-service costs depend on the number of customers that Sony can support, not the actual number of customers it serves. Sony has 70 customers in 2014 and 80 customers in 2015.

Required
1. Calculate operating income of Sony Company for 2014 and 2015.
2. Calculate the growth, price-recovery, and productivity components that explain the change in operating income from 2014 to 2015.
3. Comment on your answer in requirement 2. What do these components indicate?

Solution
1. Operating income for each year is as follows:

	2014	2015
Revenue Costs (₹4,750 × ₹8,000; ₹4,000 × ₹11,000)	₹3,80,00,000	₹4,40,00,000
Direct materials costs (₹1,600 × ₹10,000; ₹1,600 × ₹11,000)	1,60,00,000	1,76,00,000
Conversion costs	1,40,00,000	1,30,00,000
Selling & customer service costs	6,75,000	8,10,000
Total costs	3,06,75,000	3,14,10,000
Operating income	₹73,25,000	₹1,25,90,000
Change in operating income		₹52,65,000 F

2. The Growth Component

$$\text{Revenue effect of growth} = \left(\begin{array}{c}\text{Actual units of} \\ \text{output sold} \\ \text{in 2015}\end{array} - \begin{array}{c}\text{Actual units of} \\ \text{output sold} \\ \text{in 2014}\end{array}\right) \times \begin{array}{c}\text{Selling} \\ \text{price} \\ \text{in 2014}\end{array}$$

$$= (11,000 - 8,000) \times ₹4,750 = ₹1,42,50,000 \text{ F}$$

$$\text{Cost effect of growth for variable costs} = \left(\begin{array}{c}\text{Units of} \\ \text{input required} \\ \text{to produce} \\ \text{2015 output} \\ \text{in 2014}\end{array} - \begin{array}{c}\text{Actual units} \\ \text{of inputs} \\ \text{used to} \\ \text{produce} \\ \text{2014 ouput}\end{array}\right) \times \begin{array}{c}\text{Input} \\ \text{price} \\ \text{in 2015}\end{array}$$

$$\begin{array}{c}\text{Cost effect of}\\\text{growth for}\\\text{fixed costs}\end{array} = \left(\begin{array}{c}\text{Actual units of capacity in}\\\text{2014 because adequate}\\\text{capacity exists to produce}\\\text{2015 output in 2014}\end{array} - \begin{array}{c}\text{Actual}\\\text{units of}\\\text{capacity}\\\text{in 2014}\end{array}\right) \times \begin{array}{c}\text{Price per unit}\\\text{of capacity}\\\text{in 2014}\end{array}$$

Direct materials that would be required in 2015 to produce 11,000 units instead of the 8,000 units produced in 2014, assuming the 2014 input-output relationship continued into 2015, equal 13,750 kits $\left(\dfrac{10,000}{8,000} \times 11,000\right)$. That is, the number of kits to produce 11,000 units is 10,000 kits ÷ 8,000 units = 1.25 kits per unit × 11,000 units = 13,750 kits. Conversion costs and selling and customer-service capacity will not change because adequate capacity exists in 2014 to support year 2015 output and customers.

The cost effects of growth component are:

Direct materials costs	(13,750 − 10,000)	× ₹1,600	= ₹60,00,000 U
Conversion costs	(14,000 − 14,000)	× ₹1,000	= 0
Selling & customer-service costs	(90 − 90)	× ₹7,500	= 0
Cost effect of growth			₹60,00,000 U

In summary, the net increase in operating income as a result of the growth component equals:

Revenue effect of growth	₹1,42,50,000 F
Cost effect of growth	60,00,000 U
Change in operating income due to growth	₹82,50,000 F

The Price-Recovery Component

$$\begin{array}{c}\text{Revenue effect of}\\\text{price - recovery}\end{array} = \left(\begin{array}{c}\text{Selling price}\\\text{in 2015}\end{array} - \begin{array}{c}\text{Selling price}\\\text{in 2014}\end{array}\right) \times \begin{array}{c}\text{Actual units}\\\text{of output}\\\text{sold in 2015}\end{array}$$

$$= (₹4,000 - ₹4,750) \times 11,000 = ₹82,50,000 \text{ U}$$

$$\begin{array}{c}\text{Cost effect of}\\\text{price - recovery for}\\\text{variable costs}\end{array} = \left(\begin{array}{c}\text{Input}\\\text{price in}\\\text{2015}\end{array} - \begin{array}{c}\text{Input}\\\text{price in}\\\text{2014}\end{array}\right) \times \begin{array}{c}\text{Units of input}\\\text{required to}\\\text{produce 2015}\\\text{output in 2014}\end{array}$$

$$\begin{array}{c}\text{Cost effect of}\\\text{price - recovery for}\\\text{fixed costs}\end{array} = \left(\begin{array}{c}\text{Price per}\\\text{unit of}\\\text{capacity}\\\text{in 2015}\end{array} - \begin{array}{c}\text{Price per}\\\text{unit of}\\\text{capacity}\\\text{in 2014}\end{array}\right) \times \begin{array}{c}\text{Actual units of capacity in}\\\text{2014 because adequate}\\\text{capacity exists to produce}\\\text{2015 output in 2014}\end{array}$$

Direct materials costs	(₹1,600 − ₹1,600)	×13,750	= ₹0
Conversion costs	(₹1,000 − ₹1,000)	×12,000	= 0
Selling & customer-service costs	(₹9,000 − ₹7,500)	× 90	= 1,35,000 U
Cost effect of price-recovery			₹1,35,000 U

In summary, the net increase in operating income as a result of the price-recovery component equals:

Revenue effect of price-recovery	₹82,50,000 U
Cost effect of price-recovery	₹1,35,000 U
Change in operating income due to price-recovery	₹83,85,000 U

The Productivity Component

$$\begin{pmatrix}\text{Cost effect of}\\\text{productivity for}\\\text{variable costs}\end{pmatrix} = \begin{pmatrix}\text{Actual units of}\\\text{input used}\\\text{to produce}\\\text{2015 output}\end{pmatrix} - \begin{pmatrix}\text{Units of input}\\\text{required to}\\\text{produce 2015}\\\text{ouput in 2014}\end{pmatrix} \times \begin{pmatrix}\text{Input}\\\text{price}\\\text{in 2015}\end{pmatrix}$$

$$\begin{pmatrix}\text{Cost effect of}\\\text{productivity for}\\\text{fixed costs}\end{pmatrix} = \begin{pmatrix}\text{Actual}\\\text{units of}\\\text{capacity}\\\text{in 2015}\end{pmatrix} - \begin{pmatrix}\text{Actual units of capacity in}\\\text{2014 because adequate}\\\text{capacity exists to produce}\\\text{2015 output in 2014}\end{pmatrix} \times \begin{pmatrix}\text{Price per}\\\text{unit of}\\\text{capacity}\\\text{in 2015}\end{pmatrix}$$

The productivity component of cost changes are

Direct materials costs	$(11,000 - 13,750) \times ₹1,600$	$= ₹44,00,000$ F
Conversion costs	$(13,000 - 14,000) \times ₹1,000$	$= 10,00,000$ F
Selling & customer-service costs	$(90 - 90) \times ₹9,000$	$= \underline{0}$
Change in operating income due to productivity		$\underline{\underline{₹54,00,000}}$ F

The change in operating income between 2014 and 2015 can be analyzed as follows:

	Income Statement Amounts in 2014 (1)	Revenue and Co st Effects of Growth Component in 2015 (2)	Revenue and Cost Effects of Price-Recovery Component in 2015 (3)	Cost Effect of Productivity Component in 2015 (4)	Income Statement Amounts in 2015 (5) = (1) + (2) + (3) + (4)
Revenues	₹3,80,00,000	₹1,42,50,000 F	₹82,50,000 U	–	₹4,40,00,000
Costs	3,06,75,000	60,00,000 U	1,35,000 U	₹54,00,000 F	3,14,10,000
Operating income	₹73,25,000	₹82,50,000 F	₹83,85,000 U	₹54,00,000 F	₹1,25,90,000
			₹52,65,000 F		

Change in operating income

3. The analysis of operating income indicates that a significant amount of the increase in operating income resulted from Sony's cost leadership strategy. The company was able to improve quality and grow sales. The price recovery component indicates that Sony reduced prices to be competitive in the market, but Sony also improved direct material productivity and reduced conversion cost capacity as rework decreased. Lower prices and higher quality boosted sales.

12-22 Analysis of growth, price-recovery, and productivity components (continuation of 12-21). Suppose that during 2015, the market for DVD players grew 10%. All increases in market share (that is, sales increases greater than 10%) and decreases in the selling price of the DVD are the result of Sony's strategic actions.

Required

Calculate how much of the change in operating income from 2014 to 2015 is due to the industry-market-size factor, product differentiation, and cost leadership. How does this relate to Sony's strategy and its success in implementation? Explain.

Solution

Effect of the industry-market-size factor on operating income

Of the 3,000-unit increase in sales from 8,000 to 11,000 units, 10% or 800 (10% ₹8,000) units are due to growth in market size, and 22,000 (3,000 − 800) units are due to an increase in market share.

The change in Sony's operating income from the industry-market size factor rather than from specific strategic actions is:

₹82,50,000 (the growth component in Exercise 12-29) ₹ $\dfrac{800}{3,000}$ ₹22,00,000 F

Effect of product differentiation on operating income

The change in operating income due to:

Increase in price of inputs (cost effect of price recovery)	₹1,35,000 U

Effect of cost leadership on operating income

The change in operating income from cost leadership is:

Productivity component	₹54,00,000 F
Decrease in selling price (revenue effect of price recovery)	82,50,000 U
Growth in market share due to cost leadership	

₹82,50,000 (the growth component in Exercise 12-29) ₹ $\dfrac{2,200}{3,000}$ 60,50,000 F

Change in operating income due to cost leadership	₹52,65,000 F

The change in operating income between 2014 and 2015 can be summarized as follows:

Change due to industry market-size	₹22,00,000 F
Change due to product differentiation	1,35,000 U
Change due to cost leadership	52,65,000 F

Sony has been successful in implementing its cost leadership strategy. The increase in operating income during 2015 was due to cost leadership through quality improvements and sales growth. It cut its prices significantly to gain market share that might also benefit it in future periods.

Sony's operating income increase in 2015 was also helped by a growth in the overall market size.

12-23 Identifying and managing unused capacity (continuation of 12-21). Refer to the information for Sony Company in Problem 12-21.

Required

1. Calculate the amount and cost of (a) unused manufacturing capacity and (b) unused selling and customer-service capacity at the beginning of 2015 based on actual production and actual number of customers served in 2015.

2. Suppose Sony can add or reduce its selling and customer-service capacity in increments of five customers. What is the maximum amount of costs that Sony could save in 2015 by downsizing selling and customer-service capacity?

3. Sony, in fact, does not eliminate any of its unused selling and customer-service capacity. Why might Sony not downsize?

Solution

1. The amount and cost of unused capacity at the beginning of year 2014 when Sony makes its capacity decisions for the year based on year 2014 production follows:

	Amount of Unused Capacity	Cost of Unused Capacity
Manufacturing, 14,000 - 11,000; (14,000 − 11,000) ₹1,000	3,000	₹30,00,000
Selling and customer service, 90 − 80; (90 − 80) × ₹9,000	10	₹90,000

2. Sony can reduce selling and customer-service capacity by another 10 customers (90 − 80 = 10 customers). Sony will save another 10 × ₹9,000 = ₹90,000. This is the maximum amount of costs Sony can save in 2015.

3. Sony may have chosen not to downsize because it projects sales increases in the near term that would lead to greater demand for and utilization of selling and customer-service capacity. It is difficult to reduce and then immediately increase capacity. Not reducing significant capacity by laying off employees boosts employee morale and keeps employees more motivated and productive.

12-24 Balanced scorecard, environmental and social performance. Nestle India Ltd makes custom-labeled, high-quality, specialty candy bars for special events and advertising purposes. The company employs several chocolatiers who were trained in Switzerland. The company offers many varieties of chocolate, including milk, semi-sweet, white, and dark chocolate. It also offers a variety of ingredients, such as coffee, berries, and fresh mint. The real appeal for the company's product, however, is its custom labeling. Customers can order labels for special occasions (for example, wedding invitation labels) or business purposes (for example, business card labels). The company's balanced scorecard for 2015 follows. For brevity, the initiatives taken under each objective are omitted.

Objectives	Measures	Target performance	Actual performance
Financial Perspective			
Increase shareholders value	Operating–income changes from price recovery	₹5,00,000	₹7,50,000
	Operating–income changes from price growth	₹1,00,000	₹1,25,000
	Cost saving due to reduced packaging size	₹20,000	₹25,000
Customer Perspective			
Increase market share	Market share of overall candy bar market	8%	7.8%
Increase the number of new product offerings	Number of new product offerings	5	7
Increase customer acquisitions due to sustainability efforts	Percentage of new customers surveyed who required recycled paper options	35%	40%
Internal-Business-Process Perspective			
Reduce time to customer	Average design time	3 days	3 days
Increase quality	Internal quality rating (10-points scale)	7 points	8 points
Increase use of recycled materials	Recycled materials used as a percentage of total materials used	30%	32%
Learning–and Growth Perspective			
Increase number of professional chocolatiers	Number of chocolatiers	5	6
Increase number of women and minorities in the workforce	Percentage of women and minorities in the workforce	40%	38%

Required
1. Was Nestle successful in implementing its strategy in 2015? Explain your answer.
2. Would you have included some measure of customer satisfaction in the customer perspective? Are these objectives critical to Nestle for implementing its strategy? Why or why not? Explain briefly.

3. Explain why Nestle did not achieve its target market share in the candy bar market but still exceeded its financial targets. Is "market share of overall candy bar market" a good measure of market share for Nestle? Explain briefly.

4. Do you agree with Nestle's decision not to include measures of changes in operating income from productivity improvements under the financial perspective of the balanced scorecard? Explain briefly.

5. Why did Nestle include balanced scorecard standards relating to environmental and social performance? Is the company meeting its performance objectives in these areas?

Solution

1. Nestle's strategy is to focus on "service-oriented customers" who are willing to pay a higher price for services. Even though candy bars are largely a commodity product, Nestle wants to differentiate itself through the service it provides with its custom labeling and high-quality product.

Does the scorecard represent Nestle's strategy? By and large it does. The focus of the scorecard is on measures of process improvement, quality, market share, and financial success from product differentiation and charging higher prices for customer service. There are some deficiencies that the subsequent assignment questions raise, but abstracting from these concerns for the moment, the scorecard does focus on implementing a product differentiation strategy.

Based on the scorecard being reasonably well designed, how has Nestle performed relative to its strategy in 2015? It appears from the scorecard that Nestle was successful in implementing its strategy in 2015. It achieved all targets in the financial, internal business, and learning and growth perspectives (other than women and minorities in the workplace). The only target it missed was the market share target in the customer perspective. At this stage, students may raise some questions about whether this is a good scorecard measure. Requirement 3 gets at this issue in more detail. The bottom line is that measuring "market share in the overall candy market" rather than in the "specialty candy" market segment is not a good scorecard measure, so not achieving this target may not be as big a miss as it may seem at first.

2. Yes, Nestle should include some measure of customer satisfaction in the customer perspective. Nestle's differentiation strategy and ability to charge a premium price is based on meeting and/or exceeding customer expectations, especially in the custom design of the labels. Unsatisfied customers will not be loyal or will be unlikely to recommend the company's product. Hence, customer satisfaction is very important to Nestle for implementing its strategy. These measures are leading indicators of whether Nestle will be able to increase its market share in the specialty candy market and should be measured on the balanced scorecard.

3. To evaluate if it has been successful in implementing its strategy, Nestle needs to measure its market share in its targeted market segment, not its market share in the overall market. Given Nestle's strategy, it should not be concerned if its market share in the candy bar segment declines. In fact, charging premium prices will probably cause its market share in this segment to decline. Nestle should replace "market share in overall candy bar market" with "market share in the specialty food/candy segment" in its balanced scorecard customer measure. If Nestle is successfully implementing its strategy, its market share in the specialty candy segment should increase.

4. Nestle is correct in not measuring changes in operating income from productivity improvements on its scorecard under the financial perspective. Nestle's strategy is to grow by charging premium prices for customer service. The scorecard measures focus on Nestle's success in implementing this strategy. Productivity gains per se are not critical to Nestle's strategy and, therefore, should not be measured on the scorecard.

5. Nestle included social and environmental performance measures in its balanced scorecard because it believes strong environmental and social performance gives it a competitive advantage by (1) attracting and inspiring outstanding employees, (2) enhancing its reputation with socially conscious customers, investors and analysts, and (3) boosting its image with governments and citizens, all of which contribute to long-run financial performance. Nestle also believes that focusing on environmental and social performance in addition to financial performance helps it to innovate in technologies, processes, products, and business models to reduce the trade-offs between financial and sustainability goals and build transformational leadership and change capabilities to implement these "triple bottom line" strategies.

Following the concept of shared value, Nestle includes social and environmental measures (together with business goals and measures) in its balanced scorecard to evaluate how well it is doing toward achieving its social and environmental goals. The balanced scorecard indicates that Nestle's social and environmental initiatives are having an effect. Nestle's increased use of recycled materials as a percentage of total materials used has resulted in attracting customers for whom using recycled materials matters, creating long-term financial benefit. Similarly, increasing the number of women and minorities employed will allow Nestle to target a larger number of talented individuals. Reducing the size of packaging both increases income and reduces waste, achieving both financial and sustainability objectives.

Not all companies believe in implementing sustainability goals, but those that do find the balanced scorecard to be a useful tool to simultaneously implement both financial and sustainability goals.

12-25 Balanced Scorecard, social performance. Oracle Company provides cable and Internet services in the greater Gurgaon area. There are many competitors that provide similar services. Oracle believes that the key to financial success is to offer a quality service at the lowest cost. Oracle currently spends a significant amount of hours on installation and post-installation support. This is one area that the company has targeted for cost reduction. Oracle's balanced scorecard for 2015 follows.

Objectives	Measures	Target Performance	Actual Performance
Financial Perspective			
Increase shareholder value	Operating-income changes from productivity	₹12,00,000	₹4,00,000
	Operating-income changes from growth	₹2,60,000	₹1,25,000
	Increase in revenue from new customer acquisition	₹25,000	₹12,000
Customer Perspective			
Increase customer satisfaction	Positive customer survey responses	70%	65%
Increase customer acquisition	New customers acquired through company sponsored community events	475	350
Internal-Business-Process Perspective			
Develop innovative services	Research and development costs as a percentage of revenue	5%	6%
Increase installation efficiency	Installation time per customer	5 hours	4.5 hours
Increase community involvement	Number of new programs with community organizations;	12	15
Decrease workplace injuries	Number of employees injured in the workplace	<3	7
Learning-and-Growth Perspective			
Increase employee competence	Number of annual training-hours per employee	10	11
Increase leadership skills	Number of leadership workshops offered	2	1
Increase employee safety awareness	Percent of employees who have completed safety certification training	100%	95%

1. Was Oracle successful in implementing its strategy in 2015? Explain.
2. Do you agree with Oracle's decision to include measures of developing innovative services (research and development costs) in the internal-business-process perspective of the balanced score-card? Explain briefly.
3. Is there a cause-and-effect linkage between the measures in the internal-business-process perspective and the customer perspective? That is, would you add other measures to the internal-business-process perspective or the customer perspective? Why or why not? Explain briefly.
4. Why do you think Oracle included balanced scorecard measures relating to employee safety and community engagement? How well is the company doing on these measures?

Solution

1. The market for cable and Internet providers is competitive. Oracle's strategy follows a cost-leadership strategy—providing quality service at low cost by being efficient, and effective.

The scorecard correctly measures and evaluates Oracle's strategy of growth through productivity gains and cost leadership. There are, however, some deficiencies that subsequent assignment questions will consider.

It appears from the scorecard that Oracle was not successful in implementing its strategy in 2015. Although it achieved targeted performance in most of the learning and growth and internal business process perspectives, it significantly missed its targets in the customer and financial perspectives. Oracle has not had the success it targeted in the market and has not been able to improve efficiency in order to reduce costs.

Oracle's scorecard does not provide an explanation of why the target customer satisfaction measure was not met in 2015. Was it due to poor quality? Higher prices? Poor post-sales service? Aggressive competitors? The scorecard is not helpful for understanding the reasons underlying the poor customer satisfaction.

2. Oracle should not include R&D costs in its internal business process perspective. It should not focus on developing innovative services because it is not following a product differentiation strategy. It needs to cut these costs and focus instead on providing customers a quality service at the lowest costs, and faster and more efficient installation, consistent with its low-cost strategy.

3. There is a cause-and-effect relationship between the installation time per customer and customer satisfaction but not between money spent in R&D and customer satisfaction. As discussed in requirement 2 above, I would drop the R&D measure. I would then add measures for the quality of the installation service to the internal business process perspective. How much time does it take to schedule an appointment after the customer calls? Does the service work flawlessly after it has been installed? Do customers call Oracle to fix problems? How much time is spent on post-installation support? The point is to add more measures to the internal business process perspective so that Oracle can get a better understanding of the reasons underlying increases and decreases in customer satisfaction.

In the customer perspective, I would add measures to track Oracle's market share in Gurgaon area. Do increases in customer satisfaction translate into higher market shares? Is Oracle correctly identifying the factors that customers care deeply about and making improvements in those areas faster than its competitors?

Although not required by the question, the instructor could ask the class what else Oracle might want to include in the learning and growth perspective to support the customer and internal business process perspectives. The learning and growth measures would then serve as leading indicators (based on cause-and-effect relationships) for the internal-business processes and customer satisfaction. For example, Oracle could include a measure related to employee satisfaction or retention. For example, higher employee satisfaction would lead to greater ownership of employees in providing a quality service. This is critical for Oracle to successfully implement its strategy.

4. Oracle included social and environmental performance measures in its balanced score-card because it believes strong environmental and social performance gives it a competitive advantage by (1) attracting and inspiring outstanding employees, (2) enhancing its reputation with socially conscious customers, investors and analysts, and (3) boosting its image with governments and citizens, all of which contribute to long-run financial performance. Oracle also believes that focusing on environmental and social performance in addition to financial performance helps it to innovate in technologies, processes, products, and business models to reduce the trade-offs between financial and sustainability goals and build transformational leadership and change capabilities to implement these "triple bottom line" strategies.

Following the concept of shared value, Oracle includes social and environmental measures (together with business goals and measures) in its balanced scorecard to evaluate how well it is doing toward achieving its social and environmental goals. The balanced scorecard indicates that Oracle's social and environmental initiatives are having mixed results. Oracle's focus on safety certification training aims to decrease workplace injuries and to reduce overall costs. So far, the safety certification goals have not been met and workplace injuries have not been reduced to their target levels. Oracle would need to consider if the safety certification training has been as effective as it was intended. Similarly, increasing the number of new programs with community organizations aims to increase the number of new customers acquired as a result of these initiatives and in turn to increase revenue from new customers. Even though the number of new programs started exceeded the target, it did not result in the targeted number of new customers nor the target revenues from new customers. Oracle would need to reevaluate the kinds of new programs it is implementing.

Not all companies believe in implementing sustainability goals, but those that do find the balanced scorecard to be a useful tool to simultaneously implement both financial and sustainability goals.

12-26 Balanced Scorecard. IndiGo is a no-frills airline that services the major cities in India. Its mission is to be the only short-haul, low-fare, high-frequency, point-to-point carrier. However, there are several large commercial carriers offering air transportation, and IndiGo knows that it cannot compete with them based on the services those carriers provide. IndiGo has chosen to reduce costs by not offering many inflight services, such as food and entertainment options. Instead, the company is dedicated to providing the highest quality transportation at the lowest fare. IndiGo's balanced scorecard measures (and actual results) for 2015 follow:

Objectives	Measures	Target performance	Actual performance
Financial Perspective			
Increase shareholders value	Operating–income changes from productivity	₹12 crore	₹14 crore
	Operating–income changes from price recovery	₹4.5 crore	₹6 crore
	Operating–income changes from growth	₹5.0 crore	₹6.6 crore
	Cost savings due to reduction in jet consumption	₹1.5 crore	₹1.8 crore
Customer Perspective			
Increase number of on time arrivals	FAA on-time arrival ranking	1st in industry	2nd in industry
Improve brand image	Percentage of customer survey with greater than 90% approval rating on company's sustainability efforts	100%	96%
Internal-Business-Process Perspective			
Reduce turnaround time	On-ground time	<25 minutes	30 minutes
Reduce CO2 emissions	Number of engineering changes that decreased CO_2 emissions	10	9
Learning–and Growth Perspective			
Align ground crews	% of ground crews stockholders	70%	68%
Acquire new energy management tool technology	Achieve ISO 50001 certificate in energy management	Acquired certificate by Dec.31	Acquired certificate by Dec.31

1. What is IndiGo's strategy? Was IndiGo successful in implementing its strategy in 2015? Explain your answer.

2. Based on the strategy identified in requirement 1 above, what role does the price-recovery component play in explaining the success of IndiGo?

3. Would you have included customer-service measures in the customer perspective? Why or why not? Explain briefly.

4. Would you have included some measure of employee satisfaction and employee training in the learning-and-growth perspective? Would you consider this objective critical to IndiGo for implementing its strategy? Why or why not? Explain briefly.

5. Why do you think IndiGo has introduced environmental measures in its balanced scorecard? Is the company meeting its performance objectives in this area?

Solution

1. IndiGo is following a cost-leadership strategy based on low-cost, no frills, and high quality. IndiGo was successful in meeting its financial targets in 2015, but it did not achieve target performance in the other three perspectives. It was therefore only partially successful in implementing its strategy. The nonfinancial measures are leading indicators of future performance. Not meeting these targets means that IndiGo may not be able to sustain its performance in future periods. In other words, while IndiGo was able to achieve its short-term goals, will it be able to achieve its long-term goals? To do so, IndiGo needs to improve its internal business and learning and growth performance.

2. Normally, the price recovery component indicates that a company has been successful in differentiating its product or service to command a price premium so that the prices of outputs rise faster than the prices of inputs. For IndiGo, the price recovery component measures the lower input prices resulting from strong negotiations with suppliers while maintaining output prices. The productivity component measures the efficiently use of input quantities and the elimination of certain inflight services. A favorable price recovery component from reducing input prices is an important part of IndiGo's strategy that contributes to its profitability.

3. I would not have included customer-service measures in IndiGo's customer perspective because it is not part of IndiGo's strategy. IndiGo does not compete with other carriers on the basis of its services. In fact, it does not offer inflight services such as food and entertainment options. It is a no-frills airline, whose strategy is to eliminate services in order to reduce costs. We are not debating the merits of the strategy. Only that given the strategy, measures of customer service should not appear on the scorecard.

4. Yes, IndiGo should include some measure of employee satisfaction and employee training in the learning and growth perspective. IndiGo's low-cost strategy is based on efficiency. The key to good, fast, and friendly customer service is well trained and satisfied employees. Untrained and dissatisfied employees have poor interactions with customers and other employees and cause the strategy to fail. Hence, training and employee satisfaction are very important for IndiGo to implement its strategy. These measures are, therefore, leading indicators of whether IndiGo will be able to successfully implement its strategy over the long term and should be measured on the balanced scorecard.

5. IndiGo included social and environmental performance measures in its balanced scorecard because it believes strong environmental and social performance gives it a competitive advantage by (1) attracting and inspiring outstanding employees, (2) enhancing its reputation with socially conscious customers, investors and analysts, and (3) boosting its image with governments and citizens, all of which contribute to long-run financial performance. IndiGo also believes that focusing on environmental and social performance in addition to financial performance helps it to innovate in technologies, processes, products, and business models to reduce the trade-offs between financial and sustainability goals and build transformational leadership and change capabilities to implement these "triple bottom line" strategies.

Following the concept of shared value, IndiGo includes social and environmental measures (together with business goals and measures) in its balanced scorecard to evaluate how well it is doing toward achieving its social and environmental goals. The balanced scorecard indicates that IndiGo's social and environmental initiatives are by and large succeeding. IndiGo has successfully obtained ISO 50001 certification in energy management. This focus has helped it to implement engineering changes that decrease CO_2 emissions. (It was to implement 10 such changes. but it made only 9.) As it made these changes, customer surveys indicated that 96% of customers approved of IndiGo's sustainability efforts, slightly lower than the 100% of customers that IndiGo had targeted. In turn, these actions resulted in cost savings in jet fuel consumption that exceeded targets. IndiGo may need to make some small changes in its sustainability and environmental performance measures and targets, but by and large it is helping IndiGo meet its long-term financial and sustainability goals.

Not all companies believe in implementing sustainability goals, but those that do find the balanced scorecard to be a useful tool to simultaneously implement both financial and sustainability goals.

12-27 Engineered and discretionary overhead costs, unused capacity, customer help desk. Wire & Wireless Ltd., a large cable television operator, had 7,50,000 subscribers in 2015. Wire & Wireless Ltd. employs five customer-help-desk representatives to respond to customer questions and problems. During 2015, each customer-help-desk representative worked 8 hours per day for 250 days at a fixed annual salary of ₹3,60,000. Wire & Wireless Ltd. received 45,000 telephone calls from its customers in 2015. Each call took an average of 10 minutes.

Required

1. Do you think customer-help-desk costs at Wire & Wireless Ltd. are engineered costs or discretionary costs? Explain your answer.

2. Where possible, calculate the cost of unused customer-help-desk capacity in 2015 under each of the following assumptions: (a) customer-help-desk costs are engineered costs and (b) customer-help-desk costs are discretionary costs. If you are unable to calculate the amount and cost of unused capacity, then indicate why not.

3. Assume that Wire & Wireless Ltd. had 9,00,000 subscribers in 2016 and that the 2015 percentage of telephone calls received to total subscribers continued in 2016. Customer-help-desk capacity in 2016 was the same as it was in 2015. Where possible, calculate the cost of unused customer-help-desk capacity in 2016 under each of the following assumptions: (a) customer-service costs are engineered costs and (b) customer-service costs are discretionary costs. If you are unable to calculate the amount and cost of unused capacity, then indicate why not.

Solution

Engineered and discretionary overhead costs, unused capacity, customer help-desk.

1. Wire & Wireless Ltd.'s customer-help-desk costs are indirect engineered costs. Over time, there is a clear cause-and-effect relationship among the output (number of subscribers or customers) and customer-help-desk representatives needed and customer-help-desk costs. The more the number of homes serviced, the greater the number of customer-service calls expected, and therefore greater is the number of customer-help-desk representatives needed.

2a. Assume customer-help-desk costs are engineered costs.

(1) Available customer-help-desk capacity	
8 hours per day × 250 days × 5 representatives	10,000 hours
(2) Customer-help-desk services actually used	
45,000 calls × $\frac{1}{6}$ hour per call	<u>7,500</u> hours
(3) 5 (1) − (2) Hours of unused customer-help-desk capacity	<u>2,500</u> hours
(4) Cost per hour, ₹3,60,000 ÷ 2,000 hours (8 hours/day × 250 days)	₹180 per hour
(5) 5 (3) × (4) Cost of unused customer-help-desk capacity in 2015	₹4,50,000

2b. Assume customer-help-desk costs are discretionary costs. In this case, cost of unused capacity in 2015 cannot be determined. The absence of a cause-and-effect relationship between homes serviced and customer-service calls means that Wire & Wireless Ltd. cannot determine the customer-help-desk resources used and, hence, the amount of unused capacity.

3. $$\frac{\text{Telephone calls received in 2015}}{\text{Total subscribers in 2015}} = \frac{45,000}{7,50,000} = 6\%$$

Applying this 6% to the 9,00,000 subscribers in 2016 means that Wire & Wireless Ltd. received 54,000 (6% × 9,00,000) calls in 2016.

  a. Assume customer-help-desk costs are engineered costs.

(1) Available customer-help-desk capacity in 2016	10,000 hours
(2) Customer-help-desk services actually used 54,000 calls × $\frac{1}{6}$ hour per call	9,000 hours
(3) 5 (1) – (2) Hours of unused customer-help-desk capacity	1,000 hours
(4) Cost per hour	₹180 per hour
(5) 5 (3) × (4) Cost of unused customer-help-desk capacity in 2016	₹1,80,000

  b. Assume customer-help-desk costs are discretionary costs. For the reasons described in 2b, the cost of unused capacity in 2016 cannot be determined.

12-28 Balanced scorecard, ethics. Ravi, division manager of the Household Products Division, a maker of kitchen dishwashers, has just seen the balanced scorecard for his division for 2016. He immediately calls Raj, the division's management accountant, into his office for a meeting. "I think the employee-satisfaction and customer-satisfaction numbers are way too low. These numbers are based on a random sample of subjective assessments made by individual managers and customer representatives. My own experience indicates that we are doing well on both these dimensions. Until we do a formal survey of employees and customers sometime next year, I think we are doing a disservice to ourselves and this company by reporting such low scores for employee and customer satisfaction. These scores will be an embarrassment for us at the division managers' meeting next month. We need to get these numbers up."

Raj knows that the employee- and customer-satisfaction scores are subjective, but the procedure he used this year is identical to the procedures he has used in the past. He knows from the comments he had asked for that the scores represent the unhappiness of employees with the latest work rules and the unhappiness of customers with late deliveries. He also knows that these problems will be corrected in time.

Required

1. Do you think that the Household Products Division should include subjective measures of employee satisfaction and customer satisfaction in its balanced scorecard? Explain.

2. What should Raj do?

Solution
Balanced scorecard, ethics.

  1. Yes, the Household Products Division (HPD) should include measures of employee satisfaction and customer satisfaction even if these measures are subjective. For a maker of kitchen dishwashers, employee- and customer satisfaction are leading indicators of future financial performance. There is a cause-and-effect linkage between these measures and future financial performance. If HPD's strategy is correct and if the scorecard has been properly designed, employee- and customer-satisfaction information is very important in evaluating the implementation of HPD's strategy.

HPD should use employee-and customer-satisfaction measures even though these measures are subjective. One of the pitfalls to avoid when implementing a balanced scorecard is not to use only objective measures in the scorecard. Of course, HPD should guard against imprecision and potential for manipulation. Raj appears to be aware of this. He has tried to understand the reasons for the poor scores, and has been able to relate these scores to other objective evidence such as employee dissatisfaction, with the new work rules and customer unhappiness with missed delivery dates.

2. Incorrect reporting of employee-and customer-satisfaction ratings to make a division's performance look good is unethical. In assessing the situation, the specific "Standards of Ethical Conduct for Management Accountants," which the management account should consider are listed below.

Competence

Clear reports using relevant and reliable information should be prepared. Preparing reports on the basis of incorrect employee-and customer-satisfaction ratings to make the division's performance look better than it is, violates competence standards. It is unethical for Raj to change the employee-and customer-satisfaction ratings to make the division's performance look good.

Integrity

The management accountant has a responsibility to avoid actual or apparent conflicts of interest and advice all appropriate parties of any potential conflict. Raj may be tempted to report better employee-and customer-satisfaction ratings to please Ravi. This action, however, violates the responsibility for integrity. The Standards of Ethical Conduct require the management accountant to communicate favorable as well as unfavorable information.

Objectivity

The management accountant's standards of ethical conduct require that information should be fairly and objectively communicated and that all relevant information should be disclosed. From a management accountant's standpoint, modifying employee-and customer-satisfaction ratings to make division performance look good would violate the standard of objectivity.

Raj should indicate to Ravi that the employee- and customer-satisfaction ratings are, indeed, appropriate. If Ravi still insists on reporting better employee- and customer-satisfaction numbers, Raj should raise the matter with one of Ravi's superiors. If, after taking all these steps, there is a continued pressure to overstate employee-and customer-satisfaction ratings, Raj should consider resigning from the company and not engage in unethical behavior.

12-29 Strategic analysis of operating income. Van Heusen Company sells women's clothing. Van Heusen's strategy is to offer a wide selection of clothes and excellent customer service, and to charge a premium price. Van Heusen presents the following data for 2014 and 2015. For simplicity, assume that each customer purchases one piece of clothing.

	2014	2015
1. Pieces of clothing purchased and sold	40,000	40,000
2. Average selling price	₹600	₹590
3. Average cost per piece of clothing	₹400	₹410
4. Selling and customer-service capacity	51,000 customers	43,000 customers
5. Selling and customer-service costs	₹35,70,000	₹29,67,000
6. Selling and customer-service capacity cost per customer (Line = , Line 4)	₹70 per customer	₹69 per customer
7. Purchasing and administrative capacity	980 designs	850 designs
8. Purchasing and administrative costs	₹24,50,000	₹20,40,000
9. Purchasing and administrative capacity cost per distinct design	₹2,500 per design	₹2,400 per design

Total selling and customer-service costs depend on the number of customers that Van Heusen has created capacity to support, not the actual number of customers that Van Heusen serves. Total purchasing and administrative costs depend on purchasing and administrative capacity that Van Heusen has created (defined in terms of the number of distinct clothing designs that Van Heusen can purchase and administer). Purchasing and administrative costs do not depend on the actual number of distinct clothing designs purchased. Van Heusen purchased 930 distinct designs in 2014 and 820 distinct designs in 2015.

At the start of 2015, Van Heusen planned to increase the operating income by 10% over the operating income in 2014.

Required

1. Is Van Heusen's strategy one of product differentiation or cost leadership? Explain.
2. Calculate Van Heusen's operating income in 2014 and 2015.
3. Calculate the growth, price-recovery, and productivity components of changes in operating income between 2014 and 2015.
4. Does the strategic analysis of operating income indicate that Van Heusen was successful in implementing its strategy in 2015? Explain.

Solution

Strategic analysis of operating income.

1. Van Heusen is following a product differentiation strategy. Van Heusen offers a wide selection of clothes and excellent customer service. Van Heusen's strategy is to distinguish itself from its competitors and to charge a premium price.
2. Operating income for each year is as follows:

	2014	2015
Revenues (₹600 × 3,40,000; ₹590 × 40,000)	₹2,40,00,000	₹2,36,00,000
Costs		
Costs of goods sold (₹400 × 40,000; ₹410 × 40,000)	1,60,00,000	1,64,00,000
Selling and customer service costs (₹70 × 51,000); ₹69 × 43,000)	35,70,000	29,67,000
Purchasing and administrative costs (₹2,500 × 980; ₹2,400 × 850)	24,50,000	20,40,000
Total costs	2,20,20,000	2,14,07,000
Operating income	. ₹19,80,000	₹21,93,000
Change in operating income	₹2,13,000 F	

2.The Growth Component

$$\text{Revenue effect of Growth} = \left(\begin{array}{c} \text{Actual units of} \\ \text{output sold in 2015} \end{array} - \begin{array}{c} \text{Actual units of} \\ \text{output sold in 2014} \end{array} \right) \times \begin{array}{c} \text{Selling price in} \\ 2014 \end{array}$$

$$= (40,000 - 40,000) \times ₹600 = ₹0$$

$$\text{Cost effect of growth for variable costs} = \left(\begin{array}{c} \text{units of Input} \\ \text{rerquired to produce} \\ \text{2015 output in 2014} \end{array} - \begin{array}{c} \text{Actual units of inputs} \\ \text{used to produce 2014} \\ \text{output} \end{array} \right) \times \begin{array}{c} \text{Input price in} \\ 2014 \end{array}$$

$$\text{Cost effect of growth for fixed costs} = \left(\begin{array}{c}\text{Actual units of capacity in}\\ \text{2014, if adequate}\\ \text{to produce 2015 output in 2014}\\ \text{OR}\\ \text{If 2014 capacity inadequate}\\ \text{to produce 2015}\\ \text{output in 2014, units}\\ \text{of capacity required to}\\ \text{produce 2015 output in 2014}\end{array} - \begin{array}{c}\text{Actual units}\\ \text{of capacity}\\ \text{in 2014}\end{array}\right) \times \begin{array}{c}\text{Price per unit}\\ \text{of capacity in}\\ \text{2014}\end{array}$$

Pieces of clothing that would be required to be purchased in 2015 would be the same as that required in 2014 because output is the same between 2014 and 2015. Purchasing and administrative costs and selling and customer-service costs will not change as adequate capacity exists in 2014 to support year 2015 output and customers.

The cost effects of growth component are:

Costs of goods sold	(40,000 − 40,000) × ₹400	=	₹0
Selling and customer-service costs	(51,000 − 51,000) × ₹70	=	0
Purchase and administrative costs	(980 − 980) × ₹2,500	=	0
Cost effect of growth			₹0

In summary, the net effect on operating income as a result of the growth component equals:

Revenue effect of growth	₹0
Cost effect of growth	0
Change in operating income due to growth	₹0

The Price-Recovery Component

$$\text{Revenue effect of price-recovery} = (\text{Selling price in 2015} - \text{Selling price in 2014}) \times \text{Actual units of output sold in 2015}$$

$$= (₹590 - ₹600) \times 40,000 = ₹4,00,000F$$

$$\text{Cost effect of price-recovery for variable costs} = \left(\begin{array}{c}\text{Input price}\\ \text{in 2015}\end{array} - \begin{array}{c}\text{Input price}\\ \text{in 2014}\end{array}\right) \times \begin{array}{c}\text{Units of input required to}\\ \text{produce 2015 output in}\\ \text{2014}\end{array}$$

$$\text{Cost effect of price-recovery for fixed costs} = \left(\begin{array}{c}\text{Price per unit}\\ \text{of capacity in}\\ \text{2015}\end{array} - \begin{array}{c}\text{Price per unit}\\ \text{of capacity in}\\ \text{2014}\end{array}\right) \times \begin{array}{c}\text{Actual units od capacity in}\\ \text{2014, if adequate}\\ \text{to produce 2015 output in 2014}\\ \text{OR}\\ \text{If 2014 capacity inadequate}\\ \text{to produce 2015}\\ \text{output in 2014, then units}\\ \text{of capacity required to}\\ \text{produce 2015 output in 2014}\end{array}$$

Costs of goods sold	(₹410 − ₹400) × 40,000	=	₹4,00,000 U
Selling and customer-service costs	(₹69 − ₹70) × 51,000	=	51,000 F
Purchase and administrative costs	(₹2,400 − ₹2,500) × 980	=	98,000 F
Cost effect of price-recovery			₹2,51,000 U

n summary, the net decrease in operating income as a result of the price-recovery component equals:

Revenue effect of price-recovery	₹4,00,000 U
Cost effect of price-recovery	2,51,000 U
Change in operating income due to price-recovery	₹6,51,000 U

The Productivity Component

The productivity component of cost changes are:

$$\begin{array}{c}\text{Cost effect of}\\\text{productivity for}\\\text{variable costs}\end{array} = \left(\begin{array}{c}\text{Actual units of}\\\text{Input to produce 2015}\\\text{output}\end{array} - \begin{array}{c}\text{Units of input}\\\text{required to produce}\\\text{2015 output in 2014}\end{array}\right) \times \begin{array}{c}\text{Input price in}\\\text{2014}\end{array}$$

$$\begin{array}{c}\text{Cost effect of}\\\text{productivity for}\\\text{fixed costs}\end{array} = \left(\begin{array}{c}\text{Actual units}\\\text{of capacity}\\\text{in 2015}\end{array} - \begin{array}{c}\text{Actual units of capacity in}\\\text{2014, if adequate}\\\text{to produce 2015 output in 2014}\\\text{OR}\\\text{If 2014 capacity inadequate}\\\text{to produce 2015}\\\text{output in 2014, then units}\\\text{of capacity required to}\\\text{produce 2015 output in 2014}\end{array}\right) \times \begin{array}{c}\text{Price per unit}\\\text{of capacity in}\\\text{2015}\end{array}$$

Costs of goods sold	(40,000 – 40,000) ×	₹410	=	0
Selling and customer-service costs	(43,000 – 51,000) ×	₹69	=	₹5,52,000 F
Purchasing and administrative costs	(850 – 980) ×	₹2,400	=	3,12,000 F
Change in operating income due to productivity				₹8,64,000 F

The change in operating income between 2014 and 2015 can be analyzed as follows:

	IncomeStatement Amounts in 2014 (1)	Revenue and Cost Effects of Growth Componentin 2015 (2)	Revenue and Cost Effects of Price-Recovery Component in 2015 (3)	Cost Effect of Productivity Component in 2015 (4)	Income Statement Amounts in 2014 (5) = (1) + (2) + (3) + (4)
Revenues	₹2,40,00,000	₹0	₹4,00,000 U	—	₹2,36,00,000
Costs	2,20,20,000	0	2,51,000 U	₹8,64,000 F	2,14,07,000
Operating income	₹19,80,000	₹0	₹6,51,000 U	₹8,64,000 F	₹21,93,000

₹2,13,000 F

Change in operating income

4. The analysis of operating income indicates that a significant amount of the increase in operating income resulted from productivity gains rather than product differentiation. The company was unable to charge a premium price for its clothes. Thus, the strategic analysis of operating income indicates that Van Heusen has not been successful at implementing its premium price, product differentiation strategy, despite the fact that

operating income increased by more than 10% between 2014 and 2015. Van Heuser could not pass on increases in purchase costs to its customers via higher prices. Var Heusen must either reconsider its product-differentiation strategy or focus managers on increasing margins and growing market share by offering better product variety and superb customer service.

12-30 Partial productivity measurement. Gable Company manufactures wallets from fabric In 2014, Gable made 21,60,000 wallets using 16,00,000 meters of fabric. In 2014, Gable has capacity to make 24,48,000 wallets and incurs a cost of ₹8,56,80,000 for this capacity In 2015, Gable plans to make 22,03,200 wallets, make fabric use more efficient, and reduce capacity.

Suppose that in 2015 Gable makes 22,03,200 wallets, uses 14,40,000 meters of fabric and reduces capacity to 22,95,000 wallets at a cost of ₹7,80,30,000.

Required

1. Calculate the partial-productivity ratios for materials and conversion (capacity costs) fo 2015, and compare them to a benchmark for 2014 calculated based on 2015 output.

2. How can Gable Company use the information from the partial-productivity calculations?

Solution

1. Gable Company's partial productivity ratios in 2015 are as follows:

$$\frac{\text{Direct materials}}{\text{partial productivity}} = \frac{\text{Quantity of output produced in 2015}}{\text{Meters of direct materials used in 2015}} = \frac{22,03,200}{14,40,000} = \frac{1.53 \text{ wallets}}{\text{per meter}}$$

$$\frac{\text{Conversion costs}}{\text{partial productivity}} = \frac{\text{Quantity of output produced in 2015}}{\text{Units of manuf. capacity in 2015}} = \frac{22,03,200}{22,95,000} = \begin{array}{c}0.96 \text{ wallets} \\ \text{per unit of} \\ \text{capacity}\end{array}$$

To compare partial productivities in 2015 with partial productivities in 2014, we first calculate the inputs that would have been used in 2014 to produce year 2015's 22,03,200 units o output assuming the year 2014 relationship between inputs and outputs.

$$\text{Direct materials} = 16,00,000 \text{ Meters (2014)} \times \frac{22,03,200 \text{ output units in 2015}}{21,60,000 \text{ output units in 2014}}$$

$$= 16,00,000 \text{ Meters } ₹1.02 = 16,32,000 \text{ Meters}$$

Alternatively, we can calculate direct materials that would have been used in year 2014 to produce year 2015's 22,03,200 output as 16,00,000 Meters ÷ 21,60,000 units = 0.74074 Meters per unit × 22,03,200 units = 16,32,000 meters.

Manufacturing capacity = 24,48,000 units of capacity, because manufacturing capacity is fixed, and adequate capacity existed in 2014 to produce year 2015 output.

Partial productivity calculations for 2014 based on year 2015 output (to make the partial productivities comparable across the two years):

$$\frac{\text{Direct materials}}{\text{partial productivity}} = \frac{\text{Quantity of output produced in 2015}}{\begin{array}{c}\text{Yards of direct materials that would} \\ \text{have been used in 2014 to produce} \\ \text{year 2015 output}\end{array}} = \frac{22,03,200}{16,32,000} = \frac{1.35 \text{ wallets}}{\text{per meter}}$$

$$\frac{\text{Conversion costs}}{\text{partial productivity}} = \frac{\text{Quantity of output produced in 2015}}{\begin{array}{c}\text{Units of manufacturing capacity} \\ \text{that would have been used in} \\ \text{2014 to produce year 2015 output}\end{array}} = \frac{22,03,200}{24,48,000} = \frac{0.9 \text{ wallets per}}{\text{unit of capacity}}$$

The calculations indicate that Gable improved the partial productivity of direct materials and conversion costs between 2014 and 2015 via efficiency improvements and by reducing unused manufacturing capacity.

2. Gable Company management can use the partial productivity measures to set targets for the next year. Partial productivity measures can easily be compared over multiple periods. For example, they may specify bonus payments if partial productivity of direct materials increases to 1.6 units of output per meters and if partial productivity of conversion costs improves to 0.98 units of output per unit of capacity. A major advantage of partial productivity measures is that they focus on a single input; hence, they are simple to calculate and easy to understand at the operations level. Managers and operators can also examine these numbers to understand the reasons underlying productivity changes from one period to the next—better training of workers, lower labor turnover, better incentives, or improved methods. Management can then implement and sustain these factors in the future.

12-31 Total factor productivity (continuation of 12-30). Refer to the data for Problem 12-30. Assume the fabric costs ₹40 per meter in 2015 and ₹41 per meters in 2014.

Required

1. Compute Gable Company's total factor productivity (TFP) for 2015.
2. Compare TFP for 2015 with a benchmark TFP for 2014 inputs based on 2015 prices and output.
3. What additional information does TFP provide that partial productivity measures do not?

Solution

1.
$$\text{Total factor productivity for 2015 using 2015 prices} = \frac{\text{Quantity of output produced in 2015}}{\text{Costs of inputs used in 2015 based on 2015 prices}}$$

$$= \frac{22,03,200}{(14,40,000 \times ₹40) + (78,03,000)}$$

$$= \frac{22,03,200}{₹5,76,00,000 + ₹7,80,30,000} = \frac{22,03,200}{₹13,56,30,000}$$

$$= 0.01624419 \text{ units of output per rupee of input}$$

2. By itself, the 2015 TFP of 0.016244 units per rupee of input is not particularly helpful. We need something to compare the 2015 TFP against. We use, as a benchmark, TFP calculated using the inputs that Gable would have used in 2014 to produce 26,48,000 units of output calculated in requirement 1 at 2015 prices. Using the current year's (2015) prices in both calculations controls for input price differences and focuses the analysis on the adjustments the manager made in the quantities of inputs in response to changes in prices.

$$\text{2015 price of capacity} = \frac{\text{Cost of capacity in 2015}}{\text{Capacity in 2015}} = \frac{₹7,80,30,000}{22,95,000 \text{ units}} = ₹34 \text{ per unit of capacity}$$

$$\text{Benchmark TFP} = \frac{\text{Quantity of output produced in 2015}}{\substack{\text{Costs of inputs that would have been used in 2014} \\ \text{to produce 2015 output at year 2015 input prices}}}$$

$$= \frac{22,03,200}{(16,32,000 \times ₹40) + (24,48,000 \times ₹34)}$$

$$= \frac{22,03,200}{₹6,52,80,000 + ₹8,32,32,000}$$

$$= \frac{22,03,200}{₹14,85,12,000}$$

$$= 0.01483516 \text{ units of output per rupee of input}$$

Using 2015 prices, total factor productivity increased 9.5% [(0.016244 − 0.014835) ÷ 0.014835] from 2014 to 2015.

3. Total factor productivity increased because Gable produced more output per rupee of input in 2015 relative to 2014, measured in both years using 2015 prices. The change in partial productivity of direct materials and conversion costs tells us that Gable used less materials and capacity in 2015 relative to output, than in 2014.

A major advantage of TFP over partial productivity measures is that TFP combines the productivity of all inputs and so measures gains from using fewer physical inputs and substitution among inputs.

Partial productivities cannot be combined to indicate the overall effect on cost as a result of these individual improvements. The TFP measure allows managers to evaluate the change in overall productivity by simultaneously combining all inputs to measure gains from using fewer physical inputs as well as substitution among inputs. Sony Company manufactures a DVD player. The company sells the player to discount stores throughout the country. This player is significantly less expensive than similar products sold by Sony's competitors, but the Sony offers just DVD playback, compared with DVD and Blu-ray playback offered by competitor LG. Furthermore, the Sony has experienced production problems that have resulted in significant rework costs. LG's model has an excellent reputation for quality.

Exercises

[*Comprehensive solutions to all exercises are available on the companion website www. pearsoned.co.in/charlesthorngren*]

12-32 Balanced scorecard. Ballarpur Industries manufactures corrugated cardboard boxes. It competes and plans to grow by producing high-quality boxes at a low cost and by delivering them to customers quickly after receiving customers' orders. There are many other manufacturers who produce similar boxes. Ballarpur Industries believes that continuously improving its manufacturing processes and having satisfied employees are critical to implementing its strategy in 2016.

Required

1. Is Ballarpur Industries's 2016 strategy one of product differentiation or cost leadership? Explain briefly.
2. AP Paper, a competitor of Ballarpur Industries, manufactures corrugated boxes with more designs and color combinations than Ballarpur Industries at a higher price. AP Paper's boxes are of high quality but require more time to produce and so have longer delivery times. Draw a simple customer preference map as in Exhibit 12-1 for Ballarpur Industries, and AP Paper using the attributes of price, delivery time, quality, and design.

12-33 Analysis of growth, price-recovery, and productivity components (continuation of 12-32). An analysis of Ballarpur Industries's operating-income changes between 2015 and 2016 shows the following:

Operating income for 2015	₹17,00,000
Add growth component	70,000
Deduct price-recovery component	(60,000)
Add productivity component	1,40,000
Operating income for 2016	₹18,50,000

The industry-market size for corrugated cardboard boxes did not grow in 2016, input prices did not change, and Ballarpur Industries reduced the prices of its boxes.

Required

1. Was Ballarpur Industries's gain in operating income in 2016 consistent with the strategy you identified in requirement 1 of Exercise 12-32?
2. Explain the productivity component. In general, does it represent savings in only variable costs, only fixed costs, or both variable and fixed costs?

12-34 Strategy, balanced scorecard, service company. Heritage Systems is a small information-systems consulting firm that specializes in helping companies implement sales-management software. The market for Heritage's products is very competitive. To compete, Heritage must deliver quality service at a low cost. Heritage bills clients in terms of units of work performed, which depends on the size and complexity of the sales-management system. Heritage presents the following data for 2014 and 2015.

		2014	2015
1	Units of work performed	60	70
2	Selling price	₹5,00,000	₹4,80,000
3	Software-implementation labor hours	30,000	32,000
4	Cost per software-implementation labor hour	₹600	₹630
5	Software-implementation support capacity (in units of work)	90	90
6	Total cost of software-implementation support	₹36,00,000	₹36,90,000
7	Software-implementation support-capacity cost per unit of work	₹40,000	₹41,000
8	Number of employees doing software development	3	3
9	Total software-development costs	₹37,50,000	₹39,00,000
10	Software-development cost per employee	₹12,50,000	₹13,00,000

Software-implementation labor-hour costs are variable costs. Software-implementation support costs for each year depend on the software-implementation support capacity (defined in terms of units of work) that Heritage chooses to maintain each year. It does not vary with the actual units of work performed that year. At the start of each year, the management uses its discretion to determine the number of software-development employees. The software-development staff and costs have no direct relationship with the number of units of work performed.

Required

1. Is Heritage Systems's strategy one of product differentiation or cost leadership? Explain briefly.
2. Describe the key elements you would include in Heritage's balanced scorecard and your reasons for doing so.

12-35 **Strategic analysis of operating income (continuation of 12-34). Refer to Exercise 12-34.**

Required

1. Calculate the operating income of Heritage Systems in 2014 and 2015.
2. Calculate the growth, price-recovery, and productivity components that explain the change in operating income from 2014 to 2015.
3. Comment on your answer in requirement 2. What do these components indicate?

12-36 **Analysis of growth, price-recovery, and productivity components (continuation of 12-35).**

Suppose that during 2015 the market for implementing sales-management software increases by 5% and that Heritage experiences a 1% decline in selling prices. Assume that any further decreases in selling price and increases in market share are strategic choices by Heritage's management to implement their strategy.

Required

Calculate how much of the change in operating income from 2014 to 2015 is due to the industry-market-size factor, cost leadership, and product differentiation. How successful has Heritage been in implementing its strategy? Explain.

12-37 **Identifying and managing unused capacity (continuation of 12-34). Refer to Exercise 12-34.**

Required

1. Where possible, calculate the amount and cost of (a) unused software-implementation support capacity and (b) unused software-development capacity at the beginning of 2015, based on units of work performed in 2015. If you are unable to calculate the amount and cost of unused capacity, then indicate why not.
2. Suppose Heritage can add or reduce its software-implementation support capacity in increments of 15 units. What is the maximum amount of costs that Heritage could save in 2015 by downsizing software-implementation support capacity?
3. Heritage, in fact, does not eliminate any of its unused software-implementation support capacity. Why might Heritage not downsize?

12-38 Balanced scorecard. Hewlett Packard (HP) manufactures various types of color laser printers in a highly automated facility with high fixed costs. The market for laser printers is competitive. The various color laser printers on the market are comparable in terms of features and price. HP believes that satisfying customers with products of high quality at low costs is key to achieving its target profitability. For 2015, HP plans to achieve higher quality and lower costs by improving yields and reducing defects in its manufacturing operations. HP will train workers, and encourage and empower them to take the necessary actions. Currently, a significant amount of HP's capacity is used to produce products that are defective and cannot be sold. HP expects that higher yields will reduce the capacity that HP needs to manufacture products. HP does not anticipate that improving manufacturing will automatically lead to lower costs because HP has high fixed costs. To reduce fixed costs per unit, HP could lay off employees and sell equipment, or it could use the capacity to produce and sell more of its current products or improved models of its current products.

HP's balanced scorecard (initiatives omitted) for the just-completed fiscal year 2015 follows:

Objectives	Measures	Target Performance	Actual Performance
Financial Perspective			
Increase shareholder value	Operating-income changes from productive improvements	₹1,00,00,000	₹40,00,000
	Operating-income changes from growth	₹1,50,00,000	₹60,00,000
Customer Perspective			
Increase market share	Market share in color laser printers	5%	4.6%
Internal-Business-Process Perspective			
Improve manufacturing quality	Yield	82%	85%
Reduce delivery time to customers	Order-delivery time	25 days	22 days
Learning-and-Growth Perspective			
Develop process skills	Percentage of employees trained in process and quality management	90%	92%
Enhance information-system capabilities	Percentage of manufacturing processes with real-time feedback	85%	87%

Required

1. Was HP successful in implementing its strategy in 2015? Explain.
2. Is HP's balanced scorecard useful in helping the company understand why it did not reach its target market share in 2015? If it is, explain why. If it is not, explain what other measures you might want to add under the customer perspective and why.
3. Would you have included some measure of employee satisfaction in the learning-and-growth perspective and new-product development in the internal-business-process perspective? That is, do you think employee satisfaction and development of new products are critical for HP to implement its strategy? Why or why not? Explain briefly.
4. What problems, if any, do you see in HP improving quality and significantly downsizing to eliminate unused capacity?

13 Pricing Decisions and Cost Management

Learning Objective 1

Discuss the three major influences on pricing decisions

... customers, competitors, and costs

Most companies carefully analyze their input costs and the prices of their products.

They know if the price is too high, customers will go to competitors; if the price is too low, the company won't be able to cover the cost of making the product. A company must also know how its customers will react to particular pricing strategies.

Major Factors that Affect Pricing Decisions

Consider for a moment how managers at Adidas might price their newest line of sneakers, or how decision makers at Comcast would determine how much to charge for a monthly subscription of Internet service. How managers price a product or a service ultimately depends on the demand and supply. Three influences on demand and supply are customers, competitors, and costs.

Customers

Customers influence price through their effect on the demand for a product or service. The demand is affected by factors such as the features of a product and its quality. Managers always examine pricing decisions through the eyes of their customers and then manage costs to earn a profit.

Competitors

No business operates in a vacuum. Managers must always be aware of the actions of their competitors. At one extreme, for companies such as Home Depot or Texas Instruments, alternative or substitute products of competitors hurt demand and cause them to lower prices. At the other extreme, companies such as Apple and Porsche have distinctive products and limited competition and are free to set higher prices. When there are competitors, managers try to learn about competitors' technologies, plant capacities, and operating strategies to estimate competitors' costs—valuable information when setting prices.

Because competition spans international borders, fluctuations in exchange rates between different countries' currencies affect costs and pricing decisions. For example, if the yuan weakens against the U.S. dollar, Chinese producers receive more yuan for each dollar of sales. These producers can lower prices and still make a profit; Chinese products become cheaper for American consumers and, consequently, more competitive in U.S. markets.

Costs

Costs influence prices because they affect supply. The lower the cost of producing a product, such as a Toyota Prius or a Nokia cell phone, the greater the quantity of product the company is willing to supply. As companies increase supply, the cost of producing an additional unit initially declines but eventually increases and companies supply products as long as the revenue from selling additional units exceeds the cost of producing them. Managers who understand the cost of producing products set prices that make the products attractive to customers while maximizing operating income.

Weighing Customers, Competitors, and Costs

Surveys indicate that managers weigh customers, competitors, and costs differently when making pricing decisions. At one extreme, companies operating in a perfectly competitive market sell very similar commodity-type products, such as wheat, rice, steel, and aluminum. The managers at these companies have no control over setting prices and must accept the price determined by a market consisting of many participants. Cost information helps a company decide only on the output level that maximizes its operating income.

In less-competitive markets, such as those for cameras, televisions, and cellular phones, products are differentiated, and all three factors affect prices: The value customers place on a product and the prices charged for competing products affect demand, and the costs of producing and delivering the product influence supply.

As competition lessens even more, such as in microprocessors and operating software, the key factor affecting pricing decisions is the customer's willingness to pay based on the value that customers place on the product or service, not costs or competitors. In the extreme, there are monopolies. A monopolist has no competitors and has much more leeway to set high prices. Nevertheless, there are limits. The higher the price a monopolist sets, the lower the demand for the monopolist's product as customers seek substitute products.

Decision Point

What are the three major influences on pricing decisions?

Costing and Pricing for the Long Run

Long-run pricing is a strategic decision designed to build long-run relationships with customers based on stable and predictable prices. Managers prefer a stable price because it reduces the need for continuous monitoring of prices, improves planning, and builds long-run buyer–seller relationships. McDonald's maintains a stable price of its fast food items. But to charge a stable price and earn the target long-run return, managers must know and manage long-run costs of supplying products to customers, which includes *all* future direct and indirect costs. Recall that *indirect costs* of a particular cost object are costs that are related to that cost object but cannot be traced to it in an economically feasible (cost-effective) way. These costs often comprise a large percentage of the overall costs assigned to cost objects such as products, customers, and distribution channels. Consider cost-allocation issues at Astel Computers. Astel manufactures two products: a server called Deskpoint and a Pentium chip–based personal computer called Provalue. The following figure illustrates six business functions in Astel's value chain.

Learning Objective 2

Understand how companies make long-run pricing decisions

Consider all future variable and fixed costs as relevant and earn a target return on investment

Research and Development	Design of Products and Processes	Production	Marketing	Distribution	Customer Service

Exhibit 13-1 illustrates four purposes of cost allocation. Different sets of costs are appropriate for different purposes described in the exhibit. When making pricing decisions for Deskpoint and Provalue, Astel's managers allocate indirect costs from all six business functions. Why? Because in the long run, it is only worthwhile to sell a product if the price customers are willing to pay for the product exceeds all costs incurred to produce and sell it while earning a reasonable return on invested capital.

Cost allocations and product profitability analyses affect the products that managers promote. Compensating salespersons on product profitability, calculated based on fully allocated costs, motivates the sales staff to promote higher-margin products. Cost allocations also influence managers' cost management decisions. For example, to manage purchasing and ordering costs, Astel's managers might ask designers to use fewer components to manufacture Provalue. These design decisions will affect costs in some, but not all, value-chain categories (manufacturing costs but not customer service costs).

Inventory valuation for income and asset measurement requires cost allocation to calculate the cost of manufacturing inventory. For this purpose, Astel allocates only manufacturing costs to products and no costs from other parts of the value chain such as R&D, marketing, or distribution.

Exhibit 13-1   Purposes of Cost Allocation

Purpose	Examples
1. To provide information for economic decisions	To decide on the selling price for a product or service To decide whether to add a new product feature
2. To motivate managers and other employees	To encourage the design of products that are simpler to manufacture or less costly to service To encourage sales representatives to emphasize high-margin products or services
3. To justify costs or compute reimbursement amounts	To cost products at a "fair" price, often required by law and government defense contracts To compute reimbursement for a consulting firm based on a percentage of the cost savings resulting from the implementation of its recommendations
4. To measure income and assets	To cost inventories for reporting to external parties To cost inventories for reporting to tax authorities

Cost allocation is another example of the different costs for different purposes theme of the book. We will discuss cost-allocation in the next several chapters. In this chapter, we focus on the role of cost allocation when making long-run pricing decisions based on costs throughout the value chain.

Calculating Product Costs for Long-Run Pricing Decisions

Astel's market research indicates that the market for Provalue is becoming increasingly competitive. Astel's managers face an important decision about the price to charge for Provalue.

The managers start by reviewing data for the year just ended, 2013. Astel has no beginning or ending inventory of Provalue and manufactures and sells 1,50,000 units during the year. Astel uses activity-based costing (ABC) to allocate costs and calculate the manufacturing cost of Provalue. Astel's ABC system has:

- Three direct manufacturing costs: direct materials, direct manufacturing labor, and direct machining costs.

- Three manufacturing overhead cost pools: ordering and receiving components, testing and inspection of final products, and rework (correcting and fixing errors and defects).

Astel considers machining costs as a direct cost of Provalue because these machines are dedicated to manufacturing Provalue.[1]

Astel uses a long-run time horizon to price Provalue. Over this horizon, Astel's management observes the following:

▤ File Edit View Insert Format Tools Data Window Help								
	A	B	C	D	E	F	G	H
1	Manufacturing cost information							
2	to produce 150,000 units of Provalue							
3	Cost Category	Cost Driver		Details of Cost Driver Quantities			Total Quantity of Cost Driver	Cost per Unit of Cost Driver (₹)
4	(1)	(2)		(3)		(4)	(5) = (3)x(4)	(6)
5	Direct Manufacturing Costs							
6	Direct materials	No. of kits	1	kit per unit	1,50,000	units	1,50,000	4,600
7	Direct manufacturing labor (DML)	DML hours	3.2	DML hours per unit	1,50,000	units	4,80,000	200
8	Direct machining (fixed)	Machine-hours					3,00,000	380
9	Manufacturing Overhead Costs							
10	Ordering and receiving	No. of orders	50	orders per component	450	components	22,500	800
11	Testing and inspection	Testing-hours	30	testing-hours per unit	1,50,000	units	45,00,000	20
12	Rework				8%	defect rate		
13		Rework-hours	2.5	rework-hours per defective unit	12,000[a]	defective units	30,000	400
14								
15	[a]8% defect rate x 150,000 units = 12,000 defective units							

---

[1] Recall that Astel makes a server, Deskpoint, and a PC, Provalue. If Deskpoint and Provalue had shared the same machines, Astel would have allocated machining costs on the basis of the budgeted machine-hours used to manufacture the two products and would have treated these costs as fixed overhead costs.

- Direct material costs vary with number of units of Provalue produced.
- Direct manufacturing labor costs vary with number of direct manufacturing labor-hours used.
- Direct machining costs are fixed costs of leasing 3,00,000 machine-hours of capacity each year for multiple years. These costs do not vary with the number of machine-hours used each year. Each unit of Provalue requires 2 machine-hours. In 2013, Astel uses the entire machining capacity to manufacture Provalue (2 machine-hours per unit × 1,50,000 units = 3,00,000 machine-hours).
- Ordering and receiving, testing and inspection, and rework costs vary with the quantity of their respective cost driver. For example, ordering and receiving costs vary with the number of orders. In the long run, Staff members responsible for placing orders can be reassigned or laid off if fewer orders need to be placed, or increased if more orders need to be processed.

The following Excel spreadsheet summarizes manufacturing cost information to produce 1,50,000 units of Provalue in 2013. Astel's managers derive the indirect cost per unit of the cost driver in column (6) by dividing the total costs in each cost pool by the quantity of cost driver calculated in column (5). (Calculations not shown.)

Exhibit 13-2 shows the total cost of manufacturing Provalue in 2013 of ₹1,020 million subdivided into the various categories of direct costs and indirect costs. The manufacturing cost per unit in Exhibit 13-2 is ₹6,800. Manufacturing, however, is just one business function in the value chain. To set long-run prices, Astel's managers must

Exhibit 13-2

Manufacturing Costs of
Provalue for 2011 Using
Activity-Based Costing

	A	B	C
		Total Manufacturing	
1		**Costs for**	**Manufacturing**
2		**1,50,000 Units**	**Cost per Unit**
3		(1)	(2) = (1) ÷ 1,50,000
4			
5	Direct manufacturing costs		
6	Direct material costs		
7	(1,50,000 kits x ₹4,600 per kit)	₹69,00,00,000	₹4,600
8	Direct manufacturing labor costs		
9	(4,80,000 DML-hours x ₹200 per hour)	9,60,00,000	640
10	Direct machining costs		
11	(3,00,000 machine-hours x ₹80 per machine-hour)	11,40,00,000	760
12	Direct manufacturing costs	90,00,00,000	6,000
13			
14	Manufacturing overhead costs		
15	Ordering and receiving costs		
16	(22,500 orders x ₹800 per order)	1,80,00,000	120
17	Testing and inspection costs		
18	(45,00,000 testing-hours x ₹20 per hour)	9,00,00,000	600
19	Rework costs		
20	(30,000 rework-hours x ₹400 per hour)	1,20,00,000	80
21	Manufacturing overhead cost	12,00,00,000	800
22	Total manufacturing costs	₹1,02,00,00,000	₹6,800

	A	B	C
		Home Insert Page Layout Formulas Data Review View	
	A	B	C
1		**Total Amounts**	
2		**for 1,50,000 Units**	**Per Unit**
3		**₹(1)**	**(2) = (1) ÷ 1,50,000**
4	Revenues	₹1,50,00,00,000	₹10,000
5	Costs of goods sold[a] (from Exhibit 13-2)	1,02,00,00,000	6,800
6	Operating costs[b]		
7	R&D costs	2,40,00,000	160
8	Design costs of product and proces	3,00,00,000	200
9	Marketing and administration costs	15,00,00,000	1,000
10	Distribution costs	9,00,00,000	600
11	Customer-service costs	3,60,00,000	240
12	Operating costs	33,00,00,000	2,200
13	Full cost of the product	1,35,00,00,000	9,000
14	Operating income	₹1,50,00,00,000	₹1,000
15			
16	[a]Cost of goods sold = Total manufacturing costs because there is no beginning or ending inventory		
17	of Provalue in 2013		
18	[b]Numbers for operating cost line-items are assumed without supporting calculations		

Exhibit 13-3

Product Profitability of Provalue for 2013 Using Value-Chain Activity-Based Costing

calculate the full cost of producing and selling Provalue by allocating costs in all functions of the value chain.

For each nonmanufacturing business function, Astel's managers trace direct costs to products and allocate indirect costs using cost pools and cost drivers that measure cause-and-effect relationships (supporting calculations not shown). Exhibit 13-3 summarizes Provalue's 2013 operating income and shows that Astel earned ₹150 million from Provalue, or ₹1,000 per unit sold in 2013.

Alternative Long-Run Pricing Approaches

How should managers at Astel use product cost information to price Provalue in 2014? Two different approaches for pricing decisions are:

1. Market-based
2. Cost-based, which is also called cost-plus

The market-based approach to pricing starts by management asking, "Given what our customers want and how our competitors will react to what we do, what price should we charge?" Based on this price, managers control costs to earn a target return on investment. The cost-based approach to pricing starts by asking, "Given what it costs us to make this product, what price should we charge that will recoup our costs and achieve a target return on investment?"

Companies operating in *competitive* markets (for example, commodities such as steel, oil, and natural gas) use the market-based approach. The products produced or services provided by one company are very similar to products produced or services provided by others. Companies in these markets must accept the prices set by the market.

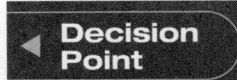

◄ Decision Point

How do companies make long-run pricing decisions?

Learning Objective 3

Price products using the target-costing approach

... target costing identifies an estimated price customers are willing to pay and then computes a target cost to earn the desired profit

Companies operating in *less competitive* markets offering products or services that differ from each other (for example, automobiles, computers, management consulting, and legal services) and can use either the market-based or cost-based approach as the starting point for pricing decisions. Some companies use the cost-based approach: They first look at costs because cost information is more easily available and then consider customers and competitors. Other companies use the market-based approach: They first look at customers and competitors and then look at costs. Both approaches consider customers, competitors, and costs. Only their starting points differ. Managers must always keep in mind market forces, regardless of which pricing approach is used. For example, building contractors often bid on a cost-plus basis but then reduce their prices during negotiations to respond to other lower-cost bids.

Companies operating in markets that are *not competitive* favor cost-based approaches. That's because these companies do not need to respond or react to competitors' prices. The margin they add to costs to determine price depends on the value customers place on the product or service.

We consider first the market-based approach.

Market-Based Approach: Target Costing for Target Pricing

Market-based pricing starts with a target price which is the estimated price for a product or service that potential customers are willing to pay. Managers base this estimate on an understanding of customers' perceived value for a product or service and how competitors will price competing products or services. In today's business context, managers need to understand customers and competitors for three reasons:

1. Lower-cost competitors continually restrain prices.
2. Products have shorter lives, which leaves companies less time and opportunity to recover from pricing mistakes, loss of market share, and loss of profitability.
3. Customers are more knowledgeable because they have easy access to price and other information online and demand high-quality products at low prices.

Understanding Customers' Perceived Value

A company's sales and marketing organization, through close contact and interaction with customers, identify customers' needs and perceptions of product value. Companies such as Toshiba and Dell also conduct market research on what customers want and the prices they are willing to pay.

Competitor Analysis

To gauge how competitors might react to a prospective price, a manager must understand competitors' technologies, products or services, costs, and financial conditions. In general, the more distinctive a product or service, the higher the price a company can charge. Where do companies obtain information about their competitors? Usually from former customers, suppliers, and employees of competitors. Some companies *reverse-engineer*— disassemble and analyze competitors' products to determine product designs and materials and to understand the technologies competitors use. At no time should a manager resort to illegal or unethical means to obtain information about competitors. For example, a manager should never bribe current employees or pose as a supplier or customer in order to obtain competitor information.

Implementing Target Pricing and Target Costing

We use the Provalue example to illustrate the five steps in developing target prices and target costs.

Step 1:   Develop a Product That Satisfies the Needs of Potential Customers. Astel's managers use customer feedback and information about competitors' products to finalize product features and design modifications for Provalue in 2014. Their market research indicates that customers do not value Provalue's extra features, such as special audio elements and designs that accommodate upgrades to make the PC run faster. Instead, customers want Astel to redesign Provalue into a no-frills but reliable PC and to sell it at a much lower price.

Step 2:   Choose a Target Price. Astel's managers expect competitors to lower the prices of PCs to ₹8,500. Astel's managers want to respond aggressively, reducing the price the company charges for Provalue by 20%, from ₹10,000 to ₹8,000 per unit. At this lower price, Astel's marketing manager forecasts an increase in annual sales from 1,50,000 to 2,00,000 units.

Step 3:   Derive a Target Cost per Unit by Subtracting Target Operating Income per Unit from the Target Price. Target operating income per unit is the operating income that a company aims to earn per unit of a product or service sold. **Target cost per unit** is the estimated long-run cost per unit of a product or service that enables the company to achieve its target operating income per unit when selling at the target price.[2] *Target cost per unit* is the target price minus *target operating income per unit*. It often needs to be lower than the existing *full cost of the product*. Target cost per unit is really just that—a target— something the company must strive to achieve.

To earn the target return on capital, Astel needs to earn 10% target operating income per unit on the 2,00,000 units of Provalue it plans to sell.

Total target revenues	= ₹8,000 per unit × 2,00,000 = ₹1,60,00,00,000
Total target operating income	= 10% × ₹1,60,00,00,000 = ₹16,00,00,000
Total operating income per unit	= ₹16,00,00,000 ÷ 2,00,000 units = ₹800 per unit
Total cost per unit	= Traget price - Target operating income per unit
	= ₹8,000 per unit - ₹800 per unit = ₹7,200 per unit
Total current full cost of provalue	= ₹1,35,00,00,000 (from Exhibit 13-2)
Current full cost per unit of provalue	= ₹1,35,00,00,000 ÷ 1,50,000 units = ₹9,000 per unit
	Exhibit 13-2

Provalue's ₹7,200 target cost per unit is ₹1,800 below its existing ₹9,000 unit cost. Astel's managers must reduce costs in all parts of the value chain, from R&D to customer service, for example, by reducing prices of materials and components while maintaining quality.

Target costs include *all* future costs, variable costs, and costs that are fixed in the short run because in the long run a company's prices and revenues must recover all its costs if it is to remain in business. In contrast, for short-run pricing or one-time-only special order decisions, managers consider only those costs that change in the short run, which are mostly, but not exclusively, variable costs.

---

[2] For a more detailed discussion of target costing, see Shahid L. Ansari, Jan E. Bell, and the CAM-I Target Cost Core Group, *Target Costing: The Next Frontier in Strategic Cost Management* (Martinsville, IN: Mountain Valley Publishing, 2009). For implementation information, see Shahid L. Ansari, Dan Swenson, and Jan E. Bell, "A Template for Implementing Target Costing," *Cost Management* (September–October 2006): 20–27.

Step 4: Perform Cost Analysis. Astel's managers analyze specific aspects of the product to target for cost reduction:

- The functions performed by different component parts, such as the motherboard, disk drives, and graphics and video cards.
- The importance customers place on different functional features. For example, Provalue's customers value reliability more than video quality.
- The relationship and tradeoffs among functional features and component parts. For example, a simpler motherboard enhances reliability but cannot support a top-of-the-line video card.

Step 5: Perform Value Engineering to Achieve Target Cost. Value engineering is a systematic evaluation of all aspects of the value chain, with the objective of reducing costs and achieving a quality level that satisfies customers. Value engineering entails improvements in product designs, changes in materials specifications, and modifications in process methods.

Decision Point ▶

How do companies determine target costs?

Value Engineering, Cost Incurrence, and Locked-In Costs

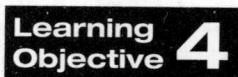

Learning Objective 4

Apply the concepts of cost incurrence

. . . when resources are consumed and locked-in costs

. . . when resources are committed to be incurred in the future

To implement value engineering, managers distinguish value-added activities and costs from nonvalue-added activities and costs. A **value-added cost** is a cost that, if eliminated, would reduce the actual or perceived value or utility (usefulness) customers obtain from using the product or service. In the Provalue example, value-added costs are costs of specific product features and attributes desired by customers, such as reliability, adequate memory, desired preloaded software, clear images on the monitor, and prompt customer service.

A **nonvalue-added cost** is a cost that, if eliminated, would not reduce the actual or perceived value or utility (usefulness) customers gain from using the product or service. Examples of nonvalue-added costs are costs of producing defective products and machine breakdowns. Companies seek to minimize non-value-added costs because they do not provide benefits to customers.

Activities and costs do not always fall neatly into value-added or non-value-added categories, so managers often have to apply judgment to classify costs. Several costs, such as supervision and production control, have both value-added and non-value-added components. When in doubt, some managers prefer to classify costs as non-value-added to focus organizational attention on cost reduction. The risk with this approach is that an organization may cut some costs that are value-adding, leading to poor customer experiences.

Despite these difficult gray areas, managers find it useful to distinguish value-added from non-value-added costs for value engineering. In the Provalue example, direct materials, direct manufacturing labor, and direct machining costs are value-added costs; ordering, receiving, testing, and inspection costs have both value-added and non-value-added components; and rework costs are non-value-added costs.

Astel's managers next distinguish cost incurrence from locked-in costs. **Cost incurrence** describes when a resource is consumed (or benefit forgone) to meet a specific objective. Costing systems measure cost incurrence. For example, Astel recognizes direct material costs of Provalue only when Provalue is assembled and sold. But Provalue's direct material cost per unit is *locked in,* or *designed in,* much earlier, when product designers choose the specific components in Provalue. **Locked-in costs,** or **designed-in costs,** are costs that have not yet been incurred but will be incurred in the future based on decisions that have already been made.

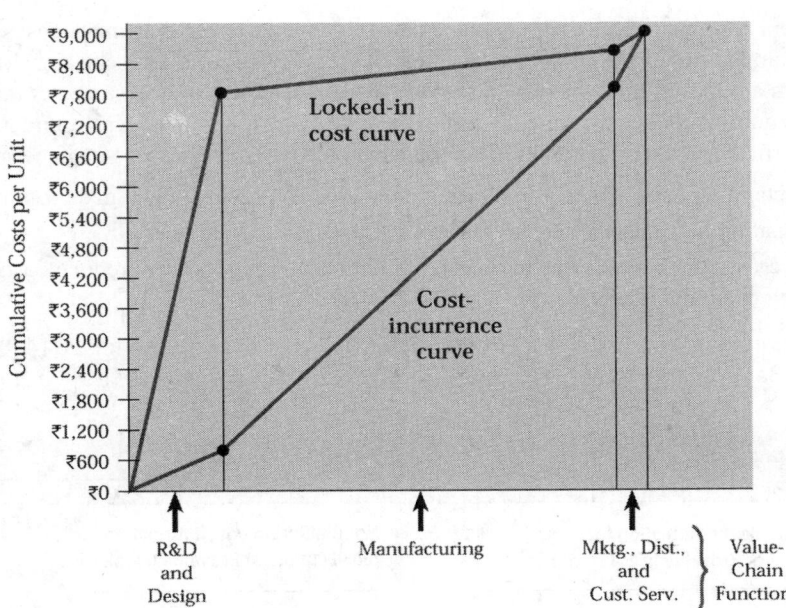

Exhibit 13-4

Pattern of Cost
Incurrence and
Locked-In Costs for
Provalue

The best opportunity to manage costs is before costs are locked in, so Astel's managers model the effect of different product design choices on costs such as scrap and rework that will only be incurred later during manufacturing. They then control these costs by making wise design choices. Similarly, managers in the software industry reduce costly and difficult-to-fix errors that appear during coding and testing through better software design and analysis.

Exhibit 13-4 illustrates the locked-in cost curve and the cost-incurrence curve for Provalue. The bottom curve uses information from Exhibit 13-3 to plot the cumulative cost per unit incurred in different business functions of the value chain. The top curve plots cumulative locked-in costs. (The specific numbers underlying this curve are not presented.) Total cumulative cost per unit for both curves is ₹9,000, but there is *wide divergence between locked-in costs and costs incurred.* For example, product design decisions lock in more than 86% (₹7,800 ÷ ₹9,000) of the unit cost of Provalue (including costs of direct materials, ordering, testing, rework, distribution, and customer service), when Astel incurs only about 4% ₹360 ÷ ₹9,000 of the unit cost!

Value-Chain Analysis and Cross-Functional Teams

A cross-functional value-engineering team consisting of marketing managers, product designers, manufacturing engineers, purchasing managers, suppliers, dealers, and management accountants redesign Provalue—called Provalue II—to reduce costs while retaining features that customers value. Some of the team's ideas are as follows:

- Use a simpler, more-reliable motherboard without complex features to reduce manufacturing and repair costs..
- Snap-fit rather than solder parts together to decrease direct manufacturing labor-hours and related costs.
- Use fewer components to decrease ordering, receiving, testing, and inspection costs.
- Make Provalue lighter and smaller to reduce distribution and packaging costs.

Management accountants use their understanding of the value chain to estimate cost savings.
The team focuses on design decisions to reduce costs before costs get locked in. However, not all costs are locked in at the design stage. Managers use *kaizen,* or *continuous improvement* techniques, to reduce the time it takes to complete a task, eliminate waste, and improve operating efficiency and productivity. To summarize, the key steps in value-engineering are:

1. Understanding customer requirements, value-added and nonvalue-added costs
2. Anticipating how costs are locked in before they are incurred
3. Using cross-functional teams to redesign products and processes to reduce costs while meeting customer needs

Exhibit 13-5 Cost-Driver Quantities and Rates for Provalue in 2013 and Provalue II for 2014 Using Activity-Based Costing

	File Edit View Insert Format Tools Data Window Help												
	A	B	C	D	E	F	G	H	I	J	K	L	M	N
1 2			Manufacturing cost information for 150,000 units of Provalue in 2011						Manufacturing cost information for 200,000 units of Provalue II for 2012					
3	Cost Category	Cost Driver	Details of Actual Cost Driver Quantities				Actual Total Quantity of Cost Driver	Actual Cost per Unit of Cost Driver (p. 000) (₹)	Details of Budgeted Cost Driver Quantities				Budgeted Total Quantity of Cost Driver	Budgeted Cost per Unit of Cost Driver (Given)(₹)
4	(1)	(2)	(3)		(4)		(5)=(3)x(4)	(6)	(7)		(8)		(9)=(7)x(8)	(10)
5	**Direct Manufacturing Costs**													
6	Direct materials	No. of kits	1	kit per unit	1,50,000	units	1,50,000	4,600	1	kit per unit	2,00,000	units	2,00,000	3,850
7	Direct manuf. labor (DML)	DML hours	3.2	DML hours per unit	1,50,000	units	4,80,000	200	2.65	DML hours per unit	2,00,000	units	5,30,000	200
8	Direct machining (fixed)	Machine-hours					3,00,000	380					3,00,000	380
9	**Manufacturing Overhead Costs**													
10	Ordering and receiving	No. of orders	50	orders per component	450	compo-nents	22,500	800	50	orders per compo-nent	425	compo-nents	21,250	800
11	Testing and inspection	Testing-hours	30	testing-hours per unit	1,50,000	units	45,00,000	20	15	testing hours per unit	2,00,000	units	30,00,000	20
12	Rework				8%	defect rate					6.5%	defect rate		
13		Rework-hours	2.5	rework-hours per defective unit	12,000[a]	defective units	30,000	400	2.5	rework-hours per defective unit	13,000[b]	defective units	32,500	400
14														
15	[a]8% defect rate x 150,000 units = 12,000 defective units													
16	[b]6.5% defect rate x 200,000 units = 13,000 defective units													

Achieving the Target Cost per Unit for Provalue

Exhibit 13-5 uses an activity-based approach to compare cost-driver quantities and rates for the 1,50,000 units of Provalue manufactured and sold in 2013 and the 2,00,000 units of Provalue II budgeted for 2014. Value engineering reduces both value-added costs (by designing Provalue II to reduce direct materials and components costs, direct manufacturing labor-hours and testing-hours) and nonvalue-added costs (by simplifying Provalue II's design to reduce the rework). Value engineering also reduces the machine-hours required to manufacture Provalue II to 1.5 hours per unit. Astel can now use the 3,00,000 machine-hours of capacity to make 2,00,000 units of Provalue II (vs. 1,50,000 units for Provalue), reducing machining cost per unit. For simplicity, we assume that value engineering will not reduce the ₹200 cost per direct manufacturing labor-hour, the ₹800 cost per order, the ₹20 cost per testing-hour, or the ₹400 cost per rework-hour. (The Problem for Self-Study, explores how value engineering can also reduce these cost-driver rates.)

Exhibit 13-6   Target Manufacturing Costs of Provalue II for 2014

	File Edit View Insert Format Tools Data Window Help				
	A	B	C	D E	F
1		PROVALUE II			PROVALUE
2		Budgeted		Budgeted	Actual Manufacturing
3		Manufacturing Costs		Manufacturing	Cost per Unit
4		for 2,00,000 Units		Cost per Unit	(Exhibit 12-1)
5		(1)		(2) = (1) ÷ 2,00,000	(3)
6	Direct manufacturing costs				
7	Direct material costs				
8	(2,00,000 kits x ₹3,850 per kit)	₹77,00,00,000		₹3,850.0	₹4,600.0
9	Direct manufacturing labor costs				
10	(5,30,000 DML-hours x ₹200 per hour)	10,60,00,000		530.0	640.0
11	Direct machining costs				
12	(3,00,000 machine-hours x ₹380 per machine-hour)	11,40,00,000		570.0	760.0
13	Direct manufacturing costs	99,00,00,000		4,950.0	6,000.0
14	Manufacturing overhead costs				
15	Ordering and receiving costs				
16	(21,250 orders x ₹800 per order)	1,70,00,000		85.0	120.0
17	Testing and inspection costs				
18	(30,00,000 testing-hours x ₹20 per hour)	6,00,00,000		300.0	600.0
19	Rework costs				
20	(32,500 rework-hours x ₹400 per hour)	1,30,00,000		65.0	80.0
21	Manufacturing overhead costs	9,00,00,000		450.0	800.0
22	Total manufaturing costs	₹1,08,00,00,000		₹5,400.0	6,800.0

Exhibit 13-6 presents the target manufacturing costs of Provalue II, using cost driver and cost-driver rate data from Exhibit 13-5. For comparison, Exhibit 13-6 also shows the actual 2013 manufacturing cost per unit of Provalue from Exhibit 13-2. Astel's managers expect the new design to reduce total manufacturing cost per unit by ₹1,400 (from ₹6,800 to ₹5,400) and cost per unit in other business functions from ₹2,200 (Exhibit 13-3) to ₹1,800 (calculations not shown) at the budgeted sales quantity of 2,00,000 units. The budgeted full unit cost of Provalue II is ₹7,200 (₹5,400 + ₹1,800), the target cost per unit. At the end of 2014, Astel's managers will compare actual costs and target costs to understand improvements they can make in subsequent target-costing efforts.

Unless managed properly, value engineering and target costing can have undesirable effects:

- Employees may feel frustrated if they fail to attain target costs.
- The cross-functional team may add too many features just to accommodate the different wishes of team members.
- A product may be in development for a long time as the team repeatedly evaluates alternative designs.
- Organizational conflicts may develop as the burden of cutting costs falls unequally on different business functions in the company's value chain, for example, more on manufacturing than on marketing.

To avoid these pitfalls, target-costing efforts should always (a) encourage employee participation and celebrate small improvements toward achieving the target cost, (b) focus on the customer, (c) pay attention to schedules, and (d) set cost-cutting targets for all value-chain functions to encourage a culture of teamwork and cooperation.

The target pricing approach is another illustration of the five-step decision-making process introduced in Chapter 1.

1. *Identify the problem and uncertainties.* The problem is the price to charge for Provalue in 2014. The uncertainties are identifying what customers want, how competitors will respond, and how to manage costs.

2. *Obtain information.* Astel's managers do market research to identify customer needs, the prices that competitors are likely to charge, and opportunities to reduce costs.

3. *Make predictions about the future.* Managers make predictions about the effect of different prices on sales volumes and how much they can reduce costs through value engineering and product redesign.

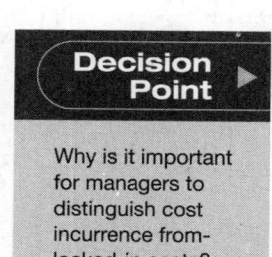

Decision Point ▶

Why is it important for managers to distinguish cost incurrence from-locked-in costs?

4. *Make decisions by choosing among alternatives.* Managers decide to reduce Provalue's price from ₹10,000 to ₹8,000, anticipating sales to increase from 1,50,000 units to 2,00,000 units in 2014.

5. *Implement the decision, evaluate performance, and learn.* Cross-functional value-engineering teams redesign Provalue to achieve a target cost of ₹7,200 per unit, considerably lower than the current cost of ₹9,000. At the end of 2014, managers will compare actual and target costs to evaluate performance and to identify ways to reduce costs even further.

Cost-Plus Pricing

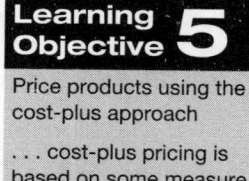

Learning Objective 5

Price products using the cost-plus approach

. . . cost-plus pricing is based on some measure of cost plus a markup

Instead of using the market-based approach for their long-run pricing decisions, managers sometimes use a cost-based approach. The general formula for setting a cost-based price adds a markup component to the cost base. Because a markup is added, cost-based pricing is often called cost-plus pricing, where the plus refers to the markup component. Managers use the cost-plus pricing formula as a starting point. The markup component is usually flexible, depending on the behavior of customers and competitors. The market conditions ultimately determine the markup component.[3]

---

[3] Exceptions are pricing of electricity and natural gas in many countries, where prices are set by the government on the basis of costs plus a return on invested capital. In these situations, products are not subject to competitive forces and cost accounting techniques substitute for markets as the basis for setting prices.

Cost-Plus Target Rate of Return on Investment

Suppose Astel uses a 12% markup on the full unit cost of Provalue II to compute the selling price. The cost-plus price is:

Cost base (full unit cost of Provalue II)	₹7,200
Markup component of 12% (0.12 × ₹7,200)	864
Prospective selling price	₹8,064

How do managers determine the markup percentage of 12% One way is to choose a markup to earn a target rate of return on investment which is the target annual operating income divided by invested capital. Invested capital can be defined in many ways. In this chapter, we define it as total assets—that is, long-term assets plus current assets. Suppose Astel's (pretax) target rate of return on investment is 18% and Provalue II's capital investment is ₹96,00,00,000. The target annual operating income for Provalue II is:

Invested capital	₹96,00,00,000
Target rate of return on investment	18%
Target annual operating income (0.18 × 96,00,00,000)	₹17,28,00,000
Target operating income per unit of Provalue II (₹17,28,00,000 ÷ 2,00,000 units)	₹864.0

This calculation indicates that Astel needs to earn a target operating income of ₹864 on each unit of Provalue II. The markup (₹864) expressed as a percentage of the full unit cost of product (₹7,200) equals 12% (₹864 ÷ ₹7,200).

Do not confuse the 18% target rate of return on investment with the 12% markup percentage.

- The 18% target rate of return on investment expresses Astel's expected annual operating income as a percentage of investment.

- The 12% markup expresses operating income per unit as a percentage of the full product cost per unit.

Astel first calculates target rate of return on investment to calculate the markup percentage.

Alternative Cost-Plus Methods

Computing the specific amount of capital invested in a product is challenging because it requires difficult and arbitrary allocations of investments in equipment and buildings to individual products. The following table uses alternative cost bases (without supporting calculations) and assumed markup percentages to set prospective selling prices for Provalue II without explicitly calculating invested capital to set prices.

Cost Base	Estimated Cost per Unit (1)	Markup Percentage (2)	Markup Component (3) ÷ (1) × (2)	Prospective Selling Price (4) = (1) + (3)
Variable manufacturing cost	₹4,750.00	65%	₹3,087.5	₹7,837.5
Variable cost of the product	5,470.00	45	2,461.5	7,931.5
Manufacturing cost	5,400.00	50	2,700.0	8,100.0
Full cost of the product	7,200.00	12	864.0	8,064.0

The different cost bases and markup percentages give four prospective selling prices that are close to each other. In practice, a company chooses a reliable cost base and a markup percentage to recover its costs and earn a target return on investment. For example, consulting companies often choose the full cost of a client engagement as their cost base because it is difficult to distinguish variable costs from fixed costs.

The markup percentages in the preceding table vary a great deal, from a high of 65% on variable manufacturing cost to a low of 12% on full cost of the product. Why the wide variation? When determining a prospective selling price, a cost base such as variable manufacturing cost that includes fewer costs requires a higher markup percentage because the price needs to be set to earn a profit margin *and* to recover fixed manufacturing costs and all nonmanufacturing costs that have been excluded from the base.

Surveys indicate that most managers use the full cost of the product for cost-based pricing decisions—that is, they include variable costs and costs that are fixed in the short run when calculating the cost per unit. Managers include fixed cost per unit in the cost base for several reasons:

1. **Full recovery of all costs of the product.** In the long run, the price of a product must exceed the full cost of the product if a company is to remain in business. Using just the variable cost as a base may tempt managers to cut prices as long as prices are above variable cost and generate a positive contribution margin. As the experience in the airline industry has shown, price wars, when airline companies cut prices as long as they exceed variable costs, have caused airlines to lose money because revenues are too low to recover the full cost of the product. Using the full cost of the product as a basis for pricing reduces the temptation to cut prices below full costs.

2. **Price stability.** Limiting the ability and temptation of salespeople to cut prices by using the full cost of a product as the basis for pricing decisions also promotes price stability. Stable prices facilitate more accurate forecasting and planning for both sellers and buyers.

3. **Simplicity.** A full-cost formula for pricing does not require the management accountant to perform a detailed analysis of cost-behavior patterns to separate costs into fixed and variable components. Variable and fixed cost components are difficult to identify for many costs such as testing, inspection, and setups.

Including fixed cost per unit in the cost base for pricing is not without problems. Allocating fixed costs to products can be arbitrary. Also, calculating fixed cost per unit requires a denominator level that is likely only an estimate of capacity or expected units of future sales. Errors in these estimates will cause actual full cost per unit of the product to differ from the estimated amount. Despite these challenges, managers generally include fixed costs when making cost-based pricing decisions.

Cost-Plus Pricing and Target Pricing

The selling prices computed under cost-plus pricing are prospective prices. Suppose Astel's initial product design results in a ₹7,500 full cost for Provalue II. Assuming a 12% markup, Astel sets a prospective price of ₹8,400 [₹7,500 + (0.12 × ₹7,500)]. In the competitive personal computer market, customer and competitor reactions to this price may force Astel to reduce the markup percentage and lower the price to, say, ₹8,000. Astel may then want to redesign Provalue II to reduce the full cost to ₹7,200 per unit, as in our example, and achieve a markup close to 12% while keeping the price at ₹8,000. The eventual design and cost-plus price must balance costs, markup, and customer reactions.

The target-pricing approach reduces the need to go back and forth among prospective cost-plus prices, customer reactions, and design modifications. In contrast to cost-plus pricing, target pricing first determines product characteristics and target price on the basis of customer preferences and expected competitor responses, and then a target cost.

Suppliers who provide unique products and services, such as accountants and management consultants, usually use cost-plus pricing. Professional service firms set prices based on hourly cost-plus billing rates of partners, managers, and associates. These prices are, however, reduced in competitive situations. Professional service firms also take a multiple-year client perspective when deciding prices because clients prefer to work with a firm over multiple periods. Certified public accountants, for example, sometimes charge a client a low price initially to get the account and recover the lower profits or losses in the initial years by charging higher prices in later years.

Service companies such as home repair services, automobile repair services, and architectural firms use a cost-plus pricing method called the *time-and-materials method*. Individual jobs are priced based on materials and labor time. The price charged for materials equals the cost of materials plus a markup. The price charged for labor represents the cost of labor plus a markup. That is, the price charged for each direct cost item includes its own markup. Companies choose the markups to recover overhead costs and earn a profit.

Decision Point

How do companies price products using the cost-plus approach?

Life-Cycle Product Budgeting and Costing

Managers sometimes need to consider target prices and target costs for a product over a multiple-year product life cycle. The **product life cycle** spans the time from initial R&D on a product to when customer service and support is no longer offered for that product. For automobile companies such as BMW, Ford, and Nissan, the product life cycle for different car models ranges from 12 to 15 years to design, introduce, and sell different car models. For pharmaceutical products, the life cycle at companies such as Pfizer, Merck, and Glaxo Smith Kline may be 15 to 20 years. For banks a product such as a newly designed savings account with specific privileges can have a life cycle of 10 to 20 years. Personal computers have a shorter life-cycle of 3 to 5 years, because rapid innovations in the computing power and speed of microprocessors that run the computers makes older models obsolete.

In **life-cycle budgeting**, managers estimate the revenues and business function costs across the entire value chain from a product's initial R&D to its final customer service and support. **Life-cycle costing** tracks and accumulates business function costs across the entire value chain from a product's initial R&D to final customer service and support. Life-cycle budgeting and life-cycle costing span several years.

Learning Objective 6

Use life-cycle budgeting and costing when making pricing decisions

. . . accumulate all costs of a product from initial R&D to final customer service for each year of its life

Life-Cycle Budgeting and Pricing Decisions

Budgeted life-cycle costs can provide useful information for strategically evaluating pricing decisions. Consider Insight, Inc., a computer software company, which is developing a new accounting package, "General Ledger." Assume the following budgeted amounts for General Ledger over a six-year product life cycle:

Years 1 and 2

	Total Fixed Costs
R&D costs	₹24,00,000
Design costs	16,00,000

Years 3 to 6

	Total Fixed Costs	Variable Cost per Package
Production costs	₹10,00,000	₹250
Marketing costs	7,00,000	240
Distribution costs	5,00,000	160
Customer-service costs	8,00,000	300

Exhibit 13-7 presents the 6-year life-cycle budget for General Ledger for three alternative selling-price/sales-quantity combinations.

Several features make life-cycle budgeting particularly important:

1. **The development period for R&D and design is long and costly.** When a company incurs a large percentage of total life-cycle costs before any production begins and any revenues are received, as in the General Ledger example, managers need to evaluate revenues and costs over the life cycle of the product in order to decide whether to begin the costly R&D and design activities.

2. **Many costs are locked in at R&D and design stages—even if R&D and design costs themselves are small.** In our General Ledger example, a poorly designed accounting software package which is difficult to install and use would result in higher marketing, distribution, and customer-service costs in several subsequent years. These costs would be even higher if the product failed to meet promised quality-performance levels. A life-cycle revenue-and-cost budget prevents Insight's managers from overlooking these multiple-year relationships among business-function costs. Life-cycle budgeting highlights costs throughout the product's life cycle and so facilitates target pricing, target costing, and value engineering at the design stage before costs are locked in. The amounts presented in Exhibit 13-7 are the outcome of value engineering.

Insight's managers decide to sell the General Ledger package for ₹4,800 per package because this price maximizes life-cycle operating income. They then compare actual costs to life-cycle budgets to obtain feedback and to learn about how to estimate costs better for subsequent products. Exhibit 13-7 assumes that the selling price per package is the same over the entire life cycle. For strategic reasons, however, Insight's managers may decide to skim the market which means the company would charge higher prices to customers eager to try General Ledger when it is first introduced and then lower prices later as the product matures. Or managers may even add new features to differentiate the product to maintain prices and sales. The life-cycle budget must then incorporate the revenues and costs of these strategies.

Managing Environmental Costs

Management of environmental costs provides another example of life-cycle costing and value engineering. Environmental laws—have introduced tougher environmental standards, imposed stringent cleanup requirements, and introduced severe penalties for polluting the air and contaminating subsurface soil and groundwater. Environmental costs that are incurred over several years of the product's life-cycle are often locked in at the product- and process-design stage. To avoid environmental liabilities, companies in industries such as oil refining, chemical processing, and automobiles do value engineering;

	Alternative Selling-Price/ Sales-Quantity Combinations		
	A	B	C
Selling price per package	₹4,000	₹4,800	₹6,000
Sales quantity in units	5,000	4,000	2,500
Life-cycle revenues			
(₹4,000 × 5,000; ₹4,800 × 4,000; ₹6,000 × 2,500)	₹2,00,00,000	₹1,92,00,000	₹1,50,00,000
Life-cycle costs			
R&D costs	24,00,000	24,00,000	24,00,000
Design costs of product/process	16,00,000	16,00,000	16,00,000
Production costs			
₹10,00,000 + (₹250 × 5,000); ₹10,00,000+			
(₹250 × 4,000); ₹10,00,000 + ₹250 × 2,500)	22,50,000	20,00,000	16,25,000
Marketing costs			
₹7,00,000 + (₹240 × 5,000); ₹7,00,000+			
(₹240 × 4,000); ₹7,00,000 + (₹240 × 2,500)	19,00,000	16,60,000	13,00,000
Distribution costs			
₹5,00,000 + (₹160 × 5,000); ₹ 5,00,000 +			
(₹160 × 4,000); ₹5,00,000 + (₹160 × 2,500)	13,00,000	11,40,000	9,00,000
Customer-service costs			
₹8,00,000 + (₹300 × 5,000); ₹8,00,000 +			
(₹300 × 4,000); ₹8,00,000 + (₹300 × 2,500)	23,00,000	20,00,000	15,50,000
Total life-cycle costs	1,17,50,000	1,08,00,000	93,75,000
Life-cycle operating income	₹82,50,000	₹84,00,000	₹56,25,000

Exhibit 13-7

Budgeting Life-Cycle Revenues and Costs for "General Ledger" Software Package of Insight, Inc.[a]

[a]This exhibit does not take into consideration the time value of money when computing life-cycle revenues or life-cycle costs. Chapter 21 outlines how this important factor can be incorporated into such calculations.

they design products and processes to prevent and reduce pollution over the product's life cycle. For example, laptop computer manufacturers like Hewlett Packard and Apple have introduced costly recycling programs to ensure that chemicals from nickel-cadmium batteries do not leak hazardous chemicals into the soil.

Customer Life-Cycle Costing

In the previous section, we considered life-cycle costs from the perspective of a product or service. **Customer life-cycle costs** focus on the total costs incurred by a customer to acquire, use, maintain, and dispose of a product or service. Customer life-cycle costs influence the prices a company can charge for its products. For example, Ford can charge a higher price and/or gain market share if its cars require minimal maintenance for 1,00,000 miles. Similarly, Maytag charges higher prices for appliances that save electricity and have low maintenance costs. Boeing Corporation justifies a higher price for the Boeing 777 because the plane's design allows mechanics easier access to different areas of the plane to perform routine maintenance, reduces the time and cost of maintenance, and significantly decreases the life-cycle cost of owning the plane.

◄ **Decision Point**

Describe life-cycle budgeting and life-cycle costing and when companies should use these techniques.

Non-Cost Factors In Pricing Decisions

In some cases, cost is not a major factor in setting prices. We explore some of the ways that market structures and laws and regulations influence price setting independent of cost.

Price Discrimination

Consider the prices airlines charge for a round-trip flight from New Delhi to Mumbai. A coach-class ticket for a flight with 7-day advance purchase is ₹4,500 if the passenger stays in Mumbai over a Saturday night. It is ₹10,000 if the passenger returns without staying over a Saturday night. Can this price difference be explained by the difference in the cost to the airline of these round-trip flights? No because it costs the same amount to transport the passenger from New Delhi to Mumbai and back, regardless of whether the passenger stays in Mumbai over a Saturday night. This difference in price is due to *price discrimination*.

Price discrimination is the practice of charging different customers different prices for the same product or service. How does price discrimination work in our airline example? The demand for airline tickets comes from two main sources: business travelers and pleasure travelers. Business travelers must travel to conduct business for their organizations, so their demand for air travel is relatively insensitive to price and airlines can earn higher operating incomes by charging business travelers higher prices. Insensitivity of demand to price changes is called *demand inelasticity*. Also, business travelers generally go to their destinations, complete their work, and return home without staying over a Saturday night. Pleasure travelers, however, usually don't need to return home during the week, and they prefer to spend weekends at their destinations. Because they pay for their tickets themselves, pleasure travelers' demand is more price-elastic, lowering prices stimulates demand. Airlines can earn higher operating incomes by charging pleasure travelers lower prices.

How can airlines keep fares high for business travelers while, at the same time, keeping fares low for pleasure travelers? Requiring a Saturday night stay discriminates between the two customer segments. The airlines price-discriminate to take advantage of different sensitivities to prices exhibited by business travelers and pleasure travelers. Price differences exist even though there is no cost difference in serving the two customer segments.

What if economic conditions weaken such that business travelers become more sensitive to price? The airlines may then need to lower the prices charged to business travelers.

Peak-Load Pricing

In addition to price discrimination, pricing decisions also consider other noncost factors such as capacity constraints. **Peak-load pricing** is the practice of charging a higher price for the same product or service when the demand for it approaches the physical limit of the capacity to produce that product or service. Prices charged during periods when demand on the production capacity is high represent what customers are willing to pay for the product or service. These prices are greater than the prices charged when slack or excess capacity is available when the goal is to utilize capacity by lowering prices to stimulate demand. Peak-load pricing occurs in the telephone, telecommunications, hotel, car rental, and electric-utility industries. When demand far exceeds capacity, the hospitality industry and airlines employ peak-load pricing to increase their profits.

International Pricing

Another example of factors other than costs affecting prices occurs when the same product is sold in different countries. Consider software, books, and medicines produced in one country and sold globally. The prices charged in each country vary much more than the costs of delivering the product to each country. These price differences arise because of differences in the purchasing power of consumers in different countries (a form of price discrimination) and government restrictions that may limit the prices that companies can charge.

Problem for Self-Study

Reconsider the Astel Computer example. Astel's marketing manager realizes that a further reduction in price is necessary to sell 2,00,000 units of Provalue II. To maintain a target profitability of ₹16,00,00,000 or ₹800 per unit, Astel will need to reduce costs of Provalue II by ₹6,00,00,000 or ₹300 per unit. Astel targets a reduction of ₹4,00,00,000, or ₹200 per unit, in manufacturing costs, and ₹2,00,00,000 or ₹100 per unit, in marketing, distribution, and customer-service costs. The cross-functional team assigned to this task proposes the following changes to manufacture a different version of Provalue, called Provalue III:

1. Reduce direct materials and ordering costs by purchasing subassembled components rather than individual components.
2. Reengineer ordering and receiving to reduce ordering and receiving costs per order.
3. Reduce testing time and the labor and power required per hour of testing.
4. Develop new rework procedures to reduce rework costs per hour.

No changes are proposed in direct manufacturing labor cost per unit and in total machining costs.

The following table summarizes the cost-driver quantities and the cost per unit of each cost driver for Provalue III compared with Provalue II.

					Manufacturing cost information for 200,000 units of Provalue II for 2010					Manufacturing cost information for 200,000 units of Provalue III for 2010		
					Budgeted Total Quantity of Cost Driver	Budgeted Cost per Unit of Cost Driver (₹)				Budgeted Total Quantity of Cost Driver	Budgeted Cost per Unit of Cost Driver (₹)
Cost Category	Cost Driver	Details of Budgeted Cost Driver Quantities					Details of Budgeted Cost Driver Quantities				
(1)	(2)	(3)	(4)	$(5)=(3)\times(4)$	(6)		(7)	(8)	$(9)=(7)\times(8)$	(10)
Direct materials	No. of kits	1 kit per unit	2,00,000 units	2,00,000	3,850		1 kit per unit	2,00,000 units	2,00,000	3,750
Direct manuf. labor (DML)	DML hours	2.65 DML hours per unit	2,00,000 units	5,30,000	200		2.65 DML hours per unit	2,00,000 units	5,30,000	200
Direct machining (fixed)	Machine-hours			3,00,000	380				3,00,000	380
Ordering and receiving	No. of orders	50 orders per component	425 components	21,250	800		50 orders per component	400 components	20,000	600
Test and inspection	Testing-hours	15 testing-hours per unit	2,00,000 units	30,00,000	20		14 testing-hours per unit	2,00,000 units	28,00,000	17
Rework			6.5% defect rate					6.5% defect rate		
	Rework-hours	2.5 rework-hours per defective unit	13,000[a] defective units	32,500	400		2.5 rework-hours per defective unit	13,000[a] defective units	32,500	320

[a]6.5% defect rate x 200,000 units = 13,000 defective units

Required

Will the proposed changes achieve Astel's targeted reduction of ₹4,00,00,000, or ₹200 per unit, in manufacturing costs for Provalue III? Show your computations.

Solution

Exhibit 13-8 presents the manufacturing costs for Provalue III based on the proposed changes. Manufacturing costs will decline from ₹1,08,00,00,000, or ₹5,400 per unit (Exhibit 13-6), to ₹1,04,00,00,000, or ₹5,200 per unit (Exhibit 13-8), and will achieve the target reduction of ₹4,00,00,000, or ₹200 per unit.

Exhibit 13-8

Target Manufacturing Costs of Provalue III for 2010 Based on Proposed Changes

	A	B	C	D
	🗏 File Edit View Insert Format Tools Data Window Help			
1		Budgeted		Budgete
2		Manufacturing Costs		Manufactu
3		for, 200,000 Units		Cost per l
4		(1)		(2) = (1) ÷ 2,0
5	Direct manufacturing costs			
6	Direct material costs			
7	(2,00,000 kits x₹3,750 per kit)	₹75,00,00,000		₹3,750
8	Direct manufacturing labor costs			
9	(5,30,000 DML-hours x₹200 per hour)	10,60,00,000		530
10	Direct machining costs			
11	(3,00,000 machine-hours x₹380 per machine-hour)	11,40,00,000		570
12	Direct manufacturing costs	97,00,00,000		4,850
13				
14	Manufacturing overhead costs			
15	Ordering and receiving costs			
16	(20,000 orders x₹600 per order)	1,20,00,000		60
17	Testing and inspection costs			
18	(28,00,000 testing-hours x₹17 per hour)	4,76,00,000		238
19	Rework costs			
20	(32,500 rework-hours x₹320 per hour)	1,04,00,000		52
21	Manufacturing overhead costs	7,00,00,000		350
22	Total manufacturing costs	₹104,00,00,000		₹5,200

Decision Points

The following question-and-answer format summarizes the chapter's learning objectives. Each decision presents a key question related to a learning objective. The guidelines are the answers to that question.

Decision

Guidelines

1. What are the three major influences on pricing decisions?

Customers, competitors, and costs influence prices through their effects on demand and supply; customers and competitors affect demand, and costs affect supply.

2. How do companies make long-run pricing decisions?

Companies consider all future costs (whether variable or fixed in the short run) and use a market-based or a cost-based pricing approach to earn a target return on investment.

3. How do companies determine target costs?	One approach to long-run pricing is to use a target price. Target price is the estimated price that potential customers are willing to pay for a product or service. Target operating income per unit is subtracted from the target price to determine target cost per unit. Target cost per unit is the estimated long-run cost of a product or service that when sold enables the company to achieve target operating income per unit. The challenge for the company is to make the cost improvements necessary through value-engineering methods to achieve the target cost.
4. Why is it important for managers to distinguish cost incurrence from locked-in costs?	Cost incurrence describes when a resource is sacrificed. Locked-in costs are costs not yet incurred but which, based on decisions that have already been made, will be incurred in the future. To reduce costs, techniques such as value engineering are most effective before costs are locked in.
5. How do companies price products using the cost-plus approach?	The cost-plus approach to pricing adds a markup component to a cost base as the starting point for pricing decisions. Many different costs, such as full cost of the product or manufacturing cost, can serve as the cost base in applying the cost-plus formula. Prices are then modified on the basis of customers' reactions and competitors' responses. Therefore, the size of the "plus" is determined by the marketplace.
6. Describe the life-cycle budgeting and life-cycle costing, and when should companies use these techniques?	Life-cycle budgeting estimates and life-cycle costing tracks and accumulates the costs (and revenues) attributable to a product from its initial R&D to its final customer service and support. These life-cycle techniques are particularly important when (a) a high percentage of total life-cycle costs are incurred before production begins and revenues are earned over several years, and (b) a high fraction of the life-cycle costs are locked in at the R&D and design stages.
7. Describe price discrimination and peak-load pricing price differences across countries.	Price discrimination is charging some customers a higher price for a given product or service than other customers. Peak-load pricing is charging a higher price for the same product or service when demand approaches physical-capacity limits. Under price discrimination and peak-load pricing, prices differ among market segments even though the cost of providing the product or service is approximately the same.

TERMS TO LEARN

The chapter and the Glossary at the end of the book contain definitions of:

cost incurrence **(p. 700)**
customer life-cycle costs **(p. 709)**
designed-in costs **(p. 700)**
life-cycle budgeting **(p. 707)**
life-cycle costing **(p. 707)**
locked-in costs **(p. 700)**
non-value-added cost **(p. 700)**

peak-load pricing **(p. 710)**
price discrimination **(p. 710)**
product life cycle **(p. 707)**
target cost per unit **(p. 699)**
target operating income per unit **(p. 699)**
target price **(p. 699)**

target rate of return on investment **(p. 705)**
value-added cost **(p. 700)**
value engineering **(p. 700)**

ASSIGNMENT MATERIAL

Questions

13-1 What are the three major influences on pricing decisions?

13-2 "Relevant costs for pricing decisions are full costs of the product." Do you agree? Explain.

13-3 Give two examples of pricing decisions with a short-run focus.

13-4 How is activity-based costing useful for pricing decisions?

13-5 Describe two alternative approaches to long-run pricing decisions.

13-6 What is a target cost per unit?

13-7 Describe value engineering and its role in target costing.

13-8 Give two examples of a value-added cost and two examples of a nonvalue-added cost.

13-9 "It is not important for a company to distinguish between cost incurrence and locked-in costs." Do you agree? Explain.

13-10 What is cost-plus pricing?

13-11 Describe three alternative cost-plus pricing methods.

13-12 Give two examples in which the difference in the costs of two products or services is much smaller than the difference in their prices.

13-13 What is life-cycle budgeting?

13-14 What are three benefits of using a product life-cycle reporting format?

13-15 Define predatory pricing, dumping, and collusive pricing.

Solved Examples

13-16 Relevant-cost approach to short-run pricing decisions. The Videocon Company is an electronics business with eight product lines. Income data for one of the products (XT-I07) for June are:

Revenues, 2,00,000 units at average price of ₹1,000		₹20,00,00,000
Variable costs		
Direct materials at ₹350 per unit	₹7,00,00,000	
Direct manufacturing labor at ₹100 per unit	2,00,00,000	
Variable manufacturing overhead at ₹50 per unit	1,00,00,000	
Sales commissions at 15% of revenues	3,00,00,000	
Other variable costs at ₹50 per unit	1,00,00,000	
Total variable costs		14,00,00,000
Contribution margin		6,00,00,000
Fixed costs		5,00,00,000
Operating income		₹1,00,00,000

Delhi Electronics an instruments company, has a problem with its preferred supplier of XT-I07 components. This supplier has had a three-week labor strike. Delhi Electronics approaches the sales representative, Sachin, of the Videocon Company about providing 3,000 units of XT-I07 at a price of ₹800 per unit. Sachin informs the XT-I07 product manager, that he would accept a flat commission of ₹60,000 rather than the usual 15% of revenues if this special order were accepted. Videocon has the capacity to produce 3,00,000 units of XT-107 each month, but demand has not exceeded 2,00,000 units in any month in the past year.

Required

1. If the 3,000-unit order from Delhi Electronics is accepted, how much will operating income increase or decrease? (Assume the same cost structure as in June.)

2. Production Manager ponders whether to accept the 3,000-unit special order. He is afraid of the precedent that might be set by cutting the price. He says, "The price is below our full cost of ₹950 per unit. I think we should quote a full price, or Delhi Electronics will expect favored treatment again and again if we continue to do business with them." Do you agree with Production Manager? Explain.

Solution

Relevant-cost approach to short-run pricing decisions.

1. Analysis of special order:

Sales, 3,000 units × ₹800		₹24,00,000
Variable costs		
Direct materials, 3,000 units × ₹350	₹10,50,000	
Direct manufacturing labor, 3,000 units × ₹100	3,00,000	
Variable manufacturing overhead, 3,000 units × ₹50	1,50,000	
Other variable costs, 3,000 units × ₹50	1,50,000	
Sales commission	60,000	
Total variable costs		17,10,000
Contribution margin		₹6,90,000

Note that the variable costs, except for commissions, are affected by production volume, not sales rupees. If the special order is accepted, operating income would be ₹1,00,00,000 × ₹6,90,000 × ₹1,06,90,000.

2. Whether Production Manager is making a correct decision depends on many factors. He is incorrect if the capacity would otherwise be idle and if his objective is to increase operating income in the short run. If the offer is rejected, Videocon, in effect, is willing to invest ₹6,90,000 in immediate gains forgone (an opportunity cost) to preserve the long-run selling-price structure. Production Manager is correct if he thinks future competition or future price concessions to customers will hurt Videocon's operating income by more than ₹6,90,000.

There is also the possibility that Delhi Electronics could become a long-term customer. In this case, is it a price that covers only short-run variable costs adequate? Would Sachin be willing to accept a ₹60,000 sales commission (as distinguished from his regular ₹3,60,000 × 15% × ₹24,00,000) for every Delhi Electronics order of this size if Delhi Electronics becomes a long-term customer?

13-17 Short-run pricing, capacity constraints. Tata Chemicals makes a specialized chemical product, Bolzene, from a specially imported material, Pyrone. To make 1 kilogram of Bolzene requires 1.5 kilogram of Pyrone. Bolzene has a contribution margin of ₹60 per kilogram. Tata has just received a request to manufacture 3,000 kilograms of Seltium, which also requires Pyrone as the material input. An analyst at Tata calculates the following costs of making 1 kilogram of Seltium:

Pyrone (2 kilograms x ₹40 per kilogram)	₹80
Direct manufacturing labor	40
Variable manufacturing overhead cost	30
Fixed manufacturing overhead cost allocated	50
Total manufacturing cost	200

Tata has adequate unused plant capacity to make Seltium.

Required

1. Suppose Tata has adequate Pyrone available to make Seltium. What is the minimum price per kilogram that Tata should charge to manufacture Seltium?

2. Now suppose Pyrone is in short supply. The Pyrone used to make Seltium will reduce the Bolzene that Tata can make and sell. What is the minimum price per kilogram that Tata should charge to manufacture Seltium?

Solution

Short-run pricing, capacity constraints.

1. With no constraints on availability of Pyrone or on plant capacity, Tata would want to charge a minimum price for Seltium that would cover its incremental costs to manufacture Seltium. (Because there is excess capacity, there is no opportunity cost.) In this case, the incremental costs are the variable costs to manufacture a kilogram of Seltium:

Pyrone (2 kilograms × ₹40 per kilogram)	₹80
Direct manufacturing labor	40
Variable manufacturing overhead costs	30
Total variable manufacturing costs	₹150

Hence, the minimum price that Tata should charge to manufacture Seltium is ₹150 per kilogram. For 3,000 kilograms of Seltium, it should charge a minimum of ₹4,50,000 (₹150 × 3,000).

2. Now Pyrone is in short supply. Using it to make Seltium reduces the Bolzene that Tata can make and sell. There is, therefore, an opportunity cost of manufacturing Seltium, the lost contribution from using the Pyrone to manufacture Bolzene. To make 3,000 kilograms of Seltium requires 6,000 (2 × 3,000) kilograms of Pyrone.

The 6,000 kilograms of Pyrone can be used to manufacture 4,000 (6,000 ÷ 1.5) kilograms of Bolzene, since each kilogram of Bolzene requires 1.5 kilograms of Pyrone.

The contribution margin from 4,000 kilograms of Bolzene is ₹2,40,000 (₹60 per kilogram × 4,000 kilograms). This is the opportunity cost of using Pyrone to manufacture Seltium. The minimum price that Tata should charge to manufacture Seltium should cover not only the incremental (variable) costs of manufacturing Seltium but also the opportunity cost:

	Costs of Manufacturing Seltium	
	Total for 3,000	Per Kilogram
Relevant Costs	Kilograms (1)	(2) = (1) ÷ 3,000
Incremental (variable) costs of manufacturing Seltium	₹4,50,000	₹150
Opportunity cost of forgoing manufacture and sale of Bolzene	2,40,000	80
Minimum cost of order	₹6,90,000	₹230

For 3,000 kilograms of Seltium, Tata should charge a minimum of ₹6,90,000. The minimum price per kilogram that Tata should charge for Seltium is ₹230 per kilogram (₹6,90,000 ÷ 3,000 kilograms).

13-18 Target prices, target costs, activity-based costing. Kajaria Tiles is a small distributor of marble tiles. Kajaria identifies its three major activities and cost pools as ordering, receiving and storage, and transporting, and reports the following details for 2015:

Activity	Cost Driver	Quantity of Driver Cost	Cost per Unit of Cost Driver
1. Placing and paying for orders of marble tiles	Number of orders	500	₹500 per order
2. Receiving and storage	Loads moved	4,000	₹300 per load
3. Transporting of marble tiles to retailers	Number of consignments	1,500	₹400 per consignment

Kajaria buys 2,50,000 marble tiles at an average cost of ₹30 per tile and sells them to retailers at an average price of ₹40 per tile. Assume Kajaria has no fixed costs.

Required

1. Calculate Kajaria's operating income for 2015.
2. For 2015, retailers are demanding a 5% discount off the 2015 price. Kajaria's suppliers are only willing to give a 4% discount. Kajaria expects to sell the same quantity of marble tiles in 2016 as in 2015. If all other costs and cost-driver information remain the same, calculate Kajaria's operating income for 2016.
3. Suppose further that Kajaria decides to make changes in its ordering and receiving and storing practices. By placing long-run orders with its key suppliers, Kajaria expects to reduce the number of orders to 200 and the cost per order to ₹250 per order. By redesigning the layout of the warehouse and reconfiguring the crates in

which the marble tiles are moved, Kajaria expects to reduce the number of loads moved to 3,125 and the cost per load moved to ₹280. Will Kajaria achieve its target operating income of ₹3 per tile in 2016 Show your calculations.

Solution

Target prices, target costs, activity-based costing.

1. Kajaria's operating income in 2015 is as follows:

	Total for 2,50,000 Tiles	Per Unit
	(1)	(2) = (1) ÷ 2,50,000
Revenues (₹40 × 2,50,000)	₹1,00,00,000	₹40
Purchase cost of tiles (₹30 × 2,50,000)	75,00,000	30
Ordering costs (₹500 × 500)	2,50,000	1
Receiving and storage (₹300 × 4,000)	12,00,000	4.8
Transporting costs (₹400 × 1,500)	6,00,000	2.4
Total costs	95,50,000	38.2
Operating income	₹4,50,000	₹1.8

2. Price to retailers in 2016 is 95% of 2015's price = 0.95 × ₹40 = ₹38; cost per tile in 2016 is 96% of 2015's cost = 0.96 × ₹30 = ₹28.8.

   Kajaria's operating income in 2016 is as follows:

	Total for 2,50,000 Tiles	Per Unit
	(1)	(2) = (1) ÷ 2,50,000
Revenues (₹38 × 2,50,000)	₹95,00,000	₹38.0
Purchase cost of tiles (₹28.8 × 2,50,000)	72,00,000	28.8
Ordering costs (₹500 × 500)	2,50,000	1.0
Receiving and storage (₹300 × 4,000)	12,00,000	4.8
Transporting costs (₹400 × 1,500)	6,00,000	2.4
Total costs	92,50,000	37.0
Operating income	₹2,50,000	₹1.0

3. Kajaria's operating income in 2016, if it makes changes in ordering and material handling, will be as follows:

	Total for 250,000 Tiles	Per Unit
	(1)	(2) = (1) ÷ 250,000
Revenues (₹38 × 250,000)	₹95,00,000	₹38.0
Purchase cost of tiles (₹28.8 × 250,000)	72,00,000	28.8
Ordering costs (₹250 × 200)	50,000	0.2
Receiving and storage (₹280 × 3,125)	8,75,000	3.5
Transporting costs (₹400 × 1,500)	6,00,000	2.4
Total costs	87,25,000	34.9
Operating income	₹7,75,000	₹3.1

Through better cost management, Kajaria will be able to achieve its target operating income of ₹3 per tile despite the fact that its revenue per tile has decreased by ₹2 (₹40 − ₹38), while its purchase cost per tile has decreased by only ₹1.2 (₹30 − ₹28.8).

13-19 Cost-plus, target pricing, working backwards. TinRoof, Limited manufactures and sells a do-it-yourself storage shed kit. In 2014, it reported the following:

Units produced and sold	3,200
Investment	₹2,40,00,000
Markup percentage on full cost	8%

Rate of return on investment	12%
Variable cost per unit	₹5,000

Required

1. What was TinRoof's operating income in 2014? What was the full cost per unit? What was the selling price? What was the percentage markup on variable cost?
2. TinRoof is considering increasing the annual spending on advertising by ₹17,50,000. The managers believe that the investment will translate into a 10% increase in unit sales. Should the company make the investment? Show your calculations.
3. Refer back to the original data. In 2015, TinRoof believes that it will only be able to sell 2,900 units at the price calculated in requirement 1. Management has identified ₹12,50,000 in fixed cost that can be eliminated. If TinRoof wants to maintain an 8% markup on full cost, what is the target variable cost per unit?

Solution

1.

Investment	₹2,40,00,000
Return on investment	12%
Operating income (12% × ₹2,40,00,000)	₹28,80,000
Operating income per unit (₹28,80,000 ÷ 3,200)	₹900
Full cost per unit (900 ÷ 0.08)	₹11,250
Selling price (₹11,250 + ₹900)	₹12,150
Markup percentage on variable cost (₹900 ÷ ₹5,000)	18%

Total fixed costs = (Full cost per unit − Variable cost per unit) × Units sold

2. Contribution margin per unit = ₹12,150 − ₹5,000 = ₹7,150

Increase in sales = 10% × 3,200 units = 320 units

Increase in contribution margin = ₹7,150 × 320 units = ₹22,88,000

Less: Advertising costs	17,50,000
Increase in operating income	₹5,38,000

TinRoof should spend ₹17,50,000 in advertising because it increases operating income by ₹5,38,000.

3.

Revenues (₹12,150 × 2,900 units)	₹3,52,35,000
Target full cost at 8% markup (₹3,52,35,000 ÷ 1.08)	₹3,26,25,000
Less: Target total fixed costs (₹2,00,00,000 − ₹12,50,000)	1,87,50,000
Target total variable costs	₹1,38,75,000
Divided by number of units	÷ 29,000 units
Target variable cost per unit	₹4,784.50

13-20 Target costs, effect of product-design changes on product costs. Medical Instruments uses a manufacturing costing system with one direct-cost category (direct materials) and three indirect-cost categories:

a. Setup, production order, and materials-handling costs that vary with the number of batches

b. Manufacturing operations costs that vary with machine-hours

c. Costs of engineering changes that vary with the number of engineering changes made

In response to competitive pressures at the end of 2015, Medical Instruments employed value engineering techniques to reduce manufacturing costs. Actual information for 2015 and 2016 are:

	2015	2016
Setup, production-order, and materials-handling cost per batch	₹8,000	₹7,500
Total manufacturing operating cost per machine-hour	55	50
Cost per engineering change	12,000	10,000

The management of Medical Instruments wants to evaluate whether value engineering has succeeded in reducing the target manufacturing cost per unit of one of its products, HJ6, by 10%. Actual results for 2015 and 2016 for HJ6 are

	Actual Results for 2015	Actual Results for 2016
Units of HJ6 produced	3,500	4,000
Direct material cost per unit of HJ6	₹1,200	₹1,100
Total number of batches required to produce HJ6	70	80
Total machine-hours required to produce HJ6	21,000	22,000
Number of engineering changes made	14	10

Required

1. Calculate the manufacturing cost per unit of HJ6 in 2015.
2. Calculate the manufacturing cost per unit of HJ6 in 2016.
3. Did Medical Instruments achieve the target manufacturing cost per unit for HJ6 in 2016 Explain.
4. Explain how Medical Instruments reduced the manufacturing cost per unit of HJ6 in 2016.

Solution

Target costs, effect of product-design changes on product costs.

   1. and **2.** Manufacturing costs of HJ6 in 2015 and 2016 are as follows:

	2015 Total (1)	2015 Per Unit (2) = (1) ÷ 3,500	2016 Total (3)	2016 Per Unit (4) = (3) ÷ 4,000
Direct materials, ₹1,200 × 3,500; ₹1,100 × 4,000	₹42,00,000	₹1,200	₹44,00,000	₹1,100
Batch-level costs, ₹8,000 × 70; ₹7,500 × 80	5,60,000	160	6,00,000	150
Manufacturing operations costs, ₹55 × 21,000; ₹50 × 22,000	11,55,000	330	11,00,000	275
Engineering change costs,; ₹12,000 × 14 ₹10,000 × 10	1,68,000	48	1,00,000	25
Total	₹60,83,000	₹1,738	₹62,00,000	₹1,550

3. Target manufacturing cost per unit of HJ6 in 2016 = Manufacturing costs per unit in 2015 × 90% = ₹1,738 × 0.90 = ₹1,564.20

   Actual manufacturing cost per unit of HJ6 in 2016 was ₹1,550. Hence, Medical Instruments did achieve its target manufacturing cost per unit of ₹1,564.20

4. To reduce the manufacturing cost per unit in 2016, Medical Instruments reduces the cost per unit of activity in each of the four cost categories—direct materials costs, batch-level costs, manufacturing operations costs, and engineering change costs. It also reduced machine-hours and number of engineering changes made—the quantities of the cost drivers. In 2015, Medical Instruments used 6 machine-hours per unit of HJ6 (21,000 machine-hours ÷ 3,500 units). In 2016, Medical Instruments used 5.5 machine-hours per unit of HJ6 (22,000 machine-hours ÷ 4,000 units). Medical Instruments reduced engineering changes from 14 in 2015 to 10 in 2016. Medical Instruments achieved these gains through value engineering activities that retained only those product features that customers wanted while eliminating activities and their costs.

13-21 Cost-plus target return on investment pricing. John is the managing partner of a business that has just finished building a 60-room motel. John anticipates that he will rent these rooms for 16,000 nights next year (or 16,000 room-nights). All rooms are similar and will rent for the same price. John estimates the following operating costs for next year:

Variable operating costs   ₹30 per room-night
Fixed costs

Salaries and wages	₹17,50,000
Maintenance of building and pool	3,70,000
Other operating and administration costs	14,00,000
Total fixed costs	₹35,20,000

The capital invested in the motel is ₹96,00,000. The partnership's target return on investment is 25%. John expects demand for rooms to be uniform throughout the year. He plans to price the rooms at full cost plus a markup on full cost to earn the target return on investment.

Required

1. What price should John charge for a room-night? What is the markup as a percentage of the full cost of a room-night?

2. John's market research indicates that if the price of a room-night determined in requirement 1 is reduced by 10%, the expected number of room-nights John could rent would increase by 10%. Should John reduce prices by 10%? Show your calculations.

Solution

Cost-plus target return on investment pricing.

1. Target operating income = Target return on investment × Invested capital

Target operating income (25% × ₹96,00,000)	₹24,00,000	
Total fixed costs	35,20,000	
Target contribution margin	₹59,20,000	
Target contribution margin per room, (₹59,20,000 ÷ 16,000)	₹370	
Add variable costs per room	30	
Price to be charged per room	₹400	
Proof		
Total room revenues (₹400 × 16,000 rooms)		₹64,00,000
Total costs		
Variable costs (₹30 × 16,000)	₹4,80,000	
Fixed costs	35,20,000	
Total costs		40,00,000
Operating income		₹24,00,000

The full cost of a room = variable cost per room + fixed cost per room
The full cost of a room = ₹30 + (₹35,20,000 ÷ 16,000) = ₹30 + ₹220 = ₹250
Markup per room   = Rental price per room − Full cost of a room
              = ₹400 − ₹250 = ₹150
Markup percentage as a fraction of full cost = ₹150 ÷ ₹250 = 60%

2. If price is reduced by 10%, the number of rooms John could rent would increase by 10%.

The new price per room would be 90% × ₹400	₹360
The number of rooms John expects to rent is 110% of 16,000	17,600
The contribution margin per room would be ₹360 − ₹30	₹330
Contribution margin (₹330 × 17,600)	₹58,08,000

Because the contribution margin of ₹58,08,000 at the reduced price of ₹360 is less than the contribution margin of ₹59,20,000 at a price of ₹400, John should not reduce the price of the rooms. Note that the fixed costs of ₹35,20,000 will be the same under the ₹400 and the ₹360 price alternatives and are, hence, irrelevant to the analysis.

13-22 Life-cycle budgeting and costing. Blue star Ltd, Inc., plans to develop a new industrial-powered vacuum sweeper for household use that runs exclusively on rechargeable batteries. The product will take 6 months to design and test. The company expects the vacuum sweeper to sell 10,000 units during the first 6 months of sales; 20,000 units per year over the following 2 years; and 5,000 units over the final 6 months of the product's life cycle. The company expects the following costs:

Period	Cost	Total Fixed Cost for the Period	Variable Cost per Unit
Months 0-6	Design costs	₹50,00,000	
Months 7-12	Production	₹1,30,00,000	₹900 per unit
	Marketing	₹1,00,00,000	
	Distribution	₹20,00,000	₹100 per unit
Months 13-36	Production	₹4,90,00,000	₹700 per unit
	Marketing	₹2,32,50,000	
	Distribution	₹70,00,000	₹80 per unit
Months 37-42	Production	₹80,00,000	₹600 per unit
	Marketing	₹47,50,000	
	Distribution	₹10,00,000	₹70 per unit

Ignore time value of money.

Required

1. If Blue star prices the sweepers at ₹3,750 each, how much operating income will the company make over the product's life cycle? What is the operating income per unit?
2. Excluding the initial product design costs, what is the operating income in each of the three sales phases of the product's life cycle, assuming the price stays at ₹3,750?
3. How would you explain the change in budgeted operating income over the product's life cycle? What other factors does the company need to consider before developing the new vacuum sweeper?
4. Blue star is concerned about the operating income it will report in the first sales phase. It is considering pricing the vacuum sweeper at ₹4,250 for the first 6 months and decreasing the price to ₹3,750 thereafter. With this pricing strategy, Blue star expects to sell 9,500 units instead of 10,000 units in the first 6 months, 19,000 each year over the next 2 years, and 5,000 over the last 6 months. Assuming the same cost structure given in the problem, which pricing strategy would you recommend? Explain.

Solution

1.

Projected Life Cycle Income Statement

Revenues [₹3,750 × (10,000 + 40,000 + 5,000)]	₹20,62,50,000
Variable costs:	
Months 7–12 (₹1,000 × 10,000)	1,00,00,000
Months 13–36 (₹780 × 40,000)	3,12,00,000
Months 37–42 (₹670 × 5,000)	33,50,000
Total variable costs	4,45,50,000
Fixed costs:	
Design costs	50,00,000
Production (₹1,30,00,000 + ₹4,90,00,000 + ₹80,00,000)	7,00,00,000
Marketing (₹1,00,00,000 + ₹2,32,50,000 + ₹47,50,000)	3,80,00,000

Distribution (₹20,00,000 + ₹70,00,000 + ₹10,00,000)   1,00,00,000
     Total fixed costs   12,30,00,000
Life cycle operating income   ₹3,87,00,000

Average profit per sweeper = ₹3,87,00,000/(10,000 + 40,000 + 5,000) = ₹703.6

2.

Projected Life Cycle Income Statement
Months 7–12

Revenues (₹3,750 × 10,000)	₹3,75,00,000
Variable costs:	
Months 7–12 (₹1,000 × 10,000)	1,00,00,000
Fixed costs:	
Production	1,30,00,000
Marketing	1,00,00,000
Distribution	20,00,000
Total fixed costs	2,50,00,000
Operating income	₹25,00,000

Average profit per sweeper = ₹25,00,000/10,000 = ₹250

Projected Life Cycle Income Statement
Months 13–36

Revenues (₹3,750 × 40,000)	₹15,00,00,000
Variable costs:	
Months 13-36 (₹780 × 40,000)	3,12,00,000
Fixed costs:	
Production	4,90,00,000
Marketing	2,32,50,000
Distribution	70,00,000
Total fixed costs	7,92,50,000
Operating income	₹3,95,50,000

Average profit per sweeper = ₹3,95,50,000/40,000 = ₹988.80

Projected Life Cycle Income Statement
Months 37–42

Revenues (₹3,750 × 5,000)	₹1,87,50,000
Variable costs:	
Months 37–42 (₹670 × 5,000)	33,50,000
Fixed costs:	
Production	80,00,000
Marketing	47,50,000
Distribution	10,00,000
Total fixed costs	1,37,50,000
Operating income	₹16,50,000

Average profit per sweeper = ₹16,50,000/5,000 = ₹330

3. In analyzing the relative profitability of the product during the three sales phases of its life cycle, the results are as expected. During the initial growth phase, all fixed costs,

including marketing, are higher in order to successfully launch the new product. In addition, variable costs are higher per unit because the company has not yet capitalized on economies of scale. As the product moves into its maturity phase, the company begins to see the benefits of economies of scale and leaner production practices. The results are lower variable and fixed costs. Also, the company will likely not need to spend as much on marketing because the product in now well established. This phase results in the highest profit per unit. Lastly, in the decline phase, variable costs per unit are the lowest because the company is maximizing its efficiencies. Marketing is at its lowest because the company is expecting to phase out the product. However, during this final phase of the product's life cycle, fixed costs per unit are higher than in the maturity phase because the company is not maximizing its production volume. The company is producing fewer units, which leads to higher fixed cost per unit. The product is still more profitable than in the growth phase, but not as profitable as in maturity.

The company may need to analyze the probability that the price will be able to remain constant through the product's entire life cycle. Because technology is rapidly changing, this product may become obsolete sooner than expected. The company also has not accounted for the time value of money, which may make a big difference in the desired outcome, depending on the company's required rate of return. In addition, the company has not budgeted for all possible expenses such as warranty claims and returns. These should be considered as well in the overall plan. Lastly, the company may want to investigate possible methods of value engineering to gain even more efficiencies and profitability over the life of the product.

4.

Projected Life Cycle Income Statement

Revenues [₹4,250 × 9,500 + ₹3,750 × (38,000 + 5,000)]	₹20,16,25,000
Variable costs:	
Months 7–12 (₹1,000 × 9,500)	95,00,000
Months 13–36 (₹780 × 38,000)	2,96,40,000
Months 37–42 (₹670 × 5,000)	33,50,000
Total variable costs	4,24,90,000
Fixed costs:	
Design costs	50,00,000
Production (₹1,30,00,000 + ₹4,90,00,000 + ₹80,00,000)	7,00,00,000
Marketing (₹1,00,00,000 + ₹2,32,50,000 + ₹47,50,000)	3,80,00,000
Distribution (₹20,00,000 + ₹70,00,000 + ₹10,00,000)	1,00,00,000
Total fixed costs	12,30,00,000
Life cycle operating income	₹3,61,35,000

Average profit per sweeper = ₹3,61,35,000/(9,500 + 38,000 + 5,000) = ₹688.3

Blue star earns more profit under its original plan (₹3,87,00,000) than it does if it increases the price to ₹4,250 for the first six months (₹3,61,35,000). The decline in sales as a result of increasing the price reduces operating income. Therefore, Blue star should price the seepers at ₹3,750 for the first six months rather than increase the price to ₹4,250.

13-23 Considerations other than cost in pricing decisions. Fun Stay Express operates a 100-room hotel near a busy amusement park. During June, a 30-day month, Fun Stay Express experienced a 65% occupancy rate from Monday evening through Thursday evening (weeknights). On Friday through Sunday evenings (weekend nights), however, occupancy increases to 90%. (There were 18 weeknights and 12 weekend nights in June.) Fun Stay Express charges ₹850 per night for a suite. The company recently hired Reema to manage the hotel to increase the hotel's profitability. The following information relates to Fun Stay Express' costs:

	Fixed Cost	Variable Cost
Depreciation	₹2,50,000 per month	
Administrative costs	₹3,80,000 per month	
Housekeeping and supplies	₹1,60,000 per month	₹300 per room-night
Breakfast	₹1,20,000 per month	₹60 per breakfast served

Fun Stay Express offers free breakfast to guests. In June, there were an average of two breakfasts served per room-night on weeknights and 4 breakfasts served per room-night on weekend nights.

Required

1. Calculate the average cost per room-night for June. What was Fun Stay Express' operating income or loss for the month?

2. Reema estimates that if Fun Stay Express decreases the nightly rates to ₹750, weeknight occupancy will increase to 75%. She also estimates that if the hotel increases the nightly rate on weekend nights to ₹1,050, occupancy on those nights will remain at 90%. Would this be a good move for Fun Stay Express? Show your calculations.

3. Why would the guests tolerate a ₹300 price difference between weeknights and weekend nights?

4. A discount travel clearinghouse has approached Fun Stay Express with a proposal to offer last-minute deals on empty rooms on both weeknights and weekend nights. Assuming that there will be an average of three breakfasts served per night per room, what is the minimum price that Fun Stay Express could accept on the last-minute rooms?

Solution

1.

Guest nights on weeknights:
  18 weeknights × 100 rooms × 65% = 1,170
Guest nights on weekend nights:
  12 weekend nights × 100 rooms × 90% = 1,080
Total guest nights in June = 1,170 + 1,080 = 2,250
Breakfasts served:
  1,170 weeknight guest nights × 2 = 2,340
  1,080 weekend guest nights × 4 = 4,320
Total breakfasts served in June = 2,340 + 4,320 = 6,660
Total costs for June:

Depreciation	₹2,50,000
Administrative costs	3,80,000
Fixed housekeeping and supplies	1,60,000
Variable housekeeping and supplies (2,250 × ₹300)	6,75,000
Fixed breakfast costs	1,20,000
Variable breakfast costs (6,660 × ₹60)	3,99,600
Total costs for June	₹19,84,600
Cost per guest night (₹19,84,600 ÷ 2,250)	₹882.00
Revenue for June (₹850 × 2,250)	₹19,12,500
Total costs for June	19,84,600
Operating income/(loss)	₹(72,100)

2.

New weeknight guest nights
  18 weeknights × 100 rooms × 75% = 1,350
New weekend guest nights
  12 weeknights × 100 rooms × 90% = 1,080

Total guest nights in June I = 1,350 + 1,080 = 2,430
Breakfasts served:
   1,350 weeknight guest nights × 2 = 2,700
   1,080 weekend guest nights × 4 = 4,320
Total breakfasts served in June = 2,700 + 4,320 = 7,020
Total costs for June:

Depreciation	₹2,50,000
Administrative costs	3,80,000
Fixed housekeeping and supplies	1,60,000
Variable housekeeping and supplies (2,430 × ₹300)	7,29,000
Fixed breakfast costs	1,20,000
Variable breakfast costs (7,020 × ₹60)	4,21,200
Total costs	₹20,60,200
Revenue [(1,350 × ₹750) + (1,080 × ₹1,050)]	₹21,46,500
Total costs for June	20,60,200
Operating income	₹86,300

Yes, this pricing arrangement would increase operating income by ₹1,58,400 from an operating loss of ₹72,100 to an operating income of ₹86,300 (₹86,300 + ₹72,100 = ₹1,58,400).

3. Guests typically do not come to the amusement park on weekdays because adults are busy at work and children have to attend school. The weeknight guests are families who stay at the hotel for convenience. They are willing to consider other hotel options or even not travel at all if the price is high and unaffordable. Reducing the weeknight price is important to entice families to try to come to the amusement park on weekdays. The demand of weeknight guests is elastic.

In contrast, weekends are really the only time when families can conveniently come to the amusement park given their busy weekday schedules. The demand of pleasure travelers on weekends is inelastic. Because of the differences in preferences of the weeknight and weekend guests, Fun Stay Express can price discriminate between these guests by charging ₹300 more on weekends than on weeknights and still have weekend travelers stay at the hotel.

4. Fun Stay Express would need to charge a minimum of ₹480 per night for the last-minute rooms, an amount equal to the variable cost per room. Variable cost per room night = ₹300 per room night + ₹60 × 3 breakfasts = ₹480. Any price above ₹480 would increase its operating income.

13-24 Cost-plus, target pricing, working backward. The new CEO of Small Robust Manufacturing has asked for a variety of information about the operations of the firm from last year. The CEO is given the following information, but with some data missing:

Total sales revenue	?
Number of units produced and sold	5,00,000 units
Selling price	?
Operating income	1,80,000
Total investment in assets	22,50,000
Variable cost per unit	₹4.00
Fixed costs for the year	₹25,00,000

Required

1. Find (a) total sales revenue, (b) selling price, (c) rate of return on investment, and (d) markup percentage on full cost for this product.
2. The new CEO has a plan to reduce fixed costs by ₹2,25,000 and variable costs by ₹0.30 per unit while continuing to produce and sell 5,00,000 units. Using the same markup percentage as in requirement 1, calculate the new selling price.

3. Assume the CEO institutes the changes in requirement 2 including the new selling price. However, the reduction in variable cost has resulted in lower product quality resulting in 5% fewer units being sold compared with before the change. Calculate operating income (loss).

4, What concerns, if any, other than the quality problem described in requirement 3, do you see in implementing the CEO's plan? Explain briefly.

Solution

1. In the following table, work backward from operating income to calculate the selling price.

Selling price	₹9.36
Less: Variable cost per unit	4.00
Unit contribution margin	₹5.36
Number of units produced and sold	× 5,00,000 units
Contribution margin	₹26,80,000
Less: Fixed costs	25,00,000
Operating income	₹1,80,000

a) Total sales revenue = ₹9.36 × 5,00,000 units = ₹46,80,000

b) Selling price = ₹9.36 (from above)

Alternatively,

Operating income	₹1,80,000
Add fixed costs	25,00,000
Contribution margin	26,80,000
Add variable costs (₹4.0 × 5,00,000 units)	20,00,000
Sales revenue	₹46,80,000

$$\text{Selling price} = \frac{\text{Sales revenue}}{\text{Units sold}} = \frac{₹46,80,000}{5,00,000} = ₹9.36$$

c) Rate of return on investment = $\dfrac{\text{Operating income}}{\text{Total investment in assets}} = \dfrac{₹1,80,000}{₹22,50,000} = 8\%$

d) Markup % on full cost

Total cost = (₹4 × 5,00,000 units) + ₹25,00,000 = ₹45,00,000

$$\text{Unit cost} = \frac{₹45,00,000}{5,00,000 \text{ units}} = ₹9.00$$

$$\text{Markup \%} = \frac{₹9.36 - ₹9.00}{₹9.00} = 4\%$$

$$\text{Or } \frac{₹46,80,000 - ₹45,00,000}{₹45,00,000} = 4\%$$

2.
New fixed costs	= ₹25,00,000 – ₹2,25,000 = ₹22,75,000
New variable costs	= ₹4.00 – ₹0.30 = ₹3.70
New total costs	= (₹3.70 × 5,00,000 units) + ₹22,75,000 = ₹41,25,000
New total sales (4% markup)	= ₹41,25,000 × 1.04 = ₹42,90,000
New selling price	= ₹42,90,000 ÷ 5,00,000 units = ₹8.58
Alternatively,	
New unit cost	= ₹41,25,000 ÷ 5,00,000 units = ₹8.25
New selling price	= ₹8.25 × 1.04 = ₹8.58

3. New units sold = 5,00,000 units × 95% = 4,75,000 units

Budgeted Operating Income
for the Year Ending December 31, 20xx

Revenues (₹8.58 × 4,75,000 units)	₹40,75,500
Variable costs (₹3.70 × 4,75,000 units)	17,57,500
Contribution margin	23,18,000
Fixed costs	22,75,000
Operating income	₹43,000

4. The CEO has not considered customers in these pricing decisions. Will customers continue to want the product at these prices? What are competitors doing? The CEO should take a more market-based approach to pricing.

The CEO should also think about the effect of cost cutting on employee participation and morale and whether the cuts are falling disproportionately on any specific value-chain function.

13-25 Value engineering, target pricing, and target costs. Lakme Cosmetics manufactures, and sells a variety of makeup and beauty products. The company has come up with its own patented formula for a new anti-aging cream The company president wants to make sure the product is priced competitively because its purchase will also likely increase sales of other products. The company anticipates that it will sell 4,00,000 units of the product in the first year with the following estimated costs:

Product design and licensing	₹1,00,00,000
Direct materials	1,80,00,000
Direct manufacturing labor	1,20,00,000
Variable manufacturing overhead	60,00,000
Fixed manufacturing overhead	2,00,00,000
Fixed marketing	3,00,00,000

Required

1. The company believes that it can successfully sell the product for ₹380 a bottle. The company's target operating income is 40% of revenue. Calculate the target full cost of producing the 4,00,000 units. Does the cost estimate meet the company's requirements? Is value engineering needed?

2. A component of the direct materials cost requires the nectar of a specific plant in South India. If the company could eliminate this special ingredient, the materials cost would drop by 45%. However, this would require design changes of ₹30,00,000 to engineer a chemical equivalent of the ingredient. Will this design change allow the product to meet its target cost?

3. The company president does not believe that the formula should be altered for fear it will tarnish the company's brand. She prefers that the company spend more on marketing and increase the price. The company's accountants believe that if marketing costs are increase by ₹40,00,000 then the company can achieve a selling price of ₹420 per bottle without losing any sales. At this price, will the company achieve its target operating income of 40% of revenue?

4. What are the advantages and disadvantages of pursuing alternative 2 and alternative 3 above?

Solution

1.

Product design and licensing	₹1,00,00,000
Direct materials	1,80,00,000
Direct manufacturing labor	1,20,00,000

Variable manufacturing overhead	60,00,000
Fixed manufacturing overhead	2,00,00,000
Fixed marketing	3,00,00,000
Total cost	₹9,60,00,000
Cost per unit (₹9,60,00,000 ÷ 4,00,000)	₹240
Target cost per unit (₹380 × 0.60)	₹228

The original cost estimate of ₹9,60,00,000 does not meet the company's requirements. Value engineering will be needed to reduce the cost per unit to the target cost. Lakme's operating income will be ₹5,60,00,000 (₹380 × 4,00,000 – ₹9,60,00,000)

2.

Total cost	₹9,60,00,000
Less: Reduction in material costs (₹1,80,00,000 × 45%)	(81,00,000)
Add: Increase in design costs	30,00,000
Total costs of redesigned table	₹9,09,00,000
Revised cost per unit (₹9,09,00,000 ÷ 4,00,000 units)	₹227.125
Target cost per unit (₹380 × 0.60)	₹228

The design change allows the table to meet its goal of target costs less than 60% of revenue and target operating income greater than 40% of revenue. The cost of materials is a locked-in cost because they are designed into the product formula.

3.

Total cost	₹9,60,00,000
Add: Increase in marketing costs	40,00,000
Total costs of redesigned table	₹10,00,00,000
Revised cost per unit (₹10,00,00,000 ÷ 4,00,000 units)	₹250
Target cost per unit (₹420 × 0.60)	₹252

Yes, this proposal does allow the company to meet its goal of target costs less than 60% of revenue and target operating income greater than 40% of revenue.

2. The company has many considerations, both quantitative and qualitative, when deciding between the preceding requirements 2 and 3 . Although both options meet the target costing objectives, they will provide different amounts of income in both the short and potentially long term. In the short term, the alternative in requirement 2 will result in income of (₹380 × 4,00,000) – ₹9,09,00,000 = ₹6,11,00,000. The alternative in requirement 3 will provide a higher income of (₹420 × 4,00,000) – ₹10,00,00,000 = ₹6,80,00,000 and will be preferred.

In the long run, however, there are other considerations that might favor the alternative in requirement 2 and using the chemical equivalent of the nectar obtained from the plant in South India. For example, will the nectar become more expensive in future periods? If so, could the product be reengineered at a later time or are the materials locked-in with the design for the full product life cycle. If the company chemically engineers the material, will this tarnish the quality of the product or more importantly, the company's brand image? How might this affect the price in future periods and/or the sales of other products within the company?

13-26 Cost-plus, time and materials, ethics. A & L Mechanical sells and services plumbing, heating, and air-conditioning systems. A & L's cost accounting system tracks two cost categories: direct labor and direct materials. A & L uses a time-and-materials pricing system, with direct labor marked up 80% and direct materials marked up 60% to recover indirect costs of support staff, support materials, and shared equipment and tools and to earn a profit.

During a hot summer day, the central air conditioning in Shveta's home stops working. A & L technician arrives at Shveta's home and inspects the air conditioner. He considers two options: replace the compressor or repair it. The cost information available to technician follows:

	Labor	Materials
Repair option	7 hrs	₹1,200
Replace option	4 hrs	₹2,300
Labor cost	₹450 per hr.	

Required

1. If technician presents Shveta with the replace or repair options, what price would he quote for each?
2. If the two options were equally effective for the 3 years that Shveta intends to live in the home, which option would she choose?
3. If technician's objective is to maximize profits, which option would he recommend to Shveta? What would be the ethical course of action?

Solution

1. As shown in the table below, Technician will tell Shveta that she will have to pay ₹7,590 to get the air conditioning system repaired and ₹6,920 to get it replaced.

COST	Labor	Materials	Total Cost
Repair option (7 hrs. × ₹450 per hr.; ₹1,200)	₹3,150	₹1,200	₹4,350
Replace option (4 hrs. × ₹450 per hr.; ₹2,300)	1,800	2,300	4,100
PRICE (100% markup on labor cost; 60% markup on materials)	**Labor**	**Materials**	**Total Price**
Repair option (₹3,150 × 1.8; ₹1,200 × 1.6)	₹5,670	₹1,920	₹7,590
Replace option (₹1,800 × 1.8; ₹2,300 × 1.6)	3,240	3,680	6,920

2. If the repair and replace options are equally effective, Shveta will choose to get the air conditioning system replaced for ₹6,920 (rather than spend ₹7,590 on repairing it).
3. A&L Mechanical will earn a greater contribution toward overhead in the repair option (₹3,240 = ₹7,590 − ₹4,350) than in the replace option (₹2,820 = ₹6,920 − ₹4,100). Therefore, Technician will recommend the repair option to Shveta, which is not the one she would prefer. Recognizing this conflict, Technician may even present only the repair option to Shveta. Of course, he runs the risk of Shveta walking away and thinking of other options (at which point, he could present the replace option as a compromise). The problem is that Technician has superior information about the repairs needed but his incentives may cause him to not reveal his information and instead use it to his advantage. It is only the seller's desire to build a reputation, to have a long-term relationship with the customer, and to have the customer recommend the seller to other potential buyers of the service, that encourages an honest discussion of the options.

The ethical courve their employees act ethically, organizations do not reward employees on the basis of the profits earned on various jobs. They also develop codes of conduct and core values and beliefs that specify appropriate and inappropriate behaviors.

13-27 Cost-plus and market-based pricing. (CMA, adapted) Quick Test Laboratories evaluates the reaction of materials to extreme increases in temperature. Much of the company's early growth was attributable to government contracts, but recent growth has come from expansion into commercial markets. Two types of testing at Quick Test are Heat Testing (HTT) and Arctic-Condition Testing (ACT). Currently, all of the budgeted operating costs are collected in a single overhead pool. All of the estimated testing-hours are also collected in a single pool. One rate per test-hour is used for both types of testing. This hourly rate is marked up by 30% to recover administrative costs and taxes and to earn a profit.

Anand, Quick Test's controller, believes that there is enough variation in the test procedures and cost structure to establish separate costing rates and billing rates at a 30% markup. He also believes that the inflexible rate structure the company is currently using is inadequate in today's competitive environment. After analyzing the company data, he has divided operating costs into the following three cost pools:

Labor and supervision	₹43,68,000
Setup and facility costs	35,18,200
Utilities	43,56,000
Total budgeted costs for the period	₹1,22,42,200

Anand budgets 1,12,000 total test-hours for the coming period. Test-hours is also the cost costs is 700 setup hours. The budgeted quantity of cost driver for utilities is 12,000 machine-hours.

Anand has estimated that HTT uses 70% of the test-hours, 20% of the setup-hours, and half the machine-hours.

Required

1. Find the single rate for operating costs based on test-hours and the hourly billing rate for HTT and ACT.
2. Find the three activity-based rates for operating costs.
3. What will the billing rate for HTT and ACT be based on the activity-based costing structure? State the rates in terms of test-hours. Referring to both requirements 1 and 2, which rates make more sense for Quick Test?
4. If Quick Test's competition all charge ₹230 per hour for arctic testing, what can Quick Test do to stay competitive?

Solution

1. Single rate $= \dfrac{₹1,22,42,200}{1,12,000 \text{ testing hours}} = ₹109.3$ per test-hour (TH)

   Hourly billing rate for HTT and ACT $= ₹109.30 \times 1.30 = ₹142.10$

2. Labor and supervision $= \dfrac{₹43,68,000}{1,12,000 \text{ test - hours}} = ₹39$ per test-hour

   Setup and facility costs $= \dfrac{₹35,18,200}{700 \text{ setup hours}} = ₹5,026$ per setup-hour

   Utilities $= \dfrac{₹43,56,000}{12,000 \text{ machine - hours}} = ₹363$ per machine-hour (MH)

3.

	HTT	ACT	Total
Labor and supervision (₹39 × 78,400; 33,600 test-hours)[1]	₹30,57,600	₹13,10,400	₹43,68,000
Setup and facility cost (₹5,026 × 140; 560 setup-hours)[2]	7,03,640	28,14,560	35,18,200
Utilities (₹363 × 6,000; 6,000 machine-hours)[3]	21,78,000	21,78,000	43,56,000
Total cost	₹59,39,240	₹63,02,960	₹1,22,42,200
Number of testing hours (TH)	÷ 78,400 TH	÷ 33,600 TH	
Cost per testing hour	₹75.8 per TH	₹187.60 per TH	
Mark-up	× 1.30	× 1.30	
Billing rate per testing hour	₹98.50 per TH	₹243.90 per TH	

[1]1,12,000 test-hours × 70% = 78,400 test-hours; 1,12,000 test-hours × 30% = 33,600 test-hours
[2]700 setup-hours × 20% = 140 setup-hours; 700 setup-hours × 80% = 560 setup-hours
[3]12,000 machine-hours × 50% = 6,000 machine-hours; 12,000 machine-hours × 50% = 6,000 machine-hours

The billing rates based on the activity-based cost structure make more sense. These billing rates reflect the ways the testing procedures consume the firm's resources.

5. To stay competitive, Quick Test needs to be more efficient in arctic testing. Roughly 45% of arctic testing's total cost $\left(\dfrac{₹28,14,560}{₹63,02,960} = 45\% \right)$ occurs in setups and facility costs. Perhaps the setup activity can be redesigned to achieve cost savings. Quick Test should also look for savings in the labor and supervision cost per test-hour and the total number of test-hours used in arctic testing, as well as the utility cost per machine-hour and the total number of machine hours used in arctic testing. This may require redesigning the test, redesigning processes, and achieving efficiency and productivity improvements.

13-28 Life-cycle costing. Maximum Metal Recycling and Salvage receives the opportunity to salvage scrap metal and other materials from an old industrial site. The current owners of the site will sign over the site to Maximum at no cost. Maximum intends to extract scrap metal at the site for 24 months and then will clean up the site, return the land to useable condition, and sell it to a developer. Projected costs associated with the project follow:

		Fixed	Variable
Months 1-24	Metal extraction and processing	₹20,000 per month	₹800 per ton
Months 1-27	Rent on temporary buildings	₹10,000 per month	
	Administration	₹60,000 per month	
Months 25-27	Clean-up	₹2,00,000 per month	
	Land restoration	₹2,30,000 total	
	Cost of selling land	₹8,00,000 total	

Ignore time value of money.

Required

1. Assuming that Maximum expects to salvage 70,000 tons of metal from the site, what is the total project life cycle cost?

2. Suppose Maximum can sell the metal for ₹1,100 per ton and wants to earn a profit (before taxes) of ₹300 per ton. At what price must Maximum sell the land at the end of the project to achieve its target profit per ton?

3. Now suppose Maximum can only sell the metal for ₹1,000 per ton and the land at ₹11,00,000 less than what you calculated in requirement 2. If Maximum wanted to maintain the same markup percentage on total project life-cycle cost as in requirement 2, by how much would the company have to reduce its total project life-cycle cost?

Solution

1.

Total Project Life-Cycle Costs	
Variable costs:	
Metal extraction and processing (₹800 per ton × 70,000 tons)	₹5,60,00,000
Fixed costs:	
Metal extraction and processing (₹20,000 × 24 months)	4,80,000
Rent on temporary buildings (₹10,000 × 27 months)	2,70,000
Administration (₹60,000 × 27 months)	16,20,000
Clean-up (₹2,00,000 × 3 months)	6,00,000
Land restoration	2,30,000
Selling land	8,00,000
Total life-cycle cost	₹6,00,00,000

2.

Projected Life Cycle Income Statement	
Revenue (₹1,100 per ton × 70,000 tons)	₹7,70,00,000
Sale of land (plug after inputting other numbers)	40,00,000
Total life-cycle cost	(6,00,00,000)
Life-cycle operating income (₹300 per ton × 70,000 tons)	₹2,10,00,000

$$\text{Mark-up percentage on project life-cycle cost} = \frac{\text{Life cycle operating income}}{\text{Total life} - \text{cycle cost}}$$

$$= \frac{₹2,10,00,000}{₹6,00,00,000} = 35\%$$

The company would have to sell the land for ₹40,00,000.

3.

Revenue (₹1,000 per ton × 70,000 tons)	₹7,00,00,000
Sale of land	29,00,000
Total revenue	₹7,29,00,000
Total life-cycle cost at mark-up of 35%	
(₹72,90,000 ÷ 1.35)	₹5,40,00,000
The company would need to reduce total life-cycle costs by	
(₹6,00,00,000 − ₹5,40,00,000)	₹60,00,000
Check	
Revenue	₹7,00,00,000
Sale of land	29,00,000
Total life-cycle cost	(5,40,00,000)
Life-cycle operating income	₹1,89,00,000

$$\text{Mark-up percentage} = \frac{₹1,89,00,000}{₹5,40,00,000} = 35\%$$

13-29 Airline pricing, considerations other than cost in pricing. Northern Airways is about to introduce a daily round-trip flight from Delhi to Mumbai and is determining how to price its round-trip tickets.

The market research group at Northern Airways segments the market into business and pleasure travelers. It provides the following information on the effects of two different prices on the number of seats expected to be sold and the variable cost per ticket, including the commission paid to travel agents:

		Number of Seats Expected to BE Sold	
Price Charged	Variable Cost per Ticket	Business	Pleasure
₹8,000	₹850	300	150
18,000	1,950	285	30

Pleasure travelers start their travel during one week, spend at least one weekend at their destination, and return the following week or thereafter. Business travelers usually start and complete their travel within the same work week. They do not stay over weekends.

Assume that round-trip fuel costs are fixed costs of ₹2,47,000 and that fixed costs allocated to the round-trip flight for airplane-lease costs, ground services, and flight-crew salaries total ₹18,30,000.

Required

1. If you could charge different prices to business travelers and pleasure travelers, would you? Show your computations.

2. Explain the key factor (or factors) for your answer in requirement 1.
3. How might Northern Airways implement price discrimination? That is, what plan could the airline formulate so that business travelers and pleasure travelers each pay the price the airline desires?

Solution

1. If the fare is ₹8,000,
   a. Northern Airways would expect to have 300 business and 150 pleasure travelers.
   b. Variable costs per passenger would be ₹850.
   c. Contribution margin per passenger = ₹8,000 − ₹850 = ₹7,150.
   If the fare is ₹18,000,
   a. Northern Airways would expect to have 285 business and 30 pleasure travelers.
   b. Variable costs per passenger would be ₹1,950.
   c. Contribution margin per passenger = ₹18,000 − ₹1,950 = ₹16,050.

   Contribution margin from business travelers at prices of ₹8,000 and ₹18,000, respectively, follow:

   At a price of ₹8,000: ₹7,150 × 300 passengers   = ₹21,45,000
   At a price of ₹18,000: ₹16,050 × 285 passengers = ₹45,74,250

   Northern Airways would maximize contribution margin and operating income by charging business travelers a fare of ₹18,000.

   Contribution margin from pleasure travelers at prices of ₹8,000 and ₹18,000, respectively, follow:

   At a price of ₹8,000: ₹7,150 × 150 passengers   = ₹10,72,500
   At a price of ₹18,000: ₹16,050 × 30 passengers = ₹4,81,500

   Northern Airways would maximize contribution margin and operating income by charging pleasure travelers a fare of ₹8,000.

   Northern Airways would maximize contribution margin and operating income by a price differentiation strategy, where business travelers are charged ₹18,000 and pleasure travelers ₹8,000.

   In deciding between the alternative prices, all other costs such as fuel costs, allocated annual lease costs, allocated ground services costs, and allocated flight crew salaries are irrelevant. Why? Because these costs will not change whatever price Northern Airways chooses to charge.

2. The elasticity of demand of the two classes of passengers drives the different demands of the travelers. Business travelers are relatively price insensitive because they must get to their destination during the week (exclusive of weekends) and their fares are paid by their companies. A 225% increase in fares from ₹8,000 to ₹18,000 will deter only 5% of the business passengers from flying with Northern Airways.

   In contrast, a similar fare increase will lead to an 80% drop in pleasure travelers who are paying for their own travels, unlike business travelers, and who may have alternative vacation plans they could pursue instead.

3. Because business travelers often want to return within the same week, while pleasure travelers often stay over weekends, a requirement that a Saturday night stay is needed to qualify for the ₹8,000 discount fare would discriminate between the passenger categories. This price discrimination is legal because airlines are service companies rather than manufacturing companies and because these practices do not, nor are they intended to, destroy competition.

13-30 Value engineering, target pricing, and Rahman locked-in costs. Wood Creations designs, manufactures, and sells modern wood sculptures. Rahman is an artist for the company. Rahman has spent much of the past month working on the design of an intricate abstract piece. Faraz, product development manager, likes the design. However, he wants to make sure that the sculpture can be priced competitively. Ankit, Wood's cost accountant, presents Faraz with the following cost data for the expected production of 75 sculptures:

Design cost	₹80,000
Direct materials	3,20,000
Direct manufacturing labor	3,80,000
Variable manufacturing overhead	3,20,000
Fixed manufacturing overhead	2,60,000
Marketing	1,40,000

Required

1. Faraz thinks that Wood Creations can successfully market each piece for ₹25,000. The company's target operating income is 25% of revenue. Calculate the target full cost of producing the 75 sculptures. Does the cost estimate Ankit developed meet Wood's requirements? Is value engineering needed?

2. Faraz discovers that Rahman has designed the sculpture using the highest-grade wood available, rather than the standard grade of wood that Wood Creations normally uses. Replacing the grade of wood will lower the cost of direct materials by 60%. However, the redesign will require an additional ₹11,000 of design cost, and the sculptures will be sold for ₹24,000 each. Will this design change allow the sculpture to meet its target cost? Is the cost of wood a locked-in cost?

3. Rahman insists that the higher-grade wood is a necessity in terms of the sculpture's design. He believes that spending an additional ₹30,000 on better marketing will allow Wood Creations to sell each sculpture for ₹27,000. If this is the case, will the sculptures' target cost be achieved without any value engineering?

4. Compare the total operating income on the 75 sculptures for requirements 2 and 3. What do you recommend Wood Creations do, based solely on your calculations? Explain briefly.

5. What challenges might managers at Wood Creations encounter in achieving the target cost and how might they overcome these challenges?

Solution

1.

Design cost	₹80,000
Direct materials	3,20,000
Direct manufacturing labor	3,80,000
Variable manufacturing overhead	3,20,000
Fixed manufacturing overhead	2,60,000
Marketing	1,40,000
Total cost	₹15,00,000
Cost per unit (₹15,00,000 ÷ 75)	₹20,000
Target cost per unit (₹25,000 × 0.75)	₹18,750
Profit per unit (₹25,000 – ₹20,000)	₹5,000

The cost estimate developed by Ankit does not meet Wood Creations' requirements. Value engineering will be needed to reduce the cost per unit to the target cost.

2.

Total costs (requirement 1)	₹15,00,000
Less: Reduction in material costs (₹3,20,000 × 60%)	(1,92,000)
Add: Increase in design costs	11,000
Total costs of redesigned table	₹13,19,000
Revised cost per unit (₹13,19,000 ÷ 75)	₹17,586.67

| Revised target cost per unit (₹24,000 × 0.75) | ₹18,000 |
| Profit per unit (₹24,000 − ₹17,586.67) | ₹6,413.33 |

The design change allows the sculpture to meet Wood Creations' requirements for target costing. The cost of materials is a locked-in cost once the design is finalized.

3.

Revised total cost (₹15,00,000 + ₹30,000)	₹15,30,000
Revised cost per unit (₹15,30,000 ÷ 75)	₹20,400
Revised target cost per unit (₹27,000 × 0.75)	₹20,250
Profit per unit (₹27,000 − ₹20,400)	₹6,600

No, this proposal does not allow the sculpture to meet Wood Creations' requirements for target costing. Value engineering will be needed to reduce the cost per unit to the target cost.

4.

	Requirement 2	Requirement 3
Revenue (₹24,000 × 75; ₹27,000 × 75)	₹18,00,000	₹20,25,000
Total costs	13,19,000	15,30,000
Operating income	₹4,81,000	₹4,95,000

Even without value engineering, Wood Creations should implement the actions in requirement 3. It should spend ₹30,000 on marketing if it can achieve a price higher than ₹27,000 even though it does not achieve the target cost because it earns a higher overall operating income. Doing value engineering will help it increase operating income even more relative to requirement 2.

5. The challenges that Wood Creations might encounter in achieving the target cost are mostly employee related. If the employees resist the changes, or struggle with the implementation of the improvements, the target cost will be in danger of not being met. Wood Creations might counter these struggles by adapting its incentive program to reward the desired effects of the changes and improvements.

Wood Creations would also need to think about the customer and whether reducing material costs would reduce demand. For example, the customer may prefer the highest grade of wood that Rahman has used rather than the standard grade of wood that Wood Creations might use to achieve the target cost.

Exercises

[*Comprehensive solutions to all exercises are available on the companion website www. pearsoned.co.in/charlesthorngren*]

13-31 Relevant-cost approach to pricing decisions, special order. The following financial data apply to the videotape production plant of the HMV for October:

Budgeted Manufacturing Cost per Video Tape

Direct material	₹15
Direct manufacturing labor	8
Variable manufacturing overhead	7
Fixed manufacturing overhead	10
Total manufacturing cost	₹40

Variable manufacturing overhead varies with the number of units produced. Fixed manufacturing overhead of ₹10 per tape is based on budgeted fixed manufacturing overhead of ₹15,00,000 per month and budgeted production of 1,50,000 tapes per month. The HMV sells each tape for ₹50.

Marketing costs have two components:

- Variable marketing costs (sales commissions) of 5% of revenues
- Fixed monthly costs of ₹6,50,000

During October, Ravi, a HMV salesperson, asked the president for permission to sell 1,000 tapes at ₹38 per tape to a customer not in HMV's normal marketing channels. The president refused this special order because the selling price was below the total budgeted manufacturing cost.

Required

1. What would have been the effect on monthly operating income of accepting the special order?
2. Comment on the president's "below manufacturing costs" reasoning for rejecting the special order.
3. What other factors should the president consider before accepting or rejecting the special order?

13-32 Target operating income, value-added costs, service company. Architecture Associates prepares architectural drawings to conform to local structural safety codes. Its income statement for April-June is:

Revenues	₹6,80,000
Salaries of professional staff (8,000 hours x ₹50 per hour)	4,00,000
Travel	18,000
Administrative and support costs	1,60,000
Total costs	5,78,000
Operating income	₹1,02,000

Following is the percentage of time spent by professional staff on various activities:

Doing calculations and preparing drawings for clients	75%
Checking calculations and drawings	4
Correcting errors found in drawings (not billed to clients)	7
Making changes in response to client requests (billed to clients)	6
Correcting own errors regarding building codes (not billed to clients)	8
Total	100%

Assume administrative and support costs vary with professional labor costs.

Consider each requirement independently.

Required

1. How much of the total costs in April-June are value-added, nonvalue-added, or in the gray area in between? Explain your answers briefly. What actions can Architecture Associates take to reduce its costs?
2. Suppose Architecture Associates could eliminate all errors so that it did not have any need to spend time making corrections and, as a result, could proportionately reduce professional labor costs. Calculate Architecture Associates's operating income.
3. Now suppose Architecture Associates could take on as much business as it could get done, but it could not add more professional staff. Assume that Architecture Associates could eliminate all errors so that it does not need to spend any time correcting errors. Assume Architecture Associates could use the time saved to increase revenues proportionately. Assume travel costs will remain at ₹18,000. Calculate Architecture Associates's operating income.

13-33 Cost-plus and target pricing. (S. Sridhar, adapted) Babloo Toys, manufactures and sells 15,000 units of Teddy Bear toy (TB), in 2015. The full cost per unit is ₹200. Babloo Toys earns a 20% return on an investment of ₹18,00,000 in 2015.

Required

1. Calculate the selling price and the markup percentage on the full cost per unit of TB toy in 2015.

2. If the selling price in requirement 1 represents a markup percentage of 40% on variable cost per unit, calculate the variable cost per unit of TB toy in 2015.

3. Calculate Babloo Toys's operating income if it had increased the selling price to ₹230. At this price Babloo Toys would have sold 13,500 units of TB toy. Assume no change in total fixed costs. Should Babloo Toys increase the selling price of TB toy to ₹230?

4. In response to competitive pressures, Babloo Toys must reduce the price of TB toy to ₹210 in 2016, in order to achieve sales of 15,000 units. Babloo Toys plans to reduce its investment to ₹16,50,000. If Babloo Toys wants to maintain a 20% return on investment, what is the target cost per unit in 2016?

13-34 Relevant-cost approach to pricing decisions. Best Foods Bakery sells biscuits to food distributors. All costs are classified as either manufacturing or marketing. Best prepares monthly budgets. The March budgeted absorption-costing income statement is as follows:

Revenues (1,000 packets × ₹100 a packet)	₹1,00,000
Cost of goods sold	60,000
Gross margin	40,000
Marketing costs	30,000
Operating income	₹10,000

Normal markup percentage:
₹40,000; – ₹60,000 = 66.7% of absorption cost

Monthly costs are classified as fixed or variable (with respect to the number of packets produced for manufacturing costs and with respect to the number of packets sold for marketing costs):

	Fixed	Variable
Manufacturing	₹20,000	₹40,000
Marketing	16,000	14,000

Best has the capacity to produce 1,500 packets per month. The relevant range in which monthly fixed manufacturing costs will be "fixed" is from 500 to 1,500 packets per month.

Required

1. Calculate the markup percentage based on total variable costs.

2. Assume that a new customer approaches Best to buy 200 packets at ₹55 per packet for cash. The customer does not require additional marketing effort. Additional manufacturing costs of ₹2,000 (for special packaging) will be required. Best believes that this is a one-time only special order because the customer is discontinuing business in six weeks' time. Best is reluctant to accept this 200-packet special order because the ₹55 per packet price is below the ₹60 per packet absorption cost. Do you agree with this reasoning? Explain.

3. Assume that the new customer decides to remain in business. How would this longevity affect your willingness to accept the ₹55 per packet offer? Explain.

13-35 Cost-plus and market-based pricing. Reliable Labour Supplying Company, supplies contract labor to building construction companies. For October, Reliable Labour Supplying Company has budgeted to supply 80,000 hours of contract labor. Its variable costs are ₹12 per hour, and its fixed costs per month are ₹2,40,000. Anwar, the general manager, has proposed a cost-plus approach for pricing labor at full cost plus 20%.

Required

1. Calculate the price per hour that Reliable Labour Supplying Company should charge based on Anwar's proposal.

2. The marketing manager supplies the following information on demand levels at different prices:

Price per Hour	Demand (Hours)
₹16	1,20,000
7	1,00,000
18	80,000
19	70,000
20	60,000

Reliable Labour Supplying Company can meet any of these demand levels. Fixed costs will remain unchanged for all the demand levels. On the basis of this additional information, calculate the price per hour that Reliable Labour Supplying Company should charge.

3. Comment on your answers to requirements 1 and 2. Why are they the same or different?

13-36 Product costs, activity-based costing. IBM manufactures and sells computers and computer peripherals to several nationwide retail chains. Vishal is the manager of the printer division. Its two best-selling printers are P-41 and P-63.

The manufacturing cost of each printer is calculated using IBM's activity-based costing system. IBM has one direct-manufacturing cost category (direct materials) and the following five indirect-manufacturing cost pools:

Indirect-Manufacturing Cost Pool	Quantity of Allocation Base	Allocation Rate
1. Materials handling	Number of parts	₹12 per part
2. Assembly management	Hours of assembly time	₹400 per hour of assembly time
3. Machine insertion of parts	Number of machine-inserted parts	₹7 per machine-inserted part
4. Manual insertion of parts	Number of manually inserted parts	₹21 per manually inserted part
5. Quality testing	Hours of quality testing time	₹250 per testing-hour

Product characteristics of P-41 and P-63 are as follows:

	P-41	P-63
Direct material costs	₹,4075	₹2,921
Number of parts	85 parts	46 parts
Hours of assembly time	3.2 hours	1.9 hours
Number of machine-inserted parts	49 parts	31 parts
Number of manually inserted parts	36 parts	15 parts
Hours of quality testing	1.4 hours	1.1 hours

Required What is the manufacturing cost of P-41 and P-63?

13-37 Target cost, activity-based costing (continuation of 13-36). Assume all the information in Exercise 13-36. A foreign competitor has introduced products very similar to P-41 and P-63. Given their announced selling prices, Vishal estimates the P-41 clone to have a manufacturing cost of approximately ₹6,800 and the P-63 clone to have a manufacturing cost of approximately ₹3,900. He calls a meeting of product designers and manufacturing personnel. They all agree to use the ₹6,800 and ₹3,900 figures as target costs for redesigned versions of EP's P-41 and P-63, respectively. Product designers examine alternative ways of designing printers with comparable performance but lower cost. They come up with the following revised designs for P-41 and P-63 (called P-41 REV and P-63 REV, respectively):

	P-41 REV	P-63 REV
Direct material costs	₹3,812	₹2,631
Number of parts	71 parts	39 parts
Hours of assembly time	2.1 hours	1.6 hours
Number of machine-inserted parts	59 parts	29 parts
Number of manually inserted parts	12 parts	10 parts
Hours of quality testing	1.2 hours	0.9 hours

1. What is a target cost per unit?
2. Using the activity-based costing system outlined in Problem 13-36, compute the manu-facturing costs of P-41 REV and P-63 REV. How do these costs compare with the ₹6,800 and ₹3,900 target costs per unit?
3. Explain the differences between P-41 and P-41 REV and between P-63 and P-63 REV.
4. Assume now that Vishal has achieved major cost reductions in one activity. As a result, the allocation rate in the assembly-management activity will be reduced from ₹400 to ₹280 per assembly-hour. How will this activity-cost reduction affect the manufacturing costs of P-41 REV and P-63 REV? Comment on the results.

13-38 **Target prices, target costs, value engineering, cost incurrence, locked-in costs, activity-based costing.** Videocon makes a radio-cassette player. CE100, which has 80 components. Videocon sells 7,000 units each month for ₹700 each. The costs of manufacturing CE100 are ₹450 per unit, or ₹31,50,000 per month. Monthly manufacturing costs incurred are:

Direct material costs	₹18,20,000
Direct manufacturing labor costs	2,80,000
Machining costs (fixed)	3,15,000
Testing costs	3,50,000
Rework costs	1,40,000
Ordering costs	33,600
Engineering costs (fixed)	2,11,400
Total manufacturing costs	₹31,50,000

Videocon's management identifies the activity cost pools, the cost drivers for each activity, and the cost per unit of the cost driver for each overhead cost pool as follows:

Manufacturing Activity	Description of Activity	Cost Driver	Cost per Unit of Cost Driver
1. Machining costs	Machining components	Machine-hours of capacity	₹45 per machine-hour
2. Testing costs	Testing components and final product (Each unit of CE100 is tested individually.)	Testing-hours.	₹20 per testing-hour
3. Rework costs	Correcting and fixing errors and defects	Units of CE100 reworked	₹200 per unit
4. Ordering costs	Ordering of components	Number of orders	₹210 per order
5. Engineering costs	Designing and managing of products and processes	Capacity of engineering-hours	₹350 per engineering hour

Videocon's management views direct material costs and direct manufacturing labor costs as variable with respect to the units of CE100 manufactured. Over a long-run horizon, each of the overhead costs described in the preceding table varies, as described, with the chosen cost drivers.

The following additional information describes the existing design:

a. Testing and inspection time per unit is 2.5 hours.
b. 10% of the CE100s manufactured are reworked.
c. Videocon places two orders with each component supplier each month. Each component is supplied by a different supplier.
d. It currently takes 1 hour to manufacture each unit of CE100.

In response to competitive pressures, Videocon must reduce its price to ₹620 per unit and its costs by ₹80 per unit. No additional sales are anticipated at this lower price. However, Videocon stands to lose significant sales if it does not reduce its price. Manufacturing has been asked to reduce its costs by ₹60 per unit. Improvements in manufacturing efficiency are expected to yield a net savings of ₹15 per radio-cassette player, but that is not enough. The chief engineer has proposed a new modular design that reduces the number of components to 50 and also simplifies testing. The newly designed radio-cassette player, called "New CE100" will replace CE100. The expected effects of the new design are as follows:

a. Direct material costs for the New CEI00 are expected to be lower by ₹22 per unit.

b. Direct manufacturing labor costs for the New CE100 are expected to be lower by ₹5 per unit.

c. Machining time required to manufacture the New CE100 is expected to be 20% less, but machine-hour capacity will not be reduced.

d. Time required for testing the New CE100 is expected to be lower by 20%.

e. Rework is expected to decline to 4% of New CE100s manufactured.

f. Engineering-hours capacity will remain the same.

Assume that the cost per unit of each cost driver for CE100 continues to apply to New CEI00.

Required

1. Calculate Videocon's manufacturing cost per unit of New CE100.

2. Will the new design achieve the per unit cost reduction targets that have been set for the manufacturing costs of New CE100? Show your calculations.

3. The problem describes two strategies to reduce costs: (a) improving manufacturing efficiency and (b) modifying the design. Which strategy has a bigger impact on Videocon's costs? Why? Explain briefly.

13-39 Cost-plus pricing. (CMA, adapted) Dr Reddy specializes in packaging bulk drugs. Batra Hospital has asked Dr Reddy to bid on the packaging of one million doses of medication at full cost plus a return on full cost of no more than 9% after income taxes. Batra defines cost as including all variable costs of performing the service, a reasonable amount of fixed overhead, and incremental administrative costs. The hospital will supply all packaging materials and ingredients. Batra has indicated that any bid over ₹0.70 per dose will be rejected.

Director of cost accounting at the Dr Reddy, has accumulated the following information prior to the preparation of the bid:

Variable direct manufacturing labor cost	₹160/direct manufacturing labor-hour
Variable overhead cost	₹90/direct manufacturing labor-hour
Fixed overhead cost	₹300/direct manufacturing labor-hour
Incremental administrative costs	₹50,000 for the order
Production rate	1,000 doses/direct manufacturing labor-hour

Dr Reddy is subject to an income tax rate of 40%.

Required

1. Calculate the minimum price per dose that Dr Reddy could bid for the Batra job without changing Dr Reddy's net income.

2. Calculate Dr Reddy's bid price per dose using the full-cost criterion and the maximum allowable return specified by Batra.

3. Without considering your answer to requirement 2, assume that the price per dose that Dr Reddy calculated using the cost-plus criterion specified by Batra is greater than the maximum bid of ₹0.70 per dose allowed by Batra. Discuss the factors that Dr Reddy should consider before deciding whether to submit a bid at the maximum price of ₹0.70 per dose.

13-40 Considerations other than cost in pricing. In an advertisement in a Times of India newspaper, three hotel chains published their weekend and weekday daily room rates for various cities in India.

Daily Rate

Hotel	City	Weekend	Weekday
Holiday Inn	New Delhi	₹1,490	₹3,190
Taj Palace	Agra	890	2,390
Sheraton	Bangalore (airport)	1,090	2,190
Sheraton	Jaipur	890	2,090
Meridean	Udaipur	750	1,690
Meridean	Baroda	890	2,090

Weekend rates required Friday and/or Saturday night stay.

Explain the reason(s) why the hotels charge lower rates for Friday and Saturday nights.   **Required**

13-41 Target prices, target costs, value engineering. Sona Koya, manufactures component parts. One component part, P-100, has annual sales of 50,000 units and sells for ₹406 per unit. Sona includes all R&D and design costs in engineering costs. Sona has no marketing, distribution, or customer-service costs.

Direct costs of P-100 including long-run fixed cost of machine capacity dedicated to P-100 are:

Direct material costs (variable)	₹85,00,000
Direct manufacturing labor costs (variable)	30,00,000
Direct machining costs (fixed, 50,000 hr × ₹30/hr)	15,00,000

Sona's management identifies the following activity cost pools, cost drivers for each activity, and the cost per unit of each cost driver:

Activity	Cost Driver	Cost per Unit of Cost Driver
Setup	Setup-hours	₹250 per setup-hour
Testing	Testing-hours	₹20 per testing-hour
Engineering	Complexity of product and process	Costs assigned to products by special study

Over a long-run horizon, management views indirect costs as variable with respect to their chosen cost drivers. For example, setup costs vary with the number of setup-hours. Additional data for P-100 are

Production batch size	500 units
Setup time per batch	12 hours
Testing and inspection time per unit of product produced	2.5 hours
Engineering costs incurred on P-100	₹17,00,000

Facing competitive pressures, Sona wants to reduce the price of P-100 to ₹348, well below its current price of ₹406. The reduction in price will allow Sona to maintain its current unit sales. If Sona does not reduce price, it will lose sales. The challenge for Sona is to reduce the cost of P-100. Sona's engineers have proposed product design and process improvements for the "New P-100" to replace P-100.

The expected effects of the new design relative to P-100 are as follows:

a. Direct material costs for New P-100 are expected to decrease by ₹30 per unit.

b. Direct manufacturing labor costs for New P-100 are expected to decrease by ₹7.5 per unit.

c. New P-100 will take 6 setup-hours for each setup.

d. Time required for testing each unit of New P-100 is expected to be reduced by 0.5 hour.

e. Engineering costs will be unchanged.

Assume that the batch sizes are the same for New P-100 as for P-100. If Sona requires additional resources to implement the new design, it can acquire these resources in the quantities needed. Further assume the cost per unit of each cost driver for the New P-100 is the same as for P-100.

1. Calculate the full cost per unit for P-100 using activity-based costing.
2. What is the markup percentage on the full cost per unit for P-100?
3. What is Sona's target cost per unit for New P-100 if it is to maintain the same markup percentage on the full cost per unit as for P-100?
4. Will the New P-100 design achieve the target cost calculated in requirement 3? Explain.
5. What price will Sona charge for New P-100 if it uses the same markup percentage on the full cost per unit for New P-100 as for P-100?

14 Cost Allocation, Customer-Profitability Analysis, and Sales-Variance Analysis

Learning Objective 1

Discuss why a company's revenues and costs differ across customers

...revenues differ because of differences in quantities purchased and price discounts while costs differ because of different demands placed on a company's resources

Companies desperately want to make their customers happy.

But how far should they go to please them, and at what price? Should a company differentiate among its customers and not treat all customers the same?

Customer-Profitability Analysis

Customer-profitability analysis is the reporting and assessment of revenues earned from customers and the costs incurred to earn those revenues. An analysis of customer differences in revenues and costs reveals why differences exist in the operating income earned from different customers. Managers use this information to ensure that customers making large contributions to the operating income of a company receive a high level of attention from the company and that loss-making customers do not use more resources than the revenues they provide. As described at the start of this chapter, at Starwood Hotels, managers use customer-profitability analysis to segment customers into profitable customers who stay frequently at the hotel and are given many perks and other customers who are much less profitable and are given less service.

Consider again Astel Computers from Chapter 13. Recall that Astel has two divisions: the Deskpoint Division manufactures and sells servers, and the Provalue Divison manufactures and sells Pentium chip-based personal computers (PCs). Exhibit 14-1, which is the same as Exhibit 13-3, presents data for the Provalue Division of Astel Computers for the year ended 2013. Astel sells and distributes Provalue through two channels: (1) wholesalers who sell Provalue to retail outlets and (2) direct sales to business customers. Astel sells the same Provalue computer to wholesalers and to business customers, so the full manufacturing cost of Provalue, ₹6,800, is the same regardless of where it is sold. Provalue's listed selling price in 2013 was ₹11,000, but price discounts reduced the average selling price to ₹10,000. We focus on customer-profitability for the Provalue Division's 10 wholesale distributors.

Customer-Revenue Analysis

Consider revenues from four of Provalue's 10 wholesale customers in 2013:

Two variables explain revenue differences across these four wholesale customers: (1) the number of computers they purchased and (2) the magnitude of price discounting. A **price discount** is the reduction in selling price below list selling price to encourage customers to purchase more quantities.

	A	B	C	D	E
1			**CUSTOMER**		
2		A	B	G	J
3	Units of Provalue sold	₹30,000	25,000	5,000	₹4,000
4	List selling price	₹11,000	₹11,000	₹11,000	11,000
5	Price discount	1,000	₹500	₹1,500	—
6	Invoice price	₹10,000	₹10,500	₹9,500	₹11,000
7	Revenues (Row 3 x Row 6)	₹30,00,00,000	₹26,25,00,000	₹4,75,00,000	₹4,40,00,000

Exhibit 14-1 Profitability of Provalue Division for 2013 Using Value-Chain Activity-Based Costing

	A	B	C
1		**Total Amounts**	
2		**for 1,50,000 Units**	**Per Unit**
3		(1)	(2) = (1) ÷ 1,50,000
4	Revenues	₹1,50,00,00,000	₹10,000
5	Costs of goods sold[a] (from Exhibit 13-2)	1,02,00,00,000	6,800
6	Operating costs[b]		
7	R&D costs	2,40,00,000	160
8	Design costs of product and process	3,00,00,000	200
9	Marketing and administration costs	15,00,00,000	1,000
10	Distribution costs	9,00,00,000	600
11	Customer-service costs	3,60,00,000	240
12	Operating costs	33,00,00,000	2,200
13	Full cost of the product	1,35,00,00,000	9,000
14	Operating income	₹15,00,00,000	₹1,000
15			
16	[a]Cost of goods sold = Total manufacturing costs because there is no beginning or ending inventory		
17	of Provalue in 2013		
18	[b]Numbers for operating cost line-items are assumed without supporting calculations		

Companies that record only the final invoice price in their information system cannot readily track the magnitude of their price discounting.[1]

Price discounts are a function of multiple factors, including the volume of product purchased (higher-volume customers receive higher discounts) and the desire to sell to a customer who might help promote sales to other customers. In some cases, discounts result from poor negotiating by a salesperson or the unwanted effect of a company's incentive plan based only on revenues.

Tracking price discounts by customer and by salesperson helps improve customer profitability. For example, the Provalue Division managers may decide to strictly enforce its volume-based price discounting policy. The company may also require its salespeople to obtain approval for giving large discounts to customers who do not normally qualify for them. In addition, the company could track future sales to customers who have received sizable price discounts on the basis of their "high growth potential." For example, managers should track future sales to Customer G to see if the ₹1,500-per-computer discount translates into higher future sales.

Customer revenues are one element of customer profitability. The other, equally important element is the cost of acquiring, serving, and retaining customers.

Customer-Cost Analysis

We apply to customers the cost hierarchy discussed in Chapter 5 (page 211). A **customer-cost hierarchy** categorizes costs related to customers into different cost pools on the basis of different types of cost drivers, or cost-allocation bases, or different degrees of difficulty in determining cause-and-effect or benefits-received relationships. The Provalue Division customer costs are composed of (1) marketing and administration costs, ₹15,00,00,000; (2) distribution costs, ₹9,00,00,000; and (3) customer-service costs, ₹3,60,00,000 (see Exhibit 14-1). Managers identify five categories of indirect costs in its customer-cost hierarchy:

1. **Customer output unit-level costs**—costs of activities to sell each unit (computer) to a customer. An example is product-handling costs of each computer sold.

2. **Customer batch-level costs**—costs of activities related to a group of units (computers) sold to a customer. Examples are costs incurred to process orders or to make deliveries.

3. **Customer-sustaining costs**—costs of activities to support individual customers, regardless of the number of units or batches of product delivered to the customer. Examples are costs of visits to customers or costs of displays at customer sites.

4. **Distribution-channel costs**—costs of activities related to a particular distribution channel rather than to each unit of product, each batch of product, or specific customers. An example is the salary of the manager of the Provalue Division's wholesale distribution channel.

5. **Division-sustaining costs**—costs of division activities that cannot be traced to individual customers or distribution channels. The salary of the Provalue Division manager is an example of a division-sustaining cost.

---

[1] Further analysis of customer revenues could distinguish gross revenues from net revenues. This approach highlights differences across customers in sales returns. Additional discussion of ways to analyze revenue differences across customers is in Robert S. Kaplan and Robin Cooper, *Cost and Effect: Using Integrated Cost Systems to Drive Profitability and Performance* (Boston: Harvard Business School Press, 1998), Chapter 10; and Gary Cokins, *Activity-Based Cost Management: An Executive's Guide* (New York: Wiley, 2001), Chapter 3.

Note from these descriptions that four of the five levels of Provalue Division's cost hierarchy closely parallel the cost hierarchy described in Chapter 5 except that the Provalue Division focuses on *customers* whereas the cost hierarchy in Chapter 5 focused on *products*. The Provalue Division has one additional cost hierarchy category, distribution-channel costs, for the costs it incurs to support its wholesale and business-sales channels.

Customer-Level Costs

Exhibit 14-2 summarizes details of the costs incurred in marketing and administration, distribution, and customer service by activity. The exhibit also identifies the cost driver (where appropriate), the total costs incurred for the activity, the total quantity of the cost driver, the cost per unit of the cost driver, and the customer cost-hierarchy category for each activity.

Exhibit 14-2   Marketing, Distribution, and Customer Service Activities, Costs, and Cost Driver Information for Provalue Division in 2013

Home	Insert	Page Layout	Formulas	Data	Review	View	
A	B	C	D	E	F	G	H
		Marketing, Distribution, and Customer Service Costs for 150,000 units of Provalue in 2013					
Activity Area	Cost Driver	Total Cost of Activity	Total Quantity of Cost Driver		Rate per Unit of Cost Driver		Cost Hierarchy Category
(1)	(2)	(3)	(4)		(5) = (3) ÷ (4)		(6)
Marketing and Administration							
Sales order	Number of sales orders	₹6,75,00,000	6,000	sales orders	₹11,250	per sales order	Customer batch-level costs
Customer visits	Number of customer visits	4,20,00,000	750	customer visits	₹56,000	per customer visit	Customer-sustaining costs
Wholesale channel marketing		80,00,000					Distribution-channel costs
Business-sales channel marketing		1,35,00,000					Distribution-channel costs
Provalue division administration		1,90,00,000					Division-sustaining costs
Total marketing & administration costs		₹15,00,00,000					
Distribution							
Product handling	Number of cubic feet moved	₹4,50,00,000	3,00,000	cubic feet	₹150	per cubic foot	Customer output unit-level costs
Regular shipments	Number of regular shipments	3,75,00,000	3,000	regular shipments	₹12,500	per regular shipment	Customer batch-level costs
Rush shipments	Number of rush shipments	75,00,000	150	rush shipments	₹50,000	per rush shipment	Customer batch-level costs
Total distribution costs		₹9,00,00,000					
Customer Service							
Customer service	Number of units shipped	₹3,60,00,000	1,50,000	units shipped	₹240	per unit shipped	Customer output unit-level costs

- ₹6,75,00,000 on the sales order activity, which includes negotiating, finalizing, issuing, and collecting on 6,000 sales orders at a cost of 11,250 (₹6,75,00,000 ÷ 6,000) per sales order. Recall that sales-order costs are customer batch-level costs because these costs vary with the number of sales orders issued and not with the number of Provalue computers in a sales order.

- ₹4,20,00,000 for customer visits, which are customer-sustaining costs. The amount per customer varies with the number of visits rather than the number of units or batches of Provalue delivered to a customer.

- ₹80,00,000 on managing the wholesale channel, which are distribution-channel costs.

- ₹1,35,00,000 on managing the business-sales channel, which are distribution-channel costs.

- ₹1,90,00,000 on general administration of the Provalue Division, which are division-sustaining costs.

The Provalue Division managers are particularly interested in analyzing *customer-level indirect costs*—costs incurred in the first three categories of the customer-cost hierarchy: customer output unit–level costs, customer batch-level costs, and customer-sustaining costs. Managers want to work with customers to reduce these costs because they believe customer actions will have more impact on customer-level (indirect) costs than on distribution-channel and division-sustaining costs. Information on the quantity of cost drivers used by each of four representative wholesale customers follows:

	Home	Insert	Page Layout	Formulas	Data	Review	View
	A		B	C	D	E	F
1						CUSTOMER	
2	**Activity**		**Quantity of Cost Driver**	**A**	**B**	**G**	**J**
3	**Marketing**						
4	Sales orders		Number of sales orders	1,200	1,000	600	300
5	Customer visits		Number of customer visits	150	100	50	25
6	**Distribution**						
7	Product handling		Number of cubic feet moved	60,000	50,000	10,000	8,000
8	Regular shipments		Number of regular shipments	600	400	300	120
9	Rush shipments		Number of rush shipments	25	5	20	3
10	**Customer Service**						
11	Customer service		Number of units shipped	30,000	25,000	5,000	4,000

Exhibit 14-3 shows customer-level operating income for the four wholesale customers using information on customer revenues previously presented (page 745) and customer-level indirect costs, obtained by multiplying the rate per unit of cost driver (from Exhibit 14-2) by the quantities of the cost driver used by each customer (in the table above). Exhibit 14-3 shows that the Provalue Division is losing money on Customer G (the cost of resources used by Customer G exceeds revenues) while it makes money on Customer J on smaller revenues. The Provalue Division sells fewer computers to Customer B compared to Customer A but has higher operating income from Customer B than Customer A.

The Provalue Division's managers can use the information in Exhibit 14-3 to work with customers to reduce the quantity of activities needed to support them. Consider, for example, a comparison of Customer G and Customer J. Customer G purchases 25% more computers than Customer J purchases (5,000 versus 4,000) but the company offers Customer G significant price discounts to achieve these sales. Compared with Customer J, Customer G places twice as many sales orders, requires twice as many customer visits, and generates two-and-a-half times as many regular shipments and almost seven times as many rush shipments. Selling smaller quantities of units is profitable, provided the Provalue Division's salespeople limit the amount of price discounting and customers do not use large amounts of Provalue Division's resources. For example, by implementing an additional charge for customers who use large amounts of marketing and distribution services, managers might be able to prevail upon Customer G to place fewer but larger sales orders and require fewer customer visits, regular shipments, and rush shipments while looking to increase sales in the future. The Provalue Division's managers would perform a similar analysis to understand the reasons for the lower profitability of Customer A relative to Customer B.

Relegare a distributor of medical supplies to hospitals, follows this approach. Relegare strategically prices each of its services separately. For example, if a hospital wants a rush delivery or special packaging, Relegare charges the hospital an additional price for each particular service. How have its customers reacted? Hospitals that value these services

Exhibit 14-3   Customer-Profitability Analysis for Provalue Division's Four Wholesale Channel Customers for 2013

	A	B	C	D	E
1		**A**	**B**	**G**	**J**
2	Revenues at list price	₹33,00,00,000	₹27,50,00,000	₹5,50,00,000	₹4,40,00,000
3	Price discount	3,00,00,000	1,25,00,000	75,00,000	-
4	Revenues	30,00,00,000	26,25,00,000	4,75,00,000	4,40,00,000
5					
6	Cost of goods sold[a]	20,40,00,000	17,00,00,000	3,40,00,000	2,72,00,000
7					
8	Gross margin	9,60,00,000	9,25,00,000	1,35,00,000	1,68,00,000
9					
10	Customer-level costs				
11	Marketing costs				
12	Sales orders[b]	1,35,00,000	1,12,50,000	67,50,000	33,75,000
13	Customer visits[c]	84,00,000	56,00,000	28,00,000	14,00,000
14	Distribution costs				
15	Product handling[d]	90,00,000	75,00,000	15,00,000	12,00,000
16	Regular shipments[e]	75,00,000	50,00,000	37,50,000	1,50,000
17	Rush shipments[f]	12,50,000	2,50,000	10,00,000	1,50,000
18	Customer service costs				
19	Customer service[g]	72,00,000	60,00,000	12,00,000	9,60,000
20					
21	Total customer-level costs	4,68,50,000	3,56,00,000	1,70,00,000	85,85,000
22					
23	Customer-level operating income	₹4,91,50,000	₹5,69,00,000	₹(35,00,000)	₹82,15,000
24	[a]₹6,800 x 30,000; 25,000; 5,000; 4,000 [b]₹11,250 x 1,200; 1,000; 600; 300 [c]₹56,000 x 150; 100; 50; 25 [d]₹150 x 60,000;				
25	50,000; 10,000; 8,000 [e]₹12,500 x 600; 400; 300; 120 [f]₹50,000 x 25; 5; 20; 3 [g]₹240 x 30,000; 25,000; 5,000; 4,000				

continue to demand and pay for them, while hospitals that do not value these services stop asking for them, saving Relegare some costs. This pricing strategy influences customer behavior in a way that increases Relegare's revenues or decreases its costs.

The ABC system also highlights a second opportunity for cost reduction. The Provalue Division's managers can reduce the costs of each activity by applying the same value-engineering process described in Chapter 13 to nonmanufacturing costs. For example, improving the efficiency of the ordering process (such as by having customers order electronically) reduces sales order costs even if customers place the same number of orders.

Simplifying the design and reducing the weight of the newly designed Provalue II for 2014 reduces the cost per cubic foot of handling Provalue and total product-handling costs. By influencing customer behavior and improving marketing, distribution, and customer service operations, Provalue Division's managers aim to reduce the nonmanufacturing cost of Provalue to ₹1,800 per computer and achieve the target cost of ₹7,200 for Provalue II.

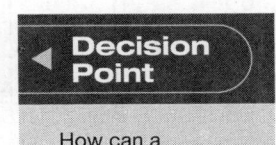

◄ **Decision Point**

How can a company's revenues and costs differ across customers?

Customer Profitability Profiles

Customer-profitability profiles are a useful tool for managers. Exhibit 14-4 ranks the Provalue Division's 10 wholesale customers based on customer-level operating income. (We analyzed four of these customers in Exhibit 14-3.)

Column 4, computed by adding the individual amounts in column 1, shows the cumulative customer-level operating income. For example, Customer C shows a cumulative income of ₹13,26,00,000 in column 4. This ₹13,26,00,000 is the sum of ₹5,69,00,000 for Customer B, ₹4,91,50,000 for Customer A, and ₹2,65,50,000 for Customer C.

Column 5 shows what percentage the ₹13,26,00,000 *cumulative* total for customers B, A, and C is of the total customer-level operating income of ₹15,02,75,000 earned in the wholesale distribution channel from all 10 customers. The three most profitable customers contribute 88% of total customer-level operating income. These customers deserve the highest service and priority. Companies try to keep their best customers happy in a number of ways, including special phone numbers and upgrade privileges for elite-level frequent flyers and free usage of luxury hotel suites and big credit limits for high rollers at casinos. In many companies, it is common for a small number of customers to contribute a high percentage of operating income. Microsoft uses the phrase "not all revenue dollars are endowed equally in profitability" to stress this point.Column 3 shows the profitability per rupee of revenue by customer. This measure of customer profitability indicates that, although Customer A contributes the second-highest operating income, the profitability per rupee of revenue is lowest among the top six customers because of high price discounts and higher customer-level costs. Provalue Division managers would like to increase profit

Exhibit 14-4 Cumulative Customer-Profitability Analysis for Provalue Division's Wholesale Channel Customers: Astel Computers, 2013

	A	B	C	D	E	F
1	Retail Customer Code	Customer-Level Operating Income	Customer Revenue	Customer-Level Operating Income Divided by Revenue	Cumulative Customer-Level Operating Income	Cumulative Customer-Level Operating Income as a % of Total Customer-Level Operating Income
2		(1)	(2)	(3) = (1) ÷ (2)	(4)	(5) = (4) ÷ ₹15,02,75,000
3	B	₹5,69,00,000	₹26,25,00,000	21.7%	₹5,69,00,000	38%
4	A	4,91,50,000	30,00,00,000	16.4%	10,60,50,000	71%
5	C	2,65,50,000	13,00,00,000	20.4%	13,26,00,000	88%
6	D	1,44,50,000	7,25,00,000	19.9%	14,70,50,000	98%
7	F	98,60,000	5,10,00,000	19.3%	15,69,10,000	104%
8	J	82,15,000	4,40,00,000	18.7%	16,51,25,000	110%
9	E	10,00,000	1,80,00,000	5.6%	16,61,25,000	111%
10	G	(35,00,000)	4,75,00,000	−7.4%	16,26,25,000	108%
11	H	(53,50,000)	2,40,00,000	−22.3%	15,72,75,000	105%
12	I	(70,00,000)	2,60,00,000	−26.9%	15,02,75,000	100%
13	Total	₹15,02,75,000	₹97,55,00,000			

margins for Customer A by decreasing price discounts or saving customer-level costs while maintaining or increasing sales. Customers D, F, and J have high profit margins but low total sales. The challenge with these customers is to maintain margins while increasing sales. With Customers E, G, H, and I, managers have the dual challenge of boosting profits and sales.

Presenting Profitability Analysis

Exhibit 14-5 illustrates two common ways of displaying the results of customer-profitability analysis. Managers often find the bar chart presentation in Panel A (based on Exhibit 14-4, Column 1) to be an intuitive way to visualize customer profitability because

Exhibit 14-5	Panel A: Bar Chart of Customer-Level Operating Income for Provalue Division's Wholesale Channel Customers in 2013
	Panel B: The Whale Curve of Cumulative Profitability for Provalue Division's Wholesale Channel Customers in 2013

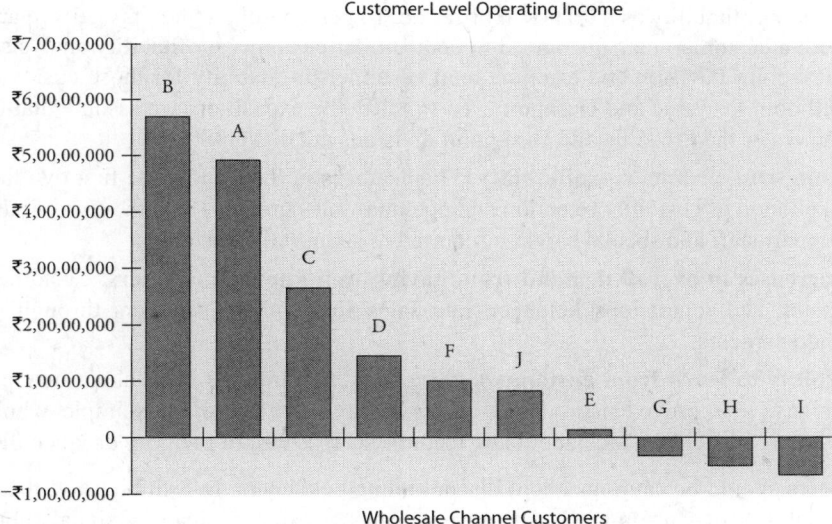

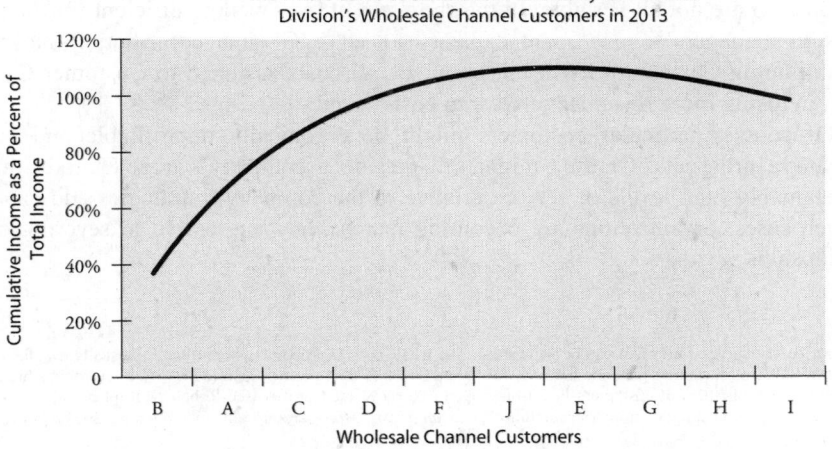

(1) the highly profitable customers clearly stand out and (2) the number of "unprofitable" customers and the magnitude of their losses are apparent. Panel B of Exhibit 14-5 is a popular alternative way to express customer profitability. It plots the contents of column 5 in Exhibit 14-4. This chart is called the **whale curve** because it is backward-bending at the point where customers start to become unprofitable and thus resembles a humpback whale.[2]

The Provalue Division managers must explore ways to make unprofitable customers profitable. Exhibits 14-2 to 14-5 emphasize annual customer profitability. Managers should also consider other factors when allocating resources among customers, including:

- **Likelihood of customer retention.** The more likely a customer will continue to do business with a company, the more valuable the customer, for example, wholesalers who have sold Provalue each year over the last several years. Customers differ in their loyalty and their willingness to frequently "shop their business."

- **Potential for sales growth.** The higher the likely growth of the customer's sales, the more valuable the customer. Moreover, customers to whom a company can cross-sell other products profitably are more desirable, for example, wholesalers willing to distribute both Astel's Provalue and Deskpoint brands. The analysis has focused on customer profitability as it relates to Provalue. To get the full picture of Astel's relationship with a customer, managers need to do a similar customer profitability analysis for the Deskpoint Division and examine total customer profitability for those customers that sell both Provalue and Deskpoint. To simplify the exposition, we assume that the customers of the Provalue and Deskpoint divisions are distinct.

- **Long-run customer profitability.** This factor is influenced by the first two factors— likelihood of customer retention and potential sales growth—and the cost of customer-support staff and special services required to support the customer.

- **Increases in overall demand from having well-known customers.** Customers with established reputations help generate sales from other customers through product endorsements.

- **Ability to learn from customers.** Customers who provide ideas about new products or ways to improve existing products are especially valuable, for example, wholesalers who give Astel feedback about key features such as size of memory or video displays.

Managers should be cautious about discontinuing customers. In Exhibit 14-4, the current unprofitability of Customer G, for example, may provide misleading signals about G's profitability in the long run. Moreover, as in any ABC-based system, the costs assigned to Customer G are not all variable. In the short run, it may well be efficient for the Provalue Division managers to use spare capacity to serve G on a contribution-margin basis. Discontinuing Customer G will not eliminate all costs assigned to Customer G and may result in losing more revenues relative to costs saved.

Of course, particular customers might be chronically unprofitable and hold limited future prospects. Or they might fall outside a company's target market or require unsustainably high levels of service relative to the company's strategies and capabilities. In such cases, organizations are becoming increasingly aggressive in severing customer relationships.

---

[2] In practice, the curve of the chart can be quite steep. The whale curve for cumulative profitability usually reveals that the most profitable 20% of customers generate between 150% and 300% of total profits, the middle 70% of customers break even, and the least profitable 10% of customers lose from 50% to 200% of total profits (see Robert S. Kaplan and V. G. Narayanan, "Measuring and Managing Customer Profitability," *Journal of Cost Management* (September/October 2001): 1–11).

Using the Five-Step Decision-Making Process to Manage Customer Profitability

In this section, we apply the five-step decision-making process (introduced in Chapter 1) to help understand how managers use different types of customer analyses to allocate resources across customers.

1. *Identify the problem and uncertainties.* The problem is how to manage and allocate resources across customers.

2. *Obtain information.* Managers identify past revenues generated by each customer and customer-level costs incurred in the past to support each customer.

3. *Make predictions about the future.* Managers estimate the revenues they expect from each customer and the customer-level costs they will incur in the future. In making these predictions, managers consider the effects that future price discounts will have on revenues, the effect that pricing for different services (such as rush deliveries) will have on the demand for these services by customers, and ways to reduce the cost of providing services. For example, Deluxe Corporation, a leading printer, initiated process modifications to rein in its cost to serve customers by opening an electronic channel to shift customers from paper to automated ordering.

4. *Make decisions by choosing among alternatives.* Managers use the customer-profitability profiles to identify the small set of customers who deserve the highest service and priority and also to identify ways to make less-profitable customers (such as Astel's Customer G) more profitable. Banks, for example, often impose minimum balance requirements on customers. Distribution firms may require minimum order quantities or levy a surcharge for smaller or customized orders. In making resource-allocation decisions, managers also consider long-term effects, such as the potential for future sales growth and the opportunity to leverage a particular customer account to make sales to other customers.

5. *Implement the decision, evaluate performance, and learn.* After the decision is implemented, managers compare actual results to predicted outcomes to evaluate the decision they made, its implementation, and ways in which they might improve profitability.

◀ **Decision Point**

How do customer-profitability profiles help managers?

Cost Hierarchy-Based Operating Income Statement

Our analysis so far has focused on customer-level costs—costs of activities that the Provalue Division managers can work with customers to influence such as sales orders, customer visits, and shipments. We now consider other costs of the Provalue Division (such as R&D and design costs, costs to manage different distribution channels, and costs of division administration) and corporate costs incurred by Astel Computers (such as corporate brand advertising and general administration costs). Customer actions do not influence these costs, which raises two important questions: (1) Should these costs be allocated to customers when calculating customer profitability, and (2) if they are allocated, on what basis should they be allocated given the weak cause-and-effect relationship between these costs and customer actions? We start by considering the first question and introduce the cost-hierarchy-based operating income statement, which does not allocate the noncustomer-level costs.

Exhibit 14-6 shows an operating income statement for the Provalue Division for 2013. The customer-level operating income of Customers A and B in Exhibit 14-3 is shown in

Learning Objective 3

Understand the cost-hierarchy-based operating income statement

. . . allocate only those costs that will be affected by actions at a particular hierarchica

Exhibit 14-6   Income Statement of Provalue Division for 2013 Using the Cost Hierarchy

	A	B	C	D	E	F	G	H	I	J	K	L	M	N	O
1											CUSTOMER DISTRIBUTION CHANNELS				
2				Wholesale Customers							Business-Sales Customers				
3		Total	Total	A**		B**		A3			Total	A	B	C	
4		(1) = (2) + (7)	(2)	(3)		(4)		(5)	(6)		(7)	(8)	(9)	(10)	(11
5	Revenues (at actual prices)	₹1 50,00,00,000	₹97,55,00,000	₹30,00,00,000		₹26,25,00,000		-	-		₹52,45,00,000	₹7,00,00,000	₹6,25,00,000	-	-
6	Cost of goods sold plus customer-level costs	1,25,55,00,000*	82,52,25,000	25,08,50,000 ᵃ		20,56,00,000		-	-		43,02,75,000	5,38,50,000	4,76,00,000	-	-
7	Customer-level operating income	24,45,00,000	15,02,75,000	₹4,91,50,000		₹5,69,00,000		-	-		9,42,25,000	₹1,61,50,000	₹1,49,00,000	-	
8	Distribution-channel costs	2,15,00,000	80,00,000								1,35,00,000				
9	Distribution-channel-level operating income	22,30,00,000	₹14,22,75,000								₹8,07,25,000				
10	Division-sustaining costs														
11	Administration costs	1,90,00,000													
12	R&D Costs	2,40,00,000													
13	Design Costs	3,00,00,000													
14	Total division-sustaining costs	7,30,00,000													
15	Division operating income	₹15,00,00,000													
16	*Cost of goods sold, ₹1,02,00,00,000 (Exhibit 14-1) + Sales order costs, ₹6,75,00,000 + Customer visit costs, ₹4,20,00,000 + Product handling costs, ₹4,50,00,000 + Regular shipment costs, ₹3,75,00,000 + Rush shipment costs, ₹75,00,000 + Customer service costs, ₹3,60,00,000 (all from Exhibit 14-2)														
17	**Full details are presented in Exhibit 14-3														
18	ᵃCost of goods sold + total customer-level costs from Exhibit 14-3 for Customer A = ₹20,40,00,000 + ₹4,68,50,000 = ₹25,08,50,000.														

columns 3 and 4 in Exhibit 14-6. The format of Exhibit 14-6 is based on the Provalue Division's cost hierarchy. As described in Exhibit 14-2, some costs of serving customers, such as the salary of the wholesale distribution-channel manager, are not customer-level costs and are therefore not allocated to customers in Exhibit 14-6. Managers identify these costs as distribution-channel costs because changes in customer behavior will have no effect on these costs. Only decisions pertaining to the channel, such as a decision to discontinue wholesale distribution, will influence these costs. Managers also believe that salespeople responsible for managing individual customer accounts would lose motivation if sales bonuses were adversely affected as a result of allocating to customers distribution-channel costs over which they had minimal influence.

Next, consider division-sustaining costs such as R&D and design costs and administration costs of the Provalue Division. Managers believe there is no direct cause-and-effect relationship between these costs and customer or sales manager's actions. Under this view, allocating division-sustaining costs serves no useful purpose in decision making, performance evaluation, or motivation. Suppose, for example, that the Provalue Division allocates the ₹7,30,00,000 of division-sustaining costs to its distribution channels and that in some subsequent period this allocation results in the business-sales channel showing a loss. Should the Provalue Division shut down the business-sales distribution channel? Not if (as we discussed in Chapter 11) division-sustaining costs are unaffected by shutting down the business-sales distribution channel. Allocating division-sustaining costs to distribution channels gives the misleading impression that potential cost savings from discontinuing a distribution channel are greater than the likely amount.

In a cost hierarchy-based income statement, how should we treat the corporate costs for brand advertising, ₹1,05,00,000, and administration, ₹4,40,00,000, incurred by Astel Computers to support the Provalue and Deskpoint divisions? The Deskpoint Division has revenues of ₹2,00,00,00,000 and operating costs of ₹1,70,00,00,000. Exhibit 14-7 presents the cost hierarchy-based income statement for Astel Computers as a whole. Corporate-sustaining costs are not allocated either to divisions or to customers. That's because, as discussed earlier in the context of division-sustaining costs, there is no direct

Exhibit 14-7	Income Statement of Astel Computers for 2013 Using the Cost Hierarchy

	A	B	C	D
1	Income Statement of Astel Computers for 2013 Using the Cost Hierarchy			
2				
3		Total	Provalue Division	Deskpoint Division
4				
5	Revenues	₹3,50,00,00,000	₹1,50,00,00,000	₹2,00,00,00,000
6	Division operating costs	(3,05,00,00,000)	(1,35,00,00,000)*	(1,70,00,00,000)
7	Division operating income before corporate costs	45,00,00,000	₹15,00,00,000	₹30,00,00,000
8	Corporate advertising	(1,05,00,000)		
9	Corporate administration	(4,40,00,000)		
10	Operating income	₹39,55,00,000		
11	*1,35,00,00,000 = ₹1,25,55,00,000 + ₹2,15,00,000 + ₹7,30,00,000 all from Exhibit 14-6, Column 1			

cause-and-effect relationship between these costs and the profitability of different customers. These costs are unaffected by the actions of division managers or customers, so corporate sustaining costs are subtracted as a lump-sum amount after aggregating operating incomes of the divisions.

Other managers and management accountants advocate fully allocating all costs to distribution channels and to customers because all costs are incurred to support the sales of products to customers. Allocating all corporate costs motivates division managers to examine how corporate costs are planned and controlled. Similarly allocating division costs to distribution channels motivates the managers of the distribution channels to monitor costs incurred in the division. Managers that want to calculate the full costs of serving customers must allocate all corporate, division, and distribution channel costs to customers. These managers and management accountants argue that, in the long run, customers and products must eventually be profitable on a full-cost basis. As we discussed in Chapter 13, for some decisions such as pricing, allocating all costs ensures that long-run prices are set at a level to cover the cost of all resources used to produce and sell products. In this case, the sum of operating incomes of all customers equals companywide operating income.

Still other companies allocate only those corporate costs, division costs, or channel costs to customers that are widely perceived as causally related to customer actions or that provide explicit benefits to customer profitability. Corporate advertising is an example of such a cost. These companies exclude other costs such as corporate administration or donations to charitable foundations because the benefits to the customers are less evident or too remote. If a company decides not to allocate some or all corporate, division, or channel costs, it results in total company profitability being less than the sum of individual customer profitabilities.

For some decision purposes, allocating some but not all indirect costs to customers may be the preferred alternative. Consider the performance evaluation of the wholesale channel manager of the Provalue Division. The controllability notion (see page 290) is frequently used to justify excluding corporate costs such as salaries of the top management at corporate headquarters from responsibility accounting reports of the wholesale channel manager. Although the wholesale channel manager tends to benefit from these corporate costs, he or she has no say in ("is not responsible for") how much of these corporate resources to use or how much they cost.

Nevertheless, the value of the hierarchical format in Exhibits 14-6 and 14-7 is to distinguish among various degrees of objectivity when allocating costs so that it dovetails with the different levels at which managers make decisions and evaluate performance. The issue

Decision Point ▶

Why do managers prepare cost-hierarchy-based operating income statements?

of when and what costs to allocate is another example of the "different costs for different purposes" theme emphasized throughout this book.

In the next section, we consider what happens if Astel's managers decided to allocate distribution channel costs (such as costs of the wholesale channel), division-sustaining costs (such as costs of R&D and design), and corporate-sustaining costs (such as corporate administration costs of Astel Computers) to individual customers.

Criteria to Guide Cost Allocations

Learning Objective 4

Understand criteria to guide cost-allocation decisions

...such as identifying factors that cause resources to be consumed

Exhibit 14-8 presents four criteria managers use to guide cost-allocation decisions. These decisions affect both the number of indirect-cost pools and the cost-allocation base for each indirect-cost pool. As done throughout this book, we emphasize the superiority of the cause-and-effect and the benefits-received criteria, especially when the purpose of cost allocation is to provide information for economic decisions or to motivate managers and employees.[3] Cause and effect is the primary criterion used in activity-based costing (ABC) applications. ABC systems use the concept of a cost hierarchy to identify the cost drivers that best demonstrate the cause-and-effect relationship between each activity and the costs in the related cost pool. The cost drivers are then chosen as cost-allocation bases. Cause and effect is often difficult to determine in the case of division-sustaining and corporate-sustaining costs. In these situations, managers and management accountants interested in allocating costs use other methods summarized in Exhibit 14-8.

Exhibit 14-8 Criteria for Cost-Allocation Decisions

1. Cause and Effect. Using this criterion, managers identify the variables that cause resources to be consumed. For example, managers may use number of sales orders as the variable when allocating the costs of order taking to products and customers. Cost allocations based on the cause-and-effect criterion are likely to be the most credible to operating personnel.

2. Benefits Received. Using this criterion, managers identify the beneficiaries of the outputs of the cost object. The costs of the cost object are allocated among the beneficiaries in proportion to the benefits each receives. Consider a corporatewide advertising program that promotes the general image of the corporation rather than any individual product. The costs of this program may be allocated on the basis of division revenues; the higher the revenues, the higher the division's allocated cost of the advertising program. The rationale behind this allocation is that divisions with higher revenues apparently benefited from the advertising more than divisions with lower revenues and, therefore, ought to be allocated more of the advertising costs.

3. Fairness or Equity. This criterion is often cited in government contracts when cost allocations are the basis for establishing a price satisfactory to the government and its suppliers. Cost allocation here is viewed as a "reasonable" or "fair" means of establishing a selling price in the minds of the contracting parties. For most allocation decisions, fairness is a matter of judgment rather than an operational criterion.

4. Ability to Bear. This criterion advocates allocating costs in proportion to the cost object's ability to bear costs allocated to it. An example is the allocation of corporate administration costs on the basis of division operating income. The presumption is that the more-profitable divisions have a greater ability to absorb corporate administration costs.

---

[3] The Federal Accounting Standards Advisory Board (which sets standards for management accounting for U.S. government departments and agencies) recommends the following: "Cost assignments should be performed by: (a) directly tracing costs whenever feasible and economically practicable, (b) assigning costs on a cause-and-effect basis, and (c) allocating costs on a reasonable and consistent basis" (*FASAB*, 1995, p. 12).

The best way to allocate costs if cause and effect cannot be established is to use the benefits-received criterion by identifying the beneficiaries of the output of the cost object. Consider, for example, the cost of managing the wholesale channel for Provalue, such as the salary of the manager of the wholesale channel. There is no cause-and-effect relationship between these costs and sales made by wholesalers. But it is plausible to assume that the customers with higher revenues benefited more from the wholesale channel support than customers with lower revenues. The benefits-received criterion justifies allocating the costs of managing the wholesale channel of ₹80,00,000 to customers based on customer revenues.

Fairness and ability to bear are less frequently used and more problematic criteria than cause and effect or benefits received. It's difficult for two parties to agree on criteria for fairness. What one party views as fair another party may view as unfair.[4] For example, a university may view allocating a share of general administrative costs to government contracts for scientific and medical research as fair because general administrative costs are incurred to support all activities of the university. The government may view the allocation of such costs as unfair because the general administrative costs would have been incurred by the university regardless of whether the government contract existed. Perhaps the fairest way to resolve this issue is to understand, as well as possible, the cause-and-effect relationship between the government contract activity and general administrative costs. This is difficult. In other words, fairness is more a matter of judgment than an easily implementable choice criterion.

To get a sense of the issues that arise when using the ability-to-bear criterion, consider Customer G where customer-level costs exceed revenues before any allocation of any division-sustaining or corporate-sustaining costs. This customer has no ability to bear any of the division- or corporate-sustaining costs, so under the ability-to-bear criterion none of these costs will be allocated to Customer G. Costs are not allocated because managers are expected to reduce their dependence on these more remote division- and corporate-sustaining costs (such as administration costs) to support loss-making customers in order to bring the customer relationship back to profitability. However, if the indirect costs are not reduced but simply allocated to other customers, these other customers would be subsidizing the customer that is losing money. The ability-to-bear criterion would then result in a distorted view of lower customer and service profitability for profitable customers and the potential for incorrect actions, such as increasing prices to restore profitability, which could then invite competitors to undercut artificially higher-priced services.

Most importantly, companies must weigh the costs and benefits when designing and implementing their cost allocations. Companies incur costs not only in collecting data but also in taking the time to educate managers about cost allocations. In general, the more complex the cost allocations, the higher these education costs.

The costs of designing and implementing complex cost allocations are highly visible. Unfortunately, the benefits from using well-designed cost allocations, such as enabling managers to make better-informed sourcing decisions, pricing decisions, cost-control decisions, and so on, are difficult to measure. Nevertheless, when making cost allocations, managers should consider the benefits as well as the costs. As costs of collecting and processing information decrease, companies are building more detailed cost allocations.

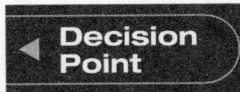

◄ **Decision Point**

What criteria should managers use to guide cost-allocation decisions?

---

[4] Kaplow and Shavell, in a review of the legal literature, note that "notions of fairness are many and varied. They are analyzed and rationalized by different writers in different ways, and they also typically depend upon the circumstances under consideration. Accordingly, it is not possible to identify a consensus view on these notions..." See Louis Kaplow and Steven Shavell, "Fairness Versus Welfare," *Harvard Law Review* (February 2001); and Louis Kaplow and Steven Shavell, *Fairness Versus Welfare* (Boston: Harvard University Press, 2002).

Fully Allocated Customer Profitability

In this section, we focus on the first purpose of cost allocation (see Exhibit 13-1): to provide information for economic decisions, such as pricing, by measuring the full costs of delivering products to different customers based on an ABC system.

We continue with the Astel Computers example introduced earlier in this chapter and focus on the fully allocated customer profitability calculations for the 10 wholesale customers in the Provalue Division. The Provalue Division also uses a direct sales channel to sell Provalue computers directly to business customers. Recall that Astel also has another division, the Deskpoint Division, that sells servers. We will use the Astel Computers example to illustrate how costs incurred in different parts of a company can be assigned, and then reassigned, to calculate customer profitability.

We summarize the cost categories as:

- **Corporate costs**—There are two major categories of corporate costs:
  1. **Corporate advertising costs**—advertising and promotion costs to promote the Astel brand, ₹1,05,00,000.
  2. **Corporate administration costs**—executive salaries, rent, and general administration costs, ₹4,40,00,000.

- **Division costs**—The Provalue Division, which is the focus of our analysis, has three indirect-cost pools—one cost pool each corresponding to the different cost drivers for allocating division costs to distribution channels: (1) cost pool 1 that aggregates all division costs that are allocated to the wholesale and business-sales channels based on revenues of each channel; (2) cost pool 2 that accumulates R&D and design costs that are allocated to the distribution channels on some fair and equitable basis; and (3) cost pool 3 that aggregates all division costs that are allocated to the wholesale and business-sales channels based on the operating incomes of each channel before such allocations (if positive). The cost pools are *homogeneous*, that is, all costs in a cost pool have the same or similar cause-and-effect, benefits-received, or fair-and-equitable relationship with the cost-allocation base. Different cost pools need different cost allocation bases to allocate the costs in the cost pools to distribution channels.

- **Channel costs**—Each distribution channel in the Provalue Division has two indirect cost pools: (1) a cost pool that aggregates all channel costs that are allocated to customers based on customer revenues and (2) a cost pool that aggregates all channel costs that are allocated to customers based on operating incomes of customers before such allocations (if positive).

Exhibit 14-9 presents an overview diagram of the allocation of corporate, division, and distribution-channel indirect costs to wholesale customers of the Provalue Division. Note that the Deskpoint Division has its own indirect-cost pools used to allocate costs to its customers. These cost pools and cost-allocation bases parallel the indirect-cost pools and allocation bases for the Provalue Division.

Implementing Corporate and Division Cost Allocations

Exhibit 14-10 allocates all overhead costs to customers based on the overview diagram in Exhibit 14-9. We describe some of the allocation choices based on the criteria for allocating costs explained in Exhibit 14-8.

1. Start at the top of Exhibit 14-9 and the allocation of corporate advertising and corporate adminisitration costs based on the demands that the Provalue Division and Deskpoint Division customers place on corporate resources. The first two columns in Exhibit 14-10 present the allocation of corporate advertising and corporate administration costs to the Provalue and Deskpoint divisions.

Exhibit 14-9   Overview Diagram for Allocating Corporate, Division, and Channel Indirect Costs to Wholesale Customers of Provalue Division

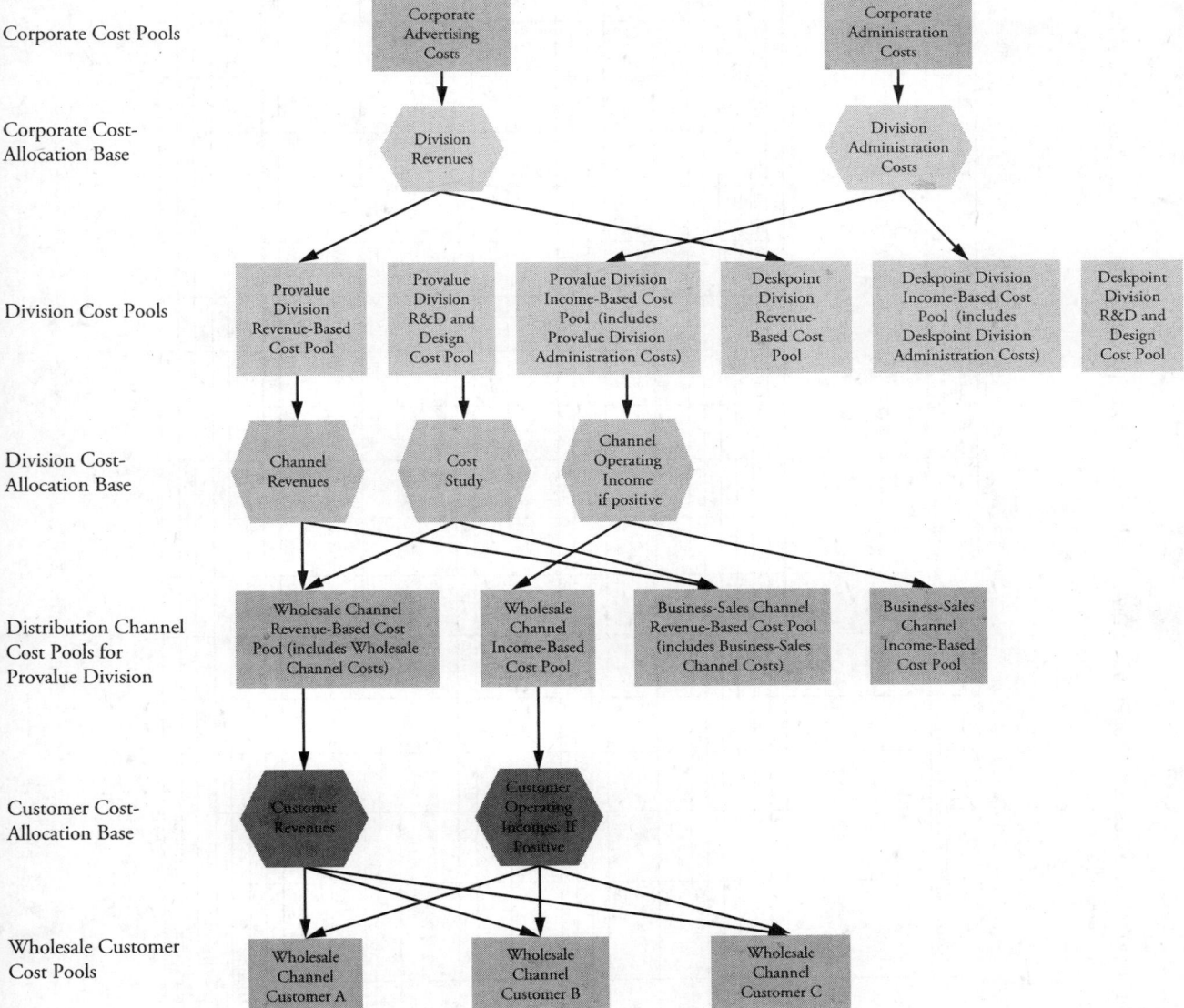

a. Astel allocates a total of ₹1,05,00,000 of corporate advertising costs to the two divisions on the basis of the revenues of each division (benefits received). It is plausible to assume that customers with higher revenues benefited more from corporate advertising costs than customers with lower revenues (see Exhibit 14-7 for information on revenues of each division):

$$\text{Provalue Division} : ₹1,05,00,000 \times \frac{₹1,50,00,00,000}{₹50,00,00,000 + ₹2,00,00,00,000} = ₹45,00,000$$

$$\text{Deskpoint Division} : ₹1,05,00,000 \times \frac{₹2,00,00,00,000}{₹1,50,00,00,000 + ₹2,00,00,00,000} = ₹60,00,000$$

Exhibit 14-10

Profitability of Wholesale Customers of Provalue Division After Fully Allocating Corporate, Division, and Channel Indirect Costs (in thousands, rounded)

Home   Insert   Page Layout   Formulas   Data   Review   View

	Astel Corporation Cost Pools		Provalue Division Cost Pools			Distribution Channel Cost Pools				Wholesale Channel Customers									
	Costs Allocated Based on Division Revenues	Costs Allocated Based on Division Administration Costs	Costs Allocated Based on Channel Revenues	R&D and Design Cost Allocation Pool	Costs Allocated Based on Channel Operating Incomes	Wholesale Channel Costs Allocated Based on Customer Revenues	Business-Sales Channel Costs Allocated Based on Customer Revenues	Wholesale Channel Costs Allocated Based on Customer Operating Incomes	Business-Sales Channel Costs Allocated Based on Customer Operating Incomes	A	B	C	D	E	F	G	H	I	J
Revenues (Exhibit 14-4)										₹3,00,000	₹2,62,500	₹1,30,000	₹72,500	₹18,000	₹51,000	₹47,500	₹24,000	₹26,000	₹44,000
Customer-level costs (Exh. 14-4, Col 2–Col.1)										(2,50,860)	(2,05,600)	(1,03,450)	(58,050)	(17,000)	(41,140)	(51,000)	(29,350)	(33,000)	(35,780)
Customer-level operating income (Exh. 14-4)										49,150	56,900	26,560	14,450	1,000	9,860	(3,500)	(5,350)	(7,000)	8,220
Astel corporate advertising costs	₹(10,500)																		
Astel corporate administration costs		₹(44,000)																	
Allocate corporate advertising costs to divisions based on division revenues[1]	10,500		₹(4,500)																
Allocate corporate administration costs to divisions based on division administration costs[2]		44,000			₹(20,900)														
R&D costs				₹(24,000)															
Design costs				(30,000)															
Division administration costs					(19,000)														
Allocate corporate advertising costs from Provalue Division to wholesale channel based on channel revenues[3]			4,500			₹(2,930)	₹(1,570)												
Allocate R&D and Design costs to channels based on fairness[4]				54,000		(27,000)	(27,000)												
Distribution channel costs						(8,000)	(13,500)												
Allocate division administration costs from Provalue division to wholesale channel based on channel operating incomes[5]					39,900			₹(27,250)	₹(12,650)										
Allocate wholesale channel costs to customers based on customer revenues						37,930				(11,660)	(10,210)	(5,050)	(2,820)	(700)	(1,960)	(1,850)	(930)	(1,010)	(1,720)
Operating income before allocation of division and corporate administration										37,490	46,690	21,500	11,630	300	7,880	(5,350)	(6,280)	(8,010)	6,500
Allocate wholesale channel costs to customers based on customer operating income, if positive (ability to bear)								27,250		(7,740)	(9,640)	(4,440)	(2,400)	(60)	(1,630)				(1,340)
Fully allocated customer profitability										₹29,750	₹37,050	₹17,060	₹9,230	₹240	₹6,250	₹(5,350)	₹(6,280)	₹(8,010)	₹5,160

[1] ₹10,500 × ₹15,00,000 / (₹15,00,000 + ₹20,00,000) = ₹4,500

[2] ₹44,000 × ₹19,000 / (₹19,000 + ₹21,000) = ₹20,900

[3] ₹4,500 × ₹9,75,500 / ₹15,00,000 = ₹2,930; ₹4,500 × ₹5,24,500 / ₹15,00,000 = ₹1,570

[4] ₹54,000 / 2 = ₹27,000

[5] ₹39,900 × ₹1,12,350 / ₹1,64,500 = ₹27,250; ₹39,900 × ₹52,150 / ₹1,64,500 = ₹12,650

b. Using the benefits-received criterion, Astel allocates corporate administration costs of ₹4,40,00,000 to each division on the basis of division-administration costs because corporate administration's main role is to support division administration. Exhibit 14-6 shows division-administration costs for Provalue Division of ₹1,90,00,000. Division administration costs for Deskpoint Division are ₹2,10,00,000. The allocations are:

$$\text{Provalue Division: } ₹4,40,00,000 \quad \times \quad \frac{₹1,90,00,000}{₹1,90,00,000 + ₹2,10,00,000} = ₹2,09,00,000$$

$$\text{Deskpoint Division: } ₹4,40,00,000 \quad \times \quad \frac{₹2,10,00,000}{₹1,90,00,000 + ₹2,10,00,000} = ₹2,31,00,000$$

2. Next, drop down one level in Exhibit 14-9 and focus on the allocation of costs from the division cost pools to the distribution-channel cost pools for the Provalue Division. The three columns labeled "Provalue Division Cost Pools" in Exhibit 14-10 show the allocations of the Provalue Division costs to the wholesale channel and the business-sales channel.

   a. Using the benefits-received criterion, the corporate advertising cost of ₹45,00,000 that had been allocated to the Provalue Division is now reallocated to the wholesale channel and the business-sales channel on the basis of the revenues of each channel (see Exhibit 14-6).

$$\text{WholeSales Channel: } ₹45,00,000 \times \frac{₹97,55,00,000}{₹97,55,00,000 + ₹52,45,00,000} = ₹29,26,500$$

$$\text{Business Sales Channel: } ₹45,00,000 \times \frac{₹52,45,00,000}{₹52,45,00,000 + ₹97,55,00,000} = ₹15,73,500$$

   b. The R&D costs and design costs are aggregated into one homogeneous cost pool and allocated to channels on the basis of a study analyzing the demand for R&D and design resources by the wholesale and business-sales channels. A significant amount of the R&D and design costs arise as a result of modifications to the Provalue computer demanded by the more sophisticated business customers. Using the results of the study and the fairness criterion, the Provalue Division allocates half of the R&D and design costs to the business-sales channel (and half to the wholesale channel) even though the business-sales channel accounts for only about one-third of the total sales of the Provalue Division. Exhibit 14-10 shows that the Provalue Division allocates ₹2,70,00,000 (₹5,40,00,000/2) each to the wholesale and business-sales channels.

   c. Each division adds the allocated corporate-administration costs to the division-administration cost pool. The costs in this cost pool are facility-sustaining costs and do not have a cause-and-effect relationship with any of the activities in the distribution channels. Astel, however, allocates all costs to products so that managers are aware of all costs when making pricing and other decisions. The Provalue Division allocates the total costs of ₹3,99,00,000 in the Provalue Division Administration cost pool to the wholesale channel and business-sales channel based on operating incomes of the wholesale and business-sales channels, representing the ability of each channel to bear division-administration costs (including allocated corporate-administration costs). The lower the operating income of a channel, the lower the division costs allocated to it. As described earlier in the chapter, the rationale for the ability-to-bear criterion is that divisions with lower incomes would work hard to reduce these overhead costs if they could manage these costs. From Exhibit 14-10, the operating income of the wholesale channel after subtracting all costs that have been allocated to it thus far is ₹11,23,48,500 (₹15,02,75,000 (Cell R7)

− ₹29,26,500 (Cell G15) − ₹2,70,00,000 (Cell G16) − ₹80,00,000 (Cell G17)) while the operating income of the business-sales channel is ₹5,21,51,500 (calculations not shown).

$$\text{WholeSales Channel : } ₹3,99,00,000 \times \frac{₹11,23,48,500}{₹11,23,48,500 + ₹5,21,51,500} = ₹2,72,50,490$$

$$\text{Business Sales Channel : } ₹3,99,00,000 \times \frac{₹5,21,51,500}{₹11,23,48,500 + ₹5,21,51,500} = ₹1,26,49,510$$

3. Finally, focus on the bottom rows in Exhibit 14-9 and the allocation of costs from the distribution channel cost pools for the Provalue Division to individual wholesale channel customers. The four columns labeled "Provalue Division Distribution Channel Cost Pools" in Exhibit 14-10 show that the costs accumulated in the wholesale channel and the business-sales channel are allocated to customers. Exhibit 14-10 only presents the allocation of wholesale channel costs to wholesale customers.

   a. Some of the wholesale channel costs are allocated to individual wholesale customers on the basis of revenues because revenues are a good measure of how individual customers benefit from these costs. The costs in this cost pool total ₹3,79,26,500 and are composed of three costs: (1) ₹29,26,500 of corporate advertising costs allocated to the wholesale channel in step 2a, (2) ₹2,70,00,000 of R&D and design costs allocated to the wholesale channel in step 2b, and (3) ₹80,00,000 of costs of the wholesale-distribution channel itself (Exhibit 14-6). In Exhibit 14-10, the costs allocated to Customer A and Customer B are:

$$\text{Customer A : } ₹3,79,26,500 \times \frac{₹30,00,00,000}{₹97,55,00,000} = ₹1,16,63,710$$

$$\text{Customer B : } ₹3,79,26,500 \times \frac{₹26,25,00,000}{₹97,55,00,000} = ₹1,02,05,740$$

   b. The second wholesale channel cost pool is composed of ₹2,72,50,490 of the division-administrative costs allocated to the wholesale channel in step 2c. These costs are allocated to individual wholesale customers on the basis of operating incomes (if positive) (see Exhibit 14-10, row 21) because operating incomes represent the ability of customers to bear these costs. In Exhibit 14-10, the sum of all the positive amounts in row 20 equals ₹13,19,59,220. The costs allocated to Customer A and Customer B are:

$$\text{Customer A : } ₹2,72,50,490 \times \frac{₹3,74,86,290}{₹13,19,59,220} = ₹77,41,170$$

$$\text{Customer B : } ₹2,72,50,490 \times \frac{₹4,66,94,260}{₹13,19,59,220} = ₹96,42,690$$

Issues in Allocating Corporate Costs to Divisions and Customers

Astel's management team makes several choices when accumulating and allocating corporate costs to divisions. We present two such issues next.

1. When allocating corporate costs to divisions, should Astel allocate only costs that vary with division activity or assign fixed costs as well? Managers allocate both variable and fixed costs to divisions and then to customers because the resulting costs are useful for

making long-run strategic decisions, such as which customers to emphasize and what prices to offer. To make good long-run decisions, managers need to know the cost of all resources (whether variable or fixed in the short run) required to sell products to customers. Why? Because in the long run, firms can manage the levels of virtually all of their costs; very few costs are truly fixed. Moreover, to survive and prosper in the long run, firms must ensure that the revenues received from a customer exceed the total resources consumed to support the customer, regardless of whether these costs are variable or fixed in the short run.

At the same time, companies that allocate corporate costs to divisions must carefully identify relevant costs for specific decisions. Suppose a division is profitable before any corporate costs are allocated but "unprofitable" after allocation of corporate costs. Should the division be closed down? The relevant corporate costs in this case are not the allocated corporate costs but those corporate costs that will be saved if the division is closed. If division profits exceed the relevant corporate costs, the division should not be closed.

2. When allocating costs to divisions, channels, and customers, how many cost pools should Astel use? One extreme is to aggregate all costs into a single cost pool. The other extreme is to have numerous individual cost pools. As discussed in Chapter 5, a major consideration is to construct **homogeneous cost pools** so that all of the costs in the cost pool have the same or a similar cause-and-effect or benefits-received relationship with the cost-allocation base.

For example, when allocating corporate costs to divisions, Astel can combine corporate advertising costs and corporate administration costs into a single cost pool if both cost categories have the same or similar cause-and-effect relationship with the same cost-allocation base. If, however, as is the case here, each cost category has a cause-and-effect or benefits-received relationship with a different cost-allocation base (for example, revenues of each division affect corporate advertising costs whereas division-administration costs of each division affect corporate administration costs), the company will prefer to maintain separate cost pools for each of these costs. Determining homogeneous cost pools requires judgment and should be revisited on a regular basis.

Managers must balance the benefit of using a multiple cost-pool system against the costs of implementing it. Advances in information-gathering technology make it more likely that multiple cost-pool systems will pass the cost–benefit test.

> ◀ **Decision Point**
>
> What are two key decisions managers must make when collecting costs in indirect-cost pools?

Using Fully Allocated Costs for Decision Making

How might Astel's managers use the fully allocated customer-profitability analysis in Exhibit 14-10? As we discussed in Chapter 13 when discussing product pricing, managers frequently favor using the full cost of a product when making pricing decisions. There are similar benefits to calculating fully allocated customer costs.

Consider, for example, Customer E, who shows a profitability of ₹2,40,000 in Exhibit 14-10. If this customer demanded a price reduction of ₹5,00,000, how should the Provalue Division respond? Based on the analysis in Exhibit 14-4, Customer E shows a profitability of ₹10,00,000 and it would appear that even a ₹5,00,000 reduction in price would still leave Customer E as a profitable customer. But in the long run, Customer E must generate sufficient profits to recover all the division-support costs of the Provalue Division and the corporate costs of Astel. A ₹5,00,000 reduction in price may not be sustainable in the long run. As the Provalue Division begins making plans for Provalue II (see Chapter 13), it simultaneously must consider what it can do to better manage its customers to improve profitability.

Another advantage of allocating costs to customers is that it highlights opportunities to manage costs. For example, the manager of the wholesale channel might want to probe whether the amounts spent on corporate advertising or on R&D and design help in promoting sales to wholesale customers. These discusssions might prompt a reevalaution of the amount and type of advertising, R&D, and design activity.

Sales Variances

The customer-profitability analysis in the previous section focused on the actual profitability of individual customers within a distribution channel (wholesale, for example) and their effect on the Provalue Division's profitability for 2013. At a more strategic level, however, recall that Provalue Division sells Provalues in two different markets: wholesale and directly to businesses. The operating margins in the business-sales market are higher than the operating margins in the wholesale market. In 2013, the Provalue Division had budgeted to sell 60% of its Provalues through wholesalers and 40% directly to businesses. It sold more Provalues in total than it had budgeted, but its actual sales mix (in computers) was 66.67% to wholesalers and 33.33% directly to businesses. Regardless of the profitability of sales to individual customers within each of the wholesale and business-sales channels, the Provalue Division's actual operating income, relative to the master budget, is likely to be positively affected by the higher number of Provalues sold and negatively affected by the shift in mix toward the less profitable wholesale customers. Sales-quantity and sales-mix variances can identify the effect of each of these factors on the Provalue Division's profitability. Companies such as Cisco, GE, and Hewlett-Packard perform similar analyses because they sell their products through multiple distribution channels like the Internet, over the telephone, and retail stores.

The Provalue Division classifies all customer-level costs, other than fixed machining costs of ₹11,40,00,000, as variable costs and distribution-channel and corporate-sustaining costs as fixed costs. To simplify the sales-variance analysis and calculations, we assume that all of the variable costs are variable with respect to Provalue computers sold. (This means that average batch sizes remain the same as the total number of Provalue computers sold vary.) Without this assumption, the analysis would become more complex and would have to be done using the ABC-variance analysis approach described in Chapter 8, pages 407–412. The basic insights, however, would not change.

Budgeted and actual operating data for 2013 are as follows:

Budget Data for 2013

	Selling Price (1)	Variable Cost per Unit (2)	Contribution Margin per Unit (3) = (1) – (2)	Sales Volume in Units (4)	Sales Mix (Based on Units) (5)	Contribution Margin (6) = (3) × (4)
Wholesale channel	₹9,800	₹7,550	₹2,250	93,000	60%[a]	₹20,92,50,000
Business-sales channel	10,500	7,750	2,750	62,000	40%	17,05,00,000
Total				1,55,000	100%	₹37,97,50,000

[a]Percentage of unit sales to wholesale channel = 93,000 units, 1,55,000 total unit = 60%.

Actual Results for 2013

	Selling Price (1)	Variable Cost per Unit (2)	Contribution Margin per Unit (3) = (1) – (2)	Sales Volume in Units (4)	Sales Mix (Based on Units) (5)	Contribution Margin (6) = (3) × (4)
Wholesale channel	₹9,755	₹7,492.25	₹2,262.75	1,00,000	66.67%[a]	₹22,62,75,000
Business-sales channel	1,049.00	7,845.50	2,644.50	50,000	33.33%	13,22,25,000
Total				1,50,000	100.00%	₹35,85,00,000

[a]Percentage of unit sales to wholesale channel = 1,00,000 units, 1,50,000 total unit = 66.67%.

The budgeted and actual fixed distribution-channel costs, division costs, and corporate-level costs are the same (see Exhibit 14-6, page 754, and Exhibit 14-7, page 755).

Recall that the levels of detail introduced in Chapter 7 (pages 333–339) included the static-budget variance (level 1), the flexible-budget variance (level 2), and the sales-volume variance (level 2). The sales-quantity and sales-mix variances are level 3 variances that sub-divide the sales-volume variance.[5]

Static-Budget Variance

The *static-budget variance* is the difference between an actual result and the corresponding budgeted amount in the static budget. Our analysis focuses on the difference between actual and budgeted contribution margins (column 6 in the preceding tables). The total static-budget variance is ₹2,12,50,000 (actual contribution margin of ₹35,85,00,000 – budgeted contribution margin of ₹37,97,50,000). Exhibit 14-11 (columns 1 and 3) uses the columnar format introduced in Chapter 7 to show detailed calculations of the static-budget variance. Managers can gain more insight about the static-budget variance by subdividing it into the flexible-budget variance and the sales-volume variance.

Flexible-Budget Variance and Sales-Volume Variance

The *flexible-budget variance* is the difference between an actual result and the corresponding flexible-budget amount based on actual output level in the budget period. The flexible budget contribution margin is equal to budgeted contribution margin per unit times actual units sold of each product. Exhibit 14-11, column 2, shows the flexible-budget calculations. The flexible budget measures the contribution margin that the Provalue Division would have budgeted for the actual quantities of cases sold. The flexible-budget variance is the difference between columns 1 and 2 in Exhibit 14-11. The only difference between columns 1 and 2 is that actual units sold of each product is multiplied by actual contribution margin per unit in column 1 and budgeted contribution margin per unit in column 2. The ₹40,00,000 U total flexible-budget variance arises because actual contribution margin on business sales of ₹2,644.50 per Provalue is lower than the budgeted amount of ₹2,750 per Provalue and offsets the slightly higher actual contribution margin of ₹2,262.75 versus the budgeted contribution margin of ₹2,250 on wholesale channel sales. The Provalue Division managers are aware that the lower contribution margin of ₹105.50 (₹2,750 – ₹2,644.50) per computer on business sales resulted from higher variable ordering and testing costs and have put in place action plans to reduce these costs in the future.

The *sales-volume variance* is the difference between a flexible-budget amount and the corresponding static-budget amount. In Exhibit 14-11, the sales-volume variance shows the effect on budgeted contribution margin of the difference between actual quantity of units sold and budgeted quantity of units sold. The sales-volume variance of ₹1,72,50,000 U is the difference between columns 2 and 3 in Exhibit 14-11. In this case, it is unfavorable overall because while wholesale channel sales of Provalue were higher than budgeted, business sales, which are expected to be more profitable on a per computer basis, were below budget. Provalue Division managers can gain substantial insight into the sales-volume variance by subdividing it into the sales-mix variance and the sales-quantity variance.

---

[5] The presentation of the variances in this chapter draws on teaching notes prepared by J. K. Harris.

| **Exhibit 14-11** | Flexible-Budget and Sales-Volume Variance Analysis of Provalue Division for 2013 |

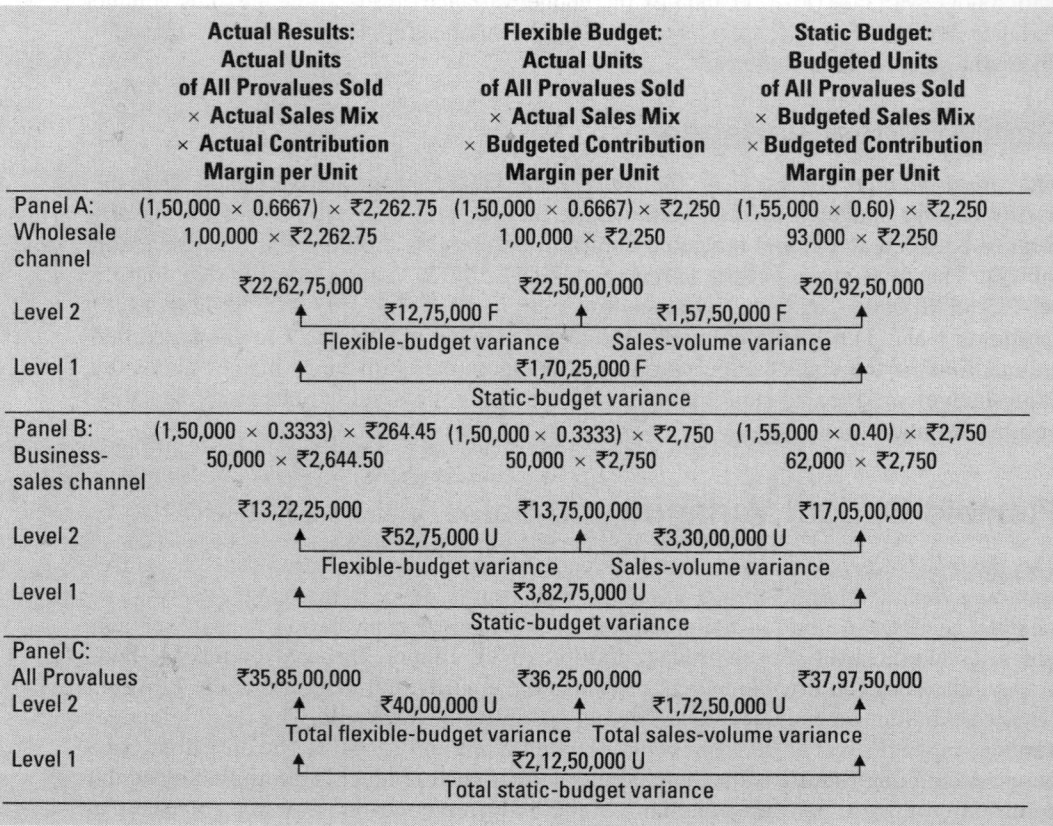

Sales-Mix Variance

The **sales-mix variance** is the difference between (1) budgeted contribution margin for the *actual sales mix* and (2) budgeted contribution margin for the *budgeted sales mix*. The formula and computations (using data from page 764) are as follows:

	Actual Units of All Products Sold	×	$\begin{pmatrix} \text{Actual} & \text{Budgeted} \\ \text{Sales - mix} - \text{Sales - Mix} \\ \text{Percentage} & \text{Percentage} \end{pmatrix}$	×	Budgeted Contribution Margin per Unit	=	Sales-Mix Variance
Wholesale	1,50,000 units	×	(0.66667 − 0.60)	×	₹2,250 per unit	=	₹2,25,00,000 F
Business-Sales	1,50,000 units	×	(0.33333 − 0.40)	×	₹2,750 per unit	=	2,75,00,000 U
Total sales-mix variance							₹50,00,000 U

A favorable sales-mix variance arises for the wholesale channel because the 66.67% actual sales-mix percentage exceeds the 60% budgeted sales-mix percentage. In contrast, the business-sales channel has an unfavorable variance because the 33.33% actual sales-mix percentage is less than the 40% budgeted sales-mix percentage. The total sales-mix variance is unfavorable because actual sales mix shifted toward the less profitable wholesale channel relative to budgeted sales mix.

The concept underlying the sales-mix variance is best explained in terms of composite units. A **composite unit** is a hypothetical unit with weights based on the mix of individual units. Given the budgeted sales for 2013, the composite unit consists of 0.60 units of sales to the wholesale channel and 0.40 units of sales to the business-sales channel. Therefore, the budgeted contribution margin per composite unit for the budgeted sales mix is as follows:

$$0.60 \times ₹2,250 + 0.40 \times ₹2,750 = ₹2,450^6$$

Similarly, for the actual sales mix, the composite unit consists of 0.66667 units of sales to the wholesale channel and 0.33333 units of sales to the business-sales channel. The budgeted contribution margin per composite unit for the actual sales mix is therefore:

$$0.66667 \times ₹2,250 + 0.33333 \times ₹2,750 = ₹2,416.667$$

The impact of the shift in sales mix is now evident. The Provalue Division obtains a lower budgeted contribution margin per composite unit of ₹33.333 (₹2,450 − ₹2,416.667). For the 1,50,000 units actually sold, this decrease translates to a ₹50,00,000 U sales-mix variance (₹33.333 per unit 1,50,000 units).

Managers should probe why the ₹50,00,000 U sales-mix variance occurred in June 2016. Is the shift in sales mix because, as the analysis in the previous section showed, profitable retail customers proved to be more difficult to find? Is it because of a competitor in the retail channel providing better service at a lower price? Or is it because the initial sales-volume estimates were made without adequate analysis of the potential market?

Exhibit 14-10 uses the columnar format to calculate the sales-mix variance and the sales-quantity variances.

Sales-Quantity Variance

The **sales-quantity variance** is the difference between (1) budgeted contribution margin based on *actual units sold of all products* at the budgeted mix and (2) contribution margin in the static budget (which is based on *budgeted units of all products to be sold* at budgeted mix). The formula and computations (using data from page 764) are as follows:

Actual total Provalues sold – Budgeted total Provalues sold			×	Budgeted Sales-Mix Percentages	×	Budgeted Contribution Margin per Unit	=	Sales-Quantity Variance
Wholesale	(1,50,000 units − 1,55,000 units)		×	0.60	×	₹2,250 per unit	=	₹67,50,000 U
Business sales	(1,50,000 units − 1,55,000 units)		×	0.40	×	₹2,750 per unit	=	₹55,00,000 U
Total sales-quantity variance								₹1,22,50,000 U

This variance is unfavorable when actual units of all products sold are less than the budgeted units of all products sold. The Provalue Division sold 5,000 fewer Provalues than were budgeted, resulting in a ₹1,22,50,000 sales-quantity variance (also equal to budgeted contribution margin per composite unit for the budgeted sales mix times fewer units sold, ₹2,450 × 5,000). Managers would want to probe the reasons for the decrease in sales. Did lower sales come as a result of a competitor's aggressive marketing? Poorer customer service? Or decline in the overall market? Managers can gain additional insight into the causes

---

[6] Budgeted contribution margin per composite unit can be computed in another way by dividing total budgeted contribution margin of ₹37,97,50,000 by total budgeted units of 1,55,000 (page 570): ₹37,97,50,000 ÷ 15,50,000 units = ₹2,450 per unit.

| **Exhibit 14-12** | Sales mix and Sales-Volume Variance Analysis of Provalue Division for 2013 |

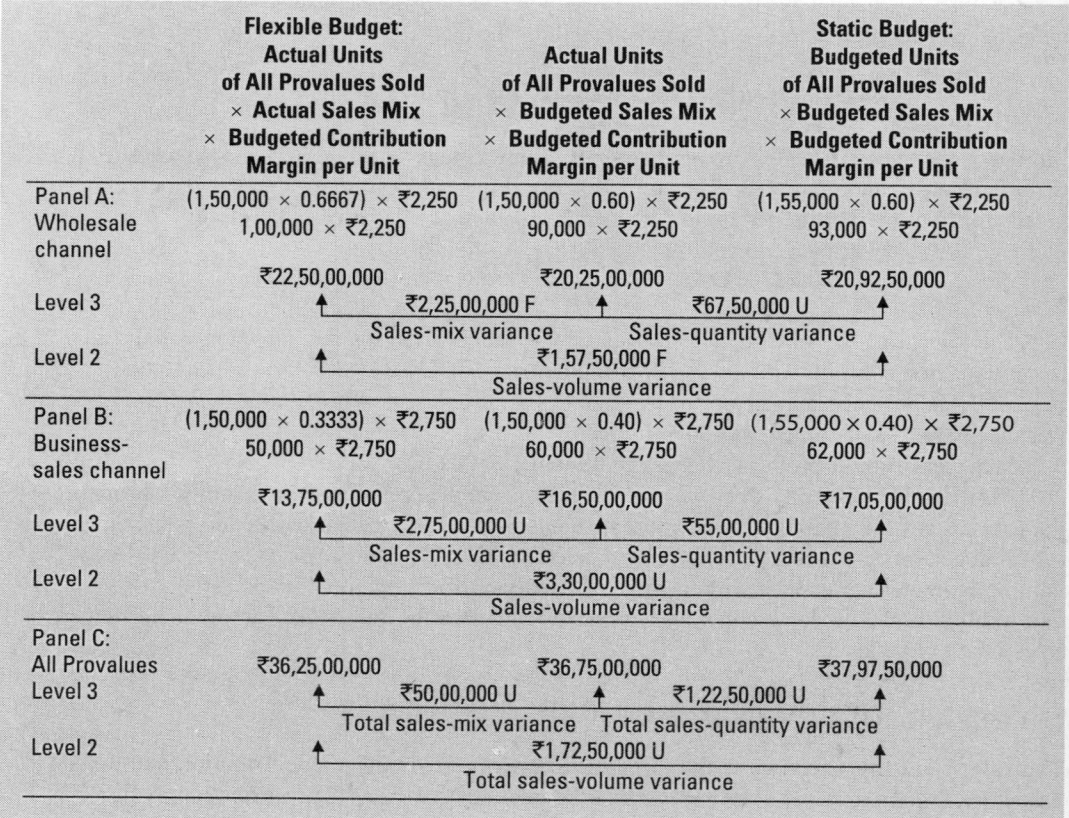

of the sales-quantity variance by analyzing changes in Provalue Division's share of the total industry market and in the size of that market. The sales-quantity variance can be decomposed into market-share and market-size variances, as we describe in the next section.

Market-Share and Market-Size Variances

The total quantity of Provalues sold depends on overall demand for similar computers in the market, as well as Provalue Division's share of the market. Assume that the Provalue Division derived its total unit sales budget of 1,55,000 Provalue computers for 2013 from a management estimate of a 20% market share and a budgeted industry market size of 7,75,000 units ($0.20 \times 7,75,000$ units = 1,55,000 units). For 2013, actual market size was 800,000 units and actual market share was 18.75% (1,50,000 units ÷ 8,00,000 units = 0.1875 or 18.75%).Exhibit 14-13 shows the columnar presentation of how the Provalue Division's sales-quantity variance can be decomposed into market-share and market-size variances.

Market-Share Variance

The market-share variance is the difference in budgeted contribution margin for actual market size in units caused solely by actual market share being different from budgeted market share. The formula for computing the market-share variance is as follows:

| **Exhibit 14-13** | Market-Share and Market-Size Variance Analysis of Provalue Division of Astel Computers for 2013[a] |

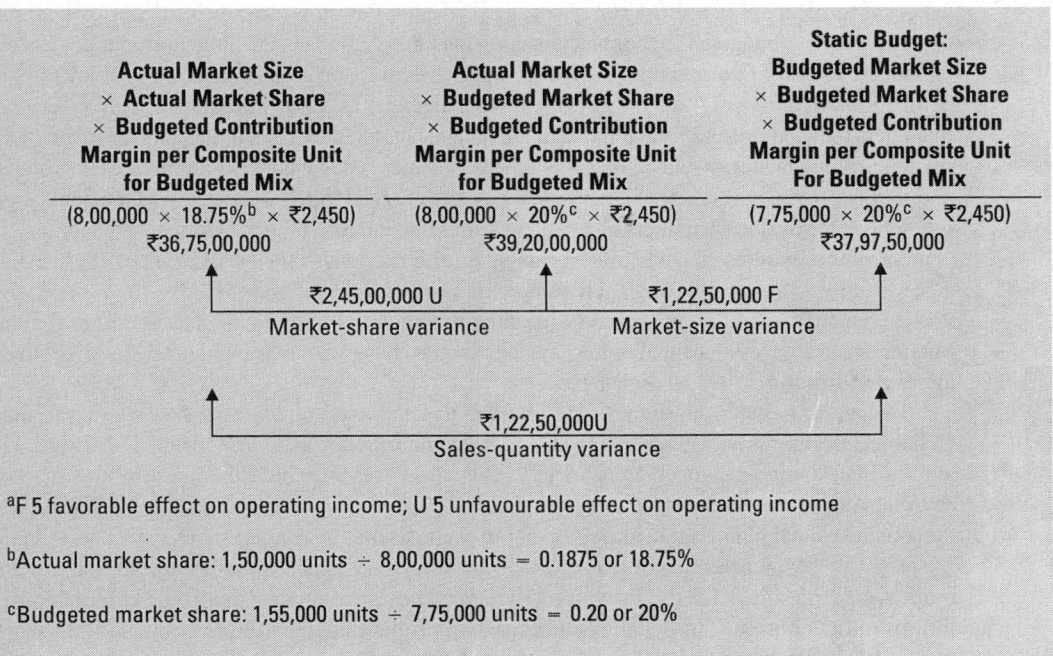

Actual Market Size × Actual Market Share × Budgeted Contribution Margin per Composite Unit for Budgeted Mix
(8,00,000 × 18.75%[b] × ₹2,450)
₹36,75,00,000

Actual Market Size × Budgeted Market Share × Budgeted Contribution Margin per Composite Unit for Budgeted Mix
(8,00,000 × 20%[c] × ₹2,450)
₹39,20,00,000

Static Budget: Budgeted Market Size × Budgeted Market Share × Budgeted Contribution Margin per Composite Unit For Budgeted Mix
(7,75,000 × 20%[c] × ₹2,450)
₹37,97,50,000

₹2,45,00,000 U
Market-share variance

₹1,22,50,000 F
Market-size variance

₹1,22,50,000U
Sales-quantity variance

[a]F 5 favorable effect on operating income; U 5 unfavourable effect on operating income

[b]Actual market share: 1,50,000 units ÷ 8,00,000 units = 0.1875 or 18.75%

[c]Budgeted market share: 1,55,000 units ÷ 7,75,000 units = 0.20 or 20%

$$\text{Market-share variance} = \text{Actual market size in units} \times \left(\text{Actual market share} - \text{Budgeted market share}\right) \times \text{Budgeted contribution margin per composite unit for budgeted mix}$$

$$= 8{,}00{,}000 \text{ units} - (0.1875 - 0.20) \times ₹2{,}450 \text{ per unit}$$

$$= ₹2{,}45{,}00{,}000 \text{ U}$$

The Provalue Division lost 1.25 market-share percentage points—from the 20% budgeted share to the actual share of 18.75%. The ₹2,45,00,000 U market-share variance is the decline in contribution margin as a result of those lost sales.

Market-Size Variance

The **market-size variance** is the difference in budgeted contribution margin at budgeted market share caused solely by *actual market size in units* being different from *budgeted market size in units*. The formula for computing the market-size variance is as follows:

$$\text{Market size variance} = \left(\text{Actual market size} - \text{Budgeted market size}\right) \times \text{Budgeted market share} \times \text{Budgeted contribution margin per composite unit for budgeted mix}$$

$$= 18{,}00{,}000 \text{ units} - 7{,}75{,}000 \text{ units} \times 0.20 \times ₹2{,}450 \text{ per units}$$

$$= ₹1{,}22{,}50{,}000 \text{ F}$$

The market-size variance is favorable because actual market size increased 3.23% [(8,00,000 − 7,75,000) / 7,75,000 = 0.0323, or 3.23%] compared to budgeted market size.

Managers should probe the reasons for the market-size and market-share variances for 2013. Is the ₹1,22,50,000 F market-size variance because of an increase in market size that can be expected to continue in the future? If yes, the Provalue Division has much to gain by attaining or exceeding its budgeted 20% market share. Was the ₹2,45,00,000 unfavorable market-share variance because of competitors providing better offerings or greater value to customers? Did competitors aggressively cut prices to stimulate market demand? Although Provalue Divison managers reduced prices a little relative to the budget, should they have reduced prices even more, particularly for business-sales customers where Provalue sales were considerably below budget and selling prices significantly higher than the prices charged to wholesalers? Was the quality and reliability of Provalue computers as good as the quality and reliability of competitors?

Some companies place more emphasis on the market-share variance than the market-size variance when evaluating their managers. That's because they believe the market-size variance is influenced by economy-wide factors and shifts in consumer preferences that are outside the managers' control, whereas the market-share variance measures how well managers performed relative to their peers.

Be cautious when computing the market-size variance and the market-share variance. Reliable information on market size and market share is not available for all industries. The automobile, computer, and television industries are cases in which market-size and market-share statistics are widely available. In other industries, such as management consulting and personal financial planning, information about market size and market share is far less reliable.

Exhibit 14-14 presents an overview of the sales-mix, sales-quantity, market-share, and market-size variances for the Provalue Division. These variances can also be calculated in a multiproduct company, in which each individual product has a different contribution margin per unit. The Problem for Self-Study presents such a setting.

Decision Point ▶

What are the two components of the sales-volume variance and two components of the sales-quantity variance?

Exhibit 14-14   Overview of Variances for Provalue Division for 2013

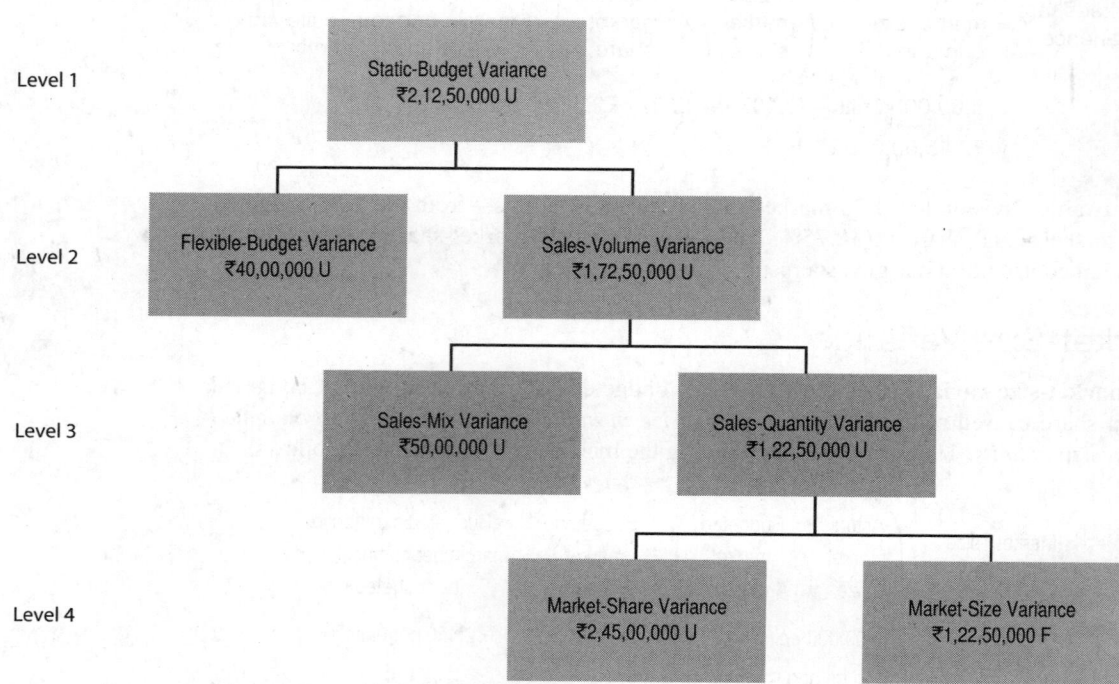

Level 1

Static-Budget Variance
₹2,12,50,000 U

Level 2

Flexible-Budget Variance
₹40,00,000 U

Sales-Volume Variance
₹1,72,50,000 U

Level 3

Sales-Mix Variance
₹50,00,000 U

Sales-Quantity Variance
₹1,22,50,000 U

Level 4

Market-Share Variance
₹2,45,00,000 U

Market-Size Variance
₹1,22,50,000 F

F = favorable effect on operating income; U = unfavorable effect on operating income

Problem for Self-Study

The SB Enterprises manufactures two types of vinyl flooring. Budgeted and actual operating data for 2013 are as follows:

	Static Budget			Actual Results		
	Commercial	Residential	Total	Commercial	Residential	Total
Unit sales in rolls	20,000	60,000	80,000	25,200	58,800	84,000
Contribution margin	₹10,00,00,000	₹24,00,00,000	₹34,00,00,000	₹11,97,00,000	₹24,69,60,000	₹36,66,60,000

In late 2016, a marketing research firm estimated industry volume for commercial and residential vinyl flooring for 2016 at 8,00,000 rolls. Actual industry volume for 2016 was 7,00,000 rolls.

1. Compute the sales-mix variance and the sales-quantity variance by type of vinyl flooring and in total. (Compute all variances in terms of contribution margins.)
2. Compute the market-share variance and the market-size variance.
3. What insights do the variances calculated in requirements 1 and 2 provide about SB Enterprises performance in 2013?

Solution

1. Actual sales-mix percentage:

   Commercial = 25,200 ÷ 84,000 = 0.30, or 30%

   Residential = 58,800 ÷ 84,000 = 0.70, or 70%

   Budgeted sales-mix percentage:

   Commercial = 20,000 ÷ 80,000 = 0.25, or 25%

   Residential = 60,000 ÷ 80,000 = 0.75, or 75%

   Budgeted contribution margin per unit:

   Commercial = ₹10,00,00,000 ÷ 20,000 units = ₹5,000 per unit

   Residential = ₹24,00,00,000 ÷ 60,000 units = ₹4,000 per unit

	Actual Units of All Products Sold ×	(Actual Sales Mix Percentage	− Budgeted Sales Mix Percentage	Budgeted Contribution Margin × per Unit)	= Sales-Mix Variance
Commercial	84,000 units ×	(0.30 − 0.25)		× ₹5,000 per unit	= ₹2,10,00,000 F
Residential	84,000 units ×	(0.70 − 0.75)		× ₹4,000 per unit	= ₹1,68,00,000 U
Total sales-mix variance					₹4,20,00,000 F

	(Actual Units of All Products Sold	− Budgeted Units of All Products Sold)	Budgeted × Sales-Mix Percentage ×	Budgeted Contribution Margin per Unit	= Sales-Quantity Variance
Commercial	(84,000 units − 80,000 units)		× 0.25	× ₹5,000 per unit	= ₹50,00,000 F
Residential	(84,000 units − 80,000 units)		× 0.75	× ₹4,000 per unit	= ₹1,20,00,000 F
Total sales-quantity variance					₹1,70,00,000 F

2. Actual market share = 84,000 ÷ 7,00,000 = 0.12, or 12%
   Budgeted market share = 80,000 ÷ 8,00,000 units = 0.10, or 10%

Budgeted contribution margin
   per composite unit = ₹34,00,00,000 ÷ 80,000 units = ₹4,250 per unit
   of budgeted mix

Budgeted contribution margin per composite unit of budgeted mix can also be calculated as follows:

Commercial : 5,000 per unit × 0 25   =   ₹1250
Residential : 4,000 per unit × 0.75   =   3,000
Budgeted contribution margin per composite unit = ₹4250

$$\text{Market-share variance} = \text{Actual market size in units} \times \left(\text{Actual market share} - \text{Budgeted market share} \right) \times \text{Budgeted contribution margin per composite unit for budgeted mix}$$

$$= 7,00,000 \text{ units} \times (0.12 - 0.10) \times ₹4,250 \text{ per unit}$$
$$= ₹5,95,00,000 \text{ F}$$

$$\text{Market-share variance} = \left(\text{Actual market share} - \text{Budgeted market share} \right) \times \text{Budgeted market share} \times \text{Budgeted contribution margin per composite unit for budgeted mix}$$

$$= 7,00,000 \text{ units} - 8,00,000 \text{ units}) \times 0.10 \times ₹4,250 \text{ per unit}$$
$$= ₹4,25,00,000 \text{ U}$$

Note that the algebraic sum of the market-share variance and the market-size variance is equal to the sales-quantity variance: ₹5,95,00,000 F + ₹4,25,00,000U = ₹1,70,00,000 F.

3. Both the total sales-mix variance and the total sales-quantity variance are favorable. The favorable sales-mix variance occurred because the actual mix was composed of more of the higher-margin commercial vinyl flooring. The favorable total sales-quantity variance occurred because the actual total quantity of rolls sold exceeded the budgeted amount.

The company's large favorable market-share variance is due to a 12% actual market share compared with a 10% budgeted market share. The market-size variance is unfavorable because the actual market size was 1,00,000 rolls less than the budgeted market size. Payne's performance in 2013 appears to be very good. Although overall market size declined, the company sold more units than budgeted and gained market share.

Decision Points

The following question-and-answer format summarizes the chapter's learning objectives. Each decision presents a key question related to a learning objective. The guidelines are the answer to that question.

Decision	Guidelines
1. How can a company's revenues and costs differ across customers?	Revenues differ because of differences in the quantity purchased and price discounts. Costs differ because different customers place different demands on a company's resources in terms of processing sales orders, making deliveries, and customer support.
2. How do customer-profitability profiles help managers?	Companies should be aware of and devote sufficient resources to maintaining and expanding relationships with customers who contribute significantly to profitability and design incentives to change behavior patterns of unprofitable customers. Customer-profitability profiles often highlight that a small percentage of customers contributes a large percentage of operating income.
3. Why do managers prepare cost-hierarchy-based operating incomes statements?	Cost-hierarchy-based operating income statements allocate only those costs that will be affected by actions at a particular hierarchical level. For example, costs such as sales-order costs and shipment costs are allocated to customers because customer actions can affect these costs, but costs of managing the wholesale channel are not allocated to customers because changes in customer behavior will have no effect on these costs.
4. What criteria should managers use to guide cost-allocation decisions?	Managers should use the cause-and-effect and the benefits-received criteria to guide most cost-allocation decisions. Other criteria are fairness or equity and ability to bear.
5. What are two key decisions managers must make when collecting costs in indirect-cost pools?	Two key decisions related to indirect-cost pools are the number of indirect-cost pools to form and the individual cost items to be included in each cost pool to make homogeneous cost pools. Generally, managers allocate both variable costs and costs that are fixed in the short-run.
6. What are the two components of the sales-volume variance and two components of the sales-quantity variance?	The two components of sales-volume variance are (a) the difference between actual sales mix and budgeted sales mix (the sales-mix variance) and (b) the difference between actual unit sales and budgeted unit sales (the sales-quantity variance). The two components of the the sales-quantity variance are (a) the difference between the actual market share and the budgeted market share (the market-share variance) and (b) the difference between the actual market size in units and the budgeted market size in units (the market-size variance).

TERMS TO LEARN

The chapter and the Glossary at the end of the book contain definitions of the following important terms:

composite unit **(p. 767)**
customer-cost hierarchy **(P. 746)**
customer-profitability
  analysis **(p. 74)**

homogeneous cost pools **(p. 763)**
market-share variance **(p. 768)**
market-size variance **(p. 769)**
price discount **(p. 744)**

sales-mix variance **(p. 766)**
sales-quantity
  variance **(p. 767)**
whale curve **(p. 752)**

ASSIGNMENT MATERIAL

Questions

14-1 "I am going to focus on the customers of my business and leave cost-allocation issues to my accountant." Do you agree with this comment by a division president? Why?

14-2 A given cost may be allocated for one or more purposes. List four purposes.

14-3 What criteria might be used to guide cost-allocation decisions? Which are the dominant criteria?

14-4 "A company should not allocate all of its corporate costs to its divisions." Do you agree? Explain.

14-5 "Once a company allocates corporate costs to divisions, these costs should not be reallocated to the indirect-cost pools of the division." Do you agree? Explain.

14-6 Why is customer-profitability analysis a vitally important topic to managers?

14-7 How can the extent of price discounting be tracked on a customer-by-customer basis?

14-8 "A customer-profitability profile highlights those customers who should be dropped to improve profitability." Do you agree? Explain.

14-9 Give examples of three different levels of costs in a customer-cost hierarchy.

14-10 Show how managers can gain insight into the causes of a sales-volume variance by subdividing the components of this variance.

14-11 How can the concept of a composite unit be used to explain why an unfavorable total sales-mix variance of contribution margin occurs?

14-12 Explain why a favorable sales-quantity variance occurs.

14-13 Distinguish between a market-share variance and a market-size variance.

14-14 Why might some companies not compute market-size and market-share variances?

14-15 Explain how the direct materials mix and yield variances provide additional information about the direct materials efficiency variance.

Solved Examples

14-16 Cost allocation and motivation. Reliance Petroleum Company is engaged in all phases of exploring, refining, and marketing of oil and petrochemical products. To ensure full compliance with all applicable laws, the company has a legal department staffed by lawyers who have expertise in a variety of legal areas. The top management of Reliance wants to motivate all operating managers to seek legal counsel from the in-house lawyers whenever necessary to avoid violation of any laws during the course of its operations.

Currently, users of the legal Department are allocated cost at a ₹400 standard hourly rate based on actual usage. The chief financial officer has suggested that department managers would make more use of the Legal Department services, and thus avoid potential legal pitfalls, if the service was provided free of cost to their departments.

Comment on the proposal of the chief financial officer. Do you have any alternative suggestion(s)?

Solution

Cost allocation and motivation.

Because corporate policy encourages line managers to seek legal counsel on pertinent issues from the Legal Department, any step in the direction of reducing costs of legal department services would be consistent with the corporate policy.

Currently a user department is charged a standard fee of ₹400 per hour based on actual usage. It is possible that some managers may not be motivated to seek the legal counsel they need due to the high allocated cost of the service. It is also possible that those managers whose departments are currently experiencing budgetary cost overruns may be disinclined to make use of the service; it would save them from the Legal Department's cost allocation. However, it could potentially result in much costlier penalties for Reliance later if the corporation inadvertently engaged in some activities that violated one or more laws.

It is quite likely that the line managers would seek legal counsel, whenever there were any pertinent legal issues, if the service were free. Making the service of the Legal Department free, however, might induce some managers to make excessive use of the service. To avoid any potential abuse, Reliance may want to adjust the rate downward considerably, perhaps at a level lower than what it would cost if outside legal services were sought, but not eliminate it altogether. As long as the managers know that their respective departments would be charged for using the service, they would be disinclined to make use of it unnecessarily. However, they would be motivated to use it when necessary because it would be considered a "good value" if the standard hourly rate was low enough.

14-17 Cost allocation to divisions. J. K. Paper Corporation has three divisions: Fibers, Paper, and Pulp. As J. K. Paper's new controller, you are reviewing the basis to be used for allocating fixed overhead costs to the three divisions in 2016. The following information is available for 2015:

	Pulp	Paper	Fibers
Revenue	₹85,00,000	₹1,75,00,000	₹2,40,00,000
Administrative costs	₹12,00,000	₹18,00,000	₹30,00,000
Number of employees	300	250	450
Floor space (square feet)	30,000	24,000	66,000
Segment margin	₹32,00,000	₹71,00,000	₹97,00,000

In the past, J. K. Paper has allocated fixed overhead costs to the division using segment margin percentages. A review of the fixed overhead costs indicates that they consist of the following:

Human resource management	₹18,00,000
Facility	27,00,000
Corporate administration	45,00,000
Total	₹90,00,000

After considering the nature of the fixed-cost items, you decide to make the allocations in 2016 using the following bases:

Human resource management	Number of employees
Facility	Floor space
Corporate administration	Divisional administrative costs

Required

1. Allocate 2015 indirect costs to the three divisions using segment margin percentages.
2. Allocate 2015 indirect costs to the three divisions using the bases you have selected.
3. Discuss the reason(s) why your approach is preferable.

Solution

Cost allocation to divisions.

1.

	Pulp	Paper	Fibers
Segment margin	₹32,00,000	₹71,00,000	₹97,00,000
Percentages	16.0%	35.5%	48.5%
Allocation (₹90,00,000 × 16.0%, 35.5%, 48.5%)	₹14,40,000	₹31,95,000	₹43,65,000

2. Percentages for new bases of allocation

	Pulp	Paper	Fibers
Number of employees	300	250	450
Percentages	30%	25%	45%
Floor space (square feet)	30,000	24,000	66,000
Percentages	25%	20%	55%
Divisional administrative	₹12,00,000	₹18,00,000	₹30,00,000
Percentages	20%	30%	50%

Allocation of indirect costs

	Pulp	Paper	Fibers
Human resource management	₹5,40,000	₹4,50,000	₹8,10,000
(₹18,00,000 × 30%, 25%, 45%)			
Facility (₹27,00,000 × 25%, 20%, 55%)	6,75,000	5,40,000	14,85,000
Corporate administration	9,00,000	13,50,000	22,50,000
(₹45,00,000 × 20%, 30%, 50%)			
Total	₹21,15,000	₹23,40,000	₹45,45,000

3. The new approach is preferable because it is based on cause-and-effect relationships between costs and their respective cost drivers in the long run.

Human resource management costs are allocated using the number of employees in each division because the costs for recruitment, training, etc., are mostly related to the number of employees in each division. Facility costs are mostly incurred on the basis of space occupied by each division. Corporate administration costs are allocated on the basis of divisional administrative costs because these costs are incurred to provide support to divisional administrations.

14-18 Customer profitability, service company. Instant Service (IS) repairs printers and photocopiers for five multisite companies in a tristate area. IS's costs consist of the cost of technicians and equipment that are directly traceable to the customer site and a pool of office overhead. Until recently, IS estimated customer profitability by allocating the office overhead to each customer based on share of revenues. For 2015, IS reported the following results:

	A	B	C	D	E	F	G
1		Anoop	Om	White	Gopal	Devi	Total
2	Revenues	26,00,000	₹20,00,000	₹32,20,000	₹12,20,000	₹21,20,000	₹1,11,60,000
3	Technician and equipment cost	18,20,000	17,50,000	22,50,000	10,70,000	17,80,000	86,70,000
4	Office overhead allocated	3,18,590	2,45,070	3,94,570	1,49,490	2,59,780	13,67,500
5	Operating income	₹4,61,410	₹4,930	₹5,75,430	₹510	₹80,220	₹11,22,500

Seema, IS's new controller, notes that office overhead is more than 10% of total costs, so she spends a couple of weeks analyzing the consumption of office overhead resources by customers. She collects the following information:

	I	J	K
	Home Insert Page Layout Formulas Data Review		
1	**Activity Area**		**Cost Driver Rate**
2	Service call handling	₹750	per service call
3	Parts ordering	₹800	per Web-based parts order
4	Billing and collection	₹500	per bill (or reminder)
5	Customer database maintenance	₹100	per service call

	A	B	C	D	E	F
	Home Insert Page Layout Formulas Data Review View					
8		**Anoop**	**Om**	**White**	**Gopal**	**Devi**
9	Number of service calls	150	240	40	120	180
10	Number of Web-based parts orders	120	210	60	150	150
11	Number of bills (or reminders)	30	90	90	60	120

Required

1. Compute customer-level operating income using the new information that Seema has gathered.
2. Prepare exhibits for IS similar to Exhibits 14-4 and 14-5. Comment on the results.
3. What options should IS consider, with regard to individual customers, in light of the new data and analysis of office overhead?

Solution

1.

	Anoop	Om	White	Gopal	Devi
Revenues	₹26,00,000	₹20,00,000	₹32,20,000	₹12,20,000	₹21,20,000
Technician and equipment cost	18,20,000	17,50,000	22,50,000	10,70,000	17,80,000
Gross margin	7,80,000	2,50,000	9,70,000	1,50,000	3,40,000
Service call handling (₹750 × 150; 240; 40; 120; 180)	1,12,500	1,80,000	30,000	90,000	1,35,000
Web-based parts ordering (₹800 × 120; 210; 60; 150; 150)	96,000	1,68,000	48,000	1,20,000	1,20,000
Billing/Collection (₹500 × 30; 90; 90; 60; 120)	15,000	45,000	45,000	30,000	60,000
Database maintenance (₹100 × 150; 240; 40; 120; 180)	15,000	24,000	4,000	12,000	18,000
Customer-level operating income	₹5,41,500	₹(1,67,000)	₹8,43,000	₹(1,02,000)	₹7,000

2. Customers Ranked on Customer-Level Operating Income

Customer Code	Customer-Level Operating Income (1)	Customer Revenue (2)	Customer-Level Operating Income as a % of Revenue (3) = (1) ÷ (2)	Cumulative Customer-Level Operating Income (4)	Cumulative Customer-Level Operating Income as a % of Total Customer-Level Operating Income (5) = (4) ÷ ₹11,22,500
White	₹8,43,000	₹32,20,000	26.18%	₹8,43,000	75%
Anoop	5,41,500	26,00,000	20.83%	13,84,500	123%
Devi	7,000	21,20,000	0.33%	13,91,500	124%
Gopal	(1,02,000)	12,20,000	−8.36%	12,89,500	115%
Om	(1,67,000)	20,00,000	−8.35%	11,22,500	100%
	₹11,22,500	₹1,11,60,000			

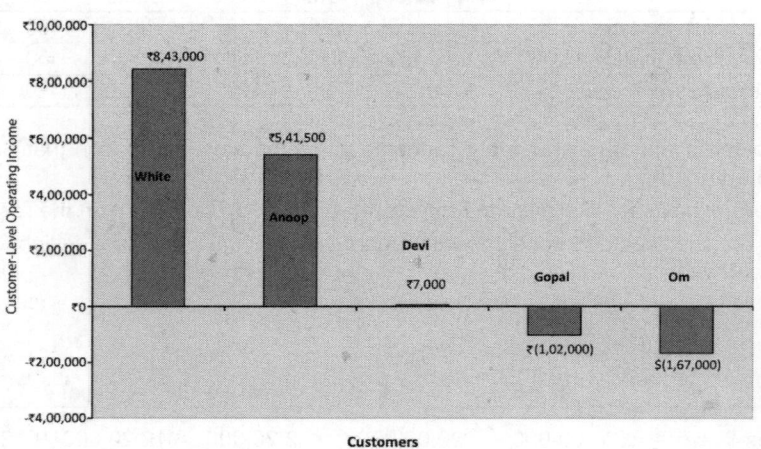

Customer-Level Operating

The table and graph above present the summary results.

The following is the whale curve of cumulative profitability for Instantw Service's customers.

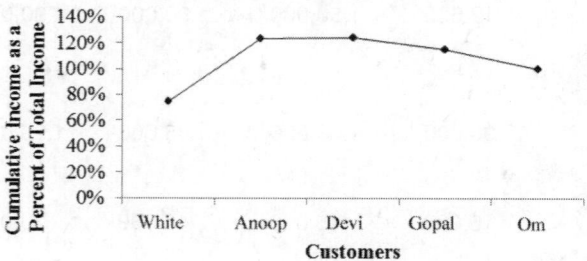

Whale Curve of Cumulative Profitability for Instant Service's Customers

White, the most profitable customer, provides 75% of total operating income. The three best customers provide 124% of IS's operating income, and the other two, by incurring losses for IS, erode the extra 24% of operating income down to IS's operating income.

3. The options that IS should consider include:

   a. Increase the attention paid to White and Anoop. These are "key customers," and every effort has to be made to ensure they retain IS. IS may well want to suggest a minor price reduction to signal how important it is in their view to provide a cost-effective service to these customers.

   b. Seek ways of reducing the costs or increasing the revenues of the problem accounts— Om and Gopal. For example, are the copying machines at those customer locations outdated and in need of repair? If yes, an increased charge may be appropriate. Can IS provide better on-site guidelines to users about ways to reduce breakdowns?

   c. As a last resort, IS may want to consider dropping particular accounts. For example, if Gopal (or Om) will not agree to a fee increase but has machines continually break-ing down, IS may well decide that it is time not to bid on any more work for that customer. But care must then be taken to otherwise use or get rid of the excess fixed capacity created by "firing" unprofitable customers.

14-19 Cost allocation and decision making. Greenbold Manufacturing has four divisions named after its locations: Delhi, Bangalore, Kolkata, and Chennai. Corporate headquarters is in Mumbai. Greenbold corporate headquarters incurs ₹84,00,000 per period, which is an indirect cost of the divisions. Corporate headquarters currently allocates this cost to the divisions based on the revenues of each division. The CEO has asked each division manager to suggest an allo-cation base for the indirect headquarters costs from among revenues, segment margin, direct costs, and number of employees. The following is relevant information about each division:

	Delhi	Bangalore	Kolkata	Chennai
Revenues	₹1,17,00,000	₹1,27,50,000	₹93,00,000	₹82,50,000
Direct costs	79,50,000	61,50,000	64,50,000	69,00,000
Segment margin	₹37,50,000	₹66,00,000	₹28,50,000	₹13,50,000
Number of employees	3,000	6,000	2,250	750

Required

1. Allocate the indirect headquarters costs of Greenbold Manufacturing to each of the four divisions using revenues, direct costs, segment margin, and number of employees as the allocation bases. Calculate operating margins for each division after allocating headquarters costs.

2. Which allocation base do you think the manager of the Chennai division would prefer? Explain.

3. What factors would you consider in deciding which allocation base Greenbold should use?

4. Suppose the Greenbold CEO decides to use direct costs as the allocation base. Should the Chennai division be closed? Why or why not?

Solution

1. Allocations based on revenues.

	Delhi	Bangalore	Kolkata	Chennai	Total
1. Revenues	₹1,17,00,000	₹1,27,50,000	₹93,00,000	₹82,50,000	₹4,20,00,000
2. % revenues (1,17,00,000; 1,27,50,000; 93,00,000; 82,50,000 ÷ 4,20,00,000)	27.86%	30.36%	22.14%	19.64%	100%
3. Allocated headquarter cost (Row 2 × ₹84,00,000)	₹23,40,240	₹25,50,240	₹18,59,760	₹16,49,760	₹56,00,000

	Delhi	Bangalore	Kolkata	Chennai	Total
Segment margin	₹37,50,000	₹66,00,000	₹28,50,000	₹13,50,000	₹1,45,50,000
Less: Headquarter costs	23,40,240	25,50,240	18,59,760	16,49,760	84,00,000
Division margin	₹14,09,760	₹40,49,760	₹9,90,240	₹(2,99,760)	₹61,50,000

2. Allocations based on direct costs.

	Delhi	Bangalore	Kolkata	Chennai	Total
1. Direct Costs	₹79,50,000	₹61,50,000	₹64,50,000	₹69,00,000	₹2,74,50,000
2. % direct costs ₹79,50,000; ₹61,50,000; ₹64,50,000; ₹69,00,000 ÷ ₹2,74,50,000	28.96%	22.40%	23.50%	25.14%	100%
(Row 2 × ₹84,00,000)	₹24,32,640	₹18,81,600	₹19,74,000	₹21,11,760	₹84,00,000

3. Allocated headquarter cost

	Delhi	Bangalore	Kolkata	Chennai	Total
Segment margin	₹37,50,000	₹66,00,000	₹28,50,000	₹13,50,000	₹1,45,50,000
Less: Headquarter costs	24,32,640	18,81,600	19,74,000	21,11,760	84,00,000
Division margin	₹13,17,360	₹47,18,400	₹8,76,000	₹(7,61,760)	₹61,50,000

4. Allocations based on segment margin.

	Delhi	Bangalore	Kolkata	Chennai	Total
1. Segment Margins	₹37,50,000	₹66,00,000	₹28,50,000	13,50,000	₹1,45,50,000
2. % segment margins ₹37,50,000; ₹66,00,000; ₹28,50,000; ₹13,50,000 ÷ ₹1,45,50,000	25.77%	45.36%	19.59%	9.28%	100%
3. Allocated headquarter cost (Row 2 × ₹84,00,000)	₹21,64,680	₹38,10,240	₹16,45,560	₹7,79,520	₹84,00,000

	Delhi	Bangalore	Kolkata	Chennai	Total
Segment margin	₹37,50,000	₹66,00,000	₹28,50,000	₹13,50,000	₹1,45,50,000
Less: Headquarter costs	21,64,680	38,10,240	16,45,560	7,79,520	84,00,000
Division margin	₹15,85,320	₹27,89,760	₹12,04,440	₹5,70,480	₹61,50,000

5 Allocations based on number of employees.

	Delhi	Bangalore	Kolkata	Chennai	Total
1. Number of Employees	3,000	6,000	2,250	750	12,000
2. % Number of employees 3,000; 6,000; 2,250; 750 ÷ 12,000	25%	50%	18.75%	6.25%	100%
3. Allocated headquarter cost (Row 2 × ₹84,00,000)	₹21,00,000	₹42,00,000	₹15,75,000	₹5,25,000	₹84,00,000

	Delhi	Bangalore	Kolkata	Chennai	Total
Segment margin	₹37,50,000	₹66,00,000	₹28,50,000	₹13,50,000	₹1,45,50,000
Less: Headquarter costs	21,00,000	42,00,000	15,75,000	5,25,000	84,00,000
Division margin	₹16,50,000	₹24,00,000	₹12,75,000	₹8,25,000	₹61,50,000

2. The Chennai Division manager will prefer to use the number of employees as the allocation base because it results in the highest operating margin for the division.

3. The Delhi Division and the Kolkata Division receive roughly the same percentage allocation of headquarter costs regardless of the allocation base used (Delhi range = 25%–29%; Kolkata range = 18.75%–23.5%). However, the Bangalore Division and the Chennai Division vary widely (Bangalore range = 22.4%–50%; Chennai range = 6.25%–25.1%). All four methods are reasonable options, but none clearly meets the cause-and-effect criterion for selecting the allocation base. If larger divisions tend to consume more of headquarters' resources, then using division revenues or number of employees seem to be the best choices. Without compelling reason to change, Greenbold should stay with the division revenues as the allocation base.

Another alternative is to use segment margin as the allocation base on the grounds that this best captures the ability of different divisions to bear corporate overhead costs.

4. If Greenbold elects to use direct costs as the allocation base, the Chennai Division will appear to have a ₹7,61,760 operating loss. Even so, the Chennai Division generates a ₹13,50,000 segment margin before allocating the cost of the corporate headquarters. As seen in the analysis in requirement 1, different allocation bases yield different operating incomes for the Chennai Division, with the direct cost allocation base being the lowest. The Chennai Division should not be closed because (1) the choice of allocation base is not based on a cause-and-effect relation (i.e., it is arbitrary), and (2) the division earns positive segment margin, which contributes to covering the cost of the corporate headquarters. The Chennai Division should only be closed if closing it will save more than ₹7,61,760 in corporate headquarter costs—a highly unlikely scenario.

14-20 Purposes of cost allocation Vandana recently started a job as an administrative assistant in the cost accounting department of a new Manufacturing firm producing small components used in computer. New to the area of cost accounting, Vandana is puzzled by the fact that one of its manufactured products, SR460, has a different cost depending on who asks for it. When the marketing department requested the cost of SR460 in order to determine pricing for the new catalog, Vandana was told to report one amount, but when a request came in the very next day from the financial reporting department for the cost of SR460, she was told to report a very different cost. Vandana runs a report using firm's cost accounting system, which produces the following cost elements for one unit of SR460:

Direct materials	₹57.00
Direct manufacturing labor	32.70
Variable manufacturing overhead	17.52
Allocated fixed manufacturing overhead	65.68
Research and development costs specific to SR460[a]	12.40
Marketing costs[a]	11.90
Sales commissions[a]	22.80
Allocated administrative costs of production department	10.76
Allocated administrative costs of corporate headquarters	37.20
Customer service costs[a]	6.10
Distribution costs[a]	17.60

[a]These costs are specific to SR460, but would not be eliminated if SR460 were purchased from an outside supplier. Allocated costs would be reallocated elsewhere in the company should the company cease production of SR460.

Required

1 Explain to Vandana why the cost given to the marketing and financial reporting departments would be different.

2 Calculate the cost of one unit of SR460 to determine the following:
   a. The selling price of SR460
   b. The cost of inventory for financial reporting
   c. Whether to continue manufacturing SR460 or to purchase it from an outside source (Assume that SR460 is used as a component in one of Firm's other products.)
   e. The ability of Firm's production manager to control costs

Solution

1. Financial reporting is guided by GAAP when determining the cost of a product such as SR460. Therefore, only inventoriable costs, such as direct materials, direct labor, and manufacturing overhead, are included in the cost of SR460 that are given to the financial reporting department. In contrast, managers at Firm will include any relevant costs when making internal decisions, such as pricing for the new catalog. Typically, pricing decisions are based on full costing or all of the costs related to the product.

2. For the four different purposes considered in the question, the cost of one unit of SR460 would be determined as follows:

	A	B	C	D
Direct materials	₹57.00	₹57.00	₹57.00	₹57.00
Direct manufacturing labor	32.70	32.70	32.70	32.70
Variable manufacturing overhead	17.52	17.52	17.52	17.52
Allocated fixed manufacturing overhead	65.68	65.68		65.68
Research and development costs specific to SR460	12.40			
Marketing costs	11.90			
Sales commissions	22.80			
Allocated administrative costs of production depart.	10.76			10.76
Allocated administrative costs of corporate headquarters	37.20			
Customer service costs	6.10			
Distribution costs	17.60			
Total	₹29,166	₹17,290	₹10,722	₹18,366

14-21 Cost allocation and decision making. Greenbold Manufacturing has four divisions named after its locations: Arizona, Colorado, Delaware, and Florida. Corporate headquarters is in Minnesota. Greenbold corporate headquarters incurs ₹84,00,000 per period, which is an indirect cost of the divisions. Corporate headquarters currently allocates this cost to the divisions based on the revenues of each division. The CEO has asked each division manager to suggest an allocation base for the indirect headquarters costs from among revenues, segment margin, direct costs, and number of employees. The following is relevant information about each division:

	Delhi	Bangalore	Kolkatta	Chennai
Revenues	₹11,700,000	₹12,750,000	₹93,00,000	₹82,50,000
Direct costs	79,50,000	6,150,000	64,50,000	69,00,000
Segment margin	₹37,50,000	₹66,00,000	₹28,50,000	₹13,50,000
Number of employees	3,000	6,000	2,250	750

Required

1. Allocate the indirect headquarters costs of Greenbold Manufacturing to each of the four divisions using revenues, direct costs, segment margin, and number of employees as the allocation bases. Calculate operating margins for each division after allocating headquarters costs.

2. Which allocation base do you think the manager of the Chennai division would prefer? Explain.

3. What factors would you consider in deciding which allocation base Greenbold should use?

4. Suppose the Greenbold CEO decides to use direct costs as the allocation base. Should the Chennai division be closed? Why or why not?

14-22 Market-share and market-size variances (continuation of 14-21). Coca Cola prepared for 2006 assuming a 10 percent market share based on total sales in the Western region of India. The total soft drinks market was estimated to reach sales of 250 lakh cartons in the region. However, actual total sales volume in the Western region was 240 lakh cartons.

Calculate the market-share and market-size variances for Coca Cola in 2015. (Report all variances in terms of contribution margin.) Comment on the results.

Solution

Market-share and market-size variances (continuation of 14-21).

	Actual	Budgeted
Western region	240 lakh	250 lakh
Coca cola	30 lakh	25 lakh
Market share	12.5%	10%

Average budgeted contribution margin per unit = ₹21.08 (₹5,27,00,000 × 25,00,000)

Solution Exhibit 14-22 presents the sales-quantity variance, market-size variance, and market-share variance for 2015.

$$\text{Market-share variance} = \begin{pmatrix} \text{Actual} \\ \text{market size} \\ \text{in units} \end{pmatrix} \times \begin{pmatrix} \text{Actual} \\ \text{market} \\ \text{share} \end{pmatrix} - \begin{pmatrix} \text{Budgeted} \\ \text{market} \\ \text{share} \end{pmatrix} \times \begin{pmatrix} \text{Budgeted} \\ \text{contribution margin} \\ \text{per composite unit} \\ \text{for budgeted mix} \end{pmatrix}$$

= 2,40,00,000 × (0.125 − 0.10) × ₹21.08

= 2,40,00,000 × .025 × ₹21.08

= ₹1,26,48,000 F

$$\text{Market-size variance} = \begin{pmatrix} \text{Actual} \\ \text{market size} \\ \text{in units} \end{pmatrix} - \begin{pmatrix} \text{Budgeted} \\ \text{market size} \\ \text{in units} \end{pmatrix} \times \begin{pmatrix} \text{Budgeted} \\ \text{market} \\ \text{share} \end{pmatrix} \times \begin{pmatrix} \text{Budgeted} \\ \text{contribution margin} \\ \text{per composite unit} \\ \text{for budgeted mix} \end{pmatrix}$$

= (2,40,00,000 − 2,50,00,000) × 0.10 × ₹21.08

= −10,00,000 × 0.10 × ₹21.08

= ₹21,08,000 U

The market share variance is favorable because the actual 12.5% market share was higher than the budgeted 10% market share. The market size variance is unfavorable because the market size decreased 4% [(2,50,00,000 − 2,40,00,000) ÷ 2,50,00,000].

While the overall total market size declined (from 250 lakh to 240 lakh), the increase in market share meant a favorable sales-quantity variance.

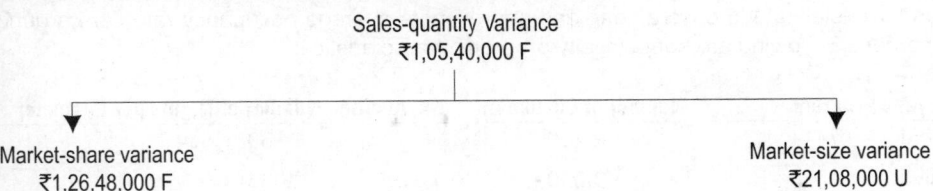

Sales-quantity Variance
₹1,05,40,000 F

Market-share variance
₹1,26,48,000 F

Market-size variance
₹21,08,000 U

Solution Exhibit 14-22

Market-Share and Market-Size Variance Analysis for 2015

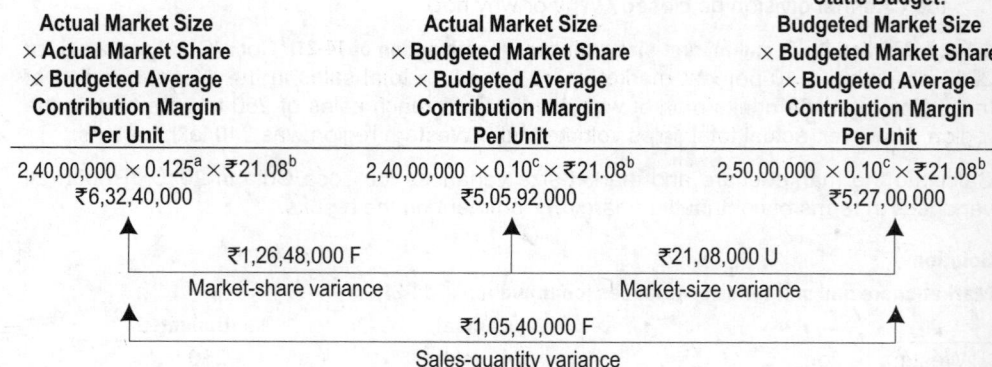

Actual Market Size × Actual Market Share × Budgeted Average Contribution Margin Per Unit	Actual Market Size × Budgeted Market Share × Budgeted Average Contribution Margin Per Unit	Static Budget: Budgeted Market Size × Budgeted Market Share × Budgeted Average Contribution Margin Per Unit
$2,40,00,000 \times 0.125^a \times ₹21.08^b$	$2,40,00,000 \times 0.10^c \times ₹21.08^b$	$2,50,00,000 \times 0.10^c \times ₹21.08^b$
₹6,32,40,000	₹5,05,92,000	₹5,27,00,000

₹1,26,48,000 F
Market-share variance

₹21,08,000 U
Market-size variance

₹1,05,40,000 F
Sales-quantity variance

F = favorable effect on operating income; U = unfavorable effect on operating income

[a]Actual market share: 30,00,000 units × 2,40,00,000 units = 0.125, or 12.5%

[b]Budgeted average contribution margin per unit ₹5,27,00,000 × 25,00,000 units = ₹21.08 per unit

[c]Budgeted market share: 25,00,000 units × 2,50,00,000 units = 0.10, or 10%

14-23 Customer loyalty clubs and profitability analysis. The Taj Group of Hotels chain embarked on a new customer loyalty program in 2015. The 2015 year-end data have been collected, and it is now time for you to determine whether the loyalty program should be continued, discontinued, or perhaps altered to improve loyalty and profitability levels at Taj.

Taj's loyalty program consists of three different customer loyalty levels. All new customers can sign up for the Taj Bronze Card. This card provides guests with a complimentary bottle of beer per night (cost to the chain is ₹50 per bottle) and ₹200 in restaurant coupons each night (cost to the chain is ₹100). Bronze customers also receive a 10 percent discount off the nightly rate. The program enables the chain to track a member's stays and activities. Once customers have stayed and paid for 20 nights at any of the chain's locations worldwide, they are upgraded to Silver Customer status. Silver benefits include the bottle of beer (cost to the chain is ₹50 per bottle per night), ₹300 in restaurant coupons per night (cost to the chain is ₹150), and a 20 percent off every night from the 21st night on. A customer who reaches the 50.night level is upgraded to Gold Customer status. Gold status increases the nightly discount to 30 percent and replaces the ₹50 bottle of beer with a bottle of champagne per night (cost to the chain is ₹200 per bottle). As well, ₹400 in restaurant coupons per night are granted (cost to the chain is ₹200). Assume all bottles and coupons offered are used.

The average full price for one night's stay is ₹2,000. The chain incurs variable costs of ₹650 per night, exclusive of loyalty program costs. Total fixed costs for the chain are ₹1,40,58,00,000. Taj operates 10 hotels, with, on average, 500 rooms each. All hotels are open for business 365 days a year, and approximate average occupancy rates are around 80 percent. Following are some loyalty program characteristics:

Loyalty Program	Number of Customers	Average Number of Nights per Customer
Gold	2,430	60
Silver	8,340	35
Bronze	80,300	10
No program	2,19,000	1

Note that a Gold Customer would have received the 10 percent discount for his or her first 20 stays, received the 20 percent discount for the next 30 stays, and the 30 percent discount only for the last 10 nights. Assume that all program members signed on to the program the first time they stayed with one of the chain's hotels. Also, assume the restaurants are managed by a 100 percent-owned subsidiary of Taj.

Required

1. Calculate the program contribution margin for each of the three programs, as well as for the customers not subscribing to the loyalty program. Which of the programs is the most profitable? Which is the least profitable? Do not allocate fixed costs to individual rooms or specific loyalty programs.

2. Prepare an income statement for Taj for the year ended December 31, 2015.

3. What is the average room rate per night3 What are average variable costs per night inclusive of the loyalty program?

4. Explain what drives the profitability (or lack thereof) of Taj's loyalty program.

Solution

Customer loyalty clubs and profitability analysis.

1.

Gold Program

Revenues

2,430 × 20 × (₹2,000 × 0.90)	₹8,74,80,000
2,430 × 30 × (₹2,000 × 0.80)	11,66,40,000
2,430 × 10 × (₹2,000 × 0.70)	3,40,20,000
Total revenues	23,81,40,000

Variable Costs

Hotel variable costs, 2,430 × 60 × ₹650	9,47,70,000
Beer Costs	
2,430 × 50 × ₹50	60,75,000
2,430 × 10 × ₹200	48,60,000
Restaurant costs	
2,430 × 20 × ₹100	48,60,000
2,430 × 30 × ₹150	1,09,35,000
2,430 × 10 × ₹200	48,60,000
Total variable costs	12,63,60,000
Contribution margin	₹11,17,80,000

Silver Program

Revenues

8,340 × 20 × (₹2,000 × 0.90)	₹30,02,40,000
8,340 × 15 × (₹2,000 × 0.80)	20,01,60,000
Total revenues	50,04,00,000

Variable Costs

Hotel variable costs, 8,340 × 35 × ₹650	18,97,35,000
Beer costs, 8,340 × 35 × ₹50	1,45,95,000
Restaurant Costs	
8,340 × 20 × ₹100	1,66,80,000
8,340 × 15 × ₹150	1,87,65,000
Total variable costs	23,97,75,000
Contribution margin	₹26,06,25,000

Bronze Program

Revenues, 80,300 × 10 × (₹2,000 × 0.90)	₹1,44,54,00,000
Variable costs	

Hotel variable costs, 80,300 × 10 × ₹650	52,19,50,000
Beer costs 80,300 × 10 × ₹50	4,01,50,000
Restaurant costs 80,300 × 10 × ₹100	8,03,00,000
Total variable costs	64,24,00,000
Contribution margin	₹80,30,00,000
No Program	
Revenues, 2,19,000 × 1 × ₹2,000	₹43,80,00,000
Variable costs, 2,19,000 × 1 × ₹650	14,23,50,000
Contribution margin	₹29,56,50,000

Loyalty program	Total Revenues	Variable Costs	Contribution Margin	Contribution Margin Total Revenues
Gold	₹23,81,40,000	₹12,63,60,000	₹11,17,80,000	46.94%
Silver	50,04,00,000	23,97,75,000	26,06,25,000	52.08
Bronze	1,44,54,00,000	64,24,00,000	80,30,00,000	55.56
No program	43,80,00,000	14,23,50,000	29,56,50,000	67.50
Total	₹2,62,19,40,000	₹1,15,08,85,000	₹1,47,10,55,000	

The no-program group of customers has the highest contribution margin per revenue rupee. However, it comprises only 16.71% (₹43,80,00,000 × ₹2,62,19,40,000) of total revenues. The gold program has the lowest contribution margin per revenue rupee. However, it is misleading to evaluate each program in isolation. A key aim of loyalty programs is to promote a high frequency of return business. The contribution margin to total revenue ratio of each program in isolation does not address this issue.

2.

Revenues	₹2,62,19,40,000
Variable costs	1,15,08,85,000
Contribution margin	1,47,10,55,000
Fixed costs	1,40,58,00,000
Operating income	₹6,52,55,000

3. Number of room nights

Gold, 2,430 × 60	1,45,800
Silver, 8,340 × 35	2,91,900
Bronze, 80,300 × 10	8,03,000
No program, 2,19,000 × 1	2,19,000
	14,59,700

Average room rate per night: $\dfrac{₹2,62,19,40,000}{14,59,700} = ₹796.22$

Average variable cost per night: $\dfrac{₹1,15,08,85,000}{14,59,700} = ₹788.44$

4. Taj Group of Hotels has fixed costs of ₹1,40,58,00,000. A key challenge is to attract a high number of repeat business customers. Loyalty programs aim to have customers return to Taj multiple times. Their aim is increasing the revenues beyond what they would be without the program. It is to be expected that the higher the level of nights stayed, the greater the inducements necessary to keep attracting the customer to return. However, given the low level of variable costs to room rates, there is considerable cushion available for Taj Group of Hotels to offer high inducements for frequent stayers.

Taj Group of Hotels could adopt a net present value analysis of customers who are in the different loyalty clubs. It would be informative for Taj Group of Hotels to have information on how much of each customer's total lodging industry expenditures it captures. It may well want to give higher levels of inducements to frequent stayers if the

current program attracts only, say, 30% of each of its frequent customer's total business in cities where it has lodging properties available.

14-24 Customer profitability in a manufacturing firm. Bajaj Electricals makes a component
called A1030. This component is manufactured only when ordered by a customer, so Bajaj
keeps no inventory of A1030. The list price is ₹115 per unit, but customers who place "large"
orders receive a 12% discount on price. The customers are manufacturing firms. Currently,
the salespeople decide whether an order is large enough to qualify for the discount. When
the product is finished, it is packed in cases of 10. If the component needs to be exchanged
or repaired, customers can come back within 10 days for free exchange or repair.

The full cost of manufacturing a unit of A1030 is ₹95. In addition, Bajaj incurs customer-
level costs.

Customer-level cost-driver rates are:

Order taking	₹360 per order
Product handling	₹15 per case
Rush order processing	₹560 per rush order
Exchange and repair	₹50 per unit

Information about Bajaj's five biggest customers follows:

	A	B	C	D	E
Number of units purchased	5,400	1,800	1,200	4,400	8,100
Discounts given	12%	12%	0	12%	12% on half the units
Number of orders	8	16	52	20	16
Number of cases	540	180	120	440	810
Number of rush orders	1	6	1	0	5
Number of units exchanged/repaired	14	72	16	40	180

All customers except E ordered units in the same order size. Customer E's order quantity
varied, so E got a discount part of the time but not all the time.

Required

1. Calculate the customer-level operating income for these five customers. Use the format
   in Exhibit 14-3. Prepare a customer-profitability analysis by ranking the customers from
   most to least profitable, as in Exhibit 14-4.
2. Discuss the results of your customer-profitability analysis. Does Bajaj have unprofitable
   customers? Is there anything Bajaj should do differently with its five customers?

Solution

1. Calculation of customer profitability by customer:

	Customer				
	A	B	C	D	E
Revenues at list price					
₹115 × 5,400; 1,800; 1,200; 4,400; 8,100	₹6,21,000	₹2,07,000	₹1,38,000	₹5,06,000	₹9,31,500
Price discount					
12% × ₹6,21,000; 12% × ₹2,07,000; 0; 12% × ₹5,06,000; 12% × (8,100 × 50%) × ₹115	74,520	24,840	0	60,720	55,890
Revenues (actual price)	5,46,480	1,82,160	1,38,000	4,45,280	8,75,610
Cost of goods sold					
₹95 × 5,400; 1,800; 1,200; 4,400; 8,100	5,13,000	1,71,000	1,14,000	4,18,000	7,69,500
Gross margin	33,480	11,160	24,000	27,280	1,06,110

Customer-level costs:
Order taking

₹360 × 8; 16; 52; 20; 16	2,880	5,760	18,720	7,200	5,760
Product handling					
₹15 × 540; 180; 120; 440; 810	8,100	2,700	1,800	6,600	12,150
Rush order processing					
₹560 × 1; 6; 1; 0; 5	560	3,360	560	0	2,800
Exchange and repair					
₹50 × 14; 72; 16; 40; 180	700	3,600	800	2,000	9,000
Total customer-level costs	12,240	15,420	21,880	15,800	29,710
Customer-level operating income	21,240	(4,260)	2,120	11,480	76,400

Customer ranking

Customer Code	Customer-Level Operating Income (1)	Customer Revenue (2)	Customer-Level Operating Income Divided by Revenue (3) = (1) ÷ (2)	Cumulative Customer-Level Operating Income (4)	Cumulative Customer-Level Operating Income as a % of Total Customer-Level Operating Income (5) = (4) ÷ ₹1,06,980
E	₹76,400	₹8,75,610	8.73%	₹76,400	71.42%
A	21,240	5,46,480	3.89%	₹97,640	91.27%
D	11,480	4,45,280	2.58%	₹1,09,120	102.00%
C	2,120	1,38,000	1.54%	₹1,11,240	103.98%
B	(4,260)	1,82,160	−2.34%	₹1,06,980	100.0%
Total	₹1,06,980	₹21,87,530			

2. Customer B is Bajaj's only unprofitable customer. All other customers are profitable in line with revenue.

If Customer B were not being given price discounts, B would be profitable. The salesperson is giving discounts on orders, even though the size of the order is small. It is costing Bajaj money to process many small orders as opposed to a few large orders. To turn Customer B into a profitable customer, Bajaj needs to encourage Customer B to place fewer, larger orders and offer a price discount only if Customer B changes behavior, rather than as a reward for repeat business.

Customer B has many rush orders in proportion to total number of orders. Bajaj should work with Customer B to find a production schedule that would meet its needs without having to rush the order.

Customer E also has many rush orders and large number of units exchanged/repaired that are costly to Bajaj. Bajaj should work with Customer E to align its production schedule to Customer E's needs and reduce the number of units exchanged/repaired.

Customer C has a low operating income and operating income as a percentage of revenues. Customer C places a large number of small orders and gets no price discounts. Bajaj could work with Customer C to reduce the number of orders by encouraging Customer C to take price discounts on large orders. Bajaj should also work with Customer C to reduce the number of units exchanged/repaired.

The exchange and repair rate for customers with rush orders is higher than for other customers. Bajaj should explore whether rushing an order reduces attention to quality. Either reducing the number of rush orders (which would also save Bajaj money) or working toward increasing the quality of rush orders would help to reduce these costs.

The three most profitable customers (E, A, and D) generate 102% of the customer-level operating income. These customers are valued customers and should receive the highest level of customer service.

14-25 Variance analysis, multiple products. Parle, operates a chain of cookie stores. Budgeted and actual operating data of its three stores for August are as follows:

Budget for August

	Selling Price per Pound	Variable Cost per Pound	Contribution Margin per Pound	Sales Volume in Pounds
Chocolate chip	₹45.0	₹25.0	₹20.0	45,000
Oatmeal raisin	50.0	27.0	23.0	25,000
Coconut	55.0	29.0	26.0	10,000

Budget for August (continued)

	Selling Price per Pound	Variable Cost per Pound	Contribution Margin per Pound	Sales Volume in Pounds
White chocolate	60.0	30.0	30.0	5,000
Macadamia nut	65.0	34.0	31.0	15,000
				1,00,000

Actual for August

	Selling Price per Pound	Variable Cost per Pound	Contribution Margin in Pounds	Sales Volume per Pound
Chocolate chip	₹45.0	₹26.0	₹19.0	57,600
Oatmeal raisin	52.0	29.0	23.0	18,000
Coconut	55.0	28.0	27.0	9,600
White chocolate	60.0	34.0	26.0	13,200
Macadamia nut	70.0	40.0	30.0	21,600
				1,20,000

Required

Parle's focuses on contribution margin in its variance analysis.
1. Compute the total sales-volume variance for August.
2. Compute the total sales-mix variance for August.
3. Compute the total sales-quantity variance for August.
4. Comment on your results in requirements 1,2, and 3.

Solution

Variance analysis, multiple products.

1, 2, and 3. Solution Exhibit 14-25 presents the sales-volume, sales-quantity, and sales-mix variances for each type of cookie and in total for Parle in August.

The sales-volume variances can also be computed as:

$$\text{Sales - volume variance} = \left(\begin{array}{c} \text{Actual sales} \\ \text{quantity in pounds} \end{array} - \begin{array}{c} \text{Budgeted sales} \\ \text{quantity in punds} \end{array} \right) \times \begin{array}{c} \text{Budgeted contribution} \\ \text{margin per pound} \end{array}$$

The sales-volume variances are:

Chocolate chip = (57,600 – 45,000) × ₹20 =		₹2,52,000 F
Oatmeal raisin = (18,000 – 25,000) × ₹23 =		1,61,000 U
Coconut = (9,600 – 10,000) × ₹26 =		10,400 U
White chocolate = (13,200 – 5,000) × ₹30 =		2,46,000 F
Macadamia nut = (21,600 – 15,000) × ₹31 =		2,04,600 F
All cookies		₹5,31,200 F

The sales-quantity variance can also be computed as:

$$\text{Sales-quantity variance} = \left(\begin{array}{c}\text{Actual pounds of all} \\ \text{cookies sold}\end{array} - \begin{array}{c}\text{Budgeted pounds of all} \\ \text{cookies sold}\end{array}\right) \times \begin{array}{c}\text{Budgeted sales-Budgeted contribution} \\ \text{mix percentage} \times \text{margin per pound}\end{array}$$

Chocolate chip	= (1,20,000 – 1,00,000) × 0.45 × ₹20 =	₹1,80,000 F
Oatmeal raisin	= (1,20,000 – 1,00,000) × 0.25 × ₹23 =	1,15,000 F
Coconut	= (1,20,000 – 1,00,000) × 0.10 × ₹26 =	52,000 F
White chocolate	= (1,20,000 – 1,00,000) × 0.05 × ₹30 =	30,000 F
Macadamia nut	= (1,20,000 – 1,00,000) × 0.15 × ₹31 =	93,000 F
All cookies		₹4,70,000 F

The sales-mix variance can also be computed as:

$$\text{Sales-mix variance} = \left(\begin{array}{c}\text{Actual sales-} \\ \text{mix percentage}\end{array} - \begin{array}{c}\text{Budgeted sales-} \\ \text{mix percentage}\end{array}\right) \times \begin{array}{c}\text{Actual pounds of all} \\ \text{cookies sold}\end{array} \times \begin{array}{c}\text{Budgeted contribution} \\ \text{margin per pound}\end{array}$$

The sales-mix variances are:

Chocolate chip	= (0.48 – 0.45) × 1,20,000 × ₹20	= ₹72,000 F
Oatmeal raisin	= (0.15 – 0.25) × 1,20,000 × ₹23	= 2,76,000 U
Coconut	= (0.08 – 0.10) × 1,20,000 × ₹26	= 62,400 U
White chocolate	= (0.11 – 0.05) – 1,20,000 × ₹30	= 2,16,000 F
Macadamia nut	= (0.18 – 0.15) × 1,20,000 × ₹31	= 1,11,600 F
All cookies		₹61,200 F

A summary of the variances is:

Sales-Volume Variance

Chocolate chip	₹2,52,000 F
Oatmeal raisin	1,61,000 U
Coconut	10,400 U
White chocolate	2,46,000 F
Macadamia nut	2,04,600 F
All cookies	₹5,31,200 F

Sales-Mix Variance		Sales-Quantity Variance	
Chocolate chip	₹72,000 F	Chocolate chip	₹1,80,000F
Oatmeal raisin	2,76,000 U	Oatmeal raisin	1,15,000F
Coconut	62,400 U	Coconut	52,000F
White chocolate	2,16,000 F	White chocolate	30,000F

Macadamia nut	1,11,600 F	Macadamia nut	93,000F
All cookies	₹61,200 F	All cookies	₹4,70,000F

4. Parle shows a favorable sales-quantity variance because it sold more cookies in total than was budgeted. Together with the higher quantities, Parle also sold more of the high-contribution margin white chocolate and macadamia nut cookies relative to the budgeted mix–hence, Parle also showed a favorable total sales-mix variance.

Solution Exhibit 14-25

Columnar Presentation of Sales-Volume, Sales-Quantity, and Sales-Mix Variances: for Parle

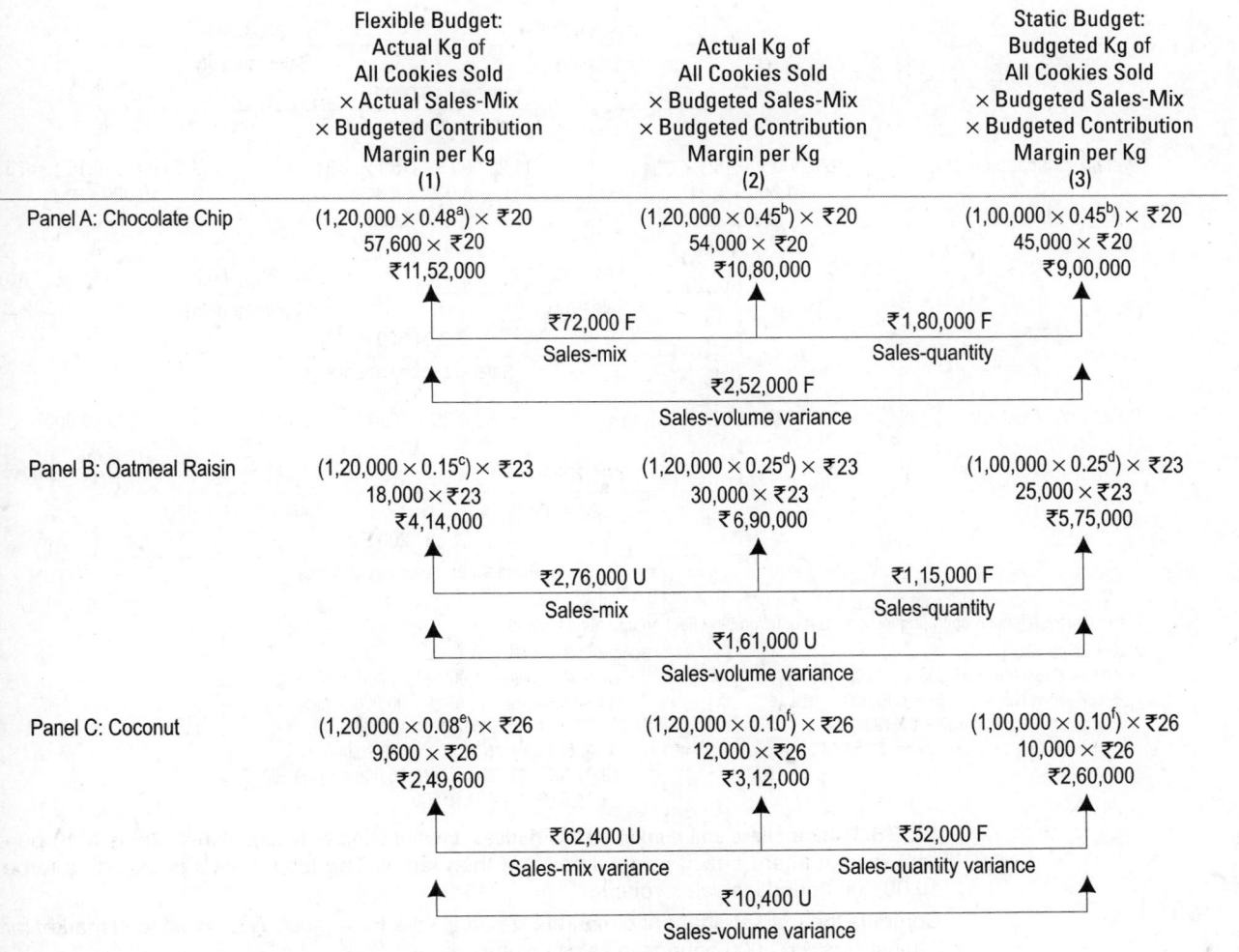

F = favorable effect on operating income; U = unfavorable effect on operating income.

Actual Sales Mix:
[a]Chocolate Chip = 57,600 ÷1,20,000 = 48%
[c]Oatmeal Raisin = 18,000 ÷1,20,000 = 15%
[e]Coconut   = 9,600 ÷1,20,000 = 8%

Budgeted Sales Mix:
[b]Chocolate Chip = 45,000 ÷1,00,000 = 45%
[d]Oatmeal Raisin = 25,000 ÷1,00,000 = 25%
[f]Coconut   = 10,000 ÷1,00,000 = 10%

Solution Exhibit 14-25

Columnar Presentation of Sales-Volume, Sales-Quantity, and Sales-Mix Variances for Parle:

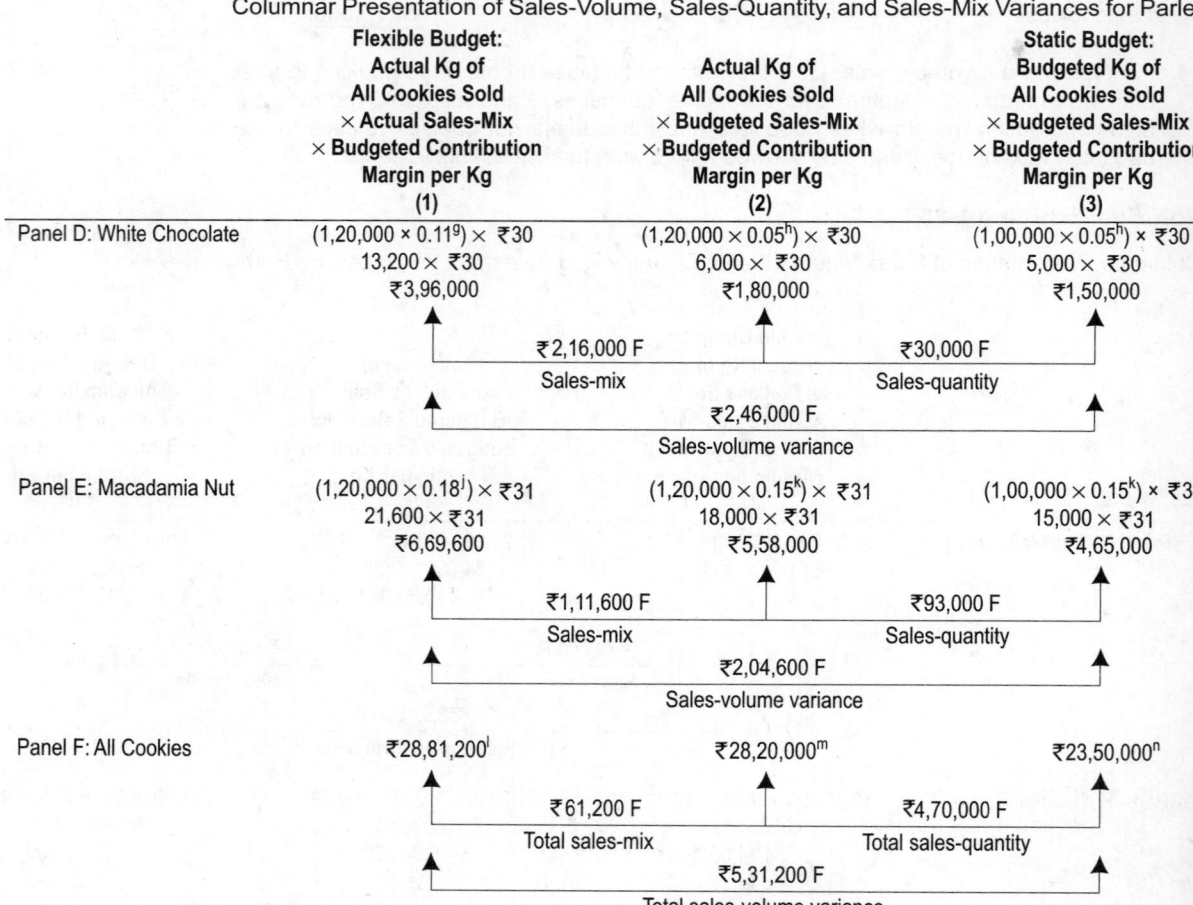

	Flexible Budget: Actual Kg of All Cookies Sold × Actual Sales-Mix × Budgeted Contribution Margin per Kg (1)	Actual Kg of All Cookies Sold × Budgeted Sales-Mix × Budgeted Contribution Margin per Kg (2)	Static Budget: Budgeted Kg of All Cookies Sold × Budgeted Sales-Mix × Budgeted Contribution Margin per Kg (3)
Panel D: White Chocolate	$(1,20,000 \times 0.11^g) \times ₹30$ $13,200 \times ₹30$ ₹3,96,000	$(1,20,000 \times 0.05^h) \times ₹30$ $6,000 \times ₹30$ ₹1,80,000	$(1,00,000 \times 0.05^h) \times ₹30$ $5,000 \times ₹30$ ₹1,50,000

₹2,16,000 F   ₹30,000 F
Sales-mix   Sales-quantity

₹2,46,000 F
Sales-volume variance

| Panel E: Macadamia Nut | $(1,20,000 \times 0.18^j) \times ₹31$ $21,600 \times ₹31$ ₹6,69,600 | $(1,20,000 \times 0.15^k) \times ₹31$ $18,000 \times ₹31$ ₹5,58,000 | $(1,00,000 \times 0.15^k) \times ₹31$ $15,000 \times ₹31$ ₹4,65,000 |

₹1,11,600 F   ₹93,000 F
Sales-mix   Sales-quantity

₹2,04,600 F
Sales-volume variance

| Panel F: All Cookies | ₹28,81,200[l] | ₹28,20,000[m] | ₹23,50,000[n] |

₹61,200 F   ₹4,70,000 F
Total sales-mix   Total sales-quantity

₹5,31,200 F
Total sales-volume variance

F = favorable effect on operating income; U = unfavorable effect on operating income.

Actual Sales Mix:

[g] White Chocolate = $13,200 \div 1,20,000 = 11\%$

[j] Macadamia Nut = $21,600 \div 1,20,000 = 18\%$

[l] ₹11,52,000 + ₹4,14,000 + ₹2,49,600 + ₹3,96,000 + ₹6,69,600 = ₹28,81,200

Budgeted Sales Mix:

[h] White Chocolate = $5,000 \div 1,00,000 = 5\%$

[k] Macadamia Nut = $15,000 \div 1,00,000 = 15\%$

[m] ₹10,80,000 + ₹6,90,000 + ₹3,12,000 + ₹1,80,000 + ₹5,58,000 = ₹28,20,000

[n] ₹9,00,000 + ₹5,75,000 + ₹2,60,000 + ₹1,50,000 + ₹4,65,000 = ₹23,50,000

14-26 Market-share and market-size variances (continuation of 14-25). Parle attains a 10 percent market share based on total sales of the market. The total market is expected to be 10,00,000 pounds in sales volume

Compute the market-share and market-size variances for August. The actual total market for August was 9,60,000 pounds in sales volume.

Required

Compute the market-share and market-size variances for Parle in August. Report all variances in contribution-margin terms. Comment on the results.

Solution

Market-share and market-size variances (continuation of 14-25).

1.

	Actual	Budgeted
Market size	9,60,000	10,00,000
Parle's share	1,20,000	1,00,000
Market share	0.125	0.100

The budgeted average contribution margin per unit (also called budgeted contribution margin per composite unit for budgeted mix) is ₹23.5:

	Budgeted Contribution Margin per Pound	Budgeted Sales Volume in Pounds	Budgeted Contribution Margin
Chocolate chip	₹20	45,000	₹9,00,000
Oatmeal raisin	23	25,000	5,75,000
Coconut	26	10,000	2,60,000
White chocolate	30	5,000	1,50,000
Macadamia nut	31	15,000	4,65,000
All cookies		1,00,000	₹23,50,000

$$\text{Budgeted average contribution margin per unit} = \frac{₹23,50,000}{1,00,000} = ₹23.5$$

$$\begin{array}{l}\text{Market - size variance}\\ \text{in contribution margin}\end{array} = \left(\begin{array}{l}\text{Actual market}\\ \text{size in units}\end{array} - \begin{array}{l}\text{Budgeted market}\\ \text{size in units}\end{array}\right) \times \begin{array}{l}\text{Budgeted}\\ \text{market share}\end{array} \times \begin{array}{l}\text{Budgeted average}\\ \text{contribution margin per unit}\end{array}$$

$$= (9,60,000 \times 10,00,000) \times 0.100 \times ₹23.5$$
$$= ₹94,000 \ U$$

$$\begin{array}{l}\text{Market - size variance}\\ \text{in contribution margin}\end{array} = \begin{array}{l}\text{Actual market}\\ \text{size in units}\end{array} \times \left(\begin{array}{l}\text{Atual}\\ \text{market share}\end{array} - \begin{array}{l}\text{Budgeted}\\ \text{market share}\end{array}\right) \times \begin{array}{l}\text{Budgeted average}\\ \text{contribution margin per unit}\end{array}$$

$$= 9,60,000 \times (0.125 - 0.100) \times ₹23.5$$
$$= ₹5,64,000 \ F$$

By increasing its actual market share from the 10% budgeted to the actual 12.50%, Parle has a favorable market-share variance of ₹5,64,000. There is a smaller offsetting unfavorable market-size variance of ₹94,000 due to the 40,000 unit decline in the total market (from 10,00,000 budgeted to an actual of 9,60,000). Solution Exhibit 14-26 presents the sales-quantity, market-share, and market-size variances for Parle in August.

Solution Exhibit 14-26

Market-Share and Market-Size Variance Analysis of Parle for August

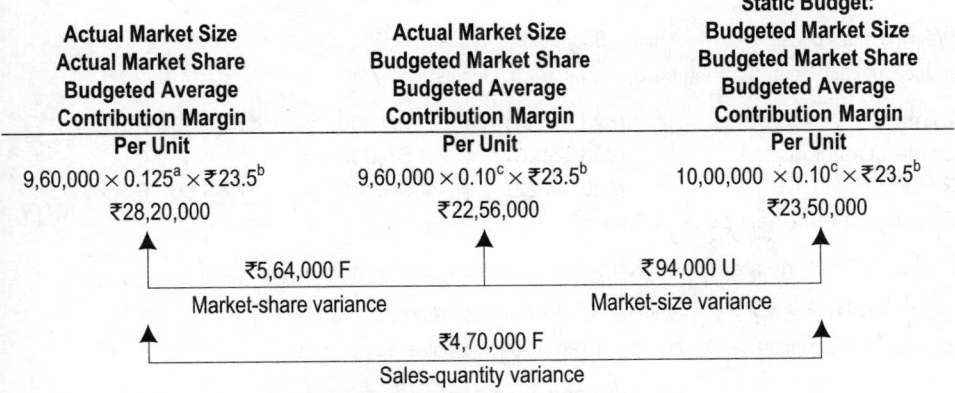

F = favorable effect on operating income; U = unfavorable effect on operating income
[a]Actual market share: 1,20,000 units ÷ 9,60,000 units = 0.125, or 12.5%
[b]Budgeted average contribution margin per unit: ₹ 23,50,000 ÷ 10,00,000 units = ₹23.5 per unit
[c]Budgeted market share: 1,00,000 units ÷ 10,00,000 units = 0.10, or 10%

An overview of Solved Problems 13-25 and 13-26 is:

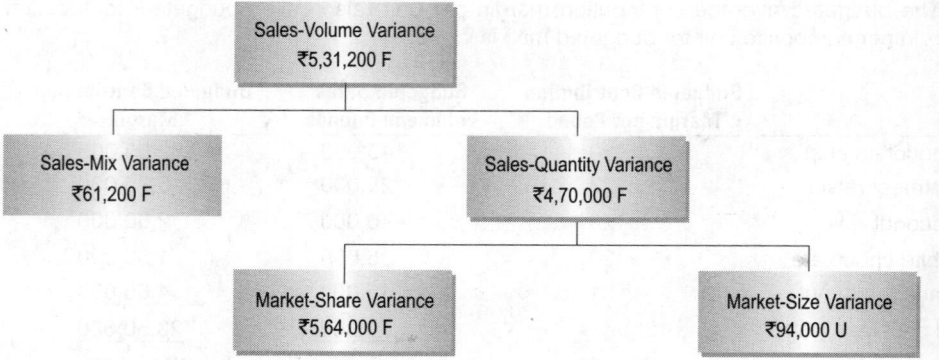

14-27 Direct materials price, efficiency, mix and yield variances. Himachal Foods, manufactures apple products such as apple jelly and applesauce. It makes applesauce by blending Tolman, Golden Delicious, and Ribston apples. Budgeted costs to produce 1,00,000 kg of applesauce in November are as follows:

45,000 kg of Tolman apples at ₹30 per kg	₹13,50,000
1,80,000 kg of Golden Delicious apples at ₹26 per kg	46,80,000
75,000 kg of Ribston apples at ₹22 per kg	16,50,000

Actual costs in November are

62,000 kg of Tolman apples at ₹28 per kg	₹17,36,000
1,55,000 kg of Golden Delicious apples at ₹26 per kg	40,30,000
93,000 kg of Ribston apples at ₹20 per kg	18,60,000

Required

1. Calculate the total direct materials price and efficiency variances for November.
2. Calculate the total direct materials mix and yield variances for November.
3. Comment on your results in requirements 1 and 2.

Solution

Direct Materials Price, Efficiency, Mix and Yield Variances

1. Solution Exhibit 14-27A presents the total price variance (₹3,10,000F), the total efficiency variance (₹2,56,000U), and the total flexible-budget variance (₹54,000F). Total direct materials price variance can also be computed as:

$$\text{Direct materials price variance for each input} = \left(\begin{array}{c}\text{Actual} \\ \text{price}\end{array} - \begin{array}{c}\text{Budgeted} \\ \text{price}\end{array}\right) \times \begin{array}{c}\text{Actual} \\ \text{Inputs}\end{array}$$

Tolman	=	(₹28 – ₹30)	×	62,000 =	₹1,24,000 F
Golden Delicious	=	(₹26 – ₹26)	×	1,55,000 =	0
Ribston	=	(₹20 – ₹22)	×	93,000 =	1,86,000 F
Total direct materials price variance					₹3,10,000 F

Total direct materials efficiency variance can also be computed as:

$$\text{Direct materials efficiency variance for each input} = \left(\begin{array}{c}\text{Actual} \\ \text{inputs}\end{array} - \begin{array}{c}\text{Budgeted inputs allowed} \\ \text{for actual outputs achieved}\end{array}\right) \times \begin{array}{c}\text{Budged} \\ \text{prices}\end{array}$$

Tolman	=	(62,000 – 45,000)	×	₹30	=	₹5,10,000 U
Golden Delicious	=	(1,55,000 – 1,80,000)	×	₹26	=	6,50,000 F
Ribston	=	(93,000 – 75,000)	×	₹22	=	3,96,000 U
Total direct materials efficiency variance						₹2,56,000 U

Solution Exhibit 14-27A

Columnar Presentation of Direct Materials Price and Efficiency Variances for Himachal Foods for November:

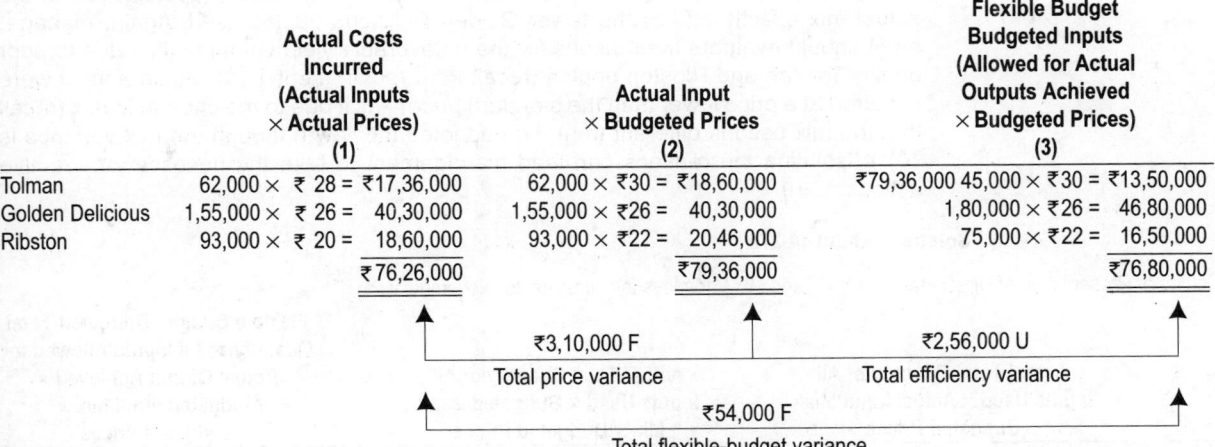

	Actual Costs Incurred (Actual Inputs × Actual Prices) (1)	Actual Input × Budgeted Prices (2)	Flexible Budget Budgeted Inputs (Allowed for Actual Outputs Achieved × Budgeted Prices) (3)
Tolman	62,000 × ₹ 28 = ₹17,36,000	62,000 × ₹30 = ₹18,60,000	₹79,36,000 45,000 × ₹30 = ₹13,50,000
Golden Delicious	1,55,000 × ₹ 26 = 40,30,000	1,55,000 × ₹26 = 40,30,000	1,80,000 × ₹26 = 46,80,000
Ribston	93,000 × ₹ 20 = 18,60,000	93,000 × ₹22 = 20,46,000	75,000 × ₹22 = 16,50,000
	₹76,26,000	₹79,36,000	₹76,80,000

↑ ₹3,10,000 F Total price variance ↑ ₹2,56,000 U Total efficiency variance ↑

↑ ₹54,000 F Total flexible-budget variance ↑

F = favorable effect on operating income; U = unfavorable effect on operating income

2. Solution Exhibit 14-27B presents the total direct materials yield and mix variances for Himachal Foods for November.

   The total direct materials yield variance can also be computed as the sum of the direct materials yield variances for each input:

$$\text{Direct materials yield variance for each input} = \left(\begin{array}{c} \text{Actual total quantity of all direct materials inputs used} - \text{Budgeted total quantity of all direct materials inputs allowed for acutal output achieved} \end{array} \right) \times \begin{array}{c} \text{Budgeted direct materials input mix percentage} \end{array} \times \begin{array}{c} \text{Budgeted price of direct materials inputs} \end{array}$$

Tolman	= (3,10,000 – 3,00,000) × 0.15 × ₹30 = 10,000 × 0.15 × ₹30 =	₹45,000U
Golden Delicious	= (3,10,000 – 3,00,000) × 0.60 × ₹26 = 10,000 × 0.60 × ₹26 =	1,56,000U
Ribston	= (3,10,000 – 3,00,000) × ₹25 × ₹22 = 10,000 × 0.25 × ₹22 =	55,000U
Total direct materials efficiency variance		₹2,56,000U

The total direct materials mix variance can also be computed as the sum of the direct materials mix variances for each input:

$$\text{Direct materials mix variance for each input} = \left(\begin{array}{c} \text{Actual direct materials input mix percentange} - \text{Budgeted direct materials input mix percentage} \end{array} \right) \times \begin{array}{c} \text{Actual total quantity of all direct materials inputs} \end{array}$$

Tolman	= (0.20 – 0.15) × 3,10,000 × ₹30 = 0.05 × 3,10,000 × ₹30 =	₹4,65,000 U
Golden Delicious	= (0.50 – 0.60) × 3,10,000 × ₹26 = –0.10 × 3,10,000 × ₹26 =	8,06,000
Ribston	= (0.30 – 0.25) × 3,10,000 × ₹22 = 0.05 × 3,10,000 × ₹22 =	3,41,000
Total direct materials mix variance		₹0 U

3. Himachal Foods paid less for Tolman and Ribston apples and, so, had a favorable direct materials price variance of ₹3,10,000. It also had an unfavorable efficiency variance of ₹2,56,000. Himachal Foods would need to evaluate if these were unrelated events or if the lower price resulted from the purchase of apples of poorer quality that affected efficiency. The net effect in this case from the cost standpoint was favorable– the savings in price being greater than the loss in efficiency. Of course, if the apple-sauce is of poorer quality, Himachal Foods must also evaluate the potential effects on

current and future revenues that have not been considered in the variances described in requirements 1 and 2. The unfavorable efficiency variance is entirely attributable to an unfavorable yield. The actual mix does deviate from the budgeted mix but at the budgeted prices, the greater quantity of Tolman and Ribston apples used in the actual mix exactly offsets the fewer Golden Delicious apples used. Again, management should evaluate the reasons for the unfavorable yield variance. Is it due to poor quality Tolman and Ribston apples (recall from requirement 1 that these apples were acquired at a price lower than the standard price) × Is it due to the change in mix (recall that the mix used is different from the budgeted mix, even though the mix variance is ₹0) × Isolating the reasons can lead management to take the necessary corrective actions.

Solution Exhibit 14-27B

Columnar Presentation of Direct Materials Yield and Mix Variances for Himachal for November:

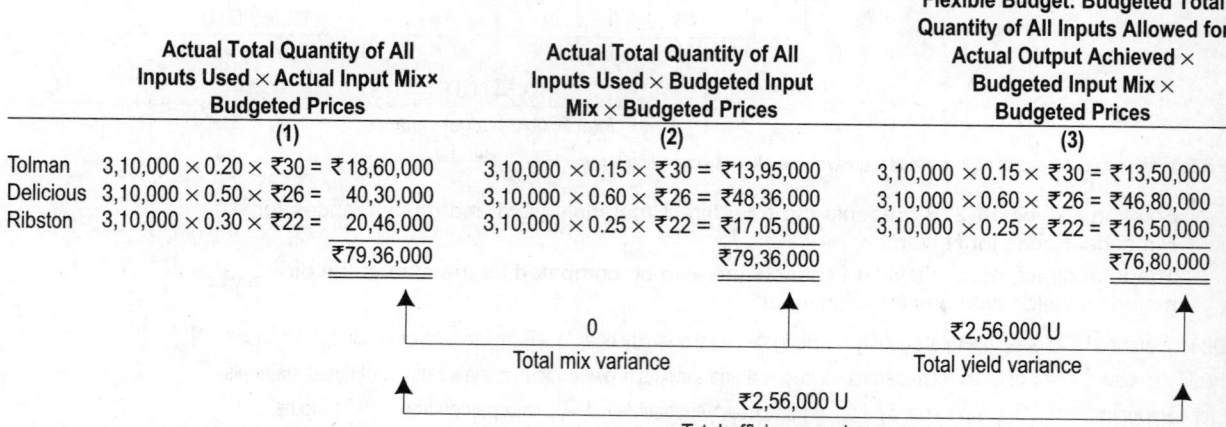

	Actual Total Quantity of All Inputs Used × Actual Input Mix× Budgeted Prices	Actual Total Quantity of All Inputs Used × Budgeted Input Mix × Budgeted Prices	Flexible Budget: Budgeted Total Quantity of All Inputs Allowed for Actual Output Achieved × Budgeted Input Mix × Budgeted Prices
	(1)	(2)	(3)
Tolman	$3,10,000 \times 0.20 \times ₹30 = ₹18,60,000$	$3,10,000 \times 0.15 \times ₹30 = ₹13,95,000$	$3,10,000 \times 0.15 \times ₹30 = ₹13,50,000$
Delicious	$3,10,000 \times 0.50 \times ₹26 = 40,30,000$	$3,10,000 \times 0.60 \times ₹26 = ₹48,36,000$	$3,10,000 \times 0.60 \times ₹26 = ₹46,80,000$
Ribston	$3,10,000 \times 0.30 \times ₹22 = 20,46,000$	$3,10,000 \times 0.25 \times ₹22 = ₹17,05,000$	$3,10,000 \times 0.25 \times ₹22 = ₹16,50,000$
	₹79,36,000	**₹79,36,000**	**₹76,80,000**

0	₹2,56,000 U
Total mix variance	Total yield variance

₹2,56,000 U
Total efficiency variance

F = favorable effect on operating income; U = unfavorable effect on operating income.

Exercises

[*Comprehensive solutions to all exercises are available on the companion website www.pearsoned.co.in/charlesthorngren*]

14-28 Customer profitability, service company. Instant Service (IS) is a repair-service company specializing in the rapid repair of photocopying machines. Each of its 10 clients pays a fixed monthly service fee (based on the type of photocopying machines owned by that client and the number of employees at that site). IS keeps records of the time technicians spend at each client's location and the cost of the equipment used to repair each photocopying machine. IS recently decided to compute the profitability of each customer. The following data (in thousands) pertain to May:

	Customer Revenues	Customer Costs
Avery Group	₹2,600	₹1,820
Duran Systems	1,800	1,840
Retail Systems	1,630	1,780
Ernst & Young	3,220	2,250
IIT Delhi	2,350	3,080
Grainger Services	800	740
Software Partners	1,740	1,000
Problem Solvers	760	1,080
Business Systems	1,370	1,100
Consultancy Enterprises	3,730	2,310

Required

1. Compute the operating income of each customer. Prepare exhibits for Instant Service that are Patterned after Exhibits 14-7 and 14-8. Comment on the results.

2. What options regarding individual customers should Instant Service consider in light of your customer profitability analysis in requirement 1?

3. What problems might Instant Service encounter in accurately estimating the operating costs of each customer

14-29 Variance analysis, multiple products. The Shimla Penguins play in the Indian Ice Hockey League. The Penguins play in Downtown Arena, (owned and managed by the City of Shimla, which has a capacity of 15,000 seats (5,000 lower-tier seats and 10,000 upper-tier seats). The Downtown Arena charges the Penguins per ticket charge for use of their facility. All tickets are sold by the Reservation Network, which charges the Penguin's a reservation fee per ticket. The Penguins' budgeted contribution margin for each type of ticket in 2015 is computed as follows:

	Lower-Tier Tickets	Upper-Tier Tickets
Selling price	₹350	₹140
Downtown Arena fee	100	60
Reservation Network fee	50	30
Contribution margin per ticket	200	50

The budgeted and actual average attendance figures per game in the 2014 season are

	Budgeted Seats Sold	Actual Seats Sold
Lower tier	4,000	3,300
Upper tier	6,000	7,700
Total	10,000	11,000

There was no difference between the budgeted and actual contribution margin for lower-tier or upper-tier seats.

The manager of the Penguins was delighted that actual attendance was 10 percent above budgeted attendance per game.

Required

1. Compute the sales-volume variance for each type of ticket and in total for the Shimla Penguins in 2015 (Calculate all variances in terms of contribution margins.)

2. Compute the sales-quantity and sales-mix variances for each type of ticket and in total in 2015.

3. Present a summary of the variances in requirements 1 and 2. Comment on the results.

14-30 Variance analysis, working backward. The Yera Glasses sells two brands of wine glasses: Plain and Chic. Yera provides the following information for sales in the month of June:

Static-budget total contribution margin	₹56,000
Budgeted units to be sold of all glasses in June	2,000 units
Budgeted contribution margin per unit of Plain	₹20 per unit
Budgeted contribution margin per unit of Chic	₹60 per unit
Total sales-quantity variance	₹14,000 U
Actual sales-mix percentage of Plain	60 percent

All variances are to be computed in contribution-margin terms.

Required

1. Calculate the sales-quantity variances for each product for June.

2. Calculate the individual product and total sales-mix variances for June. Calculate the individual product and total sales-volume variances for June.

3. Briefly describe the conclusions you would draw from the variances.

14-31 Allocation of central corporate costs to divisions. Times Group has four geographically dispersed divisions:

- Book publishing
- Broadcasting

- Print Media
- Multimedia

Under the current allocation system, costs incurred at Times Group corporate headquarters are collected in a single pool and allocated to eacl1 division on the basis of its revenues. The central corporate costs for 2015 are:

Interest on debt	₹1,00,00,000
Human resource management	15,00,00,000
Corporate administration	5,00,00,000
Research and development	10,00,00,000
Advertising	20,00,00,000
	₹51,00,00,000

Summary data (in lakh of rupees) related to the divisions for 2015 are:

	Multimedia	Broadcasting	Print Media	Book Publishing
Revenues	₹14,000	₹45,000	₹25,000	₹16,000
Direct costs	7,500	35,000	20,000	10,000
Segment margin	₹6,500	₹10,000	₹5,000	6,000

The following information on the four divisions is also available.

	Multimedia	Broadcasting	Print Media	Book Publishing
Floor space (square feet)	40,000	1,60,000	2,00,000	1,00,000
Number of employees	1,000	3,000	2,500	1,500
Divisional administrative costs (in lakh of rupees)	₹1,500	₹4,000	₹2,500	₹2,000

A review of the central corporate costs for divisions reveals the following:

- Out of the total ₹100 lakh interest on debt, ₹65 lakh is for the debt to purchase a building for the Broadcasting division. The remaining ₹35 lakh interest cost is on the borrowings for the purchase of equipment for the Multimedia division.
- No research and development work is done for the Print Media division. The director of research and development estimates that 40 percent of the work in his responsibility area is done for the Multimedia division, and the remaining 60 percent is done equally for the Broadcasting and Book Publishing divisions.
- Advertising campaigns sponsored at the central corporate level are to boost the overall corporate image. It is assumed that the benefits to the divisions are in proportion to their revenues.
- The resources expended by human resource management on recruiting, training, and so forth for the divisions are approximately in proportion to the number of employees.
- To support divisional managers, the corporate management works very closely with them. The divisional administrative costs are a good indicator of the relative size of each division's management team.

Required Allocate the central corporate costs to divisions that are consistent with cause-and-effect or benefits received criteria.

14-32 Customer profitability, distribution. Efficient Distribution has decided to analyze the profitability of five new customers. It buys bottled water at ₹12 per unit and sells to retail customers at a list price of ₹14.40 per unit. Data pertaining to five customers for the recent quarter are:

	Customer				
	P	Q	R	S	T
Bottels sold	2,080	8,750	60,800	31,800	3,900
List selling price	₹14.40	₹14.40	₹14.40	₹14.40	₹14.40

Actual selling price	₹14.40	₹14.16	₹13.20	₹13.92	12.96
Number of purchase orders	15	25	30	25	30
Number of customer visits	2	3	6	2	3
Number of deliveries	10	30	60	40	20
Miles traveled per delivery	14	4	3	8	40
Number of expedited deliveries	0	0	0	0	1

Its five activities and their cost drivers are:

Activity	Cost Driver Rate
Order taking	₹100 per purchase order
Customer visits	₹80 per customer visit
Deliveries	₹2 per delivery mile traveled
Product handling	₹0.50 per bottle sold
Expedited deliveries	₹300 per expedited delivery

Required

1. Compute the customer-level operating income of each of the five retail customers now being examined (P, Q, R, S, and T). Comment on the results.
2. What insights are gained by reporting both the list selling price and the actual selling price for each customer?
3. What factors should Efficient Distribution consider in deciding whether to drop one or more of the five customers?

14-33 Customer profitability, customer cost hierarchy. Surya Electronics has two retail customers and two wholesale customers. Pertinent information relating to each customer for 2015 follows (all amounts are in thousands of rupees):

	Wholesale North India Wholesaler	South India Wholesaler	Retail Ramesh Electronics	Shyam Electricals
Cost of goods sold	₹3,25,000	₹4,90,000	₹1,12,000	₹92,000
Delivery costs				
Regular	300	450	150	80
Expedited	120	200	10	5
Order processing	800	1,000	200	130
Product handling	5,000	6,000	800	900
Sales visits	480	550	240	165
Revenues at list prices	4,00,000	6,00,000	1,30,000	1,00,000
Discounts from list prices	30,000	50,000	7,000	0

Surya's distribution-channel costs are ₹300 lakh for wholesale customers and ₹100 lakh for retail customers. Its corporate-sustaining costs are ₹600 lakh.

Required

1. Calculate customer-level operating income using the format in Exhibit 14-5.
2. Prepare a customer cost hierarchy report, using the format in Exhibit 14-6.

14-34 Variance analysis, sales-mix and sales-quantity variances. ABC company adopts a standard costing system. It produces three products (A,B and C). You are Company's senior vice-president of marketing. The CEO has discovered that the total contribution margin came in lower than budget, and it is your responsibility to explain to him why actual results are different from the budget. Budgeted and actual operating data for the company's third quarter (2015) are as follows:

Budgeted Operating Data, Third Quarter 2015

	Selling Price	Variable Cost per Unit	Contribution Margin per Unit	Sales Volume in Units
A	₹379	₹182	₹197	12,500
B	269	98	171	37,500
C	149	65	84	50,000
				1,00,000

Actual Operating Data, Third Quarter 2015

	Selling Price	Variable Cost per Unit	Contribution Margin per Unit	Sales Volumein Units
A	₹349	₹178	₹171	11,000
B	285	92	193	44,000
C	102	73	29	55,000
				1,10,000

Required

1. Compute the actual and budgeted contribution margins in rupees for each product and in total.
2. Calculate the actual and budgeted sales mixes for the three products.
3. Calculate total sales-volume, sales-mix, and sales-quantity variances for the third quarter of 2015.
4. Write a brief note explaining why actual results were not as good as the budgeted amounts.

14-35 Market-share and market-size variances (continuation of 14-34). ABC senior vice-president of marketing prepared his budget at the beginning of the third quarter assuming a 25 percent market share based on total sales. The total market was estimated by Market Research unit of the Company to reach sales of 4,00,000 units worldwide in the third quarter. However, actual sales were 5,00,000 units.

Required

1. Calculate the market-share and market-size variances for ABC in the third quarter of 2015 (report all variances in terms of contribution margins).
2. Explain what happened based on the market-share and market-size variances.
3. Calculate the actual market size, in units, that would have led to no market-size variance (again using budgeted contribution margin per unit). Use this market-size figure to find the actual market share that would have led to a zero market-share variance.

14-36 Direct materials efficiency, mix, and yield variances. (CMA adapted) The Energy Products Company produces a gasoline additive, Gas Gain, that increases engine efficiency and improves gasoline mileage. The actual and budgeted quantities (in gallons) of materials required to produce Gas Gain and the budgeted prices of materials in August are as follows:

Chemical	Actual Quantity	Budgeted Quantity	Budgeted Price
Echol	24,080	25,200	₹2.0
Protex	15,480	16,800	4.5
Benz	36,120	33,600	1.5
CT-40	10,320	8,400	3.0

Required

1. Calculate the total direct materials efficiency variance for August.
2. Calculate the total direct materials mix and yield variances for August.
3. What conclusions would you draw from the variance analysis?

14-37 Customer profitability, credit-card operations. The Freedom Card is a credit card that competes with national credit cards such as Visa and Master Card. Freedom Card is marketed by the City Bank. Anwar is manager of the Freedom Card division. He is seeking to develop a customer-profitability reporting system. He collects the following information on four users of the Freedom Card during 2015:

	A	B	C	D
Annual purchases at retail merchants	₹80,000	₹26,000	₹34,000	₹8,000
Customer transactions at retail merchant	800	520	272	200
Annual fee	50	0	50	0
Average annual outstanding balance on credit card on which				
interest is paid to City Bank	6,000	0	2,000	100
Inquiries to City Bank	6	12	8	2
Credit-card replacement due to loss or theft	0	2	1	0

Customer B pays no membership fee because his card was issued under a special "lifetime promotion program," in which annual fees are waived as long as the card is used at least once a year. Customer D is a student. City Bank does not charge an annual fee to student credit-card holders at select universities.

City Bank has an ABC system that Anwar can use in his analysis. The following data apply to 2015:

a. Each customer transaction with a retail merchant costs City Bank ₹0.50 to process.
b. Each customer inquiry to City Bank costs ₹5.
c. Replacing a lost card costs ₹120.
d. Annual cost to City Bank of maintaining a credit-card account is ₹108 (includes sending out monthly statements).

City Bank receives 2.0 percent of the purchase amount from retail merchants when the Freedom Card is used. Bad debts of the Freedom Card in 2015 were 0.5 percent of the total purchases at retail merchants. Thus, City Bank nets 1.5 percent of the total purchases made using the Freedom Card.

City Bank had an interest spread of 9 percent in 2015 on the average outstanding balances on which interest is paid by its credit-card holders. An interest spread is the difference between what City Bank receives from card holders on outstanding balances and what it pays to obtain the funds so used. Thus, on a ₹500 average annual outstanding balance in 2015, City Bank would receive ₹45 in interest revenues (9 percent × ₹500).

Required

1. Compute the customer profitability of the four representative credit-card users of the Freedom Card for 2015.

2. Develop profiles of (a) profitable card holders and (b) unprofitable card holders for City Bank.

3. Should City Bank charge its card holders for making inquiries (such as outstanding balances or disputed charges) or for replacing lost or stolen cards?

4. Anwar has an internal proposal that City Bank discontinue a sizable number of the low-volume creditcard customers. What factors should he consider in evaluating and responding to this proposal?

5. Anwar seeks your group's advice on an ethical issue he is facing. A chain of gambling Shopping Centres (Lucky Roller) has offered to provide Freedom Card holders with money advances of up to ₹500 at its Shopping Centres. Anwar observes that from a strictly financial perspective, providing money advances to its customers would be highly profitable. Should Freedom Card holders be able to obtain money advances at Lucky Roller gambling Shopping Centres? Explain.

Allocation of Support-Department Costs, Common Costs, and Revenue

How a company allocates its overhead and internal support costs—costs related to marketing, advertising, and other internal services—among its various production departments or projects can have a big impact on how profitable those departments or projects are.

While the allocation may not affect the firm's profit as a whole, if the allocation isn't done properly, it can make some departments and projects (and their managers) look better or worse than they should profit-wise.

Allocating Support Department Costs Using the Single-Rate and Dual-Rate Methods

Companies distinguish operating departments (and operating divisions) from support departments. An operating department, also called a production department, directly adds value to a product or service. Examples are manufacturing departments where products are made. **A support department**, which is also called a **service department**, provides the services that assist other internal departments (operating departments and other support departments) in the company. Examples of support departments are information systems, production control, materials management, and plant maintenance. Managers face two questions when allocating the costs of a support department to operating departments or divisions: (1) Should fixed costs of support departments, such as the salary of the department manager, be allocated to operating divisions? (2) If fixed costs are allocated, should variable and fixed costs of the support department be allocated in the same way? With regard to the first question, most companies believe that fixed costs of support departments should be allocated because the support department needs to incur these fixed costs to provide operating divisions with the services they require. Depending on the answer to the first question, there are two approaches to allocating support-department costs: the *single-rate cost-allocation method and the dual-rate cost-allocation method.*

Single-Rate and Dual-Rate Methods

The **single-rate method** does not distinguish between fixed and variable costs. It allocates costs in each cost pool (support department in this section) to cost objects (operating divisions in this section) using the same rate per unit of a single allocation base. By contrast, the **dual-rate method** partitions the cost of each support department into two pools, a variable-cost pool and a fixed-cost pool, and allocates each pool using a different cost-allocation base. When using either the single-rate method or the dual-rate method, managers can allocate support-department costs to operating divisions based on either a *budgeted* rate or the eventual *actual* cost rate. The latter approach is neither conceptually preferred nor widely used in practice (we explain why in the next section). Accordingly, we illustrate the single-rate and dual-rate methods next based on the use of *budgeted* rates.

We continue the HEC Company example first presented in Chapter 4. Recall that HEC manufactures and installs specialized machinery for the paper-making industry. In Chapter 4 we used a single manufacturing overhead cost pool with direct manufacturing labor-hours as the cost-allocation base to allocate all manufacturing overhead costs to jobs. In this chapter, we present a more detailed accounting system to take into account the different operating and service departments within Robinson's manufacturing department.

Robinson has two operating departments—the Machining Department and the Assembly Department—where production occurs and three support departments—Plant Administration, Engineering and Production Control, and Materials Management—that provide essential services to the operating departments for manufacturing the specialized machinery.

- The Plant Adminstration Department is responsible for managing all activities in the plant. That is, its costs are incurred to support, and can be considered part of the supervision costs of, all the other departments.

- The Engineering and Production Control Department supports all the engineering activity in the other departments. In other words, its costs are incurred to support the engineering costs of the other departments and so can be considered part of the engineering costs of those departments.

- The Materials Management Department is responsible for managing and moving materials and components required for different jobs. Each job at HEC is different and requires small quantities of unique components to be machined and assembled. Materials Management Department costs vary with the number of material-handling labor-hours incurred to support each department. The Materials Management Department invests a substantial number of material-handling labor-hours in support of the Assembly Department.

The specialized machinery that HEC manufactures does not go through the service departments and so the costs of the service departments must be allocated to the operating departments to determine the full cost of making the specialized machinery. Once costs are accumulated in the operating departments, they can be absorbed into the different specialized machines that HEC manufactures. Different jobs need different amounts of machining and assembly resources. Each operating department has a different overhead cost driver to absorb overhead costs to machines produced: machine-hours in the Machining Department and assembly labor-hours in the Assembly Department.

We first focus on the allocation of the Materials Management Department costs to the Machining Department and the Assembly Department. The following data relate to the 2013 budget:

Practical capacity	4,000 hours
Fixed costs of the materials management department in the 3,000 labor-hour to 4,000 labor-hour relevant range	₹14,40,000
Budgeted usage (quantity) in labor-hours:	
Machining department	800 hours
Assembly department	2,800 hours
Total	3,600 hours
Budgeted variable cost per material-handling labor-hour in the 3,000 labor-hour to 4,000 labor-hour relevant range	₹300 per hour used
Actual usage in 2013 in labor-hours:	
Machining department	1,200 hours
Assembly department	2,400 hours
Total	3,600 hours

The budgeted rates for materials management department costs can be computed based on either the demand for materials-handling services or the supply of materials-handling services. We consider the allocation of materials management department costs based first on the demand for (or usage of) materials-handling services and then on the supply of materials-handling services.

Allocation Based on the Demand for (or Usage of) Computer Services

We present the single-rate method followed by the dual-rate method.

Single-rate method In this method, a combined budgeted rate is used for fixed and variable costs. The rate is calculated as follows.

Budgeted usage	3,600 hours
Budgeted total cost pool: ₹14,40,000 + (3,600 hours × ₹300/hour)	₹25,20,000
Budgeted total rate per hour: hours ₹25,20,000 ÷ (3,600 hours)	₹700 per hour used
Allocation rate for machining department	₹700 per hour used
Allocation rate for assembly department	₹700 per hour used

Note that the budgeted rate of ₹700 per hour is substantially higher than the ₹300 budgeted *variable* cost per hour. That's because the ₹700 rate includes an allocated amount of ₹400 per hour (budgeted fixed costs, ₹14,40,000 ÷ budgeted usage, 3600 hours) for the *fixed* costs of operating the facility.

Under the single-rate method, departments are charged the budgeted rate for each hour of *actual* use of the central facility. Applying this to our example, HEC allocates materials management department costs based on the ₹700 per hour budgeted rate and the actual hours the operating departments use. The support costs allocated to the two departments under this method are as follows:

Machining department: ₹700 per hour × 1,200 hours	₹8,40,000
Assembly department: ₹700 per hour × 2,400 hours	₹16,80,000

Dual-rate method When a company uses the dual-rate method, managers must choose allocation bases for both the variable and fixed-cost pools of the materials management department. As in the single-rate method, variable costs are assigned based on the *budgeted* variable cost per hour of ₹300 for *actual* hours each department uses. However, fixed costs are assigned based on *budgeted* fixed costs per hour and the *budgeted* number of hours for each department. Given the budgeted usage of 800 hours for the machining department and 2,800 hours for the assembly department, the budgeted fixed-cost rate is ₹400 per hour (₹14,40,000 ÷ 3,600 hours), as before. Because this rate is charged on the basis of the *budgeted* usage, however, the fixed costs are effectively allocated in advance as a lump sum based on the relative proportions of the materials management facilities the operating departments expect to use.

The costs allocated to the machining department in 2013 under the dual-rate method would be as follows:

Fixed costs: ₹400 per hour × 800 (budgeted) hours	₹3,20,000
Variable costs: ₹300 (actual) hours × 1,200 (actual) hours	3,60,000
Total costs	₹6,80,000

The costs allocated to the assembly department in 2013 would be as follows:

Fixed costs: ₹400 per hour × 2800 (budgeted) hours	₹11,20,000
Variable costs: ₹300 per hour × 2400 (actual) hours	7,20,000
Total costs	₹18,40,000

Note that each operating department is charged the same amount for variable costs under the single-rate and dual-rate methods (₹30 per hour multiplied by the actual hours of use). However, the overall assignment of costs differs under the two methods because the single-rate method allocates fixed costs of the support department based on actual usage of materials-handling resources by the operating departments, whereas the dual-rate method allocates fixed costs based on budgeted usage.

We next consider the alternative approach of allocating materials management department costs based on the capacity of materials-handling services supplied.

Allocation Based on the Supply of Capacity

We illustrate this approach using the 4,000 hours of practical capacity of the materials management department. The budgeted rate is then determined as follows:

Budgeted fixed-cost rate per hour, ₹4,40,000 ÷ 4,000 hours	₹360 per hour
Budgeted variable-cost rate per hour	300 per hour
Budgeted total-cost rate per hour	₹660 per hour

Using the same procedures for the single-rate and dual-rate methods as in the previous section, the Materials Management Department costs allocated to the operating departments are as follows:

Single-Rate Method

Machining department: ₹660 per hour × 1,200 (actual) hours	₹7,92,000
Assembly department: ₹660 per hour × 2,400 (actual) hours	15,84,000
Fixed costs of unused materials-handling capacity:	
₹360 per hour × 400 hours[a]	1,44,000

[a]400 hours = Practical capacity of 4,000 − (1,200 hours used by machining department + 2,400 hours used by assembly department).

Dual-Rate Method

Machining department

Fixed costs: ₹360 per hour × 800 (budgeted) hours	₹2,88,000
Variable costs: ₹300 per hour × 1,200 (actual) hours	3,60,000
Total costs	₹6,48,000

Assembly department

Fixed costs: ₹360 per hour × 2,800 (budgeted) hours	₹10,08,000
Variable costs: ₹300 per hour × 2,400 (actual) hours	7,20,000
Total costs	₹17,28,000

Fixed costs of unused materials-handling capacity:

₹360 per hour × 400 hours[b]	₹1,44,000

[b]400 hours = Practical capacity of 4,000 hours – (800 hours budgeted to be used by machining department + 2,800 hours budgeted to be used by assembly department).

When a company uses practical capacity to allocate costs, the single-rate method allocates only the actual fixed-cost resources used by he machining and assembly departments, while the dual-rate method allocates the budgeted fixed-cost resources to be used by the operating departments. Unused materials management department resources are highlighted but usually not allocated to the departments.[1]

The advantage of using practical capacity to allocate costs is that it focuses management's attention on managing unused capacity (described in Chapter9, pages 470–471, and Chapter 12, pages 655–656). Using practical capacity also avoids burdening the user departments with the cost of unused capacity of the materials management department. In contrast, when costs are allocated on the basis of the demand for materials-handling services, all ₹14,40,000 of budgeted fixed costs, including the cost of unused capacity, are allocated to user departments. If costs are used as a basis for pricing, then charging user departments for unused capacity could result in the downward demand spiral (see page 346).

Recently, the dual-rate method has been receiving more attention. Resource Consumption Accounting (RCA), an emerging management accounting system, employs an allocation procedure similar to a dual-rate system. For each cost/resource pool, cost assignment rates for fixed costs are based on practical capacity supplied, while rates for proportional costs (i.e., costs that vary with regard to the output of the resource pool) are based on planned quantities.[2]

There are advantages and disadvantages of using the single-rate and dual-rate methods. We discuss these next.

Advantages and Disadvantages of Single-Rate Method

Advantages (1) The single-rate method is less costly to implement because it avoids the often expensive analysis necessary to classify the individual cost items of a department into

---

[1] In our example, the costs of unused capacity under the single-rate and the dual-rate methods coincide (each equals ₹14,400). This occurs because the total actual usage of the facility matches the total expected usage of 3,600 hours The budgeted cost of unused capacity (in the dual-rate method) can be either greater or lower than the actual cost (in the single-rate method), depending on whether the total actual usage is lower or higher than the budgeted usage.

[2] Other salient features of Resource Consumption Accounting (RCA) include the selective use of activity-based costing, the nonassignment of fixed costs when causal relationships cannot be established, and the depreciation of assets based on their replacement cost. RCA has its roots in the nearly fifty-year-old German cost accounting system called Grenzplankostenrechnung (GPK), which is used by organizations such as Mercedes-Benz, Porsche, and Stihl. For further details, as well as illustrations of the use of RCA and GPK in organizations, see S. Webber and B. Clinton, "Resource Consumption Accounting Applied: The Clopay Case," *Management Accounting Quarterly* (Fall 2004) and B. Mackie, "Merging GPK and ABC on the Road to RCA," *Strategic Finance* (November 2006).

fixed and variable categories. **(2) It offers user departments some operational control over the charges they bear** by conditioning the final allocations on the actual usage of support services, rather than basing them solely on uncertain forecasts of expected demand.

Disadvantage The single-rate method may lead operating department managers to make sub-optimal decisions that are in their own best interest but that may be inefficient from the standpoint of the organization as a whole. This occurs because under the single-rate method, the allocated fixed costs of the support department appear as variable costs to the operating departments. Consider the setting where managers make allocations based on the demand for materials-handling services. In this case, each user department is charged ₹700 per hour under the single-rate method (recall that ₹400 of this charge relates to the allocated fixed costs of the materials management department). Suppose an external provider offers the machining department material-handling labor services at a rate of ₹550 per hour, at a time when the materials management department has unused capacity. The machining department's managers would be tempted to use this vendor because it would lower the department's costs (₹550 per hour instead of the ₹700 per hour internal charge for materials-handling services). In the short run, however, the fixed costs of the materials management department remain unchanged in the relevant range (between 3,000 hours of usage and the practical capacity of 4,000 hours). Robinson will therefore incur an additional cost of ₹250 per hour if the managers were to take this offer—the difference between the ₹550 external purchase price and the true internal variable cost of ₹300 of using the materials management department.

The divergence created under the single-rate method between Robinson's interests and those of its department managers is lessened when allocation is based on practical capacity. The variable cost per hour the operating department managers perceive is now ₹660 (rather than the ₹700 rate when allocation is based on budgeted usage). However, any external offer above ₹30 (HEC's true variable cost) and below ₹660 (the single-rate charge per hour) will still result in the user manager preferring to outsource the service at the expense of HEC's overall profits.

Advantages and Disadvantages of Dual-Rate Method

Advantages (1) The dual-rate method guides department managers to make decisions that benefit both the organization as a whole and each department because it signals to department managers how variable costs and fixed costs behave differently. For example, using an external provider of materials-handling services that charges more than ₹300 per hour would result in Robinson's being worse off than if its own materials management department were used because the latter has a variable cost of ₹300 per hour. Under the dual-rate method, neither department manager has an incentive to pay more than ₹300 per hour for an external provider because the internal charge for materials-handling services is precisely that amount. By charging the fixed costs of resources budgeted to be used by the departments as a lump sum, the dual-rate method succeeds in removing fixed costs from the department managers' consideration when making marginal decisions to outsource services. The dual-rate method therefore avoids the potential conflict of interest that can arise under the single-rate method. **(2) Allocating fixed costs based on budgeted usage helps user departments with both short-run and long-run planning because user departments know the costs allocated to them in advance.** Companies commit to infrastructure costs (such as the fixed costs of a support department) on the basis of a long-run planning horizon; budgeted usage measures the long-run demands of the user departments for support-department services.

Disadvantages (1) The dual-rate method requires managers to distinguish variable costs from fixed costs, which is often a challenging task. (2) The dual-rate

method does not indicate to operating managers the cost of fixed support department resources used because fixed costs are allocated to operating departments based on budgeted rather than actual usage. Thus, the Machining Department manager is allocated fixed costs of the Materials Management Department based on the budgeted usage of 800 labor-hours even though the Machining Department actually uses 1,200 labor-hours. **(3) Allocating fixed costs on the basis of budgeted long-run usage may tempt some managers to underestimate their planned usage.** Underestimating will result in their departments bearing a lower percentage of fixed costs (assuming all other managers do not similarly underestimate their usage). If all user department managers underestimate usage, it might also lead to HEC underestimating its total support department needs. To discourage such underestimates, some companies offer bonuses or other rewards—the "carrot" approach—to managers who make accurate forecasts of long-run usage. Other companies impose cost penalties—the "stick" approach—for underestimating long-run usage. For instance, a higher cost rate is charged after a department exceeds its budgeted usage.

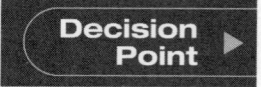

Decision Point ▶

When should manager use the dual-rate method over the single-rate method?

Budgeted Versus Actual Costs and the Choice of Allocation Base

The allocation methods previously outlined follow specific procedures in terms of the support department costs that are considered as well as the manner in which costs are assigned to the operating departments. In this section, we examine these choices in greater detail and consider the impact of alternative approaches. We show that the decision whether to use actual or budgeted costs, as well as the choice between actual and budgeted usage as allocation base, has a significant impact on the cost allocated to each operating department and the incentives of the operating department managers.

Learning Objective **2**

Understand how the choice between allocation based on budgeted and actual rates,

. . . budgeted rates provide certainty to users about charges and motivate the support division to engage in cost control

and budgeted and actual usage can affect the incentives of division managers

. . . budgeted usage helps in planning and efficient utilization of fixed resources, actual usage controls consumption of variable resources

Budgeted Versus Actual Rates

In both the single-rate and dual-rate methods, HEC uses budgeted rates to assign support department costs (fixed as well as variable costs). An alternative approach would involve using the actual rates based on the support costs realized during the period. This method is much less common because of the level of uncertainty it imposes on user departments. When allocations are made using budgeted rates, managers of departments to which costs are allocated know with certainty the rates to be used in that budget period. Users can then determine the amount of the service to request and—if company policy allows—whether to use the internal source or an external vendor. In contrast, when actual rates are used for cost allocation, user departments are not informed of their charges until the end of the budget period.

Budgeted rates also help motivate the manager of the support (or supplier) department (for example, the materials management department) to improve efficiency. During the budget period, the support department, not the user departments, bears the risk of any unfavorable cost variances. That's because user departments do not pay for any costs or inefficiencies of the supplier department that cause actual rates to exceed budgeted rates.

The manager of the supplier department would likely view the budgeted rates negatively if unfavorable cost variances occur due to price increases outside of his or her control. Some organizations try to identify these uncontrollable factors and relieve the support department manager of responsibility for these variances. In other organizations, the supplier department and the user department agree to share the risk (through an explicit formula) of a large, uncontrollable increase in the prices of inputs used by the supplier department. This procedure avoids imposing the risk completely on either the supplier department (as when budgeted rates are used) or the user department (as in the case of actual rates).

For the rest of this chapter, we will continue to consider only allocation methods that are based on budgeted rates.

Budgeted Versus Actual Usage

In both the single-rate and dual-rate methods, the variable costs are assigned on the basis of budgeted rates and actual usage. Because the variable costs are directly and causally linked to usage, charging them as a function of the actual usage is appropriate. Moreover, allocating variable costs on the basis of budgeted usage would provide the user departments with no incentive to control their consumption of support services.

What about the fixed costs? Consider the budget of ₹4,40,000 fixed costs at the Materials Management Department of HEC Company. Recall that budgeted usage is 800 hours for the Machining Department and 2,800 hours for the Assembly Department. Assume that actual usage by the Machining Department is always equal to budgeted usage. We consider three cases:

Case 1: When actual usage by the Assembly Department equals budgeted usage.

Case 2: When actual usage by the Assembly Department is greater than budgeted usage.

Case 3: When actual usage by the Assembly Department is lower than budgeted usage.

Fixed Cost Allocation Based on Budgeted Rates and Budgeted Usage

This is the dual-rate procedure outlined in the previous section. When budgeted usage is the allocation base, regardless of the actual usage of facilities (i.e., whether Case 1, 2, or × occurs), user departments receive a preset lump-sum fixed-cost charge. If rates are based on expected demand of ₹400 per hour (₹14,40,000 ÷ 3,600 hours), the Machining Department is assigned ₹3,20,000 (₹40 per hour × 800 hours) and the Assembly Department, ₹11,20,000 (₹40 per hour × 2,800 hours). If rates are set using practical capacity of ₹360 per hour (₹4,40,000 ÷ 4,000 hours), the Machining Department is charged ₹2,88,000 (₹360 per hour × 800 hours) , the Assembly Department is allocated ₹10,08,000 (₹360 per hour × 2,800 hours), and the remaining ₹14,40,000 (₹360 per hour × 400 hours) is the unallocated cost of excess capacity.

Fixed Cost Allocation Based on Budgeted Rates and Actual Usage

Column 2 of Exhibit 15-1 shows the allocations when the budgeted rate is based on expected demand (₹400 per hour), while column 3 shows the allocations when practical capacity is used to derive the rate (₹360 per hour). Note that each operating department's fixed-cost allocation varies based on its actual usage of support facilities. However, variations in actual usage in one department do not affect the costs allocated to the other department. The Machining Department is allocated either ₹3,20,000 or ₹2,88,000, depending on the budgeted rate chosen, independent of the Assembly Department's actual usage.

Note, however, that this allocation procedure for fixed costs is exactly the same as that under the single-rate method. The procedure therefore shares the advantages of the single-rate method, such as advanced knowledge of budgeted rates, as well as control over the costs charged to them based on actual usage.[3] The procedure also shares the disadvantages of the single-rate method discussed in the previous section, such as charging excessively high costs, including the cost of unused capacity, when rates are based on expected usage. In Case 1, for example, actual usage equals budgeted usage of 3,600 materials-handling labor-hours and is less than the practical capacity of 4,000 labor-hours. However, all ₹14,40,000 of fixed costs of the Materials Management Department are allocated to the operating departments even though the Materials Handling Department has idle capacity. On the other hand, when actual usage (4,000 labor-hours) is more than the budgeted amount (3,600 labor-hours) as in Case 2, a total of ₹16,00,000 is allocated, which is more than the fixed costs of ₹14,40,000. This results in overallocation of fixed costs requiring end-of period adjustments, as discussed in Chapters 4 and 8.

Allocating fixed costs based on practical capacity avoids these problems by explicitly recognizing the costs of unused capacity. However, as we have discussed earlier, allocating fixed-cost rates based on actual usage induces conflicts of interest between the user departments and the firm when evaluating outsourcing possibilities.

Allocating Budgeted Fixed Costs Based on Actual Usage

Finally, consider the impact of having actual usage as the allocation base when the firm assigns total budgeted fixed costs to operating departments (rather than specifying budgeted fixed-cost rates, as we have thus far). If the budgeted fixed costs of ₹14,40,000 are allocated using budgeted usage, we are back in the familiar dual-rate setting. On the other hand, if the actual usage of the facility is the basis for allocation, the charges would equal the amounts in Exhibit 15-1, column 4:

- In Case 1, the fixed-cost allocation equals the amount based on budgeted usage (which is also the same as the charge under the dual-rate method based on demand for material-handling services).

Exhibit 15-1   Effect of Variations in Actual Usage on Fixed-Cost Allocation to Operating Divisions

	(1) Actual Usage		(2) Budgeted Rate Based on Expected Demand[a]		(3) Budgeted Rate Based on Practical Capacity[b]		(4) Allocation of Budgeted Total Fixed Cost	
Case	Mach. Dept.	Assmb. Dept.	Mach. Dept. (₹)	Assmb. Dept. (₹)	Mach. Dept. (₹)	Assmb. Dept. (₹)	Mach. Dept. (₹)	Assmb. Dept. (₹)
1	800 hours	2,800 hours	3,20,000	11,20,000	2,88,000	10,08,000	3,20,000[c]	11,20,000[d]
2	800 hours	3,200 hours	3,20,000	12,80,000	2,88,000	11,52,000	2,88,000[e]	11,52,000[f]
3	800 hours	2,400 hours	3,20,000	9,60,000	2,88,000	8,64,000	3,60,000[g]	10,80,000[h]

a $\dfrac{₹14,40,000}{(800 + 2,800)\ \text{hours}} = ₹400\ \text{per hour}$ b $\dfrac{₹14,40,000}{4,000\ \text{hours}} = ₹360\ \text{per hour}$ c $\dfrac{800}{(800 + 2,800)} \times ₹14,40000$ d $\dfrac{2,800}{(800 + 2,800)} \times ₹14,40,000$

e $\dfrac{800}{(800 + 3,200)} \times ₹14,40,000$ f $\dfrac{3,200}{(800 + 3,200)} \times ₹14,40,000$ g $\dfrac{800}{(800 + 2,400)} \times ₹14,40,000$ h $\dfrac{2,400}{(800 + 2,400)} \times ₹14,40,000$

---

[3] The total amount of fixed costs allocated to divisions will in general not equal the actual realized costs. Adjustments for overallocations and underallocations would then be made using the methods discussed previously in chapter 4, 7 and 8.

- In Case 2, the fixed-cost allocation is ₹3,20,000 less to the Machining Department than the amount based on budgeted usage (₹2,88,000 versus ₹3,20,000).
- In Case 3, the fixed-cost allocation is ₹40,000 more to the Machining Department than the amount based on budgeted usage (₹3,60,000 versus ₹3,20,000).

Why does the Machining Department receive ₹40,000 more in costs in Case 3, even though its actual usage equals its budgeted usage? Because the total fixed costs of ₹14,40,000 are now spread over 400 fewer hours of actual total usage. In other words, the lower usage by the Assembly Department leads to an increase in the fixed costs allocated to the Machining Department. When budgeted fixed costs are allocated based on actual usage, user departments will not know their fixed-cost allocations until the end of the budget period. This method therefore shares the same flaw as those methods that rely on the use of actual cost rates rather than budgeted cost rates.

To summarize, there are excellent economic and motivational reasons to justify the precise forms of the single-rate and dual-rate methods considered in the previous section and, in particular, to recommend the dual-rate allocation procedure.

◄ **Decision Point**

What factors should managers consider when deciding between allocation based on budgeted and actual rates, and budgeted and actual usage?

Allocating Costs of Multiple Support Departments

In the previous section, we examined general issues that arise when allocating costs from one support department to operating departments. In this section, we examine the special cost-allocation problems that arise when two or more of the support departments whose costs are being allocated provide reciprocal support to each other as well as to operating departments. An example of reciprocal support is HEC's Materials Management Department providing material-handling labor services to all other departments, including the Engineering and Production Control Department, while also utilizing the services of the Engineering and Production Control Department for managing material-handling equipment and scheduling materials movement to the production floor. More accurate support-department cost allocations result in more accurate product, service, and customer costs.

Exhibit 15-2, column 6, provides details of HEC's total budgeted manufacturing overhead costs of ₹1,12,00,000 for 2013 (see page 812), for example, supervision salaries, ₹20,00,000; depreciation and maintenance, ₹19,30,000; indirect labor, ₹19,50,000; and rent, utilities and insurance, ₹16,00,000. HEC allocates the ₹1,12,00,000 of total budgeted manufacturing overhead costs to the Machining and Assembly Departments in several steps.

Learning Objective 3

Allocate multiple support-department costs using the direct method,

. . . allocate support-department costs directly to operating departments the step-down method,

. . . partially allocates support-department costs to other support departments and the reciprocal method

. . . fully allocates support-department costs to other support departments

Step A: Trace or Allocate Each Cost to Various Support and Operating Departments. Exhibit 15-2, columns (1) through (5), show calculations for this step. For example, supervision salaries are traced to the departments in which the supervisors work. As described on page 37, supervision costs are an indirect cost of individual jobs because supervisory costs cannot be traced to individual jobs. They are a direct cost of the different departments, however, because they can be identified with each department in an economically feasible way. Rent, utilities, and insurance costs cannot be traced to each department because these costs are incurred for all of HEC's manufacturing facility. These costs are therefore allocated to different departments on the basis of the square feet area—the cost driver for rent, utilities, and insurance costs.

Step B: Allocate Plant Administration Costs to Other Support Departments and Operating Departments. Plant adminstration supports supervisors in each department, so plant administration costs are allocated to departments on the basis of supervision costs.

Some companies prefer not to allocate plant adminstration costs to jobs, products, or customers because these costs are fixed and independent of the level of activity in the plant.

Exhibit 15-2 Details of Budgeted Manufacturing Overhead at HEC Company for 2013 and Allocation of Plant Administration Department Costs

	A	B	C	D	E	F	G
1		Support Departments			Operating Departments		
2	**Step A**	**Plant Administration Department** (1)	**Engineering and Production Control Department** (2)	**Materials Management Department** (3)	**Machining Department** (4)	**Assembly Department** (5)	**Total** (6)
3	Plant manager's salary	₹9,20,000					₹9,20,000
4	Supervision salaries (traced to each department)		₹4,80,000	₹4,00,000	₹5,20,000	₹6,00,000	20,00,000
5	Engineering salaries (traced to each department)		11,00,000	3,60,000	6,00,000	2,40,000	2,30,000
6	Depreciation and maintenance (traced to each department)		3,90,000	5,50,000	7,90,000	2,00,000	19,30,000
7	Indirect materials (traced to each department)		2,00,000	1,20,000	1,10,000	70,000	5,00,000
8	Indirect labor (traced to each department)		4,30,000	7,70,000	3,70,000	3,80,000	19,50,000
9	Rent, utilities, and insurance (allocated to each department based on square feet area; ₹80[1]×1,000; 2,000; 3,000; 8,000; 6,000 sq. ft.)	80,000	1,60,000	2,40,000	6,40,000	4,80,000	16,00,000
10	Total	₹10,00,000	₹27,60,000	₹24,40,000	₹30,30,000	₹19,70,000	₹1,12,00,000
11							
12	**Step B**						
13	Allocation of plant administration costs 0.50[2] × ₹48,000; ₹40,000; ₹52,000; ₹60,000	(10,00,000)	2,40,000	2,00,000	2,60,000	3,00,000	
14		₹0	₹30,00,000	₹26,40,000	₹32,90,000	₹27,70,000	
15	[1]₹16,00,000 ÷ 20,00,000 total square feet area = ₹80 per square foot						
16	Plant administration cost-allocation rate $= \dfrac{\text{Total plant administration costs}}{\text{Total supervision salaries}} = \dfrac{₹10,00,000}{₹20,00,000} = 0.50$						

However, most companies, like HEC, allocate plant adminstration costs to departments and jobs, products, or customers because allocating all costs allows companies to calculate the full manufacturing costs of products. HEC calculates the plant administration cost-allocation rate as follows:

$$\text{Plant administration cost-allocation rate} = \frac{\text{Total plant administration costs}}{\text{Total supervision salaries}} = \frac{₹10,00,000}{₹20,00,000} = 0.50$$

The bottom part of Exhibit 15-2 shows how HEC uses the 0.50 cost-allocation rate and supervision salaries to allocate plant adminstration costs to the other support and operating departments.

Step C: Allocate Engineering and Production Control and Materials Management Costs to the Machining and Assembly Operating Departments. Note that the two support departments whose costs are being allocated—Engineering and Production Control and Materials Management—provide reciprocal support to each other as well as support to the operating departments. That is, the Engineering and Production Control Department provides services to the Materials Management Department (for example, engineering services for material-handling equipment and scheduling material movement to the production floor), while the

Materials Management Department provides services to the Engineering and Production Control Department (for example, delivering materials).

Consider again the Materials Management Department. As we saw in the previous section, this department is budgeted to provide 800 hours of materials-handling labor services to the Machining Department and 2,800 hours of materials-handling labor services to the Assembly Department. In this section, we further assume that the Materials Handling Department provides an additional 400 hours of materials-handling labor services to the Engineering and Production Control Department. Recall from the previous section that the Materials Management Department has budgeted fixed costs (for example, plant administration, depreciation, and rent) of ₹14,40,000 and budgeted variable costs (for example, indirect materials, indirect labor, and maintenance) of ₹300 per labor-hour. Thus, for the analysis in this section the total budgeted costs of the Materials Management Department equal ₹26,40,000 [₹14,40,000 + ₹1,300 × (800 + 2,800 + 400) labor-hours] as shown in Exhibit 15-2.[4]

Exhibit 15-3 displays the data for budgeted overhead costs from Exhibit 15-2 after allocating Plant Administration Department costs but before any further interdepartment cost allocations and the services provided by each support department to the other departments. To understand the percentages in this exhibit, consider the Engineering and Production Control Department. This department supports the engineering activity in the other departments and so the costs of this department are allocated based on engineering salaries in each of the other departments. From Exhibit 15-2, budgeted engineering salaries are ₹3,60,000 in the Materials Management Department, ₹6,00,000 in the Machining Department, and ₹2,40,000 in the Assembly Department for a total of ₹12,00,000 (₹3,60,000 + ₹6,00,000 × ₹2,40,000). Thus, the Engineering and Production Control

Exhibit 15-3   Data for Allocating Support Department Costs at HEC Company for 2013

A	B	C	D	E	F	G
	SUPPORT DEPARTMENTS			OPERATING DEPARTMENTS		
	Engineering and Production Control	Materials Management		Machining	Assembly	Total
3 Budgeted overhead costs						
4 before any interdepartment cost allocations	₹30,00,000	₹26,40,000		₹32,90,000	₹22,70,000	₹1,12,00,000
5 Support work furnished:						
6 By Engineering and Production Control						
7 Budgeted engineering salaries	—	₹3,60,000		₹6,00,000	₹2,40,000	₹12,00,000
8 Percentage	—	30%		50%	20%	100%
9 By Materials Management						
10 Budgeted material-handling labor-hours	400	—		800	2,800	4,000
11 Percentage	10%	—		20%	70%	100%

[4] The previous section assumed that the Materials Management Department only provided services to the Machining and Assembly Departments and not to the Engineering and Production Control Department, resulting in total budgeted costs of ₹25,20,000 [₹14,40,000 + ₹300 × (800 + 2,800) labor-hours].

Department provides support of 30% (₹3,60,000 ÷ ₹12,00,000 = 0.30) to the Materials Management Department, 50% (₹16,00,000 ÷ ₹12,00,000 = 0.50) to the Machining Department, and 20% (₹2,40,000 ÷ ₹16,00,000 = 0.20) to the Assembly Department. Similarly, the Materials Management Department provides a total of 4,000 material-handling labor-hours of support work: 10% (400 ÷ 4,000 = 0.10) for the Engineering and Production Control Department, 20% (800 ÷ 4,000 = 0.20) for the Machining Department, and 70% (2,800 ÷ 4,000 = 0.70) for the Assembly Department.

We describe three methods of allocating budgeted overhead costs from the support departments to the Machining Department and the Assembly Department: *direct, step-down, and reciprocal.* Throughout this section, we use budgeted costs and budgeted hours. Why? Because our goal is to determine the budgeted costs of the operating departments (Machining and Assembly) after HEC allocates the budgeted costs of the support departments (Materials Management and Engineering and Production Control) to the operating departments. The budgeted costs of the Machining Department will be divided by the budgeted machine-hours in the Machining Department and the budgeted costs of the Assembly Department will be divided by the budgeted direct manufacturing labor-hours in the Assembly Department to calculate the budgeted overhead allocation rates in each operating department. These overhead rates will be used to allocate overhead costs to each job as it passes through an operating department based on the actual number of machine-hours used in the Machining Department and the actual number of direct manufacturing labor-hours used in the Assembly Department. To simplify the explanation and to focus on concepts, we use the single-rate method to allocate the costs of each support department. (The Problem for Self-Study illustrates the dual-rate method for allocating reciprocal support-department costs.)

Direct Method

The direct method allocates each support-department's costs to operating departments only. The direct method does not allocate support department costs to other support departments. Exhibit 15-4 illustrates this method using the data in Exhibit 15-3. The base used to allocate Engineering and Production Control costs to the operating departments is the budgeted engineering salaries in the operating departments: ₹6,00,000 + ₹2,40,000 = ₹8,40,000. This amount excludes the ₹3,60,000 of budgeted engineering salaries representing services to be provided by Engineering and Production Control to Materials Management. Similarly, the base used for allocation of Materials Management costs to the operating departments is 800 + 2,800 = 3,600 budgeted material-handling labor-hours, which excludes the 400 hours of budgeted support time provided by Materials Management to Engineering and Production Control.

An equivalent approach to implementing the direct method involves calculating a budgeted rate for each support department's costs. For example, the rate for the Engineering and Production Control Department costs is (₹30,00,000 ÷ ₹8,40,000, or 357.143%. The Machining Department is then allocated ₹21,42,860 (357.143% × ₹6,00,000), while the Assembly Department is allocated ₹8,57,140 (357.143% × ₹2,40,000). For ease of explanation throughout this section, we will use the fraction of the support department services used by other departments, rather than calculate budgeted rates, to allocate support department costs.

Most managers adopt the direct method because it is easy to use. The benefit of the direct method is simplicity. Managers do not need to predict the usage of support department services by other support departments. A disadvantage of the direct method is that it ignores information about reciprocal services provided among support departments and can therefore lead to inaccurate estimates of the cost of operating departments. We now

Exhibit 15-4   Direct Method of Allocating Support-Department Costs at HEC Company for 2013

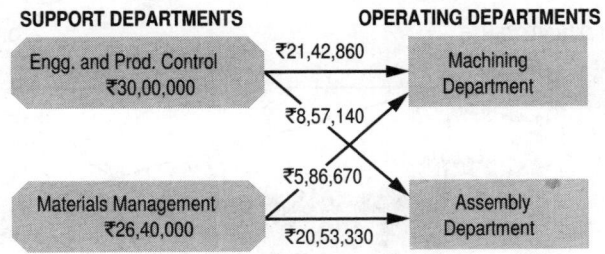

	Engineering and Production Control	Materials Management		Machining	Assembly	Total
	SUPPORT DEPARTMENTS			**OPERATING DEPARTMENTS**		
3 Budgeted overhead costs						
4 before any interdepartment cost allocations	₹30,00,000	₹26,40,000		₹32,90,000	₹22,70,000	₹1,12,00,000
5 Allocation of Engg. And Prod. Control (5/7, 2/7)[a]	(30,00,000)			21,42,860	8,57,140	
6 Allocation of Materials Management (2/9, 7/9)[b]		(26,40,000)		5,86,670	20,53,330	
7						
8 Total budgeted overhead of operating departments	₹0	₹0		₹60,19,530	₹51,80,470	₹1,12,00,000
9						
10 [a] Base is (₹6,00,000 + ₹2,40,000), or ₹8,40,000; ₹6,00,000 ÷ ₹ 8,40,000 = 5/7; ₹2,40,000 ÷ ₹8,40,000 = 2/7.						
11 [b] Base is (800 + 2,800), or 3,600 hours; 800 ÷ 3,600 = 2/9; 2,800 ÷ 3,600 = 7/9.						

examine a second approach, which partially recognizes the services provided among support departments.

Step-Down Method

Some organizations use the step-down method—also called the sequential allocation method—which allocates support-department costs to other support departments and to operating departments in a sequential manner that partially recognizes the mutual services provided among all support departments.

Exhibit 15-5 shows the step-down method. The Engineering and Production Control costs of ₹30,00,000 are allocated first. Exhibit 15-3 shows that Engineering and Production Control provides 30% of its services to Materials Management, 50% to Machining, and 20% to Assembly. Therefore, ₹9,00,000 is allocated to Materials Management (30% of ₹30,00,000), ₹15,00,000 to Machining (50% of ₹30,00,000), and ₹6,00,000 to Assembly (20% of ₹30,00,000). The Materials Management Department costs now total ₹35,40,000: budgeted costs of the Materials Management Department before any interdepartmental cost allocations, ₹26,40,000, plus ₹9,00,000 from the allocation of Engineering and Production Control costs to the Materials Management Department. The ₹35,40,000 is then only allocated between the two operating departments based on the proportion of the Materials Management Department services provided to Machining and

Exhibit 15-5   Step-Down Method of Allocating Support-Department Costs at HEC Company for 2013

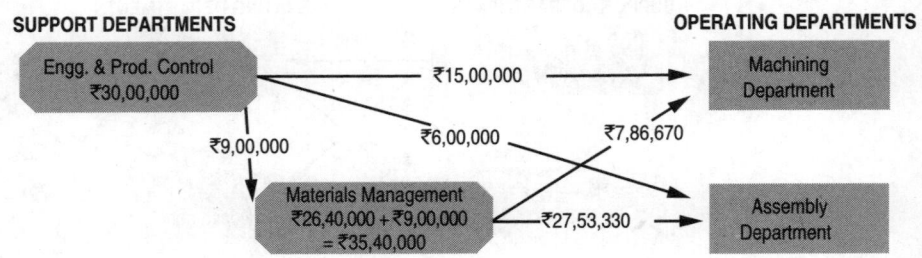

		SUPPORT DEPARTMENTS			OPERATING DEPARTMENTS		
		A	**B**	**C**	**D**	**E**	**F**	**G**
1			**SUPPORT DEPARTMENTS**			**OPERATING DEPARTMENTS**		
2			**Engineering and Production Control**	**Materials Management**		**Machining**	**Assembly**	**Total**
3	Budgeted overhead costs before any							
4	interdepartment cost allocations	₹30,00,000	₹26,40,000		₹32,90,000	₹22,70,000	₹1,12,00,000
5	Allocation of Engg. and Prod. Control (3/10, 5/10, 2/10)[a]	(30,00,000)	9,00,000		15,00,000	6,00,000	
6			35,40,000				
7	Allocation of Materials Management (2/9, 7/9)[b]		(35,40,000)		7,86,670	27,53,330	
8							
9	Total budgeted overhead of operating departments	₹0	₹0		₹55,76,670	₹56,23,330	₹1,12,00,000
10							
11	[a] Base is (₹3,60,000 + ₹6,00,000 + ₹2,40,000), or ₹12,00,000 ; ₹3,60,000 ÷ ₹12,00,000 = 3/10; ₹6,00,000 ÷ ₹12,00,000 = 5/10; ₹2,40,000 ÷ ₹12,00,000 = 2/10.						
12	[b] Base is (800 + 2,800), or 3,600 hours; 800 ÷ 3,600 = 2/9; 2,800 ÷ 3,600 = 7/9.						

Assembly. From Exhibit 15-3, the Materials Management Department provides 20% of its services to Machining and 70% to Assembly, so ₹7,86,670 (2/93× ₹35,40,000) is allocated to Machining and ₹27,53,330 (7/93× ₹354,000) is allocated to Assembly.

Note that this method requires managers to rank (sequence) the support departments in the order that the step-down allocation is to proceed. In our example, the costs of the Engineering and Production Control Department were allocated first to all other departments, including the Materials Management Department. The costs of the Materials Management support department were allocated second, but only to the two operating departments. Different sequences will result in different allocations of support-department costs to operating departments—for example, if the Materials Management Department costs had been allocated first and the Engineering and Production Control Department costs second. A popular step-down sequence begins with the support department that renders the highest percentage of its total services to other support departments. The sequence continues with the department that renders the next-highest percentage, and so on, ending with the support department that renders the lowest percentage.[5] In our example, costs of the

---

[5] An alternative approach to selecting the sequence of allocations is to begin with the support department that renders the highest dollar amount of services to other support departments. The sequence ends with the allocation of the costs of the department that renders the lowest dollar amount of services to other support departments.

Engineering and Production Control Department were allocated first because it provides 30% of its services to the Materials Management Department, whereas the Materials Management Department provides only 10% of its services to the Engineering and Production Control Department (see Exhibit 15-3).

Under the step-down method, once a support department's costs have been allocated, no subsequent support-department costs are allocated back to it. Once the Engineering and Production Control Department costs are allocated, it receives no further allocation from other (lower-ranked) support departments. The result is that the step-down method does not recognize the total services that support departments provide to each other. The reciprocal method fully recognizes all such services, as you will see next.

Reciprocal Method

The reciprocal method allocates support-department costs to operating departments by fully recognizing the mutual services provided among all support departments. For example, the Engineering and Production Control Department provides engineering services to the Materials Management Department. Similarly, Materials Management handles materials for Engineering and Production Control. The reciprocal method fully incorporates interdepartmental relationships into the support-department cost allocations.

Exhibit 15-6 presents one way to understand the reciprocal method as an extension of the step-down method. First, Engineering and Production Control costs are allocated to all other departments, including the Materials Management support department (Materials Management, 30%; Machining, 50%; Assembly, 20%). The costs in the Materials Management Department then total ₹35,40,000 (₹26,40,000 + ₹90,000 from the first-round allocation), as in Exhibit 15-5. The ₹35,40,000 is then allocated to all other departments that the Materials Management Department supports, including the Engineering and Production Control support department—Engineering and Production Control, 10%; Machining, 20%; and Assembly, 70% (see Exhibit 15-3). The Engineering and Production Control costs that had been brought down to 0 now have ₹3,54,000 from the Materials Management Department allocation. These costs are again reallocated to all other departments, including Materials Management, in the same ratio that the Engineering and Production Control costs were previously assigned. Now the Materials Management Department costs that had been brought down to ₹0 have ₹1,06,200 from the Engineering and Production Control Department allocations. These costs are again allocated in the same ratio that the Materials Management Department costs were previously assigned. Successive rounds result in smaller and smaller amounts being allocated to and reallocated from the support departments until eventually all support department costs are allocated to the Machining Department and the Assembly Department.

An alternative way to implement the reciprocal method is to formulate and solve linear equations. This implementation requires three steps.

Step 1:   Express Support Department Costs and Reciprocal Relationships in the Form of Linear Equations. Let EPC be the complete reciprocated costs of Engineering and Production Control and MM be the complete reciprocated costs of Materials Management. By complete reciprocated costs, we mean the support department's own costs plus any interdepartmental cost allocations. We then express the data in Exhibit 15-3 as follows:

$$EPC = ₹30,00,000 + 0.1\ MM \qquad (1)$$
$$MM = ₹26,40,000 + 0.3\ EPC \qquad (2)$$

The $0.1MM$ term in equation (1) is the percentage of the Materials Management services *used by* Engineering and Production Control. The $0.3EPC$ term in equation (2) is the percentage of Engineering and Production Control services *used by* Materials Management. The complete reciprocated costs in equations (1) and (2) are sometimes called the artificial costs of the support departments.

Exhibit 15-6	Reciprocal Method of Allocating Support-Department Costs Using Repeated Iterations at HEC Company for 2013

	Home	Insert	Page Layout	Formulas	Data	Review	View			

	A	B	C	D	E	F	G
1, 2		Engineering and Production Control	Materials Management		Machining Department	Assembly Department	Total
3	Budgeted overhead costs before any						
4	interdepartment cost allocations	₹30,00,000	₹26,40,000		₹32,90,000	₹22,70,000	₹1,12,00,000
5	1st Allocation of Engg. and Prod. Control (3/10,5/10,2/10)[a]	(30,00,000)	9,00,000		15,00,000	6,00,000	
6			35,40,000				
7	1st Allocation of Materials Management (1/10,2/10,7/10)[b]	3,54,000	(35,40,000)		7,08,000	24,78,000	
8	2nd Allocation of Engg. and Prod. Control (3/10,5/10,2/10)[a]	(3,54,000)	1,06,200		1,77,000	70,800	
9	2nd Allocation of Materials Management (1/10,2/10,7/10)[b]	10,620	(1,06,200)		21,240	74,340	
10	3rd Allocation of Engg. and Prod. Control (3/10,5/10,2/10)[a]	(10,620)	3,190		5310	2,120	
11	3rd Allocation of Materials Management (1/10,2/10,7/10)[b]	320	(3190)		630	2,240	
12	4th Allocation of Engg. and Prod. Control (3/10,5/10,2/10)[a]	(320)	100		160	60	
13	4th Allocation of Materials Management (1/10,2/10,7/10)[b]	10	(100)		20	70	
14	5th Allocation of Engg. and Prod. Control (3/10,5/10,2/10)[a]	(10)	0		10	00	
15							
16	Total budgeted overhead of operating departments	₹0	₹0		₹5,70,237	5,49,763	₹1,12,00,000
17							
18	Total support department amounts allocated and reallocated (the numbers in parentheses in the first two columns):						
19	Engineering and Production Control: ₹30,00,000 + ₹3,54,000 + ₹10,620 + ₹320 + ₹10 = ₹33,64,950						
20	Materials Management: ₹35,40,000 + ₹1,06,200 + ₹3,190 + ₹100 = ₹36,49,490						
21							
22	[a]Base is ₹3,60,000 + ₹6,00,000 + ₹2,40,000 = ₹12,00,000; ₹3,60,000 ÷ ₹12,00,000 = 3/10;₹6,00,000 ÷ ₹12,00,000 = 5/10; ₹2,40,000 ÷ ₹12,00,000 = 2/10						
23	[b]Base is 400 + 800 + 2,800 = 4,000 labor-hours; 400 ÷ 4,000 = 1/10; 800 ÷ 4,000 = 2/10; 2,800 ÷ 4,000 = 7/10						

Step 2: Solve the Set of Linear Equations to Obtain the Complete Reciprocated Costs of Each Support Department. Substituting equation (1) into (2):

$$MM = ₹26,40,000 + [0.3\,(₹30,00,000 + 0.1\,MM)]$$
$$MM = ₹26,40,000 + ₹9,00,000 + 0.03\,MM$$
$$0.97\,MM = ₹35,40,000$$
$$MM = ₹36,49,490$$

Substituting this into equation (1):

$$EPC = ₹30,00,000 + 0.1\,(₹36,49,490)$$
$$EPC = ₹30,00,000 + ₹3,64,950 = ₹33,64,950$$

The complete reciprocated costs or artificial costs for the Materials Management Department are ₹36,49,490 and for the Engineering and Production Control Department are ₹33,64,950. The complete-reciprocated-cost figures also appear at the bottom of Exhibit 15-6 as the total amounts allocated and reallocated. When there are more than two support departments with reciprocal relationships, managers can use software such as Excel to calculate the complete reciprocated costs of each support department. Because the calculations involve finding the inverse of a matrix, the reciprocal method is also sometimes referred to as the matrix method.[6]

Step 3: Allocate the Complete Reciprocated Costs of Each Support Department to All Other Departments (Both Support Departments and Operating Departments) on the Basis of the Usage Percentages (Based on Total Units of Service Provided to All Departments). Consider the Materials Management Department. The complete reciprocated costs of ₹36,49,490 are allocated as follows:

To Engineering and Production Control (1/10) × ₹36,49,490	=	₹3,64,950
To Machining (2/10) × ₹36,49,490	=	₹7,29,900
To Assembly (7/10) × ₹36,49,490	=	₹25,54,640
Total		₹36,49,490

Similarly, the ₹33,64,950 in reciprocated costs of the Engineering and Production Control Department are allocated to the Materials Management Department (3/10), Machining Department (5/10), and Assembly Department (2/10).

Exhibit 15-7 presents summary data based on the reciprocal method.

Robinson's ₹70,14,440 complete reciprocated costs of the support departments exceeds the budgeted amount of ₹56,40,000.

Support Department	Complete Reciprocated Costs	Budgeted Costs	Difference
Engineering and Production Control	₹33,64,950	₹30,00,000	₹3,64,950
Materials Management	36,49,490	26,40,000	10,09,490
Total	₹70,14,440	₹56,40,000	₹13,74,440

Each support department's complete reciprocated cost is greater than the budgeted amount because it takes into account that support costs are allocated to all departments using its services and not just to operating departments. This step ensures that the reciprocal method fully recognizes all interrelationships among support departments, as well as relationships between support and operating departments. The difference between complete reciprocated costs and budgeted costs for each support department reflects the costs allocated among support departments. The total costs allocated to the operating departments under the reciprocal method are still only ₹56,40,000 (₹16,82,470 + ₹6,72,990 allocated from the Engineering and Production Control Department and ₹7,29,900 + ₹25,54,640 allocated from the Materials Management Department, see Exhibit 15-7).

Overview of Methods

The amount of manufacturing overhead costs allocated to the Machining and Assembly Departments will differ depending on the method used to allocate support-department costs. Differences among the three methods' allocations increase (1) as the magnitude of the reciprocal allocations increases and (2) as the differences across operating departments' usage of each support department's services increase. Note that while the final allocations under the reciprocal method are in between those under the direct and step-down methods in our example (see page 820), in general, there is no relationship between the amount of costs allocated to the operating departments under the different methods. The method of allocation becomes particularly important in the case of cost-reimbursement contracts that require allocation of support-department costs. To avoid disputes, managers should always clarify the method to be used for allocation. For example, Medicare

---

[6] If there are n support departments, then Step + will yield n linear equations. Solving the equations to calculate the complete reciprocated costs then requires finding the inverse of an n × n matrix.

Exhibit 15-7 Reciprocal Method of Allocating Support-Department Costs Using Linear Equations at HEC Company for 2013

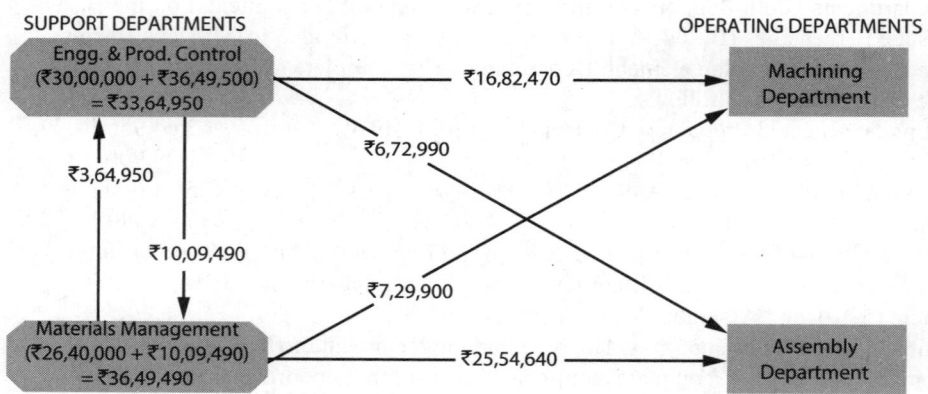

	B	C	D	E	F	G
	SUPPORT DEPARTMENTS			OPERATING DEPARTMENTS		
	Engineering and Production Control	Materials Management		Machining	Assembly	Total
3 Budgeted overhead costs before any						
4 interdepartment cost allocations	₹30,00,000	₹26,40,000		₹32,90,000	₹22,70,000	₹1,12,00,000
5 Allocation of Engg. & Prod. Control (3/10, 5/10, 2/10)[a]	30,00,000	10,09,490		16,82,470	6,72,990	
6 Allocation of Materials Management (1/10, 2/10, 7/10)[b]	3,64,950	(36,49,490)		7,29,900	25,54,640	
7						
8 Total budgeted overhead of operating departments	₹0	₹0		₹57,02,370	₹54,97,630	₹1,12,00,000

[a]Base is (₹3,60,000 + ₹6,00,000 + ₹2,40,000), or ₹12,00,000 ; ₹3,60,000 ÷ ₹12,00,000 = 3/10; ₹6,00,000 ÷ ₹12,00,000 = 5/10; ₹2,40,000 ÷ ₹12,00,000 = 2/10.

[b]Base is (400 + 800 + 2,800), or 4,000 hours; 400 ÷ 4,000 = 1/10; 800 ÷ 4,000 = 2/10; 2,800 ÷ 4,000 = 7/10.

reimbursements and central government research contracts with universities that pay for the recovery of indirect costs typically mandate use of the step-down method, with explicit requirements about the costs that can be included in the indirect cost pools.

The reciprocal method is conceptually the most precise method because it considers the mutual services provided among all support departments. The advantage of the direct and step-down methods is that they are simple for mangers to compute and understand relative to the reciprocal method. If the costs allocated to the operating departments using the direct or step-down methods closely approximate the costs allocated using the reciprocal method, managers should use the simpler direct or step-down methods. However, as computing power to perform repeated iterations (as in Exhibit 15-6) or to solve sets of simultaneous equations (as on pages 817–818) increases, more companies find the reciprocal method easier to implement.

Another advantage of the reciprocal method is that it highlights the complete reciprocated costs of support departments and how these costs differ from budgeted or actual costs of the departments. Knowing the complete reciprocated costs of a support department is a key input for decisions about whether to outsource all the services that the support department provides.

Suppose all of HEC's support-department costs are variable over the period of a possible outsourcing contract. Consider a third party's bid to provide, say, all services currently provided by the Materials Management Department. Do not compare the bid to the ₹26,40,000 costs reported for the Materials Management Department. The complete reciprocated costs of the Materials Management Department, which include the services the Engineering and Production Control Department provides the Materials Management Department, are ₹36,49,490 to deliver 4,000 hours of material-handling labor to other departments at HEC. The complete reciprocated costs for material-handling labor are ₹912.4 per hour (₹36,49,490 ÷ 4,000 hours). Other things being equal, an external pro vider's bid to supply the same materials management services as HEC's internal department at less than ₹36,49,490, or ₹912.4 per hour (even if much greater than ₹26,40,000) would improve HEC's operating income.

To see this point, note that the relevant savings from shutting down the Materials Management Department are ₹26,40,000 of Materials Management Department costs plus 10,09,490 of Engineering and Production Control Department costs. By closing down the Materials Management Department, HEC will no longer incur the 30% of reciprocated Engineering and Production Control Department costs (equal to ₹10,09,490) that were incurred to support the Materials Management Department. Therefore, the total cost savings are ₹36,49,490 (₹26,40,000 + 10,09,490).[7] Neither the direct nor the step-down method can provide this relevant information for outsourcing decisions.

Calculating the Cost of Job WPP 298

HEC uses the budgeted costs of each operating department (Machining and Assembly) to compute the rate per unit of each cost-allocation base used to allocate the indirect costs to a job (Step 5 in a job costing system, see Chapter 4). HEC budgets 20,000 direct labor-hours for the Assembly Department (of the 28,000 total direct manufacturing labor-hours) and 10,000 machine-hours for the Machining Department.

The budgeted overhead allocation rates for each operating department by allocation method are:

Support Department Cost-Allocation Method	Total Budgeted Overhead Costs After Allocation of All Support-Department Costs		Budgeted Overhead Rate per Hour for Product-Costing Purposes	
	Machining	Assembly	Machining (10,000 machine-hours)	Assembly (20,000 labor-hours)
Direct	₹60,19,530	₹51,80,470	₹602.0	₹259.0
Step-down	55,76,670	56,23,330	555.7	281.2
Reciprocal	57,02,370	54,97,630	570.2	274.9

The next step in a job-costing system (Step 6, see Chapter 4) is to compute the indirect costs allocated to a job. For the WPP 298 job, HEC uses 42 labor-hours in the Assembly Department (out of 88 direct manufacturing labor-hours) and 46 machine-hours in the Machining Department. The overhead costs allocated to the WPP 298 job under the three methods would be

---

[7] Technical issues when using the reciprocal method in outsourcing decisions are discussed in Robert S. Kaplan and Anthony A. Atkinson, *Advanced Management Accounting*, 3rd ed. (Upper Saddle River, NJ: Prentice Hall, 1998, pp. 73–81).

Direct:	₹38,570 (46 × ₹602.0 + 42 × ₹259.0)	
Step-down:	₹37,460 (46 × ₹557.7 + 42 × ₹281.2)	
Reciprocal:	₹37,780 (46 × ₹570.2 + 42 × ₹274.9)	

The manufacturing overhead costs allocated to WPP298 differ only a little under the three methods because the WPP 298 job requires roughly equal amounts of machine-hours and assembly labor-hours. These differences would be larger if a job required many more machine-hours than assembly hours or vice versa.

Using normal costing and multiple cost-allocation bases also results in higher indirect manufacturing costs allocated to Job WPP 298, ₹37,780 (under the reciprocal method) compared to ₹35,200 allocated using direct manufacturing labor-hours as the sole allocation base in Chapter 4 (page 147). Two cost-allocation bases—machine-hours and assembly labor-hours—are better able to model the drivers of manufacturing overhead costs.

The final step (Step 7, see Chapter 4) computes the total cost of the job by adding all direct and indirect costs assigned to the job. Under the reciprocal method, the total manufacturing costs of the WPP 298 job are as follows:

Direct manufacturing costs		
Direct materials	₹46,060	
Direct manufacturing labor	15,790	₹61,850
Manufacturing overhead costs		
Machining Department		
(₹570.2 per machine-hour × 46 machine-hours)	26,230	
Assembly Department		
(₹274.9 per labor-hour × 42 labor-hour)	11,550	37,780
Total manufacturing costs of job WPP 298		₹99,630

Note that the costs in Step 7 have four dollar amounts, each corresponding respectively to the two direct-cost and two indirect-cost categories in the costing system.

At the end of the year, actual manufacturing overhead costs of the Machining Department and the Assembly Department would be compared to the manufacturing overhead allocated for each department. To calculate the actual manufacturing overhead costs of the Machining and Assembly Departments, HEC would need to allocate the actual costs of the Materials Management and Engineering and Production Control Departments to the Machining and Assembly Departments using the methods described in this chapter. Management accountants would then make end-of-year adjustments (pages 158–164) separately for each cost pool for under- or overallocated overhead costs.

We now consider common costs, another special class of costs for which management accountants have developed specific allocation methods.

Learning Objective 4

Allocate common costs using the stand-alone method

. . . uses cost information of each user as a separate entity to allocate common costs and the incremental method

. . . allocates common costs primarily to one user and the remainder to other users

Allocating Common Costs

A **common cost** is a cost of operating a facility, activity, or like cost object that is shared by two or more users. Common costs arise because each user obtains a lower cost by sharing than the separate cost that would result if each user operated independently.

The goal is to allocate common costs to each user in a reasonable way. Consider Rajeev Anand, a graduating senior in New Delhi who has been invited to a job interview with an employer in Mumbai. The round-trip New Delhi–Mumbai airfare costs ₹12,000. A week later, Rajeev is also invited to an interview with an employer in Bangalore. The New Delhi–Bangalore round-trip airfare costs ₹8,000. Rajeev decides to combine the two recruiting trips into a New Delhi–Mumbai–Bangalore–New Delhi trip that will cost ₹15,000 in airfare. The prospective employers will reimburse Rajeev for the airfare. The ₹15,000 is a common cost that benefits both prospective employers because it is less than the ₹20,000 (₹12,000 + ₹8,000) that the two employers would have to pay if they operated independently.

What is a reasonable way to allocate the common costs of ₹15,000? Two methods of allocating this common cost between the two prospective employers are the stand-alone method and the incremental method.

Stand-Alone Cost-Allocation Method

The **stand-alone cost-allocation method** determines the weights for cost allocation by considering each user of the cost as a separate entity. For the common-cost airfare of ₹1,5000, information about the separate (stand-alone) round-trip airfares (₹12,000 and ₹8,000) is used to determine the allocation weights:

$$\text{Mumbai employer:} \frac{₹12,000}{₹12,000 + ₹8,000} \times ₹15,000 = 0.60 \times ₹15,000 = ₹9,000$$

$$\text{Bangalore employer:} \frac{₹8,000}{₹8000 + ₹12,000} \times ₹15,000 = 0.40 \times ₹15,000 = ₹6,000$$

Advocates of this method often emphasize the fairness or equity criterion described in Exhibit 13-1 (page 694). The method is viewed as reasonable because each employer bears a proportionate share of total costs in relation to the individual stand-alone costs.

Incremental Cost-Allocation Method

The **incremental cost-allocation method** ranks the individual users of a cost object in the order of users most responsible for the common cost and then uses this ranking to allocate cost among those users. The first-ranked user of the cost object is the *primary user* (also called the *primary party*) and is allocated costs up to the costs of the primary user as a stand-alone user. The second-ranked user is the *first incremental user* (*first incremental party*) and is allocated the additional cost that arises from two users instead of only the primary user. The third-ranked user is the *second incremental user* (*second incremental party*) and is allocated the additional cost that arises from three users instead of two users, and so on.

To see how this method works, consider again Rajeev Anand and his ₹15,000 airfare cost. Assume the Mumbai employer is viewed as the primary party. Rajeev's rationale is that he had already committed to go to Mumbai before accepting the invitation to interview in Bangalore. The cost allocations would be as follows:

Party	Costs Allocated	Cumulative Costs Allocated
Mumbai (primary)	₹12,000	₹12,000
Bangalore (incremental)	3,000 (₹15,000 − ₹12,000)	₹15,000
Total	₹15,000	

The Mumbai employer is allocated the full New Delhi–Mumbai airfare. The unallocated part of the total airfare is then allocated to the Bangalore employer. If the Bangalore employer had been chosen as the primary party, the cost allocations would have been Bangalore ₹8,000 (the stand-alone round-trip Mumbai–Bangalore airfare) and Mumbai ₹7,000 (₹15,000 − ₹8,000). When there are more than two parties, this method requires them to be ranked from first to last (such as by the date on which each employer invited the candidate to interview).

Under the incremental method, the primary party typically receives the highest allocation of the common costs. If the incremental users are newly formed companies or subunits, such as a new product line or a new sales territory, the incremental method may enhance their chances for short-run survival by assigning them a low allocation of the common costs. The difficulty with the method is that, particularly if a large common cost is involved, every user would prefer to be viewed as the incremental party!

One approach managers can use to avoid disputes in such situations is to use the stand-alone cost-allocation method. Another approach is to use the *Shapley value*, which considers each party as first the primary party and then the incremental party. From the calculations shown earlier, the Mumbai employer is allocated ₹12,000 as the primary party and ₹7,000 as the incremental party, for an average of ₹9,500 [(₹12,000 + ₹7,000) ÷ 2]. The Bengaluru employer is allocated ₹8,000 as the primary party and ₹3,000 as the incremental party, for an average of ₹5,500 [(₹8,000 + ₹3,000) ÷ 2]. The Shapley value method allocates, to each employer, the average of the costs allocated as the primary party and as the incremental party: ₹9,500 to the Mumbai employer and ₹5,500 to the Bangalore employer.[8]

As our discussion suggests, allocating common costs is not clear-cut and can generate disputes. Whenever feasible, managers should specify the rules for such allocations in advance. If this is not done, then, rather than blindly follow one method or another, managers should exercise judgment when allocating common costs by thinking carefully about allocation methods that appear fair to each party. For instance, Rajeev must choose an allocation method for his airfare cost that is acceptable to each prospective employer. He cannot, for example, exceed the maximum reimbursable amount of airfare for either firm. The next section discusses the role of cost data in various types of contracts, another area where disputes about cost allocation frequently arise.

Decision Point ▶

What methods can managers use to allocate common costs to two or more users?

Learning Objective 5

Understand how bundling of products

...two or more products sold for a single-price

causes revenue allocation issues

...allocating revenues to each product in the bundle to evaluate managers of individual products

and the methods managers use to allocate revenues

...using the stand-alone method or the incremental method

Bundled Products and Revenue Allocation Methods

Allocation issues can also arise when revenues from multiple products (for example, different software programs or cable and Internet packages) are bundled together and sold at a single price. The methods for revenue allocation parallel those described for common-cost allocations.

Bundling and Revenue Allocation

Revenues are inflows of assets (almost always cash or accounts receivable) companies receive for products or services provided to customers. Similar to cost allocation, **revenue allocation** occurs when revenues are related to a particular *revenue object* but cannot be traced to it in an economically feasible (cost-effective) way. A **revenue object** is anything for which a separate measurement of revenue is desired. Examples of revenue objects include products, customers, and divisions. We illustrate revenue-allocation issues for Dynamic Software Corporation, which develops, sells, and supports three software programs:

1. WordMaster, a word-processing program, released 36 months ago
2. DataMaster, a spreadsheet program, released 18 months ago

---

[8] For further discussion of the Shapley value, see Joel S. Demski, "Cost Allocation Games," in Joint Cost Allocations , ed. Shane Moriarity (University of Oklahoma Center for Economic and Management Research, 1981); Lech Kruś and Piotr Bronisz, "Cooperative Game Solution Concepts to a Cost Allocation Problem," *European Journal of Operational Research* 122:2 (April 16, 2000): 258–271.

3. FinanceMaster, a budgeting and cash-management program, released six months ago with a lot of favorable media attention

Dynamic Software sells these three products individually as well as together as bundled products.

A **bundled product** is a package of two or more products (or services) that is sold for a single price but whose individual components may be sold as separate items at their own "stand-alone" prices. The price of a bundled product is typically less than the sum of the prices of the individual products sold separately. For example, banks often provide individual customers with a bundle of services from different departments (cheques, safety-deposit box, and investment advisory) for a single fee. A resort hotel may offer, for a single amount per customer, a weekend package that includes services from its lodging (the room), food (the restaurant), and recreational (golf and tennis) departments. When department managers have revenue or profit responsibilities for individual products, the bundled revenue must be allocated among the individual products in the bundle.

Dynamic Software allocates revenues from its bundled product sales (called "suite sales") to individual products. Individual-product profitability is used to compensate software engineers, developers, and product managers responsible for developing and managing each product.

How should Dynamic Software allocate suite revenues to individual products? Consider information pertaining to the three "stand-alone" and "suite" products in 2013:

	Selling Price	Manufacturing Cost per Unit
Stand-alone		
WordMaster	₹1,250	₹180
SpreadMaster	1,500	₹200
FinanceMaster	2,250	₹250
Suite		
Word + Spread	₹2,200	
Word + Finance	2,800	
Finance + Spread	3,050	
Word + Finance + Spread	3,800	

Just as we saw in the section on common-cost allocations, the two main revenue-allocation methods are the stand-alone method and the incremental method.

Stand-Alone Revenue-Allocation Method

The **stand-alone revenue-allocation method** uses product-specific information on the products in the bundle as weights for allocating the bundled revenues to the individual products. The term *stand-alone* refers to the product as a separate (nonsuite) item. Consider the Word + Finance suite, which sells for ₹2,800. Three types of weights for the stand-alone method are as follows:

1. **Selling prices**. Using the individual selling prices of ₹1,250 for WordMaster and ₹2,250 for FinanceMaster, the weights for allocating the ₹2,800 suite revenues between the products are:

$$\text{WordMast} \quad \frac{₹1,250}{₹1,250 + ₹2,250} \times ₹2,800 = 0.357 \times ₹2,800 = ₹1,000$$

$$\text{FinanceMaster:} \quad \frac{₹2,250}{₹1,250 + ₹2,250} \times ₹280 = 0.643 \times ₹2,800 = ₹1,800$$

2. **Unit costs**. This method uses the costs of the individual products (in this case, manufacturing cost per unit) to determine the weights for the revenue allocations.

$$\text{WordMaster:} \quad \frac{₹180}{₹180 + ₹250} \times ₹2,800 = 0.419 \times ₹2,800 = ₹1,170$$

$$\text{FinanceMaster:} \quad \frac{₹250}{₹180 + ₹250} \times ₹2,800 = 0.581 \times ₹2,800 = ₹1,630$$

3. **Physical units**. This method gives each product unit in the suite the same weight when allocating suite revenue to individual products. Therefore, with two products in the Word + Finance suite, each product is allocated 50% of the suite revenues.

$$\text{WordMaster:} \quad \frac{1}{1+1} \times ₹2,800 = 0.419 \times ₹2,800 = ₹1,400$$

$$\text{FinanceMaster:} \quad \frac{1}{1+1} \times ₹2,800 = 0.581 \times ₹2,800 = ₹1,400$$

These three approaches to determining weights for the stand-alone method result in very different revenue allocations to the individual products:

Revenue-Allocation Weights	WordMaster	FinanceMaster
Selling prices	₹1,000	₹1,800
Unit costs	1,170	1,630
Physical units	1,400	1,400

Which method do managers prefer? The selling prices method is best because the weights explicitly consider the prices customers are willing to pay for the individual products. Weighting approaches that use revenue information better capture "benefits received" by customers than unit costs or physical units.[9] The physical-units revenue-allocation method is used when managers cannot use any of the other methods (such as when selling prices are unstable or unit costs are difficult to calculate for individual products).

Incremental Revenue-Allocation Method

The **incremental revenue-allocation method** ranks individual products in a bundle according to criteria determined by management—such as the product in the bundle with the most sales—and then uses this ranking to allocate bundled revenues to individual products. The first-ranked product is the *primary product* in the bundle. The second-ranked product is the *first incremental product*, the third-ranked product is the *second incremental product*, and so on.

How do companies decide on product rankings under the incremental revenue-allocation method? Some organizations survey customers about the importance of each of the individual products to their purchase decision. Others use data on the recent stand-alone sales performance of the individual products in the bundle. A third approach is for top managers to use their knowledge or intuition to decide the rankings.

Consider again the Word + Finance suite. Assume WordMaster is designated as the primary product. If the suite selling price exceeds the stand-alone price of the primary prod-

---

[9] The Federal Acquisition Regulation (FAR), issued in March 2005 (see www.acquisition.gov/far/current/pdf/FAR.pdf) includes the following definition of *allocability* (in FAR 31.201-4): "A cost is allocable if it is assignable or chargeable to one or more cost objectives on the basis of relative benefits received or other equitable relationship. Subject to the foregoing, a cost is allocable to a Government contract if it: (a) Is incurred specifically for the contract; (b) Benefits both the contract and other work, and can be distributed to them in reasonable proportion to the benefits received; or (c) Is necessary to the overall operation of the business, although a direct relationship to any particular cost objective cannot be shown."

uct, the primary product is allocated 100% of its *stand-alone* revenue. Because the suite price of ₹2,800 exceeds the stand-alone price of ₹1,250 for WordMaster, WordMaster is allocated revenues of ₹1,250, with the remaining revenue of ₹1,550 (₹2,800 − ₹1,250) allocated to FinanceMaster:

Product	Revenue Allocated	Cumulative Revenue Allocated
WordMaster	₹1,250	₹1250
FinanceMaster	1,550 (₹2,800 − ₹1,250)	₹2,800
Total	₹2,800	

If the suite price is less than or equal to the stand-alone price of the primary product, the primary product is allocated 100% of the suite revenue. All other products in the suite receive no allocation of revenue.

Now suppose FinanceMaster is designated as the primary product and WordMaster as the first incremental product. Then, the incremental revenue-allocation method allocates revenues of the Word + Finance suite as follows:

Product	Revenue Allocated	Cumulative Revenue Allocated
FinanceMaster	₹2,250	₹2,250
WordMaster	550 (₹2,800 − ₹2,250)	₹2,800
Total	₹2,800	

If Dynamic Software sells equal quantities of WordMaster and FinanceMaster, then the Shapley value method allocates to each product the average of the revenues allocated as the primary and first-incremental products:

$$\text{WordMaster:} \quad (₹1,250 + ₹550) \div 2 = ₹1,800 \div 2 = \quad ₹900$$
$$\text{FinanceMaster:} \quad (₹2,250 + ₹1,550) \div 2 = ₹3,800 \div 2 = \quad 1,900$$
$$\text{Total} \qquad\qquad\qquad\qquad\qquad\qquad\qquad\qquad ₹2,800$$

What happens if the firm sells 80,000 units of WordMaster and 20,000 units of FinanceMaster in the most recent quarter? Because Dynamic Software sells four times as many units of WordMaster, its manage believe that the sales of the Word + Finance *weighted Shapley value method* takes this fact into account. It assigns four times as much weight to the revenue allocations when WordMaster is the primary product as when FinanceMaster is the primary product, resulting in the following allocations:

$$\text{WordMaster:} \quad (₹1,250 \times 4 + ₹550 \times 1) \div (4 + 1) = ₹5,550 \div 5 = ₹1,110$$
$$\text{FinanceMaster:} \quad (₹2,250 \times 1 + ₹1,550 \times 4) \div (4 + 1) = ₹8,450 \div 5 = \quad 1,690$$
$$\text{Total} \qquad\qquad\qquad\qquad\qquad\qquad\qquad\qquad\qquad\qquad ₹2,800$$

When there are more than two products in the suite, the incremental revenue-allocation method allocates suite revenues sequentially. Assume WordMaster is the primary product in Supersoft's three-product suite (Word + Finance + Spread). FinanceMaster is the first incremental product, and SpreadMaster is the second incremental product. This suite sells for ₹3,800. The allocation of the ₹3,800 suite revenues proceeds as follows:

Product	Revenue Allocated	Cumulative Revenue Allocated
WordMaster	₹1,250	₹1,250
FinanceMaster	₹1,550 (₹2,800 − ₹1,250)	₹2,800 (price of Word + Finance suite)
SpreadMaster	1,000 (₹3,800 − ₹2,800)	₹3,800 (price of Word + Finance + Spread suite)
Total	₹3,800	

Now suppose WordMaster is the primary product, SpreadMaster is the first incremental product, and FinanceMaster is the second-incremental product.

Product	Revenue Allocated	Cumulative Revenue Allocated
WordMaster	₹1,250	₹1,250
SpreadMaster	950 (₹2,200 − ₹1,250)	₹2,200 (price of Word + Spread suite)
FinanceMaster	1,600 (₹3,800 − ₹2,200)	₹3,800 (price of Word + Spread + Finance suite)
Total	₹3,800	

Decision Point ▶

What is product bundling and how can managers allocate revenues of a bundled product to individual products in the package?

The ranking of the individual products in the suite determines the revenues allocated to them. Product managers at Supersoft likely would differ on how they believe their individual products contribute to sales of the suite products. In fact, each product manager would claim to be responsible for the primary product in the Word + Finance + Spread suite![10] Because the stand-alone revenue-allocation method does not require rankings of individual products in the suite, this method is less likely to cause debates among product managers.

Problem for Self-Study

This problem illustrates how costs of two corporate support departments are allocated to operating divisions using the dual-rate method. Fixed costs are allocated using budgeted costs and budgeted hours used by other departments. Variable costs are allocated using actual costs and actual hours used by other departments.

Computer Horizons budgets the following amounts for its two central corporate support departments (legal and personnel) in supporting each other and the two manufacturing divisions, the Laptop Division (LTD) and the Work Station Division (WSD):

			A				B		C		D		E		F		G
	File Edit View Insert Format Tools Data Window Help																
			A				B		C		D		E		F		G
1							SUPPORT						OPERATING				
2							Legal Department		Personnel Department				LTD		WSD		Total
3	**BUDGETED USAGE**																
4	Legal (hours)						—		250				1,500		750		2,500
5	(Percentages)						—		10%				60%		30%		100%
6	Personnel (hours)						2,500		—				22,500		25,000		50,000
7	(Percentages)						5%		—				45%		50%		100%
8																	
9	**ACTUAL USAGE**																
10	Legal (hours)						—		400				400		1,200		2,000
11	(Percentages)						—		20%				20%		60%		100%
12	Personnel (hours)						2,000		—				26,600		11,400		40,000
13	(Percentages)						5%		—				66.50%		28.5%		100%
14	Budgeted fixed overhead costs before any																
15	interdepartment cost allocations						₹36,00,000		₹47,50,000				—		—		₹83,50,000
16	Actual variable overhead costs before any																
17	interdepartment cost allocations						₹20,00,000		₹60,00,000				—		—		₹80,00,000

---

[10] Details on the Cost Accounting Standards Board are available at www.whitehouse.gov/omb/procurement/casb.html. The CASB is part of the Office of Federal Procurement Policy, U.S. Office of Management and Budget.

What amount of support-department costs for legal and personnel will be allocated to LTD and WSD using (a) the direct method, (b) the step-down method (allocating the Legal Department costs first), and (c) the reciprocal method using linear equations?

Exhibit 15-8   Alternative Methods of Allocating Corporate Support-Department Costs to Operating Divisions of Computer Horizons: Dual-Rate Method

File   Edit   View   Insert   Format   Tools   Data   Window   Help

	A	B	C	D	E	F	G
		CORPORATE SUPPORT DEPARTMENTS			OPERATING DIVISIONS		
20							
21	Allocation Method	Legal Department	Personnel Department		LTD	WSD	Total
22	A. DIRECT METHOD						
23	Fixed Costs	₹36,00,000	₹47,50,000				
24	Legal (1,500 ÷ 2,250; 750 ÷ 2,250)	(36,00,000)			₹24,00,000	₹12,00,000	
25	Personnel (22,500 ÷ 47,500; 25,000 ÷ 47,500)		(47,50,000)		22,50,000	25,00,000	
26	Fixed support dept. cost allocated to operating divisions	₹0	₹0		₹46,50,000	₹37,00,000	₹83,50,000
27	Variable Costs	₹20,00,000	₹60,00,000				
28	Legal (400 ÷ 1,600; 1,200 ÷ 1,600)	(20,00,000)			₹5,00,000	15,00,000	
29	Personnel (26,600 ÷ 38,000; 11,400 ÷ 38,000)		(60,00,000)		42,00,000	18,00,000	
30	Variable support dept. cost allocated to operating divisions	₹0	₹0		₹47,00,000	₹33,00,000	₹80,00,000
31	B. STEP-DOWN METHOD						
32	(Legal Department First)						
33	Fixed Costs	₹36,00,000	₹47,50,000				
34	Legal (250 ÷ 2,500; 1,500 ÷ 2,500; 750 ÷ 2,500)	(36,00,000)	3,60,000		₹21,60,000	₹10,80,000	
35	Personnel (22,500 ÷ 47,500; 25,000 ÷ 47,500)		(51,10,000)		24,20,530	26,89,470	
36	Fixed support dept. cost allocated to operating divisions	₹0	₹0		₹45,80,530	₹37,69,470	₹83,50,000
37	Variable Costs	₹20,00,000	₹60,00,000				
38	Legal (400 ÷ 2,000; 400 ÷ 2,000; 1,200 ÷ 2,000)	(20,00,000)	4,00,000		₹4,00,000	₹12,00,000	
39	Personnel (26,600 ÷ 38,000; 11,400 ÷ 38,000)		(64,00,000)		44,80,000	19,20,000	
40	Variable support dept. cost allocated to operating divisions	₹0	₹0		₹48,80,000	₹31,20,000	₹80,00,000
41	C. RECIPROCAL METHOD						
42	Fixed Costs	₹36,00,000	₹47,50,000				
43	Legal (250 ÷ 2,500; 1,500 ÷ 2,500; 750 ÷ 2,500)	(38,56,780)[a]	3,85,680		₹23,14,070	₹11,57,030	
44	Personnel (2,500 ÷ 50,000; 22,500 ÷ 50,000; 25,000 ÷ 50,000)	2,56,780	(51,35,680)[a]		23,11,060	25,67,840	
45	Fixed support dept. cost allocated to operating divisions	₹0	₹0		₹46,25,130	₹37,24,870	₹83,50,000
46	Variable Costs	₹20,00,000	₹60,00,000				
47	Legal (400 ÷ 2,000; 400 ÷ 2,000; 1,200 ÷ 2,000)	(23,23,230)[b]	4,64,650		₹4,64,650	₹13,93,930	
48	Personnel (2,000 ÷ 40,000; 26,600 ÷ 40,000; 11,400 ÷ 40,000)	3,23,230	(64,64,650)[b]		42,98,990	18,42,430	
49	Variable support dept. cost allocated to operating divisions	₹0	₹0		₹47,63,640	₹32,36,360	₹80,00,000
50							
51	[a] FIXED COSTS		[b] VARIABLE COSTS				
52	Letting LF = Legal Department Fixed Costs, and PF = Personnel Department Fixed Costs, the simultaneous equations for the reciprocal method for fixed costs are		Letting LF = Legal Department Variable Costs, and PV = Personnel Department Variable Costs, the simultaneous equations for the reciprocal method for variable costs are				
53	$LF = ₹36,00,000 + 0.05\ PF$		$LV = ₹20,00,000 + 0.05\ PV$				
54	$PF = ₹47,50,000 + 0.10\ LF$		$PV = ₹60,00,000 + 0.20\ LV$				
55	$LF = ₹36,00,000 + 0.05\ (₹47,50,000 + 0.10\ LF)$		$LV = ₹20,00,000 + 0.05\ (₹60,00,000 + 0.20\ LV)$				
56	$LF = ₹38,56,780$		$LV = ₹23,23,230$				
57	$PF = ₹47,50,000 + 0.10\ (₹38,56,780) = ₹51,35,680$		$PV = ₹60,00,000 + 0.20\ (₹23,23,230) = ₹64,64,650$				

Solution

Exhibit 15-8 presents the computations for allocating the fixed and variable support-department costs. A summary of these costs follows:

	Laptop Division (LTD)	Work Station Division (WSD)
(a) Direct Method		
Fixed costs	₹46,50,000	₹37,00,000
Variable costs	47,00,000	33,00,000
	₹93,50,000	₹70,00,000
(b) Step-Down Method		
Fixed costs	₹45,80,530	₹37,69,470
Variable costs	48,80,000	31,20,000
	₹94,60,530	₹68,89,470
(c) Reciprocal Method		
Fixed costs	₹46,25,130	₹37,24,870
Variable costs	47,63,640	32,36,360
	₹93,88,770	₹69,61,230

Decision Points

The following question-and-answer format summarizes the chapter's learning objectives. Each decision presents a key question related to a learning objective. The guidelines are the answer to that question.

Decision	Guidelines
1. When should managers use the dual-rate method over the single-rate method?	The single-rate method aggregates fixed and variable costs and allocates them to objects using a single allocation base and rate. Under the dual-rate method, costs are grouped into separate variable cost and fixed cost pools; each pool uses a different cost-allocation base and rate. If costs can be easily separated into variable and fixed costs, managers should use the dual-rate method because it provides better information for making decisions.
2. What factors should managers consider when deciding between allocation based on budgeted and actual rates and between budgeted and actual usage?	Using budgeted rates enables managers of user departments to have certainty about the costs allocated to them and insulates users from inefficiencies in the supplier department. Charging budgeted variable cost rates to users based on actual usage is causally appropriate and promotes control of resource consumption. Charging fixed cost rates on the basis of budgeted usage helps user divisions with planning and leads to goal congruence when considering outsourcing decisions.
3. What methods can managers use to allocate costs of multiple support departments to operating departments?	The three methods managers can use are the direct, the step-down, and the reciprocal methods. The direct method allocates each support department's costs to operating departments without allocating a support department's costs to other support departments. The step-down method allocates support-department costs to other support departments and to operating departments in a sequential manner that partially recognizes the mutual services provided among all support departments. The reciprocal method fully recognizes mutual services provided among all support departments.

4. What methods can managers use to allocate common costs to two or more users?

Common costs are the costs of a cost object (such as operating a facility or performing an activity) that are shared by two or more users. The stand-alone cost-allocation method uses information pertaining to each user of the cost object to determine cost-allocation weights. The incremental cost-allocation method ranks individual users of the cost object and allocates common costs first to the primary user and then to the other incremental users. The Shapley value method considers each user, in turn, as the primary and the incremental user.

5. How can contract disputes over reimbursement amounts based on costs be reduced?

Disputes can be reduced by making the cost-allocation rules as explicit as possible and including them in the contract. These rules should include details such as the allowable cost items, the acceptable cost-allocation bases, and how differences between budgeted and actual costs are to be accounted for.

6. What is product bundling, and how can managers allocate revenues of a bundled product to individual products in the package?

Bundling occurs when a package of two or more products (or services) is sold for a single price. Revenue allocation of the bundled price is required when managers of the individual products in the bundle are evaluated on product revenue or product operating income. Revenues can be allocated for a bundled product using the stand-alone method, the incremental method, or the Shapley value method.

TERMS TO LEARN

This chapter and the Glossary at the end of the book contain definitions of the following important terms:

bundled product **(p. 825)**
common cost **(p. 822)**
complete reciprocated
  costs **(p. 817)**
direct method **(p. 814)**
dual-rate
  method **(p. 802)**
incremental cost-allocation
  method **(p. 823)**

incremental revenue-allocation
  method **(p. 826)**
matrix method **(p. 819)**
operating department **(p. 816)**
production department **(p. 816)**
reciprocal method **(p. 817)**
revenue allocation **(p. 824)**
revenue object **(p. 824)**
service department **(p. 802)**

single-rate method **(p. 802)**
sequential allocation
  method **(p. 815)**
stand-alone cost-allocation
  method **(p. 823)**
stand-alone revenue-allocation
  method **(p. 825)**
step-down method **(p. 815)**
support department **(p. 802)**

ASSIGNMENT MATERIAL

Questions

15-1 Distinguish between the single-rate and the dual-rate methods.

15-2 Describe how the dual-rate method is useful to division managers in decision making.

15-3 How do budgeted cost rates motivate the support-department manager to improve efficiency?

15-4 Give examples of allocation bases used to allocate support-department cost pools to operating departments.

15-5 Why might a manager prefer that budgeted rather than actual cost-allocation rates be used for costs being allocated to his or her department from another department?

15-6 "To ensure unbiased cost allocations, fixed costs should be allocated on the basis of estimated long-run use by user-department managers." Do you agree? Why?

15-7 Distinguish among the three methods of allocating the costs of support departments to operating departments.

15-8 What is conceptually the most defensible method for allocating support-department costs? Why?

15-9 Distinguish between two methods of allocating common costs.

15-10 What role does the Cost Accounting Standards Board play when companies contract with the U.S. government?

15-11 What is one key way to reduce cost-allocation disputes that arise with government contracts?

15-12 Describe how companies are increasingly facing revenue-allocation decisions.

15-13 Distinguish between the stand-alone and the incremental revenue-allocation methods.

15-14 Identify and discuss arguments that individual product managers may put forward to support their preferred revenue-allocation method.

15-15 How might a dispute over the allocation of revenues of a bundled product be resolved?

Solved Examples

15-16 Single-rate versus dual-rate allocation methods, support department. The Indian Engineering Company which owns epower plant that services all manufacturing departments of the Company has a budget for the coming year. This budget has been expressed in the following terms on a monthly basis:

Manufacturing Department	Needed at Practical Capacity Production Level (Kilowatt-Hours)	Average Expected Monthly Usage (Kilowatt-Hours)
A	10,000	8,000
B	20,000	9,000
C	12,000	7,000
D	8,000	6,000
Totals	50,000	30,000

The expected monthly costs for operating the power plant during the budget year are ₹15,00,000: ₹6,00,000 variable and ₹9,00,000 fixed.

Required

1. Assume that a single cost pool is used for the power plant costs. What amounts will be allocated to each manufacturing department if (a) the rate is calculated based on practical capacity and costs are allocated based on practical capacity and (b) the rate is calculated based on expected monthly usage and costs are allocated based on expected monthly usage.

2. Assume that dual-rate method is used with separate cost pools for the variable and fixed costs. Variable costs are allocated on the basis of expected monthly usage. Fixed costs are allocated on the basis of practical capacity. What amount in rupee will be allocated to each manufacturing department? Why might you prefer the dual-rate method?

Solution

Single-rate versus dual-rate allocation methods, support department.

Bases available (kilowatt hours):

	A	B	C	D	Total
Practical capacity	10,000	20,000	12,000	8,000	50,000
Expected monthly usage	8,000	9,000	7,000	6,000	30,000

1a. Single-rate method based on practical capacity:

Total costs in pool	= ₹6,00,000 + ₹9,00,000 = ₹15,00,000
Practical capacity	= 50,000 kilowatt hours
Allocation rate	= ₹15,00,000 ÷ 50,000 = ₹30 per hour of capacity

	A	B	C	D	Total
Practical capacity in hours	10,000	20,000	12,000	8,000	50,000
Costs allocated at ₹30 per hour	₹3,00,000	₹6,00,000	₹3,60,000	₹2,40,000	₹15,00,000

1b. Single-rate method based on expected monthly usage:

Total costs in pool	= ₹6,00,000 + ₹9,00,000 = ₹15,00,000
Expected usage	= 30,000 kilowatt hours
Allocation rate	= ₹15,00,000 ÷ 30,000 = ₹50 per hour of expected usage

	A	B	C	D	Total
Expected monthly usage in hours	8,000	9,000	7,000	6,000	30,000
Costs allocated at ₹50 per hour	₹4,00,000	₹4,50,000	₹3,50,000	₹3,00,000	₹15,00,000

2. Variable-Cost Pool:

Total costs in pool	= ₹6,00,000
Expected usage	= 30,000 kilowatt hours
Allocation rate	= ₹20 per hour of expected usage

Fixed-Cost Pool:

Total costs in pool	= ₹9,00,000
Practical capacity	= 50,000 kilowatt hours
Allocation rate	= ₹18 per hour of capacity

	A	B	C	D	Total
Variable-cost pool					
₹20 × 8,000; 9,000; 7,000, 6,000	₹1,60,000	₹1,80,000	₹1,40,000	₹1,20,000	₹6,00,000
Fixed-cost pool					
₹18 × 10,000; 20,000; 12,000, 8,000	1,80,000	3,60,000	2,16,000	1,44,000	9,00,000
Total	₹3,40,000	₹5,40,000	₹3,56,000	₹2,64,000	₹15,00,000

The dual-rate method permits a more refined allocation of the power department costs; it permits the use of different allocation bases for different cost pools. The fixed costs result from decisions most likely associated with the practical capacity level. The variable costs result from decisions most likely associated with monthly usage.

15-17 Allocation of common costs. Mayank and Raghav are students at Delhi university. They share an apartment that is owned by Raghav. Raghav is considering subscribing to an Internet provider that has the following packages available:

Package	Per Month
Internet access	₹750
Phone services	250
Internet access + phone services	900

Mayank spends most of his time on the Internet ("everything can be found online now"). Raghav prefers to spend his time talking on the phone rather than using the Internet ("going online is a waste of time"). They agree that the purchase of the ₹900 total package is a "win–win" situation.

Required

1. Allocate the ₹900 between Mayank and Raghav using (a) the stand-alone cost-allocation method, (b) the incremental cost-allocation method, and (c) the Shapley value method.

2. Which method would you recommend they use and why?

Solution

1. Three methods of allocating the ₹900 are:

	Mayank	Raghav
Stand-alone	₹675	₹225
Incremental (Raghav primary)	650	250
Incremental (Mayank primary)	750	150
Shapley value	700	200

a. Stand-alone cost allocation method.

Mayank: $\dfrac{₹750}{₹750 + ₹250} \times ₹900 = \dfrac{3}{4} \times ₹900 = ₹675$

Raghav: $\dfrac{₹250}{₹750 + ₹250} \times ₹900 = \dfrac{1}{4} \times ₹900 = ₹225$

b. Incremental cost allocation method.

Assume Raghav (the owner) is the primary user and Mayank is the incremental user:

User	Costs Allocated	Cumulative Costs Allocated
Raghav	₹250	₹250
Mayank	650 (₹900 – ₹250)	₹900
Total	₹900	

This method may generate some dispute over the ranking. Notice that Mayank pays only ₹650 despite his prime interest in the more expensive Internet access package. Raghav could make the argument that if Mayank were ranked first he would have to pay ₹750 because he is the major Internet user. Then, Raghav would only have to pay ₹150.

Assume Mayank is the primary user and Raghav is the incremental user:

User	Costs Allocated	Cumulative Costs Allocated
Mayank	₹750	₹750
Raghav	150 (₹900 – ₹750)	₹900
Total	₹900	

c. Shapley value (average over costs allocated as the primary and incremental user).

User	Costs Allocated
Mayank	(₹650 + ₹750) ÷ 2 = ₹700
Raghav	(₹250 + ₹150) ÷ 2 = ₹200

2. The Shapley value approach is recommended. It is fairer than the incremental method because it avoids considering one user as the primary user and allocating more of the common costs to that user. It also avoids disputes about who is the primary user. It allocates costs in a manner that is close to the costs allocated under the stand-alone method but takes a more comprehensive view of the common cost allocation problem by considering primary and incremental users that the stand-alone method ignores.

More generally, other criteria to guide common cost allocations include the following:

a. Cause and effect. It is not possible to trace individual causes (either Internet access or phone services) to individual effects (uses by Mayank or Raghav). The ₹900 total package is a bundled product.

b. Benefits received. There are various ways of operationalizing the benefits received:

(i) Monthly service charge for their prime interest—Internet access for Mayank (₹750), and phone services for Raghav (₹250). This measure captures the services available to each person.

(ii) Actual usage by each person. This would involve keeping a record of usage by each person and then allocating the ₹900 on a percent usage time basis. This measure captures the services actually used by each person, but it may prove burdensome, and it would be subject to honest reporting by Mayank and Raghav.

c. Ability to pay. This criterion requires that Mayank and Raghav agree upon their relative ability to pay.

d. Fairness or equity. This criterion is relatively nebulous. One approach would be to split the ₹900 using the Shapely value or the stand-alone method.

15-18 Single-rate cost-allocation method, budgeted versus actual costs and quantities. Dabur Food Company, processes orange juice at its Orange Juice Division and grapefruit juice at its Grapefruit Juice Division. It purchases oranges and grapefruit from growers' cooperatives at Nagpur. It owns its own trucking fleet. Each plant is the same distance from Nagpur. The trucking fleet is operated as a cost center. Each plant is billed for the direct and indirect costs of each round-trip.

The trucking fleet costs include direct costs (labor costs of drivers, fuel, and toll charges) and indirect costs. Indirect costs include depreciation on tires and the vehicle, insurance, and state registration fees.

At the start of 2015, the Orange Juice Division budgeted for 150 round-trips and the Grapefruit Juice Division budgeted for 100 round-trips. Based on these 250 budgeted trips (equal to the practical capacity of the trucking fleet), the budgeted indirect costs of the trucking fleet were ₹28,75,000. The following actual results occurred:

Trucking fleet indirect costs	₹24,18,750
Number of round-trips,	150
Number of round-trips	75

The trucking fleet division uses the single-rate method when allocating indirect trucking costs.

Required

1. What is the indirect cost rate per round-trip when (a) budgeted costs and budgeted round-trips are used and (b) when actual costs and actual round-trips are used?

2. What are the effects of using the rate based on budgeted costs/budgeted round-trips rather than the rate based on actual costs/actual round-trips to allocate costs to the Orange Juice Division using the actual number of round trips.

Solution

Single-rate cost allocation method, budgeted versus actual costs and ouantities.

1.a. Budgeted indirect costs = ₹28,75,000 ÷ ₹11,500 per round-trip

Budgeted trips = 250 trips

b. Actual indirect costs = ₹24,18,750 ÷ ₹10,750 per round-trip

Actual trips = 225 trips

2. When budgeted costs/budgeted quantities are used, the Orange Juice Division knows at the start of 2015 that it will be charged a rate of ₹11,500 per trip. This enables it to make operating decisions knowing the rate it will have to pay for transportation. In contrast, when actual costs/actual quantities are used, the Orange Juice Division must wait until year-end to know its transportation charges.

The use of actual costs/actual quantities makes the costs allocated to one user a function of the actual demand of other users. In 2014, the actual usage was 225 trips, which is 25 trips below the 250 trips budgeted. The Orange Juice Division used all the 150 trips it had budgeted. The Grapefruit Juice Division used only 75 of the 100 trips budgeted. When costs are allocated based on actual costs and actual quantities, the same fixed costs are spread over fewer trips resulting in a higher rate than if the Grapefruit Division had used 100 trips. The Orange Juice Division then bears a proportionately higher share of the fixed costs.

Using actual costs/actual rates also means then any efficiencies or inefficiencies of the trucking division gets passed along to the user divisions. In general, this will have the effect of making the trucking division less sensitive about its costs, although in 2015, the trucking division appears to have managed its costs well leading to a lower cost per roundtrip relative to the budgeted cost per round trip.

15-19 Dual-rate cost-allocation method, budgeted versus actual costs, and practical capacity versus actual quantities (continuation of 15-18). Dabur Food Company decides to examine the effect of using the dual-rate method for allocating indirect trucking costs to each round-trip. At the start of 2015, the budgeted indirect costs were:

Variable indirect cost per round-trip	₹7,500
Fixed indirect costs	₹10,00,000

The actual results for the 225 round-trips made in 2015 were:

Variable indirect costs	₹15,18,750
Fixed indirect	9,00,000
	₹24,18,750

Assume all other information to be the same as in example 15-18.

Required

1. What is the indirect cost rate per round-trip with the dual-rate method when budgeted costs and bud- geted round-trips are used? Total costs are computed using budgeted rate times actual usage (trips) for variable costs and budgeted rate times practical capacity usage for fixed costs.

2. From the viewpoint of the Orange Juice Division, what are the effects of using the dual-rate method rather than the single-rate methods?

Solution
Dual-rate cost-allocation method, budgeted versus actual costs, and practical capacity vs actual quanti- ties (continuation of 15-19).

1. Charges with dual rate method

Variable indirect cost rate	= ₹7,500 per trip
Fixed indirect cost rate	$= \dfrac{₹10,00,000 \text{ budgeted costs}}{250 \text{ trips at practical capacity}}$
Orange Juice Division	= ₹4,000 per trip at practical capacity
Variable indirect costs, ₹7,500 × 150	₹11,25,000
Fixed indirect costs, ₹4,000 × 150	6,00,000
	₹17,25,000
Grapefruit Juice Division	
Variable indirect costs, ₹7,500 × 75	₹5,62,500
Fixed indirect costs, ₹4,000 × 100	4,00,000
	₹9,62,500

2. The dual-rate changes according to the fixed indirect cost component treatement. By using budgeted trips made, the Orange Juice Division is unaffected by changes from its own budgeted usage or that of other divisions.

15-20 Revenue allocation, bundled products. Essence Company blends and sells designer fragrances. It has a Men's Fragrances Division and a Women's Fragrances Division, each with different sales strategies, distribution channels, and product offerings. Essence is now considering the sale of a bundled product called Sync consisting of one bottle of Him, a men's cologne, and one bottle of Her, a women's perfume. For the most recent year, Essence reported the following:

	A	B
1	**Product**	**Retail Price**
2	Him	₹250
3	Her	₹500
4	Sync (Him and Her)	₹600

1 Allocate revenue from the sale of each unit of Sync to Him and Her using the following: **Required**

  a. The stand-alone revenue-allocation method based on selling price of each product

  b. The incremental revenue-allocation method, with Him ranked as the primary product

  c. The incremental revenue-allocation method, with Her ranked as the primary product

  d. The Shapley value method, assuming equal unit sales of Him and Her

2. Of the four methods in requirement 1, which one would you recommend for allocating Sync's revenues to Him and Her? Explain.

Solution

1a. Under the stand-alone revenue-allocation method based on selling price, Him will be allocated 33.33% of all revenues, or ₹200 of the bundled selling price, and Her will be allocated 66.67% of all revenues, or ₹400 of the bundled selling price, as shown below.

Stand-alone method, based on selling prices	Him	Her	Total
Selling price	₹250	₹500	₹750
Selling price as a % of total (₹250 ÷ ₹750; ₹500 ÷ ₹750)	33.33%	66.67%	100%
Allocation of ₹600 bundled selling price (33.33% × ₹600; 66.67% × ₹600)	₹200	₹400	₹600

1b. Under the incremental revenue-allocation method, with Him ranked as the primary product, Him will be allocated ₹250 (its own stand-alone selling price), and Her will be allocated ₹350 of the ₹600 selling price, as shown below.

Incremental Method (Him rank 1)	Him	Her
Selling price	₹250	₹500
Allocation of ₹600 bundled selling price (250;350 = 600 − 250)	₹250	₹350

1c. Under the incremental revenue-allocation method, with Her ranked as the primary product, Her will be allocated ₹500 (its own stand-alone selling price) and Him will be allocated ₹100 of the ₹600 selling price, as shown below.

Incremental Method (Her rank 1)	Him	Her
Selling price	₹250	₹500
Allocation of ₹600 bundled selling price (₹100 = ₹600 − ₹500; ₹500)	₹100	₹500

1d. Under the Shapley value method, each product will be allocated the average of its allocations in 1b and 1c, i.e., the average of its allocations when it is the primary product and when it is the secondary product, as shown below.

Shapley Value Method	Him	Her
Allocation when Him = Rank 1; Her = Rank 2 (from 1b.)	₹250	₹350
Allocation when Her = Rank 1; Him = Rank 2 (from 1c.)	₹100	₹500
Average of allocated selling price (₹250 + ₹100) ÷ 2; (₹350 + ₹500) ÷ 2	₹175	₹425

2. A summary of the allocations based on the four methods in requirement 1 is shown below.

	Stand-alone (Selling Prices)	Incremental (Him first)	Incremental (Her first)	Shapley
Him	₹200	₹250	₹100	₹175
Her	400	350	500	425
Total for Sync	₹600	₹600	₹600	₹600

If there is no clear indication of which product is the more "important" product, or if it can be reasonably assumed that the two products are equally important to the company's strategy, the Shapley value method is the fairest of all the methods because it averages the effect of product rank. In this particular case, note that the allocations from the stand-alone method based on selling price are reasonably similar to the allocations from the Shapley value method, so the managers at Essence may well want to use the much simpler stand-alone method. The stand-alone method also does not require ranking the products in the suite, and so it is less likely to cause debates among product managers in the Men's and Women's Fragrance divisions. If, however, one of the products (Him or Her) is clearly the product that is driving sales of the bundled product, then that product should be considered the primary product or weighted more heavily (rather than equally) when applying the Shapley value method.

15-21 Allocation of common costs. Aggarwal Auto Sales uses all types of media to advertise its products (television, radio, newspaper, and so on). At the end of 2014, the company president, Mr Aggarwal, decided that all advertising costs would be incurred by corporate headquarters and allocated to each of the company's four sales locations based on number of vehicles sold. Aggarwal was confident that his corporate purchasing manager could negotiate better advertising contracts on a corporate-wide basis than each of the sales managers could on their own. Aggarwal budgeted total advertising cost for 2015 to be ₹170 lakh. He introduced the new plan to his sales managers just before the New Year.

The manager of the east sales location, Mr Sharma, was not happy. He complained that the new allocation method was unfair and would increase his advertising costs significantly over the prior year. The east location sold high volumes of low-priced used cars and most of the corporate advertising budget was related to new car sales.

Following Mr Sharma's complaint, Mr Aggarwal decided to take another hard look at what each of the divisions was paying for advertising before the new allocation plan. The results were as follows:

Sales Location	Actual Number of Cars sold in 2014	Actual Advertising Cost Incurred in 2014
East	4,620	₹26,16,000
West	1,120	39,24,000
North	3,220	69,76,000
South	5,040	82,84,000
	14,000	₹2,18,00,000

Required

1. Using 2014 data as the cost bases, show the amount of the 2015 advertising cost (₹170 lakh) that would be allocated to each of the divisions under the following criteria:

   a. Aggarwal's allocation method based on number of cars sold

   b. The stand-alone method

   c. The incremental-allocation method, with divisions ranked on the basis of amount spent on advertising in 2014

2. Which method do you think is most equitable to the divisional sales managers? What other options might President Mr Aggarwal have for allocating the advertising costs?

Solution

1. a. Aggarwal's method based on number of cars sold:

Sales Location (1)	Number of cars sold (2)	Percentage (3) = (2) ÷ 14,000	Joint Cost (4)	Allocation (5) = (3) × (4)
East	4,620	4,620 ÷ 14,000 = 0.33	₹1,70,00,000	₹56,10,000
West	1,120	1,120 ÷ 14,000 = 0.08	1,70,00,000	13,60,000
North	3,220	3,220 ÷ 14,000 = 0.23	1,70,00,000	39,10,000
South	5,040	5,040 ÷ 14,000 = 0.36	1,70,00,000	61,20,000
	14,000			₹1,70,00,000

1. b. Stand-alone method:

Sales Location (1)	Stand-alone cost (2)	Percentage (3) = (2) ÷ ₹2,180	Joint Cost (4)	Allocation (5) = (3) × (4)
East	₹26,10,600	₹261.6 ÷ ₹2,180 = 0.12	₹1,70,00,000	₹20,40,000
West	39,24,000	₹392.4 ÷ ₹2,180 = 0.18	1,70,00,000	30,60,000
North	69,76,000	₹697.6 ÷ ₹2,180 = 0.32	1,70,00,000	54,40,000
South	82,84,000	₹828.4 ÷ ₹2,180 = 0.38	1,70,00,000	64,60,000
	₹2,18,00,000			₹1,70,00,000

1. c. Incremental method (locations ranked in order of largest advertising amount to smallest advertising amount):

Sales Location	Allocated Cost	Cost Remaining to Allocate
South	₹82,84,000	(₹1,70,00,000 – ₹82,84,000 = ₹87,16,000)
North	69,76,000	(₹87,16,000 – ₹69,76,000 = ₹17,40,000)
West	17,40,000	(₹17,40,000 – ₹17,40,000 = ₹0)
East	0	
	₹1,70,00,000	

2. In this situation, the stand-alone method is probably the best method because the weights it uses for allocation are based on the individual advertising cost for each location as a separate entity. Therefore, each entity gets the same relative proportion of advertising costs, and each location will have lower total advertising costs. The sales managers would likely not consider the incremental method fair because the locations with the higher advertising costs would be subsidizing the locations with the lower advertising costs (especially the East location, which would pay nothing in advertising). If the East sales manager is correct in his assertion that most of the advertising cost is for new car sales and not used car sales (the majority of the East location's business), then Aggarwal's method of allocating costs based on number of cars sold would be particularly unfair to East, which would pay ₹56,10,000 of the ₹1,70,00,000 in total advertising cost. Aggarwal could alternatively separate the total ₹1,70,00,000 of advertising cost into two cost pools: one for new car advertising and one for used car advertising and allocate on the basis of new cars sold and used cars sold, to make this method more equitable to the various sales locations.

15-22 Single-rate, dual-rate, and practical capacity allocation. Shopper's Stop has a free gift-wrapping service for the customers who want to get their purchases gift wrapped. It has a monthly practical capacity to gift wrap 8,000 items that it allocates among its different departments. Monthly fixed practical capacity costs of the gift-wrapping service are ₹60,000. Average budgeted variable cost to gift wrap an item is ₹6. Though the service is free to the customers, the department where the customer made the purchase is allocated gift-wrapping service costs.

Various departments' actual use of the gift-wrapping service during the current month and their respective needs at practical capacity follows:

Department	Actual Number of Gifts Wrapped	Number of Gifts That Can Be Wrapped at Practical Capacity
Gifts	2,200	2,800
Men's Wear	750	1,000
Women's Wear	1,600	2,100
Footwear	450	700
China	650	900
Linen	350	500

Required

1. Allocate the costs for the gift-wrapping service to each department using a single-rate method based on actual number of gifts wrapped.

2. Compute the amount allocated to each department using the dual-rate method when fixed costs are allocated based on practical capacity and variable costs are allocated using actual usage.

3. Comment on your results in requirements 1 and 2.

Solution

Single-rate, dual-rate, and practical capacity allocation.

1. Actual number of gifts wrapped = 6,000

   Practical capacity fixed costs = ₹60,000

   Average fixed capacity cost per item = ₹60,000 ÷ 6,000 =₹10

   Average budgeted variable cost per item =   6

   Total cost per item   ₹16

   Allocation:

Gifts (2,200 × ₹16)	₹35,200
Men's Wear (750 × ₹16)	12,000
Women's Wear (1,600 × ₹16)	25,600
Footwear (450 × ₹16)	7,200
China (650 × ₹16)	10,400
Linen (350 × ₹16)	5,600
Total	₹96,000

2. Rate for fixed costs $= \dfrac{\text{Fixed Costs}}{\text{Practical Capacity}}$

   $= \dfrac{₹60,000}{80,000} = ₹7.5 \text{ per item}$

   Rate for variable costs = ₹6 per item

   Allocation:

Department	Variable Costs	Fixed Costs	Total
Gifts	2,200 × ₹6 = ₹13,200	2,800 × ₹7.5 = ₹21,000	₹34,200
Men's Wear	750 × ₹6 = 4,500	1,000 × ₹7.5 = 7,500	12,000

Women's Wear	1,600 × ₹6 =	9,600	2,100 × ₹7.5 = 15,750	25,350
Footwear	450 × ₹6 =	2,700	700 × ₹7.5 = 5,250	7,950
China	650 × ₹6 =	3,900	900 × ₹7.5 = 6,750	10,650
Linen	350 × ₹6 =	2,100	500 × ₹7.5 = 3,750	5,850
Total		₹36,000	₹60,000	₹96,000

3. The dual-rate method has two major advantages over the single-rate method:

   a. Fixed costs are allocated proportionately to the departments causing the incurrence of those costs based on the capacity of each department.

   b. The costs allocated to a department are not affected by the usage by other departments.

Note: If capacity costs are the result of a long-term decision by top management, it may be desirable to allocate to each department the cost of capacity used based on actual usage. The users are then not allocated the costs of unused capacity.

15-23 Cost allocation, actual versus budgeted usage. (CMA, revised) Reliance Industries, is a large manufacturing company that runs its own electrical power plant from the excess steam produced in its manufacturing process. Power is provided to two production departments: Department A and Department B. The capacity of the power plant was originally determined by the expected peak demands of the two production departments. The expected normal usages are, respectively, 60% and 6,00,00,000 kilowatt-hours (kwh) for Department A, and 40% and 4,00,00,000 kwh for Department B.

The budgeted monthly costs of producing power, based on normal usage of 10,00,00,000 kwh, are ₹3,00,00,000 in fixed costs and ₹7,50,00,000 in variable costs. For November, the actual kilowatt-hours used were 6,00,00,000 by Department A and 2,00,00,000 by Department B. Actual fixed costs were ₹30,00,00,000, and actual variable costs were ₹7,50,00,000.

The Finance Controller of Reliance Industries prepared the following monthly report:

Reliance Industries Monthly Allocation Report November

Power plant usage	8,00,00,000 kwh
Actual costs:	
Variable	₹7,50,00,000
Fixed	30,00,00,000
Total	₹37,50,00,000
Rate per kwh (₹37,50,00,000 ÷ 8,00,00,000 kwh)	₹4.6875
Allocations:	
To Department A (6,00,00,000 kwh × ₹4.6875)	₹28,12,50,000
To Department B (2,00,00,000 kwh × ₹4.6875)	9,37,50,000
Total allocated	₹37,50,00,000

Finance Controller fully allocated all power plant costs on the basis of actual kilowatt-hours used by each production department. This report will be submitted to the two production-department operating managers.

Required

1. Discuss at least two problems with the monthly allocation report prepared by Finance Controller for November.

2. Prepare a revised monthly allocation report for November using a flexible-budget approach. Use budgeted rates times actual usage for variable costs and budgeted rates assuming budgeted (normal) usage for fixed costs.

3. Discuss the behavioral implication of Finance Controller's monthly allocation report for November on the production manager of Department B.

Solution

Cost allocation, actual versus budgeted usage

1. Problems with the monthly allocation report include:

   a. The single-rate method used does not distinguish between fixed vs variable costs.

   b. Actual costs and actual quantities are used. This results in managers not knowing cost rates until year-end.

   c. Monthly time periods are used to determine cost rates. The use of a monthly time period can result in highly variable cost rates depending on seasonality, days in a month, demand surges and so on.

2. Budgeted variable cost (based on normal usage):

Monthly Allocation Report November

Allocations of Variable Costs (based on budgeted rate × actual usage)*

To Department A: 6,00,00,000 × ₹0.75	₹4,50,00,000
To Department B: 2,00,00,000 × ₹0.75	1,50,00,000
	₹6,00,00,000

*There will be ₹1,50,00,000 of unallocated variable costs for November.

Allocation of fixed costs (Based on budgeted usage 3 budgeted amount)

To Department A: 60% × ₹30,00,00,000	₹1,80,00,0000
To Department B: 40% × ₹30,00,00,000	1,20,00,0000
Total	₹3,00,00,0000

Or alternatively,

$$\text{Budgeted fixed cost rate} = \frac{\text{Budgeted fixed costs}}{\text{Budgeted kwh}} = \frac{₹30,00,00,000}{6,00,00,000 + 4,00,00,000} = ₹3 \text{ per kwh}$$

Allocation of fixed costs (based on budgeted usage)

To Department A: ₹3 × 6,00,00,000 kwh =	₹18,00,00,000
To Department B: ₹3 × 4,00,00,000 kwh =	12,00,00,000
Total	₹30,00,00,000
Department A allocation of costs	
Variable costs	₹4,50,00,000
Fixed costs	18,00,00,000
Total	₹22,50,00,000
Department B allocation of costs	
Variable costs	₹1,50,00,000
Fixed costs	12,00,00,000
Total	₹13,50,00,000

3. Under Finance Controller's allocation report, the production manager has both risk-exposure and uncertainty concerns:

   Risk-exposure—Changes in the demand for energy by Department A affects the costs Finance Controller will report for Department B. Increase in demand by A will reduce B's cost per kwh and vice-versa. Department B's production manager may seek to curtail production in periods when Departments A's production declines. This could create an ever-diminishing cycle of production. Alternatively, Department B may sub-contract outside to avoid a higher energy rate, even if it is not in Reliance Industries's best interest to subcontract.

   Uncertainty—When actual costs are used, managers cannot plan costs with certainty. Managers typically have less ability to bear uncertainty than do companies. The result is that managers may reject alternatives that are good risks from Reliance Industries's perspective but not attractive risks for themselves.

Exercises

[*Comprehensive solutions to all exercises are available on the companion website www. pearsoned.co.in/charlesthorngren*]

15-24 Support department cost allocation; direct and step-down methods. Avalon Consulting provides outsourcing services and advice to both government and corporate clients. For costing purposes, Avalon classifies its departments into two support departments (Administrative/ Human Resources and Information Systems) and two operating departments (Government Consulting and Corporate Consulting). For the first quarter of current year, Avalon incurs the following costs in its four departments:

Administrative/Human Resources (A/H)	₹6,00,000
Information Systems (IS)	24,00,000
Government Clients (GOVT)	87,56,000
Corporate Clients (CORP)	1,24,52,000

The actual level of support relationships among the four departments for the first quarter was:

		Used By		
Supplied By	**A/H**	**IS**	**GOVT**	**CORP**
A/H	—	25%	40%	35%
IS	10%	—	30%	60%

The Administrative/Human Resources support percentages are based on head count. The Information Systems support percentages are based on actual computer time used.

Required

1. Allocate the two support department costs to the two operating departments using the following methods:
   a. Direct method
   b. Step-down method (allocate A/H first)
   c. Step-down method (allocate IS first)
2. Compare and explain differences in the support department costs allocated to each operating department.
3. What approaches might be used to decide the sequence in which to allocate support departments when using the step-down method? What approach would you recommend Avalon 1 to 3 use if, on government consulting jobs, it is required to use the step-down method?

15-25 Support department cost allocation, reciprocal method (continuation of 15-24). Refer to the data given in Exercise 15-24.

Required

1. Allocate the two support department costs to the two operating departments using the reciprocal method. Use (a) linear equations and (b) repeated iterations.
2. Compare and explain differences in requirement 1 with those in requirement 1 of Exercise 15-25. Which method do you prefer? Why?

15-26 Revenue allocation, bundled products. Taj Group operates a five-star hotel with a world-recog- nized championship golf course. It has a decentralized management structure. These are three divisions:

- Lodging (rooms, conference facilities)
- Food (restaurants and in-room service)
- Recreation (golf course, tennis courts, and so on)

Starting next month, Taj will offer a two-day, two-person "getaway package" deal for ₹7,000. This deal includes:

- Two nights' stay for two in an ocean-view room—separately priced at ₹6,400 (₹3,200 per night for two).
- Two rounds of golf separately priced at ₹3,000(₹1,500 per round). One person can do two rounds, or two people can do one round each.
- Candlelight dinner for two at the exclusive Taj Restaurant—separately priced at ₹800 per person. Sudhir, president of the Recreation Division, recently asked the CEO of Taj Group how his division would

share in the ₹7,000 revenue from the package. The golf course was operating at 100% capacity (and then some). Under the "getaway package" rules, participants who booked one week in advance were guaranteed access to the golf course. Sudhir noted that every "getaway" booking would displace a ₹1,500 booking. He stressed that the high demand reflected the devotion of his team to keeping the golf course rated in the "Best 10 Courses in the World" listings in Golf Monthly. As an aside, he also noted that the Lodging and Food divisions only had to turn away customers on "peak-season events such as the New Year's period."

Required

1. With selling prices as the weights, allocate the ₹7,000 "getaway package" revenue to the three divisions using:
   a. The stand-alone revenue-allocation method
   b. The incremental revenue-allocation method (with Recreation first, then Lodging, and then Food)
2. What are the pros and cons of a and b in requirement 1?

15-27 Revenue allocation, bundled products, additional complexities (continuation of 15-26). The individual items in the "getaway package" deal at Taj Group are not fully used by each guest. Assume that 10% of the "getaway package" users in its first month do not use the golfing option, and 5% do not use the food option. The lodging option has a 100% usage rate.

How should Taj Group recognize this nonuse factor in its revenue sharing of the ₹7,000 package across the Lodging, Food, and Recreation divisions? Explain.

15-28 Single-rate, dual-rate, and practical capacity allocations. Raymond, has its own power plant, which has two users, Cutting Department and Welding Department. When the plans were prepared for the power plant, top management decided that its practical capacity should be 1,50,000 machine-hours (MH). Annual budgeted practical capacity fixed costs are ₹45,00,000, and budgeted variable costs are ₹20 per machine-hour. The following data are available:

	Cutting Department	Welding Department	Total
Actual usage in 2015 (MH)	60,000	40,000	1,00,000
Practical capacity for each department (MH)	90,000	60,000	1,50,000

Required

1. Allocate the power plant's costs to the Cutting and the Welding departments using a single-rate method in which the budgeted rate is calculated using practical capacity and costs are allocated based on actual usage.
2. Allocate the power plant's costs to the Cutting and Welding departments using the dual-rate method in which the fixed costs are allocated based on practical capacity and variable costs are allocated based on actual usage.
3. Allocate the power plant's costs to the Cutting and Welding departments using the dual-rate method in which the fixed-cost rate is calculated using practical capacity but fixed costs are allocated to the Cutting and Welding departments based on actual usage. Variable costs are allocated based on actual usage.
4. Comment on your results in requirements 1, 2, and 3.

15-29 Allocating costs of support departments; step-down and direct methods. The Central Valley Company has prepared department overhead budgets for April for normal-volume levels before allocations as follows:

Support departments:		
Building and grounds	₹10,000	
Personnel	1,000	
General factory administration	26,090	
Cafeteria operating loss	1,640	
Storeroom	2,670	
Total		₹41,400
Operating departments:		
Machining	₹34,700	
Assembly	48,900	
Total		83,600
Total for support and operating departments		₹1,25,000

Management has decided that the most appropriate inventory costs are achieved by using individual department overhead rates. These rates are developed after support department costs are allocated to operating departments.

Bases for allocation are to be selected from the following:

Department	Direct Manufacturing Labor-Hours	Number of Employees	Square Feet of Floor Space Occupied	Manufacturing Labor-Hours	Number of Requisitions
Building and grounds	0	0	0	0	0
Personnela	0	0	2,000	0	0
General plant administration	0	35	7,000	0	0
Cafeteria operating loss	0	10	4,000	1,000	0
Storeroom	0	5	7,000	1,000	0
Machining	5,000	50	30,000	8,000	2,000
Assembly	15,000	100	50,000	17,000	1,000
Total	20,000	200	1,00,000	27,000	3,000

aBasis used is number of employees.

Required

1. Using a worksheet, allocate support department costs by the step-down method. Develop overhead rates per direct manufacturing labor-hour for machining and assembly. Allocate the costs of the support departments in the order given in this problem. Use the allocation base for each support department you think is most appropriate.

2. Using the direct method, rework requirement 1.

3. Based on the following information about two jobs, determine the total overhead costs for each job by using rates developed in (a) requirement 1 and (b) requirement 2.

	Direct Manufacturing Machining	Labor-Hours Assembly
Job 88	18	2
Job 89	3	17

4. The company evaluates performance of operating departments' managers on the basis of how well they managed their total costs, including allocated costs. As the manager of the Machining Department, which allocation method would you prefer from the results obtained in requirements 1 and 2? Explain.

15-30 Common costs. Mohan and Sohan would like to lease an office building to open their separate audit offices. The building has a total of 1,500 square feet of office space. They need 900 square feet and 600 square feet, respectively. If each rents the space on his own, the rent will be ₹100 per square foot. If they rent the space together, the rent will decrease to ₹80 per square foot.

Required

1. Calculate their respective share of the rent under the stand-alone cost-allocation method.
2. Do requirement 1 using the incremental cost-allocation method. Assume Mohan to be the primary party.
3. What method would you recommend Mohan and Sohan use to share the rent?

15-31 Revenue allocation, bundled products. Indian Sandal Company (IS) manufactures and sells upscale perfumes. In recent months, IS has started selling its products in bundled form, as well as in individual form. Sales in 2015 of three products that have been sold individually are as follows:

Stand-alone	Retail Price	Units Sold
Axe	₹100	20,000
Rexona	80	37,500
Sandal	250	20,000
Suite		
Axe + Rexona	150	
Axe + Sandal	280	

Each of the products is manufactured by a separate division.

1. Compute the weights for allocating revenues to each division for each of the bundled products using:
   a. The stand-alone revenue-allocation method based on total revenues of individual products
   b. The incremental revenue-allocation method, with Sandal ranked 1; Rexona, 2; and Axe, 3; based on retail prices of individual products. According to this ranking, the primary product in a suite has the highest rank, and so on.
2. What method would you recommend for allocating revenues to each division for each of the bundled products?

15-32 Overhead disputes. (Suggested by Howard Wright) The Essar Shipping Company works on Indian Navy vessels and commercial vessels. General yard overhead (for example, the cost of the Purchasing Department) is allocated to the jobs on the basis of direct labor costs.

In 2015, Essar Shipping's total ₹15 crore of direct labor costs consisted of ₹5 crore Navy and ₹10 crore commercial. The general yard overhead was ₹3 crore.

Navy auditors periodically examine the records of defense contractors. The auditors investigated a nuclear submarine contract, which was based on cost-plus-fixed-fee pricing. The auditors claimed that the Navy was entitled to a refund because of double-counting of overhead in 2015.

The government contract included the following provision related to direct costs:

A direct cost is any cost that can be identified specifically with a particular cost object. Direct costs are not limited to items that are incorporated in the end product such as material or labor. Costs identified specifically with the contract are direct costs of the contract and are to be charged directly thereto. Costs identified specifically with other work of the contractor are direct costs of that work and are not to be charged to the contract directly or indirectly. When items ordinarily chargeable as indirect costs are charged to the contract as direct costs, the cost of like items applicable to other work must be eliminated from indirect costs allocated to the contract.

Essar Shipping formed a special expediting purchasing group, the ES group, to join with the central purchasing group to obtain materials solely for the nuclear submarine. Their direct costs, ₹50 lakh, were included as direct labor of the nuclear work. Accordingly, overhead was allocated to the contracts in the usual manner. The ES cost of ₹50 lakh was not included in the general yard overhead. The auditors claimed that no overhead should have been allocated to these ES costs.

1. Compute the amount of the refund that the Navy would claim.
2. Suppose the Navy also discovered that ₹40 lakh of general yard overhead was devoted exclusively to commercial engine-room purchasing activities. Compute the additional refund that the Navy would claim. (Note: This ₹40 lakh was never classified as direct labor. Furthermore, the Navy would claim that it should be reclassified as a direct cost but not as direct labor.)

16 Cost Allocation: Joint Products and Byproducts

Learning Objectives ▼

1. Identify the splitoff point in a joint-cost situation and distinguish joint products from byproducts

2. Explain why joint costs are allocated to individual products

3. Allocate joint costs using four methods

4. Identify situations when the sales value at splitoff method is preferred when allocating joint costs

5. Explain why joint costs are irrelevant in a sell-or-process-further decision

6. Account for byproducts using two methods

Learning Objective 1

Identify the splitoff point in a joint-cost situation

. . . the point at which two or more products become separately identifiable

and distinguish joint products

. . . products with high sales values

from byproducts

. . . products with low sales values

Many companies, such as petroleum refiners, produce and sell two or more products simultaneously.

Similarly, some companies, such as health care providers, sell or provide multiple services. The question is, "How should these companies allocate costs to 'joint' products and services?" Knowing how to allocate joint product costs isn't something that only companies need to understand. It's something that farmers have to deal with, too, especially when it comes to the lucrative production of corn to make billions of gallons of ethanol fuel.

Joint-Cost Basics

Joint costs are the costs of a production process that yields multiple products simultaneously. Consider the distillation of coal, which yields coke, natural gas, and other products. The costs of this distillation are joint costs. The **splitoff point** is the juncture in a joint production process when two or more products become separately identifiable. An example is the point at which coal becomes coke, natural gas, and other products. **Separable costs** are all costs—manufacturing, marketing, distribution, and so on—incurred beyond the splitoff point that are assignable to each of the specific products identified at the splitoff point. At or beyond the splitoff point, decisions relating to the sale or further processing of each identifiable product can be made independently of decisions about the other products.

As the examples in Exhibit 16-1 show, the production processes in many industries simultaneously yields two or more products, either at the splitoff point or after further processing. In each of these examples, no individual product can be produced without the accompanying products appearing, although in some cases the proportions can be varied. Joint costing allocates costs to individual products that are eventually sold.

The outputs of a joint production process can be classified into two general categories: outputs with a positive sales value and outputs with a zero sales value.[1] For example, offshore processing of hydrocarbons yields oil and natural gas, which have positive sales value, and it also yields water, which has zero sales value and is recycled back into the ocean. The term **product** describes any output that has a positive total sales value (or an output that enables a company to avoid incurring costs, such as an intermediate chemical product used as input in another process). The total sales value can be high or low.

When a joint production process yields one product with a high total sales value, compared with total sales values of other products of the process, that

---

[1] Some outputs of a joint production process have "negative" revenue when their disposal costs (such as the costs of handling nonsalable toxic substances that require special disposal procedures) are considered. These disposal costs should be added to the joint production costs that are allocated to joint or main products.

Industry	Separable Products at the Splitoff Point
Agriculture and	
Food Processing Industries	
Cocoa beans	Cocoa butter, cocoa powder, cocoa drink mix, tanning cream
Lambs	Lamb cuts, tripe, hides, bones, fat
Hogs	Bacon, ham, spare ribs, pork roast
Raw milk	Cream, liquid skim
Lumber	Lumber of varying grades and shapes
Turkeys	Breast, wings, thighs, drumsticks, digest, feather meal, and poultry meal
Extractive Industries	
Coal	Coke, gas, benzol, tar, ammonia
Copper ore	Copper, silver, lead, zinc
Petroleum	Crude oil, natural gas
Salt	Hydrogen, chlorine, caustic soda
Chemical Industries	
Raw LPG (liquefied petroleum gas)	Butane, ethane, propane
Crude oil	Gasoline, kerosene, benzene, naphtha
Semiconductor Industry	
Fabrication of silicon-wafer chips	Memory chips of different quality (as to capacity), speed, life expectancy, and temperature tolerance

Exhibit 16-1

Examples of Joint-Cost Situations

product is called a **main product**. When a joint production process yields two or more products with high total sales values relative to the total sales values of other products, those products are called **joint products**. In contrast, the products of a joint production process that have low total sales values relative to the total sales value of the main product or of joint products are called **byproducts**.

Consider some examples. If timber (logs) is processed into standard lumber and wood chips, standard lumber is a main product and wood chips are the byproduct because standard lumber has a high total sales value compared with wood chips. If, however, logs are processed into fine-grade lumber, standard lumber, and wood chips, fine-grade lumber and standard lumber are joint products, and wood chips are the byproduct. That's because both fine-grade lumber and standard lumber have high total sales values when compared with wood chips.

Distinctions among main products, joint products, and byproducts are not so definite in practice. Companies use different thresholds for determining whether the relative sales value of a product is high enough for it to be considered a joint product. Consider kerosene, obtained when refining crude oil. Based on a comparison of its sales value to the total sales values of gasoline and other products, some companies classify kerosene as a joint product whereas others classify it as a byproduct. Moreover, the classification of products—main, joint, or byproduct—can change over time, especially for products such as lower-grade semiconductor chips, whose market prices can increase or decrease by, say, 30% or more in a year. When prices of lower-grade chips are high, they are considered joint products together with higher-grade chips; when prices of lower-grade chips fall considerably,

Decision Point

What do the terms joint cost and splitoff point mean, and how do joint products differ from byproducts?

849

they are considered byproducts. In practice, it is important to understand how a specific company classifies products.

Allocating Joint Costs

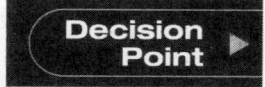

Before a manager is able to allocate joint costs, she must first look at the context for doing so. Joint costs must be allocated to individual products or services for several purposes including the following:

- Computing inventoriable costs and the cost of goods sold for external and internal reporting purposes. Recall from Chapter 9 that absorption costing is required for financial accounting and tax reporting. This necessitates the allocation of joint manufacturing or processing costs to products for calculating ending inventory values. In addition, many firms use internal accounting data based on joint cost allocations to analyze the profitability of their various divisions and evaluate the performance of division managers.

- Reimbursing companies that have some, but not all, of their products or services reimbursed under cost-plus contracts with, say, a government agency. For example, the joint costs incurred when multiple organs are removed from a single donor must be allocated to various organ centers in order to determine reimbursement rates for transplants into Medicare patients. In such cases, stringent rules typically specify the way in which joint costs are assigned to the products or services covered by the agreements.

- Regulating the rates or prices of one or more of the jointly produced products or services. This issue is critical in the extractive and energy industries, in which output prices are regulated to yield a fixed return on a cost basis that includes joint cost allocations. In telecommunications, a firm with significant market power has some products subject to price regulation (e.g., interconnection) and other activities that are unregulated (such as equipment rentals to end-users). In this case, joint costs must be allocated to ensure that costs are not transferred from unregulated services to regulated ones.

- For any commercial litigation or insurance settlement situation in which the costs of joint products or services are key inputs.

Approaches to Allocating Joint Costs

Two approaches are used to allocate joint costs.

- **Approach 1.** Allocate joint costs using *market-based* data such as revenues. This chapter illustrates three methods that use this approach:
  1. Sales value at splitoff method
  2. Net realizable value (NRV) method
  3. Constant gross-margin percentage NRV method

- **Approach 2.** Allocate joint costs using *physical measures*, such as the weight, quantity (physical units) or volume of the joint products.

In preceding chapters, we used the cause-and-effect and benefits-received criteria for guiding cost-allocation decisions (see Exhibit 14-2). Joint costs do not have a cause-and-effect relationship with individual products because the production process simultaneously yields multiple products. Using the benefits-received criterion leads to a preference for methods under approach 1 because revenues are, in general, a better indicator of benefits received than physical measures. Mining companies, for example, receive more benefits from 1 ton of gold than they do from 10 tons of coal.

In the simplest joint production process, the joint products are sold at the splitoff point without further processing. Example 1 illustrates the two methods that apply in this case: the sales value at splitoff method and the physical-measure method. Then we introduce joint production processes that yield products that require further processing beyond the splitoff point. Example 2 illustrates the NRV method and the constant-gross margin percentage NRV method. To help you focus on key concepts, we use numbers and amounts in all examples in this chapter that are much smaller than the numbers that are typically found in practice.

The exhibits in this chapter use the following symbols to distinguish a joint or main product from a byproduct:

Joint Product or Main Product   Byproduct

To compare methods, we report gross-margin percentages for individual products under each method.

Example 1: Mother Dairy purchases raw milk from individual farms and processes it until the splitoff point, when two products—cream and liquid skim—emerge. These two products are sold to an independent company, which markets and distributes them to supermarkets and other retail outlets.

In May 2014, Mother Dairy processes 1,10,000 gallons of raw milk. During processing, 10,000 gallons are lost due to evaporation and spillage, yielding 25,000 gallons of cream and 75,000 gallons of liquid skim. The data are summarized below:

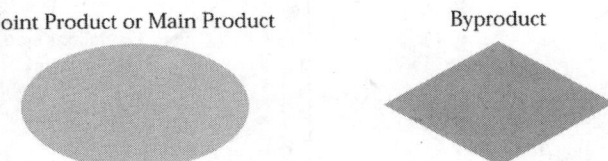

	A	B	C
		Joint Costs	
2	Joint costs (costs of 1,10,000 gallons raw milk and processing to splitoff point)	₹40,00,000	
3			
4		**Cream**	**Liquid Skim**
5	Beginnning inventory (gallons)	0	0
6	Production (gallons)	25,000	75,000
7	Sales (gallons)	20,000	30,000
8	Ending inventory (gallons)	5,000	45,000
9	Selling price per gallons	₹80	₹40

Exhibit 16-2 depicts the basic relationships in this example.

How much of the ₹40,00,000 joint costs should be allocated to the cost of goods sold of 20,000 gallons of cream and 30,000 gallons of liquid skim, and how much should be allocated to the ending inventory of 5,000 gallons of cream and 45,000 gallons of liquid skim? We begin by illustrating the two methods that use the properties of the products at the splitoff point: the sales value at splitoff method and the physical-measure method.

Exhibit 16-2

Example 1: Overview of
Mother Dairy

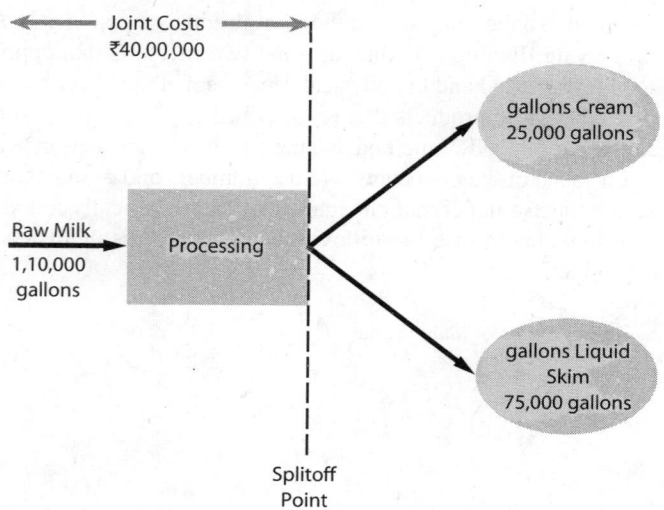

Sales Value at Splitoff Method

The **sales value at splitoff method** allocates joint costs to joint products produced during
the accounting period on the basis of the relative total sales value at the splitoff point.
Using this method for Example 1, Exhibit 16-3, Panel A, shows how joint costs are allocated to individual products to calculate cost per gallon of cream and liquid skim for
valuing ending inventory. This method uses the sales value of the *entire production of the*
accounting period (25,000 gallons of cream and 75,000 gallons of liquid skim), not just
the quantity sold (20,000 gallons of cream and 30,000 gallons of liquid skim). The reason
is that the joint costs were incurred on all units produced, not just the portion sold during the current period. Exhibit 16-3, Panel B, presents the product-line income statement
using the sales value at splitoff method. Note that the sales value at splitoff method allocates joint costs to each product in proportion to sales value of total production (cream:
₹16,00,000 ÷ ₹20,00,000 = 80%; liquid skim: ₹24,00,000 ÷ ₹30,00,000 = 80%).
Therefore, the gross-margin percentage for each product manufactured in May 2014 is
the same: 20%.[2]

Note how the sales value at splitoff method follows the benefits-received criterion of
cost allocation: Costs are allocated to products in proportion to their revenue-generating
power (their expected revenues). The cost-allocation base (total sales value at splitoff) is
expressed in terms of a common denominator (the amount of revenues) that is systematically recorded in the accounting system. To use this method, selling prices must exist for all
products at the splitoff point.

Physical-Measure Method

The **physical-measure method** allocates joint costs to joint products produced during the
accounting period on the basis of a *comparable* physical measure, such as the relative
weight, quantity, or volume at the splitoff point. In Example 1, the ₹40,00,000 joint costs

---

[2] Suppose Mother Dairy has beginning inventory of cream and liquid milk in May 2014. Suppose further that when this inventory
is sold, Mother Dairy earns a gross margin different from 20%. Then the gross-margin percentage for cream and liquid skim
will not be the same. The gross-margin percentage will depend on how much of the sales of each product came from beginning
inventory and how much came from current-period production.

Exhibit 16-3   Joint-Cost Allocation and Product-Line Income Statement Using Sales Value at Splitoff Method: Mother Dairy for May 2014

	File Edit View Insert Format Tools Data Window Help			
	A	B	C	D
1	PANEL A: Allocation of Joint Costs Using Sales Value at Splitoff Method	Cream	Liquid Skim	Total
2	Sales value of total production at splitoff point			
3	(25,000 gallons x ₹80 per gallon; 75,000 gallons x ₹40 per gallon)	₹20,00,000	₹30,00,000	₹50,00,000
4	Weighting (₹20,00,000 ÷ ₹50,00,000; ₹30,00,000 ÷ 55,00,000	4.0	0.60	
5	Joint costs allocated (0.40 x ₹40,00,000; 0.60 x ₹40,00,000)	₹16,00,000	₹24,00,000	₹40,00,000
6	Joint production cost per gallon			
7	(₹16,00,000 ÷ 25,000 gallons; ₹24,00,000 ÷ 75,000 gallons)	₹64	₹32	
8				
9	PANEL B: Product-Line Income Statement Using Sales Value at Splitoff Method for May 2012	Cream	Liquid Skim	Total
10	Revenues (20,000 gallons x ₹80 per gallon; 30,000 gallons x ₹40 per gallon)	₹16,00,000	₹12,00,000	₹28,00,000
11	Cost of goods sold (joint costs)			
12	Production costs (0.40 x ₹40,00,000; 0.60 x ₹40,00,000)	16,00,000	24,00,000	40,00,000
13	Deduct ending inventory (5,000 gallons x ₹64.0 per gallon; 45,000 gallons x ₹ 32.0 per gallon)	3,20,000	14,40,000	17,60,000
14	Cost of goods sold (joint costs)	12,80,000	9,60,000	22,40,000
15	Gross margin	₹3,20,000	₹2,40,000	₹5,60,000
16	Gross margin percentage (₹3,20,000 ÷ ₹16,00,000; ₹2,40,000 ÷ ₹12,00,000; ₹5,60,000 ÷ ₹28,00,000)	20%	20%	20%

produced 25,000 gallons of cream and 75,000 gallons of liquid skim. Using the number of gallons produced as the physical measure, Exhibit 16-4, Panel A, shows how joint costs are allocated to individual products to calculate the cost per gallon of cream and liquid skim.

Because the physical-measure method allocates joint costs on the basis of the number of gallons, cost per gallon is the same for both products. Exhibit 16-4, Panel B, presents the product-line income statement using the physical-measure method. The gross-margin percentages are 50% for cream and 0% for liquid skim.

Exhibit 16-4   Joint-Cost Allocation and Product-Line Income Statement Using Physical-Measure Method: Mother Dairy for May 2014

	File Edit View Insert Format Tools Data Window Help			
	A	B	C	D
1	PANEL A: Allocation of Joint Costs Using Physical-Measure Method	Cream	Liquid Skim	Total
2	Physical measure of total production (gallons)	2,50,000	7,50,000	10,00,000
3	Weighting (25,000 gallons ÷ 100,000 gallons; 75,000 gallons ÷ 100,000 gallons)	2.5	7.5	
4	Joint costs allocated (0.25 x ₹40,00,000; 0.75 x ₹40,00,000)	₹10,00,000	₹30,00,000	₹40,00,000
5	Joint production cost per gallons (₹10,00,000 ÷ 25,000 gallons; ₹30,00,000 ÷ 75,000 gallons)	₹40	₹40	
6				
7	PANEL B: Product-Line Income Statement Using Physical-Measure Method for May 2014	Cream	Liquid Skim	Total
8	Revenues (20,000 gallons x ₹80 per gallon; 30,000 gallons x ₹40 per gallon)	₹16,00,000	₹12,00,000	₹28,00,000
9	Cost of goods sold (joint costs)			
10	Production costs (0.25 x ₹40,00,000; 0.75 x ₹40,00,000)	10,00,000	30,00,000	40,00,000
11	Deduct ending inventory (5,000 gallons x ₹40 per gallon; 45,000 gallons x ₹40 per gallon)	2,00,000	18,00,000	20,00,000
12	Cost of goods sold (joint costs)	8,00,000	12,00,000	20,00,000
13	Gross margin	₹8,00,000	₹0	₹8,00,000
14	Gross margin percentage (₹8,00,000 ÷ ₹16,00,000; ₹0 ÷ ₹12,00,000; ₹8,00,000 ÷ ₹28,00,000)	50%	0	28.6%

Under the benefits-received criterion, the physical-measure method is much less desirable than the sales value at splitoff method. Why? Because the physical measure of the individual products may have no relationship to their respective revenue-generating abilities. Consider a gold mine that extracts ore containing gold, silver, and lead. Use of a common physical measure (tons) would result in almost all costs being allocated to lead the product that weighs the most but has the lowest revenue-generating power. This method of cost allocation is inconsistent with the main reason the mining company is incurring mining costs—to earn revenues from gold and silver, not lead. When a company uses the physical-measure method in a product-line income statement, products that have a high sales value per ton, like gold and silver, would show a large "profit," and products that have a low sales value per ton, like lead, would show sizable losses.

Obtaining comparable physical measures for all products is not always straightforward. Consider the joint costs of producing oil and natural gas; oil is a liquid and gas is a vapor. To use a physical measure, the oil and gas need to be converted to the energy equivalent for oil and gas, British thermal units (BTUs). Using some physical measures to allocate joint costs may require assistance from technical personnel outside of accounting.

Determining which products of a joint process to include in a physical-measure computation can greatly affect the allocations to those products. Outputs with no sales value (such as dirt in gold mining) are always excluded. Although many more tons of dirt than gold are produced, costs are not incurred to produce outputs that have zero sales value. Byproducts are also often excluded from the denominator used in the physical-measure method because of their low sales values relative to the joint products or the main product. The general guideline for the physical-measure method is to include only the joint-product outputs in the weighting computations.

Net Realizable Value (NRV) Method

In many cases, products are processed beyond the splitoff point to bring them to a marketable form or to increase their value above their selling price at the splitoff point. For example, when crude oil is refined, the gasoline, kerosene, benzene, and naphtha must be processed further before they can be sold. To illustrate, let's extend the Mother Dairy example.

Example 2: Assume the same data as in Example 1 except that both cream and liquid skim can be processed further:

- Cream → Buttercream: 25,000 gallons of cream are further processed to yield 20,000 gallons of buttercream at additional processing costs of ₹28,00,000. Buttercream, which sells for ₹250 per gallon, is used in the manufacture of butter-based products.
- Liquid Skim Condensed Milk: 75,000 gallons of liquid skim are further processed to yield 50,000 gallons of condensed milk at additional processing costs of ₹52,00,000. Condensed milk sells for ₹220 per gallon.
- Sales during May 2014 were 12,000 gallons of buttercream and 45,000 gallons of condensed milk.

Exhibit 16-5, Panel A, depicts how (a) raw milk is converted into cream and liquid skim in the joint production process, and (b) how cream is separately processed into buttercream and liquid skim is separately processed into condensed milk. Panel B shows the data for Example 2.

Exhibit 16-5	Example 2: Overview of Mother Dairy

PANEL A: Graphical Presentation of Process for Example 2

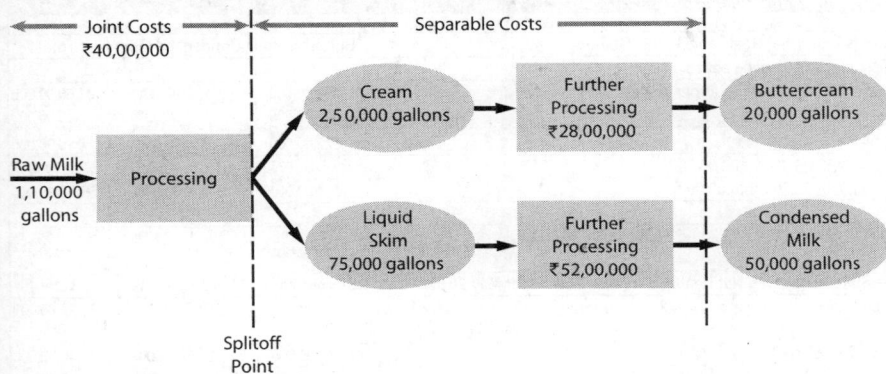

PANEL B: Data for Example 2

	A	B	C	D	E
	⁝▣⁞ File Edit View Insert Format Tools Data Window Help				
1		Joint Costs		Buttercream	Condensed Milk
2	Joint costs (costs of 1,10,000 gallons raw milk and processing to splitoff point)	₹4,000,000			
3	Separable cost of processing 25,000 gallons cream into 20,000 gallons buttercream			₹28,00,000	
4	Separable cost of processing 75,000 gallons liquid skim into 50,000 gallons condensed milk				₹52,00,000
5					
6		Cream	Liquid Skim	Buttercream	Condensed Milk
7	Beginning inventory (gallons)	0	0	0	0
8	Production (gallons)	25,000	75,000	20,000	50,000
9	Transfer for further processing (gallons)	25,000	75,000		
10	Sales (gallons)			12,000	45,000
11	Ending inventory (gallons)	0	0	8,000	5,000
12	Selling price per gallon	₹80	₹40	₹250	₹220

The **net realizable value (NRV) method** allocates joint costs to joint products on the basis of relative NRV—final sales value minus separable costs. The NRV method is typically used in preference to the sales value at splitoff method only when selling prices for one or more products at splitoff do not exist. Using this method for Example 2, Exhibit 16-6, Panel A, shows how joint costs are allocated to individual products to calculate cost per gallon of buttercream and condensed milk. Panel B presents the product-line income statement using the NRV method. The gross-margin percentages are 22.0% for buttercream and 26.4% for condensed milk.

The NRV method is often implemented using simplifying assumptions. For example, even when selling prices of joint products vary frequently, companies implement the NRV method using a given set of selling prices throughout the accounting period. Similarly, even though companies may occasionally change the number or sequence of processing steps beyond the splitoff point in order to adjust to variations in input quality or local conditions, they assume a specific constant set of such steps when implementing the NRV method.

Exhibit 16-6	Joint-Cost Allocation and Product-Line Income Statement Using NRV Method: Mother Dairy for May 2014

	A	B	C	D
		Buttercream	Condensed Milk	Total
1	PANEL A: Allocation of Joint Costs Using Net Realizable Value Method	Buttercream	Condensed Milk	Total
2	Final sales value of total production during accounting period			
3	(20,000 gallons x ₹250 per gallon; 50,000 gallons x ₹220 per gallon)	₹50,00,000	₹1,10,00,000	₹1,60,00,000
4	Deduct separable costs	28,00,000	52,00,000	80,00,000
5	Net realizable value at splitoff point	₹22,00,000	₹58,00,000	₹80,00,000
6	Weighting (₹22,00,000 ÷ ₹80,00,000; ₹58,00,000 ÷ ₹80,00,000)	.275	0.725	
7	Joint costs allocated (0.275 x ₹40,00,000; 0.725 x ₹40,00,000)	₹11,00,000	₹29,00,000	₹40,00,000
8	Production cost per gallon			
9	([₹11,00,000 + ₹28,00,000] ÷ 20,000 gallons; [₹29,00,000 + ₹52,00,000] ÷ 50,000 gallons	₹195	₹162	
10				
11	PANEL B: Product-Line Income Statement Using Net Realizable Value Method for May 2014	Buttercream	Condensed Milk	Total
12	Revenues (12,000 gallons x 250 per gallon; 45,000 gallons x ₹220 per gallon)	₹30,00,000	₹99,00,000	₹1,29,00,000
13	Cost of goods sold			
14	Joint costs (0.275 x ₹40,00,000; 0.725 x ₹40,00,000)	11,00,000	29,00,000	40,00,000
15	Separable costs	28,00,000	52,00,000	80,00,000
16	Production costs	39,00,000	81,00,000	1,20,00,000
17	Deduct ending inventory (8,000 gallons x195.0 per gallon; 5,000 gallons x ₹162.0 per gallon)	15,60,000	8,10,000	23,70,000
18	Cost of goods sold	23,40,000	72,90,000	96,30,000
19	Gross margin	₹6,60,000	₹26,10,000	₹32,70,000
20	Gross margin percentage (₹6,60,000 ÷ ₹30,00,000; ₹26,10,000 ÷ ₹99,00,000; ₹32,70,000 ÷ ₹1,29,00,000)	22.0%	26.4%	25.3%

Constant Gross-Margin Percentage NRV Method

The **constant gross-margin percentage NRV method** allocates joint costs to joint products produced during the accounting period in such a way that each individual product achieves an identical gross-margin percentage. The method works backward in that the overall gross margin is computed first. Then, for each product, this gross-margin percentage and any separable costs are deducted from the final sales value of production in order to back into the joint cost allocation for that product. The method can be broken down into three discrete steps. Exhibit 16-7, Panel A, shows these steps for allocating the ₹40,00,000 joint costs between buttercream and condensed milk in the Mother Dairy example. Refer to the Panel for an illustration of the each step, as we describe it.

Step 1: Compute overall gross margin percentage. The overall gross-margin percentage for all joint products together is first calculated. This is based on the final sales value of *total production* during the accounting period, not the *total revenues* of the period. Note, Exhibit 16-7, Panel A, uses ₹1,60,00,000, the final expected sales value of the entire output of buttercream and condensed milk, not the ₹1,29,00,000 in actual sales revenue for the month of May.

Step 2: Compute total production costs for each product. The gross margin (in rupees) for each product is computed by multiplying the overall gross-margin percentage by the product's final sales value of total production. The difference between the final sales value of total production and the gross margin then yields the total production costs that the product must bear.

Step 3: Compute allocated joint costs. As the final step, the separable costs for each product are deducted from the total production costs that the product must bear to obtain the joint-cost allocation for that product.

Exhibit 16-7, Panel B, presents the product-line income statement for the constant gross-margin percentage NRV method.

Exhibit 16-7 Joint-Cost Allocation and Product-Line Income Statement Using Constant Gross-Margin Percentage NRV Method: Mother Dairy for May 2014

	A	B	C	D
1	**PANEL A: Allocation of Joint Costs Using Constant Gross-Margin Percentage NRV Method**			
2	**Step 1**			
3	Final sales value of total production during accounting period: (20,000 gallons x ₹250 per gallon) + (50,000 gallons x ₹220 per gallon)	₹1,60,00,000		
4	Deduct joint and separable costs (₹40,00,000 + ₹28,00,000 + ₹52,00,000)	1,20,00,000		
5	Gross margin	₹40,00,000		
6	Gross margin percentage (₹40,00,000 ÷ ₹1,60,00,000)	25%		
7		**Buttercream**	**Condensed Milk**	**Total**
8	**Step 2**			
9	Final sales value of total production during accounting period: (20,000 gallons x ₹250 per gallon; 50,000 gallons x ₹220 per gallon)	₹50,00,000	₹1,10,00,000	₹1,60,00,000
10	Deduct gross margin, using overall gross-margin percentage (25% x ₹50,00,000; 25% x ₹1,10,00,000)	12,50,000	27,50,000	40,00,000
11	Total production costs	37,50,000	82,50,000	1,20,00,000
12	**Step 3**			
13	Deduct separable costs	28,00,000	52,00,000	80,00,000
14	Joint costs allocated	₹9,50,000	₹30,50,000	₹40,00,000
15				
16	**PANEL B: Product-Line Income Statement Using Constant Gross-Margin Percentage NRV Method for May 2012**	**Buttercream**	**Condensed Milk**	**Total**
17	Revenues (12,000 gallons x ₹250 per gallon ; 4 5,000 gallons x ₹220 per gallon)	₹30,00,000	₹99,00,000	₹1,29,00,000
18	Cost of goods sold			
19	Joint costs (from Panel A)	9,50,000	30,50,000	40,00,000
20	Separable costs	28,00,000	52,00,000	80,00,000
21	Production costs	37,50,000	82,50,000	1,20,00,000
22	Deduct ending inventory			
23	(8,000 gallons x ₹187.5 per gallon[a]; 5,000 gallons x ₹165 per gallon)[b]	15,00,000	82,50,000	23,25,000
24	Cost of goods sold	22,50,000	74,25,000	96,75,000
25	Gross margin	₹7,50,000	₹24,75,000	₹32,25,000
26	Gross margin percentage (₹7,50,000 ÷ 3,00,000; ₹24,75,000 ÷ ₹99,00,000; ₹32,50,000 ÷ ₹1,29,00,000)	25%	25%	25%
27				
28	[a]Total production costs of buttercream ÷ Total production of buttercream = ₹37,50,000 ÷ 20,000 gallons = ₹187.5 per gallon.			
29	[b]Total production costs of condensed milk ÷ Total production of condensed milk = ₹82,50,000 ÷ 50,000 gallons = ₹165 per gallon.			

The constant gross-margin percentage NRV method is the only method whereby products can receive negative allocations. This may be required in order to bring the gross-margin percentages of relatively unprofitable products up to the overall average. The constant gross-margin percentage NRV method also differs from the other two market-based joint-cost-allocation methods described earlier in another fundamental way. Neither the sales value at splitoff method nor the NRV method takes account of profits earned either before or after the splitoff point when allocating the joint costs. In contrast, the constant gross-margin percentage NRV method allocates both joint costs and profits: The gross margin is allocated to the joint products in order to determine the joint-cost allocations so that the resulting gross-margin percentage for each product is the same.

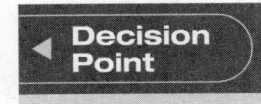

◄ Decision Point

What methods can be used to allocate joint costs to individual products?

Choosing an Allocation Method

Which method of allocating joint costs should be used? When selling-price data exist at the splitoff point, the sales value at splitoff method is preferred, even if further processing is done. The following are reasons why:

Learning Objective **4**

Identify situations when the sales value at split-off method is preferred when allocating joint costs

. . . because it objectively measures the benefits received by each product

1. **Measures of benefits received.** The sales value at splitoff is the best measure of the benefits received by joint products relative to all other methods of allocating joint costs. It is a meaningful basis for allocating joint costs because generating revenues is the reason why a company incurs joint costs in the first place. It is also sometimes possible to vary the physical mix of final output and thereby produce more or less market value by incurring more joint costs. In such cases, there is a clear causal link between total cost and total output value, thereby further validating the use of the sales value at splitoff method.[3]

2. **Independent of further processing decisions.** The sales value at splitoff method does not require information on the processing steps after splitoff, if there are any. In contrast, the NRV and constant gross-margin percentage NRV methods require information on (a) the specific sequence of further processing decisions, (b) the separable costs of further processing, and (c) the point at which individual products will be sold.

3. **Common allocation basis.** As with other market-based approaches, the sales value at splitoff method (as well as other market-based methods) has a common basis to allocate joint costs to products, which is revenue. In contrast, the physical-measure at splitoff method may lack an easily identifiable common basis for costs allocation.

4. **Simplicity.** The sales value at splitoff method is simple. In contrast, the NRV and constant gross-margin percentage NRV methods can be complex for operations with multiple products and multiple splitoff points. This complexity increases when managers makes frequent changes to the sequence of post-splitoff processing decisions or to the point at which individual products are sold.

When the selling prices of all products at the splitoff point are unavailable, the NRV method is the best alternative. It attempts to approximate sales value at splitoff by subtracting from selling prices separable costs incurred after the splitoff point. The NRV method assumes that all the markup (the profit margin) is attributable to the joint process and none of the markup is attributable to the separable costs. This is unrealistic if, for example, a firm uses a special patented technology in its separable process or innovative marketing that enables it to generate significant profits. Despite this limitation, the NRV method is commonly used when selling prices at splitoff are not available as it provides a better measure of the benefits received than either the constant gross-margin percentage NRV method or the physical-measure method.

The constant gross-margin percentage NRV method treats the joint products as though they comprise a single product. This method calculates the aggregate gross-margin percentage, applies this percentage to each product, and views the residual after separable costs are accounted for as the amount of joint costs assigned to each product. Consequently, unlike the NRV method, the benefits received by each of the joint products at the splitoff point don't have to be measured. Also, the constant gross-margin percentage method recognizes that the profit margin is not just attributable to the joint process but is also derived from the costs incurred after splitoff. The drawback of the method is that it assumes that the profit margin is identical across products; that is, all products are assumed to have the same ratio of cost to sales value. Recall from our discussion of activity-based costing (ABC) in Chapter 5 that such a situation is uncommon when companies offer a diverse set of products.

---

[3] In the semiconductor industry, for example, the use of cleaner facilities, higher quality silicon wafers, and more sophisticated equipment (all of which require higher joint costs) shifts the distribution of output to higher-quality memory devices with more market value. For details, see J. F. Gatti and D. J. Grinnell, "Joint Cost Allocations: Measuring and Promoting Productivity and Quality Improvements," *Journal of Cost Management* (2000). The authors also demonstrate that joint cost allocations based on market value are preferable for promoting quality and productivity improvements.

Although there are difficulties in using the physical-measure method—such as lack of congruence with the benefits-received criterion—there are instances when it may be preferred. In settings where end prices are volatile or the process after splitoff is long or uncertain, the presence of a comparable physical measure at splitoff would favor use of the method. This is true, for instance, in the chemical and oil refining industries. The physical-measure method is also useful when joint cost allocations are used as the basis for setting market prices, as in rate regulation. It avoids the circular reasoning of using selling prices to allocate the costs on which prices (rates) are based.

Not Allocating Joint Costs

Some companies choose to not allocate joint costs to products due to the complexity of their production or extraction processes and the difficulty of gathering sufficient data to allocate the costs correctly.

Rather than allocating joint costs, some firms simply subtract them directly from total revenues in the management accounts. If substantial inventories exist, the firms carry their product inventories at NRV. Companies in the meatpacking, canning, and mining industries often use variations of this approach. Accountants do not ordinarily record inventories at NRV because this practice recognizes the income on each product at the time it is completed but *before* it is sold. To deal with this problem, some of these companies carry their inventories at NRV minus an estimated operating income margin. When any end-of-period inventories are sold in the next period, the cost of goods sold then equals this carrying value. This approach is akin to the "production method" of accounting for byproducts, which we describe later in this chapter.

Decision Point

When is the sales value at splitoff method considered preferable for allocating joint costs to individual products and why?

Why Joint Costs are Irrelevant for Decision Making

Chapter 11 introduced the concepts of *relevant revenues*, expected future revenues that differ among alternative courses of action, and *relevant costs*, expected future costs that differ among alternative courses of action. These concepts can be applied to decisions on whether a joint product or main product should be sold at the splitoff point or processed further.

Learning Objective 5

Explain why joint costs are irrelevant in a sell-or-process-further decision

. . . because joint costs are the same whether or not further processing occurs

Sell-or-Process-Further Decisions

Consider Mother' Dairy's decision to either sell the joint products, cream and liquid skim, at the splitoff point or to further process them into buttercream and condensed milk. The decision to incur additional costs for further processing should be based on the incremental operating income attainable beyond the splitoff point. Example 2 assumed it was profitable for both cream and liquid skim to be further processed into buttercream and condensed milk, respectively. The incremental analysis for the decision to process further is:

Further Processing Cream into Buttercream

Incremental revenues

(₹250/gallon × 20,000 gallons) − (₹80/gallon × 25,000 gallons) ₹30,00,000	
Deduct incremental processing costs	28,00,000
Increase in operating income from buttercream	₹2,00,000

Further Processing Liquid Skim into Condensed Milk

Incremental revenues

(₹220/gallon × 50,000 gallons) − (₹40/gallon × 75,000 gallons)	₹80,00,000
Deduct incremental processing costs	52,00,000
Increase in operating income from condensed milk	₹28,00,000

In this example, operating income increases for both products, so the manager decides to process cream into buttercream and liquid skim into condensed milk. *Note that the 40,00,000 joint costs incurred before the splitoff point are irrelevant in deciding whether to process further.* Why? Because the joint costs of 40,00,000 are the same whether the products are sold at the splitoff point or processed further. What matters is the incremental income from additional processing.

Incremental costs are the additional costs incurred for an activity, such as further processing. *Do not assume all separable costs in joint-cost allocations are always incremental costs.* Some separable costs may be fixed costs, such as lease costs on buildings where the further processing is done; some separable costs may be sunk costs, such as depreciation on the equipment that converts cream into buttercream; and some separable costs may be allocated costs, such as corporate costs allocated to the condensed milk operations. None of these costs will differ between the alternatives of selling products at the splitoff point or processing further; therefore, they are irrelevant.

Decision Making and Performance Evaluation

The potential conflict between cost concepts used for decision making and cost concepts used for evaluating the performance of managers often arise when sell-or-process-further decisions are being made. To see how, let us continue with Example 2. Suppose *allocated* fixed corporate and administrative costs of further processing cream into buttercream equal ₹3,00,000 and that these costs will be allocated only to buttercream and to the manager's product-line income statement if buttercream is produced. How might this policy affect the decision to process further?

As we have seen, on the basis of incremental revenues and incremental costs, Mother Dairy's operating income will increase by ₹2,00,000 if it processes cream into buttercream. However, producing the buttercream also results in an additional charge for allocated fixed costs of ₹3,00,000. If the manager is evaluated on a full-cost basis (that is, after allocating all costs), processing cream into buttercream will lower the manager's performance-evaluation measure by ₹1,00,000 (incremental operating income, ₹2,00,000 − allocated fixed costs, ₹3,00,000). Therefore, the manager may be tempted to sell cream at splitoff and not process it into buttercream.

A similar conflict can also arise with joint products. Consider again Example 1, suppose Mother Dairy has the option of selling raw milk at a profit of ₹2,00,000. From a decision-making standpoint, the company would maximize operating income by processing raw milk into cream and liquid skim because the total revenues from selling both joint products (₹50,00,000) exceed the joint costs (₹40,00,000) by ₹10,00,000, which is greater than the ₹2,00,000 profit from selling the raw milk. Suppose, however, the cream and liquid-skim product lines are managed by different managers, each of whom is evaluated based on a product-line income statement. If the physical-measure method of joint-cost allocation is used and the selling price per gallon of liquid skim falls below ₹40 per gallon, the liquid-skim product line will show a loss (from Exhibit 16-4, revenues will be less than ₹12,00,000, but cost of goods sold will be unchanged at ₹12,00,000). The manager of the liquid-skim line will therefore prefer, from his performance-evaluation standpoint, to not produce liquid skim but rather to sell the raw milk.

Mother Dairy's, performance evaluation will be less severe if it uses any of the market-based methods of joint-cost allocations—sales value at splitoff, NRV, or constant gross-margin percentage NRV because each of these methods allocates costs using revenues, which generally leads to a positive income for each joint product.

Pricing Decisions

Firms should be wary of using the full cost of a joint product (that is, the cost after joint costs are allocated) as the basis for making pricing decisions. Why? Because in many situations, there is no direct cause-and-effect relationship that identifies the resources demanded by each joint product that can then be used as a basis for pricing. In fact, the use of the sales value at splitoff or the net realizable value method to allocate joint costs results in a reverse effect: The selling prices of joint products drive joint-cost allocations, rather than cost allocations serving as the basis for the pricing of joint products! Of course, the principles of pricing covered in Chapter 13 apply to the joint process taken as a whole. Even if the firm cannot alter the mix of products generated by the joint process, it must ensure that the joint products generate sufficient combined revenue in the long run to cover the joint costs of processing.

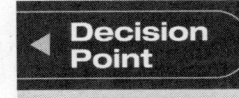

Decision Point

Are joint costs relevant in a sell-or-process-further decision?

Accounting for Byproducts

Joint production processes can yield not only joint products and main products but also byproducts. Although their total sales values are relatively low, the byproducts in a joint production process can affect the allocation of joint costs. Moreover, byproducts can be quite profitable for a firm. Wendy's, the fast food chain, uses surplus hamburger patties in its "rich and meaty" chili and, because it cooks meat specifically for the chili only 10% of the time, makes great margins even at a price of ₹9.90 for an eight-ounce serving of chili. Let's consider a two-product example consisting of a main product and a byproduct.

Learning Objective 6

Account for byproducts using two methods

. . . recognize in financial statements at time of production or at time of sale

> Example 3: The Westlake Corporation processes timber into fine-grade lumber and wood chips that are used as mulch in gardens and lawns. Information about these products follows:

■ Fine-grade lumber (the main product)—sells for ₹60 per board foot (b.f.)

■ Wood chips (the byproduct)—sells for ₹10 per cubic foot (c.f.)

The data for July 2014 are:

	Beginning Inventory	Production	Sales	Ending Inventory
Fine-grade lumber (b.f.)	0	50,000	40,000	10,000
Wood chips (c.f.)	0	4,000	1,200	2,800

The joint manufacturing costs for these products in July 2014 were ₹25,00,000. They consist of ₹15,00,000 for direct materials and ₹10,00,000 for conversion costs. Both products are sold at the splitoff point without further processing, as Exhibit 16-8 shows.

We present two byproduct accounting methods: the production method and the sales method. The production method recognizes byproducts in the financial statements at the

Exhibit 16-8

Example 3: Overview of Westlake Corporation

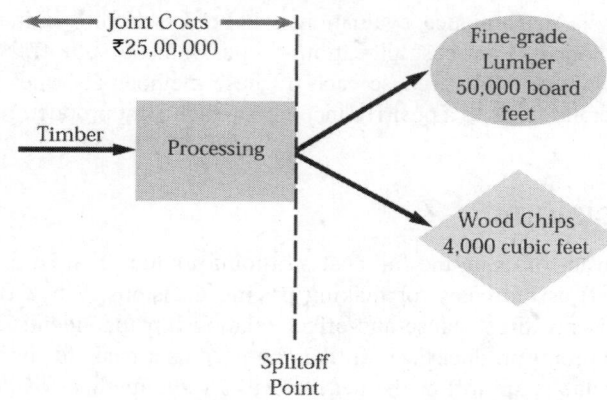

Exhibit 16-9

Income Statements of Westlake Corporation for July 2014 Using the Production and Sales Methods for Byproduct Accounting

	Production Method	Sales Method
Revenues		
Main product: Fine-grade lumber (40,000 b.f. ×₹60 per b.f.)	₹24,00,000	₹24,00,000
Byproduct: Wood chips (1,200 c.f. × ₹10 per c.f.)	–	12,000
Total revenues	₹24,00,000	24,12,000
Cost of goods sold		
Total manufacturing costs	₹25,00,000	25,00,000
Deduct byproduct revenue (4,000 c.f. ×₹10 per c.f.)	(40,000)	–
Net manufacturing costs	24,60,000	25,00,000
Deduct main-product inventory	(4,92,000)[a]	(5,00,000)[b]
Cost of goods sold	19,68,000	20,00,000
Gross margin	₹4,32,000	₹4,12,000
Gross-margin percentage (₹4,32,000 ÷₹24,00,000; ₹4,12,000 ÷ ₹24,12,000)	18.00%	17.08%
Inventoriable costs (end of period):		
Main product: Fine-grade lumber	₹4,92,000	₹5,00,000
Byproduct: Wood chips (2,800 c.f. ×10 per c.f.)[c]	28,000	0

[a](10,000 ÷ 5 0,000) × net manufacturing cost = (10,000 ÷50,000) ×₹24,60,000 = ₹4,92,000.

[b](10,000 ÷ 5 0,000) × total manufacturing cost = (10,000 ÷50,000) ×₹25,00,000 = ₹5,00,000.

[c]Recorded at selling prices.

time production is completed. The sales method delays recognition of byproducts until the time of sale.[4] Exhibit 16-9 presents the income statement of Westlake Corporation under both methods.

Production Method: Byproducts Recognized at Time Production Is Completed

This method recognizes the byproduct in the financial statements—the 4,000 cubic feet of wood chips—in the month it is produced, July 2014. The NRV from the byproduct

---

[4] For a discussion of joint cost allocation and byproduct accounting methods, see P. D. Marshall and R. F. Dombrowski, "A Small Business Review of Accounting for Primary Products, Byproducts and Scrap," The National Public Accountant (February/ March 2003): 10–13.

produced is offset against the costs of the main product. The following journal entries illustrate the production method:

1. Work in Process   15,00,000
   Accounts Payable   15,00,000
   To record direct materials purchased and used in production during July.
2. Work in Process   10,00,000
   Various accounts such as Wages Payable and
       Accumulated Depreciation   10,00,000
   To record conversion costs in the production process during
   July; examples include energy, manufacturing supplies, all
   manufacturing labor, and plant depreciation.
3. Byproduct Inventory—Wood Chips (4,000 c.f. × ₹10 per c.f.)   40,000
   Finished Goods—Fine-grade Lumber (₹25,00,000 – ₹40,000)   24,60,000
       Work in Process (₹15,00,000 + ₹10,00,000)   25,00,000
   To record cost of goods completed during July.
4a. Cost of Goods Sold [(40,000 b.f. ÷ 50,000 b.f.) × ₹24,60,000]   19,68,000
    Finished Goods—Fine-grade Lumber   19,68,000
    To record the cost of the main product sold during July.
4b. Cash or Accounts Receivable (40,000 b.f. × ₹60 per b.f.)   24,00,000
    Revenues—Fine-grade Lumber   24,00,000
    To record the sales of the main product during July.
5. Cash or Accounts Receivable (1,200 c.f. × ₹10 per c.f.)   12,000
   Byproduct Inventory—Wood Chips   12,000
   To record the sales of the byproduct during July.

The production method reports the byproduct inventory of wood chips in the balance sheet at its ₹10 per cubic foot selling price [(4,000 cubic feet – 1,200 cubic feet) × ₹10 per cubic foot = ₹28,000].

One variation of this method would be to report byproduct inventory at its NRV reduced by a normal profit margin, say 20%: (₹28,000 – 20% × ₹28,000 = ₹22,400, assuming a normal profit margin of 20%).[5] When byproduct inventory is sold in a subsequent period, the income statement will match the selling price, ₹28,000, with the "cost" reported for the byproduct inventory, ₹22,400, resulting in a byproduct operating income of ₹5,600 (₹28,000 – ₹22,400).

Sales Method: Byproducts Recognized at Time of Sale

With this method, no journal entries are made for byproducts until they are sold. At that time, the byproduct revenues are reported in the income statement. These revenues are either grouped with other sales, included as other income, or are deducted from cost of goods sold. In the Westlake Corporation example, byproduct revenues in July 2014 are ₹12,000 (1,200 cubic feet × ₹10 per cubic foot) because only 1,200 cubic feet of wood chips are sold in July (of the 4,000 cubic feet produced). The journal entries are:

1. and 2.   *Same as for the production method.*
   Work in Process   15,00,000
   Accounts Payable   15,00,000
   Work in Process   10,00,000
       Various accounts such as Wages Payable
           and Accumulated Depreciation   10,00,000

---

[5] One way to make this calculation is to assume all products have the same "normal" profit margin like the constant gross-margin percentage NRV method. Alternatively, the company might allow products to have different profit margins based on an analysis of the margins earned by other companies that sell these products individually.

3.	Finished Goods—Fine-grade Lumber	25,00,000	
	Work in Process		25,00,000
	To record cost of main product completed during July.		
4a.	Cost of Goods Sold [(40,000 b.f. ÷ 50,000 b.f.) × 25,00,000]	20,00,000	
	Finished Goods—Fine-grade Lumber		20,00,000
	To record the cost of the main product sold during July.		
4b.	Same as for the production method.		
	Cash or Accounts Receivable (40,000 b.f. × ₹60 per b.f.)	24,00,000	
	Revenues—Fine-grade Lumber		24,00,000
5.	Cash or Accounts Receivable	12,000	
	Revenues—Wood Chips		12,000
	To record the sales of the byproduct during July.		

Which method should a company use? The production method is conceptually correct in that it is consistent with the matching principle and is the preferred method. This method recognizes byproduct inventory in the accounting period in which it is produced and simultaneously reduces the cost of manufacturing the main or joint products, thereby better matching the revenues and expenses from selling the main product. However, the sales method is simpler and is often used in practice, primarily because the rupee amounts of byproducts are immaterial. The drawback of the sales method is that it allows a firm to "manage" its reported earnings by timing the sale of byproducts. For example, to boost its revenues and income slightly, a firm might store the byproducts for several periods and then sell them when the revenues and profits from the main product or joint products are low.

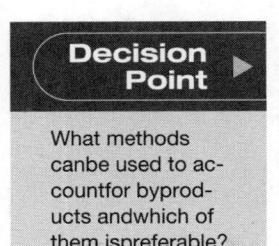

Decision Point ▶

What methods canbe used to accountfor byproducts andwhich of them ispreferable?

Problem for Self-Study

Inorganic Chemicals (IC) processes salt into various industrial products. In July 2014, IC incurred joint costs of ₹10,00,000 to purchase salt and convert it into two products: caustic soda and chlorine. Although there is an active outside market for chlorine, IC processes all 800 tons of chlorine it produces into 500 tons of PVC (polyvinyl chloride), which is then sold. There were no beginning or ending inventories of salt, caustic soda, chlorine, or PVC in July. Information for July 2014 production and sales follows:

	A	B	C	D
	File Edit View Insert Format Tools Data Window Help			
1		**Joint Costs**		**PVC**
2	Joint costs (costs of salt and processing to splitoff point)	₹10,00,000		
3	Separable cost of processing 800 tons chlorine into 500 tons PVC			₹2,00,000
4				
5		**Caustic Soda**	**Chlorine**	**PVC**
6	Beginning inventory (tons)	0	0	0
7	Production (tons)	1,200	800	500
8	Transfer for further processing (tons)		800	
9	Sales (tons)	1,200		500
10	Ending inventory (tons)	0	0	0
11	Selling price per ton in active outside market (for products not actually sold)		₹750	
12	Selling price per ton for products sold	₹500		₹2,000

1. Allocate the joint costs of ₹10,00,000 between caustic soda and PVC under (a) the sales value at splitoff method and (b) the physical-measure method.
2. Allocate the joint costs of ₹10,00,000 between caustic soda and PVC under the NRV method.
3. Under the three allocation methods in requirements 1 and 2, what is the gross-margin percentage of (a) caustic soda and (b) PVC?
4. Lifetime Swimming Pool Products offers to purchase 800 tons of chlorine in August 2014 at ₹750 per ton. Assume all other production and sales data are the same for August as they were for July. This sale of chlorine to Lifetime would mean that no PVC would be produced by IC in August. How would accepting this offer affect IC's August 2014 operating income?

Solution

The following picture provides a visual illustration of the main facts in this problem.

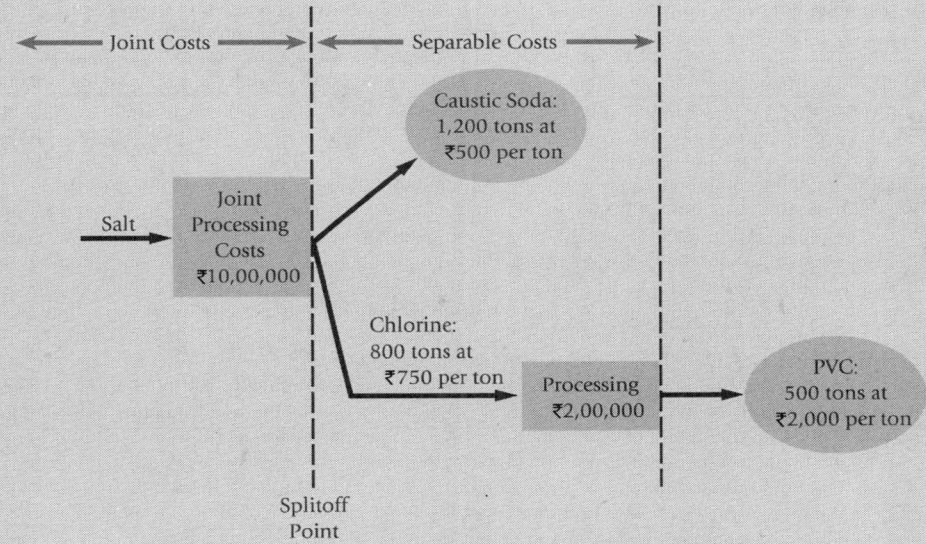

Note that caustic soda is sold as is while chlorine, despite having a market value at split-off, is sold only in processed form as PVC. The goal is to allocate the joint costs of 10,00,000 to the final products—caustic soda and PVC. However, since PVC exists only in the form of chlorine at the splitoff point, we use chlorine's sales value and physical measure as the basis for allocating joint costs to PVC under the sales value at splitoff and physical measure at splitoff methods. Detailed calculations are shown next.

   1a. Sales value at splitoff method
   1b. Physical-measure method

	File Edit View Insert Format Tools Data Window Help			
	A	B	C	D
1	**Allocation of Joint costs using Sales Value at Splitoff Method**	**Caustic Soda**	**PVC / Chlorine**	**Total**
2	Sales value of total production at splitoff point			
3	(1,200 tons x ₹500 per ton; 800 x ₹750 per ton)	₹6,00,000	₹6,00,000	₹12,00,000
4	Weighting (₹6,00,000 ÷ ₹12,00,000; ₹6,00,000 ÷ ₹12,00,000)	0.50	0.50	
5	Joint costs allocated (0.50 x ₹10,00,000; 0.50 x ₹10,00,000)	₹5,00,000	₹5,00,000	₹10,00,000

2. Net realizable value (NRV) method

	A	B	C	D
8	**Allocation of Joint Costs using Physical-Measure Method**	**Caustic Soda**	**PVC / Chlorine**	**Total**
9	Physical measure of total production (tons)	1,200	800	2,000
10	Weighting (1,200 tons ÷ 2,000 tons; 800 tons ÷ 2,000 tons)	0.60	0.40	
11	Joint cost allocated (0.60 x ₹10,00,000; 0.40 x ₹10,00,000)	₹6,00,000	₹4,00,000	₹10,00,000

3a. Gross-margin percentage of caustic soda

	A	B	C	D
14	**Allocation of Joint Costs using Net Realizable Value Method**	**Caustic Soda**	**PVC**	**Total**
15	Final sales value of total production during accounting period			
16	(1,200 tons x ₹500 per ton; 500 tons x ₹2,000 per ton)	₹6,00,000	₹10,00,000	₹16,00,000
17	Deduct separable costs to complete and sell	0	2,00,000	2,00,000
18	Net realizable value at splitoff point	₹6,00,000	₹8,00,000	₹14,00,000
19	Weighting (₹6,00,000 ÷ ₹14,00,000; ₹8,00,000 ÷ ₹14,00,000)	3/7	4/7	
20	Joint costs allocated (3/7 x ₹10,00,000; 4/7 x ₹10,00,000)	₹4,28,570	₹5,71,430	₹10,00,000

3b. Gross-margin percentage of PVC

	A	B	C	D
		Sales Value at Splitoff Point	**Physical Measure**	**NRV**
23	**Caustic Soda**			
24	Revenues (1,200 tons x ₹500 per ton)	₹6,00,000	₹6,00,000	₹6,00,000
25	Cost of goods sold (joint costs)	5,00,000	6,00,000	4,28,570
26	Gross margin	₹1,00,000	₹0	₹1,71,430
27	Gross margin percentage (₹1,00,000 ÷ ₹6,00,000; ₹0 ÷ ₹6,00,000; ₹1,71,430 ÷ ₹6,00,000)	16.67%	0.00%	28.57%

4.

	A	B	C	D
		Sales Value at Splitoff Point	**Physical Measure**	**NRV**
30	**PVC**			
31	Revenues (500 tons x ₹2,000 per ton)	₹10,00,000	₹10,00,000	₹10,00,000
32	Cost of goods sold			
33	Joint costs	5,00,000	4,00,000	5,71,430
34	Separable costs	2,00,000	2,00,000	2,00,000
35	Cost of goods sold	7,00,000	6,00,000	7,71,430
36	Gross margin	₹3,00,000	₹4,00,000	₹2,28,570
37	Gross margin percentage (₹3,00,000 ÷ ₹10,00,000; ₹4,00,000 ÷ ₹10,00,000; ₹2,28,570 ÷ ₹10,00,000)	30.00%	40.00%	22.86%

If IC sells 800 tons of chlorine to Lifetime Swimming Pool Products instead of further processing it into PVC, its August 2014 operating income will be reduced by ₹2,00,000.

File Edit View Insert Format Tools Data Window Help	
A	B
Incremental revenue from processing 800 tons of chlorine into 500 tons of PVC	
(500 tons x ₹2,000 per ton) – (800 tons x ₹750 per ton)	₹4,00,000
Incremental cost of processing 800 tons of chlorine into 500 tons of PVC	2,00,000
ncremental operating income from further processing	₹2,00,000

Decision Points

The following question-and-answer format summarizes the chapter's learning objectives. Each decision presents a key question related to a learning objective. The guidelines are the answer to that question.

Decision	**Guidelines**
1. What do the terms joint cost and and splitoff point mean, and how do joint products differ from by products?	A joint cost is the cost of a single production process that yields multiple products simultaneously. The splitoff point is the juncture in a joint production process when the products become separately identifiable. Joint products have high total sales values at the splitoff point. A byproduct has a low total sales value at the splitoff point relative to the total sales value of a joint or main product.
2. Why are joint costs allocated to individual products?	The purposes for allocating joint costs to products include inventory costing for financial accounting and internal reporting, cost reimbursement, insurance settlements, rate regulation, and product-cost litigation.
3. What methods can be used to allocate joint costs to individual products?	The methods to allocate joint costs to products are the sales value at splitoff, physical measure, NRV, and constant gross-margin percentage NRV methods.
4. When is the sales value at splitoff method considered preferable for allocating joint costs to individual products and why?	The sales value at splitoff method is preferred when market prices exist at splitoff because using revenues is consistent with the benefits-received criterion; further, the method does not depend on subsequent decisions made about further processing and is simple.
5. Are joint costs relevant in a sell-or-process-further decision?	No, joint costs and how they are allocated are irrelevant because they are the same regardless of whether further processing occurs.
6. What methods can be used to account for byproducts, and which of them is preferable?	The production method recognizes byproducts in financial statements at the time of their production, whereas the sales method recognizes byproducts in financial statements at the time of their sale. The production method is conceptually superior, but the sales method is often used in practice because the dollar amounts of byproducts are immaterial.

TERMS TO LEARN

This chapter and the Glossary at the end of the book contain definitions of the following important terms:

byproducts **(p. 848)**

constant gross-margin percentage NRV method **(p. 856)**

joint costs **(p. 848)**

joint products **(p. 848)**

main product **(p. 848)**

net realizable value (NRV) method **(p. 855)**

physical-measure method **(p. 852)**

product **(p. 848)**

sales value at splitoff method **(p. 852)**

separable costs **(p. 848)**

splitoff point **(p. 848)**

ASSIGNMENT MATERIAL

Questions

16-1 Give two examples of industries in which joint costs are found. For each example, what are the individual products at the splitoff point?

16-2 What is a joint cost? What is a separable cost?

16-3 Distinguish between a joint product and a byproduct.

16-4 Why might the number of products in a joint-cost situation differ from the number of outputs? Give an example.

16-5 Provide three reasons for allocating joint costs to individual products or services.

16-6 Why does the sales value at splitoff method use the sales value of the total production in the accounting period and not just the revenues from the products sold?

16-7 Describe a situation in which the sales value at splitoff method cannot be used but the NRV method can be used for joint-cost allocation.

16-8 Distinguish between the sales value at splitoff method and the NRV method.

16-9 Give two limitations of the physical-measure method of joint-cost allocation.

16-10 How might a company simplify its use of the NRV method when final selling prices can vary sizably in an accounting period and management frequently changes the point at which it sells individual products?

16-11 Why is the constant gross-margin percentage NRV method sometimes called a "joint-cost-allocation and a profit-allocation" method?

16-12 "Managers must decide whether a product should be sold at splitoff or processed further. The sales value at splitoff method of joint-cost allocation is the best method for generating the information managers need for this decision." Do you agree? Explain.

16-13 "Managers should consider only additional revenues and separable costs when making decisions about selling at splitoff or processing further." Do you agree? Explain.

16-14 Describe two major methods to account for byproducts.

16-15 Why might managers seeking a monthly bonus based on attaining a target operating income prefer the sales method of accounting for byproducts rather than the production method?

Solved Examples

16-16 Net realizable value method. Hindustan Oil produces two joint products, cooking oil and soap oil, from a single vegetable-oil refining process. In July, the joint costs of this process were ₹2,40,00,000. Separable processing costs beyond the splitoff point were cooking oil, ₹3,00,00,000, and soap oil, ₹75,00,000. Cooking oil sells for ₹50 per litre. Soap oil sells for ₹25 per litre. Hindustan Oil produced and sold 10,00,000 litres of cooking oil and 5,00,000 litres of soap oil. There are no beginning or ending inventories of cooking oil or soap oil.

Allocate the ₹2,40,00,000 joint costs using the NRV method.

Required

Solution

Net realizable value method.

A diagram of the situation is in Solution Exhibit 16-16 (all numbers are in thousands).

	Cooking Oil (CO)	Soap Oil (SO)	Total
Final sales value of total production, CO, 1,000 × ₹50; SO, 500 × ₹25	₹50,000	₹12,500	₹62,500
Deduct separable costs to complete and sell	30,000	7,500	37,500
Net realizable value at splitoff point	₹20,000	₹5,000	₹25,000
Weighting	$\dfrac{₹20,000}{₹25,000}$ = 0.8	$\dfrac{₹5,000}{₹25,000}$ = 0.2	
Joint costs allocated, CO, 0.8 × ₹24,000; SO, 0.2 × ₹24,000	₹19,200	₹4,800	₹24,000

Solution Exhibit 16-16 (all numbers are in thousands)

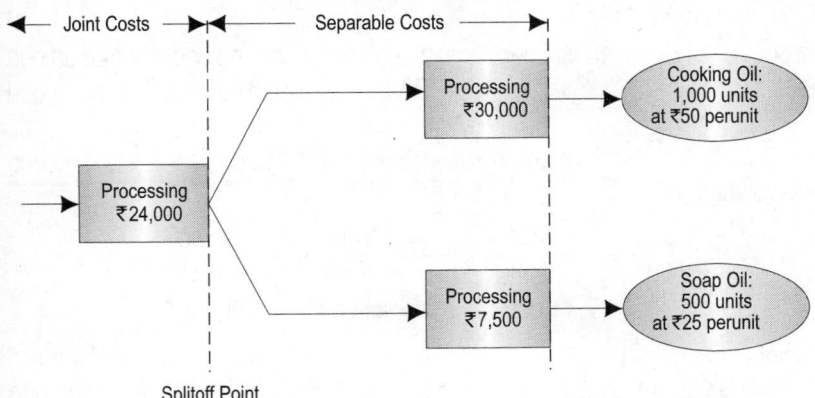

16-17 Alternative methods of joint-cost allocation, ending inventories. The Indraprastha Chemicals operates a simple chemical process to convert a single material into three separate items, referred to here as X, Y, and Z. All three end products are separated simultaneously at a single splitoff point.

Products X and Y are ready for sale immediately upon splitoff without further processing or any other additional costs. Product Z, however, is processed further before being sold. There is no available market price for Z at the splitoff point.

The selling prices quoted here are expected to remain the same in the coming year. During 2014, the selling prices of the items and the total amounts sold were:

- X—120 tons sold for ₹15,000 per ton
- Y—340 tons sold for ₹10,000 per ton
- Z—475 tons sold for ₹7,000 per ton

The total joint manufacturing costs for the year were ₹40,00,000. An additional ₹20,00,000 was spent to finish product Z.

There were no beginning inventories of X, Y, or Z. At the end of the year, the following inventories of completed units were on hand: X, 180 tons; Y, 60 tons; Z, 25 tons. There was no beginning or ending work in process.

Required

1. Compute the cost of inventories of X, Y, and Z for balance sheet purposes and the cost of goods sold for income statement purposes as of December 31, 2015, using
   a. NRV method of joint-cost allocation
   b. Constant gross-margin percentage NRV method of joint-cost allocation
2. Compare the gross-margin percentages for X, Y, and Z using the two methods given in requirement 1.

Solution

Alternative methods of joint-cost allocation, ending inventories.

Total production for the year was:

	Sold	Ending Inventories	Total Production
X	120	180	300
Y	340	60	400
Z	475	25	500

A diagram of the situation is in Solution Exhibit 16-17.

1. a. Net realizable value (NRV) method:

	X	Y	Z	Total
Final sales value of total production X 300 × ₹15,000; Y 400 × ₹10,000; Z 500 × ₹7,000	₹45,00,000	₹40,00,000	₹35,00,000	₹1,20,00,000
Deduct separable costs	–	–	20,00,000	20,00,000
Net realizable value at splitoff point	₹45,00,000	₹40,00,000	₹15,00,000	₹1,00,00,000
Weighting	₹450 / ₹1,000 = 0.45	₹400 / ₹1,000 = 0.40	₹150 / ₹1,000 = 0.15	
Joint costs allocated 0.45; 0.40; 0.15 × ₹40,00,000	₹18,00,000	₹16,00,000	₹6,00,000	₹40,00,000

Ending Inventory Percentages

	X	Y	Z
Ending inventory	180	60	25
Total production	300	400	500
Ending inventory percentage	60%	15%	5%

Income Statement

	X	Y	Z	Total
Revenues X 120 × ₹15,000; Y 340 × ₹10,000; Z 475 × ₹7,000	₹18,00,000	₹34,00,000	₹33,25,000	₹85,25,000
Cost of goods sold				
Joint costs allocated	18,00,000	16,00,000	6,00,000	40,00,000
Separable costs	–	–	20,00,000	20,00,000
Cost of goods	18,00,000	16,00,000	26,00,000	60,00,000

available for sale

Deduct ending inventory

X 60%; Y 15%; Z 5%	10,80,000	2,40,000	1,30,000	14,50,000
Cost of goods sold	7,20,000	13,60,000	24,70,000	45,50,000
Gross margin	₹10,80,000	₹20,40,000	₹8,55,000	₹39,75,000
Gross-margin percentage	60%	60%	25.71%	

b. Constant gross-margin percentage NRV method:

Step 1:

Final sales value of prodn. (300 × ₹15,000) + (400 × ₹10,000) + (500 × ₹7,000)	₹1,20,00,000
Deduct joint and separable costs ₹40,00,000 + ₹20,00,000	60,00,000
Gross margin	₹60,00,000
Gross-margin percentage ₹60,00,000 ÷ ₹1,20,00,000	50%

	X	Y	Z	Total
Final sales value of total production				
X 300 × ₹15,000; Y 400 × ₹10,000;				
Z 500 × ₹7,000	₹45,00,000	₹40,00,000	₹35,00,000	₹1,20,00,000
Step 2: Deduct gross margin using overall				
gross-margin percentage of sales 50%	22,50,000	20,00,000	17,50,000	60,00,000
Step 3: Deduct separable costs	–	–	20,00,000	20,00,000
Joint costs allocated	₹22,50,000	₹20,00,000	₹(2,50,000)	₹40,00,000

The negative joint-cost allocation to Product Z illustrates one "unusual" feature of the constant gross-margin percentage NRV method. Some products may receive negative cost allocations in order that all individual products have the same gross-margin percentage.

Income Statement

	X	Y	Z	Total
Revenues X 120 × ₹15,000;				
Y 340 × ₹10,000;				
Z 475 × ₹7,000	₹18,00,000	₹34,00,000	₹33,25,000	₹85,25,000
Cost of goods sold:				
Joint costs allocated	22,50,000	20,00,000	(2,50,000)	40,00,000
Separable costs	–	–	20,00,000	20,00,000
Cost of goods available for sale	22,50,000	20,00,000	17,50,000	60,00,000
Deduct ending inventory				
X 60%; Y 15%; Z 5%	13,50,000	3,00,000	87,500	17,37,500
Cost of goods sold	9,00,000	17,00,000	16,62,500	42,62,500
Gross margin	₹9,00,000	₹17,00,000	₹16,62,500	₹42,62,500
Gross-margin percentage	50%	50%	50%	50%

Summary

	X	Y	Z	Total
a. Estimated NRV method:				
Inventories on balance sheet	₹10,80,000	₹2,40,000	₹1,30,000	₹14,50,000
Cost of goods sold on income statement	7,20,000	13,60,000	24,70,000	45,50,000
				₹60,00,000
b. Constant gross-margin percentage NRV method				
Inventories on balance sheet	₹13,50,000	₹3,00,000	₹87,500	₹17,37,500
Cost of goods sold on income statement	9,00,000	17,00,000	16,62,500	42,62,500
				₹60,00,000

2. Gross-margin percentages:

	X	Y	Z
Estimated NRV method	60%	60%	25.71%
Constant gross-margin percentage NRV	50%	50%	50.00%

Solution Exhibit 16-17

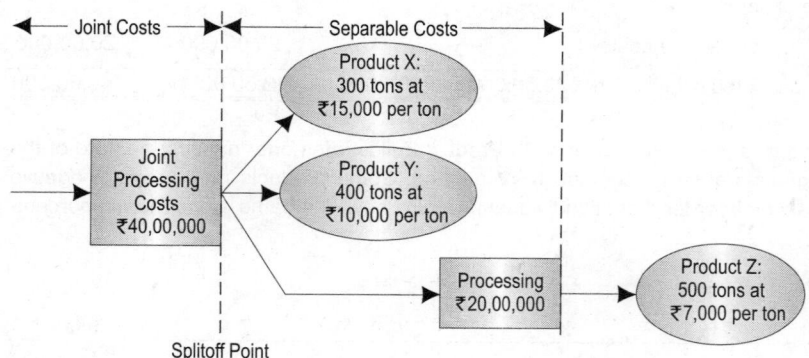

16-18 Joint cost allocation: sell immediately or process further. Soy Products Ltd.(SP) buys soybeans and processes them into other soy products. Each ton of soybeans that SP purchases for ₹34,000 can be converted for an additional cost, ₹19,000 into 575 pounds of soy meal and 160 gallons of soy oil. A pound of soy meal can be sold at split off for ₹124 and soy oil can be sold in bulk for ₹425 per gallon.

SP can process the 575 pounds of soy meal into 725 pounds of soy cookies at an additional cost of ₹38,000. Each pound of soy cookies can be sold for ₹224 per pound. The 160 gallons of soy oil can be packaged at a cost of ₹24,000 and made into 640 quarts of Soyola. Each quart of Soyola can be sold for ₹135.

Required

1. Allocate the joint cost to the cookies and the Soyola using the following:
   a. Sales value at splitoff method
   b. NRV method
2. Should SP have processed each of the products further? What effect does the allocation method have on this decision?

Solution

1.

   a. Sales value at splitoff method:

	Cookies/Soymeal	Soyola/Soy Oil	Total
Sales value of total production at splitoff,			
575 Pounds × ₹124; 160 gallons × ₹425	₹71,300	₹68,000	₹1,39,300
Weighting, ₹71,300; ₹68,000 ÷ ₹1,39,300	0.512	0.488	
Joint costs allocated,			
0.512; 0.488 × ₹53,000	₹27,100	₹25,900	₹53,000

   b. Net realizable value method:

	Cookies	Soyola	Total
Final sales value of total production,			
725 Pounds × ₹224; 640 qts × ₹135	₹1,62,400	₹86,400	₹2,48,800
Deduct separable costs	38,000	24,000	62,000
Net realizable value	₹1,24,400	₹62,400	₹1,86,800
Weighting, ₹1,24,400; ₹62,400 ÷ ₹1,86,800	0.666	0.334	
Joint costs allocated,			
0.666; 0.334 × ₹53,000	₹35,300	₹17,700	₹53,000

2.

	Cookies/Soy Meal	Soyola/Soy Oil
Revenue if sold at splitoff	₹71,300[a]	₹68,000[b]
Process further NRV	1,24,400[c]	62,400[d]
Profit (Loss) from processing further	₹53,100	₹(5,600)

[a] 575 pounds × ₹124 = ₹71,300
[b] 160 gal × ₹425 = ₹68,000
[c] 725 pounds × ₹224 − ₹38,000 = ₹1,24,400
[d] 640 qts × ₹135 − ₹24,000 = ₹62,400

SP should process the soy meal into cookies because that increases profit by ₹53,100 (₹1,24,400 − ₹71,300). However, SP should sell the soy oil as is, without processing it into the form of Soyola, because profit will be ₹5,600 (₹68,000 − ₹62,400) higher if they do. Because the total joint cost is the same under both allocation methods, it is not a relevant cost to the decision to sell at splitoff or process further.

16-19 Accounting for a main product and a byproduct. (Cheatham and Green, adapted) Ahmed is the owner and operator of Parle Bottling, a soft-drink producer. A single production process yields two soft drinks: Rainbow Dew (the main product) and Resi-Dew (the byproduct). Both products are fully processed at the splitoff point, and there are no separable costs.

   For September, the cost of the soft-drink operations is ₹1,20,000. Production and sales data are as follows:

	Production (in litres)	Sales (in litres)	Selling Price per litre
Main product: Rainbow Dew	10,000	8,000	₹20
Byproduct: Resi-Dew	2,000	1,400	2

There were no beginning inventories on September 1.

Required

1. What is the gross margin for Parle Bottling under methods A and B of byproduct accounting described in this chapter?

2. What are the inventory costs reported in the balance sheet on September 30, for Rainbow Dew and Resi-Dew under the two methods of byproduct accounting in requirement 1?

Solution

Accounting for a main product and a byproduct.

	Method A, Recognized at Production	Method B, Recognized at Sale
1. Revenues:		
Main product	₹1,60,000[a]	₹1,60,000
Byproduct	–	2,800[d]
Total revenues	1,60,000	1,62,800
Cost of goods sold		
Total manufacturing costs	1,20,000	1,20,000
Deduct byproduct revenue	4,000[b]	0
Net manufacturing costs	16,000	1,20,000
Deduct main product inventory	23,200[c]	24,000[e]
Cost of goods sold	92,800	96,000
Gross margin	₹67,200	₹66,800

[a]8,000 × ₹20.00   [d]1,400 × ₹2.00

[b]2,000 × ₹2.00   [e]$\left(\dfrac{2,000}{10,000} \times ₹1,16,000\right) = ₹23,200$

[c]$\left(\dfrac{2,000}{10,000} \times ₹1,20,000\right) = ₹24,000$

	Method A, Recognized at Production	Method B, Recognized at Sale
2. Rainbow Dew:	₹23,200	₹24,000
Resi-Dew	1,200[a]	0

[a]Ending inventory shown at unrealized selling price.

BI + Production – Sales = EI

0 + 2,000 – 1,400 = 600 litres

Ending inventory = 600 litres × ₹2 per litre = ₹1,200

16-20 Joint costs and byproducts. Sterlite Industries processes an ore in Department 1, from which comes three products, L, W, and X. Product L is processed further in Department 2. Product W is sold with- out further processing. Product X is considered a byproduct and is processed further in Department 3. Costs in Department 1 are ₹8,00,000, Department 2 costs are ₹1,00,000, and Department 3 costs are ₹50,000. Processing 6,00,000 kg in Department 1 results in 50,000 kg of product L, 3,00,000 kg of product W, and 1,00,000 kg of product X.

Product L sells for ₹10 per kg. Product W sells for ₹2 per kg. Product X sells for ₹3 per kg. The company wants to make a gross margin of 10% of revenues on product X and needs to allow 25% of revenues for marketing costs on product X.

Required

1. Compute unit costs per kg for products L, W, and X, treating X as a byproduct. Use the NRV method for allocating joint costs. Deduct the NRV of the byproduct produced from the joint cost of products L and W.

2. Compute unit costs per kg for products L, W, and X, treating all three as joint products and allocating costs by the NRV method.

Solution
Joint costs and byproducts.

1. Computing byproduct deduction to joint costs:

Revenues from X, 1,00,000 × ₹3	₹3,00,000
Deduct: Gross margin, 10% of revenues	30,000
Marketing costs, 25% of revenues	75,000
Department 3 separable costs	50,000
Net realizable value (less gross margin) of X	₹1,45,000
Joint costs	₹8,00,000
Deduct byproduct contribution	1,45,000
Net joint costs to be allocated	₹6,55,000

	Quantity	Unit Sales Price	Deduct Final Sales Value	Net Separable Processing Cost	Realizable Value at Splitoff	Weighting	Allocation of ₹6,55,000 Joint Costs
L	50,000	₹10	₹5,00,000	₹1,00,000	₹4,00,000	40%	₹2,62,000
W	3,00,000	2	6,00,000	—	6,00,000	60%	3,93,000
Totals			₹11,00,000	₹1,00,000	₹10,00,000		₹6,55,000

	Joint Costs Allocation	Add Separable Processing Costs	Total Costs	Units	Unit Cost
L	₹2,62,000	₹1,00,000	₹3,62,000	50,000	₹7.24
W	3,93,000	—	3,93,000	3,00,000	1.31
Totals	₹6,55,000	₹1,00,000	₹7,55,000	₹3,50,000	

Unit cost for X: ₹1.45 (₹1,45,000 ÷ 1,00,000) + ₹0.50 (₹50,000 ÷ 1,00,000) = ₹1.95, or ₹3.00 − ₹0.30 (10% × ₹3) − ₹0.75 (25% × ₹3) = ₹1.95.

2. If all three products are treated as joint products:

	Quantity	Unit Sales Price	Deduct Final Sales Value	Net Separable Processing Cost	Realizable Value at Splitoff	Weighting	Allocation of ₹1,80,000 Joint Costs
L	50,000	₹10	₹5,00,000	₹1,00,000	₹4,00,000	400/1,175	₹2,72,340
W	3,00,000	2	6,00,000	—	6,00,000	600/1,175	4,08,511
X	1,00,000	3	3,00,000	1,25,000	1,75,000	175/1,175	1,19,149
Totals			₹14,00,000	₹2,25,000	₹11,75,000		₹6,55,000

	Joint Costs Allocation	Add Separable Processing Costs	Total Costs	Units	Unit Cost
L	₹2,72,340	₹1,00,000	₹3,72,340	50,000	₹7.45
W	4,08,511	—	4,08,511	3,00,000	1.36
X	1,19,149	50,000	1,69,149	1,00,000	1.69
Totals	₹8,00,000	₹1,50,000	₹9,50,000	₹4,50,000	

It is important to note that there are different unit "costs" resulting from the two assumptions about the relative importance of Product X. The point is that costs of individual products depend heavily on which assumptions are made and which accounting methods and techniques are used.

Solution Exhibit 16-20

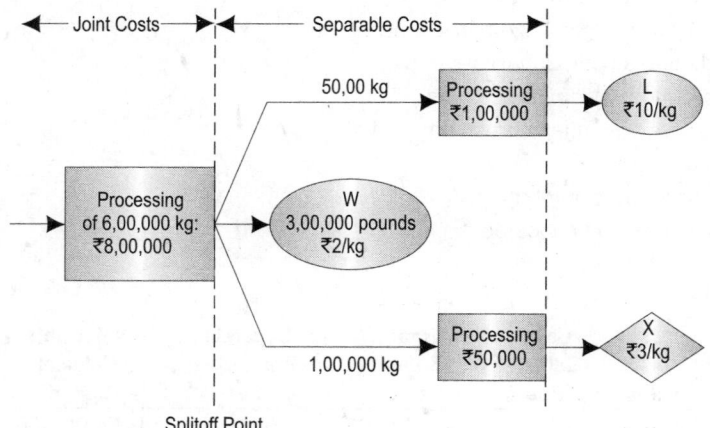

Splitoff Point

16-21 Methods of joint-cost allocation, ending inventory. Cipla produces a drug used for the treatment of hypertension. The drug is produced in batches. Chemicals costing ₹6,00,000 are mixed and heated, creating a reaction; a unique separation process then extracts the drug from the mixture. A batch yields a total of 2,500 gallons of the chemicals. The first 2,000 gallons are sold for human use while the last 500 gallons, which contain impurities, are sold to veterinarians.

The costs of mixing, heating, and extracting the drug amount to ₹9,00,000 per batch. The output sold for human use is pasteurized at a total cost of ₹12,00,000 and is sold for ₹5,850 per gallon. The product sold to veterinarians is irradiated at a cost of ₹100 per gallon and is sold for ₹4,100 per gallon.

In March, Cipla, which had no opening inventory, processed one batch of chemicals. It sold 1,700 gallons of product for human use and 300 gallons of the veterinarian product. Cipla uses the net realizable value method for allocating joint production costs.

Required

1. How much in joint costs does Cipla allocate to each product?
2. Compute the cost of ending inventory for each of Cipla's products.
3. If Cipla were to use the constant gross-margin percentage NRV method instead, how would it allocate its joint costs?
4. Calculate the gross margin on the sale of the product for human use in March under the constant gross-margin percentage NRV method.
5. Suppose that the separation process also yields 300 pints of a toxic byproduct. Cipla currently pays a hauling company ₹50,000 to dispose of this byproduct. Cipla is contacted by a firm interested in purchasing a modified form of this byproduct for a total price of ₹60,000. Cipla estimates that it will cost about ₹300 per pint to do the required modification. Should Cipla accept the offer?

Solution

1. Net realizable value of human product:

   (2,000 gallons × ₹5,850) – ₹12,00,000 = ₹1,05,00,000

   Net realizable value of veterinarian product:

   500 gallons × (₹4,100 – ₹100) = ₹20,00,000

   Joint costs: ₹6,00,000 + ₹9,00,000 = ₹15,00,000

Joint costs charged to human product: $\dfrac{1,05,00,000}{1,25,00,000} \times ₹15,00,000 = ₹12,60,000$

Joint costs charged to veterinarian product: $\dfrac{20,00,000}{1,25,00,000} \times ₹15,00,000 = ₹2,40,000$

2.

	Human Product	Vet Product	Total
Separable costs,			
₹12,00,000; 500 × ₹100	₹12,00,000	₹50,000	₹12,50,000
Joint costs (from above)	12,60,000	2,40,000	15,00,000
Total costs	₹24,60,000	₹2,90,000	₹27,50,000
Units produced (gallons)	2,000	500	2,500
Cost per gallon			
₹24,60,000 ÷ 2,000; ₹2,90,000 ÷ 500	₹1,230	₹580	₹1,100
Units in ending inventory (gallons)	300	200	500
Cost of ending inventory	₹3,69,000	₹1,16,000	₹4,85,000
₹1,230 × 300; ₹580 × 200			

3. Final gross margin: NRV (Human) + NRV (Vet) – Joint costs

$\qquad = ₹1,05,00,000 + ₹20,00,000 - ₹15,00,000 = ₹1,10,00,000$

Final sales revenues: $(2,000 \times ₹5,850) + (500 \times ₹4,100) = ₹1,37,50,000$

Final gross margin percentage: $\dfrac{₹1,10,00,000}{₹1,37,50,000} = 80\%$

By applying this constant gross margin percentage of 80% to both products, we can identify the amount of joint costs allocated to each product, as shown below.

Constant gross-margin percentage NRV method	Human Product	Vet Product	Total
Final sales value of production			
₹20,000 × 585; ₹4,100 × 500	₹1,17,00,000	₹20,50,000	₹1,37,50,000
Gross Margin (80%)	93,60,000	16,40,000	1,10,00,000
Total costs	₹23,40,000	₹4,10,000	₹27,50,000
Separable costs	12,00,000	50,000	12,50,000
Joint costs	₹11,40,000	₹3,60,000	₹15,00,000

4. In March, Cipla sold 1,700 gallons for human use for a sales revenue of:

$\qquad 1,700 \times ₹5,850 = ₹99,45,000$

Under the constant gross-margin percentage NRV method, each product is provided a gross margin of 80%. Therefore, the gross margin for the sale of human product in March is:

$\qquad ₹99,45,000 \times 80\% = ₹79,56,000$

5. Revenue from accepting the offer: ₹60,000

Cost of modification (300 pints × ₹300): 90,000

$\qquad\qquad\qquad$ Net Inflow: (₹30,000)

Add: Cost saving from not having to dispose of

$\qquad$ toxic byproduct 50,000

$\qquad\qquad$ Total benefit from offer: ₹20,000

Cipla should therefore accept the offer because its net income will increase by ₹20,000 as a result.

16-22 Comparison of alternative joint-cost-allocation methods, further-processing decision, chocolate products. Nestle manufactures chocolates and distributes chocolate products. It purchases cocoa beans and processes them into two intermediate products:

- Chocolate-powder liquor base
- Milk-chocolate liquor base

These two intermediate products become separately identifiable at a single splitoff point. Every 500 kg of cocoa beans yields 50 litres of chocolate-powder liquor base and 75 litres of milk-chocolate liquor base.

The chocolate-powder liquor base is further processed into chocolate powder. Every 50 litres of chocolate-powder liquor base yield 200 kg of chocolate powder. The milk-chocolate liquor base is further processed into milk chocolate. Every 75 litres of milk-chocolate liquor base yield 340 kg of milk chocolate.

An overview of the manufacturing operations at Nestle Chocolates follows:

Production and sales data for August are:

- Cocoa beans processed, 5,000 kg
- Costs of processing cocoa beans to splitoff point (including purchase of beans) = ₹5,00,000

	Production	Sales	Selling Price
Chocolate powder	2,000 kg	2,000 kg	₹200 per kg
Milk chocolate	3,400 kg	3,400 kg	₹250 per kg

The August separable costs of processing chocolate-powder liquor base into chocolate powder are ₹2,12,500. The August separable costs of processing milk-chocolate liquor base into milk chocolate are ₹4,37,500.

Nestle fully processes both of its intermediate products into chocolate powder or milk chocolate. There is an active market for these intermediate products. In August, Nestle could have sold the chocolate-powder liquor base for ₹420 a litre and the milk-chocolate liquor base for ₹520 a litre.

Required

1. Calculate how the joint costs of ₹5,00,000 would be allocated between the chocolate-powder and milk-chocolate liquor bases under the following methods:
   a. Sales value at splitoff
   b. Physical measure (litres)
   c. NRV
   d. Constant gross-margin percentage NRV
2. What are the gross-margin percentages of the chocolate-powder and milk-chocolate liquor bases under each of the methods in requirement 1?

Solution

Comparison of alternative joint-cost allocation methods, further-process decision, chocolate products.

1 a. Sales value at splitoff method:

	Chocolate-Powder Liquor Base	Milk-Chocolate Liquor Base	Total
Sales value of prodn. at splitoff, $500^a \times ₹420$; $750^b \times ₹520$	₹2,10,000	₹3,90,000	₹6,00,000
Weighting (in proportion of sales value at splitoff)	$\dfrac{₹2,10,000}{₹6,00,000} = 0.35$	$\dfrac{₹3,90,000}{₹6,00,000} = 0.65$	
Joint costs allocated, $0.35 \times ₹5,00,000$; $0.65 \times ₹5,00,000$	₹1,75,000	₹3,25,000	₹5,00,000

$^a(50/500) \times 5,000$ $^b(75/500) \times 5,000$

1. b. Physical-measure method:

	500 litres	750 litres	1,250 litres
Weighting	$500/1250 = 0.40$	$750/1250 = 0.60$	

Joint costs allocated, 0.40 × ₹5,00,000; 0.60 × ₹5,00,000	₹2,00,000	₹3,00,000	₹5,00,000

1. c. Net realizable value (NRV) method:

	Chocolate-Powder Liquor Base	Milk-Chocolate Liquor Base	Total
Final sales value of total production, 2,000 × ₹200; 3,400 × ₹250	₹4,00,000	₹8,50,000	₹12,50,000
Deduct separable costs to complete and sel	2,12,500	4,37,500	6,50,000
Net realizable value at splitoff point	₹1,87,500	₹4,12,500	₹6,00,000

Weighting
(in proportion of NRV at splitoff point) $\dfrac{₹1,87,500}{₹6,00,000} = 0.3125$ $\dfrac{₹4,12,500}{₹6,00,000} = 0.6875$

Joint costs allocated, 0.3125 × ₹5,00,000; 0.6875 × ₹5,00,000	₹1,56,250	₹3,43,750	₹5,00,000

d. Constant gross-margin percentage NRV method:

Step 1:

Final sales value of total production, (2,000 × ₹200) + (3,400 × ₹250)		₹12,50,000
Deduct joint and separable costs, (₹5,00,000 + ₹2,12,500 + ₹4,37,500)		11,50,000
Gross margin		₹1,00,000
Gross-margin percentage (₹1,00,000 ÷ ₹12,50,000)		8%

Step 2:

	Chocolate-Powder Liquor Base	Milk-Chocolate Liquor Base	Total
Final sales value of total production (2,000 × ₹200); (3,400 × ₹250)	₹4,00,000	₹8,50,000	₹12,50,000
Deduct gross margin, using overall gross-margin percentage of sales (8%)	32,000	68,000	1,00,000
Cost of goods available for sale	3,68,000	7,82,000	11,50,000
Step 3:			
Deduct separable costs to complete and sell	2,12,500	4,37,500	6,50,000
Joint costs allocated	₹1,55,500	₹3,44,500	₹5,00,000

2.

	Chocolate-Powder Liquor Base	Milk-Chocolate Liquor Base	Total
a. Revenues	₹4,00,000	₹8,50,000	₹12,50,000
Joint costs	1,75,000	3,25,000	5,00,000
Separable costs	2,12,500	4,37,500	6,50,000
Total costs	3,87,500	7,62,500	11,50,000
Gross margin	₹12,500	₹87,500	₹1,00,000
Gross-margin percentage	3.125%	10.294%	8%

b.	Revenues	₹4,00,000	₹8,50,000	₹12,50,000
	Joint costs	2,00,000	3,00,000	5,00,000
	Separable costs	2,12,500	4,37,500	6,50,000
	Total costs	4,12,500	7,37,500	11,50,000
	Gross margin	(12,500)	1,12,500	1,00,000
	Gross-margin percentage	(3.125%)	13.235%	8%
c.	Revenues	₹4,00,000	₹8,50,000	₹12,50,000
	Joint costs	1,56,250	3,43,750	5,00,000
	Separable costs	2,12,500	4,37,500	6,50,000
	Total costs	3,68,750	7,81,250	11,50,000
	Gross margin	31,250	68,750	1,00,000
	Gross-margin percentage	7.812%	8.088%	8%
d.	Revenues	₹4,00,000	8,50,000	12,50,000
	Joint costs	1,55,500	3,44,500	5,00,000
	Separable costs	2,12,500	4,37,500	6,50,000
	Total costs	3,68,000	7,82,000	11,50,000
	Gross margin	32,000	68,000	1,00,000
	Gross-margin percentage	8%	8%	8%

16-23 Joint-cost allocation, process further or sell. (CMA, adapted) Assam Sawmill, Limited (ASL), purchases logs from independent timber contractors and processes the logs into three types of lumber products:

- Studs for residential building (walls, ceilings)
- Decorative pieces (fireplace mantels, beams for cathedral ceilings)
- ·Posts used as support braces (mine support braces, braces for exterior fences around ranch properties)

These products are the result of a joint sawmill process that involves removal of bark from the logs, cutting the logs into a workable size (ranging from 8 to 16 feet in length), and then cutting the individual products from the logs, depending on the type of wood (pine, oak, walnut, or maple) and the size (diameter) of the log.

The joint process results in the following costs and outputs of products for a typical quarter:

Direct materials (rough timber logs)	₹50,00,000
Debarking (labor and overhead)	5,00,000
Sizing (labor and overhead)	20,00,000
Product cutting (labor and overhead)	25,00,000
Total joint costs	₹1,00,00,000

Product yields and average sales values on a per unit basis from the joint process are as follows:

Product	Monthly Output of Materials at Splitoff Point	Fully Processed Selling Price
Studs	75,000 units	₹80
Decorative pieces	5,000 units	1,000
Posts	20,000 units	200

The studs are sold as rough-cut lumber after emerging from the sawmill operation without further processing by ASL. Also, the posts require no further processing beyond the splitoff point. The decorative pieces must be planed and further sized after emerging from the sawmill. This additional processing costs ₹10,00,000 per month and normally results in a loss of 10% of the units entering the process. Without this lanning and sizing process, there is still an active intermediate market for the unfinished decorative pieces in which the selling price averages ₹600 per unit.

Required

1. Based on the information given for Assam Sawmill Limited, allocate the joint processing costs of ₹1,00,00,000 to each of the three product lines using:

   a. Sales value at splitoff method

   b. Physical-measures method (volume in units)

   c. NRV method

2. Preapre an analysis for Assam Sawmill Limited, that compares processing the decorative pieces further, as they currently do, with selling them as a rough-cut product immediately at splitoff.

3. Assume Assam Sawmill Limited, announced that in six months it will sell the rough-cut product at spiltoff due to increasing competitive pressure. Identify at least three types of likely behavior that will be demonstrated by the skilled labor in the planning and sizing process as a result of this announcement. Include in your discussion how this behavior could be improved by management.

Solution

Joint-cost allocation, process further or sell (CMA, adapted).

1.

   a. Sales value at splitoff method:

	Monthly Unit Output	Selling Price Per Unit	Sales Value at Splitoff	% of Sales	Joint Costs Allocated
Studs (Building)	75,000	₹80	₹60,00,000	46.1539%	₹46,15,390
Decorative Pieces	5,000	600	30,00,000	23.0769	23,07,690
Posts	20,000	200	40,00,000	30.7692	30,76,920
Total			1,30,00,000	100.0000%	1,00,00,000

   b. Physical measure method at splitoff:

	Physical Unit Volume	% of Total Unit Volume	Joint Costs Allocated
Studs (Building)	75,000	75.00%	₹75,00,000
Decorative Pieces	5,000	5.00	5,00,000
Posts	20,000	20.00	20,00,000
Total	1,00,000	100.00%	1,00,00,000

   c.   Net realizable value method:

	Monthly Unit Output	Fully Processed Selling Price per Unit	Estimated Net Realizable Value	% of Sales	Joint Costs Allocated
Studs (Building)	75,000	₹80	₹60,00,000	44.4445%	₹44,44,450
Decorative Pieces	4,500[a]	100	35,00,000[b]	25.9259	25,92,590
Posts	20,000	20	40,00,000	29.6296	29,62,960
Total			1,35,00,000	1,00.0000%	1,00,00,000

Notes:

[a]5,000 monthly units of output – 10% normal spoilage = 4,500 good units.

[b]4,500 good units × ₹1,000 = ₹45,00,000 – Further processing costs of ₹10,00,000 = ₹35,00,000

2. Presented below is an analysis for Assam Sawmill Limited comparing the processing of decorative pieces further versus selling the rough-cut product immediately at split-off.

	Units	Amount
Monthly unit output	5,000	
Less: Normal further processing shrinkage	500	
Units available for sale	4,500	
Final sales value (4,500 units × ₹1,000 per unit)		₹45,00,000
Less: Sales value at splitoff		30,00,000
Incremental revenue		15,00,000
Less: Further processing costs		10,00,000
Additional contribution from further processing		₹5,00,000

3. Assuming Assam Sawmill Limited announces that in six months it will sell the rough-cut product at split-off, due to increasing competitive pressure, at least three types of likely behavior that will be demonstrated by the skilled labor in the planing and sizing process includes the following.

- Poorer quality.
- Reduced motivation and morale.
- Job insecurity, leading to nonproductive employee time looking for jobs elsewhere.

Management actions that could improve this behavior include the following.

- Improve communication by giving the workers a more comprehensive explanation as to the reason for the change so they can better understand the situation and bring out a plan for future operation of the rest of the plant.
- The company can offer incentive bonuses to maintain quality and production and align rewards with goals.
- The company could provide job relocation and internal job transfers.

Solution Exhibit 16-23

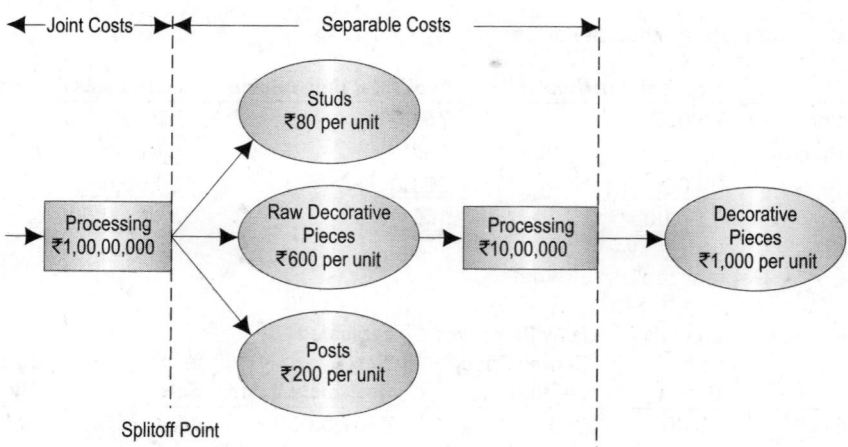

16-24 NRV method, byproducts. (CMA, adapted) Himachal Apples Ltd. (HAL) grows, processes, packages, and sells three joint apple products: (a) sliced apples that are used in frozen pies, (b) applesauce, and (c) apple juice. The outside skin of the apple, processed as animal feed, is treated as a byproduct. HAL uses the NRV method to allocate costs of the joint process to its joint products. The byproduct is inventoried at its estimated selling price when produced. The NRV of the byproduct is used to reduce the joint production costs before the splitoff point. The following details of HAL production process are available:

- The apples are washed and the outside skin is removed in the Cutting Department. The apples are then cored and trimmed for slicing. The three joint products and the byproduct are recognizable after processing in the Cutting Department. Each product is then transferred to a separate department for final processing.
- The trimmed apples are moved to the Slicing Department, where they are sliced and frozen. Any juice generated during the slicing operation is frozen with the slices.
- The pieces of apple trimmed from the fruit are processed into applesauce in the Crushing Department. The juice generated during this operation is used in the applesauce.
- The core and any surplus apple pieces generated from the Cutting Department are pulverized into a liquid in the Juicing Department. There is a loss equal to 8% of the weight of the good output produced in this department.
- The outside skin is chopped into animal feed and packaged in the Feed Department. It can be kept in cold storage until needed.

A total of 2,70,000 kg of apples were processed in the Cutting Department during November. The following schedule shows the costs incurred in each department, the proportion by weight transferred to the four final-processing departments, and the selling price of each end product:

Processing Data and Costs for November:

Department	Costs Incurred	Proportion of Product by Weight Transferred to	Selling Price per Kg of Final Product
Cutting	₹60,00,000		
Slicing	11,28,000	33%	₹80
Crushing	8,55,000	30	55
Juicing	3,00,000	27	40
Feed	70,000	10	10
Total	₹83,53,000	100%	

For the month of November, calculate:

Required

1. The output of apple slices, applesauce, apple juice, and animal feed, in kg
2. The NRV at the splitoff point of each joint product
3. The amount of Cutting Department costs assigned to each joint product and the amount assigned to the byproduct following HAL' cost-allocation method described above
4. The gross margin in rupees for each joint product

Solution

NRV method, byproducts (CMA, adapted).

1. For the month of November, HAL output was:

• apple slices	89,100
• apple sauce	81,000
• apple juice	67,500
• animal feed	27,000

These amounts were calculated as follows:

Product	Input	Proportion	Total Kg	Kg Lost	Net Kg
Slices	2,70,000 kg	0.33	89,100	–	89,100
Sauce	2,70,000	0.30	81,000	–	81,000
Juice	2,70,000	0.27	72,900	5,400	67,500[a]
Feed	2,70,000	0.10	27,000	–	27,000
		1.00	2,70,000	5,400	2,64,600

[a]Net kg: = 72,900 − (0.08 × net kg)

1.08 net kg = 72,900

Net kg   = 67,500

2. The net realizable value for each of the three main products is calculated below:

Product	Net Kg	Price	Revenue	Separable Costs	Value	Net Realizable
Slices	89,100	₹80	₹71,28,000	₹11,28,000	₹60,00,000
Sauce	81,000	55	44,55,000	8,55,000	36,00,000
Juice	67,500	40	27,00,000	3,00,000	24,00,000
			₹1,42,83,000	₹22,83,000	₹1,20,00,000

3. and 4.

The net realizable value of the byproduct is deducted from the production costs prior to allocation to the joint products, as presented below:

Allocation of Cutting Department Costs to Joint Products and Byproducts

Net realizable value (NRV) of byproduct = Byproduct revenue − Separable costs

= ₹10 (27,000 kg) − ₹70,000

= ₹2,70,000 − ₹70,000

= ₹2,00,000

Costs to be allocated = Joint costs − NRV of byproduct

= ₹60,00,000 − ₹2,00,000

= ₹58,00,000

Product	Revenue	Separable Costs	Joint Costs[a]	Gross Margin
Slices	₹71,28,000	₹11,28,000	₹29,00,000	₹31,00,000
Sauce	44,55,000	8,55,000	17,40,000	18,60,000
Juice	27,00,000	3,00,000	11,60,000	12,40,000
	₹1,42,83,000	₹22,83,000	₹58,00,000	₹62,00,000

[a]Allocated using NRV of the three joint products from requirement b:

Slices (₹60,00,000 ÷ ₹1,20,00,000) × ₹58,00,000 = ₹29,00,000

Sauce (₹36,00,000 ÷ ₹1,20,00,000) × ₹58,00,000 = 17,40,000

Juice (₹24,00,000 ÷ ₹1,20,00,000) × ₹58,00,000 = 11,60,000

16-25 Joint-cost allocation with a byproduct. Apollo Tyres also purchases old tires and recycles them to produce rubber floor mats and car mats. The company washes, shreds, and molds the recycled tires into sheets. The floor and car mats are cut from these sheets. A small amount of rubber shred remains after the mats are cut. The rubber shreds can be sold to use as cover for paths and playgrounds. The company can produce 25 floor mats, 75 car mats, and 40 kilograms of rubber shreds from 100 old tires.

In May, Apollo Tyres, which had no beginning inventory, processed 1,25,000 tires and had joint production costs of ₹60,00,000. Apollo Tyres sold 25,000 floor mats, 85,000 car mats, and 43,000 kilograms of rubber shreds. The company sells each floor mat for ₹120 and each car mat for ₹60. The company treats the rubber shreds as a byproduct that can be sold for ₹7 per kg.

Required

1. Assume that Apollo Tyres allocates the joint costs to floor mats and car mats using the sales value at splitoff method and accounts for the byproduct using the production method. What is the ending inventory cost for each product and gross margin for Apollo Tyres?

2. Assume that Apollo Tyres allocates the joint costs to floor mats and car mats using the sales value at splitoff method and accounts for the byproduct using the sales method. What is the ending inventory cost for each product and gross margin for Apollo Tyres?

3. Discuss the difference between the two methods of accounting for byproducts, focusing on what conditions are necessary to use each method.

Solution

1. Sales value at splitoff method: Byproduct recognized at time of production method

	Floor Mats	Car Mats	Rubber Shreds (kgs)
Products manufactured	31,250[a]	93,750[b]	50,000[c]
Products sold	25,000	85,000	43,000
Ending inventory	6,250	8,750	7,000

[a] 25 floor mats/100 tires = 0.25 floor mats per tire × 1,25,000 tires = 31,250 floor mats
[b] 75 car mats/100 tires = 0.75 car mats per tire × 1,25,000 tires = 93,750 car mats
[c] (1,25,000 tires/100) × 40 kgs = 50,000 kgs rubber shreds

Joint cost to be charged to joint products = Joint Cost − NRV of Byproduct

$$= ₹60,00,000 − (50,000 \text{ kgs} × ₹7 \text{ per kg})$$
$$= ₹60,00,000 − ₹3,50,000$$
$$= ₹56,50,000$$

	Floor Mats	Car Mats	Total
Sales value of mats at splitoff, 31,250 × ₹120; 93,750 × ₹60	₹37,50,000	₹56,25,000	₹93,75,000
Weighting, ₹37,50,000; ₹56,25,000 ÷ ₹93,75,000	0.40	0.60	
Joint costs allocated, 0.40; 0.60 × ₹56,50,000	₹22,60,000	₹33,90,000	₹56,50,000

	Floor Mats	Car Mats	Total
Revenues, 25,000 × ₹120; 85,000 × ₹60	₹30,00,000	₹51,00,000	₹81,00,000
Cost of goods sold:			
Joint costs allocated, 0.40; 0.60 × ₹56,50,000	₹22,60,000	₹33,90,000	₹56,50,000
Less: Ending inventory	(4,52,000)[b]	(3,16,400)[c]	(7,68,400)
Cost of goods sold	₹18,08,000	₹30,73,600	₹48,81,600
Gross margin	₹11,92,000	₹20,26,400	₹32,18,400

[b] 6,250 × ₹22,60,000/31,250 = ₹4,52,000
[c] 8,750 × ₹33,90,000/93,750 = ₹3,16,400

The ending inventory of rubber shreds is reported at its estimated market value of ₹49,000 (7,000 kgs × ₹7).

2. Sales value at splitoff method: Byproduct recognized at time of sale method
Joint cost to be charged to joint products = Joint Cost = ₹60,00,000

	Floor Mats	Car Mats	Total
Sales value of mats at splitoff, 31,250 × ₹120; 93,750 × ₹60	₹37,50,000	₹56,25,000	₹93,75,000
Weighting, ₹37,50,000; ₹56,25,000 ÷ ₹93,75,000	0.40	0.60	
Joint costs allocated, 0.40; 0.60 × ₹60,00,000	₹24,00,000	₹36,00,000	₹60,00,000

	Floor Mats	Car Mats	Rubber Shreds	Total
Revenues, 25,000 × ₹120; 85,000 × ₹60	₹30,00,000	₹51,00,000	₹3,01,000[d]	₹84,01,000
Cost of goods sold:				
Joint costs allocated, 0.40; 0.60 × ₹60,00,000	₹24,00,000	₹36,00,000		₹60,00,000

Less: Ending inventory	(4,80,000)[e]	(3,36,000)[f]		(8,16,000)
Cost of goods sold	₹19,20,000	₹32,64,000		₹51,84,000
Gross margin	₹10,80,000	₹18,36,000	₹3,01,000	₹32,17,000

[d] 43,000 kgs × ₹7 per kg.= ₹3,01,000

[e] 6,250 × ₹24,00,000/31,250 = ₹4,80,000

[f] 8,750 × ₹36,00,000/93,750 = ₹3,36,000

3. The production method of accounting for the byproduct is only appropriate if Apollo Tyres is positive that it can sell the byproduct at the expected selling price. Moreover, it should view the byproduct's contribution to the firm as material enough to find it worthwhile to record and track any inventory that may arise. The sales method is appropriate if either the disposition of the byproduct is unsure or the selling price is unknown, or if the amounts involved are so negligible as to make it economically infeasible for The Apollo Tyres to keep track of byproduct inventories.

16-26 Byproduct-costing journal entries (continuation of 16-25). The Apollo Tyres's accountant needs to record the information about the joint and byproducts in the general journal, but is not sure what the entries should be. The company has hired you as a consultant to help its accountant.

Required

1. Show journal entries at the time of production and at the time of sale assuming Apollo Tyres accounts for the byproduct using the production method.

2. Show journal entries at the time of production and at the time of sale assuming the Apollo Tyres accounts for the byproduct using the sales method.

Solution

1. Byproduct—production method journal entries

i). At time of production:

Work-in-process Inventory	₹60,00,000	
Accounts Payable, etc.		₹60,00,000
For Byproduct:		
Finished Goods Inv – Shreds	3,50,000	
Work-in-process Inventory		3,50,000
For Joint Products		
Finished Goods Inv – Floor	22,60,000	
Finished Goods Inv – Car	33,90,000	
Work-in-process Inventory		56,50,000

ii). At time of sale:

For Byproduct		
Cash or A/R	3,01,000	
Finished Goods Inv – Shreds		3,01,000
For Joint Products		
Cash or A/R	81,00,000	
Sales Revenue – Floor		30,00,000
Sales Revenue – Car		51,00,000
Cost of goods sold – Floor	18,08,000	
Cost of goods sold – Car	30,73,600	
Finished Goods Inv – Floor		18,08,000
Finished Goods Inv – Car		30,73,600

2. Byproduct—sales method journal entries

i).   At time of production:

Work-in-process Inventory	₹60,00,000	
Accounts Payable, etc.		₹60,00,000
For Byproduct:		
No entry		
For Joint Products		
Finished Goods Inv – Floor	24,00,000	
Finished Goods Inv – Car	36,00,000	
Work-in-process Inventory		60,00,000

ii).   At time of sale

For Byproduct		
Cash or A/R	₹3,01,000	
Sales Revenue – Shreds		₹3,01,000
For Joint Products		
Cash or A/R	81,00,000	
Sales Revenue – Floor		30,00,000
Sales Revenue – Car		51,00,000
Cost of goods sold – Floor	19,20,000	
Cost of goods sold – Car	32,64,000	
Finished Goods Inv – Floor		19,20,000
Finished Goods Inv – Car		32,64,000

16-27 Methods of joint-cost allocation, comprehensive. Gulabgandi Cosmetics purchases flowers in bulk and processes them into perfume. From a certain mix of petals, the firm uses Process A to generate Seduction, its high-grade perfume, as well as a certain residue. The residue is then further treated, using Process B, to yield Romance, a medium-grade perfume. An ounce of residue typically yields an ounce of Romance.

In July, the company used 11,000 kilograms of petals. Costs involved in Process A, i.e., reducing the petals to Seduction and the residue, were:

Direct Materials – ₹4,40,000; Direct Labor - ₹2,20,000; Overhead Costs - ₹1,10,000.

The additional costs of producing Romance in Process B were:

Direct Materials - ₹22,000; Direct Labor - ₹50,000; Overhead Costs - ₹40,000.

During July, Process A yielded 7,000 ounces of Seduction and 49,000 ounces of residue. From this, 5,000 ounces of Seduction were packaged and sold for ₹109.50 an ounce. Also, 28,000 ounces of Romance were processed in Process B and then packaged and sold for ₹31.5 an ounce. The other 21,000 ounces remained as residue. Packaging costs incurred were ₹1,37,500 for Seduction and ₹1,96,000 for Romance. The firm has no beginning inventory on July 1.

If it so desired, the firm could have sold unpackaged Seduction for ₹56 an ounce and the residue from Process A for ₹24 an ounce.

Required

1. What is the joint cost of the firm to be allocated to Seduction and Romance?
2. Under the physical measure method, how would the joint costs be allocated to Seduction and Romance?
3. Under the sales value at splitoff method, what portion of the joint costs would be allocated to Seduction and Romance, respectively?
4. What is the estimated net realizable value per ounce of Seduction and Romance?
5. Under the net realizable value method, what portion of the joint costs would be allocated to Seduction and Romance, respectively?

6. What is the gross margin percentage for the firm as a whole?

7. Allocate the joint costs to Seduction and Romance under the constant gross-margin percentage NRV method.

8. If you were the manager of Gulabgandi Cosmetics, would you continue to process the petal residue into Romance perfume? Explain your answer.

Solution

1. Joint costs for Gulabgandi include ₹4,40,000 in direct materials, ₹2,20,000 in direct labor, and ₹1,10,000 in overhead costs, for a total of ₹7,70,000.

2. At splitoff, the relative weights of the two perfumes are 7,000 ounces of Seduction and 49,000 ounces of Romance (in the form of residue) respectively. Accordingly, the allocation of joint costs under the physical measure method would be in the ratio of 1:7, or as follows:

Seduction: $\left(\dfrac{1}{8}\right) \times ₹7,70,000 = ₹96,250$

Romance: $\left(\dfrac{7}{8}\right) \times ₹7,70,000 = ₹6,73,750.$

3. The relative sales values of production at splitoff are as follows:

Seduction: 7,000 × ₹56 per ounce = ₹3,92,000
Romance: 49,000 × ₹24 per ounce = ₹11,76,000

The ratio of the sales values is 392:1,176, or 1:3. Accordingly, the joint costs are allocated as:

Seduction: $\left(\dfrac{1}{4}\right) \times ₹7,70,000 = ₹1,92,500$

Romance: $\left(\dfrac{3}{4}\right) \times ₹7,70,000 = ₹5,77,500.$

4. Estimated net realizable value per ounce of Seduction perfume:

Selling price per unit:	₹109.50
(−) Unit packaging cost: ₹1,37,500/5,000 =	27.50
Estimated NRV per ounce:	₹82.00

Estimated net realizable value per ounce of Romance perfume:

Selling price per unit:	₹31.50
(−) Unit packaging cost: ₹1,96,000/28,000 =	7.00
(−) Unit processing cost in B: ₹1,12,000/28,000 =	4.00
Estimated NRV per ounce:	₹20.50

5. The estimated net realizable values of the two perfumes are as follows:

Seduction: 7,000 × ₹82 per ounce = ₹5,74,000
Romance: 49,000 × ₹20.50 per ounce = ₹10,04,500

The ratio of the ENRVs is 5,74,000:10,04,500, or 4:7. Accordingly, the joint costs are allocated as:

Seduction: $\left(\dfrac{4}{11}\right) \times ₹7,70,000 = ₹2,80,000$

Romance: $\left(\dfrac{7}{11}\right) \times ₹7,70,000 = ₹4,90,000.$

6. The gross margin for Gulabgandi Cosmetics as a whole is the sum of the expected net realizable values from Seduction and Perfume, less the joint costs incurred. From the calculations in requirement 5, this is given by:

ENRV of Seduction (₹5,74,000) + ENRV of Romance (₹10,04,500) – Joint Costs (₹7,70,000)

$$= ₹8,08,500.$$

The final sales value of the total production is:

Seduction (7,000 × ₹109.50) + Romance (49,000 × ₹31.50) = ₹23,10,000.

The gross margin percentage for the firm as a whole is therefore:

$$\frac{₹8,08,500}{₹23,10,000} = 35\%.$$

7. The joint cost allocations to Seduction and Romance under the constant gross-margin percentage NRV method are given as follows:

	Seduction	Romance	Total
Final sales value of production			
7,000 × ₹109.50; 49,000 × ₹31.50	₹7,66,500	₹15,43,500	₹23,10,000
Gross Margin (35%)	2,68,275	5,40,225	8,08,500
Total costs	₹4,98,225	₹10,03,275	₹15,01,500
Separable costs			
7,000 × ₹27.50; 49,000 × ₹11	1,92,500	5,39,000	7,31,500
Joint costs	₹3,05,725	₹4,64,275	₹7,70,000

8. No.Selling the residue earns Gulabgandi ₹24 per ounce.Selling Romance perfume yields (from the calculations in requirement 4) ₹20.50 per ounce, which is lower.The manager of Gulabgandi Cosmetics could earn an extra ₹3.50 per ounce by selling residue rather than Romance.

16-28 Byproduct, disposal costs, ethics. Imperial Chemicals, Inc., is a multinational company. One of its subsidiaries is located in India. The country has only a few environmental protection laws, and even those are not enforced so as "to encourage rapid industrialization." The subsidiary's three major products emerge at splitoff point from a common input. The joint costs are allocated to each product using the sales values at splitoff method. In addition to the three joint products, another product that emerges at splitoff point is a hazardous material. The hazardous material can be dumped into the Gulf at zero cost to the company. Alternatively, it can be processed further and sold as a cleaning liquid.

The cost accountant responsible for joint-cost allocation presented the following comparative analysis to you, the controller:

	Alternatives	
	Dump into the Gulf	**Process Further**
Revenue	₹0	₹5,00,000
Costs:		
Further processing	0	3,00,000
Allocated joint costs	0	2,50,000
Marketing and distribution	0	50,000
Total costs	0	6,00,000
Net realizable value	₹0	₹(1,00,000)

Required

1. Comment on the comparative analysis prepared by the cost accountant purely from a financial perspective. Show any supporting computations.

2. Assume, regardless of your conclusions in requirement 1, that adopting the process-further alternative would lead to a decrease in the company's operating income. Disposal of the hazardous waste in a manner different than dumping it into the Gulf would also be costly. Discuss the legal and ethical implications of dumping the hazardous material into the Gulf.

Solution

Byproduct, disposal costs, ethics.

1. The comparative analysis prepared by the cost accountant is flawed. In the process further alternative, he has erroneously included the ₹2,50,000 allocated joint costs. Allocated joint costs are irrelevant because they are not incremental costs of the alternative being considered. If the joint costs allocated are taken out, it becomes clear that financially it would be to the advantage of the company to process further the product as it would increase the operating income by ₹1,50,000 [₹5,00,000 − (₹3,00,000 + ₹50,000)]. Furthermore, the dumping alternative does not consider potential future costs that may arise from environmental liabilities.

2. It appears that there would be no legal ramifications if the company decided to dump the hazardous product into the Gulf. The country either may have no laws against such dumping, or even if they exist, they are not enforced in accordance with the government policy. A more important consideration, however, is the ethical implications. To knowingly dump a hazardous material into the Gulf would certainly result in water pollution. This is an unacceptable action from a societal standpoint. It is important to remember that an act that does not violate any laws is not necessarily an ethical act. Ethical considerations go beyond legal considerations. In different parts of the world, legal systems are imperfect and not comprehensive. It is the responsibility of top management to take a broader, societal view when making decisions. In other words, a business should take its social responsibility seriously, by making it an integral part of the decision making process. In the long run it is in the best interest of all stakeholders as well as the business itself.

Exercises

[Comprehensive solutions to all exercises are available on the companion website www. pearsoned.co.in/charlesthorngren]

16-29 Joint-cost allocation, insurance settlement. Indian Small Manufacturing company produces a product. Each product can be disassembled into five main parts. The Company's management wants to assess profitability if parts are sold instead of full product. Information pertaining to production (in parts) for the month of July is:

Parts	Number of Parts	Wholesale Selling Price per Part When Production is Complete
A	1,000	₹11
B	200	4.0
C	400	7.0
D	800	2.0
E	100	1.0

Joint cost of production in July was ₹10,000.

A special consignment of 200 parts of A and 100 parts of B has been destroyed in a fire. The Company's insurance policy provides for reimbursement for the cost of the parts destroyed. The insurance company permits the Company to use a joint-cost-allocation method. The splitoff point is assumed to be at the end of the production line.

Required

1. Compute the cost of the special consignment destroyed using
   a. Sales value at splitoff method
   b. Physical-measure method (parts of finished parts)
2. Determine the profitability of each part under both the methods.

16-30 Joint products and byproducts (continuation of 16-29). The small Manufacturing company is computing the ending inventory values for its July 31, balance sheet. Ending inventory amounts on July 31 are 100 parts of A, 40 parts of B, 30 parts of C, 50 parts of D, and 20 parts of E.

The Company wants to use the sales value at splitoff point method. However, they want you to explore the effect on ending inventory values of classifying one or more products as a byproduct rather than a joint product.

1. Assume the Company classifies all five products as joint products. What are the ending inventory values of each product on July 31,?

2. Assume the Company uses a byproduct method that recognizes byproducts in the financial statements at the time production is completed. The total revenues to be received from the sale of byproducts produced dueing that period are offset against the joint cost of production of the joint products. What are the ending inventory values for each joint products on July 31, assuming A and C are the joint products and B, D, and E are byproducts?

3. Comment on differences in the results in requirements 1 and 2.

16-31 Alternative joint-cost-allocation methods, further-process decision. The Wood Spirits Company produces two products, turpentine and methanol (wood alcohol), by a joint process. Joint costs amount to ₹12,00,000 per batch of output. Each batch totals 10,000 litres: 25% methanol and 75% turpentine. Both products are processed further without gain or loss in volume. Separable processing costs are methanol, ₹30 per litre; turpentine, ₹20 per litre. Methanol sells for ₹210 per litre. Turpentine sells for ₹140 per litre.

1. How much joint costs per batch should be allocated to turpentine and methanol, assuming that joint costs are allocated on a physical-measure (number of litres at splitoff point) basis?

2. If joint costs are to be assigned on an NRV basis, how much joint cost should be assigned to turpentine and methanol?

3. Prepare product-line income statements per batch for requirements 1 and 2. Assume no beginning or ending inventories.

4. The company has discovered an additional process by which the methanol (wood alcohol) can be made into a pleasant-tasting alcoholic beverage. The selling price of this beverage would be ₹600 a litre. Additional processing would increase separable costs ₹90 per litre (in addition to the ₹30 per litre separable cost required to yield methanol). The company would have to pay excise taxes of 20% on the selling price of the beverage. Assuming no other changes in cost, what is the joint cost applicable to the wood alcohol (using the NRV method)? Should the company produce the alcoholic beverage? Show your computations.

16-32 Process further or sell. (R. Capettini, adapted) HLL produces joint products A, B, and C, from a single joint process with a fixed cost of ₹50,000 and a variable cost of ₹20 per input unit. Each product can be either processed further or, at the splitoff point, it can be sold or disposed of at a cost. Out of each input unit, HLL produces one unit of product A, three units of product B, and two units of product C.

1. Use the following data to decide whether HLL should process each product further or dispose of it (or sell it) at the splitoff point if HLL inputs 5,000 units. For each product, show how much better off HLL would be if it followed your advice versus making the alternative decision. Assume that if HLL does not further process a product, it does not incur any of the further processing costs.

Product	Selling Price per Unit at Splitoff Point	Cost per Unit to Dispose of Product at Splitoff Point	Further Processing Costs Fixed per unit	Variable	Selling Price per Unit After Further Processing
A	–	₹2.0	₹60,000	₹9.0	₹15
B	₹5	–	10,000	10.0	15
C	–	9.0	1,00,000	11.0	54

2. What is HLL's gross margin at the 5,000-unit input level?

16-33 Alternative methods of joint-cost allocation, product-mix decision. Indigo Lumber processes lumber products for sale to lumber wholesalers. Its most popular line is oak products. Oak tree growers sell Indigo Lumber whole trees. These trees are jointly processed up to the splitoff point at which raw select oak, raw white oak, and raw knotty oak become separable products. Each raw product is then separately further processed by Indigo Lumber into finished products (select oak, white oak, and knotty oak) that are sold to lumber wholesalers. Data for August are:

a. Joint processing costs (including cost of oak trees) –₹30,00,000
b. Separable product at splitoff point

- Raw select oak, 30,000 board-feet
- Raw white oak, 50,000 board-feet
- Raw knotty oak, 20,000 board-feet

c. Final product produced and sold

- Select oak, 25,000 board feet at ₹160 per board-foot
- White oak, 40,000 board feet at ₹90 per board-foot
- Knotty oak, 15,000 board feet at ₹70 per board-foot

d. Separable processing costs

- For select oak, ₹6,00,000
- For white oak, ₹9,00,000
- For knotty oak, ₹1,50,000

There is an active market for raw oak products. Selling prices available in August were raw select oak, ₹80 per board-foot; raw white oak, ₹40 per board-foot; and raw knotty oak, ₹30 per board-foot.

There were no beginning or ending inventories for August.

Required

1. Allocate the joint costs to the three products using
   a. Sales value at splitoff method
   b. Physical-measures method
   c. NRV method

2. Assume that not all final products produced in August were sold. Ending inventory for August was select oak, 1,000 board-feet; white oak, 2,000 board-feet; and knotty oak, 500 board-feet. What would be the ending inventory values in the August 31 balance sheet under each product for the three methods in requirement 1?

3. Is Indigo Lumber maximizing its total August operating income by fully processing each raw oak product into its finished product form? Show your computations.

16-34 Alternative methods of joint-cost allocation, product-mix decisions. The Sunshine Oil Company buys crude vegetable oil. Refining this oil results in four products at the splitoff point: A, B, C, and D. Product C is fully processed at the splitoff point. Products A, B, and D can individually be further refined into Super A, Super B, and Super D. In the most recent month (December), the output at the splitoff point was:

- Product A, 3,000 litres
- Product B, 1,000 litres
- Product C, 500 litres
- Product D, 500 litres

The joint costs of purchasing and processing the crude vegetable oil were ₹1,00,000. Sunshine had no beginning or ending inventories. Sales of product C in December were ₹50,000. Products A, B, and D were further refined and then sold. Data related to December are:

Separable Processing Costs to Make Super Products Revenues		
Super A	₹2,00,000	₹3,00,000
Super B	80,000	1,00,000

Sunshine had the option of selling products A, B, and D at the splitoff point. This alternative would have yielded the following revenues for the December production:

- Product A, ₹50,000
- Product B, ₹30,000
- Product D, ₹70,000

Required

1. Compute the gross-margin percentage for each product sold in December, using the following methods for allocating the ₹1,00,000 joint costs:
   a. Sales value at splitoff
   b. Physical measure
   c. NRV

2. Could Sunshine have increased its December operating income by making different decisions about the further processing of products A, B, or D? Show the effect on operating income of any changes you recommend.

16-35 Joint and byproducts, NRV method. (CPA) The Harrison Limited produces three products: Alpha, Beta, and Gamma. Alpha and Gamma are joint products, and Beta is a byproduct of Alpha. No joint costs are to be allocated to the byproduct. The production processes for a typical month are as follows:

a. In Department 1, 110,000 kg of direct material, are processed at a total cost of ₹12,00,000. After processing in Department 1, 60% of the units are transferred to Department 2, and 40% of the units (now Gamma) are transferred to Department 3.

b. In Department 2, the material is further processed at a total additional cost of ₹3,80,000. Then 70% of the units (now Alpha) are transferred to Department 4; and 30% emerge as Beta, the byproduct, to be sold at ₹12 per kg. Separable marketing costs for Beta are ₹81,000.

c. In Department 4, Alpha is processed at a total additional cost of ₹2,36,600. After this processing, Alpha is ready for sale at ₹50 per kg.

d. In Department 3, Gamma is processed at a total additional cost of ₹16,50,000. In this department, a normal loss of units of Gamma occurs, which equals 10% of the good units of output. The remaining good units of output are then sold for ₹120 per kg.

Required

1. Prepare a schedule showing the allocation of the ₹12,00,000 joint costs between Alpha and Gamma using the NRV method. The NRV of Beta should be treated as an addition to the sales value of Alpha.

2. Independent of your answer to requirement 1, assume that ₹10,20,000 of total joint costs were appropriately allocated to Alpha. Assume, also that there were 48,000 kg of Alpha and 20,000 kg of Beta available to sell. Prepare an income statement through the gross-margin line item for Alpha using the following facts:
   a. During the year, sales of Alpha were 80% of the kg available for sale. There was no beginning inventory.
   b. The NRV of Beta available for sale is to be deducted from the cost of producing Alpha. The ending inventory of Alpha is to be based on the net costs of production.
   c. All other cost and selling-price data are listed in (a) through (d) above.

16-36 Process further or sell, byproduct. (CMA, adapted) Coal India Limited (CIL) produces and sells bulk raw coal to other coal companies and exporters. CIL mines and stockpiles the coal. The coal is then passed through a one-step crushing process before being loaded onto river barges for shipment to customers. The annual output of 10 million quintals, which is expected to remain stable, has an average cost of ₹200 per quintal with an average selling price of ₹270 per quintal.

Management is currently evaluating the possibility of further processing the coal by sizing and cleaning to expand markets and enhance product revenues. Management has rejected the possibility of constructing a large sizing and cleaning plant because of the significant long-term capital investment required.

Ahmed, controller of CIL, asks Karim, mining engineer (with finance background), to develop cost and revenue projections for further processing the coal using a variety of contractual arrangements. After extensive discussions with vendors and contractors, Karim prepares the following projections of incremental costs of sizing and cleaning CIL's annual output:

Coal India Limited Sizing and Cleaning Processes

Incremental Costs

Direct labor	₹60,00,000	per year
Supervisory personnel	₹10,00,000	per year
Heavy equipment rental, operating, and maintenance costs	₹2,50,000	per month
Contract sizing and cleaning	₹35	per quintal
Outbound rail freight (per 600-quintals rail car)	₹2,400	per car

In addition to the preceding cost information, market samples obtained by Karim show that electrical utilities enter into contracts for sized and cleaned coal at an expected average price of ₹360 per quintal.

Karim has learned that 5% of the raw bulk output that enters the sizing and cleaning process will be lost as a primary product. Normally, 75% of this product loss can be salvaged as coal fines, which are small pieces ranging from dustlike particles up to pieces two inches in diameter. Coal fines are too small for use by electrical utilities but are frequently sold to steel manufacturers for use in blast furnaces.

Unfortunately, the price for coal fines frequently fluctuates between ₹140 and ₹240 per quintal (F.O.B.), and the timing of market volume is erratic. Although companies generally sell all their coal fines during a year, it is not unusual to stockpile this product for several months before making any significant sales.

Required

1. Prepare an analysis that shows whether it is more profitable for Coal India Limited (CIL) to continue to sell the raw bulk coal or to process it further through sizing and cleaning. (Note: Ignore any value related to the coal fines in your analysis.)

2. Now consider the potential value of the coal fines and prepare an addendum that shows how their value affects the results of your analysis prepared in requirement 1.

3. What other factors should be considered in evaluating a sell-or-process-further decision?

16-37 Joint-cost allocation, process further or sell. (CMA, adapted) Ranbaxy Pharmaceutical Company manufactures three joint products from a joint process: Altox, Lorex, and Hycol. Data regarding these products for the typical fiscal year ended March 31, are as follows:

	Altox	Lorex	Hycol
Units produced	1,70,000	5,00,000	3,30,000
Selling price per unit at splitoff	₹3.50	–	₹2.00
Separable costs	–	₹14,00,000	–
Final selling price per unit	–	₹5.00	–

The joint production cost up to the splitoff point at which Altox, Lorex, and Hycol become separable products is ₹18,00,000.

The president of Ranbaxy is reviewing an opportunity to change the way in which these three products are processed and sold. Proposed changes for each product are as follows:

- Altox is currently sold at the splitoff point to a manufacturer of vitamins. Altox can also be processed into a blood pressure medication. However, this additional processing causes a loss of 20,000 units of Altox. The separable costs to further process Altox are estimated to be ₹2,50,000 annually. The blood pressure medication sells for ₹5.50 per unit.

- Lorex is currently processed further after the splitoff point and is sold by Ranbaxy as a cold remedy. The company has received an offer from another pharmaceutical company to purchase Lorex at the splitoff point for ₹2.25 per unit.
- Hycol is an oil produced from the joint process and is currently sold at the splitoff point to a cosmetics manufacturer. Ranbaxy's Research Department has suggested that the company process this product further and sell it as an ointment to relieve muscle pain. The additional processing would cost ₹75,000 annually and would result in 25% more units of product. The ointment sells for ₹1.80 per unit.

Required

1. Allocate the ₹18,00,000 joint production cost to Altox, Lorex, and Hycol using the NRV method.
2. Identify which of the three joint products Ranbaxy Pharmaceutical Company should sell at the splitoff point in the future and which of the three the company should process further to maximize operating income. Support your decisions with appropriate computations.

17 Process Costing

Learning Objectives ▼

1. Identify the situations in which process-costing systems are appropriate

2. Understand the basic concepts of process-costing and compute average unit costs

3. Describe the five steps in process costing and calculate equivalent units

4. Use the weighted-average method and first-in, first-out (FIFO) method of process costing

5. Apply process-costing methods to situations with transferred-in costs

6. Understand the need for hybrid-costing systems such as operation-costing

Many companies use mass-production techniques to produce identical or similar units of a product or service:

Apple (smartphones), Coca-Cola (soft drinks), ExxonMobil (gasoline), JP MorganChase (processing of checks), and Novartis (pharmaceuticals). Managerial accountants at companies like these use process costing because it helps them (1) determine how many units of the product the firm has on hand at the end of an accounting reporting period, (2) evaluate the units' stages of completion, and (3) assign costs to units produced and in inventory. There are different methods for process costing (for example, the FIFO or weighted-average methods) that are based on different assumptions about the flow of product costs. As you learned in your financial accounting class, the choice of method results in different operating income and affects the taxes a company pays and the performance evaluation of managers. At times, variations in international rules and customs also determine the method chosen.

Illustrating Process Costing

Before we examine process costing in more detail, let's briefly review the distinction between job costing and process costing explained in Chapter 4. Job-costing and process-costing systems are best viewed as ends of a continuum:

Learning Objective 1

Identify the situations in which process-costing systems are appropriate

. . . when masses of identical or similar units are produced

Job-costing system	Process-costing system
Distinct, identifiable units of a product or service (for example, custom-made machines and houses)	Masses of identical or similar units of a product or service (for example, food or chemical)

In a *process-costing system*, the unit cost of a product or service is obtained by assigning total costs to many identical or similar units. In other words, unit costs are calculated by dividing total costs incurred by the number of units of output from the production process. In a manufacturing process-costing setting, each unit receives the same or similar amounts of direct material costs, direct manufacturing labor costs, and indirect manufacturing costs (manufacturing overhead).

The main difference between process costing and job costing is the *extent of averaging* used to compute unit costs of products or services. In a job-costing system, individual jobs use different quantities of production resources, so it would be incorrect to cost each job at the same average production cost. In contrast, when identical or similar units of products or services are mass-produced, rather than processed as individual jobs, process costing is used to calculate an average production cost for all units produced. Some processes such as clothes manufacturing have aspects of both process costing (cost per unit of each operation, such as cutting or sewing, is identical) and job costing (different materials are used in different batches of clothing, say, wool versus cotton). The final section this chapter describes "hybrid" costing systems that combine elements of both job and process costing.

Consider the following example: Suppose that Pacific Electronics manufactures a variety of cell phone models. These models are assembled in the Assembly Department. Upon completion, units are transferred to the Testing Department. We focus on the Assembly Department process for one model, SG-40. All units of SG-40 are identical and must meet a set of demanding performance specifications. The process-costing system for SG-40 in the Assembly Department has a single direct-cost category—direct materials—and a single indirect-cost category—conversion costs. Conversion costs are all manufacturing costs other than direct material costs, including manufacturing labor, energy, plant depreciation, and so on. As the following figure shows, direct materials , such as a phone's circuit board, antenna, and microphone, are added at the beginning of the Assembly process. Conversion costs are added evenly during assembly.

The following graphic represents these facts:

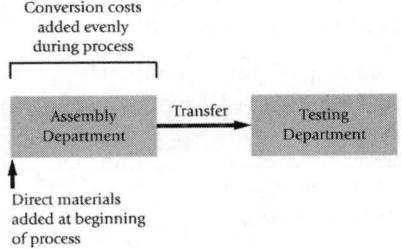

Process-costing systems separate costs into cost categories according to *when costs are introduced into the process*. Often, as in our Pacific Electronics example, only two cost classifications—direct materials and conversion costs—are necessary to assign costs to products. Why only two? Because *all* direct materials are added to the process at one time and all conversion costs generally are added to the process evenly through time sometimes the situation is different.

1. If, two different direct materials —such as the circuit board and microphone—were added to the process at different times, two different direct-materials categories would be needed to assign these costs to products.

2. If manufacturing labor costs were added to the process at a different time from when the other conversion costs were added, an additional cost category—direct manufacturing labor costs—would be needed to separately assign these costs to products.

We illustrate process using three cases, of increasing complexity:

- **Case 1**—Process costing with zero beginning and zero ending work-in-process inventory of SG-40 (that is, all units are started and fully completed within the accounting period). *This case presents the most basic concepts of process costing and illustrates the feature of averaging of costs.*

- **Case 2**—Process costing with zero beginning work-in-process inventory and some ending work-in-process inventory of SG-40. (That is, some units of SG-40 started during the accounting period are incomplete at the end of the period). *This case introduces the five steps of process costing and the concept of equivalent units.*

- **Case 3**—Process costing with both some beginning and some ending work-in-process inventory of SG-40. *This case adds more complexity and illustrates the effect of weighted-average and first-in, first-out (FIFO) methods have on cost of units completed and cost of work-in-process inventory.*

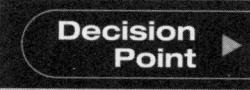
Case 1: Process Costing with No Beginning or Ending Work-in-Process Inventory

On January 1, 2014, there was no beginning inventory of SG-40 units in the Assembly Department. During the month of January, Pacific Electronics started, completely assembled, and transferred 400 units to the Testing Department.

Data for the Assembly Department for January 2014 are as follows:

Physical Units for January 2014	
Work in process, beginning inventory (January 1)	0 units
Started during January	400 units
Completed and transferred out during January	400 units
Work in process, ending inventory (January 31)	0 units

Physical units refer to the number of output units, whether complete or incomplete. In January 2014, all 400 physical units started were completed.

Total Costs for January 2014	
Direct material costs added during January	₹3,20,000
Conversion costs added during January	2,40,000
Total Assembly Department costs added during January	₹5,60,000

Pacific Electronics records direct materials costs and conversion costs in the assembly department as these costs are incurred. The cost per unit is then calculated by dividing the total costs incurred in a given accounting period by the total units produced in that period. So, the assembly department cost of an SG-40 is ₹5,60,000 ÷ 400 units = ₹1,400 per unit:

Direct material cost per unit (₹3,20,000 ÷ 400 units)	₹800
Conversion cost per unit (₹2,40,000 ÷ 400 units)	600
Assembly Department cost per unit	₹1,400

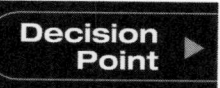
Case 1 applies whenever a company produces a homogeneous product or service but has no incomplete units when each accounting period ends, which is a common situation in service-sector organizations. For example, a bank can adopt this process-costing approach to compute the unit cost of processing 1,00,000 customer deposits, made in a month because each deposit is processed in the same way regardless of the amount of deposit.

Case 2: Process Costing with Zero Beginning and Some Ending Work-in-Process Inventory

Learning Objective 3

Describe the five steps in process costing

. . . to assign total costs to units completed and to units in work in process

In February 2014, Pacific Electronics places another 400 units of SG-40 into production. Because all units placed into production in January were completely assembled, there is no beginning inventory of partially completed units in the Assembly Department on February 1. Some customers order late, so not all units started in February are completed by the end of the month. Only 175 units are completed and transferred to the Testing Department.

Data for the Assembly Department for February 2014 are:

	File Edit View Insert Format Tools Data Window Help				
	A	B	C	D	E
1		Physical Units (SG-40s) (1)	Direct Materials (2)	Conversion Costs (3)	Total Costs (4) = (2) + (3)
2	Work in process, beginning inventory (February 1)	0			
3	Started during February	400			
4	Completed and transferred out during February	175			
5	Work in process, ending inventory (February 28)	225			
6	Degree of completion of ending work in process		100%	60%	
7	Total costs added during February		₹3,20,000	₹1,86,000	₹5,06,000

The 225 partially assembled units as of February 28, 2014, are fully processed with respect to direct materials because all direct materials in the Assembly Department are added at the beginning of the assembly process. Conversion costs, however, are added evenly during assembly. The Assembly Department supervisor estimates that the partially assembled units are, on average, 60% complete with respect to conversion costs.

The accuracy of the completion estimate of conversion costs depends on the care, skill, and experience of the estimator and the nature of the conversion process. Estimating the degree of completion is usually easier for direct material costs than for conversion costs because the quantity of direct materials needed for a completed unit and the quantity of direct materials in a partially completed unit can be measured more accurately. In contrast, the conversion sequence usually consists of a number of basic operations each for a specified period of time at various steps in the production process.[1] The degree of completion for conversion costs depends on the proportion of the total conversion costs needed to complete one unit (or one batch of production) that has already been incurred on the units still in process.

Department supervisors and line managers are most familiar with the conversion process, so they most often estimate completion rates for conversion costs. However, in some industries, such as semiconductor manufacturing, no exact estimate is possible because manufacturing occurs inside sealed environments that can be opened only when the process is complete. In other settings, such as the textile industry, vast quantities of unfinished products such as shirts and pants make the task of estimation too costly. In these cases, to calculate the conversion costs, managers assume that all work in process in a department is complete to some preset degree (for example, one-third, one-half, or two-thirds).

Because some units are fully assembled and some are only partially assembled, a common metric is needed to compare the work that's been done on them and, more

---

[1] For example, consider the conventional tanning process for converting hide to leather. Obtaining 250–300 kg of leather requires putting one metric ton of raw hide through as many as 15 steps: from soaking, liming, and pickling to tanning, dyeing, and fatliquoring, the step in which oils are introduced into the skin before the leather is dried.

importantly, obtain a total measure of the work done. The concept we will use in this regard is that of *equivalent units*. We will explain this concept in greater detail next as part of the set of five steps required to calculate (1) the cost of fully assembled units in February 2014 and (2) the cost of partially assembled units still in process at the end of that month, for Pacific Electronics. The five steps of process costing are as follows:

Step 1: Summarize the flow of physical units (of output).

Step 2: Compute output in terms of equivalent units.

Step 3: Summarize total costs to account for.

Step 4: Compute cost per equivalent unit.

Step 5: Assign total costs to units completed and to units in ending work in process.

Summarising the Physical Units and Equivalent Units (Steps 1 and 2)

In Step 1, managers track the physical units of output. Recall that physical units are the number of output units, whether complete or incomplete. The physical-units column of Exhibit 17-1 tracks where the physical units came from (400 units started) and where they went (175 units completed and transferred out, and 225 units in ending inventory). Remember that when there is no begining inventory, the number of units started must equal the sum of units transfered out and ending inventory

Because not all 400 physical units are fully completed, in step 2, managers compute the output in *equivalent units*, not in *physical units*. Equivalent units are a derived measure of output calculated by (1) taking the quantity of each input (factor of production) in units completed and in incomplete units of work in process and (2) converting the quantity of input into the amount of completed output units that could be produced with that quantity of input. To see what is meant by equivalent units, suppose that during a month, 50 physical units were started but not completed. Managers estimate that the 50 units in ending inventory are 70% complete for conversion costs. Now, suppose all the conversion costs represented in these units were used to make fully completed units instead. How many completed units would that have resulted in? The answer is 35 units. Why? Because the conversion costs incurred to produce 50 units that are each 70% complete could have instead generated 35 (0.70×50) units that are 100% complete. The 35 units are referred to as *equivalent units* of output. That is, in terms of the work done on them, the 50 partially completed units are considered equivalent to 35 completed units.

Note that equivalent units are calculated separately for each input (such as direct materials and conversion costs). Moreover, every completed unit, by definition, is composed of one equivalent unit of each input required to make it. This chapter focuses on equivalent-unit calculations in manufacturing settings, but the calculations can be used in nonmanufacturing settings as well. For example, universities convert their part-time student enrollments into "full-time student equivalents" to get a better measure of faculty–student ratios over time. Without this adjustment, an increase in part-time students would lead to a lower faculty– student ratio. This would erroneously suggest a decline in the quality of instruction when, in fact, part-time students take fewer academic courses and do not need the same number of instructors as full-time students do.

When calculating the equivalent units in step 2, focus on quantities. Disregard rupee amounts until after equivalent units are computed. In the Pacific Electronics example, all 400 physical units—the 175 fully assembled units and the 225 partially assembled units— are 100% complete with respect to direct materials because all direct materials are added in the Assembly Department at the start of the process. Therefore, Exhibit 17-1 shows that output is 400 *equivalent units* for direct materials: 175 equivalent units for the 175 physical

Exhibit 17-1

Steps 1 and 2:
Summarize Output
in Physical Units and
Compute Output in
Equivalent Units for
Assembly Department
of Pacific Electronics for
February 2014

	(Step 1)	(Step 2)	
		Equivalent Units	
Flow of Production	Physical Units	Direct Materials	Conversion Costs
Work in process, beginning	0		
Started during current period	400		
To account for	400		
Completed and transferred out during current period	175	175	175
Work in process, ending[a]	225		
(225 x 100%; 225 x 60%)		225	135
Accounted for	400		
Work done in current period only		400	310

[a]Degree of completion in this department; direct materials, 100%; conversion costs, 60%.

File   Edit   View   Insert   Format   Tools   Data   Window   Help

units assembled and transferred out, and 225 equivalent units for the 225 physical units in ending work-in-process inventory.

The 175 fully assembled units have also incurred all of their conversion costs. The 225 partially assembled units in ending work in process are 60% complete (on average). Therefore, their conversion costs are *equivalent* to conversion costs incurred by 135 fully assembled units ($225 \times 60\% = 135$). Hence, Exhibit 17-1 shows that output is a total of 310 *equivalent units* for the conversion costs: 175 equivalent units for the 175 physical units assembled and transferred out and 135 equivalent units for the 225 physical units in ending work-in-process inventory.

Calculating Product Costs (Steps 3, 4, and 5)

Exhibit 17-2 shows steps 3, 4, and 5. Together, they are called the *production cost worksheet*. In Step 3, managers summarize total costs to account for. Because the beginning balance of work-in-process inventory is zero on February 1, total costs to account for (that is, the total charges or debits to the Work in Process—Assembly account) consist only of costs added during February: direct materials of ₹3,20,000 and conversion costs of ₹1,86,000, for a total of ₹5,06,000.

In Step 4, managers calculate the cost per equivalent unit separately for the direct materials costs and conversion costs. This is done by dividing the direct material costs and conversion costs added during February by their related quantities of equivalent units of work done in February (as calculated in Exhibit 17-1).

To see why it is important to understand equivalent units in unit-cost calculations, compare the conversion costs for January and February 2014. The ₹1,86,000 in total conversion costs for the 400 units worked on during February are lower than the ₹2,40,000 in total conversion costs for the 400 units worked on in January. However, the conversion costs to fully assemble a unit are the same: ₹600 per unit in both January and February. Total conversion costs are lower in February because fewer equivalent units of conversion- costs work were completed in that month than in January (310 in February versus 400 in January). Note that using physical units instead of equivalent units would have resulted in a conversion cost per unit of just ₹465.0 (₹1,86,000 ÷ 400 units) for February, which is down from ₹600 in January. This incorrect costing might lead the firm's managers to believe that the assembly department achieved efficiencies that lowered the conversion costs of the SG-40 when in fact the costs had not declined.

Once the cost per equivalent unit is calculated for both the direct materials and conversion costs, managers can move to Step 5: assigning the total direct materials and conversion costs to the units completed and transferred out and to the units still in process at the end

Exhibit 17-2   Summarize Total Costs to Account For, Compute Cost per Equivalent Unit, and Assign Costs to Units Completed and Units in Ending Work in Process for the Assembly Department for February 2014

	File Edit View Insert Format Tools Data Window Help			
	A	B	C	D	E
1			Total Production Costs	Direct Materials	Conversion Costs
2	(Step 3)	Costs added during February	₹5,06,000	₹3,20,000	₹1,86,000
3		Total costs to account for	₹5,06,000	₹3,20,000	₹1,86,000
4					
5	(Step 4)	Costs added in current period	₹5,06,000	₹3,20,000	₹1,86,000
6		Divide by equivalent units of work done in current period (Exhibit 17-1)		÷ 400	÷ 310
7		Cost per equivalent unit		₹800	₹600
8					
9	(Step 5)	Assignment of costs:			
10		Completed and transferred out (175 units)	₹2,45,000	(175[a] x ₹800)+	(175[a] x ₹600)
11		Work in process, ending (225 units):	2,61,000	(225[b] x ₹800)+	(135[b] x ₹600)
12		Total costs accounted for	₹5,06,000	₹3,20,000+	₹1,86,000
13					
14	[a]Equivalent units completed and transferred out from Exhibit 17-1, step 2.				
15	[b]Equivalent units in ending work in process from Exhibit 17-1, step 2.				

of February 2014. As Exhibit 17-2 shows, this is done by multiplying the equivalent output units for each input by the cost per equivalent unit. For example, the total costs (direct materials and conversion costs assigned to the 225 physical units in ending work-in-process inventory are as follows:

Direct material costs of 225 equivalent units (Exhibit 17-1, step 2) ×
₹800 cost per equivalent unit of direct materials calculated in step 4   ₹1,80,000
Conversion costs of 135 equivalent units (Exhibit 17-1, step 2) ×
₹600 cost per equivalent unit of conversion costs calculated in step 4   81,000
Total cost of ending work-in-process inventory   ₹2,61,000

Note that total costs to account for in step 3 (₹5,06,000) equal total costs accounted for in step 5.

Journal Entries

Journal entries in process-costing systems are similar to the entries made in job-costing systems with respect to direct materials and conversion costs. The main difference is that, when process costing is used, there is one Work-in-Process account for each process. In our example, there are accounts for (1) Work in Process—Assembly and (2) Work in Process—Testing. Pacific Electronics purchases direct materials as needed. These materials are delivered directly to the Assembly Department. Using amounts from Exhibit 17-2, the summary journal entries for February are:

1. Work in Process—Assembly   3,20,000
    Accounts Payable Control   3,20,000
    To record direct materials purchased and used in
       production during February.
2. Work in Process—Assembly   1,86,000
    Various accounts such as Wages Payable Control and
       Accumulated Depreciation   1,86,000
    To record conversion costs for February; examples include energy,
       manufacturing supplies, all manufacturing labor, and plant depreciation.
3. Work in Process—Testing   2,45,000
    Work in Process—Assembly   2,45,000
    To record cost of goods completed and transferred from
       Assembly to Testing during February.

Exhibit 17-3 shows a general framework for the flow of costs through T-accounts. Notice how entry 3 for ₹2,45,000 follows the physical transfer of goods from the Assembly to the Testing Department. The T-account Work in Process—Assembly shows February 2014's ending balance of ₹2,61,000, which is the beginning balance of Work in Process—Assembly in March 2014. It is important to ensure that all costs have been accounted for and that the ending inventory of the current month is the beginning inventory of the following month.

Earlier, we discussed the importance of accurately estimating the completion percentages for conversion costs. We can now calculate the effect of incorrect estimates of the degree of completion of units in ending work in process. Suppose, for example, that Pacific Electronics' managers overestimate the degree of completion for conversion costs at 80% instead of 60%. The computations would change as follows:

Exhibit 17-1, Step 2

Equivalent units of conversion costs in ending Work in Process—Assembly = 80% × 225 = 180

Equivalent units of conversion costs for work done in the current period = 175 + 180 = 355

Exhibit 17-2, Step 4

Cost per equivalent unit of conversion costs = ₹1,86,000 ÷ 3550 = ₹523.90

Cost per equivalent unit of direct materials is the same, ₹800

Exhibit 17-2, Step 5

Cost of 175 units of goods completed and transferred out = 175 × ₹800 + 175 × ₹523.90 = ₹2,31,682.50

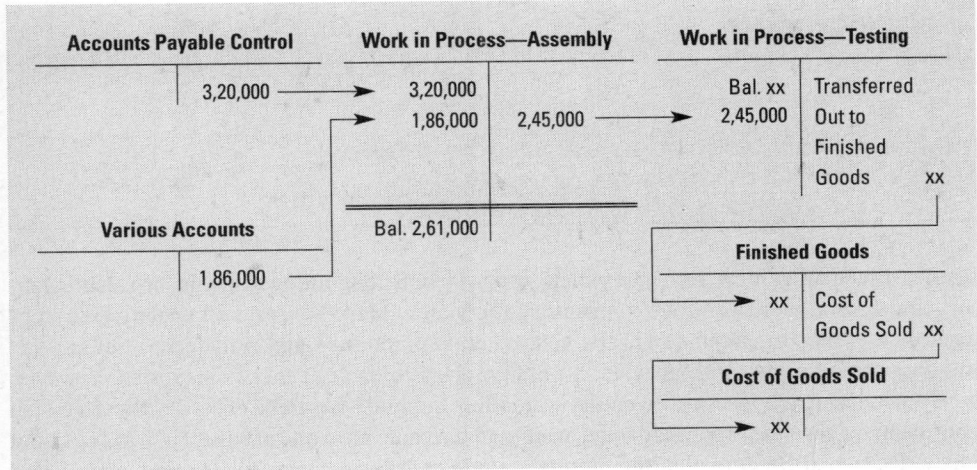

Exhibit 17-3

Flow of Costs in a Process-Costing System for the Assembly Department for February 2014

This amount is lower than the ₹2,45,000 of costs assigned to goods completed and transferred out calculated in Exhibit 17-2. Overestimating the degree of completion decreases the costs assigned to goods transferred out and eventually to cost of goods sold and increases operating income.

Managers must ensure that department supervisors avoid introducing personal biases into estimates of degrees of completion. To show better performance, for example, a department supervisor might report a higher degree of completion resulting in overstated operating income. If performance for the period is very good, the department supervisor may be tempted to report a lower degree of completion, reducing income in the current period. This has the effect of reducing the costs carried in ending inventory and the costs carried to the following year in beginning inventory. In other words, estimates of degree of completion can help to smooth earnings from one period to the next.

To guard against the possibility of bias, managers should ask supervisors specific questions about the process they followed to prepare estimates. Top management should always emphasize obtaining the correct answer, regardless of how it affects reported performance. This emphasis drives ethical actions throughout the organization.

Learning Objective 4

Use the weighted-average method of process costing

. . . assigns costs based on total costs and equivalent units completed to date

and the first-in, first-out (FIFO) method of process costing

. . . to assign costs based on costs and equivalent units of work done in the current period

Case 3: Process Costing with Some Beginning and Some Ending Work-in-Process Inventory

At the beginning of March 2014, Pacific Electronics had 225 partially assembled SG-40 units in the Assembly Department. It started production of another 275 units in March. Data for the Assembly Department for March are as follows:

	A	Physical Units (SG-40s) (1)	Direct Materials (2)	Conversion Costs (3)	Total Costs (4) = (2) + (3)
2	Work in process, beginning inventory (March 1)	225	₹1,80,000[a]	₹81,000[a]	₹2,61,000
3	Degree of completion of beginning work in process		100%	60%	
4	Started during March	275			
5	Completed and transferred out during March	400			
6	Work in process, ending inventory (March 31)	100			
7	Degree of completion of ending work in process		100%	50%	
8	Total costs added during March		₹1,98,000	₹1,63,800	₹3,61,800
9					
10					
11	[a]Work in process, beginning inventory (equals work in process, ending inventory for February)				
12	Direct materials: 225 physical units x 100% completed x ₹800 per unit = ₹1,80,000				
13	Conversion costs: 225 physical units x 60% completed x ₹600 per unit = ₹81,000				

Pacific Electronics now has incomplete units in both beginning work-in-process inventory and ending work-in-process inventory for March 2014. We can still use the five steps described earlier to calculate (1) the cost of units completed and transferred out and (2) the cost of ending work in process. To assign costs to each of these categories, however, we first need to choose an inventory-valuation method. We next describe the five-step approach for two key methods—the weighted-average method and the first-in, first-out method. These different valuation methods produce different costs for the units completed and for the ending work in process when the unit cost of inputs changes from one period to the next.

Weighted-Average Method

The **weighted-average process-costing method** calculates cost per equivalent unit of all work done to date (regardless of the accounting period in which it was done) and assigns this cost to equivalent units completed and transferred out of the process and to equivalent units in ending work-in-process inventory. The weighted-average cost is the total of all costs entering the Work in Process account (whether they are from beginning work in process or from work started during the current period) divided by total equivalent units of work done to date. We now describe the weighted-average method using the five-step procedure.

Step 1: Summarize the Flow of Physical Units. The physical-units column in Exhibit 17-4 shows where the units came from—225 units from beginning inventory and 275 units started during the current period—and where the units went—400 units completed and transferred out and 100 units in ending inventory.

Step 2: Compute Output in Terms of Equivalent Units. We use the relationship shown in the equation below.

$$\begin{array}{c} \text{Equivalent units} \\ \text{in beginning work} \\ \text{in process} \end{array} + \begin{array}{c} \text{Equivalent units} \\ \text{of work done in} \\ \text{current period} \end{array} = \begin{array}{c} \text{Equivalent units} \\ \text{completed and transferred} \\ \text{out in current period} \end{array} + \begin{array}{c} \text{Equivalent units} \\ \text{in ending work} \\ \text{in process} \end{array}$$

Although we are interested in calculating the left side of the preceding equation, it is easier to calculate this sum using the equation's right-side of the preceding equation: (1) the equivalent units completed and transferred out in the current period plus (2) the equivalent units in ending work in process. *Note that the stage of completion of the current-period beginning work in process is not used in this computation.*

The equivalent-units columns in Exhibit 17-4 show equivalent units of work done to date: 500 equivalent units of direct materials and 450 equivalent units of conversion costs.

File Edit View Insert Format Tools Data Window Help			
A	B	C	D
1	(Step 1)	(Step 2)	
2		Equivalent Units	
3 **Flow of Production**	**Physical Units**	**Direct Materials**	**Conversion Costs**
4 Work in process, beginning	225		
5 Started during current period	275		
6 To account for	500		
7 Completed and transferred out during current period	400	400	400
8 Work in process, ending[a]	100		
9 (100 x 100%; 100 x 50%)		100	50
10 Accounted for	500		
11 Work done to date		500	450
12			
13 [a]Degree of completion in this department; direct materials, 100%; conversion costs, 50%.			

Exhibit 17-4

Summarize Flow of Physical Units and Compute Output in Equivalent Units Using Weighted-Average Method for the Assembly Department for March 2014

Exhibit 17-5	Steps 3, 4 and 5: Summarize Total Costs to Account For, Compute Cost per Equivalent Unit, and Assign Total Costs to Units Completed and to Units in Ending Work in Process Using Weighted-Average Method of Process Costing for Assembly Department of Pacific Electronics for March 2014

	File Edit View Insert Format Tools Data Window Help			
	A	B	C	D	E
1			**Total Production Costs**	**Direct Materials**	**Conversion Costs**
2	**(Step 3)**	Work in process, beginning	₹2,61,000	₹1,80,000	₹81,000
3		Costs added in current period	3,61,800	1,98,000	1,63,800
4		Total costs to account for	₹6,22,800	₹3,78,000	₹2,44,800
5					
6	**(Step 4)**	Costs incurred to date		₹3,78,000	₹2,44,800
7		Divide by equivalent units of work done to date (Exhibit 17-4)		÷ 500	÷ 450
8		Cost per equivalent unit of work done to date		₹756.0	₹544.0
9					
10	**(Step 5)**	Assignment of costs:			
11		Completed and transferred out (400 units)	5,20,000	(400[a] × ₹756.0) +	(400[a] × ₹544.0)
12		Work in process, ending (100 units):	1,02,800	(100[b] × ₹756.0) +	(50[a] × ₹544.0)
13		Total costs accounted for	₹6,22,800	₹3,78,000 +	₹2,44,800
14					
15	[a]Equivalent units completed and transferred out from Exhibit 17-4, step 2.				
16	[b]Equivalent units in ending work in process from Exhibit 17-4, step 2.				

All completed and transferred-out units are 100% complete as to both direct materials and conversion costs. Partially completed units in ending work in process are 100% complete as to direct materials (because direct materials are introduced at the beginning of the process) and 50% complete as to conversion costs, based on estimates made by the Assembly Department manager.

Step 3:   Summarize Total Costs to Account For. Exhibit 17-5 presents step 3. The total costs to account for in March 2014 are described in the example data on the next page:

Beginning work in process (direct materials, ₹1,80,000 + conversion costs, ₹81,000)	₹2,61,000
Costs added during March (direct materials, ₹1,98,000 + conversion costs, ₹1,63,800)	3,61,800
Total costs to account for in March	₹6,22,800

Step 4:   Compute Cost per Equivalent Unit. Exhibit 17-5, step 4, shows the computation of weighted-average cost per equivalent unit for direct materials and conversion costs. The weighted-average cost per equivalent unit is obtained by dividing the sum of costs for beginning work in process plus costs for work done in the current period by total equivalent units of work done to date.

Total conversion costs (beginning work in process, ₹81,000 + work done in current period, ₹1, 63,800)	₹2,44,800
Divided by the total equivalent units of work done to date (equivalent units of conversion costs in beginning work in process and in work done in current period)	÷ 450
Weighted-average cost per equivalent unit	₹544.0

Step 5:   Assign Costs to Units Completed and to Units in Ending Work in Process Inventory. Step 5 in Exhibit 17-5 takes the equivalent units completed and transferred out and equivalent units in ending work in process (calculated in Exhibit 17-4, step 2) and assigns rupee amounts to them using the weighted-average cost per equivalent unit for direct materials and conversion costs calculated in step 4. For example, total costs of the 100 physical units in ending work in process are:

Direct materials:	
100 equivalent units × weighted-average cost per equivalent unit of ₹756	₹75,600
Conversion costs:	
50 equivalent units × weighted-average cost per equivalent unit of ₹544	27,200
Total costs of ending work in process	₹1,02,800

The following table summarizes total costs to account for (₹6,22,800) and how they are accounted for in Exhibit 17-5. The arrows indicate that the costs of units completed and transferred out and units in ending work in process are calculated using weighted-average total costs obtained after merging costs of beginning work in process and costs added in the current period.

Costs to Account For			Costs Accounted for Calculated on a Weighted-Average Basis	
Beginning work in process	₹2,61,000		Completed and transferred out	₹5,20,000
Costs added in current period	3,61,800		Ending work in process	1,02,800
Total costs to account for	₹6,22,800		Total costs accounted for	₹6,22,800

Before proceeding, review Exhibits 17-4 and 17-5 to check your understanding of the weighted-average method. Note: Exhibit 17-4 deals with only physical and equivalent units, not costs. Exhibit 17-5 shows the cost amounts.

Using amounts from Exhibit 17-5, the summary journal entries under the weighted-average method for March 2014 at Pacific Electronics are:

1. Work in Process—Assembly	1,98,000	
Accounts Payable Control		1,98,000
To record direct materials purchased and used in production during March.		
2. Work in Process—Assembly	1,63,800	
Various accounts such as Wages Payable		
Control and Accumulated Depreciation		1,63,800
To record conversion costs for March; examples include energy, manufacturing supplies, all manufacturing labor, and plant depreciation.		
3. Work in Process—Testing	5,20,000	
Work in Process—Assembly		5,20,000
To record cost of goods completed and transferred from Assembly to Testing during March.		

The T-account Work in Process—Assembly, under the weighted-average method, shows:

Work in Process—Assembly			
Beginning inventory, March 1	2,61,000	③ Completed and transferred	
① Direct materials	1,98,000	out to Work in Process—	5,20,000
② Conversion costs	1,63,800	Testing	
Ending inventory, March 31	1,02,800		

First-In, First-Out Method

The **first-in, first-out (FIFO) process-costing method** (1) assigns the cost of the previous accounting period's equivalent units in beginning work-in-process inventory to the first units completed and transferred out of the process; and (2) assigns the cost of equivalent units worked on during the *current* period first to complete beginning inventory, next to start and complete new units, and finally to units in ending work-in-process inventory. The FIFO method assumes that the earliest equivalent units in work in process are completed first.

A distinctive feature of the FIFO process-costing method is that work done on beginning inventory before the current period is kept separate from work done in the current period. The costs incurred and units produced in the current period are used to calculate cost per equivalent unit of work done in the current period. In contrast, the equivalent-unit and cost-per-equivalent-unit calculations under the weighted-average method *merge* units and costs in beginning inventory with units and costs of work done in the current period.

We now describe the FIFO method using the five-step procedure introduced earlier.

Step 1: Summarize the Flow of Physical Units. Exhibit 17-6, step 1, traces the flow of physical units of production and explain how they are calculated under the FIFO method.

- The first physical units assumed to be completed and transferred out during the period are 225 units from beginning work-in-process inventory.
- The March data on page 904 indicate that 400 physical units were completed during March. The FIFO method assumes that of these 400 units, 175 units (400 units − 225 units from beginning work-in-process inventory) must have been started and completed during March.
- The ending work-in-process inventory consists of 100 physical units—the 275 physical units started minus the 175 units that were started and completed.
- The physical units "to account for" equal the physical units "accounted for" (500 units).

Exhibit 17-6

Summarize the Flow of Physical Units and Compute Output in Equivalent Units Using FIFO Method of Process Costing for Assembly Department for March 2014

	A	B	C	D
		(Step 1)	**(Step 2)**	
2			**Equivalent Units**	
3	**Flow of Production**	**Physical Units**	**Direct Materials**	**Conversion Costs**
4	Work in process, beginning	225	(work done before current period)	
5	Started during current period	275		
6	To account for	500		
7	Completed and transferred out during current period:			
8	From beginning work in process[a]	225		
9	[225 x (100% - 100%); 225 x (100%-60%)]		0	90
10	Started and completed	175[b]		
11	(175 x 100%; 175 x 100%)		175	175
12	Work in process, ending[c]	100		
13	(100 x 100%; 100 x 50%)		100	50
14	Accounted for	500		
15	Work done in current period only		275	315
16				
17	[a]Degree of completion in this department; direct materials, 100%; conversion costs, 60%.			
18	[b]400 physical units completed and transferred out minus 225 physical units completed and			
19	transferred out from beginning work-in-process inventory.			
20	[c]Degree of completion in this department: direct materials, 100%; conversion costs, 50%.			

Step 2: Compute the Output in Terms of Equivalent Units. Exhibit 17-6 also presents the computations for step 2 under the FIFO method. *The equivalent-unit calculations for each cost category focus on equivalent units of work done in the current period (March) only.*

Under the FIFO method, equivalent units of work done in March on the beginning work-in-process inventory equal 225 physical units times *the percentage of work remaining to be done in March to complete these units:* 0% for direct materials, because beginning work in process is 100% complete for direct materials, and 40% for conversion costs, because the beginning work in process is 60% complete for conversion costs. The results are 0 (0% × 225) equivalent units of work for direct materials and 90 (40% × 225) equivalent units of work for conversion costs.

The equivalent units of work done on the 175 physical units started and completed equals 175 units times 100% for both direct materials and conversion costs, because all work on these units is done in the current period.

The equivalent units of work done on the 100 units of ending work in process equal 100 physical units times 100% for direct materials (because all direct materials for these units are added in the current period) and 50% for conversion costs (because 50% of conversion-costs work on these units is done in the current period).

Step 3: Summarize the Total Costs to Account For. Exhibit 17-7 presents step 3 and summarizes the ₹6,22,800 in total costs to account for in March 2014 (the costs of the beginning work in process, ₹2,61,000, and costs added in the current period, ₹3,61,800).

Exhibit 17-7 Summarize the Total Costs to Account For, Compute the Cost per Equivalent Unit, and Assign Total Costs to Units Completed and to Units in Ending Work in Process Using FIFO Method of Process Costing for Assembly Department for March 2014

	A	B	C	D	E
			Total Production Costs	Direct Material	Conversion Costs
1					
2	(Step 3)	Work in process, beginning	₹2,61,000	₹1,80,000	₹81,000
3		Costs added in current period	3,61,800	1,98,000	₹1,63,800
4		Total costs to account for	₹6,22,800	₹3,78,000	₹2,44,800
5					
6	(Step 4)	Costs added in current period		₹1,98,000	₹1,63,800
7		Divide by equivalent units of work done in current period (Exhibit 17-6)		÷ 275	÷ 315
8		Cost per equivalent unit of work done in current period		₹720	₹520
9					
10	(Step 5)	Assignment of costs:			
11		Completed and transferred out (400 units):			
12		Work in process, beginning (225 units)	₹2,61,000	₹1,80,000 +	₹81,000
13		Costs added to beginning work in process in current period	46,800	0ᵃ×₹720) +	(90ᵃ x ₹520)
14		Total from beginning inventory	3,07,800		
15		Started and completed (175 units)	2,17,000	175ᵇ×₹720) +	(175ᵇ x ₹520)
16		Total costs of units completed and transferred out	5,24,800		
17		Work in process, ending (100 units):	98,000	(100ᶜ x₹720) +	(50ᶜ x ₹520)
18		Total costs accounted for	₹6,22,800	₹3,78,000 +	₹2,44,800
19					
20		ᵃEquivalent units used to complete beginning work in process from Exhibit 17-6, step 2.			
21		ᵇEquivalent units started and completed from Exhibit 17-6, step 2.			
22		ᶜEquivalent units in ending work in process from Exhibit 17-6, step 2.			

Step 4: Compute Cost per Equivalent Unit. Exhibit 17-7 shows the step 4 computation of the cost per equivalent unit for *work done in the current period only* for direct materials and conversion costs. For example, conversion cost per equivalent unit of ₹520 is obtained by dividing current-period conversion costs of ₹1,63,800 by current-period conversion-costs equivalent units of 315.

Step 5: Assign Costs to the Units Completed and to Units in Ending Work in Process Inventory. Exhibit 17-7 shows the assignment of costs under the FIFO method. The costs of work done in the current period are assigned (1) first to the additional work done to complete the beginning work in process, then (2) to work done on units started and completed during the current period, and finally (3) to ending work in process inventory. *Step 5 takes each quantity of equivalent units calculated in Exhibit 17-6, step 2, and assigns rupee amounts to them (using the cost-per-equivalent-unit calculations in step 4).* The goal is to use the cost of work done in the current period to determine total costs of all units completed from beginning inventory and from work started and completed in the current period, and costs of ending work in process inventory.

Of the 400 completed units, 225 units are from beginning inventory and 175 units are started and completed during March. The FIFO method starts by assigning the costs of beginning work-in-process inventory of ₹2,61,000 to the first units completed and transferred out. As we saw in step 2, an additional 90 equivalent units of conversion costs are needed to complete these units in the current period. The current-period conversion cost per equivalent unit is ₹520, so ₹46,800 (90 equivalent units × ₹520 per equivalent unit) of additional costs are incurred to complete beginning inventory. The total production costs for units in beginning inventory are ₹2,61,000 + ₹46,800 = ₹3,07,800. The 175 units started and completed in the current period consist of 175 equivalent units of direct materials and 175 equivalent units of conversion costs. These units are costed at the cost per equivalent unit in the current period (direct materials, ₹720, and conversion costs, ₹520) for a total production cost of ₹2,17,000 [175 × (₹720 + ₹520)].

Under FIFO, ending work-in-process inventory comes from units that were started but not fully completed during the current period. The total costs of the 100 partially assembled physical units in ending work in process are as follows:

Direct materials:		
100 equivalent units × ₹720 cost per equivalent unit in March		₹72,000
Conversion costs:		
50 equivalent units × ₹520 cost per equivalent unit in March		26,000
Total cost of work in process on March 31		₹98,000

The following table summarizes the total costs to account for and the costs accounted for under FIFO which are ₹6,22,800 in Exhibit 17-7. Notice how the FIFO method keeps the layers of beginning work in process and the costs added in the current period. The arrows indicate where the costs in each layer go—that is, to units completed and transferred out or to ending work in process. Be sure to include costs of beginning work in process (₹2,61,000) when calculating the costs of units completed.

Costs to Account for			Costs Accounted for Calculated on a FIFO Basis	
Beginning work in process	₹2,61,000	→	Completed and transferred out	
Costs added in current period	3,61,800	→	Beginning work in process	₹2,61,000
		→	Used to complete beginning work in process	46,800
		→	Started and completed	2,17,000
			Completed and transferred out	5,24,800
			Ending work in process	98,000
Total costs accounted for	₹6,22,800		Total costs to account for	₹6,22,800

Before proceeding, review Exhibits 17-6 and 17-7 to check your understanding of the FIFO method. Note: Exhibit 17-6 deals with only physical and equivalent units, not costs. Exhibit 17-7 shows the cost amounts.

The journal entries under the FIFO method are identical to the journal entries under the weighted-average method except for one difference. The entry to record the cost of goods completed and transferred out would be ₹5,24,800 under the FIFO method instead of ₹5,20,000 under the weighted-average method.

Keep in mind that FIFO is applied within a department to compile the cost of units *transferred out*. As a practical matter, however, units *transferred in* during a given period usually are carried at a single average unit cost. For example, in the preceding example, the Assembly Department uses FIFO to distinguish between monthly batches of production. The resulting cost of each SG-40 unit transferred out of the assembly department is ₹5,24,800 ÷ 400 units = ₹1,312. The Testing, department, how ever, costs these units (which consist of costs incurred in both February and March) at one average unit cost (₹1,312 in this example). If this averaging were not done, the attempt to track costs on a pure FIFO basis throughout a series of processes would be cumbersome. As a result, the FIFO method should really be called a *modified* or *department* FIFO method.

Comparing the Weighted-Average and FIFO Methods

Consider the summary of the costs assigned to units completed and to units still in process under the weighted-average and FIFO process-costing methods in our example for March 2014:

	Weighted Average (from Exhibit 17-5)	FIFO (from Exhibit 17-7)	Difference
Cost of units completed and transferred out	₹5,20,000	₹5,24,800	+₹4,800
Work in process, ending	1,02,800	₹98,000	−₹4,800
Total costs accounted for	₹6,22,800	₹6,22,800	

The weighted-average ending inventory is higher than the FIFO ending inventory by ₹ 4,800, or 4.9% (₹4,800 ÷ ₹98,000 = 0.049, or 4.9%). This would be a significant difference when aggregated over the many thousands of products Pacific Electronics makes. When completed units are sold, the weighted-average method in our example leads to a lower cost of goods sold and, therefore, higher operating income than the FIFO method does. To see why, recall the data on page 904. For the beginning work-in-process inventory, the direct material cost per equivalent unit is ₹800, and conversion cost per equivalent unit is ₹600. These costs are greater, respectively, than the ₹720 direct materials cost and the ₹520 conversion cost per equivalent unit of work done during the current period. The current-period costs could be lower due to a decline in the prices of direct materials and conversion-cost inputs, or as a result of Pacific Electronics becoming more efficient in its processes by using smaller quantities of inputs per unit of output, or both.

FIFO assumes that (1) all the higher-cost units from the previous period in beginning work in process are the first to be completed and transferred out of the process and (2) the ending work in process consists of only the lower-cost current-period units. The weighted-average method, however, smooths out cost per equivalent unit by assuming that (1) more of the lower-cost units are completed and transferred out and (2) some of the higher-cost units are placed in ending work in process. The decline in the current-period cost per equivalent unit results in a lower cost of units completed and transferred out and a higher ending work-in-process inventory under the weighted-average method relative FIFO.

Managers use information from process-costing systems to make pricing and product-mix decisions and understand how well a firm's processing are performing. FIFO provides managers with information about changes in costs per unit from one period to the next. Managers can use this data to adjust selling prices based on current conditions (for example, based on the ₹720 direct material cost and ₹520 conversion cost in March). The managers can also more easily evaluate performance relative to either a budget or the previous period (for example, both unit direct material and conversion costs have declined relative to the prior period). By focusing on the work done and the costs of work done during the current period, the FIFO method provides useful information for these planning and control purposes.

The weighted-average method merges unit costs from different accounting periods, obscuring period-to-period comparisons. For example, the weighted-average method would lead managers at Pacific Electronics to make decisions based on the ₹756 direct materials and ₹544 conversion costs, rather than the costs of ₹720 and ₹520 prevailing in the current period. Advantages of the weighted-average method, however, are its relative computational simplicity and its reporting of a more-representative average unit cost when input prices fluctuate markedly from month to month.

The cost of units completed and, hence, a firm's operating income differ materially between the weighted-average and FIFO methods when (1) the direct materials or conversion cost per equivalent unit varies significantly from period to period and (2) the physical-inventory levels of the work in process are large relative to the total number of units transferred out of the process. As changes in unit costs and inventory levels across periods decrease, the difference in the costs of units completed under the weighted-average and FIFO methods also decreases.[2]

When the cost of units completed under the weighted-average and FIFO methods differs substantially, which method should a manager choose? In a period of falling prices, as in the Pacific Electronics case, the higher cost of goods sold under the FIFO method will lead to lower operating income and lower tax payments, saving the company cash and increasing the company's value. FIFO is the preferred choice, but managers may not make this choice. If the manager's compensation, for instance, is based on operating income, the manager may prefer the weighted-average method, which increases operating income even though it results in higher tax payments. Top managers must carefully design compensation plans to encourage managers to take actions that increase a company's value. For example, the compensation plan might reward after-tax cash flow metrics, in addition to operating income metrics, to align decision making and performance evaluation.

---

[2] For example, suppose the beginning work-in-process inventory for March was 125 physical units (instead of 225), and suppose the costs per equivalent unit of work done in the current period (March) were direct materials, ₹750, and conversion costs, ₹550. Assume that all other data for March are the same as in our example. In this case, the cost of units completed and transferred out would be ₹5,28,330 under the weighted-average method and ₹5,30,000 under the FIFO method. The work-in-process ending inventory would be ₹1,04,170 under the weighted-average method and ₹1,02,500 under the FIFO method (calculations not shown). These differences are much smaller than in the chapter example. The weighted-average ending inventory is higher than the FIFO ending inventory by only ₹1,670 (₹1,04,170 − ₹1,02,500), or 1.6% (₹1,670 ÷ ₹1,02,500 = 0.016), compared with 4.9% higher in the chapter example.

Occasionally, choosing a process-costing method can be more difficult. Suppose, for example, that by using FIFO a company would violate its debt covenants (agreements between a company and its creditors that the company will maintain certain financial ratios) resulting in its loans coming due. In this case, a manager may prefer the weighted-average method even though it results in higher taxes because the company does not have the liquidity to repay its loans.

In a period of rising prices, the weighted-average method will decrease taxes because cost of goods sold will be higher and operating income lower.

Finally, how is activity-based costing related to process costing? Like activity-based processing, each process—assembly, testing, and so on—can be considered a different (production) activity. However, no additional activities need to be identified within each process to use process costing. That's because products are homogeneous and use the resources of each process in a uniform way. The bottom line is that activity-based costing has less applicability in process-costing environments, especially when compared to the significant role it plays in job costing.

Decision Point

What are the weighted-average and first-in, first-out (FIFO) methods of process costing? Under what conditions will they yield different levels of operating income?

Transferred-In Costs in Process Costing

Many process-costing systems have two or more departments or processes in the production cycle. As units move from department to department, the related costs are also transferred by monthly journal entries. **Transferred-in costs** (also called **previous-department costs**) are costs incurred in previous departments that are carried forward as the product's cost when it moves to a subsequent process in the production cycle.

We now extend our Pacific Electronics example to the Testing Department. As the assembly process is completed, the Assembly Department of Pacific Electronics immediately transfers SG-40 units to the Testing Department. Conversion costs are added evenly during the Testing Department's process. At the *end* of the testing process, the units receive additional raw materials including crating and other packing materials to prepare them for shipment. As units are completed in Testing, they are immediately transferred to Finished Goods. The testing Department costs consists of transferred-in costs, as well as direct materials and conversion costs added in Testing.

The following diagram represents these facts:

Learning Objective 5

Apply process-costing methods to situations with transferred-in costs

. . . using weighed-average and FIFO methods

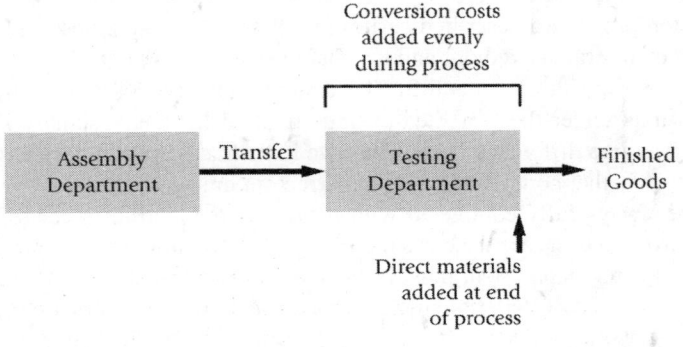

Data for the Testing Department for March 2014 are:

	A	B	C	D	E
1		Physical Units (SG-40s)	Transferred-in Costs	Direct Materials	Conversion Costs
2	Work in process, beginning inventory (March 1)	240	₹3,36,000	₹0	₹1,80,000
3	Degree of completion of beginning work in process		100%	0%	62.5%
4	Transferred in during March	400			
5	Completed and transferred out during March	440			
6	Work in process, ending inventory (March 31)	200			
7	Degree of completion of ending work in process		100%	0%	80 %
8	Total costs added during March				
9	Direct materials and conversion costs			₹1,32,000	₹4,86,000
10	Transferred in (Weighted-average from Exhibit 17-5)ᵃ		₹5,20,000		
11	Transferred in (FIFO from Exhibit 17-7)ᵃ		₹5,24,800		
12					
13	ᵃThe transferred-in costs during March are different under the weighted-average method (Exhibit 17-5) and the FIFO method (Exhibit 17-7). In our example, beginning work-in-process inventory, ₹5,16,000 (₹3,36,000 + ₹0 + ₹1,80,000) is the same under both the weighted-average and FIFO inventory methods because we assume costs per equivalent unit to be the same in both January and February. If costs per equivalent unit had been different in the two months, work-in-process inventory at the end of February (beginning of March) would be costed differently under the weighted-average and FIFO methods. The basic approach to process costing with transferred-in costs, however, would still be the same as what we describe in this section.				

The transferred-in costs are treated as if they are a separate type of direct material added at the beginning of the process. That is, the transferred costs are always 100% complete at the beginning of the process in the new department. When successive departments are involved, transferred units from one department become all or a part of the direct materials of the next department; however, they are called transferred-in costs, not direct material costs.

Transferred-In Costs and the Weighted-Average Method

To examine the weighted-average process-costing method with transferred-in costs, we use the five-step procedure described earlier to assign costs of the Testing Department to units completed and transferred out and to units in ending work in process.

Exhibit 17-8 shows steps 1 and 2. The computations are similar to the calculations of equivalent units under the weighted-average method for the Assembly Department in Exhibit 17-4. The one difference here is that we have transferred-in costs as an additional input. All units, whether completed and transferred out during the period or in ending work in process, are always fully completed with respect to transferred-in costs. The reason is that the transferred-in costs are the costs incurred in the assembly department, and any units received in the testing department must have first been completed in the assembly department. However, the direct material costs have a zero degree of completion in both beginning and ending work-in-process inventories because, in the Testing, department direct materials are introduced at the *end* of the process.

Exhibit 17-9 describes steps 3, 4, and 5 for the weighted-average method. Beginning work in process and work done in the current period are combined for purposes of computing cost per equivalent unit for transferred-in costs, direct material costs, and conversion costs.

Exhibit 17-8 Summarize the Flow Physical Units and Compute Output in Equivalent Units Using Weighted-Average Method of Process Costing for Testing Department for March 2014

	A	B	C	D	E
		(Step 1)		(Step 2)	
				Equivalent Units	
	Flow of Production	Physical Units	Transferred-in Costs	Direct Materials	Conversion Costs
4	Work in process, beginning	240			
5	Transferred in during current period	400			
6	To account for	640			
7	Completed and transferred out during current period	440	440	440	440
8	Work in process, ending[a]	200			
9	(200 x 100%; 200 x 0%; 200 x 80%)		200	0	160
10	Accounted for	640			
11	Work done to date		640	440	600
12					
13	[a]Degree of completion in this department; transferred-in costs, 100%; direct materials, 0%; conversion costs, 80%.				

Exhibit 17-9 Summarize the Total Costs to Account For, Compute Cost per Equivalent Unit, and Assign Total Costs to Units Completed and to Units in Ending Work in Process Inventory Using Weighted-Average Method of Process Costing for Testing Department for March 2014

	A	B	C	D	E	F
1			Total Production Costs	Transferred-in Costs	Direct Materials	Conversion Costs
2	(Step 3)	Work in process, beginning	₹5,16,000	₹3,36,000	₹0	₹1,80,000
3		Costs added in current period	11,38,000	5,20,000	1,32,000	4,86,000
4		Total costs to account for	₹16,54,000	₹8,56,000	₹1,32,000	₹6,66,000
5						
6	(Step 4)	Costs incurred to date		₹8,56,000	₹1,32,000	₹6,66,000
7		Divide by equivalent units of work done to date (Exhibit 17-11)		÷ 640	÷ 440	÷ 600
8		Cost per equivalent unit of work done to date		₹1,337.5	₹300.0	₹1,110.0
9						
10	(Step 0)	Assignment of costs:				
11		Completed and transferred out (440 units)	₹12,08,900	(440[a] x ₹1,337.5) +	(440[a] x ₹300) +	(440[a] x ₹1,110)
12		Work in process, ending (200 units):	4,45,100	(200[b] x ₹1,337.5) +	(0[b] x ₹300) +	(160[b] x ₹1,110)
13		Total costs accounted for	₹16,54,000	₹8,56,000 +	₹1,32,000 +	₹6,66,000
14						
15	[a]Equivalent units completed and transferred out from Exhibit 17-11, step 2.					
16	[b]Equivalent units in ending work in process from Exhibit 17-11, step 2.					

The journal entry for the transfer from Testing to Finished Goods (see Exhibit 17-9) is:

Finished Goods Control	12,08,900	
Work in Process—Testing		12,08,900
To record cost of goods completed and transferred from Testing to Finished Goods.		

Entries in the Work in Process—Testing account (see Exhibit 17-9) are:

Work in Process—Testing

Beginning inventory, March 1	5,16,000	Transferred out	12,08,900
Transferred-in costs	5,20,000		
Direct materials	1,32,000		
Conversion costs	4,86,000		
Ending inventory, March 31	4,45,100		

Transferred-In Costs and the FIFO Method

To examine the FIFO process-costing method with transferred-in costs, we again use the five-step procedure. Exhibit 17-10 shows steps 1 and 2. Other than considering transferred-in costs, computing the equivalent units is the same as under the FIFO method for the Assembly Department (see Exhibit 17-6).

Exhibit 17-11 describes steps 3, 4, and 5. In step 3, the ₹16,58,800 in total costs to account for under the FIFO method differs from the total amount under the weighted-aver-

Exhibit 17-10   Summarize the Flow of Physical Units and Compute Output in Equivalent Units Using FIFO Method of Process Costing for Testing Department for March 2014

	A	B	C	D	E
1		**(Step 1)**		**(Step 2)**	
2				**Equivalent Units**	
3	**Flow of Production**	**Physical Units**	**Transferred-in Costs**	**Direct Materials**	**Conversion Costs**
4	Work in process, beginning	240	(work done before current period)		
5	Transferred in during current period	400			
6	To account for	640			
7	Completed and transferred out during current period:				
8	From beginning work in process[a]	240			
9	[240 x (100% – 100%); 240 x (100% – 0%); 240 x (100% – 62.5%)]		0	240	90
10	Started and completed	200[b]			
11	(200 x 100%; 200 x 100%; 200 x 100%)		200	200	200
12	Work in process, ending[c]	200			
13	(200 x 100%; 200 x 0%; 200 x 80%)		200	0	160
14	Accounted for	640			
15	Work done in current period only		400	440	450
16					
17	[a]Degree of completion in this department: Transferred-in costs, 100%; direct materials, 0%; conversion costs, 62.5%.				
18	[b]440 physical units completed and transferred out minus 240 physical units completed and transferred out from beginning				
19	work-in-process inventory.				
20	[c]Degree of completion in this department: Transferred-in costs, 100%; direct materials, 0%; conversion costs, 80%.				

age method which are ₹16,54,000. This is because of different in the costs of completed units transferred in from the Assembly Department under the two methods—₹5,24,800 under FIFO and ₹5,20,000 under weighted average method. The cost per equivalent unit for the current period in step 4 is calculated on the basis of costs transferred in and work done in the current period only. Step 5 then accounts for the total costs of ₹16,55,800 by assigning them to the units transferred out and those in ending work in process inventory. Again, other than considering transferred-in costs, the calculations mirror those under the FIFO method for the Assembly Department (in Exhibit 17-7).

Remember that in a series of interdepartmental transfers, each department is regarded as separate and distinct for accounting purposes. The journal entry for the transfer from Testing to Finished Goods (see Exhibit 17-11) is as follows:

Finished Goods Control	12,23,600	
Work in Process—Testing		12,23,600
To record cost of goods completed and transferred from Testing to Finished Goods.		

The entries in the Work in Process—Testing account (see Exhibit 17-11) are as follows:

Work in Process—Testing			
Beginning inventory, March 1	5,16,000	Transferred out	12,23,600
Transferred-in costs	5,24,800		
Direct materials	1,32,000		
Conversion costs	4,86,000		
Ending inventory, March 31	4,35,200		

Exhibit 17-11 Summarize the Total Costs to Account For, Compute Cost per Equivalent Unit, and Assign Costs to Units Completed and to Units in Ending Work in Process Inventory Using FIFO Method of Process Costing for Testing Department for March 2014.

	A	B	C	D	E	F
			Total Production Costs	Transferred-in Cost	Direct Material	Conversion Costs
1						
2	(Step 3)	Work in process, beginning	₹5,16,000	₹3,36,000	₹0	₹1,80,000
3		Costs added in current period	11,42,800	5,24,800	1,32,000	4,86,000
4		Total costs to account for	₹16,58,800	₹8,60,800	₹1,32,000	₹6,66,000
5						
6	(Step 4)	Costs added in current period		₹5,24,800	₹1,32,000	₹4,86,000
7		Divide by equivalent units of work done in current period (Exhibit 17-13)		÷ 400	÷ 440	÷ 450
8		Cost per equivalent unit of work done in current period		₹1,312.0	₹300	₹1,080
9						
10	(Step 5)	Assignment of costs:				
11		Completed and transferred out (440 units)				
12		Work in process, beginning (240 units)	₹5,16,000	₹3,36,000 +	₹0 +	₹1,80,000
13		Costs added to beginning work in process in current period	1,69,200	(0[a] × ₹1,312.0) +	(240[a] × ₹300)+	(90[a] × ₹1,080)
14		Total from beginning inventory	6,85,200			
15		Started and completed (200 units)	5,38,400	(200[b] × ₹1,312.0) +	(200[b] × ₹300)+	(200[b] × ₹1,080)
16		Total costs of units completed and transferred out	12,23,600			
17		Work in process, ending (200 units):	4,35,200	(200[c] × ₹1,312.0)+	(0[a] × ₹300)+	(160[c] × ₹1,080)
18		Total costs accounted for	₹16,58,800	₹8,60,800 +	₹1,32,000 +	₹6,66,000
19						
20	[a]Equivalent units used to complete beginning work in process from Exhibit 17-13, step 2.					
21	[b]Equivalent units started and completed from Exhibit 17-13, step 2.					
22	[c]Equivalent units in ending work in process from Exhibit 17-13, step 2.					

Points to Remember About Transferred-In Costs

Some points to remember when accounting for transferred-in costs are as follows:

1. Be sure to include transferred-in costs from previous departments in your calculations.

2. When calculating the costs to be transferred using the FIFO basis, do not overlook costs assigned in the previous period to units that were in process at the beginning of the current period but are now included in the units transferred. For example, do not overlook the ₹5,16,000 in Exhibit 17-11.

3. Unit costs may fluctuate between periods. Therefore, transferred units may contain batches accumulated at different unit costs. For example, the 400 units transferred in at ₹5,24,800 in Exhibit 17-11 using the FIFO method consist of units that have different unit costs of direct materials and conversion costs when these units were worked on in the Assembly Department (see Exhibit 17-7). Remember, however, that when these units are transferred to the Testing Department, they are costed at one average unit cost of ₹1,312 (₹5,24,800 ÷ 400 units), as in Exhibit 17-11.

4. Units may be measured in different denominations in different departments. Consider each department separately. For example, unit costs could be based on kilograms in the first department and litres in the second department. Accordingly, as units are received in the second department, their measurements must be converted to litres.

Decision Point ▶

How are the weighted-average and FIFO process-costing methods applied to transferred-in costs?

Hybrid Costing Systems

Learning Objective 6

Understand the need for hybrid-costing systems such as operation-costing

. . . when product-costing does not fall into job-costing or process-costing categories

Product-costing systems do not always fall neatly into either job-costing or process-costing categories. Many production systems are hybrid systems in which both mass production and customization occur. Consider Ford Motor Company. Automobiles may be manufactured in a continuous flow (suited to process costing), but individual units may be customized with different engine sizes, transmission, music system, and so on (which requires job costing). A **hybrid-costing system** blends characteristics from both job-costing and process-costing systems. Managers must design product-costing systems to fit the particular characteristics of different production systems. Firms that manufacture closely related standardized products (for example, various types of televisions, dishwashers, washing machines, and shoes) tend to use hybrid-costing systems. They use process costing to account for the conversion costs and job costing for the material and customizable components. Consider Nike, which has a message for shoppers looking for the hottest new shoe design: Just do it . . . yourself! Athletic apparel manufacturers have long individually crafted shoes for professional athletes. Now, Nike is making it possible for other customers to design their own shoes and clothing. Using the Internet and mobile applications, Nike's customers can personalize with their own colors and patterns for Jordan-brand sneakers and other apparel.

Overview of Operation-Costing Systems

An **operation** is a standardized method or technique that is performed repetitively, often on different materials, resulting in different finished goods. Multiple *operations* are usually conducted within a department. For instance, a suit maker may have a cutting operation and a hemming operation within a single department. The term operation, however, is often used loosely. It may be a synonym for a department or process. For example, some companies may call their finishing department a finishing process or a finishing operation.

An **operation-costing system** is a hybrid-costing system applied to batches of similar, but not identical, products. Each batch of products is often a variation of a single design, and it proceeds through a sequence of operations. Within each operation, all product units are treated exactly alike, using identical amounts of the operation's resources. A key point in the operation system is that each batch does not necessarily move through the same operations as other batches. Batches are also called production runs.

In a company that makes suits, managers may select a single basic design for every suit to be made, but depending on specifications, each batch of suits varies somewhat from other batches. Batches may vary with respect to the material used or the type of stitching. Semiconductors, textiles, and shoes are also manufactured in batches and may have similar variations from batch to batch.

An operation-costing system uses work orders that specify the needed direct materials and step-by-step operations. Product costs are compiled for each work order. Direct materials that are unique to different work orders are specifically identified with the appropriate work order, as in job costing. However, each unit is assumed to use an identical amount of conversion costs for a given operation, as in process costing. A single average conversion cost per unit is calculated for each operation. This is done by dividing the total conversion costs for that operation by the number of units that pass through it. This average cost is then assigned to each unit passing through the operation. Units that do not pass through an operation are not allocated any costs for that operation. There are only two cost categories—direct materials and conversion costs in the examples we have discussed. However, operation costing can have more than two cost categories. The costs in each category are identified with specific work orders using job-costing or process-costing methods as appropriate.

Managers find operation costing useful in cost management because operation costing focuses on control of physical processes, or operations, of a given production system. For example, in clothing manufacturing, managers are concerned with fabric waste, how many fabric layers that can be cut at one time, and so on. Operation costing measures, in financial terms, how well managers have controlled physical processes.

Illustrating an Operation-Costing System

The Raymond Clothing Company, a clothing manufacturer, produces two lines of blazers for department stores: those made of wool and those made of polyester. Wool blazers use better-quality materials and undergo more operations than polyester blazers do. The operations information on work order 423 for 50 wool blazers and work order 424 for 100 polyester blazers is as follows:

	Work Order 423	**Work Order 424**
Direct materials	Wool	Polyester
	Satin full lining	Rayon partial lining
	Bone buttons	Plastic buttons
Operations		
1. Cutting cloth	Use	Use
2. Checking edges	Use	Do not use
3. Sewing body	Use	Use
4. Checking seams	Use	Do not use
5. Machine sewing of collars and lapels	Do not use	Use
6. Hand sewing of collars and lapels	Use	Do not use

The cost data for these work orders, started and completed in March 2014, are as follows:

	Work Order 423	Work Order 424
Number of blazers	50	100
Direct material costs	₹60,000	₹30,000
Conversion costs allocated:		
Operation 1	5,800	11,600
Operation 2	4,000	—
Operation 3	19,000	38,000
Operation 4	5,000	—
Operation 5	—	8,750
Operation 6	7,000	—
Total manufacturing costs	₹1,00,800	₹88,350

As in process costing, all product units in any work order are assumed to consume identical amounts of conversion costs of a particular operation. Raymond's operation-costing system uses a budgeted rate to calculate the conversion costs of each operation. The budgeted rate for Operation 1 (amounts assumed) is as follows:

$$\text{Operation 1 budgeted conversion-cost rate for 2014} = \frac{\text{Operation 1 budgeted conversion costs for 2014}}{\text{Operation 1 budgeted product units for 2014}}$$

$$= \frac{₹23,20,000}{20,000 \text{ units}}$$

$$= ₹116 \text{ per unit}$$

The budgeted conversion costs of Operation 1 include labor, power, repairs, supplies, depreciation, and other overhead of this operation. If some units have not been completed (so all units in Operation 1 have not received the same amounts of conversion costs), the conversion-cost rate is computed by dividing budgeted conversion costs by *equivalent units* of conversion costs, as in process costing.

As the company manufactures blazers, managers allocate the conversion costs to the work orders processed in Operation 1 by multiplying the ₹116 conversion cost per unit by the number of units processed. Conversion costs of Operation 1 for 50 wool blazers (work order 423) are ₹116 per blazer × 50 blazers = ₹5,800, and for 100 polyester blazers (work order 424) are ₹116 per blazer × 100 blazers = ₹11,600. When equivalent units are used to calculate the conversion-cost rate, costs are allocated to work orders by multiplying conversion cost per equivalent unit by number of equivalent units in the work order.

The direct material costs of ₹60,000 for the 50 wool blazers (work order 423) and ₹ 30,000 for the 100 polyester blazers (work order 424) are specifically identified with each order, as in job costing. The basic point of operation costing is this: Operation unit costs are assumed to be the same regardless of the work order, but direct material costs vary across orders when the materials for each work order vary.

Journal Entries

Actual conversion costs for Operation 1 in March 2014—assumed to be ₹2,44,000, including actual costs incurred for work order 423 and work order 424—are entered into a Conversion Costs Control account:

1. Conversion Costs Control   2,44,000
     Various accounts (such as Wages Payable
     Control and Accumulated Depreciation)   2,44,000

Summary journal entries for assigning costs to polyester blazers (work order 424) follow. Entries for wool blazers would be similar. Of the ₹30,000 of direct materials for work order 424, ₹29,750 are used in Operation 1, and the remaining ₹250 of materials are used in another operation. The journal entry to record direct materials used for the 100 polyester blazers in March 2012 is as follows:

2. Work in Process, Operation 1	29,750	
Materials Inventory Control		29,750

The journal entry to record the allocation of conversion costs to products uses the budgeted rate of ₹116 per blazer times the 100 polyester blazers processed, or ₹11,600:

3. Work in Process, Operation 1	11,600	
Conversion Costs Allocated		11,600

The journal entry to record the transfer of the 100 polyester blazers (at a cost of ₹29,750 + ₹11,600) from Operation 1 to Operation 3 (polyester blazers do not go through Operation 2) is as follows:

4. Work in Process, Operation 3	41,350	
Work in Process, Operation 1		41,350

After posting these entries, the Work in Process, Operation 1, account appears as follows:

Work in Process, Operation 1

② Direct materials	29,750	④ Transferred to Operation 3	41,350
③ Conversion costs allocated	11,600		
Ending inventory, March 31	0		

The costs of the blazers are transferred through the operations in which blazers are worked on and then to finished goods in the usual manner. Costs are added throughout the fiscal year in the Conversion Costs Control account and the Conversion Costs Allocated account. Any overallocation or underallocation of conversion costs is disposed of in the same way as overallocated or underallocated manufacturing overhead in a job-costing system.

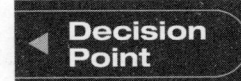

◄ Decision Point

What is an operation-costing system and when is it a better approach to product costing?

Problem for Self-Study

Allied Chemicals operates a thermo-assembly process as the second of three processes at its plastics plant. Direct materials in thermo-assembly are added at the end of the process. Conversion costs are added evenly during the process. The following data pertain to the Thermo-Assembly Department for June 2014:

	A	B	C	D	E
		Physical Units	Transferred-in Costs	Direct Materials	Conversion Costs
2	Work in process, beginning inventory	50,000			
3	Degree of completion of beginning work in process		100%	0%	80%
4	Transferred in during current period	2,00,000			
5	Completed and transferred out during current period	2,10,000			
6	Work in process, ending inventory	?			
7	Degree of completion of ending work in process		100%	0%	40%

File   Edit   View   Insert   Format   Tools   Data   Window   Help

Required   Compute equivalent units under (1) the weighted-average method and (2) the FIFO method.

Solution

1. The weighted-average method uses equivalent units of work done to date to compute cost per equivalent unit. The calculations of equivalent units follow:

	A	B	C	D	E
	File Edit View Insert Format Tools Data Window Help				
1		**(Step 1)**		**(Step 2)**	
2				**Equivalent Units**	
3	**Flow of Production**	**Physical Units**	**Transferred-in Costs**	**Direct Materials**	**Conversion Costs**
4	Work in process, beginning (given)	50,000			
5	Transferred in during current period (given)	2,00,000			
6	To account for	2,50,000			
7	Completed and transferred out during current period	2,10,000	2,10,000	2,10,000	2,10,000
8	Work in process, ending[a]	40,000[b]			
9	(40,000 x 100%; 40,000 x 0%; 40,000 x 40%)		40,000	0	16,000
10	Accounted for	2,50,000			
11	Work done to date		2,50,000	2,10,000	2,26,000
12					
13	[a]Degree of completion in this department: Transferred-in costs, 100%; direct materials, 0%; conversion costs, 40%.				
14	[b]2,50,000 physical units to account for minus 2,10,000 physical units completed and transferred out				

2. The FIFO method uses equivalent units of work done in the current period only to compute cost per equivalent unit. The calculations of equivalent units follow:

	A	B	C	D	E
	File Edit View Insert Format Tools Data Window Help				
1		**(Step 1)**		**(Step 2)**	
2				**Equivalent Units**	
3	**Flow of Production**	**Physical Units**	**Transferred-in Costs**	**Direct Materials**	**Conversion Costs**
4	Work in process, beginning (given)	50,000			
5	Transferred in during current period (given)	2,00,000			
6	To account for	2,50,000			
7	Completed and transferred out during current period:				
8	From beginning work in process[a]	50,000			
9	[50,000 x (100% – 100%); 50,000 x (100% – 0%); 50,000 x (100% – 80%)]		0	50,000	10,000
10	Started and completed	1,60,000[b]			
11	(1,60,000 x 100%; 1,60,000 x 100%; 1,60,000 x 100%)		1,60,000	1,60,000	1,60,000
12	Work in process, ending[c]	40,000[d]			
13	(40,000 x 100%; 40,000 x 0%; 40,000 x 40%)		40,000	0	16,000
14	Accounted for	2,50,000			
15	Work done in current period only		2,00,000	2,10,000	1,86,000
16					
17	[a]Degree of completion in this department: Transferred-in costs, 100%; direct materials, 0%; conversion costs, 80%.				
18	[b]2,10,000 physical units completed and transferred out minus 50,000 physical units completed and transferred out from beginning work-in-process inventory.				
19	[c]Degree of completion in this department: Transferred-in costs, 100%; direct materials, 0%; conversion costs, 40%.				
20	[d]2,50,000 physical units to account for minus 2,10,000 physical units completed and transferred out.				

Decision Points

The following question-and-answer format summarizes the chapter's learning objectives. Each decision presents a key question related to a learning objective. The guidelines are the answer to that question.

Decision	Guidelines
1. Under what conditions is a process-costing system used?	A process-costing system is used to determine cost of a product or service when masses of identical or similar units are produced. Industries using process-costing systems include the food, textiles, and oil-refining industries.
2. How are average unit costs computed when no inventories are present?	Average unit costs are computed by dividing the total costs in a given accounting period by the total units produced in that period.
3. What are the five steps in a process-costing system, and how are equivalent units calculated?	The five steps in a process-costing system are (1) summarize the flow of physical units of output, (2) compute the output in terms of equivalent units, (3) summarize the total costs to account for, (4) compute the cost per equivalent unit, and (5) assign the total costs to units completed and to units in ending work-in-process inventory.
	An equivalent unit is a derived measure of output that (a) takes the quantity of each input (factor of production) in units completed or in incomplete units in work in process and (b) converts the quantity of input into the amount of completed output units that could be made with that quantity of input.
4. What are the weighted-average and first-in, first-out (FIFO) methods of process costing? Under what conditions will they yield different levels of operating income?	The weighted-average method computes unit costs by dividing total costs in the Work in Process account by total equivalent units completed to date and assigns this average cost to units completed and to units in ending work-in-process inventory.
	The first-in, first-out (FIFO) method computes unit costs based on costs incurred during the current period and equivalent units of work done in the current period.
	Operating income can differ materially between the two methods when (1) direct material or conversion cost per equivalent unit varies significantly from period to period and (2) physical-inventory levels of work in process are large in relation to the total number of units transferred out of the process.
5. How are the weighted-average and FIFO process-costing methods applied to transferred-in costs?	The weighted-average method computes transferred-in costs per unit by dividing the total transferred-in costs to date by the total equivalent transferred-in units completed to date and assigns this average cost to units completed and to units in ending work-in-process inventory. The FIFO method computes the transferred-in costs per unit based on the costs transferred in during the current period and equivalent units of transferred-in costs of work done in the current period. The FIFO method assigns transferred-in costs in the beginning work-in-process inventory to units completed and costs transferred in during the current period first to complete the beginning inventory, next to start and complete new units, and finally to units in ending work-in-process inventory.
6. What is an operation-costing system, and when is it a better approach to product costing?	Operation costing is a hybrid-costing system that blends characteristics from both job-costing (for direct materials) and process-costing systems (for conversion costs). It is a better approach to product costing when production systems share some features of custom-order manufacturing and other features of mass-production manufacturing.

TERMS TO LEARN

The chapter and the Glossary at the end of the book contain definitions of the following important terms:

equivalent units **(p. 900)**
first-in, first-out (FIFO) process-
  costing method **(p. 908)**
hybrid-costing system **(p. 918)**

operation **(p. 918)**
operation-costing system **(p. 918)**
previous-department
  costs **(p. 913)**

transferred-in costs **(p. 913)**
weighted-average
  process-costing method
  (p. 905)

ASSIGNMENT MATERIAL

Questions

17-1 Give three examples of industries that use process-costing systems.

17-2 In process costing, why are costs often divided into two main classifications?

17-3 Explain equivalent units. Why are equivalent-unit calculations necessary in process costing?

17-4 What problems might arise in estimating the degree of completion of semiconductor chips in a semiconductor plant?

17-5 Name the five steps in process costing when equivalent units are computed.

17-6 Name the three inventory methods commonly associated with process costing.

17-7 Describe the distinctive characteristic of weighted-average computations in assigning costs to units completed and to units in ending work in process.

17-8 Describe the distinctive characteristic of FIFO computations in assigning costs to units completed and to units in ending work in process.

17-9 Why should the FIFO method be called a modified or department FIFO method?

17-10 Identify a major advantage of the FIFO method for purposes of planning and control.

17-11 Identify the main difference between journal entries in process costing and job costing.

17-12 "The standard-costing method is particularly applicable to process-costing situations." Do you agree? Why?

17-13 Why should the accountant distinguish between transferred-in costs and additional direct material costs for each subsequent department in a process-costing system?

17-14 "Transferred-in costs are those costs incurred in the preceding accounting period." Do you agree? Explain.

17-15 "There's no reason for me to get excited about the choice between the weighted-average and FIFO methods in my process-costing system. I have long-term contracts with my materials suppliers at fixed prices." Do you agree with this statement made by a plant controller? Explain.

Solved Examples

17-16 Equivalent units, zero beginning inventory. Indian Electronics manufactures microchips in large quantities. Each microchip undergoes assembly and testing. The total assembly costs during the typical month of January were:

Direct materials used	₹72,00,000
Conversion costs	76,00,000
Total manufacturing costs	₹1,48,00,000

1. Assume there was no beginning inventory on January 1. During January, 10,000 microchips were placed into production and all 10,000 were fully completed at the end of the month. What is the unit cost of an assembled microchip in January?
2. Assume that during February 10,000 microchips are placed into production. Further assume the same total assembly costs for January are also incurred in February, but only 9,000 microchips are fully completed at the end of the month. All direct materials have been added to the remaining 1,000 microchips. However, on average, these remaining 1,000 microchips are only 50% complete as to conversion costs. (a) What are the equivalent units for direct materials and conversion costs and their respective equivalent-unit costs for February? (b) What is the unit cost of an assembled microchip in the following month, February?
3. Explain the difference in your answers to requirements 1 and 2.

Solution

Equivalent units, zero beginning inventory.

1. Direct materials cost per unit (₹72,00,000 ÷ 10,000)   ₹720
    Conversion cost per unit (₹76,00,000 ÷ 10,000)   760
    Assembly Department cost per unit   ₹1,480

2. a. Solution Exhibit 17-16A calculates the equivalent units of direct materials and conversion costs in the Assembly Department of International Electronics in February. Solution Exhibit 17-16B computes equivalent units costs.

2. b. Direct materials cost per unit   ₹720
    Conversion cost per unit   800
    Assembly Department cost per unit   ₹1,520

3. The difference in the Assembly Department cost per unit calculated in requirements 1 and 2 arises because the costs incurred in January and February are the same but fewer equivalent units of work are done in February relative to January. In January, all 10,000 units introduced are fully completed resulting in 10,000 equivalent units of work done with respect to direct materials and conversion costs. In February, of the 10,000 units introduced, 10,000 equivalent units of work is done with respect to direct materials but only 9,500 equivalent units of work is done with respect to conversion costs. The Assembly Department cost per unit is, therefore, higher.

Solution Exhibit 17-16A

Steps 1 and 2: Summarize Output in Physical Units and Compute Equivalent units: Assembly Department of Indian Electronics for February:

Flow of Production	(Step 1) Physical Units	(Step 2) Equivalent Units Direct Materials	(Step 2) Equivalent Units Conversion Costs
Work in process, beginning	0		
Started during current period	10,000		
To account for	10,000		
Completed and transferred out during current period	9,000	9,000	9,000
Work in process, ending*	1,000		
1,000 × 100%; 1,000 × 50%		1,000	500
Accounted for	10,000		
Work done in current period only		10,000	9,500

*Degree of completion in this department: direct materials, 100%; conversion costs, 50%.

Solution Exhibit 17-16B

Compute Equivalent Unit Costs, Assembly Department of Indian Electronics for February:

		Total Production Costs	Direct Materials	Conversion Costs
Step 3	Costs added during February	₹1,48,00,000	₹72,00,000	₹76,00,000
	Divide by equivalent units of work done in current period (Solution Exhibit 17-I6A)		÷ 10,000	÷ 9,500
	Cost per equivalent unit		₹720	₹800

17-17 Journal entries (continuation of 17-16). Refer to requirement 2 of Example 17-16.

Required

Prepare summary journal entries for the use of direct materials and incurrence of conversion costs. Also prepare a journal entry to transfer out the cost of goods completed. Show the postings to the Work-in-Process account.

Solution

Journal entries (continuation of 17-16).

		₹	₹
1.	Work in Process—*Assembly*	72,00,000	
	Accounts Payable		72,00,000
	To record ₹72,00,000 of direct materials purchased and used in production during February		
2.	Work in Process—*Assembly*	76,00,000	
	Various accounts		76,00,000
	To record ₹76,00,000 of conversion costs for February; examples include energy, manufacturing supplies, all manufacturing labor, and plant depreciation		
3.	Work in Process—Testing	1,36,80,000	
	Work in Process—*Assembly*		1,36,80,000

To record 9,000 units completed and transferred from Assembly to Testing during February at ₹1,520 × 9,000 units = ₹1,36,80,000

Postings to the Work in Process—Assembly account follow.

Work in Process — Assembly Department			
Beginning inventory, Feb. 10		*3. Transferred out to*	
1. Direct materials	₹72,00,000	Work in Process—Testing	₹1,36,80,000
2. Conversion costs	76,00,000		
Ending inventory, Feb.	11,20,000		

17-18 Weighted-average method, equivalent units. Consider the following data for the Satellite Assembly Division of Aerospatiale:

The Satellite Assembly Division uses the weighted-average method of process costing.

	Physical Units (Satellites)	Direct Materials	Conversion Costs
Beginning work in process (May 1)[a]	8	₹49,33,600	₹9,10,400
Started in May	50		
Completed during May	46		
Continued			

	Physical Units (Satellites)	Direct Materials	Conversion Costs
Ending work in process (May 31)[b]	12		
Costs added during May		₹3,22,00,000	₹1,39,20,000

[a]Degree of completion: direct materials, 90%; conversion costs, 40%.
[b]Degree of completion: direct materials, 60%; conversion costs, 30%.

Required

Compute equivalent units for direct materials and conversion costs. Show physical units in the first column of your schedule.

Solution

Weighted-average method, equivalent units.

Under the weighted-average method, equivalent units are calculated as the equivalent units of work done to date. Solution Exhibit 17-18 shows equivalent units of work done to date for the Satellite Assembly Division of Aerospatiale for direct materials and conversion costs.

Solution Exhibit 17-18

Steps 1 and 2: Summarize Output in Physical Units and Compute Equivalent Units
Weighted-Average Method of Process Costing, Satellite Assembly Division of Aerospatiale for May:

Flow of Production	(Step 1) Physical Units (given)	(Step 2) Equivalent Units Direct Materials	Conversion Costs
Work in process beginning	8		
Started during current period	50		
To account for	58		
Completed and transferred out during current period	46	46.0	46.0
Work in process, ending*	12	7.2	3.6
(12 × 60%; 12 × 30%)			
Accounted for	58		
Work done to date		53.2	49.6

*Degree of completion in this department: direct materials, 60%; conversion costs, 30%.

Required

17-19 Weighted-average method, assigning costs (continuation of 17-18).
For the data in Solved example 17-18, calculate cost per equivalent unit for direct materials and conversion costs, summarize total costs to account for, and assign these costs to units completed and transferred out and to units in ending work in process.

Solution

Weighted-average method, assigning costs (continuation of 17-18).
Solution Exhibit 17-19 calculates cost per equivalent unit of work done to date in the Assembly Department of Aerospatiale, summarizes total costs to account for, and assigns costs to units completed and to units in ending work-in-process inventory.

Solution Exhibit 17-19

Steps 3, 4, and 5: Compute Equivalent Unit Costs, Summarize Total Costs to Account For, and Assign Costs to Units Completed and to Units in Ending Work in Process
Weighted-Average Method of Process Costing, Satellite Assembly Department of Aerospatiale for May:

		Total Production Costs	Direct Materials	Conversion Costs
(Step 3)	Work in process, beginning (given)	₹58,44,000	₹49,33,600	₹9,10,400
	Costs added in current period (given)	4,61,20,000	3,22,00,000	1,39,20,000
	Costs incurred to date		₹3,71,33,600	₹1,48,30,400
	Divide by equivalent units of work done to date (Solution Exhibit 17-18)		÷ 53.2	÷ 49.6
	Cost per equivalent unit of work done to date		₹6,98,000	₹2,99,000
(Step 4)	Total costs to account for	5,19,64,000		
(Step 5)	Assignment of costs:			
	Completed and transferred out (46 units)	4,58,62,000	(46* × ₹6,98,000) + (46* × ₹2,99,000)	
	Work in process, ending (12 units)			

Direct materials	50,25,600	$7.2^† \times ₹6,98,000$
Conversion costs	10,76,400	$3.6^† \times ₹2,99,000$
Total work in process	61,02,000	
Total costs accounted for	₹5,19,64,000	

*Equivalent units completed and transferred out from Solution Exhibit 17-18, Step 2.
†Equivalent units in work in process, ending from Solution Exhibit 17-18, Step 2.

17-20 FIFO method, equivalent units. Refer to the information in Solved example 17-18. Suppose the Satellite Assembly Division uses the FIFO method of process costing instead of the weighted-average method.

Required

Compute equivalent units for direct materials and conversion costs. Show physical units in the first column of your schedule.

Solution

FIFO method, equivalent units.

Under the FIFO method, equivalent units are calculated as the equivalent units of work done in the current period only. Solution Exhibit 17-20 shows equivalent units of work done in May in the Assembly Department of Aerospatiale for direct materials and conversion costs.

Solution Exhibit 17-20

Steps 1 and 2: Summarize Output in Physical Units and Compute Equivalent Units
FIFO Method of Process Costing, Satellite Assembly Division of Aerospatiale for May:

	(Step 1)	(Step 2) Equivalent Units	
Flow of Production	**Physical Units**	**Direct Materials**	**Conversion Costs**
Work in process, beginning (given)	8 (work done before current period)		
Started during current period (given)	50		
To account for	58		
Completed and transferred out during current period:			
From beginning work in process§ 8 (100% – 90%); 8 (100% – 40%)	8	0.8	4.8
Started and completed 38 100%, 38 100%	38†	38.0	38.0
Work in process, ending* (given) 12 60%; 12 30%	12	7.2	3.6
Accounted for	58		
Work done in current period only		46.0	46.4

§Degree of completion in this department: direct materials, 90%; conversion costs, 40%.
†46 physical units completed and transferred out minus 8 physical units completed and transferred out from beginning work-in-process inventory.
*Degree of completion in this department: direct materials, 60%; conversion costs, 30%.

Required

17-21 FIFO method, assigning costs (continuation of 17-20).

For the data in Example 17-18, use the FIFO method to calculate cost per equivalent unit for direct materials and conversion costs, summarize total costs to account for, and assign these costs to units completed and transferred out and to units in ending work in process.

Solution

FIFO method, assigning costs (continuation of 17-20).

Solution Exhibit 17-21 calculates cost per equivalent unit of work done in May in the Assembly Department of Aerospatiale, summarizes total costs to account for, and assigns costs to units completed and to units in ending work-in-process inventory.

Solution Exhibit 17-21

Steps 3, 4, and 5: Compute Equivalent Unit Costs, Summarize Total Costs to Account For, and Assign Costs to Units Completed and to Units in Ending Work in Process

FIFO Method of Process Costing, Satellite Assembly Division of Aerospatiale for May:

		Total Production Costs	Direct Materials	Conversion Costs
	Work in process beginning	₹58,44,000	(costs of work done before current period)	
	(₹49,33,600 ÷ ₹9,10,400)			
(Step 3)	Costs added in current period (given)	4,61,20,000	₹3,22,00,000	₹1,39,20,000
	Divide by equivalent units of work done in current period			
	(Solution Exhibit 17-21)		÷ 446	÷ 446.4
	Cost per equivalent unit of work done in current period		₹7,00,000	₹3,00,000
(Step 4)	Total costs to account for	₹5,19,64,000		
(Step 5)	Assignment of costs:			
	Completed and transferred out (46 units):			
	Work in process beginning (8 units)	₹58,44,000		
	Direct materials added in current period	5,60,000	0.8* × ₹7,00,000	
	Conversion costs added in current period	14,40,000		4.8* × ₹3,00,000
	Total from beginning inventory	78,44,000		
	Started and completed (38 units)	3,80,00,000	(38† × ₹7,00,000) +	(38† × ₹3,00,000)
	Total costs of units completed & transf. out	4,58,44,000		
	Work in process ending (12 units)			
	Direct materials	50,40,000	7.2# × ₹7,00,000	
	Conversion costs	10,80,000		3.6# × ₹3,00,000
	Total work in process ending	61,20,000		
	Total costs accounted for	₹5,19,64,000		

*Equivalent units used to complete beginning work in process from Solution Exhibit 17-20, Step 2.
†Equivalent units started and completed from Solution Exhibit 17-20, Step 2.
#Equivalent units in work in process, ending from Solution Exhibit 17-20, Step 2.

17-22 Operation costing. Everbake Bakery needs to determine the cost of two work orders for the month of June. Work order 215 is for 2,400 packages of dinner rolls, and work order 216 is for 2,800 loaves of multigrain bread. Dinner rolls are mixed and cut into individual rolls before being baked and then packaged. Multigrain loaves are mixed and shaped before being baked, sliced, and packaged. The following information applies to work order 215 and work order 216:

	Work Order 215	Work Order 216
Quantity (packages)	2,400	2,800
Operations		
1. Mix	Use	Use
2. Shape loaves	Do not use	Use
3. Cut rolls	Use	Do not use
4. Bake	Use	Use
5. Slice loaves	Do not use	Use
6. Package	Use	Use

Selected budget information for June follows:

	Dinner Rolls	Multigrain Loaves	Total
Packages	9,600	13,000	22,600
Direct material costs	₹52,800	₹1,17,000	₹1,69,800

Budgeted conversion costs for each operation for June follow:

Mixing	₹1,80,800
Shaping	32,500
Cutting	14,400
Baking	1,46,900
Slicing	13,000
Packaging	1,69,500

Required

1. Using budgeted number of packages as the denominator, calculate the budgeted conversion-cost rates for each operation.
2. Using the information in requirement 1, calculate the budgeted cost of goods manufactured for the two June work orders.
3. Calculate the cost per package of dinner rolls and multigrain loaves for work order 215 and 216.

Solution

1. To obtain the conversion-cost rates, divide the budgeted cost of each operation by the number of packages that are expected to go through that operation.

	Budgeted Conversion Cost	Budgeted Number of Packages	Conversion Cost per Package
Mixing	₹1,80,800	22,600	₹8.0
Shaping	32,500	13,000	2.5
Cutting	14,400	9,600	1.5
Baking	1,46,900	22,600	6.5
Slicing	13,000	13,000	1.0
Packaging	1,69,500	22,600	7.5

2.

	Work Order #215	Work Order #216
Bread type:	Dinner Roll	Multigrain Loaves
Quantity:	2,400	2,800
Direct Materials	₹13,200	₹25,200
Mixing	19,200	22,400
Shaping	0	7,000
Cutting	3,600	0
Baking	15,600	18,200
Slicing	0	2,800
Packaging	18,000	21,000
Total	₹69,600	₹96,600

The direct materials costs per unit vary based on the type of bread (₹52,800 ÷ 9,600 = ₹5.5 for the dinner rolls, and ₹1,17,000 ÷ 13,000 = ₹9.0 for the multigrain loaves). Conversion costs are charged using the rates computed in part (1), taking into account the specific operations that each type of bread actually goes through.

3.

Work order #215 (Dinner rolls):		Work order #216 (Multigrain loaves):	
Total cost	₹69,600	Total cost:	₹96,600
Divided by number of packages:	÷2,400	Divided by number of packages:	÷2,800
Cost per package of dinner rolls:	₹29	Cost per package of multigrain loaves:	₹34.55

17-23 Operation costing. Purex produces three different types of detergents: Breeze, Fresh, and Joy. The company uses four operations to manufacture the detergents: spray drying, mixing, blending, and packaging. Breeze and Fresh are produced in powder form in the mixing department, while Joy is produced in liquid form in the blending department. The powder detergents are packed in 50-ounce paperboard cartons, and the liquid detergent is packed in 50-ounce bottles made of recycled plastic.

Purex applies conversion costs based on labor-hours in the spray drying department. It takes 1½ minutes to mix the ingredients for a 50-ounce container for each product. Conversion costs are applied based on the number of containers in the mixing and blending departments and on the basis of machine-hours in the packaging department. It takes 0.3 minutes of machine time to fill a 50-ounce container, regardless of the product.

The budgeted number of containers and expected direct materials cost for each type of detergent are as follows:

	Breeze	Fresh	Joy
Number of 50-ounce containers	11,000	8,000	21,000
Direct materials cost	₹2,14,500	₹2,00,000	₹5,25,000

The budgeted conversion costs for each department for July are as follows:

Department	Budgeted Conversion Cost
Spray Drying	₹80,000
Mixing	2,28,000
Blending	3,04,500
Packaging	10,000

Required

1. Calculate the conversion cost rates for each department.
2. Calculate the budgeted cost of goods manufactured for Breeze, Fresh, and Joy for the month of July.
3. Calculate the cost per 50-ounce container for each type of detergent for the month of July.

Solution

1. Calculate the conversion cost rates for each department:

	Breeze	Fresh	Joy	Total
Budgeted 50-oz. containers	11,000	8,000	21,000	40,000
Budgeted labor hours	275[a]	200[c]	525[e]	1,000
Budgeted machine hours	55[b]	40[d]	105[f]	200

[a] 11,000 × 1.5 minutes ÷ 60 minutes/hour = 275 hours
[b] 11,000 × 0.3 minutes ÷ 60 minutes/hour = 55 hours
[c] 8,000 × 1.5 minutes ÷ 60 minutes/hour = 200 hours
[d] 8,000 × 0.3 minutes ÷ 60 minutes/hour = 40 hours
[e] 21,000 × 1.5 minutes ÷ 60 minutes/hour = 525 hours
[f] 21,000 × 0.3 minutes ÷ 60 minutes/hour = 105 hours

	Budgeted Conversion Cost	Cost Driver	Budgeted Quantity of Cost Driver	Conversion Cost Rate
Spray Drying	₹80,000	Labor hours	1,000	₹80 per labor hour
Mixing	2,28,000	# of containers	19,000	₹12 per container
Blending	3,04,500	# of containers	21,000	₹14.50 per container
Packaging	10,000	Machine hours	200	₹50.0 per machine hour

2. Budgeted cost of goods manufactured:

	Breeze	Fresh	Joy
Direct Materials	₹2,14,500	₹2,00,000	₹5,25,000
Spray Drying	22,000	16,000	42,000
Mixingh	1,32,000	96,000	0
Blending	0	0	3,04,500
Packaging	2,750	2,000	5,250
Total	₹3,71,250	₹3,14,000	₹8,76,750

g ₹80 per labor hour × (275; 200; 525 labor hours)
h ₹12 per container × (11,000; 8,000 containers)
i ₹50 per machine hour × (55; 40; 105 machine hours)

3. Budgeted cost per container

	Breeze	Fresh	Joy
Total budgeted costs	₹3,71,250	₹3,14,000	₹8,76,750
Number of containers	11,000	8,000	21,000
Budgeted cost per container	₹33.75	₹39.25	₹41.75

17-24 Equivalent units, comprehensive. Lovely Sports manufactures baseball bats for use by players in the major leagues. A critical requirement for elite players is that each bat they use have an identical look and feel. As a result, Lovely uses a dedicated process to produce bats to each player's specifications.

One of firm's key clients produces bats. Producing his bat involves the use of three materials—ash, cork, and ink—and a sequence of 20 standardized steps. Materials are added as follows:

Ash: This is the basic wood used in bats. Eighty percent of the ash content is added at the start of the process; the rest is added at the start of the 16th step of the process.

Cork: This is inserted into the bat in order to increase its bat speed. Half of the cork is introduced at the beginning of the seventh step of the process; the rest is added at the beginning of the 14th step.

Ink: This is used to stamp its name on the finished bat and is added at the end of the process.

Of the total conversion costs, 6% are added during each of the first 10 steps of the process, and 4% are added at each of the remaining 10 steps.

On May 1, 2016, Lovely sports had 100 bats in inventory. These bats had completed the ninth step of the process as of April 30, 2016. During May, Lovely sports put another 60 bats into production. At the end of May, Lovely sports was left with 40 bats that had completed the 12th step of the production process.

1. Under the weighted-average method of process costing, compute equivalent units of work done for each relevant input for the month of May.

2. Under the FIFO method of process costing, compute equivalent units of work done for each relevant input for the month of May.

Solution

1. Summarize the Flow of Physical Units and Compute Output in Equivalent Units; Weighted-Average Method of Process Costing, Lovely Sports for May 2016.

	(Step 1)	(Step 2) Equivalent Units			
Flow of Production	Physical Units	Ash	Cork	Ink	Conversion Costs
Work in process, beginning (given)	100				
Started during current period (given)	60				
To account for	160				
Completed and transferred out during current period	120	120	120	120	120
Work in process, ending* (given)	40				
40 × 80%; 50%; 0%; 68%		32	20	0	27.2
Accounted for	160				
Equivalent units of work done to date		152	140	120	147.2

*Degree of completion in this department: Step 12 of production process: Ash, 80%; Cork, 50%; Ink, 0%; Conversion costs, (6% × 10 steps) + (4% × 2 steps) = 68%.

2. Summarize the Flow of Physical Units and Compute Output in Equivalent Units; FIFO Method of Process Costing, Lovely Sports for May 2016.

	(Step 1)	(Step 2) Equivalent Units			
Flow of Production	Physical Units	Ash	Cork	Ink	Conversion Costs
Work in process, beginning (given)	100				
Started during current period (given)	60				
To account for	160				
Completed and transferred out during current period:					
From beginning work in process§	100				
100 × 20%; 50%; 100%; 46%		20	50	100	46
Started and completed†	20				
20 × 100%; 100%; 100%; 100%		20	20	20	20
Work in process, ending* (given)	40				
40 × 80%; 50%; 0%; 68%		32	20	0	27.2
Accounted for	160				
Equivalent units of work done in May		72	90	120	93.2

§ Degree of completion in this department: Step 9 of production process: Ash, 80%; Cork, 50%; Ink, 0%; conversion costs, 6% × 9 steps = 54%. The difference between 100% and these numbers represents the amount of work done to complete the beginning work in process in this period.

† 120 bats completed and transferred out minus 100 bats completed and transferred out from beginning work-in-process inventory.

* Degree of completion in this department: Step 12 of production process: Ash, 80%; Cork, 50%; Ink, 0%; conversion costs, (6% × 10 steps) + (4% × 2 steps) = 68%.

17-25 Transferred-in costs, weighted average. Pearson, Inc., has two departments: printing and binding. Each department has one direct-cost category (direct materials) and one indirect-cost category (conversion costs). This problem focuses on the binding department. Books that have undergone the printing process are immediately transferred to the binding department. Direct material is added when the binding process is 70% complete. Conversion costs are added evenly during binding operations. When those operations are done, the books are immediately transferred to Finished Goods. Pearson, Inc., uses the weighted-average method of process costing. The following is a summary of the April 2016 operations of the binding department.

	Home Insert Page Layout Formulas Data Review View				
	A	B	C	D	E
1		Physical Units (books)	Transferred-In Costs	Direct Materials	Conversion Costs
2	Beginning work in process	1,260	₹3,90,600	₹0	₹1,63,800
3	Degree of completion, beginning work in process		100%	0%	50%
4	Transferred in during April 2016	2,880			
5	Completed and transferred out during April	3,240			
6	Ending work in process (April 30)	900			
7	Degree of completion, ending work in process		100%	0%	70%
8	Total costs added during April		₹15,55,200	₹2,81,880	₹8,42,400

Required

1. Summarize total binding department costs for April 2016, and assign these costs to units completed (and transferred out) and to units in ending work in process.
2. Prepare journal entries for April transfers from the printing department to the binding department and from the binding department to Finished Goods.

Solution

1. Solution Exhibit 17-25A computes the equivalent units of work done to date in the Binding Department for transferred-in costs, direct materials, and conversion costs.

   Solution Exhibit 17-25B summarizes total Binding Department costs for April 2016, calculates the cost per equivalent unit of work done to date in the Binding Department for transferred-in costs, direct materials, and conversion costs, and assigns these costs to units completed and transferred out and to units in ending work in process using the weighted-average method.

2. Journal entries:

   a. Work in Process— Binding Department   15,55,200
         Work in Process—Printing Department   ₹15,55,200
      Cost of goods completed and transferred out
         during April from the Printing Department
         to the Binding Department

   b. Finished Goods   26,47,080
         Work in Process— Binding Department   26,47,080
      Cost of goods completed and transferred out
         during April from the Binding Department
         to Finished Goods inventory

Solution Exhibit 17-25A

Summarize the Flow of Physical Units and Compute Output in Equivalent Units; Weighted-Average Method of Process Costing, Binding Department of Pearson, Inc., for April 2016.

	(Step 1)	(Step 2) Equivalent Units		
Flow of Production	Physical Units	Transferred-in Costs	Direct Materials	Conversion Costs
Work in process, beginning (given)	1,260			
Transferred-in during current period (given)	2,880			
To account for	4,140			
Completed and transferred out during current period:	3,240	3,240	3,240	3,240
Work in process, endinga (given)	900			
(900 × 100%; 900 × 0%; 900 × 70%)		900	0	630
Accounted for	4,140			
Equivalent units of work done to date		4,140	3,240	3,870

aDegree of completion in this department: transferred-in costs, 100%; direct materials, 0%; conversion costs, 70%.

Solution Exhibit 17-25B

Summarize the Total Costs to Account for, Compute the Cost per Equivalent Unit, and Assign Costs to the Units Completed and Units in Ending Work-in-Process Inventory; Weighted-Average Method of Process Costing, Binding Department of Pearson, Inc., for April 2016.

		Total Production Costs	Transferred-in Costs	Direct Materials	Conversion Costs
(Step 3)	Work in process, beginning (given)	₹5,54,400	₹3,90,600	₹0	₹1,63,800
	Costs added in current period (given)	26,79,480	1 5,55,200	2,81,880	8,42,400
	Total costs to account for	₹32,33,880	₹19,45,800	₹2,81,880	₹10,06,200
(Step 4)	Costs incurred to date		₹19,45,800	₹2,81,880	₹10,06,200
	Divide by equivalent units of work done to date (Solution Exhibit 17-38A)		÷ 4,140	÷ 3,240	÷ 3,870
	Cost per equivalent unit of work done to date		₹470	₹87	₹260
(Step 5)	Assignment of costs:				
	Completed and transferred out (3,240 units)	₹26,47,080	(3,240a × ₹470) + (3,240a × ₹87) + (3,240a × ₹260)		
	Work in process, ending (900 units):	5,86,800	(900b × ₹470) + (0b × ₹87) + (630b × ₹260)		
	Total costs accounted for	₹32,33,880	₹19,45,800 + ₹2,81,880 + ₹10,06,200		

a Equivalent units completed and transferred out from Sol. Exhibit 17-25A, step 2.
b Equivalent units in ending work in process from Sol. Exhibit 17-25A, step 2.

17-26 Transferred-in costs, FIFO method (continuation of 17-25). Refer to the information in Problem 17-25. Suppose that Pearson, Inc., uses the FIFO method instead of the weighted-average method in all of its departments. The only changes to Problem 17-25 under the FIFO method are that total transferred-in costs of beginning work in process on April 1 are ₹4,41,000 (instead of ₹3,90,600) and that total transferred-in costs added during April are ₹14,97,600 (instead of ₹15,55,200).

1. Using the FIFO process-costing method, complete Problem 17-25.
2. If you did Problem 17-25, explain any difference between the cost of work completed and transferred out and the cost of ending work in process in the binding department under the weighted-average method and the FIFO method.

Solution

1. Solution Exhibit 17-26A calculates the equivalent units of work done in April 2016 in the Binding Department for transferred-in costs, direct materials, and conversion costs.

   Solution Exhibit 17-26B summarizes total Binding Department costs for April 2016, calculates the cost per equivalent unit of work done in April 2016 in the Binding Department for transferred-in costs, direct materials, and conversion costs, and assigns these costs to units completed and transferred out and to units in ending work in process using the FIFO method.

   Journal entries:
   a. Work in Process— Binding Department .... ₹14,97,600
         Work in Process—Printing Department .... ₹14,97,600
      Cost of goods completed and transferred out during April from the Printing Department to the Binding Department.
   b. Finished Goods 25,94,880
         Work in Process— Binding Department 25,94,880
      Cost of goods completed and transferred out during April from the Binding Department to Finished Goods inventory.

2. The equivalent units of work done in beginning inventory is as follows: Transferred-in costs, 1,260 × 100% = 1,260; direct materials, 1,260 × 0% = 0; and conversion costs, 1,260 × 50% = 630. The cost per equivalent unit of beginning inventory and of work done in the current period are

	Beginning Inventory	Work Done in Current Period
Transferred-in costs (weighted average)	₹310 (₹3,90,600 ÷ 1,260)	₹540 (₹15,55,200 ÷ 2,880)
Transferred-in costs (FIFO)	₹350 (₹4,41,000 ÷ 1,260)	₹520 (₹14,97,600 ÷ 2,880)
	—	₹87
Direct materials	₹260 (₹1,63,800 ÷ 630)	₹260
Conversion costs		

The following table summarizes the costs assigned to units completed and those still in process under the weighted-average and FIFO process-costing methods for the Binding Department.

	Weighted Average (Solution Exhibit 17-25B)	FIFO (Solution Exhibit 17-26B)	Difference
Cost of units completed and transferred out	₹26,47,080	₹25,94,880	–₹52,200
Work in process, ending	5,86,800	6,31,800	+₹45,000
Total costs accounted for	₹32,33,880	₹32,26,680	

The FIFO ending inventory is higher than the weighted-average ending inventory by ₹45,000. This is because FIFO assumes that all the lower-cost prior-period units in work in process (resulting from the lower transferred-in costs in beginning inventory) are the first to be completed and transferred out while ending work in process consists of only the higher-cost current-period units. The weighted-average method, however, smoothes out cost per equivalent unit by assuming that more of the higher-cost units are completed and transferred out, while some of the lower-cost units in beginning work in process are placed in ending work in process. Hence, in this case, the weighted-average method results in a higher cost of units completed and transferred out and a lower ending work-in-process inventory relative to FIFO. Note that the difference in cost of units completed and transferred out (−₹52,200) does not exactly offset the difference in ending work-in-process inventory (+₹45,000). This is because the FIFO and weighted-average methods result in different values for transferred-in costs with respect to both beginning inventory and costs transferred in during the period.

Solution Exhibit 17-26A

Summarize the Flow of Physical Units and Compute Output in Equivalent Units; FIFO Method of Process Costing, Binding Department of Pearson, Inc., for April 2016.

	(Step 1)	(Step 2) Equivalent Units		
Flow of Production	Physical Units	Transferred-in Costs	Direct Materials	Conversion Costs
Work in process, beginning (given)	1,260	(work done before current period)		
Transferred-in during current period (given)	2,880			
To account for	4,140			
Completed and transferred out during current period:				
From beginning work in process[a]	1,260			
[1,260 × (100% − 100%); 1,260 × (100% − 0%); 1,260 × (100% − 50%)]		0	1,260	630
Started and completed	1,980[b]			
(1,980 × 100%; 1,980 × 100%; 1,980 × 100%)		1,980	1,980	1,980
Work in process, ending[c] (given)	900			
(900 × 100%; 900 × 0%; 900 × 70%)		900	0	630
Accounted for	4,140			
Equivalent units of work done in current period		2,880	3,240	3,240

[a] Degree of completion in this department: Transferred-in costs, 100%; direct materials, 0%; conversion costs, 50%.

[b] 3,240 physical units completed and transferred out minus 1,260 physical units completed and transferred out from beginning work-in-process inventory.

[c] Degree of completion in this department: transferred-in costs, 100%; direct materials, 0%; conversion costs, 70%.

Solution Exhibit 17-26B

Summarize the Total Costs to Account for, Compute the Cost per Equivalent Unit, and Assign Costs to the Units Completed and Units in Ending Work-in-Process Inventory; FIFO Method of Process Costing, Binding Department of Pearson, Inc., for April 2016.

		Total Production Costs	Transferred-in Costs	Direct Materials	Conversion Costs
(Step 3)	Work in process, beginning (given)	₹6,04,800	₹4,41,000	₹0	₹1,63,800
	Costs added in current period (given)	26,21,880	14,97,600	2,81,880	8,42,400
	Total costs to account for	₹32,26,680	₹19,38,600	₹2,81,880	₹10,06,200
(Step 4)	Costs added in current period		₹14,97,600	₹2,81,880	₹8,42,400
	Divide by equivalent units of work done in current period (Sol. Exhibit 17-39A)		÷2,880	÷3,240	÷3,240
	Cost per equivalent unit of work done in current period		₹520	₹87	₹260
(Step 5)	Assignment of costs:				
	Completed and transferred out (3,240 units)				
	Work in process, beginning (1,260 units)	₹6,04,800	₹4,41,000 + ₹0 + ₹1,63,800		
	Costs added to beginning work in process in current period	2,73,420	$(0^a \times ₹520) + (1,260^a \times ₹87) + (630^a \times ₹260)$		
	Total from beginning inventory	8,78,220			
	Started and completed (1,980 units)	17,16,660	$(1,980^b \times ₹520) + (1,980^b \times ₹87) + (1,980^b \times ₹260)$		
	Total costs of units completed and transferred out	25,94,880			
	Work in process, ending (900 units):	6,31,800	$(900^c \times ₹520) + (0^c \times ₹87) + (630^c \times ₹260)$		
	Total costs accounted for	₹32,26,680	₹19,38,600	+ ₹2,81,880	+ ₹10,06,200

[a] Equivalent units used to complete beginning work in process from Solution Exhibit 17-26A, step 2.
[b] Equivalent units started and completed from Solution Exhibit 17-26A, step 2.
[c] Equivalent units in ending work in process from Solution Exhibit 17-26A, step 2.

17-27 Standard-costing method. Hi-sense Technologies produces stripped-down phones for sale to customers in frontier economies. The firm purchases used or obsolete models of specific smartphone models. It removes nonstandard applications, installs open source Android software, and unlocks the phone so it can operate on GSM networks. Hi-sense's most popular offering is the iZoom phone.

Given the importance of scaling and cost control for the success of its business model, Hi-sense uses a standard-costing system. The following information is available for the second quarter of 2016 (April 1–June 30):

Physical and Equivalent Units for iZoom
For the Second Quarter of 2016

	Physical Units	Equivalent Units	
		Direct Materials	Conversion Costs
Completion of beginning work in process	11,58,000	—	5,21,100
Started and completed	10,14,000	10,14,000	10,14,000
Work on ending work in process	21,80,400	21,80,400	13,08,240
Units to account for	43,52,400	31,94,400	28,43,340

	Costs
Cost of units completed from beginning work in process	₹92,06,10,000
Cost of new units started and Completed	80,61,30,000
Cost of units completed in the second quarter	1,72,67,40,000
Cost of ending work in process	1,46,30,48,400
Total costs accounted counted for	₹3,18,97,88,400

Required

1. What are the completion percentages of iZoom phones in beginning work-in-process inventory with respect to the two inputs?
2. What are the completion percentages of iZoom phones in ending work-in-process inventory with respect to the two inputs?
3. What are the standard costs per unit for direct materials and conversion costs?
4. What is the total cost of work-in-process inventory as of April 1, 2016 (the start of the second quarter)?

Solution

1. Because there was no additional work needed on the beginning inventory with respect to materials, the phones in inventory must have been 100% complete with respect to materials. For conversion costs, the work done to complete the opening inventory was 5,21,100 ÷ 11,58,000 = 45%. Therefore, the unfinished phones in opening inventory must have been 55% complete with respect to conversion costs.

2. It is clear that the ending WIP is also 100% complete with respect to direct materials (21,80,400 ÷ 21,80,400), and it is 60% (13,08,240 ÷ 21,80,400) complete with regard to conversion costs.

3. We can first obtain the total standard costs per unit. The number of units started and completed during August is 10,14,000, and a total cost of ₹80,61,30,000 is attached to them. The per unit standard cost is therefore (₹80,61,30,000 ÷ 10,14,000) = ₹795. If x and y represent the per unit cost for direct materials and conversion costs, respectively, we know that:

$$x + y = 795$$

We also know that the ending inventory is costed at ₹1,46,30,48,400 and contains 21,80,400 equivalent units of materials and 13,08,240 equivalent units of conversion costs. This provides a second equation:

$$21,80,400\, x + 13,08,240\, y = 1,46,30,48,400.$$

Solving these two equations reveals that the direct materials cost per unit, x, is ₹485, while the conversion cost per unit, y, is ₹310.

4. The opening WIP inventory contained 1,158,000 equivalent units of materials and (11,58,000 − 5,21,100) = 6,36,900 equivalent units of conversion costs. Applying the standard costs computed in step (3), the cost of the opening inventory must have been:

$$(11,58,000 \times ₹485) + (6,36,900 \times ₹310) = ₹75,90,69,000$$

17-28 Operation costing, equivalent units. (CMA, adapted) Supreme Industries manufactures plastic molded chairs. The three models of molded chairs, all variations of the same design, are Standard, Deluxe, and Executive. The company uses an operation-costing system.

Supreme has extrusion, form, trim, and finish operations. Plastic sheets are produced by the extrusion operation. During the forming operation, the plastic sheets are molded into chair seats and the legs are added. The Standard model is sold after this operation. During the trim operation, the arms are added to the Deluxe and Executive models and the chair edges are smoothed. Only the Executive model enters the finish operation, in which padding is added. All of the units produced receive the same steps within each operation.

The May units of production and direct materials costs incurred are as follows:

	Units Produced	Extrusion Materials	Form Materials	Trim Materials	Finish Materials
Standard model	6,000	₹7,20,000	₹2,40,000	₹0	₹0
Deluxe model	3,000	3,60,000	1,20,000	90,000	0
Executive model	2,000	2,40,000	80,000	60,000	1,20,000
	11,000	₹13,20,000	₹4,40,000	₹1,50,000	₹1,20,000

The total conversion costs for the month of May are:

	Extrusion Operation	Form Operation	Trim Operation	Finish Operation
Total conversion costs	₹26,95,000	₹13,20,000	₹6,90,000	₹4,20,000

Required

1. For each product produced by Supreme Industries during May, determine (a) the unit cost and (b) the total cost. Support your answer with appropriate calculations.
2. Now consider the following information for June. All unit costs in June are identical to the May unit costs calculated in 1(a). At the end of June, 1,000 units of the Deluxe model remained in work in process. These units were 100% complete as to materials costs and 60% complete in the trim operation. Determine the cost of the Deluxe model work-in-process inventory at the end of June.

Solution

Operation costing, equivalent units.

1. Materials and conversion costs of each operation, the total units produced, and the material and conversion cost per unit for the month of May are as follows:

	Extrusion	Form	Trim	Finish
1. Units produced	11,000	11,000	5,000	2,000
2. Materials costs	₹13,20,000	₹4,40,000	₹1,50,000	₹1,20,000
3. Materials cost per unit (2 ÷ 1)	120	40	30	60
4. Conversion costs	26,95,000	13,20,000	6,90,000	4,20,000
5. Conversion cost per unit (4 ÷ 1)	245	120	138	210

The unit cost and total costs in May for each product are as follows:

Cost Elements	Standard Model	Deluxe Model	Executive Model
Extrusion materials	₹120	₹120	₹120
Form materials	40	40	40
Trim materials	—	30	30
Finish materials	—	—	60
Extrusion conversion	245	245	245
Form conversion	120	120	120
Trim conversion	—	138	138
Finish conversion	—	—	210
Total unit cost	₹525	₹693	₹963
Multiply by units produced	× 6,000	× 3,000	× 2,000
Total product costs	₹31,50,000	₹20,79,000	₹19,26,000

2.

	Unit Cost	Equivalent Units	Total Costs
Deluxe model work-in process costs at the trim operation			
Extrusion material (100% complete when transferred in)	₹120	1,000	₹1,20,000
Extrusion conversion (100% complete when transferred in)	245	1,000	2,45,000
Form material (100% complete when transferred in)	40	1,000	40,000
Form conversion (100% complete when transferred in)	120	1,000	1,20,000
Trim material (100% complete)	30	1,000	30,000
Trim conversion (60% complete)	138	600*	82,800
Work-in-process costs			₹6,37,800

*1,000 units × 60% complete

Exercises

[Comprehensive solutions to all exercises are available on the companion website www. pearsoned.co.in/charlesthorngren]

17-29 Zero beginning inventory, materials introduced in middle of process. Vaasa Chemicals has a Mixing Department and a Refining Department. Its process-costing system in the Mixing Department has two direct materials cost categories (Chemical P and Chemical Q) and one conversion costs pool. The following data pertain to the Mixing Department for July of the current year:

Units	
Work in process, July 1	0
Units started	50,000
Completed and transferred to Refining Department	35,000
Costs	
Chemical P	₹25,00,000
Chemical Q	7,00,000
Conversion costs	13,50,000

Chemical P is introduced at the start of operations in the Mixing Department, and chemical Q is added when the product is three-fourths completed in the Mixing Department. Conversion costs are added evenly during the process. The ending work in process in the Mixing Department is two-thirds complete.

Required

1. Compute the equivalent units in the Mixing Department for July for each cost category.
2. Compute (a) the cost of goods completed and transferred to the Refining Department during July and (b) the cost of work in process as of July 31.

17-30 Weighted-average method, assigning costs. The Asian Chemicals Company makes a water-treatment chemical in a single processing department. Direct materials are added at the start of the process. Conversion costs are added evenly during the process. Asian Chemicals uses the weighted-average method of process costing. The following information for July related to current year is available:

		Equivalent Units	
	Physical Units	Direct Materials	Conversion Costs
Work in process, July 1	10,000[a]	10,000	7,000
Started during July	40,000		
Completed and transferred out during July	34,000	34,000	34,000
Work in process, July 31	16,000[b]	16,000	8,000

[a]Degree of completion: direct materials, 100%; conversion costs, 70%.
[b]Degree of completion: direct materials, 100%; conversion costs, 50%.

Total Costs for July	
Work in process, beginning	
Direct materials	₹6,00,000

Conversion costs	7,00,000	₹13,00,000
Direct materials added during July		28,00,000
Conversion costs added during July		37,10,000
Total costs to account for		₹78,10,000

Required

1. Calculate cost per equivalent unit for direct materials and conversion costs.
2. Summarize total costs to account for, and assign these costs to units completed (and transferred out) and to units in ending work in process.

17-31 FIFO method, assigning costs.

Required

Do Exercise 17-30 using the FIFO method. Note that you first need to calculate the equivalent units of work done in the current period (for direct materials and conversion costs) to complete beginning work-in process, to start and complete new units, and to produce ending work in process.

17-32 Standard-costing method, assigning costs. Refer to the information in Exercise 17-30. Suppose Asian Chemicals determines standard costs of ₹65 per equivalent unit for direct materials and ₹103 per equivalent unit for conversion costs for both beginning work in process and work done in the current period.

Required

1. Do Exercise 17-30 using the standard-costing method. Note that you first need to calculate the equivalent units of work done in the current period (for direct materials and conversion costs) to complete beginning work in process, to start and complete new units, and to produce ending work in process.
2. Compute the total direct materials and conversion costs variances for July.

17-33 Operation Costing. Feather Light Shoe Company manufactures two styles of men's shoes: Designer and Regular. Designer style is made from leather, and Regular style uses synthetic materials. Three operations—cutting, sewing and packing—are common to both styles, but only Designer style passes through a lining operation. The conversion cost rates for 2015 are:

	Cutting	Sewing	Lining	Packing
Rate per unit (pair)	₹100	₹150	₹80	₹20

Details of two work orders processed in August are:

	Work Order 815	Work Order 831
Number of units (pairs)	1,000	5,000
Direct materials costs	₹3,00,000	₹5,00,000
Style	Designer	Regular

Required

Calculate the total costs and the total cost per unit of work order 815 and work order 831.

17-34 Weighted-average method. Indian Defence, Limited is a manufacturer of military equipment. Its Orissa plant manufactures the Interceptor Missile under contract to the U.S. government and friendly countries. All Interceptors go through an identical manufacturing process. Every effort is made to ensure that all Interceptors are identical and meet many demanding performance specifications. The process-costing system at the Orissa plant has a single direct-cost category (direct materials) and a single indirect-cost category (conversion costs). Each Interceptor passes through two departments: the Assembly Department and the Testing Department. Direct materials are added at the beginning of the process in Assembly. Conversion costs are added evenly during the Assembly Department's process. When the Assembly Department finishes work on each Interceptor, it is immediately transferred to Testing.

Indian Defence uses the weighted-average method of process costing. Data for the Assembly Department for October of the recent year are:

	Physical Units (Missiles)	Direct Materials	Conversion Costs
Work in process, October 1[a]	20	₹46,00,000	₹12,00,000
Started during October	80		
Completed during October	90		

Work in process, October 31[b]	10		
Costs added during October		₹2,00,00,000	₹93,50,000

[a]Degree of completion: direct materials, ?%; conversion costs, 60%.
[b]Degree of completion: direct materials, ?%; conversion costs, 70%.

Required

1. For each cost element, compute equivalent units in the Assembly Department. Show physical units in the first column of your schedule.
2. For each cost element, calculate costs per equivalent unit.
3. Summarize total Assembly Department costs for October and assign these costs to units completed and transferred out and to units in ending work in process.

17-35 Journal entries (continuation of 17-34).

Required

Prepare a set of summarized journal entries for all October transactions affecting Work in Process– Assembly. Set up a T-account for Work in Process –Assembly, and post your entries to it.

17-36 FIFO method (continuation of 17-34 and 17-35).

Required

Do Exercise 17-37 using the FIFO method of process costing. Explain any difference between the costs per equivalent unit in the Assembly Department under the weighted-average method and the FIFO method.

17-37 Transferred-in costs, weighted average method (related to 17-34 to 17-36). Indian Defence, Limited, as you know, manufactures the Interceptor Missile at its Orissa plant. It has two departments: Assembly Department and Testing Department. This problem focuses on the Testing Department. (Problems 17-34 to 17-36 focused on the Assembly Department.) Direct materials are added when the Testing Department process is 90% complete. Conversion costs are added evenly during the Testing Department's process. As work in Assembly is completed, each unit is immediately transferred to Testing. As each unit is completed in Testing, it is immediately transferred to Finished Goods.

Indian Defence uses the weighted-average method of process costing. Data for the Testing Department for October are

	Physical Units (Missiles)	Transferred-In Costs	Direct Materials	Conversion Costs
Work in process October 1[a]	30	₹98,58,000	₹0	₹33,18,000
Transferred-in during October	?			
Completed during October	105			
Work in process October 31[b]	15			
Costs added during October		₹3,19,28,660	₹3,88,50,000	₹1,58,10,000

[a]Degree of completion: transferred-in costs, ?%; direct materials, ?%; conversion costs, 70%.
[b]Degree of completion: transferred-in costs, ?%; direct materials, ?%; conversion costs, 60%.

Required

1. What is the percentage of completion for (a) transferred-in costs and direct materials in beginning work-in-process inventory, and (b) transferred-in costs and direct materials in ending work-in-process inventory?
2. For each cost category, compute equivalent units in the Testing Department. Show physical units in the first column of your schedule.
3. For each cost category, calculate the cost per equivalent unit, summarize total Testing Department costs for October, and assign these costs to units completed (and transferred out) and to units in ending work in process.
4. Prepare journal entries for October transfers from the Assembly Department to the Testing Department and from the Testing Department to Finished Goods.

17-38 Transferred-in costs, FIFO method (continuation of 17-37).

Required

Using the FIFO process-costing method, do the requirements of Exercise 17-37. Under the FIFO method, the transferred-in costs for the beginning work in process in the Testing Department on October 1 are ₹98,00,600, and costs transferred in during October to the Testing Department are ₹3,18,80,000. All other data are unchanged.

17-39 Transferred-in costs, weighted-average and FIFO methods. Frito-Lay, Limited manufactures convenience foods, including potato chips and corn chips. Production of corn chips occurs in four departments: cleaning, mixing, cooking, and drying and packaging. Consider the Drying and Packaging Department, where direct materials (packaging) are added at the end of the process. Conversion costs are added evenly during the process. The accounting records of a Frito-Lay plant provides the following information for corn chips in its Drying and Packaging Department during a weekly period (week 37):

	Physical Units (Cases)	Transferred-In Costs	Direct Materials	Conversion Costs
Beginning work in process[a]	1,250	₹29,000	₹0	₹9,060
Transferred-in during week 37 from Cooking Department	5,000			
Completed during week 37	5,250			
Ending work in process, week 37[b]	1,000			
Costs added during week 37		₹96,000	₹25,200	₹38,400

[a]Degree of completion: transferred-in costs, 100%; direct materials, ?%; conversion costs, 80%.
[b]Degree of completion: transferred-in costs, 100%; direct materials, ?%; conversion costs, 40%.

Required

1. Using the weighted-average method, summarize the total Drying and Packaging Department costs for week 37, and assign these costs to units completed (and transferred out) and to units in ending work in process.
2. Assume that the FIFO method is used for the Drying and Packaging Department. Under FIFO, the transferred-in costs for work-in-process beginning inventory in week 37 are ₹28,920, and the transferred-in costs during week 37 from the Cooking Department are ₹94,000. All other data are unchanged. Summarize the total Drying and Packaging Department costs for week 37, and assign these costs to units completed and transferred out and to units in ending work in process using the FIFO method.

17-40 Standard costing with beginning and ending work in process. The Agrotech Food Limited uses the standard-costing method for its process-costing system. Standard costs for the Cooking Process are ₹60 per equivalent unit for direct materials and ₹30 per equivalent unit for conversion costs. All direct materials are introduced at the beginning of the process, and conversion costs are added evenly during the process. The operating summary for the month of May include the following data for the Cooking Process:

Work-in-process inventories:
    May 1, 3,000 units[a]
      (direct materials, ₹18,000; conversion costs, ₹54,000)
    May 31, 5,000 units[b]
    Units started in May, 20,000
Units completed and transferred out of cooking in May: 18,000
Additional actual costs incurred for cooking during May:
    Direct materials, ₹12,50,000
    Conversion costs, ₹5,70,000

[a]Degree of completion: direct materials, 100%; conversion costs, 60%.
[b]Degree of completion: direct materials, 100%; conversion costs, 50%.

Required

1. Compute the total standard costs of units transferred out in May and the total standard costs of the May 31 inventory of work in process.
2. Compute the total May variances for direct materials and conversion costs.

17-41 Transferred-in costs, equivalent-unit costs, working backward. Nilkamal Plastics has two processes: extrusion and thermo-assembly. Consider the June data for physical units in the thermo-assembly process: beginning work in process, 15,000 units; transferred in from the

Extruding Department during June, 9,000; ending work in process, 5,000. Direct materials are added when the process in the Thermo-assembly Department is 80% complete. Conversion costs are added evenly during the process. Nilkamal Plastics uses the FIFO method of process costing. The following information is available:

	Transferred-In Costs	Direct Materials	Conversion Costs
Beginning work in process	₹9,00,000	–	₹4,50,000
Percentage completion of beginning work in process	100%	–	60%
Costs added in current period	₹5,85,000	₹5,70,000	₹5,72,000
Cost per equivalent unit of work done in current period	₹65	₹30	₹52

Required

1. For each cost category, compute equivalent units of work done in the current period.
2. For each cost category, compute separately the equivalent units of work done to complete beginning work-in-process inventory, to start and complete new units, and to produce ending work in process.
3. For each cost category, calculate the percentage of completion of ending work-in-process inventory.
4. Summarize total costs to account for, and assign these costs to units completed (and transferred out) and to units in ending work in process.

18 Spoilage, Rework, and Scrap

Learning Objectives ▼

1. Understand the definitions of spoilage, rework, and scrap

2. Identify the differences between normal and abnormal spoilage

3. Account for spoilage in process costing using the weighted-average method and the first-in, first-out (FIFO) method

4. Account for spoilage at various stages of completion in process costing

5. Account for spoilage in job costing

6. Account for rework in job costing

7. Account for scrap

Learning Objective 1

Understand the definitions of spoilage,

. . . unacceptable units of production

rework,

. . . unacceptable units of production subsequently repaired

and scrap

. . . leftover material

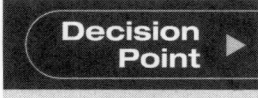

Decision Point ▶

What are spoilage, rework, and scrap?

When a product doesn't meet specification but is subsequently repaired and sold, it is called rework.

Firms try to minimize rework, as well as spoilage and scrap, during production. Why? Because higher-than-normal levels of spoilage and scrap can have a significant negative effect on a company's profits. Rework can also cause substantial production delays.

Defining Spoilage, Rework and Scrap

The following terms used in this chapter may seem familiar to you, but be sure you understand them in the context of management accounting.

Spoilage refers to units of production—whether fully or partially completed—that do not meet the specifications required by customers for good units and that are discarded or sold at reduced prices. Some examples of spoilage are defective shirts, jeans, shoes, and carpeting sold as "seconds," or defective aluminum cans sold to aluminum manufacturers for remelting to produce other aluminum products.

Rework refers to units of production that do not meet the specifications required by customers but which are subsequently repaired and sold as good finished units. For example, defective units of products (such as pagers, computers, and telephones) detected during or after the production process but before units are shipped to customers can sometimes be reworked and sold as good products.

Scrap is residual material that results from manufacturing a product. Examples are short lengths from woodworking operations, edges from plastic molding operations, and frayed cloth and end cuts from suit-making operations. Scrap can sometimes be sold for relatively small amounts. In that sense, scrap is similar to byproducts, which we studied in Chapter 16. The difference is that scrap arises as a residual from the manufacturing process, and is not a product targeted for manufacture or sale by the firm.

A certain amount of spoilage, rework, or scrap are inherent in many production processes. For example, semiconductor manufacturing is so complex and delicate that some spoiled units are inevitable due to dust adhering to wafers in the wafer production process and crystal defects in the silicon substrate. Usually, the spoiled units cannot be reworked. In the manufacture of high-precision machine tools, spoiled units can be reworked to meet standards, but only at a considerable cost. And in the mining industry, companies process ore that contains varying amounts of valuable metals and rock. Some amount of rock, which is scrap, is inevitable.

Two Types of Spoilage

Accounting for spoilage includes determining the magnitude of spoilage costs and distinguishing between the costs of normal and abnormal spoilage.[1] To manage, control, and reduce spoilage costs, companies need to highlight them, not bury them as an unidentified part of the costs of good units manufactured.

To illustrate normal and abnormal spoilage, consider Mendonza Plastics, which uses plastic injection molding to make casings for the iMac computer. In January 2014, Mendonza incurs costs of ₹3,07,50,000 to produce 20,500 units. Of these 20,500 units, 20,000 are good units and 500 are spoiled units. Mendonza has no beginning inventory and no ending inventory that month. Of the 500 spoiled units, 400 units are spoiled because the injection molding machines are unable to manufacture good casings 100% of the time. That is, these units are spoiled even though the machines were run carefully and efficiently. The remaining 100 units are spoiled because of machine breakdowns and operator errors.

Learning Objective 2

Identify the differences between normal spoilage

. . . spoilage inherent in an efficient production process

and abnormal spoilage

. . . spoilage that would not arise under efficient operation

Normal Spoilage

Normal spoilage is spoilage inherent in a particular production process. In particular, it arises even when the process is operated in an efficient manner. The costs of normal spoilage are typically included as a component of the costs of good units manufactured because good units cannot be made without also making some defective units. For this reason, normal spoilage costs are inventoried, that is, they are included in the cost of the good units completed. The following calculations show how Mendoza Plastics accounts for the cost of the 400 units normal spoilage:

Manufacturing cost per unit, ₹3,07,50,000 ÷ 20,500 units = ₹1,500

Manufacturing costs of good units alone, ₹1,500 per unit × 20,000 units	₹3,00,00,000
Normal spoilage costs, ₹1,500 per unit × 400 units	6,00,000
Manufacturing costs of good units completed (includes normal spoilage)	₹3,06,00,000

$$\text{Manufacturing cost per goods unit} = \frac{₹3,06,00,000}{20,000 \text{ units}} = ₹1,530$$

Normal spoilage rates are computed by dividing the units of normal spoilage by total *good units completed*, not total *actual units started* in production. At Mendoza Plastics, the normal spoilage rate is therefore computed as 400 ÷ 20,000 = 2%. There is a tradeoff between the speed of production and the normal spoilage rate. Managers make a conscious decision about how many units to produce per hour with the understanding that, at the chosen rate, a certain level of spoilage is unavoidable.

Abnormal Spoilage

Abnormal spoilage is spoilage that is not inherent in a particular production process and would not arise under efficient operating conditions. At Mendonza, the 100 units spoiled due to machine breakdowns and operator errors are abnormal spoilage. (If Mendoza had set 100% good units as its goal, then all 500 units of spoilage would be considered abnormal.)

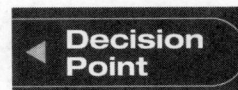

◄ **Decision Point**

What is the distinction between normal and abnormal spoilage?

---

[1] The helpful suggestions of Samuel Laimon, University of Saskatchewan, are gratefully acknowledged.

Abnormal spoilage is usually regarded as avoidable and controllable. Line operators and other plant personnel generally can decrease or eliminate abnormal spoilage by identifying the reasons for machine breakdowns, operator errors, and so forth, and by taking steps to prevent their recurrence. To highlight the effect of abnormal spoilage costs, companies calculate the units of abnormal spoilage and record the cost in the Loss from Abnormal Spoilage account, which appears as a separate line item in the income statement. That is, unlike normal spoilage, the costs of abnormal spoilage are not considered inventoriable and are written off as a period expense. At Mendonza, the loss from abnormal spoilage is ₹1,50,000 (₹1,500 per unit × 100 units).

Issues about accounting for spoilage arise in both process-costing and job-costing systems. We discuss both instances next, beginning with spoilage when process-costing is used.

Spoilage in Process Costing Using Weighted-Average and FIFO

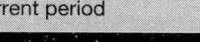

Learning Objective 3

Account for spoilage in process costing using the weighted-average method

. . . spoilage cost based on total costs and equivalent units completed to date

and the first-in, first-out (FIFO) method

. . . spoilage cost based on costs of current period and equivalent units of work done in current period

How do process-costing systems account for spoiled units? We have already said that units of abnormal spoilage should be counted and recorded separately in a Loss from Abnormal Spoilage account. But what about units of normal spoilage? The correct method is to count these units when computing both physical and equivalent output units in a process-costing system. The following example and discussion illustrate this approach.

Count All Spoilage

Example 1: Chipmakers, Ltd., manufactures computer chips for television sets. All direct materials are added at the beginning of the production process. To highlight issues that arise with normal spoilage, we assume there's no beginning inventory and focus only on direct material costs. The following data are for May 2014.

	A	B	C
	File Edit View Insert Format Tools Data Window Help		
1		**Physical Units**	**Direct Materials**
2	Work in process, beginning inventory (May 1)	0	
3	Started during May	10,000	
4	Good units completed and transferred out during May	5,000	
5	Units spoiled (all normal spoilage)	1,000	
6	Work in process, ending inventory (May 31)	4,000	
7	Degree of completion of ending work in process		100%
8	Direct material costs added in May		₹27,00,000

Spoilage is detected upon completion of the process and has zero net disposal value.

An **inspection point** is the stage of the production process at which products are examined to determine whether they are acceptable or unacceptable units. Spoilage is typically assumed to occur at the stage of completion where inspection takes place. As a result, the spoiled units in our example are assumed to be 100% complete for direct materials.

	A	B
1		**Approach Counting Spoiled Units When Computing Output in Equivalent Units**
2	Costs to account for	₹27,00,000
3	Divide by equivalent units of output	÷ 10,000
4	Cost per equivalent unit of output	₹270
5	Assignment of costs:	
6	Good units completed (5,000 units x ₹270 per unit)	₹13,50,000
7	Add normal spoilage (1,000 units x ₹270 per unit)	2,70,000
8	Total costs of good units completed and transferred out	16,20,000
9	Work in process, ending (4,000 units x ₹270 per unit)	10,80,000
10	Costs accounted for	₹27,00,000

Exhibit 18-1

Effect of Recognizing Equivalent Units in Spoilage for Direct Material Costs Chipmakers, Ltd., for May 2014

Exhibit 18-1 calculates and assigns cost per unit of direct materials used to produce both good units and units of normal spoilage. Overall, Chipmakers generated 10,000 equivalent units of output: 5,000 equivalent units in good units completed (5,000 physical units × 100%), 4,000 units in ending work in process (4,000 physical units × 100%), and 1,000 equivalent units in normal spoilage (1,000 physical units × 100%). Given total direct material costs of ₹27,00,000 in May, this yields an equivalent-unit cost of ₹270. The total cost of good units completed and transferred out, which includes the cost of normal spoilage, is then ₹16,20,000 (6,000 equivalent units × ₹270), The ending work in process is assigned a cost of ₹10,80,000 (4,000 equivalent units × ₹270).

Notice that the 4,000 units in ending work in process are not assigned any of the costs of normal spoilage because they have not yet been inspected. Undoubtedly some of the units in ending work in process will be found to be spoiled after they are completed and inspected in the next accounting period. At that time, their costs will be assigned to the good units completed in that period. Notice too that Exhibit 18-1 delineates the cost of normal spoilage as ₹2,70,000. By highlighting the magnitude of this cost, the approach helps to focus management's attention on the potential economic benefits of reducing spoilage.

Five-Step Procedure for Process Costing with Spoilage

Example 2: Anzio Company manufactures a recycling container in its Forming Department. Direct materials are added at the beginning of the production process. Conversion costs are added evenly during the production process. Some units of this product are spoiled as a result of defects, which are detectable only upon inspection of finished units. Normally, spoiled units are 10% of the finished output of good units. That is, for every 10 good units produced, there is 1 unit of normal spoilage. Summary data for July 2014 are as follows:

We can slightly modify the five-step procedure for process costing used in Chapter 17 to include the costs of Anzio Company's spoilage.

Step 1: Summarize the Flow of Physical Units. Identify the number of units of both normal and abnormal spoilage.

	File Edit View Insert Format Tools Data Window Help				
	A	B	C	D	E
1		Physical Units (1)	Direct Materials (2)	Conversion Costs (3)	Total Costs (4) = (2) + (3)
2	Work in process, beginning inventory (July 1)	1,500	₹1,20,000	₹90,000	₹2,10,000
3	Degree of completion of beginning work in process		100%	60%	
4	Started during July	8,500			
5	Good units completed and transferred out during July	7,000			
6	Work in process, ending inventory (July 31)	2,000			
7	Degree of completion of ending work in process		100%	50%	
8	Total costs added during July		₹7,65,000	₹8,91,000	₹16,56,000
9	Normal spoilage as a percentage of good units	10%			
10	Degree of completion of normal spoilage		100%	100%	
11	Degree of completion of abnormal spoilage		100%	100%	

$$\text{Total Spoilage} = \left(\begin{array}{c}\text{Units in beginning} \\ \text{work-in-process inventory}\end{array} + \begin{array}{c}\text{Units} \\ \text{started}\end{array}\right) - \left(\begin{array}{c}\text{Good units} \\ \text{completed and} \\ \text{transferred out}\end{array} + \begin{array}{c}\text{Units in ending} \\ \text{work-in-process} \\ \text{inventory}\end{array}\right)$$

$$= (1,500 + 8,500) - (7,000 + 2,000)$$
$$= 10,000 - 9,000$$
$$= 1,000 \text{ units}$$

Recall that anzio company's normal spoilage is 10% of good output. So the number of units of, normal spoilage equals 10% of the 7,000 units of good output or 700 units. With this information ,we can calculate the number of units of abnormal spoilage:

$$\text{Abnormal spoilage} = \text{Total spoilage} - \text{Normal spoilage}$$
$$= 1,000 \text{ units} - 700 \text{ units}$$
$$= 300 \text{ units}$$

Step 2:   Compute Output in Terms of Equivalent Units. Managers compute the equivalent units for spoilage the same way they compute equivalent units for good units. All spoiled units are included in the computation of output units. Because Anzio's inspection point is at the completion of production, the same amount of work will have been done on each spoiled and each completed good unit.

Step 3:   Summarize the Total Costs to Account For. The total costs to account for are all the costs debited to Work in Process. The details for this step are similar to step 3 in Chapter 17.

Step 4:   Compute Cost per Equivalent Unit. This step is similar to step 4 in Chapter 17.

Step 5:   Assign Costs to Units Completed, to Spoiled Units, and Units in Ending Work in Process Inventory. This step now includes computation of the cost of spoiled units and the cost of good units.

We illustrate these five steps of process costing for the weighted-average and FIFO methods next.

Weighted-Average Method and Spoilage

Exhibit 18-2, Panel A, presents steps 1 and 2 to calculate equivalent units of work done to date and includes calculations of equivalent units of normal and abnormal spoilage.

Exhibit 18-2, Panel B, presents steps 3, 4, and 5 (together called the production-cost worksheet).

In Step 3 managers summarize the total costs to account for. In Step 4 they calculate the cost-per-equivalent-unit using the weighted-average method. Note how, for each cost category, the costs of beginning work in process and the costs of work done in the current period are totaled and divided by equivalent units of all work done to date to calculate the weighted-average cost per equivalent unit. In the final Step, managers assign the total costs to completed units, normal and abnormal spoiled units, and ending inventory by multiplying the equivalent units calculated in step 2 by the cost per equivalent unit calculated in step 4. Also note that the ₹1,38,250 costs of normal spoilage are added to the costs of the related good units completed and transferred out.

$$\frac{\text{Cost per good units}}{\text{completed and transferred}} = \frac{\text{Total cost transferred out (including normal spoilage)}}{\text{Number of good units produced}}$$
$$= ₹15,20,750 \div 7,000 \text{ good units} \times ₹217.25 \text{ per good unit}$$

This amount is not equal to ₹197.5 per good unit, the sum of the ₹88.5 cost per equivalent unit of direct materials plus the ₹109 cost per equivalent unit of conversion costs. That's because the cost per good unit equals the sum of the direct material and conversion costs per equivalent unit, which is ₹197.5, plus a share of normal spoilage, ₹19.75 (₹1,38,250 ÷ 7,000 good units), for a total of ₹217.25 per good unit. The ₹59,250 costs of abnormal spoilage are charged to the Loss from Abnormal Spoilage account and do not appear in the costs of good units.[2]

FIFO Method and Spoilage

Exhibit 18-3, Panel A, presents steps 1 and 2 using the FIFO method, which focuses on equivalent units of work done in the current period. Exhibit 18-3, Panel B, presents steps 3, 4, and 5. Note how when assigning costs, the FIFO method keeps the costs of the beginning work in process separate and distinct from the costs of work done in the current period. All spoilage costs are assumed to be related to units completed during this period, using the unit costs of the current period.[3]

Chapter 17 highlighted taxes, performance evaluation, and accounting-based covenants as some of the elements managers must take into account when choosing between the FIFO and weighted-average methods. It also stressed the importance of making careful estimates of degrees of completion in order to avoid misstating operating income. All of these considerations apply equally well to the material in this chapter. In addition, a new issue that arises with spoilage is that of estimating the normal spoilage percentage in an unbiased manner. A supervisor who wishes to show better performance might categorize more of the spoilage as normal, thereby reducing the amount that must be written off against income as the loss from abnormal spoilage. Managers must stress the value of consistent and unbiased estimates of completion and normal spoilage percentages and drive home the importance of pursuing ethical actions and reporting the correct income figures, regardless of the short-term consequences of doing so.

---

[2] The actual costs of spoilage (and rework) are often greater than the costs recorded in the accounting system because the opportunity costs of disruption of the production line, storage, and lost contribution margins are not recorded in accounting systems. Chapter 19 discusses these opportunity costs from the perspective of cost management.

[3] To simplify calculations under FIFO, spoiled units are accounted for as if they were started in the current period. Although some of the beginning work in process probably did spoil, all spoilage is treated as if it came from current production.

Exhibit 18-2

Weighted-Average Method of Process Costing with Spoilage
Forming Department for July 2014

PANEL A: Steps 1 and 2—Summarize Output in Physical Units and Compute Equivalent Units

	File Edit View Insert Format Tools Data Window Help			
	A	B	C	D	E
1			(Step 1)	(Step 2)	
2				Equivalent Units	
3		Flow of Production	Physical Units	Direct Materials	Conversion Costs
4		Work in process, beginning	1,500		
5		Started during current period	8,500		
6		To account for	10,000		
7		Good units completed and transferred out during current period	7,000	7,000	7,000
8		Normal spoilage[a]	700		
9		(700 x 100%; 700 x 100%)		700	700
10		Abnormal spoilage[b]	300		
11		(300 x 100%; 300 x 100%)		300	300
12		Work in process, ending[c]	2,000		
13		(2,000 x 100%; 2,000 x 50%)		2,000	1,000
14		Accounted for	10,000		
15		Work done to date		10,000	9,000
16					
17	[a]Normal spoilage is 10% of good units transferred out: 10% x 7,000 = 700 units. Degree of completion of normal spoilage				
18	in this department: direct materials, 100%; conversion costs, 100%.				
19	[b]Abnormal spoilage = Total spoilage – Normal spoilage = 1,000 – 700 = 300 units. Degree of completion of abnormal spoilage				
20	in this department: direct materials, 100%; conversion costs, 100%.				
21	[c]Degree of completion in this department: direct materials, 100%; conversion costs, 50%.				

PANEL B: Summarize the Total Costs to Account For, Compute the Cost per Equivalent Unit, and Assign Costs to the Units Completed, Spoiled Units, and Units in Ending Work-in-Process Inventory

			Total Production Costs	Direct Materials	Conversion Costs
23					
24	(Step 3)	Work in process, beginning	₹2,10,000	₹1,20,000	₹90,000
25		Costs added in current period	16,56,000	7,65,000	8,91,000
26		Total costs to account for	₹18,66,000	₹8,85,000	₹9,81,000
27	(Step 4)	Costs incurred to date		8,85,000	₹9,81,000
28		Divided by equivalent units of work done to date		÷10,000	÷ 9,000
29		Cost per equivalent unit		₹88.5	₹109.0
30	(Step 5)	Assignment of costs:			
31		Good units completed and transferred out (7,000 units)			
32		Costs before adding normal spoilage	13,82,500	(7,000[d] x ₹88.5)	+(7,000[d] x ₹109.0)
33		Normal spoilage (700 units)	1,38,250	(700[d] x ₹88.5)	+ (700[d] x ₹109.0)
34	(A)	Total costs of good units completed and transferred out	15,20,750		
35	(B)	Abnormal spoilage (300 units)	59,250	(300[d]x ₹88.5)	+(300[d] x ₹109.0)
36	(C)	Work in process, ending (2,000 units)	2,86,000	(2,000[d]x ₹88.5)	+ 1000[d]x₹109.0)
37	(A)+(B)+(C)	Total costs accounted for	₹18,66,000	₹8,85,000 +	₹9,81,000
38					
39	[d]Equivalent units of direct materials and conversion costs calculated in step 2 in Panel A.				

Exhibit 18-3	First-In, First-Out (FIFO) Method of Process Costing with Spoilage Forming Department for July 2014

PANEL A: Steps 1 and 2—Summarize Output in Physical Units and Compute Equivalent Units

	File Edit View Insert Format Tools Data Window Help			
	A	B	C	D	E
1			(Step 1)	(Step 2)	
2				Equivalent Units	
3		Flow of Production	Physical Units	Direct Materials	Conversion Costs
4		Work in process, beginning	1,500		
5		Started during current period	8,500		
6		To account for	10,000		
7		Good units completed and transferred out during current period:			
8		From beginning work in process[a]	1,500		
9		[1,500 x (100% – 100%); 1,500 x (100% –60%)]		0	600
10		Started and completed	5,500[b]		
11		(5,500 x 100%; 5,500 x 100%)		5,500	5,500
12		Normal spoilage[c]	700		
13		(700 x 100%; 700 x 100%)		700	700
14		Abnormal spoilage[d]	300		
15		(300 x 100%; 300 x 100%)		300	300
16		Work in process, ending[e]	2,000		
17		(2,000 x 100%; 2,000 x 50%)		2,000	1,000
18		Accounted for	10,000		
19		Equivalent units of work done in current period only		8,500	8,100
20					
21	[a]Degree of completion in this department: direct materials, 100%; conversion costs, 60%.				
22	[b]7,000 physical units completed and transferred out minus 1,500 physical units completed and transferred out from beginning work-in-process inventory.				
23	[c]Normal spoilage is 10% of good units transferred out: 10% x 7,000 = 700 units. Degree of completion of normal spoilage in this department: direct materials, 100%; conversion costs, 100%.				
24	[d]Abnormal spoilage = Actual spoilage – Normal spoilage = 1,000 – 700 = 300 units. Degree of completion of abnormal spoilage in this department: direct materials, 100%; conversion costs, 100%.				
25	[e]Degree of completion in this department: direct materials, 100%; conversion costs, 50%.				

PANEL B: Steps 3, 4, and 5—Summarize Total Costs to Account For, Compute Cost per Equivalent Unit, and Assign Total Costs to Units Completed, to Spoiled Units, and to Units in Ending Work in Process

26			Total Production Costs	Direct Materials	Conversion Costs
27	(Step 3)	Work in process, beginning	₹2,10,000	₹1,20,000	₹90,000
28		Costs added in current period	16,56,000	7,65,000	8,91,000
29		Total costs to account for	₹18,66,000	₹8,85,000	₹9,81,000
30	(Step 4)	Costs added in current period		₹7,65,000	₹8,91,000
31		Divided by equivalent units of work done in current period		÷ 8,500	÷ 8,100
32		Cost per equivalent unit		₹90.0	₹110.0
33	(Step 5)	Assignment of costs:			
34		Good units completed and transferred out (7,000 units)			
35		Work in process, beginning (1,500 units)	₹2,10,000	₹1,20,000 +	₹90,000
36		Costs added to beginning work in process in current period	66,000	(0[f]x₹90) +	(600[f]x₹110)
37		Total from beginning inventory before normal spoilage	2,76,000		
38		Started and completed before normal spoilage (5,500 units)	11,00,000	(5,500[f]x₹90) +	(5,500[f]x₹110)
39		Normal spoilage (700 units)	1,40,000	(700[f]x₹90) +	(700[f]x₹110)
40	(A)	Total costs of good units completed and transferred out	15,16,000		
41	(B)	Abnormal spoilage (300 units)	60,000	(300[f]x₹90) +	(300[f]x₹110)
42	(C)	Work in process, ending (2,000 units)	2,90,000	(2,000[f]x₹90) +	(2,000[f]x₹110)
43	(A)+(B)+(C)	Total costs accounted for	₹18,66,000	₹8,85,000 +	₹9,81,000
44					
45					
46					
47	[f]Equivalent units of direct materials and conversion costs calculated in step 2 in Panel A.				

Decision Point ▶

How do the weighted-average and FIFO methods of process costing calculate the costs of good units and spoilage?

Journal Entries

The information from Panel B in Exhibits 18-2 and 18-3 supports the following journal entries to transfer good units completed to finished goods and to recognize the loss from abnormal spoilage.

	Weighted Average		FIFO	
Finished Goods	1,52,075		1,51,600	
Work in Process—Forming		1,52,075		1,51,600
To record transfer of good units completed in July.				
Loss from Abnormal Spoilage	5,925		6,000	
Work in Process—Forming		5,925		6,000
To record abnormal spoilage detected in July.				

Inspection Points and Allocating Costs of Normal Spoilage

Learning Objective 4

Account for spoilage at various stages of completion in process costing

... spoilage costs vary based on the point at which inspection is carried out

Spoilage might actually occur at various stages of the production process, but it is typically detected only at one or more inspection points. The cost of spoiled units equals all costs incurred in producing spoiled units up to the point of inspection. When spoiled goods have a disposal value (for example, carpeting sold as "seconds"), we compute a net cost of spoilage by deducting the disposal value from the costs of the spoiled goods.

The unit costs of normal and abnormal spoilage are the same when the two are detected at the same inspection point. This is the case in our Anzio Company example, where inspection occurs only upon completion of the units. However, situations may arise when abnormal spoilage is detected at a different point than normal spoilage. Consider shirt manufacturing. Normal spoilage in the form of defective shirts is identified upon inspection at the end of the production process. Now suppose a faulty machine causes many defective shirts to be produced at the halfway point of the production process. These defective shirts are abnormal spoilage and occur at a different point in the production process than normal spoilage. Then the per unit cost of the abnormal spoilage, which is based on costs incurred up to the halfway point of the production process, differs from the per unit cost of normal spoilage, which is based on costs incurred through the end of the production process.

The costs of abnormal spoilage are separately accounted for as losses of the accounting period in which they are detected. However, recall that normal spoilage costs are added to the costs of good units, which raises an additional issue: Should normal spoilage costs be allocated between completed units and ending work-in-process inventory? *The common approach is to presume that normal spoilage occurs at the inspection point in the production cycle and to allocate its cost over all units that have passed that point during the accounting period.*

Anzio Company inspects units only at the end of the production process. So, the units in ending work-in-process inventory are not assigned any costs of normal spoilage. Suppose Anzio were to inspect units at an earlier stage. Then, if the units in ending work in process have passed the inspection point, the costs of normal spoilage would be allocated to units in ending work in process as well as to completed units. For example, if the inspection point is at the halfway point of production, then any ending work in process that is at least 50% complete would be allocated a full measure of normal spoilage costs, and those spoilage costs would be calculated on the basis of all costs incurred up to the inspection point. If ending work in process is less than 50% complete, however, no normal spoilage costs would be allocated to it.

To better understand these issues, assume Anzio Company inspects units at various stages in the production process. How does this affect the amount of normal and abnormal spoilage? As before, consider the forming department, and recall that direct materials are added at the start of production, while conversion costs are added evenly during the process.

	Home	Insert	Page Layout	Formulas	Data	Review	View		

	A	B	C	D
1		— Physical Units: Stage of Completion at Which Inspection Occurs		
2	**Flow of Production**	**20%**	**55%**	**100%**
3	Work in process, beginning[a]	1,500	1,500	1,500
4	Started during July	8,500	8,500	8,500
5	To account for	10,000	10,000	10,000
6	Good units completed and transferred out			
7	(10,000 – 1,000 spoiled – 2,000 ending)	7,000	7,000	7,000
8	Normal spoilage	750[c]	550[d]	700[e]
9	Abnormal spoilage (1,000 – normal spoilage)	250	450	300
10	Work in process, ending[b]	2,000	2,000	2,000
11	Accounted for	10,000	10,000	10,000
12				
13	[a]Degree of completion in this department: direct materials, 100%; conversion costs, 60%.			
14	[b]Degree of completion in this department: direct materials, 100%; conversion costs, 50%.			
15	[c]10% × (8,500 units started – 1,000 units spoiled), because only the units started passed the 20% completion			
16	inspection point in the current period. Beginning work in process is excluded from this calculation because,			
17	being 60% complete at the start of the period, it passed the inspection point in the previous period.			
18	[d]10% × (8,500 units started – 1,000 units spoiled – 2,000 units in ending work in process). Both beginning and			
19	ending work in process are excluded since neither was inspected this period.			
20	[e]10% × 7,000, because 7,000 units are fully completed and inspected in the current period.			

Consider three different cases: Inspection occurs at (1) the 20%, (2) the 55%, or (3) the 100% completion stage. The last option is the one we have analyzed so far (see Exhibit 18-2). Assume that normal spoilage is 10% of the good units passing inspection. A total of 1,000 units are spoiled in all three cases. Normal spoilage is computed on the basis of the number of *good units* that pass the inspection point *during the current period*. The following data are for July 2014. Note how the number of units of normal and abnormal spoilage changes, depending on when inspection occurs.

The following diagram shows the flow of physical units for July and illustrates the normal spoilage numbers in the table. Note that 7,000 good units are completed and transferred out—1,500 from beginning work in process and 5,500 started and completed during the period—while 2,000 units are in ending work in process.

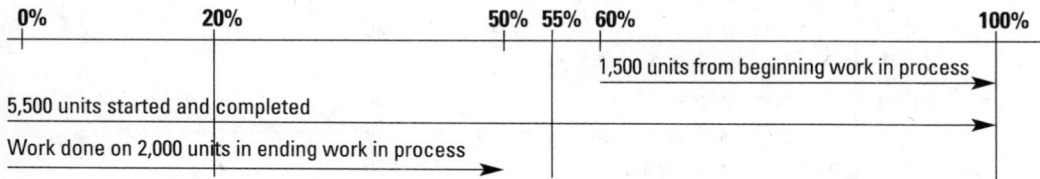

To see the number of units passing each inspection point, consider in the diagram the vertical lines at the 20%, 55%, and 100% inspection points. Note that the vertical line at 20% crosses two horizontal lines—5,500 good units started and completed and 2,000 units in ending work in process—for a total of 7,500 good units. (The 20% vertical line does not cross the line representing work done on the 1,500 good units completed from beginning work in process, because these units are already 60% complete at the start of the period and, hence, are not inspected this period.) Normal spoilage equals 10% of 7,500 = 750 units. On the other hand, the vertical line at the 55% point crosses just the second horizontal line, indicating that only 5,500 good units pass this point. Normal spoilage in this case is 10% of 5,500 = 550 units. At the 100% point, normal spoilage = 10% of 7,000 (1,500 + 5,500) good units = 700 units.

Exhibit 18-4 shows equivalent units are computed under the weighted-average method, if units are inspected at the 20% completion stage. The calculations depend on the direct materials and conversion costs incurred to get the units to this inspection point. The spoiled units have 100% of their direct materials and a 20% of their conversion costs. Because the ending work in process has passed the inspection point, these units are assigned the normal spoilage costs, just like the units that have been completed and transferred out. For example, the conversion costs of units completed and transferred out include conversion costs for 7,000 good units produced plus 20% × (10% × 5,500) = 110 equivalent units of normal spoilage. *We multiply by 20% to obtain the equivalent units of normal spoilage because conversion costs are only 20% complete at the inspection point.* The conversion costs of ending work in process include conversion costs of 50% of 2,000 = 1,000 equivalent good units plus 20% × (10% × 2,000) = 40 equivalent units of normal spoilage. Thus, the equivalent units of normal spoilage accounted for are 110 equivalent units related to units completed and transferred out plus 40 equivalent units related to units in ending work in process, for a total of 150 equivalent units, as Exhibit 18-4 shows.

Early inspections can help prevent any further costs being wasted on units that are already spoiled. For example, suppose the units can be inspected when units are 70% rather than 100% complete. If the spoilage occurs prior to the 70% point, a company can avoid incurring the final 30% of conversion costs on the spoiled units. While not applicable in the Anzio example, more generally a company can also save on the packaging or other direct materials that are added after the 70% stage. The downside to conducting inspections at too early a stage is that units spoiled at later stages of the process may go undetected. It is for

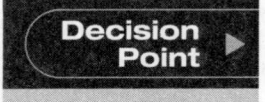

Decision Point ▶

How does inspection at various stages of completion affect the amount of normal and abnormal spoilage?

Exhibit 18-4

Computing Equivalent Units with Spoilage Using Weighted-Average Method of Process Costing with Inspection at 20% of Completion for Forming Department for July 2014

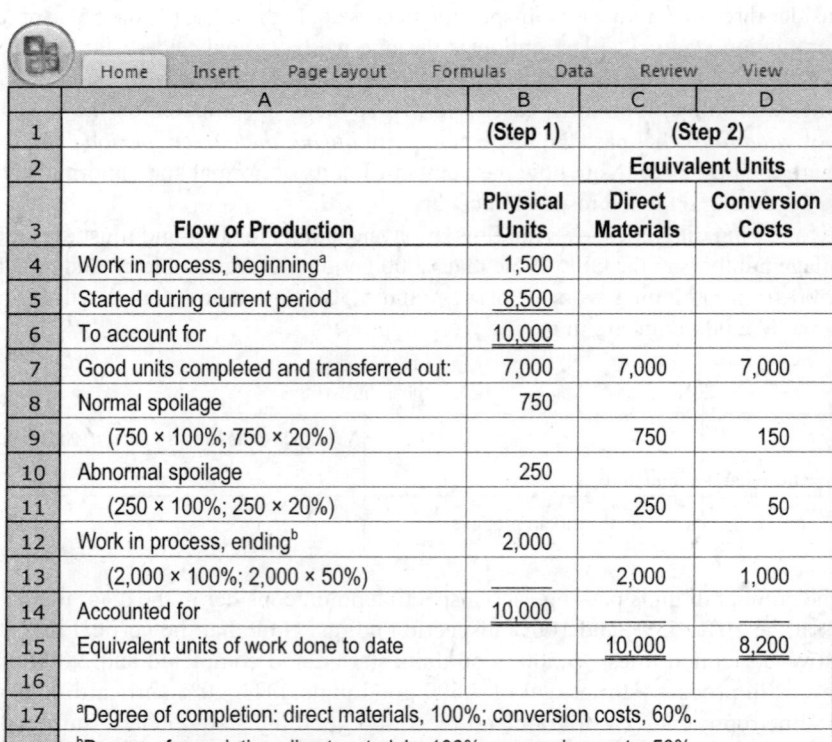

	A	B	C	D
		(Step 1)	**(Step 2)**	
			Equivalent Units	
	Flow of Production	**Physical Units**	**Direct Materials**	**Conversion Costs**
4	Work in process, beginning[a]	1,500		
5	Started during current period	8,500		
6	To account for	10,000		
7	Good units completed and transferred out:	7,000	7,000	7,000
8	Normal spoilage	750		
9	(750 × 100%; 750 × 20%)		750	150
10	Abnormal spoilage	250		
11	(250 × 100%; 250 × 20%)		250	50
12	Work in process, ending[b]	2,000		
13	(2,000 × 100%; 2,000 × 50%)		2,000	1,000
14	Accounted for	10,000		
15	Equivalent units of work done to date		10,000	8,200
16				
17	[a]Degree of completion: direct materials, 100%; conversion costs, 60%.			
18	[b]Degree of completion: direct materials, 100%; conversion costs, 50%.			

these reasons that firms often conduct multiple inspections and also empower workers to identify and resolve defects on a timely basis.

Job Costing and Spoilage

The concepts of normal and abnormal spoilage also apply to job-costing systems. Companies attempt to identify abnormal spoilage separately so they can work to eliminate it altogether. The costs of abnormal spoilage are not considered to be inventoriable costs and are written off as costs of the accounting period in which the abnormal spoilage is detected. Normal spoilage costs in job-costing systems—as in process-costing systems—are inventoriable costs, although increasingly companies are tolerating only small amounts of spoilage as normal. When assigning costs, job-costing systems generally distinguish *normal spoilage attributable to a specific job from normal spoilage common to all jobs.*

We describe accounting for spoilage in job costing using the following example.

> Example 3:   In the Harshad Machine Shop, 5 aircraft parts out of a job lot of 50 aircraft parts are spoiled. The costs assigned prior to the inspection point are ₹20,000 per part. When the spoilage is detected, the spoiled goods are inventoried at ₹6,000 per part, the net disposal value.

Our presentation here and in subsequent sections focuses on how the ₹20,000 cost per part is accounted for.

Normal spoilage attributable to a specific job   When normal spoilage occurs because of the specifications of a particular job, that job bears the cost of the spoilage minus the disposal value of the spoilage. The journal entry to recognize disposal value is as follows (items in parentheses indicate subsidiary ledger postings):

Materials Control (spoiled goods at current net disposal value):
    5 units × ₹6,000 per unit   30,000
        Work-in-Process Control (specific job): 5 units × ₹6,000 per unit   30,000

Note that, the Work-in-Process Control (for the specific job) has already been debited (charged) ₹1,00,000 for the spoiled parts (5 spoiled parts × ₹20,000 per part). So the net cost of normal spoilage is ₹70,000 (₹1,00,000 − ₹30,000), which is an additional cost of the 45 (50 − 5) good units produced. Therefore, total cost of the 45 good units is ₹9,70,000: ₹9,00,000 (45 units × ₹20,000 per unit) incurred to produce the good units plus the ₹70,000 net cost of normal spoilage. Cost per good unit is ₹21,555.6 (₹9,70,000 ÷ 45 good units).

Normal spoilage common to all jobs   In some cases, spoilage may be considered a normal characteristic of the production process. The spoilage inherent in production will, of course, occur when a specific job is being worked on. However, the spoilage is not attributable to, and hence is not charged directly to, the specific job. Instead, the spoilage is allocated indirectly to the job as manufacturing overhead because the spoilage is common to all jobs. The journal entry is as follows:

Materials Control (spoiled goods at current disposal value):
    5 units × ₹6,000 per unit   30,000
Manufacturing Overhead Control (normal spoilage):
    (₹1,00,000 − ₹30,000)   70,000
        Work-in-Process Control (specific job): 5 units × ₹20,000 per unit   1,00,000

Learning Objective 5

Account for spoilage in job costing

. . . normal spoilage assigned directly or indirectly to job; abnormal spoilage written off as a loss of the period

When normal spoilage is common to all jobs, the budgeted manufacturing overhead rate includes a provision for normal spoilage cost. The normal spoilage cost is spread, through overhead allocation, over all jobs rather than allocated to a specific job.[4] For example, if Harshad produced 140 good units from all jobs in a given month, the ₹70,000 of normal spoilage overhead costs would be allocated at the rate of ₹500 per good unit (₹70,000 ÷ 140 good units). Normal spoilage overhead costs allocated to the 45 good units in the job would be ₹22,500 (₹500 × 45 good units). Total cost of the 45 good units is ₹9,22,500: ₹9,00,000 (45 units × ₹20,000 per unit) incurred to produce the good units plus ₹22,500 of normal spoilage overhead costs. Cost per good unit is ₹20,500 (₹9,22,500 ÷ 45 good units).

Abnormal spoilage If the spoilage is abnormal, the net loss is charged to the Loss from Abnormal Spoilage account. Unlike normal spoilage costs, abnormal spoilage costs are not included as a part of the cost of good units produced. The total cost of the 45 good units is ₹9,00,000 (45 units × ₹20,000 per unit). The cost per good unit is ₹20,000 (₹9,00,000 ÷ 45 good units).

Materials Control (spoiled goods at current disposal value):		
5 units × ₹6,000 per unit	30,000	
Loss from Abnormal Spoilage (₹1,00,000 – ₹30,000)	70,000	
Work-in-Process Control (specific job): 5 units × ₹20,000 per unit		1,00,000

Decision Point ▶

How do job-costing systems account for spoilage?

Even though, for external reporting purposes, abnormal spoilage costs are written off in the accounting period and are not linked to specific jobs or units, companies often identify the particular reasons for abnormal spoilage, and, when appropriate, link abnormal spoilage with specific jobs or units for cost management purposes.

The accounting treatment described above highlights the potential impact of misclassifying the nature of the spoilage. Normal spoilage costs are inventoriable and are added to the cost of good units produced, while abnormal spoilage costs are expensed in the accounting period in which they occur. So, when inventories are present, classifying spoilage as normal rather than abnormal results in an increase in current operating income. In the above example, if the 45 parts remain unsold at the end of the period, such misclassification would boost income for that period by ₹70,000. As with our discussion of completion percentages, it is important for managers to verify that spoilage rates and spoilage categories are not manipulated by department supervisors for short-term benefits.

Job Costing and Rework

Learning Objective 6

Account for rework in job costing

. . . normal rework assigned directly or indirectly to job; abnormal rework written off as a loss of the period

Rework refers to units of production that are inspected, determined to be unacceptable, repaired, and sold as acceptable finished goods. We again distinguish (1) normal rework attributable to a specific job, (2) normal rework common to all jobs, and (3) abnormal rework.

Consider the Harshad Machine Shop data in Example 3 on p. 770. Assume the five parts are reworked. The journal entry for the ₹1,00,000 of total costs (the details of these costs are assumed) assigned to the five spoiled units before considering rework costs is as follows:

---

[4] Note that costs already assigned to products are charged back to Manufacturing Overhead Control, which generally accumulates only costs incurred, not both costs incurred and costs already assigned.

Work-in-Process Control (specific job)	1,00,000	
Materials Control		40,000
Wages Payable Control		40,000
Manufacturing Overhead Allocated		20,000

Assume the rework costs equal ₹38,000 (₹8,000 in direct materials, ₹20,000 in direct man-ufacturing labor, and ₹10,000 in manufacturing overhead).

Normal rework attributable to a specific job   If the rework is normal but occurs because of the requirements of a specific job, the rework costs are charged to that job. The journal entry is as follows:

Work-in-Process Control (specific job)	38,000	
Materials Control		8,000
Wages Payable Control		20,000
Manufacturing Overhead Allocated		10,000

Normal rework common to all jobs   The cost of rework when it is normal and not attributable to a specific job, are charged to manufacturing overhead and are spread, through overhead allocation, over all jobs.

Manufacturing Overhead Control (rework costs)	38,000	
Materials Control		8,000
Wages Payable Control		20,000
Manufacturing Overhead Allocated		10,000

Abnormal rework   If the rework is abnormal, it is charged to a loss account.

Loss from Abnormal Rework	38,000	
Materials Control		8,000
Wages Payable Control		20,000
Manufacturing Overhead Allocated		10,000

Accounting for rework in a process-costing system also requires abnormal rework to be distinguished from normal rework. Process costing accounts for abnormal rework in the same way as job costing. Accounting for normal rework follows the accounting described for normal rework common to all jobs (units) because masses of identical or similar units are being manufactured.

   Costing rework focuses managers' attention on the resources wasted on activities that would not have to be undertaken if the product had been made correctly. The cost of rework prompts managers to seek ways to reduce rework, for example, by designing new products or processes, training workers, or investing in new machines. To eliminate rework and to simplify the accounting, some companies set a standard of zero rework. All rework is then treated as abnormal and is written off as a cost of the current period.

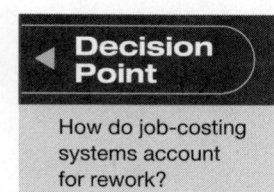

Decision Point

How do job-costing systems account for rework?

Accounting for Scrap

Scrap is residual material that results from manufacturing a product; it has low total sales value compared with the total sales value of the product. No distinction is made between

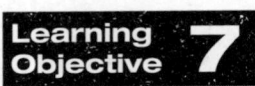

Learning Objective 7

Account for scrap

. . . reduces cost of job either at time of sale or at time of production

normal and abnormal scrap because no cost is assigned to scrap. The only distinction made is between scrap attributable to a specific job and scrap common to all jobs.

There are two aspects of accounting for scrap:

1. Planning and control, including physical tracking
2. Inventory costing, including when and how scrap affects operating income

Initial entries to scrap records are commonly in physical terms. In various industries, companies quantify items such as stamped-out metal sheets or edges of molded plastic parts by weighing, counting, or some other measure. Scrap records not only help measure efficiency, but also help keep track of scrap, and so reduce the chances of theft. Companies use scrap records to prepare periodic summaries of the amounts of actual scrap compared with budgeted or standard amounts. Scrap is either sold or disposed of quickly or it is stored for later sale, disposal, or reuse.

To carefully track their scrap, many companies maintain a distinct account for scrap costs somewhere in their accounting system. The issues here are similar to the issues in Chapter 16 regarding the accounting for byproducts:

- When should the value of scrap be recognized in the accounting records—at the time scrap is produced or at the time scrap is sold?
- How should revenues from scrap be accounted for?

To illustrate, we extend our Harshad example. Assume the manufacture of aircraft parts generates scrap and that the scrap from a job has a net sales value of ₹9,000.

Recognizing Scrap at the Time of Its Sale

When the rupee amount of scrap is immaterial, it is simplest is to record the physical quantity of scrap returned to the storeroom and to regard the revenues from the sale of scrap as a separate line item in the income statement. In this case, the only journal entry is as follows:

Sale of scrap:

Cash or Accounts Receivable	9,000	
Scrap Revenues		9,000

When the rupee amount of scrap is material and it is sold quickly after it is produced, the accounting depends on whether the scrap is attributable to a specific job or is common to all jobs.

Scrap attributable to a specific job   Job-costing systems sometimes trace scrap revenues to the jobs that yielded the scrap. This method is used only when the tracing can be done in an economically feasible way. For example, the Harshad Machine Shop and its customers, may reach an agreement that provides for charging specific jobs with all rework or spoilage costs and then crediting these jobs with all scrap revenues that arise from the jobs. The journal entry is as follows:

Scrap returned to storeroom: No journal entry.
[Notation of quantity received and related job entered in the inventory record]

Sale of scrap:

Cash or Accounts Receivable	9,000	
Work-in-Process Control		9,000

Posting made to specific job cost record.

Unlike spoilage and rework, there is no cost assigned to the scrap, so no distinction is made between normal and abnormal scrap. All scrap revenues, whatever the amount, are credited to the specific job. Scrap revenues reduce the costs of the job.

Scrap common to all jobs   The journal entry in this case is as follows:

Scrap returned to storeroom:	No journal entry.		
	[Notation of quantity received and related job entered in the inventory record]		
Sale of scrap:	Cash or Accounts Receivable	9,000	
	Manufacturing Overhead Control		9,000
	Posting made to subsidiary ledger— "Sales of Scrap" column on department cost record.		

Because scrap is not linked with any particular job or product, all products bear its costs without any credit for scrap revenues except in an indirect manner: the expected scrap revenues are considered when setting the budgeted manufacturing overhead rate. Thus, the budgeted overhead rate is lower than it would be otherwise. This method of accounting for scrap is also used in process costing when the rupee amount of scrap is immaterial because the scrap in process costing is common to the manufacture of all the identical or similar units produced (and cannot be identified with specific units).

Recognizing Scrap at the Time of Its Production

Our preceding illustrations assume that scrap returned to the storeroom is sold quickly, so it is not assigned an inventory cost figure. Sometimes, as in the case with edges of molded plastic parts, the value of scrap is not immaterial, and the time between storing it and selling or reusing it can be long and unpredictable. In these situations, the company assigns an inventory cost to scrap at a conservative estimate of its net realizable value so that production costs and related scrap revenues are recognized in the same accounting period. Some companies tend to delay sales of scrap until its market price is attractive. Volatile price fluctuations are typical for scrap metal. In these cases, it's not easy to determine some "reasonable inventory value."

Scrap attributable to a specific job   The journal entry in the Harshad example is as follows:

Scrap returned to storeroom:	Materials Control	9,000	
	Work-in-Process Control		9,000

Scrap common to all jobs   The journal entry in this case is as follows:

Scrap returned to storeroom:	Materials Control	9,000	
	Manufacturing Overhead Control		9,000

Notice that the Materials Control account is debited in place of Cash or Accounts Receivable. When the scrap is sold, the journal entry is as follows:

Sale of scrap:	Cash or Accounts Receivable	9,000	
	Materials Control		9,000

Scrap is sometimes reused as direct material rather than sold as scrap. In this case, Materials Control is debited at its estimated net realizable value and then credited when the scrap is reused. For example, the entries when the scrap is common to all jobs are as follows:

Scrap returned to storeroom:	Materials Control	9,000	
	Manufacturing Overhead Control		9,000
Reuse of scrap:	Work-in-Process Control	9,000	
	Materials Control		9,000

Accounting for scrap under process costing is like the accounting under job costing when scrap is common to all jobs. That's because the scrap in process costing is common to the manufacture of masses of identical or similar units.

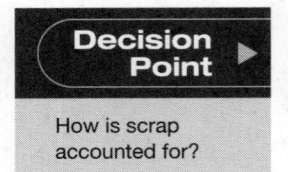

Decision Point ▶

How is scrap accounted for?

Managers focus their attention on ways to reduce scrap and to use it more profitably, especially when the cost of scrap is high. For example, General Motors has redesigned its plastic injection molding processes to reduce the scrap plastic that must be broken away from its molded products. General Motors also regrinds and reuses the plastic scrap as direct material, saving substantial input costs.

Problem for Self-Study

Bhilwara Textiles has some spoiled goods that had an assigned cost of ₹4,00,000 and zero net disposal value.

Required

Prepare a journal entry for each of the following conditions under (a) process costing (Department A) and (b) job costing:

1. Abnormal spoilage of ₹4,00,000
2. Normal spoilage of ₹4,00,000 regarded as common to all operations
3. Normal spoilage of ₹4,00,000 regarded as attributable to specifications of a particular job

Solution

(a) Process Costing	(b) Job Costing

1. Loss from Abnormal Spoilage 4,00,000
    Work in Process—Dept. A 4,00,000
	Loss from Abnormal Spoilage 4,00,000
	    Work-in-Process Control (specific job)
	    4,00,000

2. No entry until units are
   completed and transferred
   out. Then the normal spoilage
   costs are transferred as part
   of the cost of good units.
  Work in Process—Dept. B 4,00,000
    Work in Process—Dept. A 4,00,000
	Manufacturing Overhead Control 4,00,000
	    Work-in-Process Control (specific job)
	    4,00,000

3. Not applicable	No entry. Normal spoilage cost remains in Work-in-Process Control (specific job)

Decision Points

The following question-and-answer format summarizes the chapter's learning objectives. Each decision presents a key question related to a learning objective. The guidelines are the answer to that question.

Decision	Guidelines
1. What are spoilage, rework, and scrap?	Spoilage is units of production that do not meet the specifications required by customers for good units and that are discarded or sold at reduced prices. Spoilage is generally divided into normal spoilage, which is inherent to a particular production process, and abnormal spoilage, which arises because of inefficiency in operations. Rework is unacceptable units that are subsequently repaired and sold as acceptable finished goods. Scrap is residual material that results from manufacturing a product; it has low total sales value compared with the total sales value of the product.
2. What is the distinction between normal and abnormal spoilage?	Normal spoilage is inherent in a particular production process and arises when the process is done in an efficient manner. Abnormal spoilage, on the other hand, is not inherent in a particular production process and would not arise under efficient operating conditions. Abnormal spoilage is usually regarded as avoidable and controllable.
3. How do the weighted-average and FIFO methods of process costing calculate the costs of good units and spoilage?	The weighted-average method combines the costs of beginning inventory with the costs of the current period when determining the costs of good units, which include normal spoilage, and the costs of abnormal spoilage, which are written off as a loss of the accounting period.
	The FIFO method keeps the costs of beginning inventory separate from the costs of the current period when determining the costs of good units (which include normal spoilage) and the costs of abnormal spoilage, which are written off as a loss of the accounting period.
4. How does inspecting at various stages of completion affect the amount of normal and abnormal spoilage?	The cost of spoiled units is assumed to equal all costs incurred in producing spoiled units up to the point of inspection. Spoilage costs therefore vary based on different inspection points.
5. How do job-costing systems account for spoilage?	Normal spoilage specific to a job is assigned to that job or, when common to all jobs, is allocated as part of manufacturing overhead. The cost of abnormal spoilage is written off as a loss in the accounting period.
6. How do job-costing systems account for rework?	Normal rework specific to a job is assigned to that job or, when common to all jobs, is allocated as part of manufacturing overhead. Cost of abnormal rework is written off as a loss of the accounting period.
7. How is scrap accounted for?	Scrap is recognized in a firm's accounting records either at the time of its sale or at the time of its production. If the scrap is immaterial, it is recognized as revenue when it's sold. If it's not immaterial, the net realizable value of the scrap when it's sold reduces the cost of a specific job or, when common to all jobs, reduces Manufacturing Overhead Control.

TERMS TO LEARN

The chapter and the Glossary at the end of the book contain definitions of the following important terms:

abnormal spoilage **(p. 947)**   normal spoilage **(p. 947)**   scrap **(p. 946)**

inspection point **(p. 948)**   rework **(p. 946)**   spoilage **(p. 946)**

ASSIGNMENT MATERIAL

Questions

18-1 Why is there an unmistakable trend in manufacturing to improve quality?

18-2 Distinguish among spoilage, rework, and scrap.

18-3 "Normal spoilage is planned spoilage." Discuss.

18-4 "Costs of abnormal spoilage are losses." Explain.

18-5 "What has been regarded as normal spoilage in the past is not necessarily acceptable as normal spoilage in the present or future." Explain.

18-6 "Units of abnormal spoilage are inferred rather than identified." Explain.

18-7 "In accounting for spoiled units, we are dealing with cost assignment rather than cost incurrence." Explain.

18-8 "Total input includes abnormal as well as normal spoilage and is, therefore, inappropriate as a basis for computing normal spoilage." Do you agree? Explain.

18-9 "The inspection point is the key to the allocation of spoilage costs." Do you agree? Explain.

18-10 "The unit cost of normal spoilage is the same as the unit cost of abnormal spoilage." Do you agree? Explain.

18-11 "In job costing, the costs of normal spoilage that occur while a specific job is being done are charged to the specific job." Do you agree? Explain.

18-12 "The costs of rework are always charged to the specific jobs in which the defects were originally discovered." Do you agree? Explain.

18-13 "Abnormal rework costs should be charged to a loss account, not to manufacturing overhead." Do you agree? Explain.

18-14 When is a company justified in inventorying scrap?

18-15 How do managers use information about scrap?

Solved Examples

18-16 Normal and abnormal spoilage in units. The following data, in physical units, describe a grinding process for January:

Work in process, beginning	18,600
Started during current period	189,000
To account for	207,600
Spoiled units	12,600
Good units completed and transferred out	170,000
Work in process, ending	25,000
Accounted for	207,600

Inspection occurs at the 100% completion stage. Normal spoilage is 4% of the good units passing inspection.

1. Compute the normal and abnormal spoilage in units.
2. Assume that the equivalent-unit cost of a spoiled unit is ₹11. Compute the amount of potential savings if all spoilage were eliminated, assuming that all other costs would be unaffected. Comment on your answer.

Solution

1. Total spoiled units	12,600
Normal spoilage in units, 4% × 1,70,000	6,800
Abnormal spoilage in units	5,800

2. Abnormal spoilage, 5,800 × ₹11	₹63,800
Normal spoilage, 6,800 × ₹11	74,800
Potential savings, 12,600 × ₹11	₹1,38,600

Regardless of the targeted normal spoilage, abnormal spoilage is nonrecurring and avoidable. The targeted normal spoilage rate is subject to change. Many companies have reduced their spoilage to almost zero, which would realize all potential savings. Of course, zero spoilage usually means higher-quality products, more customer satisfaction, more employee satisfaction, and various beneficial effects on nonmanufacturing (for example, purchasing) costs of direct materials.

18-17 Spoilage and job costing. (L. Bamber) Vegetarian Kitchens produces a variety of items in accordance with special job orders from hospitals, plant cafeterias, and university dormitories. An order for 2,500 cases of mixed vegetables costs ₹60 per case: direct materials, ₹30; direct manufacturing labor, ₹20; and manufacturing overhead allocated, ₹10. The manufacturing overhead rate includes a provision for normal spoilage. Consider each requirement independently.

1. Assume that a laborer dropped 200 cases. Suppose part of the 200 cases could be sold to a nearby prison for ₹2,000 cash. Prepare a journal entry to record this event. Calculate and explain briefly the unit cost of the remaining 2,300 cases.
2. Refer to the original data. Tasters at the company reject 200 of the 2,500 cases. The 200 cases are disposed of for ₹4,000. Assume that this rejection rate is considered normal. Prepare a journal entry to record this event, and calculate the unit cost if
   a. The rejection is attributable to exacting specifications of this particular job.
   b. The rejection is characteristic of the production process and is not attributable to this specific job.
   c. Are unit costs the same in requirements 2a and 2b? Explain your reasoning briefly.
3. Refer to the original data. Tasters rejected 200 cases that had insufficient salt. The product can be placed in a vat, salt can be added, and the product can be reprocessed into jars. This operation, which is considered normal, will cost ₹200. Prepare a journal entry to record this event and calculate the unit cost of all the cases if
   a. This additional cost was incurred because of the exacting specifications of this particular job.
   b. This additional cost occurs regularly because of difficulty in seasoning.
   c. Are unit costs the same in requirements 3a and 3b? Explain your reasoning briefly.

Solution

Spoilage and job costing

		₹	₹
1.	Cash	2,000	
	Loss from Abnormal Spoilage	10,000	
	Work-in-Process Control		12,000

Loss = (₹60 × 200) − ₹2,000 = ₹10,000
Remaining cases cost = ₹60 per case. The cost of these cases is unaffected by the loss from abnormal spoilage.

2. a. Cash   4,000
    Work-in-Process Control   4,000

The cost of the remaining good cases = [(₹60 × 2,500) − ₹4,000] = ₹1,46,000
The unit cost of a good case now becomes ₹1,46,000 ÷ 2,300 = ₹63.478

b. Cash   4,000
Manufacturing Department Overhead Control   8,000
    Work-in-Process Control   12,000

The unit cost of a good case remains at ₹60.

c. The unit cost in the cases 2a and 2b is different because in case 2a, the normal spoilage cost, due to the exacting specifications of this particular job, is charged as a cost of this job. In case 2b, the normal spoilage is due to the production process (not the particular attributes of this specific job). These costs are, therefore, charged as part of manufacturing overhead. The manufacturing overhead cost of ₹10 per case already includes a provision for normal spoilage.

3. a. Work-in-Process Control   2,000
    Materials Control, Wages Payable Control, Manufacturing   2,000
    Overhead Allocated

The cost of the good cases = [(₹60 × 2,500) + ₹2,000] = ₹1,52,000
The unit cost of a good case is ₹1,52,000 ÷ 2,500 = ₹60.8

b. Manufacturing Department Overhead Control   2,000
    Materials Control, Wages Payable Control, Manufacturing   2,000
    Overhead Allocated

The unit cost of a good case = ₹60 per case

c. The unit cost in the cases 3a and 3b is different because in case 3a, the normal rework cost, due to the exacting specifications of this particular job, is charged as a cost of this job. In case 3b, the normal rework is due to the production process (not the particular attributes of this specific job). These costs are, therefore, charged as part of manufacturing overhead. The manufacturing overhead cost of ₹10 per case already includes a provision for this normal rework.

18-18 Reworked units, costs of rework. Whirpool India Limited assembles washing machines at its Auburn plant. In December 2006, 60 tumbler units that cost ₹44 each (from a new supplier who subsequently went bankrupt) were defective and had to be disposed of at zero disposal value. Whirpool India Limited was able to rework all 60 washing machines by substituting new tumbler units purchased from one of its existing suppliers. Each replacement tumbler cost ₹50.

Required

1. What alternative approaches are there to account for the material costs of reworked units?

2. Should Whirpool India Limited use the ₹44 tumbler or ₹50 tumbler to calculate the costs of materials reworked? Explain.

3. What other costs might Whirpool India Limited include in its analysis of the total costs of rework due to the tumbler units purchased from the (now) bankrupt supplier?

Solution

Reworked units, costs of rework.

1. The two alternative approaches to account for the materials costs of reworked units are:

   a. To charge the costs of rework to the current period as a separate expense item as abnormal rework. This approach would highlight to Whirpool India Limited the costs of the supplier problem.

   b. To charge the costs of the rework to manufacturing overhead as normal rework.

2. The ₹50 tumbler cost is the cost of the actual tumblers included in the washing machines. The ₹44 tumbler units from the new supplier were eventually never used in any washing machine and that supplier is now bankrupt. The units must now be disposed of at zero disposal value.

3. The total costs of rework due to the defective tumbler units include:

    a. The labor and other conversion costs spent on substituting the new tumbler units.

    b. The costs of any extra negotiations to obtain the replacement tumbler units.

    c. Any higher price the existing supplier may have charged to do a rush order for the replacement tumbler units.

    d. Ordering costs for the replacement tumbler units.

18-19 Weighted-average method, spoilage. Royal Company produces handbags from leather of moderate quality. It distributes the product through outlet stores and department store chains. At Kanpur's facility in U.P, direct materials (primarily leather hides) are added at the beginning of the process, while conversion costs are added evenly during the process. Given the importance of minimizing product returns, spoiled units are detected upon inspection at the end of the process and are discarded at a net disposal value of zero.

Company uses the weighted-average method of process costing. Summary data for April 2016 are as follows:

		Home	Insert	Page Layout	Formulas	Data	Review	View	

	A	B	C	D
1		Physical Units	Direct Materials	Conversion Costs
2	Work in process, beginning inventory (April 1)	2,400	₹2,12,400	₹1,33,320
3	Degree of completion of beginning work in process		100%	50%
4	Started during April	12,000		
5	Good units completed and transferred out during April	10,800		
6	Work in process, ending inventory (April 30)	2,160		
7	Degree of completion of ending work in process		100%	75%
8	Total costs added during April		₹9,75,600	₹11,14,080
9	Normal spoilage as a percentage of good units	10%		
10	Degree of completion of normal spoilage		100%	100%
11	Degree of completion of abnormal spoilage		100%	100%

Required

1. For each cost category, calculate equivalent units. Show physical units in the first column of your schedule.

2. Summarize the total costs to account for; calculate the cost per equivalent unit for each cost category; and assign costs to units completed and transferred out (including normal spoilage), to abnormal spoilage, and to units in ending work in process.

Solution

1. Solution Exhibit 18-19, Panel A calculates equivalent units of work done to date for direct materials and conversion costs.

2. Solution Exhibit 18-19, Panel B summarizes total costs to account for, calculates the costs per equivalent unit for direct materials and conversion costs, and assigns total costs to units completed and transferred out (including normal spoilage), to abnormal spoilage, and to units in ending work in process, using the weighted-average method.

Solution Exhibit 18-19

Weighted-Average Method of Process Costing with Spoilage,
Royal Company for April 2016

PANEL A: Summarize the Flow of Physical Units and Compute Output in Equivalent Units

	(Step 1)	(Step 2) Equivalent Units	
Flow of Production	**Physical Units**	**Direct Materials**	**Conversion Costs**
Work in process, beginning (given)	2,400		
Started during current period (given)	12,000		
To account for	14,400		
Good units completed and tsfd. out during current period:	10,800	10,800	10,800
Normal spoilage[a]	1,080		
(1,080 × 100%; 1,080 × 100%)		1,080	1,080
Abnormal spoilage[b]	360		
(360 × 100%; 360 × 100%)		360	360
Work in process, ending[c] (given)	2,160		
(2,160 × 100%; 2,160 × 75%)		2,160	1,620
Accounted for	14,400		
Equivalent units of work done to date		14,400	13,860

[a]Normal spoilage is 10% of good units transferred out: 10% × 10,800 = 1,080 units.
Degree of completion of normal spoilage
in this department: direct materials, 100%; conversion costs, 100%.

[b]Total spoilage = Beg. units + Units started - Good units transferred out − Ending units = 2,400 + 12,000 − 10,800 − 2,160 = 1,440; Abnormal spoilage = Total spoilage − Normal spoilage = 1,440 − 1,080 = 360 units. Degree of completion of abnormal spoilage in this department: direct materials, 100%; conversion costs, 100%.

[c]Degree of completion in this department: direct materials, 100%; conversion costs, 75%.

PANEL B: Summarize the Total Costs to Account for, Compute the Cost per Equivalent Unit, and Assign Costs to the Units Completed, Spoiled Units, and Units in Ending Work-in-Process Inventory

		Total Production Costs	**Direct Materials**	**Conversion Costs**
(Step 3)	Work in process, beginning (given)	₹3,45,720	₹2,12,400	₹1,33,320
	Costs added in current period (given)	20,89,680	9,75,600	11,14,080
	Total costs to account for	₹24,35,400	₹11,88,000	₹12,47,400
(Step 4)	Costs incurred to date		₹11,88,000	₹12,47,400
	Divide by equivalent units of work done to date		÷14,400	÷13,860
	Cost per equivalent unit		₹82.5	₹90
(Step 5)	Assignment of costs			
	Good units completed and transferred out (10,800 units)			
	Costs before adding normal spoilage	₹18,63,000	(10,800[d] × ₹82.5) + (10,800[d] × ₹90)	
	Normal spoilage (1,080 units)	1,86,300	(1,080[d] × ₹82.5) + (1,080[d] × ₹90)	
(A)	Total costs of good units completed and transferred out	20,49,300		

(B)	Abnormal spoilage (360 units)	62,100	$(360^d \times ₹82.5) + (360^d \times ₹90)$
(C)	Work in process, ending (2,160 units):	3,24,000	$(2,160^d \times ₹82.5) + (1,620^d \times ₹90)$
(A) + (B) + (C)	Total costs accounted for	₹24,35,400	₹11,88,000 + ₹12,46,800

^{d}Equivalent units of direct materials and conversion costs calculated in step 2 of Solution Exhibit 18-21A.

18-20 FIFO method, spoilage.

Required

1. Do Exercise 18-19 using the FIFO method.
2. What are the managerial issues involved in selecting or reviewing the percentage of spoilage considered normal? How would your answer to requirement 1 differ if all spoilage were viewed as normal?

Solution

1. Solution Exhibit 18-20, Panel A calculates equivalent units of work done in the current period for direct materials and conversion costs.

   Solution Exhibit 18-20, Panel B summarizes total costs to account for, calculates the costs per equivalent unit for direct materials and conversion costs, and assigns total costs to units completed and transferred out (including normal spoilage), to abnormal spoilage, and to units in ending work in process, using the FIFO method.

Solution Exhibit 18-20

First-in, first-out (FIFO) Method of Process Costing with Spoilage,
Royal Company for April 2016

PANEL A: Summarize the Flow of Physical Units and Compute Output in Equivalent Units

	(Step 1)	(Step 2) Equivalent Units	
Flow of Production	Physical Units	Direct Materials	Conversion Costs
Work in process, beginning (given)	2,400		
Started during current period (given)	12,000		
To account for	14,400		
Good units completed and transferred out during current period:			
From beginning work in process^l	2,400		
$2,400 \times (100\% - 100\%); 2,400 \times (100\% - 50\%)$		0	1,200
Started and completed	8,400#		
$8,400 \times 100\%; 8,400 \times 100\%$		8,400	8,400
Normal spoilage*	1,080		
$1,080 \times 100\%; 1,080 \times 100\%$		1,080	1,080
Abnormal spoilage†	360		
$360 \times 100\%; 360 \times 100\%$		360	360
Work in process, ending‡	2,160		
$2,160 \times 100\%; 2,160 \times 75\%$		2,160	1,620
Accounted for	14,400		
Equivalent units of work done in current period		12,000	12,660

^{l}Degree of completion in this department: direct materials, 100%; conversion costs, 50%.
#10,800 physical units completed and transferred out minus 2,400 physical units completed and transferred out from beginning work-in-process inventory.

*Degree of completion of normal spoilage in this department: direct materials, 100%; conversion costs, 100%.

†Degree of completion of abnormal spoilage in this department: direct materials, 100%; conversion costs, 100%.

‡Degree of completion in this department: direct materials, 100%; conversion costs, 75%.

PANEL B: Summarize the Total Costs to Account for, Compute the Cost per Equivalent Unit, and Assign Costs to the Units Completed, Spoiled Units, and Units in Ending Work-in-Process Inventory

		Total Production Costs	Direct Materials	Conversion Costs
(Step 3)	Work in process, beginning (given)	₹3,45,720	₹2,12,400	₹1,33,320
	Costs added in current period (given)	20,89,680	9,75,600	11,14,080
	Total costs to account for	₹24,35,400	₹11,88,000	₹12,47,400
(Step 4)	Costs added in current period		₹9,75,600	₹11,14,080
	Divided by equivalent units of work done in current period		÷12,000	÷ 12,660
	Cost per equivalent unit		₹81.3	₹88
(Step 5)	Assignment of costs:			
	Good units completed and transferred out (10,800 units)			
	Work in process, beginning (2,400 units)	₹3,45,720	₹2,12,400 + ₹1,33,320	
	Costs added to beg. work in process in current period	1,05,600	(0[a] × ₹81.3) + (1,200[a] × ₹88)	
	Total from beginning inventory before normal spoilage	4,51,320		
	Started and completed before normal spoilage (8,400 units)	14,22,120	(8,400[a] × ₹81.3) + (8,400[a] × ₹88)	
	Normal spoilage (1,080 units)	1,82,840	(1,080[a] × ₹81.3) + (1,080[a] × ₹88)	
(A)	Total costs of good units completed and transferred out	20,56,280		
(B)	Abnormal spoilage (360 units)	60,950	(360[a] × ₹81.3) + (360a × ₹88)	
(C)	Work in process, ending (2,160 units)	3,18,170	(2,160[a] × ₹81.3) + (1,620[a] × ₹88)	
(A)+(B)+(C)	Total costs accounted for	₹24,35,400	₹11,88,000 + ₹12,47,400	

[a] Equivalent units of direct materials and conversion costs calculated in Step 2 in Panel A.

2. The issues related to the determination of the percentage of spoilage considered normal are similar to the factors discussed in Chapter 17 regarding the importance of verifying the estimated completion percentages of ending work-in-process, especially with regard to conversion costs. A supervisor who wants to show better operating income performance might categorize more of the spoilage as normal, thereby reducing the amount that must be written off against income as the loss from abnormal spoilage. Managers must stress the value of consistent and unbiased estimates of normal spoilage percentages and drive home the importance of pursuing ethical actions and reporting the correct income figures, regardless of the short-term consequences of doing so.

In the above example, if all 1,440 units spoiled were considered normal spoilage, then the cost of goods completed and transferred out would increase to ₹21,17,230 (₹20,56,280 + ₹60,950), while ending work-in-process would stay unchanged at ₹3,18,170. Of course, the ₹60,950 would no longer be written off as a period expense by the Kanpur facility in U.P.

18-21 Spoilage, journal entries. Safeclear, Ltd. is the leading manufacturer of automotive glass components such as windshields. The company uses a process-costing system to account for its work-in-process inventories. When Job 26, an order for windshields for Mr Akash, was being processed, a piece of laminated sheet glass was off-center in the cutting machine and two windshields were spoiled. Because this problem occurs periodically, it is considered normal spoilage and is consequently recorded as an overhead cost. Because this step comes first in the process of making the windshields, the only costs incurred were ₹32,500 for direct materials. Assume the laminated glass cannot be sold, and its cost has been recorded in work-in-process inventory.

Prepare the journal entries to record the spoilage incurred.

Required

Solution

Spoilage represents the amount of resources that go into the process but do not result in finished product. A simple way to account for spoilage in process costing is to calculate the amount of direct material that was spoiled. The journal entry to record the spoilage incurred in Safeclear's production process is as follows:

Manufacturing overhead control (normal spoilage)	₹32,500	
Work-in-process inventory (cost of spoiled laminated glass)	₹32,500	

18-22 Recognition of loss from spoilage. Bajaj Electronics manufactures universal power adapters. The company provides you with the following information regarding operations for April 2016:

Total power adapters manufactured	10,000
Adapters rejected as spoiled units	375
Total manufactured cost	₹40,00,000

Assume the spoiled units have no disposal value.

Required

1. What is the unit cost of making the 10,000 universal power adapters?
2. What is the total cost of the 375 spoiled units?
3. |If the spoilage is considered normal, what is the increase in the unit cost of good adapters manufactured as a result of the spoilage?
4. If the spoilage is considered abnormal, prepare the journal entries for the spoilage incurred.

Solution

1. The unit cost of making the 10,000 power adapters is:
   ₹40,00,000 ÷ 10,000 units = ₹400 per unit
2. The total cost of the 375 spoiled units is:
   ₹400 × 375 units = ₹1,50,000
3. The increase in the per-unit cost of goods sold as a result of the normal spoilage is:
   ₹1,50,000 ÷ 9,625 good units = ₹15.6

   Unit cost of goods sold for units remaining after the spoilage = ₹400 + ₹15.6 = ₹415.6.
   (Or ₹40,00,000 ÷ 9,625 = ₹41

4. The ₹1,50,000 cost for the 375 spoiled units is taken out of manufacturing costs and expensed in the period of the spoilage. The journal entry to record the abnormal spoilage incurred is:

Loss from abnormal spoilage	₹1,50,000	
Work-in-process control	₹1,50,000	

18-23 Weighted-average method, spoilage. WaferCo is a fast-growing manufacturer of computer chips. Direct materials are added at the start of the production process. Conversion costs are added evenly during the process. Some units of this product are spoiled as a result of defects not detectable before inspection of finished goods. Spoiled units are disposed of at zero net disposal value. WaferCo uses the weighted-average method of process costing.

Summary data for September 2016 are as follows:

	A	B	C	D
	Home Insert Page Layout Formulas Data Review View			
1		Physical Units (Computer Chips)	Direct Materials	Conversion Costs
2	Work in process, beginning inventory (September 1)	1,200	₹14,23,210	₹1,63,140
3	Degree of completion of beginning work in process		100%	30%
4	Started during September	2,257		
5	Good units completed and transferred out during September	2,300		
6	Work in process, ending inventory (September 30)	520		
7	Degree of completion of ending work in process		100%	20%
8	Total costs added during September		₹57,32,780	₹25,73,760
9	Normal spoilage as a percentage of good units	15%		
10	Degree of completion of normal spoilage		100%	100%
11	Degree of completion of abnormal spoilage		100%	100%

Required

1. For each cost category, compute equivalent units. Show physical units in the first column of your schedule.

2. Summarize the total costs to account for; calculate the cost per equivalent unit for each cost category; and assign costs to units completed and transferred out (including normal spoilage), to abnormal spoilage, and to units in ending work in process.

Solution

1. Solution Exhibit 18-23, Panel A, calculates the equivalent units of work done to date for each cost category in September 2016.

2. Solution Exhibit 18-23, Panel B, summarizes total costs to account for, calculates the costs per equivalent unit for each cost category, and assigns total costs to units completed (including normal spoilage), to abnormal spoilage, and to units in ending work in process using the weighted-average method.

Solution Exhibit 18-23

Weighted-Average Method of Process Costing with Spoilage,
WaferCo for September 2016

PANEL A: Summarize the Flow of Physical Units and Compute Output in Equivalent Units

	(Step 1)	(Step 2) Equivalent Units	
Flow of Production	Physical Units	Direct Materials	Conversion Costs
Work in process, beginning (given)	1,200		
Started during current period (given)	2,257		
To account for	3,457		
Good units completed and transferred out during current period:	2,300	2,300	2,300
Normal spoilage*	345		
345 × 100%; 345 × 100%		345	345
Abnormal spoilage†	292		
292 × 100%; 292 × 100%		292	292
Work in process, ending‡ (given)	520		
520 × 100%; 520 × 20%		520	104
Accounted for	3,457		
Equivalent units of work done to date		3,457	3,041

*Normal spoilage is 15% of good units transferred out: 15% × 2,300 = 345 units. Degree of completion of normal spoilage in this department: direct materials, 100%; conversion costs, 100%.

†Total spoilage = 1,200 + 2,257 − 2,300 − 520 = 637 units; Abnormal spoilage = Total spoilage − Normal spoilage = 637 − 345 = 292 units. Degree of completion of abnormal spoilage in this department: direct materials, 100%; conversion costs, 100%.

‡Degree of completion in this department: direct materials, 100%; conversion costs, 20%.

PANEL B: Summarize the Total Costs to Account for, Compute the Cost per Equivalent Unit, and Assign Costs to the Units Completed, Spoiled Units, and Units in Ending Work-in-Process Inventory.

		Total Production Costs	Direct Materials	Conversion Costs
(Step 3)	Work in process, beginning (given)	₹15,86,350	₹14,23,210	₹1,63,140
	Costs added in current period (given)	83,06,540	57,32,780	25,73,760
	Total costs to account for	₹98,92,890		
			₹71,55,990	₹27,36,900
(Step 4)	Costs incurred to date	————	₹71,55,990	₹27,36,900
	Divided by equivalent units of work done to date		÷ 3,457	÷ 3,041
	Cost per equivalent unit		₹2,070	₹900
(Step 5)	Assignment of costs			
	Good units completed and transferred out (2,300 units)			
	Costs before adding normal spoilage	₹68,31,000	(2,300# × ₹2,070) + (2,300# × ₹900)	
	Normal spoilage (345 units)	10,24,650	(345# × ₹2,070) + (345# × ₹900)	
(A)	Total cost of good units completed and transferred out	78,55,650		
(B)	Abnormal spoilage (292 units)	8,67,240	(292# × ₹2,070) + (292# × ₹900)	
(C)	Work-in-process, ending (520 units)	11,70,000	(520# × ₹2,070) + (104# × ₹900)	
	(A)+(B)+(C) Total costs accounted for	₹98,92,890	₹71,55,990	₹27,36,900

Equivalent units of direct materials and conversion costs calculated in Step 2 in Panel A.

18-24 FIFO method, spoilage. Refer to the information in Exercise 18-23.

Required

1. Do Exercise 18-23 using the FIFO method of process costing.
2. Should WaferCo's managers choose the weighted-average method or the FIFO method? Explain briefly.

Solution

1. Solution Exhibit 18-24, Panel A, calculates the equivalent units of work done in the current period for each cost category in September 2016.

   Solution Exhibit 18-24, Panel B, summarizes WaferCo's production costs for September 2014, calculates the costs per equivalent unit for each cost category, and assigns total costs to units completed and transferred out (including normal spoilage) to abnormal spoilage and to units in ending work in process under the FIFO method.

Solution Exhibit 18-24

First-in, First-out (FIFO) Method of Process Costing with Spoilage, WaferCo for September 2016

PANEL A: Summarize the Flow of Physical Units and Compute Output in Equivalent Units

	(Step 1)	(Step 2) Equivalent Units	
Flow of Production	**Physical Units**	**Direct Materials**	**Conversion Costs**
Work in process, beginning (given)	1,200		
Started during current period (given)	2,557		
To account for	3,457		
Good units completed and transferred out during current period:			
From beginning work in process‖	1,200		
1,200 × (100% − 100%); 1,200 × (100% − 30%)		0	840
Started and completed	1,100#		
1,100 × 100%; 1,100 × 100%		1,100	1,100
Normal spoilage*	345		
345 × 100%; 345 × 100%		345	345
Abnormal spoilage†	292		
292 × 100%; 292 × 100%		292	292
Work in process, ending‡	520		
520 × 100%; 520 × 20%		520	104
Accounted for	3,457		
Equivalent units of work done in current period		2,257	2,681

‖Degree of completion in this department: direct materials, 100%; conversion costs, 30%.

#2,300 physical units completed and transferred out minus 1,200 physical units completed and transferred out from beginning work in process inventory.

*Normal spoilage is 15% of good units transferred out: 15% × 2,300 = 345 units. Degree of completion of normal spoilage in this department: direct materials, 100%; conversion costs, 100%.

†Abnormal spoilage = Actual spoilage − Normal spoilage = 637 − 345 = 292 units. Degree of completion of abnormal spoilage in this department: direct materials, 100%; conversion costs, 100%.

‡Degree of completion in this department: direct materials, 100%; conversion costs, 20%.

PANEL B: Summarize the Total Costs to Account for, Compute the Cost per Equivalent Unit, and Assign Costs to the Units Completed, Spoiled Units, and Units in Ending Work-in-Process Inventory

		Total Production Costs	**Direct Materials**	**Conversion Costs**
(Step 3)	Work in process, beginning (given)	₹15,86,350	₹14,23,210	₹1,63,140
	Costs added in current period (given)	83,06,540	57,32,780	25,73,760
	Total costs to account for	₹98,92,890	₹71,55,990	₹27,36,900
(Step 4)	Costs added in current period		₹57,32,780	₹25,73,760
	Divided by equivalent units of work done in current period		÷ 2,257	÷ 2,681
	Cost per equivalent unit		₹2,540	₹960

(Step 5)   Assignment of costs:

Good units completed and transferred out (2,300 units)

	Work in process, beginning (1,200 units)	₹15,86,350	₹14,23,210 + ₹1,63,140
	Costs added to beg. work in process in current period	8,06,400	(0§ × ₹2,540) + (840§ × ₹960)
	Total from beginning inventory before normal spoilage	23,92,750	
	Started and completed before normal spoilage (1,100 units)	38,50,000	(1,100§ × ₹2,540) + (1,100§ × ₹960)
	Normal spoilage (345 units)	12,07,500	(345§ × ₹2,540) + (345§ × ₹960)
(A)	Total costs of good units completed and transferred out	74,50,250	
(B)	Abnormal spoilage (292 units)	10,22,000	(292§ × ₹2,540) + (292§ × ₹960)
(C)	Work in process, ending (520 units)	14,20,640	(520§ × ₹2,540) + (104§ × ₹960)
(A)+(B)+(C)	Total costs accounted for	₹98,92,890	₹71,55,990 ₹27,36,900

§Equivalent units of direct materials and conversion costs calculated in Step 2 in Panel A.

2. The cost per equivalent unit of beginning inventory and of work done in the current period differ substantially:

	Beginning Inventory	Work Done in Current Period
Direct materials	₹1,186 (₹14,23,210 ÷ 1,200 equiv. units)	₹2,540
Conversion costs	453.2 (₹1,63,140 ÷ 360 equiv. units)	960
Total cost per unit	₹1,639.20	₹3,500

	Direct Materials	Conversion Costs
Cost per equivalent unit (weighted-average)	₹2,070*	₹900*
Cost per equivalent unit (FIFO)	₹2,540**	₹960**

* from Solution Exhibit 18-25, Panel B
** from Solution Exhibit 18-26, Panel B

The cost per equivalent unit differs between the two methods because each method uses different costs as the numerator of the calculation. FIFO uses only the costs added during the current period whereas weighted-average uses the costs from the beginning work-in-process as well as costs added during the current period. Both methods also use different equivalent units in the denominator.

The following table summarizes the costs assigned to units completed and those still in process under the weighted-average and FIFO process-costing methods for our example.

	FIFO (Solution Exhibit 18-24B)	Wtd.-Avg. (Solution Exhibit 18-24B)	Difference
Cost of units completed and transferred out	₹74,50,250	₹78,55,650	– ₹4,05,400
Abnormal spoilage	10,22,000	8,67,240	+ ₹1,54,760
Work in process, ending	14,20,640	11,70,000	+ ₹2,50,640
Total costs accounted for	₹98,92,890	₹98,92,890	

The FIFO ending inventory is higher than the weighted-average ending inventory by ₹2,50,640. This is because FIFO assumes that all the lower-cost prior-period units in work in process are the first to be completed and transferred out while ending work in process consists of only the higher-cost current-period units. The weighted-average method, in contrast, smoothes the cost per equivalent unit by assuming that more of the higher-cost units are completed and transferred out, while some lower-cost units in beginning work in process are placed in ending work in process. It similarly costs the abnormal spoilage incurred during the period using a blended cost rate rather than the higher current-period cost (as in the FIFO method, which assigns ₹1,54,760 more in costs to that spoilage). As a result, the FIFO method results in a relatively lower cost of units completed and transferred out and a higher ending work-in-process inventory.

WaferCo's managers should consider the weighted-average method because it leads to a higher cost of goods completed and transferred (and sold), thereby lowering taxes. The managers may have an incentive, however, to use the FIFO method and show a higher level of current income if their compensation increases with higher operating income or if there are debt covenants that would be violated by showing lower income. WaferCo's managers may also consider advantage of the FIFO method, which is that it provides better information for managing the business because it keeps separate the costs of the current period from costs incurred in previous periods.

18-25 Standard-costing method, spoilage. Refer to the information in Exercise 18-23. Suppose WaferCo determines standard costs of ₹2,400 per equivalent unit for direct materials and ₹1,000 per equivalent unit for conversion costs for both beginning work in process and work done in the current period.

Required

1. Do Exercise 18-23 using the standard-costing method.
2. What issues should the manager focus on when reviewing the equivalent units calculation?

Solution

1. Solution Exhibit 18-24, Panel A, shows the computation of the equivalent units of work done in September 2016 for direct materials (2,257 units) and conversion costs (2,681 units). (This computation is the same for FIFO and standard-costing.)

The direct materials cost per equivalent unit of beginning work in process and of work done in September 2016 is the standard cost of ₹2,400 given in the problem.

The conversion cost per equivalent unit of beginning work in process and of work done in September 2016 is the standard cost of ₹1,000 given in the problem.

Solution Exhibit 18-25 summarizes the total costs to account for and assigns these costs to units completed (including normal spoilage), to abnormal spoilage, and to units in ending work in process using the standard costing method.

Solution Exhibit 18-25

Summarize the Total Costs to Account for, Compute the Cost per Equivalent Unit, and Assign Costs to the Units Completed, Spoiled Units, and Units in Ending Work-in-Process Inventory;

Standard Costing Method of Process Costing with Spoilage,

WaferCo for September 2016

		Total Production Costs	Direct Materials	Conversion Costs
(Step 3)	Work in process, beginning*	₹32,40,000	(1,200 × ₹2,400)	(360 × ₹1,000)
	Costs added in current period at standard prices	80,97,800	(2,257 × ₹2,400)	(2,681 × ₹1,000)
	Costs to account for	₹1,13,37,800	₹82,96,800	₹30,41,000
(Step 4)	Standard costs per equivalent unit (given)	₹3,400	₹2,400	₹1,000

(Step 5) Assignment of costs at standard costs:

	Good units completed and transferred out (2,100 units)		
	Work in process, beginning (1,200 units)*	₹32,40,000	(1,200 × ₹2,400) + (360 × ₹1,000)
	Costs added to beg. work in process in current period	8,40,000	$(0^{\S} × ₹2,400) + (840^{\S} × ₹1,000)$
	Total from beginning inventory before normal spoilage	40,80,000	
	Started and completed before normal spoilage (1,100 units)	37,40,000	$(1,100^{\S} × ₹2,400) + (1,100^{\S} × ₹1,000)$
	Normal spoilage (345 units)	11,73,000	$(345^{\S} × ₹2,400) + (345^{\S} × ₹1,000)$
(A)	Total costs of good units completed and transferred out	89,93,000	
(B)	Abnormal spoilage (292 units)	9,92,800	$(292^{\S} × ₹2,400) + (292^{\S} × ₹1,000)$
(C)	Work in process, ending (520 units)	13,52,000	$(520^{\S} × ₹2,400) + (104^{\S} × ₹1,000)$
(A)+(B)+(C)	Total costs accounted for	₹1,13,37,800	₹82,96,800 + ₹30,41,000

*Work in process, beginning has 1,200 equivalent units (1,200 physical units × 100%) of direct materials and 360 equivalent units (1,200 physical units × 30%) of conversion costs.

§Equivalent units of direct materials and conversion costs calculated in Step 2 in Solution Exhibit 18-25, Panel A.

2. To show better performance, a department supervisor might report a higher degree of completion resulting in understated cost per equivalent unit and overstated operating income. If performance for the period is very good, the department supervisor may be tempted to report a lower degree of completion reducing income in the current period. This has the effect of reducing the costs carried in ending inventory and the costs carried to the following year in beginning inventory. In other words, estimates of degree of completion can help to smooth earnings from one period to the next.

To guard against the possibility of bias, managers should ask supervisors specific questions about the process they followed to prepare estimates. Top management should always emphasize obtaining the correct answer, regardless of how it affects reported performance. This emphasis drives ethical actions throughout the organization.

18-26 Weighted-average method, spoilage. The Seafood Company is a food-processing firm. It operates under the weighted-average method of process costing and has two departments: cleaning and packaging. For the cleaning department, conversion costs are added evenly during the process, and direct materials are added at the beginning of the process. Spoiled units are detected upon inspection at the end of the process and are disposed of at zero net disposal value. All completed work is transferred to the packaging department. Summary data for May follow:

	A	B	C	D
		Home Insert Page Layout Formulas Data Review View		
1	The Seafood Company: Cleaning Department	Physical Units	Direct Materials	Conversion Costs
2	Work in process, beginning inventory (May 1)	3,600	₹53,160	₹19,530
3	Degree of completion of beginning work in process		100%	60%
4	Started during May	30,000		
5	Good units completed and transferred out during May	24,600		
6	Work in process, ending inventory (May 31)	5,040		
7	Degree of completion of ending work in process		100%	30%
8	Total costs added during May		₹5,55,000	₹4,46,590
9	Normal spoilage as a percentage of good units	10%		
10	Degree of completion of normal spoilage		100%	100%
11	Degree of completion of abnormal spoilage		100%	100%

Required

For the cleaning department, summarize the total costs to account for and assign those costs to units completed and transferred out (including normal spoilage), to abnormal spoilage, and to units in ending work in process.

Solution

Solution Exhibit 18-26 summarizes total costs to account for, calculates the equivalent units of work done to date for each cost category, and assigns total costs to units completed (including normal spoilage), to abnormal spoilage, and to units in ending work in process using the weighted-average method.

Solution Exhibit 18-26

Weighted-Average Method of Process Costing with Spoilage,
Cleaning Department of the Seafood Company for May

PANEL A: Summarize the Flow of Physical Units and Compute Output in Equivalent Units;

		(Step 1)	(Step 2) Equivalent Units	
Flow of Production		Physical Units	Direct Materials	Conversion Costs
Work in process, beginning (given)		3,600		
Started during current period (given)		30,000		
To account for		33,600		
Good units completed and transferred out during current period:		24,600	24,600	24,600
Normal spoilage*				
2,460 × 100%; 2,460 × 100%		2,460	2,460	2,460
Abnormal spoilage[†]				
1,500 × 100%; 1,500 × 100%		1,500	1,500	1,500
Work in process, ending[‡] (given)				
5,040 × 100%; 5,040 × 30%		5,040	5,040	5,040
Accounted for				
Equivalent units of work done to date		33,600	33,600	30,072

*Normal spoilage is 10% of good units transferred out: 10% × 24,600 = 2,460 units. Degree of completion of normal spoilage in this department: direct materials, 100%; conversion costs, 100%.

[†]Total spoilage = 3,600 + 30,000 − 24,600 − 5,040 = 3,960 units; Abnormal spoilage = 3,960 − 2,460 = 1,500 units. Degree of completion of abnormal spoilage in this department: direct materials, 100%; conversion costs, 100%.

[‡]Degree of completion in this department: direct materials, 100%; conversion costs, 30%.

PANEL B: Summarize the Total Costs to Account for, Compute the Cost per Equivalent Unit, and Assign Costs to the Units Completed, Spoiled Units, and Units in Ending Work-in-Process Inventory

		Total Production Costs	Direct Materials	Conversion Costs
(Step 3)	Work in process, beginning (given)	₹72,690	₹53,160	₹19,530
	Costs added in current period (given)	10,01,590	5,55,000	4,46,590
	Total costs to account for	₹10,74,280	₹6,08,160	₹4,66,120

(Step 4)	Costs incurred to date		₹6,08,160	₹4,66,120
	Divided by equivalent units of work done to date		÷33,600	÷30,072
	Cost per equivalent unit		₹18.1	₹15.50
(Step 5)	Assignment of costs			
	Good units completed and transferred out (24,600 units)			
	Costs before adding normal spoilage	₹8,26,560 82,660	(24,600# × ₹18.1) + (2,460# × ₹18.1) +	(24,600# × ₹15.50) (2,460# × ₹15.50)
	Normal spoilage (2,460 units)			
(A)	Total costs of good units completed and transferred out	9,09,220		
(B)	Abnormal spoilage (1,500 units)	50,400	(1,500# × ₹18.1) +	(1,500# × ₹15.50)
(C)	Work in process, ending (5,040 units)	1,14,660	(5,040# × ₹18.1) +	(1,512# × ₹15.50)
(A)+(B)+(C)	Total costs accounted for	₹10,74,280	₹6,08,160 +	₹4,66,120

#Equivalent units of direct materials and conversion costs calculated in Step 2 in Panel A above.

18-27 FIFO method, spoilage. Refer to the information in Problem 18-26.

Required

Do Problem 18-26 using the FIFO method of process costing.

Solution

For the Cleaning Department, Solution Exhibit 18-27 summarizes the total costs for May, calculates the equivalent units of work done in the current period for direct materials and conversion costs, and assigns total costs to units completed and transferred out (including normal spoilage), to abnormal spoilage, and to units in ending work in process under the FIFO method.

Solution Exhibit 18-27 First-in, First-out (FIFO) Method of Process Costing with Spoilage,
Cleaning Department of the Seafood Company for May
PANEL A: Summarize the Flow of Physical Units and Compute Output in Equivalent Units

Flow of Production	(Step 1) Physical Units	(Step 2) Equivalent Units Direct Materials	Conversion Costs
Work in process, beginning (given)	3,600		
Started during current period (given)	30,000		
To account for	33,600		
Good units completed and transferred out during current period:			
From beginning work in process‖	3,600		
3,600 × (100% − 100%); 3,600 × (100% − 60%)		0	1,440
Started and completed	21,000#		
21,000 × 100%; 21,000 × 100%		21,000	21,000
Normal spoilage*	2,460		
2,460 × 100%; 2,460 × 100%		2,460	2,460
Abnormal spoilage†	1,500		

			1,500	1,500
	1,500 × 100%; 1,500 × 100%			
	Work in process, ending‡	5,040		
	5,040 × 100%; 5,040 × 30%		5,040	1,512
	Accounted for	33,600		
	Equivalent units of work done in current period		30,000	27,912

‖ Degree of completion in this department: direct materials, 100%; conversion costs, 60%.

#24,600 physical units completed and transferred out minus 3,600 physical units completed and transferred out from beginning work-in-process inventory.

*Normal spoilage is 10% of good units transferred out: 10% × 24,600 = 2,460 units. Degree of completion of normal spoilage in this department: direct materials, 100%; conversion costs, 100%.

†Total spoilage = 3,600 + 30,000 − 24,600 − 5,040 = 3,960 units; Abnormal spoilage = 3,960 − 2,460 = 1,500 units. Degree of completion of abnormal spoilage in this department: direct materials, 100%; conversion costs, 100%.

‡Degree of completion in this department: direct materials, 100%; conversion costs, 30%.

PANEL B: Summarize the Total Costs to Account for, Compute the Cost per Equivalent Unit, and Assign Costs to the Units Completed, Spoiled Units, and Units in Ending Work-in-Process Inventory

		Total Production Costs	Direct Materials	Conversion Costs
(Step 3)	Work in process, beginning (given)	₹72,690	₹53,160	₹19,530
	Costs added in current period (given)	10,01,590	5,55,000	4,46,590
	Total costs to account for	₹10,74,280	₹6,08,160	₹4,66,120
(Step 4)	Costs added in current period		₹5,55,000	₹4,46,590
	Divided by equivalent units of work done in current period		÷30,000	÷27,912
	Cost per equivalent unit		₹18.5	₹16.0
(Step 5)	Assignment of costs:			
	Good units completed and transferred out (24,600 units)			
	Work in process, beginning (3,600 units)	72,690	₹53,160 +	₹19,530
	Costs added to beg. work in process in current period	23,040	(0§ × ₹18.5) + (1,440§ × ₹16)	
	Total from beginning inventory before normal spoilage	95,730		
	Started and completed before normal spoilage (21,000 units)	7,24,500	(21,000§ × ₹18.5) + (21,000§ × ₹16)	
	Normal spoilage (2,460 units)	84,870	(2,460§ × ₹18.5) + (2,460§ × ₹16)	
(A)	Total costs of good units completed and transferred out	9,05,100		
(B)	Abnormal spoilage (1,500 units)	51,750	(1,500§ × ₹18.5) + (1,500§ × ₹16)	
(C)	Work in process, ending (5,040 units)	1,17,430	(5,040§ × ₹18.5) + (1,512§ × ₹16)	
(A)+(B)+(C)	Total costs accounted for	10,74,280	₹6,08,160 + ₹4,66,120	

§Equivalent units of direct materials and conversion costs calculated in Step 2 in Panel A.

18-28 Weighted-average method, Packaging Department (continuation of 18-27). In the Seafood Company's packaging department, conversion costs are added evenly during the process, and direct materials are added at the end of the process. Spoiled units are detected upon inspection at the end of the process and are disposed of at zero net disposal value. All completed work is transferred to the next department. The transferred-in costs for May equal the total cost of good units completed and transferred out in May from the cleaning department, which were calculated in Problem 18-27 using the weighted-average method of process costing. Summary data for May follow.

	A	B	C	D	E
		Physical Units	Transferred-In Costs	Direct Materials	Conversion Costs
1	**The Seafood Company: Packaging Department**				
2	Work in process, beginning inventory (May 1)	12,600	₹3,36,980	₹0	₹2,34,750
3	Degree of completion of beginning work in process		100%	0%	70%
4	Started during May	24,600			
5	Good units completed and transferred out during May	26,400			
6	Work in process, ending inventory (May 31)	8,400			
7	Degree of completion of ending work in process		100%	0%	40%
8	Total costs added during May		?	₹57,600	₹4,08,450
9	Normal spoilage as a percentage of good units	8%			
10	Degree of completion of normal spoilage			100%	100%
11	Degree of completion of abnormal spoilage			100%	100%

Required

For the packaging department, use the weighted-average method to summarize the total costs to account for and assign those costs to units completed and transferred out (including normal spoilage), to abnormal spoilage, and to units in ending work in process.

Solution

For the Packaging Department, Solution Exhibit 18-28 summarizes total costs to account for, calculates the equivalent units of work done to date for each cost category, and assigns costs to units completed (including normal spoilage), to abnormal spoilage, and to units in ending work in process using the weighted-average method.

Solution Exhibit 18-28

Weighted-Average Method of Process Costing with Spoilage,
Packaging Department of the Seafood Company for May
PANEL A: Summarize the Flow of Physical Units and Compute Output in Equivalent Units

	(Step 1)	(Step 2) Equivalent Units		
Flow of Production	Physical Units	Transferred-in Costs	Direct Materials	Conversion Costs
Work in process, beginning (given)	12,600			
Started during current period (given)	24,600			
To account for	37,200			
Good units completed and transferred out during current period:	26,400	26,400	26,400	26,400
Normal spoilage*	2,112			
2,112 × 100%; 2,112 × 100%; 2,112 × 100%		2,112	2,112	2,112
Abnormal spoilage†	288			
288 × 100%; 288 ×100%, 288 × 100%		288	288	288
Work in process, ending‡ (given)	8,400			
8,400 × 100%; 8,400 × 0%; 8,400 × 40%		8,400	0	3,360
Accounted for	37,200			
Equivalent units of work done to date		37,200	28,800	28,800

*Normal spoilage is 8% of good units transferred out: 8% × 26,400 = 2,112 units. Degree of completion of normal spoilage in this department: transferred-in costs, 100%; direct materials, 100%; conversion costs, 100%.

†Total spoilage = 12,600 + 24,600 − 26,400 − 8,400 = 2,400 units. Abnormal spoilage = 2,400 − 2,112 = 288 units. Degree of completion of abnormal spoilage in this department: transferred-in costs, 100%; direct materials, 100%; conversion costs, 100%.

‡Degree of completion in this department: transferred-in costs, 100%; direct materials, 0%; conversion costs, 40%.

PANEL B: Summarize the Total Costs to Account for, Compute the Cost per Equivalent Unit, and Assign Costs to the Units Completed, Spoiled Units, and Units in Ending Work-in-Process Inventory

		Total Production Costs	Transferred-in Costs	Direct Materials	Conversion Costs
(Step 3)	Work in process, beginning (given)	₹5,13,380	₹3,36,980	₹0	₹2,34,750
	Costs added in current period (given)	14,33,620	9,09,220*	57,600	4,08,450
	Total costs to account for	₹19,47,000	₹12,46,200	₹57,600	₹6,43,200
(Step 4)	Costs incurred to date		12,46,200	57,600	6,43,200
	Divided by equivalent units of work done to date		÷ 37,200	÷ 28,800	÷ 32,160
	Cost per equivalent unit		₹33.5	₹2.0	₹20.0
(Step 5)	Assignment of costs				
	Good units completed and transferred out (26,400 units)				
	Costs before adding normal spoilage	₹14,65,200	26,400# × (₹33.5 + ₹2.0 + ₹20)		
	Normal spoilage (2,112 units)	1,17,220	2,112# × (₹33.5 + ₹2.0 + ₹20)		
(A)	Total cost of good units completed and transferred out	15,82,420			
(B)	Abnormal spoilage (288 units)	15,980	288# × (₹33.5 + ₹2.0 + ₹20)		
(C)	Work in process, ending (8,400 units)	3,48,600	(8,400# × ₹33.5) + (0# × ₹2.0) + (3,360# × ₹20)		
(A)+(B)+(C)	Total costs accounted for	₹19,47,000	₹12,46,200 + ₹57,600 + ₹6,43,200		

*Total costs of good units completed and transferred out in Panel B (Step 5) of Solution Exhibit 18-31.

#Equivalent units of direct materials and conversion costs calculated in Step 2 in Panel A above.

18-29 FIFO method, Packaging Department (continuation of 18-28). Refer to the information in Problem 18-28 except that the transferred-in costs of beginning work in process on May 1 are ₹3,30,900 (instead of ₹3,36,980). Transferred-in costs for May equal the total cost of good units completed and transferred out in May from the cleaning department, as calculated in Problem 18-28 using the FIFO method of process costing.

Required   For the packaging department, use the FIFO method to summarize the total costs to account for and assign those costs to units completed and transferred out (including normal spoilage), to abnormal spoilage, and to units in ending work in process.

Solution

Solution Exhibit 18-29 summarizes the total Packaging Department costs for May, shows the equivalent units of work done in the Packaging Department in the current period for transferred-in costs, direct materials, and conversion costs, and assigns total costs to units completed and transferred out (including normal spoilage), to abnormal spoilage, and to units in ending work-in-process under the FIFO method.

Solution Exhibit 18-29

First-in, First-out (FIFO) Method of Process Costing with Spoilage,
Packaging Department of the Seafood Company for May

PANEL A: Summarize the Flow of Physical Units and Compute Output in Equivalent Units

	(Step 1)	(Step 2) Equivalent Units		
Flow of Production	Physical Units	Transferred-in Costs	Direct Materials	Conversion Costs
Work in process, beginning (given)	12,600			
Started during current period (given)	24,600			
To account for	37,200			
Good units completed and transferred out during current period:				
From beginning work in process‖	12,600			
12,600 × (100% − 100%); 12,600 (100% − 0%); 12,600 × (100% − 70%)		0	12,600	3,780
Started and completed	13,800#			
13,800 × 100%; 13,800 × 100%; 13,800 × 100%		13,800	13,800	13,800
Normal spoilage*	2,112			
2,112 × 100%; 2,112 × 100%; 2,112 × 100%		2,112	2,112	2,112
Abnormal spoilage†	288			
288 × 100%; 288 × 100%; 288 × 100%		288	288	288
Work in process, ending‡	8,400			
8,400 × 100%; 8,400 × 0%; 8,400 × 40%		8,400	0	3,360
Accounted for	37,200			
Equivalent units of work done in current period		24,600	28,800	23,340

‖Degree of completion in this department: transferred-in costs, 100%; direct materials, 0%; conversion costs, 70%.

#26,400 physical units completed and transferred out minus 12,600 physical units completed and transferred out from beginning work-in-process inventory.

*Normal spoilage is 8% of good units transferred out: 8% × 26,400 = 2,112 units. Degree of completion of normal spoilage in this department: transferred-in costs, 100%; direct materials, 100%; conversion costs, 100%.

†Total spoilage = 12,600 + 24,600 − 26,400 − 8,400 = 2,400 units.

Abnormal spoilage = 2,400 − 2,112 = 288 units. Degree of completion of abnormal spoilage in this department: transferred-in costs, 100%; direct materials, 100%; conversion costs, 100%.

‡Degree of completion in this department: transferred-in costs, 100%; direct materials, 0%; conversion costs, 40%.

PANEL B: Summarize the Total Costs to Account for, Compute the Cost per Equivalent Unit, and Assign Costs to the Units Completed, Spoiled Units, and Units in Ending Work-in-Process Inventory

		Total Production Costs	Transferred-in Costs	Direct Materials	Conversion Costs
(Step 3)	Work in process, beginning (given)	₹5,65,650	₹3,30,900	₹0	₹2,34,750
	Costs added in current period (given)	13,71,150	9,05,100*	57,600	4,08,450
	Total costs to account for	₹19,36,800	₹12,36,000	₹57,600	₹6,43,200

(Step 4)	Costs added in current period	₹9,05,100	₹57,600	₹4,08,450
	Divided by equivalent units of work done in	÷ 24,600	÷ 28,800	÷ 23,340
	current period	₹36.79	₹2.0	₹17.5
	Cost per equivalent unit			

(Step 5) Assignment of costs:

Good units completed and transferred out
(26,400 units)

	Work in process, beginning (12,600 units)	₹5,65,650	₹3,30,900 + ₹0 + ₹2,34,750
	Costs added to beg. work in process in current period	91,350	$(0 \times ₹36.79) + (12,600^§ \times ₹2.0) + (3,780^§ \times ₹17.5)$
	Total from beginning inventory before normal spoilage	6,57,000	
	Started and completed before normal spoilage (13,800 units)	7,76,800	$13,800^§ \times (₹36.79 + ₹2.0 + ₹17.5)$
	Normal spoilage (2,112 units)	1,18,880	$2,112^§ \times (₹36.79 + ₹2.0 + ₹17.5)$
(A)	Total costs of good units completed and transferred out	15,52,680	
(B)	Abnormal spoilage (288 units)	16,210	$288^§ \times (₹36.79 + ₹2.0 + ₹17.5)$
(C)	Work in process, ending (8,400 units)	3,67,840	$(8,400^§ \times ₹36.79) + (0^§ \times ₹2.0) + (3,360^§ \times ₹17.5)$
(A)+(B)+(C)	Total costs accounted for	₹19,36,730+	₹13,92,330 + ₹57,600 + ₹6,43,200

*Total costs of good units completed and transferred out in Step 5, Panel B of Solution Exhibit 18-32.

§Equivalent units of direct materials and conversion costs calculated in Step 2 in Panel A.

+ Difference of ₹70 (₹19,36,730 relative to ₹19,36,800) due to rounding.

18-30 Physical units, inspection at various levels of completion, weighted-average process costing. SunEnergy produces solar panels. A key step in the conversion of raw silicon to a completed solar panel occurs in the assembly department, where lightweight photovoltaic cells are assembled into modules and connected on a frame. In this department, materials are added at the beginning of the process and conversion takes place uniformly.

At the start of November 2016, SunEnergy's assembly department had 2,400 panels in beginning work in process, which were 100% complete for materials and 40% complete for conversion costs. An additional 12,000 units were started in the department in November, and 3,600 units remain in work in process at the end of the month. These unfinished units are 100% complete for materials and 70% complete for conversion costs.

The assembly department had 1,800 spoiled units in November. Because of the difficulty of keeping moisture out of the modules and sealing the photovoltaic cells between layers of glass, normal spoilage is approximately 12% of good units. The department's costs for the month of November are as follows:

	Beginning WIP	Costs Incurred During Period
Direct materials costs	₹76,80,000	₹2,40,00,000
Conversion costs	1,23,00,000	12,00,00,000

1. Using the in text, compute the normal and abnormal spoilage in units for November, assuming the inspection point is at (a) the 30% stage of completion, (b) the 60% stage of completion, and (c) the 100% stage of completion.

2. Refer to your answer in requirement 1. Why are there different amounts of normal and abnormal spoilage at different inspection points?

3. Now assume that the assembly department inspects at the 60% stage of completion. Using the weighted-average method, calculate the cost of units transferred out, the cost of abnormal spoilage, and the cost of ending inventory for the assembly department in November.

Solution

1.

	Inspection at 30%	Inspection at 60%	Inspection at 100%
Work in process, beginning (40%)*	2,400	2,400	2,400
Started during November	12,000	12,000	12,000
To account for	14,400	14,400	14,400
Good units completed and transferred out	9,000[a]	9,000[a]	9,000[a]
Normal spoilage	1,224[b]	1,512[c]	1,080[d]
Abnormal spoilage (1,800 − normal spoilage)	576	288	720
Work in process, ending (70%)*	3,600	3,600	3,600
Accounted for	14,400	14,400	14,400

*Degree of completion for conversion costs at the dates of the work-in-process inventories

[a]2,400 beginning inventory + 12,000 started − 1,800 spoiled − 3,600 ending inventory = 9,000.

[b]12% × (12,000 units started − 1,800 units spoiled) = 12% × 10,200 = 1,224; beginning work-in-process inventory is excluded because it was already 40% complete at November 1 and past the inspection point.

[c]12% × (14,400 units − 1,800) = 12% × 12,600 = 1,512 because all units passed the 60% completion inspection point in November.

[d]12% × 9,000 = 1,080 because 9,000 units are fully completed and inspected during November.

2. There are different amounts of normal and abnormal spoilage because the spoilage is detected at different points in the process. At the 30% inspection point, the beginning work-in-process inventory has already passed inspection and consists entirely of good units. At the 60% inspection point, the beginning work in process as well as units started this period must pass through the inspection point in the month of November. At the 100% inspection point, only the finished units have been inspected. Those in ending work in process have not yet been inspected. The finished units that are transferred out are good, but the others have not been inspected yet. Of course, in all three cases the total spoilage is 1,800 units (given in the problem).

3. Solution Exhibit 18-35 summarizes total costs to account for, calculates the equivalent units of work done to date for each cost category, and assigns total costs to units completed (including normal spoilage), to abnormal spoilage, and to units in ending work in process using the weighted-average method.

Solution Exhibit 18-30

Weighted-Average Method of Process Costing with Spoilage,
Assembly Department of SunEnergy for November 2016

PANEL A: Summarize the Flow of Physical Units and Compute Output in Equivalent Units

		(Step 1)	(Step 2) Equivalent Units	
Flow of Production		**Physical Units**	**Direct Materials**	**Conversion Costs**
Work in process, beginning (given)		2,400		
Started during current period (given)		12,000		
To account for		14,400		
Good units completed and transferred out during current period:		9,000	9,000	9,000
Normal spoilage (at 60% inspection point)				
1,512 × 100%; 1,512 × 60%		1,512	1,512	1,512
Abnormal spoilage (at 60% inspection point)				
288 × 100%; 288 × 60%		288	288	172.8
Work in process, ending‡ (given)				
3,600 × 100%; 3,600 × 70%[a]		3,600	3,600	2,520
Accounted for				
Equivalent units of work done to date		14,400	14,400	12,600

[a]Degree of completion in this department: direct materials, 100%; conversion costs, 70%.

PANEL B: Summarize the Total Costs to Account for, Compute the Cost per Equivalent Unit, and Assign Costs to the Units Completed, Spoiled Units, and Units in Ending Work-in-Process Inventory

		Total Production Costs	Direct Materials	Conversion Costs
(Step 3)	Work in process, beginning (given)	₹1,99,80,000	₹76,80,000	₹1,23,00,000
	Costs added in current period (given)	14,44,00,000	2,40,00,000	12,00,00,000
	Total costs to account for	₹16,39,80,000	₹3,16,80,000	₹13,23,00,000
(Step 4)	Costs incurred to date		₹3,16,80,000	₹13,23,00,000
	Divided by equivalent units of work done to date		÷14,400	÷ 12,600
	Cost per equivalent unit		₹2,200	₹10,500
(Step 5)	Assignment of costs			
	Good units completed and transferred out (9,000 units)			
	Costs before adding normal spoilage	₹11,43,00,000	(9,000 × ₹2,200) + (9,000 ×₹10,500)	
	Normal spoilage (1,512# units, 907.2# units)	1,28,52,000	(1,512 × ₹2,200) + (907.2 × ₹10,500)	
(A)	Total costs of good units completed and transferred out	12,71,52,000		
(B)	Abnormal spoilage (288# units, 172.8# units)	24,48,000	(288 × ₹2,200) + (172.8 × ₹10,500)	
(C)	Work in process, ending (3,600# units, 2,520# units)	3,43,80,000	(3,600 × ₹2,200) + (2,520 × ₹10,500)	
(A)+(B)+(C)	Total costs accounted for	₹16,39,80,000	₹3,16,80,000 + ₹13,23,00,000	

#Equivalent units of direct materials and conversion costs calculated in Step 2 in Panel A.

18-31 Physical units, inspection at various stages of ompletion. Superb Furniture manufactures plastic lawn furniture in a continuous process. The company pours molten plastic into molds and then cools the plastic. Materials are added at the beginning of the process, and conversion is considered uniform through the period. Occasionally, the plastic does not completely fill a mold because of air pockets, and the chair is then considered spoiled. Normal spoilage is 6% of the good units that pass inspection. The following information pertains to March 2016:

Beginning inventory	2,200units(100%completeformaterials;20% complete for conversion costs)
Units stared	21,000
Units in ending work in process	1,900 (100% complete for materials; 70% complete for conversion costs)

Superb furniture had 1,800 spoiled units in March 2016

Required

Using the format given in text, compute the normal and abnormal spoilage in units, assuming the inspection point is at (a) the 15% stage of completion, (b) the 40% stage of completion, and (c) the 100% stage of completion.

Solution

	Inspection at 15%	Inspection at 40%	Inspection at 100%
Work in process, beginning (20%)*	2,200	2,200	2,200
Started during March	21,000	21,000	21,000
To account for	23,200	23,200	23,200
Good units completed and transferred out	19,500[a]	19,500[a]	19,500[a]
Normal spoilage	1,152[b]	1,284[c]	1,170[d]
Abnormal spoilage (1,800 − Normal spoilage)	648	516	630
Work in process, ending (70%)*	1,900	1,900	1,900
Accounted for	23,200	23,200	23,200

*Degree of completion for conversion costs at the dates of the work-in-process inventories
[a]2,200 beginning inventory + 21,000 − 1,800 spoiled − 1,900 ending inventory = 19,500.
[b]6% × (21,000 units started − 1,800 units spoiled) = 6% × 19,200 = 1,152; beginning work-in-process inventory is excluded because it was already 20% complete at March 1 and past the inspection point.
[c]6% × (23,200 units − 1,800) = 6% × 21,400 = 1,284 because all units passed the 40% completion inspection point in March.
[d]6% × 19,500 = 1,170 because 19,500 units are fully completed and inspected during March.

18-32 Job costing, rework. Royal Corporation manufactures a sophisticated controller that is compatible with a variety of gaming consoles. Excluding rework costs, the cost of manufacturing one controller is ₹22,000. This consists of ₹12,000 in direct materials, ₹2,400 in direct manufacturing labor, and ₹7,600 in manufacturing overhead. Maintaining a reputation for quality is critical to Royal. Any defective units identified at the inspection point are sent back for rework. It costs Royal ₹7,200 to rework each defective controller, including ₹2,400 in direct materials, ₹1,800 in direct manufacturing labor, and ₹3,000 in manufacturing overhead.

In August 2016, Royal manufactured 1,000 controllers, 80 of which required rework. Of these 80 controllers, 50 were considered normal rework common to all jobs and the other 30 were considered abnormal rework.

Required

1. Prepare journal entries to record the accounting for both the normal and abnormal rework.

2. What were the total rework costs of controllers in August 2016?

3. Suppose instead that the normal rework is attributable entirely to Job #9, for 200 controllers intended for export. In this case, what are the total and unit costs of the good units produced for that job in August 2016? Prepare journal entries for the manufacture of the 200 controllers, as well as the normal rework costs.

Solution

1.

Manufacturing Overhead Control (rework costs)	₹3,60,000	
Materials Control (₹2,400 × 50)		₹1,20,000
Wages Payable (₹1,800 × 50)		90,000
Manufacturing Overhead Allocated (₹3,000 × 50)		1,50,000

Normal rework on 50 units but not attributable to any specific controller

Loss from Abnormal Rework (₹7,200 × 30)	2,16,000	
Materials Control (₹2,400 × 30)		72,000
Wages Payable (₹1,800 × 30)		54,000
Manufacturing Overhead Allocated (₹3,000 × 30)		90,000

Total costs of abnormal rework on 30 controllers

(Abnormal rework = Actual rework − Normal rework
= 80 − 50 = 30 controllers)

2. Total rework costs for controllers in August 2016 are as follows:

Normal rework costs allocated to controllers	₹3,60,000
Abnormal rework costs for controllers	2,16,000
Total rework costs	₹5,76,000

3. Manufacturing costs of job #9 before rework:

200 units × (₹12,000 + ₹2,400 + ₹7,600)	₹44,00,000
Add: Normal rework costs	3,60,000
Total cost of job #9	₹47,60,000
Unit cost of job (Total /200 units)	₹23,800

Work-in-Process Control (Job #9)	₹44,00,000	
Materials Control (₹12,000 × 200)		₹24,00,000
Wages Payable (₹2,400 × 200)		4,80,000
Manufacturing Overhead Allocated (₹7,600 × 200)		15,20,000

Manufacturing costs for 200 controllers on Job #9

Work-in-Process Control (Job #9)	₹3,60,000	
Materials Control (₹2,400 × 50)		₹1,20,000
Wages Payable (₹1,800 × 50)		90,000
Manufacturing Overhead Allocated (₹3,000 × 50)		1,50,000

Normal rework for 50 controllers attributable to Job #9

18-33 Job costing, spoilage, ethics. (CMA, adapted) Jindal Company manufactures products that often require specification changes or modifications to meet its customers' needs. Still, Jindal has been able to establish a normal spoilage rate of 2.5% of normal input. Normal spoilage is recognized during the budgeting process and classified as a component of manufacturing overhead when determining the overhead rate.

Peter, one of Jindal's inspection managers, obtains the following information for Job No. N1192-122, which was recently completed, just before the end of Jindal's current accounting year. The units will be delivered early in the next accounting year. A total of 1,22,000 units were started, and 5,000 spoiled units were rejected at final inspection, yielding 1,17,000 good units. Rejected units were sold at ₹7 per unit. Peter indicates that all rejects were related to this specific job.

The total costs for all 1,22,000 units of Job No. N1192-122 follow. The job has been completed, but the costs are yet to be transferred to Finished Goods.

Direct materials	₹21,96,000
Direct manufacturing labor	18,30,000
Manufacturing overhead	29,28,000
Total manufacturing costs	₹69,54,000

Required

1. Calculate the unit quantities of normal and abnormal spoilage.
2. Prepare the journal entry (or entries) to account for Job No. N1192-122, including spoilage, disposal of spoiled units, and transfer of costs to the Finished Goods account.
3. Jindal Company has small profit margins and is anticipating very low operating income for the year. The controller, tells the management accountant responsible for Job No. N1192-122, the following, "This was an unusual job. I think all 5,000 spoiled units should be considered normal." The management accountant knows that Jindal's normal spoilage rate has been a good measure of normal spoilage levels on similar jobs in the past and that the spoilage levels for Job N1192-122 were much greater. He feels the controller made these comments because he wants to show higher operating income for the year.
   a. Prepare the journal entry (or entries), similar to the journal entry (or entries) prepared in requirement 2, to account for Job No. N1192-122 if all spoilage were considered normal. By how much will Jindal's operating income be affected if all spoilage is considered normal?
   b. What should the management accountant do?

Solution

Job costing, spoilage, ethics

1. Analysis of the 5,000 units rejected by Jindal Company for Job No. N1192-122 yields the following breakdown between normal and abnormal spoilage:

	Units
Normal spoilage*	3,000
Abnormal spoilage (5,000 – 3,000)	2,000
Total units rejected	5,000

*Normal spoilage   = 0.025 of normal input
When output equals   1,17,000 units,
Normal input   = 1,17,000 ÷ (1 – 0.025)
  = 1,20,000 units
Normal spoilage = 1,20,000 × 0.025
  = 3,000 units

2. The journal entries required to properly account for Job No. N1192-122 are presented below and use an average cost per unit of ₹57 (₹69,54,000 ÷ 1,22,000):

	₹	₹
Accounts Receivable or Cash[1]	35,000	
Abnormal loss[2]	1,00,000	
WIP Control[3]		1,35,000
To account for 5,000 units rejected.		
Finished Good Control	68,19,000	
WIP Control		68,19,000

To transfer 1,17,000 units to finished goods inventory (costs incurred on job and debited to WIP Control, ₹ 69,54,000, minus ₹1,35,000 credited to WIP control).
[1]Units sold 5,000 units sold at ₹7 each.
[2]Loss from abnormal spoilage: 2,000 units at ₹57   ₹1,14,000
Cost recovery (2,000 × ₹7)   (14,000)
                                                           ₹1,00,000

[3]WIP control:
2,000 abnormal spoilage units at ₹57   ₹1,14,000
3,000 normal spoilage units at ₹7   21,000
                                                           ₹1,35,000

3. a. If all spoilage were considered normal, the journal entries to account for Job No. N1192-122 would be as follows:

Accounts Receivable or Cash   35,000
  WIP Control   35,000

To account for 5,000 units of normal spoilage, credited to WIP Control at ₹35,000 (5,000 units × ₹7).

Finished Goods Control   69,19,000
  WIP Control   69,19,000

To transfer 1,17,000 units to finished-goods inventory (costs incurred on job and debited to WIP Control, ₹69,54,000, minus ₹35,000 credited to WIP Control).

By considering all spoilage as normal, Jindal will show no abnormal loss of ₹1,00,000 (see requirement 2) but instead will add ₹1,00,000 to the finished-goods inventory [₹69,19,000 (in requirement 3a) minus ₹68,19,000 (in requirement 2)]. Hence, showing all spoilage as normal will increase Jindal's operating income by ₹1,00,000.

3. b. Incorrect reporting of spoilage as normal instead of abnormal with the goal of increasing operating income is unethical.

The management accountant should indicate to the controller that the classification of normal and abnormal spoilage established by Jindal Company is, indeed, appropriate. If the controller still insists on modifying the spoilage classification for this job to report higher operating income figures, The management accountant should raise the matter with one of the controller's superiors. If, after taking all these steps, there is continued pressure to overstate operating income, The management accountant should consider resigning from the company, and not engage in unethical behavior.

Exercises

[*Comprehensive solutions to all exercises are available on the companion website www.pearsoned.co.in/charlesthorngren*]

18-34 Weighted-average method, spoilage. Godrej Manufacturing Company uses the weighted-average method of process costing. All direct materials are added at the beginning of the process, and conversion costs are added evenly during the process. Spoiled units are detected upon inspection at the end of the process and are disposed of at zero net disposal value. Summary data for March are:

	Physical Units	Direct Materials	Conversion Costs
Work in process, March 1[a]	30,000	₹24,00,000	₹18,00,000
Started in March	50,000		
Good units completed and transferred out during March	40,000		
Normal spoilage	6,000		
Abnormal spoilage	2,000		
Work in process, March 31[b]	32,000		
Costs added during March		₹42,00,000	₹58,32,000

[a]Degree of completion: direct materials, 100%; conversion costs, 60%.
[b]Degree of completion: direct materials, 100%; conversion costs, 75%.

Required

1. For each cost category, compute equivalent units. Show physical units in the first column of your schedule.
2. For each cost category, calculate cost per equivalent unit.
3. Summarize total costs to account for, and assign these costs to units completed and transferred out (including normal spoilage), to abnormal spoilage, and to units in ending work in process.

18-35 FIFO method, spoilage. Refer to the information in 18-34.

Required

Do Exercise 18-34 using the FIFO method. Note that you first need to calculate the equivalent units of work done in the current period (for direct materials and conversion costs) to complete beginning work in process, to start and complete new units, for normal and abnormal spoilage units, and to produce ending work in process.

18-36 Standard-costing method, spoilage. Refer to the information in Exercise 18-34. Suppose Godrej determines standard costs of ₹80 per equivalent unit for direct materials and ₹100 per equivalent unit for conversion costs for both beginning work in process and work done in the current period.

Required

Do Exercise 18-34 using the standard-costing method. Note that you first need to calculate the equivalent units of work done in the current period (for direct materials and conversion costs) to complete beginning work in process, to start and complete new units, for normal and abnormal spoilage units, and to produce ending work in process.

18-37 Weighted-average method, spoilage. Superchip specializes in the manufacture of microchips for aircraft. Direct materials are added at the start of the production process. Conversion costs are added evenly during the process. Some units of this product are spoiled as a result of defects not detectable before inspection of finished goods. Normally, the spoiled units are 15% of the good units transferred out. Spoiled units are disposed of at zero net disposal value. Superchip uses the weighted-average method of process costing. Summary data for September are:

	Physical Units (Microchips)	Direct Materials	Conversion Costs
Work in process, September 1[a]	400	₹6,40,000	₹1,02,000
Started in September	1,700		
Good units completed and transferred out during September	1,400		
Work in process, September 30[b]	300		
Costs added during September		₹37,80,000	₹15,36,000

[a]Degree of completion: direct materials, 100%; conversion costs, 30%.
[b]Degree of completion: direct materials, 100%; conversion costs, 40%.

Required

1. For each cost category, compute equivalent units. Show physical units in the first column of your schedule.
2. For each cost category, calculate cost per equivalent unit.
3. Summarize total costs to account for, and assign these costs to units completed and transferred out (including normal spoilage), to abnormal spoilage, and to units in ending work in process.

18-38 FIFO method, spoilage. Refer to the information in Exercise 18-37.

Required

Do Exercise 18-37 using the FIFO method of process costing.

18-39 Standard-costing method, spoilage. Refer to the information in Exercise 18-38. Suppose Superchip determines standard costs of ₹2,050 per equivalent unit for direct materials and ₹80 per (equivalent) unit for conversion costs for both beginning work in process and work done in the current period.

Required

Do Exercise 18-40 using the standard-costing method.

18-40 Scrap, job costing. The Jindal Company has an extensive job-costing facility that uses a variety of metals. Consider each requirement independently.

1. Job 372 uses a particular metal alloy that is not used for any other job. Assume that scrap is material in amount and sold quickly after it is produced. The scrap is sold for ₹490. Prepare the journal entry.
2. The scrap from Job 372 consists of a metal used by many other jobs. No record is maintained of the scrap generated by individual jobs. Assume that scrap is accounted for at the time of sale of scrap. Scrap totaling ₹4,000 is sold. Prepare two alternative journal entries that could be used to account for the sale of scrap.
3. Suppose the scrap generated in requirement 2 is returned to the storeroom for future use and a journal entry is made to record the scrap. A month later, the scrap is reused as direct material on a subsequent job. Prepare the journal entries to record these transactions.

18-41 Job-costing, spoilage and scrap. (F. Mayne) Mahalaxmi Metal Fabricators Limited, has a large job, No. 2734, that calls for producing various ore bins, chutes, and metal boxes for enlarging a copper concentrator. The following charges were made to the job in November:

Direct materials	₹2,69,510
Direct manufacturing labor	1,50,760
Manufacturing overhead	75,380

The contract with the customer called for the total price to be based on a cost-plus approach. The contract defined cost to include direct materials, direct manufacturing labor costs, and manufacturing overhead to be allocated at 50% of direct manufacturing labor costs. The contract also provided that the total costs of all work spoiled were to be removed from the billable cost of the job and that the benefits from scrap sales were to reduce the billable cost of the job.

1. In accordance with the stated terms of the contract, prepare journal entries for the following two items:
   a. A cutting error was made in production. The up-to-date job cost record for this batch of work showed materials of ₹6,500, direct manufacturing labor of ₹5,000, and allocated overhead of ₹2,500. Because fairly large pieces of metal were recoverable, the company believed that the scrap value was ₹6,000 and that the materials recovered could be used on other jobs. The spoiled work was sent to the warehouse.
   b. Small pieces of metal cuttings and scrap in November amounted to ₹12,500, which was the price quoted by a scrap dealer. No journal entries were made with regard to the scrap until the price was quoted by the scrap dealer. The scrap dealer's offer was immediately accepted.
2. Consider normal and abnormal spoilage. Suppose the contract described above had contained the clause "a normal spoilage allowance of 1% of the job costs will be included in the billable costs of the job."
   a. Is this clause specific enough to define exactly how much spoilage is normal and how much is abnormal? Explain.
   b. Repeat requirement 1a with this "normal spoilage of 1%" clause in mind. You should be able to provide two slightly different journal entries.

18-42 Weighted-average method, inspection at 80% completion. (A. Atkinson) Delhi Manufacturing produces a plastic toy in a two-stage molding and finishing operation. The company uses the weighted-average method of process costing. During June, the following data were recorded for the Finishing Department:

Units of beginning inventory	10,000
Percentage completion of beginning units	25%
Cost of direct materials in beginning work in process	₹0
Units started	70,000
Units completed	50,000

Units in ending inventory	20,000
Percentage completion of ending units	95%
Spoiled units	10,000
Costs added during current period:	
Direct materials	₹6,55,200
Direct manufacturing labor	₹6,35,600
Manufacturing overhead	₹6,16,000
Work in process, beginning:	
Transferred-in costs	₹82,900
Conversion costs	₹42,000
Cost of units transferred in during current period	₹6,47,500

Conversion costs are incurred evenly during the process. Direct materials costs are incurred when production is 90% complete. The inspection point is at the 80% stage of production. Normal spoilage is 10% of all good units that pass inspection. Spoiled units are disposed of at zero net disposal value.

Required

For June, summarize total costs to account for, and assign these costs to units completed and transferred out (including normal spoilage), to abnormal spoilage, and to units in ending work in process.

18-43 FIFO method, spoilage, working backward. The Cooking Department of Haldiram Foods, uses a process-costing system. Direct materials are added at the beginning of the cooking process. Conversion costs are added evenly during the cooking process. Consider the following data for the Cooking Department for January:

	Physical Units	Direct Materials	Conversion Costs
Work in process, January 1[a]	10,000	₹2,20,000	₹30,000
Started in January	74,000		
Good units completed and transferred out during January	61,000		
Spoiled units	8,000		
Work in process, January 31	15,000		
Costs added during January		₹14,80,000	₹9,42,000
Cost per equivalent unit of work done in January		₹20	₹12

[a]Degree of completion: direct materials, 100%; conversion costs, 25%.

Haldiram Foods uses the FIFO method of process costing. Inspection occurs when production is 100% complete. Normal spoilage is 11% of good units completed and transferred out during the current period.

Required

1. For each cost category, compute equivalent units of work done in the current period (January).
2. For each cost category, compute separately the equivalent units of work done to complete beginning work-in-process inventory, to start and complete new units, for normal and abnormal spoilage, and to produce ending work-in-process inventory.
3. For each cost category, calculate the percentage of completion of ending work-in-process inventory.
4. Summarize total costs to account for, and assign these costs to units completed and transferred out (including normal spoilage), to abnormal spoilage, and to units in ending work in process.

19 Balanced Scorecard: Quality and Time

Learning Objective 1

Explain the four cost categories in a costs-of-quality program

. . . prevention, appraisal, internal failure, and external failure costs

To satisfy ever-increasing customer expectations, managers at companies such as Samsung, Sony, Texas Instruments, and Toyota find cost-effective ways to continuously improve the quality of their products and services and shorten response times.

They balance the costs of achieving these improvements against the benefits from higher performance. Improving quality and decreasing customer-response times are hard work, but when companies do not make these improvements, the losses can be substantial.

Quality as a Competitive Tool

The American Society for Quality defines **quality** as the total features and characteristics of a product or a service made or performed according to specifications to satisfy customers at the time of purchase and during use. Many companies throughout the world—like, Cisco Systems, Motorola, British Telecom, Fujitsu, Toyota and Samsung—emphasize quality as an important strategic initiative. These companies have found that focusing on the quality of a product or service generally builds expertise in producing it, lowers the costs of providing it, creates higher satisfaction for customers using it, and generates higher future revenues for the company selling it. Several high-profile awards are given to companies that have produced high-quality products and services.

International quality standards have also emerged. ISO 9000, developed by the International Organization for Standardization, is a set of five international standards for quality management adopted by more than 85 countries. The standards help companies to monitor, document and certify the elements of their production processes that lead to quality. To ensure that their suppliers deliver high-quality products at competitive costs, companies such as DuPont and General Electric require their suppliers to obtain ISO 9000 certification. ISO 9000 certification has become a necessary condition for competing in the global marketplace.

Companies are also using quality management and measurement practices to find cost-effective ways to reduce the environmental and economic costs of air pollution, wastewater, oil spills, and hazardous waste disposal. ISO 14000, also developed by the International Organization for Standardization, are standards designed to encourage organizations to develop (1) environmental management systems to reduce environmental costs and (2) environmental auditing and performance-evaluation systems to review and monitor their progress toward their environmental goals. Quality and environmental issues came together in a big way when British Petroleum's Deepwater Horizon platform exploded in the Gulf of Mexico in 2010 while drilling for oil. Eleven workers died as a result of the explosion, and over the course of approximately three months, nearly 5 million gallons of oil spilled out into the Gulf, causing an environmental catastrophe.

Product quality can also be an important engine for environmental progress. For example, Stonyfield Farm, the world's leading organic yogurt company, provides high-quality, all-natural products while educating customers and suppliers about sustainable farming and protecting the environment. As Stonyfield Farm transitioned to organic production, it developed quality control capabilities, performing more than 900 quality checks daily to ensure that its yogurt justified the higher costs of organic milk, fruit, and sugar. Automated systems accomplish quality compliance electronically. Plant processes are interlocked so elements of production cannot move forward unless the product passes inspection at every stage of the process. The quality focus has allowed Stonyfield to grow at a 23% annual rate for more than 18 years, while its use of organic ingredients has kept more than 1,80,000 farm acres free of pesticides and chemical fertilizers.

We focus on two basic aspects of quality: design quality and conformance quality. **Design quality** refers to how closely the characteristics of a product or service meet the needs and wants of customers. **Conformance quality** is the performance of a product or service relative to its design and product specifications. Apple Inc. has built a reputation for design quality by developing many innovative products such as the iPod, iPhone, and iPad that have uniquely met customers' music, telephone, entertainment, and business needs. Apple's products have also had excellent conformance quality; rarely do the products fail to do what they were supposed to do. In the case of the iPhone 5, however, the problems with the map application were an example of good design quality but poor conformance quality because maps were a feature desired by customers but the map application itself did not perform according to its specifications. The following diagram illustrates that actual performance can fall short of customer satisfaction because of design-quality failure and because of conformance-quality failure.

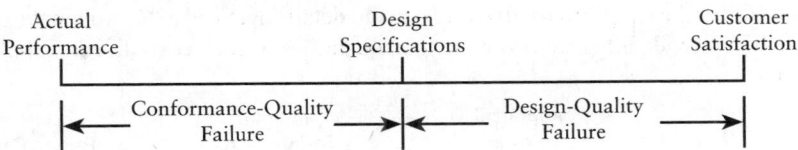

We illustrate the issues in managing quality—computing the costs of quality, identifying quality problems, and taking actions to improve quality—using Photon Corporation. While Photon makes many products, we will focus only on Photon's photocopying machines, which earned an operating income of ₹240 million on revenues of ₹3,000 million (from sales of 20,000 copiers) in 2013.

Quality has both financial and nonfinancial components relating to customer satisfaction, improving internal quality processes, reducing defects, and the training and empowering of workers. To provide some structure, we discuss quality from the four perspectives of the balanced scorecard: financial in the next section and customer, internal business process, and learning and growth in the following section.

The Financial Perspective: The Costs of Quality

Financial measures include measures affected by quality, such as revenues and operating income growth. The most direct financial measure of quality, however, is the *costs of quality*. The **costs of quality (COQ)** are the costs incurred to prevent the production of a low-quality product or the costs arising as a result of such products. These costs are classified into the following four categories, and examples for each category are listed in Exhibit 19-1.

1. **Prevention costs**—costs incurred to preclude the production of products that do not conform to specifications.

2. **Appraisal costs**—costs incurred to detect which of the individual units of products do not conform to specifications.

3. **Internal failure costs**—costs incurred on defective products before they are shipped to customers.

4. **External failure costs**—costs incurred on defective products after they have been shipped to customers.

The items in Exhibit 19-1 arise in all business functions of the value chain, and they are broader than the internal failure costs of spoilage, rework, and scrap described in Chapter 18.

Photon determines the COQ of its photocopying machines by adapting the seven-step activity-based costing approach described in Chapter 5.

Step 1: Identify the Product That Is the Chosen Cost Object. The cost object is the quality of photocopying machine that Photon made and sold in 2013. Photon's goal is to calculate the total costs of quality of these 20,000 machines.

Step 2: Identify the Direct Costs of Quality of the Product. The photocopying machines have no direct costs of quality because there are no resources such as inspection or repair workers dedicated to managing the quality the photocopying machines.

Step 3: Select the Activities and Cost-Allocation Bases to Use for Allocating Indirect Costs of Quality to the Product. Column 1 of Exhibit 19-2, Panel A, classifies the activities that result in prevention, appraisal, and internal and external failure costs of quality at Photon Corporation and the business functions of the value chain in which these costs occur. For example, the inspection activity results in appraisal costs and occurs in the manufacturing function. Photon identifies the number of inspection-hours (across all products) as the cost-allocation base for the inspection activity. (To avoid details not needed to explain the concepts here, we do not provide information on the total quantities of each cost-allocation base.)

Exhibit 19-1				
Items Pertaining to Costs-of-Quality Reports	**Prevention Costs**	**Appraisal Costs**	**Internal Failure Costs**	**External Failure Costs**
	Design engineering	Inspection	Spoilage	Customer support
	Process engineering	Online products	Rework	Manufacturing/
	Supplier evaluations	manufacturing	Scrap	process
	Preventive equipment	and process	Machine repairs	engineering
	maintenance	inspection	Manufacturing/	for external
	Quality training	Product testing	process	failures
	Testing of new		engineering on	Warranty repair
	materials		internal failures	costs
				Liability claims

Step 4: Identify the Indirect Costs of Quality Associated with Each Cost-Allocation Base. These are the total costs (variable and fixed) incurred for each of the costs-of-quality activities, such as inspections, across all of Photon's products. (To avoid details not needed to understand the points described here, we do not provide information about these total costs.)

Exhibit 19-2 Analysis of Activity-Based Costs of Quality (COQ) for Photocopying Machines at Photon Corporation

File Edit View Insert Format Tools Data Window Help

	A	B	C	D	E	F	G
1	**PANEL A: COQ REPORT**						**Percentage of**
2		**Cost Allocation**		**Quantity of Cost**		**Total**	**Revenues**
3	**Cost of Quality and Value-Chain Category**	**Rate[a] (₹)**		**Allocation Base**		**Costs**	**(5) = (4) ÷**
4	**(1)**	**(2)**		**(3)**		**(4) = (2) x (3)**	**₹3,00,00,00,000**
5	*Prevention costs*						
6	Design engineering (R&D/Design)	800	per hour	40,000 hours		₹3,20,00,000	1.1%
7	Process engineering (R&D/Design)	600	per hour	45,000 hours		2,70,00,000	0.9%
8	Total prevention costs					5,90,00,000	2.0%
9	*Appraisal costs*						
10	Inspection (Manufacturing)	400	per hour	2,40,000 hours		9,60,00,000	3.2%
11	Total appraisal costs					9,60,00,000	3.2%
12	*Internal failure costs*						
13	Rework (Manufacturing)	1,000	per hour	1,00,000 hours		10,00,00,000	3.3%
14	Total internal failure costs					10,00,00,000	3.3%
15	*External failure costs*						
16	Customer support (Marketing)	500	per hour	12,000 hours		60,00,000	0.2%
17	Transportation (Distribution)	2,400	per load	3,000 loads		72,00,000	0.2%
18	Warranty repair (Customer service)	1,100	per hour	1,20,000 hours		13,20,00,000	4.4%
19	Total external failure costs					14,52,00,000	4.8%
20	Total costs of quality					₹40,02,00,000	13.3%
21							
22	[a]Amounts assumed.						
23							
24	**PANEL B: OPPORTUNITY COST ANALYSIS**						
25						**Total Estimated**	**Percentage**
26						**Contribution**	**of Revenues**
27	**Cost of Quality Category**					**Margin Lost (₹)**	**(3) = (2) ÷**
28	**(1)**					**(2)**	**₹300,00,00,000**
29	*External failure costs*						
30	Estimated forgone contribution margin						
31	and income on lost sales					12,00,00,000[b]	4.0%
32	Total external failure costs					12,00,00,000	4.0%
33							
34	[b]Calculated as total revenues minus all variable costs (whether output-unit, batch, product-sustaining, or facility-sustaining) on						
35	lost sales in 2008. If poor quality causes Photon to lose sales in subsequent years as well, the opportunity costs will be						
36	even greater.						

Step 5: Compute the Rate per Unit of Each Cost-Allocation Base. For each activity, the total costs (identified in step 4) are divided by total quantity of the cost-allocation base (calculated in step 3) to compute the rate per unit of each cost-allocation base. Column 2 in Exhibit 19-2, Panel A, shows these rates (without supporting calculations).

Step 6: Compute the Indirect Costs of Quality Allocated to the Product. The indirect costs of quality of the photocopying machines, shown in Exhibit 19-2, Panel A, column 4, equal the cost-allocation rate from Step 5 (column 2) multiplied by the total quantity of the cost-allocation base used by the photocopying machines for each activity (column 3). For example, the inspection costs for ensuring the quality of the photocopying machines are ₹9,60,00,000 (₹400 per hour × 2,40,000 inspection-hours).

Step 7: Compute the Total Costs of Quality by Adding All Direct and Indirect Costs of Quality Assigned to the Product. Photon's total costs of quality in the COQ report for photocopying machines is ₹400.2 million (Exhibit 19-2, Panel A, column 4), or 13.3% of current revenues (column 5).

As we have seen in Chapter 11, opportunity costs are not recorded in financial accounting systems. Yet, a very significant component of costs of quality is the opportunity cost of the contribution margin and income forgone from lost sales, lost production, and lower prices resulting from poor design and conformance quality. Photon's market research department estimates that design and conformance quality problems experienced by some customers resulted in lost sales of 2,000 photocopying machines in 2013 and forgone contribution margin and operating income of ₹120 million (Exhibit 19-2, Panel B). The total costs of quality, including opportunity costs, equal ₹520.2 million (₹400.2 million recorded in the accounting system and shown in Panel A plus ₹120 million of opportunity costs shown in Panel B), or 17.3% of current revenues. Opportunity costs account for 23.1% (₹120 million ÷ ₹520.2 million) of Photon's total costs of quality.

We turn next to the leading indicators of the costs of quality, the nonfinancial quality measures for Photon's photocopiers.

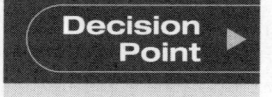

Decision Point ▶

What are the four cost categories of a costs-of-quality program?

Using Nonfinancial Measures to Evaluate and Improve Quality

Companies such as Unilever, FedEx, and TiVo use nonfinancial measures to manage quality. Almost always, the first step is to look at quality through the eyes of customers. Managers then turn their attention inward toward their organizations to develop processes that help improve quality and corporate cultures that help sustain it.

Learning Objective 2

Develop nonfinancial measures

. . . customer satisfaction measures such as number of customer complaints, internal-business process measures such as percentage of defective and reworked products, and learning and growth measures such as employee empowerment and training

and methods to improve quality

. . . control charts, Pareto diagrams, and cause-and-effect diagrams

The Customer Perspective: Nonfinancial Measures of Customer Satisfaction

Photon's managers track the following measures of customer satisfaction:

- Market research information on customer preferences for and customer satisfaction with specific product features (to measure design quality)
- Market share
- Percentage of highly satisfied customers
- Number of defective units shipped to customers as a percentage of total units shipped
- Number of customer complaints (Companies estimate that for every customer who actually complains, there are 10 to 20 others who have had bad experiences with the product or service but did not complain.)
- Percentage of products that fail soon after delivery

- Average delivery delays (difference between the scheduled delivery date and the date requested by the customer)
- On-time delivery rate (percentage of shipments made on or before the scheduled delivery date)

Photon's management monitors whether these numbers improve or deteriorate over time. Higher customer satisfaction should lead to lower external failure costs, lower costs of quality and higher future revenues due to greater customer retention, loyalty, and positive word-of-mouth advertising. Lower customer-satisfaction indicates that external failure costs and costs of quality will likely increase in the future. We next discuss internal business processes to identify and analyze quality problems that help to improve quality and increase customer satisfaction.

The Internal-Business-Process Perspective: Analyzing Quality Problems and Improving Quality

We present three techniques for identifying and analyzing quality problems: control charts, Pareto diagrams, and cause-and-effect diagrams.

Control Charts

Statistical quality control (SQC), also called statistical process control (SPC), is a formal means of distinguishing between random and nonrandom variations in an operating process. Random variations occur, for example, when chance fluctuations in the speed of equipment cause defective products to be produced, such as copiers that produce fuzzy and unclear copies or copies that are too light or too dark. Nonrandom variations occur when defective products are produced as a result of a systematic problem such as an incorrect speed setting, a flawed part design, or mishandling of a component part. A **control chart**, an important SQC tool, is a graph of a series of successive observations of a particular step, procedure, or operation taken at regular intervals of time. Each observation is plotted relative to specified ranges that represent the limits within which observations are expected to fall. Observations that fall outside the control limits are regarded as nonrandom and worth investigating.

Exhibit 19-3 presents control charts for the daily defect rates (defective copiers divided by the total number of copiers produced) observed at Photon's three photocopying-machine pro-

Exhibit 19-3   Statistical Quality Control Charts: Daily Defect Rate for Photocopying Machines at Photon Corporation

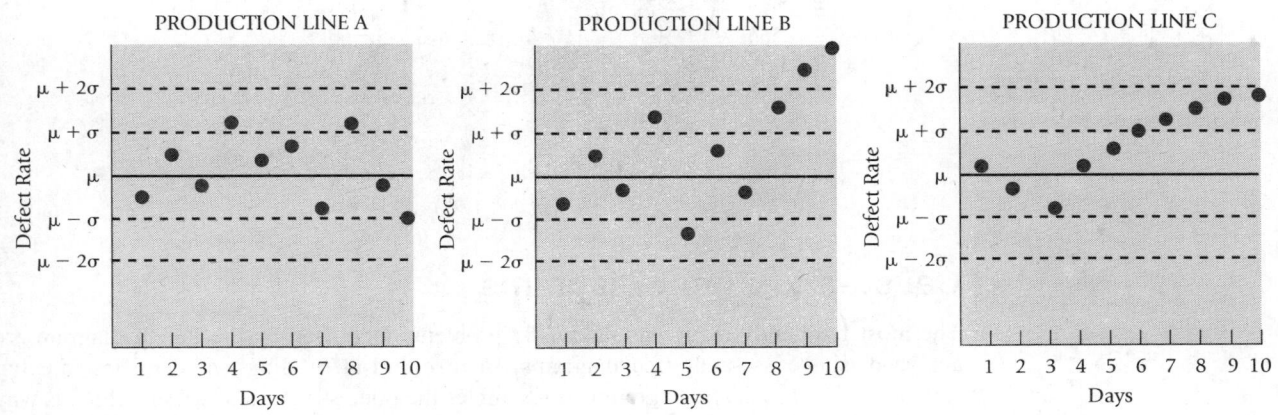

duction lines. The defect rates in the prior 60 days for each production line provide a basis upon which to calculate the distribution of daily defect rates. The arithmetic mean (μ, read as "mu") and standard deviation (σ, read as "sigma," how much an observation deviates from the mean) are the two parameters of the distribution that are used in the control charts in Exhibit 19-3. On the basis of experience, the company decides that managers should investigate any observation outside the $\mu \pm 2\sigma$ range.

For production line A, all observations are within the range of $\mu \pm 2\sigma$, so managers believe no investigation is necessary. For production line B, the last two observations signal that a much higher percentage of copiers are not performing as they should, indicating that the problem is probably because of a nonrandom, out-of-control occurrence such as an incorrect speed setting or mishandling of a component part. Given the $\pm 2\sigma$ rule, both observations would be investigated. Production line C illustrates a process that would not prompt an investigation under the $\pm 2\sigma$ rule but that may well be out of control. Why? Because the last eight observations show a clear pattern: Over the last 6 days, the percentage of defective copiers increased and got further and further away from the mean. The pattern could be due, for example, to the tooling on a machine wearing out, resulting in poorly machined parts. As the tooling deteriorates further, the trend in producing defective copiers is likely to persist until the production line is no longer in statistical control. Statistical procedures have been developed using the trend as well as the variation to evaluate whether a process is out of control.

Pareto Diagrams

Observations outside control limits serve as inputs for Pareto diagrams. A **Pareto diagram** is a chart that indicates how frequently each type of defect occurs, ordered from the most frequent to the least frequent. Exhibit 19-4 presents a Pareto diagram of quality problems for all observations outside the control limits at the final inspection point in 2013. Copiers that produce fuzzy and unclear copies are the most frequently recurring problem, and they result in high rework costs. Sometimes problems such as these are detected at customer sites and result in high warranty and repair costs and low customer satisfaction.

Exhibit 19-4

Pareto Diagram for Photocopying Machines at Photon Corporation

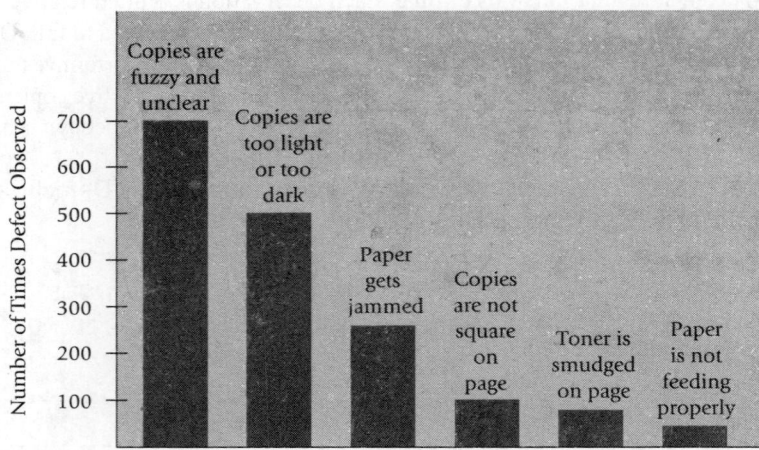

Cause-and-Effect Diagrams

The most frequently recurring and costly problems identified by the Pareto diagram are analyzed using cause-and-effect diagrams. A **cause-and-effect diagram** identifies potential causes of defects using a diagram that resembles the bone structure of a fish (which is why the diagrams are also called *fishbone diagrams*).[1] Exhibit 19-5 presents the cause-and-effect diagram describing potential reasons for fuzzy and unclear copies. The "backbone" of the diagram represents the problem being examined. The large "bones" coming off the backbone represent the main categories of potential causes of failure. The exhibit identifies four of these: human factors, methods and design factors, machine-related factors, and materials and components factors. Photon's engineers identify the materials and components factor as an important reason for the fuzzy and unclear copies. Additional arrows, or bones, are added to provide more detailed reasons for each higher-level cause. For example, Photon's engineers determine that two potential causes of material and component problems are variations in purchased components and incorrect component specifications. The engineers quickly determine that Photon's component specifications are correct, so variations in the purchased components or mishandling of them is the likely cause. Further analysis leads Photon to conclude that mishandling of the steel frame that holds in place various components of the copier such as drums, mirrors, and lenses results in the misalignment of these components and causes fuzzy and unclear copies.

Manufacturers use automated equipment and computers to record the number and types of defects and the operating conditions that existed at the time the defects occurred. Using these inputs, computer programs simultaneously and iteratively prepare control charts, Pareto diagrams, and cause-and-effect diagrams with the goal of continuously reducing the mean defect rate, μ, and the standard deviation, σ.

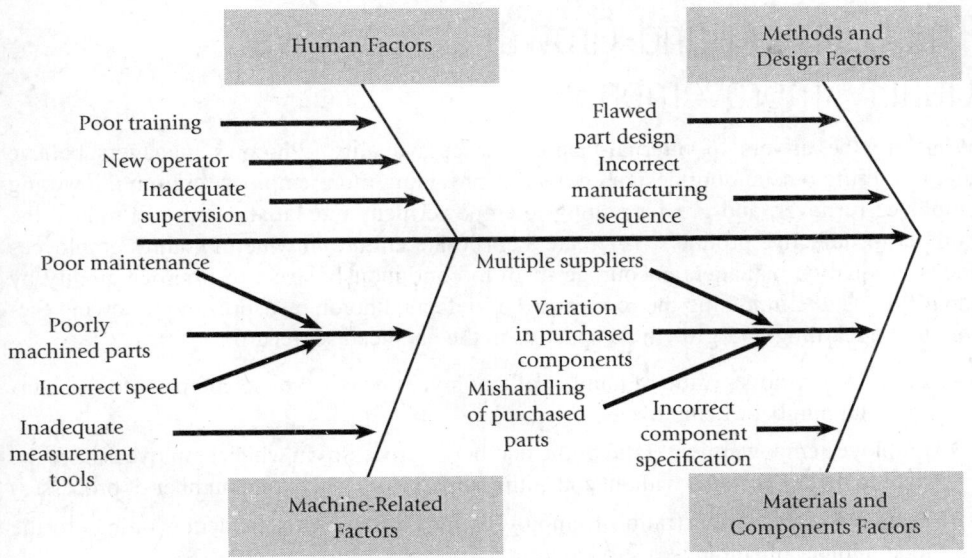

Exhibit 19-5

Cause-and-Effect Diagram for Fuzzy and Unclear Photocopies at Photon Corporation

Six Sigma Quality The ultimate goal of quality programs at companies such as Motorola, Honeywell, and General Electric is to achieve Six Sigma quality.[2] This means that the process is so well-understood and tightly controlled that the mean defect rate, μ, and the standard deviation, σ, are both very small. As a result, the upper and lower control limits in Exhibit 19-3 can be set at a distance of 6σ (six sigma) from the mean (μ). The implication of controlling a process at a Six Sigma level is that the process produces only 3.4 defects per million products produced.

To implement Six Sigma, companies use techniques such as control charts, Pareto diagrams, and cause-and-effect diagrams to define, measure, analyze, improve, and control processes to minimize variability in manufacturing and achieve almost zero defects.

---

[1] See P. Clark, "Getting the Most from Cause-and-Effect Diagrams," *Quality Progress* 33:6 (June 2000).
[2] Six Sigma is a registered trademark of Motorola Inc.

Critics of Six Sigma argue that it emphasizes incremental rather than dramatic or disruptive innovation. Nevertheless, companies report substantial benefits from Six Sigma initiatives.

Nonfinancial Measures of Internal-Business-Process Quality

Companies routinely use nonfinancial measures to track the quality improvements they are making. Photon's managers use the following nonfinancial measures of internal-business-process quality:

- Percentage of defective products
- Percentage of reworked products
- Number of different types of defects analyzed using control charts, Pareto diagrams, and cause-and-effect diagrams
- Number of design and process changes made to improve design quality or reduce costs of quality

Photon's managers believe that improving these measures will lead to greater customer satisfaction, lower costs of quality, and better financial performance.

The Learning-and-Growth Perspective: Quality Improvements

What are the drivers of internal-business-process quality? Photon's managers believe that recruiting outstanding design engineers, providing more employee training, lowering employee turnover, and greater employee empowerment and satisfaction will reduce the number of defective products. To create a corporate culture in which Photon's employees focus on quality, managers encourage them to continuously strive to improve quality by identifying and eliminating the root causes of defects. Photon measures the following factors in the learning-and-growth perspective in the balanced scorecard:

- Employee turnover (ratio of number of employees who leave the company to the average total number of employees)
- Employee empowerment (ratio of the number of processes in which employees have the right to make decisions without consulting supervisors to the total number of processes)
- Employee satisfaction (ratio of employees indicating high satisfaction ratings to the total number of employees surveyed)
- Employee training (percentage of employees trained in different quality-enhancing methods)

Decision Point ▶

What nonfinancial measures and methods can managers use to improve quality?

Learning Objective 3

Use costs of quality measures to make decisions

... identify relevant incremental costs and benefits and opportunity costs to evaluate trade offs

Weighing the Costs and Benefits of Improving Quality

Recall that the cause-and-effect diagram reveals that the steel frame (or chassis) of the copier is often mishandled as it travels from a supplier's warehouse to Photon's warehouse and then to the production line. The frame must meet very precise specifications or else copier components (such as drums, mirrors, and lenses) will not fit exactly on the frame. Mishandling frames during transport causes misalignment and results in fuzzy and unclear copies.

A team of engineers offers two solutions: (1) electronically inspect and test the frames immediately before production starts or (2) redesign and strengthen the frames and their shipping containers to withstand mishandling during transportation. The cost structure of the cost of quality for 2014 is expected to be the same as the cost structure for 2013 presented in Exhibit 19-2.

To evaluate each alternative versus the status quo, managers identify the relevant costs and benefits for each solution by focusing on *how total costs and total revenues will change under each alternative*. Relevant-cost and relevant-revenue analysis ignores allocated costs (see Chapter 11).

Photon uses only a one-year time horizon (2014) for the analysis because it plans to introduce a completely new line of copiers at the end of 2014. The new line is so different that the choice of either the inspection or the redesign alternative will have no effect on the sales of copiers in future years.

Exhibit 19-6 shows the relevant costs and benefits for each alternative.

1. **Estimated incremental costs:** ₹40,00,000 for the inspection alternative; ₹46,00,000 for the redesign alternative (₹30,00,000 for process engineering, ₹16,00,000 for design engineering, and ₹20,00,000 for the frames).

2. **Cost savings from less rework, customer support, and repairs:** Exhibit 19-6, line 10, shows that reducing rework saves of ₹400 per hour of rework. However, Exhibit 19-2, Panel A, column 2, line 13, shows that the total rework cost per hour of ₹1,000, not 400. Why is the difference? Because as it improves quality, Photon will only save the ₹400 variable cost per rework-hour, not the ₹600 fixed cost per rework-hour. Exhibit 19-6, line 10, shows Photon will save ₹96,00,000 (₹400 per hour × 24,000 rework-hours saved) if it inspects the frames versus ₹1,28,00,000 (₹400 per rework-hour × 32,000 rework-hours saved) if it redesigns the frames. The cost-benefit choice is clear for Photon's managers: Redesigning the frames and eliminating the root cause of the problem is better than trying to detect defective units later. Toyota has instituted a similar line of reasoning: Always emphasize defect prevention ("front of the pipe solutions") over defect inspection ("back of the pipe solutions"). Exhibit 19-6 also shows Photon's expected variable-cost savings for customer support (line 11), transportation (line 12), and warranty repair (line 13) for the two alternatives.

3. **Increased contribution margin from higher sales as a result of building a reputation for quality and performance:** Exhibit 19-6, line 14, shows ₹1,50,00,000

Exhibit 19-6 Estimated Effects of Quality-Improvement Actions on Costs of Quality for Photocopying Machines at Photon Corporation

		Home	Insert	Page Layout	Formulas	Data	Review	View			

	A	B	C	D	E	F	G	H	I	J
1						Relevant Costs and Benefits of				
2				Further Inspecting Incoming Frames				Redesigning Frames		
3	Relevant Items	Relevant Benefit per Unit (₹)		Quantity		Total Benefits		Quantity		Total Benefits
4	(1)	(2)		(3)		(4)		(5)		(6)
5	Additional inspection and testing costs			₹40,00,000						
6	Additional process engineering costs									(₹30,00,000)
7	Additional design engineering costs									(16,00,000)
8										
9						(2) × (3)				(2) × (5)
10	Savings in rework costs	400 per hour		24,000 hours		₹96,00,000		32,000 hours		₹1,28,00,000
11	Savings in customer-support costs	200 per hour		2,000 hours		4,00,000		2,800 hours		5,60,000
12	Savings in transportation costs for repair parts	1,800 per load		500 loads		9,00,000		700 loads		12,60,000
13	Savings in warranty repair costs	450 per hour		20,000 hours		90,00,000		28,000 hours		1,26,00,000
14	Total contribution margin from additional sales	60,000 per copier		250 copiers		1,50,00,000		300 copiers		1,80,00,000
15										
16	Net cost savings and additional contribution margin					₹3,09,00,000				₹3,86,20,000
17										
18	Difference in favor of redesigning frames (J16) – (F16)						₹77,20,000			

in higher contribution margins from selling 250 more copiers under the inspection alternative and ₹1,80,00,000 in higher contribution margin from selling 300 more copiers under the redesign alternative. Management should always look for opportunities to generate higher revenues, not just cost reductions, from quality improvements.

Exhibit 19-6 shows that both the inspection and the redesign alternatives yield net benefits relative to the status quo. However, consistent with value engineering, design for manufacturing, and Kaizen or continuous improvement that emphasize eliminating the root causes of defects, Photon expects the net benefits from the redesign alternative to be ₹77,20,000 greater.

Note how quality improvements affect the costs of quality. Redesigning the frame increases Photon's prevention costs (the costs of process engineering, design engineering, and frames increase), but decreases the firm's internal failure costs (rework) and external failure costs (customer support costs, transportation costs, and warranty repairs). Improving quality also results in greater sales and higher contribution margins. COQ reports provide more insight about quality improvements and allow managers to compare trends over time. In successful quality programs, companies decrease costs of quality and, in particular, internal and external failure costs as a percentage of revenues. Many companies, such as Hewlett-Packard, go further and believe they should eliminate all failure costs and have zero defects.

Decision Point ▶

How do managers identify the relevant costs and benefits of quality-improvement programs?

Evaluating a Company's Quality Performance

Because each offers different benefits, Photon's managers use both financial (COQ) and nonfinancial measures to evaluate the firm's quality performance

Learning Objective 4

Use financial and nonfinancial measures to evaluate quality

... nonfinancial measures are leading indicators of future costs of quality

Advantages of COQ Measures

- COQ measures focus managers' attention on how poor quality affects operating income.
- Total costs of quality help managers aggregate costs to evaluate the tradeoffs of incurring prevention costs and appraisal costs to eliminate internal and external failure costs.
- COQ measures assist in problem solving by comparing costs and benefits of different quality-improvement programs and by setting priorities for cost reduction.

Advantages of Nonfinancial Measures of Quality

- Nonfinancial measures of quality are often easy to quantify and understand.
- Nonfinancial measures direct attention to physical processes that help managers identify the precise problem areas that need improvement.
- Nonfinancial measures, such as number of defects, provide immediate short-run feedback on whether quality-improvement efforts are succeeding.
- Nonfinancial measures such as measures of customer satisfaction and employee satisfaction are useful indicators of long-run performance.

Decision Point ▶

How do managers use financial and nonfinancial measures to evaluate quality?

COQ measures and nonfinancial measures complement each other. Without financial quality measures, companies could be spending more money on improving nonfinancial quality measures than the effort is worth. Without nonfinancial quality measures, quality problems might not be identified until it is too late. Most organizations use both types of measures to gauge how well their firms are performing in terms of quality. McDonald's pays "mystery shoppers" to score individual restaurants on quality, cleanliness, service, and value measures. The company then evaluates each restaurant's performance across these dimensions over time and against other restaurants. In its balanced scorecard, Photon evaluates whether improvements in various nonfinancial quality measures eventually lead to improvements in financial measures.

Time as a Competitive Tool

Companies increasingly view time as a driver of strategy. For example, Capital One has increased the business on its Web site by promising home-loan approval decisions in 30 minutes or less. Companies such as AT&T, General Electric, and Walmart attribute not only higher revenues but also lower costs to doing things faster and on time. These firms claim, for example, that they need to carry fewer inventories because they are able to respond rapidly to customer demands.

Managers need to measure time to manage it properly. In this section, we focus on two *operational measures of time*: *customer-response time*, which reveals how quickly companies respond to customers' demands for their products and services, and *on-time performance*, which indicates how reliably companies meet their scheduled delivery dates. We also show how managers measure the causes and costs of delays.

Customer-Response Time and On-Time Performance

Customer-response time is how long it takes from the time a customer places an order for a product or service to the time the product or service is delivered to the customer. Quickly responding to customers is strategically important in many industries including construction, banking, car rental, and fast food industries. Some companies, such as Airbus, have to pay penalties to compensate their customers (airline companies) for lost revenues and profits (from being unable to operate flights) as a result of delays in delivering products to them.

Exhibit 19-7 describes the components of customer-response time. *Receipt time* is how long it takes the Marketing Department to specify to the Manufacturing Department the exact requirements in the customer's order. **Manufacturing cycle time** (also called **manufacturing lead time**) is how long it takes from the time an order is received by Manufacturing to the time a finished good is produced. Manufacturing cycle time is the sum of waiting time and manufacturing time for an order. For example, an aircraft order received by Airbus may need to wait for components before the plane can be assembled. *Delivery time* is how long it takes to deliver a completed order to a customer.

Some companies evaluate their response time improvement efforts using a measure called **manufacturing cycle efficiency** (MCE):

$$MCE = (\text{Value-Added manufacturing time} \div \text{Total manufacturing})$$

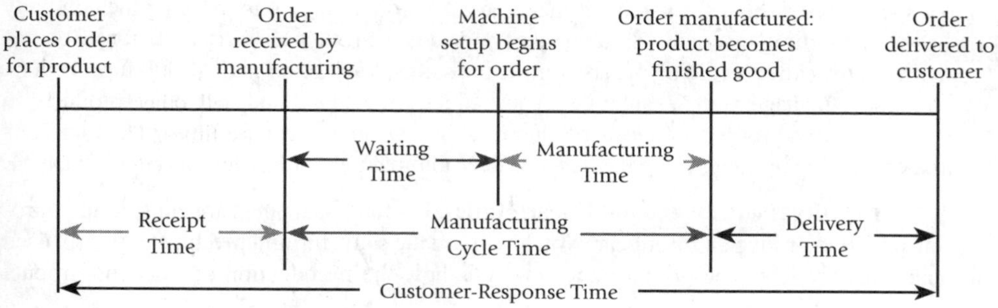

Learning Objective 5

Describe customer-response time

... time between receipt of customer order and product delivery

and on-time performance

...delivery of product at the time it is scheduled

and why delays occur

... uncertainty about the timing of customer orders and limited capacity

Exhibit 19-7

Components of Customer-Response Time

| Customer places order for product | Order received by manufacturing | Machine setup begins for order | Order manufactured: product becomes finished good | Order delivered to customer |

Value-added manufacturing activities (see Chapter 13) are activities that customers perceive as adding value or utility to a product. The time spent efficiently assembling the product is value-added manufacturing time. The rest of manufacturing cycle time, such as the time the product spends waiting for parts or for the next stage in the production process, and being repaired, is nonvalue-added manufacturing time. Identifying and minimizing the sources of non-value-added manufacturing time increases a firm's responsiveness to its customers and reduces its costs.

Similar measures apply to service-sector companies. Consider a 40-minute doctor's office visit. Suppose a patient spends 9 of those minutes on administrative tasks such as filling out forms, 20 minutes waiting in the reception area and examination room, and 11 minutes with a nurse or doctor. The service cycle efficiency for this visit equals 11 ÷ 40, or 0.275. In other words, only 27.5% of the 40 minutes added value to the patient/customer. Minimizing their non-value-added service times has allowed hospitals such as Kailash Medical Center in Noida to treat more patients in less time.

On-time performance is the delivery of a product or service by the time it is scheduled to be delivered. Consider FedEx, which specifies a price per package and a next-day delivery time of 10:30 a.m. for its overnight courier service. FedEx measures the on-time performance of the service based on how often the firm meets that standard. Commercial airlines gain loyal passengers as a result of consistent on-time service. But there is a tradeoff between a customer's desire for a shorter response time and better on-time performance. Scheduling longer customer-response times, such as airlines lengthening scheduled arrival times, displeases customers on the one hand but increases customer satisfaction on the other hand by improving the airline's on-time performance.

Bottlenecks and Time Drivers

Managing customer-response time and on-time performance requires managers to understand the causes and costs of delays that occur, for example, at a machine in a manufacturing plant or at a checkout counter in a store. A **time driver** is any factor that causes a change in the speed of an activity when the factor changes. Two time drivers are:

1. **Uncertainty about when customers will order products or services.** For example, the more randomly Airbus receives orders for its airplanes, the more likely queues will form and delays will occur.

2. **Bottlenecks due to limited capacity.** A **bottleneck** occurs in an operation when the work to be performed approaches or exceeds the capacity available to do it. For example, a bottleneck results and causes delays when products that must be processed at a particular machine arrive while the machine is being used to process other products. Bottlenecks can also occur on the Internet, for example, when many users try to operate wireless mobile devices at the same time.

Many banks, grocery stores, and entertainment parks, actively work to reduce queues and delays to better serve their customers.

Consider again Photon Corporation, which uses one turning machine to convert steel bars into a special fuser roller for its copier machines. The roller is the only product the company makes on the turning machine. Photon makes and sells the rollers as spare parts for its photocopier machines after receiving orders from wholesalers. Each order is for 1,000 fuser rollers.

Photon's managers are examining opportunities to produce and sell other products to increase the firm's profits without sacrificing its short customer-response times. The managers examine these opportunities using the five-step decision-making process introduced in Chapter 1.

Step 1. Identify the Problem and Uncertainties. Photon's managers are considering introducing a second product, a fuser gear, which will use the same turning machine currently used to make fuser rollers. The primary uncertainty is how the introduction of a second product will affect the manufacturing cycle times for rollers. (We focus on Photon's manufacturing cycle time because the receipt time and delivery time for the rollers and gears are minimal.)

Step 2.   Obtain information. Managers gather data on the number of orders for rollers Photon has received in the past, the time it takes to manufacture them, the available capacity, and their average manufacturing cycle time. Photon typically receives 30 orders for rollers each year, but it could receive 10, 30, or 50 orders. Each order is for 1,000 units and takes 100 hours of manufacturing time (8 hours of setup time to clean and prepare the machine that makes the rollers and 92 hours of processing time). The annual capacity of the machine is 4,000 hours. If Photon receives the 30 orders it expects, the total amount of manufacturing time required on the machine is 3,000 hours (100 hours per order x 30 orders), which is less than the available machine capacity of 4,000 hours. Queues and delays still occur because wholesalers can place their orders at any time, even while the machine is processing an earlier order.

Average waiting time, the average amount of time that an order waits in line before the machine is set up and the order is processed, equals,[3]

$$\frac{\begin{array}{c}\text{Annual average}\\\text{number of}\\\text{orders for rollers}\end{array} \times \left(\begin{array}{c}\text{Manufacturing}\\\text{time per order}\\\text{for rollers}\end{array}\right)^2}{2 \times \left[\begin{array}{c}\text{Annual machine}\\\text{capacity}\end{array} - \left(\begin{array}{c}\text{Annual average number}\\\text{of orders for rollers}\end{array} \times \begin{array}{c}\text{Manufacturing}\\\text{time per order for rollers}\end{array}\right)\right]}$$

$$= \frac{30 \times (100)^2}{2 \times [4{,}000 - (30 \times 100)]} = \frac{30 \times 10{,}000}{2 \times (4{,}000 - 3{,}000)} = \frac{3{,}00{,}000}{2 \times 1{,}000} = \frac{3{,}00{,}000}{2{,}000}$$

$$= 150 \text{ hours per order (for rollers)}$$

Therefore, the average manufacturing cycle time for an order is 250 hours (150 hours of average waiting time + 100 hours of manufacturing time). Note that manufacturing time per order is a squared term in the numerator. It indicates the disproportionately large impact manufacturing time has on waiting time. As the manufacturing time lengthens, there is a much greater chance that the machine will be in use when an order arrives, leading to longer delays. The denominator in this formula is a measure of the unused capacity, or cushion. As the unused capacity becomes smaller, the chance that the machine is processing an earlier order becomes more likely, leading to greater delays.

The formula describes only the *average* waiting time. A particular order might arrive when the machine is free, in which case manufacturing will start immediately. In another situation, Photon may receive an order while two other orders are waiting to be processed, which means the delay will be longer than 150 hours.

Step 3.   Make predictions about the future. The manager makes the following predictions about gears: Photon expects to receive 10 orders for gears, each order for 1,600 units, in the coming year. Each order will take 50 hours of manufacturing time, comprising 3 hours for setup and 47 hours of processing. The expected demand for rollers will be unaffected by whether Photon introduces and sells gears.

The average waiting time *before* the machine setup begins is expected to be (the formula is an extension of the preceding formula for the single-product case) as follows:

Producing gears will cause the average waiting time for an order to more than double, from 150 hours to 325 hours. The waiting time increases because the production of gears

---

[3] The technical assumptions are (a) that customer orders for the product follow a Poisson distribution with a mean equal to the expected number of orders (30 in our example), and (b) that orders are processed on a first-in, first-out (FIFO) basis. The Poisson arrival pattern for customer orders has been found to be reasonable in many real-world settings. The FIFO assumption can be modified. Under the modified assumptions, the basic queuing and delay effects will still occur, but the precise formulas will be different.

$$\left[\text{Annual average number of orders for rollers} \times \left(\text{Manufacturing time per order for rollers}\right)^2\right] + \left[\text{Annual average number of orders for gears} \times \left(\text{Manufacturing time per order for gears}\right)^2\right]$$

$$2 \times \left[\text{Annual machine capacity} - \left(\text{Annual average number of orders for rollers} \times \text{Manufacturing time per order for rollers}\right) - \left(\text{Annual average number of orders for gears} \times \text{Manufacturing time per order for gears}\right)\right]$$

$$= \frac{[30 \times (100)^2] + [10 \times (50)^2]}{2 \times [4{,}000 - (30 \times 100) - (10 \times 50)]} = \frac{(30 \times 10{,}000) + (10 \times 2{,}500)}{2 \times (4{,}000 - 3{,}000 - 500)}$$

$$= \frac{3{,}00{,}000 + 25{,}000}{2 \times 500} = \frac{3{,}25{,}000}{1{,}000} = 325 \text{ hours per order (for rollers and gears)}$$

will cause the machine's unused capacity to shrink, increasing the probability that new orders will arrive while current orders are being manufactured or waiting to be manufactured. The average waiting time is very sensitive to the shrinking of unused capacity.

If Photon's manager decides to make gears as well as rollers, the average manufacturing cycle time will be 425 hours for a roller order (325 hours of average waiting time + 100 hours of manufacturing time), and 375 hours for a gear order (325 hours of average waiting time + 50 hours of manufacturing time). A roller order will spend 76.5% (325 hours ÷ 425 hours) of its manufacturing cycle time just waiting for manufacturing to start!

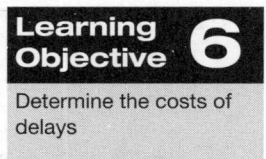

Decision Point

What is customer response time and what are the reasons for delays?

Step 4. Make decisions by choosing among alternatives. Should Photon produce gears given how much it would slow down the manufacturing cycle time for rollers? To help the company's managers make a decision, the management accountant identifies and analyzes the relevant revenues and relevant costs of producing gears and, in particular, the cost of delays on all products. The next section focuses on this step.

Relevant Revenues and Costs of Delays

Learning Objective 6

Determine the costs of delays

...lower revenues and higher inventory carrying costs

To determine the relevant revenues and costs of producing gears under Step 4, the management accountant prepares the following additional information:

Product	Annual Average Number of Orders	Average Selling Price per Order If Average Manufacturing Lead Time per Order Is		Direct Material Cost per Order	Inventory Carrying Cost per Order per Hour
		Less Than 300 Hours	More Than 300 Hours		
Gears	30	₹2,20,000	₹2,15,000	₹1,60,000	₹10.0
Pistons	10	1,00,000	96,000	80,000	5.0

Manufacturing cycle times affect both revenues and costs. Revenues are affected because customers are willing to pay a higher price for faster delivery. On the cost side, direct material costs and inventory carrying costs are the only relevant costs of introducing gears (all other costs are unaffected, and hence irrelevant). Inventory carrying costs equal the opportunity costs of investment tied up in inventory (see Chapter 11) and the relevant costs of storage, such as space rental, spoilage, deterioration, and materials handling. Usually, companies calculate inventory carrying costs on a per-unit, per-year basis. To simplify the calculations, the management accountant calculates inventory carrying costs on a per-order, per-hour basis. Also, Photon acquires direct materials at the time the order is received by manufacturing, and, therefore, calculates inventory carrying costs for the duration of the manufacturing cycle time.

Exhibit 19-8 presents relevant revenues and relevant costs for the "introduce gears" and "do not introduce gears" alternatives. Photon's managers decide not to introduce gears, even though they have a positive contribution margin of ₹16,000 (₹96,000 – ₹80,000) per order and Photon has the capacity to make them. If it produces gears, Photon will, on average, use only 3,500 (Rollers: 1,000 hours per order × 30 orders + Gears: 50 hours per order × 10 orders) of the available 4,000 machine-hours. So why is Photon better off to not introduce gears? *Because of the negative effects that producing them will have on the existing product, rollers.* The following table presents the *costs of time*, the expected loss in revenues and expected increase in carrying costs as a result of delays that manufacturing the gears would cause.

| | Effect of Increasing Average Manufacturing Cycle Time | | Expected Loss in Revenues Plus Expected Increase |
| | Expected Loss in Revenues for Gears (₹) | Expected Increase in Carrying Costs for All Products | in Carrying Costs of Introducing Gears |
Product	(1)	(2)	(3) = (1) + (2)
Gears	1,50,000[a]	₹52,500[b]	₹2,02,500
Pistons	—	18,750[c]	18,750
Total	1,50,000	₹71,250	₹2,21,250

[a](₹2,20,000 – ₹2,15,000) per order × 30 expected orders = ₹1,50,000.
[b](425 – 250) hours per order × ₹10 per hour × 30 expected orders = ₹52,500.
[c](375 – 0) hours per order × ₹5 per hour × 10 expected orders = ₹18,750.

Introducing gears causes the average manufacturing cycle time of rollers to increase from 250 hours to 425 hours. Longer manufacturing cycle times increase the inventory carrying costs of rollers and decrease roller revenues (the average manufacturing cycle time for rollers exceeds 300 hours so the average selling price per order decreases from ₹2,20,000 to ₹2,15,000). Together with the inventory carrying cost of the gears, the expected cost of introducing the gears, ₹2,21,250 exceeds the expected contribution margin of ₹1,60,000 (₹16,000 per order × 10 expected orders) from selling gears by ₹61,250 (the difference calculated in Exhibit 19-8).

Relevant Items	Alternative 1: Introduce Gears (₹) (1)	Alternative 2: Do Not Introduce Gears (2)	Difference (3) = (1) – (2)
Expected revenues	74,10,000[a]	₹66,00,000[b]	₹8,10,000
Expected variable costs	56,00,000[c]	48,00,000[d]	(8,00,000)
Expected inventory carrying costs	1,46,250[e]	75,000[f]	(71,250)
Expected total costs	57,46,250	48,75,000	8,71,250
Expected revenues minus expected costs	16,63,750	₹17,25,000	₹(61,250)

Exhibit 19-8

Determining Expected Relevant Revenues and Relevant Costs for Photon's Decision to Introduce Gears

[a](₹2,15,000×30)+(₹96,000×10) = ₹74,10,000; average manufacturing lead time will be more than 300 hours.
[b](₹2,20,000×30) = ₹66,00,000; average manufacturing lead time will be less than 300 hours.
[c](₹1,60,000×30)+(₹80,000 × 10) = ₹56,00,000.
[d](₹1,60,000×30 = ₹48,00,000.
[e](Average manufacturing lead time for gears× Unit carrying cost per order for gears × Expected number of orders for gears) + (Average manufacturing lead time for pistons × Unit carrying cost per order for pistons × Expected number of orders for pistons) = (425 ×₹10 ×30) + (375 + ₹5 × 10) ₹1,27,500 + ₹18, 750 + ₹1,46,250
[f]Average manufacturing lead time for gears × Unit carrying cost per order for gears × Expected number of orders for gears = 250 × ₹10×30 = ₹75,000.

Decision Point ▶

What are relevant revenues and costs of delays?

This simple setting illustrates that when demand uncertainty is high, some unused capacity is desirable.[4] Increasing the capacity of a bottleneck resource reduces manufacturing cycle times and delays. One way to increase capacity is to reduce the time it takes for setups and processing. Another way to increase capacity is to invest in new equipment, such as flexible manufacturing systems that can be programmed to switch quickly from producing one product to producing another. Delays can also be reduced by carefully scheduling production, such as by batching similar jobs together for processing.

Balanced Scorecard and Time-Based Measures

Learning Objective **7**

Use financial and nonfinancial measures of time

…nonfinancial measures are leading indicators of future financial effects of delays

In this section, we focus on the final step of the five-step decision-making process—**implement the decision, evaluate performance, and learn**—by tracking changes in time-based measures, evaluating and learning whether these changes affect financial performance, and modifying decisions and plans to achieve the company's goals. We use the structure of the balanced scorecard perspectives—financial, customer, internal business processes, and learning and growth—to summarize how financial and nonfinancial measures of time relate to one another, reduce delays, and increase output of bottleneck operations.

Financial measures
Revenue gains or price increases from fewer delays
Carrying cost of inventories

Customer measures
Customer-response time (the time it takes to fulfill a customer order)
On-time performance (delivering a product or service by the scheduled time)

Internal-business-process measures
Average manufacturing time for key products
Manufacturing cycle efficiency for key processes
Defective units produced at bottleneck operations
Average reduction in setup time and processing time at bottleneck operations

Learning-and-growth measures
Employee satisfaction
Number of employees trained in managing bottleneck operations

To see the cause-and-effect linkages across these balanced scorecard perspectives, consider the example of the Bell Group, a designer and manufacturer of equipment for the jewelry industry. A key financial measure was to achieve a higher profit margin on a specific product line. In the customer-measure category, the company set a goal of a 2-day turnaround time on all orders for the product. To achieve this goal, an internal-business-process measure required a bottleneck machine to be operated 22 hours per day, 6 days a week. Finally, in the learning-and-growth measures category, the company trained new employees to carry out nonbottleneck operations to free experienced employees to operate the bottleneck machine. The Bell Group's emphasis on time-related measures in its balanced scorecard has allowed the company to substantially increase manufacturing throughput and decrease customer-response times, leading to higher revenues and increased profits.

Decision Point ▶

What financial and nonfinancial measures of time can managers use in the balanced scorecard?

Managers use both financial and nonfinancial measures to manage the performance of their firms along the time dimension. They use revenue and cost measures to evaluate the financial effects of increases or decreases in customer-response times. Nonfinancial measures help managers evaluate how well they have done on goals such as improving manufacturing cycle times and customer-response times.

---

[4] Other complexities, such as analyzing a network of machines, priority scheduling, and allowing for uncertainty in processing times, are beyond the scope of this book. In these cases, the basic queuing and delay effects persist, but the precise formulas are more complex.

Problem for Self-Study

The Motika Roadlines transports household goods from one city to another within North India. It measures quality of service in terms of (1) time required to transport goods, (2) on-time delivery (within two days of agreed-upon delivery date), and (3) number of lost or damaged shipments. Motika is considering investing in a new scheduling-and-tracking system costing ₹16,00,000 per year, which should help it improve performance with respect to items (2) and (3). The following information describes Motika's current perfor mance and the expected performance if the new system is implemented:

	Current Performance	Expected Future Performance
On-time delivery performance	85%	95%
Variable cost per carton lost or damaged	₹600	₹600
Fixed cost per carton lost or damaged	₹400	₹400
Number of cartons lost or damaged per year	3,000 cartons	1,000 cartons

Motika expects each percentage point increase in on-time performance to increase revenue by ₹2,00,000 per year. Motika's contribution margin percentage is 45%.

Required

1. Should Motika acquire the new system? Show your calculations.
2. Motika is very confident about the cost savings from fewer lost or damaged cartons as a result of introducing the new system but unsure about the increase in revenues. Calculate the minimum amount of increase in revenues needed to make it worthwhile for Motika to invest in the new system.

Solution

1. Additional costs of the new scheduling-and-tracking system are ₹16,00,000 per year. Additional annual benefits of the new scheduling-and-tracking system are as follows:

Additional annual revenues from a 10% improvement in on-time performance, from 85% to 95%,		
₹2,00,000 per 1% × 10 percentage points		₹20,00,000
45% contribution margin from additional annual revenues		
(0.45 × ₹20,00,000)	₹9,00,000	
Decrease in costs per year from fewer cartons lost or damaged		
(only variable costs are relevant)		
[₹600 per carton × (3,000 − 1,000) cartons]		12,00,000
Total additional benefits		₹21,00,000

Because the benefits of ₹21,00,000 exceed the costs of ₹16,00,000, Motika should invest in the new system.

2. As long as Motika earns a contribution margin of ₹4,00,000 (to cover incremental costs of ₹16,00,000 minus relevant variable-cost savings of ₹12,00,000) from additional annual revenues, investing in the new system is beneficial. This contribu tion margin corresponds to additional revenues of ₹4,00,000 ÷ 0.45 = ₹8,88,890.

Decision Points

The following question-and-answer format summarizes the chapter's learning objectives. Each decision presents a key question related to a learning objective. The guidelines are the answer to that question.

Decision	Guidelines
1. What are the four cost categories of a costs-of-quality program?	Four cost categories in a costs-of-quality program are prevention costs (costs incurred to prevent the production of products that do not conform to specifications), appraisal costs (costs incurred to detect which of the individual units of products do not conform to specifications), internal failure costs (costs incurred on defective products before they are shipped to customers), and external failure costs (costs incurred on defective products after they are shipped to customers).
2. What nonfinancial measures and methods can managers use to improve quality?	Nonfinancial quality measures managers can use include customer satisfaction measures such as the number of customer complaints and percentage of defective units shipped to customers; internal-business-process measures such as the percentage of defective and reworked products; and learning-and-growth measures such as the percentage of employees trained in and empowered to use quality principles.
	Three methods to identify quality problems and to improve quality are (a) control charts to distinguish random from nonrandom variations in an operating process; (b) Pareto diagrams to indicate how frequently each type of failure occurs; and (c) cause-and-effect diagrams to identify and respond to potential causes of failure.
3. How do managers identify the relevant costs and benefits of quality-improvement programs?	The relevant costs of quality-improvement programs are the expected incremental costs to implement the program. The relevant benefits are the cost savings and the estimated increase in contribution margin from the higher revenues expected from quality improvements.
4. How do managers use financial and nonfinancial measures to evaluate quality?	Financial measures help managers evaluate the tradeoffs among prevention costs, appraisal costs, and failure costs. Nonfinancial measures identify problem areas that need improvement and serve as indicators of future financial performance.
5. What is customer-response time and what are the reasons for delays?	Customer-response time is how long it takes from the time a customer place an order for a product or service to the time the product or service to the time the product or service is delivered to the customer. Delays occur because of (a) uncertainty about when customers will order products or services and (b) bottlenecks due to limited capacity. Bottlenecks are operations at which the work to be performed approaches or exceeds avaliable capacity
6. What are relevant revenues and costs of delays?	Relevant revenues and costs of delays include lower revenues and higher inventory carrying costs.
7. What financial and nonfinancial measures of time can managers use in the balanced scorecard?	Examples of financial and nonfinancial measures managers can use in the balanced scorecard to evaluate a company's performance related to time are revenue losses from delays, customer-response time, on-time performance, average manufacturing cycle time, and number of employees trained to manage bottleneck operations.

TERMS TO LEARN

This chapter and the Glossary at the end of the book contain definitions of the following important terms:

appraisal costs **(p. 996)**
average waiting time **(p. 1007)**
bottleneck **(p. 1006)**
cause-and-effect
  diagram **(p. 1000)**
conformance quality **(p. 995)**
control chart **(p. 999)**
costs of quality (COQ) **(p. 996)**

customer-response time **(p. 1005)**
design quality **(p. 995)**
external failure costs **(p. 996)**
internal failure costs **(p. 996)**
manufacturing cycle efficiency
  (MCE) **(p. 1005)**
manufacturing cycle
  time **(p. 1005)**

manufacturing lead
  time **(p. 1005)**
on-time
  performance **(p. 1006)**
Pareto diagram **(p. 1000)**
prevention costs **(p. 996)**
quality **(p. 994)**
time driver **(p. 1006)**

ASSIGNMENT MATERIAL

Questions

19-1 Describe two benefits of improving quality.

19-2 How does conformance quality differ from design quality? Explain.

19-3 Name two items classified as prevention costs.

19-4 Distinguish between internal failure costs and external failure costs.

19-5 Describe three methods that companies use to identify quality problems.

19-6 "Companies should focus on financial measures of quality because these are the only measures of quality that can be linked to bottom-line performance." Do you agree? Explain.

19-7 Give two examples of nonfinancial measures of customer satisfaction relating to quality in a balanced scorecard.

19-8 Give two examples of nonfinancial measures of internal-business-process quality in a balanced scorecard.

19-9 Distinguish between customer-response time and manufacturing lead time.

19-10 "There is no trade-off between customer-response time and on-time performance." Do you agree? Explain.

19-11 Give two reasons why delays occur.

19-12 "Companies should always make and sell all products whose selling prices exceed variable costs." Assuming fixed costs are irrelevant, do you agree? Explain.

19-13 Describe the three main measures used in the theory of constraints.

19-14 Describe the four key steps in managing bottleneck operations.

19-15 Describe three ways to improve the performance of a bottleneck operation.

Solved Examples

19-16 Costs of quality analysis. Safe Travel produces car seats for children from newborn to 2 years old. The company is worried because one of its competitors has recently come under public scrutiny because of product failure. Historically, Safe Travel's only problem with its car seats was stitching in the straps. The problem can usually be detected and repaired during an internal inspection. The cost of the inspection is ₹50 per car seat, and the repair cost is ₹10 per car seat. All 2,00,000 car seats were inspected last year, and 5% were found to have problems with the stitching in the straps during the internal inspection. Another 1% of the 2,00,000 car seats had problems with the stitching, but the internal inspection did not discover them. Defective units that were sold and shipped to customers needed to be shipped back to Safe Travel and repaired. Shipping costs are ₹80 per car seat, and repair costs are ₹10 per car seat. However, the out-of-pocket costs (shipping and repair) are not the only costs of defects not discovered in the internal inspection. Negative publicity will result in a loss of future contribution margin of ₹1,000 for each external failure.

1. Calculate appraisal cost.
2. Calculate internal failure cost.
3. Calculate out-of-pocket external failure cost.
4. Determine the opportunity cost associated with the external failures.
5. What are the total costs of quality?
6. Safe Travel is concerned with the high up-front cost of inspecting all 2,00,000 units. It is considering an alternative internal inspection plan that will cost only ₹30 per car seat inspected. During the internal inspection, the alternative technique will detect only 3.5% of the 2,00,000 car seats that have stitching problems. The other 2.5% will be detected after the car seats are sold and shipped. What are the total costs of quality for the alternative technique?
7. What factors other than cost should Safe Travel consider before changing inspection techniques?

Solution

1. Appraisal cost = Inspection cost

$$= ₹50 \times 2,00,000 \text{ car seats}$$
$$= ₹1,00,00,000$$

2. Internal failure cost = Rework cost

$$= 5\% \times 2,00,000 \times ₹10$$
$$= 10,000 \times ₹10 = ₹1,00,000$$

3. Out of pocket external failure cost = Shipping cost + Repair cost

$$= 1\% \times 2,00,000 \times (₹80 + ₹10)$$
$$= 2,000 \times ₹90 = ₹1,80,000$$

4. Opportunity cost of external failure = Lost future profits

$$= (1\% \times 2,00,000) \times ₹1,000$$
$$= 2,000 \text{ car seats} \times ₹1,000 = ₹20,00,000$$

5. Total cost of quality control = ₹1,00,00,000 + ₹1,00,000 + ₹1,80,000 + ₹20,00,000

$$= ₹1,22,80,000$$

6. Quality control costs under the alternative inspection technique:

   Appraisal cost = ₹30 × 2,00,000 = ₹60,00,000

   Internal failure cost = 3.5% × 2,00,000 × ₹10 = ₹70,000

   Out-of-pocket external failure cost = 2.5% × 2,00,000 × (₹80 + ₹10)

$$= 5,000 \times ₹90 = ₹4,50,000$$

   Opportunity cost of external failure = (2.5% × 2,00,000) × ₹1,000

$$= 5,000 \text{ car seats} \times ₹1,000 = ₹50,00,000$$

   Total cost of quality control = ₹60,00,000 + ₹70,000 + ₹4,50,000 + ₹50,00,000

$$= ₹1,15,20,000$$

7. In addition to the lower costs under the alternative inspection plan, Amron should consider a number of other factors:

   a. There could easily be serious reputation effects if the percentage of external failures increases by 250% (from 1% to 2.5%). This rise in external failures may lead to costs greater than ₹5,000 per failure due to lost profits.
   b. Higher external failure rates may increase the probability of lawsuits.
   c. Government intervention is a concern with the chances of government regulation increasing with the number of external failures.

19-17 Cost of quality analysis, ethical considerations Refer to information in Exercise 19-16 in answering this question. Safe Travel has discovered a more serious problem with the plastic core of its car seats. An accident can cause the plastic in some of the seats to crack and break, resulting in serious injuries to the occupant. It is estimated that this problem will affect about 200 car seats in the next year. This problem could be corrected by using a higher quality of plastic that would increase the cost of every car seat produced by ₹100. If this problem is not corrected, Safe Travel estimates that out of the 200 car seats affected, customers will realize that the problem is due to a defect in the seats in only three cases. Safe Travel's legal team has estimated that each of these three cases would result in a lawsuit that could be settled for about ₹50,00,000. All lawsuits settled would include a confidentiality clause, so Safe Travel's reputation would not be affected.

Required

1. Assuming that Safe Travel expects to sell 2,00,000 car seats next year, what would be the cost of increasing the quality of all 2,00,000 car seats?
2. What will be the total cost of the lawsuits next year if the problem is not corrected?
3. Suppose Safe Travel has decided not to increase the quality of the plastic because the cost of increasing the quality exceeds the benefits (saving the cost of lawsuits). What do you think of this decision? (Note: Because of the confidentiality clause, the decision will have no effect on Safe Travel's reputation.)
4. Are there any other costs or benefits that Safe Travel should consider?

Solution

1. Cost of improving quality of plastic = ₹100 × 2,00,000 = ₹20,00,00,000
2. Total cost of lawsuits = 3 × ₹50,00,000 = ₹1,50,00,000
3. Although economically this may seem like a good decision, qualitative factors should be more important than quantitative factors when it comes to protecting customers from harm and injury. If a product can cause a customer serious harm and injury, an ethical and moral company should take steps to prevent that harm and injury. The company's code of ethics should guide this decision.
4. In addition to ethical considerations, the company should consider the societal cost of this decision, reputation effects if word of these problems leaks out at a later date, and governmental intervention and regulation.

19-18 Costs of quality, quality improvements. Cell Design produces cell phone covers for all makes and models of cell phones. Cell Design sells 10,50,000 units each year at a price of ₹100 per unit and a contribution margin of 40%.

A survey of Cell Design customers over the past 12 months indicates that customers were very satisfied with the products but a disturbing number of customers were disappointed because the products they purchased did not fit their phones. They then had to hassle with returns and replacements.

Cell Design's managers want to modify their production processes to develop products that more closely match Cell Design's specifications because the quality control in place to prevent ill-fitting products from reaching customers is not working very well.

The current costs of quality are as follows:

Preventions costs	₹21,00,000
Appraisal costs	10,00,000
Internal failure costs	
Rework	42,00,000
Scrap	2,10,000
External failure costs	
Product replacement	31,50,000
Lost sales from customer returns	78,75,000

The QC manager and controller have forecast the following additional costs to modify the production process.

CAD design improvement	15,00,000
Improve machine calibration to specifications	13,75,000

Required

1. Which cost of quality category are managers focusing on? Why?
2. If the improvements result in a 60% decrease in customer replacement cost and a 70% decrease in customer returns, what is the impact on the overall COQ and the company's operating income? What should Cell Design do? Explain.
3. Calculate prevention, appraisal, internal failure, and external failure costs as a percentage of total quality costs and as a percentage of sales before and after the change in the production process. Comment briefly on your results.

Solution

1. Cell Design's managers plan to increase spending on CAD design improvement improving machine calibrations to achieve product specifications. These are prevention activities. Cell Design's managers plan to increase prevention costs to improve quality. This is consistent with much of the research on quality. Preventing defects from occurring in the first place generally gives the best cost to benefit gains from quality improvement.

2. Cost of making quality improvements = ₹15,00,000 + ₹13,75,000 = ₹28,75,000
   Benefits of quality improvements:
   (1) 70% decrease in lost sales from customer returns = 70% × ₹78,75,000 = ₹55,12,500
   Increase in contribution margin = Contribution margin % × Increase in sales
   $$= 40\% \times ₹55,12,500 = ₹22,05,000$$
   (2) 60% decrease in customer replacement costs = 60% × ₹31,50,000 = ₹18,90,000
   Total benefit = 22,05,000 + 18,90,000 = 40,95,000

   The benefits of making the quality improvements exceed the costs by ₹12,20,000 (₹40,95,000 − ₹28,75,000), so Cell Design should implement the changes to improve quality.

3. The following table shows the actual costs of quality at Cell Design, as a percentage of total costs of quality, and as a percentage of revenues, before the change in the production process. Note that sales revenues = ₹100 × 10,50,000 units = ₹10,50,00,000.

Description (1)	Amount (2)	Percentage of Total Costs of Quality (3) = (2) ÷ ₹1,38,10,000	Percentage of Revenues (4) = (2) ÷ ₹10,50,00,000
Prevention costs	₹21,00,000	15.2%	2.0%
Appraisal costs	10,00,000	7.3%	1.0%
Internal failure costs			
Rework	42,00,000		
Scrap	2,10,000		
Total internal failure costs	44,10,000	31.9%	4.2%
External failure costs			
Customer replacements	31,50,000		
Lost contr. margin from customer returns1	31,50,000		
Total external failure costs	63,00,000	45.6%	6.0%
Total costs of quality	₹1,38,10,000	100.0%	13.2%

[1]Lost contribution margin from customer returns = 40% × Lost sales from customer returns.
$$= 40\% \times ₹7,87,500$$
$$= ₹3,15,000$$

The following table shows the actual costs of quality at Cell Design, as a percentage of total costs of quality, and as a percentage of revenues, after the change in the production process. Note that as a result of these changes, lost sales from customer returns decrease by 70% × ₹78,75,000 = ₹55,12,500, so sales revenues increase by the same amount. Sales revenues in this case = ₹10,50,00,000 + ₹55,12,500 = ₹11,05,12,500

Description (1)	Amount (2)	Percentage of Total Costs of Quality (3) = (2) ÷ ₹1,25,90,000	Percentage of Revenues (4) = (2) ÷ ₹11,05,12,500
Prevention costs1	₹49,75,000	39.5%	4.5%
Appraisal costs	10,00,000	8.0%	0.9%
Internal failure costs			
Rework	42,00,000		
Scrap	2,10,000		
Total internal failure costs	44,10,000	35.0%	4.0%
External failure costs			
Customer replacement costs2	12,60,000		
Lost contr. margin from customer returns3	9,45, 000		
Total external failure costs	22,05,000	17.5%	2.0%
Total costs of quality	₹1,25,90,000	100.0%	11.4%

[1]Prevention costs = Existing prevention costs + CAD design improvement costs + Machine calibration costs

$$= ₹21,00,000 + ₹15,00,000 + ₹13,75,000 = ₹49,75,000$$

[2]Customer replacement costs = ₹31,50,000 × (1 − 0.60) = ₹12,60,000

[3]Lost contribution margin from customer returns = 40% × Lost sales from customer returns

$$= 40\% × ₹78,75,000 × (1 − 0.70)$$
$$= 40\% × ₹23,62,500 = ₹9,45,000$$

As a result of implementing the changes in the production process, prevention costs, which are 15.2% of the total costs of quality and 2% of revenues, will become 39.5% of the total costs of quality and 4.5% of revenues. External failure costs, which are 45.6% of the total costs of quality and 6% of revenues, will become 17.5% of the total costs of quality and 2% of revenues. The changes also result in a decrease in the total costs of quality. The preceding calculations assume that overall sales revenues (other than the additional sales from fewer returns) will be unaffected by the change in the production process. But quality improvements could well result in an increase in sales, providing further benefit to Cell Design.

Improvements in the production process could also decrease rework costs resulting in even more benefits from quality improvement. Better quality could also have other advantages such as making employees proud to work for Cell Design and increasing employee morale.

19-19 Quality improvement, relevant costs, relevant revenues. City Park Conference and Catering Center is a conference center and restaurant facility that hosts more than 300 national and international events each year attended by 50,000 professionals. Due to increased competition and soaring customer expectations, the company has been forced to revisit its quality standards. In the company's 25-year history, customer demand has never been greater for high-quality products and services. Nitin has the following budgeted fixed and variable costs for 2015:

	Total Conference Center Fixed costs	Variable costs per Conference Attendee
Building and facilities	₹4,32,00,000	
Management salaries	₹1,68,00,000	
Customer support and services personnel		₹660

Food and drink	₹1,200
Conference materials	₹420
Incidental products and services	₹180

The company's budgeted operating income is ₹4,20,00,000.

After conducting a survey of 3,000 conference attendees, the company has learned that its customers would most like to see the following changes in the quality of the company's products and services: (1) more menu options and faster service, (2) more incidental products and services (wireless access in all meeting rooms, computer stations for Internet use, free local calling, and so on), and (3) upscale and cleaner meeting facilities. To satisfy these customer demands, the company would be required to increase fixed costs by 50% per year and increase variable costs by ₹120 per attendee as follows:

Customer support and service personnel	₹40
Food and drink	50
Conference materials	0
Incidental products and services	30

Nitin believes that the preceding improvements in product and service quality would increase overall conference attendance by 40%.

1. What is the budgeted revenue per conference attendee?
2. Assuming budgeted revenue per conference attendee is unchanged, should Nitin implement the proposed changes?
3. Assuming budgeted revenue per conference attendee is unchanged, what is the variable cost per conference attendee at which Nitin would be indifferent between implementing and not implementing the proposed changes?

Solution

1.

Budgeted variable cost per attendee:		
Customer support and service personnel	₹660	
Food and drink	1,200	
Conference materials	420	
Incidental products and services	180	
Total budgeted variable cost per attendee		₹2,460
Total budgeted variable cost (₹2,460 × 50,000 attendees)		₹12,30,00,000
Budgeted fixed costs:		
Building and facilities	₹4,32,00,000	
Management salaries	1,68,00,000	
Total budgeted fixed costs		6,00,00,000
Total budgeted costs		18,30,00,000
Budgeted operating income		4,20,00,000
Budgeted revenues		₹22,50,00,000
Budgeted revenue per conference attendee (₹22,50,00,000 ÷ 50,000)		₹4,500

The budgeted revenue per conference attendee is ₹4,500.

2. Quality improvements: additional menu items; additional incidental products and services; improved facilities.

Budgeted variable cost per attendee:

Customer support and service personnel (₹660 + ₹40)	₹700	
Food and drink (₹1,200 + ₹50)	1,250	
Conference materials (₹420 + ₹0)	420	
Incidental products and services (₹180 + ₹30)	210	
Total budgeted variable cost per attendee		₹2,580
Budgeted revenues (₹4,500 per attendee × 70,000 attendees)		₹31,50,00,000
Total budgeted variable costs (₹2,580 × 70,000 attendees)		18,06,00,000
Budgeted fixed costs:		
Building and facilities (₹4,32,00,000 × 1.50)	₹6,48,00,000	
Management salaries (₹1,68,00,000 × 1.50)	2,52,00,000	
Total budgeted fixed costs		9,00,00,000
Total budgeted costs		27,06,00,000
Budgeted operating income		₹4,44,00,000

The improvements above would increase operating income from ₹4,20,00,000 to ₹4,44,00,000. Moreover, improving the company's meeting facilities could also lead to long-term growth.

3. Using information from requirement 2,

Revenues	₹31,50,00,000
Fixed costs	₹9,00,00,000

Denote total variable costs by ₹x

$$₹31,50,00,000 - ₹x - ₹9,00,00,000 = ₹4,20,00,000$$
$$₹x = ₹31,50,00,000 - ₹9,00,00,000 - ₹4,20,00,000$$
$$= ₹18,30,00,000$$

Total variable costs = ₹18,30,00,000

Variable cost per conference attendee = ₹18,30,00,000 ÷ 70,000 = ₹2,614.29

At a variable cost per conference attendee of ₹2,614.29, Nitin would be indifferent between implementing and not implementing the proposed changes.

19-20 Theory of constraints, throughput contribution, relevant costs. The Delite India manufactures filing small cabinets in two operations: machining and finishing. It provides the following information:

	Machining	Finishing
Annual capacity	1,00,000 units	80,000 units
Annual production	80,000 units	80,000 units
Fixed operating costs (excluding direct materials)	₹64,00,000	₹40,00,000
Fixed operating costs per unit produce (₹64,00,000 ÷ 80,000; ₹40,00,000 ÷ 80,000)	₹80 per unit	₹50 per unit

Each cabinet sells for ₹720 and has direct material costs of ₹320 incurred at the start of the machining operation. Delite has no other variable costs. Delite can sell whatever output it produces. The following requirements refer only to the preceding data. There is no connection between the requirements.

1. Delite is considering using some modern jigs and tools in the finishing operation that would increase annual finishing output by 1,000 units. The annual cost of these jigs and tools is ₹3,00,000. Should Delite acquire these tools? Show your calculations.

2. The production manager of the Machining Department has submitted a proposal to do faster setups that would increase the annual capacity of the Machining Department by 10,000 units and would cost ₹50,000 per year. Should Delite implement the change? Show your calculations.

3. An outside contractor offers to do the finishing operation for 12,000 units at ₹100 per unit, double the ₹50 per unit that it costs Delite to do the finishing in-house. Should Delite accept the subcontractor's offer? Show your calculations.

4. The Indian Corporation offers to machine 4,000 units at ₹40 per unit, half the ₹80 per unit that it costs Delite to do the machining in-house. Should Delite accept Indian corporation offer? Show your calculations.

Solution

Theory of constraints, throughput contribution, relevant costs.

1. Finishing is a bottleneck operation. Therefore, producing 1,000 more units will generate additional throughput contribution and operating income.

Increase in throughput contribution (₹720 – ₹320) × 1,000	₹4,00,000
Incremental costs of the jigs and tools	₹3,00,000
Net benefit of investing in jigs and tools	₹1,00,000

Delite should invest in the modern jigs and tools because the benefit of higher throughput contribution of ₹4,00,000 exceeds the cost of ₹3,00,000.

2. The Machining Department has excess capacity and is not a bottleneck operation. Increasing its capacity further will not increase throughput contribution. There is, therefore, no benefit from spending ₹50,000 to increase the Machining Department's capacity by 10,000 units. Delite should not implement the change to do setups faster.

3. Finishing is a bottleneck operation. Therefore, getting an outside contractor to produce 12.000 units will increase throughout contribution:

Increase in throughput contribution (₹720 – ₹320) × 12,000	₹48,00,000
Incremental contracting costs ₹100 × 12,000	12,00,000
Net benefit of contracting 12,000 units of finishing	₹36,00,000

Delite should contract with an outside contractor to do 12,000 units of finishing at ₹100 per unit because the benefit of higher throughput contribution of ₹48,00,000 exceeds the cost of ₹12,00,000. The fact that the cost of ₹100 per unit is double Delite's finishing cost of ₹50 per unit is irrelevant.

4. Operating costs in the Machining Department of ₹64,00,000, or ₹80 per unit, are fixed costs. Delite will not save any of these costs by subcontracting machining of 4,000 units to Indian Corporation. Total costs will be greater by ₹1,60,000 (₹40 per unit × 4,000 units) under the subcontracting alternative. Machining more filing cabinets will not increase throughput contribution, which is constrained by the finishing capacity. Delite should not accept Indian's offer. The fact that Indian Corporation's costs of machining per unit are half of what it costs Delite in-house is irrelevant.

19-21 Theory of constraints, throughput contribution, quality. Refer to the information in Exercise 19-20 in answering the following requirements. There is no connection between the requirements.

1. Delite produces 2,000 defective units at the machining operation. What is the cost to Delite of the defective items produced? Explain your answer briefly.

2. Delite produces 2,000 defective units at the finishing operation. What is the cost to Delite of the defective items produced? Explain your answer briefly.

Solution

Theory of constraints, throughput contribution, quality.

1. Cost of defective unit at machining operation which is not a bottleneck operation is the loss in direct materials (variable costs) of ₹320 per unit. Producing 2,000 units of defectives doe not result in loss of throughput contribution. Despite the defective production, machining can produce and transfer 80.000 units to finishing. Therefore, cost of 2,000 defective units at the machining operation is ₹320 × 2,000 = ₹6,40,000.

2. A defective unit produced at the bottleneck finishing operation costs Delite materials costs plus the opportunity cost of lost throughput contribution. Bottleneck capacity not wasted in producing defective units could be used to generate additional sales and throughput contribution. Cost of 2,000 defective units at the finishing operation is:

Loss of direct materials ₹320 × 2,000	₹6,40,000
Forgone throughput contribution (₹720 – ₹320) × 2,000	8,00,000
Total cost of 2,000 defective units	₹14,40,000

Alternatively, the cost of 2,000 defective units at the finishing operation can be calculated as the lost revenue of ₹720 × 2,000 = ₹14,40,000. This line of reasoning takes the position that direct materials costs of ₹320 × 2,000 = ₹6,40,000 and all fixed operating costs in the machining and finishing operations would be incurred anyway whether a defective or good unit is produced. The cost of producing a defective unit is the revenue lost ₹14,40,000.

19-22 Quality improvement, relevant costs, and relevant revenues. The Puralator Corporation sells 3,00,000 V262 valves to the automobile and truck industry. Thomas has a capacity of 1,10,000 machine-hours and can produce 3 valves per machine-hour. V262's contribution margin per unit is ₹80. Thomas sells only 3,00,000 valves because 30,000 valves (10% of the good valves) need to be reworked. It takes 1 machine-hour to rework 3 valves, so 10,000 hours of capacity are used in the rework process. Puralator's rework costs are ₹21,00,000. Rework costs consist of:

■ Direct materials and direct rework labor (variable costs): ₹30 per unit
■ Fixed costs of equipment, rent, and overhead allocation: ₹40 per unit

Puralator's process designers have developed a modification that would maintain the speed of the process and ensure 100% quality and no rework. The new process would cost ₹31,50,000 per year. The following additional information is available:

■ The demand for Puralator's V262 valves is 3,70,000 per year.
■ The Jackson Corporation has asked Puralator to supply 22,000 T971 valves (another product) if Puralator implements the new design. The contribution margin per T971 valve is ₹100. Puralator can make two T971 valves per machine-hour with 100% quality and no rework.

Required

1. Suppose Puralator's designers implement the new design. Should Puralator accept Jackson's order for 22,000 T971 valves? Show your calculations.
2. Should Puralator implement the new design? Show your calculations.
3. What nonfinancial and qualitative factors should Puralator consider in deciding whether to implement the new design?

Solution

Quality improvement, relevant costs, and relevant revenues.

One way to present the alternatives is via a decision tree as shown below.

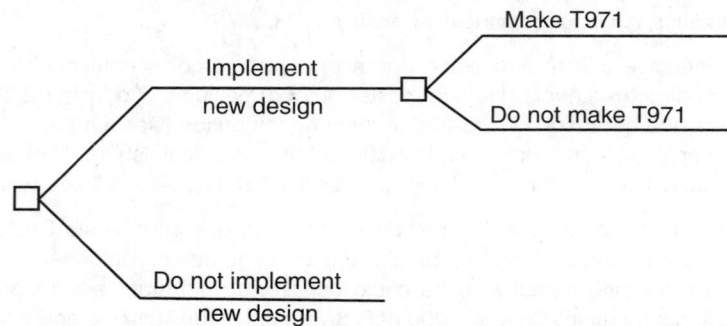

The idea is first evaluate the best action that Puralator should take if it implements the new design (that is, make or not make T971). Puralator can then compare the best mix of products to produce if it implements the new design against the status quo of not implementing the new design.

1. Puralator has capacity constraints. Demand for V262 valves (3,70,000 valves) exceeds production capacity of 330,000 valves (3 valves per hour × 1,10,000 machine-hours). Since capacity is constrained, Puralator will choose to sell the product that maximizes contribution margin per machine-hour (the constrained resource).

   Contribution margin per
   machine-hour for V262 = ₹80 per valve × 3 valves per hour = ₹240

   Contribution margin per
   machine-hour for T971 = ₹100 per valve × 2 valves per hour = ₹200.

   Puralator should reject Jackson Corporation's offer and continue to manufacture only V262 valves.

2. Now compare the alternatives of (a) not implementing the new design versus (b) implementing the new design. By implementing the new design, Puralator will save 10,000 machine-hours of rework time. This time can then be used to make and sell 30,000 (3 valves per hour × 10,000 hours) additional V262 valves. The relevant costs and benefits of implementing the new design follow:

The relevant costs of implementing the new design	₹31,50,000
Relevant benefits:	
a. Savings in rework costs (₹30[a] per V262 valve × 30,000 valves)	9,00,000
b. Additional contribution margin from selling another	
30,000 V262 valves (3 valves per hour × 10,000 hours)	
because capacity previously used for rework is freed up	
₹80 per valve × 30,000 units)	24,00,000
Net relevant benefit	₹1,50,000

   [a]Note that the fixed rework costs of equipment rent and allocated overhead are irrelevant, because these costs will be incurred whether Puralator implements or does not implement the new design.

   Puralator should implement the new design since the relevant benefits exceed the relevant costs by ₹1,50,000.

3. Puralator Corporation should also consider other benefits of improving quality. For example, the process of quality improvement will help Puralator's managers and workers gain expertise about the product and the manufacturing process that may lead to further cost reductions in the future. Improving quality within the plant is also likely to translate into delivering better quality products to customers. The increased reputation and customer goodwill may well lead to higher future revenues through greater unit sales and higher sales prices.

19-23 Waiting time. Kitty Wonderland (KW) makes toys for cats and kittens. KW's managers have recently learned that they can calculate the average waiting time for an order from the time an order is received and the time it is manufactured. They have asked for your help and have provided the following information.

Expected number of orders for the product: 2,000

Manufacturing time per order: 4 hours

Annual machine capacity in hours: 10,000

Required

1. Calculate the average waiting time per order.
2. After learning about the average waiting time, KW's managers are confused. They do not understand why, if annual machine capacity is greater than the average number of orders for the product, there would be any waiting time at all. Write a memo to clarify the situation.
3. The managers have asked for your suggestions on what they can do to minimize or eliminate waiting time. How would you respond?
4. Management is expecting sales to increase. Will average waiting time increase or decrease? Explain briefly.

Solution

1.

$$\text{Average waiting time} = \frac{\left(\begin{array}{c}\text{Annual average}\\\text{number of orders}\end{array}\right) \times \left(\begin{array}{c}\text{Manufacturing}\\\text{time per order}\end{array}\right)^2}{2 \times \left[\begin{array}{c}\text{Annual machine}\\\text{capacity}\end{array} - \left[\left(\begin{array}{c}\text{Annual average}\\\text{number of orders}\end{array}\right) \times \left(\begin{array}{c}\text{Manufacturing}\\\text{time per order}\end{array}\right)\right]\right]}$$

$$= \frac{2,000 \times (4)^2}{2 \times \left[10,000 - \left[2,000 \times 4\right]\right]}$$

$$= \frac{32,000}{2 \times \left[10,000 - 8,000\right]} = 8 \text{ hours}$$

2. To: Management of Kitty Wonderland

   Subject: Explanation of waiting times

Even though Kitty Wonderland expects to utilize only 8,000 hours of the 10,000 hours of capacity available to it, queues can form for two reasons. (1) Kitty Wonderland expects to receive 2,000 orders, but it may receive fewer (say 1,800 orders) or more (say 2,200) orders. (2) Kitty Wonderland may receive orders while it is processing other orders. For example, Kitty Wonderland may receive three orders as soon as it starts processing an order. In this case, the first order would have to wait four hours till manufacturing of the current order is completed; the second order would have to wait another four hours till the first order is completed for a total of eight hours; the third order would have to wait yet another four hours till the second order is completed for a total of 12 hours.

   The denominator in the formula is a measure of the unused capacity, or cushion. As the unused capacity becomes smaller as a result of Kitty Wonderland receiving more orders, the chance that the machine is processing an earlier order when an order arrives becomes more likely, leading to greater delays.

3. Management can take a number of actions to reduce wait times.
   a. Increase the annual capacity by purchasing another machine. This will, of course, increase costs.
   b. Work with customers to smooth the receipt of orders throughout the year or produce for inventory rather than only when an order is received. This will increase inventory holding costs.
   c. Work with process engineering to reduce manufacturing time.

In each case, management would have to consider the benefits of reducing wait times against the costs.

4. If sales increase, the average wait time will increase because the cushion provided by unused capacity will become smaller and the chance that the machine is processing an earlier order when another order arrives becomes more likely, resulting in greater delays.

19-24 Compensation linked with profitability, waiting time, and quality measures. Max Healthcare operates two medical groups, one in Delhi and one in Mumbai. The semi-annual bonus plan for each medical group's president has three components:

a. Profitability performance. Add 1% of operating income.

b. Average patient waiting time. Add ₹50,000 if the average waiting time for a patient to see a doctor after the scheduled appointment time is less than 15 minutes. If average patient waiting time is more than 15 minutes, add nothing.

c. Patient satisfaction performance. Deduct ₹50,000 if patient satisfaction (measured using a survey asking patients about their satisfaction with their doctor and their overall satisfaction with Max Healthcare) falls below 70 on a scale from 0 (lowest) to 100 (highest). No additional bonus is awarded for satisfaction scores of 70 or more.

Semi-annual data for 2015 for Delhi and Mumbai groups are as follows:

	File Edit View Insert Format Tools Data Window Help		
	A	B	C
1		**January-June**	**July-December**
2	**Delhi**		
3	Operating income	₹1,06,50,000	₹1,06,00,000
4	Average waiting time	14 minutes	16 minutes
5	Patient satisfaction	79	82
6			
7	**Mumbai**		
8	Operating income	₹90,00,000	₹9,50,000
9	Average waiting time	17 minutes	14.5 minutes
10	Patient satisfacation	66	70

Required

1. Compute the bonuses paid in each half year of 2015 to the Delhi and Mumbai medical group presidents.

2. Discuss the validity of the components of the bonus plan as measures of profitability, waiting time performance, and patient satisfaction. Suggest one shortcoming of each measure and how it might be overcome (by redesign of the plan or by another measure).

3. Why do you think Max Healthcare includes measures of both operating income and waiting time in its bonus plan for group presidents? Give one example of what might happen if waiting time was dropped as a performance measure.

Solution

Compensation linked with profitability, on-time delivery, and external quality-performance measures.

1.

	Jan.-June	July-Dec.
Delhi		
Add: Profitability		
1% of operating income	₹1,06,500	₹1,06,000
Add: Average waiting time		
₹50,000 if < 15 minutes	50,000	0

Deduct: Patient satisfaction		
₹50,000 if < 70	0	0
Total: Bonus paid	₹1,56,500	₹1,06,000
Mumbai		
Add: Profitability		
1% of operating income	₹90,000	₹9,500
Add: Average waiting time		
₹50,000 if < 15 minutes	0	50,000
Deduct: Patient satisfaction		
₹50,000 if < 70	(50,000)	0
Total: Bonus paid	₹40,000	₹59,500

2. **Operating income as a measure of profitability**

Operating income captures revenue and cost-related factors. However, there is no rec-ognition of investment differences between the two groups. If one group is substantially bigger than the other, differences in size alone give the president of the larger group the opportunity to earn a bigger bonus. An alternative approach would be to use return on investment (perhaps relative to the budgeted ROI).

15 minute benchmark as a measure of patient response time

This measure reflects the ability of Max Healthcare to meet a benchmark for patient response time. Several concerns arise with this specific measure:

a. It is a yes-or-no cut-off. A 16 minute waiting time earns no bonus, but neither does a two hour wait. Moreover, no extra bonus is paid for additional waiting time reductions below 15 minutes. An alternative is to have the bonus that increases with greater waiting time improvements.

b. It can be manipulated. Doctors might quickly make initial contact with a patient to meet the benchmark, but then leave the patient sitting in the examination room for a more detailed examination or procedure to take place.

c. It reflects performance relative only to the initial waiting time. It does not consider other time-related issues such as the wait for an appointment or the time needed to fill out forms.

Problems in (b) and (c) can be overcome by measuring total patient response time (such as how long it takes from the time a patient makes an appointment to the time the actual appointment is concluded), in addition to average waiting time to meet the doctor.

Patient satisfaction as a measure of quality

This measure represents a common method for assessing quality. However, there are sev-eral concerns with its use:

a. Patient satisfaction is likely to be influenced by a number of factors that are outside the groups' control, such as how sick the patients are when coming in or the extent to which they follow doctors' orders,

b. It is influenced by the questions asked in the survey and the survey methodology. As a result, is likely to be "noisy" or very sensitive to assumptions.

c. Patient satisfaction is not the same as patient health outcomes, an important measure of healthcare quality. A combination of measures may work well as a composite mea-sure of quality.

3. Most companies use both financial and nonfinancial measures to evaluate performance, sometimes presented in a single report such as a balanced scorecard. Using multiple measures of performance enables top management to evaluate whether lower-level managers have improved one area at the expense of others. For example, did the bet-ter average waiting time (and patient satisfaction) between July and December in the Mumbai group result from significantly higher expenditures that contributed to the dra-matic reduction m operating income?

An important issue is the relative importance to place on the different measures. If waiting time is not used for performance evaluation, managers will concentrate on increasing operating income and give less attention to waiting time, even if waiting time has a significant influence on whether customers choose Max Healthcare or another healthcare provider when given the choice. However, the president of the Mumbai group received a larger bonus in the second half of the year due in part to lower average waiting time, even though operating profits dropped by nearly 90%. Companies must understand the relative importance of different financial and nonfinancial objectives when using multiple measures for performance evaluation.

19-25 Waiting time, service industry. The registration advisors at a Vidyamandir University (VU) help 4,200 students develop their class schedules and register for classes each semester. Each advisor works for 10 hours a day during the registration period. VU currently has 10 advisors. While advising an individual student can take anywhere from 2 to 30 minutes, it takes an average of 12 minutes per student. During the registration period, the 10 advisors see an average of 300 students a day on a first-come, first-served basis.

Required

1. Using the formula (given in text), calculate how long the average student will have to wait in the advisor's office before being advised.

2. The head of the registration advisors would like to increase the number of students seen each day because at 300 students a day it would take 14 working days to see all of the students. This is a problem because the registration period lasts for only 2 weeks (10 working days). If the advisors could advise 420 students a day, it would take only 2 weeks (10 days). However, the head advisor wants to make sure that the waiting time is not excessive. What would be the average waiting time if 420 students were seen each day?

3. VU wants to know the effect of reducing the average advising time on the average wait time. If VU can reduce the average advising time to 10 minutes, what would be the average waiting time if 420 students were seen each day?

Solution

1. If VU's advisors expect to see 300 students each day and it takes an average of 12 minutes to advise each student, then the average time that a student will wait can be calculated using the following formula:

$$\text{Wait time} = \frac{\left(\substack{\text{Average number} \\ \text{of students per day}}\right) \times \left(\substack{\text{Time taken to} \\ \text{advise a student}}\right)^2}{2 \times \left[\substack{\text{Maximum amount} \\ \text{of time available}} - \left[\left(\substack{\text{Average number} \\ \text{of students per day}}\right) \times \left(\substack{\text{Time taken to} \\ \text{advise a student}}\right)\right]\right]}$$

$$= \frac{300 \times (12)^2}{2 \times \left[10 \text{ advisors} \times 10 \text{ hours} \times 60 \text{ minutes} - \left[300 \times 12\right]\right]}$$

$$= \frac{43,200}{2 \times \left[6,000 - 3,600\right]} = 9 \text{ minutes}$$

2. At 420 students seen a day,

$$\text{Wait time} = \frac{\left(\substack{\text{Average number} \\ \text{of students per day}}\right) \times \left(\substack{\text{Time taken to} \\ \text{advise a student}}\right)^2}{2 \times \left[\substack{\text{Maximum amount} \\ \text{of time available}} - \left[\left(\substack{\text{Average amount} \\ \text{of students per day}}\right) \times \left(\substack{\text{Time taken to} \\ \text{advise a student}}\right)\right]\right]}$$

$$= \frac{420 \times (12)^2}{2 \times \left[10 \text{ advisors} \times 10 \text{ hours} \times 60 \text{ minutes} - \left[420 \times 12\right]\right]}$$

$$= \frac{60,480}{2 \times \left[6,000 - 5,040\right]} = 31.5 \text{ minutes}$$

3. If the average time to advise a student is reduced to 10 minutes, then the average wait time would be

$$= \frac{\left(\begin{array}{c}\text{Average number}\\\text{of students per day}\end{array}\right) \times \left(\begin{array}{c}\text{Time taken to}\\\text{advise a student}\end{array}\right)^2}{2 \times \left[\begin{array}{c}\text{Maximum amount}\\\text{of time available}\end{array} - \left[\left(\begin{array}{c}\text{Average amount}\\\text{of students per day}\end{array}\right) \times \left(\begin{array}{c}\text{Time taken to}\\\text{advise a student}\end{array}\right)\right]\right]}$$

$$= \frac{420 \times (10)^2}{2 \times \left[10 \text{ advisors } \times 10 \text{ hours} \times 60 \text{ minutes} - \left[420 \times 10\right]\right]}$$

$$= \frac{42,000}{2 \times \left[6,000 - 4,200\right]} = 11.67 \text{ minutes}$$

19-26 Waiting time, cost considerations, and customer satisfaction (continued from 19-25) Refer to the information presented in Exercise 19-25. The head of the registration advisors at VU has decided that the advisors must finish their advising in 2 weeks and therefore must advise 420 students a day. However, the average waiting time given a 12-minute advising period will result in student complaints, as will reducing the average advising time to 10 minutes. VU is considering two alternatives:

a. Hire two more advisors for the 2-week (10-working day) advising period. This will increase the available number of advisors to 12 and therefore lower the average waiting time.

b. Increase the number of days that the advisors will work during the 2-week registration period to 6 days a week. If VU increases the number of days worked to 6 per week, then the 10 advisors need only see 350 students a day to advise all of the students in 2 weeks.

Required

1. What would the average wait time be under alternative A and under alternative B?
2. If advisors earn ₹2,000 per day, which alternative would be cheaper for VU (assume that if advisors work 6 days in a given work week, they will be paid time and a half for the sixth day)?
3. From a student satisfaction point of view, which of the two alternatives would be preferred? Why?

Solution

1. **a)** If VU hires two more advisors, then the average wait time will be

$$= \frac{\left(\begin{array}{c}\text{Average number}\\\text{of students per day}\end{array}\right) \times \left(\begin{array}{c}\text{Time taken to}\\\text{advise a student}\end{array}\right)^2}{2 \times \left[\begin{array}{c}\text{Maximum amount}\\\text{of time available}\end{array} - \left[\left(\begin{array}{c}\text{Average amount}\\\text{of students per day}\end{array}\right) \times \left(\begin{array}{c}\text{Time taken to}\\\text{advise a student}\end{array}\right)\right]\right]}$$

$$= \frac{420 \times (12)^2}{2 \times \left[12 \text{ advisors} \times 10 \text{ hours } \times 60 \text{ minutes} - \left[420 \times 12\right]\right]}$$

$$= \frac{60,480}{2 \times \left[7,200 - 5,040\right]} = 14 \text{ minutes}$$

b) If VU has its current employees work six days a week and has them advise 350 students a day, then the average wait time will be

$$= \frac{\left(\begin{array}{c}\text{Average number}\\ \text{of students per day}\end{array}\right) \times \left(\begin{array}{c}\text{Time taken to}\\ \text{advise a student}\end{array}\right)^2}{2 \times \left[\begin{array}{c}\text{Maximum amount}\\ \text{of time available}\end{array} - \left[\left(\begin{array}{c}\text{Average amount}\\ \text{of students per day}\end{array}\right) \times \left(\begin{array}{c}\text{Time taken to}\\ \text{advise a student}\end{array}\right)\right]\right]}$$

$$= \frac{350 \times (12)^2}{2 \times \left[10 \text{ advisors} \times 10 \text{ hours} \times 60 \text{ minutes} - \left[350 \times 12\right]\right]}$$

$$= \frac{(50,400)}{2 \times \left[6,000 - 4,200\right]} = 14 \text{ minutes}$$

2. **a)** Cost if VU hires two extra advisors for the registration period:

Advisor salary cost = 12 advisors × 10 days × ₹2,000 = ₹2,40,000

b) Cost if VU has its 10 advisors work six days a week for the registration period:

Advisor salary cost = (10 advisors × 10 days × ₹2,000) + (10 advisors × 2 days × ₹3,000) = ₹2,60,000

Alternative (a) is less costly for VU.

3. Hiring two extra advisors has the same waiting time and a lower cost than extending the workweek to six days during the registration period. However, the quality of the advising may not be as high. The temporary advisors may not be as familiar with the requirements of the university. They may also be unaware of how to work within the system (i.e., they may not be aware of alternatives that may be available to help students). Therefore, from a student satisfaction standpoint, it would be better to have the regular advisors work an extra day in the week and pay them overtime. This alternative will be more costly for VU, but it is likely to result in better student advising.

19-27 Nonfinancial measures of quality and time. Global Cell Phones (GCP) has developed a cell phone that can be used anywhere in the world (even countries like Japan that have a relatively unique cell phone system). GCP has been receiving complaints about the phone. For the past two years, GCP has been test-marketing the phones and gathering nonfinancial information related to actual and perceived aspects of the phone's quality. The company expects that, given the lack of competition in this market, increasing the quality of the phone will result in higher sales and thereby higher profits.

Quality data for 2012 and 2013 include the following:

	2012	2013
Cell phones produced and shipped	3,000	15,000
Number of defective units shipped	150	600
Number of customer complaints	225	375
Units reworked before shipping	180	1,050
Manufacturing cycle time	15 days	16 days
Average customer-response time	30 days	28 days

Required

1. For Each Year, 2012 And 2013, Calculate The Following:
   a. Percentage Of Defective Units Shipped
   b. Customer Complaints As A Percentage Of Units Shipped
   c. Percentage Of Units Reworked During Production
   d. Manufacturing Cycle Time As A Percentage Of Total Time From Order To Delivery
2. Referring To The Information Computed In Requirement 1, Explain Whether Gcp's Quality And Timeliness Have Improved.

3. Why Would Manufacturing Cycle Time Have Increased While Customer-Response Time Decreased? (It May Be Useful To First Describe What Is Included In Each Time Measurement—See Exhibit 19-7, Page 1005.)

Solution

1.

	2012	2013
Percentage of defective units shipped	$\dfrac{150}{3,000} = 5\%$	$\dfrac{600}{15,000} = 4\%$
Customer complaints as a percentage of units shipped	$\dfrac{225}{3,000} = 7.5\%$	$\dfrac{375}{15,000} = 2.5\%$
Percentage of units reworked during production	$\dfrac{180}{3,000} = 6\%$	$\dfrac{1,050}{15,000} = 7\%$
Manufacturing cycle time as a percentage of total time from order to delivery	$\dfrac{15\ \text{days}}{30\ \text{days}} = 50\%$	$\dfrac{16\ \text{days}}{28\ \text{days}} = 57\%$

2. Quality has by and large improved. The percentage of defects has decreased by 1 percentage point and the number of customer complaints has decreased by 5 percentage points. The former indicates an increase in the quality of the cell phones being produced. The latter has positive implications for future sales. However, the percentage of units reworked has also increased. Nokia should look into the reason for the increase. One possible explanation is the fivefold increase in production that may have resulted in a higher percentage of errors. Nokia should do a root-cause analysis to identify reasons for the additional rework. Finally, the average time from order placement to order delivery has decreased. So customers are receiving their orders on a timelier basis. But manufacturing cycle time is a higher fraction of customer response time. Nokia should seek ways to reduce manufacturing cycle time. For example, process improvements could reduce both rework and manufacturing cycle time. Any reduction in manufacturing cycle time would help to further reduce customer response time.

3. Manufacturing cycle time = wait time + manufacturing time. Producing 15,000 cell phones in 2013 may have required more wait time for each order than the wait time from producing 3,000 cell phones in 2012. Manufacturing cycle time may have increased as more time was spent on making products with fewer defects and reducing rework activities.

Customer response time = receipt time + manufacturing cycle time + delivery time. Manufacturing cycle time is a subset of customer response time. Lower customer response time times is due to order processing efficiency and/or delivery efficiency and not manufacturing cycle time.

19-28 Theory of constraints, contribution margin, sensitivity analysis. Barbic Toys (BT) produces dolls in two processes: molding and assembly. Barbic Toys is currently producing two models: Chatty Akshita and Talking Ayera. Production in the Molding Department is limited by the amount of materials available. Production in the Assembly Department is limited by the amount of trained labor available. The only variable costs are materials in the Molding Department and labor in the Assembly Department. Following are the requirements and limitations by doll model and department.

	Molding Materials	Assembly Time	Selling Price
Chatty Akshita	1.5 pounds per doll	20 minutes per doll	₹350 per doll
Talking Ayera	2 pounds per doll	30 minutes per doll	₹450 per doll
Materials/Labor Available	30,000 pounds	8,400 hours	
Cost	₹100 per pound	₹120 per hour	

Required

1. If Barbic Toys sold only one type of doll, which doll would it produce? How many of these dolls would it make and sell?

2. If Barbic Toys can sell two Chatty Akshitas for each Talking Ayera, how many dolls of each type would it produce and sell? What would be the total contribution margin?

3. How much would production and contribution margin increase if the Molding Department could buy 10 more pounds of materials for ₹100 per pound?

4. How much would production and contribution margin increase if the Assembly Department could get 10 more labor hours at ₹120 per hour?

5. Using the production level in requirement 2, how many pounds of materials are left? How many labor hours are left?

Solution

Theory of constraints, contribution margin, sensitivity analysis

1. Assuming only one type of doll is produced, the maximum production in each department given their resource constraints is:

	Molding Department	Assembly Department	Contribution Margin
Chatty Akshita	$\dfrac{30{,}000 \text{ lbs}}{1.5 \text{ lbs}} = 20{,}000$	$\dfrac{8{,}400 \text{ hours}}{1/3 \text{ hours}} = 25{,}200$	₹350 − 1.5 × ₹100 − 1/3 × 120 = ₹160
Talking Ayera	$\dfrac{30{,}000 \text{ lbs}}{2 \text{ lbs}} = 15{,}000$	$\dfrac{8{,}400 \text{ hours}}{1/2 \text{ hours}} = 16{,}800$	₹450 − 2 × ₹100 − 1/2 × 120 = ₹190

For both types of dolls, the constraining resource is the availability of material since this constraint causes the lowest maximum production.

If only Chatty Akshita is produced, BT can produce 20,000 dolls with a contribution margin of 20,000 × ₹160 = ₹32,00,000

If only Talking Ayera is produced, BT can produce 15,000 dolls with a contribution margin of 15,000 × ₹190 = ₹28,50,000

BT should produce Chatty Akshitas

2. As shown in Requirement 1, available material in the Molding department is the limiting constraint.

If BT sells two Chatty Akshitas for each Talking Ayera, then the maximum number of Talking Ayera dolls the Molding Department can produce (where the number of Talking Ayera dolls is denoted as T) is:

$$(T \times 2 \text{ lbs.}) + ([2 \times T] \times 1.2 \text{ lbs.}) = 30{,}000 \text{ lbs.}$$
$$2T + 3T = 30{,}000$$
$$5T = 30{,}000$$
$$T = 6{,}000$$

The Molding Department can produce 6,000 Talking Ayera dolls, and 2 × 6,000 (or 12,000) Chatty Akshita dolls.

Since BT can only produce 6,000 Talking Ayera and 12,000 Chatty Akshitas before it runs out of ingredients, the maximum contribution margin (CM) is:

$$CM = 12{,}000 \times ₹160 + 6{,}000 + ₹190$$
$$= ₹30{,}60{,}000$$

3. With 10 more pounds of materials, BT would produce more dolls. Using the same technique as in Requirement 2, the increase in production is:

$$(T \times 2 \text{ lbs.}) + ([2 \times T] \times 1.5 \text{ lbs.}) = 10 \text{ lbs.}$$
$$2T + 3T = 10$$
$$T = 2$$

LTT would produce 2 extra Talking Ayera dolls and 4 extra Chatty Akshita dolls. Contribution margin would increase by

$$4 \times ₹160 + 2 \times ₹190 = ₹1,020$$

4. With 10 more labor hours, production would not change. The limiting constraint is pounds of material, not labor hours. BT already has more labor hours available than it needs.

19-29 Manufacturing cycle time, manufacturing cycle efficiency, nonfinancial measures of quality. (CMA, adapted) Reliance Manufacturing evaluates the performance of its production managers based on a variety of factors, including cost, quality, and cycle time. The following are nonfinancial measures for quality and time for 2014 and 2015 for its only product:

Nonfinancial Quality Measures	2014	2015
Number of returned goods	750	915
Number of defective units reworked	2,200	1,640
Annual hours spent on quality training per employee	38	44
Number of units delivered on time	24,820	29,935
Annual totals	**2014**	**2015**
Units of finished goods transported	28,480	33,668
Average total hours worked per employee	2,000	2,000

The following information relates to the average amount of time needed to complete an order:

Time to Complete an order	2014	2015
Wait time		
From customer placing order being received by production	15	14
From order received by production to machine set up for production	13	12
Inspection time	4	2
Process time	8	8
Move time	4	4

Required

1. Compute the manufacturing cycle efficiency for an order for 2014 and 2015.
2. For each year 2014 and 2015, calculate the following:
   a. Percentage of goods returned
   b. Defective units reworked as a percentage of units shipped
   c. Percentage of on-time deliveries
   d. Percentage of hours spent by each employee on quality training
3. Evaluate management's performance on quality and timeliness in 2014 and 2015.

Solution

1. Manufacturing cycle time = Total time from receipt of an order by production until its completion.

> Manufacturing cycle time for 2014 = (13 + 4 + 8 + 4) days = 29 days
> Manufacturing cycle time for 2015 = (12 + 2 + 8 + 4) days = 26 days

Manufacturing cycle efficiency (MCE) is defined as follows:

> MCE = Value-added manufacturing time ÷ Manufacturing cycle time
> MCE for Reliance Manufacturing for 2014 is:
> MCE = 8 days of processing time ÷ 29 days manufacturing cycle time = 0.28
> MCE for Reliance Manufacturing for 2015 is:
> MCE = 8 days of processing time ÷ 26 days manufacturing cycle time = 0.31

It may be argue d that a part of inspection time is also value-added time. Reliance reduced inspection time to two days in 2015, so if we think of two days of inspection as value-added time in 2014 (out of four days) and in 2015:

MCE in 2011 = (8 + 2) days ÷ 29 days = 10 ÷ 29 = 0.34

MCE in 2012 = (8 + 2) days ÷ 26 days = 10 ÷ 26 = 0.38

Reliance has become more efficient in its value-added manufacturing time as a percentage of total manufacturing time during the last year.

Reliance has also shortened its lead time, which means that customers had less time to wait between placing their order and receiving their shipment. This improvement in timeliness will likely lead to greater customer satisfaction.

Some students might ask if inspection has been excessively reduced or simply become more efficient. The key is to improve processes and only then reduce inspection so that the percentage of goods returned does not increase.

2.

Non-Financial Quality Measure	2014	2015
Percentage of goods returned (as a percentage of units shipped) (750 ÷ 28,480; 915 ÷ 33,668)	2.63%	2.72%
Defective units reworked as a percentage of units shipped (2,200 ÷ 28,480; 1,640 ÷ 33,668)	7.72%	4.87%
Percentage of on-time deliveries (24,820 ÷ 28,480; 29,935 ÷ 33,668)	87.15%	88.91%
Percentage of hours spent by each employee on quality training (38 ÷ 2,000; 44 ÷ 2,000)	1.90%	2.20%

3. Reliance has become more efficient in its value-added manufacturing time as a percentage of manufacturing cycle time and has improved the company's lead time. This improved efficiency should result in cost savings for the company as well as greater customer satisfaction.

It is important to evaluate the other nonfinancial quality measures in relation to annual totals (total units sold, etc.) rather than as absolute values. For example, the total number of on-time deliveries increased from 24,820 to 29,935 during 2015. This is an improvement in the timeliness of the company's deliveries. As a percentage of total units delivered, the percentage of on-time deliveries increased from 87.15% to 88.88%.

Management also had two noteworthy areas of improvement related to the nonfinancial quality measures above. The first is the reduction in the total number of defective units reworked. This is a significant improvement compared to the prior year. However, it should be noted that a greater percentage of goods were returned in 2015 than in 2014. Reliance may want to investigate if the reduction in rework led to more defective units being sold to the end consumer. Second, the company spent an increased amount of time per employee on quality training. Because quality training programs are considered lead measures of performance, it is likely that the company will, as a result, see improvements in the quality of its output in the future.

19-30 Statistical quality control. MTR Foods produces a wide variety of breakfast products. The company's three best-selling breakfast products are Idli, Upma, and Uttpam. Each box of a particular type of product is required to meet pre-determined weight specifications, so that no single box contains more or less product than another. The company measures the mean weight per production run to determine if there are variances over or under the company's specified upper- and lower-level control limits. A production run that falls outside of the specified control limit does not meet quality standards and is investigated further by management to determine the cause of the variance. The three MTR Foods products had the following weight standards and production run data for the month of March:

Quality standards: Mean Weight per Production Run

Idli	Upma	Uttpam
17.97 ounce	14 ounce	16.02 ounce

Actual Mean Weight per Production Run (Ounces)

Production Run	Idli	Upma	Uttpam
1	18.23	14.11	15.83
2	18.14	14.13	16.11
3	18.22	13.98	16.24
4	18.30	13.89	15.69
5	18.10	13.91	15.95
6	18.05	14.01	15.50
7	17.84	13.94	15.86
8	17.66	13.99	16.23
9	17.60	14.03	16.15
10	17.52	13.97	16.60
Standard Deviation	0.28	0.16	0.21

Required

1. Using the $\pm 2\sigma$ rule, what variance investigation decisions would be made?
2. Present control charts for each of the three breakfast products for March. What inferences can you draw from the charts?
3. What are the costs of quality in this example? How could MTR employ Six Sigma programs to improve quality?

Solution

1. The $\pm 2\sigma$ rule will trigger a decision to investigate when mean weight per production run is outside the control limit:

   Idli: Mean $\pm 2\sigma = 17.97 \pm (2 \times 0.28)$ or 17.41 to 18.53 oz.

   Upma: Mean $\pm 2\sigma = 14 \pm (2 \times 0.16)$ or 13.68 to 14.32 oz.

   Uttpam: Mean $\pm 2\sigma = 16.02 \pm (2 \times 0.21)$ or 15.60 to 16.44 oz.

Any weight less than the lower control limit or greater than the upper control limit will trigger an investigation by management.

The only product weights outside the specified $m \pm 2s$ control limit were Uttpam on production runs #6 and #10.

2. Solution Exhibit 19-30 presents the SQC charts for each of the three breakfast products.

Idli had no observations outside the control limits. Each of the production runs is considered to be in conformance with quality standards. However, there is an apparent trend from the SQC that the mean of each of the later production runs gets nearer to the lower control limit. Even though this product has not violated the quality requirements, management should investigate the trend to learn if there is faulty equipment or flawed processes that are causing subsequent runs to result in less product per box on average.

Upma also has no observations outside of the control limits. In fact, this product seems to be following the quality specifications most closely. Also, variations appear random in nature and no trends are apparent from the SQC that warrant further investigation by management.

Uttpam has two observations outside the control limits. One falls below the lower control limit and one above the upper control limit. These two production runs would not be in conformance with quality standards. The wide fluctuation in weight variances should be investigated further by management to determine the failure to comply with quality standards.

3. The costs of quality include

   (1) Prevention costs—Costs of designing the process, maintaining equipment, and employee training to operate the production line.
   (2) Appraisal costs—Costs of inspection to check the weight of product boxes.
   (3) Internal failure costs—Costs of refilling product boxes that do not meet specifications; costs to identify causes of failure such as machine calibration, material variability, or human error; costs of reconfiguring manufacturing processes to prevent errors in filling product boxes.

(4) External failure costs—Costs of customer ill-will if they discover that product boxes are underfilled; costs of returning and replacing incorrectly filled boxes.

Six Sigma quality is a standard of excellence that requires a strict understanding of both customer expectations and reasons for manufacturing defects to improve current quality performance. The statistical term Six Sigma translates to 3.4 defects per 1 lakh incidents, or near perfection in quality variability. Key aspects of Six Sigma are to Define, Measure, Analyze, Improve, and Control processes. MTR Foods could employ Six Sigma programs to reduce variability in box weights. The company would first need to (1) define the quality problem (i.e., variability in weight per product box); (2) measure the incidents of defect using statistical quality control tools; (3) analyze potential reasons for variability in the weight per product box (machine calibration, material variability, human error, etc.); (4) assuming the variability is due to machines, the company may choose to better calibrate the existing machines, purchase new machines that are more precise, or investigate other engineering alternatives; (5) finally, once improvements have been made to the existing machines, the company needs to monitor the improvements to ensure that the variability problem has been resolved.

Solution Exhibit 19-30

Plots of Mean Weight per Production Run for MTR Foods

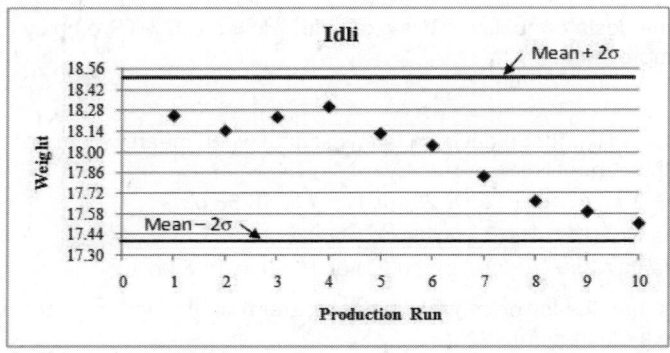

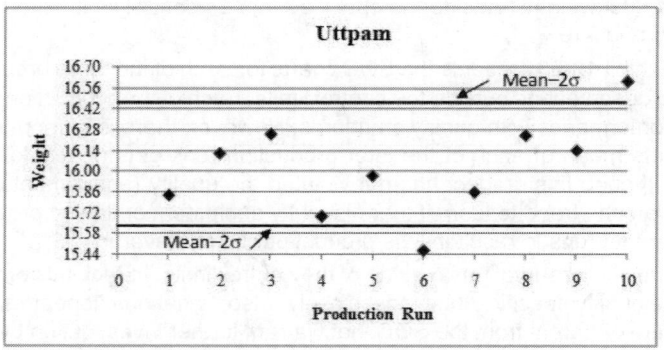

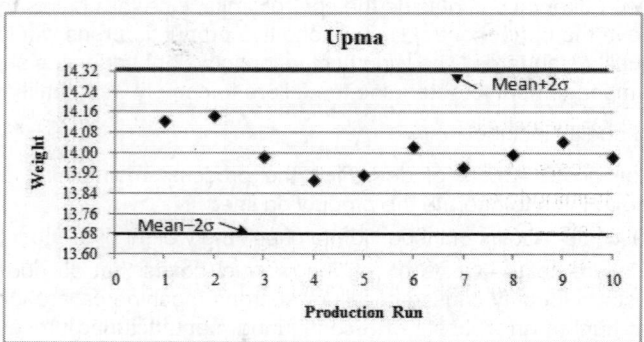

19-31 Quality improvement, Pareto diagram, cause-and-effect diagram. Domino's Pizza has recently begun collecting data on the quality of its customer order processing and delivery. Domino's made 1,800 deliveries during the first quarter of 2015. The following quality data pertain to first-quarter deliveries:

Type of Quality Failure	Quality Failure Incidents, first quarter 2015
Late delivery	50
Damaged or spoiled products delivered	5
Incorrect order delivered	12
Service complaints by customer of delivery personnel	8
Failure to deliver incidents items with order (drinks, side items, etc.)	18

Required

1. Draw a Pareto diagram of the quality failures experienced by Domino's Pizza.
2. Give examples of prevention activities that could reduce the failures experienced by Domino's.
3. Draw a cause-and-effect diagram of possible causes for late deliveries.

Solution

1. Solution Exhibit 19-31A presents a Pareto diagram for the quality incidents observed by Domino's Pizza.

Solution Exhibit 19-31A

Quality improvement, Pareto diagram, cause-and-effect diagram

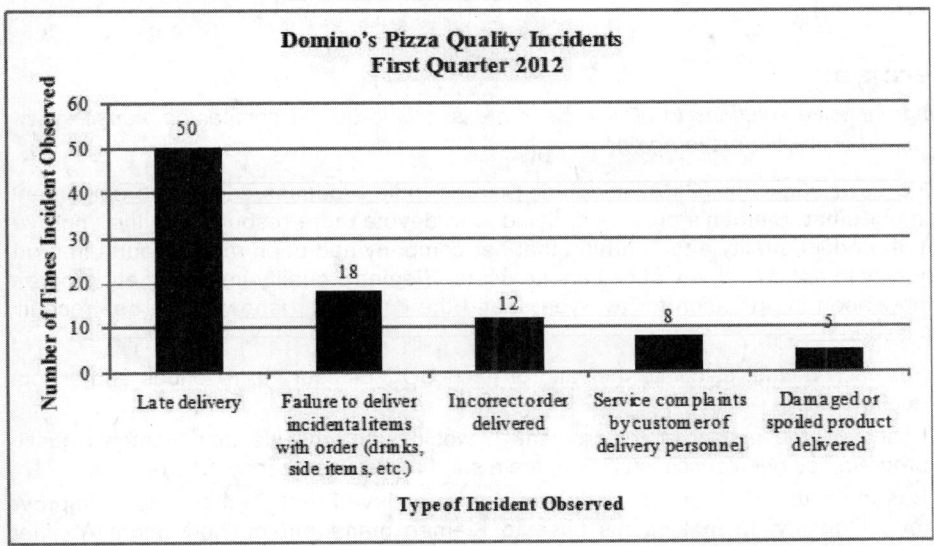

2. Prevention activities that could reduce failures in Domino's Pizza deliveries could include the following:
   a. Better staff training
   b. Improved technology for order processing
   c. Additional time for delivery personnel to review orders prior to pick-up
   c. Additional procedure checks to ensure all order items are included and that delivery pick-up matches order
   d. Incentives offered to staff and delivery personnel for lower rates of quality failure to avoid delivery of damaged or spoiled products and to reduce service complaints by customers

3. Solution Exhibit 19-31B presents a cause-and-effect or fishbone diagram for the problem of "late deliveries."

Solution Exhibit 19-31B

Cause-and-Effect Diagram for incidents of "late delivery" to customer at Domino's Pizza

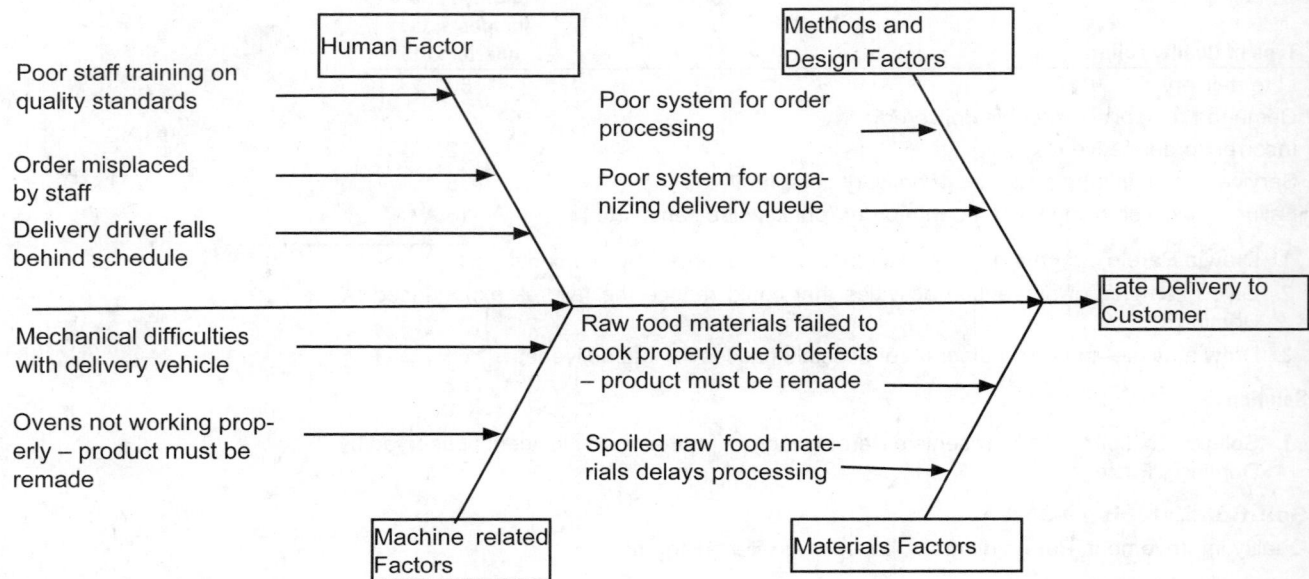

Exercises

[*Comprehensive solutions to all exercises are available on the companion website www.pearsoned.co.in/charlesthorngren*]

19-32 Costs of quality. (CMA, adapted) Siemen India produces cell phone equipment. Abhinav Kumar, Siemen's president, decided to devote more resources to the improvement of product quality after learning that her company had been ranked fourth in product quality in a 2014 survey of cell phone users. Siemen's quality-improvement program has now been in operation for two years, and the cost report shown here has recently been issued.

Required

1. For each period, calculate the ratio of each COQ category to revenues and to total quality costs.

2. Based on the results of requirement 1, would you conclude that Siemen's quality program has been successful? Prepare a short report to present your case.

3. Based on the 2014 survey, Abhinav Kumar believed that Siemen had to improve product quality. In making his case to Siemen management, how might Abhinav have estimated the opportunity cost of not implementing the quality-improvement program?

19-33 Nonfinancial measures of quality and time. Nokia has developed a cell phone that can be used anywhere in the world (even countries like Japan that have a relatively unique cell phone system). Nokia has been receiving complaints about the phone. For the past two years, Nokia has been test marketing the phones and gathering nonfinancial information related to actual and perceived aspects of the phone's quality. They expect that, given the lack of competition in this market, increasing the quality of the phone will result in higher sales and thereby higher profits.

	A	B	C	D	E
	File Edit View Insert Format Tools Data Window Help				
1	Semi-annual COQ report, Siemen India				
2	(In thousands)				
3		30/6/2014	31/12/2014	30/6/2015	31/12/2015
4	Prevention costs				
5	Machine maintenance	₹440	₹440	₹390	₹330
6	Supplier training	20	100	50	40
7	Design reviews	50	214	210	200
8	Total prevention costs	510	754	650	570
9	Appraisal costs				
10	Incoming inspections	108	123	90	63
11	Final testing	332	332	293	203
12	Total appraisal costs	440	455	383	266
13	Internal failure costs				
14	Rework	231	202	165	112
15	Scrap	124	116	71	67
16	Total internal failure costs	355	318	236	179
17	External failure costs				
18	Warranty repairs	165	85	72	68
19	Customer returns	570	547	264	188
20	Total external failure costs	735	632	336	256
21	Total quality costs	₹2,040	₹2,159	₹1,605	₹1,271
22					
23	Total revenues	₹8,240	₹9,080	₹9,300	₹9,020

Quality data for 2014 and 2015 include the following:

	2014	2015
Cell phones produced and shipped	2,000	10,000
Number of defective units shipped	100	400
Number of customer complaints	150	250
Units reworked before shipping	120	700
Manufacturing lead time	15 days	16 days
Average customer response time	30 days	28 days

Required

1. For each year, 2014 and 2015, calculate:

   a. Percentage of defective units shipped.

   b. Customer complaints as a percentage of units shipped.

   c. Percentage of units reworked during production.

   d. Manufacturing lead time as a percentage of total time from order to delivery.

2. Referring to the information computed in requirement 1, explain whether Nokia's quality and timeliness have improved.

3. Why would manufacturing lead time have increased while customer response time decreased?

19-34 Nonfinancial quality measures, on-time delivery. Domino's Pizza promises to deliver pizzas in twenty-five minutes or less. If pizzas are not delivered on time, then the customer receives ₹100 off the price of the order. Some store managers, who receive bonuses based on store profits, believe that the guarantee is a win-win situation for Domino's. Because the average pizza sells for ₹180 but has a marginal cost of ₹45, the store makes a profit no matter what the delivery time. If a pizza is delivered on time, then the store earns ₹135 (₹180 − ₹45) per pizza. If a pizza is delivered late, then the store still earns ₹35 (₹180 − ₹100 − ₹45) per pizza. If more than one pizza is ordered, then Domino's makes even more money because it only gives one ₹100 discount per order.

The head of the Domino's chain is worried that this perceived win-win situation may encourage a complacent attitude in store managers with respect to on-time deliveries. While short-run profits are still earned with late deliveries, repeated late deliveries could lead to annoyance on the part of customers and eventually to a loss of customers. Therefore, the Domino's corporate headquarters has decided to gather information about late deliveries and customer satisfaction. It has developed a survey that asks delivery customers to rate their satisfaction based on three attributes: delivery service, value for money, and overall satisfaction with Domino's. Responses can range from 1 to 5, where 1 is "Awful" and 5 is "Excellent." The following responses were gathered from stores in a single city.

	Store 1	Store 2	Store 3	Store 4
Percentage of deliveries that were late	10%	5%	12%	25%
Average rating of delivery service	4	4.5	3.8	2
Average rating of value received	3.5	4.1	3.5	1.5
Average overall satisfaction	3.6	4	3	2

Required

1. Examine the relationship between the percentage of deliveries that were late and average responses to the three survey questions. Do the data provide any support for Domino's headquarters' concerns?

2. Using the high-low method estimate the effect of changes in the late delivery percentage on average overall satisfaction with Domino's. Use the customer satisfaction score as the dependent variable. Based on this analysis, compute the impact of a change from 5% late deliveries to 7% late deliveries on overall customer satisfaction.

3. What factors would Domino's need to consider when determining whether the delivery guarantee is actually beneficial for the company?

19-35 Manufacturing cycle time, manufacturing cycle efficiency. (CMA, adapted) Torrance Manufacturing evaluates the performance of its production managers based on a variety of factors, including cost, quality, and cycle time. The following information relates to the average amount of time needed to complete an order for its one product:

- Wait time:
  - From order being placed to start of production — 8 days
  - From start of production to completion — 6 days
- Inspection time — 2 days
- Process time — 4 days
- Move time — 2 days

Required

1. Compute the manufacturing cycle efficiency for an order.
2. Compute the manufacturing cycle time (or lead time) for an order.

19-36 Quality improvement, relevant costs, and relevant revenues. The Surya India uses multicolor molding to make plastic lamps. The molding operation has a capacity of 2,00,000 units per year. The demand for lamps is very strong. Surya will be able to sell whatever output quantities it can produce at ₹400 per lamp.

Surya can start only 2,00,000 units into production in the Molding Department because of capacity constraints on the molding machines. If a defective unit is produced at the molding operation, it must be scrapped at a net disposal value of zero. Of the 2,00,000 units started at the molding operation, 30,000 defective units (15%) are produced. The cost of a defective unit, based on total (fixed and variable) manufacturing costs incurred up to the molding operation, equals ₹250 per unit, as follows:

Direct materials (variable)	₹160 per unit
Direct manufacturing labor, setup labor, and materials-handling labor (variable)	30 per unit
Equipment, rent, and other allocated overhead, including inspection and testing costs on scrapped parts (fixed)	60 per unit
Total	₹250 per unit

Surya's designers have determined that adding a different type of material to the existing direct materials would result in no defective units being produced, but it would increase the variable costs by ₹40 per lamp in the Molding Department.

1. Should Surya use the new material? Show your calculations.
2. What nonfinancial and qualitative factors should Surya consider in making the decision?

19-37 Waiting times, manufacturing lead times. The Neelkamal Plastics Limited (NPL) uses an injection molding machine to make a plastic product, Z39. NPL makes products only after receiving firm orders from its customers. NPL estimates that it will receive 50 orders for Z39 (each order is for 1,000 units) during the coming year. Each order of Z39 will take 80 hours of machine time. The annual capacity of the machine is 5,000 hours.

1. Calculate (a) the average amount of time that an order for Z39 will wait in line before it is processed and (b) the average manufacturing lead time per order for Z39.
2. NPL is considering introducing a new product, Y28. NPL expects it will receive 25 orders of Y28 (each order for 200 units) in the coming year. Each order of Y28 will take 20 hours of machine time. The average demand for Z39 will be unaffected by the introduction of Y28. Calculate (a) the average waiting time for an order received and (b) the average manufacturing lead time per order for each product, if NPL introduces Y28.

19-38 Waiting times, relevant revenues, and relevant costs (continuation of 19-37). NPL is still deciding whether it should introduce Y28. The following table provides information on selling prices, variable costs, and inventory carrying costs for Z39 and Y28. NPL will incur additional variable costs and inventory carrying costs for Y28 only if it introduces Y28. Fixed costs equal to 40% of variable costs are allocated to all products produced and sold during the year.

| Product | Annual Average Number of Orders | Selling Price per Order If Average Manufacturing Lead Time per Order Is | | Variable Cost per Order | Inventory Carrying Cost per Order per Hour |
		Less Than 320 Hours	More Than 320 Hours		
Z39	50	₹27,000	₹26,500	₹15,000	₹0.75
Y28	25	8,400	8,000	5,000	0.25

1. Should NPL manufacture and sell Y28? Show your calculations.
2. Should NPL manufacture and sell Y28 if the data in Problem 19-37 are changed as follows: Selling price per order is ₹6,400, instead of ₹8,400, if average manufacturing lead time per order is less than 320 hours; and ₹6,000, instead of ₹8,000, if average manufacturing lead time per order is more than 320 hours? All other data for Y28 are the same.

19-39 Theory of constraints, throughput contribution, quality, relevant costs. Sun Pharmaceuticals manufactures pharmaceutical products in two departments: Mixing and Tablet-Making. Additional information on the two departments follows. Each tablet contains 0.5 gram of direct materials.

	Mixing	Tablet Making
Capacity per hour	150 grams	200 tablets
Monthly capacity		
(2,000 hours available in each department)	3,00,000 grams	4,00,000 tablets
Monthly production	2,00,000 grams	3,90,000 tablets
Fixed operating costs (excluding direct materials)	₹1,60,000	₹3,90,000
Fixed operating cost per tablet		
(₹1,60,000 ÷ 2,00,000 grams;		
₹3,90,000 ÷ 3,90,000 tablets)	₹0.8 per gram	₹1.0 per tablet

The Mixing Department makes 2,00,000 grams of direct materials mixture (enough to make 4,00,000 tablets) because the Tablet-Making Department has only enough capacity to process 4,00,000 tablets. All direct material costs are incurred in the Mixing Department. Sun incurs ₹1,56,000 in direct material costs. The Tablet-Making Department manufactures only 3,90,000 tablets from the 2,00,000 grams of mixture processed; 2.5% of the direct materials mixture is lost in the tablet-making process. Each tablet sells for ₹10. All costs other than direct material costs are fixed costs. The following requirements refer only to the preceding data. There is no connection between the requirements.

Required

1. An outside contractor makes the following offer: If Sun will supply the contractor with 10,000 grams of mixture, the contractor will manufacture 19,500 tablets for Sun (allowing for the normal 2.5% loss of the mixture during the tablet-making process) at ₹0.12 per tablet. Should Sun accept the contractor's offer? Show your calculations.

2. Another company offers to prepare 20,000 grams of mixture a month from direct materials Sun supplies. The company will charge ₹0.70 per gram of mixture. Should Sun accept the company's offer? Show your calculations.

3. Sun's engineers have devised a method that would improve quality in the Tablet-Making Department. They estimate that the 10,000 tablets currently being lost would be saved. The modification would cost ₹7,000 a month. Should Sun implement the new method? Show your calculations.

4. Suppose that Sun also loses 10,000 grams of mixture in its Mixing Department. These losses can be reduced to zero if the company is willing to spend ₹9,000 per month in quality-improvement methods. Should Sun adopt the quality-improvement method? Show your calculations.

5. What are the benefits of improving quality in the Mixing Department compared with improving quality in the Tablet-Making Department?

19-40 Quality improvement, Pareto diagram, cause-and-effect diagram. The Xerox India manufactures, sells, and installs photocopying machines. Xerox India has placed heavy emphasis on reducing defects and failures in its production operations. Xerox India wants to apply the same total quality management principles to manage its accounts receivable.

Required

1. On the basis of your knowledge and experience, what would you classify as failures in accounts receivable?

2. Give examples of prevention activities that could reduce failures in accounts receivable.

3. Draw a Pareto diagram of the types of failures in accounts receivable and a cause-and-effect diagram of possible causes of one type of failure in accounts receivable.

19-41 Ethics and quality. Information from a quality report for 2015 prepared by Nitin Gupta, assistant controller of Crompton Greaves a manufacturer of electric motors, is as follows:

Revenues	₹1,00,00,000
Inspection of production	₹90,000
Warranty liability	₹2,60,000
Product testing	₹2,10,000
Scrap	₹2,30,000
Design engineering	₹2,00,000
Percentage of customer complaints	5%
On-time delivery rate	93%

Salman Khan, the plant manager of Crompton, is eligible for a bonus if the total costs of quality as a percentage of revenues are less than 10%, the percentage of customer complaints is less than 4%, and the on-time delivery rate exceeds 92%. Salman is unhappy about the customer complaints of 5% because, when preparing her report, Arun actually surveyed customers regarding customer satisfaction. Salman khan expected Arun to be less proactive and to wait for customers to complain. Salman Khan concern with Arun's approach is that it introduces subjectivity into the results and also fails to capture the seriousness of customers' concerns. "When you wait for a customer to complain, you know he is complaining because it is something important. When you do customer surveys, customers mention whatever is on their mind, even if it is not terribly important."

Aamir Khan, the controller, asks Arun to see him. He tells him about Salman's concerns. "I think Salman has a point. See what you can do." Arun is confident that the customer complaints are genuine and that customers are concerned about quality and service. He believes it is important for Crompton to be proactive and obtain systematic and timely customer feedback, and then to use this information to make improvements. He is also well aware that Crompton has not done customer surveys in the past, and that, except for his surveys, Salman would probably be eligible for the bonus. He is confused about how to handle Aamir's request.

Required

1. Calculate the ratio of each cost-of-quality category (prevention, appraisal, internal failure, and external failure) to revenues in 2015. Are the total costs of quality as a percentage of revenues less than 10%?

2. Would it be unethical for Arun to modify his analysis? What steps should Arun take to resolve this situation?

 **Inventory Management, Just-in-Time, and Simplified Costing Methods**

Suppose you could receive a large quantity discount for a product that you regularly use, but the discount requires you to buy a year's supply and necessitates a large up-front expenditure.

Would you take the quantity discount? Companies face similar decisions because firms pay a price for tying up money in inventory sitting on their shelves or elsewhere. Money tied up in inventory is a particularly serious problem when times are tough. When faced with these circumstances, companies work very hard to better manage their inventories.

Inventory Management in Retail Organizations

Inventory management includes planning, coordinating, and controlling activities related to the flow of inventory into, through, and out of an organization. Consider this breakdown of operations for three major retailers for which cost of goods sold constitutes their largest cost item.

	Modern	Bharati	Wal-Mart
Revenues	100.0%	100.0%	100.0%
Deduct costs:			
Cost of goods sold	75.8%	87.7%	75.8%
Selling and administration costs	18.9%	9.5%	18.4%
Other costs, interest, and taxes	3.6%	1.0%	2.2%
Total costs	98.3%	98.2%	96.4%
Net income	1.7%	1.8%	3.6%

The low percentages of net income to revenues means that improving the purchase and management of goods for sale can cause dramatic percentage increases in net income.

Costs Associated with Goods for Sale

There are a number of different types of costs associated with inventory other than the cost of the actual goods purchased. The costs associated with inventory fall into the following six categories:

1. **Purchasing costs** are the cost of goods acquired from suppliers, including incoming freight costs. These costs usually make up the largest cost category of goods in inventory. Discounts for various purchase-order sizes and supplier payment terms affect purchasing costs.

1042

2. **Ordering costs** are the costs of preparing and issuing purchase orders, receiving and inspecting the items included in the orders, and matching invoices received, purchase orders, and delivery records to make payments. Ordering costs include the cost of obtaining purchase approvals, as well as other special processing costs.

3. **Carrying costs** are the costs that arise while goods are being held in inventory. Carrying costs include the opportunity cost of the investment tied up in inventory (see Chapter 11) and the costs associated with storage, such as space rental, insurance, and obsolescence.

4. **Stockout costs** are the costs that arise when a company runs out of a particular item for which there is customer demand, a *stockout*. The company must act quickly to replenish inventory to meet that demand or suffer the costs of not meeting it. A company may respond to a stockout by expediting an order from a supplier, which can be expensive because of additional ordering and manufacturing costs plus any associated transportation costs. Or the company may lose sales due to the stockout. In this case, the opportunity cost of the stockout includes lost contribution margin on the sale not made plus any contribution margin lost on future sales due to customer ill will.

5. **Costs of Quality** are the costs incurred to prevent and appraise, or the costs arising as a result of, quality issues. Quality problems arise, for example, because products get spoiled or broken or are mishandled while products are moved in and out of the warehouse. As discussed earlier in Chapter 19, there are four categories of quality costs: prevention costs, appraisal costs, internal failure costs, and external failure costs.

6. **Shrinkage costs** result from theft by outsiders, embezzlement by employees, misclassifications, and clerical errors. Shrinkage is measured by the difference between (a) the cost of the inventory recorded on the books (after correcting errors), and (b) the cost of inventory when physically counted. Shrinkage can often be an important measure of management performance. Consider, for example, the grocery business, where operating income percentages hover around two percent. With such small margins, it is easy to see why one of a store manager's prime responsibilities is controlling inventory shrinkage. A ₹10,000 increase in shrinkage will erase the operating income from sales of ₹5,00,000 (2% × ₹5,00,000 = ₹10,000).Because shrinkage costs generally increase when a firm's inventory increases, most firms try not to hold more inventory than necessary.

Note that not all inventory costs are available in financial accounting systems. For example, opportunity costs are seldom recorded in these systems and are a significant component in several of these cost categories.

Information-gathering technology increases the reliability and timeliness of inventory information and reduces the costs related to inventory. For example, bar-coding technology allows a scanner to record individual units purchased and sold. As soon as a unit is scanned, a record of its movements is created which helps a firm better manage its purchasing, carrying, and stockout costs. In the next several sections, we consider how relevant costs are computed for different inventory-related decisions in merchandising companies.

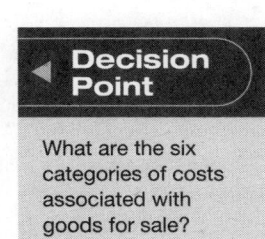

◄ Decision Point

What are the six categories of costs associated with goods for sale?

The Economic-Order-Quantity Decision Model

How much should a firm order of a given product? The **economic order quantity (EOQ)** is a decision model that, under a given set of assumptions, calculates the optimal quantity of inventory to order.

- The simplest version of an EOQ model assumes there are only ordering and carrying costs because these are the most common costs of inventory.
- The same quantity is ordered at each reorder point.
- Demand, ordering costs, and carrying costs are known with certainty. The **purchase-order lead time**, the time between placing an order and its delivery—is also known with certainty.
- The purchasing cost per unit is unaffected by the quantity ordered. This assumption makes purchasing costs irrelevant to determining EOQ because purchasing price is the same, whatever the order size.
- No stockouts occur. The basis for this assumption is that the costs of stockouts are so high that managers maintain adequate inventory to prevent them.
- When deciding on the size of a purchase order, managers consider the costs of quality and shrinkage costs only to the extent that these costs affect ordering or carrying costs.

Note that EOQ analysis ignores purchasing costs, stockout costs, costs of quality, and shrinkage costs. Also recall from Chapter 11 that manage
only consider relevant costs when making decisions. In a later section we will discuss how to identify the relevant ordering and carrying costs. At this point, we simply note that EOQ is the order quantity that minimizes the sum of a company's relevant ordering and carrying costs. The sum of the costs is the firm's *relevant total ordering and carrying costs* of inventory. The relevant total costs are calculated as follows:

Relevent total costs = Relevants ordeing costs + Relevents carrying costs

We use the following notations:

D = Demand in units for a specified period (one year in this example)
Q = Size of each order (order quantity)

$$\text{Number of purchase orders per period (one year)} = \frac{\text{Demand in units for a period (one year)}}{\text{Size of each order (order quantity)}} = \frac{D}{Q}$$

Average inventory in units $= \dfrac{Q}{2}$, because each time the inventory goes down to 0, an order for Q units is received. The inventory varies from Q to 0 so the average inventory is $\dfrac{0 + Q}{2}$.

P = Relevant ordering cost per purchase order
C = Relevant carring cost of one unit in stock for the time period used for D (one year)

For any order quantity, Q,

$$\text{Annual relevant ordering costs} = \left(\begin{array}{c} \text{Number of} \\ \text{purchase orders} \\ \text{per year} \end{array} \times \begin{array}{c} \text{Relevant ordering} \\ \text{cost per} \\ \text{purchase order} \end{array} \right) = \left(\frac{D}{Q} \times P \right)$$

$$\text{Annual relevant carrying costs} = \left(\begin{array}{c} \text{Average inventory} \\ \text{in units} \end{array} \times \begin{array}{c} \text{Annual} \\ \text{relevant carrying} \\ \text{cost per unit} \end{array} \right) = \left(\frac{Q}{2} \times C \right)$$

$$\text{Annual relevant total costs} = \begin{array}{c} \text{Annual} \\ \text{relevant ordering} \\ \text{costs} \end{array} + \begin{array}{c} \text{Annual} \\ \text{relevant carrying} \\ \text{costs} \end{array} = \left(\frac{D}{Q} \times P \right) + \left(\frac{Q}{2} \times C \right)$$

The order quantity that minimizes annual relevant total costs is

$$EOQ = \sqrt{\frac{2DP}{C}}$$

The EOQ model is solved using calculus but the key intuition is that relevant total costs are minimized when relevant ordering costs equal relevant carrying costs. If carrying costs are less (greater) than ordering costs, total costs can be reduced by increasing (decreasing) the order quantity. To solve for EOQ, we set

$$\left(\frac{Q}{2} \times C\right) = \left(\frac{D}{Q} \times P\right)$$

Multiplying both sides by $\frac{2Q}{C}$, we get $Q^2 = \frac{2DP}{C}$

$$Q = \sqrt{\frac{2DP}{C}}$$

The formula indicates that EOQ increases with higher demand and/or higher ordering costs and decreases with higher carrying costs.

Let's see how EOQ analysis works. Glare Shade sells sunglasses. This problem focuses on Glare Shade's basic sunglasses, UX1. Glare Shade purchases the UX1s from Sontek at ₹140 a unit. Sontek pays for all incoming freight. No inspection is necessary at Glare Shade because Sontek supplies quality merchandise. Glare Shade's annual demand is 13,000 units of UX1s, at a rate of 250 units per week. Glare Shade requires a 15% annual rate of return on investment. Relevant ordering cost per purchase order is ₹2,000.

The relevant carrying cost per unit per year is as follows:

Required annual return on investment, 0.15 × ₹140	₹21
Relevant costs of insurance, materials handling, breakage, shrinkage, and so on, per year	31
Total	₹52

What is the EOQ for ordering UX1 sunglasses?

Substituting $D = 13,000$ units per year, $P = ₹2000$ per order, and $C = ₹52.0$ per unit per year, in the EOQ formula, we get

$$EDO = \sqrt{\frac{2 \times 13,000 \times ₹2,000}{₹52}} = \sqrt{₹10,00,000} = 1,000 \text{units}$$

Purchasing 1,000 units per order minimizes total relevant ordering and carrying costs. Therefore, the number of deliveries each period (one year in this example) is as follows:

$$\frac{D}{EDO} = \frac{13,000}{1,000} = 13 \text{deliveries}$$

Recall the annual relevant total costs (RTC) $= \left(\frac{D}{Q} \times P\right) + \left(\frac{Q}{2} \times C\right)$
For $Q = 1,000$ units,

$$RTC = \frac{13,000 \times ₹2000}{1,000} + \frac{1,000 \times ₹52}{2}$$

$$= ₹26,000 + ₹26,000 = ₹52,000$$

Exhibit 20-1 graphs the annual relevant total costs of ordering (DP/Q) and carrying inventory ($QC/2$) under various order sizes (Q), and it illustrates the trade-off between these two types of costs. The larger the order quantity, the lower the annual relevant ordering costs, but the higher the annual relevant carrying costs. *The annual relevant total costs are at a minimum at the EOQ at which the relevant ordering and carrying costs are equal.*

When to Order, Assuming Certainty

The second decision Glare Shade's managers face is *when to order* the units. The **reorder point** is the quantity level of inventory on hand that triggers a new purchase order. The reorder point is simplest to compute when both demand and purchase-order lead time are known with certainty:

$$\text{Reorder point} = \frac{\text{Number of units sold}}{\text{per units of time}} \times \frac{\text{Purchase-order}}{\text{lead time}}$$

Suppose the purchase-order lead time for UX1 is 2 weeks:

Economic order quantity	1,000 units
Number of units sold per week	250 units per week (13,000 units ÷ 52 weeks)
Purchase-order lead time	2 weeks

Reorder point = 250 units per week × 2 weeks = 500 units

Glare Shade will order 1,000 units of UX1 each time inventory stock falls to 500 units.[1] Exhibit 20-2 shows the behavior of the inventory level of UX1 units, assuming demand occurs uniformly during each week. If purchase-order lead time is two weeks, a new order will be placed when the inventory level falls to 500 units, so the 1,000 units ordered will be received at the precise time that inventory reaches zero.

Exhibit 20-1	Graphic Analysis of Ordering Costs and Carrying Costs for U×1 Sunglasses at Glare Shade

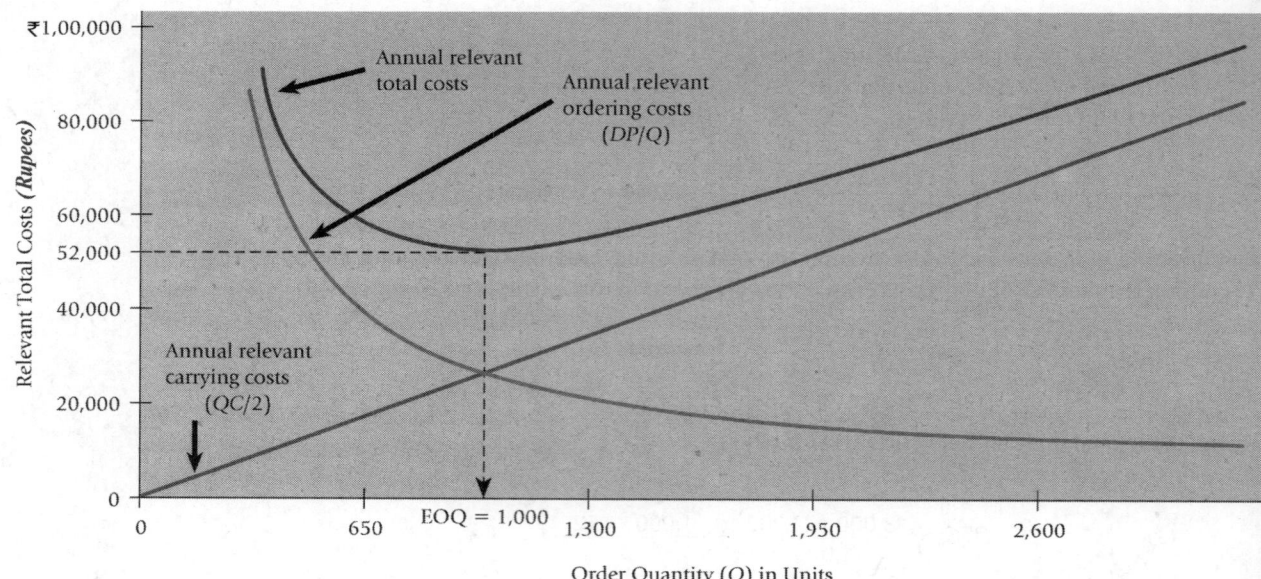

---

[1] This handy but special formula does not apply when receipt of the order fails to increase inventory to the reorder-point quantity (for example, when lead time is three weeks and the order is a one-week supply). In these cases, orders will overlap.

Safety Stock

If Glare Shade's managers are uncertain about demand or the purchase-order lead time or if they are uncertain about the quantities of UX1s Sontek can provide, they will hold safety stock. **Safety stock** is inventory held at all times regardless of the quantity of inventory ordered using the EOQ model. Companies use safety stock as a buffer against unexpected increases in demand, uncertainty about lead time, and unavailability of stock from suppliers. Suppose Glare Shade's managers are uncertain about demand. They expect the demand for UX1s to be 250 units per week, but it could be as high as 400 units per week or as low as 100 units per week. If stockout costs are very high, the managers will want to hold a safety stock of 300 units and incur higher carrying costs. The 300 units equal the maximum excess demand of 150 (400 − 250) units per week times the 2 weeks of purchase-order lead time. If stockout costs are minimal, no safety stock will be held to avoid incurring the additional carrying costs.

Managers use a frequency distribution based on prior daily or weekly levels of demand forms the basis for computing safety-stock levels. Assume that one of the following levels of demand will occur over the two-week purchase-order lead time at CD World.

Total Demand for 2 Weeks	200 Units	300 Units	400 Units	500 Units	600 Units	700 Units	800 Units
Probability (sums to 1.00)	0.06	0.09	0.20	0.30	0.20	0.09	0.06

We see that 500 units is the most likely level of demand for two weeks because it has the highest probability of occurrence. We see also a 0.35 probability that demand will be 600, 700, or 800 units (0.20 + 0.09 + 0.06 = 0.35).

If a customer wants to buy U × 1 and the store has none in stock, Glare Shade can "rush" them to the customer at an additional cost to Glare Shade of ₹40 per unit. The relevant stockout costs in this case are ₹40 per unit. The optimal safety-stock level is the quantity of safety stock that minimizes the sum of annual relevant stockout and carrying costs. Note that Glare Shade will place 13 orders per year for UX1 and will incur the same ordering costs whatever level of safety stock it chooses. Therefore, ordering costs are irrelevant for the safety-stock decision. Recall that the relevant carrying cost for UX1 is ₹52 per unit per year.

Exhibit 20-2

Inventory Level of UX1 Sunglasses at Glare Shade[a]

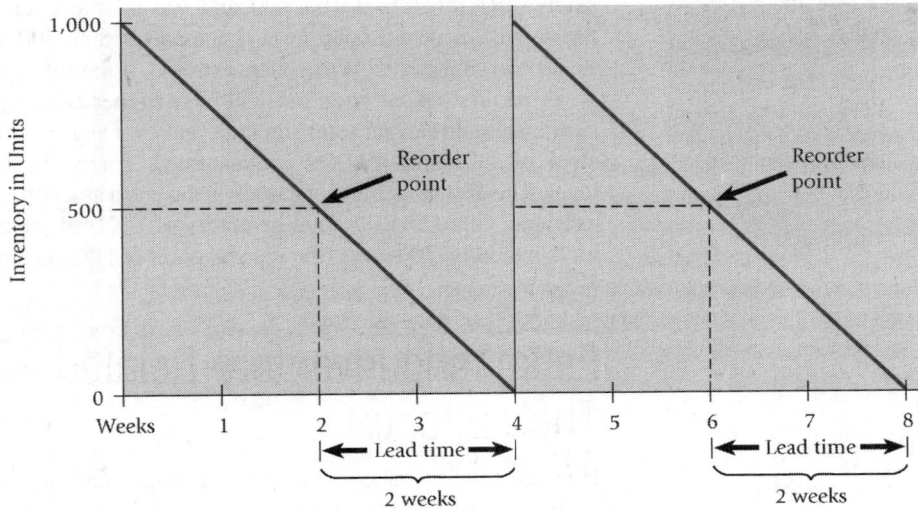

[a] This exhibit assumes that demand and purchase-order lead time are certain:
Demand = 250 UX1 sunglasses per week
Purchase-order lead time = 2 weeks

Exhibit 20-3   Computation of Safety Stock for Glare Shade When Reorder Point Is 500 Units

	A	B	C	D	E	F	G	H	I
	File Edit View Insert Format Tools Data Window Help								
1	Safety	Demand							
2	Stock	Levels			Relevant	Number of	Expected	Relevant	Relevant
3	Level	Resulting	Stockout	Probability	Stockout	Orders	Stockout	Carrying	Total
4	in Units	in Stockouts	in Units^a	of Stockout	Costs^b	per Year^c	Costs^d	Costs^e (₹)	Costs (₹)
5	(1)	(2)	(3) = (2) − 500 − (1)	(4)	(5) = (3) × ₹40	(6)	(7) = (4) × (5) × (6)	(80) = (1) × ₹52	(9) = (7) + (8)
6	0	600	100	0.20	₹4,000	13	₹10,400		
7		700	200	0.09	8,000	13	9,360		
8		800	300	0.06	12,000	13	9,360		
9							₹29,120	0	29,120
10	100	700	100	0.09	4,000	13	₹4,680		
11		800	200	0.06	8,000	13	6,240		
12							₹10,920	5,200	16,120
13	200	800	100	0.06	4,000	13	₹3,120	10,400	13,520
14	300	–	–	–	–	–	₹0^f	15,600	15,600
15									
16	^a Demand level resulting in stockouts – Inventory available during lead time (excluding safety stock), 500 units – Safety stock.								
17	^b Stockout in units x Relevant stockout costs of ₹40 per unit.								
18	^c Annual demand, 13,000 ÷ 1,000 EOQ = 13 orders per year.								
19	^d Probability of stockout x Relevant stockout costs x Number of orders per year.								
20	^e Safety stock x Annual relevant carrying costs of ₹52 per unit (assumes that safety stock is on hand at all times and that there is no overstocking								
21	caused by decreases in expected usage).								
22	^f At a safety stock level of 300 units, no stockout will occur and, hence, expected stockout costs = ₹0								

Exhibit 20-3 tabulates the annual relevant total stockout and carrying costs when the reorder point is 500 units. Over the 2-week purchase-order lead time, stockouts can occur if demand is 600, 700, or 800 units because these levels exceed the 500 units in stock at the time Glare Shade places the purchase orders. Consequently, Glare Shade only evaluates safety stock levels of 0, 100, 200, and 300 units of UX1s. If the safety stock is 0 units, Glare Shade will incur stockout costs if demand is 600, 700, or 800 units but will have no additional carrying costs. At the other extreme, if the safety stock is 300 units, Glare Shade will never incur stockout costs but will have higher carrying costs. As Exhibit 20-3 shows, the firm's annual relevant total stockout and carrying costs are lowest (₹13,520) when a safety stock of 200 units of UX1s is maintained. Therefore, 200 units is the optimal safety-stock level. The 200 units of safety stock is the extra stock that Glare Shade always maintains. For example, Glare Shade's total inventory of UX1s at the time of reordering its EOQ of 1,000 units would be 700 units (the reorder point of 500 units plus safety stock of 200 units).

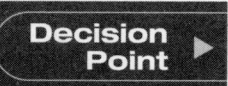

Decision Point ▶

What does the EOQ decision model help managers do and how do managers decide on the safety stock levels?

Estimating Inventory-Related Relevant Costs and Their Effects

How do Glare Shade's managers calculate the annual relevant inventory-related costs, such as the relevant carrying, stockout, and ordering costs?

We start by discussing the relevant inventory carrying costs of ₹52.0 per unit per year, which consist of the *relevant incremental costs* plus the *relevant opportunity cost of capital*.

What are the *relevant incremental costs* of carrying inventory? Only those costs, such as warehouse rent, warehouse workers' salaries, costs of obsolescence, costs of shrinkage, costs of breakage, and costs of insurance, that change with the quantity of inventory held. The salaries paid to clerks, stock keepers, and materials handlers are irrelevant if they are unaffected by changes in inventory levels. Suppose, however, that as inventories increase (decrease), total salary costs increase (decrease) as clerks, stock keepers, and materials handlers are added (transferred to other activities or laid off). In this case, the salaries paid are relevant costs of carrying inventory. Similarly, costs of storage space owned that cannot be used for other profitable purposes when inventories decrease are irrelevant. But if the space has other profitable uses or if total rental cost is tied to the amount of space occupied, storage costs are relevant costs of carrying inventory.

What is the *relevant opportunity cost of capital*? It is the return forgone by investing capital in inventory rather than elsewhere. It is calculated as the required rate of return multiplied by the per-unit costs of acquiring inventory, such as the purchase price of units, incoming freight, and incoming inspection. Opportunity costs are also computed on investments (say, in equipment) if these investments are affected by changes in inventory levels.

In the case of stockouts, the relevant incremental cost is the cost of expediting an order from a supplier. The relevant opportunity cost is (1) the lost contribution margin on sales forgone because of the stockout and (2) lost contribution margin on future sales forgone as a result of customer ill will.

The relevant ordering costs are only those ordering costs that change with the number of orders placed (for example, costs of preparing and issuing purchase orders and receiving and inspecting materials).

Learning Objective 3

Identify the effect of errors that can arise when using the EOQ decision model

. . . errors in predicting parameters have a small effect on costs

and ways to reduce conflicts between the EOQ model and models used for performance evaluation

. . . by making the two models congruent

Cost of a Prediction Error

Predicting relevant costs is difficult and seldom flawless, which raises the question, "What is the cost when actual relevant costs differ from the estimated relevant costs used for decision making"?

Suppose Glare Shade's relevant ordering costs per purchase order for UX1 are ₹1,000, but the manager predicts them to be ₹2,000 when calculating the order quantity. We can calculate the cost of this "prediction" error using a three-step approach.

Step 1: Compute the Monetary Outcome from the Best Action That Could Be Taken, Given the *Actual* Amount of the Cost Input (Cost per Purchase Order). This is the benchmark—that is, the decision the manager would have made if the manager had known the correct ordering cost against which actual performance can be measured. Using $D = 13,000$ units of UX1 per year, $P = ₹1,000$, and $C = ₹52.0$ per units per year,

$$EDQ = \sqrt{\frac{2DP}{C}}$$

$$= \sqrt{\frac{2 \times 13,000 \times ₹1,000}{₹52}} = \sqrt{5,00,000}$$

$$= 707 \text{ packages (rounded)}$$

Glare Shade's annual relevant total costs when the EOQ = 707 packages are as follows:

$$RTC = \frac{DP}{Q} + \frac{QC}{2}$$

$$= \frac{13,000 \times ₹1,000}{707} + \frac{707 \times ₹52}{2}$$

$$= ₹18,390 + ₹18,380 = ₹36,770$$

Step 2:   Compute the Monetary Outcome from the Best Action Based on the Incorrect *Predicted* **Amount of the Cost Input (Cost per Purchase Order).** In this step, the manager calculates the order quantity based on the prediction (that later proves to be wrong) that the ordering cost is ₹2,000. When this is the case, the best action is to purchase 1,000 units in each order. However, the actual cost of the purchase order is only ₹1,000. Consequently, the actual annual relevant total costs when $D = 13,000$, units per year, $Q = 1,000$ units, $P = ₹1,000$, and $C = ₹52.0$, per unit per year are as follows:

$$RTC = \frac{13,000 \times ₹1,000}{1,000} + \frac{1,000 \times ₹52}{2}$$
$$= ₹13,000 + ₹26,000$$
$$= 39,000$$

Step 3:   Compute the Difference Between the Monetary Outcomes from step 1 and step 2.

	Monetary Outcome
Step 1	₹36,770
Step 2	39,000
Difference	₹(2,230)

The cost of the prediction error, ₹2,230, is less than 7% of the relevant total costs of ₹36,770. Note that the annual relevant-total-costs curve in Exhibit 20-1 is somewhat flat over the range of order quantities from 700 to 1,300 units. That is, the annual relevant cost is roughly the same even if misestimating the relevant carrying and ordering costs results in an EOQ quantity of 1,000 plus 30% (1,300) or 1,000 minus 30% (700). *The square root in the EOQ model diminishes the effect of estimation errors because it results in the effects of the incorrect numbers becoming smaller.*

In the next section, we consider a planning-and-control and performance-evaluation issue that frequently arises when managing inventory.

Conflicts Between the EOQ Decision Model and Managers' Performance Evaluation

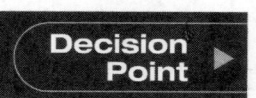

Decision Point ▶

How do errors in predicting the parameters of the EOQ model affect costs? How can companies reduce the conflict between the EOQ decision model and models used for performance evaluation?

What happens if the order quantity based on the EOQ decision model differs from the order quantity managers would choose to make their own performance look best? Consider, for example, opportunity costs. As we have seen, the EOQ model takes into account opportunity costs because these costs are relevant costs when calculating inventory carrying costs. However, managers evaluated on financial accounting numbers, which is often the case, will ignore opportunity costs. Why? Because financial accounting only records actual transactions,not the costs of opportunities forgone (see Chapter 11). Managers interested in making their own performance look better will only focus on measures used to evaluate their performance. Conflicts will then arise between the EOQ model's optimal order quantity and the order quantity that managers regard as optimal.

As a result of ignoring some of the carrying costs (the opportunity costs), managers will be inclined to purchase larger lot sizes of materials than the lot sizes calculated according to the EOQ model, particularly if larger lot sizes result in lower purchase prices. As we discussed in the previous section, the cost of these suboptimal choices is small if the quantities purchased are close to the EOQ. However, if the lot sizes become much greater, the cost to the company can be quite large. Moreover, if we consider other costs, such as costs of quality and shrinkage of holding large inventories, the cost to the company of purchasing in large lot sizes is even greater. To achieve congruence between the EOQ decision model and managers' performance evaluations, companies such as Walmart design performance-evaluation systems that charge managers responsible for managing inventory levels with carrying costs that include a required return on investment.

Just-in-Time Purchasing

Just-in-time (JIT) purchasing is the purchase of materials (or goods) so that they are delivered just as needed for production (or sales). Consider Hewlett-Packard's (HP's) JIT purchasing. HP has long-term agreements with suppliers for the major components of its printers. Each supplier is required to make frequent deliveries of small orders directly to the production floor, based on the production schedule HP provides them. The suppliers work hard to keep their commitments because any failure on their part will result in HP's assembly plant not meeting its own scheduled deliveries of printers.

Learning Objective **4**
Describe why companies are using just-in-time purchasing
. . . high carrying costs, low ordering costs, high-quality suppliers, and reliable supply chains

JIT Purchasing and EOQ Model Parameters

Suppose Glare Shade's managers believe that the current purchasing policies might result in the carrying costs of the firm's inventories (parameter C in the EOQ model) being much greater than what they had estimated because of higher warehousing, handling, insurance, and equipment costs. Suppose they also believe that the cost of placing a purchase order (parameter P in the EOQ model) is likely to decrease because of the following:

■ Glare Shade is establishing long-term purchasing agreements that define the price and quality terms it has with its suppliers over an extended period. No additional negotiations need to take place before supplies can be ordered.

■ New electronic systems allow Glare Shade to place purchase orders, tally delivery records, and make payments to suppliers more cost effectively.

■ Glare Shade is using purchase-order cards (similar to consumer credit cards such as VISA and MasterCard). As long as purchasing personnel stay within preset total and individual-transaction dollar limits, traditional labor-intensive procurement-approval procedures are not required.

File Edit View Insert Format Tools Data Window Help

	A	B	C	D	E	F	G
1				Economic Order Quantity in Units			
2				At Different Ordering and Carrying Costs			
3	Annual Demand (D) =	13,000	units				
4							
5	Relevant Carrying Costs			Relevant Ordering Costs per Purchase Order (P)			
6	Per Package per Year (C)			₹2,000	₹1,500	₹1,000	₹300
7	₹52			10,000	8,660	7,070	3,870
8	70			8,620	7,460	6,090	3,340
9	100			7,210	6,240	5,100	2,790
10	150			5,890	5,100	4,160	2,280

Exhibit 20-4

Sensitivity of EOQ to Variations in Relevant Ordering and Carrying Costs for U×1 Sunglasses

Exhibit 20-4 tabulates the sensitivity of the EOQ to changes in carrying and ordering costs of UX1s. Exhibit 20-4 supports moving toward JIT purchasing because, as the company's relevant carrying costs increase and relevant ordering costs per purchase order decrease, the EOQ decreases and ordering frequency increases.

Relevant Costs of JIT Purchasing

JIT purchasing is not guided solely by the EOQ model because that model only emphasizes the tradeoff between relevant carrying and ordering costs. Inventory management, however, also includes accounting for a company's purchasing costs, stockout costs, costs of quality, and shrinkage costs. Glare Shade's managers are concerned that ordering and storing large quantities of UX1 units have contributed to defective and broken units and shrinkage. So, the company begins implementing JIT purchasing by asking the supplier of UX1 units to make more frequent deliveries of smaller sizes. Glare Shade has recently established an Internet business-to-business purchase-order link with its supplier, Sontek. Glare Shade triggers a purchase order for UX1s by a single computer entry. Payments are made electronically for batches of deliveries, rather than for each individual delivery. These changes reduce the company's ordering costs from ₹2,000 to only ₹20 per purchase order! Glare Shade will use the Internet purchase-order link whether or not it shifts to JIT purchasing. We next evaluate the effect JIT purchasing has on quality and costs.

Description of item	Current Purchasing Practice	JIT Purchasing Practice
Deliveries	1,000 units purchased 13 times per year	100 unit purchased 130 times per year (5 times every 2 weeks)
Purchasing costs	₹140 per unit	₹140.2 per unit (Note: Many companies do not pay a higher price for more frequent deliveries.)
Inspection of units	Units inspected at time of receipt at a cost of ₹0.5 per unit to identify that need to be returned	Units not inspected because Sontek ensures that quality UX1 sunglasses are delivered to support Glare Shade's JIT purchasing.
Required rate of return on investment	15%	15%
Relevent carrying cost of insurance, materials handling, storage, etc.	₹31.0 per unit of average inventory per year	₹30 per unit of average inventory per year (lower insurance, materials handling and storage rates)
Customer return costs	₹100 for shipping and processing a defective unit returned by a customer. The high quality of units supplied by Sontek and Glare will result in no units being returned by customers.	₹100 for shipping and processing a defective unit returned by a customer. The high quality of units supplied by Sontek will result in no units being result in no units being returned by customer.
Stockout costs	No stockout costs because demand and purchase order lead times during each 4-week period (52 weeks ÷ 13) delivery are know with certainty.	More stockouts because demand variation and delays in supplying units are more likely in the short time intervals between orders under JIT purchasing. Glare Shade expects to incur stockout costs on 150 units of UX1 per year under the JIT purchasing policy. When a stockout occurs, Glare Shade must rush-order units at an additional cost of ₹40 per unit.

Should Glare Shade implement the JIT purchasing option of 130 deliveries of UX1 per year? Exhibit 20-5 compares Glare Shade's relevant total costs under the current purchasing policy and the JIT policy. It shows net cost savings of ₹19,010 per year by shifting to a JIT purchasing policy. The benefits of JIT purchasing arise from lower carrying and inspection costs as a result of better quality. JIT purchasing gives Glare Shade's managers immediate feedback about quality problems by reducing the "safety net" large quantities of inventory afford.

Supplier Evaluation and Relevant Costs of Quality and Timely Deliveries

Companies that implement JIT purchasing choose their suppliers carefully and develop long-term supplier relationships. Some suppliers are better positioned than others to support JIT purchasing. For example, the corporate strategy of Brittania, a supplier of potato chips and other snack foods, emphasizes service, consistency, freshness, and quality of the delivered products. As a result, Brittania makes deliveries to retail outlets more frequently than many of its competitors.

What are the relevant total costs when choosing suppliers? Consider again the UX1 units purchased by Glare Shade. Denton Corporation, another supplier of UX1 sunglasses, offers to supply all the units that Glare Shade needs. Glare Shade requires the supplier to deliver 100 units 130 times per year (5 times every 2 weeks). Glare Shade will establish an Internet-based purchase-order link with whichever supplier it chooses, trigger a purchase order for UX1 units by a single computer entry, and make payments electronically for batches of deliveries, rather than for each individual delivery. As discussed earlier, the company's ordering costs will be only ₹20 per purchase order. The following table provides information about Denton versus Sontek. Sontek charges a higher price than Denton but also supplies higher-quality UX1s. The information about Sontek is the same as that presented earlier under JIT purchasing in Exhibit 20-5.

Exhibit 20-5 Annual Relevant Costs of Current Purchasing Policy and JIT Purchasing Policy for UX1 Sunglasses

	Relevant Cost per Unit (₹) (2)		Quantity per Year (3)	Total Costs (4) = (2) × (3)		Relevant Cost per Unit (₹) (5)		Quantity per Year (6)	Total Costs (7) = (5) × (6)
		Current Purchasing Policy					**JIT Purchasing Policy**		
Relevant Items (1)									
Purchasing costs	140	per unit	13,000	₹18,20,000		140.2	per unit	13,000	₹18,22,600
Ordering costs	20	per order	13	260		20.0	per order	130	2,600
Inspection costs	0.5	per unit	13,000	6,500		-	per unit	-	-
Opportunity carrying costs	21[a]	per unit of average inventory per year	500[b]	10,500		21.0[a]	per unit of average inventory per year	50[c]	1,050
Other carrying costs (insurance, materials handling, etc.)	31	per unit of average inventory per year	500[b]	15,500		30.0	per unit of average inventory per year	50[c]	1,500
Customer return costs	100	per unit returned	0	0		100.0	per unit returned	0	0
Stockout costs	40	per unit	0	0		40.0	per unit	150	6,000
Total annual relevant costs				₹18,52,760					₹18,33,750
Annual difference in favor of JIT Purchasing					₹19,010				

[a]Purchasing cost per unit × 0.15 per year
[b]Order quantity/2 = 1,000/2 = 500 units
[c]Order quantity/2 = 100/2 = 50 units

Description of Item	Purchasing Terms from Rytek	Purchasing Terms from Denton
Purchasing costs	₹140.2 per unit	₹138.0 per unit
Inspection of UX1s	Glare Shade has bought UX1s from Rytek in the past and knows that it will deliver quality UX1s on time. UX1s supplied by Rytek require no inspection.	Denton does not enjoy a sterling reputation for quality, so Glare Shade plans to inspect UX1s at a cost of ₹0.5 per UX1.
Required rate of return on investment	15%	15%
Relevant carrying cost of insurance, materials handling, storage, etc.	₹30.0 per unit per year	₹29.0 per unit per year because of lower purchasing costs
Customer return costs	Glare Shade estimates ₹100 for shipping and processing a defective UX1 unit returned by a customer. Fortunately, the high quality of units supplied by Rytek will result in no units being returned by customers.	Glare Shade estimates ₹100 for shipping and processing a defective UX1 unit returned by a customer and product returns of 2.5% of all units sold.
Stockout costs	Glare Shade expects to incur stockout costs on 150 UX1 units each time resulting in a rush-order at a cost of ₹40 per unit.	Denton has less control over its processes, so Glare Shade expects to incur stockout costs on 360 UX1 units each time initiating rush orders at a cost of ₹40 per unit

Exhibit 20-6 shows the relevant total costs of purchasing from Sontek and Denton. Even though Denton is offering a lower price per unit, there is a net cost savings of ₹18,730 per year by purchasing UX1s from Sontek because of lower inspection, customer returns, and stockout costs. The benefit of purchasing from Sontek could be even greater if purchasing high-quality UX1s from Sontek enhances Glare Shade's reputation and increases customer goodwill,leading to higher sales and profitability in the future.

JIT Purchasing, Planning and Control, and Supply-Chain Analysis

Retailers inventory levels depend on the demand patterns of their customers and supply relationships with their distributors and manufacturers, the suppliers to their manufacturers, and so on. *The supply chain* describes the flow of goods, services, and information from the initial sources of materials and services to the delivery of products to consumers, regardless of whether those activities occur in the same company or in other companies. Retailers can purchase inventories on a JIT basis only if activities throughout the supply chain are properly planned, coordinated, and controlled.

Procter and Gamble's (P&G's) experience with its Pampers product illustrates the gains from supply-chain coordination. Retailers selling Pampers found that the weekly demand for the product varied because families purchased disposable diapers randomly. Anticipating even more demand variability and lacking information about available inventory with P&G, retailers' orders to P&G became more variable. This, in turn, increased variability of orders at P&G's suppliers resulting in high levels of inventory at all stages in the supply chain.

How did P&G respond to these problems? By sharing information and planning and coordinating activities throughout the supply chain with retailers Sharing sales information reduced the level of uncertainty that P&G and its suppliers had about retail demand for the product and led to (1) fewer stockouts at the retail level, (2) reduced manufacturing of Pampers not immediately needed by retailers, (3) fewer manufacturing orders that had to be "rushed" or "expedited," and (4) lower inventories held by each company in the supply chain. The benefits of supply chain coordination at P&G have been so great that retailers such as Wal-Mart have contracted with P&G to manage their retail inventories on a just-in-time basis.

Exhibit 20-6 Annual Relevant Costs of JIT Purchasing for UX1 Sunglasses From Sontek and Denton

	File Edit View Insert Format Tools Data Window Help								
	A	B	C	D	E	F	G	H	I	J

	A	B	C	D	E	F	G	H	I	J
1					Relevant Cost of Purchasing From					
2			Sontek					Denton		
3	Relevant Items	Relevant Cost per Unit		Quantity Per Year	Total Costs		Relevant Cost per Unit		Quantity Per Year	Total Costs
4	(1)	(2)		(3)	(4) = (2) × (3)		(5)		(6)	(7) = (5) × (6)
5	Purchasing costs	₹140.2	per unit	13,000	₹18,22,600		138.0	per unit	13,000	₹17,94,000
6	Ordering costs	20.0	per order	130	2,600		20.0	per order	130	2,600
7	Inspection costs	0.5	per unit	0	0		0.5	per unit	13,000	6,500
8	Opportunity carrying costs	21.0[a]	per unit of average inventory per year	50[b]	1,050		20.7[a]	per unit of average inventory per year	50[b]	1,030
9	Other carrying costs (insurance, materials handling, and so on)	30.0	per unit of average inventory per year	50[b]	1,550		30.0	per unit of average inventory per year	50[b]	1,500
10	Customer return costs	100.0	per unit returned	0	0		100.0	per unit returned	325[c]	32,500
11	Stockout costs	40.0	per unit	150	6,000		40.0	per unit	360	14,400
12	Total annual relevant costs				₹18,33,800					₹18,52,530
13	Annual difference in favor of Sontek					₹18,730				
14										
15	[a]Purchasing cost per unit x 0.15 per year									
16	[b]Order quantity ÷ 2 = 100 ÷ 2 = 50 units									
17	[c]2.5% of units returned x 13,000 units									

This practice is called *supplier-or vendor-managed inventory*. Coordinating supply chains, however, can be difficult because supply-chain partners don't always share accurate and timely information about their sales, inventory levels, and sales forecasts with one another. Some of the reasons for these challenges are communication problems, trust issues between the companies, incompatible information systems, and limited people and financial resources.

Inventory Management and MRP, and JIT Production

We now turn our attention from purchasing to managing the production inventories of manufacturing companies. Two of the most widely used systems to plan and implement inventory activities within plants are materials requirements planning (MRP) and just-in-time (JIT) production.

Materials Requirements Planning

A materials requirements planning (MRP) system is a "push-through" system that manufactures finished goods for inventory on the basis of demand forecasts. Companies such as Guidant, which manufactures medical devices, and Philips, which makes consumer electronic products, use MRP systems. To determine outputs at each stage of production, MRP uses (1) the demand forecasts for final products; (2) a bill of materials detailing the materials, components, and subassemblies for each final product; and (3) information about a company's inventories of materials, components, and products. Taking into account the lead time required to purchase materials and to manufacture components and finished products, a master production schedule specifies the quantity and timing of each item to be produced. Once production starts as scheduled, the output of each department is pushed through the production line.

Maintaining accurate inventory records and costs is critical in an MRP system. For example, after becoming aware of the full costs of carrying finished goods inventory in its MRP system, National Semiconductor contracted with FedEx to airfreight its microchips from a central location in Singapore to customer sites worldwide instead of storing the chips at geographically dispersed warehouses.

Just-in-Time (JIT) Production

Decision Point ▶

How do materials requirements planning (MRP) systems differ from just-in-time (JIT) production systems?

In contrast, JIT production is a "demand-pull" approach, which is used by companies such as Toyota in the automobile industry, Dell in the computer industry, and Braun in the appliance industry. **Just-in-time (JIT) production,** which is also called **lean production,** is a "demand-pull" manufacturing system that manufactures each component in a production line as soon as, and only when, needed by the next step in the production line. Demand triggers each step of the production process, starting with customer demand for a finished product at the end of the process and working all the way back to the demand for direct materials at the beginning of the process. In this way, demand pulls an order through the production line. The demand-pull feature of JIT production systems results in close coordination among workstations and smooths the flow of goods, despite low quantities of inventory. JIT production systems help companies meet the demand for high-quality products on time and at the lowest possible cost.

Features of JIT Production Systems

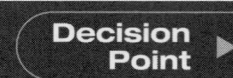

Identify the features of a just-in-time production system

. . . for example, organizing work in manufacturing cells, improving quality, reducing manufacturing lead time

A JIT production system has these features:

- Production is organized in **manufacturing cells,** which are work areas with the different types of equipment grouped together to make related products. Materials move from one machine to another, and various operations are performed in sequence, minimizing materials-handling costs.

- Workers are hired and trained to be multiskilled and capable of performing a variety of operations and tasks, including minor repairs and routine equipment maintenance.

- Defects are aggressively eliminated. Because of the tight links between workstations and the minimal inventories at each workstation, defects arising at one workstation quickly affect other workstations in the line. JIT creates an urgency for solving problems immediately and eliminating the root causes of defects as quickly as possible. Low levels of inventories allow workers to trace problems to and solve problems at earlier workstations in the production process, where the problems likely originated.

- *The setup time,* the time required to get equipment, tools, and materials ready to start the production of a component or product and the, *manufacturing cycle time,* the time from when an order is received by manufacturing until it becomes a finished good, are reduced. Setup costs correspond to the ordering costs P in the EOQ model. Reducing setup time and its costs makes production in smaller batches economical, which in turn reduces inventory levels. Reducing the manufacturing cycle time enables a company to respond faster to changes in customer demand.

- Suppliers are selected on the basis of their ability to deliver quality materials in a timely manner. Most companies implementing *JIT production* also implement *JIT purchasing.* JIT plants expect JIT suppliers to make timely deliveries of high-quality goods directly to the production floor.

We next present a relevant-cost analysis for deciding whether to implement a JIT production system.

Costs and Benefits of JIT Production

As we have seen, JIT production clearly lowers a company's carrying costs of inventory. But there are other benefits of lower inventories: heightened emphasis on improving quality by eliminating the specific causes of rework, scrap, and waste, and lower manufacturing cycle times. It is important, therefore, when computing the relevant benefits and costs of reducing inventories in JIT production systems, the cost analyst should take into account all benefits and all costs.

Consider Naman Metal Works, a manufacturer of brass fittings. Naman is considering implementing a JIT production system. To implement JIT production, Naman must incur ₹10,00,000 in annual tooling costs to reduce setup times. Naman expects that JIT will reduce its average inventory by ₹50,00,000 and that the relevant costs of insurance, storage, materials handling, and setup will decline by ₹3,00,000 per year. The company's required rate of return on its inventory investments is 10% per year. Should Naman implement a JIT production system? On the basis of the information provided, we would be tempted to say "no" because the annual relevant cost savings amount to ₹8,00,000 [(10% of ₹50,00,000) + ₹3,00,000)], which is less than the additional annual tooling costs of ₹10,00,000.

Our analysis, however, is incomplete. We have not considered the other benefits of lower inventories in JIT production. Naman estimates that implementing JIT will improve quality and reduce rework on 500 units each year, resulting in savings of ₹500 per unit. Also, better quality and faster delivery will allow Naman to charge ₹20 more per unit on the 20,000 units that it sells each year.

The annual relevant benefits and costs from implementing JIT equal the following:

Incremental savings in insurance, storage, materials handling, and set up	₹3,00,000
Incremental savings in inventory carrying costs (10% × ₹50,00,000)	5,00,000
Incremental savings from reduced rework (₹500 per unit × 500 units)	2,50,000
Additional contribution margin from better quality and faster delivery (₹20 per unit × 20,000 units)	4,00,000
Incremental annual tooling costs	(10,00,000)
Net incremental benefit	₹4,50,000

Therefore Hudson should implement a JIT production system.

JIT in Service Industries

JIT purchasing and production methods can be applied in service industries as well. For example, inventories and supplies, and the associated labor costs to manage them, represent more than a third of the costs in most hospitals. By implementing a JIT purchasing and distribution system, Sir Ganga Ram Hospital, New Delhi reduced its inventories and supplies by 90 percent in 18 months. McDonald has adapted JIT production practices to making hamburgers.[2] Before, McDonald's precooked a batch of hamburgers that were placed under heat lamps to stay warm until ordered. If the hamburgers didn't sell within a specified period of time, they were discarded, resulting in high inventory holding costs and spoilage costs. Moreover, the quality of hamburgers deteriorated the longer they sat under the heat lamps. A customers placing a special order for a hamburger (such as a hamburger with no cheese) had to wait a long time for it to be cooked. Now McDonald cooks hamburgers only when they are ordered. By increasing the quality of hamburgers and reducing the time needed for special orders JIT has improved customer satisfaction.

We next turn our attention to planning and control in JIT production systems.

Enterprise Resource Planning (ERP) Systems[3]

Enterprise resource planning systems are frequently used in conjunction with JIT production. An **enterprise resource planning (ERP) system** is an integrated set of software modules covering a company's accounting, distribution, manufacturing, purchasing, human resources, and other functions. Real-time information is collected in a single database and

---

[2] Charles Atkinson, "McDonald's, A Guide to the Benefits of JIT," *Inventory Management Review*, inventorymanagementreview.org/2005/11/mcdonalds_a_gui.html, accessed May 2, 2007.

[3] For an excellent discussion, see T. H. Davenport, "Putting the Enterprise into the Enterprise System," *Harvard Business Review*, July–August 1998; also see A. Cagilo, "Enterprise Resource Planning Systems and Accountants: Towards Hybridization?" *European Accounting Review*, May 2003.

simultaneously fed into all of the software applications, giving personnel greater visibility into the company's end-to-end business processes. For example, using an ERP system, a salesperson can generate a contract for a customer in Germany, verify the customer's credit limits, and place a production order. The system will then use this same information to schedule manufacturing in, say, Brazil, requisition materials from inventory, order components from suppliers, and schedule shipments. Simultaneously the system credits the salesperson with his or her commission and records all the costing and financial accounting information. An ERP system also allows a company to shift its manufacturing and distribution plans rapidly in response to changes in supply and demand.

Companies believe that an ERP system is essential to support JIT initiatives because of the effect it has on lead times. Using an ERP system, Autodesk, a maker of computer-aided design software, reduced order lead time from 2 weeks to 1 day; Fujitsu reduced lead time from 18 to 1.5 days.

ERP systems are large and unwieldy. Because of its complexity, suppliers of ERP systems such as SAP and Oracle provide software packages that are standard, but that can be customized, although at considerable cost. Without some customization, unique and distinctive features that confer strategic advantage will not be available. The challenge when implementing ERP systems is to strike the right balance between the lower cost of standardized systems and the strategic benefits that accrue from customization.

Performance Measures and Control in JIT Production

In addition to personal observation, managers use financial and nonfinancial measures to evaluate and control JIT production. We now describe these measures and indicate the effect that JIT systems are expected to have on these measures.

1. Financial performance measures, such as inventory turnover ratio (Cost of goods sold ÷ Average inventory), which is expected to increase
2. Nonfinancial performance measures of time, inventory, and quality, such as the following:
   - Manufacturing cycle time, expected to decrease
   - Units produced per hour, expected to increase
   - Number of days of inventory on hand, expected to decrease
   - $\dfrac{\text{Total setup time for machines}}{\text{Total manufacturing time}}$, expected to decrease
   - $\dfrac{\text{Number of units scrapped or requiring rework}}{\text{Total number of units started and completed}}$, expected to decrease

Personal observation and nonfinancial performance measures provide the most timely, intuitive, and easy to understand measures of manufacturing performance. Rapid, meaningful feedback is critical because the lack of inventories in a demand-pull system makes it urgent to detect and solve problems quickly.

Effect of JIT Systems on Product Costing

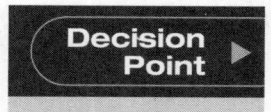

Decision Point ▶

What are the features and benefits of a JIT production system?

By reducing materials handling, warehousing, and inspection, JIT systems reduce overhead costs. JIT systems also aid in direct tracing of some costs usually classified as indirect. For example, the use of manufacturing cells makes it cost-effective to trace materials handling, machine operating inspection costs to specific products or product families made in these cells. These costs then become direct costs of those products. Also, the use of multiskilled workers in these cells allows the costs of setup, maintenance, and quality inspection to be traced as direct costs. These changes have prompted some companies using JIT to adopt simplified product costing methods that dovetail with JIT production and that are less costly to operate than the traditional costing systems described in Chapters 4, 7, 8, and 17. We examine two of these methods next: backflush costing and lean accounting.

Backflush Costing

Organizing manufacturing in cells,reducing defects and manufacturing cycle time, and ensuring timely delivery of materials, enables purchasing, production, and sales to occur in quick succession with minimal inventories. The absence of inventories makes choices about cost-flow assumptions (such as weighted-average or first-in, first-out) or inventory-costing methods (such as absorption or variable costing) unimportant: All manufacturing costs of the accounting period flow directly into cost of goods sold. The rapid conversion of direct materials into finished goods that are immediately sold greatly simplifies the costing system.

Simplified Normal or Standard Costing Systems

Traditional normal and standard-costing systems (Chapters 4, 7, 8, and 17) use **sequential tracking**, which is a costing system in which recording of the journal entries occurs in the same order as actual purchases and progress in production. Costs are tracked sequentially as products pass through each of the following four stages:

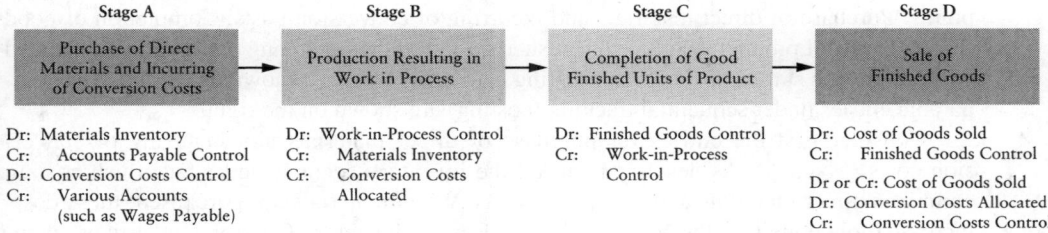

Stage A	Stage B	Stage C	Stage D
Purchase of Direct Materials and Incurring of Conversion Costs	Production Resulting in Work in Process	Completion of Good Finished Units of Product	Sale of Finished Goods

Dr: Materials Inventory
Cr: Accounts Payable Control
Dr: Conversion Costs Control
Cr: Various Accounts
        (such as Wages Payable)

Dr: Work-in-Process Control
Cr: Materials Inventory
Cr: Conversion Costs
        Allocated

Dr: Finished Goods Control
Cr: Work-in-Process
        Control

Dr: Cost of Goods Sold
Cr: Finished Goods Control
Dr or Cr: Cost of Goods Sold
Dr: Conversion Costs Allocated
Cr: Conversion Costs Control

A sequential-tracking costing system has four *trigger points*, corresponding to stages A, B, C, and D. A **trigger point** is a stage in the cycle, from the purchase of direct materials and incurring of conversion costs (stage A) to the sale of finished goods (stage D) at which journal entries are made in the accounting system. The journal entries (with Dr representing debits and Cr. representing credits) for each stage are displayed below the box for that stage (as described in Chapter 4).

An alternative approach to sequential tracking is backflush costing. **Backflush costing** is a costing system that omits recording some of the journal entries relating to the stages from purchase of direct materials to the sale of finished goods. When journal entries for one or more stages are omitted,the journal entries for a subsequent stage use normal or standard costs to work backward to "flush out" the costs in the cycle for which journal entries were *not* made.When inventories are minimal, as in JIT production systems, backflush costing simplifies the costing system without losing much information.

Consider the following data for the month of April for Silicon Valley Computer (SVC), which produces keyboards for personal computers.

- There are no beginning inventories of direct materials and no beginning or ending work-in-process inventories.
- SVC has only one direct manufacturing cost category (direct materials) and one indirect manufacturing cost category (conversion costs). All manufacturing labor costs are included in conversion costs.
- From its bill of materials and an operations list (description of operations to be undergone), SVC determines that the standard direct m aterial cost per keyboard unit is ₹190 and the standard conversion cost is ₹120.
- SVC purchases ₹1,95,00,000 of direct materials. To focus on the basic concepts, we assume SVC has no direct materials variances. Actual conversion costs equal ₹1,26,00,000. SVC produces 1,00,000 good keyboard units and sells 99,000 units.
- Any underallocated or overallocated conversion costs are written off to cost of goods sold at the end of April.

We use three examples to illustrate backflush costing. *They differ in the number and placement of trigger points.*

Example 1: The three trigger points for journal entries are Purchase of direct materials and incurring of conversion costs (Stage A), Completion of good finished units of product (Stage C), and Sale of finished goods (Stage D).

Note that there is no journal entry for Production resulting in work in process (Stage B) because this method is used when work-in-process inventory is minimal (units started are quickly converted to finished goods).

SVC records two inventory accounts:

Type	Account Title
Combined materials inventory and materials in work in process	Materials and In-Process Inventory Control
Finished goods	Finished Goods Control

Exhibit 20-7, Panel A, summarizes the journal entries for Example 1 with three trigger points: Purchase of direct materials and incurring of conversion costs, Completion of good finished units of product, and Sale of finished goods (and recognizing under-or overallocated costs). For each stage, the backflush costing entries for SVC are shown on the left. The comparable entries under sequential tracking (costing) are shown on the right.

Consider first the entries for purchase of direct materials and incurring of conversion costs (Stage A). As described earlier, the inventory account under backflush costing combines direct materials and work in process. When materials are purchased, these costs increase (are debited to) the Materials and In-Process Inventory Control. Under the sequential tracking approach, the direct materials and work in process accounts are separate, so the purchase of direct materials is debited to Materials Inventory Control. Actual conversion costs are recorded as incurred under backflush costing, just as in sequential tracking, and they increase (are debited to) Conversion Costs Control.

Next consider the entries for production resulting in work in process (Stage B). Recall that 1,00,000 units were started into production in April and that the standard cost for the units produced is ₹310 (₹190 direct materials + ₹120 conversion costs) per unit. Under backflush costing, no entry is recorded in Stage B because work-in-process inventory is minimal and all units are quickly converted to finished goods. Under sequential tracking, work-in-process inventory is increased as manufacturing occurs and later decreased as manufacturing is completed and the product becomes a finished good.

The entries to record completion of good finished units of product (Stage C) gives backflush costing its name. The costs have not been recorded sequentially with the flow of product along its production route through work in process and finished goods. Instead, the output trigger point reaches *back* and pulls ("*flushes*") the standard direct material costs from Materials and In-Process Inventory Control and the standard conversion costs for manufacturing the finished goods. Under the sequential tracking approach, Finished Goods Control is debited (increased) and Work-in-Process Control is credited (decreased) as manufacturing is completed and finished goods are produced. The net effect of Stages B and C under sequential tracking is the same as the effect under backflush costing (except for the name of the inventory account).

Finally consider entries to record the sale of finished goods (and under-or overallocated conversion costs) (Stage D). The standard cost of 99,000 units sold in April equals ₹3,06,90,000 (99,000 units × ₹310 per unit). The entries to record the cost of finished goods sold are exactly the same under backflush costing and sequential tracking.

Actual conversion costs may be underallocated or overallocated in an accounting period. Chapter 4 discussed various ways to dispose of underallocated or overallocated manufacturing overhead costs. Companies that use backflush costing typically have low inventories, so

Exhibit 20-7	Journal Entries and General Ledger Overview for Backflush Costing and Journal Entries for Sequential Tracking with Three Trigger Points: Purchase of Direct Materials and Incurring of Conversion Costs, Completion of Good Finished Units of Product, and Sale of Finished Goods

PANEL A: Journal Entries

Backflush Costing			Sequential Tracking		

Stage A: Record Purchase of Direct Materials and Incurring of Conversion Costs

1. Record Direct Materials Purchased.

Entry (A1)	Materials and In-Process Inventory Control	1,95,00,000		Materials Inventory Control	1,95,00,000	
	Accounts Payable Control		1,95,00,000	Accounts Payable Control		1,95,00,000

2. Record Conversion Costs Incurred.

Entry (A2)	Conversion Costs Control	1,26,00,000		Conversion Costs Control	1,26,00,000	
	Various accounts (such as Wages			Various accounts (such as Wages		1,26,00,000
	Payable Control)		1,26,00,000	Payable Control)		

Stage B: Record Production Resulting in Work in Process.

Entry (B1)	No Entry Recorded			Work-in-Process Control	₹3,10,00,000	
				Materials Inventory Control		1,90,00,000
				Conversion Costs Allocated		1,20,00,000

Stage C: Record Cost of Good Finished Units Completed.

Entry (C1)	Finished Goods Control	₹3,10,00,000		Finished Goods Control	₹3,10,00,000	
	Materials and In-Process Inventory Control		1,90,00,000	Work-in-Process Control		₹3,10,00,000
	Conversion Costs Allocated		1,20,00,000			

Stage D: Record Cost of Finished Goods Sold (and Under- or Overallocated Conversion Costs).

1. Record Cost of Finished Goods Sold.

Entry (D1)	Cost of Goods Sold	₹3,06,90,000		Cost of Goods Sold	₹3,06,90,000	
	Finished Goods Control		₹3,06,90,000	Finished Goods Control		₹3,06,90,000

2. Record Underallocated or Overallocated Conversion Costs.

Entry (D2)	Conversion Costs Allocated	₹1,20,00,000		Conversion Costs Allocated	₹1,20,00,000	
	Cost of Goods Sold	6,00,000		Cost of Goods Sold	6,00,000	
	Conversion Costs Control		1,26,00,000	Conversion Costs Control		1,26,00,000

PANEL B: General Ledger Overview for Backflush Costing

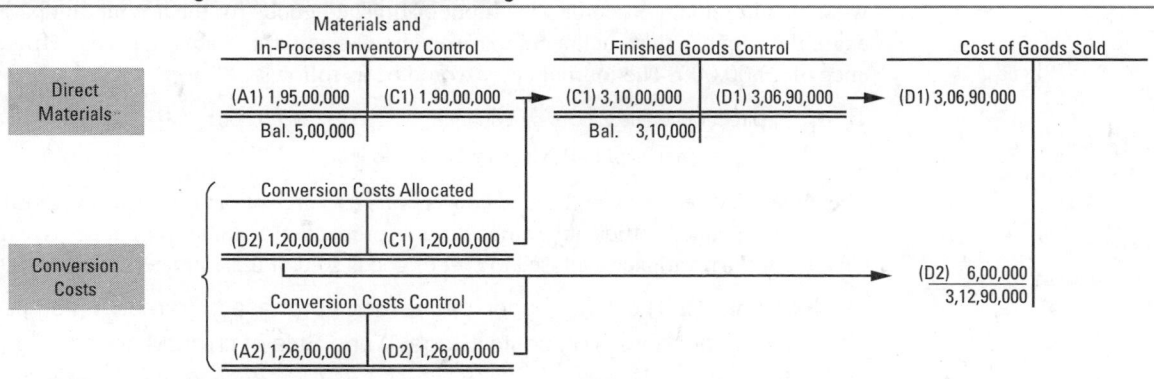

The coding that appears in parentheses for each entry indicates the stage in the production process that the entry relates to as presented in the text.

prorating underallocated or overallocated conversion costs between work in process, finished goods, and cost of goods sold is seldom necessary. Generally, companies write off underallocated or overallocated conversion costs to cost of goods sold only at the end of the fiscal year. Other companies, like SVC, record the write-off monthly. The journal entry to dispose of the difference between actual conversion costs incurred and standard conversion costs allocated is exactly the same under backflush costing and sequential tracking.

The April 30 ending inventory balances under backflush costing are as follows:

Materials and In-Process Inventory Control (₹1,95,00,000 − ₹1,90,00,000)	₹5,00,000
Finished Goods Control, 1,000 units × ₹310/unit (₹3,10,00,000 − ₹3,06,90,000)	3,10,000
Total	₹8,10,000

The April 30 ending inventory balances under sequential tracking would be exactly the same except that the inventory account would be Materials Inventory Control. Exhibit 20-7, Panel B, provides a general-ledger overview of this version of backflush costing.

The elimination of the typical Work-in-Process Control account reduces the amount of detail in the accounting system. Units on the production line may still be tracked in physical terms, but there is "no assignment of costs" to specific work orders while they are in the production cycle. In fact, there are no work orders or labor-time records in the accounting system.

The three trigger points to make journal entries in Example 1 will lead SVC's backflush costing system to report costs that are similar to the costs reported under sequential tracking when SVC has minimal work-in-process inventory. In Example 1, any inventories of direct materials or finished goods are recognized in SVC's backflush costing system when they are acquired or produced (as would be done in a costing system using sequential tracking). International Paper Company uses a method similar to Example 1 in its specialty papers plant.

Accounting for Variances Accounting for variances between actual and standard costs is basically the same under all standard-costing systems. The procedures are described in Chapters 7 and 8. Suppose that in Example 1, SVC had an unfavorable direct materials price variance of ₹4,20,000. Then the journal entry would be as follows:

Materials and In-Process Inventory Control	₹1,95,00,000	
Direct Materials Price Variance	4,20,000	
Accounts Payable Control		1,99,20,000

Direct material costs are often a large proportion of total manufacturing costs, sometimes well over 60%. Consequently, many companies measure the direct materials efficiency variance in total by physically comparing what remains in direct materials inventory against what should remain based on the output of finished goods for the accounting period. In our example, suppose that such a comparison showed an unfavorable materials efficiency variance of ₹3,00,000. The journal entry would be as follows:

Direct Materials Efficiency Variance	₹3,00,000	
Materials and In-Process Inventory Control		₹3,00,000

The underallocated or overallocated conversion costs are split into various overhead variances (spending variance, efficiency variance, and production-volume variance), as explained in Chapter 8. Each variance is closed to cost of goods sold, if it is immaterial in amount.

Example 2: The two trigger points are Purchase of direct materials and incurring of conversion costs (Stage A) and Sale of finished goods (Stage D).

This example uses the SVC data to illustrate a backflush costing that differs more from sequential tracking than the backflush costing in Example 1. This example and Example 1 have the same first trigger point, purchase of direct materials and incurring of conversion costs. But the second trigger point in Example 2 is the sale, not the completion, of finished goods. *Note that in this example, there is no journal entry for Production resulting in work in progress (Stage B) and Completion of good finished units of product (Stage C) because this method is used when there are minimal work-in-process and finished goods inventories (units started are quickly converted into finished goods that are immediately sold).*

In this example, there is only one inventory account: direct materials, whether they are in storerooms, in process, or in finished goods.

Type	Account Title
Combines direct materials inventory and any direct materials in work-in-process and finished goods inventories	Inventory Control

Exhibit 20-8, Panel A, summarizes the journal entries for Example 2 with two trigger points: Purchase of direct materials and incurring of conversion costs, and Sale of finished goods (and recognizing under-or overallocated costs). As in Example 1, for each stage, the backflush costing entries for SVC are shown on the left. The comparable entries under sequential tracking are shown on the right.

The entries for direct materials purchased and conversion costs incurred (Stage A) are the same as in Example 1, except that the inventory account is called Inventory Control. As in Example 1, no entry is made to record production of work-in-process inventory (Stage B) because work-in-process inventory is minimal. When finished goods are completed (Stage C), no entry is recorded because the completed units are expected to be sold quickly and finished goods inventory is expected to be minimal. As finished goods are sold (Stage D), the cost of goods sold is calculated as 99,000 units sold × ₹310 per unit = ₹3,06,90,000, which is composed of direct material costs (99,000 units × ₹190 per unit = ₹1,88,10,000) and conversion costs allocated (99,000 units × ₹120 per unit = ₹1,18,80,000). This is the same Cost of Goods Sold calculated under sequential tracking as described in Example 1.

Under this method of backflush costing, conversion costs are not inventoried because no entries are recorded when finished goods are produced in Stage C. That is, compared with sequential tracking, Example 2 does not assign ₹1,20,000 (₹120 per unit × 1,000 units) of conversion costs to finished goods inventory produced but not sold. Of the ₹1,26,00,000 in conversion costs, ₹1,18,80,000 is allocated at standard cost to the units sold. The remaining ₹7,20,000 (₹1,26,00,000 − ₹1,18,80,000) of conversion costs is underallocated compared to ₹6,00,000 under sequential tracking. Entry (D2) presents the journal entry if SVC, like many companies, writes off these underallocated costs monthly as additions to cost of goods sold.

The April 30 ending balance of Inventory Control is ₹6,90,000 (₹1,95,00,000 − ₹1,18,80,000). This balance represents the ₹5,00,000 direct materials still on hand + ₹1,90,000 direct materials embodied in the 1,000 good finished units manufactured but not sold during the period. Finished goods inventory under sequential tracking is: direct materials, ₹1,90,000 + conversion costs, ₹1,20,000 for a total of ₹3,10,000. Exhibit 20-8, Panel B, provides a general-ledger overview of Example 2. The approach described in Example 2 closely approximates the costs computed using sequential tracking when a company holds minimal work-in-process and finished goods inventories.

Toyota's cost accounting system is similar to this example. Two advantages of this system are (1) it removes the incentive for managers to produce for inventory because conversion costs are recorded as period costs instead of inventoriable costs and (2) it focuses managers on sales.

Example 3: The two trigger points are Completion of good finished units of product (Stage C) and Sale of finished goods (Stage D).

Exhibit 20-8	Journal Entries and General Ledger Overview for Backflush Costing and Journal Entries for Sequential Tracking with Two Trigger Points: Purchase of Direct Materials and Incurring of Conversion Costs and Sale of Finished Goods

PANEL A: Journal Entries

	Backflush Costing			**Sequential Tracking**	

Stage A: Record Purchase of Direct Materials and Incurring of Conversion Costs

1. Record Direct Materials Purchased.

Entry (A1)	Inventory: Control	1,95,00,000		Materials Inventory Control	1,95,00,000	
	Accounts Payable Control		1,95,00,000	Accounts Payable Control		1,95,00,000

2. Record Conversion Costs Incurred.

Entry (A2)	Conversion Costs Control	1,26,00,000		Conversion Costs Control	1,26,00,000	
	Various accounts (such as Wages			Various accounts (such as Wages		1,26,00,000
	Payable Control)		1,26,00,000	Payable Control)		

Stage B: Record Production Resulting in Work in Process.

Entry (B1)	No Entry Recorded			Work-in-Process Control	3,10,00,000	
				Materials Inventory Control		1,90,00,000
				Conversion Costs Allocated		1,20,00,000

Stage C: Record Cost of Good Finished Units Completed.

Entry (C1)	No Entry Recorded			Finished Goods Control	3,10,00,000	
				Work-in-Process Control		3,10,00,000

Stage D: Record Cost of Finished Goods Sold (and Under- or Overallocated Conversion Costs).

1. Record Cost of Finished Goods Sold.

Entry (D1)	Cost of Goods Sold	3,06,90,000		Cost of Goods Sold	3,06,90,000	
	Inventory Control		1,88,10,000	Finished Goods Control		3,06,90,000
	Conversion Costs Allocated		1,18,80,000			

2. Record Underallocated or Overallocated Conversion Costs.

Entry (D2)	Conversion Costs Allocated	1,18,80,000		Conversion Costs Allocated	1,20,00,000	
	Cost of Goods Sold	7,20,000		Cost of Goods Sold	6,00,000	
	Conversion Costs Control		1,26,00,000	Conversion Costs Control		1,26,00,000

PANEL B: General Ledger Overview for Backflush Costing

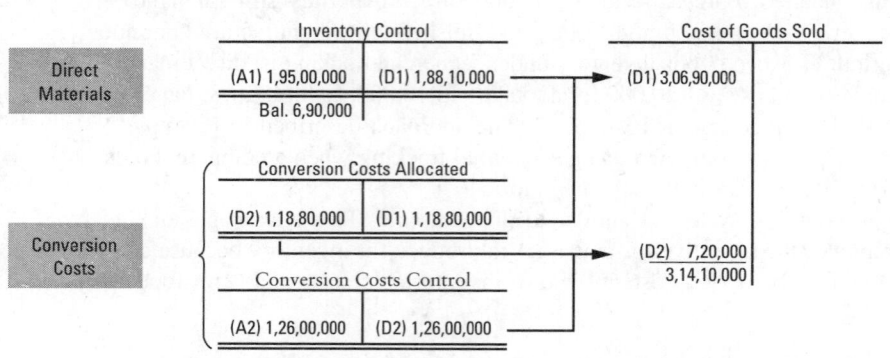

The coding that appears in parentheses for each entry indicates the stage in the production process that the entry relates to as presented in the text.

This example has two trigger points. In contrast to Example 2, the first trigger point in Example 3 is delayed until Stage C, SVC's completion of good finished units of product. *Note that there are no journal entries for Purchase of direct materials and incurring of conversion costs (Stage A) and Production resulting in work in process (Stage B) because this method is used when there are minimal direct materials and work-in-process inventories (direct materials purchased are quickly placed into production and then quickly converted into finished goods).*

Exhibit 20-9, Panel A, summarizes the journal entries for Example 3 with two trigger points: Completion of good finished units of product and Sale of finished goods (and recognizing under-or overallocated costs). As in Examples 1 and 2, for each stage, the backflush costing entries for SVC are shown on the left. The comparable entries under sequential tracking are shown on the right.

No entry is made for direct materials purchases of ₹1,95,00,000 (Stage A) because the acquisition of direct materials is not a trigger point in this form of backflush costing. As in Examples 1 and 2, actual conversion costs are recorded as incurred and no entry is made to record production resulting in work-in-process inventory (Stage B). The cost of 1,00,000 good finished units completed (Stage C) is recorded at standard cost of ₹310 (₹190 direct materials + ₹120 conversion costs) per unit as in Example 1 except that Accounts Payable Control is credited (instead of Materials and In-Process Inventory Control) because no entry had been made when direct materials were purchased in Stage A. Note that at the end of April, ₹5,00,000 of direct materials purchased have not yet been placed into production (₹1,95,00,000 − ₹1,90,00,000 = ₹5,00,000), nor have the cost of those direct materials been entered into the inventory-costing system. The Example 3 version of backflush costing is suitable for a JIT production system in which both direct materials inventory and work-in-process inventory are minimal. As finished goods are sold (Stage D), the cost of goods sold is calculated as 99,000 units sold × ₹310 per unit = ₹3,06,90,000. This is the same Cost of Goods sold calculated under sequential tracking. The Finished Goods Control has a balance of ₹3,10,000 under both this form of backflush costing and sequential tracking. The journal entry to dispose of the difference between actual conversion costs incurred and standard conversion costs allocated is the same under backflush costing and sequential tracking. The only difference between this form of backflush costing and sequential tracking is that direct materials inventory of ₹5,00,000 (and the corresponding Accounts Payable Control) is not recorded, which is no problem if direct materials inventories are minimal. Exhibit 20-9, Panel B, provides a general-ledger overview of Example 3.

Extending Example 3, backflush costing systems could use the sale of finished goods as the only trigger point. This version of backflush costing is most suitable for a JIT production system with minimal direct materials, work-in-process, and finished goods inventories. That's because this backflush costing system maintains no inventory accounts.

Special Considerations in Backflush Costing

The accounting procedures illustrated in Examples 1, 2, and 3 do not strictly adhere to generally accepted accounting principles (GAAP). For example, work in process inventory, which is an asset, exists but it is not recognized in the financial statements. Advocates of backflush costing, however, cite the generally accepted accounting principle of materiality in support of the various versions of backflush costing. As the three examples illustrate, backflush costing can approximate the costs that would be reported under sequential tracking by varying the number of trigger points and where they are located. If significant amounts of direct materials inventory or finished goods inventory exist, adjusting entries can be incorporated into backflush costing (as explained next).

Suppose there are material differences in operating income and inventories based on a backflush costing system and a conventional standard-costing system. A journal entry

Exhibit 20-9   Journal Entries and General Ledger Overview for Backflush Costing and Journal Entries for Sequential Tracking with Two Trigger Points: Completion of Good Finished Units of Product and Sale of Finished Goods

---

PANEL A: Journal Entries

Backflush Costing			Sequential Tracking		

Stage A: Record Purchase of Direct Materials and Incurring of Conversion Costs.

1. Record Direct Materials Purchased.

| Entry (A1) | No Entry Recorded | | Materials Inventory Control | 1,95,00,000 | |
| | | | Accounts Payable Control | | 1,95,00,000 |

2. Record Conversion Costs Incurred.

| Entry (A2) | Conversion Costs Control | 1,26,00,000 | Conversion Costs Control | 1,26,00,000 | |
| | Various accounts (such as Wages Payable Control) | 1,26,00,000 | Various accounts (such as Wages Payable Control) | | 1,26,00,000 |

Stage B: Record Production Resulting in Work in Process.

Entry (B1)	No Entry Recorded		Work-in-Process Control	3,10,00,000	
			Materials Inventory Control		1,90,00,000
			Conversion Costs Allocated		1,20,00,000

Stage C: Record Cost of Good Finished Units Completed.

Entry (C1)	Finished Goods Control	3,10,00,000	Finished Goods Control	3,10,00,000	
	Accounts Payable Control	1,90,00,000	Work-in-Process Control		3,10,00,000
	Conversion Costs Allocated	1,20,00,000			

Stage D: Record Cost of Finished Goods Sold (and Under- or Overallocated Conversion Costs).

1. Record Cost of Finished Goods Sold.

| Entry (D1) | Cost of Goods Sold | 3,06,90,000 | Cost of Goods Sold | 3,06,90,000 | |
| | Finished Goods Control | 3,06,90,000 | Finished Goods Control | | 3,06,90,000 |

2. Record Underallocated or Overallocated Conversion Costs.

Entry (D2)	Conversion Costs Allocated	1,20,00,000	Conversion Costs Allocated	1,20,00,000	
	Cost of Goods Sold	6,00,000	Cost of Goods Sold	6,00,000	
	Conversion Costs Control	1,26,00,000	Conversion Costs Control		1,26,00,000

PANEL B: General Ledger Overview for Backflush Costing

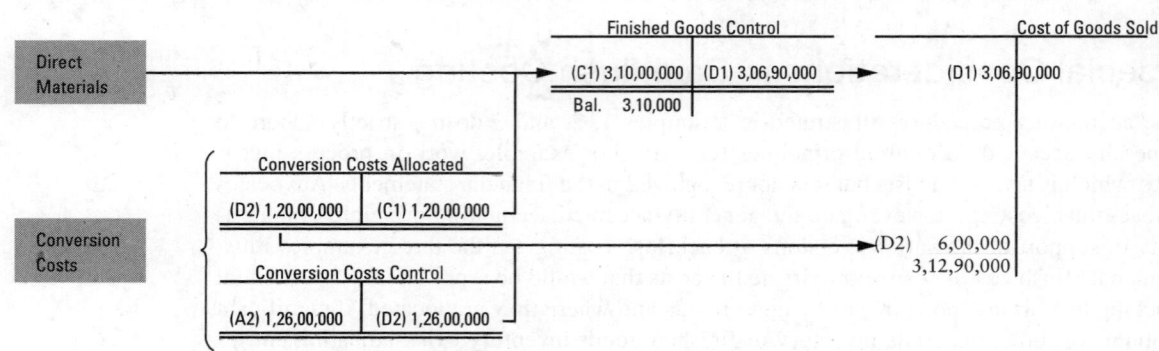

The coding that appears in parentheses for each entry indicates the stage in the production process that the entry relates to as presented in the text.

can be recorded to adjust the backflush number to comply with GAAP. For example, the backflush entries in Example 2 would result in expensing all conversion costs to Cost of Goods Sold (₹1,18,80,000 at standard costs + ₹7,20,000 write-off of underallocated conversion costs = ₹1,26,00,000). But suppose conversion costs were regarded as sufficiently material in amount to be included in Inventory Control. Then entry (D2) in Example 2, closing the Conversion Costs accounts, would change as follows:

Original entry (D2) Conversion Costs Allocated	1,18,80,000	
Cost of Goods Sold	7,20,000	
Conversion Costs Control		1,26,00,000
Revised entry (D2) Conversion Costs Allocated	1,18,80,000	
Inventory Control (1,000 units × ₹12)	1,20,000	
Cost of Goods Sold	6,00,000	
Conversion Costs Control		1,26,00,000

Critics say backflush costing leaves no audit trails—the ability of the accounting system to pinpoint the uses of resources at each step of the production process. However, the absence of large amounts of materials inventory and work-in-process inventory means managers can keep track of operations by personal observations, computer monitoring, and nonfinancial measures.

What are the implications of JIT and backflush costing systems for activity-based costing (ABC) systems? Simplifying the production process, as in a JIT system, makes more of the costs direct and reduces the extent of overhead cost allocations. Simple ABC systems are often adequate for companies implementing JIT. These simple ABC systems work well with backflush costing. Costs from ABC systems yield more-accurate budgeted conversion cost per unit for different products in the backflush costing system. The activity-based cost information is also useful for product costing, decision making, and cost management.

> ◄ **Decision Point**
>
> How does backflush costing simplify traditional inventory costing?

Lean Accounting

Another simplified product costing system that can be used with JIT (or lean production) systems is *lean accounting*. When a company utilizes JIT production, it has to focus on the entire value chain of business functions (from suppliers to manufacturing to customers) in order to reduce inventories, lead times, and waste. The improvements throughout the value chain that result have led some companies with JIT systems to develop organizational structures and costing systems that focus on **value streams,** which are all the value-added activities needed to design, manufacture, and deliver a given product or product line to customers. For example, a value stream can include the activities needed to develop and engineer products, advertise and market those products, process orders, purchase and receive materials, manufacture and ship orders, bill customers, and collect payments. The use of manufacturing cells in JIT systems helps keep a company focused on its value streams.

> **Learning Objective 8**
>
> Understand the principles of lean accounting
>
> . . . focus on costing value streams rather than products, and limit arbitrary allocations

Lean accounting is a costing method that focuses on value streams, as distinguished from individual products or departments, thereby eliminating waste in the accounting process.[4] If a company makes multiple, related products in a single value stream, it does not compute product costs for the individual products. Instead, it traces many actual costs directly to the value stream. Tracing more costs as direct costs to value streams is possible

---

[4] See B. Baggaley, "Costing by Value Stream," *Journal of Cost Management* (May–June 2003).

because companies using lean accounting often dedicate resources to individual value streams. We now illustrate lean accounting for Manuela Corporation.

	Toner Cartridges		Ink Cartridges	
	Model A	Model B	Model C	Model D
Revenues	₹60,00,000	₹70,00,000	₹80,00,000	₹55,00,000
Direct materials	34,00,000	40,00,000	41,00,000	27,00,000
Direct manufacturing labor	7,00,000	7,80,000	10,50,000	8,20,000
Manufacturing overhead costs (e.g., equipment lease, supervision, and unused facility costs)	11,20,000	13,00,000	12,80,000	10,30,000
Rework costs	1,50,000	1,70,000	1,40,000	1,00,000
Design costs	2,00,000	2,10,000	2,40,000	1,80,000
Marketing and sales costs	3,00,000	3,30,000	4,00,000	2,80,000
Total costs	58,70,000	67,90,000	72,10,000	51,10,000
Operating income	₹1,30,000	₹2,10,000	₹7,90,000	₹3,90,000
Direct materials purchased	₹35,00,000	₹42,00,000	₹43,00,000	₹28,50,000
Unused facility costs	₹2,20,000	₹3,80,000	₹1,80,000	₹1,50,000

Using lean accounting principles, Manuela's managers calculate the value-stream operating costs and operating income for toner cartridges and ink cartridges, not individual models, as follows:

	Purses	Wallets
Revenues (₹60,00,000 + ₹70,00,000; ₹80,00,000 + ₹55,00,000)	₹1,30,00,000	₹1,35,00,000
Direct material purchases (₹34,00,000 + ₹40,00,000; ₹41,00,000 + ₹27,00,000)	74,40,000	68,00,000
Direct manufacturing labor (7,00,000 + ₹7,80,000; ₹10,50,000 + ₹8,20,000)	14,80,000	18,70,000
Manufacturing overhead (after deducting unused facility costs) (₹11,20,000 – ₹2,20,000) + (₹13,00,000 – ₹3,80,000); (₹12,80,000 – ₹1,80,000) + ₹10,30,000 – ₹1,50,000)	18,20,000	19,80,000
Design costs (₹2,00,000 + ₹2,10,000; ₹2,40,000 + ₹1,80,000)	4,10,000	4,20,000
Marketing and sales costs (₹3,00,000 + ₹3,30,000; ₹4,00,000 + ₹2,80,000)	6,30,000	6,80,000
Total value stream operating costs	1,20,40,000	1,21,00,000
Value stream operating income	₹12,60,000	₹17,50,000

To gain insights, Manuela's lean accounting system, like many lean accounting systems, compares value-stream costs against costs that include costs of all purchased materials. Doing so keeps the company focused on reducing its direct materials and work-in-process inventory. In our example, the cost of direct material purchases exceeds the cost of direct materials used.

Manuela allocates its facility costs (such as depreciation, property taxes, and leases) to value streams based on the square footage each value stream uses. This encourages managers to use less space for production and for holding and moving inventory. Note that Manuela does not consider unused facility costs when calculating its manufacturing overhead costs of value streams. Instead, it treats these costs as plant or business unit expenses. Manuela excludes unused facility costs because it only includes in its value-stream costs those costs that add value. Increasing the visibility of unused capacity costs creates incentives to reduce these costs or to find alternative uses for the company's capacity. Manuela also excludes rework costs when calculating its value-stream costs and operating income because these costs are non-value-added costs. Companies also exclude from value-stream costs common costs such as corporate or support-department costs that cannot reasonably be assigned to value streams.

The analysis shows that although the total cost of the toner cartridges based on direct materials purchases rather than direct materials used is ₹1,29,60,000 [₹58,70,000 + ₹67,90,000 + (₹35,00,000 − ₹34,00,000) + (₹42,00,000 − ₹40,00,000)], the value−stream cost using lean accounting is ₹1,17,40,000 (90.6% × ₹1,29,60,000). The difference between the two indicates that there are opportunities for improving the company's profitability by reducing unused facility and rework costs and by purchasing direct materials only as needed for production. Making improvements is particularly important because Manuela's value−stream operating income is only 9.7% (₹12,60,000 ÷ ₹1,30,00,000) of its revenues. Manuela's ink cartridges portray a different picture. The total cost for ink cartridges based on direct materials purchases rather than direct materials used is ₹1,26,70,000 [₹72,10,000 + ₹51,10,000 + (₹43,00,000 − ₹41,00,000) + (₹28,50,000 − ₹27,00,000)], whereas the value−stream cost using lean accounting is ₹1,17,50,000 (92.7% × ₹1,26,70,000). The ink car tridges value stream has low unused facility and rework costs and is more efficient. Moreover, the ink cartridges also have higher value−stream operating income profitabil ity of 13% (₹17,50,000 ÷ ₹1,35,00,000).

Lean accounting is much simpler than traditional product costing. Why? Because calculating actual product costs by value streams requires less overhead allocation. Consistent with JIT and lean production, lean accounting emphasizes improvements in the value chain from suppliers to customers. Lean accounting encourages practices—such as reducing direct materials and work-in-process inventories, improving quality, using less space, and eliminating unused capacity—that reflect the goals of JIT production.

Critics of lean accounting charge that it does not compute the costs of individual products, which makes it less useful for making decisions. Proponents of lean accounting argue that the lack of individual product costs is not a problem because most decisions are made at the product line level rather than the individual product level and that pricing decisions are based on the value created for the customer (market prices) and not product costs.

Another criticism of lean accounting is that it excludes certain support costs and unused capacity costs. As a result, the decisions based on only value-stream costs will look profitable because they do not consider all costs. Proponents of lean accounting argue that the method overcomes this problem by adding a larger markup on value-stream costs to compensate for some of these excluded costs. Moreover, in a competitive market, prices will eventually settle at a level that represents a reasonable markup above a product's value-stream costs because customers will be unwilling to pay for non-value-added costs. The goal must therefore be to eliminate non-value-added costs.

A final criticism of lean accounting is that, like backflush costing, it does not correctly account for inventories under Generally Accepted Accounting Principles (GAAP). However, the method's proponents are quick to point out that in lean accounting environments, work-in-process and finished goods inventories are immaterial from an accounting perspective.

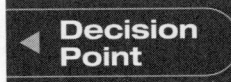

◄ Decision Point

How is lean accounting different from traditional costing systems?

Problem for Self-Study

Problem 1

Lee Company has a Mumbai plant that manufactures MP3 players. One component is an XT chip. Expected demand is for 5,200 of these chips in March 2013. Lee estimates the ordering cost per purchase order to be ₹2,500. The monthly carrying cost for one unit of XT in stock is ₹50.

Required

1. Compute the EOQ for the XT chip.
2. Compute the number of deliveries of XT in March 2013.

Solution

$$EOQ = \sqrt{\frac{2 \times 5,200 \times ₹2,500}{₹50}}$$

= 721 chips (rounded)

$$\text{Number of deliveries} = \frac{5,200}{721}$$

= 8 (rounded)

Problem 2

Littlefield Company uses a backflush costing system with three trigger points:

■ Purchase of direct materials
■ Completion of good finished units of product
■ Sale of finished goods

There are no beginning inventories. Information for April 2013 is as follows:

Direct materials purchased	₹88,00,000	Conversion costs allocated	₹40,00,000
Direct materials used	₹85,00,000	Costs transferred to finished goods	₹1,25,00,000
Conversion costs incurred	₹42,20,000	Cost of goods sold	₹1,19,00,000

Required

1. Prepare journal entries for April (without disposing of underallocated or overallocated conversion costs). Assume there are no direct materials variances.
2. Under an ideal JIT production system, how would the amounts in your journal entries differ from the journal entries in requirement 1?

Solution

1. Journal entries for April are as follows:

Entry (A1) Inventory: Materials and In-Process Control	88,00,000	
Accounts Payable Control		88,00,000
(direct materials purchased)		
Entry (A2) Conversion Costs Control	42,20,000	
Various accounts (such as Wages Payable Control)		42,20,000
(conversion costs incurred)		
Entry (C1) Finished Goods Control	1,25,00,000	

Inventory: Materials and In-Process Control		85,00,000
Conversion Costs Allocated		40,00,000
(standard cost of finished goods completed)		
Entry (D1) Cost of Goods Sold	1,19,00,000	
Finished Goods Control		1,19,00,000
(standard costs of finished goods sold)		

2. Under an ideal JIT production system, if the manufacturing lead time per unit is very short, there would be zero inventories at the end of each day. Entry (C_1) would be ₹1,19,00,000 finished goods production [to match finished goods sold in entry (D_1)], not ₹1,25,00,000. If the Marketing Department could only sell goods costing ₹1,19,00,000, the JIT production system would call for direct materials purchases and conversion costs of lower than ₹88,00,000 and ₹42,20,000, respectively, in entries (A_1) and (A_2).

Decision Points

The following question-and-answer format summarizes the chapter's learning objectives. Each decision presents a key question related to a learning objective. The guidelines are the answer to that question.

Decision	**Guidelines**
1. What are the six categories of costs associated with goods for sale?	The six categories are purchasing costs (costs of goods acquired from suppliers), ordering costs (costs of preparing a purchase order and receiving goods), carrying costs (costs of holding inventory of goods for sale), stockout costs (costs arising when a customer demands a unit of product and that unit is not on hand), costs of quality (prevention, appraisal, internal failure, and external failure costs), and shrinkage costs (the costs resulting from theft by outsiders, embezzlement by employees, misclassifications, and clerical errors).
2. What does the EOQ decision model help managers do, and how do managers decide on the safety-stock levels?	The economic-order-quantity (EOQ) decision model helps managers to calculate the optimal quantity of inventory to order by balancing ordering costs and carrying costs. The larger the order quantity, the higher are the annual carrying costs and the lower the annual ordering costs. The EOQ model includes costs recorded in the financial accounting system as well as opportunity costs of carrying inventory that are not recorded in the financial accounting system. Managers choose a level of safety stock to minimize the stockout costs and the carrying costs of holding more inventory.
3. How do errors in predicting the parameters of the EOQ model affect costs? How can companies reduce the conflict between the EOQ decision model and models used for performance evaluation?	The cost of prediction errors when using the EOQ model is small. To reduce the conflict between the EOQ decision model and the performance evaluation model, companies should include the opportunity cost of investment in inventory when evaluating managers. The opportunity cost of investment tied up in inventory is a key input in the EOQ decision model that is often ignored in the performance-evaluation model.

4. Why are companies using just-in-time (JIT) purchasing?	Just-in-time (JIT) purchasing is making purchases in small order quantities just as needed for production (or sales). JIT purchasing is a response to high carrying costs and low ordering costs. JIT purchasing increases the focus of companies and suppliers on quality and timely deliveries. Companies coordinate their activities and reduce inventories throughout the supply chain, from the initial sources of materials and services to the delivery of products to consumers.
5. How do materials requirements planning (MRP) systems differ from just-in-time (JIT) production systems?	Materials requirements planning (MRP) systems use a "push-through" approach whereby finished goods are manufactured on the basis of demand forecasts. Just-in-time (JIT) production systems use a "demand-pull" approach in which goods are manufactured only after receiving customer orders.
6. What are the features and benefits of a just-in-time (JIT) production system?	JIT production systems (a) organize production in manufacturing cells, (b) hire and train multiskilled workers, (c) emphasize total quality management, (d) reduce manufacturing lead time and setup time, and (e) build strong supplier relationships.
	The benefits of JIT production include lower costs and higher margins from better flow of information, higher quality, and faster delivery as well as simpler accounting systems.
7. How does backflush costing simplify traditional inventory costing?	Traditional inventory-costing systems use sequential tracking, in which recording of the journal entries occurs in the same order as actual purchases and progress in production. Most backflush costing systems do not record journal entries for the work-in-process stage of production. Some backflush costing systems also do not record entries for either the purchase of direct materials or the completion of finished goods.
8. How is lean accounting different from traditional costing systems?	Lean accounting assigns costs to value streams rather than to products. Non-value-added costs, unused capacity costs, and costs that cannot be easily traced to value streams are not allocated but instead expensed.

TERMS TO LEARN

This chapter and the Glossary at the end of the book contain definitions of the following important terms:

backflush costing **(p. 1059)**
carrying costs **(p. 1043)**
economic order quantity
  (EOQ) **(p. 1044)**
enterprise resource planning (ERP)
  system **(p. 1057)**
inventory
  management **(p. 1042)**
just-in-time (JIT)
  production **(p. 1056)**

just-in-time (JIT)
  purchasing **(p. 1051)**
lean accounting **(p. 1067)**
lean production **(p. 1056)**
manufacturing cells **(p. 1056)**
materials requirements planning
  (MRP) system **(p. 1055)**
ordering costs **(p. 1043)**
purchase-order lead
  time **(p. 1044)**

purchasing
  costs **(p. 1042)**
reorder point **(p. 1046)**
safety stock **(p. 1047)**
sequential
  tracking **(p. 1059)**
shrinkage costs **(p. 1043)**
stockout costs **(p. 1043)**
trigger point **(p. 1059)**
value streams **(p. 1067)**

ASSIGNMENT MATERIAL

Questions

20-1 Why do better decisions regarding the purchasing and managing of goods for sale frequently cause dramatic percentage increases in net income?

20-2 Name six cost categories that are important in managing goods for sale in a retail company.

20-3 What assumptions are made when using the simplest version of the economic-order-quantity (EOQ) decision model?

20-4 Give examples of costs included in annual carrying costs of inventory when using the EOQ decision model.

20-5 Give three examples of opportunity costs that typically are not recorded in accounting systems, although they are relevant when using the EOQ model.

20-6 What are the steps in computing the cost of a prediction error when using the EOQ decision model?

20-7 Why might goal-congruence issues arise when an EOQ model is used to guide decisions on how much to order?

20-8 Describe JIT purchasing and its benefits.

20-9 What are three factors causing reductions in the cost to place purchase orders for materials?

20-10 "You should always choose the supplier who offers the lowest price per unit." Do you agree? Explain.

20-11 What is supply-chain analysis, and how can it benefit manufacturers and retailers?

20-12 What are the main features of JIT production?

20-13 Distinguish inventory-costing systems using sequential tracking from those using backflush costing.

20-14 Describe three different versions of backflush costing.

20-15 Discuss the differences between lean accounting and traditional cost accounting.

Solved Examples

20-16 Economic order quantity for retailer. Delhi Sports (DS) operates a megastore featuring sports merchandise. It uses an EOQ decision model to make inventory decisions. It is now considering inventory decisions for its new Vest product line. This is a highly popular item. Data for 2015 are:

- Expected annual demand for Vests: 10,000
- Ordering costs for purchase order: ₹225
- Carrying costs per year: ₹10 per Vest

Each Vest costs DS ₹40 and sells for ₹75. The ₹10 carrying cost per Vest per year comprises the required return on investment of ₹4.80 (12% × ₹40 purchase price) plus ₹5.20 in relevant insurance, handling, and theft-related costs. The purchasing lead time is 7 days. DS is open 365 days a year.

Required

1. Calculate the EOQ.
2. Calculate the number of orders that will be placed each year.
3. Calculate the reorder point.

Solution

Economic order quantity for retailer.

1. $D = 10,000$, $P = ₹225$, $C = ₹10$

$$EPQ = \sqrt{\frac{2DP}{C}} = \sqrt{\frac{2 \times 10,000 \times ₹20}{10}}$$

$$= 670.82 \cong 671 \text{ Vests.}$$

2. Number of orders per year $= \dfrac{D}{EOQ} = \dfrac{10,000}{671}$

$$= 14.90 \cong 15 \text{ orders.}$$

3. $=$ Demand each working day $= \dfrac{D}{\textit{Number of working days}}$

$$= \frac{10,000}{365}$$

$$= 27.40 \text{ Vests per day}$$

Purchase lead time $= 7$ days

Reorder point $= 27.40 \times 7$

$$= 191.80 \cong 192 \text{ Vests.}$$

20-17 Economic order quantity, effect of parameter changes (continuation of 20-16). Athletic Products (AP) manufactures the Vests that Delhi Sports (DS) sells to its customers. AP has recently installed computer software that enables its customers to conduct "one-stop" purchasing using state-of-the-art web site technology. DS's ordering cost per purchase order will be ₹20 using this new technology.

Required

1. Calculate the EOQ for the Vests using the revised ordering cost of ₹20 per purchase order. Assume all other data from Exercise 20-16 are the same. Comment on the result.

2. Suppose AP proposes to "assist" DS. AP will allow DS's customers to order directly from the AP web site. AP would transport directly to these customers. AP would pay ₹10 to DS for every Vest purchased by one of DS's customers. How would this offer affect inventory management at DS? Should DS accept AP's proposal? Explain.

Solution

Economic order quantity, effect of parameter changes (continuation of 20-16).

1. $D = 10{,}000$, $P = ₹20$, $C = ₹10$

$$\text{EOQ} = \sqrt{\frac{2DP}{C}} = \sqrt{\frac{2 \times 10{,}000 \times ₹20}{10}}$$

$$= 200 \text{ Vests}$$

The sizable reduction in ordering cost (from ₹225 to ₹20 per purchase order) has reduced the EOQ from 671 to 200.

2. The AP proposal has both upsides and downsides. The upside is potentially higher sales. DS customers may purchase more online than if they have to physically visit a store. DS would also have lower administrative costs and lower inventory holding costs with the proposal.

The downside is that AP could capture DS's customers. Repeat customers to the AP Web site need not be classified as DS customers. DS would have to establish enforceable rules to make sure it captures ongoing revenues from customers it directs to the AP Web site.

There is insufficient information to determine whether DS should accept AP's proposal. Much depends on whether DS views AP as a credible, "honest" partner.

20-18 EOQ for manufacturer. CG Electronics makes air conditioners. It purchases 12,000 units of a particular type of compressor part, LG29, each year at a cost of ₹500 per unit. CG Electronics requires a 12% rate of return on investment. In addition, relevant carrying costs (for insurance, materials handling, breakage, and so on) are ₹20 per unit per year. Relevant costs per purchase order are ₹1,200.

Required

1. Calculate CG Electronics's EOQ for LG29.
2. Calculate CG Electronics's total relevant ordering and carrying costs.
3. Assume that demand is uniform throughout the year and is known with certainty. The purchasing lead time is half a month. Calculate CG Electronics's reorder point for LG29.

Solution

EOQ for manufacturer.

1. Relevant carrying costs per part per year:

Required annual return on investment 12% × 500 =	₹60
Relevant insurance, materials handling, breakage, etc. costs per year	20
Relevant carrying costs per part per year	₹80

With D = 12,000; P = ₹1,200; C = ₹80, EOQ for manufacturer is:

$$\sqrt{\frac{2DP}{C}} = \sqrt{(2 \times 12,000 \times ₹1,200)/₹80} = 600 \text{ units}$$

2. Total relevant ordering $= \left(\frac{D}{Q} \times P\right) + \left(\frac{Q}{2} \times C\right)$

and carrying costs

$$= \left(\frac{12,000}{600} \times ₹1,200\right) + \left(\frac{600}{2} \times ₹80\right)$$

$$= ₹24,000 + ₹24,000 = ₹48,000$$

where Q = 600 units, the quantity ordered.

3. Purchase order lead time is half a month

Monthly demand is 12,000 units ÷ 12 months = 1,000 units per month.

Demand in half a month is $\frac{1}{2}$ × 1,000 units or 500 units.

Hence, CG Electronics should reorder when inventory of LG29 falls to 500 units.

20-19 Sensitivity of EOQ to changes in relevant ordering and carrying costs. Hawkin's annual demand for its only product, cooker, is 10,000 units. Hawkin is currently analyzing possible combinations of relevant carrying cost per unit per year and relevant ordering cost per purchase order, depending on the company's choice of supplier and average levels of inventory. This table presents three possible combinations of carrying and ordering costs.

Relevant Carrying Cost per Unit per year	Relevant Ordering Cost per Purchase Order
₹10	₹400
₹20	₹200
₹40	₹100

1. For each of the relevant ordering and carrying-cost alternatives, determine (a) EOQ and (b) annual relevant total costs. **Required**

2. How does your answer to requirement 1 give insight into the impact of changes in relevant ordering and carrying costs on EOQ and annual relevant total costs? Explain briefly.

3. Suppose the relevant carrying cost per unit per year was ₹20 and the relevant ordering cost per purchase order was ₹200. Suppose further that Hawkin calculates EOQ after incorrectly estimating relevant carrying cost per unit per year to be ₹10 and relevant ordering cost per purchase order to be ₹400. Calculate the actual annual relevant total costs of Hawkin's EOQ decision. Compare this cost to the annual relevant total costs that Hawkin would have incurred if it had correctly estimated the relevant carrying cost per unit per year of ₹20 and the relevant ordering cost per purchase order of ₹200 that you have already calculated in requirement 1. Calculate and comment on the cost of the prediction error.

Solution

1. A straightforward approach to the requirement is to construct the following table for EOQ at relevant carrying and ordering costs. Annual demand is 10,000 units. The formula for the EOQ model is:

$$EOQ = \sqrt{\frac{2DP}{C}} \text{ and for Relevant Total Costs (RTC)} = \frac{DP}{Q} + \frac{QC}{2}$$

where   D = demand in units per year

           P = relevant ordering costs per purchase order

           C = relevant carrying costs of one unit in stock for the time period used for D (one year in this problem.

Relevant Carrying Costs per Unit per Year (C)	Relevant Ordering Costs per Purchase Order (P)			
₹10	₹400	EOQ $= \sqrt{\dfrac{2 \times 10{,}000 \times ₹400}{₹10}} = 895$,	RTC $= \dfrac{10{,}000 \times ₹400}{895} + \dfrac{895 \times ₹10}{2} = ₹8{,}944$
₹20	₹200	EOQ $= \sqrt{\dfrac{2 \times 10{,}000 \times ₹200}{₹20}} = 447$,	RTC $= \dfrac{10{,}000 \times ₹200}{447} + \dfrac{447 \times ₹20}{2} = ₹8{,}944$
₹40	₹100	EOQ $= \sqrt{\dfrac{2 \times 10{,}000 \times ₹100}{₹40}} = 224$,	RTC $= \dfrac{10{,}000 \times ₹100}{224} + \dfrac{224 \times ₹40}{2} = ₹8{,}944$

2. For a given demand level, as relevant carrying costs increase and relevant ordering costs decrease, EOQ becomes smaller. That is EOQ decreases to compensate for increases in carrying costs and to take advantage of decreases in ordering costs. That is, the EOQ offsets the effect on total costs of the increase in carrying costs and the decrease in ordering costs.

In this example, the change in EOQ results in relevant total costs (RTC) being the same across all three cases. The fact that the total costs are the same is a function of the specific numbers chosen in this example. For example, in the last combination, if relevant carrying costs per unit per year were ₹35 instead of ₹40 and relevant ordering costs per purchase order remained at ₹100, the relevant total costs would equal ₹8,367.

$$EOQ = \sqrt{\dfrac{2 \times 10{,}000 \times ₹100}{₹35}} = 239, \quad RTC = \dfrac{10{,}000 \times ₹100}{239} + \dfrac{239 \times ₹35}{2} = ₹8{,}367$$

3. If Alpha estimates C = ₹10 per unit per year and P = ₹400 per order, then from requirement 1,

EOQ = 224 units and Relevant Total Cost (RTC) = ₹8,944

For EOQ = 224 units, C = ₹20 per unit per year and P = ₹200 per order,

$$Relevant\ total\ costs\ (RTC) = \dfrac{DP}{Q} + \dfrac{QC}{2}$$

$$= \dfrac{10{,}000 \times ₹200}{224} + \dfrac{224 \times ₹20}{2}$$

$$= ₹8{,}929 + ₹2{,}240 = ₹11{,}169$$

The prediction error equals ₹11,169 − ₹8,944 = ₹2,225, which is 25% (₹2,225 ÷ ₹8,944) of the relevant total cost had there been no prediction error. The error in prediction results in a significantly higher cost but is still limited, given that the estimate of the carrying cost was half the actual amount and the estimate of the ordering cost was twice the actual amount. The square root function dampens the effect of the errors.

20-20 Purchase-order size for retailer, EOQ, just-in-time purchasing. The 24-Hour Mart operates a chain of supermarkets. Its best-selling soft drink is Frooti. Demand (D) in April for Frooti at its Gurgaon supermarket is estimated to be 6,000 cases (24 cans in each case). In March, the Gurgaon supermarket estimated the ordering costs per purchase order (P) for Frooti to be ₹150. The carrying costs (C) of each case of Frooti in inventory for a month were estimated to be ₹5. At the end of March, the Gurgaon 24-Hour Mart reestimated its carrying costs to be ₹7.5 per case per month to take into account an increase in warehouse-related costs.

During March, 24-Hour Mart restructured its relationship with suppliers. It reduced the number of suppliers from 600 to 180. Long-term contracts were signed only with those suppliers that agreed to make product-quality checks before supplying. Each purchase order will now be made by linking into the suppliers' computer network. The Gurgaon 24-Hour Mart estimated that these changes will reduce the ordering costs per purchase order to ₹25. The 24-Hour Mart is open 30 days in April.

Required

1. Calculate the EOQ in April for Frooti. Assume in turn:
   a. D = 6,000; P = ₹150; C = ₹5   c. D = 6,000; P = ₹25; C = ₹7.5
   b. D = 6,000; P = ₹150; C = ₹7.5
2. How does your answer to requirement 1 give insight into the retailer's movement toward JIT purchasing policies?

Solution

Purchase-order size for retailer, EOQ, just-in-time purchasing.

1. $EOQ = \sqrt{\dfrac{2DF}{C}}$

   a. D = 6,000; P = ₹150; C = ₹5

   $EOQ = \sqrt{(2 \times 6,000 \times 150)/₹5} \times \sqrt{3,60,000} = 600$ cases.

   b. D = 6,000; P = ₹150; C = ₹7.5

   $EOQ = \sqrt{(2 \times 6,000 \times 150)/₹7.5} \times \sqrt{2,40,000} = 489.9$ cases $\cong 490$ cases.

   c. D = 6,000; P = ₹25; C = ₹7.5

   $EOQ = \sqrt{(2 \times 6,000 \times 25)/₹7.5} \times \sqrt{40,000} = 200$ cases.

2. A just-in-time purchasing policy involves the purchase of goods or materials such that their delivery immediately precedes their demand or use. Given the purchase order sizes calculated in requirement 1, the number of purchase orders placed each month is: (D ÷ EOQ):

   a. $\dfrac{D}{EOQ} = \dfrac{6,000}{600} = 10$ orders per month or $\cong 1$ every 3 days.

   b. $\dfrac{D}{EOQ} = \dfrac{6,000}{490} = 12.25$ orders per month or $\cong 1$ every 2.45 days.

   c. $\dfrac{D}{EOQ} = \dfrac{6,000}{200} = 30$ orders per month or $\cong 1$ every day.

   An increase in C and a decrease in P lead to increase in the optimal frequency of orders. The 24-Hour Mart has increased the frequency of delivery from every third day (1a: P = ₹150; C = ₹5) to a delivery every day (1c: P = ₹25; C = ₹7.5). There is a reduction of 200 cases in the average inventory level: (600 − 200) ÷ 2 = 200.

20-21 JIT production, relevant benefits, relevant costs. The Harrisons Company manufactures specialty brass door handles at its Pune plant. Harrisons is considering implementing a JIT production system. The following are the estimated costs and benefits of JIT production:
   a. Annual additional tooling costs would be ₹2,00,000.
   b. Average inventory would decline by 80% from the current level of ₹20,00,000.
   c. Insurance, space, materials-handling, and setup costs, which currently total ₹6,00,000 annually, would decline by 25%.
   d. The emphasis on quality inherent in JIT production would reduce rework costs by 30%. Harrisons currently incurs 4,00,000 in annual rework costs.
   e. Improved product quality under JIT production would enable Harrison's to raise the price of its product by ₹8 per unit. Harrisons sells 40,000 units each year.
Harrisons's required rate of return on inventory investment is 15% per year.

1. Calculate the net benefit or cost to Harisson's if it adopts JIT production at the Pune plant.
2. What nonfinancial and qualitative factors should Harrisons consider when making the decision to adopt JIT production?
3. Suppose Harrisons implements JIT production at its Pune plant. Give examples of performance measures Harrisons could use to evaluate and control JIT production. What would be the benefit of Harrisons implementing an enterprise resource planning (ERP) system?

Solution

1. Solution Exhibit 20-21 presents the annual net benefit of ₹6,30,000 to Harrisons Company of implementing a JIT production system.
2. Other nonfinancial and qualitative factors that Harrisons should consider in deciding whether it should implement a JIT system include:
   a. The possibility of developing and implementing a detailed system for integrating the sequential operations of the manufacturing process. Direct materials must arrive when needed for each subassembly so that the production process functions smoothly.
   b. The ability to design products that use standardized parts and reduce manufacturing time.
   c. The ease of obtaining reliable vendors who can deliver quality direct materials on time with minimum lead time.
   d. Willingness of suppliers to deliver smaller and more frequent orders.
   e. The confidence of being able to deliver quality products on time. Failure to do so would result in customer dissatisfaction.
   f. The skill levels of workers to perform multiple tasks such as minor repairs, maintenance, quality testing and inspection.
3. Personal observation by production line workers and managers is more effective in JIT plants than in traditional plants. A JIT plant's production process layout is streamlined. Operations are not obscured by piles of inventory or rework. As a result, such plants are easier to evaluate by personal observation than are cluttered plants where the flow of production is not logically laid out.

Besides personal observation, nonfinancial performance measures are the dominant methods of control. Nonfinancial performance measures provide most timely and easy to understand measures of plant performance. Examples of nonfinancial performance measures of time, inventory, and quality include the following:

- Manufacturing lead time
- Units produced per hour
- Machine setup time ÷ manufacturing time
- Number of defective units ÷ number of units completed

In addition to personal observation and nonfinancial performance measures, financial performance measures are also used. Examples of financial performance measures include the following:

- Cost of rework
- Ordering costs
- Stockout costs
- Inventory turnover (cost of goods sold ÷ average inventory)

The success of a JIT system depends on the speed of information flows from customers to manufacturers to suppliers. The Enterprise Resource Planning (ERP) system has a single database and gives lower-level managers, workers, customers, and suppliers access to operating information. This benefit, accompanied by tight coordination across business func-

tions, enables the ERP system to rapidly transmit information in response to changes in supply and demand so that manufacturing and distribution plans may be revised accordingly.

Solution Exhibit 20-21
Annual Relevant Costs of Current Production System and JIT Production System
for Harrisons Company

Relevant Items	Relevant Costs under Current Production System	Relevant Costs under JIT Production System
Annual tooling costs	–	₹2,00,000
Required return on investment:		
15% per year × ₹20,00,000 of average inventory per year	₹3,00,000	
15% per year × ₹4,00,000[a] of average inventory per year		60,000
Insurance, space, materials handling, and setup costs	6,00,000	4,50,000[b]
Rework costs	4,00,000	2,80,000[c]
Incremental revenues from higher selling prices		(3,20,000)[d]
Total net incremental costs	₹13,00,000	₹6,70,000
Annual difference in favor of JIT production		₹6,30,000

[a] ₹20,00,000 × (1 – 80%) = ₹4,00,000
[b] ₹6,00,000 × (1 – 0.25) = ₹4,50,000
[c] ₹4,00,000 × (1 – 0.30) = ₹2,80,000
[d] ₹8 × 40,000 units = ₹3,20,000

20-22 Effect of different order quantities on ordering costs and carrying costs, EOQ. Jagdish
Stores retails a broad line of Indian merchandise at its Preet Vihar store. It sells 26,000 ABC
linen bedroom packages (two sheets and two pillow cases) each year. Jagdish Stores pays
ABC Limited, ₹1,040 per package. Its ordering costs per purchase order are ₹720. The carrying costs per package are ₹104 per year.

Hans, manager of the Preet Vihar store, seeks your advice on how ordering and carrying
costs vary with different order quantities. ABC Merchandise guarantees the ₹1,040 purchase
cost per package for the 26,000 units budgeted to be purchased in the coming year.

Required

1. Compute the annual ordering costs, the annual carrying costs, and their sum for
   purchase-order quantities of 300, 500, 600, 700, and 900. What is the EOQ? Comment
   on your results.
2. Assume that ABC Merchandise introduces a computerized ordering network for its
   customers. Hans estimates that Jagdish Stores's ordering costs will be reduced to
   ₹400 per purchase order. How will this reduction in ordering costs affect the EOQ for
   Jagdish Stores on their linen bedroom packages?

Solution
Effect of different order quantities on ordering costs and carrying costs, EOQ.

1. A straightforward approach to this requirement is to construct the following table for
   different purchase-order quantities:

D: Demand	26,000	26,000	26,000	26,000	26,000
Q: Order quantity	300	500	600	700	900
Q/2: Average inventory in units	150	250	300	350	450
D/Q: Number of purchase orders	86.67	52	43.33	37.14	28.89
(D/Q) × P: Annual ordering costs	₹62,400	₹37,440	₹31,200	₹26,740	₹20,800

(Q/2) × C: Annual carrying costs	15,600	26,000	31,200	36,400	46,800
Total relevant costs of ordering and carrying inventory	₹78,000	₹63,440	₹62,400	₹63,140	₹67,600

$$\neq$$

Minimum Cost

D = 26,000 units

Q = order quantity

P = ₹720

C = ₹104

$$EOQ = \sqrt{\frac{2DP}{C}} = \sqrt{\frac{2 \times 26,000 \times ₹720}{₹104}} = \sqrt{3,60,000} = 600 \text{ packages}$$

The shape of the total relevant cost function for Jagdish Stores is relatively flat from order quantities 500 to 700.

2. When the ordering cost per purchase order is reduced to ₹400:

$$EOQ = \sqrt{\frac{2 \times 26,000 \times ₹400}{₹104}} = \sqrt{2,00,000} = 447.2 \text{ packages or 447 packages (rounded)}$$

The EOQ drops from 600 packages to 447 packages when Jagdish Stores's ordering cost per purchase order drops from ₹720 to ₹400.

20-23 EOQ, uncertainty, safety stock, reorder point. Action shoes produces and sells an excellent-quality walking shoe. After production, the shoes are distributed to 20 warehouses around the country. Each warehouse services approximately 100 stores in its region. Action shoes uses an EOQ model to determine the number of pairs of shoes to order for each warehouse from the factory. Annual demand for Warehouse OR2 is approximately 1,20,000 pairs of shoes. The ordering cost is ₹250 per order. The annual carrying cost of a pair of shoes is ₹2.40 per pair.

Required

1. Use the EOQ model to determine the optimal number of pairs of shoes per order.
2. Assume each month consists of approximately 4 weeks. If it takes 1 week to receive an order, at what point should warehouse OR2 reorder shoes?
3. Although OR2's average weekly demand is 2,500 pairs of shoes (1,20,000 ÷ 12 months ÷ 4 weeks), demand each week may vary with the following probability distribution:

Total demand for 1 week	2,000 pairs	2,250 pairs	2,500 pairs	2,750 pairs	3,000 pairs
Probability (sums to 1.00)	0.04	0.20	0.52	0.20	0.04

If a store wants shoes and OR2 has none in stock, OR2 can "rush" them to the store at an additional cost of ₹2 per pair. How much safety stock should Warehouse OR2 hold? How will this affect the reorder point and reorder quantity?

Solution

1. $$EOQ = \sqrt{\frac{2DP}{C}} = \sqrt{\frac{2 \times 1,20,000 \times ₹250}{₹2.40}}$$

   = 5,000 pairs of shoes

2. Weekly demand = Monthly demand ÷ 4

   = 10,000 ÷ 4 = 2,500 pairs of shoes per week

   Purchasing lead time = 1 week

   Reorder point = 2,500 pairs of shoes per week × 1 week = 2,500 pairs of shoes

3. Solution Exhibit 20-23 presents the safety stock computations for Warehouse OR2 when the reorder point excluding safety stock is 2,500 pairs of shoes. The exhibit shows that annual relevant total stockout and carrying costs are the lowest ₹1,080) when a safety

stock of 250 pairs of shoes is maintained. Therefore, Warehouse OR2 should hold a safety stock of 250 pairs. As a result, Reorder point with safety stock = 2,500 pairs + 250 pairs = 2,750 pairs. Reorder quantity is unaffected by the holding of safety stock and remains the same as calculated in requirement 1.

Reorder quantity = 5,000 pairs

Warehouse OR2 should order 5,000 pairs of shoes each time its inventory of shoes falls to 2,750 pairs.

Solution Exhibit 20-23

Computation of Safety Stock for Warehouse OR2 When Reorder Point is 2,500 Units

Safety Stock Level in Units (1)	Demand Levels Resulting in Stockouts (2)	Stockout in Units[a] (3) = (2) − 2,500 − (1)	Probability of Stockouts (4)	Relevant Stockout Costs[b] (5) = (3) × ₹2	Number of Orders per Year[c] (6)	Expected Stockout Costs[d] (7) = (4) × (5) × (6)	Relevant Carrying Costs[e] (8) = (1) × ₹2.4	Relevant Total Costs (9) = (7) + (8)
0	2,750	250	0.20	₹500	24	₹2,400		
	3,000	500	0.04	1,000	24	960		
						₹3,360	₹0	₹3,360
250	3,000	250	0.04	500	24	₹480	₹600	₹1,080
500	–	–	–	–	–	₹0[f]	₹1,200	₹1,200

[a]Demand level resulting in stockouts – Inventory available during lead time (excluding safety stock), 2,500 units – Safety stock.

[b]Stockout in units × Relevant stockout costs of ₹2.00 per unit.

[c]Annual demand, 1,20,000 ÷ 5,000 EOQ = 24 orders per year.

[d]Probability of stockout × Relevant stockout costs × Number of orders per year.

[e]Safety stock × Annual relevant carrying costs of ₹2.4 per unit (assumes that safety stock is on hand at all times and that there is no overstocking caused by decreases in expected usage).

[f]At a safety stock level of 500 units, no stockout will occur and, hence, expected stockout costs = ₹0.

20-24 EOQ, uncertainty, safety stock, reorder point. Maruti Suzuki India is a major automobile manufacturer. It purchases steering wheels from Sona Kap Steering. Annual demand is 10,400 steering wheels per year or 200 steering wheels per week. The ordering cost is ₹100 per order. The annual carrying cost is ₹13 per steering wheel. It currently takes 1.5 weeks to supply an order to the assembly plant.

Required

1. What is the optimal number of steering wheels that Maruti's managers should order according to the EOQ model?
2. At what point should managers reorder the steering wheels, assuming that both demand and purchase-order lead time are known with certainty?
3. Now assume that demand can vary during the 1.5-week purchase-order lead time. The following table shows the probability distribution of various demand levels:

Total Demand for Steering Wheels for 1.5 Weeks	Probability of Demand (sums to 1)
100	0.15
200	0.20
300	0.40
400	0.20
500	0.05

If Maruti runs out of stock, it would have to rush order the steering wheels at an additional cost of ₹9 per steering wheel. How much safety stock should the assembly plant hold? How will this affect the reorder point and reorder quantity.

Solution

1. $EOQ = \sqrt{\dfrac{2\,DP}{C}} = \sqrt{\dfrac{2 \times 10,400 \times ₹100}{₹13}}$

   EOQ = 400 steering wheels

2. Average weekly demand = 10,400 ÷ 52 weeks = 200 steering wheels per week

   Purchasing lead time = 1.5 weeks

   Reorder point at each plant = 200 steering wheels × 1.5 weeks = 300 steering wheels

3. Solution Exhibit 20-24 presents the safety stock computations for a given assembly plant when the reorder point excluding safety stock is 300 steering wheels. The exhibit shows that annual relevant total stockout and carrying costs are the lowest (₹2,470) when a safety stock of 100 steering wheels is maintained. Therefore, a given assembly plant should hold a safety stock of 100 steering wheels. As a result, Reorder point with safety stock = 300 steering wheels + 100 steering wheels = 400 steering wheels. Reorder quantity is unaffected by the holding of safety stock and remains the same as calculated in requirement 1.

   Reorder quantity = 400 steering wheels

A given assembly plant should order 400 steering wheels each time its inventory falls to 400 steering wheels.

Solution Exhibit 20-24

Computation of Safety Stock for the assembly plant when Reorder Point is 300 Units

Safety Stock Level in Units (1)	Demand Levels Resulting in Stockouts (2)	Stockout in Unitsa (3) = (2) − 300 − (1)	Probability of Stockouts (4)	Relevant Stockout Costsb (₹) (5) = (3) × ₹9	Number of Orders per Yearc (6)	Expected Stockout Costsd (7) −(4) × (5) × (6)	Relevant Carrying Costse (₹) (8) = (1) × ₹13	Relevant Total Costs (₹) (9) = (7) + (8)
0	400	100	0.20	900	26	₹4,680		
	500	200	0.05	1,800	26	2,340		
						₹7,020	0	7,020
100	500	100	0.05	900	26	₹1,170	1,300	2,470
200	–	–	–	–	–	₹0f	2,600	2,600

[a]Demand level resulting in stockouts – Inventory available during lead time (excluding safety stock), 300 units – Safety stock.

[b]Stockout in units × Relevant stockout costs of ₹9.00 per unit.

[c]Annual demand, 10,400 ÷ 400 EOQ = 26 orders per year.

[d]Probability of stockout × Relevant stockout costs × Number of orders per year.

[e]Safety stock × Annual relevant carrying costs of ₹13 per unit (assumes that safety stock is on hand at all times and that there is no overstocking caused by decreases in expected usage).

[f]At a safety stock level of 200 units, no stockout will occur and, hence, expected stockout costs = ₹0.

20-25 Supply chain effects on total relevant inventory costs. Lenovo Computer Co. outsources the production of wireless mouse for its computers. It is currently deciding which of two suppliers to use: Alpha or Beta. Due to differences in the product failure rates in the two companies, 5% of wireless mouse purchased from Alpha will be inspected and 25% of wireless mouses purchased from Beta will be inspected. The following data refer to costs associated with Alpha and Beta:

	Alpha	Beta
Number of orders per year	50	50
Annual mouses demanded	10,000	10,000
Price per mouse	₹1,080	₹1,050
Ordering cost per order	₹130	₹100
Inspection cost per unit	₹60	₹60
Average inventory level	100 units	100 units
Expected number of stockouts	100	300
Stockout cost (cost of rush order) per stockout	₹40	₹60
Units returned by customers for replacing wireless mouses	50	500
Cost of replacing each mouse	₹300	₹300
Required annual return on investment	10%	10%
Other carrying cost per unit per year	₹35	₹35

Required

1. What is the relevant cost of purchasing from Alpha and Beta?
2. What factors other than cost should Lenovo consider?

Solution

1. The relevant costs of purchasing from Alpha and Beta are:

Cost Category	Alpha	Beta
Purchase costs		
10,000 wireless mouses × ₹1,080 per unit	₹1,08,00,000	
10,000 wireless mouses × ₹1,050 per unit		₹1,05,00,000
Ordering costs		
50 orders × ₹130 per order	6,500	
50 orders × ₹100 per order		5,000
Inspection costs		
10,000 wireless mouses × 5% × ₹60 per unit	30,000	
10,000 wireless mouses × 25% × ₹60 per unit		1,50,000
Required annual return on investment		
100 wireless mouses × ₹1,080 per unit × 10%	10,800	
100 wireless mouses × ₹1,050 per unit × 10%		10,500
Stock out costs		
100 wireless mouses × ₹40 per unit	4,000	
300 wireless mouses × ₹60 per unit		18,000
Return costs		
50 wireless mouses × ₹300 per unit	15,000	
500 wireless mouses × ₹300 per unit		1,50,000
Other carrying costs		
100 wireless mouses × ₹35 per unit per year	3,500	
100 wireless mouses × ₹35 per unit per year		3,500
Total Cost	₹1,08,69,800	₹1,08,37,000

2. Although Beta will save Lenovo ₹32,800 (₹1,08,69,800 − ₹1,08,37,000), Lenovo may still choose to use Alpha for the following reasons:
   a. The savings are less than 1% of the total cost of the wireless mouses.

b. With 10 times the number of returns, Beta will probably have a negative effect on Lenovo's reputation.

c. With Beta's higher stock outs, Lenovo's reputation for availability and on time delivery will be effected.

d. The increased number of inspections may necessitate the hiring of additional personnel and the need for additional factory space and equipment.

20-26 Supply chain effects on total relevant inventory costs. Everbake orders specially-made sandwich buns from two different suppliers: Gold Star Breads and Grandma's Bakery. Everbake would like to use only one of the suppliers in the future. Due to variations in quality, Everbake would need to inspect 30% of Gold Star's buns and 60% of Grandma's. The following data refer to costs associated with the two suppliers.

	Gold star	Grandma's
Number of orders per year	100	100
Annual buns demanded	2,400	2,400
Price per bun	₹25	₹20
Ordering cost per order	₹100	₹120
Inspection cost per bun	₹5	₹5
Average inventory level	200	200
Expected number of stockouts	10	10
Stockout cost of rush order	₹100	₹30
Estimated sandwiches returned by customers because of defective buns	60	100
Cost of fixing sandwiches returned by customers because of defective buns	₹15	₹15
Opportunity cost of investment	12%	12%
Other carrying costs per bun per year	₹5	₹5

Required

1. What is the relevant cost of purchasing from Gold Star and Grandma's?
2. What factors other than cost should Everbake consider?

Solution

1. The relevant costs of purchasing from Gold Star Breads and Grandma's Bakery are:

Cost Category	Gold Star Breads	Grandma's Bakery
Purchase costs		
2,400 buns × ₹25 per bun	₹60,000	
2,400 buns × ₹20 per bun		₹48,000
Ordering costs		
100 orders × ₹100 per order	10,000	
100 orders × ₹120 per order		12,000
Inspection costs		
2,400 buns × 30% × ₹5 per bun	3,600	
2,400 buns × 60% × ₹5 per bun		7,200
Opportunity cost of investment		
200 buns × ₹25 per bun × 12%	600	
200 buns × ₹20 per bun × 12%		480
Stockout costs		
10 buns × ₹100 per bun	1,000	
10 buns × ₹30 per bun		300

Return costs

60 buns × ₹15 per sandwich	900	
100 buns × ₹15 per sandwich		1,500
Other carrying costs		
200 buns × ₹5 per bun	1,000	
200 buns × ₹5 per bun		1,000
Total Cost	₹77,100	₹70,480

2. Grandma's Bakery will save Everbake ₹6,620 (₹77,100 – ₹70,480). However, Everbake may still consider using Gold Star Breads for the following reasons:

   a. The taste of the product may be different and be perceived differently by the customer. If Gold Star Breads is preferred by consumers, Everbake may lose business in the future if it switches to Grandma's Bakery product. In addition, it may be able to charge more for its sandwiches if customers prefer the Gold Star Breads brand.

   b. The additional returns of sandwiches due to the defective Grandma's Bakery product may result in additional lost sales that cannot be quantified.

20-27 Lean accounting. Reliable Security Devices (RSD) has introduced a just-in-time production process and is considering the adoption of lean accounting principles to support its new production philosophy. The company has two product lines: Mechanical Devices and Electronic Devices. Two individual products are made in each line. Product-line manufacturing overhead costs are traced directly to product lines and then allocated to the two individual products in each line. The company's traditional cost-accounting system allocates all plant-level facility costs and some corporate overhead costs to individual products. The latest accounting report using traditional cost accounting methods included the following information (in thousands of rupees):

	Mechanical Devices		Electronic Devices	
	Product A	Product B	Product C	Product D
Sales	₹1,400	₹1,000	₹1,800	₹900
Direct material (based on quantity used)	400	200	500	150
Direct manufacturing labor	300	150	400	120
Manufacturing overhead (equipment lease, supervision, production control)	180	240	400	190
Allocated plant-level facility costs	100	80	160	60
Design and marketing costs	190	100	210	84
Allocated corporate overhead costs	30	20	40	16
Operating income	₹200	₹210	₹90	₹280

RSD has determined that each of the two product lines represents a distinct value stream. It has also determined that out of the ₹4,00,000 (₹1,00,000 + ₹80,000 + ₹1,60,000 + ₹60,000) plant-level facility costs, product A occupies 22% of the plant's square footage, product B occupies 18%, product C occupies 36%, and product D occupies 14%. The remaining 10% of square footage is not being used. Finally, RSD has decided that in order to identify inefficiencies, direct material should be expensed in the period it is purchased, rather than when the material is used. According to purchasing records, direct material purchase costs during the period were as follows:

	Mechanical Devices		Electronic Devices	
	Product A	Product B	Product C	Product D
Direct material (purchases)	₹420	₹240	₹500	₹180

Required

1. What are the cost objects in RSD's lean accounting system?
2. Compute operating income for the cost objects identified in requirement 1 using

lean accounting principles. What would you compare this operating income against? Comment on your results.

Solution

1. The cost object in lean accounting is the value stream, not the individual product. RSD has identified two distinct value streams: Mechanical Devices and Electronic Devices. All direct costs are traced to the value streams. However, not all plant-level overhead costs are allocated to the value streams when computing operating income. Value streams are only charged for the percentage of space they actually use; only 90% of the ₹4,00,000 plant facility costs are charged to the two value streams. The remaining 10%, or ₹40,000, is not used to compute value stream profits, and neither are other corporate-level overhead costs. In addition, RSD's lean accounting system accounts for direct materials as expenses in the period the materials are purchased.

2. Operating income under lean accounting are the following (in thousands of rupees):

	Mechanical Devices	Electronic Devices
Sales (₹1,400 + ₹1,000; ₹1,800 + ₹900)	₹2,400	₹2,700
Costs		
Direct materials purchased		
(₹420 + ₹240; ₹500 + ₹180)	660	680
Direct manufacturing labor		
(₹300 + ₹150; ₹400 + ₹120)	450	520
Equipment lease, supervision, prod. control		
(₹180 + ₹240; ₹400 + ₹190)	420	590
Design and marketing costs		
(₹190 + ₹100; ₹210 + ₹84)	290	294
Plant facility costs		
(₹4,00,000 × 40%; ₹4,00,000 × 50%)	160	200
Total value-stream costs	1,980	2,284
Value stream operating income	₹420	₹416

I would compare the operating income under lean accounting with the following income computation.

	Mechanical Devices	Electronic Devices
Sales (₹1,400 + ₹1,000; ₹1,800 + ₹900)	₹2,400	₹2,700
Costs		
Direct materials purchased		
(₹420 + ₹240; ₹500 + ₹180)	660	680
Direct manufacturing labor		
(₹300 + ₹150; ₹400 + ₹120)	450	520
Equipment lease, supervision, prod. control		
(₹180 + ₹240; ₹400 + ₹190)	420	590
Design and marketing costs		
(₹190 + ₹100; ₹210 + ₹84)	290	294
Plant level facility costs		
(₹100 + ₹80; ₹160 + ₹60)	180	220
Total plant-level costs	2,000	2,304
Plant-level operating income	₹400	₹396

For Mechanical Devices, the total plant-level costs are ₹20,00,000, while the total value stream costs are ₹19,80,000 (99% of ₹20,00,000). For Electronic Devices, the total plant-level costs are ₹23,04,000, while the total value stream costs are ₹22,84,000 (99.1% of ₹23,04,000). The difference between the total value-stream costs and the total plant-level costs is very small, indicating that the main opportunity for improving efficiency to reduce costs and improve profitability is reducing unused plant-level facility costs.

The value-stream operating income as a percentage of revenues for Mechanical Devices is 17.5% (₹4,20,000 ÷ ₹24,00,000) and for Electronic Devices is 15.4% (₹4,16,000 ÷ ₹27,00,000). Mechanical Devices has higher value stream operating income as a percentage of revenue than Electronic Devices but both value streams can improve profitability by being more efficient in their purchases of direct materials. Mechanical Devices purchases ₹60,000 (₹6,60,000 − ₹6,00,000) more direct materials than it uses while Electronic Devices purchases ₹30,000 (₹6,80,000 − ₹6,50,000) more. If Mechanical Devices had purchased ₹60,000 less direct materials, its value-stream operating income would be ₹4,80,000 (₹4,20,000 + ₹60,000) and its profitability percentage would be 20% (₹4,80,000 ÷ ₹24,00,000). If Electronic Devices had purchased ₹30,000 less direct materials, its value-tream operating income would be ₹4,46,000 (₹4,16,000 + ₹30,000) and its profitability percentage would be 16.5% (₹4,46,000 ÷ ₹27,00,000). Given that Electronic Devices is less profitable than Mechanical Devices, it is more urgent for Mechanical Devices to make efficiency improvements.

Value-stream operating income analyses ignore allocated corporate overhead costs because these costs cannot be controlled or influenced by plant-level managers. The following factors explain the differences between traditional operating income and lean accounting income for the two value streams (in thousands of rupees):

	Mechanical Devices	Electronic Devices
Traditional operating income		
(₹200 + ₹210; ₹90 + ₹280)	₹410	₹370
Additional cost of direct materials purchased over direct materials used		
(₹660 − ₹400 − ₹200; ₹680 − ₹500 − ₹150)	(60)	(30)
Decrease in allocated plant-level overhead		
(₹100 + ₹80 − ₹160; ₹160 + ₹60 − ₹200)	20	20
Add back allocated corporate overhead costs		
(₹30 + ₹20; ₹40 + ₹16)	50	56
Value stream operating income	₹420	₹416

20-28 JIT production, relevant benefits, relevant costs, ethics. Hyundai India is considering implementing a JIT production system. The new system would reduce current average inventory levels of ₹40,00,000 by 75%, but it would require a much greater dependency on the company's core suppliers for on-time deliveries and high-quality inputs. The company's operations manager Rohan, is opposed to the idea of a new JIT system because he is concerned that the new system (a) will be too costly to manage; (b) will result in too many stockouts; and (c) will lead to the layoff of his employees, several of whom are currently managing inventory. He believes that these layoffs will affect the morale of his entire production department. The management accountant, Preeti, is in favor of the new system because of its likely cost savings. Rohan wants Preeti to rework the numbers because he is concerned that top management will give more weight to financial factors and not give due consideration to nonfinancial factors such as employee morale. In addition to the reduction in inventory described previously, Preeti has gathered the following information for the upcoming year regarding the JIT system:

- Annual insurance and warehousing costs for inventory would be reduced by 60% of current budgeted level of ₹7,00,000.

- Payroll expenses for current inventory management staff would be reduced by 15% of the budgeted total of ₹12,00,000.
- Additional annual costs for JIT system implementation and management, including personnel costs, would equal ₹4,40,000.
- The additional number of stockouts under the new JIT system is estimated to be 5% of the total number of consignments annually. Ten thousand consignments are budgeted for the upcoming year. Each stockout would result in an average additional cost of ₹500.
- Hyundai's required rate of return on inventory investment is 10% per year.

Required

1. From a financial perspective, should Hyundai adopt the new JIT system?
2. Should Preeti rework the numbers?
3. How should she manage Rohan's concerns?

Solution

1. Solution Exhibit 20-28 presents the annual net benefit of ₹2,10,000 to Hyundai India of implementing a JIT production system.
2. As part of the IMA's Standards of Ethical Professional Practice, Preeti, the management accountant, has an obligation under the competence standard to "provide decision support information and recommendations that are accurate, clear, concise and timely." Therefore, she must provide the cost benefit analysis to Hyundai's senior management in a timely fashion, even if it could result in layoffs for some employees. The credibility standard also requires her to disclose any relevant information that could be expected to influence an intended user's decision. This would indicate that she has an ethical obligation to disclose the potential cost/benefits of the new JIT system to management.
3. It is understandable that Rohan, the company's operations manager, would be concerned about potential layoffs in his department and the resulting morale issues. However, recommendations could include (1) fully engaging the production staff in the upcoming changes to minimize negative morale issues; (2) retraining existing staff to manage the new JIT production and purchasing system so as to avoid as many potential layoffs, as possible; (3) and relocating existing staff to other production and or administrative positions wherever possible to minimize layoffs. As for Rohan's other concerns, the new system will be costly to implement and maintain and there is a likelihood for additional stock outs, but the financial benefits clearly outweigh the costs.

Solution Exhibit 20-28
Annual Relevant Costs and Benefits of new JIT Production System for Hyundai India

Relevant Items	Relevant Benefits under JIT Production System	Relevant Costs under JIT Production System
Annual additional costs for JIT system implementation and management		₹4,40,000
Additional expected stock out costs 10,000 × 5% × ₹500		2,50,000
Required return on investment:		
10% per year × ₹40,00,000 × 75% of average inventory	₹3,00,000	
Insurance and warehousing costs 60% per year × ₹7,00,000	4,20,000	
Reduction in payroll expense for current inventory management staff 15% per year × ₹12,00,000	1,80,000	
Total net incremental benefits/costs	₹9,00,000	₹6,90,000
Annual difference in favor of JIT production	₹2,10,000	

20-29 Backflush costing, income manipulation, ethics. BV Rajesh, the chief financial officer of Bangalore Computer (BC) is an enthusiastic advocate of JIT production. The BC's Keyboard Division, which produces keyboards for personal computers, has made dramatic improvements in its operations with a highly successful JIT implementation. The Keyboard Division president now wants to adopt backflush costing.

Rajesh discusses the backflush costing proposal with Harish, the controller of BC's. Harish is totally opposed to backflush costing. He argues that it will open up "Pandora's box," by allowing division managers to manipulate reported division operating income. A member of Harish's group outlines the three possible variations of backflush costing. Harish notes that none of these three methods tracks work in process. He asserts that this omission would allow managers to "artificially change" reported operating income by manipulating work-in-process levels. He is especially scathing about the backflush costing in which no entries are made until a sale occurs.

"Suppose the division has already met its target operating income and wants to shift some of this year's income to next year," he says. "Under backflush costing with sale of finished goods as the trigger point, the division will have an incentive to not make sales this year of goods produced this year. This is a bizzare incentive. I rest my case about why we should stay with a job-costing system using sequential tracking."

Harish concludes that as long as reported accounting numbers are central to BC's performance and bonus reviews, backflush costing should never be adopted.

Required

1. What factors should BC's consider in deciding whether to adopt a version of backflush costing?
2. Are Harish's concerns about income manipulation sufficiently important for BC's to not adopt backflush costing?
3. What other ways does BC's have to motivate managers to not "artificially change" reported income?

Solution

Backflush costing, income manipulation, ethics.

1. Factors BC's should consider in deciding whether to adopt a version of backflush costing include:
   a. Effects on decision making by managers. There is a loss of information with backflushing. Supporters of backflushing maintain, however, that nonfinancial information and observation of production provide sufficient inputs to monitor production and management costs at the shop-floor level.
   b. Costs of maintaining sequential tracking vis-à-vis backflush costing.
   c. Materiality of the differences. If the production lead time is short (say, less than one day) and inventory levels are minimal (as one would anticipate with JIT), the differences between sequential tracking and backflush may be minimal.
   d. Opportunity for managers to manipulate reported numbers.
2. Harish's concerns certainly warrant consideration. Much depends on the corporate culture at BC's. If the culture is that quarterly or monthly reported numbers are pivotal to evaluations, and that managers "push the accounting system to facilitate meeting the numbers," Harish should raise these issues with Rajesh. Adopting an accounting system with an obvious opportunity for manipulation (backflush with sale as the trigger point) may well send managers the wrong message.

   Harish's concerns, however are not by themselves sufficient to cause BC's to not adopt backflush costing. The factors mentioned in requirement 1 may well be compelling enough to support adoption of backflush costing. Rajesh has alternative ways to address Harish's quite legitimate concerns (see requirement 3).
3. Ways to motivate managers to not "artificially change" reported income include:
   a. Adopting long-term measures that reduce the importance of short-run financial targets.
   b. Increasing the weight on nonaccounting-based variables-e.g., more use of stock options or customer-satisfaction measures.

c. Penalize heavily (the "stick approach") managers who are found out to have "artificially changed" reported income. This can include withdrawal of bonuses or even termination of employment.

Exercises

[*Comprehensive solutions to all exercises are available on the companion website www.pearsoned.co.in/charlesthorngren*]

20-30 EOQ for a retailer. The Cloth Center buys and sells fabrics to a wide range of industrial and consumer users. One of the products it carries is denim cloth used in the manufacture of jeans and carrying bags. The supplier for the denim cloth pays all incoming freight. No incoming inspection of the denim is necessary because the supplier has a track record of delivering high-quality merchandise. The purchasing officer of the Cloth Center has collected the following information:

Annual demand for denim cloth	20,000 yards
Ordering costs per purchase order	₹200
Carrying costs per year	10% of purchase costs
Safety stock requirements	None
Cost of denim cloth	₹80 per yard

The purchasing lead time is 2 weeks. The Cloth Center is open 250 days a year (50 weeks for 5 days a week).

Required

1. Calculate the EOQ for denim cloth.
2. Calculate the number of orders that will be placed each year.
3. Calculate the reorder point for denim cloth.

20-31 Backflush costing and JIT production. HCL Limited assembles handheld computers that have scaled-down capabilities of laptop computers. Each handheld computer takes 6 hours to assemble. HCL Limited uses a JIT production system and a backflush costing system with three trigger points:

- Purchase of direct (raw) materials
- Sale of finished goods
- Completion of good finished units of product

There are no beginning inventories of materials or finished goods. The following data are for August:

Direct (raw) materials purchased	₹2,75,40,000	Conversion costs incurred	₹72,36,000
Direct (raw) materials used	2,73,36,000	Conversion costs allocated	75,04,000

HCL Limited records direct materials purchased and conversion costs incurred at actual costs. When finished goods are sold, the backflush costing system "pulls through" standard direct materials costs (₹1,020 per unit) and standard conversion costs (₹280 per unit). HCL Limited produced 26,800 finished units in August and sold 26,400 units. The actual direct materials cost per unit in August was ₹1,020, and the actual conversion cost per unit was ₹270.

Required

1. Prepare summary journal entries for August (without disposing of under-or overallocated conversion costs).
2. Post the entries in requirement 1 to T-accounts for applicable Inventory: Direct and In-Process, Conversion Costs Control, Conversion Costs Allocated, and Cost of Goods Sold.
3. Under an ideal JIT production system, how would the amounts in your journal entries differ from those in requirement 1?

20-32 Backflush costing, two trigger points, materials purchase and sale (continuation of 20-31). Assume the same facts as in Exercise 20-31, except that HCL Limited now uses a backflush costing system with the following two trigger points:

- Purchase of direct (raw) materials
- Sale of finished goods

The Inventory Control account will include direct materials purchased but not yet in production, materials in work in process, and materials in finished goods but not sold. No conversion costs are inventoried. Any under/or overallocated conversion costs are written off monthly to cost of goods sold.

Required

1. Prepare summary journal entries for August, including the disposition of under/or over-allocated conversion costs.
2. Post the entries in requirement 1 to T-accounts for Inventory Control, Conversion Costs Control, Conversion Costs Allocated, and Cost of Goods Sold.

20-33 Backflush costing, two trigger points, completion of production and sale (continuation of 20-32). Assume the same facts as in Exercise 20-32, except now HCL Limited uses only two trigger points, the completion of good finished units of product and the sale of finished goods. Any under-or overallocated conversion costs are written off monthly to Cost of Goods Sold.

Required

1. Prepare summary journal entries for August, including the disposition of under/or over-allocated conversion costs.
2. Post the entries in requirement 1 to T-accounts for Finished Goods Control, Conversion Cost Control, Conversion Costs Allocated, and Cost of Goods Sold.

20-34 EOQ, cost of prediction error. Harvinder is the owner of a truck repair shop. He uses an EOQ model for each of his truck parts. He initially predicts the annual demand for heavy-duty tires to be 2,000. Each tire has a purchase price of ₹1,000. The incremental ordering costs per purchase order are ₹800. The incremental carrying costs per year are ₹80 per tire plus 10% of the supplier's purchase price per tire.

Required

1. Calculate the EOQ for tires, along with the sum of annual relevant ordering costs and relevant carrying costs.
2. Suppose Harvinder is correct in all his predictions except the purchase price. If he had been a faultless predictor, he would have foreseen that the purchase price would drop to ₹600. What is the cost of the prediction error?

20-35 JIT purchasing, relevant benefits, relevant costs. (CMA adapted) The Omax Auto is an automotive supplier that uses automatic turning machines to manufacture precision parts from steel bars. Omax's inventory of raw steel averages ₹60,00,000. The president of Omax, and Omax's Controller, are concerned about the costs of carrying inventory. The steel supplier is willing to supply steel in smaller lots at no additional charge. The Controller identified the following effects of adopting a JIT inventory program to virtually eliminate steel inventory:

- Without scheduling any overtime, lost sales due to stockouts would increase by 35,000 units per year. However, by incurring overtime premiums of ₹4,00,000 per year, the increase in lost sales could be reduced to 20,000 units. This would be the maximum amount of overtime that would be feasible for Omax.
- Two warehouses currently used for steel bar storage would no longer be needed. Omax rents one warehouse from another company under a cancelable leasing arrangement at an annual cost of ₹6,00,000. The other warehouse is owned by Omax and contains 12,000 square feet. Three-fourths of the space in the owned warehouse could be rented for ₹15 per square foot per year. Insurance and property tax costs totaling ₹1,40,000 per year would be eliminated.

Long-term capital investments by Omax are expected to produce an annual rate of return of 20%. Omax Auto Budgeted Income Statement for the Year Ending December 31, 2014, (in thousands) is as follows:

Revenues (9,00,000 units)		₹1,08,000
Cost of goods sold		
Variable costs	₹40,500	

Fixed costs	14,500	
Total costs of goods sold		55,000
Gross margin		53,000
Marketing and distribution costs		
Variable costs	₹9,000	
Fixed costs	15,000	
Total marketing and distribution costs		24,000
Operating income		₹29,000

Required

1. Calculate the estimated savings (loss) for the Omax Auto that would result in 2014 from the adoption of the JIT inventory-control method.

2. Identify and explain other factors that Omax should consider before deciding whether to install a JIT system.

20-36 Relevant benefits and costs of JIT purchasing. Maharishi Medical Instruments is considering JIT implementation in 2015. Maharishi's annual demand for product XJ-200, a surgical scalpel, is 20,000 units. If Maharishi implements JIT, the purchase price of the scalpel is expected to increase from ₹100 to ₹100.5 because of frequent deliveries by Apollo Manufacturing, Limited. Apollo enjoys a sterling reputation for quality and reliability. Ordering costs will remain at ₹50 per order. However, the annual number of orders placed will be 200 instead of the current 20. As a result of frequent ordering, Maharishi's order size will decrease proportionally. Maharishi's required rate of return on investment is 20%. Other carrying costs (insurance, materials handling, and so on) will remain at ₹45 per unit. Currently Maharishi has no stockout costs. Lower inventory levels from implementing JIT will lead to ₹30 per unit stockout costs on 100 units during the year.

Required

1. Calculate the estimated savings (loss) for Maharishi Medical Instruments from the adoption of JIT purchasing using the format of Exhibit 20-5.

2. Under what conditions would it be beneficial for Maharishi to have Apollo manage all inventories in the supply chain?

20-37 Supplier evaluation and relevant costs of quality and timely deliveries (continuation of 20-36) Maharishi Medical Instruments installed a JIT purchasing system in 2015 and selected Apollo Manufacturing, Limited, as its supplier. Batra Manufacturing Company also manufactures XJ-200. It offers to supply all of Maharishi's XJ-200 needs at a price of ₹97.5 per unit (less than Apollo's price of ₹100.5) under the same JIT delivery terms that Apollo offers. Maharishi's relevant carrying costs of insurance, material handling, and so on would be ₹44 per unit per year if it purchases from Batra. Due to the lower quality of Batra's product, Maharishi anticipates the following negative consequences of purchasing from Batra:

- Maharishi would incur inspection costs of ₹0.80 per unit.
- Average stockouts of 800 units per year would occur from late deliveries, requiring rush orders at a cost of ₹30 per unit.
- Customers would likely return 10% of all units sold due to poor quality of the product. Maharishi estimates its additional costs to handle each returned unit are ₹60.

Required

Calculate the relevant costs of purchasing (1) from Apollo and (2) from Batra. From whom should Maharishi buy XJ-200?

20-38 Backflush costing and JIT production. National Electric Appliances Company (NEA) manufactures electrical meters. For August, there were no beginning inventories of direct materials and no beginning or ending work in process. NEA uses a JIT production system and backflush costing with three trigger points for making entries in the accounting system:

- Purchase of direct materials-debited to Inventory: Direct and In-Process Control
- Completion of good finished units of product-debited to Finished Goods Control
- Sale of finished goods

NEA's August standard cost per meter is direct materials, ₹250; and conversion costs, ₹200. The following data apply to August manufacturing:

Direct materials purchased	₹55,00,000	Number of finished units manufactured	21,000
Conversion costs incurred	₹44,00,000	Number of finished units sold	20,000

Required

1. Prepare summary journal entries for August (without disposing of under-or overallo-cated conversion costs). Assume no direct materials variances.
2. Post the entries in requirement 1 to T-accounts for Inventory: Direct and In-Process Control, Conversion Costs Control, Conversion Costs Allocated, and Cost of Goods Sold.

20-39 Backflush, two trigger points, materials purchase and sale (continuation of 20-38). Assume that the second trigger point for NEA company is the sale-rather than the production-of finished goods. Also, the inventory account is confined solely to direct materials, whether these materials are in a storeroom, in work in process, or in finished goods. No conversion costs are inventoried. They are allocated to the units sold at standard costs. Any under/or overallocated conversion costs are written off monthly to Cost of Goods Sold.

Required

1. Prepare summary journal entries for August, including the disposition of under-or over-allocated conversion costs. Assume no direct materials variances.
2. Post the entries in requirement 1 to T-accounts for Inventory Control, Conversion Costs Control, Conversion Costs Allocated, and Cost of Goods Sold.

20-40 Backflush, two trigger points, completion of production and sale (continuation of 20-38). Assume the same facts as in Problem 20-38 except now there are only two trigger points: the completion of good finished units of product and the sale of finished goods.

Required

1. Prepare summary journal entries for August, including the disposition of under-or over-allocated conversion costs. Assume no direct materials variances.
2. Post the entries in requirement 1 to T-accounts for Finished Goods Control, Conversion Costs Control, Conversion Costs Allocated, and Cost of Goods Sold.

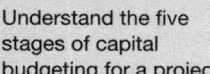

Learning Objective 1

Understand the five stages of capital budgeting for a project

. . . identify projects, obtain information, make predictions, make decisions, and implement the decision, evaluate performance, and learn

Should Honda open a new plant in China or India?

Should Sony invest in developing the next generation of PlayStation consoles? Should the Gap discontinue its children's clothing line and expand its women's athletic clothing line? Working closely with accountants, top executives have to figure out how and when to best allocate the firm's financial resources among alternative opportunities to create future value for the company. Because it's hard to know what the future holds and how much projects will ultimately cost, this can be a challenging task, but it's one that managers must constantly confront. To meet this challenge, companies such as Target and Chevron have developed special groups to make project-related capital budgeting decisions. This chapter explains the different methods managers use to get the "biggest bang" for the firm's "buck" in terms of the projects they undertake.

Stages of Capital Budgeting

Capital budgeting is the process of making long-run planning decisions for investments in projects. In much of accounting, income is calculated on a period-by-period basis. In choosing investments, however, managers make a selection from among a group of multiple projects, each of which may span several periods. Exhibit 21-1 illustrates these two different, yet intersecting, dimensions of cost analysis: (1) horizontally across, as the *project dimension*, and (2) vertically upward, as the *accounting-period dimension*. Each project is represented as a horizontal rectangle starting and ending at different times and stretching over time spans longer than one year. The vertical rectangle for the 2015 accounting period, for example, represents the dimensions of income determination and routine annual planning and control that cuts across all projects that are ongoing that year.

To make capital budgeting decisions, managers analyzes each project by considering all the lifespan cash flows from its initial investment through its termination. This process is analogous to life-cycle budgeting and costing (Chapter 13). For example, when Honda considers producing a new model of automobiles, it begins by estimating all potential revenues from the new line as well as any costs that will be incurred along its life cycle, which may be as long as 10 years. Only after examining the potential costs and benefits across all of the business functions in the value chain, from research and development (R&D) to customer service, across the entire lifespan of the new-car project, does Honda decide whether the new model is a wise investment.

Managers use capital budgeting as a decision-making and a control tool. Like the five-step decision process that we have emphasized throughout this book, there are five stages to the capital budgeting process:

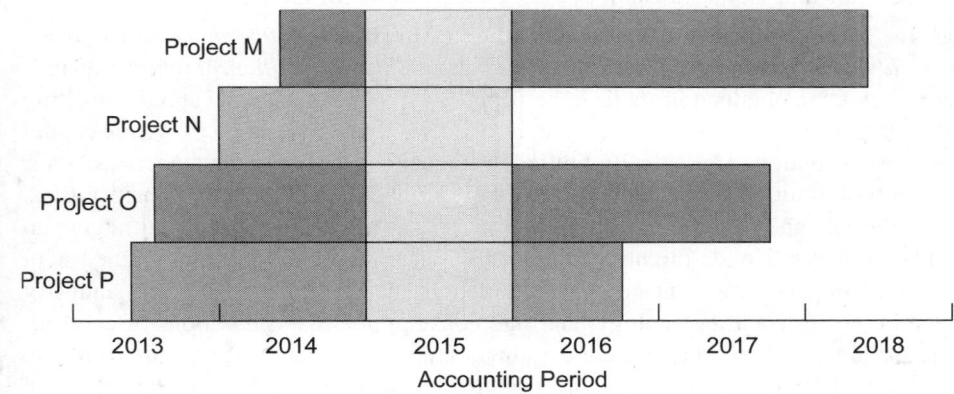

Exhibit 21-1

The Project and Time
Dimensions of Capital
Budgeting

Stage 1:   Identify Projects *Identify potential capital investments that agree with the organization's strategy.* For example, Nike, an industry leader in product differentiation, makes significant investments in product innovation, engineering, and design, hoping to develop the next generation of high-quality sportswear. Alternatively, managers could promote products that improve productivity and efficiency as a cost-leadership strategy. For example, Dell's strategy of cost leadership includes outsourcing certain components to lower-cost contract manufacturing facilities located overseas. Identifying which types of capital projects to invest in is largely the responsibility of a firm's top managers.

Stage 2:   Obtain Information *Gather information from all parts of the value chain to evaluate alternative projects.* Returning to the new car example at Honda, in this stage, the firm's top managers ask the company's marketing managers for potential revenue numbers, plant managers for assembly times, and suppliers for prices and the availability of key components. Lower-level managers are asked to validate the data provided and to explain the assumptions underlying them. The goal is to encourage open and honest communication that results in accurate estimates so that the best investment decisions are made. Some projects will be rejected at this stage. For example, suppose Honda learns that the car cannot be built using existing plants. It may then opt to cancel the project altogether.

Stage 3:   Make Predictions *Forecast all potential cash flows attributable to the alternative projects.* A new project generally requires a firm to make a substantial initial outlay of capital, which is recouped over time through annual cash inflows and the disposal value of the project's assets after it is terminated. Consequently, investing in a new project requires the firm to forecast its cash flows several years into the future. BMW, for example, estimates yearly cash flows and sets its investment budgets accordingly using a 12-year planning horizon. Because of the significant uncertainty associated with these predictions, firms typically analyze a wide range of alternate circumstances. In the case of BMW, the marketing group is asked to estimate a band of possible sales figures within a 90% confidence interval. Firms also attempt to ensure that estimates, especially for the later years of a project, are grounded in realistic scenarios. It is tempting for managers to introduce biases into these projections in order to drive the outcome of the capital budgeting process to their preferred choice. This effect is exacerbated by the fact that managers may not expect to be employed at the firm during those years and therefore cannot be held accountable for their estimates.

Stage 4:   Make Decisions by Choosing Among Alternatives *Determine which investment yields the greatest benefit and the least cost to the organization.* Using the quantitative information obtained in stage 3, the firm uses any one of several capital budgeting methodologies to determine which project best meets organizational goals. While capital budgeting calculations are typically limited to financial information, managers use their judgment and intuition to factor in qualitative information and strategic considerations as well. For example, even if a proposed new line of cars meets its financial targets on a standalone basis, Honda might decide not to pursue the line if it is not aligned with the strategic imperatives of the company on matters such as brand positioning, industry leadership in safety and technology, and fuel consumption. Considerations of environmental sustainability might also favor certain projects that currently appear unprofitable. For example, UPS relaxes the company's minimum rate of return on vehicles that have the potential to reduce fuel use and costs. Similarly, Sealed Air is willing to accept projects with a lower projected return if they look promising with regard to reducing greenhouse gas emissions. Finally, managers spend a significant amount of time assessing the risks of a project, in terms of both the uncertainty of the estimated cash flows as well as the potential downside risks of the project (as well as to the firm as a whole) if the worst-case scenario were to occur.

Stage 5:   Implement the Decision, Evaluate Performance, and Learn Given the complexities of capital investment decisions and the longer time horizon they span, this stage can be separated into two phases:

- *Obtain funding and make the investments selected in stage 4.* The sources of funding include internally generated cash flow as well as equity and debt securities sold in capital markets. Making capital investments is often an arduous task, laden with the purchase of many different goods and services. If Honda opts to build a new car, it must order steel, aluminum, paint, and so on. If some of the materials are unavailable, managers must determine the economic feasibility of using alternative inputs.

- *Track realized cash flows, compare against estimated numbers, and revise plans if necessary.* As the cash outflows and inflows begin to accumulate, managers can verify whether the predictions made in stage 3 agree with the actual flows of cash from the project. When the BMW group initially released the new Mini Cooper, its sales were substantially higher than the original demand estimates. BMW responded by manufacturing more cars. It also decided to expand the Mini line to include convertibles and the larger Clubman model.

  It is equally important for a company to abandon projects that are performing poorly relative to expectations. A natural bias for managers is to escalate their commitment to a project they chose to implement for fear of revealing they made an incorrect capital budgeting decision. It is in the firm's and the managers' long-term interest, however, to acknowledge the mistake when it is clear that the project is not financially sustainable.

To illustrate capital budgeting, consider Jaipur Golden Transport. Jaipur operates bus lines throughout the country, often providing transportation services on behalf of local transit authorities. Several of Jaipur Golden's buses are nearing the end of their useful lives and are requiring increased operating and maintenance costs. Customers have also complained that the buses lack adequate storage, flexible seating configurations, and newer amenities such as wireless Internet access. The firm has made a commitment to act in an environmentally responsible manner and will only pursue projects that do minimal harm to the ecosystem. Accordingly, in stage 1, Jaipur Golden's managers decide to look for replacement buses that generate low emissions. In the information-gathering stage (stage 2), the company learns that as early as 2014, it could feasibly begin purchasing and using diesel electric hybrid buses that have Wi-Fi and also offer greater comfort and storage. After collecting additional data, Jaipur Golden begins to forecast its future cash flows if it invests in the new buses (stage 3). Jaipur Golden estimates that it can purchase a hybrid bus with a useful life of 5 years for a net after-tax initial investment of ₹64,89,000, which is calculated as follows:[1]

Cost of new hybrid bus	₹66,00,000
Investment in working capital	3,00,000
Cash flow from disposing of existing bus (after-tax)	(4,11,000)
Net initial investment for new bus	₹64,89,000

Working capital refers to the difference between current assets and current liabilities. New projects often require additional investments in current assets such as inventories and receivables. In the case of Jaipur Golden, the purchase of the new bus is accompanied by an incremental outlay of ₹3,00,000 for supplies, replacement batteries, and spare parts inventory. At the end of the project, the ₹3,00,000 in current assets is liquidated, resulting in a cash inflow. However, because of the rapid nature of improvements in hybrid technology, the bus itself is believed to have no terminal disposal value after 5 years.

Managers estimate that by introducing the new hybrid buses, operating cash inflows (cash revenues minus cash operating costs) will increase by ₹18,00,000 (after tax) in the first 4 years and by ₹15,00,000 in year 5. This arises from higher ticket prices and increases in ridership because of new customers who are drawn to the amenities of the hybrid bus, as well as savings in fuel, maintenance, and operating costs. To simplify the analysis, suppose that all cash flows occur at the end of each year. Note that cash flow at the end of the fifth year also increases by ₹18,00,000, ₹15,00,000 in operating cash inflows and ₹3,00,000 in working capital. Management next calculates the costs and benefits of the proposed project (stage 4). This chapter discusses four capital budgeting methods to analyze financial information: (1) net present value (NPV), (2) internal rate-of-return (IRR), (3) payback, and (4) accrual accounting rate-of-return (AARR). Both the net present value (NPV) and internal rate-of-return (IRR) methods use discounted cash flows, which we discuss in the next section.

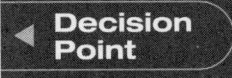

Decision Point

What are the five stages of capital budgeting?

Discounted Cash Flow

Discounted cash flow (DCF) methods measure all expected future *cash* inflows and outflows of a project discounted back to the present point in time. The key feature of DCF

---

[1] For the purposes of exposition, we study the capital budgeting problem for replacing one bus, rather than a fleet of buses.

methods is the **time value of money,** which means that a rupee (or any other monetary unit) received today is worth more than a rupee received at any future time. The reason is that ₹10 received today can be invested at, say, 10% per year so that it grows to ₹11 at the end of one year. The time value of money is the opportunity cost (the return of ₹1 forgone per year) from not having the money today. In this example, ₹100 received one year from now is worth ₹10 ÷ 11 = ₹0.9091 today. Similarly, ₹1,000 received 1 year from now will be weighted by 0.9091 to yield a discounted cash flow of ₹909.10, which is today's value of that ₹1,000 next year. In this way, discounted cash flow methods explicitly measure *cash* flows in terms of the time value of money. Note that DCF focuses exclusively on *cash* inflows and outflows rather than on operating income as calculated under accrual accounting.

The compound interest tables and formulas used in DCF analysis are in Appendix A. If you are unfamiliar with compound interest, do not proceed until you have studied Appendix A, as the tables in Appendix A will be used frequently in this chapter.

The two DCF methods we describe are the **net present value (NPV) method** and the **internal rate-of-return (IRR)** method. Both DCF methods use what is called the **required rate of return (RRR)**, the minimum acceptable annual rate of return on an investment. The RRR is internally set, usually by upper management, and typically reflects the return that an organization could expect to receive elsewhere for an investment of comparable risk. The RRR is also called the **discount rate**, **hurdle rate**, **cost of capital**, or **opportunity cost of capital**. Let us suppose that the CFO at Jaipur Golden has set the required rate of return for the firm's investments at 8% per year.

Net Present Value Method

The **net present value (NPV) method** calculates the expected monetary gain or loss from a project by discounting all expected future cash inflows and outflows back to the present point in time using the required rate of return. To use the NPV method, apply the following three steps:

Step 1: Draw a Sketch of Relevant Cash Inflows and Outflows. The right side of Exhibit 21-2 shows arrows that depict the cash flows of the new hybrid bus. *Note that parentheses denote relevant cash outflows throughout all exhibits in this Chapter.* Exhibit 21-2 includes the outflow for the acquisition of the new bus at the start of year 1 (also referred to as end of year 0) and the inflows over the subsequent 5 years. The NPV method specifies cash flows regardless of their source, such as from operations, purchase or sale of equipment, or investment in or recovery of working capital. However, accrual-accounting concepts such as sales made on credit or noncash expenses are not included because the focus is on cash inflows and outflows.

Step 2: Discount the Cash Flows Using the Correct Compound Interest Table from Appendix A and Sum Them. In the Jaipur Golden example, we can discount each year's cash flow separately using Table 2, or we can compute the present value of an annuity, a series of equal cash flows at equal time intervals, using Table 4. (Both tables are in Appendix A). If we use Table 2, we find the discount factors for periods 1 through 5 under the 8% column. Approach 1 in Exhibit 21-2 uses the five discount factors. To obtain the present value amount, multiply each discount factor by the corresponding amount represented by the arrow on the right in Exhibit 21-2 (−₹64,89,000 × 1.000; ₹18,00,000 × 0.926; and so on to ₹18,00,000 × 0.681). Because the investment in the new bus produces an annuity, we may also use Table 4. Under Approach 2, we find that the annuity factor for five periods under the 8% column is 3.993, which is the sum of the five discount factors used in Approach 1. We multiply the uniform

Exhibit 21-2   Net Present Value Method: Jaipur Golden Hybrid Bus

	Home	Insert	Page Layout	Formulas	Data	Review	View		
	A	B	C	D	E	F	G	H	I
1			Net initial investment	₹64,89,000					
2			Useful life	5 years					
3			Annual cash flow	₹18,00,000					
4			Required rate of return	8%					
5									
6		**Present Value**	**Present Value of**		**Sketch of Relevant Cash Flows at End of Each Year**				
7		of Cash Flow	₹10 Discounted at 8%	0	1	2	3	4	5
8	**Approach 1: Discounting Each Year's Cash Flow Separately**[a]								
9	Net initial investment	₹(64,89,000) ◄	1.000 ◄	₹(64,89,000)					
10		1,66,6800 ◄	0.926 ◄		₹18,00,000				
11		1,54,2600 ◄	0.857 ◄			₹18,00,000			
12	Annual cash inflow	1,42,9200 ◄	0.794 ◄				₹18,00,000		
13		1,32,3000 ◄	0.735 ◄					₹18,00,000	
14		1,22,5800 ◄	◄						₹18,00,000
15	NPV if new bus purchased	₹6,98,400							
16									
17	**Approach 2: Using Annuity Table**[b]								
18	Net initial investment	₹(64,89,000) ◄	1.000 ◄	₹(64,89,000)					
19					₹18,00,000	₹18,00,000	₹18,00,000	₹18,00,000	₹18,00,000
20									
21	Annual cash inflow	7,187,400 ◄	3.993 ◄						
22	NPV if new bus purchased	₹6,98,400							
23									
24	*Note:* Parentheses denote relevant cash outflows throughout all exhibits in Chapter 21.								
25	[a] Present values from Table 2, Appendix A, at the end of the book. For example, $0.857 = 1 \div (1.08)^2$.								
26	[b] Annuity present value from Table 4, Appendix A. The annuity value of 3.993 is the sum of the individual discount rates 0.926 + 0.857 + 0.794 + 0.735 + 0.681.								

annual cash inflow by this factor to obtain the present value of the inflows (₹71,87,400 = ₹18,00,000 x 3.993). Subtracting the initial investment then reveals the NPV of the project as ₹6,98,400 (₹6,98,400 = ₹71,87,400 − ₹64,89,000).

Step 3:   Make the Project Decision on the Basis of the Calculated NPV. An NPV that is zero or positive suggest that from a financial standpoint, the company should accept the project because its expected rate of return equals or exceeds the required rate of return. If the NPV is negative, the company should reject the project because its expected rate of return is below the required rate of return.

Exhibit 21-2 calculates an NPV of ₹6,98,400 at the required rate of return of 8% per year. The project is acceptable based on financial information. The cash flows from the project are adequate (1) to recover the net initial investment in the project and (2) to earn a return greater than 8% per year on the investment tied up in the project over its useful life.

Managers must also weigh nonfinancial factors such as the effect that purchasing the bus will have on Jaipur Golden's brand. This is a nonfinancial factor because the financial benefits that accrue from Jaipur Golden's brand are very difficult to estimate. Nevertheless, managers must consider brand effects before reaching a final decision. Suppose, for example, that the NPV of the hybrid bus is negative. Jaipur Golden's managers might still decide to buy the bus if it maintains Jaipur Golden's technological image and reputation for environmental responsibility. These are factors that could increase Jaipur Golden's financial outcomes in the future, such as by attracting more riders or generating additional contracts from government transit agencies.

Pause here. Do not proceed until you understand what you see in Exhibit 21-2. Compare approach 1 with approach 2 in Exhibit 21-2 to see how Table 4 in Appendix A merely aggregates the present value factors of Table 2. That is, the fundamental table is Table 2. Table 4 simply reduces calculations when there is an annuity.

Internal Rate-of-Return Method

The **internal rate-of-return (IRR) method** calculates the discount rate at which an investment's present value of all expected cash inflows equals the present value of its expected cash outflows. That is, the IRR is the discount rate that makes NPV = ₹0. Exhibit 21-3 shows the cash flows and the NPV of Jaipur Golden's hybrid project using a 12% annual discount rate. At a 12% discount rate, the NPV of the project is ₹0. Therefore, the IRR is 12% per year.

Exhibit 21-3 Internal Rate-of-Return Method: Jaipur Golden's Hybrid Bus[a]

	Home	Insert	Page Layout	Formulas	Data	Review	View		
	A		B	C	D	E	F	G	H	I
1				Net initial investment	₹64,89,000					
2				Useful life	5 years					
3				Annual cash flow	₹18,00,000					
4				Annual discount rate	12%					
5										
6			Present Value	Present Value of		Sketch of Relevant Cash Flows at End of Each Year				
7			of Cash Flow	₹10 Discounted at 12%	0	1	2	3	4	5
8	Approach 1: Discounting Each Year's Cash Flow Separately[b]									
9	Net initial investment		₹(64,89,000) ◄───	1.000 ◄───	₹(64,89,000)					
10			16,07,400 ◄───	0.893 ◄───		₹18,00,000				
11			14,34,600 ◄───	0.797 ◄───			₹18,00,000			
12	Annual cash inflow		12,81,600 ◄───	0.712 ◄───				₹18,00,000		
13			11,44,800 ◄───	0.636 ◄───					₹18,00,000	
14			10,20,600 ◄───	0.567 ◄───						₹18,00,000
15	NPV if new bus purchased		₹0							
16	(the zero difference proves that									
17	the internal rate of return is 12%)									
18										
19	Approach 2: Using Annuity Table[c]									
20	Net initial investment		₹(64,89,000) ◄───	1.000 ◄───	₹(648,90,00)					
21						₹18,00,000	₹18,00,000	₹18,00,000	₹18,00,000	₹18,00,000
22										
23	Annual cash inflow		64,89,000 ◄───	3.605 ◄───						
24	NPV if new bus purchased		₹0							
25										
26	Note: Parentheses denote relevant cash outflows throughout all exhibits in Chapter 21.									
27	[a]The internal rate of return is computed by methods explained on pp. 808–809.									
28	[b]Present values from Table 2, Appendix A, at the end of the book.									
29	[c]Annuity present value from Table 4, Appendix A. The annuity table value of 3.605 is the sum of the individual discount rates 0.893 + 0.797 + 0.712 + 0.636 + 0.567 subject to rounding.									

Managers or analysts solving capital budgeting problems typically use a calculator or computer program to provide the internal rate of return. The following trial-and-error approach can also provide the answer.

Step 1:   Use a discount rate and calculate the project's NPV.

Step 2:   If the calculated NPV is less than zero, use a lower discount rate. (A *lower* discount rate will *increase* NPV. Remember that we are trying to find a discount rate for which NPV = ₹0.) If NPV exceeds zero, use a higher discount rate to lower NPV. Keep adjusting the discount rate until NPV = ₹0. In the Jaipur Golden example, a discount rate of 8% yields an NPV of + ₹6,98,400 (see Exhibit 21-2). A discount rate of 14% yields an NPV of − ₹3,09,600 (3.433, the present value annuity factor from Table 4 × ₹18,00,000 minus ₹64,89,000). Therefore, the discount rate that makes the NPV equal ₹0 must lie between 8% and 14%. We use 12% and get NPV = ₹0. Hence, the IRR is 12% per year.

Computing the IRR is easier when the cash inflows are constant, as in our Jaipur Golden example. Information from Exhibit 21-3 can be expressed as follows:

₹64,89,000 = Present value of annuity of ₹18,00,000 at *X*% per year for 5 years

Or what factor *F* in Table 4 (in Appendix A) will satisfy this equation?

$$₹64,89,000 = ₹18,00,000F$$
$$F = ₹64,89,000 ÷ ₹18,00,000 = 3.605$$

On the five-period line of Table 4, find the percentage column that is closest to 3.605. It is exactly 12%. If the factor (*F*) falls between the factors in two columns, straight-line interpolation is used to approximate IRR. This interpolation is illustrated in the Problem for Self-Study.

Managers accept a project only if IRR equals or exceeds required rate of return (RRR). In the Jaipur Golden example, the hybrid bus has an IRR of 12%, which is greater than the RRR of 8%. On the basis of financial factors, Jaipur Golden should invest in the new bus. In general, the NPV and IRR decision rules result in consistent project acceptance or rejection decisions. If IRR exceeds RRR, then the project has a positive NPV (favoring acceptance). If IRR equals RRR, NPV = ₹0, so the company is indifferent between accepting and rejecting the project. If IRR is less than RRR, NPV is negative (favoring rejection). Obviously, managers prefer projects with higher IRRs to projects with lower IRRs if all other things are equal. The IRR of 12% means the cash inflows from the project are adequate to (1) recover the net initial investment in the project and (2) earn a return of exactly 12% on the investment tied up in the project over its useful life.

Comparing the Net Present Value and Internal Rate-of-Return Methods

The NPV method is the preferred method for selecting projects because its use leads to shareholder value maximization. At an intuitive level, this occurs because the NPV measure for a project captures the value, in today's rupees, of the surplus the project generates for the firm's shareholders, over and above the required rate of return.[2] Next, we highlight some of the limitations of the IRR method relative to the NPV technique.

---

[2] More detailed explanations of the preeminence of the NPV criterion can be found in corporate finance texts.

One advantage of the NPV method is that it's expressed in rupees, not in percentages. Therefore, we can sum NPVs of individual projects to calculate an NPV of a combination or portfolio of projects. In contrast, of individual projects cannot be added or averaged to represent the IRR of a combination of projects.

A second advantage of NPV is that it can be expressed as a unique number. From the sign and magnitude of this number, the firm can then make an accurate assessment of the financial consequences of accepting or rejecting the project. Under the IRR method, it is possible that more than one IRR may exist for a given project. In other words, there may be multiple discount rates that equate the NPV of a set of cash flows to zero. This is especially true when the signs of the cash flows switch over time; that is, when there are outflows, followed by inflows, followed by additional outflows and so forth. In such cases, it is difficult to know which of the IRR estimates should be compared to the firm's required rate of return.

A third advantage of the NPV method is that it can be used when the RRR varies over the life of a project. Suppose Jaipur Golden's management sets an RRR of 10% per year in years 1 and 2 and 14% per year in years 3, 4, and 5. Total present value of the cash inflows can be calculated as ₹63,37,800 (computations not shown). It is not possible to use the IRR method in this case. That's because different RRRs in different years mean there is no single RRR that the IRR (a single figure) can be compared against to decide if the project should be accepted or rejected.

Finally, in some situations, the IRR method is prone to indicating erroneous decisions. This can occur when comparing mutually exclusive projects with unequal lives or unequal levels of initial investment are being compared to one another. The reason is that the IRR method implicitly assumes that project cash flows can be reinvested at the *project's* rate of return. The NPV method, in contrast, accurately assumes that project's cash flows can be reinvested at the *company's* required rate of return.

Despite its limitations, the IRR method is widely used.[3] Why? Probably because managers find the percentage return computed under the IRR method easy to understand and compare. Moreover, in most instances where a single project is being evaluated, their decisions would likely be unaffected by using IRR or NPV.

Sensitivity Analysis

To present the basics of the NPV and IRR methods, we have assumed that the expected values of cash flows will occur *for certain*. In reality, there is substantial uncertainty associated with the prediction of future cash flows. To examine how a result will change if the predicted financial outcomes are not achieved or if an underlying assumption changes, managers can use *sensitivity analysis*, a "what-if" technique introduced in Chapter 3.

A common way to apply sensitivity analysis in capital budgeting decisions is to vary each of the inputs to the NPV calculation by a certain percentage and assess the effect of the change on the project's NPV. Sensitivity analysis can take various forms. Suppose a manager at Jaipur Golden believes the firm's forecasted cash flows are difficult to predict. She asks, "What are the minimum annual cash inflows that make the investment in a new hybrid bus acceptable—that is, what inflows lead to an NPV = ₹0?" For the data in Exhibit 21-2, let A = annual cash flow and let the NPV = ₹0. The net initial investment is ₹64,89,000, and the present value factor at the 8% required annual rate of return for a five-year annuity of ₹1 is 3.993. Then:

---

[3] In a recent survey, John Graham and Campbell Harvey found that 75.7% of CFOs always or almost always used IRR for capital budgeting decisions, while a slightly smaller number, 74.9%, always or almost always used the NPV criterion.

$$
\begin{aligned}
NPV &= ₹0 \\
3.993A - ₹64,89,000 &= ₹0 \\
3.993A &= ₹64,89,000 \\
A &= ₹16,25,090
\end{aligned}
$$

At the discount rate of 8% per year, the annual (after tax) revenue growth can decrease to ₹16,25,090 (a decline of ₹18,00,000 − ₹16,25,090 = ₹1,74,910) before the NPV falls to ₹0. If the manager believes she can attain annual revenue growth of at least ₹16,25,090, she can justify investing in the hybrid bus on financial grounds.

Exhibit 21-4 shows that variations in the annual cash inflows or the RRR significantly affect the NPV of the hybrid bus project. NPVs can also vary with different useful lives of a project. Sensitivity analysis helps managers to focus on decisions that are most sensitive to different assumptions and to worry less about decisions that are not so sensitive.

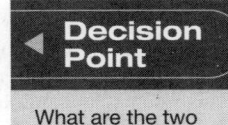

Decision Point

What are the two primary discounted cash flow (DCF) methods for project evaluation?

File Edit View Insert Format Tools Data Window Help					
1	**Required**	**Annual Cash Flows (₹)**				
2	**Rate of Return**	**14,00,000**	**16,00,000**	**18,00,000**	**20,00,000**	**22,00,000**
3	8%	(8,98,800)	(1,00,200)	6,98,400	14,97,000	22,95,600
4	10%	(11,81,600)	(4,23,400)	3,34,800	10,93,000	18,51,200
5	12%	(14,42,000)	(7,21,000)	0	7,21,000	14,42,000
6						
7	[a]All calculated amounts assume the project's useful life is five years.					

Exhibit 21-4

Net Present Value Calculations for Jaipur Golden's Hybrid Bus Under Different Assumptions of Annual Cash Flows and Required Rates of Return[a]

Payback Method

We now consider the third method for analyzing the financial aspects of projects. The **payback method** measures the time it will take to recoup, in the form of expected future cash flows, the net initial investment in a project. Like the NPV and IRR methods, the payback method does not distinguish among the sources of cash flows, such as those from operations, purchase or sale of equipment, or investment or recovery of working capital. As you will see, payback is simpler to calculate when a project has uniform cash flows than when cash flows are uneven over time.

Learning Objective 3

Use and evaluate the payback method

. . . to calculate the time it takes to recoup the investment

Uniform Cash Flows

The hybrid bus Jaipur Golden is considering buying costs ₹64,89,000 and generates a uniform ₹18,00,000 in cash flow every year of its 5-year expected useful life. The payback period is calculated as follows:

$$
\text{Payback period} = \frac{\text{Net initial investment}}{\text{Uniform increase in annual future cash flows}}
$$

$$
\frac{₹64,89,000}{₹18,00,000} = 3.6 \text{ years}^4
$$

---

[4] Cash inflows from the new hybrid bus occur uniformly throughout the year, but for simplicity in calculating NPV and IRR, we assume they occur at the end of each year. A literal interpretation of this assumption would imply a payback of 4 years because Vector will only recover its investment when cash inflows occur at the end of year 4. The calculations shown in the chapter, however, better approximate Vector's payback on the basis of uniform cash flows throughout the year.

The payback method highlights liquidity, a factor that often plays a role in capital budgeting decisions, particularly when the investments are large. Managers prefer projects with shorter payback periods (projects that are more liquid) to projects with longer payback periods, if all other things are equal. Projects with shorter payback periods give an organization more flexibility because funds for other projects become available sooner. Also, managers are less confident about cash flow predictions that stretch far into the future, again favoring shorter payback periods.

Unlike the NPV and IRR methods where managers select a RRR, under the payback method, managers chooses a cutoff period for a project. Projects with a payback period that is less than the cutoff period are considered acceptable, and those with a payback period that is longer than the cutoff period are rejected, Japanese companies favor the payback method over other methods and use cutoff periods ranging from three to five years depending on the risks involved with the project. In general, modern risk management calls for using shorter cutoff periods, the riskier the project. If Jaipur Golden's cutoff period under the payback method is three years, it will reject the new bus.

The payback method is easy to understand. As in DCF methods, the payback method is not affected by accrual accounting conventions such as depreciation. Payback is a useful measure when (1) preliminary screening of many proposals is necessary, (2) interest rates are high, and (3) the expected cash flows in later years of a project are highly uncertain. Under these conditions, companies give much more weight to cash flows in early periods of a capital budgeting project and to recovering the investments they have made, thereby making the payback criterion especially relevant.

Two weaknesses of the payback method are that (1) it fails to explicitly incorporate the time value of money and (2) it does not consider a project's cash flows after the payback period. Consider an alternative to the ₹64,89,000 hybrid bus. Another hybrid bus, with a three-year useful life and no terminal disposal value, requires only a ₹54,00,000 net initial investment and will also result in cash inflows of ₹18,00,000 per year. First, compare the payback periods:

$$\text{Bus 1} = \frac{₹64,89,000}{₹18,00,000} = 3.6 \text{ years}$$

$$\text{Bus 2} = \frac{₹54,00,000}{₹18,00,000} = 3.0 \text{ years}$$

The payback criterion favors bus 2, which has a shorter payback. If the cutoff period were three years, bus 1 would fail to meet the payback criterion.

Consider next the NPV of the two investment options using Jaipur Golden's 8% required rate of return for the hybrid bus investment. At a discount rate of 8%, the NPV of bus 2 is − ₹7,61,400 (2.577, the present value annuity factor for three years at 8% per year from Table 4, times ₹18,00,000 = ₹46,38,600 minus net initial investment of ₹54,00,000). Bus 1, as we know, has a positive NPV of ₹6,98,400 (from Exhibit 21-2). The NPV criterion suggests Jaipur Golden should acquire Bus 1. Bus 2, with a negative NPV, would fail to meet the NPV criterion.

The payback method gives a different answer from the NPV method in this example because the payback method ignores cash flows after the payback period and ignores the time value of money. Another problem with the payback method is that choosing too short a cutoff period can lead to projects with high short-run cash flows being selected. Projects with long-run, positive NPVs will tend to be rejected. Despite these differences, companies find it useful to look at both NPV and payback when making capital investment decisions.

Nonuniform Cash Flows

When cash flows are not uniform, the payback computation takes a cumulative form: The cash flows over successive years are accumulated until the amount of net initial investment is recovered. Suppose Venture Law Group is considering the purchase of video conferencing equipment for ₹15,00,000. The equipment is expected to provide a total cash savings of ₹34,00,000 over the next five years, due to reduced travel costs and more effective use of associates' time. The cash savings occur uniformly throughout each year, but are not uniform across years.

Year	Cash Savings	Cumulative Cash Savings	Net Initial Investment Unrecovered at End of Year
0	—	—	₹15,00,000
1	₹5,00,000	₹5,00,000	10,00,000
2	5,50,000	10,50,000	4,50,000
3	6,00,000	16,50,000	—
4	8,50,000	25,00,000	—
5	9,00,000	34,00,000	—

The chart shows that payback occurs during the third year. Straight-line interpolation within the third year reveals that the final ₹4,50,000 needed to recover the ₹15,00,000 investment (that is, ₹15,00,000 − ₹10,50,000 recovered by the end of year 2) will be achieved halfway through year 3 (in which ₹6,00,000 of cash savings occur):

$$\text{Payback period} = 2 \text{ years} + \left(\frac{₹4,50,000}{₹8,00,000} \times 1 \text{ year} \right) = 2.75 \text{ years}$$

It is relatively simple to adjust the payback method to incorporate the time value of money by using a similar cumulative approach. The **discounted payback method** calculates the amount of time required for the discounted expected future cash flows to recoup the net initial investment in a project. For the videoconferencing example, we can modify the preceding chart by discounting the cash flows at the 8% required rate of return.

Year (1)	Cash Savings (2)	Present Value of ₹10 Discounted at 8% (3)	Discounted Cash Savings (4) = (2) × (3)	Cumulative Discounted Cash Savings (5)	Net Initial Investment Unrecovered at End of Year (6)
0	—	1.000	—	—	₹15,00,000
1	₹5,00,000	0.926	₹4,63,000	₹4,63,000	10,37,000
2	5,50,000	0.857	4,71,350	9,34,350	5,65,650
3	6,00,000	0.794	4,76,400	14,10,750	89,250
4	8,50,000	0.735	6,24,750	20,35,500	—
5	9,00,000	0.681	6,12,900	28,48,400	—

The fourth column represents the present values of the future cash savings. It is evident from the chart that discounted payback occurs between years 3 and 4. At the end of the third year, ₹89,250 of the initial investment is still unrecovered. Comparing this to the ₹6,24,750 in present value of savings achieved in the fourth year, straight-line interpolation then reveals that the discounted payback period is exactly one-seventh of the way into the fourth year:

$$\text{Discounted payback period} = 3 \text{ years} + \left(\frac{89,250}{6,24,750} \times 1 \text{ year} \right) = 3.14 \text{ years}$$

The discounted payback does incorporate the time value of money, but it is still subject to the other criticism of the payback method—cash flows beyond the discounted payback period are ignored, resulting in a bias toward projects with high short-run cash flows. Companies such as Hewlett-Packard value the discounted payback method (HP refers to it as "breakeven time") because they view longer-term cash flows as inherently unpredictable in high-growth industries, such as technology.

Finally, the videoconferencing example has a single cash outflow of ₹15,00,000 in year 0. When a project has multiple cash outflows occurring at different points in time, these outflows are first aggregated to obtain a total cash-outflow figure for the project. For computing the payback period, the cash flows are simply added, with no adjustment for the time value of money. For calculating the discounted payback period, the present values of the outflows are added instead.

Accrual Accounting Rate-of-Return Method

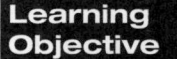

We now consider a fourth method for analyzing the financial aspects of capital budgeting projects. The **accrual accounting rate of return (AARR)** method divides the average annual (accrual accounting) income of a project by a measure of the investment in it. We illustrate this method for Jaipur Golden using the project's net initial investment as the amount in the denominator:

$$\text{Accrual accounting rate of return} = \frac{\text{Increase in expected average annual after-tax operating income}}{\text{Net initial investment}}$$

If Jaipur Golden purchases the new hybrid bus, its net initial investment is ₹64,89,000. The increase in expected average annual after-tax operating cash inflows is ₹17,40,000. This amount is the expected after-tax total operating cash inflows of ₹87,00,000 (₹18,00,000 for four years and ₹15,00,000 in year 5), divided by the time horizon of five years. Suppose that the new bus results in additional depreciation deductions of ₹12,00,000 per year (₹13,20,000 in annual depreciation for the new bus, relative to ₹1,20,000 per year on the existing bus).[5] The increase in expected average annual after-tax income is therefore ₹5,40,000 (the difference between the cash flow increase of ₹17,40,000 and the depreciation increase of ₹12,00,000). The AARR on net initial investment is computed as:

$$\text{AARR} = \frac{₹17,40,000 - ₹12,00,000}{₹64,89,000} = \frac{₹5,40,000 \text{ per year}}{₹64,89,000} = 0.083, \text{ or } 8.3\% \text{ per year}$$

The 8.3% figure for AARR indicates the average rate at which a rupee of investment generates after-tax operating income. The new hybrid bus has a low AARR for two reasons: (1) the use of net initial investment as the denominator, and (2) the use of income as the numerator, which necessitates deducting depreciation charges from the annual operating cash flows. To mitigate the first issue, many companies calculate AARR using an average level of investment. This alternative procedure recognizes that the book value of the investment declines over time. In its simplest form, average investment for Jaipur Golden is calculated as the arithmetic mean of the net initial investment of ₹64,89,000 and the net terminal cash flow of ₹3,00,000 (terminal disposal value of bus equal to ₹0 and terminal recovery of working capital of ₹3,00,000) is

---

[5] We provide further details on these numbers in the next section; see next page.

$$\text{Average investment over five years} = \frac{\text{Net initial investment} + \text{Net terminal cash flow}}{2}$$

$$= \frac{₹64,89,000 + ₹3,00,000}{2} = ₹33,94,500$$

The AARR on average investment is then calculated as follows:

$$AARR = \frac{₹5,40,000}{₹33,94,500} = 0.159, \text{ or } 15.9\% \text{ per year}$$

Our point here is that companies vary in how they calculate AARR. There is no uniformly preferred approach. Be sure you understand how AARR is defined in each individual situation. Projects with AARR that exceeds a specified hurdle required rate of return are regarded as acceptable (the higher the AARR, the better the project is considered to be).

The AARR method is similar to the IRR method in that both methods calculate a rate-of-return percentage. The AARR method calculates the return using operating-income numbers after considering accruals and taxes, whereas the IRR method calculates the return on the basis of after-tax cash flows and the time value of money. Because cash flows and time value of money are central to capital budgeting decisions, the IRR method is regarded as better than the AARR method.

AARR computations are easy to understand, and they use numbers reported in the financial statements. The AARR gives managers an idea of how the accounting numbers they will report in the future will be affected if a project is accepted. Unlike the payback method, which ignores cash flows after the payback period, the AARR method considers income earned *throughout* a project's expected useful life. Unlike the NPV method, the AARR method uses accrual accounting income numbers, it does not track cash flows, and it ignores the time value of money. Critics of the AARR method argue that these are drawbacks.

Overall, keep in mind that companies frequently use multiple methods for evaluating capital investment decisions. When different methods lead to different rankings of projects, more weight should be given to the NPV method because the assumptions made by the NPV method are most consistent with making decisions that maximize company value.

◄ **Decision Point**

What are the strengths and weaknesses of the accrual accounting rate-of-return (AARR) method for evaluating long-term projects?

Relevant Cash Flows in Discounted Cash Flow Analysis

Learning Objective 5

Identify relevant cash inflows and outflows for capital budgeting decisions

. . . the differences in expected future cash flows resulting from the investment

So far, we have so far examined methods for evaluating long-term projects in settings where the expected future cash flows of interest were assumed to be known. One of the biggest challenges in capital budgeting, particularly DCF analysis, is determining which cash flows are relevant in making an investment selection. Relevant cash flows are the differences in expected future cash flows as a result of making the investment. In the Jaipur Golden example, the relevant cash flows are the differences in expected future cash flows that will result from continuing to use one of the firm's old buses versus purchasing a new hybrid bus. *When reading this section, focus on identifying expected future cash flows and the differences in expected future cash flows.*

To illustrate relevant cash flow analysis, consider a more complex version of the Jaipur Golden example with these additional assumptions:

■ Jaipur Golden is a profitable company. The income tax rate is 40% of operating income each year.

- The before-tax additional revenues from the hybrid bus are ₹22,00,000 in years 1 through 4 and ₹17,00,000 in year 5.
- For tax purposes, Jaipur Golden uses the straight-line depreciation method and assumes there is no terminal disposal value of the bus.
- Gains or losses on the sale of depreciable assets are taxed at the same rate as ordinary income.
- The tax effects of cash inflows and outflows occur at the same time that the cash inflows and outflows occur.
- Jaipur Golden uses an 8% required rate of return for discounting after-tax cash flows.

The data for the buses follow:

	Old Bus	New Hybrid Bus
Purchase price	–	₹66,00,000
Current book value	₹6,00,000	–
Current disposal value	2,85,000	Not applicable
Terminal disposal value 5 years from now	0	0
Annual depreciation	1,20,000[a]	13,20,000[b]
Working capital required	60,000	3,60,000

[a]₹6,00,000 ÷ 5 years = ₹1,20,000 annual depreciation.

[b]₹66,00,000 ÷ 5 years = ₹13,20,000 annual depreciation.

Relevant After-Tax Flows

We use the concepts of differential cost and differential revenue introduced in Chapter 11. We compare (1) the after-tax cash outflows as a result of replacing the old bus with (2) the additional after-tax cash inflows generated from using the new bus rather than the old bus.

As Benjamin Franklin said, "Two things in life are certain: death and taxes." Income taxes are a fact of life for most corporations and individuals. It is important first to understand how income taxes affect cash flows in each year. Exhibit 21-5 shows how investing in the new bus will affect Jaipur Golden's cash flow from operations and its income taxes in year 1. Recall that Jaipur Golden will generate ₹22,00,000 in before-tax additional operating cash flows by investing in the new bus but it will record additional depreciation of ₹12,00,000 (₹13,20,000 − ₹1,20,000) for tax purposes.

Panel A shows, using two methods based on the income statement, that the year 1 cash flow from operations, net of income taxes, equals ₹18,00,000. The first method focuses on cash items only, the ₹22,00,000 operating cash inflows minus income taxes of ₹4,00,000. The second method starts with the ₹6,00,000 increase in net income (calculated after subtracting the ₹12,00,000 additional depreciation deductions for income tax purposes) and adds back that ₹12,00,000, because depreciation is an operating cost that reduces net income but is a noncash item itself.

Panel B of Exhibit 21-5 describes a third method frequently used to compute the cash flow from operations, net of income taxes. The easiest way to interpret the third method is to think of the Government as a 40% (equal to the tax rate) partner in Jaipur Golden. Each time Jaipur Golden obtains operating cash inflows, C, its income is higher by C, so it will pay 40% of the operating cash inflows, C (0.40C) in taxes. This results in additional after-tax cash operating flows of C − 0.40C, which in this example is ₹22,00,000 − (0.40 x ₹22,00,000) = ₹13,20,000, or ₹22,00,000 x (1 − 0.40) = ₹13,20,000.

PANEL A: Two Methods Based on the Income Statement

Exhibit 21-5

Effect on Cash Flow from Operations, Net of Income Taxes, in Year 1 for Jaipur golden's Investment in the New Hybrid Bus

R	Operating cash inflows from investment in bus	₹22,00,000
D	Additional depreciation deduction	12,00,000
OI	Increase in operating income	10,00,000
T	Income taxes (Income tax rate $t \times OI$) =	
	40% × ₹10,00,000	4,00,000
NI	Increase in net income	₹3,00,000
	Increase in cash flow from operations, net of income taxes	
	Method 1: $C - T$ = ₹22,00,000 − ₹4,00,000 = ₹18,00,000 or	
	Method 2: $NI + D$ = ₹6,00,000 + ₹12,00,000 = ₹10,00,000	

PANEL B: Item-by-Item Method

	Effect of cash operating flows	₹22,00,000
C	Operating cash inflows from investment in bus	
$t \times C$	Deduct income tax cash outflow at 40%	8,80,000
$C - (1 \times t)$	After-tax cash flow from operations	13,20,000
$= (1 - t) \times R$	(excluding the depreciation effect)	
	Effect of depreciation	
D	Additional depreciation deduction, ₹12,00,000	
$t \times D$	Income tax cash savings from additional depreciation	
	deduction at 40% × ₹12,00,000	4,80,000
$C \times (1\text{-}t) + t \times D$	Cash flow from operations, net of income taxes	₹18,00,000

To achieve the higher operating cash inflows, C, Jaipur Golden incurs higher depreciation charges, D, from investing in the new bus. Depreciation costs do not directly affect cash flows because depreciation is a noncash cost, but higher depreciation cost *lowers* Jaipur Golden's taxable income by D, saving income tax cash outflows of $0.40D$, which in this example is $0.40 \times ₹12,00,000 = ₹4,80,000$.

Letting t = tax rate, cash flow from operations, net of income taxes, in this example equals the operating cash inflows, C, minus the tax payments on these inflows, $t \times C$, plus the tax savings on depreciation deductions, $t \times D$: ₹22,00,000 − (0.40 × ₹22,00,000) + (0.40 × ₹12,00,000) = ₹22,00,000 − ₹8,80,000 + ₹4,80,000 = ₹18,00,000.

By the same logic, each time Jaipur Golden has a gain on the sale of assets, G, it will show tax outflows, $t \times G$; and each time Jaipur Golden has a loss on the sale of assets, L, it will show tax benefits or savings, $t \times L$.

Categories of Cash Flows

A capital investment project typically has three categories of cash flows: (1) the net initial investment in the project, which includes the acquisition of assets and any associated additions to working capital, minus the after-tax cash flow from the disposal of existing assets; (2) the after-tax cash flow from operations (including income tax cash savings from annual depreciation deductions) each year; and (3) the after-tax cash flow from terminal disposal of an asset and recovery of working capital invested at the termination of the project. We use the Jaipur Golden example to discuss these three categories.

As you work through the cash flows in each category, refer to Exhibit . This exhibit sketches the relevant cash flows for Jaipur Golden's decision to purchase the new bus as described in items 1 through 3 here. Note that the total relevant cash flows for each year equal the relevant cash flows used in Exhibits 21-2 and 21-3 to illustrate the NPV and IRR methods.

Exhibit 21-6	Relevant Cash Inflows and Outflows for Jaipur golden's Hybrid bus

	File Edit View Insert Format Tools Data Window Help							
	A	B	C	D	E	F	G	H
1				**Sketch of Relevant Cash Flows at End of Year**				
2			**0**	**1**	**2**	**3**	**4**	**5**
3	**1a.**	Initial hybrid bus investment	₹(66,00,000)					
4	**1b.**	Initial working-capital investmen	(3,00,000)					
5	**1c.**	After-tax cash flow from current disposal						
6		of old bus	4,11,000					
7	Net initial investment		₹(64,89,000)					
8	**2a.**	Annual after-tax cash flow from operations						
9		(excluding the depreciation effect)		₹13,20,000	₹13,20,000	₹13,20,000	₹13,20,000	10,20,000
10	**2b.**	Income tax cash savings from annual						
11		depreciation deductions		4,80,000	4,80,000	4,80,000	4,80,000	4,80,000
12	**3a.**	After-tax cash flow from terminal disposal						
13		of bus						0
14	**3b.**	After-tax cash flow from recovery of						
15		working capital						30,00,000
16	Total relevant cash flows,							
17	as shown in Exhibits 21-2 and 21-3		₹(64,89,000)	₹18,00,000	₹18,00,000	₹18,00,000	₹18,00,000	₹18,00,000
18								

1. **Net Initial Investment** Three components of net-initial-investment cash flows are (a) the cash outflow to purchase the hybrid bus, (b) the cash outflow for working capital, and (c) the after-tax cash inflow from current disposal of the old bus.

   1a. *Initial bus investment.* These outflows, made for purchasing plant and equipment, occur at the beginning of the project's life and include cash outflows for transporting and installing the equipment. In the Jaipur Golden example, the ₹66,00,000 cost (including transportation and initial preparation) of the hybrid bus is an outflow in year 0. These cash flows are relevant to the capital budgeting decision because they will be incurred only if Jaipur Golden decides to purchase the new bus.

   1b. *Initial working-capital investment.* Initial investments in plant and equipment are usually accompanied by additional investments in working capital. These additional investments take the form of current assets, such as accounts receivable and inventories, minus current liabilities, such as accounts payable. Working-capital investments are similar to plant and equipment investments in that they require cash. The magnitude of the investment generally increases as a function of the level of additional sales generated by the project. However, the exact relationship varies based on the nature of the project and the operating cycle of the industry. For a given rupee of sales, a maker of heavy equipment, for example, would require more working capital support than Jaipur Golden, which in turn has to invest more in working capital than a retail grocery store.

   The Jaipur Golden example assumes a ₹3,00,000 additional investment in working capital if the hybrid bus is acquired. The additional working-capital investment is the difference between working capital required to operate the new bus (₹3,60,000) and working capital required to operate the old bus (₹60,000).

The ₹3,00,000 additional investment in working capital a consequence of the higher cost of replacement batteries and spare parts for the technologically advanced new bus is a cash outflow in year 0 and is returned, that is, becomes a cash inflow, at the end of year 5.

1c. *After-tax cash flow from current disposal of old bus.* Any cash received from disposal of the old bus is a relevant cash inflow (in year 0) because it is a cash flow that differs between the alternatives of investing and not investing in the new bus. Jaipur Golden will it dispose of the old bus for ₹2,85,000 only if it inverts in the new hybride bus. Recall that the book value (which is original cost minus accumulated depreciation) of the old equipment is irrelevant to the decision because it is a past, or sunk, cost. However, when tax considerations are included, the book value does play a role because it determines the gain or loss on the sale of the bus and, therefore, the taxes paid (or saved) on the transaction.

Consider the tax consequences of disposing of the old bus. We first have to compute the gain or loss on disposal:

Current disposal value of old bus	₹2,85,000
Deduct current book value of old bus	6,00,000
Loss on disposal of bus	₹(3,15,000)

Any loss on the sale of assets lowers taxable income and results in tax savings. The after-tax cash flow from disposal of the old bus equals:

Current disposal value of old bus	₹2,85,000
Tax savings on loss (0.40 × ₹3,35,000)	1,26,000
After-tax cash inflow from current disposal of old bus	₹4,11,000

The sum of items **1a**, **1b**, and **1c** appears in Exhibit 21-6 as the year 0 net initial investment for the new hybrid bus. It equals to ₹64,89,000 (initial bus investment, ₹66,00,000, plus additional working-capital investment, ₹3,00,000, minus after-tax cash inflow from current disposal of the old bus, ₹4,11,000).[6]

2. **Cash Flow from Operations** This category includes the difference between each year's cash flow from operations under the two alternatives. Organizations make capital investments to generate future cash inflows. These inflows may result from producing and selling additional goods or, as for Jaipur Golden, from savings in fuel, maintenance, and operating costs and the additional revenue from higher ticket prices as well as new customers who wish to take advantage of the greater comfort and accessibility of the hybrid bus. The annual cash flow from operations can be net outflows in some years. For example, Chevron periodically upgrades its oil extraction equipment, and when it does, the cash flow from operations tends to be negative for the site being upgraded. However, in the long run, the upgrades are NPV positive. Always focus on the cash flow from operations, not on revenues and expenses under accrual accounting.

Jaipur Golden's additional operating cash inflows—₹22,00,000 in each of the first 4 years and ₹17,00,000 in the fifth year—are relevant because they are expected future cash flows that will differ depending on whether the firm purchases the new bus. The after-tax effects of these cash flows follow.

2a. *Annual after-tax cash flow from operations (excluding the depreciation effect).* The 40% tax rate reduces the benefit of the ₹22,00,000 additional operating cashflow

---

[6] To illustrate the case when there is a gain on disposal, suppose that the old bus could be sold now for ₹7,00,000 instead. Then, the firm would record a gain on disposal of ₹1,00,000 (₹7,00,000 less the book value of ₹6,00,000), resulting in additional tax payments of ₹40,000 (0.40 tax rate × ₹1,00,000 gain). The after-tax cash inflow from current disposal would therefore equal ₹6,60,000 (the disposal value of ₹7,00,000, less the tax payment of ₹40,000).

for years 1 through 4 with the new hybrid bus. The after-tax cash flow (excluding the depreciation effect) is:

Annual cash flow from operations with new bus	₹22,00,000
Deduct income tax payments (0.40 × ₹22,00,000)	6,80,000
Annual after-tax cash flow from operations	₹13,20,000

For year 5, the after-tax cash flow (excluding the depreciation effect) is as follows:

Annual cash flow from operations with new bus	₹17,00,000
Deduct income tax payments (0.40 × ₹10,50,000)	6,80,000
Annual after-tax cash flow from operations	₹10,20,000

Exhibit 21-6, item **2a**, shows that the after-tax cash flows are ₹13,20,000 in each of the years 1 through 4 and ₹10,20,000 for year 5.

To reinforce the idea about focusing on cash flows, consider the following additional fact about Jaipur Golden. Suppose its total administrative costs will not change whether the company purchases a new bus or keeps the old one. The administrative costs are allocated to individual buses—Jaipur Golden has several—on the basis of the costs for operating each bus. Because the new hybrid bus would have lower operating costs, the administrative costs allocated to it would be ₹3,00,000 less than the amount allocated to the bus it would replace. How should Jaipur Golden incorporate the ₹3,00,000 decrease in allocated administrative costs in the relevant cash flow analysis?

To answer that question, we need to ask, "Do total administrative costs decrease at Jaipur Golden Transport as a result of acquiring the new bus?" In our example, they do not. They remain the same whether or not the new bus is acquired. Only the administrative costs allocated to individual buses change. The administrative costs allocated to the new bus are ₹3,00,000 less than the amount allocated to the bus it would replace. This ₹3,00,000 difference in costs would be allocated to other buses in the company. That is, no cash flow savings in total costs would occur. Therefore, the ₹3,00,000 should not be included as part of the annual cash savings from operations.

Next consider the effects of depreciation. The depreciation line item is itself irrelevant in a DCF analysis. That's because depreciation is a noncash allocation of costs, whereas DCF is based on inflows and outflows of cash. If a DCF method is used, the initial cost of equipment is regarded as a lump-sum outflow of cash in year 0. Deducting depreciation expenses from operating cash inflows would result in counting the lump-sum amount twice. However, depreciation results in income tax cash savings. These tax savings are a relevant cash flow.

2b. *Income tax cash savings from annual depreciation deductions.* Tax deductions for depreciation, in effect, partially offset the cost of acquiring the new hybrid bus. By purchasing the new bus, Jaipur Golden is able to deduct ₹13,20,000 in depreciation each year, relative to the ₹1,20,000 depreciation on the old bus. The additional annual depreciation deduction of ₹1,20,000 results in incremental income tax cash savings of 1,20,000 × 0.4, or ₹4,80,000 annually. Exhibit 21-6, item **2b**, shows that the after tax cash flows ₹13,20,000 in each of the years 1 through 4 and ₹10,20,000 for year 5.[7]

For economic-policy reasons, usually to encourage (or in some cases, discourage) investments, tax laws specify which depreciation methods and which depreciable lives are permitted. Suppose the government permitted accelerated

---

[7] If Jaipur Golden were a nonprofit foundation not subject to income taxes, cash flow from operations would equal ₹22,00,000 in years 1 through 4 and ₹17,00,000 in year 5. The revenues would not be reduced by 40%, nor would there be income tax cash savings from the depreciation deduction.

depreciation to be used, allowing for higher depreciation deductions in earlier years. Should Jaipur Golden then use accelerated depreciation? Yes, because there is a general rule in tax planning for profitable companies such as Jaipur Golden: When there is a legal choice, take the depreciation (or any other deduction) sooner rather than later. Doing so causes the (cash) income tax savings to occur earlier, which increases a project's NPV.

3. **Terminal Disposal of Investment.** The disposal of an investment generally increases cash inflow of a project at its termination. An error in forecasting the disposal value is seldom critical for a long-duration project because the present value of the amounts to be received in the distant future is usually small. For Jaipur Golden, the two components of the terminal disposal value of an investment are (a) the after-tax cash flow from the terminal disposal of buses and (b) the after-tax cash flow from recovery of working capital.

3a. *After-tax cash flow from terminal disposal of buses.* At the end of the useful life of the project, the bus's terminal disposal value is usually considerably less than the net initial investment (and sometimes zero). The relevant cash inflow is the difference in the expected after-tax cash inflow from terminal disposal at the end of 5 years under the two alternatives. Disposing of both the existing and the new bus will result in a zero after-tax cash inflow in year 5. Hence, there is no difference in the disposal-related after-tax cash inflows of the two alternatives.

Because both the existing and new bus have disposal values that equal their book values at the time of their disposal (in each case, this value is ₹0), there are no tax effects for either alternative. What if either the existing or the new bus had a terminal value that differed from its book value at the time of disposal? In that case, the approach for computing the terminal inflow is identical to that for calculating the after-tax cash flow from current disposal illustrated earlier in part 1c.

3b. *After-tax cash flow from terminal recovery of working-capital investment.* The initial investment in working capital is usually fully recouped when the project is terminated. At that time, inventories and accounts receivable necessary to support the project are no longer needed. Jaipur Golden receives cash equal to the book value of its working capital. Thus, there is no gain or loss on working capital and, hence, no tax consequences. The relevant cash inflow is the difference in the expected working capital recovered under the two alternatives. At the end of year 5, Jaipur Golden recovers ₹3,60,000 cash from working capital if it invests in the new hybrid bus versus ₹60,000 if it continues to use the old bus. The relevant cash inflow at the end of year 5 if Jaipur Golden invests in the new bus is thus ₹3,00,000 (₹3,60,000 − ₹60,000).

Some capital investment projects *reduce* working capital. Assume that a computer-integrated manufacturing (CIM) project with a 7-year life will reduce inventories and, hence, working capital by ₹200 million from, say, ₹500 million to ₹300 million. This reduction will be represented as a ₹200 million cash *inflow* for the project in year 0. At the end of 7 years, the recovery of working capital will show a relevant incremental cash outflow of ₹200 million. That's because, at the end of year 7, the company recovers only ₹300 million of working capital under CIM, rather than the ₹500 million of working capital it would have recovered had it not implemented CIM.

Exhibit 21-6 shows items 3a and 3b in the "year 5" column. The relevant cash flows in Exhibit 21-6 serve as inputs for the four capital budgeting methods described earlier in the chapter.

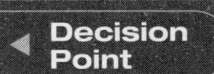

Decision Point

What are the relevant cash inflows and outflows for capital budgeting decisions? How should accrual accounting concepts be considered?

Project Management and Performance Evaluation

We have so far looked at ways to identify relevant cash flows and appropriate techniques for analyzing them. The final stage (stage 5) of capital budgeting begins with implementing the decision, or managing the project.[8] This includes management control of the investment activity itself, as well as management control of the project as a whole.

Capital budgeting projects, such as purchasing a hybrid bus or videoconferencing equipment, are easier to implement than projects that involve building shopping malls or manufacturing plants. The building projects are more complex, so monitoring and controlling the investment schedules and budgets are critical to successfully completing the investment activity. This leads to the second dimension of stage 5 in the capital budgeting process: *evaluate performance and learn*.

Post-Investment Audits

A post-investment audit provides managers with feedback about the performance of a project so they can compare the actual results to the costs and benefits expected at the time the project was selected. Suppose the actual outcomes (such as the additional operating cash flows from Jaipur Golden's purchase of a new hybrid bus) are much lower than expected. Managers must then determine if this result occurred because the original estimates were overly optimistic or because of implementation problems. Either of these explanations is a concern.

Optimistic estimates can result in managers accepting a project they should reject. To discourage unrealistic forecasts, companies such as DuPont maintain records comparing the actual results of the firm's projects to the estimates individual managers either made or signed off on when seeking approval for capital investments. Post-investment audits prevent managers from overstating the expected cash inflows from projects and accepting projects they should reject. Implementation problems, such as weak project management, poor quality control, or inadequate marketing, are also a concern. Post-investment audits help to alert senior management to these problems so they can be quickly corrected.

Companies should perform post-investment audits with thought and care, and only after the outcomes of projects are fully known. Performing audits too early can be misleading. In addition, obtaining actual results to compare against estimates is often difficult. For example, in any particular period, macroeconomic factors, such as the weather and changes in fuel prices, can greatly affect the ridership on buses and the costs of running them. Consequently, the overall additional net revenues from Jaipur Golden's new hybrid bus may not be immediately comparable to the estimated revenues. A better evaluation would look at the average revenues across a couple of seasons.

Performance Evaluation

As the preceding discussion suggests, ideally one should evaluate managers on a project-by-project basis and look at how well managers achieve the amounts and timing of forecasted cash flows. In practice, however, companies often evaluate managers based on aggregate information, especially when multiple projects are under way at any point in time. It is important then for companies to ensure that the method of evaluation does not conflict with the use of the NPV method for making capital budgeting decisions. For example, suppose Jaipur Golden uses the accrual accounting rate of return generated in each period to assess its managers. We know the managers should purchase the hybrid bus because it has a positive NPV of ₹6,98,400. However, they may reject the project if the AARR of 8.3% on the net initial investment is lower than the minimum accounting rate of return Jaipur Golden requires them to achieve.

---

[8] In this section, we do not consider the different options for financing a project (refer to a text on corporate finance for details).

There is an inconsistency between promoting the NPV method as best for capital budgeting decisions and then using a different method to evaluate performance. Even though the NPV method is best for capital budgeting decisions, managers will be tempted to make those decisions based on the method on which they are being evaluated. The temptation becomes more pronounced if managers are frequently transferred (or promoted) or if their bonuses are affected by the level of year-to-year income earned under accrual accounting.

Other conflicts between decision making and performance evaluation persist even if a company uses similar measures for both purposes. If the AARR on the hybrid bus exceeds the minimum required AARR but is below Jaipur Golden's current AARR in the region, the manager may still be tempted to reject purchase of the hybrid bus because the lower AARR of the hybrid bus will reduce the AARR of the entire region and hurt the manager's reported performance. Or consider an example where the cash inflows from the hybrid bus occur mostly in the later years of the project. Then, even if the project's AARR exceeds the current AARR of the projects overseen by the manager (as well as the minimum required return), the manager may still reject the purchase because for the first few years it will have a negative effect on the rate of return earned under accrual accounting. In Chapter 23, we study these conflicts in greater depth and describe how performance evaluation models such as economic value added (EVA®) help lessen these conflicts.

> **◄ Decision Point**
>
> What conflicts can arise between using DCF methods for capital budgeting decisions and accrual accounting for performance evaluation? How can these conflicts be reduced?

Strategic Considerations in Capital Budgeting

Managers consider a company's strategic goals when making capital budgeting decisions. Strategic decisions by United Airlines, Westin Hotels, FedEx, and Pizza Hut to expand in Europe and Asia required capital investments in several countries. The strategic decision by Barnes & Noble to support book sales over the Internet required capital investments creating barnesandnoble.com and an Internet infrastructure. AOL's desire to create an enhanced digital destination with greater appeal for consumers and advertisers led to its purchase of The Huffington Post, as well as increased investment in editorial staff and sales representatives and higher marketing expenses. AstraZeneca's decision to develop Nexium as a patented replacement drug for its blockbuster Prilosec to prevent the formation of gastric acid led to major investments in R&D and marketing. Toyota's decision to offer a line of hybrids across both its Toyota and Lexus platforms required start-up investments to form a hybrid division and ongoing investments to fund the division's continuing research efforts.

> **Learning Objective 7**
>
> Explain how managers can use capital budgeting to achieve their firms' strategic goals
>
> ...make critical investments aligned with the firm's objectives but whose benefits are uncertain or difficult to estimate

Capital investment decisions that are strategic in nature require managers to consider a broad range of factors that may be difficult to estimate. Consider some of the difficulties of justifying investments made by companies such as Mitsubishi, Sony, and Audi in computer-integrated manufacturing (CIM) technology. In CIM, computers give instructions that quickly and automatically set up and run equipment to manufacture many different products. Quantifying these benefits requires some notion of how quickly consumer demand will change in the future. CIM technology also increases worker knowledge of and experience with automation; however, the benefit of this knowledge and experience is difficult to measure. Managers must develop judgment and intuition to make these decisions.

Investment in Research and Development

Companies such as GlaxoSmithKline, in the pharmaceutical industry, and Intel, in the semiconductor industry, regard research and development (R&D) projects as important strategic investments. The distant payoffs from R&D investments, however, are more uncertain than other investments such as new equipment purchases. On the positive side, R&D investments are often staged: As time unfolds, companies can increase or decrease the resources committed to a project based on how successful it has been up to that point. This option feature of R&D investments, called real options, is an important aspect of R&D investments and increases the NPV of these investments, because a company can limit its losses when things are going badly and take advantage of new opportunities when things are going well. As an example, a pharmaceutical company can increase or decrease its investment in an R&D joint venture based on the progress of the clinical trials of new drugs being developed by the venture.

Customer Value and Capital Budgeting

Finally, note that managers can use the framework described in this chapter to both evaluate investment projects and to make strategic decisions regarding which customers to invest in. Consider Potato Supreme, which makes potato products for sale to retail outlets. It is currently analyzing two of its customers: Shine Stores and Always Open. Potato Supreme predicts the following cash flow from operations, net of income taxes (in thousands), from each customer account for the next five years:

	2014	2015	2016	2017	2018
Shine Stores	₹14,500	₹13,050	₹11,750	₹10,580	₹9,500
Always Open	6,900	11,600	19,000	29,500	41,600

Which customer is more valuable to Potato Supreme? Looking at only the current period, 2014, Shine Stores provides more than double the cash flow compared to Always Open (₹14,500 versus ₹6,900). A different picture emerges, however, if you look at the entire five-year horizon. Potato Supreme anticipates Always Open's orders to increase; meanwhile, it expects Shine Stores' orders to decline. Using Potato Supreme's 10% RRR, the NPV of the Always Open customer is ₹76,100, compared with ₹45,910 for Shine Stores (computations not shown). Note how NPV captures in its estimate of customer value the future growth of Always Open. Potato Supreme uses this information to allocate more resources and sales-persons to service the Always Open account. Potato Supreme can also use NPV calculations to examine the effects of alternative ways of increasing customer loyalty and retention, such as introducing frequent-purchaser cards.

A comparison of year-to-year changes in customer NPV estimates highlights whether managers have been successful in maintaining long-run profitable relationships with their customers. Suppose the NPV of Potato Supreme's customer base declines 15% in one year. The firm's managers can then examine the reasons for the decline, such as aggressive pricing by competitors, and devise new-product development and marketing strategies for the future.

Capital One, a financial-services company, uses NPV to estimate the value of differ-ent credit-card customers. Cellular telephone companies such as Cellular One and Verizon Wireless attempt to sign up customers for multiple years of service. The objective is to prevent "customer churn,"—that is, customers switching frequently from one company to another. The higher the probability is of customer switching, the lower the Jaipur Golden customer's NPV.

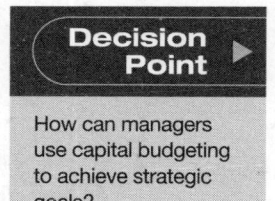

Decision Point

How can managers use capital budgeting to achieve strategic goals?

Problem for Self-Study

PART A

Returning to the Jaipur Golden hybrid bus project, assume that Jaipur Golden is a *non profit organization* and that the expected additional operating cash inflows are ₹24,00,000 in years 1 through 4 and ₹21,00,000 in year 5. The net initial investment is ₹66,15,000 (new bus, ₹66,00,000 plus additional working capital, ₹3,00,000 minus terminal dis-posal value of old bus, ₹2,85,000). All other facts are unchanged: a five-year useful life, no terminal disposal value, and an 8% RRR. Year 5 cash inflows are ₹24,00,000, which includes a ₹3,00,000 recovery of working capital.

Calculate the following:

1. Net present value
2. Internal rate of return
3. Payback
4. Accrual accounting rate of return on net initial investment

Solution

1. NPV = ₹24,00,000 × 3.993) – ₹66,15,000
     = ₹95,83,200 – ₹66,15,000 = ₹29,68,200

2. There are several approaches to computing IRR. One is to use a calculator with an IRR function. This approach gives an IRR of 23.8%. Another approach is to use Table 4 in Appendix A at the end of the text:

$$₹66,15,000 = ₹24,00,000\,F$$

$$F = \frac{₹66,15,000}{₹24,00,000} = 2.756$$

On the five-period line of Table 4, the column closest to 2.756 is 24%. To obtain a more-accurate number, use straight-line interpolation:

	Present Value Factors	
22%	2.864	2.864
IRR	—	2.756
24%	2.745	—
Difference	0.199	0.108

$$IRR = 22\% + \frac{0.108}{0.119}\ (2\%) = 23.8\%\ \text{per year}$$

3. $Payback\ period = \dfrac{\text{Net initial investment}}{\text{Uniform increase in annual future cash flows}}$

     = ₹66,15,000 ÷ ₹24,00,000 = 2.76 years

4. $$AARR = \frac{\text{Increase in expected average annual operating income}}{\text{Net initial investment}}$$

Increase in expected average annual operating cash inflows = [(₹24,00,000 × 4) + ₹21,00,000] ÷ 5 years

= ₹1,17,00,000 ÷ 5 + ₹23,40,000

Increase in annual depreciation = ₹12,00,000 (₹13,20,000 – ₹1,20,000)

Increase in expected average annual operarating income = ₹23,40,000 – ₹12,00,000 = ₹11,40,000

$$AARR = \frac{₹11,40,000}{₹66,15,000} = 17.2\%\ \text{per year}$$

PART B

Assume that Jaipur Golden is subject to income tax at a 40% rate. All other information from Part A is unchanged. Compute the NPV of the new hybrid bus project.

Solution

To save space, Exhibit 21-7 shows the calculations using a format slightly different from the format used in this chapter. Item **2a** is where the new cash flow assumption affects the NPV analysis (compared with Exhibit 21-6). All other amounts in Exhibit 21-7 are identical to the corresponding amounts in Exhibit 21-6. For years 1 through 4, after-tax cash flow (excluding the depreciation effect) is as follows :

Annual cash flow from operations with new bus	₹24,00,000
Deduct income tax payments (0.40 × ₹24,00,000)	9,60,000
Annual after-tax cash flow from operations	₹14,40,000

For year 5, after-tax cash flow (excluding the depreciation effect) is as follows:

Annual cash flow from operations with new bus	₹21,00,000
Deduct income tax payments (0.40 × ₹21,00,000)	8,40,000
Annual after-tax cash flow from operations	₹12,60,000

NPV in Exhibit 21-7 is ₹12,59,280. As computed in Part A, NPV when there are no income taxes is ₹29,68,200. The difference in these two NPVs illustrates the impact of income taxes in capital budgeting analysis.

Exhibit 21-7 — Net Present Value Method Incorporating Income Taxes: Jaipur Golden's Hybrid Bus with Revised Annual Cash Flow from Operations

		Home	Insert	Page Layout	Formulas	Data	Review	View			
	A	B	C	D	E	F	G	H	I	J
1			Present Value	Present Value of		Sketch of Relevant Cash Flows at End of Year				
2			of Cash Flow	₹10 Discounted at 8%	0	1	2	3	4	5
3	1a.	Initial hybrid bus investment	₹(66,00,000)	10.000	₹(66,00,000)					
4										
5	1b.	Initial working-capital investment	(3,00,000)	10.000	₹(3,00,000)					
6	1c.	After-tax cash inflow from current disposal								
7		of old bus	4,11,000	10.000	₹4,11,000					
8	Net initial investment		(64,89,000)							
9	2a.	Annual after-tax cash flow from operations								
10		(excluding the depreciation effect)								
11		Year 1	13,33,440	0.926		₹14,40,000				
12		Year 2	12,34,080	0.857			₹14,40,000			
13		Year 3	11,43,360	0.794				₹14,40,000		
14		Year 4	10,58,400	0.735					₹14,40,000	
15		Year 5	8,58,060	0.681						₹12,60,000
16	2b.	Income tax cash savings from annual								
17		depreciation deductions								
18		Year 1	4,44,480	0.926		₹4,80,000				
19		Year 2	4,11,360	0.857			₹4,80,000			
20		Year 3	3,81,120	0.794				₹4,80,000		
21		Year 4	3,52,800	0.735					₹4,80,000	
22		Year 5	3,26,880	0.681						₹4,80,000
23	3.	After-tax cash flow from recovery of								
24		a. Terminal disposal of bus	0	0.681						₹0
25		b. Recovery of working capital	2,04,300	0 681						₹(3,00,000)
26	NPV if new hybrid bus purchased		₹12,59,280							
27										

Decision Points

The following question-and-answer format summarizes the chapter's learning objectives. Each decision presents a key question related to a learning objective. The guidelines are the answer to that question.

Decision	Guidelines
1. What are the five stages of capital budgeting?	Capital budgeting is long-run planning for proposed investment projects. The five stages of capital budgeting are as follows: (1) Identify projects: Identify potential capital investments aligned with the organization's strategy; (2) Obtain information: Gather information from all parts of the value chain to evaluate alternative projects; (3) Make predictions: Forecast all potential cash flows attributable to the alternative projects; (4) Choose among alternatives: Determine which investment yields the greatest benefit and the least cost to the organization; and (5) Implement the decision, evaluate performance, and learn: Obtain funding and make the investments selected in stage 4; track the realized cash flows, compare them against estimated numbers, and revise plans if necessary.
2. What are the two primary discounted cash flow (DCF) methods for project evaluation?	The two main DCF methods are the net present value (NPV) method and the internal rate-of-return (IRR) method. The NPV method calculates the expected net monetary gain or loss from a project by discounting to the present all expected future cash inflows and outflows, using the required rate of return. A project is acceptable in financial terms if it has a positive NPV. The IRR method computes the rate of return (also called the discount rate) at which a project's present value of expected cash inflows equals the present value of its expected cash outflows. A project is acceptable in financial terms if its IRR exceeds the required rate of return. DCF is the best approach to capital budgeting. It explicitly includes all project cash flows and recognizes the time value of money. The NPV method is the preferred DCF method.
3. What are the payback and discounted payback methods? What are their main weaknesses?	The payback method measures the time it will take to recoup, in the form of cash inflows, the total cash amount invested in a project. The payback method neglects the time value of money and ignores cash flows beyond the payback period. The discounted payback method measures the time taken for the present value of cash inflows to equal the present value of cash outflows. It adjusts for the time value of money but overlooks cash flows after the discounted payback period.
4. What are the strengths and weaknesses of the accrual accounting rate-of-return (AARR) method for evaluating long-term projects?	The accrual accounting rate of return (AARR) divides an accrual accounting measure of average annual income from a project by an accrual accounting measure of its investment. AARR gives managers an idea of how accepting a project will affect a firm's future reported accounting profitability. However, AARR uses accrual accounting income numbers, does not track cash flows, and ignores the time value of money.
5. What are the relevant cash inflows and outflows for capital budgeting decisions? How should accrual accounting concepts be considered?	Relevant cash inflows and outflows in a DCF analysis are the differences in expected future cash flows as a result of making the investment. Only cash inflows and outflows matter; accrual accounting concepts are irrelevant for DCF methods. For example, the income taxes saved as a result of depreciation deductions are relevant because they decrease cash outflows, but the depreciation itself is a noncash item.

6. What conflicts can arise between using DCF methods for capital budgeting decisions and accrual accounting for performance evaluation? How can these conflicts be reduced?	Using accrual accounting to evaluate the performance of a manager may create conflicts with the use of DCF methods for capital budgeting. Frequently, the decision made using a DCF method will not report good "operating income" results in the project's early years under accrual accounting. For this reason, managers are tempted to not use DCF methods even though the decisions based on them would be in the best interests of the company as a whole over the long run. This conflict can be reduced by evaluating managers on a project-by-project basis and by looking at their ability to achieve the amounts and timing of forecasted cash flows.
7. How can managers use capital budgeting to achieve strategic goals?	A company's strategy is the source of its strategic capital budgeting decisions. Such decisions require managers to consider a broad range of factors that may be difficult to estimate. Managers must develop judgment and intuition to make these decisions. R&D projects, for example, are important strategic investments, with distant and usually highly uncertain payoffs.

TERMS TO LEARN

This chapter and the Glossary at the end of the book contain definitions of the following important terms:

accrual accounting rate-of-return (AARR) method (p. 1106)

capital budgeting (p. 1094)

cost of capital (p. 1098)

discount rate (p. 1098)

discounted cash flow (DCF) methods (p. 1097)

discounted payback method (p. 1105)

hurdle rate (p. 1098)

internal rate-of-return (IRR) method (p. 1098, 1100)

net present value (NPV) method (p. 1098)

opportunity cost of capital (p. 1098)

required rate of return (RRR) (p. 1098)

time value of money (p. 1098)

ASSIGNMENT MATERIAL

Questions

21-1 "Capital budgeting has the same focus as accrual accounting." Do you agree? Explain.

21-2 List and briefly describe each of the five stages in capital budgeting.

21-3 What is the essence of the discounted cash flow methods?

21-4 "Only quantitative outcomes are relevant in capital budgeting analyses." Do you agree? Explain.

21-5 How can sensitivity analysis be incorporated in DCF analysis?

21-6 What is the payback method? What are its main strengths and weaknesses?

21-7 Describe the accrual accounting rate-of-return method. What are its main strengths and weaknesses?

21-8 "The trouble with discounted cash flow methods is that they ignore depreciation." Do you agree? Explain.

21-9 "Let's be more practical. DCF is not the gospel. Managers should not become so enchanted with DCF that strategic considerations are overlooked." Do you agree? Explain.

21-10 "All overhead costs are relevant in NPV analysis." Do you agree? Explain.

21-11 Bill Watts, president of Western Publications, accepts a capital budgeting project proposed by Division X. This is the division in which the president spent his first 10 years with the company. On the same day, the president rejects a capital budgeting project proposal from Division Y. The manager of Division Y is incensed. She believes that the Division Y project has an internal rate of return at least 10 percentage points higher than the Division X project. She comments, "What is the point of all our detailed DCF analysis? If Watts is panting over a project, he can arrange to have the proponents of that project massage the numbers so that it looks like a winner." What advice would you give the manager of Division Y?

21-12 Distinguish different categories of cash flows to be considered in an equipment replacement decision by a taxpaying company.

21-13 Describe three ways income taxes can affect the cash inflows or outflows in a motor vehicle-replacement decision by a taxpaying company.

21-14 How can capital budgeting tools assist in evaluating a manager who is responsible for retaining customers of a cellular telephone company?

21-15 Distinguish the nominal rate of return from the real rate of return.

Solved Examples

21-16 Exercises in compound interest, no income taxes. To be sure that you understand how to use the tables in Appendix A at the end of this book, solve the following exercises. Ignore income tax considerations. The correct answers, rounded to the nearest rupee, appear at the end of chapter.

Required

1. You have just won ₹10,000. How much money will you accumulate at the end of 10 years if you invest it at 8% compounded annually? At 10%?

2. Ten years from now, the unpaid principal of the mortgage on your house will be ₹1,54,900. How much do you need to invest today at 4% interest compounded annually to accumulate the ₹1,54,900 in 10 years?

3. If the unpaid mortgage on your house in 10 years will be ₹1,54,900, how much money do you need to invest at the end of each year at 10% to accumulate exactly this amount at the end of the 10th year?

3. You plan to save ₹7,500 of your earnings at the end of each year for the next 10 years. How much money will you accumulate at the end of the 10th year if you invest your savings compounded at 8% per year?

4. You have just turned 65 and an endowment insurance policy has paid you a lump sum of ₹2,50,000. If you invest the sum at 8%, how much money can you withdraw from your account in equal amounts at the end of each year so that at the end of 10 years (age 75) there will be nothing left?

5. You have estimated that for the first 10 years after you retire you will need a cash inflow of ₹65,000 at the end of each year. How much money do you need to invest at 8% at your retirement age to obtain this annual cash inflow? At 12%?

7. The following table shows two schedules of prospective operating cash inflows, each of which requires the same net initial investment of ₹10,000 now:

Annual Cash Inflows

Year	Plan A	Plan B
1	₹3,000	₹1,000
2	5,000	2,000
3	2,000	3,000
4	3,000	4,000
5	2,000	5,000
Total	₹15,000	₹15,000

The required rate of return is 8% compounded annually. All cash inflows occur at the end of each year. In terms of net present value, which plan is more desirable? Show your computations.

Solution

The answers to these exercises are printed after the last problem, at the end of the chapter.

21-17 New equipment purchase, income taxes. Everbake Bakery plans to purchase a new oven for its store. The oven has an estimated useful life of 4 years. The estimated pretax cash flows for the oven are as shown in the table that follows, with no anticipated change in working capital. Everbake Bakery has a 14% after-tax required rate of return and a 35% income tax rate. Assume depreciation is calculated on a straight-line basis for tax purposes using the initial oven investment and estimated terminal disposal value of the oven. Assume all cash flows occur at year-end except for initial investment amounts.

	Home	Insert	Page Layout	Formulas	Data	Review	View	
	A		B	C	D	E	F
1				Relevant Cash Flows at End of Each Year			
2			0	1	2	3	4
3	Initial machine investment		₹(1,86,000)				
4	Annual cash flow from operations (excluding the depreciation effect)			₹77,000	₹77,000	₹77,000	₹77,000
5	Cash flow from terminal disposal of oven						₹6,000

Required

1. Calculate (a) net present value, (b) payback period, and (c) internal rate of return.
2. Calculate accrual accounting rate of return based on net initial investment.

Solution

1. The after-tax cash inflow per year is ₹65,000 (₹50,050 + ₹15,750), as shown below:

Annual cash flow from operations	₹77,000
Deduct income tax payments (0.35 × ₹36,000)	26,950
Annual after-tax cash flow from operations	₹50,050
Annual depreciation on machine	
[(₹1,86,000 – ₹6,000) ÷ 4]	₹45,000
Income tax cash savings from annual depreciation deductions	
(0.35 × ₹45,000)	₹15,750

a. Solution Exhibit 21-17 shows the NPV computation. NPV = ₹9,228

b. Payback = ₹1,86,000 ÷ (₹50,050 + ₹15,750) = 2.83 years

c. For a ₹1,86,000 initial outflow, the project generates ₹65,800 (₹50,050 + ₹15,750) in after-tax cash flows at the end of each of years one through four and an additional ₹6,000 at the end of year 4.

Using either a calculator or Excel, the internal rate of return for this stream of cash flows is found to be 16.38%.

2. Accrual accounting rate of return based on net initial investment:

Net initial investment = ₹1,86,000

Annual after-tax operating income = ₹65,800 – ₹45,000 depreciation

= ₹20,800

Accrual accounting rate of return = $\dfrac{₹20,800}{₹1,86,000}$ = 11.18%.

Solution Exhibit 21-17

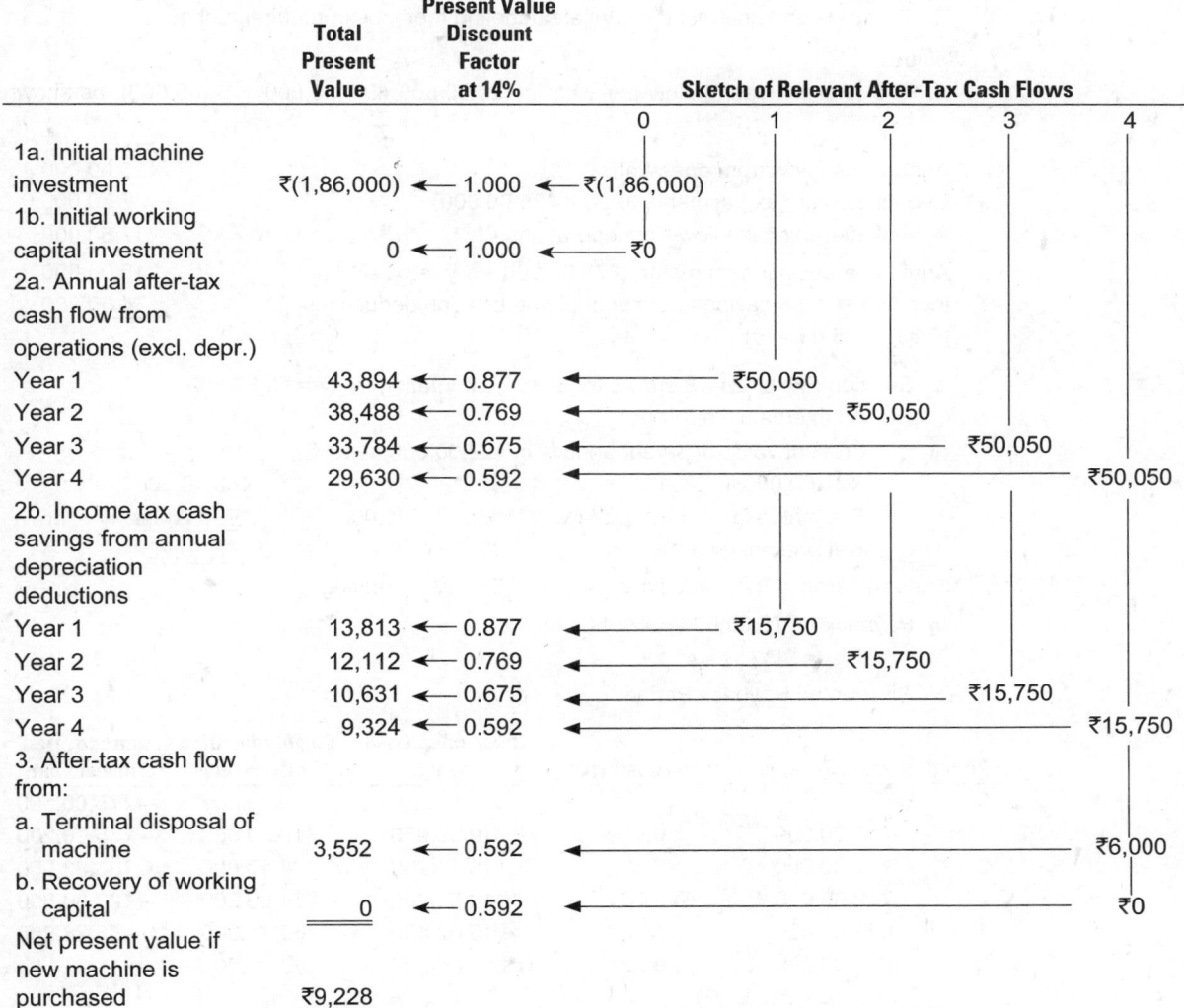

	Total Present Value	Present Value Discount Factor at 14%	Sketch of Relevant After-Tax Cash Flows				
			0	1	2	3	4
1a. Initial machine investment	₹(1,86,000) ←	1.000 ←	₹(1,86,000)				
1b. Initial working capital investment	0 ←	1.000 ←	₹0				
2a. Annual after-tax cash flow from operations (excl. depr.)							
Year 1	43,894 ←	0.877 ←		₹50,050			
Year 2	38,488 ←	0.769 ←			₹50,050		
Year 3	33,784 ←	0.675 ←				₹50,050	
Year 4	29,630 ←	0.592 ←					₹50,050
2b. Income tax cash savings from annual depreciation deductions							
Year 1	13,813 ←	0.877 ←		₹15,750			
Year 2	12,112 ←	0.769 ←			₹15,750		
Year 3	10,631 ←	0.675 ←				₹15,750	
Year 4	9,324 ←	0.592 ←					₹15,750
3. After-tax cash flow from:							
a. Terminal disposal of machine	3,552 ←	0.592 ←					₹6,000
b. Recovery of working capital	0 ←	0.592 ←					₹0
Net present value if new machine is purchased	₹9,228						

21-18 New equipment purchase, income taxes. Tata motors. is considering the purchase of a new industrial electric motor to improve efficiency at its Pune plant. The motor has an estimated useful life of 5 years. The estimated pretax cash flows for the motor are shown in the table that follows, with no anticipated change in working capital. Tata motors has a

10% after-tax required rate of return and a 30% income tax rate. Assume depreciation is calculated on a straight-line basis for tax purposes. Assume all cash flows occur at year-end except for initial investment amounts.

	A	B	C	D	E	F	G
			Relevant Cash Flows at End of Each Year				
1			0	1	2	3	4	5
2			**0**	**1**	**2**	**3**	**4**	**5**
3	Initial motor investment	₹(75,00,000)					
4	Annual cash flow from operations (excluding the depreciation effect)		₹25,00,000	₹25,00,000	₹25,00,000	₹25,00,000	₹25,00,000
5	Cash flow from terminal disposal of motor						₹0

Required

1. Calculate (a) net present value, (b) payback period, (c) discounted payback period, and (d) internal rate of return.

2. Compare and contrast the capital budgeting methods in requirement 1.

Solution

1. The after-tax cash inflow per year is ₹22,00,000 (₹17,50,000 + ₹4,50,000), as shown below:

Annual cash flow from operations	₹25,00,000
Deduct income tax payments (0.30 × ₹25,00,000)	7,50,000
Annual after-tax cash flow from operations	₹17,50,000
Annual depreciation on motor (₹75,00,000 ÷ 5 years)	₹15,00,000
Income tax cash savings from annual depreciation deductions (0.30 × ₹15,00,000)	₹4,50,000

a. Solution Exhibit 21-18 shows the NPV computation. NPV = ₹8,37,600
   An alternative approach:
   Present value of 5-year annuity of ₹22,00,000 at 10%

₹22,00,000 × 3.791	₹83,40,200
Present value of cash outlays, ₹75,00,000 × 1.000	75,00,000
Net present value*	₹8,40,200

* Minor difference from solution exhibit 21-25 due to rounding.

b. Payback = ₹75,00,000 ÷ ₹22,50,000
   = 3.33 years

c. Discounted Payback Period

Period	Cash Savings	Disc Factor (10%)	Discounted Cash Savings	Cumulative Disc Cash Savings	Unrecovered Investment
0					– ₹75,00,000
1	₹22,00,000	0.909	₹19,99,800	₹19,99,800	– ₹55,00,200
2	₹22,00,000	0.826	₹18,17,200	₹38,17,000	– ₹36,83,000
3	₹22,00,000	0.751	₹16,52,200	₹54,69,200	– ₹20,30,800
4	₹22,00,000	0.683	₹15,02,600	₹69,71,800	– ₹5,28,200
5	₹22,00,000	0.621	₹13,66,200	₹83,38,000	

₹5,28,200/₹13,66,200 = .39

Discounted Payback Period = 4.39 years

d. For a ₹75,00,000 initial outflow, the project generates ₹22,00,000 in after-tax cash flows at the end of each of years one through five.

Using either a calculator or Excel, the internal rate of return for this stream of cash flows is found to be 14.29%.

2. Both the net present value and internal rate of return methods use the discounted cash flow approach in which all expected future cash inflows and outflows of a project are measured as if they occurred at a single point in time. The net present value approach computes the surplus generated by the project in today's rupees, while the internal rate of return attempts to measure its effective return on investment earned by the project.

The payback method, by contrast, considers nominal cash flows (without discounting) and measures the time at which the project's expected future cash inflows recoup the net initial investment in a project. The payback method thus ignores the profitability of the project's entire stream of future cash flows. The discounted payback method shares this last defect but looks at the time taken to recoup the initial investment based on the discounted present value of cash inflows. The two payback methods are becoming increasingly important in the global economy. When the local environment in an international location is unstable and therefore highly risky for a potential investment, a company would likely pay close attention to the payback period for making its investment decision. In general, the more unstable the environment, the shorter the payback period desired.

Solution Exhibit 21-18

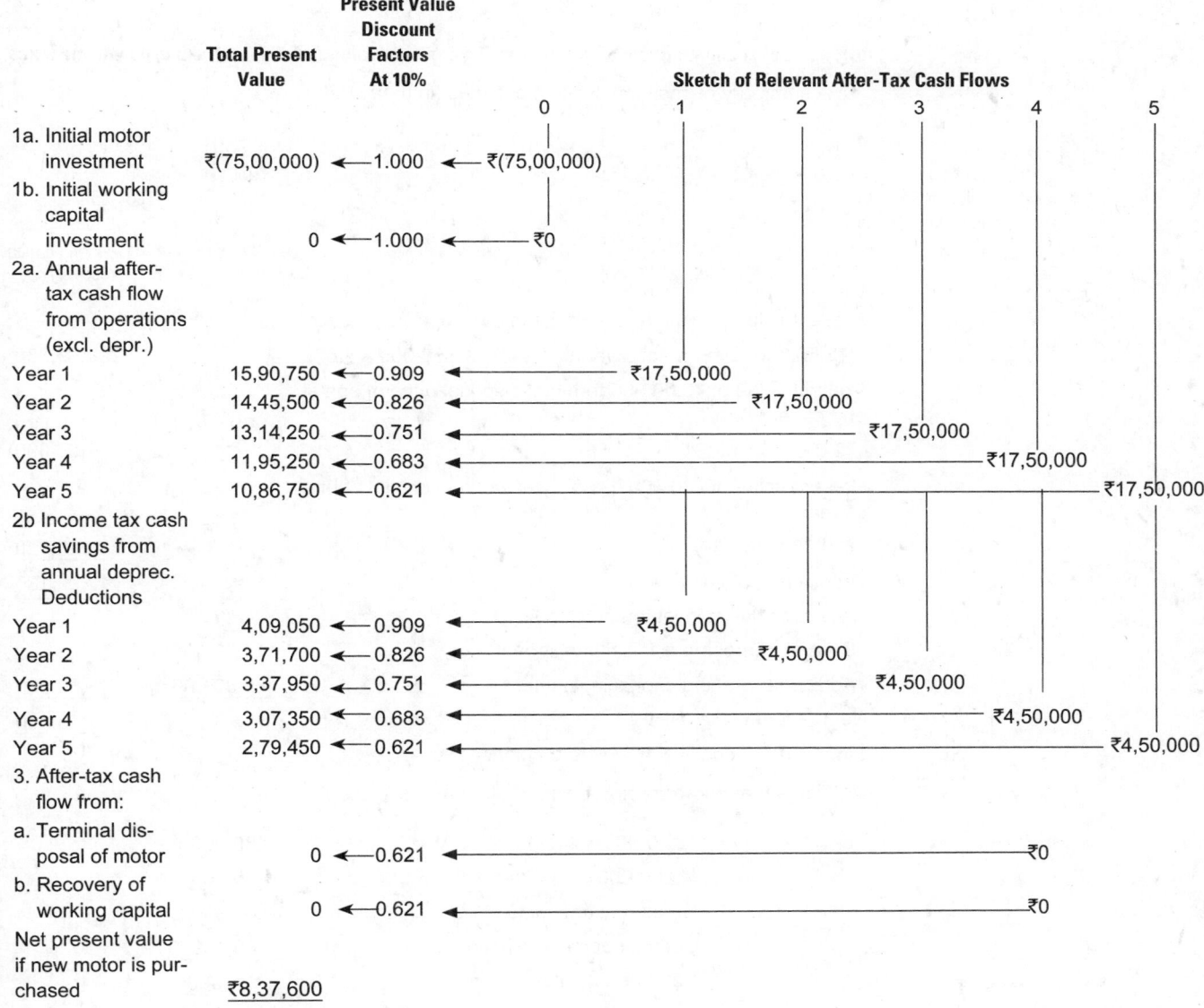

	Total Present Value	Present Value Discount Factors At 10%	Sketch of Relevant After-Tax Cash Flows					
			0	1	2	3	4	5
1a. Initial motor investment	₹(75,00,000) ◀—1.000		◀— ₹(75,00,000)					
1b. Initial working capital investment	0 ◀—1.000		◀— ₹0					
2a. Annual after-tax cash flow from operations (excl. depr.)								
Year 1	15,90,750 ◀—0.909		◀—	₹17,50,000				
Year 2	14,45,500 ◀—0.826		◀—		₹17,50,000			
Year 3	13,14,250 ◀—0.751		◀—			₹17,50,000		
Year 4	11,95,250 ◀—0.683		◀—				₹17,50,000	
Year 5	10,86,750 ◀—0.621		◀—					₹17,50,000
2b Income tax cash savings from annual deprec. Deductions								
Year 1	4,09,050 ◀—0.909		◀—	₹4,50,000				
Year 2	3,71,700 ◀—0.826		◀—		₹4,50,000			
Year 3	3,37,950 ◀—0.751		◀—			₹4,50,000		
Year 4	3,07,350 ◀—0.683		◀—				₹4,50,000	
Year 5	2,79,450 ◀—0.621		◀—					₹4,50,000
3. After-tax cash flow from:								
a. Terminal disposal of motor	0 ◀—0.621		◀—					₹0
b. Recovery of working capital	0 ◀—0.621		◀—					₹0
Net present value if new motor is purchased	₹8,37,600							

21-19 DCF, accrual accounting rate of return, working capital, evaluation of performance, no income taxes. Supreme Manufacturing Company has been offered a special-purpose metal-cutting bus for ₹11,00,000. The bus is expected to have a useful life of eight years, with a terminal disposal value of ₹3,00,000. Savings in cash operating costs are expected to be ₹2,50,000 per year. However, additional working capital is needed to keep the bus running efficiently and without stoppages. Working capital includes such items as filters, lubricants, bearings, abrasives, flexible exhaust pipes, and belts. These items must continually be replaced, so an investment of ₹80,000 must be maintained in them at all times, but this investment is fully recoverable (will be "cashed in") at the end of the useful life. Supreme's required rate of return is 14%. Ignore income taxes in your analysis.

Required

1. Compute net present value.
2. Compute internal rate of return.
3. Compute accrual accounting rate of return based on net initial investment. Assume straight-line depreciation.
4. You have the authority to make the purchase decision. Why might you be reluctant to base your decision on the DCF methods?

Solution

DCF, accrual accounting rate of return, working capital, evaluation of performance, no income taxes.

1. A summary of cash inflows and outflows (in thousands) are:

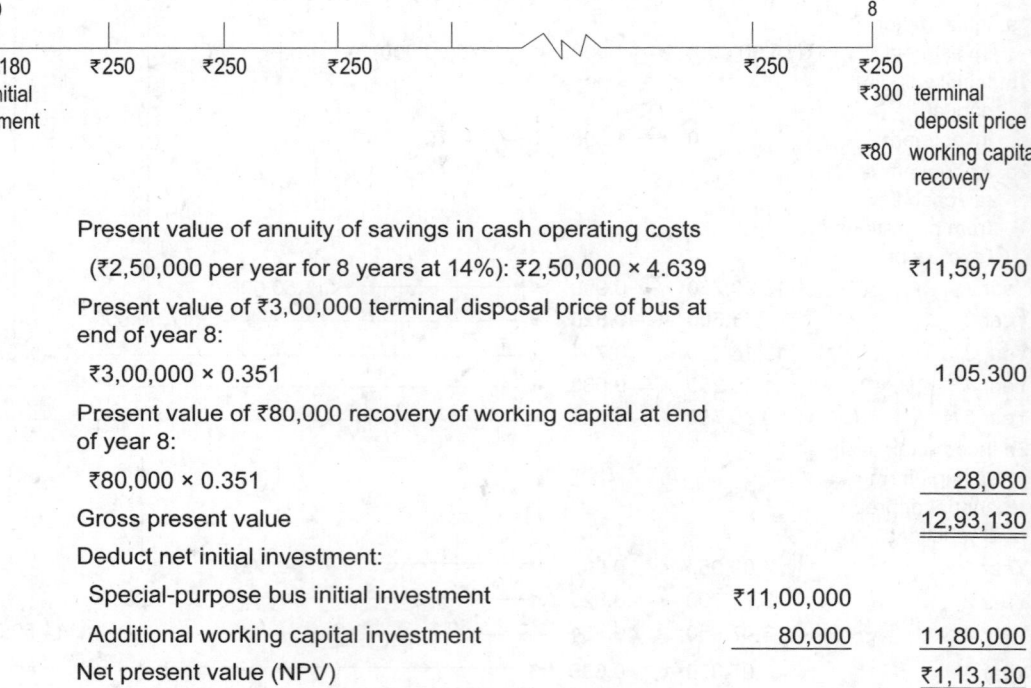

Present value of annuity of savings in cash operating costs (₹2,50,000 per year for 8 years at 14%): ₹2,50,000 × 4.639	₹11,59,750
Present value of ₹3,00,000 terminal disposal price of bus at end of year 8:	
₹3,00,000 × 0.351	1,05,300
Present value of ₹80,000 recovery of working capital at end of year 8:	
₹80,000 × 0.351	28,080
Gross present value	12,93,130
Deduct net initial investment:	
Special-purpose bus initial investment	₹11,00,000
Additional working capital investment	80,000
	11,80,000
Net present value (NPV)	₹1,13,130

Since NPV is positive, IRR is to be higher than 14%.

2. Use a trial-and-error approach. First try a 16% discount rate:

₹2,50,000 × 4.344	₹10,86,000
(₹3,00,000 + ₹80,000) × 0.305	1,15,900
Gross present value	12,01,900
Deduct net initial investment	(11,80,000)
Net present value	₹21,900

Second try an 18% discount rate:

₹2,50,000 × 4.078	₹10,19,500
(₹3,00,000 – ₹80,000) × .266	1,01,080
Gross present value	11,20,580
Deduct net initial investment	(11,80,000)
Net present value	₹(59,420)

By interpolation:

$$\text{Internal rate of return} = 16\% + \left(\frac{21,000}{21,900 + 59,420} \right) \times 2\%$$

$$= 16\% + (.2693 \times 2\%)$$

$$= 16.54\%$$

3. Accrual accounting rate of return based on net initial investment:

Net initial investment	$= ₹11,00,000 + ₹80,000$
	$= ₹11,80,000$
Annual depreciation	
(₹11,00,000 – ₹3,00,000) ÷ 8 years	$= ₹1,00,000$
Accrual accounting rate of return	$= \dfrac{₹2,50,000 - ₹1,00,000}{₹11,80,000} = 12.71\%.$

4. If your decision is based on the DCF model, the purchase would be made because the net present value is positive, and the 16.54% internal rate of return exceeds the 14% required rate of return. However, you may believe that your performance may actually be measured using accrual accounting. This approach would show a 12.71% return on the initial investment, which is below the required rate. Your reluctance to make a "buy" decision would be quite natural unless you are assured of reasonable consistency between the decision model and the performance evaluation method.

21-20 Equipment replacement, no income taxes. Superfast Chips manufactures and delivers prototype chips to customers within 24 hours. The current production facility was set up when the company began operations in 2004. It is outdated and constrains future growth. Next year, in 2016, Superfast expects to deliver 460 prototype chips at an average price of ₹80,000 per prototype. Superfast's marketing vice president forecasts growth of 50 prototype chips per year through 2022. That is, demand is 460 in 2016, 510 in 2017, 560 in 2018, and so on.

The current facility cannot produce more than 450 prototypes annually. To meet future demand, Superfast must either modernize the current facility or replace it. The old equipment is fully depreciated and can be sold for ₹30,00,000. If the current facilities are modernized, such costs are to be capitalized and depreciated over the useful life of the updated facility. The old equipment is retained as part of the modernize alternative. Following is some data on the two options available to Superfast:

	Modernize	Replace
Initial investment in 2016	₹2,80,00,000	₹4,90,00,000
Terminal disposal price in 2022	₹50,00,000	₹1,20,00,000
Useful life	7 years	7 years
Total annual cash operating costs per prototype	₹62,000	₹56,000

Superfast uses straight-line depreciation for income reporting, assuming zero terminal disposal value. For simplicity, we assume no change in prices or costs in future years. The investment will be made at the beginning of 2016, and all transactions thereafter occur on the last day of the year. Superfast's required rate of return is 12%.

There is no difference between the modernize and replace alternatives in terms of required working capital. Superfast Chips has a special waiver on income taxes until 2022.

Required

1. Sketch the cash inflows and outflows of the modernize and replace alternatives over the 2016 to 2022 period.
2. Compute payback period for the modernize and replace alternatives.
3. Compute net present value of the modernize and replace alternatives.
4. What factors should Superfast Chips consider in choosing between the alternatives?

Solution

Equipment replacement, no income taxes.

1. Cash flows for modernizing alternative:

Year (1)	Units Sold (2)	Net Cash Contributions (3) = (2) × ₹18,000[a]	Initial Investments (4)	Sale of Equip. at Termination (5)
Jan. 1, 2016	–	–	₹(2,80,00,000)	–
Dec. 31, 2016	460	82,80,000		
Dec. 31, 2017	510	91,80,000		
Dec. 31, 2018	560	1,00,80,000		
Dec. 31, 2019	610	1,09,80,000		
Dec. 31, 2020	660	1,18,80,000		
Dec. 31, 2021	710	1,27,80,000		
Dec. 31, 2022	760	1,36,80,000		₹50,00,000

[a]₹80,000 – ₹62,000 = ₹18,000 cash contribution per prototype.

Cash flows for replacement alternative:

Year (1)	Units Sold (2)	Net Cash Contributions (3) = (2) × ₹24,000[b]	Initial Investments (4)	Sale of Equip. at Termination (5)
Jan. 1, 2016	–	–	₹(4,90,00,000)	₹30,00,000
Dec. 31, 2016	460	1,10,40,000		
Dec. 31, 2017	510	1,22,40,000		
Dec. 31, 2018	560	1,34,40,000		
Dec. 31, 2019	610	1,46,40,000		
Dec. 31, 2020	660	1,58,40,000		
Dec. 31, 2021	710	1,70,40,000		
Dec. 31, 2022	760	1,82,40,000		₹1,20,00,000

[b]₹80,000 – ₹56,000 = ₹24,000 cash contribution per prototype.

2. Payback period calculations for modernizing alternative:

Year (1)	Cash Inflow (2)	Cumulative Cash Inflow (3)	Net Initial Investment Yet to be Recovered at Year End (4)
Jan. 1, 2016	–	–	₹2,80,00,000
Dec. 31, 2016	₹82,80,000	₹82,80,000	1,97,20,000
Dec. 31, 2017	91,80,000	1,74,60,000	1,05,40,000

| Dec. 31, 2018 | 1,00,80,000 | 2,75,40,000 | 4,60,000 |
| Dec. 31, 2019 | 1,09,80,000 | | |

$$\text{Payback} = \times + \frac{₹4,60,000}{₹1,09,80,000} = 3.04 \text{ years}$$

Payback period calculations for replacement alternative:

Year (1)	Cash Inflow (2)	Cumulative Cash Inflow (3)	Net Initial Investment Yet to be Recovered at Year End (4)
Jan. 1, 2016	—	—	₹4,60,00,000
Dec. 31, 2016	₹1,10,40,000	₹1,10,40,000	3,49,60,000
Dec. 31, 2017	1,22,40,000	2,32,80,000	2,27,20,000
Dec. 31, 2018	1,34,40,000	3,67,20,000	92,80,000
Dec. 31, 2019	1,46,40,000		

$$\text{Payback} = \times + \frac{₹92,80,000}{₹1,46,40,000} = 3.06 \text{ years}$$

3. Modernizing alternative:

Year	Present Value Discount Factors At 12%	Net Cash Flow	Total Present Value
Jan. 1, 2016	1.000	₹(2,80,00,000)	₹(2,80,00,000)
Dec. 31, 2016	0.893	82,80,000	73,94,040
Dec. 31, 2017	0.797	91,80,000	73,16,460
Dec. 31, 2018	0.712	1,00,80,000	71,76,960
Dec. 31, 2019	0.636	1,09,80,000	69,83,280
Dec. 31, 2020	0.567	1,18,80,000	67,35,960
Dec. 31, 2021	0.507	1,27,80,000	64,79,460
Dec. 31, 2022	0.452	1,86,80,000	84,43,360
			₹2,25,29,520

Replace Alternative:

Year	Present Value Discount Factors At 12%	Net Cash Flow	Total Present Value
Jan. 1, 2016	1.000	₹(4,60,00,000)	₹(4,60,00,000)
Dec. 31, 2016	0.893	1,10,40,000	98,58,720
Dec. 31, 2017	0.797	1,22,40,000	97,55,280
Dec. 31, 2018	0.712	1,34,40,000	95,69,280
Dec. 31, 2019	0.636	1,46,40,000	93,11,040
Dec. 31, 2020	0.567	1,58,40,000	89,81,280
Dec. 31, 2021	0.507	1,70,40,000	86,39,280
Dec. 31, 2022	0.452	3,02,40,000	1,36,68,480
			₹2,37,83,360

4. The NPV amounts are based on best estimates. Superfast Chips could examine the sensitivity of the NPV amounts to variations in the estimates.

Nonfinancial qualitative factors could include the quality of the prototypes produced by the modernize and replace alternatives. These alternatives may differ in capacity and their ability to meet surges in demand beyond the estimated amounts. The alternatives may also differ in how workers increase their shop floor-capabilities. Such differences could provide labor force externalities that can be the source of future benefits to Superfast.

21-21 Equipment replacement, income taxes (continuation of 21-20). Assume the same facts as in Example 21-20, except that Superfast has no special waiver on income taxes. It pays a 30% tax rate on all income. Proceeds from sale of equipment above book value are taxed at the same 30% rate.

Required

1. Sketch the after-tax cash inflows and outflows of the modernize and replace alternatives over the 2016 to 2022 period.
2. Compute net present value of the modernize and replace alternatives.
3. Suppose Superfast is planning to build several more plants. It wants to have the most advantageous tax position possible. It has been approached by Spain, Malaysia, and Australia to construct a plant in their country. Briefly describe income tax features that would be attractive and advantageous to Superfast You should discuss the magnitude and timing of cost deductions in your description.

Solution

Equipment replacement, income taxes

1. & 2. Income tax rate = 30%

Modernize Alternative

Annual depreciation:

₹2,80,00,000 ÷ 7 years = ₹40,00,000 a year.

Income tax cash savings from annual depreciation deductions:

₹40,00,000 × 0.30 = ₹12,00,000 a year.

Terminal disposal of equipment = ₹50,00,000.

After-tax cash flow from terminal disposal:

₹50,00,000 × 0.70 = ₹35,00,000.

The NPV components are:

		NPV
1. Initial investment:		
₹(2,80,00,000) × 1.000		₹(2,80,00,000)

2a. Annual after-tax cash flow from operations (excluding depreciation):

Dec. 31, 2016	82,80,000 × 0.70 × 0.893	51,75,828
2017	91,80,000 × 0.70 × 0.797	51,21,522
2018	1,00,80,000 × 0.70 × 0.712	50,23,872
2019	1,09,80,000 × 0.70 × 0.636	48,88,296
2020	1,18,80,000 × 0.70 × 0.567	47,15,172
2021	1,27,80,000 × 0.70 × 0.507	45,35,622
2022	1,36,80,000 × 0.70 × 0.452	43,28,352

2b. Income tax cash savings from annual depreciation deductions (annuity of ₹12,00,000 for 7 years):

₹12,00,000 × 4.564	54,76,800

3. After-tax cash flow from terminal sale of equipment:

₹35,00,000 × 0.452	15,82,000
Net present value	₹1,28,47,464

Replace alternative

Initial bus replacement = ₹4,90,00,000

Sale in Jan. 1, 2016, of equipment = ₹30,00,000

After-tax cash flow from sale:

₹30,00,000 × 0.70 = ₹21,00,000

Net after-tax initial investment

₹4,90,00,000 − ₹21,00,000 = ₹4,69,00,000

Annual depreciation

₹4,90,00,000 ÷ 7 years = ₹70,00,000 a year

Income-tax cash savings from annual depreciation deductions

₹70,00,000 ÷ 0.30 = ₹21,00,000

Terminal disposal of equipment = ₹1,20,00,000

After-tax cash flow from terminal disposal

₹1,20,00,000 × 0.70 = ₹84,00,000

The NPV components are:

1. Net after-tax initial investment

₹(4,69,00,000) x 1.000		₹(4,69,00,000)

2a. Annual after-tax cash flow from operations (excluding depreciation)

Dec. 31, 2016	₹1,10,40,000 × 0.70 × 0.893	69,01,104
2017	1,22,40,000 × 0.70 × 0.797	68,28,696
2018	1,34,40,000 × 0.70 × 0.712	66,98,496
2019	1,46,40,000 × 0.70 × 0.636	65,17,728
2020	1,58,40,000 × 0.70 × 0.567	62,86,896
2021	1,70,40,000 × 0.70 × 0.507	60,47,496
2022	1,82,40,000 × 0.70 × 0.452	57,71,136

2b. Income tax cash savings from annual depreciation deductions (annuity of ₹21,00,000 for 7 years)

₹21,00,000 × 4.564	95,84,400

2c. After-tax cash flow from terminal sale of equipment

₹84,00,000 × 0.452	37,96,800
Net present value	₹1,15,32,752

3. Superfast would prefer to:

  a. have lower tax rates,

  b. have revenue exempt from taxation,

  c. recognize taxable revenues in later years rather than earlier years,

  d. recognize taxable cost deductions greater than actual outlay costs, and

  e. recognize cost deductions in earlier years rather than later years (including accelerated amounts in earlier years).

21-22 NPV of JIT, income taxes (CMA, adapted). Robust Furniture Company produces office furniture and sells it wholesale to furniture distributors. Robust's management is reviewing a proposal to purchase a just-in-time inventory (JIT) system to better serve its customers. The JIT system will include a computer system and materials-handling equipment. The decision will be based on whether the new JIT system is cost effective to the organization for the next five years.

The computer system, including hardware and software, will initially cost ₹12,50,000. Materials-handling equipment will cost ₹4,50,000. Both groups of equipment will have a five-year useful life for tax reporting of depreciation (straight-line) calculated assuming a ₹0 terminal disposal value. At the end of the five years, the newly acquired materials-handling equipment is expected to be sold for ₹1,50,000. The computer system will have a ₹0 terminal disposal value at the end of five years.

Other factors to be considered over the next five years for this proposal include the following:

• Due to the service improvement resulting from this new JIT system, Robust will realize a ₹8,00,000 increase in revenues during the first year. Robust expects this initial ₹8,00,000 revenue increase to continue to grow by 10% per year thereafter.

• The contribution margin is 60% .

• Annual material-ordering costs will increase ₹50,000 due to a greater level of purchase orders.

- There will be a one-time decrease in working-capital investment of ₹1,50,000 at the end of the first year.
- There will be a 20% savings in warehouse rent due to less space being needed. The current annual rent is ₹3,00,000.

Robust uses an after-tax required rate of return of 10% and is subject to an income tax rate of 40%. Assume that all cash flows occur at year-end for tax purposes except for any initial purchase amounts.

Required

1. Prepare an analysis of the after-tax effects for the purchase of the JIT system at Robust using the net present value method for evaluating capital expenditures.

2. Determine whether Robust should purchase the JIT system. Explain your answer.

Solution

NPV of JIT, income taxes (CMA adapted).

1. Initial investment (Year 0):

Computer system	₹12,50,000
Materials handling equipment	4,50,000
Total initial investment	₹17,00,000

Working-capital investment:

Reduced working capital of	₹1,50,000 at end of Year 1.
Increased working capital of	₹1,50,000 at end of Year 5.

Depreciation on initial investment:

₹17,00,000 ÷ 5 years = ₹3,40,000 per year

Income tax cash savings from annual depreciation deductions:

₹3,40,000 × 0.40 = ₹1,36,000

After-tax flow from disposal of materials-handling equipment at end of Year 5:

₹1,50,000 × 0.60 = ₹90,000

Annual after tax flow from operations:

	Year 1	Year 2	Year 3	Year 4	Year 5
Revenue	₹8,00,000	₹8,80,000	₹9,68,000	₹10,64,800	₹11,71,280
Contribution margin, 60%	4,80,000	5,28,000	5,80,800	6,38,880	7,02,768
Rent savings	60,000	60,000	60,000	60,000	60,000
Materials ordering cost	(50,000)	(50,000)	(50,000)	(50,000)	(50,000)
Annual cash inflow from operation	4,90,000	5,38,000	5,90,800	6,48,880	7,12,768
Income tax, 40%	1,96,000	2,15,200	2,36,320	2,59,552	2,85,107
After-tax annual cash inflow	₹2,94,000	₹3,22,800	₹3,54,480	₹3,89,328	₹4,27,661

from operations

Solution Exhibit 21-22 reports the net present value to be ₹2,46,111.

2. Robust will have a NPV of ₹2,46,111 with the new JIT system. Based on financial quantitative factors, this is an attractive investment. Qualitative factors could make the

JIT system even more attractive. For example, if a competitor adopts JIT but Robust does not, Robust could be at a sizable competitive disadvantage. Not adopting JIT does not mean the status quo will remain. Robust's workers can also gain additional shop-floor expertise when using the JIT system that can be beneficially employed on other Robust projects.

Solution Exhibit 21-22

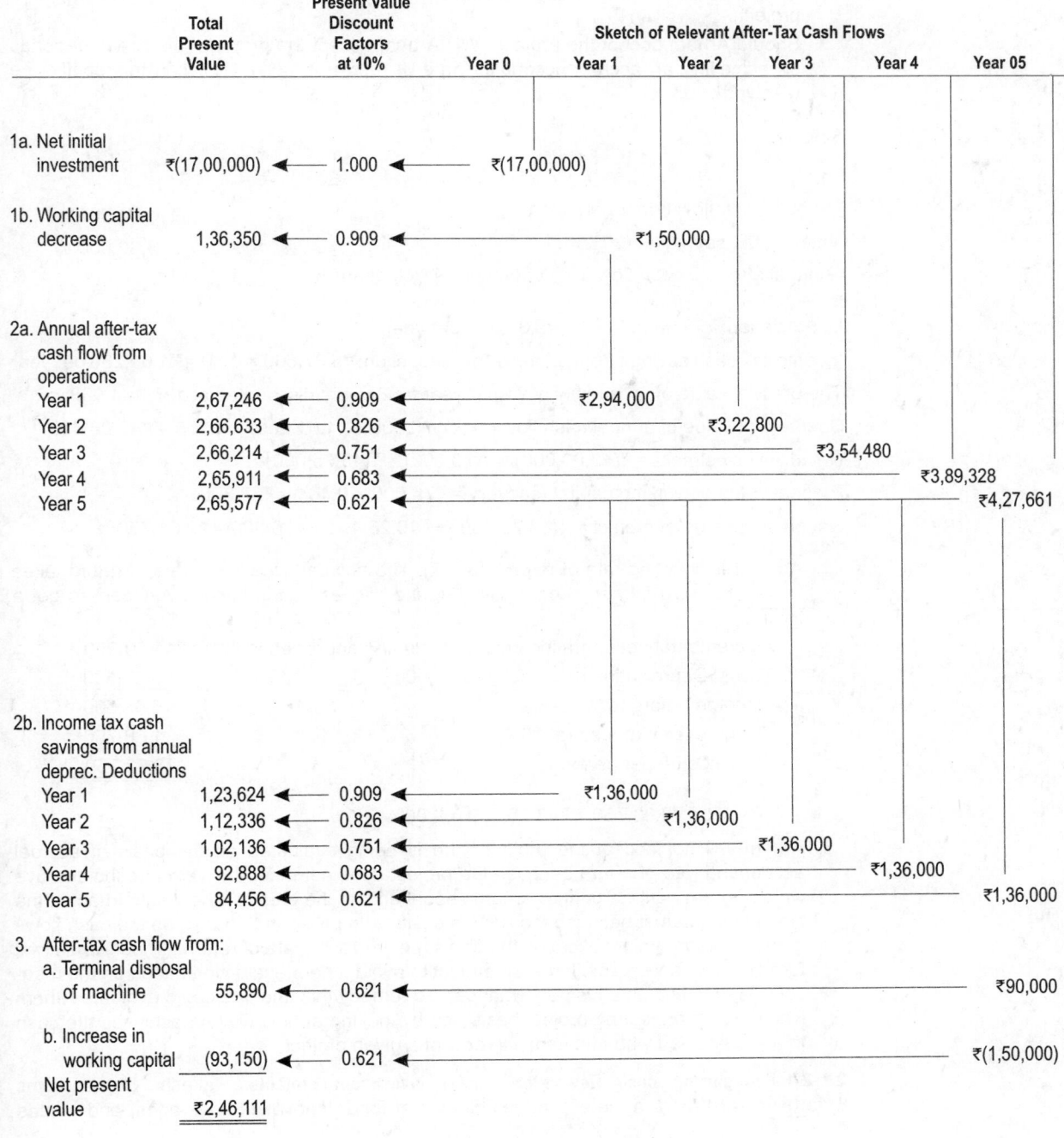

	Total Present Value	Present Value Discount Factors at 10%	Year 0	Year 1	Year 2	Year 3	Year 4	Year 05
1a. Net initial investment	₹(17,00,000)	1.000	₹(17,00,000)					
1b. Working capital decrease	1,36,350	0.909		₹1,50,000				
2a. Annual after-tax cash flow from operations								
Year 1	2,67,246	0.909		₹2,94,000				
Year 2	2,66,633	0.826			₹3,22,800			
Year 3	2,66,214	0.751				₹3,54,480		
Year 4	2,65,911	0.683					₹3,89,328	
Year 5	2,65,577	0.621						₹4,27,661
2b. Income tax cash savings from annual deprec. Deductions								
Year 1	1,23,624	0.909		₹1,36,000				
Year 2	1,12,336	0.826			₹1,36,000			
Year 3	1,02,136	0.751				₹1,36,000		
Year 4	92,888	0.683					₹1,36,000	
Year 5	84,456	0.621						₹1,36,000
3. After-tax cash flow from:								
a. Terminal disposal of machine	55,890	0.621						₹90,000
b. Increase in working capital	(93,150)	0.621						₹(1,50,000)
Net present value	₹2,46,111							

21-23 NPV and AARR, goal-congruence issues. Arham Jain, a manager of the Plate Division for the Stone Ware Manufacturing company, has the opportunity to expand the division by investing in additional machinery costing ₹43,00,000. He would depreciate the equipment using the straight-line method and expects it to have no residual value. It has a useful life of 8 years. The firm mandates a required after-tax rate of return of 12% on investments. Arham estimates annual net cash inflows for this investment of ₹11,00,000 before taxes and an investment in working capital of ₹75,000. The tax rate is 30%.

Required

1. Calculate the net present value of this investment.
2. Calculate the accrual accounting rate of return based on net initial investment for this project.
3. Should Arham accept the project? Will Arham accept the project if his bonus depends on achieving an accrual accounting rate of return of 12%? How can this conflict be resolved?

Solution

1.

Annual cash flow from operations	₹11,00,000
Income tax payments (30%)	3,30,000
Annual after-tax cash flow from operations (excl. deprn.)	₹7,70,000

Depreciation: ₹43,00,000 ÷ 8 = ₹5,37,500 per year

Income-tax cash savings from depreciation deduction: ₹5,37,500 × 0.30 = ₹1,61,250 per year

The present value of an annuity of ₹1 per year for 8 years discounted at 12% = 4.968.

So, present value of annual cash flows = (₹7,70,000 + ₹1,61,250) × 4.968 = ₹46,26,450

Net initial investment = ₹(43,00,000) + ₹(75,000) = ₹(43,75,000)

Present value of working capital recovery = ₹75,000 × 0.404 = ₹30,300

Net present value of project = ₹(43,75,000) + ₹46,26,450 + ₹30,300 = ₹2,81,750

2. Accrual accounting rate of return (AARR): The accrual accounting rate of return takes the annual accrual net income after tax and divides by the initial investment to get a return.

Incremental net operating income excluding depreciation	₹11,00,000
Less: Depreciation expense (₹43,00,000 ÷ 8)	5,37,500
Income before tax	5,62,500
Income tax expense (at 30%)	1,68,750
Net income per period	₹3,93,750

AARR = ₹3,93,750 ÷ ₹43,75,000 = 9.00%.

3. Arham will not accept the project if he is being evaluated on the basis of accrual accounting rate of return because the project does not meet the 12% threshold above which Arham earns a bonus. Arham should accept the project if he wants to act in the firm's best interest because the NPV is positive, implying that, based on the cash flows generated, the project exceeds the firm's required 12% rate of return. Thus, Arham will turn down an acceptable long-run project to avoid a poor evaluation based on the measure used to evaluate his performance. To remedy this, the firm could evaluate Arham instead on a project-by-project basis and by looking at how well he achieves the cash flows forecasted when he chose to accept a given project.

21-24 Recognizing cash flows for capital investment projects. Rakesh Gupta owns Entertainment World, a place that combines fast food, innovative beverages, and arcade games. Worried about the shifting tastes of younger audiences, Rakesh contemplates bringing in new simulators and virtual reality games to maintain customer interest.

As part of this overhaul, Rakesh is also looking at replacing his old Guitar Hero equipment with a Rock Band Pro machine. The Guitar Hero setup was purchased for ₹2,52,000 and has accumulated depreciation of ₹2,30,000, with a current trade-in value of ₹27,000. It currently costs Rakesh ₹6,000 per month in utilities and another ₹50,000 a year in maintenance to run the Guitar Hero equipment. Rakesh feels that the equipment could be kept in service for another 11 years, after which it would have no salvage value.

The Rock Band Pro machine is more energy-efficient and durable. It would reduce the utilities costs by 30% and cut the maintenance cost in half. The Rock Band Pro costs ₹4,90,000 and has an expected disposal value of ₹50,000 at the end of its useful life of 11 years.

Rakesh charges an entrance fee of ₹50 per hour for customers to play an unlimited number of games. He does not believe that replacing Guitar Hero with Rock Band Pro will have an impact on this charge or materially change the number of customers who will visit Entertainment World.

Required

1. Rakesh wants to evaluate the Rock Band Pro project using capital budgeting techniques. To help him, read through the problem and separate the cash flows into four groups: (1) net initial investment cash flows, (2) cash flow savings from operations, (3) cash flows from terminal disposal of investment, and (4) cash flows not relevant to the capital budgeting problem.
2. Assuming a tax rate of 40%, a required rate of return of 8%, and straight-line depreciation over the remaining useful life of equipment, should Rakesh purchase Rock Band Pro?

Solution

1. Partitioning relevant cash flows into categories:

   (1) Net initial investment cash flows

   —The ₹4,90,000 cost of the new Rock Band Pro

   —The disposal value of Guitar Hero, ₹27,000, is a cash inflow.

   —The book value of Guitar Hero ₹22,000 (₹2,52,000 − ₹2,30,000), relative to the disposal value of ₹27,000, yields a taxable gain of ₹5,000 (₹27,000 − ₹22,000) that leads to a cash outflow for taxes of ₹5,000 × Tax Rate.

   (2) Cash flow savings from operations

   —The 30% savings in utilities cost per year of ₹21,600 (30% × ₹6,000 per month × 12 months) results in cash inflow from operations after tax of ₹21,600 × (1 − Tax Rate).

   —The savings of half the maintenance costs per year of ₹25,000 (50% × ₹50,000) results in a cash inflow from operations after tax of ₹25,000 × (1 − Tax Rate).

   —Annual depreciation of (₹4,90,000 − ₹50,000) ÷ 11 years = ₹40,000 on Rock Band Pro, relative to the (₹22,000 − ₹0) ÷ 11 years = ₹2,000 depreciation on current Guitar Hero leads to additional tax savings of ₹38,000 × Tax Rate.

   (3) Cash flows from terminal disposal of investment

   —The ₹50,000 salvage value of Rock Band Pro minus the ₹0 salvage value of the old Guitar Hero equipment is a terminal cash flow at the end of Year 11. There are no tax effects because both systems are planned to be disposed of at book value.

   (4) Data not relevant to the capital budgeting decision

   —The ₹50 per hour charge for customers, since it would not change whether or not Rakesh got the new machine

   —The ₹2,52,000 original cost of the Guitar Hero setup

2. Net present value of the investment:

<u>Net initial investment</u>

Initial investment in Rock Band Pro	₹(4,90,000)
Current disposal value of Guitar Hero	27,000
Tax on gain on sale of Guitar Hero, 40% × ₹5,000	(2,000)
Net initial investment	₹(4,65,000)

<u>Annual after-tax cash flow from operations (excl. deprn. effects)</u>

After-tax savings in utilities costs, ₹21,600 × (1 − 0.40)	₹12,960
After-tax savings in maintenance costs, ₹25,000 × (1 − 0.40)	15,000
Annual after-tax cash flow from operations	₹27,960
Income-tax cash savings from annual additional depreciation deductions (₹40,000 − ₹2,000) × 40%	₹15,200
After-tax cash flow from terminal disposal of machines	₹50,000

These four amounts can be combined to determine the NPV at an 8% discount rate.

Present value of net initial investment, ₹(4,65,000) × 1.000	₹(4,65,000)
Present value of 11-year annuity of annual after-tax cash flow from operations (excl. deprcn. effects), ₹27,960 × 7.139	1,99,610
Present value of 11-year annuity of income-tax cash savings from annual depreciation deductions, ₹15,200 × 7.139	1,08,510
Present value of after-tax cash flow from terminal disposal of machines, ₹50,000 × 0.429	21,450
Net present value	₹(1,35,430)

At the required rate of return of 8%, the net present value of the investment in the Rock Band Pro machine is substantially negative. Rakesh should therefore not make the investment.

21-25 NPV, inflation and taxes. Haldiram Foods is considering replacing all 10 of its old cash registers with new ones. The old registers are fully depreciated and have no disposal value. The new registers cost ₹8,99,640 (in total). Because the new registers are more efficient than the old registers, Haldiram will have annual incremental cash savings from using the new registers in the amount of ₹1,92,000 per year. The registers have a 7-year useful life and no terminal disposal value and are depreciated using the straight-line method. It requires an 8% real rate of return.

Required

1. Given the preceding information, what is the net present value of the project? Ignore taxes.
2. Assume the ₹1,92,000 cost savings are in current real rupees and the inflation rate is 5.5%. Recalculate the NPV of the project.
3. Based on your answers to requirements 1 and 2, should Haldiram buy the new cash registers?
4. Now assume that the company's tax rate is 30%. Calculate the NPV of the project assuming no inflation.
5. Again assuming that the company faces a 30% tax rate, calculate the NPV of the project under an inflation rate of 5.5%.
6. Based on your answers to requirements 4 and 5, should Haldiram buy the new cash registers?

Solution

1. Without inflation or taxes, this is a simple net present value problem using an 8% discount rate

Present value of initial investment, ₹(8,99,640) × 1.000	₹(8,99,640)
Present value of 7-year annuity of annual cash savings:	
₹1,92,000 × 5.206	9,99,552
Net present value	₹99,912

2. With inflation, we adjust each year's cash flow for the inflation rate to get nominal cash flows and then discount each cash flow separately using the nominal discount rate.

Nominal rate = (1 + real rate) × (1 + inflation rate) − 1
Nominal rate = (1.08) × (1.055) − 1 = 1.1394 − 1 = 0.1394 or 14% (approx.)

Period	Cash Flow (Real Rupees) (1)	Cumulative Inflation Rate (2)	Cash Inflows (Nominal Rupees) (3) = (1) × (2)	Present Value Factor, 14% (4)	Present Value (5) = (3) × (4)
1	₹1,92,000	1.055	₹2,02,560	0.877	₹1,77,645
2	1,92,000	1.1131	2,13,696	0.769	1,64,332
3	1,92,000	1.174	2,25,408	0.675	1,52,150
4	1,92,000	1.239	2,37,888	0.592	1,40,830
5	1,92,000	1.307	2,50,944	0.519	1,30,240
6	1,92,000	1.379	2,64,768	0.456	1,20,734
7	1,92,000	1.455	2,79,360	0.400	1,11,744

Total present value of annual net cash inflows in nominal rupees	9,97,675
Present value of initial investment, ₹(8,99,640) × 1.000	(8,99,640)
Net present value	₹98,035

[1]1.113 = (1.055)^2

3. Both the unadjusted and adjusted NPV are positive. Based on financial considerations alone, Haldiram Foods should buy the new cash registers. However, the effect of taxes should also be considered, as well as any pertinent nonfinancial issues, such as potential improvements in customer response time from moving to the new cash registers.

4.

Initial equipment investment		₹(8,99,640)
Annual cash flow from operations (excl. deprn. effects)	₹1,92,000	
Deduct income tax payments (0.30 × ₹1,92,000)	57,600	
Annual after-tax cash flow from operations (excl. deprn. effects)		₹1,34,400
Income tax cash savings from annual depreciation deductions		
(0.30 × ₹1,28,520)[1]		₹38,556

[1] Depreciation deductions = (₹8,99,640 − ₹0)/7 = ₹1,28,520

The terminal disposal price of the equipment is equal to the book value at disposal = ₹0, so the above three amounts suffice to determine the NPV at a 8% discount rate.

Present value of net initial investment, ₹(8,99,640) × 1.000	₹(8,99,640)
Present value of 7-year annuity annual after-tax cash flow from operations, ₹1,34,400 × 5.206	6,99,686
Present value of 7-year annuity of income tax cash savings from annual depreciation deductions, ₹38,556 × 5.206	2,00,723
Net present value	₹769

5. As in the previous section, with inflation, we adjust each year's cash flow for the inflation rate to get nominal cash flows and then discount each cash flow separately using the nominal discount rate.

Nominal rate = (1 + real rate) × (1 + inflation rate) − 1

Nominal rate = (1.08) (1.055) − 1 = 1.1394 − 1 = .1394 or 14% (approx.)

Period	Cash Flow (Real Rupees) (1)	Cumulative Inflation Rate (2)	Cash Inflows (Nominal Rupees) (3) = (1) × (2)	Present Value Factor, 14% (4) = 0.7 × (3)	Present Value (5)	Present Value (6) = (4) × (5)
1	₹1,92,000	1.055	₹2,02,560	0.877	₹1,77,645	₹1,24,352
2	1,92,000	1.1131	2,13,696	0.769	1,64,332	1,15,033
3	1,92,000	1.174	2,25,408	0.675	1,52,150	1,06,505
4	1,92,000	1.239	2,37,888	0.592	1,40,830	98,581
5	1,92,000	1.307	2,50,944	0.519	1,30,240	91,168
6	1,92,000	1.379	2,64,768	0.456	1,20,734	84,514
7	1,92,000	1.455	2,79,360	0.400	1,11,744	78,221

Total present value of annual net cash inflows (excl. depreciation. effects)	₹6,98,374
Present value of 7-year annuity of income-tax cash savings from annual depreciation deductions, ₹38,556 × 5.206	2,00,723
Present value of initial investment ₹(8,99,640) × 1.000	(8,99,640)
Net present value	₹(543)

6. Without inflation, we obtain a positive NPV; however, with inflation NPV is negative, and Haldiram Foods would be better off not purchasing the new registers. Negative NPV is obtained with an inflation estimate of 5.5%. If a careful review of this forecasted inflation rate results in a lower rate of inflation, Haldiram Foods should recalculate the NPV to determine whether the purchase of the registers is in its best interest.

21-26 NPV of information system, income taxes. Saina Supplies leases and sells materials, tools, and equipment and also provides add-on services such as ground maintenance and waterproofing to construction and mining sites. The company has grown rapidly over the past few years. The owner, Saina Torrance, feels that for the company to continue to scale, it needs to install a professional information system rather than relying on intuition and Excel analyses. After some research, Saina's CFO reports back with the following data about a data warehousing and analytics system that she views as promising:

- The system will cost ₹7,50,000. For tax purposes, it can be depreciated straight-line to a zero terminal value over a 5-year useful life. However, the CFO expects that the system will still be worth ₹50,000 at that time.

- There is an additional ₹75,000 annual fee for software upgrades and technical support from the vendor.
- The ability to provide better services and to target and reach more clients as a result of the new system will directly result in a ₹5,00,000 increase in revenues for Saina in the first year after installation. Revenues will grow by 5% each year thereafter. Saina's contribution margin is 60%.
- Due to greater efficiency in ordering and dispatching supplies, as well as in collecting receivables, the firm's working-capital requirements will decrease by ₹1,00,000.
- Saina will also be able to reduce the amount of warehouse space it currently leases, saving ₹40,000 annually in the process.
- Saina Supplies pays an income tax of 30% and requires an after-tax rate of return of 12%.

Assume that all cash flows occur at year-end except for initial investment amounts.

Required

1. If Saina decides to purchase and install the new information system, what is the expected incremental after-tax cash flow from operations during each of the 5 years?
2. Compute the net present value of installing the information system at Saina Supplies.
3. In addition to the analysis in requirement 2, what nonfinancial factors you would consider in making the decision about the information system?

Solution

1. Initial investment (Year 0):   ₹7,50,000

        Working-capital investment:

                Reduced working capital of   ₹1,00,000 at end of Year 0.

                Increased working capital of   ₹1,00,000 at end of Year 5.

Depreciation on initial investment: ₹7,50,000 ÷ 5 years = ₹1,50,000 per year

Income tax cash savings from annual depreciation deductions: ₹1,50,000 × 0.30 = ₹45,000

After-tax cash flow from disposal of JIT system at end of Year 5: ₹50,000 × (1 − 0.30) = ₹35,000

Annual after-tax cash flow from operations:

	Year 1	Year 2	Year 3	Year 4	Year 5
Incremental revenues					
(5% annual growth)	₹5,00,000	₹5,25,000	₹5,51,250	₹5,78,813	₹6,07,753
Incremental contribution margin					
(60% × incremental revenues)	₹3,00,000	₹3,15,000	₹3,30,750	₹3,47,288	₹3,64,652
Rent savings	40,000	40,000	40,000	40,000	40,000
Deduct increase in software upgrades and tech support costs	(75,000)	(75,000)	(75,000)	(75,000)	(75,000)
Annual pre-tax incremental cash inflow from operations	2,65,000	2,80,000	2,95,750	3,12,288	3,29,652
Deduct income tax payments (30%)	79,500	84,000	88,725	93,686	98,896
Annual after-tax incremental cash inflow from operations	₹1,85,500	₹1,96,000	₹2,07,025	₹2,18,602	₹2,30,756

2. Solution Exhibit 21-26 reports the net present value to be ₹2,14,506.

3. Saina will have a NPV of ₹2,14,506 with the new data warehousing and analytics system. Based on financial quantitative factors, this is an attractive investment. Qualitative factors could make the system even more attractive. For example, if a competitor

adopts the new information system but Saina does not, Saina could be at a sizable competitive disadvantage. Not adopting the information system does not mean the status quo will remain. Saina's workers can also gain additional expertise when using the data warehousing and analytics system that can be beneficially employed on other projects.

Solution Exhibit 21-26

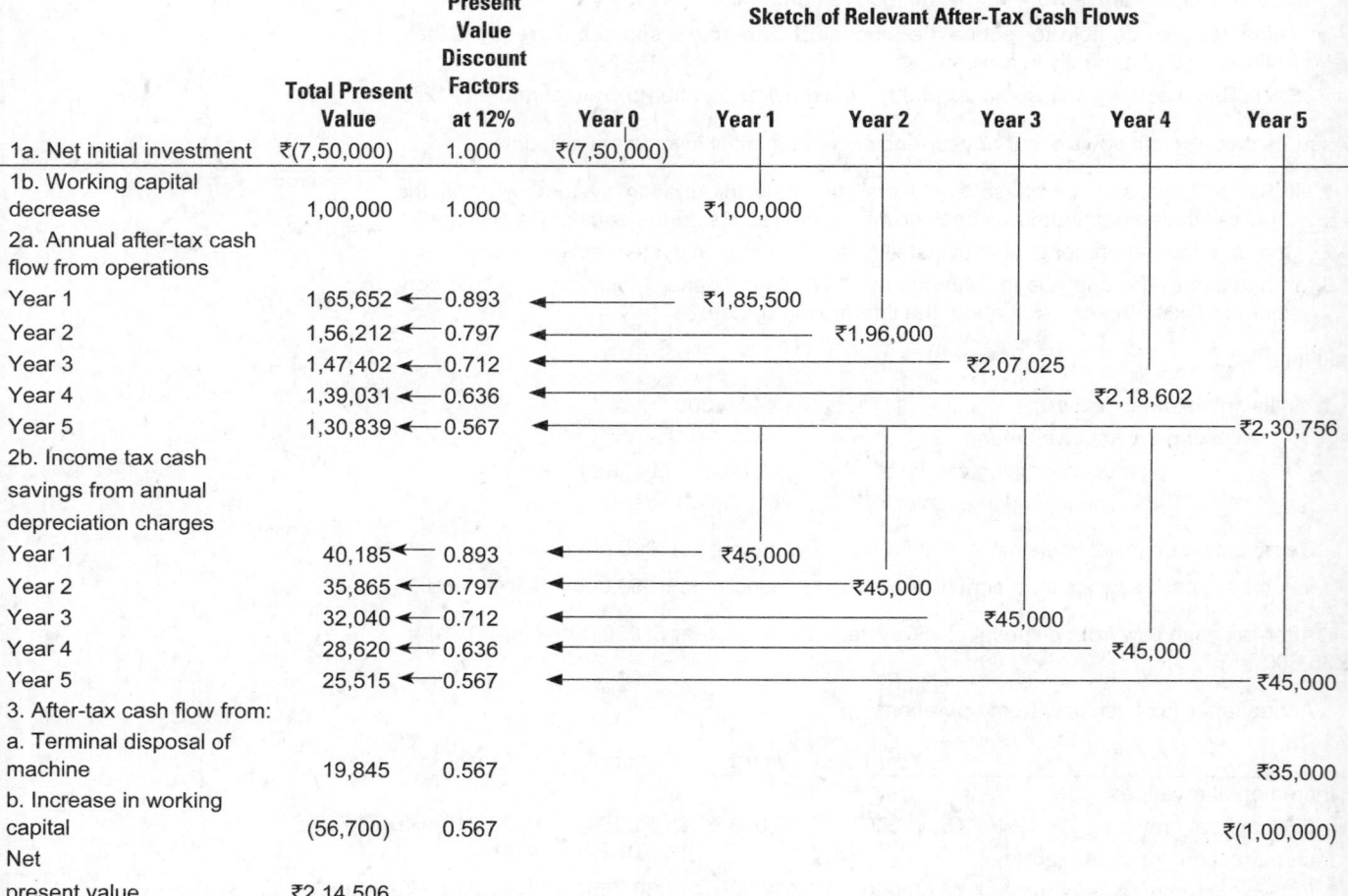

	Total Present Value	Present Value Discount Factors at 12%	Year 0	Year 1	Year 2	Year 3	Year 4	Year 5
					Sketch of Relevant After-Tax Cash Flows			
1a. Net initial investment	₹(7,50,000)	1.000	₹(7,50,000)					
1b. Working capital decrease	1,00,000	1.000		₹1,00,000				
2a. Annual after-tax cash flow from operations								
Year 1	1,65,652 ← 0.893			₹1,85,500				
Year 2	1,56,212 ← 0.797				₹1,96,000			
Year 3	1,47,402 ← 0.712					₹2,07,025		
Year 4	1,39,031 ← 0.636						₹2,18,602	
Year 5	1,30,839 ← 0.567							₹2,30,756
2b. Income tax cash savings from annual depreciation charges								
Year 1	40,185 ← 0.893			₹45,000				
Year 2	35,865 ← 0.797				₹45,000			
Year 3	32,040 ← 0.712					₹45,000		
Year 4	28,620 ← 0.636						₹45,000	
Year 5	25,515 ← 0.567							₹45,000
3. After-tax cash flow from:								
a. Terminal disposal of machine	19,845	0.567						₹35,000
b. Increase in working capital	(56,700)	0.567						₹(1,00,000)
Net present value	₹2,14,506							

Answers to Exercises in compound interest (Exercise 21-16)

The general approach to these exercises centers on a key question: which of the four basic tables in Appendix A should be used? No computations should be made until this basic question has been answered with confidence

1. **Form table 1.** The ₹10,000 is the present value P of your Winnings. Their future value S in 10 years will be as follows:

   $S = P(1 + r)^n$

   The conversion, $(1 + r)^n$, is on line 10 of Table 1

   Substituting at 8%: S = ₹10,000 (2.159) = ₹21,590

   Substituting at 10%: S = ₹10,000 (2.594) = ₹25,940

2. **Form table 2.** The ₹1,54,900 is a future value. You want the present value of that amount $P = S \div (1+r)n$. the conversion factor, $1 \div (1 + r)^n$ is on line 10 of table 2. Substituting

   $$P = ₹1,54,900 (.676) = ₹1,04,172.40$$

3. **Form table .3** The ₹1,54,900 is a Future value. You are seeking the uniform (annuity) to set aside annually. Note that ₹1 invested each year for 10 year at 10% has a future value of ₹15.937 after 10 years, form line 10 of table 3

   ₹1,54,900/15,937 = ₹9,719.52

4. **Form table 3.** You need to find the future value of an annuity of ₹7,500 per year. Note that ₹1 invested each year for 10 years at 8% has a future value of ₹14.487 after 10 years.

   ₹7,500 (14.487) = ₹1,08,652.50

5. **Form table. 4.** when you reach age 65 you will get ₹2,50,000 a present value at that time. You need to find the annuity that will exactly exhaust the invested principal in 10 years. To pay yourself ₹1 each year for 10 years when the interest rate is 8% requires you to have ₹6.710 today, form line 10 of table 4

   ₹2,50,000/6.710 = ₹37,257.82

6. **Form Table 4.** You need to find the present value of an annuity for 10 years at 8% and at 12%

   8%: ₹65,000(6.710) = ₹4,36,150.00

   12%: ₹65,000(5.650) = ₹3,67,250,00

7 Plan A is preferable. The NPV of plan A exceeds that of plan B by ₹851

Year	PV Factor at 8%	Plan A Cash inflows	Plan A PV cash inflows	Plan B Cash inflows	Plan B PV of Cash inflows
0	1.000	₹(10,000)	₹(10,000)	₹(10,000)	₹(10,000)
1	0.926	3,000	2,778	1,000	926
2	0.587	5,000	4,285	2,000	1,714
3	0.794	2,000	1,588	3,000	2,382
4	0.735	3,000	2,205	4,000	2,940
5	0.681	2,000	1,362	5,000	3,405
			₹2,218		₹1,367

Even though plans A and B have the same total cash inflows over the 5 years, plan A is preferred because it was greater cash inflows occurring earlier

Exercises

[*Comprehensive solutions to all exercises are available on the companion website www. pearsoned.co.in/charlesthorngren*]

21-27 Capital budgeting with uneven cash flows, no income taxes. Village Soft Drink Company is considering the purchase of a special purpose bottling bus for ₹2,30,000. It is expected to have a useful life of four years with a ₹0 terminal disposal value. The plant manager estimates the following savings in cash operating costs:

Year	Amount
1	₹1,00,000
2	80,000
3	60,000
4	50,000
Total	₹2,90,000

Village Soft Drink Company uses a required rate of return of 16% in its capital budgeting decisions. Ignore income taxes in your analysis.

Compute the following:

Required

1. Net present value
2. Payback period
3. Internal rate of return

4. Accrual accounting rate of return based on net initial investment (Assume straight-line depreciation. Use the average annual savings in cash operating costs when computing the numerator of the accrual accounting rate of return.)

21-28 Payback and NPV methods, no income taxes (CMA, adapted). Royal Manufacturing is a small company currently analyzing capital expenditure proposals for the purchase of equipment. The capital budget is limited to ₹5,00,000, which Royal believes is the maximum capital it can raise.

A consulting company is preparing an analysis of four projects that Royal is considering. The consulting company has projected the future cash flows for each potential purchase. The information concerning the four projects is as follows:

	Project A	Project B	Project C	Project D
Projected cash outflow				
Net initial investment	₹2,00,000	₹1,90,000	₹2,50,000	₹2,10,000
Projected cash inflows				
Year 1	₹50,000	₹40,000	₹75,000	₹75,000
Year 2	50,000	50,000	75,000	75,000
Year 3	50,000	70,000	60,000	60,000
Year 4	50,000	75,000	80,000	40,000
Year 5	50,000	75,000	1,00,000	20,000

Required

1. Because Royal Manufacturing's cash is limited, its CEO thinks the payback method for calculating investments would be the best method for choosing capital budgeting projects. (a) Explain what the payback method measures and how it is used. Include in your explanation several benefits and limitations of the method. (b) Calculate the payback period for each of the four projects. Ignore income tax considerations.

2. The consulting company would like to compare the projects using the net present value method. The required rate of return for Royal is 12%. All cash flows occur at the end of the year. Calculate the net present value for each project. Ignore income tax considerations.

3. Which projects, if any, would you recommend funding? Briefly state your reasons.

21-29 New equipment purchase, income taxes. Presentation Graphics prepares slides and other aids for individuals making presentations. It estimates it can save ₹3,50,000 a year in cash operating costs for the next five years if it buys a special-purpose color-slide workstation at a cost of ₹7,50,000.

The workstation will have a ₹0 terminal disposal value at the end of year 5. No change in working capital will be required. Presentation Graphics has a 12% after-tax required rate of return. Its income tax rate is 40%.

Required

1. Assume that Presentation Graphics uses straight-line depreciation on its tax return. Compute (a) net present value, (b) payback period, and (c) internal rate of return.

2. Compare and contrast the capital budgeting methods in requirement 1.

21-30 Selling a plant, income taxes (CMA, adapted). Raymond, a clothing manufacturer, has a plant that will become idle on December 31, 2015. The corporate controller, has been asked to look at two options regarding the plant.

- Option 1: The plant, which has been fully depreciated for tax purposes can be sold immediately for ₹90,00,000.

- Option 2: The plant can be leased to Arvind Mills, one of Raymond's suppliers, for four years. Under the lease terms, Arvind would pay Raymond ₹24,00,000 rent per year (payable at year-end) and would grant Raymond a ₹4,74,000 annual discount off the normal price of fabric purchased by Raymond (assume discount received at year-end for each of the four years). Arvind would bear all of the plant's ownership costs. Raymond expects to sell this plant for ₹20,00,000 at the end of the four-year lease.

Raymond treats all cash flows as if they occur at the end of the year, and it uses an after-tax required rate of return of 12%. Raymond is subject to a 40% income tax rate.

Required

Calculate net present value of each of the options and determine which option Raymond should select using the NPV criterion.

21-31 NPV and customer profitability, no income taxes. National Granite sells granite counter-tops to the construction industry. National has three customers: X, Y, and Z. Following are National Granite's revenue and cost data by customer for the year ended December 31, 2014:

	X	Y	Z
Revenues	₹45,000	₹3,25,000	₹8,60,000
Cost of goods sold	22,000	1,80,000	5,50,000
Operating costs	10,000	75,000	2,35,000

Jay National, the owner, estimates that revenue and costs will increase as follows on an annual basis:

	X	Y	Z
Revenues	5%	6%	8%
Cost of goods sold	4%	4%	4%
Operating costs	4%	4%	4%

National Granite's required rate of return is 10%. Assume that (a) all transactions occur at year-end, (b) all revenues are cash inflows, and (c) all costs are cash outflows. Ignore income tax considerations.

Required

1. Calculate operating income per customer for 2014 and for each year of the 2015 to 2019 period.

2. National estimates the value of each customer by calculating the customer's projected net present value over the next five years (2015 to 2019). Use the operating incomes calculated in requirement 1 to compute the value of each of its three customers.

3. Recently, customer Y has been threatening to switch suppliers. Y demands a 20% price discount on the revenues for 2015 to 2019 that were estimated for Y in requirement 1 above, if it is to continue using National as a supplier. What is the five-year NPV of Y after incorporating the 20% discount? What other factors should National consider before making its final decision?

21-32 Replacement of a bus, income taxes, sensitivity (CMA, adapted). Rainbow Company operates a snack-food center at the heart of city. On January 1, 2012, Rainbow purchased a special cookie-cutting bus, which has been used for three years. Rainbow is considering purchasing a newer, more-efficient bus. If purchased, the new bus would be acquired today, January 1, 2015. Rainbow expects to sell 3,00,000 cookies in each of the next four years. The selling price of each cookie is expected to average ₹5.

Rainbow has two options: (1) continue to operate the old bus or (2) sell the old bus and purchase the new bus. The seller of the new bus offered no trade-in. The following information has been assembled to help management decide which option is more desirable:

	Old Machine	New Machine
Initial purchase costs of bus	₹8,00,000	₹12,00,000
Terminal disposal value at the end of useful life assumed for depreciation purposes	₹1,00,000	₹2,00,000
Useful life from date of acquisition	7 years	4 years
Expected annual cash operating costs:		
Variable cost per cookie	₹2.0	₹1.4
Total fixed costs	₹1,50,000	₹1,40,000
Depreciation method used for tax purposes	Straight-line	Straight-line
Estimated disposal prices of buss:		
January 1, 2015	₹4,00,000	₹12,00,000
December 31, 2018	₹70,000	₹2,00,000

Rainbow is subject to a 40% income tax rate. Assume that any gain or loss on the sale of buss is treated as an ordinary tax item and will affect the taxes paid by Rainbow in the year in which it occurs. Rainbow has an after-tax required rate of return of 16%.

1. Use the net present value method to determine whether Rainbow should retain the old bus or acquire the new bus.

2. How much more or less would the recurring after-tax cash operating savings have to be for Rainbow to exactly earn the 16% after-tax required rate of return? Assume all other data about the investment do not change.

3. Assume that the financial differences between the net present values of the two options are so slight that Rainbow is indifferent between the two proposals. Identify and discuss the nonfinancial and qualitative factors that Rainbow should consider.

21-33 Relevant costs, outsourcing, capital budgeting, income taxes. The Indian Electrical appliances (IEA) Company currently makes as many units of Part No. 789 as it needs. David, general manager of the IEA Company, has received a bid from the Philips for supplying Part No. 789. Current plans call for Philips to supply 10,000 units of Part No. 789 per year at ₹50 a unit. Philips can begin supplying on January 1, 2015, and continue for five years, after which time IEA will not need the part. Philips can accommodate any change in IEA's demand for the part and will supply it for ₹50 a unit, regardless of quantity.

The management accountant of IEA Company reports the following costs for manufacturing 10,000 units of Part No. 789:

Direct materials	₹2,20,000
Direct manufacturing labor	1,10,000
Variable manufacturing overhead	70,000
Depreciation on bus	1,00,000
Product and process engineering	40,000
Rent	20,000
Allocation of general plant overhead costs	50,000
Total costs	₹6,10,000

The following additional information is available:

a. Part No. 789 is made on a bus used exclusively for the manufacture of Part No. 789. The bus was acquired on January 1, 2014, at a cost of ₹6,00,000. The bus has a useful life of six years and ₹0 terminal disposal value. Depreciation is calculated on the straight-line method.

b. The bus could be sold today for ₹1,50,000.

c. Product and process engineering costs are incurred to ensure that the manufacturing process for Part No. 789 works smoothly. Although these costs are fixed in the short run with respect to units of Part No. 789 produced, they can be saved in the long run if this part is no longer produced. If Part No. 789 is outsourced, product and process engineering costs of ₹40,000 will be incurred for 2015 but not thereafter.

d. Rent costs of ₹20,000 are allocated to products on the basis of the floor space used for manufacturing the product. If Part No. 789 is discontinued, the space currently used to manufacture it would become available. The company could then use the space for storage and save ₹10,000 currently paid for outside storage.

e. General plant overhead costs are allocated to each department on the basis of direct manufacturing labor costs. These costs will not change in total, but no general plant overhead will be allocated to Part No. 789 if the part is outsourced.

Assume that IEA requires a 12% required rate of return for this project.

Should David outsource Part No. 789? Prepare a quantitative analysis using the net present value method. Assume all cash flows other than disposal of bus occur at the end of each year.

Transfer pricing is the price one subunit of a company charges for the services it provides another subunit of the same company.

At Ford, for example, automotive components, vehicles, and assembly services are bought and sold internally across divisions. The intellectual property patents of many pharmaceutical companies, such as Merck, are usually held by foreign subsidiaries, making the transfer price to these subsidiaries a critical factor in how much income is recognized in various tax jurisdictions.

Firms use transfer prices (1) to focus managers' attention on the performance of their own subunits and (2) to plan and coordinate the actions of different subunits to maximize the company's income as a whole. Transfer prices can lead to disagreements, however, because managers of different subunits often have very different preferences about how transfer prices should be set. For example, some managers prefer the prices be based on market prices. Others prefer the prices be based on costs alone. Controversies also arise when multinational corporations seek to reduce their overall income tax burden by charging high transfer prices to units located in countries with high tax rates. Many countries, including the United States, attempt to restrict this practice.

Management Control Systems

A **management control system** is a means of gathering and using information to aid and coordinate the planning and control decisions throughout an organization and to guide the behavior of its managers and other employees. Some companies design their management control system around the concept of the balanced scorecard. For example, ExxonMobil's management control system contains financial and nonfinancial information in each of the four perspectives of the balanced scorecard (see Chapter 12 for details). Well-designed management control systems use information both from within the company, such as net income and employee satisfaction, and from outside the company, such as stock price and customer satisfaction data.

Formal and Informal Systems

Management control systems consist of formal and informal control systems. The formal management control system of a company includes explicit rules, procedures, performance measures, and incentive plans that guide the behavior of its managers and other employees. The formal control system is comprised of several systems, such as:

- The management accounting system provides information regarding costs, revenues, and income.

- The human resources systems provide information on recruiting, training, absenteeism, and accidents.

- The quality systems provide information on yield, defective products, and late deliveries to customers.

The informal management control system includes the shared values, loyalties, and mutual commitments among members of the company, the company's culture, and the unwritten norms about acceptable behavior for managers and other employees. Examples of company slogans that reinforce values and loyalties are "At Ford, Quality Is Job 1," and "At Home Depot, Low Prices Are Just the Beginning."

Effective Management Control

Learning Objective 1

Describe a management control system

. . . gathers information for planning and control decisions

and its three key properties

. . . aligns with strategy, supports organizational responsibility of managers, and motivates employees

To be effective, management control systems should be closely aligned with the company's strategies and goals. Two examples of strategies at Exxon-Mobil are (1) providing innovative products and services to increase market share in key customer segments (by targeting customers who are willing to pay more for faster service, better facilities, and well-stocked convenience stores) and (2) reducing costs and targeting price-sensitive customers. Suppose Exxon-Mobil decides, to pursue the former strategy. The management control system must then reinforce this goal, and Exxon-Mobil should tie managers' rewards to achieving the targeted measures.

Management control systems should also be designed to support the organizational responsibilities of individual managers. Different levels of management at Exxon-Mobil need different kinds of information to perform their tasks. For example, top management needs stock-price information to evaluate how much shareholder value the company has created. The stock price, however, is less important for line managers supervising individual refineries. Those managers are more concerned with obtaining information about the firm's on-time delivery of gasoline, equipment downtime, product quality, number of days lost to accidents and environmental problems, cost per gallon of gasoline, and employee satisfaction. Similarly, marketing managers are more concerned with information about the service at gas stations, customer satisfaction, and market share.

Effective management control systems should also motivate managers and other employees. **Motivation** is the desire to attain a selected goal (the *goal-congruence* aspect) combined with the resulting pursuit of that goal (the *effort* aspect).

Goal congruence exists when individuals and groups work toward achieving the organization's goals—that is, managers working in their own best interest take actions that align with the overall goals of top management. Suppose the goal of Exxon-Mobil's top management is to maximize operating income. If the management control system evaluates the refinery manager *only* on the basis of costs, the manager may be tempted to make decisions that minimize cost but overlook product quality or timely delivery to retail stations. This oversight probably won't maximize operating income of the company as a whole. In this case, the management control system will not achieve goal congruence.

Effort is the extent to which managers strive or endeavor in order to achieve a goal. Effort goes beyond physical exertion, such as a worker producing at a faster rate, to include mental actions as well. For example, effort includes the diligence or acumen with which a manager gathers and analyzes data before authorizing a new investment. It is impossible

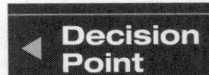
Decision Point

What is a management control system and how should it be designed?

to directly observe or reward effort. As a result, management control systems motivate employees to exert effort by rewarding them for the achievement of tangible goals, such as profit targets or stock returns. This induces managers to exert effort because higher levels of effort increase the likelihood that the goals are achieved. The rewards can be monetary (such as cash, shares of company stock, use of a company car, or membership in a club) or nonmonetary (such as a better title, greater responsibility, or authority over a larger number of employees). Management control systems must be aligned with an organization's structure. An organization with a decentralized structure will have different issues to consider when designing its management control system than a firm with a centralized structure.

Decentralization

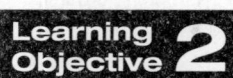

Learning Objective 2

Describe the benefits of decentralization

. . . responsiveness to customers, faster decision making, management development

and the costs of decentralization

. . . loss of control, duplication of activities

Until the mid-20th century, many firms were organized in a centralized, hierarchical fashion. Centralization is an organizational structure in which power is concentrated at the top and there is relatively little freedom for managers at the lower levels to make decisions. Perhaps the most famous example of a highly centralized structure is the Soviet Union, prior to its collapse in the late 1980s.

Today, organizations are far more decentralized and many companies have pushed decision-making authority down to subunit managers. Decentralization is an organizational structure that gives managers at lower levels the freedom to make decisions. Autonomy is the degree of freedom to make decisions. The greater the freedom, the greater the autonomy. As we discuss the issues of decentralization and autonomy, we use the term *subunit* to refer to any part of an organization. A subunit may be a large division, such as the refining division of ExxonMobil, or a small group, such as a two-person advertising department of a local clothing chain.

Examples of firms with decentralized structures include Nucor, the U.S. steel giant, which gives the general managers of its plants a substantial amount of operational autonomy, and Tesco, Britain's largest retailer, which offers great latitude to its store managers. Of course, no firm is completely decentralized. Nucor's top managers are still responsible for the firm's overall strategic planning, financing, setting of base salary levels and bonus targets, and so on. How much decentralization is optimal? Companies try to choose the degree of decentralization that maximizes benefits over costs. We next discuss the key benefits and costs of decentralization.

Benefits of Decentralization

Supporters of decentralizing decision making claim the following benefits from granting responsibilities to managers of subunits:

1. **Creates greater responsiveness to the needs of a subunit's customers, suppliers, and employees.** Good decisions cannot be made without good information. Compared with top managers, subunit managers are better informed about their competitors, suppliers, and employees, as well as about local factors that affect performance, such as ways to decrease costs, improve quality, and better respond to customers. Flextronics, a global supply chain solutions company, uses decentralization to reduce bureaucracy and increase responsiveness. Managers can use the company's worldwide information technology to solve a local customer's problem or send a project to other managers without going through red tape.

2. **Leads to gains from faster decision making by subunit managers.** Decentralization speeds decision making, creating a competitive advantage over centralized organizations. Centralization slows down decision making because the decisions must be pushed upward through layer after layer of management before they are finalized. Interlake Mecalux, a leading provider of materials-handling solutions and storage products, cites this benefit of decentralization: "We have distributed decision-making powers more broadly to the

cutting edge of product and market opportunity." Interlake's storage system solutions must often be customized to fit the needs of customers. Delegating decision making to the sales force allows Interlake to respond faster to changing customer requirements.

3. **Assists management development and learning.** Subunit managers are more motivated and committed when they can exercise initiative. Moreover, giving managers more responsibility helps a company develop an experienced pool of talent to fill higher-level management positions and weed out people unlikely to be successful top managers. According to Tektronix, an electronics company based in Oregon, "Decentralized units provide a training ground for general managers and a visible field of combat where product champions can fight for their ideas."

4. **Sharpens the focus of subunit managers, broadens the reach of top management.** In a decentralized setting, the manager of a subunit has a concentrated focus. The head of Yahoo Japan, for example, can develop country-specific knowledge and expertise (local advertising trends, cultural norms, payment forms, etc.) and focus attention on maximizing Yahoo's profits in Japan. At the same time, this relieves Yahoo's top management in Sunnyvale, CA from the burden of controlling day-to-day operating decisions in Japan. The American managers can now spend more time and effort on strategic planning for the entire organization.

Costs of Decentralization

Advocates of more-centralized decision making believe decentralizing is costly because it does the following:

1. **Leads to suboptimal decision making.** If the subunit managers do not have the necessary expertise or talent to make major decisions, the company, as a whole, is worse off because its top managers have relinquished their responsibility for doing so. Even if subunit managers are sufficiently skilled, **suboptimal decision making**—also called **incongruent decision making** or **dysfunctional decision making**—occurs when a decision's benefit to one subunit is more than offset by the costs to the organization as a whole. This is most prevalent when the subunits of the company are highly interdependent, such as when the end product of one subunit is used or sold by another subunit. For example, suppose Nintendo's marketing group receives a rush order for additional Wii consoles in Australia following the release of some popular new games. A manufacturing manager in Japan who is evaluated on the basis of costs may be unwilling to arrange this rush order because altering production schedules invariably increases manufacturing costs. From Nintendo's viewpoint, however, supplying the consoles may be optimal, both because the Australian customers are willing to pay a premium price and because the current shipment is expected to stimulate future orders for other Nintendo games and consoles.

2. **Leads to unhealthy competition.** In a decentralized setting, subunit managers may regard themselves as competing with managers of other subunits in the same company as if they were external rivals. This pushes them to view the relative performance of the subunit as more important than the goals of the company. Consequently, managers may be unwilling to assist other subunits (as in the Nintendo example) or share important information. The 2010 Congressional hearings on the recall of Toyota vehicles revealed that it was common for Toyota's Japan unit to not share information about engineering problems or reported defects between its United States, Asian, and European operations. Toyota has since asserted that it will change this dysfunctional behavior.

3. **Results in duplication of output.** If subunits provide similar products or services, their internal competition could lead to failure in the external markets. The reason is that divisions may find it easier to steal market share from one another, by mimicking each other's successful products, rather than those of competing firms. Eventually, this leads to confusion in the minds of customers and the loss of each division's

distinctive strengths. A classic example is General Motors, which eventually dissolved its Oldsmobile, Pontiac, and Saturn divisions. Similarly, Condé Nast Publishing's initially distinct food magazines *Bon Appétit* and *Gourmet* eventually ended up chasing the same readers and advertisers, to the detriment of both. *Gourmet* magazine stopped publication in November 2009.[1]

4. **Results in duplication of activities.** Even if the subunits operate in distinct markets, several individual subunits of the company may undertake the same activity separately. In a highly decentralized company, each subunit may have personnel to carry out staff functions such as human resources or information technology. Centralizing these functions helps to streamline and use fewer resources for these activities and eliminates wasteful duplication. For example, ABB of Switzerland, a global leader in power and automation technology, is decentralized but has generated significant cost savings of late by centralizing its sourcing decisions across business units for parts, such as pipe pumps and fittings, as well as engineering and erection services. Having subunits share services such as information technology and human resources is becoming popular with companies because it saves 30–40% of the cost of having each subunit purchase these services on its own.

Comparing Benefits and Costs

Top managers must compare the benefits and costs of decentralization, often on a function-by-function basis, when choosing an organizational structure. Surveys of U.S. and European companies report that the decisions made most frequently at the decentralized level are related to product mix and advertising. In these areas, subunit managers develop their own operating plans and performance reports and make faster decisions based on local information. Decisions related to the type and source of long-term financing are made least frequently at the decentralized level. Corporate managers have better information about financing terms in different markets and can obtain the best terms. Likewise, centralizing its income tax strategies allows the organization to optimize across subunits, for example by offsetting the income in one subunit with losses in others.

Decentralization in Multinational Companies

Multinational companies—companies that operate in multiple countries—are often decentralized because centralizing the control of their subunits around the world can be physically and practically impossible. Also, language, customs, cultures, business practices, rules, laws, and regulations vary significantly across countries. Decentralization enables managers in different countries to make decisions that exploit their knowledge of local business and political conditions and enables them to deal with uncertainties in their individual environments. For example, Philips, a global electronics company headquartered in the Netherlands, delegates marketing and pricing decisions for its television businesses in India and Singapore to the managers in those countries. Multinational corporations often rotate managers between foreign locations and corporate headquarters. Job rotation combined with decentralization helps develop the ability of managers to operate in the global environment.

There are drawbacks to decentralizing multinational companies. One of the most important is the lack of control and the resulting risks. In 1995, Barings PLC, a British investment banking firm, went bankrupt and had to be sold when one of its traders in Singapore caused the firm to lose more than ₹10 billion on unauthorized trades that went undetected. Similarly, in 2011, a London trader working for UBS, Switzerland's largest bank, circumvented the bank's risk controls and made unauthorized trades that resulted in a ₹23.0 billion loss for the company. UBS's CEO and other top managers resigned because of the scandal. Multinational

---

[1] For an intriguing comparison of the failure of decentralization in these disparate settings, see Jack Shafer's article, "How Condé Nast Is Like General Motors: The Magazine Empire as Car Wreck," Slate (October 5, 2009). http://www.slate.com/ id/2231177/.

corporations that implement decentralized decision making usually design their management control systems to measure and monitor the performance of divisions. Information and communications technology helps the flow of information for reporting and control.

Choices About Responsibility Centers

Recall from Chapter 6 that a responsibility center is a segment or subunit of the organization whose manager is accountable for a specified set of activities. To measure the performance of subunits in centralized or decentralized companies, the management control system uses one or a mix of the four types of responsibility centers:

1. *Cost center*—the manager is accountable for costs only.
2. *Revenue center*—the manager is accountable for revenues only.
3. *Profit center*—the manager is accountable for revenues and costs.
4. *Investment center*—the manager is accountable for investments, revenues, and costs.

Each type of responsibility center can be found in either centralized or decentralized companies.

A common misconception is that profit center—and, in some cases, *investment center*—is a synonym for a decentralized subunit, and cost center is a synonym for a centralized subunit. *Profit centers can be coupled with a highly centralized organization, and cost centers can be coupled with a highly decentralized organization.* For example, managers in a division organized as a profit center may have little freedom in making decisions. They may need to obtain approval from corporate headquarters for introducing new products and services or to make expenditures over some preset limit. When Michael Eisner ran Walt Disney Company, the giant media and entertainment conglomerate, from 1984 until 2005, the firm's strategic-planning division scrutinized business proposals so closely that managers were reluctant to pitch new ideas.[2] In other companies, divisions such as information technology may be organized as cost centers, but their managers may have great latitude to make capital expenditures and purchase materials and services. In short, the labels "*profit center*" and "*cost center*" are independent of the degree of centralization or decentralization in a company.

> ◀ **Decision Point**
>
> What are the benefits and costs of decentralization?

Transfer Pricing

In decentralized organizations, much of the decision-making power resides in its individual subunits. Often, the subunits interact by supplying goods or services to one another. In these cases, top management uses *transfer prices* to coordinate the actions of the subunits and to evaluate the performance.

A **transfer price** is the price one subunit (department or division) charges for a product or service supplied to another subunit of the same organization. If, for example, a car manufacturer like BMW or Ford has a separate division that manufactures engines, the transfer price is the price the engine division charges when it transfers engines to the car assembly division. The transfer price creates revenues for the selling subunit (the engine division in our example) and purchase costs for the buying subunit (the assembly division in our example), affecting each subunit's operating income. These operating incomes can be used to evaluate subunits' performances and to motivate their managers. The product or service transferred between subunits of an organization is called an intermediate product.

> **Learning Objective 3**
>
> Explain transfer prices
>
> . . . price one subunit charges another for product
>
> and four criteria used to evaluate them
>
> . . . goal congruence, management effort, subunit performance evaluation, and subunit autonomy

---

[2] When Robert Iger replaced Eisner as CEO in 2005, one of his first acts was to disassemble the strategic-planning division, thereby giving more authority to Disney's business units (parks and resorts, consumer products, and media networks).

The receiving unit (the assembly division in the engine example) may work on the product further or the product may be transferred from production to marketing and sold directly to an external customer.

In one sense, transfer pricing is a curious phenomenon. Activities within an organization are clearly nonmarket in nature; products and services are not bought and sold as they are in open-market transactions. Yet, establishing prices for transfers among subunits of a company has a distinctly market flavor. The rationale for transfer prices is that when subunit managers (such as the manager of the engine division), make decisions, they need only focus on how their decisions will affect their subunit's performance without evaluating their impact on companywide performance. In this sense, transfer prices ease the subunit managers' information-processing and decision-making tasks. In a well-designed transfer-pricing system, manager focus on optimizing the performance of there sub-units and in so doing optimizes the performance of the company as a whole.

Criteria for Evaluating Transfer Prices

To help a company achieve its goals, transfer prices should meet four key criteria:

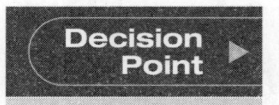

1. Promote goal congruence, so that division managers acting in their own interest will take actions that are aligned with the objectives of top management.
2. Induce managers to exert a high level of effort. Subunits selling a product or service should be motivated to hold down their costs; subunits buying the product or service should be motivated to acquire and use inputs efficiently.
3. Help top managers evaluate the performance of individual subunits.
4. Preserve autonomy of subunits if top managers favor a high degree of decentralization. A subunit manager seeking to maximize the operating income of the subunit should have the freedom to transact with other subunits of the company (on the basis of transfer prices) or to transact with external parties.

Calculating Transfer Prices

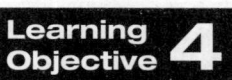

There are three broad categories of methods top managers can use to determine transfer prices. They are as follows:

1. **Market-based transfer prices.** Top managers may choose to use the price of a similar product or service publicly listed in, say, a trade association Web site. Or they may select, for the internal price, the external price that a subunit charges to outside customers.
2. **Cost-based transfer prices.** Top management may choose a transfer price based on the cost of producing the product being transferred. Examples include the variable production cost, variable and fixed production costs, and full cost of the product. The full cost of the product includes all production costs plus costs from other business functions (R&D, design, marketing, distribution, and customer service). The cost used in cost-based transfer prices can be actual cost or budgeted cost. Sometimes, the cost-based transfer price includes a markup or profit margin that represents a return on subunit investment.
3. **Hybrid transfer prices.** Hybrid transfer prices take into account both cost and market information. Top managers may set the prices by specifying a transfer price that is an average of the cost of producing and transporting the product internally and the market price for comparable products. At other times, a hybrid transfer price may allow

for the revenue recognized by the selling unit to differ from the cost recognized by the buying unit. The most common form of hybrid prices arises via negotiation—the subunit managers are asked to negotiate the transfer price between them and to decide whether to buy and sell internally or deal with external parties. Negotiated transfer prices are often employed when market prices are volatile. Thus, managers need current information about the costs and prices of products to participate in the bargaining process.

Under what circumstances should each of these options be used? To answer this question, we next demonstrate how each of the three transfer-pricing methods works and highlight the differences among them. We examine transfer pricing at Horizon Petroleum against the four criteria of promoting goal congruence, motivating management effort, evaluating subunit performance, and preserving subunit autonomy.

An Illustration of Transfer Pricing

Hindustan Petroleum has two divisions, each operating as a profit center. The Transportation Division purchases crude oil in Ankleshwar, Gujarat, and transports it from Ankleshwar to Mathura, U.P. The Refining Division processes crude oil into gasoline. For simplicity, we assume gasoline is the only salable product the Mathura refinery makes and that it takes two barrels of crude oil to yield one barrel of gasoline.

The Variable costs of each division are associated with single cost driver: barrels of crude oil transported by the Transportation Division, and barrels of gasoline produced by the Refining Division. The fixed cost per unit is based on the budgeted annual fixed costs and practical capacity of crude oil that can be transported by Transportation, as well the budgeted fixed costs and practical capacity of gasoline that can be produced by the Refining division.

- The Transportation Division has obtained rights to certain oil fields in the Ankleshwar area. It has a long-term contract to purchase crude oil produced from these fields at ₹720 per barrel. The division transports the oil to Mathura and then "sells" it to the Refining Division. The pipeline from Ankleshwar to Mathura has the capacity to carry 40,000 barrels of crude oil per day.

- The Refining Division has been operating at capacity (30,000 barrels of crude oil a day), using oil supplied by Hindustan Petroleum's Transportation Division (an average of 10,000 barrels per day) and oil bought from another producers and delivered to the Mathura refinery (an average of 20,000 barrels per day at ₹850 per barrel).

- The Refining Division sells the gasoline it produces to outside parties at ₹1,900 per barrel.

Exhibit 22-1 summarizes Hindustan Petroleum's variable and fixed costs per barrel of crude oil in the Transportation Division and variable and fixed costs per barrel of gasoline in the Refining Division, the external market prices of buying crude oil, and the external market price of selling gasoline. What's missing in the exhibit is the actual transfer price from the Transportation Division to the Refining Division. This transfer price will vary depending on the transfer-pricing method used. The transfer prices from the Transportation Division to the Refining Division under each of the three methods are as follows:

1. A market-based transfer price of ₹850 per barrel of crude oil based on the competitive market price in Mathura.

2. A cost-based transfer prices at, say, 105% of full cost, where full cost is the cost of the crude oil purchased in Ankleshwar plus the Transportation Division's own variable and fixed costs (from Exhibit 22-1): $1.05 \times (₹720 + ₹10 + ₹30) = ₹798$.

Exhibit 22-1   Operating Data for Hindustan Petroleum

	File Edit View Insert Format Tools Data Window Help						
	A	B	C	D	E	F	G	H
1								
2				**Transportation Division**				
3	Contract price per barrel of crude oil supplied in Ankleshwar			Variable cost per barrel of crude oi l	₹10			
4		= ₹720 →		Fixed cost per barrel of crude oil	30			
5				Full cost per barrel of crude oil	₹40			
6								
7								
8				Barrels of crude oil transferred				
9								
10								
11				**Refining Division**				
12	Market price per barrel of crude oil supplied to Mathura refinery			Variable cost per barrel of gasoline	₹80		Market price per barrel of gasoline sold to external parties	
13		= ₹ 850 →		Fixed cost per barrel of gasoline	60	→		= ₹1,900
14				Full cost per barrel of gasoline	₹140			
15								

3. A hybrid transfer price of, say, ₹820 per barrel of crude oil, which is between the market-based and cost-based transfer prices. We describe later in this section the various ways in which hybrid prices can be determined.

Exhibit 22-2 presents division operating incomes per 100 barrels of crude oil purchased under each transfer-pricing method. Transfer prices create income for the selling division and corresponding costs for the buying division that cancel out when division results are consolidated for the company as a whole. The exhibit assumes all three transfer-pricing methods yield transfer prices that are in a range that does not cause division managers to change the business relationships shown in Exhibit 22-1. That is, Hindustan Petroleum's total operating income from purchasing, transporting, and refining the 100 barrels of crude oil and selling the 50 barrels of gasoline is the same (₹12,000) *regardless of the internal transfer prices used.*

$$\text{Operating income} = \text{Revenues} - \begin{array}{c}\text{Cost of crude}\\\text{oil purchases}\\\text{in Ankleshwar}\end{array} - \begin{array}{c}\text{Transportation}\\\text{cost}\end{array} - \begin{array}{c}\text{Refining}\\\text{costs}\end{array}$$

= (₹1,900 × 50 barrels of gasoline) – (₹720 × 100 barrels of crude oil)
   (– ₹40 × 100 barrels of crude oil) – (₹140 × 50 barrels of gasoline)

= ₹95,000 – ₹72,000 – ₹4,000 – ₹7,000 = ₹12,000

Note further that under all three methods, summing the two division operating incomes equals Hindustan Petroleum's total operating income of ₹12,000. By keeping total operating income the same, we focus attention on the effects of different transfer-pricing methods on the operating income of each division. Subsequent sections of this chapter show that different transfer-pricing methods can cause managers to take different actions leading to different total operating incomes.

Consider the two methods in the first two columns of Exhibit 22-2. The operating income of the Transportation Division is ₹5,200 more (₹9,000 – ₹3,800) if transfer prices are based on market prices rather than on 105% of the full cost. The operating income of the Refining Division is ₹5,200 more (₹8,200 − ₹3,000) if transfer prices are based on 105% of full cost rather than market prices. If the Transportation Division's sole criterion were to maximize its own division operating income, it would favor transfer prices at market prices. In contrast, the Refining Division would prefer transfer prices at 105% of full cost to maximize its own division operating income. The hybrid transfer price of ₹820 negotiated by the Transportation and Refining Division managers is between the 105% of full cost and market-based transfer prices. It splits the ₹12,000 of operating income equally between the divisions. This price could arise as a result of negotiations between the transportation and refining division managers.

It's not surprising that subunit managers especially those managers whose compensation or promotion directly depends on subunit operating income, take considerable interest in setting transfer prices. To reduce the excessive focus of subunit managers on their own

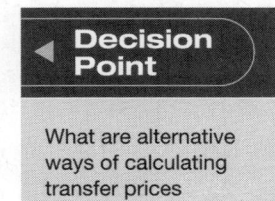

Decision Point

What are alternative ways of calculating transfer prices

Exhibit 22-2 — Division Operating Income of Hindustan Petroleum for 100 Barrels of Crude Oil Under Alternative Transfer-Pricing Methods

	A	B	C	D	E	F	G	H
1	**Production and Sales Data**							
2	Barrels of crude transferred	= 100						
3	Barrels of gasoline sold	= 50						
4								
5		**Internal Transfers**			**Internal Transfers at**		**Internal Transfers at**	
6		**at Market Price of**			**105% of Full Cost =**		**Negotiated Price of**	
7		**₹850**			**₹798**		**₹820**	
8		**per barrel**			**per barrel**		**per barrel**	
9	**Transportation Division**							
10	Revenues, ₹210, ₹176, ₹192.5 × 100 barrels of crude oil	₹85,000			₹79,800		₹82,000	
11	Costs							
12	Crude oil purchase costs,							
13	₹120 × 100 barrels of crude oil	72,000			72,000		72,000	
14	Division variable costs,							
15	₹10 × 100 barrels of crude oil	1,000			1,000		1,000	
16	Division fixed costs,							
17	₹30 × 100 barrels of crude oil	3,000			3,000		3,000	
18	Total division costs	76,000			76,000		76,000	
19	Division operating income	₹9,000			₹3,800		₹6,000	
20								
21	**Refining Division**							
22	Revenues, ₹580 × 50 barrels of gasoline	₹95,000			₹95,000		₹95,000	
23	Costs							
24	Transferred-in costs, ₹210, ₹176, ₹192.5							
25	× 100 barrels of crude oil	85,000			79,800		82,000	
26	Division variable costs,							
27	₹80 × 50 barrels of gasoline	4,000			4,000		4,000	
28	Division fixed costs,							
29	₹60 × 50 barrels of gasoline	3,000			3,000		3,000	
30	Total division costs	92,000			86,800		89,000	
31	Division operating income	₹3,000			₹8,200		6,000	
32								
33	Operating income of both divisions together	₹12,000			₹12,000		₹12,000	

subunits, many companies compensate subunit managers on the basis of both the operating incomes earned by their respective subunits and the company as a whole.

We next examine market-based, cost-based, and negotiated transfer prices in more detail. We show how the choice of transfer-pricing method combined with managers' sourcing decisions can determine the size of the companywide operating-income pie itself.

Market-Based Transfer Prices

Transferring products or services at market prices generally leads to optimal decisions when three conditions are satisfied: (1) The market for the intermediate product is perfectly competitive, (2) interdependencies of subunits are minimal, and (3) there are no additional costs or benefits to the company as a whole from buying or selling in the external market instead of transacting internally.

Perfectly-Competitive-Market Case

Learning Objective 5

Illustrate how market-based transfer prices promote goal congruence in perfectly competitive markets

... division managers transacting internally are motivated to take the same actions as if they were transacting externally

A **perfectly competitive market** exists when there is a homogeneous product with buying prices equal to selling prices and no individual buyers or sellers can affect those prices by their own actions. By using market-based transfer prices in perfectly competitive markets, a company can (1) promote goal congruence, (2) motivate management effort, (3) evaluate the performance of subunits, and (4) preserve their autonomy.

Consider Hindustan Petroleum again. Assume there is a perfectly competitive market for crude oil in the Mathura area. As a result, the Transportation Division can sell and the Refining Division can buy as much crude oil as each wants at ₹850 per barrel. Hindustan would prefer its managers to buy or sell crude oil internally. Think about the decisions that Hindustan's division managers would make if each had the autonomy to sell or buy crude oil externally. If the transfer price between Hindustan's Transportation and Refining Divisions is set below ₹850, the manager of the Transportation Division will be motivated to sell all crude oil to external buyers in the Mathura area at ₹850 per barrel. If the transfer price is set above ₹850, the manager of the Refining Division will be motivated to purchase all crude oil requirements from external suppliers. Only a ₹850 transfer price will motivate the Transportation Division and the Refining Division to buy and sell internally. That's because neither division profits by buying or selling in the external market.

Suppose Hindustan evaluates its division managers on the basis of their individual division's operating income. The Transportation Division will sell, either internally or externally, as much crude oil as it can profitably transport, and the Refining Division will buy, either internally or externally, as much crude oil as it can profitably refine. A ₹850-per-barrel transfer price achieves goal congruence—the actions that maximize each division's operating income are also the actions that maximize operating income of Hindustan Petroleum as a whole. Furthermore, because the transfer price is not based on costs, it motivates each division manager to exert management effort to maximize his or her own division's operating income. Market prices also serve to evaluate the economic viability and profitability of each division individually. For example, if under market-based transfer prices, the Refining Division consistently shows small or negative profits, Hindustan may decide to shut down the Refining Division and simply transport and sell the oil to other refineries in the Mathura area.

Distress Prices

When supply outstrips demand, market prices may drop well below their historical averages. If the drop in prices is expected to be temporary, these low market prices are sometimes called "distress prices." Deciding whether a current market price is a distress price is often difficult. Prior to the world-wide spike in commodity prices in the 2006–2008 period, the market prices of several mineral agricultural commodities, including nickel, uranium, and wheat stayed for many years at what many people initially believed were temporary distress levels!

Which transfer price should be used for judging performance if distress prices prevail? Some companies use the distress prices themselves, but others use long-run average prices, or "normal" market prices. In the short run, the manager of the selling subunit should supply the product or service at the distress price as long as it exceeds the incremental costs of supplying the product or service. If the distress price is used as the transfer price, the selling division will show a loss because the distress price will not exceed the full cost of the division. If the long-run average market price is used, forcing the manager to buy internally at a price above the current market price will hurt the buying division's short-run operating income. But the long-run average market price will provide a better measure of the long-run profitability and viability of the supplier division. Of course, if the price remains low in the long run, the company should use the low market price as the transfer price. If this price is lower than the variable and fixed costs that can be saved if manufacturing facilities are shut down, the production facilities of the selling subunit should be sold, and the buying subunit should purchase the product from an external supplier.

Imperfect Competition

If markets are not perfectly competitive, selling prices affect the quantity of product sold. Consider an auto dealer: In order to move more new or used cars off the lot, the dealer has to reduce the price of the vehicles. A similar situation applies to industries ranging from toilet paper and toothpaste to software. Faced with an imperfectly competitive market, the manager of the selling division will choose a price and quantity combination for the intermediate product that maximizes the division's operating income. If the transfer price is set at this price, the buying division may find that acquiring the product is too costly and results in a loss and decide not to purchase the product. Yet, from the point of view of the company as a whole, it may well be that profits are maximized if the selling division transfers the product to the buying division for further processing and sale. For this reason, when the market for the intermediate good is imperfectly competitive, the transfer price must generally be set below the external market price (but above the selling division's variable cost) in order to induce efficient transfers.[3]

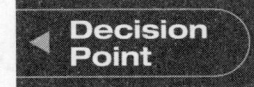

Decision Point

Under what market conditions do market-based transfer prices promote goal congruence?

Cost-Based Transfer Prices

Cost-based transfer prices are helpful when market prices are unavailable, inappropriate, or too costly to obtain, such as when markets are not perfectly competitive, when the prod-

---

[3] Consider a firm where division S produces the intermediate product. S has a capacity of 15 units and a variable cost per unit of ₹20. The imperfect competition is reflected in a downward-sloping demand curve for the intermediate product—if S wants to sell Q units, it has to lower the market price to $P = 20 - Q$. The division's profit function is therefore given by $Q \times (20 - Q) - 2Q = 18Q - Q^2$. Simple calculus reveals that it is optimal for S to sell 9 units of the intermediate product at a price of ₹110, thereby making a profit of ₹810. Now, suppose that division B in the same firm can take the intermediate product, incur an additional variable cost of ₹40 and sell it in the external market for ₹120. Since S has surplus capacity (it only uses 9 of its 15 units of capacity), it is clearly in the firm's interest to have S make additional units and transfer them to B. The firm makes an incremental profit of ₹120 − ₹20 − ₹40 = ₹60 for each transferred unit. However, if the transfer price for the intermediate product were set equal to the market price of ₹110, B would reject the transaction since it would lose money on it (₹120 − ₹110 − ₹40 = − ₹30 per unit).

To resolve this conflict, the transfer price should be set at a suitable *discount* to the external price in order to induce the buying division to seek internal transfers. In our example, the selling price must be greater than S's variable cost of ₹20, but less than B's contribution margin of ₹80. That is, the transfer price has to be discounted relative to the market price (₹110) by a minimum of ₹30. We explore the issue of feasible transfer pricing ranges further in the section on hybrid transfer prices.

uct is specialized, or when the internal product is different from the products available externally in terms of quality and customer service provided for it.

Full-Cost Bases

In practice, many companies use transfer prices based on full cost. To approximate market prices, cost-based transfer prices are sometimes set at full cost plus a margin. These transfer prices, however, can lead to suboptimal decisions. Suppose Hindustan Petroleum makes internal transfers at 105% of the full cost. Recall that the Refining Division purchases, on average, 20,000 barrels of crude oil per day from a local Mathura supplier, who delivers the crude oil to the refinery at a price of ₹850 per barrel. To reduce its crude oil costs, the Refining Division has located an independent producer in Ankleshwar—Reliance Petroleum—that is willing to sell 20,000 barrels of crude oil per day at ₹790 per barrel, delivered to Hindustan's pipeline in Ankleshwar. Given Hindustan's organization structure, the Transportation Division would purchase the 20,000 barrels of crude oil in Ankleshwar from Reliance Petroleum, transport it to Mathura, and then sell it to the Refining Division. The pipeline has unused capacity and can ship the 20,000 barrels per day at its variable cost of ₹10 per barrel without affecting the shipment of the 10,000 barrels of crude oil per day acquired under its existing long-term contract arrangement. Will Hindustan Petroleum incur lower costs by purchasing crude oil from Reliance Petroleum in Ankleshwar or by purchasing crude oil from the Mathura supplier? Will the Refining Division show lower crude oil purchasing costs by acquiring oil from Reliance Petroleum or by acquiring oil from its current Mathura supplier?

The following analysis shows that Hindustan Petroleum's operating income would be maximized by purchasing oil from Reliance Petroleum. The analysis compares the incremental costs in both divisions under the two alternatives. The analysis assumes the fixed costs of the Transportation Division will be the same regardless of the alternative chosen. That is, the Transportation Division cannot save any of its fixed costs if it does not transport Reliance's 20,000 barrels of crude oil per day.

- **Alternative 1:** Buy 20,000 barrels from the Mathura supplier at ₹850 per barrel. The total costs to Hindustan Petroleum are 20,000 barrels × ₹850 per barrel = ₹1,70,00,000.
- **Alternative 2:** Buy 20,000 barrels in Ankleshwar at ₹790 per barrel and transport them to Mathura at a variable cost of ₹10 per barrel. The total costs to Hindustan Petroleum are 20,000 barrels × (₹790 + ₹10) per barrel = ₹1,60,00,000.

There is a reduction in total costs to Hindustan Petroleum of ₹10,00,000 (₹1,70,00,000 − ₹1,60,00,000) by acquiring oil from Reliance.

Suppose the Transportation Division's transfer price to the Refining Division is 110% of the full cost. The Refining Division will see its reported division costs increase if the crude oil is purchased from Reliance:

$$\text{Transfer price} = 1.05 \times \left(\begin{array}{c} \text{Purchase price} \\ \text{from} \\ \text{Reliance} \end{array} + \begin{array}{c} \text{Variable cost per unit} \\ \text{of Transportation} \\ \text{Division} \end{array} + \begin{array}{c} \text{Fixed cost per unit} \\ \text{of Transportation} \\ \text{Division} \end{array} \right)$$

$$= 1.05 \times (₹790 + ₹10 + ₹30) = 1.05 \times ₹830 = ₹871.5 \text{ per barrel}$$

- **Alternative 1:** Buy 20,000 barrels from Mathura supplier at ₹850 per barrel. The total costs to Refining Division are 20,000 barrels × ₹850 per barrel = ₹1,70,00,000.

- **Alternative 2:** Buy 20,000 barrels from the Transportation Division of Hindustan Petroleum that were purchased from Reliance. The total costs to Refining Division are 20,000 barrels × ₹871.5 per barrel = ₹1,74,30,000.

As a profit center, the Refining Division can maximize its short-run division operating income by purchasing from the Mathura supplier.

The Refining Division looks at each barrel that it obtains from the Transportation Division as a variable cost of ₹871.5 per barrel; if 10 barrels are transferred, it costs the Refining Division ₹8,715; if 100 barrels are transferred, it costs ₹87,150. In fact, the variable cost per barrel is ₹800 (₹790 to purchase the oil from Reliance plus ₹10 to transport it to Mathura). The remaining ₹71.5 (₹871.5 − ₹800) per barrel is the Transportation Division's fixed cost and markup. *The full cost plus a markup transfer-pricing method causes the Refining Division to regard the fixed cost (and the 50% markup) of the Transportation Division as a variable cost and leads to goal incongruence.*

Should Hindustan's top management interfere and force the Refining Division to buy from the Transportation Division? Doing so would undercut the philosophy of decentralization, so Hindustan's top managers would probably view the decision by the Refining Division to purchase crude oil from external suppliers as an inevitable cost of decentralization and not interfere. Of course, some interference may occasionally be necessary to prevent costly blunders. But recurring interference and constraints would simply transform Hindustan Petroleum from a decentralized company into a centralized company.

What transfer price will promote goal congruence for both the Transportation and Refining divisions? The minimum transfer price is ₹800 per barrel. A transfer price below ₹800 does not provide the Transportation Division with an incentive to purchase crude oil from Reliance in Ankleshwar because it is below the transport division's incremental costs. The maximum transfer price is ₹850 per barrel. A transfer price above ₹850 will cause the Refining Division to purchase crude oil from the external market in Mathura rather than from the Transportation Division. A transfer price between the minimum and maximum transfer prices of ₹800 and ₹850 will promote goal congruence: Each division will increase its own reported operating income while increasing Hindustan Petroleum's operating income if the Refining Division purchases crude oil from Reliance in Ankleshwar.

In the absence of a market-based transfer price, senior Hindustan Petroleum's top managers cannot easily determine the profitability of the investment made in the Transportation Division and hence whether Hindustan should keep or sell the pipeline. Furthermore, if the transfer price had been based on the actual costs of the Transportation Division, it would provide the division with no incentive to control costs. That's because all cost inefficiencies of the Transportation Division would get passed along as part of the actual full-cost transfer price. In fact, every additional rupee of cost arising from wastefulness in the transportation division would generate an additional five paise in profit for the division under the "105% of full cost" rule!

Surveys by accounting firms and researchers indicate that, despite its limitations, managers generally prefer to use full-cost-based transfer prices because (1) they represent relevant costs for long-run decisions, (2) they facilitate external pricing based on variable and fixed costs, and (3) they are the least costly to administer. However, full-cost transfer pricing does raise many issues. How are each subunit's indirect costs allocated to products? Have the correct activities, cost pools, and cost-allocation bases been identified? Should the chosen fixed-cost rates be actual or budgeted? The issues here are similar to the issues that arise in allocating fixed costs, which were introduced in Chapter 14. Many companies determine the transfer price based on budgeted rates and practical capacity because it overcomes the problem of inefficiencies in actual costs and costs of unused capacity getting passed along to the buying division.

Variable-Cost Bases

Transferring 20,000 barrels of crude oil from the Transportation Division to the Refining Division at the variable cost of ₹800 per barrel achieves goal congruence, as shown in the preceding section. The Refining Division would buy from the Transportation Division because the Transportation Division's variable cost is less than the ₹850 price charged by external suppliers. Setting the transfer price equal to the variable cost has other benefits. Knowing the variable cost per barrel of crude oil helps the Refining Division make many decisions such as the short-run pricing decisions discussed in Chapters 11. However, at the ₹800-per-barrel transfer price, the Transportation Division would record an operating loss, and the Refining Division would show large profits because it would be charged only for the variable costs of the Transportation Division. One approach to addressing this problem is to have the Refining Division make a lump-sum transfer payment to cover fixed costs and generate some operating income for the Transportation Division while the Transportation Division continues to make transfers at variable cost. The fixed payment is the price the Refining Division pays for using the capacity of the Transportation Division. The income earned by each division can then be used to evaluate the performance of each division and its manager.

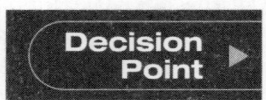

Decision Point

What problems can arise when full cost plus a markup is used as the transfer price?

Hybrid Transfer Prices

Consider again Hindustan Petroleum. As we saw earlier, the transportation division has unused capacity it can use to transport oil from Ankleshwar to Mathura at an incremental cost of ₹800 per barrel. Hindustan Petroleum, as a whole, maximizes operating income if the refining division purchases crude oil from the transportation division rather than from the Mathura market (incremental cost per barrel of ₹800 versus price per barrel of ₹850). Both divisions would be interested in transacting with each other (and the firm achieves goal congruence) if the transfer price is between ₹800 and ₹850.

For any internal transaction, there is generally a minimum transfer price the selling division will not go below, based on its cost structure. In the Hindustan Petroleum example, the minimum price acceptable to the transportation division is ₹800. There is also a maximum price the buying division will not wish to exceed, which is determined by the lower of two quantities—the eventual contribution it generates from an internal transaction and the price of purchasing a comparable intermediate product from an outside party. For the refining division, each barrel of gasoline sold to external parties generates ₹1,820 in contribution (the ₹1,900 price less the ₹80 variable cost of refining). Because it takes two barrels of crude oil to generate a barrel of gasoline, this is equivalent to a contribution of ₹910 per barrel of crude. For any price higher than ₹910, the refining division would lose money for each barrel of crude it takes from the transportation division. On the other hand, the refining division can purchase crude oil on the open market for ₹850 rather than having it transported internally. The maximum feasible transfer price is thus the lower of ₹910 and ₹850, or ₹850 in this instance. We saw previously that a transfer price between the minimum price (₹800) and the maximum (₹850) would promote goal congruence. We now describe three different ways in which firms attempt to determine the specific transfer price within these bounds.

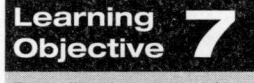

Learning Objective 7

Describe the range of feasible transfer prices when there is unused capacity

. . . from variable cost to market price of the product transferred

and alternative methods- for arriving at the eventual hybrid price

. . . proration, negotiation between divisions, and dual pricing

Prorating the Difference Between Maximum and Minimum Transfer Prices

One approach that Hindustan Petroleum could pursue is to choose a transfer price that splits, on some fair basis, the ₹50 difference between the ₹850-per-barrel maximum transfer price the Refining Division is willing to pay and the ₹800-per-barrel variable cost-based minimum price the transportation division wants to receive. An easy solution is to split the difference equally, resulting in a transfer price of ₹825. However, this solution ignores the relative costs incurred by the two divisions and might lead to disparate profit margins on the work contributed by each division to the final product. As an alternative approach, Hindustan Petroleum could allocate the ₹50 difference on the basis of the variable costs of the two divisions. Using the data in Exhibit 22-1 (p. 1154), variable costs are as follows:

Transportation Division's variable costs to transport 100 barrels of crude oil (₹10 × 100)	₹1,000
Refining Division's variable costs to refine 100 barrels of crude oil and produce 50 barrels of gasoline (₹80 × 50)	4,000
Total variable costs	₹5,000

Of the ₹50 difference, the Transportation Division gets to keep (₹1,000 ÷ ₹5,000) × ₹50 = ₹10 and the Refining Division gets to keep (₹4,000 ÷ ₹5,000) × ₹50 = ₹40. That is, the transfer price is ₹810 per barrel of crude oil (₹790 purchase cost + ₹10 variable cost + ₹10 that the Transportation Division gets to keep). In effect, this approach results in a budgeted variable-cost-plus transfer price. The "plus" indicates the setting of a transfer price above variable cost.

To decide on the ₹10 and ₹40 allocations of the ₹50 incremental benefit to total company operating income per barrel, the divisions must share information about their variable costs. In effect, each division does not operate (at least for this transaction) in a totally decentralized manner. Furthermore, each division has an incentive to overstate its variable costs to receive a more-favorable transfer price. In the preceding example, suppose the transportation division claims a cost of ₹20 per barrel to ship crude oil to Mathura. This increased cost raises the variable cost-based minimum price to ₹790 + ₹20 = ₹810 per barrel; the maximum price remains ₹850. Of the ₹40 difference between the minimum and maximum, the transportation division now gets to keep (₹2,000 ÷ (₹2,000 + ₹4,000)) × ₹40 = ₹13.3, resulting in a higher transfer price of ₹823.3. The refining division similarly benefits from asserting that its variable cost to refine 100 barrels of crude oil is greater than ₹4,000. As a consequence, proration methods either require a high degree of trust and information exchange among divisions or include provisions for objective audits of cost information in order to be successful.

Negotiated Pricing

Negotiated pricing is the most common hybrid method. Under this approach, top managers do not administer a specific split of the eventual profits across the transacting divisions. Rather, the eventual transfer price results from a bargaining process between the selling and buying subunits. In the Hindustan Petroleum's case, for example, the transportation division and the refining division would be free to negotiate a price that is mutually acceptable to both.

Recall that the minimum and maximum feasible transfer prices are ₹800 and ₹850, respectively, per barrel of crude oil. Where between ₹800 and ₹850 will the transfer price per barrel be set? Under a negotiated transfer price, the answer depends on several things: the bargaining strengths of the two divisions; information the transportation division has about the price minus incremental marketing costs of supplying crude oil to outside refineries; and the information the refining division has about its other available sources of crude oil. The negotiations become particularly sensitive because Hindustan Petroleum can now evaluate each division's performance on the basis of its operating income. The price negotiated by the two divisions will, in general, have no specific relationship to either costs or market price. But cost and price information is often the starting point in the negotiation process.

Consider the following situation: Suppose the refining division receives an order to supply specially processed gasoline. The incremental cost to purchase and supply crude oil is still ₹800 per barrel. However, suppose the refining division will profit from this order only if the transportation division can supply crude oil at a price not exceeding ₹820 per barrel.[4] In this case, the transfer price that would benefit both divisions must be greater than ₹800 but less than ₹820. Negotiations would allow the two divisions to achieve an acceptable transfer price. By contrast, a rule-based transfer price, such as a market-based price of ₹850 or a 105% of full-cost-based price of ₹871.5, would result in Hindustan passing up a profitable opportunity.

A negotiated transfer price strongly preserves the autonomy of divisions, and the division managers are motivated to put forth effort to increase the operating income of their divisions. Surveys have found that approximately 15%–20% of firms set transfer prices based on negotiation among divisions. Firms that do not use negotiated prices believe the time and energy spent by managers haggling over transfer prices make the method too costly.

Dual Pricing

There is seldom a single transfer price that simultaneously meets all the criteria we have discussed (achieving goal congruence, motivating managerial effort, evaluating the performance of subunits, and preserving their autonomy). As a result, some companies choose **dual pricing,** using two separate transfer-pricing methods to price each transfer from one subunit to another. An example of dual pricing arises when the selling division receives a full-cost-based price and the buying division pays the market price for the internally transferred products. Assume Hindustan Petroleum purchases crude oil from Reliance Petroleum in Ankleshwar at ₹790 per barrel. One way of Recording the journal entry for the transfer between the Transportation Division and the Refining Rivision is as follows:

1. Debit the Refining Division (the buying division) with the market-based transfer price of ₹850 per barrel of crude oil.

2. Credit the Transportation Division (the selling division) with the 105%-of-full-cost transfer price of ₹871.5 per barrel of crude oil.

3. Debit a corporate cost account for the ₹21.5 (₹871.5 − ₹850) per barrel difference between the two transfer prices.

Decision Point ▶

Within a range of feasible transfer prices, what are alternative ways for firms to arrive at the eventual hybrid price?

The dual-pricing system promotes goal congruence because it makes the Refining Division no worse off if it purchases the crude oil from the Transportation Division rather than from the external supplier at ₹850 per barrel. The Transportation Division receives a corporate subsidy. As a result, the operating income for Hindustan Petroleum as a whole under dual pricing is less than the sum of the operating incomes of the divisions.

Dual pricing is not widely used in practice. One concern with dual pricing is that it leads to disputes about which price should be used when computing the taxable income of subunits located in different tax jurisdictions, such as in our example, where the transportation division is taxed in Mexico while the refining division is taxed in the United States. A second concern is that dual pricing insulates managers from the realities of the marketplace because costs, not market prices, affect the revenues of the supplying division.

---

[4] For example, suppose a barrel of specially processed gasoline could be sold for ₹2,000 but also required a higher variable cost of refining of ₹360 per barrel. In this setting, the incremental contribution to the refining division is ₹1,640 per barrel of gasoline, which implies that it will pay at most ₹820 for a barrel of crude oil (since two barrels of crude are required for one barrel of gasoline).

A General Guideline for Transfer-Pricing Situations

Exhibit 22-3 summarizes the properties of market-based, cost-based, and negotiated transfer-pricing methods using the criteria described in this chapter. As the exhibit indicates, it is difficult for a transfer-pricing method to meets all criteria. The transfer price a company will eventually choose depends on the economic circumstances and the decision at hand. Surveys of company practice indicate that the full-cost-based transfer price is generally the most frequently used transfer-pricing method around the world, followed by market-based transfer price and negotiated transfer price.

   Our discussion so far highlight that, barring settings in which a perfectly competitive market exists for the intermediate product, there is generally a range of possible transfer prices that would promote goal congruence. The following formula provides a general guideline for determining the minimum transfer price in that range:

$$\text{Minimum transfer price} = \begin{array}{c}\text{Incremental cost}\\\text{per unit}\\\text{incurred up}\\\text{to the point of transfer}\end{array} + \begin{array}{c}\text{Opportunity cost}\\\text{per unit}\\\text{to the selling subunit}\end{array}$$

The incremental cost in the formula is the additional cost of producing and transferring the product or service. The opportunity cost is the maximum contribution margin forgone by the selling subunit if the product or service is transferred internally. For example, if the selling subunit is operating at capacity, the opportunity cost of transferring a unit internally rather than selling it externally is equal to the market price minus variable cost. That's because by transferring a unit internally, the subunit forgoes the contribution margin it could have obtained by selling the unit in the external market. We distinguish the incremental cost from the opportunity cost because the financial accounting system typically records incremental

Exhibit 22-3	Comparison of Different Transfer-Pricing Methods		
Criteria	**Market-Based**	**Cost-Based**	**Negotiated**
Achieves goal congruence	Often, but not always are competitive	Yes, when markets	Yes
Useful for evaluating subunit performance	Yes, when markets are competitive	Difficult unless transfer price exceeds full cost and even then is somewhat arbitrary	Yes, but transfer prices are affected by bargaining strengths of the buying and selling divisions
Motivates management effort	Yes	Yes, when based on budgeted costs; less incentive to control costs if transfers are based on actual costs	Yes
Preserves subuni autonomy	Yes, when markets are competitive	No, because it is rule-based	Yes, because it is based on negotiations between subunits
Other factors	Market may not exist, or markets may be imperfect or in distress	Useful for determining full cost of products and services; easy to implement	Bargaining and negotiations take time and may need to be reviewed repeatedly as conditions change

cost but not opportunity cost. The guideline measures a *minimum* transfer price because it represents the selling unit's cost of transferring the product. We illustrate the general guideline in some specific situations using data from Hindustan Petroleum.

1. **A perfectly competitive market for the intermediate product exists, and the selling division has no unused capacity.** If the market for crude oil in Mathura is perfectly competitive, the Transportation Division can sell all the crude oil it transports to the external market at ₹850 per barrel, and it will have no unused capacity. The Transportation Division's incremental cost (as shown in Exhibit 22-1) is ₹730 per barrel (purchase cost of ₹720 per barrel plus variable transportation cost of ₹10 per barrel) for oil purchased under the long-term contract or ₹800 per barrel (purchase cost of ₹790 plus variable transportation cost of ₹10) for oil purchased at current market prices from Reliance Petroleum. The Transportation Division's opportunity cost per barrel of transferring the oil internally is the contribution margin per barrel forgone by not selling the crude oil in the external market: ₹120 for oil purchased under the long-term contract (market price, ₹850, minus variable cost, ₹730) and ₹50 for oil purchased from Reliance (market price, ₹850, minus variable cost, ₹800). In either case,

$$\begin{array}{c} \text{Minimum transfer price} \\ \text{per barrel} \end{array} = \begin{array}{c} \text{Incremental cost} \\ \text{per barrel} \end{array} + \begin{array}{c} \text{Opportunity cost} \\ \text{per barrel} \end{array}$$

$$= ₹730 + ₹120 = ₹850$$

$$= ₹800 + ₹50 = ₹850$$

2. **An intermediate market exists that is not perfectly competitive, and the selling division has unused capacity.** In markets that are not perfectly competitive, companies can increase their capacity utilization only by decreasing prices. Unused capacity exists because decreasing prices is often not worthwhile—it decreases operating income.

   If the Transportation Division at Hindustan Petroleum has unused capacity, its opportunity cost of transferring the oil internally is zero because the division does not forgo any external sales or contribution margin from internal transfers. In this case,

$$\begin{array}{c} \text{Minimum transfer price} \\ \text{per barrel} \end{array} = \begin{array}{c} \text{Incremental cost} \\ \text{per barrel} \end{array} = \begin{array}{c} \text{₹730 per barrel for oil purchased under the} \\ \text{long-term contract or ₹800 per barrel for oil} \\ \text{purchased from Reliance Petroleum in Ankleshwar} \end{array}$$

   In general, when markets are not perfectly competitive, the potential to influence demand and operating income through prices complicates the measurement of opportunity costs. The transfer price depends on constantly changing levels of supply and demand. There is not just one transfer price. Rather, the transfer prices for various quantities supplied and demanded depend on the incremental costs and opportunity costs of the units transferred.

3. **No market exists for the intermediate product.** This situation would occur if the crude oil transported by the Transportation Division could be used only by the Mathura refinery (due to, say, its high tar content) and would not be wanted by external parties. Here, the opportunity cost of supplying crude oil internally is zero because it can't be sold externally so no contribution margin is forgone. For the Transportation Division,

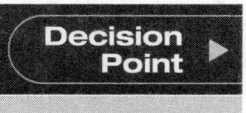

Decision Point ▶

What is the general guideline for determining a minimum transfer price?

the minimum transfer price under the general guideline is the incremental cost per barrel (either ₹730 or ₹800). As in the previous case, any transfer price between the incremental cost and ₹850 will achieve goal congruence.

How Multinationals Use Transfer Pricing to Minimize their Taxes

Transfer pricing is an important accounting priority for managers around the world. A 2010 Ernst & Young survey of multinational enterprises in 25 countries found that 74% of parent firms and 76% of subsidiary respondents believed that transfer pricing was "absolutely critical" or "very important" to their organizations. The reason is that parent companies can save large sums of money in taxes depending on the transfer pricing methods they use. Consider Google, which earned £6 billion in advertising revenues in the United Kingdom from 2004 to 2010. The UK's corporate income tax rate is 28%, yet Google UK paid just £8 million in taxes during that time. How is that possible? To start with, Google has licensed the offshore rights to its intellectual property to Google Ireland Holdings, an Irish company that is managed from Bermuda, thereby exempting it from Irish taxes. When Google earns revenue from a customer in Britain, that amount is credited to a different Irish entity, Google Ireland Limited, located in Dublin. About 88% of Google's non-U.S. revenues flow through this entity. However, it records almost no pretax profit because it pays a royalty fee to the Bermuda/Irish company for the use of Google's intellectual property. Rather than pay the amount directly, which would trigger an Irish withholding tax, the money is routed through Google Netherlands Holdings BV (Amsterdam).[5] These techniques are estimated to have saved Google about ₹1 billion a year. Facebook, Microsoft, and Forest Laboratories, a pharmaceutical company headquartered in New York City, have used similar transfer-pricing practices. Such profit-shifting arrangements are estimated to save companies as much as ₹600 billion annually.[6]

Learning Objective 9

Incorporate income tax considerations in multinational transfer pricing

. . . Set transfer prices to minimize tax payments to the extent permitted by tax authorities

| Transfer-Pricing Method | Operating Income for 100 Barrels of Crude Oil | | | Income Tax on 100 Barrels of Crude Oil | | |
	Transportation Division (India) (1)	Refining Division (United States) (2)	Total (6) = (4) + (5)	Transportation Division (India) (4) = 0.30 × (1)	Refining Division (United States) (5) = 0.20 × (2)	Total (3) = (1) + (2)
Market price	₹9,000	₹3,000	₹12,000	₹2,700	₹600	₹3,300
105% of full costs	3,800	8,200	12,000	1,140	1,640	2,780
Hybrid price	6,000	6,000	12,000	1,800	1,200	3,000

---

[5] Netherlands Holdings BV has no employees—it is simply a legal entity through which money is routed. This arrangement, which involves transfers between two Irish entities via the Netherlands, is referred to by tax planners as "Double Irish" or "Dutch Sandwich." For a detailed description of Apple's use of this structure, see http://www.nytimes.com/ interactive/2012/04/28/business/Double-Irish-With-A-Dutch-Sandwich.html?ref=business.

[6] It is important to understand that U.S. companies pay no taxes to the IRS until profits are repatriated back to the United States. As a result, the incentive for top management is to keep and reinvest cash overseas rather than in the United States. According to Apple CFO Peter Oppenheimer, "We think that the current tax laws provide a considerable economic disincentive to U.S. companies that might otherwise repatriate." As of April 2013, Apple had ₹1,450 billion in cash, but chose to borrow ₹170 billion in order to finance a payout to shareholders. The reason—about ₹1,020 billion of Apple's cash sits overseas, and bringing that "home" would trigger close to a 35% repatriation tax. Such actions led to the recent bipartisan Senate probe that resulted in Apple CEO Tim Cook testifying to Congress on allegations that Apple had used transfer pricing and other loopholes to avoid paying U.S. taxes on ₹440 billion in offshore income between 2009 and 2012.

Transfer prices affect not just income taxes, but also payroll taxes, customs duties, tariffs, sales taxes, value-added taxes, environment-related taxes, and other government levies. Our aim here is to highlight tax factors, and in particular income taxes, as important considerations for managers when determining transfer prices.

Consider the Hindustan Petroleum data in Exhibit 22-2. Assume that the transportation division based in India pays income taxes at 30% of operating income and that the refining division based in the United States pays income taxes at 20% of operating income. Hindustan Petroleum would minimize its total income tax payments with the 105%-of-full-cost transfer-pricing method, as shown in the following table, because this method minimizes income reported in India, where income is taxed at a higher rate than in the United States.

Minimizing a firm's income taxes can sometimes conflict with the other objectives the firm's top managers hope to achieve via transfer pricing. Suppose the market for crude oil in Mathura is perfectly competitive. In this case, the market-based transfer price achieves goal congruence, provides incentives for management effort, and helps Hindustan Petroleum to evaluate the economic profitability of the transportation division. But it is costly from the perspective of income taxes. To minimize its income taxes, Hindustan Petroleum would favor using 105% of the full cost for tax reporting. But the tax laws in the United States and India limit this option. India's tax authorities would challenge any attempt by Hindustan Petroleum to shift income to the refining division through an unreasonably low transfer price

Consequently, if the market for crude oil is perfectly competitive, Hindustan would be required to calculate taxes using the market price of ₹850 for transfers from the transportation division to the refining division. Hindustan might successfully argue that the transfer price should be set below the market price because the transportation division incurs no marketing and distribution costs when selling crude oil to the refining division. For example, if marketing and distribution costs equal ₹20 per barrel, Hindustan could set the transfer price at ₹830 (₹850 − ₹20) per barrel, the selling price net of marketing and distribution costs. Under the U.S. Internal Revenue Code, Hindustan could obtain advanced approval of the transfer-pricing arrangements from the tax authorities, called an advanced pricing agreement (APA). The APA is a binding agreement for a specified number of years. The goal of the APA program is to avoid costly transfer-pricing disputes between taxpayers and tax authorities. As of the end of 2012, the APA program had completed 1,155 APAs since inception and had pending requests for another 391 new APAs. In 2012 alone, there were a record 140 APAs executed, of which 103 were bilateral agreements with other tax treaty countries. Walmart, for example, signed the first bilateral APA between the United States and China in 2007.

The number of countries that have imposed transfer-pricing regulations approximately quadrupled from 1995 to 2007, according to a 2008 KPMG report. The last global recession pushed even more governments around the world to impose tighter trading rules and aggressively pursue tax revenues. Foreign businesses formerly enjoyed favorable treatment in China. But officials there recently issued new rules requiring multinationals to submit extensive transfer-pricing documentation. Countries such as India, Canada, Turkey, and Greece have brought greater scrutiny to bear on transfer pricing, focusing in particular on intellectual-property values, the costs of back-office functions, and losses of any type. In the United States, the Obama administration plans to shrink a "tax gap" the IRS estimates may be as high as ₹3450 billion by restricting or closing several widely used tax loopholes. While the plan does not directly address transfer-pricing practice, the IRS has become more aggressive with enforcement. The agency has added hundreds of additional people to its international staff. In 2011, the IRS named its first director of transfer pricing and, in early 2012, raised inquiries or disputes with a variety of technology firms, including

Amazon, Adobe, Juniper Networks, and Yahoo. The IRS has proposed Amazon pay a ₹15 billion tax increase related to transfer pricing for the period 2005–2012. In 2006, the agency won the largest settlement ever in a transfer-pricing dispute, getting GlaxoSmithKline, a UK-based pharmaceutical and health care company, to pay ₹34 billion to cover back taxes and interest for the period 1989–2005.

The tariffs and customs duties governments levy on imports of products into a country also affect the transfer pricing practices of multinationals. The issues here are similar to income tax considerations. Companies will have incentives to lower the transfer prices of products they are exporting into a country to reduce the tariffs and customs duties charged on those products. The restrictions some countries place on dividend- or income-related payments to parties outside their national borders also affect how firms set their transfer prices. By increasing the prices of goods or services transferred into divisions in these countries, companies can increase the cash paid out of these countries without violating dividend- or income-related restrictions.

Transfer Prices Designed for Multiple Objectives

At times, one transfer price will not satisfy all of a firm's objectives, such as minimizing its income taxes, achieving goal congruence, and motivating managers' effort. As a result, a company may choose to keep one set of accounting records for tax reporting and a second set for internal management reporting. Of course, it is costly to maintain two sets of books. Some companies, such as Case New Holland, a world leader in the agricultural and construction equipment business, oppose doing so based on the principle that statutory and internal reporting systems must reflect the same information. However, a survey by the AnswerThink Consulting Group of large companies (more than ₹20 billion in revenues) found that 77% of companies considered to follow "best practices" used separate reporting systems to track internal pricing information, compared with about 25% of companies outside that group.

Microsoft, for example, believes in "delinking" transfer prices and employs an internal measurement system (Microsoft Accounting Principles, or MAPs) that uses a separate set of company-designed rules and accounts.[7] A key aspect of management control at Microsoft is holding product and division managers accountable for the profitability of products and establishing appropriate sales and marketing spending levels for every product line. To establish these sales and spending levels, the firm creates a profitability statement for every product in every region and allocates R&D and administrative costs across sales divisions in ways that aren't necessarily the most tax efficient.

Even if a company does not have separated reporting systems, a firm can still informally adjust its transfer prices to satisfy the tradeoff between minimizing its taxes and incentivizing its managers. Consider a multinational firm that makes semiconductor products that it sells through its sales organization in a higher-tax country. To minimize the firm's taxes, the parent company sets a high transfer price, thereby lowering the operating income of the foreign sales organization. It would be inappropriate to penalize the country sales manager for this low income because the sales organization has no say in determining the transfer price. As an alternative, the company can evaluate the sales manager on the direct contribution (revenues minus marketing costs) incurred in the country. That is, the transfer price incurred to acquire the semiconductor products is omitted for performance-evaluation purposes. Of course, this is not a perfect solution. By ignoring the cost of acquiring the products, the sales manager has an incentive to overspend on local marketing relative to what would be optimal from the firm's perspective. If the dysfunctional effects are suitably large, corporate managers must then step in, evaluate the situation, and dictate specific

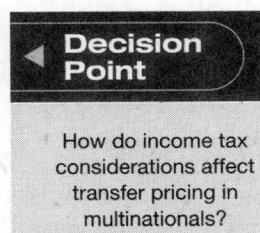

Decision Point

How do income tax considerations affect transfer pricing in multinationals?

---

[7] For further details, see I. Springsteel, "Separate but Unequal," *CFO Magazine* (August 1999).

operational decisions and goals for the manager. More generally, when a firm adopts a tax-compliant transfer pricing policy, it needs nonfinancial performance indicators (such as production yields, number of on-time deliveries, or customer response times) at lower management levels in order to better evaluate and reward performance.[8]

Problem for Self-Study

The Pillercat Corporation is a highly decentralized company. Each division manager has full authority for sourcing decisions and selling decisions. The Machining Division of Pillercat has been the major supplier of the 2,000 crankshafts that the Tractor Division needs each year.

The Tractor Division, however, has just announced that it plans to purchase all its crankshafts in the forthcoming year from two external suppliers at ₹2,000 per crankshaft. The Machining Division of Pillercat recently increased its selling price for the forthcoming year to ₹2,200 per unit (from ₹2,000 per unit in the current year).

Juàn Gomez, manager of the Machining Division, feels that the 10% price increase is justified. It results from a higher depreciation charge on some new specialized equipment used to manufacture crankshafts and an increase in labor costs. Gomez wants the president of Pillercat Corporation to force the Tractor Division to buy all its crankshafts from the Machining Division at the price of ₹2,200. The following table summarizes the key data.

	File Edit View Insert Format Tools Data Window Help	
	A	B
1	Number of crankshafts purchased by Tractor Division	2,000
2	External supplier's market price per crankshaft	₹2,000
3	Variable cost per crankshaft in Machining Division	₹1,900
4	Fixed cost per crankshaft in Machining Division	₹200

Required

1. Compute the advantage or disadvantage in terms of annual operating income to the Pillercat Corporation as a whole if the Tractor Division buys crankshafts internally from the Machining Division under each of the following cases:
   a. The Machining Division has no alternative use for the facilities used to manufacture crankshafts.
   b. The Machining Division can use the facilities for other production operations, which will result in annual cash operating savings of ₹2,90,000.
   c. The Machining Division has no alternative use for its facilities, and the external supplier drops the price to ₹1,850 per crankshaft.

2. As the president of Pillercat, how would you respond to Juan Gomez's request that you force the Tractor Division to purchase all of its crankshafts from the Machining Division? Would your response differ according to the three cases described in requirement 1? Explain.

---

[8] Cools et al. "Management control in the transfer pricing tax compliant multinational enterprise," *Accounting, Organizations and Society*, August 2008 provides an illustrative case study of this issue in the context of a semiconductor product division of a multinational firm.

Solution

1. Computations for the Tractor Division buying crankshafts internally for one year under cases a, b, and c are as follows:

	A	B	C	D
	File Edit View Insert Format Tools Data Window Help			
1			Case	
2		a	b	c
3	Number of crankshafts purchased by Tractor Division	2,000	2,000	2,000
4	External supplier's market price per crankshaft	₹2,000	₹2,000	₹1,850
5	Variable cost per crankshaft in Machining Division	₹1,900	₹1,900	₹1,900
6	Opportunity costs of the Machining Division supplying crankshafts to the Tractor Division	-	₹2,90,000	-
7				
8	Total purchase costs if buying from an external supplier			
9	(2,000 shafts x ₹2,000, ₹2,000, ₹1,850 per shaft)	₹40,00,000	₹40,00,000	₹37,00,000
10	Incremental cost of buying from the Machining Division			
11	(2,000 shafts x ₹1,900 per shaft)	38,00,000	38,00,000	38,00,000
12	Total opportunity costs of the Machining Division	-	2,90,000	-
13	Total relevant costs	38,00,000	40,90,000	38,00,000
14	Annual operating income advantage (disadvantage) to			
15	Pillercat of buying from the Machining Division	₹2,00,000	₹(90,000)	₹(1,00,000)

The general guideline that was introduced in the chapter as a first step in setting a transfer price can be used to highlight the alternatives:

	A	B	C	D	E	F	G
	File Edit View Insert Format Tools Data Window Help						
1	Case	Incremental Cost per Unit Incurred to Point of Transfer	+	Opportunity Cost per Unit to the Supplying Division	=	Transfer Price	External Market Price
2	a	₹1,900	+	₹0	=	₹1,900	₹2,000
3	b	₹1,900	+	₹145[a]	=	₹2,045	₹2,000
4	c	₹1,900	+	₹0	=	₹1,900	₹1,850
5							
6	[a]Opportunity cost per unit	=	Total opportunity costs	÷	Number of crankshafts	= ₹2,90,000 ÷ 2,000 = ₹145	
7							

Comparing transfer price to external-market price, the Tractor Division will maximize annual operating income of Pillercat Corporation as a whole by purchasing from the Machining Division in case **a** and by purchasing from the external supplier in cases **b** and **c**.

2. Pillercat Corporation is a highly decentralized company. If no forced transfer were made, the Tractor Division would use an external supplier, a decision that would be in the best interest of the company as a whole in cases **b** and **c** of requirement 1 but not in case **a**.

Suppose in case **a**, the Machining Division refuses to meet the price of ₹2,000. This decision means that the company will be ₹2,00,000 worse off in the short run. Should top management interfere and force a transfer at ₹2,000? This interference would undercut the philosophy of decentralization. Many top managements would not interfere because they would view the ₹2,00,000 as an inevitable cost of a suboptimal decision that can occur under decentralization. But how high must this cost be before the temptation to interfere would be irresistible? ₹3,00,000? ₹4,00,000?

Any top management interference with lower-level decision making weakens decentralization. Of course, Pillercat's management may occasionally interfere to prevent costly mistakes. But recurring interference and constraints would hurt Pillercat's attempts to operate as a decentralized company.

Decision Points

The following question-and-answer format summarizes the chapter's learning objectives. Each decision presents a key question related to a learning objective. The guidelines are the answer to that question.

Decision	Guidelines
1. What is a management control system, and how should it be designed?	A management control system is a means of gathering and using information to aid and coordinate the planning and control decisions throughout the organization and to guide the behavior of managers and other employees. Effective management control systems (a) are closely aligned to the organization's strategy, (b) support the organizational responsibilities of individual managers, and (c) motivate managers and other employees to give effort to achieve the organization's goals.
2. What are the benefits and costs of decentralization?	The benefits of decentralization include (a) greater responsiveness to local needs, (b) gains from faster decision making, (c) greater management development and learning, and (d) sharpened focus of subunit managers. The costs of decentralization include (a) suboptimal decision making, (b) excessive focus on the subunit rather than the company as a whole, (c) increased costs of information gathering, and (d) duplication of activities.
3. What are transfer prices, and what criteria do managers use to evaluate them?	A transfer price is the price one subunit charges for a product or service supplied to another subunit of the same organization. Transfer prices seek to (a) promote goal congruence, (b) motivate management effort, (c) help evaluate subunit performance, and (d) preserve subunit autonomy (if desired).
4. What are alternative ways of calculating transfer prices?	Transfer prices can be (a) market-based, (b) cost-based, or (c) hybrid. Different transfer-pricing methods produce different revenues and costs for individual subunits and, so, different operating incomes for the subunits.

5. Under what market conditions do market-based transfer prices promote goal congruence?

In perfectly competitive markets, there is no unused capacity, and division managers can buy and sell as much of a product or service as they want at the market price. In such settings, using the market price as the transfer price motivates division managers to transact internally and to take exactly the same actions as they would if they were transacting in the external market.

6. What problems can arise when full cost plus a markup is used as the transfer price?

A transfer price based on the full cost plus a markup may lead to suboptimal decisions because it leads the buying division to regard the fixed costs and the markup of the selling division as a variable cost. The buying division may then purchase products from an external supplier and expect cost savings that will not occur.

7. Within a range of feasible transfer prices, what are alternative ways for firms to arrive at the eventual hybrid price?

When there is unused capacity, the transfer-price range lies between the minimum price at which the selling division is willing to sell (its variable cost per unit) and the maximum price the buying division is willing to pay (the lower of its contribution or price at which the product is available from external suppliers). Methods for arriving at a price in this range include proration (such as splitting the difference equally or on the basis of relative variable costs), negotiation between divisions, and dual pricing.

8. What is the general guideline for determining a minimum transfer price?

The general guideline states that the minimum transfer price equals the incremental cost per unit incurred up to the point of transfer plus the opportunity cost per unit to the selling division.

9. How do income tax considerations affect transfer pricing in multinationals?

A firm can use transfer pricing to lower its income tax payments by reporting more income in low-tax-rate countries and less income in high-tax-rate countries. However, the tax regulations of different countries restrict the transfer prices that companies can use.

TERMS TO LEARN

This chapter and the Glossary at the end of the book contain definitions of the following important terms:

Cost-based transfer prices (p. 1152)

decentralization (p. 1150)

dual pricing (p. 1162)

dysfunctional decision
 making (p. 1148)

effort (p. 1147)

goal congruence (p. 1147)

incongruent decision
 making (p. 1148)

intermediate product (p. 1151)

management control
 system (p. 1146)

motivation (p. 1147)

perfectly competitive
 market (p. 1156)

suboptimal decision
 making (p. 1149)

transfer price (p. 1151)

ASSIGNMENT MATERIAL

Questions

22-1 What is a management control system?

22-2 Describe three criteria you would use to evaluate whether a management control system is effective.

22-3 What is the relationship among motivation, goal congruence, and effort?

22-4 Name three benefits and two costs of decentralization.

22-5 "Organizations typically adopt a consistent decentralization or centralization philosophy across all their business functions." Do you agree? Explain.

22-6 "Transfer pricing is confined to profit centers." Do you agree? Explain.

22-7 What are the three methods for determining transfer prices?

22-8 What properties should transfer-pricing systems have?

22-9 "All transfer-pricing methods give the same division operating income." Do you agree? Explain.

22-10 Under what conditions is a market-based transfer price optimal?

22-11 What is one potential limitation of full-cost-based transfer prices?

22-12 Give two reasons why the dual-pricing system of transfer pricing is not widely used.

22-13 "Cost and price information play no role in negotiated transfer prices." Do you agree? Explain.

22-14 "Under the general guideline for transfer pricing, the minimum transfer price will vary depending on whether the supplying division has unused capacity or not." Do you agree? Explain.

22-15 How should managers consider income tax issues when choosing a transfer-pricing method?

Solved Examples

22-16 Decentralization, responsibility centers. Phillips India manufactures and sells lighting products. Phillips's sales and marketing divisions are organized along product lines—wall sconces, recessed lights, track lights, and so on. The Manufacturing Division produces lighting products for all the sales and marketing divisions.

During the planning process, each sales and marketing division specifies the quantity of each style of light to be manufactured. Senior management then assigns the task of manufacturing the lights to different plants in the Manufacturing Division. Because manufacturing capacity is limited, some of the production is also outsourced. Senior management determines the manufacturing schedule on the basis of detailed studies that have been done to measure the time and cost of manufacturing different types of lighting products. Manufacturing managers are evaluated based on achieving target output within budgeted costs.

Required

1. Are the manufacturing plants in the Manufacturing Division cost centers or profit centers? Explain.

2. Phillips India is considering decentralizing its marketing and manufacturing decisions by letting manufacturing and marketing managers directly negotiate the prices for manufacturing various products.

   a. How should Phillips evaluate manufacturing plant managers under this proposal?

   b. Would you recommend that Phillips India decentralize its marketing and manufacturing decisions? Explain.

Solution

Decentralization, responsibility centers.

1. The manufacturing plants in the Manufacturing Division are cost centers. Senior management determines the manufacturing schedule based on the quantity of each type of lighting product specified by the sales and marketing division and detailed studies of the time and cost to manufacture each type of product. Manufacturing managers are accountable only for costs. They are evaluated based on achieving target output within budgeted costs.

2a. If manufacturing and marketing managers were to directly negotiate the prices for manufacturing various products, Phillips should evaluate manufacturing plant managers as profit centers—revenues received from marketing minus the costs incurred to produce and sell output.

2b. Phillips India would be better off decentralizing its marketing and manufacturing decisions and evaluating each division as a profit center. Decentralization would encourage plant managers to increase total output to achieve the greatest profitability, and motivate plant managers to cut their costs to increase margins.

Manufacturing managers would be motivated to design their operations according to the criteria that meet the marketing managers' approval, thereby improving cooperation between manufacturing and marketing.

Under Phillips's existing system, manufacturing managers had every incentive not to improve. Manufacturing managers' incentives were to get as high a cost target as possible so that they could produce output within budgeted costs. Any significant improvement could result in the target costs being lowered for the next year, increasing the possibility of not achieving budgeted costs. By the same line of reasoning, manufacturing managers would also try to limit their production so that production quotas would not be increased in the future. Decentralizing manufacturing and marketing decisions overcomes these problems.

22-17 Benefits and costs of decentralization. Big Bazaar, a chain of traditional supermarkets, is interested in gaining access to the organic and health food retail market by acquiring a regional company in that sector. Big Bazaar intends to operate the newly acquired stores independently from its supermarkets.

One of the prospects is Reliance Fresh, a chain of 20 stores. Buying for all 20 stores is done by the company's central office. Store managers must follow strict guidelines for all aspects of store management in an attempt to maintain consistency among stores. Store managers are evaluated on the basis of achieving profit goals developed by the central office.

The other prospect is Store 99, a chain of 30 stores .Its managers are given significant flexibility in product offerings, allowing them to negotiate purchases with local organic farmers. Store managers are rewarded for exceeding self-developed return-on-investment goals with company stock options. Some managers have become significant shareholders in the company and have even decided on their own to open additional store locations to improve market penetration. However, the increased autonomy has led to competition and price cutting among its stores within the same geographic market, resulting in lower margins.

Required

1. Would you describe Store 99 as having a centralized or a decentralized structure? Explain.

2. Would you describe Store 99 as having a centralized or a decentralized structure? Discuss some of the benefits and costs of that type of structure.

3. Would stores in each chain be considered cost centers, revenue centers, profit centers, or investment centers? How does that tie into the evaluation of store managers?

4. Assume that Big Bazaar chooses to acquire Store 99. What steps can Big Bazaar take to improve goal congruence between store managers and the larger company?

Solution

1. Reliance Fresh has a centralized structure. Individual managers have little autonomy in decision making.

2. Store 99 has a decentralized structure. Store managers have significant autonomy. They are able to customize product offerings, negotiate purchases with local farmers, and can even influence store expansion decisions.

Benefits of a decentralized structure include: greater responsiveness to local needs and local opportunities, gains from faster decision making, increased motivation and personal commitment of store managers, and freedom of corporate managers to concentrate on strategic planning.

Costs of a decentralized structure include: potential for suboptimal decision making, shift of store managers' focus away from company as a whole, increased cost of information gathering, and duplication of effort.

3. The stores in Store 99 chain would be considered profit centers. Store managers are responsible for store revenues and costs, and as such, would be evaluated based on operating income. Store 99 store managers would be considered investment center

managers, as they also make, or at least influence, capital investment decisions. They would be evaluated based on return on investment or residual income.

4. Big Bazaar must be attentive to the fact that Store 99 managers have enjoyed significant freedom to make decisions about their own stores. Big Bazaar will need to carefully blend the two corporate cultures, and communicate to store managers that their input and efforts are valued. Bonuses and other rewards must be aligned with the company's best interests. Specifically, Big Bazaar should discourage price competition between stores and encourage cooperation among store managers. For example, store managers should be rewarded based on achieving both store-specific and corporate-wide profitability goals.

22-18 Effect of alternative transfer-pricing methods on division operating income. Balrampur Sugar Mills is a sugar cooperative that operates two divisions, a harvesting division and a processing division. Currently, all of harvesting's output is converted into cranberry juice by the processing division, and the juice is sold to large beverage companies that produce cranberry juice blends. The processing division has a yield of 500 gallons of juice per 1,000 pounds of cranberries. Cost and market price data for the two divisions are as follows:

	A	B	C	D	E
1	**Harvesting Division**			**Processing Division**	
2	Variable cost per pound of cranberries	$0.14		Variable processing cost per gallon of juice produced	$0.32
3	Fixed cost per pound of cranberries	$0.26		Fixed cost per gallon of juice produced	$0.50
4	Selling price per pound of cranberries in outside market	$0.58		Selling price per gallon of juice	$2.15

Required

1. Compute Balrampur's operating income from harvesting 4,20,000 pounds of cranberries during June 2016 and processing them into juice.

2. Balrampur rewards its division managers with a bonus equal to 3% of operating income. Compute the bonus earned by each division manager in June 2016 for each of the following transfer pricing methods:

   a. 150% of full cost

   b. Market price

3. Which transfer-pricing method will each division manager prefer? How might Balrampur resolve any conflicts that may arise on the issue of transfer pricing?

Solution

1.

Pounds of cranberries harvested		4,20,000
Gallons of juice processed (500 gals per 1,000 pounds.)		2,10,000
Revenues (2,10,000 gals. × $2.15 per gal.)		$4,51,500
Costs		
Harvesting Division		
Variable costs (4,20,000 pounds. × $0.14 per pound.)	$58,800	
Fixed costs (4,20,000 pounds. × $0.26 per pound.)	1,09,200	
Total Harvesting Division costs		1,68,000
Processing Division		
Variable costs (2,10,000 gals. × $0.32 per gal.)	$67,200	
Fixed costs (2,10,000 gals. × $0.50 per gal.)	1,05,000	
Total Processing Division costs		1,72,200
Total costs		3,40,200
Operating income		$1,11,300

2.

	150% of Full Costs	Market Price
Transfer price per pound [($0.14 + $0.26) × 1.5; $0.58]	$0.60	$0.58

1. Harvesting Division

Revenues (4,20,000 pounds. × $0.60; $0.58)	$2,52,000	$2,43,600
Costs		
Division variable costs (4,20,000 pounds. × $0.14 per pound.)	58,800	58,800
Division fixed costs (4,20,000 pounds. × $0.26 per pound.)	1,09,200	1,09,200
Total division costs	1,68,000	1,68,000
Division operating income	$84,000	$75,600
Harvesting Division manager's bonus (3% of operating income)	$2,520	$2,268

2. Processing Division

Revenues (2,10,000 gals. × $2.15 per gal.)	$4,51,500	$4,51,500
Costs		
Transferred-in costs	2,52,000	2,43,600
Division variable costs (2,10,000 gals. × $0.32 per gal.)	67,200	67,200
Division fixed costs (2,10,000 gals. × $0.50 per gal.)	1,05,000	1,05,000
Total division costs	4,24,200	4,15,800
Division operating income	$27,300	$35,700
Processing Division manager's bonus (3% of operating income)	$819	$1,071

3. Bonus paid to division managers at 3% of division operating income is computed above and summarized below:

	Internal Transfers at 150% of Full Costs	Internal Transfers at Market Prices
Harvesting Division manager's bonus (3% × $84,000; 3% × $75,600)	$2,520	$2,268
Processing Division manager's bonus (3% × $27,300; 3% × $35,700)	$819	$1,071

The Harvesting Division manager will prefer to transfer at 150% of full costs because this method gives a higher bonus. The Processing Division manager will prefer transfer at market price for its higher resulting bonus.

Balrampur may resolve or reduce transfer pricing conflicts by the following:

- Base division managers' bonuses on overall Company profits in addition to division operating income. This will motivate each manager to consider what is best for Balrampur overall and not be concerned with the transfer price alone.
- Let the two divisions negotiate the transfer price between themselves. However, this may result in constant renegotiation between the two managers each accounting period.
- Use dual transfer prices. However, a cost-based transfer price will not motivate cost control by the Harvesting Division manager. It will also insulate that division from the discipline of market prices.

22-19 Goal congruence problems with cost-plus transfer-pricing methods, dual pricing system (continuation of 22-18). Assume that Nitin Jain, CEO of Balrampur, had mandated a transfer price equal to 150% of full cost. Now he decides to decentralize some management decisions and sends around a memo that states the followisng: "Effective immediately, each division of Balrampur is free to make its own decisions regarding the purchase of direct materials and the sale of finished products."

Required

1. Give an example of a goal-congruence problem that will arise if Balrampur continues to use a transfer price of 150% of full cost and Nitin's decentralization policy is adopted.

2. Nitin feels that a dual transfer-pricing policy will improve goal congruence. He suggests that transfers out of the harvesting division be made at 150% of full cost and transfers into the processing division be made at market price. Compute the operating income of each division under this dual transfer-pricing method when 4,20,000 pounds of cranberries are harvested during June 2016 and processed into juice.

3. Why is the sum of the division operating incomes computed in requirement 2 different from Balrampur's operating income from harvesting and processing 4,20,000 pounds of cranberries?

4. Suggest two problems that may arise if Balrampur implements the dual transfer prices described in requirement 2.

Solution

1. Two examples of goal congruence problems that arise if a transfer price of 150% of full costs is mandated and Nitin's decentralization policy is adopted are as follows:

   a. The Processing Division manager will prefer to buy cranberries from an external supplier at $0.58 per pound, incurring some extra purchasing costs and lowering Balrampur's overall operating income. Balrampur will incur costs of $0.58 per pound and save variable costs of only $0.14 per pound.

   b. The Harvesting Division manager is forced to sell to an outside purchaser (because the Processing Division prefers to purchase from an external supplier) when it is better for Balrampur Products to process internally.

2. *Transfer into buying division at market price*

Harvesting Division to Processing Division = $0.58 per pound of cranberries

Transfer out of selling division at 150% of full costs

Harvesting Division to Processing Division = 1.5 × ($0.14 + $0.26) = $0.60 per pound of cranberries

As calculated in Requirement 2 of 22-18 and also shown on the following page, under the dual transfer-pricing policy, the Harvesting Division will earn an operating income of $84,000 and the Processing Division will earn an operating income of $35,700.

	150% of Full Costs	Market Price
Harvesting Division		
Revenues (4,20,000 pounds. × $0.60 per pound.)	2,52,000	
Costs		
Division variable costs (4,20,000 pounds. × $0.14 per pound.)	58,800	
Division fixed costs (4,20,000 pounds. × $0.26 per pound.)	1,09,200	
Total division costs	1,68,000	
Division operating income	$84,000	
Processing Division		
Revenues (2,10,000 gals. × $2.15 per gal.)		$4,51,500
Costs		
Transferred in costs (4,20,000 pounds. × $0.58 per pound.)		2,43,600
Division variable costs (4,20,000 gals. × $0.32 per gal.)		67,200
Division fixed costs (2,10,000 gals. × $0.50 per gal.)		1,05,000
Total division costs		4,15,800
Division operating income		$35,700

3. Under the dual transfer pricing policy,

	Division Operating Income
Harvesting Division	$84,000
Processing Division	35,700
Balrampur Products	$1,19,700

The overall company operating income from harvesting and processing 4,20,000 pounds of cranberries is $1,11,300 (see Problem 22-29, requirement 1).

A dual transfer-pricing method entails using different transfer prices for transfers into the buying division and transfers out of the supplying division. As a result, the sum of division operating incomes does not equal the total company operating income.

4. Problems which may arise if Balrampur uses the dual transfer-pricing system include:

  a. It may reduce the incentives of the supplying division to control costs because every $1 of cost of the supplying division is transferred out to the buying division at $1.50.

  b. A dual transfer-pricing system does not provide clear signals to the individual divisions about the level of decentralization top management seeks.

  c. It insulates the Harvesting Division manager from the frictions and the discipline of the marketplace because costs, not market prices, affect the revenues of the supplying division.

22-20 General guideline, transfer-price range. The BPL Ltd. manufactures and sells television sets. The Assembly Division assembles the television sets. It buys the screens for the television sets from the Screen Division. The Screen Division is operating at capacity. The incremental cost of manufacturing the screens is ₹700 per unit. The Screen Division can sell as many screens as it wants in the outside market at a price of ₹1,100 per screen. If it sells screens in the outside market, the Screen Division will incur variable marketing and distribution costs of ₹40 per unit. Similarly, if the Assembly Division purchases screens from outside suppliers, it will incur variable purchasing costs of ₹20 per screen.

Required

1. Using the general guideline presented in the chapter, what is the minimum transfer price at which the Screen Division will sell screens to the Assembly Division?

2. Suppose division managers act autonomously to maximize their own division's operating income, either by transacting internally or buying and selling in the market. If the two division managers were to negotiate a transfer price, what is the range of acceptable transfer prices?

Solution

General guideline, transfer price range.

1. If the Screen Division sells screens in the outside market, it will receive, for each screen, the market price of the screen minus variable marketing and distribution costs per screen = ₹1,100 − ₹40 = ₹1,060. The incremental cost of manufacturing each screen is ₹700. The Screen Division is operating at capacity. Hence, the opportunity cost per screen of selling the screen to the Assembly Division rather than in the outside market is the contribution margin the Screen Division would forgo if it transferred screens internally rather than sold them in the outside market.

Contribution margin per screen = ₹1,060 − ₹700 = ₹360.

Using the general guideline,

$$\text{Minimum transfer price per screen} = \text{Incremental costs per screen up to the point of transfer} + \text{Opportunity costs per screen to the selling division}$$

That is, Minimum transfer price per screen = ₹700 + ₹360 = ₹1,060

2. If the two division managers were to negotiate a transfer price, the range of possible transfer prices is between ₹1,060 and ₹1,120 per screen. As calculated in requirement 1, the Screen Division will be willing to supply screens to the Assembly Division only if the transfer price equals or exceeds ₹1,060 per screen.

   If the Assembly Division were to purchase the screens in the outside market, it will incur a cost of ₹1,120, the cost of the screen equal to ₹1,100 plus variable purchasing costs of ₹20 per screen. Hence, the Assembly Division will be willing to buy screens from the Screen Division only if the price does not exceed ₹1,120 per screen. Within the price range of ₹1,060 and ₹1,120 per screen, each division will be willing to transact with the other. The exact transfer price between ₹1,060 and ₹1,120 will depend on the bargaining strengths of the two divisions.

22-21 Transfer-pricing dispute. The Escorts Ltd., manufacturer of tractors and other heavy farm equipment, is organized along decentralized lines, with each manufacturing division operating as a separate profit center. Each division manager has been delegated full authority on all decisions involving the sale of that division's output both to outsiders and to other divisions of Escorts Ltd.. Division C has in the past always purchased its requirement of a particular tractor-engine component from Division A. However, when informed that Division A is increasing its selling price to ₹1,500, Division C's manager decides to purchase the engine component from outside suppliers.

Division C can purchase the component for ₹1,350 in the open market. Division A insists that, because of the recent installation of some highly specialized equipment and the resulting high depreciation charges, it will not be able to earn an adequate return on its investment unless it raises its price. Division A's manager appeals to top management of Escorts Ltd. for support in the dispute with Division C and supplies the following operating data:

C's annual purchases of the tractor-engine component	1,000 units
A's variable costs per unit of the tractor-engine component	₹1,200
A's fixed costs per unit of the tractor-engine component	₹200

Required

1. Assume that there are no alternative uses for internal facilities. Determine whether the company as a whole will benefit if Division C purchases the component from outside suppliers for ₹1,350 per unit. What should the transfer price for the component be set at so that division managers acting in their own divisions' interests take actions that are in the best interest of the company as a whole?

2. Assume that internal facilities of Division A would not otherwise be idle. By not producing the 1,000 units for Division C, Division A's equipment and other facilities would be used for other production operations that would result in annual cash-operating savings of ₹1,80,000. Should Division C purchase from outside suppliers? Show your computations.

3. Assume that there are no alternative uses for Division A's internal facilities and that the price from outsiders drops ₹200. Should Division C purchase from outside suppliers? What should the transfer price for the component be set at so that division managers acting in their own divisions' interests take actions that are in the best interest of the company as a whole?

Solution

Transfer-pricing dispute.

This problem is similar to the Problem for Self-Study in the chapter.

1. Company as a whole will not benefit if Division C buys on the outside market:

Purchase costs from outsider, 1,000 units × ₹1,350	₹13,50,000
Deduct: Savings in variable costs by reducing	
Division A output, 1,000 units × ₹1,200	12,00,000
Net cost (benefit) to company as a whole by	
buying from outside	₹1,50,000

Any transfer price between ₹1,200 to ₹1,350 per unit will achieve goal congruence. Divisionmanagers acting in their own best interests will take actions that are in the best interests of the company as a whole.

2. Company will benefit if C purchases from the outsider supplier:

Purchase costs from outsider, 1,000 units × ₹1,350		₹13,50,000
Deduct: Savings in variable costs,		
1,000 units × ₹1,200	₹12,00,000	
Savings due to A's equipment and		
facilities assigned to other operations	1,80,000	13,80,000
Net cost (benefit) to company as a whole by		
buying from outside		₹(30,000)

Division C should purchase from outside suppliers.

3. Company will benefit if C purchases from the outside supplier:

Purchase costs from outsider, 1,000 units × ₹1,150	₹11,50,000
Deduct: Savings in variable costs by reducing	
Division A output, 1,000 units × ₹1,200	12,00,000
Net cost (benefit) to company as a whole by	
buying from outside	₹(50,000)

The three requirements are summarized below (in thousands):

	(1)	(2)	(3)
Total purchase costs from outsider	₹1,350	₹1,350	₹1,150
Total relevant costs if purchased from Division A			
Total incremental (outlay) costs if purchased from A	1,200	1,200	1,200
Total opportunity costs if purchased from A	–	180	–
Total relevant costs if purchased from A	1,200	1,380	1,200
Operating income advantage (disadvantage) to			
company as a whole by buying from A	₹150	₹(30)	₹(50)

Goal congruence would be achieved if the transfer price is set equal to the total relevant costs of purchasing from Division A.

22-22 Transfer-pricing problem (continuation of 22-21). Refer to Example 22-21. Assume that Division A can sell the 1,000 units to other customers at ₹1,550 per unit, with variable marketing costs of ₹50 per unit.

Determine whether Escorts Ltd. will benefit if Division C purchases the 1,000 components from outside suppliers at ₹1,350 per unit. Show your computations.

Required

Solution

Transfer-pricing problem (continuation of 22-20).

The company as a whole would benefit in this situation if C purchased from outside suppliers. The ₹1,50,000 disadvantage to the company as a whole by purchasing from the outside supplier would be more than offset by the ₹3,00,000 contribution margin of A's sale of 1,000 units to other customers.

Purchase costs from outside supplier, 1,000 units × ₹1,350		₹13,50,000
Deduct variable cost savings, 1,000 units × ₹1,200		12,00,000
Net cost to company as a whole by buying units from outside		₹1,50,000
A's sales to other customers, 1,000 units × ₹1,550		₹15,50,000
Deduct:		
Variable manufacturing costs, ₹1,200 × 1,000 units	₹12,00,000	
Variable marketing costs, ₹50 × 1,000 units	50,000	
Total variable costs		12,50,000
Contribution margin from selling units to other customers		₹3,00,000

22-23 Multinational transfer pricing, effect of alternative transfer-pricing methods, global income tax minimization. Tech Friendly Computer, Inc., with headquarters Bangalore, manufactures and sells a desktop computer. Tech Friendly has three divisions, each of which is located in a different country:

a. China division—manufactures memory devices and keyboards

b. South Korea division—assembles desktop computers using locally manufactured parts, along with memory devices and keyboards from the China division

c. U.S. division—packages and distributes desktop computers

Each division is run as a profit center. The costs for the work done in each division for a single desktop computer are as follows:

China division	Variable cost = 900 yuan
	Fixed cost = 1,980 yuan
South Korea division	Variable cost = 3,50,000 won
	Fixed cost = 4,70,000 won
U.S. division	Variable cost = $125
	Fixed cost = $325

- Chinese income tax rate on the China division's operating income: 40%
- South Korean income tax rate on the South Korea division's operating income: 20%
- U.S. income tax rate on the U.S. division's operating income: 30%

Each desktop computer is sold to retail outlets in the United States for $3,800. Assume that the current foreign exchange rates are as follows:

$$9 \text{ yuan} = \$1 \text{ U.S.}$$

$$1,000 \text{ Won} = \$1 \text{ U.S.}$$

Both the China and the South Korea divisions sell part of their production under a private label. The China division sells the comparable memory/keyboard package used in each Tech Friendly desktop computer to a Chinese manufacturer for 4,500 yuan. The South Korea division sells the comparable desktop computer to a South Korean distributor for 13,40,000 won.

Required

1. Calculate the after-tax operating income per unit earned by each division under the following transfer-pricing methods: (a) market price, (b) 200% of full cost, and (c) 350% of variable cost. (Income taxes are not included in the computation of the cost-based transfer prices.)

2. Which transfer-pricing method(s) will maximize the after-tax operating income per unit of Tech Friendly Computer?

Solution

1. This is a three-country, three-division transfer-pricing problem with three alternative transfer-pricing methods. Summary data in U.S. dollars are as follows:

China Plant

Variable costs:	900 Yuan ÷ 9 Yuan per $ = $100 per subunit
Fixed costs:	1,980 Yuan ÷ 9 Yuan per $ = $220 per subunit

South Korea Plant

Variable costs:	3,50,000 Won ÷ 1,000 Won per $ = $350 per unit
Fixed costs:	4,70,000 Won ÷ 1,000 Won per $ = $470 per unit

U.S. Plant

Variable costs:	= $125 per unit
Fixed costs:	= $325 per unit

Market prices for private-label sale alternatives:

China Plant: 4,500 Yuan ÷ 9 Yuan per $ = $500 per subunit
South Korea Plant: 13,40,000 Won ÷ 1,000 Won per $ = $1,340 per unit

The transfer prices under each method are:

a. Market price
   - China to South Korea = $500 per subunit
   - South Korea to U.S. Plant = $1,340 per unit
b. 200% of full costs
   - China to South Korea
        2.0 × ($100 + $220) = $640 per subunit
   - South Korea to U.S. Plant
        2.0 × ($640 + $350 + $470) = $2,920 per unit
c. 350% of variable costs
   - China to South Korea
        3.5 × $100 = $350 per subunit
   - South Korea to U.S. Plant
        3.5 × ($350 + $350) = $2,450 per unit

	Method A Internal Transfers at Market Price	Method B Internal Transfers at 200% of Full Costs	Method C Internal Transfers at 350% of Variable Costs
1. China Division			
Division revenue per unit	$500	$640	$350
Cost per unit:			
Division variable cost per unit	100	100	100
Division fixed cost per unit	220	220	220
Total division cost per unit	320	320	320
Division operating income per unit	180	320	30
Income tax at 40%	72	128	12
Division net income per unit	$108	$192	$18
2. South Korea Division			
Division revenue per unit	$1,340	$2,920	$2,450
Cost per unit:			
Transferred-in cost per unit	500	640	350
Division variable cost per unit	350	350	350
Division fixed cost per unit	470	470	470
Total division cost per unit	1,320	1,460	1,170
Division operating income per unit	20	1,460	1,280
Income tax at 20%	4	292	256
Division net income per unit	$16	$1,168	$1,024
3. United States Division			
Division revenue per unit	$3,800	$3,800	$3,800
Cost per unit:			
Transferred-in cost per unit	1,340	2,920	2,450
Division variable cost per unit	125	125	125

Division fixed cost per unit	325	325	325
Total division cost per unit	1,790	3,370	2,900
Division operating income per unit	2,010	430	900
Income tax at 30%	603	129	270
Division net income per unit	$1,407	$301	$630

2. Division net income:

	Market Price	200% of Full Costs	350% of Variable Costs
China Division	$108	$192	$18
South Korea Division	16	1,168	1,024
U.S. Division	1,407	301	630
Tech Friendly Computer, Inc.	$1,531	$1,661	$1,672

Tech Friendly will maximize its net income by using the third method, 350% of variable costs, as the transfer price. This is because this method sources relatively little income in China, the country with the highest income tax rate.

22-24 Multinational transfer pricing, global tax minimization. The Questron Company manufactures telecommunications equipment at its plant in Scranton, Pennsylvania. The company has marketing divisions throughout the world. A Questron marketing division in Hamburg, Germany, imports 1,00,000 broadband routers from the United States. The following information is available:

U.S. income tax rate on the U.S. division's operating income	35%
German income tax rate on the German division's operating income	40%
German import duty	15%
Variable manufacturing cost per router	$275
Full manufacturing cost per router	$400
Selling price (net of marketing and distribution costs) in Germany	$575

Suppose the United States and German tax authorities only allow transfer prices that are between the full manufacturing cost per unit of $400 and a market price of $475, based on comparable imports into Germany. The German import duty is charged on the price at which the product is transferred into Germany. Any import duty paid to the German authorities is a deductible expense for calculating German income taxes.

Required

1. Calculate the after-tax operating income earned by the United States and German divisions from transferring 1,00,000 broadband routers (a) at full manufacturing cost per unit and (b) at market price of comparable imports. (Income taxes are not included in the computation of the cost-based transfer prices.)

2. Which transfer price should the Questron Company select to minimize the total of company import duties and income taxes? Remember that the transfer price must be between the full manufacturing cost per unit of $400 and the market price of $475 of comparable imports into Germany. Explain your reasoning.

Solution

1. Solution Exhibit 22-23 shows the after-tax operating incomes earned by the U.S. and German divisions from transferring 1,00,000 broadband routers using (a) full manufacturing cost per unit, and (b) market price of comparable imports as transfer prices.

2. There are many ways to proceed, but the first thing to note is that the transfer price that minimizes the total of company import duties and income taxes will be either the full manufacturing cost or the market price of comparable imports.

Consider what happens every time the transfer price is increased by $1 over, say, the full manufacturing cost of $400. This results in the following change for each unit:

a.	an increase in U.S. taxes of 35% × $1	$0.35
b.	an increase in import duties paid in Germany, 15% × $1	0.15
c.	a decrease in German taxes of 40% × $1.15 (the $1 increase in transfer price + $0.15 paid by way of import duty)	(0.46)
	Net effect is an increase in import duty and tax payments of:	$0.04

To verify this solution, note that if the transfer price changes from $400 to $475, the net effect is an increase in import duty and tax payments of ($475 − $400) × $0.04 = $3 per unit. Across 1,00,000 units, this implies a decrease in total profits of (1,00,000) × $3 = $3,00,000, which corresponds exactly to the $3,00,000 difference in total after-tax operating incomes documented in Solution Exhibit 22-23.

Therefore, Questron Company will minimize import duties and income taxes by setting the transfer price at its minimum level of $400, the full manufacturing cost.

Solution Exhibit 22-23

Division Incomes of U.S. and German Divisions from Transferring 1,00,000 broadband routers

Particulars	Method A Internal Transfers at Full Manufacturing Cost	Method B Internal Transfers at Market Price
U.S. Division		
Revenues:		
$400, $475 × 1,00,000 units	$4,00,00,000	$4,75,00,000
Costs:		
Full manufacturing cost:		
$400 × 1,00,000 units	4,00,00,000	4,00,00,000
Division operating income	0	75,00,000
Division income taxes at 35%	0	26,25,000
Division after-tax operating income	$0	$48,75,000
German Division		
Revenues:		
$575 × 1,00,000 units	$5,75,00,000	$5,75,00,000
Costs:		
Transferred-in costs:		
$400 × 1,00,000, $475 × 1,00,000 units	4,00,00,000	4,75,00,000
Import duties at 15% of transferred-in price		
$60 × 1,00,000, $71.25 × 1,00,000 units	60,00,000	71,25,000
Total division costs	4,60,00,000	5,46,25,000
Division operating income	1,15,00,000	28,75,000
Division income taxes at 40%	46,00,000	11,50,000
Division after-tax operating income	$69,00,000	$17,25,000

Sum of divisional after-tax operating incomes $69,00,000 $66,00,000

22-25 Multinational transfer pricing, goal congruence (continuation of 22-24). Suppose that the U.S. division could sell as many broadband routers as it makes at $450 per unit in the U.S. market, net of all marketing and distribution costs.

1. From the viewpoint of the Questron Company as a whole, would after-tax operating income be maximized if it sold the 1,00,000 routers in the United States or in Germany? Show your computations.

2. Suppose division managers act autonomously to maximize their division's after-tax operating income. Will the transfer price calculated in requirement 2 in Exercise 22-23 result in the U.S. division manager taking the actions determined to be optimal in requirement 1 of this exercise? Explain.

3. What is the minimum transfer price that the U.S. division manager would agree to? Does this transfer price result in the Questron Company as a whole paying more import duty and taxes than the answer to requirement 2 in Exercise 22-23? If so, by how much?

Solution

1. After-tax operating income if Questron Company sells all 1,00,000 broadband routers in the United States:

Revenues, $450 × 1,00,000 units	$4,50,00,000
Full manufacturing costs, $400 × 1,00,000 units	4,00,00,000
Operating income	50,00,000
Income taxes at 35%	17,50,000
After-tax operating income	$32,50,000

From Exercise 22-23, requirement 1, Questron Company's after-tax operating income if it transfers 1,00,000 broadband routers to Germany at full manufacturing cost and sells the units in Germany is $69,00,000. Therefore, Questron should sell the 1,00,000 units in Germany.

2. Transferring broadband routers at the full manufacturing cost of the U.S. Division minimizes import duties and taxes (Exercise 22-23, requirement 2) but creates zero operating income for the U.S Division. Acting autonomously, the U.S. Division manager would maximize division operating income by selling routers in the U.S. market, which results in $32,50,000 in after-tax division operating income as calculated in requirement 1, rather than by transferring routers to the German division at full manufacturing cost. Thus, the transfer price calculated in requirement 2 of Exercise 22-23 will not result in actions that are optimal for Questron Company as a whole.

3. The minimum transfer price at which the U.S. Division manager acting autonomously will agree to transfer broadband routers to the German Division is $450 per unit. Any transfer price less than $450 will leave the U.S. Division's performance worse than if it were to sell directly in the U.S. market. Because the U.S. Division can sell as many routers as it makes in the U.S. market, there is an opportunity cost of transferring the product internally equal to $175 (selling price $450 - variable manufacturing costs, $275).

$$\begin{matrix} \text{Minimumtransfer} \\ \text{price per unit} \end{matrix} = \begin{matrix} \text{Incremental cost per} \\ \text{unit up to the point of} \\ \text{transfer} \end{matrix} + \begin{matrix} \text{Opportunity cost per} \\ \text{unit to the selling} \\ \text{(U. S.) division} \end{matrix}$$

$$= \$275 + \$175 = \$450$$

This transfer price will result in Questron Company as a whole paying more import duties and taxes than the answer to Exercise 22-23, requirement 2, as calculated below:

U.S. Division

Revenues, $450 × 1,00,000 units	$4,50,00,000
Full manufacturing costs	4,00,00,000
Division operating income	50,00,000
Division income taxes at 35%	17,50,000
Division after-tax operating income	$32,50,000

German Division

Revenues, $575 × 1,00,000 units	$5,75,00,000
Transferred in costs, $450 × 1,00,000 units	4,50,00,000
Import duties at 15% of transferred-in price,	
$67.50 × 1,00,000 units	67,50,000
Division operating income	57,50,000
Division income taxes at 40%	23,00,000
Division after-tax operating income	$34,50,000

Total import duties and income taxes at transfer prices of $400 and $450 per unit for 1,00,000 broadband routers are given below:

	Transfer Price of $400 per Unit (Exercise 22-23, Requirement 2)	Transfer Price of $450 per Unit
(a) U.S. income taxes	$0	$17,50,000
(b) German import duties	60,00,000	67,50,000
(c) German income taxes	46,00,000	23,00,000
	$1,06,00,000	$1,08,00,000

The minimum transfer price that the U.S. Division manager, acting autonomously, would agree to results in Questron Company paying $2,00,000 in additional import duties and income taxes.

A student who has done the calculations shown in Exercise 22-23, requirement 2, can calculate the additional taxes from a $450 transfer price more directly, as follows:

Every $1 increase in the transfer price per unit over $400 results in additional import duty and taxes of $0.04 per unit, so a $50 increase ($450 – $400) per unit will result in additional import duty and taxes of $0.04 × 50 = $2.00. For 1,00,000 units transferred, this equals $2.00 × 1,00,000 = $2,00,000.

22-26 General guideline, transfer pricing. The Sony Company manufactures and sells television sets. Its assembly division (AD) buys television screens from the screen division (SD) and assembles the TV sets. The SD, which is operating at capacity, incurs an incremental manufacturing cost of $65 per screen. The SD can sell all its output to the outside market at a price of $100 per screen, after incurring a variable marketing and distribution cost of $8 per screen. If the AD purchases screens from outside suppliers at a price of $100 per screen, it will incur a variable purchasing cost of $7 per screen. Sony's division managers can act autonomously to maximize their own division's operating income.

Required

1. What is the minimum transfer price at which the SD manager would be willing to sell screens to the AD?
2. What is the maximum transfer price at which the AD manager would be willing to purchase screens from the SD?
3. Now suppose that the SD can sell only 70% of its output capacity of 20,000 screens per month on the open market. Capacity cannot be reduced in the short run. The AD can assemble and sell more than 20,000 TV sets per month.

a. What is the minimum transfer price at which the SD manager would be willing to sell screens to the AD?

b. From the point of view of Sony's management, how much of the SD output should be transferred to the AD?

c. If Sony mandates the SD and AD managers to "split the difference" on the minimum and maximum transfer prices they would be willing to negotiate over, what would be the resulting transfer price? Does this price achieve the outcome desired in requirement 3b?

Solution

1. The minimum transfer price that the SD would demand from the AD is the net price it could obtain from selling its screens on the outside market: $100 minus $8 marketing and distribution cost per screen, or $92 per screen. The SD is operating at capacity. The incremental cost of manufacturing each screen is $65. Therefore, the opportunity cost of selling a screen to the AD is the contribution margin the SD would forgo by transferring the screen internally instead of selling it on the outside market.

$$\text{Contribution margin per screen} = \$92 - \$65 = \$27$$

Using the general guideline,

$$\begin{array}{l}\text{Minimum transfer} \\ \text{price per screen}\end{array} = \begin{array}{l}\text{Incremental cost per} \\ \text{screen incurred up to} \\ \text{the point of transfer}\end{array} + \begin{array}{l}\text{Opportunity cost per} \\ \text{screen to the} \\ \text{selling division}\end{array}$$

$$= \$65 + \$27 = \$92$$

2. The maximum transfer price the AD manager would be willing to offer SD is its own total cost for purchasing from outside, $100 plus $7 per screen, or $107 per screen.

3a. If the SD has excess capacity (relative to what the outside market can absorb), the minimum transfer price using the general guideline is as follows: for the first 6,000 units (or 30% of output), $65 per screen because opportunity cost is zero; for the remaining 14,000 units (or 70% of output), $92 per screen because opportunity cost is $27 per screen.

3b. From the point of view of Sony's management, all of the SD's output should be transferred to the AD. This would avoid the $7 per screen variable purchasing cost that is incurred by the AD when it purchases screens from the outside market, and it would also save the $8 marketing and distribution cost the SD would incur to sell each screen to the outside market.

3c. If the managers of the AD and the SD could negotiate the transfer price, they would settle on a price between the minimum transfer price the SD will accept (from requirement 3a) and $107 per screen (the maximum transfer price the AD would be willing to pay). Any price in this range would be acceptable to both divisions for all of the SD's output and would also be optimal from Sony's point of view. This would obviously apply to the "split the difference" price as well. When the SD has excess capacity, this rule would suggest a price of ($65 + $107)/2 = $86; for the other 70% of output that SD can sell externally, the rule indicates a price of ($92 + $107)/2 = $99.5. From a practical standpoint, note that the latter price also works when SD has excess capacity; as a result, the firm might prefer it as a stable benchmark price, keeping in mind of course that it credits SD with too high a profit even at times of unused capacity.

22-27 Transfer pricing, external market, goal congruence. Pony India produces and sells high-quality scissors made of stainless steel. The firm consists of two divisions, UP and DOWN. The UP division manufactures 30,000 pairs of scissors per year. It incurs variable manufacturing costs of $9 per unit and total annual fixed manufacturing costs of $60,000. The UP division sells 10,000 units externally at a price of $16 each, mostly to office supplies stores.

It transfers the remaining 20,000 units internally to the DOWN division, which modifies the units, adds a titanium plasma coating, and sells them for use by salon professionals in the United States.

Pony India has adopted a market-based transfer pricing policy. For each pair of scissors it receives from the UP division, the DOWN division pays the weighted-average external price the UP division charges its customers outside the company. The current transfer price is accordingly set at $16.

Abhishek, the manager of the UP division, receives an offer from Jean-Georges, an international hair salon supplier. Jean-Georges offers to buy 4,000 pairs of scissors at a price of $12.50 each, knowing that the entire scissors industry (including Pony India) has excess capacity at this time. The variable manufacturing cost to UP for the units Jean-Georges is requesting is $9, and there are no additional costs associated with this offer. Accepting Jean-Georges' offer would not affect the current price of $16 charged to existing external customers.

1. Calculate the UP division's current annual level of profit (without the new order). **Required**
2. Compute the change in the UP division's profit if it accepts Jean-Georges' offer. Will Abhishek accept this offer if her aim is to maximize the UP division's profit?
3. Would the top management of Pony India want the UP division to accept the offer? Compute the change in firm wide profit associated with Jean-Georges' offer.
4. Pony India. is considering changing its policy. Henceforth, the transfer price will be set at a fixed percentage discount from the weighted-average price charged by UP on external sales. At what percentage discount would the goal incongruence identified in your answer to requirements 2 and 3 no longer be a problem?

Solution

1. The UP division's current level of profit is as follows:

Sales to external customers:	10,000 × $16 = $1,60,000
Sales to DOWN division:	20,000 × $16 = 3,20,000
Sales Revenues:	4,80,000
Variable manufacturing costs:	30,000 × $9 = 2,70,000
Fixed manufacturing costs:	60,000
Operating Income:	$1,50,000

2. With the new order, the UP division generates additional contribution margin from the 4,000 units it sells to Jean Georges (note that fixed costs are irrelevant because of the presence of excess capacity). At a price of $12.50, the incremental contribution from the order is:

$$4,000 \text{ units} \times (\$12.50 - \$9) = \$14,000$$

However, the weighted average external price is no longer $16, but rather

$$\frac{(10,000 \times \$16) + (4,000 \times \$12.50)}{10,000 + 4,000} = \$15.$$

As a result, the transfer price realized by UP for internal sales is lowered from $16 to $15, reducing UP's sales revenues by (20,000 units) × $1 = $20,000.

The net effect therefore is that UP's operating income would decrease by $6,000 ($20,000 – $14,000) overall. As manager of the UP division, Abhishek would therefore choose to reject the offer from Jean Georges.

3. Yes, because the new order from Jean Georges results in an additional contribution margin to Abhishek of $14,000, and the same amount in higher firm-wide profit. The

additional effect identified in requirement 2, namely the effect on the internal transfer price, has no relevance in evaluating the value of the order to the firm as a whole.

4. Let d be the percentage discount from the weighted average market price that is used to set the internal transfer price. To eliminate the goal incongruence identified in requirements 1 and 2, we have to solve for the value of d at which the UP division makes the same profit both with and without the new order from Jean Georges. Note that we can ignore the sales revenues from external customers, the variable manufacturing costs for the initial 30,000 units and the fixed manufacturing costs as none of these amounts are affected by the new external order or the transfer price. The rest of UP division's profits are given by:

Without order: 20,000 units × $16 × (1 − d)
With order: 20,000 units × $15 × (1 − d) + $14,000

Setting these quantities equal, we see that:

$$1 - d = \frac{\$14,000}{\$20,000} = 0.70, \text{ or } d = 0.30.$$

So, by setting the transfer price at a 30% discount from the weighted average price of external sales, the manager of the UP division, Abhishek, will have the right incentives to take the outside offer that is in the firm's best interest. Of course, any discount greater than 30% will provide Abhishek even greater motivation to accept the offer from Jean Georges.

22-28 International transfer pricing, taxes, goal congruence. Castor, a division of Hindalco Ltd, is located in the United States. Its effective income tax rate is 30%. Another division of Hindalco, Pollux, is located in Canada, where the income tax rate is 40%. Pollux manufactures, among other things, an intermediate product for Castor called Alumina. Pollux operates at capacity and makes 15,000 units of Alumina for Castor each period, at a variable cost of $56 per unit. Assume that there are no outside customers for Alumina. Because the Alumina must be shipped from Canada to the United States, it costs Pollux an additional $8 per unit to ship the Alumina to Castor. There are no direct fixed costs for Alumina. Pollux also manufactures other products.

A product similar to Alumina that Castor could use as a substitute is available in the United States for $77 per unit.

Required

1. What is the minimum and maximum transfer price that would be acceptable to Castor and Pollux for Alumina, and why?
2. What transfer price would minimize income taxes for Hindalco Ltd as a whole? Would Castor and Pollux want to be evaluated on operating income using this transfer price?
3. Suppose Hindalco uses the transfer price from requirement 2 and each division is evaluated on its own after-tax division operating income. Now suppose Pollux has an opportunity to sell 8,000 units of Alumina to an outside customer for $62 each. Pollux will not incur shipping costs because the customer is nearby and offers to pay for shipping. Assume that if Pollux accepts the special order, Castor will have to buy 8,000 units of the substitute product in the United States at $77 per unit.
   a. Will accepting the special order maximize after-tax operating income for Hindalco Ltd as a whole?
   b. Will Castor want Pollux to accept this special order? Why or why not?
   c. Will Pollux want to accept this special order? Explain.
   d. Suppose Hindalco Ltd wants to operate in a decentralized manner. What transfer price should Hindalco set for Alumina so that each division acting in its own best interest takes actions with respect to the special order that are in the best interests of Hindalco Ltd as a whole?

Solution

1. The minimum transfer price would be $64 to cover the variable production ($56 per unit) and shipping ($8 per unit) costs because Pollux would want, at a minimum, zero

contribution margin. The opportunity cost is $0 because there are no external custom-ers for Alumina. The maximum transfer price would be the $77 market price that Castor would have to pay to acquire a product similar to Alumina from the external market in the United States.

2. To minimize income taxes, Hindalco should use a transfer price of $64. Canada has a higher tax rate so goods coming from Canada should have the lowest transfer price. Pollux would not like a transfer price of $64 because it would report no operating income from the transfer. Castor would like a transfer price of $64 because it is lower than the outside market price of $77.

3a. It is easiest to see the solution to this problem if we assume a selling price for the prod-uct that Castor manufactures, for example, $120. (The actual selling price you choose is irrelevant.)

Pollux's after-tax income on each unit from accepting the special order is as follows:

Revenue per unit	$62.00
Variable cost per unit	56.00
Contribution margin per unit	6.00
Income taxes (0.40 × $6)	2.40
Increase in division income per unit after tax	$3.60

Castor's after-tax income on each unit if Pollux accepts the special order and Castor buys the substitute product for Alumina in the United States for $77 per unit is as follows:

Revenue per unit	$120.00
Variable cost per unit	77.00
Contribution margin per unit	43.00
Income taxes (0.30 × $43)	12.90
Increase in division income per unit after tax	$30.10

Hindalco's total net income on each unit from Pollux accepting the special order is therefore $3.60 + $30.10 = $33.70.

If Pollux rejects the special order and instead transfers the units internally to Castor at $64 per unit, Pollux's after-tax income would be as follows:

Revenue per unit	$64
Variable cost per unit	64
Contribution margin per unit	0
Income taxes	0
Increase in division income per unit after tax	$0

Castor's after-tax income on each unit is as follows:

Revenue per unit	$120.00
Variable cost per unit	64.00
Contribution margin per unit	56.00
Income taxes (0.30 × $56)	16.80
Increase in division income per unit after tax	$39.20

Hindalco's total net income on each unit as a result of Pollux rejecting the special order and transferring units of Alumina to Castor at $64 per unit is therefore $39.20 per unit. As this is higher than $33.70, accepting the special order does not maximize after-tax operating income. After-tax operating income is maximized by rejecting the special order.

3b. Castor will not want Pollux to accept the special order. It is more costly to buy from the external market than from Pollux.

3c. Pollux will want to accept the special order because Pollux's income per unit after-tax increases by $3.60 per unit by accepting the special order rather than transferring Alumina to Castor at $64 per unit and earning $0 operating income.

3d. Hindalco should set the transfer price at $70 per unit. This will result in each division taking actions in its own best interest that are also in the best interest of Hindalco as a whole acting as a decentralized organization.

The opportunity cost of transferring Alumina internally is $6 ($62 − $56) per unit for the first 8,000 units and $0 per unit thereafter.

Using the general guideline,

$$\begin{array}{c}\text{Minimum transfer} \\ \text{price}\end{array} = \begin{array}{c}\text{Incremental cost per} \\ \text{unit incurred up to} \\ \text{the point of transfer}\end{array} + \begin{array}{c}\text{Opportunity cost per} \\ \text{unit to the} \\ \text{selling subunit}\end{array}$$

$$\begin{array}{c}\text{So, minimum} \\ \text{transfer price}\end{array} = \$64 + \$6 = \$70 \text{ per unit for the first 8,000 units}$$

$$\$64 + \$0 = \$64 \text{ per unit for the next 7,000 units}$$

Hindalco should use these minimum transfer prices because they are also (reasonably) tax-efficient.

At a transfer price of $70 per unit for the first 8,000 units, Pollux is indifferent between accepting the special order or transferring internally. Pollux earns $6 per unit if it accepts the special order. It also earns $6 per unit if it transfers Alumina to Castor ($70 − $64 variable cost per unit).

Castor will prefer to "buy" Alumina from Pollux because the transfer price of $70 is less than the $77 price it would pay to buy a product similar to Alumina in the United States.

The increase in Hindalco's income will be as follows:

From Pollux:

Revenue per unit	$70.00
Variable cost per unit	64.00
Contribution margin per unit	6.00
Income taxes (0.40 × $6)	2.40
Increase in division income per unit after tax	$3.60

From Castor:

Revenue per unit	$120.00
Transfer price per unit	70.00
Contribution margin per unit	50.00
Income taxes (0.30 × $50)	15.00
Increase in division income per unit after tax	$35.00

Increase in Hindalco's income = $3.60 + $35.00 = $38.60

This net income is greater than the $33.70 net income that Hindalco would earn if Pollux accepted the special order. It is less than the $39.20 that Hindalco would earn if Pollux had transferred Alumina at $64 per unit. Of course, if the transfer price is set at $64 per unit, Pollux would accept the special order, which would lead to a lower net income of $33.70. If Hindalco wants to get the benefits of decentralization, it must be willing to suffer the consequences of higher taxes that Pollux would have to pay.

Note that Hindalco would not want to set the transfer price any higher than $70, the minimum transfer price that would induce Pollux to transfer internally to Castor. Why? Because setting the transfer price any higher would result in exactly the same action (transferring Alumina internally) but at a higher cost because of the higher taxes that Pollux would have to pay in Canada. Consider for example a transfer price of $75 per unit. The increase in Hindalco's income will be as follows:

From Pollux:

Revenue per unit	$75.00
Variable cost per unit	64.00
Contribution margin per unit	11.00
Income taxes (0.4 × $11)	4.40
Increase in division income per unit after tax	$6.60

From Castor:

Revenue per unit	$120.00
Transfer price per unit	75.00
Contribution margin per unit	45.00
Income taxes (0.30 × $45)	13.50
Increase in division income per unit after tax	$31.50

Increase in Hindalco's income is $6.60 + $31.50 = $38.10, which is less than the $38.60 Hindalco earns if the transfer price is set at $70 per unit. A transfer price of $70 is the most tax-efficient transfer price consistent with Hindalco operating as a decentralized organization. Note also that the transfer price cannot be set above $77 per unit because then Castor would buy a product similar to Alumina in the United States rather than from Pollux.

22-29 Transfer pricing, goal congruence, ethics. Ballarpur Industries manufactures cardboard containers (boxes) made from recycled paper products. The company operates two divisions, paper recycling and box manufacturing, as decentralized entities. The recycling division is free to sell recycled paper to outside buyers, and the box manufacturing division is free to purchase recycled paper from other sources. Currently, however, the recycling division sells all of its output to the manufacturing division, and the manufacturing division does not purchase materials from outside suppliers.

The recycled paper is transferred from the recycling division to the manufacturing division at 110% of full cost. The recycling division purchases recyclable paper products for $0.075 per pound. The recycling division uses 100 pounds of recyclable paper products to produce one roll of recycled paper. The division's other variable costs equal $6.35 per roll, and fixed costs at a monthly production level of 10,000 rolls are $2.15 per roll. During the most recent month, 10,000 rolls of recycled paper were transferred between the two divisions. The recycling division's capacity is 15,000 rolls.

With the increase in demand for sustainably made products, the manufacturing division expects to use 12,000 rolls of paper next month. JK Corp has offered to sell 2,000 rolls of recycled paper next month to the manufacturing division for $17.00 per roll.

Required

1. Compute the transfer price per roll of recycled paper. If each division is considered a profit center, would the manufacturing manager choose to purchase 2,000 rolls next month from J.K. Corporation?

2. Is the purchase in the best interest of Ballarpur Industries? Show your calculations. What is the cause of this goal incongruence?

3. The manufacturing division manager suggests that $17.00 is now the market price for recycled paper rolls and that this should be the new transfer price. Ballarpur's corporate management tends to agree. The paper recycling manager is suspicious. J.K.'s prices have always been much higher than $17.00 per roll. Why the sudden price cut? After further investigation by the recycling division manager, it is revealed that the $17.00 per roll price was a one-time-only offer made to the manufacturing division due to excess inventory at J.K.. Future orders would be priced at $18.50 per roll. Comment on the

validity of the $17.00 per roll market price and the ethics of the manufacturing manager. Would changing the transfer price to $17.00 matter to Ballarpur Industries?

Solution

1. The transfer price is 110% of the full cost per unit:

   1.10 [($0.075 × 100) + $6.35 + $2.15] = $17.60

Because $17.00 is below the transfer price of $17.60, the manufacturing division manager would choose to purchase the 2,000 rolls from J.K..

2. The purchase is not in the best interest of Ballarpur Industries because, if produced internally, the additional 2,000 rolls would only cost the company $27,700 ($13.85 of variable cost per unit × 2,000 rolls). Because there is available capacity, fixed costs would be unaffected. If purchased from J.K., the paper would cost $34,000. The cause of this goal incongruence is two-fold: setting a transfer price based on full cost treats fixed costs as variable, and setting the price above full cost (in this case 110%) artificially inflates the cost to the purchasing division.

3. $17.00 is not a valid market price because it could not be replicated on future orders. $18.50 is a more appropriate market price. The manufacturing manager was not acting ethically in this situation because he or she was withholding pertinent information from both upper management and the recycling division manager and was even promoting a position known to be false. If the transfer price had been changed to $17.00, it would not have affected the company overall, but profit incentive rewards would have been shifted away from the recycling division manager and to the manufacturing manager.

22-30 Transfer pricing, perfect and imperfect markets. Rallis India has three divisions (R, S, and T), organized as decentralized profit centers. Division R produces the basic chemical Ranbax (in multiples of 1,000 pounds) and transfers it to Divisions S and T. Division S processes Ranbax into the final product Syntex, and Division T processes Ranbax into the final product Termix. No material is lost during processing.

Division R has no fixed costs. The variable cost per pound of Ranbax is $0.18. Division R has a capacity limit of 10,000 pounds. Divisions S and T have capacity limits of 4,000 and 6,000 pounds, respectively. Divisions S and T sell their final product in separate markets. The company keeps no inventories of any kind.

The *cumulative* net revenues (i.e., total revenues – total processing costs) for divisions S and T at various output levels are summarized below.

Division S				
Pounds of Ranbax processed in S	1,000	2,000	3,000	4,000
Total net revenues ($) from sale of Syntex	$ 500	$ 850	$1,100	$1,200

Division T					
Pounds of Ranbax processed in T	1,000	2,000	3,000	4,000	5,000	6,000
Total net revenues ($) from sale of Termix	$ 600	$1,200	$1,800	$2,100	$2,250	$2,350

Required

1. Suppose there is no external market for Ranbax. What quantity of Ranbax should the Rallis India produce to maximize overall income? How should this quantity be allocated between the two processing divisions?

2. What range of transfer prices will motivate Divisions S and T to demand the quantities that maximize overall income (as determined in requirement 1), as well as motivate Division R to produce the sum of those quantities?

3. Suppose that Division R can sell any quantity of Ranbax in a perfectly competitive market for $0.33 a pound. To maximize Rallis's income, how many pounds of Ranbax should Division R transfer to Divisions S and T, and how much should it sell in the external market?

4. What range of transfer prices will result in Divisions R, S, and T taking the actions determined as optimal in requirement 3? Explain your answer.

Solution

Solution Exhibit 22-37A

	1,000	2,000	3,000	4,000
Pounds of Ranbax Processed in S				
Total Net Revenues ($) from Sale of Syntex	$500	$850	$1,100	$1,200
Incremental net revenues from processing next 1,000 pounds of Ranbax in S	$500	$350	$250	$100
Incremental net revenues per pound from processing next 1,000 pounds of Ranbax in S	$0.50	$0.35	$0.25	$0.10

Solution Exhibit 22-37B

	1,000	2,000	3,000	4,000	5,000	6,000
Pounds of Ranbax Processed in T						
Total Net Revenues ($) from Sale of Termix	$600	$1,200	$1,800	$2,100	$2,250	$2,350
Incremental net revenues from processing next 1,000 pounds of Ranbax in T	$600	$600	$600	$300	$150	$100
Incremental net revenues per pound from processing next 1,000 pounds of Ranbax in T	$0.60	$0.60	$0.60	$0.30	$0.15	$0.10

1. The variable cost per pound of Ranbax is $0.18. From the last row of Solution Exhibit 22-37a, it is evident that for the first 3,000 pounds of Ranbax processed in S, the incremental net revenue per pound exceeds $0.18. However, the next 1,000 pounds following that generate only $0.10 per pound when converted to Syntex, which is below the variable cost of $0.18. Similarly, from the last row of Solution Exhibit 22-37b, it is in Rallis 's interest to transfer 4,000 pounds of Ranbax to T to be processed into Termix.

   Rallis India should therefore produce 7,000 pounds of Ranbax overall and send 3,000 pounds to S and 4,000 pounds to T.

2. Division R will produce and ship Ranbax of any quantity up to its capacity of 10,000 pounds provided it gets a price not lower than its variable cost of $0.18 per pound.

   From Solution Exhibit 22-37a, Division S will be motivated to acquire exactly 3,000 pounds of Ranbax if the transfer price lies between $0.10 and $0.25 per pound.

   From Solution Exhibit 22-37b, Division T will be motivated to acquire exactly 4,000 pounds of Ranbax if the transfer price lies between $0.15 and $0.30 per pound.

   The set of transfer prices that will induce all three divisions to implement the plan found to be optimal in requirement 1 is given by the intersection of these three ranges. In other words, the transfer price must lie between $0.18 and $0.25 per pound of Ranbax.

3. If R can sell any quantity of Ranbax in a competitive market for $0.33 per pound, Rallis India will choose to have Ranbax processed further into Syntex or Termix only to the extent the incremental net revenue per pound exceeds $0.33.

   From Solution Exhibits 22-37a and 22-37b, Rallis India would therefore like to process 2,000 pounds of Ranbax into Syntex and 3,000 pounds of Ranbax into Termix.

   Because the variable cost of producing Ranbax is $0.18 less than the market price of $0.33, Rallis India will now choose to have Division R operate at capacity. The final 5,000 pounds of Ranbax will then be sold in the external market.

4. The presence of a competitive external market with a price higher than $0.18 implies that Division R will operate at capacity. Further, R must receive a transfer price of at least $0.33 per pound in order to transfer any units internally.

From Solution Exhibit 22-37a, Division S will be motivated to acquire exactly 2,000 pounds of Ranbax if the transfer price lies between $0.25 and $0.35 per pound.

From Solution Exhibit 22-37b, Division T will be motivated to acquire exactly 3,000 pounds of Ranbax if the transfer price lies between $0.30 and $0.60 per pound.

The set of transfer prices that will induce all three divisions to implement the plan found to be optimal in Requirement 3 is given by the intersection of these three ranges. This implies that the transfer price must lie between $0.33 and $0.35 per pound of Ranbax.

Of course, if the market is truly competitive, in the sense that Divisions S and T can also purchase Ranbax externally for $0.33 per pound, then there is a unique optimal transfer price, given by the market price of $0.33 per pound!

Exercises

[*Comprehensive solutions to all exercises are available on the companion website www. pearsoned.co.in/charlesthorngren*]

22-31 Decentralization, goal congruence, responsibility centers. Jubilant Chemicals consists of seven operating divisions that operate independently. The operating divisions are assisted by a number of support groups, such as R&D, human resources, and environmental management. The environmental management group consists of 20 environmental engineers. These engineers must seek business from the operating divisions that is, the projects they work on must be mutually agreed to and paid for by one of the operating divisions. Under Jubilant's rules, the environmental group is required to charge the operating divisions for environmental services at cost.

Required

1. Is the environmental management group centralized or decentralized?
2. What type of responsibility center is the environmental management group?
3. What benefits and problems do you see in structuring the environmental management group in this way? Does it lead to goal congruence and motivation? Explain.

22-32 Transfer pricing, general guideline, goal congruence (CMA, adapted). Tata, operates as a decentralized multidivision company. The Igo Division of Tata purchases most of its airbags from the Airbag Division. The Airbag Division's incremental costs for manufacturing the airbags are ₹1,100 per unit. The Airbag Division is currently working at 80% of capacity. The current market price of the airbags is ₹1,400 per unit.

Required

1. Using the general guideline presented in the chapter, what is the minimum price at which the Airbag Division would sell airbags to the Igo Division?
2. Suppose that Tata requires that whenever divisions with idle capacity sell products internally, they must do so at incremental costs. Evaluate this transfer-pricing policy using the criteria of goal congruence, evaluating division performance, motivating management effort, and preserving division autonomy.
3. If the two divisions were to negotiate a transfer price, what is the range of possible transfer prices? Evaluate this negotiated transfer-pricing policy using the criteria of goal congruence, evaluating division performance, motivating management effort, and preserving division autonomy.
4. Do you prefer the transfer-pricing policy in requirement 2 or requirement 3? Explain your answer briefly.

22-33 Multinational transfer pricing and taxation (Richard Lambert, adapted). Anita Corporation, headquartered in India, manufactures state-of-the-art milling machines in India. It has two marketing subsidiaries, one in Brazil and one in Switzerland, that sell its products. Anita is building one new machine, at a cost of ₹5,00,000. There is no market for the equipment in India. The equipment can be sold in Brazil for ₹10,00,000, but the Brazilian subsidiary would incur transportation and modification costs of ₹2,00,000. Alternatively, the equipment can be sold in Switzerland for ₹9,50,000, but the Swiss subsidiary would incur transportation and modification costs of ₹2,50,000. The Indian company can sell the equipment to either its Brazilian or its Swiss subsidiary, but not to both. The Anita Corporation and its subsidiary companies operate in a very decentralized manner. Managers in each company have considerable autonomy, with managers interested in maximizing their own company's income.

Required

1. From the viewpoint of Anita and its subsidiaries taken together, should the Anita Corporation manufacture the equipment? If it does, where should it sell the equipment to maximize total operating income? What would the operating income for Anita and its subsidiaries be from the sale? Ignore any income tax effects.

2. What range of transfer prices will result in achieving the actions determined to be optimal in requirement 1? Explain your answer.

3. The effective income tax rates are as follows: 40% in India, 60% in Brazil, and 15% in Switzerland. The tax authorities in the three countries are uncertain about the cost of the intermediate product and will allow any transfer price between ₹500,000 and ₹700,000. If Anita and its subsidiaries want to maximize after-tax operating income, (a) should the equipment be manufactured, and (b) where and at what price should it be transferred and sold? Show your computations.

4. Now suppose managers act autonomously to maximize their own subsidiary's after-tax operating income. The tax authorities will allow transfer prices only between ₹5,00,000 and ₹7,00,000. Which subsidiary will get the product and at what price? Is your answer the same as your answer in requirement 3? Explain why or why not.

22-34 Transfer pricing, utilization of capacity (J. Patell, adapted). The Banagalore Instrument Company (BIC) consists of the Semiconductor Division and the Process-Control Division, each of which operates as an independent profit center. The Semiconductor Division employs craftsmen who produce two different electronic components, the new high-performance Super-chip and an older product called Okay-chip. These two products have the following cost characteristics:

	Super-chip	Okay-chip
Direct materials	₹20	₹10
Direct manufacturing labor 2 hours × ₹140; 0.5 hour × ₹140	280	70

Annual overhead in the Semiconductor Division totals ₹4,00,000, all fixed. Due to the high skill level necessary for the craftsmen, the Semiconductor Division's capacity is set at 50,000 hours per year.

One customer orders a maximum of 15,000 Super-chips per year, at a price of ₹600 per chip. If BIC cannot meet this entire demand, the customer curtails its own production. The rest of the Semiconductor Division's capacity is devoted to the Okay-chip, for which there is unlimited demand at ₹120 per chip.

The Process-Control Division produces only one product, a process-control unit, with the following cost structure:

• Direct materials (circuit board): ₹600
• Direct manufacturing labor (5 hours × ₹100): ₹500

Fixed overhead costs of the Process-Control Division are ₹8,00,000 per year. The current market price for the control unit is ₹1,320 per unit.

A joint research project has just revealed that a single Super-chip could be substituted for the circuit board currently used to make the process-control unit. Using Super-chip would require an extra one hour of labor per control unit for a new total of six hours per control unit.

Required

1. Calculate the contribution margin per hour of selling Super-chip and Okay-chip. If no transfers of Super-chip were made to the Process-Control Division, how many Super-chips and Okay-chips should the Semiconductor Division sell? Show your computations.

2. The Process-Control Division expects to sell 5,000 control units this year. From the viewpoint of Bangalore Instruments as a whole, should 5,000 Super-chips be transferred to the Process-Control Division to replace circuit boards? Show your computations.

3. If demand for the control unit is certain to be 5,000 units but its price is uncertain, what should the transfer price of Super-chip be to ensure that the division managers' actions maximize operating income for BIC as a whole? (All other data are unchanged.)

4. If demand for the control unit is certain to be 12,000 units, but its price is uncertain, what should the transfer price of Super-chip be to ensure that the division managers' actions maximize operating income for BIC as a whole? (All other data are unchanged.)

22-35 Goal congruence, income taxes, different market conditions. The KSM Pumps makes water pumps. The Engine Division makes the engines and supplies them to the Assembly Division, where the pumps are assembled. KSM Pumps is a successful and profitable company that attributes much of its success to its decentralized operating style. Each division manager is compensated on the basis of division operating income.

The Assembly Division currently acquires all its engines from the Engine Division. The Assembly Division manager could purchase similar engines in the market for ₹4,000 each.

The Engine Division is currently operating at 80% of its capacity of 4,000 units and has the following costs:

Direct materials (₹1,250 per unit × 3,200 units)	₹40,00,000
Direct manufacturing labor (₹500 per unit × 3,200 units)	16,00,000
Variable manufacturing overhead costs (₹250 per unit × 3,200 units)	8,00,000
Fixed manufacturing overhead costs	52,00,000

All the Engine Division's 3,200 units are currently transferred to the Assembly Division. No engines are sold in the outside market.

The Engine Division has just received an order for 2,000 units at ₹3,750 per engine that would utilize half the capacity of the plant. The order must either be taken in full or rejected. The order is for a slightly different engine than what the Engine Division currently makes, but it takes the same amount of manufacturing time. To produce the new engine would require direct materials per unit of ₹1,000, direct manufacturing labor per unit of ₹400, and variable manufacturing overhead costs per unit of ₹250.

Required

1. From the viewpoint of the KSM Pumps as a whole, should the Engine Division accept the order for the 2,000 units? Show your computations.

2. What range of transfer prices will result in achieving the actions determined to be optimal in requirement 1 if division managers act in a decentralized manner?

3. The manager of the Assembly Division has proposed a transfer price for the engines equal to the full costs of the engines, including an allocation of overhead costs. The Engine Division allocates overhead costs to engines on the basis of the total capacity of the plant used to manufacture the engines.

   a. Calculate the transfer price for the engines transferred to the Assembly Division under this arrangement.

   b. Do you think that the transfer price calculated in requirement 3a will result in achieving the actions determined to be optimal in requirement 1 if division managers act in a decentralized manner?

   c. Comment in general on one advantage and one disadvantage of using full costs of the producing division as the basis for setting transfer prices.

4. Now consider the effect of income taxes.

   a. Suppose the Assembly Division is located in a state that imposes a 10% tax on income earned within its boundaries, and the Engine Division is located in a state that imposes no tax on income earned within its boundaries. What transfer price would be chosen by the KSM Pumps to minimize state income tax payments for the corporation as a whole? Assume that only transfer prices that are greater than or equal to full manufacturing costs and less than or equal to the market price of "substantially similar" engines are acceptable to the tax authorities.

    b. Suppose that the KSM Pumps announces the transfer price computed in requirement 4a to price all transfers between the Engine and Assembly divisions. Each division manager then acts autonomously to maximize division operating income. Will division managers acting in a decentralized manner achieve the actions determined to be optimal in requirement 1? Explain.

5. Consider your responses to requirements 1 through 4 and assume the Engine Division will continue to have opportunities for outside business as described in requirement 1. What transfer-pricing policy would you recommend KSM Pumps use, and why? Would you continue to evaluate division performance on the basis of division operating incomes? Explain.

Performance Measurement, Compensation, and Multinational Considerations

When you complete this course, you'll receive a grade that represents a measure of your performance in it.

Your grade will likely consist of four elements—homework, quizzes, exams, and class participation. Do some of these elements better reflect your knowledge of the material than others? Would the relative weights placed on the various elements when determining your final grade influence how much effort you expend to improve your performance on the different elements? Would it be fair if you received a good grade regardless of your performance? The following article about former AIG chief executive Martin Sullivan examines that very situation in a corporate context. Sullivan continued to receive performance bonuses despite pushing AIG to the brink of bankruptcy. By failing to link pay to performance, AIG's board of directors rewarded behavior that led to a government takeover of the firm.

Financial and Nonfinancial Performance Measures

As you have learned, many organizations record financial and nonfinancial performance measures for their subunits on a *balanced scorecard*. The scorecards of different organizations emphasize different measures, but the measures are always derived from a company's strategy. Consider the case of Mayur Inns, a chain of hotels. Mayur Inns' strategy is to provide excellent customer service and to charge a higher room rate than its competitors. Mayur Inns uses the following measures in its balanced scorecard:

1. **Financial perspective**—the firm's stock price, net income, return on sales, return on investment, economic value added

2. **Customer perspective**—market share in different geographic locations, customer satisfaction, brand image, and average number of repeat visits

3. **Internal-business-process perspective**—customer-service time for making reservations, for check-in, and restaurants services; cleanliness of hotel and room, room service and restaurant quality; time taken to clean rooms; reductions in waste output and energy and water consumption; number of new services provided to customers (wireless Internet, video games, and so on); and the time taken to plan and build new hotels.

4. **Learning-and-growth perspective**—the education, skill and satisfaction levels of the firm's employees; employee turnover and hours of employee training; and the company's achievement of ISO 14001:2004 certification for environment management

As in all balanced scorecard implementations, the goal is to make improvements in the learning-and-growth perspective that will lead to improvements in the internal-business-process perspective that, in turn, will result in improvements in the customer and financial perspectives. Mayur Inns also uses balanced scorecard measures to evaluate and reward the performance of its managers.

Some performance measures, such as the time it takes to plan and build new hotels, have a long time horizon. Other measures, such as time taken to check in or quality of room service, have a short time horizon. In this chapter, we focus on *organization subunits'* most widely used performance measures that cover an intermediate-to-long time horizon. These are internal financial measures based on accounting numbers routinely reported by organizations. In later sections, we describe why companies use both financial and nonfinancial measures to evaluate performance.

Designing accounting-based performance measures requires several steps:

Step 1: Choose Performance Measures That Align with Top Management's Financial Goals. For example, is operating income, net income, return on assets, or revenues the best measure of a subunit's financial performance?

Step 2: Choose the Details of Each Performance Measure in Step 1. Once a firm has chosen a specific performance measure, it must make a variety of decisions about the precise way in which various components of the measure are to be calculated. For example, if the chosen performance measure is return on assets, should it be calculated for one year or for a multiyear period? Should assets be defined as total assets or net assets (total assets minus total liabilities)? Should assets be measured at historical cost or current cost?

Step 3: Choose a Target Level of Performance and Feedback Mechanism for Each Performance Measure in Step 1. For example, should all subunits have identical targets, such as the same required rate of return on assets? Should performance reports be sent to top management daily, weekly, or monthly?

The decisions made in these steps don't have to be sequential. The issues considered in each step are interdependent, and top management will often proceed through these steps several times before deciding on one or more accounting-based performance measures. At each step, the answers to the questions raised depend on top management's beliefs about how well each alternative measure fulfills the behavioral criteria of promoting goal congruence, motivating management effort, evaluating subunit performance, and preserving subunit autonomy (discussed in Chapter 2).

Accounting-Based Measures for Business Units

Companies commonly use four measures to evaluate the economic performance of their subunits. We illustrate these measures for Mayur Inns.

Mayur Inns owns and operates three hotels—one each in Mumbai, Kolkata, and New Delhi. Exhibit 23-1 summarizes data for each hotel for 2014. At present, Mayur Inns does not allocate the total long-term debt of the company to the three separate hotels. The exhibit indicates that the New Delhi hotel generates the highest operating income, ₹51,00,000, compared with Kolkata's ₹30,00,000 and Mumbai's ₹24,00,000. But does this comparison mean the

◀ **Decision Point**

What financial and nonfinancial performance measures do companies use in their balanced scorecards?

Learning Objective 2

Examine accounting-based measures for evaluating business unit performance, including return on investment (ROI),

. . . return on sales times investment turnover

residual income (RI),

. . . income minus a dollar amount for required return on investment

and economic value added (EVA®)

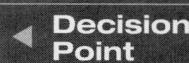

. . . a variation of residual income

New Delhi hotel is the most "successful"? The main weakness of comparing operating incomes alone is that it ignores the differences in *the size of the investment* in each hotel. **Investment** refers to the resources or assets used to generate income. The real question is whether a division generates sufficient operating income relative to the investment made to earn it

Three of the approaches to measuring performance include a measure of investment: return on investment, residual income, and economic value added. A fourth approach, return on sales, does not measure investment.

Return on Investment

Return on investment (ROI) is an accounting measure of income divided by an accounting measure of investment.

$$\text{Return on investment} = \frac{\text{Income}}{\text{Investment}}$$

Return on investment is the most popular approach to measure performance for two reasons: (1) it blends all the ingredients of profitability—revenues, costs, and investment—into a single percentage; and (2) it can be compared with the rate of return on opportunities elsewhere, inside or outside the company. As with any single performance measure, however, managers should use ROI cautiously and in conjunction with other measures.

ROI is also called the *accounting rate of return* or the *accrual accounting rate of return* (Chapter 21). Managers usually use the term ROI when evaluating the performance of an organization's subunit and the term accrual accounting rate of return when using an ROI measure to evaluate a project. Companies vary in the way they define income in the numerator and investment in the denominator of the ROI calculation. Some companies use operating income for the numerator; others prefer to calculate ROI on an after-tax basis and use net income. Some companies use total assets in the denominator; others prefer to focus on

Exhibit 23-1

Financial Data for
Mayur Inns for 2014
(in Thousands)

		Mumbai Hotel	Kolkata Hotel	New Delhi Hotel	Total
2	Hotel revenues	₹1,20,00,000	₹1,40,00,000	₹3,18,50,000	₹5,78,50,000
3	Hotel variable costs	31,00,000	37,50,000	99,50,000	1,68,00,000
4	Hotel fixed costs	65,00,000	72,50,000	1,68,00,000	3,05,50,000
5	Hotel operating income	₹24,00,000	₹30,00,000	₹51,00,000	₹1,05,00,000
6	Interest costs on long-term debt at 10%				45,00,000
7	Income before income taxes				60,00,000
8	Income taxes at 30%				18,00,000
9	Net income				42,00,000
10	Net book value at the end of 2014:				
11	Current assets	₹40,00,000	₹50,00,000	₹66,00,000	₹1,56,00,000
12	Long-term assets	60,00,000	1,50,00,000	2,34,00,000	4,44,00,000
13	Total assets	₹1,00,00,000	₹2,00,00,000	₹3,00,00,000	₹6,00,00,000
14	Current liabilities	₹5,00,000	₹15,00,000	₹30,00,000	₹50,00,000
15	Long-term debt				4,50,00,000
16	Stockholders' equity				1,00,00,000
17	Total liabilities and stockholders' equity				₹6,00,00,000
18					

only those assets financed by long-term debt and stockholders' equity and use total assets minus current liabilities.

Consider the ROIs of each of the three Mayur hotels in Exhibit 23-1. For our calculations, we use the operating income of each hotel for the numerator and total assets of each hotel for the denominator.

Using these ROI figures, the Mumbai hotel appears to make the best use of its total assets.

Hotel	Operating Income (₹)	÷	Total Assets (₹)	=	ROI
Mumbai	24,00,000	÷	1,00,00,000	=	24%
Kolkata	30,00,000	÷	2,00,00,000	=	15%
New Delhi	51,00,000	÷	3,00,00,000	=	17%

Each manager can increase his or her hotel's ROI, by increasing its revenues or decreasing it's costs (each of which increases the numerator), or by decreasing investment in the hotel (which decreases the denominator). Even when a hotel operating income falls, the manager can increase its ROI by reducing its total assets by a greater percentage. Suppose, for example, that operating income of the Kolkata hotel decreases by 4% from ₹30,00,000 to ₹28,80,000 [₹30,00,000 × (1 − 0.04)] and its total assets decrease by 10% from ₹2,00,00,000 to ₹1,80,00,000 [₹2,00,00,000 × (1 − 0.10)]. The ROI of the Kolkata hotel would then increase from 15% to 16% (₹28,80,000 ÷ ₹1,80,00,000).

ROI can provide more insight into performance when it is represented as two components:

$$\frac{\text{Income}}{\text{Investment}} = \frac{\text{Income}}{\text{Revenues}} \times \frac{\text{Revenues}}{\text{Investment}}$$

which is also written as,

ROI = Return on sales × Investment turnover

This approach is known as the *DuPont method of profitability analysis*. The DuPont method recognizes the two basic ingredients in profit-making: increasing income per rupee of revenues and using assets to generate more revenues. An improvement in either ingredient without changing the other increases the ROI.

Assume that top Mayur Inns managers adopt a 30% target ROI for the Mumbai hotel. How can this return be attained? Using Dupont method, the following example shows three ways the managers of the hotel can increase its ROI from 24% to 30%.

	Operating Income (₹) (1)	Revenues (₹) (2)	Total Assets (₹) (3)	Operating Income / Revenues (4)	×	Revenues / Total Assets (5) = (2) ÷ (3)	=	Operating Income / Total Assets (6) = (4) × (5)
Current ROI **Alternatives**	24,00,000	1,20,00,000	1,00,00,000	20%	×	1.2	=	24%
A. Decrease assets (such as receivables), keeping revenues and operating income per rupee of revenue constant	24,00,000	1,20,00,000	80,00,000	20%	×	1.5	=	30%
B. Increase revenues (via higher occupancy rate), keeping assets and operating income per rupee of revenue constant	30,00,000	1,50,00,000	1,00,00,000	20%	×	1.5	=	30%

C. Decrease costs (via, say, efficient maintenance) to increase operating income per rupee of revenue, keeping revenue and assets constant

| 30,00,000 | 1,20,00,000 | 1,00,00,000 | | 25% | × | 1.2 | = | 30% |

Other alternatives, such as increasing the selling price per room, could increase both the revenues per rupee of total assets and the operating income per rupee of revenues.

ROI makes clear the benefits that managers can obtain by reducing their investment in current or long-term assets. Most managers know they need to boost revenues or to control costs, but they pay less attention to reducing their investment base. Reducing the investment base involves decreasing idle cash, managing credit judiciously, determining proper inventory levels, and spending carefully on long-term assets.

Residual Income

Residual income (RI) is an accounting measure of income minus a rupee amount for required return on an accounting measure of investment.

Residual income (RI) = Income × (Required rate of return × Investment)

The required rate of return multiplied by the investment is the *imputed cost of the investment*. **The imputed costs** of the investment is a cost recognized in particular situations but not incorporated in financial accounting systems because it is an opportunity cost. In this situation, the imputed cost refers to the return Mayur Inns could have obtained by making an alternative investment with similar risk characteristics.

Assume that each hotel faces similar risks and that Mayur Inns has a required rate of return of 12% of total assets:

Hotel	Operating Income (₹)	−	Required Rate of Return	×	Investment (₹)	=	Residual Income (₹)
Mumbai	24,00,000	−	(12%	×	1,00,00,000)	=	12,00,000
Kolkata	30,00,000	−	(12%	×	2,00,00,000)	=	6,00,000
New Delhi	51,00,000	−	(12%	×	3,00,00,000)	=	15,00,000

Note that the New Delhi hotel has the best RI. In general, RI is influenced by size: For a given level of performance, larger divisions generate higher RI.

Some companies favor the RI measure because managers will concentrate on maximizing an absolute amount, such as rupees of RI, rather than a percentage, such as ROI. The objective of maximizing RI means that as long as a subunit earns a return in excess of the required return for investments, that subunit should continue to invest.

The objective of maximizing ROI may induce managers of highly profitable subunits to reject projects that, from the viewpoint of the company as a whole, should be accepted. Suppose Mayur Inns is considering upgrading room features and furnishings at the Mumbai hotel. The upgrade will increase operating income of the Mumbai hotel by ₹7,00,000 and increase its total assets by ₹40,00,000. The ROI for the expansion is 17.5% (₹7,00,000 ÷ ₹40,00,000), which is attractive to Mayur Inns because it exceeds the required rate of return of 12%. By making this expansion, however, the Mumbai hotel's ROI will decrease:

$$\text{Preupgrade ROI} = \frac{₹24,00,000}{₹1,00,00,000} = 0.24, \text{ or } 24\%$$

$$\text{Preupgrade ROI} = \frac{₹24,00,000 + ₹7,00,000}{₹1,00,00,000 + ₹40,00,000} = \frac{₹31,00,000}{₹1,40,00,000} = 0.221, \text{ or } 22.1\%$$

The annual bonus paid to the Mumbai manager may decrease if ROI affects the bonus calculation and the upgrading option is selected. Consequently, the manager may shun the expansion. In contrast, if the annual bonus is a function of RI, the Mumbai manager will favor the expansion:

Preupgrade RI $= ₹24,00,000 - (0.12 \times ₹1,00,00,000) = ₹12,00,000$
Preupgrade RI $= ₹31,00,000 - (0.12 \times ₹1,40,00,000) = ₹14,20,000$

So, it is more likely that a firm will achieve goal congruence if it uses RI rather than ROI to measure the subunit manager's performance.

To see that this is a general result, notice that the post-upgrade ROI is a weighted average of the pre-upgrade ROI and the ROI of the project under consideration. Therefore, whenever a new project has a return higher than the required rate of return (12% in our example) but below the current ROI of the division (24% in our example), the division manager is tempted to reject it even though it is a project the shareholders would like to pursue.[1] On the other hand, RI is a measure that aggregates linearly, that is, the post-upgrade RI always equals the pre-upgrade RI plus the RI of the project under consideration. To verify this in the preceding example, observe that the project's RI is $₹7,00,000 - (12\% \times ₹40,00,000) = ₹2,20,000$, which is the difference between the post-upgrade and pre-upgrade RI amounts. As a result, a manager who is evaluated on residual income will choose a new project if and only if it has a positive RI. But this is exactly the criterion shareholders want the manager to employ; in other words, RI achieves goal congruence.

Economic Value Added[2]

Economic value added (EVA®) is a variation of RI used by many companies.[3] It is calculated as follows:

$$\begin{array}{l} \text{Economic value} \\ \text{added (EVA)} \end{array} = \begin{array}{l} \text{After-tax} \\ \text{operating income} \end{array} - \left[\begin{array}{l} \text{Weighted} \\ \text{average} \\ \text{cost of captial} \end{array} \times \left(\begin{array}{l} \text{Total} \\ \text{assets} \end{array} - \begin{array}{l} \text{Current} \\ \text{liabilities} \end{array} \right) \right]$$

That is, EVA substitutes the following numbers in the RI calculations:

1. Income: After-tax operating income,
2. Required rate of return: (After-tax) weighted-average cost of capital, and
3. Investment: Total assets minus current liabilities.[3]

We use the Mayur Inns data in Exhibit 23-1 to illustrate the basic EVA calculations. The weighted-average cost of capital (WACC) equals the *after-tax* average cost of all the long-term funds by Mayur Inns uses. The company has two sources of long-term funds: (a) long-term debt with a market value and book value of ₹45 million issued at an interest rate of 10%, and (b) equity capital that also has a market value of ₹45 million (but a book

---

[1] Analogously, the manager of an underperforming division with an ROI of 7%, say, may wish to accept projects with returns between 7% and 12% even though these opportunities do not meet the shareholders' required rate of return.

[2] S. O'Byrne and D. Young, *EVA and Value-Based Management: A Practical Guide to Implementation* (New York: McGraw-Hill, 2000); J. Stein, J. Shiely, and I. Ross, *The EVA Challenge: Implementing Value Added Change in an Organization* (New York: John Wiley and Sons, 2001).

[3] When implementing EVA, companies make several adjustments to the operating income and asset numbers reported under generally accepted accounting principles (GAAP). For example, when calculating EVA, costs such as R&D, restructuring costs, and leases that have long-run benefits are recorded as assets (which are then amortized), rather than as current operating costs. The goal of these adjustments is to obtain a better representation of the economic assets, particularly intangible assets, used to earn income. Of course, the specific adjustments applicable to a company will depend on its individual circumstances.

value of ₹10 million).[4] Because interest costs are tax-deductible and the income tax rate is 30%, the after-tax cost of debt financing is 0.10 × (1 − Tax rate) = 0.10 × (1 − 0.30) = 0.10 × 0.70 = 0.07, or 7%. The cost of equity capital is the opportunity cost to investors of not investing their capital in another investment that is similar in risk to Mayur Inns. Mayur Inns' cost of equity capital is 14%.[5] The WACC computation, which uses market values of debt and equity, is as follows:

$$
\begin{aligned}
WACC &= \frac{(7\%\ Market\ value\ of\ deb + (14\%\ Market\ value\ equity)}{Market\ value\ of\ debt + Market\ value\ of\ equity} \\
&= \frac{(0.07 \times ₹4,50,00,000 + (0.14 \times ₹4,50,00,000)}{₹4,50,00,000 + ₹4,50,00,000} \\
&= \frac{₹94,50,000}{₹9,00,00,000} = 0.105,\ or\ 10.5\%
\end{aligned}
$$

The company applies the same WACC to all its hotels because each hotel faces similar risks. Total assets minus current liabilities (see Exhibit 23-1) can also be computed as:

Total assets−Current liabilities = Long-term assets + Current assets − Current liabilities

= Long-term assets + Working capital

where

Working capital = Current assets − Current liabilities

After-tax hotel operating income is:

$$
\begin{array}{ccc}
\text{Hotel operating} & & \text{Hotel operating} & & \text{Hotel operating} \\
\text{income} & \times (1 - \text{Tax rate}) = & \text{income} & \times (1 - 0.30) = & \text{income} & \times 0.70
\end{array}
$$

EVA calculations for Mayur Inns are as follows:

Hotel	After-Tax Operating Income (₹)	−	[WACC ×	(Total Assets−Current Liabilities) (₹)]	=	EVA
Mumbai	24,00,000 × 0.70	−	[10.50% ×	(1,00,00,000 − 5,00,000)]	=	6,82,500
Kolkata	30,00,000 × 0.70	−	[10.50% ×	(2,00,00,000 − 15,00,000)]	=	1,57,500
New Delhi	51,00,000 × 0.70	−	[10.50% ×	(3,00,00,000 − 30,00,000)]	=	7,35,000

The New Delhi hotel has the highest EVA. Economic value added, like residual income, charges managers for the cost of their investments in long-term assets and working capital. Value is created only if after-tax operating income exceeds the cost of investing the capital. To improve EVA, managers can, for example, (a) earn more after-tax operating income with the same capital, (b) use less capital to earn the same after-tax operating income, or (c) invest capital in high-return projects.[6]

---

[4] The market value of Mayur Inns' equity exceeds book value because book value, based on historical cost, does not measure the current value of the company's assets and because various intangible assets, such as the company's brand name, are not shown at current value in the balance sheet under GAAP.

[5] In practice, the most common method of calculating the cost of equity capital is by applying the capital asset pricing model (CAPM). For details, see Jonathan Berk and Peter DeMarzo, *Corporate Finance*, 3rd ed. (Upper Saddle River, NJ: Prentice Hall, 2013).

[6] Observe that the sum of the divisional after-tax operating incomes used in the EVA calculation, (₹24,00,000 + ₹30,00,000 + ₹51,00,000) × 0.7 = ₹73,50,000, exceeds the firm's net income of ₹42,00,000. The difference is due to the firm's after-tax interest expense on its long-term debt, which amounts to ₹45,00,000 × 0.7 = ₹31,50,000. Because the EVA measure includes a charge for the weighted average cost of capital, which includes the after-tax cost of debt, the income figure used in computing EVA should reflect the after-tax profit before interest payments on debt are considered. After-tax operating income (often referred to in practice as NOPAT, or net operating profit after taxes) is thus the relevant measure of divisional profit for EVA calculations.

Companies such as Briggs and Stratton (a leading producer of gasoline engines), Coca-Cola, Equifax, and FMC, a specialty chemical company, use EVA to guide their decisions. CSX, a railroad company, credits EVA for decisions such as to run trains with three locomotives instead of four and to schedule arrivals just in time for unloading rather than having trains arrive at their destination several hours in advance. The result? Higher income because of lower fuel costs and lower capital investments in locomotives. Division managers find EVA helpful because it allows them to incorporate the cost of capital, which is generally only available at the company-wide level, into the decisions they make. Comparing the actual EVA achieved to the estimated EVA is useful for evaluating the performance of subunits and their managers.

Return on Sales

The income-to-revenues ratio (or sales ratio), often called *return on sales* (*ROS*), is a frequently used financial performance measure. As we have seen, ROS is one component of ROI in the DuPont method of profitability analysis. To calculate ROS for each of Mayur's hotels, we divide operating income by revenues:

Hotel	Operating Income (₹)	÷	Revenues (Sales) (₹)	=	ROS
Mumbai	24,00,000	÷	1,20,00,000	=	20%
Kolkata	30,00,000	÷	1,40,00,000	=	21.4%
New Delhi	51,00,000	÷	3,18,50,000	=	16.0%

The Kolkata hotel has the highest ROS, but its performance is rated worse than the other hotels using measures such as ROI, RI, and EVA.

Comparing Performance Measures

The following table summarizes the performance of each hotel and ranks it (in parentheses) under each of the four performance measures:

Hotel	ROI	RI (₹)	EVA (₹)	ROS
Mumbai	24% (1)	12,00,000 (2)	6,82,500 (2)	20.0% (2)
Kolkata	15% (3)	6,00,000 (3)	1,57,500 (3)	21.4% (1)
New Delhi	17% (2)	15,00,000 (1)	7,35,000 (1)	16.0% (3)

The RI and EVA rankings are the same. They differ from the ROI and ROS rankings. Consider the ROI and RI rankings for the Mumbai and New Delhi hotels. The New Delhi hotel has a smaller ROI. Although its operating income is only slightly more than twice the operating income of the Mumbai hotel—₹51,00,000 versus ₹24,00,000—its total assets are three times as large—₹30 million versus ₹10 million. The New Delhi hotel has a higher RI because it earns a higher income after covering the required rate of return on investment of 12%. The high ROI of the Mumbai hotel indicates that its assets are being used efficiently. Even though each rupee invested in the New Delhi hotel does not give the same return as the Mumbai hotel, this large investment creates considerable value because its return exceeds the required rate of return. The Kolkata hotel has the highest ROS but the lowest ROI. The high ROS indicates that the Kolkata hotel has the lowest cost structure per rupee of revenues of all of Mayur Inns' hotels. Kolkata has low ROI because it generates very low revenues per rupee of assets invested. Is any one method better than the others for measuring performance? No, because each evaluates a different aspect of performance.

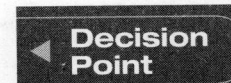

Decision Point

What are the relative merits of return on investment (ROI), residual income (RI), and economic value added (EVA) as performance measures for subunit managers?

ROS measures how effectively costs are managed. To evaluate overall aggregate performance, ROI, RI, or EVA measures are more appropriate than ROS because they consider both income and investment. ROI indicates which investment yields the highest return. RI and EVA measures overcome some of the goal-congruence problems of ROI. Some managers favor EVA because of the accounting adjustments related to the capitalization of investments in intangibles. Other managers favor (pretax) RI because it is easier to calculate and because, in most cases, it leads to the same conclusions as EVA does. Generally, companies use multiple financial measures to evaluate performance.

Choosing the Details of the Performance Measures

Learning Objective 3

Analyze the key measurement choices in the design of each performance measure

. . . choice of time horizon, alternative definitions, and measurement of assets

It is not sufficient for a company to identify the set of performance measures it wishes to use. The company has to decide how to compute the measures. This includes deciding on the time frame over which the measures are computed, defining key terms such as *investment,* and agreeing on how to calculate the components of each performance measure.

Alternative Time Horizons

An important element in designing accounting-based performance measures is choosing the time horizon of the performance measures. The ROI, RI, EVA, and ROS calculations represent the results for a single period, one year in our example. Managers could take actions that cause short-run increases in these measures but that conflict with the long-run interest of the company. For example, managers may curtail R&D and plant maintenance in the last three months of a fiscal year to achieve a target level of annual operating income. For this reason, many companies evaluate subunits on the basis of ROI, RI, EVA, and ROS over multiple years.

Another reason to evaluate subunits over multiple years is that the benefits of actions taken in the current period may not show up in short-run performance measures, such as the current year's ROI or RI. For example, an investment in a new hotel may adversely affect ROI and RI in the short run but positively affect them in the long run.

A multiyear analysis highlights another advantage of the RI measure: The net present value of all cash flows over the life of an investment equals the net present value of the RIs.[7]

---

[7] This equivalence, often referred to as the "Conservation Property" of residual income, was originally articulated by Gabriel Preinreich in 1938. To see the equivalence, suppose the ₹40,00,000 investment in the Mumbai hotel increases operating income by ₹7,00,000 per year as follows: Increase in operating cash flows of ₹15,00,000 each year for five years minus depreciation of ₹8,00,000 (₹40,00,000 ÷ 5) per year, assuming straight-line depreciation and ₹0 terminal disposal value. Depreciation reduces the investment amount by ₹8,00,000 each year. Assuming a required rate of return of 12%, net present values of cash flows and residual incomes are as follows:

Year	0	1	2	3	4	5	Net Present Value
(1) Cash flow	− ₹40,00,000	₹15,00,000	₹15,00,000	₹15,00,000	₹15,00,000	₹15,00,000	
(2) Present value of ₹1 discounted at 12%	1	0.89286	0.79719	0.71178	0.63552	0.56743	
(3) Present value: (1) × (2)	− ₹40,00,000	₹13,39,290	₹11,95,780	₹10,67,670	₹9,53,820	₹8,51,140	₹14,07,160
(4) Operating income		₹7,00,000	₹7,00,000	₹7,00,000	₹7,00,000	₹7,00,000	
(5) Assets at start of year		₹40,00,000	₹32,00,000	₹24,00,000	₹16,00,000	₹8,00,000	
(6) Capital charge: (5) × 12%		₹4,80,000	₹3,84,000	₹2,88,000	₹1,92,000	₹96,000	
(7) Residual income: (4) −(6)		₹2,20,000	₹3,16,000	₹4,12,000	₹5,08,000	₹6,04,000	
(8) Present value of RI: (7) × (2)		₹1,96,430	₹2,51,910	₹2,93,250	₹3,22,840	₹3,42,730	₹14,07,160

This means that if managers use the net present value method to make investment decisions (as Chapter 21 advocates), then using a multiyear RI to evaluate managers' performances achieves goal congruence.

Another way to motivate managers to take a long-run perspective is by compensating them on the basis of changes in the market price of the company's stock because stock prices incorporate the expected future effects of a firm's current decisions.

Alternative Definitions of Investment

Companies use a variety of definitions for measuring investment in their divisions. Four common alternative definitions used in the construction of accounting-based performance measures are as follows:

1. **Total assets available**—includes all assets, regardless of their intended purpose.

2. **Total assets employed**—total assets available minus the sum of idle assets and assets purchased for future expansion. For example, if the New Delhi hotel in Exhibit 23-1 has unused land set aside for potential expansion, the total assets employed by the hotel would exclude the cost of that land.

3. **Total assets employed minus current liabilities**—total assets excluding assets financed by short-term creditors. One negative feature of defining investment in this way is that it may encourage subunit managers to use an excessive amount of short-term debt because short-term debt reduces the amount of investment.

4. **Stockholders' equity**—calculated by assigning liabilities among subunits and deducting these amounts from the total assets of each subunit. One drawback of this method is that it combines operating decisions made by hotel managers with financing decisions made by top management.

Companies that use ROI or RI generally define investment as the total assets available. When a firm directs a subunit manager to carry extra or idle assets, the total assets employed (used) can be more informative than total assets available. Companies that use EVA define investment as total assets employed minus current liabilities and the long-term assets employed in the subunit. Managers are responsible for generating an adequate return on both components.

Alternative Asset Measurements

To design accounting-based performance measures, we must consider different ways to measure assets included in the investment calculations. Should assets be measured at historical cost or current cost? Should gross book value (that is, original cost) or net book value (original cost minus accumulated depreciation) be used for depreciable assets?

Current Cost

Current cost is the cost of purchasing an asset today identical to the one currently held, or the cost of purchasing an asset that provides services like the one currently held if an identical asset cannot be purchased. Of course, measuring assets at current costs will result in different ROIs than the ROIs calculated on the basis of historical costs.

We illustrate the current-cost ROI calculations using the data for Mayur Inns (Exhibit 23- 1) and then compare current-cost-based ROIs and historical-cost-based ROIs. Consider the following information about the long-term assets of each hotel:

	Mumbai	Kolkata	New Delhi
Age of facility in years (at end of 2014)	8	4	2
Gross book value (original cost)	₹1,40,00,000	₹2,10,00,000	₹2,73,00,000
Accumulated depreciation	80,00,000	60,00,000	39,00,000
Net book value (at end of 2014)	60,00,000	1,50,00,000	2,34,00,000
Depreciation for 2014	10,00,000	15,00,000	19,50,000

Mayur Inns assumes a 14-year estimated useful life, zero terminal disposal value and straight-line depreciation.

An index of construction costs indicating how the cost of construction has changed over the eight-year period that Mayur Inns has been operating (2006 year-end = 100) is as follows:

Year	2007	2008	2009	2010	2011	2012	2013	2014
Construction cost index	110	122	136	144	152	160	174	180

Earlier in this chapter, we computed an ROI of 24% for Mumbai, 15% for Kolkata, and 17% for New Delhi. One possible explanation of the high ROI for the Mumbai hotel is that its long-term assets are expressed in 2006 construction-price levels—prices that prevailed eight years ago—and the long-term assets for the Kolkata and New Delhi hotels are expressed in terms of higher, more-recent construction-price levels, which depress ROIs for these two hotels.

Exhibit 23-2 illustrates a step-by-step approach for incorporating current-cost estimates of long-term assets and depreciation expense into the ROI calculation. We make these calculations to approximate what it would cost today to obtain assets that would produce the same expected operating income that the subunits currently earn. (For RI and EVA calculations, similar adjustments to represent the current costs of capital employed and depreciation expense can also be made.) The current-cost adjustment reduces the ROI of the Mumbai hotel by more than half.

	Historical-Cost ROI	Current-Cost ROI
Mumbai	24%	10.8%
Kolkata	15%	11.1%
New Delhi	17%	14.7%

Adjusting assets to recognize current costs negates differences in the investment base caused solely by differences in construction-price levels. The current-cost ROI better measures the current economic returns from the investment than the historical-cost ROI does. If Mayur Inns were to invest in a new hotel today, investing in one like the New Delhi hotel offers the best ROI.

Current cost estimates may be difficult to obtain for some assets. Why? Because the estimate requires a company to consider, in addition to increases in price levels, technological advances and processes that could reduce the current cost of assets needed to earn today's operating income.

Long-Term Assets: Gross or Net Book Value?

The historical cost of assets is often used to calculate ROI. There has been much discussion about whether managers should use gross book value or net book value of assets. Using the data in Exhibit 23-1, we calculate ROI using net and gross book values of plant and equipment:

Exhibit 23-2   ROI for Mayur Inns: Computed Using Current-Cost Estimates as of the End of 2014 for Depreciation Expense and Long-Term Assets

	File Edit View Insert Format Tools Data Window Help

	A	B	C	D	E	F	G	H	I	J
1	Step 1: Restate long-term assets from gross book value at historical cost to gross book value at current cost as of the end of 2014.									
2		Gross book value of long-term assets at historical cost (₹)	x	Construction cost index in 2014	÷	Construction cost index in year of construction	=	Gross book value of long-term assets at current cost at end of 2014 (₹)		
3	Mumbai	1,40,00,000	x	(180	÷	100)	=	2,52,00,000		
4	Kolkata	2,10,00,000	x	(180	÷	144)	=	2,62,50,000		
5	New Delhi	2,73,00,000	x	(180	÷	160)	=	3,07,12,500		
6										
7	Step 2: Derive net book value of long-term assets at current cost as of the end of 2014 (Assume estimated useful life of each hotel is 14 years.)									
8		Gross book value of long-term assets at current cost at end of 2014 (₹)	x	Estimated remaining useful life	÷	Estimated total useful life	=	Net book value of long-term assets at current cost at end of 2014 (₹)		
9	Mumbai	2,52,00,000	x	(6	÷	14)	=	1,08,00,000		
10	Kolkata	2,62,50,000	x	(10	÷	14)	=	1,87,50,000		
11	New Delhi	3,07,12,500	x	(12	÷	14)	=	2,63,25,000		
12										
13	Step 3: Compute current cost of total assets in 2014 (Assume current assets of each hotel are expressed in 2014 rupees.)									
14		Current assets at end of 2014 (from Exhibit 23-1) (₹)	+	Long-term assets from Step 2 above (₹)	=	Current cost of total assets at end of 2014 (₹)				
15	Mumbai	40,00,000	+	1,08,00,000	=	1,48,00,000				
16	Kolkata	50,00,000	+	1,87,50,000	=	2,37,50,000				
17	New Delhi	66,00,000	+	2,63,25,000	=	3,29,25,000				
18										
19	Step 4: Compute current-cost depreciation expense in 2014 rupees.									
20		Gross book value of long-term assets at current cost at end of 2014 (from Step 1) (₹)	÷	Estimated total useful life	=	Current-cost depreciation expense in 2014 rupees (₹)				
21	Mumbai	2,52,00,000	÷	14	=	18,00,000				
22	Kolkata	2,62,50,000	÷	14	=	18,75,000				
23	New Delhi	3,07,12,500	÷	14	=	21,93,750				
24										
25	Step 5: Compute 2014 operating income using 2014 current-cost depreciation expense.									
26		Historical-cost operating income (₹)	−	Current-cost depreciation expense in 2014 rupees (from Step 4) (₹)	−	Historical-cost depreciation expense (₹)	=	Operating income for 2014 using current-cost depreciation expense in 2014 rupees (₹)		
27	Mumbai	24,00,000	−	(18,00,000	−	10,00,000)	=	16,00,000		
28	Kolkata	30,00,000	−	(18,75,000	−	15,00,000)	=	26,25,000		
29	New Delhi	51,00,000	−	(21,93,750	−	19,50,000)	=	48,56,250		
30										
31	Step 6: Compute ROI using current-cost estimates for long-term assets and depreciation expense.									
32		Operating income for 2014 using current-cost depreciation expense in 2014 rupees (from Step 5) (₹)	÷	Current cost of total assets at end of 2014 (from step 3) (₹)	=	ROI using current-cost estimate (₹)				
33	Mumbai	16,00,000	÷	1,48,00,000	=	10.8%				
34	Kolkata	26,25,000	÷	2,37,50,000	=	11.1%				
35	New Delhi	48,56,250	÷	3,29,25,000	=	14.7%				

	Operating Income (from Exhibit 23-1) (1)	Net Book Value of Total Assets (from Exhibit 23-1) (2)	Accumulated Depreciation (3)	Gross Book Value of Total Assets (4) = (2) + (3)	2014 ROI Using Net Book Value of Total Assets (calculated earlier) (5) = (1) ÷ (2)	2014 ROI Using Gross Book Value of Total Assets (6) = (1) ÷ (4)
Mumbai	₹24,00,000	₹1,00,00,000	₹80,00,000	₹1,80,00,000	24%	13.3%
Kolkata	30,00,000	2,00,00,000	60,00,000	2,60,00,000	15%	11.5%
New Delhi	5,10,000	3,00,00,000	39,00,000	3,39,00,000	17%	15.0%

Decision Point ▶

Over what time frame should companies measure performance, and what are the alternative choices for calculating the components of each performance measure?

Using gross book value, the 13.3% ROI of the older Mumbai hotel is lower than the 15.0% ROI of the newer New Delhi hotel. Those who favor using gross book value claim it enables a firm to compare ROI across its subunits more accurately. For example, using gross-book-value calculations, the return on the original plant-and-equipment investment is higher for the newer New Delhi hotel than for the older Mumbai hotel. This difference probably reflects the decline in earning power of the Mumbai hotel. Using the net book value masks this decline in earning power because the constantly decreasing investment base results in a higher ROI for the Mumbai hotel—24% in this example. This higher rate may mislead decision makers into thinking that the earning power of the Mumbai hotel has not decreased.

The proponents of using net book value as an investment base maintain it is less confusing because (1) it is consistent with the amount of total assets shown in the conventional balance sheet, and (2) it is consistent with income computations that include deductions for depreciation expense. Surveys report that the net book value is the measure of assets most commonly used by companies for internal performance evaluation.

Target Levels of Performance and Feedback

Now that we have covered the different types of measures and how to choose them, let us turn our attention to how mangers set and measure target levels of performance.

Learning Objective 4

Study the choice of performance targets and design of feedback mechanisms

. . . carefully crafted budgets and sufficient feedback for timely corrective action

Choosing Target Levels of Performance

Historical-cost-based accounting measures are usually inadequate for evaluating economic returns on new investments, and in some cases, they create disincentives for expansion. Despite these problems, managers can use historical-cost ROIs to evaluate current performance by establishing *target* ROIs. For Mayur Inns, we need to recognize that the hotels were built in different years, which means they were built at different construction-price levels. The firm could adjust the target historical-cost-based ROIs accordingly, say, by setting Mumbai's ROI at 26%, Kolkata's at 21%, and New Delhi's at 19%.

This useful alternative of comparing actual results with targeted, or budgeted, results is often overlooked, but should not be. *Companies should tailor and negotiate a budget for a particular subunit, a particular accounting system, and a particular performance measure while keeping in mind the pitfalls of using historical-cost accounting.* For example, many problems related to valuing assets and measuring income can be resolved if top managers can get subunit managers to focus on what is attainable in the forthcoming budget period—whether ROI, RI, or EVA is used and whether the financial measures are based on historical costs or some other measure, such as current costs.

A popular way to establish targets is to set continuous improvement targets. If a company is using EVA as a performance measure, the firm can evaluate operations on year-to-year changes in EVA, rather than on absolute measures of EVA. Evaluating performance on the basis of *improvements* in EVA makes the initial method of calculating EVA less important.

Companies using the balanced scorecard establish targets for financial performance measures, while simultaneously setting targets in the customer, internal-business-process, and learning-and-growth perspectives. For example, Mayur Inns will establish targets for employee training and employee satisfaction, customer-service time for reservations and check-in, the quality of room service, and customer satisfaction that each hotel must reach to achieve its ROI and EVA targets.

Choosing the Timing of Feedback

A final step in designing accounting-based performance measures is the timing of performance feedback which depends largely on (a) how critical the information is for the success of the organization, (b) the level of management receiving the feedback, and (c) the sophistication of the organization's information technology. For example, hotel managers responsible for room sales want information on the number of rooms sold (rented) on a daily or weekly basis because a large percentage of hotel costs are fixed costs, Achieving high room sales and taking quick action to reverse any declining sales trends are critical to the financial success of each hotel. Supplying managers with daily information about room sales is much easier if Mayur Inns has a computerized room-reservation and check-in system. The company's top managers, however, may look at information about daily room sales only on a monthly basis unless there is a problem, like the low sales-to-total-assets ratio of the Kolkata hotel has.

Similarly, human resources managers at each hotel measure employee satisfaction annually because satisfaction is best measured over a longer horizon. However, housekeeping-department managers measure the quality of room service over much shorter time horizons, such as a week. That's because poor levels of performance in these areas for even a short period of time can harm a hotel's reputation for a long period. Moreover, housekeeping problems can be detected and resolved over a short time period.

> ◄ **Decision Point**
>
> What targets should companies use and when should they give feedback to managers regarding their performance relative to these targets?

Performance Measurement in Multinational Companies

Our discussion so far has focused on performance evaluation of different divisions of a company operating within a single country. We next discuss the additional difficulties created when the performance of divisions of a company operating in different countries is compared. Several issues arise.[8]

- The economic, legal, political, social, and cultural environments differ significantly across countries. Operating a division in an open economy like Singapore is very different from operating in a closed economy such as Venezuela, where many prices are controlled and there is a constant threat of nationalization.

- Import quotas and tariffs range widely from country to country, and it's not unusual for countries to impose tariffs and custom duties to restrict the imports of certain goods.

- The availability of materials and skilled labor as well as the costs of materials, labor, and infrastructure (power, transportation, and communication) also differ significantly across countries. Companies operating in Indonesia, for example, must spend 30% of

> **Learning Objective 5**
>
> Indicate the difficulties that occur when the performance of divisions operating in different countries is compared
>
> . . . adjustments needed for differences in inflation rates and changes in exchange rates

---

[8] See M. Z. Iqbal, *International Accounting—A Global Perspective* (Cincinnati: South-Western College Publishing, 2002).

their total production costs on transportation, whereas these costs account for just 12% of total spending in China.

■ Divisions operating in different countries account for their performance in different currencies, and inflation and fluctuations in foreign-currency exchange rates affect performance measurement. For example, fast-growing economies such as Paraguay, Nigeria, and Vietnam suffer from double-digit inflation, which dampens the performance of divisions in those countries when their results are measured in dollars.

As a result of these differences, adjustments need to be made to accurately compare the performance of divisions in different countries.

Calculating a Foreign Division's ROI in the Foreign Currency

Suppose Mayur Inns invests in a hotel in Mexico City. The investment consists mainly of the costs of buildings and furnishings. Also assume the following:

■ The exchange rate at the time of Mayur's investment on December 31, 2013, was 10 pesos = ₹10.

■ During 2014, the Mexican peso suffered a steady decline in its value. The exchange rate on December 31, 2014, is 15 pesos = ₹10.

■ The average exchange rate during 2014 is [(10 + 15) ÷ 2] = 12.5 pesos = ₹10.

■ The investment (total assets) in the Mexico City hotel is 3,00,00,000 pesos.

■ The operating income of the Mexico City hotel in 2014 is 60,00,000 pesos.

What is the historical-cost-based ROI for the Mexico City hotel in 2014?

To answer this question, Mayur Inns' managers first have to determine: if they calculate the ROI in pesos or in rupees. If they calculate the ROI in rupees, what exchange rate should they use? The managers may also be interested in how the ROI of Mayur Inns Mexico City (MIMC) compares with the ROI of Mayur Inns New Delhi (MIND), which is also a relatively new hotel of approximately the same size. The answers to these questions yield information that will be helpful when making future investment decisions.

$$\text{MIMC's } ROI \text{ (calculated using pesos)} = \frac{\text{Operating incomes}}{\text{Total assets}} = \frac{60,00,000 \text{ pesos}}{3,00,00,000 \text{ pesos}} = 0.20, \text{ or } 20\%$$

MIMC's ROI of 20% is higher than MIND's ROI of 17% (page 1059). Does this mean that MIMC outperformed MIND based on the ROI criterion? Not necessarily. That's because MIMC operates in a very different economic environment than MIND.

The peso has declined in value relative to the rupee in 2014. This decline has led to higher inflation in Mexico than in India. As a result of the higher inflation in Mexico, MIMC will charge higher prices for its hotel rooms, which will increase MIMC's operating income and lead to a higher ROI. Inflation clouds the real economic returns on an asset and makes historical-cost-based ROI higher. Differences in inflation rates between the two countries make a direct comparison of MIMC's peso-denominated ROI with MIND's rupee-denominated ROI misleading.

Calculating the Foreign Division's ROI in Indian Rupees

One way to make a comparison of historical-cost-based ROIs more meaningful is to restate MIMC's performance in Indian rupees. But what exchange rate should be used to make the comparison meaningful? Assume HIMC's operating income was earned evenly throughout

2014. Mayur Inns' managers should use the average exchange rate of 12.5 pesos = ₹10 to convert operating income from pesos to rupees: 60,00,000 pesos ÷ 12.5 pesos per rupee = ₹48,00,000. The effect of dividing the operating income in pesos by the higher pesos-to-rupee exchange rate prevailing during 2014, rather than the 10 pesos = ₹10 exchange rate prevailing on December 31, 2013, is that any increase in operating income in pesos as a result of inflation during 2014 is eliminated when converting back to rupees.

At what rate should MIMC's total assets of 3,00,00,000 pesos be converted? They should be converted at the 10 pesos = ₹10 exchange rate which was the exchange rate prevailing when the assets were acquired on December 31, 2013. That's because MIMC's assets are recorded in pesos at the December 31, 2013. Why? Because assets are recorded in pesos at the December 31,2013 cost, and the assets are not revalued as a result of inflation in Mexico in 2014. Because subsequent inflation does not affect the cost of assets in HIMC's financial accounting records, managers should use the exchange rate prevailing on the date the assets were acquired to convert the assets into rupees. Using exchange rates after December 31, 2013, would be incorrect because these exchange rates incorporate the higher inflation in Mexico in 2014. HIMC's total assets are therefore ₹3,00,00,000 (3,00,00,000 pesos ÷ 10 pesos per dollar).

Then,

$$\text{MIMC's } \textit{ROI} \text{ (calculated using rupess)} = \frac{\text{Operating income}}{\text{Total assets}} = \frac{₹48,00,000}{₹3,00,000} = 0.16, \text{ or } 16\%$$

As we have discussed, these adjustments make the historical-cost-based ROIs of the Mexico City and New Delhi hotels comparable because they negate the effects of any differences in inflation rates between the two countries. Now MIMC's ROI is less than MIND's ROI (16% versus HINO's ROI of 17%).

Calculating residual income in pesos poses the same problems as calculating the ROI does. Calculating MIMC's ROI in rupees adjusts for changes in exchange rates and makes for more-meaningful comparisons with Mayur's other hotels:

$$\text{MIMC's RI} = ₹48,00,000 - (0.12 \times ₹3,00,00,000)$$
$$= ₹48,00,000 - ₹36,00,000 = ₹12,00,000$$

which is also less than MIND's RI of ₹15,00,000.

Keep in mind that MIMC's and MIND's ROIs and RIs are historical-cost-based calculations. However, both hotels are relatively new, so this of a concern.

Decision Point

How can companies compare the performance of divisions operating in different countries?

Distinguishing The Performance Of Managers From The Performance Of Their Subunits[9]

Learning Objective 6

Understand the roles of salaries and incentives when rewarding managers

. . . balancing risk and performance-based rewards

Our focus has been on how to evaluate the performance of a subunit of a company, such as a division. However, is evaluating the performance of a subunit manager the same as evaluating the performance of the subunit? If the subunit performed well, does it mean the manager performed well? In this section, we argue that a company should distinguish between the performance evaluation of a *manager* and the performance evaluation of that manager's *subunit*. For example, companies often put the most skillful division manager in charge of the division producing the poorest economic return in an

---

[9] The presentations here draw (in part) from teaching notes prepared by S. Huddart, N. Melumad, and S. Reichelstein.

attempt to improve it. But this may take years and the relative underperformance of the division during that time is no reflection of the performance of the manager.

As another example, consider again the Mayur Inn Mexico City (MIMC) hotel. Suppose, despite the high inflation in Mexico, MIMC could not increase room prices because of price-control regulations imposed by the government. MIMC's performance in rupee terms would be very poor because of the decline in the value of the peso. But should top management conclude from MIMC's poor performance that the MIMC manager performed poorly? Probably not. The poor performance of MIMC is largely the result of regulatory factors beyond the manager's control.

In the following sections, we show the basic principles for evaluating the performance of an individual subunit manager. These principles apply to managers at all organization levels. Later sections consider the principles that apply to rank-and-file employees and those apply to top executives. We illustrate these principles using the RI performance measure.

The Basic TradeOff: Creating Incentives versus Imposing Risk

How companies measure and evaluate the performance of managers and other employees affects their rewards. Compensation arrangements range from a flat salary with no direct performance-based incentive (or bonus), as in the case of many government employees, to rewards based on only performance, as in the case of real estate agents who receive no salary and are compensated via commissions paid on the properties they sell. Most managers' total compensation includes some combination of salary and performance-based incentive. In designing compensation arrangements, we need to consider the *tradeoff between creating incentives and imposing risk*. We illustrate this tradeoff in the context of our Mayur Inns example.

Sandeep Sharma owns the Mayur Inns chain of hotels. Roshan Bhatt manages the Mayur Inns Mumbai (MIM) hotel. Assume Sharma uses RI to measure performance. To improve hotel's RI, Sharma would like Bhatt to increase its sales, control its costs, provide prompt and courteous customer service, and reduce the hotel's working capital. But even if Bhatt did all those things, a high RI is not guaranteed. That's because MIM's RI is affected by many factors beyond Sharma's and Bhatt's control, such as a recession in the Mumbai economy or near the hotel that would make it difficult for customers to get it.

As an entrepreneur, Sharma expects to bear risk. But Bhatt does not like being subject to risk. One way of "insuring" Bhatt against risk is to pay Bhatt a flat salary, regardless of the actual amount of RI the hotel earns. Sharma would then bear all of the risk. This arrangement creates a problem, however, because Bhatt's effort is difficult to monitor. The absence of performance-based compensation means that Bhatt has no direct incentive to work harder or to undertake extra physical and mental effort beyond what is necessary to hold onto his job.

Moral hazard describes a situation in which an employee prefers to exert less effort compared with the effort the owner desires because the owner cannot accurately monitor and enforce the employee's effort.[10] Moral hazard also occurs when an employee reports inaccurate or distorted information for personal benefit because the owner cannot monitor the validity of the reported information. Repetitive jobs, as in electronic assembly, are relatively straightforward to monitor and so are less subject to moral hazard. However, a manager's job, which is to gather and interpret information and exercise judgment on the basis of the information obtained, is more difficult to monitor.

---

[10] The term *moral hazard* originated in insurance contracts to represent situations in which insurance coverage caused insured parties to take less care of their properties than they might otherwise. One response to moral hazard in insurance contracts is the system of deductibles (that is, the insured pays for damages below a specified amount).

Paying no salary and rewarding Bhatt *only* on the basis of some performance measure—RI in our example—raises different concerns. In this case, Bhatt would be motivated to strive to increase RI because his rewards would increase with increases in RI. But compensating Bhatt on RI also subjects him to risk is because MIM's RI depends not only on Bhatt's effort, but also on factors such as local economic conditions over which Bhatt has no control.

Bhatt does not like being subject to risk. To compensate Bhatt for taking risk, Sharma must pay him extra compensation. That is, using performance-based bonuses will cost Sharma more money, *on average*, than paying Bhatt a flat salary. Why "on average"? Because Sharma's compensation payment to Bhatt will vary with RI outcomes. When averaged over these outcomes, the RI-based compensation will cost Sharma more than paying Bhatt a flat salary. The motivation for having some salary and some performance-based bonus in compensation arrangements is to balance the benefit of incentives against the extra cost of imposing risk on the manager.

Intensity of Incentives and Financial and Nonfinancial Measurements

What affects the intensity of incentives? That is, how large should the incentive component of a manager's compensation be relative to the salary component? To answer these questions, we need to understand how much the performance measure is affected by actions the manager takes to further the owner's objectives.

Preferred performance measures are those that are sensitive to or that change significantly with the manager's performance. They do not change much with changes in factors that are beyond the manager's control. Sensitive performance measures motivate the manager as well as limit the manager's exposure to risk, reducing the cost of providing incentives. Less-sensitive performance measures are not affected by the manager's performance and fail to induce the manager to improve. The more owners have access to sensitive performance measures, the more they can rely on incentive compensation for their managers.

The salary component of compensation dominates when performance measures that are sensitive to managers' actions are not available. This is the case, for example, for some corporate staff and government employees. A high salary component, however, does not mean incentives are completely absent. Promotions and salary increases do depend on some overall measure of performance, but the incentives are less direct. The incentive component of compensation is high when sensitive performance measures are available and when monitoring the employee's effort is difficult, such as in real estate agencies.

To evaluate Bhatt, Sharma uses measures from multiple perspectives of the balanced scorecard because nonfinancial measures on the balanced scorecard—employee satisfaction and the time taken for check-in, cleaning rooms, and providing room service—are more sensitive to Bhatt's actions. Financial measures such as RI are less sensitive to Bhatt's actions because they are affected by external factors such as local economic conditions beyond Bhatt's control. Residual income may be a very good measure of the economic viability of the hotel, but it is only a partial measure of Bhatt's performance.

In addition to considerations of sensitivity and risk, another reason for using nonfinancial measures is that these measures follow Hospitality Inns' strategy and are drivers of future performance. Evaluating managers on these nonfinancial measures motivates them to take actions that will sustain the long-run performance of the firm's hotels while meeting the company's environmental and social goals. Therefore, evaluating performance in all four perspectives of the balanced scorecard promotes both short- and long-run actions. The relative weight placed on the various measures in the scorecard is ideally aimed at achieving congruence between the extent to which the manager is motivated to maximize each performance metric and its importance in generating the long-run objective the firm wishes to achieve. The tradeoff between considerations of sensitivity and risk, on the one hand, and the congruence of goals, on the other, determines the effective intensity of incentives placed on each measure of performance.

Benchmarks and Relative Performance Evaluation

Owners often use financial and nonfinancial benchmarks to evaluate performance. The benchmarks, which are metrics that correspond to the "best practice" of organizations may be available inside or outside an organization. For MIM, benchmarks could be from similar hotels, either within or outside the Mayur Inns chain. Suppose Bhatt has responsibility for revenues, costs, and investments. In evaluating Bhatt's performance, Sharma would want to use as a benchmark a hotel of a similar size influenced by the same uncontrollable factors— for example, location, demographic trends, and economic conditions—that affect MIM. If all these factors were the same, *differences* in performances of the two hotels would occur only because of differences in the two managers' performances. Benchmarking, which is also called *relative performance evaluation*, filters out the effects of the common uncontrollable factors.

Can the performance of two managers responsible for running similar operations within a company be benchmarked against each other? Yes, but this approach could create a problem: It could reduce the managers' incentives to help one another. When managers do not cooperate, the company suffers. In this case, using internal benchmarks for performance evaluation may not lead to goal congruence.

Performance Measures at the Individual Activity Level

Managers need to do two things when designing the measures used to evaluate the performance of individual employees:

1. Design performance measures for activities that require multiple tasks and
2. Design performance measures for activities done in teams

Performing Multiple Tasks

Most employees perform more than one task as part of their jobs. Marketing representatives sell products, provide customer support, and gather market information. Manufacturing workers are responsible for both the quantity and quality of their output. Employers want employees to allocate their time and effort intelligently among various tasks or aspects of their jobs.

Consider mechanics at an auto repair shop. Their jobs have two distinct aspects: repair work—performing more repair work generates more revenues for the shop—and customer satisfaction—the higher the quality of the job, the more likely the customer will be pleased. If the employer wants an employee to focus on both aspects, then the employer must measure and compensate performance on both aspects.

Suppose the employer can easily measure the quantity, but not the quality, of auto repairs. If the employer rewards workers on a by-the-job rate, which pays workers only on the basis of the number of repairs actually performed, mechanics will likely increase the number of repairs they make and quality will suffer. Saran Auto Center experienced this problem when it introduced by-the-job rates for its mechanics. To resolve the problem, Saran's managers took three steps to motivate workers to balance both quantity and quality: (1) The company dropped the by-the-job rate system and paid mechanics an hourly salary, a step that deemphasized the quantity of repairs. Managers determined mechanics' bonuses, promotions, and pay increases on the basis of an assessment of each mechanic's overall quantity and quality of repairs. (2) Saran evaluated employees, in part, using the number of dissatisfied customers, the number of customer complaints and data collected from customers participication surveys (3) Finally, Saran used staff from an independent outside agency to randomly monitor whether the repairs performed were of high quality.

Team-Based Compensation Arrangements

Many manufacturing, marketing, and design problems can be resolved when employees with multiple skills, knowledge, experiences, and perceptions pool their talents. A team achieves better results than individual employees acting alone.[11] Many companies reward individuals on a team based on team performance. Team-based incentives encourage individuals to help one another as they strive toward a common goal.

The specific forms of team-based compensation vary across companies. Colgate Palmolive rewards teams on the basis of each team's performance. Novartis, the Swiss pharmaceutical company, rewards teams on companywide performance: Some team-based bonuses are paid only if the company reaches certain goals. To encourage the development of team skills, Tennessee Eastman, a chemical manufacturer, rewards team members using a checklist of team skills, such as communication and willingness to help one another. Whether team-based compensation is desirable depends, to a large extent, on the culture and management style of a particular organization. One criticism of team-based compensation is that, it diminishes the incentives of individual employees, which can harm a firm's overall performance. Another problem is how to manage team members who are not productive contributors to the team's success but who, nevertheless, share in the team's rewards.

Executive Performance Measures and Compensation

The principles of performance evaluation described in the previous sections also apply to executive compensation plans. These plans are based on both financial and nonfinancial performance measures and consist of a mix of (1) base salary; (2) annual incentives, such as a cash bonus based on achieving a target annual RI; (3) long-run incentives, such as stock options (described later in this section) based on stock's performance over, say, a five-year period; and (4) other benefits, such as medical benefits, pensions plans, and life insurance.

Well-designed plans use a compensation mix that balances risk (the effect of uncontrollable factors on the performance measure and hence compensation) with short-run and long-run incentives. For example, an evaluation based on a firm's annual EVA sharpens an executive's short-run focus. Using EVA and stock option plans over, say, five years motivates the executive to take a long-run view as well.

Stock options give executives the right to buy company stock at a specified price (called the exercise price) within a specified period. Suppose that on September 16, 2014, Mayur Inns gave its CEO the option to buy 2,00,000 shares of the company's stock at any time before June 30, 2019, at the September 16, 2014, market price of ₹490 per share. Let's say Mayur Inns' stock price rises to ₹690 per share on March 24, 2019, and the CEO exercises his options on all 2,00,000 shares. The CEO would earn ₹200 (₹690 − ₹490)

◀ Decision Point

Why are managers compensated based on a mix of salary and incentives?

---

[11] *Teams That Click: The Results-Driven Manager Series* (Boston: Harvard Business School Press, 1995).

per share on 2,00,000 shares, or ₹40 million. If Mayur Inns' stock price stays below ₹490 during the entire period, the CEO will simply forgo his right to buy the shares. By linking CEO compensation to increases in the company's stock price, the stock option plan motivates the CEO to improve the company's long-run performance and stock price.

Strategy and Levers of Control[12]

Learning Objective 7

Describe the four levers of control and why they are necessary

. . . boundary, belief, and interactive control systems counterbalance diagnostic control systems

Financial and nonfinancial performance-evaluation measures help managers track progress toward achieving a company's strategic goals. Because these measures help diagnose whether a company is performing to expectations, they are collectively called **diagnostic control systems**. Companies motivate managers by holding them accountable for and by rewarding them for meeting these goals. It's not unusual for managers to cut corners and misreport numbers to make their performance look better than it is, as happened at companies such as Enron, WorldCom. To prevent unethical and outright fraudulent behavior, companies need to balance the push for performance resulting from diagnostic control systems, the first of four levers of control, with three other levers: *boundary systems, belief systems,* and *interactive control systems.* This will ensure that proper business ethics, inspirational values, and attention to future threats and opportunities are not sacrificed while achieving business results.

Boundary Systems

Boundary systems describe standards of behavior and codes of conduct expected of all employees, especially actions that are off-limits. Ethical behavior on the part of managers is paramount. In particular, numbers that subunit managers report should not be tainted by "cooking the books." The books should be free of, for example, overstated assets, understated liabilities, fictitious revenues, and understated costs.

Codes of business conduct signal appropriate and inappropriate individual behaviors. The following is from Caterpillar Tractor's "Code of Worldwide Business Conduct and Operating Principles":

> *While we conduct our business within the framework of applicable laws and regulations, for us, mere compliance with the law is not enough. We strive for more than that.... We must not engage in activities that create, or even appear to create, conflict between our personal interests and the interests of the company.*

Division managers who fail to adhere to legal or ethical accounting policies and procedures often rationalize their behavior by claiming they were under enormous pressure from top managers "to make the budget." A healthy amount of motivational pressure is desirable, as long as the "tone from the top" and the code of conduct simultaneously communicate the absolute need for all managers to behave ethically at all times. Managers should train employees to behave ethically. They should promptly and severely reprimand unethical conduct, regardless of the benefits that might accrue to the company from unethical actions. Some companies, such as Lockheed-Martin, emphasize ethical behavior by routinely evaluating employees against a business code of ethics.

Many organizations also set explicit boundaries precluding actions that harm the environment. Environmental violations (such as water and air pollution) carry heavy fines and prison terms under the laws of India and other countries.

---

[12] For a more-detailed discussion see R. Simons, *Levers of Control: How Managers Use Innovative Control Systems to Drive Strategic Renewal* (Boston: Harvard Business School Press, 1995).

In many companies, the environmental responsibilities of employees extend beyond legal requirements. Some companies, such as DuPont, make environmental performance a line item on every employee's salary appraisal report. Duke Power Company appraises employees on measures such as reducing solid waste, cutting emissions and discharges, and implementing environmental plans. Socially responsible companies such as Best Buy, Campbell Soup, and Intel set aggressive environmental goals and measure and report their performance against them. German, Swiss, and Scandinavian companies report on environmental performance as part of a larger set of social responsibility disclosures (such as employee welfare and community development activities). In 2012, Dutch financial services giant ING began incorporating social, ethical, and environmental objectives as part of its top management's pay structure. Other firms in the Netherlands—including chemical company Akzo Nobel, life sciences group DSM, and mail operator TNT—also tie executive compensation to environmental improvement.

Belief Systems

Belief systems articulate the mission, purpose, and core values of a company. They describe the accepted norms and patterns of behavior expected of all managers and other employees when interacting with one another, shareholders, customers, and communities. For example, Johnson & Johnson describes its values and norms in a credo statement that is intended to inspire all managers and other employees to do their best.[13] Belief systems play to employees' *intrinsic motivation*, the desire to achieve self-satisfaction from good performance regardless of external rewards such as bonuses or promotion. Intrinsic motivation comes from being given greater responsibility, doing interesting and creative work, having pride in doing that work, making commitment to the organization, and developing personal bonds with one's coworkers. High intrinsic motivation enhances a firm's performance because managers and workers have a sense of achievement in doing something important, feel satisfied with their jobs, and see opportunities for personal growth.

Interactive Control Systems

Interactive control systems are formal information systems managers use to focus the company's attention and learning on key strategic issues. Managers use interactive control systems to create an ongoing dialogue around these key issues and to personally involve themselves in the decision-making activities of subordinates. An excessive focus on diagnostic control systems and critical performance variables can cause an organization to ignore emerging threats and opportunities—changes in technology, customer preferences, regulations, and industry competition that can undercut a business. Interactive control systems help prevent this problem by highlighting and tracking strategic uncertainties businesses face, such as the emergence of digital imaging in the case of Kodak and Fujifilm, airline deregulation in the case of Indian Airlines and the shift in customer preferences toward open-source Android operating systems in the case of BlackBerry. The key to this control lever is frequent face-to-face communications among managers and employees regarding these critical uncertainties. The result is ongoing discussion and debate about assumptions and action plans. New strategies emerge from the dialogue and debate surrounding the interactive process. Interactive control systems force busy managers to step back from the actions needed to manage the business today and to shift their focus forward to positioning the organization for the opportunities and threats of tomorrow.

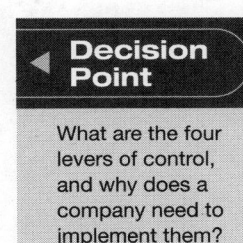

Decision Point

What are the four levers of control, and why does a company need to implement them?

---

[13] A full statement of the credo can be accessed at www.jnj.com/about-jnj/jnj-credo.

Problem for Self-Study

The Baseball Division of Home Run Sports manufactures and sells baseballs. Assume production equals sales. Budgeted data for February 2014 are:

Current assets	₹40,00,000
Long-term assets	60,00,000
Total assets	₹1,00,00,000
Production output	2,00,000 baseballs per month
Target ROI (Operating income ÷ Total assets)	30%
Fixed costs	₹40,00,000 per month
Variable cost	₹40 per baseball

Required

1. Compute the minimum selling price per baseball necessary to achieve the target ROI of 30%.
2. Using the selling price from requirement 1, separate the target ROI into its two components using the DuPont method.
3. Compute the RI of the Baseball Division for February 2014, using the selling price from requirement 1. Home Run Sports uses a required rate of return of 12% on total division assets when computing division RI.
4. In addition to her salary, Anita Kapoor, the division manager, receives 3% of the monthly RI of the Baseball Division as a bonus. Compute Anita's bonus. Why do you think Anita is rewarded using both salary and a performance-based bonus? Anita does not like bearing risk.

Solution

1.

$$\text{Target operating income} = 30\% \text{ of } ₹1,00,00,000 \text{ of total assets}$$
$$= ₹30,00,000$$
$$\text{Let } P = \text{Selling price}$$
$$\text{Revenues} - \text{Variable costs} - \text{Fixed costs} = \text{Operating income}$$
$$2,00,000P - (2,00,000 \times ₹40) - ₹40,00,000 = ₹30,00,000$$
$$2,00,000P = ₹30,00,000 + ₹80,00,000 + ₹40,00,000$$
$$= ₹1,50,00,000$$
$$P = ₹75 \text{ baseball}$$

Proof:		
	Revenues, 2,00,000 baseballs × ₹75 baseball	₹1,50,00,000
	Variable costs, 2,00,000 baseballs × ₹40 baseball	₹80,00,000
	Contribution margin	₹70,00,000
	Fixed costs	₹40,00,000
	Operating income	₹30,00,000

2. The DuPont method describes ROI as the product of two components: return on sales (income ÷ revenues) and investment turnover (revenues ÷ investment).

$$\frac{\text{Income}}{\text{Revenues}} \times \frac{\text{Revenues}}{\text{Investment}} = \frac{\text{Income}}{\text{Investment}}$$

$$\frac{₹30,00,000}{₹1,50,00,000} \times \frac{₹1,50,00,000}{₹1,00,00,000} = \frac{₹30,00,000}{₹1,00,00,000}$$

$$0.2 \times 1.5 = 0.30, \text{ or } 30\%$$

3. RI = Operating income − Requied return on investment

   = ₹30,00,000 − (0.12 × ₹1,00,00,000)

   = ₹30,00, 000 − ₹12,00,000

   = ₹18,00,000

4. Anita's bonus = 3% of RI

   = 0.03 × ₹18,00,000 = ₹54,000

The Baseball Division's RI is affected by many factors, such as general economic conditions, beyond Anita's control. These uncontrollable factors make the Baseball Division's profitability uncertain and risky. Because Anita does not like bearing risk, paying her a flat salary, regardless of RI, would shield her from this risk. But there is a moral-hazard problem with this compensation arrangement. Because Anita's effort is difficult to monitor, the absence of performance-based compensation will provide her with no incentive to undertake extra physical and mental effort beyond what is necessary to retain her job or to uphold her personal values.

Paying no salary and rewarding Anita only on the basis of RI provides her with incentives to work hard but also subjects her to excessive risk because of uncontrollable factors that will affect RI and hence Anita's compensation. A compensation arrangement based only on RI would be more costly for Home Run Sports because it would have to compensate Anita for taking on uncontrollable risk. A compensation arrangement that consists of both a salary and an RI-based performance bonus balances the benefits of incentives against the extra costs of imposing uncontrollable risk

Decision Points

The following question-and-answer format summarizes the chapter's learning objectives. Each decision presents a key question related to a learning objective. The guidelines are the answer to that question.

Decision	**Guidelines**
1. What financial and nonfinancial performance measures do companies use in their balanced scorecards?	Financial measures such as the return on investment and residual income measure aspects of the performance of organizations, their subunits, managers, and employees. In many cases, financial measures are supplemented with nonfinancial measures of performance based on the customer, internal-business-process, and learning-and-growth perspectives of the balanced scorecard—for example, customer satisfaction, quality of products and services, employee satisfaction, and the achievement of environmental objectives.
2. What are the relative merits of return on investment (ROI), residual income (RI), and economic value added (EVA) as performance measures for subunit managers?	Return on investment (ROI) is the product of two components: income divided by revenues (return on sales) and revenues divided by investment (investment turnover). Managers can increase ROI by increasing revenues, decreasing costs, and decreasing the investment. But ROI may induce the managers of highly profitable divisions to reject projects in the firm's best interest because accepting the project reduces the ROI for their divisions.
	Residual income (RI) is income minus a dollar amount of required return on investment. RI is more likely than ROI to promote goal congruence. Evaluating managers on RI is also consistent with using the net present value method to choose long-term projects.
	Economic value added (EVA) is a variation of the RI calculation. It equals after-tax operating income minus the product of the (after-tax) weighted-average cost of capital and total assets minus current liabilities.

3. Over what time frame should companies measure performance, and what are the alternative choices for calculating the components of each performance measure?

A multiyear measure gives managers the incentive to consider the long-term consequences of their actions and prevents a myopic focus on short-run profits. When constructing accounting-based performance measures, firms must first define what constitutes investment. They must also choose whether the assets included in the investment calculations are measured at historical cost or current cost and whether depreciable assets are calculated at gross or net book value.

4. What targets should companies use, and when should they give feedback to managers regarding their performance relative to the targets?

Companies should tailor a budget to a particular subunit, a particular accounting system, and a particular performance measure. In general, asset valuation and income measurement problems can be overcome by emphasizing budgets and targets that stress continuous improvement. Timely feedback enables managers to implement actions that correct deviations from the target performance.

5. How can companies compare the performance of divisions operating in different countries?

Comparing the performance of divisions operating in different countries is difficult because of legal, political, social, economic, and currency differences. ROI and RI calculations for subunits operating in different countries need to be adjusted for differences in inflation between the two countries and changes in exchange rates.

6. Why are managers compensated based on a mix of salary and incentives?

Companies create incentives by rewarding managers on the basis of performance. But managers face risk because factors beyond their control may also affect their performance. Owners choose a mix of salary and incentive compensation to trade off the incentive benefit against the cost of imposing risk.

7. What are the four levers of control, and why does a company need to implement them?

The four levers of control are diagnostic control systems, boundary systems, belief systems, and interactive control systems. Implementing the four levers of control helps a company simultaneously strive for performance, behave ethically, inspire employees, and respond to strategic threats and opportunities.

TERMS TO LEARN

This chapter and the Glossary at the end of the book contain definitions of:

belief systems **(p. 1219)**
boundary systems **(p. 1218)**
current cost **(p. 1207)**
diagnostic control
  systems **(p. 1218)**

economic value added
  (EVA®) **(p. 1203)**
imputed costs **(p. 1202)**
interactive control
  systems **(p. 1219)**

investment **(p. 1200)**
moral hazard **(p. 1214)**
residual income (RI) **(p. 1202)**
return on investment
  (ROI) **(p. 1200)**

ASSIGNMENT MATERIAL

Questions

23-1 Give examples of financial and nonfinancial performance measures that can be found in each of the four perspectives of the balanced scorecard.

23-2 What are the six steps in designing accounting-based performance measures?

23-3 What factors affecting ROI does the DuPont method of profitability analysis highlight?

23-4 "RI is not identical to ROI, although both measures incorporate income and investment into their computations." Do you agree? Explain.

23-5 Describe EVA.

23-6 Give three definitions of investment used in practice when computing ROI.

23-7 Distinguish between measuring assets based on current cost and historical cost.

23-8 What special problems arise when evaluating performance in multinational companies?

23-9 Why is it important to distinguish between the performance of a manager and the performance of the organization subunit for which the manager is responsible? Give an example.

23-10 Describe moral hazard.

23-11 "Managers should be rewarded only on the basis of their performance measures. They should be paid no salary." Do you agree? Explain.

23-12 Explain the role of benchmarking in evaluating managers.

23-13 Explain the incentive problems that can arise when employees must perform multiple tasks as part of their jobs.

23-14 Describe two disclosures required by the SEC with respect to executive compensation.

23-15 Describe the four levers of control.

Solved Examples

23-16 Analysis of return on invested assets, comparison of two divisions, DuPont method. Brilliant Classes has two divisions: Test Preparation and Language Arts. Results (in lakh of rupees) for the past three years are partially displayed here:

	A	B	C	D	E	F	G
		Operating Income	Operating Revenues	Total Assets	Operating Income/ Operating Revenues	Operating Revenues/ Total Assets	Operating Income/ Total Assets
2	Test Preparation Division						
3	2013	₹680	₹7,960	₹1920	?	?	?
4	2014	840	?	?	10%	?	42%
5	2015	1,160	?	?	11%	5	?
6	Language Arts Department						
7	2013	₹620	₹2,360	₹1,280	?	?	?
8	2014	?	3,000	1,800	22%	?	?
9	2015	?	?	2,340	?	2	25%
10	Brilliant Classes						
11	2013	₹1,300	₹10,320	₹3,200	?	?	?
12	2014	?	?	?	?	?	?
13	2015	?	?	?	?	?	?

Required

1. Complete the table by filling in the blanks.

2. Use the DuPont method of profitability analysis to explain changes in the operating-income-to-total-assets ratios over the 2013 through 2015 period for each division and for Brilliant Classes as a whole. Comment on the results.

Solution

Analysis of return on invested assets, comparison of two divisions, DuPont method (Amount in ₹lakh)

1.

	Operating Income	Operating Revenues	Total Assets	Operating Income 4 Operating Revenues	Operating Revenues 4 Total Assets	Operating Income 4 Total Assets
Test Preparation Division						
2013	₹680	₹7,960	₹1920	8.5%	4.1	35.4%
2014	840	₹840 ÷ 10% = ₹8,400	₹840 ÷ 42% = ₹2,000	10%	4.2	42%
2015	1,160	₹1,160 ÷ 11% = ₹10,545	₹10,545 ÷ 5 = ₹2,109	11%	5	55%
Language Arts Department						
2013	₹620	₹2,360	₹1,280	26.3%	1.8	48.4%
2014	₹3,000 × 22% = ₹660	3,000	1,800	22%	1.7	36.7
2015	₹2,340 × 25% = ₹585	₹2,340 × 2 = ₹4,680	2,340	12.5%	2	25%
Brilliant Classes						
2013	₹1,300	₹10,320	₹3,200	12.6%	3.2	40.6%
2014	₹840 + ₹660 = ₹1,500	₹8,400 + ₹3,000 = ₹11,400	₹2,000 + ₹18,00 = ₹3,800	13.2%	3	39.5%
2015	₹1.160 + ₹585 = ₹1,745	₹19,545 + ₹4,680 = ₹15,225	₹2,109 + ₹2,340 = ₹4,449	11.5%	3.4	39.2%

2. Based on re.venues, Test Preparation is about twice as big as Language Arts. The Language Arts Department earns higher margins (operating income as a percent of operating revenues); the Test Preparation Division turns over its assets at more than twice the rate of the Language Arts Department (operating revenues as a multiple of total assets).

The net result is that the ROI of the two divisions was similar (in the 30–50% range). But whereas the ROI of the Test Preparation Division has been increasing from 2013 to 2015, the ROI of the Language Arts Department has been falling. Overall, this has resulted in Brilliant Classes showing stable ROI over the past three years.

23-17 ROI and RI with manufacturing costs. Superior Motor Company makes electric cars and has only two products, the Simplegreen and the Superiorgreen. To produce the Simplegreen, Superior Motor employed assets of ₹13,50,00,000 at the beginning of the period, and ₹13,40,00,000 of assets at the end of the period. Other costs to manufacture the Simplegreen include:

Direct materials	₹30,000 per unit
Setup	₹13,000 per setup hour
Production	₹4,150 per machine hour

General administration and selling costs total ₹7,34,00,000 for the period. In the current period, Superior Motor produced 10,000 Simplegreen cars using 6,000 setup hours and ₹1,75,200 machine hours. Superior Motor sold these cars for ₹1,20,000 each.

Required

1. Assuming that Superior Motor defines investment as average assets during the period, what is the return on investment for the Simplegreen division?
2. Calculate the residual income for the Simplegreen if Superior Motor has a required rate of return of 12% on investments.

Solution

ROI and RI with manufacturing costs.

1. The operating income is:

Sales revenue (₹1,20,000 × 10,000)		₹1,20,00,00,000
Less:		
Direct materials (₹30,000 × 10,000)	₹30,00,00,000	

Setup (₹13,000 × 6,000)	7,80,00,000	
Production (₹4,150 × 1,75,200)	72,70,80,000	110,50,80,000
Gross margin		₹9,49,20,000
Selling and administration		7,34,00,000
Operating income		₹2,15,20,000

Average invested capital is (₹13,50,00,000 + ₹13,40,00,000) ÷ 2 = ₹13,45,00,000

$$\text{ROI} = \frac{₹2,15,20,000}{₹13,45,00,000} = 16\%$$

2. Residual income = operating income − (12% × Invested capital)

$$= ₹2,15,20,000 − (12\% × ₹13,45,00,000)$$
$$= ₹2,15,20,000 − ₹1,61,40,000$$
$$= ₹53,80,000$$

23-18 Financial and nonfinancial performance measures, goal congruence. (CMA, adapted) GE Equipment specializes in the manufacture of medical equipment, a field that has become increasingly competitive. Approximately two years ago, Pradeep Goel, president of GE, decided to revise the bonus plan (based, at the time, entirely on operating income) to encourage division managers to focus on areas that were important to customers and that added value without increasing cost. In addition to a profitability incentive, the revised plan includes incentives for reduced rework costs, reduced sales returns, and on-time deliveries. Bonuses are calculated and awarded semiannually on the following basis: A base bonus is calculated at 2% of operating income; this amount is then adjusted as follows:

a. (i)   Reduced by excess of rework costs over and above 2% of operating income
   (ii) No adjustment if rework costs are less than or equal to 2% of operating income
b. (i)   Increased by ₹50,000 if more than 98% of deliveries are on time, and by ₹20,000 if 96% to 98% of deliveries are on time
   (ii) No adjustment if on-time deliveries are below 96%
c. (i)   Increased by ₹30,000 if sales returns are less than or equal to 1.5% of sales
   (ii) Decreased by 50% of excess of sales returns over 1.5% of sales

Note: If the calculation of the bonus results in a negative amount for a particular period, the manager simply receives no bonus, and the negative amount is not carried forward to the next period.

Results for GE's Charter Division and Mesa Division for 2015, the first year under the new bonus plan, follow. In 2014, under the old bonus plan, the Charter Division manager earned a bonus of ₹2,70,600 and the Mesa Division manager, a bonus of ₹2,24,400.

	Charter Division		Mesa Division	
	January 1, 2015 to June 30, 2015	**July 1, 2015 to Dec. 31, 2015**	**January 1, 2015 to June 30, 2015**	**July 1, 2015 to Dec. 31, 2015**
Revenues	₹4,20,00,000	₹4,40,00,000	₹2,85,00,000	₹2,90,00,000
Operating income	₹46,20,000	₹44,00,000	₹34,20,000	₹40,60,000
On-time delivery	95.4%	97.3%	98.2%	94.6%
Rework costs	₹1,15,000	₹1,10,000	₹60,000	₹80,000
Sales returns	₹8,40,000	₹7,00,000	₹4,47,500	₹4,25,000

Required

1. Why did Pradeep Goel need to introduce these new performance measures? That is, why does Pradeep Goel need to use these performance measures in addition to the operating-income numbers for the period?

2. Calculate the bonus earned by each manager for each six-month period and for 2015.

3. What effect did the change in the bonus plan have on each manager's behavior? Did the new bonus plan achieve what Pradeep Goel desired? What changes, if any, would you make to the new bonus plan?

Solution

Financial and nonfinancial performance measures, goal congruence.

1. Operating income is a good summary measure of short-term financial performance. By itself, however, it does not indicate whether operating income in the short run was earned by taking actions that would lead to long-run competitive advantage, For example, GE's division might be able to increase short-run operating income by producing more product while ignoring quality or rework. Pradeep, however, would like to see division managers increase operating income without sacrificing quality. The new performance measures take a balanced scorecard approach by evaluating and rewarding managers on the basis of direct measures (such as rework costs, on-time delivery performance, and sales returns). This motivates managers to take actions that Pradeep believes will increase operating income now and in the future. The nonoperating income measures serve as surrogate measures of future profitability.

2. The semiannual instalments and total bonus for the Charter Division are calculated as follows:

Charter Division Bonus Calculation
For Year Ended December 31, 2015
January 1, 2015 to June 30, 2015

Profitability	(0.02 × ₹46,20,000)	₹92,400
Rework	(0.02 × ₹46,20,000) − ₹1,15,000	(22,600)
On-time delivery	No bonus—under 96%	0
Sales returns	[(0.015 × ₹4,20,00,000) − ₹8,40,000] × 50%	(1,05,000)
Semiannual instalment		₹(35,200)
Semiannual bonus awarded		₹0

July 1, 2015 to December 31, 2015

Profitability	(0.02 × ₹44,00,000)	₹88,000
Reword	(0.02 × ₹44,00,000) − ₹1,10,000	(22,000)
On-time delivery	96% to 98%	20,000
Sales returns	[(0.015 × ₹4,40,00,000) − ₹7,00,000] × 50%	(20,000)
Semiannual instalment		₹66,000
Semiannual bonus awarded		₹(66,000)
Total bonus awarded for the year		₹66,000

The semiannual instalments and total bonus for the Mesa Divison are calculated as follows:

Mesa Division Bonus Calculation
For Year Ended December 31, 2015
January 1, 2015 to June 30, 2015

Profitability	(0.02 × ₹34,20,000)	₹68,400
Rework	(0.02 × ₹34,20,000) − ₹60,000	0
On-time delivery	Over 98%	50,000
Sales returns	[(0.015 × ₹2,85,00,000) − ₹4,47,500] × 50%	(10,000)
Semiannual bonus instalment		₹1,08,400
Semiannual bonus awarded		₹1,08,400

July 1, 2015 to December 31, 2015

Profitability	(0.02 × ₹40,60,000)	₹81,200
Rework	(0.02 × ₹40,60,000) − ₹80,000	0
On-time delivery	No bonus—under 96%	0
Sales returns	[(0.015 × ₹2,90,00,000) − ₹4,25,000]	
	which is greater than zero, yielding a bonus	30,000
Semiannual bonus instalment		₹1,11,200
Semiannual bonus awarded		1,11,200
Total bonus awarded for the year		2,19,600

3. The manager of the Charter Divison is likely to be frustrated by the new plan, as the division bonus has fallen by more than ₹2,00,000 compared to the bonus of the previous year. However, the new performance measures have begun to have the desired effect—both on-time deliveries and sales returns improved in the second half of the year, while rework costs were relatively even. If the division continues to improve at the same rate, the Charter bonus could approximate or exceed what it was under the old plan.

The manager of the Mesa Division should be as satisfied with the new plan as with the old plan, as the bonus is almost equivalent. On-time deliveries declined considerably in the second half of the year and rework costs increased. However, sales returns decreased slightly. Unless the manager institutes better controls, the bonus situation may not be as favorable in the future. This could motivate the manager to improve in the future but currently, at least, the manager has been able to maintain his bonus with showing improvement in only one area targeted by Pradeep.

Pradeep's revised bonus plan for the Charter Division fostered the following improvements in the second half of the year despite an increase in sales:

- An increase of 1.9% in on-time deliveries.
- A ₹5,000 reduction in rework costs.
- A ₹1,40,000 reduction in sales returns.

However, operating income as a percent of sales ahs decreased (11% to 10%).

The Mesa division's bonus has remained at the status quo as a result of the following effects:

- An increase of 2.0% in operating income as a percent of sales (12% to 14%).
- A decrease of 3.6% in on-time deliveries.
- A ₹20,000 increase in rework costs.
- As ₹22,500 decrease in sales returns.

This would suggest that revisions to the bonus plan are needed. Possible changes include:

- increasing the weights put on on-time deliveries, rework costs, and sales returns in the performance measures while decreasing the weight put on operating income;
- a reward structure for rework costs that are below 2% of operating income that would encourage managers to drive costs lower;
- reviewing the whole year in total. The bonus plan should carry forward the negative amounts for one six-month period into the next six-month period incorporating the entire year when calculating a bonus; and
- developing benchmarks, and then giving rewards for improvements over prior periods and encouraging continuous improvement.

23-19 ROI, RI, EVA. Bajaj Allianz is a reinsurance and financial services company. It strongly believes in evaluating the performance of its standalone divisions using financial metrics such as ROI and residual income. For the year ended December 31, 2015, Its CFO received the following information about the performance of divisions Y:

Sales revenues	₹1,20,00,000
Operating income	20,00,000
Total assets	1,25,00,000
Current liabilities	25,00,000
Debt (interest rate:6.25%)	60,00,000
Common equity	40,00,000

For the purposes of divisional performance evaluation, Bajaj defines investment as total assets and income as operating income (that is, income before interest and taxes). The firm pays a flat rate of 20% in taxes on its income.

Required

1. What was the net income after taxes of the division Y?
2. What was the division's ROI for the year?
3. Based on Bajaj Allianz's required rate of return of 10%, what was the division's residual income for 2015?
4. Bajaj Allianz's CFO has heard about EVA and is curious about whether it might be a better measure to use for evaluating division managers. Its four divisions have similar risk characteristics. Its debt trades at book value while its equity has a market value approximately twice that of its book value. The company's cost of equity capital is 12%. Calculate each of the following components of EVA for the division Y, as well as the final EVA figure:
   a. Net operating profit after taxes
   b. Weighted-average cost of capital
   c. Investment, as measured for EVA calculations

Solution

1. The after-tax net income (Division Y is:

Operating income	₹20,00,000
Less:	
Interest expense (₹60,00,000 × 6.25%)	3,75,000
Income after interest and before taxes	₹16,25,000
Income taxes (₹16,25,000 × 20%)	3,25,000
Net income after taxes	₹13,00,000

2. Investment = Total assets = ₹1,25,00,000

   Income = Operating income = ₹20,00,000

   $$ROI = \frac{₹20,00,000}{₹1,25,00,000} = 16\%$$

3. Income = Operating income = ₹20,00,000

   Imputed cost of investment = Investment (₹1,25,00,000) × Required rate of return (10%)

   = ₹12,50,000

   Residual income = Income – Imputed cost of investment

   = ₹20,00,000 – ₹12,50,000

   = ₹7,50,000

4.a. Net operating profit after taxes = Operating income × (1 – Tax rate)

   = ₹20,00,000 × (1 – 0.2)

   = ₹16,00,000

   b. Market value of debt = ₹60,00,000

   After-tax cost of debt = 6.25% × (1 – Tax rate) = 6.25% × 80% = 5%

Market value of equity = ₹40,00,000 × 2 = ₹80,00,000

Cost of equity capital   = 12%

$$\text{Weighted-average cost of capital} = \frac{(5\% \times ₹60,00,000) + (12\% \times ₹80,00,000)}{₹60,00,000 + ₹80,00,000} = 9\%$$

c. Investment = Total Assets – Current Liabilities = ₹1,25,00,000 – ₹25,00,000
= ₹1,00,00,000

Therefore, EVA = ₹16,00,000 – 9% × ₹1,00,00,000 = ₹7,00,000.

23-20 Capital budgeting, RI. Ritu Jain, a new associate at Aggarwal Partners, has compiled the following data for a potential venture:

Investment: ₹20,00,000

5 year useful life, with no salvage value

Annual sales revenues = ₹10,00,000

Annaul cash costs = ₹4,20,000

Firm faces a 20% tax rate on income and knows that the tax authorities will only permit straight-line depreciation for tax purposes. Its after-tax required rate of return is 10%.

Required

1. Based on net present value considerations, is this a project Aggarwal Partners would want to take?
2. Aggarwal Partners use straight-line depreciation for internal accounting and measure investment as the net book value of assets at the start of the year. Calculate the residual income in each year if the project were adopted.
3. Demonstrate that the conservation property of residual income, as described in text, holds in this example.
4. If Ritu is evaluated on the residual income of the projects she undertakes, would she take this project? Explain.

Solution

1. Annual depreciation = ₹20,00,000/5 years = ₹4,00,000

   Annual cash flows = Sales revenues – Cash costs – Cash taxes

   = ₹10,00,000 – ₹4,20,000 – 20% × (₹10,00,000 – ₹4,20,000 – ₹4,00,000)

   = ₹5,44,000

   Net present value = – ₹20,00,000 + ₹5,44,000 × PV of ₹1 Annuity (5 years, 10%)

   = ₹62,304.

   The project has a positive net present value at the required rate of return of 10% and so is a project Aggarwal Partners would want to take.

2. The annual after-tax accounting income from the project is:

   80% × (₹10,00,000 – ₹4,20,000 – ₹4,00,000) = ₹1,44,000

   The residual incomes in each period are given by:

	Year 1	Year 2	Year 3	Year 4	Year 5
Investment	₹20,00,000	₹16,00,000	₹12,00,000	₹8,00,000	₹4,00,000
Capital charge (10%)	2,00,000	1,60,000	1,20,000	80,000	40,000
After-tax income	1,44,000	1,44,000	1,44,000	1,44,000	1,44,000
Residual income1	₹(56,000)	₹(16,000)	₹24,000	₹64,000	₹1,04,000

[1]After-tax income – Capital charge

3. To verify the conservation property, we have to check whether the net present value of the stream of residual incomes equals the net present value of the project. At the required rate of return of 10%, the present value of the residual incomes identified in requirement 2 is:

$$\frac{-₹56,000}{1.1} - \frac{₹16,000}{(1.1)^2} + \frac{₹24,000}{(1.1)^3} + \frac{₹64,000}{(1.1)^4} + \frac{₹1,04,000}{(1.1)^5} = ₹62,188$$

This is identical to the net present value of the project, which was calculated in requirement 1 as ₹62,188. Therefore, the conservation property of residual income does in fact hold.

4. Not necessarily. From requirement 3, the conservation property guarantees that over the lifetime of the project, it will generate the equivalent in residual incomes of its net present value. However, the project generates negative residual income figures over its first two years (see requirement 2). Therefore, if Ritu is not committed to staying with Aggarwal Partners for the project's lifetime of five years (and in particular if she expects to leave after the first two years), she would choose to reject the project rather than take the hit to her residual income performance figures. The conservation property, while a truly remarkable identity, does not solve the horizon problem: When compensated via residual income, managers with a different time horizon than the firm, or those who discount the future at a different rate than the firm's shareholders, may not have the incentive to take the right decisions on behalf of the shareholders.

23-21 ROI performance measures based on historical cost and current cost. Dabur India operates three divisions that process and bottle natural fruit juices. The historical-cost accounting system reports the following information for 2015:

	Orange Division	Pineapple Division	Mango Division
Revenues	₹1,00,00,000	₹1,40,00,000	₹2,20,00,000
Operating costs (excluding plant depreciation)	60,00,000	76,00,000	1,20,00,000
Plant depreciation	14,00,000	20,00,000	24,00,000
Operating income	₹26,00,000	₹44,00,000	₹76,00,000
Current assets	₹40,00,000	₹50,00,000	₹60,00,000
Long-term assets—plant	28,00,000	1,80,00,000	2,64,00,000
Total assets	₹68,00,000	₹2,30,00,000	₹3,24,00,000

Dabur estimates the useful life of each plant to be 12 years, with no terminal disposal value. The straight-line depreciation method is used. At the end of 2014, the Orange plant is 10 years old, the Pineapple plant is 3 years old, and the Mango plant is 1 year old. An index of construction costs over the 10-year period that Dabur has been operating (2005 year-end = 100) is:

2005	2013	2014	2015
100	136	160	170

Given the high turnover of current assets, management believes that the historical-cost and current-cost measures of current assets are approximately the same.

Required

1. Compute the ROI ratio (operating income to total assets) of each division using historical-cost measures. Comment on the results.

2. Use the approach in Exhibit 23-2 to compute the ROI of each division, incorporating current-cost estimates as of 2014 for depreciation expense and long-term assets. Comment on the results.

3. What advantages might arise from using current-cost asset measures as compared with historical-cost measures for evaluating the performance of the managers of the three divisions?

Solution
ROI performance measures based on historical cost and current cost.

1. ROI using historical cost measures:

Orange Fruit	₹26,00,000 ÷ ₹68,00,000	=	38.24%
Pineapple Fruit	₹44,00,000 ÷ ₹2,30,00,000	=	19.13%
Mango Fruit	₹76,00,000 ÷ ₹3,24,00,000	=	23.46%

The Orange Fruit Division appears to be considerably more efficient than the Pineapple Fruit and Mango Fruit Divisions.

2. The gross book values (i.e., the original costs of the plants) under historical cost are calculated as the useful life of each plant (12 years) × the annual depreciation:

Orange Fruit	12 × ₹14,00,000	=	₹1,68,00,000
Pineapple Fruit	12 × ₹20,00,000	=	₹2,40,00,000
Mango Fruit	12 × ₹24,00,000	=	₹2,88,00,000

Step 1: Restate long-term assets from gross book value at historical cost to gross book value at current cost as of the end of 2015:

(Gross book value of long-term assets at historical cost) × (Construction cost index in 2015 ÷ Construction cost index in year of construction).

Orange Fruit	₹1,68,00,000 × (170 ÷ 100)	=	₹2,85,60,000
Pineapple Fruit	₹2,40,00,000 × (170 ÷ 136)	=	₹3,00,00,000
Mango Fruit	₹2,88,00,000 × (170 ÷ 160)	=	₹3,06,00,000

Step 2: Derive net book value of long-term assets at current cost as of the end of 2015. (Estimated useful life of each plant is 12 years.)

(Gross book value of long-term assets at current cost at the end of 2015) × (Estimated remaining useful life ÷ Estimated total useful life)

Orange Fruit	₹2,85,60,000 × (2 ÷ 12)	=	₹47,60,000
Pineapple Fruit	₹3,00,00,000 × (9 ÷ 12)	=	₹2,25,00,000
Mango Fruit	₹3,06,00,000 × (11 ÷ 12)	=	₹2,80,50,000

Step 3: Compute current cost of total assets at the end of 2015. (Assume current assets of each plant are expressed in 2015 rupees.)

(Current assets at the end of 2015 [given]) + (Net book value of long-term assets at current cost at the end of 2015 [Step 2])

Orange Fruit	₹40,00,000 + ₹47,60,000	=	₹87,60,000
Pineapple Fruit	₹50,00,000 + ₹2,25,00,000	=	₹2,75,00,000
Mango Fruit	₹60,00,000 + ₹2,80,50,000	=	₹3,40,50,000

Step 4: Compute current-cost depreciation expense in 2015 rupees.

Gross book value of long-term assets at current cost at the end of 2015 (from Step 1) ÷ 12

Orange Fruit	₹2,85,60,000 ÷ 12	=	₹23,80,000
Pineapple Fruit	₹3,00,00,000 ÷ 12	=	₹25,00,000
Mango Fruit	₹3,06,00,000 ÷ 12	=	₹25,50,000

Step 5: Compute 2015 operating income using 2015 current-cost depreciation expense.

(Historical-cost operating income − [Current-cost depreciation expense in 2015 rupees (Step 4)− Historical-cost depreciation expense])

Orange Fruit	₹26,00,000 − (₹23,80,000 − ₹14,00,000)	=	₹16,20,000
Pineapple Fruit	₹44,00,000 − (₹25,00,000 − ₹20,00,000)	=	₹39,00,000
Mango Fruit	₹76,00,000 − (₹25,50,000 − ₹24,00,000)	=	₹74,50,000

Step 6: Compute ROI using current-cost estimates for long-term assets and depreciation expense (Step 5 ÷ Step 3).

Orange Fruit	₹16,20,000 ÷ ₹87,60,000	=	18.49%
Pineapple Fruit	₹39,00,000 ÷ ₹2,75,00,000	=	14.18%
Mango Fruit	₹74,50,000 ÷ ₹3,40,50,000	=	21.88%

	ROI: Historical Cost	ROI: Current Cost
Orange Fruit	38.24%	18.49%
Pineapple Fruit	19.13	14.18
Mango Fruit	23.46	21.88

Use of current cost results in the Mango Fruit Division appearing to be the most efficient. The Orange Fruit ROI reduced substantially when the ten-year-old plant is restated for the 70% increase in construction costs over the 2005 to 2015 period.

3. Use of current costs increases the comparability of ROI measures across divisions' operating plants built at different construction cost price levels. Use of current cost also will increase the willingness of managers, evaluated on the basis of ROI, to move between divisions with assets purchased many years ago and divisions with assets purchased in recent years.

23-22 Evaluating managers, ROI, DuPont method, value-chain analysis of cost structure. IBM Computer Corporation is the largest personal computer company in the world. The CEO of IBM is retiring, and the board of directors is considering external candidates to fill the position. The board's top two choices are CEOs Sudhir Goenka (current CEO of Dell) and Kapil Singhania (current CEO of Hewlett Packard (HP)). As a board member on the search committee, you collect the following information (in ₹Crore):

	A	B	C	D	E
		Dell		Hewlett Packard (HP)	
1		2010	2011	2010	2011
2					
3	Revenues	₹600.0	₹480.0	₹300.0	₹525.0
4	Costs				
5	R&D	71.2	40.2	35.9	76.1
6	Production	132.6	145.6	107.6	128.2
7	Marketing and distribution	173.2	193.7	96.4	153.8
8	Customer service	65.5	40.0	30.4	67.6
9	Total costs	442.5	419.5	270.3	425.7
10	Operating income	₹157.5	₹60.5	₹29.7	₹99.3
11	Total assets	₹540.00	₹510.0	₹240.0	₹360.0

In early 2015, a leading computer magazine gave HP's main product five stars, its highest rating. Dell's main product received three stars, down from five stars a year earlier. In the same article, HP's new products received praise; Dell's new products were judged as "mediocre."

Required

1. Use the DuPont method to calculate Dell's and HP's ROIs in 2013 and 2014. Comment on the results. What can you tell from the DuPont analysis that you might have missed from calculating ROI itself?

2. Compute the percentage of costs in each of the four business-function cost categories for Dell and HP in 2013 and 2014. Comment on the results.

3. Relate the results of requirements 1 and 2 to the comments made by the computer magazine. Of Goenka and Singhania, whom would you suggest to be the new CEO of IBM?

Solution

Evaluating managers, ROI, DuPont method, value-chain analysis of cost structure. (Amount in ₹crore)

1.

	$\dfrac{\text{Revenues}}{\text{Total Assets}}$ ×	$\dfrac{\text{Operating Income}}{\text{Revenues}}$ =	ROI = $\dfrac{\text{Operating Income}}{\text{Total Assets}}$
Dell			
2013	1.11 (₹600 ÷ ₹540)	0.26 (₹157.5 ÷ ₹600)	0.29 (₹157.5 ÷ ₹540)
2014	0.94 (₹480 ÷ ₹510)	0.13 (₹60.5 ÷ ₹480)	0.12 (₹60.5 ÷ ₹510)
Hewlett packard			
2013	1.25 (₹300 ÷ ₹240)	0.10 (₹29.7 ÷ ₹300)	0.12 (₹29.7 ÷ ₹240)
2014	1.46 (₹525 ÷ ₹360)	0.19 (₹99.3 ÷₹525)	0.28 (₹99.3 ÷ ₹360)

Dell's ROL has declined sizably from 2013 to 2014 largely because of a decline in operating income to revenues (return on sales or ROS). On point's ROI has more than doubled from 2013 to 2014, in large part due to an increase in operating income to revenues (return on sales or ROS). The DuPont analysis tells us that Dell's ROI decline arises from a serious degradation in its ROS, and not from any significant problem in assets turns, i.e., its management should probably examine and try to fix its eroding margins. This insight would not be available from a direct calculation of ROI.

2.

	Dell		Hewlett packard	
Business Function	**2013**	**2014**	**2013**	**2014**
Research and development[a]	16%	10%	13%	18%
Production	30	35	40	30
Marketing & Distribution	39	46	36	36
Customer Service	15	10	11	16
Total costs*	100%	100%	100%	100%

[a] For example, ₹71.2 ÷ ₹442.5; ₹40.2 ÷ ₹419.5; ₹35.9 ÷ ₹270.3; ₹76.1 ÷ ₹425.37

* May sum to more than 100% due to rounding.

Business functions with increases/decreases in the percentage of total costs from 2013 to 2014 are:

	Dell	Hewlett Packard
Increases	Production	Research and development
	Marketing & Distribution	Customer service
Decreases	Research and development	Production
	Customer service	

Dell has decreased expenditures in two key business functions that are critical in the computer industry—research and development and customer service. These costs are discretionary and they can be reduced in the short run without any short-run effect on customers, but such action is likely to create serious problems in the long run. Hewlett Packard, on the other hand, increased its percentage of total costs in these two areas.

3. Based on the information provided, Singhania is the better candidate for president of IBM Computer. Both Dell and HP are in the same industry. Singhania has been CEO of HP at a time when it has considerably outperformed Dell:

   a. The ROI of HP has increased from 2013 to 2014, while that of Dell has decreased.

   b. The computer magazine has given the highest ranking to HP's main product, while Dell's received a lower ranking.

c. HP has received high marks for new products (the lifeblood of a computer company), while Dell's new-product introductions have been described as "mediocre".

It is likely that HP's better rating for its current product is based on customer service and its better rating for its new product is based on research and development spending.

23-23 ROI, RI and Multinational Firms. Konekopf Corporation has a division in the United States, and another in France. The investment in the French assets was made when the exchange rate was $1.2 per euro. The average exchange rate for the year was $1.3 per euro. The exchange rate at the end of the fiscal year was $1.38 per euro. Income and investment for the two divisions are:

	United States	France
Investment in assets	$34,90,000	24,00,000 euros
Income for current year	$3,83,900	2,66,400 euros

Required

1. The required return for Konekopf is 10%. Calculate ROI and RI for the two divisions. For the French division, calculate these measures using both dollars and euros. Which division is doing better?

2. What are the advantages and disadvantages of translating the French division information from euros to dollars?

Solution

ROI, RI, and multinational firms.

1. Calculation of ROI and RI before currency translation:

	United States	France
Investment in assets	$34,90,000	24,00,000 eu
Income for current year	$3,83,900	2,66,400 eu
ROI ($3,83,900 ÷ $34,90,000; 2,66,400 eu ÷ 24,00,000 eu)	11.0%	11.1%
RI ($3,83,900 − 0.10 × $34,90,000; 2,66,400 eu − 0.10 × 24,00,000 eu)	$34,900	26, 400 eu

	United States	France
Investment in assets	$34,90,000	$28,80,000 (24,00,000 eu × $1.20)
Income for current year	$3,83,900	$346,320 (2,66,400 eu × $1.30)
ROI ($3,83,900 ÷ $34,90,000; $3,46,320 ÷ $28,80,000)	11.0%	12.0%
RI ($3,83,900 − 0.10 × $34,90,000; $3,46,320 − 0.10 × $28,80,000)	$34,900	$58,320

Without currency translation, the ROIs in the United States and France are similar, but after currency translation the ROI of France is substantially higher. Residual income is not comparable before currency translation given the different currencies used by the units. After translation, RI is higher in France. Together with the higher ROI, the RI results suggest that performance was better in France than in the United States.

2. Adjusting for differences in currency values makes the comparison of performance between foreign countries more meaningful since the accounting measures being examined are more comparable. However, changes in relative currency values can lead to misleading performance evaluations if interdependencies exist across units in different countries.

23-24 ROI, measurement alternatives for performance measures. Sagar Ratna's owns and operates a variety of casual dining restaurants in three cities: Delhi, Mumbai, and Chennai. Each geographic market is considered a separate division. The Delhi division includes four restaurants, each built in early 2004. The Mumbai division consists of three restaurants, each built in January 2008. The Chennai division is the newest, consisting of three restaurants built 4 years ago. Division managers at Sagar Ratna's are evaluated on the basis of ROI. The following information refers to the three divisions at the end of 2015:

	Home	Insert	Page Layout	Formulas	Data	Review	View	
	A				B	C	D	E
1					Delhi	Mumbai	Chennai	Total
2	Division revenues				₹1,73,36,000	₹1,20,50,000	₹1,08,90,000	₹4,02,76,000
3	Division expenses				1,58,90,000	1,10,42,000	99,58,000	3,68,90,000
4	Division operating income				14,46,000	10,08,000	9,32,000	33,86,000
5	Gross book value of long-term assets				90,00,000	75,00,000	81,00,000	2,46,00,000
6	Accumulated depreciation				66,00,000	35,00,000	21,60,000	1,22,60,000
7	Current assets				19,99,600	15,36,400	16,49,200	51,85,200
8	Depreciation expense				6,00,000	5,00,000	5,40,000	16,40,000
9	Construction cost index for year of construction				100	110	118	

Required

1. Calculate ROI for each division using net book value of total assets.
2. Using the technique in Exhibit 23-2, compute ROI using current-cost estimates for long-term assets and depreciation expense. The construction cost index for 2015 is 122. Estimated useful life of operational assets is 15 years.
3. How does the choice of long-term asset valuation affect management decisions regarding new capital investments? Why might this choice be more significant to the Delhi division manager than to the Chennai division manager?

Solution

1. ROI = Operating income ÷ Net book value of total assets

Delhi ROI	= ₹14,46,000 ÷ (₹90,00,000 − ₹66,00,000 + 19,99,600)
	= ₹14,46,000 ÷ ₹43,99,600
	= 32.87%
Mumbai ROI	= ₹10,08,000 ÷ (₹75,00,000 − ₹35,00,000 + 15,36,400)
	= ₹10,08,000 ÷ ₹55,36,400
	= 18.21%
Chennai ROI	= ₹9,32,000 ÷ (₹81,00,000 − ₹21,60,000 + 16,49,200)
	= ₹9,32,000 ÷ ₹75,89,200
	= 12.28%

2.

Step 1:

	Gross book value of long-term assets at historical cost	×	Construction cost index in 2015	÷	Construction cost index in year of construction	=	Gross book value of long-term assets at current cost at end of 2014
Delhi	₹90,00,000	×	(122	÷	100)	=	₹1,09,80,000
Mumbai	₹75,00,000	×	(122	÷	110)	=	₹83,18,182
Chennai	₹81,00,000	×	(122	÷	118)	=	₹83,74,576

Step 2:

	Gross book value of long-term assets at historical cost	×	Estimated remaining useful life	÷	Estimated useful life	=	Net book value of long-term assets at current cost at end of 2015
Delhi	₹1,09,80,000	×	(4	÷	15)	=	₹29,28,000
Mumbai	₹83,18,182	×	(8	÷	15)	=	₹44,36,364
Chennai	₹83,74,576	×	(11	÷	15)	=	₹61,41,356

Step 3:

	Current assets at end of 2015	+	Long-term assets (from Step 2, above)	=	Current cost of total assets at end of 2015
Delhi	₹19,99,600	+	₹29,28,000	=	₹49,27,600
Mumbai	₹15,36,400	+	₹44,36,364	=	₹59,72,764
Chennai	₹16,49,200	+	₹61,41,356	=	₹77,90,556

Step 4:

	Gross book value of long-term assets at current cost at end of 2015	+	Estimated total useful life	=	Current-cost depreciation expense in 2015 Rupees
Delhi	₹1,09,80,000	+	15	=	₹7,32,000
Mumbai	₹83,18,182	+	15	=	₹5,54,545
Chennai	₹83,74,576	+	15	=	₹5,58,305

Step 5:

	Historical-cost operating income	−	Current-cost depreciation expense in 2015 Rupees	−	Historical-cost depreciation expense	=	Operating income for 2015 using current-cost depreciation expense in 2015 Rupees
Delhi	₹14,46,000	−	(₹7,32,000	−	₹6,00,000)	=	₹13,14,000
Mumbai	₹10,08,000	−	(₹5,54,545	−	₹5,00,000)	=	₹9,53,454
Chennai	₹9,32,000	−	(₹5,58,305	−	₹5,40,000)	=	₹9,13,695

Step 6:

	Operating income for 2015 using current-cost depreciation expense in 2015 Rupees	÷	Current cost of total assets at end of 2014	=	ROI using current-cost estimate
Delhi	₹13,14,000	+	₹49,27,600	=	26.67%
Mumbai	₹9,53,454	+	₹59,72,764	=	15.96%
Chennai	₹9,13,695	+	₹77,90,556	=	11.73%

3. Adjusting assets to recognize current costs negates differences in the investment base caused solely by differences in construction-price levels. Compared with historical-cost ROI, current cost ROI better measures the current economic returns from the investment. Because the Delhi assets are older, there is a more significant difference between historical cost and current cost.

23-25 ROI, RI, DuPont method, investment decisions, balanced scorecard. Times Group has two major divisions: Print and Internet. Summary financial data (in lakh rupees) for 2014 and 2015 are as follows:

	File Edit View Insert Format Tools Data Window Help								
	A	B	C	D	E	F	G	H	I
1		Operating Income			Revenues			Total Assets	
2		2014	2015		2014	2015		2014	2015
3	Print	₹3,780	₹4,620		₹18,900	₹19,320		₹18,480	₹20,580
4	Internet	546	672		25,200	26,880		11,340	12,600

The two division managers' annual bonuses are based on division ROI (defined as operating income divided by total assets). If a division reports an increase in ROI from the previous year, its management is automatically eligible for a bonus; however, the management of a division reporting a decline in ROI has to present an explanation to the Times Group board and is unlikely to get any bonus.

Arvind, manager of the Print Division, is considering a proposal to invest ₹800 lakh in a new computerized news reporting and printing system. It is estimated that the new system's state-of-the-art graphics and ability to quickly incorporate late-breaking news into papers will increase 2015 division operating income by ₹120 lakh. Times Group uses a 15% required rate of return on investment for each division.

Required

1. Use the DuPont method of profitability analysis to explain differences in 2015 ROIs between the two divisions. Use 2015 total assets as the investment base.
2. Why might Arvind be less than enthusiastic about accepting the investment proposal for the new system, despite her belief in the benefits of the new technology?
3. Ashish, CEO of Times Group, is considering a proposal to base division executive compensation on division RI.
   a. Compute the 2015 RI of each division.
   b. Would adoption of an RI measure reduce Arvind's reluctance to adopt the new computerized system investment proposal?
4. Ashish is concerned that the focus on annual ROI could have an adverse long-run effect on News Times Group's customers. What other measurements, if any, do you recommend that Ashish use? Explain briefly.

Solution

ROI, RI, DuPont method, investment decisions, balanced scorecard. (Amount in ₹Lakh)

1.

2015	$\dfrac{\text{Revenues}}{\text{Total Assets}}$	×	$\dfrac{\text{Operating Income}}{\text{Revenues}}$	=	ROI = $\dfrac{\text{Operating Income}}{\text{Total Assets}}$
Print	0.939 (₹19,320 ÷ ₹20,580)		0.239 (₹4,620 ÷ ₹19,320)		0.224 (₹4,620 ÷ ₹20,580)
Internet	2.133 (₹26,880 ÷ ₹12,600)		0.025 (₹672 ÷ ₹26.880)		0.053 (₹672 ÷ ₹12,600)

The Print Division has a relatively high ROI because of its high income margin relative to Internet. The Internet Division has a low ROI despite a high investment turnover because of its very low income margin.

2. Although the proposed investment is small, relative to the total assets invested, it earns less than the 2011 return on investment (0.224) (Amount in ₹Lakh):

$$\text{2015 ROI (before proposal)} = \frac{₹4,620}{₹20,580} = 0.224$$

$$\text{Investment proposal ROI Y} = \frac{₹120}{₹800} = 0.150$$

$$\text{2015 ROI (with proposal)} = \frac{₹4,620 + ₹120}{₹20,580 + ₹800} = 0.222$$

Given the existing bonus plan, any proposal that reduces the ROI is unattractive.

3a. Residual income for 2015 (before proposal, in ₹lakh):

	Operating Income		Imputed Interest Charge		Division Residual Income
Print	₹4,620	−	₹2,470 (0.12 × ₹20,580)	=	₹2,150
Internet	672	−	1,512 (0,12 × ₹12,600)	=	(840)

3b. Residual income for proposal (in ₹lakh):

	Operating Income		Imputed Interest Charge		Residual Income
	₹120	−	₹120 (0.15 × ₹800)	=	₹0

Investing in the fast-speed printing press will have no effect on the Print Division's residual income. As a result, if Arvind is evaluated using a residual income measure, Arvind would be indifferent to adopting the printing press proposal.

4. As discussed in requirement 3b, Ashish could consider using RI. The use of RI motivates managers to accept any project that makes a positive contribution to net income after the cost of the invested capital is taken into account. Making such investments will have a positive effect on Times Group's customers.

Ashish may also want to consider nonfinancial measures such as newspaper subscription levels, internet audience size, repeat purchase patterns, and market share. These measures will require managers to invest in areas that have favorable long-run effects on Times Group's customers.

23-26 Division managers' compensation, levers of control (continuation of 23-25). Ashish seeks your advice on revising the existing bonus plan for division managers of Times Group. Assume division managers do not like bearing risk. Ashish is considering three ideas:

- Make each division manager's compensation depend on division RI.
- Make each division manager's compensation depend on companywide RI.
- Use benchmarking, and compensate division managers on the basis of their division's RI minus the RI of the other division.

Required

1. Evaluate the three ideas Ashish has put forth using performance-evaluation concepts described in this chapter. Indicate the positive and negative features of each proposal.

2. Ashish is concerned that the pressure for short-run performance may cause managers to cut corners. What systems might Ashish introduce to avoid this problem? Explain briefly.

3. Ashish is also concerned that the pressure for short-run performance might cause managers to ignore emerging threats and opportunities. What system might Ashish introduce to prevent this problem? Explain briefly.

Solution

Division manager's compensation, levers of control.

1. Consider each of the three proposals that Ashish is considering:

a. *Compensate managers on the basis of division RI.*

The benefit of this arrangement is that managers would be motivated to put in extra effort to increase RI because managers' rewards would increase with increases in RI. But compensating managers largely on the basis of RI subjects the managers to excessive risk, because each division's RI depends not only on the manager's effort but also on random factors over which the manager has no control. A manager may put in a great deal of effort, but the division's RI may be low because of adverse factors (high interest, recession) that the manager cannot control.

To compensate managers for taking on uncontrollable risk, Ashish must pay them additional amounts within the structure of the RI-based arrangement. Thus, using mainly performance-based incentives will cost Ashish more money, on average, than paying a flat salary. The key question is whether the benefits of motivating additional effort justify the higher costs of performance-based rewards. The motivation for having some salary and some performance-based bonus in compensation arrangements is to balance the benefits of incentives against the extra costs of imposing uncontrollable risk on the manager.

Finally, rewarding a manager only on the basis of division RI will induce managers to maximize the division's RI even if taking such actions are not in the best interests of the company as a whole.

b. *Compensate managers on the basis of companywide RI.*

Rewarding managers on the basis of companywide RI will motivate managers to take actions that are in the best interests of the company rather than actions that maximize a division's RI.

A negative feature of this arrangement is that each division manager's compensation will now depend not only on the performance of that division manager but also on the performance of the other division managers. For example, the compensation of Arvind, the manager of the Print Division, will depend on how well the manager of Internet performs, even though Arvind himself may have little influence over the performance of these divisions. Therefore, compensating managers on the basis of companywide RI will impose extra risk on each division manager, and will raise the cost of compensating them, on average.

c. *Compensate managers using the other division's RI as a benchmark,*

The benefit of benchmarking or relative performance evaluation is to cancel out the effects of common noncontrollable factors that affect a performance measure. Taking out the effects of these factors provides better information about a manager's performance. What is critical, however, for benchmarking and relative performance evaluation to be effective is that similar noncontrollable factors affect each division. It is not clear that the same noncontrollable factors that affect the performance of the Print Division (cost of newsprint paper, for example) also affect the performance of the Internet division. If the noncontrollable factors are not the same, then comparing the RI of one division to the RI of the other division will not provide useful information for relative performance evaluation.

A second factor for Ashish to consider is the impact that benchmarking and relative performance evaluation will have on the incentives for the division managers of the Print and Internet Divisions to cooperate with one another. Benchmarking one division against another means that a division manager will look good by improving his or her own performance or by making the performance, of the other division manager look bad.

2. Using measures like RI and ROI—diagnostic levers of control—can cause managers to cut corners and take other actions that boost short-run performance but harm the company in the long run. Ashish can guard against such problems by introducing and upholding strong boundary and belief systems of control within the company. Strict codes of conduct should govern what employees cannot do. Ashish should also foster a culture where employees have a deep belief in the value of the company's journalistic mission.

3. Another potential problem of an excessive focus on diagnostic measures is a myopic disregard for emerging threats and opportunities. Interactive control systems, based on debate and discussion and regular review of strategic uncertainties and the corripetitive landscape can help overcome this problem. Ashish should not only ask for regular reports on ROI, RI, etc., he should meet regularly with division managers, discuss 5- and 10-year strategic plans, and obtain their field-based inputs. Such regular dialogues will help surface emerging threats and opportunities, and the action plans that need to be taken in response.

23-27 ROI, RI, decision making. The following data refer to the successful Munger division of Buffett, Inc. Munger makes and sells high-end cordless drills. The drills sell for $80 each, and Munger expects sales of 3,00,000 units in 2016. Munger's annual fixed costs are $4 million. The variable cost per drill is $48.

Buffett evaluates Munger based on residual income. The total investment attributed to Munger is $16 million, and Buffett has a required rate of return on investment of 20%.

Ignore taxes and depreciation expense. Answer each of the following parts independently, unless otherwise stated.

Required

1. What is the expected residual income in 2016?

2. Munger receives an external special order for 1,00,000 units at $60 each. If the order is accepted, Munger will have to incur incremental fixed costs of $8,50,000 and invest an additional $2 million in various assets.

   What is the effect on Munger's residual income of accepting the order?

3. One of the components Munger manufactures for its drill has a variable cost of ₹4. An outside vendor has offered to supply the 3,00,000 units required at a cost of ₹5.25 per unit. If the component is purchased outside, fixed costs will decline by ₹2,00,000 and assets with a book value of ₹7,60,000 will be sold at book value.

   Will Munger decide to make or buy the component? Explain your answer.

4. One of Munger's regular customers asks for a special drill made of tempered steel. The customer requires 15,000 drills. Munger estimates its variable cost for these special units at ₹54 apiece. Munger will also have to undertake new investment of ₹15,00,000 to produce the drills.

   What is the minimum selling price that will make the deal acceptable to Munger?

5. Assume the same facts as in requirement 4. Also suppose that the customer has offered ₹82 for each special drill. In addition, the customer has indicated that its purchases of the existing product will drop by 6,000 units.

   a. What is the net change in Munger's residual income from taking the offer, relative to its planned 2016 situation?

   b. At what drop in unit sales of the regular drill would Munger be indifferent to the offer?

Solution

1. Annual income = 3,00,000 × ($80 − $48) − $40,00,000 = $56,00,000
   Capital charge = 20% × $1,60,00,000 = $32,00,000
   Residual income = $56,00,000 - $32,00,000 = $24,00,000

2. Additional income = 1,00,000 × ($60 − $48) − $8,50,000 = $3,50,000
   Additional capital charge = 20% × $20,00,000 = $4,00,000
   Additional residual income = $3,50,000 − $4,00,000 = ($50,000)
   Munger's residual income would decrease by $50,000 if the order were accepted.

3. If Munger accepts the order, its performance measures would look as follows:
   Annual income = 3,00,000 × ($80 − $44 − $5.25) − $38,00,000 = $54,25,000
   Capital charge = 20% × $1,52,40,000 = $30,48,000
   Residual income = $54,25,000 − $30,48,000 = $23,77,000

   Relative to the status quo residual income of $24,00,000 (see requirement 1), accepting this offer lowers Munger's residual income by $23,000. Munger will therefore decide to make the component in-house rather than buy it externally.

4. The minimum selling price, p, is one at which Munger is indifferent to taking on the deal, in the sense that it yields $0 in residual income. The residual income from the deal is given by

   $$15,000 × (p − \$54) − (20\% × \$15,00,000)$$
   $$= 15,000 × (p − \$54 − \$20)$$

   Setting this to equal zero reveals that the minimum selling price is p = $74.

5a. At a price of $82, the residual income from the special tempered steel drills is
   15,000 × ($82 − $54) − (20% × $15,00,000) = $1,20,000

The loss in residual income from the lost sales of 6,000 original cordless drills is

6,000 × ($80 − $48) = $1,92,000.

Overall, Munger's residual income is reduced by $72,000 ($1,92,000 − $1,20,000) as a result of the transaction related to the special tempered steel drills.

5b. For each original drill that Munger does not sell, it loses a residual income (or, equivalently, contribution margin) of $32 per unit ($80 − $48). From requirement 5a, the residual income from the new tempered steel drills is $1,20,000. Therefore, the drop in unit sales of the regular drill that would leave Munger indifferent to the offer is

$$\frac{₹1,20,000}{₹32} = 3,750 \text{ regular drills.}$$

23-28 RI, EVA, measurement alternatives, goal congruence. Refresh Resorts, Ltd., operates health spas in Key West, Florida; Phoenix, Arizona; and Carmel, California. The Key West spa was the company's first and opened in 1988. The Phoenix spa opened in 2001, and the Carmel spa opened in 2010. Refresh Resorts has previously evaluated divisions based on RI, but the company is considering changing to an EVA approach. All spas are assumed to face similar risks. Data for 2014 are:

	Home	Insert	Page Layout	Formulas	Data	Review	View	
	A			B	C	D	E	
1				Key West	Phoenix	Carmel	Total	
2	Revenues			$41,00,000	$43,80,000	$32,30,000	$1,17,10,000	
3	Variable costs			16,00,000	16,30,000	9,55,000	41,85,000	
4	Fixed costs			12,80,000	15,60,000	9,80,000	38,20,000	
5	Operating income			12,20,000	11,90,000	12,95,000	37,05,000	
6	Interest costs on long-term debt at 8%			3,68,000	4,16,000	4,40,000	12,24,000	
7	Income before taxes			8,52,000	7,74,000	8,55,000	24,81,000	
8	Net income after 35% taxes			5,53,800	5,03,100	5,55,750	16,12,650	
9								
10	Net book value at 2014 year-end:							
11	Current assets			$12,80,000	$ 8,50,000	$ 6,00,000	$ 27,30,000	
12	Long-term assets			48,75,000	54,62,000	68,35,000	1,71,72,000	
13	Total assets			61,55,000	63,12,000	74,35,000	1,99,02,000	
14								
15	Current liabilities			3,30,000	2,65,000	84,000	6,79,000	
16	Long-term debt			46,00,000	52,00,000	55,00,000	1,53,00,000	
17	Stockholders' equity			12,25,000	8,47,000	18,51,000	39,23,000	
18	Total liabilities and stockholders' equity			61,55,000	63,12,000	74,35,000	1,99,02,000	
19								
20	Market value of debt			$46,00,000	$52,00,000	$55,00,000	$1,53,00,000	
21	Market value of equity			24,00,000	26,60,000	25,90,000	76,50,000	
22	Cost of equity capital						14%	
23	Required rate of return						11%	
24	Accumulated depreciation on long-term assets			$22,00,000	$15,10,000	$2,20,000		

1. Calculate RI for each of the spas based on operating income and using total assets as the measure of investment. Suppose that the Key West spa is considering adding a new group of saunas from Finland that will cost $2,25,000. The saunas are expected to bring in operating income of $22,000. What effect would this project have on the RI of the Key West spa? Based on RI, would the Key West manager accept or reject this project? Why? Without resorting to calculations, would the other managers accept or reject the project? Why?

2. Why might Refresh Resorts want to use EVA instead of RI for evaluating the performance of the three spas?

3. Refer back to the original data. Calculate the WACC for Refresh Resorts.

4. Refer back to the original data. Calculate EVA for each of the spas, using net book value of long-term assets. Calculate EVA again, this time using gross book value of long-term assets. Comment on the differences between the two methods.

5. How does the selection of asset measurement method affect goal congruence?

Solution

1.

Spa	Operating Income	−	Required Rate of Return	×	Investment	=	Residual Income
Key West	$12,20,000	−	(11%	×	61,55,000)	=	$5,42,950
Phoenix	11,90,000	−	(11%	×	63,12,000)	=	4,95,680
Carmel	12,95,000	−	(11%	×	74,35,000)	=	4,77,150

The residual income from the new saunas would be:

$22,000 operating income − ($2,25,000 investment × 11% required rate) = ($2,750)

Because the RI of the project is negative, the rate of return on the project is less than the required rate of 11%, and the Key West manager would reject the project. Other managers would also reject the project because they all face a required rate of return of 11%.

2. Refresh Resorts may want to use EVA instead of RI because EVA explicitly takes into consideration both the weighted-average cost of capital and the effect of income taxes. EVA also uses long-term assets and working capital in its calculation as opposed to the use of total assets in the RI calculation. When performance is evaluated using EVA, managers must either earn more after-tax operating income with the same capital, use less capital to earn the same after-tax operating income, or invest capital in high-return projects. EVA is considered a stricter standard by which to gauge performance.

3. WACC =

$$\frac{8\% \times (1-35\%) \times \$1,53,00,000 + (14\% \times \$76,50,000)}{\$1,53,00,000 + \$76,50,000} = \frac{\$18,66,600}{\$2,29,50,000} = 8.13\%$$

4.

EVA = After-tax operating income − [WACC × (Total assets − current liabilities)]

Using net book value of assets:

Key West EVA	= ($12,20,000 × 65%) − [8.13% × ($61,55,000 − $3,30,000)]
	= $7,93,000 − $4,73,573
	= $3,19,427
Phoenix EVA	= ($11,90,000 × 65%) − [8.13% × ($63,12,000 − $2,65,000)]
	= $7,73,500 − $4,91,621
	= $2,81,879

Carmel EVA $\quad$ = ($12,95,000 × 65%) – [8.13% × ($74,35,000 – $84,000)]

$\qquad\qquad\qquad$ = $8,41,750 – $5,97,636

$\qquad\qquad\qquad$ = $2,44,114

Using gross book value of assets:

Key West EVA $\quad$ = ($12,20,000 × 65%) – [8.13% × ($83,75,000a – $3,30,000)]

$\qquad\qquad\qquad$ = $7,93,000 – $6,54,059

$\qquad\qquad\qquad$ = $1,38,941

Phoenix EVA $\quad$ = ($11,90,000 × 65%) – [8.13% × ($78,22,000a – $2,65,000)]

$\qquad\qquad\qquad$ = $7,73,500 – $6,14,384

$\qquad\qquad\qquad$ = $1,59,116

Carmel EVA $\quad$ = ($12,95,000 × 65%) – [8.13% × ($76,55,000a – $84,000)]

$\qquad\qquad\qquad$ = $8,41,750 – $6,15,522

$\qquad\qquad\qquad$ = $2,26,228

aTotal assets + Accumulated depreciation

Using net book value of assets, Key West, the oldest spa, shows the highest EVA, and Carmel shows the lowest. This is understandable, as the Key West assets have been more fully depreciated. This technique, however, can lead management to make false assumptions about the earning power of the Key West spa. Using the gross book value method, Carmel shows the highest EVA, while Key West shows the lowest. This method unmasks the decline in earning power of older spa assets.

5. If Refresh Resorts chooses to use gross book value of assets in its EVA calculation, it may achieve greater goal congruence, as spa managers will be less reluctant otherwise to invest in newer assets that will produce higher future revenue. If a company measures assets using net book value, a manager will reject replacing older, fully depreciated, less profitable assets with newer ones because the initial effect will be lower EVA, even though the replacement may have positive long-term effects for the company.

23-29 Ethics, levers of control. (R. Madison, adapted, Strategic Finance, January 2000). Plywood Forest Products (PFP) is a large timber and wood processing plant. PFP's performance-evaluation system pays its managers substantial bonuses if the company achieves annual budgeted profit numbers. In the last quarter of 2014, Amita, PFP's controller, noted a slight increase in output and a significant decrease in the purchase cost of raw timber.

One day when Amita was at the log yard where timber is received and scaled (weighed and checked for quality) to determine what PFP pays for it, she noted that a timber contractor was quite aggravated when he was given the scale report (board feet and quality). When she asked one of the scale employees what was bothering the contractor, he revealed that the scalers had received instructions from their supervisors to deliberately "lowball" evaluations of timber quantity and quality. This reduced the price paid to timber suppliers, which also reduced direct material costs, helping PFP to meet its profit target.

Required

1. What should Amita do? You may want to refer to Standards of Ethical Conduct for Management Accountants and Resolution of Ethical Conflict.

2. Which lever of control is PFP emphasizing? What changes, if any, should be made?

Solution

Ethics, levers of control.

1. If Amita "turns a blind eye" toward what she has just observed at the PFP log yard, she will be violating the competence, integrity, and objectivity standards for management accountants.

Competence

• Performs professional duties in accordance with technical standards

Integrity

- Communicate unfavorable as well favorable information and professional judgments or opinions
- Refrain from engaging in or supporting any activity that would discredit the profession

Credibility

- Communicate information fairly and objectively
- Discolse fully all relevant information that could reasonably be expected to influence an intended user's understanding of the reports, comments, and recommendations.

Amita should:

a Try to follow established PFP policies to try to bring the issue to the attention of PFP management through regular channels; then, if necessary,

b Discuss the problem with the immediate superior who is not involved in the understatement of quality and costs.

c Clarify relevant ethical issues with an objective advisor, preferably a professional person outside PFP.

d If all the above channels fail to lead to a correction in the organization, she may have to resign and become a "whistle-blower" to bring PFP to justice.

2. PFP is clearly emphasizing profit, driving managers to find ways to keep profits strong and increasing. This is a diagnostic measure, and over-emphasis on diagnostic measures can cause employees to do whatever is necessary—including unethical actions—to keep the measures in the acceptable range, not attract negative senior management attention and possibly improve compensation and job reviews.

To avoid problems like this in the future, PFP needs to establish some strong boundary systems and codes of conduct. There should be a clear message from upper management that unethical behavior will not be tolerated. Training, role-plays, and case studies can be used to raise awareness about these issues, and strong sanctions should be put in place if the rules are violated. An effective boundary system is needed to keep managers "on the right path."

PFP also needs to articulate a belief system of core values. The goal is to inspire managers and employees to do their best, exercise greater responsibility, take pride in their work, and do things the right way.

23-30 ROI, RI, division manager's compensation, balanced scorecard. Key information for the Peoria Division (PD) of Ballarpur Industries for 2015 follows.

Revenues	₹15,00,00,000
Operating income	₹1,80,00,000
Total assets	₹10,00,00,000

PD's managers are evaluated and rewarded on the basis of ROI defined as operating income divided by total assets. Ballarpur Industries expects its divisions to increase ROI each year.

Next year, 2016, appears to be a difficult year for PD. PD had planned a new investment to improve quality but, in view of poor economic conditions, has postponed the investment. ROI for 2016 was certain to decrease if PD had made the investment.

Management is now considering ways to meet its target ROI of 20% for next year. It anticipates revenues to be steady at ₹15,00,00,000 in 2016.

Required

1. Calculate PD's return on sales (ROS) and ROI for 2015.
2. **a.** By how much would PD need to cut costs in 2016 to achieve its target ROI of 20%, assuming no change in total assets between 2015 and 2016?
   b. By how much would PD need to decrease total assets in 2016 to achieve its target ROI of 20%, assuming no change in operating income between 2015 and 2016?
3. Calculate PD's RI in 2015 assuming a required rate of return on investment of 15%.

4. PD wants to increase RI by 50% in 2016. Assuming it could cut costs by ₹4,50,000 in 2016, by how much would PD need to decrease total assets in 2016?

5. Ballarpur Industries is concerned that the focus on cost cutting, asset sales, and no new investments will have an adverse long-run effect on PD's customers. Yet Ballarpur wants PD to meet its financial goals. What other measurements, if any, do you recommend that Ballarpur use? Explain briefly.

Solution

ROI, RI, division manager's compensation, balanced scorecard.

1. $\text{ROS} = \dfrac{\text{Operating Income}}{\text{Sales}} = \dfrac{₹1,80,00,000}{₹15,00,00,000} = 12\%$

   $\text{ROI} = \dfrac{\text{Operating Income}}{\text{Total Assets}} = \dfrac{₹1,80,00,000}{₹10,00,00,000} = 18\%$

2a. $\text{ROI} = 20\% = \dfrac{\text{Operating Income}}{\text{Total Assets}} = \dfrac{X}{₹10,00,00,000}$

   Hence, operating income = 20% × ₹10,00,00,000 = ₹2,00,00,000

   Operating income = Revenue − Costs

   Therefore, Costs = ₹15,00,00,000 − ₹2,00,00,000 = ₹13,00,00,000

   Currently,

   Costs = Revenues − Operating income = ₹15,00,00,000 − ₹1,80,00,000 = ₹13,20,00,000

   Costs need to be reduced by ₹20,00,000 (₹13,20,00,000 − ₹13,00,00,000).

2b. $\text{ROI} = 20\% = \dfrac{\text{Operating Income}}{\text{Total assets}} = \dfrac{₹1,80,00,000}{X}$

   Hence X = ₹1,80,00,000 ÷20% = ₹9,00,00,000

   PD would need to decrease total assets in 2012 by ₹1,00,00,000 (₹10,00,00,000 − ₹9,00,00,000).

3. RI = Income − (Required rate of return × Investment)

   = ₹1,80,00,000 − (0.15 × ₹10,00,00,000)

   = ₹30,00,000

4. PD wants RI to increase by 50% × ₹30,00,000 = ₹15,00,000

   That is, PD wants RI in 2012 to be ₹30,00,000 + ₹15,00,000 = ₹45,00,000

   If PD cuts costs by ₹4,50,000 its operating income will increase to

   ₹1,80,00,000 + ₹4,50,000 = ₹1,84,50,000

   RI_{2012} = ₹45,00,000 = ₹1,84,50,000 − (0.15 × Assets)

   ₹1,39,50,000 = 0.15 × Assets

   Assets = ₹1,39,50,000 ÷ 0.15 = ₹9,30,00,000

PD would need to decrease total assets by ₹70,00,000 (₹10,00,00,000 − ₹9,30,00,000).

Ballarpur could focus more on revenues and ROS. Then, it will focus less on cutting costs and reducing assets and put more emphasis on customers, actual revenues, and how they translate into operating income.

Ballarpur may also want to consider nonfinancial measures such as customer satisfaction and market share, quality, yield, and on-time performance as well as monitor employee satisfaction and the development of employee skills. Maintaining high performance along these measures will have a favorable long-run effect on PD's customers.

Exercises

[Comprehensive solutions to all exercises are available on the companion website www. pearsoned.co.in/charlesthorngren]

23-31 ROI, comparisons of three companies. (CMA, adapted) Return on investment (ROI) is often expressed as follows:

$$\frac{\text{Income}}{\text{Investment}} = \frac{\text{Income}}{\text{Revenues}} \times \frac{\text{Revenues}}{\text{Investment}}$$

Required

1. What advantages are there in the breakdown of the computation into two separate components?

2. Fill in the following blanks:

	Companies in Same Industry		
	A	B	C
Revenues	₹10,00,000	₹5,00,000	?
Income	₹1,00,000	₹50,000	?
Investment	₹5,00,000	?	₹50,00,000
Income as a percentage of revenues	?	?	0.5%
Investment turnover	?	?	2
ROI	?	1%	?

After filling in the blanks, comment on the relative performance of these companies as thoroughly as the data permit.

23-32 ROI and RI. (D. Kleespie, adapted) The Outdoor Sports Company produces a wide variety of outdoor sports equipment. Its newest division, Golf Technology, manufactures and sells a single product: AccuDriver, a golf club that uses global positioning satellite technology to improve the accuracy of golfers' shots. The demand for AccuDriver is relatively insensitive to price changes. The following data are available for Golf Technology, which is an investment center for Outdoor Sports:

Total annual fixed costs	₹3,00,00,000
Variable cost per AccuDriver	₹500
Number of AccuDrivers sold each year	1,50,000
Average operating assets invested in the division	₹4,80,00,000

Required

1. Compute Golf Technology's ROI if the selling price of AccuDrivers is ₹720 per club.

2. If management requires an ROI of at least 25% from the division, what is the minimum selling price that the Golf Technology Division should charge per AccuDriver club?

3. Assume that Outdoor Sports judges the performance of its investment centers on the basis of RI rather than ROI. What is the minimum selling price that Golf Technology should charge per AccuDriver if the company's required rate of return is 20%?

23-33 Goal incongruence and ROI. Godrej Industries manufactures furniture in several divisions, including the Patio Furniture division. The manager of the Patio Furniture division plans to retire in two years. The manager receives a bonus based on the division's ROI, which is currently 11%. Godrej Industry's weighted average cost of capital is 6%.

One of the machines that the Patio Furniture division uses to manufacture the furniture is rather old, and the manager must decide whether to replace it. The new machine would cost ₹3,00,000 and would last 10 years. It would have no salvage value. The old machine is fully depreciated and has no trade-in value. Godrej uses straight-line depreciation for all assets. The new machine, being new and more efficient, would save the company ₹50,000 per year in cash operating costs. The only difference between cash flow and net income is depreciation. The internal rate of return of the project is 11%.

1. Should Godrej Industries replace the machine? Why or why not?

2. Assume that "investment" is defined as average net long-term assets after depreciation. Compute the project's ROI for each of its first five years. If the Patio Furniture manager is interested in maximizing his bonus, would he replace the machine before he retires? Why or why not?

3. What can Godrej do to entice the manager to replace the machine before retiring?

23-34 ROI, RI, measurement of assets. (CMA, adapted) Royal Plastics recently announced a bonus plan to be awarded to the manager of the most profitable division. The three division managers are to choose whether ROI or RI will be used to measure profitability. In addition, they must decide whether investment will be measured using gross book value or net book value of assets. Royal Plastics defines income as operating income and investment as total assets. The following information is available for the year just ended:

Division	Gross Book Value of Assets	Accumulated Depreciation	Operating Income
Drums	₹12,00,000	₹6,45,000	₹1,42,050
Buckets	₹11,40,000	₹6,15,000	₹1,37,550
Trays	₹7,50,000	₹4,20,000	₹92,100

Royal uses a required rate of return of 12% on investment to calculate RI.

Each division manager has selected a method of bonus calculation that ranks his or her division Number 1. Identify the method for calculating profitability that each manager selected, supporting your answer with appropriate calculations. Comment on the strengths and weaknesses of the methods chosen by each manager.

23-35 Risk sharing, incentives, benchmarking, multiple tasks. The Battery Division of Exide Industries sells car batteries. Exide's corporate management gives Battery management considerable operating and investment autonomy in running the division. Exide Industries is considering how it should compensate Praveen Tiwari, the general manager of the Battery Division. Proposal 1 calls for paying Praveen a fixed salary. Proposal 2 calls for paying Praveen no salary and compensating him only on the basis of the division's ROI, calculated based on operating income before any bonus payments. Proposal 3 calls for paying Praveen some salary and some bonus based on ROI. Assume that Praveen does not like bearing risk.

1. Evaluate the three proposals, specifying the advantages and disadvantages of each.

2. Suppose that Exide' competes against Supreme Batteries in the car battery business. Supreme is approximately the same size as the Battery Division and operates in a business environment that is similar to Battery's. The top management of Exide is considering evaluating Praveen on the basis of Exide's ROI minus Supreme's ROI. Praveen complains that this approach is unfair because the performance of another company, over which he has no control, is included in his performance-evaluation measure. Is Praveen's complaint valid? Why or why not?

3. Now suppose that Praveen has no authority for making capital-investment decisions. Corporate management makes these decisions. Is ROI a good performance measure to use to evaluate Praveen? Is ROI a good measure to evaluate the economic viability of the Battery Division? Explain.

4. Battery's salespersons are responsible for selling and providing customer service and support. Sales are easy to measure. Although customer service is important to Battery in the long run, it has not yet implemented customer-service measures. Praveen wants to compensate his sales force only on the basis of sales commissions paid for each unit of product sold. He cites two advantages to this plan: (a) It creates strong incentives for the sales force to work hard, and (b) the company pays salespersons only when the company itself is earning revenues. Do you like his plan? Why or why not?

23-36 Multinational firms, differing risk, comparison of profit, ROI and RI. Suzlon Energy has divisions in the United States, Germany, and New Zealand. The U.S. division is the oldest and most established of the three, and has a cost of capital of 6%. The German division was started three years ago when the exchange rate for euros was 1 euro = $1.25. Although it is a large and powerful division of Suzlon Energy its cost of capital is 10%. The New Zealand division was started this year, when the exchange rate was 1 New Zealand Dollar (NZD) = $$0.64. Its cost of capital is 13%. Average exchange rates for the current year are 1 euro=$1.32 and 1 New Zealand dollar = $0.67. Other information for the three divisions includes:

	United States	Germany	New Zealand
Long term assets	$1,48,45,000	98,56,000 euros	90,72,917 NZD
Operating revenues	$1,04,79,000	52,00,000 euros	48,00,000 NZD
Operating expenses	$72,10,000	34,00,000 euros	34,00,000 NZD
Income expense	$3,00,000	2,00,000 euros	1,00,000 NZD
Income tax rate	40%	30%	20%

Required

1. Translate the German and New Zealand information into dollars. Find the net income for each division and compare the profits.
2. Calculate ROI using net income. Compare among divisions.
3. Use the individual cost of capital of each division to calculate residual income and compare.
4. Redo requirement 2 using pretax operating income instead of net income. Why is there a big difference, and what does it mean for performance evaluation?

23-37 Executive compensation, balanced scorecard. HDFC Bank recently introduced a new bonus plan for its business unit executives. The company believes that current profitability and customer satisfaction levels are equally important to the bank's long-term success. As a result, the new plan awards a bonus equal to 1% of salary for each 1% increase in net income or 1% increase in the company's customer satisfaction index. For example, increasing net income from ₹3 crore to ₹3.3 crore (or 10% from its initial value) leads to a bonus of 10% of salary, while increasing the bank's customer satisfaction index from 70 to 73.5 (or 5% from its initial value) leads to a bonus of 5% of salary. There is no bonus penalty when net income or customer satisfaction declines. In 2014 and 2015, HDFC Bank's three business units reported the following performance results:

	Retail Banking		Business Banking		Credit Cards	
	2014	2015	2014	2015	2014	2015
Net income	₹2,80,00,000	₹3,22,00,000	₹2,90,00,000	₹3,01,60,000	₹2,75,00,000	₹2,72,25,000
Customer satisfaction	73	73	70	75.6	69	79.35

Required

1. Compute the bonus as a percent of salary earned by each business unit executive in 2015.
2. What factors might explain the different improvement rates for net income and customer satisfaction in the three units?
3. HDFC Bank's board of directors is concerned that the 2015 bonus awards may not actually reflect the executives' overall performance. In particular, it is concerned that executives can earn large bonuses by doing well on one performance dimension but underperforming on the other. What changes can it make to the bonus plan to prevent this from happening in the future? Explain briefly.

23-38 Ethics, manager's performance evaluation. (A. Spero, adapted) Tarla Semiconductors manufactures specialized chips that sell for ₹200 each. Tarla's manufacturing costs consist of variable cost of ₹20 per chip and fixed costs of ₹9,00,00,000. Tarla also incurs ₹40,00,000 in fixed marketing costs each year.

Tarla calculates operating income using absorption costing—that is, Tarla calculates manufacturing cost per unit by dividing total manufacturing costs by actual production. Tarla costs all units in inventory at this rate and expenses the costs in the income statement at the time when the units in inventory are sold. Next year, 2016, appears to be a difficult year for Tarla. It expects to sell only 5,00,000 units. The demand for these chips fluctuates considerably, so Tarla usually holds minimal inventory.

Required

1. Calculate Tarla's operating income in 2016 (a) if Tarla manufactures 5,00,000 units and (b) if Tarla manufactures 6,00,000 units.

2. Would it be unethical for Sunil Jalan, the general manager of Tarla Semiconductors, to produce more units than can be sold in order to show better operating results? Jalan's compensation has a bonus component based on operating income. Explain your answer.

3. Would it be unethical for Jalan to ask distributors to buy more product than they need? Tarla follows the industry practice of booking sales when products are transported to distributors. Explain your answer.

Appendix: Notes on Compound Interest and Interest Tables

Interest is the cost of using money. It is the rental charge for funds, just as renting a building and equipment entails a rental charge. When the funds are used for a period of time, it is necessary to recognize interest as a cost of using the borrowed ("rented") funds. This requirement applies even if the funds represent ownership capital and if interest does not entail an outlay of cash. Why must interest be considered? Because the selection of one alternative automatically commits a given amount of funds that could otherwise be invested in some other alternative.

Interest is generally important, even when short-term projects are under consideration. Interest looms correspondingly larger when long-run plans are studied. The rate of interest has significant enough impact to influence decisions regarding borrowing and investing funds. For example, ₹1,00,000 invested now and compounded annually for 10 years at 8% will accumulate to ₹2,15,900; at 20%, the ₹1,00,000 will accumulate to ₹6,19,200.

Interest Tables

Many computer programs and pocket calculators are available that handle computations involving the time value of money. You may also turn to the following four basic tables to compute interest.

Table 1—Future Amount of ₹1

Table 1 shows how much ₹1 invested now will accumulate in a given number of periods at a given compounded interest rate per period. Consider investing ₹1,000 now for three years at 8% compound interest. A tabular presentation of how this ₹1,000 would accumulate to ₹1,259.70 follows:

Year	Interest per Year	Cumulative Interest Called Compound Interest	Total at End of Year
0	₹—	₹—	₹1,000.00
1	80.00 (0.08 × ₹1,000)	80.00	1,080.00
2	86.40 (0.08 × ₹1,080)	166.40	1,166.40
3	93.30 (0.08 × ₹1,166.40)	259.70	1,259.70

This tabular presentation is a series of computations that could appear as follows, where S is the future amount and the subscripts 1, 2, and 3 indicate the number of time periods.

$$S_1 = ₹1,000(1.08)^1 = ₹1,080$$
$$S_2 = ₹1,080(1.08) = ₹1,000(1.08)^2 = ₹1,166.40$$
$$S_3 = ₹1,166.40 \times (1.08) = ₹1,000(1.08)^3 = ₹1,259.70$$

The formula for the "amount of 1," often called the "future value of ₹1" or "future amount of ₹1," can be written

$$S = P(1 + r)^n$$
$$S = ₹1,000(1 + .08)^3 = ₹1,259.70$$

S is the future value amount; P is the present value, ₹1,000 in this case; r is the rate of interest; and n is the number of time periods.

Fortunately, tables make key computations readily available. A facility in selecting the *proper* table will minimize computations. Check the accuracy of the preceding answer using Table 1.

Table 2—Present Value of ₹1

In the previous example, if ₹1,000 compounded at 8% per year will accumulate to ₹1,259.70 in 3 years, then ₹1,000 must be the present value of ₹1,259.70 due at the end of 3 years. The formula for the present value can be derived by reversing the process of *accumulation* (finding the future amount) that we just finished.

if

$$S = P(1 + r)^n$$

then

$$P = \frac{S}{(1 + r)^n}$$

$$P = \frac{₹1,259.70}{(1.08)^3} = ₹1,000$$

Use Table 2 to check this calculation.

When accumulating, we advance or roll forward in time. The difference between our original amount and our accumulated amount is called *compound interest*. When discounting, we retreat or roll back in time. The difference between the future amount and the present value is called *compound discount*. Note the following formulas (where $P = ₹1,000$):

$$\text{Compound interest} = P[(1 + r)^n - 1] = ₹259.70$$

$$\text{Compound discount} = S\left[1 - \frac{1}{(1 + r)^n}\right] = ₹259.70$$

Table 3—Compound Amount of (Future Value) Annuity of ₹1

An (ordinary) *annuity* is a series of equal payments (receipts) to be paid (or received) at the end of successive periods of equal length. Assume that ₹1,000 is invested at the end of each of 3 years at 8%:

0	1	2	3

End of Year		Amount
1st payment	₹1,000.00 → ₹1,080.00 →	₹1,166.40, which is ₹1,000(1.08)²
2nd payment	₹1,000,00 →	1,080.00, which is ₹1,000(1.08)¹
3rd payment		1,000.00
Accumulation (future amount)		₹3,246.40

The preceding arithmetic may be expressed algebraically as the amount of an ordinary annuity of ₹1,000 for 3 years $= ₹1,000(1 + r)^2 + ₹1,000(1 + r)^1 + ₹1,000$.

We can develop the general formula for S_n, the amount of an ordinary annuity of ₹1, by using the example above as a basis where $n = 3$ and $r = 0.08$:

1. $S_n = 1 + (1 + r)\,1 + (1 + r)^2$
2. Substitute: $S_n = 1 + (1.08)^1 + (1.08)^2$
3. Multiply (2) by $(1 + r)$: $(1.08)S_n = (1.08)^1 + (1.08)^2 + (1.08)^3$
4. Subtract (2) from (3): $(1.08)S_n - S_n = (1.08)^3 - 1$
   Note that all terms on
   the right-hand side are
   removed except $(1.08)^3$

in equation (3) and 1 in equation (2).

$$S_n(1.08 - 1) = (1.08)^3 - 1$$

5. Factor (4):

$$S_n = \frac{(1.08)^3 - 1}{1.08 - 1} = \frac{(1.08)^3 - 1}{.08}$$

6. Divide (5) by (1.08 - 1):

$$S_n = \frac{(1 + r)^n - 1}{r} \text{ or } \frac{\text{Compound interest}}{\text{Rate}}$$

7. The general formula for the amount of an ordinary annuity of ₹1 becomes:

This formula is the basis for Table 3. Look at Table 3 or use the formula itself to check the calculations.

Table 4—Present Value of an Ordinary Annuity of ₹1

Using the same example as for Table 3, we can show how the formula of P_n, *the present value of an ordinary annuity,* is developed.

End of Year			0	1	2	3
1st payment	$\frac{1,000}{(1.08)^1}$ =	₹926.14 ←		₹1,000		
2nd payment	$\frac{1,000}{(1.08)^2}$ =	₹857.52 ←			₹1,000	
3rd payment	$\frac{1,000}{(1.08)^3}$ =	₹794.00 ←				₹1,000
Total present value		₹2,577.66				

For the general case, the present value of an ordinary annuity of ₹1 may be expressed as:

1.

$$P_n = \frac{1}{1 + r} + \frac{1}{(1 + r)^2} + \frac{1}{(1 + r)^3}$$

2. Substitute

$$P_n = \frac{1}{1.08} + \frac{1}{(1.08)^2} + \frac{1}{(1.08)^3}$$

3. Multiply by

$$P_n = \frac{1}{1.08} = \frac{1}{(1.08)^2} + \frac{1}{(1.08)^3} + \frac{1}{(1.08)^4}$$

4. Subtract (3) from (2):

$$P_n - P_n\frac{1}{1.08} = \frac{1}{1.08} - \frac{1}{(1.08)^4}$$

5. Factor:

$$P_n\left(1 - \frac{1}{(1.08)}\right) = \frac{1}{1.08}\left[1 - \frac{1}{(1.08)^3}\right]$$

6. or

$$P_n\left(\frac{.08}{1.08}\right) = \frac{1}{1.08}\left[1 - \frac{1}{(1.08)^3}\right]$$

7. Multiply by $\frac{1.08}{.08}$

$$P_n = \frac{1}{.08}\left[1 - \frac{1}{(1.08)^3}\right]$$

The general formula for the present value of an annuity of ₹1.00 is:

$$P_n = \frac{1}{r}\left[1 - \frac{1}{(1 + r)^n}\right] = \frac{\text{Compound discount}}{\text{Rate}}$$

Solving,

$$P_n = \frac{.2062}{.08} = 2.577$$

The formula is the basis for Table 4. Check the answer in the table. The present value tables, Tables 2 and 4, are used most frequently in capital budgeting.

The tables for annuities are not essential. With Tables 1 and 2, compound interest and compound discount can readily be computed. It is simply a matter of dividing either of these by the rate to get values equivalent to those shown in Tables 3 and 4.

Table 1

Compound Amount of ₹1.00 (The Future Value of ₹1.00)

$S = P(1 + r)^n$. In this table $P = ₹1.00$

Periods	2%	4%	6%	8%	10%	12%	14%	16%	18%	20%	22%	24%	26%	28%	30%	32%	40%	Periods
1	1.020	1.040	1.060	1.080	1.100	1.120	1.140	1.160	1.180	1.200	1.220	1.240	1.260	1.280	1.300	1.320	1.400	1
2	1.040	1.082	1.124	1.166	1.210	1.254	1.300	1.346	1.392	1.440	1.488	1.538	1.588	1.638	1.690	1.742	1.960	2
3	1.061	1.125	1.191	1.260	1.331	1.405	1.482	1.561	1.643	1.728	1.816	1.907	2.000	2.097	2.197	2.300	2.744	3
4	1.082	1.170	1.262	1.360	1.464	1.574	1.689	1.811	1.939	2.074	2.215	2.364	2.520	2.684	2.856	3.036	3.842	4
5	1.104	1.217	1.338	1.469	1.611	1.762	1.925	2.100	2.288	2.488	2.703	2.932	3.176	3.436	3.713	4.007	5.378	5
6	1.126	1.265	1.419	1.587	1.772	1.974	2.195	2.436	2.700	2.986	3.297	3.635	4.002	4.398	4.827	5.290	7.530	6
7	1.149	1.316	1.504	1.714	1.949	2.211	2.502	2.826	3.185	3.583	4.023	4.508	5.042	5.629	6.275	6.983	10.541	7
8	1.172	1.369	1.594	1.851	2.144	2.476	2.853	3.278	3.759	4.300	4.908	5.590	6.353	7.206	8.157	9.217	14.758	8
9	1.195	1.423	1.689	1.999	2.358	2.773	3.252	3.803	4.435	5.160	5.987	6.931	8.005	9.223	10.604	12.166	20.661	9
10	1.219	1.480	1.791	2.159	2.594	3.106	3.707	4.411	5.234	6.192	7.305	8.594	10.086	11.806	13.786	16.060	28.925	10
11	1.243	1.539	1.898	2.332	2.853	3.479	4.226	5.117	6.176	7.430	8.912	10.657	12.708	15.112	17.922	21.199	40.496	11
12	1.268	1.601	2.012	2.518	3.138	3.896	4.818	5.936	7.288	8.916	10.872	13.215	16.012	19.343	23.298	27.983	56.694	12
13	1.294	1.665	2.133	2.720	3.452	4.363	5.492	6.886	8.599	10.699	13.264	16.386	20.175	24.759	30.288	36.937	79.371	13
14	1.319	1.732	2.261	2.937	3.797	4.887	6.261	7.988	10.147	12.839	16.182	20.319	25.421	31.691	39.374	48.757	111.120	14
15	1.346	1.801	2.397	3.172	4.177	5.474	7.138	9.266	11.974	15.407	19.742	25.196	32.030	40.565	51.186	64.359	155.568	15
16	1.373	1.873	2.540	3.426	4.595	6.130	8.137	10.748	14.129	18.488	24.086	31.243	40.358	51.923	66.542	84.954	217.795	16
17	1.400	1.948	2.693	3.700	5.054	6.866	9.276	12.468	16.672	22.186	29.384	38.741	50.851	66.461	86.504	112.139	304.913	17
18	1.428	2.026	2.854	3.996	5.560	7.690	10.575	14.463	19.673	26.623	35.849	48.039	64.072	85.071	112.455	148.024	426.879	18
19	1.457	2.107	3.026	4.316	6.116	8.613	12.056	16.777	23.214	31.948	43.736	59.568	80.731	108.890	146.192	195.391	597.630	19
20	1.486	2.191	3.207	4.661	6.727	9.646	13.743	19.461	27.393	38.338	53.358	73.864	101.721	139.380	190.050	257.916	836.683	20
21	1.516	2.279	3.400	5.034	7.400	10.804	15.668	22.574	32.324	46.005	65.096	91.592	128.169	178.406	247.065	340.449	1171.356	21
22	1.546	2.370	3.604	5.437	8.140	12.100	17.861	26.186	38.142	55.206	79.418	113.574	161.492	228.360	321.184	449.393	1639.898	22
23	1.577	2.465	3.820	5.871	8.954	13.552	20.362	30.376	45.008	66.247	96.889	140.831	203.480	292.300	417.539	593.199	2295.857	23
24	1.608	2.563	4.049	6.341	9.850	15.179	23.212	35.236	53.109	79.497	118.205	174.631	256.385	374.144	542.801	783.023	3214.200	24
25	1.641	2.666	4.292	6.848	10.835	17.000	26.462	40.874	62.669	95.396	144.210	216.542	323.045	478.905	705.641	1033.590	4499.880	25
26	1.673	2.772	4.549	7.396	11.918	19.040	30.167	47.414	73.949	114.475	175.936	268.512	407.037	612.998	917.333	1364.339	6299.831	26
27	1.707	2.883	4.822	7.988	13.110	21.325	34.390	55.000	87.260	137.371	214.642	332.955	512.867	784.638	1192.533	1800.927	8819.764	27
28	1.741	2.999	5.112	8.627	14.421	23.884	39.204	63.800	102.967	164.845	261.864	412.864	646.212	1004.336	1550.293	2377.224	12347.670	28
29	1.776	3.119	5.418	9.317	15.863	26.750	44.693	74.009	121.501	197.814	319.474	511.952	814.228	1285.550	2015.381	3137.935	17286.737	29
30	1.811	3.243	5.743	10.063	17.449	29.960	50.950	85.850	143.371	237.376	389.758	634.820	1025.927	1645.505	2619.996	4142.075	24201.432	30
35	2.000	3.946	7.686	14.785	28.102	52.800	98.100	180.314	327.997	590.668	1053.402	1861.054	3258.135	5653.911	9727.860	16599.217	130161.112	35
40	2.208	4.801	10.286	21.725	45.259	93.051	188.884	378.721	750.378	1469.772	2847.038	5455.913	10347.175	19426.689	36118.865	66520.767	700037.697	40

Table 2 (Place a clip on this page for easy reference.)

Present Value of ₹1.00

$$P = \frac{S}{(1 + r)^n}. \text{ In this table } S = ₹1.00$$

Periods	2%	4%	6%	8%	10%	12%	14%	16%	18%	20%	22%	24%	26%	28%	30%	32%	40%	Periods
1	0.980	0.962	0.943	0.926	0.909	0.893	0.877	0.862	0.847	0.833	0.820	0.806	0.794	0.781	0.769	0.758	0.714	1
2	0.961	0.925	0.890	0.857	0.826	0.797	0.769	0.743	0.718	0.694	0.672	0.650	0.630	0.610	0.592	0.574	0.510	2
3	0.942	0.889	0.840	0.794	0.751	0.712	0.675	0.641	0.609	0.579	0.551	0.524	0.500	0.477	0.455	0.435	0.364	3
4	0.924	0.855	0.792	0.735	0.683	0.636	0.592	0.552	0.516	0.482	0.451	0.423	0.397	0.373	0.350	0.329	0.260	4
5	0.906	0.822	0.747	0.681	0.621	0.567	0.519	0.476	0.437	0.402	0.370	0.341	0.315	0.291	0.269	0.250	0.186	5
6	0.888	0.790	0.705	0.630	0.564	0.507	0.456	0.410	0.370	0.335	0.303	0.275	0.250	0.227	0.207	0.189	0.133	6
7	0.871	0.760	0.665	0.583	0.513	0.452	0.400	0.354	0.314	0.279	0.249	0.222	0.198	0.178	0.159	0.143	0.095	7
8	0.853	0.731	0.627	0.540	0.467	0.404	0.351	0.305	0.266	0.233	0.204	0.179	0.157	0.139	0.123	0.108	0.068	8
9	0.837	0.703	0.592	0.500	0.424	0.361	0.308	0.263	0.225	0.194	0.167	0.144	0.125	0.108	0.094	0.082	0.048	9
10	0.820	0.676	0.558	0.463	0.386	0.322	0.270	0.227	0.191	0.162	0.137	0.116	0.099	0.085	0.073	0.062	0.035	10
11	0.804	0.650	0.527	0.429	0.350	0.287	0.237	0.195	0.162	0.135	0.112	0.094	0.079	0.066	0.056	0.047	0.025	11
12	0.788	0.625	0.497	0.397	0.319	0.257	0.208	0.168	0.137	0.112	0.092	0.076	0.062	0.052	0.043	0.036	0.018	12
13	0.773	0.601	0.469	0.368	0.290	0.229	0.182	0.145	0.116	0.093	0.075	0.061	0.050	0.040	0.033	0.027	0.013	13
14	0.758	0.577	0.442	0.340	0.263	0.205	0.160	0.125	0.099	0.078	0.062	0.049	0.039	0.032	0.025	0.021	0.009	14
15	0.743	0.555	0.417	0.315	0.239	0.183	0.140	0.108	0.084	0.065	0.051	0.040	0.031	0.025	0.020	0.016	0.006	15
16	0.728	0.534	0.394	0.292	0.218	0.163	0.123	0.093	0.071	0.054	0.042	0.032	0.025	0.019	0.015	0.012	0.005	16
17	0.714	0.513	0.371	0.270	0.198	0.146	0.108	0.080	0.060	0.045	0.034	0.026	0.020	0.015	0.012	0.009	0.003	17
18	0.700	0.494	0.350	0.250	0.180	0.130	0.095	0.069	0.051	0.038	0.028	0.021	0.016	0.012	0.009	0.007	0.002	18
19	0.686	0.475	0.331	0.232	0.164	0.116	0.083	0.060	0.043	0.031	0.023	0.017	0.012	0.009	0.007	0.005	0.002	19
20	0.673	0.456	0.312	0.215	0.149	0.104	0.073	0.051	0.037	0.026	0.019	0.014	0.010	0.007	0.005	0.004	0.001	20
21	0.660	0.439	0.294	0.199	0.135	0.093	0.064	0.044	0.031	0.022	0.015	0.011	0.008	0.006	0.004	0.003	0.001	21
22	0.647	0.422	0.278	0.184	0.123	0.083	0.056	0.038	0.026	0.018	0.013	0.009	0.006	0.004	0.003	0.002	0.001	22
23	0.634	0.406	0.262	0.170	0.112	0.074	0.049	0.033	0.022	0.015	0.010	0.007	0.005	0.003	0.002	0.002	0.000	23
24	0.622	0.390	0.247	0.158	0.102	0.066	0.043	0.028	0.019	0.013	0.008	0.006	0.004	0.003	0.002	0.001	0.000	24
25	0.610	0.375	0.233	0.146	0.092	0.059	0.038	0.024	0.016	0.010	0.007	0.005	0.003	0.002	0.001	0.001	0.000	25
26	0.598	0.361	0.220	0.135	0.084	0.053	0.033	0.021	0.014	0.009	0.006	0.004	0.002	0.002	0.001	0.001	0.000	26
27	0.586	0.347	0.207	0.125	0.076	0.047	0.029	0.018	0.011	0.007	0.005	0.003	0.002	0.001	0.001	0.001	0.000	27
28	0.574	0.333	0.196	0.116	0.069	0.042	0.026	0.016	0.010	0.006	0.004	0.002	0.002	0.001	0.001	0.001	0.000	28
29	0.563	0.321	0.185	0.107	0.063	0.037	0.022	0.014	0.008	0.005	0.003	0.002	0.001	0.001	0.001	0.000	0.000	29
30	0.552	0.308	0.174	0.099	0.057	0.033	0.020	0.012	0.007	0.004	0.003	0.002	0.001	0.001	0.000	0.000	0.000	30
35	0.500	0.253	0.130	0.068	0.036	0.019	0.010	0.006	0.003	0.002	0.001	0.001	0.000	0.000	0.000	0.000	0.000	35
40	0.453	0.208	0.097	0.046	0.022	0.011	0.005	0.003	0.001	0.001	0.000	0.000	0.000	0.000	0.000	0.000	0.000	40

Table 3

Compound Amount of Annuity of ₹1.00 in Arrears* (Future Value of Annuity)

$$S_n = \frac{(1 + r)^n - 1}{r}$$

Periods	2%	4%	6%	8%	10%	12%	14%	16%	18%	20%	22%	24%	26%	28%	30%	32%	40%	Periods
1	1.000	1.000	1.000	1.000	1.000	1.000	1.000	1.000	1.000	1.000	1.000	1.000	1.000	1.000	1.000	1.000	1.000	1
2	2.020	2.040	2.060	2.080	2.100	2.120	2.140	2.160	2.180	2.200	2.220	2.240	2.260	2.280	2.300	2.320	2.400	2
3	3.060	3.122	3.184	3.246	3.310	3.374	3.440	3.506	3.572	3.640	3.708	3.778	3.848	3.918	3.990	4.062	4.360	3
4	4.122	4.246	4.375	4.506	4.641	4.779	4.921	5.066	5.215	5.368	5.524	5.684	5.848	6.016	6.187	6.362	7.104	4
5	5.204	5.416	5.637	5.867	6.105	6.353	6.610	6.877	7.154	7.442	7.740	8.048	8.368	8.700	9.043	9.398	10.946	5
6	6.308	6.633	6.975	7.336	7.716	8.115	8.536	8.977	9.442	9.930	10.442	10.980	11.544	12.136	12.756	13.406	16.324	6
7	7.434	7.898	8.394	8.923	9.487	10.089	10.730	11.414	12.142	12.916	13.740	14.615	15.546	16.534	17.583	18.696	23.853	7
8	8.583	9.214	9.897	10.637	11.436	12.300	13.233	14.240	15.327	16.499	17.762	19.123	20.588	22.163	23.858	25.678	34.395	8
9	9.755	10.583	11.491	12.488	13.579	14.776	16.085	17.519	19.086	20.799	22.670	24.712	26.940	29.369	32.015	34.895	49.153	9
10	10.950	12.006	13.181	14.487	15.937	17.549	19.337	21.321	23.521	25.959	28.657	31.643	34.945	38.593	42.619	47.062	69.814	10
11	12.169	13.486	14.972	16.645	18.531	20.655	23.045	25.733	28.755	32.150	35.962	40.238	45.031	50.398	56.405	63.122	98.739	11
12	13.412	15.026	16.870	18.977	21.384	24.133	27.271	30.850	34.931	39.581	44.874	50.895	57.739	65.510	74.327	84.320	139.235	12
13	14.680	16.627	18.882	21.495	24.523	28.029	32.089	36.786	42.219	48.497	55.746	64.110	73.751	84.853	97.625	112.303	195.929	13
14	15.974	18.292	21.015	24.215	27.975	32.393	37.581	43.672	50.818	59.196	69.010	80.496	93.926	109.612	127.913	149.240	275.300	14
15	17.293	20.024	23.276	27.152	31.772	37.280	43.842	51.660	60.965	72.035	85.192	100.815	119.347	141.303	167.286	197.997	386.420	15
16	18.639	21.825	25.673	30.324	35.950	42.753	50.980	60.925	72.939	87.442	104.935	126.011	151.377	181.868	218.472	262.356	541.988	16
17	20.012	23.698	28.213	33.750	40.545	48.884	59.118	71.673	87.068	105.931	129.020	157.253	191.735	233.791	285.014	347.309	759.784	17
18	21.412	25.645	30.906	37.450	45.599	55.750	68.394	84.141	103.740	128.117	158.405	195.994	242.585	300.252	371.518	459.449	1064.697	18
19	22.841	27.671	33.760	41.446	51.159	63.440	78.969	98.603	123.414	154.740	194.254	244.033	306.658	385.323	483.973	607.472	1491.576	19
20	24.297	29.778	36.786	45.762	57.275	72.052	91.025	115.380	146.628	186.688	237.989	303.601	387.389	494.213	630.165	802.863	2089.206	20
21	25.783	31.969	39.993	50.423	64.002	81.699	104.768	134.841	174.021	225.026	291.347	377.465	489.110	633.593	820.215	1060.779	2925.889	21
22	27.299	34.248	43.392	55.457	71.403	92.503	120.436	157.415	206.345	271.031	356.443	469.056	617.278	811.999	1067.280	1401.229	4097.245	22
23	28.845	36.618	46.996	60.893	79.543	104.603	138.297	183.601	244.487	326.237	435.861	582.630	778.771	1040.358	1388.464	1850.622	5737.142	23
24	30.422	39.083	50.816	66.765	88.497	118.155	158.659	213.978	289.494	392.484	532.750	723.461	982.251	1332.659	1806.003	2443.821	8032.999	24
25	32.030	41.646	54.865	73.106	98.347	133.334	181.871	249.214	342.603	471.981	650.955	898.092	1238.636	1706.803	2348.803	3226.844	11247.199	25
26	33.671	44.312	59.156	79.954	109.182	150.334	208.333	290.088	405.272	567.377	795.165	1114.634	1561.682	2185.708	3054.444	4260.434	15747.079	26
27	35.344	47.084	63.706	87.351	121.100	169.374	238.499	337.502	479.221	681.853	971.102	1383.146	1968.719	2798.706	3971.778	5624.772	22046.910	27
28	37.051	49.968	68.528	95.339	134.210	190.699	272.889	392.503	566.481	819.223	1185.744	1716.101	2481.586	3583.344	5164.311	7425.699	30866.674	28
29	38.792	52.966	73.640	103.966	148.631	214.583	312.094	456.303	669.447	984.068	1447.608	2128.965	3127.798	4587.680	6714.604	9802.923	43214.343	29
30	40.568	56.085	79.058	113.263	164.494	241.333	356.787	530.312	790.948	1181.882	1767.081	2640.916	3942.026	5873.231	8729.985	12940.859	60501.081	30
35	49.994	73.652	111.435	172.317	271.024	431.663	693.573	1120.713	1816.652	2948.341	4783.645	7750.225	12527.442	20188.966	32422.868	51869.427	325400.279	35
40	60.402	95.026	154.762	259.057	442.593	767.091	1342.025	2360.757	4163.213	7343.858	12936.535	22728.803	39792.982	69377.460	120392.883	207874.272	1750091.741	40

*Payments (or receipts) at the end of each period.

Table 4 (Place a clip on this page for easy reference.)

Present Value of Annuity ₹1.00 in Arrears*

$$P_n = \frac{1}{r}\left[1 - \frac{1}{(1+r)^n}\right]$$

Periods	2%	4%	6%	8%	10%	12%	14%	16%	18%	20%	22%	24%	26%	28%	30%	32%	40%	Periods
1	0.980	0.962	0.943	0.926	0.909	0.893	0.877	0.862	0.847	0.833	0.820	0.806	0.794	0.781	0.769	0.758	0.714	1
2	1.942	1.886	1.833	1.783	1.736	1.690	1.647	1.605	1.566	1.528	1.492	1.457	1.424	1.392	1.361	1.331	1.224	2
3	2.884	2.775	2.673	2.577	2.487	2.402	2.322	2.246	2.174	2.106	2.042	1.981	1.923	1.868	1.816	1.766	1.589	3
4	3.808	3.630	3.465	3.312	3.170	3.037	2.914	2.798	2.690	2.589	2.494	2.404	2.320	2.241	2.166	2.096	1.849	4
5	4.713	4.452	4.212	3.993	3.791	3.605	3.433	3.274	3.127	2.991	2.864	2.745	2.635	2.532	2.436	2.345	2.035	5
6	5.601	5.242	4.917	4.623	4.355	4.111	3.889	3.685	3.498	3.326	3.167	3.020	2.885	2.759	2.643	2.534	2.168	6
7	6.472	6.002	5.582	5.206	4.868	4.564	4.288	4.039	3.812	3.605	3.416	3.242	3.083	2.937	2.802	2.677	2.263	7
8	7.325	6.733	6.210	5.747	5.335	4.968	4.639	4.344	4.078	3.837	3.619	3.421	3.241	3.076	2.925	2.786	2.331	8
9	8.162	7.435	6.802	6.247	5.759	5.328	4.946	4.607	4.303	4.031	3.786	3.566	3.366	3.184	3.019	2.868	2.379	9
10	8.983	8.111	7.360	6.710	6.145	5.650	5.216	4.833	4.494	4.192	3.923	3.682	3.465	3.269	3.092	2.930	2.414	10
11	9.787	8.760	7.887	7.139	6.495	5.938	5.453	5.029	4.656	4.327	4.035	3.776	3.543	3.335	3.147	2.978	2.438	11
12	10.575	9.385	8.384	7.536	6.814	6.194	5.660	5.197	4.793	4.439	4.127	3.851	3.606	3.387	3.190	3.013	2.456	12
13	11.348	9.986	8.853	7.904	7.103	6.424	5.842	5.342	4.910	4.533	4.203	3.912	3.656	3.427	3.223	3.040	2.469	13
14	12.106	10.563	9.295	8.244	7.367	6.628	6.002	5.468	5.008	4.611	4.265	3.962	3.695	3.459	3.249	3.061	2.478	14
15	12.849	11.118	9.712	8.559	7.606	6.811	6.142	5.575	5.092	4.675	4.315	4.001	3.726	3.483	3.268	3.076	2.484	15
16	13.578	11.652	10.106	8.851	7.824	6.974	6.265	5.668	5.162	4.730	4.357	4.033	3.751	3.503	3.283	3.088	2.489	16
17	14.292	12.166	10.477	9.122	8.022	7.120	6.373	5.749	5.222	4.775	4.391	4.059	3.771	3.518	3.295	3.097	2.492	17
18	14.992	12.659	10.828	9.372	8.201	7.250	6.467	5.818	5.273	4.812	4.419	4.080	3.786	3.529	3.304	3.104	2.494	18
19	15.678	13.134	11.158	9.604	8.365	7.366	6.550	5.877	5.316	4.843	4.442	4.097	3.799	3.539	3.311	3.109	2.496	19
20	16.351	13.590	11.470	9.818	8.514	7.469	6.623	5.929	5.353	4.870	4.460	4.110	3.808	3.546	3.316	3.113	2.497	20
21	17.011	14.029	11.764	10.017	8.649	7.562	6.687	5.973	5.384	4.891	4.476	4.121	3.816	3.551	3.320	3.116	2.498	21
22	17.658	14.451	12.042	10.201	8.772	7.645	6.743	6.011	5.410	4.909	4.488	4.130	3.822	3.556	3.323	3.118	2.498	22
23	18.292	14.857	12.303	10.371	8.883	7.718	6.792	6.044	5.432	4.925	4.499	4.137	3.827	3.559	3.325	3.120	2.499	23
24	18.914	15.247	12.550	10.529	8.985	7.784	6.835	6.073	5.451	4.937	4.507	4.143	3.831	3.562	3.327	3.121	2.499	24
25	19.523	15.622	12.783	10.675	9.077	7.843	6.873	6.097	5.467	4.948	4.514	4.147	3.834	3.564	3.329	3.122	2.499	25
26	20.121	15.983	13.003	10.810	9.161	7.896	6.906	6.118	5.480	4.956	4.520	4.151	3.837	3.566	3.330	3.123	2.500	26
27	20.707	16.330	13.211	10.935	9.237	7.943	6.935	6.136	5.492	4.964	4.524	4.154	3.839	3.567	3.331	3.123	2.500	27
28	21.281	16.663	13.406	11.051	9.307	7.984	6.961	6.152	5.502	4.970	4.528	4.157	3.840	3.568	3.331	3.124	2.500	28
29	21.844	16.984	13.591	11.158	9.370	8.022	6.983	6.166	5.510	4.975	4.531	4.159	3.841	3.569	3.332	3.124	2.500	29
30	22.396	17.292	13.765	11.258	9.427	8.055	7.003	6.177	5.517	4.979	4.534	4.160	3.842	3.569	3.332	3.124	2.500	30
35	24.999	18.665	14.498	11.655	9.644	8.176	7.070	6.215	5.539	4.992	4.541	4.164	3.845	3.571	3.333	3.125	2.500	35
40	27.355	19.793	15.046	11.925	9.779	8.244	7.105	6.233	5.548	4.997	4.544	4.166	3.846	3.571	3.333	3.125	2.500	40

*Payments (or receipts) at the end of each period.

Glossary

Abnormal spoilage. Spoilage that would not arise under efficient operating conditions; it is not inherent in a particular production process. (947)

Absorption costing. Method of inventory costing in which all variable manufacturing costs and all fixed manufacturing costs are included as inventoriable costs. (452)

Account analysis method. Approach to cost function estimation that classifies various cost accounts as variable, fixed, or mixed with respect to the identified level of activity. Typically, qualitative rather than quantitative analysis is used when making these cost-classification decisions. (517)

Accrual accounting rate-of-return (AARR). Capital budgeting method that divides an accrual accounting measure of average annual income of a project by an accrual accounting measure of its investment. See also *return on investment (ROI)*. (1106)

Activity. An event, task, or unit of work with a specified purpose. (8)

Activity-based budgeting (ABB). Budgeting approach that focuses on the budgeted cost of the activities necessary to produce and sell products and services. (276)

Activity-based costing (ABC). Approach to costing that focuses on individual activities as the fundamental cost objects. It uses the costs of these activities as the basis for assigning costs to other cost objects such as products or services. (208)

Activity-based management (ABM). Method of management decision-making that uses activity-based costing information to improve customer satisfaction and profitability. (220)

Actual cost. Cost incurred (a historical or past cost), as distinguished from a budgeted or forecasted cost. (36)

Actual costing. A costing system that traces direct costs to a cost object by using the actual direct-cost rates times the actual quantities of the direct-cost inputs and allocates indirect costs based on the actual indirect-cost rates times the actual quantities of the cost allocation bases. (149)

Actual indirect-cost rate. Actual total indirect costs in a cost pool divided by the actual total quantity of the cost-allocation base for that cost pool. (150)

Adjusted allocation-rate approach. Restates all overhead entries in the general ledger and subsidiary ledgers using actual cost rates rather than budgeted cost rates. (159)

Appraisal costs. Costs incurred to detect which of the individual units of products do not conform to specifications. (996)

Artificial costs. See *complete reciprocated costs*. (817)

Autonomy. The degree of freedom to make decisions. (1148)

Average cost. See *unit cost*. (44)

Average waiting time. The average amount of time that an order will wait in line before the machine is set up and the order is processed. (1007)

Backflush costing. Costing system that omits recording some of the journal entries relating to the stages from purchase of direct materials to the sale of finished goods. (1059)

Balanced scorecard. A framework for implementing strategy that translates an organization's mission and strategy into a set of performance measures. (634)

Batch-level costs. The costs of activities related to a group of units of products or services rather than to each individual unit of product or service. (211)

Belief systems. Lever of control that articulates the mission, purpose, norms of behaviors, and core values of a company intended to inspire managers and other employees to do their best. (1219)

Benchmarking. The continuous process of comparing the levels of performance in producing products and services and executing activities against the best levels of performance in competing companies or in companies having similar processes. (350)

Book value. The original cost minus accumulated depreciation of an asset. (594)

Bottleneck. An operation where the work to be performed approaches or exceeds the capacity available to do it. (1006)

Boundary systems. Lever of control that describes standards of behavior and codes of conduct expected of all employees, especially actions that are off-limits. (1218)

Breakeven point (BEP). Quantity of output sold at which total revenues equal total costs, that is where the operating income is zero. (93)

Budget. Quantitative expression of a proposed plan of action by management for a specified period and an aid to coordinating what needs to be done to implement that plan. (10)

1257

Budgetary slack. The practice of underestimating budgeted revenues, or overestimating budgeted costs, to make budgeted targets more easily achievable. (292)

Budgeted cost. Predicted or forecasted cost (future cost) as distinguished from an actual or historical cost. (36)

Budgeted indirect-cost rate. Budgeted annual indirect costs in a cost pool divided by the budgeted annual quantity of the cost allocation base. (144, 147)

Budgeted performance. Expected performance or a point of reference to compare actual results. (332)

Bundled product. A package of two or more products (or services) that is sold for a single price, but whose individual components may be sold as separate items at their own "stand-alone" prices. (825)

Business function costs. The sum of all costs (variable and fixed) in a particular business function of the value chain. (574)

Byproducts. Products from a joint production process that have low total sales values compared with the total sales value of the main product or of joint products. (848)

Capital budgeting. The making of long-run planning decisions for investments in projects. (1094)

Carrying costs. Costs that arise while holding inventory of goods for sale. (1043)

Cash budget. Schedule of expected cash receipts and disbursements. (276)

Cause-and-effect diagram. Diagram that identifies potential causes of defects. Four categories of potential causes of failure are human factors, methods and design factors, machine-related factors, and materials and components factors. Also called a *fishbone diagram*. (1000)

Chief financial officer (CFO). Executive responsible for overseeing the financial operations of an organization. Also called *finance director*. (14)

Common cost. Cost of operating a facility, activity, or like cost object that is shared by two or more users. (822)

Complete reciprocated costs. The support department's own costs plus any interdepartmental cost allocations. Also called the *artificial costs* of the support department. (817)

Composite unit. Hypothetical unit with weights based on the mix of individual units. (767)

Conference method. Approach to cost function estimation on the basis of analysis and opinions about costs and their drivers gathered from various departments of a company (purchasing, process engineering, manufacturing, employee relations, and so on). (516)

Conformance quality. Refers to the performance of a product or service relative to its design and product specifications. (995)

Constant. The component of total cost that, within the relevant range, does not vary with changes in the level of the activity. Also called *intercept*. (512)

Constant gross-margin percentage NRV method. Method that allocates joint costs to joint products in such a way that the overall gross-margin percentage is identical for the individual products. (856)

Constraint. A mathematical inequality or equality that must be satisfied by the variables in a mathematical model. (587)

Continuous budget. See *rolling budget*. (275)

Contribution income statement. Income statement that groups costs into variable costs and fixed costs to highlight the contribution margin. (88)

Contribution margin. Total revenues minus total variable costs. (88)

Contribution margin per unit. Selling price minus the variable cost per unit. (88)

Contribution margin percentage. Contribution margin per unit divided by selling price. Also called *contribution margin ratio*. (89)

Contribution margin ratio. See *contribution margin percentage*. (89)

Control. Taking actions that implement the planning decisions, deciding how to evaluate performance, and providing feedback and learning that will help future decision making. (11)

Control chart. Graph of a series of successive observations of a particular step, procedure, or operation taken at regular intervals of time. Each observation is plotted relative to specified ranges that represent the limits within which observations are expected to fall. (999)

Controllability. Degree of influence that a specific manager has over costs, revenues, or related items for which he or she is responsible. (290)

Controllable cost. Any cost that is primarily subject to the influence of a given responsibility center manager for a given period. (290)

Controller. The financial executive primarily responsible for management accounting and financial accounting. Also called *chief accounting officer*. (14)

Conversion costs. All manufacturing costs other than direct material costs. (53)

Cost. Resource sacrificed or forgone to achieve a specific objective. (29)

Cost accounting. Measures, analyzes, and reports financial and nonfinancial information relating to the costs of acquiring or using resources in an organization. It provides information for both management accounting and financial accounting. (4)

Cost accumulation. Collection of cost data in some organized way by means of an accounting system. (4)

Cost allocation. Assignment of indirect costs to a particular cost object. (38)

Cost-allocation base. A factor that links in a systematic way an indirect cost or group of indirect costs to a cost object. (139)

Cost-application base. Cost-allocation base when the cost object is a job, product, or customer. (139)

Cost assignment. General term that encompasses both (1) tracing accumulated costs that have a direct relationship to a cost object and (2) allocating accumulated costs that have an indirect relationship to a cost object. (38)

Cost–benefit approach. Approach to decision-making and resource allocation based on a comparison of the expected benefits from attaining company goals and the expected costs. (12)

Cost center. Responsibility center where the manager is accountable for costs only. (289)

Cost driver. A variable, such as the level of activity or volume, that causally affects costs over a given time span. (41)

Cost estimation. The attempt to measure a past relationship based on data from past costs and the related level of an activity. (514)

Cost function. Mathematical description of how a cost changes with changes in the level of an activity relating to that cost. (510)

Cost hierarchy. Categorization of indirect costs into different cost pools on the basis of the different types of cost drivers, or cost-allocation bases, or different degrees of difficulty in determining cause-and-effect (or benefits received) relationships. (211)

Cost incurrence. Describes when a resource is consumed (or benefit forgone) to meet a specific objective. (700)

Cost leadership. Organization's ability to achieve lower costs relative to competitors through productivity and efficiency improvements, elimination of waste, and tight cost control. (631)

Cost management. The approaches and activities of managers to use resources to increase value to customers and to achieve organizational goals. (4)

Cost object. Anything for which a measurement of costs is desired. (36)

Cost of capital. See *required rate of return (RRR)*. (1098)

Cost of goods manufactured. Cost of goods brought to completion, whether they were started before or during the current accounting period. (49)

Cost pool. A grouping of individual cost items. (139)

Cost predictions. Forecasts about future costs. (514)

Cost tracing. Describes the assignment of direct costs to a particular cost object. (37)

Costs of quality (COQ). Costs incurred to prevent, or the costs arising as a result of, the production of a low-quality product. (996)

Cost–volume–profit (CVP) analysis. Examines the behavior of total revenues, total costs, and operating income as changes occur in the units sold, the selling price, the variable cost per unit, or the fixed costs of a product. (86)

Cumulative average-time learning model. Learning curve model in which the cumulative average time per unit declines by a constant percentage each time the cumulative quantity of units produced doubles. (529)

Current cost. Asset measure based on the cost of purchasing an asset today identical to the one currently held, or the cost of purchasing an asset that provides services like the one currently held if an identical asset cannot be purchased. (1207)

Customer-cost hierarchy. Hierarchy that categorizes costs related to customers into different cost pools on the basis of different types of cost drivers, or cost-allocation bases, or different degrees of difficulty in determining cause-and-effect or benefits-received relationships. (746)

Customer life-cycle costs. Focuses on the total costs incurred by a customer to acquire, use, maintain, and dispose of a product or service. (709)

Customer-profitability analysis. The reporting and analysis of revenues earned from customers and the costs incurred to earn those revenues. (74)

Customer relationship management (CRM). A strategy that integrates people and technology in all business functions to deepen relationships with customers, partners, and distributors. (6)

Customer-response time. Duration from the time a customer places an order for a product or service to the time the product or service is delivered to the customer. (1005)

Customer service. Providing after-sale support to customers. (6)

Decentralization. The freedom for managers at lower levels of the organization to make decisions. (1150)

Decision model. Formal method for making a choice, often involving both quantitative and qualitative analyses. (570)

Degree of operating leverage. Contribution margin divided by operating income at any given level of sales. (102)

Denominator level. The denominator in the budgeted fixed overhead rate computation. (391)

Denominator-level variance. See *production-volume variance*. (398)

Dependent variable. The cost to be predicted. (519)

Design of products and processes. The detailed planning and engineering of products and processes. (5)

Design quality. Refers to how closely the characteristics of a product or service meet the needs and wants of customers. (995)

Designed-in costs. See *locked-in costs*. (700)

Diagnostic control systems. Lever of control that monitors critical performance variables that help managers track progress toward achieving a company's strategic goals. Managers are held accountable for meeting these goals. (1218)

Differential cost. Difference in total cost between two alternatives. (579)

Differential revenue. Difference in total revenue between two alternatives. (579)

Direct costing. See *variable costing*. (452)

Direct costs of a cost object. Costs related to the particular cost object that can be traced to that object in an economically feasible (cost-effective) way. (37)

Direct manufacturing labor costs. Include the compensation of all manufacturing labor that can be traced to the cost object (work in process and then finished goods) in an economically feasible way. (46)

Direct materials costs. Acquisition costs of all materials that eventually become part of the cost object (work in process and then finished goods), and that can be traced to the cost object in an economically feasible way. (46)

Direct materials inventory. Direct materials in stock and awaiting use in the manufacturing process. (46)

Direct method. Cost allocation method that allocates each support department's costs to operating departments only. (814)

Discount rate. See *required rate of return (RRR)*. (1098)

Discounted cash flow (DCF) methods. Capital budgeting methods that measure all expected future cash inflows and outflows of a project as if they occurred at the present point in time. (1097)

Discounted payback method. Capital budgeting method that calculates the amount of time required for the discounted expected future cash flows to recoup the net initial investment in a project. (1105)

Discretionary costs. Arise from periodic (usually annual) decisions regarding the maximum amount to be incurred and have no measurable cause-and-effect relationship between output and resources used. (655)

Distribution. Delivering products or services to customers. (6)

Downsizing. An integrated approach of configuring processes, products, and people to match costs to the activities that need to be performed to operate effectively and efficiently in the present and future. Also called *rightsizing*. (656)

Downward demand spiral. Pricing context where prices are raised to spread capacity costs over a smaller number of output units. Continuing reduction in the demand for products that occurs when the prices of competitors' products are not met and, as demand drops further, higher and higher unit costs result in more and more reluctance to meet competitors' prices. (470)

Dual pricing. Approach to transfer pricing using two separate transfer-pricing methods to price each transfer from one subunit to another. (1162)

Dual-rate method. Allocation method that classifies costs in each cost pool into two pools (a variable-cost pool and a fixed-cost pool) with each pool using a different cost-allocation base. (802)

Dysfunctional decision making. See *suboptimal decision making*. (1148)

Economic order quantity (EOQ). Decision model that calculates the optimal quantity of inventory to order under a set of assumptions. (1044)

Economic value added (EVA®). After-tax operating income minus the (after-tax) weighted-average cost of capital multiplied by total assets minus current liabilities. (1203)

Effectiveness. The degree to which a predetermined objective or target is met. (348)

Efficiency. The relative amount of inputs used to achieve a given output level. (348)

Efficiency variance. The difference between actual input quantity used and budgeted input quantity allowed for actual output, multiplied by budgeted price. Also called *usage variance*. (342)

Effort. Exertion toward achieving a goal. (1147)

Engineered costs. Costs that result from a cause-and-effect relationship between the cost driver, output, and the (direct or indirect) resources used to produce that output. (654)

Enterprise resource planning (ERP) system. An integrated set of software modules covering a company's accounting, distribution, manufacturing, purchasing, human resources, and other functions. (1057)

Equivalent units. Derived amount of output units that (a) takes the quantity of each input (factor of production) in units completed and in incomplete units of work in process and (b) converts the quantity of input into the amount of completed output units that could be produced with that quantity of input. (900)

Experience curve. Function that measures the decline in cost per unit in various business functions of the value chain, such as manufacturing, marketing, distribution, and so on, as the amount of these activities increases. (529)

External failure costs. Costs incurred on defective products after they are shipped to customers. (996)

Facility-sustaining costs. The costs of activities that cannot be traced to individual products or services but support the organization as a whole. (212)

Factory overhead costs. See *indirect manufacturing costs.* (46)

Favorable variance. Variance that has the effect of increasing operating income relative to the budgeted amount. Denoted F. (334)

Finance director. See *chief financial officer (CFO).* ((p. 14)

Financial accounting. Measures and records business transactions and provides financial statements that are based on generally accepted accounting principles. It focuses on reporting to external parties such as investors and banks. (p. 3)

Financial budget. Part of the master budget that focuses on how operations and planned capital outlays affect cash. It is made up of the capital expenditures budget, the cash budget, the budgeted balance sheet, and the budgeted statement of cash flows. (276)

Financial planning models. Mathematical representations of the relationships among operating activities, financial activities, and other factors that affect the master budget. (287)

Finished goods inventory. Goods completed but not yet sold. (46)

First-in, first-out (FIFO) process-costing method. Method of process costing that assigns the cost of the previous accounting period's equivalent units in beginning work-in-process inventory to the first units completed and transferred out of the process, and assigns the cost of equivalent units worked on during the current period first to complete beginning inventory, next to start and complete new units, and finally to units in ending work-in-process inventory. (908)

Fixed cost. Cost that remains unchanged in total for a given time period, despite wide changes in the related level of total activity or volume. (39)

Fixed overhead flexible-budget variance. The difference between actual fixed overhead costs and fixed overhead costs in the flexible budget. (397)

Fixed overhead spending variance. Same as the fixed overhead flexible-budget variance. The difference between actual fixed overhead costs and fixed overhead costs in the flexible budget. (397)

Flexible budget. Budget developed using budgeted revenues and budgeted costs based on the actual output in the budget period. (335)

Flexible-budget variance. The difference between an actual result and the corresponding flexible-budget amount based on the actual output level in the budget period. (336)

Full costs of the product. The sum of all variable and fixed costs in all business functions of the value chain (R&D, design, production, marketing, distribution, and customer service). (574)

Goal congruence. Exists when individuals and groups work toward achieving the organization's goals. Managers working in their own best interest take actions that align with the overall goals of top management. (1147)

Gross margin percentage. Gross margin divided by revenues. (108)

Growth component. Change in operating income attributable solely to the change in the quantity of output sold between one period and the next. (647)

High-low method. Method used to estimate a cost function that uses only the highest and lowest observed values of the cost driver within the relevant range and their respective costs. (520)

Homogeneous cost pool. Cost pool in which all the costs have the same or a similar cause-and-effect or benefits-received relationship with the cost-allocation base. (763

Hurdle rate. See *required rate of return (RRR).* (1098)

Hybrid-costing system. Costing system that blends characteristics from both job-costing systems and process-costing systems. (918)

Idle time. Wages paid for unproductive time caused by lack of orders, machine breakdowns, material shortages, poor scheduling, and the like. (55)

Imputed costs. Costs recognized in particular situations but not incorporated in financial accounting records. (1202)

Incongruent decision making. See *suboptimal decision making.* (1148)

Incremental cost. Additional total cost incurred for an activity. (579)

Incremental cost-allocation method. Method that ranks the individual users of a cost object in the order of users most responsible for the common cost and then uses this ranking to allocate cost among those users. (823)

Incremental revenue. Additional total revenue from an activity. (579)

Incremental revenue-allocation method. Method that ranks individual products in a bundle according to criteria determined by management (for example, sales), and then uses this ranking to allocate bundled revenues to the individual products. (826)

Incremental unit-time learning model. Learning curve model in which the incremental time needed to produce the last unit declines by a constant percentage each time the cumulative quantity of units produced doubles. (529)

Independent variable. Level of activity or cost driver used to predict the dependent variable (costs) in a cost estimation or prediction model. (519)

Indirect costs of a cost object. Costs related to the particular cost object that cannot be traced to that object in an economically feasible (cost-effective) way. (37)

Indirect manufacturing costs. All manufacturing costs that are related to the cost object (work in process and then finished goods) but that cannot be traced to that cost object in an economically feasible way. Also called *manufacturing overhead costs* and *factory overhead costs*. (46)

Industrial engineering method. Approach to cost function estimation that analyzes the relationship between inputs and outputs in physical terms. Also called *work measurement method*. (516)

Insourcing. Process of producing goods or providing services within the organization rather than purchasing those same goods or services from outside vendors. (578)

Inspection point. Stage of the production process at which products are examined to determine whether they are acceptable or unacceptable units. (948)

Interactive control systems. Formal information systems that managers use to focus organization attention and learning on key strategic issues. (1219)

Intercept. See *constant*. (512)

Intermediate product. Product transferred from one subunit to another subunit of an organization. This product may either be further worked on by the receiving subunit or sold to an external customer. (1151)

Internal failure costs. Costs incurred on defective products before they are shipped to customers. (996)

Internal rate-of-return (IRR) method. Capital budgeting discounted cash flow (DCF) method that calculates the discount rate at which the present value of expected cash inflows from a project equals the present value of its expected cash outflows. (1098, 1100)

Inventoriable costs. All costs of a product that are considered as assets in the balance sheet when they are incurred and that become cost of goods sold only when the product is sold. (46)

Inventory management. Planning, coordinating, and controlling activities related to the flow of inventory into, through, and out of an organization. (1042)

Investment. Resources or assets used to generate income. (1200)

Investment center. Responsibility center where the manager is accountable for investments, revenues, and costs. (289)

Job. A unit or multiple units of a distinct product or service. (140)

Job-cost record. Source document that records and accumulates all the costs assigned to a specific job, starting when work begins. Also called *job-cost sheet*. (144)

Job-cost sheet. See *job-cost record*. (144)

Job-costing system. Costing system in which the cost object is a unit or multiple units of a distinct product or service called a job. (140)

Joint costs. Costs of a production process that yields multiple products simultaneously. (848)

Joint products. Two or more products that have high total sales values compared with the total sales values of other products yielded by a joint production process. (848)

Just-in-time (JIT) production. Demand-pull manufacturing system in which each component in a production line is produced as soon as, and only when, needed by the next step in the production line. Also called *lean production*. (1056)

Just-in-time (JIT) purchasing. The purchase of materials (or goods) so that they are delivered just as needed for production (or sales). (1051)

Kaizen budgeting. Budgetary approach that explicitly incorporates continuous improvement anticipated during the budget period into the budget numbers. (294)

Labor-time record. Source document that contains information about the amount of labor time used for a specific job in a specific department. (146)

Lean accounting. Costing method that supports creating value for the customer by costing the entire value stream, not individual products or departments, thereby eliminating waste in the accounting process. (1067)

Lean production. See *just-in-time (JIT) production*. (1056)

Learning. Involves managers examining past performance and systematically exploring alternative ways to make better-informed decisions and plans in the future. (p. 11)

Learning curve. Function that measures how labor-hours per unit decline as units of production increase because workers are learning and becoming better at their jobs. (529)

Life-cycle budgeting. Budget that estimates the revenues and business function costs of the value chain attributable to each product from initial R&D to final customer service and support. (707)

Life-cycle costing. System that tracks and accumulates business function costs of the value chain attributable to each product from initial R&D to final customer service and support. (707)

Line management. Managers (for example, in production, marketing, or distribution) who are directly responsible for attaining the goals of the organization. (p. 14)

Linear cost function. Cost function in which the graph of total costs versus the level of a single activity related to that cost is a straight line within the relevant range. (510)

Locked-in costs. Costs that have not yet been incurred but, based on decisions that have already been made, will be incurred in the future. Also called *designed-in costs*. (700)

Main product. Product from a joint production process that has a high total sales value compared with the total sales values of all other products of the joint production process. (848)

Make-or-buy decisions. Decisions about whether a producer of goods or services will insource (produce goods or services within the firm) or outsource (purchase them from outside vendors). (578)

Management accounting. Measures, analyzes, and reports financial and nonfinancial information that helps managers make decisions to fulfill the goals of an organization. It focuses on internal reporting. (p. 3)

Management by exception. Practice of focusing management attention on areas not operating as expected and giving less attention to areas operating as expected. (332)

Management control system. Means of gathering and using information to aid and coordinate the planning and control decisions throughout an organization and to guide the behavior of its managers and employees. (1146)

Manufacturing cells. Grouping of all the different types of equipment used to make a given product. (1056)

Manufacturing cycle efficiency (MCE). Value-added manufacturing time divided by manufacturing cycle time. (1005)

Manufacturing cycle time. See *manufacturing lead time*. (1005)

Manufacturing lead time. Duration between the time an order is received by manufacturing to the time a finished good is produced. Also called *manufacturing cycle time*. (1005)

Manufacturing overhead allocated. Amount of manufacturing overhead costs allocated to individual jobs, products, or services based on the budgeted rate multiplied by the actual quantity used of the cost-allocation base. Also called *manufacturing overhead applied*. (153)

Manufacturing overhead applied. See *manufacturing overhead allocated*. (153)

Manufacturing overhead costs. See *indirect manufacturing costs*. (46)

Manufacturing-sector companies. Companies that purchase materials and components and convert them into various finished goods. (45)

Margin of safety. Amount by which budgeted (or actual) revenues exceed breakeven revenues. (99)

Marketing. Promoting and selling products or services to customers or prospective customers. (6)

Market-share variance. The difference in budgeted contribution margin for actual market size in units caused solely by actual market share being different from budgeted market share. (768)

Market-size variance. The difference in budgeted contribution margin at the budgeted market share caused solely by actual market size in units being different from budgeted market size in units. (769)

Master budget. Expression of management's operating and financial plans for a specified period (usually a fiscal year) including a set of budgeted financial statements. Also called *pro forma statements*. (272)

Master-budget capacity utilization. The expected level of capacity utilization for the current budget period (typically one year). (467)

Materials requirements planning (MRP). Push-through system that manufactures finished goods for inventory on the basis of demand forecasts. (1055)

Materials-requisition record. Source document that contains information about the cost of direct materials used on a specific job and in a specific department. (145)

Matrix method. See *reciprocal method*. (819)

Merchandising-sector companies. Companies that purchase and then sell tangible products without changing their basic form. (45)

Mixed cost. A cost that has both fixed and variable elements. Also called a *semivariable cost*. (512)

Moral hazard. Describes situations in which an employee prefers to exert less effort (or to report distorted information) compared with the effort (or accurate information) desired by the owner because the employee's effort (or validity of the reported information) cannot be accurately monitored and enforced. (1214)

Motivation. The desire to attain a selected goal (the goal-congruence aspect) combined with the resulting pursuit of that goal (the effort aspect). (1147)

Multiple regression. Regression model that estimates the relationship between the dependent variable and two or more independent variables. (522)

Net income. Operating income plus nonoperating revenues (such as interest revenue) minus nonoperating costs (such as interest cost) minus income taxes. (95)

Net present value (NPV) method. Capital budgeting discounted cash flow (DCF) method that calculates the expected monetary gain or loss from a project by discounting all expected future cash inflows and outflows to the present point in time, using the required rate of return. (1098)

Net realizable value (NRV) method. Method that allocates joint costs to joint products on the basis of final sales value minus separable costs of total production of the joint products during the accounting period. (855)

Nonlinear cost function. Cost function in which the graph of total costs based on the level of a single activity is not a straight line within the relevant range. (527)

Non-value-added cost. A cost that, if eliminated, would not reduce the actual or perceived value or utility (usefulness) customers obtain from using the product or service. (700)

Normal capacity utilization. The level of capacity utilization that satisfies average customer demand over a period (say, two to three years) that includes seasonal, cyclical, and trend factors. (467)

Normal costing. A costing system that traces direct costs to a cost object by using the actual direct-cost rates times the actual quantities of the direct-cost inputs and that allocates indirect costs based on the budgeted indirect-cost rates times the actual quantities of the cost-allocation bases. (144)

Normal spoilage. Spoilage inherent in a particular production process that arises even under efficient operating conditions. (947)

On-time performance. Delivering a product or service by the time it is scheduled to be delivered. (1006)

One-time-only special order. Orders that have no long-run implications. (573)

Operating budget. Budgeted income statement and its supporting budget schedules. (276)

Operating department. Department that directly adds value to a product or service. Also called a *production department* in manufacturing companies. (816)

Operating income. Total revenues from operations minus cost of goods sold and operating costs (excluding interest expense and income taxes). (52)

Operating-income volume variance. The difference between static-budget operating income and the operating income based on budgeted profit per unit and actual units of output. (406)

Operating leverage. Effects that fixed costs have on changes in operating income as changes occur in units sold and hence in contribution margin. (102)

Operation. A standardized method or technique that is performed repetitively, often on different materials, resulting in different finished goods. (918)

Operation-costing system. Hybrid-costing system applied to batches of similar, but not identical, products. Each batch of products is often a variation of a single design, and it proceeds through a sequence of operations, but each batch does not necessarily move through the same operations as other batches. Within each operation, all product units use identical amounts of the operation's resources. (918)

Opportunity cost. The contribution to operating income that is forgone or rejected by not using a limited resource in its next-best alternative use. (581)

Opportunity cost of capital. See *required rate of return (RRR)*. (1098)

Ordering costs. Costs of preparing, issuing, and paying purchase orders, plus receiving and inspecting the items included in the orders. (1043)

Organization structure. Arrangement of lines of responsibility within the organization. 289)

Output unit–level costs. The costs of activities performed on each individual unit of a product or service. (211)

Outsourcing. Process of purchasing goods and services from outside vendors rather than producing the same goods or providing the same services within the organization. (578)

Overabsorbed indirect costs. See *overallocated indirect costs*. (159)

Overallocated indirect costs. Allocated amount of indirect costs in an accounting period is greater than the actual (incurred) amount in that period. Also called *overapplied indirect costs* and *overabsorbed indirect costs*. (158)

Overapplied indirect costs. See *overallocated indirect costs*. (159)

Overtime premium. Wage rate paid to workers (for both direct labor and indirect labor) in excess of their straight-time wage rates. (54)

Pareto diagram. Chart that indicates how frequently each type of defect occurs, ordered from the most frequent to the least frequent. (1000)

Payback method. Capital budgeting method that measures the time it will take to recoup, in the form of expected future cash flows, the net initial investment in a project. (1103)

Peak-load pricing. Practice of charging a higher price for the same product or service when the demand for it approaches the physical limit of the capacity to produce that product or service. (710)

Perfectly competitive market. Exists when there is a homogeneous product with buying prices equal to selling prices and no individual buyers or sellers can affect those prices by their own actions. (1156)

Period costs. All costs in the income statement other than cost of goods sold. (46)

Physical-measure method. Method that allocates joint costs to joint products on the basis of the relative weight, volume, or other physical measure at the splitoff point of total production of these products during the accounting period. (852)

Planning. Selecting organization goals, predicting results under various alternative ways of achieving those goals, deciding how to attain the desired goals, and communicating the goals and how to attain them to the entire organization. (10)

Practical capacity. The level of capacity that reduces theoretical capacity by unavoidable operating interruptions such as scheduled maintenance time, shutdowns for holidays, and so on. (467)

Prevention costs. Costs incurred to preclude the production of products that do not conform to specifications. (996)

Previous-department costs. See *transferred-in costs*. (913)

Price discount. Reduction in selling price below list selling price to encourage increases in customer purchases. (744)

Price discrimination. Practice of charging different customers different prices for the same product or service. (710)

Price-recovery component. Change in operating income attributable solely to changes in prices of inputs and outputs between one period and the next. (647)

Price variance. The difference between actual price and budgeted price multiplied by actual quantity of input. Also called *rate variance*. (341)

Prime costs. All direct manufacturing costs. (52)

Pro forma statements. Budgeted financial statements. (272)

Process-costing system. Costing system in which the cost object is masses of identical or similar units of a product or service. (140)

Product. Any output that has a positive total sales value (or an output that enables an organization to avoid incurring costs). (848)

Product cost. Sum of the costs assigned to a product for a specific purpose. (56)

Product-cost cross-subsidization. Costing outcome where one undercosted (overcosted) product results in at least one other product being overcosted (undercosted). (201)

Product differentiation. Organization's ability to offer products or services perceived by its customers to be superior and unique relative to the products or services of its competitors. (631)

Product life cycle. Spans the time from initial R&D on a product to when customer service and support is no longer offered for that product. (707)

Product-mix decisions. Decisions about which products to sell and in what quantities. (585)

Product overcosting. A product consumes a low level of resources but is reported to have a high cost per unit. (201)

Product-sustaining costs. The costs of activities undertaken to support individual products regardless of the number of units or batches in which the units are produced. (211)

Product undercosting. A product consumes a high level of resources but is reported to have a low cost per unit. (201)

Production. Acquiring, coordinating, and assembling resources to produce a product or deliver a service. (6)

Production department. See *operating department*. (816)

Production-volume variance. The difference between budgeted fixed overhead and fixed overhead allocated on the basis of actual output produced. Also called *denominator-level variance*. (398)

Productivity component. Change in costs attributable to a change in the quantity of inputs used in the current period relative to the quantity of inputs that would have been used in the prior period to produce the quantity of current period output. (647)

Profit center. Responsibility center where the manager is accountable for revenues and costs. (289)

Proration. The spreading of underallocated manufacturing overhead or overallocated manufacturing overhead among ending work in process, finished goods, and cost of goods sold. (160)

Purchase-order lead time. The time between placing an order and its delivery. (1044)

Purchasing costs. Cost of goods acquired from suppliers including incoming freight or transportation costs. (1042)

PV graph. Shows how changes in the quantity of units sold affect operating income. (95)

Qualitative factors. Outcomes that are difficult to measure accurately in numerical terms. (572)

Quality. The total features and characteristics of a product made or a service performed according to specifications to satisfy customers at the time of purchase and during use. (994)

Quantitative factors. Outcomes that are measured in numerical terms. (572)

Rate variance. See *price variance*. (341)

Reciprocal method. Cost allocation method that fully recognizes the mutual services provided among all support departments. Also called *matrix method*. (817)

Reengineering. The fundamental rethinking and redesign of business processes to achieve improvements in critical measures of performance, such as cost, quality, service, speed, and customer satisfaction. (632)

Refined costing system. Costing system that reduces the use of broad averages for assigning the cost of resources to cost objects (jobs, products, services) and provides better measurement of the costs of indirect resources used by different cost objects—no matter how differently various cost objects use indirect resources. (206)

Regression analysis. Statistical method that measures the average amount of change in the dependent variable associated with a unit change in one or more independent variables. (522)

Relevant costs. Expected future costs that differ among alternative courses of action being considered. (572)

Relevant range. Band of normal activity level or volume in which there is a specific relationship between the level of activity or volume and the cost in question. (42)

Relevant revenues. Expected future revenues that differ among alternative courses of action being considered. (572)

Reorder point. The quantity level of inventory on hand that triggers a new purchase order. (1046)

Required rate of return (RRR). The minimum acceptable annual rate of return on an investment. Also called the *discount rate*, *hurdle rate*, *cost of capital*, or *opportunity cost of capital*. (1098)

Research and development (R&D). Generating and experimenting with ideas related to new products, services, or processes. (5)

Residual income (RI). Accounting measure of income minus a dollar amount for required return on an accounting measure of investment. (1202)

Residual term. The vertical difference or distance between actual cost and estimated cost for each observation in a regression model. (523)

Responsibility accounting. System that measures the plans, budgets, actions, and actual results of each responsibility center. (289)

Responsibility center. Part, segment, or subunit of an organization whose manager is accountable for a specified set of activities. (289)

Return on investment (ROI). An accounting measure of income divided by an accounting measure of investment. See also *accrual accounting rate of return method*. (1200)

Revenue allocation. The allocation of revenues that are related to a particular revenue object but cannot be traced to it in an economically feasible (cost-effective) way. (824)

Revenue center. Responsibility center where the manager is accountable for revenues only. (289)

Revenue driver. A variable, such as volume, that causally affects revenues. (92)

Revenue object. Anything for which a separate measurement of revenue is desired. (824)

Revenues. Inflows of assets (usually cash or accounts receivable) received for products or services provided to customers. (46)

Rework. Units of production that do not meet the specifications required by customers for finished units that are subsequently repaired and sold as good finished units. (946)

Rightsizing. See *downsizing*. (656)

Rolling budget. Budget or plan that is always available for a specified future period by adding a period (month, quarter, or year) to the period that just ended. Also called *continuous budget or rolling forecast*. (275)

Safety stock. Inventory held at all times regardless of the quantity of inventory ordered using the EOQ model. (1047)

Sales mix. Quantities of various products or services that constitute total unit sales. (104)

Sales-mix variance. The difference between (1) budgeted contribution margin for the actual sales mix, and (2) budgeted contribution margin for the budgeted sales mix. (766)

Sales-quantity variance. The difference between (1) budgeted contribution margin based on actual units sold of all products at the budgeted mix and (2) contribution margin in the static budget (which is based on the budgeted units of all products to be sold at the budgeted mix). (767)

Sales value at splitoff method. Method that allocates joint costs to joint products on the basis of the relative total sales value at the splitoff point of the total production of these products during the accounting period. (852)

Sales-volume variance. The difference between a flexible-budget amount and the corresponding static-budget amount. (336)

Scrap. Residual material left over when making a product. (946)

Selling-price variance. The difference between the actual selling price and the budgeted selling price multiplied by the actual units sold. (338)

Semivariable cost. See *mixed cost*. (512)

Sensitivity analysis. A what-if technique that managers use to calculate how an outcome will change if the original predicted data are not achieved or if an underlying assumption changes. (99)

Separable costs. All costs (manufacturing, marketing, distribution, and so on) incurred beyond the splitoff point that are assignable to each of the specific products identified at the splitoff point. (848)

Sequential allocation method. See *step-down method*. (815)

Sequential tracking. Approach in a product-costing system in which recording of the journal entries occurs in the same order as actual purchases and progress in production. (1059)

Service department. See *support department*. (802)

Service-sector companies. Companies that provide services or intangible products to their customers. (46)

Service-sustaining costs. The costs of activities undertaken to support individual services. (211)

Shrinkage costs. Costs that result from theft by outsiders, embezzlement by employees, misclassifications, and clerical errors. (1043)

Simple regression. Regression model that estimates the relationship between the dependent variable and one independent variable. (522)

Single-rate method. Allocation method that allocates costs in each cost pool to cost objects using the same rate per unit of a single allocation base. (802)

Slope coefficient. Coefficient term in a cost estimation model that indicates the amount by which total cost changes when a one-unit change occurs in the level of activity within the relevant range. (511)

Source document. An original record that supports journal entries in an accounting system. (144)

Splitoff point. The juncture in a joint-production process when two or more products become separately identifiable. (848)

Spoilage. Units of production that do not meet the specifications required by customers for good units and that are discarded or sold at reduced prices. (946)

Staff management. Staff (such as management accountants and human resources managers) who provide advice and assistance to line management. (14)

Stand-alone cost-allocation method. Method that uses information pertaining to each user of a cost object as a separate entity to determine the cost-allocation weights. (823)

Stand-alone revenue-allocation method. Method that uses product-specific information on the products in the bundle as weights for allocating the bundled revenues to the individual products. (825)

Standard. A carefully determined price, cost, or quantity that is used as a benchmark for judging performance. It is usually expressed on a per unit basis. (340)

Standard cost. A carefully determined cost of a unit of output. (340)

Standard costing. Costing system that traces direct costs to output produced by multiplying the standard prices or rates by the standard quantities of inputs allowed for actual outputs produced and allocates overhead costs on the basis of the standard overhead-cost rates times the standard quantities of the allocation bases allowed for the actual outputs produced. (389)

Standard input. A carefully determined quantity of input required for one unit of output. (340)

Standard price. A carefully determined price that a company expects to pay for a unit of input. (340)

Static budget. Budget based on the level of output planned at the start of the budget period. (334)

Static-budget variance. Difference between an actual result and the corresponding budgeted amount in the static budget. (334)

Step cost function. A cost function in which the cost remains the same over various ranges of the level of activity, but the cost increases by discrete amounts (that is, increases in steps) as the level of activity changes from one range to the next. (527)

Step-down method. Cost allocation method that partially recognizes the mutual services provided among all support departments. Also called *sequential allocation method*. (815)

Stockout costs. Costs that result when a company runs out of a particular item for which there is customer demand. The company must act to meet that demand or suffer the costs of not meeting it. (1043)

Strategic cost management. Describes cost management that specifically focuses on strategic issues. (4)

Strategy. Specifies how an organization matches its own capabilities with the opportunities in the marketplace to accomplish its objectives. (4)

Strategy map. A diagram that describes how an organization creates value by connecting strategic objectives in explicit cause-and-effect relationships with each other in the financial, customer, internal business process, and learning and growth perspectives. (634)

Suboptimal decision making. Decisions in which the benefit to one subunit is more than offset by the costs or loss of benefits to the organization as a whole. Also called *incongruent decision making* or *dysfunctional decision making*. (1149)

Sunk costs. Past costs that are unavoidable because they cannot be changed no matter what action is taken. (572)

Super-variable costing. See *throughput costing*. (464)

Supply chain. Describes the flow of goods, services, and information from the initial sources of materials and services to the delivery of products to consumers, regardless of whether those activities occur in the same organization or in other organizations. (7)

Support department. Department that provides the services that assist other internal departments (operating departments and other support departments) in the company. Also called a *service department*. (802)

Sustainability. The development and implementation of strategies to achieve long-term financial, social, and environmental goals. (8)

Target cost per unit. Estimated long-run cost per unit of a product or service that enables the company to achieve its target operating income per unit when selling at the target price. Target cost per unit is derived by subtracting the target operating income per unit from the target price. (699)

Target operating income per unit. Operating income that a company aims to earn per unit of a product or service sold. (699)

Target price. Estimated price for a product or service that potential customers will pay. (699)

Target rate of return on investment. The target annual operating income that an organization aims to achieve divided by invested capital. (705)

Theoretical capacity. The level of capacity based on producing at full efficiency all the time. (467)

Theory of constraints (TOC). Describes methods to maximize operating income when faced with some bottleneck and some nonbottleneck operations. (587)

Throughput costing. Method of inventory costing in which only variable direct material costs are included as inventoriable costs. Also called *super-variable costing*. (464)

Throughput margin. Revenues minus the direct material costs of the goods sold. (587)

Time driver. Any factor in which a change in the factor causes a change in the speed of an activity. (1006)

Time value of money. Takes into account that a dollar (or any other monetary unit) received today is worth more than a dollar received at any future time. (1098)

Total-overhead variance. The sum of the flexible-budget variance and the production-volume variance. (405)

Total quality management (TQM). An integrative philosophy of management for continuously improving the quality of products and processes. (8)

Transfer price. Price one subunit (department or division) charges for a product or service supplied to another subunit of the same organization. (1151)

Transferred-in costs. Costs incurred in previous departments that are carried forward as the product's costs when it moves to a subsequent process in the production cycle. Also called *previous department costs*. (913)

Trigger point. Refers to a stage in the cycle from purchase of direct materials to sale of finished goods at which journal entries are made in the accounting system. (1059)

Uncertainty. The possibility that an actual amount will deviate from an expected amount. (101)

Underabsorbed indirect costs. See *underallocated indirect costs*. (159)

Underallocated indirect costs. Allocated amount of indirect costs in an accounting period is less than the actual (incurred) amount in that period. Also called *underapplied indirect costs* or *underabsorbed indirect costs*. (158)

Underapplied indirect costs. See *underallocated indirect costs*. (159)

Unfavorable variance. Variance that has the effect of decreasing operating income relative to the budgeted amount. Denoted U. (334)

Unit cost. Cost computed by dividing total cost by the number of units. Also called *average cost*. (44)

Unused capacity. The amount of productive capacity available over and above the productive capacity employed to meet consumer demand in the current period. (654)

Usage variance. See *efficiency variance*. (341)

Value-added cost. A cost that, if eliminated, would reduce the actual or perceived value or utility (usefulness) customers obtain from using the product or service. (700)

Value chain. The sequence of business functions in which customer usefulness is added to products or services of a company. (5)

Value engineering. Systematic evaluation of all aspects of the value chain, with the objective of reducing costs and achieving a quality level that satisfies customers. (700)

Value streams. All valued-added activities needed to design, manufacture, and deliver a given product or product line to customers. (1067)

Variable cost. Cost that changes in total in proportion to changes in the related level of total activity or volume. (39)

Variable costing. Method of inventory costing in which only all variable manufacturing costs are included as inventoriable costs. Also called *direct costing*. (452)

Variable overhead efficiency variance. The difference between the actual quantity of variable overhead cost-allocation base used and budgeted quantity of variable overhead cost-allocation base that should have been used to produce actual output, multiplied by budgeted variable overhead cost per unit of cost-allocation base. (393)

Variable overhead flexible-budget variance. The difference between actual variable overhead costs incurred and flexible-budget variable overhead amounts. (392)

Variable overhead spending variance. The difference between actual variable overhead cost per unit and budgeted variable overhead cost per unit of the cost-allocation base, multiplied by actual quantity of variable overhead cost-allocation base used for actual output. (394)

Variance. The difference between actual result and expected performance. (332)

Weighted-average process-costing method. Method of process costing that assigns the equivalent-unit cost of the work done to date (regardless of the accounting period in which it was done) to equivalent units completed and transferred out of the process and to equivalent units in ending work-in-process inventory. (905)

Whale curve. A typically backward-bending curve that represents the results from customer profitability analysis by first ranking customers from best to worst and then plotting their cumulative profitability level. (752)

Work-in-process inventory. Goods partially worked on but not yet completed. Also called *work in progress*. (46)

Work in progress. See *work-in-process inventory*. (46)

Work-measurement method. See *industrial engineering method*. (516)

Index